When we think of archaeology, most of us think first of its many spectacular finds: the legendary city of Troy, Tutankhamun's golden tomb, the three-million-year-old footprints at Laetoli, the mile-high city at Machu Picchu, the cave paintings at Lascaux. But as marvelous as these discoveries are, the ultimate goal of archaeology, and of archaeologists, is something far more ambitious. Indeed, it is one of humanity's great quests: to recapture and understand our human past, across vast stretches of time, as it was lived in every corner of the globe. Now, in *The Oxford Companion to Archaeology*, readers have a comprehensive and authoritative overview of this fascinating discipline, in a book that is itself a rare find, a treasure of up-to-date information on virtually every aspect of the field.

The range of subjects covered here is breathtaking—everything from the domestication of the camel, to Egyptian hieroglyphics, to luminescence dating, to the Mayan calendar, to Koobi Fora and Olduvai Gorge. Readers will find extensive essays that illuminate the full history of archaeology—from the discovery of Herculaneum in 1783, to the recent finding of the "Ice Man," and the ancient city of Uruk—and engaging biographies of the great figures in the field, from Gertrude Bell, Paul Emile Botta, and Louis and Mary Leakey, to V. Gordon Childe, Li Chi, Heinrich Schliemann, and Max Uhle. The *Companion* offers extensive coverage of the methods used in archaeological research, revealing how archaeologists find sites (remote sensing, aerial photography, ground survey), how they map excavations and report findings, and how they analyze artifacts (radiocarbon dating, dendrochronology, stratigraphy, mortuary analysis). Of course, archaeology's great subject is humanity and human culture, and there are broad essays that examine human evolution—ranging from our early primate ancestors, to *Australopithecus* and the Cro-Magnons, to *Homo erectus* and the Neanderthals—and explore the many general facets of culture, from art and architecture, to arms and armor, to beer and brewing, to astronomy and religion. And perhaps most important, the contributors provide insightful coverage of human culture as it has been expressed in every region of the world. Here entries range from broad overviews, to treatments of particular themes, to discussions of peoples, societies, and particular sites. Thus, anyone interested in North America would find articles that

THE OXFORD COMPANION TO
Archaeology

THE OXFORD COMPANION TO
Archaeology

Editor in Chief
Brian M. Fagan

Editors
Charlotte Beck   George Michaels
Chris Scarre   Neil Asher Silberman

New York   Oxford
OXFORD UNIVERSITY PRESS
1996

OXFORD UNIVERSITY PRESS

Oxford   New York
Athens Auckland Bangkok Bogota Bombay
Buenos Aires Calcutta Cape Town Dar es Salaam
Delhi Florence Hong Kong Istanbul Karachi
Kuala Lumpur Madras Madrid Melbourne
Mexico City Nairobi Paris Singapore
Taipei Tokyo Toronto

and associated companies in
Berlin   Ibadan

Published by Oxford University Press, Inc.
198 Madison Avenue, New York, New York 10016

Oxford is a registered trademark of Oxford University Press

Maps created by Mapping Specialists, Ltd.
Tables and charts created by Hadel Studio
Maps, tables, and charts copyright © 1996 Oxford University Press, Inc.
"Archaeologist" is printed with the permission of John Drexel.

Library of Congress Cataloging-in-Publication Data
The Oxford companion to archaeology / editor, Brian M. Fagan.
p. cm.   Includes bibliographical references and index.
ISBN 0-19-507618-4
1. Archaeology—Dictionaries. I. Fagan, Brian M.
CC70.096   1996
930.1'03—dc20   96-30792

1 3 5 7 9 8 6 4 2

Printed in the United States of America
on acid-free paper

CONTENTS

Archaeologist

Those who have patience to learn his patience
as he digs into the past with patient hands
will learn to accept his patience and his reticence,
the artifacts retrieved from shifting sands:

which is to say, the feel of history
in its alien, unaltered state,
the unworn emblems of memory
that lie beneath the truth of what we write,
rough and untutored.

See: our lives have not been wholly severed
from all that matters
and has mattered:
piece by blessed piece he'll gather,
piece each piecemeal part together.
In time we'll learn to recognize the patterns.

—John Drexel

INTRODUCTION

Archaeology in the popular imagination is the stuff of which dreams are made, a world of adventure, intrigue, and romance, of golden pharaohs and long-vanished civilizations. Many people still believe archaeologists are tough, pith-helmet-clad men and women slashing their way through clinging jungle or penetrating the secrets of ancient pyramids. In the movies, Indiana Jones searches for the Ark of the Covenant, the Holy Grail, and other treasures, while detective novels weave complex tales of discovery, like Agatha Christie's *Murder in Mesopotamia*, about a not-so-fictional dig at Sumerian Ur in Iraq. There was a lot of truth in these tired stereotypes a century or more ago, for to discover an early civilization was to venture far off the beaten track. Englishman Austen Henry Layard unearthed Assyrian Nineveh in the 1840s. John Lloyd Stephens and Frederick Catherwood revealed the ancient Maya of the Central American rainforest to an astonished world in the same decade. And the archaeologist's life was not without danger—as late as 1924, English excavator Leonard Woolley repelled a raid on his camp at Ur with rifle fire, killing at least one marauder. Much Victorian archaeology was indeed an unbridled treasure hunt, an undignified scramble for spectacular and preferably valuable artifacts. But by the time Woolley discovered the Royal Cemetery at Ur in 1927, archaeology had moved a long way from its treasure hunting days—although armed guards watch the tombs of the gold-laden Lords of Sipán in Peru even today. The transformation of archaeology from an amateur pastime into a sophisticated, multidisciplinary area of study is one of the great triumphs of twentieth-century science.

The Oxford Companion to Archaeology celebrates this remarkable metamorphosis with a comprehensive look at archaeology and archaeologists. Like all *Oxford Companions*, it strives to make specialized knowledge available and accessible to a wide range of audiences, including interested nonspecialists. An encyclopedic survey of the field written by established experts is long overdue, for the dramatic advances in archaeological methods and both the spectacular and not-so-well known discoveries of recent years have often passed by the world at large. These pages offer a global assessment of archaeology's achievements, scientists' reconstruction of the past, and archaeologists' contributions to society, at a time when the precious archives of the human past are vanishing rapidly under the onslaught of modern industrial development, systematic looting, and intensive agriculture. This volume offers a particularly timely reminder of the importance of the past to the present and future.

The *Companion* is a book of contemporary science with strong roots in the humanities and social sciences, written by active scholars with broad experience in the field and the laboratory. They present the latest advances and discoveries in archaeology. For example, contributors discuss the spectacular Moche royal burials from Sipán, Peru; the "Ice Man" corpse from Similaun, high in the Austrian Alps; and the latest underwater finds. One can learn about experimental archaeology, fission-track dating, and settlement pattern analysis, all recent developments in the field.

The past described within this book is the common past, a past revealed through the application of multidisciplinary science, historiography, and disciplined inquiry from scholars in every field from chemistry to linguistics to zoology. Such a past is the intellectual property of all humankind, progressively modified by each generation of scholarship, excavation, and analysis. To archaeologists, the human past is owned by no one. It represents the cultural heritage of everyone who has ever lived on Earth or will live on it in the future. Archaeology puts all human societies on an equal footing.

APPROACH

From the very beginning, the editors and advisers intended *The Oxford Companion to Archaeology* as an overview of archaeology from a global perspective. Early archaeology centered on Europe and the Near East, and in the Americas on the Midwest, the Southwest, and the Maya lowlands; the scope of this book reflects the dramatic widening of archaeological inquiry during the twentieth century to all corners of the world. The *Companion* also covers the entire spectrum of human existence, from the Australopithecines and human origins more than 2.5 million years ago to the important discoveries made in the heart of modern cities like London, New York, and Rome.

Many people still think archaeologists do little more than excavate and count artifacts, when, in fact, they make full use of the remarkable technologies of contemporary science. The *Companion* describes how modern archaeology works: how archaeologists call on high technology and techniques from many disciplines to study the minutest details of the past. Theoretical or conceptual frameworks used by archaeologists are also an important component of the *Companion*. For generations, archaeologists were content to describe local artifacts and specific ancient cultures, what is called "culture history," without answering larger questions about the past. Why did humans evolve in tropical Africa and not in some more temperate climate? Why did the Mesopotamians, the Egyptians, and the Maya, of all the world's peoples, develop cities and writing systems, entire civilizations? The past half-century has seen archaeologists pay closer attention to answering questions like these, interpreting the meaning of the archaeological record rather than merely describing it, while descriptive culture history remains an important and powerful force in archaeology.

The Oxford Companion to Archaeology aims at comprehensive coverage, although we realize that most subjects warranted more thorough treatment than was possible in a one-volume work with nearly seven hundred entries. The references at the end of most entries provide an avenue for the reader to explore a specific subject in more depth. The *Companion* is a starting point, the trunk of a complicated and ever-growing tree that sprouts and branches ever larger as each generation of archaeologists builds on the research of its predecessors. More than four hundred contributors speak largely with their own voices to preserve the enthusiasm and originality of their individual perspectives and styles of presentation, which not only imparts an engaging diversity to the volume, but also permits the reader to appreciate the variety of approaches to the past.

A cumulative science merits a broad framework of comprehension; the *Companion* is organized theoretically around five broad, interconnected themes:

- *How archaeology began and developed.* Current archaeology is a product not only of modern science, but of its own history. The *Companion* summarizes the general history of archaeology from its beginnings in the Renaissance, recorded in the context of wider intellectual and historical developments. Every science is a product of its times and reflects the thinking of its own historical period; archaeology is no exception.

- *How archaeology works.* How old is the artifact? How do archaeologists know where to dig? The *Companion* offers insights on how archaeologists find and excavate sites; how they date archaeological sites; and how they reconstruct prehistoric environments and ancient lifeways. Entries cover the entire spectrum of archaeological method, from radiocarbon dating, zooarchaeology, and plant flotation to carbon isotope analysis of prehistoric diet and the study of ancient scripts. Descriptions of the methods and high-tech approaches of archaeological research are also found in many entries; for example, the entry on "Olduvai Gorge" in East Africa points out that the site is not only famous for its early human remains, but also for the use of potassium-argon methods to date these fossils.

- *How archaeologists explain the past.* Archaeologists do far more than describe and reconstruct the past; they attempt to explain what happened in ancient times. The entries representing this theme explore such topics as cultural ecology, multilinear evolution, processual and post-processual archaeology, structural archaeology, and Marxist approaches—the all important theories of modern archaeology—and some of the sophisticated and not-so-sophisticated ways in which archaeologists have explained developments like the beginnings of agriculture and the origins of civilization.

- *Archaeology and the human past.* Archaeology is the most effective discipline to study human evolution and changes in human behavior over immensely long time periods. The cultures and societies archaeologists examine are known from surviving artifacts and other material remains. Artifacts, structures, food remains, and other kinds of archaeological evidence provide a broad picture of day-to-day ordinary human behavior, rather than a narrowly focused view of rulers and their policies. Nonetheless, the great public buildings, grandiose sculptures, and elaborate glyphs studied often boast of the achievements of ancient rulers. Such monuments were intended to be powerful political statements and as propagandistic self-aggrandizement.

What archaeology tells us about the past can be organized conceptually into a series of subdivisions covering the entire spectrum of human experience, coinciding with broad slices across prehistoric and historic time. These subdivisions have emerged from generations of archaeological research, and entries in this volume are organized to reflect them.

- *World prehistory.* Thanks to sophisticated dating techniques, which allow comparative dating of cultural developments on a global basis, and to recent excavations in every corner of the world, we can now examine human prehistory not from a narrowly American or European perspective, but as a truly global phenomenon. Archaeology is a means of studying people who may lack written history, which thereby places every society on an equal historical basis. The *Companion* explores major sites, cultures, and civilizations, and the series of overarching developments all over the world that determined the course of human history. Human origins, the search for our beginnings, drives much research, as does the study of human biological evolution, the emergence of fully modern human forms.

The spread of humanity across the Old World and into the Americas occupies the earlier eras of the prehistoric past that unfolded during more than 1.5 million years of fluctuating Ice Age climate and ended in massive global warming after 15,000 years ago. The major climate changes at the end of the Ice Age coincided with major developments in human history, with the beginnings of farming and animal husbandry (as discussed in the entries "Domestication of Animals" and "Domestication of Plants"). Such recent advances as the Accelerator Mass Spectrometry (AMS) radiocarbon dating of maize cobs, described here, are revolutionizing the early history of agriculture.

- *The origins of civilization.* Archaeology maintains an intense focus on the dramatic cultural changes in a number of geographic areas accompanying the appearance of the first civilizations. Pre-industrial civilizations appeared in the Near East and later in other parts of the Eastern Mediterranean, in Asia, and the Americas; all are discussed in separate entries in this volume. The first cities and their development are traced through writing, trade, and new religious beliefs, as described in entries on the Sumerians and ancient Egyptians, Harappans, Myceneans and Minoans, Shang lords, and the beginnings of civilization in Central and South America. Entries in the *Companion* answer such questions as: Why did civilizations develop in some areas and not in others? Why did civilizations rise and collapse so rapidly? What caused human societies to achieve much greater complexity in the first place?

  The entries in the *Companion* also carry one out of prehistoric into historic times, into a more complicated world where civilizations were part of larger regional patterns and where states functioned not in isolation, but in close interdependence.

- *States and civilizations.* The *Companion*'s global perspective allows the exploration of the increasingly sophisticated and interdependent civilizations of the past three millennia. Entries provide thorough coverage of Classical and Biblical archaeology, the early empires, Teotihuacán and Maya civilization in the New World, and cultural developments in all parts of the world.

- *Historical archaeology.* The *Companion* explores the way in which archaeologists add new dimensions to our understanding of more recent history, from Medieval times onward. Coverage includes Anglo-Saxon, Viking, and Medieval archaeology (on cities, villages, monasteries and other religious buildings) in Europe; historic archaeological sites in the Americas; industrial archaeology; and the study of sites dating to the European colonization of Africa, Australia, and other continents. Seafaring and the age of exploration, evidence for the end of prehistory, and European colonization of the world are all examined. Each such entry shows the unique perspectives archaeology brings to our understanding of centuries rich in historical documentation; together, they provide the reader with a cross-cultural perspective on how archaeology sheds light on complex pre-industrial and industrial civilizations and on contemporary societies elsewhere in the world. For example, the entry "Historical Archaeology" describes how archaeologists have used artifacts to examine the lifeways of anonymous groups within historic American society, such as African-American slaves.

- *Archaeology in the late twentieth century.* The *Companion* takes a unique look at archaeology in the modern world. It examines the ethics of collecting, the crisis in archaeology caused by widespread looting and vandalism, and the wholesale destruction of the past that threatens the very future of the science. How can we stem the tidal wave of destruction? How do different nations protect their past, and what strategies are successful in reducing looting and vandalism? Also examined are the contributions archaeology makes to solving the problems of today's world (for example, garbage studies and waste management, reconstructing ancient agricultural systems, and game conservation). Some important entries such as "Nationalism" and "Non-Western Societies, Archaeology and " explore the role of archaeology in establishing ethnic and national identities, as well as political uses of the past. The *Companion* examines the archaeology of gender and alternative worldviews, different perspectives on the past espoused by women, Native Americans, Australian Aborigines, and other groups or peoples. For example,

"Reburial and Repatriation" discusses the recent and ongoing controversies about the excavation of Native American burials by archaeologists.

The Oxford Companion to Archaeology aims to define archaeology as a critical intellectual phenomenon of the late-twentieth-century world, as one of the seminal ways in which humankind can achieve a better understanding of our common roots, differences, and similarities. To consult theses pages is to take a fascinating journey through the human past as seen through the eyes of those who study it. One can read about Adena earthworks in the North American Midwest, peruse a summary of the archaeology of New Zealand, or learn about the history of archaeological research in Europe from 1900 to 1950. There are articles on Pompeii and Herculaneum, on remote sensing, and on rock art. Tourism, archaeological theory, and Old Kingdom Egypt are covered, as are the Aztec Empire, Neanderthals, and ancient disease. Even a cursory examination of these pages will reveal how archaeology plays an essential role in the study of societies past and present.

HOW TO USE THIS COMPANION

This alphabetically arranged volume is designed for specific reference and sustained browsing. Wide exploration of related topics is encouraged by several features.

- *The index* is a good starting point for investigation, for it offers a useful way to discover the wide variety of archaeologists, sites, and topics covered in the book. If one is interested in, say, Austen Henry Layard or John Lloyd Stephens, one can turn to the alphabetical entry on this individual. From there, a search can be broadened to sites discovered and excavated by these archaeologists, or to a general discussion of Assyrian or Maya civilization, writing systems, or decipherment.

- *Blind entries* appear within the alphabetical range of headwords and, for synonyms, related subjects, and inverted terms, refers one to the entry under which the topic is discussed. For example, the blind entry "Iron Age" refers one to the article on "Three-Age System." In some cases, the blind entry will refer to another entry that discusses the topic as part of a broader rubric.

- *Asterisks* are used in the body of an article to denote cross-references. Topics marked in this way will be found elsewhere in the book as separate entries. For example, in the entry "Mesopotamia: Sumer and Akkad," the city of Ur is marked with an asterisk, indicating that it is treated as a separate entry. This allows the reader to look up related entries as he or she goes along.

- *Cross-references* are also made at the end or the entry. For example, "Trade, African" is cross-referenced to, among other topics, "Africa: The Rise of Kingdoms and States," for trading activities were an integral part of that development.

Many pieces feature references for further reading at the end of entry that may be useful to learn more about the topic. The length of the reading lists varies from one entry to the next, with the longest usually attached to the most comprehensive essays. While every effort has been made to include nontechnical and widely available works, inevitably some topics require more specialized reading and their bibliographies reflect this reality. Finally, the entry contributor's name appears either at the end of the text or after the reference list. A section in the front of the book lists individual contributors and their current institutional affiliations.

Archaeologists often work in obscure places; maps and chronological tables are essential. The *Companion* includes maps and chronological tables, placed at the end of the book for the reader's reference, that cover every major area of the world and the entire timespan of the human past.

DATES

Dates throughout this volume are given according to the following long-established conventions:

Dates in millions of years are sometimes shortened to Mya, millions of years ago. By the same token, Kya is thousands of years ago. *Dates prior to 12,000 years ago* are given in years before present (B.P.), "present" being A.D. 1950 by internationally agreed usage.

Dates after 12,000 years ago are given in years A.D. and B.C., as this is the common practice in archaeology. Unless otherwise stated, all radiocarbon dates more recent than about 6000 B.C. are calibrated with tree rings.

ACKNOWLEDGMENTS

My first and greatest debt is to the devoted Section Editors: Charlotte Beck (The Americas), George Michaels (Methods and Theory in Archaeology; Asia), Chris Scarre (Europe), and Neil Silberman (Near East; Eastern Mediterranean; Historical Archaeology). Their support, encouragement, and hard work from the moment when the *Companion* was little more than a six-page proposal have been deeply appreciated. This book is a tribute to their tenacious devotion and unflinching intellectual standards. Members of the Advisory Board gave us invaluable advice and encouragement when the book was taking shape in its conceptual stages. Many other colleagues suggested authors, reviewed entries, and provided moral support. Although they are too numerous to mention here, I hope they will accept this brief acknowledgment as a salute to their cooperation. We owe much to our more than four hundred contributors. We thank them for providing us with a unique and authoritative portrait of archaeology, and only hope they forgive our importunate faxes, e-mail messages, and phone calls.

The staff at Oxford University Press, who commissioned the book, then supported the endeavor at every stage of the way, were vital members of our team. Linda Halvorson Morse provided inspirational leadership and was an invaluable catalyst from the beginning. John Drexel led us through the complex process of entry development with infinite patience, while Liza Ewell and Ann Toback were deeply involved in the early stages of the book. Margaret Hogan and Anita Vanca have carried the project through to fruition. Efficient, always good humored, and maestros of even the smallest detail, they kept the project always on track. Their diligence has helped to ensure the accuracy and accessibility of the text. They have saved me, my fellow editors, and the contributors from many inadvertent errors, large and small. This is as much their book as ours, as it is our devoted copyeditors and proofreaders Angie Miccinello (Miccinello Associates), Douglas Goertzen, Jacqueline Remlinger, and Steve Brauer.

Brian M. Fagan
Santa Barbara, California
May 1996

CONTRIBUTORS

David R. Abbott, *Adjunct Professor of Anthropology, Arizona State University, Tempe*

Michael A. Adler, *Assistant Professor, Department of Anthropology, Southern Methodist University, Dallas, Texas*

J. M. Adovasio, *Director, Anthropology, Archaeology, and Geology Departments; Professor of Anthropology and Archaeology; Executive Director of Mercyhurst College Archaeological Institute, Erie, Pennsylvania*

Leslie C. Aiello, *Reader in Biological Anthropology, University College London, England*

Mark Aldenderfer, *Associate Professor of Anthropology, University of California, Santa Barbara*

Abbas Alizadeh, *Research Assistant, The Oriental Institute, University of Chicago, Illinois*

James P. Allen, *Associate Curator of Egyptian Art, The Metropolitan Museum of Art, New York*

Jim Allen, *Professor of Archaeology, La Trobe University, Melbourne, Australia*

Mitchell Allen, *Publisher, AltaMira Press, Walnut Creek, California*

Kenneth M. Ames, *Professor of Anthropology, Portland State University, Portland, Oregon*

David G. Anderson, *Archaeologist, National Park Service, Atlanta, Georgia*

Carol A. R. Andrews, *Assistant Keeper, Department of Egyptian Antiquities, British Museum, London, England*

Peter Andrews, *Head, Human Origin Program, Department of Palaeontology, Natural History Museum, London, England*

Carla M. Antonaccio, *Associate Professor of Classical Studies, Wesleyan University, Middletown, Connecticut*

George Armelagos, *Professor of Anthropology, Emory University, Atlanta, Georgia*

James A. Armstrong, *Assistant Curator of Collections, Semitic Museum, Harvard University, Cambridge, Massachusetts*

Béat Arnold, *Docteur ès Lettres, Université de Neuchâtel, Switzerland*

Anthony F. Aveni, *Russell B. Colgate Professor of Astronomy and Anthropology, Colgate University, Hamilton, New York*

Dan Bahat, *Lecturer of History and Archaeology of Jerusalem at Bar-Ilan University, Ramat-Gan, Israel*

Paul G. Bahn, *Freelance Archaeologist, Hull, England*

Miriam S. Balmuth, *Professor of Classics, Archaeology, and Art History, Tufts University, Medford, Massachusetts*

Douglas B. Bamforth, *Associate Professor of Anthropology, University of Colorado, Boulder*

E. B. Banning, *Associate Professor of Archaeology, Department of Anthropology, University of Toronto, Canada*

Uzi Baram, *Department of Anthropology, University of Massachusetts at Amherst*

Gina L. Barnes, *Senior Researcher in Far Eastern Archaeology, St. John's College, Cambridge, England*

John C. Barrett, *Reader in Archaeology, University of Sheffield, England*

Joseph John Basile, *Assistant Professor of Art History, Maryland Institute, College of Art, Baltimore*

Charlotte Beck, *Associate Professor of Anthropology, Hamilton College, Clinton, New York*

Mary Anne Beecher, *Assistant Professor of Art and Design, Iowa State University, Ames*

Peter Bellwood, *Reader in Archaeology, Australian National University at Canberra*

Glenn W. Berger, *Research Professor, Quaternary Sciences Center, Reno, Nevada*

Robert L. Bettinger, *Professor of Anthropology, University of California at Davis*

Cynthia Ann Bettison, *Director, Western New Mexico University Museum; Adjunct Assistant Professor of Anthropology, Western New Mexico University at Silver City*

Bruce W. Bevan, *Owner, Geosight, Pitman, New Jersey*

Robert Steven Bianchi, *New York, New York*

Robin Birley, *Director, Vindolanda Trust, Northumberland, England*

Richard E. Blanton, *Professor of Anthropology, Purdue University, West Lafayette, Indiana*

Edward Bleiberg, *Associate Professor of Egyptology, Institute of Egyptian Art and Archaeology, The University of Memphis, Tennessee*

Peter Bogucki, *Assistant Dean for Undergraduate Affairs, School of Engineering and Applied Science, Princeton University, Princeton, New Jersey*

Larissa Bonfante, *Professor of Classics, New York University, New York*

Mark Bowden, *Field Officer, Royal Commission on the Historical Monuments of England, Newcastle upon Tyne, England*

John Bower, *Research Associate, Archaeometry Laboratory, University of Minnesota, Duluth; Professor Emeritus, Iowa State University, Ames*

Richard Bradley, *Professor of Archaeology, Reading University, England*

Steven A. Brandt, *Associate Professor of Anthropology, University of Florida at Gainesville*

Geoffrey E. Braswell, *Adjunct Professor, Department of Anthropology, Tulane University, New Orleans, Louisiana*

Günter Bräuer, *Professor of Anthropology, University of Hamburg, Germany*

David J. Breeze, *Chief Inspector of Ancient Monuments, Scotland; Visiting Professor, Deparment of Archaeology, University of Durham, Scotland*

José Proenza Brochado, *Professor of Archaeology, Pontifícia Universidade Católica do Rio Grande do Sul at Porto Alegre, Brasil*

Cyprian Broodbank, *Lecturer in Aegean Archaeology, Institute of Archaeology, University College London, England*

Don Brothwell, *Professor of Human Palaeoecology, University of York, England*

David L. Browman, *Professor of Anthropology and Chairman, Department of Archaeology, Washington University, St. Louis, Missouri*

Vaughn M. Bryant, Jr., *Professor and Department Head, Department of Anthropology, Texas A & M University, College Station*

Anthony A. M. Bryer, *Professor of Byzantine Studies, University of Birmingham, England*

R. Angus Buchanan, *Professor of the History of Technology, University of Bath, England*

Aubrey Burl, *Former Principal Lecturer in Archaeology, Hull College of Higher Education, Yorkshire, England*

David L. Carlson, *Associate Professor of Anthropology, Texas A & M University, College Station*

Martin Carver, *Professor of Archaeology, University of York, England*

Timothy Champion, *Reader in Archaeology, University of Southampton, England*

John Chapman, *Senior Lecturer in Archaeology, University of Newcastle upon Tyne, England*

Robert Chapman, *Reader in Archaeology, Reading University, England*

Thomas H. Charlton, *Professor of Anthropology, University of Iowa, Iowa City*

Arlen F. Chase, *Professor of Anthropology, Department of Sociology and Anthropology, University of Central Florida, Orlando*

Diane Z. Chase, *Professor of Anthropology, Department of Sociology and Anthropology, University of Central Florida, Orlando*

Christopher Chippindale, *Senior Assistant Curator, Cambridge University Museum of Archaeology and Anthropology, England*

Catherine Clark, *Inspector of Ancient Monuments, English Heritage, London, England*

John E. Clark, *Assistant Professor of Anthropology, Brigham Young University, Provo, Utah; Director, New World Archaeological Foundation*

Henry Cleere, *World Heritage Coordinator, International Council on Monuments and Sites, Paris, France*

Angela E. Close, *Associate Professor of Anthropology, Ohio State University, Columbus*

Michael D. Coe, *Charles J. MacCurdy Professor of Anthropology, Emeritus, Yale University, New Haven, Connecticut*

Herbert M. Cole, *Professor of Art History, University of California at Santa Barbara*

Bryony Coles, *Reader in Prehistoric Archaeology, University of Exeter, England*

John Collis, *Professor of Archaeology, University of Sheffield, England*

Robin A. E. Coningham, *Lecturer in South Asian Archaeology, University of Bradford, England*

Graham Connah, *Emeritus Professor of Archaeology and Palaeoanthropology, University of New England at New South Wales, Australia*

C. Wesley Cowan, *Curator of Archaeology, Cincinnati Museum of Natural History, Ohio*

Paul T. Craddock, *Department of Scientific Research, The British Museum, London, England*

Gary W. Crawford, *Professor of Anthropology, University of Toronto, Canada*

T. Patrick Culbert, *Professor of Anthropology, University of Arizona at Tucson*

Terence N. D'Altroy, *Associate Professor of Anthropology, Columbia University, New York, New York*

William S. Dancey, *Associate Professor of Anthropology, Ohio State University, Columbus*

Ken Dark, *Research Fellow, Clare Hall, University of Cambridge, England*

Janet Davidson, *Curator of Pacific Collections, Museum of New Zealand Te Papa Tongarewa, Wellington*

Hester A. Davis, *Professor of Anthropology, University of Arkansas, Fayetteville; State Archeologist, Arkansas Archeological Survey*

Alastair G. Dawson, *Reader in Quaternary Science, Coventry University, England*

Petra Day, *Fellow, Department of Geography, University of Reading, England*

Frans De Corte, *Research Director, Belgian National Fund for Scientific Research; Guest Professor, Institute for Nuclear Sciences, University of Gent, Belgium*

H. J. Deacon, *Professor of Archaeology, University of Stellenbosch, Matieland, South Africa*

Jeffrey S. Dean, *Professor of Dendrochronology, University of Arizona, Tucson*

Christopher R. DeCorse, *Assistant Professor of Anthropology, Syracuse University, Syracuse, New York*

Paola Demattè, *Assistant Curator, Los Angeles County Natural History Museum, Los Angeles, California*

D. Bruce Dickson, Jr., *Professor of Anthropology and Archaeology, Texas A & M University, College Station*

Richard A. Diehl, *Professor of Anthropology, University of Alabama, Tuscaloosa*

Tom D. Dillehay, *Professor of Anthropology, University of Kentucky, Lexington*

Marcia-Anne Dobres, *Research Associate, Archaeological Research Facility, Department of Anthropology, University of California at Berkeley*

Aidan Dodson, *Freelance Egyptologist, London, England*

Corinne Duhig, *Research Student, Faculty of Oriental Studies, Wolfson College, Cambridge, England*

Philip Duke, *Professor of Anthropology and Associate Director of the Center of Southwest Studies, Fort Lewis College, Durango, Colorado*

Don E. Dumond, *Professor Emeritus of Anthropology, University of Oregon, Eugene*

Stephen L. Dyson, *Professor of Classics, State University of New York at Buffalo*

Mark Edmonds, *Lecturer in Department of Archaeology and Prehistory, University of Sheffield, England*

George Eogan, *Professor of Archaeology, University College Dublin, Ireland*

Clark L. Erickson, *Associate Professor of Anthropology; Associate Curator University Museum, University of Pennsylvania, Philadelphia*

Charles R. Ewen, *Associate Professor of Anthropology, East Carolina University, Greenville, North Carolina*

Brian M. Fagan, *Professor of Anthropology, University of California at Santa Barbara*

Kenneth L. Feder, *Professor of Anthropology, Central Connecticut State University, New Britain*

Gary M. Feinman, *Professor of Anthropology, University of Wisconsin, Madison*

Paul R. Fish, *Curator of Archaeology, Arizona State Museum; Research Professor, Anthropology, University of Arizona, Tucson*

Kent V. Flannery, *James B. Griffin Professor of Anthropological Archaeology, University of Michigan, Ann Arbor*

Robert Foley, *University Lecturer in Biological Anthropology, University of Cambridge, England*

David Frankel, *Reader in Archaeology, La Trobe University, Bundoora, Australia*

David H. French, *Director (RTD), British Institute of Archaeology at Ankara, Turkey*

Elizabeth B. French, *Director, British School at Athens 1989–1994; Field Director and Publication Editor, Mycenae Excavations*

Edward Friedman, *Federal Preservation Officer, Bureau of Reclamation, Denver, Colorado*

Chris Gaffney, *Partner, Geophysical Surveys of Bradford, England*

Janine Gasco, *Research Associate, Institute for Archaeology, University of California at Los Angeles*

Yan Ge, *Curatorial Assistant, East Asian Art, Philadelphia Museum of Art, Pennsylvania*

Joan M. Gero, *Associate Professor of Anthropology, University of South Carolina at Columbia*

Egon Gersbach, *Assistant Professor Emeritus of Archaeology, Institut für Ur- und Frühgeschichte der Universität Tübingen, Germany*

Guy Gibbon, *Professor of Anthropology, University of Minnesota, Minneapolis*

Jon L. Gibson, *Professor of Anthropology, University of Southwestern Louisiana at Lafayette*

Douglas R. Givens, *Professor of Anthropology, St. Louis Community College, Meramec, Missouri*

William D. Glanzman, *Instructor, Department of Classical, Near Eastern, and Religious Studies, University of British Columbia, Vancouver, Canada*

Ogden Goelet, *Assistant Professor of Egyptian Language and Literature, New York University, New York*

Lynne Goldstein, *Professor and Chair of Anthropology, University of Wisconsin, Milwaukee*

Jack Golson, *Professor Emeritus of Prehistory, Australian National University at Canberra*

Albert C. Goodyear, *Associate Director for Research, South Carolina Institute of Archaeology and Anthropology, University of South Carolina, Columbia*

Paul Gorecki, *Senior Lecturer in Anthropology and Archaeology, James Cook University, Townsville, Australia*

Richard A. Gould, *Professor of Anthropology, Brown University, Providence, Rhode Island*

John A. J. Gowlett, *Reader in Archaeology, University of Liverpool, England*

David F. Graf, *Professor of Ancient History, University of Miami, Coral Gables, Florida*

Michael W. Graves, *Professor of Anthropology, University of Hawaii, Manoa*

Roger C. Green, *Emeritus Professor in Prehistory, University of Auckland, New Zealand*

Joseph A. Greene, *Assistant Director, Semitic Museum, Harvard University, Cambridge, Massachusetts*

Timothy E. Gregory, *Professor of History, Ohio State University, Columbus*

James Greig, *English Heritage Contractor, Archaeobotany, Birmingham University, England*

David C. Grove, *Professor of Anthropology and Jubilee Professor of Liberal Arts and Sciences, University of Illinois at Urbana-Champaign*

Jonathan Haas, *MacArthur Curator of North American Anthropology, The Field Museum, Chicago, Illinois*

Erika Hagelberg, *Lecturer in Molecular Anthropology, University of Cambridge, England*

Martin Hall, *Professor of Historical Archaeology, University of Cape Town, South Africa*

Richard A. Hall, *Deputy Director, York Archaeological Trust for Education and Research, York, England*

Donny L. Hamilton, *Associate Professor of Anthropology; Head, Nautical Archaeology Program, Texas A & M University at College Station*

Sheila Hamilton-Dyer, *Independent scholar, Southampton, England*

Anthony F. Harding, *Professor of Archaeology, University of Durham, England*

Edward Cecil Harris, *Director, Bermuda Maritime Museum, Bermuda*

Elvin Hatch, *Professor of Anthropology, University of California at Santa Barbara*

Joyce L. Haynes, *Resident Associate, Department of Ancient Egyptian, Nubian and Near Eastern Art, The Museum of Fine Arts, Boston, Massachusetts*

Lotte Hedeager, *Institute of Archaeology, University of Lünd, Sweden*

Thomas R. Hester, *Professor of Anthropology, University of Texas at Austin; Director, Texas Archaeological Research Laboratory, Austin*

Charles Higham, *Professor of Anthropology, University of Otago, New Zealand*

Catherine Hills, *Lecturer in Post-Roman Archaeology, University of Cambridge, England*

Peter Hiscock, *Senior Lecturer, Northern Territory University at Darwin, Australia*

A. Trevor Hodge, *Professor of Classics, Carleton University, Ottawa, Canada*

Jack L. Hofman, *Assistant Professor of Anthropology, University of Kansas at Lawrence*

Diane L. Holmes, *Honorary Research Fellow, Institute of Archaeology, University College London, England*

Frank L. Holt, *Associate Professor of Ancient History, University of Houston, Texas*

Mark Horton, *Lecturer in Archaeology, University of Bristol, England*

Dorothy Hosler, *Associate Professor of Archaeology and Ancient Technology, Department of Materials Science and Engineering, Massachusetts Institute of Technology, Cambridge, Massachusetts*

Kenneth Hudson, *Director, European Museum of the Year Award, Bristol, England*

Terry L. Hunt, *Associate Professor of Anthropology, University of Hawaii, Manoa*

John G. Hurst, *Former Assistant Chief Inspector of Ancient Monuments, English Heritage, London, England (retired)*

William D. Hyder, *Director, Social Sciences Computing, University of California at Santa Cruz*

Geoffrey Irwin, *Professor of Archaeology, University of Auckland, New Zealand*

William H. Isbell, *Professor of Anthropology, State University of New York at Binghamton*

Edward James, *Department of History, University of Reading, England*

Matthew Johnson, *Lecturer in Archaeology, University of Durham, England*

John Ellis Jones, *Senior Lecturer in Classical Studies, University of Wales, Bangor, North Wales*

John G. Jones, *Smithsonian Post-Doctoral Fellow, Smithsonian Tropical Research Institute, Balboa, Republic of Panama*

Lisa C. Kahn, *Visiting Assistant Professor of Art History, University of Oklahoma, Tulsa*

John Kantner, *Department of Anthropology, University of California at Santa Barbara*

David H. Kelley, *Professor Emeritus of Archaeology, University of Calgary, Alberta, Canada*

Douglas J. Kennett, *Department of Anthropology, University of California at Santa Barbara*

Susan Kent, *Associate Professor of Anthropology, Old Dominion University, Norfolk, Virginia*

Adam Kessler, *Curator, Los Angeles County Natural History Museum, Los Angeles, California*

John E. Kicza, *Professor of Latin American History, Washington State University, Pullman, Washington*

Thomas W. Killion, *Archaeologist, Department of Anthropology, National Museum of Natural History, Smithsonian Institution, Washington, D.C.*

Eleanor M. King, *College Archivist, Gwynedd-Mercy College, Gwynedd Valley, Pennsylvania; Department of Anthropology, University of Pennsylvania, Philadelphia*

Leo S. Klejn, *Professor of Archaeology and Anthropology, St. Petersburg State University, Russia*

Alexandra M. Ulana Klymyshyn, *Adjunct Professor of Anthropology, Multicultural Center, Central Michigan University at Mt. Pleasant*

Vernon James Knight, *Associate Professor of Anthropology, University of Alabama, Tuscaloosa*

Marc Kodack, *Archaeologist, U.S. Army Corps of Engineers, St. Louis, Missouri*

Ian Kuijt, *Visiting Lecturer in Anthropology, University of California at Berkeley*

Patricia M. Lambert, *Visiting Research Instructor, Department of Anthropology, University of North Carolina at Chapel Hill*

John R. Lanci, *Assistant Professor of Religious Studies, Stonehill College, North Easton, Massachusetts*

Eleanor Winsor Leach, *Professor of Classical Studies, Indiana University, Bloomington*

Stephen H. Lekson, *Senior Research Fellow, Crow Canyon Archaeological Center, Cortez, Colorado*

Robert D. Leonard, *Associate Professor of Anthropology, University of New Mexico, Albuquerque*

Mark P. Leone, *Professor of Anthropology, University of Maryland, College Park*

Marsha A. Levine, *Fellow of the McDonald Institute for Archaeological Research, Department of Archaeology, Cambridge University, England*

Thomas E. Levy, *Professor of Anthropology, University of California at San Diego*

David Lewis-Williams, *Professor of Cognitive Archaeology, Director, Rock Art Research Unit, University of the Witwatersrand, South Africa*

Katheryn M. Linduff, *Research Professor, University Center for International Studies, Department of Art History and Department of Anthropology, University of Pittsburgh, Pennsylvania*

Shelly Lowenkopf, *Adjunct Professor, Master's in Professional Writing Program, University of Southern California, Los Angeles*

Thomas F. Lynch, *Director, Brazos Valley Museum of Natural History, Bryan, Texas; Adjunct Professor, Catholic University of the North, Chile*

Kevin C. MacDonald, *Lecturer in African Archaeology, Institute of Archaeology, University College London, England*

Torsten Madsen, *Lecturer of Archaeology, University of Aarhus, Moesgaard, Denmark*

Jodi Magness, *Assistant Professor of Classical and Near Eastern Archaeology, Tufts University, Medford, Massachusetts*

J. P. Mallory, *Senior Lecturer, Department of Archaeology and Palaeoecology, Queen's University of Belfast, Northern Ireland*

Paul S. Martin, *Professor Emeritus of Geoscience, University of Arizona, Tucson*

Herbert D. G. Maschner, *Assistant Professor of Anthropology, University of Wisconsin, Madison*

Christopher Matthews, *Faculty Research Associate, Department of Anthropology, University of Maryland, College Park*

David J. Mattingly, *Reader in Roman Archaeology, School of Archaeological Studies, University of Leicester, England*

Patricia A. McAnany, *Associate Professor of Archaeology, Boston University, Massachusetts*

Emily McClung de Tapia, *Professor of Archaeology, Instituto de Investigaciones Antropologicas, Universidad Nacional Autónoma de Mexico*

Brian E. McConnell, *Research Investigator, Center for Old World Archaeology and Art, Brown University, Providence, Rhode Island*

Bonnie G. McEwan, *Director of Archaeology, San Luis Archaeological and Historic Site, Tallahassee, Florida*

Robert McGhee, *Curator of Arctic Archaeology, Canadian Museum of Civilization, Hull, Quebec*

Seán McGrail, *Professor of Maritime Archaeology, Institute of Archaeology, University of Oxford, England*

Randall H. McGuire, *Professor of Anthropology, State University of New York at Binghamton*

Roderick J. McIntosh, *Professor of Anthropology, Rice University, Houston, Texas*

Susan Keech McIntosh, *Professor of Anthropolgy, Rice University, Houston, Texas*

Paul Mellars, *Reader in Archaeology, University of Cambridge, England*

John L. Meloy, *Department of History, University of Chicago, Illinois*

David J. Meltzer, *Professor of Anthropology, Southern Methodist University, Dallas, Texas*

Phyllis Messenger, *Senior Education Archaeologist, Institute for Minnesota Archaeology, Minneapolis*

Karen Bescherer Metheny, *Department of Archaeology, Boston University, Massachusetts*

Demetrios Michaelides, *Associate Professor of Classical Archaeology, Archaeological Research Unit, University of Cyprus, Nicosia*

George Michaels, *Instructional Consultant, Office of Instructional Consultation, University of California at Santa Barbara*

George R. Milner, *Associate Professor of Anthropology, Pennsylvania State University, University Park*

Paul E. Minnis, *Associate Professor of Anthropology, University of Oklahoma, Norman*

Steven Mithen, *Lecturer in Archaeology, University of Reading, England*

Eduardo Matos Moctezuma, *Director, Professor of Archaeology, Museum del Templo Mayor, Mexico City, Mexico*

Christine E. Morris, *Leventis Lecturer in Greek History and Archaeology, Trinity College, Dublin, Ireland*

Ian Morris, *Professor of Classics and History, Stanford University, Palo Alto, California*

Michael E. Moseley, *Professor of Anthropology, University of Florida, Gainesville*

Ivan Munhamu Murambiwa, *Senior Curator, National Museums and Monuments of Zimbabwe, Masvingo*

Francis B. Musonda, *Director of Lusaka National Museum, Zambia*

Webber Ndoro, *Lecturer, Department of History, University of Zimbabwe, Harare*

Sarah Milledge Nelson, *Professor and Chair, Department of Anthropology, University of Denver, Colorado*

Mark Nesbitt, *Research Assistant, Institute of Archaeology, University College London, England*

Sarah W. Neusius, *Associate Professor of Anthropology, Indiana University of Pennsylvania, Indiana, Pennsylvania*

Deborah L. Nichols, *Associate Professor of Anthropology, Dartmouth College, Hanover, New Hampshire*

Susan A. Niles, *Associate Professor of Anthropology, Lafayette College, Easton, Pennsylvania*

Ivor Noël-Hume, *Foundation Archaeologist, Colonial Williamsburg (retired)*

Francisco S. Noelli, *Pontifícia Universidade Católica do Rio Grande do Sul, Porto Alegre, Brasil*

Jarl Nordbladh, *Assistant Professor, Head of Department of Archaeology, Göteborg University, Sweden*

M. O'Connor, *Associate Professor of Hebrew and Hebrew Bible, Union Theological Seminary, New York, New York*

John H. Oakley, *Chancellor Professor of Classical Studies, College of William and Mary, Williamsburg, Virginia*

John W. Olsen, *Professor of Anthropology, University of Arizona, Tuscon*

Charles E. Orser, Jr., *Professor of Anthropology, Illinois State University at Normal*

Robin Osborne, *University Lecturer in Ancient History and Fellow of Corpus Christi College, Oxford, England*

John K. Papadopoulos, *Associate Curator of Antiquities, The J. Paul Getty Museum, Santa Monica, California*

John Parkington, *Professor of Archaeology, University of Cape Town, South Africa*

Deborah M. Pearsall, *Associate Professor of Anthropology, University of Missouri, Columbia*

Michael Parker Pearson, *Lecturer in Archaeology, University of Sheffield, England*

Alan A. D. Peatfield, *College Lecturer in Greek Archaeology, University College Dublin, Ireland*

Steven R. Pendery, *Archaeologist, Cultural Resources Center, National Park Service, Lowell, Massachusetts*

Timothy K. Perttula, *Assistant Director for Antiquities Review, Department of Antiquities Protection, Austin, Texas*

David W. Phillipson, *Curator of the Museum of Archaeology and Anthropology, Reader in African Prehistory, Cambridge University, England*

Jean-Luc Pilon, *Curator of Ontario Archaeology; Archaeological Survey of Canada, Canadian Museum of Civilization*

Mark G. Plew, *Professor of Anthropology, Boise State University, Boise, Idaho*

John M. D. Pohl, *Research Associate, Fowler Museum of Cultural History, University of California at Los Angeles*

Gregory L. Possehl, *Curator of South Asian Archaeology and Professor of Anthropology, University of Pennsylvania, Philadelphia*

Marvin A. Powell, *Distinguished Research Professor of History, Northern Illinois University at DeKalb, Illinois*

William F. Powell, *Associate Professor, History of Chinese Religions, University of California at Santa Barbara*

Wm. Roger Powers, *Professor of Anthropology, University of Alaska, Fairbanks*

Shelia Pozorski, *Associate Professor of Anthropology, Department of Psychology and Anthropology, University of Texas–Pan American, Edinburg*

Thomas Pozorski, *Professor of Anthropology, Department of Psychology and Anthropology, University of Texas–Pan American, Edinburg*

Adrian Praetzellis, *Assistant Professor of Anthropology and Director of Anthropological Studies Center, Sonoma State University, Rohnert Park, California*

Gilbert Pwiti, *Lecturer in Archaeology, History Department, University of Zimbabwe*

K. Anne Pyburn, *Assistant Professor of Anthropology, Indiana University—Purdue University at Indianapolis*

Jeffrey Quilter, *Director of Pre-Columbian Studies and Curator of the Pre-Columbian Collection, Dumbarton Oaks, Washington, D.C.*

Barry Raftery, *Associate Professor of Celtic Archaeology, University College Dublin, Ireland*

Ann F. Ramenofsky, *Associate Professor of Archaeology, University of New Mexico, Albuquerque*

W. L. Rathje, *Professor of Anthropology, Director, The Garbage Project, University of Arizona, Tucson*

Marcus Rautman, *Associate Professor of Art History and Archaeology, University of Missouri at Columbia*

Jane M. Renfrew, *Vice President, Lucy Cavendish College, University of Cambridge, England*

Tim Reynolds, *Associate Lecturer, Department of Archaeology, University of Cambridge, England; Manager, Archaeological Field Unit, Cambridgeshire County Council, Cambridge, England*

Song Nai Rhee, *Adjunct Professor of Anthropology, Korean Prehistory, and Culture, University of Oregon, Eugene*

Robin Francis Rhodes, *Principal Investigator, The Greek Stone Architecture, Corinth Excavations, American School of Classical Studies at Athens, Greece*

Thom Richardson, *Keeper of Oriental Armour, The Royal Armouries, London, England*

Mario A. Rivera, *Adjunct Professor of Anthropology, Beloit College, Beloit, Wisconsin; Research Associate, Field Museum of Chicago, Illinois*

Derek A. Roe, *University Lecturer in Prehistoric Archaeology and Honorary Director of the Donald Baden-Powell Quaternary Research Centre, Oxford University, England*

Anna Curtenius Roosevelt, *Professor of Anthropology, University of Illinois at Chicago; Curator of Archaeology, Field Museum of Chicago, Illinois*

Mark J. Rose, *Managing Editor, Archaeology Magazine, New York, New York*

Steven A. Rosen, *Senior Lecturer, Archaeology Division, Department of Bible and Ancient Near East, Ben-Gurion University of the Negev, Beersheva, Israel*

Julie Ruiz-Sierra, *Independent scholar, Fremont, California*

Curtis Runnels, *Associate Professor of Archaeology, Department of Archaeology, Boston University, Massachusetts*

Leona Glidden Running, *Professor Emerita of Biblical Languages, Seminary, Andrews University, Berrien Springs, Missouri*

Jeremy A. Sabloff, *Charles K. Williams II Director, University of Pennsylvania Museum of Archaeology and Anthropology, Philadelphia*

Ross Samson, *Editor-in-Chief, Cruithne Press, Glasgow, Scotland*

Carleen D. Sanchez, *Department of Anthropology, University of California at Santa Barbara*

Daniel H. Sandweiss, *Assistant Professor of Anthropology and Quaternary Studies, University of Maine, Orono*

Chris Scarre, *Acting Assistant Director, The McDonald Institute for Archaeological Research, Cambridge, England*

Polly Schaafsma, *Research Associate, Museum of Indian Arts and Culture, Laboratory of Anthropology, Museum of New Mexico, Santa Fe*

Kathy D. Schick, *Associate Professor of Anthropology and Co-Director, CRAFT Research Center, Indiana University, Bloomington*

Robert Schick, *Professor of Islamic Archaeology, Institute of Islamic Archaeology at Al-Quds University, Jerusalem, Israel*

Michael Brian Schiffer, *Professor of Anthropology, University of Arizona, Tucson*

Sarah H. Schlanger, *Curator of Archaeology, Laboratory of Anthropology and Museum of Indian Arts and Culture, Museum of New Mexico, Santa Fe*

Denise Schmandt-Besserat, *Professor of Middle Eastern Studies, University of Texas at Austin*

Keith N. Schoville, *Professor of Hebrew and Semitic Studies, University of Wisconsin, Madison*

Katharina J. Schreiber, *Associate Professor of Anthropology, University of California at Santa Barbara*

Angela M. H. Schuster, *Associate Editor, Archaeology Magazine, New York, New York*

Robert L. Schuyler, *Associate Professor of Anthropology and Curator in Charge, History of Archaeology Section, University Museum, University of Pennsylvania, Philadelphia*

David A. Scott, *Head, Museum Services, GCI Museum Laboratory, J. Paul Getty Museum, Malibu, California*

Douglas D. Scott, *Chief, Rocky Mountain Research Division, Midwest Archaeological Center, National Park Service, Lincoln, Nebraska*

Elizabeth M. Scott, *Archaeological Consultant, Zooarch Research; Research Associate, Illinois State Museum*

Julie M. Segraves, *Executive Director, Asian Art Coordinating Council; Lecturer, University of Denver, Colorado*

H. A. Shapiro, *Professor of Classics, University of Canterbury, Christchurch, New Zealand*

Niall M. Sharples, *Inspector of Ancient Monuments, Historic Scotland, Edinburgh, Scotland*

Payson Sheets, *Professor of Anthropology, University of Colorado, Boulder*

Colin Shell, *Professor of Archaeology, University of Cambridge, England*

Andrew Sherratt, *Department of Antiquities, Ashmolean Museum, University of Oxford, England*

P. L. Shinnie, *Professor Emeritus of Archaeology, University of Calgary, Alberta, Canada*

Michael J. Shott, *Associate Professor of Anthropology, University of Northern Iowa, Cedar Falls*

Neil Asher Silberman, *Independent scholar, Branford, Connecticut*

Steven R. Simms, *Associate Professor of Anthropology, Utah State University, Logan*

Anthony Sinclair, *Lecturer in Archaeological Theory and Method, University of Liverpool, England*

Paul J. J. Sinclair, *Associate Professor of Archaeology, Uppsala University, Sweden*

Theresa A. Singleton, *Associate Curator, National Museum of Natural History, Smithsonian Institution, Washington, D.C.*

Carla M. Sinopoli, *Assistant Professor of Anthroplogy and Assistant Curator of Asian Archaeology, University of Michigan, Ann Arbor*

Andrew B. Smith, *Associate Professor of Archaeology, University of Cape Town, South Africa*

Michael E. Smith, *Associate Professor of Anthropology and Director, Institute for Mesoamerican Studies, State University of New York at Albany*

Dean R. Snow, *Professor of Anthropology, State University of New York at Albany*

Olga Soffer, *Professor of Anthropology, University of Illinois at Champaign-Urbana*

Marie Louise Stig Sørensen, *University Lecturer, Department of Archaeology, Cambridge University, England*

Donald B. Spanel, *Assistant Curator, Egyptian Department, The Brooklyn Museum, New York*

Brian A. Sparkes, *Professor of Classical Archaeology, University of Southampton, England*

Charles Stanish, *Associate Curator, Middle and South American Anthropology, Department of Anthropology, Field Museum of Natural History, Chicago, Illinois*

Mark D. Stansbury-O'Donnell, *Chair and Assistant Professor of Art History, University of St. Thomas, St. Paul, Minnesota*

Julie K. Stein, *Professor of Anthropology, Curator of Archaeology, University of Washington, Seattle*

Vincas P. Steponaitis, *Professor of Anthropology and Director, Research Laboratories of Anthropology, University of North Carolina, Chapel Hill*

Tammy Stone, *Assistant Professor of Anthropology, University of Colorado, Denver*

Rebecca Storey, *Associate Professor of Anthropology, University of Houston, Texas*

Andrew L. Sussman, *Department of Anthropology, University of New Mexico, Albuquerque*

John E. G. Sutton, *Director of the British Institute in Eastern Africa, Nairobi, Kenya*

James L. Swauger, *Curator Emeritus, Anthropology, Carnegie Museum of Natural History, Pittsburgh, Pennsylvania*

Joseph A. Tainter, *Project Leader, Cultural Heritage Research, Rocky Mountain Forest and Range Experiment Station, Albuquerque, New Mexico*

Ron E. Tappy, *Assistant Professor of Archaeology and Literature of Ancient Israel, Westmont College, Santa Barbara, California*

Maisie Taylor, *Wisbech, Cambridgeshire, England*

R. E. Taylor, *Professor of Anthropology, Director, Radiocarbon Laboratory, University of California at Riverside*

Tim Taylor, *Lecturer in Archaeology, Department of Archaeologica Sciences, University of Bradford, England*

Patrice Teltser, *Assistant Professor of Anthropology, Lehigh University, Bethlehem, Pennsylvania*

David Hurst Thomas, *Curator of Anthropology, American Museum of Natural History, New York, New York*

Michael W. Thompson, *Former Head of Ancient Monuments in Wales, Cardiff (retired)*

Christopher Tilley, *Reader in Material Culture, Department of Anthropology and Institute of Archaeology, University College London, England*

Malcolm Todd, *Professor of Archaeology, University of Exeter, England*

Theresa Lange Topic, *Professor of Anthropology, Trent University, Peterborough, Ontario, Canada*

Robin Torrence, *Australian Research Council Fellow, Australian Museum, Sydney*

Nicholas Toth, *Professor of Anthropology and Co-Director, CRAFT Research Center, Indiana University, Bloomington*

David A. Traill, *Professor of Classics, University of California at Davis*

Ruth Tringham, *Professor of Anthropology, University of California at Berkeley*

Erik Trinkaus, *Professor of Anthropology, University of New Mexico, Albuquerque*

Pierre-Jean Trombetta, *Ingénieur de Recherche, Ministère de la Culture, Charge de Cours Archéologie Urbaine, Université de Paris, France*

Anne P. Underhill, *Visiting Scholar, Fairbank Center for East Asian Research, Harvard University, Cambridge, Massachusetts*

Gary Urton, *Professor of Anthropology, Colgate University, Hamilton, New York*

Mary Van Buren, *Assistant Professor of Anthropology, Trinity University, San Antonio, Texas*

Peter Van den haute, *Senior Research Associate, Belgian National Fund for Scientific Research, University of Gent, Belgium*

Ulrich Veit, *Wissenschafflicher Assistent für Ur- und Frühgeschichte, Institut für Ur- und Frühgeschichte der Universität Tübingen, Germany*

Alan G. Vince, *Assistant Director, City of Lincoln Archaeology Unit, England*

Barbara Voorhies, *Professor and Chair, Department of Anthropology, University of Colorado at Boulder*

Michael J. Walsh, *Doctoral Student, Department of Religious Studies, University of California at Santa Barbara*

David Webster, *Professor of Anthropology, Department of Anthropology, Pennsylvania State University, University Park*

Colin M. Wells, *T. Frank Murchison Distinguished Professor of Classical Studies, Trinity University, San Antonio, Texas*

John W. Weymouth, *Professor Emeritus of Physics, University of Nebraska, Lincoln*

Robert Whallon, *Professor of Anthropology and Curator of the Museum of Anthropology, University of Michigan, Ann Arbor*

Donald S. Whitcomb, *Research Associate, The Oriental Institute, University of Chicago, Illinois*

Joyce C. White, *Research Specialist, Asian Section, University of Pennsylvania Museum, Philadelphia*

Tim D. White, *Professor of Integrative Biology, University of California at Berkeley*

David Whitehouse, *Director, The Corning Museum of Glass, Corning, New York*

William D. Whitt, *Independent scholar, Durham, North Carolina*

James D. Wilde, *Archaeologist, Headquarters Air Force Center for Environmental Excellence, Brooks Air Force Base, San Antonio, Texas*

Richard R. Wilk, *Associate Professor of Anthropology, Indiana University, Bloomington*

Bruce B. Williams, *Independent scholar, Chicago, Illinois*

W. H. Wills, *Associate Professor of Anthropology, University of New Mexico, Albuquerque*

R.J.A. Wilson, *Professor of Archaeology, University of Nottingham, England*

Samuel M. Wilson, *Associate Professor of Anthropology, University of Texas at Austin*

Bonnie L. Wisthoff, *Near Eastern Studies Department, University of Arizona, Tucson*

James C. Wright, *Professor of Classical and Near Eastern Archaeology, Bryn Mawr College, Pennsylvania*

Fikret K. Yegül, *Professor of the History of Architecture, University of California at Santa Barbara*

James A. Zeidler, *Research Associate, Deptartment of Anthropology, University of Illinois at Urbana-Champaign*

Larry J. Zimmerman, *Distinguished Regents Professor of Anthropology, University of South Dakota, Vermillion*

Mattanyah Zohar, *Researcher, Institute of Archaeology, Hebrew University, Jerusalem, Israel*

A

ACHEULEAN TRADITION. A major facies of the Old World Lower Paleolithic whose stone tool assemblages include certain large cutting tool types, especially hand axes and cleavers, the Acheulean Tradition takes its name from Saint-Acheul (Amiens, France), where it was first recognized during the nineteenth century. Acheulean sites are widely distributed in the Old World, from India in the east to Britain in the northwest, including all of Africa, the Near East, and Europe, especially the western half. This broad spatial distribution of the Acheulean Tradition (often simply called "the Acheulean") is matched by the long period of time over which it persists: The oldest assemblages date from about 1.4 million years ago, while the youngest are perhaps 100,000 years old. It is no longer believed, as formerly, that the whole of the Acheulean was produced by a single human population, which gradually migrated over much of the Old World. Rather, it is one version of a general level of technological achievement, which proved entirely adequate to support the needs of human hunter-gatherers in many regions, over what seems to us a surprisingly long period of time. If one examines in detail the Acheulean lithic assemblages of any one area, it is immediately apparent that there are substantial differences between them, and also changes and developments, as time passed, in the ways in which the tools were made. But even so, the general stability within the Acheulean Tradition remains remarkable, which is exactly why the term continues to be used.

Acheulean Stone Tools. Hand axes, widely regarded as the hallmark of the Acheulean, are large cutting tools, with various carefully fashioned planforms, the commonest being oval, pear-shaped, lanceolate, and triangular. The cutting edges, convex, concave, or straight, occupy much or all of their circumferences. Many hand axes also have a more or less sharp point, and some have a heavy hammerlike butt. They are usually worked bifacially, that is, both main faces have been flaked during the often symmetrical shaping of the implement. Cleavers are more axlike, with a broad transverse or oblique cutting edge as the main feature and less emphasis on cutting edges at the sides. Because hand axes and cleavers are so readily recognizable, they tend to dominate our perception of Acheulean stone tool kits, which in fact also contain a considerable range of other implements, made by retouching simple flakes of suitable size to make points, knives, and scrapers. Many flakes were also used without formal retouch.

As for technological changes through time in the Acheulean, it is broadly true that in the earliest industries the hand axes tend to be thicker and less symmetrical, made by the removal of relatively few flakes with a hard stone hammer. Later, they are often flat and elegantly shaped by the use of a softer hammer (of bone, antler, or wood), which could remove thin trimming flakes, leaving straight and regular cutting edges. Later Acheulean knappers also often show awareness of the "prepared core" flaking methods, such as Levallois technique, which characterize most Middle Paleolithic industries. There is, however, a wide technological range throughout the Acheulean everywhere, rather than a simple, inviolable progression from "crude" to "refined" industries. The implement types made, and the knapping techniques used, are always profoundly influenced by the types of rock locally obtainable, which varied in hardness, grain size, and manner of fracture. Flint and the purer forms of chert are easiest to work, but are not available everywhere. In sub-Saharan Africa, for example, quartzites and many kinds of volcanic rocks, especially fine-grained lavas, were frequently used.

Origins and Spread of the Acheulean. The genesis of the Acheulean Tradition certainly lies in sub-Saharan Africa. Its oldest-known occurrences include sites EF-HR and MLK in Middle Bed II at *Olduvai Gorge (Tanzania), Peninj (Tanzania, west of Lake Natron), and Konso-Gardula (southern Ethiopia); dating, mainly by the potassium-argon method, suggests a time range of 1.2 to 1.4 million years. They appear quite suddenly, after over a million years of the Oldowan Tradition, which had only simple tools made from pebbles and flakes. A major technological difference between the two was the Acheulean workers' ability to strike large flakes from boulders, as the blanks from which their hand axes and cleavers were fashioned, rather than depending on whole cobbles or pebbles. This enabled large, broad tools with relatively thin cutting edges to be regularly achieved. It may be no coincidence that Acheulean industries first appeared soon after the emergence of a new hominid type, *Homo erectus, larger in both stature and brain than *Homo habilis, widely regarded as the maker of the Oldowan.

Between about 1.8 and 1.2 million years ago, the first movement of humans out of sub-Saharan Africa occurred. The migration was begun by *H. erectus* humans, but as time passed, physical evolution and adaptation to new geographical situations brought these early people to a stage that we refer to generally as *Homo sapiens,* though within it there is considerable local variability: For example, in Europe the early *H. sapiens* people developed into the well-known Neanderthal population—a process already discernible a quarter of a million years ago and complete by about 120,000 B.P. Sub-Saharan Africa retained its own hominid population during and after the first human migration to other parts of the Old World, and it was apparently here that the development took place from *H. erectus,* via an early *H. sapiens* stage, to anatomically modern humans (*H. sapiens sapiens*), who, by around 100,000 years ago, had themselves spread out of Africa and reached the Near East.

The foregoing clearly implies that, over time, several

different human types must have made Acheulean industries. Some of the people involved in the first *Homo erectus* movement out of sub-Saharan Africa were certainly hand-axe makers, since stone tool manufacture in the mainstream Acheulean Tradition spread during the Early and Middle Pleistocene to North Africa and the Near East, into southern and western Europe, and eastward to the Indian subcontinent, though arrival dates are not clear everywhere. There was little penetration of Central or northern Asia at this time, and none of Australasia or the Americas. China and Southeast Asia, however, have many important Lower Paleolithic sites, but their stone artifacts do not belong to the Acheulean Tradition as described here. If the first humans to penetrate east of India were Acheuleans, they would have found few rocks suitable for hand-axe manufacture, and would have had to content themselves with stone tools of less sophisticated design to fulfill the same functions; other materials, such as bamboo, could also have provided highly effective points and cutting edges (though without surviving in the archaeological record). Accordingly, we need not assume that the earliest humans of the Far East had a separate ultimate origin from those who spread the Acheulean Tradition so widely elsewhere: Quite different artifact types could easily have become and remained the fashion in the Far East, especially since there is little sign of subsequent contact with Lower Paleolithic peoples away to the west, during the Middle Pleistocene.

The Acheulean, however, is rarely alone in any area where it occurs: There are often contemporary lithic assemblages from which the typical hand axes and cleavers are quite absent. Examples of this phenomenon include the Soan Tradition of India, the later stages of the Oldowan in East Africa, the flake-tool industries of central Europe, and the Clactonian in Britain. The explanation need not always be the same. Particular human groups must often have produced specialized tool kits to deal with the many different activities undertaken by hunter-gatherers, exploiting seasonal resources of food and raw materials over territorial ranges comprising very variable landscapes: The classic hand axes and cleavers will not always have been the most advantageous tools. But there also remains the possibility of distinct contemporary human groups, maintaining their own separate tool-making traditions, for whatever reasons, with room enough for all, in any given region.

Acheulean Settlements. Acheulean sites mainly occur as scatters of the typical stone artifacts, associated with the channels or floodplains of streams and rivers, or with lake margins. Early humans favored such locations for settlement, but the traces they left were liable to subsequent hydraulic disturbance. Structures, hearths, and fragile materials like wood or plant remains only rarely survive in association with the stone artifacts. At a few sites, such as *Torralba (Spain), Kalambo Falls (Zambia), and Gesher Benot Ya'aqov (Israel), waterlogging has preserved traces of worked wood. The remains of bone at many sites, sometimes with cut marks left by stone implements, make clear that the Acheulean people exploited the carcasses of large and small animals, whether as hunters or scavengers. They occasionally used caves or rock shelters as habitations or working places, a few examples being Montagu Cave and Cave of the Hearths (South Africa), Tabun Cave (Israel), Lazeret Cave (southern France), and Pontnewydd Cave (northern Wales). Sometimes they occupied coastal locations, as at Boxgrove (Sussex, England) or *Terra Amata (Nice, France), though there is little evidence for their ex-

ploiting marine fish or shellfish. Occasional finds on higher ground, for example, the chalk downlands of southern England, testify to their use of the land around and between their main campsites. No unequivocal evidence relating to Acheulean beliefs or ritual has yet been discovered.

The End of the Acheulean Tradition. The late Acheulean lasts into the Upper Pleistocene, but from around 180,000 B.P. the late Lower Paleolithic and earlier Middle Paleolithic overlap in time and to some extent blend together, as hand axes and cleavers lose importance in many areas, while specialized tools and projectile points, made by retouching specially struck flakes, increase. In the Micoquian industries of central Europe, the Jabrudian of the Near East, and the Fauresmith of southern Africa, varying examples of changing tool kits during the passage from a hand-ax-making Lower Paleolithic to a flake-tool-making Middle Paleolithic can be seen. Such terminology, however, really only reflects the efforts of archaeologists to label their current understanding of dynamic and varied processes of change in human circumstances, for which only parts of the imperishable segment of the evidence survive.

The final use of the term "Acheulean Tradition" is for the *Moustérien de tradition acheuléenne* (MTA), one of the many different Middle Paleolithic industries made by the Neanderthal population of Atlantic Europe during the early and middle stages of the last glaciation, about 75,000 to 35,000 years ago. It includes finely made bifacial hand axes, of cordiform and subtriangular shapes, whose inspiration may well come ultimately from the final pure Acheulean industries of the same region and whose makers must themselves have been *Neanderthals.

[See also PALEOLITHIC: LOWER AND MIDDLE PALEOLITHIC.]

■ Derek A. Roe, *The Lower and Middle Palaeolithic Periods in Britain* (1981). John J. Wymer, *The Palaeolithic Age* (1982). John A. J. Gowlett, *Ascent to Civilization: The Archaeology of Early Man* (1985). Richard G. Klein, *The Human Career: Human Biological and Cultural Origins* (1989).

Derek A. Roe

ADENA CULTURE. The term "Adena" refers to a burial ceremonial complex in the middle Ohio River area of mid-continent North America. It was discovered and named in 1901 when W. C. Mills of the Ohio State Museum excavated a 26-foot- (8-m-) tall burial mound on the Adena Estate of Governor Thomas Worthington in Chillicothe, Ohio. Differences in artifact style compared to the *Hopewell culture were noted leading to the identification of Adena as a new culture type. As currently defined, Adena consists of a pattern of burial in which the individual is placed in a shallow sealed grave or a log tomb, or is simply laid out on the surface and then covered with earth. Most burials are single, extended inhumations, although cremations and bundle burials are known, as are instances of multiple burial (two to three individuals). As the same spot was used for new burials, an Adena cemetery grew vertically. On the average, the burial mounds rarely exceed 17 feet (5 m) in height and more than half of the known mounds were less than 10 feet (3 m) high. Two are known, however, that reached roughly 65 feet (20 m) in height and must have grown over many generations. These are the Grave Creek Mound in West Virginia on the Ohio River and the Miamisburg Mound on a high hill overlooking Dayton on the Great Miami River. Adena burial ceremonialism originates during the late Early Woodland Period around 500 B.C. and lasts to A.D. 200 in the Middle Woodland.

Artifacts distinctive of Adena include a tubular pipe style, mica cutouts, copper bracelets and cutouts, incised tablets, stemmed projectile points, oval bifaces, concave and reel-shaped gorgets, and thick ceramic vessels decorated with incised geometric designs. At the type site, a tubular pipe was found that had been carved in the form of a dwarfed male who appears to be dressed in ritual garb.

Adena incised tablets contain stylized raptorial bird designs similar to those of the Hopewell and along with pipe smoking and a preference for copper, shell, and mica argue strongly that Adena is ancestral to Hopewell, at least within the middle Ohio Valley. The nonlocal materials, such as mica and copper, were obtained through a pan-regional exchange system that originated in the previous Late Archaic Period and became elaborated in the Middle Woodland. Several other Adena practices foreshadowed Hopewell developments. These include building circular earthworks and enclosing burials within a protective fence or shelter.

Adena spatial distribution was greater than that of Ohio Hopewell and temporally it continued alongside Hopewell around the edges of the middle and upper Ohio River. Two areas where the practice continued into the middle Woodland Period are The Plains in Athens County, Ohio, and northern Kentucky.

Adena ceremonial sites included circular earthworks with interior ditches. Most often these do not contain burial mounds and are considered nonmortuary ritual centers. In several instances, excavation has revealed a ring of post molds forming a circular structure, possibly a fence or screen, around the edge of the ditch. Circular structures like this have been found under mounds as well. Some burial mounds are surrounded by an enclosure and interior ditch, which may mean that under some circumstances the earthworks, also known as "sacred circles," became burial sites.

Burial included both cremation and inhumation. The initial graves in the earliest of Adena burial mounds were sealed subsurface pits. This practice gave way to aboveground, reusable tombs that housed the dead until someone else came along, at which time the previous occupant was bundled up and reinterred in another part of the mound area. In addition to graves, Adena burial mounds often contained caches of artifacts or raw materials, another practice that continued into Hopewell.

Little is known about Adena settlements. No evidence has been found of villages containing all or most of a community's households. What evidence exists consists of scattered, small household clusters suggesting that the settlement pattern was one of household dispersion. It was once thought that the circular post-mold patterns under mounds were the houses of important individuals who had been buried at home. Scholarly studies, however, cast doubt on this reconstruction and suggest specialized ritual facilities instead, leaving the nature of Adena domestic architecture unknown. Rock shelter deposits at this time contain remains of local plants that exhibit properties of domestication. Included are *Helianthus annuus* (sunflower), *Chenopodium berlandieri* (goosefoot), *Polygonum erectum* (erect knotweed), *Phalaris caroliniana* (maygrass), *Iva annua* (marsh elder), and *Hordeum pusillum* (little barley), which form the core of a suite of cultivated woodland plants sometimes referred to as the Eastern Agricultural Complex. The presence of cultivated plants speaks of at least a semblance of settlement permanence, although seasonal movement of the entire community is suspected in many local areas.

The archaeological record suggests that the Adena practiced a hunter-gatherer-horticultural subsistence strategy within small territories and lived in household groups of unknown stability. A large enclosure in northern Kentucky, the Peter Enclosure, may have served a special purpose, possibly related to galena processing, within the local area. Burials represent veneration of ancestors and acknowledgment of position of status within the community. Their distribution indicates the nature of intercommunity relationships just as intracemetery burial comparison reflects community structure. Most likely there was no permanent social hierarchy; leaders may have come forth when needed, but their role did not become institutionalized.

[*See also* NORTH AMERICA: THE EASTERN WOODLANDS AND THE SOUTH; NORTH AMERICA, ORIGINS OF FOOD PRODUCTION IN.]

■ Don Dragoo, *Mounds for the Dead* (1963). Robert Silverberg, *The Mound Builders* (1970). William S. Webb and Charles E. Snow, *The Adena People* (1974).

William S. Dancey

AEGEAN CULTURES

Overview
Cycladic Culture
Minoan Culture
Helladic (Mycenaean) Culture
Mycenae

OVERVIEW

The Bronze Age civilizations of the Aegean basin, rediscovered in the late nineteenth century by the pioneering excavations of Heinrich *Schliemann at *Troy and Mycenae and in the early twentieth century by Arthur *Evans at *Knossos, have offered scholars a unique new perspective on the economic and cultural developments in the region that preceded the rise of the classical Greek world. From the evidence of the Neolithic period at Knossos and other sites of the fifth and fourth millennia B.C. throughout the Aegean, archaeologists have been able to chart the main outlines of a system of agriculture, resource exploitation, and trade that provided the material basis for the later Minoan and Mycenaean palace economies.

In the sections that follow, the development of the Minoan civilization of Crete will be described, with its long-lasting impact on the artistic and religious traditions of the region. The rise of the subsequent Mycenaean culture, centered on the mainland, will also be traced in its putative connection to the world described in the Homeric epics, in its commercial expansion throughout the entire Eastern Mediterranean, and in its seemingly catastrophic break up in the twelfth century B.C.

From the time of their modern rediscovery, these archaeologically reconstructed Aegean cultures have formed an important field of investigation within classical studies. Yet in recent years, with the excavation of Aegean-style palaces in Egypt and Israel and with ever-widening evidence of the distribution of Minoan and Mycenaean trade goods, scholars have come to recognize that the international connections of the Aegean Bronze Age cultures were far deeper and more diverse than ever before imagined.

[*See also* MEDITERRANEAN WORLD: THE RISE OF AEGEAN AND MEDITERRANEAN STATES.]

Neil Asher Silberman

CYCLADIC CULTURE

Cycladic culture can be understood in several senses. At a general level it comprises the material remains of the societies that have inhabited the Cycladic islands in the southern Aegean from the period of their earliest settlement onward. As such, Cycladic culture can be informatively compared with that of other island clusters. In common with most Mediterranean islands the Cyclades are small in size, with a semiarid environment, and lie fairly close to other islands and adjacent mainland coasts. They are poor prospects in terms of agriculture, but they possess important metallic and obsidian resources and are rich in marbles. Geographical location and mineral resources have enabled them to participate in networks of maritime interaction and trade from an early date, and many aspects of Cycladic culture might be understood in terms of such networks, which bound together groups in the marginal conditions of these islands and provided the means by which islanders could gain in wealth and prestige by trading in many raw and manufactured materials. Such networks also acted as a conduit for the inflow and dissemination of exotic objects, practices, ideas, and people from beyond the island world. In a narrower sense, however, "Cycladic culture" is commonly taken to define the material associated with early inhabitants of the Cyclades, before the influence of external powers became a dominant factor. The periods of relevance here are the Aegean later Neolithic (ca. 5200–3200 B.C.) and Early Bronze Age (ca. 3200–2100 B.C.). Grave goods from cemeteries of the latter period have provided us with a range of objects in pottery, marble, and metal that are exhibited in museums in many countries, and which constitute the most familiar Cycladic material for the nonspecialist. From the aesthetic appreciation of this material, especially the well-known marble figurines, by the leaders of twentieth-century Modernism such as Picasso, Moore, and Brancusi, stems a third perception of Cycladic culture, one that emphasizes its products as works of art to be investigated and admired within the frameworks of connoisseurship and art history. The impact of this on the desirability of Cycladic figurines for collectors has led to the looting of Cycladic sites (and a faking of Cycladic material) that has devastated the archaeology of these islands and tragically impeded our understanding of early Cycladic life. Cycladic culture is therefore prone to multiple interpretations and has become a phenomenon of contested contemporary significance.

The current archaeological evidence suggests that the Cyclades were first settled at the end of the sixth millennium B.C., as part of the wider process of island colonization in the southern Aegean during the later Neolithic. Prior to this there is evidence of visits by special-purpose groups, in the form of finds of obsidian from sources on the Cycladic island of Melos in early contexts on the Greek mainland and in Crete. Neolithic settlers practiced a mixed farming economy, augmented by hunting and fishing, as illustrated by a small village excavated on Saliagos near Antiparos. Their material culture resembles that of the later Neolithic throughout much of the Aegean, with elaborate painted pottery and steatopygous figurines. Burials close to the settlement at Kephala on Kea constitute the first formal cemetery, presaging a major aspect of Cycladic culture in the Early Bronze Age. It is uncertain how completely and successfully these Neolithic groups settled the Cyclades, and several islands apparently remained empty until the Early Bronze Age. The transition to the Early Bronze Age therefore remains tenuous in many respects, although some continuous occupation is now fairly certain.

The general pattern of Early Bronze Age settlement is one of dispersed farming hamlets with nearby cemeteries of cist graves, each of which contained a single body or, less frequently, multiple inhumations. From these graves come most of the objects that we associate with Cycladic culture. These include marble anthropomorphic figurines and vessels, decorated pottery in forms such as the so-called sauceboats and frying pans, the latter often bearing a sun or canoe motif, and a variety of silver, copper, and lead ornaments, tools and, by the later phases, daggers and spearheads. It is the figurines that have attracted most attention from modern scholars. The majority represent females. In the earlier phase, violin-shaped and schematic forms predominate, with a shift toward more fully anthropomorphic types during the period, coalescing in the folded-arm form. Rarer are seated figures, harpists and other musicians, and a male hunter / warrior type. The sizes of the figurines range from examples a few centimeters tall to a limited number of large, almost life-sized examples. Although these figurines are now admired for the purity of their white marble, it is obvious from traces of red and blue paint that they were originally brightly colored, with renditions of the hair, eyes, bracelets, and necklaces, as well as facial designs indicating tattoos or body paint. Finds of pigment, grinders, and application tools in Cycladic graves leave no doubt that the human body itself comprised a field for decoration. Yet unfortunately, despite the prominence of the figurines in our perceptions of Cycladic culture, we have little clue as to their meaning, not least because the ravages of looters have ensured that 90 percent have no archaeological context. Most were found in graves, but several settlement finds have also been made. Although of fairly certain symbolic significance, there is as yet no secure evidence to suggest that they acted as the foci of religious practices, even though interpretations as divine images or votives are, as so often, popular among archaeologists and the public.

The exceptions to this pattern of small sites are a number of larger settlements whose focal location and wealth of finds argues that they acted as centers for maritime interaction, possibly not unlike the specialist island trading communities known from the recent past in Melanesia. Notable among these centers are Chalandriani on Syros and Ayia Irini on Kea. From the former comes a series of depictions of many-paddled war canoes incised on "frying pans," which are both among the earliest illustrations of seagoing vessels in the world and a testimony to the importance of control of the sea to Cycladic societies. Another spectacular but more enigmatic site is Dhaskaleio-Kavos on the tiny island of Keros. This has been devastated by looters, but the unprecedented number of finds of prestige material, notably in marble, argues for a prominent position within Cycladic society. Explanations in terms of a ritual site or an inter-island trading center have been put forward. It was centers such as these that assuredly organized the longer-range voyages beyond the Cyclades that are documented by finds of Cycladic material in other parts of the Aegean and even (although in most instances the evidence is ambivalent) by possible examples of Cycladic enclaves abroad. One motivation for such voyages is sure to have been a trade in Cycladic metals, although such business is liable to have been embedded in wider patterns of social interaction. It is in this sense interesting to note that the links between the Cyclades and western Anatolia that develop in the later Early Bronze Age are evidenced by both the adoption of new metallurgical traditions, not least the working of tin bronze instead of arsenical copper, and by the simultaneous spread of drinking vessel shapes associated with new social practices.

In the late third millennium B.C. this complex system collapsed during the period of transformation that accompanied the end of the Early Bronze Age, the rise of palatial civilizations on Crete, and the advent of long-range sailing ships that replaced the earlier canoe traffic. The extent of the hiatus in the Cyclades is hotly debated, but by the early second millennium B.C. the pattern of Cycladic culture and society had changed radically. For the remainder of the Bronze Age, people lived mainly in substantial nucleated villages or towns, often fortified and sometimes with a central building and communal shrine (Phylakopi on Melos is an example of the type). Material culture, although displaying many distinctive characteristics, was increasingly influenced by styles and practices originating in Minoan Crete or, later, the Mycenaean mainland. Minoan culture influence reached its height in the middle of the second millennium B.C., when a string of island towns on the shipping route linking Crete to the metal resources of Attica become so heavily "Minoanized" that the possibility of a Cretan element in the population cannot be ruled out. The most remarkable instance is Akrotiri on the island of Thera. Here, the Bronze Age town was buried in an eruption of the Thera volcano in the mid-second millennium B.C., preserving a major settlement that seems to have acted as a hub of trade in the southern Aegean, with links also to the Levant. Although only a tiny percentage of this unique site has been excavated so far, the finds of astonishingly well-preserved wall paintings depicting a wide range of ritual and other themes, some of a maritime nature, together with numerous other finds, demonstrate a firm generic link to Crete, although the probability that Akrotiri acted as a major center in its own right is strong. This period of alignment with Minoan and Mycenaean culture ended during the demise of Bronze Age civilization in the late second millennium B.C. Different patterns emerged in the first millennium B.C, notably the rise of Delos as a major religious center, but during this period the Cyclades again became increasingly dominated by external powers, culminating in the effective demise of independent island cultures through their incorporation into the wider structures of the classical Hellenistic and Roman worlds.

[See also MEDITERRANEAN TRADE; MEDITERRANEAN WORLD, articles on THE MEDITERRANEAN PRE-BRONZE AGE, THE RISE OF AEGEAN AND MEDITERRANEAN STATES.]

■ Colin Renfrew, The Emergence of Civilisation: The Cyclades and the Aegean in the Third Millennium BC (1972). Christos G. Doumas, Early Bronze Age Burial Habits in the Cyclades (1977). Christos G. Doumas, Thera: Pompeii of the Ancient Aegean (1983). R.L.N. Barber, The Cyclades in the Bronze Age (1987). Jack L. Davis, "Perspectives on the Prehistoric Cyclades: An Archaeological Introduction," in Early Cycladic Art in North American Collections, ed. P. Getz-Preziosi (1987), pp. 4–45. P. Getz-Preziosi, Sculptors of the Cyclades (1987). Cyprian Broodbank, "Ulysses without Sails: Trade, Distance, Knowledge and Power in the Early Cyclades," World Archaeology 24 (1993): 315–331. David Gill and Christopher Chippindale, "Material and Intellectual Consequences of Esteem for Cycladic Figures," American Journal of Archaeology 97 (1993): 601–659.

Cyprian Broodbank

MINOAN CULTURE

"Minoan" is the term applied to the prehistoric Bronze Age civilization of Crete, to distinguish it from the Greek Mainland (Helladic) and the islands (Cycladic). The name, derived from the mythical king Minos, was coined by Arthur *Evans, the excavator of the palace of *Knossos. Evans's comprehensive analysis of Minoan civilization, The Palace of Minos at Knossos, finished in 1935, laid the foundation from which further study of the Minoans progresses.

The island of Crete lies at the center of the East Mediterranean, strategically located to absorb influences from Egypt, the Near East, and Europe. The Cretan terrain is mountainous, with limited fertile land; most cultivatable land is marginal. Crete has a typical Mediterranean ecology and its agricultural exploitation is dominated by the cereal-olive-vine triad.

The earliest human settlement of Crete was in the Aceramic Neolithic Period, around 6000 B.C., after which there was a long period of relative stability until the start of the Bronze Age, around 3000 B.C. The chronological parameters of the Bronze Age / Minoan Period are normally taken to be roughly 3000 to 1000 B.C., with key events (the foundation of Knossos 1900 B.C.; the eruption of Thera 1500 B.C.; the destruction of Knossos 1375 B.C.) given absolute dates through links with Egyptian objects dateable from the Egyptian calenders. Absolute chronology, however, is currently under review; thus the approximate, conventional dates given here.

More useful are the systems of relative chronology. Evans's framework was based on the fine details of ceramic typology, dividing the period into Early (EM), Middle (MM), and Late Minoan (LM), each further subdivided into I, II, and III. Though useful for stratigraphic dating, this system does not entirely reflect Minoan cultural development. The highpoint of Minoan civilization was a centralized palace-dominated state, and the Greek archaeologist Nikolas Platon therefore developed an alternative chronology: Prepalatial (EM I–MM I), Protopalatial (MM I–MM III), Neopalatial (MM III–LM II [LM IIIa at Knossos]), and Postpalatial (LM III).

The technological advances that mark the beginning of the Bronze Age are thought to have been brought to Crete by foreign migrants from the Troad area of Asia Minor—if new pottery styles and shapes are conclusive evidence. While Prepalatial material culture is sufficiently similar all over the island to justify the name Minoan, the degree of regional variation suggests that the society was divided into a series of small politically and economically independent units. The evidence of EM settlements is sparse. Excavated sites such as Vasilike, Myrtos (Phournou Koryphi), and Debla are small, with crudely built rough-stone structures. The material provides little evidence for social hierarchy or an organized economic structure.

The contemporary tombs, by contrast, were clearly the main focus for conspicuous material consumption. The tholos (circular) tombs of the Mesara (south Crete) and the rectangular "house-tombs" of central and east Crete were stone-built, the more elaborate incorporating cut masonry. The earliest examples were single-chamber structures, where the dead were laid with their offerings. The later tombs were more elaborate, with additional rooms used as ossuaries and for storage. The multiple burials reveal that the tombs were reused over many generations, probably by kinship groups.

The offerings with the dead vary from personal possessions (weapons, jewelry, and toiletry implements) to ritual vases and even cult images in the form of vessel figurines. The fineness of many artifacts, the use of precious materials such as imported gold, and bone and ivory seals suggest a developing economic infrastructure, controlled by an emerging hierarchy, at least from EM II. This is further indicated by some burials, for example at Mochlos and Gournia, where the elite tombs form a cemetery separate from the poorer tombs.

The pace of cultural progress accelerated until the emergence of the palaces in MM Ib. The canonical form of the Minoan palace, an agglomerative structure around a central court, with a second court to the west, was established at the three palaces of Knossos, Phaistos, and Mallia. Though the details of their Protopalatial arrangements are obscured by later constructions, the palaces were already controlling fully developed centralized states, economically linked, though politically independent. Easily identifiable are storage rooms (magazines), lined with enormous pithoi (storage jars), where the palaces stored huge reserves of surplus agricultural produce. They also supported specialist craftsmen, working in gold and faience, and producing the fine, polychrome "Kamares" pottery which defines the MM period. The existence of an administrative system is suggested by stone seals and clay sealings, where elaborate designs are accompanied by a hieroglyphic script, still undeciphered, but including pictograms, phonetic symbols, and numerals.

The Protopalatial Period ended with an earthquake (MM III) which devastated Crete. The succeeding Neopalatial Period is the zenith of Minoan civilization—the Minoans rebuilt their palaces and society on an even larger and richer scale.

The palaces continued the process of economic centralization. Control of the countryside and its resources was extended through a network of villas as subsidiary regional centers. Most villas have extensive storage magazines, and one, at Vathypetro, preserves a complete winepress. The larger of these villas, such as Ayia Triadha and Tylissos, emulate palatial architectural and decorative features to indicate their hierarchical status. Furthermore, at one preexisting coastal town, Zakro, a fourth palace was founded, probably under Knossian influence, to control the overseas trade. Other towns, like Gournia and Palaikastro, also built chieftains' "palaces" or aristocratic townhouses. The presence of recurring seal designs, and the development of a more sophisticated script, Linear A (also undeciphered), demonstrate the complex administrative system into which these sites were integrated.

During this period the Minoans developed extensive overseas contacts with Egypt, Cyprus, and the Near East. Within Greece the cultural dominance of Minoans meant their art was copied and adapted by the island (e.g., Thera and Melos) and mainland elites (e.g., Mycenae and Pylos).

The palaces themselves were the main cultural foci. The monumental exterior masonry was matched by lavish internal decoration. Knossos, the leading palace, was decorated with an elaborate program of pictorial frescoes. This pictorial interest is manifest in other art forms such as carved stone vases, stone seals, and gold rings. Much of this material expresses the Minoans' sensitive aesthetic appreciation of Nature. The more complex scenes involving people are narrative and interactive, and provide evidence for Minoan religion.

From the ubiquity of religious material, cult images, and equipment (double axes and rhyta-vases for liquid offerings) as well as ritual scenes (depicting sacrifice or divine epiphany), it seems that religion played a pervasive role in Minoan society. As befitted an agrarian society, Minoan religion celebrated the fertility of Nature and its seasonal cycle. Ritual scenes are given a rural context, and the main communal shrines were in the countryside and associated with natural features, such as caves or springs. The largest group of rural sanctuaries were set on mountain peaks, appropriate symbols of the religious unity of the mountainous island. Scholars disagree whether Minoan religion was polytheist or monotheist, but the main deity was certainly female, in a variety of guises: the Minoan Goddess. In the social context, religion provided the ideology by which the Minoan elites sustained their position. Parts of the palaces were surmounted by architectural horns-of-consecration to mark sacred precincts. In the Neopalatial Period public access to palace shrines was restricted and the peak sanctuaries were centralized. This palatial control of religion was celebrated by religious iconography, the dominance of the urban palatial elite expressed in the symbolism of the rural, natural world.

The end of the Neopalatial Period (ca. 1450 B.C. / LM Ib) is marked by fire destructions at the main settlements, from which they did not recover. These destructions are suggestive of warfare, rather than natural disaster. Knossos, alone among the palaces, continued, though on a reduced scale. The introduction of new grave types (the "Warrior Graves"), non-Minoan vase forms, and, most significant, the development of Linear B script (deciphered as Mycenaean Greek), suggests a foreign, Mycenaean component among the Knossian ruling elite during its final phase. The final destruction of Knossos, in 1375 B.C. / LM IIIa, is attributed to a Minoan overthrow of the rule of "Mycenaean" Knossos.

Knossos was not reoccupied, except by squatters, and this was the end of Minoan palatial society. Nevertheless Postpalatial Minoan civilization still enjoyed several centuries of prosperity until the end of the Bronze Age around 1000 B.C. Artistic regionalism suggests an increasing political and economic fragmentation, the beginning of the process by which the later city-states emerged. Postpalatial Crete participated in the trading koine which the Mycenaeans imposed on the East Mediterranean. Kydonia in west Crete, for instance, was the source of Linear B-marked stirrup jars which were exported as oil containers throughout the Aegean area.

Crete did not escape the catastrophes at the end of the Bronze Age. Displaced Minoans and Mycenaeans were among the Sea Peoples who threatened Egypt; defeated in 1191 B.C. by pharaoh Rameses III, they settled and became the Philistines. On Crete, insecurity forced the Minoans to establish defensible refuge settlements in the mountains. The best-known site is Karphi, high in the Lasithi mountains of central Crete. When Karphi was abandoned around 1050 B.C., the people left behind the cult images, the goddesses-with-upraised-arms, which were the final manifestations of the Minoan Goddess. This was an appropriate symbolic end to Minoan civilization.

[See also MEDITERRANEAN WORLD, articles on THE MEDITERRANEAN PRE-BRONZE AGE, THE RISE OF AEGEAN AND MEDITERRANEAN STATES.]

Alan A. D. Peatfield

HELLADIC (MYCENAEAN) CULTURE

The Mycenaeans are commonly thought to have been a warlike society. They lived within fortified citadels on mainland Greece and conquered the supposedly peaceful Minoans, whose society was centered in palaces at places like *Knossos. Many believe that myths, such as that of Theseus and the Minotaur, and legends, such as those about the House of Atreus and the Trojan War, record actual events of the Mycenaean era. Some scholars think that Homer's poems provide a historical background to the Mycenaean civilization. Our archaeological knowledge of the Mycenaeans, however, though lacking the excitement of the epic poems, presents a different yet fascinating picture of this society.

The Mycenaeans originated on the mainland of Greece between approximately 1700 and 1600 B.C. By around 1400 B.C. their influence had extended throughout the islands of the Aegean Sea and along the coast of Asia Minor. Between roughly 1200 and 1100 B.C. the Mycenaeans disappeared, at the same time that the Hittite empire collapsed, cities in Cyprus and the Levant were destroyed, and Egypt repulsed foreign invaders.

The Mycenaeans largely inhabited the Peloponnese and central Greece. They also reached north to Thessaly, west to the Ionian islands, and east into the Aegean islands. At their greatest extent Mycenaean artifacts are distributed from the west coast of *Anatolia into its central plateau; throughout Cyprus; along the coastal margins of Syro-Palestine; along the Nile in Egypt and even into *Nubia; in southern Italy, *Sicily, and surrounding islands; and on Sardinia.

The rise of the New Palaces in Crete probably stimulated the emergence of a distinct Mycenaean society in Greece. This occurred around 1650 to 1600 B.C., the period known as Late Bronze Age I or Late Helladic I (LH I) in pottery terms. Between 1425 B.C. and 1365 B.C. (LH II and IIIA:1) Mycenaean society evolved into a state, recognized by the advent of palaces and a written script, Linear B. The palaces reached their acme during LH IIIA:2 and IIIB:1, roughly 1365 B.C. to 1300 B.C. Thenceforth the Mycenaeans went into a gradual decline that culminated in the destruction of their palaces around 1200 B.C. There followed approximately 150 years of recession in economy and in social and political organization.

The recognition of Mycenaean society began in the last half of the 19th century with the excavations of Heinrich *Schliemann at *Troy, Mycenae, Tiryns, and Orchomenos. Homer's *Iliad* and *Odyssey* stimulated his interest, and his excavations attempted to show the historicity of Homer by linking the legends in the epics to the archaeological remains. His successor, Wilhelm Dörpfeld, and many other scholars of Europe and North America (notably Chrestos Tsountas and Alan Wace at Mycenae and Carl Blegen at the palace of Pylos in Messenia) continued the tradition of Schliemann's work. Their discoveries, however, shifted attention from the supposed literary sources to the actual archaeological ones. Since the decipherment of Mycenaean Greek in the 1950s, a more detailed reconstruction of Mycenaean society has been possible. Thousands of documents written on clay tablets have turned up at many sites on the mainland of Greece and on Crete. In addition to this, increasing knowledge of events in the eastern Mediterranean has focused attention on the role of the Mycenaeans in the international arena of the late second millennium. Espe-cially important in this regard are Cyprus, Syro-Palestine, and Egypt.

Specific current issues in Mycenaean studies are the origins of the Mycenaeans; the evolution of their palatial society; the role of external forces, notably Minoan Crete, in that evolution; the reconstruction of Mycenaean religion; the nature of Mycenaean industry and trade; and the nature of Mycenaean political organization. The first three issues are largely archaeological whereas the others are equally epigraphical, since the texts provide abundant information about them.

There also continues to be a strong interest in the relationship between the archaeologically known Mycenaeans and the Greeks attested to in the Homeric epics. Some Greek scholars still insist that Homer's writing has a certain historical validity whereas many archaeologists view the issue in terms of evidence for cultural continuity between the Mycenaeans and the early Greeks. Much current scholarship focuses on post-palatial (ca. 1200–1050 B.C.) and Dark Age (ca. 1050–700 B.C.) Greece. Scholars are investigating the legacy of Mycenaean society in terms of physical remains (fortifications, buildings, and tombs) and religious and political institutions. This area of research is fundamental for those interested in the origins of historic Greek society.

Today scholars generally acknowledge that Mycenaean culture is primarily an amplification of that of the Middle Bronze Age on the mainland, known as Middle Helladic. A central problem in this regard is understanding the process of the arrival of Greek-speaking *Indo-Europeans. Traditionally these people have been thought to have entered Greece en masse at the end of the Early Bronze Age, but recent research suggests it is more likely that the spread of Indo-European–speaking peoples occurred piecemeal over the entire Middle Bronze Age. Aside from linguistic evidence, a minority of scholars argues that the archaeological traces of the horse and the chariot allow the likelihood that some highly mobile, well-armed Indo-European speakers arrived in Greece toward the end of the Middle Helladic Period. Most scholars claim the transformation of early Mycenaean society from a scatter of regional agricultural subsistence villages to a system of relatively uniform early states centered at fortified citadels, many with palaces and literate administrators, is the result of systemic changes in Middle Helladic society brought on by increasing contact with Crete and the islands during the New Palace Period. Whatever the ultimate truth of this problem, the basic assumption that the culture of the Middle Helladic Period evolves into Mycenaean is sound, for all artifact forms, from pottery to architecture, show continuities. The rest of this short account will consider the evidence and interpretation of Mycenaean society during three successive stages: Formative (Middle Bronze Age, ca. 2100–1700 B.C.); Transitional (Late MH through LH II, ca. 1700–1400 B.C.); and Palatial, divided into Early Palatial (LH IIIA, ca. 1400–1340 B.C.), Late Palatial (LH IIIB, ca. 1340–1185 B.C.), and Post-Palatial (LH IIIC, ca. 1185–1065 B.C.).

Formative. Survey work in several regions of mainland Greece has demonstrated a paucity of settlement during the Middle Bronze Age. Sites of the period are small hamlets or villages. Evidence of industry is negligible, though throughout this period some sites (e.g., Lerna) display continuous contact with the Cyclades and Crete. Excavation of settlements has disclosed remarkable coherence in pottery decorations and shapes, but it is important to stress the regional variation apparent in the overall picture of artifacts. The architecture, too, is generally uniform, with a preference for curvilinear (apsidal, oval, and round) structures. Linear and axial arrangements are common and, toward the end of the period, predominate in the form of a freestanding rectangular dwelling, dubbed the "megaron." Inhumation is the standard burial custom, but burial facilities vary from rectangular "cist" graves to mounds containing cists and jar burials. Multiple burials and cemeteries occur rarely, though increasingly at the end of the period. Some important Middle Bronze Age sites are Eutresis in Boeotia, Lerna and Argos in the Argolid, and Kolonna on Aigina.

Transitional. The transitional Middle Helladic / Late Helladic Period is marked by increasing contact with Crete, the islands of the Aegean and, indirectly, Europe. Settlements become more complex with larger and more numerous dwellings, simple fortifications at a few sites, and elaborate burials. Much of what is known of this era comes from graves, which display the evidence for a stratified society. The chamber tomb, a hillside burial carved into the rock, becomes common, used for consecutive interments over many generations. The wealthiest graves contain imported luxury artifacts of precious metals, decorative stone, faience, and ivory. Bronze vessels, implements, and weapons appear. The iconography and origin of a majority of these artifacts is Minoan, and it is clear that some Mycenaean chiefs established special relations with rulers in Crete. Major settlements begin to emerge at Mycenae, Tiryns, Argos, Dendra-Midea, Vapheio, Pylos, Orchomenos, and Thebes.

During this time many chiefs began to consolidate control over their surroundings. They commemorated their power by erecting monumental burial chambers, notably the tholos, a large underground stone-corbelled tomb. It is likely that toward the end of this period some of the chiefdoms were sufficiently strong to absorb neighboring ones. This led directly to the founding of the first palaces.

Early Palatial. The first palaces for which we have evidence were built at the beginning of the Late Helladic III Period, around 1400 (LH IIIA:1). This phase probably marks the introduction of an incipient state form of government, with an administrative system that utilized Linear B, a syllabic script derived from the Linear A of the Minoans to record economic, religious, and political activities. Industries began to specialize in textile and oil production, and markets were sought throughout the Aegean and beyond. An active trade in copper, silver, and lead, established earlier in the Late Bronze Age, flourished with the exploitation of Cypriot copper deposits. In this manner the Mycenaeans participated in a major international exchange system which linked the entire eastern Mediterranean. There is substantial evidence that Mycenaean goods were prized in Cyprus, the Levant, and Egypt, and there are possible references to the Mycenaeans in some Egyptian and Hittite documents. The shipwreck at Ulu Burun (Kaş) off the southwest coast of Turkey is an excellent example of the international nature of trade at this time.

In Crete, conflict brought the Mycenaean palace at Knossos to ruin around 1365 B.C., and on the mainland the rulers at the major palace centers began to expend great effort on fortifications. At the same time they engaged in an active systematic interpalatial trading network, recorded in transport vessels and clay sealings inscribed in Linear B. The palaces at Mycenae, Tiryns, Pylos, Orchomenos, and

presumably elsewhere where they are not preserved, were centered on a monumental megaron, the seat of authority of the ruler who was known as the *wanax*. At the center of the megaron was a monumental sacred hearth. The first palaces lacked recognizable shrines or temples.

Late Palatial. Toward the end of the fourteenth century (LH IIIB:1) and continuing for at least a century, major sites like Mycenae, Tiryns, Thebes, and Pylos witnessed massive projects with the rebuilding of their palaces, enlargement of their fortifications, and the diversion of water for agriculture, as at Gla in Boeotia.

The palaces were marked by uniformity in plan and construction techniques and were decorated with frescoes. By this time there had evolved a standard Mycenaean iconography and style, derived from the Minoan, but with Mycenaean subjects (such as combat and hunting scenes and fantastic animals) and forms (as exemplified in the shapes and decoration of pottery). Scripts of texts written at different sites are in the same language, and names and places document extensive geographic and economic interaction. Land tenure, a taxation structure, craft groups, administrative and religious officials, and names of deities readable as, for example, Zeus, Athena, Hephaistos, and Dionysos, are recorded in the texts. An established Mycenaean religion began to be evident in the production of figurines and small statuettes of women, men, and bulls in fresco scenes, and in the founding of humble shrine buildings at the edges of the citadels.

Post-Palatial. Perhaps as a result of disruptions in the trade in scarce resources such as metal ores, imbalances in the political geography of the Eastern Mediterranean world, and contradictions in the internal social order, the Mycenaean palace-states began to be unstable during the later thirteenth century. This situation culminated in the destruction of all the palaces in around 1200 B.C. There followed a general upheaval resulting in the establishment of new settlements in montane, coastal, and insular areas, while core areas were depopulated or abandoned. Life at the major palace centers continued, but without any signs of an administrative authority and with a greatly decreased level of craft activity. Linear B ceased to be written. Settlements seem to have returned to a village level of organization. This situation persisted throughout the Post-Palatial phase, marked by continuity in pottery production, settlement, and worship at primary centers, until around 1050 B.C. when most of the distinctive signs of Mycenaean culture disappeared. There ensued a long period of economic decline, marked by subsistence-level settlements, very little craft production, and general signs of depopulation until the late eighth century B.C. when the classical Greek *poleis* (city-states) began to emerge.

[*See also* MEDITERRANEAN WORLD, *articles on* THE MEDITERRANEAN PRE-BRONZE AGE, THE RISE OF AEGEAN AND MEDITERRANEAN STATES.]

■ Michael Ventris and John Chadwick, *Documents in Mycenaean Greek*, 2nd ed. (1973). John Chadwick, *The Mycenaean World* (1976). Katie Demakopoulou, *The Mycenaean World* (1988). Sara A. Immerwahr, *Aegean Painting in the Bronze Age* (1990). William A. McDonald and Carol G. Thomas, *Progress into the Past: The Rediscovery of Mycenean Civilization*, 2nd ed. (1990). Noel H. Gale, ed., *Bronze Age Trade in the Mediterranean*, Studies in Mediterranean Archaeology 90 (1991). Stuart W. Manning, *The Absolute Chronology of the Aegean Early Bronze Age: Archaeology, Radiocarbon, and History*, Monographs in Mediterranean Archaeology I (1993). Jeremy B. Rutter, "Review of Aegean Prehistory II: The Prepalatial Bronze Age of the Southern and Central Greek Mainland," *American Journal of Archaeology* 97 (1993): 745–797. Oliver Dickinson, *The Aegean Bronze Age* (1994).

James C. Wright

MYCENAE

Mycenae, a rocky acropolis with remains of an extensive surrounding town, lies in the northeast corner of the Argive Plain, 7 miles (11 km) from Argos and 9 miles (15 km) from the sea, among the foothills bridging the divide between arable land and pasture and guarding the routes and roads to Corinth. The adjacent territory is fertile; a copious spring 1,300 feet (400 m) away gives water to the acropolis. This site has always been known and commented on by travellers, ancient and more recent, as that described by Homer as Agamemnon's capital. The first major excavation was started by *Schliemann in 1874 following his work at *Troy and has been continued notably by Tsountas, by Wace, by Mylonas, and currently by Iakovides.

Occupation began in the Early Neolithic Period (6500 B.C.) but was of little import until the Late Middle Bronze Age (1650 B.C.) when Mycenae rose to power, overtaking nearby Argos as the principal center of the region. It gave its name to the distinctive Late Bronze Age of Greece, which is known as the Mycenaean Period. The warrior chieftains who dominated Mycenae at this time were buried in the Shaft Graves of the two Grave Circles. The earlier Grave Circle B, lying well outside the later walls, gives evidence of this increase of power and wealth; Grave Circle A, which was deliberately encircled by the later extension of the Citadel wall, contained six major graves of very great wealth. Early in the Late Bronze Age these chieftains adopted the built "tholos" tomb for their burials; six tholoi arranged in three groups, possibly relating to separate clan territories, date to 1550 to 1450 B.C. They also constructed a "palace" on the summit of the acropolis of which reconstruction during the fourteenth century destroyed all but a few traces. The populace was buried in groups of rock-cut chamber tombs (over two hundred documented) on the surrounding hills. Other major building of the fourteenth to thirteenth centuries included, as well as the Palace, the last three tholos tombs (again in the three groups) and a massive "Cyclopean" citadel wall in two phases, (the second including the famous Lion Gate).

Also to this period belong extensive areas of "houses" (residences, craft workshops, and storage facilities) inside the citadel and outside along the Panagia Ridge to the west and on the lower slopes of Mt. Aghios Elias to the north. Recent work has identified a Cult Center comprising possibly four distinct shrines with ancillary structures on the western slope within the Citadel; important cult paraphernalia were recovered. Late in the thirteenth century the citadel walls were extended eastward to incorporate protection for the water supply. The discovery of a small number of clay tablets inscribed in the Linear B script shows that the bureaucratic administration known from *Knossos and Pylos was in force here. Present archaeological evidence suggests that the site suffered a severe earthquake (accompanied in places by burning) ca. 1250 B.C.; not all areas were repaired and those that were suffered very heavy burning ca. 1200 B.C. At this point the palace-organized bureaucratic economy seems to have ceased, though parts of the citadel continued to be well inhabited until at least 1050 B.C.

Sporadic occupation is attested at Mycenae during the Protogeometric and Geometric Periods; in the Archaic Period a temple was built on the summit (of doubtful dedication) and there is considerable evidence of other cult activity, probably connected with local heroes. During the Persian invasion of Greece (480 B.C.), the town sent a contingent to fight at Thermopylae and at Plataea; some ten years later (ca. 468 B.C.) it was captured by Argos, who disabled the fortifications. In Hellenistic times Mycenae was revived by Argos as a "koma," or fortified settlement; the citadel walls were repaired, the lower town enclosed by a wall, the temple rebuilt, a theater constructed, and extensive workshops (possibly for the wool trade) put into use. This town gradually declined and by the time Pausanias wrote his guidebook to Greece (second century A.D.) the main site was deserted.

Mycenae is only one of at least five fortified Late Bronze Age citadels in the Argive plain. It is generally considered to have been the capital of Mycenaean Greece, largely because of Homer's description. Agamemnon, King of Mycenae, was overall leader of the Greek forces in the expedition against Troy (as recounted in the *Iliad* by Homer). The archaeological evidence confirms that the site is atypical in wealth and influence by the contents of the Shaft Graves, the number of Tholos Tombs, the level of craft production, the presence of stone sculpture, and its central place in networks both of trade and of roads and bridges. The relation of Mycenae to the other citadels is not clear, however, and the site hierarchy of the region and of Late Bronze Age Greece as a whole is complex.

[*See also* MEDITERRANEAN WORLD: THE RISE OF AEGEAN AND MEDITERRANEAN STATES.]

■ Heinrich Schliemann, *Mycenae* (1878). Christos Tsountas and J. Irving Manatt, *The Mycenaean Age* (1897, rep. 1969). Alan J. B. Wace, *Mycenae, an Archaeological History and Guide* (1949). George E. Mylonas, *Mycenae and the Mycenaean Age* (1966). Spiridon Iavokides, "The Present State of Research at the Citadel of Mycenae," *Bulletin of the Institute of Archaeology*, 14 (1977): 99–141. William D. Taylour, Elizabeth B. French, Kenneth A. Wardle, *Well Built Mycenae, the Helleno-British Excavations within the Citadel at Mycenae 1959–69; Fascicule 1: The Excavations* (1981).

Elizabeth B. French

AFAR. The lowland area of eastern Ethiopia is called the Afar Triangle, or Afar Depression. Named after the people living there, the area today is an equatorial desert of approximately 80,000 square miles (200,000 sq km). Not worked as intensively or for as long as other regions, the Afar has produced some of Africa's most important early hominid remains. Most discoveries have been made at Hadar and in the Middle Awash.

The first geological reconnaissance of the Middle Awash was in 1938, but French geologist Maurice Taieb discovered the paleoanthropological potential of the Afar in the late 1960s. In 1971 and 1972, Taieb was joined by Donald Johanson, Yves Coppens, and Jon Kalb in an exploratory survey in an area of the Afar known as Hadar, just north of the Middle Awash. Radiometric dating and biochronology in the Hadar Formation indicates that its hominid fossils span the period ca. 2.9 to 3.4 million years ago.

By 1977 nearly six thousand fossils representing eighty-seven species were recovered at Hadar. In November 1974, Don Johanson and Tom Gray discovered the partial skeleton of a small hominid, which they nicknamed "Lucy" after the Beatles' song "Lucy in the Sky with Diamonds." The following year Locality 333 yielded hundreds of hominid fragments derived from at least thirteen hominid individuals, including children.

In 1978, Johanson, Tim White, and Yves Coppens named the Hadar fossils *Australopithecus afarensis*. According to Johanson and White, this bipedal species was the common ancestor to all later hominids. Their functional and phylogenetic interpretations were, and still are, controversial. Work resumed in 1990 and is ongoing. Many new hominid fossils have been discovered.

The Hadar deposits were searched for archaeological remains. No stone tools were found in the area despite the abundant hominid remains. In 1976 and 1977, however, Qldowan tools were recovered in situ from an excavation by Jack Harris in the West Gona area, west of the main hominid-bearing Hadar succession. These tools are stratigraphically above and therefore younger than the youngest *Australopithecus afarensis* fossils. The tools are estimated to date to 2.6 million years ago, making them among the oldest on earth.

The Middle Awash study area lies south of Hadar along both eastern and western sides of the Awash River. Jon Kalb surveyed the Middle Awash until 1978, and his team recovered a massive Middle Pleistocene hominid cranium from Bodo. Further study of this late *Homo erectus* revealed cutmarks made by stone tools when the bone was fresh. In 1981 and in the early 1990s, Middle Awash research was conducted by a team led by Desmond Clark and Tim White. Discoveries made in 1992 and 1993 in the Aramis catchment of the Middle Awash led to the description of the earliest known hominid genus and species, *Ardipithecus ramidus*, dating to ca. 4.4 million years. The Middle Awash team followed this with the recovery of a partial skeleton of an adult individual of this species at the same site in 1994. Geological and paleontological work at Aramis has established tight chronological control and detailed knowledge of the Aramis paleoenvironment. This work has shown that *Ardipithecus ramidus* occupied a wooded rather than an open savanna habitat.

Middle Awash research is proceeding on several younger sites. In addition to Aramis, some of the more important sites and the hominid fossils found in them include: Maka (*Australopithecus afarensis*), Matabaietu (early *Homo*), Bouri (*Homo erectus*), and Bodo (advanced *Homo erectus*). Archaeological remains are found at most of the sites younger than two million years. These occurrences include early and late Acheulean assemblages as well as abundant Middle Stone Age artifacts at Aduma.

[*See also* AUSTRALOPITHECUS AND HOMO HABILIS; HUMAN EVOLUTION: THE ARCHAEOLOGY OF HUMAN ORIGINS.]

■ Donald C. Johanson, Maurice Taieb, and Yves Coppens, "Pliocene Hominids from the Hadar Formation, Ethiopia (1973–1977): Stratigraphic, Chronologic and Paleoenvironmental Contexts, with Notes on Hominid Morphology," *American Journal of Physical Anthropology* 57 (1982): 373–402. Jon E. Kalb, et al., "Fossil Mammals and Artefacts from the Middle Awash Valley, Ethiopia," *Nature* 298 (1982): 25–29. J. Desmond Clark, et al., "Paleoanthropological Discoveries in the Middle Awash Valley, Ethiopia," *Nature* 307 (1984): 423–428. Tim D. White et al., "*Australopithecus ramidus*, A New Species of Early Hominid from Aramis, Ethiopia," *Nature* 371 (1994): 306–312.

Tim D. White

AFRICA

INTRODUCTION

Victorian biologist Charles *Darwin pointed to Africa as the cradle of humankind, because the closest primate relatives of humans lived there. A century and a half of intensive palaeoanthropological research has shown he was right. The archaeological record of human activity is longer in tropical Africa than anywhere else in the world, extending back more than 2.5 million years. At present, the evidence for very early human evolution comes from eastern and southern Africa. Tim White describes the earliest Australopithecines and hominids from Ethiopia, Kenya, and Tanzania, an area where the increasingly diverse primate fossil record now extends back to 4 million years. Bipedalism dates back far earlier than the first appearance of stone artifacts and other protohuman culture, which first appear in archaeological sites like those at *Koobi Fora on the eastern shore of Lake Turkana in northern Kenya about 2.5 million years ago. These earliest sites are little more than transitory scatters of crude stone artifacts and fractured animal bones, located in dry stream beds, where there was shade and water. In this section, Nicholas Toth and Kathy Schick describe the stone technology behind this earliest of human tool kits, reconstructed from controlled experiments and replications of the first hominid stoneworking. Much of the evidence for very early human behavior comes from the now-classic sites in Bed I at *Olduvai Gorge in northern Tanzania, excavated by Louis and Mary *Leakey. Dating to just under 2 million years ago, these small artifact and bone scatters have been the subject of much controversy, but they are now regarded not as campsites but as places where early hominids cached meat and ate flesh scavenged from predator kills. The earliest human lifeway was much more apelike than human, with *Homo habilis*, and probably other hominids, relying heavily on both edible plants and scavenged game meat.

Homo erectus, a more advanced human, seems to have evolved about 1.8 million years ago in Africa from earlier hominid stock. By that time, too, some *Homo erectus* populations were living in Southeast Asia. So if these archaic humans evolved in Africa, they must have radiated rapidly out of Africa into other tropical regions. Leslie Aiello analyzes what we know about *Homo erectus* from a very sketchy fossil record and shows that these humans evolved slowly toward more modern forms over a period of more than 1.5 million years. Africa provides good evidence for animal butchery and the domestication of fire by *Homo erectus*, especially by about 750,000 years ago, with some experts arguing that fire originated on the East African savanna. To what extent *Homo erectus* relied on big-game hunting as opposed to scavenging for meat supplies is a matter for controversy. However, more diverse tool kits, some of them surprisingly lightweight, argue for improved hunting skills throughout Africa, at a time when humans were adapting to all manner of moist and arid tropical environments.

Most authorities also believe that anatomically modern humans evolved in Africa from a great diversity of archaic *Homo sapiens* forms, which in turn evolved from much earlier human populations. As Gunter Bräuer points out, two main hypotheses pit those who believe Africa was the

homeland of modern humans against those who argue for
the evolution of *Homo sapiens sapiens* in Africa, Asia, and
other regions more or less simultaneously. The evidence for
an African origin is in large part derived from mitochondrial DNA, but the fossil record from *Klasies River
Cave, Omo, and other locations provides at least some
evidence for anatomically modern humans as early, if not
earlier, than in the Near East. According to the out-of-Africa
hypothesis, modern humans evolved south of the Sahara,
then radiated northward across the desert at a time when it
was moister than today, appearing in the Near East at least
100,000 years ago. But, while the case for an African origin
for modern humans is compelling, the actual scientific evidence to support it is still inadequate.

During the last glaciation, the Sahara was extremely dry,
effectively isolating the African tropics from the Mediterranean. Despite this isolation, Africans developed sophisticated foraging cultures, adapted not only to grassland and
woodland savanna but to dense rain forest and semiarid
and desert conditions. We know little of these adaptations,
except from increasingly specialized tool kits, many of them
based on small stone flakes and blades. The ultimate roots
of the Stone Age foraging cultures of relatively recent millennia and centuries lie in the many late Stone Age groups
that flourished throughout tropical Africa for more than
10,000 years, as societies in the Near East, Europe, and Asia
were experimenting with agriculture and animal domestication. Some of these Late Stone Age groups, especially
the ancestors of the modern-day San of southern Africa, are
celebrated for their lively cave paintings and engravings,
which, as David Lewis-Williams tells us, have deep symbolic meaning.

As Steven Brandt and Andrew Smith recount, farming
and animal domestication came to tropical Africa very
late in prehistoric times. Cereal agriculture may have
been introduced into the Nile Valley by 6000 B.C., or crops
may have been domesticated there indigenously, but the
question is still unresolved. At the time, the Sahara Desert
was still moister than today, supporting scattered groups
of cattle herders by 5000 B.C. While ancient Egyptian
civilization was based on the annual floods of the Nile
River, the Saharans had no such dependable water supplies. As the desert dried up after 4000 B.C., they moved
to the margins of the desert, into the Nile Valley, and onto
the West African Sahel, where both cattle herding and the
cultivation of summer rainfall crops were well established
by 2000 B.C. About this time, some pastoralist groups also
penetrated on the East African highlands. But the spread
of agriculture and herding into tropical regions was inhibited by widespread tsetse fly belts and, perhaps, by the
lack of tough-edged axes for forest clearance. It was not
until after 1000 B.C. that the new economies spread from
northwest of the Zaire forest and from the southern
Sahara into eastern, central, and southern Africa. These
lifeway changes may have connected with the introduction of ironworking technology, which was well established in West Africa in the first millennium B.C., having
been introduced from either North Africa or the Nile
along desert trade routes. Once ironworking spread, especially through the Zaire forest, agriculture spread rapidly.
By A.D. 500, mixed farming cultures were well established
throughout tropical Africa, except in areas like the Kalahari Desert, where any form of farming or herding was
marginal. The rapid spread of farming may have also coincided, in general terms, with the spread of Bantu lan-

guages throughout tropical Africa from somewhere
northwest of the Zaire forest.

With the spread of food production throughout tropical
Africa, many general patterns of architecture; metal, wood,
and clay technology; and subsistence were established
south of the Sahara. These simple farming cultures achieved
great elaboration during the ensuing two millennia, largely
as a result of African responses to economic and political
opportunities outside the continent.

Ancient Egyptian civilization was one of the earliest and
most long-lived of all preindustrial civilizations. The Nile
Valley from the Mediterranean Sea to the First Cataract at
Aswan was unified under the pharaoh Narmer about 3100
B.C., in a state that had entirely indigenous roots, even if
some innovations, like writing, may have arrived in Egypt
from elsewhere in the Near East. There is no evidence that
ancient Egypt was a black African civilization, as some
scholars have claimed, even if there was constant interaction between the land of the pharaohs and Nubia, upstream
of the First Cataract, for more than 3,000 years. The Old
Kingdom pharaohs explored Nubian lands for their exotic
raw materials. When the Egyptian state passed through a
period of political weakness, Nubian leaders assumed
greater control and power over the vital trade routes that
passed through the Land of Kush. Middle and New Kingdom pharaohs conquered, garrisoned, then colonized
Kush, which survived as a powerful kingdom in its own
right after 1000 B.C., reaching the height of its power when
Nubian kings briefly ruled over Egypt in the seventh century B.C. After being driven from Egypt and chivied as far as
their Napatan homeland, the Nubian kings withdrew far
upstream to *Meroe, where they founded an important
kingdom at the crossroads between Saharan, Red Sea, and
Nile trade routes. Meroe became an important trade center,
especially with the domestication of the *camel in the late
first millennium B.C., also a major center for ironworking,
going into decline only in the fifth century B.C., when it was
overthrown by the kings of the rival kingdom Aksum in the
Ethiopian highlands. Like Meroe, Aksum prospered off the
Red Sea trade, emerging into prominence with the Mediterranean and India. It reached the height of its power in the
eleventh century B.C., after Christianity reached Ethiopia.

Two developments had a profound effect on the course
of tropical African history. The first was the domestication
of the camel, which opened up the trade routes of the
Sahara Desert. The second was the discovery by Greek
navigators about the time of Jesus of the Monsoon winds of
the Indian Ocean. These two developments brought Africa
into the orbit of much larger, and rapidly developing, global
economic systems, which were to link China, Southeast
Asia, Africa, and the Mediterranean and European worlds
into a giant web of interconnectedness.

Camels were not used for Saharan travel in the Roman
colonies in North Africa, although they may have penetrated south of the desert on several occasions. The Saharan
camel trade in gold, salt, and other commodities developed
in the first millennium A.D., especially after the spread of
Islam into North Africa. Indigenous West African kingdoms developed in the Saharan Sahel, at the southern extremities of the caravan routes, as local leaders exercised
close control over the mining and bartering of gold and
other tropical products. By A.D. 1000, Islam was widespread
in the Sahel, and the Sahara, the West African savanna, and
the forests to the south were linked by close economic ties.
Ghana, Mali, and Songhai in turn dominated the southern

end of the Saharan trade between 900 and 1500, during centuries when most of Europe's gold came from West Africa. Small kingdoms also developed in the West African forest, as the institution of kingship assumed great importance, associated as it was with long-distance trade, important ancestor cults, and indigenous terra-cotta and bronze sculpture and art traditions that flourished long after European contact in the late fifteenth century.

The monsoon winds linked not only the Red Sea and Arabia with India, but the Land of Zanj, on the East African coast, as well. During the first millennium, Arabian merchants visited the villages and towns of the coast regularly, trading gold, ivory, hut poles, and other products for textiles, porcelain, glass vessels, glass beads, and other exotic products. By 1100, a series of small ports and towns dotted the coast from present-day Somalia to Kilwa in the south. This was a cosmopolitan African civilization, with strong indigenous roots and close ties to Arabia. Its merchants obtained gold, ivory, and other interior products from kingdoms far from the coast, notably from the Shona chiefdoms between the Limpopo and Zambezi Rivers in southern Africa. Archaeological evidence shows how a series of powerful cattle kingdoms developed in this highland region, kingdoms that prospered from their connections with long-distance trade routes that linked them with the port of Sofala on the Mozambique coast. During the fifteenth century, *Great Zimbabwe, the seat of the Mutapa Dynasty, was at the height of its importance. Zimbabwe's imposing stone ruins are among Africa's most important archaeological sites, for the settlement was abandoned just before Europeans landed at the Cape of Good Hope.

African kingdoms developed out of indigenous roots, especially in areas where local leaders could control important resources such as grazing grass, salt sources, and copper or gold mines. A series of such chiefdoms flourished south of the Zaire forest in the Kisale region at the end of the first millennium. Richly adorned graves testify to the great economic power and far-flung trading contacts in the region. Cultural influences from these kingdoms spread far and wide over central and southern Africa before the fifteenth century.

A seminal event in African history came with the Portuguese capture of the important Islamic trading city of Ceuta in Morocco in 1415. In the 1430s and 1440s, Prince Henry the Navigator of Portugal sent ships on long journeys of exploration down the West African coast, trying to outflank the Islam-controlled Saharan gold routes. By 1480, the Portuguese were well established along the West African coast, while Vasco da Gama rounded the Cape of Good Hope, explored the East African towns, and crossed the Indian Ocean to Goa, opening up a southern route for the spice trade. European contact with Africa brought new economic opportunities for Africans, who took full advantage of them. These opportunities were manifested in the Atlantic slave trade, which began early in the Portuguese exploration of African coasts and reached a crescendo in the late eighteenth and early nineteenth centuries. Christopher DeCorse summarizes the emerging field of historical archaeology, which is documenting not only the European presence in Africa but some of the cultural interactions resulting from the slave trade and other developments.

[See also AFAR; AFRICA, ORIGINS OF FOOD PRODUCTION IN; ANTIQUITY OF HUMANKIND: ANTIQUITY OF HUMANKIND IN THE OLD WORLD; AUSTRALOPITHECUS AND HOMO HABILIS; EAST AFRICA; EGYPT AND AFRICA; HOLOCENE: HOLOCENE ENVIRONMENTS IN AFRICA; HUMAN EVOLUTION, *articles on* INTRODUCTION, FOSSIL EVIDENCE FOR HUMAN EVOLUTION, THE ARCHAEOLOGY OF HUMAN ORIGINS; HUMANS, MODERN: ORIGINS OF MODERN HUMANS; HUNTER-GATHERERS, AFRICAN; NUBIA; PASTORALISTS, AFRICAN; ROCK ART: ROCK ART OF SOUTHERN AFRICA; TRADE: AFRICAN; WEST AFRICAN FOREST KINGDOMS; WEST AFRICAN SAVANNA KINGDOMS; WEST AFRICAN SCULPTURE.]

Brian M. Fagan

PREHISTORY OF AFRICA

Africa occupies a unique place in world prehistory. Its archaeological sequence is of unparalleled length, for the simple reason that it was almost certainly in this continent that hominids and their distinctive behavior first evolved. In the sub-Saharan regions, because literacy has been restricted to the last few centuries, archaeology is a prime source of information about even comparatively recent periods. The great environmental diversity of the African continent, ranging from snow-capped glaciated mountains, to torrid rain forests, to arid deserts totally devoid of vegetation, provides an unparalleled opportunity to observe human ingenuity and adaptation through time. These environments have, in many instances, survived into modern times comparatively unmodified by large-scale industrialization or mechanized cultivation. Thus, continuing traditional African lifestyles can provide exceptionally informative guidelines to the interpretation of the archaeological record.

The significance of African archaeology extends far beyond Africa, yet it is hardly surprising that research in this field can rarely be a high priority for the developing nations of that continent. Despite their huge potential and importance, archaeological researches in many parts of Africa remain in their infancy. While intensive investigations have been carried out in several areas, major regions remain almost completely unexplored archaeologically.

Discoveries relating to the earliest periods of human activity have been made in eastern Africa (from Ethiopia southward to Tanzania and inland as far as the western branch of the Rift Valley) and in South Africa. Conditions in these areas have been favorable not only to the preservation of the earliest hominids' bones and of the stone tools that they made, but also to their subsequent exposure for discovery whether by natural erosion or by quarrying. The concentrations of archaeological discoveries thus do not necessarily mean that the earliest hominids were restricted to these particular parts of Africa, and it seems likely that their ranges in the east and in the south were continuous. However, environmental conditions in this general region were probably better suited to these creatures' lives and activities than those farther to the west.

Recognition in the archaeological record of the earliest evidence for humanity involves a degree of necessarily arbitrary definition. In evolving populations whose scanty representations in the fossil record display a wide range of physical variation, where does one choose to recognize the transition to human status? Given the difficulties in interpreting the simplest and most ancient traces of technology, which survive only in the form of unstandardized stone tools, archaeologists have increasingly sought evidence for human behavioral traits, such as social cooperation, planning, and food sharing. Recent research, especially in East Africa, has made some progress in elucidating these aspects of the past.

More intensive use of particular foodstuffs, both plant and animal, led eventually to the seasonal exploitation of different environments. Such, indeed, may have been the practice in very early times, but its clear attestation in the archaeological record requires the preservation of organic material such as is provided by cave deposits and water-logged occurrences. Study of prehistoric resource exploitation on a regional basis has enabled archaeologists to demonstrate shifting reliance on, for example, marine foods, plants, and land animals at differing seasons of the year.

In Africa, as in many other parts of the world, a tendency toward reduced tool size is apparent through all periods of prehistory before the invention of metallurgy. This led ultimately to the appearance in virtually all parts of the continent of *microliths—implements so tiny that they must have been used hafted, often several together, as composite tools. A variety of cutting and scraping tools were formed in this way, but most characteristic were pointed and barbed arrows; probably the bow and arrow was an African invention. These microliths, with their characteristic steep retouch, were widespread in Africa by about 20,000 B.P., but had first appeared in South Africa significantly earlier, perhaps as much as 100,000 years ago.

Two overall trends in stone-tool technology may thus be discerned through the immensely long duration of the African Stone Age. There was a progressive increase in specialization, indicated by the production of more different standardized tools for particular purposes; and there was a steadily more economical use of more carefully selected raw material.

The African microlithic industries were the work of people who were fully modern in the anatomical sense: *Homo sapiens sapiens*. Precisely where and when such people first evolved is not yet known, but it is significant that the oldest known fossils generally accepted as being of this type come from sites in South Africa, where they seem to date to about 100,000 years ago. These, if correctly attributed, are the most ancient remains of fully modern people anywhere in the world, and they support genetic evidence that, although controversial, suggests that it may have been in sub-Saharan Africa that *Homo sapiens sapiens* first developed.

As people became more adaptable and specialized, they were able to respond more readily to changing environmental opportunities. A particularly significant instance of this, and one which had far-reaching consequences, occurred in what is now the southern Sahara and in parts of East Africa during the period 10,000 to 6000 B.C. This period, which corresponded with the final retreat of the northern-hemisphere ice sheets and consequent worldwide adjustments in sea level, saw the establishment of lakes and rivers in a region that was previously (as again today) too arid to support regular human habitation. Beside these waters, previously nomadic groups established semipermanent habitations that were supported by the rich year-round supplies of fish that the lakes provided, supplemented by hunting for meat and by collecting wild vegetable foods. Sites of these settled peoples are characterized by the barbed-bone heads of the harpoons with which they fished and by the pottery of which their settled lifestyle enabled them to make use.

Between 5000 and 3000 B.C. the climate in the southern Sahara once again deteriorated. Sources of fish became depleted, many wild animal herds moved southward to better-watered regions, and plant foods were fewer and less reliable. It was at this general time that we find the first evidence that people in this part of Africa were taking steps to control the plants and animals upon which they depended—steps that led ultimately to the development of farming.

The extent to which the domestication of animals and plants was an indigenous African development, rather than one due to stimuli from outside that continent, has for long been a matter of controversy. The question may be clarified, if not finally resolved, by considering the different species involved and the geographical distributions of their wild forms. Of the continent's most important domestic animals, sheep and goats are not known to have occurred wild in Africa, and they were presumably introduced already domesticated from the Near East. Wild cattle, on the other hand, were common in much of the Sahara during the period of high lake levels noted above. In the case of plants, a markedly contrasting situation is apparent. Wheat and barley, probably of ultimate Near Eastern origin, were grown in North Africa and Ethiopia, but virtually all the cereals traditionally cultivated south of the Sahara are of species that occur wild in what is now the southern Sahara and the Sahel. Other crops are of highland Ethiopian origin or, as in the case of yams, from the northern fringes of the equatorial forest.

Convincing archaeological evidence for the initial stages of African farming is scanty, but what there is tends to confirm the geographical conclusions summarized above. Rock paintings in the Sahara, tentatively dated between 7000 and 3000 B.C., provide numerous representations of domestic cattle, indicating, among other features, the importance that was attached to body markings and the configuration of horns. Later art in the Nile Valley, and undated examples in the eastern Sahara, show that attempts were made to constrain or tame many other species, including giraffe and ostrich, that were never successfully domesticated. Bones of domestic cattle come from several sites, notably in Libya, Algeria, Niger, and Sudan, dated mostly the fifth or fourth millennia B.C. Firm data about the cultivation of plants are much more rarely available. Large numbers of heavily used grindstones on fourth-millennium-B.C. sites in the Sudanese Nile Valley probably indicate use of cereals, but actual remains of the grains themselves are rarely preserved, and the extent to which they were formally cultivated is still uncertain. However, by 1200 B.C., if not before, bulrush millet was intensively cultivated in the western Sahara of Mauritania.

The initial stages of African farming development thus almost certainly took place in the same general area as was occupied by the harpoon fishers, and at the time when these peoples' established lifestyle was subject to considerable stress through the lowering of water levels. It is easy to visualize how, in such circumstances, settled people would have exercised control over the herds of formerly wild cattle and begun to protect, to care for, and then to cultivate plant foods in order to maintain their supplies in the face of reduced availability of fish. Data are not yet available for Ethiopia and the forest fringes: we do not know whether farming began in these areas at the same general period as it did in the southern Sahara. It is, however, important to emphasize that, other than in a very restricted area of the

East African highlands, there is no evidence from any part of Africa south of the equator for the practice of any form of farming prior to the start of ironworking late in the last millennium B.C.

[*See also* AFRICA, ORIGINS OF FOOD PRODUCTION IN; HUMAN EVOLUTION: THE ARCHAEOLOGY OF HUMAN ORIGINS; HUMANS, MODERN: ORIGINS OF MODERN HUMANS.]

■ J. Desmond Clark, ed., *The Cambridge History of Africa, Vol. 1* (1982). J. Desmond Clark and Steven A. Brandt, eds., *From Hunters to Farmers: The Causes and Consequences of Food Production in Africa* (1984). David W. Phillipson, *African Archaeology* (1985; 2nd ed., 1993).

David W. Phillipson

EARLY IRON-AGE SETTLEMENT OF SUB-SAHARAN AFRICA

It is reasonable to conclude, although the archaeological evidence remains extremely scant, that during the last two thousand years B.C. the peoples of the northern savanna belt between the southern fringes of the Sahara Desert and the northern margin of the equatorial forest turned increasingly to settled life and farming as a prime means of subsistence. To the south of the forest, however, the hunter-gatherer lifestyle of previous millennia continued. There is no evidence whatsoever that cultivation or herding was practiced at this time in any part of Africa south of a line running from the lower Congo to the Serengeti Plain in what is now northern Tanzania: In this vast southern region settled villages were unknown and pottery is not represented in the artifact assemblages. By around 1000 to 500 B.C. there was thus a pronounced distinction between the northern and subequatorial zones of sub-Saharan Africa not only in the domestic economy and settlement pattern but also in material culture.

It is noteworthy that, unlike most other parts of the Old World, sub-Saharan Africa generally lacked a distinct "Bronze Age" when the softer metals could be worked but techniques of dealing with iron had not yet been developed. The only probable exceptions to this generalization are found in parts of Niger and Mauritania where there is evidence that copper tools may have been made during the middle centuries of the last millennium B.C. Claims for even earlier copper working in these regions are not now credited and it is no longer regarded as certain that copper has been known there for longer than iron.

It is in the savanna country north of the equatorial forest that, during the third quarter of the first millennium B.C., occurred the earliest working of iron in Africa south of the Sahara. The evidence for this comes primarily from the Jos Plateau of Nigeria, from sites that have also yielded the remarkable Nok terra-cotta sculptures. Further evidence for iron working more than two thousand years ago has been recovered around Lake Victoria, primarily on its western shore in northwestern Tanzania, and it may be that future research will show that early metallurgy was widespread between these two regions.

The precise chronology of these phenomena is hard to establish for two reasons: known fluctuations in levels of the radiocarbon on which dating largely depends, and the tendency for smelters to use dense heartwood as fuel for their furnaces rather than new growth, the date of which would more accurately reflect the age of the site. In both Nigeria and Tanzania the complex and sophisticated smelting technology shows little sign of local antecedents, and it has frequently been suggested that knowledge of how to smelt iron was introduced from more northerly areas, perhaps from the Carthaginian colonies of western Mediterranean Africa or via the Nile Valley. No clear evidence for such long-distance connection has, however, been cited, and recent research gives little support for a Nile Valley source of early East African metallurgy.

In the southern half of Africa the beginnings of farming and of metal working seem to have been broadly concurrent. Indeed, through most of the savanna country south and east of the equatorial forest there was a major discontinuity in cultural development during the first few centuries of the Christian era. In territory previously inhabited solely by stone-tool-using mobile hunter-gatherer peoples there were established villages of settled farmers—cultivators of plant foods and herders of domestic animals—who worked metals and made pottery, both artifact types that previously were unknown in these regions. The pottery of these early farming communities appears to belong to a common stylistic tradition, probably related to that of the early ironworkers in the Lake Victoria region. This stylistic uniformity and the apparent speed with which the new lifestyle was begun over an enormous area, together with its marked contrast with what had gone before, has led archaeologists to link this change to a rapid influx of new people.

Many scholars subscribe to the view that these newcomers may have been speakers of Bantu languages ancestral to those that are ubiquitous in the region today. The closely interrelated Bantu languages may be shown to be derived from a common ancestral tongue that was formerly spoken, perhaps some three thousand years ago, in the area that now comprises the borderland between Cameroon and eastern Nigeria. It is no longer believed that the spread of Bantu speech into more southerly latitudes need have occurred through a mass migration; rather the new language and lifestyle (if, indeed, they were linked) could have been introduced by relatively small numbers of migrants who dispersed rapidly through the southern savanna in search of grazing land and microenvironmental circumstances suitable for their cultivation practices.

Recent research suggests that herding peoples may have penetrated certain areas of subequatorial Africa somewhat earlier than was previously believed. The evidence for this comes primarily from the upper Zambezi valley in Zambia, and also from southwestern Zimbabwe, where domestic animals appear to have been kept as early as the third or second century B.C. It was probably from this source area that domestic sheep and knowledge of ceramic technology reached southwesternmost Africa around the beginning of the Christian era.

By about the third century A.D., farming peoples had established themselves alongside, and had begun gradually to absorb or to replace, the hunter-gatherer populations of most of southern Africa wherever environmental conditions were suitable for the cultivation of African cereal crops (excluding, that is, the arid southwestern regions and the extreme south where a summer rainfall pattern prevails). In few areas has archaeological research on this period been conducted on a scale adequate for illustrating details of the sites' structure or of the societies that they supported. We thus rarely know precisely how the newcomers settled or how they interacted with the earlier inhabitants, although both archaeological and linguistic studies suggest that interaction was prolonged and that the indigenes made a significant contribution to the farming cultures that arose in subequatorial Africa during the middle centuries of the first millennium A.D.

Archaeological research into these farming cultures has so far concentrated on pioneering studies of technology, distribution, chronology, and domestic economy. We know relatively little about the sociopolitical or belief systems that prevailed at this time. Attention should, however, be drawn to the remarkable series of life-sized terra-cotta sculptures of human heads from a village site of the fifth century A.D. at Lydenburg in the Transvaal. These heads share many technological and stylistic features with the contemporary domestic pottery, and one of them is surmounted by a figurine of a cow, perhaps suggesting that cattle already occupied a significant place, not only in the economy but also in the belief system of the site's inhabitants. If this proves to have been the case, it follows that the great and varied importance that is attached to cattle by several recent Bantu-speaking peoples of southeastern Africa represents a very ancient tradition.

[See also AFRICA, ORIGINS OF FOOD PRODUCTION IN; HUNTER GATHERERS, AFRICAN.]

■ J. D. Fage, ed., *The Cambridge History of Africa, Vol. 2* (1978). Christopher Ehret and Merrick Posnansky, eds., *The Archaeological and Linguistic Reconstruction of African History* (1982). David W. Phillipson, *African Archaeology* (1985; 2nd ed., 1993). Thurstan Shaw et al., eds., *The Archaeology of Africa* (1993).

David W. Phillipson

THE RISE OF KINGDOMS AND STATES IN AFRICA

Although many people considering African civilization would immediately think of Egypt, the overwhelming diversity and richness of subsequent sub-Saharan chiefdoms and states must truly claim pride of place in any discourse on the subject. Suffice it to note that the great civilization of *Egypt developed between Mediterranean and African spheres of influence out of a long tradition of incipient stratified social systems already boasting well-organized agro-pastoral economies, ceremonial architecture, and sailing craft (the Predynastic, 5500–3100 B.C.). Between 3100 and 331 B.C., Egyptian dynastics would profoundly influence socioeconomic developments in northeast Africa and southwest Asia, and forever alter the landscape of Egypt with some of the most impressive monuments known to humanity.

Northern Africa. In the third millennium B.C., a broad swath of cultures economically dominated by *pastoralism would stretch across the African Sahel, from modern Sudan to Mauritania. The small stone and earthen tumuli left in their wake attest to a degree of social ranking probably based on the accumulation of livestock and widely traded polished stone objects. In two places, environmental and external social factors crystallized these mobile societies into more sedentary and complex politics: Kerma and Dhar Tichitt.

Kerma, potentially the first Nubian state, prospered between the third and fourth cataracts of the Nile from ca. 2500 to 1500 B.C. During Kerma's earliest development, its cultural influences were undeniably sub-Saharan, manifested in round-hut dwellings and ceremonial structures as well as distinctive circular tumuli featuring livestock sacrifices. Over time, however, the cultural proximity of Egypt becomes increasingly visible in linear-walled, fired mud-brick architecture, more elaborate burial practices, and prestige goods imported from the lower Nile (Middle to Final Kerma, ca. 2050–1500 B.C.). Kerma's economy appears

to have been based upon external trade in ivory, diorite, and gold to the north, with its subsistence base founded upon pastoralism and an as yet unverified grain component. After the collapse of Kerma, other Nubian states would arise in the same region, most important those of Napata (ca. 900–300 B.C.) and *Meroe (ca. 300 B.C.–A.D. 350). All of these polities would appear to have been the result of indigenous responses to the proximity of Egyptian civilization to the north.

Meanwhile, far to the west, the first substantial masonry structures in Africa outside the Nile Valley were being built. At Dhar Tichitt and Dhar Oualata, in modern Mauritania, a pristine chiefdom developed (ca. 2000–800 B.C.) in a deteriorating environment where arable land and pasturage were at a premium. Remote sensing has revealed a four-tier settlement hierarchy, with the largest regional centers exceeding 220 acres (90 ha) in area. The evolution of Tichitt-Oualata society remains unclear, obscured by thin stratigraphy at deflated settlement sites, and competing hypotheses include long-term in situ development, rapid evolution, or immigration from elsewhere. The presence of large stone-walled corral areas and numerous granary foundations points to the importance of mixed farming; definite evidence demonstrates the existence of domestic millet, cattle, sheep, and goats. Inorganic wealth resided in the same objects valued by contemporary pastoral nomad cultures: carnelian and amazonite beads, polished bracelets of siltstone, and a plethora of small stone axes. Unfortunately, none of the region's many tumuli have yet been excavated. It would appear that the collapse of Tichitt-Oualata around 800 B.C. was brought about both by regional dessication and increasing harassment from Berber interlopers.

Trade Networks. During the first millennium B.C., the advent of *metallurgy added further impetus to the growth of complex societies south of the Sahara. Indeed, precious metals were to play a key role in international trade between West Africa and the Mediterranean world, and between East Africa and Asia throughout late first and early second millennia A.D. At a more regional level, iron and copper would play a crucial part as the source of both practical and prestige objects. Coupled with ivory and the slave trade, the control of metallurgical commodities supplanted mere subsistence as the power basis of African elites from the beginning of the first millennium A.D.

By the time Arab geographers began to write of West Africa in the eight century A.D., the empire of Ghana—described as a "land of gold"—was already in existence (Al-Fazari, *Bilad-as-Sudan*, 773). The origins of Ghana, and even its extent, remains unclear. The ruins of one of its capitals, Kumbi-Saleh, lie in southeastern Mauritania; yet the most substantive settlement clusters known from the first millennium A.D. rest within the bounds of the Middle Niger in the neighboring republic of Mali. Earlier scholarly thought placed Ghana as a puppet state founded by Arab traders, but recent research has emphasized the indigenous development of regional trade webs long before the Arab conquest of North Africa (ca. A.D. 750).

Undoubtedly, the Middle Niger's best-excavated sequence is that of Jenné-Jeno (250 B.C. to A.D. 1400). At this tell site, trade with adjoining regions in commodities such as copper, iron, and sandstone is in evidence by A.D. 500. Additionally, by A.D. 800, local craft specialization and a regional site hierarchy centered on Jenné-Jeno point to an urban status for the site. It must be stressed, however, that Jenné-Jeno is only one of many impressive settlements now known from the Middle Niger. The occupation of such sites continued through the time of Ghana's Islamic successor states, the empire of Mali (A.D. 1250–1600) and the empire of Songhai (A.D. 1375–1600). It is expected that future work will confirm the view that the heart of the empire of Ghana, like that of the Malinke empire of Mali, lay not in its trade entrepots in the Sahara but closer to the resource centers of the Middle Niger.

West Africa. During Jenné-Jeno's floruit, spectacular developments were also afoot in the West African forest. Although limited excavations have only begun to hint at the political organization of Nigerian societies during the late first millennium A.D., their richness and artistic expertise have been well demonstrated at the site of Igbo-Ukwu. From this site, an elaborate burial and a storehouse of regalia have been excavated, both holding superb brass castings made by the lost-wax method and thousands of glass trade beads. The presence of such wealth hints at a well-organized system of trade, craft specialists, and a wealthy elite, but we know little of settlements in the region until the emergence of the state of Ife around A.D. 1100.

Ife, perched at the edge of Nigeria's tropical forest, is thought to have come to prominence by the control of local products (ivory, gold, pepper, kola nuts) in external trade. By A.D. 1300, its walled capital was at the peak of its wealth, with many shrines featuring elaborate potsherd pavements scattered throughout the city and a rich sculptural tradition, steeped in realism, represented in brass and terracotta. In sculptures, personages are depicted richly adorned in ceremonial regalia. Shrines featuring such depictions may point to the historical existence of a form of divine kingship in the region. To support this large elite and artisan population, Ife's subsistence base appears to have been based upon vegeculture and small livestock. Around A.D. 1500, the city of Ife declined, and the region's center of power shifted to Benin without any appreciable break in cultural tradition.

East Africa. Along the East African littoral, during the first millennium A.D., coastal trade was to play a role in the elaboration of local social hierarchies, just as trans-Saharan trade was doing in the west. Although the *Periplus of the Erythraean Sea,* an anonymous document written in Greek and Egyptian around A.D. 50, cites the presence of a trading city (Rhapta) along the coast of Kenya or Tanzania, we are without archaeological evidence for East African polities until the ninth century. The Red Sea coast is another matter, however, with Axumite civilization blossoming from the first century A.D.—itself established upon an intrusive Pre-Axumite (ca. 500 B.C.–A.D. 100) polity of south Arabian origin. *Aksum, famed for the massive stone stelae of its capital's royal cemetery, supplied African luxury goods to the Red Sea trade and received in return precious metals, glass, cloth, wine, and spices from Arabia and the Byzantine world. Between the third and the eighth centuries, at its height as a trade entrepot, Aksum minted its own coinage and conquered portions of southern Arabia. A Coptic Christian state beginning in the fourth century, the country has retained its religion in the successor states that emerged in the wake of the Islamic expansion of the late first millennium A.D.

From A.D. 800, Swahili trading cities dotted the East African coast, fusing Islamic *religion and architecture with indigenous sociopolitical organization and commercial acumen. In this area the Indian Ocean served as a trade corridor to the Far East, with lateen and square-rigged dhows stocking the menageries of Chinese emperors and carrying silks and porcelain to African merchants and their sultans. At an incipient level, Swahili civilization arose out of coastal agro-pastoral societies, whose gradual mastery of the sea lanes made them ideal intermediaries with foreign mariners. In occupation sequences such as that of Shanga, mud and thatch indigenous architecture in the ninth century gives way rapidly to a local mutation of Islamic mortar and stone buildings in the eleventh century, with evidence for long-distance trade present throughout. At its apex, however, the Swahili coast had a lavish Islamic veneer, with impressive palaces and mosques distributed among sites such as *Kilwa and Gedi.

Interior and South Africa. During the time of the Swahili civilization, numerous complex societies and states grew in the interior, often as trade-item consolidators for the coastal trade. Farthest from the coast were the wealthy societies of Zaire's Upemba Depression, the neighboring Kisalian and Katotian polities (A.D. 700 and 1300). Both are known for their sumptuous graves, with those of the Kisalian suggesting wealth deriving from an intra-African trade (copper, iron, and ivory) and those of the Katotian suggesting firmer links with Indian Ocean commerce (cowries, conus shells, and glass beads).

Farther to the south, trading states developed where Bantu agro-pastoralists had already established transient chiefdoms based upon the manipulation of livestock wealth. The first of these states, *Mapungubwe (ca. A.D. 1000–1200), grew up in the South African Limpopo River basin. Here, an intermediary role in the coastal trade fossilized existing, and otherwise transient, social hierarchies based upon cattle wealth. A further elaboration of such hierarchies, but over a greater zone of influence, can be seen in the state of *Great Zimbabwe (ca. A.D. 1150–1400). Known for the unique drystone masonry architecture of its impressive settlements Great Zimbabwe, like Mapungubwe, consolidated the gold and animal product wealth of its hinterland as a powerful bargaining chip in the competitive coastal trade. At its height in the thirteenth century, Great Zimbabwe's capital was home to as many as 18,000 people. *Subsistence to support such population concentrations remained crucial, and it is likely that cattle and agricultural surplus continued to play a highly visible role in the maintenance of power.

In summary, a recurring pattern may be observed in the formation of African states during the past two millennia. From Ghana to Great Zimbabwe, rich excursions into international trade elevated already robust internal exchange networks to the complexity of full-fledged states and empires.

[See also AKSUM; GREAT ZIMBABWE; MAPUNGUBWE AND TOUTSWEMOGALA.]

■ Peter Garlake, *Great Zimbabwe* (1973). Peter Garlake, *The Kingdoms of Africa* (1978). Francis Van Noten, ed., *The Archaeology of Central Africa* (1982). A. Holl, "Background to the Ghana Empire: Archaeological Investigations on the Transition to Statehood in the Dhar Tichitt Region (Mauritania)," *Journal of Anthropological Archaeology* 4 (1985): 73–115. Graham Connah, *African Civilizations, Precolonial Cities and States in Tropical Africa: An Archaeological Perspective* (1987). Martin Hall, *The Changing Past: Farmers, Kings and Traders in Southern Africa 200–1860* (1987). B. Kemp, *Ancient Egypt: Anatomy of a Civilization* (1989). John Sutton, *A Thousand Years of East Africa* (1990). David O'Connor, *Ancient Nubia, Egypt's Rival in Africa* (1993). Susan Keech McIntosh, ed., *Excavations at Jenné-Jeno, Hambarketolo, and Kaniana (Inland Niger Delta, Mali), the 1981 Season* (1995).

Kevin McDonald

HISTORICAL ARCHAEOLOGY OF AFRICA

The historical record in Africa began with snippets of information about people and their ways of life that can now be interpreted with the archaeological record. For example, the "Periplus of the Erythraen Sea," apparently written by a Greek merchant living in Egypt in the first century A.D., describes trade from *Alexandria through the Red Sea to the Indian Ocean, and contacts with the Yemen and down the East African coast to a port called Rhapta, probably located on the Tanzanian coast. From about A.D. 700 this East African route was used regularly by Arab traders who called their southern clients the Zanj, the area of modern Mozambique the land of Sofala, and the vaguely defined country beyond, Waqwaq.

By A.D. 1100, substantial Muslim settlements had been established on the East African coast, often on offshore islands for ease of defense. Several of these coastal cities have been excavated. Mandy (near Lamu, on the Kenyan coast) had a massive sea wall, some stone buildings, and an extensive town of clay and thatch houses. Its main export was probably ivory, while large quantities of imported Persian ceramics and Chinese porcelain attest to the wealth that was once accumulated here. *Kilwa, to the south, was a small settlement that grew into a powerful city-state governed by the Muslim Shirazi dynasty. At its center were the Great Mosque and the stone houses of those close to the seat of power, built from coral cut from reefs at low tide. Again, fortunes rested on trade, in this case with places such as *Great Zimbabwe.

The wealth of the Arab states attracted the Portuguese, and in 1488 Bartolomeu Dias opened a sea route to the Indian Ocean by rounding the Cape of Good Hope. There have yet been few excavations of sites linked to this initial phase of European colonization; an exception is the fortified settlement at Massangaro, at the junction of the Luenha and Zambezi Rivers. First built in the mid-seventeenth century, Massangaro comprised houses and storerooms within a wooden stockade.

Arab traders were as interested in West Africa as they were in the Indian Ocean littoral, although the "sea" to be crossed in this case was the Sahara Desert. Medieval travelers described towns and cities in the savannas on the far side of the desert sands, and it has been possible to correlate some of these places with archaeological traces, disproving the earlier historical interpretation of the West African savanna cities as products of external trade contact. The West African coast was described by the Portuguese from the mid-fifteenth century onward. Again, an issue has been the antiquity of urban centers—cities such as Ijebu-Ode and Benin (both in Nigeria). Was urbanization a consequence of European contact, or were West African cities in existence prior to their historical description? Again, archaeology has demonstrated their antiquity. For example, excavations at towns of the Ghanaian Akan states have shown that some of them date back to the eleventh century. In Nigeria the city of Ife (where, according to Yoruba tradition, the world was created) is known for its terra-cottas, bronzes, and stone sculptures. The first mud walls and domestic buildings date back to the late first millennium. Benin City was probably founded in the late thirteenth century, and has extensive archaeological deposits that span the historic period of interaction between the indigenous urban community and European colonial settlers.

Elmina (Ghana) was the first European trade post in West Africa, although there was a large town at the site before the arrival of the Portuguese (and the construction of the Caste) in the mid-fifteenth century. Fieldwork has shown a town of more than one thousand tightly packed stone buildings close to the castle, and extensive artifactual evidence for interaction between the new arrivals and the local population. Elmina was also a point of contact with global networks of trade. Captured by the Dutch in the mid-seventeenth century, Elmina and Dutch West Africa were governed from Brazil, where slaves were taken to work sugar plantations and South American mines.

Portuguese control of West and East Africa depended on scattered garrisons with tenuous links to one another and the outside world, and it is surprising that this colonial foothold survived for more than a century. But the rise of the great Dutch chartered companies from the early seventeenth century led to most of the western side of Africa falling within the monopoly of the Dutch West India Company and the far south, important as a waystation in the long journey to Indonesia, coming into the keep of the Dutch East India Company.

Table Bay, a sheltered anchorage with fresh water, halfway between Amsterdam and Batavia (Jakarta), was fortified by the Dutch in 1652 and, by the end of the century, was an established town. Archaeological excavations in modern Cape Town have provided a wealth of information that illuminates everyday life in the colony: ceramics, food remains, personal possessions, as well as details of houses and other structures. Other techniques of historical archaeology—particularly the study of inventories and associated documents—have widened this understanding of colonial material culture. The countryside has been less fully explored, but excavations of outposts at Paradise (on the far side of Table Mountain) and Oudepost (on the coast to the north), along with several farm buildings, show what life was like on the expanding colonial frontiers.

At the close of the eighteenth century, when the Dutch East India Company had finally sunk beneath the weight of its own corruption and inefficiency, southern Africa became part of the British Empire with consequent changes in material culture, whether ceramics or architectural style. Archaeological research in the Eastern Cape has shown how British ideals of identity and gentility were adopted and adapted in the new colonial village of Salem, inviting parallels with the archaeology of colonial North America. Other studies have begun to explore the historical archaeology of the Transvaal and Natal, as well as the material culture of racial segregation, the legacy of which has for many years divided South African archaeological work from research in the rest of the continent.

[See also TRADE, AFRICAN.]

■ Peter Shinnie, *Meroe: A Civilization of the Sudan* (1967). H. N. Chittick, *Kilwa: An Islamic Trading City on the East African Coast*, 2 vols., (1974). Graham Connah, *African Civilizations: Precolonial Cities and States in Tropical Africa—An Archaeological Perspective* (1987). Martin Hall, "The Archaeology of Colonial Settlement in Southern Africa," *Annual Review of Anthropology* 22 (1993). Ann Markell and Martin Hall, eds., "Historical Archaeology in the Western Cape," *South African Archaeological Society Goodwin Series* 7 (1993).

Martin Hall

AFRICA, Origins of Food Production in. "Food production" is an umbrella term covering a wide variety of economic activities that yield not only edible material, such as grain, fruit, meat, and dairy goods, but also fibers, hides, and other substances used in fabricating clothing and shelter. The common denominator that underlies all such activities is the domestication of the relevant plant and animal species. For this reason, food production is distinguished from food gathering, wherein resource exploitation is confined to wild plants and animals, and economic productivity is thus restricted to the limits imposed by nature's bounty.

The geographic distribution of modern domesticates and their wild progenitors suggests that prehistoric domestication occurred in a number of areas scattered around the world. However, because food production played a crucial role in the emergence of early civilizations, archaeological studies of plant and animal domestication have tended to focus geographically on the homelands of early civilization, such as southwestern Asia, China, and Mesoamerica. Such studies are simultaneously engaged in two basic cultural developments: the beginnings of food production and the beginnings of civilization.

Until recently, Africa's potential for contributing to our understanding of such beginnings has been thought to be limited. Outside of the Egyptian part of the Nile Valley, African civilizations are not evident much before 2,000 years ago. In general, the earliest occurrences of food production in Africa are also relatively late and have been regarded as largely derivative, involving the importation of domesticated species, as well as perhaps the idea of domestication, from other continents. Such considerations have tended to dampen interest in the origins of African food production.

Also contributing to the "backwater" status of research on early African food production is its slow rate of progress, largely because of the many intrinsic obstacles to investigation. One is simply the scale of the research agenda, which is such as to pit a handful of investigators against questions that not only span enormous areas but also entail a remarkably diverse assortment of cultural and ecological situations. Any reasonably detailed vegetation map of Africa will reveal an extraordinary variety of biomes, as well as the vast size of the continent, whose area is about three times that of the forty-eight contiguous states in the United States. What will not be apparent is the repeated transformation of such biomes over time in response to changes in precipitation. This not only alters the ecology of food production but also determines whether some areas are habitable by certain types of societies (e.g., by affecting the distribution of tsetse fly, whose presence virtually blocks occupation by cattle herders) or indeed practically all kinds of societies (for example, by creating deserts).

Yet, despite the many hindrances that impede the study of early African food production, this line of research is beginning to generate important results, some of which are being viewed with interest by archaeologists engaged in early food production in various parts of the world. This is partly because of a growing recognition that a full understanding of the origins of food production requires knowing why it did not occur, or did not occur early, in some areas. It is also partly because of an increasing awareness that the domestication of plants and animals in Africa was, in many cases, essentially an original process. More generally, the burgeoning interest in early African food production reflects a potential for helping to explain the origins of food production globally.

Taking these points in reverse order, there is an emerging theoretical perspective that sees the shift from food gathering to food production as taking place largely among relatively settled societies that exploited a wide range of wild species in resource-rich environments. From this perspective, domestication can be explained as a process aimed at establishing a food reserve as insurance against the recurrent unavailability of one or more important wild resources. Alternatively, such food reserves may have served to consolidate patron-client relationships in moderately stratified, basically food-gathering societies, in which clients depended on their patrons for some food resources. In fact, these explanations may be linked, since patron-client relationships themselves may have functioned as mechanisms for insuring the availability of reserve foods during times of resource deficiency.

What is particularly interesting about the origins of African food production in this connection is that it seems to have occurred initially among relatively mobile cultures inhabiting resource-poor environments. This is especially true of Africa north of the equator, where the earliest traces of a food-producing way of life were often exhibited by nomadic people who generally occupied environments ranging from deserts to semiarid savannas. Although it is possible that such societies may have domesticated species as a kind of food reserve, they would have done so under ecological circumstances that differed radically from those experienced by the types of societies implicated in the model for the origins of domestication mentioned earlier. This underscores the difficulty of constructing a single explanatory model for the origins of food production on a global scale.

Turning to the matter of plant and animal domestication in Africa, one can point to several noteworthy features. Perhaps the most striking is the extremely limited number of animal species that were domesticated in a continent whose rich and varied fauna contains a substantial range of creatures that are clearly domesticable, including several ungulates. For example, modern experiments in domesticating Thomson's gazelle (*Gazella thomsoni*) and eland (*Taurotragus oryx*) have been generally successful. Yet, the only animal that can be said with virtual certainty to have been domesticated in Africa is the guinea fowl. There is strong evidence for African domestication of the donkey and a substantially weaker case for the domestication of cattle in Africa. Beyond that, there is no clear evidence for African domestication of any animal that was an important source of food, fabric, or traction.

In contrast, a large and varied ensemble of plant species was domesticated in Africa. Thus, while various crops from southwestern Asia, including emmer wheat, barley, lentils, and peas, were imported into the Nile Valley by about 7,000 B.P. and have persisted as major components of North African subsistence regimes into the present, the earliest agricultural economies of sub-Saharan Africa were based entirely on African domesticates. These included numerous species from the savanna zone south of the Sahara, such as sorghum, pearl millet, African rice, and groundnuts; others from lowland forest habitats bordering the savanna zone, such as yams, oil palm, okra, and cola nut; and still others from the Ethiopian highlands, such as tef (*Eragrostis tef*, a cereal), finger millet, coffee, and enset (*Ensete ventricosum*, false banana).

Unfortunately, while the major areas where plant domestication occurred are reasonably well established, its chronology is poorly documented. There is virtually no evidence regarding the time of domestication of yams, which are a staple of the forest margin zone, and the limited chronological data concerning the principal cereals of the savanna zone point toward a range of time for domestication from about 4,000–3,000 B.P. Two things seem clear: While plant domestication in sub-Saharan Africa occurred relatively late, it was not derivative in the sense discussed earlier; and the earliest food production in many parts of Africa seems to have been based on domesticated animals (cattle, sheep, and goats) rather than plants, which is opposite to what occurred in most other parts of the world. Thus, it appears that early food production in Africa offers a unique perspective on the global picture of the shift from food gathering to food production.

[*See also* AGRICULTURE; AFRICA, *articles on* PREHISTORY OF AFRICA, EARLY IRON-AGE SETTLEMENT OF SUB-SAHARAN AFRICA.]

■ J. Desmond Clark, ed., *The Cambridge History of Africa, Vol. I: From the Earliest Times to c. 500 B.C.* (1982). Francis Van Noten, *The Archaeology of Central Africa* (1982). J. Desmond Clark and Steven A. Brandt, eds., *From Hunters to Farmers: The Causes and Consequences of Food Production in Africa* (1984). Angela E. Close, ed., *Prehistory of Arid North Africa* (1987). C. J. Cowan and P. J. Watson, eds., *The Origins of Agriculture. An International Perspective* (1992). A. B. Smith, *Pastoralism in Africa: Origins and Development Ecology* (1992). T. Shaw et al., eds., *The Archaeology of Africa: Food, Metals and Towns* (1993).
John Bower

AGRICULTURE. Archaeologists have long recognized the critical importance of farming as a primary source of food, fibers, and raw materials in most past societies, and in all complex, urban societies. Since the 1960s both the techniques by which past agricultural practices can be studied, and the conceptual frameworks within which agricultural change can be understood, have been vigorously debated.

Archaeological Evidence for Agriculture. Agricultural systems, unlike pottery or architecture for example, are sets of processes that leave no direct traces. Past farming can, however, be studied through its impact on three key classes of material remains: the husbanded plants and animals, the landscape in which they were managed, and the humans for which they were the diet. Animal and plant remains of some form—bones, seeds, phytoliths, pollen—are abundant in archaeological deposits of virtually all agricultural settlements. They can be used to address two main questions: (1) which species of plants or animals were husbanded? and (2) how were they managed? Although species can usually be identified relatively easily, as indicators of agricultural systems and change they are difficult to interpret unless evidence for husbandry practices is also obtained. In the case of crops the associated weed floras can identify irrigation, manuring, or weeding practices; for animals, ageing and sexing of bones are among the tools that can be used to reconstruct herding practices.

Evidence of environmental manipulation—especially the cultivation of fields—can be found in the physical changes in the landscape, such as field patterns, the construction of raised fields, or the construction of irrigation canals. Pollen from lake cores, geoarchaeological fieldwork, and charcoal from excavations can pick up environmental changes associated with agriculture such as deforestation or erosion. Human diet—not a direct index of agricultural practice, but obviously linked—is recorded in bone chemistry and pathological conditions of human skeletal remains, as well as in occasional finds of coprolites and preserved stomach contents.

No single type of evidence is adequate in itself; animal and plant remains are often open to varying interpretations of their economic implications, and landscape archaeology is difficult to date. An approach which first seeks to integrate different types of agricultural evidence, and then seeks to integrate these with other types of archaeological evidence (e.g., changing settlement patterns) for wider cultural change, is ideal but rarely achieved. As with archaeological evidence for other processes, the study of long-term change in agricultural patterns is vital in seeking causal explanations. All too often, the archaeological record of agriculture in a given region consists of a small collection of key sites at which adequate evidence for ancient agriculture has been recovered and published, separated by long gaps in distance and time.

Agricultural Ecology. Basic features of the earth's climate and topography circumscribe agricultural options in many regions. In areas of low rainfall or high altitude, crop production may be very difficult, and pastoralism is the dominant form of agriculture. Examples include the high altitude grasslands of the Andes, at over 13,123 feet (4,000 m), on which llamas and alpacas are herded, the arid steppic interiors of the Near East and Africa, where pastoralists herd sheep, goats, and cattle, and the reindeer herders of northern Asia. In arid areas with major river systems, irrigation agriculture is essential for the support of any settlement, for example in Egypt, the Indus valley and lower Mesopotamia.

Global patterns of insolation and rainfall do result in global patterns of crop types: for example, tuber crops are predominant in equatorial regions. These may have been of great significance at the origins of agriculture, but although the specific technology in a given system is partly determined by climate and topography, they have changed relatively little since the beginnings of agriculture. Explanations for the major changes that have occurred in agricultural systems must be sought in human actions.

Early Agriculture. Agriculture is one end of a gradient of human interaction with plants and animals. Ethnographic studies have shown that procurement of food by hunter-gatherers often involves different degrees of manipulation of organisms and their environments. These may range from almost incidental effects such as the dispersal of yam tubers during harvesting by Australian aborigines, to large-scale environmental manipulation by burning vegetation to increase yields of game or seeds, recorded ethnographically in Australia, Africa, and the Americas. Small-scale cultivation of wild plants is also known. Agricultural systems differ in that manipulation of resources extends beyond the environment, to the manipulation of plant and animal populations. Human interference in the reproductive behavior of managed plants and animals results in the fundamental genetic changes in the behavior and structure of plants and animals that are defined as domestication. The package of environmental manipulation with domesticated plants and animals is often seen as representing a major discontinuity in the gradient of human interaction with the environment.

Ethnographic and archaeological evidence shows that the appearance of agricultural systems is usually linked to the appearance of sedentary villages. This is not a simple case of cause and effect: sedentary hunter-gatherer villages are known from a number of resource-rich areas such as the Pacific coast of North America and the *Natufian period of the Levant, and some hunter-gatherer societies have engaged in small-scale cultivation without significant effects on their overall economy. It is generally true, however, that the introduction of agriculture is linked to an increase in population and in the number and size of sedentary villages. This is particularly clear in the case of the spread of the Neolithic package of crops and domesticated animals from the Near East into Europe. Although the reasons for the spread of agriculture are still the subject of speculation, there is no doubt that agriculture has the potential to be more productive than foraging. In this case, productivity is not only a matter of yield, but also of producing predictable crops that can be easily stored. Agricultural systems also have the important property of spreading easily, even into areas that are marginal for the wild ancestors of the crops and animals concerned: for example, wheat and barley have spread over most of the temperate world, although their wild ancestors are restricted to their Near Eastern homeland. Agriculture has therefore had an important role both in supporting higher populations and in extending areas of human settlement.

Understanding of the early history of agricultural systems is handicapped by limited archaeological data on any aspect of early societies, particularly in the Americas and southeast Asia. This is reflected in the controversy that surrounds basic questions on the date and area of domestication of the main crops. In the case of both North and South America, however, small-scale cultivation of domesticated crops (domesticated animals were less important than in Eurasia) as part of a hunter-gatherer economy seems to have continued over several millennia, prior to the development of fully agricultural societies. In North America, bottle gourd, sumpweed, sunflower, and other species entered part-time horticulture between the third and first millennia B.C. and in Mesoamerica and the Andes, crops such as maize, beans, squash, potato, and cotton may have been domesticated by 6000 B.C. It is increasingly clear that earlier models for the emergence of agriculture, which draw heavily on Nikolai Vavilov's concept of seven narrowly delineated centers of origin, do not take account of what is a much more complex and geographically widespread set of processes.

Identifying agricultural change in early, preurban societies and linking it to wider socioeconomic patterns is still a major challenge for archaeologists. There are two main reasons for this: first, that early archaeological sites and the evidence they contain are usually less well preserved and difficult to date; second, that there are relatively few excavated sites over what are usually long periods of prehistory. In general, for these early periods, attention has focused on the origins of agriculture rather than its subsequent development. There is evidence from a number of areas, such as late Jomon Japan, that agriculture can initially form a relatively minor part of food procurement systems, and key variables associated with agriculture, such as population increase, only come into play once agriculture has been more fully adopted. In contrast, agriculture in the Near East seems to have spread fast, as an identifiable Neolithic "package." Clearly generalizations about the impact of agriculture on hunter-gatherer societies may be hard to sustain on a cross-cultural basis.

Agricultural Intensification. Agricultural intensification is often cited as a key factor in the evolution of complex—often urban—societies. Intensification—a concept drawn from agricultural economics—can be a nebulous term, but usually means a great input of resources—especially labor—into a given area of land, or in other words, a high input, high output system. The appearance of

new crop species or new agricultural techniques in the archaeological record is often interpreted as evidence of intensification.

Cases in which new crops apparently correlate with the beginnings of complex society include the spread of maize into lowland areas of Mesoamerica during the Formative period (2500 B.C. onward), of summer-season crops such as sorghum and cotton into India in the second millennium B.C., maize and the development of hierarchical societies in the Amazon in the first millennium B.C., rice into Japan at the beginning of the Yayoi period (300 B.C.), and the appearance of domesticated grape and other tree fruits at the beginning of the Bronze Age in the Aegean, which has been linked to the beginnings of urban civilization there.

Three key examples of intensification are irrigation, the engineering of fields, and the introduction of the plow. Where radial canals have been constructed to carry water from rivers to fields, surface traces of canals often exist that can be dated by comparing their path with the distribution of settlements of known dates. In Mesopotamia, field surveys have traced the development of canal systems from sites such as Choga Mami, dating to about 5000 B.C. through to the Medieval period. In areas such as the Indus Valley and the Nile Valley where irrigation occurs from the annual flooding of the river, traces of the system of dikes and basins that held back the water are buried under alluvium. Even though direct evidence for irrigation may be lacking, however, the aridity of these areas means that agriculture must have depended on irrigation. The beginnings of urban civilization in all three areas in the third millennium B.C. are often thought to be causally linked to the necessity for central administrative structures with which to operate large-scale irrigation systems.

Elsewhere, irrigation has often been linked to the development of specialized forms of fields. In the tropical zone, raised fields have the advantage of allowing drainage in poor soils as well as irrigation. Raised-field systems are most frequent in Middle and South America. Major civilizations of Mesoamerica such as the *Maya and *Teotihuacán were fed by irrigated raised-field systems. That the Maya culture was thought to have depended on slash-and-burn agriculture until the late 1970s is an indication of the difficulties in locating field systems in what is now tropical forest. Terracing of fields is another form of agricultural development with high labor input for construction and maintenance. Such terraces are also very difficult to date, but are a major feature of the landscape in the eastern Mediterranean and form a crucial part of irrigation systems in the wet-rice agriculture of southeast Asia. In temperate Eurasia the introduction of the animal-drawn plow is often cited as evidence of a form of intensification. The plow seems to have spread from the periphery of the Near East to much of Europe around 3000 B.C. allowing expansion of population into previously uncultivable areas.

Those agricultural changes that can be identified as intensification are obviously linked to increased population: this both creates the demand for intensification to occur, and provides the increased labor that most forms of intensification require. The issue of causality remains controversial: does the introduction of a new crop really destabilize and change an existing agricultural system, or will new crops be drawn into cultivation by increasing demand? To what extent does a successful agricultural system remain stable? Is the rise of a complex society always linked to major shifts in agricultural production—in temperate Eurasia, for example? It is likely that the answers to such questions cannot be framed in simple terms of one or two active agents, but approaches that consider systems as a whole can be complex and difficult to quantify. In the formation of the great irrigated civilizations, trade seems to have played as vital a role as agriculture.

Similar issues have to be considered when discussing the subject of agricultural decline or collapse. In view of the obvious, close relationship between complex societies and intensive agriculture, archaeologists are quick to point to mismanagement by farmers as the cause of collapse of a civilization. Empirical evidence does not support such arguments: traditional systems of agriculture today, whether intensive or extensive, have proved to be stable and adaptable. Agricultural systems tend to break down owing to interference by sociopolitical disruption. The causes of agricultural change cannot be sought in agriculture alone; farming is one part—a very important part—of a wider society.

[See also AFRICA: ORIGINS OF FOOD PRODUCTION IN; ASIA, ORIGINS OF FOOD PRODUCTION IN, *articles on* ORIGINS OF FOOD PRODUCTION IN SOUTH ASIA, ORIGINS OF FOOD PRODUCTION IN SOUTHEAST ASIA; CHINA; EUROPE: THE EUROPEAN NEOLITHIC PERIOD; MESOAMERICA, ORIGINS OF FOOD PRODUCTION IN; THE NEAR EAST: THE NEOLITHIC AND CHALCOLITHIC (PRE-BRONZE AGE) PERIODS IN THE NEAR EAST; PLANT REMAINS, ANALYSIS OF.]

■ D. B. Grigg, *The Agricultural Systems of the World* (1974). I. S. Farrington, ed., *Prehistoric Intensive Agriculture in the Tropics* (1985). Juliet Clutton-Brock, ed., *The Walking Larder: Patterns of Domestication, Pastoralism and Predation* (1988). David R. Harris and Gordon C. Hillman, eds., *Foraging and Farming: The Evolution of Plant Exploitation* (1989). Charles B. Heiser, *Seed to Civilization: The Story of Food*, new ed. (1990). L. T. Evans, *Crop Evolution, Adaptation and Yield* (1993). Thurstan Shaw, Paul Sinclair, Bassey Andah, and Alex Okpoko, eds., *The Archaeology of Africa: Food, Metals and Towns* (1993). Daniel Zohary and Maria Hopf, *Domestication of Plants in the Old World*, 2d ed. (1993). Jon G. Hather, ed., *Tropical Archaeobotany* (1994). Bruce D. Smith, *The Emergence of Agriculture* (1995).

Mark Nesbitt

AKSUM. The city of Aksum lies on the fertile plateau of Tigray in northern Ethiopia, at an altitude of over 7,220 feet (2,200 m) above sea level. Although there is evidence for earlier settlement in the vicinity, Aksum itself does not appear to have been occupied before the first century A.D. At that time, however, it rapidly gained importance as the capital of one of the most prosperous states in sub-Saharan Africa, exploiting local agricultural resources and raw materials—notably ivory and gold—which were fed, through the port of Adulis, into the Red Sea trade network linking the Roman Empire with regions as far distant as India.

Archaeological research at Aksum has so far emphasized the major monuments, notably the elite residences or palaces, and the (presumably royal) graves that were marked by elaborately carved stelae. The first substantial investigations were undertaken in 1906 by a German expedition led by E. Littmann. Other excavators worked at Aksum between 1937 and 1970 but, sadly, their results have been very imperfectly published. Research was resumed from 1972 to 1974 and from 1993 onward by the British Institute in Eastern Africa. The main burial area, near the center of ancient Aksum, was in use from the first or second century A.D. By the third century, burials of great wealth were taking place: one tomb of this period, although disturbed in ancient times, has yielded abundant pottery, glass, elaborate metal-

work, and finely carved ivory. The largest of the stelae, 98 feet (30 m) high and some 517 tons in weight, marked two monumental tombs of great size and architectural sophistication. This complex probably dates from just before the adoption of Christianity as the state religion under King Ezana, during the second quarter of the fourth century.

[See also AFRICA: THE RISE OF KINGDOMS AND STATES IN AFRICA; EAST AFRICA.]

■ E. Littmann, *Deutsche Aksum-Expedition* (1913). S. Munro-Hay, *Excavations at Aksum* (1989). D. Phillipson, "The Significance and Symbolism of Aksumite Stelae," *Cambridge Archaeological Journal* 4 (1994): 189–210.

David W. Phillipson

ALBRIGHT, W. F. (1891–1971). Eldest of four sons and two daughters of a Wesleyan missionary couple in Chile, William Albright was educated in their home school until their return to Iowa in 1903. He graduated in 1912 from Upper Iowa University, Fayette, and spent the next year as principal of the high school in Menno, South Dakota. His lifelong severe myopia and crippled left hand, resulting from a farm accident during furlough in 1896, had forced him to turn to his father's library. Having taught himself Hebrew and Akkadian, he wrote an article on an Akkadian word for a German scholarly journal and sent a copy of its proof with his application to Johns Hopkins University. Recognizing Albright's potential, Professor Paul Haupt provided modest scholarships for Albright's doctoral study and subsequent teaching. In 1919, Albright was able to use the Thayer Fellowship he had won to begin a career of study and exploration in Palestine. He married a fellow scholar, Ruth Norton, at the end of August 1921 in Jerusalem.

As director of the American School of Oriental Research (now the W. F. Albright Institute of Archaeological Research) Albright established the modern discipline of Biblical Archaeology, in which the realia of ancient Near Eastern material culture were used to illustrate and deepen scholarly understanding of the biblical text. Among Albright's major archaeological undertakings were Tell el-Fûl (1922 and 1933); Tell Beit Mirsim (four seasons, between 1926 and 1932, during which he established pottery chronology for western Palestine); Beth-Zur (1931); Bethel (1934); the Sinai expedition (1947–48); and South Arabia (1950).

From 1929 until retirement in 1958, he was chairman of the Oriental Seminary, Johns Hopkins; from 1930 to 1968 he edited the *Bulletin of the American Schools of Oriental Research*. His lifetime bibliography contains over eleven hundred books, articles, reviews, and chapters. He recognized and publicized the great discoveries of the Ugaritic tablets (1929 to 1930) and the *Dead Sea Scrolls (1947 on), and cofounded the Anchor Bible Project with D. N. Freedman. Thirty honorary doctorates, several *Festschriften*, and many other awards acknowledged his enduring contributions to archaeology and ancient history.

[See also HISTORY OF ARCHAEOLOGY FROM 1900 TO 1950: NEAR EASTERN ARCHAEOLOGY.]

■ W. F. Albright, *From the Stone Age to Christianity* (1940). W. F. Albright, *Yahweh and the Gods of Canaan* (1968). Leona Glidden Running and David Noel Freedman, *William Foxwell Albright: A Twentieth-Century Genius* (1975; centennial ed. 1991). David Noel Freedman, ed., *The Published Works of William Foxwell Albright* (1975).

Leona Glidden Running

ALEXANDRIA. Located in Egypt's northwestern delta on the limestone shelf between Lake Mareotis and the Mediterranean Sea, the site was inhabited in pharaonic times, perhaps as early as the New Kingdom period. The town continued to be inhabited into the fourth century B.C. when Alexander the Great arrived. He is said to have laid out the ground plan of the city—which he dedicated on April 7, 331 B.C.—in the form of a Greek *chlamys*, or riding cape, symbolizing its founding as a purely Greek, not a pharaonic Egyptian, polis. Its broad avenues and boulevards intersected at right angles in accordance with the gridiron plan attributed to Hippodamus of Miletus. Alexander also connected the island of the Pharos, known to Homer, to the mainland by means of a causeway, the Heptastadion, thereby forming two harbors, the Great Port in the east which served the city's mercantile interests, and the smaller Port of Safe Return in the west.

The city continued to expand under the reign of Ptolemy I Soter and his son Ptolemy II Philadelphus, both of whom may have jointly founded the Museion within which was the Great Library. During the reign of the latter, the famous Lighthouse was erected. The body of Alexander the Great was moved from Memphis to Alexandria for burial, then subsequently reburied by Ptolemy IV Philopator.

Of the ancient city, very little remains today. The sites of the royal palaces, the Great Library, and the tomb of Alexander the Great have yet to be identified. Nevertheless, remains of the Lighthouse, one of the seven wonders of the ancient world, are still visible in the rebuilt fifteenth-century citadel, known as the Fort of Qait Bey. The center of the city has been converted into an archaeological park featuring an *odeon* and a bath complex of Roman Imperial date. In the section of the modern city known as Qarmouz, one can visit the site of the Temple of Serapis, dominated by a single column, erected to commemorate the Roman Emperor Diocletian's visit to the city during which he unleashed a massacre of the population. Alexandria still boasts several cisterns of Roman date and a number of cemeteries, the earliest at Hadra, which is much eroded, and at Mustapha Pasha, whose lavishly decorated tombs recall those at Vergina in Macedonia. The tombs of Anfouchy are somewhat later, but their painted decoration is unsurpassed, as are the cavernous subterranean passages at Kom *esch-Chugafa* of Roman Imperial date, the relief sculpture of which is without precedent in the ancient world.

[*See also* GREECE: THE HELLENISTIC AGE; NEAR EAST: LATE ANTIQUITY IN THE NEAR EAST.]

■ E. M. Foster, *Alexandria. A History and a Guide* (1961). P. M. Fraser, *Ptolemaic Alexandria*, Vols. I–III (1972).

Robert Steven Bianchi

ALTAMIRA. Located 1.2 miles (2 km) south of Santillana del Mar (Santander), on the north coast of Spain, the cave of Altamira, nicknamed the "Sistine Chapel of Cave Art," was decorated at various times between approximately 14,000 and 12,000 B.C. First discovered by a hunter in 1868, it was visited in 1876 by a local landowner, Don Marcelino Sanz de Sautuola, who noticed some black painted signs on a wall, but thought little of them. In 1879 he returned to do some excavating, and in November of that year he was digging in the cave floor, searching for prehistoric tools and portable art of the kind he had seen displayed at a Paris exhibition. His daughter Maria was playing in the cavern when she spotted the cluster of great polychrome bison paintings on the ceiling.

The figures seemed to be done with a fatty paste, and de Sautuola noticed the close similarity in style between these huge figures and the small portable depictions he had seen in Paris; he therefore deduced that the cave art was of similar age, but his attempts to convince the academic establishment met with widespread rejection and accusations of naiveté or fraud. De Sautuola died prematurely in 1888, a sad and disillusioned man.

Altamira is 971 feet (296 m) in length, being divided into different chambers and passages, and ending in a very long, narrow section. Although the site always calls to mind the great painted bison, it would be classed as a major decorated cave even without that ceiling, since its galleries are filled with an abundance of engravings, including some particularly fine deer heads identical to some found on deer shoulder blades in the occupation layers of the cave. There are also meandering finger tracings, some of which form a bovine head. One remarkable feature is a series of "masks," where natural rock shapes were turned into humanoid faces by the addition of eyes and other details; most of these can only be noticed when leaving, rather than entering, the cave.

The "great hall," with its high vault, has engravings and red compartmentalized quadrilateral "signs," akin to those of the cave of El Castillo in the same region. The cave also has black paintings (black figures often occur in different zones from red figures), stenciled hands, and (far rarer) positive painted hand prints.

To the left, as one enters Altamira, is the great hall of paintings, measuring about 65.6 by 33 feet (20 m by 10 m). The floor has been lowered in order to allow visitors easier access and viewing of the very low ceiling on which a score of large painted animals are spread: there are eighteen bison, a horse, and a hind, the latter 8.2 feet (2.5 m) in length. They are polychromes, done in ochre, manganese, and charcoal. Most animals are standing, but a few natural "bulges" in the ceiling are occupied by curled-up bison which thus appear three-dimensional. Two or three painted figures on the ceiling have been described as boars (a very rare animal in Palaeolithic art) but are now seen as streamlined bison (especially as one has horns).

The curled-up bison on the bulges have been described as sleeping, wounded or dying, falling down a cliff, or giving birth. Currently the dominant view is that they are males (even though one of them has an udder!), rolling in dust impregnated with their urine, in order to rub their scent on territorial markers. In fact, they may simply be bison drawn to fit the bulges—they have the same volume, form, and dorsal line as those standing around them, but their legs are bent and their heads are down. Some researchers see this chamber as a symbolic pound, with a bison drive depicted on the ceiling (the curled-up animals at the center are dead, while those around them stand and face the hunters—there are male humans engraved at the edge); another interpretation is that the ceiling is a depiction of a bison herd in rutting season.

Although the Altamira ceiling has sometimes been taken as a single accumulated composition, it actually comprises a series of superimpositions: researchers have distinguished five separate phases of decoration, beginning with continuous-line engravings, followed by figures in red flat-wash, then multiple-line engravings, black figures, and finally the famous polychromes. The multiple-line figures are identical to portable specimens from the cave, dated to 13,550 B.C., so it is clear that the two earlier phases predate them, while the black figures and polychromes are younger. Charcoal used in three polychrome bison at the center of the painted ceiling has produced radiocarbon dates of 12,380, 11,990, and 11,620 B.C. The cave was probably blocked shortly after this period.

De Sautuola saw the ceiling as a unified work, and *Breuil always insisted that one artist of genius could have done all the cave's polychromes. Recent detailed observation has confirmed these intuitions that one expert artist was probably responsible for at least all the bison on the ceiling. The different radiocarbon dates may indicate subsequent retouching.

The occupation layers at Altamira have yielded material from several phases: the Mousterian; the Solutrean, including classic shouldered points and the engraved deer shoulder blades; and the early Magdalenian, with perforated antler batons and antler spear points with complex decorative motifs. The Magdalenian fauna is dominated by red deer, and has abundant seashells reflecting the proximity of the coast; seal bones occurred in the Solutrean layers. Altamira's wealth of occupational material and of portable and parietal art suggests strongly that it was an important regional focus at times, perhaps the scene of seasonal or periodic aggregations when people from a wide area might meet for ritual, economic, and social activities.

[See also PALEOLITHIC: UPPER PALEOLITHIC; ROCK ART: PALEOLITHIC ART.]

■ Emile Cartailhac and Henri Breuil, *La caverne d'Altamira à Santillane, près Santander (Espagne)* (1906). Henri Breuil and Hugo Obermaier, *The Cave of Altamira at Santillana del Mar, Spain* (1935).

Paul G. Bahn

AMERICAS, First Settlement of the

Settlement of the Americas Before 12,500 B.C.
Settlement of the Americas After 12,000 B.C.

SETTLEMENT OF THE AMERICAS BEFORE 12,500 B.C.

Around 11,500 years ago, according to long-held archaeological theory, small groups of Clovis hunters crossed the now-submerged land bridge between Asia and Alaska and became the first humans to enter the New World. Upon entering this world these groups had to traverse several hundred miles of forbidding frigid terrain of the Late Pleistocene Ice Age before reaching the hospitable temperate environs of the southern latitudes.

Archaeologists have long believed that the hunters pioneered these landscapes in pursuit of bison, horse, mammoth, caribou, musk ox, and other now extinct big game. Eventually they entered the Great Plains of central North America, where large stocks of prey existed. A human population explosion presumably resulted, and in a matter of a few decades the hunters helped drive species such as mastodons, mammoths, camelids, and tapirs into extinction. In order to survive, the hunters rapidly moved farther south in an endless pursuit of game, eventually reaching South America and finally Tierra de Fuego.

This dramatic theory of "big-game" hunters has been stoutly defended by North American archaeologists for half a century. But is it correct?

Due to a series of recent archaeological discoveries in North and South America, many aspects of the accepted migration hypothesis are under intense scrutiny. New data from sites in Alaska and Pennsylvania in the north and Brazil and Chile in the south offer challenging fresh insights on the initial peopling of the Americas. This challenge is not new. In every decade since the 1950s a group of controversial sites with early radiocarbon dates—a few hinting at settlement prior to 15,000 B.P., 50,000 B.P., and even 300,000 B.P.—have challenged many of the old assumptions of the extant theory.

At the root of the debate on the peopling of the Americas is the entry date of humans. The timing question has been hotly debated among archaeologists. More than an academic disagreement, the date of the first human presence in the New World has a crucial impact on our understanding of how it happened. Each chronological possibility involves entirely different episodes of Late Pleistocene climate, styles of life, and human technological skills. Even if the migration occurred a mere two or three thousand years before the traditional 11,500-year benchmark, it would imply a drastic new perspective of the peopling of the Americas. Instead of specialized big-game hunters traveling rapidly down from the north as they tracked prey and killed them with Clovis spearheads, the earlier dates indicate more generalized populations feeding off of all sizes of animals, a wide variety of plants, and other food types in a multitude of open and forested environments. It also is possible that splinter groups subsisted primarily on sea life by following a Pacific strip now submerged by rising ocean.

No one seriously doubts the source population and the entry place of the first South Americans. North American populations must have passed through the Panamanian Isthmus and Colombia before reaching Tierra del Fuego. No hard evidence exists to suggest that people from other continents ever came across the Pacific or Atlantic Ocean. There also is no evidence to show that humans first arrived in South America and then migrated north.

Exactly when early humans first entered the Southern Hemisphere is still quite uncertain. It has been believed for many years that the first South Americans did not predate 10,000 B.P., and that there was no sure evidence of tool traditions of very much greater antiquity. For decades, archaeologists had believed that the die-hard Clovis hunters moved rapidly southward, reaching Fell's Cave, Palli Aike, Cueva del Medio, Mylodon Cave, and other sites in southern Patagonia by 11,000 to 10,500 B.P., if not earlier.

This hypothesis has flaws, however. It is very unlikely that prehistoric people, even the highly skilled and effective Clovis hunters, could have populated the entire New World in a mere five hundred years, the maximum span between the time of the presumed land migration in North America and the time by which the first humans reached Tierra del Fuego. This means, of course, that humans would have moved at an incredibly rapid rate across unknown, and at times daunting, landscapes to reach the far end of the Americas. There is no precedent in human history for this kind of blitzkrieg migration, to use the term coined by Paul S. Martin. Even more problematic are signs of possible earlier cultures at a handful of North American and South American localities.

One of the candidates for early occupancy is the site of Pedra Furada, located in a dry *caatinga* thorn forest with high sandstone cliffs in arid northeastern Brazil. A stratified series of hearths and stones in a rock shelter dating back to at least 12,000 B.P. make this site a plausible candidate. Many of the rock surfaces of the cliffs are covered with ancient paintings, rendered in vivid red, yellow, black, and white pigments. They depict deer, armadillos, lizards, and jaguars, as well as people. There are scenes suggesting hunting, sexual relations, and childbirth. Extensive burned layers have been dated back to 45,000 B.P., but no animal bones, plant remains, and other secure indicators of human activity are associated with these features. Nor are the possible stone tools in the early layers obviously distinguishable from natural quartz flakes, which are present in the local rock debris and could well have fallen from cliffs overhead. Neide Guidon, who directs the Pedra Furada Project, is not without her skeptics who claim that the burned areas and the broken stones are all natural occurrences.

As reported in more detail below, at the *Monte Verde site in southern Chile, where the author has been excavating since 1977, a human campsite was inhabited between 12,800 and 12,300 years ago. Usually archaeologists find stone tools and the bone remains of extinct megafauna in Late Pleistocene sites. At Monte Verde, due to a muddy peat layer that formed after the site was occupied by humans, perishable materials were mummified and preserved. The organic remains included chunks of meat, wild potatoes, seaweed and other plants, wooden tools, and architectural remains. Buried deeper in another area of the site is an older possible culture that is associated with stone tools, clay-lined pits, and radiocarbon dates reaching back to 33,000 B.P. Although the younger cultural component is securely human in nature, the older, deeper material is inconclusively related to human activity.

Located in an ancient water hole called Taima-Taima in northern Venezuela are the bone remains of a young mastodon, a pointed projectile point, and several stone tools. The site, excavated intermittently by Jose Cruxent, Ruth Gruhn and Alan Bryan, dates between 13,000 to 12,500 B.P. Some archaeologists believe that the bones and stone tools are from different geological periods and are mixed by rising water. Even so, the projectile point is remarkably similar to those found at Monte Verde.

The gateway to South America is Colombia, where in the past twenty years a series of rockshelter and open-air sites have been excavated by several researchers and dated from 14,000 to 11,000 B.P. years ago. These sites are Tequendama, Tibito, Sueva, and El Abra. Each of these sites are characterized by the association of the bone remains of extinct animals, primarily mastodon, horse, deer, and other megafauna, and unifacial stone tools. More radiocarbon dates and detailed publications are needed for these localities before they can be accepted confidently.

In addition to these localities, there is a small handful of other sites that contain traces of early cultural materials. These are Los Toldos in Argentina, several caves and rockshelters in Brazil, and Quereo in Chile, among others. Although most of these sites are beset with problems such as questionable human artifacts, radiocarbon dates, or reliable geological contexts, some of the data cannot easily be explained by the extant model. Collectively, these and sites such as Monte Verde, Pedra Furada, and Taima-Taima hint at settlements prior to 11,500 B.P. and at lifestyles different from those of highly mobile big-game hunters, thus forcing many archaeologists throughout the Americas to rethink their old assumptions.

There is another important aspect of the early human record that plagues us—the absence of ice-age human skeletal remains. Human skeletal remains from reliable contexts are rare occurrences in the early archaeological record. The difficulty in finding these remains may be related to the high mobility of foraging groups who may have buried their dead along the trail, so to speak. If so, archaeologists may only fortuitously find isolated burials. The absence also may be related to mortuary practices or to preservation factors. Whatever the reasons may be, the recovery of these remains holds many important clues to our understanding of the biological and genetic make-up of the early populations.

We still do not know for certain when the first South Americans arrived. We do know, however, that cultural diversity on the continent was widespread at least by 11,000 B.P. This diversity accelerated very rapidly once humans entered the continent. The triggering mechanisms of this cultural explosion are not known, but may be related to the procurement of food and other resources in the highly productive tropical environments in the south and to the growing sophistication of a migrating *Homo sapiens*. Ancient lifestyles in the Amazonian forests, Andean mountains, and Patagonian plains would certainly have been very different from those in areas such as the Rocky Mountains and the Great Plains of North America. Once we know more about these landscapes we may hope to establish a broad picture of when and how humans spread to Tierra del Fuego. The migration to the southernmost inhabitable point on Earth marked the final destination of a worldwide trip by Ice Age humans. While scholars from several disciplines and nationalities are studying this migration, they are far from a consensus, but the outline of a new picture of the first South Americans is emerging.

[See also ANTIQUITY OF HUMANKIND: ANTIQUITY OF HUMANKIND IN THE AMERICAS; MEGAFAUNAL EXTINCTION.]

■ C. Vance Haynes, "The Earliest Americans," *Science* 166: 709–715. Alan Bryan, "Paleoenvironments and Cultural Diversity in Late Pleistocene South America," *Quaternary Research* 3 (1973): 237–256. Paul S. Martin, "The Discovery of America," *Science* 179 (1973): 969–974. Thomas F. Lynch, "The Paleo-Indians," in *Ancient South Americans*, ed. Jesse D. Jennings (1983), pp. 87–137. Brian Fagan, *The Great Journey: The Peopling of Ancient America* (1987). Warwick Bray, "The Paleoindian Debate," *Nature* 332 (1988): 150–152. Richard Carlisle, ed., *Americas Before Columbus: Ice-Age Origins,* Ethnology Monographs, no. 12 (Department of Anthropology, University of Pittsburgh, 1988). Tom Dillehay, Gerardo Ardila Calderón, Gustavo Politis, and Maria da Conceicao de Moraes Coutinho Beltrão, "Earliest Hunters and Gatherers of South America," *Journal of World Prehistory* 6:2 (1993): 145–204. David J. Meltzer, *Search for the First Americans* (1993).

Tom D. Dillehay

SETTLEMENT OF THE AMERICAS AFTER 12,000 B.C.

Regardless of the ongoing controversy over whether the first Americans arrived before 12,000 B.P., it is certain that Clovis and related Paleo-Indians were present in the millennium after 12,000 B.P. Their distinctive fluted points are found throughout North America south of the Late Wisconsin glacial margin, and into northern Mesoamerica. Despite their wide distribution, these remains fall into a relatively narrow slice of time: The earliest radiocarbon dated Clovis assemblages occur in the North American Southwest and High Plains between 11,200 B.P. and 10,900 B.P. In eastern North America comparable assemblages date between 10,600 and 10,200 B.P., making them contemporaneous with post-Clovis (Folsom) occupations on the High Plains. Nearly all fluted-point finds in far-western North America are surface sites, and though their age is largely unknown, it is suspected to be comparable to Clovis and fluted-point sites elsewhere.

The seemingly rapid spread of fluted-point groups

across the many and varied environments of North America shapes views of their origins and adaptations. In the traditional model, Clovis groups were the first Americans, crossing the Bering Land Bridge from Siberia and arriving in central Alaska around 11,300 B.P.—their arrival marked by the Nenana Complex sites, the artifacts and assemblages of which are similar to those of Clovis, yet lack typical Clovis fluted points. From there, groups traveled south through the corridor between the Cordilleran and Laurentide glaciers (roughly the present British Columbia and Alberta borders), which was just then becoming habitable. They are seen as hunters—their prey including mammoth, mastodon, and other Pleistocene megafauna—and the pursuit of game is thought to have enabled them to move rapidly across ecological boundaries, and propelled them south as prey became depleted. In an extreme variation on that theme, intense Paleo-Indian predation is blamed for driving some thirty-five genera of Pleistocene megafauna to extinction.

While that traditional model prevails, it is nonetheless being revised in light of new archaeological evidence, which reveals that although these Late Pleistocene hunter-gatherers were historically related, their adaptations varied, as did aspects of the archaeological record they left behind.

That variation is most conspicuous in their economy. Clovis groups did occasionally target big game, successfully hunting mammoth at sites such as Lehner (Arizona), and Blackwater Locality No. 1 (the Clovis type site in New Mexico), and mastodon at Kimmswick (Missouri). Yet, almost as often as the hunt was unsuccessful: The Naco site (Arizona), for example, yielded remains of a lone mammoth that was stabbed repeatedly but escaped to die alone and unbutchered by Clovis hunters. Further, fewer than twenty sites in North America yield artifacts directly associated with megafaunal remains. Nearly all are in the west, contain only mammoth, and in many cases the animals died young and near water, leading Gary Haynes to surmise most were enfeebled and died naturally, their carcasses later scavenged by Paleo-Indians. That, of course, considerably weakens the case for a human role in Pleistocene *megafaunal extinction.

Fluted-point groups hunted other, smaller animals, their prey varying by region: Bison were taken at several sites in the west (including Murray Springs [Arizona], which also yielded mammoth bones), along with pronghorn, jack rabbit, muskrat, and several birds. Caribou and reindeer are the known or suspected prey at sites in northeastern North America, from Nova Scotia (Debert site) to the upper Great Lakes (Udora, Ontario), along with deer, beaver, hare, and fox; in the southeast deer, small mammals, fish, and birds were likely taken.

Only one group of animals consistently appears in both eastern and western sites: turtles. Their remains were found, for example, in a roasting pit at Blackwater Locality No. 1, and a large, now-extinct Pleistocene tortoise, *Geochelone crassicutata*, was found upended and skewered at Little Salt Springs (Florida). Sometimes large, and always easily exploited, Pleistocene turtles may prove to have been one of the staples of the Paleo-Indian diet.

These groups were likely gatherers as well, but direct evidence for plant use is rare, either because it has not survived or because recovery strategies have been inadequate. At Shawnee-Minisink (Pennsylvania), however, intensive flotation yielded the seeds of almost ten species of plants. Circumstantial evidence of plant use appears in grinding stones from several sites east and west (including mammoth kill sites), and knives with a sheen or polish derived from repeated plant (especially grass) harvesting. On the High Plains, Great Basin, and far west, isolated fluted points are often found alongside ancient lakes, indicating the use of lakeside and marsh plants and animals.

Most High Plains Clovis sites are mammoth kills or scavenging locales, but this pattern may be biased by the high visibility of the bones they contain. In northeastern North America, kill sites are rare and small, and large residential sites are more common. Based on several lines of evidence, Dena Dincauze hypothesizes these large sites reflect population aggregations rather than periodic reoccupations. In the southeast, habitation sites are rare, and usually occur near stone quarries; the Flint Run Complex (Virginia), for instance, included habitation, hunting, and manufacturing stations around a large jasper outcrop. Continentwide, remarkably few fluted points have been found in caves or rock shelters, though whether that reflects archaeological search strategies or the unfamiliarity of fluted-point groups with their new landscape remains to be tested.

Because these groups were on a vast, largely unexplored, and virtually empty landscape with few constraints on movement, and where one had to travel long distances to maintain ties with kith and kin, they were widely mobile. Their mobility is tracked archaeologically by their preference for high-quality chert, jasper, obsidian, and other durable, easily knapped, fine-grained stone (in rare cases points were fashioned of quartz crystal, an extremely difficult stone to work). Since the stone was customarily obtained from outcrops (rather than secondary gravel sources), the distance between the outcrop and the site where the stone was finally discarded provides a measure of the scale of mobility. It reveals that trips of over 190 miles (300 km) were common in western and northern North America, which at that time were relatively open landscapes (grassland and northern parkland). By contrast, in the rich southeastern forests of North America the scale of mobility was lower by an order of magnitude. This difference likely reflects the greater density of food, stone, and other resources in the forests.

Available radiocarbon dates would suggest fluted-point groups spread across the continent in just three hundred years. But that pace is far more rapid than documented at any other time or place in human prehistory, and unexpected of pioneering groups entering exotic habitats where they had to locate water, stone, and other vital resources, identify the edible (and toxic) plants, and learn the behavior of native animals. Colonizing new habitats could not have been sped up even if they were predominantly hunters. As George Frison observes, knowledge of a particular animal in one region is not necessarily transferrable to potential animal prey in another. Ultimately, more radiocarbon dates are needed to ascertain whether the expansion took longer than now appears. If pre-Clovis claims prove correct, they will raise the additional possibility that the sudden widespread appearance of fluted points may not mark population movement, but instead the diffusion of a distinctive technology across an extant population (although currently there is scarce evidence of trade among these groups).

Befitting wide-ranging hunter-gatherers who lacked animal transport and were able to carry only limited provisions, they often cached stone for later use. Five are known from western North America; like the Fenn (Utah) and

Richey-Roberts (Washington) caches, they can contain scores of completed artifacts, and large biface preforms ready to be made into one or more finished tools. Human bone fragments were found with the Anzick (Montana) cache, making it one of the very few sites in North America with Clovis-age human skeletal remains (the scarcity of such remains is variously attributed to their low population density, high mobility, or burial practices).

Meat was also cached: at Adkins (Maine), and Colby (Wyoming), where two piles of mammoth bones were carefully stacked; one contained articulated ribs and shoulder bones, with a projectile point at the base and a mammoth skull perched on top. Frison, who excavated Colby, believes the meat was frozen (not dried), and helped Clovis groups survive harsh, northern winters.

The gear that was carried included a small number of readily adaptable tools that were carefully curated and resharpened to prolong their usefulness, which also explains the preference for high-quality, longer-lasting stone. The tool kit derived from bifacial tool and flake manufacture (blades are rare), and though it varied by region it generally included knives, end and side scrapers, gravers, drills, wedges, flake cutting tools, and lanceolate projectile points (many of which doubled as knives), made by percussion and pressure flaking, and marked by that uniquely American knapping feature—fluting. Fluting is the removal of a basal thinning flake, typically extending from the base to midway up the blade, creating a channel (flute) that resembles the groove on a bayonet, which led to early speculation that flutes served to intensify bleeding of stabbed prey. That idea fell into disfavor when it was realized the flutes were sandwiched between foreshafts or embedded in sockets that attached the point to a spear shaft.

Those foreshafts or sockets were likely fashioned of wood, bone, or ivory, but so far only the latter two have been found. Other bone and ivory artifacts include cylindrical and beveled projectile points, awls or punches, bone beads, and at Murray Springs a mammoth bone wrench—possibly used for straightening green wood, fresh bone, or ivory. In rare instances these artifacts were decorated: two of the cylindrical, bipointed and bibeveled bone rods from the Richey-Roberts cache were marked by small nicks and scored lines. Generally, fluted-point assemblages have little of the elaborate artistry characteristic of Upper Paleolithic Europe and western Asia, although like their Old World counterparts they sometimes sprinkled or smeared red ocher (hematite) over their artifacts, especially those in caches.

Clovis and related fluted points vary greatly in style, particularly in eastern North America. The greater number and diversity of styles in this region has led to the suggestion that groups were here in greater numbers, lasted longer, or perhaps even developed the distinctive Clovis culture in this region, then spread elsewhere. Current radiocarbon evidence does not support the latter hypothesis, though some see it as bolstered by an unfluted lanceolate—a possible Clovis point forerunner—in the disputed pre-Clovis levels at *Meadowcroft Rockshelter (Pennsylvania).

Whether their origins are in earlier sites south of the Late Wisconsin glacial margin, or somewhere between Alaska's Nenana Valley and the contiguous United States, these historically related, but regionally distinctive fluted point groups represent the first—and last—pan-continental occupation of the Americas.

[See also ANTIQUITY OF HUMANKIND: ANTIQUITY OF HUMANKIND IN THE AMERICAS.]

■ J. Willig, C. M. Aikens, and J. L. Fagan, eds., *Early Human Occupation in Far Western North America* (1988). R. Bonnichsen and K. Turnmire, eds., *Clovis: Origins and Adaptations* (1991). G. Frison, *Prehistoric Hunters of the High Plains* (1991). G. Haynes, *Mammoths, Mastodonts, and Elephants: Biology, Behavior, and the Fossil Record* (1991). O. Soffer and N. Praslov, eds., *From Kostenki to Clovis* (1993). D. K. Grayson, *The Desert's Past: A Natural Prehistory of the Great Basin* (1993). D. J. Meltzer, *Search for the First Americans* (1993).

David J. Meltzer

AMERICAS, Introduction of Diseases Into the. When, in 1492, Columbus left Seville for points east, he did not intend to change the course of Native American history. Yet, that was exactly what happened. The most devastating of the changes for Native Americans was the loss of human life, and the primary cause of death was not warfare or enslavement, but infectious diseases.

Within a decade of discovery, the Taino and Carib Indians of the Caribbean were extinct. These extinctions, in turn, paved the way for the development of the African slave trade. Between 1520 and 1550, Aztecs living in the Basin of Mexico suffered a population loss of at least forty percent. And this was only the beginning. Over the next half-century, they would experience at least four such catastrophes, each of which carried a death rate equal to that of the European Black Plague. When Pizarro marched into Cuzco to conquer the Inca empire, he found that smallpox had preceded him. Huayna Capac and his son, the imperial heads of the empire, as well as thousands of other Inca had already died in a microbial battle.

Why did Amerindians experience such devastation from Old World diseases? A hundred years ago it was commonly believed that Native Americans were intellectually, morally, and spiritually inferior to Europeans. This inherent inferiority created weak constitutions and explained the catastrophic loss of life. Fortunately, such racist beliefs are no longer accepted nor acceptable. Indeed, one of the lasting contributions of anthropology is the destruction of these erroneous beliefs. Explanations of the demographic catastrophe of Native Americans lie deep in evolutionary history. Archaeology is helping unravel the story.

The twelve or so diseases that killed Native Americans in such numbers range from the mundane to the exotic, from mumps or whooping cough to typhus and plague. Although very diverse, these diseases share a few important traits.

As anyone who has had mumps knows, you only get sick from this disease once. In epidemiological terms, exposure and recovery from the mumps virus gives the person lifelong immunity. Although permanent immunity is good news for people, it is bad news for the mumps virus. If the microbe is to reproduce and survive, it must find a fresh victim to attack. Thus, mumps is called a crowd infection.

All introduced diseases are crowd infections. Because individuals develop permanent immunity, the organisms survive indefinitely in cities where people are concentrated. Measles, for instance, requires a population of about 300,000 to survive. When the population size drops below this threshold, the virus can cause illness and death, but after one epidemic, the virus itself dies out. In a population of at least 300,000, there are enough births each year for the measles virus to find a new victim. Over time and in large cities, a balance between people and their microbes develops.

Because there are no fossils of microorganisms, we do not know absolutely the evolutionary histories of these crowd diseases. Currently, similar forms of the human crowd afflictions are found among herd animals; it seems likely that these animals were the source of the human diseases. Tuberculosis, for instance, can spread from cattle or pigs to humans; there is also a swine form of influenza. Cowpox, the bovine form of smallpox, was the first source of human vaccinations against this deadly disease.

Permanent immunity, cities, and herd animals created the historical context in which the human crowd infections evolved. Crowds of people counteracted permanent immunity of the individual and insured the survival of the disease; herds of animals were the source of the infections. The evolution of smallpox may have accidentally occurred when a human milked a cow infected with cowpox.

Although both cities and herd animals were present in both the Old and New Worlds, they coexisted only in the Old World. Humans began to domesticate cattle, horses, sheep, and goats about 10,000 years ago in the Old World. Shortly thereafter, humans began living together in villages and towns. This nucleation process eventually resulted in the development of such cities as Uruk, Ninevah, and Babylon. By the third millennium B.C., then, humans and animals had been living in close proximity for at least five thousand years. The time depth and the right mix of people and animals created the context that resulted in the development of human crowd diseases.

In the Americas, by contrast, herd animals and people in cities did not overlap; they were separated by millennia. The Pleistocene, or last Ice Age, began about 750,000 years ago. At that time there were ancestral horses, cattle, and even elephants in the Americas. But there were no human populations. By the end of the Pleistocene, roughly 10,000 years ago, just about the time that Paleo-Indians were entering the New World, most herd animals had either become extinct or had migrated west into Asia. Much later in Native American prehistory when people began building such substantial cities as *Tenochtitlán, there were no domesticated herd animals to trigger the evolution of human crowd diseases. Without the diseases, native immunities could not develop. Without immunity, Native Americans were defenseless against Old World microbes, and the results were catastrophic. Old World crowd diseases winnowed native populations by upwards of eighty percent.

In the end, understanding and explaining the demographic collapse of Native Americans involves two facts: the absence of herd animals to serve as sources for the evolution of human diseases and the number of diseases introduced. Each new introduction created new waves of illness and death: the combination of all diseases made the scale of Native American depopulation unique in human history.

[See also AZTEC CIVILIZATION: THE SPANISH CONQUEST OF THE AZTECS; DISEASE; INCA CIVILIZATION: PIZARRO AND THE CONQUEST OF THE INCAS.]

■ A. F. Ramenofsky, *Vectors of Death: The Archaeology of European Contact* (1987). David H. Thomas, *Columbian Consequences: The Spanish Borderlands in Pan American Perspective*, Vol. 3 (1992). Thomas M. Whitmore, *Disease and Death in Early Colonial Mexico: Simulating Amerindian Depopulation* (1992). Kenneth F. Kiple, *The Cambridge World History of Human Disease* (1993). Randolph M. Neese and George C. Williams, *Why We Get Sick* (1994).

Ann R. Ramenofsky

ANALYSIS, Methods of. Methods of analysis in archaeology cover a broad range of areas of expertise and all stages of the process of archaeology from initial planning to final report and curation. For our purposes, analysis in archaeology can be divided into three broad categories: spatial analyses, chronological analyses, and artifact analyses. There is often considerable overlap between these categories in reality, and all three typically employ a significant component of statistical or quantitative analysis as part of their practice.

Spatial analysis refers to methods of determining patterns of distribution of significant archaeological units across a landscape. The archaeological units and spatial scale can vary in size and scope from clusters of related sites in a large geographic region down to the distribution of a single artifact type within a feature at a site. Whatever the scale, the goal of all spatial analyses is to discover underlying patterns of association or disassociation of archaeological entities in space that may relate to patterns of human behavior as they were expressed at some time in the past.

Chronological analyses are those analyses that pertain to dating archaeological materials and sites. As spatial analysis is concerned with discovering patterns of association in space, chronological analysis is concerned with discovering patterns of association in time. Archaeologists have a large number of techniques for determining and assessing chronological relationships. These include techniques of both relative dating and absolute dating. Relative dating techniques rely on the relative vertical or chronological relationships between artifacts to provide a sense of the sequence of events. Absolute dating techniques rely on various chemical and nuclear properties of materials to allow analysts to place a specific date on an artifact or stratum.

Artifact analysis can be divided into two important subcategories: material analysis and technological analysis. The material analysis of artifacts pertains to the study of the physical and chemical properties of artifacts. For example, trace element analysis of obsidian tools has been used extensively to determine the source locations for the raw material as well as to determine the patterns of distribution or trade in those tools prehistorically. The technological analysis of artifacts refers to the study of the ways in which artifacts were made, used, and discarded. A good example of the application of technological analysis is the analysis of stone-tool manufacturing debris, debitage, to determine the stages in the production and use of various types of stone tools.

The process of archaeological analysis proceeds in a series of interlocking stages from particularistic analyses of individual entities to composite analyses of groups of entities in both the spatial and chronological dimensions. While one can easily get lost in the minutia of the lower-order analyses, the goal of all archaeological analyses is the same, the interpretation of past human behavior on the basis of the material remains. The results of the painstaking lower-order analyses conducted by archaeologists and other specialists they call in must themselves be analyzed within the framework of hypothetical models constructed by archaeologists. These hypothetical models, based on the theoretical orientation of the archaeologist conducting the research, form the critical point of contact between method and theory in archaeology. Neither of the two domains of archaeology, method and theory, is sufficient in and of itself, but the two domains are complementary components that serve to drive the discipline forward. New developments in analytical techniques can be just as important as new theory in revealing previously unrecognized patterns in the material record of past human behavior. It is the dynamic interaction of methods and theory, analysis and hypothesis, that continues to make archaeology the stimulating and challenging discipline that it is.

[See also ARTIFACT DISTRIBUTION ANALYSIS; CERAMICS: INTRODUCTION; DATING THE PAST; LITHICS: INTRODUCTION; METALS: INTRODUCTION; SETTLEMENT-PATTERN ANALYSIS; WOOD: INTRODUCTION.]

George Michaels

ANASAZI CULTURE. The word "Anasazi" refers to the prehistoric agricultural people of the *American Southwest who inhabited what is now known as the four-corners region of Utah, Colorado, New Mexico, and Arizona. In general, the Anasazi were restricted to the semiarid area known geologically as the Colorado Plateau from approximately A.D. 600 to historic times. Early travelers of European descent were drawn to the spectacular ruins of the Anasazi, and today many of these ruins are protected as popular national parks and monuments. The best-known examples include the spectacular cliff dwellings at *Mesa Verde (Colorado) and the Great Houses of Chaco Canyon (New Mexico).

The first conceptual framework used to understand the Anasazi was developed by archaeologists brought together by A. V. *Kidder at Pecos Pueblo, New Mexico, in 1927. Kidder and his contemporaries sought to create an overall scheme for prehistoric development in the Southwest, as well as to solve problems of typology (see Seriation) and nomenclature. The conceptual product of the conference is called the Pecos Classification. Archaeologists now recognize that the general scheme fits only the four-corners region, not the entire Southwest, and that there are a number of other problems as well. Regardless, the general framework is still employed with modifications.

Kidder and his contemporaries began the Anasazi sequence with a hypothesized Basketmaker I period. The period was hypothesized because at the time nothing was known of either the antecedents or the beginnings of the Anasazi. Today we recognize that the Anasazi arose out of what is called the Archaic adaptation of small bands of roving hunter-gatherers found throughout the area. The term "Basketmaker I" is no longer used, with "Archaic" being the preferred term.

Basketmaker II refers to the first peoples of the area for whom corn formed a large part of the diet. As might be expected, the Basketmaker II peoples are well known for their use of basketry, much of which has been recovered from rock shelters in the Kayenta, Arizona, area. Black Mesa, Arizona, has perhaps the best-known Basketmaker II occupation in the Southwest, as hundreds of sites have been located and dozens excavated in the area. These sites are predominantly open sites, that is, not in rock shelters, and consist largely of pit-house villages with abundant underground storage pits and abundant chipped stone.

Basketmaker III is perhaps best known from the Dolores area of southwestern Colorado, but may be found throughout the four-corners area. Basketmaker III adaptations are very similar to Basketmaker II, with the exception that ceramics, predominantly gray wares, become more important. It is also believed that dependence on agriculture is increased, as well as increased sedentism. Many Basketmaker III occupations are situated in lowland floodplain areas.

Pueblo I sites are abundant, but surprisingly few have been excavated. The Puebloan I way of life is a continuation of the Basketmaker lifestyle, with the exception that we commonly see small above-ground structures made of sandstone and adobe along with pit structures. Black-on-white ceramics are common, and redware appears in some places at this time. It appears that long-distance trade—as far as the Gulf of Mexico and Pacific coasts—served an important economic function during this and subsequent time periods. It is during this time period that the Chaco regional system emerged.

Pueblo II times are dominated, in the opinion of many archaeologists, by developments in the San Juan Basin area of New Mexico centered in Chaco Canyon. While many archaeologists have historically seen the numerous large Great Houses as a local phenomenon restricted to Chaco Canyon proper, most archaeologists today see Chaco as a regional phenomenon that extended throughout the entire Anasazi world, albeit centered at Chaco Canyon. Throughout the area architecture in the form of masonry styles, Great Houses, and large subterranean ritual structures called Great Kivas has a clear influence from the canyon. Many of the outlying sites, some called Great Houses as well, are also connected to the Great Houses of Chaco Canyon by clearly visible prehistoric "roads" (see Land Transportation: Roads and Tracks). The nature of relationship between the canyon and outlying settlements, however, is unknown. Many archaeologists see Chaco Canyon as the center of a broad economic redistribution center (see Social Organization, Prehistoric) to which goods from outlying settlements flowed. Others see the Great Houses, Great Kivas, and roads as evidence of a shared religious identity, and see the connections as not necessarily explained in terms of material needs. Still others view the outlying settlements as having been largely independent economically but influenced by events in the canyon. Regardless of these relationships, the Pueblo II period can be characterized as a period of great expansion, as many areas that had few occupants before were well populated during this time period. Despite the success of this regional system, archaeologists estimate that it collapsed sometime during the period between 1140 and 1200. Reasons offered for this collapse are many, ranging from warfare to disease, but most archaeologists consider that below-average rainfall during the period 1140–1190 played a role.

Pueblo III times reflect a reorganization after the Chacoan collapse, and highly varied adaptations are seen throughout the area. In many areas post-Chacoan Great Houses and Great Kivas can be observed, often surrounded by smaller settlements. In other areas, aggregation into many-roomed, multistoried pueblos begins. In the Mesa Verde area, large settlements, perhaps housing as many as 1,200 to 2,500 people, emerge, as do the spectacular cliff dwellings for which the area is famous. Between 1275 and 1300, much of the Anasazi world was affected by what has been called the "Great Drought." Many areas were abandoned, with major occupations either continuing or being established in the northern Rio Grande area, the area surrounding the Hopi Mesas of Arizona, and the Zuñi in western New Mexico and eastern Arizona, among other locales.

By Pueblo IV times (1300 to historic times), aggregation was complete, and settlement by the Anasazi and their descendants was largely restricted to the Rio Grande Valley, Hopi, Acoma, and Zuñi. It is at the beginning of this time period when archaeologists see the establishment of kachina societies that are so important to the religious life of contemporary Puebloan peoples. Prior to the arrival of the Spanish in 1539, diseases brought by Europeans decimated Native American populations, and their numbers were much reduced by the time the Spanish arrived. Regardless of the impact of Europeans, the resilient adaptation crafted for millennia in the harsh environments of the Southwest by Native Americans served them well in their interactions with Europeans, as the descendants of the Anasazi occupy the contemporary pueblos and cities of the North American Southwest today.

[See also CHACOAN PHENOMENON; HISTORY OF ARCHAEOLOGY FROM 1900 TO 1950: ARCHAEOLOGY OF THE AMERICAS; KIDDER, ALFRED; MESA VERDE; NORTH AMERICA: NORTH AMERICAN SOUTHWEST.]

Robert D. Leonard

ANATOLIA (from the Greek "Land of the Rising Sun") is a mountainous plateau, once covered by lakes and forests, and comprises the peninsula of Asia Minor. It is surrounded by the Pontic Mountains to the north and the Taurus Mountains to the south, which meet in the east around Mount Ararat forming an alpine landscape continuing into the Transcaucasian and Iranian highlands. In the west, the central plateau opens into wide river valleys that descend toward the Aegean Sea. As part of the Fertile Crescent, Anatolia participated in the cultural development of the ancient Near East, as well as being a physical and cultural bridge linking Asia and Europe.

The Neolithic and Chalcolithic Periods. From the ninth millennium B.C., sedentism and incipient food production developed in southeastern Anatolia. Aceramic Neolithic villages, such as Cafer Höyük and Gritille in the Euphrates Valley, contained rectangular houses built in timber and mud bricks on stone foundations, an architectural tradition surviving into the present. At Çayönü near Ergani in the upper Tigris area, large houses contained remains of locally domesticated cereals, sheep and goat bones, and some of the earliest copper artifacts ever discovered. The obsidian and flint tools of this period are closely related to the Syro-Mesopotamian variant of the Pre-Pottery Neolithic B tradition. In the central Anatolian lake district, Hacilar, Can Hasan III, and Suberde III have mud-brick houses with red-painted floors, fixed-hearth ovens, and intramural burials, as well as a locally developed flint tool tradition.

The nature of the transition to the Ceramic Neolithic (ca. 6500–5500 B.C.) is still unclear. Tepecik and Kumartepe in the southeast, Mersin and Tarsus in Cilicia, all closely related with the Amuq phases A and B, Hacilar IX–V, Can Hasan I, Erbaba I–II, and, above all, *Catal Hüyük in central Anatolia are the most outstanding sites of this period, with their characteristic architecture and abundant plastic art.

Late Neolithic traditions continue into the Chalcolithic Period (5500–3200 B.C.) at sites such as Can Hasan, Beycesultan, Mersin, and Tarsus. Tools, weapons, and jewelry were increasingly made of copper. The first fortified settlements were built at this time, but art declined, except on painted pottery.

Southeastern Anatolia was constantly exposed to cultural stimuli from Mesopotamia. At Samsat and Mevkii Karatut, traces of the Sumerian Uruk expansion along the Euphrates (3600–3400 B.C.) were found. That contact apparently prepared the ground for the urbanization of Anatolia.

The Bronze Age (3300–1200 B.C.). The first flowering of civilization during the Early Bronze Age (3200–1900 B.C.) brought a network of independent city-states, centered on fortified towns dominated by palaces and temples. Excavated sites are Lidar, Kurban Höyük, Arslantepe, Norsuntepe, and Tarsus in the southeast, Ikiztepe in the north, and Troy I and II in the northwest. Their economy was based on trade and metalworking, particularly arsenical copper. The simple painted pottery was increasingly wheel-made and burnished.

During this period eastern Anatolia was drawn into the cultural sphere of the Transcaucasian Kura-Araxes culture, characterized by its handmade, highly polished red-black pottery. From the middle of the third millennium B.C. a constant trickle of pastoral groups from the steppes north of the Black Sea entered Anatolia, forming a new elite. Their tombs at Alaca Höyük, Horoztepe, and Mahmutlar contained exquisite bronze and gold artifacts showing cultural connections with Eurasia and Iran. From ca. 2400 B.C., however, many towns declined and were destroyed, probably as the result of internecine warfare and bids by invading groups, such as the ancestors of the Hurrians and the Indo-European Luwians and Hittites.

The Middle Bronze Age (ca. 2000–1600 B.C.) basically continued the material culture of the Early Bronze Age, but tools and weapons were increasingly made of tin bronze. The cuneiform archives found in the Assyrian trading colonies established outside some native towns, in particular Karum Kanes/Kultepe (1950–1750 B.C.), provide historical information on the period immediately preceding the establishment of the Hittite Old Kingdom.

The political unification of Anatolia by the Hittites, from the beginning of the Late Bronze Age (ca. 1600 B.C.) on, and campaigns abroad brought wealth to the capital Hattusas/Bogazkale and towns such as Alaca Höyük, Acemhoyuk, Masat, and Tilmen Höyük. Excavations of monumental palaces and temple storerooms yielded a staggering amount of highly burnished red pottery, bronze weapons, art objects, ceremonial artifacts, and cuneiform archives informing us about the rituals and history of the empire. The monumental sculptures such as the Sphinx Gate at Alaca Höyük and the Lions, Sphinx and King's Gate at Hattusas display Egyptian artistic influence. At the same time, the growing importance of Hurrian religion is reflected in the rock reliefs of Yazilikaya. It was found that in the thirteenth century B.C., Hattusas expanded into a vast city of temples, surrounded by elaborate fortifications. The contemporary layers of Beycesultan and Troy in the western parts of Anatolia show a similar cultural horizon and close contacts with the Aegean world during the second millennium B.C.

A hypothesized climatic crisis ca. twelfth–thirteenth centuries B.C., political turmoil, and the invasion of the Sea Peoples apparently contributed to the collapse of the Hittite empire. The destruction of Hattusas around 1200 B.C. marks the end of the Bronze Age.

The Iron Age and the Classical Periods (1200–30 B.C.). Following the tumultuous period at the end of the Late Bronze Age, the survivors of the Hittite aristocracy founded the Neo-Hittite kingdoms in southeastern Anatolia, at Carchemish, Zincirli, Malatya, and Karatepe. Farther east, excavations at Tushpa/Van, Cavustepe, and Altintepe/Erzincan provide testimony of the sophisticated bronze technology and the civil and military architecture of that time in the kingdom of Urartu, established by the descendants of the Hurrians.

In central Anatolia, the excavations at Gordion, the capital of the kingdom of Phrygia during the ninth and eighth centuries B.C., at Midas City and the tumulus at Elmali, have recovered intricately painted dark-on-light pottery, ivory and wood carvings, and exquisite bronze implements. After the destruction of Phrygia by the Cimmerians around 700 B.C., Lydia and its capital, Sardis, where coinage was invented, rose to political and economic power.

In the west, the Greeks reoccupied the former Mycenaean settlements at Troy, Ephesos, Miletos, and other sites. On the ruins of the Bronze Age civilizations, a new and vigorous Greek culture was born, documented in the excavations of the Protogeometric, Geometric, and Archaic ages at Smyrna/Bayrakli and Erythrai.

While the Persian conquest in 546 B.C. and the violent suppression of the revolt of Miletos in 496 B.C. forstalled the participation of western Anatolia in the achievements of classical Greece, the conquest of Alexander the Great revitalized the Greek civilization in Anatolia during the Hellenistic period (330–30 B.C.). The art of Pergamon was of paramount importance for the development of Roman art. Ephesus, Priene, Miletos, Halicarnassos, Aphrodisias, and dozens of other sites typify the achievements of Hellenistic civilization of Anatolia during the Roman and Byzantine periods.

[See also GREECE: THE HELLENISTIC AGE; NEAR EAST, articles on THE NEOLITHIC AND CHALCOLITHIC (PRE-BRONZE-AGE) PERIODS IN THE NEAR EAST, THE BRONZE AGE IN THE NEAR EAST, IRON AGE CIVILIZATIONS OF THE NEAR EAST; ROMAN EMPIRE: THE EASTERN PROVINCES OF THE ROMAN EMPIRE.]

■ O. R. Gurney, *The Hittites* (1952). E. Akurgai and M. Hirmer, *The Art of the Hittites* (1962). J. Cook, *The Greeks in Ionia and the East* (1965). C. Blegen, *Troy and the Trojans* (1966). S. Lloyd, *Early Highland Peoples of Anatolia* (1967). J. Mellaart, *Catal Hoyuk* (1967). B. B. Piotrowski, *Urartu* (Archaeologia Mundi) (1969). E. Akurgal, *Ancient Civilisations and Ruins in Turkey* (1970). K. Bittel, *Hattusa, the Capital of the Hittites* (1970). *Architektur Kleinasiens von thren Anfangen bis zum Ende der hethitischen Zeit* (1971). M. J. Mellink, "Anatolian Chronology," in *Chronologies in Old World Archaeology*, ed. R. W. Ehrich, R. Naumann (1993).

Mattanyah Zohar

ANDEAN PRE-INCA CIVILIZATIONS, The Rise of

Introduction
Effects of El Niño on Peruvian
 Civilization
Maritime Foundations of Pre-Inca
 Civilization

INTRODUCTION

In the more than three thousand years between the introduction of ceramic technology and the emergence of the great Inca Empire, numerous civilizations rose and fell in the Andean region of South America. The chronological sequence began with the Initial Period, which designated the introduction of ceramic technology. This period was followed by three Horizons (Early, Middle, and Late), periods during which a single artistic style was widespread

throughout the region. Between Horizons were Intermediate Periods (Early and Late), during which numerous regional cultures with distinctive styles of artifacts arose.

During the Initial Period (1800 B.C. to 800 B.C.) subsistence shifted from primarily hunting and gathering, with some limited cultivation of cotton and gourds, to a system in which people relied on domesticated plants and animals for their food. In the highlands llamas were domesticated as pack animals and for their meat, alpacas were used for their wool, and guinea pigs were bred for food. Highland food crops included many varieties of potatoes, beans, and quinoa. On the coast, subsistence also included peanuts, squash, and a variety of other fruits and vegetables. People adopted a sedentary lifestyle, and lived in villages that gradually increased in size.

On the central and north coasts of Peru the Initial Period also saw the first constructions of monumental religious architecture and the emergence of major ceremonial centers. On the central coast the architecture sometimes was arranged in a U-shaped configuration: a large temple mound with long flanking mounds on either side. El Paraíso in the Chillon Valley is an example of this type of site, as is Garagay in the Rimac Valley. Farther north the sites tended to be laid out in a more linear fashion, also including large temple mounds, and also incorporating semi-subterranean circular courts. The site of Las Haldas, on the coast near the Casma Valley, conforms to this arrangement.

In the highlands, the Kotosh Religious Tradition emerged, best known from the sites of Kotosh, Huaricoto, and La Galgada in the northcentral highlands of Peru. People of this tradition erected small square temple structures, with perimeter benches and a central fire pit. After a period of use, such temples were carefully filled and covered over with earth, and new temples were erected on or near them. Elsewhere in the highlands people lived in small villages and grew potatoes, but did not develop distinctive religious or political complexes.

During the Early Horizon (800 B.C. to A.D. 1) it is thought that the highland site of *Chavín de Huantar became very influential and was the center of dispersal for the widespread styles of artifacts seen at this time. Many of the coastal ceremonial centers were suddenly abandoned at the end of the Initial Period, perhaps due to catastrophic effects of particularly strong El Niños. At about the same time, Chavín was erected in the north highlands. The site was originally laid out as a U-shaped temple complex, with a sunken circular court within the wings of the complex. Inside the main temple structure at the base of the U is still seen a monumental stone carving of the deity that may have been worshipped in the temple. The figure is a human, with a feline mouth and fangs, and hair depicted as snakes. After a time the Old Temple was expanded, and new wings were built to create a much larger New Temple, with a sunken rectangular court.

Chavín seems to have functioned as a pilgrimage center. People journeyed from distant regions to make offerings at the site. The Gallery of the Offerings was filled with broken pottery brought in from many different parts of the Andes. It seems most likely that the horizon style was dispersed by pilgrims who copied the designs and styles they saw there, and perhaps even by missionaries who established branch temples in other areas. For example, textiles painted with pure Chavín designs have been found on the south coast of Peru, near the Ica Valley.

Styles that show some similarity to Chavín are found in

the north Peruvian highlands, and on much of the coast. On the north coast the Cupisnique style prevailed, and was closely related to Chavín. On the south coast, the Paracas culture adopted some elements of Chavín style, depicting the designs by incising them on their ceramics in their own distinctive manner. The Paracas culture is also known for the extensive cemeteries found on the Paracas peninsula, which gives its name to the culture. Two styles of burial, the Necropolis and Cavernas styles, are found there.

The central and south highlands of Peru, and the highlands of Bolivia, seem to have been only very indirectly influenced by Chavín, if at all. By about 200 B.C. Chavín was abandoned, and the religious cult diminished. The last two centuries of the Early Horizon were characterized by increased warfare and the emergence of regional styles: Recuay in the north highlands, Gallinazo on the north coast, La Pena on the south coast.

In the Early Intermediate Period (A.D. 1 to 750) several major regional cultures emerged, including Moche and Nasca, perhaps the best known of the pre-Inca civilizations. Moche was located on the north coast of Peru, centered around the Moche Valley and its capital at Cerro Blanco. The site includes two well-known structures: the Huaca del Sol (Pyramid of the Sun), perhaps the largest structure in the New World at the time, and the Huaca de la Luna (Pyramid of the Moon) with fabulous polychrome friezes decorating its walls. Moche influence extended south to the Nepena Valley, and north to Lambayeque. Moche, whose influence seems to take the form of direct political control, was perhaps the first Andean civilization that can be defined as a true state-level society. Warfare seems to have played an important role in Moche control.

Much is known of Moche life from depictions on ceramic artifacts. Some Moche pottery is modeled in the form of animals, plants, humans, or supernatural creatures. Some of the best-known forms include portrait pots, depicting the heads of individuals, and erotic pottery, depicting a variety of sexual activities. Other Moche pottery is decorated with fine red lines on a buff-colored background. These fine-line vessels depict elaborate scenes, including burial scenes, battles, sacrifices, and various ceremonies. All Moche art can be seen to pertain to a total of about fifteen separate themes; many modeled vessels are actually elements from the more elaborate themes.

Recently a series of extraordinary Moche tombs was excavated at *Sipan, in the Lambayeque region of the north. In these tombs a royal personage was buried in an elaborate coffin, filled with textiles and metal art, and placed in a tomb along with several other individuals, as well as dozens of other artifacts.

On the south coast of Peru another complex civilization arose, centered in the Nasca Valley. The Nasca civilization began as a rather simple society: people lived in small scattered villages in the Andean foothills, but they produced some of the most elaborate ceramic and textile art ever seen in the Andes. Ceramics were painted in up to sixteen colors, depicting natural life as well as supernatural beings and events. During the Early Nasca phase (A.D. 1 to 500) they built a major ceremonial center at Cahuachi, out on the desert plain, far from their villages, and surrounded by enormous cemeteries. Cahuachi seems to have served as a pilgrimage center, much as Chavín had, but on a much smaller scale; there is no evidence that people lived permanently at the site. Around A.D. 500 there began a series of devastating droughts: construction ceased at Cahuachi, and

in Late Nasca times (A.D. 500 to 750) people aggregated into large towns. Warfare increased at this time, as did political complexity. Hydraulic technology was developed to allow the people of Nasca to tap underground water and free them from their reliance on meager river water.

Elsewhere in the Andean region there arose smaller, distinctive cultures, most of which are still known only on the basis of the distribution of artifact styles: the Lima culture on the central coast, Pucara in southern Peru, Chiripa in northern Bolivia. The site of Tiwanaku emerged in Bolivia toward the end of the EIP; it was a vast complex of ceremonial structures that revived some of the old Chavín images, and probably also served as a major pilgrimage center as well. Toward the end of the Early Intermediate there seems to have been an increase in interaction between the various cultures, perhaps due to the deteriorating climate and the concomitant disruption of their subsistence systems.

In the Middle Horizon (A.D. 750 to 1000) the site of Wari in central Peru grew suddenly to urban proportions, and began a series of conquests that resulted in one of the first true empires in the Andes. At the same time Tiwanaku may also have expanded its political control, also becoming an empire. Archaeological research in Peru has demonstrated the existence of an extensive system of administrative centers, roads, and economic and political control overseen by Wari. Few Tiwanaku provincial centers are known, but the few that are known suggest a strong religious component to Tiwanaku control, very different from that of Wari. The architecture of Wari sites is designed to keep people out; the architecture of Tiwanaku sites is designed to bring large numbers of people together.

These empires lasted only a few centuries, and in the aftermath of their collapse there arose again a series of distinctive local cultures in the Late Intermediate Period (A.D. 1000 to 1476). The most complex of these was the *Chimu state of the north coast. From their capital at *Chanchan in the Moche Valley, the Chimu controlled a territory from the Casma Valley in the south, north through Lambayeque. The site of Chanchan comprises nine or ten large rectangular compounds called ciudadelas. Each compound served as the residence and administrative offices of a Chimu ruler; upon his death it then served as his mausoleum, while the next ruler erected his own compound.

On the southcentral coast of Peru, the Chincha Valley was the center of a culture that was known for its long-distance trade networks. Although there is little evidence of major political centralization and control in and around Chincha, they built balsa rafts and sailed up and down the coastline, carrying textiles and metals north as far as Ecuador, and bringing warm-water shells such as Spondylus south. In the highlands there emerged a series of small polities including Cajamarca in the north, the Wankas in the central highlands, the Chankas in the southcentral highlands, the Incas in the Cuzco region, and the Colla and Lupaqa in the Titicaca Basin.

In the mid-fifteenth century the Incas began a series of conquests that was to culminate in the largest empire ever known in the New World.

[See also CHAVÍN CULTURE; MOCHE CULTURE; NASCA LINES; NASCA STATE; SOUTH AMERICA, articles on THE RISE OF COMPLEX SOCIETIES IN SOUTH AMERICA, HIGHLANDS CULTURES OF SOUTH AMERICA; SOUTH AMERICA, ORIGINS OF FOOD PRODUCTION IN; TIAHUANACO EMPIRE; WARI EMPIRE.]

■ Wendell C. Bennett and Junius B. Bird, *Andean Culture History*, 2nd edition (1949). Luis G. Lumbreras, *The Peoples and Cultures of Ancient Peru* (1974). Richard W. Keatinge, ed., *Peruvian Prehistory* (1988). Michael E. Moseley, *The Incas and Their Ancestors* (1992).

Katharina Schreiber

EFFECTS OF EL NIÑO ON PERUVIAN CIVILIZATION

El Niño is part of a global climatic perturbation that causes tremendous changes in the desert coast and adjacent highlands of western South America. During certain years, the warm, south-flowing, coastal current known as El Niño pushes the normal, cold, north-flowing Humboldt Current seaward, bringing rain to the desert and altering life in the ocean.

For the inhabitants of the north coast of Peru, El Niño can be a true disaster. Cold-water marine animals die or migrate south, to be replaced by less abundant warm-water species. Torrential rains in the desert cause massive flooding and erosion, damaging or destroying sites as well as the irrigation systems on which coastal agriculture has depended for three millennia. El Niño is often accompanied by tropical diseases and pests. In the southern highlands of Peru and Bolivia, El Niño years are often drought years.

The intensity, duration, and extent of El Niño vary from event to event. On the coast, the effects decrease to the south, so El Niño is not uniformly negative. On the central and southern coast of Peru, many of the fish migrating southward come inshore where they are easier to catch from the beach or in small, prehispanic-type watercraft. During the last serious event (1982–1983), there was a boom in the scallop population south of Lima, Peru. After the rains, much of the desert blooms, though only temporarily.

Strong to moderate El Niños occur irregularly, about once every seven to fifteen years; major events take place about twice per century. Some evidence suggests that El Niño began only five thousand years ago, but this idea is still being debated. For the last five millennia, at least, El Niño has been an important factor in the development of Peruvian civilization. Studies of its effects are just beginning, and most concentrate on identifying when El Niño occurred in the past. Ancient El Niños are recognized in archaeological sites by studying erosion, flood deposition, changes in plant and animal species collected by a site's inhabitants, and changes in the growth pattern and chemistry of mollusks. For more recent times, independent climate records such as annual levels from Andean glaciers provide data on El Niño occurrences. Cultural interpretations have been suggested on the basis of correlations between El Niño events and cultural changes, but must still be tested.

The first monumental architecture on the Peruvian coast was built during the Late Preceramic Period (4450–3800 B.P.), signaling an increase in social complexity. El Niño may have played a role in this development by stimulating storage or other responses to cyclical resource fluctuation.

Richard Burger argues that during the Early Horizon (2450–2150 B.P.), the highland Chavín cult abruptly replaced the coastal religion of northern Peru around 2450 B.C., perhaps due in part to destabilization caused by a major El Niño event.

The largest and best-known prehistoric event is the mega-Niño, which took place sometime between A.D. 1000 and 1100. Archaeological evidence for this event is found in several valleys on the Peruvian north coast. The mega-Niño coincided with a number of significant cultural changes, and the destruction it caused may have been partially re-sponsible for them. In the Lambayeque valley of northern Peru, the center of power apparently shifted from the religious center at Batán Grande to the possibly more secular monumental site of Tucume. At the same time, the *Chimu state of the Moche valley began expanding to the north and south.

In historic times, El Niño has seriously disrupted life in Peru, as it certainly did in the prehistoric past. As archaeologists learn more about when past El Niños occurred, they may better understand the effects on ancient lifeways.

[*See also* SOUTH AMERICA: THE RISE OF COMPLEX SOCIETIES IN SOUTH AMERICA.]

■ Thomas Y. Canby, "El Niños Ill Wind," *National Geographic Magazine* 165:2 (1984): 144–184. Michael E. Moseley, "Punctuated Equilibrium: Searching the Ancient Record for El Niño," *The Quarterly Review of Archaeology* 8:3 (1987): 7–10. Richard Burger, "Unity and Heterogeneity within the Chavín Horizon," in *Peruvian Prehistory*, ed. Richard W. Keatinge (1988), pp. 99–144. David B. Enfield, "El Niño, Past and Present," *Reviews of Geophysics* 27 (1989): 159–187.

Daniel H. Sandweiss

MARITIME FOUNDATIONS OF PRE-INCA CIVILIZATION

The coast of Peru is an environment of stark contrasts. On land, one of the world's driest deserts is broken only by the narrow rivers that descend from the adjacent Andean highlands. In front of the desert, however, is one of the world's richest maritime ecosystems. Archaeologists have long been concerned with how complex societies emerged in this striking context.

In 1975, Michael Moseley offered a controversial hypothesis on the origin of early complex society on the Peruvian coast. He proposed that the first such societies were supported by maritime fishing and gathering, at a time when most archaeologists believed that such phenomena could arise only when agriculture, and particularly irrigation agriculture, dominated the subsistence economy. Although drawing on earlier work, especially that of Edward Lanning, Moseley's hypothesis set off a continuing debate.

Moseley based his original formulation of the Maritime Hypothesis on his excavations in the Ancón-Chillón region, on the coast north of Lima, Peru. Originally he thought that marine mollusks provided the bulk of the food; however, he soon realized that small, netted fish such as anchovetas were the mainstay of the diet. According to the hypothesis, agriculture was known but used primarily for "industrial" crops such as cotton (for fishing nets) and gourds (for net floats). The few food plants known to be present were considered a minor component of the diet. Irrigation agriculture was not yet in use.

Moseley's early maritime societies date to the Late Preceramic Period (2500–1750 B.C.) on the central and north-central coast of Peru. The sites contain monumental architecture, such as platform mounds, which was thought to require significant planning and labor. It is this monumental architecture that is most often interpreted as evidence of complex society. The largest site is El Paraíso, near Lima; it has at least eight major buildings and covers over 123 acres (50 ha). Other important sites include Aspero in the Supe Valley, the Late Preceramic component of Las Haldas near Casma, and Salinas de Chao.

Moseley's hypothesis generated vociferous counterarguments. Some authors pointed to the instability of maritime resources on the Peruvian coast as a result of the aperiodic incursions of the warm-water El Niño current, which happens on average every seven to fifteen years but is truly devastating only about twice per century. What these authors failed to consider is that El Niño is a disaster only on the north coast. On the central coast, where most Late Preceramic monumental centers occur, El Niño is more often a benefit than a catastrophe: The fish that flee south from the warm water come close inshore on the central coast and are easier to catch than normal, while the torrential rains that flood the northern valleys become gentler to the south, where they aid agriculture rather than destroy it.

Another counterargument is that marine foods alone are incapable of supporting the populations necessary for early complex society. Ethnographic data suggest that this idea is not strictly true. Finally, several archaeologists have suggested that particular cultivated plants were the true staple of the diet, despite their near absence in the archaeological record for the coastal Late Preceramic Period. Archaeologist David Wilson hypothesized that maize (*Zea mays*) was the basis of subsistence, as it was later in prehistory; however, no maize has been found in any of the Late Preceramic monumental centers, and its reported occurrence in a small site of that period has been seriously questioned. A more intriguing possibility was raised by another archaeologist, Scott Raymond, who proposed that the root crop achira (*Canna edulis*) provided the calories that marine foods lacked. Achira is found in small quantities in Late Preceramic sites; as an edible root, few remains would be expected in an archaeological context.

More recent fieldwork by Jeffrey Quilter and associates at El Paraíso, the principal Late Preceramic monumental center, has provided the best empirical evidence on the subsistence of these sites. The bulk of the meat consumed at the site came from the sea: Fish were most important, but mollusks, crabs, sea urchins, and other marine organisms were eaten as well. Plants were also crucial to the diet. Cultivated species included squash, beans, achira, jicama (*Pachyrrhizus tuberosus*), and a variety of tree fruits. Most archaeologists now accept this synthesis of marine protein and terrestrial plant carbohydrates (but not maize) as the basic subsistence pattern supporting the Late Preceramic societies.

When Moseley first formulated the Maritime Hypothesis, archaeologists still believed that prehistoric Peruvians did not use marine resources until about 3000 B.C. and that the development of complex society followed shortly thereafter. We now know that maritime lifeways in Peru extend back to at least 8000 B.C. It may be that the crucial factor in supporting Late Preceramic monumental construction was not the maritime resources alone but rather the combination of these resources with terrestrial cultigens, as witnessed at El Paraíso.

The debate on the origins of complex society on the Peruvian coast has now moved beyond subsistence. Some scholars have begun searching the archaeological record for antecedents to the monumental architecture of the Late Preceramic Period. Others argue that the pyramid platforms of the Late Preceramic and succeeding Initial period were built in increments by egalitarian societies, not by complex societies usually considered necessary for planning and executing such structures. Regardless of its ultimate resolution, the Maritime Hypothesis has already proven to be one of the most stimulating ideas in Andean prehistory, responsible for two decades of frontline research with more to come.

[*See also* EARLY PREHISTORY OF SOUTH AMERICA; SOUTH AMERICA, ORIGINS OF FOOD PRODUCTION IN; SOUTH AMERICA: THE RISE OF COMPLEX SOCIETIES IN SOUTH AMERICA; STATES: THEORIES OF THE ORIGINS OF STATES.]

■ Edward P. Lanning, *Peru before the Incas* (1967). Michael E. Moseley, *The Maritime Foundations of Andean Civilization* (1975). J. Scott Raymond, "The Maritime Foundations of Andean Civilization: A Reconsideration of the Evidence," *American Antiquity* 46 (1981): 806–821. David Wilson, "Of Maize and Men: A Critique of the Maritime Hypothesis of State Origins on the Coast of Peru," *American Anthropologist* 83 (1981): 93–120. Jeffrey Quilter et al., "Subsistence Economy of El Paraíso, An Early Peruvian Site," *Science* 251 (1991): 277–283. Daniel H. Sandweiss, ed., *Andean Past 3* (1992).
Daniel H. Sandweiss

ANGKOR, THE EMPIRE OF. *See* KHMER CIVILIZATION AND THE EMPIRE OF ANGKOR.

ANIMAL REMAINS, Analysis of. The study of animal remains from archaeological sites constitutes a major discipline within the field of archaeology. Also referred to as archaeozoology and *zooarchaeology, this discipline is concerned with the identification and interpretation of food refuse and other types of animal remains from archaeological contexts. The questions addressed through the analysis of faunal remains generally pertain to four major topics: prehistoric subsistence, paleoenvironmental conditions, processes of animal domestication, and season(s) of occupation.

Anthropological interest in prehistoric faunal remains can be traced back to the mid-1800s, when European scientists turned to the evidence of stone tools in association with extinct fauna to establish the antiquity of humankind. There were also some early uses of animal remains for documenting cultural sequences and paleoenvironmental change. In the first half of the twentieth century, researchers began to tackle questions of animal domestication, studies that accelerated with growing interest in agricultural origins around 1950. Since that time, the study of animal remains has become an increasingly important part of archaeological research.

The animal remains found in archaeological deposits are in most cases those of animals that lived around, and that were used by, the site inhabitants. These may include species of mammals, birds, fish, reptiles, amphibians, shellfish, and insects. Generally, it is the hard components that are preserved: the bones, teeth, antlers, and horns of mammals; bird bones; the bones, teeth, otoliths (ear stones), and dermal structures of fish; the bones and teeth of reptiles and amphibians; and the shells of terrestrial, freshwater, and marine invertebrates. In cases of exceptional preservation, such as dry caves or anaerobic peat deposits, skins, hairs, feathers, scales, and even the eggs of intestinal parasites may also be preserved.

Once retrieved, washed, and sorted, the taxonomic identification of archaeological faunal remains is accomplished through the use of modern comparative material. Study collections are comprised of the disarticulated skeletons of animals of known age and sex from taxa likely to be encountered in a particular region. Ideally, a comparative collection contains a minimum of several individuals of each species so that the range of variation within a given species can be assessed.

One essential task of the faunal analyst is to identify and separate cultural from noncultural materials. An important source of noncultural bone in archaeological deposits is burrowing rodents. These animals thrive in uncompacted cultural soils, dying naturally in their burrows long after humans actually occupied the site. Fortunately, it is often possible to identify such intrusive animals by the relative completeness of their skeletons and the fresh appearance of their bones.

The separation of cultural from noncultural bone is a more central issue in early African hominid studies. Ancient faunal assemblages created by carnivores such as hyenas and leopards may be difficult to distinguish from those created by hominids. Because meat-eating behavior is a central issue in studies of early humans, it is important for researchers to be able to distinguish hominid from non-hominid bone accumulations. Since the late 1970s, when the significance of the problem first became apparent, a considerable amount of effort has been directed at elucidating the signatures (cutmarks, tooth marks, water-worn surfaces, etc.) of the different processes that result in bone accumulations.

Once cultural remains are identified, there are several methods used in their quantification. These methods are particularly useful when attempting to assess the relative dietary contribution of different taxa. The most common method for assessing the composition of a collection is the determination of the minimum number of individuals (MNI). Since archaeological collections are comprised of hundreds or thousands of mixed-up fragments, MNIs are determined by counting the most frequent side of the most frequent skeletal element of each taxon. Size differences and age indicators may also be taken into account in these calculations. Weight measures also provide several methods for quantifying relative abundance. These include the following: estimates based on the cumulative bone or shell weight for each taxonomic grouping; estimates that translate bone or shell weight into corresponding meat weight; estimates based on the average live weight of the minimum number of individuals; and those based on size-specific weight estimates of identified individuals. The weight conversion factors used in these calculations are sometimes obtained through experimental and ethnographic studies, but may also derive from government fish and game reports or other published sources.

Each method used to quantify faunal remains has its benefits and problems. A good source of information on the limitations of different techniques can be found in Donald Grayson's treatise *Quantitative Zooarchaeology* (1984).

Age and sex determinations constitute another important component of faunal analysis. For mammals, age is usually determined from tooth eruption, tooth wear, and epiphyseal fusion, the sequences of which are known from studies of modern animals. Size and annual growth rings are better determinants of age for fish and shellfish species. Sex may be determined by the presence of sex-specific elements such as carnivore bacula (penis bones) or ungulate horns and antlers, but is often implied by size differences. If the sample is relatively large, age and sex data can be used to construct population profiles that inform on the nature of animal acquisition. For example, in their book *The Analysis of Animal Bones from Archaeological Sites* (1984), Klein and Cruz-Uribe interpret the high frequency of very young and very old Cape buffalo remains in two South African cave sites to reflect the judicious behavior of human hunters in acquiring the meat of an ill-tempered and powerful beast. On the other hand, they interpret the high frequency of juvenile domestic sheep remains from another,

much later cave deposit to reflect the culling behavior of herders. These examples illustrate the potential of faunal analysis for understanding the decision-making processes of prehistoric hunters and herders.

Because different types of animals are associated with different landscapes and climates, animal remains can also provide important clues about the paleoenvironment. For example, the remains of cold-adapted species such as reindeer and lemmings in archaeological deposits in France are evidence that the climate during the occupation of these sites was substantially colder than it is today. The replacement of certain fauna, or changes in the average size of a species, may also indicate a change in climatic regime.

Even the season of occupation can be investigated through the analysis of faunal remains. Two very useful methods for studying season through the analysis of shellfish are profiled in Margaret Deith's article "Seasonality from Shells" in *Paleobiological Investigations* (1985). Both methods involve the study of annual, temperature-regulated growth bands. The vertebrae, scales, and otoliths of fish provide similar records of growth that can be analyzed for seasonal information. Other faunal indicators of season include the presence of migratory birds, the growth stages of impermanent elements such as antlers and deciduous (milk) teeth, and birth-season indicators such as the presence of newborn animals. Seasonality studies are important because they enable the archaeologist to reconstruct settlement patterns by providing information on the timing and duration of site occupations.

A range of other topics including living conditions, trade and exchange, differential access to protein resources, and the processes of domestication have been successfully investigated through the analysis of animal remains from archaeological sites. As our understanding of the processes that result in archaeological faunal assemblages increases, so will our ability to interpret ancient human cultures through their animal refuse.

[*See also* DOMESTICATION OF ANIMALS; PALEOENVIRONMENTAL RECONSTRUCTION.]

■ Louis R. Binford, *Bones: Ancient Men and Modern Myths* (1981). C. K. Brain, *The Hunters or the Hunted* (1981). Betty Meehan, *Shell Bed to Shell Midden* (1982). N.R.J. Fieller, D. D. Gilbertson and N.G.A. Ralph, *Palaeobiological Investigations* (1985). B. Miles Gilbert, Larry D. Martin, and Howard G. Savage, *Avian Osteology* (1985). Simon J. M. Davis, *The Archaeology of Animals* (1987). Alwyne Wheeler and Andrew K. G. Jones, *Fishes* (1989). B. Miles Gilbert, *Mammalian Osteology* (1993). Jean Hudson, ed., *From Bones to Behavior* (1993).

Patricia M. Lambert

ANIMALS, Domestication of. *See* DOMESTICATION OF ANIMALS.

ANTIQUITY OF HUMANKIND

Overview
Antiquity of Humankind in the Old World
Antiquity of Humankind in the Americas

OVERVIEW

Prior to the mid-nineteenth century, both archaeology and paleontology were bound by the rigid confines of Christian dogma, which held that the first chapter of Genesis was the literal historical truth. In 1650, Archbishop James Ussher had used the genealogies in the Old Testament to date the

Creation to 4,004 B.C., allowing a mere six thousand years for all human history.

The first entry describes the establishment of human antiquity in Europe, and shows how advances in stratigraphic geology resulting from the Industrial Revolution led to the theory of uniformitarianism. Meanwhile, Charles *Darwin and Alfred Wallace grappled with biological evolution. Their research culminated in the publication of Darwin's *Origin of Species* in 1859. In the same year, English scholars John Evans and Joseph Prestwich visited French archaeologist Boucher de *Perthes in the Somme Valley. They observed prehistoric stone axes eroding from the same gravel layers as the bones of extinct Ice Age animals—field evidence for human antiquity.

David Meltzer describes how American archaeologists searched for sites as early as those in Europe. Their search soon faltered, for no unquestionably early artifacts were found. Today, the earliest well-documented human settlement in the New World dates to about twelve thousand years ago.

Brian M. Fagan

ANTIQUITY OF HUMANKIND IN THE OLD WORLD

Until the late eighteenth century, most scientists believed in the literal historical truth of Genesis, Chapter 1. God had created the world and its inhabitants in six days. The story of Adam and Eve provided an entirely consistent explanation for the creation of humankind and the peopling of the world. Seventeenth-century cleric Archbishop James Ussher of Armagh, Ireland, used Old Testament genealogies to calculate the world was created on the night preceding October 23, 4004 B.C. Ussher's chronology became theological dogma, allowing only 6,000 years for all of human history.

The eighteenth century saw an explosion of scientific inquiry, which coincided with the Industrial Revolution. French scientist George Cuvier (1769–1832) spent a lifetime studying fossil animals, distinguishing hundreds of species and founding the science of paleontology. Cuvier laid out a geological history of the world, using dozens of fossil animals as type indicators for different geological layers and epochs. He discovered a period when great dinosaurs had been the dominant creatures on Earth. Throughout his long career, Cuvier persisted in explaining massive extinctions of animals like dinosaurs as the result of giant cataclysms, the last of which was the biblical flood.

Geologists were in the forefront of the new science, studying the deep cuts in the earth's layers made by large-scale railroad and canal building. William "Strata" Smith (1769–1839) was one of many field observers, studying not only geological strata, but the fossil animals in them, which appeared and disappeared at the same time everywhere on Earth. Smith emphasized the rocks of the earth had been formed by continuous natural processes—earthquakes, wind action, floods, and all the phenomena that still modified the landscape. Thus, as James Hutton argued in his *Theory of the Earth* (1784), the earth was formed not by divine intervention or by catastrophic floods, but by entirely natural geological processes. Hutton's and Smith's theories of "uniformitarianism" attacked the very essence of the Ussherian chronology and caused a furor, for they appeared to deny divine creation. The new theories already enjoyed wide acceptance when Charles Lyell's *Principles of Geology* appeared in 1830–1833. Locality by locality, stratum by stratum, Lyell summarized the findings of the new geology, giving uniformitarianism a solid foundation in field evidence from many parts of Europe. *Principles of Geology* was read not only by a wide public, but by scientists in many fields, among them an obscure naturalist, Charles *Darwin.

In his book, Lyell used a generalized philosophy of gradual change in describing the types of fossils found in successive strata of the earth. His book appeared as Charles Darwin left England on the H.M.S. *Beagle* on a five-year voyage (1831–1836). As Darwin began his classic observations in South America that led him toward his theories of evolution and natural selection, he read Lyell's great work. From that moment on, he looked at the earth with new eyes, as a continuously changing world formed and modified by natural geological processes. On his return to England, Darwin started the first of a series of notebooks on what he called "the species question," ways in which species had changed with time. In 1838 he read Thomas Henry Malthus's famous *Essay on the Principle of Population* (1798). He immediately realized he was close to an important hypothesis. Malthus argued that human reproductive capacity far exceeds the available food supply. In other words, people must compete with one another for the necessities of life. Similar competition occurs among all living organisms. Darwin wondered if new forms had in part been formed by this "struggle for existence," in which the well-adapted individuals survive and the ill-adapted are eliminated. The doctrine of evolution was nothing new at the time. Many scientists before Darwin, including Jean Lamarck, Georges-Louis Buffon, and even Darwin's own grandfather Erasmus, had suggested animals and plants had not remained unaltered through the ages, but had changed continuously. They had hinted that all organisms, including human beings, were modified descendants of previously existing forms of life. Using uniformitarianism, Malthus's ideas, and his own field observations of fossil and living organisms, Darwin converted evolution from mere speculation into active theory by showing how change could occur.

Darwin was a timid man who sat on his ideas for twenty years. He realized his new theory, like uniformitarianism, flew in the face of theological canon. Evolution and natural selection would allow not only for a human history far longer than a mere 6,000 years. Darwin knew, also, many people would be horrified by his assumption that humans were descended from apelike ancestors. In 1858, another naturalist, Alfred Wallace, forced his hand, sending him an essay in which he reached much the same conclusions. The following year, Charles Darwin published *On the Origin of Species*, a "preliminary sketch" of the theory of evolution by natural selection.

Darwin's book was greeted with both acclaim and vicious controversy, as scientists and theologians took sides in a debate that lasted for generations, and persists in extreme forms to this day. Evolution by natural selection gave a theoretical explanation for the diversity of both fossil and living forms, and for the complex biological changes in humankind. It also provided an explanation for discoveries of humanly manufactured stone artifacts in the same geological strata as long extinct animals.

In 1797, an English country squire named John Frere recovered some beautifully made flint axes from a Suffolk lake bed containing hippopotamus bones. In his report on the find to the Society of Antiquaries, Frere remarked that the circumstances of the find tempted him to refer them to "a remote period indeed, even beyond that of the present world." Frere's discovery caused little excitement at the time, for most people accepted the biblical creation as historical fact. Soon more finds of extinct animals and stone tools came from caves and rock shelters in France and Belgium, but mostly in the hands of amateur diggers, distrusted by the scientific establishment. Between 1824 and 1829, English Catholic priest J. MacEnery unearthed extinct animal bones and stone tools from the lower levels of Kent's Cavern near Torquay in southwestern England. Both bones and tools were sealed under a layer of stalagmite, a concretelike cave earth. Even then, some scientists insisted the tools came from ancient British ovens dug through the cemented layer into earlier strata.

Jacques Boucher de *Perthes (1788–1868) was a customs officer at Abbeville in the Somme Valley of northern France with a passion for geology and fossils. In 1837, he began collecting not only fossils but stone tools from the same river gravels. Immediately, he found humanly made artifacts and extinct animals in the same sealed gravel beds in such numbers he was convinced he had found pre–biblical flood people. Unfortunately, de Perthes was rather pompous, with a long-winded prose style. Few people read his books from cover to cover. His fellow collectors and scientists scorned his revolutionary ideas and ignored his thousands of fossils and stone axes. His rambling Antiquités Celtiques et Antédiluviennes (1847) claimed humanity was much earlier than the 6,000 years in Old Testament genealogies. Most of de Perthes's contemporaries considered him a nuisance.

In 1856, quarrymen unearthed a strange skull in a long-sealed cave in the Neander Valley in western Germany. The cranium, with its huge, beetling brow ridges, thick walls, and squat shape, puzzled all who examined it. Some experts dismissed the Neanderthal find as a pathological idiot, or even the remains of a Cossack from the Napoleonic Wars. But a minority believed the find was a primitive human being, perhaps the maker of the crude stone tools found not only in the Somme Valley, but in caves and rock shelters throughout Europe.

Meanwhile, the Royal Society had commissioned new excavations at Kent's Cavern and at nearby Brixham Cave, where archaeologist William Pengelly found the bones of extinct animals and stone tools sealed in a thick stalagmite layer. By this time, news of de Perthes's discoveries had drifted across the English Channel to the scientific establishment in London. In 1859, archaeologist John *Evans and geologist William Falconer visited de Perthes and examined his collections and the quarry sites. Evans himself actually found a stone hand axe in the same level as the bones of a hippopotamus. The sheer quantity of the finds convinced Evans and archaeologist Joseph Prestwich that here, at last, was scientific proof for the great antiquity of humankind, something the new theories of uniformitarianism and evolution had made intellectually possible. In June 1859, John Evans addressed the Society of Antiquaries in London and stated: "This much appears established beyond doubt, that in a period of antiquity remote beyond any of which we have hitherto found traces, this portion of the globe was peopled by man" (Evans 1860).

There followed rapid and fairly general acceptance of the idea, as a scientific fact, that human beings had been living on this earth longer than 6,000 years. The great biologist Thomas *Huxley (1825–1895) took up the cudgels on behalf of Darwin's ideas, saying that evolution "will extend by long epochs the most liberal estimate that had yet been made of the Antiquity of Man." In his classic work Man's Place in Nature (1863), Huxley compared the Neanderthal skull with those of chimpanzees and gorillas. He also posed the "question of questions for mankind . . . , the ascertainment of the place which man occupies in nature." Modern paleoanthropologists still wrestle with this question.

The spectacular social and economic changes generated by the Industrial Revolution in the early nineteenth century engendered great interest in ideas of human progress. In 1850, sociologist Herbert Spencer (1820–1903) declared: "Progress is not an accident, but a necessity." And the establishment of human antiquity gave archaeologists the open-ended time scale for measuring such progress. The oldest finds were de Perthes's Somme Valley stone axes, while later prehistoric peoples settled in the sheltered river valleys of southwestern France, at a time when reindeer, not hippopotami, were living in western Europe. There followed the celebrated Swiss lake dwellings, villages occupied by much later farming peoples, and then the familiar civilizations of Egypt, Greece, and Rome. This simple, almost linear, framework has long been supplanted by far more elaborate formulations, which assume human biological and cultural evolution has proceeded along many, diverse paths throughout the world. A century and a half after John Evans and Joseph Prestwich visited the Somme Valley, modern archaeological science has vindicated their conclusion that the frontiers of human history lay far beyond the narrow confines of biblical chronology.

[See also HISTORY OF ARCHAEOLOGY BEFORE 1900: EUROPEAN ARCHAEOLOGY.]

■ John Evans, "On the Occurrence of Flint Implements in Undisturbed Beds of Gravel, Sand, and Clay," Archaeologia 38 (1860): 280–308. Thomas Huxley, Man's Place in Nature (1863). Glyn Daniel, A Short History of Archaeology (1981). Donald K. Grayson, The Establishment of Human Antiquity (1983).

Brian M. Fagan

ANTIQUITY OF HUMANKIND IN THE AMERICAS

The discovery of America was a profound jolt to European thinkers. Of its people and their origins, the Bible said nothing. Yet here was a continent whose natives spoke a baffling number of languages, showed surprising variation in physical type, and displayed an array of distinct cultural practices, all of which, Thomas Jefferson supposed in his Notes on the State of Virginia (1787), implied a long period of divergence from a common Asian ancestor. Longer, perhaps, than the six thousand years of history recorded in the Bible.

An American Paleolithic? But the possibility of a deep human antiquity in the Americas could only be seriously considered after 1859, with the discovery in Europe of human remains associated with extinct Pleistocene mammals. That demonstration of a human prehistory antedating the Bible and secular histories spurred American scientists. After all, the geological histories of Europe and America were supposedly similar, so why shouldn't America also yield traces of ancient Stone Age (Paleolithic) peoples?

As their European counterparts had done, American scientists searched for human artifacts in cave and river deposits that bore the bones of now extinct Pleistocene mammals (in those preradiocarbon days, the surest proof of great antiquity was to find artifacts directly associated with animals known to have become extinct long before historic times). But no such associations were found.

So in the 1870s, Trenton, New Jersey, naturalist and archaeologist Charles C. Abbott (1843–1919) took another tack: all that was necessary to demonstrate a deep human antiquity in the Americas, he argued, was to find artifacts that looked "primitive" and that resembled genuine European paleoliths. If they looked like primitive artifacts from Europe, he reasoned, then they must be just as old. Certainly, he thought they were distinctly more primitive than any of the artifacts made and used by more recent, stone-working Native Americans.

It was a compelling argument, coupled as it was with Abbott's claim that he was finding American Paleolithic artifacts deep in the Trenton gravels, which were apparently laid down in the final retreat of the Pleistocene glaciers. Others soon followed suit: through the 1880s, American paleoliths were reported at dozens of sites, from Washington, D.C., to Little Falls, Minnesota. On occasion, the artifacts came from geological settings suggestive of a great antiquity, but mostly their age was fixed by their resemblance to European paleoliths.

From this mounting evidence a consensus emerged in articles and books of the late 1880s—especially those of Oberlin theologian and geologist Reverend George Frederick Wright (1838–1921). They heralded an American Paleolithic, the proof that the first Americans had arrived thousands (if not tens of thousands) of years before Columbus, when North America was buried under Pleistocene ice. Some even pushed the American Paleolithic into the Pliocene.

But in less than a year that consensus was under withering fire. The attack came from government scientific bureaus, and was led by William Henry Holmes (1846–1933), whose extraordinary artistic talents had captured the grandeur of the Grand Canyon for the United States Geological Survey (USGS), but who in 1889 transferred to the Bureau of American Ethnology (BAE) and turned his attention to archaeology. That autumn, Holmes began research at the Piney Branch site in Washington, D.C., a prehistoric stone quarry where quartzite cobbles had been flaked into artifacts and tools. Holmes learned at Piney Branch that an artifact might appear "primitive" because it was unfinished or discarded in the manufacturing process, and not because (as Abbott assumed) it was old. An artifact's age, therefore, had to be determined by its geological context.

Over the next several years Holmes examined American Paleolithic sites, Abbott's Trenton gravels included, concluding at each that the paleoliths were merely the debris of recent Native American flint knapping, and where they had been found in Pleistocene deposits it was only because they had fallen there long after those deposits had formed. Proponents of the American Paleolithic were utterly unconvinced. Abbott insisted Holmes's quarry debris was completely unlike any genuine paleoliths, while Wright accused Holmes of exaggerating the ease by which artifacts on the surface might slip to deeper, older deposits.

The debate came to an ugly head in the winter of 1892, when Wright's newly published *Man and the Glacial Period* (1892) reasserted his belief in the American Paleolithic. The BAE's W. I. McGee (1853–1912) called Wright "a betinseled charlatan whose potions are poison," and the battle lines emerged between the well-funded BAE and USGS on one side, and state and local museums on the other. Archaeological issues were lost in a cross fire of accusations of

government intimidation, scientific incompetence, and intellectual dishonesty.

By the spring of 1893, the discussion of the American Paleolithic had mired, and stayed so until August 1897, at a joint meeting of the American and British Associations, when Sir John Evans, dean of European Paleolithic archaeologists, examined a set of artifacts from the Trenton gravels and dismissed them as Neolithic, not Paleolithic. Proponents of the American Paleolithic were badly shaken, and thereafter few new finds of paleoliths were made. But in the waning days of the old century the dispute took a new turn.

Harvard University's Frederic Ward Putnam (1839–1915), staking his reputation and part of his museum's annual budget on a deep human antiquity in America, for nearly a decade employed Ernst Volk (1845–1919) to monitor railroad cuts, sewer lines, and deep exposures around Trenton. Finally, December 1, 1899, Volk found a human femur in the Trenton gravels. It was the first of nearly a dozen finds of human skeletal remains in apparent Pleistocene deposits, all of which ultimately came under the close scrutiny of Ales Hrdlicka (1869–1943).

Hrdlicka, a physician-turned-physical anthropologist, began his career under Putnam, but soon moved (1903) to Holmes's employ at the Smithsonian Institution. There, he amassed an unrivaled collection of human skeletal material on the basis of which he could argue, with supreme authority, whether a purported Pleistocene skeleton showed the necessary traits of great antiquity (i.e., resembled Neanderthals or other Pleistocene-age humans found in the Old World), or whether it fit within the variability seen in historic New World populations.

The argument was structured like Abbott's (if a skeleton is old, it should look primitive), but for Hrdlicka it worked. He was able to demonstrate—at Trenton, at Lansing, Kansas (1902–1903), at Gilder Mound, Nebraska (1906–1907), at Vero, Florida (1916), and a host of lesser sites—that these allegedly ancient human fossils were anatomically identical to (and thus no older than) recent Native Americans. Following Holmes's lead, he even argued that since humans routinely bury their dead, any skeletons found in ancient geologic deposits were almost certainly interred there long after the deposits formed.

Again, proponents of a deep human antiquity were unrepentant, but again their rebuttals were unsuccessful. Few had the expertise to combat Hrdlicka's knowledge of human anatomy, and their efforts to make the case solely on geological grounds met sharp opposition from Hrdlicka's (and Holmes's) formidable allies in geology. Thomas C. Chamberlin (1843–1928), for example, longtime chief of the USGS Glacial Division and founder of the Department of Geology at the University of Chicago, personally examined the ground at Lansing, then declared that the deposits yielding the human remains were not true Pleistocene-age loess, but loess-like deposits reworked in Recent times. As before, the dispute dissolved in irreconcilable rancor, so much so that Alfred V. *Kidder (1885–1963) afterward claimed many were actually frightened away from searching for evidence of a deep human antiquity in America.

A Paleo-Indian Presence. But resolution was nearing. In 1924, a freelance fossil collector excavating an extinct Pleistocene bison in the banks of Lone Wolf Creek (Texas) for the Colorado Museum of Natural History, uncovered several artifacts with the bones. But he paid these no mind. Learning of them afterward, but appreciating their significance, Harold Cook (1887–1962)—the museum's paleontologist—

declared the artifacts "definite evidence" of a Pleistocene human presence. Few accepted Cook's claim: the artifacts had not been found in place, raising serious doubts they were contemporaneous with the fossil bison.

Two years later, at Folsom, New Mexico, a similar scenario: the Colorado Museum, excavating a late Pleistocene bison for museum display, uncovered fluted projectile points with the bones. Once more these were not found *in situ* but Jesse Figgins (1867–1944), the museum's director, took them to Washington the spring of 1927 to show Holmes and Hrdlicka. Hrdlicka advised Figgins that if any points were found next to the bison bones, they should be left in place for other scientists to verify. Just such an association was uncovered in August of 1927, and Figgins fired off telegrams announcing the find.

Frank Roberts (1897–1966) responded on behalf of the BAE, and brought Kidder along. Together, they concluded that the points entered the deposit in the carcass of the freshly killed bison, and thus Folsom proved that humans were inhabiting the Americas by late Pleistocene times: 15,000 years ago, in Kidder's opinion. And because Kidder was then at the height of his considerable powers, his opinion carried considerable weight. Neither Holmes nor Hrdlicka challenged Folsom, as they had every other purportedly ancient site the previous forty years.

The details of Folsom's exact age remained to be worked out (it was younger than Kidder thought), but it nonetheless resolved the human antiquity debate. As a kill site, with points embedded in the skeletons of late Pleistocene-age bison, there was no possibility the artifacts and bones were fortuitously associated. Folsom showed that North American Paleo-Indians arrived in the late Pleistocene, but it was not a past comparable to the deep human antiquity of Paleolithic Europe.

Within a decade, dozens more Paleo-Indian sites were found, including Clovis, New Mexico, where in 1933 larger and less delicately made fluted points were found alongside mammoth bones. With the advent of radiocarbon dating twenty years later, Clovis proved to be just over 11,000 years old—slightly older than Folsom. Clovis became the anchor of American prehistory.

But were these Paleo-Indians the first Americans? In 1953, worried that Clovis was already becoming the maximum-allowable antiquity, Alex Krieger (1911–1991) listed half a dozen sites he believed broke the Clovis barrier. By 1964, he upped that total to fifty sites in North and South America. Yet, not many on the list were compelling—their artifacts were suspect, their ages unreliable, or they possessed some other flaw—and few accepted the claims.

Besides, C. Vance Haynes (b. 1928) had just shown that radiocarbon dates for the appearance of Clovis coincided neatly with the opening of a passageway between the vast North American glaciers that for 15,000 years (as was then believed) separated Alaska and the coterminous United States. That correlation seemed strong evidence the first Americans arrived just at Clovis times or (less likely given the sites on Krieger's list) over 25,000 years ago. Even so, in 1964 neither Haynes nor anyone else denied the latter possibility.

Since then, glacial and Clovis chronologies have been refined, and there have been dozens more pre-Clovis claims—some of which, like *Meadowcroft Rockshelter (Pennsylvania) and *Monte Verde (Chile), may yet break the Clovis barrier. But, so far, that barrier remains intact.

[*See also* HISTORY OF ARCHAEOLOGY BEFORE 1900: ARCHAEOLOGY OF THE AMERICAS.]

■ C. C. Abbott, *Primitive Industry* (1881). W. H. Holmes, *Stone Implements of the Potomac-Chesapeake Tidewater Province* (1897). A. Hrdlicka, *Skeletal Remains Suggesting or Attributed to Early Man in North America* (1907). T. C. Chamberlin, ed., "Symposium on the Age and Relations of the Fossil Human Remains Found at Vero, Florida," *Journal of Geology* 25 (1917): 1–62. J. D. Figgins, "The Antiquity of Man in America," *Natural History* 27 (1927): 229–239. A. Krieger, "Early Man in the New World," in *Prehistoric Man in the New World*, ed. J. Jennings and E. Norbeck (1964), pp. 23–81. C. V. Haynes, "Fluted Projectile Points: Their Age and Dispersion," *Science* 145 (1964): 1408–1413. D. J. Meltzer, *Search for the First Americans* (1993).

David J. Meltzer

ANURADHAPURA, capital of Sri Lanka from 437 B.C. to A.D. 1017, is situated in the north-central plains of the island's dry zone. The site, a thirty-three-foot-high (ten-meter-high) mound covering 25 acres (100 hectares), is surrounded by parkland containing reservoirs, Buddhist monasteries, and stupas. Although abandoned as a capital a millennium ago, it attracts thousands of pilgrims annually.

Details of Anuradhapura's foundation and early history are documented by the *Mahavamsa*, an ancient Buddhist chronicle, but research-oriented archaeological investigation has taken place only in the last twenty-five years.

It was first occupied ca. 3500 B.C. by microlith-using hunter-gatherers whose presence is evidenced by tool scatters. Nineteenth-century analogies from Sri Lanka's Vedda hunter-gatherers suggest interpretation as seasonal camps exploiting the perennial water of the Malvatu-Oya.

Earliest sedentary occupation began (ca. 700 B.C.) with a settlement of round houses covering 45 acres (18 ha). Black and red ware ceramics, domestic cattle, iron objects, and sherds bearing nonscriptural symbols place the site within the Iron Age technocomplex of peninsular India. It is likely that the inhabitants practiced slash-and-burn cultivation (*see* Agriculture). The next period (ca. 450–350 B.C.) saw the site grow to 64 acres (26 ha). Iron slag and semiprecious stone waste shows increasing exploitation of the island's raw materials and the increasing role of the site as a center of manufacture and distribution. Although artifacts are still linked with the peninsula, sherds inscribed with Brahmi script suggest contact with a wider network.

During the third period (ca. 350–275 B.C.) the site grew to 181 acres (66 ha). This coincided with the construction of a rampart and a one hundred and thirty-two-foot-wide (forty-meter-wide) moat around the site, rectangular cardinally oriented houses, and the appearance of coins. There is also evidence for the first manipulation of water resources in the region for irrigation agriculture. Lapis lazuli from Afghanistan and carnelian from western India indicate access to wide South Asian trade links. Toward the end of this period rouletted ware is found, further linking Anuradhapura with the contemporary civilizations of northern India.

During the following period (ca. 275 B.C.–A.D. 150) the site reached a maximum size of 25 acres (100 ha). Wattle-and-daub structures were replaced by ones of brick and tile. Anuradhapura's position within trade networks on an international scale and finds of eastern Hellenistic ceramics, Indo-Greek ivory work, and Indo-Roman coins confirm the city's upper status on the island. Throughout the next millennium, the foundations of wealth were established, and monumental reservoirs, monasteries, and stupas were constructed.

[See also ASIA: PREHISTORY AND EARLY HISTORY OF SOUTH ASIA; INDUS CIVILIZATION.]

■ R.A.E. Coningham and F. R. Allchin, "The Rise of Cities in Sri Lanka," in *The Archaeology of Early Historic South Asia: The Emergence of Cities and States,* ed. F. R. Allchin (in press).

Robin A. E. Coningham

ANYANG, a modern city of Henan Province in northern China, is situated in a once-fertile plain at about 36° north latitude and 114° longitude. Not until the end of the nineteenth century, when hundreds of oracle bones were found near the city, did Anyang become greatly interesting to archaeologists. Beginning in 1928, the Academic Sinica and then archaeologists of the Chinese Academy of Social Sciences excavated there. With evidence from more than seventeen sites covering approximately 9 miles (24 sq km), Anyang has proven to be a capital of the Shang dynasty (sixteenth to eleventh centuries B.C.).

Immense remains of architecture and thousands of artifacts were uncovered at Anyang. They attest to the linkage of Shang with the Neolithic cultures previous to the dynasty, and reveal aspects of city life. The excavations in Xiaotun, the ritual center of the city, yielded fifty-three large stamp-earth foundations of aboveground architecture, including the largest measuring approximately 230 by 131 ft. (70 by 40 m). These platforms are the remains of palaces and temples which must have lined the city streets. Less magnificent aboveground and semisubterranean structures are identified as residential dwellings and workshops. They exemplify the life of commoners and highly specialized industries including bronze casting, jade and stone carving, pottery making, and bone working. The underground structures include more than twelve lavishly furnished and stately mausoleums mainly located at the cemetery site, Xibeigang. Among them, one intact tomb, Tomb Five, yielded more than sixteen hundred artifacts, encompassing bronze ritual objects and weapons, jade works, and other precious items. Of the more than 100,000 inscribed oracle bones discovered at Anyang, approximately 33,500 were scientifically excavated. They exhibit a well-developed writing system primarily used for divination. Significantly, the names of several kings repeatedly appear in the inscriptions. According to late literature, these kings were the rulers of Yin, the capital of late Shang (ca. 1300 to 1045 B.C.). That information identifies Anyang as Yinxu, or, the "Ruins of Yin," the remains of the last of seven or so capitals of the dynasty. Very likely, these sites constitute the remains of the ritual and burial sections of Yin.

The discoveries in Anyang indicate that the area around the city was the locus for a sophisticated Bronze Age civilization characterized by writing, bronze and jade industries, monumental architecture, distinctive ritual practices, and a social structure that interwove kinship, lineage, and administrative systems. The splendor of the monuments and the massive uses of natural resources suggest that the Shang was sustained by a complex network of trading and military and political domination over a vast area far beyond this culture.

[See also ASIA: PREHISTORY AND EARLY HISTORY OF EAST ASIA; CHINA: SHANG CIVILIZATION.)

■ Li Chi, *Anyang: A Chronicle of the Discovery, Excavation, and Reconstruction of the Ancient Capital of the Shang Dynasty* (1977). Kwangchih Chang, *Shang Civilization* (1980).

Yan Ge

ARABIA AND THE PERSIAN/ARABIAN GULF. The Arabian Peninsula is a roughly triangular tectonic plate bordered by water on three sides and attached to Asia at its northern tip along the border between Saudi Arabia and Jordan, Iraq, and Kuwait. Mountains hug the western coastline and rise steeply from north to south along the Red Sea toward Aden; there they turn and diminish eastward, toward the Straits of Hormuz, where they rise again. The eastern coastline along the Arabian / Persian Gulf by contrast is a long, gently sloping terrain often culminating in a *sabkha* (salt marsh / swamp).

Few places around those boundaries have perennial water sources. *Wadis* (dried-up river and stream beds) bisect the coastline and trail from the mountains on the hinterland side, providing water only during the rainy season, which coincides with the summer *monsoon*. Annual rainfall is meager, less than ca. 8 inches (200 mm). Oases dot the vast arid expanse of the interior, and springs emanate from mountains within the interior and especially along the western and southern coastal ranges. These water sources were increasingly important to the cultural development of Arabia from Neolithic times, when the last major desiccation occurred, promoting desert development and isolating the inhabitants in antiquity. The coastal ranges are impassable in most places, a factor which also contributed to isolation in southern Arabia. For these reasons the orientation of cultural development in eastern Arabia takes a different course than elsewhere from the fifth millennium B.C., when cultural influence from Mesopotamia and Central Asia was strong.

Prehistory. Evidence of the earliest human occupation has so far been found only in Saudi Arabia, where flaked pebble tools, equivalent to Developed Oldowan A in eastern Africa, have been dated between 1.6 million and 1.3 million B.P. and associated with *Homo erectus*. Although no human remains have yet to be found, it is possible that *Homo erectus* could have crossed over the Red Sea near the Bab al-Mandab on rafts. Hand axes of Acheulean type, characteristic of the Lower Paleolithic (ca. 200,000 to 80,000 B.P.), are found throughout the peninsula. Functional analysis of these and associated lithic tools suggests a variety of activities, including chopping, butchering, hide scraping, lithic tool manufacture, woodworking, bone working, and even plant gathering or processing by early hunter-gatherer groups. Tool assemblages of the Middle Paleolithic (ca. 80,000 to 40,000 B.P.) are best known in central and western Saudi Arabia, where they are characterized by a wider variety of tools and blade production by Levalloiso-Mousterian techniques.

The Upper Paleolithic (ca. 40,000 to 10,000 B.C.) is poorly attested, whereas the Epi-Paleolithic (ca. 10,000 to 8000 B.C.) is characterized by the presence of small bladelets that once were hafted, forming the composite tool, the sickle. This new tool reflects exploitation of wild stands of grain.

The "Neolithic" Period is difficult to isolate from a "Chalcolithic" Period in the peninsula. The material culture of western and central Arabia from ca. 8000 to 2900 B.C. differs from that of eastern Arabia, where a narrow coastal strip reflects an intensive interaction between indigenous folk and foreigners from Mesopotamia, Central Asia, and the Indus Valley. The aceramic Neolithic phase (ca. 8000 to 5000 B.C.) is characterized by the appearance of a long, slender bifacially flaked point, similar to points of the Pre-Pottery Neolithic B (PPNB) of Palestine and Transjordan. A few oval- or elliptical-shaped huts outlined in stone are associated with these points; they are probably the outlines of a tentlike structure supported by stakes and branches. Associated faunal remains attest to hunting, gathering, and fishing activities. The widespread occurrence of this phase is due more to moist conditions from ca. 10,000 to 6000 B.P., when numerous ancient lakes dotted the landscape. Desiccation occurred ca. 6000 B.P., and the loss of traditionally exploited resources seems to have become an impetus toward the domestication of plants and animals.

A later phase of the Neolithic is indicated by the appearance of a squat point exhibiting fine flaking technology and having pronounced barbs or tangs. Faunal remains, especially sheep, goat, pig, and camel, were intensively exploited, though wild species also occur. In eastern Arabia mortars and pestles were then common, indicating an increased reliance on processing grains, including domestic grain sorghum. Two kinds of distinctive pottery now appeared: an organic-tempered plain red ware, and painted wares that compositional analyses demonstrate were imported from southern Mesopotamia (Ubaid 2, 3, and 4 wares). The red ware is felt to be the product of local interaction with Mesopotamian fishermen and traders. A few poorly preserved burials occurred within pits surmounted by stone-built cairns.

During the fourth millennium B.C. desiccation again prevailed and the sea level dropped; eastern coastal sites were abandoned. By the third millennium a brief increase in precipitation enabled a return to coastal habitation. Numerous cemetery sites now appeared, and their grave goods demonstrate a renewed contact with Mesopotamia. Wheelmade and painted jars imported from Mesopotamia were common, but their chronological position is debated: either Jamdat Nasr, ca. 3200 to 3000 B.C., or as late as Early Dynastic (ED) III, ca. 3000 to 2500 B.C. Copper artifacts also occur. Also found are bowls carved from a soft schist (e.g., chlorite and steatite) and decorated with animals and palm tree motifs; this is the Intercultural Style of soft stone vessels, found throughout Mesopotamia and Iran. Quarry sites in central Arabia were exploited to produce some examples. Few domestic structures from this period are known, yet there is evidence of early cultivation of the domestic date palm.

In eastern Arabia the third millennium B.C. represents a period of cultural fluorescence and widespread trade contacts. Circular stamp seals depicting animals foreign to the region, and words, perhaps personal names, in Indus Valley script appear here and in Mesopotamia. The island of Bahrain (identified as the land of "Dilmun" in contemporary Mesopotamian texts) now was home to several urban centers, temples, and especially massive cemeteries. Burials were made in tightly packed clusters of small, beehivelike, slab-built stone structures encircled by ring walls and pierced by an entryway. Single and collective burials are present.

In the Omani Peninsula, third-millennium sites are widespread, and furnaces and slag heaps derived from copper smelting and melting activities are common. Copper artifacts (e.g., fishhooks, knives, pins) abound at occupation and burial sites, often in association with wheelmade black-painted wares with decoration schemes similar to wares in Iran and Afghanistan. Soft-stone vessels resemble types found throughout eastern Arabia, Central Asia, and Mesopotamia. Tombs are circular, built of unworked slabs surrounded by a ring wall; some larger tombs have well-cut limestone blocks with animal and human forms cut in low relief. Most tombs have collective burials and many associated artifacts.

During the second millennium B.C. eastern Arabia's main developments occurred on Bahrain and in the Omani Peninsula. The cities and temple complexes continued, as do cemeteries. Graves are single- or multiple-chambered, stone-built tombs with a conical shape, covered with a tumulus. Burials, usually single, occur in a stone-lined chamber on the interior. "Dilmun" seals now appeared in a shape reminiscent of Indus Valley seals but with Mesopotamian iconography (human and animal). References to Dilmun abound in Mesopotamian texts of the Isin-Larsa and Old Babylonian periods, and the principal deity of Dilmun, Inzak, even had a sanctuary in the Elamite center, Susa. Trade with Dilmun extended to *Mari in eastern Syria.

A "Bronze Age" culture (ca. 2900/2700 to 2000/1800 B.C.) has recently come to light in northern Yemen. Several villages are known in the highland plateau region. Houses consist of several contiguous circular rooms often clustered into a circular village arrangement. Some rooms have internal pillar supports. Specialized activity areas are found in many rooms, including butchery and cooking areas. Domestic sheep, goat, cattle, and pig are among the faunal remains alongside wild mammals, indicating a reliance upon domestic species but supplemented with wild game. Various nonlocal stone artifacts reflect long-distance trade; copper/bronze artifacts also occur but are relatively rare. Pottery vessels similar in shape to certain Early Bronze Age (EB) III and IV wares of Palestine and Transjordan are present, but their decorations resemble later East African decorated wares. Geological and geomorphological studies indicate abandonment at the end of the period followed seismic uplifting, coincidental with interrupted rainfall patterns, rendering highland plateau agriculture untenable.

Protohistory. A "protohistoric" phase of cultural development follows in the Yemen, where several sites recently have revealed occupation datable ca. 1500 to 1200/1000 B.C. It is here that the famous "spice kingdoms" arose, reputed homeland of the biblical Queen of Sheba and of the Arabian frankincense and myrrh trees whose resin and its products enticed even Rome's emperors. The chronological order of appearance of those kingdoms is an unsettled matter, although excavations at Shabwa in the Wadi Hadhramaut and at a large mound near the modern village of Jubat al-Jadidah near Marib, demonstrate the presence of protohistoric communities upon which the historic kingdoms built. The pottery from the earliest deposits attest to continuity with the Bronze Age culture. These wares are organic-tempered and handmade; both features are characteristic of the subsequent historic period.

Historic Pre-Islamic Times. Five kingdoms developed in early historic times: Saba, with its capital at Marib; Qataban, with its capital at Timna'; Hadhramaut, with its capital at Shabwa; Ma'in, with its capital at Qarnaw; and Ausan. Another power, Himyar, with its capital at Zafar, arose close to the beginning of the Common Era. Collectively, these kingdoms comprise South Arabian civilization. Regional developments are evident from protohistoric times onward, a fact which has yet to be correlated with differences in the dialects written and spoken in each of the kingdoms, and in their respective deities.

The question of when writing, the hallmark of civilization, appeared in South Arabia is still debated. The earliest inscriptions occurred as letters and monograms applied and incised on pottery vessels. While opinions vary on absolute chronology, it is clear that writing, and therefore some degree of literacy, appeared at least by the eight century B.C. This date agrees well with the earliest mention of a king (*malik*) for the Sabaeans in Late Assyrian annals of the eighth and seventh centuries B.C. That term, however, appears in South Arabian texts rather late, perhaps by the fifth century B.C. Its precursor is *mukarrib,* usually translated "priest-king."

Though the late Jacqueline Pirenne favored a late sixth or fifth century date for the introduction of writing into South Arabia, it is now clear that literate Sabaean, Qatabanian, and Hadhramitic kingdoms arose by the eight century. The visit of the unnamed Queen of Sheba to King Solomon's court in the late tenth century B.C. (I Kings 10, II Chronicles 9) may reflect the rise of South Arabia's commercial interests in markets around the Mediterranean Basin, and some scholars associate that visit with the introduction of the alphabet into South Arabia.

Strabo (writing before A.D. 21) and Pliny the Elder (writing ca. A.D. 54 to 68) ascribe the wealth and indeed the *raison d'être* of South Arabian civilization to the harvest and trafficking of frankincense and myrrh. However, this view is one of outsiders looking in to Arabia; the South Arabian texts themselves make no mention of this trade. The most important facet of the economy seems to have been the erection and maintenance of irrigation systems; for remains of irrigation structures and their inscriptions abound. Most of these structures relate to barrage dams deflecting *seil* (flash flood) waters into field plots. The largest and most famous of these is the ancient Marib Dam. The dams are sophisticated engineering feats, and are often built of large, finely cut masonry blocks. Large sluice gates controlled the flow of water into fields, where smaller dams and dirt channels directed the *seil* into individual plots.

Throughout the region major urban sites were surrounded by a city wall, usually built in a series of offset-inset segments, and sometimes having more than one city gate. Early city walls were built of huge unworked boulders (megalithic construction), whereas later city walls had finely cut ashlar blocks with different decorative finishes.

Temple construction seems to have varied with respect to kingdom, era, and perhaps deity. One common feature, however, was the use of monolithic four-sided stone pillars and beams. Inscriptions mentioning the ruler under whose authority the structure was built (or rebuilt) were often cut at prominent, visible portions of walls and gates. These records were obviously meant for public display, such as on the famous Mahram Bilqis ("sacred precinct of Bilqis," legendary name for the Queen of Sheba) at Marib. A few large private dwellings also employed the same building techniques and carried inscriptions attached to walls.

Ancient South Arabian religion centered on a pantheon of numerous, presumably local and tribal deities. Lunar, solar, and stellar deities were common, suggesting to some scholars the presence of a "holy trinity": 'Athtar, associated with Venus; Ilumquh (Saba), Sin (Hadhramaut), and 'Amm (Qataban), associated with the moon; and a sun god. While some of these deities are invoked by name in inscriptions, certain symbols also were used to indicate a deity in South Arabian art (e.g., the bull's head symbolizes the lunar deity). The lunar deity, in particular, controlled the all-important *seil,* and for that reason is one of the most frequently encountered deities.

Many different burial customs are attested. Of great antiquity and longevity (Neolithic to sixth century A.D.) is the stone-built cairn. Another common tomb type is the rock-cut chamber, sometimes with carved benches and niches. Recent excavations in southern Yemen also reveal "sacrificial" camel burials, a practice widespread in the peninsula. In Qataban another type of tomb occurs: a stone-built rectangular structure with rows and tiers of burial slabs off to either side of a central aisle.

From the surviving material culture of ancient South Arabia, we see a very high technological expertise in various arts and crafts. Stone masonry and carving were highly developed. Besides decorative massive constructions and masonry finishes, friezes of bull, ibex, and plant motifs adorned walls of various temples and palaces, and recessed niches similar to Egyptian "false doors" are found inside temples. As elsewhere in Late Iron Age or Roman times in the Near East, many different column and capital arrangements are found. Alabaster, a locally available stone, was used to produce small lidded jars, tripod offering dishes, distinctive squat funerary sculpture, votive plaques, and "sacrificial tables." These latter may be plain or decorated and bear inscriptions; their shape is virtually identical to "sacrificial tables" associated with temples in pharaonic Egypt. Bronze sculpture is another field in which South Arabian craftsmen excelled producing votive offerings, statuary (human and animal), and decorative affixes to monumental architecture. The styles of human statuary are unique but show some influences from the Levant and Greece from Iron Age through Hellenistic times.

Transport, Trade, and the Decline of South Arabian Civilization. Camels were likely used as beasts of burden, as today, in addition to a meat source. The arid interior of Arabia is crossed by well-worn camel tracks, many of which pass by springs and wells. Only the camel is suited for travel under such harsh conditions. While the date of the origin for overland camel caravan trade is still debated, the presence of the camel from Neolithic times on suggests a long history of its exploitation as a beast of burden. Because of the importance of camel transport, many scholars have attempted to equate the decline and fall of South Arabian civilization with the rise in maritime trade between the Mediterranean Basin and India in the Roman Period, most likely in the first century A.D. A few scholars have tried to tie in the abandonment of Timna' (ca. A.D. 10 to 15), following a conflagration, with the rise in maritime trade. Excavations at the oasis of Qaryat al-Fau in central Saudi Arabia, however, have demonstrated that camel caravan traffic flourished well beyond the end of Timna'. Excavations at Shabwa, Qana, and Khor Rori point to an active maritime trade from the first century B.C. to at least the fourth century A.D. Imported Mediterranean *amphorae,* Roman *terra sigillata,* painted Nabataean fine wares, and Parthian / Sasanian blue-green glazed wares occur at all of those sites.

Those and other imported wares show up at many sites along eastern Arabia's coast, such as at Failaka and Thaj. Failaka, ancient Ikaros at the headwaters of the Arabian / Persian Gulf, functioned as both a settlement and a major sanctuary site. Thaj, a large walled city north of Qatar and south of Kuwait, is considered by most scholars to be ancient Gerrha, the region's most important mainland port. It is connected by the overland route with Qaryat al-Fau, and excavations reveal a strong tie also with Persia. Thus, the archaeological evidence is clear; maritime and overland camel caravan commerce in Arabia were integrated from the Hellenistic through the Roman Period, ca. 325 B.C.

through the fourth century A.D. The supplanting of one by the other was clearly not a cause of South Arabia's decline.

Archaeological and epigraphic evidence suggests a gradual decline during a period of increased militancy between the various kingdoms. Written sources indicate that a confederation grew after ca. 115 to 110 B.C. when the kingdom of Himyar emerged as a significant rival to Saba. By the second century A.D. Hadharmaut had swallowed up Qataban, and Saba's power dwindled with changes in dynastic rule. At the end of the third century, Sabaeo-Himyaritic rule grew to encompass all of South Arabia in a larger confederation, "Saba and Dhu Raydan [former Qataban] and Hadhramaut and Yamanat," which continued for about two hundred years. Tribal movements from southern into northern Arabia occurred during this time, while Sasanid Persian domination of the Arabian/Persian Gulf spread as far as eastern Oman. Pressure on the Sabaeo-Himyarite confederation may account for the abandonment of its port at Khor Rori, while Shabwa and the port of Qana continued for two centuries. Migration northward into Byzantine territory and eastward into Oman occurred at the same time as the Marib Dam began to fail. Campaigns against Ethiopia's Abyssinians, who had taken territory as far east as Zafar, and a Christian community at Najran, now took place. Social and political tensions ran high, and the economic burden of successive repairs to the Marib Dam and its extensive field systems apparently became too great to bear. By A.D. 597/8 the Sasanids declared Arabia a *satrapy* (province) within their empire under Khosrau II (590 to 628). After A.D. 628 the victorious forces of Islam spread out from the Hijaz, eventually uniting the peninsula, and the history of Pre-Islamic Arabia came to an end.

[See also CAMEL, DOMESTICATION OF THE; NEAR EAST: IRON AGE CIVILIZATIONS OF THE NEAR EAST.]

■ Wendell Phillips, *Qataban and Sheba* (1955). Gus W. Van Beek, *Hajar Bin Humeid: Investigations at a Pre-Islamic Site in South Arabia* (1969). T. Geoffrey Bibby, *Looking for Dilmun* (1970). James B. Pritchard, ed., *Solomon & Sheba* (1974). Abdul Rahman al-Ansary, *Qaryat al-Fau: A Portrait of Pre-Islamic Civilisation in Saudi Arabia* (1982). D. Brian Doe, *Monuments of South Arabia* (1983). Maurizio Tosi, "The Emerging Picture of Prehistoric Arabia," *Annual Review of Anthropology* 15 (1986): 461–490. Walter Daum, ed., *Yemen: 3000 Years of Art and Civilisation in Arabia Felix* (1988). Daniel T. Potts, *The Arabian Gulf in Antiquity*, 2 vols. (1990).

William D. Glanzman

ARCHAEOLOGY AS A DISCIPLINE. Archaeology is the sole discipline in the social sciences concerned with reconstructing and understanding human behavior on the basis of the material remains left by our prehistoric and historic forebears. Although the theories archaeologists employ for framing their questions of the past have changed dramatically in the short hundred years of its existence as a discipline and the current goals of archaeology are hotly debated, all archaeologists are concerned at some level with using the analysis of past material remains, in conjunction with other bodies of information, to either reconstruct or interpret the behaviors and events that resulted in the final disposition of those remains.

In the United States, archaeology has traditionally been viewed as one of the four classic subdisciplines of anthropology, along with cultural anthropology, physical anthropology, and linguistics. This was a result of Franz Boas's early realization that no ethnographic study of New World peoples could be complete without a thorough understanding of their present culture, their past culture, their biology,

and their language. In Europe, where archaeology as an academic pursuit has a somewhat longer history, archaeology has traditionally been considered a separate discipline owing to its roots in the study of the remains of Classical Greek, Roman, and Egyptian culture and history. As currently practiced throughout the world, one can fairly conveniently divide the major domains of archaeology into prehistoric, historical, classical, and industrial archaeology.

*Prehistoric archaeology is concerned with testing anthropological theories of human behavior and evolution against the archaeological record of societies that left no known written record of themselves. *Historical archaeology attempts to use archaeological data both to test hypotheses about the operation of historically known societies and to fill in the historical gaps concerning the more mundane, but crucially important, aspects of the day-to-day operation of those societies. *Classical archaeology is very similar to historical archaeology in its methods and goals, since it too attempts to study historically known societies. The difference between classical archaeology and general historical archaeology is the suite of societies in which classical archaeologists are primarily interested—the Classical Period circum-Mediterranean cultures (e.g., the Greeks, Phoenicians, Romans, Egyptians, etc.). *Industrial archaeology is also related to historical archaeology, but is primarily concerned with the study of Western European and American societies during the Industrial Revolution and the rise of modern urban society as we know it.

These four general divisions of archaeology are discussed at length in other portions of this volume. With respect to these general divisions, the reader must realize that there are a multitude of differences in the goals, theoretical biases, and analytical methods employed by the archaeologists whose research interests place them in one or the other of the four groups. The sections on archaeological* method and *theory in this volume are intended to help the reader see and understand the breadth and depth of those differences. Differences aside, however, archaeology has been, and remains, singular among the social sciences in its general goal of understanding the how, what, and why of past human behavior largely on the basis of the physical remains left behind.

George Michaels

ARCHAEOLOGY IN THE CONTEMPORARY WORLD. Archaeology is the study of the past as evident in the material remains available to us. To some people, this makes it a marginal activity in the Western world today. It is harmless, to be sure—pottering about in the earth to turn up broken shards of pottery, the bones of animals and (sometimes) of humans, and rarely, real golden treasure. But does it change who we are or how we see ourselves?

As the twenty-first century nears, Western society is largely persuaded that the world is—or should be—a rational place directed by the logic of scientific reasoning and based on the tested facts of gathered data. One prefers to think today's Western society is neither driven by emotion nor controlled by history. We are in charge of ourselves, not determined by where we come from, nor driven by the beliefs we have carried along. A few obvious, agreeable bits of history are possessed as "heritage"; the rest, we think, is just something that happened a long time ago and has not much to do with the real and contemporary world.

Current Place of Archaeology. The small place permitted history in the contemporary world is largely occupied by written history, the past as is read from the recorded words of documents. Physical history in its several forms—the history of buildings, artifacts, and landscapes—is secondary in status and in standing to the written word.

So what is the place of archaeology in the contemporary world? On the surface, its small place is clear enough. Archaeology consists of noticing, preserving, and rescuing buried fragments from ancient and not-so-ancient times, and then striving to understand earlier peoples and societies from those fragments. The mechanics of archaeology—finding old sites, preserving them, digging and recording, and interpreting what is found—are the routine procedures of a field science. The people who perform these tasks—academics in universities, bureaucrats in historic preservation offices, field workers out in the mud—are engaged in the routine of work in our society. The means of communicating their findings—archives, database records, specialized books, magazine articles, television programs—are the routine ways of dealing with knowledge.

Underneath this, beyond this, archaeology has a larger ambition, which can be considered the real place of archaeology in the contemporary world.

Purpose of Archaeology. Archaeology stands for where we have come from, for our history in the broad sense and in a direct way that documentary history often cannot do. Writing is a comparatively recent invention, if one looks at the whole story of human life on earth; it began only some five or six thousand years ago, while the human presence goes back about a million years ago. For most of that five or six thousand years, writing was the province of a small and restricted class of society—the scribes who served kings and princes, keeping the records of trade and tribute. Even in the present century, whole classes and groups of people are visible scarcely or not at all in the common pattern of written history.

Archaeology, on the other hand, is about the physical. There is a directness in physical contact with the object. Around the globe, the characteristic artifact of the earlier species of human beings, *Homo erectus*, is a big chunky thing, generally called a hand axe, flakes out of stone. We do not know what it was for—the name "hand axe" is a nineteenth-century guess at its function. We do not know how human the human being who made the hand axe was; whether *Homo erectus* had language is disputed, and there seem to be no pictures drawn by *Homo erectus*. Yet one can hold a hand axe and know, "In my hand is something that was made by human beings who are 200 or 400 thousand years or more remote from me; it sits comfortably in my palm, as once it may have sat in theirs."

Archaeology stands for the Other, for the alien, in a way that other people and other cultures cannot do in a homogenized world where hardly anyone is more than a few hundred meters from a can of Coca-Cola. It has been the traditional role of anthropology to study other cultures. Now that practically the whole world has been enveloped in a single world system and the prestige artifacts that stand for the West and for progress are to be found everywhere, we all seem to belong, in one or another variant, within a common culture. Archaeology preserves a knowledge of those "other" cultures, those "other" manners of human existence, that are wholly or nearly extinct now in their full differentness. Such cultures may include the world of *Homo erectus*; the world of hunter-gatherers, which was all of human experience until only nine thousand years ago; or the world of early states and empires, whether in ancient China, the Near East, the Maya realm of Central America, or other regions.

It is hard to grasp other human experiences, even in our own time and culture. How is one to imagine what it was like to live in Neolithic Europe? We "recognize" many of the objects of Neolithic Europe—axes, scrapers, arrowheads, houses. But do we know what they meant, how they were experienced, what they were called? The creatures were the same—sheep, pigs, mice, people, bears—but what were their names and what did they stand for? What was it like to be a mobile hunter-gatherer in ancient Australia, or to be an aged person, though not thirty years old, without possessions beyond a favorite digging stick and what was carried in a little bag—perhaps a few finger and toe bones kept as tokens of kinship to a son who had perished many years earlier? These things we cannot know by direct experience, but archaeology is a good, or the only, route to such knowledge of them as we can reach.

Archaeology is humbling. The golden palaces of the ancient East are today traced from ruins of mud brick, washed down and so blended back into the soil that it is hard to see where wall ends and earth starts. In the mud are the broken fragments, the scraps and excreta, of ancient greatness. In our own time, the enduring monuments we will leave are not the high-rise palaces of commerce and finance, but the landfills. Long after the modern city of Chicago has fallen into ruin beneath the earth, there will stand the rolling artificial mounds, strung out along the interstate highway, where Chicago threw out its garbage. It is by their garbage that we know ancient civilizations; it is by our garbage, and by the view of ourselves that the garbage displays, that we shall be known. The bones that endure from a human life fit into quite a small box; the ash that endures from a human cremation is only enough to fill a hat—and if it is scattered, it leaves a phosphate smear in the soil not immediately distinguishable from a moderate manuring.

Archaeology is rooted in place. The last centuries have seen populations move within and between countries and continents on a scale never before experienced. We are wanderers, and with wandering we become lost regarding our sense of place. Yet archaeology is all about place, and the particular place: *here* Ice Age hunters speared a mammoth bogged in the tundra; *here* the Chumash of the California coast venerated the spirit of the swordfish; *here* the alchemists of Bronze Age Europe wrought their smelting magic to make great swords; from *here* noble Caesar ruled all of the known world. The sense of place, and of the particular place, that our shifting, rootless world no longer knows is held in the direct link to past experience that archaeology forges.

Archaeology stands for the mystery in our artificial world of artifacts, the things we believe we create with good sense and purpose. The richer contemporary Western societies have more material objects than those other and older societies ever possessed. We have or want to have countless material things; we even persuade ourselves that we actually need them and tell ourselves stories as to why we need them. The human story in museums is one of technical progress and improvement: from hand axes to farming to ironworking to cathedrals to railways to space rockets to personal computers.

The question is, who is in charge? Is it us? Or is it the artifacts? Biologists tell us that human beings reproduce themselves by means of DNA, yet one can say as well that the DNA reproduces itself by means of human beings! From the human cell to DNA, from DNA to the human cell. Who is to say which is primary, which is secondary? Consider the parallels with our relationship to artifacts—all the possessions Westerners have, all that people in poorer lands wish to acquire. It is said that workers in an industrial society spend far more time a their labor than hunter-gatherers are known to have spent. Do we shape the artifacts to suit the way we want to spend our lives? Or are our lives shaped to suit the artifacts—not just the little things, the door handle that doesn't quite fit your hand, the seat that you cannot sit comfortably in, but deep down such as psychologically or ethically, as well? This is where archaeology may shed some light.

Archaeologists want to study past human lives, but those lives are gone. We see them only by proxy; they are shadows we strain to see from the artifacts, so often worn and broken, they chanced to leave behind. What we know of *Homo erectus* is what we can read from the hand axes. The archaeologist's is a strange view of the world, with its odd basis of looking at artifacts in quest of the essence of human lives. It is a view congruent with our society—so cluttered by artifacts, yet so uncertain and so ignorant of how those artifacts may direct our lives.

[See also CULTURAL RESOURCE MANAGEMENT: GLOBAL ISSUES; DESTRUCTION OF THE PAST; FUTURE OF THE PAST.]

Christopher Chippindale

ARCHAEOMETRY is the application of various analytical techniques from the physical sciences and engineering to archaeological materials. The term "archaeometry" is very broad and encompasses a wide range of interdisciplinary studies. Examples of archaeometry in modern archaeology are many. Applying trace element analyses to learn the source of obsidian used to manufacture artifacts is one example. Chemical analysis of the growth rings of marine shells to detect seasonal changes in local temperature over time is another example.

Much of what we consider modern archaeology would not be possible without archaeometry. The sections on excavation techniques, remote sensing, dating methods, and various techniques used in artifact and ecofact analysis that occur throughout this volume contain many examples of archaeometry in common use in archaeology. Modern archaeometry has its roots in the development and acceptance of *radiocarbon dating in the 1950s. Since then fruitful collaborations between archaeologists and various physical scientists and engineers have dramatically increased the arsenal of tools available to archaeologists to decipher the details of past human lifeways.

In the future, archaeometry's importance in archaeology will expand, driven by increasing constraints on new excavation and demands to extract more information from existing artifact collections. Continuing trends toward higher levels of specialization in archaeology will also expand the ranks of archaeometricians, as the ranks of general archaeologists decline. It is through the efforts of dedicated specialists in archaeometry, coupled with powerful computer-based data analysis and storage tools to manage the masses of minute details that future developments in archaeometry will produce, that will allow the next generation of archaeologists to develop more refined interpretations of past human behavior.

[See also ARCHAEO-PALEOMAGNETIC DATING; CERAMICS: TECHNOLOGICAL ANALYSIS OF CERAMICS; DENDROCHRONOLOGY; FISSION-TRACK DATING; LITHICS: TECHNOLOGICAL ANALYSIS OF LITHICS; LUMINESCENCE DATING; METALS: ANALYSIS OF METALS; METHOD, ARCHAEOLOGICAL; OBSIDIAN HYDRATION DATING; PALEOBOTANY; PLANT REMAINS, ANALYSIS OF; POTASSIUM-ARGON DATING; RADIOCARBON DATING; SITE LOCATION: REMOTE SENSING AND GEOPHYSICAL PROSPECTION; SUBSURFACE TESTING, *articles on* SOIL RESISTIVITY SURVEY, MAGNETOMETER SURVEY, GROUND PENETRATING RADAR; WOOD: ANALYSIS OF WOOD; ZOOARCHAEOLOGY.]

George Michaels

ARCHAEO-PALEOMAGNETIC DATING. These two dating techniques rely on the fact that the Earth's magnetic field varies through time. Eddies in the semimolten core of the planet cause the strength of the magnetic field to vary, and the magnetic north pole to shift position. Geologists interested in the Earth's magnetic field developed techniques for measuring the ancient movements of the pole after World War II, and archaeologists began using these techniques for dating in the late 1960s.

Paleomagnetic and archaeomagnetic dating measure the remnant magnetism in samples to plot the location of the magnetic pole in the past. When iron-bearing minerals are heated above a certain temperature, their Curie point, they will align with magnetic north, just as a compass needle does. As the material cools below the Curie point this alignment will be frozen in place until the sample is again heated above the Curie point, or physically displaced. Chemical changes can also create remnant magnetism, and fine iron mineral particles settling in still water will align with the magnetic pole.

Paleomagnetism. Paleomagnetic dating is a geological technique that dates rock based on the occurrence of polar reversals. A reversal occurs when the magnetic pole moves to the opposite end of the globe. During a reversal a compass needle would point south, instead of north. Such reversals have occurred at irregular intervals of hundreds of thousands of years throughout the history of the earth. Geologists collect samples for paleomagnetic dating by drilling a core into bedrock, and marking the top of the core with a line pointing to the modern magnetic pole. They then measure the sample in a laboratory magnetometer to determine the orientation of the pole when the rock was hot. Geologists have compiled a master chronology of global reversals, and calibrated it using *potassium-argon dating.

Paleomagnetic dating is only useful for dating deposits that are hundreds of thousands, or millions of years old. Archaeologists employ the technique in early hominid research. Commonly, researchers use potassium-argon dating and fossils to establish the broad temporal placement of a stratigraphic column. They can then use paleomagnetism to more precisely place layers in time. The technique has been used to date *Ramapithecus* remains in the Siwalki Hills of India, *Australopithicus* remains at *Olduvai Gorge in Kenya, and the Lucy skeleton in the Hadar region of Ethiopia.

Archaeomagnetism. Archaeomagnetism measures the polar wandering of the North Pole. The position of the magnetic pole is not stable and it moves around the geographical north pole. When clay is heated to the Curie point, the iron mineral in it will align to the magnetic pole. If the clay is undisturbed it will preserve the position of the pole at the time of its firing. Thus, clay used to line fire pits, plaster walls, or house floors can be used for this technique, but ceramic artifacts cannot. Researchers use other chronometric dating techniques such as *radiocarbon dating and *dendrochronology to date the fired clay. They can then plot a master curve of the movement of the North Pole over time. With a master curve, undated archaeomagnetic samples can be assigned dates based on where their remnant magnetism shows the magnetic pole to have been. Due to large scale ripples in the earth's magnetic field, archaeologists must develop separate master curves for each geographical region. Master curves going back several thousand years exist for the southwestern and southeastern United States, Japan, Mesoamerica, Germany, France, and England among other regions.

Archaeologists use a complex and tedious procedure to cut out pieces of clay, mark their orientation, encase them in plaster, and return them to the laboratory to be measured on a magnetometer. The procedure requires special training and equipment, and the skill of the collector will affect the precision of the date.

The precision possible with archaeomagnetic dating also depends upon the technique and number of samples used to calibrate the master curve. In the southwestern United States, where dendrochronology has been used to calibrate the curve, dates may be given within a range of fifty years. The technique is widely used in this region because it usually gives more precise dates than radiocarbon dating. In the late 1980s archaeologists used archaeomagnetic dating to resolve a fifty-year-old controversy about the chronology of the Hohokam tradition of southern Arizona. Master curves calibrated with radiocarbon give dates with ranges considerably larger than a fifty-year range and are more imprecise than radiocarbon dating.

[See also DATING THE PAST.]

■ J. L. Eighmy, *Archaeomagnetic Dating: A Handbook for Archaeologists* (1980). J. L. Eighmy and R. S. Sternberg, eds., *Archaeomagnetic Dating* (1990). R. F. Butler, *Paleomagnetism: Magnetic Domains to Geologic Terrans* (1992).

Randall H. McGuire

ARCHAEOZOOLOGY. *see* ZOOARCHAEOLOGY.

ARCHIVAL MANAGEMENT OF ARCHAEOLOGICAL RECORDS. The archival management of records means caring for them in a way that promotes their long-term survival. Preserving archaeological records is particularly important because they contain invaluable cultural and scientific information that would otherwise be lost. Excavation destroys. Thus, the only record of an excavated site lies in the field notes, drawings, and photographs that investigators keep. Similarly, survey maps and notes document prehistoric landscapes that are often later modified or obliterated by development. Even general correspondence and administrative files can contain crucial data on the genesis of scholarly ideas or the budgetary decisions that affected the structure of research. While some of this information is disseminated and perpetuated through publications, a great deal of it is not. A higher percentage of archaeological records has permanent value than, for example, business records, where typically only five percent of the total is retained.

The intrinsic value of archaeological records has been heightened by the emergence of the history of archaeology as a vigorous subdiscipline. This development is due to several factors. To begin with, the cumulative archaeological research of the last hundred years has led to a constriction of the uninvestigated prehistoric world. It is now infrequent for archaeologists to work in a pristine region, where no sites have been surveyed or dug. The records of past archaeological work, therefore, become critical, not just for

providing background historical information, but also for understanding cultural patterns in the region or depositional sequences at a particular site.

The importance of such data in the United States has been further underscored by recent federal legislation. Environmental impact statements, now mandatory for many construction development projects, have led to a surge in cultural resource management (CRM) work. To cut time and costs and to establish research priorities, CRM archaeologists routinely review previous research in the area under consideration. New regulations concerning the repatriation of artifactual and skeletal collections have only intensified this need for older archaeological records.

These documents are not just being mined for their practical content, however. A new wave of professional self-examination has led archaeologists to a critical reappraisal of both the internal workings of their discipline and of the place of archaeology within its wider social and cultural contexts. Older records hold important clues for understanding the sociopolitical dynamics that helped shape archaeology's development. They also provide a means of examining and reformulating the epistemological foundations of the discipline.

The recent emphasis on archaeology's legacy has highlighted the sad fact that many older records are now lost or missing. It has also made archaeologists realize that unless they take proper care of the documents they are currently creating, these too will suffer a similar fate. Many institutions sponsoring archaeological work have begun requiring the deposition of project records in designated archives to ensure their permanent retention. Additionally, government regulations may dictate that copies of field records be placed in approved repositories. These various rules do not govern all projects, however, nor do they cover personal papers and other documents that might have enduring value. By and large, it is still up to individual archaeologists to ensure the preservation of their important records.

The best way to promote permanence is to follow archival principles of records management. Specialized skills are not required. Rather, an awareness of the need for preservation and a willingness to do something about it is necessary. Archivists have two primary concerns when looking at scientific collections: one is that the record of the work be as complete as possible; the other is that it be in good physical condition. Archaeologists can help ensure this dual outcome by adhering to a few guidelines.

Most importantly, researchers should plan to preserve from the beginning, otherwise key records may be lost and funding may be short. The first step is to determine what kind of documentation will be needed for a particular piece of research. One should consider how someone from the outside might reconstruct the development of a scholarly theory or a project's trajectory from planning through field work and analysis to publication. It is important to look beyond such obvious documents as field notes and conference papers to correspondence, administrative memos, and other kinds of records that might contain significant information. Including non-paper records like film and computer files in the inventory is also crucial. Reviewing record keeping at the completion of each stage of the research helps ensure that all relevant documents are present. It is essential to begin building funds for preservation early, so that money is available for duplication and conservation at critical stages. Finally, ascertaining in advance where the records will go is also helpful. If an employer or government regulations do not specify an archive, then one should be selected in consultation with local archivists.

Equally important are environmental considerations. Extremes of temperature or humidity are damaging to all types of records, regardless of physical format. Even more harmful are constant fluctuations in atmospheric conditions. While few archaeologists can control their physical surroundings in the office or in the field, they can avoid storing their records in environmentally hazardous places such as car trunks, attics, and basements. Protecting records from light, dirt, dust, and food residues, which attract document-eating pests, will also prolong their longevity. Segregating records used only a few times a year from those that are actively used also helps. Semi-active records should be moved, if possible, from offices and laboratories to a long-term storage facility, where environment and access may be monitored more securely.

Finally, it is essential to check on the condition of important documents regularly and preserve them as necessary. Different information-storage media degrade at different rates. Color film, for instance, fades faster than black and white, and film is usually, but not always, more unstable than paper. Establishing a regular reviewing schedule will help catch any deterioration before it becomes serious. Records can then be conserved or duplicated as warranted. Archaeologists should be especially careful of computer disks, whose long-term stability has not been established. Particularly problematic for all machine-readable records are technological advances that rapidly make specific formats obsolete. Who now, for instance, has access to a punch-card reader? In planning for the long-term preservation of these documents, researchers should make sure they are routinely upgraded or translated into a more permanent medium.

By following these basic procedures, archaeologists can expect to turn over a complete and reasonably well-conserved record of their research to a receiving archive. In so doing, they will have taken an important step in preserving the past for the future.

[See also CULTURAL RESOURCE MANAGEMENT.]

■ Mary-Anne Kenworthy, Eleanor M. King, Mary Elizabeth Ruwell, and Trudy Van Houten, *Preserving Field Records. Archival Techniques for Archaeologists and Anthropologists* (1985). Jane Mohlhenrich, *Preservation of Electronic Formats & Electronic Formats for Preservation* (1993). Mary Lynn Ritzenthaler, *Preserving Archives and Manuscripts* (1993). The Society of American Archivists, brochures on *Donating Your Personal or Family Papers to a Repository* and *Donating Your Organizational Records to a Repository* (1994). Henry Wilhelm with contributing author Carol Brower, *The Permanence and Care of Color Photographs: Traditional and Digital Color Prints, Color Negatives, Slides, and Motion Pictures* (1994). Sydel Silverman and Nancy J. Parezo, eds., *Preserving the Anthropological Record*, 2nd ed. (1995).
Eleanor M. King

ARMS AND ARMOR. It is likely that the first tools used by humans fall into the category of arms and armor: hand and hafted axes, spearheads, and, later, arrowheads. It is easy to see the hunt as the principal use for these weapons, and arms for the hunt have remained very important throughout the history of arms and armor. However, arms and armor for war have long played a part in human history too. The earliest evidence for warfare seems to be datable to ca. 8000 B.C., in the rock paintings of Arnhem Land in the Northern Territory of Australia, in which combat with spears, shields, and boomerangs is depicted. Ever since then, a great deal of man's effort and ingenuity worldwide have been expended on the production of arms and armor, principally for war. Weapons and armor have in many societies been used to symbolize the social status of the wearer, and have almost always been of prime importance in society.

The great mass of historical arms and armor that survives has been preserved in arsenals, churches, and other collections; the fact that most arms and armor are formed of iron or steel makes them particularly vulnerable to oxidation and decomposition in the soil. Furthermore, most of the surviving archaeological material from the ground has come from chance finds, and very little has come from organized excavations. Arms and armor survive in the soil in three principal ways: as the result of accidental loss; as the result of the collapse of arsenals or stores, from which the material housed was never rescued; and as a result of burial. The latter is of most importance both for the quantity and the quality of the artifacts.

An important aspect of the study of historical arms and armor is the study of fakes. The demand from collectors of arms and armor, particularly of medieval European material, has caused the manufacture of a great number of fake objects, from the Gothic revival of the 1830s to the present day. This is not irrelevant to the study of arms and armor in archaeology, for very many of these fakes were provided with archaeological provenances.

The demand in Europe for the artifacts of classical antiquity caused the excavation of innumerable tombs in Greece and, most significantly, Italy, for the sale of the finds to collectors. Most of the surviving Greek arms and armor came from tombs robbed in this way in the eighteenth and nineteenth centuries. The provenances of this material are usually suspect, for the pieces required provenances for their eventual owners and were supplied with them. As the trade was illicit, such information was impossible to check.

Surprisingly little of the arms and armor of the ancient Near Eastern civilizations has survived. A small number of Assyrian helmets, shields, and weapons are known, but few of these come from satisfactorily stratified contexts. A recent find that is datable to the sixth century B.C. is an iron helmet from Sardis, reconstructed by the Royal Armouries at London.

Some of the most important organized excavations have produced a wealth of Hellenistic material. Most noteworthy among these are the excavations of the royal tombs at Vergina in Macedonia, which have produced a cuirass of iron scales covered with fabric, as well as an important series of spearheads and butt spikes. An example from the far end of the Hellenistic world is the excavation of the collapsed arsenal at Aï Khanoum in Afghanistan, where an important group of armor pieces for a cataphract cavalryman, as well as some useful shield covers, were recovered. Cataphract cavalry were heavy cavalry provided with armor for man and horse, introduced to the Seleucids and Romans in the west by the Parthians.

The study of Roman armor has been revolutionized by the analysis of excavated material. Finds of mail shirts have made it abundantly clear that sculptures showing Roman legionaries, cavalry, and auxiliaries thought in the nineteenth century to be shown in leather defenses, in fact depict defenses of mail. The plate body defenses developed in the Principate, called the *lorica segmentata*, were very poorly understood before H. R. Robinson's reconstructions of these defenses (1975) based on the excavated examples from Corbridge and Housesteads. The evidence for later Roman armor comes from a number of sources. An important hoard, principally containing fragments of scale defenses, was excavated from the Danubian frontier site at Carnuntum by the German archaeologist M. von Groller. There is also an extensive series of late Roman helmets from a number of finds, notably Intercisa, Duerne, and Berkasovo.

In contrast to the Greek and Roman worlds, where our knowledge of arms, armor, and military history comes principally from literature, we depend almost entirely on archaeology for any understanding of the military hardware of the Celtic and Germanic worlds. Mail, composed of interlocking iron links, seems to have been a Celtic invention that went on to be the most extensively used type of armor in western Europe until the fifteenth century. One of the very earliest examples, datable to the third century B.C., was excavated in Kirkburn, West Yorkshire. The high quality of Celtic armor can be seen in examples such as the Battersea shield, found near Battersea in the River Thames.

Likewise, our knowledge of the arms and armor of the Saxons and Vikings comes mainly from archaeological deposits. The famous ship burial at *Sutton Hoo provided a wide spectrum of military remains, including he sword with its associated furniture, the shield fittings, the shoulder clasps possibly from a mail shirt, and the famous helmet. Another important helmet of the period is that from Coppergate, in Viking York, but these English finds are overshadowed by the wealth of material from Valsgarde, Vendel, and many other sites in Sweden.

Our knowledge of Near Eastern armor in the Parthian Period (third century B.C. to third century A.D.) rests principally on the excavations carried out by Yale University at the fortified town of Dura Europos on the Euphrates. Here the collapse of an arsenal in one of the mural towers preserved an extensive set of horse armor, as well as an important helmet, painted late Roman shields, and woven cane Parthian shields. From the later Sasanian Period (third to seventh centuries A.D.) in Persia come a number of swords and helmets, and a single, fragmentary lamellar coat.

The vast majority of surviving European medieval arms and armor made before 1400 comes from archaeological provenances. The most important groups of excavated material are largely unpublished. These include the hoard of swords and other material from the site of the battle of Castillon in Spain, and the extensive group of early to mid-fifteenth-century armor from Chalkis on the island of Euboea. One important excavated group that has been fully published is the mass burial of participants in the battle of Wisby in 1356 in Sweden. The excavation of this site produced the largest corpus of coats of plate, the type of body armor that preceded the solid plate breastplate in Europe. Some chance finds have had scholarly implications beyond their apparent importance. A small group of plates from a sixteenth-century jack of plate from Beeston Castle in Cheshire, England, gave rise to a seminal scholarly article on the history of the jack of plate and the brigandine.

Most later European arms and armor from archaeological contexts has been recovered from underwater sites. Underwater archaeology has contributed a great deal to our knowledge of artillery from the Middle Ages to the present, especially because the organic objects that are always associated with artillery equipment (carriages, rammers, buckets, etc.) are preserved for study. An extensive group of wrought iron ordnance of ca. 1520 from the Molasses Reef wreck, situated off an isolated reef near the Caicos Bank, the Turks and Caicos Islands, in the British West Indies, has

been studied in great detail. One of the most famous excavations of shipwrecks is that of the flagship of King Henry VIII, the *Mary Rose*, which sank off Portsmouth in 1545. The military finds include the largest collection of surviving English longbows, as well as arrows and numerous other pieces such as gun shields and cannon. The remains of field carriages aboard *La Trinidad Valencera*, a Spanish Armada vessel shipwrecked in Kinnagoe Bay, County Donegal, in 1588, and discovered in 1971, have provided important information about these fugitive elements of ordnance. Later wrecks—for instance, that of the Dutch East Indiaman *Batavia*, sunk in 1629 off the coast of western Australia—have provided important insights into the nature of naval ordnance.

The arms and armor of the early historic period in central Asia are very poorly understood in the West. Many excavations of burial sites were undertaken under Soviet rule, however, and the material uncovered from these is of immense importance. A fine series of arms and armor from Scythian tombs (sixth to fourth centuries B.C.), including swords and their scabbards, quiver covers, scale armor, and helmets, is preserved in the Hermitage Museum, St Petersburg. The later material from the Kirghiz sites of the tenth to twelfth centuries is also important. It includes, for example, what seem to be the earliest curved cavalry sabers. These finds greatly assist interpretation of the equally important frescoes of military subjects from the silk road towns of Pjandjikent, Turfan, and others, which are known because of their wholesale removal to the West by Albert von le Coq and others.

Chinese archaeologists have uncovered large quantities of arms and armor in extensive excavations since 1967. In particular, our understanding of Zhou Dynasty armor has been advanced by excavations at Huhehot and Leigudun, where series of important laced plate armors were discovered. The terra-cotta army of the emperor Qinshihuangdi is most important for the study of Chinese armor, and fragments of laced plate armor corresponding with the terra-cotta sculptures there have also been found. The figures, life-size and arranged within a series of huge pits, were originally equipped with weapons of bronze, but these were removed by tomb robbers very soon after the burial of the emperor. A few examples of bronze swords and crossbow bolt heads nonetheless survived the pillaging. Han Dynasty material has been recovered from various sites, the most important of which is *Mawangdui, which yielded a particularly well-preserved scale coat, and many halberds, swords, and daggers. Chinese arms and armor of later periods is much less plentiful. A number of swords of the Tang period are known, but these have been excavated from sites in Japan. One of the few sources of Ming arms and armor is the tomb of the Wanli emperor, which contained his armor and a sword.

Most of the surviving early arms and armor of Japan have been preserved in Shinto shrines, notably those of the Oyamazumi Jinja on Omishima Island and the Itsukushima Jinja near Hiroshima, as well as in the imperial repository, the Shosoin, at Nara. The excavation of burial mounds of the early historical period has produced important evidence of the importation of Chinese swords of high quality and of Chinese, Korean, or Mongolian lamellar armor. Both of these types of arms and armor were the continental precursors of the later Japanese types, which established unique styles and high standards of excellence in production in the historical period.

[See also BATTLEFIELD ARCHAEOLOGY OF NORTH AMERICA; BRITISH ISLES, articles on CELTIC IRELAND, MEDIEVAL BRITAIN, THE ANGLO-SAXONS, VIKING RAIDS AND SETTLEMENT IN BRITAIN AND IRELAND; CHINA: HAN EMPIRE; EUROPE, articles on THE EUROPEAN BRONZE AGE, THE EUROPEAN IRON AGE; MAIDEN CASTLE; TRAFFICKING IN ANTIQUITIES.]

■ B. Thordeman, Armour from the Battle of Wisby (1939–40). H. R. Robinson, The Armour of Imperial Rome (1975). R. R. Brown and R. D. Smith, "Guns from the Sea: Ship's Armaments in the Age of Discovery," The International Journal of Nautical Archaeology and Underwater Exploration 17 (1988): 1–111. I.D.D. Eaves, "Notes on the Excavation of a Jack of Plate from Beeston Castle, Cheshire," Journal of the Arms and Armour Society XIII (1989): 81–154. I. Stead, Iron Age Cemeteries in East Yorkshire, English Heritage archaeological reports 22 (1991). C. H. Greenwood and A. M. Heywood, "A Helmet of the Sixth Century B.C. from Sardis," Basor 285 (1992): 1–31. D. Tweddle, The Anglian Helmet from Coppergate (1992).

Thom Richardson

ART exists in every present-day human society and apparently in every ancient one too, back to at least 40,000 years ago and probably much further. Yet it is a phenomenon that is notoriously difficult to define, not least because it encompasses such a vast array of activities and products. Further, in many societies art is not perceived as a separate entity but merely as an inherent part of normal social or religious life, and just as there are no clear boundaries between the secular and the religious, so there are none between the aesthetic and the practical.

Hence, a common perception of art as "an achievement of human skill the aim of which is to give pleasure rather than utility" is of little use in archaeology, where the aim of most art—particularly in prehistoric periods—remains unknown. Some archaeologists go so far as to reject the word *art* altogether, or at least place it between quotation marks, because the term is seen to presume the aesthetic and because it lumps together such a huge variety of material into a single, monolithic category.

Perhaps the simplest and most sensible course, therefore, is to use the centuries-old definition of art as "the work of people as opposed to that of nature," thus avoiding any differentiation of the diversity of forms, content, or intention. In other words, art is art, regardless of the variety in its meaning and function, whether it is prehistoric, Greek, Assyrian, or whatever. Many of the images and objects in question have a (sometimes intentional) aesthetic impact for us, and their continued use through centuries and civilizations continually gives them new meanings. Our own ideas about what art is are continually changing, so how can we possibly understand the art of thousands of years ago and other parts of the world? Yet the art of the past speaks to us, even though no longer in the language of its creators.

Archaeologists need to be wary of using an aesthetic approach and to look beyond any beauty or formal qualities they may perceive in the art of the past, in order to try to recreate the perception and use of images of ancient peoples. It is important to remember that in remote periods (and in traditional societies today), some images were considered the work of the supernatural, not merely products of the human mind. They were seen as more or less direct manifestations of the divine and sometimes even as spontaneous miracles, like the image on the Turin Shroud. For example, many Australian rock engravings and paintings were (and in some areas still are) interpreted by the Aborigines as imprints left on the rock by the Dreamtime heroes. In other cases, ancient artists were anonymous go-betweens, conveying the decisions of the spirits and interceding between them and the people, whereas today artists in most cultures have lost their social and religious function.

Quite apart from the impossibility of truly understanding the art of the ancient past, the archaeologist is faced with some fundamental problems in its study. In common with every other category of archaeological evidence, art has reached us in a highly distorted and incomplete sample. Except in sites with special conditions of preservation—the frozen, the arid, or the waterlogged—where objects made of fragile organic materials can survive, the art of the past is dominated by the materials that are the most durable: stone, pottery, metal, and so forth. In other words, the art objects that we have from the past, especially the remote past, represent only the tip of the iceberg.

It is certain that a huge amount of artistic activity involving perishable materials has gone forever—work in wood, bark, fibers, feathers, or hides; figures made in mud, sand, or snow; and of course, body painting and tattooing, which probably have very distant origins. In addition, dance and song leave no traces at all, and most ancient musical instruments have disintegrated.

Even the durable objects that have reached us often provide no more than a pale shadow, and indeed, a false image, of their former selves. For example, it is known from traces on them that many Ice Age portable art objects, together with most Ice Age bas-relief sculpture on cave walls, were originally painted, often in gaudy colors, as were Greek and Roman statuary, Aztec temples, and the medieval cathedrals of Europe. To our modern eyes, such coloring would probably ruin them, whereas the original artists and their contemporaries might well be horrified at the present uncolored state of the works.

Another basic problem for archaeology is the origins of art—not so much the why and wherefore, about which debate will probably continue forever, but the appearance of proto-art. At present, art is traditionally seen as an invention of fully modern *humans, its rise coinciding with their arrival in Europe and elsewhere over 40,000 years ago. Since fully modern humans are now thought by some researchers to have been in Africa and the Near East at least 100,000 years ago, however, one wonders why art took so long to emerge. A more realistic approach is to acknowledge the growing number and variety of apparently nonfunctional objects and examples of incipient decoration that are being discovered for earlier periods, produced by *Neanderthals and even by *Homo erectus, extending back some 200,000 or 300,000 years. This problem is linked to that of when tools moved beyond the strictly utilitarian into a symmetry that was perhaps more aesthetically pleasing than functionally necessary: many researchers would point to the highly symmetrical hand axes of the Middle Pleistocene, several hundred thousand years ago, as the first visible example of this behavior.

Conversely, it is quite possible that not only these early tools but also many later artifacts were primarily conceived in terms of practical use and that any aesthetic effect they may have on us was unintended or at best incidental. For example, much of the simplest "decoration" of tools and weapons, such as incisions near the base, was probably intended to strengthen the adherence to the shaft and to improve the user's grip: this has been called "technical aesthetics." Apparently, nonfigurative art—motifs that convey nothing to our eyes other than patterning—has existed from the beginning; in fact, it often dominates the art of the *Pleistocene, and its study is one of the long-neglected challenges of archaeology.

Figurative images are more easily recognized as "artistic," though once again they may well be utilitarian rather than simply decorative. Theoretically, "art for art's sake" may have occurred in any culture, but in most cases individual artistic inspiration was subject to some more widespread system of thought and had messages to convey—signatures, ownership, warnings, exhortations, demarcations, commemorations, narratives, myths, and metaphors. The function of most art was probably to affect the knowledge or behavior of the people who could read those messages. We cannot read ancient art in the same way as its intended public, and the way all aspects were combined into an experience has gone forever. (Much cave art, for example, was intensely private, meant to be seen only by the artist and perhaps by some deity; it was the act of producing the image and its location that seem to have been important.) Without informants, we can use art only as a source of hypotheses. Without the artists or, in later cultures, the presence of some explanatory label or writing, our chances of interpreting correctly the content and meaning of ancient art are small. Meaning can only be conjured in our imaginations, or more reliably, through comparisons with images from historic cultures.

Art is of supreme importance in archaeology not because of the vast numbers of objects and images from the past that our twentieth-century eyes consider beautiful or striking, but because it is art alone that gives humankind its true dimension, by showing that human activities hold meanings other than those of a purely utilitarian kind.

[See also BYZANTINE CULTURE: BYZANTINE DECORATIVE ARTS; CELTIC ART; GREEK ART AND ARCHITECTURE, CLASSICAL, articles on CLASSICAL GREEK POTTERY, CLASSICAL GREEK SCULPTURE, CLASSICAL GREEK ARCHITECTURE; IDEOLOGY AND ARCHAEOLOGY; RELIGION; ROCK ART; ROMAN DECORATIVE ARTS: OVERVIEW; VENUS FIGURINES; WEST AFRICAN SCULPTURE.]

■ L. Adam, Primitive Art, rev. ed. (1949). E. H. Gombrich, Art and Illusion: A Study in the Psychology of Pictorial Representation (1960). J. Macquet, Introduction to Aesthetic Anthropology (1979). R. Layton, The Anthropology of Art (1981). P. G. Bahn and J. Vertut, Images of the Ice Age (1988). P. G. Bahn, The Cambridge Illustrated History of Prehistoric Art (forthcoming).

Paul G. Bahn

ARTIFACT DISTRIBUTION ANALYSIS.

The analysis of the distribution of artifacts across site surfaces is commonly called *intrasite spatial analysis*. This distinguishes it from *intersite spatial analysis*, which also may concern the study of artifact distributions, but on a regional or larger scale. Although there is some overlap in the statistical techniques used, these two types of analysis are largely different in approach, methodology, and history of development within archaeology.

Intrasite spatial analysis was conceived in the 1960s, largely within the context of the American "New Archaeology" and, specifically, the Bordes-Binford debate over the nature and meaning of variability in Mousterian stone-tool assemblages. Binford argued essentially that statistical covariation among tool types from site to site was the result of Mousterian use of more than one kind of tool for certain, common tasks. The tools thus presumably used together were called a "tool kit." It was felt that, if it were possible to demonstrate the existence of such tool kits as spatially de-

finable concentrations within sites, this "functional" interpretation of Mousterian assemblage variability would be confirmed, or at least greatly strengthened.

Intrasite artifact distribution analysis is useful in studying and interpreting an archaeological site when the materials to be analyzed come from levels that are believed to represent former land "'surfaces" on which the artifacts were originally scattered. Such probable, former surfaces often are called "occupation floors (or surfaces)" or "living floors." If other data, observations, or analyses appear to indicate that post-depositional processes have not substantially disturbed the archaeological materials lying on such a surface, spatial analysis may reveal patterns of distribution that can be interpreted in terms of the human activities or other processes that created the site, or a particular level within the site.

The methods used for artifact distribution analysis are primarily statistical in nature, although various cartographic methods have been used, and simple visual inspection of distribution maps or plans can be adequate in cases of particularly strong and uncomplicated spatial patterning. Although the statistical methods used for artifact distribution analysis were at first borrowed from other disciplines, the most useful approaches now used have been developed by archaeologists themselves to deal with the specific questions and problems of archaeological sites and data.

The first factor determining what methods may be applicable in a given case is whether the spatial distribution of the archaeological materials was recorded in terms of exact two- or three-dimensional coordinates for each artifact, or whether the data are in the form of counts per grid square or quadrat. The literature cited in the bibliography gives thorough, technical overviews of all the methods mentioned below, as well as of some less frequently applied methods.

Among the first methods to be used were nearest neighbor analysis for absolute coordinate data and the variance/mean ratio for grid-count data. Dimensional analysis of variance was another early technique used on grid-count data. These methods are still occasionally applied, in particular various forms of nearest neighbor analysis. However, all of these methods are severely limited, either in terms of their ability to deal with more than one artifact type at a time or by various constraints on their ability to detect spatial clusters of different sizes, shapes, densities, positions, orientations, or composition.

Currently, two major approaches dominate the methodology of artifact distribution analysis. K-means clustering, or "pure locational clustering," can be used for absolute coordinate data. Unconstrained clustering can be used both for absolute coordinate and for grid-count data. Both of these approaches still have limitations on their abilities to reveal all the details and intricacies of artifact distributions. K-means clustering has a tendency to constrain the shape of the spatial clusters that it defines, and it can not take composition, in terms of the artifact types that make up a cluster, into account in defining clusters. However, it is otherwise particularly effective in the definition of spatial location and size of artifact clusters. Unconstrained clustering is strong in the definition of clusters on the basis of their artifactual composition, and it places no constraints on the shapes of clusters, but its results are also, therefore, potentially weak in terms of the precision of spatial definition and the spatial integrity of the clusters it defines. Although in practice archaeologists often seem wedded to one or the other of these two major approaches, the most effective current practice is to apply both, with final conclusions drawn and interpretations based on their areas of mutual corroboration and divergence.

It is important to keep in mind that the results of any artifact distribution analysis are nothing more than static descriptions of the spatial patterning (or lack thereof) of artifacts over an area. These results always leave open the question of what processes created such patterned distributions. The interpretation of each individual situation will depend, therefore, on a wide range of ancillary information and knowledge about the site, and cannot be derived directly from distributional analysis itself.

Thus, with the emergence of these two complementary and effective approaches to analysis, interest is beginning to turn to attempts to understand the many processes that can create patterned artifact distributions over archaeological sites. The first, and still the primary, reason for archaeological interest in artifact distributions is, of course, that they may allow us to infer prehistoric patterns of human behavior. A good deal of ethnoarchaeological research has been undertaken specifically to develop guides for the interpretation of artifact distributional patterns in these terms. There is, however, a growing awareness of the importance and the difficulty of identifying and disentangling the effects of both human behavior and of other possible causes for observed artifact distributional patterns. Geological processes are among the main nonhuman processes that produce patterned artifact distributions, but other postdepositional processes, such as animal scavenging, may be quite significant.

In its current state of development, artifact distribution analysis, or intrasite spatial analysis, has begun to take its place in archaeology as a useful set of methods for the description of certain kinds of archaeological sites, where its results may, with adequate information and understanding from other sources, allow a fuller interpretation and reconstruction of human activities in the past.

[See also SITE LOCATION: SITE ASSESSMENT.]

■ John E. Yellen, *Archaeological Approaches to the Present* (1977). Harold Hietala, *Intrasite Spatial Analysis in Archaeology* (1984). Susan Kent, ed., *Method and Theory for Activity Area Research: An Ethnoarchaeological Approach* (1987). Keith W. Kintigh, "Intrasite Spatial Analysis: A Commentary on Major Methods," in *Mathematics and Information Science in Archaeology: A Flexible Framework*, ed. Albertus Voorrips (1990), pp. 165–200. Hans Peter Blankholm, *Intrasite Spatial Analysis in Theory and Practice* (1991).

Robert Whallon

ASIA

INTRODUCTION

The prehistory and early history of Asia is a grand tapestry woven on an enormous geographic and chronological scale. For this article, Asia is considered to consist of the Indian subcontinent or southern Asia, eastern and central Asia, mainland Southeast Asia, and the peninsular region of Korea and Japan. Island Southeast Asia is discussed separately as part of Oceania and the Pacific. Within Asia are included the highest mountains in the world, some of the largest and driest deserts in the world, extensive temperate plains, and equally extensive tropical lowland rain forest. In short, the region has an enormous diversity of local and regional environments and plant, animal, and mineral resources. Chronologically, this overview covers the past two million years in the region, from the first evidence of *Homo erectus* through the late historic period. Over this vast time span, the archaeological record has preserved the full panoply of human cultural development, rich with local innovations and remarkable evidence of interregional contact with *diffusion through trade and, later, through empire building.

Paleolithic. The earliest occupations of Asia were by *Homo erectus* from about two million years ago and, arguably, lasting to about 200,000 to 58,000 years ago in most regions. While fossil remains of *Homo erectus* are relatively rare, sites containing the now classic Lower Paleolithic stone tool assemblage occur in all regions during this time period. Notable fossil sites for *H. erectus* include Modjokerto (1.8 mya B.P.), Lantian in China (800,000–760,000 B.P.), and locality I at *Zhoukoudian cave in China (500,000–230,000 B.P.).

The appearance of Archaic *Homo sapiens* in Asia is currently problematic. While there are a number of sites in China (Dali, Jinniushan, Hexian, Dingcun, Maba) dating between 280,000 and 100,000 B.P. where claims have been made for transitional Archaic *H. sapiens* fossils, the data are sparse and far from convincing at this time. In addition to the Chinese sites, there are also three cave sites in Korea (Yonggok-dong, Daehyun-dong, and Dokch'on) dating between 200,000 and 50,000 B.P. where Archaic *H. sapiens* fossil remains have been found, although the remains are more conclusive from the upper levels than the lower levels at these sites. Fossil remains aside, there is a long-lasting chopper–chopping tool tradition, with local variations, throughout Asia during this time period.

Significant changes began to occur throughout Asia at about 50,000 years ago, with occupations of anatomically modern *H. sapiens*. Technologically this transition is marked by the appearance of stone tools manufactured on blades followed by microblades used in the construction of multicomponent tools. A generalized hunting-gathering economy appears to have been typical, based on data from cave and rockshelter sites from Sri Lanka (Sanghao cave, 38,000–18,000 B.P.) in the south to the Mongolian steppes (Sjaraosso-gol, 50,000–30,000 B.P.) in the north, and a substantial number of sites in Japan (50,000–12,000 B.P.) in the east. In most cases, excellent preservation in cave and rockshelter deposits indicate a very sophisticated material culture based on compound tools.

The botanical and faunal remains indicate seasonal exploitation of wild plant foods, large and small animals, fish, and shellfish. This economic tradition appears to have lasted much longer in the coastal areas of Southeast Asia and in Japan than in southern Asia, inland Southeast Asia, or the Korean peninsula. The *Jomon tradition in Japan, for example, essentially continued the hunting-gathering tradition of the Upper Paleolithic, with the addition of simple pottery at around 12,000 B.P. and lasted until 2,200 B.P., when rice cultivation and *metallurgy were introduced from the Korean peninsula. Similar patterns of stable adaptation are also recorded in Southeast Asian cave sites such as Spirit Cave (14,000–7,600 B.P.), Banyan Valley Cave (7,600–450 B.P.), and the series of Vietnamese sites that demark the *Hoabinhian culture (13,000–7,200 B.P.).

The transition from food collecting to food producing occurred in several locations in southern Asia and China starting sometime after about 14,000 B.P. This transition to an agricultural economy based on different plant and animal domesticates in the different areas was essentially complete by 9,000 B.P., after which diffusion to Southeast Asia, peninsular eastern Asia, and the rest of southern Asia began to occur.

Neolithic. In China the earliest Neolithic phase is dated between 12,000 and 10,000 B.P. This phase includes an early period with preceramic sites followed by a later period in which the sites contain primitive ceramics. Sites dating to this phase have been found in southern, western, and northern China. The Middle Neolithic phase in China dates from 10,000 B.P. to 7,000 B.P. This phase was marked by the proliferation of settlements, advancements in pottery technology, and the cultivation of millet in the northern parts of China. There is some controversy as to whether rice was also being cultivated in the Pengtoushan area of southern China at the same time. Some evidence of the beginnings of monumental architecture also exists, for instance, at Qin'an Dadiwan (7,000 B.P.) and the Xinglongwa sites in Inner Mongolia. The Late Neolithic in China is dated from 7,000 to 5,500 B.P. During this time, millet agriculture was firmly established in the north and long grain rice agriculture was standard in the south. The end of this period saw a remarkable increase in both the numbers and the sizes of communities throughout China. Early use of metals in China also dates to the end of the Late Neolithic at about 5,500 B.P., and is firmly established during the Longshan culture period (4,600–4,100 B.P.). During this period, there were a number of important identifiable culture areas in China, including the Yangshao (7,000–5,000 B.P.), the Hongshan (6,500–5,000 B.P.) and the Liangzhu (5,000–3,700 B.P.).

The transition to food production occurred at roughly the same time in southern Asia, with four separate traditions. The earliest and least understood is the East Indian Neolithic tradition, which is dated between 10,000 and 9,000 B.P. From what is known of this tradition, it appears to be similar to beginning agricultural traditions known in Southeast Asia, specifically Spirit Cave (13,000–7,500 B.P.) in Thailand and the Padah Lin caves of Burma. Chronologically following the East Indian Neolithic are the remarkable developments preserved in the early deposits at Mehrgarh in the Indus Valley of Pakistan. While the occupation at Mehrgarh has been divided into seven periods, the first three relate to the transition to agriculture. The earliest deposits of Mehrgarh contain no *ceramics but do provide ample evidence of the cultivation of domesticated barley and wheat. During this earliest period, the inhabitants appear to have been exploiting the wild animals of the Kachi Plain, but by the beginning of the ceramic period (ca. 7,500 B.P.), the faunal assemblage reflects a significant shift to domesticated sheep, cattle, and goat. By 6,500 B.P. the city of Mehrgarh had expanded to its maximum size, and the deposits for this time period provide ample evidence of well-developed, specialized craft production of painted, wheel-thrown ceramics, ceramic figurines, steatite beads, and smelted copper tools. The later periods at Mehrgarh overlap with the establishment of the Indus or Harappan civilization (5,200–3,400 B.P.) in northern India, centered on the large cities of Harappa, Mohenjo-daro, and Chirand—

roughly the same time that the first state level society was appearing in China (Erlitou, 4,050–3,800 B.P.). It was also during this later time period that the two other agricultural traditions of southern Asia, the northern Neolithic in Kashmir and the southern Neolithic in India, were gaining momentum, although based on different suites of plant and animal domesticates.

The transition to *agriculture in Southeast Asia was clearly influenced by climatic changes and the diffusion of rice cultivation from southern China. The interior uplands were occupied by broad-spectrum foragers collectively known as the Hoabinhian culture. The rich coastal areas of north and central Vietnam were occupied by a variety of groups inhabiting sedentary villages with an economy based on exploiting the rich estuarine resources, and included the manufacture of pottery and polished stone adzes. For example, the site of Nong Nor (4,500 B.P.) contains a shell midden and evidence of fishing and pottery production, but no indication of agricultural activities. It is not until 500 years later, at the site of Khok Phanom Di (4,000–3,500 B.P.), that clear evidence appears for rice agriculture and the use of domesticated cattle and pigs, as well as for extensive trade networks (in the form of burials containing exotic items). Thus, at the time that the Harrapan civilization was giving way to a period of dispersed farming communities in southern Asia and the first states were forming in China, agricultural expansion and the formation of complex chiefdoms was occurring in central southeast Asia.

In Korea, the ceramic Chulmun Period (8,000–3,300 B.P.) sites only show evidence of agriculture and animal domestication at the end of the sequence, with millet cultivation appearing at the sites of Hokok and Odong at about 3,500 B.P. This was probably introduced from northern China. Evidence for rice cultivation appears at the site of Namkyong around 3,000 B.P. As Korea was influenced by China during this period, by 2,200 B.P. Korean immigrants to Japan introduced rice agriculture and metallurgy, thus ending the long-lived Jomon tradition.

States. In the following centuries, the prehistory and history of Asia forms a complex web of emerging chiefdoms and states vying for power, in part fueled by an even more complex and extensive network of trade routes. Around 3,400 B.P. the Chinese Shang dynasty had begun developing *writing, its earliest form being that of glyphs inscribed on "oracle bones." In southern Asia, the Rig Vedas were written around 3,100 B.P. The Chinese writing system later influenced the development of both Korean and Japanese writing systems. Also around 3,000 B.P., iron manufacturing became widespread throughout Asia, supplanting bronze for the manufacture of tools.

The expansion of the Chinese empire began after final consolidation during the Western Han dynasty (2,200–2,000 B.P.; Eastern Han, 2,000–1,800 B.P.). Part of this expansion took the form of military garrisons in Korea, further influencing the development of later states there and in Japan. The Han also struck south, consolidating their borders in Southeast Asia and extending significant cultural influence in central Southeast Asia. The Han were also intensely interested in expanding trade, and forged new maritime trade routes along the Southeast Asian coast, sending expeditions as far west as India. In addition, the Silk Route from Chang'an through central Asia to Antioch and *Constantinople was begun during the Han dynasty, providing contact with all cultures along the route as well as with the *Roman Empire to the west.

During this time, southern Asia experienced an upsurge in the growth of cities, with the Second Urbanization beginning around 2,600 B.P. and the formation of the Mauryan empire in 2,300 B.P. Large port cities such as Arikamedu participated in what was the first world economy, documented by evidence for trade with Rome, China, and Africa.

In the period between 2,000 and 1,000 B.P. the various Chinese dynasties became more inward oriented than had the Han. The Chinese withdrawal from much of Southeast Asia opened up opportunities for the founding of the Indian-influenced Khmer Civilization (1,400–575 B.P.). In Korea, the Three Kingdoms Period (1,700–1,300 B.P.) ended with the formation of the United Shilla empire, with a centralized government based on the Chinese system. Japan witnessed the formation of the Yamato State (1,375 B.P.), whose structure was also influenced by the Chinese model; this state formed the foundation of Japan's feudal society until recent historic times. In southern Asia, this period witnessed the formation, prosperity, and decline of a series of great city-states, such as Pollonnaruwa in Sri Lanka and *Vijayangara. This episode finally ended with the formation of the Mughal empire in 1600.

The entire history and prehistory of Asia is one of varied local innovations and developments that resulted, as time went on, in a rich interweaving of cultural traditions and technological innovations. Based on the archaeological and historical evidence, the world economy as we have come to understand it had its beginnings over 2,000 years ago in the varied cultural and material commerce begun by the early state societies of southern Asia, China, and Southeast Asia. History and archaeology are fundamental guides to a full understanding of the modern political, religious, and cultural realities in this crucial and complex region of the world.

[See also ASIA, ORIGINS OF FOOD PRODUCTION IN, articles on ORIGINS OF FOOD PRODUCTION IN SOUTH ASIA, ORIGINS OF FOOD PRODUCTION IN SOUTHEAST ASIA; BANYAN CAVE; CHANG'AN; CHINA, articles on STONE AGE CULTURES OF CHINA, HAN EMPIRE, TANG AND SUNG DYNASTIES; DONG SUN CULTURE; FUNAN CULTURE; GREAT WALL OF CHINA; HARAPPA; HEMUDU; HISTORY OF ARCHAEOLOGY FROM 1900 TO 1950; INDUS CIVILIZATION; JAPAN AND KOREA, articles on INTRODUCTION, EARLY STATES OF JAPAN AND KOREA; KHMER CIVILIZATION AND THE EMPIRE OF ANGKOR; KHOK PHANOM DI; MAWANGDUI; MEHRGARH; MOHENJO-DARO; NON NOK THA; PENGTOUSHAN; SILK ROUTE; SOUTHEAST ASIA, KINGDOMS AND EMPIRES OF; SPIRIT CAVE; YANGSHAO CULTURE; ZHENGZHOU.]

George Michaels

PREHISTORY AND EARLY HISTORY OF SOUTH ASIA

The earliest settlement of humans in South Asia is not well defined. It is known that important evidence of human evolution is documented by the appearance of large apelike (hominoid) creatures in the Miocene of the Siwalik Hills. For the past twenty years research has been conducted in Pakistan, Kashmir, and Hari Talyanagar. Fossil apes are of the genus *Sivapithecus* and *Ramapithecus*, a subgroup of the *Sivapithicines*. They are closely related to the modern gibbon and can be considered a form of *Dryopithecus*. *Gigantopithecus* sometimes occurs, also. These fossils date to a period between about 11.8 million years B.P. and 7.2 million years B.P.

*Pleistocene finds have been well summarized by K.A.R. Kennedy (1973). The best-documented fossil human is an archaic *Homo sapiens* from the bed of the Narmada River. A second hominid fossil was found in Afghanistan at Dara-i Kur in association with a Middle Palaeolithic stone tool assemblage, probably *Homo sapiens sapiens*.

The abundance of Lower Palaeolithic artifacts in South Asia contrast sharply with the spotty human fossil record. There are hundreds of sites that contain core bifaces, choppers, and chopping tools. Lower Palaeolithic tools are reported from most of the major regions of South Asia; the exceptions are Southern Sind, Baluchistan, Bangladesh and Sri Lanka. Tools dating to two million years B.P. are reported at Riwat on the Potwar Plateau, a claim being clarified by continuing research. Systematic excavations at Chirki and Paisra have unearthed, *in situ*, living and working floors. Research at Didwana in Rajasthan produced environmental data, plus masses of artifacts.

Eastern India has evidence that *Hoabinhian tool making extended into the Subcontinent.

The South Asian Middle Paleolithic is abundantly documented by sites but there is no association with human fossils, except for the Dara-I Kur find. This is a flake industry, with limited evidence for the Levallois technique. Middle Paleolithic sites are known from most major regions of South Asia. The exceptions are Baluchistan and the Eastern Indian States. There is considerable topological diversity in this body of material.

The Upper *Palaeolithic of South Asia is not as well documented as the Middle Paleolithic. Sites appear in some numbers in Gujarat, Rajasthan, the hilly tracts of central and eastern India, and on the Potwar Plateau of Pakistan, most notably at Sanghao Cave. Some contain long, narrow blades taken from prismatic cores. At other sites, Sanghao Cave for example, the artifacts consist of small irregular flakes. A series of radiocarbon dates from this cave, run by Oxford, yielded consistent results and dated the deeply stratified deposits between about 20,000 and 40,000 years B.P., which overlaps the dates for microlithic tool technology in Sri Lanka.

The South Asian Mesolithic has been documented best in Sri Lanka where a series of thirty-two radiocarbon dates from the sites of Batadomba Lena Cave and Beli-lena Kitulgala date a microlithic chipped stone tool industry to around 28,500 to 10,000 B.P. The earliest anatomically modern *Homo sapiens* in South Asia comes from Batadomba Lena Cave and is associated with the levels dated to around 28,500 B.P. There are also early dates for human fossils from Fa Hien Cave in Sri Lanka that could push this date back to 31,000 B.P.

The South Asian Mesolithic assemblages include microblades, lunates, crescents, triangles, trapezes, and the rest of the microlithic tool kit. Some come from sites of hunter-gathering peoples, contemporary with the end of the last glacial period and the early Holocene. The microlithic tool kit, used by many peoples who were not just hunter-gatherers, has a long history in the Subcontinent. By the sixth millennium B.C. microlithic tool users were herding cattle, sheep, and goats.

Adaptive strategies are apparent at sites with microlithic technology: herding, hunting and gathering, primitive cultivation, and the keeping of domesticated animals. There are assemblages that suggest a symbiotic relationship of South Asian hunter-gatherers with nearby settled, agricultural and herding communities. Not all sties with microlithic assemblages and adaptive strategies can be considered "Mesolithic."

The Beginnings of Food Production. The food-producing economy associated with Pakistan and much of India today, originated in the uplands of the Iranian Plateau and Afghanistan and is based on the wheat/barley and sheep/goat/cattle constellation of domesticated plants and animals. This is clearly related to the Near Eastern pattern of early food production. It was this complex of plants and animals on which the Harappan and Mesopotamian civilizations were based. The earliest manifestation of this tradition in South Asia comes from the site of *Mehrgarh, on the Kachi Plains of the Indus Valley in Pakistan.

Period IA at Mehrgarh is an aceramic Neolithic with mud brick houses. There is a rich, complex collection of palaeobotanical remains, most of which is from thousands of impressions in the mud bricks of the period. The dominant plant of Period I is domesticated naked six-row barley (*Hordeum vulgare* subspecies *vulgare* variety *nudum*) representing 90 percent of identified plant remains. Domesticated hulled six-row and two-row barley and domesticated einkorn, emmer, and hard wheat were also there.

In Period IA the animal economy was dominated by twelve species of large ungulates: gazelle, swamp deer, nilgai, blackbuck, onager, chital, water buffalo, wild sheep, wild goat, wild cattle, wild pig, and elephant. Richard Meadow takes this to indicate that the first inhabitants of aceramic Mehrgarh I exploited the Kachi Plain and the surrounding hills. By the end of the aceramic period the faunal assemblage is different. Remains are from sheep, goat, or cattle, domestic animals of great importance in the Middle East and South Asia today.

The radiocarbon determinations for Mehrgarh I are inconsistent. The best estimate for its beginnings is around 7000 B.C. Mehrgarh I compares well in cultural development with sites in the Near East.

There is a second food-producing cultural tradition in the northern regions of the Subcontinent that is called the Northern Neolithic, dating to around 3000 B.C. Most of the sites are found in Kashmir, but there are also settlements on the plains, as at Sarai Khola, near Taxila. These sites have cord-impressed pottery, ground stone knives and ring stones, a rich bone tool industry, dog burials, and semisubterranian houses. They represent the southernmost expression of a North Asian complex with a cultural tradition that has its roots in inner Asia.

A third cultural tradition of early food producers is found in eastern India, and probably Bangladesh. It relates to Southeast Asian traditions found at places like *Spirit Cave in northwestern Thailand and the Padah Lin Caves in Burma. These archaeological assemblages may be early, around 8000 to 7000 B.C.

Finally, there is the Southern Neolithic of peninsular India. The antecedents of these farmers and herders are not entirely clear, but the sites appear to date to the late third and early second millennia B.C. These peoples used two forms of gram as well as millets, and were cattle herders. There is evidence for keeping domesticated sheep and goats, whose derivations are in the Indus Valley and the Iranian Plateau.

By about 2500 B.C. the Indus or Harappan civilization emerged from the food-producing communities of the Indus Valley and surrounding areas. Excavations at the great cities of *Mohenjo-daro and *Harappa have demonstrated that some of these people were literate, were craft specialists, lived in cities with a complex society, and engaged in long-distance trade. The *Indus civilization covered an immense area; over one million square kilometers. The Mature or Urban Harappan, lasted only about 500 years (ca. 2500–2000 B.C.). Although the Indus civilization was different from the archaic states of the Near East there were shared traits. Plants and animals used in the subsistence systems are largely the same. They all made extensive use of brick in their buildings, most of which are rectilinear. Wheel-thrown pottery, usually fired in an oxidizing atmosphere producing red to buff in color, was made. A substantial portion was slipped or decorated with mineral paints applied prior to firing. Walter Fairservis (1961) noted that the Indus civilization reached the eastern limits for the practical cultivation of wheat and barley. These observations suggest that the Indus civilization is the easternmost expression of a very large, heterogeneous pattern of ancient urbanization that stretches from northwestern India, through Pakistan to the Mediterranean Sea. An interaction sphere of considerable proportions that involved overland and maritime trade, commerce, and diplomacy, was probably embodied across the entire area.

The cities of the Indus civilization were abandoned as functioning urban centers around 2000 B.C. The reasons are unclear, but invading Aryan tribes or the natural damming of the Indus River were probably not factors. There is also cultural continuity between the Indus civilization and succeeding Early Iron Age of the Painted Grey Ware in northern India, as documented at Bhagwanpura in Haryana and other sites in the region. There are still gaps in the sequences in Gujarat, Sind, and the West Punjab, which no doubt will be filled in once systematic exploration and excavation are completed.

Central India, in 2000 B.C., was home to diverse peoples, documented best by distinctive pottery styles such as Ahar, Kayatha, Malwa, and Jorwe. They were wheat and millet farmers who herded cattle, sheep, and goats. There is continuity in Central India and Southern India between the earliest farming/herding peoples (Malwa-Jorwe and the Southern Neolithic) and the succeeding Early Iron Age of the Peninsular Indian Megalithic Complex.

There is evidence, though infrequent, for the occurrence of smelted iron in the South Asian Bronze Age at several sites. The widespread use of iron occurs in South Asia at about 1000 B.C., which is close to the beginnings of the Iron Age in a broad band of regions stretching from the Mediterranean Sea to Southeast Asia and China. There is considerable regionalization in the Early Iron Age in India.

The earliest texts in ancient India are the so-called Vedas, consisting of four books, each a collection of hymns. The first is the Rgveda, composed and codified to enable Vedic priests to perform the sacrificial rite necessary for the proper ordering of the life of the Aryan people. The other texts are the Samaveda, the Yajurveda, and the Atharvaveda. The date of the Rgveda is not clear, although the relative chronological sequence for the composition of the texts seems certain: Rgveda/Samaveda, the Yajurveda, and finally the Atharvaveda. The date is based on an analysis of the Sanskrit employed in the texts. The best estimate is that the Rgveda was codified between 1200 and 800 B.C. Most western scholars favor the later date.

There is some geographical information in the Rgveda that has been relatively well studied. Rivers mentioned in the text can be equated with modern streams of the Punjab (Indus, Jhelum, Chenab, Ravi, Sutlej). Some, like the ancient Sarasvati, are now largely dry. The people who composed these hymns were familiar with the Punjab, which they called, "land of the seven rivers." This is the territory from the Indus in the west to the Yamuna in the east and from the mountains of the north to the panjnad in the south. Sindh, the Ganges Valley, and Peninsular India were almost unknown to them.

References are made to gold, silver, lead, copper, and probably bronze, but not iron. However, iron was known by the time of the Atharvaveda which suggests that the Rgveda was codified prior to the widespread use of iron in northern India and Pakistan and that the Atharvaveda was written after 1000 B.C.

The peoples of the Rgveda were cattle pastoralists who engaged in some farming. They were a tribal people whose only specialists were chiefs and priests. There are no archaeological sites that can be linked to the Vedic texts, but if the dating is correct, the Painted Grey Ware sites of the Punjab and Haryana would have been occupied by someone of that time.

Other bodies of ancient writing called the Brahmanas, Aryanakas, and Upanishads form the balance of the literature that is called "Vedic." These and other texts reveal a great deal about the growing complexity of ancient Indian society with the emergence of the Second Urbanization on the Plains of the Ganges by about 500 B.C. The geographical focus of the literature gradually moves east, down the Ganges, and there are increasing references to Sind in Pakistan and Peninsular India. Archaic states are mentioned; Vatsa, Avanti, Kalinga of modern Orissa, Kasi, now Beneres or Varanasi, and Magada in southern Bihar with its famous city of Pataliputra, modern Patna. They tell of kings, states with elaborate bureaucracies, armies, taxes, and law codes. In this context Buddhism and Jainism were born and spread into Southeast Asia, China, and Japan. Widespread writing returned to South Asia in the fourth century B.C., with the edicts of the first great King, Asoka. Two scripts were employed, Kharoshti in the west, a derivative of Aramaic writing, and Brahmi in the east, thought to be related to Aramaic, but a more doubtful association than Kharoshti.

The archaeology of the second urbanization of northern South Asia is documented by excavations at a number of early cities: Taxila, Charsada, Hastinapura, Ahichchhatra, and Sisulpulgarh. The subject has been brought together by Ghosh (1973), Erdosy (1987), and F. R. Allchin (1990).

It is surprising that Sind and Baluchistan are mentioned infrequently in the ancient literature of South Asia, but the Deccan and South India were not neglected, although urbanization and sociocultural complexity were relatively late there. Literacy is associated with the so-called Tamil-Brahmi inscriptions of the early centuries B.C. These and other texts note kings, states, and political conflicts. The era coincides generally with the reopening of sea trade between South Asia and the west, and eventually Rome. There is an implication that this economic stimulation and competition is intimately involved with the growth of sociocultural complexity in South India.

The archaeological study of South India at the time of Christ involves a consideration of the latest Iron Age Megalithic burials and settlements, and the great coastal ports like Arikamedu and Kauveripattinam. Roman coins in Megalithic burials and the presence of terra sigillata and amphorae in many sites make a strong case for commerce. There is also a robust set of documents that guide archaeological research, especially L. Casson's *The Periplus of the Erythraean Sea* (1989).

[*See also* ANURADHAPURA; ASIA, ORIGINS OF FOOD PRODUCTION IN: ORIGINS OF FOOD PRODUCTION IN SOUTH ASIA; NINDOWARI; VIJAYANGARA.]

■ Walter A. Fariservis, Jr., "The Harappan Civilization: New Evidence and More Theory," *Novitates* No. 2055 (1961). Arthur L. Basham, *The Wonder That Was India,* 3rd ed. (1967). Chester Gorman, "Excavations at Spirit Cave, North Thailand," *Asian Perspectives* 13 (1970): 79–107. A. Ghosh, *The City in Early Historical India* (1973). Kenneth A. R. Kennedy, "The Search for Fossil Man in India," in *Physical Anthropology and Its Expanding Horizons: Professor S. S. Sarkar Memorial Volume,* ed. A. Basu (1973): 25–44. Walter A. Fairservis, Jr., *The Roots of Ancient India,* 2nd ed. (1975). Chester Gorman, "A Priori Models and Thai Prehistory: A Reconsideration of the Beginnings of Agriculture in Southeastern Asia," in *Origins of Agriculture,* ed. C. A. Reed (1977): 321–355. Gregory L. Possehl and Kenneth A. R. Kennedy, "Hunter-gatherer / Agriculturalist Exchange in Prehistory: An Indian Example," *Current Anthropology* 20 (1979): 592–593. Jim G. Shaffer, "Bronze Age Iron from Afghanistan: Its Implications for South Asian Protohistory," in *Studies in the Archaeology and Palaeoanthropology of South Asia,* eds. K.A.R. Kennedy and G. L. Possehl (1984): 41–62. J. C. Barry, "A Review of the Chronology of the Siwalik Hominoids," in *Primate Evolution,* eds. J. G. Else and P. C. Lee (1986): 93–105. George Erdosy, "Early Historic Cities in India," *South Asian Studies* 3 (1987): 1–23. R. W. Dennell, H. Rendell, and E. Hailwood, "Early Tool-Making in Asia: Two-million-year Old Artefacts in Pakistan," *Antiquity* 62 (1988): 98–104. L. Casson, *The Periplus Maris Erythraei* (1989). Kenneth A. R. Kennedy, "Fossil Remains of 28,000-year-old Hominids from Sri Lanka," *Current Anthropology* 30 (1989): 394–399. F. R. Allchin, "Patterns of City Formation in Early Historic South Asia," *South Asian Studies* 6 (1990): 163–174. Arthur L. Basham, *The Origins and Development of Classical Hinduism* (1990). Dilip K. Chakrabarti, *The Early Use of Iron in India* (1992).

Gregory L. Possehl

PREHISTORY AND EARLY HISTORY OF SOUTHEAST ASIA

Southeast Asia has no rigid boundaries, and may be defined in more than one way. Politically, it could be seen as the territory lying between the subcontinent of India to the west and China to the north. But Chinese imperial expansion began only in the late first millennium B.C., and there is no reason why southern China should not be included as part of Southeast Asia. This receives support if one employs a climatic criterion, for the valleys of the Xijiang and Yangtze enjoy the same monsoonal conditions as the more traditional core incorporating Thailand, Vietnam, Laos, and Cambodia. There is also the issue of island against mainland Southeast Asia, but again there are problems, for the main islands were formed only with the sharp rise in the mid-Holocene sea level. An ethnic rationale for defining Southeast Asia would founder due to the extraordinary diversity of the peoples and languages encountered: four major language families are present, Sino-Tibetan, Austro-Tai, Austroasiatic and Austronesian.

This essay concentrates on the mainland, and in particular the valleys of the Red, Mekong, and Chao Phraya Rivers and the intervening uplands because we now recognize a pattern of prehistoric and early historic adaptation differing sharply from that of the islands to the south and China to the north. This must be considered within a framework of marked environmental variability, distribution of resources, and means of communication.

The high temperatures and abundant rainfall during the wet season (May to November) encourage a luxuriant vegetation, particularly in the uplands. During the dry season, however, certain lowland areas are subjected to a desiccation, particularly those lying in a rains shadow, such as the

Khorat plateau of northeastern Thailand, and the forest cover is partially deciduous. The conjunction of the rainy season with the spring melt of snow in the headwaters of the Mekong and Red Rivers also leads to flooding in the lower reaches, and a high water table discourages tree growth. On the coast, with its abundant marine food resources, seasonal climatic change has less of an impact.

Southeast Asia is rich in food resources. Rice grows as a wild marsh grass; the lakes, rivers, and coasts provide an abundance of fish; and the tropical estuary is the richest habitat known. There is also a wide range of high-quality stone, a number of major copper, lead, and iron ore deposits, and the world's richest source of tin.

Archaeology in the area began well over a century ago, in the wake of French colonial expansion. Excavations and surface collections dating from the 1870s revealed a sequence that parallels the same time in Europe. Yet to this day, there is no agreed cultural framework for easy reference, and some chronological issues are unresolved.

The Late Pleistocene is little known, but recent research at Lang Rongrien by D. Anderson has shown that from about 37,000 B.P., this rock shelter in peninsular Thailand was intermittently occupied at a time when the sea level was much lower and the climate probably cooler and drier. It continued to attract settlement when the sea rose in the Holocene, and the climate became warmer and moister. Sites belonging to this same Late Pleistocene context are also found in northern Vietnam, where they are known as the Son Vi culture. At the site of Con Moong, a Son Vi stone industry is stratified below material ascribed to the *Hoabinhian.

The Hoabinhian culture was originally defined following the excavation of a number of rock shelters in northern Vietnam. Madeleine Colani recovered a stone industry that included cobbles flaked on one side, a vigorous bone industry, and a subsistence economy based on collecting, fishing, and hunting. Its initial stages have been dated to about 11,000 B.C., and toward the end of its span in the uplands surrounding the Red River, dated to about 5000 B.P., there was a trend to edge grinding and polishing stone axes and making pottery. However, no convincing evidence has been encountered for any form of food production.

Fieldwork since the initial discoveries has identified similar sites, usually in the form of upland rock shelters, in southern China, Thailand, and Cambodia. Clearly there were many local groups of forest foragers adapted to the canopied forest of the uplands. *Spirit Cave in northern Thailand was the first to reveal, through Gorman's screening procedure, the presence of many plant remains that reflect a close relationship between these foragers and their forested habitat, but the presence of many animal bones at nearby Steep Cliff Cave reminds us that hunting wild cattle, deer, and buffalo also occurred.

Some of the Vietnamese sites contain marine shellfish, reflecting the wealth of the coastal habitat. There are many sea-level curves for various parts of Southeast Asia, and these vary with local conditions. All agree that by about 4000 B.C., a shore was established several meters higher than at present. There followed local fluctuations, but these raised beaches harbor a series of prehistoric settlements revealing an adaptation to marine conditions. While it cannot be demonstrated archaeologically, it is highly likely that the drowned landscape formed as the sea rose and contains sites that would demonstrate a long period of marine adaptation with roots in the Pleistocene.

The settlements on the raised beaches are particularly well known in central and northern Vietnam. These are ascribed to regional cultures, the best-documented being named after the sites of Cai Beo, Da But, Quynh Van, and Bau Du. Each has its own characteristics and internal development. Cai Beo, which is located on an island in Ha Long Bay, reveals a stone industry similar to that of the inland Hoabinhian, in association with pottery decorated with basketry impressions. At Da But, which covers less than a quarter of a hectare, twelve burials interred in a seated position and abundant evidence for an estuarine setting have been found. Again, pottery was basketry-impressed, and some of the stone adzes were polished. Quynh Van sites also contain seated, flexed burials and pottery decorated with comb impressions, but no evidence for edge grinding stone tools has been found. Bau Du, dated to 3500–3000 B.C., reveals an estuarine habitat but no pottery. The only site that might correspond to these Vietnamese settlements in the region of the Gulf of Siam is Nong Nor. Dated to 2500 B.C., this site was formerly located on the edge of a shallow marine embayment. The occupants fished, collected shellfish, and made pottery vessels.

The Vietnamese call these sites Neolithic. This might be justified in technological terms, for most yield pottery and polished stone tools. But sites are relatively small, and hitherto no biological evidence has been published that indicates the domestication of plants. This does not, of course, rule out the possibility that plants were cultivated, but the alternative, that these settlements reflect an adaptation by hunter-gatherer-fishers to the rich marine habitat, must also be considered.

We do not know when rice cultivation became established in Southeast Asia, but it was apparently widespread by the later third millennium B.C. Pollen spectra taken from cores in the vicinity of *Khok Phanom Di, central Thailand, show phases of burning and rises in the pollen counts for grasses and weeds associated today with rice cultivation dating from the fifth millennium B.C., but such episodes could equally have been caused by forest fires. Further research on pollen and phytolith remains promises to resolve this problem, but the earliest rice remains to be identified positively as coming from a cultivated plant have been recovered from Khok Phanom Di, dated between 2000 and 1500 B.C. This is a large five-hectare settlement and cemetery that was located on the estuary of a major river. The mortuary record, which spans about twenty generations, reveals a community that tapped the rich local marine resources, cultivated rice, and made a range of superb pottery vessels. Exchange in stone, pottery, and shell items took place, and the rich female potters whose graves have been found suggest that women made ceramic vessels, and attained personal status through feeding them into their exchange network.

The pots at Khok Phanom Di were decorated by burnishing and incising parallel lines infilled with impressions. This style is found, albeit with regional variations, in many sites that represent the earliest known sedentary communities in the interior river valleys of Southeast Asia. In the Red River Valley, these sites belong to the Phung Nguyen culture. Many have been excavated and reveal mastery in the manufacture of polished stone artifacts, including stone adze heads and bracelets. Rice was used as a temper in the manufacture of pottery vessels, and inhumation graves at Lung Hoa reveal much energy expenditure, one being a little more than 16 feet (5 m) deep. Only twelve graves have been excavated, but there are hints that some individuals were differentially wealthy. The few radiocarbon dates available suggest a time span between 2000 and 1500 B.C. for this culture.

The situation on the Khorat plateau of northeastern Thailand is less clear. The two principal excavated sites, *Non Nok Tha and *Ban Chiang, are both cemeteries without a widely accepted chronological framework. This reflects the rarity with which charcoal has been found in undisturbed contexts. Both sites include early interments devoid of copper-based artifacts as grave offerings. Again, some of the pottery vessels from these early contexts were tempered with rice chaff. Domestic cattle, pigs, and dogs were found among the grave goods, for animal sacrifice was a widespread part of mortuary ritual. The date of Non Nok Tha has only recently been established through the AMS (Accelerator Mass Spectroscopy) dating of rice chaff from provenanced pottery, and it is evident that it belongs within the period 1500–1000 B.C. Careful appraisal of the radiocarbon dates from Ban Chiang also suggest occupation in the region from about 2000 B.C.

There are two radiocarbon dates for the initial settlement of Non Pa Wai, central Thailand, where the same incised and impressed pottery has been found in association with a cemetery in which no metal artifacts have been recovered despite the later use of the site to process copper ore. These suggest that the site was occupied by agriculturalists between 2400 and 2000 B.C.

There is a growing body of evidence that the later third millennium B.C. saw an expansion of rice agriculturalists in the lowlands of Southeast Asia that originated ultimately in the basin of the Yangtze River. This phenomenon of rapid population growth and the expansion of human settlement is familiar following the establishment of sedentary communities concerned with food production. It is found in the Yangtze and Huanghe Valleys, Mesoamerica, the Near East, and Europe. In the case of Southeast Asia, it is clear that the people in question participated in widespread exchange networks linking the interior with the coast, following riverine routes.

It was within the context of these villages that copper and tin smelting originated. The best evidence for the date of this development, the Bronze Age in Southeast Asia, comes from two mining and smelting complexes, Phu Lon and Non Pa Wai. The former is located on the southern edge of the Mekong River, and the latter near Lopburi in central Thailand. Initial metalworking at both dates to about 1500 B.C. Non Pa Wai covers five hectares, and is part of one of the largest complexes of copper working in East Asia. The copper ores were crushed, smelted, and cast into ingots, which entered the established exchange network.

Many cemeteries, remote from the ore sources, received such ingots or finishes artifacts. The vast majority of copper-based artifacts before about 500 B.C. comprise bracelets, but there are also socketed axe heads, arrowheads, spears, and ear ornaments. Several sites in northeastern Thailand, such as Ban Na Di, Non Nok Tha, and Ban Chiang, have furnished ceramic crucibles, stone or ceramic molds or furnaces for liquefying the metal before casting. The preferred alloy at such sites was bronze, which included about 10 percent tin. Similar techniques and artifacts are found at the same time in the Dong Dau culture of northern Vietnam and along the coast of southern China.

For the first millennium of the Bronze Age, there appears to have been very little social change over the preceding period. The extensively excavated cemetery of Nong Nor, for example, dated between 1200 and 800 B.C., does not contain any graves markedly richer than some of those from Khok Phanom Di about 9 miles (14 km) to the north. Ban Na Di in northeastern Thailand, and the later mortuary phases at Non Nok Tha, reveal that bronze ornaments and some tools took their place among grave goods, but were found only in a small proportion of graves. There was, however, a significant change from about 500 B.C., a period that has been variously described as the Late Bronze Age, High Bronze Age, and the Iron Age.

This late part of the prehistoric sequence saw the development of iron forging and a great proliferation of bronzes, within a social context involving a higher echelon in society. These have been described as chiefdoms, high chiefdoms, or even states. One of the best known, and certainly the richest in terms of bronzes, is known as the Dian culture after the lake in Yunnan that was a focus for the major sites. Of these, Shizhaishan has furnished the remains of the ruling line, for one grave contains a golden seal bestowed on the ruler by the Han emperor. This polity was clearly organized along class lines, and the bronzes include scenes, cast with masterly skill, of meetings, houses, sacrifices, and warfare in which the aristocrats were portrayed larger than life and gilded. Some such scenes are found in cowrie containers, and remind us that the most direct route from the sea to Yunnan is by the valley of the Red River.

The delta of that river saw the development of the *Dong Son culture from local roots, and its bronze tradition, while not as varied as that of Dian, stands out for its exquisite bronze drums, body plaques, and weapons. In central Thailand, similar intensification is seen at the site of Ban Don Ta Phet, where early exchange with India is evident in the jewelry and local manufacture of high tin bronze bowls.

It was upon the foundations of these rich, ranked societies that the subsequent civilizations were built, but the impact of the expanding Chinese empire and growing trade with India must be considered. Dian and Dong Son rulers fell to the expanding Han Chinese in the later first millennium B.C., and their regions were incorporated as provinces of the Han Empire. To the south, however, beyond the pale of Chinese expansion, local groups reacted to contact with India, and to the increasing availability of iron, by increasing nucleation into statelike polities. Their overlords selectively adopted Indian legal and political practices, took Sanskrit names, and identified themselves with the gods of the Hindu pantheon. From the second century A.D., they began to emerge from the obscurity of prehistory; we can identify polities in Cambodia where the local language was Khmer, and in the Chao Phraya Valley, where Mon was spoken. On the coast of central Vietnam, the language was Cham. The first two are Austroasiatic; the last is Austronesian. Austroasiatic languages are now thought to belong to the Austric Phylum, which includes the Austronesian languages spoken today over much of Island Southeast Asia. The most economical way of interpreting the present distribution of these languages is to relate them to the expansion of agricultural communities from the Yangtze Valley. This would have introduced rice cultivation into Southeast Asia at least by the mid-third millennium B.C. and possibly earlier.

[See also ASIA, ORIGINS OF FOOD PRODUCTION IN: ORIGINS OF FOOD PRODUCTION IN SOUTHEAST ASIA; CHINA: HAN EMPIRE; KHMER CIVILIZATION AND THE EMPIRE OF ANGKOR; SOUTHEAST ASIA; KINGDOMS AND EMPIRES OF.]

■ P. Bellwood, *Southeast Asia Before History,* in N. Tarling, ed., *The Cambridge History of Southeast Asia* (1992), pp. 51–136. K. W. Taylor, "The Early Kingdoms." In N. Tarling, ed., *The Cambridge History of Southeast Asia* (1992), pp. 137–181. C.F.W. Higham and R. Thosarat. *Khok Phanom Di: Prehistoric Adaptation to the World's Richest Habitat* (1994). C.F.W. Higham, *The Bronze Age of Southeast Asia* (1996).

Charles Higham

PREHISTORY AND EARLY HISTORY OF EAST ASIA

East Asia, bounded by the South China Sea and the Himalayas to the south, the Ordos grasslands and the Amur River to the north, the Tienshan Mountains to the west, and the Pacific Ocean to the east, has been the traditional home of Chinese, Manchus, Koreans, and Japanese. In this vast Asian continent humans first appeared more than a million years ago, and in time achieved great civilizations, first in the Yellow Sea region of northern China and later in its surrounding regions.

Paleolithic Period. So far, archaeological investigations indicate that the earliest human existence in East Asia occurred in northern China, and evidence of early habitation has been found in other parts of China as well as Japan and Korea.

First humans: **Homo erectus** *(1 million years–200,000 B.P.).* Chronology for the earliest human occupation of East Asia is not firmly established yet, but current archaeological research reveals that *Homo erectus,* the first toolmaking hominids of East Asia, initially appeared ca. 750,000–800,000 years ago at Lantian in northern China in the middle reaches of the Yellow River. (Even earlier dates, up to 1.5 million years, have been claimed for *Homo erectus* fossils from Xihoudu, also in northern China, but their paleomagnetic readings are viewed with skepticism.)

Tools of the earliest *Homo erectus* of East Asia consisted of pebble and flake implements, including heavy pointed tools such as choppers, chopping tools, and hand axes as well as scrapers, blades, and stone balls. Similar tools have been found at other Early Paleolithic sites in the north, such as Kehe and Sanmensha.

The most well-known Middle Pleistocene site in north China is that of *Zhoukoudian Locality 1, near Beijing, a cave continuously inhabited by the now-famous Peking humans (the "Peking Man") for over 200,000 years, between 460,000 and 220,000 B.P. The Peking humans, considered late *Homo erectus,* used a hammer technique to make choppers and flake tools such as scrapers, engravers, points, awls, and balls. They also made fire and cooked deer meat as well as elephant, rhinoceros, camel, leopard, cave bear, boar, horse, and water buffalo, among other game.

In central and southwestern China, Middle Pleistocene *Homo erectus* fossils have been reported from central Anhwei as well as from Yuanmou, Yunnan Province. The Yuanmou stone tool assemblage included scrapers and points similar to those of the Peking people.

Moving to the east, evidence for *Homo erectus* comes from various Middle Pleistocene sites in Korea, including Kommonmoru (cave) and Yonggok-dong (cave) in the northwest and Chŏngok-ni (open), Sŏkch'ang-ni (open), and Turubong (cave) in the south-central region. Lithic artifacts include heavy-duty tools such as choppers, picks, hand axes, cleavers, and polyhedrals. Excavators of the Chŏngok-ni site have reported Acheulian-like hand axes.

In the Japanese archipelago, Early Paleolithic tools comprising choppers, chopping tools, picks, points, and proto–hand axes have been reported from the Sozudai site in Kyushu and the Hoshino site in central Japan. With wide-ranging dates of 400,000 B.P. to 80,000 B.P., these sites have been correlated to the chopper–chopping tool tradition of Zhoukoudian.

Human fossils representing a transitional stage between *Homo erectus* and early *Homo sapiens* come from Jinniushan in the southern part of Lioning Province (Manchuria).

Early **Homo sapiens** *(200,000–50,000 B.P.).* Human fossils of the Middle Paleolithic from Dali and Dingcun indicate that archaic *Homo sapiens* appeared in northern China around 200,000 years ago. The Dali cranium's interparietal distance of 5 inches (130 mm) and its parietobasal index of 91.3 clearly suggest that Dali humans were similar to other early *Homo sapiens.* According to faunal remains, the early *Homo sapiens* appeared during a time of warm and humid climate.

Tools of early *Homo sapiens* were markedly different from those of *Homo erectus.* Instead of pebbles and quartzite, they used flint as the primary raw material, and made tools much smaller and finer than those of *Homo erectus.* For lithic technology, the early *Homo sapiens* at Dingcun employed bifacial flaking, prepared cores, and striking platforms. They also used parallel-sided flaking, considered a precursor of later blade technology.

Middle Paleolithic human fossils have also been reported from south China at Maba (Mapa) in Guangdong Province. Elsewhere in East Asia, they have been found in the caves of Yonggok-dong, Daehyun-dong, and Dokch'on in northwest Korea. Tools of Yonggok-dong cave included choppers, protobifaces, and scrapers made of quarts cobbles.

Modern humans: **Homo sapiens sapiens** *(50,000–12,000 B.P.).* During the Late Paleolithic, which began around 50,000 years ago, modern humans occupied all parts of East Asia. This was a period when at least on three occasions (50,000 B.P., 37,000 B.P., and 18,000 B.P.), the glaciation of the earth's northern latitudes turned the Yellow Sea between China and Korea into expansive plains and linked the Japanese archipelago to the continent, enabling the migration of humans and big game animals such as elephants, moose, rhinoceroses, and bison to the easternmost regions of East Asia.

Late Paleolithic sites of East Asia abound. Moving from the west to the east, major sites include Sjara-osso-gol (50,000–30,000 B.P.) and Shuidonggou (40,000–32,000 B.P.) in the Ordos regions of China's northwest grasslands; Shiyu (28,000 B.P.) and Xiachuan (23,000–16,000 B.P.) in the Shaanxi loessic plateau; Zhoukoudian Upper Cave (20,000–10,000 B.P.), Xiaonanhai (24,000–10,000 B.P.), and Xiachuan (20,000–10,000 B.P.) in the northern China plains; Jianping and Jinniushan in southwest Manchuria; Antu and Yushu in eastern Manchuria; and Ang-ang-xi and Djalai-nor (12,000–11,000 B.P.) in northern Manchuria.

On the Korean peninsula, Late Paleolithic sites have been found at Kulpori and Dŏksan in the northeast; Mandal-li and Dŏkch'ŏn in the northwest; Sangsi (40,000–30,000 B.P.), Sŏkch'ang-ni Dwelling (21,000 B.P.), Suyanggae, Changnae, Myung'o-ri, and Kumgul in the south-central region. On the Japanese islands, the Late Paleolithic sites (50,000–12,000 B.P.) are found throughout the entire archipelago, at Shukubai-Sankakuyama, Kamishihoro-Shimagi, Shirataki-Hattoridai, and Tachikaru-Shunai in Hokkaido; Nakazanya, Nishinodai, Iwajuku, Kou, and Nogawa; and Hykkadai and Fukui Rockshelter in Kyushu.

In lithic technology, many of the earlier heavy tools such as choppers, chopping tools, and picks continued to be used. Artifacts also varied from region to region, but on the whole, Late Paleolithic stone implements tended to become more complex and diversified. Tools aimed at a variety of special functions became predominant, including scrapers, blades, engravers, points, awls, and burins. Bone and antler tools as well as composite tools made of bone/antler shaft and small blades also came into use.

In lithic technology, East Asia's Late Paleolithic inhabitants employed prepared cores and a striking platform to obtain flake tools, as in the case of their west European counterparts. The most prominent feature, however, was the increasing emphasis on microlithic tools. First appearing at Xiachuan (23,000–16,000 B.P.) in the northern China plains, microliths spread westward as well as eastward to Manchuria, eastern Siberia, Korea, and Japan, where an elaborate microblade industry based on microcores, such as the Yubetsu technique, developed.

Late Paleolithic humans in East Asia were primarily mobile hunters, depending on a variety of game animals such as deer, moose, bison, elephants, and horses as well as on edible plants and seeds. For religious and ceremonial purposes, they made rock engravings and human figurines. They also adorned themselves with ornaments made of bones, animal teeth, and perforated pebbles.

Emerging Sedentism and Early Villages (9000–3000 B.P.). As the last major ice age came to an end around 10,000 years ago, the climate of East Asia became increasingly mild, warm, and moist, making green vegetation grow all across the landscape. Modern humans began to settle around rivers and lakes and along coastlines to maximize the natural resources provided by them.

China. Between 7000 B.C. and 5000 B.C., the early settlements were transformed into permanent farming villages and subsequently into several Neolithic culture complexes. Cishan-Peiligang, Laoguantai-Baijia, and Lijia cultures in northern China; Xing-long-wa and Xin-le cultures in the Liao River basin of southwestern Manchuria; Beixin culture in the Shandong region; *Hemudu, Chengbeixi, and Zhoashi cultures in the Yangtze River basin; Zengpiyan culture in southern China.

The early Neolithic cultures of northern China engaged in dryland cultivation of foxtail millet (*Setaria italica*) and broomcorn millet (*Panicum miliaceum*). They also domesticated pigs, dogs, chickens, and possibly sheep. Their tools included stone mortars and pestles as well as stone sickles. They made and used simple, low-fired pottery vessels (all handmade) mostly for cooking, eating, drinking, and storing purposes, often decorated with linear incised, rocker-stamped, or cord-marked designs. In the Zengpiyan Neolithic culture of southern China, radiocarbon-dated from 7160+/−930 B.P. to 10370+/−870 B.P., cord-marked pottery was predominant, linking southern Chinese Neolithic culture more closely with the Southeast Asian tradition.

Almost at the same time, in the middle and lower reaches of the Yangtze River in central China, rice cultivation commenced, as evidenced by rice remains from the Pentushan site in Hunan and Hemudu site in Zhejiang, dated 7000 B.C. and 5000 B.C., respectively. Rice remains at Hemudu included both *Oryza sativa-hsien*, or *indica*, and *Oryza sativa-keng*, or *japonica*, and were found along with many agricultural implements, such as wooden spades related to paddy-field rice cultivation. By 4000 B.C. rice began to appear in the Yangshao culture zone in northern China as well.

Between 5000 B.C. and 3000 B.C., the early Neolithic cultures reached a new height in different regions of China, with regional pottery traditions: *Yangshao culture in the central plains; Dawenko culture in the Shandong region; Majiayao culture in the upper reaches of the Yellow River; Hongshan culture in the upper Liao River drainage of southwestern Manchuria; and Qinglian'gang and Majiabang cultures in the lower Yangtze River basin.

By 4000 B.C., lifeways in Neolithic China were becoming increasingly complex, sophisticated, and stratified. Along with highly diversified stone, wood, bamboo, and bone tools as well as refined ceramic vessels, the Neolithic cultures valued aesthetic and ceremonial dimensions, as reflected in artistic designs on pottery vessels, jade and ivory ornaments, and anthropoid or zoomorphic figurines. Villages, often built on river terraces, consisted of up to 100 round, square, or rectangular semisubterranean houses, and were planned around a central plaza. Hongshan monumental architecture included impressive ritual installations and mounded tombs. These suggest that by 3500 B.C., social stratification had emerged.

Korea and Japan. While the advent of *agriculture, sedentism, and pottery all coincided in Neolithic China, this did not happen elsewhere in East Asia. In Korea and Japan, the sedentism and pottery long preceded agriculture, by about 5,000 years in the former and by nearly 10,000 years in the latter.

In Japan, pottery appeared ca. 10,000 B.C. Initially of an appliqué ware tradition, it was soon replaced by a new pottery characterized by complex cord-marked, or *jomon*, surface designs, suggesting a link with Southeast Asia. As Jomon pottery evolved, it assumed new forms in shape and decorative design.

Korea's earliest pottery, dated to ca. 6,000 B.C., was also of the appliqué ware tradition (*yungki-mun*). This was soon replaced by pottery distinguished by surface impressions similar to comb-tooth marks, or *chulmun*. By 5,000 B.C., the Chulmun pottery, all handmade, was a distinct tradition with regional variations.

Both in Japan and in Korea, the early sedentary groups chose resource-rich coastal areas as well as sites along rivers. They lived in semisubterranean pit-houses and engaged in hunting, fishing, and gathering nuts, berries, and shellfish. Their tools were made of stone, bone, and antler. Stone tools included ground adzes, picks, polished stone arrowheads, saddle guerns, net sinkers, and compound fish hooks. Bone and antler implements included digging sticks, fish hooks, barbed harpoons, spearheads, awls, and needles. The foraging economy of Korea's Chulmun society persisted until ca. 1500 B.C., while Japan's *Jomon tradition endured as late as ca. 200 B.C.

Emerging Complex Society. With sedentary lifeways came greater concentrations of human population and increasing social complexity; over time, settlements evolved from chiefdoms to early states.

China. By 3000 B.C., long cultural interaction among the regionally developing Neolithic traditions had led China's sociocultural evolution to a new height, namely the era of complex chiefdoms of the *Longshan Period, ca. 3000 B.C.–2000 B.C.

Appearing almost simultaneously in various parts of the Yellow River basin, the Longshan culture had a number of common characteristics: large walled towns occupying an area of 2 to 25 acres (1 to 10 ha) (Wangchenggang, Haojiatai, Pingliangtai, Hougang, Bianxianwang); fortifications (the town wall plus moats, guardhouses, and gates); frequent and violent warfare; differentiated housing within walled towns; differentiated burials; use of rammed or stamped earth foundations for large structures; a new pottery tradition employing a wheel technique and emphasizing black painting, tripod cooking pots, high-pedestaled *dou* vessels, and *zeng* steamers; ritual objects such as *zong* jade tubes and *bi* jade rings; scapulamancy; rice cultivation; and incipient bronze and copper metallurgy (toward the end of the Longshan Period). In every respect, these cultural elements suggest that during the third millennium B.C., China's prehistory had reached the threshold of civilization. And indeed, out of various Longshan settlement centers emerged China's first states.

China's earliest state-level society has been uncovered among the ruins of Erlitou, in the central plains of northern China. First discovered in 1957, Erlitou (with radiocarbon dates of ca. 1800–2100 B.C.) has revealed remains of palatial buildings, royal tombs, bronze foundry, paved roads, storage pits, human sacrificial burials, animal shoulder blades used for divination, as well as valued jade ritual objects, including *zong* tubes, long knives, and axes, among others. Similar impressive cultural remains, of slightly later date, have been found at *Zhengzhou, also in Hunan. Of particular significance was the highly advanced bronze technology present at these sites, used to produce all sorts of ritual bronze vessels and bronze tools.

Erlitous and Zhengzhou are regarded by some as the early and middle capital of Shang, China's first state-level society. But writing was still absent, and China had to wait until Yin Shang, the next cultural stage, to see the beginnings of its early historical period.

Korea and Japan. In Korea, the incipient agriculture of the late Chulmun Period continued to expand, resulting in the growth of farming communities and population throughout the peninsula. These in turn led to increasing societal complexity centering around numerous polities forming in major river valleys during the first millennium B.C. (Korea's Bronze and early Iron Age). Enhancing this process was the ever-increasing political and cultural influence of Han China, beginning in the first century B.C. During the first three centuries of the Christian era, the prehistoric polities became the basis for Korea's early states, Koguryo in the north, Paekche in the south-central region, and Shilla in the southeast region.

In Japan, beginning around 300 B.C., the 8,000-year-old Jomon hunting-fishing-gathering lifeways rapidly came to an end with the introduction of wet-rice agriculture from the continent. As in Korea, with the advent of agriculture, population increased, and with it societal complexity, during the Yayoi period (ca. 300 B.C.–A.D. 300). And during the Kofun period (A.D. 300–700), under increasing cultural influence from Korea, social stratification was intensified, as evidenced in the appearance of differentiated burials throughout Japan. Various polities emerging in this period became the basis for Japan's first state.

[See also ASIA: PREHISTORY AND EARLY HISTORY OF SOUTH ASIA, PREHISTORY AND EARLY HISTORY OF SOUTHEAST ASIA; ASIA: ORIGINS OF FOOD PRODUCTION IN; CHINA: STONE AGE CULTURES OF CHINA, EARLY CIVILIZATIONS OF CHINA, SHANG CIVILIZATION; JAPAN AND KOREA: INTRODUCTION, EARLY STATES OF JAPAN AND KOREA.]

■ C. Melvin Aikens and Takayasu Higuchi, *Prehistory of Japan* (1982). David N. Keightley, ed., *The Origin of Chinese Civilization* (1983). K.-C. Chang, *The Archaeology of Ancient China* (1986). C. Melvin Aikens and Song N. Rhee, eds., *Pacific Northeast Asia in Prehistory* (1992). Gina Barnes, *China, Korea, and Japan: The Rise of Civilization in East Asia* (1993). Sarah M. Nelson, *The Archaeology of Korea* (1993).

Song Nai Rhee

HISTORICAL ARCHAEOLOGY OF ASIA

In the New World the phrase "historical archaeology" is traditionally restricted to the study of the Euroamerican period. Historic archaeology has a much wider application throughout Asia, where it refers to research on indigenous literate civilizations as well as to the study of the post-fifteenth-century European presence. Thus, in China, history begins with the Shang civilization of the second millennium B.C., while in South Asia, the historic period commences with the earliest sacred texts of the sixth century B.C. (the untranslated script of the Indus civilization is referred to as belonging to the "protohistoric" period). Asian historical archaeology thus spans a vast area and time span, and includes practitioners working from a range of theoretical and methodological perspectives—including art history, epigraphy, numismatics, and anthropology. Much work has focused on documenting individual monuments and attempting to support or verify historical accounts of particular sites or polities. Increasingly, however, Asian historical archaeologists are seeking to examine the material evidence of people and activities that seldom appear in written accounts, through the study of domestic artifacts and a range of large and small archaeological site types. In this brief essay I attempt to outline recent research and major discoveries from China, South Asia, and Southeast Asia.

China. Found first engraved on metal, stone, and bone, and later on bamboo and paper, Chinese writings can be traced back to the Shang dynasty (ca. 1766–1122 B.C.). Excavations have been conducted at the late Shang capital of *Anyang and at other Shang cities. The tomb of Fu Hao, a member of the Shang royal family, was discovered in 1976, and contained more than two hundred ceremonial bronze vessels and over seven hundred pieces of jade.

The 1974 discovery of the grave of the first emperor of China, *Shihuangdi (246–210 B.C.) is one of the most exciting archaeological discoveries of recent decades. This royal grave as a vast underground city. A large mount 250 feet (76 m) high and 1,591 by 1,689 feet (485 by 515 m) at its base, covered the royal tomb. Beyond the walled precincts of the mound area are four enormous pits containing over 6,000 life-sized terra-cotta figurines and more than 1,400 wooden chariots and ceramic cavalry figures, with 9,000-plus weapons, including swords, bows, spears, and knives. These detailed and finely sculpted figures were arranged in military formations. Their highly individualized faces, uniforms, and hairstyles provide evidence of the ethnic and social diversity of the empire.

Several royal tombs from the Han dynasty (ca. 200 B.C.–A.D. 200), though smaller in scale, provide additional evidence for the elaborate treatment of the elite dead, and contain an array of ceramic, jade, lacquer, and bronze objects. Han imperial cities, such as *Chang'an (Xi'an, Western Han) and Luoyang (Eastern Han) have also been the focus of archaeological investigation.

Along with the Great Pyramids of Giza, the *Great Wall of China is one of the most instantly recognizable archaeological sites in the world. This dramatic feature stands 29.5 feet (9 m) high in parts and the "Great Wall" is actually comprised of a number of massive walls built over two millennia (third century B.C. to seventeenth century A.D.) as part of defenses against invasions by nomadic populations from the north.

South Asia. In the island nation of Sri Lanka work has focused on the major political centers of *Anuradhapura (first century B.C. to tenth century A.D.) and Pollonnaruwa (sixth to thirteenth century A.D.). The many Buddhist monasteries, stupas, and images found at these sites have been a particular emphasis of study. Important recent archaeological work in Sri Lanka has sought to examine the island's participation in international maritime commerce. Ceramic and other artifacts recovered in excavations at the ports of Mantai and Vanakalai and at other sites, have provided evidence for contacts with northern India from roughly 600 B.C., with the Hellenistic and Roman world in the early centuries A.D., and with China and Southeast Asia from the fifth century A.D.

Vast numbers of historic sites and monuments have been documented throughout India; spanning from the beginnings of the historic period up to the Mughal Empire (sixteenth to eighteenth centuries). The earliest historic remains in South Asia are located in the Ganges River valley and associated with the ceramic ware known as Northern Black Polished Ware. Archaeological research has focused on urban sites and inscriptions of the Mauryan empire (ca. 324–184 B.C., Pataliputra, Kausambi, and Sarnath), as well as sites associated with the life of the Buddha.

The site of Arikamedu in Tamil Nadu is a harbor town of the first and second centuries A.D.; excavations in the 1940s and 1980s have revealed evidence of local occupation and industrial activities as well as significant quantities of Mediterranean artifacts, including Roman amphoras, terra sigillata, and coins.

Excavation and documentation projects studying late Indian states and empires have focused largely on major political centers, including Champaner, Daulatabad, Fatehpur Sikri, Agra, and *Vijayanagara. At Vijayanagara in southern India (fourteenth to sixteenth century A.D.), recent archaeological work has focused on the monumental remains of the city's administrative center, as well as an elite residential zone, inscriptions, and utilitarian ceramics from across the city. Systematic archaeological survey in the city's suburbs has sought to document nonelite remains and activities, including rural settlements, craft production locales, and evidence for massive agricultural systems.

An important early historic site in Pakistan is Taxila, located in northern Pakistan along a major route between Central and South Asia. The site contains evidence for occupation by a sequence of local and foreign occupants, and was reportedly occupied by Alexander the Great in 326 B.C.

Southeast Asia. Historic developments in Southeast Asia were influenced by interaction with both China and India, and historic temples and other features have been documented throughout mainland and island southeast Asia. The *Khmer civilization, dating from around A.D. 600 to 1450 produced some of the greatest historical architecture of the region in the lush tropical lowlands of modern Cambodia. Numerous Khmer sites are known, and the development of Khmer architecture can be traced at the temples of Bakong, Phnom Bekhent, Prè-Rup, Bantéay Srei, Ta Kèo and others. The culmination of this development is seen in the famous temple complex of Angkor Wat (built ca. 1130–1150), a massive architectural complex in the ancient Khmer capital. The structures of Angkor Wat are surrounded by a large moat enclosing an area of approximately 0.8 square mile (2 sq km). The elevated temple is contained within three walled cruciform enclosures or galleries, each ornately sculpted. The outermost enclosure is entered via a causeway that leads to three large towered gateways (gopura). A raised walkway lined by structures and large basins leads to the second cruciform gallery, which rims a platform 372 by 235 yards (340 × 215 m) in dimension. Scenes from Hindu epics are sculpted along the gallery interior. Only priests and kings could pass through the second inner gallery, and only the king and high priest could pass through the third gallery, inside which was the 71-yard- (65 m) high towered sanctuary of the god and its four surrounding towers. In recent decades Angkor and many other major archaeological sites of Cambodia have been threatened by war and the tropical environment. Angkor Wat has been the focus of a large scale international conservation project since the late 1980s.

Numerous other important historic sites are found throughout Southeast Asia. Major sites include the late Khmer capital of Angkor Thom, the Buddhist temple at Borobudor (eighth–ninth century A.D.) and the Hindu temple of Prambanam (tenth century A.D.) in central Java, sites of the Sukhothai (1287–1353) and Ayuthia (1347–1767) periods in Thailand, and the Buddhist center of Pagan (ca. 1000–1287) in Burma (Mayanmar).

[See also CHINA, *articles on* SHANG EMPIRE, HAN CIVILIZATION; INDUS CIVILIZATION; SOUTHEAST ASIA, KINGDOMS AND EMPIRES OF.]

■ R. N. Mehta, *Medieval Archaeology* (1979). Caroline Blunden and M. Elvin, *Cultural Atlas of China* (1983). Institute of Archaeology, *Recent Archaeological Discoveries in the People's Republic of China* (1984). Henri Stierlin, *The Cultural History of Angkor* (1984). S. Bandaranayake et al., eds., *Sri Lanka and the Silk Road of the Sea* (1990). A. Waldron, *The Great Wall of China: From History to Myth* (1990).

Carla M. Sinopoli

ASIA, Origins of Food Production in

Overview
Origins of Food Production in South Asia
Origins of Food Production in Southeast Asia
Origins of Food Production in China

OVERVIEW

Determining the origins of food production in Asia is an enormous and complex problem. Part of the complexity arises from the huge geographic scale involved, the resulting variety of climates, physiographic zones, environments, and microenvironments. The biological and cultural diversity promoted by this range of environmental factors is then further compounded by an extremely long-time depth for human habitation in various parts of Asia. In an effort to make the syntheses of research results on the origins of food production more comprehensible, this topic has been divided into separate articles in this volume: South Asia, Southeast Asia, and China. What follows is a very brief synopsis of those larger articles.

In South Asia, a wide variety of plant and animal domesticates came into use in different ways in different areas at different times and with different rates of acceptance. Some of the earliest evidence of domestication in South Asia occurs at Mehrgarh in western Pakistan in deposits dating to 7000 B.C. Domesticates found there include barley, wheat, sheep, goat, and cattle.

The histories of domestication in China and Southeast Asia are intimately linked. On the basis of research in both areas to date, it seems clear that rice cultivation, accompanied by domestication of pigs and cattle, began in the central lakes region of the Yangzi River valley around 6500 B.C. Over the next 5,000 years rice cultivation spread south down the major rivers of southern China and into Southeast Asia. While there may have been an independent development of rice cultivation in the area between the Red and Chao Phraya rivers on the Indochina Peninsula, the evidence is not conclusive and postdates developments in the Yangzi Valley by almost 4,000 years.

[See also ASIA, articles on PREHISTORY AND EARLY HISTORY OF SOUTH ASIA, PREHISTORY AND EARLY HISTORY OF SOUTHEAST ASIA.]

George Michaels

ORIGINS OF FOOD PRODUCTION IN SOUTH ASIA

Understanding of the origins of food production in South Asia changed dramatically in the 1970s and 1980s as a result of new archaeological research at major sites in India and Pakistan. Prior to that time, scholars had assumed that domestic resources arrived in South Asia from the Middle East or East Asia in the late fourth or early third millennia B.C. Recent excavations at *Mehrgarh in western Pakistan have, however, provided evidence for domestic plants and animals and settled village life from as early as the seventh millennium B.C. Domesticates appear somewhat later in other regions of South Asia, and in any discussion of food production it is important to recognize the broad ecological and historic diversity of the region. A wide range of domesticates became important in distinct regions at widely different times, and were incorporated into local subsistence patterns in varied ways. South Asia is characterized by extreme variations in rainfall, temperature, and seasonality, which have significant impact on cropping patterns and resources. Variations in the history and intensity of archaeological research across South Asia also play an important role in current knowledge of agricultural origins. This discussion will be organized by broad geographic region, following a brief discussion of the most important domesticates.

Resources. Domesticated plant and animal resources in South Asia include a range of species of indigenous and exotic origin. Major cereal species include rice, wheat, and millets. Rice was probably locally domesticated, and the local domestication of wheat and barley is argued by some scholars, though others argue for a west Asian origin of these crops. Millets including *Setaria italica* and *Eleusine coracana* may have originated in Southeast Asia and Africa, respectively. Other important domestic food plants include a wide variety of pulses, fruits and vegetables, cotton, and spices important in internal trade throughout late prehistory and historic periods. Important domesticated animal species include humped cattle (*Bos indicus*), water buffalo (*Bubalus bubalis*), sheep, goat, pig, fowl, dog, cat, and horse, with cattle the numerically most important species in most regions and periods.

Pakistan. Excavations at the site of *Mehrgarh were initiated in 1974 by the French Archaeological Mission, directed by Jean-Francoise Jarrige, in cooperation with the Pakistan Department of Archaeology. Located in the Kacchi Plain of northwest Pakistan, the site consists of a series of mounds extending along the Bolan River in a region transitional between the eastern Iranian plateau and the Indus River valley. Mehrgarh has been divided into seven stratigraphic periods, of which the earliest three are relevant here. Remains from the Aceramic Period I (seventh to early sixth millennium B.C.) include abundant wild plant and animal resources, as well as domestic barley, wheat, sheep, goat, and cattle. Also found are rectilinear mud-brick structures, subfloor burials, and flaked stone tools. Domestic plants and animals increase in importance in period II (mid-sixth to early fifth millennia B.C.), with South Asian zebu cattle and water buffalo especially common. Handmade ceramics appear near the end of this period, which is characterized by compartmentalized mud-brick buildings interpreted as storage features. Mehrgarh reached its maximal extent of approximately 185 acres (75 ha) during period III (late fifth millennium B.C.). There is extensive evidence for specialized craft production in period III; craft goods include elaborately painted wheelmade ceramics, ceramic figurines, steatite beads, and smelted copper implements.

The early phases of occupation at Mehrgarh are unique in South Asia; no comparable seventh or sixth millennia sites are currently known. However, the presence of a large suite of domesticates comparable in date to the Near Eastern Neolithic suggests that traditional views of late agricultural expansion into South Asia can no longer be accepted. Instead, it is most appropriate to view Mehrgarh in particular, and northwest Pakistan in general, as both a locus of domestication and participant in a vast interregional interaction network.

By the fifth millennium B.C., several other agricultural communities are known in Pakistan. Kili Ghul Muhammed is a small single mound 1.2 acres (0.5 ha) site located near the Quetta valley, occupied from the mid-fifth through the mid-fourth millennia B.C. Remains from the site include domestic sheep and cattle, wattle and daub and later, mud-brick architecture, and late in the occupation, painted wheelmade ceramics. By the mid-fourth millennium B.C. (the Early Indus Period), agricultural towns and villages were widespread throughout the greater Indus region, which was soon to witness the emergence of South Asia's earliest state level society—the *Indus or Harappan Civilization (ca. 2600–1900 B.C.).

Kashmir. A number of early agricultural settlements are known from the Valley of Srinigar in the Himalayan mountains. Chronologically, these are much later than Mehrgarh and date to the third millennium B.C. The most thoroughly excavated site of the Kashmiri Neolithic is Burzahom (ca. 2500–1500 B.C.), a settlement and cemetery site, with two phases of Neolithic occupation (periods IA and IB). The earliest remains from the site (period IA) include semisubterranean pit dwellings, handmade ceramics, and an array of groundstone and bone and antler tools. Faunal remains include domestic sheep and many wild species. No plant remains were recovered from the site, but numerous grinding stones attest to their importance. In period IB, pit dwellings were replaced by mud-brick and wooden rectilinear structures, and the faunal assemblage includes domestic sheep, dog, cattle, and buffalo, as well as wild species.

Gufkral, a second important Kashmiri site, contains evidence for three Neolithic phases of occupation (periods IA–IC). In period IA (ca. 2800–2500 B.C.), pit houses and ground stone and bone tools resemble those from Burzahom IB. Domestic sheep and goat, as well as wild cattle, red deer, and ibex are found, along with domestic wheat and barley. Handmade ceramics appear in period IB (ca. 2500–2000 B.C.), as do domestic cattle and fowl. In period IC, (ca. 2000–

1500 B.C.), domestic fauna substantially outnumber hunted resources.

Northern India. Recent work in the Belan, Son, and Ganges valleys of northern India has led to the identification of an agricultural tradition dating from around 4000 to 1200 B.C. Important excavated sites include Chopani-Mando, Koldihwa, and Mahagara in the Belan Valley, and Mahadaha in the Ganges. These sites show continuous developments from pre-agricultural Mesolithic periods, and are characterized by ground stone technology and impressed and burnished ceramic wares. The sites of Koldihwa and Mahagara, located south of modern Allahabad, contain stratified early agricultural deposits from the second millennium B.C. Remains include circular huts defined by posthole patterns, ground stone axes, chipped stone blades, bone tools, and handmade pottery. The coarsely made cord-impressed pottery contains impressions of domestic rice husks. A cattle pen was identified at Koldihwa, with post holes and cattle hoof impressions. Faunal materials include domestic sheep, goat, and cattle, as well as wild cattle, pig, and deer. Although there are two earlier radiocarbon dates from Koldihwa these are controversial and most dates from the two sites belong to the mid-second millennium B.C. (ca. 1770–1375 B.C.).

The most thoroughly excavated site in the eastern Ganges valley is Chirand, a small mound located near the confluence of the Ghaggra and Ganges Rivers. The early village site contains roughly 10 feet (3 m) of stratified remains from the early second millennium B.C. The settlement consisted of small round houses, identified by pits and postholes. Artifacts include numerous bone and antler tools, ground stone axes and grinding stones, stone blades and microliths, and gray and red handmade ceramics. Plant remains include domestic rice, as well as wheat, barley, and lentils. Fish bones predominate in the faunal remains.

The above discussion has focused on the emergence of agricultural villages whose occupants exploited domestic plant and animal resources, along with wild resources. Still earlier evidence for the exploitation of domestic animals comes from sites in Rajasthan and the Narmada River valley. The site of Bagor in Rajasthan contains evidence for domestic fauna from its earliest phase, which has been dated from around 5000 to 3000 B.C. In this level, microlithic tools occur in association with small huts and large numbers of faunal remains including domesticated sheep, goat, and cattle, as well as several wild species. Similar remains are found in the subsequent period (ca. 2800–600 B.C.), with the addition of ceramics and copper objects. No plant remains are known from this site, and it is not clear whether this is because the inhabitants of Bagor, or of sites such as Adamgarh in the Narmada Valley, did not produce domestic crops or because the crops have yet to be identified. Certainly, the interaction of nomadic or seminomadic pastoralists with settled agricultural communities is well known from later periods of South Asian history, including perhaps the Harappan period; more evidence is required to determine the origins of such a pattern.

Southern India. Communities dependent on domestic resources appear in South India in the late third millennium. The characteristic site type of the "Southern Neolithic" (ca. 2800–1500 B.C.) is the ash mound site, found in the modern state of Karnataka. These sites consist of low mounds of consolidated ash composed of burnt cattle dung. They have been interpreted as the remains of cattle pens, which were burned and rebuilt over several phases. Bones

from domestic cattle are common at excavated sites such as Utnur and Kodekal, as are grinding stones and axes, chipped stone blades, and handmade ceramics. The Neolithic settlement site of Piklihal in Raichur District of northern Karnataka has two Neolithic phases dating from the late third to the early second millennium. Domestic cattle remains are common at this site, and remains of sheep, goat, tortoises, and shellfish are also found. Tekkalakota, dating to the first half of the second millennium, contains the remains of circular hut foundations and domestic cattle. Seven burials were recovered; artifacts include hand and wheelmade ceramics, beads, copper implements, and gold ear ornaments. South Indian Neolithic rock paintings on the faces of stone outcrops and in rock shelters near Tekkalakota and Piklihal depict humans, bulls, dogs, and wild fauna.

The archaeological evidence for the origins of food production in South Asia presents a complex mosaic, with transitions to a food-producing economy occurring in different regions at widely different times. Plant and animal resources and their relative importance to subsistence also show considerable variation. There therefore can be no single explanation for this process that will be applicable to all of South Asia. Factors that must be considered in each region include population densities (at present poorly understood for much of South Asia), climatic conditions, the availability and distribution of resources, and interregional interaction and diffusion of resources, technology, and people.

[*See also* ASIA: PREHISTORY AND EARLY HISTORY OF SOUTH ASIA; DOMESTICATION OF PLANTS.]

■ F. R. Allchin, *Neolithic Cattle Keepers of the Deccan* (1963). G. R. Sharma, *Beginnings of Agriculture: From Hunting and Food Gathering to Domestication of Plants and Animals* (1980). J.-F. Jarrige, "Chronology of the Earlier Periods of the Greater Indus as Seen from Mehrgarh, Pakistan," in *South Asian Archaeology, 1981* ed. Bridget Allchin (1984), pp. 21–28. B. and F. R. Allchin, *The Rise of Civilization in India and Pakistan* (1988). B. P. Sahu, *From Hunters to Breeders* (1988). G. L. Possehl and P. C. Rissman: "The Chronology of Prehistoric India: From Earliest Times to the Iron Age," in *Chronologies in Old World Archaeology*, ed. R. W. Ehrich (1992), vol. 1, pp. 465–490, vol. 2, pp. 447–474.

Carla M. Sinopoli

ORIGINS OF FOOD PRODUCTION IN SOUTHEAST ASIA

No sensible discussion of the origins of food production in Southeast Asia could take place without reference to the archaeological sequence in the Yangtze (Yangzi) valley. Indeed, there are grounds for including China south of this river within greater Southeast Asia for it has a monsoon climate, is home to wild rice, and only two millennia have elapsed since it was incorporated by force of arms within the borders of modern China. Southeast Asia including southern China accounts for over 700 million people, representing a sixth of humanity. This concentration of population rests on a diet dominated by rice and fish.

Effects of Climate. Climatic variations in this region increase with latitude. While there was relatively slight change in the tropical parts of Southeast Asia with the end of the *Pleistocene, there was a continuous record of quite serious fluctuations in the Yangtze valley. The mean temperature there increased by seven degrees Celsius between 11,150 and 10,400 B.C. and the sea level rose from -272 to -174 feet (-83 to -53 m). This warming phase was followed by the

Younger Dryas, involving increased cold between 9000 and 8000 B.C., but conditions thereafter reverted to another warm phase until 6500 B.C., and then another period of relative cold.

During the warm phases, there would also have been increased rainfall, and wild rice could have flourished in the extensive marshes and lake margins of the middle Yangtze valley. It is also highly likely that analogous low-lying marshy conditions would have been present on the extensive offshore habitat now drowned by the sea. It was during the period between 8000 and 6500 B.C. that the south Chinese archaeological sequence saw the establishment of communities, which show signs of permanent, sedentary settlement. Xianrendong, for example, was a riverine site settled during the warm phase that followed the Younger Dryas. The inhabitants consumed fish, shellfish, and crabs, and made cord-marked pottery. Large, perforated stones have been interpreted as weights for digging sticks. Baozitou was sited on a river terrace, and its material culture includes pottery, ground stone adzes, and pestles. Chang has suggested that it was the base for a group of sedentary, broad-spectrum foragers. Zengpiyan, which belongs to the same period, has yielded a cemetery containing at least eighteen burials. It seems likely that some communities chose a sedentary aquatic lifestyle which took advantage of a warming trend in the climate.

Archaeological Evidence. This amelioration would have encouraged wild rice to grow in the middle reaches of the Yangtze, a region still known for its extensive lakes. It was indeed here that we encounter the earliest evidence for the consumption of rice. *Pengtoushan represents a new and highly significant settlement form which could have developed from the preceding small riverine sites. It is a 13-foot (4-m) high mound which covers about one hectare. It is located on the Liyang plain close to the northern shore of Lake Dongting, and was occupied between about 6500 and 5800 B.C. Excavations have revealed the foundations of houses covering 333 square feet (30 sq m), and a cemetery in which individuals were interred with grave goods including pottery vessels tempered with rice chaff. Other artifacts include flaked stone implements, but polished axes or adzes were rare. None of the tools thought to reflect rice cultivation and processing have been found, but there are some small stone implements that could have been used for rice husking.

No evidence has yet been published which shows that the rice was cultivated rather than collected from wild stands. This is a difficult exercise, because the chaff commonly used as a tempering agent in pottery does not easily permit separation between wild and cultivated varieties. However, Pengtoushan was clearly a village community, permanently occupied, which included rice in the diet. It stands at the threshold of a major population expansion in the Yangtze valley represented by many similar villages that grew rapidly in size, number, and cultural complexity. Moreover, this initial trend occurred during the cold phase that commenced about 6500 B.C. It might not be coincidental that millet cultivation in the Huanghe valley, 311 miles (500 km) to the north, began at this same juncture.

In the sequel, sites of the Daxi (4500–3000 B.C.) and Qujialing cultures (3300–2600 B.C.) proliferated in the middle Yangtze, and the material culture incorporated stone spades and reaping knives of shell and stone. Villages were occupied over many centuries, and the presence of exotic jade, ivory, and shell ornaments reveals participation in extensive exchange networks. Again, a long and rich cultural sequence is evident in the lower reaches of the Yangtze. The sequence here began later than in the central lake area, probably because initial trends occurred on the inundated continental shelf. By the initial settlement of *Hemudu (5000 B.C.), rice was already a key component of the diet. The remains of rhinoceros and alligator and pollen from plants which do not now extend further north than Taiwan and Guangdong attest to favorably mild and swampy conditions. The inhabitants of Hemudu had easy access to lake fishing and fowling as well as raising domestic pigs and water buffalo. Artifacts include many bone spades, and the abundant remains of cultivated rice leave no doubt that it played a central role in the diet of the inhabitants of a site occupied for about one thousand years.

Once again, we find evidence for an expansion of settlement both in terms of the area involved, and the number of villages. There was some expansion to the south, but as one proceeds down the coast and the river valleys that flow north into the Yangtze, village sites become fewer and later. Shixia, for example, dates to the third millennium B.C. Chang has recognized a number of broad affinities in terms of pottery forms and personal ornaments within these agricultural villages, and links them into a common interaction sphere.

Sites that clearly belong to this general grouping diminish in number by the time one enters the Xijiang valley, and in the heartland of Southeast Asia we encounter a different archaeological sequence. The forested uplands were home to small groups of broad-spectrum foragers known as *Hoabinhian after the Vietnamese province in which they were first investigated. The rich coastal environment of northern and central Vietnam was home to a series of distinct groups, which have in common a preference for estuarine conditions, fishing and shellfish collecting, and the manufacture of pottery and polished stone adzes. The dead were often interred in an upright, crouched position. Although Vietnamese archaeologists call these groups Neolithic, no biological evidence for the cultivation of plants has been described. These sites, which date from the period of a high sea level (ca. 4000 B.C.), surely reflect a mature maritime adaptation lost to archaeology as the sea rose.

It is possible that some of these groups took to cultivating rice. The sequence on the old coastlines behind the present Gulf of Siam is centered on two sites. Nong Nor is a small site dated to 2500 B.C., the layers of which are dominated by a shell midden which also contains evidence for fishing and pottery manufacture. But again, there is no evidence for agriculture. Five centuries later, the much larger site of Khok Phanom Di has provided undoubted remains of cultivated rice as well as shell-harvesting knives.

It is during the period 2500 to 1500 B.C. that we encounter a major settlement expansion in the valleys of the Red, Mekong, and Chao Phraya rivers that involved agricultural villages. The remains of rice and domestic cattle and pigs reveal a fully developed Neolithic economy, and the cemeteries contain exotic items revealing wide exchange contacts.

There are at least two alternatives to account for the different sequences described above. The first would see initial rice cultivation and animal domestication in the Yangtze valley that was to expand, over the ensuing five thousand years, over the lowlands of all Southeast Asia. The second favors at least two separate transitions, the earlier in the Yangtze and the later between the Red and Chao Phraya valleys.

There is no doubt that the earliest such development was centered in the Yangtze valley. Several factors can be identified that might have contributed to it. These include a preceding period of sedentary settlement by fishing and gathering groups during a warm phase. Where wild rice was collected, it is likely that a climatic deterioration would have encouraged the manipulation of this plant, for example by removing competitors, in order to assure the food supply for a permanent population. This procedure would have been encouraged by sickle or knife harvesting rather than beating the seed heads into a receptacle, because the act of cutting the stalk would have selected for plants with a stronger than normal point of attachment between the seed and the pedicel. Under natural conditions, the seeds are quickly dispersed by the wind as the brittle rachis shatters. Rice agriculture was clearly a contributing factor to the establishment and expansion of village communities.

But climatic change can hardly have been a factor in a second such transition in hot, tropical Southeast Asia. A feature of the coastal habitat there is the formation of river levées as a consequence of wet-season flooding, and the development of freshwater swamps or lagoons as streams bank up. Dry season burning to remove competing plants there, allied with sickle harvesting could have been instrumental in rice becoming increasingly prominent in the diet. A sedentary lifestyle in the rich coastal habitat would have been an initial condition, and the protection of the rice stands from competitors, such as birds, pigs, and deer, would have further stimulated sedentism.

Current Research. While we remain largely ignorant of the origins and timing of early agriculture in this southern region, moves are afoot to redress the situation. Research on distinguishing between wild and domestic rice on the basis of phytoliths is underway, lake sediments are being sampled in order to retrieve and date their pollen and phytolith remains, and rice isozymes are being studied in order to seek any differences that exist between the rice strains initially cultivated in the Yangtze valley and in tropical Southeast Asia. DNA sequencing of prehistoric rice remains is another promising avenue of research.

At present, the most promising source of information comes from comparative linguistics. The languages spoken in southern China and Southeast Asia fall into three major families. Sino-Tibetan need not detain us; it results from a relatively recent expansion to the south from the Huanghe valley. Austronesian languages are found from Taiwan south into island Southeast Asia, and Austroasiatic languages are distributed from eastern India to Vietnam. Only recently, these two have been linked into the Austric phylum, although their separation has such a time depth few if any cognates survive. It is, nevertheless, highly likely that rice was originally brought into cultivation in the upper or middle Yangtze valley, from which speakers of proto-Austroasiatic languages moved down the major rivers into India and Southeast Asia.

[*See also* ASIA: PREHISTORY AND EARLY HISTORY OF SOUTHEAST ASIA.]

■ Yan Wenming, "China's Earliest Rice Agriculture Remains," *Bulletin of the Indo-Pacific Prehistory Association* 10 (1991): 118–26. P. Bellwood, "Foraging Towards Farming: A Decisive Transition or a Millennial Blur?," *The Review of Archaeology* 11 (1991): 14–24. C.F.W. Higham, "The Transition to Rice Cultivation in Southeast Asia," in *Last Hunters—First Farmers: New Perspectives on the Prehistoric Transition to Agriculture,* ed. T. D. Price and A. B. Gebauer (1995), pp. 127–55.

Charles Higham

ORIGINS OF FOOD PRODUCTION IN CHINA

Evidence of food production in China dates back at least to the seventh millennium B.C., found in village settlements with pottery and stone tools. Early food production has been claimed for sites with rice, sites with millets, and sites with pigs. Since new and earlier sites are announced every year or so, it is important not to be doctrinaire about which kinds of food were first produced, but it is possible to say that food production began early in the Holocene. In terms of grains, China is divided roughly into southern and northern halves between the Yellow and Yangtze (Yangzi) Rivers, with the southern half featuring rice and the northern half millets. This division relates most prominently to climate, and the native plants that grew in the regions which were available for early experiments in domestication. Pigs believed to be domesticated were found without grains at Zengbiyan, and pigs occur in sites with grains wherever there is developed agriculture in China. They were clearly important for the agricultural complex. Dogs are almost ubiquitous in Chinese Neolithic sites, and may represent a food source. Other domesticated animals, such as chickens, cattle and water buffalo, and sheep, vary according to region.

Rice. Rice (*Oryza sativa*) is the most widely grown and most-valued grain in Asia today. Because it is a swamp plant that grows in standing water, and because its wild relatives are adapted to wet tropical areas, it is reasonable to seek its origin as a domesticate in coastal regions with warm, rainy climates. The two major strains of rice are known as indica and japonica. Japonica is adapted to cooler weather and shorter growing seasons, and is found in the mountains of South and Southeast Asia as well as northern China, Korea, and Japan. The grains of japonica are shorter and rounder than indica grains. Rice cultivation may have occurred independently in various parts of this region, or domesticated rice could have spread out from a single center. Until a great many more sites are found and dated it will be impossible to settle this question.

The earliest site in China with likely domesticated rice is *Pengtoushan, in Li County, Hunan, in the middle reaches of the Changjiang (Yangtze) river. C–14 dates collected from this site suggest occupation between 7000 and 5500 B.C. Rice is associated with these layers of the site beyond doubt, since rice husks are found in the pottery. The rice has not been identified as to species, and on that account there are some who are skeptical about its status as a domesticate, but it is reported as domesticated rice on the basis of large grains which are much like the present indica type. Sites in this region with similar pottery containing rice grains and husks have been located, leading to speculation that rice farming was common, but other sites have not yet been excavated to confirm this suspicion.

It seems that rice became a staple of the southern Chinese diet very quickly. The site of *Hemudu, south of Hangzhou Bay in Zhejiang province, which is dated in the sixth to fifth millennia B.C., demonstrates the next stage in rice cultivation. Very abundant remains of rice have been found at the site—it has been estimated that the quantity is 120 tons. This intensive and successful rice production cannot be seen as the first domestication, for it is surely based on long experience with rice cultivation. Other plants were also important. In addition to rice, plants such as bottle gourd, acorns, and water chestnut were identified, and cordage was made from a kind of nettle called ramie. Agricultural implements made of wood also abound from this water-logged site—a reminder not to assume that agriculture was not present merely because the stone tool inventory seems inadequate for the tasks of cultivation and preparation of plant foods. Domesticated dogs, pigs, and water buffalo were found, along with many kinds of wild animals, birds, reptiles, and fish. Some two dozen other sites of the Hemudu culture have also been located in this region.

Luojiajiao, another large site with rice, north of Hangzhou Bay in Zhejiang province, confirms that rice was important at this early stage in southern China. The C–14 dates fall in the sixth millennium B.C., approximately the same as those of Hemudu. Similar to Hemudu in several respects, Luojiajiao has wooden building posts, abundant stone and bone artifacts, and about 50,000 pot sherds. More than 2,204 pounds (1,000 kg) of animal bones include oxen, pig, and dog as the most common species.

The Yangtze valley continued to be an important center for rice cultivation in the middle Neolithic. Sites grouped into the Majiabang culture in the delta of the Yangtze River are somewhat later, and still later related cultures farther to the north, were all based on rice as the staple food. Settlements were on low mounds near rivers, and water buffalo bones are found along with those of pig and dog.

Rice is not found so early in the north, although the japonica variety can be grown as far north as the Manchurian plain. It was claimed by Andersson (*Children of the Yellow Earth*, 1934) for the Yangshao site, but this was based on slim evidence, and is generally disregarded. Rice is not otherwise present in northern China before Shang times.

Millet Cultivation. In the north of China, in the Yellow River basin and beyond, the staple today is wheat, appearing in favored foods such as noodles (*mian*), stuffed buns, and wrapped fillings (*baozi* and *jiaozi*). However, wheat is rarely (if at all) found in Neolithic China, and was not important even in Shang times. It has replaced the earlier millets, which were the Neolithic staples in northern China. There has been little botanical study of these grains, and the identification of specific millets at particular sites is often vague. Both foxtail millet (*Setaria italica*) and broomcorn millet (*Panicum miliaceum*) have been identified in northern Chinese sites. *Echinochloa villosa* (sometimes referred to as glutinous millet) has been identified in the Xituanshan culture of the Warring States period, and very likely was domesticated much earlier. All three millets were probably domesticated from native grasses of northern China.

Peiligang and Cishan are the names given to the earliest farming cultures in the north. Most of the sites are dated from 6500 to 5000 B.C., only slightly later than those of the first rice cultivation in the south. Actual remains of foxtail and broomcorn millets, as well as stone tools frequently associated with agriculture, are found at these sites, along with bones of domesticated pigs and dogs and many pig figurines. Chicken bones (*Gallus gallus domesticus*) were also present at some sites. Other possibly cultivated plant remains identified as cabbage, walnut, hazelnut, jujube, and celtis were found at one or more sites of these cultures.

The Manchurian plain is another location where early farming cultures are found. For example, Chahai near Fuxin in Liaoning province, dated around 7000 B.C., had stone tools suggestive of agriculture, and a settled village, with substantial houses erected in rows. Pottery beakers covered with rocker-stamping were made in various sizes, and an incipient jade industry is evident in polished slit earrings. Nuts have been found, but so far no grains have been

identified. However, it is likely that this region, which was warmer and wetter than the present, also had domesticated plants. Xinglongwa in western Liaoning probably also had early millet cultivation, along with pigs. An ash circle surrounding the site may be the remains of an encircling palisade. Other sites and cultures with rocker-stamped beakers dated somewhat later, such as Lower Xinle near Shenyang, Houwa near Dandong, and sites on the Liaodong peninsula, are clearly millet and pig-raising societies.

By the time of the Yangshao sites with painted pottery, once thought to be the beginning of the Chinese Neolithic, farming was thoroughly established in both north and south China.

Other Domesticated Plants. The soybean (*Glycine max*) has wild relatives which are indigenous to northern China, Korea, Japan, and eastern Siberia. It is an important protein source in China today, both as fermented sauce and as *dofu*, bean cakes. The storability of these soy products was probably an important survival factor in the nongrowing season in the north.

Chinese cabbage (*Brassica sp.*) is found in Yangshao sites, and no doubt other vegetables, especially storable root crops, were domesticated as well.

Plants such as hemp (*Cannabis sativa*) and ramie, a more southern plant, were probably domesticated for their fibers, and hemp in addition has seeds from which oil can be extracted. Impressions of textiles in various Neolithic sites, and the presence of needles and spindle whorls, show that some type of textile industry had arisen. The mulberry tree (*Morus alba*) had to be planted in order to raise silkworms, an activity that is attested at the Yangshao site of Xiyincun in Shanxi province.

Domesticated Animals. Pigs and dogs appear to be the earliest domesticated animals in China. At Zengbiyan near Guilin on the Li River in southern China, bones of sixty-seven individual pigs were found, of which most were killed before they were two years old. This selective pattern of "harvesting" pigs suggests domestication. Pottery and stone tools are common at Zengbiyan, but evidence of plant domestication in the lower levels is lacking. The earliest dates from the site are around 7000 B.C.

The centrality of pigs in the Neolithic scheme is hard to overlook. At *Banpo, on the Yellow River, most trash pits contain pig bones, and in the later Neolithic, pig skulls or whole pigs are common burial accompaniments. Pig figurines are also frequently found.

Cattle were probably used more for traction animals than as a source of food. Dairy products have never been utilized in China, and beef is not a traditional food. This is not to say that cattle were not sometimes eaten, but that their primary use was for transportation or plowing. Water buffalo are found where there is rice cultivation, and oxen occur in northern sites. A large stone tool found in Hongshan sites in Liaoning province is interpreted as a plow, and it is likely that wooden plows were used in the rice paddies of the south.

Sheep and goats appear to be late additions. Grazing animals are not appropriate for most of China's climate and terrain, except for parts of the north and northwest. Sheep appear in Hongshan sites, on the edge of the Inner Mongolian grasslands, in the fourth millennium B.C. Goats are not found until after 2000 B.C. in the Qijia culture in Gansu province, suggesting an import from central Asia. The Mongolian horse (*Equus przwalski*) appears in some Neolithic sites, but does not appear to have been an important domesticate.

[*See also* ASIA: PREHISTORY AND EARLY HISTORY OF EAST ASIA; CHINA: EARLY CIVILIZATIONS OF CHINA; YANGSHAO CULTURE.]

■ Ping-ti Ho, *The Cradle of the East* (1975). Hui-lin Li, "The Domestication of Plants in China: Ecogeographical Consideration," in *The Origins of Chinese Civilization*, ed. David N. Keightly (1983), pp. 21–63. Te-Tzu Chang, "The Origins and Early Cultures of the Cereal Grains and Food Legumes," in *The Origins of Chinese Civilization*, ed. David N. Keightly (1983), pp. 65–94. K. C. Chang, *The Archaeology of Ancient China* (1986). Richard Pearson and Anne Underhill, "The Chinese Neolithic: Recent Trends in Research," *American Anthropologist* 89:1 (1987): 807–822. Sarah M. Nelson, "The Neolithic of Northeastern China and Korea," *Antiquity* 64 (1990): 234–248. Yan Wenming, "China's Earliest Rice Agriculture Remains," in *Indo-Pacific Prehistory 1990*, vol. 1, pp. 118–126. Guo Da-shun, "Hongshan and Related Cultures," in *Beyond the Great Wall: The Archaeology of Northeast China*, ed. Sarah M. Nelson (1994).

Sarah Milledge Nelson

ASTRONOMY

Astronomy in the Old World
Astronomy in the Americas

ASTRONOMY IN THE OLD WORLD

Most of our knowledge of ancient astronomy comes from written texts: Babylonian cuneiform tablets and copied and recopied manuscripts from Greece and the Islamic world. These consist mainly of recorded observations of celestial bodies and accompanying astrological omens. But there is an unwritten record as well. The coming together of archaeological data and questions of astronomical practice by ancient civilizations first occurred in Great Britain and Egypt with the work of astronomer Sir Norman Lockyer in the 1890s. He proposed that many Egyptian temples were aligned with the sun and bright stars, and he revitalized the old idea that the axis of Stonehenge had been deliberately directed toward midsummer sunrise. But his attempt to date ancient structures astronomically (e.g., by computing the time when they would have aligned most precisely with astronomical bodies), along with his wild speculations about the astral nature of Egyptian religion, constituted a callous disregard for historical and archaeological chronology and history that ultimately led to a rejection of his ideas by the scholarly community.

In the 1960s a popular spate of works on *Stonehenge brought to light the ongoing meticulous investigations of Scottish engineer Alexander Thom. He had carefully surveyed and mapped hundreds of Neolithic and Bronze Age (fourth–second millennium B.C.) stone structures in the British Isles and concluded that an enduring civilization he called "megalithic man" erected these great monuments to align precisely with key seasonal positions of the sun, including the northern and southern standstills at the horizon. He also contended that these people charted the long-term horizon limits of the moon, often by employing notches on the horizon as precise indicators, thus showing an interest in predicting eclipses. Moreover, Thom alleged, a fundamental measuring unit, the Megalithic Yard (ca. 2.7 ft. (0.8 m)), was employed in the design of many of these structures, which builders often deliberately distorted into egg and elliptical shapes. Thom's "megalithic man" was, like the modern western scientist, apparently motivated by curiosity to understand the universe for its own sake.

Since the 1970s this archetypal view of "megalithic man" as philosopher and scientist has largely faded. First, the archaeological record reveals that many different traditions had existed in the period from the fourth to the first millennium B.C., and second, early investigators like Thom may have been reading too much into the data. An inherent difficulty with precision calendrics is that it must be shown to be consistent with the needs of the simple farming communities that had begun to be established in approximately 4000 B.C. Third, in addition to the place of astronomy in a given culture, one also needs to consider the level of skill and the time required to collect enough data to make a precise calendar. A new generation of interdisciplinary scholars, trained in or allied with the methods of the archaeological sciences, have reexamined Thom's data and arguments, and collected data of their own. They have concluded that the appearance of the sky was but one among a number of factors in site selection and orientation that may have included the existence of holy places and directions, proximity to resources or occupation units, geographic features such as hills or bends in rivers, perhaps even personal reasons, such as where an individual of high social rank was born, won a battle, or died.

There are many classes of prehistoric stone structures in Europe. Newgrange, a passage grave in Ireland dating from about 3000 B.C., offers one possible astronomically significant orientation. Around the time of the winter solstice, sunlight admitted via a roof box penetrates the 62-foot (19m) length of the passage to illuminate the main chamber. It would not at all have been out of character for a chief to have had himself buried in alignment with a purported solar deity on the day the sun reached its lowest noontime position in the sky. Indeed, Christmas is patterned after this very concept, derived from pagan religion, with Christ representing the resurrected solar light that fades from the midwinter sky. Analyzed statistically as a class of objects, however, chambered tombs do not align with astronomical bodies. Furthermore, most of them have been built over and altered in structure and perhaps in religious meaning.

*Stone circles and alignments (there are more than a thousand in the British Isles alone) like Stonehenge and *Avebury may have employed large standing stones as backsights and distant natural horizon features as foresights to mark the approximate limits of the sun and moon. When archaeologically similar groups of such circles (e.g., recumbent stone circles) are analyzed statistically, their astronomical function appears more likely to have played a role in acquiring the proper conditions of illumination to conduct a ritual, such as the full moon rising in time to meet the setting sun at the winter solstice, or sunlight being conducted along the accessway and perhaps through the gate leading to an assembly area within the circular enclosure—rather than as a precise observatory in the modern scientific sense. Kintraw in Argyil, Scotland, is an excellent example of a possible test of celestial alignment via excavation. It consists of a triple set of sights: a hilltop, a single standing stone, and a notch in which the sun disappears at the winter solstice. Was there a platform with cultural remains on the hilltop? Excavations to date leave the matter unresolved among the archaeological community.

In the 1980s and '90s interdisciplinary studies of astronomy in the unwritten record (usually labeled archaeoastronomy) have spread throughout Europe and have even begun to transcend the prehistoric record. As it is impossible to point out all of these results here, we will mention only a selected sample of the areas studied and leave the reader to peruse the bibliography.

Reexamination of the Egyptian architecture reveals that many of the temples (e.g., the Temple of Amun at Thebes) align with the midwinter sunrise. In Italy, both solar extremes are evident in the *motte* (conical mounds with access ramps) and *castellieri* (quadrangular earthworks) of the Veneto-Friuli area of northern Italy as well as in early Iron Age (1500–1000 B.C.) *Tombe dei Giganti,* megalithic burial structures on Sardinia. Lunar orientations are claimed as well but these are less certain. In Minorca the *talayots* (large stone towers built of marble and often containing windows) and *taulas* (upright worked stone slabs 6.5–13 feet (2–4 m) tall capped by a single flat tabular stone) exhibit nonrandom directions. Stellar orientations claimed for some of these are difficult to evaluate statistically. The same can be said for complex multichambered "temples" in Malta. On the other hand, an extensive study of more than two thousand Neolithic graves in Central Europe revealed strong orientation trends along cardinal axes. This was likely achieved by sighting the sun at culmination (its high point) or by the position of the celestial pole as the approximate center of motion of the night sky. East–west would then be obtained either by spotting the annual midpoint of the sun at horizon or by bisecting the north–south axis geometrically. In the Golan Heights (today Israel) a unique structure called Rujm el Hiri dating from the Chalcolithic (ca. 3000 B.C.) to the Late Bronze Age (down to 1500 B.C.) consists of five concentric walls made of material ranging from small boulders up to multiton megaliths. It measures over 328 feet (100 m) in diameter and centers on a (later) burial cairn 66 feet (20 m) wide. Astronomy may have played a role in its design. The main astronomic feature is an accessway aligned with the June solstice sunrise. Other alignments include the equinox sunrise and a precise north geographic indicator. Radial walls that make up the spaces between circles are also best explained as alignment devices to celestial and terrestrial features.

That the Old World archaeological record harbors many astronomical orientations seem clear. The real question is why? Given all the religiously motivated effort (e.g., the computation of the Paschal date) that lies behind the revisions of our own modern calendar, it would not be surprising to find a knowledge of astronomy incorporated in religious architecture. Indeed, many of the cathedrals and churches of medieval Europe exhibit such astronomical arrangements. For example, unusual openings in the lower cathedral of St. Lizier in France were likely used to mark the solstices and equinoxes. One motive may have been to allow the bishop to cite errors in the Julian calendar when fixing the ecclesiastical year. One study of nineteen churches in Central Europe revealed such axial directions as sunrise on the Easter festival in the founding year (A.D. 1075). In all cases the orientation axes fit within the extremes of solar declination.

There is a well-known tradition in Islam that all good Muslims must face Mecca when praying. But how to know which way to turn? In medieval Islam it is written that the *Qibla,* or sacred direction, was originally determined in an approximate way by wind direction or by having the sun on the side of one's face. Later it was formalized in the architecture of the *Ka'ba,* the pre-Islamic pagan shrine, via astronomical orientation to objects at the local horizon. Solstices, the lunar standstills and the bright star Canopus have all been implicated. Later, medieval Islamic astronomical methods became more abstract and mathematically based. In medieval India the city of *Vijayanagara, and in China

ancient Beijing were two among many cities that reflected the harmony of the cosmos. Like Egyptian pyramids built four thousand years before them, each possessed precise cardinal axes, a habit that also can be found in the remains of capitals of ancient New World empires. From what the historical record tells us about the divine rulers of these impressive places (e.g., the Chinese emperor was called the Son of Heaven) it would have been to their advantage to legitimize and strengthen their positions by offering concrete visible evidence to their subjects that indeed their power was ordained in the sky.

In sum, in the absence of other evidence, the archaeological record alone cannot provide a firm basis for testing astronomic hypotheses. Where no historical or other written record exists, one is forced to rely on statistical evidence alone. Used as a dating technique the theory of astronomical alignments suffices only when archaeological dating schemes are there to back it up. At its worst archaeoastronomy is tarnished by having managed to attract wild speculation, often engendered by inquirers who are oblivious to what is already known or can be known from studies undertaken in disciplines with which they are unfamiliar. But at its best, as an interdisciplinary enterprise, it offers a viable method both for formulating and testing hypotheses that inquire into ancient astronomical practice and that attempt to place astronomical ideas, along with other notions about the structure and purpose of the natural world, in a social context.

■ A. Pannekoek, *A History of Astronomy* (1961). F. Hodson, ed. *The Place of Astronomy in the Ancient World* (1974). D. Heggie, ed. *Archaeoastronomy in the Old World* (1982). C. Ruggles, ed. *Records in Stone: Papers in Memory of Alexander Thom* (1988). C. Ruggles, "Recent Developments in Megalithic Astronomy" in *World Archaeoastronomy,* ed. A. Aveni (1989), pp. 13–26. A. Aveni, *Ancient Astronomers* (1993). C. Ruggles and N. Saunders, eds. *Astronomies and Cultures* (1993).

Anthony F. Aveni

ASTRONOMY IN THE AMERICAS

Interdisciplinary studies of archaeological sites have helped reveal a knowledge of the nature and uses of astronomy among the indigenous cultures of the Americas. Especially in those areas where no written record exists, investigations have made extensive use of site plans, orientations, and the iconography associated with standing architecture, along with the post-contact ethnohistoric record. In a few instances, such as the remote regions of the Andes, Amazonia, and the Guatemalan rain forest, some of these data can be linked to still-living traditions that are observed by field anthropologists. Here we shall review representative contributions to astronomical knowledge both by types of remains and methods of studying them.

One artifact that relates to astronomy and calendar keeping consists of a double circle centered on a cross. More than seventy examples of this symbol have been excavated since 1950. It is found pecked into the floors of buildings and on rock outcrops all over Mesoamerica from Chalchihuites, a Xolalpan phase (A.D. 600) Teotihuacán outpost in the Northwest of Mexico, to Maya Uaxactun (A.D. 300) in the rain forest of Guatemala. At *Teotihuacán certain of these markers were likely used to fix the skewed (15½° E of N) orientation of the city so that it aligned appropriately with the cosmos (see Astronomy in the Old World). The east–west axis of the site, defined by an 18-mile (3-km) line between a pair of such petroglyphs, aligned with the setting point of the Pleiades star group about the time the city was erected (A.D. 150). Moreover, the first annual predawn appearance of the Pleiades took place on the same day that the sun passed the zenith or overhead point. Commencing the year with a solar zenith passage and using the Pleiades as a stellar timing device to coordinate the calendar were widespread habits in the tropical regions of the Americas in later times. For example, the Aztec chronicler Sahagun states that the Aztec fifty-two-year cycle, the commensuration of the two major time cycles employed throughout Mesoamerica (the 260-day ritual count and the 365-day seasonal cycle), was commenced by a zenith observation of the Pleiades at midnight from the Hill of the Star, a promontory jutting out into Lake Texcoco. That such a functional stellar–solar timing device might be incorporated into a city plan seems quite plausible.

The pecked circle may also have been used as a time-keeping device as evidenced by its similarity to quadripartite calendars found in both Mayan and Central Mexican codices. Counting the elements along quadrants and especially axes of the petroglyph, one usually finds numbers that functioned in the Mesoamerican counting system (e.g., 20, 13, and its multiples). Archaic tally schemes, many of them implicating time counts, appear on rock outcrops at sites in northwestern Mexico, for example, Presa de la Mula and Icamole. In some of these cases counts of a few up to seven lunar months (as measured by the phases) raise the possibility that hunter-gatherers employed rudimentary calendars to help formalize their itineraries through this relatively hostile area of the northern Sierra Madre.

Other artifacts of ancient astronomy consist of specialized architectural assemblages often taking on unusual shapes or orientations with respect to neighboring structures. For example, at Uaxactun the Group E complex was an orientation device used to formally mark out the annual course of the rising sun. It consists of a pyramidal structure on the west side of an open plaza, from which the sun can be observed to rise over three smaller structures on the east side at the solstices and equinoxes. Just as the Teotihuacán orientation seems to have been copied all over central Mexico and beyond, so too did architects at neighboring sites in the central Petén create Group E–type complexes. In many instances, however, the copies follow the form though not the function of the archetype in precisely the same way. This raises the question whether cosmic axes formalized early on by donor cultures do not retain the same meaning as they are incorporated into the foundations of the built environment of later cultures who receive these ideas. Indeed the Group E complex at Uaxactun has itself been traced from an earlier nonastronomically related form.

Other specialized astronomical buildings in Mesoamerica include the Caracol of *Chichén Itzá (ca. A.D. 1000), a Maya-Toltec round building that incorporates in its base, as well as in narrow horizontal shafts in its turret, alignments to the sunset at the equinox as well as to the Venus extremes on the horizon (i.e., the Venusian analogue of the solstice); Building J at *Monte Albán (ca. 250 B.C.), a five-sided building, the skewed axis of which aligns with a solar zenith sighting tube in nearby Building P—remains of a similar vertical sun-watching device have been found at the ruins of Xochicalco (ca. A.D. 600); the House of the Governor at Uxmal (ca. A.D. 850), the axis of which aligns with the southernmost "Venustice"; and Temple 22 at *Copán (ca. A.D. 750), which possesses a single slot-like window through which Venus appearances correspond to the commencement of the rainy season in the Valley of Copán. Iconography on the latter two buildings contain Venus-related symbolism, including a hieroglyph for Venus also found in the Venus prediction table in the Dresden Codex.

In the case of the Maya, a sophisticated, now mostly deciphered, writing system enabled the art of astronomical prediction to scale great heights. The few surviving precontact codices provide us with tables for predicting Venus and Mars appearances, the course of the moon in the zodiac, eclipses, and seasonal limits. By the eighth century, these astronomical capabilities became fully articulated in stone and served both as a baseline for recording dynastic history and as the philosophical underpinning for a cosmic world view in which the right to rule was believed to have descended from celestial deities. It is in the enactment of cosmically based rituals organized by the ruling class (i.e., bloodletting by a ruler as a way of communicating with ancient gods and ancestors), rather than as precise observatories, that these specialized buildings likely functioned.

Studies of the dates on monumental inscriptions and of recently excavated mural paintings at Cacaxtla (A.D. 650–900), and the murals at Bonampak (ca. A.D. 650–800) suggest the proliferation of a Venus cult relating to the paraphernalia and rituals of warfare. This may have descended from the so-called Tlaloc-related warfare iconography of Teotihuacán. Thus advances in Mesoamerican astronomy parallel the continuity of culture.

On the South American continent the precise equinoctial orientation of the Kalassasaya of Tiahuanaco (ca. A.D. 1000) has long been known and many Inca outposts along the northwest coast of Peru seem to be oriented in the same direction. Such a custom probably originated in the southern highland capital of *Cuzco (ca. 14th–15th century). Numerous chronicles also refer to calendar keeping in the northern capital (Quito) of the Inca empire. Pillars on the horizon (in some cases mountains themselves) marked the solstices, possibly the equinoxes, and the days of passage of the sun through the zenith and its reciprocal date, the antizenith. The latter date, corresponding to our mid-August in the calendar of Cuzco, closely matches the location of a set of four pillars on Cerro Picchu, a hill immediately overlooking the city on its west-northwest. According to one chronicler, as the setting sun filed past the array, over the course of about a month, planting was initiated in progressively lower altitudes in order to adjust to the differential time that crops took to ripen. Unfortunately, no writing system, save for the largely undecoded *quipu* or knotted string counting device, supports these arguments. And no remains of the pillars have been discovered by Andean archaeologists. Moreover, uncertainties about the locations of the huacas or sacred shrines of the ceque system (the radial arrangement of huacas worshipped by various kinship classes) of which the pillars are said to have been a part, leave details about the astronomical record in the cityscape of Cuzco in a state of incompleteness.

Also without a decipherable writing system, the native cultures of North America offer little more than archaeological evidence as a way of generating hypotheses about the native practice of astronomy. Statistical approaches cast considerable doubt on earlier claims that the medicine wheels of the Rocky Mountain states and western Canada possess astronomical orientations to solstices and bright stars. But we can be sure that the Hopi-Navajo created solar orientation calendars at the horizon. Such information was communicated to early ethnologists and now the archaeological record has disclosed some of the sunwatchers' shrines. These consist of both foresights and backsights employed by the keepers of the calendar who set the festal dates. Like Teotihuacán, many of the kivas and roads of Chaco Canyon incorporated cosmic axes as part of their design. A special petroglyph at Fajada Butte (ca. A.D. 1000) may have been used to set the approximate limits of the year via the image of the sun moving over it in the shape of a dagger of light. Other solar light and shadow phenomena indicating an interest in charting out the sun's annual course have been reported in the architecture at Hovenweep and at other Pueblo sites. Early Hopewellian tribes of the Ohio Valley (ca. A.D. 400–200) incorporated solar and possibly lunar orientations into their octagon earthworks of Ohio; and *Cahokia (ca. A.D. 1200) likely also preserves solar orientations in the major axes of some of its mounds.

The archaeological record reveals that cultures as diverse as urban Tenochtitlán and Cuzco on the one hand and hunter-gatherer groups of the Amazon and California on the other, employed observations and made predictions concerning sky events as a way of formalizing the civic and religious calendar. Artifacts like Teotihuacán's pecked circle and Chaco's sun dagger developed into more elaborate mechanisms promoting social action. In *Tenochtitlán, in which the mandate of the people was concerned with keeping the sun in motion through military action and human sacrifice, the structure of the city became a microcosm of the cosmos. And astronomy, as a practical day-keeping and date-reaching enterprise, grew to become part and parcel of an ideology that prescribed good behavior for its citizens. The sacred precinct of Tenochtitlán, like the center of *Stonehenge, the giant trapezoids on Nasca's pampa, the plaza fronting the group of the Cross at *Palenque, and the octagon mounds of Ohio—all likely were places of assembly where people worshiped their ancestors and the gods of nature. Thus the archaeological record in the Americas has contributed significantly to our understanding of relatively esoteric and elusive concepts, such as religion, cosmology, and world view, that structure human culture.

■ R. Zuidema, "The Inca Calendar" in *Native American Astronomy*, ed. A. Aveni (1977), pp. 219–259. A. Aveni, H. Hartung, and B. Buckingham, "The Pecked Cross Symbol in Ancient Mesoamerica" *Science* 202 (1978): 267–271. A. Aveni, *Skywatchers of Ancient Mexico* (1980). W. Breen Murray, "Calendrical Petroglyphs of Northern Mexico" in *Archeoastronomy in the Old World*, ed. A. Aveni (1982), pp. 195–204. A. Aveni and H. Hartung, "Uaxautun, Guatemala, Group E and Similar Assemblages: An Archaeoastronomical Reconsideration" in *World Archaeoastronomy*, ed. A. Aveni (1989), pp. 441–61. M. Zeilik, "Keeping the Sacred and Planting Calendar: Archaeoastronomy in the Pueblo Southwest" in *World Archaeoastronomy*, ed. A. Aveni (1989), pp. 143–66. A. Aveni, *Ancient Astronomers* (1993). R. Hively and R. Horn, "Geometry & Astronomy in Prehistoric Ohio," *Archaeoastronomy* 13(4), pp. S1–S20.

Anthony F. Aveni

ATHABASKAN CULTURES OF THE AMERICAN SOUTHWEST.

According to the Navajo, their ancestors, along with the Anasazi (prehistoric Pueblo Indians), came from the fourth underworld. After a series of adventures, the Navajo emerged on earth, where they planted seeds brought from below. According to archaeologists, Navajo, along with their Athabaskan cousins the Apaches, were at one time part of the larger Athabaskan group currently occupying southwestern Canada. Navajo and Apache ancestors were nomadic hunter-gatherers who, for reasons not entirely understood, migrated south. The volcanic White River ash fall might have encouraged migration. There are sites on the high plains east of the Rocky Mountains attributable to migrating Athabaskans. However, some archaeologists suggest a few groups arrived by a more western route.

The arrival of the first Athabaskans in the American Southwest remains controversial. While a minority of archaeologists still hold to an early date of entry (ca. A.D. 1200) in order to implicate Athabaskans in the depopulation of the *Mesa Verde Anasazi region, most favor a later date between A.D. 1450 and 1500. The relationship between Athabaskan immigrants and indigenous Puebloan peoples at this time is also controversial. Some archaeologists suggest a volatile relationship including raids on villages by the nomadic newcomers. Others see the relationship as primarily peaceful and based on trade. Early ethnohistorical sources indicate peaceful trade between nomadic and sedentary peoples. Both Juan Vásquez de Coronado in A.D. 1541 and Juan de Oñate sixty years later, encountered groups of nomadic Plains Apaches engaged in peaceful trading of bison meat with Rio Grande Puebloans for domestic products. When Spaniards entered the Southwest with their European diseases, guns, horses, livestock, and sociopolitical domination, they disrupted trading relationships, and Athabaskans became raiders who were feared by the Puebloans as well as by the Spanish.

Different waves of Athabaskans migrating into the Southwest were probably at first indistinguishable, at least between Navajos and Apaches (the latter including the Chiricahua, Mescalero, Jicarilla, Lipan, and Western Apache). Navajos interacted and intermarried more with Puebloans than did other Apacheans, resulting in a slightly different culture, although linguistically all southern Athabaskan languages are mutually intelligible. Cultural merging intensified between Athabaskans and Puebloans just before and after the Pueblo revolt of 1680 against the Spanish, when many Puebloans fled to northern New Mexico, then occupied by southern Athabaskans. Some never returned, and became part of the emerging Navajo society. The melding of two ways of life produced early Navajo culture. Contemporary Athabaskan groups referred to as Apaches were less influenced by the Puebloans. In contrast to the Navajos, and as a generalization, Apaches emphasized hunting and gathering over horticulture and sheep/goat pastoralism.

The original Navajo homeland, called Dinetah, is located in northern New Mexico, east of present-day Farmington. Because early Athabaskan sites are extremely ephemeral, often consisting of only a small lithic scatter, they are difficult to locate and even more difficult to identify as Athabaskan. Nevertheless, there are sites in the Dinetah area that have been classified as early Navajo. They belong to the Dinetah Phase tentatively dated from A.D. 1450 to 1690. Traits associated with this period are those thought to have been brought with the Athabaskans to the Southwest. Sites consist of forked-stick hogans and associated lithics and Dinetah Gray pottery.

The Gobernador Phase, dating from about A.D. 1691–1775, depending on the investigator, is a time of profound change, which features the amalgamation of Athabaskan and Pueblo society. Athabaskan clans deriving from Pueblo origins were established during this time. Other introduced Puebloan traits, such as rock art and curing ceremonial paraphernalia, including masked dancers, dry paintings, and prayer sticks, date to this period. Pueblitos (or small pueblos) are the characteristic feature of Gobernador sites.

In addition to a small one- to ten-room masonry building, sites include forked-stick or masonry hogans, hearths, storage bins and pits, ramadas or shades, and middens with outlying sweat lodges, ovens, corrals, and occasionally rock art panels and burials. Associated pottery types include Dinetah Gray and Gobernador Polychrome, in addition to a low frequency of Puebloan wares. Lithics and historic artifacts, such as metal or glass objects acquired from the Spanish, are common at some sites (e.g., pueblitos). It is interesting that kivas are missing from pueblito sites. Although hunting remained important, horticulture and small livestock were added to Athabaskan subsistence endeavors. Most southern Athabaskan groups during this time period adopted a pattern termed "subsistence raiding," wherein they continuously appropriated food, horses, livestock, and variety of objects from Pueblo and Spanish communities, although not all archaeologists agree on such an early timing of this raiding.

The Raiding Period (the Cabezon Phase) lasted from about A.D. 1776 to 1863. It represented a time of increased raiding activities on all sides: Navajos and Apaches plundered for livestock, corn, and slaves to sell; Spanish and later Euro-Americans raided for slaves and punitive revenge; other Indians, particularly Utes, raided one another and the European/Euro-Americans for goods and slaves. Many Navajos were taken to Hispanic settlements as slaves; twentieth-century Navajo women's dress is thought to date to this period, when they adopted their masters' style of clothing. This was a time of increasing local variation in Navajo and Apache culture, perhaps partly caused by local variation in the intensity of interaction with non-Athabaskan neighboring groups. The turmoil of this period continued into the Bosque Redondo Period (A.D. 1863–1868). Euro-Americans imprisoned Navajos and Apaches at Bosque Redondo near Fort Sumner on the Pecos River (called "The Long Walk"). Some avoided capture by fleeing to isolated areas; others fled to the Pueblos, including Jemez, whose inhabitants had sought refuge with the Athabaskans from the Spanish almost 200 years before. The Reservation Phase spans from A.D. 1868 to the present and is characterized by a rapidly changing culture; a mixed economy including goat/sheep and cattle ranching; maize, bean, and alfalfa agriculture; wage work; welfare; tribal cash-generating enterprises; a blending of Christian and Navajo/Apachean beliefs; and a decline in the use of hogans (among Navajos) and wickiups (among Apaches) in favor of Euro-American-style houses and material culture. Today, the southern Athabaskans of the American Southwest represent a fascinating merging of Native American and Western culture, as they continue to adapt to rapidly changing conditions by combining elements of the past with those of the present.

[See also NORTH AMERICA: THE NORTH AMERICAN SOUTHWEST.]

■ William Workman, "The Significance of Vulcanism in the Prehistory of Subarctic Northwest North America," Paper Presented at the Society for American Archaeology, New Orleans, LA (1977). David Brugge, Navajos in the Catholic Church Records of New Mexico—1694–1875 (1985). Michael Marshall, "The Pueblito as a Site Complex: Archaeological Investigations in the Dinetah District," in ed. Michael Marshall and Patrick Hogan, Rethinking Pueblitos (1991), pp. 1–282. Richard Perry, Western Apache Heritage: People of the Mountain Corridor (1991). Judith Habicht-Mauche, "Coronado's Querechos and Teyas in the Archaeological Record of the Texas Panhandle," Plains Anthropologist 37 (1992): 247–259. David Brugge, "Thoughts on the Significance of Navajo Traditions in View of the Newly Discovered Early Athabaskan Archaeology North of the San Juan River," in ed. Meliha Duran and David Kirkpatrick, Why Museums Collect: Papers in Honor of Joe Ben Wheat (1993), pp. 31–38.
Susan Kent

ATHENS. The importance of Athens, occupied since the Neolithic, lies chiefly in the period from the end of the Bronze Age (1200 B.C.) to its sack by the Herulians in A.D. 267. From this period the city has yielded a quantity and quality of archaeological data unmatched by any other mainland Greek site. Furthermore, because of the amount of surviving Athenian literature mapping both political and cultural developments, it offers the archaeologist unique literary control on the interpretation of the artifactual evidence.

Athens is located at the upper corner of a small coastal plain on the western side of the peninsula of Attica. The site is sheltered by the mountain ranges of Aigaleos to the north and Hymettos to the south, and is dominated by the Acropolis. Neolithic settlement is known from the Acropolis and the area below the Acropolis to the north. There is only exiguous evidence of Early Bronze Age settlement but plentiful Middle Helladic evidence, and in the Late Bronze Age (Mycenaean Period) the Acropolis acquired a palace and impressive fortifications. Graves of that period are rich and numerous in areas both north and south of the Acropolis. Athens was perhaps simply one of several political centers in Attica during this period, but from the Dark Ages onward it was the most important settlement in Attica, and politically dominant.

Athens was one of few sites in Greece continuously occupied through the Dark Ages of the eleventh through the ninth centuries B.C. and one of the first to develop new links with the wider world. It seems to have been at Athens that the Proto-Geometric style of pottery, involving use of the multiple-brush compass, was first developed, although it spread quickly to other parts of the Greek world. It was Athens, too, that developed the most sophisticated figured style of late Geometric pottery. The continuously used cemetery of the Kerameikos has provided not only a rich sequence of Athenian pottery but also evidence for detailed changes in Athenian burial customs. These included the proportion of the child and adult population that was buried in an archaeologically visible way, the method of disposal of the body, the nature of the grave goods, and the nature of the grave markers. On the basis of these changes recent scholars have attempted to trace changes in Athenian social organization, as Athens moved from being impoverished but relatively egalitarian to being a society in which wealth was concentrated in few hands, only to become, in the second half of the eighth century B.C., much more inclusive.

The seventh century B.C. at Athens is not well known, but the sixth century B.C. sees the beginnings of monumental temple building on the Acropolis. It also saw a tradition of monumental sculpture, both limestone architectural sculpture and free-standing sculpture in marble, most notably the dedication of a series of korai (maidens). The first clearly civic buildings in the agora were built during this period, and Athenian black-figure pottery of high artistic quality was developed and came to be widely distributed through the Mediterranean world. Black-figure pottery was succeeded about 500 B.C. by a new red-figure style, also developed at Athens. The sack of Athens by the Persians in 480 B.C. both destroyed (and therefore preserved for us) the archaic sculpture and architecture of the Acropolis and created the blank sheet and the imperial base that made possible a massive program of public building in marble to create a civic and religious center without parallel in the Greek world of the time. Outstanding among fifth-century B.C. monuments are the Parthenon and Erechtheum on the Acropolis, both of which were architecturally innovative in the way in which they articulated the Doric and Ionic orders, respectively. They were also sculpturally innovative: The Parthenon not only housed a chryselephantine statue of Athena that cost as much as the temple itself, but carried more architectural sculpture than any previous Greek temple, far surpassing the Temple of Zeus at Olympia. The sculptures may have formed part of a single program, the key element of which was the continuous frieze showing a religious procession. These sculptures, mostly acquired by Lord Elgin and housed in the British Museum, have largely determined the popular view of classical Greece and its art.

After the defeat of Athens by Sparta in the Peloponnesian War (432–404 B.C.), state building nearly ceased. From the fourth century B.C. onward the notable monuments were financed by individuals, by Athenian citizens commemorating victories in public competitions for poetic performance in the fourth century B.C. (notably the Choregic Monument of Lysicrates), and by Hellenistic rulers and Roman philhellenes in subsequent centuries. Thus the whole eastern side of the agora was filled in the second century B.C. by a stoa financed by Attalos, King of Pergamum. Ptolemy VI, the emperor Hadrian, and others built libraries, and Caesar and Augustus provided a second, initially commercial agora. In the first century B.C., Andronicus built the famous, and very influential, Tower of the Winds to house a twenty-four-hour water clock, and in the second century A.D. the emperor Hadrian completed an enormous temple to Olympian Zeus that had been started in the sixth century B.C. The traveler Pausanias has left us an invaluable account of what there was to see in second-century A.D. Athens in the first book of his *Guide to Greece*, although he tends to turn a blind eye to recent monuments.

The artistic and architectural achievements of Athens in the sixth, fifth, and fourth centuries B.C. have distracted attention from other aspects of the archaeological record, but the extensive excavations in the agora and surrounding area have shed considerable light on Athenian public and political life and also on Athens the industrial city.

[*See also* GREECE, *articles on* THE RISE OF GREEK CITY-STATES, CLASSICAL GREECE, THE HELLENISTIC AGE; GREEK ART AND ARCHITECTURE, CLASSICAL: CLASSICAL GREEK ARCHITECTURE; MEDITERRANEAN WORLD: THE DOMINANCE OF GREECE AND ROME.]

■ John Travlos, *Pictorial Dictionary of Ancient Athens* (1971). Robert Cook, *Greek Painted Pottery*, 2nd ed. (1972). R. E. Wycherley, *The Stones of Athens* (1978). John Camp, *The Athenian Agora* (1986). Ian Morris, *Burial and Ancient Society* (1987). L. Schneider and C. Höcker, *Die Akropolis von Athen* (1990).

Robin Osborne

ATLANTIS. *See* PSEUDO-ARCHAEOLOGY: LOST CONTINENTS (ATLANTIS AND MU).

AUSTRALIA AND NEW GUINEA

INTRODUCTION

Australia and New Guinea were settled comparatively late in human prehistory. The archaeological evidence for first settlement is still virtually nonexistent, but it seems likely that human occupation of offshore Southeast Asia had to await the development of at least rudimentary watercraft. As far as is known, no archaic humans ever crossed even narrow ocean straits, so crossings to New Guinea and Australia did not occur until anatomically modern humans had evolved or settled on the Asian mainland. If this hypothesis is correct, then first settlement took place during the late Ice Age, when sea levels were much lower than today. At the height of the glacial maximum, some 18,000 years ago, a wide continental shelf intersected by large rivers joined Sumatra to Borneo, forming a land mass called Sunda. Nearly nineteen miles (31 km) of open water separated the mainland from Wallacea, the modern islands of Sulawesi and Timor. A further sixty-two-mile (100 km) strait divided Wallacea from Sahul, a combination of New Guinea, Australia, and what is now the shallow Arafura Sea between them. While sea levels were higher during much of the late Ice Age, even at the height of the last cold snap people would have had to cross sizable bodies of water. These were, of course, more benign waters than those of the icy Bering Sea or the Atlantic Ocean, so the first watercraft may have been simple rafts that carried people to new lands, either by accident or on deliberate voyages. Whatever the process of colonization, it involved island hopping downwind, using the prevailing currents. The actual date of first settlement is hotly debated, especially in Australia. Jim Allen points out that human settlement in New Guinea may date to at least 40,000 years ago, while even earlier dates are sometimes proposed, controversially, for Australia. But, as Allen also shows, the number of reliably dated archaeological sites in Australia increases after 35,000 years ago, with well-established wallaby-hunting groups in the extreme south, in bitterly cold Tasmania, by 30,000 years ago. What is in little doubt is the early colonization of the Solomon Islands and other archipelagos within line-of-sight navigation of mainland New Guinea. Stone Age groups were living in the Solomons 28,000 years ago, while there was widespread trade in fine-grained toolmaking stone in the Bismarck Archipelago region of the southwestern Pacific by 18,000 years ago. Settlement of more offshore islands had to await the development of easily stored root crops and domesticated animals and the refinement of the double-hulled offshore canoe and navigational techniques, which were effective out of sight of land.

A second major controversy in New Guinea archaeology revolves around the origins of agriculture. Did food production spread into New Guinea, and from there into the Pacific from mainland Asia, or were the densely forested New Guinea highlands an independent center of early agriculture? There is said to be archaeological evidence for diversion of water into the fields from the *Kuk Basin in the highlands dating to about 7000 B.C., with clear pollen evidence for taro or yam cultivation by 3000 to 4000 B.C., with highly developed agricultural drainage systems a millennium later. But the evidence for independent development or introduction remains uncertain. Certainly, taro and yam cultivation was widespread throughout the southwestern Pacific by 1500 B.C., when the *Lapita complex flourished on the islands and began colonizing Melanesia.

The modern environment of Australia was established

by 4000 B.C., but foraging continued to be the staple throughout the continent until historic times. While tool kits appear to become smaller and more efficient after that date, opinions differ as to why this change took place. Was it due to rising population densities and a need for more effective ways of exploiting food resources? Or does the increased number of archaeological sites reflect a higher survival rate for more recent settlements? As Frankel argues, many such changes may document small-scale local adaptations to purely local events, as Australian Aborigines responded to different circumstances in a wide variety of ways.

With European settlement in 1788, millennia of aboriginal culture were disrupted with bewildering rapidity. Graham Connah describes how historical archaeologists are using the archaeological record of recent times to study not only the evolution of European architecture but also relationships and interactions between aborigines and newcomers, and between different segments of colonial society. Recent excavations have also shown how settler culture developed fundamental differences from those of the many homelands from which the immigrants came.

[See also LAPITA COMPLEX; NEW GUINEA, ORIGINS OF FOOD PRODUCTION IN; PACIFIC ISLANDS; SETTLEMENT OF MELANESIA AND MICRONESIA; ROCK ART: AUSTRALIAN ROCK ART.]
Brian M. Fagan

FIRST SETTLEMENT OF SUNDA AND SAHUL

Humans colonized Australia and New Guinea during the Late *Pleistocene period. Currently, views on the general timing of first landfall range from 40,000 B.P. to beyond 120,000 B.P. A review of the data and arguments for these chronologies is best set in a context of the behavioral achievement of this colonization.

Until the seas rose after the last glaciation New Guinea, Australia, and Tasmania formed a single Pleistocene continent, popularly called either Sahul or Greater Australia. This continent stretched from almost at the equator to about 40 degrees south and across almost 40 degrees of latitude at its widest point. Although it is characterized by low physical relief, its very size presented human arrivals with a great diversity of environments, from tropical coasts and islands in the north, through continental deserts at its center, to periglacial and glacial uplands in its southeastern extremes. However, glaciations had fewer direct effects on human settlement than associated climate changes and, most particularly, changing sea levels.

Water Barriers and Sailing Efficiency. Greater Australia has been physically separated from Southeast Asia for some fifty million years. Even at the times of lowest sea levels, water crossings of at least ninety kilometers provided an effective barrier to terrestrial animal migration in either direction; rats and bats are the only placental mammals to have managed the crossing independent of human intervention. When humans crossed this divide they moved into a region populated by marsupials rather than the primates, elephants, carnivores, and ungulates of Asia. This barrier also excluded earlier hominids. *Homo erectus* reached Java well over a million years ago but could not move farther through the transition zone of the present-day eastern Indonesian islands, also called Wallacea, after Alfred Russel Wallace, who first recognized this biogeographical boundary in 1860.

The marine barrier to entry into Greater Australia has dominated reconstructions of initial human colonization.

Two possible routes have been favored, a northern route into the western end of present-day New Guinea, which presented the shortest sea crossings, and a southern route from Java through Flores and Timor. There is presently no archaeological evidence to favor either route above the other. Earlier minimalist views concluded that landfalls must have been both accidental and rare. More recent views, based on reconstructions of wind and water currents, intervisibility between islands, and the sizes of target islands, all coupled with computer-simulated voyages, have tempered this view. It was always possible to reach Greater Australia from Southeast Asia and to see the next island before leaving the occupied one; however, when sailing from New Britain (on the eastern side of Papua New Guinea) to the Solomon Islands, one cannot see the target island from the shore of the occupied island. This last crossing was achieved by 29,000 B.P. As well, obsidian was being regularly moved 218 miles (350 kms) from New Britain to New Ireland by 20,000 B.P., a journey that involved a 19-mile (30-km) water crossing. While a direct and conclusive demonstration of the frequency and purposeful nature of early human arrivals into Greater Australia may not be forthcoming, such evidence as exists suggests that Wallacea provided perhaps the earliest voyaging nursery in the world.

Choosing between deliberate and frequent landings on the one hand and rare and accidental ones on the other carries many implications for understanding the nature of the early colonization of Greater Australia. Whether Pleistocene human fossils in Greater Australia represent two separate groups, one physically robust and the other gracile, or merely a variation within a single group might be resolved by knowing how often and from more precisely where early colonists arrived. Unfortunately, at present the human fossil record in Australia dates only to perhaps 30,000 years after the earliest landfall, so that external comparisons are difficult. There is no suggestion, however, that Greater Australia was not settled by anatomically modern humans. As well, previous efforts to calculate the smallest biologically viable group of initial colonists are obviated if regular external additions to the population were the norm. Finally, deliberate voyages imply purposeful watercraft; the levels of technological competence that watercraft connote take on greater significance as the antiquity for humans in Greater Australia increases.

The Timing of Initial Colonization. The identification of increased amounts of charcoal in pollen cores taken at several locations across Greater Australia has led some geomorphologists to argue that more frequent fires on the landscape reflect human presence in Greater Australia by or before 120,000 B.P. Similarly, a riverine shell accumulation near Warrnambool in Victoria, thought to date at least to 80,000 B.P., has also been attributed to humans. However, no direct archaeological evidence supports these claims. Such an antiquity, if demonstrated, would demand many reassessments including, perhaps, the accepted modernity of the earliest colonists.

Most archaeological sites in Greater Australia have been dated using the radiocarbon method. An initial antiquity dating to 10,000 B.P. in the early 1960s had increased fourfold by the early 1980s. During the last decade, radiocarbon dates between 34,000 B.P. and 37,000 B.P. have been determined for archaeological sites in the farthest corners of the Pleistocene continent—from the north coast and offshore islands of Papua New Guinea to the periglacial uplands of southwest Tasmania and from the southwest and northwest of Western Australia to northern Queensland. The lack of time gradients in this distribution argues for rapid dispersal of perhaps only several thousand years after initial human occupation into all areas except the central desert region, where the oldest radiocarbon date yet established is about 29,000 B.P.

By 1990 the thermoluminescence technique had been used to date a New Guinean site on the Huon Peninsula to about 40,000 B.P., and a gravel bed near Sydney, thought to contain human artifacts, to between 40,000 B.P. and 47,000 B.P., but the association of dates and artifacts, especially of the latter site, are at least arguable. These dates did not extend the chronology of settlement much beyond the projected dates of radiocarbon, allowing for possible underestimations by that technique. However, since 1990, thermoluminescence and optical luminescence techniques have been used to date the earliest occupations at Malakunanja II and Nauwalabila I, two rock shelters in western Arnhem Land, in the north of Australia, to between 52,000 B.P. and 60,000 B.P.

The older antiquity proposed by luminescence dating is not fully accepted in Australia, because of the great gap between it and that provided by radiocarbons. Arguments by proponents of the luminescence chronology that radiocarbon ages in Greater Australia are at the limits of the technique seem improbable, given that many radiocarbon determinations for geological sites exceed 37,000 B.P. and reach beyond 50,000 B.P. Resolving the discrepancy between these techniques is of primary importance. If the luminescence chronology is verified, it may be that there is a longer chronology for humans in the north but not in the south, which would refute the radiocarbon notion of rapid dispersal of humans as part of the initial colonization. Alternatively a longer chronology may prevail over most of the continent. Greater Australia in the Late Pleistocene lacked extinct faunal successions and temporally and regionally distinctive stone artifact types that elsewhere provide relative chronological structures for reconstructing prehistory. Instead radiometric dating has provided the fundamental framework in which to interpret the past, and radical changes to the chronology will affect many existing interpretations.

Population Dispersal in Greater Australia. While determining rates of human dispersal in Greater Australia relies in part on future chronological clarification, there is also no consensus on other determinants such as the probable rates of demographic growth or the occurrence of frequency of subsequent human migrations into Greater Australia. Internal routes of dispersal have also been argued theoretically, but available data are too few to choose between options, especially since these are equally linked with chronology and demography. A popular model of colonization involving initial movement around the coasts and up the major river systems has been weakened over the last decade with the location of many of the oldest sites well inland, with the few Pleistocene coastal sites to have survived the last marine transgression returning no older dates.

Essentially, however, these are the questions of earlier generations. Current research emphasizes early local adaptations to a wide range of environments and the degree of variability in the nature of settlement in different regions. Overall there is clearer understanding of the human achievement of settling a previously empty Pleistocene continent where adaptation to a foreign flora and fauna was fundamental. Individual achievements now documented

have corrected an earlier view that saw the region as one of the most unenterprising parts of the Late Pleistocene world. The lack of elaborate Pleistocene lithic industries in Greater Australia is offset by the inventiveness of other technologies, which are as early or earlier than elsewhere. Mention has been made of Pleistocene maritime technology and long-distance movements of commodities like obsidian; in addition there is now evidence for waisted (and thus presumably hafted) axes for forest clearance on the Huon Peninsula, Papua New Guinea, at ca. 40,000 B.P.; marine fishing at Matenkupkum Cave, New Ireland, at ca. 35,000 B.P.; the use of ocher for personal decoration and/or cave art at Nauwalabila I Rockshelter, Northern Territory, at ca. 53,000 B.P.; twenty-three shell beads used as personal decoration from Mandu Mandu Creek Rockshelter, Western Australia, at ca. 32,000 B.P.; an ocher-decorated burial from Lake Mungo, New South Wales, at ca. 26,000 B.P.; and structured wallaby hunting in the periglacial uplands of southwest Tasmania from ca. 35,000 B.P. onward. The colonization of Greater Australia carries important implications for Late Pleistocene world prehistory.

■ Jim Allen, Jack Golson, and Rhys Jones, eds., *Sahul and Sunda: Prehistoric Studies in Southeast Asia, Melanesia and Australia* (1977). J. Peter White, with James F. O'Connell, *A Prehistory of Australia, New Guinea and Sahul* (1982). Josephine Flood, *Archaeology of the Dreamtime* (1983, rev. ed. 1989). John Dodson, ed., *The Naive Lands* (1992). Geoffrey Irwin, *The Prehistoric Exploration and Colonization of the Pacific* (1992). John Ross, ed., *Chronicle of Australia* (1993). Mike A. Smith, Matthew Spriggs, and Barry Fankhauser, eds., *Sahul in Review* (1993). Matthew Spriggs et al., eds., *A Community of Culture: The People and Prehistory of the Pacific* (1993).

Jim Allen

ABORIGINAL PEOPLES OF AUSTRALIA

Australian prehistory is entirely that of mobile or semisedentary hunter-gatherer peoples. The majority of archaeological sites are surface scatters of stone tools, shell middens, or rock shelters. Ecological conditions play an important role in most archaeological analysis, at both continental and site-specific scales.

There is a wide array of climates and environments across the approx 3.1 million square miles (8 million sq. km) of the Australian continent. Apart from the north-south variation from tropics to cool temperate regimes, a dominant factor is the contrast between the arid center and the better-watered coastal fringe. The extent and structure of ecological zones fluctuated with changes in global climate. During glacial periods lower sea levels exposed the continental shelf, periodically linking the mainland with the large islands of Tasmania to the south and New Guinea to the north. At no time was this enlarged area (called Sahul) joined to any lands to the north.

There are two competing theories on the origins of the first Australians, based on different weighting given to observed variation in skeletal remains and alternative views of the origin and spread of fully modern humans. One model, requiring a contemporaneous evolution of *Homo sapiens* in different regions, emphasizes differences within the Australian material, and derives a robust series of crania (such as those found at Kow Swamp) from ancestral populations in Java and a gracile series (as at Keilor and Mungo) from a Chinese ancestry. These two racial types are regarded as maintaining their distinct form until after the end of the Pleistocene (about 10,000 years ago). An increasingly favored alternative is of a common source population with variation developing within Australia as a result of particular patterns of settlement and social interaction.

All movement into Australia involved substantial voyages across open ocean. The date of first arrival and the timing and nature of initial colonization of different parts of the continent form a major focus of interest. There is general agreement that people arrived in Australia from the Indonesian region by 40,000 B.P., with some suggestion of earlier material. Early dates are reported from a variety of sites and environments in the tropical north: from mainland New Guinea (Huon Peninsula, 40,000 B.P.); New Ireland (Matenkupkum, 33,000 B.P.), and northern Australia (Malakununja II, 52,000 B.P.; Nurrabullgin, 37,000 B.P.). Early sites are also known from southern regions: in Western Australia (Upper Swan, 38,000 B.P.); the Willandra Lakes region in western New South Wales (36,000 B.P.); and southwestern Tasmania (Warreen, 35,000 B.P.). The varied location, structure, and contents of these sites provide evidence for a rapid spread into very different environments. Early Australians made use of both coastal and inland regions, with associated adaptations to local conditions in all the better favored parts of the continent. The arid areas of central Australia may not have been inhabited until considerably later (Puritjarra, 22,000 B.P.), although there is mounting evidence that rock engravings in semiarid areas may be over 30,000 years old.

Some Australian archaeologists maintain an artificial division between the Holocene (the last 10,000 years) and the earlier Pleistocene periods. They regard the entire Pleistocene as having a low population density; a common, very generalized economic strategy; and a uniform stone tool technology characterized by large core tools and steepedged scrapers (the Core Tool and Scraper Tradition). It is increasingly recognized that there was always a great variety in all these aspects, with local adaptations to different and changing environmental conditions.

Conditions from about 32,000 B.P. to 24,000 B.P. were particularly favorable. Campsites on the shores of inland lakes in western New South Wales (Mungo and other lakes of the Willandra system) and inland caves in southwest Tasmania (Warreen, ORS 7, Nunamira) show long periods of regular and uniform use of these very different regions. People in western New South Wales developed an economy based largely on the resources of the lakes (fish, shellfish, and the plants and animals from the surrounding region). Burials and cremations beside Lake Mungo provide evidence of early funerary customs. Contemporary Tasmanians maintained a specialized strategy based in part on hunting red-necked wallabies in the southern highlands. Similar well-established local adaptations may be suggested for other regions.

From 22,000 B.P., with the onset of the last glaciation, there was increasing aridity accompanied by colder and windier conditions. By the time of the glacial maximum, about 18,000 B.P., the inland lakes had dried up, resulting in a redistribution of population and new social and economic patterns of land use. Most of the population probably lived on the expanded coastal plains, but there is some evidence of continued occupation in highland regions of New Guinea, Tasmania, and New South Wales, as well as parts of the more arid interior.

After 15,000 B.P. warmer, wetter conditions returned, but areas such as western New South Wales remained semiarid, and the extensive lake systems of earlier times never refilled. From about 12,000 B.P. the post-Pleistocene rise in sea level began to flood the continental shelf, restructuring

coastal environments and incidentally submerging all traces of earlier coastal economies. By 8,000 B.P. New Guinea and Tasmania were permanently cut off from the mainland. The effects of these major changes on local ecology and resource availability are well documented in art sites in tropical Arnhem Land, where different species are depicted at different times.

By the mid-Holocene (6,000–5,000 B.P.) conditions were broadly the same as those of the present, although there have been constant fluctuations in local climate and resources. There are two main approaches to explaining archaeological changes in the last few thousand years. One approach emphasizes local variation and diversity, explained as short-term responses to changes in the immediate environment. The other emphasizes common elements and a related series of developments.

Eastern South Australia and Victoria provide an example of one regional sequence for the last 10,000 years. Until about 8,000 B.P. there were two regional stone tool traditions (the Kartan and the Gambieran) along the eastern coast of South Australia. The economy was based partly on coastal resources, including seals, with a reliance on inland swamps. The earliest known wooden artifacts (spears, digging sticks, and boomerangs) come from Wyrie Swamp, together with Gambieran tools dated to about 10,000 B.P. Contemporary burials at Kow Swamp on the Murray River are of a robust population, which some trace back to a Javanese ancestry but which can more plausibly be related to later burials to show the development of local genetic groupings as a result of long-lasting patterns of interaction along the course of this major river.

There is comparatively little archaeological evidence for the period between about 8,000 and 5,000 B.P. in this and many other areas of temperate Australia. After this time there are increasing numbers of dated sites, especially coastal shell middens. During the last few thousand years in Victoria new types of sites appear, including low earth mounds (in some areas the by-product of earth ovens and in others representing a change in housing). Facilities such as fish and eel traps are also known, and the distribution of greenstone hatchet heads from favored quarries demonstrates extensive intergroup relationships.

From 4,000 B.P. new stone tool types, particularly *microliths, appear in this and other areas. These are often seen as components of the Small Tool Tradition, although the unity and significance of this tradition has been seriously questioned. Some of the new formal types, such as the Bondi Point (a microlithic-backed blade) are found across much of temperate Australia. At about the same time the dingo (a distinctive breed of domestic dog) first appears in Australia. While many archaeologists assume an association between the advent of the Small Tool Tradition and the dingo, their spread involves very different mechanisms. The dingo was certainly imported, but they may have spread through the continent on their own. The new tool types were probably developed in Australia, and their distribution must have involved connections between different regions. Some archaeologists argue for a link between these new elements and the increase in site numbers, which they take to be a direct reflection of a growth in population. They see these changes as part of an intensification of production and an increase in the scale of social interaction. This model of widespread intensification has been adopted for many areas, imposing a common, unilineal view of evolutionary change, leading directly to the social systems observed by Europeans in the late eighteenth and nineteenth centuries.

Another view of recent Australian prehistory rejects the idea that an increase in numbers of sites means an increase in population. It is, instead, the result of the greater survival of recent sites. This is especially true for coastal shell middens. Other changes reflect small-scale local adaptations to particular circumstances. Aboriginal lifeways of the nineteenth century need not be the result of a directional trend toward greater social and economic complexity. Rather they are the accidental result of local events and illustrate the diversity of responses by Australian hunter-gatherers to different circumstances.

The European invasion of Australia was very rapid. Within fifty years of first colonization in 1788 Aboriginal people in the southern temperate regions had suffered massive disruption and, in some areas, almost complete annihilation. In the tropics and the arid regions populations were less speedily and less drastically affected.

[See also HUMANS, MODERN: PEOPLING OF THE GLOBE.]

■ J. Peter White and James F. O'Connell, *A Prehistory of Australia, New Guinea and Sahul* (1982). D. John Mulvaney and J. Peter White, eds., *Australians to 1788* (1987). Josephine Flood, *Archaeology of the Dreamtime*, 2nd ed. (1989). David Frankel, *Remains to Be Seen: Archaeological Insights into Australian Prehistory* (1991). John Dodson, ed., *The Naive Lands* (1992). Michael A. Smith, Matthew Spriggs, and Barry Fankhauser, eds., *Sahul in Review: Pleistocene Archaeology in Australia, New Guinea and Island Melanesia* (1993).

David Frankel

THE ARCHAEOLOGY OF EUROPEAN SETTLEMENT IN AUSTRALIA

Although Dutch and British ships had been wrecked on the coasts of Australia during the seventeenth and eighteenth centuries, it was only in 1788 that European settlement commenced. This was at Sydney, and the first to arrive was a large number of British convicts, together with guards and officials. Transported convicts contributed substantially to the European settlement of Australia until after the middle of the nineteenth century, but free settlers also arrived in increasing numbers, particularly after gold was discovered in the 1850s. Although most nineteenth-century settlers came from the British Isles, large numbers of Germans went to South Australia; many Chinese worked on the gold fields, although most eventually returned home. The total population remained small until the middle of the twentieth century, when there was a substantial immigration of Italians, Greeks, various other European nationalities, and, more recently, people from Southeast Asia. Settlement continued to concentrate in the southeastern corner of Australia, but by 1900 settlers had penetrated, although often only thinly, nearly every part of the continent. This extraordinarily rapid settlement of such a large landmass, compared with the relatively slow occupation of the United States, was probably because the settlement of Australia commenced late enough to benefit from the technological advances brought about by Europe's so-called Industrial Revolution.

The documentary sources for the European settlement of Australia are very extensive and often very detailed, but they tend to be official records or accounts by people some way up the socioeconomic ladder. Convicts of both sexes, free settlers trying to carve out a living for themselves, Aborigines trying to survive the impact of European expansion, and many more were either illiterate, semiliterate, or too busy to have left much for us to read. In addition, the cultural adaptation that resulted from history's longest-known mass migration can be studied more readily from material evidence than from written sources. For these and other reasons, including the opportunity to test archaeological methods and theories in controlled situations, archaeologists have developed since the 1970s a considerable interest in the physical traces of European settlement in Australia. Some of these remains require excavation, particularly where former structures were made of perishable materials or have been subsequently demolished, but much of the evidence is above ground and is often in a fairly complete state.

Thus the historical archaeologist in Australia is able to study the evolution of the Australian house and other buildings, the growth of cities and towns, the failure and disappearance of some settlements, the prisons in which the convicts lived and the public works that they labored on, the impact of pastoral and arable agriculture on the varied landscapes, the depredations of past mining, the remnants of defunct secondary industries, the development of communications, the achievements of the engineers, and the countless movable artifacts of iron, glass, ceramic, and other materials that litter the surface of the continent as witness to the burgeoning production of British, European, American, and Australian factories. Study of this huge variety of physical evidence can shed light on those aspects of Australia's historical past that are neglected in the documents and beyond the reach of living memory. It can do more than supplement historical evidence, however; it has the capacity to generate new and important questions about the character of European settlement in Australia. Of these, perhaps the most important are those that seek detailed information about the environmental consequences of European settlement or about the character of the colonization process. Furthermore, in the archaeological records one can trace the gradual emergence of Australian culture as something distinct and different from the cultures of the settlers' homelands. One can also investigate the tragic consequences of the sudden contact between European agriculturalists and Aboriginal hunter-gatherers.

Australian historical archaeology is a new area of scholarship, but already there is a growing body of published research work; particularly for the states of New South Wales, Victoria, and Tasmania. Much of this work results from the demands of cultural resource management, for there is an increasing public concern for the conservation of Australia's historical heritage. In addition, because of the character of the evidence, research in Australian historical archaeology frequently requires collaboration with historians, geographers, architects, engineers, metallurgists, soil scientists, agronomists, botanists, industrial chemists, and many other specialists. Nevertheless, archaeology is beginning to provide a fuller, richer picture of the European settlement of Australia than is available from documents alone.

[See also PACIFIC ISLANDS: EUROPEAN VOYAGERS AND THE END OF PREHISTORY IN THE PACIFIC ISLANDS.]

■ J. Birmingham, I. Jack, and D. Jeans, *Australian Pioneer Technology: Sites and Relics* (1979). D. Denholm, *The Colonial Australians* (1979). D. N. Jeans and P. Spearritt, *The Open Air Museum: The Cultural Landscape of New South Wales* (1980). J. Birmingham, I. Jack, and D. Jeans, *Industrial Archaeology in Australia: Rural Industry* (1983). D. N. Jeans, ed., *Australian Historical Landscapes* (1984). G. Henderson, *Maritime Archaeology in Australia* (1986). G. Connah, *The Archae-*

ology of Australia's History (1993). R. I. Jack and A. Cremin, Australia's Age of Iron: History and Archaeology (1994).

Graham Connah

AUSTRALOPITHECUS AND HOMO HABILIS. The African genus *Australopithecus* includes several species of early human ancestors and collateral relatives. Sometime before two million years ago one of these species gave rise to humans via the earliest, most primitive species of our genus, *Homo habilis.*

History of Discovery and Interpretation. In 1925 Raymond *Dart named a new genus and species, *Australopithecus africanus.* Dart proposed that the fossilized child's skull from Taung, South Africa, represented a bipedal species ancestral to later humans. Other authorities challenged this interpretation. More complete cranial and postcranial remains of *Australopithecus africanus* were found by paleontologist Robert Broom at Sterkfontein in the 1930s and 1940s. In 1938, Broom added another species to the genus, recovering a partial skull with a larger face and jaw from Kromdraai, South Africa. Broom named it *Paranthropus robustus* (most authorities include this species in *Australopithecus,* and have dropped the genus name). In 1948 Broom and John Robinson began to recover additional examples of *Australopithecus robustus* at nearby Swartkrans. For the first time they demonstrated two contemporary hominid species in Plio-Pleistocene times—early *Homo* and robust *Australopithecus.* Robinson's work on fossils of *Australopithecus africanus* and *Australopithecus robustus* led him to a to a formulate a "dietary hypothesis," whereby the former species had humanlike proportions of front and back teeth indicating an omnivorous diet, and the robust species had huge teeth and jaws indicative of a vegetarian diet.

In 1959, after an intermittent search of over twenty-five years, Mary Leakey, wife of Louis Leakey, found a hominid cranium at *Olduvai Gorge in eastern Africa. Unlike the difficult-to-interpret, poorly dated *Australopithecus*-bearing cave infillings in South Africa, Olduvai's strata were arranged in an orderly fashion, with interbedded volcanic strata amenable to radiometric dating. Bed I, low in the gorge, yielded the massive, robust hominid cranium that Leakey named *Zinjanthropus boisei.* Most workers immediately recognized this specimen as a northern cousin of *Australopithecus robustus,* but Louis Leakey insisted that he had found a direct human ancestor dating to 1.8 million years ago. Further excavations in Bed I revealed the contemporary fragmentary remains of a juvenile hominid whose larger braincase and smaller teeth made it a better candidate for human ancestry. Leakey joined Phillip Tobias and John Napier in naming a new, initially disputed species, *Homo habilis,* in 1964, relegating *Australopithecus boisei* to a collateral position.

Beginning with Olduvai, much new work took place in eastern Africa's rift. During the late 1960s and early 1970s Clark Howell, Yves Coppens, and colleagues recovered hominid fossils spanning the period 1 to 3.4 million years from the Omo Valley of southern Ethiopia. Richard Leakey's work at *Koobi Fora in Kenya established the validity of *Homo habilis* as a taxon distinct from *Australopithecus africanus.* The work of Mary Leakey's team at Laetoli in Tanzania, and the efforts of Maurice Taieb, Don Johanson, and their colleagues in Ethiopia's *Afar Triangle at Hadar led to the discovery of even more ancient fossil hominids. These remains were attributed by Johanson, Tim White, and Coppens to a primitive species of *Australopithe-*cus, *A. afarensis* in 1978. In the 1980s the validity of *Australopithecus aethiopicus* was confirmed at West Turkana in Kenya. Associated cranial and postcranial remains of *Homo habilis* were found at Olduvai. Excavations at Sterkfontein yielded a large sample of hominids and fauna. In the early 1990s continuing work by White and his colleague Desmond Clark in the Middle Awash resulted in the recovery of fossil hominids that predate four million years. These fossils, the earliest hominid ancestors, were placed by T. White, Gen Suwa, and Berhane Asfaw into a new species of *Australopithecus, Australopithecus ramidus,* in 1994, and into a new genus *Ardipithecus* in 1995. The earliest species of *Australopithecus* is *A. anamensis,* named in 1995 by Meave Leakey and Alan Walker.

Australopithecus Today. *Australopithecus* appears in the record at about 4 million years ago, but slightly older jaw and limb fragments may also belong to the genus. The youngest *Australopithecus* specimens are from deposits a little beyond one million years ago and are contemporary with *Homo erectus.* Comparisons between the DNA of modern humans and living great apes of Africa (the chimpanzees and the gorilla) have shown that these creatures, the pongids, are our closest living relatives. *Australopithecus* was neither an ape nor a human. All *Australopithecus* species had skeletons consistent with upright, striding bipedalism, and this unique hominid mode of locomotion is indicated in many parts of the skeleton. The fossilized Laetoli footprints attributed to this species are consistent with this interpretation of the skeletal anatomy. The genus is therefore included in our own zoological family, the Hominidae. Virtually all bones of the body are known for *A. afarensis* and *A. africanus,* but skeletal parts for *A. robustus* and *A. boisei* are more poorly known, and *A. aethiopicus* is unknown below the cranium.

There is much body size variation in all known species of *Australopithecus,* much of this probably attributable to sexual dimorphism. Some aspects of early *Australopithecus* postcranial skeletal anatomy such as long, curved finger and toe phalanges may be holdovers of primitive traits from an ape ancestor. Alternatively, some workers consider such traits to indicate semiarboreal existence. The fundamental musculoskeletal differences between *Australopithecus* and pongids in the foot, the knee, and the pelvis, however, indicate abandonment of the arboreal substrate and commitment to terrestrial bipedalism.

All *Australopithecus* species lacked the strongly projecting, pointed canines seen in great apes. Another generic trait is the large size of the teeth relative to the body size, a phenomenon known as megadontia. This suggests that *Australopithecus* consumed low-quality foods requiring heavy chewing. This is particularly true of the extremely megadont, specialized robust *Australopithecus* species. None of the *Australopithecus* species had substantially enlarged braincases, and most known cranial capacities lie between 25 and 37 cubic inches (400 and 600 cu cm)—about a third as large as the braincases of modern people. *Australopithecus* is therefore a creature whose body had evolved toward the human condition considerably sooner than its brain did—a good example of "mosaic evolution."

The genus *Australopithecus* was exclusively African, and intermittent claims for its presence in China and Java have usually been based on fragmentary remains belonging to early *Homo. Australopithecus* fossils have been found in eastern and southern Africa but this is not an accurate characterization of genus distribution. Other parts of Africa have not been so well explored or do not have depositional environments conducive to the preservation of ancient skeletal remains. The earliest *Australopithecus* populations were ecologically widespread, from the dry, upland wooded savannah at Laetoli to the more bushy, highland lakeside environment at Hadar. Given these wide ecological tolerances, it is likely that even the earliest *Australopithecus* populations were very widespread in Africa.

Possibly as a response to his critics' dismissal of *Australopithecus africanus* as a hominid ancestor, Raymond Dart spent much of his career investigating the bones found intermingled with hominid fossils in South African cave breccias. Concentrating on the Makapansgat site, Dart interpreted antelope bone disproportions and fragmentation as evidence for hominid modification. He imagined a pre-stone-tool culture for *Australopithecus africanus* in which bone, teeth, and horn were used for implements. Dart called this the "osteodontokeratic" culture, and he described *Australopithecus africanus* as an omnivorous hunting species. These ideas have been tested by actualistic research on modern human and nonhuman carnivore bone accumulations, and cast into doubt by C. K. Brain and others.

Despite concentrated searches in appropriate contexts, no recognizable stone or bone implements, nor any other evidence of materially based cultural activity such as cut marks on bones, has yet been found with the earliest species of *Australopithecus*. Modern chimpanzees, however, make and use tools of perishable materials, and this suggests a sort of minimal baseline against which early *Australopithecus* cultural behaviors might be judged. Evidence for material culture in later *Australopithecus* is even more clouded by the presence of at least one other contemporary hominid lineage that evolves into humans. The earliest stone tools in the fossil record are Oldowan assemblages from about 2.6 million years ago. This is a period from which there is evidence of a robust *Australopithecus* as well as at least one other lineage leading to *Homo habilis* in eastern Africa. It is widely assumed that members of the latter lineage were authors of the stone tools, but there is anatomically nothing that would have prevented members of both lineages from making and using stone tools.

The earliest and most apelike of six widely recognized *Australopithecus* species is *A. anamensis* from Kenya. It was the ancestor of *Australopithecus afarensis*, which is, in turn, widely considered to be the ancestor of all later hominids. *A. anamensis* descended from *Ardipithecus ramidus* sometime after 4.4 million years ago. One evolving lineage in eastern Africa links *A. afarensis* with the descendant species *A. aethiopicus* (ca. 2.3–2.6 million years ago [Myr]) and *A. boisei* (ca. 1–2 Myr). The latter went extinct. *Australopithecus africanus* (ca. 2.5–2.8 Myr) may have been the exclusive ancestor to either *Homo habilis* (ca. 1.7–2.3 Myr) or to *A. robustus* (ca. 1.8 Myr). Alternatively, it might have been a common ancestor to both, or an evolutionary dead end. Species distinctions and phylogenetic reconstructions within *Australopithecus* are based on comparisons of the cranial and dental anatomy.

Many controversial issues persist in the study of *Australopithecus* and *Homo habilis*. There is debate over whether the three species *A. afarensis*, *A. africanus*, and *Homo habilis* should each be broken into smaller species because of the large variation in size and morphology seen in each. There is debate over the mode and tempo of evolution in the various species, and there is heated controversy over the evolutionary relationships among them. Also unresolved is the question of which or how many of these taxa were responsible for manufacturing stone tools, and how the various species members subsisted and locomoted. Some of these problems, like species recognition, are intrinsic to the fossil record. Most of the problems and ongoing debates result from an inadequate fossil record, but accelerated fossil recovery has established the presence of *Australopithecus* in human ancestry and revealed a more complex and interesting picture of our origins and evolution than was once thought possible.

[See also AFRICA: PREHISTORY OF AFRICA; GENETICS IN ARCHAEOLOGY; HUMAN EVOLUTION.]

■ Lewis R. Binford, *Bone: Ancient Men and Modern Myths* (1981). Charles K. Brain, *The Hunters or the Hunted?* (1981). John Reader, *Missing Links* (1981). Eric Delson, ed., *Ancestors: The Hard Evidence* (1985). Roger Lewin, *Bones of Contention* (1987). Frederick E. Grine, *Evolutionary History of the "Robust" Australopithecines* (1988). Richard G. Klein, *The Human Career* (1989).

Tim D. White

AVEBURY. A very large enclosure and complex of stone settings, Avebury is a Late Neolithic ritual site in central-southern England that is so well preserved in its earth-built features that it shows well the grandeur of these places in their original scale.

At Avebury, a roughly circular area some 985 feet (300 m) in diameter is enclosed by a deep ditch, dug into the chalk. The spoil dug out from it was piled into a bank, set outside the ditch. Even today, after some 4,500 years of erosion, the crest of the bank stands up to 26 feet (8 m) above the ditch floor. Originally the bank was higher, and the ditch was nearly twice its present depth; a photograph from the excavations at the turn of the twentieth century shows the workmen standing on the giant steps that they had cut, one above another, deep into the accumulated fill. As is characteristic of the henge monuments of which Avebury is a very splendid and very large example, the bank is on the outside, where it would give attackers the advantage over defenders inside; for this reason the henges are not thought to be defensive in intent.

Round the inner edge of the enclosed circular area runs a setting of well-spaced and unshaped sarsen stones, one of the largest of British stone circles. There were further stone settings inside, more circles, and a "cove" constructed of three great slabs that stood together to make an open-ended box. From one of the original four entrances, an "avenue" made of paired upright stones ran along a valley for .6 miles (1 km) to the sanctuary, a small stone circle recorded by William Stukeley in the eighteenth century before a farmer broke the stones up. The stones of the main Avebury circles were, for the most part, buried or broken up either in medieval times or about Stukeley's day. The ones seen now were for the most part excavated and reerected in position in the 1920s and 1930s. The many eighteenth- and nineteenth-century houses in the modern village of Avebury that are built of broken sarsen blocks are further memorials to what has gone. Air photography has detected some sites flattened completely by plowing; nearby, another great circular enclosure, demarcated by a palisade fence of close-set posts, came to light in the 1980s.

In the environs of Avebury are many other important sites of the Neolithic and Bronze Age. The most famous and puzzling is Silbury Hill, a giant flat-topped barrow that is the largest artificial mound of prehistoric Europe; its exploration by shaft and by tunnel in the nineteenth and twentieth centuries has found no burial at its center. The nature and purpose of Silbury Hill, which dates a little later than Avebury and broadly contemporary with *Stonehenge, remains unknown. Above Avebury, on the summit of Windmill Hill, is a smaller, slighter, and older circular causewayed enclosure which may have functioned as its predecessor.

This ritual landscape of sacred and ceremonial sites around Avebury echoes the similar complex around Stonehenge, about 19 miles (30 km) to the south. Avebury, reckoned to date a few hundred years earlier than Stonehenge, shares many features with its more famous sister monument. Each has settings of stone circles within a bank and ditch, and the entrance approach to each is marked by a long avenue. Yet the particulars are different. Avebury is very large, and Stonehenge is small. The Avebury stone circles, made of the same sarsen rock, are unshaped, well spaced, and have no horizontal lintels, whereas the Stonehenge sarsens are shaped, close-set, and support lintels. The Avebury avenue is of parallel lines of stones, and the Stonehenge avenue is of parallel banks of earthy chalk. The same goes for the ritual landscapes of their environs, which have a profusion of burial mounds in common, and other earth, wood, and stone structures each peculiar to that particular complex.

[See also BRITISH ISLES: PREHISTORY OF THE BRITISH ISLES; CAMPS AND ENCLOSURES, CAUSEWAYED; STONE CIRCLES AND ALIGNMENTS.]

■ Aubrey Burl, *Prehistoric Avebury* (1979).

Christopher Chippindale

AZTEC CIVILIZATION

Introduction
The Rise of Aztec Civilization
Economic Organization of Aztec Civilization
The Spanish Conquest of the Aztecs

INTRODUCTION

According to their own accounts, the Aztecs originally composed seven Chichimec tribes who called themselves the people of Aztlan, or Land of the Heron, a legendary place of origin located in western Mexico. Drawn by their marginal participation in trading networks dominated by the Toltecs who controlled the Valley of Mexico from A.D. 950 to 1150, the Aztecs migrated to the Valley of Mexico between the twelfth and fourteenth centuries. Many encountered tremendous hostility from their Toltec hosts, who attempted to exterminate them, while others were eventually assimilated.

One tribe, called the Mexica, discovered that they could affect the balance of power in the region by lending their support to one or the other of the Tolteca-Chichimeca factions that were continually embroiled in struggles around the southern end of Lake Texcoco. Despite early setbacks, including exile to an island in Lake Texcoco, the Mexica skillfully exploited their military prowess and eventually admitted themselves into local alliance networks by electing a ruler, who claimed descent from the Toltec line of Culhuacan, named Acamapichtli (1372–1391).

Early attempts to consolidate the region militarily by the city-state of Azcapotzalco eventually met with disaster at the hands of an alliance between the cities of Texcoco and *Tenochtitlán, the Mexica capital. The latter two allies then incorporated their former enemy and created the powerful Triple Alliance. Under the expert leadership of a succession of six Mexica emperors, the Triple Alliance embarked on a program of military expansion by first dominating the basin of Mexico and then expanding into the states of Morelos, Guerrero, Veracruz, Puebla, and Oaxaca. Attempts to penetrate the Tarascan Empire to the west failed with a crushing defeat. Tlaxcala on the other hand was simply surrounded and cut off from assistance by any of their former confederates.

The city of Tenochtitlán, together with neighboring Tlatelolco, boasted a population of nearly 200,000, making it one of the largest cities in the world. The wealth that flowed into this capital from hundreds of tributary city-states allowed the Aztecs to engage in the construction of massive public works, including the erection of miles of aqueducts that brought fresh water into the city daily, a protective dike across Lake Texcoco, and a massive system of raised fields called *chinampas* that increased the agricultural potential of their island city 1,000-fold. Under the able guidance of two emperors, Nezahualcoyotl and Nezahualpilli, Texcoco not only enriched itself but became a renowned center of learning.

By 1500, Aztec social organization had become extremely complicated, fusing elements of both the old Toltec city-state and Chichimec tribal organizations together with a new imperial order. The emperor, or *huey tlatoani*, was an elected position with preference given to nephews. A system of checks and balances to his authority were incorporated into a priesthood supervised by the Cihuacoatl, or Snakewoman, who headed the war council and governed the city when the emperor was personally commanding the army in the field. The upper classes were dominated by noblemen called *tetecuhtin* (sing. *tecuhtli*), who resided on their own estates, which were worked by slaves or serfs; Tenochtitlán was also organized into residential districts called *calpulli*, whose members claimed a clanlike affiliation that they believed to be derived from an old Chichimec custom. Each *calpulli* owned their lands communally, elected their own civic leaders, worshiped their own gods, and fought together as military units. A special class of merchants resided at Tlatelolco.

The ceremonial and religious headquarters of the Triple Alliance Empire was located within a great ceremonial precinct in the center of Tenochtitlán. The excavations of successive building constructions of the temples dedicated to the gods Huitzilopochtli and Tlaloc by Mexican archaeologists under the direction of Eduardo Matos Moctezuma have confirmed much of the Aztecs' own history about their origins, as well as uncovered exquisitely crafted works of monumental art.

Upon the death of the emperor Ahuitzotl in 1502, control of the empire fell to Moctezuma Xocoyotzin. By 1519, hostilities between the Triple Alliance and Tlaxcala had reached a feverish pitch as Moctezuma sought to declare himself ruler of the known world. It was at this fateful point in time that an army of Spaniards led by Hernando Cortés landed on the coast of Veracruz.

Employing the political strategies that had served them so well during the Italian Renaissance wars together with cavalry and guns, the Spaniards marched inland unopposed and allied themselves with the Tlaxcalan city-states. Faced with dissent within his administration and unable to raise an army, Moctezuma opted for a diplomatic solution and invited Cortés to Tenochtitlán. The city rose in rebellion to Moctezuma, elected a new emperor, and Moctezuma was killed. The Spaniards fled to Tlaxcala. Then in 1521 an Indian-Spanish allied army laid siege to Tenochtitlán, bringing to an end the rule of the greatest military empire North America had ever known.

[See also MESOAMERICA, articles on INTRODUCTION, POST-CLASSIC PERIOD IN MESOAMERICA.]

■ Nigel Davies, The Aztecs (1973). Benardino Sahagún, Florentine Codex: General History of the Things of New Spain, tr. and ed. by Arthur J. O. Anderson and Charles E. Dibble (1982). Brian Fagan, The Aztecs (1984). Johanna Broda, Davíd Carrasco, and Eduardo Matos Moctezuma, The Great Temple of Tenochtitlán: Center and Periphery in the Aztec World (1987). Diego Durán, The History of the Indies of New Spain, tr. by Doris Heyden (1994).

John M. D. Pohl

THE RISE OF AZTEC CIVILIZATION

Aztec civilization was the last in a series of urban societies that flourished in central Mexico before the arrival of Spanish conquerors in A.D. 1519. Although the term "Aztec" is sometimes used to refer exclusively to the Mexica people of Tenochtitlán, most scholars use the term in the wider sense of the Nahuatl-speaking peoples of central Mexico in the centuries prior to 1519. Information on the rise of Aztec civilization comes from both archaeology and native histories. The archaeological record of the Aztecs covers the Mesoamerican Post-Classic era, and is divided into three periods: early Post-Classic (A.D. 950–1150), Middle Post-Classic (1150–1350), and Late Post-Classic (1350–1550). Aztec native history is culled from pictorial documents and oral accounts told to early Spanish writers. Major elements in this historical record include the Aztlan migrations, Toltec civilization, the growth of city-states, and the expansion of the Aztec Empire. While the general correspondence between the archaeological record and native history is clear, the detailed correlation of the two is an area of active research and debate.

Origins (A.D. 900–1175). The Aztec peoples traced their origins to Aztlan, a semimythical place north of central Mexico. Native histories mention several tribes of hunter-gatherers who migrated south, some of whom settled in the basin of Mexico (for example, the Acolhua, Tepaneca, Chalca, and Mexica peoples), while others settled in surrounding highland valleys (such as the Tlaxcalteca, Tlahuica, and Matlatzinca). These named peoples all spoke Nahuatl and shared a common culture, yet they maintained their ethnic distinctiveness throughout the Post-Classic era. Nahuatl, a language with ties to native languages in the southwestern United States, was intrusive in central Mexico, and the native historical dates for the arrival of the Aztlan migrants correlate with linguistic data for the inception of the Nahuatl language in central Mexico.

The Aztlan groups passed close to the Toltec city of *Tula (A.D. 700–1175) as they entered central Mexico from the north, but the nature of their interactions with the Toltecs is uncertain. In the later Aztec native histories the Toltecs were described as great priests, artists, intellectuals, warriors, and statesmen who invented most of Mesoamerican culture. The Toltecs, however, inherited much from the earlier civilization of *Teotihuacán (A.D. 150–750). Archaeological fieldwork has shown that Tula was a far more modest urban center than the Toltec capital described by the Aztecs.

Growth of City-States (A.D. 1175–1350). The *Toltec Empire collapsed around 1175, close to the date of arrival of the Aztlan migrants in central Mexico (the possible role of the Aztlan peoples in the Toltec collapse is unknown). Nearly all of the major Aztec cities were founded during the following 150 years, and the new rulers traced their genealogy and legitimacy back to the Toltec kings. Tenochtitlán, later to become the imperial capital, was founded in 1325. The relations among the new city-states were both friendly and antagonistic. On the one hand, polities interacted through royal marriage alliances and trade, while on the other, wars were common, as city-states tried to conquer their neighbors.

Archaeological research has identified distinct, local stylistic traditions within a common central Mexican cultural pattern. During the Middle Post-Classic Period (1150–1350), each region had its own easily recognizable style of decorated pottery, and site inventories show an active trade in ceramics, obsidian, and other goods. Certain architectural features exhibited a uniformity across large areas of central Mexico. The most spectacular of these is the double-stair pyramid temple. Examples have been excavated and restored at the sites of Tenayuca in the basin of Mexico and Teopanzolco in Morelos (an area immediately south of the basin); this style was later employed in the Templo Mayor of Tenochtitlán. Other Middle Post-Classic archaeological sites that have been surveyed or excavated include Chalco, Culhuacan, Huexotla, Otumba, and Xaltocan in the basin of Mexico; and Calixtlahuaca, Capilco, Tepozteco, Tetla, Tula, and Yautepec in surrounding valleys of central Mexico.

Political and Economic Expansion (1350–1428). One of the most dramatic changes that occurred in Post-Classic central Mexico was a major population surge from the thirteenth through fifteenth centuries. The full-coverage archaeological survey of the basin of Mexico by William Sanders, Jeffrey Parsons, and colleagues revealed a tremendous jump in the numbers and sizes of sites between the Middle and Late Post-Classic periods. The population surge was accompanied by agricultural intensification, growth of market trade, urbanization, and political expansion. To feed the millions of people in central Mexico, irrigation systems and agricultural terraces were built in many areas and the swampy southern lakes of the basin of Mexico were turned into highly productive agricultural fields through the construction of chinampas, or raised fields. Trade increased greatly, craft specialization flourished, and cities grew. A major theme of archaeological research at Late Post-Classic sites has been the nature of these changes and their impact on households and communities. Excavations and surface collections addressing this topic have been carried out at the sites of Chalco, Huexotla, Otumba, Siguatecpan, and Xaltocan in the basin of Mexico, and at Capilco, Coatlan, Cuexcomate, and Yautepec in Morelos.

Political rivalries among city-states escalated as several polities succeeded in conquering their neighbors to establish small tributary empires. By 1428, the most powerful of these was the Tepanec Empire centered at Azcapotzalco in the western basin of Mexico. The Mexica, who would later dominate much of Mesoamerica, served as vassals and mercenaries for the Tepanec king. Their capital, Tenochtitlán, grew in size and importance as the Mexica grew in population and military strength.

The Aztec Empire (1428–1519). In 1428 the Mexica joined with the Acolhua of Texcoco and a dissident Tepanec faction to overthrow the Tepanec Empire. The Aztec, or Triple Alliance, Empire was formed when the three allies agreed jointly to conquer other areas in order to generate tribute. The empire subdued the remaining areas of the basin of Mexico and then its armies moved out from the basin eventually to conquer much of Mesoamerica by 1519. As the empire grew, the Mexica assumed an increasingly dominant role. In comparative terms, the Aztec Empire was a hegemonic empire relying upon indirect rule in the provinces. So long as tribute was delivered, local rulers and institutions were generally left alone, and the Aztecs built only a few imperial installations in the provinces. Two of the known examples of Aztec military settlements—Oztuma in Guerrero and Quauhtochco in Veracruz—have been excavated, and recent archaeological projects have investigated the local effects of Aztec imperialism in provincial areas.

The impact of imperial expansion on Tenochtitlán was dramatic. Both ethnohistorical accounts and archaeological excavations reveal a thriving city whose economy was fueled by massive amounts of tribute that arrived from all over Mesoamerica. Excavations at the Templo Mayor uncovered many rich offerings of luxury goods obtained from the provinces through both tribute and trade.

When the Spanish conqueror Hernando Cortés entered Tenochtitlán in 1519, the Aztec Empire was at the height of its power and glory. The Spanish conquest of the Aztecs brought to an end a dynamic civilization whose success was due to the creative blending of two disparate sociocultural traditions: an ancient tradition of urban society extending back through the Toltecs to Teotihuacán, and a newer tradition of Nahuatl-speaking migrants from Aztlan.

[See also MESOAMERICA: THE POST-CLASSIC PERIOD MESO-AMERICA.]

■ Nigel Davies, *The Aztecs: A History* (1973). Nigel Davies, *The Toltecs Until the Fall of Tula* (1977). William T. Sanders, Jeffrey R. Parsons, and Robert S. Santley, *The Basin of Mexico: Ecological Processes in the Evolution of a Civilization* (1979). Nigel Davies, *The Toltec Heritage: From the Fall of Tula to the Rise of Tenochtitlan* (1980). Frances F. Berdan, *The Aztecs of Central Mexico: An Imperial Society* (1982). Richard A. Diehl, *Tula: The Toltec Capital of Ancient Mexico* (1983). Mary G. Hodge and Michael E. Smith, eds., *Economies and Polities in the Aztec Realm* (1994). Frances F. Berdan et al., *Aztec Imperial Strategies* (1995). Michael E. Smith, *The Aztecs* (1996).

Michael E. Smith

ECONOMIC ORGANIZATION OF AZTEC CIVILIZATION

Human labor, together with a largely Neolithic technology, supplied the energy for agriculture, craft production, and transportation in pre-Hispanic Mesoamerica, which lacked large domestic animals for food, plowing, or transportation. Despite these energetic and technological constraints, the Aztec economy supported large, dense, and highly urbanized populations and distributed a wide array of goods both within and without the empire's borders.

The Aztec economy rested on a foundation of labor-intensive agricultural systems that took advantage of the micro-environmental diversity characteristic of the heartland of the empire, the basin of Mexico, and the surrounding, more temperate highlands to the east, west, and south and coastal lowlands. Hundreds of varieties of plants were cultivated, but the most important staple food crop throughout the empire was maize (corn); other significant commestibles included beans, squash, chia, amaranth, and maguey (a cactus used for food and fiber). Some crops could be grown only in particular environments—most notable were cacao (chocolate) from the lowlands and cotton from the temperate highlands and tropical lowlands.

Because of the high costs of transporting goods overland by human bearers, staple foods were rarely exchanged over distances greater than 93–155 miles (150–250 km). Thus the breadbasket (or more correctly, tortilla and tamale basket) for the imperial capital, *Tenochtitlán, was the basin of Mexico and the adjoining regions. By the sixteenth century most arable land in the basin was under cultivation. Various land-use techniques were employed, including dry farming, which on the lower mountain slopes was often done in conjunction with terracing. Where possible, farmers reduced the risk of crop losses from early fall frosts or delayed or insufficient summer rains with irrigation. Small flood-water irrigation networks tapped the seasonal runoff produced by high-intensity summer rainstorms to irrigate piedmont slopes and alluvial plains. A limited number of perennial water sources—springs and rivers—provided water for relatively large-scale permanent irrigation networks.

The most intensive form of agriculture practiced in the basin was the *chinampa* system, misnamed "floating gardens," but are more accurately, raised fields. This is a type of drained-field agriculture that entails the conversion of swampy land into highly productive agricultural plots by a system of drainage ditches that control the level of the water table. Although requiring substantial labor, *chinampas* can be kept in continuous cultivation and produce as many as seven crops a year. By the sixteenth century, most of the western shore of Lake Texcoco and the southern Lake Chalco-Xochimilco had been converted to *chinampas* that produced an annual surplus equivalent to approx. 44 million pounds (20 million kg) of maize.

Much of this surplus was eventually exchanged in the marketplace of Tenochtitlán for goods and services provided by urban specialists. Highly developed craft specialization was another hallmark of the Aztec economy, and Tenochtitlán was the largest center of craft specialization in Mesoamerica. This city of 150,000–200,000 people was occupied almost exclusively by nonagriculturalists. Specialists in particular crafts tended to reside together in the city as members of the same *calpulli*, or ward. Artisans who crafted luxury goods—lapidaries, feather workers, gold and silver workers—were organized into guilds, and they, along with the professional long-distance merchants, *pochteca*, formed a middle class above the commoners and below the nobles. Tenochtitlán was also home to an array of other occupational specialists—tax collectors, judges, professional warriors, priests—as the expansion of the empire fueled a concomitant expansion in religious, military, and political institutions sustained by the tribute from conquered regions.

Craft specialization was not restricted to Tenochtitlán. It was once thought that the capital towns and cities of the formerly independent city-states in the basin were centers of craft production and distribution similar to Tenochtitlán. Recent archaeological work has revealed a more complicated picture, however. It now appears that, following the expansion of the Aztec Empire in the fifteenth century, the economies of city-states near Tenochtitlán were restructured to emphasize agricultural production and deemphasize craft production because of the increased volume of goods coming into Tenochtitlán and the ease of transport provided by the lake system. On the periphery of the basin city-states retained their marketing systems, and craft production may have even intensified with the growth of the empire. Some communities specialized in the production of goods from natural resources with restricted distributions;

remains of salt-production workshops can still be found along the northern and eastern shores of Lake Texcoco.

While the production of luxury goods in the major cities was done by full-time specialists, commoners often working on a part-time basis in household workshops, made most other goods. In addition, all women spun and wove cloth, and not just for use by their own families. Cloth played a multifaceted role in Aztec society. *Textiles, some elaborately decorated, represent the most common item on Aztec tribute lists, and cloth also served as a medium of exchange in markets.

Craft specialists and surplus production were integrated in the Aztec economy through complex exchange networks that involved both tribute and marketplaces. All conquered areas paid tribute to the empire, which by 1519 encompassed 77,000 square miles (200,000 sq. km) and a total population of 5 million to 6 million people. The Aztec nobility was exempt from paying tribute, but commoners in the basin of Mexico supplied goods and provided labor for public works and military campaigns. By collecting and redistributing vast quantities of goods, the Aztec state had become a major economic institution.

Tribute goods included staple food from nearby areas, luxury foods from more distant territories (such as honey), basic items (wood, mats, warrior costumes, and other textiles), and luxury or ceremonial items (rubber, precious stones and jewelry, and incense). These goods were used to support the imperial palace, the imperial administration, and the military and were given as gifts to warriors, merchants, and others, including on occasion, conquered nobles in return for their service and loyalty to the empire.

Goods were also exchanged through a well-developed system of open-air marketplaces. Most towns had a market every five days (one Aztec week). Goods were arranged by type, and most were exchanged by barter, although cotton mantles, cacao beans, and a few other items were used as money. The largest market in the empire was the one at Tlatelolco, which served Tenochtitlán; 20,000–25,000 people attended this market each day to buy and sell goods from all over Mesoamerica—precious stones, foodstuffs from maize to honey cakes, animal skins, timber, furniture, paper, pitchpine, and sandals, to name just a few of the items. Luxury goods were sold by professional merchants (*pochteca*) who conducted most of the long-distance trade within and beyond the empire's borders. In addition to supplying luxury goods to the nobility, the *pochteca* also acted as spies for the Aztec ruler, who sometimes funded major trading expeditions.

The Aztec economy combined state control with a market sector, although significant differences of opinion exist about the significance of the private sector. Not only was the economy of the Aztec Empire complex, but through recent archaeological surveys and excavations and ethnohistoric studies of local documents, it has become clear that the imperial economy overlaid diverse economic institutions and relations at the local and regional levels.

[See also MESOAMERICA: POST-CLASSIC PERIOD IN MESOAMERICA.]

■ Bernardino de Sahagún, *Florentine Codex: General History of the Things of New Spain* (1950–1969). Jacques Soustelle, *Daily Life of the Aztecs on the Eve of the Spanish Conquest* (1961). Jeffrey R. Parsons, "The Role of Chinampa Agriculture in the Food Supply of Aztec Tenochtitlan," in ed. Charles E. Cleland, *Cultural Change and Continuity* (1976). William T. Sanders, Jeffrey R. Parsons, and Robert S. Santley, *The Basin of Mexico: Ecological Processes in the Evolution of a Civilization* (1979). Francis E. Berdan, *The Aztecs of Central Mexico* (1982). Ross Hassig, *Trade, Tribute, and Transportation* (1985). Mary Hodge and Michael Smith, eds., *Economies and Polities in the Aztec Realm* (1994).

Deborah L. Nichols

THE SPANISH CONQUEST OF THE AZTECS

Hernando Cortés, under the auspices of Governor Velásquez of Cuba, sailed from Havana on 10 February 1519 with 11 ships, 450 men, and 16 horses to explore the coast of Mexico. Within a week the expedition reached Cozumel Island off the coast of Yucatán, where they took on supplies and Jerónimo de Aguilar, a Spaniard stranded there earlier, whose knowledge of Yucatec Maya proved a valuable asset to Cortés.

The expedition sailed up the coast to Tabasco, where local Maya engaged the Spaniards in battle. Unable to defeat the Spanish troops, whose horses, along with crossbows, cannons, and harquebuses, gave them a decisive advantage, Maya nobles pledged their support to Cortés. As a symbol of their subordination they gave Cortés gifts, including women, one of whom, Malinche, spoke both Yucatec Maya and Nahuatl, the language of the Aztecs. With Malinche and Aguilar as translators, Cortés was able to communicate with both Maya and Aztecs. Cortés needed native allies for transportation and supplies and to expand his fighting force.

The expedition proceeded along the coast to central Veracruz, a Totanac region controlled by the Aztec Empire. Here, emissaries of the Aztec ruler Moctezuma met Cortés, gave him gifts, and gathered information. A second group of emissaries brought even more lavish gifts, and requested that the Spaniards not attempt to come to *Tenochtitlán, capital of the Aztec Empire.

The Spaniards remained on the coast for five months and, disobeying orders from Governor Velásquez, established a settlement. To prevent persons loyal to Velásquez from returning to Cuba, Cortés burned his ships and marched inland to the Totanac town of Cempoalla, where he forged alliances with Totanac rulers, who were unhappy about paying tribute to the Aztec Empire. As he would elsewhere, Cortés removed images of Totanac gods from their temple and replaced them with the Catholic cross as part of a forced conversion to Christianity. He persuaded the Totanacs to capture Aztec tribute collectors, a serious offense, which cemented the Totanacs' alliance with Cortés.

Spurred by the prospect of greater gold, the Spaniards and their native allies began their march to Tenochtitlán in central Mexico by traveling through the state of Tlaxcalla that had not been conquered by the Aztecs. The Tlaxcallans and Spaniards fought a series of battles. Unable to defeat the Spaniards—whose firepower reduced the effectiveness of native military tactics—the Tlaxcallan rulers agreed to ally with Cortés partly out of self-interest, since Tlaxcalla was surrounded by Aztec-controlled provinces.

Moctezuma was aware of these developments but took no action against Cortés. His failure to attack the foreigners might have stemmed from uncertainty about the supernatural status of the Spaniards, the Aztecs' weak control over tributary provinces, or the problem of raising a large army during the growing season when peasants engaged in agriculture, the basis of the Aztec economy.

Cortés and his Tlaxcallan allies moved on to Cholula, a major city under Aztec control. After being granted permission to enter the city, they massacred 4,000–5,000 people, including the king. Cortés and his troops arrived on the outskirts of Tenochtitlán on 8 November 1519. Emissaries of Moctezuma brought lavish gifts to persuade Cortés to turn back. When he refused, Moctezuma sent Cacama, his nephew and king of Texcoco, to escort the Spanish into Tenochtitlán, where Cortés and Moctezuma met for the first time. Shortly thereafter, the Aztecs attacked Cortés's Totanac allies on the Gulf coast for refusing to pay tribute. Fearing defection of his native allies, Cortés seized Moctezuma, who did not resist, and held him hostage.

The arrival of Spanish forces sent by Governor Velásquez to Veracruz to capture Cortés forced him to return to the coast. He left Pedro de Alvarado in charge in Tenochtitlán. Soon after Cortés departed, thousands of Aztec nobles came to the Great Temple in Tenochtitlán to honor their war god, Huitzilopochtli, in a religious ceremony that involved human sacrifice. Perhaps because he felt threatened, Alvarado massacred possibly as many as 8,000–10,000 nobles. The massacre began a rebellion, and Cortés returned to Tenochtitlán to find the Spaniards under siege in the palace where they had been housed. Moctezuma was killed during the fighting, probably by Spaniards; he was succeeded by his younger brother, Cuitlahua. Unable to defeat the Aztecs, Cortés and his troops escaped from Tenochtitlán on the night of 30 June 1520; they fought their way around the northern basin and engaged in a major battle outside the town of Otumba before reaching Tlaxcallan territory.

The Spaniards remained in Tlaxcalla for more than five months, securing their control over the region, obtaining reinforcements of Spanish soldiers and arms, and building ships suitable for transport on the lakes that surrounded Tenochtitlán. During this time smallpox carried by a Spanish soldier spread into central Mexico with devastating consequences for the indigenous populations, who had never been exposed to the disease and thus had no immunity. Included among its victims was Cuitlahua, the Aztec king, who died in early December 1520 and was replaced by Cuauhtemoc.

In late December, Cortés, along with 10,000 Tlaxcallan troops, marched on the basin of Mexico. They made alliances with towns and cities surrounding Tenochtitlán, including Texcoco, the second-largest city, which became Cortés's base of operations. Cortés began his attack on Tenochtitlán on 28 April 1521, but after his troops failed to capture the city through direct combat, they blockaded the island and cut it off from supplies. Thousands of Aztecs died of starvation and lack of drinking water in the city. The siege lasted seventy-five days, but by 1 August the Spaniards and their allies had taken control of Tenochtitlán's marketplace at Tlatelolco, and they captured Cuauhtemoc on 13 August. The city was sacked, and only about 60,000 of the original 300,000 defenders survived.

Many reasons have been given for the success of Cortés and his small force, but the most important factors were disease, military technology and tactics, and the loose integration of conquered regions into the Aztec Empire. Even before the capture of Tenochtitlán thousands died from smallpox, the first in a series of epidemics of European diseases. On the battlefield steel swords offered clear advantages over wooden shields in hand-to-hand fighting. Cavalry charges with mounted lancers were especially effective against the open formation of the Aztecs in battle, which was better suited to taking prisoners for sacrifice than vanquishing the enemy, as was the Spaniards' goal.

The loose hegemonic structure of the Aztec Empire allowed Tenochtitlán to exact tribute without the high cost of imperial infrastructure, but the lack of integration made it possible for Cortés to form alliances with conquered nobles who saw these alliances as a way of removing the Aztecs. Their payment of tribute to Cortés acknowledged subordination, but conquered groups in Mesoamerica had previously been left alone with regard to internal affairs. European notions of complete domination were alien and unforeseen.

The defeat of Tenochtitlán represented only the beginning of the Spanish conquest of Mesoamerica. Spanish domination lasted for nearly 350 years, but the heritage of the Aztec Empire remains a vibrant part of the identity of indigenous people and the nation-state of Mexico.

[*See also* AMERICAS, INTRODUCTION OF DISEASES INTO THE; MESOAMERICA: SPANISH SETTLEMENT IN MESOAMERICA.]

■ Bernal Díaz del Castillo, *The Conquest of New Spain* (1963, originally written 1560s). Patricia de Fuentes, ed., *The Conquistadors: First Person Accounts of the Conquest of Mexico* (1963). Hernán Cortés, *Letters from Mexico* (1971). Arthur J. O. Anderson and Charles Dibble, trans. and eds., *The War of Conquest: How It Was Waged Here in Mexico* (1978). Frances F. Berdan, *The Aztecs of Central Mexico* (1982). Eduardo Matos Moctezuma, *The Great Temple of the Aztecs* (1988). Ross Hassig, *Mexico and the Spanish Conquest* (1994).

Deborah L. Nichols

B

BABYLON lies 56 miles (90 km) south of Baghdad on the outskirts of the city of Hilla. Though it was abandoned in the second century, the city's location was never completely forgotten. Its ancient name was preserved as Babil, the name of one of the site's several mounds. The Greek name Babylon represents the Akkadian *bab ilani*, or "gate of the gods." Earlier, the city was called *bab illm*, or "gate of the god," a Semiticized rendering of an original non-Semitic (and non-Sumerian) name, the meaning of which is unknown.

Babylon existed as a city from the latter part of the third millennium B.C., and was originally rather insignificant. Under Hammurabi (1792–1750 B.C.), however, it emerged to lead a kingdom comprising all of southern Mesopotamia. Although Hammurabi's attempt at hegemony was short-lived, Babylon continued as the preeminent city in the south, remaining the seat of succeeding dynasties and growing to become the unrivaled religious and cultural center of the country. The city reached the zenith of its power and prestige during the reign of Nebuchadnezzar II (604–562 B.C.). Shortly thereafter, however, the Persian conquest cost Babylon its political independence forever. The founding of Seleucia-on-the-Tigris around 300 B.C. sealed the city's fate, and it slowly began to die.

From medieval times travelers had visited and commented upon the ruins of Babylon. In 1899, long-term excavations began, led by Robert *Koldewey for the Deutsche Orient-Gesellschaft and Berlin's Königliche Museen. The Germans worked at the site until 1917, digging year-round and employing up to 250 laborers. Koldewey's goal was the systematic excavation of the city as a whole, not merely the retrieval of artifacts. In accomplishing this his team set a new standard for archaeological excavation. After 1917 efforts focused mostly on the conservation and restoration of structures already exposed by the Germans. Since the 1970s, the Iraqi Department of Antiquities and Heritage has engaged in an ambitious program of new excavations and large-scale restoration of the site.

The earliest remains thus far identified at Babylon consist of third-millennium B.C. pottery found on the site's surface. Koldewey was able to reach seventeenth-century levels when the nearby bed of the Euphrates was dry and the water table was low. However, the Babylon we know today is essentially that of Nebuchadnezzar II and those who came after him.

Nebuchadnezzar's Babylon occupied a 1 by 1.5 foot (1.5 by 2.5 km) rectangle, divided in two parts by the Euphrates and enclosed by a massive triple wall. Excavation has concentrated on the east side of the river, the heart of the ancient city, where the major palaces and temples have been found. A second great wall, 5 miles (8 km) long, enclosed a roughly triangular area east of the river, protecting some of the suburban districts and providing an additional line of defense for the city's institutional heart.

The principal street in the eastern part of the city was the Processional Way, which connected the Esagila, temple of the chief god Marduk, with the *akitu* temple outside the city, where the god sojourned during the New Year's festival. Along the walls on either side of the street ran a frieze of lions in relief composed of multicolored glazed bricks. The street passed through the Ishtar Gate, whose sides were also decorated with glazed animals in relief dragons, emblematic of Marduk, and bulls. The glazed walls of the gate were built on unglazed walls bearing the same arrangement of dragons and bulls in relief. It remains unclear whether these are an earlier version of the gate or simply its foundations.

The so-called Northern and Southern Palaces lay near the Ishtar Gate, between the Processional Way and the river. The Northern Palace, where the Lion of Babylon and other trophies were kept, guarded the northwestern corner of the inner city. The Southern Palace held Nebuchadnezzar's principal throne room, adorned with lions and stylized trees in glazed brick. A group of storerooms in this palace were long considered to be the substructure of the Hanging Gardens. That identification is generally rejected, so the location of the fabulous gardens remains a mystery. The so-called Summer Palace was north of the inner city, protected by the outer wall where it met the river.

Esagila, the temple of Marduk, and Etemenanki, the city's ziggurat, known from Herodotus and the Bible as the Tower of Babel, faced each other across the southern end of the Processional Way. These, the two most important religious edifices of the city, are still not completely understood. The temple lies under more than twenty meters of later deposition and could be only partially explored, while the fabled tower, robbed of its valuable baked-brick facing, exists only as an eroded mud-brick mass encircled by a reed-filled sump of brackish groundwater.

Between the ziggurat and the Southern Palace lay the temple of Nabu, god of scribes. When it was excavated and restored by the Iraqis in the 1970s and 1980s the temple was virtually intact, its interior walls still bearing painted black-and-white designs. Across the Processional Way from this temple lay a district of large houses, homes to wealthier residents of the city.

Babylon continued to thrive for some time after Nebuchadnezzar II. Among its later monuments are a Greek theater and palestra of the Seleucid era.

[*See also* ASSYRIAN EMPIRE; MESOPOTAMIA, *articles on* THE RISE OF URBAN CULTURE, SUMER AND AKKAD, BABYLONIA; NEAR EAST: IRON AGE CIVILIZATIONS OF THE NEAR EAST; WRITING: CUNEIFORM.]

■ Joan Oates, *Babylon*, rev. ed. (1986). Robert Koldewey, *Das wieder erstehende Babylon*, 5th ed. (1990).

James A. Armstrong

BAN CHIANG is a prehistoric site in northeastern Thailand at least 20 acres (8 hectares) in size, dating between 3600 B.C. and A.D. 500. The site, which gives its name to a regional culture known as the Ban Chiang Cultural Tradition, is renowned for the depth of its sequence, its elegant ceramics, early metallurgy, and controversial chronology. At the time of the site's major excavations in the 1970s, Southeast Asia had seen little archaeological research. Establishing a chronology for the site to serve as a benchmark for the region has been a priority. A "best fit" approach to the thirty-three radiocarbon dates from the University of Pennsylvania/Fine Arts Department of Thailand excavations put initial settlement of the site by rice cultivators in the fourth millennium B.C. and bronze metallurgy beginning about 2000 B.C. This controversial chronology, which places the appearance of bronze in Southeast Asia 1,500 years earlier than formerly thought and close to its date for more advanced civilizations in China, is being reassessed by AMS dating of rice husks in mortuary pottery.

The cultural deposits at the site include both mortuary and habitation remains. Habitation deposits consist primarily of pits, postholes, and dense concentrations of refuse and fragmentary artifacts. These deposits reveal the development of many aspects of life typical of Southeast Asian villages today, including pile-built dwellings, fishing, growing rice, raising pigs, cattle, water buffalo, and chickens, and making pottery using a paddle-and-anvil technique.

Ban Chiang is especially known for its human burials and associated grave goods. The superimposed mortuary deposits, which in places reach depths of over 13 feet (4 m) and span 2,000–4,000 years, include remains from premetal, bronze, and iron periods, making this site unusually informative of the Southeast Asian cultural sequence. Artifactual remains include a diverse assemblage of ceramics with many beautiful and distinctive styles of vessels, bronze and iron implements and personal ornaments, and, late in the sequence, glass beads. Stone and shell ornaments and tools demonstrate that Ban Chiang Tradition villages participated in extensive trade networks extending as far as the Gulf of Siam.

Mortuary ritual changed over time and includes a first-millennium B.C. practice of smashing as many as twenty large graceful pottery vessels over the bodies. Grave contents indicate some variation in wealth among individuals but no evidence for a distinct hereditary elite. Overall the site documents a flourishing, relatively peaceful, and technologically precocious village society.

[*See also* ASIA: PREHISTORY AND EARLY HISTORY OF SOUTHEAST ASIA.]

■ Joyce C. White, *Ban Chiang: Discovery of a Lost Bronze Age* (1982). Joyce C. White, *A Revision of the Chronology of Ban Chiang and Its Implications for the Prehistory of Northeast Thailand* (1986).

Joyce C. White

BANDELIER, Adolph (1840–1914), historian, ethnologist, and archaeologist, was a primary force in the early ethnology and archaeology of the American Southwest, Mexico, and Peru. Born in Switzerland of upper-middle-class parents, Bandelier spent the first half of his life in Highland, Illinois, being trained in banking and investments. Bandelier offset his dissatisfaction with business by reading and translating accounts of early Spanish explorations in the Americas. Formal training for ethnologists was nonexistent at the time, but Bandelier developed an intense interest in native cultures of the Americas. He was profoundly influenced by Lewis Henry *Morgan (1818–1881), one of the most powerful figures in nineteenth-century anthropology. The lengthy letters from Bandelier to Morgan that followed their first meeting in 1873 afford invaluable insights into Bandelier's research as well as the conceptual bases prevalent in early American anthropology. The correspondences reveal Bandelier's gradual conversion to Morgan's belief that early European historiography was not a trustworthy source for ethnographic information. The letters comprise one of the first extensive debates between an ethnohistorian (Bandelier) and an ethnographer (Morgan) in American anthropology.

Throughout his life Bandelier was a scholar without an institution. Bandelier was forty years old before he broke free of his business past and first traveled to the American Southwest. Through Morgan's influence, the American Institute for Archaeology funded Bandelier from 1880 to 1885 to study prehistoric and living Native American cultures, allowing Bandelier to investigate his own theory that the Aztec of central Mexico were descendants of prehistoric puebloan groups of the American Southwest. Bandelier later abandoned this idea based upon his extensive travels through the Rio Grande and Zuñi regions. In 1886 his friend and noted ethnographer Frank Cushing (1857–1900) arranged to have Bandelier join the Hemenway expedition as its official historiographer. Financed by Henry Villard in 1892, Bandelier spent the next decade extending his expertise to the early history of South America. Throughout his publications Bandelier apologized for his inability to utilize documentary sources in Spain. His yearning to investigate the archives in Seville ended in 1913, when he sailed for Spain. The following year Bandelier died and was buried in Seville.

[*See also* HISTORY OF ARCHAEOLOGY BEFORE 1900: ARCHAEOLOGY OF THE AMERICAS.]

■ Adolph F. Bandelier, *On the Social Organization and Mode of Government of the Ancient Mexicans*, Twelfth Annual Report, Peabody Museum, Cambridge, pp. 557–699 (1879). Adolph F. Bandelier, "Final Report of the Investigations among the Indians of the Southwestern United States, Carried on Mainly in the Years from 1880 to 1885," Parts I and II, in *Papers of the Archaeological Institute of America*, American Series III and IV (1890–1892). Leslie A. White, *Pioneers in American Anthropology: The Bandelier–Morgan Letters, 1873–1883*, 2 vols. (1957).

Michael A. Adler

BANDKERAMIK is the term that embraces the first farming cultures of central Europe. In the 1880s, the German prehistorian Friedrich Klopfleisch identified the *Linearbandkeramik* on the basis of its distinctive curvilinear incised decoration. Later, the successor to the Linearbandkeramik in much of central Europe, the *Stichbandkeramik*, was differentiated by its stroked ornamentation. The two groups together could be called the Bandkeramik Tradition. Over the past century, *Bandkeramik* has been referred to by a variety of different names. V. Gordon *Childe called Linearbandkeramik "Danubian I" and Stichbandkeramik "Danubian II" in his sequence of prehistoric European cultures. In English-language texts, the term "Linear Pottery culture" and "Stroke-Ornamented Pottery culture" are frequently used, as is the abbreviation *LBK*. Finally, there are a variety of national names across Europe, including *Céramique Rubané* in France and *Ceramika Wstegowa* in Poland. In general but imprecise usage, *Bandkeramik* is often used interchangeably with *Linearbandkeramik*.

Bandkeramik sites are distributed across central Europe from Slovakia and the western Ukraine to eastern France and Belgium. They are found primarily along the rivers and streams of the rolling uplands of central Europe in basins filled with loess soil, which is very fertile but also rather dry except along watercourses. Bandkeramik sites typically occur in small clusters, called "settlement cells," separated from nearby clusters by some distance. In the loess belt, these sites typically occur in the landscape zone where the floodplain meets the adjoining watershed. Farther north, Bandkeramik cells also occur on the glacial soils of the northern European plain in the lower Vistula and Oder drainages.

Beginning on the Hungarian plain and spreading through Slovakia, the Czech lands, Austria, Germany, and Poland into the Low Countries and eastern France, the expansion of the Bandkeramik is one of the most remarkable phenomena in prehistoric Europe, taking place over only a few centuries between approximately 5400 and 4900 B.C. (according to calibrated carbon-14 datings). It appears, for several reasons, to represent a colonization process rather than an *in situ* development. First, Bandkeramik material culture is extraordinarily uniform over wide areas, particularly in the earliest phases. Second, there is no preexisting tradition of pottery manufacture in central Europe, although the recent identification of two anomalous pottery types (Limburg and La Hoguette) in the western part of the Bandkeramik realm suggests the involvement of indigenous peoples in some regions. Third, Bandkeramik flint technology is quite different from tool types used by local foraging populations. Fourth, the cereals and some of the livestock used by Bandkeramik communities have no native counterparts in central Europe. Finally, *Bandkeramik* house forms are completely unlike anything found in central Europe before 5400 B.C.

Perhaps the most distinctive characteristic of the Bandkeramik was its large longhouses, up to 148 feet (45 m) in length—the largest buildings in the world at this time. They were multipurpose structures, providing shelter for humans and livestock, as well as storage and working space. Linearbandkeramik longhouses were built from massive timber posts, which usually occur in five rows, two forming the exterior walls and three providing the interior support for the roof. They have rectangular plans, between 23 and 148 feet (7 and 45 m) long and 16 to 23 feet (5 to 7 m) wide. In the exterior walls, the space between the posts was filled with wooden wattle (woven twigs and branches) and plastered with mud taken from elongated pits dug alongside the walls. In the Stichbandkeramik period, houses were somewhat more lightly constructed, without the massive interior posts, and took on a wedge-shaped plan, sometimes with the wall lines bulging outward.

Recent studies have indicated that Bandkeramik longhouses were rebuilt on the same locations over time to create a palimpsest of house outlines in the loess subsoil. Another recent development is the discovery that a number of *Bandkeramik* settlements were enclosed by ditches and palisades, particularly in northern and western areas.

The key distinguishing characteristic of the *Bandkeramik* is its pottery, particularly the fine ware decorated with incised lines, strokes, and indentations. Most Bandkeramik decorated vessels from Slovakia to eastern France take the form of a three-quarter-spherical bowl. The largest are 24 to 28 inches (60 to 70 cm) in diameter, but most are considerably smaller, 8 to 16 inches (20 to 40 cm) across. Decorated Bandkeramik vessels are made from high-quality clay, rarely tempered. A stylus was used to make curvilinear incised lines, in simple designs in the earlier phases, becoming progressively more complex as time went on. During the last phases of the Bandkeramik, many decorative dots or strokes were made in parallel rows using a denticulated spatula. On Bandkeramik coarse ware, often in the form of large flasks, patterns of fingernail impressions and concave bosses provide modest ornamentation.

Bandkeramik chipped stone tools are based on blades, from which were made a variety of knives, sickle blades, borers, burins, and scrapers. High-quality flint was sought, including Jurassic and "chocolate" flint from southern Poland and Rijkholt flint from the Netherlands. Obsidian, traded over long distances, was used to make sharp blades. Ground stone tools, particularly adzes, are common on Bandkeramik sites. They are commonly made from amphibolites and basalts from the uplands of central Europe. The "shoe-last celts" of the Bandkeramik are chisel-like implements, long and slender with oblong cross-sections, perhaps used in the carpentry work involved in the construction of longhouses.

The Bandkeramik subsistence economy was based on crop agriculture and animal husbandry. Emmer and einkorn wheat, peas, lentils, and linseed were grown throughout the Bandkeramik area, while barley has an unusual distribution limited to the eastern, northern, and western periphery. Several sites in the western part of the Bandkeramik distribution have yielded traces of poppyseed, which has a Mediterranean origin. Although animal bones are poorly preserved in the loess soil, those of cattle comprise the largest portion of Bandkeramik samples, usually over 70 percent. It is likely that the cattle were used for dairy products in addition to meat. Sheep and goat are also present in smaller quantities, while pig bones are relatively rare, particularly on Linear Pottery sites. Bones of wild animals occur sporadically, but not in quantities that indicate that hunting made a significant contribution to the diet.

For many years, it had been thought that Bandkeramik farmers practiced a form of slash-and-burn agriculture, which quickly exhausted soil fertility and necessitated constant relocation of settlements. Recently, this idea has been largely abandoned in favor of the long-term occupation of settlements and cultivation of small fields located in the fertile zone where the floodplain meets the watershed. Carbonized seeds of shade-loving plants suggest that the fields were surrounded by trees. Grain was harvested by cutting off the ears with a flint sickle.

Bandkeramik communities buried their dead in cemeteries located a short distance from their settlements. The dead were usually placed in separate graves in a contracted position, sometimes with a small quantity of grave goods. Typical offerings include adzes, ceramic vessels, arrowheads and other flint tools, and beads and bracelets made from shells of the marine mollusk *Spondylus gaedoropus*, which is found in the Mediterranean and Black Seas. The remarkable aspect of the distribution of *Spondylus* ornaments is that many are found far from the coasts where the raw material was obtained, even as distant as eastern France. Clearly some sort of trade mechanism was involved, perhaps to cement alliances or to demonstrate prestige.

Analysis of cemetery data suggests that Bandkeramik social organization was relatively egalitarian, with some degree of prestige based on age and sex. There is increasing evidence of long-distance connections for the exchange of obsidian and *Spondylus*. Finally, while there is some evidence for contacts with indigenous hunter-gatherer populations, the nature of this interaction remains to be determined.

[*See also* EUROPE: THE EUROPEAN NEOLITHIC PERIOD.]

■ Alasdair Whittle, "Neolithic Settlement Patterns in Temperate Europe: Progress and Problems," *Journal of World Prehistory* 1 (1987): 5–52. Peter Bogucki, *Forest Farmers and Stockherders: Early Agriculture and Its Consequences in North-Central Europe* (1988). Jens Lüning, "Frühe Bauern in Mitteleuropa im 6. und 5. Jahrtausend v. Chr.," *Jahrbuch des Römisch-Germanischen Zentralmuseums Mainz* 35 (1988): 27–93. P.J.R. Modderman, "The Linear Pottery Culture: Diversity in Uniformity," *Berichten van de Rijksdienst voor het Oudheidkundig Bodemonderzoek* 38 (1988): 63–139. Sarunas Milisauskas and Janusz Kruk, "Neolithic Economy in Central Europe," *Journal of World Prehistory* 3 (1989): 403–446. Ian Hodder, *The Domestication of Europe* (1990). Peter Bogucki and Ryszard Grygiel, "The First Farmers of Central Europe: A Survey Article," *Journal of Field Archaeology* 20 (1993).

Peter Bogucki

BANPO is a large Neolithic village on a tributary of the Wei River, which joins the Yellow River outside Xian, Shansi Province. It is dated in the earlier part of the *Yangshao culture, covering a time span of 5000 to 4000 B.C. The site covers 60,000 square meters and is divided into three areas. The central region has houses, storage pits, and a large central building, all surrounded by a wide ditch. Beyond the ditch, a pottery-producing area with six kilns was found to the east, and burial grounds were discovered north of the village. Among the 250 burials excavated, about one-third were infants, given urn burial under the house floors. Adults were buried in various groupings, often several persons of the same sex and age in a single grave, in a cemetery. The rectangular central building covers an area of 300 square yards (250 sq m), while the smaller houses, either round or rectangular, have floor areas of only 10 to 30 sq. yards (10 to 25 sq m). The earlier round houses are semisubterranean, with entrances on the south and a small porch on the front. Central square hearths are characteristic, and the floors and walls are plastered with mud and straw. The later oblong houses are larger and their interior space is divided into sections with rows of slender posts. Hearths are gourd-shaped and deeper. The ditch surrounding the settlement is V-shaped, up to 20 feet (6 m) wide at the top and 20 feet (6 m) deep.

The quantity of artifacts recovered is overwhelming, including 8,000 stone and bone tools and half a million potsherds. More than half the pottery was coarse, surface-roughened with cord marks, impressing, or incising, and was used for cooking and storage. Finer painted pottery was used for food and water vessels. Most of the designs are geometric, but some are zoomorphic (especially fish) or anthropomorphic. Clay figurines of humans and animals are also found. Stone tools, made by both chipping and grinding, include hoes, spades, grinding stones, and perforated stone discs. Small projectile points were made from both bone and stone. The main cultivated crop was foxtail millet, but nuts and other gathered foods were also prominent. Pigs and dogs were domesticated, and deer bones and other wild species are also common. Evidence of hemp has been found, and of silkworm cultivation. Bone needles with eyes further attest to a textile industry, and basketry impressions were left on pottery. Imported raw materials include nephrite and serpentine.

[*See also* ASIA: PREHISTORY AND EARLY HISTORY OF EAST ASIA; CHINA: INTRODUCTION.]

■ K.-C. Chang, *The Archaeology of Ancient China* (1986).

Sarah Milledge Nelson

BANYAN CAVE is a prehistoric site in the karstic Golden Triangle area of northern Thailand close to the border with Burma. It was discovered during a site survey and excavated by Chester Gorman in 1972. Cultural remains indicate two major cultural periods: a lower period with primary affinities to Southeast Asia's later *Hoabinhian Stone Age, and an upper period in which a lithic flake tool kit co-occurs with ground-stone tools and *ceramics. The lower level produced a calibrated C-14 date in the second half of the fifth millennium B.C., and the upper level produced a calibrated date in the second half of the first millennium A.D.

The cultural sequence appears to be related to the later part of the *Spirit Cave sequence, another cave site excavated by Gorman in northwest Thailand. The material culture in the lower period is dominated by flake debitage and some core tools, including the Hoabinhian type tool, the Sumatralith: a water-worn river cobble flaked unifacially around its circumference. However, low frequencies of ceramic sherds were found in the lower deposits, as was an edge-ground slate knife. The combination of edge grinding and ceramics within a predominantly flaked-core tool industry and the associated fifth millennium date support Gorman's view that a later facies of the Hoabinhian included intrusive elements of a technologically more advanced culture.

In the assemblage of cultural remains from the upper period, the pebble-tool element is absent and the flakes are thinner, with less of the dorsal step flaking characteristic of Hoabinhian debitage. Ceramic sherds, edge-ground tools, and prepared blanks for ground tools increase in prominence. One piece of iron was recovered.

The fauna recovered from the site indicate a broad-spectrum economic strategy exploiting a range of environmental zones, and include large to small mammals, fish, shellfish, birds, and crustaceans. Bones of larger species are battered, and bones of all species have evidence of burning. A greater variety of species as well as over twenty hearths in the lower period levels suggest intensive and repeated use of the site, probably to exploit upland and forest resources.

Plant macrofossils generally support the picture of species exploitation at Spirit Cave, and include annual legumes, cucurbits, and *Lagenaria*, as well as *Canarium* tree nuts and *Prunus* during the earlier period. Wild rice was found in the upper level. The overall significance of Banyan Cave is its evidence for specialized exploitation of upland areas lasting for a prolonged period of time in Southeast Asia, from the Stone Age well into the historic Metal Age.

[*See also* ASIA: PREHISTORY AND EARLY HISTORY OF SOUTHEAST ASIA; ASIA, ORIGINS OF FOOD PRODUCTION IN: ORIGINS OF FOOD PRODUCTION IN SOUTHEAST ASIA.]

■ Douglas E. Yen, "Hoabinhian Horticulture? The Evidence and the Questions from Northwest Thailand," in *Sunda and Sahul: Prehistoric Studies in Southeast Asia, Melanesia and Australia*. Ed. J. Allen, J. Golson, and R. Jones (1977), pp. 567–599. Timothy E. G. Reynolds, "Excavations at Banyan Valley Cave, Northern Thailand: A Report on the 1972 Season," *Asian Perspectives* 31 (1992): 77–97.

Joyce C. White

BAT CAVE is a complex of large and small rockshelters containing evidence of human use from ca. 10,000 B.P. to the present, but is best known as one of the oldest maize-producing archaeological sites in North America. Two projects have conducted excavations in the Bat Cave complex, the first in 1948 and 1950 (Dick, 1965) and the second in 1981 and 1983 (Wills, "Early Agriculture and Sedentism in the American Southwest"; *Early Prehistoric Agriculture in the American Southwest*). Located in a volcanic cliff adjacent to the San Augustine Plains, a large enclosed basin within the montane Mogollon Highlands of western New Mexico, the Bat Cave site was discovered in the late 1940s by graduate students from the University of New Mexico searching for localities that might produce stratigraphic contexts for Paleo-Indian material (Hurt and McKnight, 1947). Limited test excavations in 1946 revealed abundant maize macrofossils (cobs and kernels) in preceramic horizons.

*Radiocarbon dating of charcoal obtained during the 1948 investigations produced age estimates of 6000 to 4000 B.P. for the lowest levels at the site. Since maize was found in these levels, investigators assumed that cultivation began in this area during the mid-Holocene. Subsequent research in the Mogollon Highlands failed to find other sites with maize in the range of 6000 to 4000 B.P. and in fact, the next oldest maize, from Tularosa Cave, just 19 miles (30 km) west of Bat Cave, was dated approximately 2300 B.P. This temporal discrepancy concerned many archaeologists, who worried that maize dates from Bat Cave might be in error, particularly since the maize had not been directly dated. Results from fieldwork and reanalysis of original collections, including direct dating of many maize specimens found in 1948, indicated that the earliest maize at Bat Cave was 3,500 to 3,000 years old. The use of arbitrary 12-inch (4.7-cm) excavation levels during the 1948 and 1950 fieldwork had inadvertently mixed cultural material of different ages, a problem compounded by prehistoric pits that intruded into lower site deposits, introducing younger material (including cultigens) to older (premaize) sediments.

Despite the revised estimates of its age, the oldest maize recovered from Bat Cave is still the oldest yet recorded in *North America. However, maize and squash from other sites in New Mexico and Arizona also date to the interval between 3500 and 3000 B.P. indicating that the adoption of these domesticates from *Mesoamerica was a phenomenon that took place widely throughout the American Southwest at approximately the same time.

[*See also* COCHISE CULTURE; NORTH AMERICA: THE NORTH AMERICAN SOUTHWEST.]

■ Wesley R. Hurt and Daniel McKnight, "Archaeology of the San Augustine Plains: A Preliminary Report," *American Antiquity* 3 (1947): 172–194. Herbert W. Dick, *Bat Cave* (1965). W. H. Wills, "Early Agriculture and Sedentism in the American Southwest: Evidence and Interpretations," *Journal of World Prehistory* 2 (1988): 445–488; *Early Prehistoric Agriculture in the American Southwest* (1988).
W. H. Wills

BATTLEFIELD ARCHAEOLOGY OF NORTH AMERICA. The study of military and battlefield sites can provide an important means of analyzing the behavioral patterns and cultural expressions of status in American society. Because military sites are easily defined archaeologically, and are usually relatively compact social, cultural, and physical units, they are ideal for intensive survey and excavation. The archaeological analysis of military sites can also offer unique perspectives on the behavioral aspects of cultures in conflict.

Military sites, particularly forts and fortifications, have long been of interest to North American archaeologists. There are a plethora of published site reports detailing the results of investigations at these American military sites. The investigations have often been conducted as ancillary studies to preservation, restoration, reconstruction, or interpretation efforts of local, state, or national agencies. Recently, another type of military site, the battlefield, has become the subject of archaeological investigations.

While the explanation of battlefield sites was once considered useful only for locating the opposing armies' cannon positions or recovering war relics for museum displays, recent battlefield archaeology at the American Revolutionary War site of Saratoga, New York, and at the famous 1876 Battle of the Little Bighorn ("Custer's Last Stand"), Montana, have demonstrated a far wider usefulness of battlefield archaeology.

Battlefield Research. Until recently, battlefield archaeology concentrated on uncovering or tracing fortification, particularly earthworks. Archaeological investigations by Lee Hanson in 1968 of the American Civil War Water Battery at Fort Donnelson was oriented toward the identification of gun emplacements, including determining what type of guns were placed at each embrasure. Another Civil War earthwork, at Causton's Bluff, Georgia, revealed, through archaeological work by Lawrence Babits in 1986, otherwise unknown details of the construction of bomb-proof shelters.

The first intensive archaeological study of an open battlefield site took place at the Little Bighorn Battlefield National Monument in southeastern Montana, from 1985 to 1989. The site yielded thousands of cartridge cases, bullets, army equipment, clothing fragments, Sioux and Cheyenne artifacts, and some skeletal remains of the soldiers who died 25 June 1876. The computer-assisted analysis of the distribution of artifacts on the battlefield yielded information about how the combatant groups utilized the terrain. Firearms identification analysis of thousands of recovered bullets added substantial knowledge about the role of firearms in the battle. The archaeological investigations demonstrated in considerable detail how George Custer's Seventh Cavalry was outnumbered, out-gunned, and outfought by Native American adversaries.

Since the completion of the Little Bighorn investigations, several other battlefield sites have been studied using metal-detecting techniques and artifact-patterning analysis. The earliest battlefield site studied was the 1846 Mexican-American War site of Palo Alto, Texas. Charles Hacker's 1993 investigations succeeded in finding the battlefield, which was believed lost, and he definitively located both United States and Mexican troop battlelines. His findings have modified the traditionally held historical view of a Mexican rout with the archaeological data clearly showing it was a pitched battle with extensive movement by the Mexican troops. The defeated Mexican army left behind a wealth of uniform and equipment artifacts that archaeologically demonstrate a valiant fight by a poorly armed and equipped army facing a much better equipped and armed United States Army.

Several American Civil War battlefields have also been investigated with the metal-detecting technique. The most intensively studied to date are by William Lees. One was the Honey Springs, Oklahoma, 1863 battle that pitted Federal black, Native American, and white troops against Confederate Native American and white troops. The second was Mine Creek, Kansas, the site of an 1864 battle during Confederate general Sterling Price's raid into Missouri. The Mine Creek investigations show that historians have incorrectly identified the battle site. Lees' work defined much of the actual battle site and determined positions and movement of both combatant groups, which was unrecorded or poorly documented in the historic record. Another Civil War battle site, recently investigated by Douglas D. Scott, is Monroe's Crossroads, North Carolina. This 1865 cavalry battle is little recorded in the historic record and archaeological investigation was the primary means to recover the site's history. The battle site, located on modern Fort Bragg, will be used by the army as a staff ride site for in-field small unit leadership training exercises.

Aside from the Little Bighorn, other United States Indian War battlefields have also been investigated. Douglas D. Scott studied the 1877 Nez Perce War battle site of Big Hole, Montana. There, archaeology revealed information that supported Nez Perce oral history and interpretation of the battle events and demonstrated that U.S. Army battle accounts were somewhat exaggerated. One of the U.S. Army's 1881 Apache campaign sites, K-H Butte, Arizona, has also been investigated by Larry Ludwig and James Shute.

Battlefield Theory. Because of the structured and ranked nature of military forces, battlefields have proved to be excellent locales for finding archaeologically definable behavioral patterns. Those who engage in combat usually fight in established manners and patterns in which they have been trained. It is precisely this training in proper battlefield or combat behavior that results in the deposition of artifacts that can be recovered by archaeological means and interpreted in an anthropological perspective.

Although interest in behavioral dynamics is not new in historical archaeology, battlefield archaeology is a relatively new area of study. The battlefield model developed by Richard Fox and Douglas Scott (1991) asserts that individual, unit, and battlefield movements can be reconstructed using pattern recognition techniques. The model also predicts certain types of depositional patterns depending on the culture, training, and organization of the combatant groups.

Battlefield studies can yield information on combatant positions used during the course of the battle as well as details of dress, equipage, and, in some cases, individual movements. Archaeological investigations can also retrieve information on troop deployment, firing positions, fields of fire, and weapon types present. Studies of artifact patterning can also reveal unit or individual movement during the battle, weapon trajectory, and range of firing by determining forces of projectile impact. Viewed in an anthropological context battlefields are the physical and violent expression of the culture or cultures in conflict.

Battlefield Recovery and Analytical Techniques. Archaeological remains of military equipment and firearms are among the most important classes of battlefield evidence. However, the ability to translate patterning of these artifacts into behavioral dynamics, particularly through the use of modern firearms identification procedures, constitutes an important advance over the traditional, nonsystematic recovery of battlefield relics.

The comparative study of ammunition components, known as firearms identification analysis, was first devel-

oped by law-enforcement agencies as an aid in solving crimes. Firearms, in their discharge, leave behind distinctive metallic "fingerprints," or signatures, on the ammunition components. These signatures, also called class characteristics, allow the determination of the types of guns used in a given situation.

Further, this analytical technique allows the identification of individual weapons by comparing the unique qualities of individual firearm signatures. This capability is very important because coupled with the precise artifact locations, identical individual characteristics can be used to identify specific areas of firearms use and individual movement. Analysis of a series of individual movements can, in turn, define unit deployment, and a series of unit deployments can be used to determine overall combatant tactics and the application of battle doctrine.

It is not enough to know where artifacts are found on a battlefield; archaeologists must also determine where they are not found. A primary goal of most battlefield research is therefore to define the limits of the battlefield. Faced with examining a large area, and assuming that most artifacts of war are either metallic or associated with metal, metal detectors have been successfully employed to define the full extent of the battlefield. As was the case at the Little Bighorn Battlefield National Monument, the use of metal detecting by experienced operators proved its value. It enables archaeologists to uncover artifacts with minimal disturbance and to point-plot each artifact location for precise mapping. Precise artifact location information is essential to revealing the behavioral patterns that are crucial to understanding the combat events.

Battlefield archaeology is a relatively new field of study, yet it has demonstrated its utility in correcting errors in the historical record and in adding new information. Recovered battlefield artifacts, as the physical evidence of the event, are also useful for interpretive purposes. More important, the artifactual data and the archaeological context provide new and independent sources of evidence for analysis of conflict situations and the broader study of the anthropology of war.

[*See also* FRONTIER SITES OF THE AMERICAN WEST; NORTH AMERICA: HISTORICAL ARCHAEOLOGY OF NORTH AMERICA.]

■ Julian Hatcher, Frank J. Jury, and Jac Weller, *Firearms Investigation, Identification and Evidence* (1977). Dean R. Snow, "Battlefield Archaeology," *Early Man* 3 (1981): 18–21. Gwynne Dyer, *War* (1985). Douglas D. Scott and Melissa A. Conner, "Post-Mortem at the Little Bighorn," *Natural History* 95 (1986): 46–55. Douglas D. Scott and Richard A. Fox Jr., *Archaeological Insights into the Custer Battle* (1987). Douglas D. Scott et al., *Archaeological Perspectives on the Battle of the Little Bighorn* (1989). Richard A. Fox Jr. and Douglas D. Scott, "The Post-Civil War Battlefield Pattern: An Example from the Custer Battlefield," *Historical Archaeology* 95 (1991): 92–103.

Douglas D. Scott

BEAKERS. The term *beaker (Becher, gobelet)* has traditionally been used by European prehistorians to designate a handleless drinking vessel, usually holding a pint or so of liquid, several varieties of which became widespread in northern and western Europe in the later Copper Age and earlier Bronze Age, between 4000 and 2000 B.C. The careful manufacture and decoration of such cups has given them a particular prominence in the archaeological record, and several cultures have been named after varieties of them, principally the funnel-beaker, the protruding-foot beaker, and the bell-beaker.

The distinctiveness of the shape arises from the contrast

with preceding Neolithic cultures of Bandkeramik derivation in this area, which might be designated *bowl cultures* (a term used by J.G.D. Clark) in that they used largely round-based vessels of open shapes, without any evidently privileged form of drinking vessel. Assemblages of *ceramics from the various beaker cultures, by contrast, are generally flat based, and often contain a range of specialized shapes for handling and pouring liquids—globular or tall-necked amphorae (two-lugged jars), flasks, or jugs—among which the beakers increasingly stand out because of the care and elaboration of their decoration. It thus seems likely that the appearance of these new types of vessels relates to changes in diet and cuisine, and specifically to serving practices accompanying a socially privileged consumption ritual—broadly analogous to the introduction of cups for tea and coffee at the time of the introduction of these beverages to Europe in the early modern period.

The appearance of beakers in northern and western Europe can only be understood in relation to the transformation of pottery assemblages in southeast and central Europe from the fourth millennium onward, in the Baden and related cultures. This transformation encompassed both shape and appearance: the introduction of shapes for the manipulation of liquids, and methods of manufacture and surface treatment (gray polished surfaces with channeling, omphalos bases, strap handles) derived from sheet-metal originals. A. Sherratt has suggested that this change reflects the introduction at this time of fermentation practices from western Asia and the social privileges symbolized by the consumption of alcohol. That these changes were often combined with other innovations is suggested by the occurrence of such drinking sets in elite graves (e.g., with paired cattle as accompaniments) and cups in the form of wagons (Budakalasz, Szigetszentmarton, both in Hungary). A comparable set of finely finished vessels in a complementary combination is characteristic of the early TRB culture (named after its cup, the funnel-beaker *Trichter[rand]becher*), which is associated with the first appearance of farming in areas of northern Europe beyond the loess after 4000 B.C. Such vessels, in combination with specific types of amphorae and of collared flask, commonly occur in individual graves, especially under earthen long barrows in newly settled areas, from eastern Poland to Jutland. These, again, suggest a context of ritual consumption.

The particular emphasis on drinking equipment continued in the east of the North European Plain in the Globular Amphora culture (named after one of the complementary vessels), and it decisively reappeared in Scandinavia and northern Germany after 3000 B.C. with the spread of the Corded Ware culture. The name *corded ware* describes a decorative technique, used earlier on the steppes, in which twisted cord was impressed on the surface of the pot, typically in parallel rows on the upper half of a beaker. These drinking vessels (especially in the west) have a protruding foot, hence the term Protruding-Foot Beaker (PFB) or *Standfußbecher*. Such vessels (and often globular amphorae) occur characteristically with individual burials of adult males accompanied by stone battle-axes in single graves under round mounds. Again, the specific form of consumption represented by the beaker seems to have been symbolic and socially privileged, in the same way as possession of a weapon. This symbolism and its burial rite extended over a vast area of northern Europe, from the mouth of the Rhine as far east as Moscow. At the western end of the North European Plain, where this rite replaced burial in a mega-

lith, it was associated with a radical shift in settlement patterns and a dispersal of population into smaller and more mobile units less rooted to individual locations than the megalith builders. This has been seen as part of an ideological realignment at a time of economic and political change, as the implications of plow-based farming and livestock keeping became apparent and contradictions accumulating within the existing social system were resolved in revolutionary change. The drinking ritual was a badge of solidarity amongst the new, mobile elites.

This background helps to put in perspective the phenomenon symbolized by the best-known type of beaker, the Bell-beaker (*Glockenbecher, Gobelet campaniforme*, so called after its shape when inverted). These distinctive and highly decorated vessels, distributed over an area from Scotland to Sicily and often accompanied by archery equipment in graves, were recognized by nineteenth-century prehistorians as constituting a classic puzzle—to which the traditional answer was a dispersal of the "Beaker Folk" from Iberia along the Atlantic facade, perhaps as metalworkers, warriors, or herdsmen. In a wider context, however, the Bell-beaker phenomenon can be seen as an extension of the Corded Ware social and cultural pattern into those parts of western Europe—like Britain and the Atlantic coastlands—where megalith-building societies still prevailed and where many Copper Age innovations were still unknown: metallurgy, horses, woolly breeds of sheep and woollen textiles, alcohol. As in Scandinavia, the introduction of these new features was often seriously destabilizing to older indigenous patterns of organization, and seems to have been temporarily resisted in areas of the British Isles such as Wessex. The Bell-beaker complex probably had its genesis at the mouth of the Rhine, where certain Corded Ware groups began to explore the seaways, perhaps using leather boats, reaching Brittany and the British Isles and penetrating down to Portugal. At a time when *metallurgy was just beginning in western Europe, these contacts provided a channel for the flow of novelties—flint, metal, livestock, wool, drinking recipes and ingredients—in several directions. Such contacts led to the propagation of Bell-beaker habits and equipment, initially by sea and then inland along the river networks as far as central Europe (hence there are maritime or pan-European beaker styles). Symbolic of membership of this club was use of the appropriate vessel for consuming what can now, from the evidence of pollen analysis, be reconstructed as a herb-flavored mead. Later Bell-beakers came to be ornamented in an increasing variety of complicated zoned patterns (which themselves hint at the potential importance of textiles in trade), and in southwest Europe these motifs were sometimes transferred to other pottery, especially bowls. The trade networks became especially important in linking two sets of commodities: western *metals (copper, gold, and later, tin) and eastern livestock (especially horses and woolly sheep, both spreading from the steppes via central Europe). Bell-beaker communities exploited their unique, though temporary, advantage in linking east and west, north and south.

On a global scale, it is not unusual for a particular decorative style applied to a specific form of container to achieve a widespread distribution at a time of extensive trading activity. New drinks, consumed with appropriate ritual to connote membership in a newly formed community, are characteristic of periods of enlarged contacts. A prehistoric analogy might be Lapita ware in second-millennium B.C. Melanesia (perhaps already used for drinking *kava*); a more recent one would, of course, be Coca-Cola. These examples suggest that Copper Age beakers of all kinds may have played a similar role in opening up the European continent.

[See also EUROPE: THE EUROPEAN COPPER AGE.]

■ Richard J. Harrison, *The Beaker Folk: Copper Age Archaeology in Western Europe* (1980). Andrew Sherratt, "Cups that Cheered," in *Bell-Beakers of the West Mediterranean,* ed. William Waldren and R. C. Kennard (1987), pp. 81–106. Andrew Sherratt, "Alcohol and Its Alternatives: Symbol and Substance in Pre-Industrial Cultures," in *Peculiar Substances: Essays in the History and Anthropology of Psychoactive Products,* ed. Jordan Goodman, Paul Lovejoy, and Andrew Sherratt (1995), pp. 11–46.

Andrew Sherratt

BEER AND BREWING. Beer has long been known to have played an important part in the history of civilization, but only recently has an interdisciplinary view of its role in social, agricultural, economic, religious, and dietary developments begun to emerge. The archaeological record suggests that beer has served both as a beverage of choice and, more importantly, as a dietary supplement of great significance for perhaps the last 10,000 years.

The preparation of grains, specifically barley and wheat, can be documented in the Near East as early as the Neolithic Period. Wild varieties of these grains were utilized by the hunters and gatherers of the *Natufian culture, as indicated by the discovery of grinding tools, sickle blades, and seeds at many Natufian sites. In order for the grain to have nutritional value, however, it had to be processed. It was the processing of the grain that led the way to brewing beer.

Earliest types of beer were more like a gruel than a beverage, since soaking grain in water was the simplest way to prepare the cereal for digestion. It was a small step to the process of malting, the germination of the grain. By controlled soaking, diastase converted part of the starch into maltose and dextrose. The maltose gave the grain a sweet taste. Malt could be dried or ground into a flour. If the malted product was crushed and sieved, the hulls could be removed.

The nutritional value of cereals could be further enhanced through the introduction of yeast, the ingredient furnishing the enzyme maltase for the conversion of the starch (maltose) to dextrose. While both bread and beer offered this possibility, the simple step of adding diastase, the enzyme that converted the starch into alcohol and carbon dioxide, made a beverage with far more than just nutritional importance.

Scholars have recently proposed that the Neolithic revolution, the turn toward the *domestication of plants, was primed by a cultural preference for beer. The appearance of seeds of domesticated wheat and barley at about 8000 B.C. on sites in the Levant such as Tell Aswad, *Jericho, and Nahal Oren attests to the importance of the processed grain. Archaeologists Soloman Katz and Mary Voight attribute the development of settled agriculture to the desire to brew beer. According to their theory, the social and religious impact of alcohol on the Neolithic societies, in addition to the nutritional benefits of cereal consumption, brought about the demand for the continual production of alcoholic beverages. A sedentary lifestyle would have been more suitable for beer production, which required specific grains as well as precise preparation to ensure a consistent product.

Mesopotamia. By the Sumerian period, beer production was regulated and its usage controlled. Temple inscriptions from the third millennium reflect a regulatory system wherein beer was rationed according to status as pay for workmen and both lower and higher officials. The earliest recorded recipe for beer is, in fact, Sumerian.

From the inscriptional evidence for beer in *Mesopotamia, it is possible to distinguish at least eight types of beer brewed from barley, eight brewed from emmer wheat, and another three mixed types. Both filtered and unfiltered beers were brewed. Because the unfiltered beer had grain husks floating on its surface, it was consumed through a pipe or reed. Visual representations of people drinking through long straws inserted into wide-mouthed, pointed-bottom vessels are known from cylinder and stamp seals. The earliest known example is a stamp seal from Tepe Gawra, dated to ca. 4000 B.C. A drinking straw made from gold was found in the tomb of a wealthy woman at *Ur.

While many terms to describe beer are known from the Sumerian texts, there is not a distinctive term for yeast. The word *s'rm*, introduced ca. 2000 B.C., may denote yeast, but it can also be translated as "dregs" or "lees." Because yeast was originally airborne, the ancient brewers did not fully realize its existence. They did know, however, that if left exposed, the brew would ferment. They could control the quality of a new mix by adding some previously brewed beer. It was also possible to transfer yeast cells from one batch to the next by reusing jars. While it is debatable whether ancient brewers used aromatics such as hops or spices to flavor their beers, Louis F. Hartman and A. L. Oppenheim suggested that the use of such additives is attested to in the pictographic sign for beer at about 1000 B.C. In earlier times, the prominent role of women in beer brewing was indicated by the fact that it was the only Mesopotamian profession with female deities as patronesses.

Egypt. Beer brewing in ancient *Egypt is also well attested, beginning with beer residues found in the bottoms of predynastic jars. Inscriptions from the Third Dynasty and representations in tomb paintings and tomb models from the Fifth Dynasty document the production of beer in the Old Kingdom. Apparently the Egyptian beer was somewhat different from the Mesopotamian types, since it was made by grinding the grain into a flour. This flour was then made into a dough, yeast was added, and it was allowed to rise. It was then baked into thick loaves. The yeast in at least one sample from ca. 1500 B.C. appears to have been almost pure and was probably processed. The baking was at fairly low temperatures, allowing for the survival of many yeast cells. The loaves were broken into a vessel containing water and allowed to ferment. Fermentation could be accelerated by the heating of this mixture, but the air temperatures in the Near East would usually have been sufficient. Evidence for aromatic additives in Egypt is questionable, although ingredients such as lupin, skirret, rue, safflower, bitter orange peel, and resin may have been brewed in for medicinal purposes. In Egypt the pharmaceutical importance of beer was long acknowledged, as was its cultic role, with beer used as divine and mortuary offerings. As in Mesopotamia, beer was at first home-brewed by women and later became commercially prepared and controlled by men.

Europe. In ancient *Europe, the Celts, Germans, Britons, and Iberians had their own characteristic methods of brewing. The Roman writer Pliny in his *Natural History* recorded that beverages were made from cereals in Gaul and that these were not mixed as wine was. He also related how an intoxicating drink was made with water and how, when the grain was steeped to make the beer, the foam that arose on the surface was skimmed and used as leaven to bake exceptionally light bread. This process is depicted in the workshop scenes on a number of sculpted reliefs from the Gallo-Roman sanctuary site of Grand (Vosges, France).

[See also AGRICULTURE; NEAR EAST: THE NEOLITHIC AND CHALCOLITHIC (PRE-BRONZE-AGE) PERIODS IN THE NEAR EAST; WINE: INTRODUCTION.]

■ A. Lucas, *Ancient Egyptian Materials and Industries,* 2nd ed. (1934). Louis F. Hartman and A. L. Oppenheim, "On Beer and Brewing Techniques in Ancient Mesopotamia According to the XXIII Tablet of the Series HAR.ra=Habullu," *Supplement to the Journal of the American Oriental Society* 10 (1950). R. J. Forbes, *Studies in Ancient Technology,* vol. 3 (1955). Charles Singer, E. J. Holmyard, A. R. Hall, and Trevor I. Williams, eds., *A History of Technology,* vol. 2 (1967). Albert Neuburger, *The Technical Arts and Sciences of the Ancients,* trans. Henry L. Brose (1969). Anna M. Macleod, "Beer," in *Alcoholic Beverages,* ed. A. H. Rose, vol. 1 (1977), pp. 43–137. Solomon H. Katz and Mary M. Voigt, "Bread and Beer: The Early Use of Cereals in the Human Diet," *Expedition* 28 (1986): 23–34.

Lisa C. Kahn

BELL, Gertrude (1868–1926), archaeologist who founded the Iraq Museum and laid the groundwork for modern research in Mesopotamia. Bell was the daughter of a well-known northern England iron manufacturer. She attended Oxford University in 1886, where she developed a taste for mountaineering and travel. In 1902, she traveled to Palmyra and Petra, developing a passion for desert travel and archaeology. She worked on excavations in Turkey and studied Byzantine monuments in northern Syria and Cilicia in 1905. In 1909 she published a major study of the Byzantine Thousand and One Churches at Birbinkilise in *Anatolia, a unique record of sites that no longer exist. Next she journeyed from Aleppo across the desert to the Euphrates River, spending four days surveying the walled Abbasid Palace of Ukhaidir, a huge castle with a fortified enclosure described in her most famous book, *Amurath to Amurath* (1911). Bell's knowledge of *Arabia brought her to Cairo, then Basra on the Persian Gulf in 1915, where she served in the Arab Intelligence Bureau. Eventually she became Chief Political Officer to the British Resident in the Gulf, a position of considerable importance. In 1918, she became the new government of Iraq's Director of Antiquities, responsible for founding the Iraq Museum and for foreign excavations. Bell filled the museum with finds from Leonard *Woolley's excavations at *Ur and from digs at other major sites. Lonely and increasingly isolated politically, Bell buried herself ever deeper in archaeological matters. Worried about her deteriorating health and future, she committed suicide in 1926.

Gertrude Bell was a learned archaeologist with a powerful personality. Her surveys at Birbinkilise and Ukhaidir were of considerable scientific value, but her greatest contribution was the Iraq Museum. Her reputation in Iraq itself is somewhat tarnished. Many Iraqis think she was too generous to foreign excavators. But this remarkable woman laid the legal and conservationist foundations for modern archaeological research in *Mesopotamia.

[See also HISTORY OF ARCHAEOLOGY FROM 1900 TO 1950: NEAR EASTERN ARCHAEOLOGY.]

■ Gertrude Bell, *The Desert and the Sown* (1907). Gertrude Bell, *Amurath to Amurath* (1911). Lady Bell, *The Letters of Gertrude Bell* (1927). H.W.V. Winstone, *Gertrude Bell* (1978).

Brian M. Fagan

BELZONI, Giovanni, (1778–1822), tomb robber who collected notable Egyptian relics for posterity. Belzoni was the son of a Padua barber. He became an actor and strong-arm performer on the English stage, performing at London's Sadler's Wells Theater as the *Patagonian Samson* in 1803. After the Napoleonic Wars, Belzoni's wanderlust took him to *Malta, then *Egypt, in 1815. British consul Henry Salt hired Belzoni to recover a head of Ramesses II from the Ramesseum near Thebes, a seemingly impossible task he performed with ease. Belzoni journeyed upstream to the temple of Abu Simbel, collecting numerous antiquities along the way. A second trip in 1817 had Belzoni befriending the tomb robbers of Qurna and Thebes, acquiring dozens of intact mummies and papyri. He returned to Abu Simbel and cleared the temple entrance. In the *Valley of the Kings, he located several royal tombs, notably the richly painted sepulchre of Seti I. In 1818, Belzoni penetrated the Pyramid of Khafra, one of the *pyramids of Giza, becoming the first person to do so since medieval times. The energetic and successful Belzoni aroused the jealousy of his rivals. He returned from a desert journey to Berenice on the Red Sea to have his life threatened. After another journey to the Fayum Depression and other oases in the western desert, Belzoni and his wife left Egypt in early 1820. They opened an imposing and well-received exhibition in London's Egyptian Hall in May 1821. But Belzoni soon became restless and set off in search of the source of the Niger River in West Africa. He died of fever near Benin a week after landing.

Giovanni Belzoni was a tomb robber who did untold damage to Egyptian antiquities. But he was more responsible than his peers, recording Seti's tomb paintings for posterity. His finds are in the British Museum, the Louvre, the Turin Museum, and other major European collections.

[See also HISTORY OF ARCHAEOLOGY BEFORE 1900: NEAR EASTERN ARCHAEOLOGY.]

■ Giovanni Battista Belzoni, *Narrative of the Operations and Recent Discoveries within the Pyramids, Temples, Tombs, and Excavations, in Egypt and Nubia* (1822). Maurice Wilson Disher, *Pharaoh's Fool* (1957). Stanley Mayes, *The Great Belzoni* (1961).

Brian M. Fagan

BILZINGSLEBEN is an open-air Lower Paleolithic lakeshore site at Steinrinne in eastern Germany, near the confluence of the Wipper and Wirbelbach rivers. It first became known as an old quarry with tuffs containing fossil bones and plant impressions of the Middle *Pleistocene. A few artifacts were found at the start of the twentieth century, but it was only in 1969 that Dietrich Mania discovered an important archaeological layer and began investigations at the site. Over 980 square feet (900 sq m) have since been exposed.

More than 100,000 stone artifacts have been recovered, mostly very small tools of flint, such as denticulates, awls, and side-scrapers. They are accompanied by some voluminous choppers and chopping tools of quartzite and limestone. This constitutes firm evidence for a Lower Paleolithic industry without hand axes in central Europe. Many deer antlers also seem to have been used as tools, and there are also large retouched bone flakes and some bone points with worn ends, as well as some remains of wooden tools.

The excavations have exposed what appear to be three simple oval dwellings, each ca. 10 by 13 feet (3 by 4 m), the outlines of which were recognized from the peripheral accumulations of stone and large bones. The presence of abundant charcoal, heated stones, and burnt bones marks the position of a fireplace in this lakeside camp. There are also a number of areas for the working of stone, bone, and wood, some of them with centrally placed stone anvils. In the center of the area in front of the dwellings, about 20 feet (6 m) away from them, is a roughly circular floor of small pebbles and bone debris.

The fauna is varied and includes straight-tusked elephant, rhinoceros, bear, deer, aurochs, horse, and beaver. Some of the animals may have been hunted, and many of the bones are fractured. The remarkable conditions of preservation have also ensured that eggshells, freshwater mollusks, nuts, and fruits have survived.

The artifacts were buried in spring deposits that have been dated by the Uranium/Thorium method to ca. 230,000 years ago, though occupation at the site stretches back to ca. 350,000 B.P. These dates place Bilzingsleben in the Holsteinian Interglacial, while plant impressions and mollusk shells indicate quite a warm episode within that period.

Ten fragments of human skull, together with seven molars, were found in the 1970s and display a mixture of *Homo erectus* and *Homo sapiens* traits. Of potentially even greater importance is the presence of some animal bones bearing incised lines arranged in rhythmic sequences that appear to be nonfunctional and hence represent some form of systematic pattern—in other words, of incipient *art.

[See also ACHEULEAN TRADITION; EUROPE; THE EUROPEAN PALEOLITHIC PERIOD.]

■ D. Mania and T. Weber, *Bilzingsleben III* (1986). D. Mania and E. Ulcek, "*Homo erectus* from Bilzingsleben (GDR). His Culture and His Environment," *Anthropologie* 25 (1987): 1–45. D. Mania and U. Mania, "Deliberate Engravings on Bone Artifacts of *Homo erectus*," *Rock Art Research* 5 (1988): 91–107. H. Schwarcz et al., "The Bilzingsleben Archaeological Site: New Dating Evidence, *Archaeometry* 30 (1988): 5–17. D. Mania, "The Zonal Division of the Lower Paleolithic Open-Air Site Bilzingsleben," *Anthropologie* 29 (1991): 17–24.

Paul G. Bahn

BISKUPIN is the site of a fortified stockade lying in west central Poland in the lake area near the town of Znin, in the valley of the river Warta. It belongs to a late phase of the Lausitz culture and dates to the beginning of the Iron Age. The site was discovered in 1933 by Walenty Szwajcer (Schweitzer), the local schoolmaster, and excavated from 1934 by Jozef Kostrzewski and Zdzislaw Rajewski of Poznan University. Because of its waterlogged state, *wood was well preserved; this led to the recovery of an exceptional quantity and quality of information, though also to many problems of preservation. Today most of the excavation has been filled in to protect the remains, and a set of reconstructions (houses, gateway, palisaded rampart) erected. It has become a major visitor center and also a center for *experimental archaeology.

The site lies on a peninsula in the Biskupin lake, and was probably originally an island about 525 by 656 feet (160 x 200 m) in extent. This area was enclosed by a palisade of rows of stakes driven into the ground at an angle, to serve also as a breakwater, and by a box-framed rampart of wood filled with earth and sand. A single entrance lay in the southwestern sector and was protected by a gate tower with twin gates. A wooden road ran around the inside of the rampart, enclosing a street system of eleven streets made of logs laid side by side, corduroy style. Along the streets lay houses, over 100 in number; they were typically 26 by 30 feet (8 x 9 m) in extent, built of walls of horizontal logs keyed into uprights, which were then reinforced by pegs. The floor was made of bundles of small branches. Each house

had an anteroom and a main room with hearth; a loft ran over part of the main room and was reached by ladder. Smaller animals were probably housed underneath, and a couple of cattle could have been accommodated in the anteroom. There were two main phases of occupation on the site. In the first, almost all the structural timber was oak, but in the second, pine was mainly used—presumably because of a shortage of oak in the vicinity of the site. Since there were over 35,000 stakes in the palisade alone, and 10,500 cubic yards (8,000 cu m) of timber in each phase of the site, it is clear that its construction represented a major drain on local woodland and a major effort in terms of labor input and organization.

The material from the site constitutes a standard domestic assemblage of the late Lausitz culture. Large quantities of pottery, numerous bone and stone tools, clay weights, wooden tools including a *wheel, hoes, plowshares, and paddles, and other organic materials such as bundles of flax were found. Metal objects were not so numerous, but both bronze and iron are represented, and bronze was worked on site. Analysis of this material indicates that the occupation belonged to Hallstatt C, which is the beginning of the Iron Age, probably eighth to seventh centuries B.C. The destruction of the site may reflect internal economic and social pressures arising from the cramped conditions and overexploitation of critical resources, but intergroup conflict probably also played a part.

[See also EUROPE: THE EUROPEAN IRON AGE; HALLSTATT.]

■ Z. Rajewski, *Biskupin, Poland's Iron Age Town* (1957).

Anthony F. Harding

BLACK DEATH, The. An English nursery rhyme recalls the still-fearsome plague: the "Ring-o-ring o' roses" is the pink rash that is an early symptom. Characterized by the black, agonizing swellings in groin and armpit called buboes and by fever and hemorrhages, the bubonic form causes death in five days or less, the pneumonic form is fatal in less than three days, and the septicemic in twenty-four hours. Rodents—in Europe usually the black ship rat—harbor the virulent causative bacillus *Pasteurella pestis*, which is conveyed to humans by flea bites and then easily transmitted in confined and insanitary conditions by human fleas, the clothing and bedding of victims, and in the pneumonic form, by coughing and sneezing ("atishoo, atishoo, we all fall down").

Pestilences, some probably plague, are described by Latin authors. The Plague of Justinian beginning A.D. 541, the first known pandemic, described by Procopius, traveled from Africa via Pelusium to the Byzantine Empire and killed 10,000 each day in Byzantium. Outbreaks followed for another two hundred years. The Black Death, the second pandemic, came from central Asia. It was supposedly introduced to the Crimea in 1347, when the Kipchaks catapulted infected corpses of their besieging army into a Genoese-held city, but was probably carried by Italian ships trading with the East. It reached Mediterranean ports in the same year, then spread inland, attacking a population already reduced by famine earlier in the century. In rural areas maximum mortality was reached within six months, but in densely populated cities, winter lulls were followed by spring resurgences. In the next five years, the plague overran all of Europe except Poland (which closed its borders), reaching eastward beyond Moscow and northward into southern Scandinavia.

Probably one third of the population, approximately 20

to 25 million, died in Europe, principally the poor because of their unhealthy conditions of life. The wealthy—like Boccaccio's young Florentines of the *Decameron*—were to some extent able to shut themselves away from infection. Certain cities established quarantines, and the heartlessly practical Milanese Visconti protected their city by walling up entire infected households, but most of those fleeing the disease simply carried it further. Doctors, unable to save lives, could not even relieve suffering, although Guy de Chauliac, physician to Pope Clement VI, attributed his own recovery to his medical expertise. Bodies were dumped in plague pits, the haste of disposal suggested by the chaotic conditions frequently found on excavation; unburied corpses were thrown in ditches and piled up in streets, increasing infection.

Despite the pronouncement by the University of Paris that the sickness was due to a malign conjunction of planets, for most people it was inexplicable. Its disgusting and horrific symptoms, the prospect of almost certain death, and the collapse of social order produced despair and hysteria and increased the endemic cruelty of the time: "the cruelty of heaven and to a great degree of man." Blame on Jews for supposedly poisoning wells led to massacres that, with the plague itself, almost eradicated Jews in Germany and the Low Countries, and restrictive enactments reduced their once-important position to marginal. The Church's view that the plague was God's judgment against sinful humankind enriched it by bequests. It also produced groups such as the Flagellants, who aspired to expiate the world's sins by their penance but whose leaders increasingly encouraged aggressive anticlericalism in the people. Their processions unwittingly carried the disease from town to town.

By the end of the fourteenth century, further resurgences of plague had reduced the population of Europe by nearly half. Many villages were abandoned, their manor houses, homesteads, streets, and fields disappearing, to await modern archaeological investigation. Some landowners gave over arable fields to sheep grazing, although others remitted rents and fees to secure their reduced agricultural labor force. Although there were new opportunities for both peasants and artisans to demand higher wages, these were frequently offset by higher taxes and food prices. Repressive legislation, such as the English and French statutes of 1381 limiting wage rises and controlling mobility, was to contribute to later popular risings such as the Jacquerie and the Peasants' Revolt. The Black Death was not solely responsible for the century's "strange and great perils and adversities"—which derive from such diverse causes as diminishing trade, widespread debasement of coinages, financial failures in Italian city-states, the breakdown of political alliances, and the depredations of mercenary armies—but it contributed both to societal decline and to a compensatory spirit of inquiry and search for new truths, which produced fresh religious, artistic, and intellectual developments.

[*See also* DISEASE; MEDIEVAL EUROPE, *articles on* TOWNS AND CITIES OF MEDIEVAL EUROPE, DESERTED VILLAGES OF MEDIEVAL EUROPE.]

■ Philip Ziegler, *The Black Death* (1969). Barbara W. Tuchman, *A Distant Mirror* (1978). Nancy Duin and Jenny Sutcliffe, *A History of Medicine* (1992).

Corinne Duhig

BOG BODIES. The bogs, particularly of western Europe, have provided a special environment for the preservation of human remains. Not only are the waterlogged anaerobic conditions conducive to the preservation of human soft tissue, but it is thought that sphagnan, a chemical component of sphagnum moss, may have further preservative and antimicrobial properties. The only detrimental affect of acid bogs is that they are likely to lead to the decalcification of the skeleton and teeth, so bodies can appear to be eroded or flattened and distorted by the pressure of the overlying peat that has formed.

Surveys of the individual reports of bog bodies, especially from Denmark, Germany, Holland, Britain, and Ireland, suggest that over 700 bodies have been found over the past 200 years or so. Famous examples include *Tollund Man and Grauballe in Denmark, and Lindow Moss in Britain. Both males and females are well represented but not younger children—with a few exceptions. From the evidence of the clothing and other associated finds, it is clear that some are of medieval or postmedieval date. However, the most interesting series have associated radiocarbon dates ranging from ca. 800 B.C. to A.D. 200, corresponding to the European Iron Age, but extending into Roman times.

With the introduction of peat-cutting machinery in commercial enterprises and the growing pressures in societies to conserve wetlands it is unlikely that many more bodies will be found in the future. An example of the devastation caused by such peat-cutting machinery is provided by the discovery of the third body from Lindow Moss, near Manchester, England. This was identified in cut peat as numerous separate pieces of body, representing a major forensic problem in terms of reconstruction.

Why were these bodies placed in bogs? While a few may be the result of accidental deaths in very waterlogged bogs, and others perhaps normal burial in wetland areas, there is little doubt that there are other explanations for perhaps the majority. More recent cases very probably include victims of murder, conveniently hidden away in these deposits; historical evidence suggests that at least a few were suicides excluded from normal Christian burial. In the case of the Iron Age and Roman burials, the bodies may include executions, and in some instances the nature of the injuries gives support to the view that they were ritual killings. In particular, the very well-preserved Grauballe Man from Denmark (ca. 55 B.C.) not only displayed a deeply cut throat on discovery, but also skull injuries and other trauma. In the case of Lindow Man (ca. 300 B.C.), the second of the discoveries from Lindow Moss, evidence of head injuries, a cut throat, asphyxiation caused by a tightened thong, as well as chest and neck trauma was found.

The recently reexamined Huldre Fen Woman (ca. A.D. 95) had an arm hacked off (causing bleeding that surely led to her death), as well as multiple deep cuts to her legs. In the latter case, most of the injuries were revealed only by a detailed restudy, which emphasizes the need for further investigations to be carried out on some of the earlier finds, some of which received only very superficial examination. In many instances the cause of death is not known; the cause of death of other subjects originally appeared to be clear, but alternative possibilities need to be ruled out. Thus, in the case of the Borre Fen Man (ca. 840 B.C.) head injuries seem to have caused his death, but the hemp rope around his neck may well have hanged or strangled him.

In the case of the more recent bog bodies, buried within the last few hundred years, the garments were often coarse country wear, sometimes patched and mended. They were rarely of the fine quality exemplified by the seventeenth-century Irish bog body find at Tawnamore, with fine woollen clothes, felt hat, greatcoat, breeches, jacket, knitted stockings, and shoes of good hide. In some contrast, the late prehistoric or early historic bodies were varyingly clothed, from largely unmodified skins to more complete dress. Lindow Man was naked except for a fox-fur armband, while the Borre Fen III Woman wore a voluminous woollen skirt. The Huldre Fen Woman was apparently better dressed, with a checkered skirt, lambskin cape, and head scarf, as well as amber beads on a string and a horn comb. In some cases the clothing is in a crumpled state and generally the bodies cannot be said to have been laid out for funerary rites. The hair may also suggest rather different treatment before or at death. There are cases where the hair is closecropped, as with Borre Fen II and the Huldre Fen Women. It is well trimmed on Lindow Man, but longer on the Grauballe individual. In a few instances the hair is clearly long but dishevelled.

This evidence seems to confirm that various factors led to the depositing of these bodies in the bogs. The Roman historian Tacitus (ca. A.D. 55–120) noted that contemporary Germanic peoples punished adulterous wives by cutting off their hair, stripping them naked, parading them through their home village, and flogging them. But how much more violent could such punishments be? Tacitus also calls our attention to other tribal habits that are relevant to a full interpretation of bog bodies. He states that "traitors and deserters are hanged on trees; cowards, shirkers and sodomites are pressed down under a wicker hurdle into the slimy mud of a bog." Other writings of this kind confirm that human sacrifices were made in these northern Iron Age cultures, and it is thus no great surprise to find bodies appearing in bogs.

A new impetus to research on bog bodies was provided by the discoveries in May 1983 and August 1984 of parts of two bog bodies at Lindow Moss in Cheshire. Subsequently, further discoveries were made at this site of fragments that probably represented yet another body. No clothing is associated with these individuals. Radiocarbon dates suggest a time range between 300 B.C. and A.D. 300. Unlike previous discoveries, it was possible to excavate much of the second body (Lindow Man) from the peat in laboratory conditions. It was also possible to assemble a team of specialists and equipment to investigate a wide range of problems, from the animal species represented by the armband, and the ABO blood group, of the body itself, to the insects and pollen in the peat directly surrounding the corpse.

In the study of Lindow Man, it was also possible to check the degree of preservation of internal organs by CT (computerized tomographic) scanning, as well as by conventional X-rays and xeroradiography. These revealed bone damage, decomposing brain material, parts of the intestinal tract, and evidence of long-established minor trauma to the vertebrae (Schmorl's nodes). Forensic experts were called in to advise on the knots in the thong around the neck, as well as the nature of the injuries. A separate and highly specialized line of investigation was undertaken on the parasite eggs (Ascaris and Trichuris) and the food residue from the lower intestinal tract. This kind of work was pioneered by Hans Helbaek on Danish bog body food residues, and these new discoveries provided further material for detailed evaluation. The food being digested by Lindow Man at death was probably mainly cereals (emmer and spelt wheats, barley, and oats). It was notable for the small range of species represented, and contrasts markedly with the more varied "muesli" in the gut of Grauballe Man, which contained over sixty plant species (although some may have been accidental inclusions in the form of crop weeds). The parasitic worms (revealed by the presence of their eggs) had not posed a serious health problem, and have been found in other bog bodies. In terms of new techniques being applied to such bog bodies, however, it was disappointing to find no human DNA, which might have provided the first genetic information on northern Iron Age people.

[See also EUROPE, articles on THE EUROPEAN IRON AGE, ROMAN AND POST-ROMAN EUROPE; TOLLUND MAN.]

■ P. V. Glob, (1969). The Bog People: Iron-Age Man Preserved (1969). I. M. Stead, J. B. Bourke, and D. Brothwell (eds), Lindow Man: The Body in the Bog (1986). R. C. Turner and R. G. Scaife (eds), Bog Bodies: New Discoveries and New Perspectives (1995).

Don Brothwell

BOTTA, Paul Emile (1807–1870), the first archaeologist to uncover an Assyrian palace. Botta was the son of a well-known Italian historian, an experienced traveler who entered the service of Pasha Mohammed Ali of Egypt as a physician. In 1833, he was appointed French consul in Alexandria and traveled deep into Yemen. The French government transferred him to Mosul in northern modern Iraq in 1840, with instructions to excavate on the ancient city of *Nineveh across the Tigris River from the town. Botta excavated briefly into Nineveh's mounds and found nothing in the overburden. When one of his workmen found carved horsemen under his house at nearby Khorsabad, the consul moved his operations there, promptly uncovering the palace of Assyrian King Sargon II. Unable to read cuneiform inscriptions, Botta claimed wrongly that he had unearthed Nineveh. The French government responded magnificently, sending out artist Eugène Napoléon Flandin to draw and record the precious alabaster reliefs from the palace before it was too late. Botta continued to dig into Khorsabad with as many as three hundred men until 1844, recovering much of the floor plan of Sargon II's palace and barracks, built in the eighth century B.C. Unfortunately, his *excavation methods were too crude to trace mud-brick structures successfully, but he acquired enormous quantities of bas-relief and spectacular artifacts, including human-headed and winged bulls that guarded the palace doorways. Botta and Flandin published the sumptuous four-volume *Monuments de Ninive* between 1846 and 1850. After the excitement of the Khorsabad excavations, Botta was transferred to a minor diplomatic post in Lebanon, where he died in 1870.

By all accounts a pleasant and easy going man, Botta was the first archaeologist to excavate an Assyrian palace. Inevitably his discoveries were eclipsed by those of his contemporary Austen Henry *Layard. The galleries of the Louvre bear testimony to his researches.

[See also HISTORY OF ARCHAEOLOGY BEFORE 1900: NEAR EASTERN ARCHAEOLOGY.]

■ Paul Emile Botta and Eugène Napoléon Flandin, Monuments de Nineve, 4 vols. (1846–1850). Brian Fagan, Return to Babylon. (1979). Seton Lloyd, Foundations in the Dust (1980).

Brian M. Fagan

BOYNE VALLEY, or Brugh na Bóinne, is situated in the valley of the river Boyne in eastern Ireland. Bounded on three sides by the river, the complex of sites and monuments is approximately 3 miles (4.8 km) long and close to 2 miles (3.2 km) in maximum width. The first mention of any aspect of Brugh na Bóinne goes back to 1699 when the keeper of the Ashmolean Museum in Oxford described the megalithic tomb of Newgrange. Major and planned programs of excavation commenced in 1960, and these are still continuing. It can now be demonstrated that there was a long sequence of use and settlement at Brugh na Bóinne beginning close to 6000 years ago, when an early Neolithic farming family or families settled on the hilltop at Knowth. Occupation continued, with interruptions, down to post-medieval times. In all, nine main cultural phases can be detected.

Earliest Neolithic Stage (ca. 4000–3500 B.C.). A small group of farmers arrived at Knowth, cleared an area in the woodland, and commenced mixed farming. They lived in a rectangular wooden house 26 by 20 feet (8 m by 6 m) with a limited range of articles consisting of flint scrapers and pottery vessels with round bases and simple rims.

Developed Early Neolithic (ca. 3500–3000 B.C.). The homestead was again the rectangular wooden house, but a progression to nucleated settlement is evident at Knowth, where the remains of a palisaded enclosure up to 379 feet (100 m) in diameter has come to light. By now it can be assumed that more intensive farming was under way and that there was an increase in population as well as a greater dispersal in population.

Passage Tomb Builders (ca. 3000–2400 B.C.). This was an exceedingly vigorous phase at Knowth. External influence was strong, notably from the Atlantic lands of Europe to the south (Brittany and Western Iberia), but there were also influences from Britain, especially in artifacts such as pottery. Evidence comes from both settlement and *burial.

The best evidence for settlement is provided by the sites of Townley Hall and Knowth. There are two sites at Townley Hall, with circular houses constructed from a framework of stakes that were covered by skins or thatch. Site 2 was particularly rich in finds. These included different varieties of pottery, especially Carrowkeel and Sandhills wares, but also a range of flint artifacts, predominantly rounded and hollow scrapers.

The other important area of settlement was at Knowth. This was much larger, extending over an area of approximately 140 square feet (1,250 sq m). Evidence for at least fourteen houses came to light, and though not all were in simultaneous use, at one place there was evidence for at least six houses.

The passage tombs constitute the most spectacular aspect of the archaeology of Brugh na Bóinne, as among them are Europe's greatest prehistoric monuments. Altogether, there are approximately forty tombs forming a large cemetery, with clusters within it. The most notable concentration is at Knowth, with up to twenty tombs; Newgrange and Ballincrad have four each, and it is likely that there was a similar cluster at Dowth.

A feature of all four clusters is a major and dominating mound. That at Ballincrad is badly damaged, but seems to be approximately 235 feet (70 m) in diameter. Dowth is approx. 285 (85 m) feet in diameter and covers 1 acre (.4 ha). It is known to contain two tombs, both of which open on the western side of the mound. The Newgrange cairn varies between 265 and 285 feet (79 and 85 m) in diameter and covers approximately 1 acre (.4 ha). It is delimited by ninety-seven curbstones. The passage, approximately 63 feet (19 m) long, leads into a cruciform-shaped chamber with a corbelled roof rising to a height of 20 feet (6 m). The principal mound at Knowth is the largest of all the Brugh na Bóinne mounds, measuring approximately 316 by 266 feet

(95 m by 80 m) and covering approximately 1.5 acres (.6 ha). It is delimited by 127 curbstones and contains two tombs, placed back-to-back and opening respectively to west and east. The western tomb is 80 feet (24.2 m) in total length and ends in a bottle-shaped chamber. The eastern tomb is the larger and more elaborate. It consists of a parallel-sided passage approximately 3 feet (1 m) in width and 133 feet (40 m) long leading into a cruciform-shaped chamber roofed, as at Newgrange, by corbelling and reaching a height of 20 feet (6 m).

Where information is available through excavation, the dominant rite was cremation, and this was communal and successive. It was the practice to place grave goods with the remains, especially items of personal adornment such as beads, pendants of stone, and pins of bone and antler.

Another remarkable aspect of the tombs is their art. At present up to 410 individual stones are known, but many more await discovery, while others have been destroyed without record. They constitute the greatest concentration of megalithic art known. In the creation of the *rock art, two main techniques were used—incision and picking (or pocking). The art is nonrepresentational and consists of abstract motifs such as circle spirals, rectilinear designs, and lozenges/triangles. The circular art is mainly external and is the "public" art, probably having a role in processions of the laity around the sites. The other two main forms were placed internally and as such probably played a role in tomb ceremonies. The rectilinear art occurs toward the inner end of the passage and could indicate a special place where ceremonies took place before entering the chamber. The angular art concentrates in the chamber, and here may have been the most important art of all, as an accompaniment to the burials.

The passage tomb stage represents a period of outstanding development at Brugh na Bóinne. By now there were large tracts of open countryside, and these could have supported large numbers of farming families. The construction of the larger megalithic tombs was a major undertaking, a huge commitment from the contemporary population involving various grades of society, from laborers to highly skilled individuals who were the equivalent of structural engineers, quantity surveyors, and architects.

The Grooved Ware Stage (ca. 2400–2200 B.C.). The evidence for this stage is provided by the remains of domestic activity at Knowth and Newgrange but especially by large earthen enclosures and a ritual wooden structure at Knowth.

Beaker Folk (ca. 2200–1900 B.C.). This stage is represented by areas of settlement occupation at Knowth and Newgrange. The building and use of large ritual earthen enclosures continued, as is demonstrated by the finds from the Monknewtown enclosure. The freestanding stone circle from Newgrange may also have been erected by Beaker people.

Apart from a flat axe from Newgrange and a food-vessel burial, there is practically no evidence for activity at Brugh na Bóinne during the Bronze and Early Iron Ages (1900 B.C.–0).

Late Iron Age (Early Centuries A.D.). The most definite evidence for the revival of activity in the Late Iron Age is provided by a series of inhumation burials in simple pit graves at Knowth. About a dozen of these contained grave goods, such as necklaces or bracelets of small blue glass beads or occasionally other objects—in one instance a set of stone game pieces, bone dice and bone pegs. It may also have been at this time that the main mound at Knowth was transformed into a well-protected settlement site by the digging of two penannular ditches, one at the base, the other around the summit. The site became a significant homestead, possibly that of a prominent person and his family.

Newgrange also emerged as a place of prominence, seemingly of a ritual nature. There is one inhumation burial, but fuller evidence is provided by the discovery of objects from Roman Britain close to the entrance of Newgrange tomb. These finds can be explained as offerings close to what still must have been considered a sacred site.

Mature Early Christian Period (ca. A.D. 800–1100). During the ninth, tenth, and into the eleventh centuries, another new and vigorous stage emerged. This is shown by the construction of protected farmsteads ("ring-forts") in Knowth and Newgrange town lands and by an underground storage chamber that was inserted into the western edge of the Dowth mound. But the main focus of activity was at Knowth. That site became the focus of a prominent rural settlement with rectangular houses and souterrains. During the ninth century it became an important political center, the royal residence of the kings of Northern Brega, but by the eleventh century its importance was diminishing, and its significance had virtually faded by the twelfth.

Cistercian-Norman (ca. Latter Half of the Twelfth Century to the Fourteenth Century). Around the middle of the twelfth century, Knowth passed out of native hands and was incorporated into the newly acquired domains of the recently arrived Cirstercians, who in 1157 established the nearby monastery of Mellifont. The site became a grange, with the main occupation on top of the large mound, where a rectangular-shaped area was enclosed by a wall. An important interlude took place about 1169, when the site was occupied by the Normans and played a part in the Norman Conquest of Meath. The Cistercian grange was finally abandoned in the fourteenth century.

Postmedieval (ca. Seventeenth Century). Evidence for postmedieval settlement at Brugh na Bóinne was limited to a couple of small rectangular dwelling houses.

[See also BEAKERS; BRITISH ISLES: CELTIC IRELAND; MEGA-LITHIC TOMBS; STONE CIRCLES AND ALIGNMENTS.]

George Eogan

BREUIL, Henri. French prehistorian, the leading authority on Paleolithic art during his lifetime, trained as a priest in his youth, but although he remained a priest till his death, it was only a title. He was allowed to devote his whole existence to prehistory, undertook virtually no religious duties, and made almost no contribution to the reconciliation of prehistory's findings with religious teachings. Breuil's determination to be both priest and scientist was aided by the fact that one teacher at the seminary, the abbé Guibert, not only encouraged his bent toward natural history but even expounded the theory of evolution and lent him the works of Gabriel de Mortillet, the anticlerical prehistorian.

Breuil had the supreme good fortune, as a young man with a talent for drawing animals, to make the acquaintance of Edouard Piette and Emile Cartailhac, two of France's greatest prehistorians, who needed help with the study and illustration of Paleolithic portable and cave *art, respectively. His association with these men eventually led Breuil to become the world's leading authority of his era on Paleolithic art. He discovered many decorated caves or galleries and copied their art; by his own reckoning he spent about seven hundred days of his life underground. Although now seen as excessively subjective and incomplete, his tracings

are nevertheless recognized as remarkable for their time. For some caves, they constitute our only record of figures that have since faded or disappeared.

In the Second World War, Breuil began a long campaign of copying rock art in parts of southern Africa. He had also visited Zhoukoudian, China, in the 1930s, after the discoveries there of fossil hominids and their tools. His greatest contributions to tool typology, however, were in France, where he won the "Aurignacian battle," establishing once and for all that the Aurignacian preceded the Solutrean. He set out the first detailed description of the characteristic tools of each French Paleolithic period, dividing the Magdalenian into six phases on the basis of changing tool types. This scheme was durable and influential, but has now been replaced by a simpler and more flexible Early / Middle / Upper Magdalenian.

In the same way, his concept of two cycles in the development of Paleolithic art, the Aurignaco-Perigordian followed by the Solutreo-Magdalenian—two essentially similar but independent cycles, each progressing from simple to complex forms in engraving, sculpture, and painting—was inconsistent and unsatisfactory. Eventually it was replaced by Andre *Leroi-Gourhan's four styles, themselves now in the course of being abandoned. Breuil saw Paleolithic art primarily in terms of hunting magic, thanks to a simplistic use of selected ethnographic analogies, and he generally considered decorated caves to be accumulations of single figures, unlike Leroi-Gourhan, who saw them as carefully planned compositions.

An irascible and egotistical man, Breuil nevertheless had a lasting influence on numerous devoted friends and pupils. So ingrained was his image as the Pope of Prehistory that he was often thought virtually infallible. It is only in recent years that it has become possible in France to criticize openly and reexamine his work like that of any other scholar. His huge legacy of publications and tracings has been found to contain many errors and misjudgments, but also an abundance of profound insights that are only now being supported by new finds.

[See also HISTORY OF ARCHAEOLOGY BEFORE 1900: EURO-PEAN ARCHAEOLOGY; ROCK ART: PALEOLITHIC ART.]

■ Alan Brodrick, *The Abbé Breuil, Prehistorian: A Biography* (1963). Eduardo Ripoll, *El Abate Henri Breuil (1877–1961)* (1994).

Paul G. Bahn

BRITISH ISLES

OVERVIEW

The British Isles are archaeologically one of the best-known regions of the world, and they contain a number of well-known sites and monuments including *Stonehenge and *Hadrian's Wall. Lying off the northwest corner of the European mainland, this island group benefits from the effects of the warm North Atlantic currents which make them much less inclement in winter than their northerly latitude would otherwise imply. This has not always been the case, however, and during the cold phases of the Pleistocene the British Isles presented a harsh environment, visited only by migratory bands of hunter-gatherers making summer forays at the northern edge of their annual range. On the mainland of Britain there are nevertheless signs of human activity as long as 500,000 years ago, notably the recently discovered skeletal remains of Boxgrove Man in Sussex. The scouring effect of the ice sheets and the extreme cold mean however that there are few *in situ* archaeological deposits before the later stages of the last ice age, around 20,000 years ago.

The warmer climate of the postglacial period encouraged human settlement of the whole of Britain, including Scotland and (from around 7000 B.C.) Ireland. During the earlier postglacial era, the rising sea level meant that Britain itself was connected to mainland Europe across the low-lying area later occupied by the North Sea. Sites such as *Star Carr in Yorkshire relate closely to similar hunter-gatherer encampments in northern Germany. The flooding of the North Sea in around 6500 B.C. severed Britain's land-link with the continent and converted it into the island it has remained ever since. The same is not true of Ireland, however, since deep water channels ensured that the latter was never accessible from Britain without water transport, and this no doubt accounts for the absence of Irish evidence of Paleolithic occupation.

The prehistoric communities of Britain and Ireland first began to use domestic plants and animals in about 4000 B.C., in a move which conventionally marks the transition from Mesolithic to Neolithic. Neolithic Britain and Ireland are perhaps best known for their ritual monuments, including henges, stone circles, and burial mounds, some of these last containing chamber tombs of timber or megalithic construction. The most elaborate British ritual monuments belong to the later stages of the Neolithic and the following Early Bronze Age, and include *Avebury, Stonehenge, and Silbury Hill. Another salient feature of the British Isles during the Neolithic was the widespread trade in axes of polished hard stone quarried in northern Ireland and the mountainous regions of northern and western Britain. The transition to the Early Bronze Age (ca. 2500 B.C.) is associated with the appearance of Beaker pottery (*see* Beakers), illustrating the existence of long-distance contacts which brought with them the use of copper, gold, and bronze.

The second millennium B.C. marks a major transformation of prehistoric Britain with the appearance of the first substantial settlements and field systems, indicating a greater commitment to agriculture, a growing population, and a developing social hierarchy. This leads directly to the hill fort society of the Iron Age (ca. 700 B.C. to A.D. 43), characterized by hilltop fortresses and nascent tribal groupings. By the first century B.C. there were kingdoms in southern Britain, encountered by Julius Caesar in his invasions of 55 through 54 B.C. and Claudius in the full-scale Roman Conquest of A.D. 43.

Britain under Roman rule was a heavily militarized province with a troublesome northern frontier. Despite several attempts, the Romans never completed the conquest of Scotland and never attempted the conquest of Ireland, where traditional Celtic culture and society continued to develop. Hadrian attempted to resolve the frontier problem by the building of his famous wall, which gave a measure of security. Britain passed out of Roman control early in the fifth century, however, when the western provinces were

taken over by incoming Germanic groups. Southern and eastern Britain was seized by Anglo-Saxons from Scandinavia and northern Germany who settled in sufficient numbers to change the language from Latin or Celtic to English and established a series of kingdoms. The early Anglo-Saxons were non-Christians who introduced their own burial traditions, seen most impressively in the *Sutton Hoo cemetery, but during the seventh century, missionaries gradually converted Anglo-Saxon England to Christianity. The Anglo-Saxon kingdoms came under fierce assault from Scandinavian war bands (the Vikings) in the ninth through the eleventh centuries, but Vikings also stimulated the growth of towns and trade and the Anglo-Saxon response led to the formation of a unified kingdom of England.

The Norman Conquest of 1066 marks the end of Anglo-Saxon England and the beginning of the Medieval Period. The twelfth and thirteenth centuries saw the expansion of English political control into Ireland and Wales, and the attempted conquest of Scotland, but each region maintained much of its distinctive cultural identity into recent times. Prosperity continued to rise during the Late Middle Ages and Tudor period, but the great change in economy and society came with the Industrial Revolution of the eighteenth and nineteenth centuries, leading to new industries, new and larger cities, and the extensive use of water power and fossil fuel for transport and manufacturing. Many impressive remains and installations still survive from the Industrial Revolution, including workers' housing, factories, and machines, and *industrial archaeology is today one of the growth areas of British archaeology.

[*See also* CAMPS AND ENCLOSURES, CAUSEWAYED; CELTIC ART; CELTS; EUROPE: INTRODUCTION; HILL FORTS; STONE CIRCLES AND ALIGNMENTS.]

Chris Scarre

PREHISTORY OF THE BRITISH ISLES

Properly speaking, British prehistory did not begin until about 6500 B.C., when Britain itself became an island. Before then, the country had been at the extreme limits of habitable land, and occupation during the Paleolithic Period had fluctuated according to the movement of the ice caps. During the Upper Paleolithic and Early Mesolithic phases the flint industries found in Britain resemble those known from adjacent areas of the European continent, but after Britain was separated from the mainland, the material culture of the two areas diverged.

In practice it is difficult to work out to what extent the British sequence was distinct from wider developments in continental Europe. The next point of contact came at the start of the Neolithic Period, about 4000 B.C., but the adoption of monuments and material culture of continental character took place against an uncertain background because so little is known about the last thousand years of Mesolithic activity. The latest reliably dated Mesolithic assemblages have been found mostly on the coastline of northern Britain. This was an area of isostatic uplift where the original shoreline survives, but in southern England the Mesolithic coast has been lost. If settlement had focused on such areas, the last hunter-gatherer occupation sites would no longer survive.

Neolithic Period. It is difficult to establish whether Neolithic material culture was introduced to Britain by substantial immigration or whether the main contribution was made by acculturated natives. Three points do seem to be clear. The main food resources—wheat, barley, sheep, and probably domesticated cattle—were not native to the country and had to be introduced. British Neolithic culture seems to be an amalgam of influences drawn from widely separated areas of continental Europe; there is no one source of inspiration. At the same time, the first Neolithic in Britain belongs to a later period than the intensive settlement of the loess epitomized by the Linear Pottery culture. It began during a phase in which settlements are harder to detect and in which the economy may have been more diversified.

Neolithic Britain is in any case more easily characterized by its public monuments than by the introduction of agriculture, the true extent of which remains conjectural. The period can be divided into two phases, each of them represented by a different group of monuments. The Early Neolithic is typified by collective burials beneath long mounds and by ceremonial enclosures. Although a small number of houses have been identified in excavation, these were isolated structures, and there is little to suggest a pattern of nucleated settlement. Human effort seems to have been directed as much into ritual and ceremony as into any form of intensive food production. Two major developments can be identified during this phase. The first is a gradual change from collective burials to the burial of individuals accompanied by grave goods, and the second is the superimposition of fortified settlements on earlier ceremonial enclosures. Both hint at a process of social differentiation. Certainly, conditions were not entirely peaceful, for a few of those fortified sites were attacked and destroyed.

The Late Neolithic continues some of these trends, but with a stronger emphasis on individual burials, mainly in northern England. Settlement may have been more extensive, but its character remains little known. New developments most probably began on the Atlantic seaboard about 3000 B.C., and are evidenced by a range of interconnections between Ireland and Orkney. In the latter area these links involved a new style of *megalithic tombs and a series of ceremonial enclosures known as henge monuments. Between 3000 and 2400 B.C., such enclosures were adopted over wide areas of the British Isles, with the largest—and some of the latest—examples in *Wessex. These earthworks contained circles of posts or upright stones and often provide evidence of feasting and the exchange of nonlocal artifacts. In areas in which henge monuments were less conspicuous, there is more evidence for individual burials beneath circular mounds.

Bronze Age. Individual burials had always been associated with occasional finds of weapons and ornaments, but it was only from about 2400 B.C. that they came to include material of continental origin or inspiration. Two developments are especially important. These graves are among the earliest contexts to include Beaker pottery (see Beakers), and they can also be found with the first metal artifacts in the country. In addition, Beaker pottery is sometimes associated with the levels of the henges. At this time some of the timber circles inside these enclosures were replaced with stone, but with the exception of *Stonehenge, their period of use was rather brief, and the major monuments of the Early Bronze Age are the burial mounds. Once again, occupation sites remain poorly documented, and the pattern of settlement may not have been entirely sedentary.

The burial mounds dominate the other evidence dating from this period. Only a small proportion of the population could be commemorated by monuments, and some archaeologists suggest the evolution of chiefdoms during this phase. Individual graves were sometimes lavishly provided with elaborately decorated pottery and both weapons and ornaments in a variety of nonlocal materials, including copper, bronze and gold, jet, amber, and faience. They evidence a range of contacts extending from Brittany through central Europe to the Mycenaean world, although the strength of some of these connections can be exaggerated. This is commonly referred to as a period of "single" burial, but there might be as many as twenty of these graves in any one mound, and individual graves could also be reopened to receive new burials. Some of the mounds occur singly, but more are found in cemeteries of as many as forty. They tend to be located around already established ceremonial monuments. The earlier burials were mostly inhumations, but the later mounds also include cremations.

Nearly all these developments ended between about 1500 and 1200 B.C., when new traditions emerged. Some can be defined in negative terms—the building of large mounds seems to have lapsed, and so did the provision of elaborate grave goods—but most important was the development of an agricultural landscape. *Agriculture was characterized for the first time by *field systems, land boundaries, domestic enclosures, and archaeologically detectable houses. These seem to suggest a more stable pattern of settlement. In the occupation sites we find evidence of ponds and grain storage pits, and some of the field systems extended over considerable areas. Human effort seems to have been directed toward food production, and the large ceremonial monuments built during earlier phases lost their significance. They were apparently abandoned and a few were even plowed out. At first, small cremation cemeteries were created alongside the newly built settlements, but later even this evidence for the treatment of the dead disappears.

That is not to say that evidence for ritual activity is lacking. From this time onward there is evidence for the formal deposition of metal objects in bogs and rivers. It was a tradition that extended from the Middle Bronze at the end of the Iron Age. The main items deposited were weapons, some of them types related to those placed in earlier graves. They may also have been funeral offerings, and for that reason it is not surprising that there are occasional discoveries of human skulls from the same locations.

The settlement pattern became more diversified during the Late Bronze Age, when we find evidence for new kinds of sites. In some areas large tracts of land were enclosed by boundary ditches, and within such territories in central southern England there were large open settlements. Specialized sites were established beside major rivers; these engaged in large-scale craft production. It is in the same period that we encounter the first evidence of *hill forts. In western Britain a number of hilltop settlements were established, some of them defended by elaborate stone and timber ramparts. These sites are sometimes associated with evidence of the production of *metals, but they also contain concentrations of circular houses and raised store-buildings, probably granaries. In eastern England, smaller circular enclosures were constructed, some of them defined by ramparts of similar character, but in this case the main internal feature was a large circular house, perhaps a public building. These sites provide more evidence of bronze working, including the manufacture of weapons.

Iron Age. Most of the metal itself was imported into Britain, and it was not until the long-distance movement of bronze was curtailed around 800 B.C. that iron technology had any impact. The lapse in long-distance exchange came at the same time as important developments in the pattern of settlement. There was an increase in the number of occupation sites and in the scale of food production. Field systems were created over larger areas, and a new range of agricultural tools came into use. More of the settlements were enclosed, and we also see an increase in the building of hill forts, although these are less common along the North Sea coast. These sites also contain a significant number of houses, but their chief characteristic may be that they include numerous storage pits and raised granaries. Their interpretation remains extremely controversial: some archaeologists claim that they were high-status settlements, while others prefer to see them as agricultural villages, centers for craft production and redistribution, communal grain stores, or even ritual sites. There is much regional diversity, and most of these interpretations have some merit in individual areas. There is little evidence, however, for the use of these sites in warfare, and in the one area with evidence of weapon burials, the Yorkshire Wolds, hill forts seem to be absent.

During most of the Iron Age, British society had a distinctly local character, illustrated by the dense distribution of fortified enclosures. There is only limited evidence of long-distance exchange. During the closing years of the period, however, areas of southern Britain were drawn into wider international exchange networks extending across the English Channel and along the Atlantic coastline It is during this final phase, between about 100 B.C. and A.D 50, that we find evidence of stronger contacts between Britain and continental Europe. With the expansion of Roman power, Britain was increasingly involved in a wider sphere of political relations. British mercenaries fought in the Gallic Wars, and Julius Caesar twice invaded southern England, in 55 and 54 B.C. During the period between his second expedition and Claudius's conquest of Britain in A.D. 43, larger political units seemed to have formed as a result of contacts with the Roman world. In southern England the hill forts were gradually abandoned in favor of much larger, open settlements. Royal dynasties, issuing their own coins, developed in the south, and lowland Britain was drawn into the politics of the Roman frontier. In the early first century A.D., relations between Britain and continental Europe became so close that its incorporation into the *Roman Empire seemed increasingly inevitable. Where Caesar had failed, the emperor Claudius succeeded. The Roman Conquest of A.D. 43 came as the culmination of almost a century of economic and diplomatic contact.

[See also BURIAL AND TOMBS; CAMPS AND ENCLOSURES, CAUSEWAYED; EUROPE, articles on THE EUROPEAN PALEOLITHIC PERIOD, THE EUROPEAN MESOLITHIC PERIOD, THE EUROPEAN NEOLITHIC PERIOD, THE EUROPEAN COPPER AGE, THE EUROPEAN BRONZE AGE, THE EUROPEAN IRON AGE; STONE CIRCLES AND ALIGNMENTS.]

■ Vincent Megaw and Derek Simpson, Introduction to British Prehistory (1979). Colin Burgess, The Age of Stonehenge (1980). Richard Bradley, The Social Foundations of Prehistoric Britain (1984). David Clarke, Trevor Cowie, and Andrew Foxon, Symbols of Power at the Time of Stonehenge (1985). Timothy Darvill, Prehistoric Britain (1987). Barry Cunliffe, Iron Age Communities in Britain, 3rd ed. (1991). Michael Parker Pearson, Bronze Age Britain (1993).

Richard Bradley

ROMAN BRITAIN

Britannia is archaeologically one of the most thoroughly investigated provinces of the Roman Empire. Although ancient literary sources are meager, the detailed nature of the archaeological data allows a reasonably coherent historical narrative to be written and illuminates many aspects of everyday life. The British province was unique in certain respects, however, being the most northerly and the most heavily militarized region in the empire, and one of the least successfully urbanized. The archaeology of Roman Britain thus offers important testimony on the workings and impact of imperialism in a frontier region.

Military Aspects. Roman involvement in Britain began with two risky and only moderately successful campaigns of Julius Caesar from 55 to 54 B.C. Subsequently, Rome maintained diplomatic contacts with the British tribes until the emperor Claudius launched a major invasion in A.D. 43. The motive was partly personal prestige for Claudius, but the intention was clearly to create a new province, with Britain's suspected mineral wealth an incentive. The conquest was hard fought and both long and drawn out, facing fierce resistance from Welsh tribes during A.D. 47 to 77 and Scottish ones from the 70s onward. Several revolts, most notably that of Queen Boudicca of A.D. 60 to 61, provided further setbacks. Only in ca. A.D. 83, following the remarkable series of campaigns conducted by Julius Agricola, were the tribes of the Scottish Highlands defeated, allowing Rome to confirm, some forty years after the Claudian invasion, that Britain was indeed an island.

Rome's objective would appear to have been total conquest, in the hope that the large size of the military establishment in Britain might eventually be scaled down (as in Spain, for instance). The pacification and provincialization of Britain, however, never reached its logical conclusion. Instead of being transformed into a civil zone of urban-based local government, much of western Britain remained a militarized zone, and the conquest of a substantial part of northern Scotland was relinquished in the late first century in favor of a heavily garrisoned frontier zone.

Britain is undeniably one of the best places to study the archaeology of the Roman army. In the second century A.D., Britain had a garrison of ca. 50,000 men, comprised of three legions (with fortresses at Caerleon, Chester, and *York) and a huge force of auxiliary troops. This army of occupation, variously estimated at between 10 and 12 percent of the entire imperial army, is a key distinguishing characteristic of Roman Britain, being by far the heaviest density of troops for a comparable area of territory. Air photography has been an important tool in the discovery of many fortifications, and numerous sites have been excavated. These range from turf and timber constructions of the later first century, such as the forts at Elginhaugh and Vindolanda I (a site that has also yielded a remarkable archive of *writing tablets) or the legionary fortress at Inchtuthil, to stone examples of the second century such as the Housesteads, or the legionary fortresses at Caerleon and Chester. Late Roman fortifications along the eastern and southern coast of Britain are also well preserved (notably Richborough, Pevensey, and Portchester).

*Hadrian's Wall (constructed from A.D. 122) ran for 80 Roman miles from the Tyne to the Solway and consisted of a broad ditch backed by a stone or turf wall, sixteen forts, and a regular sequence of fortlets (milecastles) and turrets. A further complex earthwork (the vallum) lay to the south, limiting access from that direction to a few controlled crossing points. A second frontier line (the Antonine Wall), comprising a ditch backed by a turf wall, ran 40 Roman miles from the Forth to the Clyde in Lowland Scotland. It was constructed in the early 140s, abandoned briefly in the mid-150s, then reoccupied for a few years before the frontier was pulled back definitively to Hadrian's Wall, ca. 163.

The courses of many separate campaigns from the late first to fourth centuries can be partially reconstructed from the evidence of hundreds of temporary camps north of the frontier. Roman battle groups erected these each night when on the march. Other camps can be identified as practice works, designed to keep the troops in training for actual campaigning. The effectiveness of Roman siege warfare is well attested at *hill forts stormed in the 40s (Hod Hill and *Maiden Castle), but practice siege-works (Burnswark) show that the capability was carefully maintained in later centuries.

The impact of the army on both military and civil zones must have been considerable, as a result of its policing work, maneuvers, supervision of native peoples, construction projects, recruiting, and provisioning needs.

Administration and Government. Because of the size of its garrison, Britain was governed by a legate appointed directly by the emperor, normally from among senior senators with military experience. His primary function was the maintenance of justice and the conduct of military affairs. An imperial financial official (or procurator) was responsible for taxation and the exploitation of mines and other state-controlled resources in the province. Both these officials were based in the provincial capital at London (Londinium). Local government was delegated to towns, organized along Romanized lines but based in many cases on tribal groupings (civitates). Urban development was slow, however, and only partial in western and northern Britain, and the military zone presumably remained under martial law in areas where no towns developed. Three colonies were established at Colchester, Gloucester, and Lincoln for veterans from the legions serving in Britain, and York and probably London were eventually promoted to this rank. There is scant evidence that the civitas capitals received promotion to the intermediate rank of chartered town (municipia), a fact that may indicate the limited success of urbanization in Roman Britain.

The province of Britain was subdivided in the early third century and again in the late third or early fourth to create two, then four, separate provinces, with a fifth province perhaps added by a further subdivision in the late fourth century. There was thus a tendency over time toward increasing bureaucracy, while conversely, the overall size and efficiency of the army had declined markedly by the later fourth century. When the British provinces decided to rebel from the control of a usurper to the imperial throne in 409, they were never recovered by the legitimate emperor Honorius, who sent a well-known rescript in 410 acknowledging that the former British provinces were to see to their own affairs as best they could.

Towns. The proto-urban development of some sites in Late Iron Age Britain is not in doubt, but it is equally apparent that the form of urbanism promoted by Rome after the conquest represented a profound change for the indigenous peoples. There were about twenty-two main towns in Britain (generally with well-planned street grids), with over one hundred other sites classifiable broadly as small towns. Some of the towns were laid out on the sites of abandoned Roman fortresses or forts, but many succeeded Iron Age settlements. Archaeology has demonstrated that even the major towns took many years to acquire their full complement of Romanized amenities (forum and basilica complexes, baths, aqueducts, theaters, amphitheaters, etc.), and such features are rare in the small towns. The scale and ornamentation of many of the urban monuments, though impressive in terms of the pre-Roman architectural tradition, are not exceptional in the overall context of Roman imperial architecture. The most extensively excavated towns are Silchester, Caerwent, and St. Albans (Calleva Atrebatum, Venta Silurum, and Verulamium), but important excavations have been carried out at many other sites. A notable result of this work is the important information gained about techniques of timber construction both for some early public buildings and for many residential or commercial properties.

The provision of defenses for most towns from the second century onward illustrates the frontier character of the province. Although sometimes ascribed to particular moments of crisis, the construction and subsequent elaboration of urban defenses may simply reflect a long-term concern for security. Defenses were also provided for many small towns, which seem to have reached the peak of their prosperity by the later third century, when the principal towns were already slipping into decline, as indicated by the dereliction of many public buildings before 409.

Countryside. Much attention has focused on the Romanized houses or villas frequently encountered in the civil zone. The "palace" of Fishbourne is the best-known luxury villa and was built in the first century A.D., possibly for a Roman official or, more likely, for the British client King Cogidubnus who was for a time left in control of part of southern Britain. With a few other exceptions (Woodchester, Bignor, Castor, etc.), however, Romano-British villas were not all that grandiose. Most so-called villas were essentially modest farmhouses, many succeeding Iron Age farms on the same sites and growing gradually in size, complexity, and comfort. Their numbers peaked in the later third and early fourth centuries, but their elite status is shown by the fact that they always formed a minority of the rural settlements (with a large part of the population continuing to live in farmsteads and villages of Celtic form). By the fourth century, numerous villas were furnished with mosaic or tessellated pavements, painted wall plaster, underfloor heating systems (hypocausts), and sometimes bathsuites. Villa estates were, above all, functional farms, a point exemplified by recent excavations (as at Gorhambury or Stanwick) of the numerous ancillary buildings that stood alongside the Romanized residential blocks.

Religion, Culture, and Economy. Most epigraphic evidence for religious practice in Britain relates to the activities of imperial officials, soldiers, or high-ranking Britons who chose to emulate the habits of the former. Celtic cults were often conflated with the Roman pantheon by these groups, pairing (syncretizing) the name of a Celtic deity with a convenient Roman one (illustrated by the temple and sacred spring of Sulis Minerva at Bath). The towns and army bases were undoubtedly the most notable centers of Romanization. The religious practices of the bulk of the population are far harder to gauge, but the prevalence of Romano-Celtic types of temples (Uley, Hayling Island) instead of Roman ones, the lack of widespread evidence for the adoption of classical cults or imagery, and the absence of Latin dedications from many shrines all seem to point to considerable passive resistance to acculturation.

The population of Roman Britain was extremely heterogeneous, with native Britons coexisting alongside army units and officials brought from all parts of the empire and supplemented by foreign traders, artisans, and slaves. Some of the outsiders took up permanent residence, notably in the three veteran colonies and cities such as London. By the second century, however, it is likely that most of the recruitment for the army was done within the province and that many of the elite who sat on the town councils and owned the rural villas were of British origin. Estimates of the population of Roman Britain lack precision, but a peak figure between three and four million is now widely accepted, of which about 90 percent probably lived in the countryside, the remaining 10 percent being split between the army and the towns. Burial practices and demographic trends are explored by cemetery excavations as in Ciencester, Poundbury, and Winchester.

The economic worth of Britain was founded on its mineral resources and its farming. Rome exploited the former through direct operation or regulation of the numerous mining sites known in the military zone (e.g., Dolaucothi, gold, Charterhouse-on-Mendip, silver-lead; Anglesey, copper). The late burgeoning of the villa system suggests that the economy of the civil zone was relatively underdeveloped in the first centuries of Roman occupation but eventually became more self-sufficient. Pottery manufacture has been minutely studied, revealing much about the province's marketing patterns, though its products were rarely exported. Quantified studies of imported pottery demonstrate the incredible reach of Roman material culture despite the peripheral position of the province in relation to the major trade routes. In its economic development, as in other areas, Roman Britain is, however, as interesting for its limitations and failures as for its successes.

[See also CELTS; EUROPE: ROMAN AND POST-ROMAN EUROPE; ROMAN EMPIRE: THE ROMAN FRONTIER.]

■ A. R. Birley, *The People of Roman Britain* (1979). A.L.F. Rivet and C. Smith, *The Place-Names of Roman Britain* (1979). S. S. Frere and J. K. St-Joseph, *Roman Britain from the Air* (1983). S. S. Frere, *Britannia*, 3rd ed. (1987). Richard Hingley, *Romano British Rural Settlement* (1989). Malcolm Todd, ed., *Research on Roman Britain 1960–89* (1989). Barri Jones and David Mattingly, *An Atlas of Roman Britain* (1990). Martin Millett, *The Romanization of Britain: An Essay in Archaeological Interpretation* (1990). Peter Salway, *The Oxford Illustrated History of Roman Britain* (1993). Martin Millet, *Roman Britain* (1995). John Wacher, *The Towns of Roman Britain* (1995).

David J. Mattingly

THE ANGLO-SAXONS

At the beginning of the fifth century A.D., Britain ceased to be part of the Roman Empire. Peoples from northern Germany and Scandinavia, including Angles and Saxons, attacked eastern and southern Britain and settled in sufficient numbers for their culture and language to become dominant. Britain disintegrated into many small, warring territories, under British control in the west, Anglo-Saxon in the east. To this period belongs any historical reality behind the story of King Arthur, leader of the British against the invaders. Fewer, larger kingdoms emerged by the seventh century, when the conversion of the Anglo-Saxons to Christianity brought renewed contacts with the Mediterranean world. From the end of the eighth century, Viking raids brought instability again until Alfred of Wessex (849–899) and his successors created a new, consolidated English kingdom. From 1016–1042, England was part of a Danish empire, and in 1066 Anglo-Saxon rule was ended by the conquest of Duke William of Normandy.

Written records provide an opportunity for both a richer and a more detailed understanding of the Anglo-Saxon period than for prehistory as well as a control on conclusions based on archaeological evidence alone. Scholars, however, have come to this field primarily by way of Anglo-Saxon literature or art history or as excavators of Anglo-Saxon sites. They have less often been trained as theoretical archaeologists, and have been unwilling to depart from accepted historical frameworks. Even for the earlier centuries, where archaeology is the main source, it has often been seen simply as a means of expanding the historical narrative, principally through *typological analysis of grave goods. A larger database, no longer confined to cemeteries, and an increased awareness of theoretical issues are now providing the basis for new interpretations.

New Perspectives on the Anglo-Saxon Migration. The migration of the Anglo-Saxons has been considered a classic example of the replacement of one people by another, the Britons only surviving, if at all, as slaves. Historical, archaeological, and linguistic evidence seemed to support this version of events. But this has been questioned in light of the recognition that invasion is not the only mechanism for culture change and that interpretation of the past has been colored by subsequent ideologies. The supposed foundation of the English Constitution in an ancestral Anglo-Saxon love of democracy and freedom may have biased accounts of the original Anglo-Saxon migration.

Archaeological evidence does partly sustain the traditional story. Seaborne threats to the Roman province existed and were met by a system of coastal fortifications, which ultimately failed. Roman institutions and their physical expression—masonry buildings, mosaics, coins and wheel-thrown pottery, roads, and systems for water supply—disappeared during the fifth century. Towns were abandoned or lost their urban functions. At the same time burials, artifacts, and timber buildings with close continental parallels appeared in England. Cemeteries such as Spong Hill in Norfolk or Loveden Hill in Lincolnshire included thousands of cremations. Human and animal bones were buried in handmade decorated pots with fragments of burnt equipment and sets of miniature toilet implements. This can be precisely paralleled in northern Germany, especially in Schleswig-Holstein, traditional homeland of the Angles. The sunken-featured buildings found on settlement sites such as Mucking in Essex, and West Stow, Suffolk, are also a Germanic house type, although these are now seen as ancillary buildings. At West Heslerton in Yorkshire, they are interpreted as having had industrial or storage functions.

But field and aerial survey has shown a density of Romano-British settlement—and therefore population—comparable with that of a much later medieval date. This large native population could not easily have disappeared and must have outnumbered the immigrants, who did not, as once thought, come in such numbers as to leave their homelands empty. Environmental evidence shows that farmland did not revert to woods, crop and animal species did not change, and in some areas field boundaries and even settlement patterns survived from Roman or earlier periods into recent centuries. Incoming Saxons did not find an empty forest but a settled landscape. They may have taken over ownership by force or treaty, but the people farming the land are as likely to have remained as to have fled or been killed. Not all aspects of Germanic culture arrived in England. The continental longhouse, a narrow-aisled building with human habitation at one end and animal stalls at the other, does not appear. Instead, there is a wider, larger type of structure, which might owe something to Romano-British traditions or be a new creation by a mixed population.

There is also the problem of archaeological visibility. In the Roman Period a complex society produced many durable remains: stone buildings, roads, quantities of wheel-thrown pottery. This disappears both in the areas that remained British and in those that fell under Anglo-Saxon control. In western Britain there are few sites dated to this period, mostly high-status strongholds like South Cadbury and Tintagel, which have produced sherds of pottery imported from the Mediterranean rather than identifiable local products. Ordinary people have left little trace. In eastern England Britons might have been similarly invisible. Or they might have taken on the material culture of their new leaders, so that "Anglo-Saxons" of later centuries might have had more British ancestors than they or later writers believed.

Social and Religious Change. Inhumation cemeteries have been analyzed in terms of chronology and social structure. Clear gender and regional differences can be seen in the jewelry and weapon types buried with the dead, but there is also much local and individual variation. Social hierarchy is elusive until the emergence of a few very wealthy *burials at a time when grave goods were generally declining, during the seventh century. This has been interpreted as evidence for the emergence of more powerful elites, ruling territories that can be seen as the nuclei of the historical kingdoms, of which the most important were to be Kent, East Anglia, Northumbria, Mercia, and *Wessex. At Yeavering, in Northumberland, a series of very large timber halls has been excavated, together with part of an arena or grandstand, burials, and possibly both a pagan temple and a Christian church. This has been interpreted as a residence of the kings of Northumbria. At *Sutton Hoo in Suffolk, the lavishly furnished ship burial from Mound 1, excavated in 1939, showed that considerable local resources and widespread foreign contacts were available to the rulers of seventh-century East Anglia. Investigation of this site in the 1980s produced more burials, some of them possibly human sacrifices. The whole cemetery may represent a political statement, an affirmation of the pagan, Germanic northern affiliation of the East Anglian rulers as opposed to the continental, Christian orientation of Kent. It was in Kent that King Aethelbert, married to a Christian Frankish princess, in 597 received the mission sent by Pope Gregory and led by St. Augustine that was to begin the conversion of the Anglo-Saxons.

Accounts of the conversion depend on the *Ecclesiastical History of the English People,* completed in 732 by Bede, a monk at Jarrow in northern England. The archaeological evidence shows how considerable an impact on material culture religious change can cause, without mass migration. Christianity brought the reintroduction of Mediterranean art styles, literacy, the use of Latin, and masonry buildings. It coincided with, but probably did not cause, the abandonment of the practice of furnishing burials with grave goods. In Britain and Ireland, sculpture and illuminated manuscripts show a combination of Germanic, Mediterranean, and Celtic art styles to produce works like the Lindisfarne Gospels, the Ardagh chalice, and the stone crosses of Northumbria and Ireland. So complete was the conversion that the Anglo-Saxons could send a mission to convert the still heathen Germans of their traditional homelands. The ar-

chaeology of the church begins with the remains of Augustine's churches at Canterbury and Bede's at Jarrow. Many existing parish churches incorporate remnants of their original Anglo-Saxon fabric.

The consolidation of larger political units is represented archaeologically by the growth of towns, coinage, and territorial boundaries. Trading centers developed at new coastal sites such as Southampton and Ipswich, and also outside the walls of former Roman towns such as *London and *York. They were part of a network around the North Sea, including places such as Dorestad in the Netherlands and Ribe in Denmark. Excavation has produced evidence of local craft manufacture and imports. Pottery produced at Ipswich was distributed throughout the kingdom of East Anglia and also along waterborne routes further afield.

Historical accounts show the kings of Mercia, Aethelbald, and Offa dominating southern Britain for much of the eighth century. The linear earthwork that forms a boundary between England and Wales has been attributed to King Offa since the ninth century and reveals the scale of resources that could be mobilized by a strong ruler at this time. Offa's coinage includes an imitation of an Arab dirhem: by this time Britain had once again become part of a complex European economy.

The Later Anglo-Saxon Period. The Viking raids and settlements of the ninth century are directly witnessed archaeologically only by a few burials, including the dramatic mass burial at Repton, Derbyshire; hoards of silver buried as loot or for safekeeping; and weapons, especially swords, dropped or thrown into rivers. Scandinavian art styles appear on metalwork and sculpture. A response to attack is visible in the system of forts and fortified towns, the "burhs" developed by the West Saxon kings across Wessex. These included refurbished Roman towns, like Winchester, and new foundations like Wallingford.

Most major preindustrial cities of England developed during the later Anglo-Saxon period, either built on Roman foundations like Winchester, York, and London, or appearing for the first time, like Norwich. Extensive excavations at many of these towns have produced a detailed picture of life in the tenth and eleventh centuries. There has also been large-scale investigation of the rural landscape, like the project at Raunds in Northamptonshire or investigation of the earlier phases of deserted medieval villages like *Wharram Percy in Yorkshire.

Later Anglo-Saxon England was a wealthy country with a complex system of government, literature, art, skilled craftsmen, and a productive agricultural base. It was an attractive target for attackers—Vikings, Danish kings, and finally the Duke of Normandy. The Norman invasion is not apparent in the archaeological record of everyday life. House types, burial practices, and pottery did not change, and even the coinage continued—with a new king's portrait. But the scale and destructive character of the construction of new buildings, which disregarded ancient shrines and ordinary houses, combined with the spread of castles across the country, do speak of conquest. Yet Anglo-Saxon England did not disappear completely. *Domesday Book* is a Norman record of an Anglo-Saxon system of taxation, and the best account of the Norman Conquest is that shown in the Bayeux tapestry worked by English needlewomen.

[*See also* CELTS; GERMANS AND GERMANIC INVASIONS.]

■ Steven Bassett, ed., *The Origins of Anglo-Saxon Kingdoms* (1989). Richard Hodges, *The Anglo-Saxon Achievement* (1989). Martin Carver, ed., *The Age of Sutton Hoo: The Seventh Century in North-*

Western Europe (1992). Nicholas Higham, *Rome, Britain and the Anglo-Saxons* (1992). Martin Welch, *Anglo-Saxon England* (1992).

Catherine Hills

CELTIC IRELAND

As history begins to dawn in fifth century A.D., Ireland, in its language, culture, and institutions, emerges as a country that we may legitimately describe as Celtic. How and when this came about is uncertain. For some, notably philologists, only immigration on a significant scale will explain the Celticization of Ireland. The archaeological record of the last pre-Christian millennium is, however, equivocal on this, for there are few convincing indications of major cultural change during this period.

The introduction of iron working in the seventh or sixth centuries B.C. and the appearance of a scattering of *Hallstatt artifacts, mainly bronze swords, at about the same time are sometimes seen as linked to the appearance of Celtic cultural elements in the land. The limited extent of this material and its overwhelmingly indigenous character make this unlikely. It is not until about 300 B.C., with the appearance of material of *La Tène aspect, that a cultural horizon of more decidedly Celtic character begins to be recognizable. This material is concentrated in the northeast region of the country and scattered in a discontinuous band across the center of Ireland from Meath in the east to Galway in the west. Southern areas of the country, inexplicably, are largely devoid of La Tène artifacts, so that the nature of society in these regions during the last centuries B.C. is obscure.

The scattered La Tène artifacts are generally stray finds devoid of archaeological contexts. Most frequently they are found in rivers, lakes, and bogs. In attempting to reconstruct Irish society on the basis of this material, we must be cautious because so many of the finds are high-status, prestige items that were doubtless the trappings of an elite stratum of society. They are thus not necessarily representative of society as a whole, so in this respect the archaeological record is defective. The finished products do, however, inform us that influences from Britain, from parts of Gaul, and from as far away as the middle Danube contributed to the genesis of the Irish La Tène horizon.

We can assume that the bulk of the population consisted of people who lived by means of mixed farming and were dispersed on farmsteads in rural areas. Everyday life probably differed little from that depicted in the early historic literature, with cattle-rearing a dominant activity of the masses. Kings and petty kings existed, and there were numerous grades of nobles who owed allegiance to the kings and who received it from the lesser members of society. Druids and seers held important positions in society, and skilled craftsmen, especially blacksmiths, were particularly well regarded. Society was based on a system of mutual obligation, each member with his specific duties, each with his honor price based on his social status and his value to the community.

We have few details about the economy of the ordinary people in pagan Celtic Ireland because of the dearth of excavated settlement sites. We can take it that their houses were round and they may, on occasion, have lived on fortified hilltops. Their domestic equipment would, in general, have differed little from contemporary peasant communities elsewhere. The appearance of the rotary quern at this time, however, was an important innovation. Warriors fought with short iron swords and spears and carried rectangular shields of leather-covered wood for protection in combat. The many bronze bridle bits found in the country must have been for the horses of mounted aristocrats. Some, occurring in pairs, indicate the existence of wheeled transport, possibly even chariots. A range of often finely fashioned items of personal ornament testify to the well-documented Celtic predilection for personal ostentation. Most spectacular are the gold neck ornaments, especially that known as the Clonmacnois torc (though actually found at Knock, County Roscommon) and the superbly decorated Broighter torc, found with other gold objects in a presumed votive deposit in County Derry.

The archaeological record is dominated by metalwork objects, notably those of bronze. Indeed, in casting and in working sheet bronze, the Irish craftsmen were at least the equals of their contemporaries in other countries. The great, curving sheet-bronze trumpets in particular represent a tour de force of Celtic metalworking in Ireland in the period around the birth of Christ. In two dimensions and in the round they produced a local version of the pan-Celtic La Tène art style which, in certain instances, rose to peaks of great technical and artistic sophistication. On bone flakes and on ritual standing stones, they were equally adept at creating this *art.

At least six bronze trumpets have been found in lakes, in presumed votive contexts, emphasizing once more the Celtic veneration for wet places. Four of these were found, in apparent association with human skulls, in a small lake at Loughnashade, County Armagh. Overlooking the lake, on the summit of a low drumlin, is the hilltop enclosure of Navan Fort (Emain Macha), the political and religious center of ancient Celtic Ulster. A large circular temple of wood stood on the summit before it was deliberately burnt, presumably in the course of some ritual ceremony, and covered by a mound of stones and earth. Through dendrochronology the construction of this building has been dated to 95 B.C. The exceptional importance of Emain Macha in the late prehistoric period is highlighted by the discovery there of the skull of a north African Barbary ape, which must have been imported to the site live, perhaps as a gift to an Ulster king from a Phoenician trader.

Other important Celtic royal hilltop centers are Dún Ailinne, County Kildare, and Tara, County Meath, where, in each instance, remains of circular timber-built enclosures have been revealed by excavation. West of the Shannon River was Cruachain, the capital of Celtic Connacht. Today this consists of a large complex of varying earthworks as yet untested by significant excavation.

While the hilltop enclosures mark the foci of tribal power, the perimeters of the tribal area also seem to have been marked, in certain instances—notably in southern Ulster—by conspicuous earthworks: linear dikes. These were discontinuous lengths of bank-and-ditch construction and can hardly have been frontiers in the modern sense. They may have been attempts to protect specific routeways or to hinder large-scale cattle rustling. They could also have had a more symbolic significance intended, through massive works of ostentation, to proclaim the limits of tribal hegemony.

The contemporaneity of the dikes with royal centers has been clearly established. Thus it seems that during the last centuries B.C., especially the second, there was a phase of major construction that involved building communal works of considerable magnitude. The building of a 1.2-

mile (2-km)-long roadway of massive oak planks across a bog at Corlea, County Longford, in 148 B.C. is a further example of the large-scale undertakings of this period. The broad contemporaneity of such works suggests that this might have been a time of tribal consolidation or expansion that could well have witnessed the formation of Ireland's political geography, which was to endure into the historic period.

In contrast to these massive works, the burials of late prehistoric Ireland are simple and unostentatious. Initially, it seems, the dead were cremated. The ashes were placed in simple pits that were sometimes inserted into preexisting barrows, sometimes placed in freshly-built ringbarrows, or within circular ditched or embanked enclosures. Later, perhaps through Roman influences, inhumation gradually replaced cremation as the normal burial rite. Grave goods, when they occur, generally consist of a few items of personal adornment such as pins, bracelets, or beads. In a unique, recent discovery the burnt remains, accompanied by a bronze brooch and glass beads, were contained within a bronze box.

Roman contacts in the early centuries A.D. influenced but did not radically alter the character of Celtic, Iron Age society in Ireland. Unconquered by Rome and untouched by the folk movements that followed the collapse of the empire, Ireland preserved an archaic Iron Age culture for centuries after it had elsewhere ceased to exist. But it was the skills and traditions of pagan Iron Age craftsmanship which, following the introduction of Christianity, laid the foundations for the golden age of Irish artistic achievement in the seventh and eighth centuries after Jesus.

[See also CELTIC ART; CELTS.]

■ B. Raftery, *La Tène in Ireland: Problems of Origin, Development and Chronology* (1984). "Focus on the Origins of the Irish," *Emania* 9 (1991). B. Raftery, *Pagan Celtic Ireland: The Enigma of the Irish Iron Age* (1994).

Barry Raftery

VIKING RAIDS AND SETTLEMENT IN BRITAIN AND IRELAND

Contemporary records, most important among them the *Anglo-Saxon Chronicle* and various Irish *Annals,* provide a historical framework for Viking raids and Scandinavian settlement in the British Isles.

Early Activity. The earliest recorded raid, on the island monastery of Lindisfarne, off the northeast coast of England, was in 793. For half a century afterward, surprise seaborne attacks on vulnerable coastal sites, mostly monasteries, occurred quite frequently. Although no archaeological trace of destruction has been found that can definitely be attributed to these raids, some of the insular metalwork found in Scandinavian graves may represent Viking booty. By ca. 850 the nature of Viking activity in Britain was changing. Subsequent developments varied considerably from region to region. Only Wales, a relatively poor area with much harsh terrain, saw comparatively little Viking activity.

Scotland. There is no historical record of the Scandinavians' settlement of Scotland. Their land taking in the Northern and Western Isles, in Caithness in northern mainland Scotland, and in Argyll to the west continued successfully, but outside the notice of contemporary writers, until the eleventh century. It is known through Old Norse influence on place names (great in Orkney and Shetland,

less important elsewhere) and through the discovery of their farmsteads and burial places. Most Viking graves in Scotland, as elsewhere in Britain, have been found by chance, and few have been excavated scientifically. They are recognized by objects of typically Scandinavian form, normally jewelry, tools, or weapons, which may date the burial to within approximately fifty years. Some burials, for example, one excavated in 1991 at Scar on Sanday, Orkney, used a boat as a container for the corpse; others used stone settings, cairns, or mounds to mark the grave.

The few farm sites that have been investigated in Scotland typically include a relatively long, rectangular house, with stone walls that may have incorporated turf sods; they may have been timbered on the inside, with a sod or thatched roof. Some incorporated cattle stalls, and there were usually outhouses. The settlements were normally for a single family, though perhaps with several generations living together. They exploited whatever resources were most readily available. At Jarlshof at the southern tip of Shetland, perhaps the most famous of these sites, fish, shellfish, sea birds, and their eggs were dietary mainstays.

Throughout Scotland, silver, the standard and gauge of contemporary wealth, is not found in anything like the quantities recovered from Scandinavian settlements in Ireland or England, and there was never any attempt to mint an independent Viking coinage in Scotland, as there was elsewhere. Yet the Earls of Orkney, in particular, were important socially and politically, and the Northern Isles generally formed a series of ports of call for Viking seafarers plying between Scandinavia, the British Isles, and the North Atlantic settlements.

Both the rise of the earldoms and the institution of Christianity in about 1000 helped to integrate the Scandinavian settlers of outer Scotland into the politically more coherent world of the eleventh and later centuries. Even at this late date, Norse characteristics appear in the archaeological record, for example, the remarkable series of runic inscriptions carved in the Neolithic passage grave at Maes Howe, Orkney, a site also mentioned in *Orkneyinga Saga*. Most archaeological remains, however, do not show the Scandinavian inheritance. The cathedral church of St. Magnus, built in Kirkwall, Orkney, in 1137, or indeed the relics of the murdered St. Magnus himself, rediscovered there in 1919, reflect mainstream western European influences. Yet in political terms, the Scandinavian link continued; the Western Isles were finally incorporated into the Kingdom of Scotland in 1266, while the Northern Isles remained Norwegian property until 1469.

Isle of Man. The history of Viking settlement on the Isle of Man is obscure, although the island clearly benefitted from its nodal position in the Irish Sea, where it could exploit all the surrounding territories. By the later eleventh century, it was bound up with lordship of the Scottish Isles, but an earlier Viking presence is clearly manifest. There are the institution and siting of a Scandinavian-style *thing* (assembly) at Tynwald; place names derived from Old Norse; an important series of cross slabs carved in slate, which preserve some of the earliest surviving representations of Norse myths; and a number of Viking graves, including cases of boat burial and, possibly, human sacrifice. In the early to middle eleventh century, Manx Vikings issued silver coins based on those struck in Dublin.

Ireland. In Ireland, the Vikings established coastal encampments, called *longphorts,* mostly during the period ca. 850 to 900. Some were at sites that later developed into towns, such as Wexford, Waterford, Cork, Limerick, and Dublin. No *longphort* has been traced through archaeology, although a cemetery that may represent the warriors of the Dublin *longphort* was found in the mid-nineteenth century at Islandbridge/ Kilmainham, 1.2 miles (2 km) upriver of the modern city center. It is the largest group of pagan graves in Britain or Ireland, represented by decorated swords, spearheads, axes and shields, and some tools and other gear, but there is evidence for just a handful of female graves.

Only the documents provide evidence for the raiding that at this stage continued to be the Vikings' principal activity. The Vikings gradually became a part of the tribal warfare between rival Irish kings, making and breaking alliances and even fighting each other. Their *longphorts* provided protection yet also constrained them, making them more vulnerable than when they had been hit-and-run raiders. This vulnerability led to the expulsion of the Dublin Vikings in 902. Some settled in northwest England, but by 917 Vikings had returned and refounded Dublin. Viking kings, albeit in thrall to Irish overlords, ruled in Dublin until the Anglo-Normans invaded and conquered in 1169–1170.

The investigation of tenth- to twelfth-century Viking towns, first Dublin and then Waterford and Wexford, has been one of the triumphs of Irish archaeology since the 1960s. In each of these places the buildup of anaerobic deposits has allowed the preservation of organic materials. The timber buildings survive, as do leather and textiles as well as items of stone, metal, bone, and other less common resources. Viking Age Dublin is now recognized as a 25-acre (10-ha)-defended settlement on the edge of the river Liffey. Natural topography, not rigid planning, dictated the street plan. Tenement plots were established, and normally maintained exactly the same boundaries. Post-and-wattle buildings of a distinctive "nave-and-aisles" form stood near the street frontage on each plot. There is abundant evidence for manufacturing, with raw materials, debris, waste, and finished products from a wide range of crafts and industries. There is also clear evidence of contacts with England. Scandinavian-derived art styles, artifact forms, and raw materials confirm the settlement's origins, but there is also a distinctive Irish element, and overall the material culture exhibits many characteristics common to northwest European towns.

From 997 the Dublin kings issued their own coins, initially using recut English coin dies. A considerable quantity of silver, including coins, jewelry, and hacksilver, has been found in the hinterland of the towns, especially Dublin and Limerick. There is currently much debate about whether the Vikings introduced or merely modified the use of silver-based currency. Dublin and its coastal cousins seem to have operated as points of entry for exotic goods and as centers of industry. These towns supplied their Irish-controlled rural hinterlands with items that otherwise were not so readily available. Scandinavians were therefore ultimately accepted as a welcome component of the Irish political scene.

England. In England, a Viking "great army" arrived in 865 and campaigned each summer until 880. They overwintered each year in a defensible base. Their camp of 873–874 at Repton (Derbyshire), incorporating an important Mercian church into a D-shaped earthwork by the river Trent, has recently been discovered. Nearby was a mass grave of 249 individuals, mostly males aged 16 to 40, who may have been Viking warriors. They, and later Viking invaders, can

sometimes be traced through discoveries of silver hoards buried for protection and not recovered. The largest such hoard in England, from Cuerdale, Lancashire, was deposited ca. 905 and contained about 7,000 silver coins and over 1,300 items of silver, mainly jewelry and ingots.

Unable to subdue King Alfred in *Wessex, the last stronghold of English power, the Viking army settled in Yorkshire, the east Midlands, and East Anglia from 876 to 880. This area became known as the Danelaw. Place-names with Scandinavian elements, for example, -by and -thorpe, and personal-name elements like the *Grim* in *Grimston* confirm the ultimate linguistic impact of this settlement, although the number of settlers involved has been hotly disputed. As yet there is very little archaeological evidence for these rural settlements.

Viking graves are rarities, although there are some, from churchyards, which show the adoption of local burial customs. The new Scandinavian landlords also adopted and popularized the erection of stone crosses and grave markers, introducing Scandinavian motifs to their designs and instituting new forms, notably the so-called hogback gravestone. These Viking Age carved stones, most of them broken up later for use as building rubble for churches, are among the best surviving indicators of contemporary settlement. At their finest, as at Gosforth (Cumbria), they are both works of art and important references to the merging of the Scandinavian pantheon with Christian belief. Others, like those at Middleton (Yorkshire), carry representations of warriors or contorted animals in interlaced designs.

The Vikings took over existing focal points, such as the few contemporary trading centers and both royal and ecclesiastical manors. These places became the heart of Viking administration, power, influence, and commerce, and some developed into shire towns. But by 918 Alfred's successors had recaptured most of the Danelaw, including the Five Boroughs of Derby, Leicester, Lincoln, Nottingham, and Stamford. Only *York held out a little longer, although by 927 it too was in English hands.

York had been transformed under Viking control from a largely derelict Roman fortress and walled town into a major manufacturing center. Its coinage had been upgraded and its trading links widened to an unprecedented extent, using the tidal inland port on the river Ouse. Most far-reaching was its new layout of streets and tenement plots, defined by the preexisting natural and human-made topography. Excavations on one of these new Viking Age streets, Coppergate, where anaerobic conditions allowed the preservation of organic remains, have confirmed that the modern layout of property boundaries originated in ca. 900. The plots each had a post-and-wattle building near the street frontage; associated objects show that these were both houses and workshops. Many different trades were practiced at an industrial scale of manufacture.

England suffered a second wave of Viking attacks from the 980s, culminating in the acceptance of the Dane Cnut as king in 1016. This introduced new Scandinavian artistic influences, seen on gravestones from St. Paul's churchyard, *London, and on southern English metalwork. Cnut's dynasty failed in 1042 and the Norwegian King Harald Hadraada's attempt to conquer England in 1066 was the conclusive rebuff for Scandinavian invaders.

[*See also* NORSE IN NORTH AMERICA; SCANDINAVIA: SCANDINAVIA IN THE VIKING AGE.]

■ E. Roesdahl, J. Graham-Campbell, P. Connor, and K. Pearson, eds., *The Vikings in England* (1981). C. Fell, P. Foote, J. Graham-

Campbell, and R. Thomson, eds., *The Viking Age in the Isle of Man* (1983). B. Crawford, *Scandinavian Scotland* (1987). J. Bradley, "The Interpretation of Scandinavian Settlement in Ireland," in *Settlement and Society in Medieval Ireland*, ed. J. Bradley (1988), pp. 49–78. W. Davies, *Patterns of Power in Early Wales* (1990). R. A. Hall, *Viking Age Archaeology in Britain and Ireland* (1990). M. Ryan, "The Vikings," in *The Illustrated Archaeology of Ireland*, ed. M. Ryan (1991), pp. 153–70. A. Ritchie, *Viking Scotland* (1993). R. A. Hall, *Viking Age York* (1994).
Richard A. Hall

MEDIEVAL BRITAIN

In the Middle Ages, Britain was not a single kingdom but comprised three distinct realms: England, Scotland, and Wales. England and Wales were united in 1282, but Scotland remained independent throughout the period.

Documentation. From the eleventh century onward, medieval England is documented by a rich and extensive corpus of written evidence. These writings include those produced by the state—such as legal and administrative documents —and those produced by the church. There were also works of literature and scholarship, most famously those by Chaucer. These texts were written in English (of which the medieval form is known as Middle English), in French, and in Latin, and survive in such quantities as to provide the basis for detailed narrative histories, economic studies, and reconstructions of social organization. Along with documents relating to taxation, such as the famous Norman *Domesday Book* (compiled in 1086), and maps, these sources can be used to produce detailed geographies of medieval England.

For Scotland and Wales, other—only slightly less rich—documentation exists, written in the Celtic languages spoken in these areas as well as in Latin. Like medieval England, medieval Scotland had its own sets of annals, year-by-year notes of important events, such as the birth and death of kings, the appointment of bishops, wars, and plagues. In Wales, one of the most celebrated sources for this period is the Laws of Hywel Dda, today surviving in a thirteenth-century form. These reveal a very different society and economy from that in medieval England, relating to the Celtic past rather than to continental Europe. In medieval England, the Anglo-Saxon and Viking settlement had almost completely expunged traces of Celtic culture and law in all but a few areas, such as Cornwall, and it was Germanic and Scandinavian foundations that formed the British background of Norman England.

Norman Period. One of the most famous dates in English history is 1066, when the Normans, led by William the Conqueror, invaded England. The Anglo-Saxons under King Harold were defeated at Hastings soon after the invasion, and resistance elsewhere was swiftly suppressed. The Norman Conquest resulted in the rule of a new elite over a substantially Anglo-Saxon population. The Normans who formed this elite were descendants of Vikings who had settled in northwest France in the early tenth century. By the Conquest period, they had become culturally very similar to the Carolingian Franks within whose kingdom they had settled, and had adopted French as their language. In England, their linguistic and cultural differences set them apart from the local population, and the distance was emphasized by the establishment of a network of new castles throughout the lands that they controlled. Although William's principal castle in *London (the Tower of London) did have a mortared stone keep (central defensive tower), most of these castles were built of wood. Typically, a castle comprised an outer earthen bank topped by a wooden palisade (the bailey) looping around a conical earthern mound (the motte), with a wooden tower on its summit. This type of castle, known as motte and bailey, was to be found throughout Norman Britain. Recent excavations have examined one such castle, Hen Domen, on the border between Norman England and what was then the independent kingdom of Wales. Here, in addition to the defensive features, the outer enclosure was packed with architecturally sophisticated rectangular timber buildings. This evidence helps us to realize the motte-and-bailey castles, as well as serving as fortresses, were domestic settlements with sizeable populations living within their walls.

It is a mistake to suppose that timber castles were necessarily either less architecturally advanced or earlier in date than those built of stone. Motte-and-bailey castles continued to be built well into the Middle Ages, while the Tower of London was not alone among early stone castles. After the twelfth century, however, the majority of English castles were built in stone. Designs became increasingly complex, from the simple rectangular form of a twelfth-century castle such as Norwich to the concentric rings of the great thirteenth-century castles built to consolidate the English conquest of Wales, such as Beaumaris, Conway, and Caernarvon.

In the eleventh century, motte-and-bailey castles formed a major focus of the new social and economic order introduced by the Conquest. In feudal society, where social ranks were strictly defined—hierarchical and rigid—these castles were the bases of Norman landowners, among whom the lands of the conquered Anglo-Saxons were distributed. Alongside the new castles came innovations in religious architecture. None of the Anglo-Saxon cathedrals long survived the Conquest; all were demolished by the Normans and replaced with their own buildings in the Norman variant of Romanesque style.

Feudal Period. The Norman period laid the foundation for feudal medieval England. The twelfth and thirteenth centuries witnessed economic growth, including an expansion in urbanism. This growth led to increased elite activity in the countryside also, such as the setting aside of large areas for hunting. Even in peasant households, however, the material standard of living was, to modern eyes, surprisingly high, with evidence of a well-nourished population with access to traded goods from overseas.

Major setbacks occurred at the end of the thirteenth century and continued into the fourteenth, when population expansion and declining crop yields coincided with a devastating and widespread plague, the *Black Death (1348–1349). This had a major impact on population numbers—which dramatically declined—and on both society and economy. Immediately following an economic crisis, a period of crop failure, and an intensification of criminal activity (which may, perhaps, have been linked to fluctuations in food prices), the plague was devastating in its effects, and forms a turning point in the history of medieval England. Nor was the Black Death an isolated event; further pestilence struck in the 1360s, accentuating the problems.

Economic Recovery. While social disorder increased following the plague, and discontent with feudalism spread among the lower social classes (breaking into open revolt in the 1380s), the relationship of social unrest to the economic recovery of the fourteenth and fifteenth centuries is uncertain. It is no longer widely assumed that plague was the simple cause, as these were trends detectable before the plague years. Nor, today, would we attribute every deserted medieval village to this period, as was once the fashion.

Deserted medieval villages have themselves been a major theme of research since the start of excavations at *Wharram Percy (Yorkshire). This site, the subject of long and extensive excavations, has revealed the wealth of information about everyday life and rural economy that may be gained by studies of this sort. The archaeology of medieval villages, whether deserted or beneath modern settlements, is now an important part of British archaeology. Foremost among its results are the realizations that the reasons for and chronologies of settlement desertion in the Middle Ages are so varied as to preclude any single explanation and that the material standard of living in the medieval countryside was higher than that which may be surmised from written sources alone.

By the fifteenth century, a new wealth is detectable, whether in written or archaeological sources. It is in this period that a series of grandiose but militarily useless castles were constructed, such as Bodiam in Sussex, attesting to a newly rich and secure aristocracy. In the towns, industry and trade formed the basis of an urban middle class, whose guilds also exhibited the new prosperity. The Guildhall in London was rebuilt at considerable cost at the very start of the fifteenth century.

Cathedrals, Churches, and Monasteries. Since the Norman invasion, the church had occupied a central position in medieval British society and economy. Apart from the large and urban-based Jewish community, which included some of the wealthiest individuals in medieval England, almost the entire population was Christian and within the Roman Catholic church. For everyone, from the king to the most lowly feudal serf, churches and monasteries formed a focus of religious devotion, and the clergy played a role in the life of every community. At the heart of the major cities were the cathedrals, in most cases still surviving today as working buildings. Although this continuing use makes it difficult to excavate either within or around the majority of medieval cathedrals, major projects have been undertaken at both *York and Canterbury and at other sites, such as Wells Cathedral in Somerset. It has proved possible to trace long sequences of building plans, cemetery use, and even characteristics of internal organization (locations of altars, etc.) within major churches still in use by careful excavation during building work and structural improvements.

Many local parish churches existed in both towns and countryside. Some of these, too, have been the subject of modern excavations, as at Rivenhall, Hadstock, and Asheldham in Essex and in towns at St. Nicholas Shambles (London) and St. Helen on the Walls (York). Often the earliest phases of rural churches were built of timber.

Another feature of town and countryside was the monastery, housing a community of monks or nuns. Again, these have often been the subject of archaeological research, but the archaeology of monasteries was, until the 1960s, limited both by the use of inadequate excavation techniques and by an overemphasis on the principal buildings (those of the cloister). The large-scale excavation of Bordesley Abbey (Warwickshire) using modern techniques opened a new phase in the investigation of monastic sites. This involved not merely the application of the latest fieldwork methods but an examination of those parts of the monastery situated away from the main buildings. As these areas included zones used for industrial activities and food production, a much clearer picture of the monastic economy could be built up. Similar work has now been conducted on monastic sites throughout Britain.

Impact of Protestantism. During the Middle Ages, dissatisfaction with some of the institutions and doctrines of the medieval Roman Catholicism was widespread, and England produced some notable reformers, such as John Wycliffe. This dissatisfaction formed a background for the revolutionary changes of the sixteenth century, which brought the period to an end. Following the lead of Martin Luther in Germany, Protestantism swept across Europe. The decision of the English king Henry VIII to break with the Papacy and establish a Protestant Church in England led to the Reformation of the English Church in the sixteenth century. This ultimately transformed the structure of rural and urban life, by abolishing the monasteries. The Reformation was also closely connected with the demise of feudalism. These changes, signaling the end of the medieval period in Britain, illustrate that the history of England throughout these centuries was closely linked to that of Continental Europe.

[*See also* MEDIEVAL EUROPE.]

■ Colin Platt, *Medieval England* (1978). Helen Clarke, *The Archaeology of Medieval England* (1984).

Ken Dark

THE INDUSTRIAL REVOLUTION

The realization that an Industrial Revolution was transforming Britain occurred to some perceptive observers in the nineteenth century: Frederick Engels related it to the formation of an urban proletariat in Manchester in 1844, and Arnold Toynbee delivered his seminal *Lectures on the Industrial Revolution in England* at Oxford in 1884. By the early twentieth century, historians were firmly committed to the idea and applied it confidently to the years between 1750 and 1830. More recently, however, some historians have questioned the adequacy of the idea to explain an evolutionary, cumulative process, and others have diminished its precision by drawing attention to alternative "industrial revolutions" both before and after the period that has come to be regarded as conventional in textbooks.

The Process of Transformation. This critical discussion has made it necessary to use the term *Industrial Revolution* with some reservation, but it has also served to clarify the essential historical qualities of the concept. For one thing, it is now generally agreed that a process of industrialization has transformed the Western world in the last three centuries. Even though the roots of this process can be traced back at least to the mercantile expansion of Europe in the sixteenth and seventeenth centuries, raising questions about the date of its onset, the fact of the transformation is beyond serious doubt. It is apparent in the rising population sustained at a standard of life comfortably above the subsistence level, in the more abundant and varied food and drink, in the greater availability of consumer goods, and in the control of debilitating diseases, in the facilities for rapid transport and instantaneous communication, and in the spread of urban culture and secularization. The transformation bears comparison with the Neolithic revolution and urban revolution of the ancient world in terms of the profound changes that it caused in the living conditions of human societies.

The second certainty about the Industrial Revolution is that it occurred first in Britain. There were many historical reasons for this. Britain was well endowed with the natural resources—especially coal—that were essential for the early stages of industrialization. But of more immediate importance was the fact that Britain had a more open society than its rivals in the eighteenth century, offering more freedom for industrial enterprise and greater social rewards for those who demonstrated such enterprise. Other countries were anxious to follow the British example, and by the end of the nineteenth century several of them were already pulling ahead in certain respects. But for a hundred years, from the mid-eighteenth to the mid-nineteenth century, Britain was unchallenged as the first industrial nation and the workshop of the world.

The third certainty is that, even as Britain was overtaken by other nations in Europe and North America, the process of industrialization continued without abatement. Indeed, it can be argued that the social transformation brought by the internal combustion engine and electricity—arising from use of the automobile, the airplane, atomic power, rocketry, the cinema, electronics, television, and so forth— has been even more extensive than that achieved in the period of British supremacy. The continuing process of industrialization has, however, effected a more widely shared series of changes, and for that reason the process has been more easily taken for granted.

Impact of the Revolution. The Industrial Revolution that began in Britain in the eighteenth century began in the heavy coal and iron industries and quickly spread to *textiles and other consumer industries. It was accompanied by an agricultural revolution, which enabled the farmers to produce more food and drink for the expanding population, and by a transport revolution that promoted improvements in the methods of conveying people and goods around the country. Industrialization began in the areas of north and midland Britain and Scotland where the coal and iron industries were already established and also in *London, which had been an outstanding mass-consumption market for several centuries. Some traditional industrial areas like the Weald of Kent and Sussex, long associated with the process of smelting iron in charcoal-fired blast furnaces, languished in competition with those parts of the country possessing easy access to coal, the new staple fuel of industry. One of many territorial transitions promoted by industrialization was the dominant trend away from rural locations, where much early industry had developed, toward the coalfields—for fuel and power, especially after the introduction of the steam engine—and toward the towns for labor and markets.

This increasing concentration and urbanization encouraged the mechanization of industrial processes and the search for improved means of transport. By the middle of the nineteenth century, the thriving industrial towns of the midlands and north had become linked by a network of roads, canals, and railways. These towns flourished on the basis of large labor forces employed in factories driven by steam engines, with both employers and employed living close to the places of work and expecting to work long hours. The conditions of life were, by modern standards, poor, but they were better than any alternatives that were available to the masses who had to earn a living. And as the productivity of the industrial processes steadily increased, so an improved standard of life trickled down to the workers, with restrictions placed on the more laborious activities (e.g., in mines and factories, the curtailment of the employment of women and children), shorter working hours, paid holidays, and the widening recreational prospects made possible by increasing prosperity. The society that emerged in the new conditions of industrialization was dominated by class divisions and strongly influenced by a materialist and secular ideology. But as far as the physical well-being of its members was concerned, it was a tremendous improvement on previous societies.

Industrial Archaeological Research. The process of industrialization has left a wealth of artifacts and monuments, many of them completely obsolete and only surviving because they exist in neighborhoods where nobody has an interest in demolishing them. Others have survived because of the active intervention of the state to list and schedule them under the available conservation legislation or because preservationists have undertaken to protect and restore them. The abundance of industrial monuments in Britain reflects its achievement as the first industrial nation and calls for interpretation. Archaeology has been a major tool in interpreting the British Industrial Revolution. The investigation has taken place at several levels. First, excavation has been a valuable means of discovering the provenance of many early processes, such as those of metalworking and the manufacture of glass, pottery, soap, and other chemical products. Much information has been recovered from the careful excavation of industrial sites. Second, the artifacts discovered during excavation, such as ceramic shards, metallic waste, and fragments of tools, have greatly enlarged the historical understanding of the manufacturing processes, craft techniques, and trade in the products. Third, machines associated with industrial plants—especially steam engines and other prime movers—survive plentifully but selectively, and the analysis of these remains has significantly enlightened historians concerned with the adoption of new sources of power and mechanical innovations. Fourth, industrial history is rich in standing buildings, and the study of these has made possible the establishment of factory and workshop typologies, even when the buildings have been abandoned or converted to new uses. The record of textile mill buildings, for example, has proved to be a rewarding resource for understanding the development of the wool, cotton, linen, and silk industries in Britain.

Systematic analysis of this wealth of physical evidence has provided many insights into the history of industrialization that could not have been achieved by documentary research alone. A few of the instances in which industrial archaeological research has promoted a more thorough understanding of the processes concerned include the location and development of tin and copper mining in Cornwall and of lead mining in the Mendips and Yorkshire dales, the evolution of factory organization in the textile industry and elsewhere, the exploitation and application of Welsh slate, the incremental improvements in steam engines, the disposition and social impact of the Staffordshire pottery industry, and the transition of the iron and steel industry from areas like the Weald and Shropshire to the Black Country and south Yorkshire.

Some of the fruits of this research have been harvested by industrial museums, particularly the large open-air museums such as Beamish in County Durham and *Ironbridge in Shropshire, and the standards of collection and presentation in British museums generally have been revitalized by this new emphasis on industrial artifacts. The interest in *industrial archaeology, which only began to express itself in an organized way in the 1960s, has acquired a substantial institutional existence in a plethora of local societies and conservation groups as well as in national bodies such as the Association for Industrial Archaeology, with its headquarters at Ironbridge. This organization produces its own journal, *Industrial Archaeology Review*, which maintains a high standard of coverage of current research. It is hardly too much to claim that through the application of archaeological perceptions and skills to the interpretation of industrial monuments, the understanding of the British Industrial Revolution has been, if not revolutionized, at least provided with a dimension that it previously lacked.

[*See also* INDUSTRIAL ARCHAEOLOGY; IRONBRIDGE.]

■ Frederick Engels, *The Condition of the Working Class in England in 1844* (1845). Arnold Toynbee, *Lectures on the Industrial Revolution in England* (1884). Paul Mantoux, *The Industrial Revolution in the Eighteenth Century* (1928). T. S. Ashton, *The Industrial Revolution 1760–1830* (1948). R. M. Hartwell, *The Causes of the Industrial Revolution in England* (1967). David Landes, *The Unbound Prometheus*, (1969). P. Mathias, *The First Industrial Nation* (1969). R. M. Hartwell, *Industrial Revolution and Economic Growth*, London, (1971). R. A. Buchanan, *Industrial Archaeology in Britain* (1972). R. A. Buchanan, *The Power of the Machine* (1992).

R. Angus Buchanan

BRONZE AGE. *See* THREE-AGE SYSTEM.

BRUGH NA BÓINNE. *See* BOYNE VALLEY.

BURIAL AND TOMBS. Cultural practices with regard to treatment of the dead can be an important window into the past. Just as there are no singular or unitary set of beliefs with regard to treatment of the corpse, to time of mourning, or to the afterlife in the contemporary world, many variations in patterns of mortuary activity are found in antiquity. Variability in mortuary practices exists both within and among cultures and is useful for both descriptions of single cultures and comparisons among societies.

Prehistoric mortuary practices are extremely diverse. The remains of individuals may be found in cemeteries, in funerary structures, below the floors of houses, or within garbage. Individuals may have their final resting place directly in the ground, in a tomb, on a scaffold, or in water; people may be interred by themselves or with others. Corpses may be immediately deposited in the archaeological record or processed in some way first; thus, interments may be "primary" or "secondary." And, bodies may be interred with or without offerings.

Regardless of where they are encountered, the investigation of human remains are best undertaken by specialists fully aware not only of procedures for careful investigation and analysis but also of their legal responsibilities. Excavation of human skeletal remains may not always be possible. Laws and traditions concerning the appropriateness of digging and analyzing human remains are somewhat divergent. In certain areas, nearly immediate reburial of human bone is undertaken following excavation; in other situations, skeletal material may be the source of continued study.

Human burials have been used to infer many different aspects of ancient life including health and demography, status differentiation, belief systems, and ethnic differences; however, there are no absolute correlations between burial customs and specific cultural practices. Peter Ucko (*World Archaeology* 1 [1969]: 262–280) used ethnographic examples from contemporary societies to demonstrate that there may be several possible reasons for a specific mortuary practice

and that common assumptions about mortuary activity may be incorrect. For example, a lack of grave offerings may not always be an indicator of low material wealth; increased tomb size may not necessarily correlate with high status. Nevertheless, analysis of mortuary activities can provide an extremely useful means for viewing ancient cultures.

There are many classifications of mortuary information and variability. Important clues for the interpretation of mortuary patterns may be found in several areas—from analysis of the osteological remains themselves to a consideration of the manner of "disposal" of the corpse to a study of grave offerings. Analysis of human remains is particularly significant for biological information. In the arid conditions of ancient Egypt or in the frozen tundra of the Arctic where organic remains are likely to be preserved, analyses can be conducted to ascertain diverse information regarding blood type, DNA, and/or the presence of parasites. When all that remains of a human corpse are fragmentary pieces of bone, even determinations of an individual's sex, age at death, or evidence of disease may prove difficult. However, new techniques of analysis are making it possible to look at increasingly complex issues, even with poorly preserved bone. Human remains also are critical in establishing how many individuals are present in an interment and how the corpse(s) was/were prepared after death — whether the deposition of the body was primary, closely following death, or secondary, succeeding activities such as defleshing, cremation, or exposure to the elements.

Intentional symbolic burial has often been equated with the existence of human culture and belief systems. Early hominid skeletal remains of *Australopithecines* (dating from 1 million to 4.5 million years ago) have been found in situations that do not suggest intentional interment. Finds are generally of incomplete individuals. It has been suggested that South African *Australopithecine* finds at sites like Swartkrans, where some bones may actually show evidence of carnivore tooth marks, were preserved in underground caves only because these remains were dropped by predators. The first examples of intentional burials have been correlated with *Neanderthals and date between 125,000 and 40,000 years ago at sites such as La Chapelle-aux-Saints, France, where a grave filled with flint tools and animal bones contained an adult male with a bison leg on his chest, and La Ferrassie, France, where the graves of two adults and six children were found in close proximity and may represent a family cemetery.

Excavations at more recent sites generally lead to larger samples of skeletal remains and greater possibilities for using these interments to make statements not about the existence of human culture, but about the nature of the culture itself. In certain cases burial analysis may indicate that there was little if any social distinction among people other than that correlated with age, sex, or possibly lifetime skills. Even in these cases, however, osteological materials and burial patterns have been used to show ethnic distinctions, kinship relationships, and residence patterns.

Burials are not always correlated with single individuals or single events. Numerous examples exist worldwide of staged burials and so-called double funerals, in which individuals are not immediately interred in their final resting places. Secondary burial may accompany a secondary funeral, held either a short time or many years after an initial interment. Factors determining the timing of these events may include practical considerations such as the length of time necessary to accumulate the finances to pay for a second ceremony or for flesh to decay from the bones. In certain cultures, however, secondary burial may be an episodic communitywide event. All of the individuals who have died during a given period of time (often years) may be buried together in a communal grave in conjunction with a specific ceremony.

Studies formulated to identify social stratification have focused primarily on differentiating among grave offerings and/or on distinguishing differences in the effort or energy expended in the entire mortuary process. Such studies have used burial information to demonstrate both the contemporary and the temporal variability in mortuary activity that exists within single cultures. Burial information also has been used to identify the existence of rank or stratified, as opposed to egalitarian, societies and to examine changes in social differentiation over time.

The Maya area of Mesoamerica provides a clear demonstration of the large amount of variability of mortuary activity that can exist not only within a single culture area but also within a single site or even within a single residential group. The Classic Maya (A.D. 250–950) had a series of possible ways of dealing with a corpse. Human remains have been found in contexts that do not indicate intentional burial, such as when burnt and broken human bones are discovered in garbage (possibly suggesting cannibalism). Sometimes bodies are intentionally placed in trash or directly in construction layers. Human remains are also found intentionally interred in a variety of containers, ranging from simple graves to cists to crypts to tombs. Individuals within Maya tombs are often accompanied by elaborate grave offerings, including jadeite, shell, and pottery artifacts. The percentage of individuals that were interred in the most elaborate tomb contexts vary site by site, but generally include only a small portion of Maya society. An increase in the number of individuals interred in tombs (as well as in the number of tombs themselves) occurred during the Late Classic Period (A.D. 550–950) at Caracol, Belize, and has been correlated with increased prosperity among this population, in contrast to its neighbors. Multiple individuals were often placed inside a single burial chamber at Caracol, and single tombs were used repeatedly; thus, the increased proportion of this kind of burial may also correlate with the massive population increases noted for the site during this era.

Perhaps the best-known examples of burial in tombs derive from ancient Egypt. Excavations have shown that the tombs of the pharaohs were extremely elaborate funerary monuments, the construction of which was often begun by a specific ruler years before his death. While the tombs of Egyptian rulers have been popularized worldwide, recent scientific excavations have focused on the burial patterns of other members of Egyptian society. Although the use of tombs may have been limited to the most high ranking of individuals in early dynastic history, by 1300 B.C. the artisans who created the pharaoh's tombs were building their own (albeit less elaborate) chapels and tombs in their village outside of Thebes; at about the same time, temple-tombs were also being constructed for administrators, army officials, and craftsmen in the area around Memphis. Many of these tombs have scenes and texts painted on their walls that have been extremely useful for interpretations concerning day-to-day activities in ancient Egypt as well as for explicating beliefs concerning the Egyptian afterlife.

Finally, studies of mortuary activity have not been limited to the physical excavation of burial sites, but have also been conducted without digging through viewing variation visible in monuments such as burial markers. The study of gravestones in eighteenth- and nineteenth-century New England by James Deetz and Edwin Dethlefsen (*Natural History* 76 [1967]: 29–37) is not only an example of the potential use of style as a dating tool but also a demonstration of mortuary activities that both correlate with and reflect wider societal patterns and changes.

[*See also* HUMAN REMAINS, ANALYSIS OF; MEGALITHIC TOMBS; MORTUARY ANALYSIS; PALEOPATHOLOGY; REBURIAL AND REPATRIATION; URNFIELDS.]

■ R. Chapman, I. Kinnes, and K. Randsborg, *The Archaeology of Death* (1981). S. C. Humphreys and H. King, *Mortality and Immortality* (1981). M. Bloch and J. Parry, *Death and the Regeneration of Life* (1982). J. O'Shea, *Mortuary Variability* (1984). J. Romer, *Ancient Lives* (1984). G. Martin, *The Hidden Tombs of Memphis* (1991). P. Metcalf and R. Huntington, *Celebrations of Death* (1991). D. Chase and A. Chase, *Studies in the Archaeology of Caracol, Belize* (1994).

Diane Z. Chase

BYZANTINE CULTURE

Byzantine Decorative Arts
Byzantine Fortifications
Ancient Synagogues
Byzantine Monasteries

BYZANTINE DECORATIVE ARTS

Byzantium's decorative arts developed within the context of the late Roman world. The variable starting points assigned to Byzantine history reflect this essential continuity, which maintained Roman artistic means and ideas and only gradually defined a distinctive artistic style. The earliest phase of Byzantine material culture (fourth through seventh centuries) has received the greatest archaeological attention, as a result of excavations conducted at classical sites that were continuously inhabited into Byzantine times. Lacking comparable study of Byzantium's Dark Age (eighth through ninth centuries) and later years (tenth through fifteenth centuries), traditional scholarship has focused on the artistic production of *Constantinople and has emphasized formalist approaches to the study of later Byzantine art. Recent scholarly interest has also included the cultural life of small settlements in the provinces and their interaction with neighboring states. Special attention has been paid to understanding how the arts functioned within contemporary society and the relationship between visual and literary images.

Byzantine decorative arts encompass objects used in daily life as well as in civil and religious ceremonies. The most common artifacts are ceramic and glass vessels, lamps, and other domestic objects. On archaeological sites, the best-dated Byzantine objects are fine red-slipped ceramic tablewares, which in the early Byzantine period originated in north Africa, western Asia Minor, and *Cyprus. Common forms include broad dishes and plates stamped with vegetal and animal images and religious symbols. The subsequent development of glazed wares led to distinctive pottery styles that flourished in the east Mediterranean during the tenth through fifteenth centuries. Regional workshops produced wares with different patterns of incised and glazed decoration representing fanciful animals and floral motives as well as stylized human figures. Thin-walled glass vessels for table use were manufactured throughout the empire. Small oil-burning lamps usually were made of ceramic and glass. Terracotta mold-made lamps were typically disc- or slipper-shaped with raised decoration. Glass lamps were often goblet-shaped and suspended in bronze stands or hanging chandeliers.

Metal objects also figured prominently in Byzantine daily life. Heavy iron implements were used primarily for building and as tools for commerce, industry, and warfare. Bronze was widely used for such household furnishings as tables and stands as well as lamps, braziers, and censers. Elaborately decorated pieces of silverplate and gold signified high social rank and were often donated for church use; they are known primarily from buried hoards and literary descriptions. Items of personal adornment included finely worked pins, fibulae, buckles, strap ends, and jewelry of bronze, silver, and gold, depending on the status of the owner. These highly mobile and intrinsically ornamental objects helped spread new ideas from the Byzantine borderlands, including the animal motives and polychrome style of northern migrating peoples and Arab decorative themes. The working of gems in Constantinople was complemented by a sophisticated enamel-working tradition that flourished during the tenth through twelfth centuries.

Apart from literary descriptions, Byzantine *textiles have survived primarily in Egypt and in west European church treasuries. Curtains were woven of linen, wool, and silk, and were hung as wall decoration and as partitions between rooms. Preserved fragments reflect the special popularity of repeated floral patterns enclosing animal or figural scenes. Items of everyday dress included the tunic and short cloak; contemporary mosaics and illuminated manuscripts depict elaborately woven and embroidered garments that were worn by churchmen and officials at court.

Other important categories of Byzantine decorative arts include small-scale sculpture in bone, ivory, and stone. Cosmetic implements and toys carved of bone and ivory have been excavated in residential contexts. Much less common were early Byzantine ivory reliefs or diptychs, which were often carved with portraits and decorative scenes to commemorate religious and political events among high-ranking families and officeholders. In the tenth through twelfth centuries, ivory workshops provided aristocratic families with small boxes, carved with mythological and other figural scenes, as well as devotional plaques and triptychs. Books and illuminated manuscripts for aristocratic and ecclesiastical patrons were produced in cities and monasteries across the empire. Early surviving examples include fifth- and sixth-century editions of classical and biblical literature, while the production of gospel and liturgical books was especially popular during the later empire.

Byzantine culture may be best known for its monumental painting and mosaics. Popular classical themes, including architectural moldings, floral patterns, and vegetal borders, continued to appear in early Byzantine floor mosaics and in wall mosaics and paintings through the fifteenth century. The illusionistic representational techniques of late Roman artists were combined in the fifth and sixth centuries with a hieratic formality to produce a distinctive means of visual communication that both influenced and was shaped by contemporary Christianity. This process is best documented by the icon, or painted devotional panel depicting a religious person or event. Debate over the spiritual properties of religious images led to their official banishment during the Iconoclastic Period (726–843). The restoration of such images in the midninth century fostered the development of complex programs of decoration that evolved to-

gether with ecclesiastical architecture. The synthesis of these two traditions in the body of the Byzantine church constitutes one of the most distinctive features of the cultural landscape of modern Greece.

[See also ROMAN DECORATIVE ARTS: ROMAN MOSAICS.]

■ Cyril Mango, *Art of the Byzantine Empire, 312–1453: Sources and Documents* (1972). Ernst Kitzinger, *Byzantine Art in the Making* (1977). John Beckwith, *Early Christian and Byzantine Art*, 2nd ed. (1979). Kurt Weitzmann, ed., *Age of Spirituality, Late Antique and Early Christian Art*, exhibition catalog (1979). Eunice Dauterman Maguire, Henry P. Maguire, and Maggie J. Duncan-Flowers, *Art and Holy Powers in the Early Christian House*, exhibition catalog (1989). Lyn Rodley, *Byzantine Art and Architecture: An Introduction* (1994).

Marcus Rautman

BYZANTINE FORTIFICATIONS

Byzantine fortifications vary in type according to their date, geographical location, the type of settlement they protected, topographical conditions, sources of funding, and the building materials used. The Byzantines inherited and maintained Roman military works, but modified them over the course of time. The regular layouts and low lying positions of Roman towns and military posts reflected the Romans' military superiority over their enemies. Changes began in the third century A.D., with the end of the period of general security throughout the *Roman empire and the transition to the more unsettled conditions of Late Antiquity. Settlements throughout the eastern Mediterranean moved up to more easily defensible hilltop locations, and many were now fortified for the first time. Towers were added to curtain walls in response to increasingly aggressive and sophisticated enemies and siege tactics.

Over the course of time, the area encompassed by walls tended to shrink, due to the decreasing size of urban populations. There were also changes in the building materials used in fortifications. Roman walls were typically constructed of ashlar masonry or bricks facing a core of lime mortar and stone rubble. Bands of brick courses were carried at intervals through the core of the wall to provide stability. From the sixth century A.D. on, mortared rubble replaced the facing as the primary component in walls. The wall was faced with whatever material was available, especially reused marble architectural or sculptural fragments (*spolia*) and old bricks. Small stones were used to fill the empty spaces, and the surface was sometimes covered with a coat of lime plaster. There was a tendency throughout the Byzantine Period to alternate courses of stone facing with brick bands.

In order to protect the borders of the Byzantine empire, Justinian I (527–565) and his successors established a series of frontier posts and renovated the fortifications of older settlements. The frontier posts usually consisted of a square or rectangular area rarely larger than 200 by 260 feet (61 by 79 m). They often served as monasteries, fortified garrisons, and caravanserais, protecting either isolated strategic points or the outskirts of settlements. The fortification walls were up to 25 feet (7.6 m) high and from 9 to 33 feet (3 to 10 m) thick, with square or round towers at the corners and on either side of the single main gate. The barracks were located against the inner face of the wall, and there was often a church dedicated to the Virgin Mary. St. Catherine's Monastery at the foot of Mount Sinai was erected by Justinian as part of this defensive system. The fortification wall is still preserved to its original height on three sides of the monastery. The main gate, in the center of the wall's northwest side, consisted of a large portal and a postern to the left of it.

The fortified posts of the sixth century provided a model that was employed by later monasteries such as the one at Kaisariani in Greece, which was founded in the eleventh century A.D.

The land walls of *Constantinople provide one of the best-preserved examples of Byzantine fortifications. They were constructed during the reign of Theodosius II in 412/413 A.D., and their 4½-mile (2.8 km) course effectively isolates the peninsula on which the city is located. The walls were constantly maintained and repaired throughout the Byzantine period, but no fundamental changes were made except for some adaptations to changing techniques of warfare. The 30-foot- (9 m) high inner wall was 16 feet (4.8 m) thick, and had 96 square or polygonal towers and six main gates. A parapet ran along the inside of the curtain. The towers had a windowless lower story that could be used for storage or for garrisoning soldiers. The upper stories of the towers, which were accessible from the parapet, had windows from which soldiers could fire upon the enemy. A flight of steps led from the second-story rooms of the towers to the roof, where heavy artillery could be placed. A second, outer line of wall was constructed 50 to 65 feet (15 to 20 m) in front of the inner wall. The terrace between the two walls (the Peribolos) accommodated the troops that defended the outer wall. The outer wall consisted of a solid lower part that supported the Peribolos and an arcaded upper portion with stone facing on the exterior that rose about 10 feet (3 m) above the level of the Peribolos. The towers in the outer wall alternated with those in the larger inner wall. Another terrace, 60 feet (18 m) wide, lay outside the outer wall, and beyond it was a moat that was originally over 60 feet deep.

The scale of Constantinople's fortifications reflect its position as the capital city of the Byzantine empire. The fortifications of other cities tended to be smaller in scale and much less elaborate.

■ George H. Forsyth and Kurt Weitzmann, *The Church and Fortress of Justinian* (1973). Richard Krautheimer, *Early Christian and Byzantine Architecture*, 3rd ed. (1979). Byron C. P. Tsangadas, *The Fortifications and Defense of Constantinople* (1980). Malgorzata Biernacka-Lubanska, *The Roman and Early-Byzantine Fortifications of Lower Moesia and Northern Thrace* (1982). Clive Foss and David Winfield, *Byzantine Fortifications, an Introduction* (1986).

Jodi Magness

ANCIENT SYNAGOGUES

The origins of the synagogue as an institution are obscure, though many scholars believe that they developed during the period of the Babylonian exile (586–539 B.C.). In Egypt, synagogues are mentioned (as *proseuchai*, or Houses of Prayer) in papyri of the third century B.C. They are also mentioned in Philo, Josephus, and the New Testament. Though the precise function of the earliest synagogues is debated among scholars, they certainly served as centers for the reading and study of Torah, and as hostels for pilgrims on their way to the Temple in *Jerusalem.

The oldest known synagogue is perhaps a structure of the first century B.C. found on the island of Delos. An inscription associated with it mentions Zeus Hypsistos (the God most high), which may refer to the Jewish God, but could also be a Samaritan or pagan Greek epithet. The first indisputable archaeological evidence for a synagogue is a dedicatory inscription from Jerusalem mentioning the synagogue of Theodotos, son of Vettenos, dating to the first century A.D.

The earliest excavated synagogue buildings are located in Israel, where remains have been found at several sites dating to the time of the First Jewish Revolt against the Romans (66–74 A.D.). These include Herodian structures at *Masada and Herodium which were converted by the Jewish rebels to halls of assembly by the addition of benches along the walls. The synagogue at Gamla is slightly earlier in date, having been constructed before the outbreak of the revolt in A.D. 66. All these structures have a colonnaded hall with benches around the walls, yet they lack a set place for the Torah Shrine, any distinctive Jewish iconography, or standard orientation.

With the destruction of the Second Temple in A.D. 70 and the end of the Bar-Kokhba Revolt in A.D. 135, synagogues acquired added importance in Jewish religious and social life, as prayer services replaced the sacrifices formerly offered in the Temple. Over 100 ancient synagogues have been found so far in Israel and Transjordan, most of them located in Galilee, where the Jewish population was concentrated following the Bar-Kokhba Revolt. Archaeologists working in Israel have divided these synagogues into a series of types based on an evolution of architectural styles. The second- and third-century A.D. Galilean synagogues, as they are called, had a large rectangular hall built of ashlar masonry. The facade, oriented toward Jerusalem, was richly decorated with carved stone reliefs including geometric, floral, and figured designs. Three doorways in the facade provided access to the interior, which was divided by three rows of columns into a nave surrounded by three aisles. There was either a clerestory or a gallery level, and there may or may not have been a set place for the Torah Shrine. Examples of Galilean synagogues include those at Capernaum, Chorazin, and Kfar Bar'am.

During the fourth century A.D., synagogues underwent some changes. These transitional synagogues had a niche or platform for the Torah Shrine in the wall facing Jerusalem, with the entrance in another wall. The plan was often of the broad-room type. Mosaics sometimes decorated the floors of these synagogues; the most famous example is that at Hammath Tiberias, where the central part of the nave contains a zodiac cycle surrounding the sun god Helios in his chariot.

These trends in layout and decoration crystallized by the fifth and sixth centuries A.D. in the Byzantine synagogues. Rubble walls replaced ashlar masonry, and mosaic floors covered the interior of the building. These synagogues had a courtyard (atrium), porch (narthex), and hall (basilica) with an apse, mirroring the layout of contemporary Christian churches. These features can be seen in the synagogues at Beth Alpha and Na'aran, where the center of the nave is again decorated with a zodiac cycle, accompanied by biblical scenes such as the offering of Isaac and Daniel in the lions' den.

Why these ancient synagogues were decorated with figured and even pagan designs, in contrast to the aniconic Jewish art of the Second Temple period, and what significance the decorative motifs might have had is a hotly debated issue among scholars. By the seventh to eighth centuries the figurative trend in Jewish art seems to have disappeared, as evidenced by the ancient synagogue at *Jericho, whose mosaic floor is decorated with simple geometric motifs.

The typology of ancient Palestinian synagogues presented here, however, has recently been brought into question. One problem concerns the Galilean synagogue at Capernaum, where recent excavations have turned up large quantities of coins dating to the fourth and early fifth centuries A.D. under the stone pavement of the interior. Many scholars now agree that the development of ancient synagogue types needs to be reevaluated, taking into account such factors as regionalism and building materials.

Archaeological evidence for ancient synagogues has also been found outside Palestine, at Priene, Miletos, Corinth, and Ostia, among other places. Two of the most famous Diaspora synagogues are located at Dura Europos on the Euphrates River in northeast Syria and at Sardis in Asia Minor. At Dura Europos, which was destroyed in A.D. 256, the walls were covered with an elaborate program of wall paintings depicting biblical scenes. The synagogue at Sardis, used by an affluent Jewish community from the fourth to early seventh centuries A.D., was a monumental structure within a Roman bath and gymnasium complex.

[See also NEAR EAST: LATE ANTIQUITY IN THE NEAR EAST; ROMAN EMPIRE: THE EASTERN PROVINCES OF THE ROMAN EMPIRE.]

■ Eliezer L. Sukenik, Ancient Synagogues in Palestine and Greece (1934). Herschel Shanks, Judaism in Stone, the Archaeology of Ancient Synagogues (1979). Joseph Gutmann, Ancient Synagogues: The State of Research (1981). Lee I. Levine, ed., Ancient Synagogues Revealed (1981). Marilyn J. S. Chiat, Handbook of Synagogue Architecture (1982). Lee I. Levine, ed., The Synagogue in Late Antiquity (1987).

Jodi Magness

BYZANTINE MONASTERIES

The word "monastery," from the Greek "to live alone," defines a building complex housing members of a religious community living apart from the world and devoting themselves to asceticism and prayer. In the Byzantine world from the fourth to fifteenth centuries A.D. in the eastern Mediterranean, monasteries took several forms of general organization, and archaeological evidence for all of them has been recovered in excavations and surveys.

A cenobitic monastery, from the Greek for "communal life," was one in which the monks, under the authority of an abbot, led a communal life, with a shared daily routine of worship, work, and meals. By contrast, a Lavra, from the Greek for "lane"—referring to the path linking the cells with the church—was a monastery composed of a group of scattered cells inhabited by individual eremitic monks associated with a central church and a variety of service buildings. The monks, under the authority of an abbot, lived alone during the week in their cells but assembled each Saturday and Sunday for common worship and to obtain supplies for the following week. Throughout the Byzantine period, there were also isolated hermits and wandering monks.

The number of monks throughout the Byzantine Empire was sizable, though in Byzantium there were no monastic "orders" as in the west. Each monastery had its own unique organization described in its foundation document (in Greek, Typikon). There were many more monasteries for men than for women. The size of the monastic communities varied from fewer than ten monks to several hundred. Some monasteries proved to be ephemeral, scarcely lasting beyond the lifetimes of their founders, but others, such as St. Catherine's at Mount Sinai, have remained in constant use throughout the centuries. Monasteries were found everywhere—in cities, towns, and the countryside. Some monasteries, especially in the Holy Land, were built next to memorial churches to serve the needs of pilgrims.

Some one thousand Byzantine monasteries are attested in written sources, and the archaeological remains of monasteries have been found all over the territory of the empire.

Concentrations of monasteries are known from the capital *Constantinople, with around seventy attested in the mid-sixth century, the holy mountains of Mt. Athos in northern Greece and Mt. Olympus in Turkey, and the Judean desert east of Jerusalem, where there were perhaps more than two thousand monks in some sixty-five monasteries in the fifth and sixth centuries A.D.

The first monasteries developed organically when disciples gathered around a well-known ascetic, such as the pioneering eremetic monk Antony (died A.D. 356), who withdrew into the desert of Egypt. Pachomius (died A.D. 346) established the basic cenobitic form of Egyptian monasticism, which soon spread to Palestine and elsewhere, while Basil (died A.D. 379) developed influential sets of rules for monks who favored the cenobitic over the eremitic type of monasticism. The reforms of Theodore (died A.D. 826) of the Stoudios monastery in Constantinople served as a later model of monastic organization. Throughout the centuries a great many hagiographic lives of monks and collections of edifying anecdotes were written, along with a vast literature on monastic spirituality. Some monks were especially noted for their ascetic practices, such as Simeon (died A.D. 459), the pioneer stylite pillar saint, who lived for decades on the top of a column in northern Syria. After his death, a major pilgrimage site developed around his column at Qal'at Saman.

Byzantine monasteries have fairly standardized architecture. They were enclosed within walls, while the individual cells in a lavra would be more spread out than in the more compact cenobitic type. Since the monasteries took care of all aspects of the monks' lives, the complex included the religious elements of a main church and secondary chapels, and burial places—often including the venerated tomb of the founder—and the everyday service facilities of water supply systems, enclosure walls, gates, towers, the refectory and kitchen, a hospice for visitors, cells for the monks, an infirmary, and gardens and agricultural fields. The archaeological remains of monasteries are normally easily identifiable, especially if they are isolated. However, it is sometimes difficult for archaeologists to distinguish between monasteries and memorial or parish churches surrounded by service buildings.

Numerous monasteries have been excavated throughout Byzantine territory, and excavation reports of individual sites abound. The investigation of thousands of eremetic cells at Kellia and Esna in Egypt warrant special mention. The monasteries of the Judean desert have been the object of intensive survey and excavation in recent decades. However, the exposure and documentation of architecture remain the principal focus of most excavation projects, and rapid clearance of sites remains all too common. Projects with wide-ranging research goals and rigorous excavation methodology are, regrettably, far less common.

[See also CHRISTIANITY, EARLY; NEAR EAST: LATE ANTIQUITY IN THE NEAR EAST.]

■ A. K. Orlandos, Monasteriake architetonike, 2nd ed. (1958). Jean Jacquet and Serge Sauneron, Les Ermitages Chrétiens du Désert d'Esna (1972). C. C. Walter, Monastic Archaeology in Egypt (1974). Ignace Peña, Pascal Castellana, and Romuald Fernandez, Les Stylites Syrien (1975). Rodolphe Kasser, Kellia 1965 (1977). Ignace Peña, Pascal Castellana, and Romuald Fernandez, Les Reclus Syriens (1980). Ignace Peña, Pascal Castellana, and Romuald Fernandez, Les Cénobites Syriens (1983). Lyn Rodley, Cave Monasteries of Byzantine Cappadocia (1985). Yizhar Hirschfeld, The Judean Desert Monasteries in the Byzantine Period (1992).

Robert Schick

C

CACHES. *See* HOARDS AND HOARDING.

CAHOKIA was the largest pre-Columbian town in what is now the United States. It covered about 5 square miles (13 sq km) of unevenly occupied Mississippi River bottomland and included over one hundred earthen mounds. First described two centuries ago, much of Cahokia has been destroyed by urban expansion near East St. Louis, Illinois, although the core of the site is now preserved as a park.

Cahokia began to develop into the region's preeminent settlement during the Emergent Mississippian Period at the close of the first millennium A.D. The site's greatest elaboration in monumental architecture and internal organization took place shortly after 1000 in the Early Mississippian Period. Strong leaders enjoyed disproportionate access to labor and to prestige-denoting objects made from raw materials, including marine shell and copper. People gravitated toward bottomland settings near Cahokia, which by this time was the principal settlement of a powerful chiefdom. In the twelfth century, however, a defensive palisade was erected at the site and a depopulation of Cahokia and the surrounding floodplain was under way. The number of people in this part of the valley continued to drop thereafter, until it was nearly abandoned.

Human labor built the mounds at Cahokia. They vary widely in size and shape, with most being conical, flat-topped rectangles or long ridges. Some mounds enclosed the tombs of high-ranking people, their retainers, or sacrificial victims; other mounds served as elevated platforms for their buildings. The largest of them all, Monks Mound, rises to a height of 98 feet (30 m), covers about 17 acres (7 ha), and has four terraces. Monks Mound occupies the northern end of a quadrangle of mounds that were the most important part of the site. These mounds enclosed an intentionally leveled area, and the central precinct was surrounded by a wall of stout logs. Large special-function structures were built in several areas and on top of some mounds. Several circles or arcs consisting of regularly spaced large posts were erected for calendric purposes.

Much of the site area was at one time covered by buildings, storage pits, and other features. Most residential structures were rectangular, floors were sunken in shallow basins, and walls were made from thatch-covered poles. Construction details changed somewhat during the occupation of the site, as did the dimensions of domestic structures, which became larger later in time. The average sizes of commoners' houses, however, were always similar to contemporaneous buildings at other sites in the valley, including farmsteads.

Topographic relief influenced the internal configuration of Cahokia. People preferred the highest and best-drained land because much of the valley was often flooded. Many mounds and habitation areas lined an abandoned river channel that extends through the northern part of Cahokia. The crest of the south bank, in particular, supported many buildings, several of which were of unusually large size. The density of structure remnants in excavations generally decreases southwards away from the slough margin. Land near the principal mound group was especially valued by the site's inhabitants. Excavations west of the central mound quadrangle encountered signs of several special-purpose wooden constructions. Many mounds were located nearby, including several built immediately north of Monks Mound in flood-prone ground.

During its heyday, Cahokia probably was occupied by several thousand people who lived in separate residential areas that were often, but not always, accompanied by mounds. All prime areas, however, did not support the same density of occupation during the several centuries' history of the site. The residential areas were positioned to take advantage of reasonably well-drained, fertile soils for farming and resource-rich wetlands.

[*See also* MISSISSIPPIAN CULTURE; MOUNDS OF EASTERN NORTH AMERICA; MOUNDVILLE; NORTH AMERICA: THE EASTERN WOODLANDS AND THE SOUTH.]

■ Charles J. Bareis and James W. Porter, eds., *American Bottom Archaeology* (1984). Mikels Skele, *The Great Knob: Interpretations of Monks Mound* (1988). Melvin Fowler, *The Cahokia Atlas: A Historical Atlas of Cahokia Archaeology* (1989). George R. Milner, "The Late Prehistoric Cahokia Cultural System of the Mississippi River Valley: Foundations, Florescence, and Fragmentation," *Journal of World Prehistory* 4 (1990): 1–43.

George R. Milner

CAMEL, Domestication of the. The domestication of the camel, like the horse, seems to have occurred much later than that of sheep, goat, and cattle. The camel is inferior to the horse in warfare and is further disadvantaged by slow reproduction and an intolerance of wet climates. Camels are superior pack animals in arid regions, however, and their usefulness in long-distance trade may be a major reason for the timing of their domestication.

There are two species of camel: the one-humped dromedary, *Camelus dromedarius,* admirably suited to the hot dry deserts of North Africa and the Near East, and the two-humped Bactrian camel, *Camelus bactrianus,* better suited to the cold deserts of Central Asia. Both probably evolved from a common Pleistocene ancestor. Camelid bones have been found in Pleistocene deposits in India, western Asia, and North Africa.

As in the case of the horse, it is difficult to establish whether any truly wild camels now exist. All one-humped camels are directly controlled by humans or are feral descendants of domesticated animals, but there may still be genuinely wild two-humped camels in the Gobi Desert. The superb adaptation of both camels to extreme conditions has made them useful to desert peoples with very little further selection.

Evidence of early domestication of the camel is difficult to interpret. Camel dung, hair, and bones, probably of the Bactrian variety, have been found in deposits of ca. 2600 B.C. at Shar-i Sokhta in Iran. Farther north in southern Turkmenia, camel bones are found from the fourth millennium B.C. Since the bones of camel do not change at domestication in the manner seen in other species, it is difficult to determine whether these were domestic or merely the residue of camel hunting. Artifacts, such as figurines and reliefs, or the discovery of camel dung at occupation sites, provides surer evidence of domestication than bones alone.

The dromedary appears first to have been domesticated in the southern Arabian Peninsula. Between 3000 and 2500 B.C., it is suggested that coastal peoples there switched from hunting camels to herding them for their milk. The camel subsequently spread to Somalia between 2500 and 1500 B.C., and then northward and across to Egypt in the first millennium B.C. This expansion may have been connected with the growth of the incense trade.

The evidence thus seems to indicate that by the beginning of the second millennium B.C. both species of Old World camel had been domesticated, the Bactrian in eastern Iran, the dromedary in southern Arabia.

Remains comparable with the dromedary are reported from Tell Jemmeh near Gaza in deposits of the fourteenth and thirteenth centuries B.C. and later. The quantity increases after 675 B.C., when the Assyrians invaded Egypt. Assyrian inscriptions and representations indicate that both dromedaries and Bactrian camels were in use by this time. Farther east, the Bactrian camel was used for long-distance trade along the *Silk Route to China, though the use of dromedaries in the Baghdad region led after a time to the development of hybrids that supplemented the Bactrian in the western parts of Central Asia.

The camel saddle was a critical part of the equation. The early southern Arabian saddle carried the weight behind the hump. Some time before 100 B.C., a revolutionary new type of saddle was developed in northern Arabia. This had a wooden frame surrounding the hump, which enabled the rider to fight while securely mounted above the hump. The invention of the northern Arabian saddle was probably a major factor in the rise of Arab power and influence.

With the Arab expansion, camel usage spread from Egypt and the Sudan across the whole of the Sahara, greatly affecting the society and economy of the region. Here, however, a different type of saddle was invented, located in front of the hump. This was efficient for riding but not for carrying a pack, and the northern Arabian saddle continued to be used for the important trans-Saharan trade. With the new saddle designs and the decay of the roads after the end of the Roman Empire, dromedaries almost entirely supplanted wheeled transport in North Africa and the Near East. They remained the principal method of travel in these regions until the present century.

[See also DOMESTICATION OF ANIMALS; HORSE, DOMESTICATION OF THE.]

■ F. E. Zeuner, A History of Domesticated Animals (1963). Richard W. Bulliet, The Camel and the Wheel (1975). Hilde Gauthier-Pilters and Anne Innis Dagg, The Camel, Its Evolution, Ecology, Behaviour and Relationship to Man (1981). Juliet Clutton-Brock, A Natural History of Domesticated Mammals (1987). Simon J. M. Davis, The Archaeology of Animals (1987).

Sheila Hamilton-Dyer

CAMPS AND ENCLOSURES, Causewayed. Causewayed enclosures are one of the major classes of field monument dating from the Neolithic Period in southern Britain. Similar enclosures are also present in continental Europe, notably in eastern France, the Rhineland, and southern Scandinavia. They consist of an open space enclosed by one or more ditches, which are interrupted by a series of breaks, known as causeways. In Britain, they are also referred to as causewayed camps or interrupted-ditch enclosures. Early investigators were struck by the number of causeways; they are more numerous than would be expected if their function was simply to give access to the interior of the site. This feature also sets them clearly apart from later kinds of enclosures, such as *hill forts, some of which occupy the same, or very similar, locations.

The first causewayed enclosures to be discovered were in southern Britain, notably on the chalk lands of Sussex and *Wessex, where, in the absence of heavy plowing, traces of their ditches and banks survived as surface features. Within the last fifty years, however, aerial photography has led to the discovery of many more of these enclosures, reduced to crop marks or soil marks on cultivated land. Examination of aerial photographs has shown that causewayed enclosures were not limited to chalk lands, for evidence of them occurs also on river gravels and other kinds of subsoil. They are now known in most parts of the British Isles, with the possible exception of Scotland.

In plan, causewayed enclosures display considerable variety. The basic conception is of one or more ditches, each with a bank on its inner side. The frequent interruptions in the ditch, the causeways, do not in all cases seem to have corresponded with a break in the bank. Furthermore, not only was the bank more continuous than the ditch, but postholes show that it was usually surmounted by a palisade, which again should have closed off access to the interior. The causeways, therefore, do not correspond to separate entrances. One possible explanation for the frequency of breaks in the ditch is that each section of ditch was allocated to a different labor gang, the principal aim of the work being not the ditch, which was left discontinuous, but the bank behind.

Some enclosures have only a simple ditch, while others have two or more, sometimes closely spaced and parallel to each other but in other cases more widely separated. In a few cases, the "enclosure" appears to have been left open along one side. Causewayed enclosures also vary considerably in size, from less than 3 acres (1 ha) to well in excess of 25 acres (10 ha). One of the best-known is that at Windmill Hill in southern Britain, which covers an area of 20 acres (8 ha). Estimates have shown that almost 50,000 hours of work would have been required for its construction. This in itself suggests that causewayed enclosures were built not by individual communities but by several communities working together.

Functions of Causewayed Enclosures. Early theories regarded causewayed enclosures as the Neolithic antecedents of Iron Age hill forts. According to this model they were places of refuge in times of unrest, fortified strongholds into which the local people could withdraw themselves and their livestock. The evidence for a defensive function is weak, however, and most recent accounts have transferred attention to their role as ritual or ceremonial centers. A ritual dimension is illustrated by finds of pottery, stone axes, and animal bones in pots within the enclosure or at particular points in the enclosure ditches, especially beside enclosure entrances. The nature of these deposits suggests that they were not merely discarded refuse but were intentionally placed as part of some ritual act. On the other hand, dense deposits of material that clearly is refuse are also found in some parts of the ditches; these have been interpreted as evidence of communal feasting. The causewayed enclosures may indeed have been gathering places for small communities from the whole of the surrounding area.

Another important category of evidence links the causewayed enclosures to death and mortuary rituals. Most of the sites have yielded scattered human remains, and at some enclosures, such as Hambledon Hill in southwestern England, human skulls had been carefully placed on the floor of the ditch. The skulls concerned lacked their mandibles, and must already have been defleshed when they were put in position. At the causewayed enclosure of Etton in eastern England, one part of the interior was particularly rich in deposits of human and animal bone. Discoveries such as these have suggested that these enclosures were places where bodies were exposed after death, perhaps on raised timber platforms, until the flesh had decayed. Once that stage was reached, the bones would have been removed for final disposal elsewhere.

The clear conclusion to be drawn from all of the evidence is that causewayed enclosures performed multiple functions. They may have been feasting venues and places for the exposure of corpses. The abundance of polished stone axe remains suggests that at these sites highly prized axes from different parts of the British Isles were bargained for and exchanged. And the carefully placed deposits of pots and other artifacts in the ditch ends illustrates something of the pattern of ritual practices and observances associated with the use of the enclosures.

The causewayed enclosures of southern Britain belong to the earlier Neolithic, between ca. 3500 B.C. and 3000 B.C. They are one element in a larger series of early Neolithic monuments that also includes long barrows, long mortuary enclosures, and cursus monuments. Occasionally, several of these different kinds of monuments occur together, forming ritual complexes such as that at Dorchester–on–Thames in the Thames valley. The tradition of field monuments continues in southern Britain into the later Neolithic (after 3000 B.C.) in the form of henge monuments and stone circles.

Neolithic Enclosures in Europe. The causewayed enclosures of the British Isles are not an isolated phenomenon but form part of a wider western European tradition of enclosures. The group that most closely resembles the British examples in form and function are the enclosures of southern Scandinavia. In one of the best examples, at Sarup in Denmark, a curving length of double ditch, broken by numerous gaps, cuts across the neck of a promontory. In the interior were pits containing ritual deposits. Access across most of the causeways was blocked by a substantial timber palisade, but the pits within the enclosure suggest that this was as much a ceremonial as a defensive site. The enclosures of southern Scandinavia are contemporary with those of the British Isles.

Other Neolithic enclosures are found in the area of the initial *Bandkeramik agricultural colonization, focused on central Europe but extending as far west as the Paris basin.

The earliest appear to be enclosures of late Bandkeramik or immediately post-Bandkeramik date (ca. 4500–4000 B.C.), such as Langweiler in Germany or Berry-au-Bac in the Paris basin. These have many fewer causeways or entrance gaps than the British or southern Scandinavian examples, and the purpose for which they were intended was far from uniform. The Berry-au-Bac enclosure was a defended settlement site. Here the enclosure ditch was backed by a trench in which a substantial palisade had been constructed, with only a single narrow entrance. Against the rear of the palisade was an earthen rampart, in the shelter of which a series of rectangular timber buildings had stood. The Rhineland enclosures, on the other hand, appear to have delimited a communal open space within the settlement. At Langweiler Site 9, the subrectangular earthwork enclosure was constructed in the free space between two clusters of timber longhouses. The material from pits within the enclosed space suggests that it was reserved for certain specialized activities, such as flint working.

These early enclosures date to the fifth millennium B.C., but the idea of enclosure became much more widespread in the following millennium. The later Neolithic enclosures are more substantial than their predecessors, and some may have had a serious defensive purpose. Late Neolithic enclosures in southern Britain, such as the latest phase of Crickley Hill, appear also to have had a defensive function. In this they may be compared to the stone-walled enclosures of Mediterranean Europe, and notably to the fortresslike structures of southeastern Spain and central Portugal.

The relative abundance and variety of earthwork enclosures in Neolithic and post-Neolithic Europe make it necessary to consider how far those in the interrupted-ditch category form part of a single phenomenon. The idea of enclosure itself may have originated in the late Bandkeramik and been carried from central Europe to the north, the west, and the British Isles along with other features of Neolithic ideology, such as the long mound. Interrupted-ditch enclosures do indeed seem to belong to a particular phase in the development of early European farming societies, a stage that may be bracketed in chronological terms between 4800 B.C. and 3500 B.C. Later enclosures tend to conform more closely either to the category of specialized ritual monuments, such as the henges of southern Britain, or to the category of defended enclosures, such as those found in southern Germany or western France in the fourth millennium B.C. These in their own way form part of a separate but less homogenous grouping that reaches its culmination in the hill forts and *oppida of the European Iron Age.

[See also BRITISH ISLES: PREHISTORY OF THE BRITISH ISLES; EUROPE: THE EUROPEAN NEOLITHIC PERIOD; STONE CIRCLES AND ALIGNMENTS.]

■ C. Burgess, P. Topping, C. Mordant, and M. Maddison, eds., *Enclosures and Defences in the Neolithic of Western Europe*. (1988). R. Bradley, *Altering the Earth: The Origins of Monuments in Britain and Continental Europe*. (1993).

Chris Scarre

CARBON DATING. *See* RADIOCARBON DATING.

CAREERS. In 1961 John Howland Rowe, an American archaeologist trained in Latin American history, anthropology, and classical archaeology, surveyed the career choices and outlook for prospective archaeologists. His conclusion was grim: "Employment opportunities are few, the competition for them is heavy, and the salaries are comparatively low." Nearly three decades later an assessment of career opportunities in Great Britain was no more encouraging: "Universities have been cruel to dangle the mirage of archaeology as a career when it can never be anything more than a career for a very small fortunate minority."

This bleak outlook is still true for traditional archaeological careers in academic or museum settings that focus on teaching, research, and curation. While there has been increasing diversity and specialization in the field—specialties within archaeology may be based on different time periods, particular ancient cultures, and specialized techniques or interdisciplinary training—the number of available positions has not increased significantly. As a result, numbers of ever more highly specialized archaeologists are competing for a limited number of positions. Although these specializations are worthwhile, they do not always conform to the core needs of universities or museums. There are some brighter prospects, particularly in private or government agencies involved with cultural resource management (CRM). Other career possibilities that may grow include public-oriented heritage projects, like the Jorvik Viking Center in York, England, or Colonial Williamsburg, Virginia, and international projects such as those of the World Monuments Fund.

With the rise of cultural resource management, archaeology is no longer an academic luxury but a mainstream part of planning and development. More than half the archaeologists employed in the United States are involved in CRM, either in state, city, or federal agencies or in university-based or private consulting firms. These apply, however, primarily to projects that are federally funded or licensed or are on federal land. In Britain most archaeologists are employed in regionally based "units" initially funded by the Department of the Environment, but are now independent or within county governments or universities.

The growing emphasis on CRM has raised the question of professionalism. Concerns over the quality of archaeological work in the United States prompted the founding of the Society of Professional Archeologists, which has attempted to define professional qualifications and standards for archaeology. These include a graduate degree in archaeology, anthropology, history, classics, or another pertinent discipline with a specialization in archaeology; substantial laboratory analysis or fieldwork including supervision of excavations; and the design and completion of research as evidenced by a thesis or equivalent research report. The Institute of Field Archaeologists in Britain has a similar goal of establishing and maintaining high standards of professional practice.

There is a growing divergence in the qualifications required for traditional university and museum positions and those for resource management. While a doctorate remains a necessity for academic positions, a master's degree with greater practical experience may be more appropriate for those in resource management.

A survey in 1991 revealed that more than half of all archaeological positions in Britain are temporary, that 75 percent of archaeologists receive less than the national average salary, and that 90 percent of those in temporary jobs are paid below average. Funding, according to the survey, came half from developers and half from national and local governments. The situation in the United States is similar, and archaeologists are more dependent on the general economic climate than ever before. Even in times of economic growth, competitive bidding for developer-funded projects may result in pressure to keep wages low.

Change in the career prospects for archaeologists can come about only through increased public awareness of the importance of archaeology, archaeologists, and their work. To accomplish this archaeologists must press for change both in the public's perception of the field and in terms of collegial responsibilities. Academic archaeologists who have relied on student labor and the contributed time of specialists to undertake and complete their research must reconsider their actions. Archaeologists must be fairly compensated for their work, and fellow archaeologists should be the first to recognize this. Academic archaeologists also have the responsibility to prepare their students for adequately paid permanent positions. Archaeology curricula need to be reoriented to match the current need for specialists in cultural resource management and historic preservation. The necessity of cultivating and maintaining good relations with the public should be explicitly taught and the stigma of "popularization" removed. Outside the university, developer-financed and government projects are usually underfunded in terms of postexcavation work. The analysis of remains by specialists, which takes more time than the excavation itself, and full publication of sites must be supported.

[See also CULTURAL RESOURCE MANAGEMENT: INTRODUCTION; EDUCATION IN ARCHAEOLOGY: PROFESSIONAL TRAINING.]

■ John Howland Rowe, "Archaeology as a Career," *Archaeology* 14 (1961): 45–55. Andrew Selkirk, "Diary," *Current Archaeology* 112 (1988): 151; Paul Spoerry, "Structure and Funding in British Archaeology: Some Points Raised by 'The Rescue Questionnaire 1990–91,'" *Rescue News* 54 (1991): 2. Robert Sharer and Wendy Ashmore, *Archaeology: Discovering Our Past*, 2nd ed. (1993).

Mark J. Rose

CARIBBEAN, Archaeology of the. The islands of the Caribbean archipelago extend from near the South American mainland in Venezuela in the southeast to the Gulf of Mexico in the northwest. To the north, the Bahamas reach up to within about 50 miles (80 km) of Florida, and to the west, Cuba lies 62 miles (100 km) from the Yucatán peninsula. The Caribbean islands were first occupied by people about six thousand years ago, and subsequently experienced several large migrations of people from the surrounding mainlands as well as considerable movement and interaction among peoples within the archipelago. By about one thousand years ago, large populations lived in the Greater Antilles (Cuba, Jamaica, Haiti, Dominican Republic, and Puerto Rico) and had begun to form complex chiefdoms with centralized political authority and social stratification.

Caribbean archaeologists have focussed their attention on several issues: the migrations of people throughout the Caribbean over time, the new and continuing adaptations that had to be made to the island environments, patterns of trade and interaction within and beyond the archipelago, and the emergence of complex societies in the Greater Antilles.

The earliest evidence for human colonization of the Caribbean is found in Cuba and Hispaniola (Haiti and the Dominican Republic), where sites have been dated to around 4000 B.C. The similarities between the flaked-stone assemblages at these sites and those of the Yucatán peninsula suggest that the earliest migrants came from the west across the Yucatán Channel, or via other routes from Central America. The assemblages from these sites have been called Casimiroid after the site of Casimira in the Dominican Republic. Related assemblages are named in regional sequences for other contemporary sites (Barrera-Mordán, Cabaret, Seboruco).

The movement from the mainland to the Antilles required substantial changes in people's economic adaptations. As is the case in most island settings, the island fauna were very different from that of the mainland (e.g., there were no large mammals). Subsequent immigrants faced the problem of adapting to the distinctive island ecosystems as well. The earliest Greater Antillean colonists were non-horticultural: they depended on hunting, fishing, and collecting wild marine and terrestrial foods.

By 2000 B.C. a number of regional archaeological variants had developed in Cuba and Hispaniola, a process which also occurred later in Puerto Rico. The economics of these varying developments were still based on wild resources, but with perhaps greater movement between the coast and interior to exploit seasonal resources. Their material culture included an elaborate ground stone tradition, with decorated bowls, pendants, axes, and other objects.

Another group of non-horticultural migrants moved into the Caribbean sometime before 2000 B.C., this time from the northeast coast of South America. They moved through the islands of the Lesser Antilles and into Puerto Rico. Their small settlements are scattered through many of the Lesser Antilles and raw materials such as chert are widely distributed, demonstrating their competence in ocean travel. There are concentrations of settlements on some islands (e.g., Antigua). This occupation, never large, may have persisted until the Lesser Antilles were colonized by new migrants from South America.

Between 500 and 250 B.C., horticulturalists who used ceramics moved into the Lesser Antilles and Puerto Rico. They came from the Orinoco drainage and the river systems of South America's northeast coast. It is likely that this migration involved more than one mainland group and place of origin, but within a few centuries a relatively homogenous Caribbean culture had emerged. The ceramics of this culture, called Saladoid after the Venezuelan site of Saladero, were decorated with striking white-on-red painting and incised cross-hatching. Some of the portable art (including triangular, carved stone and shell objects called *zemis*) symbolized aspects of their ideological system, and the long continuity of the use of such symbols, even at the time of European contact, argues that later groups descended from Saladoid ancestors. The Saladoid immigrants brought dogs and the agouti (*Dasyprocta sp.* or *Myoprocta sp.*) with them, as well as a lowland South American suite of domesticates emphasizing root crops like manioc (*Manihot sp.*). These domesticates were complemented with wild foods from terrestrial and marine habitats. Through time they relied less heavily on terrestrial resources like land crabs and more on marine species from the deep reef and open sea.

Saladoid people settled extensively on the large and rich island of Puerto Rico, occupying sites near the coast on the major rivers. Saladoid settlement also extended to the eastern end of Hispaniola, where Saladoid people lived in contact with the island's longtime inhabitants. From the few Saladoid sites where large-area excavations have been undertaken, it appears that Saladoid villages typically consisted of several large—over 33 feet (10 m) in diameter—houses built of poles and thatch, similar to those known ethnographically from lowland South America. The houses surrounded a central plaza, and most sites have substantial midden deposits.

Between A.D. 500 and 1000 a series of changes took place which are manifest in settlement organization, economy, pottery manufacture, and evidence for population growth. Settlements became more numerous in the Lesser Antilles and the descendants of the Saladoid people (whose ceramic series is termed Ostionoid) colonized the upland interior of Puerto Rico. They also moved beyond the small Saladoid foothold on Hispaniola throughout that island, and into Cuba and Jamaica. Populations of hunting and gathering people already lived in many of these areas, and they apparently incorporated themselves into the newly emerging society, for later archaeological evidence shows stylistic continuities with both groups. People also began colonizing the Bahamas archipelago, which extends between Hispaniola and Florida. Beginning with the rapid expansion of ceramics-using horticultural people through most of the Greater Antilles, there is evidence for rapid population growth and the beginnings of the emergence of more complex forms of social and political integration.

After A.D. 800 the predecessors of the historic Taino people developed a number of regional ceramic traditions, and throughout the Greater Antilles, especially between A.D. 1000 and 1492, there is evidence of emerging social hierarchies and political complexity. Stone-lined ball courts and ceremonial plazas were built and a flamboyant tradition of ceramic production and carving in stone and wood emerged. Accounts written at the time of the Spanish conquest of the islands show the Taino as a series of complex chiefdoms—polities encompassing as many as one hundred villages and tens of thousands of people. Villages of two to three thousand people are described, with intensive forms of agriculture and specialization in food production. There was a clear hierarchy of social status, with elites, commoners, and slaves, and other special categories such as religious specialists and healers. Among the elite, complex rules governed inheritance and succession within the matrilineal lineages. Elites from the different cacicazgos or chiefdoms interacted with each other through trade, warfare, intermarriage, and the ball game. Oceangoing canoes that could carry as many as one hundred people extended this interaction among the islands of the Greater Antilles, northern Lesser Antilles, and Bahamas.

In 1492 the indigenous people of the Caribbean comprised an ethnic mosaic of different groups through the Lesser Antilles, Greater Antilles, and Bahamas. Nearly all were speakers of Arawakan languages, although with several mutually unintelligible variants, and nearly all were descendants of the Saladoid immigrants of the last centuries B.C. Centuries of divergent development, and different experiences with both the preceramic groups who occupied the islands before their arrival and with mainland populations, contributed to the Caribbean peoples' diversity.

[*See also* SOUTH AMERICA: LOWLANDS CULTURES OF SOUTH AMERICA.]

■ Samuel M. Wilson, *Hispaniola: Caribbean Chiefdoms in the Age of Columbus* (1990). Peter L. Drewett, *Prehistoric Barbados* (1991). William F. Keegan, *The People who Discovered Columbus: The Prehistory of the Bahamas* (1992). Irving Rouse, *The Tainos* (1992).

Samuel Wilson

CARNAC in southern Brittany (France) stands at the heart of a territory rich in prehistoric monuments, dating mainly to the Neolithic Period (ca. 5000–2500 B.C.). The monuments are as remarkable for their diversity as for their number, and include passage graves, long mounds (most notably the spectacular Carnac mounds), and standing stones, or menhirs, placed either singly or in parallel rows. These show that the Carnac region was the center of an active tradition of monument building extending over a period of more than 2,000 years.

Recent discoveries have shown that large standing stones are among the earliest of the Carnac monuments. The most famous is the Grand Menhir Brisé at Locmariaquer, an enormous granite pillar now fallen and broken into four separate fragments. When complete it would have stood more than 66 feet (20 m) high. Nearby is the low mound of Er Grah, 394 feet (120 m) long, which contains a megalithic chamber in its central section. This is one of a series of monuments known as Carnac mounds, which are unique to this part of southern Brittany. They are distinguished both by their size and by the objects of turquoise, jasper, and jadeite from the stone-built chambers within them. The largest of all is the Tumulus Saint-Michel, measuring 410 feet (125 m) long, 197 feet (60 m) wide, and 33 feet (10 m) high, with a later Christian chapel built on the summit. The Carnac mounds were probably constructed in the late fifth or early fourth millennium B.C.

The Carnac area is also famous for the passage graves of La Table des Marchand at Locmariaquer and Gavrinis on a small island in the Gulf of Morbihan. These were built around 3200 B.C. The Gavrinis passage grave is especially notable for the richness of the carved decoration in the passage and chamber, including curved lines and concentric semicircles. A remarkable recent discovery has been that the capstones of these tombs consist of adjoining sections of the same standing stone, which must have been felled and broken up intentionally for this purpose. The Grand Menhir Brisé may have also been toppled as part of the same destruction episode.

Probably the most famous of the Carnac monuments are the stone rows, notably those of Kermario and Le Menec. These were erected probably in the course of the third millennium B.C. The Kermario rows are long with 1,029 surviving stones arranged in seven principal lines running cross-country for 3,700 feet (1,128 m). Neither they nor the Le Menec rows run in an exact straight line, but incorporate several changes of direction, and may have been altered and extended on a number of occasions. Each of them ends in an oval enclosure of standing stones known as a *cromlech*. The purpose of the Carnac alignments has excited much debate, but has never been satisfactorily explained.

[See also EUROPE: THE EUROPEAN NEOLITHIC PERIOD; MEGALITHIC TOMBS.]

■ A. Burl., *Megalithic Brittany* (1985).

Chris Scarre

CARTHAGE. Carthage (Qrthdst [="New Town"]; Latin Carthago), a Phoenician colony founded from Tyre, and later a major Roman city, is situated on the coast of northeastern Tunisia on part of a peninsula which stretches eastward from lagoons into the Gulf of Tunis. The site, dominated by the Byrsa hill, provided anchorage and supplies for Phoenician ships trading in the western Mediterranean for gold, silver, and tin. Its convenient position, fertile hinterland, and adequate harbor soon made Carthage the preeminent Phoenician colony in the west.

The traditional foundation date is 814–813 B.C., but no archaeological evidence has yet been found earlier than the second half of the eighth century B.C. Scanty remains of houses of this date have been found, at one point up to 1150 feet (350 m) from the shore, suggesting that the settlement was already then of considerable size; but the original nucleus, if there really was a colony here from the later ninth century, has yet to be found.

Early contact with the Greek world is shown by the presence of Attic amphorae (of "SOS" type) in the earliest levels. Little is known of the archaic topography, but surface finds and necropolises to the north and west suggest that the city covered at least 136 acres (55 ha). Pottery kilns and metal-working quarters have also been identified, as well as the *tophet*, where child sacrifice to Baal and Tanit took place; the sanctuary was in continuous use from the later eighth century down to 146 B.C.

Carthage, an oligarchy ruled by two annually elected "judges" (in Latin *suffetes*), controlled much of the trade in the western Mediterranean, setting its own trading posts in addition to those founded by the Phoenicians. Carthaginian influence in its heyday in the fifth and fourth centuries B.C. extended from Tripolitania in Libya to Morocco, as well as to western Sicily, Sardinia, and southern Spain. In the late fifth century B.C. massive fortifications, 17 feet (5.20 m) wide, were erected with projecting towers and gates; Livy says that they were 20 miles (32 km) long. Substantial houses, some with peristyles and simple tessellated floors, are known from the Hellenistic period, when the city reached its greatest extent: a new area of housing, for example, was laid out on the slopes of the Byrsa hill soon after 200 B.C., covering an archaic necropolis. Also to the last Punic phase belong the two artificial harbors to the south near the *tophet*, one approximately rectangular, the other circular around a central island. The first was the commercial harbor, and the latter housed the warships of the Carthaginian navy: Appian reports a shipshed capacity of 220 vessels here. Little is known of the disposition of the harbor(s) at an earlier date.

With Rome Carthage had concluded treaties in 508 and 348, in which it guarded its maritime interests in the western Mediterranean while agreeing not to interfere in Italy. But in 264 B.C. Sicilian politics brought the two states into open conflict: Carthaginian intervention on the side of the Mamertines at Messina in 264 precipitated the first of the Punic wars between Rome and Carthage, which culminated in the total destruction of the latter in 146 B.C. Rome decreed that the defenses, houses and crops of Carthage should never rise again. The site, however, was too attractive to remain permanently unoccupied, and it was newly colonized by Augustus in the second decade B.C., when it became the capital of the Roman province of Africa Proconsularis.

Roman Carthage has suffered greatly from stone robbing, but the regular Augustan street grid centered on the Byrsa hill is known in detail, as well as the position of the principal public buildings, including the amphitheater on the western outskirts, the circus on the southwest, the theater, and the odeum. The second century saw the apogee of the city's prosperity, when Carthage became the second city to Rome in the western Mediterranean, and was a major exporter to Italy of grain and other foodstuffs, as well as animals for the amphitheater. A forum and basilica, the biggest known outside Rome, was erected on the Byrsa in Antonine times, and also Antonine is the huge and lavish bathhouse down by the sea, designed on a symmetrical layout like the great imperial baths of Rome. Carthage's 82-mile (132-km) aqueduct, the longest known in the Roman world, was probably built to supply it. The Byrsa forum was not the first: work since 1990 near the coast, midway between the Antonine baths and the harbors, has revealed part of what is probably the Augustan forum, with below it a Punic temple, perhaps that of Apollo (Appian says it bordered the Punic agora). Prosperity continued in the third century, when the export of olive oil massively increased; attractive polychrome mosaics, the product of local workshops, became particularly numerous in the third and fourth centuries. The city early embraced Christianity: numerous extramural churches are known from the fourth, fifth, and sixth centuries. A massive new defensive circuit was erected around A.D. 425 on the landward side; despite it the city fell easily to the Vandals in 439, and became the capital of their king Geiseric and his successors. Several houses of the fifth and sixth centuries are known, and survey work in the Carthaginian hinterland shows rural settlement at its densest now, matching and even outstripping that of the second and third centuries. But Carthage itself shows signs of being increasingly run down as the fifth century progressed, and decline continued in earnest under Byzantine rule after a brief respite under Justinian. Although Carthage beat off the earlier Moslem invasions, the city was captured by Arabs in 697.

[*See also* MEDITERRANEAN TRADE; MEDITARRANEAN WORLD: THE DOMINANCE OF GREECE AND ROME.]

■ A. Audollent, *Carthage romaine, 146 avant J.-C.–698 après J.-C.* (1901). E. Lipinski, ed., *Studia Phoenica VI: Carthago* (1988). M. H. Fantar, *Carthage: Approche d'une civilisation,* 2 vols. (1993). Serge Lancel, *Carthage: A History* (1995; French original 1992). *Carthage: l'histoire, sa trace et son écho* (1995) (Paris exhibition catalogue). UNESCO-sponsored excavations since 1973: J. G. Pedley, ed., *New Light on Ancient Carthage* (1980). A. Ennabli, ed., *Pour sauver Carthage* (1992), with full bibliography.

R.J.A. Wilson

CASAS GRANDES, also known as Paquimé, was once one of the largest and most influential communities in the American Southwest and northern Mexico. Casas Grandes is located in northwestern Chihuahua at the foot of the Sierra Madre Occidental Mountains near the headwaters of the Casas Grandes River.

The site covers (89 acres (36 ha) and is estimated to have had two thousand rooms. Paquimé was the center of a complex society. There is evidence of elites (special burial practices), wealth accumulation (e.g., storerooms with over four million shell artifacts), economic specialization (such as of scarlet macaw parrots, turkeys, shell artifacts, agave, and possibly copper artifacts), a sophisticated water distribution system, and a diversity of public ritual architecture (ball courts and earthen mounds). Hundreds of villages surrounding Paquimé probably were part of the Casas Grandes polity.

Casas Grandes was first reported by European explorers in 1565. Only sporadic and limited archaeological study was conducted in northwestern Chihuahua until the Joint Casas Grandes Expedition in 1958–1961. Directed by Dr. Charles C. Di Peso of the Amerind Foundation in collaboration with the Instituto Nacional de Antropología e Historia, this project conducted excavations and wall stabilization at

Paquimé and did limited research at other nearby sites. The resulting eight-volume *Casas Grandes: A Fallen Trading Center of the Gran Chichimeca,* (by Di Peso), is the baseline for all understanding of the area's prehistory.

The height of Paquimé's influence occurred during the Medio period, and was originally dated by Di Peso to A.D. 1060–1350 and is now more securely dated to A.D. 1200–1450. The Casas Grandes–dominated culture then disintegrated and early Spanish explorers reported the presence of only small farming villages and nomadic hunter-gatherers in northwestern Chihuahua.

Major controversy surrounds the interpretation of Casas Grandes. Di Peso suggested that Paquimé was founded by long-distance traders from Mesoamerica for the exploitation of the American Southwest and northern Mexico to the benefit of states in central Mexico. Others argue that while Paquimé was not founded by Mesoamerican traders, this site was a major center of Mesoamerican and southwestern relationships. Some question these views, believing that the connections between Paquimé and Mesoamerica were minimal. Rather they argue that the strongest relationships were between Casas Grandes and its surrounding communities and adjacent cultural regions to the north and west.

Currently, there are several international teams investigating the internal organization of the Casas Grandes regional system in northwestern Chihuahua. The Mexican government has increased stabilization efforts and is constructing a new archaeological museum at the site.

[*See also* NORTH AMERICA: THE NORTH AMERICAN SOUTHWEST.]

Paul E. Minnis

CATAL HÜYÜK. The mound of Catal Hüyük in central *Anatolia, about fifty kilometers southeast of Konya, lies on a river entering a wide plain once covered by a lake, reduced now to a salt lake, the Tuz Gölü. James Mellaart's excavations, from 1961 to 1964, revealed fourteen building levels; beneath the lowest layer excavated by Mellaart (XII), a thick layer of cultural deposits awaits further exploration.

The excavated levels, carbon dated to about 6300 to 5500 B.C., fall into the Ceramic Neolithic Period, contemporary with the Pre-Pottery Neolithic of the Levant and phases Amuq A and B in Syria. Catal Hüyük's cultural development is remarkably homogeneous, showing only minor evolutionary adjustments. The wealth of artifacts and art objects is unparalleled in the Neolithic Period of the Near East.

Residential Structures. Each dwelling at the site had a standardized main room of approximately 19.5 by 13 feet (6 by 4 m), accessible through an opening in the roof using ladders, and one or two smaller storerooms reached from the main room through a small doorway or a raised porthole. Some abandoned rooms probably served as courtyards or as rubbish dumps. The pattern of tightly packed houses—each of which had its own roof, plastered mudbrick, and timber walls leaning against each other—showed no evidence of streets or open places; all traffic apparently moved at roof level.

The houses were equipped with plastered clay niches, benches, raised platforms, and flat-domed ovens. Many storerooms contained grain bins, often with charred remains of cereals. The lime-plaster floors showed impressions of reed mats. The walls of the main rooms were painted with red panels that were frequently renewed.

Some rooms, though not structurally different, had elaborate wall paintings, plastic depictions incorporating skulls of animals, and other ceremonial objects that justify Mellaart's characterization of them as shrines.

The extensive use of timber in the house construction in the early levels decreased over time, and the later houses were entirely built of mud brick. This reduced the danger of fire, yet indicates a diminishing wood supply.

Mortuary Customs. The dead of the community were probably left in the open to be picked by vultures (as depicted on wall paintings) or temporarily buried. The bare bones were then wrapped in cloth or mats and entombed beneath the sleeping platforms of the houses and shrines. Except for a few personal ornaments, mainly shell or stone necklaces, anklets, and wristbands, there were no funerary goods. Some skeletons showed signs of ocher, and the shrines contained high-status burials accompanied by stone vessels, obsidian mirrors, or other precious objects and food offerings—but never pottery or figurines.

With each new burial, the older bones were usually disturbed and rearranged. In a burial of level VII, cowrie shells were set into the eye sockets, similar to the contemporary practice at Jericho and Tell Ramadi.

Material Culture. Catal Hüyük's chipped stone industry was among the most elegant in the Near East. Mellaart distinguished some fifty different types of tools and weapons, mostly made from local obsidian or imported flint. Bifacial, pressure-flaked flat retouch is typical; some items were polished on one side. They include arrowheads, with or without tangs and barbs, double-pointed spearheads and daggers with lengths up to 8 inches (20 cm), scrapers, knives, and a plethora of other implements for daily or ceremonial use, while some were clearly prestige objects.

Other stone tools, such as mortars, pestles, querns, handstones, axes, adzes, and maceheads, were made from a variety of colored rocks, often imported from distant sources. Cosmetic palettes of sandstone or schist were sometimes found together with ocher. A speciality of Catal Hüyük were polished obsidian mirrors. However, a marked decline in stone tools is observed in the later levels dated to the middle of the sixth millennium B.C., when copper came into use.

Some tools and jewelry were made of bone, including awls, needles, spatulae, toggles, knife hafts, cosmetic pins, forks, hairpins, beads, and a beautifully carved fishhook. A variety of well-carved wooden bowls and boxes with lids were found at the site, as well as baskets, leather bags, and textiles.

Pottery was present in all excavated levels and was always monochrome and purely functional. The earliest ceramic vessels were coil-made with some straw tempering, cream colored or a mottled gray, burnished, and fired in low to medium temperatures. Occasionally, a red wash was applied, or knob handles or ledge handles were added for easy handling. Painted or plastic decorations on vessels are lacking except a few incised lines or a few animal heads adorning the rim of a bowl.

In levels VI to II, terra-cotta stamp seals with geometric designs of spirals or meanders occurred, probably used to apply color to cloth or perhaps indicating that the notion of private ownership was already developed.

Artistic Expression. The art objects from Catal Hüyük are most remarkable. There are a variety of figurines, ranging from aniconic to naturalistic female figures and animals of clay or stone. Crude female figurines with pointed legs, rodlike bodies, and beaked heads are commonly found in crevices of buildings. Figurines of cattle, goats, and boars often show stab marks, suggesting magic hunting rites.

Shrines contained more elaborately modeled or carved statuettes of females in association with broken-off stalagmites or stalactites. These include the famous large goddess giving birth on a throne of leopards, a schist plaque with two embracing couples, and some outstanding representations of voluptuous naked women sitting, kneeling, or reclining, undoubtedly the ancestors of the Great Mother venerated in Anatolia and all over the ancient Mediterranean world.

Wall paintings, also mostly in shrines and executed in a variety of mineral and organic paints on plaster, range from plain panels or kelimlike geometric patterns to a landscape with volcanoes erupting over a settlement, scenes of vultures devouring human corpses, and the celebration of animal games with bulls, stags, boars, lions, or leopards (sometimes with leopard skulls in the plaster), and dancing or stalking human figures clad in leopard skins.

The inhabitants of Catal Hüyük engaged in active trade, particularly in obsidian from the nearby Hasan Dag volcano, which was exchanged all over southern Anatolia and the Levant. Luxury items, often made of precious exotic materials imported from the Iranian highlands, Syria, and the Levant also bear testimony to a sophisticated society of accomplished traders, craftspeople, and artists.

[*See also* DOMESTICATION OF ANIMALS; DOMESTICATION OF PLANTS; NEAR EAST: THE NEOLITHIC AND CHALCOLITHIC (PRE-BRONZE-AGE) PERIODS IN THE NEAR EAST.]

■ E. Anati, "Anatolia's Earliest Art," *Archaeology* 21 (1968): 22–35. J. L. Angel, "Early Neolithic Skeletons from Catal Hoyuk: Demography and Pathology," *Anatolian Studies* XXI (1971): 77–98. P. Bialor, "The Chipped Stone Industry of Catal Hoyuk," *Anatolian Studies* XII (1962): 67–110. H. Burnham, "Catal Hoyuk: The Textiles and Twine Fabrics," *Anatolian Studies* XV (1965): 169–174. D. Ferembach, "Les hommes du gisement neolithique de Catal Hoyuk," *VII Turk Tarini Kongresi [1970]* (1972). H. Helbaek, "First Impressions of the Catal Hoyuk Plant Husbandry," *Anatolian Studies* XIV (1964): 121–123. J. Mellaart, "Excavations at Catal Hoyuk, First to Fourth Preliminary Reports," *Anatolian Studies* XII (1962): 41–65, XIII (1963): 43–103, XIV (1964): 39–119, XVI (1966): 165–191. J. Mellaart, *Catal Hoyuk, a Neolithic Town in Anatolia* (1967). J. Mellaart, *The Neolithic of the Near East* (1975). M. J. Mellink, "Anatolian Chronology," in *Chronologies of Old World Archaeology*, 3rd ed. (1993). R. W. Ehrich, D. Perkins Jr., "Fauna of Catal Hoyuk," *Science* 164 (1969): 177–179.

Mattanyah Zohar

CELTIC ART designates at least two things: (1) art of any type that was or is done by or used by people called Celts and (2) a distinctive art style originated by or associated at some stage with Celts, but which can be made and appreciated within wider ethnic contexts. The constituent elements of the terms *Celtic* and *art* are each problematic in themselves. In the broadest terms, art relates to expressive human behavior and to notions of beauty. When attached to an ethnonym, as in "Greek art," "Indian art," or "Celtic art," the implications are twofold: first, that such art is stylistically characterizable through its relationship to a particular tradition of production; second, that such production will tend to incorporate or express something of the specific worldview of the society in question. For Celtic art this represents a particular problem, as the extent to which Celtic society or culture can be clearly defined as a homogeneous entity in any given place and time is doubtful. The ethnic term *Celtic* has a wide range of meanings, both in common parlance and in the academic discourses of, among other things, archaeologists, biological anthropologists, classicists, historians, linguists, mythographers, and students of comparative religion. Not only does the definition of *Celtic* differ between specializations, but there are different focuses within them, for example, some linguistic approaches focus on poetry and song in extant Celtic languages while others are concerned with underlying and ancient Indo-European roots; archaeological definitions may focus on continental Iron Age weaponry, on late pre-Roman Gaulish coinages, on insular medieval manuscript illumination, and so on. Celtic art is also a living tradition that embraces jewelry, music, calligraphy, tattooing, weaving, and story-writing. Some of this is produced as a conscious reproduction or reconstruction of ancient Celtic material, some is inspired by such material, and some, done by artists who define themselves as ethnic Celts, must be thought of as genuine or "living" Celtic art, with its proximal roots in the Celtic revival movement of the nineteenth and early twentieth centuries; Markale argued that the work of the Impressionists and of Picasso and Kandinsky was part of this revival.

Celtic art today is seen as connecting to Celtic spirituality, which involves mystical and sometimes esoteric knowledge that opposes modern materialism and empiricism.

The idea of Celtic art as almost timeless goes back to the work of Sir John Rhye, who attributed similarities in Irish and Indian mythologies to the preservation of a distinctively Indo-European culture from the time of the original putative dispersion of Indo-European people from their homeland, sometime in the Bronze Age. This theme was taken up by Georges Dumézil, whose theory of trifunctionality presented the Indo-European cosmos as constructed on three levels, reflected in the organization of all Indo-European societies into priest-kings, warriors, and farmers (or, in Caesar's Formulation for the Celts, *druides*, *equites*, and *plebes*) with their specific deities. However, despite the widespread use of tripling in Celtic visual imagery, no convincing connection between Dumézil's theory and Celtic artistic expression can be demonstrated. The connections that do exist between Celtic and Oriental art and mythology can be better explained in terms of human and material mobility at particular times, such as tribal migrations and campaigns, mercenary activities, mobile craftspeople, diplomatic marriages, fosterage, looting, trading, and a range of less direct influences; the article in this volume on the *Gundestrup cauldron outlines this for the late first millennium B.C.; similarities between stories in the *Mahabharata* and in the Welsh *Mabinogion*, the latter formalized in the twelfth century A.D., may represent a refreshment of shared thematic material by wandering balladeers and itinerant craftspeople with Indian links, such as the Gypsies, whose precise history in the period A.D. 1000–1500 is as yet poorly known.

A tribe called *Celts is first mentioned historically in the works of Hecataeus (ca. 500 B.C.) and Herodotus (ca. 450 B.C.), who locate them inland of the colony of Massalia (modern Marseilles), between the source of the Danube and the Pyrenees, and possibly extending into Iberia; in the following centuries, Celtic war bands went on the rampage, sacking Rome in the period 390–387 B.C. and Delphi in 279 B.C. establishing themselves in Thracian southeastern Europe and western Anatolia, and fighting in Sarmatia and points farther east. For most prehistorians, Celtic art dates no earlier than the fifth century B.C., and relates most centrally to the distinctive *La Tène style in metalwork, the

presence of which in graves corroborates the historical data on Celtic adventurism beyond central and western Europe. The style is named after a Swiss lake site, discovered in 1857, occupied between 275 and 60 B.C., from which a large number of swords and torcs have been recovered; evidence for human sacrifice in and around the site suggests a religious character to the deposition. Paul Jacobsthal, in his monumental work *Early Celtic Art* (1944), suggested a four-fold division of La Tène art. The Early Style, fifth to early fourth centuries B.C., is characterized by classical and Oriental influences: a good example is a bronze wine flagon from a rich female grave at Kleinaspergle, Baden-Württemburg, which follows a basic Etruscan form, with curiously lobed and slightly vegetal human and animal forms grafted on. The Waldalgesheim Style emerged around 350 B.C., following the raids on Italy, and was named after a rich double burial in the Hunsrück, where a gold torc, bracelets, and chariot mounts all demonstrate a new, swirled vegetal style, through which human and animal faces peer (Jacobsthal also used the phrase "Cheshire-cat style" to describe this). The latest styles were the Plastic Style and the Hungarian Sword Style; the former is marked by chunky, bossed, curved, and faceted pieces with unexpected, teetering symmetries, marking a complete integration of iconic content with decorative motifs; the latter is represented by a mainly central-eastern European distribution of engraved iron sword scabbards, influenced by Hellenistic art. Jacobsthal's division has been tweaked here and there and chronologies and influences revised and discussed by, among others, P. M. Duval and J.V.S. Megaw. The style sequence is ultimately not convincing, and whole areas, such as the little-known material from southeastern Europe and southern Russia, and the better-known "Celt-Iberian" art of Spain and British "Insular La Tène" do not fit well in the sequence. Very little convincing work of a contextual nature has been done, integrating art-style analysis with broader archaeological and anthropological approaches. Although some remarkable La Tène jewelry was created for high-ranking women, most of it seems to have been for men of warrior status.

It is possible to argue that Celtic art has no clear coherence; however, taking a broad, Eurasiatic view, the material is clearly distinctive. This is probably most easily seen in decorative metalwork. When compared with preceding European prehistoric art, it is possible to sensibly distinguish La Tène Celtic and its medieval and modern continuation and development. Within a European frame, La Tène appears as a sudden freeing of motifs from the technocentric rigidity of the preceding *Hallstatt period art, with its symmetric circles and compass work related to advances in particular areas of engineering, such as wagon construction. In La Tène there is a total transformation of the natural world. The clumsily fused composite beasts of the orientalizing period give way to apparently free-form fantastic shapes and creatures and allow the effortless grafting of plant and animal motifs. Each piece of La Tène art is different, involving a unique nexus of curving lines that converge and diverge. Artists had tried sometimes maintaining and sometimes releasing the developing trajectories of edges, so as to always keep the motifs from becoming over-geometric, stylized, or, indeed, replicable. This is quite clear in the difference between Thraco-Scythian four-armed whirligig appliqués (*tetraskeles*) and the choice of the three-armed *triskele* in Celtic art. The latter obviously breaks cardinal point symmetry, and the angles are not easy to calculate or judge. These threefold designs are held in a marvelous balance between symmetry and its breakdown. Shapes are allowed to grow and echo, but never in an obvious way (cf. Egyptian art of Art Deco, where there is "echoing" in bilateral symmetry, but more predictably). There is much scope for an investigation of the social dimensions of Celtic art— the status of craftspeople as virtuoso performers and, perhaps, ritual specialists, and the reception and use of the art objects, such as the relationship between male adornment and warfare.

[See also CELTS; EUROPE: THE EUROPEAN IRON AGE.]

Tim Taylor

CELTS were one of the major peoples of central and western Europe in later prehistory. They are seen as the ancestors of later peoples on the western fringe of Europe, and of modern peoples such as the Irish, Welsh, and Bretons. Information about the Celts comes from a variety of sources: literary references in Greek and Roman authors; the written records of the early Medieval period; linguistic evidence from prehistoric place-names, personal names, and rare inscriptions, as well as medieval and modern languages; and the prehistoric and early historic record of archaeology. Interpretation of each of these separate strands of evidence has become intertwined, and ideas about the Celts both among the classical writers and in more modern times owe much to contemporary concepts of ethnicity and attitudes toward other peoples. Modern critiques are beginning to question the stereotyped image of the Celts, and even the ethnic or cultural homogeneity of the people referred to by that name. Instead, more attention is being paid to the processes by which ideas about the Celts have been constructed.

The first references to the Celts are in Greek authors from as early as the fifth century B.C. They are placed rather vaguely in western France, or at the headwaters of the Danube. At that time Greek knowledge of western Europe was still slight, though it improved later with closer contact. Greek use of the term "Celts" at this time must be understood in the context of their perception of the world; "Celts" may be no more than a general geographical term for the people to the west, rather as the word "Indians" was applied to all indigenous peoples in North America, masking much cultural diversity.

From the early fourth century B.C., migrations are recorded from central Europe to the south and southeast. To the Roman historians these people were known as the Gauls, and this term was taken to be synonymous with "Celts." The Gauls invaded Italy in the early fourth century B.C. and sacked *Rome, a traumatic event in its history. They settled in large numbers in northern Italy and were a continual source of conflict until finally defeated by Rome in 225 B.C. Other groups of Celts moved to the southeast, confronting Alexander the Great in 335 B.C., and sacking Delphi in 279 B.C. They established the kingdom of Tylis, probably in modern Bulgaria, and some groups moved farther southeast into Asia Minor: Here again they were a source of conflict until defeated by Attalus of Pergamum.

One dominant image of the Celts and Gauls was, therefore, as a military threat; Celts also served as mercenaries in the armies of various Mediterranean states. They were widely characterized for their warlike nature and their bravery in battle. There are also many classical representations of the Celts in sculpture, mostly as warriors, such as *The Dying Gaul* from Pergamum.

This closer contact with the Celts, both through military confrontation and later in Rome's northward expansion into Europe, provided better knowledge of them. Unfortunately, some of the major works on the Celts, such as an ethnography by Posidonius, survive only in fragmentary quotations, but others, such as Caesar's account of his conquest of Gaul, provide valuable information. The Celts were seen as tall and blond, brave and reckless, much given to the aggressive defense of their honor, and to feasting and drinking; the classical world was particularly appalled at their habit of drinking wine neat, that is, not diluted with water in the civilized manner.

We also have some details of the organization of Celtic society. The main political group was the tribe, which comprised nobles and a much larger number of common people. An important institution was clientage; nobles acted as patrons to clients, offering protection and status in return for support and service. Power and authority within the tribe was hotly contested and claims were based on a combination of descent, success in battle, wealth in cattle and gold, and number of clients. Classical authors described the tribal leader as a king. By the first century B.C. in central France, some tribes were beginning to adopt a different form of organization, involving annually elected magistrates and a council of elders.

In addition to the nobles and commoners, there was a learned class with special skills and knowledge, including bards, seers, and druids. These last were an intellectual and religious elite, the guardians of sacred and ritual knowledge, and possibly also exercised a judicial function.

The other source of historical evidence for the Celts is the literary record of the early medieval period, especially in Ireland. There is a large quantity of written documents, including many law tracts, that cast light on Celtic society. Though in some ways similar to the classical picture of prehistoric Celtic society, there are important differences. The primary social group (the *tuath*) was much smaller, and political power was much more fragmented. Kingship was universal, and kings were elected from within the noble lineages of the group. There was a clear distinction between nobles and commoners, and the laws describe a finely graded series of ranks within society. Each individual had an honor price, which established the compensation payable for any injury suffered: The oath of one person was outweighed by that of another with a higher honor price. Particularly high status was attributed to those with special skills or learning, such as poets, musicians, lawyers, genealogists, craftsmen in wood and metal, priests, prophets, and others with ritual knowledge. Irish society was changing fast at this time under the impact of Christianity, with the decline of a kin-based society and the emergence of larger political groupings, and it is possible that the Irish laws and other writings give an idealized and schematized picture of Irish society rather than describing it as it actually was.

The Celts were largely forgotten in the medieval period until the revival of classical learning. This was followed in the late seventeenth century by developments in linguistic scholarship. It was realized that some of the languages surviving in the periphery of Europe were related to the language of pre-Roman western Europe. This family of languages was called Celtic. The modern Celtic languages comprise two groups: Goidelic (Irish, Scots Gaelic, and Manx) and Brythonic (Welsh, Cornish, and Breton). They show a strong connection to the Gaulish and other related languages known from prehistoric names and a small number of inscriptions. A linguistic descent was thus established from later prehistory to modern times, and the importance placed on the role of language as a marker of ethnic identity led to the belief in a similar continuity of the ethnic identity of the Celts. Subsequent discussions were heavily influenced by a belief in an innate ethnicity determined by birth, and coinciding with differences in language and culture.

In the eighteenth century archaeological knowledge was not sufficiently advanced to be able to identify with any certainty the material record of the Celtic-speaking inhabitants of later prehistoric western Europe. The Celts, however, became the objects of Romantic fascination. Many monuments were attributed to them; *Stonehenge was seen as a druidic temple. The material of the later Iron Age, now assigned to the La Tène culture and attributed to the Celts, was thought to be Roman or Etruscan.

It was not until the middle of the nineteenth century that the archaeological record of the Iron Age was clarified and the material of the immediately pre-Roman population recognized. The *La Tène culture of the later Iron Age comprises a range of artifact types, especially weapons and personal ornaments, a broadly homogeneous set of burial rites, and a distinctive art style. These are found in central and western Europe, though the distribution patterns of different elements of the culture are by no means identical; some, such as brooches and versions of the art style, are found much more widely than others, such as the burials. Nevertheless, the La Tène culture was identified as the characteristic material of the Celts. So close is this identification that in some contexts the terms "La Tène" and "Celtic" are interchangeable; the La Tène art style in particular is regularly known as Celtic art.

Some features of the archaeology matched well the historical record of the Celts. The weaponry deposited in many male graves suited a heroic warrior people, and the concern for ornament and decoration and the presence of drinking vessels in richer graves confirmed the picture. Iron Age archaeology has traditionally devoted much scholarly attention to the study of these characteristic features, especially to Celtic art, as well as to the evidence for Celtic religion.

The archaeological record for the Celts of early medieval Ireland lacks a comparable burial tradition and its associated grave goods, but does have a similar tradition of fine decorated metalwork. Though some of the techniques may derive from a Roman craft milieu, several of the decorative motifs are remarkably similar to those of La Tène art, even though it is difficult to demonstrate unbroken continuity of practice.

Thus the historical, linguistic, and archaeological evidence has been amalgamated to produce a picture of a heroic barbarian people who expanded to dominate much of Europe before being overcome by the Romans but who survived on the fringes. Such a picture rests on a belief in a fixed ethnic identity based on descent, and in language and culture as distinctive ethnic markers. It does, however, pose several serious problems. The distributions of the various elements of La Tène culture are not all coterminous, and there is therefore a problem in explaining the presence of some items, but not all, in peripheral regions. Furthermore, some of the known Celtic areas, such as the kingdom of Tylis, have no obvious archaeological manifestation in La Tène material, even if the classical authors are rightly interpreted as using the term "Celtic" in an ethnic sense rather than as a generalized description of people from western

Europe. The development of language and material culture in later prehistoric Europe has been tied to an ethnic interpretation that relies on population movements to explain all change.

Again, the belief in an unchanging ethnic identity suggests that the Celts of the La Tène culture should have ancestral Celts who could be recognized in earlier forms of distinctive archaeological material. There has, therefore, been an argument, not resolved and perhaps misconceived, about whether earlier cultures in European prehistory should be identified as Celtic.

Modern criticism would question the concept of ethnic continuity and the assumption that ethnic boundaries will be shared by language and culture. It would emphasize the role of others in constructing their image, whether classical authors inventing the warrior barbarians, or modern scholars reinterpreting them in the light of contemporary social and political concerns, either as artistic but disorganized, or as the civilized precursors of a hoped-for unified Europe.

[See also BRITISH ISLES, *articles on* CELTIC IRELAND, PREHISTORY OF THE BRITISH ISLES; CELTIC ART; EUROPE: THE EUROPEAN IRON AGE; EUROPE: ROMAN AND POST-ROMAN EUROPE; ROMAN EMPIRE: THE ROMAN FRONTIER.]

■ S. Piggott, *The Druids,* 2nd ed. (1975). H. D. Rankin, *Celts and the Classical World* (1987). M. Chapman, *The Celts: The Construction of a Myth* (1992). C. Eluère, *The Celts: First Masters of Europe* (1993). S. James, *Exploring the World of the Celts* (1993).

Timothy Champion

CENTRAL AMERICA, Archaeology of. The area between Guatemala and Colombia is usually referred to as the Intermediate Area, the Mesoamerican Frontier, the Southeast Maya Periphery, or Lower Central America to distinguish it from the high civilizations of Mesoamerica and South America. Central American societies—seen as lacking in highly stylized art, sculpture, and mystery—are often typified as the poor cousins of their more advanced northern and southern neighbors. Nevertheless, prehistoric societies of this region demonstrate significant variability in social organization, religion, and material culture, reflecting a commingling of varying degree of Mesoamerican, South American, and indigenous cultural developments.

Although far from being a region of cultural homogeneity, Central America can be divided into two general areas. First, the Southeastern Maya Periphery or Frontier includes western Honduras and eastern, if not all of, El Salvador. Second, eastern Honduras, Nicaragua, Costa Rica, and Panama are designated as Lower Central America. Environmentally, the more tropical, wetter Atlantic side of the isthmus contrasts with the drier Pacific side. Highland valleys, which were significant focal areas in Mesoamerica for the development of complex societies, are generally lacking in Central America. For reasons that are still not fully understood, Central American cultures never developed into state-level societies and most were at the low or intermediate chiefdom stage.

Although research in the Southeast Maya Periphery has been conducted for at least the last one hundred years, other areas in Lower Central America are almost unknown archaeologically, particularly western Honduras and Nicaragua. As a result, our understanding of the prehistory of Central America has significant temporal and spatial gaps, which, hopefully, will be addressed in the coming years.

For Central America a six-period regional chronology was developed in 1984—in part to provide a common temporal framework for the area, and also to avoid bias by utilizing Mesoamerican terms. For Periods I and II, the Paleo-Indian and Tropical Archaic Periods (ca. 8000 to 4000 B.C.), the archaeological evidence consists of isolated projectile points or lithic scatters. These have mostly been surface finds and no datable material has been recovered. As a result the first settlement of the region is still unknown. Nevertheless, peoples of these times probably pursued a hunter-gatherer subsistence mode, exploiting a wide range of coastal and inland resources. After these time periods, it appears that the cultures of this region diversify and distinct "culture areas" can be distinguished.

Southeast Periphery. The cultural development of this region has been conceptualized as subordinate to the Classic Period Maya world. Indeed, the periphery is often described by what it lacks in terms of Mesoamerican traits rather than what it is on its own terms. Furthermore, assigning this area peripheral status occults the fact that regional interaction and cultural development in this area was not static through neither time nor space. Indeed, eastern El Salvador and eastern Honduras are better seen as a "soft" boundary of fluid intercultural relations.

Period III (4000 to 1000 B.C.) was a time of expansion and diversification. Again, the archaeological record is poor for this period. The first good evidence for human occupation comes from sediment cores extracted from Lake Yojoa in central Honduras. An increase in carbon and maize pollen indicate that by about 3000 B.C. the area was being cleared and farmed by slash-and-burn horticulturalists.

Period IV (1000 B.C. to A.D. 500) was a time of significant change. By the beginning of this period, permanent agricultural settlements had been established throughout the region. Some of these settlements quickly expanded in population and political complexity, the largest being Chalchuapa in western El Salvador, Quelepa in eastern El Salvador, and Yarumela in central Honduras. By about 300 B.C. these sites boasted monumental architecture, settlement systems indicative of centralized authority, and a shared ceramic style (Usulutan), suggesting significant regional interaction. This interaction sphere, called Uapala, was also linked with the Mesoamerican Formative site of Kaminaljuyu (Guatemala). Nevertheless, it appears that in this early period, this region developed chiefdom-level organization out of indigenous conditions.

By Period V (A.D. 500 to 1000) the Uapala interaction sphere had disintegrated, perhaps as a result of the brutal eruption of the Ilopango volcano in El Salvador in A.D. 250. Sites in other areas, notably around Lake Yojoa and the Ulua Valley, increased in size and complexity. The dominant ceramic style, the Ulua-Yojoa polychromes, is often described as "Mayoid." Although some vessels resemble Maya polychromes, these vessels are found in domestic rather than ritual contexts indicating that although some design elements were adopted from the Maya, the function and meaning of these vessels were adapted to the local system. Other Ulua-Yojoa polychromes, particularly the Bold Geometric tradition, were the result of local stylistic developments. Recent analysis suggests that polychrome ceramics developed out of a long indigenous bichrome tradition, rather than as the result of Maya influence.

Period VI (A.D. 1000 to 1550) corresponds with the Mesoamerican Post-Classic Period. In the first half of this period, western and central Honduran sites experienced declining population and site abandonment. Disruption of Maya so-

ciety is seen as a possible cause for the destabilization of these groups. Period VI sites of this region include artifacts from Lower Central America indicating that interaction had turned to the south. The Naco Valley (northwestern Honduras), however, grew in importance through the development of maritime exchange extending to Yucatan. Northeastern Honduras experienced significant change during Period VI. Recovered ceramics and stone sculptures demonstrate affinity with southern traditions, while other artifacts such as copper bells, obsidian, and plumbate pottery probably originated in Mesoamerica. The Northeast, then, was derived mostly from non-Mesoamerican traditions, yet maintained interaction with the North.

Lower Central America. This area is a mosaic of relatively small environmental zones. Although the Pacific and Atlantic coasts vary most significantly from one to another, these two zones can be used to discuss human adaptation to the region.

Sometime between Periods III and IV the first ceramics and evidence for settled villages are found. The earliest ceramics, the La Montana complex found in the Turrialba Valley in Costa Rica, are similar to ceramics found in South America. A slightly later complex, Chaparron, appears related to Mesoamerican ceramics. This indicates that Lower Central America was an area of fluctuating interaction between Mesoamerica and South America. For both ceramic complexes (ca. 1000 to 500 B.C.), simple villages were the norm suggesting egalitarian tribal societies.

Between 300 B.C. and A.D. 500 Lower Central America experienced a surge in population, particularly along the Atlantic watershed, culminating in chiefly societies. Monumental architecture and large public works are not found, but grave goods indicate the development of ranked society.

In Costa Rica, the early part of Period V (A.D. 500 to 1000) is known as the Early Polychrome Period, which includes the Nicoya Polychrome Tradition. Large-scale stone sculpture became important during this period. Interestingly, the stone sculpture of Lower Central America predominantly found in Costa Rica is fully three-dimensional. Maya stoneworkers, by contrast, eschewed sculpting in the round. By A.D. 700 gold and copper metallurgy appeared.

By the beginning of Period VI (A.D. 1000 to 1520) more complex chiefdoms had developed. The changes were tangible in the form of platform constructions, stone causeways, fortified sites, hydraulic management, and settlement hierarchies of two or three tiers. Small amounts of obsidian entered into Lower Central America from El Salvador, Honduras, and Guatemala, indicating at least low levels of interaction with the North. Population continued to expand with a coastal orientation, perhaps focused on near-shore trade and salt production.

The Late Polychrome Period (A.D. 1350 to 1520) settlement was focused on the northwestern coast of Costa Rica and in the Gulf of Nicoya. The close of this period is marked by the Spanish Conquest and the destruction of Native American cultures through conquest and disease.

[See also MAYA CIVILIZATION: INTRODUCTION; MESOAMERICA, *articles on* THE FORMATIVE PERIOD IN MESOAMERICA, THE CLASSIC PERIOD IN MESOAMERICA, THE POSTCLASSIC PERIOD IN MESOAMERICA; SOUTH AMERICA, *articles on* THE AMAZON, LOWLANDS CULTURES OF SOUTH AMERICA.]

■ Frederick W. Lange and Doris Z. Stone, eds., *The Archaeology of Lower Central America* (1984). Doris Stone, *Pre-Columbian Man Finds Central America: The Archaeological Bridge* (1972).

Carleen Sanchez

CERAMICS

INTRODUCTION

Ceramic artifacts, made from fired clay, and stone tools are the most durable objects created by prehistoric peoples. While archaeologically durable, ceramics have another attribute that makes them invaluable to archaeologists—they break or wear out during use, thus entering the archaeological record fairly soon after manufacture. These two important characteristics of ceramics have garnered them a long and enduring role as primary data in archaeological inquiry. The archaeologist surrounded in the laboratory by thousands of pot sherds sorted into meaningful piles on long lab tables is an image that is bound to be with the discipline for as long as it is practiced.

The art of manufacturing pottery was discovered about 12,000 years ago in the Old World and about 5,000 years ago in the New World. Pottery manufacture generally accompanied the transition to food production and increasing sedentism in the prehistory of most parts of the world. Pottery has been of enormous benefit to humanity in the form of the most common everyday objects—water carriers, food storage vessels, cooking vessels, and serving vessels. Precisely because of the intimate relationship among everyday activities such as food storage, preparation, and consumption, pottery has long been one of the primary types of artifacts collected by archaeologists. Ceramics are not limited to utilitarian wares, however, and include fine wares for ceremonial functions and trade as well as other types of objects such as figurines, jewelry, and even toys. One of the enduring benefits of clay as a raw material is its plasticity, allowing the artisan to shape and form it to myriad functional and imaginative requirements. In addition to formal and functional characteristics derived from the plasticity of the raw material, pottery often conveys additional information about its makers and users in the form of painted designs and illustrations. From simple geometric patterns to the elaborate illustrative decorations of Maya or Chinese ceramics, artisans added important stylistic and even political and mythological information to their pottery for millennia. To this day, few people fail to be stirred by the wonderful painted decorations of Classical Grecian urns or the marvelous zoomorphic creatures on Mimbres pots. From their first invention and on through the ages, ceramic objects served crucial functional, aesthetic, and informational purposes for peoples all around the world.

All of the attributes of ceramic artifacts—shape, size, type of clay, type of temper, surface treatment, and painting, to name a few—serve as a rich and varied set of data for archaeologists intent on reconstructing past human lifeways. There are essentially four types of analyses that archaeologists perform on ceramic artifacts in order to obtain the data contained within them: experimental studies, form and function analysis, stylistic analysis, and technological analysis.

Experimental studies consist of controlled experiments used to replicate prehistoric ceramic manufacturing processes. From these studies, archaeologists gain valuable information on firing techniques, firing temperatures, and the properties of various tempers, glazes, and paints. In addition to replicative experimentation, archaeologists have also taken advantage of ethnographic observations of traditional pottery manufacturing from societies around the world to better understand the manufacture, use, and reuse of pottery in traditional cultures.

Form and function analyses are based on the study of the shapes of pots and other ceramic vessels. The assumption underlying these studies is that form follows function. Of course, many factors that would negate this assumption can come into play, including the material properties of the clay used, the technology of manufacture available, and various cultural factors that constrain the technology of manufacture, the forms produced, and the uses to which the pottery may be put. Thus simple correlations between shape and assumed function based on ethnographic analogy must be weighed against other contextual data obtained from a site before any veracity can be attached to them. These types of studies, when well conducted, can provide valuable insights into changes in economic behavior over time, units of measure used by prehistoric peoples, estimates of household food production and consumption, and even average household size.

Stylistic analysis is perhaps the most common form of analysis applied to ceramic artifacts. This form of analysis focuses on the decorative styles present on ceramic vessels in the form of painted designs, postfiring incising, prefiring embossing and appliques, and other surface treatments. Since decoration, in contrast to form and function, is more likely to be wholly culturally determined, it is assumed that an analysis of style tends to be more sensitive to culturally bound explicit and implicit information encoded on the pots. On the basis of this assumption, archaeologists worldwide developed quite complex classification models used to trace social change through time. In the best cases, these models were tested against other archaeological data to determine their validity. Efforts to standardize the way in which stylistic analyses are conducted are fairly recent, but have resulted in a hierarchical type-variety system of classification. In this system, small numbers of easily identified attributes are recorded. Based on the clustering of sets of these attributes, types and then varieties of ceramics are identified. Types are the super order and varieties are the subordinate order in this scheme. Thus a type may be identifiable throughout a geographic region or over a certain time period, with consistent variations categorized as varieties of that type. While this kind of analysis has proven invaluable to archaeology from its beginnings, significant work remains to be done to make it more rigorous and consistent across regions and time periods.

The technological analysis of ceramics focuses on the materials from which ceramic objects are made. In technological analysis, the chemical composition of the clay and tempering materials as well as the proportions of clay to temper are of primary interest. The results of technological analysis are useful for interpreting variations between vessel forms, for enhancing classification systems, and for tying pots to the source locations of their clays or tempers or both. Determining source locations is invaluable to archaeologists seeking to understand the nature and extent of *prehistoric trade routes. Not only were pots themselves exchanged as part of these regional systems of trade, but pots were often the primary transport vessels for other valuable commodities such as grain, oils, wine, and salt. Thus knowing the origin of the pot can provide valuable information on the origin of other traded commodities as well. Typical technological analysis of ceramics involves some sort of trace element analysis of either the clay or the temper or both. The trace element analysis can be conducted using any of a number of techniques, including neutron activation analysis, X-ray diffraction, and ceramic petrology. Such studies, combined with other, similar analyses of regional clay and temper sources, provide archaeologists with invaluable information on the production, distribution, use, and final discard of prehistoric and historic ceramic artifacts.

In many ways the lowly potsherd has been and will continue to be of immense utility to archaeologists. While not applicable to the earliest human habitation of the planet, ceramic data provide a rich source of information about the sedentary societies that have taken advantage of the marvelous properties of simple clay.

[See also LUMINESCENCE DATING; SERIATION; TYPOLOGICAL ANALYSIS.]

■ J. S. Olin and A. D. Franklin, *Archaeological Ceramics* (1982). Prudence M. Rice, *Pots and Potters. Current Approaches in Ceramic Archaeology* (1984). Prudence M. Rice, *Pottery Analysis: A Sourcebook* (1987).

George Michaels

TECHNOLOGICAL ANALYSIS OF CERAMICS

There are two kinds of technological analysis of ceramics that commonly are undertaken in archaeology. The first attempts to understand the physical and mechanical properties of ceramic vessels and their constituent clays in order to better understand the manufacturing decision-making process. Analysts investigate aspects of thermal shock, tensile strength, and crack propagation in vessels. Also, the impact of various surface treatments, including texturing, slips, and polishing, on the performance of the vessel in storage and cooking activities is investigated. Most of this work is carried out through *experimental archaeology in which various clays, temper types, surface treatments, and vessel forms are exposed to these stresses in a controlled manner.

The second type of technological analysis is concerned with identifying the types of clay and tempering material present in the ceramic assemblage to determine whether the raw materials from which the vessels were made were available locally or were imported into the area. Sourcing studies of ceramics can occur on both the mineralogical and elemental level. Mineralogical analysis is easier to interpret from a geologic perspective. It is also less accurate and less sensitive to slight differences in geologic sources, and thus production locale, however, than elemental techniques. The two most commonly used mineralogical techniques are petrographic analysis and X-ray defraction (XRD). Petrographic analysis microscopically examines thin section samples of the ceramic under polarizing filters and identifies the minerals used as temper by their optical and morphological qualities. XRD analyzes the mineralogical makeup of the clay matrix by bombarding the sample with X rays. As the rays hit the molecular structure of the clay, they are defracted. Because the molecular structure of minerals differ, the way in which the ray is defracted also differs. Therefore, the minerals present can be identified by identifying the direction and wave length of the defracted ray.

Clays can be examined on an elemental level using a variety of techniques including optical emission spectroscopy (OES), inductively coupled plasma spectroscopy (ICP), X-ray fluorescence (XRF), neutron activation (NA), proton-induced X-ray emission (PIXE), microprobe analysis, and atomic absorption spectroscopy (AAS). All of these methods identify the elements present by calculating the wavelength of the energy that is either emitted or absorbed when the electrons, protons, or neutrons present in the atomic structure of the clay are excited or displaced. Differences in the wavelengths are related to differences in the atomic structure, and thus, the elements present in the sample. In each of these techniques, the intensity of energy associated with each wavelength also can be measured, indicating the amount of the element present.

OES and ICP both use a spectrometer to identify the elemental makeup of a clay body, but they prepare and process the samples in different ways. In both, the sample is powdered and put into a solution. The solutions are heated, which results in the outer electrons of the atoms in the sample becoming excited. When the heat is removed and the atoms return to a normal state, energy in the form of light is released. The light is refracted through a prism and projected onto a spectrometer. The different wavelengths result in different colors on the light spectrum, allowing the elements present to be identified.

In ICP analysis the powdered sample is put into a hydrochloric acid solution that is then sprayed into a flame of argon plasma—argon atoms whose outer electrons have been removed inductively by passing through a radio frequency coil—to excite the electrons. In OES, an aqueous solution is used and passed through either an open flame or an electric arc.

XRF displaces one of the inner electrons in the atom by bombarding the sample with primary X rays. When the inner electron is displaced, the outer electrons drop down to fill the inner level. When this occurs, energy is released in the form of secondary X rays. The elements present can be identified by the wavelength of the secondary X rays that are emitted.

A combination of XRF technology and a scanning electron microscope (SEM) is used in microprobe analysis. The use of the SEM allows the researcher to concentrate a beam of electrons to a particular place on the surface of the sherd. This area is bombarded with high-energy electrons, resulting in the production of secondary X rays, which can be analyzed in a manner similar to XRF.

NA and PIXE identify the elements present by exciting the nuclei of the atom. The sample is bombarded with neutrons or protons, respectively, which makes the nuclei unstable. The nuclei starts a decay process to form a more stable atom. When this occurs, radiation, in the form of gamma rays with NA and X rays with PIXE, are emitted. The rays associated with each element differ in wavelength and therefore can be identified.

Rather than measuring the wavelength of the energy emission, AAS is concerned with the wavelengths of light that are absorbed by a sample. The sample is put into solution and then sprayed into a flame. At the same time, a light beam, of a wavelength that corresponds to the element being tested for, is passed through the flame. If the element is present, some of the light from the beam will be absorbed. This process can test for one wavelength at a time and must be repeated for each element of concern.

[See also SOURCING ARCHAEOLOGICAL MATERIALS.]

■ Anna O. Shepard, *Ceramics for the Archaeologist* (1976). J. S. Olin and A. D. Franklin, eds., *Archaeological Ceramics* (1982). David P. Braun, "Pots as Tools," in *Archaeological Hammers and Theories*, eds. James A. Moore and Arthur S. Keene (1983), pp. 107–134. Prudence Rice, *Pottery Analysis, A Sourcebook* (1987).

Tammy Stone

CONSERVATION OF CERAMICS

While ceramics have been manufactured since the Neolithic, the first archaeological evidence for ceramic conservation is found in Sumerian deposits dated 5000 B.C. Conservation is the slowing or prevention of deterioration through environmental control, cleaning, consolidation, reinforcing, bonding, or the replacement of lost material.

Whether found through excavation or survey, ceramics are well preserved. Excellent preservation is due to the firing process, which makes ceramics chemically stable. However, ceramics are still prone to a large number of degenerative processes.

First and foremost, ceramics are vulnerable to everyday wear and tear during their use-life. This includes breakage; abrasion from serving food, cleaning, or dish stacking; food stains; encrustations; mold growth; and carbon residues and thermal damage from cooking. Acids contained in foodstuffs can also react chemically with the ceramic surface, causing damage.

Before recovery by an archaeologist, ceramic objects are susceptible to breaking, cracking, and surface flaking as a result of freeze-thaw action, root action, absorption and recrystallization of soluble salts, earthquake, flood, fire, and the trampling of animals. Surface discoloration can occur from metals in the dirt and calcium carbonate encrustations. Acidic and alkaline soils, organic residues, and water can chemically damage the fabric and surface of ceramics.

Once recovered, ceramics are inclined to break and scratch from improper handling, storage, and transport. Soluble salts can recrystallize, flaking off portions of the ceramic body. Glues, coatings, and resins used before the late nineteenth century can break down under improper environmental conditions and react chemically with the original object.

People have repaired broken ceramics for millennia, using everything from sinew to starch pastes, natural gums and resins, protein binders, and beeswax. Early adhesives included bitumen, gelatin, animal glue, shellac, and Portland cement. Ceramics were also rejoined with a variety of mechanical bindings, including jointing with molten metal, riveting, tying, and dowelling. Many of these materials and methods are not used by modern conservators due to unacceptable color, messy application, nonreversibility, and subsequent chemical reaction with or physical damage to the original ceramic from the early treatment.

Today, ceramic conservators will avoid, whenever possible, the need for direct treatment by using noninterventive methods such as creating a stable storage and display environment. This is accomplished by limiting the temperature range; stabilizing humidity; reducing ultraviolet radiation, illuminance, and particle pollution; stabilizing objects to prevent vibration; and minimizing human handling.

When direct treatment is necessary, the conservator must first examine the object thoroughly to determine the cause and extent of damage, the composition and characteristics of the ceramic body, and the presence and types of decoration. These observations are essential to determining the course of conservation treatment. Exacting records of the examination and treatments followed are kept for future reference.

Current conservation treatment regimes include cleaning of harmful soluble salts and grease stains, consolidation or reinforcing to restore strength, and bonding to prevent further loss of material or breakage. Objects can be cleaned either mechanically or chemically. The choice of cleaning agent depends on the nature of the dirt and deposits and the strength of their attachment to the ceramic surface. Mechanical methods, such as dusting or ultrasonic cleaning, are easily controlled, but they are not always powerful enough for the task. Chemical cleaning methods such as acid, water, or alkali baths, while powerful, are not easily controlled, and there is a danger of etching, abrading, or otherwise damaging the fabric of the ceramic.

When ceramics are very friable, the first step is to temporarily reinforce or consolidate the object to restore structural strength. Ceramics are reinforced by bandaging. Consolidation is the addition of a material that will bind the crumbling object together. Unfortunately, once an object has been subjected to consolidation, the treatment cannot be reversed.

Ceramic objects that are broken are repaired by using bonding agents to prevent further breakage and loss of material. There are many different adhesives available for use on ceramics, but the choice of adhesive is dependent on the type of ceramic object; its composition, form, and dimensions; the condition of the object; and the environmental and handling demands that will be made on the object once repaired. Modern bonding agents include epoxy resins, polyester resins, polyvinyl acetate emulsions, and cellulose nitrate and acrylic adhesives. The disadvantages of bonding include nonreversibility, appearance, and use of toxic substances.

When an object has sustained large losses of material, the conservator may choose to replace the lost material with a filler. The filler must permit the application of surface treatments; must adhere to the ceramic; must be of similar strength and density; must be durable, reversible, and safe to use; must not contaminate the ceramic or shrink or cure with age; and must have a thermal expansion compatible with the ceramic. The ideal filler should meet these criteria but be distinguishable from the original ceramic body.

After replacing lost material, the next step is retouching or restoring the object. Retouching cannot be considered a conservation technique, however, because it does not slow or prevent the deterioration of the object; instead, it restores the aesthetic value to the object.

■ Garry Thompson, *The Museum Environment* (1986). N. Williams, "Ancient Methods of Repairing Pottery and Porcelain" in *Early Advances in Conservation*, ed. V. Daniels (1988). Susan Buys and Victoria Oakley, *The Conservation and Restoration of Ceramics* (1993).

Cynthia Ann Bettison

CEREN. The Ceren site was a thriving southern Mesoamerican village, some 1,400 years ago, in what is now El Salvador. It was highly organized, with most buildings and crops oriented 30 degrees east of north. Four functional zones have been discovered to date: a domestic zone for households, various agricultural zones, a public zone, and a religious zone. The site is highly unusual because it did not experience the natural and cultural degradation of the archaeological record that occurs when people gradually and deliberately abandon their settlements.

The reason for the exceptional preservation at Ceren was the sudden eruption of Loma Caldera volcano, located less than a kilometer to the north, which buried the site under 16 feet (5 m) of volcanic ash, sealing the buildings and their contents in time. The site was first discovered by accident in 1976 by bulldozers leveling a low hill. It was not recognized as an archaeological site until two years later when a University of Colorado team explored it.

The domestic zone of the site consists of at least four known households, of which two are largely excavated. Each household constructed a domicile building for sleeping and daytime activities, a storehouse, a kitchen, and certain other specialized buildings around a patio. Construction of most buildings began with an earthen platform that was fired to form a hard floor; then wattle-and-daub walls were constructed that supported the roof. The interlocked elements result in a highly seismically resistant architecture.

Households had considerable roofed space, over 111 square yards (93 sq m), and within it they stored a surprising abundance of artifacts. Household 1, the poorest of the households excavated so far, had seventy complete ceramic vessels, including elegant polychrome pottery. Based on the material indices of square meters, housing, quantity and variety of foods stored, and possessions, the quality of life at Ceren was high. Sadly, it was higher than most households living in the area today.

Each household had a kitchen garden and maize field nearby, but the majority of food must have been grown in outfields. The following foods were found stored in households and growing in gardens: maize, beans, squash, chiles, avocado, manioc, cacao, nance, guayabo, and various wild fruits and nuts.

The civic portion of the site is composed of at least two large solid-walled buildings that border a formal plaza. The civic buildings were not as seismically resistant as domestic buildings, and they had far fewer artifacts.

Although the ritual zone of the village is not completely excavated, structure 12 appears to be where a shaman practiced. The building has numerous vertical niches and small rooms, with artifacts apparently left as offerings. Structure 10 apparently served as the storehouse for domestic and ritual items, including a deer-skull headdress painted white and red, with a string for attachment to a person's head during rituals.

Research is continuing, and many decades more of research at the site are anticipated. The research is multidisciplinary, with volcanology, remote sensing, geophysics, ethnobotany, ethnoarchaeology, and other disciplines contributing to knowledge about the site and environs.

[See also MAYA CIVILIZATION: MAYA VILLAGE LIFE; MESOAMERICA: CLASSIC PERIOD IN MESOAMERICA.]

■ Payson Sheets, ed., *Archeology and Volcanism in Central America: The Zapotitan Valley of El Salvador* (1983). Payson Sheets, *The Ceren Site: A Prehistoric Village Buried by Volcanic Ash in Central America* (1992).

Payson Sheets

CHACOAN PHENOMENON. The ruins at Chaco Canyon, in northwestern New Mexico, have been called a "phenomenon" for two reasons. First, they represent a unique development in the prehistory of the Pueblo Indian peoples, and second, the term *phenomenon*, in its vagueness, reflects the archaeological ambiguity about the nature of that development. We know that, from A.D. 850 to 1130, Chaco was an important—probably transforming—episode in Pueblo prehistory, but we do not know exactly what Chaco was.

There are ten huge ruins in Chaco Canyon, and hundreds of smaller buildings. The large sites have been referred to as pueblos (from their resemblance to the compact villages of the modern Pueblo Indians), great pueblos, or—most commonly— great houses. The two largest great houses, Pueblo Bonito and Chetro Ketl, each cover over 2.5 acres (about 1 ha). At each, over five hundred rooms are terraced from a one-story front row up to a four- or five-story rear that surrounds central plazas or public open spaces. *Kivas*—circular, subterranean chambers reminiscent of Pueblo Indian ceremonial rooms of that name—surround the plaza with an extraordinarily large 55 feet (about 16 m) in diameter great kiva at its center.

Chaco buildings were massively built. Sandstone masonry walls were almost 3 feet (1 m) wide on the ground floors, and battered in on each successive story. Curiously, the elaborate, ornamental coursing patterns of alternating thick and thin sandstone slabs were hidden beneath layers of mud plaster. Ceiling and roof timbers were carefully smoothed trunks, brought by human labor from forests up to 75 miles (about 125 km) distant. It has been conservatively estimated that over 200,000 beams were required for all the large buildings at Chaco Canyon. Everything about Chaco construction was labor intensive. Building during Chaco's peak, between A.D. 1075 and 1110, required an average of about 450,000 person days per decade.

Ground plans were simple, but formal. They are often described by letters: "E-shaped," "D-shaped," "O-shaped," and so on. The architectural geometry apparently incorporated sophisticated astronomical alignments, with the major walls oriented to celestial phenomena.

Geometric formality extends to the larger canyon area. Rather than the individual ruins representing independent, self-sufficient farming villages (as implied by the term *pueblo*), they were in fact buildings incorporated into a larger 6 mile (about 10 km) long settlement capable of housing over five thousand inhabitants. Chaco Canyon was the ancient Pueblo region's closest approach to a city.

Chaco achieved an architectural quality unequaled in other Pueblo building—earlier, later, or contemporary. Indeed, much of Chaco's "phenomenal" quality is comparative. From A.D. 850 to 1150, when Chaco was being built, the typical ancestral Pueblo house was much more modest: a five- to six-room unit, built to an ad hoc plan with much simpler masonry, with a small kiva in front. A complete household unit could fit within a single room at Pueblo Bonito. Over the contiguous quarters of Arizona, Utah, Colorado, and New Mexico, hundreds of thousands of these small units, differing only in minor details, constituted the Pueblo family home.

Dozens of these small units formed variably dispersed communities. Most (and perhaps all) communities had at their core a great kiva (much like those at Chaco Canyon) and a small version of the big buildings at Chaco, that is, a small great house. Built with the same, unmistakable Chaco construction technology, the same scale, and the same geometric formality of the Chaco Canyon great houses, these so-called outliers were simply small versions of the Chaco Canyon buildings, one-twentieth the size of Pueblo Bonito.

The remarkable thing about smaller, Chacoan great houses is their geographic extent. Minimally, they are found over an area of 20,000 square miles (about 52,000 sq km), and many archaeologists argue that great houses are found over an area six to eight times larger, covering almost all of the ancestral Pueblo area. Either geographic estimate places

Chaco Canyon itself at the conceptual, if not geometric center of a region unprecedentedly large for native North America. The reality of the Chaco region is demonstrated by a network of roads—30 feet (9 m) wide, carefully constructed, and invariably straight, that connect many (or all) of the great houses with Chaco Canyon. It should be noted that, while there is abundant segmentary evidence of roads throughout the region, only a few have actually been studied and traced on the ground over their entire length from distant outliers back to Chaco Canyon.

What was the nature of this region or regional system? The answer depends on Chaco Canyon, the obvious, anomalous center. It is clear that Chaco was a central place, but its central function is not at all clear. Hypotheses range from a political and military capital to an empty ceremonial center. A likely scenario combines a number of currently competing models: Chaco began, between A.D. 650 and 900 as an economic center for redistribution of agricultural foods within a core area (often called the San Juan Basin), approximately equivalent to northwestern New Mexico, articulated by a radial network of roads. With the success of the San Juan Basin system, the ideology if not the economy of Chaco expanded to incorporate most of the ancestral Pueblo world. The peak of construction at Chaco Canyon, and coincidently the greatest expansion of the regional system, was from A.D. 1075 to 1130. Decades of disastrous drought, from A.D. 1130 to 1180, probably caused the demise, or at least redefinition of the center.

Chaco cast a long shadow. Its architecture was the archetype of the Pueblo style, continuing down through the centuries to the modern pueblos of New Mexico and Arizona. Its regional system united the ancestral Pueblo region and its dissolution shaped the later Pueblo world. The inevitable balkanization that followed the loss of the center at Chaco Canyon begins the history of modern Pueblos. Chaco was, almost certainly, the central matter of Pueblo archaeology.

[See also ANASAZI CULTURE; MESA VERDE; NORTH AMERICA: THE NORTH AMERICAN SOUTHWEST.]

■ Patricia L. Crown, and W. James Judge, eds., Chaco and Hohokam: Prehistoric Regional Systems in the American Southwest (1991). David E. Doyel, ed., Anasazi Regional Organization and the Chaco System, Anthropological Papers 5 (1992). Stephen H. Lekson, Great Pueblo Architecture of Chaco Canyon, New Mexico (1986). Robert H. Lister and Florence C. Lister, Chaco Canyon: Archaeology and Archaeologists (1981). Lynne Sebastian, The Chaco Anasazi: Sociopolitical Evolution in the Prehistoric Southwest (1992). R. Gwinn Vivian, The Chacoan Prehistory of the San Juan Basin (1990).

Stephen H. Lekson

CHAN CHAN, located in the Moche Valley on the north coast of Peru, was the capital of the *Chimu State. The city may have been established in A.D. 850 and was occupied until about 1470. The city is mentioned in Spanish chronicles and in travel accounts. Excavations were conducted under the directorship of Michael E. Moseley and Carol J. Mackey beginning in 1969; excavations continue under the auspices of the Instituto Nacional de Cultura.

Though continuous architectural remains spread over 8 square miles (20 sq km), the densely packed civic core of Chan Chan covers an area of over 2.5 square miles (6 sq km). Monumental architecture includes 10 large rectangular enclosures (up to 1,969 feet [600 m] long with surrounding adobe walls up to 30 feet [9 m] high) identified as palaces of the Chimu kings and truncated pyramids. Access into and

within the palaces, which contain plazas, smaller courts, and U-shaped structures, is highly restricted. U-shaped structures are often associated with storerooms and have been identified as administrative residences and offices. Main courts are decorated with mud friezes depicting maritime motives. Most of the palaces also contain a burial structure with a central tomb (probably for the king) and ancillary chambers for offerings. It may be that the palaces were built in pairs, reflecting possible dual rulership.

The thirty-five intermediate or elite compounds, though considerably smaller than the palaces, contain many of the same features as the palaces, but these features are always smaller and/or fewer in number. These compounds were probably the residences of the Chimu nobility.

The majority of the population lived in densely packed small, irregularly agglutinated rooms (SIAR) of perishable materials. Based on the number and size of the SIAR, Chan Chan may have had close to 30,000 inhabitants at its height. The inhabitants were mainly artisans, 10,000 of whom might have come from Lambayeque after this valley was annexed. The artisans were primarily engaged in metallurgy and weaving, as well as woodcarving and lapidary work.

The growth of the city, as well as the standardization of the layout of the palaces, large banks of storerooms guarded by U-shaped structures, and elite compounds, correlate with the kingdom's expansion. Chan Chan was the node of an unusually centralized political and economic system. After the Inca conquest, the flow of tribute into Chan Chan stopped, artisans were taken to *Cuzco, and many of the nobles probably moved back to their regions, leading to the city's abandonment.

[See also INCA CIVILIZATION: INTRODUCTION; SOUTH AMERICA, articles on RISE OF COMPLEX SOCIETIES IN SOUTH AMERICA, HIGHLANDS CULTURES OF SOUTH AMERICA.]

■ Michael E. Moseley and Kent C. Day, eds., Chan Chan: Andean Desert City (1982). John R. Topic and Michael E. Moseley, "Chan Chan: A Case Study of Urban Change in Peru," Ñawpa Pacha 21 (1983): 153–182.

Alexandra M. Ulana Klymyshyn

CHANG'AN was the capital of many dynasties in China, three of which are of primary archaeological significance, the Western Han (202 B.C.–A.D. 8), the Sui (A.D. 581–618), and the Tang (A.D. 618–907). At the end of the Tang, Chang'an was completely destroyed. The city was built on different sites in the vicinity of present-day Xi'an in Shansi Province. Foundations and pottery remains, uncovered in *Banpo to the northeast of Xi'an, indicate that this area has been inhabited since at least the fifth millennium B.C. Most excavations have been carried out since 1950. Contemporary research is currently being conducted by organizations such as Gudu Xuehui at Shansi Normal University in Xi'an, a research group founded in 1983 that studies ancient Chinese capitals.

The remains of the Western Han Chang'an are located about 6 miles (10 km) northwest of present-day Xi'an. Construction of the Han capital began under Emperor Gao Zu (206–194 B.C.). The walls were made of rammed earth and stood just over 39 feet (12 m) high with a thickness of 39 (12 m) to 52 feet (16 m). The city was divided into 160 smaller walled units. Initially, each wall had three gates, bringing the total to twelve. During excavations from 1961 to 1962, the street system was confirmed. Since 1975 further extensive excavations have uncovered the partial remains of the two palaces, Changlegong and Weiyanggong (half of the city was devoted to palatial compounds), as well as an armory and drainage system.

During the Sui dynasty, the construction of Chang'an (called Daxing at the time) was commissioned by Emperor Wen Di just slightly to the southeast of the Han Chang'an location. The city was completed on 8 February 583. The outer wall was over 22 miles (36 km) in circumference and was made of rammed earth 29.5 feet (9 m) to 39 feet (12 m) thick. When the Li family conquered the Sui in 618 thereby founding the Tang dynasty, they too used the same capital, renaming it Chang'an (Long Peace). The city was designed in the shape of a near-perfect square comprised of nine smaller squares within it. This configuration manifests itself throughout Chinese history in ancestral shrines, maps of cities, and temple designs. Chang'an was at this time, the largest city in the world with a population of roughly two million people. Chang'an was divided into 108 wards, and the streets were arranged in a grid pattern, with 14 running in a north to south direction and 11 running from east to west.

Given that Chang'an was the capital of the empire, the seat of government, and thus the residence of the emperor during three of China's most culturally rich dynasties, further archaeological and historical research on the city promises to be exceedingly fruitful.

[See also ASIA: PREHISTORY AND EARLY HISTORY OF EAST ASIA; CHINA, articles on HAN EMPIRE, TANG AND SONG DYNASTIES.]

■ Wang Zhongshu, Han Civilization, trans. K. C. Chang et al. (1982). Nancy Shatzman Steinhardt, Chinese Imperial City Planning (1990).
Michael J. Walsh

CHAVÍN CULTURE. For decades, this early culture was viewed as the first "civilization" of ancient Peru, reaching its apogee during the first millennium B.C. The culture is noted for its art style centered around feline and other animal designs that feature grimacing mouths with interlocking canines and eyes with eccentric or pendant pupils. These designs appear on spectacular stone carvings, particularly at the type site of *Chavín de Huantar, and on distinctive incised black pottery that has a wider distribution over Peru than the stone carvings themselves. The pottery also contains stamped geometric designs such as circles, concentric circles, circles and dots, and "S" shapes that have been identified with the Chavín culture.

In the 1890s, explorer Ernst Middendorf first proposed a cultural connection between Chavín de Huantar in the north-central highlands and similar-looking stone mounds along the desert coast of Peru. In the 1920s and 1930s, Julio Tello greatly expanded this idea and first proposed that the Chavín culture originated in the jungle area to the east of the Andes mountains and was the first pan-Andean civilization, a precursor to the much later Tiahuanaco and Inca civilizations. It was not until the 1940s that other Andean scholars generally accepted Tello's ideas about the Chavín culture. With the advent of radiocarbon dating in the early 1950s, it became clear that Tello was generally correct in his dating of the Chavín culture.

In the 1960s, John Rowe proposed a revised chronological system for Andean archaeology, based on periods and horizons, that is still generally followed by most scholars. Periods are relatively long spans of time that are characterized by many local and regional cultures. Horizons are relatively short periods of time that are typified by one widespread, dominant culture. In Rowe's scheme, the Chavín culture dominated the Early Horizon, which he dated between 1400 and 400 B.C. A few years later, this time range was adjusted by Edward Lanning to 900 to 200 B.C., a range that continues to be widely used today.

On the basis of his analysis of sculpture and architecture at Chavín de Huantar and of pottery from looted graves of the Paracas culture of the Peruvian south coast, Rowe also proposed that the Chavín art style could be divided into four phases—labeled AB, C, D, and EF—with the distinct possibility that phases AB and EF would later be subdivided when more material became available for study. It was hoped that a finer chronological sequence of Chavín-related material would help in understanding the growth and decline of the Chavín culture. By the early 1970s, archaeologists generally viewed the Chavín culture as a religious cult that spread out from the north-central highlands to much of the highlands and coast of Peru. The spread of cult ideas, reflected in Chavín iconography, was possibly facilitated by preexisting trade networks that linked various centers and by religious missionaries. A few scholars held that militarism was an important factor in the spread of the cult. Exposure to the Chavín cult, its art style, and architectural canons was supposed to have brought "civilization" to much of Peru.

However, the above scenario was far from certain. Problems with the definition of the Chavín culture and art style had existed since Tello's original conception. Dating remained a big problem, especially since the Chavín cult was perceived as a short-lived, widespread phenomenon, yet had a time span estimated between 400 and 1,000 years. Fortunately, fieldwork over the past 25 years has substantially helped revise views on the nature of the Chavín culture. Essentially, current data suggest that the Chavín phenomenon was much more short-lived and much less widespread than previously envisioned. Moreover, highly organized societies had already existed on the central and north coasts for hundreds of years before the appearance of the Chavín culture, thereby precluding its role as disseminator of "civilization."

Excavations at coastal sites such as Huaca de los Reyes in the Moche Valley, Pampa de las Llamas-Moxeke in the Casma Valley, Garagay in the Rimac Valley, and Cardal in the Lurin Valley have uncovered impressive U-shaped mounds decorated with mud friezes. Formerly, such remains were attributed to the Chavín culture of the Early Horizon, but associated radiocarbon dates and pottery clearly show that all these centers were built, used, and largely abandoned before 1000 or 900 B.C. during a time span known as the Initial Period. Furthermore, excavations at Chavín de Huantar established the site's main occupation between 900 and 200 B.C.—with the widespread Chavín cult pottery, typical of the Janabarriu phase at the site, occurring only between 400 and 200 B.C. Finally, recent scholarly evaluation of old and new evidence casts serious doubt on the validity of Rowe's proposed Chavín stylistic sequence.

Current evidence still supports the idea that the Chavín phenomenon was probably centered around a religious cult. However, this cult was a more limited, regional religion—one that did not exert strong influence much beyond the north-central highlands—rather than a pan-Andean phenomenon. Chavín de Huantar, adorned by dozens of stone sculptures, most likely served as an oracle center for pilgrims. The art, architecture, and pottery found at Chavín de Huantar appear to have been inspired by earlier Peruvian cultures in the highlands, in the jungle, and on the coast that date before 1800 B.C.

The precise nature of Chavín society is still a matter of debate. Some scholars contend that the Chavín culture, even in its reduced scope, still represents the first truly stratified society in the central Andes. Supporters of this position emphasize the presence of gold artifacts, imported *Spondylus* shell, and obsidian in some elite graves and marked differences in food remains associated with elite houses compared to those of common people. Others argue that the precise planning and construction of immense Initial Period stone mound sites, especially along the north and central coasts, provide proof of a stratified society that presaged the later Chavín culture.

[*See also* ANDEAN PRE-INCA CIVILIZATIONS, THE RISE OF: INTRODUCTION; SOUTH AMERICA, *articles on* THE RISE OF COMPLEX SOCIETIES IN SOUTH AMERICA, HIGHLANDS CULTURES OF SOUTH AMERICA.]

■ Gordon R. Willey, "The Chavín Problem, A Review and Critique," *Southwestern Journal of Anthropology* 7 (1951): 103–144. John H. Rowe, "Form and Meaning of Chavín Art," in *Peruvian Archaeology: Selected Readings,* eds. John H. Rowe and Dorothy Menzel (1967), pp. 72–103. Elizabeth P. Bensen, ed., *Dumbarton Oaks Conference on Chavin* (1971). Thomas Pozorski and Shelia Pozorski, "Chavín, the Early Horizon and the Initial Period," in *The Origins and Development of the Andean State,* eds. Jonathan Haas, Shelia Pozorski, and Thomas Pozorski (1987), pp. 36–46. Richard L. Burger, *Chavín and the Origins of Andean Civilization* (1992). Michael E. Moseley, *The Incas and Their Ancestors* (1992).

Shelia Pozorski and Thomas Pozorski

CHAVÍN DE HUANTAR. The site of Chavín de Huantar is characteristic of the *Chavín culture, and is situated on the eastern slopes of the Andes Mountains in the north-central highlands of Peru. The site itself is located some 2 miles (3,150 m) above sea level near the junction of the Huachesa and Mosna Rivers. Chavín de Huantar was first described by the chronicler Pedro de Cieza de León in 1553 and was subsequently visited by several travelers before the early twentieth century. Most important among these nineteenth-century visitors was Ernst Middendorf, who first envisioned a cultural connection between some of the massive stone mounds of the Peruvian coast and Chavín de Huantar.

The excavations and explorations of Chavín de Huantar and related sites by Julio Tello between 1919 and 1941 greatly expanded upon Middendorf's idea and firmly established the early chronological position of the Chavín culture in the Peruvian archaeological sequence. More recent excavations (1966–1972) at Chavín de Huantar by Luis Lumbreras uncovered a sunken circular plaza and fine ceramic collections associated with the monumental architecture of the site. Finally, in the mid-1970s, Richard Burger investigated several domestic areas away from the main architectural complex, thereby furthering understanding of nonmonumental aspects of the site.

The main prehistoric occupation of Chavín de Huantar occurred between 900 and 200 B.C. and is defined archaeologically by three ceramic phases. The last phase, Janabarriu (400–200 B.C.), represents the expansion of the site and the Chavín culture as a whole to other areas of Peru. Chavín de Huantar is dominated by a group of monumental stone mounds that collectively cover about 7.5 acres (3 ha) and habitation areas of the site covered over 99 acres (40 ha) during Janabarriu times. The stone mounds are not the largest such constructions of early prehistoric Peru, but are among the most architecturally impressive. Most of the stonework has been roughly quarried, and much of it is finely polished and carefully fitted together to make tall mound facades over 33 feet (10 m) high. The two main mounds are the "Old Temple" and the larger "New Temple." The names connote a chronological difference in the construction of the mounds; however, such a distinction has not been conclusively demonstrated at this architecturally complex site. The Old Temple is U-shaped in plan and has a sunken circular court located between the two arms of the "U." The facade of the New Temple incorporates the south wing of the Old Temple and is associated with a large sunken rectangular plaza and smaller stone mounds and staircases.

Aside from fine stonework, the Old and New Temples are also associated with numerous galleries, ventilation ducts, and water conduits within the mounds—features that are virtually unique for this period in ancient Peru. Also prominent at the site are dozens of stone carvings that vary in style from two-dimensional incisions executed on flat slabs to fully three-dimensional figures. All of the stone carvings are or were once part of the architectural decoration of the main temples.

A majority of the subjects depicted are animals such as jaguars, harpy eagles, caimans, and snakes, which reflect the religious pantheon of the Chavín culture. The Lanzón, the Raimondi Stone, the Tello Obelisk, and the Black and White Portal are the most notable among these carvings. There are also numerous three-dimensional heads, once attached by tenons to the facades of the temples. According to one theory, these tenon heads depict shamans transforming into animal intermediaries of the spirit world. The considerable variety of images depicted in the carvings most likely reflects a complex religious pantheon. Most of the carvings were visible and utilized throughout the main occupation of the site. Hypotheses concerning chronological differences among the carvings have not proved convincing.

Chavín de Huantar is best viewed as a regional oracle center for a religious cult that influenced the north-central highlands from 400 to 200 B.C. In particular, the Lanzón, still located within a main gallery of the Old Temple, is believed to be the principal deity or oracle that was consulted by visiting pilgrims from different regions of Peru. Because of its location midway between the western coast and the eastern jungle, the site also seems to have served as a communication and trade center. Communication with the jungle is reflected in the iconography of the stone sculpture and ceramics that contains animals and plants of jungle origin. Interaction with the coast is reflected in the U-shaped layout of the main temples, the sunken circular and rectangular plazas, and profile felines on the stonework—features that occur in the coastal archaeological record well before 1000 B.C. Far-reaching trade relations are reflected in exotic finds at the site of *Spondylus* shell from Ecuador and obsidian and cinnabar from the south-central highlands.

[*See also* ANDEAN PRE-INCA CIVILIZATIONS, THE RISE OF: INTRODUCTION; SOUTH AMERICA, *articles on* THE RISE OF COMPLEX SOCIETIES IN SOUTH AMERICA, HIGHLANDS CULTURES OF SOUTH AMERICA.]

■ Julio C. Tello, *Chavin, Cultura Matriz de la Civilización Andina* (1960). Luis G. Lumbreras, *The Peoples and Cultures of Ancient Peru* (1974). Luis G. Lumbreras, "Excavaciones en el Templo Antiguo de Chavin (Sector R): Informe de la Sexta Campaña," *Ñawpa Pacha* 15

(1977): 1–38. Richard L. Burger, *The Prehistoric Occupation of Chavin de Huantar, Peru* (1984). Thomas Pozorski and Shelia Pozorski, "Chavin, the Early Horizon and the Initial Period," in eds. Jonathan Haas, Shelia Pozorski, and Thomas Pozorski, *The Origins and Development of the Andean State* (1987), pp. 36–46. Richard L. Burger, *Chavin and the Origins of Andean Civilization* (1992).

Shelia Pozorski and Thomas Pozorski

CHICHÉN ITZÁ flourished in northern Yucatán during the Epiclassic and early Post-Classic Periods (ca. A.D. 800 and 1200). Its chronology and history are quite controversial, a result of the two radically different styles of art and architecture at the site. One, the Puuc style, is identical to that found at late Classic Maya centers in western Yucatán, while the other is strikingly similar to Toltec remains at *Tula, Hidalgo. There are two historical reconstructions of the Puuc style: one predates the Toltec and was replaced by it, the other assumes that Puuc and Toltec were contemporaneous. Cultural relationships between Chichén Itzá and Tula also have been interpreted in two ways: first, Chichén Itzá provided the stimulus for Toltec art and architecture at Tula, and second, Toltec merchant-warriors, perhaps as allies of Putun Maya from Campeche, either dominated commercial and social life at the Maya center or actually conquered Chichén Itzá and its hinterland. Archaeologists almost universally reject the first alternative, but the second lacks sufficient supporting data to be clearly convincing.

Chichén Itzá consists of numerous building complexes within a 12-mile (2-km) radius of a large, natural well, known as the Sacred Cenote. The imposing masonry structures include ball courts, temples, colonnaded halls, palaces, causeways, an astronomical observatory, and a cave where the Maya conducted rituals and placed offerings. Remains of ordinary residences are scattered throughout and beyond the site core.

Although it lay in ruins when the Spaniards arrived, Chichén Itzá is mentioned in several colonial documents. John L. *Stephens and Frederick Catherwood published the first modern description and drawings of the site in 1841. Today, to the general public, Chichen Itzá epitomizes Maya ruins. Unfortunately most of the basic research predated the advent of modern archaeological techniques and standards of publication. The Carnegie Institution of Washington, D.C., conducted a long-term project from 1924 to 1936; since then, Mexican government archaeologists have conducted research from time to time and today maintain an ongoing research program.

[See also MAYA CIVILIZATION, *articles on* MAYA BALL COURTS, MAYA PYRAMIDS AND TEMPLES, OVERVIEW; MESOAMERICA: POST-CLASSIC PERIOD IN MESOAMERICA; TOLTEC EMPIRE.]

■ Michael D. Coe, *The Maya*, 4th ed. (1994).

Richard A. Diehl

CHILDE, V. Gordon (1892–1957), was born in Australia and studied classical philology at Oxford University. He dabbled in Australian politics after World War I, but soon returned to his passion for ancient history. Childe's *Dawn of European Civilization* (1925), based on wide travels, established the cultural and chronological framework of European prehistory and remained the seminal work for over forty years. Childe became the first Abercromby professor of prehistoric archaeology at Edinburgh University in 1927. *The Most Ancient East* (1928) was an influential synthesis of the evidence for early farming and the rise of civilization in the Near East. Childe set these developments in the context of agricultural and urban revolutions, which soon became widely accepted frameworks for studying later prehistory. In 1946, he became director of the Institute of Archaeology at London University, a post he held until his retirement in 1956.

Childe was convinced that the social evolution of Europe could not be understood in isolation from that of the wider ancient world. He believed the transformations of the European Bronze Age were inspired by traveling bronzesmiths from Mesopotamia and by Indo-European pastoralist culture. These pioneers laid the foundations for a European society based on individual creative expression and technological enterprise that contrasted sharply with the despotism of the Near East. These contrasts were the focus of his popular books on the ancient world, such as *Man Makes Himself* (1936), written for a European audience threatened by despotism. At the time, Childe was unique among archaeologists in applying a marxist (historical materialist) analysis to the interpretation of European and Near Eastern archaeology. His marxism was not explicit, but he was trying to argue that the struggle between social classes trying to control the means of production underlay the transformations of Near Eastern and European society. These ideas were important sources of inspiration for American cultural anthropologists like Leslie White, who were seeking to understand world cultural evolution.

Childe's interests led him to ponder the nature of history and the social production of knowledge, especially technology and science. His later works, such as *Society and Knowledge* (1956), were as significant as his archaeological publications. Childe held that knowledge is progress as long as it is widely disseminated, but that it could also be turned into a powerful weapon of exploitation. As a marxist, he felt that ideology masks certain essential social relations and social actions. Thus, he felt the role of the archaeologist and historian is to reveal, through critical analysis, the true story of contradictions and exploitations of social classes.

Childe's authoritative syntheses of European and Near Eastern prehistory were undermined by the advent of radiocarbon dating in the 1950s. But archaeologists sharing his interest in critical analysis and broad trends have been rereading his philosophical works in recent years, attracted by his marxist focus on ideology and by his political activism. Vere Gordon Childe was one of the most influential archaeologists of the twentieth century. His concepts of what happened in history continue to be the subject of debate.

[See also HISTORY OF ARCHAEOLOGY FROM 1900 TO 1950, *articles on* EUROPEAN ARCHAEOLOGY, NEAR EASTERN ARCHAEOLOGY; HISTORY OF ARCHAEOLOGY, INTELLECTUAL; MARXIST THEORY.]

■ Barbara McNairn, *The Method and Theory of V. Gordon Childe* (1980). Bruce Trigger, *Gordon Childe: Revolutions in Archaeology* (1980). Sally Green, *Prehistorian: A Biography of V. Gordon Childe* (1981). Ruth Tringham, "V. Gordon Childe 25 Years After: His Relevance for the Archaeology of the Eighties," *Journal of Field Archaeology* 10 (1983): 85–100. Bruce Trigger, *A History of Archaeological Thought* (1989).

Ruth Tringham

CHIMU STATE. The earliest evidence for the Chimu state or "Kingdom of Chimor" dates to the ninth century A.D.; the kingdom was conquered by the Inca around 1470 during the reign of Topa Inca. From the capital (*Chan Chan) in the Moche Valley, the kingdom extended some 621 miles (1000 km) from Tumbes to the Chillon Valley on the north coast of Peru.

The Chimu state expanded during the Late Intermediate Period, a phase in Peruvian prehistory characterized by a series of smaller polities rather than a single unifying empire. The settlement pattern consists of the capital, several regional centers, local centers, and villages. Centers are distinguished from villages by the presence of monumental architecture or at least adobe structures. Regional centers are found in some of the larger valleys, with several local centers in each valley. The most spectacular remains may well be the intervalley irrigation systems; for example, the canal bringing water from the Chicama to the Moche Valley is 43.5 miles (70 km) long. The Chimu ceramic style— mainly burnished black ware decorated by plastic techniques—appears to have developed out of a combination of late Moche (especially the maritime themes), Wari, and Sipan influences. However, the role of these influences in the formation of the kingdom is not clear.

The historical information, contained in the chronicles written shortly after the Spanish conquest and in colonial records, has been analyzed by M. Rostworowski, P. Netherly, and S. Ramirez among others. One fragment contains information on the Chimu dynasty, founded by Tacaynamo; another records the conquest of the Jequetepeque Valley. The most notable of Tacaynamo's nine or ten (largely unnamed) successors were Ñançenpinco (who expanded the kingdom northward to the Zaña Valley and southward to the Santa Valley) and Minchançaman (who accomplished the maximum expansion of the empire before being conquered by the Inca). Several chronicles mention the Inca conquest of Chimor and subsequent events. Colonial documents, particularly legal and administrative records, provide information about various aspects of Chimu organization and beliefs.

The last twenty-five years have seen the excavation of many Chimu sites, including Chan Chan and two regional centers, Farfan and Manchan. These excavations have corroborated much of the ethnohistorical data, while also providing new information, such as the definition of stages of military expansion and expanding our knowledge of various parts of the kingdom under central rule.

Models of Chimu organization are not always in agreement. One model of Chimu sociopolitical organization based mainly on ethnohistorical information focuses on the role of local nobles and presents a decentralized view of political and economic organization, whereas another (based mainly on archaeological data) posits a highly centralized state, administered from the capital by nobles. The major evidence for the decentralized model is the information on the role of the local lords and their arguments presented in colonial courts defending their jurisdiction over lands and people. The archaeological evidence for centralization comes primarily from the settlement pattern. The regional centers are not only a fraction of Chan Chan's size, but also contain a disproportionately smaller number of storerooms and other architectural forms associated either with the dynasty or with administrative function.

Another major difference between the two views is the question of dual rulership (two kings representing moieties ruling at any one time), which is indicated by the ethnohistorical information, though the archaeological remains are not clear on this point. Other inferences about

political organization include the principle of split inheritance deduced on the basis of the sequential building and use of the palaces in Chan Chan. According to this principle, each new ruler inherited only the title, while the land and other riches stayed with the deceased king's lineage. For obvious reasons, this rule of succession necessitated the expansion of the kingdom. Both ethnohistory and archaeology agree on asymmetrical reciprocity as the defining characteristic of sociopolitical organization. Similarly, both agree on a high degree of economic specialization among both the rural and urban populations. There is some ethnohistorical evidence that women had the right of inheritance, to both property and political positions (at least on the local level).

After conquering the Chimu, the Inca appear to have purposefully broken up their empire; for example, by moving the artisans from Chan Chan to *Cuzco. They also built a new regional center in the Chicama Valley, Chiquitoy Viejo, after Chan Chan was abandoned. This policy may have started after a rebellion against the Inca on the north coast. Nonetheless, the local lords continued to administer their areas, indicating that the imperial organization may well have been an overlay superimposed on local organization.

[See also ANDEAN PRE-INCA CIVILIZATIONS, THE RISE OF, articles on INTRODUCTION, EFFECTS OF EL NIÑO ON PERUVIAN CIVILIZATION, MARITIME FOUNDATIONS OF PRE-INCA CIVILIZATION; INCA CIVILIZATION: INTRODUCTION; SOUTH AMERICA, articles on THE RISE OF COMPLEX SOCIETIES IN SOUTH AMERICA, HIGHLANDS CULTURES OF SOUTH AMERICA.]

■ John Howland Rowe, "The Kingdom of Chimor," *Acta Americana* 6 (1948): 1–2. Paul Kosok, *Life, Land and Water in Ancient Peru* (1965). Patricia J. Netherly, "The Management of Late Andean Irrigation Systems on the North Coast of Peru," *American Antiquity* 49:2 (1984): 227–254. Michael E. Moseley and Alana Cordy-Collins, *The Northern Dynasties: Kingship and Statecraft in Chimor* (1990). Geoffrey W. Conrad, "Cultural Materialism, Split Inheritance, and the Expansion of Ancient Peruvian Empires," *American Antiquity* 46 (1991): 3–26.

Alexandra M. Ulana Klymyshyn

CHINA

Introduction
Stone Age Cultures of China
Early Civilizations of China
Shang Civilization
Early Farming Cultures of China
Han Empire
Tang and Song Dynasties

INTRODUCTION

Major new discoveries in recent years have required new interpretations of Chinese archaeology. The wealth of new material is astounding, in all time periods and all regions of China. These problems and discoveries will be treated chronologically, with a brief consideration of controversy and consensus where they arise.

Paleolithic. One of the most interesting controversies in Chinese Paleolithic concerns the typology of human remains and how they should be regarded in the world scheme. For example, there is a tension between assertions that Mongoloid traits in human skulls and teeth, such as shovel-shaped incisors, absence of the third molar, and prominent cheekbones, are to be found as early as 750,000 B.P., well back into the Pleistocene, and the notion that *Homo sapiens* spread out from Africa relatively recently, perhaps only 100,000 B.P. If *Homo erectus* had some branches with Mongoloid features, did they hybridize with *H. sapiens* to become the modern Chinese? A related problem is that skeletons interpreted as *H. sapiens* are believed to coexist with those of *H. erectus* in China. For example, bones of *H. erectus* were found at Hexian and of *H. sapiens* at Chaohu, caves only 31 miles (50 km) apart in Anhui Province. Both caves have been dated by faunal analysis and by uranium series dating to about 200,000 B.P. At the site of Jinniushan in Liaoning Province, too, an almost complete skeleton identified as *H. sapiens* was dated to 300,000–230,000 B.P.

Another Paleolithic controversy involves the interpretation of stone tools. Archaeologists in China perceive two different tool traditions running in parallel since the Early Paleolithic—one with large tools such as choppers and picks, the other having smaller tools made on flakes. This pattern is quite different from that which has been identified in Europe, with progressively smaller tools making increasingly more efficient use of flint nodules. The large tools in China represent the so-called Chopper-Chopping Tool Tradition, which has been considered backward compared to the development and elaboration of reduction techniques and the variety of patterned tool types in Africa, Europe, and western Asia during the *Pleistocene. Thus, the identification of parallel traditions of large and small tools is in part a response to the charge of lack of development in China. Another response is to suggest that the relatively crude stones found in Asia are merely tools to make tools, that the real tools were probably made of bamboo, a material that is strong and will take a sharp edge, but which has disappeared from the archaeological record. Finally, it has been pointed out that there are hand axes and other large patterned tools in China, and that while there may be regional differences, it is incorrect to view the Chinese assemblages as backward. These controversies over interpretations of both human remains and tool assemblages promise more accurate and inclusive models of human evolution when they are resolved.

Neolithic. In contrast to the apparent advancement in the elaboration of stone tools in Europe and Africa, when it comes to pottery, pride of place must be granted to Asia. The earliest dated pottery vessels in the world are found in Fukui Cave, Kyushu, Japan. However, a number of Early Holocene dates are turning up in China, as well, suggesting that the spread of pottery around the edges of the China Sea was well established by the time of maximum sea level. The Japanese sites are not agricultural for several thousand years after the appearance of pottery, but the sites in China with early pottery are almost all implicated in the origins of plant and/or animal domestication.

The first site with domesticated rice is *Pengtoushan in the middle reaches of the Yangzi River, dated about 7000 B.C. This is followed by the *Hemudu culture, in which remains of rice are abundant. Pig domestication, without evidence of grains, is claimed for the site of Zengbiyan, at about the same time. In the north, millets of two or three kinds were domesticated, and pigs, dogs, and chickens were also found. For example, the sites of the Cishan and Peiligang cultures are dated to the seventh to sixth millennia B.C., with a well-established farming economy. In Manchuria, the early site of Chahai probably is also a farming village, where jade earrings and pottery beakers were made. Later Neolithic sites are increasingly complex. *Yangshao culture sites with painted pottery have large

villages with zoned areas, including houses surrounded by a deep ditch, and pottery firing kiln areas and cemeteries outside the ditch. *Longshan sites indicate the beginnings of social stratification, with elaboration of some burials in size and features of the grave itself, and quantity and quality of burial goods. The Hongshan culture in the north is the most elaborate of all, with huge tombs, ceremonial complexes, and very finely carved jade pendants. Some evidence of the use of copper and perhaps bronze in the Hongshan culture is beginning to appear.

Bronze Age. The beginning of a bronze age in China is a matter of definition, for examples of the early use of metals are found quite widely for perhaps two millennia before any obvious impact on the economy can be noted. The first sporadic appearances include knives, ornaments, mirrors, and weapons. These were all cast in simple two-piece molds. Evidence of bronze casting, in the form of molds and slag, is found as widely and as thinly as the bronzes themselves. This leads to the question of whether there were itinerant smiths, or whether bronze casting spread wherever the raw materials were available. It must be borne in mind that bronze is unlikely to have been discarded, for even broken bits are easily recycled. Therefore, discovery of bronzes except in burial contexts could be expected to be rare, even if bronze use were quite intensive. Probably for each bronze object found in sites, hundreds or even thousands were melted down.

The best-known use of bronze in China is for ceremonial containers. Although four bronze wine vessels were found at the site of Erlitou, Henan Province, now identified with the Xia dynasty by most Chinese archaeologists, the first archaeologically visible intensive use of bronze is in the Shang dynasty, when enormous amounts of bronze were used for ceremonial vessels. The burial of these objects, and the sacredness of their purpose, protected many of them from being melted down. These bronze wine and food containers with their elaborate surface decorations are among the glories of the Shang dynasty. Bronze weapons, especially the *ge* halberd, battle axes, execution axes, and knives suggest that bronze was used as an instrument of tyranny, not to make people's lives easier. Stone tools for agriculture and some kinds of manufacturing were still in use until the advent of iron in about the sixth century B.C.

Whether metallurgy was locally invented, or whether it diffused from western and Central Asia, is a matter of extensive discussion. Certain types of hafting are peculiarly Chinese, such as the rectangular holes in *ge* for riveting them to the shaft. On the other hand, socketed tools and weapons such as axes and spears have more affinity for the bronze industry of southwestern Asia. Some of the first metal objects are found in the northwest, such as the earring from Hongshan, and are almost pure copper, while other objects, somewhat later, such as the knife from Linjia, a Majiayao culture site in Gansu; Machang in Qinghai; and Qijia in Gansu have relatively large amounts of tin or zinc. A Longshan site in Jiao Xian, Shangdong Province, has two bronze awls that date to around 2000 B.C., and there are also two bronze pieces from Dachengshan, in Hebei Province. The differences in alloys may represent local copper impurities rather than deliberate experiments with alloys, or the choice may relate to the proximity of certain metals rather than others. A group of bronze weapons and ornaments in Inner Mongolia and Liaoning Province, known as the Northern Bronzes, suggests that some bronze shapes relate to the north, but the temporal priority of the northern bronzes is still in dispute.

Development of Civilizations. What any particular scholar considers to be the first Chinese civilization depends on the definition of civilization, the orientation toward history or archaeology, and the regional perspective chosen. The three dynasties of early China, called collectively the Sandai, which consisted of the Xia, Shang, and Zhou dynasties, are considered as civilizations within the histories themselves. Of these, the Shang dynasty will definitely qualify, as it is attested by both written and archaeological materials. The Xia dynasty is not entirely accepted, since no contemporary writing definitively ties the site of Erlitou to the Xia dynasty. On the other hand, there are champions for considering various archaeological cultures from well before the Sandai as civilizations, in particular the Hongshan and Longshan cultures.

Chinese legendary history includes the three sages and the five legendary emperors before the Xia, Shang, and Zhou, but there is too little specific information to attach any of these legends to particular archaeological sites. New discoveries in the Hongshan region particularly lend themselves to interpretations of civilization, with complex ceremonial sites, tomb precincts, and elaborate crafts. The Longshan culture has walled cities and elite burials, and is clearly at least on the road to civilization.

Many burial grounds of the Zhou dynasty have greatly enlarged our understanding of the varieties of cultures present in China at that time, for example, Liulihe outside of Beijing. A palace complex at Qishan in Shaanxi Province contained an unexpected cache of 17,000 archaic oracle bones. Musical instruments, especially sets of bells, found in various graves have extended the knowledge of early Chinese court music, and the archaeology of the areas surrounding the central Zhou have brought to light many facets of the Chu, the Ba, and other states. Warring States and Qin and Han dynasty archaeology have also focused on tombs. The Zhongshan kingdom in Hebei was remarkably rich, and Yan remains at Xiadu in Hebei have produced armor. The remains of the pottery army guarding the tomb of Qin *Shihuangdi are well known, but the tomb itself has not yet been excavated. Han dynasty tombs feature figurines of servants, buildings, horses, pig sties, and watchtowers—everything that could possibly be needed in the afterlife—leaving an extraordinarily rich view of Han daily life as well as the accoutrements of the elite. The jade burial suits, sewn together with gold thread, from Tushan, Jiangsu Province, are also well known, as are the Chu tombs at Mawangdui. In Yunnan Province there are bronze cowrie shell containers with three-dimensional scenes of daily life on the lids.

[See also ASIA: PREHISTORY AND EARLY HISTORY OF EAST ASIA; ASIA, ORIGINS OF FOOD PRODUCTION IN: ORIGINS OF FOOD PRODUCTION IN CHINA; ZHENGZHOU; ZHOUKOUDIAN.]

■ Qian Hao, Chen Heyi, and Ru Suichu, *Out of China's Earth* (1981). Danielle and Vadima Elisseeff, *New Discoveries in China* (1983). Wu Rukang and John Olsen, *Palaeoanthropology and Palaeolithic Archaeology in the People's Republic of China* (1985). K.-C. Chang, *The Archaeology of Early China*, 4th ed. (1986). Yan Wenming, *China's Earliest Rice Agriculture Remains, Indo-Pacific Prehistory*, Vol. 1 (1990), pp. 118–126. Zhang Yinyun, *Human Fossils from Anhui, Southeast China: Coexistence of Homo erectus and Homo sapiens, Indo-Pacific Prehistory*, Vol. 1 (1990), pp. 79–82. Lothar von Falkenhausen, *Suspended Music: Chime-Bells in the Culture of Bronze Age China* (1994).

Sarah Milledge Nelson

STONE AGE CULTURES OF CHINA

The Stone Age archaeology of China is overshadowed by the spectacular cultural developments of later times.

First Settlement and Homo erectus. There is no securely dated human settlement in China before one million years ago. Despite many years of search, no signs of *Australopithecus* have come to light in Asia. The three molars found in a southern Chinese cave and claimed by some Chinese scholars to be Australopithecine are considered by Western paleoanthropologists to be large *Homo erectus* specimens. *Australopithecus* is confined to tropical Africa, so most archaeologists believe *Homo erectus* evolved in that continent and subsequently spread into other parts of the Old World, including China. Until recently, the radiation of *H. erectus* out of Africa was dated to between a million and 700,000 years ago, but new potassium-argon dates for the Mojokerto site in Southeast Asia of about 1.8 million years ago make it possible the radiation took place much earlier.

The date of earliest settlement remains uncertain, with the earliest securely dated fossil remains from the Lantian site near the Wei River dating to between 750,000 and 800,000 years ago. Paleomagnetic dates from Xihoudu in central China and Yuanmou south of the Yangzi River place crude choppers and scrapers as early as 1.5 million years ago, but the dates are controversial. A date of about a million years for first settlement is perhaps conservative, but the timing of initial colonization and the means by which it took place are still little researched.

Homo erectus settled widely in China and is well known from many years of excavations at Locality I at *Zhoukoudian near Beijing. This important earth-filled cave has yielded the remains of at least forty individuals, more *H. erectus* fossils than any other site in the world, enabling paleoanthropologists to study variations within this species of archaic human. While the fossils are well documented, Locality I was occupied by both hyenas and humans, both of whom left the carcasses of local animals behind them. Some of these bones have been modified by humans and display signs of burning, and some of the large ash concentrations in the cave may represent hearths. The many layers at Locality I have been uranium-series dated from at least 500,000 years ago to about 230,000 years ago, with sporadic occupation of the cave coinciding with a shift from warmer conditions to colder ones, and then back to warmer.

Back in the 1940s, Harvard archaeologist Hallam Movius Jr. classified the artifacts made by Chinese *H. erectus* groups within a "chopper-chopping tool complex," quite distinct from the hand-axe cultural traditions of the West. Some researchers have pointed out that the "frontier" between hand-axe-making cultures and chopper and flake tool cultures coincides in general terms with the distribution of Asian bamboo. Since bamboo is ideal for making simple but effective spears, knives, and other weapons, the stone tool kits used in China and Southeast Asia are correspondingly simpler than those in the West, goes the argument. In fact, Movius's "frontier" is only vaguely demarcated, for some hand-axe-like artifacts occur in east Asian sites. Locality I at Zhoukoudian contains large numbers of small flakes and flake tools rather than large choppers. Small artifacts were also uncovered at Lantian and other important *H. erectus* sites. There appear to be at least two Lower Paleolithic stone tool traditions in China, the one characterized by direct percussion techniques, the other by the use of bipolar methods. Thus, the "chopper-chopping tool complex" has given way to classifications that allow for much greater and still little-understood regional variations in Lower Paleolithic culture. However, points, scrapers, and other artifacts become more standardized, especially during the Middle Paleolithic.

Appearance of Modern Humans. The controversies surrounding the evolution of *Homo sapiens sapiens* pit those who believe that modern humans originated in tropical Africa against another school of thought that argues for the development of anatomically modern people from more archaic populations in several parts of the Old World, including China. While most Western archaeologists support the Out-of-Africa hypothesis, pointing to the considerable diversity of early *Homo sapiens* fossils south of the Sahara Desert, some Chinese paleoanthropologists and a few Westerners consider that east Asian *H. erectus* populations display considerable variation, with evolutionary changes in facial features and increased brain size over time. Unfortunately, the later Chinese *H. erectus* fossils are far from accurately dated, but the Dali cranium from China's eastern Shaanxi Province may be about 200,000 years old, and another find at Hexian has uranium dates between 200,000 and 150,000 years ago. There are reports of archaic *Homo sapiens* fossils from fissures in the Jinniushan area of Liaoning Province, uranium-series dated to about 260,000 years ago. Archaic *H. sapiens* fossils in the 200,000- to 100,000-year range come from Dingcun and Dali in central China, and from Maba in the south. The human remains are mainly teeth, skull, and facial fragments, but there is said to be evidence of anatomical continuity between *H. erectus* and early *H. sapiens*, including an increase in brain size. Whether these finds are sufficient evidence for claiming that modern humans evolved independently in China is still impossible to determine. The fossil evidence is so incomplete that it is hard even to agree on what long-term traits are evidence of evolutionary continuity. And the genetic evidence strongly favors an origin for modern humans in tropical Africa.

An archaic-looking *H. sapiens* skull from the Linjiang site is uranium-series dated to about 67,000 years ago, followed by a gap in the fossil record until between 50,000 and 37,000 years ago, when some fragments of human bone from Salawusu in Mongolia are thought to be from anatomically modern people. The changeover from archaic to modern humans took place during the last glaciation, which saw a dramatic rise in Stone Age populations at about the time of the glacial maximum, after 20,000 years ago. Sea levels were so low that the modern-day Sea of Japan was a large lake, which drained through the present Korea Strait. Tundra, steppe, and boreal forests covered northern China, with temperate forests in more southern latitudes. Many Late Ice Age groups subsisted off large and small mammals, which flourished both on the tundra and on the Yellow and Seto plains, exposed by low sea levels. As was the case elsewhere in the Old World, most of these peoples were constantly on the move, which means that their archaeological signature is exiguous.

Later Cultural Traditions. The flake and heavy tool traditions of the earlier Chinese Stone Age gave way to bladelike technologies by about 30,000 years ago, perhaps earlier in the arid north of the Mongolian deserts. The Huanghe He River flowed through arid grasslands, attracting huntergatherer bands, who preyed on game of all sizes and exploited plant foods in riverine locations. Archaeologically, they form the so-called Ordosian culture, comprising a combination of Levallois and disc-core technologies with

smaller blades struck from prismatic cores. A handful of Mongolian sites document the Ordosian, and a significant reduction in artifact size between about 35,000 and 25,000 years ago, the precursor of the well-defined "microblade" traditions of later millennia.

The long-lived microblade cultures of China and northern Asia generally appeared at least 30,000 years ago, based on a technology that produced dozens of diminutive blades from wedge-shaped, conical, and cylindrical cores. These in turn became sharp-edged barbs, arrow barbs, or scraper blades. Microblade technologies may have first evolved in northern China, where the earliest sites may occur, but they eventually spread northward to the steppe-tundra of northeastern Asia, and even into North America. They represent a highly effective adaptation to highly mobile huntergatherer lifeways in open terrain.

Farther south, blade technologies appear at Shiyu, west of Zhoukoudian, by 29,000 years ago, with true microliths at the Xiachuan site north of the Wei River by 23,000 years ago. The Upper Cave at Zhoukoudian served as a burial area, where at least five adults were interred, accompanied by perforated animal teeth, drilled bone and shell fragments, and bird bone segments, which may have served as clothing ornaments.

After about 14,000 years ago, the tundra and boreal forest retreated northward, as sea levels started rising at the end of the Ice Age. Many large game animals became extinct, as they did in the Americas, so human groups turned to exploitation of a broader range of smaller game, plant foods, and maritime resources. Fishing and shellfish foraging assumed great importance in coastal and lacustrine areas, as did the deliberate manipulation of plant remains and harvesting of acorns from evergreen broadleaf and deciduous forests. Many groups exploited these harvests intensively, at a time when polished axe technology assumed considerable importance, and pottery appeared in many parts of east Asia. By the seventh millennium, perhaps considerably earlier, some Chinese hunter-gatherers had turned from foraging to millet cultivation in the north, and to rice horticulture in the warmer south.

[*See also* HOMO ERECTUS; HUMANS, MODERN: ORIGINS OF MODERN HUMANS; ZHOUKOUDIAN.]

■ Lanpo Jin, *Early Man in China* (1980). Chun Chen, "The Microlithic in China," *Journal of Anthropological Archaeology* 3 (1984): 79–115. Kwang-Chih Chang, *The Archaeology of Ancient China*, 4th ed (1984). R. Wu and J. W. Olsen, eds., *Palaeoanthropology and Palaeolithic Archaeology in the People's Republic of China* (1985). Lanpo Jin, "On Problems of the Beijing-Man Site: A Critique of New Interpretation," *Current Anthropology* 30 (1989): 201–205. Gina Barnes, *China, Korea, and Japan: The Rise of Civilization in East Asia* (1993).
Brian M. Fagan

EARLY CIVILIZATIONS OF CHINA

Chinese civilization developed from a number of diverse roots, and it is a matter of definition to decide exactly which archaeologically known culture should be considered the earliest manifestation of civilization in China. The Sandai—the three historic dynasties of Xia, Shang, and Zhou—are generally now connected with archaeological sites, although the connection of the site of Erlitou with Xia is not fully accepted everywhere. For earlier times, legends speak of the three sages and the five emperors. Although these are too nonspecific to be associated with any particular cultures or sites, it is clear that prior to the Sandai there are sites with some characteristics of civilization—cultures such as Hongshan and Lower Xiajiadian in the northeast, Dawenkou in the east, Liangzhu in the southeast, and early Sanxingdui in the southwest. In addition, cultures contemporaneous with the Sandai flourished on all sides, and should be considered a part of Chinese early civilization in a larger sense.

Before the Sandai. The Hongshan culture (4000–3000 B.C.) flourished in the far north, on the borderlands between the grasslands of Mongolia and the hills above the Manchurian plain. Hongshan has some characteristics that did not contribute to Chinese civilization, for example, female figurines, larger-than-life-size female statues, and the "goddess temple," as well as typical Chinese characteristics such as unequaled jades, outdoor earth altars, and large, complex elite burials. It is proposed as a civilization because of a three-tier elite and the perfection of the jades, long known out of context but not suspected to be so early. The jades are made to be suspended on a cord and worn on the chest, where they would be visible as status markers. Best known perhaps are circular "pig-dragons," perhaps developed from slit earrings that are found in the northeast back to the beginning of the Neolithic. Others are flat carvings of turtles, birds, and clouds, made from a variety of colors of jade and turquoise. Larger cufflike jade objects were found under or near skulls, and may be part of an elite hairstyle. Painted pottery may link Hongshan to *Yangshao culture, but most of it is ceremonial only, cylinders with no bottom that were set in rows around the central graves of larger tombs. The tombs feature one larger burial in the center and subsidiary burials, some primary and some secondary, radiating in stone slab cists around the main interment. One earring with copper wire was found in a burial context, and a mold has also been reported, leading to speculation that this may be an early site of metal casting. Two large ceremonial centers have been partially excavated, but there is no urban center as such. The contemporaneous Fuhe culture has the earliest dated oracle bone, a scapula with prepared burn holes on the back, but without writing.

After the decline of Hongshan, sites grouped into the Xiaoheyan culture show some continuity with Hongshan, but traits often associated with *Longshan also appear, such as black polished pottery and pedestal vessels. The Lower Xiajiadian culture (2400–1500 B.C.), contemporary with Xia and Shang, returned to the complexity of Hongshan and surpassed it. Lower Xiajiadian arose in the same region, but covered a larger territory, with sites that reached to the south of the Yanshan Mountains. It is characterized by painted pottery in pinks, blacks, and yellows, as well as various shades of red, with motifs of spirals and animal masks, strongly resembling those of Shang bronzes, but preceding them. Tripod ceramic wine vessels foreshadow later ones of bronze at Erlitou. The larger graves in the spectacular cemetery of Dadianzi in Aohan, with more than 800 burials, have sets of vessels that suggest burial rituals involving wine. Burials differ markedly in depth and size, as well as elaboration of grave goods. The deepest burial is almost 30 feet (9 m) below the contemporary surface. Gold earrings made of gold wire with fan-shaped endings are characteristic of the culture. Bronze artifacts are also present, in the form of weapons such as arrowheads and dagger axes, and ornaments. A pottery mold for bronze casting confirms that some of the bronze was made locally. Burials are usually accompanied by pig and dog skeletons, with several whole animals in the larger graves, and only a leg or less in the smaller ones. Dense clusters of houses are found in the settlements. Some houses have mud-brick or stone

walls, and the villages or towns are often enclosed within walls. In addition, long walls protect groups of sites, and sentry posts are found in the hills.

In the east, the Dawenkou culture (4500–2700 B.C.) in southern Shandong and northern Jiangsu Provinces, is known for walled towns and high-status burials. Elaborate pottery shapes were produced, such as tripods, pedestal bowls with cutouts in the stand, and animal shapes. The pottery was made on a wheel, and is thin and hard fired, showing considerable advances in ceramic technology. Well-carved jade is also found, along with carved ivory, tusk, and bone. Turquoise appears here as well. The burials fall into three or four different classes, depending on the size and elaboration of the grave and the amount of grave goods, showing that the social structure was pyramidal. Wooden coffins and chambers and second-level ledges came into use in the larger graves. Pig heads were commonly placed in the larger graves. As an example of differential burials in Late Dawenkou, at Chengzuyai in Shandong Province, eleven people were buried in wooden coffins with grave goods, seventeen people without coffins but with some grave goods, and fifty-four pit burials with no grave goods. Through time there is increasing evidence of armed conflict, in the form of bodies, some decapitated, thrown into wells, and other casual treatment of the dead.

The Liangzhu culture (3300–2200 B.C.) in Zhejiang and Jiangsu Provinces near Hangzhou Bay and the lower reaches of the Yangzi River is particularly well known for its jades, of which more than 5,000 pieces were found, often in sets of *bi* (flat rings) and *cong* (square tubes). In later Shang times these objects were used as ritual paraphernalia with which the kings worshiped heaven (represented as round) and earth (represented as square). The jades are decorated with monster masks in low relief, the forerunners of the *taotie* motif for which Shang bronzes are famous, and bird designs are also common. Wheel-made and polished black pottery was made, including tripod and pedestal vessels. Wooden artifacts were preserved, including boats and parts of houses. Like other cultures of the same time period, burials are strikingly unequal. At the Sidun site, one young adult male, buried under a sixty-six-foot-high (20 m) oval earthen mound, had more than a hundred jades, including a virtual blanket of *cong* and *bi*. Some of the jades showed traces of burning, and some were broken, suggesting ritual treatment. A sacrificial human skeleton was found above the coffin chamber. At the Fanshan site 90 percent of the grave goods had been placed in only eleven of the burials, including 3,200 pieces of jade. On the top of Mount Yao, 3 miles (5 km) northeast of Fanshan, a ceremonial platform contained twelve burials with 635 sets of jade. Wheel-turned black pottery is found in these sites, suggesting a pottery industry, but no traces of metal have been uncovered.

These incipient civilizations laid the groundwork for further developments in China, and merge imperceptibly into the dynastic period.

Xia and Shang. The Xia dynasty is mentioned in historical texts, but until recently it was considered to be mythical. Discoveries at Erlitou, however, seem to have uncovered the archaeological correlates of the Xia. The site is dated beginning at 2000 B.C., and the Erlitou phase lies stratigraphically between a Longshan layer and early Shang. Thus it fits as the Xia dynasty both in terms of absolute dates and stratigraphic position. It is also located in the district historically associated with the Xia dynasty. A city wall enclosed large and small houses, storage pits, wells, and roads. Most spectacularly, a stamped earth terrace 328 feet (100 m) on a side was surrounded by its own wall and contained palatial buildings with large wooden pillars to hold up the roof, and another smaller platform also had signs of architecture. Some human sacrifices are found in the foundations. Human sacrifices are also found in some graves. A pit grave 16 by 13 feet (5 by 4 m) has a second-level ledge. Traces of a lacquer coffin and a dog skeleton were all that were left by tomb robbers. The Erlitou site contains the earliest bronze vessels yet found in China. They are all wine vessels on tripod legs with long pouring spouts, which were cast in section molds. A few tools and weapons were also made of bronze. Jades are made in a variety of shapes, including the *cong* tube, and ritual weapons. Cowrie shells, lacquer on wood, and objects with turquoise inlays are other interesting finds. Oracle bones without writing also appear.

The Erligang period follows that of Erlitou. Erligang is a section of the city of *Zhengzhou, in Henan Province, but the ancient Shang remains are spread over a wider territory in Zhengzhou than just Erligang. Remains of a stamped earth wall, rectangular but with one corner angled off, are still to be found in Zhengzhou, in some places over 29.5 feet (9 m) high, with a base 118 feet (36 m) wide. The perimeter of the wall measures over 4.3 miles (7 km), surrounding an area of more than 1.2 square miles (3 sq km). Inside the wall are palaces with stamped earth foundations and large posts. Outside the wall are nonelite houses, workshops, and burials. The city represents one of the early capitals of Shang, but which capital it is is in dispute. It is usually suggested as either the first capital of Bo or the succeeding one called Ao. Many other sites of this culture have been found, spread quite widely over central China, from Beijing to the Hanshui Valley. While some of these have stylistic differences as well as typical Shang artifacts, at the site of Panlongcheng, farthest to the south, the artifact inventory, city layout, and grave treatments are indistinguishable from those of the contemporaneous central Shang.

The site of the final Shang city, known as Yin, is well known archaeologically. The last twelve kings ruled here for 273 years, according to historic accounts, and the oracle bones concur. Royal graves were largely looted before they could be properly excavated, but they are well known for their bronze vessels, many of them inscribed. The kings' graves had long ramps leading down to them, usually on all four sides. The south ramp, up to 197 feet (60 m) long, led to the bottom of the pit, where the coffin was placed inside a chamber. At the very bottom, under the middle of the coffin, was a small pit, with either a human or a dog sacrifice. The coffins were probably lacquered. Some grave goods may have been inside the coffin, but most were outside the coffin but within the wooden chamber. The other ramps reached to this level, where there were human sacrifices, with additional ones along the ramps.

Sites contemporary with Shang are found throughout China. The Liujiahe burial near Beijing in Pinggu County is an example, where gold bracelets and earrings, related to the Lower Xiajiadian culture, and bronze vessels in Shang style and jades were found in a rich grave.

In the southwest, at the site of Sanxingdui in Sichuan, remains that have been connected to the state of Shu have been excavated. Attention was drawn to this site and others because of the mixture of Shang-style bronzes and locally produced bronze heads of a type never before seen. The heads, and in some cases whole statues, have large staring eyes, ears as long as the heads, and big noses. Two rectangular pits seem to have had ritual deposits, with bronze vessels, elephant tusks, jades, and items made of gold, stone, and pottery laid neatly into the ground in layers, along with burned animal bone.

Zhou. The Zhou conquerers of the Shang came from the west, and some predynastic sites are known. In taking over the "mandate of heaven" from the Shang, the Zhou retained many of the traits already visible in the archaeology. The Zhou period is fully historical, but archaeological sites have added detail and corroboration of the histories. The early Zhou is known as the Western Zhou period, when the capital was at Luoyang. Chariot burials, complete with highly ornamented horses and charioteers, became common. Inscribed bronze vessels continued to be important, but the decoration became less ornate, while the inscriptions became longer and more informative. Palaces were composed of square buildings grouped together around a central ceremonial one. Many scraps of jade and shell at the palace site of Qishan suggest that the walls may have been covered with mosaics, as noted in historic documents. Tile roofs seem to have been invented in this period, and second stories or towers are implied by a few unusually large central posts.

The Liulihe cemetery and walled city in Fangshan County near Beijing is representative of the Yan culture. Many inscribed bronzes announce that they belonged to the Marquis of Yan. The inscriptions show that he was granted the territory of Yan by the Zhou king, but there is much discussion over whether this is a properly Chinese or a barbarian region. Glazed hard fired pottery was found. Daggers with eagle and horse heads connect these graves with the Northern Bronzes.

Cemeteries assigned to the Shanrong "barbarians," with a style unlike the Liaodong sites but also not like the Central Plain, have been excavated, revealing more than 500 burials. Animal style is present in belt hooks and a tiger with inlaid stones. Short bronze daggers are cast all in one piece, and feature openwork.

By the Spring and Autumn period the Zhou power was split, but various civilizations continued to flourish. Tombs of the elite began to take on more splendor. In the tomb of the Marquis Zhao, in the early fifth century B.C., an entire set of bells was found, and several other sets of bells are now known.

The capitals of the state of Chu have been explored, especially the city of Jinan and Ying in Hubei Province, which were walled cities in the south. There is also some archaeology from the state of Ba in the Three Gorges region of the Yangzi River, including high roads above the gorges.

Thus, the development of civilization was a long, continuous process in China that involved many regions and various threads of development. It is no longer possible to consider only sites in the Central Plain as representing a linear development of civilization; rather it is necessary to include the complex web of cultures that contributed various traits to each other and modified them in their own ways in the creation of civilization. It is probably more appropriate to speak of the origins of Chinese civilizations than to consider that a single entity arose within China.

[*See also* ASIA: PREHISTORY AND EARLY HISTORY OF EAST ASIA.]

■ K.-C. Chang, *Early Chinese Civilization* (1976). Li Chi, *Anyang* (1977). K.-C. Chang, *Shang Civilization* (1980). Wen Fong, ed., *The*

Great Bronze Age of China (1980). David N. Keightley, "The Late Shang State: When, Where, and What?," in David N. Keightley, ed., *The Origins of Chinese Civilization* (1983). K.-C. Chang, ed., *Studies of Shang Archaeology* (1986). Cho-yun Hsu and Katheryn M. Linduff, *Western Chou Civilization* (1988). Cho-yun Hsu and Katheryn M. Linduff, *Beijing Relics* (1990). Yan Ge and Katheryn Linduff, "Sanxingdui: A New Bronze Age Site in Southwest China," *Antiquity* 64 (1990): 505–513. Tsui-mei Huang, "Laingzhu—A Late Neolithic Jade-Yielding Culture in Southeastern Coastal China," *Antiquity* 66 (1992): 75–83. Roderick Whitfield, ed., *The Problem of Meaning in Early Chinese Ritual Bronzes* (1993).

Sarah Milledge Nelson

SHANG CIVILIZATION

The Shang civilization flourished in China from the eighteenth to the eleventh centuries B.C. The traditional dates of 1766 to 1122 B.C. have been questioned with reference to the archaeology as well as internal historical factors, but from an archaeological perspective precise dates are not needed, and an ending date of 1100 B.C. is acceptable. Shang was the second of the Sandai, the three dynasties that mark the beginning of Chinese history: Xia, Shang, and Zhou. Although Shang is the second of these, it is the earliest with extant contemporary written records, in the form of oracle bones and inscriptions on bronze vessels. These discoveries have had the effect of confirming some later histories formerly considered suspect, and have confirmed the historicity of the Shang kings in the Late Shang period at *Anyang.

Periodization. The Shang dynasty is divided into three periods on the basis of the history, but some controversy over matching the archaeological sites with the periods exists. One of these periods is missing in the archaeological record, but whether it is Late or Middle Shang is uncertain. The histories tell of seven moving capital cities. The first capital was Bo, and the second capital was Ao, or Xiao. The evidence for one of these capitals is at *Zhengzhou, sometimes called the Erligang phase after the first excavations in Zhengzhou to reveal Shang Period sites. Those who consider Zhengzhou to be Early Shang believe that it directly follows the Erlitou site, which at first was called Early Shang but is now assigned by most Chinese archaeologists to the Xia dynasty on the basis of carbon-14 dating. Those who believe Zhengzhou is Middle Shang point to the written record. Contemporaneous with Zhengzhou are some two dozen other Shang sites, including Panglongcheng far to the south. In any case, Late Shang is clearly at Anyang, which was the site of the final capital city of Yin, where 12 kings ruled for 273 years. The unwalled site covers 258 square feet (24 sq m), and includes palaces, temples, and royal tombs. The majority of the oracle bones have been found in this area, as well as the royal burials, almost surely those of the Anyang kings, although they were repeatedly looted before they could be excavated by archaeologists.

Bronzes. Shang bronzes, especially bronze vessels, are considered to be some of the most precisely made bronzes in the world. Each one was unique, since they were made by crafting a clay model and then constructing a multipart mold around it. Elaborate surface patterns were carved into the mold. Although animals of many kinds were the inspiration for the designs, many were composite animals, and all were covered with surface decorations of spirals and whorls. The most common motif is called the *taotie*, identified by two large eyes. Often the face is seen frontally, but the body of the animal splays out in profile view on each side, so the design can also be perceived as two animals facing each other in profile or two animals with one head.

Legend credits the Xia founder with creating nine bronze vessels, one for each of the regions of the kingdom, which were seen as representing the legitimacy of Xia rule. The vessels passed to Shang and then to Zhou as symbols of rulership, but they no longer exist. Other vessels were used in funeral ceremonies, and were placed in graves. They were made in specific shapes, especially for serving wine and the preparation and service of food. The largest known Shang vessel is a square *ding*, a food vessel on solid legs, 53 inches (133 cm) high and weighing 1,930 pounds (875 kg). It is from the Middle Yin Period at Anyang, and is inscribed from the king Wen Ding to his mother. The only intact grave from Anyang was not a royal grave, but it contained 40 food vessels, 117 wine vessels, and 60 various other vessels, allowing a glimpse of the richness of the bronze assemblages.

Burials. Many of the elaborate bronzes are without provenance, but they must have come from royal burials and other elite graves. Earlier graves at Zhengzhou and Panlongcheng provide some sense of the layout of the graves, for some were found relatively intact. Impressions of carving on the wooden coffins of patterns similar to those on bronzes suggest the splendor of the funerals. Many of the elements of the later Anyang tombs were already in place, including the small "waist pit" under the coffin containing a sacrificed dog or human, other human sacrifice, and an inner and outer chamber. At Anyang the royal graves are deep square or rectangular pits, up to 60 feet (18 m) on a side and 39 feet (12 m) deep, with one to four ramps leading down to the burial chamber. The south ramp extended to the bottom of the burial, while the others reach the ledge around the top. The longest ramp is 197 feet (60 m). Sometimes the ledges extend out in each direction, giving the graves a cruciform shape. Although the royal tombs had all been plundered, excavations showed that the chambers contained painted lacquer coffins, sometimes inlaid with ivory and turquoise. A pit below the coffin contained a sacrifice of a dog or human or both, and other dog and human sacrifices were found on the ledges and ramps. Some of the human male victims were buried with weapons and were accompanied by dogs, who may have functioned as tomb guardians. Others, possibly concubines, were placed in coffins. Some of the sacrificial victims were beheaded, and one was cut in half. Ritual bronzes were found in sets, with the wine containers in the inner chamber and food vessels between the inner and outer chambers. A pair of *ding* are often found, and seem to be part of the funeral ritual. The graves were without mounds, but may have had a temple above them for continuing rites.

The only unlooted grave to be excavated at Anyang provided a wealth of information about the arrangement of burial goods and the amount of artifacts that must have been taken from the royal tombs. Known as Tomb 5, or the grave of Fu Hao, it was astonishingly rich. For example, it contained 440 bronzes (70 inscribed), 590 jades, 560 bone artifacts, as well as other items of stone, ivory, shell, and pottery, and nearly 7,000 cowrie shells. Four bronze mirrors and knives comprise a group of artifacts similar to the Northern Bronzes of Inner Mongolia and Liaoning Province. There is some controversy over the grave occupant, but scholarly opinion suggests that she was possibly a major consort of Wu Ding, the fourth king at Anyang. To have such an elaborate tomb, she was surely an important person in her own right.

Small graves in the vicinity of the larger ones are laid out in rows oriented in the same direction. Over 1,000 of these have been excavated, and they contain both juveniles and young adults, some without their skulls. Animals also appear, including horses and elephants.

Cities. Both capitals and provincial cities have been excavated. Some of the most important include the capitals Zhengzhou and Anyang, as well as Panlongcheng in the south. Shang cities were surrounded by walls (although no city wall has been found at Anyang) and divided into districts. Cemeteries were outside the walls, as well as most of the workshops and nonelite housing. Floors of buildings interpreted as palaces and temples are found in Shang cities, often clustered together. More than fifty of these have been located in one section at Anyang. Some buildings are of enormous proportions, the longest measuring 279 by 47.5 feet (85 by 14.5 m), while the one covering the greatest area is 230 by 131 feet (70 by 40 m).

Oracle Bones. The Shang oracle bones are significant because archaic forms of the present Chinese characters were carved into them. More than 10,000 pieces of inscribed oracle bones have been recovered, mostly from Anyang. Most of these were broken, and many had to be meticulously reconstructed to be read. They were made from plastrons, and rarely carapaces, of turtles and scapulae of cattle and water buffalo. The bones were prepared by smoothing and polishing and by making hollows on the back, usually in rows. Used for divination, pits were made in the oracle bones, which were then heated. A divination question was written near a pit in the bone and then heat was applied to crack it. The shape of the crack supplied the yes or no answer, with the help of the diviner. Sometimes the answer and the correctness of the prognistication was written on the bone. Questions usually concerned future events, such as the outcome of military campaigns and pregnancies, the weather, and the harvest.

Economy. The cowrie shell was the basic monetary unit. A nonlocal product (it is a marine shell that grows in warm waters), its importation must have been controlled by the Shang elite. Nearly 7,000 cowrie shells were found in Tomb No. 5 at Anyang (Fu Hao's grave), the only intact elite burial to have been excavated. This suggests an enormous amount of shell money in circulation. Imported raw materials, such as jade, copper, tin, turtles, and ivory came from every direction. Workshops for the production of bronze, pottery, bone wares, and jade have been found in Shang cities. The organization of production and its management by an elite class is implied.

■ K.-C. Chang, *Early Chinese Civilization* (1976). Li Chi, *Anyang* (1977). K.-C. Chang, *Shang Civilization* (1980). Wen Fong, ed., *The Great Bronze Age of China* (1980). David N. Keightley, "The Late Shang State: When, Where, and What?," in David N. Keightley, ed., *The Origins of Chinese Civilization* (1980). K.-C. Chang, ed., *Studies of Shang Archaeology* (1986). Cho-yun Hsu and Katheryn M. Linduff, *Western Chou Civilization* (1988). Roderick Whitfield, ed., *The Problem of Meaning in Early Chinese Ritual Bronzes* (1993).

Sarah Milledge Nelson

EARLY FARMING CULTURES OF CHINA

While the archaeological investigation of the origins of Chinese civilization began more than seventy years ago, dramatic advances have been made since the 1970s. New finds have challenged specialists not only to reconsider traditional viewpoints but also to devise new means to evaluate coherently an increasingly complex picture of China's prehistory, which today presents 10,000 sites. For instance, in the early part of the twentieth century archaeologists focused on classifying prehistoric and early dynastic remains in central China because it was thought that Chinese civilization originated there and spread to other regions. Although archaeological work has demonstrated that central China is vital to the study of China's prehistory and particularly its early dynastic history, it is also evident that other regions throughout China played significant roles in the formation of Chinese civilization. By the 1980s, leading researchers like Xia Nai and Su Bingqi began calling upon scholars to search for the origins of Chinese civilization before the era of early dynasties and beyond the confines of central China.

Emergence of Neolithic Cultures. Neolithic cultures appear in China at the start of the Holocene era (ca. 11,000 B.P.), when the fauna of the Pleistocene became extinct. Comprehensive studies of stone tools indicate that early Chinese Neolithic cultures developed from their predecessors of the Late Paleolithic (ca. 50,000–10,000 B.P.). Some scholars now identify the earliest Chinese Neolithic cultures as "preceramic" types, maintaining that these developed directly out of the Late Paleolithic and that China experienced no Mesolithic (ca. 12,000–10,000 B.P.) transition period.

In recent years, using radiocarbon dates, pottery sequence seriation, and typological criteria as guidelines, specialists have divided the Chinese Neolithic into various approximate phases. The earliest phase of Neolithic culture in China dates from approximately 10,000 to 8000 B.C. It includes an early period of "preceramic" sites and a later phase of sites with primitive pottery remains. These remains have been uncovered in various regions of southern China with representative sites in the south (Guangdong and Guangxi), in the west (Shaanxi and Qinghai), as well as in northern China (Hebei, Shanxi, and Inner Mongolia). Such sites have yielded chipped stone tools (with little evidence of polishing) and implements indicating rudimentary agricultural activities. The pottery vessels of this phase are typically flat- or round-bottom vessels of coarse quality fired at a low temperature.

Middle Neolithic Settlements. During the Middle Neolithic phase dating from approximately 8000 to 5000 B.C., more advanced settlements flourished throughout China. Many of the pottery vessels of this period are similar in shape to their predecessors', although more advanced features of legs, spouts, and handles are found. Most stone tools retrieved from sites of this phase are finely worked and polished. Discoveries at Neolithic sites in northern Henan and southern Hebei Provinces (called the Peiligang and Cishan cultures) demonstrate that societies in the Huanghe River Valley had already developed agriculture based primarily upon millet. The discovery of the so-called Houli culture now places comparable communities in Shandong Province dating to as early as 6000 B.C. Recently, there has been much debate over evidence that rice was already cultivated in the Pengtoushan area of southern China's Changjiang River basin during this period.

Some of the more extraordinary finds from this middle phase are those at the Qin'an Dadiwan site (ca. 5000 B.C.) in Gansu Province and at the Xinglongwa culture sites in Inner Mongolia. The Dadiwan site is spread across a mountain slope and occupies a surface area of more than 1,200,000 square yards (1,000,000 sq m). The remains of the foundations of structure #901 are of particular interest. This structure, which covers an area of approximately 500 square yards (420 sq m), is divided into a front hall, a back room, and two side chambers. The front hall exhibits a pair of postholes with a diameter of 36 inches (90 cm); it is estimated that the posts used to support the original structure's walls were more than 10 feet (3 m) in height. Scholars speculate that this was originally a palace compound for tribal leaders that had ritual significance.

In the 1970s and 1980s, archaeologists excavated a series of settlements on the hilltops and in elevated flat areas near the Xilamulun River in Inner Mongolia dating approximately from 6000 B.C. The representative Xinglongwa-type settlement near Aohan Banner is spread across an area of approximately 24,000 square yards (20,000 sq m), and comprises over a hundred semisubterranean houses lined up in rows surrounded by an uneven oval-shaped protective ditch. Stone tools and pottery vessels indicate that grain was harvested; animal bones and bone tools point to the fact that these people supplemented their diet by hunting and fishing as well as practicing animal husbandry (raising mainly pigs). Of special interest among the Xinglongwa finds is a four-inch-high (10 cm) granite figurine of a kneeling woman and some of the earliest jade artifacts yet found in China.

Late Neolithic Settlements. The Late Neolithic in China dates from approximately 5000 to 3500 B.C. Starting from approximately 3500 B.C., there is evidence of incipient metal use. Scholars such as Yan Wenming have recently proposed that the period from 3500 to 2000 B.C. be referred to as the Chalcolithic (i.e., the era when copper was used along with stone tools). He further subdivides this period into an early and a late period (i.e., 3500–2600 B.C. and 2600–2000 B.C.). Most others, however, consider that the Chalcolithic commenced during the Longshan culture (ca. 2600–2100 B.C.). Archaeological finds depict an exponential growth from simpler settlements at the beginning of the Late Neolithic phase to large cities toward the end of the Chalcolithic. For example, whereas at the early Yangshao culture villages of Banpo and Jiangzhai in Shaanxi (dating from 5000 B.C.), one sees, respectively, 46 and 120 house foundations, at one of the largest Xiajiadian lower period cities in southeastern Inner Mongolia (dating from 2300 B.C.), it is estimated there were originally over 600 structures within its walls.

The growth of settlements during Late Neolithic China was accompanied by advances in material culture. By the beginning of this era, foxtail and broomcorn millet was grown in abundance in the Yellow River Valley, and long-grained and round-grained rice was grown in the Changjiang River Valley. Production increased as tools such as hoes were perfected; in some regions, such as the Tai Lake basin in the south, plows were developed. Animal domestication also gained in importance. In Dawenkou cultural sites (of Shandong Province) dating from approximately 4300 B.C., for instance, there is increased evidence of the raising of pigs, dogs, cows, and sheep.

The more remarkable finds from this phase shed some light on ritual practices. At the Puyang Xishuipo site (ca. 4000 B.C.), in the large Tomb #45 an adult man, 6 feet (1.84 m) tall, was found accompanied by three human sacrifices. Shells laid out to his right show the image of a dragon nearly 6 feet (1.78 m) in length, and to his left a tiger 4.5 feet (1.39 m) in length. The Xishuipo image is being studied together with those found on pottery and in jade at Zhaobaogou and Hongshan cultural sites in Inner Mongolia as representing some of the earliest dragon images in China. The Inner Mongolian images show a pig's head with a snakelike body.

Startling discoveries have been revealed by the archaeological exploration of Hongshan cultural sites. To date, Hongshan sites have been found in an area including parts of Hebei and western Liaoning Provinces and eastern Inner Mongolia flourishing from about 4500 to 3000 B.C. In the 1980s, at the Liaoning Dongshanzui and Niuheliang sites various remains have been uncovered that are being studied as some of China's earliest ritual obeisance altars with associated burials. At the Dongshanzui site archaeologists found round and square altars. The rectangular altar in the central part of the site is flat and approximately 33 by 40 feet (10 by 12 m). Within this area are three piles of large pointed stones with flat bottoms. In the vicinity, in addition to other kinds of pottery, there were large cylindrical vessels without bottoms that appear to have been used to store offerings of food. Also retrieved was a jade *huang* (i.e., semicircular) plaque depicting two dragon heads. In the southern part of the site is a perfectly round area 8 feet (2.5 m) in diameter surrounded by grayish-white stones. Within the circular altar and its vicinity, there were pottery statues of female deities (some naked and pregnant), varying in size from figurines less than 4 inches (10 cm) high to pieces larger than life-size. From the many animal bones uncovered it appears that animal sacrifice was carried out. Scholars are now speculating that the altars were used for the worship of heaven and Earth and ancestors.

Another important set of discoveries are those from the Liangzhu culture sites. While Liangzhu culture was centered in the region of the Tai Lake spread between Jiangsu and Zhejiang Provinces, its influence extended toward Anhui, Shandong, and Guangdong Provinces. Liangzhu culture persisted from approximately 3000 to 1700 B.C. The majority of Liangzhu sites have been uncovered on earth mounds from 6.5 to 20 feet (2 to 6 m) high in the vicinity of river basins and lakes. Some interesting discoveries have been made at the Kunshan Taishidian site in Jiangsu Province and the Wuxingxian Qianshanyang site in Zhejiang Province. At Taishidian site, a well constructed with wooden posts over 6.5 feet (2 m) long was excavated; at Qianshanyang well-preserved silk woven fabrics were retrieved from a bamboo box.

By far the most important Liangzhu finds so far were made in 1987 at the Yuhang County Anxixiang Yaoshan site in Zhejiang Province. At the Yaoshan site, archaeologists uncovered a large, flat, rectangular area approximately 24.5 by 19.5 feet (7.5 by 6 m) constructed of red-colored earth. It is surrounded by a ditch, and piles of gravel were found on its surface. Scholars suggest that this was an altar used for ritual obeisance to heaven and Earth. Eleven graves were discovered surrounding the altar. One of these graves (#12) yielded 344 jade artifacts evidencing highly sophisticated lapidary skill. These jades are comparable to work from Liangzhu tombs uncovered at the Changmingxiang site (also in Yuhang County). Among the jades retrieved in these tombs are great numbers of the so-called *cong* (a jade in a square shape with a hole in the middle) and a *bi* (a flat, round jade with a hole in the center). These discoveries are significant because they help to trace the origin of ancient Chinese ritual practices. According to Chinese records, the *cong* and *bi* were buried with the deceased as supplication to heaven and Earth.

Many advancements were made during the Late Chalcolithic, or the Longshan cultural era. While evidence of copper and incipient metallurgy was already present in the Late Neolithic phase, during this cultural era metallurgy progressed in forging and casting techniques (as represented by finds in Longshan culture sites in Shandong and the Qijia culture sites in Gansu and Qinghai Provinces). Progress in well technology during the Longshan cultural era (from ca. 2600 B.C.) helped stabilize agriculture. Also, such ready sources of water made it feasible to locate kilns nearby, thus improving pottery production. By the beginning of the Late Neolithic phase, pottery was already being made with a slow wheel and painted pottery was mass produced (e.g., pieces found in Yangshao sites such as the Banpo village). Pottery from a Dawenkou culture site appear with glyphs important to the study of the origins of Chinese writing. Moreover, at the Longshan Dinggong city site, a pottery fragment with an as yet undeciphered eleven-character inscription was retrieved. As the pottery wheel was perfected, the shapes, designs, and dimensions of pottery vessels flourished. Experimentation led to the refining of clays from coarser gray and red pottery to the so-called black "egg-shell" pottery of Shandong, which, with the invention of the vertical kiln, was fired at temperatures in excess of 1830 degrees Fahrenheit (1000 degrees Celsius). White pottery artifacts retrieved from Dawenkou cultural sites, moreover, were made of clays that contain a high percentage of natural gaolinite.

In architecture, developments in the Late Neolithic include the use of lime plaster for floors and walls, the building of stone walls (e.g., the stone city walls of the Inner Mongolia Laohushan site, ca. 2800–2300 B.C.), and the perfecting of *hangtu*, or pounded earth. Pounded earth was used primarily to construct the foundations upon which wood structures were erected—a technique still being used in China today. It was also used to build city walls, such as those of the famous Longshan era Zhangqiu County Chengziyai site in Shandong Province and the Huaiyang Pingliangtai in Henan Province. Such walls have also been uncovered at the Aohan Banner Dadianzi site (ca. 2300–1600 B.C.) in Inner Mongolia.

[See also ASIA.]

Adam Kessler

HAN EMPIRE

The legacy of one of China's longest and most powerful dynasties, the Han, can be traced to the previous dynasty, the Qin (221–207 B.C.). Legalism, a philosophy that evolved during the Warring States period (475–221 B.C.), was the foundation for this former dynasty. According to legalism, the power of the state and the self-interest of the ruler were foremost. Procuring wealth, securing military power, and direct control over the population was considered essential.

The Qin dynasty established the first centralized monarchy in China's history. In an attempt to secure its northern borders, the walls of conquered states were joined to form the Great Wall, measuring some 540 miles (868 km) in length. In addition, the Qin dynasty standardized weights, measures, coinage, script, and even chariot axle widths.

Still, the Qin was a police state. Privately owned weapons were confiscated, and all books of political significance, except the approved official history of the Qin, were burned. Moreover, Confucian followers were discredited, persecuted, and murdered for opposing the regime. Huge public works like the imperial palace and the first Qin emperor's tomb and clay army effectively emptied the treasury, exhausted the manpower, and, finally, caused the fall of the dynasty.

The first emperor of the Western Han dynasty (206 B.C.–

A.D. 8), Liu Bang, learned much from the Qin emperors' mistakes. First, he made amends for the excesses of his predecessors. Then, selectively using elements from the Qin dynasty philosophy, Liu Bang and subsequent Han emperors established a strong, centralized bureaucracy, one that served as the model for China's imperial rule up until the early twentieth century. But Confucianism, not Qin legalism, was the favored philosophy of Han emperors, as it promoted a social and political framework for a centralized monarchy emphasizing loyalty to the emperor.

Confucian followers also believed that education and culture should be attributes of the ruling class. Consequently, impressive steps were taken to develop a state bureaucracy wherein intellectual merit, rather than divine or noble descent, determined an official's post. An examination system for candidates vying for official posts was initiated in 196 B.C., and an imperial academy was established in 124 B.C. to train upcoming officials. By the end of the Western Han dynasty, over 3,000 scholars were enrolled there.

During their first sixty years of rule, the Han emperors turned their attention inward. After centuries of war and turbulence, the peaceful years of the early Western Han enabled its citizens to thrive: population increased, the economy grew, and their culture flourished. Agricultural production expanded due to the widespread use of iron tools as well as the refinement and elaboration of irrigation systems.

By the middle of the Western Han dynasty, China was at the zenith of its power. Having consolidated its sovereignty within, China's rulers changed direction and became intent on expanding their influence outside of China. A major trade route was established at the capital at *Chang'an (present-day Xi'an), passed through the Gansu corridor, then by the Tarim basin oases, through central and western Asia, finally reaching its destination—the eastern coast of the Mediterranean. Stretching for more than 1,540 miles (2,480 km), this route came to be known as the *Silk Route, named after one of China's most important trade items. Economic expansion along this and other routes caused major markets to spring up in numerous frontier towns. Sea expeditions established contacts with Japan and various Southeast and South Asian countries.

Military excursions were sent to the south, including Vietnam, and to the northeast to Manchuria and Korea. China's most taxing military excursions, however, were in Mongolia and Central Asia subduing marauding nomads. In order to pay for these campaigns, a wide variety of taxes were implemented, including property tax on merchants, a license tax on boats and carriages, and a state monopoly in wine, salt, and iron, to name a few.

During the last years of the Western Han dynasty escalating court intrigue finally resulted in Wang Mang, a prestigious minister belonging to a consort's family, seizing the throne for himself in A.D. 8. Wang Mang set out to reestablish early Zhou dynasty institutions in order to create a utopian society based on his interpretation of Confucian teachings. Although Wang Mang initiated many reforms, a Han family prince managed to restore the dynasty to power in A.D. 25.

The first Eastern Han emperor, Kuangwudi, established a new capital in eastern China at Loyang, Honan Province, in A.D. 25 near his own power base. During the first century of the Eastern Han dynasty (A.D. 25–220), succeeding rulers were both principled and forceful, and enabled China to regain its former stability and prominence. In addition, the northern nomad confederation dissolved and various tribes migrated westward, alleviating the threat to the Eastern Han. Indeed, Chinese life was as affluent and sophisticated as it had been during the height of the Western Han.

After the first century, however, the situation changed radically, as peasants were increasingly controlled by land barons. Among the common people, Daoist-inspired religious cults promoting faith healing and immortality on a higher plane became popular. The court itself was also in disarray, as palace eunuchs and ambitious consort families once again plotted for control. Moreover, the scholar class, which had dominated the civil service since Emperor Wudi's reign, was now forced to accept men who had gained positions through connections or money rather than merit. Epidemics in A.D. 173 and 179, in addition to a number of floods and locust infestations, further devastated Eastern Han rule, effectively causing its demise by A.D. 220.

Although the Han Empire itself ended, its artistic, cultural, and scientific legacies survived. Scientific innovations during the Han dynasty include the seismograph, paper, the crank handle, the wheelbarrow, methods of drilling for natural gas, the suspension bridge, the parachute, and miniature hot-air balloons, to name a few. In literature, histories of past and present dynasties were penned, rhyme-prose (*fu*) was perfected, and a new bureau of music was formed, encouraging collaboration between musicians and poets.

Many spectacular archaeological sites have yielded an abundance of artifacts documenting life during this time. One of the most important archaeological sites to date is located at *Mawangdui, near Changsha in Hunan Province. Three tombs dating from the Middle Western Han and belonging to the marquis of Dai and his family contained elaborate wooden chambers in vertical pits, a tomb style dating to the Shang dynasty (1523–1028 B.C.). An abundance of grave goods, some made specifically for burial, and other valuable items used for everyday life, was found in the tombs. Large quantities of silks, however, were perhaps the most significant grave goods: More than twenty different colors appear in various robes, gloves, socks, and other items that range from the lightest gauzes to heavier brocades and damask. Early Han lacquer ware was also found in the tombs, indicating that bronze was no longer the preferred material for vessels. Wooden and clay tomb figures representing attendants, ladies in waiting, and noblemen were also found, as well as a variety of silk manuscripts on philosophy, medicine, and divination. Additionally, a military map and a topographical map represent the oldest extant examples of Chinese cartography.

In Mancheng in Hubei Province, the extreme luxury at the imperial Han court during the latter part of the Western Han dynasty (end of second century B.C.) is documented by the tombs of Liu Sheng, king of Zhongshan, and Princess Dou Wan, his wife. These tombs were actually hollowed-out cave complexes in a hillside and illustrate an alternative type of tomb structure. Two of the most spectacular items unearthed at the Mancheng site are the jade shrouds covering both the king and his princess. Each shroud is composed of over 2,000 small jade tablets sewn together with gold wire. Most of the 3,000 articles found in these tombs were valuable personal objects used by the owners during their lifetimes, including a small pair of bronze leopards inlaid with gold, silver, and garnets, and a gilt bronze figure in the shape of a young woman attendant holding an oil lamp.

By the Eastern Han dynasty, the two older styles of tombs had given way to a new style: chambered tombs resembling houses. These tombs, made of brick and stone slabs, provided perfect mural surfaces upon which scenes were engraved. By this time a new group of patrons, the scholar-officials, eschewed elaborate personal tomb art. Instead, this group preferred tomb art that indicated rank or inspired awe, or that made a statement about issues of relevance to the public. Some of the new subjects included illustrations of famous men, episodes from the Confucian classics, and tableaus emphasizing public duty. Some of the best-known examples of this type of tomb art are found in the Wu family shrines in Shandong Province.

With the end of the Han dynasty, China entered a period of political chaos that lasted for over 350 years. With the establishment of the Sui dynasty (A.D. 581–618), China began to function as a unified nation, but it was not until the Tang dynasty (A.D. 618–907) that China once again became the most powerful and influential nation in Asia.

■ Charles O. Hucker, *China's Imperial Past* (1975). Kwang-chih Chang, *The Archaeology of Ancient China* (1977). Jessica Rawson, *Ancient China: Art and Archaeology* (1980). Michele Pirazzoli-t'Serstevens, *The Han Dynasty* (1982). Danielle and Vadime Elisseeff, *New Discoveries in China* (1983). Wang Zhongzhu, *Han Civilization* (1984). Jacques Gernet, *A History of Chinese Civilization* (1987). Martin J. Powers, *Art and Political Expression in Early China* (1991).

Julie M. Segraves

TANG AND SONG DYNASTIES

Powerful and prosperous, the Tang dynasty (A.D. 618–907) is celebrated for embracing liberal attitudes and cultural reciprocity. Early Tang emperors refined and fine-tuned various government enactments of the previous Sui dynasty (A.D. 581–618). A selective service program (as opposed to a mercenary system) was implemented to provide soldiers for China's frontiers, and a land distribution system specified that all males were eligible to receive 100 mu of land, 20 of which could be passed on as inheritance. A simplified tax system designated specific amounts of silk, grain, and corvée service owed. Thus, each peasant family had enough land to support itself, and the central government was ensured a regular labor/tax base.

Due to its location on China's famed *Silk Route, *Chang'an, the Tang capital, became the most cosmopolitan city in the world. It is estimated that among the one million city residents, 50,000 were foreigners or members of ethnic minorities. The Tang was open to exotic influences for several reasons. During the previous Sui dynasty, the northern nomadic invaders had intermarried with local Chinese resulting in many of the Tang elite, including the Tang emperors, being of mixed Chinese and Turkish blood. Then, too, after crushing their contenders and restoring peace early in the dynasty, the Tang rulers initiated one of the greatest military expansions in China's history, stretching their empire to the Caspian Sea.

Reaching its zenith in the first half of the eighth century, the Tang controlled the Silk Route, and Chang'an welcomed traders, diplomats, and clerics from Korea, Japan, Syria, Arabia, Iran, and Tibet, to name a few. The Chinese fascination with things foreign was soon reflected in the decorative arts of the period. Several Tang tombs, unearthed near the capital city, revealed an assortment of three-color glazed pottery figures depicting Central Asians, Arabians, and Africans along with Persian coins, silks with Sasanian pearl roundel designs, and metalwork decorated with floral motifs and hunting scenes reminiscent of those found in the Near East or Central Asia.

One of the most important foreign ideas imported from the West was Buddhism. Buddhism was first introduced into China during the Han dynasty, but it did not gain widespread appeal until several centuries later. By Tang times, Buddhists had become a powerful religious and economic force. Although intended to bring comfort to the soul, in reality Buddhism broadened China's intellectual horizons, affecting literature, music, sculpture, and painting. Indeed, wall paintings in cave temples from western Turkestan to Dunhuang in Gansu Province document the development of China's early Buddhist-inspired paintings, and the carved niches in Yun'gang in Shanxi Province and Longmen Caves in Henan Province contain examples of the evolving Buddhist sculptural styles.

By the mid-eighth century, the Tang suffered some critical setbacks. In 751 the Chinese army was defeated by the Arabs in Central Asia, the Thai state on the southwest border forced Chinese soldiers in that area to retreat, and threatening nomads on northern frontier borders caused the peasants to flee south. The government's power deteriorated, and the rulers were compelled to suppress an internal rebellion led by An Lushan, a military governor on China's northern frontier in 755. This rebellion was put down in 763, but the Tang never regained its central authority. In time warlords and mercenary armies replaced the selective service system. The land distribution system fell into disuse. The Buddhist church itself was persecuted in 840 and again in 845 with some 4,600 of its temples destroyed. The Tang dynasty was finally shattered by another series of internal rebellions in 875–884, thereafter ruling in name only until its final demise in 907.

Fifty years of turmoil followed until another Chinese dynasty, the Song, was established in 960. Divided into the Northern Song (960–1126) and the Southern Song (1126–1278), this dynasty is renowned for its elegant living, high intellectual pursuits, and artistic achievements.

At the Northern Song capital of Kaifeng, in Henan Province, the Song rulers set out to regain land lost after the downfall of the Tang. By 979 much of the traditional Chinese homeland was reclaimed. Notable exceptions included areas in the northwest controlled by the Xixia state and territories in the northeast seized by the Liao Empire.

The Song emperors were in no position to confront the Liao Empire, controlled by the Qidan, or the Xixia state, ruled by Tibetans. By the tenth century both of these foreign states had a Sinicized government with a strong agricultural base and well-trained armies. Thus, the Song rulers elected to pursue pacifist policies, and foreign as well as internal conflicts were regularly solved by conciliation.

Song rulers revived the Han tradition of staffing the centralized government with professional bureaucrats, scholar-officials who attained positions through competitive examinations. This system replaced staffing by aristocrats who had gained positions through financial means or family connections. The military's power was severely curtailed. Empresses, eunuchs, and imperial families who had used their influence to gain control in past dynasties, were now effectively held in check.

The Song's governing class consisted largely of rich, educated men who were contemplative and intellectual by nature. Common to these civil servants was their interest in improving China's political and social systems. A good example is Wang Anshi's edict of 1069 that presented a fifteen-point plan for sweeping military, economic, and educational reforms.

In 1113, a group of nomads called the Junjen established the Jin Empire in the northeast. They conquered the Liao state in the northwest in 1125, and finally deposed the Northern Song dynasty in 1126. The remnants of the Song court fled south and established a new capital for the Southern Song dynasty (1126–1278) at Hangzhou in Zhejiang Province. By this time, Hangzhou was already a thriving cultural and financial center. China saw tremendous economic expansion during the eleventh through the thirteenth centuries, as silk waving, printing, and metallurgy all experienced unprecedented growth. Chinese stoneware and porcelain reached perfection, and virtually every region throughout China had its own particular specialty. Major eleventh-century stoneware sites have yielded Yaozhou ceramics from Shaanxi Province and the famous white glazed Ding ware in Hebei Province. From the twelfth to the thirteenth centuries, green glazed Longquan stoneware from Zhejiang Province was popular as was the Jian stoneware made in Fujian Province. Perhaps the most highly prized wares were the porcelains made in the Jingdezhen kilns in Jiangxi Province.

Handicraft revenues coupled with income from monopolies in salt, tea, alcohol, and perfume resulted in China's principal wealth now being derived from commercial and craft endeavors, not agriculture. These goods were dispersed throughout the world via the Song's principal port at Quanzhou in Fujian Province. Aided by advances made in seafaring and the appearance of new and improved junks, Southern Song traders preferred sea routes to the overland Silk Route. Their ships were capable of carrying several thousand people and featured air-tight compartments in their holds. The remains of some of these ships, unearthed at the Quanzhou shipyards, explain why China is considered the greatest maritime power in the world during this time.

During the waning days of the Southern Song, as the empire was about to face the formidable Mongols, scholars remained dedicated to their pursuits of scholarship, literature, and art. A new Confucianism was developed by scholar Chu Hsi (1130–1200), which combined ancient Confucian political and moral values with cosmological and metaphysical concepts derived from Taoism and Buddhism. Archaeology, which had emerged at the end of the Northern Song period with the discovery of the Shang dynasty capital at Anyang, stimulated interest during the Southern Song, resulting in China's first archaeological publication exploring ancient Chinese bronze bells and vessels. China also had one of the most sophisticated painting traditions in the world. The monumental landscapes featuring the power of nature, which had been so popular during the Northern Song, gave way to smaller, more intimate landscapes featuring scholarly figures contemplating the beauty of nature.

But in spite of the Song's success in academic, artistic, literary, and commercial endeavors, the dynasty's demise was near. Mongols, under the leadership of Genghis Khan and then his grandson Kublai Khan, first attacked the Jin Empire in 1215 capturing Beijing, terminated the Xixia state in 1227, and finally took control of China itself in 1278, thus ending Chinese rule until the advent of the Ming dynasty in 1368.

■ Charles O. Hucker, *China's Imperial Past* (1975). Mary Tregear, *Song Ceramics* (1982). Danielle and Vadime Elisseeff, *New Discoveries in China* (1983). William Watson, *Tank and Liao Ceramics* (1984).

Jacques Gernet, *A History of Chinese Civilization* (1987). Ray Huang, *China: A Macro History* (1990).

Julie M. Segraves

CHINCHORRO is an unstratified burial site located on the upper marine terrace, overlooking the Chinchorro beach in Arica, northern Chile. Artifacts from this site include spear throwers, harpoons, cotton textiles, matting, basketry, and ornaments such as necklaces of shell beads. But the main feature of this site is the presence of human mummies. The practice of mummification followed at Chinchorro consisted of a complicated treatment featuring the evisceration of internal organs, defleshing of extremities, refilling of the thorax with straw and pieces of wood, and restoration of the body form including face masks using clay, wigs, and reimplanted teeth.

The site was discovered by the German archaeologist Max *Uhle probably in 1914. Based on the type of mummifications used, Uhle assigned these findings to his aborigines of Arica period. Chinchorro is considered the type site for the Chinchorro Tradition that defines the Initial Period in this region. The site itself has not been dated, but by cross-reference it is estimated to date to about 3000 B.C. However, Chinchorro as a tradition has been dated to between 5000 and 500 B.C., based on thirty-five radiocarbon dates from twenty different sites that include cemeteries, middens, and settlement sites. Thus, the mummies themselves could represent the oldest of their kind worldwide. The Chinchorro people as hunters of sea mammals were in the process of adapting themselves to the coastal environment. Marine resources allowed them some degree of permanency and economic stability, although they moved seasonally throughout the year, using a central base camp. They were organized into small groups under the inherited leadership of a chief. The custom of mummifying the bodies reveals the existence of some degree of social differentiation. Their ritual beliefs and concepts of an afterlife also suggest elaborated cosmological views.

[*See also* SOUTH AMERICA, *articles on* INTRODUCTION, HIGHLANDS CULTURES OF SOUTH AMERICA.]

■ Marvin J. Allison, "Chile's Ancient Mummies," *Natural History* October (1985): 75–80. Mario A. Rivera, "The Prehistory of Northern Chile: A Synthesis," *Journal of World Prehistory* 5 (1991): 1–47.

Mario A. Rivera

CHRISTIANITY, Early. Direct archaeological evidence for the early development of Christianity is scant and difficult to interpret. The first followers of Jesus were indistinguishable from other Jewish groups, worshiping at the Jerusalem temple and following Jewish law. When they gathered in separate assemblies, they met in private homes. Moreover, as the Jesus movement spread, it diversified and fragmented; multiple "Christianities" developed in different geographic regions, each with different beliefs, rituals, and symbols. Art and artifacts later understood as distinctively Christian, such as the cross, appear for the first time only at the end of the second century A.D. As a result, archaeological study cannot confirm the historical accuracy of biblical texts, and rarely sheds light on important early Christian figures, including Jesus and his first followers. Revered ancient shrines and artifacts, such as the Church of the Holy Sepulchre in Jerusalem, date only to post-Constantinian times. However, archaeological material has proved helpful in modern attempts to reconstruct the world out of which Christianity developed.

The Jesus Movement. Recent archaeological investigation of the region of Galilee indicates that Jesus of Nazareth was born into an area deeply influenced by Roman economic activity and culture. Excavations at Sepphoris, a regional administrative center located about 1.5 miles (2.5 km) from the village Nazareth, indicate that the city was renovated in a strongly Roman style by Herod Antipas in 6 B.C. and was connected by an extensive road system to nearby cities and villages. While life in smaller Galilean towns was probably not heavily influenced by an urban cosmopolitanism, economic disparities and heavy taxation by Roman clients such as Herod may have led to the rise of factions opposed to Roman economic and political influence. It is possible that the early Jesus movement was such a group, and that Jesus was a peasant leader who challenged the Romanization of Galilee, perhaps a cynicstyle preacher or an apocalyptic prophet who proclaimed the arrival of a new kingdom of God in the face of Roman oppression.

Archaeological material provides little testimony concerning the death of Jesus in A.D. 29–30 at the hands of the Romans. In 1961, Italian excavators discovered an inscription mentioning Pontius Pilate at Caesarea Maritima, Herod's great seaport and later the Roman administrative center for Judea. This constitutes the only archaeological evidence for the existence of the Roman prefect who passed sentence on Jesus. In 1990, the tomb of the Caiaphas family was discovered in Jerusalem. At the other end of the social spectrum, in 1968 the bones of a crucified man were found near the city, the first physical evidence for crucifixion in the region.

The site of multiple levels at Capernaum on the northwest shore of the Sea of Galilee provides one of the few clues concerning continued Christian activity in Roman Palestine in the centuries following the death of Jesus. Alleged to be the home of St. Peter (cf. Mark 1:29), it consists of a private house dating to the first century that was later renovated a number of times as a public building, perhaps a house-church. The site displays graffiti of a Christian character that has been dated by some scholars to the second and third centuries.

Jewish Christian groups apparently continued to exist in Palestine after the first Jewish revolt (A.D. 66–74), although no clear archaeological evidence of them has been found. Early Christian writers such as Irenaeus and Epiphanius refer in particular to the Ebionites and the Nazarenes, communities that maintained the importance of Jewish law and the rebuilding of the Jerusalem temple.

Pauline Missions. The letters of Paul are the earliest documentary evidence for the spread of the Jesus movement outside Palestine. These are rhetorical texts designed to argue and convince, and they must be read for historical information with caution, for they constitute only one side of a series of discussions between Paul and communities he founded or hoped to visit. Archaeology has served as an effective tool in reconstructing the social world of his correspondents.

The historical facts of Paul's life lie beyond the competence of archaeological investigation. After receiving his revelation, Paul tells us that he set off to proclaim his message among the Gentile cities of the Roman provinces of Galatia, Asia, Macedonia, and Achaia. In each area, he recruited and trained a network of associates who continued the work of preaching locally while he moved on to another region, keeping in touch with his foundations through his letters.

Archaeological study of the cities Paul visited illuminates some of the particulars of these epistles. Excavation of the Corinthian sanctuaries of Asklepios and Demeter uncovered rooms lined with couches for ritual meals, which provide a background for Paul's discussion of Christians dining in "an idol's temple" (1 Cor. 8:10). A large number of inscriptions dedicated to and by women of means in Corinth and *Ephesus, as well as evidence for ritual activity of women in Philippi, suggest a context for Paul's apparent difficulties with some of the women in his communities, despite his reliance upon them as colleagues (cf. Rom. 16:1–7).

More broadly, archaeological investigation has augmented modern understanding of the social organization of the Pauline communities and the social status of their members. As Wayne Meeks points out (*The First Urban Christians*, 1983), Paul worked to create a new social reality. His communities resembled the religious associations and voluntary clubs (*collegia*) that left inscriptions at Thessalonica and Ephesus. Members of these groups looked after one another in times of need and dined together in convivial celebration, often in honor of a local deity. However, the Christian communities differed from other associations in the diversity of their members' social status; comparison of the names mentioned in Pauline texts with similar names found in inscriptions in Greece and Asia Minor suggests that Christianity drew from a wide cross section of urban society, excluding only those of the highest echelons. Pauline Christianity may have been attractive particularly to those who experienced an inconsistency in social status, such as influential women and civic officials like Erastos, treasurer of Corinth (Rom. 16:23), who an inscription from the Corinthian theater indicates was probably a freedperson.

Late First and Second Centuries. Numerous missionaries evangelized the Greco-Roman world, and diverse Christian movements continued to develop. The original situation of each of the canonical gospels is obscure, although Matthew may have been composed in Syrian Antioch and the influential Roman Christian communities may have produced at least one of the gospels preserved in the New Testament. Suetonius (*Claudius* 25) records civil unrest among Rome's Jews at the "instigation of Chrestus"; this may be an early reference to the presence of Christians in the capital. Paul refers to Christian assemblies in private homes in Rome (Rom. 16:3–5), and ancient traditions locate Paul and Peter in the city; however, no material evidence of Christians in Rome can be dated conclusively to the first century.

Excavations at Ephesus hint at the social and political situation of Christians in parts of the eastern empire. The Temple of the *Sebastoi*, honoring a number of emperors, and an immense bath-gymnasium complex dedicated to Domitian, witness to the fact that first-century Ephesus was heavily influenced by imperial culture. Such activity, and the closer ties with Rome that it facilitated, was probably the context for the New Testament Revelation of John, now widely recognized as a discourse in opposition to the rise of Roman political and cultural influence in Asia Minor.

By the beginning of the second century, Pliny (*Epistulae* 10.96) and Tacitus (*Annales* 15.44) indicate that the Christian *superstitio* was penetrating deeply into the cities, towns, and villages of the empire. The early development of Christianity in Egypt is obscure, although the New Testament includes reference to first-century Egyptian believers (Acts 2:10; 6:9; 18:24) and tradition dates the Jesus movement in Alexandria to the evangelizing of Mark, an associate of Peter in Rome. While no architectural evidence exists for Egyptian Christianity in its first centuries, a number of documents attest to the vitality of Christian life in the region. A second-century letter of Clement of Alexandria discovered in 1958 alludes to a secret version of the Gospel of Mark, confirming that some of the canonical gospels circulated in a number of different forms for decades before being stabilized. A cache of papyrus documents buried in the fourth century and discovered near the village of Nag Hammadi in 1945 revealed fifty-two tractates from the second through the fourth centuries. These indicate the presence in Egypt of a variety of gnostic Jewish and Christian beliefs. Among the Nag Hammadi documents was a Coptic version of the Gospel of Thomas, already discovered at Oxyrhynchus in fragmentary Greek form. This important collection of the sayings of Jesus, which probably originated in late-first- or early-second-century Syria, may provide some authentic memories and sayings of Jesus not found in the New Testament.

Third and Fourth Centuries. By the end of the second century A.D., Christians throughout the empire were beginning to move toward the center of urban life and influence. They still met in private houses, but by the mid-third century they were remodeling some of these structures into public churches. One such house, discovered in the Roman military garrison of Dura-Europos on the Euphrates, was renovated in 232–233. It consists of a courtyard surrounded by a number of rooms, including an assembly hall and a baptistery decorated with images of Adam and Eve, Jesus as the Good Shepherd, and miracle stories from the Gospels. Among the few Christian sites of similar antiquity found elsewhere are several chapels and catacombs in Rome. In one of the oldest of these, the catacombs of St. Priscilla, frescoes portray a number of motifs that later become typical of early Christian art, including Noah and the ark, Daniel's three young men in the furnace, the three wise men, and the resurrection of Lazarus. Particularly interesting is the depiction of a eucharistic banquet presided over by a woman. Inscriptions from elsewhere in the empire suggest that women functioned widely in such leadership roles during the first four Christian centuries.

Roman coins minted under the reign of Constantine exhibit only intermittent Christian influence, suggesting that the emperor's conversion was a gradual process rather than a sudden revelation at the Mulvian Bridge in 312. Nevertheless, under his influence, Christian art and architecture flowered rapidly. The emperor's mother, Helena, visited the Holy Land in 326 and instigated the construction of lavish basilica churches commemorating significant events in the life of Christ. The Christian movement was well on its way to dominating the empire.

Future of Early Christian Archaeology. Much of the material associated with early rural Christian communities has yet to be studied, but work done so far throws into question much of the received wisdom concerning the nature and practice of the first Christian groups. Investigation of the Pachomian monastery at Phbow in Upper Egypt, for instance, suggests that although third- and fourth-century Christian ascetics did seek to separate themselves from the world, they remained within the Nile's green belt and engaged in farming and trade with outsiders. Inscriptions and tombs from all over the empire continue to augment our understanding of the important role of women in local Christian assemblies. Tombs and inscriptions from the Montanist communities in central Asia Minor challenge traditional understandings of orthodoxy; were such people heretics, as the church fathers claim, or were they, as the archaeological record hints, just the indigenous brand of Christianity in some sections of Phrygia? The study of magical papyri and curse tablets indicates that the distinction between Christian and "pagan" customs was not always clear, even well after the "conversion" of the Roman Empire to Christianity. The particular value, then, of archaeological investigation lies in its ability to add pieces to the mosaic of early Christianities, documenting the varieties of early Christian belief and practice of people who for various reasons were not prominent in the written historical record.

[See also EPHESUS; JERUSALEM; ROMAN EMPIRE: THE EASTERN PROVINCES OF THE ROMAN EMPIRE.]

■ Gerd Theissen, *The Social Setting of Pauline Christianity* (1982). Abraham J. Malherbe, *Social Aspects of Early Christianity*, 2nd ed. (1983). Elisabeth Schüssler Fiorenza, *In Memory of Her: A Feminist Theological Reconstruction of Christian Origins* (1983). Graydon F. Snyder, *Ante Pacem: Archaeological Evidence of Church Life Before Constantine* (1985). Richard A. Horsley, *Jesus and the Spiral of Violence: Popular Jewish Resistance in Roman Palestine* (1987). John Dominic Crossan, *The Historical Jesus: The Life of a Mediterranean Jewish Peasant* (1991). Jack Finegan, *Archaeology of the New Testament*, rev. ed. (1992). Marvin Meyer and Richard Smith, eds., *Ancient Christian Magic* (1994). Helmut Koester, *Introduction to the New Testament*, 2 vols., rev. ed. (1995).

John R. Lanci

CLASSICAL ARCHAEOLOGY focuses on the study of the physical remains of the civilizations of ancient Greece and Rome. For *Greece the time frame is the period from the rise of the Minoan and Mycenaean civilizations in the second millenium B.C. to the Christianization of Greece. For Roman civilization, it begins with the foundation of the city of *Rome and continues through the collapse of the Roman Empire. Some of the other Italic cultures, such as the *Etruscans, are normally included in classical archaeology. The geographical focus of the discipline is the Mediterranean and those parts of western Europe that were part of the Roman Empire.

Research in classical archaeology began in the Renaissance in conjunction with the revival of interest in the Greek and Roman world. Humanists, especially in Italy, began acquiring classical art works. Excavation began at classical sites. This early archaeology was closely allied with the study of the written texts. The collecting of art objects, initially by individuals and later by museums, and the emphasis on using archaeology to illustrate the Greek and Latin authors have played important roles in shaping classical archaeology since then.

Field research has concentrated on the excavation of major sites important for their literary and historical associations. The long-term excavations at Delphi, Olympia, and the Athenian Agora reflect this focus. Early excavations at sites like Halicarnassus and Pergamon aimed also at the collection of classical art objects, especially sculpture, that could be sent home to European museums. With the passage by most countries of laws against exportation, museums have lost interest in excavation and have turned increasingly to the legal and illegal antiquities markets for new acquisitions for their collections. This has led to increasing tensions between museum and field archaeologists.

These large, multiyear excavations created a distinctive classical archaeological culture. The research was traditionally financed by national governments in Europe and by rich individuals and major foundations in the United States. These excavations played an important role in the development of modern archaeological excavation and recording techniques between the world wars, but their research agendas have changed little since then. They were hierarchical in organization and relied on large staffs of specialists. Great emphasis has been placed on the classification and dating of finds and the relations of archaeological finds to historical events, and much less on the use of archaeological material to understand long-term social and economic developments. Classical archaeology in countries like Greece and Italy has also been used in the debates concerning national culture. This can be seen in the 1930s archaeological program of the Italian fascists.

Deference to the agendas of philologists has limited the research creativity of archaeologists working on the classic Greek and Roman periods. More original contributions have come in time periods or areas of ancient society, where the literary record is more limited and archaeologists can shape the research agenda. Beginning with the excavations of Heinrich *Schliemann at *Troy in the 1870s and later at sites like *Knossos and Pylos, archaeology has provided much of our information on preclassical Aegean Bronze Age civilization. Classical period archaeologists are now turning more to research areas like the Greek and Roman countryside and the ancient economy, where the literary information is limited and often misleading. Systematic archaeological surveys and rural site excavation are forcing reconsiderations of standard, text-based reconstructions of Greek and Roman agrarian history. Researchers using new techniques like *underwater archaeology and physical and chemical analysis of archaeological material like pottery have provided much new information on ancient manufacturing and trade. Roman provincial archaeologists working in countries like Britain have demonstrated that material evidence can be used to produce complex historical reconstructions even when few written records exist.

While classical archaeologists were the founders of the discipline of archaeology, classical archaeology's subordination to philological studies and close association with museum-oriented connoisseurship have meant that it did not play a major role in the theoretical debate that reshaped much of European and New World archaeology from the 1960s onward. Classical archaeologists were physically and intellectually separated from other branches of archaeology. They have generally been located in classics and art history departments at universities or in art museums rather than in anthropology departments and natural history museums and have continued to pursue traditional research projects in fields like stylistic analysis.

The discipline is slowly changing. Economics and politics have made large-scale excavations increasingly impractical. Greater emphasis is being placed on less expensive field surveys. More museums are adhering to codes that limit collecting. The younger generation of classical archaeologists increasingly uses approaches developed by anthropological archaeologists, art historians, and cultural theorists.

[See also ETHICS OF ARCHAEOLOGY AND COLLECTING; HISTORICAL ARCHAEOLOGY; HISTORY OF ARCHAEOLOGY BEFORE 1900: CLASSICAL ARCHAEOLOGY; HISTORY OF ARCHAEOLOGY FROM 1900 TO 1950: CLASSICAL ARCHAEOLOGY; HISTORY OF ARCHAEOLOGY SINCE 1950: CLASSICAL ARCHAEOLOGY; HISTORY OF ARCHAEOLOGY, INTELLECTUAL; MUSEUMS AND COLLECTING; PREHISTORIC ARCHAEOLOGY.]

■ P. MacKendrick, *The Mute Stones Speak* (1960). P. MacKendrick, *The Greek Stones Speak* (1962). D. Manacorda, *Il piccone del regime* (1985). J. Camp, *The Athenian Agora* (1986). R. Stoneman, *Land of the Lost Gods* (1987). N. A. Silberman, *Between Past and Present* (1989). W. A. McDonald and C. G. Thomas, *Progress into the Past* (1990).

Stephen L. Dyson

COCHISE CULTURE. The Cochise culture is a model developed by archaeologists in the 1940s to describe a series of geologically superimposed preceramic archaeological sites exposed by erosion in southeastern Arizona (Sayles and Antevs 1941). On the basis of associated paleoclimatic evidence, researchers reconstructed an extensive history of environmental change dating from the beginning of the Holocene Period, between approximately 12,000 and 10,000 B.P., to historic times. At many points during the Holocene the local environmental conditions in the Sonoran Desert of southeastern Arizona were quite different from today, sometimes wetter and cooler, occasionally hotter and drier. The artifacts and subsistence remains recovered from sites dating to varying climatic regimes were thought to reflect human adjustments to different ecological conditions, especially the availability of different plants and animals. Archaeologists identified long-term patterns of technological change in artifacts, especially milling stones, and used these to propose a series of three evolutionary "stages" (Sulphur Spring, Chiricahua, and San Pedro) corresponding to fundamental shifts in local economies (Sayles and Antevs 1941). Sayles (1983) later added the Cazador stage intermediate between Sulphur Spring and Chiricahua, based on research between 1950 and 1970. These stages constitute the Cochise Culture.

The Sulphur Spring stage was described as a Late Pleistocene–Early Holocene occupation of the northern Sonoran Desert, predating 10,000 B.P. and possibly ranging from 12,500 to 9,000 B.P. (Sayles 1983: 35). The type site for the Sulphur Spring stage is Double Adobe, where mammoth, horse, bison, and dire wolf bones were found associated in redeposited stream sediments with fire-cracked rock and small grinding stones. According to Sayles (1983: 88), regional hunter-gatherer groups during the Sulphur Spring stage were highly mobile and primarily dependent on plant foods for subsistence, with hunting providing a supplementary source of food.

Sayles (1983) proposed the Cazador stage as a transitional period in terms of stone tool technology. In addition to grinding stones, Cazador assemblages include chipped stone knives, scrapers, and projectile points. All associated fauna are modern, indicating a fully Holocene date, estimated at 9,000 to 8,000 B.P. Sayles (1983: 90) suggested that hunting had a greater economic role during the Cazador stage, relative to the preceding Sulphur Spring stage.

The Chiricahua stage (ca. 8,000–4,000 B.P.) is notable for two reasons. First, stone tool technology saw an increase in formal diversity and presumably an increase in the complexity of tasks for which they were used; seed grinding is thought to have become especially important. Chiricahua sites represent the first large sample of archaeological material from campsites where multiple features such as hearths were found with midden deposits resulting from discard of ash, bone, and chipped stone debris. Second, the Chiricahua stage corresponded to the Altithermal climatic period, a time of elevated temperature and aridity throughout the American Southwest. Consequently it is assumed that the apparent emphasis on seed processing and plant collec-

tion found in the technological realm was related to greater reliance on plant foods during this episode of diminished water availability (Sayles 1983: 124).

The San Pedro stage (3,500–2,000 B.P.) encompasses two major economic developments. The first is the appearance of pit house architecture in association with dense midden deposits, storage pits, and burials. In some areas, such as Matty Canyon south of Tucson, pit house density is high enough to suggest the formation of small hamlets or perhaps villages. The second development is the introduction of maize (*Zea mays*) from Mesoamerica, an event clearly related to the establishment of seasonally or annually sedentary settlements along broad alluvial plains. The original Cochise Culture model did not include maize cultivation within any stage, but fieldwork since the early 1980s has consistently recovered maize from San Pedro stage sites.

Although the initial Cochise Culture was primarily designed to synthesize observed changes in artifact form and function, subsequent applications of the Cochise Culture model often had a somewhat different goal, that being to identify ethnic affiliations on the basis of similarities in tool morphology. For example, archaeologists working in New Mexico during the 1940s and 1950s frequently described preceramic artifact assemblages as belonging to the Cochise Culture because some tools, such as metates, were much like those found in the Cochise sites. In the 1980s, a number of researchers argued that the ethnic interpretation of the Cochise Culture was inappropriate (Huckell 1984; Berry and Berry 1986) and suggested that preceramic sites simply be described as belonging to the Archaic "tradition," meaning that they represent a basic hunter-gatherer way of life and / or predate the origins of ceramic technology. These arguments have been persuasive, and currently the use of the Cochise Culture concept is fairly uncommon among archaeologists, who now generally divide the preceramic period into two broad divisions, Paleo-Indian (ca. 11,500–9,500 B.P.) and Archaic (9,500–2,000 B.P.). The archaic is often subdivided into early, middle, and late, with date ranges reflecting local or regionally established chronologies. The Cochise Culture stage names, such as San Pedro, are sometimes retained in descriptive reports, but presently do not have the same technological and economic correlates proposed by Sayles and Antevs.

[*See also* HUNTER-GATHERERS, NORTH AMERICAN ARCHAIC; NORTH AMERICA: THE NORTH AMERICAN SOUTHWEST.]

■ E. B. Sayles and Ernst Antevs, "The Cochise Culture," *Medallion Papers*, 24, (1941). E. B. Sayles, "The Cochise Cultural Sequence in Southeastern Arizona," *Anthropological Papers of the University of Arizona* 42 (1983). Bruce B. Huckell, "The Archaic Occupation of the Rosemont Area, Northern Santa Rita Mountains, Southeastern Arizona," *Archaeological Series* 147, Arizona State Museum (1984). Claudia F. Berry and Michael S. Berry, "Chronological and Conceptual Models of the Southwestern Archaic," *Anthropology of the Desert West: Essays in Honor of Jesse D. Jennings* (1986) pp. 253–327, University of Utah Anthropological Papers No. 110.

W. H. Wills

COGNITIVE ARCHAEOLOGY. Archaeology is once again facing profound reconsiderations of theoretical discourse. The positivism of processual archaeology has been critiqued by some of the more vocal post-processualists who believe that a scientific and hermeneutic archaeology is preferable to the logical empiricism that has underpinned processual archaeology. Proponents of such a perspective are known as cognitive archaeologists.

Archaeologists have traditionally focused on people/land relationships as these have been the easiest to address with archaeological data. This has led many researchers to identify the physical environment as a primary causal agent of change in human societies. Cognitive archaeologists reject this determinism and seek to develop a more informed theoretical framework by revitalizing the central concept of anthropological research: *culture. They do not dismiss the importance of prehistoric material remains but are more concerned with studying the cognitive systems that produced and created the archaeological record.

Cognitive archaeologists argue that aspects of the ideological subsystem such as status, class, gender, and kinship systems are essential components in explaining why societies became organized in particular ways. This type of analysis posits a more dynamic and diachronic notion of culture. That is, it is the purpose of cognitive archaeological research to elucidate the cultural context and logic from which social systems were constituted and to explain how such institutions were maintained and transformed over time.

James Deetz has applied the central precepts of cognitive archaeology to early Anglo-America. He identifies three distinct periods that, according to Deetz, are associated with different world views that permeate all aspects of life, from ceramics and gravestones to architecture and the organization of space. Deetz's study proposes that a utilitarian or materialist interpretation of human action may be misleading as social and technoeconomic institutions are intimately related to cultural systems of cognition. Archaeologists associated with the University of Witwatersrand, Johannesburg, have also used cognitive archaeology to further our knowledge of African Iron Age studies and hunter-gatherer research.

[See also CRITICAL THEORY; POST-PROCESSUAL THEORY; PROCESSUAL THEORY; THEORY IN ARCHAEOLOGY.]

■ James Deetz, *In Small Things Forgotten* (1977). David S. Whitley, "Prehistory and Post-Positivist Science," in *Archaeological Method and Theory*, ed. Michael B. Schiffer (1992), pp. 57–100.

Andrew L. Sussman

COLLECTING. *See* MUSEUMS AND COLLECTING.

COMMERCIAL ARCHAEOLOGY. As a relatively recent development within the field of archaeology, commercial archaeology focuses on the impact of developing technologies on culture and design. More specifically, commercial archaeologists study spaces and places of commerce as well as the material culture that is associated with the machine age, primarily that which has developed in association with the automobile and roads. Commercial archaeology also aligns itself closely with the field of culture studies.

Commercial archaeology was initiated in the mid-1970s as an outgrowth of the historic preservation movement and the recognition of value in the commonplace. Participants recognized the need for the documentation and research of twentieth-century structures and products, particularly considering the vulnerability to change to which much of roads and roadsides are subjected. In response to the inherently ephemeral quality of modern artifacts, commercial archaeologists primarily concern themselves with the documentation of roadside architecture including gas stations, roadside snack shops, restaurants and diners, and roadside lodging including tourist camps and motels. The material culture of commerce is also studied, including documents and publications such as maps, tourist guidebooks, and postcards. The iconography of commerce and transportation also falls within the realm of commercial archaeology and includes the study of nineteenth- and twentieth-century signage of all kinds.

Studies of the American roadside by Chester Liebs, Philip Langdon, and Richard Gutman are considered to exemplify the kinds of artifact-based studies typically conducted by commercial archaeologists. However, the 1980s saw the expansion of the field to include a greater emphasis on the theoretical study of the evolution of roadways through the literal and figurative excavation of transportation corridors. Issues related to the interconnectedness of culture and commerce including aspects of gender studies and symbiotics have also dominated recent works.

[See also HISTORICAL ARCHAEOLOGY; NORTH AMERICA: HISTORICAL ARCHAEOLOGY OF NORTH AMERICA; URBAN ARCHAEOLOGY.]

■ Chester Liebs, *Main Street to Miracle Mile: American Roadside Architecture* (1985). Jan Jennings, ed., *Roadside America: The Automobile in Design and Culture* (1990).

Mary Anne Beecher

CONSTANTINOPLE. The striking site of Constantinople, on land and sea crossroads between the Balkans and *Anatolia, and the Black Sea and the White Sea (now called the Aegean), thrust fame and history upon it. It was the successive capital of the East Roman (now called Byzantine) Empire (330–1453) and Ottoman Empire (1453–1923) and remains the seat of the Ecumenical Patriarchate of the Orthodox Church. But it began modestly enough as the classical Greek colony of Byzantium, founded by Megara in the seventh century B.C. The colony stood at the tip of a triangle on the European side of the Bosphorus, a tight, deep channel running from the Black Sea, where an inlet called the Golden Horn provides anchorage, before both debouch into the Sea of Marmara and through the Dardenelles on to the Aegean. But the site is not as convenient as it looks, for it is on an earthquake belt and has always had problems of supply and defense. To surmount these difficulties, the resources of the Roman Empire endowed its medieval successors with massive public works, which still characterize the city.

The birthday of the city was on 11 May 330, when emperor Constantine I "the Great" (306–337), the first Christian emperor, inaugurated it with pagan rites by its official name: New Rome (it has many others, but Greeks simply call it "The City"). The acropolis of ancient Byzantium lies under the Ottoman palace of Topkapi Sarayí: Constantine's now lost walls lay 2 miles (3.5 km) to the west. In the late fourth and fifth centuries the Theodosian dynasty furnished the city as an imperial capital, most impressively by even wider land walls (ca. 431) running 4 miles (6.5 km) from the Golden Gate, Constantinople's ceremonial "front door" on the Sea of Marmara, to the head of the Golden Horn at the sacred spring of the Blachernae. In its final form this was a triple-walled system with moat, ninety-six towers, and eight main gates. It sealed off the peninsula of Constantinople by land, and was followed by 10 miles (16 km) of sea walls on the two other sides of the triangle, embracing about 4500 acres (1,830 ha), the last and largest planned city of the ancient world. But, like medieval Baghdad or modern Brasília, it was never finished or filled. Civic planning ended with the sixth century when the city may have had a population of a half-million, grouped (like Ottoman Istanbul) into about fourteen districts on seven hills, amid intramural market gardens. Its principal industry was government; its principal export, luxury goods. Otherwise the capital was an open mouth that its empire had to feed.

The land walls of Constantinople were not breached until 1453 and remained the most awesome example of Roman military architecture until the 1990s, when restoration destroyed much of their archaeological value. But the city was still vulnerable and further "Long Walls" were built 40 miles (65 km) to the west. Comparable to Hadrian's Wall in Britain, they run 28 miles (45 km) across scrubland from the Sea of Marmara to the Black Sea, and block the approaches to Constantinople within sight of the foothills of the Balkan range. Like the Dardanelles to the south of the Sea of Marmara, the Bosphorus passage was also difficult to defend but gave enemies a stranglehold on the city.

Constantinople has little fresh water and no river. The Long Walls protected a vast and complex system of aqueducts that snaked even farther west, where invaders could cut them. They fed open reservoirs and about eighty closed cisterns in the city itself, holding over 35 million cubic feet (1 million cu. m) of water. One reservoir, of Aetios (419), is the size of two football stadiums, which it now holds; today the most accessible cistern is the Basilica or Yerebatan Sarayí, just north of the *milion*, Constantinople's surviving Milestone 0. There was local fishing, but grain was shipped in from Egypt until 618. There is today evidence of the state granaries, clustered around harbors and landings on the Golden Horn and Marmara sides of the city, where from the eleventh century Italian merchants set up trading colonies.

In the face of such natural drawbacks, fifth century New Rome was planned on a grandiose scale. From the *milion*, a *cardo* (High Street), called the Mese, ran through the Forum of Constantine to the Forum of Theodosius, where it branched northwest to the Blachernae and southwest to the Golden Gate. Here it became the Via Egnatia, the main high road across the Balkans to old Rome. It was paved, arched by tetrapylons, punctuated by columns, and lined with arcaded markets built in white marble from Proconnesus Island in the Sea of Marmara. North of the *milion* was a commercial quarter stretching to the Golden Horn. To the south was a hippodrome, embellished with classical statuary and obelisks. Between the hippodrome and the Sea of Marmara lay the inadequately excavated Great Palace, a walled city within a city, stretching almost 1.2 miles (2 km), an accumulation of palaces and barracks, ministries and monasteries, mint and silkworks, which was the heart of Byzantine government and its ceremonial until the twelfth century. To the east of the *milion* lay the cathedral of the empire, dedicated to the Holy Wisdom of God (Hagia Sophia) and inaugurated in its surviving form by Emperor Justinian I (527–565) on 27 December 537. Built fast on the living rock (which has probably saved it from earthquake), it remains the most colossal brick-domed basilica in the world. Like the Theodosian land walls, it is a final expression of Roman imperial architecture. But even in Christian terms, Constantinople was an upstart place. Constantine himself erected a church dedicated to the Holy Apostles, where emperors were buried until 1028, now beneath the Fatih Camii (1771).

Land and sea sieges (especially in 626 and 717), fire, plague, and earthquake reduced the population of the city.

Acqueducts and public baths ran dry. Constantinople recovered slowly from the ninth century, when monasteries multiplied. In the twelfth century the Comnene emperors shifted the focus of government to the Blachernae Palace, and founded as their mausoleum the still impressive monastery of the Pantocrator or Zeyrek Camii, midway between the land walls and the *milion*. During the Crusader occupation, or Latin empire (1204–1261), the Pantocrator served as the Venetian base.

The final Byzantine phase of the city (1261–1453), under the Palaeologan emperors, is marked by a number of exquisitely decorated monastery churches (like the Chora or Kariye Camii, and the Pammacaristos or Fethive Camii), while across the Golden Horn the Genoese established their own walled colony of Galata. After getting a stranglehold on first the Dardanelles and then the Bosphorus, the Ottoman Turks under the conquering sultan Mehmed II (1451–1475) finally stormed the land walls near the Blachernae on 29 May 1453. By this time Constantinople may have been reduced to about 50,000 inhabitants. Mehmed set about repopulating and rebuilding his new capital as vigorously as had Constantine. By the sixteenth century it boasted 120 mosques and other buildings designed from 1538 to 1588 by the architect Sinan alone, while the center of government moved back to the original site of Byzantium, where the Topkapi palace lies under the shadow of Justinian's cathedral, which became the imperial mosque of Ayasofya. The city was not officially renamed Istanbul until 1923, when the capital of Turkey moved to Ankara.

[*See also* BYZANTINE CULTURE, *articles on* BYZANTINE FORTIFICATIONS, ANCIENT SYNAGOGUES.]

■ Robert Janin, *Constantinople Byzantine: développement urbain et repertoire topographique* (1964). Rodolphe Guilland, *Études de topographie Byzantine, I–II* (1969). Gilbert Dagron, *Naissance d'une capitale. Constantinople et ses institutions de 330 à 451* (1974). Wolfgang Müller-Wiener, *Bildlexikon zur topographie Istanbuls* (1977). Hilary Sumner-Boyd and John Freely, *Strolling through Istanbul* (1989). Cyril Mango, *Le développement urbain de Constantinople (IVe–VIIe siècle)* (1990). Cyril Mango and Gilbert Dagron, eds., *Constantinople and Its Hinterland*, Twenty-seventh Spring Symposium of Byzantine Studies (1995).

Anthony A. M. Bryer

COPÁN is a major Classic Maya royal center on the southeastern frontier of Mesoamerica. Between A.D. 400 and 800 it was the capital of a regional polity covering several hundred square kilometers, centered on a small, highland river valley in western Honduras. Although Copán was known to Europeans since the sixteenth century, the explorations of John Stephens and Frederick Catherwood in 1839 and their subsequent publications describing its ruins and monuments drew popular and scholarly attention to the site. Systematic archaeological research by a variety of institutions began in 1889 and continued to 1946. Since 1975 renewed research by many institutions has focused both on the royal center of Copán itself and its larger sustaining region.

The Copán Main Group—the ritual/regal capital—covers approximately 54 acres (22 ha) and is famous for its superb architecture and many carved and inscribed monuments, including stelae, altars, and facade sculpture. Copán's Hieroglyphic Stairway is the longest known Classic Maya inscription/with 1,260 glyphs. Surrounding the Main Group is a one-half square mile (1 sq km) residential core that was occupied by subroyal elite groups. It is one of the densest concentrations of population known for any Classic Maya center.

Because of the intensity and variety of archaeological research we have an unusually clear picture of the growth and decline of the Copán polity. Small farming communities occupied the region prior to 1000 B.C. Population levels remained at a few thousand until at least A.D. 400. Around that time Classic Maya influences appeared in the form of art, architecture, and inscriptions, and a dynasty of local kings was founded. Considerable political consolidation occurred under the twelfth ruler, Smoke Imix (A.D. 628–695). His four successors greatly enlarged and elaborated the royal center and ruled over a growing population that eventually peaked at about 27,000 in A.D. 850. Copán's royal line came to an abrupt end shortly after A.D. 800, but lesser elites survived for several more generations. After A.D. 900 the polity experienced increasing political fragmentation and general population decline, and the valley was largely depopulated by A.D. 1200.

[See also MAYA CIVILIZATION, articles on CLASSIC MAYA COLLAPSE, INTRODUCTION, MAYA RULERS AND WARFARE; MESOAMERICA: CLASSIC PERIOD IN MESOAMERICA.]

David Webster

CRITICAL THEORY. The essence of a critical archaeology is to respond to the basic question: What is the use of doing archaeology within a democratic society? Although reading the past through the material remains excavated from archaeological sites makes immediate sense to readers of this volume as well as many members of the general public, the greater purpose of the knowledge drawn from archaeological data often remains incompletely identified. To what end does understanding how past actors lived in differing social, cultural, and environmental contexts move us? Additionally, what do funding institutions, such as the National Science Foundation (USA) or the National Endowment for the Humanities, receive in return for their support of archaeological field work and laboratory analysis? A critical archaeology responds to questions such as these.

Critical archaeology is a strain of post-modern thought that has clear Marxist roots. Though not alone, critical archaeologists have challenged the claims to objectivity in the interpretation of the past. Drawing from original work by European scholars such as Lukacs, Althusser, Foucault, members of the Frankfurt School (e.g., Adorno, Benjamin, Habermas), and also anthropologists like Barnett and Silverman, critical archaeologists have demonstrated that ideologies rooted in the present have a significant role in archaeological interpretations of the past. As described by Althusser (1971), these ideologies are, for a given society, the "taken-for-granteds," the "things that go without saying," and the "natural." Scholars who study ideology attempt to show that many unequal and exploitative relations are integral to the successful reproduction of a social order and can sustain systems of inequality, sexism, and racism. Critical archaeologists contend that such misrepresentation is active in the practice of contemporary archaeology. Their goal is to develop an archaeological perspective that identifies contemporary ideologies, demystifies them, and builds paths toward greater social consciousness within recipients of archaeological knowledge. It is assumed that these practices would free citizens to understand, challenge, and participate more equally in their own society.

Beginnings. The earliest thrust of critical archaeology was toward a clear understanding of the articulation of the present with the past. It stemmed from ethnographic studies of historical museums (e.g., Wallace, 1981), which made clear that the distinctions between past and present were being blurred in the usual depiction of prehistory and history as culminating in the present day. This was an ideological representation that removed the curator from the presentation of history, making past societies seem to move along through time and space unattended, ultimately arriving in an ever better present. This is the opposite path of a critical inquiry. The critical effort is to disclose how knowledgeable actors exist in and move through their social contexts, past and present. Critical ethnographers suggested a reflexive approach in which the central problem is not, "How did we get from the past to the present, [but] what is communicated by going from the present to the past" (Leone, 1981).

Carrying on from this point, critical archaeologists question the ideologies that stem from noncritical readings of history. In doing so, the relevance of archaeology toward the general critical inquiry becomes clear. Archaeology can do more than describe past lifeways; it can also show that the roots of modern society are arbitrary and not inevitable. From the perspective that "archaeology is capable of providing a critique of [present] society by using its history" (Leone et al., 1995), it can be understood how the taken-for-granted notions in a society came to be that way. The focus has been on modern capitalist societies and investigations that reveal how life was before the definition of the modern individual, time discipline, wage labor, and advanced capitalism. Critical archaeologists believe that modern ideologies can be challenged as arbitrary and as having origins in specific circumstances of class relations rather than being natural and timeless. This can be done by contextualizing the origins, or history, of these practices in discrete social forms and exploitative circumstances as these existed in the past.

Applications. Such work is exemplified in a series of publications of the study of historic New England undertaken by Russell G. Handsman and the American Indian Archaeological Institute (1981). In a series of articles published locally, he approached an archaeological study of sites in and around the Center Village of Canaan, Connecticut. Handsman's analysis of the formation of nucleated villages as part of the rise of capitalism and urbanization in New England reveals how objects and ideas having historical origins within distinct social structures and processes come to be taken by historians as givens or part of the *natural* social and physical landscape. The ideology Handsman recognizes is the "valuation of the individual, wealth, and the relation of persons to objects." His example is the "cultural separation" of the individual from the domain and ties of extended kinship, and how this modern construct was incorporated by historians in their understanding of the past. Handsman notes, "When modern historians assume that categories such as 'the family' or 'the individual' or 'the entrepreneur' existed in premodern [New England], they are transposing modern American categories into the historic past, making those people into us." This misrepresents New England's Native Americans, as well as European settlers of the seventeenth and early eighteenth centuries. The modern category of the individual is found throughout the transition to modern capitalist societies. The use of archaeology to study specialization and differentiation in material culture demonstrates the context of certain ways of thinking and living in modern life. By giving a history to the facets of a contemporary ideology, critical archaeology helps to disassociate the events, structures, and processes of the past from their naturalized connection with the present. According to Russell G. Handsman, a critical archaeology writes histories that show and explain "the structural continuities and . . . cultural discontinuities; bridges to the past and the breaks with it" (Handsman, 1981).

Social Consciousness. An alternative and complementary thrust of critical archaeology has been to move out from the academy into the community. In recognition of the observation that differing groups may claim differing meanings as valid or invalid, this strain of critical archaeology is a form of social activism. It supports descendent communities of unrecorded peoples and archaeology in general. This is a formal recognition that the social whole in which archaeologists exist is fragmented and weakly, if at all, cohesive, and that archaeology as political action is both a condition of, and possibly an antidote for, the modern capitalist societies in which archaeologists live. From within this context archaeologists must individually acknowledge their position. That is, archaeologists can be conscious social advocates for a plural society. Critical archaeologists suggest that students of the past can help define themselves and their work by collaborating with a living community in which they work as professionals. Those normally the subject of archaeology can define what the use of archaeology is as they define what they would like to know through their past, given their concerns about themselves in the present.

Recent work along these lines has been undertaken by Archaeology in Annapolis and some African Americans living there represented by the Banneker-Douglas Museum, the home of the State of Maryland's Commission on Afro-American History and Culture. This is a collaborative inquiry into the historical archaeology of African Americans in Annapolis. It has also been an experiment in the application of some of the ideas of Jurgen Habermas (1984). Habermas emphasizes the significance of standard speech acts and dialogues where the voices of subordinate groups are unheard in the practice of everyday life. An ideal dialogue for Habermas exists where the voices of all parties affected are heard equally without being filtered by social inequalities so that a more equal negotiation can occur. In the field of archaeology, this especially needs to be the case where competing interests concern meanings assigned to the past.

Such dialogues occurred in the development of the research design for African American archaeology in Annapolis. The first part of this process was archaeologists' recognition of the distinct relations African Americans in Annapolis have with history compared with whites. Paraphrasing Byron Rushing, African Americans want to know how and why they are here now, they want to know why there is no change for them now (Rushing as cited in Leone et al., 1995). With this in mind, a dialogue between the archaeologists and the directors of the Banneker-Douglas Museum resulted in three questions that became the guidelines for research: "Do African Americans have archaeology?" "We're tired of hearing about slavery; tell us about freedom!," and "Is there anything left from Africa?" These questions are at once archaeological, anthropological, and political since they involve the archaeologists in the struggles about beliefs and social and political values concerning contending political relationships of groups in the present to their pasts.

With the formulation of these research questions, four African American sites in Annapolis were excavated. Certain artifacts have proved informative toward understanding the experience of free blacks in Annapolis over the last 140 years. At the Gott's Court site (18AP63), a steel hot comb was excavated. Once archaeologists learned that this essentially African American artifact was used to straighten hair, it was thought that this artifact told of the assimilation of African Americans in the early twentieth century to combat racism. However, when the artifact and its interpretation were presented to the African American community, the archaeologists suffered a sobering critique. The African Americans said that the straightening comb merely gave the appearance of assimilation in the public world of Annapolis where racism was always open and potentially hostile. The archaeologists were themselves accused of racism because of their inability to recognize the conscious social strategy practiced by blacks in the past.

Archaeologists also learned of the importance of orally recounted stories to the African American community. These were especially vital to the local community as they were considered comparable to the written records maintained by the white community. Words, it became clear, were treated by African Americans as things to be cherished, guarded, and passed along through time. This may very well be additional evidence of efforts toward cultural autonomy practiced by African Americans.

The long-term outcome of the critical African American archaeology in Annapolis is clear. Notably, the relations between some of the African American community and archaeologists have been defined productively. Their fruitful collaboration is evident in the initially incorrect, but subsequently corrected, interpretations of the hot comb, the oral histories, and much of the rest of the archaeological remains.

Similar and powerful examples of the influence of some of the ideas embodied in critical thought are Baker's description of the Active Museum of Fascism and Resistance in Berlin (Baker, 1990), O'Neill's description of a community-based industrial museum in Scotland, and West's of a foundation for African American archaeology in South Carolina. Robert Layton's edited volume, *Conflict in the Archaeology of Living Traditions* (1989) contains many pieces that form the bases of an effectively critical approach to archaeological settings. Several similar conclusions have been reached by members of the Arizona State Museum (Thompson, 1991), who have given great weight to Native American concerns for some time. Some of these examples use critical theories explicitly; all illustrate a dialogue with those subject to archaeology.

Ultimately a critical archaeology is an anthropological effort exploring and hoping to affect the social consciousness of actors in the present and their relations to the past. It recognizes the variability in access to understanding the past and that multiple versions of the events of the past are likely to coexist. It hopes to confront these differing understandings by making people aware of this multiplicity and assumes that each version is an intact, valid, and internally coherent perspective. Such an approach works with descendent communities to retrieve histories from within their own perspectives. It can also provide a way to confront these different perspectives without destroying them.

[*See also* COGNITIVE ARCHAEOLOGY; CULTURAL ECOLOGY THEORY; CULTURE HISTORICAL THEORY; DARWINIAN THEORY; GENDER, ARCHAEOLOGY OF; GENERAL SYSTEMS THEORY; HIS-

TORICAL ARCHAEOLOGY; HISTORY OF ARCHAEOLOGY, INTEL-
LECTUAL; NATIONALISM; POLITICAL USES OF ARCHAEOLOGY;
POST-PROCESSUAL THEORY; PROCESSUAL THEORY; SCIENCE IN
ARCHAEOLOGY; THEORY IN ARCHAEOLOGY.]

■ Louis Althusser, "Ideology and Ideological State Apparatuses,"
in *Lenin and Philosophy* (1971), pp. 127–88. Steve Barnett and Martin
Silverman, "Separations in Capitalist Societies: Persons, Things,
Units and Relations," in *Ideology and Everyday Life* (1979), pp. 41–81.
Russell G. Handsman, "Early Capitalism and the Center Village of
Canaan, Connecticut: A Study of Transformations and Separa-
tions," *Artifacts* 9:3 (1981):1–22. Mark P. Leone, "Archaeology's
Relation to the Present and the Past," in *Modern Material Culture: The
Archaeology of Us*, ed. R. Gould and M. Schiffer (1981), pp. 5–13.
Michael Wallace, "Visiting the Past: History Museums in the United
States," *Radical History Review* 25 (1981) 63–96. Jurgen Habermas,
The Theory of Communicative Action, vol. 1, *Reason and the Rationaliza-
tion of Society* (1984). Robert Layton, ed., *Conflict in the Archaeology of
Living Traditions* (1989). Frederick Baker and Julian Thomas, eds.,
Writing the Past in the Present (1990). Raymond H. Thompson,
"Looking to the Future," *Museum News* (January/February 1991):
36–40. Mark P. Leone, Paul R. Mullins, Marian C. Creveling, Law-
rence Hurst, Barbara Jackson Nash, Lynn D. Jones, Hannah Jopling
Kaiser, George C. Logan, and Mark S. Warner, *Can an African-
American Historical Archaeology Be an Alternative Voice?* (1995).

Mark P. Leone and Christopher Matthews

CRO-MAGNONS are, in informal usage, a group among
the late Ice Age peoples of Europe. The Cro-Magnons are
identified with *Homo sapiens sapiens* of modern form, in the
time range ca. 35,000–10,000 B.P., roughly corresponding
with the period of the Upper *Paleolithic in archaeology.
The term "Cro-Magnon" has no formal taxonomic status,
since it refers neither to a species or subspecies nor to an
archaeological phase or culture. The name is not commonly
encountered in modern professional literature in English,
since authors prefer to talk more generally of anatomically
modern humans. They thus avoid a certain ambiguity in the
label "Cro-Magnon," which is sometimes used to refer to all
early moderns in Europe (as opposed to the preceding
*Neanderthals), and sometimes to refer to a specific human
group that can be distinguished from other Upper Paleolithic humans in the region. Nevertheless, the term "Cro-
Magnon" is still very commonly used in popular texts,
because it makes an obvious distinction with the Neanderthals, and also refers directly to people, rather than to
the complicated succession of archaeological phases that
make up the Upper Paleolithic. This evident practical value
has prevented archaeologists and human paleontologists—
especially in continental Europe—from dispensing entirely
with the idea of Cro-Magnons.

The Cro-Magnons take their name from a rock shelter in
the Vezere Valley in the Dordogne, within the famous village of Les Eyzies de Tayac. When the railway was being
constructed in 1868, parts of five skeletons were found
sealed in Pleistocene deposits, along with hearths and Aurignacian artifacts. Subsequently similar finds were made at
sites such as Combe Capelle and Laugerie-Basse in the
Dordogne, and Mentone and Grimaldi in Italy. Other specimens found earlier, such as Paviland in Britain and Engis in
Belgium could be set in the same group, and it became plain
that their physical makeup contrasted sharply with that of
Neanderthals discovered in other sites. Sufficient data to
build up this classic picture accumulated over a period, but
it was brought into sharp focus following the find of a
classic Neanderthal at La Chapelle in 1908. The early interpretations owe much to the French scholars Marcellin Boule
and Henri Vallois. Later research has extended the geographical distribution of similar humans and has provided
an absolute dating scale for them; however, later research
has also raised many questions about the origins of the Cro-
Magnons and their status as a coherent group.

Physical Characteristics and Adaptation. Cro-Magnons
were closely similar to modern humans, but more robust in
some features, especially of the cranium. They meet criteria
listed by Michael Day and Chris Stringer for modern humans, such as a short, high cranium and a discontinuous
supra-orbital torus (brow ridge). Many individuals were
well above present-day average in stature, often reaching
around 75 inches (190 cm). Their limbs were long, especially
in the forearms and lower legs, body proportions suggesting to some anthropologists that their origins lie in warm
climes, rather than Ice Age Europe.

Significant variability had already been recognized by
Boule, who attributed Negroid characters to some specimens from Grimaldi (placing them in a separate race). A
recent study has found that earlier specimens such as those
from Cro-Magnon and Mladec in the Czech Republic are
outside modern human range, whereas specimens later
than 26,000 B.P. generally fall within it. Emanuel Vlcek re-
gards the Mladec I finds as Cro-Magnons, but sees features
related to the Neanderthals in later Mladec II specimens
and ascribes later specimens from Dolni Vestonice and Predmosti specimens to a robust "Brno Group." Such findings
suggest that the original remains from Cro-Magnon are too
distinctive to serve as a template of identification for a race
all over Europe. If any overall trend can be picked out, it is
toward greater gracility as time progressed.

Chronology. Given the rarity of human remains, it is
easier to date the onset of the Upper Paleolithic than the first
appearance of people resembling the Cro-Magnons, which
is not necessarily the same event. Nevertheless, dates
around 40,000 B.P. seem highly likely. It is certain that populations of *Homo sapiens sapiens* became established throughout Europe in far less than 10,000 years. Since the 1950s the
chronology of these Late Pleistocene human populations
has been derived principally from radiocarbon dating. A
late Neanderthal found at St. Césaire in western France
with a Châtelperronian (initial Upper Paleolithic) industry
is dated to ca. 36,000 B.P. by thermoluminescence (TL), but
the Upper Paleolithic Aurignacian appears earlier in northern Spain at ca. 42,000–39,000 B.P., as shown by radiocarbon
and uranium series dating. It is widely assumed that the
Aurignacian is associated with modern (i.e., Cro-Magnon-
like) populations, and that the Châtelperronian, though
associated with Neanderthals, may have been triggered by
the cultural effects of modern human presence elsewhere in
the region (a so-called bow-wave phenomenon).

Thereafter the Cro-Magnons were continuously represented in Europe for 20,000 years or more. It might be
convenient to end the Cro-Magnons with the glacial maximum of 18,000 B.P., but in France their characteristics persist
in Magdalenian populations through the later part of the
glaciation until about 12,000–10,000 B.P. At this stage human
populations began to become more gracile.

Geographical Distribution. Human remains are extremely scarce in relation to the number of archaeological
sites. The earliest Upper Paleolithic in France is almost
devoid of skeletal remains; finds such as Cro-Magnon, Abri
Pataud, and Combe Capelle are probably several thousand
years later. These are a minimal sampling of a distribution
that archaeological traces strongly suggest was much
wider. Thus there are no early remains of Cro-Magnons

from Spain, Greece, or Turkey, but populations were probably present. To the north, Upper Paleolithic human remains have been found in Britain, represented by Paviland and Kent's Cavern, and in Germany, by Hahnöfersand. Farther east, burials are well represented in the Upper Paleolithic records of the Czech Republic, and in Russia at Kostenki and Sunghir. In the south numbers of finds are known from Italy.

Cultural Associations. Most of the Upper Paleolithic humans are found in deliberate burials, often single but sometimes in groups, and frequently associated with grave goods, such as necklaces of pierced teeth. Such finds are known from a sequence of archaeological phases beginning with the Aurignacian (e.g., Combe Capelle or Mladec), but the succeeding Gravettian (ca. 29,000–20,000 B.P.) is richer in burials (e.g., those of Dolni Vestonice in the Czech Republic). It has yielded fewer specimens in western Europe. In southwestern Europe the Solutrean phase is associated with similar populations. They are found again in the Magdalenian or Epi-Gravettian. By this time preserved human remains are much more numerous, and they are known from most parts of Europe. Grave goods sometimes attest to highly developed artistic abilities. The Cro-Magnons were responsible for much art, but rarely figured in their own work.

Relationship with the Neanderthals and Other Hominids. Recent work has shown that early modern humans (sometimes called Proto-Cro-Magnons) first appeared at least 100,000 B.P. They are documented in Africa, but most specifically on the cave sites of Skhul and Qafzeh in Israel in the period 100,000–90,000 B.P. The Cro-Magnon specimens of Europe must be derived ultimately from one of these ancestral populations, but the available finds show no continuity. Indeed, by 60,000 B.P. Neanderthals featured in the Middle East, and the Proto-Cro-Magnons may have been displaced to the south. It seems likely that they returned somewhere around 50,000 B.P. and flowed into Europe, although there is no documentation in the Middle East other than a burial at Ksar Akil in Lebanon. There is also no close similarity, according to most authors, between the Proto-Cro-Magnons and the Cro-Magnons. The simplicity of these hypotheses is belied by the complexity of the scarce data that we do have. Just as the St. Césaire find in France documented a late Neanderthal and placed constraints on our ideas about the distribution of the early Cro-Magnons, so one new early Cro-Magnon discovery could dramatically alter our view of their origins.

[*See also* HUMANS, MODERN, *articles on* ORIGINS OF MODERN HUMANS, PEOPLING THE GLOBE.]

■ Marcellin Boule and Henri Vallois, *Fossil Men* (1957). Paul Mellars and Chris Stringer, eds., *The Human Revolution* (1989). Paul Mellars, ed., *The Emergence of Modern Humans* (1990). Alan Bilsborough, *Human Evolution* (1992). Gunter Brauer and Fred H. Smith, eds., *Continuity or Replacement: Controversies in Homo sapiens Evolution* (1992). Martin J. Aitken, Christopher B. Stringer, and Paul A. Mellars, eds., *The Origins of Modern Humans and the Impact of Chronometric Dating* (1993). John A. J. Gowlett, *Ascent to Civilization*, 2nd ed. (1993). Chris Stringer and Clive Gamble, *In Search of the Neanderthals* (1993).

John A. J. Gowlett

CULTURAL ECOLOGY THEORY has been a fundamental perspective of American archaeology and anthropology since World War II. Its origin and development are most directly associated with Julian Steward, an anthropologist whose interests incorporated both ethnography and archaeology. Steward succinctly defined cultural ecology as "the study of the processes by which a society adapts to its environment" (1968). The term "environment" here is conceived in its broadest sense, including, for example, other social groups. As the word "adaptation" implies, cultural ecology is related conceptually to cultural evolution, and specifically to Steward's own concept of multilinear evolution, which stressed the search for regularities in independent sequences of evolutionary change.

Central to cultural ecology was Steward's idea of the culture core, those cultural features that mediate most directly between humans and their environments and that are essential to subsistence and other basic economic activities. Such features might include technological, social, political, or ideological elements of culture. Core features are most heavily determined by environmental constraints and interactions, while others not as directly linked to the core are determined by cultural-historical factors such as *diffusion or random innovation. Human culture is inextricably linked to the larger systems of the natural world.

Steward advocated cultural ecology both as a theory concerning the nature of *culture and its transformation and as a set of research methods for investigating cultural phenomena. Theoretically, the most powerful explanations of evolutionary change were to be found in the environment/culture core interaction; methodologically, research should identify and investigate core attributes of culture such as technology, subsistence, economy, the organization of work, landholding, and inheritance, since these are situated most directly at the interface between environment and culture. Steward believed that ecological analysis yielded the most powerful and straightforward results when applied to simple small-scale cultures that are technologically unsophisticated and not buffered from nature by complex supracommunity institutions. This conviction is reflected in his own predilection for the study of hunter-gatherers, particularly his classic *The Economic and Social Basis of Primitive Bands* (1936) and *Basin-Plateau Aboriginal Sociopolitical Groups* (1938).

The development of cultural ecology was partly a reaction against the atheoretical, particularistic, culturalogical, and cultural-historical approaches that dominated American anthropology and archaeology before World War II. While eschewing the environmental determinism and equally sterile "possibilism" advocated by some human geographers, Steward championed the search for causation of sociocultural phenomena, adopting an explicitly natural science perspective. He thus was among the very first materialists in American anthropology. His formulation of cultural ecology was also influenced by the work of Oswald Spengler, Max Weber, and Arnold Toynbee, as well as Karl Wittfogel, and in turn helped shape Wittfogel's theory of hydraulic civilization.

Cultural ecology had an enormous accelerating influence on archaeology beginning in the late 1940s. Until that time American archaeology had remained largely aloof from the strong tradition of ecological, *environmental, and *economic archaeology long established in Europe. Linked much more closely to anthropology than its European counterparts, archaeology was seen by most anthropologists as the poor handmaiden of ethnography, incapable of a robust identity of its own.

Ecological perspectives helped to alter this situation dramatically beginning in the late 1940s. By encouraging Gordon Willey to undertake the settlement pattern component of the archaeological investigation of the Viru Valley in 1946, Steward helped pioneer the emergence of a strong tradition of *settlement archaeology that later included the work of William T. Sanders and Robert McCormick Adams. This methodological innovation stimulated the extension of ecological and materialist perspectives to the comparative study of the evolution of complex societies. Partly under the stimulus of Steward's ideas, Robert Braidwood began his research into the origins of agriculture in the Near East, utilizing a team of natural scientists who could effectively augment the skills and interpretations of archaeologists. The issues of the agricultural transformation and the evolution of sociocultural complexity have since been dominant themes of American archaeological research.

Cultural ecology also helped to form strong linkages with scholars in related fields who developed their own interests in archaeology, most notably the geographer Karl Butzer.

Several of the basic precepts of the "New Archaeology" of the 1960s had roots in earlier formulations of cultural ecology. These include the idea of the fundamental adaptive, evolutionary functions of culture, the search for causation and explanation using overtly scientific research models, the interdependence of the archaeological and ethnographic records, and the relevance of biological anthropology.

Ecological perspectives especially dominated American archaeology between 1955 and 1980, although they increasingly diverged from the original cultural ecology perspective in important ways. New elements included sophisticated quantification, adoption of formal models from the biological sciences (e.g., energy flow), and human geography (e.g., locational analysis), as well as concern with agronomy, human fertility, demography, and nutrition. In addition, largely because of the explanatory power of settlement research, ecological investigations of complex societies have become commonplace. Steward himself had emphasized the cultural rather than ecological dimensions of cultural ecology, but by the 1970s ecological perspectives and methods were much more obtrusive, and remain so today.

Criticisms of cultural ecology focus both on Steward's original formulation and on its derived, more explicitly ecological approaches. Among the former are that Steward emphasized qualitative rather than quantitative data, and that the culture core concept is a muddled reinvention or rediscovery of much older, more useful principles devised by Karl Marx. More generally, cultural ecological research is characterized as deterministic, overly reductionist, tautological, dehumanizing, and just plain boring. Such criticisms originate most frequently from structuralists, mentalists, humanists, culture historians, and post-processual archaeologists. None of these "schools" or approaches is necessarily antithetical to ecological perspectives. Revealingly, many of those who offer such criticisms themselves conduct research that has fundamental adaptive, evolutionary, ecological implications.

Archaeology, particularly in the United States, has always been prone to intellectual fashion. Today, many scholars who would not characterize themselves as cultural ecologists in the Stewardian mold, or perhaps not even ecologists or materialists at all, have nevertheless been heavily influenced by the cultural ecology tradition begun by Steward. Ecological perspectives continue to thrive, providing a strong theoretical, scientific, and methodological core of ongoing research. Seen as a pervasive and dynamic point of view rather than an identifiable discipline or school, cultural ecology's legacy includes the convictions that humans and their cultures are integral parts of larger, natural systems, that causal, scientific explanations of cultural phenomena are possible, and that the enterprise of archaeology requires strong linkages not only with the other subfields of anthropology, but with the hard sciences as well.

[See also CRITICAL THEORY; CULTURE HISTORICAL THEORY; GENERAL SYSTEMS THEORY; MARXIST THEORY; POST-PROCESSUAL THEORY; PROCESSUAL THEORY; STRUCTURALISM; THEORY IN ARCHAEOLOGY.]

■ Julian Steward, *Cultural Ecology* (1968).

David Webster

CULTURAL RESOURCE MANAGEMENT

Introduction
Collections Management
Site Management
Global Issues

INTRODUCTION

The term "cultural resources" includes prehistoric and historic sites, any materials recovered from these sites, and places or areas of historic or religious significance. Cultural resources management involves the preservation and recovery of cultural resources that might otherwise be threatened by vandalism or construction. The legal protection for cultural resources varies greatly among countries. Within countries it varies, depending on whether the cultural resource is located on public land, on private land, or underwater.

Although the term "cultural resources" potentially includes all sites and all artifacts in the world, in practice, decisions must be made regarding which cultural resources to protect. Generally this decision entails including a cultural resource on a list of sites to be protected. In the U. S., the list is the National Register of Historic Places. In England, sites of national importance are scheduled by the Secretary of State. On the international level, in 1972 UNESCO adopted the International Convention for the Protection of the World Cultural and Natural Heritage and correspondingly created the World Heritage List.

Protecting cultural resources takes two broad forms: in-place preservation and the preservation of artifacts and site records in a museum or other collections facility. In-place preservation provides an opportunity for the future study of the cultural resource and the opportunity for public education. Preservation of artifacts and records is less desirable, but is the only option when the site has been destroyed by vandalism or construction. In either case there is a long-term obligation for the protection and conservation of the site or the collection.

In the U. S., cultural resources investigations conducted to comply with the National Historic Preservation Act of 1966 dominate archaeological research. Far more money is expended on surveys and excavations of endangered sites than on field projects funded by grants and focused on a particular research topic. The main concern created by this situation is the short time frame allotted for excavation, analysis, and the reporting of results. The sites to be excavated will usually be destroyed, so therefore research designs must be broader. One does not have the option of leaving part of the site for future investigators. Reports of these investigations are often distributed in limited quantities to a few state and federal agencies, which reduces their impact on professional and public audiences.

A second area of controversy in cultural resources management focuses on the artifacts and the question of ownership. To varying degrees, the nation, the landowner, the descendants of the site's occupants, and the person or institution in possession of the artifact all can exert claims of ownership. One principal area of controversy involves the movement of artifacts across international boundaries. In an effort to manage the problem, UNESCO drafted the Convention on the Means of Prohibiting and Preventing Illicit Import, Export, and Transfer of Ownership of Cultural Property in 1970. In the U. S., a second area of controversy involves the claims of Native American peoples to human remains and associated artifacts, a claim which has been supported by the passage of the Native American Graves and Repatriation Act in 1990 (*see* Reburial and Repatriation).

[*See also* ARCHIVAL MANAGEMENT OF ARCHAEOLOGICAL RECORDS; DESTRUCTION OF THE PAST.]

■ T. F. King, P. P. Hickman, and G. Berg, *Anthropology in Historic Preservation: Caring for Culture's Clutter* (1977). H. Cleere, ed., *Approaches to the Archaeological Heritage* (1984). L. V. Prott and P. J. O'Keefe, *Law and the Cultural Heritage. Volume 1. Discovery & Excavation. Volume 3: Movement* (1984, 1989). I. McBryde, ed., *Who Owns the Past?* (1985). P. M. Messenger, ed., *The Ethics of Collecting Cultural Property* (1989). H. Cleere, ed., *Archaeological Heritage Management in the Modern World* (1989).

David L. Carlson

COLLECTIONS MANAGEMENT

Every year archaeologists in cultural resource management and academia generate mountains of artifacts, archaeological samples, paper records, computer disks, and photographs through excavation and survey. After final analysis is complete, the material remains and associated documents are often stored in a repository located in a local museum, a local historical society, or a campus museum. Curation of these materials is essential for several reasons. First, the collections are often irreplaceable, representing the only source of information on destroyed or reburied sites. Second, as archaeology continues to change, older collections may be subjected to newer and improved analyses. Finally, archaeological collections are very useful in educating the public.

In the past, like their academic colleagues, many contract archaeologists did not consider the long-term storage needs of the wide range of different materials procured and produced through their excavations, surveys, and analyses. Collection managers and archaeologists alike perceived archaeological collections as indestructible and stable since they had survived burial in the ground. This indestructibility and stability even extended, in a figurative sense, to the associated documents. Thus, when analysis was completed the many artifacts and samples, still in their brown kraft paper bags, were simply boxed with research records. Once boxed, the accepted practice was to hand over all of the material remains and associated documentation to the state or local historical society, the natural history museum, the campus museum, the historical park, or the general-purpose regional museum. Accordingly, when a collection was transferred to the facility, archaeologists assumed that the facility was ultimately responsible for its long-term storage needs and preservation.

Within the last ten years, the accepted practice described above has changed dramatically. In the United States, the change was a result of two factors: the phenomenal growth in cultural resource management and a decrease in federal funding for new excavations. The surge in cultural resource management created large numbers of collections and an increased demand for collection storage space. Collection managers throughout the United States were faced with dwindling storage space.

The decrease in federal funding for new excavations induced many archaeologists to re-analyze stored collections. Many of these archaeologists, and collection managers, were horrified when they went to open old collections. Instead of collections preserved in a pristine state they found deteriorated maps, fading field notes, mold-encrusted reports, decaying slides and photographs, and thousands of keypunched cards for computer technology no longer in use. Artifacts from different units and levels were mixed, their original paper bags having burst and decayed with time. Portions of collections were absent as a result of collection managers' and curators' desire to make more storage space by throwing out bulk samples of ceramics, bone, soil, shell, or large artifacts such as groundstone.

The condition of stored collections led a few archaeologists and collection managers to demand that the archaeological community begin to take responsibility for preserving the past they were digging up. Turning to the museum community, these pioneers found knowledge they could readily tap regarding the environmental, storage, and curation needs of the wide range of materials recovered through excavation and produced in analyses. In the United States, Elizabeth Sanford in "Conservation of Artifacts: A Question of Survival" (*Historic Archaeology*, 1971) and Katherine Singley in "Caring for Artifacts After Excavation—Some Advice for Archaeologists" (*Historic Archaeology*, 1981) alerted the field of American archaeology to its responsibility. In Britain, during the mid-1970s and early 1980s, the government and the Archaeology Section of the United Kingdom Institute for Conservation developed standards for the packaging and storage of freshly excavated artifacts.

During the late 1980s in the United States, the voice for the preservation of archaeological records grew stronger. The federal government enacted regulations that specified the long-term curatorial capabilities required of repositories that store federally owned and administered archaeological collections. The regulations required that the repository have the capability to accession, label, catalog, store, maintain, inventory, and conserve collections on a long-term basis using common museum practices. The regulations also required the repositories themselves to meet museum environmental standards, to maintain records on collections, to protect records from fire, to dedicate requisite facilities, equipment, and space to the physical plant, to be physically secure, to have educated and trained staff, to inspect all collections regularly for damage and deterioration, and to conduct inventories periodically. This federal document, 36 CFR Part 79 (*Federal Register*, 1990), has become the standard for all repositories to set and to maintain regardless of whether or not they house federal collections.

Repository collection managers have turned to archaeologists to share the preservation burden by issuing curation guidelines to all archaeologists and cultural resource management firms wishing to store collections. The guidelines often contain explicit procedures for the cleaning, labeling, cataloging, documenting, and packaging of the collection prior to being deposited in the repository. Many guidelines also include a prorated cost for the repository's services of long-term storage and perpetual curation of archaeological collections and associated documents.

Today, archaeologists, whether in academia or in cultural resource management, are requested to consider curatorial needs early in project planning, to include costs for proper curation and perpetual storage in their project budgets, to select a curational facility, and to adequately document, clean, and stabilize the collection prior to depositing in a repository. Discussion, however, still revolves around who is fiscally responsible for the curation, preservation, and conservation of older non-federal collections, which materials are to be kept and which are to be discarded before storage, and what to do about diminishing space, staff, and funding.

[See also ARCHIVAL MANAGEMENT OF ARCHAEOLOGICAL RECORDS; DESTRUCTION OF THE PAST.]

■ Susan Pearce, Archaeological Curatorship (1990).

Cynthia Ann Bettison

SITE MANAGEMENT

Site management seeks to balance development with the preservation of archaeological information in some form, either through in-place preservation or data recovery. However, before we can discuss site management, an archaeological site needs to be defined. Professional archaeologists think of sites as locations on a landscape where past human activities occurred. Usually, but not always, these sites contain products of past human activities such as artifacts, features, architecture, or rock art. The distribution of these products is continuous across a landscape with densities varying from sparse to very dense. The enactment of laws and regulations protecting the products of past human manufacture compel archaeologists to impose artificial boundaries around areas with higher densities. We call these higher-density areas archaeological sites. We can no longer depend on ill-defined site definitions because archaeological investigations, particularly those performed as part of environmental compliance activities, require explicit site definitions.

What constitutes an archaeological site can be very different to nonarchaeologists. A site may have importance to a group because significant events occurred there, but these events may not have left any physical traces or these physical traces may no longer exist. Even sites with physical remains may be interpreted very differently by professionals and nonprofessionals. For the discussion here, a site is an area of previous human activity around which a discrete boundary can be drawn. The emphasis is placed on the presence of material remains to aid in boundary delineation.

A variety of options exist concerning the fate of a site after it is located and defined. The disposition of sites is at the core of forward-thinking site management. The oldest component of site management in the United States is site preservation. Site preservation seeks to insure the perpetual existence of a site. As populations from the eastern United States began to settle areas throughout the west in the nineteenth century, the destruction of large, prehistoric sites located in the Southwest accelerated. By 1894 Congress and the President were convinced that protecting deterio-

rating adobe structures at a site called Casa Grande located southeast of Phoenix, Arizona, was in the national interest. Less than fifteen years later, protection of all archaeological material on federal lands occurred in the landmark legislation known as the Antiquities Act of 1906.

The role and obligations of the federal government in the protection of archaeological materials throughout the United States has increased ever since. Severe criminal and civil penalties now exist. The prosecution of individuals and groups caught damaging and/or destroying archaeological sites on federal lands is just beginning. This is significant because one-third of all land in the United States is controlled by the federal government.

Modern site management can take many forms, from actual avoidance by a proposed project such as a highway or a new building, to excavation of a site to recover information through scientific investigation. In-place preservation and data recovery are options and are often used together when a portion of a site or several sites are affected by a project.

Outside of project-related impacts to sites, site management can take the form of site stewardship programs where an individual or group becomes caretakers and helps to interpret a site for visitors, and the purchase of a site with the intent to protect it from development or destruction.

Another aspect of site management, but one rarely used when the normal compliance procedures fail, is mandated site preservation. In wetlands mitigation, on which mandated site preservation is modeled, new wetlands are created or former wetlands are restored as a substitute for wetlands that are legally destroyed. The character of these new wetlands may not be the same as those they replace (e.g., species diversity, soil chemistry, and water availability), but by presidential order, total wetlands acreage is not reduced and usually is increased. Whereas wetlands can be created and destroyed, the destruction of archaeological sites results in the loss of contextual information.

No archaeologist, not even the most experienced or skillful, can ever reconstruct a site to understand past human behavior once that site is destroyed. If we fail to protect a site or sites, mandated site preservation should be available as an option to redress errors harmful to the archaeological record.

Mandated site preservation should be viewed as a flexible concept tailored to local circumstances. Thus, options could include: purchasing one or more sites to physically protect them from pending or future development; enhancing educational and/or research programs at an archaeological site; making those individuals responsible for site damage or destruction participate in archaeological projects; donating property containing a site to a nonprofit organization such as the Archaeological Conservancy; and providing financial support for the rehabilitation of existing archaeological materials and associated records. Whatever the option chosen, mandated site preservation should be conducted as close as possible to the site that is adversely affected. The support and involvement of local residents is crucial to the success of any program.

As individual sites continue to dwindle and disappear due to natural deterioration or human depredation against them, we need to ensure that those sites that remain are protected, or their information retrieved, before the opportunity to act is gone forever. Forward-thinking site management, through the use of in-place preservation, scientifically conceived and legally conducted data recovery, and a program of mandated site preservation, can ensure that the archaeological record is available for future study and educational programs.

[*See also* DESTRUCTION OF THE PAST.]

■ Don D. Fowler, "Conserving American Archaeological Resources," in *American Archaeology Past and Future*, David J. Meltzer, Don D. Fowler, and Jeremy A. Sabloff, eds. (1985): 135–162. A. Gwynn Henderson, "The Kentucky Archaeological Registry: Landowner Participation in Site Preservation," *National Park Service, Archaeological Assistance Program, Technical Brief* No. 6 (1989). Hal Rothman, *Preserving Different Paths* (1989). Sherry Hutt, Elwood W. Jones, and Martin E. McAllister, *Archaeological Resource Protection* (1993).

Marc Kodack

GLOBAL ISSUES

The preamble to the 1972 UNESCO Convention for the Protection of the World Cultural and Natural Heritage notes that "deterioration or disappearance of any item of the . . . heritage constitutes a harmful impoverishment of the heritage of all the nations of the world" (UNESCO, 1983).

The major issue confronting the preservation and management of the world's cultural heritage is that of creating favorable official and public attitudes. While every member of the United Nations has legislative protection for its antiquities and some form of official agency responsible for implementing that legislation, only in rare cases (such as the Scandinavian countries) is the concept of preservation deeply embedded in the public consciousness. No CRM system can be considered to be effective unless it has complete public sympathy and support, and for this to be achieved significant resources must be made available for education and promotion at both national and international levels.

The social and economic changes identified in the 1972 Convention as threatening the heritage are very diverse. Many threats are posed by development in various forms. Infrastructural projects, such as dams, pipelines, roads, railways, and airfields, can have disastrous effects on archaeological and historical monuments and sites. The best known example is that of the Aswan High Dam, which led to the submergence of hundreds of square miles of land rich in such monuments. In this case a UNESCO-sponsored international campaign led to the recording and rescue of the most important of these, but much was lost. In such cases it is essential that CRM specialists should be involved from the earliest stages of planning, so as to avoid direct impact on monuments and sites wherever possible. The effectiveness of this approach is vividly illustrated by the route of the natural-gas pipeline network constructed throughout Denmark between 1979 and 1986.

Mineral extraction is also a source of considerable threat to the heritage. Following the oil crisis of 1973 certain countries were faced with the need to exploit alternative energy sources. As a result, enormous areas of western Bohemia and eastern Germany were turned into lunar landscapes for the open-pit mining of lignite. Modern concrete construction is heavily dependent upon the use of sand and gravel, which are quarried in enormous quantities in all parts of the world. Peat bogs provide a unique environment for the preservation of organic archaeological artifacts, as demonstrated by the Somerset Levels in southwestern Britain, but peat is a material that is used both as fuel and fertilizer, and as a result much information is lost every year.

Traditional agricultural techniques have little impact on buried archaeological sites, but the advent of mechanized plowing techniques and the increased use of chemical fertilizers result in the destruction, both physical and chemical, of fragile buried sites. Large-scale forestry is equally destructive, in both the planting and the felling stages: the most devastating impact is undoubtedly in the Amazon Basin, where past and present are being ruthlessly eliminated.

Third World countries are especially at risk so far as the heritage is concerned. New industrial and infrastructural projects, often financed by developed countries or international agencies, are pressed forward remorselessly, taking little or no heed of their impact on cultural resources. The World Bank has taken a laudable initiative in this respect, requiring preliminary impact assessment to be carried out for all projects that it funds, but its approach is still exceptional. Many of the world's most important archaeological monuments are located in developing countries in Africa, Asia, and Latin America, which have woefully inadequate resources for their proper management. International agencies such as UNESCO have been responsible for attracting funds to restore and preserve some of these, such as Old Havana or the Cultural Triangle of central Sri Lanka (Anuradhapura, Polonnaruwa, and Sigirya). Bilateral projects have also been developed, such as those between Sweden and several countries of East Africa. However, there is a pressing need for more international aid to be allocated to this sector, particularly in the provision of technical assistance and training.

Industrialization creates another form of severe threat to cultural resources, resulting from atmospheric pollution. The Taj Mahal has suffered for many years from acid attack from the emissions from nearby factories, and it was only in 1993 that the Indian government took steps to relocate these factories. A long legal struggle was necessary before the Greek government decided not to authorize the construction of an aluminum smelter close to the great classical site of Delphi. Traffic is also a source of chemical attack on monuments in historic cities. The pollution in Athens constitutes a grave threat to the marble of the Parthenon, and the civic authorities in Rome in 1994 were still wrestling with the chemical erosion of its wealth of monuments.

Mass tourism is a phenomenon of the late twentieth century which also threatens the world's cultural resources. The physical erosion by millions of pairs of feet each year on sites such as Ephesus, Pompeii, Luxor, Great Zimbabwe, or Stonehenge calls for the introduction of more stringent control over access and routing of visitors, a field that requires urgent study. This needs to be coupled with the provision of interpretive facilities and documentation oriented toward different levels of visitor interest. Care must be taken to avoid a Disneyland approach to cultural resources, for which the "heritage industry" has been deservedly castigated in recent years. Attention should also be focused on the immediate surroundings of major monuments, to avoid the undesirable clutter of souvenir stalls and worse which disfigure the Giza plateau or the environs of Pompeii.

Another grave threat to the world's cultural resources comes from the growth in the looting of archaeological sites to satisfy the illicit trade in antiquities. The 1970 UNESCO Convention on the Means of Prohibiting and Preventing the Illicit Import, Export, and Transfer of Ownership of Cultural Property provides the appropriate legislative instrument, but it has significantly not been ratified by those countries at the center of this iniquitous trade, such as Germany, the Netherlands, Switzerland, or the United Kingdom, with the result that it has had little effect overall. It remains to be seen whether the 1992 Revised European Convention on the Protection of the Archaeological Heritage, which contains provisions relating to this traffic, will be ratified and implemented by these countries. In the meantime, the trade continues, abetted by international dealers in the flourishing black market who provide a ready outlet for the results of clandestine excavations, in countries such as Cyprus, Guatemala, Ecuador, Thailand, and Turkey. The prime object should be to stamp out the trade at the level of the dealers and auction houses that benefit from it, while at the same time making full use of national statutes such as the U.S. Archaeological Resources Protection Act of 1979, which is belatedly beginning to discourage pot hunters and metal-detector users. At the same time, serious attention should be given to the protection of historic wrecks in international waters, so as to end the plundering of such vessels as the Dutch East Indiaman *Geldermalsen* and the Spanish treasure ship *Atocha*.

Finally, there is the tragic impact of war on the heritage. Recent events such as the Gulf War and the civil strife in former Yugoslavia have shown the 1954 UNESCO Convention for the Protection of Cultural Property in the Event of Armed Conflict to be ineffective and largely ignored, even by signatory nations. Work is currently beginning to revise this Convention and give it more teeth; however, its implementation will demand a considerable effort of will on the part of its signatories. The problems created by civil war, illustrated by the destruction of the famous medieval bridge at Mostar (Croatia), will be more intractable, but this should not preclude every effort being made to draw up some enforceable international rules.

[See also DESTRUCTION OF THE PAST; ETHICS OF ARCHAEOLOGY AND COLLECTING; TRAFFICKING IN ANTIQUITIES.]

■ Karl E. Meyer, *The Plundered Past* (1973). UNESCO, *Conventions and Recommendations of UNESCO concerning the Protection of the Cultural Heritage* (1983). Joachim Reichstein, "Federal Republic of Germany," in *Approaches to the Archaeological Heritage,* ed. Henry Cleere (1984), pp. 37–47. Henry Cleere, ed., *Archaeological Heritage Management in the Modern World* (1989). Council of Europe, *European Convention on the Protection of the Archaeological Heritage (Revised)* (1992).

Henry Cleere

CULTURE, as commonly used in anthropology, refers to the way of life of a people, including patterns of both thought and behavior. The concept is rooted in the German intellectual tradition, and it came into general use among Anglo-American anthropologists in the last half of the nineteenthcentury. Its meaning underwent a fundamental change at the beginning of the twentieth century, and the meaning that developed then, with modifications, still prevails within the discipline.

The nineteenth-century meaning of the term gave a central place to both progress and reason. It was assumed by such writers as Edward *Tylor and Lewis Henry *Morgan that lower forms of culture—savagery and barbarism—eventually gave rise to the highest form—civilization—and that this came about with the progressive development of the human mind. For example, myths were conceived as mistaken attempts to explain such phenomena as storms and geological formations, but as intelligence developed,

tales of this kind were eventually replaced by science. Plural marriage, such as polygyny, originated as an attempt to rise above a life of unregulated sexual unions, but eventually the higher form of monogamy was achieved. The blood feud developed among savage peoples as an attempt to protect individual rights, but this was eventually replaced by the more prudent systems of justice of modern society. The nineteenth-century culture concept was closely linked with the notion of race: it was assumed that dark-skinned peoples not only have lower forms of culture, but are less intelligent as well.

The twentieth-century meaning of culture is closely associated with the work of Franz Boas, who emigrated to the United States from Germany in the 1880s and eventually became a towering figure in American anthropology. The changes in his usage of the term were apparent just before the turn of the century. In the concept of culture that emerged in his work, a central place was given to learning rather than reason or intelligence: culture now was conceived as a body of patterns that one learns through interaction with other members of society, and people were seen to adhere to cultural forms not because they are intelligent enough to grasp the truth or usefulness of the traits but because they have assimilated the patterns of their social milieu. This line of thought had major implications for race. Since differences among peoples now were conceived as a product of upbringing and not intelligence, the idea of racial differences in intelligence lost its force. Racial explanations for cultural diversity were discredited in the context of the new culture concept. Boas and his students actively opposed racial explanations of behavior, and their published work on this topic was influential in both professional and popular literature.

The twentieth-century concept of culture helped to redefine the nature of the human character. Whereas the nineteenth-century culture concept assumed that people are oriented largely by a process of reasoning that is universal among human beings—although some people are more intelligent and therefore able to achieve higher forms of reason than others—from the twentieth-century perspective people are oriented rather by a body of cultural patterns that are historically conditioned and learned. These patterns include both emotional and unconscious dimensions. Thus, according to the twentieth-century view, much of culture is beyond the level of conscious awareness, including such features as values and implicit assumptions about the world. Similarly, some twentieth-century anthropologists became interested in the ways in which the emotional makeup of the personality is shaped by cultural conditioning and in the differences in personality structures among societies.

The new concept of culture also had implications for the notion of progress. On one hand, it was no longer thought that history is guided by a singular process of increasing rationality, or that cultures at the same level of development and intelligence are roughly comparable, regardless of where they are situated in the world. Rather, cultural phenomena were conceived in terms of their own historicity: cultures are historically conditioned, the result of complex and variable historical processes. For example, people borrow traits from their neighbors, and this, not levels of intelligence, helps to explain the cultural inventory of a particular society. On the other hand, the notion of progress was subverted by the growth of relativism. One version of relativity holds that there are no culture-free grounds for evaluating or judging other cultures: any standard that a person might use will reflect the historically conditioned values of his or her society. According to the other version, the features of a given culture are suitable given the local context: for example, the blood feud is appropriate in certain kinds of societies in which European systems of justice would not work.

From the twentieth-century perspective, the nineteenth-century version of culture was ethnocentric, for it employed Western standards for judging other ways of life. The contrast between the two versions of culture is graphically revealed in that, in the nineteenth century, the term was used exclusively in the singular. Anthropologists wrote of different degrees of culture, and they referred to peoples as being more or less cultured. By contrast, in the twentieth-century usage, the term appears in the plural: one speaks of different cultures, all peoples being equally cultured.

Understanding cultural diversity became a central problem for anthropology once the nineteenth-century framework had been overturned: anthropologists now were faced with the problem of how to understand or account for the differences among peoples if these differences were not associated with degrees of intelligence. The major theoretical developments of twentieth-century anthropology relate to this question. The work of Ruth Benedict, one of Boas's students, is illustrative. She elaborated a cultural theory which posited that each culture tends to be characterized by a distinctive emotional theme or pattern. For example, she argued that Plains Indian culture was oriented toward a set of aggressive, individualistic values, whereas the Pueblo Indians were characterized by a configuration which emphasized the golden mean or moderation. In her view, the historical development of a culture represents the progressive elaboration of its distinctive pattern, and differences in cultural configurations constitute the essence of cultural diversity.

Functionalism is another important approach to culture that developed in the twentieth century. This approach is most closely associated in anthropology with A. R. Radcliffe-Brown and Bronislaw Malinowski, who held that such institutions as religion, magical practices, and kinship rules have very subtle beneficial effects—or functions —that are unrecognized by the members of society. For example, according to Malinowski, the function of magic is to reduce people's anxieties in the face of danger or uncertainty, and therefore to make them better able to cope. The diversity of institutions reflects the variety of ways in which the needs of both individuals and societies can be met, and the key to understanding an item of culture is to grasp the functions it performs.

A third example of the twentieth-century approaches to culture is the cultural ecology of Julian Steward. According to Steward, each society goes through a long-term process of adjustment or adaptation to the local environment, which is crucial in giving the culture its basic shape or form. Thus, cultural diversity is understood in regard to adaptive processes. For example, according to Steward, leadership patterns among hunter-gatherers vary in relation to differences in subsistence patterns, for different types of leadership are needed depending on the type of foraging in which the people engage. A number of other approaches to culture and cultural diversity have been important in the twentieth century in addition to the above—for example, culture and personality studies, French structuralism, and Marxist theory, to name a few.

Contemporary approaches to culture tend to be divided between what may be called the materialist-oriented approaches on one hand and meaning-oriented ones on the other. The materialist approaches all share the assumption that material forces drive the cultural system, and that to understand both cultural diversity and the dynamics of culture it is necessary to look to the underlying material conditions. By material conditions is meant such matters as subsistence, technology, and economic patterns in general—in short, the processes involved in making a living and in human survival. Steward's cultural ecology is an example of such an approach. Materialist approaches in archaeology tend to emphasize such matters as population pressure and competition over resources as forces that generate developments like the change from band to tribal organization and the emergence of the state.

The meaning-oriented approaches to culture take as a central principle that human beings bestow meaning on the world of experience. The world is said to be culturally constructed, by which is meant that phenomena are classified and ordered, valued, given significance, made salient, and the like, by means of cultural frames of reference. By this view, it is essential that the researcher focus on the systems of meaning of a society, for people are oriented in their everyday lives by their cultural frames of reference. Interpretive anthropology is a particularly prominent example of a meaning-oriented approach to culture. Interpretive anthropologists such as Clifford Geertz use a variety of interpretive methods or procedures, including hermeneutic methods, in understanding meaning, hence they have a good deal in common with literary critics and theorists. Interpretive studies assume that the problem of understanding the meaning underlying human behavior and human institutions is very similar in principle to the problem of understanding the meaning of a literary work such as a novel or a poem.

Materialist-oriented and meaning-oriented anthropologists disagree over the nature of culture. The former hold that what makes cultures different is that, in the past, they have faced different adaptive problems or have experienced different material forces. The meaning-oriented anthropologist does not reject this, but places more weight on systems of meaning: he or she holds that a people confront the world with different cultural points of view, hence different societies respond differently to the same objective circumstances. While the meaning-oriented anthropologist feels that the materialist approaches give too little attention to historically conditioned systems of meaning, the materialist-oriented anthropologists feel that their meaning-oriented colleagues give too little attention to the universal material forces that help shape cultures.

[See also CULTURAL ECOLOGY THEORY; CULTURE HISTORICAL THEORY; DARWINIAN THEORY; HISTORY OF ARCHAEOLOGY, INTELLECTUAL; THEORY IN ARCHAEOLOGY.]

■ Edward B. Tylor, *Primitive Culture* (1871). Lewis Henry Morgan, *Ancient Society* (1887). Ruth Benedict, *Patterns of Culture* (1934). Franz Boas, *Race, Language and Culture* (1940). Bronislaw Malinowski, *A Scientific Theory of Culture and Other Essays* (1944). A. L. Kroeber and Clyde Kluckhohn, *Culture: A Critical Review of Concepts and Definitions* (1952). A. R. Radcliffe-Brown, *Structure and Function in Primitive Society* (1952). Julian Steward, *Theory of Culture Change* (1955). George Stocking, *Race, Culture, and Evolution* (1968). Clifford Geertz, *The Interpretation of Cultures* (1973). Elvin Hatch, *Theories of Man and Culture* (1973).

Elvin Hatch

CULTURE HISTORICAL THEORY is actually a misnomer deriving more from the needs of the organization of this volume than from any historical reality. The culture historical approach was really just that, an approach to doing archaeology, a school of thought or paradigm, rather than an actual theory in any sense of the word. Culture history studies were the hallmark of archaeology through the nineteenth and early twentieth centuries. For many parts of the world today, building basic culture histories is still an essential first step toward more modern analyses of the prehistory of these regions.

Culture history studies are exactly what the name implies, the use of archaeological data to build general time lines of major events and cultural changes for the prehistoric societies of a region. The culture historical approach has its roots in nineteenth-century European notions of the inevitable march of human progress given anthropological form in the writings of Lewis Henry *Morgan (1818–1881), Sir Edward *Tylor (1832–1917), and Karl Marx (1818–1883). The notion of unilineal social evolution progressing along a series of more or less fixed stages formed the core theoretical position of archaeologists building culture histories. Their goal was to determine what stages were reached and when, for the various cultures studied in different parts of the world using archaeological remains as their guide.

The cultural historians counted essentially three primary processes as the drivers of social evolution. These processes were invention, *diffusion, and migration. Invention is the process of transforming a new idea into a tangible innovation that will survive. Inventions can either be new things or new ways of doing things. Diffusion is the process of transmitting inventions from one region or cultural group to another, often with modifications or enhancements along the way or through time. Diffusion can often trigger new inventions in a new locale. Finally, migration is the actual movement of people from one region to another, often displacing other human groups as well as increasing speed of diffusion of new ideas, tools, and ways of doing things. Early in the history of archaeology, there were wild assertions about the importance of diffusion and migration as the primary movers of inventions from hearth areas to the rest of the world (e.g., the notion that almost everything in antiquity was invented in Egypt and spread to the rest of the world by diffusion and migration), but these ideas were debunked in the early 1900s, as a more reasoned, scientific approach to archaeology came to the fore.

Two key players in the refinement of the culture historical approach were Franz Boas (1858–1942) and V. Gordon *Childe (1892–1957). Boas's influence on American archaeology was a profound one. He intimately linked archaeology with cultural anthropology, which is one of the great strengths of American archaeology, and he championed the notion that the rigorous analysis of basic archaeological and ethnographic data is fundamental to a scientific discipline of archaeology. In his view, theory must be grounded in empirical data and tested against such data. These two fundamental notions remain as important underpinnings of archaeology to this day.

Perhaps the greatest expression of Boas's emphasis on the minute analysis of archaeological data was the elaboration of the comparative method as a primary tool for building culture histories. The comparative method simply uses comparisons of artifacts, assemblages, settlement patterns, art styles, and the like to determine relative similarities and differences between geographic regions both in space and in time. Through the application of detailed artifact analysis, classification, and comparison, early archaeologists were able to build quite detailed, and in many respects quite accurate, culture histories of most of the major and minor regions of interest at the time.

One of the greatest practitioners of the culture history approach based on the comparative method was V. Gordon Childe. While Childe's models of European and Near Eastern prehistory were often controversial, there is no doubt that his influence on the nature of archaeological inquiry and the later development of archaeology were profound. His models of the diffusion of important technologies such as *metallurgy and *agriculture from eastern Asia through the filter of the Near East and thence to Europe were masterfully constructed from solid archaeological and anthropological data covering an enormous area and time depth, all without the benefit of absolute dating techniques. In and of itself, Childe's work was extremely important, providing archaeologists of the 1960s and 1970s with many important hypotheses to test through greatly refined theories and methods. Perhaps more important, Childe pushed the culture historical approach as far as it could go, to the very limits of its useful application—to the threshold that ultimately resulted in the development of the New Archaeology, or processual archaeology. Once Childe had so thoroughly reconstructed the detailed and complex history of the invention and diffusion of ideas and tools and the migrations of ancient peoples in the Near East and Europe, he was poised to start asking the next important question—what processes caused people to change, to develop new tools and techniques, and to migrate? Childe, unfortunately, did not live to see the fruit of that shift in the kinds of questions archaeologists ask.

With the development of processual archaeology in the early 1960s, the culture historical approach declined as the primary concern of archaeologists. While building culture histories ceased to be the ultimate goal of archaeologists, building culture histories is still an integral part of the process of archaeology. Regardless of one's theoretical orientation, one cannot begin to ask the difficult questions about past human behavior until one has a reasonably firm understanding of the general progression of events, trends, and changes that occurred in a region over time. Archaeology is an accretionary discipline. While the culture historical approach is no longer the central method of archaeology, it is still a vital component of archaeology.

[See also POST-PROCESSUAL THEORY; PROCESSUAL THEORY; THEORY IN ARCHAEOLOGY.]

■ Elvin Hatch, *Theories of Man and Culture* (1973). Ruth Tringham, "V. Gordon Childe 25 Years After," *Journal of Field Archaeology* 10 (1983): 85–100. Brian Fagan, *People of the Earth* (8th ed., 1995).

George Michaels

CULTURE–PEOPLE HYPOTHESIS. The culture–people model proposes that distinctive archaeological cultures, which are comprised of "packages" of artifacts repeatedly used together in a particular time and place, are the remains of distinct peoples or ethnic groups. The model became an important component of culture–historical theory that developed during the first half of the twentieth century and which, in modified form, is still the primary organizational model for the discipline.

The model is predicated on the so-called normative approach, in which it is assumed that each individual society or group makes its artifacts in a particular way. An important secondary element of the culture–people model is the direct historical approach. First used in Europe at the end of the nineteenth century, but perhaps developed to the fullest in North America during the 1920s and 1930s, the direct historical approach is based on the assumption that if, for example, a particular pottery style originated in a particular area, then this was the place of origin of the historic tribe who used it. It directly proceeds, therefore, from the assumption that a specific people is represented by diagnostic artifacts or archaeological cultures.

The culture–people model was first explicitly set out by V. Gordon *Childe (*The Danube in Prehistory,* 1929), but his arguments were based on earlier work by other European scholars, exemplified by Gustav *Kossinna. They were part of the rejection of the evolutionary archaeology of the nineteenth century, whereby the past was conceived as documenting successive stages in a unilinear cultural progression.

In Europe, the model was popularized by the search for the prehistoric origins of the Indo-Europeans made by Childe and others, and to a lesser extent by the development during the 1930s of nationalist archaeologies in Germany and the Soviet Union that attempted to document the antiquity (and cultural superiority) of the German and Russian peoples (Nazi Germany's infatuation with the racist elements of Kossinna's work has overwhelmed the significant contributions that he made in other ways to the study of European prehistory). (*See* Political uses of Archaeology.) In general, cultural change in Europe was explained by migration and diffusion, and the continent's past was seen as a mosaic of different cultures (i.e., peoples) moving across the landscape.

In North America, the model became popular alongside the proposals of the anthropologist Franz Boas, who emphasized the detailed description and study of specific areas and peoples. In that continent, archaeology became a subdiscipline of anthropology; thus, the latter's concentration on specific aboriginal groups filtered into archaeology, too. By the end of the first decade of the twentieth century, North American archaeologists were identifying cultures as the prehistoric manifestations of historic tribes such as the Iroquois. American archaeologists continued to define their archaeological cultures as lists of artifact traits (unlike Childe, who had included behavior such as subsistence in his definitions).

Despite its popularity as a means of organizing and humanizing the archaeological record, it became apparent early on that a simple correlation between a people and a distinctive archaeological culture was not always warranted. Questions on the nature of an archaeological culture and the complexity of what exactly was meant by "a people" were first posed in the late nineteenth century, and one still finds these questions addressed, both implicitly and explicitly, in the current literature. An empirical consideration of the problems with the model was made by Donald Thomson ("The Seasonal Factor in Human Culture," *Proceedings of the Prehistoric Society* 10 [1939]: 209–221), who, in an early example of *ethnoarchaeology, studied the remains of campsites used by a single Australian aboriginal group during the course of a year. Thomson showed that in using standard archaeological techniques he would be forced to conclude that different cultural groups, rather than just one, left behind the remains.

In North America, similar doubts about the model's validity were expressed; indeed some scholars have argued that the culture–people model never became as fundamental an element of North American archaeology as it did in Europe, although the work since the late 1930s, of the American archaeologist Irving Rouse (e.g., *Introduction to Prehistory,* 1972) provides one of the most explicit and sustained arguments for the ethnic basis to the archaeological culture.

The most important attack on the culture–people model was made by the processual school during the 1960s. Processualists preferred to see cultures not as normative "packages" of artifacts that represent distinct peoples, but rather as adaptive mechanisms for coping with the environment; variation in "cultures," therefore, was not the result of a change in ethnic groups. This argument stimulated a spirited debate in the 1960s between the processualist Lewis Binford and the French archaeologist François Bordes, concerning how best to explain the variation observed in assemblages belonging to the French Mousterian. During that same decade, British archaeologists like David Clarke and Colin Renfrew also began to question the assumptions behind the culture–people model and to propose more realistic approaches to identifying the particular forms of prehistoric social behavior manifested in the archaeological record.

Archaeologists now appreciate more fully the nature of archaeological cultures and the complexity of social units, and accept that although archaeological cultures represent some form of past social reality, they probably are not directly equatable with "peoples" or "ethnic groups." However, many archaeologists, for convenience, still speak of the Magdalenians or the Anasazi, for example, thereby implicating these taxa as the archaeological remains of ethnically distinct peoples, even though the discipline has accepted that this is not, in most cases, a valid inference.

[*See also* CULTURE; DARWINIAN THEORY; PROCESSUAL THEORY.]

■ Glyn Daniel, *The Idea of Prehistory* (1963). Bruce Trigger, *Time and Traditions* (1978). Colin Renfrew, *Approaches to Social Archaeology* (1984). Bruce Trigger, *A History of Archaeological Thought* (1989). Gordon Willey and Jeremy Sabloff, *A History of American Archaeology* (1993).

Philip Duke

CUNEIFORM. *See* WRITING: CUNEIFORM.

CUZCO was the capital of the Inca Empire, the political entity that dominated the Andean region of South America from the middle of the fifteenth century A.D. until the Spanish Conquest in 1532. Many traces of the Inca city remain in the Peruvian provincial capital of the same name, built on its foundations.

Our knowledge of the Inca city comes from three sources: sixteenth- and seventeenth-century accounts prepared by early Spanish visitors to Cuzco; identification of Inca foundations within the modern city; and archaeological research in the Cuzco region.

The founding of Cuzco is recounted in several Inca myths. In one version presented by the seventeenth-century chronicler Bernabé Cobo, the legendary founder of the Inca dynasty, Manco Capac, emerged from the ground along with three brothers and four sisters. In company with the sisters, he wandered to the future site of the Inca capital, established political and religious order among the savage people who then lived there, and mandated that a city be built.

The capital, as observed by Spanish visitors, was probably laid out in the middle of the fifteenth century. Several sources claim that a decisive military victory over the enemy Chanca people propelled the Inca prince Inca Yupanqui to the throne around the year 1438. Taking the name Pachacuti ("transformer of the earth"), the young king designed the city and its environs and had it rebuilt as the new capital. Additional buildings were constructed by his son and grandson, filling in the plan to create the city described in the historical accounts.

The Incas considered Cuzco to be the conceptual as well as the political capital of Tahuantinsuyu ("the Four Quarters"), as their empire was called. The main roads to each quadrant emanated from its central plaza, a space that was also used for public performance of religious rituals and military celebration. The buildings of Cuzco were similarly associated with the city's special purpose: They included palaces for each of the Inca kings and his relatives, buildings used for instructing and installing young men into the military orders, cloisters for women who served the Inca and the Sun god, and many places associated with devotional activity. The Coricancha ("Golden Enclosure"), commonly called the Temple of the Sun, was the principal religious structure of Cuzco. It displayed the tokens of the major Inca deities (Sun, Moon, Thunder, and the creator god, Viracocha), and some of the booty from important military campaigns. Most of the buildings of Cuzco—as is the case for many of the important structures in other parts of the Inca Empire—were built of stone fitted with little or no mud mortar. The Coricancha, for example, has walls of stone so carefully worked and fitted that the seams are barely visible.

In contrast to many ancient cities, there was little in the urban plan of Cuzco to suggest that it housed a large support population. Inca law restricted access to the city, and other than retainers who served in their households, its citizenry was comprised of members of the Inca royal families and those in the service of the king or the religion. Support for the capital came from tribute throughout the empire; but some immediate support would have come from the many planned farming communities that were built in the Huatanay and adjacent Vilcanota valleys. Here, estates belonging to royalty were created, with terracing, irrigation works, and housing for the populations of farmers that were settled there.

Much of the structure of ancient Cuzco is still visible in the plan of modern Cuzco: the current Plaza de Armas is the Inca main plaza; the Coricancha forms the support of the convent of Santo Domingo; many foundation walls and house walls in the central part of Cuzco show their Inca construction, as do many of the streets and waterworks in the older part of town.

The central debate about Cuzco (and, indeed, about the Incas) centers around the form of the city, and the degree to which early descriptions of it should be taken as literally true. Some early sources claim that Cuzco was built in the form of a puma, the mountain lion that was the symbol of the Inca dynasty. Indeed, a very convincing outline of such an animal can be discerned in the walls and streets of Inca Cuzco, as has been discussed by J. Rowe. This plan, as well as possible alternate readings of a feline form in the plan of the city, is discussed by Gasparini and Margolies. Others claim that any reference to Cuzco being built as a puma were intended as metaphors to describe the centrality of the Inca dynasty to the rule of the empire.

Since the 1970s, the Peruvian government has supported excavation and reconstruction of a number of Inca and Colonial sites in and around Cuzco, in order to attract tourists. In addition to the Coricancha, there is ongoing research at Sacsahuaman, an elaborate Inca fortress overlooking their capital.

[See also INCA CIVILIZATION, articles on INCA RULING DYNASTIES, INCA ECONOMIC ORGANIZATION, INCA ROADS, INCA RELIGION, AND PIZARRO AND THE CONQUEST OF THE INCAS.]

■ John H. Rowe, "An Introduction to the Archaeology of Cuzco," *Papers of the Peabody Museum of American Archaeology and Ethnology, Harvard University* 27 (2) (1944). John H. Rowe, "What Kind of Settlement was Inca Cuzco," *Nawpa Pacha* 5 (1967): 59–76. Bernabé Cobo, *History of the Inca Empire,* Roland Hamilton, trans. and ed. (1979). Graziano Gasparini and Luise Margolies, *Inca Architecture* (1980). R. Tom Zuidema, "The Lion in the City: Royal Symbols of Transition in Cuzco," in *Animal Myths and Metaphors in South America,* ed. Gary Urton (1985), pp. 183–250. Susan A. Niles, *Callachaca: Style and Status in an Inca Community* (1987). John Hyslop, *Inca Settlement Planning* (1990).

Susan A. Niles

CYPRUS is a large, mountainous island in the eastern Mediterranean, 66 miles (120 km) west of Syria and 43 miles (70 km) south of Turkey. The heavily forested Troodos massif in the southwest and the Kyrenia Range along the north coast flank the rolling central Mesaoria Plain. Elsewhere mountains partition the island into winding river valleys and narrow coastal plains. The Troodos foothills are rich in copper, and in antiquity Cyprus gave its name to the metal. The abundance of copper, the diverse yet compact landscape, and the proximity of Syro-Anatolia directly affected patterns of human settlement on Cyprus and thus, its archaeology.

The Proto-Neolithic Period (ca. 8100 B.C.), the period of earliest human contact, is known so far only at the ephemeral south coastal site of Akrotiri-Aetokremnos. Charred bones of (now extinct) pygmy hippopotami and elephants suggest that late-ninth-millennium hunters killed and cooked these animals, but these people disappeared without trace. It has been suggested that they abandoned the island after hunting the native fauna to extinction.

In the Aceramic (pre-pottery) Neolithic Period (7000–5600 B.C.), humans returned to Cyprus. The newcomers (whether from Anatolia or the Levant is uncertain) settled Cape Andreas-Kastros on the northeast coast and Khirokitia in the Vasilikos valley. They built circular mud houses, buried their dead beneath house floors, herded sheep, goats, and pigs, and cultivated cereals—all practices imported from the mainland. For unknown reasons, their settlements ended and an enigmatic thousand-year gap ensued.

In the Ceramic Neolithic period (4500–3800 B.C.), immigrants reoccupied Khirokitia and founded new sites at Philia, Vrysi, and Sotira. Like their predecessors, they cultivated cereals, herded animals, and practiced intramural burial. Their innovation was pottery—Combed Ware at Sotira, Red-on-White at Vrysi—all hand formed in a limited range of shapes. Olive and grape remains from Vrysi indicate the colonists introduced specialized horticulture to Cyprus soon after its origin on the mainland.

The Chalcolithic period (3800–2500 B.C.), a transitional era of growing social complexity and technical sophistication, is known at Erimi (south coast), Kissonerga, and Lemba (west coast). The first metal artifacts—small tools of hammered copper—occurred, but whether metalworking was an indigenous discovery or an external, possibly Anatolian, introduction is unclear. Red-on-White pottery continued with an enlarged repertoire of shapes. Storage bins in dwellings suggest increasingly efficient agriculture supported an expanding population. Cemeteries were set aside for the dead, and human sculpture—small cruciform statuettes in steatite or ceramic—appeared for the first time.

The Early Bronze Age (or Early Cypriot Period, 2500–1900 B.C.) is known mainly from cemeteries on the north coast (Lapithos, Vounous, Vasilia) and in the western Mesaoria. No settlements have yet been discovered. The graves contain quantities of implements in copper or bronze (forged or cast, not hammered), along with Red Polished pottery, a new style recalling Anatolian prototypes characterized by multitiered shapes with long curving spouts and modeled decoration. Red Polished pottery models also found in graves depict ancient life in miniature, from agricultural labor to cultic worship.

By the Middle Bronze Age (or Middle Cypriot Period, 1900–1625 B.C.), settlements were prospering at Phaneromeni (south coast) and Alambra (eastern Troodos foothills). Red Polished pottery continued while White Painted II ware, the period hallmark, began. Relations developed with Middle Bronze Syria-Palestine and Minoan Crete, and copper became an important export. Despite these foreign contacts, Cyprus remained an island of villages largely isolated from the impacts of urbanization, literacy, and state formation that swept both the Aegean and the Levant.

By the Late Bronze Age (or Late Cypriot Period 1625–1050 B.C.), Cyprus was integrated into a Mediterranean trade network. Mercantile cities flourished at Enkomi, Kition, Hala Sultan Teke, and Maroni, sustained by the island's copper wealth and its juxtaposition between the Near East and Mycenaean Greece. The Mycenaeans came first as traders, then stayed on as settlers, enriching Cypriot ceramic traditions and introducing Greek language and religion. Cyprus maintained strong Near Eastern links. *Al ashiya*, meaning either the entire island or Enkomi specifically, is named as a copper source in cuneiform texts from Ugarit, Amarna, and Bogazkoy. By 1050 B.C., the upheavals that precipitated social collapse in the Aegean, Anatolia, Syria-Palestine, and Egypt finally reached Cyprus.

In the Iron Age (1050–325 B.C.), urban society reemerged. New coastal cities grew up at Salamis, Kition, Amathus, Kourion, Palaepaphos, Soloi, and inland at Idalion, Tammasos, and Ledra (ancient Nicosia). The repopulation of the island by Phoenicians and Greeks set a pattern that persisted until the Hellenistic period: small, autonomous city-states controlling geographically limited regions and maintaining their precarious independence by relying on the island's relative remoteness to stave off mainland domination. Egyptians, Assyrians, and Persians successively claimed suzerainty over the island, but only the Persians left any archaeological traces.

In the Hellenistic, Roman, and Early Byzantine periods (325 B.C.–ca. A.D. 650) Cyprus was successively Hellenized, Romanized, and Christianized. The Iron Age city-states capitulated en masse to Alexander. Afterward, the Seleucids and Ptolemies disputed control of the island. Cyprus was then absorbed by the Romans and their heirs, the Byzantines. The Romans built monumental cities at Salamis, Kourion, and Nea Paphos. Elaborate early-third-century figural mosaics were buried intact at Nea Paphos by the violent earthquakes that leveled the city in the late fourth century. Kourion and Salamis were likewise flattened by tremors that rocked the island in late antiquity.

After 650 A.D., Byzantine Cyprus lay exposed to seaborne raids from the Muslim Levant. During the Crusades, Frankish knights under Guy de Lusignan occupied the island and erected European-style castles and churches. After Saladin's victory, Cyprus became a Crusader refuge and one of Europe's sources of sugar. (Sugarcane was earlier introduced to Cyprus from the Jordan Valley.) A well-preserved fourteenth-century sugar mill has been excavated at Palaeapaphos. In 1489 Venice annexed and fortified the island. Significant traces of Venetian fortifications are still visible at Kyrenia, Famagusta, and Nicosia. These were of no avail when the Ottomans captured Cyprus in 1571. They organized the Greek-speaking peasantry into *chifliks* (estates) controlled by military land grantees. Under the Ottomans, an influx of Anatolian immigrants set the demographic pattern of mixed Turkish/Greek villages that prevailed until the twentieth century.

Archaeological research in Cyprus has been nearly continuous for more than a century. Although the excavations of Luigi Palma di Cesnola in the 1860s through 1870s were, frankly, treasure hunts, they did draw attention to the rich antiquity of the island. After 1878, the British colonial administration of Cyprus established an archaeological service and a museum, precursors of the modern institutions. In 1899, J. L. Myres and Max Ohnefalsch-Richter collaborated on the *Catalogue of the Cyprus Museum* and in the 1920s and 1930s, the Swedish Cyprus Expedition mounted a comprehensive archaeological exploration of the island. Since then, many teams of archaeologists, both foreign and Cypriot, have investigated all aspects of Cypriot antiquity. In addition to conventional excavations, recent work has also included multiperiod regional surveys, archaeometric and geoarchaeological examinations of copper production, and ethnoarchaeological inquiries.

The Turkish invasion and occupation of the northern part of the island in 1974 prematurely ended excavations there. Displaced archaeologists turned to underexplored western Cyprus, making unexpected discoveries such as the Lemba Chalcolithic complex near Paphos. They also came to realize the adverse impact of unbridled economic development on the island's archaeological resources. The recent creation in the new University of Cyprus of an Archaeological Research Unit has opened new horizons for archaeology on Cyprus.

[See also AEGEAN CULTURES, *articles on* HELLADIC (MYCENAEAN) CULTURE, MYCENAE; MEDITERRANEAN TRADE.]

■ V. Karageorghis, *Cyprus: From the Stone Age to the Romans* (1982). V. Karageorghis, ed., *Archaeology in Cyprus, 1960–1985* (1985). E. J. Peltenburg, ed., *Early Society in Cyprus* (1989). G.R.H. Wright, *Ancient Building in Cyprus* (1992). A. T. Reyes, *Archaic Cyprus: A Study of the Textual and Archaeological Evidence* (1994).

Joseph A. Greene

D

DALTON CULTURE is a Late Paleo-Indian or very Early Archaic archaeological manifestation which existed over the southeastern United States probably from about 10,500 to 10,000 B.P. It is recognized primarily by the lanceolate Dalton point which was resharpened as a knife resulting in a characteristic narrowing of the blade length and width and in some cases a distinct alternate bevel. The lithic tool kit is essentially Paleo-Indian with the singular exception of the woodworking adze. What subsistence data that are available indicate utilization of modern plant and animal species implying that the origins of the eastern Archaic can be found in Dalton culture.

Dalton points and the culture for which they are named, were named for Judge S. P. Dalton of Jefferson City, Missouri, who had collected several of the distinctive points from a single location. The Paleo-Indian character of the points was recognized even at that time as they were thought to have been derived from a Folsom variant. In the 1950s and 1960s, excavations done in Missouri, Alabama, and North Carolina showed that Dalton points were among the oldest of projectile point types found, and they were associated with a variety of unifacial tools such as endscrapers, sidescrapers, flake blades, and gravers further substantiating their Paleo-Indian affinity. Radiocarbon dating of Dalton remains has been difficult. Two radiocarbon dates, 10,530 and 10,200 B.P., from Dalton hearths in the alluvial terrace in front of Rodgers Shelter in Missouri, are considered to be the best temporal indicators of Dalton culture.

In the 1970s, fieldwork done by the Arkansas Archaeological Survey in northeast Arkansas led to the discovery and excavation of key Dalton sites with effectively pure Dalton contexts which have provided, to date, the clearest definition of Dalton culture in the Southeast. The northeast Arkansas region has produced literally hundreds of Dalton sites and thousands of the distinctive points. In addition to points, a woodworking adze is also commonly found there as a part of an essentially Paleo-Indian tool kit. The high site and artifact density of the northeast Arkansas area marks it out from the rest of the Southeast.

The first extensively excavated northeast Arkansas Dalton site was Brand. It was a shallow, open site where numerous Dalton stone tools were found buried by Holocene windblown silt overlying ancient weathered clay subsoil. Excavations revealed artifact clusters of about the same size and shape and with nearly identical contents. These spatial concentrations were interpreted as discrete working areas probably created by males who were processing deer meat some distance from a base village. The Brand site excavation and assemblage analysis allowed a thorough definition of the Dalton tool kit and confirmed many tools suspected to be associated with Dalton.

Perhaps the most spectacular Dalton site ever excavated was that of the Sloan site located only a few miles from Brand. From an area of only 36 by 39 feet (11 by 12 m), 1.6 feet (.5 m) deep, 448 Dalton lithic artifacts were excavated, many of which were in discrete caches with the artifacts still touching. At the time of excavation, it was strongly felt that the concentrations of artifacts represented grave goods. This was subsequently confirmed by the identification of several bone fragments as human. The presence of a cemetery at this early time horizon seems remarkable in New World prehistory given that such burial treatment does not show up until a few thousand years later in the Archaic. The existence of base villages, a cemetery, and the woodworking adze was found in the northeast Arkansas Dalton manifestation, which suggests considerable sedentism and cultural complexity in the region on a Late Pleistocene time level.

The Dalton culture may also be conceived as a cultural horizon which existed about the same time across the Southeast. Stylistic variations in the point occur from east Texas to North Carolina reflected in such terms as San Patrice and Hardaway-Dalton, respectively. Wherever Dalton points occur, they are associated with a Paleo-Indian flake tool industry. Ecologically, the Dalton adaptation appears to be a continuation of the Paleo-Indian lifeway with respect to tool design, cryptocrystalline raw material selection, and extensive regional mobility. However, the economy is oriented toward modern plant and animal species native to the Southeastern hardwood forests and indicates the beginnings of the Archaic.

[See also HUNTER-GATHERERS, NORTH AMERICAN ARCHAIC; NORTH AMERICA: THE EASTERN WOODLANDS AND THE SOUTH.]

■ Carl H. Chapman, "A Preliminary Study of Missouri Archaeology, Part IV, Ancient Cultures and Sequence," *The Missouri Archaeologist* 10:4 (1948). Dan F. Morse, "Dalton Culture in Northeast Arkansas," *The Florida Anthropologist* 26 (1973): 23–38. Dan F. Morse and Albert C. Goodyear, "The Significance of the Dalton Adze in Northeast Arkansas," *Plains Anthropologist* 19 (1973): 316–322. Albert C. Goodyear, "The Brand Site: A Techno-Functional Study of a Dalton Site in Northeast Arkansas," *Arkansas Archaeological Survey, Research Series* 7 (1974). James A. Tuck, "Early Archaic Horizons in Eastern North America," *Archaeology of Eastern North America* 2 (1974): 72–80. Albert C. Goodyear, "The Chronological Position of the Dalton Horizon in the Southeastern United States," *American Antiquity* 47(2) (1982): 382–395. Dan F. Morse and Phyllis A. Morse, *Archaeology of the Central Mississippi Valley* (1983).

Albert C. Goodyear

DARWIN, Charles. Charles Robert Darwin (1809–1882) was the greatest biologist of the nineteenth century. After two years as a medical student in Edinburgh, he earned a Bachelor of Arts degree at Cambridge University in 1831, where he met the geologist Adam Sedgewick and the botanist John Henslow. Henslow recommended him for the post of naturalist on H.M.S. *Beagle*. Between 1831 and 1836, Darwin used the voyage to make the seminal observations in biology and geology which formed the basis of his entire career. He published a general account of the voyage in 1839, followed by a volume on coral reefs, another on the geology of volcanic islands, and a third on geological observations in South America. From 1846 to 1854, Darwin moved away from geology to biology, studying fossil and living barnacles. These researches clarified his thinking on the classification, variation, and origins of animal species. In 1858, naturalist Alfred Russel Wallace sent Darwin a manuscript outlining similar evolutionary thinking. Darwin then published his "abstract," *On the Origin of Species* in 1859, documenting his evidence for the operation of biological evolution. The book brought Darwin enduring fame and provided not only a fundamental general principle for biology, but also a biological theory for the antiquity of humankind. He developed his ideas on human evolution further in *The Descent of Man and Selection in Relation to Sex*, published in 1871. Darwin's theories in refined forms provide the intellectual framework for human paleontology and for the study of prehistoric archaeology.

[See also ANTIQUITY OF HUMANKIND: ANTIQUITY OF HUMANKIND IN THE OLD WORLD; DARWINIAN THEORY; HISTORY OF ARCHAEOLOGY BEFORE 1900: EUROPEAN ARCHAEOLOGY.]

■ Donald K. Grayson, *The Establishment of Human Antiquity* (1983). N. C. Gillespie, *Charles Darwin and the Problem of Creation* (1979). H. Gruber, *Darwin on Man: A Psychological Study of Scientific Creativity*, 2d ed. (1981).

Brian M. Fagan

DARWINIAN THEORY. The human species is a product of biological evolution. We were not created by divine intervention, but evolved by the same processes as other species. Of these, natural selection, as originally conceived of by Charles *Darwin in the nineteenth century and substantially refined in the twentieth century, is likely to have played a major role. Few archaeologists would question these assertions. It is when archaeologists are asked about the relevance of this knowledge to their discipline that one finds an immense range of responses covering the spectrum from total insignificance to the belief that these principles should guide the way we do archaeology.

Some archaeologists feel that the field cannot advance without a strong foundation in evolutionary theory and that any studies of culture change must make explicit reference to our biological makeup and the manner by which it evolved. For those who propose the need for a Darwinian theory of archaeology, there is much debate as to what is an appropriate Darwinian archaeology. Consensus appears remote, yet as little as twenty years ago there was little debate. From the late 1960s to the early 1980s a functionally based ecological approach to archaeology was developed, especially among archaeologists specializing in the study of hunters and gatherers. These archaeologists claimed a Darwinian theme and they frequently used such concepts as selection and adaptation. It was argued that culture was a nongenetic means of adaptation and therefore cultures must be adaptive. At the heart of this approach was the assumption that the behavior of a group was a representation of that group's adaptation to its environment, with specific reference to the balance between people and their subsistence resources. Subsistence practices, tools, social

behavior, religious practices, and even art were interpreted as functioning to "fit" the group to the availability and distribution of resources in the natural environment.

One of the problems with this approach was that it left little room for human actors. People were purely reactive, at the level of the group or more tangentially, the cultural system. Binford stated this most clearly when he argued that "selection for change occurs when the system is unable to continue previously successful tactics in the face of changed conditions in the environment" (*In Pursuit of the Past*, 1983: 203). These types of studies made invaluable contributions to our knowledge of the past. The papers in the archetypal volume *Hunter-Gatherer Economy in Prehistory* (1983) epitomize this group adaptationist approach for studies of hunter-gatherers. These articles illustrate the significant contribution that studies using this approach have made.

In the 1980s another Darwinian archaeology was developed which was explicitly advertised as the application of evolutionary theory in archaeology and is now called cultural selectionism, although that is not a term used by the proponents themselves. Perhaps the founder of this approach is Robert Dunnell, whose seminal 1980 paper "Evolutionary Theory and Archaeology" set the foundation for this perspective in archaeology.

The central theme to the cultural selectionist approach is the notion that artifacts are treated as part of the human phenotype, even though they are unattached to the human body. From this it is argued that the "fitness" of an artifact can be determined by its replication and spread through space and time and thus a selectionist or Darwinian nomenclature is the appropriate framework for interpreting the archaeological record. David Rindos provides a particularly detailed discussion of cultural selectionism and its relationship to biological evolution, and uses this to interpret the origins of agriculture in his book *The Origins of Agriculture: An Evolutionary Perspective* (1984). Michael J. O'Brien has also been one of the prime movers behind this approach and has developed much of the theory behind its use, especially in his article with T. Holland titled "Variation, Natural Selection and the Archaeological Record." Cultural selectionism remains one of the most common forms of Darwinian archaeology in the field today.

Since the later 1980s the group adaptationist and cultural selectionist approaches have been joined by three new themes claiming a Darwinian label. These include a focus on the individual; attempts to study the interaction between biological and cultural modes of inheritance and a cognitive approach that was stimulated by recent advances in the evolution of human psychology.

Those attempting to focus on the individual rather than the group claim to be attempting to conform to the biological definition of the term adaptation that they suggest requires reference to individual behavior rather than group behavior. Following evolutionary biologists, the whole notion of group adaptation is rejected unless it is conceived of as being no more than the summation of individual adaptations and, as such, would have little analytical value in itself. This marks an attempt to move away from cultural ecology to a more explicitly evolutionary ecology for past human behavior. In such works the "stable until pushed" premise of the adaptationist perspective is replaced by a view that societies are always in a state of readjustment, experimentation, and change because certain individuals within the society will be attempting to manipulate culture to their own ends.

Steve Mithen, in his important paper "Evolutionary Theory and Post-Processual Archaeology" (*Antiquity* 63, 1989), presents a very elucidating argument for the importance of individuals in archaeological interpretation. Here he contrasts a Darwinian perspective based on the individual with both the group adaptationist perspective and the 1980s version of post-processualist or post-modern archaeology. Herbert Maschner, in his Ph.D. dissertation titled *The Origins of Hunter and Gatherer Sedentism and Political Complexity: A Case Study from the Northern Northwest Coast* (1992), found that individuals working toward their own and their kinsmen's interests were perhaps the best explanation for why hunter-gatherers on the Northwest Coast became so politically complex.

Archaeologists who focus on the interaction between social learning, cultural transmission, and biological evolution are finding more widespread support, especially after the publication of Boyd and Richerson's important volume *Culture and the Evolutionary Process* (1985). The essence of this approach lies in understanding the dynamic interplay between the biological and cultural modes of inheritance. Many of the studies using this perspective have become popular because of the strong use of quantification and mathematical modeling by some of its proponents.

The third new form of Darwinian theory in archaeology is composed of those studies that make explicit reference to the human mind as a product of biological evolution. These are founded in the interaction between biological and psychological approaches to behavior—a new field called evolutionary psychology. The basic premise of this perspective is that the structure of the human mind evolved in a Pleistocene environment when our human ancestors were faced with a radically different range of problems than we face in our modern surroundings. Consequently, for many types of modern behavior, there is a limited expectation that it will be "adaptive" in any biological sense. Much of our cultural behavior, many aspects of which are not functional and may even be maladaptive, derives from the presence of a Pleistocene psychology living in an urban social setting. This theory and many of the current evolutionary psychological studies are discussed in *The Adapted Mind: Evolutionary Psychology and the Generation of Culture* (1993). A purely archaeological example of the use of cognition and the evolutionary psychological approach is Steve Mithen's *Thoughtful Foragers: A Study of Prehistoric Decision Making* (1990).

Overall there is little consensus as to what is an appropriate Darwinian archaeology. In fact, archaeologists who take a Darwinian perspective cannot agree on what is the most useful unit of measurement. Cultures, artifacts, groups, systems, individuals, and genes have all been proposed with great debate. The only true concordance among Darwinian archaeologists is that a Darwinian evolutionary approach must be adopted before a true science of archaeology can be developed.

[See also COGNITIVE ARCHAEOLOGY; CRITICAL THEORY; CULTURAL ECOLOGY THEORY; CULTURAL HISTORICAL THEORY; GENDER, ARCHAEOLOGY OF; GENERAL SYSTEMS THEORY; HISTORY OF ARCHAEOLOGY, INTELLECTUAL; MARXIST THEORY; MIDDLE RANGE THEORY; POST-PROCESSUAL THEORY; PROCESSUAL THEORY; SCIENCE IN ARCHAEOLOGY; STRUCTURALISM; THEORY IN ARCHAEOLOGY.]

■ R. Dunnell, "Evolutionary Theory and Archaeology," in *Advances in Archaeological Method and Theory*, Vol. 3, ed. M. B. Schiffer (1982), pp. 35–99. G. N. Bailey, ed., *Hunter-Gatherer Economy in Prehistory* (1983). Lewis Binford, *In Pursuit of the Past* (1983). D. Rindos, *The Origins of Agriculture: An Evolutionary Perspective* (1984). R. Boyd and P. J. Richerson, *Culture and the Evolutionary Process* (1985). S. Mithen, "Evolutionary Theory and Post-processual Archaeology," *Antiquity* 63 (1989): 483–494. S. Mithen, *Thoughtful Foragers: A Study of Prehistoric Decision Making* (1990). M. J. O'Brien and T. Holland, "Variation, Natural Selection and the Archaeological Record," in *Archaeological Method and Theory* Vol. 2, ed. M. B. Schiffer (1990), pp. 31–79. J. Barkow, L. Cosmides, and J. Tooby, eds., *The Adapted Mind: Evolutionary Psychology and the Generation of Culture* (1993). H.D.G. Maschner, *Darwinian Archaeologies* (1996).

Herbert D. G. Maschner

DATING THE PAST. Central to the process of doing archaeology is the necessity of understanding the chronological sequencing of archaeological entities and past events. Without a firm grasp of this sequencing, archaeologists would not be able to deal with issues of behavioral process and evolution. Archaeology as a discipline would be reduced to a dry cataloging of artifacts and monuments with little hope of understanding the mechanisms and rates of change in past human cultures. For this reason, dating the past has been one of the most crucial methodological problems facing archaeologists. Fortunately, the past hundred years' work on this problem has yielded a wide array of methods and techniques to allow archaeologists to extrapolate the fourth dimension (time) from the three physical dimensions (latitude, longitude, and elevation) of archaeological sites. These techniques fall into two categories—relative chronology and absolute chronology.

Relative chronology is based on the simple stratigraphic principle that older materials will be found lower in an archaeological deposit than newer materials—the law of superposition. For example, a stone tool dropped on a cave floor in 1000 B.C. will eventually be covered by deposits and possibly later human construction. Another stone tool dropped in that cave in A.D. 1000 will fall on a floor that is higher than the original floor. An archaeologist excavating that cave in 1995 will uncover the tool dropped in A.D. 1000 first because it is higher in the stratigraphic sequence. Subsequent excavation will uncover the tool dropped in 1000 B.C. in a lower level. Simply on the basis of the vertical relationship between the two tools, the archaeologist could determine that the tool found on the lower level was deposited some time before the tool found on the upper level. The archaeologist would not know when either of the two tools were deposited. Nor would he or she know how much time elapsed between the deposition of the two tools. Nevertheless, the archaeologist would be able to develop a relative chronology of the cave deposits that would accurately portray the relative sequence of depositional events that occurred in the cave. This is the first, and simplest, tool that archaeologists have for determining the temporal relationships between occupation events in archaeological sites. For many years this was the only tool that archaeologists had available to them. There are, of course, a range of human and nonhuman factors and processes that can obscure and even reverse that simple relationship, and field archaeologists must be very careful to determine what postdepositional processes have affected their deposits and adjust their relative chronologies accordingly.

Another technique of relative dating is *seriation. Seriation is based on the principle that artifacts will change in decorative style and form over time and that each style or form will follow a similar trajectory of early limited use, acceptance and increased popularity, and eventual decline in popularity tapering to final disuse. A graphical representation of this trajectory with popularity, as measured by the frequency of occurrences in a stratigraphic level, plotted as horizontal bars centered on a vertical axis representing time forms, is called a battleship curve. By plotting battleship curves for several artifact styles (usually, but not necessarily, pottery types) within a site, archaeologists can develop a relative chronology for the site. For many years prior to the development of techniques for absolute dating, seriation was the principal tool that archaeologists had for developing refined chronologies. The drawback, of course, was that this technique did not provide archaeologists with actual dates; nor did it allow archaeologists to know how long or short a period of time was represented by a battleship curve.

The great breakthrough for archaeologists came with the development of techniques of absolute dating. Absolute dating techniques allow archaeologists to assign specific calendar dates to deposits within sites and, by extension, sites within regions. The simplest of these techniques uses artifacts of known age. These are artifacts that have a date inscribed on them or artifacts for which historical records indicate the time period when they first came into use and eventually went out of use. While a valuable tool in areas such as the Classical *Mediterranean world, where dated or datable coins, tokens, jewelry, and historical records were available, the technique was simply not applicable in most of the rest of the world.

In the early part of the twentieth century in the American Southwest and later in northern Europe, archaeologists began exploring the use of tree rings to determine the age of site deposits. Thus was born the science of *dendrochronology, or tree-ring dating. Dendrochronology was a breakthrough for archaeologists working in the American Southwest, where wood was preserved by the aridity, and for those working in northern Europe, where wood was preserved in bogs and marshes, but was of little or no use in most other parts of the world.

The real explosion in the development of techniques of absolute dating began in the 1950s and 1960s. In 1952 *radiocarbon dating was developed, and for the first time a technique offered archaeologists in almost all parts of the world a way to accurately determine the actual age of the carbonized wood and bone in the deposits of their sites. Radiocarbon dating revolutionized archaeology worldwide and in large part made possible the "new" or "processual" archaeology of the 1960s and 1970s. Not only were archaeologists able to accurately date events but they could also start looking at things like the rates of cultural change, and not just on a regional basis, but on a global scale, because finally everyone was able to talk about time using the same calendar scale.

Development of new techniques to address both the temporal limitations of radiocarbon dating and the inapplicability of radiocarbon dating to certain areas or contexts blossomed in the 1960s and 1970s. Today archaeologists can look to *fission-track and *potassium-argon dating for dating extremely old deposits (on the order of millions of years) and *obsidian hydration dating, thermoluminescence dating, and archaeomagnetic dating for determining the age of deposits or sites where radiocarbon dating is not an option.

In addition to expanding the number of options that archaeologists have for dating their sites, techniques have also been developed for refining the precision of those date estimates. A variety of techniques for doing *seasonality studies, discussed elsewhere, can allow the archaeologist to determine not only the approximate year or years that a site was occupied, but the actual season or seasons of occupation.

Finally, all of these techniques can be used in conjunction through a technique known as cross-dating. In cross-dating, stratigraphic or assemblage similarities between sites within a region can be used (much in the same way that tree rings are matched) to extend known dates from one or more sites to sites where chronometric techniques might not work, allowing archaeologists to develop cohesive chronologies for exploring regional social and cultural evolution over time.

George Michaels

DEAD SEA SCROLLS. As the most important collection of ancient Hebrew and Aramaic manuscripts ever discovered, the Dead Sea Scrolls have shed important light on the textual development of the Old Testament and on religious thought in Judea in the last centuries before the Common Era and during the first century A.D. Preserved by the extreme aridity of the Dead Sea region, the collection consists of nearly eight hundred separate documents, with the vast majority being highly fragmentary texts. Only nine complete, or nearly complete, scrolls have been found. Written on parchment and papyrus, the Dead Sea Scrolls represent the theological speculations of a sect, or perhaps even a movement, within Judaism that anticipated the imminent arrival of messianic leaders and the establishment of God's kingdom on Earth. The identity of the scrolls' authors and their connections to the emergence of Early Christianity and Rabbinic Judaism have occasioned considerable scholarly discussion and debate.

The first of the Dead Sea Scroll discoveries took place in the winter of 1946 and 1947, when three members of the Taamireh bedouin tribe, grazing their flocks along the steep cliffsides of the northwestern shore of the Dead Sea near an ancient site known as Khirbet Qumran, located a cave containing a cache of ancient manuscripts contained in tall clay jars. Seven nearly complete manuscripts were recovered from this cave: two copies of the Book of Isaiah; a scroll of Thanksgiving Hymns; a detailed description of the rules and rituals of a strict religious community (initially called the Manual of Discipline, but now generally known as the Community Rule); a commentary on the Book of Habakkuk; and a description of an eschatological war to take place at the end of times between the forces of good and evil, entitled the "Scroll of the War of the Sons of Light Against the Sons of Darkness." Three of these scrolls were purchased in 1947 by Professor Eleazar Sukenik of the Hebrew University in Jerusalem. Four others were purchased in 1947 by the Syrian Orthodox archbishop of Jerusalem, Mar Athanasius Yeshue Samuel, who, in 1954, sold them through intermediaries to Professor Yigael Yadin, Sukenik's son. All seven scrolls are now kept at the Shrine of the Book in Jerusalem.

In the years that followed the scrolls' initial discovery and the annexation of the Qumran area by the Hashemite Kingdom of Jordan after the 1948 Arab-Israeli War, ten more caves containing manuscripts or manuscript fragments were discovered along the northwestern shore of the Dead Sea. Among the most important of these were Cave Three (containing, in addition to the usual parchment and papyrus fragments, an intriguing document inscribed on copper, describing hiding places for temple treasure); Cave Four, containing an enormous cache of approximately fifteen thousand manuscript fragments; and Cave Eleven, from which were retrieved a complete Psalms Scroll and the Temple Scroll.

The study and publication of the great number of fragmentary texts from Cave Four was initially undertaken in Jordan by an international team of scholars headed by Pere Roland De Vaux of the Ecole Biblique et Archeologique in Jerusalem. However, the team's slow pace of publication after the 1967 Israeli takeover of the Palestine Archeological Museum in East Jerusalem sparked an international campaign to allow open access to the Dead Sea Scrolls by scholars from all over the world. The campaign was eventually successful; in the autumn of 1991, the official monopoly of the international team came to an end.

The importance of the Dead Sea Scrolls for the study of the development of the biblical text is underlined by the fact that the oldest known Hebrew biblical manuscript before the scrolls' discovery, the Aleppo Codex, was approximately one thousand years more recent—dated to around A.D. 1000. Thus the biblical manuscripts from Qumran, which include at least fragments from every book of the Old Testament, except perhaps for the Book of Esther, provide a far older cross section of scriptural tradition than that available to scholars before. While some of the Qumran biblical manuscripts are nearly identical to the Masoretic, or traditional, Hebrew text of the Old Testament, some manuscripts of the books of Exodus and Samuel found in Cave Four exhibit dramatic differences in both language and content. In their astonishing range of textual variants, the Qumran biblical discoveries have prompted scholars to reconsider the once-accepted theories of the development of the modern biblical text from only three manuscript families: of the Masoretic text, of the Hebrew original of the Septuagint, and of the Samaritan Pentateuch. It is now becoming increasingly clear that the Old Testament scripture was extremely fluid until its canonization around A.D. 100.

The study of the Old Testament Apocrypha and Pseudepigrapha (namely, those prophetic and apocalyptic books not universally included in the official Old Testament canon) has been considerably advanced by the finds from Qumran. The Hebrew texts of works such as the Book of Jubilees and the Book of Enoch—previously known only in Greek or Ethiopic translations—have been identified among the Qumran manuscripts and have led to a far better understanding of the prominent role that apocalypticism and messianic expectation played in the evolving theology of Judaism in the last centuries before the Common Era. The study of the connections of the Jewish apocalyptic tradition to the messianism of Early Christianity, previously studied only through texts transmitted through religious tradition over the centuries, has now been greatly assisted by the discovery of original, ancient manuscripts.

The Qumran texts also include a large number of documents that were apparently the literary product of the members of a sect or theological movement within ancient Judaism—variously identified by scholars as Essenes, Sadducees, or even militant, anti-Roman followers of the so-called "zealot" movement. Though the debates on the precise identity of the authors of the Qumran literature continue, their main beliefs and rituals are expressed in documents such as the Community Rule and the Damascus Rule which set down the history of the group and describe the process of initiation, communal ceremonies, and strict regulations for behavior among the membership. Unique commentaries on the prophetic books of Habakkuk, Nahum, Isaiah, Hosea, and Micah, among others, vividly illustrate the belief of this community that the End of Times was fast approaching and that the prophecies of redemption for the Righteous Remnant of Israel applied specifically to them. However, the theological, legal, or liturgical function of such other apparently sectarian texts as the Thanksgiving Hymns, the Temple Scroll, and MMT (an important legal text known to scholars as *Miqsat Ma'asei Ha-Torah*, "Some Works of the Torah") remain matters of considerable scholarly controversy.

The general chronological framework for the composition and copying of the Dead Sea Scrolls has been provided by paleographic analysis of the handwriting of the manuscripts and by carbon-14 dating, which offer a general time frame for most of the texts, ranging from the second century B.C. to the first century A.D. Additional important information has come from the excavations of the site of Khirbet Qumran, excavated between 1952 and 1956 by a joint expedition of the Ecole Biblique and the Department of Antiquities of Jordan. The site is located at the foot of the steep cliffside in which most of the scroll caves were found and occupies the same limestone plateau as Cave Four, with its huge cache of manuscripts. Despite the lingering doubts of some scholars regarding the relation of the buildings and large cemetery of Khirbet Qumran to the manuscript caves, it now seems clear that there was a relation, at least during most of the occupational history of the site. Another archaeological site, at Ain Feshkha, two miles to the south of Qumran, has also been connected with the community that presumably produced the scrolls.

Pottery, architecture, and coins excavated at Qumran indicate that the site was founded around 125 B.C. on the ruins of a destroyed Iron Age fortress. The new settlement flourished during the early first century B.C. at the time of the great expansion of the Hasmonean Kingdom into the area of the Dead Sea. Though the original excavators of the site identified this settlement (Level Ia and Ib) as the center of a community of Essenes who had fled into the wilderness in opposition to the Hasmonean rulers of Judea, subsequent research has thrown this hypothesis into doubt. Surveys of the western coast of the Dead Sea in recent years have located a number of structures and apparent settlements founded at roughly the same time as Qumran and Ain Feshkha that were apparently connected to the Hasmonean royal activities in this area: trade, agriculture, and frontier defense. Thus it now seems plausible that Level I at Qumran be connected with Hasmonean settlement and military activity in the area, not anti-Hasmonean religious protest.

After a possible gap in occupation toward the end of the first century B.C., the site of Qumran was repaired and reoccupied, though not nearly on the same scale as before. This settlement (Level II), plausibly connected with the religious community that collected and copied the manuscripts deposited in the nearby caves, was apparently destroyed at the time of the First Jewish Revolt against Rome. This event has been plausibly linked to the campaign of Vespasian in the Jordan Valley in the spring of A.D. 68. After a brief reoccupation of the site, perhaps by a small Roman garrison guarding the area, and its later use as a fortress of the Jewish rebels during the Bar Kokhba Revolt (A.D. 132 to 135), Qumran was abandoned forever as a permanent settlement. The occupational history of the nearby site of Ain

Feshkha follows that of Qumran closely, though it seems to have been established slightly later, early in the first century B.C.

Although the Qumran area has been the focus of most scholarly attention, several other important groups of ancient manuscripts have been discovered elsewhere in the lower Jordan Valley and Dead Sea region. During the excavations of *Masada, fourteen fragmentary texts were recovered, consisting of biblical books (Genesis, Leviticus, Deuteronomy, Psalms, and Ezekiel), apocryphal works (Jubilees and the Wisdom of Ben-Sira), and, despite the contention of the excavator that the Masada rebels had no formal connection with the Qumran community, a sectarian document (Songs of the Sabbath Sacrifice), nearly identical to a text found at Qumran. Farther to the north, between Masada and Qumran, important collections of biblical texts, economic documents, and military correspondence have been found in the ravines of Wadi Murrabat, Nahal Hever, and Nahal Se'elim. Among the most significant of these documents are personal dispatches from rebel leader Shimeon Bar-Kosiba, better known as Bar-Kokhba, leader of the Second Jewish Revolt against Rome in the second century A.D. Additional scattered finds of Bar-Kokhba-period texts have been made in recent years in the vicinity of *Jericho as well.

Two other important manuscript finds have been made in the lower Jordan Valley and Dead Sea region. In caves in Wadi Daliyeh, to the north of Jericho, an important collection of legal and administrative papyri from the fourth century B.C. were discovered. And at the site of Khirbet Mird, nine miles southeast of Jerusalem, an important collection of Arabic, Greek, and Aramaic documents were found, dating from the sixth to the eighth centuries A.D., and providing important evidence on economic and religious life in Palestine during the period of transition from Byzantine to Muslim rule.

[See also RELIGION.]

■ Edmund Wilson, *The Scrolls from the Dead Sea* (1955). Yigael Yadin, *The Temple Scroll* (1985). Robert Eisenman and Michael Wise, *The Dead Sea Scrolls Uncovered* (1992). Hershel Shanks, ed., *Understanding the Dead Sea Scrolls* (1992). Florentino Garcia Martinez, *The Dead Sea Scrolls Translated* (1994). Lawrence H. Schiffman, *Reclaiming the Dead Sea Scrolls* (1994). Neil Asher Silberman, *The Hidden Scrolls* (1994). James C. VanderKam, *The Dead Sea Scrolls Today* (1994). Frank M. Cross, *The Ancient Library of Qumran* (1995). Geza Vermes, *The Dead Sea Scrolls in English* (1995).

Neil Asher Silberman

DECIPHERMENT. *See* WRITING: INTRODUCTION.

DENDROCHRONOLOGY is the scientific study of the chronological and environmental information contained in the annual growth layers of trees. The method uses accurately dated tree-ring sequences for placing past events in time and for reconstructing environmental conditions that prevailed when the rings were grown. Both aspects of this science are relevant to archaeology, the first to the exact dating of archaeological features, the second to understanding the effects of environmental variability on human societies.

Dendrochronology was created early in the twentieth century by Andrew Ellicott Douglass, an astronomer with the Lowell Observatory in Flagstaff, Arizona, as an outgrowth of his study of the effects of sunspots on terrestrial climate. Lacking weather records long enough to be tested for correlation with the twenty-two-year sunspot cycle, Douglass turned to the rings of coniferous trees in this semiarid area as potential proxy climatic indicators that could be related to sunspot activity. Building on his discovery that these trees possessed identical sequences of wide and narrow rings, he developed a continuous 450-year record of the ring-width variability common to the trees of the area and demonstrated that this variability was highly correlated with the precipitation of the winter preceding the growth year.

Archaeologists quickly recognized the potential of Douglass's method for dating abundant wood and charcoal remains in the ruins of the *Southwest. His discovery, in 1917, that archaeological samples exhibited common patterns of ring-width variability, stimulated an intensive effort to link the undated prehistoric ring sequence with the dated living-tree sequence. Twelve years' work produced a 585-year prehistoric ring series that did not overlap with the dated sequence. In 1929, the rings in a charred log from a site near Show Low, Arizona, connected the two sequences and, for the first time in North American archaeology, allowed calendar dates to be assigned to prehistoric sites. Thus, dendrochronology became the first of many independent dating techniques used in archaeology. Since that time, nearly 50,000 tree-ring dates from nearly 5,000 sites in the Southwest have produced the finest prehistoric chronological controls available in the world.

Douglass's success sparked the immediate adoption of tree-ring dating in other regions, notably Alaska, the North American Great Plains, and southern Germany. The University of Arizona recognized Douglass's achievement by creating the Laboratory of Tree-Ring Research in 1937; it remains the world's largest and most comprehensive dendrochronological research and teaching facility. After 1960, tree-ring programs were begun in virtually every area of the globe. Archaeological dating is now widely practiced in North America and Europe, and other applications of the method are pursued throughout the world.

The fundamental principle of dendrochronology is crossdating, the matching of identical patterns of variation in ring morphology among trees in a particular area. Although several ring attributes (density, trace element content, stable isotope composition, intra-annual growth bands, and others) can be used for this purpose, crossdating most commonly is expressed in the covariation of ring widths. Whether established visually, graphically, or statistically, unequivocal crossdating is the essential element of dendrochronology. The size of the area encompassed by a particular crossdating pattern varies from hundreds to hundreds of thousands of square kilometers and must be determined empirically in each case.

Chronology building is the process of averaging the annual ring widths of many crossdated samples into composite sequences of ring-size variability with each ring dated to the year in which it was grown. By incorporating overlapping ring records of varying lengths and ages, this procedure produces ring chronologies that are longer than any of their individual components. Thus, the chronology for the Southwest has been extended back to 322 B.C. by adding progressively older archaeological samples to the living-tree sequence. In addition, chronology building reduces individual tree effects and maximizes the variability common to all the trees, that is, the variability caused by large-scale external factors, primarily climate. Thousands of chronologies have been built in many regions of the world, the longest of which are an 8,700-year bristlecone pine sequence from California and a 10,000-year sequence from central Europe. Composite chronologies serve as standards for dating samples of unknown age, as records of past climatic variability, and as referents for calibrating *radiocarbon and other time scales.

Archaeological tree-ring collections yield three kinds of information: chronological, behavioral, and environmental. Dating remains dendrochronology's primary contribution to archaeology. A tree-ring date is determined by finding the unique point at which the ring-width sequence of a sample matches the pattern of a dated chronology. Tree-ring dates have two notable attributes: accuracy to the calendar year and no associated statistical error. When a sample's outer ring is the final ring grown by the tree, the date specifies the year in which the tree died, usually the year that the tree was cut for use by humans. When complicating factors can be controlled by evaluating detailed data on the provenance, function, and physical attributes of the wooden artifact from which the sample is taken, the date can be applied to the construction of features associated with the artifact. Analyses such as these produce unequaled levels of chronological control at site, locality, and regional scales.

Behavioral information results from treating tree-ring samples as artifacts rather than just sources of dates. Analyzing wooden elements in this fashion illuminates a prehistoric people's treatment of trees as a natural resource and wood as a raw material. Information on the season of tree cutting, distance of wood transport, species preferences, tree-felling and woodworking tools and techniques, dead wood use, stockpiling, beam reuse, structure repair, element shaping, and other behaviors can be acquired in this way.

Environmental information comes from two sources. When differential use of tree species by a site's inhabitants can be controlled, differences between the species assemblage of the site and the modern flora of the area can indicate major environmental changes since the site's occupation. The chief source of environmental information is variation in ring widths, which records several aspects of climatic variability. Dendroclimatology is the branch of dendrochronology concerned with environment–tree growth relationships. Dendroclimatic reconstructions are produced by establishing mathematical relationships between ring widths and climate data for the period of overlap between these two records and then using the resulting equations to reconstruct past climatic variability from the longer tree-ring record. These operations reconstruct past climate in terms of standard measures, such as millimeters of precipitation or degrees of temperature, at time scales ranging from seasons to centuries and at spatial scales ranging from localities to continents. Dendroclimatic analyses of climate-sensitive archaeological tree-ring chronologies produce accurate reconstructions of prehistoric climatic variability that can be related to past human behavior. Combining high-frequency dendroclimatic reconstructions with other paleoenvironmental indicators reveals a broad spectrum of environmental variability that would have affected prehistoric and historic human populations.

Since its creation by Douglass, dendrochronology has made important contributions to archaeology in many areas of the world. It is safe to predict that, as global interest continues to grow, archaeological applications and the spatial coverage of the method will continue to expand.

[See also DATING THE PAST; PALEOENVIRONMENTAL RECONSTRUCTION; RADIOCARBON DATING.]

■ Bryant Bannister, "Dendrochronology," in *Science in Archaeology*, ed. Don Brothwell and Eric Higgs (1963), pp. 161–176. H. C. Fritts, *Tree-Rings and Climate* (1976). Martin R. Rose, Jeffrey S. Dean, and William J. Robinson, "The Past Climate of Arroyo Hondo, New Mexico, Reconstructed from Tree-Rings," *Arroyo Hondo Archaeological Series* 4 (1981). M. G. L. Baillie, *Tree-Ring Dating and Archaeology* (1982). Jeffrey S. Dean, "Dendrochronology," in *Dating and Age Determination of Biological Materials*, ed. Michael R. Zimmerman and J. Lawrence Angel (1986), pp. 126–165. Fritz Hans Schweingruber, *Tree Rings: Basics and Applications of Dendrochronology* (1988).

Jeffrey S. Dean

DESTRUCTION OF THE PAST. Almost any activity that disturbs the surface of the earth will destroy information in an archaeological site. If the disturbance is done without any record being made of the evidence of previous human occupation, then a portion of history (or prehistory) has been destroyed. Scientific archaeology preserves the information and artifacts found in a site, while it destroys the original context of the information and artifacts; any other kind of earth disturbance at an archaeological site also destroys the original context (whether done purposely with a bulldozer, or inadvertently with a plow), but with no record being made, that small piece of the past is lost forever.

Greed and ignorance—economic greed and ignorance of laws and in general of the value of the past to the present—are the two greatest causes for destruction of archaeological sites. Despite the fact that most nations have laws which, to one degree or another, aim to protect the important vestiges of their heritage, loss of these sites continues at a much faster pace than protection, even of the most important or historically valuable of these properties.

The pace of damage to the world's archaeological heritage differs between developed and developing countries, but the causes for damage are much the same. The most obvious cause is land alteration brought about by "progress"—construction of all kinds, from small but numerous pads for new oil wells, to city malls, to new housing, to highways, to massive hydroelectric dams, power plants, and associated reservoirs. In many countries, some of this construction is preceded, by law, with archaeological investigation of the area to be affected, but often construction is proceeding faster than archaeologists can investigate or, as is the case in the United States and Canada, the construction is purely a private (nongovernmental) endeavor and no federal laws apply. In these cases, where there is also a long-standing tradition of collecting for personal benefit, and where the general public does not always appreciate the value of, much less the nature of, historic and prehistoric sites, ignorance of the fact that construction is destroying history is responsible for the loss of many sites. Even in those countries where all archaeological sites and their contents are the property of the government, as in Central and South America, the ability of government agencies responsible for protecting or investigating sites to be affected is hampered by lack of funds and lack of qualified personnel. As a consequence, and contrary to the intent of federal law, many archaeological sites are destroyed with no record, no investigation, no effort to preserve the information about the past.

Less insidious, but nonetheless destructive, are farming practices worldwide. Clearing land, deep plowing, creation of rice fields—all of this activity is necessary for life but means the death of thousands of archaeological sites.

On the other hand, since the end of World War II, efforts to bring to the attention of the public the nature and value of important national heritage sites, as well as those considered of worldwide importance, have made great headway in slowing the rate of needless destruction. These efforts should decrease the possibility that the past will be destroyed because of ignorance either of the law or of the value, even of the existence, of particularly important properties. Ignorance of the law or of the nature of archaeological sites is less and less an excuse for site destruction.

Greed as a cause for destruction of the past has been with us since the first looters entered the pyramids in Egypt only a few hundred years after the death of the pharaohs. It is compounded in modern times by the prestige of collecting antiquities as art, and by the presence of gold in many sites—in shipwrecks of the Spanish New World fleets or in tombs of powerful chiefs in Mexico, Panama, or Peru. The wholesale looting of cemeteries, which is often where the most beautiful and therefore monetarily valuable objects are found, has reached epic proportions in the last thirty years, as the selling price for these objects has made it feasible to risk obtaining them illegally. The objects taken quickly and illegally may be intact, but the information of their origin, function, and meaning to the culture that made them is lost. The cycle of greed is a vicious one, from the local looters in Central America (known as huaqueros) who carry guns and have been known to shoot-to-kill, to the dealers in antiquities who do not care about the source, to the collectors—and in some cases the museums—who do not care if a beautiful and extremely valuable object has been taken illegally from its country of origin.

So long as there is a market anywhere, so long as there are people who will buy an object regardless of how it was obtained, the huaqueros will be at work. When governments cannot (or will not) control this illicit digging, it continues, supplying the international art market and destroying more and more information about the past. Incidents such as the looting in the *Sipan Region of Peru and the robbing of prehistoric graves at the Slack Farm in Northern Kentucky may reach the popular press, and in the case of Slack Farm can be instrumental in the passage of stricter laws to protect certain kinds of sites, in this case prehistoric cemeteries.

From the destruction of Dubrovnic (a World Heritage City), to the individual with a metal detector on a Roman site in Britain, loss of the world's heritage, a nation's heritage, and local heritage continues through greed or ignorance or in the name of "progress." Making it socially unacceptable as well as illegal to own, buy, sell, or trade in illegally obtained antiquities could dry up the market and save thousands of sites. Only massive efforts at educating political leaders, school children, museum directors, and others will stem the tide of destruction of what little evidence of the past is left to us.

[See also CULTURAL RESOURCE MANAGEMENT: GLOBAL ISSUES; EDUCATION IN ARCHAEOLOGY: POPULAR EDUCATION; ETHICS OF ARCHAEOLOGY AND COLLECTING; TRAFFICKING IN ANTIQUITIES.]

■ Karl Meyer, The Plundered Past (1973). Henry Cleere, ed., Approaches to the Archaeological Heritage (1984). Jeanette Greenfield, The Return of Cultural Treasures (1989). Phyllis Mauch Messenger, ed., The Ethics of Collecting Cultural Property: Whose Culture? Whose Property? (1989).

Hester A. Davis

DEVELOPMENT, Economic. The earth's landscapes have a long history of intensive use by indigenous peoples and small farmers. These peoples have utilized agricultural technologies that permit them to make a living from what is often considered to be marginal farmland, despite pressures from the world economy, urbanism, civil unrest, and top heavy national development. Indigenous knowledge systems can provide models for sustainable uses of landscapes and a viable alternative to the economic development commonly promoted by national and international institutions.

What is often forgotten is that these indigenous knowledge systems have long histories. The deep trajectories result from dynamic, long-term interaction between humans and local environments. Indigenous knowledge systems are often fragmentary or transformed. Often they have been abandoned, as in the case of raised field agriculture in the upper Amazon of Bolivia, in the highland Andes, and the Maya lowlands of Guatemala, Belize, and Mexico. The same is true of irrigation and terrace agriculture throughout much of Latin America. Archaeology can provide a "window" into the history of indigenous knowledge systems. Ancient agricultural systems often were based on the massive transformation of local and regional landscapes. Embedded in these landscapes are the physical structure, patterning, and designs of agricultural engineering and expertise, resulting in a palimpsest of land-use strategies and knowledge systems. Many of these long-used landscapes in Latin America are presently underproductive or abandoned. Archaeological techniques, combined with a multidisciplinary approach, can provide information on the crops grown, tools utilized, field morphology, and patterning, functions, prehistoric demography, and the technical knowledge used. This long-term perspective also provides the political, demographic, social, and economic context of the ancient farming system and its evolution over time.

A small group of prehistorians are practicing what has been referred to as an "applied archaeology." Through the study of ancient indigenous knowledge systems and landscapes, archaeology can provide a practical contribution to rural economic development in the contemporary situation. Despite drastic changes in the social, economic, political, and natural environment, many ancient technologies have been demonstrated to be appropriate in contemporary rural society.

Raised Fields in Peru and Bolivia. Traces of an impressive agricultural system referred to as raised fields (waru waru, suka kollus) are found throughout the Lake Titicaca region at 12,500 feet (3,810 m) in the Andes. Raised fields are large, elevated planting platforms constructed of earth taken from adjacent canals, which improve planting conditions by doubling topsoil, aerating the soil, and providing local drainage. In addition to irrigation, the deep canals capture, produce, and recycle nutrients in the form of organic matter, algae and green manure and act as a heat sink to protect fields from frosts. Although once a highly productive landscape, the ancient fields now lie abandoned and little agriculture is practiced here because of poor soils, seasonal inundation, and harsh frosts. A number of indigenous communities in the region have worked with two archaeological projects in the rehabilitation of raised fields. In 1981, raised fields were rebuilt for experimental purposes in Huatta using information recovered from excavations of ancient fields. The results were so impressive that a number of projects have begun to promote raised fields as a sustainable alternative to capital-based western models of agriculture being introduced into the region. An estimated 741 acres (300 ha) of fields have been put back into production and over fifty communities are participating in the rehabilitation projects. A similar raised-field rehabilitation project based on the study of ancient fields has begun with native communities in the Amazon region of Bolivia.

Prehispanic Terracing in Peru. An estimated 12 million acres (5 million ha) of mountain slope were once farmed using stone-faced terrace platforms. Many of these now abandoned fields were part of elaborate irrigation canal networks which distributed water over long distances. Traditionally attributed to the Incas, archaeologists now know that these agricultural works have a long history in the Andean region. In the recent years, various multidisciplinary projects have begun to promote the rehabilitation of pre-Hispanic terraces to put these lands back into production for the benefit of local communities.

Desert Agriculture in the Negev. Archaeological investigations of the Negev Desert region of Israel located numerous large settlements in areas that today are deserted arid wastelands. A long multidisciplinary study by Michael Evenari and colleagues of the landscapes around these sites discovered engineering works which show us how these areas were farmed in the past. A sophisticated network of stone lines, ditches, and barriers above the sites were used to capture the limited rainfall in this area and the runoff was funneled into artificially leveled fields where it provided the moisture necessary to farm these marginal regions. Experiments based on the ancient design proved successful and a development project has put some of these lands back into use.

[See also ARCHAEOLOGY IN THE CONTEMPORARY WORLD; FUTURE OF THE PAST.]

■ Michael Everai, et al., *The Negev: The Challenge of a Desert* (1971). John Browder, ed., *Andenes y camellones en el Perz Andino: historia presente y futuro* (1986). John Browder, ed., *Fragile Lands in Latin America: Strategies for Sustainable Development* (1989). Clark L. Erickson, "Applied Archaeology and Rural Development: Archaeology's Potential Contribution to the Future," *Journal for the Steward Anthropological Society* 20: 1–2 (1992): 1–16. Clark L. Erickson, "Prehistoric Landscape Management in the Andean Highlands: Raised Field Agriculture and Its Environmental Impact," *Population and Environment* 13: 4 (1992): 285–300. Alan L. Kolata, *The Tiwanaku* (1993). Kathryn Gleason and Naomi Miller, eds., *The Archaeology of Garden and Field* (1994). Clark L. Erickson, "Archaeological Perspectives on Ancient Landscapes of the Llanos de Mojos in the Bolivian Amazon," in *Archaeology in the American Tropics: Current Analytical Methods and Applications*, ed. Peter Stahl (1994).

Clark L. Erickson

DIET, Reconstruction of. The acquisition of food is the first concern of all human societies. Not surprisingly, food-getting activities have played a central role in shaping the course of human history. The reconstruction of prehistoric diets is therefore an important part of modern archaeological research.

Prehistoric *subsistence first became a major subject of archaeological inquiry in the 1940s and 1950s, when archaeologists began to conduct detailed studies of the origins of agriculture in the Near East, Europe, and the Americas. It was also during these years that Grahame Clark conducted his landmark study of hunter-gatherer subsistence at the Mesolithic site of Star Carr in East Yorkshire, England. In the 1960s and 1970s, paleodietary research broadened to encompass a wide range of questions and economies. During these years archaeology began to shift from a historical discipline concerned with sequences and unique events to one of holistic inquiry into the causal relationships between culture and environment. The shift to problem-oriented research was accompanied by technological and methodological developments in data collection and analysis. Biological specialists were included in archaeological research teams to aid in the analysis of plant and animal remains. More rigorous excavation and extraction techniques were developed to insure the proper collection of food refuse.

From the late 1960s onward, archaeologists have increasingly turned to studies of modern human and nonhuman primate groups to achieve a better understanding of the benefits and limitations of different subsistence strategies. Studies of nonhuman primates have provided valuable insights into the relationship between subsistence practices and variables such as body size, group size, and mating patterns. Modern hunter-gatherer and horticultural groups have provided models for understanding the relationship between cultural attributes, environmental conditions, and economic strategies, and for interpreting the distribution of patterns of food refuse in archaeological sites.

Modern paleodietary research depends on a variety of different analytic specialties, the practitioners of which are generally trained within the discipline of archaeology. These specialties include artifact and analysis, the analysis of animal and plant remains, coprolite studies, site catchment analysis, and the study of human skeletal remains. Each line of inquiry contributes its own dimension to the study of prehistoric foodways.

The artifacts found in archaeological deposits are important sources of information about food procurement and processing techniques. Subsistence-related artifacts include such implements as manos and metates, digging sticks, hoes, fishhooks, knives, projectiles, and cooking and storage vessels. Since resource availability is a function of technological capability, the resource potential of a region must be evaluated in the context of a particular group's ability to exploit it.

Animal remains also provide a wealth of information about subsistence activities. Faunal remains that tend to be preserved in archaeological sites include the bones and teeth of vertebrates, and the shells of marine and terrestrial invertebrates. Through the analysis of these remains, it is possible to look at temporal and spatial variations in the relative importance of different animal food resources. Cut marks on bone can be used to determine when early hominids began to eat meat and provide clues on how this meat was acquired. Other research questions that have been addressed using faunal remains include differential access to protein resources and processes of animal domestication.

Plant remains are equally important in the reconstruction of prehistoric diets. Depending on conditions of preservation, these may include seeds, nut shells, rinds, pollen grains, and phytoliths. Botanical remains document the selection and use of different plant species by ancient peoples, and have been particularly valuable in documenting the origins and processes of Old and New World plant domestication.

In the rare cases where they are preserved, human coprolites (fossil / ancient feces) are the best single source of information regarding what people actually ate. Coprolites are primarily comprised of residues and undigested plant and animal food components, in roughly the same combinations (meals) in which they were ingested. Because parasites may also be preserved, it is sometimes possible to investigate the parasite load of a diet through the analysis of human waste.

By combining information derived from animal and plant remains with studies of the modern (or ancient) landscape, archaeologists can reconstruct a site's catchment—the region around the site from which resources were procured. This information can then be used to build models that predict which resources may be used in what proportions for specified sets of priorities (e.g., maximum nutrition, taste, risk minimization). A model's ability to explain prehistoric behavior can then be tested by comparing the predicted frequencies of different types of resources with those actually observed in the archaeological record. These models enable archaeologists to better understand the decision-making processes of the prehistoric people they study.

Recently, archaeologists have turned to human skeletal remains for answers to questions about the quality and quantity of different prehistoric diets. There are several different types of skeletal evidence that can be used to investigate paleonutrition. Stature, bone density, skeletal lesions, and dental pathology have all been used to examine the relationship between diet and health. Bone chemistry is proving useful in the assessment of gross dietary composition. For example, studies of inorganic trace elements and organic stable isotopes have been particularly successful in identifying the transition from hunting and gathering to maize agriculture.

Paleodietary research provides glimpses of a past shaped in large part by subsistence practices. The shift to an omnivorous diet that focused increasingly on meat consumption played a significant role in the evolution of early hominids. The origins of agriculture in the Near East, Far East, Mesoamerica, and elsewhere forever changed the relationship between humans and their environment. In the absence of agriculture, inhabitants of rich marine environments of the west coast of North America harnessed nature's bounty and followed a cultural trajectory similar in many respects to that found in agricultural areas. Diet has clearly influenced the course of human biological and cultural evolution, and future studies of prehistoric foodways promise to enhance our understanding of the nature of this relationship.

[See also ANIMAL REMAINS, ANALYSIS OF; PALEOBOTANY; PLANT REMAINS, ANALYSIS OF; ZOOARCHAEOLOGY.]

■ Elizabeth S. Wing and Antoinette B. Brown, *Paleonutrition: Method and Theory in Prehistoric Foodways* (1979). N.R.J. Fieller, D. D. Gilbertson, and N.G.A. Ralph, eds., *Palaeobiological Investigations: Research Design, Methods, and Data Analysis* (1985). Robert I. Gilbert and James H. Mielke, eds., *The Analysis of Prehistoric Diets* (1985). Brenda V. Kennedy and Genevieve M. LeMoine, eds., *Diet and Subsistence: Current Archaeological Perspectives* (1988). Wesley Cowan and Patty Jo Watson, eds., *The Origins of Plant Domestication in World Perspective* (1989). David R. Harris and Gordon C. Hillman, eds., *Foraging and Farming: The Evolution of Plant Exploitation* (1989). Kristin Sobolik, ed., *Paleonutrition: The Diet and Health of Prehistoric Americans* (1994).

Patricia M. Lambert

DIFFUSION is the transfer and transformation of innovations in ideas and material culture across space and through time. The profound effect that the diffusion of innovation has had on the distribution of people, ideas, and artifacts across the earth is well documented in the historical record. It is not surprising, therefore, to find that the archaeological record also contains abundant evidence of the operation of this process.

Diffusion of Innovation. To innovate is to create or invent something new. Innovation in cultural evolution is analogous to genetic mutation in organic evolution. Both processes contribute to adaptation by producing variations in existing arrangements that are in turn selected for or against by the material conditions in which an organism or human cultural system exists. However, there are also profound differences between the two processes.

First, while biological mutation is a random process productive of what Darwin called "chance variation," cultural innovation is seldom so. Rare is the innovator who creates something entirely new. Most innovations unite existing, hitherto unconnected, ideas or things in novel ways. Innovation is thus more often patterned than random. Second, while mutations must be transmitted genetically from one generation of organisms to the next, innovations are transmitted by learning. Innovations simply diffuse. Procreation is unnecessary for their transfer.

Simplistic reconstructions of cultural evolution posit neat stages of technical advances, each one building upon the last. Diffusion makes it possible to skip stages. The mastery of relatively simple copper and bronze metallurgy preceded the development of iron smelting in southwestern Eurasia. Following the arrival of Europeans in North America, Native Americans leapt from stone to iron tools in the space of a single generation without transit through the intervening bronze stage of tool manufacture and use.

Although ample testimony to the creative capacities of our species can be found throughout prehistory and history, innovation is not the most important source of the remarkable diversity and complexity of human culture. Greater even than our capacity to innovate is our ability (and inclination) to copy and adopt the creative work of others. Diffusion, adoption, and reconfiguration of innovation, not innovation in and of itself, have been the most important sources of cultural development and change.

Diffusion occurs either as a process of expansion or of relocation. In expansion diffusion, a phenomenon spreads through a population from one region to another. When this occurs by direct contact, as in the spread of an epidemic disease, it is known as "contagious" diffusion. More commonly, transfer takes place in a step-wise fashion along existing geographic hierarchies, for example, from a metropolis to its hinterland along its transportation network, or through existing social structures—say, from the elite to the middle classes. Transfer through expansion of this kind is known as "cascade" diffusion.

In relocation diffusion, ideas or material culture traits diminish or disappear in their source area even as they spread into their new location. Relocation diffusion takes place between centers of high cultural innovation and the regions of cultural receptivity and retardation on their peripheries. It also occurs in the course of human migration and colonization.

The Principle of Limited Possibilities. Despite the ubiquitousness of diffusion, similarities of nature, style, or function between traits in separate areas are not always due to cultural transfer. It is also possible for a trait to be independently invented at different times and places due either to "convergent development" or to what Alexander Goldenweiser called "The Principle of Limited Possibilities." Some problems in human adaptation are both universal and admissible to only a few practical solutions. As Robert Lowie put it, "How many ways of fastening a skin membrane to a drum are conceivable?" The limited ways of tipping a spear, hafting an axe head, or grinding seeds mean that mere similarity of form of such simple objects cannot be taken as proof of diffusion.

The Hägerstrand Model. The most widely recognized general model of the innovation/diffusion process was developed by Torsten Hägerstrand (1954) in the course of studying the diffusion of modern agricultural innovations in Sweden. Hägerstrand carefully specified six elements: the characteristics of the innovation, its place of origin, the nature of the area over which it diffused, the paths of its dispersal, its ultimate destination, and the time it took to get there.

Hägerstrand discovered that innovations of all kinds tend to diffuse from their points of origin in a similar, four-stage wave. In the primary stage an innovation occurs and gains acceptance at its point of origin. In the second stage, its dispersal begins to widen rapidly. In the tertiary stage adoption begins to slow. In the final saturation stage, the innovation approaches its maximum dispersal and its rate of acceptance declines or stops altogether. The simplicity of the Hägerstrand model allows its terms to be precisely specified, simulated mathematically, and measured empirically. Such studies confirm that the diffusion and adoption of an innovation over time tends to form the S-shaped curves predicted by the model: slow initial acceptance, followed by rapid dispersal that slows to an asymptotic increase.

The Hägerstrand model has been refined to include such factors as the level of communication between innovators and adopters, the complexity of both the innovation and the sociocultural system of the adopting group, the degree of congruence between the innovation and existing system, its real or perceived advantages, even individual and societal attitudes toward change.

Diffusion and Indigenism. Unfortunately, the sophisticated modeling of diffusion has not been widely appreciated by archaeologists. Perhaps this is because the systematic plotting of trait distribution, once a standard activity among archaeologists, has largely fallen out of favor. Many contemporary archaeologists regard distribution studies as possessing little explanatory power or reject diffusion altogether as an explanatory "ism."

Partly this rejection is a reaction to the excesses of the radical diffusionist school of Elliot Smith, who proposed that ancient civilization worldwide originally diffused out of Egypt. Unfortunately, the rejection of diffusionism by some archaeologists is so extreme as to become a radical "indigenism" that assumes, unless forcefully shown otherwise, that cultural traits in a given region are the result of independent invention. Informed by anthropological theory, contemporary archaeologists tend to see human cultural prehistory in evolutionary, neofunctional, ecological, and, most recently, "post-processual" terms. They tend to regard human cultures as interrelated systems and are less concerned with how an individual trait entered into such a cultural system than why it was chosen above other possibilities or how it articulates with the other parts.

Prehistorians have also rejected diffusionism because such explanations of cultural similarity are difficult to falsify by archaeological means. The absence of direct archaeological evidence of contact between two cultural traditions does not prove that such contact did not occur. Indigenism, on the other hand, is readily falsifiable. The hypothesis that

a cultural tradition developed in complete isolation from its neighbors must be rejected following the discovery of but one object of foreign manufacture or direct inspiration dating to the period in question.

Demonstrating that an archaeological object is of foreign origin is not always easy, of course, and cultural traits vary in their appropriateness for this task. As noted, traits simple enough to have been independently invented are of little use in demonstrating contact. Domesticated plants and animals are at the opposite end of the scale. As George Carter puts it, their distribution is governed by "Kilmer's Law" ("Only God can make a tree"). Therefore, the recovery of the bottle gourd, a cultivated plant of African origin, in pre-Columbian archaeological sites in the Americas must be taken as evidence of some form of contact between the Old and New Worlds in prehistory.

While the simple fact of foreign contact may be proven in this way, the significance of such contact can only be estimated by assessing the volume and variety of foreign ideas and material culture found to be present. The greater the number of traits shared by two areas, the more likely it is that the presence of these traits is due to diffusion. Viewing our bottle gourd example in these terms, the fact that no other domesticants of indisputably Old World origin have been recovered in pre-Columbian New World archaeological contexts has led many Americanists to the suspicion that the bottle gourd accidentally drifted to the New World on the Atlantic currents.

Sorting out the impact of diffusion in the archaeological record is not often easy. For example, excavation of the Valdivia site on the coast of Ecuador produced an early, sophisticated ceramic sequence that appeared around 3000 B.C., apparently without local antecedents. To explain this abrupt appearance, the excavators evoked the mechanism of trans-Pacific diffusion and proposed that storm-tossed fishermen from the Jomon culture of Japan introduced ceramic manufacture to the Americas. At the time of their discovery, the specimens from the Valdivia site were the oldest known ceramics recovered in the New World. This fact coupled with their putative Jomon attributes and the location of Valdivia on the Pacific coast strengthened the argument that the vessels were the product of diffusion despite the truly daunting nautical problems that confront drift voyagers in the Pacific. Subsequently, pottery clearly unrelated to Jomon ware was recovered from earlier strata at the Valdivia site. More recently, excavations have produced pottery dating to around 5000 and 6000 B.C. in the Brazilian Amazon and around 5000 and 4500 B.C. in northern Columbia. These finds do not eliminate the possibility that Jomon-style pottery making diffused from Japan to Ecuador. However, they dispose of the argument that ceramic technology was unknown in the Americas before 3000 B.C. and lend credence to the view that pottery developed independently in both the New and Old Worlds.

The manufacture of ceramics involves simple, perhaps self-evident, technological steps. Diffusion can be more clearly recognized in more complex traits. Fritz Graebner argued that the more complex a culture trait is, and the more secondary traits not essential to its function, the greater the likelihood that its presence in both areas was due to contact rather than independent invention. His criteria are widely, if unconsciously, applied in archaeological studies of diffusion. Iron smelting, practiced throughout much of sub-Saharan Africa in the Precolonial Period, meets Graebner's criteria. Indigenous African iron technology is complex, and associated with its practice over much of the continent are such decidedly inessential traits as the belief that blacksmiths are sorcerers. Graebner's rules are not laws, of course. In the absence of reliably dated archaeological sequences, therefore, they must be applied with special care.

[*See also* THEORY IN ARCHAEOLOGY.]

■ Robert H. Lowie, "On the Principle of Convergence in Ethnology," *Journal of American Folklore* 25 (1912): 24–42. Alexander A. Goldenweiser, "The Principle of Limited Possibilities in the Development of Culture," *Journal of American Folklore* 26 (1913): 259–290. G. Elliot Smith, *In the Beginning: The Origin of Civilization* (1932). Betty J. Meggers, Clifford Evans, and Emilo Estrada, "Early Formative Period of Coastal Ecuador: The Valdivia and Machalilla Phases," *Smithsonian Contributions to Anthropology* 1 (1965): 1–34. Thorsten Hägerstrand, *Innovation Diffusion as a Spatial Process* (1967). Colin Renfrew, "Carbon-14 and the Prehistory of Europe," *Scientific American* 225 (1971): 63–72. Everett M. Rogers and F. F. Shoemaker, *Communication of Innovations: A Cross-Cultural Approach* (1971). Lawrence A. Brown, *Innovation Diffusion: A New Perspective* (1981). D. Bruce Dickson, "Anthropological Utopias and Geographical Epidemics: Competing Models of Social Change and the Problem of the Origins of Agriculture," in *The Transfer and Transformation of Ideas and Material Culture*, ed. Peter J. Hugill and D. Bruce Dickson (1988), pp. 45–72.

D. Bruce Dickson

DISEASE, by its direct and indirect effects, has molded human lifestyles and societies from the earliest true humans to the present day. We are not, however, simply passive recipients of disease, and there is a constant reciprocity between natural processes and social practices. The historian of disease aspires to establish diagnoses, distinguishing between mortality and morbidity; produce profiles of the spatial and temporal distributions of diseases, their prevalence and specificity for age, sex, occupation, class, environmental zones, and so on (sometimes it is only this evidence that permits diagnosis); consider the causes, reinforcing and reducing factors, and the effects of each disorder, in relation to the individual, the local group, and larger, even worldwide, populations.

Evidence for the study of ancient disease is fragmentary and distorted, but our sources can be complementary. Only a small proportion of the disorders of humankind is recorded in human remains, but there are advantages in being able to examine and analyze tissue inaccessible in the living. Written history has conscious and unconscious biases. Even when authors were stringently objective, disease identification was difficult or impossible: Terminology is obscure, spurious etiologies are given (for example, "worm in the tooth" was a widespread ancient explanation for toothache), and usually only gross symptoms or those causing the greatest distress were reported. It is impossible, for example, to distinguish clearly between types of fever, although they would include familiar infectious diseases such as typhoid, cholera, and malaria. On the other hand, records often give invaluable demographic details. Archaeological evidence is restricted to material culture but can indicate cultural factors causing or produced by disease with a time depth unavailable to history, and modern ethnography provides models for comparison with the ancient world. With rare exceptions, interpretation of art tends to be most revealing of the art historian's ignorance of medicine or the doctor's misunderstanding of ancient or ethnographic iconography.

At each stage of human history, patterns of disease have changed and developed, indicating the effects of new environments, subsistence patterns and activities, social systems, and cultural practices. We bear today the stigmata of early hominid development in the spinal arthritis that affects, if not afflicts, much of the population of the world, and is due to stresses on the spine due to our upright posture, which evolved more than three million years ago. During the millennia when humankind lived in small nomadic groups, they would probably have had the same disorders as modern hunter-gatherers: ectoparasites such as lice, and infections conveyed from wild animals through insect vectors (for example, sleeping sickness and scrub typhus) or directly from bodies of prey. Recent research is seeking the origins of a range of modern diseases in mummified monkeys from Egypt.

The beginnings of agriculture and associated sedentism had a profound and largely negative effect on human health. The apparent beneficial effects of dependence on a staple crop were offset by malnutrition due to a restricted diet, a high infant death rate due to weaning on unsuitable foods, and famine when harvests failed. It is at this stage that we find signs on the skeleton of dietary deficiencies, particularly anemia—especially in the Americas, dependent on maize agriculture. These deficiencies were worsened by intestinal and other parasites, which caused bleeding and prevented nutrient absorption and were constantly reintroduced in the settled communities, endoparasite effects are described in medical papyri and are found even in very early Egyptian mummies. Domesticated animals often harbored part of the life cycle of some of these parasites, the pig tapeworm being a well-known example. They also brought their own diseases that, in the original or a mutated form, were passed to humans or kept in an animal reservoir: anthrax, mycotic (fungal) infections, sleeping sickness maintained in domestic cattle and horses, and, nowadays, pigs, which in China are a reservoir of rapidly mutating strains of influenza. Sometimes, however, these diseases were beneficial, as was the case with the relatively harmless cowpox, which provides immunity against smallpox and was used by Edward Jenner (1749–1823) in the first vaccinations. Commensal animals such as rats, which have some dependence on the human settlement, also acted as vectors of diseases, most notoriously plague. The use of low-lying land for cultivation exposed more people to the marsh-favoring mosquito and to the malaria it carries, still a major killer in Third World countries and probably the infectious disease that has affected most people throughout history. Despite the hazards of damp, fertile land—which also included the mosquito-borne yellow fever and elephantiasis—cultivation continued due to human persistence and to immunity rising from hereditary blood disorders that make blood cells inhospitable to the malaria parasite, such as sickle-cell anemia and thalassemia, found as early as the Mesolithic Period.

We know nothing of the history of medicine at this early stage, except for the numerous examples of trephination of the skull, particularly frequent in early American societies and Neolithic western Europe, which demonstrate medical skill in their successful healing. One of the uses of trephination was probably treatment of skull fractures, and this reminds us that trauma was always present in the past, as today, due to the type of activity undertaken and to violence, and that weapon injuries tend to increase with increasing population density, the types of weapons often identifiable by their effects.

With the development of urbanism, town dwellers began to suffer diseases favored by dense concentrations of population, allowing the spread of pathogens such as tuberculosis, which is endemic at high population density—the earliest examples are from ancient Egypt, but it was present in the pre-Columbian New World—and the short-duration infections that include the common bacterial and viral childhood diseases, insignificant only in the modern developed world, and smallpox, typhoid, and cholera. Diarrheal diseases and parasite infestation in modern Third World countries are exacerbated by unhygienic living conditions, and we interpret the high infant mortality of the urban stage as primarily caused by crowding, presence of refuse and fecal material of people and animals, and lack of clean water. Buffering against famine could be provided by the state or other institutions, but true famines were rare by comparison with chronic or seasonal malnutrition. Unfortunately, one result of state provision of water in Rome was lead poisoning from pipes, and much later, public water sources transmitted cholera in nineteenth-century London, although one outbreak inspired English physician John Snow's early (1854) epidemiological insight into its waterborne nature. Egyptian and Mesopotamian medicine, despite its good reputation, was primarily magico-religious; Greek and Roman medical knowledge and practice was reasonably scientific and successful, but much of their expertise, particularly in hygiene and surgery, was lost after the collapse of the Roman world.

In the medieval period a new deficiency disease, rickets, appeared, due to the absence of sunlight between the close housing and consequent lack of vitamin D, and it continued because of air pollution in early industrialized towns. Even before the Industrial Revolution, pollutants, the many infectious agents, and an inadequately nourished urban population probably offset some of the gains of industrial intensification. However, cancers, often thought to be modern disorders due to longevity, or at least appearing in the industrial period, have been present from the earliest human history. Exploration and trade was always a source of new diseases, the most notable being plague, the transmission of which was then favored by overcrowded towns and unsanitary conditions. The origin of syphilis and related diseases is still the source of intense debate, although a New World origin now appears to be impossible (there are Old World venereal syphilis cases of pre-Columbian date). Its transmission from centers in the East, however, appears to have been facilitated by the expansion of the Arabian empire in the ninth century and movements of the armies of Genghis Khan and returning Crusaders in the twelfth century, when syphilis reached epidemic proportions in western Europe; it then followed trade routes around the world.

Just as the relatively new disease of syphilis devastated Europe, the sixteenth-century introduction to the great civilizations of the Americas of infections to which they had no immunity—smallpox, measles, and chicken pox—probably had more effect on their collapse than warfare. Today, Native Americans, especially the Inuit, and indigenous peoples of Oceania and Australia suffer from diseases resulting from a diet to which they are not physically adapted. In the modern world we can observe societies at all the stages discussed above, and it is noteworthy that the great majority of the world's people still suffer the same diseases, and for much the same reasons, as our ancestors from the times of the agricultural, urban, and industrial revolutions.

[See also BLACK DEATH, THE; PALEOPATHOLOGY.]

■ Don Brothwell and A. T. Sandison, eds., *Diseases in Antiquity* (1967). Peter J. Ucko, Ruth Tringham, and G. W. Dimbleby, eds., *Man, Settlement and Urbanism* (1972). Mark Nathan Cohen and George J. Armelagos, eds., *Paleopathology at the Origins of Agriculture* (1984). Ralph Jackson, *Doctors and Diseases in the Roman Empire* (1988). Nancy Duin and Jenny Sutcliffe, eds., *A History of Medicine from Prehistory to the Year 2000* (1992). Mehmet Yaşar İşcan and Kenneth A. R. Kennedy, eds., *Reconstruction of Life from the Skeleton* (1994).

Corinne Duhig

DOMESTICATION OF ANIMALS. The domestication of animals involves a shift in the relationship between hunters and their prey. Successful hunting of wild game using traditional weapons, such as bows and arrows, spears, and traps, requires an intimate knowledge of animal behavior. Wild animals which move around in large numbers have a "herd mentality," that is, they feel secure in the herd, and because they follow each other, their behavior can be directed and controlled.

Domestication takes this control one step further, and can be defined as a manipulation of the genetic material or selective breeding for easy access to the resource. However, there is a trade-off. The point about domestication is that it is not only the animals which become domesticated, but the people as well. The freedom that hunters have to move with the wild herds becomes restricted, in the sense that they now have to consider the needs of the animals. Once the animals are in close proximity to humans they need protection and need to be taken to where water and forage are available. Ultimately the animals become wealth that requires nurturing, and may also become central in inheritance, exchange, and ritual/ceremonial systems.

An important question to ask is: if hunting was so successful, why bother with domestication? One immediate answer is that in many places hunters may have been too successful and threatened or overcome the ability of the animals to reproduce themselves, leading to local extinction. An example of this has been suggested by Tony Legge and Peter Rowley-Conwy at Tell Abu Hureyra in Syria, where the hunting of gazelles using "kites" or traps into which large numbers of animals were driven and killed was so effective that during the period 9000 to 6000 B.C. access to the animals dropped from 80 percent to 20 percent of the meat resources, to be replaced by ovicaprids (sheep/goats). The indications were that the ovicaprids were domesticates, and this controlled resource was needed to maintain an adequate meat supply for a human population that was becoming more and more sedentary with increasing reliance on domesticated plants.

This brings us to another important aspect of early animal domestication: that with sedentism human population numbers were starting to outstrip those of wild game in the vicinity of villages. This meant there were pressures to try to keep the animals close to the habitation sites, and this could be done only by controlling them.

One might further ask: why did the people of Abu Hureyra not domesticate the gazelles? The answer probably lies in the behavior of these animals. During the breeding season the males are highly territorial and compete for females which they maintain in harems. Such intense competition would have been very difficult to suppress for ease of herding by domestication. This does not mean that some of the animals which were domesticated had no similar negative behavioral characteristics from a human perspective. We can be sure that wild cattle, for example, were rather ferocious beasts, but from analogy with wild buffalo or eland, as long as the herds are mixed with both males and females the herd mentality takes over, and once humans are no longer perceived as a threat the animal behavior is capable of an increasing degree of manipulation.

Wild or Domestic Animals? How can you tell a wild from a domestic animal in the archaeological record? This is not a simple matter, since the direct evidence has to come from the bones of the animals which are found on sites during this formative period. Therefore, preservation and sample size become crucial. One of the effects of close control over animals is the restriction of the gene pool. Within a few generations this usually results in smaller animals. Also, Pollard and Drew found that the bone cavities of the foot bones of domestic llamas were larger (i.e., less well formed) than wild ones, a possible result of feeding stress under domestication. People also have aesthetic needs and will intentionally manipulate the breeding of their stock to enhance desirable characteristics, some of which can be seen in the skeleton. For example, the horns of cattle can be trained to grow in almost any direction, or the muzzle of dogs trained to become shorter.

There is some debate over how easy it is to recognize domestic animals during early domestication, since it may take quite some time before distinct morphological changes can be seen. In this case indirect evidence is used. The claims for early domesticated cattle in Egypt serve as an example. At Nabta Playa and Bir Kiseiba, a faunal record comprising up to 65 percent gazelles and 21 percent hares also included small percentages of large bovids identified as cattle. The argument for domestication of the cattle is an ecological one, stating that an environment capable of only sustaining hares and gazelles would be unlikely to support cattle without human intervention. This would be an example of the presence of an "exotic" species.

Other criteria are used, such as culling patterns. With large enough samples one can produce mortality profiles. Since only a few males are needed to service a flock of sheep, for instance, young males are killed and eaten. Ewes, on the other hand, will be kept until the end of their reproductive life. A mortality profile of such herd management would produce a bimodal graph showing mostly immature and some old animals being killed. In contrast, the exploitation of wild herds by hunters should show many more mature animals killed during their reproductive period.

Indirect evidence may also be found in changes in species frequency before and after domestication took place. An example was offered above from Tell Abu Hureyra, where a high frequency of gazelles was replaced by a similarly high frequency of ovicaprids, the latter being assumed to be domesticates.

Categories of Domesticated Animals. Turning to those animals which were domesticated, we can group them into different categories. One group of which there are few members would have been those used to assist in hunting. The most obvious is the dog, most probably derived from the wolf, *Canis lupus*, although some authors do not discount the possibility of a wild dog progenitor, or even the jackal. It is possible that the latter, while not the main progenitor, may have contributed genetic material to certain breeds (e.g., greyhounds). The earliest dog domestication probably occurred in the Near East by 10,000 B.C. In this category would also go the ferret. Where the domestication of this animal took place is uncertain, but North Africa or the Iberian Peninsula is suggested.

A second and much larger group would be the meat sources: ovicaprids, cattle, pigs, reindeer, guinea pigs, and New World dogs. In this case, the fat content of these animals, as well as controllable herd behavior, may well have been the reason for the domestication of the larger mammals. Wild sheep are found throughout the highland areas of Asia, but only one group, *Ovis orientalis*, from southwestern Iran and Turkey, has the same number of chromosomes (forty-six) as domestic sheep. Goats are probably derived from the wild *Capra aegagrus* also found in Iran and Turkey, although the ibex (*Capra ibex*) can produce viable offspring when crossed with domestic goats, as they both have the same number of chromosomes. Both sheep and goats were domesticated in southwestern Asia by 7000 B.C.

Domesticated cattle, derived from the wild *Bos primigenius*, were to be found in southwestern Asia by 6000 B.C. Whether these were the earliest domesticates is presently debated, as there are the claims mentioned above for cattle under human control from the desert regions of southwestern Egypt before 7000 B.C. This is not universally accepted, and a counterargument looks to the introduction of ovicaprids (none of which have African progenitors) after 5000 B.C. as a more likely date for the introduction of domestic stock to Africa.

The other major food domesticates are the pigs. The thirty-eight chromosomes found in domestic animals are also found in the wild pigs of Europe, as well as those of the Far East. By 6000 B.C. they were found in Near Eastern sites, but the claims by William Solheim for the antiquity of animal domestication in Southeast Asia, perhaps as long ago as 6000 B.C., should not be discounted, although they remain to be proven.

Independent domestication of mammals certainly occurred in the Americas. Small dogs were an important animal protein resource in the Valley of Mexico by 3000 B.C., replacing deer, which were overexploited and which became unavailable to the general farming population at this time. Equally, guinea pigs were domesticated by 3500 B.C., when they played a similar role among Archaic peoples of South America. Later, among the Incas of Peru they were also used for divination and religious sacrifices.

The domestication of reindeer and some pigs illustrates another aspect of the process of human/animal relationships. Reindeer have been intensively hunted in both the Old and the New Worlds since the Upper Pleistocene. Closer attachments can now be seen with the Saami of Scandinavia and the Tungus of Siberia, but many of the animals are not in any way modified by human intervention (i.e., the animals are basically wild and run free, but seem to like human company, and therefore are easily available when they are needed). At the other end of the continuum some of the animals are more intensively "tamed"; consequently, they can be used for milk or as draught animals. Like all deer they crave salt, and human urine around a camp is very attractive to them. Similarly, among the Maring of New Guinea, pigs run free, returning to human settlements to root among the garbage or to get a share of low-grade tubers.

Such examples of sociable animals becoming closely involved with human settlements have led researchers to believe that this was how animal domestication began. This has a degree of casualness about it, with bonds between animals and humans being gradually strengthened over time.

Elsewhere other mechanisms have been suggested. One is the Periphery or Marginal Area Theory where people being forced to survive on the edges of more productive regions intensified their relationships with animals. Examples of this have been suggested by Kent Flannery for the highland areas of Iran, where the possible wild progenitors of goats and sheep, as well as plants which became domesticated, still exist.

Another model, first developed by V. Gordon *Childe, has been called the Oasis or Propinquity Theory. In some ways, Childe's theory is similar to the reindeer example above, but it was formulated around the belief of severe aridification taking place in the Near East, which forced people and animals into close proximity around oases. Thus the prime mover would have been environmental change. These same pressures are indicated for North Africa and the Sahara where a dry period some 7,000 years ago may have precipitated a much closer human/animal relationship and the need not only to control local resources in a much more coherent fashion, but also to make use of potential imports from southwestern Asia.

A subgroup of the domesticated meat resources are birds. There is a general acceptance that the chicken was first domesticated in the Far East, possibly near the Thai/Burma border or in China, ca. 6000 B.C. Later it spread west to the Near East, from where it entered Africa and Europe by at least the Punic period. The turkey was independently domesticated in Mesoamerica at the beginning of the Christian era, while the guinea fowl was domesticated in Africa, although its antiquity as a domesticate is uncertain. Waterfowl are widespread domesticates throughout the Far East, as well as in Europe, but their origins are unknown. Domestic geese were certainly part of the dynastic Egyptian economy, probably by New Kingdom times.

A third category of domesticates is draught animals (which could also be eaten). These include horses, camels, donkeys, the South American camelids (llamas, alpacas) and the Tibetan yak. The horse was first used in southern Russia about 4000 B.C., while camels were domesticated in southern Arabia ca. 3000 B.C. (but not introduced to North Africa until the Roman period). Donkeys were domesticated ca. 3500 B.C. in the Near East, while the earliest domesticated llamas appeared in Peru at least by 4000 B.C. As yet, there is no data on the antiquity of the yak as a beast of burden.

Many of the animals in the last two categories have provided later secondary products: milk from cattle, ovicaprids, reindeer, and even horses; wool from sheep and llamas; and hair from goats and camels. (*See* Secondary Products Revolution.)

A final category, which all animals discussed above can at some time or another perform, is that of companions or pets. The cat is probably the best example, having been domesticated in the Near East around 6000 B.C. Cats, of course, are also "mousers" and so are useful around a settlement.

Development of Pastoralist Societies. The discussion above deals primarily with the beginnings of animal domestication (i.e., changing and intensifying human/animal relationships). Pastoral societies, on the other hand, are those in which the animals have become symbolic items in the deeper or ideological realm of social relationships. It is important to distinguish the two, since there are people, like the Basarwa hunters of Botswana, who keep goats, but basically see them as an extension of wild game and let them more or less take care of themselves around settlements. In other words, the animals have not been integrated into the symbolic realm where they might be used for ritual purposes, such as naming ceremonies, bridewealth payments, or strengthening political alliances, as they are in pastoralist societies.

On the one hand, there is a general belief among many researchers that nomadic pastoralism developed out of a mixed economy in most parts of the world. In northeast Africa, Sadr (*The Development of Nomadism in Ancient Northeast Africa,* 1991), for example, has postulated that such nomadism was closely integrated into the state administration. On the other hand, the introduction of already domesticated animals into an area occupied by aboriginal hunters poses different sets of criteria. This occurred, among other places, in southern Africa sometime at the beginning of the Christian era. It would appear that the earliest domestic animals in this area showed up on sites that can be related to incoming Iron Age farmers. The transfer of domestic stock to local hunters must have occurred, since the Khoikhoi herders of the Cape, South Africa, are genetically related to San (Bushmen) hunter-gatherers. The mechanism for exchange and the transition to pastoralism probably had to do with clientship and the integration into a more dominant society.

[*See also* ANIMAL REMAINS, ANALYSIS OF; CAMEL, DOMESTICATION OF THE; DOMESTICATION OF PLANTS; HORSE, DOMESTICATION OF THE; ZOOARCHAEOLOGY.]

■ Frederick E. Zeuner, *A History of Domesticated Animals* (1963). Eric Higgs, *Papers in Economic Prehistory* (1967). Sally and Lew Binford, *New Perspectives in Archaeology* (1968). Charles Redman, *The Rise of Civilization* (1978). Tim Ingold, *Hunters, Pastoralists and Ranchers* (1980). Juliett Clutton-Brock and Caroline Grigson, *Animals and Archaeology,* BAR Int'l. Series: 163 (1983). Simon Davis, *The Archaeology of Animals* (1987). Juliette Clutton-Brock, *The Walking Larder* (1988). Andrew Smith, *Pastoralism in Africa* (1992).

Andrew B. Smith

DOMESTICATION OF PLANTS. Soon after the end of the Pleistocene, the appearance of domesticated plants marked a fundamental change in the relationship between plants and people throughout much of the world. These domesticated plants fall into six main groups: grasses, legumes (beans of Fabaceae), roots and tubers (arums, lilies), oil plants (palms, mustards, sunflower, and relatives), fruits and nuts (rose family, butternut/walnut family), and vegetables and spices (nightshade family, gourd family, etc.). In all cases, domesticated plants share a dependence on people for their propagation and survival and have developed characteristics that ensure this dependency. For the most part, domestication makes the plant parts that are useful to people even more useful than they would be in the wild. Domesticated plants fall at one end of a continuum ranging from wild through weedy to fully dependent upon humans. The process whereby this human-plant mutualism develops has been termed coevolution. Interdisciplinary work in archeology, botany, ecology, genetics, chemistry, and physics, are contributing to our understanding of domestication, but much remains to be learned. Our understanding of these plants is important because domestication tells us a great deal about human ecology and behavior as well as about who we are in general.

No single trait differentiates domesticated plants from their wild ancestors. Most domesticated plants can still cross with their wild ancestors and produce fertile offspring. In some crops, such as maize, this crossing is essential for maintaining genetic diversity. In most cases, the domesticated plants and their wild ancestors are the same species. Traits that benefit people and are counterproductive to survival in the wild differentiate domesticated from wild forms. Usually the plant loses its natural dissemination method. For example, some plants, such as manioc, valued for its starchy tubers, no longer sets flower. Other plants, particularly grasses such as maize, wheat, and barley, keep their fruit attached to the plant and require people to go through a series of steps to free the grain from the plant. Human intervention is necessary to maintain each successive generation of plant.

Also advantageous to a human-plant mutualism are characteristics that make scheduling of planting and harvests predictable. To start, domesticated plants will generally germinate soon after planting. Dormancy is a trait that allows seeds to survive for long periods before conditions are right for growth. Thin seed coats in many domesticated plants reduce possible delays in germination. At the other end of the growth cycle, fruits of specific crop varieties will simultaneously ripen, permitting people to harvest them at one time.

The wild forms must have fruiting stems that are brittle to ensure the independent and often spontaneous dispersal of as many fruits as possible. Plant parts used by people are often enlarged. Whole plants, such as sunflower, may exhibit gigantism. Other plants, such as dwarf wheat, may be diminutive. The short stalks allow wheat to withstand heavy winds and rains without tangling and becoming impossible to harvest.

In order to determine whether domesticated plants were present in a particular time and place, archaeologists must first recover the remains of plants from the locale in which they are interested. This is done primarily by flotation of soils from archaeological sites. Other sources of data include desiccated plant remains, impressions in clay, pollen, and phytoliths or plant opals. Microscopic examination of the recovered plant parts provide the necessary clues. Sometimes biochemical traces in the remains offer insights on the domesticated status of a plant. Efforts to recover genetic information from archaeologically recovered crop remains is just beginning, but promises significant gains in our understanding of domestication. In order to fix the contexts of the remains in time, archaeologists radiocarbon date individual seeds or other relevant plant parts by the relatively new accelerator mass spectrometry technique (AMS dating). Scanning electron microscopy combined with light microscopy will often provide telltale clues of morphological changes in plants indicative of domestication.

Plant domestication occurred independently throughout the world. Significant areas to consider include the Near East, South and East Asia, Africa, eastern North America, Mexico, and South America. Some plant domestication also occurred in southwestern North America, Oceania, and the Caribbean. Domestication of plants is thus a relatively universal process and one that is no longer considered to have occurred in specific centers in the aforementioned areas. Rather, the processes were regional.

Old World. Wheat and barley were the most important of the early crops in the *Near East. Considerable botanical investigation has provided a great deal of background on these and other crops. Archaeological investigations are spotty, with large samples of plant remains coming from a very few sites. One of these is Abu Hureyra in Syria, significant because it is the first site in the Near East to produce a rich collection of plant remains spanning the time from just before agriculture through periods with evidence of agriculture. At about 9000 B.C., wild grains such as einkorn wheat were being collected. However, by 8000 B.C., after a short hiatus at the site, domesticated einkorn was accompanied by emmer wheat, barley, and rye. Bread wheat comes considerably later, by about 6000 B.C.

The sequence of wheat types makes sense, considering wheat biology. Domesticated einkorn differs from its wild form only in lacking brittleness. Wild emmer wheat is a cross between wild einkorn and a closely related grass, *Triticum speltoides*. Domesticated emmer, like einkorn, is nonshattering. Finally, bread wheat evolved as a result of a cross between emmer (and it is not known whether it was wild or domesticated emmer) and goat grass (*Triticum tauschii*). In other words, bread wheat could not have existed until emmer did. This process, unlike normal crossing, increased the number of chromosomes in each form of wheat. Thus, one would expect to see bread wheat later in the sequence.

Early domesticated barley seems to have appeared first around 7000 to 8000 B.C. at *Jericho and Ali Kosh. As with einkorn wheat, domesticated barley differs from wild barley only in brittleness. There are two alleles for nonbrittleness in barley, suggesting that barley was domesticated independently in two places. After barley's initial domestication, it further evolved so that more grains per flower stalk (inflorescence) became fertile (six instead of two). The earliest domesticated barleys are known as two-row, while the other form is six-row. Six-row barley appears not long after the two-row form was domesticated.

At one time it was presumed that domestication in the Near East took a considerable period of time. However, recent research indicates that wheat, and probably barley too, were transformed in a matter of centuries, not millennia. One model proposes that wild grains were cultivated, and then people selected for nonbrittle forms that ripened together. Domestication could have taken place in this context in a century or two.

In Africa, domestication took place in a region between the Sahara and the equator, including the upper Nile Valley. Little is known about the earliest phase of domestication in this area. We do know that several grains, including sorghum, pearl millet, African rice, tef, finger millet, and Guinea millet, originated here. In addition are several legumes, including earthpea, cowpea, and a groundnut; members of the gourd family, including bottle gourd and watermelon; as well as coffee; a few root crops, including yams; and numerous other crops. These represent at least four regional complexes. The earliest sorghum dates to about 2000 B.C., while pearl millet has been found in deposits dated to about 1200–1300 B.C. Researchers feel that these dates are much too late to represent the earliest domesticates in sub-Saharan Africa.

Northern and southern crop complexes flourished in East Asia. In the north the first to appear are foxtail and broomcorn millet, about 6500 B.C., and shortly thereafter, hemp (3500 B.C.). In the south, rice appears about 5000 B.C. The millets and rice appear fully domesticated in their earliest contexts, so it is presumed that their domestication took place much earlier. Unlike the case in the Near East, no one is carefully investigating the problems of domestication in East Asia, so almost nothing is known about how it happened. We do know that foxtail millet is a nonbrittle form of its wild relative, green foxtail grass. Broomcorn millet, on the other hand, is a hybrid of a panic grass and another, as yet unidentified, grass. Rice domestication took place as rice expanded its range from highland southeast Asia and southwest China northward and eastward into China and southeastward into island Southeast Asia. Domesticated forms are represented at *Hemudu and Luojiajiao about 5000 B.C. Just how early its domestication began, no one knows. The ancestor of domesticated rice is *Oryza rufipogon*, a weedy species with annual and perennial forms. It readily hybridizes with domesticated rice. Interestingly, long- and short-grained rice do not hybridize, and the wild ancestor is not divided into short- and long-grained forms. Much work remains in order to understand the domestication of rice.

Extending from Thailand and Vietnam to Papua New Guinea is another region with a wide range of local crops, including black pepper, Job's tears, betel, ginger, banana, cucumber, taro, yam, and sugar cane. Bottle gourd and sweet potato, although not native to the area, are plants that are significant in the archaeological record as well. Significant sites include *Spirit Cave, *Banyan Cave, and *Khok Phanom Di, all in Thailand, and *Kuk in highland New Guinea. Evidence suggests that the beginnings of domestication lie in the Early Holocene in this region. In Thailand significant changes are visible in the archaeological record by about 6000 B.C. Local agriculture may have begun at the same time or earlier in New Guinea, although 4000 B.C. marks the time when pigs, which are normally associated with plant cultivation, are common in the record. Considerable research is required to detail the Early Holocene record in the region.

New World. In the New World, plant domestication began independently in Mexico, South America, and eastern North America. Corn, common bean, tomato, squash, avocado, chile pepper, cacao, and grain amaranths are significant locally domesticated crops. The earliest domesticates may be squash and bottle gourd, whose remains are found at the *Guila Naquitz rock shelter on Oaxaca in levels dated to about 8000–7000 B.C. The next domesticated plants may not appear until about 5000 B.C. in the Tehuacán Valley, where beans and corn are reported. This sequence, long accepted by most archaeologists, is being challenged, however. Until recently, stratigraphic evidence indicated an initiation of corn domestication around 5000 B.C. However, the corn remains themselves have just been AMS dated, and surprisingly, the oldest corn is no older than 3600 B.C. It appears that the earliest domesticated bean may be younger, too. The early contexts for squash and gourd at Guila Naquitz are being questioned as well. One needs to consider seriously that domestication of plants in Mexico is much younger than had been thought only a few years ago.

How corn was domesticated is problematic. As a grass, its fruit in the form of a cob is a monstrosity. However, it fits the pattern seen for many other grasses in that a cob is a type of nonbrittle fruiting structure (or spike). Corn's closest wild relative is teosinte, a grass with which corn readily hybridizes and which is brittle and does not have a cob. As such, the generally accepted view is that teosinte is the wild ancestor of corn. There are problems with this view, however. Teosinte seems to have been rarely harvested in the Early and Middle *Holocene, for example. A view that has not been entirely defeated is that another grass, actual wild corn with a true cob, now extinct, is the true ancestor. This wild corn is not confirmed in the archaeological record.

In South America, at least thirty plants were domesticated over a large area. Plants include all the major groups mentioned above. These include two grains, amaranth and quinoa (a chenopod); legumes such as lima bean, common bean, and peanut; vegetables such as capsicum (bell) peppers and three species of squash; cotton; fruits such as avocado, pineapple, and papaya; potato, sweet potato, and manioc; and drug plants such as tobacco and coca. The earliest evidence for cultigens are from Peru, Chile, and Ecuador at *Guitarrero Cave, the Ayacucho Caves, and a number of other localities. By 3000 B.C., and perhaps as early as 5000 B.C., many of the important South American crops may have been grown. These include bean, bell pepper, bottle gourd, guava, maize, potato, quinoa, and squash. As with Mexico, stratigraphic and other problems lower confidence for the 5000–3000 B.C. period. AMS dating of these early collections should resolve the issue. Of particular interest is maize. Proposed dates for its introduction from Mexico range from 5000 B.C. to 3000 B.C.

Crop diffusion and domestication in eastern North America have been the focus of intensive research. A number of crops can claim independent origins. Among them are sunflower, sumpweed or marsh elder, chenopod, amaranth, and egg gourd or cucurbit. Data are from a series of sites in the Illinois River valley to the west, and Kentucky, Tennessee, and Arkansas to the south. Egg gourd and warty squash, plants closely related to squash and pumpkin, appear in the archaeological record in the early to mid-Holocene, but domesticated forms were probably not grown until 1000 B.C. Sumpweed, sunflower, and chenopod were domesticated by 1500 B.C. Two of these, sumpweed and chenopod, are native to the East, but the wild ancestor of sunflower is native to the Colorado Plateau. Domesticated sunflower is unknown in the Southwest at the same time. How sunflower came eastward is unknown, although human and nonhuman agencies such as bison have all been suggested. Dependence on these plants to any great extent took another 1000 years. Corn and beans did not become important in eastern North America until about A.D. 1000.

Origin and Impact. All the evidence to date indicates that plant domestication began after the end of the *Pleistocene, sometime between 10,000 and 3,000 years ago. In some areas, such as the Near East and Asia, the process began during the Early Holocene. Elsewhere, such as in eastern North America, South America, and Mexico, it had certainly commenced by the Middle Holocene. Because of this timing, research on the conditions in which humans were living at this time is critical. We are learning that during the first half of the Holocene, plant associations, particularly the expansion of forests, went through dramatic changes in much of the world. Drainage patterns that resulted in the evolution of new river systems altered the landscape. Carbon dioxide levels in the atmosphere increased substantially at the end of the Pleistocene. This in turn had a number of effects, including differentially impacting the productivity of groups of plants due to certain physiological and ecological factors, which happen to be those that eventually evolved a close relationship with people. These and other phenomena provided conditions that were right in many areas for the relationship between plants and people to change substantially.

Were these conditions sufficient to cause domestication to occur? One view holds that domestication was part of a gradual evolutionary change in the relationship between plants and people. Others contend that characteristics of domesticated plants arose only after people began to plant and manage their wild ancestors. In the case of the first domesticated barley and wheat, one scenario allows that only a century or two is necessary to change the balance of plants in a field from mostly brittle to mostly tough forms. In eastern North America, the process is seen to be more gradual.

Once domestication occurred, the consequences were enormous. The availability of generally controlled resources permitted mitigating the risks and other effects of seasonal variations by enabling the production of larger quantities of storable resources. In turn, sedentary village life was ensured in places where it either had not begun or was only beginning. Risk was not entirely reduced unless a variety of resources were maintained. Dependence on too few crops increased the risk of famine due to crop failure. Domestication also had broad ecological and health-related impacts. For example, field preparation led to wide-scale ecological disruption with changed erosion patterns. Intensive irrigation brought about soil salination in the Middle Holocene Near East. Desertification was enhanced in some regions. Health risks increased despite the year-round greater availability of energy. Higher starch content in the human diet led to poorer dental health. When people were brought together by village life, risks of viral disease increased. Domestication and the agricultural systems within which crops were produced introduced systemic changes to human life around the globe. Research on domestication is slowly revealing an understanding of one of the most important processes in the development of modern human culture.

[*See also* AGRICULTURE; AFRICA: ORIGINS OF FOOD PRODUCTION IN; ASIA, ORIGINS OF FOOD PRODUCTION IN, *articles on* SOUTH ASIA, SOUTHEAST ASIA, AND CHINA; EUROPE, ORIGINS OF FOOD PRODUCTION IN; MESOAMERICA, ORIGINS OF FOOD PRODUCTION IN; NEW GUINEA, ORIGINS OF FOOD PRODUCTION IN; NORTH AMERICA, ORIGINS OF FOOD PRODUCTION IN; PACIFIC ISLANDS, ORIGINS OF FOOD PRODUCTION IN; PLANT REMAINS, ANALYSIS OF; SOUTH AMERICA, ORIGINS OF FOOD PRODUCTION IN.]

■ David Rindos, *The Origins of Agriculture: An Evolutionary Perspective* (1984). Charles B. Heiser, Jr., *Of Plants and People* (1985). David R. Harris and Gordon C. Hillman, eds., *Foraging and Farming: The Evolution of Plant Exploitation* (1989). Jane M. Renfrew, ed., *New Light on Early Farming: Recent Developments in Palaeoethnobotany* (1991). C. Wesley Cowan and Patty Jo Watson, eds., *The Origins of Agriculture: An International Perspective* (1992). Anne Birgitte Gebauer and T. Douglas Price, eds., *Transition to Agriculture in Prehistory* (1992).
Gary W. Crawford

DONG SON CULTURE. Beginning in the middle of the first millennium B.C., Southeast Asia, including the southern fringes of China, came under the influence of a distinctive metal-using tradition called Dong Son.

The discovery of the protohistoric Dong Son culture was the first exposure to Europeans of a complex Bronze Age stratified society in mainland Southeast Asia. At the site of Dong Son, on the south bank of the Ma River near Thanh Hoa in northern Viet Nam, excavations conducted by Pajot and, later, by Janse revealed a rich cemetery complex containing objects of bronze, iron, pottery, imported semi-precious stones, and artifacts of Chinese origin (Janse, 1958). Subsequent excavations at Vietnamese sites such as Viet Khe, Lang Ca, and Lang Vac (Bellwood 1985, Tan 1980), indicate that although the type site was peripheral to the focus of Dong Son activities in the Red River delta (Higham, 1989), it is nonetheless typical of this aspect of mainland Southeast Asian Bronze Age culture in that it provides dramatic evidence of the socially stratified, semiurban nature of the culture as a whole.

Initially, the Dong Son was regarded as a distinctive Bronze Age culture principally on the basis of archaeological materials derived from burial contexts at the type site and similar localities along the eastern margin of the Southeast Asian peninsula. Subsequent excavations of habitation sites such as Co Loa in the floodplain of the Red River, near Hanoi, as well as the recovery of Dong Son–style bronzes over a much wider region of Southeast Asia, including the Indo-Malaysian archipelago, have forced a reevaluation of the nature of Dong Son culture and its geographical and temporal parameters. The bulk of recent research indicates a local Vietnamese origin for the Dong Son culture. Archaeologists are able to delineate a clear development trajectory between roughly 1000 B.C. and 1 B.C. in which stylistic elements of local Neolithic origin are gradually incorporated within the products of the Dong Son bronze-casters.

The Dong Son is best known for its bronze wares, including so-called drums (which often functioned also as cowrie-shell containers), large bucket-shaped vessels termed *situlae*, daggers, swords, and socketed axes. The scale of the metal industry indicated by these finds is an indirect measure of the complexity of Dong Son society (the bronze drum from Co Loa, for example, weighs 159 pounds (72 kg) and would have required the smelting of between 1 and 7 tons of copper ore).

Toward the end of the Dong Son sequence, during the last two centuries B.C., Chinese culture, as an exponent of the expansionist Han empire, began to exert greater and greater influence on Dong Son civilization. This influence is detectable in the form of bronze mirrors, coins, seals, halberds, and other small artifacts that regularly occur in later Don Son sites. It is also likely that it was the Chinese who introduced iron technology into the Don Son metallurgical repertoire.

Historical documents record that in A.D. 43 the Dong Son homeland in Southeast Asia finally succumbed to Chinese invasions from the north and the entire region was incorporated within the territory of the Han dynasty.

The extent to which superficially similar metal-using traditions in adjacent regions such as Thailand (e.g., the *Ban Chiang complex) and south China (e.g., the Dian civilization) should be considered an integral part of the Dong Son tradition remains to be adequately explored.

[*See also* ASIA: PREHISTORY AND EARLY HISTORY OF SOUTHEAST ASIA; CHINA: HAN EMPIRE; SOUTHEAST ASIA, KINGDOMS AND EMPIRES OF.]

■ J. M. Janse, *Archaeological Research in Indo-China. Volume III, The Ancient Dwelling Site of Dong-S'on (Thanh-Hoa, Annam)* (1958). Peter Bellwood, *Man's Conquest of the Pacific* (1979). Ha Van Tan, "Nouvelles Recherches Prehistoriques et Protohistoriques au Vietnam," *Bulletin de l'Ecole Francaise d'Extreme-Orient* 68 (1980):113–54. Peter Bellwood, *Prehistory of the Indo-Malaysian Archipelago* (1985). Charles Higham, *The Archaeology of Mainland Southeast Asia* (1989).
John W. Olsen

E

EAST AFRICA

OVERVIEW (THE EAST AFRICAN IRON AGE)

South of the Sahara there was no Bronze Age; in East Africa around 2,000 years ago the main population moved from a Late Stone Age technology (with blades and *microliths dominant) to one based on iron. The period from then till European conquest in the nineteenth century is generally called the Iron Age. The manufacture and use of iron itself was as important as the development of farming by communities dependent on that metal to clear bush and forest and to hoe the land. In most of eastern as well as west-equatorial and southern Africa, the beginning of the Iron Age marks the effective emergence and expansion of food-producing economies (*see* Agriculture) (and the gradual retreat, but not extinction, of hunter-gatherer lifeways). However, in some of the more northerly regions of eastern Africa, which had suitable pastures, the herding of cattle, goats, and sheep, and arguably the cultivation of certain crops, long preceded acquaintance with iron.

The revolutionary impact of this combination of iron and agriculture is seen most markedly in the Interlacustrine region, that lying astride the equator between Lake Victoria and the western rift valley. (This comprises much of modern Uganda together with Rwanda and Burundi and adjacent parts of Tanzania and Zaire.) Dated Early Iron Age sites with their distinctive pottery (the Urewe styles discussed below) show that it was from this productive region that the new way of living expanded across the southerly third of Africa. Instructive here is comparison with the modern language map that shows this vast zone covered almost entirely by the Bantu family; it has been argued that the spread of early Bantu speech southward and southeastward from the equatorial forest and Lake Victoria as far as the distant shores of the subcontinent was one and the same process as this Iron Age settlement of selected environments. These now began to be cleared for sorghum and other old African crops. It was a rapid expansion in which, it appears, the farmer settlers distinguished themselves from the older populations of hunter-gatherers—or at least those elements of them that they did not assimilate—by both their iron technology and their Bantu speech.

The working of iron (*see* Metallurgy) required a self-perpetuating corps of technicians who could locate ores and maintain the skills (or indeed magic) of smelting them into usable metal and then forging the necessary tools. It required also organization of labor not only for assisting at the furnace and the forge, with bellows in particular, but also for cutting wood and preparing charcoal from chosen trees. This last activity, and the large amounts of wood fuel required by the iron industry, had in regions of demand a considerable impact on the environment, adding to that caused by clearance for farming itself.

Another distinctive industry tied to the new settled agricultural life was pottery. This, like iron, required the dual manipulation of minerals and fire. From the Interlacustrine region southward through eastern and southern Africa as far as Natal and Transkei, the Early Iron Age vessels display a number of similar or related features—in their texture, their decorative patterns, and their shapes. In all these respects they contrast with the pottery of pre–Iron Age pastoral and lakeside populations of the northerly parts of East Africa and the Lake Victoria basin. Around the lake and in the rich agricultural hill country of Burundi, Rwanda, and Kivu adjoining the western rift, this distinctive Early Iron Age pottery is usually called Urewe ware (once known as "dimple-based" ware). It dates mostly to the first half of the first millennium, but on some sites on the western side it extends back to the last few centuries B.C. (For certain sites in Rwanda, Burundi, and northwestern Tanzania considerably earlier dating has been claimed for such pottery and early ironworking by treating random radiocarbon readings at their face value; but the considered view, from the range of the pottery and the run of the radiocarbon evidence, is that this complex emerges in the final centuries B.C.) Then, in the earliest centuries A.D., there began the rapid expansion of this Early Iron Age complex from this interlacustrine region through much of eastern and southern Africa. As these people settled and adapted their farming in these different environments, there emerged regional variants of this pottery tradition (for which the overall term "Mwitu" has been proposed). The variant known as Kwale, between the eastern rift valley and the coast, bears several features in common with classic Urewe. It is thought to represent the first settlement of Bantu cultivators in that region.

Before the end of the first millennium A.D. there occurred some marked changes in East African societies and their economies. Though the detail is yet poorly understood in most regions, this transition to what is called the later Iron Age is documented in the first place by various regional styles of pottery that retain few of the distinctive features of the Early Iron Age legacy. These changes accompanied important cultural and economic developments, both in the Bantu regions and in the more northerly parts in which Cushitic and later Nilotic languages came to predominate. One of these was the emergence of more efficient Iron Age cattle keeping (*see* Pastoralism), in regions with suitable grassland and free of tsetse fly, often pursued within or alongside agricultural systems. Another was the adaptation of crops for the wetter and more forested regions, most notably the banana. This crop was introduced to Africa from the far side of the Indian Ocean at least a thousand years ago. In East Africa it has been developed and diversified more than anywhere else, numerous varieties becoming the staples of life to this day, notably on the slopes of Kilimanjaro and the shores of Lake Victoria. Similarly, rice, coconuts, and several Asian fruits were introduced and became particularly popular along the East African coast. In more recent times crops of American origin have been adapted to East African conditions and have increased the versatility of many agricultural systems. These include root crops, notably cassava (manioc) and sweet potatoes, and the grain crop maize (or corn)—which in the twentieth century has replaced sorghum and other millets as the staple in many districts.

The change from early to later Iron Age is especially striking in the interlacustrine region at the end of the first millennium. Urewe ware is no longer found; the dominant pottery types of the whole second millennium are distinct, being commonly decorated with twisted and, more frequently, knotted roulettes. Indeed, around Lake Victoria and in the highlands to either side the first rouletted pottery, which is thought to derive from farther north, is taken as the most convenient archaeological marker of the later Iron Age. It is demonstrated most clearly at Ntusi in the rolling grasslands of western Uganda, a place of concentrated population combining intensive grain cultivation with specialized cattle pastoralism. Uniquely for this region and period, it may merit being called a town. Ntusi's integrated system flourished for a remarkably long period, from the tenth or eleventh century till about the fourteenth century. This chronology is established from the *stratigraphy of the large mounds on which the settlement's rubbish was piled quarter by quarter.

Culturally related to Ntusi is the celebrated earthwork system of Bigo, built along the edge of the Katonga swamp 8 miles (13 km) to the north. At its most developed stage, Bigo enclosed more than 740 acres (300 ha) within a complex of banks and ditches measuring in all over 6.2 miles (10 km). In places the ditches are dug 16 feet (5 m) into the rock. The true purpose of Bigo, as of certain smaller earthwork complexes in the region, must await further research. Limited excavations have, however, shown that it contained a settlement; it may have served as a refuge for cattle and their owners in times of raiding and warfare, and some historians would see it as a royal capital of the early second millennium. There has been speculation whether these sites, including Ntusi as well as certain ancient hilltop shrines of local fame, should be attributed to an ancient empire in this region, mentioned in legend as Kitara and ruled by an alleged dynasty called (Ba) Chwezi; this in turn has been seen as ancestral to the more recent kingdoms of the region (notably Bunyoro, Ankole, Rwanda, and Buganda) and their ruling houses. Recently, however, with more critical evaluation of the oral-historical sources as well as renewed archaeological work, the literal interpretation of the Chwezi legends and claims of simple dynastic continuity have been questioned. Ntusi and Bigo were abandoned sometime around the fifteenth century, and this grassland district of Bwera declined in importance. The later kingdoms of this interlacustrine region, both pastoral and agricultural, developed from new bases. Nevertheless, much of their cultural, social, and economic background, including the prestige of cattle keeping in suitable districts, may be foreshadowed by the Kitara period of Ntusi and Bigo.

Interaction between agriculturalists and pastoralists in the later Iron Age was not confined to the interlacustrine region and its kingdoms. To the east, in the ecologically diverse highlands and plains either side of the Great Rift Valley—largely a region where kingdoms did not emerge and where non-Bantu languages have prevailed— mixed farming systems developed; in other areas, highly specialized cultivators and cattle herders exchanged their products or provided mutual support in years of drought or dearth. Well represented archaeologically are the pastoral encampments of the Sirikwa of the high grasslands of Kenya during the middle centuries of the second millennium, and at the foot of the rift escarpment to the south, near the present border of Tanzania, the remarkable remains of irrigated field systems and associated villages are also well represented (at *Engaruka in particular). This period preceded the emergence and expansion of the Maasai as such. The success of the latter in the high equatorial grasslands was dependent, however, on the pioneering achievements of these predecessors; indeed, Maasai cattle keeping owes much to the methods, breed selection, and ecological experience of the Sirikwa, many aspects of which were assimilated into the emergent Maasai identity some three centuries ago.

Along with ironwork and ceramics, East African Iron Age specializations included livestock and agricultural products. Another item of importance for agricultural communities was salt. This commodity has been produced in numerous localities by a variety of methods (including filtering saline soils and burning particular grasses). But rich and commercial sources of fine salt are less frequent; here there developed intensive seasonal activity in obtaining the saline soil or brine, filtering it, and boiling it in coarse pots. With their essential service industries, such centers became regional markets, not for salt alone but also for food, livestock, and specialist products including ironware.

Several of these salt sources have been investigated archaeologically; they provide valuable regional Iron Age sequences. At Ivuna and Kibiro the activity stretches back some eight centuries. However, excavations at the Uvinza brine springs have yielded a much longer sequence from the Early Iron Age, with Urewe-style pottery occurring in the lowest levels, to the twentieth century.

In time, objects of longer-distance trade were incorporated into the local and regional networks. These included cloth, beads, metalware, and eventually firearms imported from overseas through the Swahili coast, especially as international demands for ivory and other East African products increased. Except in the coastal region, specific archaeological signs of the coastal and overseas trade connections remain very sparse until the nineteenth century. The interior connections of the Swahili harbor towns and city-states (see East Africa: Coastal Towns of East Africa), including *Kilwa, Mombasa, and Shanga, which developed from the ninth century, were till recent times more marked in the south, near the Zambezi basin and the gold-producing region of *Great Zimbabwe.

[See also AFRICA; articles on PREHISTORY OF AFRICA, EARLY IRON-AGE SETTLEMENT OF SUB-SAHARAN AFRICA, THE RISE OF KINGDOMS AND STATES IN AFRICA; PASTORALISTS, AFRICAN: EAST AFRICAN PASTORALISTS; TRADE, AFRICAN.]

■ Peter L. Shinnie, ed., The African Iron Age (1971). Robert C. Soper, ed., "The Iron Age in Eastern Africa," Azania 6 (1971). Cambridge

History of Africa, Vols. 2, 3, 4 (1975–1978). David W. Phillipson, *The Later Prehistory of Eastern and Southern Africa* (1977). J.E.G. Sutton, *A Thousand Years of East Africa* (1990). David W. Phillipson, *Africa Archaeology*, 2nd ed. (1993).

John E. G. Sutton

NORTHEASTERN MEDIEVAL STATES OF EAST AFRICA

The part of Africa between the Horn and the Middle Nile contains not only hot arid lowlands with sparse pastoral populations (relying mostly on goats and camels, but in suitable places, sheep and cattle, too), but also the cool fertile highland massif of Ethiopia. Here there are dense populations with an agricultural tradition several thousand years old relying on a variety of crops developed in the region. Moreover, while in a way rather isolated within its highland fastness, Ethiopia was in pre-Islamic times closely connected across the Red Sea with southern Arabia. It has retained, at least in a religious and spiritual way, a link with Egypt and Jerusalem, while sharing some of the cosmopolitan cultural experiences of the Near East through more than two millennia. Thus, the ancient religious and funerary monuments of northern Ethiopia reveal the extension of the cults of Baal and Ashtaroth this far south; then in the fourth century, King Ezana of the already powerful state of *Aksum, who was the contemporary of the Roman emperor Constantine, chose to modernize (and to symbolize his alliance with Rome) by converting to Christianity. This move is reflected pointedly in the style of the monumental tombs at Aksum: from this time the kings ceased the practice of carving and erecting the spectacular giant stelae (sometimes called obelisks) with pagan symbolisms. A similar change occurs on Ezana's coins—Aksum being the only state in Africa south of the Roman Empire to issue its own coinage (in gold, silver, and bronze)—where the old pagan symbols were replaced with the cross.

It is from then that Ethiopian Christianity, of the Monophysite persuasion and allied to the Coptic Church of Egypt, recognizes its foundation. Its own traditions claim an older, if legendary, link with the ancient Near East, by tracing the line of kings back to the issue of Solomon of Israel and Bilqis, queen of Sheba. This national tradition in turn reflects the strong Judaic element (and depth of Old Testament learning) in Ethiopian Christianity and a number of parallels in the culture, law, and ethics of Ethiopian peoples, both Cushitic and Semitic speaking. One aspect of this is the existence till the late twentieth century of "Black Jews," or Falasha, near Lake Tana, the source of the Blue Nile; another is the belief that the original Ark of the Covenant is preserved at the cathedral of Aksum, the spiritual center of the Ethiopian church.

With its cultural roots in the Early Iron Age "pre-Aksumite" Period, Aksum was established as a capital no later than the first century A.D. The twin foundations of this empire were first its agricultural base in the northern Ethiopian highlands with their light fertile soils, and second its commercial relations with the Roman Empire, especially following the latter's incorporation of Egypt by Augustus. Through its port of Adulis on the southern Red Sea, Aksum supplied African products, particularly ivory (and in this role rivaled and by the fourth century eclipsed *Meroe, the capital of Kush on the Middle Nile). Moreover, by extending its control across the Red Sea to southern Arabia, Aksum became the chief supplier of aromatics as well as middle-

man for spices and other products carried by ship from India to Egypt and the Roman Empire.

The wealth and power that accrued are indicated by monuments and inscriptions at several places between Adulis and Aksum, and at Aksum itself by the colossal stelae as well as by the rock-cut tombs and the remains of great palaces. The stelae evolved from natural rock columns erected with considerable skill and labor to rough-hewn monoliths and on to dressed and tooled examples, and from these to the carved and storied, becoming progressively more elaborate and taller. They were hauled from quarries on a hill some 2.5 miles (4 km) away. The last in the series which fell long ago, perhaps during an attempt to erect it, is 98.5 feet (30 m) long and weighs over five hundred tons. Near it stands the second largest, 79 feet (24 m) high. So far, archaeological work has concentrated on these monumental features and on the inscriptions of Ezana and other kings (in ancient Ethiopic and southern Arabian script and occasionally in Greek translation). Spectacular though the findings are, archaeologists currently working around Aksum are acutely aware of the need for a change of emphasis, with attention to the town and other Aksumite settlements as well as the rural background, in order to reconstruct the economy and culture of this civilization of late antiquity.

With the Persian empire extending its influence into the Red Sea in the late sixth century and then, in the early seventh, the conquest of Arabia, Egypt, and the Near East by the Arab armies, sea trade declined, and Ethiopia's commercial links with the Mediterranean were severed. Aksum and its empire faded rapidly. Nevertheless, Ethiopian Christianity persisted in the highlands, extending from the Tigraean-speaking region of Aksum southward into the Amharic. This is illustrated exquisitely by the tradition, perhaps to be traced from Aksumite times, of rock-carved architecture, of which the churches of Lalibela are the most famous examples. These should date early in the second millennium A.D. to the period when the medieval Ethiopian kingdom was consolidating its rule over the expanding agricultural populations of the highlands while at the same time struggling to exert suzerainty over the growing Muslim emirates between them and the coast. An important factor in this rivalry was the revival of world trade and, by the eleventh century, the effective reopening of the Red Sea. Though medieval Ethiopia, unlike ancient Aksum, could not control the harbors and shipping, which were all in Muslim hands, it could profit from products from the interior required in Egypt and beyond, notably ivory and a certain amount of gold.

The study of the medieval and later archaeology of Ethiopia has yet barely moved beyond the adulation of the spectacular historical monuments, notably the churches of Lalibela and sites of royal fame, including the castles of Gondar. The latter date to the seventeenth century and reflect in their architecture some external influences, resulting from the sojourns of Spanish and Portuguese missionaries (who tried unsuccessfully to convert the country to Catholicism). By the Gondarine Period the extent and power of the Christian Ethiopian kingdom was considerably reduced, after Muslim incursions in the early sixteenth century followed by Oromo (Gall) expansion. In the preceding period royal capitals tended to be mobile, and town sites, though known in some cases, have not yet lent themselves to archaeological attention. Clearly, however, there is enormous potential in Ethiopia for urban as well as rural archaeological studies that would contribute to the understanding of that country's cultural and economic history.

[*See also* AFRICA, *articles on* PREHISTORY OF AFRICA, THE RISE OF KINGDOMS AND STATES IN AFRICA; TRADE, AFRICAN.]

▪ A.H.M. Jones and Elizabeth Munroe, *A History of Abyssinia* (1935). *Cambridge History of Africa*, Vols. 2, 3 (1977–1978). Stuart C. Munro-Hay, *Excavations at Aksum (Directed in 1972–74 by the Late Neville Chittick)*, British Institute in Eastern Africa, Memoir 10 (1989). Stuart C. Munro-Hay, *Aksum: An African Civilisation of Late Antiquity* (1991).

John E. G. Sutton

COASTAL TOWNS OF EAST AFRICA

The East African coast lies within the monsoon wind zone of the western Indian Ocean, enabling rapid navigation both along the coast and northward to western and southern Asia. The coastal inhabitants were able to exploit their position in the long-distance trade between continental Africa and the maritime societies of the Indian Ocean and emerged at the beginning second millennium A.D. as urban communities, known as Swahili, in control of the trade along the coastal areas of Somalia, Kenya, Tanzania, Mozambique, the Comoro Archipelago, and northern *Madagascar.

These towns (of which over four hundred sets of ruins are known, mainly dating from the fourteenth to the eighteenth century) look superficially foreign. The communities were Islamic, and they often built in the locally available coral stone. Their own traditions and histories often spoke of a Middle Eastern origin, while their language, ki-Swahili, was seen as containing numerous Semitic loan words. Earlier historians and archaeologists were keen to identify these towns as the result of Asiatic colonization, established on the edge of the continent for the purpose of trade, colonies which over time became mixed in race and culture.

This view has now been completely rejected. There is no evidence for any substantial Arab settlement in East Africa before the late eighteenth century, while ki-Swahili has been placed firmly within the Northeast Coastal Bantu language group. No "Arab" colony has yet been found or excavated, and the Swahili communities are now seen as an indigenous response to emerging long-distance trade within the Indian Ocean World.

The earliest archaeological evidence for trade on the East African coast comes from Ras Hafun, a site in Somaliland, where both Egyptian and Gulf pottery has been found, spanning the first century B.C. to fourth century A.D. This site can be identified as Opone, noted in the *Periplus of the Erythrean Sea* (ca. A.D. 40) and *Geography* of Ptolemy (ca. A.D. 150). These classical sources described both trade and settlements as far south as a town called Rhapta, generally thought to be near Dar es Salaam, but as yet no convincing archaeological evidence has been discovered for contact this far south. The Early Iron Age sites, probably associated with Bantu-speaking agriculturalists, spanning the period A.D. 100 to 500, are generally found not on the coast but inland in the Kwale, Usambara, and Pare Hills and contain no evidence for long-distance trade. The only coastal occupation of this period lies along the Mozambique coast far to the south, notably the sites of Bazaruto Island, Matola, and Maputo University.

Recent survey has established that the earliest evidence for long-distance trade along the coast dates from the sixth century A.D. with radiocarbon dates from Mpiji, Unguja Ukuu, and Amboni Cave. Other trade sites of similar date

include Fukuchani and Mkokotoni on Zanzibar, Mkadini and Dar es Salaam on mainland Tanzania, and Chibuene and Inhambane in southern Mozambique. These sites are characterized by Tana tradition pottery (also known as "triangular incised ware"), shellfish and fish bones, often in middens, with evidence for ironworking, shell-bead making, and small quantities of imported pottery mainly of Gulf origin. Tana tradition pottery has a more general distribution inland. Sites are known along the Tana River, in the Usambaras, with a group along the Wami River, of which the furthest is Dakawa, about 125 miles (200 km) inland. While many of these sites are purely agricultural, some may have been supplying commodities such as ivory and gum copal to the coast.

As the makers of Tana tradition pottery were the ancestors of the later inhabitants of the coastal towns, it provides direct evidence for their origins. Two distinct theories are current. The first is that the tradition lies within the Chifanblaze complex of Early Iron Age pottery, and evolved out of Kwale ware. The second is that it is a distinct tradition, which developed on the coast through the fusion of both Early Iron Age and Pastoral Neolithic complexes. Historical linguistic evidence favors the first theory, and suggests that the Sabaki group of Northeast Coastal Bantu languages (of which ki-Swahili is a member) emerged around A.D. 500. Either (or both) agriculturalist and pastoralist groups may have moved to the coast to exploit the maritime resources, and conveniently found that they could supplement their food-procuring activities with maritime trade.

Tana tradition pottery is found in the basal levels of several coastal towns, many of which seem to have been founded in the period A.D. 750 to 825. Sequences have been obtained from Manda, Pate and Shanga (Lamu Archipelago), Ungwana and Mombasa (Kenya coast), Mtambwe Mkuu and Ras Mkumbuu (Pemba Island), Kisimani Mafia (Mafia Island), Kilwa Kisiwani (Tanzania coast), and Dembani and Sima (Comoro Islands). At Shanga, the timber architecture and spatial organization has been studied in detail. Unlike earlier sites, which were strung along beaches, Shanga lies a little inland, with an enclosure around a well, with timber houses lying beyond. Within the enclosure, trade and craft activities took place and large buildings of a ceremonial nature were also placed there.

The economic basis of these emerging towns was trade. They are poor in faunal remains, with a general absence of domesticates (except chicken) before A.D. 900, but fishing on inshore reefs, the collection of turtles and dugong, and the exploitation of shellfish is present. The manufacture of shell beads, iron forging, and sporadic copper and silver working were the main craft activities. Imported pottery is found at levels of around five percent of the ceramic assemblage, and includes large unglazed storage jars (many of which were manufactured in the kilns at Siraf, Iran), the blue alkaline-glazed jars, Islamic white-glazed wares, and more rarely Indian waterjars and Chinese stonewares, including Yue and Changsha. These assemblages suggest strong contact with the Gulf, which also acted as an entrepôt for the South Asian and Far Eastern wares.

The main products of the coast, traded to the Gulf until the tenth century, were timber, slaves, and ivory. Timber included mangrove poles, a versatile roofing material (often cut in lengths of around 8.2 feet [2.5 m]), while slaves seem to have been obtained in quantity to work the swamps of southern Mesopotamia. Ivory was greatly in demand in both China and India, and thus of particular value to ships trading with the East. From the tenth century, competition in the Indian Ocean trade resulted in direct trade with India, southern Arabia, and the Red Sea, while other high-value items such as gold, copper, and crystal were now added to the list of African commodities. Much of this material was now obtained from the later Iron Age sites in southern Africa such as K2/*Mapungubwe, Shroda, and later *Great Zimbabwe and *Ingombe Ilede, and it seems that the hinterland of the Swahili coast itself, exploited from the sixth to the tenth century, was largely abandoned.

The adoption of Islam by the coastal towns was an important factor in their development. Small communities of Muslims were present at Shanga from before A.D. 800, where both burials and series of timber mosques have been excavated. The Shanga Muslims may have been early conversions, possibly to establish reliable trading partners. There are two possible tenth-century stone mosques at Ras Mkumbuu and Unguja Ukuu; these are very much larger than the Shanga mosques and suggest substantial Muslim populations. Tenth-century Muslim burials have also been found as far south as Chibuene. Outside the major towns, Islam was adopted in the eleventh and twelfth centuries, with stone mosques known from sites such as Kaole, Kisimani Mafia, Sanje ya Kati, and *Kilwa. Coins were also minted by the emerging Muslim polities. The earliest known are from Shanga, in the ninth century, Manda in the tenth century, and Pemba, Mafia, and Kilwa from the early eleventh century onward. These coins were initially silver, but copper coins became widespread, and some gold coins were produced in the fourteenth century.

Timber buildings were replaced by stone about A.D. 900; one technique used undersea *Porites* coral, which was shaped into neat ashlar blocks. Later on, sources of coralline limestone and sandstone were employed, but these blocks were much more irregular in shape and had to be used in smaller pieces, and bonded in locally prepared lime. At Manda, both *Porites* coral and fired bricks were used for building in the tenth century, while massive coral walls were built for reclamation and the construction of wharfs.

By the fourteenth century, a style of house had emerged (examples of which continue to be built in Pate and Lamu to this day), which was built of stone, entered through a courtyard, with parallel rows of rooms, leading back into the house, with the most private areas furthest from the courtyard. These houses were often elaborately decorated internally, using cut coral or plaster. They had flat roofs and few external windows; some were on two stories. Well-preserved houses of this date are known from Ungwana, Gedi, Jumba la Mtwana, Mtwapa, Tumbatu, Kilwa, and Songo Mnara.

Mosques were likewise of a standard plan, normally a roofed rectangular prayer hall with an external washing courtyard; the mihrab was the principal decorative feature, again using cut coral, with Kufic and Naski calligraphy. The earliest surviving mihrab is at Kizimkazi (Zanzibar), dated 500 H/A.D. 1107. Mosque roofs were normally flat, but some domed roofs occur around A.D. 1300 and again in the mid-fifteenth century. Stone tombs were the third architectural element in these towns, and here there was much regional variation, with large and small enclosures, headstone, hut, and pillar tombs; decoration used cut-coral and glazed bowls could be inset into the wall. Elaborately decorated tombs, dating to the fifteenth century, are known on the northern Kenyan coast, at Ishakani and Omwe and Dondo.

Apart from mosques, the coastal towns possessed few large public buildings, palaces, or markets. Where palaces have been identified, such as at Gedi, they are in reality large houses. The absence of such buildings seems to have been a result of the social system in which families or clans remained powerful, and centralized power was strongly resisted. Trade took place inside the house, and foreign merchants were often attached to particular families. When Sultans emerged, they were often very weak, frequently deposed, and often chosen from outside the communities, for example from Arabian sharif families. Each town (and often each village) claimed its own political autonomy. With very little militarism, there was no tendency for empires to develop. The towns were, however, often in a state of intense rivalry in their attempts to obtain African commodities and to attract merchants to their ports.

The first signs of decline came in the fourteenth century, possibly brought on by the economic impact of the Black Death in Europe and the Middle East, with the abandonment of hitherto successful towns such as Shanga and Tumbatu. Even Kilwa, the supposed leader of the gold trade, fell partly into ruins. The Portuguese arrived in 1498, and in 1505 to 1506 sacked Kilwa, Mombasa, Hoja (a town near the mouth of the Tana River), and Barawa; but their impact seems to have been fairly minimal, as they concentrated their settlement in Mozambique. More serious to Swahili prosperity was the demand for African commodities, which were now obtained directly by the Portuguese from the Zambezi, or, in the case of gold, more cheaply from the New World. The Swahili towns struggled to maintain limited trade in items such as mangrove poles, ambergris, civet musk, and ivory; many abandoned trade altogether and subsisted on the rich coastal resources. Numerous towns, with poor resources, or positioned where they could be attacked by mainland pastoralists, were abandoned. The survivors were the island communities, especially with nearby coral reefs or good farming land.

In the eighteenth century the fortunes of a few towns improved, with a revival in the slave trade, supported by the French and Arabs. With Mombasa, Zanzibar, and Pemba under Arab control, large areas of the coast were opened up with plantations, using slave labor, and several towns, such as Malindi and Bagamoyo, were reoccupied. Arab influence spread along the coast in the nineteenth century, and many of the Swahili communities compiled histories to establish their supposed "Arab" origins. They lost their independence, with the installation of governors from Zanzibar and the deportation of their own rulers. In a few places, urban life survives in a traditional manner into the late twentieth century; examples include Barawa, Lamu, Pate, Wasin, and Tumbatu. Such towns provide a useful ethnoarchaeological resource with which to interpret the archaeological evidence.

[See also AFRICA; articles on THE RISE OF KINGDOMS AND STATES IN AFRICA, HISTORICAL ARCHAEOLOGY OF AFRICA; TRADE, AFRICAN.]

■ H. N. Chittick, "The East Coast, Madagascar and the Indian Ocean," in *Cambridge History of Africa Vol. 3*, ed. R. Oliver (1977), pp. 183–231. J. Middleton, *The World of the Swahili* (1992). D. Nurse and T. Hinnebusch, *Swahili and Subaki* (1993). F. Chami, *The Tanzanian Coast in the First Millenium AD: An Archaeology of the Iron-Working, Farming Communities* (1994). M. C. Horton, *Shanga: The Archaeology of a Muslim Trading Community on the Coast of East Africa* (1995).

Mark Horton

INTERIOR KINGDOMS OF EAST AFRICA

East African societies, in both recent and earlier times, have organized themselves in diverse ways. Some, especially the pastorally oriented peoples of the Rift Valley and high grasslands, have been structured along age principles, their continuity—and indeed their sense of history and identity—being enshrined in the succession at fixed intervals of named age- or generation-sets. In these societies (which include Kalenjin, Kikuyu, and Maasai)—broadly described as "democratic" by anthropologists—notions of chiefship and kingship are quite alien. Other societies, especially those with agricultural economies who identify themselves with the settlement and clearance of particular tracts of land, have regarded lineage and clan as their essential social and political entities; here leadership may be vested in family heads and clan elders, for example among many of the Lwo peoples of western Kenya, eastern and northern Uganda, and the southern Sudan. In some instances those who could exercise effective leadership, charisma, or ritual power (over the land, the crops, or the rain, say, or some special resource such as iron) became elevated to the status of chiefs, with political control over larger groups of people and their territory. Where such control became hereditary and ritualized, and incorporated people outside the real and imagined lineages, the term kingship is often appropriate—especially if the ruler could command force to exert tribute or service from the subjects and conversely to defend them, their land, their crops, and their cattle.

The most famous cluster of old kingdoms in the East African interior is that of the Interlacustrine region (encompassing southern and western Uganda, Rwanda, and adjacent countries). Lying between the Western Rift Valley with its line of lakes (Tanganyika northward to Albert) and Lake Victoria on the east, this Interlacustrine zone comprises both fertile agricultural land, for dense banana cultivation as well as grains, and fine grasslands for cattle. When this lakes region was first brought to international attention by British explorers around 1860, the latter were impressed by the power, size, organization, courts, and ritual of certain of these kingdoms, notably Bunyoro, Karagwe, and Buganda. Becoming objects of anthropological fascination (as well as of political relations), questions of these kingdoms' antiquity were naturally raised; and some of them, through their court attendants or official guardians of the oral traditions and the burial shrines, produced long lists of kings with historical details. Some of the lists run to over thirty reigns, although (since succession was not always from father to son, but could be to a brother or other relative) the number of generations would have been rather less. Even so, taken at their face value these king lists imply a history of some five hundred years, that is, back toward the middle period of the Iron Age, for Bunyoro, Buganda, Rwanda, and perhaps Ankole and Karagwe. Some more skeptical historians suspect that there may have been exaggeration of the genealogies for reasons of competition and prestige (especially during the period of British "indirect" rule in Uganda, in which respect, patronage and power were granted to "traditional" authorities who could prove their history).

The obvious test of the veracity of these traditions and of the antiquity of the Interlacustrine kingdoms is an archaeological one, in particular to locate and date the early capitals and royal graves. The results have been generally inconclusive. For one reason the royal burials (and jawbone reliquaries), being revered as shrines, cannot usually be investigated in detail or accurately dated; and it is difficult to allay entirely the suspicion that some of their shrines belong not to historical kings but to local deities and spirits of the land. Moreover, since in these essentially rural kingdoms courts were mobile as rulers fought rivals, imposed their rule over provinces, and extracted tribute—with the capitals being moved from reign to reign or even within reigns—there are no clearly visible town sites or long statigraphies. In Nkore (Ankole), a kingdom in western Uganda with a marked emphasis on cattle keeping, the occasional old royal center is visible with earthen banks, being in effect an elaborate cattle kraal rather than a metropolis.

In advocating longer chronologies for these kingdoms, historians have linked their ancestry to legends of a previous kingdom recalled as Kitara and its supposed "Chwezi" dynasty five or six centuries ago. This in turn has been correlated, speculatively, with the ancient earthwork enclosures of western Uganda, notably the extensive system of Bigo, and the large related settlement of farmers and cattle keepers nearby at Ntusi. These sites, belonging to the early part of the second millennium A.D., are discussed in the section on the East African Iron Age. Linking them to the cultural evolution of the kingdoms of later fame makes an attractive historical hypothesis, even if direct ancestry and genealogical connections are not easily demonstrated.

Such attempts to trace links between recent (if not existing) kingdoms and supposed ancient ones may appear antiquarian rather than strictly historical. Intellectually, this line relates to culture-historical theories about African civilizations and kingship generally, which would see the elements and institutions of kingdoms having diffused throughout the continent at some early date. Some of these theories assume an origin in the Nile Valley, if not in Ancient Egypt, and have cited various customs and ethnographic traits in support. In the Interlacustrine case a more immediate connection has been posited with Ethiopia. But specific historical or linguistic support seems lacking. The more recent trend of thinking has imagined the Interlacustrine kingdoms, and others in eastern Africa, as having evolved within their own region.

In many parts of Africa the control of long-distance trade and of exports valued overseas, such as ivory, has been considered important in the growth and power of kingdoms. But this argument barely applies in the Interlacustrine region, situated far in the interior and not connecting with the Indian Ocean trade (or the Swahili city-states of the east coast) in a regular way until the nineteenth century. The wealth of this region and its kingdoms was internally generated, resting on agriculture and cattle. Power and patronage were maintained by the royal houses and the administrative and aristocratic elites through control of these resources, especially cattle, and also iron and salt.

On a lesser scale the same applies to more sparsely populated kingdoms and small chiefdoms to the south in Tanzania. Some of these may be related historically to the Interlacustrine tradition; other groupings may have emerged quite independently. Being generally in less rich terrain and with fewer cattle, chiefly power and prestige are usually less spectacular here. But in the nineteenth century some developed rapidly, or enjoyed temporary wealth and power, as new trade routes, to satisfy international demands for ivory and slaves, linked the deep interior with the coast more effectively. From Usambara in the northeast of Tanzania to Usangu in the south and Unyamwezi in the west, the sites of some of these capitals and trading posts can still be seen, in some cases as fortifications with surviving walls or earthworks. As the new import and export trade latched onto the existing regional infrastructures, local resources were exploited and traded more intensively. For instance, the rulers of Uvinza, situated between Unyamwezi and Lake Tanganyika, intensified production of their fine salt for sale along the extended and more regular routes, and at the same time profited from the other trade attracted to their market. And as increased competition led to banditry and warfare, as well as enslavement, and placed greater demands on security in the settlements and the markets and on the road, the old iron industries, long integral to the agricultural economy, were given a new boost in producing greater quantities and new designs of spears and arrows—as well as repairs to firearms.

[See also AFRICA: THE RISE OF KINGDOMS AND STATES IN AFRICA; EGYPT AND AFRICA; TRADE, AFRICAN.]

■ Cambridge History of Africa, vols. 3 and 4 (1975–1977), pp. 621–699 (vol. 3), 469–536 (vol. 4). John E. G. Sutton, A Thousand Years of East Africa (1990).

John E. G. Sutton

EASTER ISLAND is a tiny (64 sq. miles or 166 sq. km) volcanic speck in the South Pacific, 2,340 miles (3,765 km) from South America and 1,400 miles (2,253 km) from Pitcairn to the northwest, which people reached in the early centuries A.D. The island is so remote that there was probably only one major influx of people, and the archaeological record certainly suggests a single unbroken development of material culture. Once settled on the island, the colonists were trapped, and it constituted their world.

The earliest known contact with the outside world occurred on Easter Sunday, 1722, when the Dutch navigator Roggeveen encountered and christened the island. A Norwegian expedition of 1955, led by Thor Heyerdahl, carried out the first stratigraphic excavations, obtaining radiocarbon dates and pollen samples, and conducting experiments in carving, moving, and erecting statues.

Every aspect of Easter Island's archaeology and anthropology points unequivocally to the northwest (Polynesia, and more specifically the Marquesas Islands) as the source of its population and culture. A few minor Amerindian traits in what are definitely Marquesas-type skulls may indicate the arrival at some point of a few lost South American fishermen.

The first colonists, probably a few dozen people in large double canoes, brought with them the domestic animals (chickens, rats, pigs, and dogs) and food plants (bananas, sweet potatoes, breadfruit) with which Polynesians transformed the environment of so many Pacific islands. Pigs and dogs did not survive long on Easter Island, and breadfruit could not grow here. The island, according to recent pollen analyses and finds of extinct snails, was covered in a rain forest dominated by enormous palm trees similar to the Chilean Wine Palm, Jubaea chilensis. Early types of ahu (platforms) were constructed, with small, relatively crude statues on or in front of them.

In the second phase of Easter Island's history, ca. A.D. 1000 to 1500, tremendous energy was devoted to the construction of more and bigger ceremonial platforms (rubble cores encased in well-cut slabs) and hundreds of large statues. At least eight hundred moai (statues) were carved, almost all in the soft volcanic tuff of the Rano Raraku crater, using basalt hammerstones. Thought to represent ancestor figures, they are human figures with prominent angular noses and chins, and often elongated ears containing discs. The bodies, ending at the abdomen, have arms held tightly to the sides, and hands held in front, with elongated fingertips meeting at a stylized loincloth. More than 230 statues were transported from the quarry to platforms around the edge of the island, where they were erected, backs to the sea, watching over the villages. It was traditionally thought that the statues were dragged horizontally to their destinations, but recent experiments suggest that the most efficient mode of transportation was upright, on a sledge and rollers.

At the most important and prestigious platforms, statues were given eyes of white coral, and a separate pukao ("topknot") of red scoria was placed on the head.

The platform statues vary from 6 feet to 33 feet (1.8 to 10 m) in height, and weigh up to 82 tons. There might be up to fifteen in a row on a single platform. But the quarry still contains over 394 statues at every stage of manufacture.

In the final phase of the island's prehistory, statues ceased to be carved, and one thousand years of peaceful coexistence were shattered by the mass production of mataa, obsidian spearheads and daggers. Conflict led to the toppling of the statues, and was resolved by the abandonment of a religion and social system based on ancestor worship for a religion featuring a warrior elite. An annual chief or "birdman" was chosen each year at the ceremonial village of Orongo, its drystone corbelled houses perched high on the cliff between the Rano Kau crater and the ocean. Orongo's rich rock art is festooned with carvings of the birdmen, sometimes holding the sooty-tern egg which symbolized fertility. This was the system that was still developing when the Europeans arrived, and which ended with the arrival of missionaries in the 1860s.

The complex causes of the island's decline can be traced to one major factor: palynology has shown that it has the most dramatic history of deforestation in the archaeological record. From at least twelve hundred years ago, there was a massive reduction in forest cover, until, by 1722, there were virtually no large trees left. The imported rats fed on the palm fruits and prevented regeneration. Without the palm trees, statues could no longer be moved; oceangoing canoes could no longer be built, thus depriving the population of the crucial protein supply of deep-sea fish (there is no coral reef or lagoon); and deforestation also caused massive soil erosion which damaged crop-growing potential. Chickens became the most precious protein source, guarded like treasure in fortified structures.

The steady growth in population—perhaps up to twenty thousand or more—plus the decline in food and the increasing importance of useless activities (platform building, statue carving, and transportation) clearly led to a collapse. Starvation led to raiding and violence, perhaps even cannibalism.

[See also PACIFIC ISLANDS; articles on INTRODUCTION, OVERVIEW, SETTLEMENT OF POLYNESIA; PACIFIC ISLANDS CHIEFDOMS; PACIFIC ISLANDS NAVIGATION AND WATERCRAFT; SOCIETY ISLANDS.]

■ Katherine Routledge, The Mystery of Easter Island (1919). Alfred Métraux, Ethnology of Easter Island (1940). Thor Heyerdahl and Edwin Ferdon, eds., Reports of the Norwegian Archaeological Expedition to Easter Island and the East Pacific, vol. 1: The Archaeology of Easter Island (1961). Paul Bahn and John Flenley, Easter Island, Earth Island (1992). Steven R. Fischer, ed., Easter Island Studies (1993).

Paul G. Bahn

EBLA, also known as Tell Mardikh, its modern name, is located in northern Syria, 35 miles (55 km) south of Alleppo. The 135-acre (55-ha) site is surrounded by a high rampart and has a central mound about 50 feet (15 m) tall. It lies in a region of low, rolling hills, where the rainfall is generally sufficient for dry farming.

Under the direction of Paolo Matthiae, the University of Rome's Italian Archaeological Mission to Syria began excavating at Tell Mardikh in 1964. The site has yielded evidence of occupation between the fourth millennium B.C. and the seventh century A.D., but the periods when it flourished were of substantially shorter duration—during the twenty-fourth century B.C. and between about 1900 and 1600 B.C. In 1968 the discovery of a fragmentary statue bearing the inscription of an early-second-millennium king of Ebla, Ibbit-Lim, suggested that Tell Mardikh was the location of that ancient city, whose name was already known from cuneiform and Egyptian sources.

This identification was overwhelmingly confirmed in the mid-1970s, when the Italians uncovered the royal archives of twenty-fourth-century-B.C. Ebla (Early Bronze Age IVa). Some two thousand whole or nearly whole cuneiform tablets were recovered from Palace G, along with fragments representing several thousand more documents. Most were found in a small chamber, where they had been filed on wooden shelves. These texts, mostly administrative in nature, but including letters, decrees, treaties, literary texts, and lexical lists, were written in Sumerian or Eblaite, a local western Semitic dialect. The tablets span a period of perhaps forty years, at the end of which the palace and its contents were destroyed and burned. The archive, unique in northern Syria, shows Ebla to have been the capital of a prosperous, administratively sophisticated state, deriving much of its wealth from its trade in textiles and metals. Ebla's destruction, originally attributed to Naram-Sin of Agade (2254–2218 B.C.), is now generally placed earlier, either shortly before Sargon, Naram-Sin's grandfather, came to power, or early in his reign (2334–2279 B.C.).

After several centuries of relative obscurity, Ebla re-emerged in the early second millennium as one in a broad continuum of Amorite-ruled states that stretched from the Mediterranean to southern Mesopotamia. The rampart surrounding the site today was constructed at this time along with several palaces and temples. Displaying a plan typical of second-millennium Syrian sanctuaries, Temple D, dedicated to Ishtar, consisted of three axially arranged chambers: a broad portico or vestibule, a broad antecella, and a long cella, or cult room, with a niche for the divine statue in the short end opposite the door. A group of tombs beneath the so-called Western Palace, apparently belonging to the rulers of the city, yielded a noteworthy collection of small finds: jewelry and other artifacts made of gold and semiprecious stones, stone vessels, and a ceremonial mace of Egyptian origin in limestone, ivory, bronze, silver, and gold. Around 1600 B.C., Ebla was destroyed, perhaps by the Hittite king Mursilis I. Although the site was subsequently reoccupied, the settlement thereafter was of only minor significance.

[See also NEAR EAST: THE BRONZE AGE IN THE NEAR EAST; WRITING: CUNEIFORM.]

■ Paolo Matthiae, *Ebla: An Empire Rediscovered* (1981). Paolo Matthiae and Alfonso Archi, "Ebla Recovered," in *Ebla to Damascus*, ed. Harvey Weiss (1985), pp. 134–148. Alfonso Archi, "The Archives of Ebla," in *Cuneiform Archives and Libraries*, ed. Klaas Veenhof (1986), pp. 72–86.

James A. Armstrong

ECONOMIC ARCHAEOLOGY. During the past thirty years, economic archaeology has become an essential subdiscipline of archaeological research throughout the world. Economic archaeology is the study of the relationships between ancient populations and their natural and cultural resources. Accordingly, economic archaeologists try to explain how societies used their natural resources; how human populations grew and diminished; and how changes in environment, technology, and production influenced cultural change.

While intellectual trends can shift rapidly in archaeology, economic archaeology has become a long-lasting and integral part of all archaeological field and research programming. This is because economic archaeology is empirically based, utilizing a wide range of biological and material sources of data that enable theoretical archaeologists, of whatever school of thought, to test their hypotheses. One of the reasons economic archaeology survives during paradigm shifts is that it is grounded in quantitative descriptions of data, making it possible to replicate the observations used in making hypotheses. Today, most interdisciplinary research projects include a wide range of specialists in subfields of economic archaeology, including *paleobotany, *zooarchaeology, petrography, geomorphology, and spatial analysis.

Economic archaeology developed as a well-defined subdiscipline in the United Kingdom in the early 1970s with the publication of *Papers in Economic Prehistory* (Cambridge University Press), edited by E. S. Higgs. This work was based on studies carried out by a diverse group of scholars who were associates of the British Academy Major Research Project in the Early History of Agriculture. The team, under Higgs's direction, included scholars in the fields of biology, genetics, plant physiology, zoology, geography, anthropology, and other subjects. It is here that the ground rules for economic archaeology, as it is practiced in the 1990s, were written. In order to test models and methods for studying the origins of agriculture and animal husbandry, these scholars developed a wide range of new methods of investigation which today are part and parcel of the scientific archaeologist's "tool box."

The techniques of the subdisciplines of economic archaeology require more care and attention to the recovery and sampling of archaeological materials than "traditional" archaeology has devoted. Zooarchaeology requires large collections of faunal remains to reconstruct kill-off patterns of herd animals and the nature of animal husbandry systems. Paleobotany, which aims at reconstructing plant-based economies, is based on the examination of microscopic and macroscopic carbonized seed remains which can only be obtained through flotation methods. Consequently, economic archaeology introduced an emphasis on dry and wet sieving of site sediments in order to procure large representative samples of faunal and botanical remains.

A wide range of sieving techniques was developed and quickly adopted by archaeologists working all over the world. New methods for retrieving botanical data were also introduced based on the flotations of ashy sediments in order to obtain carbonized seed samples. In some cases, paleobotanists produce compressed air in a large steel flotation cell to which water, a soil sample, and a mild detergent were added to float the carbonized seeds to the surface. In retrospect, these grand flotation machine designs can be seen as a reaction to the paucity of carbonized seed remains obtained in the traditional excavations. Today, most paleobotanical remains are obtained by simple flotations of sediment in an open barrel in which samples are collected by pouring the soil into the barrel of water, stirring, and skimming the carbonized remains that float to the surface of the water with a fine flour sieve. The wet and dry sieving techniques used by economic archaeologists have influenced all aspects of archaeological fieldwork, making recovery and sampling of key concern to all archaeological excavation research designs today.

■ E. S. Higgs, ed., *Papers in Economic Prehistory* (1972). F. J. Findlow and J. E. Ericson, eds., *Catchment Analysis—Essays on Prehistoric Resource Space* (1980). T. E. Levy, "Transhumance, Subsistence, and Social Evolution," in ed. O. Bar-Yosef and A. Khazanov, *Pastoralism in the Levant* (1992). D. M. Pearsall and D. R. Piperno, eds., *Current Research in Phytolithi Analysis: Applications in Archaeology and Paleoecology* (1993).

Thomas E. Levy

EDUCATION IN ARCHAEOLOGY

Professional Training
Popular Education

PROFESSIONAL TRAINING

For over 100 years archaeology has been a formal academic discipline. In the United States archaeology was traditionally treated as one of the four classic subdisciplines of anthropology along with cultural anthropology, physical anthropology, and linguistics. In much of the rest of the world archaeology is either treated as a separate discipline or as an adjunct to specialized regional or historic studies such as classical or Oriental studies. Whatever the formulation, the traditional professional outlet for most archaeologists has been the academy.

Before the post–World War II era, there were generally few professionally trained archaeologists in the world. The postwar era in the United States (but elsewhere in the industrialized world as well) brought a boom in the growth of universities, departments of anthropology/archaeology, and the number of professional archaeologists. Most of these archaeologists were employed in colleges and universities and were expected to divide their time between research and teaching archaeology. As a result, graduate programs in archaeology were geared to producing regional specialists who could conduct meaningful research in their area of interest; teach undergraduate general anthropology, general archaeology, and regional archaeology courses; and train the next generation of professionals with a mixture of field experience and graduate seminars on the history, theory, and methods of archaeology. In many respects this is the same model applied in most university departments to this day.

Several events over the past twenty years have served to underscore the need to reevaluate the goals and structure of professional training in archaeology. The two most important of these events were the university budget crises of the 1970s and 1980s and the dramatic increase in the importance of cultural resource management as an outgrowth of the environmental movement of the 1960s and 1970s.

The budget crises resulted in a significant disparity between the demand for new archaeology faculty and the supply of new professional archaeologists. In short, enrollments surged and the number of masters' and doctoral degrees awarded in archaeology increased, but the number of teaching positions available declined. Competition for faculty positions became, and continues to be, fierce.

Many new professionals, with no teaching positions available to them, found professional employment opportunities in the then-burgeoning cultural resource management (CRM) arena. Both government and the private sector were faced with new requirements for compliance with a raft of important legislation aimed at protecting cultural and historic heritage. Unfortunately, many archaeologists who went into CRM work found that they had in many ways been poorly prepared in their professional training to cope with the unique demands of this stimulating but often tense and confusing expression of archaeology.

In the academic arena, conditions have become as problematic as in CRM work. Although budgets dictated restrictions in the number of tenured faculty, enrollments continued to increase. Undergraduate class sizes swelled. Many new faculty found themselves teaching introductory classes with enrollments as high as four hundred to five hundred students. Pressure to "publish or perish" to gain tenure simply exacerbated the problems of also having to find effective ways to teach these enormous classes. As a result, the single largest point of contact between the profession and the public—the introductory undergraduate class—often suffered from a lack of training in how to manage learning for these large numbers of students.

This situation can be expected to continue for at least several academic generations. It is highly likely that there will be a permanent shift in the dominant employer of professional archaeologists from the universities to private and government CRM organizations. The result will be fewer professional archaeologists in the universities conducting "pure" research and teaching increasing numbers of students, many of whom will be returning students. Clearly the time has come for archaeologists as a professional body to recognize these trends and to organize in a way that accommodates these changing roles.

How can this be accomplished? The first thing is to recognize that most graduates with master's and doctoral degrees in archaeology will not be employed in universities. Graduate curricula should be modified to reflect this reality. Besides requisite courses in method and theory combined with field and laboratory practices, courses in personnel management, project management, environmental law, public education, collections management, database design and management, and contract law should be regularly offered as options to university positions. Graduate students intent on pursuing careers within the traditional university research role should be offered courses in large class management, effective teaching strategies, instructional design, public education, and project management. It is only with this kind of professional training that they can meet the challenges of the university of the future.

Finally, in a more subtle way, the traditional emphasis on conducting original field research as part of graduate training and part of "pure" research must be significantly modified. In general, archaeologists involved in CRM work are constantly pressed to locate, assess, mitigate damage to, and manage archaeological sites and materials, and rarely do they get the opportunity to investigate theoretically important or interesting hypotheses with the substantial quantities of data they collect. Much of that information is rarely published and merely generates an increasing body of "gray" literature. Furthermore their efforts generate collections that must be maintained in perpetuity in one form or another. Archaeology as a discipline would be better served if the two houses worked together rather than against each other. Meaningful research collaboration between professionals in the academy and those in government service or the private sector should be a goal instilled in all graduate students. As it stands, the public is ill served by the current formulation of CRM on one hand generating immense quantities of variously digested data and "pure" researchers on the other hand generating their own data. Neither group does a very good job of informing the public of the results of their inquiries on the public's behalf and generally at the public's expense.

Archaeology is a rewarding, demanding profession. It has always relied on personal integrity, intelligence, innovation, determination, and years of training. The archaeological profession of the future will be, if anything, more challenging, more rewarding, and more frustrating than it has ever been. If we are to save archaeology from devolving into the intellectual pursuit of the well-heeled, inquisitive tyro, as it once was, we must take steps now to adapt the professional training of future archaeologists to the realities of the markets and the contexts in which they must function.

[See also ARCHAEOLOGY AS A DISCIPLINE; CULTURAL RESOURCE MANAGEMENT, articles on INTRODUCTION, COLLECTIONS MANAGEMENT, SITE MANAGEMENT.]

George Michaels

POPULAR EDUCATION

Hidden mysteries of past cultures have long been a source of great fascination for the public. Today, information about archaeology and cultural heritage resources is increasingly accessible, through a wide range of television programs, books, and periodicals. Museums, parks, and interpretive centers provide on-site experiences and school-based programming.

In the United States, many archaeology education initiatives have developed on a local or state level, often inspired by a handful of dedicated individuals or the desire to preserve or study a particular site. In recent years, the alarming escalation of site looting and vandalism, as well as a heightened interest of Native American peoples and other cultural groups in the care and interpretation of their past, have contributed to new efforts to communicate and cooperate on a national and an international scale.

An important conclusion of the pivotal 1974 Airlie House Conference, sponsored by the Society for American Archaeology (SAA), was that better communication with the public was needed. "While it will always be true that archaeologists need to communicate effectively among themselves, it now is abundantly clear that unless they also communicate effectively with the general public, and with those making decisions affecting the cultural resource base, all else will be wasted effort" (McGimsey and Davis 1977: 89).

According to the 1988 amendment to the Archaeological Resources Protection Act (ARPA) of 1979: "Each Federal land manager shall establish a program to increase public awareness of the significance of the archaeological resources located on public lands and Indian lands and the need to protect such resources" (Jameson 1991). Federal agencies implementing ARPA have developed collaborative programs such as the Public Interpretation Initiative of the National Park Service, which sponsors symposia, training courses, and publications aimed at archaeologists and interpreters.

Professional organizations including the Society for Historic Archaeology, the American Anthropological Association, and the Society for American Archaeology are addressing public education issues, as well. In 1988, SAA initiated the Save the Past for the Future project and sponsored a conference in Taos, New Mexico, to study the unrelenting loss of sites and information they once contained. Conference participants concluded that there was a need for more data on looting and vandalism. They urged that more money should be spent on public education and law enforcement, and concluded that "we need a major paradigm shift in American archaeology, in which we consciously and systematically engage the public to join us in the challenge of defending the past. Engaging the public as partners in our discipline must become a fully integrated, even honored component of our professional lives" (Judge 1991: 278).

The Taos Conference led SAA to establish a Public Education Committee to promote public education about the past and to engage the public in the preservation and protection of heritage resources. The Archaeology and Public Education newsletter, as well as workshops and exhibits at professional meetings, promote archaeology education, that is, teaching about and through archaeology.

Today, opportunities for the public to participate in organized and supervised archaeological investigation have expanded from university field schools to include organizations with projects designed specifically for the public, such as Crow Canyon Archaeological Center in Cortez, Colorado, and the Center for American Archaeology in Kampsville, Illinois. The U.S. Forest Service offers short-term family-focused opportunities at excavations in national forests through the Passport in Time (PIT) Project. Many states have annual archaeology weeks offering a variety of events throughout the state. Site steward programs train volunteers to monitor sites for signs of looting or vandalism.

Many initiatives integrate archaeology into school curricula to address cultural diversity and preservation of cultural heritage, as well as encouraging hands-on application of math, science, and social studies skills. In Utah, for example, the Bureau of Land Management and other agencies developed an education program, Intrigue of the Past: Investigating Archaeology, which is being adapted for use in other regions as well.

The Archaeological Resource Center, created within the Toronto Board of Education in 1985, is a unique archaeology education initiative in Canada. Each year, an excavation on a site of heritage significance in downtown Toronto provides archaeological experiences for thousands of students, as well as summer field schools for youth groups and the public.

As archaeologists, educators, interpreters, and the public work together, issues about access to and use of sites, distribution of limited resources, and the very purpose and meaning of archaeology emerge and must be addressed thoughtfully. Such discussions promise to keep the development of public education in archaeology a lively and critical endeavor for the future.

■ Charles R. McGimsey III and Hester A. Davis, eds., *The Management of Archaeological Resources: The Airlie House Report* (1977). Karolyn E. Smardz, "Educational Archaeology: Toronto Students Dig into Their Past," *The History and Social Science Teacher* (1989): 148–155. John H. Jameson Jr., "Public Interpretation Initiative," in *Federal Archaeology Report* (1991): 1, 4–6. James W. Judge, "Saving the Past for Ourselves: The Society for American Archaeology Taos Anti-

Looting Conference," in *Protecting the Past,* ed. George S. Smith and John E. Ehrenhard (1991), pp. 277–282.

Edward Friedman and Phyllis Messenger

EGYPT

OVERVIEW

Even though it was more geographically restricted than the other great civilizations of the Eastern Mediterranean and the Near East, ancient Egypt developed a distinctive culture and society which proved to be as coherent, long lasting, and influential as any in the region. Egyptian civilization was initially derived from the many regional cultures of the Nile Valley, yet as the following sections will show, the political unification of Upper and Lower Egypt around 3000 B.C. led to the creation of a vibrant and resilient culture of centralization and to a certain extent, redistribution, focused on a national monarchy.

Through the period of the Old Kingdom, with its intensive elaboration of the status and power of the pharaoh, through the Middle Kingdom, with Egypt's first extensive exploitation of the resources of the surrounding nations, the power and prestige of the rulers of Egypt culminated in the great international empire of the New Kingdom. Centered on Thebes in Upper Egypt, the pharaohs of the eighteenth, nineteenth, and early twentieth dynasties controlled extensive territories in *Nubia, Libya, and Canaan and conducted diplomatic and material exchanges with the peoples of Mesopotamia, *Anatolia, and the Aegean world.

Though only a small number of Egyptian artifacts have been found in Mesopotamia and the Aegean, Egypt's close links to Canaan and Northern Syria are evident from the period of the Middle Kingdom to the end of New Kingdom times. Even after the political decline of Egypt and its subjugation by the Persian Empire and the successors of Alexander the Great, Egyptian funerary and temple architecture—and indeed Egyptian religion—retained its basic outlines. Though the establishment of the Macedonian Ptolemaic dynasty ended the native monarchy, the ancient culture of the indigenous population of the Nile Valley maintained much of its distinctive character until the spread of Christianity in the fourth century A.D.

[*See also* EGYPT AND AFRICA.]

Neil Asher Silberman

PREDYNASTIC CULTURES OF EGYPT

Civilization arose in Egypt shortly before 3000 B.C., following a long period during which agriculture became established in the Nile Valley, and socio-political developments led toward the creation of the world's first nation-state. This final era of Egypt's prehistoric past is known as the Predynastic Period.

The study of Predynastic Egypt goes back to the end of the nineteenth century with the work of such individuals as Sir Flinders *Petrie (1853–1942) and Jacques de Morgan (1857–1924). Petrie's tireless efforts provided the basis for our understanding of the Predynastic of Upper Egypt (i.e. the Egyptian Nile Valley south of the Nile Delta). Rather fewer early agricultural sites were known in the north of

Egypt and these were referred to as Neolithic. However, excavations carried out since the late 1970s throughout the Egyptian Nile Valley system, including the Delta and the Fayum depression, have dramatically altered our understanding of later Egyptian prehistory. The term *Predynastic* is best used in a socioeconomic sense to refer to social groups practicing a farming way of life anywhere within the Egyptian Nile Valley system (at least as far south as Edfu), prior to the start of the First Dynasty. A Neolithic phase is still recognized but it may be subsumed within the Predynastic as described below.

Predynastic Cultures of Northern Egypt. The earliest Predynastic cultures known in Egypt occur in the Nile Delta (which forms Lower Egypt) and the Fayum depression (approximately 40 miles [70 km] southwest of Cairo), and are assigned to a Neolithic phase beginning at about 5300 B.C. Compared with the Levant, where the first cereal crops were cultivated during the tenth millennium B.P., agriculture came rather late to the Nile Valley. Recent geological investigations suggest this may be due to the unsuitability of the Nile Delta for cultivation or grazing until after its fertile silts started to be deposited from around 6500 to 5500 B.C. Previously the delta was a sandy, partially vegetated plain subject to periodic destructive flooding. The delta would have been the most likely point of entry for domestic crops and animals from the Levant into the Nile Valley. However, the first Near Eastern domesticates to come into North Africa seem simply to have passed through the delta. Domestic sheep and goats are present in the Western Desert of Egypt from around 7000 B.P. Cattle, on the other hand, may well have been independently domesticated in North Africa. Cattle bones, tentatively identified as being of domestic stock, have been recovered from sites in the Western Desert dating to as much as 9500 B.P.—roughly three thousand years earlier than the appearance of domestic cattle in the Nile Valley.

The oldest northern Neolithic sites occur in the Fayum depression where there are several localities with dates in excess of 5000 B.C.—up to approximately 5200 to 5300 B.C. Although there are a number of similarities to be seen between the Neolithic sites of the north, each place has its own distinctive cultural traits. The sites in the Fayum, dating from around 5300 to shortly before 4000 B.C., belong to one cultural tradition, the Fayum Neolithic. Although the people grew wheat and barley and kept domestic animals, they also exploited a wide range of wild resources. They hunted animals such as gazelle, and caught huge quantities of fish from the then more extensive lake in the depression, the Birket Qarun. Many of the excavated sites appear to have been seasonal fishing camps. A more sedentary way of life devoted to food production is represented at the large Neolithic settlements of Merimde (ca. 4800–4300 B.C.) and El Omari (ca. 4600–4350 B.C.).

The northern sequence continues with the Maadi Cultural Complex (ca. 4000–3200 B.C.) which is represented throughout northern Egypt. The principal sites are Maadi, now a southern suburb of Cairo, and Buto in the northern delta. Maadi cultural sites indicate that northern Egypt now had regular contact with both Upper Egypt and the Levant. At Maadi, itself, there are definite imports from Upper Egypt, including rhomboidal-shaped slate palettes and black-topped pottery, as well as imports from Palestine. Objects of copper also occur and these are likely to have been acquired from copper-working communities in the Negev.

During the Neolithic and Maadi cultural phases, social organization was comparatively simple with village-based agrarian communities showing little status differentiation, at least as reflected by the impoverished character of their grave goods compared with contemporary burials in Upper Egypt. The people appear to have lived in huts made of mud-daubed reeds or wattling.

Toward the end of the Maadi culture, an increasing number of Upper Egyptian imports appear, particularly ceramics. By 3200 B.C., Upper Egyptian pottery types (often locally made but using Upper Egyptian techniques) dominate the northern ceramic inventories, and mud-brick architecture is introduced. In terms of Upper Egyptian chronology, this occurs at the very end of the Gerzean phase (ca. 3500–3200 B.C.). From then on the material cultures of Upper and Lower Egypt are virtually the same.

Predynastic Cultures of Upper Egypt. In Upper Egypt the earliest Predynastic sites date to about 4500 B.C. and belong to a tradition known as the Badarian which occurs in the Badari region near Asyut. Whether the Badarian ever extended beyond this area is unclear. It is a culture characterized by thin-walled, polished brown to reddish-brown pottery vessels with black tops—wide blackened areas around the rim, a decorative effect that was to remain characteristic throughout most of the Upper Egyptian Predynastic, in contrast to the almost exclusively monochrome wares of northern Egypt. The surfaces of many Badarian vessels also show a distinctive rippling effect. Like all Predynastic pottery, the Badarian wares were made by hand without the use of a wheel. The Badarian may have continued as a regional tradition until roughly 3800 B.C., though as yet there are few radiocarbon dates available for the Badarian and its chronological limits remain uncertain.

Elsewhere in Upper Egypt, the earliest-known Predynastic sites date to about 4000 B.C., and this marks the beginning of the Amratian (or Naqada I) phase. The Badarian and earlier Amratian, like the Neolithic and Maadi phases in the north, appear to have been characterized by simple village societies though even as early as the Badarian, there are indications that certain individuals, perhaps village headmen, were accorded a certain measure of rank which is reflected in the comparative richness of their grave goods. There are numerous Predynastic cemeteries in Upper Egypt, and these provide us with important clues to the nature of society throughout the Predynastic. Later on in the Amratian there are indications of increasing social complexity. It is likely that there were now chiefdoms ruled by powerful leaders. Some of the late Amratian grave goods suggest that craft specialists such as potters, stone workers, and flint knappers had also emerged.

Although there are similarities in Amratian grave goods from all areas of Upper Egypt, there are differences in the day-to-day utilitarian ceramic wares and flint artifacts, suggesting that ordinary objects of daily use were made locally, and effectively represent regional subtraditions within the Amratian phase. As in northern Egypt, house structures at this time are mostly represented by pits, postholes, and hearths indicating relatively lightly constructed huts.

During the succeeding Predynastic phase, the Gerzean (or Naqada II), dating between approximately 3500 and 3200 B.C., there is abundant evidence for increasing social stratification. There are comparatively rich tombs, some now lined with mud-brick, as well as poorer graves. The simplest graves were similar in many respects to Amratian burials. They consisted of oval to subrectangular pits in which the deceased was placed in a contracted position along with a few pots and other items. The most elaborate Gerzean tomb was found at Hierakonpolis near Edfu at the end of the nineteenth century. It was a 15- by 6.5-foot (5 × 2 m) rectangular pit cut into the ground and lined with mud-brick which was plastered and then painted with scenes of boats and human figures. It also had a mud-brick partition wall. Regrettably now destroyed, it represented Egypt's oldest painted tomb, and probably belonged to a local ruler. During the Gerzean, the Hierakonpolis area grew in importance, and the floodplain settlement of Nekhen, a mere village during the Amratian, became a town and the capital of an Upper Egyptian kingdom. The Hierakonpolis area also boasts a ceremonial structure of Gerzean date which probably represents the oldest-known Egyptian temple. This ceremonial site also highlights the extent of exchange networks in the Gerzean phase with goods coming from at least as far away as Canaan and *Nubia. Hierakonpolis, itself, represents the approximate southern limit of Predynastic culture in Egypt.

The succeeding Protodynastic phase (or Naqada III), beginning around 3200 B.C., saw the continuation of the political and social developments already well underway during the Gerzean. By the start of this final phase of the Predynastic, Upper and Lower Egypt had achieved a unity of material culture which may reflect political unity though this is by no means certain. Alternatively, the similarities in the artifacts of Upper and Lower Egypt may simply be a reflection of increasing cultural contact and exchange.

[See also EGYPT AND AFRICA; NEAR EAST: THE NEOLITHIC AND CHALCOLITHIC (PRE-BRONZE-AGE) PERIODS IN THE NEAR EAST.]

■ Karl W. Butzer, *Early Hydraulic Civilization in Egypt* (1976). Barbara Adams, *Predynastic Egypt* (1988). Michael A. Hoffman, *Egypt before the Pharaohs* (1979; revised and updated 1991). Angela E. Close and Fred Wendorf, "The Beginnings of Food Production in the Eastern Sahara," in *Transitions to Agriculture in Prehistory*, ed. A. B. Gebauer and T. D. Price (1992), pp. 63–72. Renée F. Friedman and Barbara Adams, eds, *The Followers of Horus: Studies Dedicated to Michael Allen Hoffman* (1992). Béatrix Midant-Reynes, *Préhistoire de l'Égypte des premiers hommes aux premiers pharaons* (1992). A. J. Spencer, *Early Egypt: The Rise of Civilisation in the Nile Valley* (1993). Daniel J. Stanley and Andrew G. Warne, "Sea Level and Initiation of Predynastic Culture in the Nile Delta," *Nature* 363 (1993): 435–438.

Diane Holmes

OLD KINGDOM EGYPT

For Old Kingdom Egypt, a history in the sense that one normally thinks of history—a recounting of events and deeds of figures of the past—cannot be written. Virtually no Old Kingdom royal inscriptions of any length have survived and private inscriptions afford only a narrow viewpoint of events. Our sense of contemporary life is derived chiefly from archaeological finds and the scenes of daily life found in the hundreds of private tombs belonging to the nobility and high officials.

"Dynasty 0" and the Unification of Egypt. From the earliest days of Egyptian history until the appearance of a strong centralized monarchy, the basic political units had been small city-states, called nomes after the term used by ancient Greek historians. As we shall see later, when the royal house weakened toward the end of the Old Kingdom, many of these ancient political divisions were to assert themselves again. According to Egyptian tradition, the first king was a certain Meni (the "Menes" of Greek sources), who reportedly united Upper and Lower Egypt and founded the capital city of Memphis. Many scholars suggest that "Menes" is a composite figure based on the achievements of several early Egyptian rulers.

In actuality, the archaeological record is so unclear about the beginnings of Egyptian history, that it has become the practice among Egyptologists when dealing with this formative period to speak of both a First Dynasty and a "Dynasty 0." The latter term helps convey the consensus among scholars that the transition between city-states and unified monarchy as well as the shift from a pre-literate to a literate culture were gradual and did not occur as a single, discrete event. One early monarch who is frequently cited as the unifier of Egypt is Narmer, who is commemorated on a large slate palette from Hierakonpolis which can be considered Egypt's earliest written document. The palette depicts Narmer on a heroic scale triumphant over enemies from the north. Because he wears the White Crown of Lower Egypt and the Red Crown of Lower Egypt on different sides of the palette, this object has been interpreted as a graphic commemoration of Narmer's unification of Egypt.

Early Dynastic Period. For the earliest historical period, the most important archaeological sites are Buto (Tel el-Fara'in), Saqqara, Abydos, and Elephantine. The remains at these sites consist primarily of temple or tomb architecture. Of the four sites mentioned, Saqqara and Abydos seem to be particularly important for they represent the necropolises of the two capital cities.

One of the most problematic aspects of the development of Egyptian culture in the period between Dynasty 0 and the Second Dynasty is the question of foreign influence. The distinctive style of recessed or niched brick architecture found at Abydos, Hierakonpolis, and Saqqara is remarkably similar to the mode of wall construction found in temples in the southern part of Mesopotamia which date to roughly the same time as the Egyptian First Dynasty. Although there are a large number of other parallels between Mesopotamian and Egyptian art, the cultural interaction was apparently one-way. Mesopotamian and Elamite sites have yielded virtually nothing which can be traced back to Egypt.

It is possible to trace the increasing power of the united Egyptian monarchy through the First and Second Dynasties in the increasing size and complexity of the royal burials in the Western Desert at the base of cliffs at Abydos. Because the Egyptians believed that there was some connection between this world and the next, tools, household utensils, games, jewelry, furniture, and even food and drink were placed in the royal tombs, offering us an invaluable insight into contemporary material culture.

Several of the First and Second Dynasty tombs at Abydos are surrounded by small graves which were intended mostly for low-status individuals, presumably the kings' servants. A large proportion of these subsidiary graves contained the bodies of robust young men, who may have been killed at the king's death, in order to accompany and serve him in the next world, a funerary practice which ended with the Second Dynasty. Another remarkable feature of the Abydos necropolis are large enclosures whose walls exhibit the same niched decoration as the facade of the royal palace. These structures were probably used for the king's mortuary cult.

During the first two dynasties, nearly every monarch buried at Abydos also had a funerary monument at Saqqara. That site, located approximately 6 miles (10 km) south of modern Cairo, served throughout the history of pharaonic Egypt as the main necropolis for Memphis, the northern capital city at the apex of the Delta. The Saqqara tombs of the First and Second Dynasties are considerably larger than their southern counterparts and their construction is more elaborate. Another reflection of the cultural difference between the two parts of Egypt is the absence of subsidiary graves of deceased servants. Yet, like the Abydos tombs, these monuments were covered pit graves sunk into the ground and lined with stone. Their upper structures also bear distinctive niching or projections on the outside walls of the tombs. The Egyptians called this type of wall decoration *serekh*, a term which roughly means "palace facade." This architectural feature was so closely connected with the kingship that it was incorporated into the official hieroglyphic writing of the pharaoh's Horus Name.

Third Dynasty. The kings of the Third Dynasty chose Saqqara as their primary burial site. Even today the southern portion of the site is dominated by the funerary monument of King Netjery-khet ("Djoser"), with its vast enclosure wall and pyramid rising in seven steps to an original height of 254 feet (77 m) (Nu). The Step Pyramid and its enclosure are the earliest examples of large-scale stone architecture in Egypt. This vast project was directed by an official named Imhotep, long identified in an inscription on the base of a royal statue as the king's chief architect.

During the Old Kingdom, the expenditure of so much effort on the king's mortuary establishment must have been undertaken with the understanding that the entire nation had a stake in the monarch's afterlife. It might be said that a construction like Netjery-khet's funerary monument symbolically expresses some of the political, religious, and economic principles underlying the Egyptian state. The oft-repeated statement that the Egyptians thought that their ruler was a god is only partially accurate. A careful reading of statuary, reliefs, and texts describing the king's interaction with the gods reveals that the pharaoh was considered a godlike mortal whose chief functions were to act as the intermediary between the divine sphere and (Egyptian) humanity and to administer Egypt on behalf of the gods.

Fourth Dynasty and the Great Pyramids. The Fourth Dynasty is certainly among the most famous of all the ruling houses of Egypt, for its kings built the *pyramids of Giza, a western suburb of Cairo. Snofru, the founder of the dynasty, erected no fewer than three pyramids, none of which, however, were at Giza. Two of these, the Maidum pyramid and the so-called Bent Pyramid at Dahshur show evidence that serious structural instabilities developed during their construction. The North Stone Pyramid at Dahshur was the last and most successful of Snofru's three pyramids, and may have served as the basis for the design of the Giza monuments.

It was probably during Snofru's reign that classical tripartite form of Egyptian pyramid complexes was developed. Each complex consists of a valley temple allowing access by boat, a covered causeway leading up to the pyramid enclosure, and finally, the pyramid enclosure itself on the desert plateau. This upper unit was walled off and the funerary cult of the king was maintained within its precincts. Often the king had members of his family buried in subsidiary pyramids near him. In order to assist the king in his travels to the next world, large boats for the afterlife journey would occasionally be buried in special pits near the pyramid enclosure.

Perhaps no aspect of Egyptian civilization has so captured the popular imagination throughout the ages as the massive pyramids of Giza. The greatest of the three Giza pyramids was made for Khufu (or Cheops as he is known in Greek sources). At the base the sides were 754 feet (230 m) long, while the structure rose to a height of 479 feet (146 m). Unfortunately, no contemporary inscription survives which describes the methods employed to build this gigantic structure. If we ascribe a fifty-year reign to Khufu and assume that the work of placing the approximately 2.3 million blocks in his pyramid continued non-stop for twelve hours a day, 365 days a year, this would still mean that a well-squared and finished block of stone would have to be put into place every ten to twelve minutes. The housing, feeding, and care of the estimated 100,000 laborers, as well as the careful planning and management of their labor is a feat of organization as impressive as the skillful engineering by which the project was accomplished.

Khufu was followed by the enigmatic Dedefre, who chose to build his pyramid at Abu Rowash, a plateau approximately 3 miles (5 km) northwest of Giza. This king did not reign long and the construction never progressed much beyond its initial stages. Khafre (or Chephren) built the second of the Giza pyramids on a scale only slightly smaller than the Great Pyramid of Khufu. Next to Khafre's valley temple was a large stone outcropping, into which was carved the famous Sphinx, a creature combining the body of a lion and the head of the pharaoh. The original purpose and meaning of the Sphinx are uncertain, but it was later identified with the god Harmaklis. The last and smallest of the Giza pyramids was erected for Menkaure (Mycerinus). As is the case with the other pyramids of Giza, there are no surviving contemporary inscriptions on either the inside or the outside of this structure except for the occasional graffiti left by the work teams. The last king of the dynasty, Shepseskaf, abandoned Giza for his funerary monument, choosing to build a tomb in the shape of a giant sarcophagus.

Although it had long been the custom for the king's lesser family members and the high officials of the realm to be buried close to the royal burial, it was only in the Fourth Dynasty that great numbers of substantial tombs belonging to the non-royal aristocracy were built. The characteristic form of the Old Kingdom private tomb is the *mastaba*, so called because it resembles the bevel-sided benches (known by the same Arabic word) that are built outside peasant houses today. Most mastaba tombs were constructed of limestone blocks surrounding a stone rubble core. The focal point of the tomb was often a cruxiform chapel with a false-door stela before which offerings could be placed. In some cases cult statues of the deceased would be placed in special chambers, called *serdabs* after the Arabic word for "cellar," so these images might also be able to receive offerings on behalf of the tomb owner. Some of the larger mastabas had additional rooms richly decorated with scenes of daily life which presumably would occur in much the same form in the world beyond the grave. For the actual burial, a deep shaft leading to a burial chamber was cut into the mastaba and down into the bedrock below.

Fifth Dynasty. The origin of the Fifth Dynasty and its relationship to the preceding ruling family are uncertain. This dynasty exhibited an unusually strong devotion to the sun god Re. The first king of the dynasty, Userkaf, built a rather modest pyramid near the northeast corner of Netjery-khet's enclosure as Saqqara. In addition to his pyramid, he also constructed a sun temple near Abu Ghurab, thus setting a pattern that was to be followed by most of the kings of the dynasty of building both a funerary monument and a sun sanctuary.

The best-preserved temple of this kind is Niuserre's sun sanctuary at Abu Ghurab. The sun sanctuary had the same tripartite division as the pyramid complex, but instead of a pyramid, the main enclosure contained a squat obelisk, an object which the Egyptians connected with both royal display and the worship of the sun. Many of the Fifth Dynasty monarchs built their pyramids slightly to the south of Abu Ghurab near Abusir, none of which are more than one-third of the height of their counterparts at Giza. A few decorated relief fragments from Sahure's mortuary temple depict what may be a trading expedition to either Syria or Canaan and a military expedition against the Libyans in the Western Desert. Two large finds of papyri from this area have given us valuable insights into how royal mortuary establishments were operated.

The last two kings of the Fifth Dynasty, Djedkare Isesi and Unas, built their funerary establishments at Saqqara. The pyramid of Unas is particularly interesting because it is the first royal monument to be inscribed with the Pyramid Texts, the first in a long tradition of Egyptian religious texts dealing with the afterlife and containing the first mention of the god Osiris.

Sixth Dynasty. Though the origins of the Sixth Dynasty are unknown, the size and number of official tombs built during this dynasty indicate that the bureaucracy was growing more powerful at the expense of the royal house, especially in the provinces. Much of the administrative, legal, and financial power of the nation was concentrated either directly or indirectly in hands of the vizier. The biographical inscription of a successful functionary called Weni at Abydos describes a close personal relationship with the ruling monarch, a harem conspiracy, and an expedition into southern Palestine. Two later biographical inscriptions of officials at Elephantine, Harkhuf, and Pepinakht provide information about Egypt's relations with the Nubian lands south of the first cataract.

By the end of the Sixth Dynasty, Egypt was involved in trade and other contacts beyond its borders with increasing frequency. Yet during the long reign of Pepi II, the last important monarch of the dynasty, a process of slow disintegration seems to have set in. There is a marked decrease in quality of the royal pyramids and private monuments and there also seems to have been a considerable expansion of the bureaucracy, which resulted in what might be termed a "title inflation," in which even minor officials granted themselves grandiose titles on their monuments.

End of the Old Kingdom and the First Intermediate Period. According to Greek sources, Pepi II may have been succeeded by a Queen named Nitokris. This tradition may be based on little more than the desire to blame the ensuing disintegration of the central government on a woman. Although the sequence of events is quite clouded, it seems relatively certain that within a short time after the death of Pepi II, various names set themselves apart as competing states, each with its own "king." The major conflict during this period appears to have been a lengthy struggle between a group of kings, the Ninth and Tenth Dynasties, which ruled from Heracleopolis near the Fayyum, and another group of monarchs, the Eleventh Dynasty, a group of nomarchs (provincial governors) from Thebes in Upper Egypt who likewise thought that they were the legitimate rulers of the entire country. Between these two centers of power were the many nomes of Middle Egypt, which apparently vacillated in their loyalties to the main competing centers. This era is known as the First Intermediate Period and lasted until the reunification of Egypt under King Nebhepetre Menthuhotep of the Theban Eleventh Dynasty. The chaos of this period left a lasting impression on the Egyptian people as an example of the disasters that can occur in the absence of a strong king ruling a unified land. By contrast, throughout the rest of their history the Egyptians looked back on the Old Kingdom as a golden age of order and prosperity.

[See also EGYPT AND AFRICA; NEAR EAST: IRON AGE CIVILIZATIONS OF THE NEAR EAST.]

■ A. Fakhry, *The Pyramids* (1961). Jean-Phillipe Lauer, *Saqqara: The Royal Cemetery of Memphis, Excavations and Discoveries since 1850* (1976). Barry J. Kemp, *Ancient Egypt: Anatomy of a Civilization* (1989). Dieter Arnold, *Building in Egypt: Pharaonic Stone Masonry* (1991). George Hart, *Pharaohs and Pyramids: A Guide Through Old Kingdom Egypt* (1991). Nicolas Grimal, *A History of Ancient Egypt* (1992). Eugen Strouhal, *The Life of the Ancient Egyptians* (1992). Miroslav Verner, *Forgotten Pharaohs, Lost Pyramids.* (1994).

Ogden Goelet

MIDDLE KINGDOM EGYPT

Consisting of the late Eleventh and Twelfth Dynasties (ca. 2040–1780 B.C.), the Middle Kingdom was a glorious renaissance. Its energetic pharaohs were responsible for what have become some of the greatest archaeological discoveries of ancient Egypt. Their accomplishments are significant because the Middle Kingdom was bracketed by the first and second of three so-called intermediate periods, which are characterized by weakened central administration; overlapping, rivalrous, and often ephemeral kings; occasional civil war; and a decline in artistic quality. The Middle Kingdom was not isolated from either intermediate period. It benefited from the first, and its own political instabilities opened the door to the second.

Historical Overview. A time of political turmoil, the First Intermediate Period (2134–2040 B.C.) began with the close of the Old Kingdom at the end of the Sixth Dynasty and lasted until the latter part of the Eleventh Dynasty. During the First Intermediate Period, two hostile royal houses governed different parts of the country. The Nile Delta and the central region of the country were loosely controlled by a line of kings centered at Nennisut (better known by its Greek appellation Heracleopolis), on the southern edge of the Faiyūm. The eight southernmost provinces, or *nomes*, were dominated by a succession of powerful pharaohs whose capital was at Thebes.

All the Heracleopolitan kings are obscure, and their monuments are extremely rare. Of the eighteen rulers the names of more than half are unknown. Two ruined pyramids remain: Merikare's at Saqqara and Khui's at Dara near Asyut in central Egypt. A third pyramid, belonging to King Iti, is known from inscriptions, but its location has not been established. The ongoing Spanish excavations at Heracleopolis itself have failed to unearth any royal works, but this situation may change. The paucity of well-dated Heracleopolitan royal material is unfortunate. In the absence of a king's name, many scholars date particular objects to the Middle Kingdom instead of the First Intermediate Period.

The geographical and chronological extent of Heracleopolitan control is uncertain. The first four kings may have had authority over all Egypt for eighty years. The southernmost areas were perhaps then relinquished to the Thebans. Or the Heracleopolitan never dominated more

than the Nile Delta and central Egypt. Whether the Heracleopolitan line consists of one dynasty (Nine or Ten) or two dynasties (Nine and Ten) remains controversial.

The six monarchs who constitute the Theban Eleventh Dynasty (2134–1991 B.C.) are all known by name, and most of their reigns are well documented. Around 2040 B.C., the fourth—King Mentuhotep II—defeated his unknown Heracleopolitan rival, laid claim to the entire country, and ushered in the Middle Kingdom. The capital of the country remained at Thebes. In the early Twelfth Dynasty, King Amenemhet I moved the capital north to Lisht, not far from Memphis, which had been the center of power in the Old Kingdom. Amenemhet I had seven successors, the last of whom, Sebeknefru, was a woman.

Her accession signifies a dynastic disruption, a break in the line of male succession, and her four-year rule marked the end of the Middle Kingdom. Despite the claims of some contemporary historians, royal legitimacy was not matrilineal. On only three other occasions in the three millennia of ancient Egyptian history did a woman become pharaoh. By Sebeknefru's time the central administration had weakened, and soon the country was divided once more into antagonistic territories presided over by contemporary kings. The Thirteenth through the Seventeenth Dynasties (1780–1500 B.C.) constitute the Second Intermediate Period. Its history is even more convoluted than that of the Heracleopolitan–Theban rivalry.

Consisting of approximately seventy kings, the Thirteenth Dynasty lasted around 140 years (1783–ca. 1640 B.C.). Although many are known by name from archaeological finds, they are mostly obscure. They were probably nonroyal, largely contemporary persons who seized power. The nature of their suzerainty is not entirely clear. Several early Thirteenth Dynasty kings had Asiatic names, such as Ameni Aamu and Khendjer. Probably from the Levant and elsewhere in the Near East, they occupied the northeastern Nile Delta.

These Asiatics were the latest of many foreigners who had migrated to Egypt since the Middle Kingdom as freepersons and captives of foreign campaigns. Many of them became completely Egyptianized. Others took advantage of the enervated monarchy and seized control in the northeastern Nile Delta. An important Asiatic settlement at what is now Tell ed Daba (known to Greek historians as Avaris) became the Asiatics' capital.

The Asiatics are known as the Hyksos, a Greek term derived from the Egyptian designation "rulers of foreign lands." It is a political term, not an ethnological description. From their base at Avaris, the Asiatics developed far-flung alliances and contacts: to the south, scattered areas of Egypt and Kush, an area in what is now the Sudan; to the north and northeast, Crete, Cyprus, and parts of Anatolia; and to the east, the Levant and possibly Mesopotamia. Minoan artists from Crete provided the most fabulous items found during the continuing Austrian excavations at Tell ed Daba: great frescoes (now fragmentary), featuring traditional Minoan bull-leaping acrobats, and Egyptian landscapes.

The main line of Hyksos domination was the Fifteenth Dynasty, which was partially coeval with the Thirteenth, Seventeenth, and even early Eighteenth Dynasties. The Fourteenth and Sixteenth Dynasties are particularly problematic. Like the Thirteenth Dynasty, they consisted of concurrent rulers. The Fourteenth Dynasty kings were the first to make Avaris their capital. The Sixteenth Dynasty sovereigns may not have resided in Egypt at all, but in Sharuhen, in what is now the southern part of Israel. Consisting entirely of native Egyptians, the Seventeenth Dynasty saw a series of ultimately victorious struggles with the last kings of the Hyksos Fifteenth Dynasty. The withdrawal of Khamudy, the final Hyksos ruler, to the Levant did not occur until the first part of the Eighteenth Dynasty, which marked the beginning of the New Kingdom (ca. 1550 B.C.).

Because of an obdurate Egyptian disdain for foreigners, some ancient texts unfairly describe the Hyksos as marauders. Localized skirmishes certainly occurred as various Asiatic leaders consolidated their claims to kingship. No evidence exists, however, for a full-scale invasion of Egypt. Archaeological excavations within the Wadi Tumilat in the northeastern delta—the point of entry for the Asiatics—have not unearthed large-scale burn levels or other evidence of massive destruction.

The bad press not only obscures the peaceful interludes of the Second Intermediate Period but also diminishes many profoundly important Asiatic legacies: new weapons; improved metalworking, weaving, and pottery techniques; and the introduction of new gods and religious beliefs. Associated with the northern Syrian weather god Baal Zephon, the Egyptian deity Seth enjoyed an unprecedented and long-lasting popularity. Ironically, one of the greatest benefits of the Asiatics came with their withdrawal. As the early kings of the Eighteenth Dynasty pushed into the Near East in pursuit of the Hyksos, they acquired a hitherto unrivaled cosmopolitanism, which set the stage for the royal greater military and trading expeditions of the New Kingdom.

General Overview. The Twelfth Dynasty is the defining phase of the Middle Kingdom. Eight pharaohs presided over a vast and efficient bureaucracy; sent many military and trading expeditions to foreign lands; and built numerous monuments, including a great array of pyramids and an impressive series of forts in the northern part of what is now the Sudan. The sculptures commissioned by Senwosret III for sites throughout the land and the jewelry belonging to various royal women found at the pyramid cemeteries of Dahshûr and Lahun rank among the finest works of Egyptian art. Likewise, the Twelfth Dynasty witnessed exponential developments in the language and literature. Nonroyal persons played a much greater role in ancient Egyptian society during the Middle Kingdom than ever before. In general, the nonroyal archaeological material of the Middle Kingdom indicates a hitherto unparalleled wealth across a broad spectrum of society. Ironically, the enhanced status of private individuals and the social dynamic behind it have not received sufficient attention in scholarly or popular literature and therefore deserve special emphasis.

The high incidence of monuments and the prominence of genealogies are two immediately apparent aspects of Middle Kingdom nonroyal archaeological data. From the various quarters of Abydos, a vast site in southern Egypt, come an immense number of stelae (commemorative inscribed tablets) that document the participation of private individuals in the festival procession of Osiris, lord of the underworld. An equally great quantity of private stelae have been found in the numerous Middle Kingdom burials at Abydos. The two sets comprise the most extensive corpus of inscriptions from a single Middle Kingdom site. These stelae specify the ancestry of the individuals as often as, if not more than, the names of the kings they served. A certain leveling of prestige had developed; lineage took on a new importance.

Actually, the status of private individuals had risen since the end of the Old Kingdom. To understand their importance in the Middle Kingdom, an important contrast must be described. The pyramids and large tombs of the Fourth Dynasty kings and their courtiers eclipse the modest tombs belonging to persons of lower rank, whose burials were relegated to the less desirable real estate on the fringe of the Giza plateau. Certain protocols dictated the decoration and even the location of tombs belonging to all nonroyal persons. No one except the king could copy the *Pyramid Texts,* the oldest collection of ancient Egyptian funerary texts. Officials of all ranks generally chose to be buried in or near the pyramid cemeteries at Giza or Saqqara, which lay in the region of Memphis.

As various strictures were relaxed at the end of the Old Kingdom and throughout the First Intermediate period, the map changed. Some officials were buried near the pyramids, but many others were laid to rest in their home provinces. Most conspicuous in the pyramid cemeteries are the small First Intermediate period and Twelfth Dynasty burials of lesser officials that intrude upon and clutter the interstices of the quadrants formed by the grand rectangular tombs of Old Kingdom courtiers. Middle Kingdom nonroyal coffins often include magical spells from the *Pyramid Texts.* A new "book" of incantations—the *Coffin Texts*—evolved sometime before the Middle Kingdom for use by private persons.

During the First Intermediate Period, the emerging confidence among private individuals manifested itself in a widespread skepticism about the Heracleopolitan sovereigns. In almost all other periods, nonroyal persons proudly cited the king they served. The inscriptions from Heracleopolitan regions are remarkably taciturn. Only in the tomb of the loyalist Kheti at Asyut is a Heracleopolitan king—Merikare—cited. Otherwise, complete silence prevails in the inscriptions at the important provincial Heracleopolitan cemeteries at Sedment, Beni Hasan, Deir el Bersheh, Meir, Naga ed Deir, and Hawawish.

Pertinent here are several extraordinary graffiti left by the First Intermediate Period nomarch (provincial governor) Neheri at the calcite quarry of Hatnub not far from Bersheh and Tell al-'Amarna in central Egypt. Neheri's account of his expeditions to Hatnub bear his name, year, and office, not those of his king. In a bolder breach of etiquette, Neheri appropriated royal epithets. Disdain for the Heracleopolitan court may explain Neheri's actions, but they were part of a wider phenomenon. Self-confidence had also developed in Theban territory, where respect for the royal court was high. Private individuals in both Heracleopolitan and Theban domains assumed other privileges that had been forbidden to them. For example, they depicted themselves in their tombs with the ankh amulet (the Egyptian emblem of life) in their hands. In the Old Kingdom this attitude had been restricted to representations of gods and kings.

Disillusionment with the monarchy may account in part for the rise in importance of private persons, but it is certainly not the only explanation. Having begun already in the late Old Kingdom, popular self-assertion may have been an inevitable sociopolitical development, independent of attitudes toward the king. Commoners were prominent in later generations when popular and powerful rulers prevailed. Their increased status did not pose a threat to the pharaohs of the Twelfth Dynasty who brought the country once again under an efficient administration that was centralized at the royal residence. Like Neheri at Hatnub, the Middle Kingdom nomarch Amenemhet inscribed the facade of his large tomb at Beni Hasan with his current year in office, but he also included the corresponding regnal year of Senwosret I. Indeed, throughout the Twelfth Dynasty, commoners prominently cited the rulers they had served.

Likewise, the cessation of large burials at provincial sites such as Beni Hasan, Bersheh, Meir, and Asyut after the reign of Senwosret III does not imply that the nomarchs had become so self-reliant that the crown had to suppress them, as many scholars have claimed. Senwosret III and his predecessors probably adopted peaceful measures that strengthened the central administration. No longer was the office of nomarch hereditary; instead, the kings allowed the positions to expire and appointed the eldest sons of the local governors to important offices at the royal court. Not coincidentally, the main period of use begins at several important cemeteries at or near Lisht in the second half of the Twelfth Dynasty. An extremely important indication of centralized control over the provinces is the widespread distribution throughout the country of pottery types that originated at Lisht. Finally, many nonroyal persons preferred burial in the Twelfth Dynasty pyramid cemeteries, which were widely scattered in regions around Lisht (Lisht itself [Amenemhet I and Senwosret I], Dahshûr [Amenemhet II and III and Senwosret III], Lahun [Senwosret II], and Hawara [a second pyramid of Amenemhet III]).

Two further precautions are necessary in discussing the prominence of private persons in the Middle Kingdom. First, the terminology of contemporary politics should be avoided. For all the gains made by private persons, the Middle Kingdom was not a time of democracy, division of power, or equality. The pharaohs and their high officials instigated the majority of important projects. To cite but one example, from Upper Egypt to Lower Nubia at sites such as Aniba, Askut, Buhen, Dabonarti, Elephantine, Faras, Ikkur, Kor, Kumma, Mirgissa, Quban, Semna, Serra, Shalfak, and Uronarti, the rulers of the Middle Kingdom either renovated or built anew many fortified stations to protect the important riverine trade in luxury products with the regions far to the south of Egypt. Likewise, popular opinion did not determine royal succession. If the pharaohs had questions, they consulted their high officials and various oracles; they did not schedule plebiscites. Although most of the Middle Kingdom pharaohs shared the monarchy in the latter years of their tenure with a junior royal partner (usually a son) known as a co-regent, who became sole ruler at the death of the senior sovereign, the distribution of authority went no further. Even within the private sector, equal opportunity was not enjoyed by all. Women did not possess the same privileges as men. Women generally held no higher religious office than priestess of Hathor. Furthermore, disparities in entitlements for women no doubt existed across social classes.

The prominence of commoners in the Middle Kingdom has no easy explanation. That said, one indication of social change is clear in a popular Middle Kingdom sculptural type—the family group. Old Kingdom versions depict the male (usually a husband) on a larger scale than the female and children. The woman embraces the man or holds his hand, but with exceedingly few exceptions, he does not return her gesture. In the Middle Kingdom, both men and women are frequently of the same stature, and the affection is mutual.

A remarkable and widely ranging textual transformation occurred at the very beginning of the Twelfth Dynasty. Individual hieroglyphs, such as the papyrus roll, that were written only occasionally in the Old Kingdom and the First Intermediate period turn up with great frequency throughout the country in more detailed forms in the reign of Amenemhet I, as if to clarify their meanings. Funerary phrases and prayers have more elaborate versions. Amenemhet I himself may not have served as copyeditor, but the sudden and pervasive changes in his reign suggest that he at least set his scribes to work. These redactions comprise the most valuable criteria for distinguishing between inscribed monuments of the First Intermediate Period and the Middle Kingdom.

A related phenomenon is the abundant literary activity during the Middle Kingdom. Previously dated to the First Intermediate Period, several of the greatest surviving ancient Egyptian narratives have been reassigned to the Twelfth Dynasty, among them *The Man Who Was Weary of Life, The Tale of the Eloquent Peasant,* and *The Instructions for King Merikare.* A Twelfth Dynasty date has long been accepted for still other masterpieces such as *The Tale of Sinuhe, The Teaching of Amenemhat I for His Son, The Prophecy of Neferti, The Story of the Shipwrecked Sailor.*

The artists of the Middle Kingdom pursued aesthetic innovations that had developed in the latter half of the Old Kingdom and had been pursued aggressively in the First Intermediate Period. Throughout Heracleopolitan and Theban territory, at such sites as Saqqara, Sedment, Beni Hasan, Bersheh, Meir, Asyut, Hawawish, Abydos, Naga ed Deir, Dendera, Coptos, Khozam, Thebes, Gebelein, Moalla, and Qubbet el Hawa, a bright polychrome palette prevails. At many of these same sites, the rendering of the human figure shows a curious elongation of the torso and limbs that had developed at Saqqara in the late Fifth Dynasty. Although the scenes are often awkwardly rendered and garishly painted, the playful imagery and the interesting juxtapositions of color are bold and imaginative experiments. They are not only the reverse of decline, but they are also important legacies to the art of the Middle Kingdom.

[See also NUBIA; PYRAMIDS OF GIZA; WRITING: EGYPTIAN HIEROGLYPHIC.]

■ Georges Posener, "Les Asiatiques en Égypte sous les XIIe et XIIIe Dynasties," *Syria* 34 (1957): 145–163. David O'Connor, "Political Systems and Archaeological Data in Egypt: 2600–1780 B.C.," *World Archaeology* 6 (1974): 15–38. William Kelly Simpson, *The Terrace of the Great God at Abydos: The Offering Chapels of Dynasties 12 and 13* (1974). Detlef Franke, *Personendaten aus dem Mittleren Reich (20.-16. Jahrhundert v. Chr.): Dossiers 1–96* (1984). Manfred Bietak, "Canaanites in the Eastern Delta," in *Egypt, Israel, Sinai: Archaeological and Historical Relationships in the Biblical Period,* ed. Anson F. Rainey (1987), pp. 41–56. Janine Bourriau, *Pharaohs and Mortals: Egyptian Art in the Middle Kingdom* (1988). Dorothea Arnold, "Amenemhat I and the Early Twelfth Dynasty at Thebes," *Metropolitan Museum Journal* 26 (1991): 5–38. Janine Bourriau, "Patterns of Change in Burial Customs During the Middle Kingdom," in *Middle Kingdom Studies,* ed. Stephen Quirke (1991), pp. 3–20. Detlef Franke, "The Career of Khnumhotep III of Beni Hasan and the so-called 'Decline of the Nomarchs,'" in *Middle Kingdom Studies,* ed. Stephen Quirke (1991), pp. 51–68. Richard Parkinson, "Teachings, Discourses, and Tales from the Middle Kingdom," in *Middle Kingdom Studies,* ed. Stephen Quirke (1991), pp. 91–122. Stephen Quirke, "Royal Power in the Thirteenth Dynasty," in *Middle Kingdom Studies,* ed. Stephen Quirke (1991), pp. 123–139. Manfred Bietak et al., "Neue Grabungsergebnisse aus Tell el Dab'a und 'Ezbet Helmi im ostlichen Nildelta 1989–1991," *Ägypten und Levante* 4 (1994): 9–81. Manfred Bietak et al., *Pharaonen und Fremde: Dynastien im Dunkel* (1994).

Donald B. Spanel

NEW KINGDOM EGYPT

The New Kingdom (ca. 1550 to 1075 B.C.) is the name Egyptologists give to the third period of unified central government in Egyptian history. It corresponds to the third century B.C. historian Manetho's Eighteenth, Nineteenth, and Twentieth Dynasties. Eduard Meyer introduced the name in his 1913 study *Geschichte des Altertums (History of Antiquity)*. English-speaking Egyptologists, who had previously referred to this period as "The Empire," later adopted this designation. This older name referred to the increased contact Egypt experienced with other parts of Africa, the Near East, and the Aegean at this time. This contact was the result of Egyptian military activity, domination, and settlement in *Nubia and the creation of an Egyptian sphere of influence in parts of the Levant. This expansion of Egyptian power led to increased wealth for the Egyptian king that is attested to in the archaeological and textual record. Temples, towns, and tombs reflect the wealth and cosmopolitan nature of New Kingdom Egypt.

Some Egyptologists have described the New Kingdom by an organic metaphor. It was born when Ahmose, Prince of Thebes, completed the expulsion of the Hyksos to their west Asian homeland. The Hyksos were foreign rulers who had dominated the Delta for approximately one hundred years. During the period's vigorous youth, Ahmose's successors expanded Egyptian influence as far as the Euphrates River in the north and to the fourth cataract of the Nile River in the south. A period of relatively peaceful middle age began under Amunhotpe III's rule. The period's midlife crisis, his son's religious revolution, succeeded it. Akhenaten abandoned Amun worship and substituted the monotheistic or henotheistic cult of Aton. The following three kings, including Tutankhamun, restored Amun worship. Each of these kings died without a male heir. The New Kingdom experienced a productive old age when Rameses I came to the throne and established a new line of kings. The most famous of these kings was his grandson, Rameses II, called "the Great," who fought the Hittites in the East to a stalemate (ca. 1294 B.C.), resulting in another period of relative peace. The New Kingdom's last burst of glory came with the reign of Rameses III, who repulsed invasions by the Sea Peoples from the north and the Libyans from the west. The successor kings, however, were unable to hold the possessions outside Egypt or even to maintain the central government. Within eighty years of the war against the Sea Peoples, Rameses XI had lost control of Upper Egypt to a former general, now the High Priest of Amun, named Herihor. The New Kingdom was dead.

In a more sophisticated view, Barry Kemp (1989) has argued that the New Kingdom was a time when the already ancient conception of divine monarchy evolved into a more pluralist state. The military and temple branches of the government possessed a variety of powers that could counterbalance the authority of the king. Kemp incorporates archival texts and the archaeological record in his analysis, which, if properly understood, add a new dimension to scholars' understanding of the New Kingdom. In his analysis of archival records, Kemp grounds his belief that there was a personal economic emancipation as the New Kingdom progressed.

New Kingdom Temples. The local temple dominated the typical Egyptian town of the New Kingdom. Ordinarily, it was the only stone building in a settlement of mud-brick structures. A New Kingdom temple was a stage set for the processional of the god's barque, the major ritual event in Egyptian religious practice. The Egyptians also conceived the temple as the *huat-netjer* or "mansion of the god." As was true of any mansion belonging to an ancient Egyptian noble, there were both private rooms accessible only to the owner and his intimates and public spaces where the common people could greet the god.

In an ideal temple plan, all the rooms were arranged symmetrically along a central axis. The massive pylon gateway in the front communicated along the axis to an open forecourt. The forecourt contained an open, sunny space and covered colonnades to the left and right. Directly opposite the pylon doorway, a central opening led to a roofed hypostyle hall, a dark room filled with columns. The forecourt and hypostyle hall corresponded to the public rooms in a nobleman's mansion. Beyond the hypostyle was at least one pronaos. It was sometimes used as storage for the god's barque. Finally a naos acted as a statue room. These rooms corresponded to the private rooms of a nobleman's house and were inaccessible to the public.

Though this is the ideal basic plan of a typical Egyptian temple of the New Kingdom, few actual temples conformed to the plan. In the best-preserved New Kingdom temples found on the east bank of the Nile in ancient Thebes (modern Luxor, about 350 miles [565 km] south of Cairo on the Nile River) constant additions and renovations distorted the original plan. The largest Theban temple is the *Ipet-isut*, ("Most Select of Places") or Temple of Amun at Karnak. A processional way links it to *Ipet-resyt* ("Southern Ipet") or Temple of Amun at Luxor. At *Karnak, kings added a total of ten pylons at the front of their predecessor's temple. The axis at Luxor is bent, rather than the ideal straight line, to accommodate buildings that were standing in front of Amunhotpe III's temple at the time when Rameses II made additions to it.

The basic plan is more clearly visible in the mortuary temples. Each king built one on the west bank of the river at Thebes for his own cult after his death. While kings added to their predecessors' work at gods' temples, mortuary temples dedicated to a king as a form of the god Amun, chief deity of the New Kingdom, were less likely to be renovated. The most famous examples of mortuary temples are Hatshepsut's mortuary temple at Deir el Bahri, the Rameseum built by Rameses II, and its close imitator, the Temple of Medinet Habu built by Rameses III.

The ritual performed at all of these temples was similar. Priests treated the statue of the god or of the divine deceased king as if it were a living nobleman. They awoke it with hymns, then washed, dressed, and fed it. The statue traveled through its mansion in the divine barque, carried by priests. At the end of the day they undressed it, washed it, and put it to sleep. They performed each step according to a prescribed ritual. Specialist priests studied ancient texts to insure that they had performed the ritual properly.

There were also many festivals during which the gods distributed food and drink to the population. In Thebes in the time of Amunhotpe III, about one day of every three was a festival. These included festivals of specific gods, observances of certain royal occasions such as the coronation or the jubilee of a reign, marking of events in the agricultural cycle including sowing and harvest, and festivals based on the calendar such as the new year, the new month, and the half month. The Festival of Opet celebrated in Karnak and Luxor Temples, and the Festival of the Valley, celebrated at the mortuary temples on the western bank of the Nile, seem to be typical. They each commemorated a ritual visit by Amun during Opet to the Luxor Temple and during the Valley festival to the mortuary temples of deceased kings. They both included a procession to the river and distribution of vast amounts of food and drink. These festivals, from an economic viewpoint, functioned as a mechanism to redistribute the vast food wealth of the gods to the people who needed it in order to survive. They served a very practical purpose arranged according to Egyptian cultural norms.

City Planning. In spite of increased research during the 1970s and 1980s, archaeologists still know the towns less well than the temples. The hieroglyph for "town" represents a walled village with two roads intersecting at a 90° angle. Reality, however, was probably less orderly. The New Kingdom town attached to eastern Thebes has not been excavated, though its probable location is east of the Karnak Temple. Tell el Amarna, the site that Akhenaten chose for his new capital, is the best-known New Kingdom town. Because Akhenaten's successors abandoned it, it has been easier to study than many other towns.

The main districts of Amarna, called Akhetaton in ancient times, included residential, ceremonial, and business quarters. The royal residence was in the north part of town, adjacent to a ceremonial palace. A residential zone separated the ceremonial palace from the Great Aton Temple. The official city bounded the temple on the south. To the west was another ceremonial palace. Further south was a residential zone for high-ranking government officials and priests. Artisans' houses and cemeteries were located in the less desirable, more arid areas to the east of the temple. At the far south was the Maru-Aton, a religious district consisting of shrines, pavilions, and artificial lakes. A broad avenue connected all areas of the town. Its plan reflected the close control that the king had over officials and his close personal contact with the courtiers.

New Kingdom Social History. Deir el-Medina, the home of the workmen who built and decorated the tombs in the Valley of the Kings, is a second well-known residential area dating to the New Kingdom. It is located in western Thebes in the hills near Qurnet Murai. It consists of seventy houses arranged along a narrow main street. A slightly later district with additional streets is found to the west. Amunhotpe I and / or Thutmose I founded the town to house the workers who constructed their tombs; tomb builders inhabited it throughout the New Kingdom. Many if not all the inhabitants of Deir el-Medina seem to have been literate, since excavations have revealed numerous written records. As a result, this village has supplied much of what Egyptologists know of workers' lives during the New Kingdom. Documents written and discovered there elucidate the education, working life, economic life, and local governance at Deir el-Medina. School texts reveal the teaching methods and classic literary compositions such as the already ancient "Story of Sinuhe," studied in scribal schools. Work records attest a ten-day work week, the division of workers into gangs to accomplish certain jobs, salaries paid in kind, and even one instance of a strike when wages were not delivered on time. Many records describe barter exchanges among the residents of the village. They bartered their specialized skills, the rental of donkeys, and the acquisitions of servants. The records of the local *qenbet* or community court describe the resolution of legal disputes among the residents. Scholars, however, should not forget that Deir el-Medina was a unique settlement. Because of the gaps in our knowledge it is tempting to describe these workers'

lives as a prototype for life in ancient Egypt. But caution must be exercised in generalizing too freely from this unique record.

Mortuary Customs. Tombs of both royalty and the nobility constitute a third body of archaeological evidence from the New Kingdom. The best-known tombs are again found at Thebes, cut into the rock at the desert edge. Archaeologists have recently rediscovered an additional group of tombs in Memphis.

The kings of the New Kingdom separated their tombs from their mortuary temples, probably as a security measure. Though kings attempted to conceal their tombs in the Valley of the Kings, only the tomb of *Tutankhamun remained intact until modern times. Tomb robbers plundered almost all the others in antiquity. This fact has increased the importance of Tutankhamun's tomb beyond any other historical importance this king might have had. The riches and variety of his grave goods, discovered by Howard Carter in 1922, are the most widely known archaeological discovery of the twentieth century. Unfortunately, because the tomb has not been fully published, Egyptologists have not been able to exploit this find to its full potential. Tutankhamun's treasures, now housed in the Egyptian Museum in Cairo, still contain secrets.

Much more information is available from the tombs of the nobles found on the western bank of the Nile at Thebes and in the Memphite New Kingdom necropolis. The rock-cut tombs of nobles at Thebes and the mastaba tombs (freestanding stone buildings) in Memphis reveal through their decoration a visual record of the official and private lives of the aristocracy and their servants. Paintings in the Theban tombs established the cosmopolitan atmosphere of the New Kingdom which Egyptologists believe characterize it. Many tombs included scenes of foreigners delivering gifts to the king during various kinds of official audiences. These so-called tribute scenes cataloged the variety of goods brought to Egypt from Nubia, the Near East, and the Aegean during the New Kingdom. These goods included oils from Anatolia, pine and cedar from Lebanon, weapons from Syria, lapis lazuli from Afghanistan, copper from Cyprus, elaborate metal vessels from the Aegean islands, ebony, gold, and exotic animals from Nubia, and incense from Punt (Somalia). This catalog includes the entire world as understood by the Egyptians. The tombs also illustrate the evolution of sophisticated clothing and hairstyles among the aristocratic class, elaborate entertainment including banquets, dancing, and music, and religious practices.

Egyptologists have not yet analyzed the full range of archaeological evidence from the New Kingdom. Much work remains to study the material that has already been unearthed. Moreover, Egypt's New Kingdom sites still undoubtedly hold finds that may provide the solution to many unresolved questions.

[See also EGYPT AND AFRICA; ROMAN EMPIRE: THE EASTERN PROVINCES OF THE ROMAN EMPIRE.]

■ Elizabeth Riefstahl, *Thebes in the Times of Amunhotep III* (1964). Charles F. Nims, *Thebes of the Pharaoh's: Pattern for Every City*, 1965. David O'Connor, "New Kingdom and Third Intermediate Period," in *Ancient Egypt: A Social History*, ed. Bruce G. Trigger et al. (1983). Barry J. Kemp, "New Kingdom Egypt: The Mature State," in *Ancient Egypt: Anatomy of a Civilization* (1989).

Edward Bleiberg

EGYPT AND AFRICA. Ancient Egypt flourished on the edge of a vast continent of the Mediterranean world yet part of Africa as well. Cosmopolitan crowds lived in its towns, shopped in its marketplaces, and participated in its religious festivals. Pharaonic civilization was nourished by constant contacts with black African civilizations up the Nile. Egypt's rulers depended on Africa for ivory and semi-precious stones, for gold for their tombs, and for mercenaries for their armies. Ancient Egypt enjoyed an ambivalent, ever-changing relationship with black Africa to the south.

Ancient Egyptian civilization developed out of a patchwork of competing chiefdoms along the Nile before 3000 B.C. The new state extended as far upstream as the First Cataract. Beyond Aswan lay Nubia, "The Land of the Blacks." During the Old Kingdom, the Egyptians traded with Nubia and sent many expeditions searching for valuable commodities like building stone and semiprecious stones. About 2100 B.C., the Old Kingdom ended in crisis as catastrophic droughts hit the Nile. The Nubians became bolder and more aggressive. The governor of Aswan, the "Keeper of the Door to the South," dealt with a patchwork of prosperous and shrewd Nubian kingdoms whose leaders were well aware of the twists and turns of Egyptian politics. Along the fertile Dongola Reach far above Aswan, the first black African states now came into being, ruled by chiefs who measured wealth not in gold and ivory, but in cattle. The rulers' power lay in their control of large herds, and in their entrepreneurial skills, their ability to manipulate the gold and ivory trade with Egypt downstream.

In about 1900 B.C., Middle Kingdom pharaoh Amenemhet raised an army and subjugated Nubian chiefs as far upstream as the Third Cataract. The Egyptians now fortified the strategic Nile reaches below the Second Cataract. Ten major forts protected a 40 mile (64 km) stretch of the Nile, from Buhen in the north to Semna in the south. Buhen was the headquarters, a rectangular fortress that enclosed not only a governor's residence, houses, and workshops, but a temple and military barracks. Semna, the southernmost of the Second Cataract forts, was the boundary between the Egyptian and African worlds during the Middle Kingdom. Upstream, the commerce was in the hands of powerful Nubian chieftains, whose territory extended from Semna far upstream to Kerma and beyond. This was the fabled Land of Kush, country so rich in gold and ivory that its fame spread throughout the eastern Mediterranean world.

The Nubian chieftains of Kush presided over a narrow strip of fertile valley, a hub for important trade routes from both east and west, and from upstream, which converged on the Dongola Reach. The families that controlled this land of cattle herders and farmers held the key to an international trade that flourished for many centuries. When the pharaohs were strong and political conditions in Egypt were stable, the rulers of Kush kept within their boundaries. But when pharaonic control weakened and soldiers were withdrawn from the Second Cataract forts, the Nubians extended their influence upstream. In the seventeenth century B.C., the Asian Hyksos invaded the Nile Delta and ruled Egypt from the far north. The Nubians took over control of most commerce upstream of Aswan. Kush's rulers dwelt at Kerma in the Dongola Reach, an important settlement as long ago as 3000 B.C., larger than its neighbors on account of the fertile soils nearby. By 1750 B.C., between 2,000 and 3,000 people lived in what had become a small town. The entire town was fortified with elaborate defenses— wide, massive walls, protected with rectangular, projecting

watchtowers, all surrounded with dry ditches to prevent undermining. Kerma's rulers were buried under large burial mounds near the town. The three largest mounds had a remarkable internal structure made up of long, parallel mud-brick walls that ran across the tumulus. Each ruler lay on a bed with his weapons and personal possessions. Dozens of sacrificial victims lay both in the chamber and in a corridor that ran across the mound. As many as 400 people perished with one ruler, one of the largest human sacrifices recorded anywhere in the ancient world. Ancient Kush was an entirely African kingdom, created by local chiefs who seized the economic and political initiative when their more powerful neighbors faltered.

In the sixteenth century B.C., the barometer of political power swung again in Egypt's favor. Once pharaoh Ahmose had expelled the Hyksos from Egypt, he turned his attention to his southern frontiers. In about 1535 B.C., he pounced on Lower Nubia and refortified Buhen. This time, Egypt needed Nubia's wealth to finance not only ambitious public works at home, but military campaigns in distant lands. Ahmose's successors Amunhotep I and the three Thutmoses sent their armies far into Upper Nubia. They crushed the rulers of Kerma and occupied Kush, extending Egyptian rule to the Fourth Cataract, and perhaps even farther beyond. Nubia became, for all intents and purposes, an Egyptian colony, a far larger conquest than all the pharaohs' Asian territories combined. By 1479 B.C., Nubia was largely pacified and occupied. The main focus of settlement was between Aniba and the Second Cataract, and upstream in the fertile Abri-Delgo Reach. Some Egyptian colonies flourished much farther upstream, in the Dongola Reach, notably at Napata near the Fourth Cataract, which later became the capital of a powerful indigenous Nubian state. Amunhotep I appointed a "King's Son of Kush," Thuwre, the commandant of Buhen, as viceroy of Kush. He and his successors were powerful men. They were tax collectors and administrators, responsible for delivering vast annual tribute assessments to Thebes. They governed through loyal Nubian chiefs, whose sons were often taken to Egypt as hostages and given an Egyptian education and rank. Nubia changed from a country of village farmers and herders into something more closely resembling a vast plantation state, whose inhabitants worked for the benefit of absentee landlords and sometimes for Nubian officials who were indistinguishable from high Egyptian nobles.

The economic and political shock waves that rolled across the eastern Mediterranean after 1200 B.C. not only overthrew the Hittites, but rippled up the Nile. Within a century, the Egyptian hold on Nubia weakened, as the center of political gravity shifted away from Thebes to the Delta. The colony of Kush was abandoned to its own devices. Many Nubians still clung to Egyptian ways, forming a new elite that created their own distinctive civilization. Much of the wealth and military power that had been Egypt's now stayed at home in Nubia. Gold and Nubian mercenaries—these were the keys to power in Upper Egypt as the imperial age of ancient Egyptian civilization waned. Far away in Upper Nubia, the end of direct Egyptian rule left a political vacuum, but the tradition of divine monarch and the cult of Amun survived, indeed flourished. The flat-topped sacred mountain named Gebel Barkal stands close to the north bank of the Nile at the Fourth Cataract, near the town of Napata. Thutmose III and Rameses II both chose this magnificent setting for a Temple of Amun. The great shrine built by Rameses, brilliantly reconstructed with three-dimensional computer graphics by archaeologist Timothy Kendall, ranks among the finest examples of its kind. It was here that the traditions of kingship and ancient religious beliefs were kept alive. And, in due time, the cult of Amun became the ideological thread that sustained Nubian civilization for more than a thousand years. A common hypothesis has it that the priests of Amun at Gebel Barkal kept alive the ancient traditions. In time, alliances formed between the priests and local chiefs, the ancestors of men who were to rule not only a new kingdom of Kush, but Egypt itself.

The first Napatan king we know by name is Kashta, at least the sixth generation of the dynasty to which he belonged. We know little of him, except that he journeyed north to Thebes, where he was confirmed as ruler by the priests of Amun. He was received with relief by the Theban priests, for Nubian mercenaries kept them in power and threats from the north in check. Kashta took the reigns of power at Thebes, but neither he nor his son Piye (Piankhi) assumed the title of pharaoh.

Piye spent the first twenty years of his reign in Nubia and apparently gave little thought to Thebes. Then came word from the priests of a threat from a Delta king named Tefnakhte, "the great chief of the Ma (Libyans)," who sought to control all Egypt. Piye marched north in about 750 B.C. and conquered the Delta. He now assumed the full title of pharaoh of Egypt and then quietly returned to Napata, where he ruled for another decade without returning to Thebes. Piye was not only a skilled general but an expert politician. Piye's successors Shabaqo and Shebitqo established the royal seat at Thebes, effectively founding the Twenty-Fifth Dynasty of Egyptian pharaohs. Now the tide was turned completely, for the servant had become the master, and the conquered, the conquerors. But there was a major difference, for the Nubian kings, unlike earlier pharaohs, were not exploiters. Perhaps they were slightly overawed by the sheer antiquity and grandeur of the civilization they now controlled. Such was their piety that they restored temples all along the Nile and sponsored a revival of ancient styles, with, however, one difference. Their artists always recorded the kings' distinctive racial differences and the Nubian costume they wore.

The Nubian pharaohs may have been devout admirers of Egyptian art and culture, but they were less adept at foreign policy. Their lack of experience led ultimately to their downfall. The Assyrians invaded Egypt in the seventh century B.C. and installed a puppet pharaoh. In 591 B.C., pharaoh Psamtik II marched on Napata. The Nubian royal family fled upstream to the safety of *Meroe on the Shendi Reach, some 300 miles (482 km) upstream around the great bend of the Nile, where navigation is difficult. They consolidated their kingdom on Meroe, so far from Egypt that no army could reach it. For nearly a thousand years, their successors kept alive an Africanized version of ancient Egyptian civilization, as they prospered off the Red Sea and Saharan caravan trade.

Ancient Egypt's influence on sub-Saharan Africa was negligible, despite the widespread incidence of institutions like divine kingship in indigenous African states. Egypt was a Nile civilization, whose relationships with black Africa were confined to Nubia and the eastern fringes of the Sahara.

[See also AFRICA: RISE OF KINGDOMS AND STATES IN AFRICA; EGYPT, *articles on* MIDDLE KINGDOM EGYPT, NEW KINGDOM EGYPT, OLD KINGDOM EGYPT, PREDYNASTIC CULTURES OF EGYPT; TRADE, AFRICAN.]

■ George Reisner, *Excavations at Kerma* (1923). W. Y. Adams, *Nubia: Corridor to Africa* (1977). Timothy Kendall, *Kush, Lost Kingdom of the Nile* (1982). Graham Connah, *African Civilizations* (1987). Torgny Save-Soderbergh, *Temples and Tombs of Ancient Nubia* (1987). John Taylor, *Egypt and Nubia* (1991). David O'Connor, *Ancient Nubia: Egypt's Rival in Africa* (1994).

Brian M. Fagan

ELM DECLINE, European. The elm decline is a widely recognized horizon in pollen sequences from northwest Europe, involving a major fall in the abundance of elm (*Ulmus*) pollen at around 5000 B.P. This decline occurred over a span of less than one hundred years, and since often it coincides with the first occurrence of pollen of cereals and weeds in a pollen sequence, it was once thought to result from the destruction of elm-rich woodland associated with the spread of agriculture across northwest Europe at the beginning of the Neolithic. The discovery of cereal pollen in pre-elm decline horizons in a number of pollen sequences indicates that this is not the case, however, and the elm decline is no longer taken to mark the onset of the Neolithic Period.

Other explanations suggested for the elm decline include climatic deterioration, depletion of soil fertility, use of elm leaves to feed stalled cattle, and disease. Of these, climatic deterioration and soil exhaustion have been dismissed as there is little independent evidence that either was important. Use of leaf fodder in an early Neolithic context is attested from archaeological evidence, such as the finding of cut twigs of a range of tree species, including ash (*Fraxinus*), lime (*Tilia*), and elm (*Ulmus*), at the settlement at Thayngen-Weier in Switzerland. Foliage-stripping would reduce pollen production of these trees by interfering with their flowering, without directly causing their death. Pollen sequences do sometimes show a decline of other trees, particularly lime, at the elm decline, and such sequences would seem to support the leaf-fodder hypothesis. It is unlikely, however, that this provides a complete explanation for the elm decline, since other trees are not always affected, and the scale of the event argues against an exclusively human cause.

The widespread occurrence, rapidity, synchrony, and selectivity of the elm decline can best be explained by disease, as has been demonstrated by the recent spread of Dutch Elm Disease across Europe. This involves infection of wood by a fungus, *Ceratocystis ulmi*, which is carried from tree to tree by a bark beetle, *Scolytus scolytus*. A similar disease may have been involved in the Neolithic elm decline, and the recent discovery of the remains of a *Scolytus* beetle in supposed pre-elm decline deposits from Hampstead Heath in London adds some support to this suggestion. Unfortunately, however, there has been no identification of the fungus itself from Neolithic wood.

Although disease seems likely to have been the primary cause of the elm decline, the variable character of associated vegetational changes suggests that human activity was also involved, at least at some sites. Indeed, this activity may have facilitated the spread of the disease, by damaging trees and thereby providing infection sites, and by moving infected material over wide areas. Conversely, the death of a large number of trees may have reduced the effort required for clearance. As Oliver Rackham has suggested, it is possible that the spread of an elm disease and the creation of open land for Neolithic agriculture were complementary processes.

[See also EUROPE: THE EUROPEAN NEOLITHIC PERIOD.]

■ O.Rachhan, *Ancient Woodland* (1980). B. Huntley and H.J.B. Birks, *An Atlas of Past and Present Pollen Maps for Europe: 1–13000 Years Ago* (1983). Maureen A. Girling, "The Bark Beetle *Scolytus scolytus* (Fabricius) and the Possible Role of Elm Disease in the Early Neolithic," in *Archaeology and the Flora of the British Isles*, ed. Martin Jones (1988), pp. 34–38.

Petra Day

ENGARUKA lies on the dry Rift Valley floor north of Lake Manyara in Tanzania, East Africa. Here, deep gorges bring water from the nearby Crater Highlands to the plain. Beginning about the fifteenth and culminating in the sixteenth and seventeenth centuries A.D., several thousand people lived at Engaruka, clustered in seven large villages on terraced hillsides above the highest fields and canals. Their fields and irrigation works covered at least 5,000 acres (2,000 ha) of the nearby foothills and flat lands.

The irrigation works depended on stone-built canals, which channeled the water from the mouths of stream gorges into grids of stone-walled, leveled fields. These canals extended for considerable distances along the base of the escarpment, through foothills, then subdivided into well-maintained furrows that watered each area of the continuous field system. The Engaruka people, like other communities elsewhere in the Rift Valley, depended on gravity for their water supplies, using simple canal-building techniques that have much in common with the larger-scale operations of the Inca of the Andes. Each Engaruka community depended on a permanent water source, yet maintained lesser canal systems to divert water from seasonal streams, and to expand cultivated lands in high rainfall years. Such irrigation systems allowed agricultural populations to rise to quite high levels within small areas, as happened at Engaruka.

Engaruka's specialized agricultural economy may have been the cause of its eventual demise. A rising population may have overgrazed the outer land, cleared woodland for firewood, and exhausted even irrigated soils, perhaps at a time when natural drought conditions and human pressure on the land reduced water flows. But even after Engaruka's abandonment, the tradition of simple irrigation agriculture survived in the East African Rift, notably among the related Sonjo people who live northwest of Lake Natron.

[*See also* EAST AFRICA: INTERIOR KINGDOMS OF EAST AFRICA.]

John E. G. Sutton

ENVIRONMENTAL ARCHAEOLOGY is a term applied to a broad range of specialized studies in archaeology that pertain to prehistoric human environment interactions. Much of the growth of what could be considered environmental archaeology dates to the early 1960s.

It was during this time that cultural ecology became a prominent theoretical school in American cultural anthropology, and exerted a powerful influence on many American archaeologists who themselves were promoting the "New Archaeology." Central to the New Archaeology was an emphasis on a general systems approach to reconstructing past human behavior coupled with a desire to test hypotheses about that behavior. The combination of these three influences caused many archaeologists to begin looking for ways in which to reconstruct past environments and the relationships between humans and important environmental variables and resources.

Trying to develop new data recovery and analysis methods, archaeologists turned to soil scientists, chemists, physicists, geologists, botanists, zoologists, and ecologists. Over time these efforts resulted in the development of such new specialties in archaeology as *paleobotany, *zooarchaeology, raw material sourcing, various forms of geophysical and geomorphological analysis, *paleoenvironmental reconstruction, and *seasonality studies to mention the most prominent.

Whatever the long-term theoretical impact of the New Archaeology on the practice of archaeology worldwide, the importance of these new environmental specialties within archaeology cannot be denied and will only grow in the future. Environmental archaeology, in all of its many forms, is an integral part of modern archaeology that has contributed many of the most important and exciting archaeological discoveries of the past thirty years. Indeed, perhaps the most enduring legacy of archaeology will be the reconstruction of the evolution of the relationship between humans and this planet we call home.

[*See also* CULTURAL ECOLOGY THEORY; GENERAL SYSTEMS THEORY; PROCESSUAL THEORY, SCIENCE IN ARCHAEOLOGY.]

George Michaels

EPHESUS is located in western Turkey, near the mouth of the Cayster River (Küçük Menderes), 60 miles (97 km) south of modern Izmir (Smyrna). Once a flourishing Aegean port, the site is now located some 5 miles (8 km) inland. An Ionian colony whose recorded history goes back to the tenth century B.C., the early Greek city was founded in the vicinity of the Sanctuary of Artemis. During the early third century B.C. Lysimachos, one of the generals of Alexander, relocated the city 1 mile (1.7 km) south of Artemision, in the valley between two small mountains, Panayirdag (Mount Pion) and Bulbuldag (Mount Lepre Akte) and their northern extension into the coastal plain. The Hellenistic city was enclosed by a 5.5-mile (9 km) long circuit wall of ashlar masonry; parts of this fine wall can be seen on the northern slopes of Bulbuldag.

Ephesus was one of the wealthiest Greek settlements during the sixth century B.C., justly famous as the site of the great sanctuary of Artemis. This important sanctuary had replaced an earlier one dedicated to Kybele, an Anatolian mother goddess. Along with the temple of Hera at Samos, the archaic Artemision was one of the largest Ionic dipteral temples of the ancient world, 181 by 377 feet (55 × 115 m). It was burned in 356 B.C. and replaced by a Hellenistic successor of equal size and splendor, one of the Seven Wonders of the World. Cult figures, votive offerings in ivory, and precious metals from the archaic Artemision are kept at Istanbul Archaeological Museum. Referred to as the Metropolis of Asia, Ephesus continued to prosper under Roman rule, and along with Smyrna and Sardis, was honored several times as "temple warden" for the imperial cult. During the Christian era Ephesus enjoyed another golden age and was the leading city of the Seven Cities of the Apocalypse. St. John's Church, a monumental domed basilica erected by Justinian (A.D. 527–565) on the Ayasoluk hill, bears witness to the importance of the city in the Early Christian period. Progressively, the ancient site was reduced in size, but not abandoned before the end of the eleventh century. The most distinctive urban connector in Ephesus was a 1.5-mile- (2.4 km) long thoroughfare stretched between the Koresian Gate on the northeast and the Magnesian Gate on the southeast. Looping around Panayirdag it followed the course of an ancient processional way and linked the city to the Sanctuary of Artemis. The colonnaded portion, which ran at the bottom of the narrow valley between the two hills, was known in late antiquity as the Embolos (also Kuretes Street in some publications). A broad colonnaded avenue, named the Arkadiane in the fourth century A.D., joined the thoroughfare at midpoint creating a plaza and connecting the harbor with the city center. The curved arms of a magnificent theater (1st–3rd century A.D.) punctuated the crossing. Although the Embolos intersected diagonally a number of streets, which created a loosely organized grid plan on both sides of the steeply sloping hills, Ephesus never developed a strictly orthogonal (or Hippodamian) plan. In its loose interpretation of a grid, Ephesus was typical of many Asian cities under the Roman Empire, where Greek theories of urban planning intersected with the Anatolian preference for organic improvisation.

Entering the city at the Magnesian Gate, one would see the great vaults of the East Bath-Gymnasium Complex, and follow the ancient street west to the large open area of the State Agora. The north wing of the Agora is occupied by a three-aisled basilica dedicated to Artemis and the emperors Augustus and Tiberius. Remains of a Hellenistic stoa have been found under the basilica. Three important civic centers are located immediately north of the basilica: the Pryteneion, a state guest house with the altar of Hestia Boulaia, where the famous statues of Artemis of Ephesus were found; a precinct with temples to the Deified Julius Caesar and Dea Roma; and the Bouleterion, with a semicircular auditorium (formerly called an odeion). Southwest of the State Agora, raised on a tall artificial terrace and overlooking a plaza is the temple of Domitian. From this plaza, the Embolos follows downhill the course of the valley bottom passing by the Nyphaeum of Trajan, the small and ornate temple of Hadrian, the baths of Scholastikia, public latrines, and an octagonal tomb of Augustan date. The bend at the north end of the Embolos is marked by the ornate aedicular facade of the second-century Library of Celsus, and the enormous quadriporticus of the Commercial Agora. On the hills on either side of the street, houses, mainly of the courtyard type, rise over terraces and overlap each other in tight groups. Several blocks (named *Hanghäuser*) have been excavated and partially restored. Their history covers the span between the first and sixth centuries; many were decorated with elaborate frescoes representing mythological scenes, muses, poets, ancient philosophers, and historians. Of particular note is a magnificent first-century portrait of Socrates identified by an inscription.

The large plain east of the harbor and north of the Arkadiane must have been occupied by public structures. Today, it is dominated by the massive ruins of the second century A.D. Harbor Bath-Gymnasium joining an immense colonnaded exercise ground, known as the Porticoes of Verulanus, from the late first century A.D. To the north of the Harbor Bath-Gymnasium was an 853-foot (260-m) -long market basilica, later rebuilt as the Church of the Virgin Mary. The stretch between the Theater Bath-Gymnasium and the Koresus Gate has been only partially excavated. The major monuments near the gate are the stadium and a second-century A.D. bath-gymnasium complex built by the wealthy Ephesian Publius Vedius Antoninus.

Ephesus was an important sculpture-production center. A rich display of Roman portraits, especially images of Augustus, Livia, Domitian, and Hadrian are displayed in several museums—Vienna, Istanbul, Izmir, and Selcuk. Some exceptionally powerful late antique heads, such as the bust of Eutropius (5th century A.D.) and full-length Early Christian statues can be mentioned. Also notable is the "Great Antonine Relief," composed of many panels with over-lifesize images of Hadrian and Antonine emperors.

The first excavations at the Artemision were conducted by the English engineer John Wood from 1863 to 1874 followed by D. G. Hogarth who found the foundation deposits of the archaic temple in 1904. Current investigations at the sanctuary site are conducted by Anton Bammer. Work in the classical site started in 1895 for the Austrian Archaeological Institute under the direction of Otto Bendorf; subsequent directors of the Austrian team have been Joseph Keil, Franz Miltner, Fritz Eichler, and Wilhelm Alzinger. The Austrian excavations in Ephesus are reaching their hundredth anniversary under the direction of Hermann Vetters.

[See also GREECE: THE HELLENISTIC AGE; ROMAN EMPIRE: THE EASTERN PROVINCES OF THE ROMAN EMPIRE.]

■ Franz Miltner, *Ephesos, Stadt der Artemis und des Johannes* (1958). George E. Bean, *Aegean Turkey* (1989, first ed. 1966). Ekrem Akurgal, *Ancient Civilizations and Ruins of Turkey* (1973, first ed. 1969). Wilhelm Alzinger, "Ephesos," in *Paulys Real-Encyclopedie der classischen Altertumwissenshaft*, ed. G. Wissowa, E. Kroll et al., Supplement 12 (1972), pp. 1588–1704. Veronika Mitsopoulou-Leon, "Ephesos," in *The Princeton Encyclopedia of Classical Sites*, ed. Richard Stillwell (1976), pp. 306–310. Volker M. Strocka, *Die Wandmalerei der Hanghäuser in Ephesos* (1977).

Fikret K. Yegül

ETHICS OF ARCHAEOLOGY AND COLLECTING.

Archaeology is a political endeavor as well as a science. Research questions are born in a political context and funded according to political agendas. Archaeology derives political clout from its ability to generate and legitimize myths about the human past that can ally people through historical commonalities or divide them with chronicles of divergence, heterogeneity, and "otherness." It is no accident that projects investigating the culture history of the West Bank or Aryans or Mexico are funded by particular governments at particular times.

In consequence of their power to create a bridge between the present and the past, archaeologists are becoming increasingly aware of the ethical implications and consequences of their work. For many archaeologists the history of this awareness begins with accusations by local or ethnic groups that a people's heritage is being stolen. While professional archaeologists are forbidden by all recognized professional societies to dig up artifacts to sell, the discipline has a poor record of communicating either this fact or the results of research to the public. Consequently, public misapprehensions abound, leading with increasing frequency to local resistance to archaeological research. In recent years, organizations like the Society of American Archaeology, the Archaeological Institute of America, and the World Archaeological Congress have concerned themselves increasingly with ethical issues.

The focus of debates about ethical principles has always been on the relationship of professional archaeologists to commercial interests and other nonarchaeological stakeholders. Many archaeologists argue that commercial sale and distribution of looted artifacts are incompatible with the charge of public responsibility and scientific integrity accepted by professional archaeologists. They condemn collaboration between professional archaeologists and commercial treasure hunters, and the use of looted artifacts in research. Some archaeologists have claimed that because only looted material exists from some cultural periods, archaeologists have a professional responsibility to record and use private collections. Others believe that scientific use of privately owned looted relics validates these pieces, increasing their market value and enhancing the incentive for further looting. The relationship between scientific evaluation of artifacts and their market value has been clearly established.

Ethical problems of balancing the archaeologist's claim to knowledge of the past with the desires and needs of other noncommercial interest groups, professions, and minorities are more complex. There are also practical issues in conducting fieldwork, including hiring practices, staff comportment in local communities, and gender bias. Many projects have begun to include ethnic representatives of groups under study in balancing commitment to curation and stewardship with destruction through development and research, though rarely are nonprofessionals involved in the development of research designs. Current professional opinion supports the treatment of problems on a case-by-case basis, guided by a combination of cultural sensitivity and scientific responsibility. In rescue or cultural resource management (CRM) archaeology these compromises are complicated by the demands of powerful interests for quick and inexpensive solutions. Archaeologists find themselves accepting the role of stewards of the archaeological record. More excavations are likely to be curtailed in favor of preservation and renewed emphasis on archival research and existing collections.

When social science acts on the perceptions and practices of living people, as do archaeologists when they educate the public about the goals of research, create tourist destinations, unwittingly attract looters to sites, and interpret evidence of other people's heritage, such work is usually considered "applied research." Archaeologists must acknowledge that responsible archaeology is applied anthropology, and must be governed by the same ethics.

[See also ARCHAEOLOGY IN THE CONTEMPORARY WORLD; CULTURAL RESOURCE MANAGEMENT: GLOBAL ISSUES; DESTRUCTION OF THE PAST; FUTURE OF THE PAST; TRAFFICKING IN ANTIQUITIES.]

■ K. D. Vitelli, "The Ethics of Collecting: Afterthoughts on the Responsibilities of Archaeologists," *Journal of Field Archaeology* 8 (1981): 88–89. R. Layton, ed., *Conflict in the Archaeology of Living Traditions* (1989a). R. Layton, ed., *Who Needs the Past? Indigenous Values and Archaeology* (1989b). L. Levy and A. Wylie, "Archaeological Ethics in Print: An Annotated Bibliography," *Public Archaeology Review* 2 (1994): 21–24. A. Wylie, "Principles of Archaeological Ethics: A Preliminary Report on the Reno Workshop on Ethics in Archaeology," *Public Archaeology Review* 2 (1994): 11–13.

K. Anne Pyburn and Richard Wilk

ETHNOARCHAEOLOGY is the use of ethnographic observations of contemporary societies to explain patterning of cultural remains in the archaeological record. Ethnoarchaeology has been conducted in a relatively unstructured way since the nineteenth century in areas as widely separated as Scandinavia and the southwestern United States. Since then, ethnoarchaeology has evolved, mainly in relation to the issue of how to convincingly apply ethnographic results to archaeological findings. The term ethnoarchaeology was first coined by J. W. Fewkes in 1900 following his archaeological work at the Tusayan Pueblo in the American Southwest. The pioneering efforts of Fewkes and his contemporaries reflected their interest in using archaeology to demonstrate the historical validity of oral traditions, along the lines of *Schliemann at Troy. For example, F. W. Hodge's discovery of prehistoric materials on the top of Enchanted Mesa in 1893 seemed to confirm the accuracy of oral traditions at the nearby modern pueblo of Acoma about the existence of an ancient settlement in this relatively inaccessible location.

Another common feature of early ethnoarchaeology was the uncontrolled use of ethnographic analogues to identify and explain prehistoric artifacts and structures and to account for patterning on a larger scale. One example was a long-standing attempt by archaeologists to relate ethnographic information about traditional hunter-gatherers like the Paiute in the Great Basin of North America, using what Julian Steward termed the "direct historical approach," continuously back through time to archaeological assemblages from early sites like Danger Cave, excavated by J. D. Jennings in the early 1950s. These studies exemplified the need to identify and control for ecosystemic variables.

Along with a recognition of the importance of human ecology, there were also attempts to develop coherent theories about the role of ethnoarchaeology. The concept of the "new analogy" by R. Ascher in 1961 introduced ecological controls into comparisons between ethnology and archaeology. Ascher argued that archaeologists should draw analogies between present and past only from cultures that adapted to similar environments in similar ways. Although much criticized, this approach had the virtue of addressing structural and systemic relationships instead of relying upon anecdotal resemblances between ethnographic and prehistoric cultures. Ascher's study initiated the modern, critical approach to the archaeological use of ethnographic information. It led directly to current debates about the role of ethnoarchaeology.

Among the more conservative theorists to build on Ascher's views is Patty Jo Watson, who has argued for the role of ethnographic analogues as a source of hypotheses for archaeological testing. Watson's approach makes no a priori assumptions about the outcome of the testing process. Unlike earlier ethnoarchaeologists, Watson's "analogies as hypotheses" do not depend upon confirmation or closeness-of-fit to an anticipated pattern in the archaeological record. This position has been challenged by claims that one cannot use the archaeological record to test ethnographically derived hypotheses, although convincing cases of such testing abound in the literature. C. White and N. Peterson's 1969 analysis of prehistoric aboriginal remains from western Arnhem Land, Australia, is a good example. Using ethnographic data on seasonal migration patterns of the Wik Munkan people of Cape York, collected by D. Thomson in 1939, White and Peterson were able to pose a convincing explanation for variability in prehistoric assemblages from Arnhem Land. Such variability could be more simply accounted for as a result of a single cultural group moving through the landscape on seasonal rounds using different tools to exploit different resources at different times of the year than as the result of several different subcultures occupying the area. White and Peterson's work is similar to Watson's and Ascher's approaches in making the assumption that given similar seasonal tropical environments in Arnhem Land and Cape York, the pattern of seasonal migration and resource exploitation of the Wik Munkan better explains the archaeological patterning in Arnhem Land than the alternative hypothesis that assumed the presence of multiple cultural, or subcultural, groups.

L. R. Binford has invoked the concept of "*middle range theory" in relation to ethnoarchaeology to identify cultural processes that transcend particular cases but still depend on defined domains of human behavior (such as hunter-gatherer mobility, or social status as reflected by mortuary assemblages). His Nunamiut Eskimo study represented an effort to identify behavioral and environmental factors that structure the use and discard of caribou meat and bone products. This example of "middle range theory" was intended to provide explicitly scientific explanations for the patterning of faunal remains in the archaeological record.

There are difficulties with this approach, particularly the requirement to link middle range theory to a body of general theory about human behavior that does not yet exist as a consensus within archaeology. Pervasive assumptions about archaeological remains as fossilized human behavior also pose problems. Binford's call for more explicit use of scientific reasoning in applying ethnographic results to the explanation of archaeological evidence has been widely, though not universally, adopted.

Assumptions about archaeological remains as fossilized human behavior do not always take into account the post-depositional effects of natural processes like weathering and erosion or the reworking of archaeological deposits through later, often unrelated, human activities. Many natural and cultural factors can intervene between the cultural system that originally produced these residues and the archaeological record. For archaeologists like M. Schiffer, these *site formation processes must be recognized and controlled far before ethnoarchaeological explanations for the patterning of cultural materials in archaeological deposits are attempted.

Perhaps the most radical ethnoarchaeological interpretations are represented by explanations based on recognition of "anomalies" from expected patterns. R. Gould and J. Yellen explain differences in their data on household spacing among the Ngatatjara Aborigines and the !Kung San of the Kalahari Desert by positing cultural patterning in the archaeological record based on similar kinds of cultures that manipulate different environments in measurably different ways. This approach is intended to generate hypotheses based on comparative differences between known ethnographic societies, where cultural and ecological variables can be controlled in detail. These hypotheses can then be tested wherever such variables are observed in the archaeological record.

A different kind of "transformational" theory is favored by I. Hodder, who adheres to the direct historical approach in order to identify changes in materials based on transformations from preexistent, culturally constructed patterns. Hodder's approach uses a historical-particularist framework to identify relationships between symbolism and material remains in specific culture-historical traditions. Claims by Hodder and others that they have inferred the cultural meaning of these remains have been criticized as lacking scientific credibility, but they continue to attract interest and to generate debate.

Ethnoarchaeology today not only embraces a broad range of theoretical positions but has also moved beyond the domain of hunter-gatherers to include a wide variety of traditional and modern societies, such as pastoral nomads, farming communities (including those embedded in complex, modern nation-states), and maritime cultures. Despite this increasing breadth, the central challenge for ethnoarchaeology remains that of presenting convincing explanations of material patterning in the archaeological record based on ethnographic observations.

[See also THEORY IN ARCHAEOLOGY.]

■ Robert Ascher, "Analogy in Archaeological Interpretation," Southwestern Journal of Anthropology (1961): 317–325. Carmel White and Nicolas Peterson, "Ethnographic Interpretations of the Prehistory of Western Arnhem Land," Southwestern Journal of Anthropology (1969): 45–67. Lewis R. Binford, Nunamiut Ethnoarchaeology (1978). Patty Jo Watson, "The Idea of Ethnoarchaeology," in Ethnoarchaeology, ed. Carol Kramer (1979), pp. 277–287. Ian Hodder, Symbols in Action (1982). Michael B. Schiffer, Formation Processes of the Archaeological Record (1987). Richard A. Gould and John E. Yellen, "Man the Hunted: Determinants of Household Spacing in Desert and Tropical Foraging Societies," Journal of Anthropological Archaeology 6 (1987): 77–103.

Richard A. Gould

ETRUSCANS. Inhabiting an area of central Italy, between the Arno and the Tiber rivers, from at least the eleventh to the first century B.C., the Etruscans gradually developed into a number of independent city-states, each with its special character, contacts, commerce, and artistic style. A loose league of twelve cities had its religious center at the Fanum Voltumnae, near Volsinii (modern Orvieto). The twelve included the chief coastal cities (Cerveteri, Veii, Tarquinia, Vulci, Vetulonia, Roselle, Populonia) as well as the central and northern cities (Volsinii, Chiusi, Arezzo, Volterra); others, like Cortona and Fiesole, joined later. Etruscan political and cultural influence extended far beyond the boundaries of Etruria proper, expanding northward into the Po Valley and southward into Campania. In the seventh and sixth centuries B.C. nearly the entire Italian peninsula had come under some form of Etruscan influence or control.

The material culture of the Iron Age "Villanovan" period (named after a site near Bologna), dating 1000 to 800 B.C., was characterized by cremation burials reminiscent of the urnfields of Europe, in biconical urns of dark impasto fabric. Villanovan material has been found at all major Etruscan sites, testifying to cultural continuity from at least 1000 B.C. and even earlier, from pre-Villanovan times. The adoption of the Greek alphabet in the Orientalizing period (following the "proto-Etruscan" Villanovan period) allows us to recognize the language of the many discovered inscriptions as Etruscan, a language unrelated to the Indoeuropean languages of Europe. The Etruscans brought literacy to many peoples of Italy, including the Romans. To the north, in Europe, their alphabet gave rise to the Germanic and Scandinavian runes.

The mineral-rich lands of southern Italy and Sicily attracted Greek colonists by the eighth century B.C. and the southern cities of Tarquinia and Caere (modern Cerveteri) became wealthy from trading contacts with Greeks and Phoenicians, as shown by their rich seventh-century B.C. graves furnished with chariots, and rich ivory, bronze, amber, and gold ornaments. Southern craftsmen specialized in goldwork decorated with "granulation," or gold globules. Excavations have revealed evidence that sizable foreign groups resided in Gravisca, the port of Tarquinia where a Greek sanctuary was found, and Pyrgi, one of Caere's ports. The discovery, in 1964, of three gold tablets from Pyrgi provided scholars with a bilingual Etruscan-Phoenician text referring to the dedication of a temple to Uni Ishtar by Thefarie Velianas, "king" of Caere.

Populonia, the only Etruscan city located directly on the sea, faced the island of Elba, from which came the copper, bronze, and iron which was worked and traded on the shore, bringing this city wealth and leaving deep layers of iron slag. The coinage of Populonia is the most distinctive and continuous of any Etruscan city. Chiusi (Clevsin, Camars in Etruscan) became one of the most powerful cities of the league, thanks to its flourishing economy, its agriculture, and its strategic position controlling the Val di Chiana and the trade routes with the north. Its king, Lars Porsenna, besieged and took Rome after Tarquin's expulsion: Roman tradition remembers the names of the Roman heroes Horatius and Cloelia, who challenged him, and descriptions of his enormous tomb at Chiusi.

The northern Etruscan cities depended on agriculture, but were also known in antiquity for their metalwork: many engraved bronze Etruscan mirrors and bronze votive statuettes were manufactured there. Arezzo, famous for its bronze statue of a chimera, gave the name used in German for metal, *Erz*; and its famous red, mold-made "Arretine" ware of Augustan times imitated metalwork. Other inland cities, such as Volterra, or Perugia (an Umbrian-speaking Etruscan city), reached their most flourishing phases in the Hellenistic Period (fourth to first centuries B.C.). Etruscan artists excelled in working terra-cotta. One of their specialities, the black bucchero of the seventh and sixth centuries B.C., imitated bronze tableware, decorated with incision (bucchero sottile, from Caere), or with molds (bucchero pesante, from Chiusi). Painted terra-cotta reliefs protected their wooden temples, which were decorated with sculpture and reliefs of Greek mythological figures. The life-size statues of Apollo and other figures found by archaeologists in the sanctuary of Veii, across the Tiber from Rome, are from the end of the sixth century B.C., a date which relates them to the workshop of Vulca of Veii, the Etruscan artist whom—according to Roman tradition—Tarquin summoned to Rome to work on the temple of Jupiter Capitoline.

The lack of any Etruscan literature, except for short or ritual inscriptions, makes the accounts by Greek and Roman authors our only written source for Etruscan history. Yet Etruscan tombs reveal much about their daily life, their art, and their houses, and something of their religion, beliefs, and society. The geology of the land determined the type of tombs used in the different cities. The soft volcanic tufa of Cerveteri and Tarquinia allowed its citizens to excavate chamber tombs out of the living rock, imitating the layout of a house. At Tarquinia, wealthier tombs were painted. In the northern cities of Populonia and Vetulonia, chamber tombs were built up of harder stone; while in the central area, the steep cliffs were carved to represent architectural structures such as temple facades as at San Giovenale, Norchia, and Sovana. Stone sculpture was reserved for funerary art such as sarcophagi and tomb guardians, while Hellenistic ash urns have been found at Volterra, Perugia, and Chiusi.

Etruscan cities are much less well known than the cemeteries, or necropoleis, but outside of Etruria proper, at Marzabotto, near Bologna, a still-unidentified city has been excavated, with an orthogonal city plan and such advanced features as sewers, metal-working facilities and terra-cotta decoration for the houses. Archaic buildings have also been excavated at Acquarossa, near Rome, and the remains of a sanctuary or palace at Murlo, near Siena.

The Etruscans adopted—and adapted—aspects of Greek civilization: the alphabet, mythology, monumental temples and sculpture, the human figure in art, the convention of Greek athletic nudity, and the institution of the symposium with all its equipment (such as vases, craters, pitchers, and cups). In fact, from the tombs of Etruria and southern Italy come 75 to 80 percent of the Greek vases in museums and private collections, including some of the finest and largest in the world. But the Etruscans never gave up their language, their religion, or their customs, and their depictions of Greek mythology were often used to express their own ideas, sometimes humorously.

Theirs was an aristocratic society, with the married couple, the husband and wife, as the basic unit. Upper-class women thus played a much more public role among the Etruscans than in contemporary Greece or Rome. Their religion included many mother goddesses (Uni, Mnerva, Cel). They specialized in techniques for learning the will of the gods; their methods of reading omens, the *haruspicina*, was adopted by the Romans. The Etruscans also held a fatalistic view of the world, believing that the Etruscan people had been allotted a limited, predestined period of time for their historical existence.

The political and cultural impact of the Etruscans on the Romans was profound. According to Roman tradition, an Etruscan dynasty ruled at Rome from 616 B.C. to 509 B.C. The exile of the last of its rulers brought on the Roman Republic. In fact we can trace much Etruscan influence on Roman music, dress, art, military symbols, and institutions to this period. Subsequent wars with the Celts to the north and with Rome to the south in the fourth century B.C. caused the Etruscan cities to retrench and build great fortification walls. At the same time, grave goods and votives from sanctuaries testify to a unified style and common subject matter, products of an artistic and cultural *koine* or community. Only the conquest of the Etruscan cities by the Romans in the late third century B.C. prompted the disintegration of Etruscan culture. Though some artistic and linguistic forms survived, most of the Etruscan aristocracy eventually became Roman citizens, abandoning their language and customs in favor of those of the then more prestigious Greco-Roman culture.

[See also MEDITERRANEAN TRADE; MEDITERRANEAN WORLD, *articles on* INTRODUCTION, THE RISE OF AEGEAN AND MEDITERRANEAN STATES, THE DOMINANCE OF GREECE AND ROME.]

■ Emeline Richardson, *The Etruscans: Their Art and Civilization* (1964). Massimo Pallottino, *The Etruscans* (1978). Otto J. Brendel, *Etruscan Art* (1978, 1995 2nd ed.). Gilda Bartoloni and Maja Sprenger, *Etruscans* (1983). Larissa Bonfante, ed., *Etruscan Life and Afterlife* (1986). Larissa Bonfante, *Reading the Past, Etruscan* (1990). Ellen Macnamara, *The Etruscans* (1990). David Ridgway, *The First Western Greeks* (1992).

Larissa Bonfante

EUROPE

INTRODUCTION

Europe is a continent of varied climate and topography, a veritable mosaic of zones and microregions such as islands, river valleys, fertile plains, and mountains. Its principal geographical features are the great plains of the north and east, from the steppe lands of the Ukraine to the boulder clays of the Baltic shores, and the mountain ranges of the south, notably the Alps, the Pyrenees, and the Carpathians. There is also a wide range of climate, from the hot, dry summers and cool, wet winters of the Mediterranean zone to the damper but more equable climate of the Atlantic coast, and the dry summers but intensely cold winters of the East European interior.

Europe is not an isolated continent but merely the western extremity of the larger Eurasian landmass, which is itself linked to Africa. The concept and name of Europe were the creation of Greek geographers of the sixth and fifth centuries B.C. Herodotus, writing in the later fifth century, argued for a tripartite division of the habitable world into Europe, Asia, and Libya (Africa). This was generally followed by later classical authors who placed the boundary between Europe and Asia along the River Don, and that between Libya and Asia along the Nile or the Isthmus of Suez. It was not until 1833 that Volger in his *Handbuch der Geographie* located the boundary between Russia in Europe and Russia in Asia at the River Ural and the Ural mountains, so fixing the eastern frontier in its present position.

It follows from this that the archaeology of Europe cannot be studied in isolation but must be seen as part of the broader Old World story. Indeed, the Mediterranean Sea which forms Europe's southern boundary has in historical times been as much of a bond as a barrier.

This raises the question of whether there was a distinctive European identity in the past, and if so, when this emerged. The British archaeologist V. Gordon *Childe, in the 1930s, developed the theory that particular forms of trade and technology had given rise to a distinctive European identity as long ago as the second millennium B.C. He drew this conclusion from the contrast between the Bronze Age societies of the Near East, where craftsmen worked under the close control of rulers, and Europe, where he envisaged itinerant bronze-smiths selling their skills to local chiefs but retaining their independence. This freedom, he thought, lay at the heart of European technological progress.

Few would follow this line today, since there is little to suggest that Bronze Age craftsmen really operated in this way nor that this would have conferred on European society an especially innovative character. Furthermore, it was only in relatively recent times that the peoples of Europe developed any special awareness of being "European"; even today, the term is geographical rather than cultural, ethnic, or economic. Nor should we forget that throughout prehistoric times many European communities were regular recipients of non-European artifacts and raw materials: threads of Chinese silk in the *Hallstatt princely burial at Hohmichele being one of the more spectacular examples that springs to mind.

Europe does, however, have one special claim in the study of the past, since the growth of the archaeological discipline in the Renaissance and later was essentially a European phenomenon. Thus it is that many parts of Europe have been subject to careful archaeological scrutiny for several centuries, resulting in the accumulation of a rich and diverse body of information. Our knowledge of the European past is still woefully inadequate, however, and chance discoveries such as *Similaun Man in the Italian Alps still have the potential to revolutionize our understanding of particular regions or periods.

The scarcity of evidence is particularly acute for the Lower and Middle *Paleolithic periods. There is still considerable disagreement about the date of the earliest colonization of Europe, some putting it around two million years ago, others arguing for an age less than half as old, around 900,000 or even 700,000 years ago. There is similar disagreement about the type of hominid concerned: *Homo erectus or archaic *Homo sapiens?

Controversy continues to surround the later stages of the Paleolithic Period when Europe was home to the *Neanderthals, a cold-adapted species also present in the Near East. The cultural and linguistic skills of the Neanderthals are hotly disputed, but many archaeologists believe that their replacement in Europe by fully modern humans between 45,000 and 35,000 B.C. marks a major change. The skills of fully modern humans are amply demonstrated by the famous discoveries of Upper Paleolithic art on the walls of caves such as *Lascaux and *Altamira.

The melting of the ice sheets, the warmer temperatures, and the spread of forest vegetation around 10,000 years ago transformed Europe and forced hunter-gatherer communities to adapt to a very different set of environments. In many coastal areas, rising sea level led to the loss of valuable coastal lowlands, one example being the flooding of the North Sea around 6500 B.C. which finally separated Britain from the continent of Europe. On the other hand, it is in the Early Holocene Period that we find the first evidence for the extensive exploitation of coastal environments by human groups, as seen for instance in the shell middens of Iberia and Scandinavia.

European societies underwent a major change in the Middle Holocene, when Neolithic village farming communities dependent on plant cultivation and animal husbandry appeared in southeastern Europe. This represented not an influx of new people but the adoption of new techniques by existing hunter-gatherer populations. They used cereals of Near Eastern origin, but steadily developed crop varieties better suited to the cooler and damper environment of temperate Europe. This eventually made possible the rapid colonization of central Europe by farmers from the Hungarian plain around 5300 B.C., associated with distinctive Bandkeramik pottery. Within a matter of centuries Bandkeramik farmers had reached the Low Countries and the Paris basin, and the farming technology they brought with them was soon adopted in Britain and Scandinavia. Meanwhile a separate axis of contact brought cereal agriculture independently to the West Mediterranean and thence northwards through Iberia and France.

During the fifth millennium B.C. the farmers of northern and western Europe (including the British Isles) developed a tradition of monumental architecture, using large stones (megaliths) or timbers to build chambered tombs covered by mounds or barrows. Similar technology was later applied to the construction of rows or circles of stone or timber uprights, such as *Carnac in Brittany, and *Avebury and *Stonehenge in southern Britain. At around the same period, eastern Europe was undergoing a different technological transition with the discovery of metals, initially copper and gold. These new materials soon became valuable and mines were sunk to extract copper ore from ever deeper layers as surface or shallow deposits were exhausted. From the use of copper this has become known as the European Copper Age or Chalcolithic, following on from the age of polished stone tools or Neolithic. Though current from around 4500 B.C. in the east, however, copper working spread only slowly to western Europe, and was not known in Britain until 2500 B.C.

The Copper Age was followed by the Bronze Age, beginning around 2800 B.C. in the Aegean and some 500 years later in western and northern Europe. The key features of this period are the rise of more complex and hierarchical societies, notably the palace-centered states of Minoan Crete and Mycenaean Greece. Elsewhere in Europe a new emphasis on agriculture and land ownership is shown by the development of *field systems. Early European bronze implements were as much for show as for use, but by the beginning of the Urnfield Period (1300 B.C.) a kind of primitive arms race was under way: much greater quantities of metal being produced and used for the manufacture of heavy bronze slashing swords, sheet metal body armor, and helmets. These betoken the emergence of a warrior aristocracy in Europe north of the Alps, parallel to but less sophisticated than the warrior kingdoms of Mycenaean Greece.

The warrior aristocracies of late Bronze Age Europe are the direct antecedents of those that are known to us through the writings of classical historians such as Herodotus and Polybius. By this time iron had replaced bronze as the metal for everyday use (around 1000 B.C. in Greece; 700 B.C. or later in western and northern Europe). Greek historians of the fifth century divided the peoples of Europe north of the Alps into *Celts in the west and Scythians in the east. Archaeologists have sought to associate each of these with a particular artistic tradition (through the definition of Celtic and Scythian art styles), though the reality that lay behind the ethnic identity of the Celts, in particular, is unclear.

During the sixth century B.C., Celtic chieftains were trading with both Greeks and *Etruscans, providing raw materials such as slaves, salt, and hides to their urbanized southern neighbors. *Hill forts such as the *Heuneburg on the Danube were the centers of small chiefdoms controlling and profiting from this trade. This earlier Celtic period (Hallstatt) gave way around 450 B.C. to the *La Tène phase and ushered in a time of less amicable relations between temperate Europe and the Mediterranean. Groups of Celts invaded northern Italy in the fourth century (sacking Rome in 390 B.C.) and eastern Europe and Asia Minor in the third. During the final centuries B.C., however, more stable conditions returned and the Celtic lands saw the development of tribal kingdoms and the appearance of "oppida," the first towns north of the Alps.

In Gaul these changes were soon submerged by the expansion of Roman power in the first century B.C., and its spread to Britain, also, in the first century A.D. The long frontier of the Roman Empire, following almost the entire length of the rivers Rhine and Danube, divided Europe in two, but did not prevent contact between Roman and non-Roman sectors. There was trading and intermittent raiding in both directions, and North European peoples (known as Germans to Roman historians) gradually adopted features of Roman technology.

Narrowing of the technology gap was one of the factors (though not the only one) that enabled Germanic invaders to take control of the western provinces of the Roman Empire in the fifth century A.D. By the end of the century Spain was held by the Visigoths, France by the Franks, Italy by the Ostrogoths, and eastern Britain by the Anglo-Saxons. These kingdoms, though reflecting the geography of the Roman provinces, were the basis from which the nation-states of modern Europe were gradually to develop. Though the formal political structure changed, however, there was con-

siderable continuity with the past, and in most areas of western Europe, Roman provincial notables continued to hold high office under the new Germanic rulers. Furthermore Christianity, which had become established throughout Europe during the third and fourth centuries A.D., remained the dominant religion into the Middle Ages; only eastern Britain (of the former Roman provinces) required concerted missionary activity to bring it back to the faith.

The archaeology of medieval Europe illustrates a gradual increase in commerce, population, and economic activity from at least the ninth century A.D. to the Renaissance. Towns, churches, and the countryside have all become subjects of major archaeological research in recent years, which has sought to trace the progress of developments from the shadowy Post-Roman Period to the well-documented Europe of the late Middle Ages. This has been encouraged by city-center redevelopments since the Second World War, which have provided new opportunities for investigations into the origins and growth of medieval towns. The next major stage came in the fifteenth century, when improvements in European maritime technology led to trade, colonization, and expansion on a global scale. Archaeological attention is increasingly being directed to European colonial settlements of the sixteenth to nineteenth centuries in Africa, Australia, and the Americas, and to the evidence of European interaction with existing inhabitants of those regions. This is essential if the archaeology of later historic Europe is to be set in its full global context. It is already clear that archaeology has much to say about the import and export of materials and manufactures which underlay the European economic expansion of the sixteenth, seventeenth, and eighteenth centuries, and about the Industrial Revolution which followed. These relatively new approaches will have much more to tell us in the years to come.

[See also BRITISH ISLES: OVERVIEW; CRO-MAGNONS; EUROPE, ORIGINS OF FOOD PRODUCTION IN; EUROPE, THE FIRST COLONIZATION OF; EUROPEAN COLONIES IN THE NEW WORLD; INDO-EUROPEANS; LAKE DWELLINGS, EUROPEAN, MEDIEVAL EUROPE: OVERVIEW; MEDITERRANEAN WORLD: INTRODUCTION; ROMAN EMPIRE: INTRODUCTION; URNFIELDS.]

■ T. Champion, C. Gamble, S. Shennan, and A. Whittle, *Prehistoric Europe* (1984). J. Collins, *The European Iron Age* (1984). K. Randsborg, *The First Millennium AD in Europe and the Mediterranean* (1991). B. Cunliffe, ed., *The Oxford Illustrated Prehistory of Europe* (1994).

Chris Scarre

THE EUROPEAN PALEOLITHIC PERIOD

The Paleolithic was the earliest period of human occupation of the European continent and coincided with glacial and interglacial climatic conditions over possibly 700,000 years, from the first colonization of Europe by early hominids to the advent of the Holocene around 10,300 B.P. During this time not all parts of Europe were constantly occupied, and the archaeological record from a number of northern areas, such as Britain, suggests cycles of depopulation and recolonization in response to changing climatic conditions and the resources available to hunter-gatherer groups. The primary evidence of human activities comprises (1) stone tools of various forms and the waste products from their manufacture, (2) animal bones, and (3) the bones of hominids themselves. These are found both in covered sites, such as caves and rockshelters, and open-air sites, often on river terraces.

Traditionally, the Paleolithic Period has been subdivided

into Lower, Middle, and Upper Paleolithic. The Lower Paleolithic begins with the first appearance of hominids in Europe some 700,000 years ago. The Middle Paleolithic is thought to have started around 250,000 B.P. The Upper Paleolithic began at approximately 35,000 to 40,000 B.P. The Paleolithic in Europe was therefore contemporary with the Middle and Upper *Pleistocene climatic periods and traditionally ended with the onset of the current interglacial environmental conditions. The archaeological period after this, although still a record of hunters and gatherers, has been called the Mesolithic. These subdivisions of Lower, Middle, and Upper Paleolithic were initially defined according to the types of stone tools produced. During the Lower Paleolithic, simple flake tools and hand-axe tools were manufactured. Beginning in the Middle Paleolithic, developed flake stone tools were produced, sometimes using a method known as the Levallois technique. The characteristic tools of the Upper Paleolithic are made on blades and are temporally and regionally distinctive.

Paleolithic Europe was colonized and occupied by a succession of hominid species. These included *Homo erectus, Archaic *Homo sapiens, *Neanderthals (Homo sapiens neanderthalis) and, finally, anatomically modern humans (Homo sapiens sapiens). Of these hominid species, it is currently thought that Homo erectus first appeared in Europe as part of the initial radiation of hominids out of Africa. The appearance of anatomically modern humans represents the second radiation of hominids out of Africa. The other hominid species, in particular the Neanderthals, are most likely to have been a local development in response to the specific environmental conditions within Europe.

Following the acceptance of the Pleistocene age of Paleolithic finds in Europe in the mid-nineteenth century, the earliest studies of the Paleolithic Period in Europe looked backward from the final record of modern humans and their developed material culture to the earliest evidence. This resulted in an evolutionary understanding that was couched in terms of gradual progression based upon a steady development in hominid abilities and refinement of technological forms. Human species became more upright, with bigger brains; tools became more delicate and definite in shape; and finally *art was produced. With general changes in our understanding of evolutionary processes, recent studies have focused more on the contemporary ecological relationships of hominids and their environments, seeing the archaeological record in terms not of what followed next but of how particular patterns of evidence can inform us about the specific patterns of adaptation of hominid groups to their environment. Interpretation is now devoted to understanding the activities of past hominid species without the bias of modern hindsight. It involves recognizing and interpreting the effects of a range of factors that shaped the lives of mobile hunter, gatherer, and scavenger populations in the changing climatic conditions of Pleistocene Europe.

Lower Paleolithic. The study of the Lower Paleolithic Period is dominated by the questions of when hominids first appeared in Europe, what they looked like, and what resources they exploited.

Despite claims for evidence of human activities from 1 million years B.P. at sites such as Vallonet in southern France, the earliest definite evidence for European colonization comes from the site of Isernia La Pineta in Italy, currently dated to 700,000 B.P., where collections of stone tools and animal bones have been found. It is only from approx-

imately 500,000 B.P., however, that there is evidence from most areas of Europe. The bones of erectus-type hominids have been found at sites such as Mauer, Steinheim, Petralona, and Arago. It was probably not just the appearance of Homo erectus–type hominids that made it possible to colonize Europe. These hominid species have been discovered in Georgia dating back to 1.5 million years B.P. Approximately 500,000 years ago, however, the structure of the large carnivore community changed. This resulted in an environment that was more similar in terms of available resources and competitors to that in which hominids had lived outside of Europe. Colonization might have been more successful in these circumstances. The seemingly late colonization of Europe is still a matter of debate.

The earliest evidence for this period comprises industries with simple, flake-based stone tools as well as industries with handaxes. The hand-axe industries are often called the *Acheulean Tradition, after the site of St. Acheul in France. Hand axes appear in a variety of shapes, including pointed and ovate forms, and in a range of sizes from small to large. Refitting studies, such as that undertaken at the site of Boxgrove in southern England, have indicated that many of these tools were produced in response to an immediate need and were discarded once that need had been satisfied. It was once thought that there was a development from simple chopper tools, found at sites such as Verte Zöllos in Hungary, to smaller, more refined flake tools, such as those recovered from the site of Ehringsdorf in southern Germany. This reinforced an idea of unilinear evolutionary development in technological ability, but dating of these sites has disproved the relationship, and it now seems clear that technology was more a varied response to local requirements.

The faunal evidence includes bones from a number of large animals, which have at times been interpreted as evidence of large game hunting by early hominids. At the site of *Torralba/Ambrona in Spain, for example, the bones of numerous elephants were found in what would have been a tar pit. Early hominids were thought to have driven these animals to their death, but new interpretations suggest that these earliest hominids in Europe may not have been big game hunters. Instead, they may have been scavengers, exploiting an ecological niche left open by the departure of other scavenging species, particularly in the winter months.

Middle Paleolithic. No definite boundary is recognized between the Lower and Middle Paleolithic. The archaeological record indicates that particular aspects of hominid behavior were developing at different rates, but recent studies are beginning to suggest that around 250,000 B.P., behavior changed to incorporate more forward planning and greater organizational effort. The period that follows, the Middle Paleolithic, has been dominated by the study of the Neanderthal-type hominids and variations in flake-based stone industries. These Middle Paleolithic stone tools and assemblages are often called Mousterian, named after the site of LeMoustier in southern France.

Middle Paleolithic stone tools are distinguished by the use of prepared cores for the production of tool blanks, the inclusion of distinct tool types that can be categorized, and the presence of recognizable variations in the composition of assemblages from different sites. The flake tools of the Middle Paleolithic were often made on prepared cores, facilitating a predetermined form and definite tool shapes. The most common cores were exploited according to a discoidal or Levallois technique, requiring specific sequences of actions. Distinctively shaped stone tools, including notches, denticulates, and various forms of side scrapers, were then made using these blanks. There are suggestions, however, that some of these "distinct" shapes may be the result of continuous use and wear of one original shape. Studies of Middle Paleolithic stone tool assemblages have revealed variations in stone tool assemblage composition. Distinctive tool types are present in certain assemblages, and the percentage of other tools varies between assemblages. These differences were originally thought to be cultural, indicating the presence of contemporary but distinct tribal groups living throughout Middle Paleolithic Europe, but are now seen as related to geographical, temporal, functional, and climatic factors.

The archaeological evidence of the Middle Paleolithic is contemporary with the Neanderthals. These hominids were a specifically European–Near Eastern phenomenon with a distribution from the Levant to Spain. They are also the first hominids to have left us a large number of skeletons, many of which seem to have been buried deliberately, as at La Ferrassie and La Chapelle aux-Saints in France. While the classic Neanderthal remains date to the period of the last glacial cycle (120,000–35,000 B.P.), there is evidence from sites such as Atapuerco in Spain for the increasing adaptation of hominids to cold European conditions from as early as 300,000 B.P. These hominids are called pre-Neanderthals. Anatomical studies suggest that Neanderthal hominids, who had large brains, large, muscular bodies, and short limbs, can be interpreted as a progressive adaptation to the rigors of a cold, glacial environment. Aging of Neanderthal skeletons has indicated that they matured young and died on average before the age of 40.

Upper Paleolithic. There appear to be a number of marked differences between the archaeological record of the Upper Paleolithic and the Middle Paleolithic. These include the manufacture of highly developed stone tools using a blade technique; the production of bone tools; the appearance of art, both painted and carved; specialization in the hunting of single animal species such as reindeer; the exploitation of new environments, such as the high mountains; and the colonization of new areas, such as the Americas. This range of features has been considered to be indicative of fully modern behavior and therefore a natural consequence of the appearance of anatomically modern humans at this time. It is, however, proving to be a complex issue, and unravelling the social and the biological in the interpretation of modern humans and their behavior is far from easy. There are examples of anatomically modern humans with archaeological evidence that is Middle Paleolithic in character, and of Neanderthals with Upper Paleolithic archaeology.

Upper Paleolithic stone tools were made using blade blanks. They exhibit a range of distinct forms, including end scrapers, borers, gravers, a range of weapon tips, and small microlithic pieces. Most tools would have been hafted, and many may have been composite tools. Spears and, later, bows and arrows were used. In addition, there are bone tools, including not only weapon tips but also eye needles, which have been interpreted as evidence for the manufacture of elaborate clothing. Studies of raw materials indicate contact over or exploitation of large geographical areas. Distinct regional groupings of tool types are possibly indicative of separate territories.

Recognizable art appears for the first time, both representational and abstract. It takes the form of mobiliary art, such as the carved female figurines from sites throughout Europe, and also the parietal art in numerous caves, primarily in southwestern Europe, such as *Lascaux and *Altamira. This art may be concerned with the symbolic communication of specific information, possibly by means of ceremonies involving the young, such as at Niaux in the Pyrenees.

Examination of sites indicates clear structure with huts, stone-lined hearths, storage pits, and activity areas clearly visible. Following the last glacial maximum, the faunal remains from these sites indicate the exploitation of upland species and concentration on the exploitation of single species, such as reindeer in France and Germany. Upper Paleolithic groups may have been the first specialist hunters.

[See also CRO-MAGNONS; EUROPE, THE FIRST COLONIZATION OF; HOLOCENE, *articles on* INTRODUCTION, HOLOCENE ENVIRONMENTS IN EUROPE; PALEOLITHIC, *articles on* LOWER AND MIDDLE PALEOLITHIC, UPPER PALEOLITHIC; ROCK ART: PALEOLITHIC ART; VENUS FIGURINES.]

▪ François Bordes, *The Old Stone Age* (1969). John Wymer, *The Palaeolithic Age* (1982). Robin Dennell, *European Economic Prehistory* (1983). Clive Gamble, *The Palaeolithic Settlement of Europe* (1986). Clive Gamble, *Timewalkers* (1993). Christopher Stringer and Clive Gamble, *In Search of the Neanderthals* (1994).

Anthony Sinclair

THE EUROPEAN MESOLITHIC PERIOD

The term *Mesolithic* refers to the Middle (=Meso) Stone Age (=lithic), having originally been coined as a contrast to the Old and the New Stone Age (the Palaeolithic and Neolithic). For many years it was thought of as a period of rather dismal cultural achievement, lacking both the cave paintings of the Paleolithic and the agriculture and pottery of the Neolithic. Such views are now beginning to change as we realize the considerable behavioral developments of the Mesolithic and the quality of its art and technology, much of which, however, was created in organic materials and has been poorly preserved.

Lying between the Paleolithic and Neolithic, the Mesolithic denotes the period following the end of the last ice age and prior to the establishment of predominantly farming economy. Both of these boundaries are extremely fuzzy. The end of the last glacial period (ca. 13,000–10,000 B.P.) was marked by a series of climatic oscillations requiring hunter-gatherers to adapt to warmer conditions, and then readapt to a late interstadial before adjusting their socioeconomic behavior to the postglacial. At the opposite end of the period there are similar problems of demarcation since many "Neolithic" traits, such as pottery and sedentism, are now firmly traced into the Mesolithic and certain early Neolithic groups appear dependent upon wild resources. As a result, the end of the Mesolithic is rather arbitrarily defined, with dates ranging from around 8000 B.P. in southeast Europe to 5000 B.P. in the northwest Atlantic fringes. In the far north a predominantly hunter-gatherer existence continued until historic times. Between these fuzzy boundaries, the Mesolithic denotes a period of postglacial hunting and gathering, with marked variability in socioeconomic organization and material culture across Europe.

Much of this behavioral diversity can be attributed to the spatial and temporal variability of the early postglacial environment. The eustatic rising of the sea level, and the isostatic rising of the land in some areas created a complex series of changes in the height of the coastline, and consequently in the topography of the landscape. During the course of the Mesolithic, large areas of coastal lowlands, which would formerly have been valuable hunting lands, were lost to the rising sea level. Consequently in many regions we lack Early Mesolithic coastal sites, although an increasing number of excellently preserved underwater sites are now being discovered and excavated (e.g., Tybrind Vig, Denmark).

The rapid global warming resulted in marked changes in vegetation and animal communities across Europe. Extensive pollen analyses have documented the transition from the late glacial open tundra of northern Europe to mixed oak woodland by 8000 B.P. Some of the large herbivores of the late glacial, such as reindeer, moved to the far north of Europe, while others, like red deer, adapted to the forested environments by living in more dispersed and smaller herds. Other large terrestrial animals, such as mammoths, became extinct, while forest-loving animals such as roe deer and wild boar extended their range. Along with changes in the large game, there was a marked increase in the abundance and diversity of small game, wildfowl, and coastal resources. In southern Europe, the changes in plant and animal communities were less dramatic and we find a much higher degree of economic continuity across the Pleistocene–Holocene interface.

The archaeological record of the Mesolithic documents the process of human exploration and exploitation of these new environments. Throughout the period we see a continuous series of technological innovations—although the extent to which this is due to the often excellent preservation conditions of the Mesolithic is contentious. The characteristic artifact type of the Mesolithic is the microlith, although these are also found in several late Palaeolithic industries. *Microliths come in a variety of shapes and sizes and have been used to create detailed cultural chronologies in areas such as southern Scandinavia where three main cultural periods have been distinguished: Maglemose, 9500 to 7600 B.P.; Kongemose, 7600 to 6500 B.P.; and Ertebølle, 6500 to 5000 B.P. Microliths have traditionally been interpreted as projectile points, although it is likely that they were used as components in a range of other tools, such as for plant processing and leather working. The bogland and underwater sites of northern Europe have preserved an array of organic artifacts, including wooden, antler, and bone harpoons and arrows, fish traps, canoes, decorated paddles, and fragments of textiles. These have provided an unprecedented view of the material culture of a prehistoric hunter-gatherer society.

The rapid environmental change during the Mesolithic, and the diversity of animal and plant communities across Europe, make it difficult to generalize about Mesolithic economies. Throughout much of Europe, large game hunting focused on red deer, probably by stalking individual animals in thick woodland with the occasional use of drives. Sites such as *Star Carr (Britain) are most likely hunting camps from which small parties stalked large terrestrial herbivores including red deer, auroch, and roe deer. Coastal resources appear to have played an increasingly important role, culminating in massive Late Mesolithic shell middens such as Ertebølle (Denmark). At the Franchthi cave (Greece), a long stratigraphic sequence documents such economic change largely as a direct response to rising sea level. Plant foods were also particularly abundant during the Mesolithic and have occasionally been well preserved. Sites including Franchthi cave and the Balma Ab-

eurador (France) suggest that incipient cultivation may have been undertaken of certain plants, notably legumes. In many areas this economic activity was organized by a complex subsistence-settlement pattern involving large base camps and a series of small, specialized activity sites, such as hunting camps and fishing stations.

At some settlement locations of the Mesolithic, the available resources appear to have been so abundant and diverse that some measure of sedentism is likely. At Skateholm (Scania) for instance, Late Mesolithic foragers had access to resources from aquatic, lagoon, and terrestrial environments. Similarly at *Lepenski Vir (Danube Valley) the construction of substantial trapezoidal houses probably reflects the abundant resources of the region. At certain of these sites, for example, Vedbaek (Denmark) and Skateholm, large cemeteries were created after approximately 6500 B.P. The diversity of burial customs in these cemeteries is often striking, as is the presence of dog burials and the richness of certain graves. It appears from cemeteries such as Oleneostrovski Mogilnik (Karelia) and Téviec and Hoëdic (France) that some Mesolithic societies may have recognized hereditary social status, in addition to the more common recognition of status achieved, for example, by hunting success. The evidence of armed combat from the burials of individuals killed by arrows, and the bounded distributions of artifact types, suggest that a complex social geography arose during the Late Mesolithic involving the definition and defense of territorial boundaries.

These social and economic developments may have been due to resource / people imbalance caused by rising sea levels and the growth of human population. In addition, it is likely that in areas of seasonally abundant resources, such as migratory fish, the availability of surpluses not only allowed economic security but created a medium for securing wealth and power. We should not be surprised, therefore, that in areas like southern Scandinavia, a hunting and gathering economy continued long after knowledge of farming techniques was acquired and trade relations were established with the farmers in northern Germany. In other regions, the spread of farming appears to have been a complex mix of incoming peoples and indigenous economic development.

The Mesolithic was one of the major periods of transformation in European prehistory. At its beginning, people were living in essentially the same fashion as when modern humans first entered Europe 35,000 years earlier. By the end of the Mesolithic, three irreversible events had occurred that served to underwrite the social and economic developments of later prehistory: ranked societies had appeared; agricultural economies had been adopted, and people had interfered with, and dramatically altered, the natural environment. But it was not simply a period of transition. From the well-preserved organic remains of northern Europe, and the reconstruction of extensive and complex subsistence settlement patterns, the Mesolithic emerges as the period when humans achieved one of the most intensive exploitations of the natural world which was possible with a hunting and gathering mode of existence.

[See also HOLOCENE: HOLOCENE ENVIRONMENTS IN EUROPE.]

■ Marek Zvelebil, ed., *Hunters in Transition* (1986). Clive Bonsall, ed., *The Mesolithic in Europe* (1989). Lars Larson, "The Mesolithic of Southern Scandinavia," *Journal of World Prehistory* 4 (1990): 257–309.

Steven Mithen

THE EUROPEAN NEOLITHIC PERIOD

The beginning of the Neolithic, or New Stone Age, in Europe is conventionally defined by the appearance of the first domestic crops and livestock. The period is also marked by the first widespread use of pottery and ground stone tools, by a substantial increase in the number of settlement sites and the quantity of material remains, and, in certain regions of Europe, by the first field monuments. These changes no doubt reflect a significant growth in population. At the same time, there is evidence of a new attitude toward the landscape, which suggests that the beginning of the Neolithic in Europe was as much a cultural revolution as an economic one. In some areas it seems that the cultural features such as pottery and field monuments, together with some domesticates, appeared many centuries before the shift to a complete reliance on domesticated plants and animals.

Southeast Europe. European Neolithic communities developed earliest in the southeast, in Greece and the Balkans. These were the areas that had the closest links with the early centers of plant and animal domestication in the Near East. The early crop regimes of Greece and the Balkans resembled those of western *Anatolia and it is likely that some of the domesticates, notably emmer wheat and sheep/goat, were brought to southeastern Europe from Anatolia. There are similarities also in the first pottery of the two regions. Whether these new elements were introduced by immigrant farmers, or simply adopted by the local indigenous population, has been much discussed, but the indigenous hypothesis currently accords best with the available evidence.

One important difference between the early farmers of Anatolia and those of southeastern Europe is in their settlement and house types. The best-known examples of early Anatolian farming settlements have rectangular houses which are built adjoining each other, whereas in southeastern Europe free-standing rectangular houses are the norm.

Spread of the Neolithic. The earliest Neolithic settlements in southeastern Europe have been dated to around 7000 B.C. or a little later. This was the starting point, both geographically and chronologically, for the spread of Neolithic features throughout the rest of the continent. We may envisage the process as a kind of dispersion, along a number of favored routes. The mechanism behind these dispersions, however, was not a uniform process of colonization, but varied from region to region. Recent research has helped to show how in each individual area of Europe the transition to the Neolithic, and the uptake of farming, followed its own particular course.

In the spread of the Neolithic through Europe, two principal routes may be identified: one leading through central Europe along the valleys of the Rhine and the Danube; the other following the southern coast. The former is associated with colonization by Bandkeramik farmers, the latter with the spread of domesticates and Impressed Ware pottery among indigenous Mediterranean communities.

Bandkeramik Farmers. By 6000 B.C., farming villages with pottery and other Neolithic features had become established throughout southeastern Europe as far north as the Danube valley and the Great Hungarian Plain. The success of these settlements in economic terms is illustrated by the fact that many of them grew to form substantial tells. These were villages of several hundred people, with continuous occupation over hundreds or thousands of years. In central Europe, the pattern of settlement was strikingly different. Here farming communities built villages of one or two massive timber longhouses in small forest clearings. These longhouses combined a number of separate functions under a single roof, including grain stores, haylofts, and cattle byres, as well as providing a living area for an extended family of ten or a dozen people. The settlements were located on the gravel terraces along the river valleys, where fertile loess soils could be farmed. The bulk of the landscape remained under forest, however, and forest-adapted animals such as pigs and cattle predominated in the livestock assemblage.

These central European farming settlements are known as *Bandkeramik, after the incised decoration used on their pottery. The Bandkeramik represents a distinct phenomenon in the European Neolithic because of the rapidity of its spread. It first emerged as a package of cultural elements (longhouse, decorated pottery, and shoe-last adze) on the edges of the Great Hungarian Plain around 500 B.C. By 5300 B.C. Bandkeramik settlement had spread along the major river valleys of central Europe, and communities of Bandkeramik farmers were established in eastern France and the Low Countries. There is little or no evidence of continuity with local Mesolithic populations, and this remarkable dispersion, associated with a strikingly uniform cultural assemblage, is usually interpreted as a movement of colonizing farmers from the southeast.

The forest-farming adaptation of the Bandkeramik exerted considerable influence on neighboring regions as they too adopted Neolithic features. The Bandkeramik longhouse, for example, may have provided the inspiration for the long mounds that were constructed as funerary monuments in northern and northwestern Europe, beyond the area of Bandkeramik colonization itself. Bandkeramik communities buried their dead in ordinary graves, which occasionally were grouped into larger cemeteries, as, for example, at Nitra in Slovakia and Elsloo in the Netherlands. The grave goods placed with the dead in these cemeteries suggest that power lay in the hands of the older males. There is no evidence that wealth or social status was heritable.

Northern Europe and the Alpine Zone. Despite the massive timbers used in the construction of the longhouses, Bandkeramik settlements did not long remain in the same locations, and did not form tells like those of southeastern Europe. Neither did the early farming settlements beyond the limits of the Bandkeramik zone, in western and northern Europe. Indeed, in many of these areas the evidence for settlement sites of any kind is slight, and the new Neolithic elements may simply have been incorporated into traditional Mesolithic lifestyles involving periodic movement between living sites.

One region where this was very clearly the case is the Alpine zone. The earliest Alpine Neolithic is represented by Egolzwil, a village site on the shore of the former Lake Wauwil in western Switzerland. This had cereals and domestic animals, rectangular timber houses, and simple round-based pottery vessels, all dated to the late fifth millennium B.C. These are classic Neolithic features, yet the economy of this and other Alpine sites was very different from that of the Neolithic villages of southeastern or central Europe. Wild foods (both plants and animals) continued to play a significant part in the Alpine diet, as they have done up to recent times. Furthermore, there is no reason to assume that these early Alpine farming villages were founded by colonizing farmers from the lower-lying areas around; they most likely represent the adoption and adaptation of Neolithic features by indigenous Mesolithic communities.

A similar process may be documented in northern Europe, where Mesolithic communities of gatherers, fishers, and hunters continued to flourish for almost a thousand years after the adoption of farming in the lands to the south. These Ertebølle-Ellerbek communities, as they are known, developed from earlier Mesolithic traditions around 5300 B.C. They adopted the use of pottery, possibly through the stimulus of contact with pottery-using farmers, and buried their dead in cemeteries. The transition to the Neolithic, with domestic livestock and cultivated plants, took place in southern Scandinavia around 4000 B.C. At the same time, there was a change in the type of pottery in use, with Ertebølle-Ellerbek varieties being replaced by the TRB (Trichterbecker), a pottery style that developed in central Europe from the earlier Bandkeramik pottery style. At about the same time, or only a little later, Danish Neolithic communities began to construct substantial field monuments, in particular mounded tombs of the long mound and passage grave varieties. The long mound, as we have noted, is probably a translation of the longhouse, which played a central role in Bandkeramik settlement.

Central Europe 4500–3500 B.C. Around 4500 B.C. the Bandkeramik Period came to a close and this relatively homogeneous phase spanning large areas of central Europe gave way to a number of more regionalized developments. These are identified and distinguished through their pottery styles, which are taken as the hallmark of particular groups or cultures. In Hungary, Czechoslovakia, and eastern Germany, the principal successor was the Lengyel culture; in the Rhineland and western Germany, it was the Rössen culture. These in turn underwent change and diversification, leading to the rise around 4200 B.C. of several new groups, including the Michelsberg in the west, and the Trichterbecker (TRB) in the east. The latter was an especially significant development since it incorporated both northern Europe and parts of the former Bandkeramik area into an interaction sphere, within which ideas and commodities were able to move over relatively long distances. It is at this time, for example, that the first copper objects appear in Denmark, at the northern periphery of the TRB, illustrating the rapid transmission of the products of the new copper metallurgy of Czechoslovakia, in the southernmost TRB area.

Alongside these particular cultural groups, it is important also to note a number of general developments which were taking place throughout this region during the late fifth and earlier fourth millennium B.C. One of the most significant was the gradual expansion of settlement beyond the river valleys which has been the principal focus of Bandkeramik activity. Another was the gradual change in house forms. The rectangular, parallel-sided Bandkeramik house was replaced by longhouses of trapezoidal plan, and then, in the Michelsberg/TRB phase, by smaller and less substantial dwellings. This shift may be related to basic social changes such as the rise of more hierarchical community structures. The same changes may be reflected in the construction during this period of hilltop-defended enclosures such as the famous TRB site of Dölauer Heide in central Germany.

Western Europe. The beginning of the Neolithic to the west of the Rhine likewise owed something to Bandkeramik influence, although here other factors also came into play. During the Late Bandkeramik Period (5000–4600 B.C.) settlements of longhouses with typical Bandkeramik pottery appeared as far west as the Paris Basin. The Bandkeramik pottery style played some part in the development of the Cerny style which is found widely through northern France in the middle and later fifth millennium B.C. This could indicate a further westward movement by colonizing farmers into Normandy and down the Loire valley to the Atlantic coast. Other evidence, however, strongly suggests that influences from Mediterranean France, where the Impressed Ware Neolithic had been established since at least 5500 B.C., also played a part in the inception of the Neolithic in western France. It is certainly clear that, as in northern Europe or the Alpine zone, it was adoption by indigenous Mesolithic groups rather than immigration or colonization that lay behind the transition to the Neolithic in this region. The same is true of Iberia and the British Isles. The use of Impressed Ware pottery along with domestic plants and animals became established in southern Iberia and Mediterranean France around the middle of the sixth millennium B.C. In the British Isles, the Neolithic began somewhat later, around 4000 B.C., under influence from neighboring regions of mainland Europe.

In western Europe as a whole the Neolithic is characterized not by substantial farming settlements comparable to those of southeastern Europe or the Bandkeramik, but by field monuments, notably megalithic tombs and causewayed enclosures. In southern Britain, burial chambers of timber or megalithic construction were often placed beneath long mounds. These British long mounds form part of the north European long mound tradition which may take its origin from the Bandkeramik longhouse. The communities that built these monuments practiced crop cultivation and livestock husbandry but may still have derived much of their sustenance from wild resources.

The two routes by which Neolithic features spread across Europe—the major river valleys and the Mediterranean coast—meet again along the Atlantic fringe. In the British Isles, the principal links were with adjacent regions of the mainland where Bandkeramik influences were strong. In Iberia, the major source of Neolithic features was the Mediterranean zone. In France, both Mediterranean and central European features appear to have played a part. But in all these west European regions, the transition to the Neolithic was a process of change and adaptation by the indigenous population rather than the work of incoming populations of farmers. Furthermore, the character of the Neolithic as a cultural as much as an economic change is highlighted in western Europe by the construction of the field monuments which are its most conspicuous surviving feature and have no parallel in central Europe or the local Mesolithic. The individuality of the western European Neolithic illustrates that, while the concept of domestication and the domestic species themselves may have been imported from adjacent regions, the communities that adopted these features created from them their own unique social and spiritual world.

[*See also* EUROPE, ORIGINS OF FOOD PRODUCTION IN.]

■ G. Barker, *Prehistoric Farming in Europe* (1985). A. Whittle, *Neolithic Europe: A Survey* (1985). I. Hodder, *The Domestication of Europe* (1990). C. Cunliffe, ed., *The Oxford Illustrated Prehistory of Europe* (1994).

Chris Scarre

THE EUROPEAN COPPER AGE

During the fifth millennium B.C., as agriculture was still spreading through Europe following its introduction to the Balkans in the seventh millennium B.C., copper came into use in the southeastern part of the continent. Although the initial development of copper metallurgy seems to have occurred in Anatolia, southeastern Europe developed a distinctive range of local forms, produced by casting in one-piece (open) molds. This metallurgical tradition lasted until the introduction of alloying and the two-piece mold in the third millennium. While its products were occasionally exported over longer distances, this copper *metallurgy was essentially confined to the Balkans and the Carpathian Basin, based on sources in the mountain chain, so that in other parts of Europe the term "Neolithic" is still applied to this period. The cultures of the Balkan–Carpathian Copper Age are celebrated not just for their often spectacular copper and gold metallurgy, but for the attractive painted wares which continued earlier traditions and still occurred in abundance on substantial settlement sites such as those of the Gumelnitsa culture in Bulgaria and Romania.

It is convenient to divide the phase of European prehistory between 4500 and 2500 B.C. into two equal parts: an earlier phase down to 3500, when European cultures developed largely in isolation; and a later phase when Europe began to form part of a larger community of plow- and wheel-using cultures in which specialized livestock rearing played an increasingly important part. In the earlier phase, western Europe saw the rise of a distinctive local phenomenon, megalith building. This grew up in several different places within the great arc surrounding the loessland cultures of central Europe that were descendants of the *Bandkeramik dispersal, and which were themselves increasingly influenced by the tell-building and copper-using cultures of the southeast. Interaction between expanding loessland populations and the indigenous inhabitants of the Atlantic and Baltic coastlands created a distinctive new pattern of settlement in which monumental earth and stone burial structures played as important a part as did substantial houses and settlement mounds in central and southeastern Europe. The cultures generated in these active outer parts of Europe spread back over the loesslands, creating new blocks of farming cultures: TRB (Funnel-beaker) in northern Europe, Michelsberg between the Rhine delta and the Alps, and Chasséen over much of France.

Within the Carpathian Basin, Lengyel and Tiszapolgár-Bodrogkeresztúr communities also placed increased emphasis on their burials: though here it was not size, but contents that counted. In their flat, inhumation cemeteries, different categories of age, gender, and status were carefully distinguished by appropriate grave goods, which in the case of elder males included shafthole copper axes. An even more spectacular equivalent was the Bulgarian coastal cemetery of *Varna, with its abundant gold- and copperwork. These portable symbols of masculinity and social status started to become more prominent items of material culture than the domestic appurtenances that distinguished the Neolithic. Eastward from the Balkans, across the Pontic steppes toward the Urals, indigenous hunting and fishing groups, which had previously acquired pottery-making skills and domestic cattle from their Neolithic neighbors, now also came to use small quantities of copper ornaments. Equally important for the future was an indigenous development: the taming and domestication of small numbers of horses as a means of hunting the extensive herds of wild animals that roamed the steppe interfluves.

In the later fourth millennium, the ultimate effects of Near Eastern urbanization and trade expansion came to be felt in Europe. These effects are most directly evident in the Carpatho-Balkan area, where pottery of the Baden and related cultures shows a radical change to dark, burnished, channelled wares, shapes and decoration of which reflect sheet-metal forms in silver. The appearance of these shapes coincides with the first evidence for wheeled vehicles and paired draft animals, echoed in the first plowmarks under burial mounds in northern Europe. Soon the metal forms, too, underwent radical change, as the arrival of two-piece mold casting and arsenical alloying caused a fundamental alteration in the design of shafthole axes. On the Pontic steppes, the spread of wheeled vehicles and new breeds of sheep enhanced the possibilities of pastoralism, and resulted in the emergence of a widespread complex called the Pit-grave culture, characterized by ochre-covered burials in chambers under round barrows, sometimes accompanied by wagon wheels.

In outer Europe, and especially in the far north and west, these innovations penetrated only slowly and did not initially change established patterns of culture. Although plowmarks demonstrate the use of this instrument (e.g., in Denmark ca. 3500), it seems initially to have promoted earlier tendencies, as megalithic monuments proliferated and now came to occupy a more or less continuous band around Atlantic Europe, including inland areas such as the Paris Basin as well as coastal areas such as Ireland and Orkney. Simple copper metallurgy, too, flourished near the abundant sources in southern Iberia, where its products occur in megalithic tombs, sometimes associated with nucleated and defended settlements like *Los Millares. Evidence of some interaction between these opposing tendencies—extensification in eastern Europe, local sedentism in the west—comes from the area of the North European Plain between Denmark and Kiev, where the Globular Amphora culture combined stone cist graves and paired-ox burials with pottery decorated with the cord impressions characteristic of the steppes. This process culminated in the appearance of the Corded Ware culture in the same region, characterized by adult male burials accompanied by pottery *beakers and stone battle-axes, beneath round barrows of steppe type (which, incidentally, often preserve traces of plowmarks in the old land surface). Occasional finds of small copper artifacts finally justify the inclusion of this group in a local north European Copper Age; and this pattern of prominent burials with weaponry and drinking vessels spread into the megalith-building Atlantic area as the Bell-beaker complex.

The Copper Age thus witnessed a fundamental transformation in the nature of European cultures: from the domestic emphasis of nucleated settlements in the Balkans or through the use of their monumental surrogates in the form of collectively used megaliths in outer Europe, to the individualism of burial under a tumulus, with the equipment for the archetypal male roles of drinking and fighting, that could be found over an area from the Atlantic to the Urals. These features were to continue in the following millennia.

■ Hermann Müller-Karpe, *Handbuch der Vorgeschichte iv (Kupferzeit)* (1971). Stephen J. Shennan, "Settlement Expansion and Socioeconomic Change 3200–2500 B.C.," in Timothy C. Champion, Clive Gamble, Stephen Shennan and Alasdair Whittle, *Prehistoric Europe* (1983), pp. 153–190. Andrew Sherratt, "The Transformation of Early

Agrarian Europe: The Later Neolithic and Copper Ages 4500–2500 B.C.," in *The Oxford Illustrated Prehistory of Europe*, ed. Barry Cunliffe (1994), pp. 167–201.

Andrew Sherratt

THE EUROPEAN BRONZE AGE

The Bronze Age in Europe lasted from around 2300 B.C. to around 800 B.C. It was the period when, as the name implies, there was a major shift in metal production toward alloys of copper, notably copper alloyed with tin to make bronze. While it is an oversimplification to see the nature of the metal used as a main criterion for the period, it is true that during the Bronze Age the scale and nature of metallurgy developed enormously, from a time where metals were relatively rare to one where huge quantities of metals—principally copper alloys, though not iron—were in common circulation.

The large and varied geographical area of Europe was host to numerous different Bronze Age peoples and cultures, though certain common features can be seen in all areas. Certainly the processes at work during the period manifest themselves widely: not only industrial processes such as the advent of new materials, but also social and economic ones. During these centuries, a marked degree of ranking developed in society, as is shown by the variable furnishing of burials and the creation of prestige bronze-ware such as sheet-metal armor. Something akin to mass production of metalwork began, with smiths turning out thousands of high-quality tools, weapons, and ornaments in well-defined forms; the number of such forms also increased markedly. There was a startling growth in population in the later centuries of the period, to judge from site and burial numbers. Exchange of goods between widely separated areas also increased greatly, with an attendant development of technology for transport by land and water. And there was a marked shift in settlement patterns, with the creation of large numbers of defended sites, often on hills, surrounded by ramparts of earth with a wooden framework.

The third millennium B.C. saw the spread of Corded Ware/Battle Axe groups and Beaker groups over much of Europe, with their highly distinctive pottery, grave form, and some use of metalworking (simple flat tanged daggers, for example). Much of central, eastern, and northern Europe was characterized by Corded Ware pottery, while western and parts of southern and southcentral Europe were characterized by the use of Beaker pottery. From about 2300 B.C. these groups started to be replaced by a variety of new, more localized material culture groupings, often continuing some of the traditions of the Copper Age (for instance in pot shapes and metal forms).

It is convenient, and the normal convention, to divide the Bronze Age into three successive parts. Early, Middle, and Late, with internal boundaries at around 1500 and 1300 B.C., respectively, for Early–Middle and Middle–Late. The most important Early Bronze Age culture is that named after the cemetery of Unetice near Prague. This serves as a model for a whole range of related groups across central Europe, from Austria and Switzerland in the south to Poland in the north. Flat cemeteries (i.e., graves in pits in the ground with no mound heaped up over them) are the rule, the bodies oriented according to sex in some areas, and frequently also arranged with respect to the points of the compass. Of the many artifact forms, particular attention may be drawn to the characteristic hourglass cup and racket-headed pin. For the most part graves were furnished quite simply, but there is a small group of richer graves found in eastern Germany and Poland—Helmsdorf, Leubingen, and Leki Male are the best-known examples—with multiple bronzes, gold objects, and other signs of exceptional provision. To the southeast, in Hungary and adjoining areas, the extensive cemetery evidence is joined by that of large settlement sites on mounds or tells, rising up out of the flat plains. On these sites excavation has recovered the remains of numerous superimposed houses, post-framed with wattle-and-daub or plank-built walls. Notable sites such as Nagyrev, Hatvan, Otomani, and Fuzesabony give their names to the cultural groups in this area. Further east again are a series of small local groups in Romania and Bulgaria, named after settlement sites at Wietenberg and Monteoru.

In Italy, much of the peninsula was occupied by a set of material culture named after its principal mountain range, the Appenines. This is mostly known from small settlement sites, though in some cases, as at Luni sul Mignone in Etruria, the sites are not so small and the houses are quite large. Appenine Italy was practically metalless. Perhaps to compensate, much attention was directed toward the production of elaborate pottery, treatment of the handles being especially complex—high handles with forked ends or wishbones being particularly favored. In the south of Italy and in Sicily, a different set of developments occurred. The Castelluccio culture of Early Bronze Age Sicily favored rock-cut tombs with elaborate facades, while on the small rocky Aeolian islands, centered on Lipari, the settlements of small round houses (such as Capo Graziano on Filicudi) were in touch with lands to the east, as is shown by the presence of imported Aegean pottery. These contacts developed much further in the ensuing centuries, and in the Middle Bronze Age Thapsos culture, eastern Sicily saw the construction of large rock-cut tombs in the Aegean style, with considerable quantities of imported Mycenaean and, in at least one case, Cypriot pottery.

In the north and northwest of Europe, we know most about the funerary rite, which was that of inhumation under a large mound or "barrow." In southern Britain the "Wessex culture" has attracted much attention because of its preference for depositing trinkets of exotic materials (gold, amber, shale, faience) in some of the graves. In Denmark, this period of barrow building is particularly important because preservation conditions in some of the oak coffins that were used to contain the burials have allowed the survival of items of clothing. Bronzes allow a division into male and female graves, and taken together this Scandinavian material offers rich insights into Bronze Age society.

Burial under barrows became the normal mode of deposition throughout much of central Europe during the Middle Bronze Age, also called the Tumulus Period. A standardized range of characteristic objects for each main area was developed, including the sword, invented now and deposited in graves that were presumably those of warriors. The change to highly visible burial must represent the effect of social developments, in particular a move toward a more ranked society. On the other hand, settlement sites are not especially elaborate; most that are known are simple agricultural villages, marked by post-built houses and pits.

Around 1300 B.C., a sea change swept across Europe; few regions were unaffected, and then not for long. This change is most manifest in the funerary practices adopted: instead of inhumation, the normal practice changed to that of cremation. The ashes generated were collected up and placed in an urn, the urn being deposited in a defined burial area or "urnfield." The Late Bronze Age or "Urnfield Period" was a time of enormous population expansion, of technological innovation, and of economic diversification. While some parts of Europe continued to maintain distinctive traditions, in general one can say that the Late Bronze Age culture of Europe was a unified one, with common bronze forms appearing widely across the continent, and the common burial rite of cremation being nearly ubiquitous.

The change to cremation is thought to imply a major change in religious beliefs, notably those concerning the fate of the body after death. One possible explanation is that there was a change of population at the start of the Late Bronze Age. References by Greek writers of the classical period, notably Herodotus, to the *Celts, Scythians, and other peoples may contain echoes of a past that harks back to the Bronze Age. In this, the timing of the arrival of the Celts in Europe is a topic of continuing importance. Iron Age Europe was largely Celtic; therefore, the Celts must either have arrived at the end of the Bronze Age or have been there previously. Since there is no good evidence for an arrival with the start of the Iron Age, which continues many of the traditions of the Urnfield Period, it is likely that Urnfield Europe was itself occupied by Celtic peoples, and one of the possible times for their arrival in Europe is the start of the Urnfield Period. The likelihood is, however, that the peoples who later became known collectively as Celts were in fact present long before that, potentially since the start of the Neolithic Period.

The European Bronze Age runs parallel to that of its more illustrious neighbors to the south and east, in Greece, Anatolia (Turkey), and the countries of the Levant, Mesopotamia, and Egypt. It did not of course develop the social and economic complexity of those civilizations, nor the devices—such as palaces and towns—to express the increasing divisions in society and organize their implementation. But there is a significant amount of evidence to show that contacts took place between east Mediterranean societies and those of Europe, especially Italy and Sicily, but also Sardinia and possibly Spain (imported Aegean pottery has recently turned up there). With exotic substances such as amber, which can be tied down to a particular source area, it is also clear that the northern world was in regular contact with the southern. This can be seen in the development of one particular substance: glass, or its primitive forerunner, faience. This material, which is a silica-based compound, was invented somewhere in the Near East probably in the fourth millennium B.C. but was widely adopted in Europe during the Early Bronze Age (late third to early second millennium B.C.). The technology was certainly derived from the Near East, and in some cases the actual objects may have been imported. The means by which such transfer took place are a matter of some controversy. What is not in doubt is that long-distance trade routes became an established fact of life during this period. This is shown not only by isolated objects such as faience but more pertinently by the large-scale movement of metal in finished or semifinished form.

The most important metal in the Bronze Age, in volume terms if not in value, was copper, and a number of mining sites are known (Mount Gabriel in southern Ireland, the Mitterberg in Austria). Shafts and adits, sometimes of considerable size, were driven into the mountainside and ore was extracted using fire setting, prying the chunks of rock out by means of wedges and picks. Smelting near the mine

sites was followed by distribution in ingot form; whereas in the East Mediterranean the favored ingot type was the so-called ox-hide ingot, elsewhere the most popular form was the plano-convex shape, rounded on the bottom and flat on the top. In central Europe in the Early Bronze Age, ingots in the form of neck rings were widely distributed.

This large volume of metal was fashioned into artifacts: tools, ornaments, and weapons. Some of the material found its way into graves, but a much larger quantity was buried in the ground in groups, sometimes very large groups of hundreds or thousands of objects. While some of these collective finds or hoards are probably the remains of industrial processes, others seem to have been deposited for reasons that we can only describe as ritual.

Bronze Age Europe was a world of small-scale societies, even though the different parts of it were increasingly in touch with each other. In its later stages one can discern sites that served as population and perhaps economic centers, but they are relatively small in extent and closely spaced in terms of distribution. Fortified sites were not therefore the centers of major population units or political forces, but they do represent the start of a tradition that found its most eloquent expression in the great forts and fortified towns of the Iron Age. In this, and in many other matters of economy and technology, the Bronze Age provides direct forebears for the world of the Celts that ran parallel to that of classical Greece and Rome.

[See also SCANDINAVIA: SCANDINAVIA IN THE BRONZE AGE; URNFIELDS.]

■ Tibor Kovacs, *The Bronze Age in Hungary* (1977). J. M. Coles and A. F. Harding, *The Bronze Age in Europe* (1979). Colin Burgess, *The Age of Stonehenge* (1980). Peter S. Wells, *Farms, Villages and Cities. Commerce and Urban Origins in Late Prehistoric Europe* (1984). Abbaye de Daoulas, *Avant les Celtes. L'Europe à l'âge du bronze. 2500–800 avant J-C* (1988). Gilles Gaucher, *Peuples de bronze. Anthropologie de la France à l'âge du bronze* (1988). Hans-Ake Nordström and Anita Knape, eds., *Bronze Age Studies* (1989). Richard Bradley, *The Passage of Arms* (1991).

Anthony F. Harding

THE EUROPEAN IRON AGE

The Iron Age represents a major turning point in European prehistory, not only because it was the period in which the foundations were laid for many of the social, political, and cultural developments of historic Europe but also because the modern perception of the European past divides Europe into separate traditions for the first time in the middle of the first millennium B.C.: the classical and the barbarian. This split tradition is represented in different disciplinary specialisms, *classical and prehistoric archaeology; some cultural groups, such as the *Etruscans and Iberians, who shared social developments with the Greeks and Romans, occupy an ambivalent position between the two traditions. This modern cultural attitude to the past has also shaped the approach to the study of the Iron Age and to the interpretation placed on the transformations of European society. The classical world has been studied within a historical paradigm, and much attention has been paid to art and architecture. This has also had an effect on the study of the Iron Age in temperate Europe, for instance, in the approach to the art of the *La Tène period, but in general Iron age studies outside the Mediterranean region have been much more open to the ideas of prehistory, in particular the theoretical developments from the 1960s onward.

The high value placed on the role of classical civilization

in Europe's perception of its own cultural tradition has also meant that the transformations of later prehistoric society have been explained as the result of influence from the classical world. By the end of the Iron Age large parts of Europe were occupied by societies that were literate, used coins, lived in towns, and had a high degree of political centralization. These processes had undoubtedly begun earliest in the eastern Mediterranean and from there had spread northward and westward. More recent accounts have rejected a simple explanation in terms of cultural diffusion and have sought to examine the processes by which temperate Europe came to be a periphery of an expanding central zone focused originally in the eastern Mediterranean. They have also sought to explain the nature of the social interactions that made the north-south relationship between Mediterranean and temperate Europe the dominant axis of social change in the Iron Age. Despite the importance of this relationship for understanding Iron Age changes, archaeologists have also stressed the contribution of local societies in Europe to their own long-term development.

Sources of Evidence. With the exception of Bronze Age Greece, the Iron Age is the first period in Europe for which there are extensive written records. The works of the Latin and Greek authors provide the basis for the historical tradition of the Mediterranean world, but they also contain many references to the remoter parts of Europe. The earliest records are sparse and of doubtful reliability, but the later ones, such as those of Julius Caesar, are much more authoritative, frequently being eyewitness accounts. As well as supplying ethnographic details of the Iron Age, these authors also provide names for the peoples of Europe such as the *Celts in the center and west or the Germans in the north, as well as many smaller groups. In addition, we know the names of individuals in later prehistory, in particular the leaders of the opposition to Roman expansion, such as Viriatus in Portugal, Vercingetorix in France, Arminius in Germany, or Boudicca in England. These historically documented groups and individuals have been exploited by modern European nations in the creation for themselves of a remote and glorious past, peopled by heroes and heroines, and apparently authenticated by archaeology.

The archaeological evidence for the Iron Age of the classical world has been well recognized since the Renaissance, and a formidable body of scholarship has developed. The material record of the Iron Age in temperate Europe, however, was first identified in the middle of the nineteenth century. Excavation of the cemetery at *Hallstatt and the votive deposits at La Tène together with research on cemeteries in Scandinavia provided the basis for an Iron Age chronology. By the 1880s a chronological scheme was widely accepted that divided the Iron Age into two phases, Hallstatt (ca. 700–450 B.C.) and La Tène (ca. 450 B.C. to the Roman Conquest), and that has been used ever since, with various regional subdivisions. Much energy has been devoted to the excavation of cemeteries in many parts of Europe, and analysis of the artifacts deposited as grave goods, especially weapons and personal ornaments, has been a major feature of Iron Age studies; particular attention has been devoted to decorated items of the La Tène period. Though many settlements are known, extensive excavation has been limited to a few regions such as Britain, Scandinavia, and the Czech Republic. More recent themes have included Iron Age agriculture, technological innovation, and the organization of production and distribution.

The Expansion of the Mediterranean World. The beginning of the Iron Age was not marked by the first appearance of iron, but the point at which it became widely used. Iron was known from at least 1700 B.C. but was not common in most of Europe until about 700 B.C. It used to be thought that iron was a material superior to bronze, to be adopted as soon as knowledge of how to work it was available. The question is more complex, however; iron was known for a long time before it was widely used, and it never replaced bronze for all purposes. Nor was it necessarily superior; as late as the third century B.C., iron swords used by the Celts buckled on impact. Iron may not have been very plentiful at first, and output increased significantly only in the final stages of the Iron Age. One of the reasons for its widespread adoption around 700 B.C. may have been prestige, given its usage for swords and vehicle fittings.

The rapid development of a dynamic urban society in the eastern Mediterranean and the Aegean in the ninth and eighth centuries B.C. sparked a wave of colonial expansion, by both Phoenicians and Greeks. The Phoenicians were primarily seeking raw materials, especially metals, and founded trading posts in *Sicily, Spain, and North Africa. The Greeks, too, founded colonies, especially in southern Italy, France, and Spain, as well as in the Black Sea region; initially established for trading purposes, colonies were later a means of settling excess population. These colonies had not only established a ring of urban societies around the Mediterranean by the sixth century B.C., they had also stimulated a new set of political and economic relationships with the external world, which resulted in rapid transformations. One major problem is the extent to which local developments were already under way. In central Italy and southern and eastern Spain, the Etruscans and Iberians developed complex, literate urban societies, with sophisticated artistic and architectural traditions owing much to eastern Mediterranean influences.

Farther north, the earliest Iron Age societies show evidence for social inequality, but contacts with the classical world offered new opportunities for augmentation of power through control of people and wealth. From France to the Ukraine a series of regional groups of rich graves, sometimes associated with the fortified residences of the elite, dominate the archaeological record of the eighth to fifth centuries B.C. The graves often contain local prestige items, such as wheeled vehicles or jewelry, as well as imported items from the Mediterranean world, including wine amphorae, fine pottery, and metalwork. The Scythian graves in the Ukraine have produced prodigious quantities of gold, and another group in the eastern Alps contained many bronze vessels. One of the most spectacular groups is the sixth-century graves of France and southern Germany, such as Vix and Eberdingen-Hochdorf. Elite settlements are also known, especially the *Heuneburg in southern Germany, which contained workshops for the production of prestige goods. In one phase the defenses of the Heuneburg were rebuilt using mud brick and incorporating bastions; both the material and the plan were derived from the south. Other finds in central Europe, such as fans and musical instruments, suggest that Mediterranean styles of clothing and behavior were also imitated by the barbarian aristocracy. Interaction with the classical world clearly comprised much more than trade, and there must have been regular political and cultural contacts of various sorts.

The effects of these contacts were felt farther north; some Mediterranean imports traveled as far north as Britain and

Scandinavia, but were not used in the same way as farther south. Localized social hierarchies are seen throughout northern Europe in the record of burials and settlements.

The Beginnings of Urban Society. By the end of the fifth century B.C. most of the rich burial traditions had ceased, especially in central and western Europe. Graves still show differences in the quantities of weapons and ornaments deposited, but the extremely rich goods, especially imports, are no longer seen. Contacts with the Mediterranean were still maintained, however, as shown by artistic borrowings and the importation of coral. The marked change in the burial record signifies not so much the cessation of trade with the Mediterranean world as a change in the nature of the contact. Barbarian mercenaries regularly served in Mediterranean armies, and Celtic migrations from central Europe are known into Italy in the fourth century B.C. to southeastern Europe in the third century B.C.

There are also signs of important developments in Iron Age society. High-value coinage was minted in gold and silver, suggesting new social uses for wealth. Technological developments included innovations such as the rotary quern, increased production of wheel-thrown pottery, and greater centralization and standardization of production, especially of pottery and iron, with an associated growth of distribution networks. Less is known about Iron Age agriculture, but *field systems and storage facilities in many regions of Europe suggest intensification of food production and increasing control over supplies. New forms of ritual activity also appeared; as less wealth was deposited in graves, more was disposed of in votive deposits such as those in the river at La Tène, Switzerland, and the temple at Gournay, France.

These processes culminated in the second and first centuries B.C., when an entirely new form of settlement system appeared, dominated by large nucleated sites. Roman authors describing these sites used the word *oppidum* (town), and indeed they show some of the features of modern towns. They were centers for the production and distribution of manufactured goods, including metal, wood, leather, and ceramic products. In central and western Europe many of the sites, such as *Manching in southern Germany, were located on good communication routes or to control valuable sources of raw materials, especially metal ores. There is, however, no clear evidence of public architecture or elite residences, and the social and political context of these towns is unclear. Farther east, many of the towns were grouped around a defended hilltop, but they show similar levels of economic activity. In several parts of central and western Europe writing systems were adopted, using versions of Latin or Greek alphabets, for record keeping, but also for religious and ceremonial purposes. These towns were the economic and political centers of the Celts and other peoples conquered by Rome from the first century B.C. onward. Many were used by the Romans as centers for political administration, and many medieval and modern towns rest on such Iron Age foundations.

Roman expansion northward in the first century B.C. set off another cycle of social change. Rich burials are found in southeastern England and northern Europe, again containing many luxury imports from the south. Towns also developed in southeastern England in the century before the Roman Conquest began in A.D. 43. Farther north still, the nature of Iron Age tribal society is shown in different ways. At Navan in Northern Ireland, the legendary royal center of Ulster, a huge wooden ceremonial structure was built in 94 B.C. At Hodde in Denmark, the successive phases of the village show the emergence of some households as wealthier than others.

Thus, by the end of the Iron Age, and before the Roman conquest, much of Europe had developed an urban literate society with a complex economic and technological organization and a high degree of political centralization.

[*See also* ARMS AND ARMOR; FEDDERSEN WIERDE; GERMANS AND GERMANIC INVASIONS; HILL FORTS; HOARDS AND HOARDING; MAIDEN CASTLE; ROMAN EMPIRE: THE ROMAN FRONTIER; SCANDINAVIA: SCANDINAVIA IN THE IRON AGE; THREE-AGE SYSTEM.]

■ P. S. Wells, *Culture Contact and Culture Change* (1980). J. Collis, *The European Iron Age* (1984). J. L. Brunaux, *The Celtic Gauls: Gods, Rites and Sanctuaries* (1988). F. Audouze and O. Büchsenschütz, *Towns, Villages and Countryside of Celtic Europe* (1989). V. Kruta, O.-H. Frey, B. Raftery, and M. Szabo, eds., *The Celts* (1991). L. Hedeager, *Iron-Age Societies: From Tribe to State in Northern Europe, 500 B.C. to A.D. 700* (1992).

Timothy Champion

ROMAN AND POST-ROMAN EUROPE

The Roman Empire was born in 27 B.C. out of the civil war which ended the Roman Republic in the mid-first century. Although not officially an empire until this date, the Roman state had already conquered most of Europe. What are now France and Spain were already under direct Roman rule and when the first emperor, Augustus, died in A.D. 14, the empire stretched from the Atlantic to the Middle East. Rome's final European conquests in the west were added by the time of Trajan, who died in A.D. 117. At this time, the Roman Empire reached its greatest extent and encompassed all of Europe west of the Rhine and south of the Danube, in addition to some outlying territories in southeastern Europe and Britain. The conquest of Britain in A.D. 43 resulted in the acquisition of almost all of what is today England and Wales, but Roman success in the north of the island was limited, resulting in the establishment of frontiers, first on or near the line of *Hadrian's Wall (built in the early second century A.D.) and later of the shortlived but more northerly Antonine Wall, running on a line approximately between modern Glasgow and Edinburgh.

The Roman frontiers in Britain and on the mainland were garrisoned by professional soldiers and furnished with forts, linear earthworks, and in some cases, stone built defenses. Behind the frontiers, other military bases, fortresses, and naval establishments, combined with efficient systems of communication and a network of paved and regularly maintained routeways, made Roman defenses especially formidable. This was all the more the case because, unlike the populations ("barbarians") to the north of the empire, the Roman army was highly trained and strictly disciplined, with a well-developed tactical and strategic understanding of military operations.

The widespread distribution of military bases and the deliberate Roman policy of encouraging local populations to adopt urban lifestyles and Roman customs ("romanization"), combined with intense economic activity by Mediterranean and other traders and entrepreneurs in newly conquered territories, led inevitably to a degree of cultural unity. Within the empire, people could travel relatively freely and were assured of the rule of Roman law and the acceptability of Roman currency. Taxation, and even prices during the later Roman Period, were maintained at a standard level by the state. This necessitated government representation in every part of Roman territory. It also encouraged an empire-wide trading network, which in turn allowed the export and import of both manufactured goods and raw materials, assisted by the efficiency of the road network and the security afforded by the "Roman peace" (Pax Romana) to seafarers.

In addition to economic standardization, the promotion of cultural values brought about the widespread adoption of romanized ways of life. This was especially true for local aristocracies, even those derived from what had been Iron Age kingdoms which had fought against the Romans, although local "Iron Age" culture and local religions persisted alongside those of Rome.

By the beginning of the third century A.D., this Europe-wide social and economic system was well established and local populations were no longer prone to anti-Roman revolts. As the century progressed, however, military disasters and economic depression severely affected almost the entire Roman Empire. Germanic peoples crossed the frontiers in a number of sectors (notably along the Rhine and Danube) and raided Roman provinces.

The third-century crisis lasted from A.D. 235 to 270 and saw the rapid demise of no fewer than fifteen emperors. Gaul, Spain, and Britain had for a while become independent under their own rulers (the "Gallic Empire") and barbarian tribes rampaged through the Roman provinces. Roman recovery began only in its 270s, and was consolidated by the emperors Diocletian and Constantine in the following decades.

Diocletian adopted unusual measures to restore stability following the retrieval of the military situation and the reunification of the empire. Using the Persian court as his model, he formalized Roman imperial court ceremony and made the role of the emperor both more like that of a king and more militarized. Formalization was now to characterize all aspects of government administration, which was expanded into a huge official bureaucracy. New laws gave the emperor, the administration, and the state far greater supervision over everyday life.

An even wider-reaching change in the culture of the Roman Empire was brought about by the Emperor Constantine in the early fourth century. Diocletian had been the pagan ruler of an officially pagan empire, and a persecutor of Christians. Constantine, however, was converted to Christianity in A.D. 312 and made this the official religion of the whole empire. This brought about sweeping religious and social changes throughout Europe, though the Church had already been established in the south (notably Italy) during the first century, and had steadily grown in size through the Roman Period.

The fourth century was a period of renewed stability and economic development, with new and more centralized industries gaining large markets for their products. At the end of the century, however, barbarian raids again began to pierce Roman defenses. A mixture of military blunder and inept policy on the part of the Roman government led to large-scale incursions into the European provinces. The fall of the west came very quickly. In A.D. 402 the Goths, a Germanic people, moved into Italy, and in 406 other Germans (Vardale, Alars, and Sueves) crossed the Rhine. In A.D. 410 Rome itself was sacked by the Goths. Other Germanic peoples gradually took control of the remaining western provinces as the fifth century progressed. The Franks seized Gaul, which henceforth became Francia (France) and one branch of the Goths (the Visigoths) took Spain. Italy fell to

another branch, the Ostrogoths, and between these two groups, the Burgundians took control of the area which still bears their name (Burgundy). So by A.D. 500 almost all of continental Europe was in "barbarian" hands, and the last Roman emperor (no more than a puppet ruler) was deposed in A.D. 476. The Roman Empire survived only in the Balkans, where the eastern emperors, based at Constantinople, still held control.

There was one exception to this generalization: In Britain, the local provincial population had unique success in holding out against the barbarian invaders. These so-called sub-Roman or Dark Age Britons formed their own kingdoms and preserved several aspects of romanized life, including Christianity, for many years. It was not until the seventh century that the majority of what had been Roman Britain came under Germanic (in this case, Anglo-Saxon) rule.

Each of these Germanic peoples preserved aspects of their indigenous heritage. They were ruled by kings and their society was based on kinship and ties of loyalty and duty. Living under their own laws and in small villages rather than towns or villas, their lifestyle was in stark contrast to the Roman provincials among whom they settled. Yet, during the course of the fifth century, they became increasingly integrated into Roman provincial life. At the same time, romanization gradually decreased among what had been provincial Roman citizens. As a result, by the end of the sixth century, the two societies—Germanic newcomers and Roman provincials—had largely converged, but at a point closer to that of the Germanic Iron Age than to Late Roman urban culture.

By the end of the sixth century, too, Christianity had spread widely among these barbarian peoples. The Anglo-Saxon kingdoms in Britain were the last to be converted, but even this had been achieved by the end of the seventh century.

From that point onward a new barbarian, but Christian, European world began to develop its own towns and economic structures. These emerged within the context of individual kingdoms, rather than a single state, although the western Church headed by the Pope at Rome bound the various kingdoms together as Western Christendom.

As this social and economic system developed, it produced both technological advances and an urban-based administrative structure. Although early medieval towns were fundamentally different from those of the Roman Empire, they, like their forerunners, served as market and administrative centers and were part of a coin-using economy articulating long-distance maritime trade.

At the end of the eighth century the developing pattern was disrupted by another period of invasions from the north. The Vikings, Scandinavian traders and warriors, began a devastating series of raids which led to the temporary establishment of Viking kingdoms in some parts of Europe, notably eastern England, Ireland, and northern France (Normandy). Socially and culturally similar to the Germanic peoples who had invaded the Late Roman Empire, the Vikings dominated the political and military affairs of Europe until the eleventh century. Unlike the barbarians of the fifth century, however, the Vikings did not destroy the existing social and economic framework but were as much involved in long-distance trade as in conquest and migration, and (especially after their conversion to Christianity) were gradually integrated into the society and culture of the European kingdoms.

Though the Vikings failed to establish any long-lasting

kingdom outside their Scandinavian homeland, their impact on the political development of Europe was as important as their economic and cultural role. Their dukedom of Normandy very rapidly developed institutions and culture based on that of the neighboring Frankish kingdom. It was a ruler of Normandy, William the Conqueror, who invaded and conquered Anglo-Saxon England in 1066.

The end of the Viking Age, in the eleventh century, marks the start of the European Middle Ages. This period saw the development of those kingdoms founded in the fifth to eleventh centuries into medieval feudal states with urban-based bureaucratic—although still monarchical—governments, written systems of laws, and a monetary market-based economy. Economic growth continued throughout the later medieval period and, spurred on by technological and cultural changes in the fourteenth and fifteenth centuries, ultimately laid the foundations for the Industrial Revolution. The European Middle Ages drew to a close in the sixteenth century with the Protestant Reformation and the High Renaissance.

[See also BRITISH ISLES, articles on ROMAN BRITAIN, THE ANGLO-SAXONS, VIKING RAIDS AND SETTLEMENT IN BRITAIN AND IRELAND, MEDIEVAL BRITAIN; FRANKS AND THE FRANKISH EMPIRE; GERMANS AND GERMANIC INVASIONS; MEDIEVAL EUROPE: OVERVIEW; ROMAN EMPIRE: THE ROMAN FRONTIER.]

■ Tim Cornell and John Matthews, Atlas of the Roman World (1982). Richard Hodges and David Whitehouse, Mohammed, Charlemagne and the Origins of Europe (1983). John Wacher, ed., The Roman World, 2 vols. (1990). Roger Collins, Early Medieval Europe 300–1000 (1991). Klavs Randsborg, The First Millennium A.D. in Europe and the Mediterranean (1991). Else Roesdahl, The Vikings (1991).

Ken Dark

HISTORICAL ARCHAEOLOGY OF EUROPE

The archaeology of the historic periods in Europe technically begins with the rise of literate societies in Bronze Age and classical Greece. Conversely, New World archaeologists refer to historical archaeology as the archaeology of colonial settlement after ca. A.D. 1500. The term "historical archaeology" is usually taken by European archaeologists, however, to mean the period after the fall of the western Roman Empire after ca. A.D. 400. This is not just a divide in time. It is also a divide between subdisciplines, between distinctive traditions of classical and medieval archaeology. The terminology used to classify the historic periods is hence often confused and contradictory.

The archaeology of the period after ca. A.D. 1000 in particular has long been a "poor relation" of prehistoric and *Classical archaeology. This is partly due to the relative youth of *historical archaeology. Though high-status buildings and works of art have long been studied, most aspects of later historic archaeology have only become a major area of inquiry since the 1950s. In some European countries this period is archaeologically still relatively unexplored.

This relative youth has resulted in a problem. We have accumulated large amounts of material in the wake of projects often related to "rescue" priorities, but we lack broad synthetic treatments of the period's archaeological problems. The problem of youth is compounded by the established nature of historical narratives. Archaeologists have tended to fit their findings around the framework of those narratives. It is therefore difficult to specify a set of broad themes that are distinctively archaeological in nature; but the following is a selection covering some of the major issues.

The Early Middle Ages and the Identity of Europe. In an age when the concept of "Europe" is under stress, do we see European origins in the Roman world or in the Germanic peoples? Related to this is the question of how we understand the nature of early medieval ethnic groups and political entities. Do these groups stand in a direct ancestry to the present?

This question is intimately bound up with that of the origins of modern nation-states. Traditional histories have given us a list of Germanic, Slavic, and Scandinavian peoples whose wanderings gave rise to the nations of Europe we know today: the Franks, Slavs, Huns, Goths, Angles, Saxons, and so on. But the archaeological record offers much more equivocal evidence on the existence and nature of such cohesive groups. Variation in different kinds of burial rite, pottery, house type, settlement form, and so on suggest that there was much continuity and intermingling with indigenous groups, as well as changes and internal differentiation within groups as they moved across Europe. The pattern is certainly far too complex to be explained simply by a list of migrations.

Central and eastern European scholars have looked at this problem in terms of the concept of "ethnogenesis," while English-speaking scholars have become steadily more skeptical of the assumption of large-scale migration by distinct ethnic groups. They often stress instead the underlying continuity of late Roman cultural forms, particularly in field systems, territorial units and the location of later towns on Roman sites. West European scholars have generally preferred to stress underlying social change rather than ethnic migrations. This debate has clear political resonance in a modern Europe caught between ethnic and national antagonisms rooted in "history" on the one hand, and centralizing cultural and economic forces on the other.

The Continuing Legacy of the Roman Empire, in Particular Christianity, and the Archaeology of the Church. The institutions of the Church survived the fall of the Roman Empire in mainland western Europe, and by the end of the millennium most of central, northern, and eastern Europe had been Christianized by either the Catholic or Orthodox Churches. Christianity brought with it more than a system of doctrine and learning. Archaeology shows that the medieval Church was an important social and economic institution. After the Benedictine Revival of the tenth century A.D., a network of monasteries acquired lands and wealth. Excavations have showed their role as industrial and agricultural centers. By contrast, the influence of Islam on the art and archaeology of Mediterranean Europe has often been ignored or forgotten.

The Rise of Medieval States and Towns in Northern Europe. Archaeology has done much to modify the "Pirenne thesis" that trade and urban life continued after the fall of the western Roman Empire, and that the key to understanding the rise of medieval states is rather in the collapse of Mediterranean trade after the Muslim expansions of the seventh and eighth centuries. Finds of Arab silver in Scandinavia have directed attention to trade across eastern Europe between the Baltic and East Mediterranean worlds.

More broadly, the seventh to eleventh centuries saw the rise of feudal states across central and northern Europe, and archaeology is playing a key role in reassessing their nature and origins. Archaeologists have excavated a network of production and trading centers or "emporia" across the North Sea and Baltic areas, centers such as Ipswich, Hamwic, Dorestad, Quentovic, Helgo, and many others. The kings who apparently controlled these centers traded prestige and other goods—quernstones, pottery, glassware—between competing kingdoms. Commodities such as wool and timber were also traded.

A new generation of urban centers in the ninth and tenth centuries in northern Europe, termed "burhs" in England, were laid out on a planned, defended basis. They may have had their immediate origin either in Viking trade or in defense against Viking attack, but they were more broadly designed to control local trade and were associated with the issuing of coins, royal authority, local markets, and tax collection.

The archaeology of rural settlement similarly indicates a restructuring and expansion between the seventh and eleventh centuries, with the replacement of often scattered and shifting settlement with permanent, nucleated villages centered around castles or manorial centers. The regularity of building plots and tenements suggests that these new villages were often partially or completely planned in form. These new forms are termed *villages perchés* in southern France, *incastillamento* in Italy, and are found in the Midlands in England and across central and eastern Europe.

Finally, excavation and field work on early castles has shown that their origins were tied up with feudal power in the tenth and eleventh centuries. Stone castles often had their antecedents in timber and earthwork enclosures. Many have argued that castles evolved more or less independently in different areas of Europe such as Normandy, central France, and the Rhineland.

Everyday Life in the High Middle Ages. Traditional historians have always appreciated the great cultural and architectural achievements of the twelfth to fourteenth centuries—the great castles, cathedrals, and so on—but know much less of the rural and urban infrastructure that they were built upon. Excavations and field work, most extensively in Britain but also in northern and Mediterranean Europe, have told us much about the lives of ordinary people. They have shown for example that peasant houses were not flimsy hovels but were often well built, that peasants often enjoyed a varied diet, and that relations between environment, people, and lords were much more complex than hitherto supposed. Analysis of topography and excavation in medieval towns has revealed a wide range of trading and industrial activities.

The Transition from Feudalism to Nascent Capitalism. This is another traditional historical problem that archaeologists are only now beginning to address. Again historians have talked much of the disaster and desertion that followed the *Black Death of 1347 to 1351 and the associated economic crises, but have not focused as much attention on the associated restructuring of European society and culture at the ordinary, peasant level. Recent advances in social theory have stressed that the feudal/capitalist transition was as much about small-scale and everyday life as large-scale transformations, a point taken up by Annales historians such as Fernand Braudel.

Archaeologists and students of material culture are beginning to respond to this challenge. They have looked at the rise of privacy and material comfort in domestic architecture, the rise of the individual as seen in eating habits, cooking and tableware, and changing patterns of treatment of the dead.

The Archaeology of Europe in the Colonies. We are beginning to study colonial landscapes, or the way in which European powers settled the land in other areas of the globe. The colonization and exploitation of the Americas and other areas outside Europe was a process that started on the fringes of Europe, arguably stretching back to the Crusades. The patterns of settlement adopted by the English in Virginia and New England have antecedents, for example, in the colonial landscapes of Wales and Ireland. Studying the archaeology of such landscapes will tell us much about material ways of life, and also about the self-perception and ideology of the European settlers and colonists.

***Industrial Archaeology.** Many of the large-scale changes of the late eighteenth and nineteenth centuries studied by industrial archaeologists were presaged by small-scale industries that developed in Europe from the later Middle Ages onward. Archaeological field work and excavation has shown that this industry was often part-time in nature. The archaeology of stone quarrying, tin, lead, and other mining and production is often found in association with upland rural settlements.

To conclude, it must be stressed that the above is a personal selection of themes. A more traditional narrative of the archaeology of the Germanic migrations, the Vikings, the Normans, and so on might equally well have been highlighted. Other questions may be asked, and the real value of the archaeology of historic Europe lies in opening up other possible stories, other narratives, and other European identities. This is particularly true as medieval archaeologists from all areas of Europe come together to debate different traditions of work and ask questions of their material outside their local context.

[*See also* MEDIEVAL EUROPE: OVERVIEW; MEDITERRANEAN, HISTORICAL ARCHAEOLOGY AND ETHNOARCHAEOLOGY OF THE.]

■ Phil Dixon, *Barbarian Europe* (1976). Klaus Ransborg, *Viking Age Denmark* (1980). Richard Hodges and David Whitehouse, *Mohammed, Charlemagne and the Origins of Europe* (1983). Donald Matthew, *Atlas of Medieval Europe* (1983). J. Chapelot and C. Fossier, *The Village and House in the Middle Ages* (1985). David Austin and Leslie Alcock, *From the Baltic to the Black Sea: Studies in Medieval Archaeology* (1990). Martin Gojda, *The Ancient Slavs: Settlement and Society* (1991). Hans Andersson, and Jes Weinberg, eds., *The Study of Medieval Archaeology* (1993). Matthew Johnson, *An Archaeology of Capitalism* (1995).

Matthew Johnson

EUROPE, The First Colonization of. In archaeology, it has been the traditional view for decades that humankind arose in Africa, and only spread to other continents at a comparatively late stage. The human ancestor known as *Homo habilis* (handy man) evolved in Africa by about 2 million years ago but never spread elsewhere. It was the later species, *Homo erectus* (erect man), which also appeared first in Africa around 1.8 million years ago, that radiated out from that continent into Europe and elsewhere around 1 million years ago.

This scenario has been challenged in recent years, not only by some (still contentious) new dates which place *Homo erectus* in Indonesia at 1.8 million years ago, and which assign similar ages to stone tools in Pakistan and Israel (Ubeidiyeh), but also by a series of finds and dates in Europe and Siberia that may yet lead to a complete revision of human prehistory.

At present, the earliest known human remains in Europe are the recently discovered (though still somewhat controversial) series of fragments found in the Orce Basin, northeast of Granada in southeast Spain, which, together with stone tools from the area, are thought to date to about 1.6 million years ago. Likewise, some collapsed cave-sites in the Sierra de Atapuerca near Burgos, in northern Spain, have recently yielded one hundred fragments from five or six individual humans, dating to between 800,000 and 1 million years ago, as well as some crude stone tools (associated with animal bones) from a lower layer estimated to be a million years old.

Such finds are far more ancient than what was previously thought to be Europe's oldest human bone, the Mauer jaw in Germany, dating to about 500,000 years ago.

In sites lacking human remains, the clues to a human presence lie in stone tools. As in Africa, however, the earliest artifacts tend to be somewhat crude and rudimentary, making it often difficult to prove that they are indeed human-worked rather than products of nature. One site containing what are agreed to be definite tools is the cave of Vallonnet in the Alpes-Maritimes of southern France, which has yielded four flakes and five pebble tools of limestone and quartzite in its center, while animal bones were pushed against the walls. The cave had no traces of fire. Its occupation is dated to about 900,000 years ago.

Archaic pebble industries are also known from a number of areas—for example the high terraces of Catalonia and Roussillon (Spain and France) and those of the Somme (France)—which are thought to date back to at least 800,000 years ago.

These remains, however, are young when compared to the claims being made for a number of sites in the Massif Central, France, a crucial region for the investigation of early occupations since its volcanic layers not only afford good conservation but also allow accurate dating. The best-known site is that of Chilhac, in the upper valley of the Allier, which is rich in early fauna but which has also yielded a very archaic pebble industry of choppers, cores, and flakes. Unfortunately its date of 1.9 million years has been obtained for the fauna rather than for the industry, but some researchers believe that the two are contemporaneous.

More recently, claims have emerged from the region that Europe may have been occupied up to 2.5 million years ago. The principal proponent of this view, the French prehistorian Eugène Bonifay, has discovered what seem to be crude tools of quartz at a site called Saint Eble, located near Langeac at the foot of Mont Coupet, an extinct volcano in the Auvergne region of the Massif Central. Several hundred flakes and chunks of quartz have been recovered from deposits that lie beneath (and are therefore older than) animal fossils known to be around 2 million years old, and also beneath debris from the volcano of about the same age.

The crucial question is whether the flakes and pebbles were worked artificially or are products of nature. Bonifay believes that at least five of the quartz pieces are of unquestioned human manufacture, though other specialists remain divided on the issue: some argue that the "tools" may in fact have been produced by volcanic eruption.

If human remains were to be found with the tools, this would be a decisive factor, but meanwhile sites in other parts of the world are accepted by many specialists simply on the evidence of stone tools. In the absence of bones, speculation as to the identity of these first European tool-makers remains just that, though most assume it was some form of *Homo erectus* or perhaps even *Homo habilis* for the earliest sites.

Some support for the European claims has also been emerging in northern Asia in recent years. In 1991, the complete and very archaic lower jaw of an adult hominid was found in the republic of Georgia, in the city of Dmanisi. It has been dated to about 1.4 million years ago, and assigned to an early *Homo erectus* or an even older hominid. It was found with archaic stone tools of volcanic tuff and some fractured faunal remains.

Moreover, in the 1980s the Russian archaeologist Yuri Mochanov discovered a very early stone-tool industry at the site of Diring in Siberia which he believes to be at least 1.8 million years old, and perhaps even 3.2 million on the basis of palaeoenvironmental data. The pebble tools are claimed to resemble those from Olduvai Gorge, Tanzania, more closely than those from any other Early Pleistocene site, and have led him to resurrect the long-ignored theory of a nontropical origin for humankind. While few researchers agree with Mochanov's earliest date, he has recently found considerable support among American specialists not only for the claim that the industry is humanly made, but also for a date of at least 500,000 years ago. In view of the Georgian jaw, a date of 1.8 million no longer seems preposterous for a site in Siberia.

In short, the traditional scenario of a rather late entrance of *Homo erectus* into Europe no more than 900,000 years ago is being gradually undermined, not only by discoveries of stone tools throughout Europe that may be at least twice as old, but also by the Dmanisi jaw in Georgia and the Diring finds in Siberia which point to a human presence in northern Asia by at least 1.4 million B.P., and perhaps far earlier. The next few years will undoubtedly produce more such claims and, one hopes, further well-dated artifacts and hominid remains which will help clarify this new version of events.

[See also EUROPE: THE EUROPEAN PALEOLITHIC PERIOD; HUMANS, MODERN: PEOPLING OF THE GLOBE; PALEOLITHIC: LOWER AND MIDDLE PALEOLITHIC.]

■ *Les Premiers Habitants de l'Europe: 1,500,000–100,000 ans.* (1982). E. Bonifay and B. Vandermeersch, eds , *Les Premiers Européens*, Actes du 114e Congrès nat. des Sociétés Savantes, Paris 1989 (1991). P. G. Bahn, "Treasure of the Sierra Atapuerca," *Archaeology* 49 (1) (1996): 45–48.

Paul G. Bahn

EUROPE, Origins of Food Production in. Food production may be taken primarily to mean the husbandry of domesticated animals and plants, although the contribution of hunting and gathering to food supplies must also be mentioned. This essay describes the origins and spread in Europe of the main domestic animals connected with food production (not the horse) and the main cultivated plants used for food (not hemp). Most of the taxa discussed were first domesticated in the Near East or elsewhere in Asia long before they arrived in Europe.

Evidence for the animals is provided principally by bones found on archaeological sites, where they probably collected as rubbish. Exact study of the bone anatomy can show the state of domestication of the individuals from which they were derived, as well as features such as age, size, nutritional state, and pathology. Such information often provides clues as to the methods of stock raising and which animal products were used.

Much of the evidence for plants comes from their charred (partially burnt) remains, especially those of cereals, since cereal ears were heated to permit threshing, and cereal products were sometimes burnt. Charred remains need special sieving and floating processes to extract them from the soil matrix. At some sites, plant remains are also preserved by waterlogging, or being kept wet enough to exclude oxygen and hence to halt decay, especially in northern Europe. There is also some evidence from pollen, although it cannot usually be identified to such an exact degree (e.g., to determine the precise species) as can larger remains.

The evidence from plants and animals is very hard to quantify, since the chance of being preserved may have had a large effect on the chance of the different remains being recovered. Relative abundance of remains is assumed, however, to have some relationship to the past abundance of the different plants and animals. The timescale is provided by uncalibrated radiocarbon dates given as years before present (B.P.). The evidence is uneven, with plenty of modern data from some parts of Europe, such as *Greece, but so far practically nothing from others, such as Albania.

Domestication in Asia. The main domestic animals used for food are cattle, sheep, goat, and pigs as well as domestic fowl (hens, geese, and ducks). Animals are versatile; cattle, sheep, and goat can provide many useful items besides meat, such as milk and cheese, wool, leather, and horn. Sheep and goat were domesticated in the *Near East around 9000 B.P., cattle before 8000 B.P., pigs around 8000 B.P., and hens around 3000 B.P., while domestication may also have occurred independently elsewhere, for example, in the Far East. Evidence of domestic status is provided by anatomical features such as decrease in size as compared with the animal's wild relatives.

The main crop plants were various primitive forms of domesticated wheat and barley, together with peas, beans, lentils, and flax (used as an oilseed as well as for the fiber). The earliest domestic cereal, cultivated einkorn wheat, has been found at sites in Syria and Jordan dated to around 10,000 B.P., and cultivation spread westward through the Near East in about 9000 B.P. The first finds of domestic emmer wheat (the principal early crop along with cultivated einkorn wheat and barley), are dated to around 9800 B.P. The first lentils are found at the same time, and peas a little later.

Domestication in Southeast Europe. The arrival of domestic animals in Europe is graphically shown by the sharp change in the range of animal remains in the levels dated to about 8000 B.P. and after at the Franchthi cave in Greece. The cave deposits span the period from roughly 14,000 to 5000 B.P. Before 6000 B.P. the bone assemblage is of wild animals such as red deer, wild cattle, horses, and wild pig; after that date, mostly of sheep and goat. It is hard to identify the latter exactly as either sheep or goat.

Evidence from charred plant remains at Franchthi cave also shows a change from undomesticated plants that had been collected, such as wild oats and barley, vetches, peas and lentils, in the levels before ca. 8000 B.P. After this, cultivated crops are present, dating to the early Neolithic. Other sites in Greece, such as Argissa, Achilleion, Gediki, and Sesklo, show similar evidence of crops such as einkorn and emmer wheats, cultivated barley, lentil, pea, and bitter vetch. They have been dated from about 9000 to 8000 B.P. Farming appears to have spread into Europe from the general area of the Bosphorus, where the sea crossing is shortest. The Mediterranean Sea seems to have provided an immigration route at a somewhat later date, when seafaring had developed.

Farming had spread throughout the Balkans and into the Danube basin by ca. 7000 B.P., reaching all of Greece, Bulgaria, Bosnia-Herzegovina, Macedonia, and Serbia. Flax joins the three cereals as a crop around 8000–7000 B.P., used for its oil as well as for linen fiber.

Domestication in Southwest Europe. Domestic animals appear between 8000 and 7000 B.P. in the western Mediterranean, for instance, in the Iberian Peninsula. The change from wild to domestic plants, dated to around 8000 B.P., is best documented by the results from the cave deposits of the Grotta del'Uzzo in northwest *Sicily, where einkorn and emmer wheats, barley, lentil, and fig were found. There is also a little evidence from the south of France. In Spain the earliest cereals, a similar selection to those just mentioned, are dated to around 6500 B.P. The somewhat later appearance of cultivated plants here as compared to the Balkans may represent the slow spread of farming westward around the Mediterranean coast, although it is only recently that much evidence has begun to appear from this region.

The Linearbandkeramik in Central Europe. The LBK, or Linear Pottery (*Bandkeramik) culture, was not the earliest Neolithic culture everywhere it is found. It was, however, one of the most widespread, distributed extensively in the north and northwest of Hungary along the Danube basin and across the plains of central Europe as far north as the Netherlands. LBK settlements are mainly on fertile loess soils, and date from around 6500 to 5500 B.P. These settlements represent the first farming in suitable loessic areas of Germany and the Netherlands; less favorable areas with other soils were farmed later. LBK farmers grew einkorn, emmer, flax, peas, and lentils, a little barley in some areas, and poppy used as an oilseed in others. Broomcorn millet, an introduction from central Asia, occurs at some LBK sites from ca. 6000 B.P. Chess (Bromus secalinus), a grass that grew as a cornfield weed, may also have been cultivated for food. The food produced by cultivation was probably supplemented by edible plants gathered from the surroundings.

Bone is not generally well preserved in the slightly acid loess soils settled by the LBK but it is clear that farmers' cattle were the most common domestic animals, followed by pigs and sheep. It is hard to tell which animal products were the most important. There is some evidence of cheesemaking equipment, which indicates dairying, though age and mortality patterns suggest slaughter of animals for meat. It is likely that everything possible was used.

Other Neolithic Cultures of Northern Europe. Later Neolithic cultures spread out from the loessic plains into other regions. Especially good evidence has been obtained from later Neolithic lakeside settlements in the Alpine region, occupied from around 6000 B.P. Here a form of bread wheat was the main crop, together with einkorn and emmer wheats, barley, and opium poppy, the latter used as an oilseed. There is evidence of sheep, goat, and cattle from ca. 5500 B.P. in the Alpine region, in place of the red deer, roe deer, aurochs, and wild boar found in Mesolithic assemblages. In the northern European plains, however, the remains from cultures such as the Ellerbek culture in northern Germany and the Ertebølle culture in Denmark show evidence of continued hunting, fishing, and gathering up to 5000 B.P.

Cereal farming spread fairly slowly into Scandinavia. The earliest finds of emmer wheat have been dated to 4600 B.P. in Denmark, where early cereal finds often occur together with quantities of wild edible plants. Further north still, the earliest cereals so far are naked barley, dated to ca.

4000 B.P. in Norway. The earliest evidence of cereals from Finland is as late as 3250 B.P., and again consists of naked barley. Finally, crops and domestic animals were brought to Iceland by the Norse settlers around 1200 B.P., making this the last part of Europe to which food production methods were introduced.

The earliest Neolithic evidence in southern Britain, around 5500 B.P., shows that cereals were grown but that large quantities of wild plants were also used, such as hazel nuts and wild apples. The sheep and goat remains represent domestic animals that had been brought to Britain, since they did not occur in the wild there. The earliest remains of cattle and pig may represent either introduced domestic stock or local wild fauna, although there are signs of domestic pig by 5000 B.P. The chicken did not arrive until 2000 B.P. Agriculture gradually spread northward, as shown by the results from Balbridie in Scotland dated ca. 4500 B.P., with emmer wheat, club wheat, barley, and flax together with wild apples and hazel nuts. There were no wild aurochs in Ireland, so cattle must have been brought there from ca. 5400 B.P.

Later Prehistoric and Early Historic Cultures in the Mediterranean. In the Mediterranean region, the olive, grape, and fig are three of the most important traditional food plants after cereals. Olives were probably first cultivated in the Near East, and the earliest appearances in Europe are at Bronze Age sites on Crete, such as Myrtos, and on the mainland of Greece at Tiryns from ca. 5000 B.P. The grape, although probably domesticated earlier in the Near East, seems to have been in cultivation in Greece at least by ca. 4000 B.P., according to the evidence from Lerna. The fig is present at a number of Neolithic sites in Greece from ca. 8000 to 7000 B.P. It is not possible to tell whether fig was cultivated, although it probably was by the time that other Mediterranean crops were. The most important Mediterranean crops, the olive, grape vine, and fig, were domesticated and spread around the Mediterranean from around 3000 B.P., probably carried by the Greeks and Phoenicians. Of these, only the grape could be grown far from its Mediterranean home, by the Romans as they moved into Europe. Other fruit, such as apples, pears, cherries, and plums, seem to have been spread through Europe by the Romans around 2000 B.P.

Later Prehistoric Cultures of North Central Europe. During the Bronze Age in northern Europe (ca. 4000–3200 B.P.), further crops came into cultivation. One of these was spelt wheat, which spread from the Caucasus, becoming important by ca. 4000 B.P. in Slovakia and by 3200 in southern Germany, where it remained an important crop. Oats, which had grown as a weed among cereals, became domesticated and cultivated from around 2000 B.P., as indicated by occasional unmixed finds that indicate it was a crop, not a weed. Finally, rye, which had been a cornfield weed, became a crop in its own right after about 2000 B.P., and more especially from 1500 B.P. Rye flourished—and has continued to flourish—particularly in areas with poor, sandy soils, where it was hardier and more productive than other cereals.

[See also AGRICULTURE; DOMESTICATION OF ANIMALS; DOMESTICATION OF PLANTS; EUROPE: THE EUROPEAN NEOLITHIC PERIOD.]

■ Simon J. M. Davis, *The Archaeology of Animals* (1987). Peter Bogucki, *Forest Farmers and Stockherders* (1988). Annie Milles, Diane Williams, and Neville Gardner, *The Beginnings of Agriculture,* British Archaeological Reports (International Series) 496 (1989). Willem van Zeist, Krystina Wasylikowa, and Karl-Ernst Behre, *Progress in Old World Palaeoethnobotany* (1991). Daniel Zohary and Maria Hopf, *Domestication of Plants in the Old World* (1993).

James Greig

EUROPEAN COLONIES IN THE NEW WORLD. Any discussion of European colonial ventures in the New World begins with "who was first?" No one can argue that it was Columbus who opened the New World to serious European colonization, but there is considerable argument as to whether or not he actually was the first European to make landfall across the Atlantic. Archaeological investigations have confirmed what historians have long suspected, but could not prove conclusively. Columbus may have opened the floodgates to European colonization, but there was definitely a European presence in the New World beforehand. Excavations at the L'Anse aux Meadows site in Newfoundland have yielded proof of a Norse occupation dating to the tenth century A.D. Archaeologists recovered a variety of Norse artifacts among the ruined foundations of several structures including a longhouse. This site demonstrates that the Vikings did not indeed attempt the settlement of "Vinland"; however, their reasons for leaving and not attempting any further colonization remain a mystery.

Sparse archaeological data corroborates the historical documentation that the European presence was fleeting prior to the sixteenth century. The exploration and exploitation of the New World began in earnest with the first voyage of Columbus. The question of where Columbus made first landfall is far from resolved with a half dozen islands vying for that honor. The location of the first settlement, La Navidad (where Columbus left the crew of the Santa Maria after it ran aground on Christmas Eve, 1492), is still questionable, although the site of En Bas Saline on the north coast of Haiti is a good candidate.

There, archaeologists have discovered what appears to be the village of Guacanagaric, the Arawak chief who befriended Columbus. Using various means of remote sensing, they have traced the perimeter of this large habitation site and found remains of European fauna and metal artifacts. The data recovered from this site is especially important in that it provides excellent information concerning the indigenous population at the point of first contact.

Spain immediately recognized the economic opportunities that the New World presented. Exploration was quickly followed by colonization. The site of Isabella on the north coast of the Dominican Republic illustrates Spain's commitment to New World colonization. Archaeologists have delineated a fortified enclave overlooking a shallow harbor as well as a large residential section nearby. The presence of a pottery kiln attests to the permanence of the settlement and the tenacity of its inhabitants in the face of unfavorable geographic conditions. Investigations at this site and the site of Puerto Real, on the other side of Hispaniola, indicate that the Spaniards wished to remain as Spanish as possible, but were not above substituting native goods for Spanish in the less visible, utilitarian aspects of their daily lives.

This same pattern of acculturation is evident at the sites of St. Augustine and Santa Elena on the coasts of north Florida and South Carolina, respectively. These two sites were founded in the mid-sixteenth century (St. Augustine in 1565, Santa Elena in 1566) to guard the northern frontier of the Spanish colonies from the encroachment of other European powers. Though of little commercial value to the

Spanish Crown, these outposts protected the Spanish treasure fleets that passed on the trade winds. Their presence discouraged the establishment of non-Spanish colonies in North America until the seventeenth century.

Another example of an early European presence in North America are the remains of a Basque whaling station at Red Bay, Labrador. The prodigious schools of cod in the North Atlantic had long drawn European fisherman to the North Atlantic. Whales also abounded in these waters. The whaling station at Red Bay (1550 to 1600) is tangible evidence of this early European commercial activity. Excavations on land and in the bay itself have recovered a wealth of well-preserved artifacts that provide revealing insights into the truly industrial nature of this processing center.

Ironically, when most people consider the Spanish presence in North America it is usually the missions of the American Southwest and California that come to mind. Even though these sites are much younger than their counterparts in the Southeastern U.S., the more durable stone and adobe structural ruins are more tangible and hence a visible reminder of the Spanish presence in the New World. They have also attracted a considerable amount of scientific research. The La Purisma mission site in central California (early nineteenth century) is one of the most thoroughly studied of these sites. Besides the usual architectural and artifact studies, the site has revealed much about the way the Spaniards interacted with the native population.

The French settlement system was somewhat different than the Spanish one, though it too had its economic underpinnings. Although the French came to control vast reaches of the New World, they never established the same presence as the Spanish or the British. Ultimately, most of New France was lost and French influence was restricted to small enclaves in the New World.

The efforts of the French to control North America is evident in the string of fortifications established during the seventeenth and eighteenth centuries. Fortress Louisbourg is an outstanding example of French military architecture. Based on the extensive archaeological work that has been carried out over the past three decades, the accurate reconstruction of this eighteenth-century fort and town is the showcase of Parks Canada.

Two interior sites in the French military strategy were Fort Michilimackinac and Fort de Chartres. A wooden fort at the northern tip of Michigan, Michilimackinac served as a trade hub in France's key North American fur trade enterprise. Fort de Chartres was an impressive stone edifice in the most remote part of New France—the Illinois country. The extensive archaeological work at these eighteenth-century forts and at smaller fur trading posts demonstrates that the French incorporated more native traits into their own cultural repertoire. This should not be too surprising given the close French and Indian alliances in conflicts with other European powers.

The most familiar colonial power to generations of American schoolchildren was, of course, England. British colonial sites have been extensively studied by North American historical archaeologists. England was as committed as Spain to a truly colonial venture, with the major difference being, at least initially, that the British launched private rather than state-sponsored ventures. Although much of the Spanish exploration and settlements were privately financed, the Spanish Crown had more of a direct hand in the governing of these earliest colonial ventures.

Ironically, later in the colonial period, the English Crown came to more thoroughly dominate her colonies.

Two early English settlements that have had extensive archaeological research associated with their public interpretation are Plimouth Plantation and the Jamestown site. Much of the work at these two coastal sites has gone into interpreting past lifeways at these seventeenth-century settlements. Both sites have active living history programs based, in part, on the data recovered from over several decades of archaeological research.

Archaeologists unearthed the grimmer aspects of seventeenth-century English colonial life at the Wolstenholme site in tidewater Virginia. Part of an area known as *Martin's Hundred, Wolstenholme provides a glimpse of the rigors of life on a colonial farm, including the consequences of conflict with the resident native population. The nearby reconstructed eighteenth-century town of Williamsburg illustrates the full-blown English colonial pattern which, with the exception of the incorporation of certain native food items, had virtually eliminated any Native American influence.

Further south, archaeological work at Bethabara and Brunswick, North Carolina, has pursued a scientific approach to colonial archaeology. Archaeological work has focused on determining patterns of trash disposal for different groups at different times as well as applying mathematical formulas to the study of material culture to better determine when sites were occupied. These methods have been applied to other colonial sites including British, French, and Spanish sites across the United States.

England, France, and Spain composed the primary European colonial powers in the New World, but certainly not the only ones. The Portuguese established colonies and missions in South America. However, little archaeological work has been reported for these sites. Likewise, the Swedes and Danes dabbled in the New World, but their efforts were relatively minor and the archaeology reflects this.

The Dutch were active in the Caribbean and archaeological projects on the islands of St. Eustasius and Curaçao have been carried out at these entrepots. The Dutch, consummate middlemen that they were, viewed the Caribbean as a purely business venture. Their presence in New York might be seen as more of a colonial venture, although the acquisition of Long Island was handled in a stereotypically shrewd business transaction. Archaeological work in New York City has uncovered significant evidence of the Dutch presence in North America.

The history of archaeological inquiry into the European colonial experience is not unlike the general history of American archaeology. Early interest in colonial sites was antiquarian in nature. Archaeological digs were designed specifically to recover artifacts for display or to assist in the reconstruction of the site. Starting in the late 1960s and early 1970s archaeological investigations took on a more anthropological orientation, studying such processes as acculturation and status variability as well as pursuing a science of material culture.

The American Bicentennial gave a huge boost to historical archaeological programs. English colonial sites received the lion's share of attention of course, although other types of colonial sites were studied as well, especially in relation to the English colonial effort. More recently, the Columbian Quincentennial has again raised the public's awareness of European colonial efforts in the New World. This time, however, much of the attention concerned the impact of European colonization on the indigenous peoples.

The impact of Old World technology and ideas on New World populations is readily detectable in the archaeological record. Although extensive historical records exist for much of the colonial period, the documentary record tends to dwell primarily on the lives of important people or events. These documents also demonstrate bias on the part of the author, who was often trying to convey his or her perspective on the events. Colonial archaeology has given voice to the common folk and illuminated their everyday lives. The stories of socially invisible, disenfranchised groups such as slaves and ethnic minorities are being told through archaeology. Far from being a scavenger hunt into a well-known era, colonial archaeology is rounding out the historical record and providing a better understanding of this crucial period in the history of the New World.

[See also CARIBBEAN, ARCHAEOLOGY IN THE; HISTORICAL ARCHAEOLOGY; MESOAMERICA: HISTORICAL ARCHAEOLOGY OF MESOAMERICA; MISSION ARCHAEOLOGY; NORSE IN NORTH AMERICA; NORTH AMERICA: HISTORICAL ARCHAEOLOGY OF NORTH AMERICA; PLANTATION LIFE IN THE SOUTHERN UNITED STATES; SOUTH AMERICA: HISTORICAL ARCHAEOLOGY OF SOUTH AMERICA.]

■ Lyle M. Stone, *Fort Michilimackinac, 1715–1781* (1974). Ivor Noël Hume, *Martin's Hundred* (1982). Kathleen Deagan, *Spanish St. Augustine* (1983). William W Fitzhugh, ed., *Cultures in Contact* (1985). Charles R. Ewen, *From Spaniard to Creole* (1991). Lisa Falk, *Historical Archaeology* (1991). John A. Walthall, ed., *French Colonial Archaeology* (1991).

Charles R. Ewen

EVANS, Arthur. Arthur John Evans (1851–1941) was the son of John Evans, a paper manufacturer and highly respected archaeologist. He inherited his love of the past from his father, using his microscopic eyesight to study coins and prehistoric jewelry. After graduating from Oxford in 1875, he spent some time wandering in the Balkans as a journalist, being thrown in jail for his pains. He became curator of Oxford's Ashmolean Museum in 1884 and spent a quarter-century reviving the fortunes of a moribund institution. At the same time, he developed an interest in Mycenaean archaeology and the undeciphered script on their seals and gemstones. These seals led him to Crete and the unexcavated *Knossos site, which he purchased in 1896. The Knossos excavations began in 1900 and continued intermittently for thirty years. Evans revealed a labyrinthlike palace and a hitherto unknown civilization, which he named Minoan, after the legendary King Minos of the Greeks. He used the family fortune to reconstruct much of the two-story royal palace and the frescoes on its walls. At the same time, he used cross-dates from dated Minoan vessels found in ancient Egyptian sites along the Nile to date Minoan civilization to between 2000 and 1250 B.C. Its origins were entirely indigenous, among simple farming communities dating to before 3000 B.C. Arthur Evans devoted the rest of his long life to the excavation and publication of the palace of Knossos, which he described in his classic monograph *The Palace of Minos*, published between 1921 and 1935. But the secrets of Minoan script eluded him, only to be partially deciphered in 1952, long after his death. Evans was an archaeologist with the rare ability to reconstruct a civilization from small clues, like the Minoan seals that led him to Knossos and archaeological immortality.

[See also HISTORY OF ARCHAEOLOGY BEFORE 1900: EUROPEAN ARCHAEOLOGY; HISTORY OF ARCHAEOLOGY FROM 1900 TO 1950: NEAR EASTERN ARCHAEOLOGY.]

■ Joan Evans, *Time and Chance* (1943). Arthur Evans, *The Palace of Minos* (1921–1935).

Brian M. Fagan

EVOLUTION. See HUMAN EVOLUTION.

EXCAVATION

Introduction
Excavation Strategies
Mapping and Recording of Excavations
Artifact Recovery in Excavations
Publication of Findings From Excavations

INTRODUCTION

Archaeological excavation is one of a number of approaches used to acquire information about human behavior in the past. In the early days of archaeology, excavation was the only technique and in practice it differed little from mining operations. Today, however, it is but one of many techniques. It is a highly refined scientific process and is employed only when justified by a formal research design because of its destructive nature.

Typically, archaeology is equated with excavation, and although this is not strictly true, excavation accounts for a significant amount of the information upon which our current knowledge of the human past is based. Alternatives to excavation include detection and recording of surface-exposed artifacts, remote sensing as in aerial photography and geophysical prospecting, and the examination of soil and plant distributions. The advantage of such approaches is that they are nondestructive and permit widespread coverage of entire landscapes. Yet, at some point in nearly every archaeological project, probing beneath the surface becomes necessary to gain access to the hidden dimensions of the archaeological record.

The allure of buried archaeological deposits lies in their removal, to some degree, from the disturbance suffered by surface exposure. In the extreme, a set of artifacts may become sealed in a deposit which preserves the exact spatial relationships of the event of which they were a part. Deliberate burial creates such conditions, as when artifacts are cached and the dead entombed. Sealed deposits may also result from accidental events such as sudden flooding, avalanches, and volcanic eruptions. Most commonly, however, burial results from the gradual accumulation of materials from geological and cultural processes. Therefore, apart from exceptional circumstances, buried deposits once were exposed and excavation always must take account of this fact.

Before planning an excavation, a site must be located, and this process may employ some of the nondestructive alternatives to excavation. Wide-ranging pedestrian surveys, inspection of remote sensing data, aerial reconnaissance, and regional scale soil survey all may be used for site discovery. Test pitting and shovel testing may also be used to find places that exhibit properties traceable to past utilization of a place. The latter are particularly prominent in cultural resource management (CRM) as it is practiced in the United States.

In planning an archaeological excavation, a process which starts with the formulation of a research problem and ends with the publication of the results of the work, intensive applications of nondestructive methods can again be helpful. For example, systematic surface collection can help define the location of subsurface deposits, at least for the uppermost strata, although it must always be remembered that such exposures point only to specialized parts of a complete occupied place, such as a dump, a collapsed structure, or a workshop. Geophysical prospecting instruments, including resistivity meters and magnetometers, can reveal the locations of structures, walls, pottery kilns, and other facilities within a site. Testing of soil samples for chemical traces of past activities may reveal parts of the original settlement that do not contain massive artifact remains, the foundations of structures, or other more visible elements. Aerial photography, and other remote sensing techniques, can also provide valuable information.

Preparation for excavation necessarily includes making a topographic map, and archaeologists must either become skilled in surveying and mapping, or be able to employ professional surveyors. Projects on sites with complicated, extensive architectural ruins typically include a surveyor and an architectural draftsman as permanent members of the staff. Skilled use of transits and alidades, to name two common surveying instruments, is essential also in the laying out of excavation grids and recording the location, or provenance, of finds.

Excavation strategy normally takes either a horizontal or vertical direction depending on whether the research problem calls for examining settlement layout or the history of occupation. Many special approaches have been developed, including the balk/debris layer, checkerboard, vertical face, isolated block, quartering, and step trenching methods.

Naturally, the specific qualities of an archaeological deposit exert a great influence on the organization and conduct of excavation. The sparse remains of small-scale societies differ greatly from the massive remains of urban civilizations. Stratified open sites present different challenges and opportunities than stratified deposits in rock shelters. Deflated desert surfaces, arctic permafrost soils, plowed fields, and waterlogged or underwater sites also require special approaches.

Tackling the job of opening a deposit, archaeologists have employed tools and equipment ranging from bulldozers to tweezers. Heavy equipment ordinarily is used only in emergency situations when time is short. Most commonly, the archaeological tool kit consists of the shovel and pick with trowels, brushes, and dental picks on hand for detailed work. Always present is a pocket ruler, plumb bob, and jack knife.

Upon discovery, archaeological remains (cultural features, cultural items, or ecofacts) must be plotted on the site map and photographed in place (in situ) as well as cataloged. With the advent of inexpensive, small-scale computers, archaeological records management is routinely computerized and hand-held units are made that permit data collection directly in the field.

Electronics has revolutionized archaeology in many ways, and it is now possible to integrate the records of topographic surveys, geophysical prospecting, remote sensing, and excavation so that field investigation and hypothesis testing can proceed hand in hand. As these technologies advance, the precision and efficiency of excavation should increase with the added benefit that more can be learned from smaller exposures. Furthermore, the ideal of preserving as much as possible of a site for future archaeologists is enhanced.

As can be seen, an archaeological expedition can engage the services of numerous specialists. Apart from the excavators, a dig might draw upon experts in all branches of science and technology. Not the least important of these specialists is the conservator. Upon removal from the ground, artifacts and other materials are instantly vulnerable to processes of deterioration to which they were immune while buried. Applying principles of materials science, the conservator sees to it that artifacts survive the trauma of excavation.

Records and collection management is a critical element of an archaeological excavation. It must be included in the advance planning right along with excavation strategy and not left to the last moment. An excavation can be considered a failure if the notes, photographs, catalogs, and labeled samples and specimens are not saved and protected. Archaeologists are professionally committed to publishing the results of their work, but having done so, the evidence cannot be abandoned. It must be accessible to other scientists and scholars so that the original conclusions can be checked and alternative hypotheses tested. Archaeological records and collections must be preserved as well so that they can be restudied as new research problems and analytical techniques emerge with the advancement of the field.

In many countries, the United States in particular, increasingly demanding antiquities legislation has forced archaeology to take stock of its ethics and practices. Advance consideration of where the products of an investigation will be housed (curated) has become a required part of developing an explicit research design. Interaction with descendants of the groups producing the archaeological remains has gained strong emphasis, as has the treatment of human remains and objects of sacred value. Internationally, laws have been enacted to govern archaeological research and to ensure that professional standards are upheld and that materials of significance remain in the country of their origin. Such legislation, along with technological advances, is moving archaeology forward as a legitimate science.

[See also CULTURAL RESOURCE MANAGEMENT, articles on COLLECTIONS MANAGEMENT, SITE MANAGEMENT; SITE LOCATION: FINDING ARCHAEOLOGICAL SITES.]

■ M. Joukowsky, A Complete Manual of Field Archaeology; Tools and Techniques of Field Work for Archaeologists. (1980). E. Harris, Principles of Archaeological Stratigraphy, 2d ed. (1989). B. G. Trigger, A History of Archaeological Thought (1989). G. R. Willey and J. Sabloff, A History of American Archaeology, 3d ed. (1993).

William S. Dancey

EXCAVATION STRATEGIES

Early archaeological excavation was little more than mining for artifacts, and engineers were frequently consulted for advice on tunneling into deep deposits. Although a minerals extraction approach such as this continues today among vandals and uneducated collectors, professional archaeology has changed radically. Where at one time little or no attention was given to the spatial relationships or context of things in an archaeological deposit, today a set of rigorous standards guides archaeological digging. At the core of these controls is the need to record finds within a local grid system and to document the soils and sediments containing the finds. Application of these standards potentially allows the excavated deposit to be reassembled from notes, photographs, and maps.

In theory, two kinds of relationships characterize an archaeological deposit: vertical and horizontal. Vertical relationships potentially have meaning for the inference of time (culture history) while horizontal relationships inform on the spatial organization of activities and elements of the built environment (settlement layout). Thus, an archaeologist interested exclusively in constructing a chronological sequence would excavate trenches. The archaeologist wanting to map the layout of a past settlement would concentrate on exposing large areas of a single occupation layer. In practice these fundamental strategies might be combined.

Vertical excavation can take several forms. Along with simple trenching, the vertical-face method has been popular in the past and was especially favored by archaeologists working in the Midwest from the 1920s through the 1940s. This approach involves lining up workers at the edge of an occupation and advancing in regular increments through a deposit. Sediments from the active trench are thrown into the previously excavated trench. Step trenching is a variation which blends with the horizontal approach. By this strategy upper layers are exposed more than lower layers, giving the effect of stair steps. The isolated block strategy, an effective but little-used approach, involves digging into pairs of intersecting trenches which upon completion define a thick column, or block, of the deposit.

In all vertical excavation the aim is to identify individual deposition units, or strata, or to remove them one by one. In deposits with no discernible stratification, or within thick strata, many archaeologists use arbitrary levels to segregate finds. If this strategy of metrical *stratigraphy is adopted, the excavator must be alert for evidence of stratification and shift to these natural units when they appear.

Horizontal excavation can be accomplished in several ways. One is by surface stripping. This strategy commonly is used in plowed fields where no evidence of stratification can be found. Ideally, the plow zone is sampled before removal. If house foundations and facility outlines are present they should show up clearly in the exposed sediments. In the case of a stratified deposit the horizontal exposure can proceed downward by level stripping. Layer by layer the excavator travels into the past.

A strategy used around the world is the Wheeler-Kenyon method, named after Sir Mortimer *Wheeler and Kathleen Kenyon, British archaeologists famous for their investigations in Britain, India, and the Middle East and for their textbooks on archaeological method. Also known as the balk/debris layer approach, this strategy calls for excavating through a deposit within stratigraphic units and leaving balks of unexcavated sediment between excavation squares. The impression created after opening a large area by this strategy is that of a beehive of square cells. Its value is that the balks retain a visible record of the deposit which can be looked back at as the excavation proceeds downward. Sites with complex stratification would be impossible to dig any other way. A variation on this method calls for excavation of alternate squares in a checkerboard pattern, which permits recording continuous profiles at half the labor cost.

The strategies described above include broad alternatives from which the archaeologist may choose when planning an excavation. However, specific site types (such as rock shelters, Middle Eastern tells, *shell middens, wet sites, and submerged sites) may set limits on which method can be used productively. Burial mounds and other aboveground monuments often are excavated by a strategy known as the quadrant method. This approach entails removing opposite quarters in order to identify internal features and

expose a continuous profile of the deposit through its center along intersecting axes.

The internal features of an archaeological deposit can be approached by adapting one of the general strategies, although special procedures have been developed in many cases. Successive house floors might be peeled back in a manner resembling level stripping and pit features can be excavated effectively by quartering or sectioning. Pits, trenches, and post molds often are excavated by removing the sediments which fill them. Finally, artifacts and features can be left in place by pedestaling while excavation continues downward around them.

[See also SUBSURFACE TESTING: INTRODUCTION.]

■ Martha Joukousky, *A Complete Manual of Field Archaeology* (1980). William S. Dancey, *Archaeological Field Methods: An Introduction* (1981).

William S. Dancey

MAPPING AND RECORDING OF EXCAVATIONS

Although archaeologists agree that sound archaeological field work requires detailed recording of data, the perception of what constitutes data varies. The evidence that archaeologists record is dependent on their research strategies and preconceptions about what constitute "interesting" or useful observations. Just as archaeologists of one hundred years ago did not anticipate modern archaeologists' interest in microscopic phytoliths, microdebitage, or the magnetic fields in burned clay, archaeologists of the future will be dismayed by omissions in our data records. Progress in the discipline inevitably attracts archaeologists to new problems, and new kinds of data are needed to solve them. Consequently, there is no single "right way" to record data from archaeological sites, whether on paper or electronically.

Even though data are theory-dependent, archaeologists routinely record some types of data by convention or because of widely shared theoretical orientations. Most archaeologists' field observations concern the "archaeological context." The dimensions of archaeological context are spatial, stratigraphic, and relational.

The distribution of artifacts, features, and other relevant items in space is one of the keys of archaeological interpretation. The scale and precision with which archaeologists measure spatial context varies with the research questions of interest. In the early twentieth century, most archaeologists were content to record that an artifact came from a particular structure, or from a particular 16 by 16 feet (5 by 5 m) square. Today, archaeologists record provenience more precisely, sometimes mapping individual artifacts in place or providing the x, y, and z coordinates of each to the nearest centimeter, relative to permanent "datum" or bench mark. In other cases, they still use grids, but at a much smaller scale.

Mapping is an important way to record spatial context. Archaeologists use equipment ranging from simple measuring tapes and plumb bobs through sophisticated laser theodolites to measure the distributions of artifacts, features, and deposits in space, and to record them on maps. They endeavor to do this with accuracy and precision, but a map is always a simplification of reality because it depicts only a selection of potential observations. Accuracy is the degree to which a given measurement approximates a "true" value, while precision describes how consistent a measurement is when repeated many times. A precise measurement can be inaccurate if there is bias in the measurement method (e.g., from an improperly calibrated tape, failure to hold the tape tightly and horizontally, or failure to measure from immovable bench marks). Accuracy is never perfect, nor is there a general rule for adequate precision, but archaeologists must decide how much precision and accuracy is appropriate, and adopt the most efficient means to achieve it. No amount of measurement effort or high technology will improve accuracy if there is no fixed datum. In fact, often the most accurate and precise way to plot provenience is by triangulating from two bench marks with tape and plumb bob. In addition, measuring to the nearest millimeter is pointless if a line thickness on the final map represents 1 centimeter (i.e., a 0.5 millimeter line at 1 : 20), or if the edges of a feature are so ambiguous that excavators cannot agree on them with better precision than 10 centimeters.

Stratigraphic context is another vital component of archaeological recording. *Site formation processes, such as dumping, alluviation, collapse of structures, pit digging, or erosion, create the deposits and interfaces that archaeologists document. Deposits are volumes of material added to an archaeological site, while interfaces are surfaces corresponding to the removal of material, as by erosion or pit digging. Archaeologists record evidence for the sequential order of deposits and interfaces, both as an aid to chronology and to understand the history of a site's formation. Although archaeologists record deposits and surfaces during their removal, they also draw and photograph "balks," or vertical sections, through the sites to document depositional histories. They often use a "Harris matrix," a kind of graph, to organize the vertical relationships between deposits and interfaces and sort them into chronological order. They also record a physical description of each deposit. Munsell charts, designed to standardize the description of soil colors, are a valuable tool for this purpose. Typically the physical description also includes the frequency, size, and kind of stones, the soil texture (sand, loam, or clay), pH, and compaction.

Every recording system has a way for each artifact, sample, or bag of artifacts to be labelled with a code describing its spatial and stratigraphic context. This allows later analysts to calculate such measures as artifact proportions and densities, and to determine whether there are patterns in their distributions.

Recording archaeological field methods and theoretical orientation is important too. Since not all archaeologists use the same research design, sampling design, or methods of measurement, it is critical that the record include details of procedures. Otherwise an apparent pattern in the data, such as the lack of fish or carbonized seeds in some contexts, may result simply from the mesh sizes of screens or from the volumes of soil subjected to flotation.

[See also STRATIGRAPHY.]

■ Philip Barker, Techniques of Archaeological Excavation, second edition (1982). Philip Barker, Understanding Archaeological Excavation (1986). Edward C. Harris, Principles of Archaeological Stratigraphy, 2nd edition (1989). Mark Monmonier, How to Lie with Maps (1991). Daniel Arroyo-Bishop, "Further Structuring of the ArchéoDATA System" in Computer Applications and Quantitative Methods in Archaeology 1991, eds. Gary Lock and Jonathan Moffet (1992), pp. 89–94. Katherine Gruel, Olivier Buchsenschutz, Jean-François Alliot and Hervé Murgalé, "Arkeoplan: A New Tool for the Archaeologist," in Computing the Past. Computer Applications and Quantitative Methods in Archaeology, eds. Jens Andresen, Torsten Madsen, and Irwin Scollar (1993), pp. 81–84.

E. B. Banning

ARTIFACT RECOVERY IN EXCAVATIONS

The goal of artifact recovery in excavations is to be sure that the context of the artifact has been clearly established and is accurately documented. Recovery of context requires careful measurement of vertical and horizontal provenience and an understanding—in the field—of a specimen's stratigraphic placement and cultural association. Artifacts must be bagged (and sometimes assigned a field number) and all relevant data recorded on the bag and in the field notes before the materials are sent to the laboratory for processing.

Different research designs will require varying artifact recovery methods, depending upon the contextual data that are required. For example, artifact recovery may be guided by "piece-plotting," the in situ documentation of all artifacts and associated debris: In sites where chipped stone was being worked, such precise recording may allow for "refitting" of flakes to cores or bifaces. Whether the archaeologist uses natural stratigraphic levels for excavation or subdivides these into arbitrary increments, the deposits are usually carefully dug with a trowel and whisk broom, and artifacts, when found, are plotted. However, the primary technique to insure total artifact recovery is screening or sifting. Usually, a screen of one-quarter-inch (60 mm) mesh ensures the recovery of most artifacts, animal bones, and other remains; however, at many sites, one-eighth of an inch (30 mm) or one-sixteenth of an inch (15 mm) mesh is preferable, to maximize recovery of smaller animal bones, snails, seeds, and tiny chipping debris. Such screens are of varying sizes; they can be mounted on sawhorses, or suspended or built with legs so they can be used as "shaker screens." The screens can also be "nested," with the quarter-inch (60 mm) over the eighth-inch (30 mm) or sixteenth-inch (15 mm); large objects can be quickly collected from the upper screen, while the fine materials on the lower can be bagged and picked at the laboratory. In any case, the goals of an excavation dictate the recovery method. The archaeologist has to plan the types of recovery methods to be used at a site, but also be willing to adapt to techniques that may prove to yield better recovery.

In excavating chipped stone workshops, such as those at Colha, Belize, a quarter-inch (60 mm) or eighth of an inch (30 mm) mesh screen is useless when there are debitage quantities of several hundred thousand flakes per cubic meter. Harry J. Shafer and Thomas R. Hester devised "sorting boards," which were table tops on which lithic debris from an excavation level could be sorted, and artifacts selected from the vast number of flakes. To quantify flakes, and to obtain an unbiased sample for technological study, large column samples were taken from unit profiles.

Artifact recovery at many sites is enhanced by water screening. Using a gasoline-driven water pump to hose down matrix during screening not only speeds up the screening process with, for example, clayey soils, but also permits better recovery of delicate objects such as animal bones without the damage that often results from conventional dry screening. Maintenance of water pumps, runoff from the water-screening process, and, of course, a reliable water source are key concerns with this technique. In some regions of the United States, local environmental regulations prohibit the kind of muddy discharge into a stream that derives from water screening.

Flotation is another technique that maximizes recovery, sometimes of artifacts, but mainly of seeds, tiny bones, and charred botanical remains. A sample of archaeological deposit is immersed in a container filled with plain water or chemically treated water. Agitating the sample causes small particles (such as charcoal) to rise to the top where they can be skimmed with a fine-screen strainer. Flotation also speeds up the separation of other small materials, which can be screened through different sizes of geologic sieves, into "fractions" of various sizes. In the field, flotation can sometimes be done at a nearby running stream or water source, using fine mesh screen to recover artifacts and other objects. Archaeologists have devised elaborate flotation systems, some using power-driven equipment. Flotation can also take the form of water separation, using a technique reported by E. M. Davis and A. B. Wesolowsky at the site of Stobi. With their "Izum" device, water flows up through the tray holding the soils, with the lighter materials carried into a second tray and the heavier earth settling in the first container.

In addition to recovering artifacts, many kinds of samples can be collected from site deposits. Matrix, or bulk soil, samples can be taken back to the laboratory to be fine-screened, and the residues painstakingly picked for tiny animal bones. The fill from hearth features should be collected. At Baker Cave in southwest Texas, R. F. Heizer and Thomas R. Hester bagged several hundred pounds of fill from a 9,000-year-old hearth. Fine-screen sieving in the lab yielded tremendous quantities of seeds, hulls, and tiny animal bones—including sixteen different species of snakes. Such materials would not be recovered by traditional field-screening methods. Charcoal samples for *radiocarbon dating should be collected with tweezers or a clean trowel and placed in envelopes made of new aluminum foil. The sample context must be clearly recorded. Even though tiny bits of charcoal can be dated today using accelerator mass spectrometry (AMS), the associations of such samples must be clear for the resulting assays to be of value.

Archaeologists take a variety of "column samples," often 1.2 cubic inches (20 cu cm) in size (this will vary given the research goals at a site). Such columns can be analyzed for pollen, or can be used for soil studies, such as grain-size analysis. Column samples are invaluable for quantifying composition of deposits, especially at shell middens, lithic workshops, or other sites with dense material accumulations. S. F. Cook, in the 1950s, pioneered the analysis of the physical composition of sites, using a 2-millimeter screen to sort the constituents. In addition, there are now specialized techniques for the analysis of soil samples for micromorphological studies (microscopic thin-section analysis to study site formation processes) and for collecting soil samples for radiocarbon dating of humates.

Artifact recovery can be extremely difficult at wet or submerged sites, where artifacts are extremely fragile and can be destroyed by rapid drying. Dry caves often preserve artifacts for thousands of years, but surviving bits of baskets or textiles may need special treatment and handling to ensure proper recovery. Archaeological conservators should be on staff for work at such sites, where fragile remains are to be expected. In addition, consultation with conservators should be part of research planning for most excavations, to be sure that current techniques and preservations are used; outdated techniques, especially involving the use of some chemicals, can prove hazardous not only to the specimens, but to the archaeologist.

While there are these basic methods of artifact and ecofact recovery, through screening, flotation, sample collec-

tion, etc., there is no simple "guide" to the proper techniques. These must be developed through careful planning as part of a project's research design. Equally important is an awareness of proper approaches to conservation of artifacts in the field. Finally, artifact recovery must be quickly followed by prompt laboratory processing, so that the full documentation of artifactual remains may be completed.

■ S. F. Cook and A. E. Treganza, "The Quantitative Investigation of Indian Mounds," *University of California Publications in American Archaeology and Ethnology* 40 (1950): 223–262. E. Mott Davis and Al B. Wesolowsky, "The Izum: A Simple Water Separation Device," *Journal of Field Archaeology* 2 (1975): 271–273. Patty Jo Watson, "In Pursuit of Prehistoric Subsistence: A Comparative Account of Some Contemporary Flotation Techniques," *Mid-Continental Journal of Archaeology* 1 (1976): 77–100. Knut R. Fladmark, *A Guide to Basic Archaeological Field Procedures* (1978). Junius Bird, "Comments on Sifters, Sifting and Sorting Procedures," in *A Complete Manual of Field Archaeology,* by Martha Joukowsky (1980), pp. 165–170. William S. Dancey, *Archaeology Field Methods: An Introduction* (1991). Catherine Sease, *A Conservation Manual for the Field Archaeologist* (1992). Thomas R. Hester, Harry J. Shafer, and Kenneth L. Feder, *Field Methods in Archaeology* (1997).

Thomas R. Hester

PUBLICATION OF FINDINGS FROM EXCAVATIONS

Excavation is destructive of the archaeological strata it investigates—always partially and often totally. The records of an excavation are therefore all that remains and must stand forever as the evidence for human activity in that place. Since the past is deemed in most modern societies to belong to the public at large, including those as yet unborn, prompt and detailed publication is seen as a moral duty for the excavator. For *Pitt-Rivers, "every detail" should be recorded—and publication was closely equated to recording. For P. A. Barker, publication is an "obligation." Excavators have striven to live up to these oft expressed ideals, both in the generation of records on site and in publication. Just as the records were seen as a substitute for the site itself, so the publication has sometimes been regarded as a substitute for the records. During the nineteenth and twentieth centuries in Europe, national and regional journals have carried what are virtually full transactions of interventions underground. The original excavation records themselves have not always survived. The back numbers of such journals therefore have constituted an "archive" from which synthetic papers were composed. Other field workers believed that a presentation which was attractive to the user, and thus carefully structured and shorn of superfluity, was more beneficial to the subject in the long term. An example is R.E.M. and T. V. Wheeler's *Maiden Castle* (London, 1943), which featured a narrative account of the events discovered at this Iron Age hill fort as it was overwhelmed by the armies of Rome. Their work was supported by carefully edited extracts from the records. The pendulum swung back from the 1960s when professionals engaged in the widespread campaign of salvage ("rescue") which had been provoked by modern redevelopment, sought to achieve a "preservation by record" of the totality of the archaeological strata encountered. The results of such campaigns have proven difficult to publish, either because of their volume, or because the exercises were empirical and lacked the motivation of research relevance.

Recent attempts to reconcile the need to maximize access to the records made with the selectivity preferred by a reader have led to a new definition of archaeological publication, which now includes a wide variety of media. A modern excavation produces copious written, drawn, and photographic records, some of which are preformatted and may be carried in computerized database management systems. These are the field records, which are now seldom published in multiple copies, but are curated in an archive. These raw data are then analyzed, using a series of routines (stratigraphic analysis, spatial analysis, seriation, assemblage analysis, finds typologies, biological analysis, scientific dating, etc.) to generate a model of the sequence of activities encountered on the site. The analyses and the synthesis drawn from them constitute the field report, which is deductive, conclusive, and fully supported by the evidence, but does not place the site in its historical context. Field reports are still sometimes published in their entirety, either as a monograph or as fascicules which contain accounts of individual analyses or groups of analyses and appear when ready. However the mood is turning against full publication of field reports because of their cost and doubtful relevance to a wide circulation. Public access to excavation data can be provided by museum archives or through electronic media such as the new journal "Internet Archaeology." Full publication in multiple hard copy can then be reserved for matters contributing to the current research debate: a newly discovered or a major redefinition of an existing one.

These syntheses are carried in a variety of media. Most countries have national journals devoted to the major periods (*Proceedings of the Prehistoric Society, Acta Archaeologica, Archaeologia Medievale,* etc.), and many of the specialist societies and government agencies have monograph series. More rarely, a commercial publisher may undertake to market an excavation synthesis where the results are seen as of exceptionally widespread interest. Some government agencies insist on the appearance of a more rigorously selective summary which must be published rapidly as a condition of grant. Excavation summaries, variously embellished, may be found in other published forms: as guide books, in newspapers, magazines, (e.g., *National Geographic Magazine*) and in educational books for children. Other media too, such as television and radio, are employed to carry the message and some of the excitement of the excavation to a wider audience. Archaeological sites themselves, if not subsequently destroyed, can be presented to the public as part of the publication venture, either as conserved monuments *(Stonehenge) or as reconstructions (The Jorvik Viking Centre, *York), both in England.

Professional and ethical difficulties occasionally arise over publication and copyright as a result of local systems of archaeological procurement. Where excavation is undertaken for governments, publication might be seen as low priority or as a government prerogative. Where, as increasingly is the case, excavation is undertaken for a private client, the results may have to be regarded as confidential. However the archaeological profession would consider as inalienable the public right of accession to field records and reports and the consequent duty of making research widely available, perhaps more in this than in any other science.

[*See also* ARCHIVAL MANAGEMENT OF ARCHAEOLOGICAL RECORDS.]

■ A.L.L. Fox Pitt-Rivers, *Excavations in Cranbourne Chase* (1887). P. A. Barker, *Techniques of Archaeological Excavation* (1977). M.O.H. Carver, "Digging for Data: Archaeological Approaches to Data Definition, Acquisition and Analyses" in *Lo Scavo Archeologico: dalla Diagnosi all'Edizione*, R. Francovich and D. Manacorda, eds. (1990), pp. 45–120.

Martin Carver

EXCHANGE. *See* TRADE, PREHISTORIC.

EXPERIMENTAL ARCHAEOLOGY refers to the application of experimental methods in data collection and description, interpretation, and explanation of the archaeological record. It is one of several increasingly important sources of archaeological analogy. It is a study by which archaeologists test the validity of assumptions made about past behavior. The usefulness of the approach is exemplified by a long history of experimentation which has its beginnings in the early nineteenth and twentieth centuries. Early examples include the work of the English archaeologists Lubbock, Joan Evans and A.H.L. Fox *Pitt-Rivers, who experimented with stone tools and digging implements in the nineteenth century as the basis for interpreting their manufacture and use.

In the twentieth century, the experimental tool tradition has been furthered by the pioneering work of Don Crabtree and François Bordes, whose work has led to the replication and identification of stages of production. Further work by the Russian scholar Semenov and a number of British and American scholars, including Lawrence Keeley, have defined methods of examining wear patterns produced on artifacts as the result of differing uses. These and other studies provide a basis for examining the relative efficiency of one tool or strategy over another. The experimental tradition has over the course of the twentieth century broadened to include the replication of features and the labor force required to construct such large and notable features as Stonehenge and the Egyptian pyramids. In some instances experimental projects have provided insights about the nature of construction, the efficiency of the technology used, and the deterioration of features after abandonment. In other instances experiments with replicated features have provided a more adequate determination of function. Yet other projects have included attempts to duplicate agricultural practices, to determine the feasibility of transoceanic travel so well exemplified by Thor Heyerdahl's Kon-Tiki voyage, and to reconstruct community lifeways.

Most experimental studies belong to one of four distinct categories. These include replication experiments, testing of methodological assumptions by applying them to known contexts, experiments involving site formation processes, and ethnoarchaeology, or the collection of ethnographic data with specific reference to archaeological problems.

The best represented are replication experiments in which artifacts or activities are reproduced. These are well exemplified by stone-tool replication as well as the reconstruction of features discussed earlier. These experiments are typically specific in design and assist the archaeologist in assessing the probable function of materials. Closely related are experiments which seek to evaluate the methodological assumptions made about the archaeological record by testing them in historical context. Test situations have included Plimouth Plantation and the investigation of the early twentieth-century village of Silcott in Washington State. Such studies make it possible to control time and space dimensions so important in archaeological interpretation. In addition, such contexts have broadened our appreciation of the lack of corroboration between historical records and archaeological data. These experiments have often caused archaeologists to consider the interrelationship of activities across communities.

An increasingly common experimental approach is that concerned with *site formation processes. The intent is to better understand the natural and behavioral processes which form archaeological sites and the subsequent alteration of deposits. One of the early and major discussants of the approach is Michael Schiffer, who introduced the idea of transformational processes, which attempts to construct the post-depositional history of archaeological sites.

In recent years an increasingly common experiment termed *"ethnoarchaeology" has involved the collection of ethnographic information to address specific archaeological problems. The approach "checks" the validity of archaeological observations or hypotheses against ethnographic data. These comparisons are often specific and, as with Longacre's and Ayers's description of an abandoned Apache wickiup, describe associated spatial relationships of artifacts and features reflecting patterns of residence and activity. In the case of the Apache wickiup, observations were compared to contemporary Apache use of such structures as a "check" on the original interpretations. Ethnoarchaeology has greatly assisted our linkage of the past with contemporary behavior.

Typically archaeologists combine more than one of the experimental components. A number of archaeologists have used the study of site formation processes and *ethnoarchaeology to effect a broader linkage of past and present through *Middle Range Theory. Binford's work among the arctic Nunamuit, and Yellen's research among the !Kung of the Kalahari Desert, have generated theories or explanations of limited relationships as the basis for examining the principles articulating more general theories. These studies link the dynamics of living cultures to their static consequences. Many good applications of this approach have been made by paleoanthropologists studying our earliest ancestors. Here the use of experimental approaches is critical. It is well exemplified by Brain's study of the accumulation of bone deposits at the South African site of Makapansgat and recently by Schick and Toth in *Making Silent Stones Speak* (1993).

As with all approaches, experimental archaeology has some limitations. In many instances, experimental evidence is negative, suggesting only that a particular phenomenon or event did not occur. Yet experimentation allows the testing of assumptions about the past by eliminating improbable hypotheses and identifying the range of possible explanations of highly variable archaeological phenomena. Increasingly over the past century, experimental archaeology has become a key element in understanding the past.

[*See also:* ETHNOARCHAEOLOGY; THEORY IN ARCHAEOLOGY.]

■ John Coles, *Archaeology by Experiment* (1973). Daniel Ingersoll, John E. Yellen, and William Macdonald, eds., *Experimental Archaeology* (1977). Richard A. Gould, ed., *Explorations in Ethnoarchaeology* (1978). Lewis R. Binford, *In Pursuit of the Past* (1983). Kathy Schick and Nickolas Toth, *Making Silent Stones Speak* (1993).

Mark G. Plew

F

FEDDERSEN WIERDE lies in the coastal marshland on the western side of the Weser estuary in northern Germany, 8.6 miles (14 km) north of Bremerhaven, and is one of numerous settlements on mounds in this region. Large-scale excavations here from 1955 to 1963 have revealed the successive phases of an Iron Age settlement, originating in the first century B.C. and continuing without break into the first half of the fifth century A.D. The site is of great significance for the study of Iron Age communities in the north European coastland and the natural environment in which they developed.

The earliest settlement was on a modest scale and is represented by a single farmstead. Arable farming had begun by the later first century B.C.; by the early first century A.D. at least four substantial aisled longhouses and their associated granaries existed. The longhouses measured up to 98 feet (30 m) in length and 32 feet (10 m) in width. Most contained stalling for animals over more than half their interior space, the remainder being devoted to human use. Striking evidence for the constructional details of walls was preserved in wet ground conditions. Steady growth of the settlement followed over the next two centuries, on a radial plan, as the site began to rise above the surrounding marsh. By the late second century, as many as fifty longhouses may have been occupied at one time, each representing a family holding.

A major internal development of the second century was the segregation of a large house and its ancillary buildings at the southeastern edge of the settlement and the demarcation of this complex by a palisade and ditch. Within this enclosure, craftsmen had been at work in several materials: wood, leather, iron, antler, and bone. This group of artisans was probably dependent on a leader whose authority extended over the entire settlement, important evidence that social differentiation had developed by the second century A.D. The leader's compound, or *Herrenhof*, remained in existence until the fourth century. The settlement as a whole continued to number at least fifty longhouses, all with animal stalling. Cattle formed a major economic resource in this marshland environment, though sheep and pigs also made a contribution to the food stock. Arable *agriculture was also pursued. Emmer wheat, barley, oats, and millet were grown; beans, brassicas, flax, and woad were also cultivated. Hunting, fishing, and the collection of seafood contributed little to the diet.

Abandonment of the site began early in the fifth century and was complete by A.D. 450. It occurred within the framework of westward migration to the Low Countries and eastern Britain at this time. A striking similarity between the latest pottery at Feddersen Wierde and the earliest Germanic material at sites in eastern Britain suggests that some settlers moved directly from the Weser estuary to Britain.

The mound at Feddersen Wierde was not occupied again after their departure.

[See also EUROPE: THE EUROPEAN IRON AGE.]

■ W. Haarnagel, *Die Grabungen Feddersen Wierde* (1979). Malcolm Todd, *The Northern Barbarians,* 2nd ed. (1987).

Malcolm Todd

FEMINIST ARCHAEOLOGY. *See* GENDER, ARCHAEOLOGY OF.

FERTILE CRESCENT. *See* NEAR EAST: THE NEOLITHIC AND CHALCOLITHIC (PRE-BRONZE-AGE) PERIODS IN THE NEAR EAST.

FIELD SYSTEMS provide much of the best evidence for early *agriculture, but, ironically, few of them have been studied until recently, and even then most examples may belong to a developed stage of the local sequence. Important investigations of Maya field systems are now in progress, there have been studies of agricultural terracing in South America, and recent years have seen pioneering research on the field systems and land divisions of New Guinea, Hawaii, and Japan. At present, however, it is only in northwest Europe that we can trace a full sequence of developments from the adoption of agriculture to the imposition of the state.

Even in northwest Europe we can say very little about the earliest land divisions. In the Rhineland, where Neolithic settlements are particularly well preserved, short lengths of fences survive which may be all that now remains of enclosed plots beside the main groups of houses. Similarly, outside the fortified settlement at Carn Brea in western England there are areas of cultivated soil and cairns that probably accumulated during land clearance. Such traces are widespread in upland Britain, but, despite the claim that they result from the first agricultural colonization of those areas, they are often impossible to date. It is in the west of Ireland that more convincing evidence can be found, for here there are clearance cairns and longer systems of walling buried below the blanket peat. In County Mayo, a system of very regular land divisions, apparently defining areas of pasture, may be associated with a number of *megalithic tombs. Very similar patterns can be observed in the Shetland Islands, where again much of the evidence is sealed by dated peat horizons, and in the Scilly Isles, off the coast of southwest England, where such claims depend on surface observation. There are hints of rather similar patterns at excavated sites in Britain and northern Europe, where cultivated surfaces and occasional field divisions have been sealed by the construction of Neolithic and Early Bronze Age burial mounds. In *Wessex there are also a very few sites at which surviving burial mounds were built on top of the earthworks of field systems.

Such evidence is surprisingly sparse, and in most cases it survives because these particular field systems were abandoned at an early stage in their history. In other areas it is possible that similar traces have been destroyed because the land has been used continuously. Even so, it is very striking that most archaeologically attested field systems do not seem to have developed until the first millennium, or, less often, the later second millennium B.C. That evidence matches the general development of the settlement pattern in different areas, with signs of agricultural intensification in the British Isles from the beginning of the Middle Bronze Age and in northern Europe from the Late Bronze Age to Early Iron Age transition. In both regions these changes seem to be reflected by the evidence of environmental archaeology.

Apart from the pre-bog field systems in the west of Ireland, the first extensive field systems in prehistoric Europe are those found on the uplands of Dartmoor in southwest England, which are dated by pottery and radiocarbon to the later second millennium B.C. Their scale is quite extraordinary, for they are laid out around a series of parallel axes which extend across country for considerable distances, taking little account of the details of the local topography. Individual land blocks may cover areas as extensive as 741 acres (300 ha). The low banks or walls that form the field boundaries are known as "reaves," and similar earthworks also follow the watersheds below the higher moorland, dividing large blocks of settled land from one another. Similar features separate the more sheltered soils from the higher ground, which may have been used only seasonally. The whole system is associated with a series of houses and enclosures. Like even older land divisions, it survives intact because it went out of use at an early stage—in this case because of worsening environmental conditions on the moor.

Such regular arrangements have been described as "coaxial" field systems. There are hints that similar systems of reaves existed elsewhere in western Britain, but the closest parallels to the arrangement on Dartmoor are found at sites on the chalkland of southern England, in some of the British river valleys and on the Fen Edge in East Anglia. In all these areas the fields are intimately connected with houses and sometimes with enclosed settlements, but the functions of these land divisions were not always the same. On the chalk, where the field edges survive as shallow terraces because of soil erosion, they were probably used for growing crops, while those in eastern England more likely provided pasture when the fens were too waterlogged to be used as grazing land.

Far more of the field systems in the British Isles can be dated to the Iron Age, and these would have been contemporary with the so-called "Celtic field systems" found in northern Germany, the Netherlands, Denmark, and southern Sweden. Although this term was adopted from British archaeology, the fields that it describes are not quite the same as those discussed so far. Most of those found in continental Europe are located on light sandy soils, where they sometimes survive in areas of modern heathland. Others are discovered as soil marks on air photographs. Like their British counterparts, they observe a surprisingly regular layout, based on a series of parallel axes. Again the fields are generally square or rectangular. They seem to have been cultivated by cross-plowing, but the individual plots are significantly smaller than those in Britain. This is probably because of the friable character of the cultivated soils, and there is experimental evidence to suggest that the spacing of the field divisions is intended to minimize wind erosion. In contrast to the shallow terraces (lynchets) that mark ancient field divisions in the British Isles, these plots are bounded by wide structureless banks of windblown soil. There is little information on the precise character of the original field boundaries in any part of Europe, although individual plots seem to have been bounded by fences, walls, ditches, hedges, or simply by narrow strips of uncleared ground. In Britain there is evidence that these boundaries were less effective as traps for eroding soil, since work on valley sediments has identified deposits of displaced plow soil which seem to have accumulated in parallel with the subdivision of the landscape.

It is not clear how far we can associate particular fields or groups of fields with individual settlements. In northern Europe, houses are generally scattered among the fields themselves. Their positions may have shifted fairly often, with the result that some of the evidence would have been removed in later episodes of cultivation. There are striking contrasts between the sites on either side of the North Sea. On the Continent (continental Europe), the predominant house style is rectangular, in contrast to the tradition of round houses found in the British Isles. One reason for this difference is that the north European houses also included cattle byres, with the result that individual fields could be regularly and intensively manured. In Britain, on the other hand, there was little if any provision for stalled animals, with the result that livestock may have been penned on fallow ground. In fact the British landscape may have been organized on an altogether larger scale. Although raised storehouses can be found in association with continental field systems, these normally accompany the individual houses. In Britain, on the other hand, they can be grouped together and are sometimes found within specialized enclosures, some of them with massive defenses. Outside the northwest Netherlands there is little sign of such a complex system on the European mainland, and no evidence for the centralized storage or redistribution of foodstuffs.

The later history of these field systems also varies considerably. In continental Europe there are major differences according to the position of the Roman frontier. Close to the frontier the small field systems that had originated during the Iron Age eventually went out of use, and more intensive practices were adopted, involving the development of a new kind of plow. By contrast, in Sweden the regular layout of the "Celtic fields" was increasingly disregarded and they were gradually replaced by individual farms whose boundaries were defined by continuous walls. Instead of a system in which resources could be allocated on a cooperative basis, there are signs that land had become a commodity that could be appropriated and owned.

Only in the British Isles were field systems of the traditional kind maintained throughout the Roman period, although they were substantially remodelled—the process may even have started in the Late Iron Age. The small rectangular plots so characteristic of earlier phases could be amalgamated to form long rectangular units, and it seems possible that they were cultivated more intensively. Fresh field systems also developed on lowland soils where they had not existed before. Some of these newer field systems were laid out, like the earlier ones, according to a coaxial pattern, and incorporated a distinctive mixture of paddocks, ditched enclosures, and roadways. Elsewhere, for example in south Wales, the population embarked upon extensive land drainage schemes. But although the scale of these initiatives is certainly impressive, there is some reason to doubt the lasting character of such developments, for only where the physical remains of these systems were too substantial to replace did elements of the older system exert much influence over the later pattern of land use. Otherwise, as in northern Europe, this impressive remodeling of the agrarian landscape had already run its course by the Early Medieval Period.

■ J. A. Brongers, *Air Photography and Celtic Field Research in the Netherlands* (1976). Roger Mercer, ed., *Farming Practice in British Prehistory* (1981). Andrew Fleming, *The Dartmoor Reaves* (1988). Françoise Audouze and Olivier Buchsenschutz, *Towns, Villages and Countryside of Celtic Europe* (1991).

Richard Bradley

FISSION-TRACK DATING is a method of absolute age determination based on the microscopic counting of micrometer-sized damage tracks that are created by the spontaneous fission of uranium (U^{238}) atoms and that accumulate with time in minerals and glasses containing uranium in minor concentrations. The method was developed in 1963–1964 by three U.S. physicists (P. B. Price, R. M. Walker, and R. L. Fleischer). Observation of the tracks under an optical microscope is possible only after special preparation of the sample (polishing and etching). The number of tracks counted per unit of surface in a mineral or glass sample is a function of its age and uranium content. In order to determine the age, a determination of the uranium content is therefore also required. This is performed by irradiating the sample with a calibrated dose of slow neutrons in a nuclear reactor, an operation that induces new (U^{235}) fission tracks, the number of which is proportional to the uranium content.

Fission tracks are thermally unstable, meaning that they fade, to disappear completely at high temperature, a process that is called track annealing. Different materials have different sensitivities with respect to track annealing, glass being more sensitive than minerals, and the annealing process depends not only upon the temperature but also upon the duration of heating. Partially annealed tracks are distinguished from fresh tracks by their smaller size.

In the geological sciences, fission-track dating has evolved to the point where an acknowledged chronometer is applied not only to determine the age of minerals (and of the rocks of which they are constituents) but also, and even more often, to study their temperature evolution with time. In archaeology, fission-track dating has remained of rather limited importance. The limitations are mainly related to the low number of fission tracks accumulated in the relatively young archaeological samples compared to the half-life of 8.2×10^{15} years for U^{238} spontaneous fission. Samples of large size or relatively high uranium content are required, and one is often confronted with lengthy counting procedures of low surface track densities, with a considerable background of spurious tracklike etch pits, deteriorating both precision and accuracy. Fission-track dating can therefore not be considered competitive with radiocarbon or thermoluminescence dating. Nevertheless, the method proved to be well suited for studying specific materials and problems.

One of the favorite materials fission-track dating has been applied to is obsidian. Artifacts such as knives and arrowheads made of natural obsidian glass found in Europe and South America can be dated if they were fired by ancient humans. The condition is that heating was sufficiently strong to completely anneal all previously stored "geological" tracks so that all tracks that are counted result from uranium fission reactions that took place after the firing. This can be checked by track size analysis. Fission-track age determinations on artifacts that were not heated normally yield the geological age of the obsidian lava flow the obsidian was extracted from. A comparison of fission-track age determinations on obsidian tools found at different localities with those of known outcrops of obsidian lava flows in Italy, Greece, and Turkey allowed researchers to determine the geographic provenance of the tools and to reconstruct in this way the ancient obsidian trade routes in the *Mediterranean world.

Fission-track dating has also been applied to man-made glass. Studies of this kind were performed on glaze covering 400- to 500-year-old Japanese bowls. Another example is a glass shard originating from a Gallo-Roman bath near Limoges, France. A correct result of A.D. 150 was found for the age of the bath, with a precision, however, as poor as twenty percent. The fluorescent green uranium-rich glassware produced in Bohemia (central Europe) during the nineteenth century has, on the other hand, been dated quite precisely.

Occasionally, pottery has been dated, if it contained suitable inclusions such as flakes of obsidian or zircon grains. Here too, all geological tracks are supposed to be erased in these inclusions during the baking process. Similar studies were carried out on fired stones and baked earth. Remarkable success was achieved in the age determination of the *Homo erectus pekinensis*. Based on ca. 100 suitable grains of sphene found in firing ashes in two layers containing human remains in the *Zhoukoudian cave near Peking, fission-track ages of 306 ± 56 and 462 ± 45 thousand years B.P. were obtained.

Some of the very early hominid sites aged around 2 million years B.P. in eastern Africa (Tanzania, Ethiopia, Kenya) have also been dated with fission tracks, supplementing potassium-argon age determinations that were often found to be problematic. Use was made of glass shards or uranium-rich mineral grains, such as zircons extracted from the volcanic tuff layers that are intercalated between the sedimentary sequences containing the hominid remains.

[*See also* ARCHAEO-PALEOMAGNETIC DATING; DATING THE PAST; DENDROCHRONOLOGY; LUMINESCENCE DATING; OBSIDIAN HYDRATION DATING; POTASSIUM-ARGON DATING; RADIOCARBON DATING; SERIATION; STRATIGRAPHY.]

■ Robert L. Fleischer, P. Buford Price, and Robert M. Walker, *Nuclear Tracks in Solids; Principles and Applications* (1975). Günther A. Wagner, "Archaeological Applications of Fission-Track Dating," *Nuclear Track Detection* 2 (1978):51–63. Günther A. Wagner and Peter Van den haute, *Fission-Track Dating* (1992).

Frans De Corte and Peter Van den haute

FLINT KNAPPING. *See* LITHICS: INTRODUCTION.

FOOD. *See* AGRICULTURE *AND* DIET, RECONSTRUCTION OF.

FRANKS AND THE FRANKISH EMPIRE. The Franks first appear in Latin sources in the third century A.D. as a Germanic people living to the east of the lower Rhine, just beyond the frontier of the Roman Empire. The name, meaning "fierce" or "bold," seems to have been applied to an amalgamation of various Germanic tribes, such as the Bructeri, the Chamavi, and the Salians. The Franks were still ruled by different tribal kings until the time of the Salian king, Clovis (481 through 511), and some of the tribal names survived until at least the eighth century.

During the fourth and fifth centuries, groups of Franks raided the Roman Empire on numerous occasions, but Franks also took service with the Roman army in large numbers, and several reached high position within the Empire. The Frank Silvanus, serving as a Roman general in Gaul, was elected emperor by his troops in 355, although he survived less than a month. Around 390 the eastern and western Roman armies were both commanded by Franks: Richomer and his nephew Arbogast.

There are a number of cemeteries from the late fourth and early fifth centuries in northern Gaul containing graves which are quite different from those of Romans: they are characterized by the burial of weapons with the men, and Germanic-style jewelry with the women. It has been suggested by H. W. Böhme that this is evidence of the wide-scale settlement by the Romans of various barbarians within the empire, to augment the defenses of Gaul. The fact that many of the weapon graves contained franciscas, the throwing axes characteristic of the Franks, suggests that Franks were the major component.

In the fifth century the effective authority of the emperors within Gaul diminished, as Visigoths settled in southwest Gaul and Burgundians in the southeast. In northern Gaul, the Franks were the major power, and seem to have worked closely with the surviving Roman authorities, including the Church. The burial of King Childeric, discovered in 1653 in Tournai, and published by Jacques Chifflet in 1655, shows something of this cooperation. Childeric (who died ca. 481 to 482) was buried with his weapons and with much of the gold-and-garnet cloisonné-decorated equipment fashionable among the military elite at the time. He wore a Roman-style seal ring with his own portrait on it and the Latin inscription CHILDERICI REGIS; he also wore a gold crossbow brooch of the type presented to Roman officials as a symbol of his office. This excavation was the foundation of early medieval archaeology; it remains the only furnished burial of the period which can be certainly associated with a known historical personage. R. Brulet's excavations on the same site in the 1980s revealed the pagan associations of Childeric's burial: three pits full of sacrificed horses.

The custom of furnished burial seems to have become common among the Franks in the period immediately after Childeric, and the spread of Frankish power across northern Gaul and into the lands beyond the Rhine is mirrored in the spread of the new burial customs. In the nineteenth century the archaeologists who discovered these cemeteries in northern France, the Low Countries, and Germany tended to imagine that when they found graves with weapons, metal and ceramic vessels, and items of personal apparel they had found the bodies of the Frankish newcomers themselves; the Frankish immigration could be traced through distribution maps of these "row-grave" (*Reihengräber*) cemeteries. It now seems much more likely that these cemeteries contain not only the graves of Franks, but also the graves of the many other people of non-Frankish descent (above all Gallo-Romans), who threw in their lot with the new political elite, adopting their customs and their way of life. The Franks, in their turn, adopted many of the customs of the Romans, above all the use of the Latin language. Only in the area immediately west of the Rhine, in what is now Flemish-speaking Belgium and Germany, was the Latin language eventually supplanted by Germanic dialects.

By his death in 511, Childeric's son Clovis had forcibly united the Frankish kingdom under his rule, and his prestige ensured that his descendants (known as the Merovingians, after his ancestor Merovech) would rule the Franks for another 250 years. Clovis defeated neighboring Germanic kingdoms, consolidated the Frankish hold on northern Gaul, and conquered the powerful Visigothic kingdom in southwest Gaul. Most significant of all, he converted to Catholic Christianity, and established a close alliance with the Gallic church. At a time when most other Germanic kings on the continent were Arian Christians, regarded as heretics by most of their Roman subjects, the Franks had a considerable political advantage.

Under Clovis's sons the Franks extended their power, and their sphere of cultural influence, over all of Gaul except the northwest peninsula (newly settled by British immigrants, who gave it its current name of Brittany) and the small strip of coast between the Pyrenees and the Rhone, which was an annex of the Visigothic kingdom of Spain. Frankish armies subjugated various German peoples east of the Rhine, notably the Thuringians, Alamans, and Bavarians; they fought, with varying degrees of success, in Spain and northern Italy; and they possibly held overlordship over part of southeast England. By the middle of the sixth century the Frankish kingdom was the most politically united, militarily successful, and economically prosperous of all the barbarian kingdoms established in the former Roman Empire. Archaeologists have discovered their dress fashions and burial fashions imitated across a wide area of western Europe.

Some of the graves of the Frankish aristocrats who profited from these successes have been found. The richest of them were under the floors of churches: the custom of richly furnished burials was not seen as incompatible with Christianity, and indeed was only adopted by the Franks at the time of the conversion of their leadership to Christianity. The most spectacular finds were made in the year 1959 under the floors of Cologne Cathedral, and the abbey of St-Denis, north of Paris. The Cologne "prince" was buried ca. 530 with a child-sized helmet and adult-sized weapons, suggesting both that status could be inherited, and that it could be denoted by the placing of particular objects in the graves. The St-Denis grave contained a ring inscribed with the name "Arnegundis": attempts have been made to associate the woman with the Aregund who was one of the wives of Clovis's son Chlothar (d. 561), but the gold jewelry and other artifacts in the grave appear to be of a later generation (ca. 600).

The heartland of Frankish power in the sixth century was Gaul, whose population was mostly Gallo-Roman by descent and, by the sixth century, very largely Christian by religion. Most of the Roman towns of Gaul had survived the turmoil of the fifth century, with their defenses and many of their public and domestic buildings intact, and the bishops and their clergy held considerable authority and influence in these towns. A rather better picture of the physical world of sixth-century Gaul can be gained from the writings of Bishop Gregory of Tours (d. 594), than from archaeology. Recently, however, excavations in a number of Roman towns, notably Geneva, Lyons, and Tours, have revealed elements of the Merovingian city, above all the churches.

The cathedral complex at Geneva excavated by C. Bonnet, consisting of several churches, a baptistery, and other ancillary buildings, is the best-known example of the extensive urban building program conducted by the Gallic church in the fifth and sixth centuries. The numerous rural monasteries founded in the seventh century have, with few exceptions (such as Nivelles), not been investigated archaeologically. Several thousand cemeteries from the period have been excavated, but only a handful of rural settlement sites, such as Brebières and Juvincourt. Programs of field walking, however, are beginning to produce results.

The descendants of Clovis remained kings of the Franks until 751, but their last century is one of decline. The aristocrats of Frankish and Roman origin, with whose help the kings had governed, gained increasing independence in their own localities, and some of them, like the rulers of Aquitaine, achieved royal status in all but name. The most powerful aristocratic family in the region between the Rhine and the Moselle were the Pippinids, who after 687 controlled the office of Mayor of the Palace for the Merovingian kings and effectively ruled in their name. The decline of royal power went hand in hand with economic advance, however, as can be seen by the growth of Channel ports in the seventh century, such as Dorestad and Quentovic, both of which have been investigated archaeologically.

The Pippinid mayor Charles Martel began the reconquest of Gaul in the name of the Frankish kings: after Charles the family became known as the Carolingians. His son Pippin and grandson Charles (Charles the Great, or Charlemagne) continued the process, and extended Frankish conquests into Muslim Spain, Lombard Italy, and eastern Europe. In 751 Pippin shut up the last Merovingian in a monastery and had himself crowned king, in the first ceremony of coronation in European history; in 800 Charlemagne was crowned emperor in Rome by the Pope, the first of a line of German Emperors which only ended with Napoleon.

The enormous wealth gained in decades of successful campaigning was partly used in massive ecclesiastical patronage: in the building of churches, the founding of monasteries, and the production of manuscripts. Alongside this went a process of ecclesiastical reform, the revival of Latin learning and the return to classical values in art, all of which has been described as the "Carolingian Renaissance." Two of its most celebrated products are probably the palace complex at Aachen, of which the palace chapel survives, and the Plan of St. Gall, a detailed map of an ideal monastery. Carolingian art is best known through sculpture and illuminated manuscripts, although work in precious metal and ivory also survives, and a small quantity of wall painting. Some palaces and churches have been investigated archaeologically, but very little has been discovered of urban or rural life in the period through excavation. The custom of burial with grave goods had disappeared throughout the Frankish world by the mid-eighth century, so Carolingian cemeteries are difficult to identify and relatively uninformative.

Louis the Pious, Charlemagne's sole surviving son, succeeded to the entire empire in 814, but his own three sons squabbled over the inheritance. Louis died in 840, and three years later, the Frankish kingdoms were split definitively into three, with Louis's youngest son Charles the Bald taking the western part (central and western France), Louis the German taking the eastern, and the eldest son, Lothar, taking the central portion, from Italy up to Belgium, and the title emperor. The crown remained in the Carolingian family in the east (Germany) until 888, and in the west (France) until 987.

[See also EUROPE: ROMAN AND POST-ROMAN EUROPE; FRÉNOUVILLE.]

■ E. James, *The Franks* (1988). N. Duval, ed., *Naissance de la France* (1993).

Edward James

FREMONT FARMERS. The archaeological culture called Fremont is found in Utah and portions of Colorado, Wyoming, Idaho, and Nevada. Its similarity to early *Anasazi culture of Arizona and New Mexico is expressed in first descriptions in the region as "Puebloan" and "Puebloid" cultures on the "Northern Periphery" of the Southwest. Similarities diminished as Anasazi became better known, and Noel Morss named the Fremont a distinct culture (*The Ancient Culture of the Fremont River in Utah*, Peabody Museum, 1931).

Fremont characteristics include round or square semi-subterranean houses; pit and surface storage structures; plain, black-painted, and corrugated gray ceramics; distinctive clay figurines and rock art figures; stone balls; deerskin moccasins, and deep-trough "Utah" style grinding stones. Some traits are not found everywhere in the region, and most traits that are found tend to vary from place to place. For example, surface structures were usually of adobe, but some Fremont areas contain buildings with masonry walls. Classic Fremont figurines come only from the Colorado Plateau in central Utah. A less-elaborate style of figurine is found in the eastern Great Basin. Only the classic style is similar to Fremont rock-art figures found throughout the region. Fremont ceramics have been categorized by temper types, but recent work shows much more variability in temper than previously thought.

The importance of these differences was debated for sixty years. Many have argued that "Fremont" should be divided into two, three, or five distinct archaeological units. Some would have "Fremont" reserved for remains on the Colorado Plateau, and "Sevier" would name Great Basin manifestations. Others have argued that "Fremont" encompasses the entire region, but that geographical "variants" better define observed differences.

Archaeologists now agree that "Fremont" seems to be a reasonable label to account for general similarity over the entire region. Most have embraced Fremont variability as a defining character. Strategies changed from place to place, and from time to time in the same places. As David Madsen says in *Exploring the Fremont* (1989), people lived in large and sedentary communities as well as in highly mobile family groups, depending on the nature of the resources in a place and in a given year.

The Fremont seem to have been consistent in farming and maintaining communities in a "core area" where the eastern Great Basin meets the western Colorado Plateau. Sedentary structures and communities were occupied in this core for the whole of the Fremont period. Flexible shifts between sedentary community life and more mobile strategies characterize areas in the outlying Fremont region. Major expansions of sedentary communities away from the core seem to have occurred between A.D. 900 and 1050, A.D. 1050 and 1200, and A.D. 1250 and 1350. Few sedentary communities were occupied outside the core between A.D. 1200 and 1250. Only one sedentary site in northwestern

Colorado dates after A.D. 1350, when Fremont culture disappeared.

Many different theories have been proposed for the demise of the Fremont. One suggests that northern groups moved to join farmers on the Great Plains. Eastern groups adopted Plains-like hunter-gatherer strategies. Southern Fremont peoples joined Anasazi migrations to the south. Other theories suggest that Fremont farmers were pushed out or exterminated by large groups of Numic-speaking ancestral Utes, Shoshones, and Paiutes who migrated into the region from southern California. Little evidence exists for these scenarios. Recent research near Great Salt and Utah lakes suggests that Fremont peoples became full-time foragers in response to climatic conditions that no longer favored farming. Fremont in other areas may have selected similar shifts in strategies, even if ancestral Numic groups invaded the region. Others may have joined the Anasazi migrations, and others may have been displaced or exterminated. The last fifty years of Fremont existence were characterized by increased variability and fragmentation.

Many important sedentary sites excavated through the 1970s have been described by Jesse Jennings in *Prehistory of Utah and the Eastern Great Basin* (1978), while Steven Simms has described a mobile foraging camp in "New Evidence for Fremont Adaptive Diversity," (*Journal of California and Great Basin Anthropology* 8(2), 1986: 204–216). Modern ecological and behavioral studies of Fremont are underway in several areas in Utah and eastern Nevada. Studies associated with highway construction in Hogan Pass, Clear Creek Canyon, and the San Rafael Swell are revealing new data on regional strategies. Research near Baker, Nevada, is providing insights into Fremont communities, trade, social structure, and possibly religion. Work around the Great Salt Lake is addressing Fremont transitions and genetic and material relations to past and present peoples.

[*See also* NORTH AMERICA: THE NORTH AMERICAN WEST.]

■ LaMar W. Lindsay, "Fremont Fragmentation," in *Anthropology of the Desert West: Essays in Honor of Jesse D. Jennings*, ed. Carol J. Condie and Don D. Fowler (1986), pp. 229–252. Richard K. Talbot and James D. Wilde, "Giving Form to the Formative: Shifting Settlement Patterns in the Eastern Great Basin and Northern Colorado Plateau," *Utah Archaeology* 2 (1989): 3–18. James D. Wilde, "Finding A Date: Some Thoughts on Radiocarbon Dating and the Baker Fremont Site in Eastern Nevada," *Utah Archaeology* 5 (1992): 39–54.
James D. Wilde

FRÉNOUVILLE (Calvados) is one of the best excavated and published of late antique and early medieval cemeteries in France, and may stand as a typical example. It is situated in western Normandy 6 miles (10 km) southeast of Caen; its placename, with its Frankish personal name prefix and *-ville* ending, is similar in construction to many found in northern France. But the excavations suggest that the development of the community buried at Frénouville may be very different from the traditional picture of Frankish conquest and settlement.

The excavations took place between 1970 and 1972: its 650 graves make it the largest in the area, although far smaller than some of the contemporary cemeteries in the Rhineland. The southern part of the site consisted of burials aligned on a north-south axis, dated to the late Roman period (third to fourth centuries); most graves, to the north, were aligned east-west, and date from the fifth to the seventh centuries. The grave cuts were made in a series of uneven rows; there were signs of some internal divisions

within the cemetery, including a fence. Some of the bodies were buried in wooden or stone coffins, but most were laid out in graves cut usually about 3 feet (1 m) into the soil.

Pilet argued from a study of the grave goods and the skeletons that there was a remarkable stability of population right through the period. Dress fashions changed, but many of the burial customs in the later graves (food offerings, and the coin placed in the dead person's mouth) were still Roman in style. There was a change of the orientation of graves in the fifth century, and in the earliest phase of the east-west graves a number of Anglo-Saxon objects are to be found: some button brooches and square-headed brooches. In the mid-sixth century some weapon burials were grouped together in one portion of the cemetery. Pilet underlines that "these arm-bearers were not strangers but the sons of those already buried." Pilet's thesis is that Frénouville saw little or no ethnic change: it was a small rural community that continued in its quiet isolation during the turmoil of the late Roman period. There were contacts, but perhaps indirect ones, with Anglo-Saxon England down to ca. 550. The appearance of warriors in the community at that point may have been due to the Frankish need to defend the area from the Bretons.

This reconstruction has been questioned by the physical anthropologist Luc Buchet. He looked at various anatomical features, such as metopism (the persistance of a cranial suture among adults) and dolichocephaly, and argued that there was the arrival, in the sixth century, of strangers in the community. The genetic changes could have been introduced by just a few individuals, or one family, perhaps a Frankish lord imposed on the community from outside.

[*See also* EUROPE: ROMAN AND POST-ROMAN EUROPE; FRANKS AND THE FRANKISH EMPIRE.]

■ Christian Pilet, *La Nécropole de Frénouville: Etude d'une population de la fin du IIIe à la fin du VIIe siècle*, 3 volumes (1980).
Edward James

FRONTIER SITES OF THE AMERICAN WEST. The cultural and economic development of western North America through the historical period in the New World contrasts sharply with those of the East Coast or Central Mexico. Starting between 1415 and 1550, and expansion of Western Europe created the first truly global world system, which eventually consisted of core areas of Old World civilizations with secondary overseas European colonial societies and large interaction zones where native and European cultures met and mutually evolved. Central Mexico and parts of eastern North America moved out of this initial interaction or "frontier" phase and rapidly, as seen in Quebec, Boston, or Mexico City, became transplanted segments of Old World civilization. However, the West, from Alaska to Northern Mexico, remained an interaction zone for well over three hundred years.

The dimensions of this West, covering thousands of miles and spanning centuries, may be too extensive and persistent to be considered simply a "frontier" or periphery. Perhaps the concept of interaction zones, which comprised most of the world between A.D. 1400 and 2000, are much more basic to understanding the origins of the Modern World. Archaeologically, interaction zones are typified by a complex pattern of archaeological sites, assemblages, and documentary (ethnohistoric) records.

From the point of initial contact in 1540 to the California Gold Rush of 1850, western North America was occupied by Native American sites (either continuing prehistoric patterns or showing varying degrees of European influence) and Euroamerican sites which, however, were in turn usually complex frontier multiethnic communities. Two well-known and easily visited sites in the American West, one spanning the sixteenth, seventeenth, and eighteenth centuries, the other limited to the nineteenth century, highlight this complexity.

Pecos. When Francisco de Coronado led the first major exploratory expedition (1540 to 1541) into the Southwest, among the largest of the numerous agricultural villages he encountered was Pecos. This pueblo of ca. 2,000 people had existed prehistorically and eventually survived until its abandonment in 1838. Decades of archaeological work at the site have revealed an architectural sequence preserving three centuries of Native American-European interaction.

Today, a visitor to Pecos National Historical Park, 25 miles (40 km) southeast of Santa Fe, New Mexico, sees the remains of a fortified residential pueblo anchored at its south end by the impressive ruins of a large Catholic church. Excavations have revealed that this complex, consisting of the church (Nuestra Señora de Porciúncula) and adjacent convento (friars' residence and work area), which dates between 1705 and the early nineteenth century, is directly superimposed over and within the massive foundations of a much larger structure (Nuestra Señora de los Angeles) dating between 1622 and 1680. The first great church with a nave 133 feet (41 m) by 40 feet (12 m) and walls 10 feet (3 m) thick and 45 feet (14 m) high was, when it was built between 1622 and 1629, the largest European structure in the present United States. There is ample archaeological evidence that this "magnificent temple" was violently destroyed by fire and demolition in the late seventeenth century, not to be replaced by the smaller church (nave 76 feet (23 m) long, and walls 5 feet (1.5 m) to 6 feet (2 m) thick) until a quarter of a century had passed. Even more telling was the discovery of a kiva, an underground Native American ceremonial chamber, built directly into the convento area.

Archaeological stratigraphy at Pecos gives detailed physical evidence of almost three hundred years of intense but changing cultural interaction. Contact in the sixteenth century was followed by colonization and missionization between 1598 and 1680, the period of the larger church. This sequence was broken in August 1680 by the Great Pueblo Revolt that drove the Spanish out of New Mexico, symbolized archaeologically by the reimposition of a kiva within the center of the destroyed Catholic complex. Reconquest came between 1692 and 1696 as seen in the eventual rebuilding of the second, smaller Nuestra Señora de Porciúncula. However, the nature of contact altered in the eighteenth century, creating a more open and mutual interaction.

Both the seventeenth- and eighteenth-century churches and the adjacent pueblo were within a defensive wall which in the eighteenth century became vital as nomads, first Apache peoples and then Comanches, alternated between trading with and raiding New Mexico. Pecos, as the most eastern pueblo, was in the cockpit of this conflict. Archaeological evidence of this Spanish-Pueblo-Plains interaction may appear after 1700 in alterations in the convento area with a growing emphasis on corrals, stables, and pens possibly tied to interregional trade. However, warfare and disease overran positive factors. The last baptism was recorded at Pecos in 1828 and ten years later the pueblo mission was abandoned.

It was not only the Spanish Southwest nor the early historic period that saw such complex contact. Such interaction spanned the West and continued into the twentieth century.

Fort Ross. Contemporaneous with the eclipse of Pecos another European frontier settlement was forming on the West Coast. Fort Ross (1812 to 1841) was the most outer link in a chain of Russian fur-trading posts extending from Siberia, across the Aleutian Islands and mainland Alaska, ending at Ross on the Pacific shore north of San Francisco. Archaeological exploration has recovered the plan of the original stockade with its two blockhouses and the enclosed Russian administration and residential quarters. More recent field work has highlighted the truly pluralistic nature of this community. Around the fort were clustered a separate Russian village, a Native Alaskan settlement, and several satellite Indian hamlets. Ethnically, Fort Ross, which served as both a fur-trade and agricultural production center, consisted of Russians (divided by class), "creoles" (products of Russian-Native Alaskan intermarriage), Native Alaskans (both Aleuts and mainland Eskimos), and local Californian peoples, especially Kashaya Pomos and Coast Miwoks.

Archaeological work within the fort on a range of former wooden structures, including a barracks, manager's house, fur warehouse, kitchen, and the Russian Orthodox Chapel, have revealed an elaborate, intruded European architecture and material culture. In contrast, surface surveys combined with ethnohistoric records have more recently located and identified four separate, distinct ethnic occupation areas around the fort. To the southeast of the palisade is the Siberian-style Russian village, while 100 feet (30 meters) south of the fort's south gate is the Native Alaskan village site containing in 1817 "fourteen Aleut Yurts made of planks." Some of its inhabitants were probably Alaskan men married to local Indian women. Testing of the village refuse deposits produced a mixed assemblage of European, Aleut, and local artifacts and faunal remains. Both sites overlooked the Fort Ross Bay. Inland, north of the stockade, surface collecting has located eight Californian native sites which obsidian hydration chronology and scattered historic artifacts place within the Russian period. These sites are residential bases where Kashaya Pomo and Coast Miwok congregated, at least during the growing season, as agricultural workers under Russian supervision. Payment was in European foodstuffs and trade goods. Since Californian Indians were hunter-gatherers, their movement into an agricultural regimen accompanied by noticeable shifts in settlement seems to indicate deep cultural change. However, preliminary survey patterns, in contrast, display strong continuities in both native diet and material culture.

Both Pecos and Fort Ross were Euroamerican frontier sites, one a mission pueblo the other a commercial entrepreneurial post. Nevertheless, between 1540 and 1850 most archaeological sites between Alaska and northern Mexico were not such European outposts but rather independent Native American communities showing varying degrees of outside world influence. Direct contact or colonization by Europeans was not necessary to cause significant change. Many North American groups became part of a world system and yet remained outside European political domination.

Even the California Gold Rush did not eliminate the Frontier West. Rather, all over western North America a greater cultural complexity evolved as Asians (archaeologically visible on many Overseas Chinese sites) and African-Americans joined Euroamericans and Native peoples. Only after 1880 did a regional railroad system give industrial society the ability to forcefully displace and encapsulate the frontier. This most recent period is, in turn, being explored through excavations at sites like Johnny Ward's Ranch (1859 through 1903) and Silcott, Washington (1900 to 1930).

Archaeology now covers the entire history of the West: its long interactive frontier period (1540 through 1880) and its more recent and quite different industrial period covering the late nineteenth and twentieth centuries.

[See also EUROPEAN COLONIES IN THE NEW WORLD; MISSION ARCHAEOLOGY; NORTH AMERICA: HISTORICAL ARCHAEOLOGY OF NORTH AMERICA.]

■ Bernard L. Fontana and J. Cameron Greenleaf, "Johnny Ward's Ranch: A Study in Historic Archaeology," *The Kiva* 28 (1962): Number 1–2. Alden C. Hayes, *The Four Churches of Pecos* (1974). William H. Adams, *Silcott, Washington: Ethnoarchaeology of a Rural American Community* (1976). Donald L. Hardesty, *Archaeology of Mining and Miners: A View from the Silver State* (1988). Robert L. Schuyler, "Historical Archaeology in the American West: The View from Philadelphia," *Historical Archaeology:* 25 (1991): 7–17. Kent G. Lightfoot, Thomas A. Wake, and Ann M. Schiff, "Native Responses to the Russian Mercantile Colony of Fort Ross, Northern California," *Journal of Field Archaeology:* 20 (1993): 159–175. Priscilla Wegars, ed., *Hidden Heritage: Historical Archaeology of the Overseas Chinese* (1993).

Robert L. Schuyler

FUNAN CULTURE. In about A.D. 250, two Chinese representatives of the Wu emperor visited a place described as Funan. Kang Dai and Zhu Ying filed a report on their return to China, which is referred to in later surviving texts. They described a country to the south ruled by a king who resided in a palace within a walled settlement. There was a taxation system involving payment in gold, silver, perfumes, and pearls, and a script which originated in India. Rice was cultivated, and the presence there of a representative of an Indian king showed that, already, trade with the West flourished.

The Chinese called this place Funan. No one can be sure of its location and attempts to identify it have suggested the area of lower Mekong or the Central Plain of Thailand. However, the flat plains surrounding the Mekong and its Bassac arm below Phnom Penh are the most likely. In the 1920s, Pierre Paris overflew this area and took a series of photographs. These revealed a network of canals crossing the landscape, and various nodal points where they met. One such junction revealed a huge enceinte demarcated by five moats and ramparts enclosing 1,112 acres (450 ha). It was here that Louis Malleret excavated in 1944.

This site is known as Oc Eo, and the research there confirmed and added an archaeological dimension to the Chinese reports. The center contained substantial brick foundations for a series of public buildings, and the range of decorative and votive items revealed an exchange network which incorporated China to the east and India, Iran, and the Roman Empire to the west. There were two Roman medallions bearing the images of Marcus Aurelius (A.D. 161 to 180) and Antoninus Pius (A.D. 138 to 161), Iranian coinage and rings and seals bearing inscriptions of the Brahmi script of India. The style of the Indian writings covers the first to fifth centuries A.D.

The area incorporating Oc Eo and associated settlements controls the lower Mekong River. River transport has traditionally been a key to communication in Southeast Asia, and the range of raw materials which were converted into or used as ornaments at Oc Eo encompasses virtually all available sources. But some local craft traditions survived alongside such introductions as glass-bead manufacture. Traditional bivalve sandstone molds, for example, continued to be used when casting tin ornaments.

This site was one center linked by the canals which served for communication and doubtless drainage in this low-lying delta terrain. We do not know if Funan was a unitary state, as the Chinese descriptions seem to suggest, or a series of competing centers. Whichever was the case, certain trends are found which were to contribute to the character of later complex polities in Southeast Asia. The handful of surviving inscriptions, for example, indicate that the local rulers adopted the Sanskrit language and took Sanskrit names. Indian religious and legal systems were adopted as well. The rulers are seen to be concerned with drainage and the reclamation of marshland, an inscription which reminds one of the extensive canal network. At Banteay Prei Nokor, a series of brick religious shrines has been identified, built in Indian style, while a further series of monumental structures are known from Angkor Borei, which lies 56 miles (90 km) north of Oc Eo, and is linked with it by canal.

These delta communities had the early advantage of direct contact with seagoing traders based in India, or with Chinese emissaries. They also controlled access to the arterial Mekong River route to the interior, with its rich mineral resources. But the land itself is prone to serious flooding, and has few important raw materials, such as iron ore. It is evident that, from about A.D. 550, the political center of gravity moved north to the Mekong Valley above Phnom Penh and the central plain of Cambodia around the Great Lake. There, another entity known to the Chinese as Zhenla developed but, again, it was probably made up of a series of competing polities each with its own court center.

[See also ASIA, *articles on* INTRODUCTION, PREHISTORY AND EARLY HISTORY OF SOUTHEAST ASIA.]

■ P. Wheatley, *Nāgara and Commandery*, University of Chicago Department of Geography Research Paper, Nos. 207–208 (1983). K. W. Taylor, "The Early Kingdoms," in *The Cambridge History of Southeast Asia* Vol. 1 (1992), pp. 137–182.

Charles Higham

G

GATECLIFF SHELTER. Throughout most of the 1970s and 1980s, the American Museum of Natural History conducted extensive archaeological excavations and reconnaissance in Monitor Valley in the Great Basin uplands of central Nevada. One key component of this research was the decade-long excavations at Gatecliff Shelter, situated in the Toquima Range, at an elevation of 7,600 feet (2,319 m).

Gatecliff Shelter contained more than 32 feet (10 m) of extraordinarily well-stratified deposits. Most of this stratigraphic column was deposited by extremely turbulent sediment-laden water, from debris flows upslope and upcanyon. Primary chronological controls derived from a sequence of 47 radiocarbon dates, spanning the last 7,000 years; evidence of the Mt. Mazama volcanic eruption was detected in the basal levels of the column. The Gatecliff Shelter sequence can be divided into 56 geological strata and 16 cultural horizons. The first evidence of human usage of Gatecliff Shelter occurs at about 5,500 B.P., and the most intensive periods of utilization took place during the last 3,200 years.

Gatecliff Shelter contained more than 400 typeable projectile points in tight stratigraphic context. This assemblage allowed a refinement of the cultural chronology for the central Great Basin. Gatecliff also contained 400+ incised limestone slabs. Although similar finds have been made elsewhere, this is the largest concentration of such artifacts in the New World. Significant parallels exist between this portable *rock art and the wall art painted inside Gatecliff and elsewhere in the Great Basin.

Three dozen hearths were found on the various living surfaces. They formed a distinctive "hearthline" approximately 13 feet (4 m) from the rear cave wall, suggesting that they were deliberately situated to create a relatively warm and smoke-free work area. The rear wall effectively served as a passive heat sink, enabling visitors to warm the inner part of this south-facing shelter with a relatively small fire.

Gatecliff Shelter was probably a short-term field camp, visited mostly by single-sex task groups working some distance from their base camp, although it is possible that small groups occasionally used Gatecliff as a residential base.

An extensive randomized and systematic archaeological survey was conducted throughout the Monitor Valley in order to place Gatecliff Shelter within its regional context. A dozen additional sites were also excavated in Monitor Valley, including Alta Toquima, an unusual alpine settlement at an elevation of 11,000 feet (3,352 m).

[*See also* HUNTER-GATHERERS, NORTH AMERICAN ARCHAIC; NORTH AMERICA: THE NORTH AMERICAN WEST.]

■ David Hurst Thomas, "How to Classify the Projectile Points from Monitor Valley, Nevada," *Journal of California and Great Basin Anthropology* 3 (1981): 7–43. David Hurst Thomas, "The Archaeology of Monitor Valley: 2. Gatecliff Shelter," *Anthropological Papers of the American Museum of Natural History* 59 (1983): 1–552.

David Hurst Thomas

GENDER, Archaeology of. The archaeology of gender is a general term that refers to an interest in the activities, the relative positions of autonomy and power, and the symbolic meanings attached to males and females in the past. It assumes that the process of survival and the production and reproduction of society have always involved a collaborative effort between men and women, and that archaeology should include an elucidation of past gender roles (what women and men do; what is considered appropriate), as well as gender ideology (what meanings are assigned to being female or male under specific sociohistoric circumstances) and gender relations (how men and women, as distinct interest groups, interact)? Moreover, it also shows how gender relations interact with other social categories such as class, age, ethnicity, religion and kin. Since gender is the single most universal social category for task divisions and the organization of social activity, as well as for the ascription of social and symbolic meanings, the archaeology of gender is integral to describing social life in past societies.

The archaeology of gender stands in contrast to other general theoretical frameworks, most notably cultural evolutionary and ecosystem approaches that focus on whole populations or whole behavioral systems as the units of analysis. Such "macro" approaches necessarily collapse the variability of personal activities, statuses, and symbolic postures within sociohistorical settings; they obscure the internal processes of social negotiation and accommodation which are not held to be significant in shaping the dynamics of social change. The archaeology of gender starts with just these rejected variables and dynamics, insisting that ideational and social variables account for and accumulate into structural change.

Within the field of an archaeology of gender, it is possible to differentiate an explicitly "feminist archaeology" from a more general "gender archaeology" approach. Gender archaeology proceeds empirically, identifying men's and women's roles, activities, spatial domains, and associated material elements (including skeletal remains), underscoring that what can be known about past gender systems is bounded by empirical evidence. Thus, gender archaeology seeks material or spatial correlatives to men's and women's presences in the past, using either gender-identified objects (e.g., hand-built pottery associated with women or projectile points associated with men) or gender-identified activity areas (e.g., cooking hearths linked with women or butchering areas with men) as a basic means of identifying the domains of past gender systems. The analogical constancy or parallelism between our modern, western sex/gender-system and the sex/gender system of past societies, while potentially problematic, is supported in either of two ways: either such gender associations (e.g., men making projectile points) are reiterated often enough in cross-cultural observations to make it statistically probable that parallel associations held in the past, and/or it is considered likely that, as with other classes of empirical archaeological evidence, we can proceed by tentatively holding a gender association as a hypothesis or assumption which a sufficient accumulation of empirical evidence will ultimately support or disprove.

Feminist archaeology, on the other hand, places women—as the too-often excluded gender—at the center of archaeological analysis in order to restore gender balance to the history of "man." Feminist archaeology is informed by an extensive literature on gender theory and research that recognizes gender not only as socially constituted and historically conditioned but as a dynamic ongoing process of negotiating changing social parameters. The result of adopting a feminist approach in archaeology is a more radical and less familiar perspective on the prehistoric past: it uses the unfamiliar perspective of women's experience to problematize conventional treatments of archaeological evidence, definitions, associations, frameworks, and identities (e.g., projectile points are not necessarily the dominant or most important material culture of the Paleolithic). Even conventional chronological periods, where defined by the adoption of a new technology believed to have been exclusively made or used by men (or women), would be challenged by a feminist archaeology as inappropriate for demarcating changes in human life (e.g., the Solutrean-Magdalenian divide, apparently based on men's hunting equipment, is rejected as representative of human change).

Admitting gender as a serious issue of prehistory, and recognizing the importance of gender categories in the constitution of all social groups, are common ground to the wide range of interests included within an archaeology of gender. While it is generally conceded that gender interests came late to archaeological theory and practice, they have quickly shifted attention to previously neglected classes of archaeological evidence such as spatial and temporal variability in cooking vessels (including the adoption or abandonment of specific attributes related to specific food preparations), grinding stones, fuels, and sizes of hearths or of areas of hide preparation, textile production, or net manufacture. The introduction of gender into archaeology similarly associates new classes of data on the basis of a presumed interdependence of gendered activities, as in considering relationships between butchering techniques and the cooking and storage requirements of meat consumption, examining frequencies and distributions of tribute-producing equipment (such as spinning whorls) at sites within a context of militaristic empires, or identifying productive activities like pottery making as sequential tasks (finding and quarrying clay, constructing vessels, decorating vessels, adding additional elements such as handles, gathering fuel for firing, etc.) in order to replace isolated, independent producers with mixed gender production units in prehistory. Finally and most significantly, an archaeology of gender promotes new models of sociopolitical change (e.g., the emergence of non-egalitarian relations or the appearance of the state), following from the view that social and political change arises out of and necessitates radical realignments of how men and women conduct their lives. These may involve a restructuring of household labor

around the production of new forms of wealth, the realignment of kin and civic relations, and/or the bestowing of ideological value on new symbols and statuses. The archaeology of gender prompts questions that underpin this view of change: what roles would have been adopted by women and men under different conditions of production, of political relations, of symbolic associations?

Despite such promising directions, the future of an archaeology of gender, and especially a feminist archaeology, remains ambiguous and full of tensions between different theoretical orientations. Can women's experiences be accommodated within traditional archaeological practices and assumptions? Will a restructuring of fundamental methods and theories be called for and admitted? Are interpretive understandings, including critical and self-reflexive thinking, admissible on an equal footing with formally testable criteria? Are sociobiological arguments, where biological sex differences are taken as foundational and largely immutable, and rules of difference are held constant for all societies, to be entertained within an archaeology of gender which insists that expressions of biological sex are socially and historically constituted? And finally, will gender considerations ultimately be marginalized by the dominant white male archaeologists who take their experiences and perspectives as the norm for all prehistory?

[*See also* HISTORY OF ARCHAEOLOGY, INTELLECTUAL; POSTPROCESSUAL THEORY; THEORY IN ARCHAEOLOGY.]

■ Margaret W. Conkey and Janet Spector, "Archaeology and the Study of Gender," *Advances in Archaeological Method and Theory* 7, pp. 1–38. Joan M. Gero and Margaret W. Conkey, eds., *Engendering Archaeology: Women and Prehistory* (1991). Roberta Gilchrist, "Women's Archaeology? Political Feminism, Gender Theory and Historical Revision," *Antiquity* 65: 495–501. Dale Walde and Noreen Willows, eds., *The Archaeology of Gender: Proceedings of the 23rd Annual Chacmool Conference* (1991). Cheryl Claassen, ed., *Exploring Gender Through Archaeology* (1992). Alison Wylie, "The Interplay of Evidential Constraints and Political Interests: Recent Archaeological Research on Gender," *American Antiquity* 57:15–35. Hilary du Cros and Laurajane Smith, eds., *Women in Archaeology: A Feminist Critique* (1993). Cheryl Claassen, ed., *Women in Archaeology* (1994). Rita Wright, ed., *Gender in Archaeology: Research in Gender and Practice* (1996).

Joan M. Gero

GENERAL SYSTEMS THEORY has had a significant impact on archaeological thought over the past three decades. Prior to the 1960s there was no well-established body of theory for exploring the prehistoric past. Traditional archaeologists were more concerned with describing the archaeological record and developing cultural chronologies. Dissatisfaction with this approach prompted a new generation of archaeologists to develop more scientific approaches for understanding and reconstructing prehistoric human behavior. General systems theory, inspired by the biologist Ludwig von Bertalanffy, was one such approach advocated by archaeologists as a means for explaining stability and change in human cultural systems. The attractiveness of the systems approach was its focus on multivariate causality and its emphasis on the interrelationships between components of prehistoric cultural systems.

A resurgence of evolutionary theory in the field of anthropology during the early 1960s set the stage for the development of a systemic view of culture and the use of systems theory in archaeology. The earliest and strongest proponents of systems theory were Lewis Binford in the United States and David Clarke in Britain. Binford conceived of culture as a system composed of technological, social, and ideological subsystems. He argued that structural relationships in prehistoric cultural systems could be investigated through the careful study of artifact assemblages related to each subsystem. Likewise, Clarke, influenced by locational analysis and general systems approaches to the New Geography, envisioned social systems as intercommunicating networks of attributes or entities forming a complex whole. The holistic approach that systems theory offered was applied to a wide array of archaeological problems from the origins of agriculture in the Southern Highlands of Mexico to the emergence of civilization in the Aegean and Mesopotamia.

The use of general systems theory in archaeology prompted debate on what actually constitutes a system. Systems are generally conceived of as a number of interrelated entities, components, and subsystems that have discrete boundaries. Information flow coordinates system components in response to internal structural changes and external stresses. Changes are either regulated to maintain equilibrium (homeostasis) or amplified to promote systemwide changes. Homeostasis is maintained by self-regulating mechanisms (negative feedback) that serve to prevent systemwide changes or collapse. Changes are caused by the amplification (positive feedback) of small perturbations within the system. These irreversible changes either cause systems to collapse or to develop until a new level of homeostasis is obtained.

As with all living systems, cultures are open to the input and output of matter, energy, and information. Therefore, cultural systems are extremely complex and have been defined by archaeologists in many different ways. Beyond recognizing the systemic nature of culture there is no real consensus among archaeologists on how to define and measure the variables, components, and subsystems within a cultural system.

General systems theory was introduced into archaeology to explain why cultures change through time. This was one of the principal goals of the "new archaeology." Unfortunately, many initial applications of systems theory focused on how cultural systems operated in equilibrium. These static models made it difficult to explain cultural change. This led many archaeologists to the unsatisfactory conclusion that change must be stimulated by stresses external to the system. As a result, archaeologists were forced to rely upon "prime movers," such as environmental changes and population increases to explain cultural change. Reliance on these "prime movers" essentially undermined the multivariate approach that systems theory allowed for. The fact is, systems theory actually describes *how* cultures change rather than explaining *why* they change.

More recently, the use of systems theory has been criticized by post-processual archaeologists for being overly mechanistic and functionalist. Post-processual archaeologists argue that an emphasis on cultural systems presupposes group adaptation and ignores the needs, aspirations, and desires of individuals within the system. They also point out that, due to the complexity of cultural systems, the same factors may have different effects depending on individual circumstances. General systems theory is, therefore, overly reductionist and inappropriate for explaining complex cultural phenomena. Unfortunately, they have not provided an alternative approach for investigating the prehistoric past.

Although in recent years there have been few studies that explicitly use general systems theory, the underlying principles of the systems approach still exist in contemporary archaeology. Most archaeologists recognize that systems theory has provided unparalleled insight into the complex ramifications of cultural process. Although the explanatory value of the systems approach is questionable, it does provide an explicit and practical framework to organize various components of a society. Coupled with recent advances in computer simulation and modeling, the systems approach may provide an effective means for investigating more complex interrelationships in human societies. If archaeologists recognize the limitations of the systems approach it can be used heuristically for exploring the prehistoric past.

[*See also* CULTURAL ECOLOGY THEORY; POST-PROCESSUAL THEORY; PROCESSUAL THEORY; THEORY IN ARCHAEOLOGY.]

■ James N. Hill, ed., *Explanation of Prehistoric Change* (1978). Merrilee Salmon, "What Can Systems Theory Do for Archaeology?," *American Antiquity* 43:2 (1978): 174–183. E. Gary Stickel, ed., *New Uses of Systems Theory in Archaeology* (1982). Patty Jo Watson, Steven A. LeBlanc, and Charles Redman, *Archaeological Explanation: The Scientific Method in Archeology* (1984). Bruce G. Trigger, *A History of Archaeological Thought* (1989).

Douglas J. Kennett

GENETICS IN ARCHAEOLOGY. Genetics is the study of inherited variation in living organisms. Inherited traits in humans, from skin color to genes, together with acquired characteristics such as language and cultural habits, can provide information about the geographical origins and ancestry of a person. Beginning with the identification of the ABO blood system in the early years of this century, the realization that the frequency of inherited characteristics could vary in different human populations had a profound impact on the application of genetics to the study of human evolutionary history.

Many genetic traits such as the blood groups are inherited in a simple fashion, and the frequency of a particular type varies markedly in different geographical areas. For instance, Native Americans carry almost exclusively blood group O, whereas the people from the Orkney Islands in the north of Scotland have a particularly high frequency of blood group B. The properties of blood groups are now known to result from small differences in the proteins found on the surface of red blood cells of different individuals. After the elucidation of the structure of the genetic material DNA (deoxyribonucleic acid) in 1953, scientists discovered that protein variants result from spontaneous changes in the sequence of the DNA, known as mutations, that generate new gene forms. These are distributed through populations by mating, natural selection, genetic drift, and migration.

The study of human genetics has undergone exciting changes with the advent of modern molecular biology techniques, and it is becoming increasingly easy to detect and analyze new polymorphic genes (genes present in slightly different forms in different people) that might have medical or anthropological interest. All humans have ancestors, so each person carries in his or her genes a record of their past history. The study of the variation of living populations can provide information about evolutionary processes and the patterns of past population expansions and migrations.

Stanford University geneticist Luca Cavalli-Sforza has pioneered the analysis of genetic variation in living human populations to infer ancient human relationships. With colleagues Paolo Menozzi and Alberto Piazza, he proposed that the spread of farming from the Near East was brought about by population expansion of Neolithic farmers into Europe rather than solely by the diffusion of new technologies. This conclusion was strengthened by the study of the distribution of Indo-European languages in Europe by Cambridge University archaeologist Colin Renfrew. Although the hypothesis is still the subject of heated debate, it has been given additional support by other findings, for example, the study of Robert Sokal and colleagues at the State University of New York at Stony Brook, who observed a close correlation between the patterns of genetic markers in European populations and the archaeological evidence for the spread of farming from the Near East in the last 9,000 years.

More recently, Cavalli-Sforza and colleagues have published an exhaustive compendium of genetic information based on the analysis of blood groups and many other classical (that is, non-DNA) markers in many modern human populations. They have interpreted these in the context of archaeological and linguistic data. In the last few years, however, the emphasis of genetic research has shifted from the study of classic genetic markers to the use of DNA analysis for detecting human variation. Studies on one particular type of DNA, mitochondrial DNA, have made a particular impact on the study of human evolutionary history.

Mitochondrial DNA (mtDNA), present outside the cell nuclei in small structures called mitochondria, has been used extensively in recent years for evolutionary studies, as it has a number of useful characteristics, including its small size, relative simplicity, and rapid rate of evolution. MtDNA is inherited through the maternal line in a manner analogous to the transmission of surnames through the male line. MtDNA does not undergo recombination (the shuffling of maternal and paternal genes that happens from one generation to the next), and it is passed on from mothers to offspring virtually unaltered except for rare changes introduced by mutations. The more alike two individuals are in their mtDNA, the nearer the relationship between them.

One of the most notable studies using human mtDNA was that of Rebecca Cann, Mark Stoneking, and the late Allan Wilson at the University of California at Berkeley. In 1987, these workers carried out an extensive survey of mtDNA variation in present-day people of Africa, Asia, Australia, New Guinea, and Europe. Their results showed that the degree of mtDNA variation in people of different parts of the world was very low, suggesting a relatively recent branching-out of living peoples. Moreover, the African mtDNAs were the most variable, consistent with the idea that the African lineages were the oldest ones. The Berkeley team proposed that all modern mtDNA types can be traced back to a single individual living in Africa approximately 200,000 years ago. This result was consistent with the Out-of-Africa model of the origin of modern humans that states that anatomically modern humans evolved in Africa relatively recently and eventually replaced archaic humans in the rest of the Old World. Although other studies have questioned the statistical validity of the team's results, most research on modern populations has shown more genetic variability in Africa than anywhere else, suggesting that African populations are more ancient than others and had more time to accumulate genetic changes.

Since this pioneering study, the usefulness of mtDNA for phylogenetic and evolutionary studies has gradually been recognized. An area of particular interest for archaeologists and anthropologists concerns the reconstruction of patterns of migration of past human populations in the Pacific and the New World. The vast expanse of Polynesia was settled recently by humans, so it provides a relatively simple scenario for studying migration patterns. There is a significant amount of archaeological, linguistic, and ethnographic data on Pacific populations, which has been augmented recently by genetic data. In their world survey of human mtDNA variation, Wilson and his colleagues identified certain mtDNA polymorphisms specific to Asian populations. Further investigation revealed that one of these informative sites was a harmless mutation consisting of the deletion of nine DNA bases from the mtDNA. This mutation is present at relatively high frequencies in individuals of Asian origin and constitutes a useful anthropological marker for Asian populations. The frequency of the mutation in the Pacific increases from west to east, reaching fixation (i.e., a frequency of 100 percent) in some Polynesian archipelagos. Several other mtDNA markers seem to be present exclusively in Polynesia and can be traced back to island Southeast Asia, providing genetic evidence for the so-called "fast train to Polynesia" model of Pacific settlement. As mtDNA is inherited through the female line only, however, care must be taken in the interpretation of results. What the mtDNA data show is that the ancestors of modern Polynesians derived ultimately from Asia and underwent a very stringent genetic bottleneck, probably somewhere in the central Pacific, during their migration into remote Oceania.

Research on genes carried in the cell nuclei (nuclear DNA), and passed on by both parents, has shed additional light on the question of Polynesian origins. John Clegg and colleagues at the Institute of Molecular Medicine in Oxford are investigating inherited blood disorders in Asian and Pacific populations, in particular the different types of thalassemias that are associated with resistance to malaria in parts of the Pacific. These anemias are caused by chance mutations in genes coding for the oxygen-carrying blood molecule hemoglobin. They persist in human populations at elevated frequencies in regions where malaria is endemic because they confer resistance to this disease. Clegg's group found that some of these globin polymorphisms can be highly informative for inferring the pattern of human movements in Oceania.

A particular mutation in the alpha-globin gene, called the $\alpha^{-3.7}$ III deletion, is present in parts of the Solomon and Bismarck Islands and in the Melanesian archipelago of Vanuatu. Interestingly, although there is no malaria and never has been malaria in the remote islands of Polynesia, the mutation is present at elevated frequencies in many parts of Polynesia, particularly in Tahiti, the Cook Islands, and among New Zealand Maories. As the existence of the mutation in Polynesia cannot be explained by the presence of malaria, Clegg and colleagues suggested that it derived from island Melanesia and was carried into remote Oceania by the proto-Polynesian settlers. This would tend to contradict the "fast train" hypothesis, and argues for a much more gradual expansion of people into the Pacific.

Although the study of genetic markers in modern populations helps to understand events that occurred in prehistory, the interpretation of the data can be obscured by the effect of multiple migrations of peoples, recent genetic bottlenecks, and genetic drift. Some of these problems can be overcome by the use of direct genetic information about the past, in the form of DNA recovered from the skeletal remains and mummified bodies of ancient peoples. This area of research, known as molecular archaeology, has grown considerably in importance in the last few years.

The first ancient human DNA sequences were reported in 1985 by Svante Pääbo at the University of Uppsala, Sweden, who extracted and characterized DNA from the skin of a predynastic Egyptian mummy. Since then, many ancient materials have been shown to contain DNA, including bones, teeth, plant remains, and insects in amber. The analysis of ancient DNA sequences has serious technical problems resulting from poor preservation, degradation of the original DNA, and contamination by microbial DNA from the soil or human DNA from people handling the remains. Some of these problems can be overcome by the use of the polymerase chain reaction (PCR). This permits the amplification of a specific segment of DNA from biological samples with very small amounts of DNA, or DNA that is modified or damaged. Pääbo used the PCR on ancient human brain tissue from a 7,000-year-old site in Florida and detected a mtDNA type not previously observed in the New World. More recently, the amplification of mtDNA from skeletal remains of fifty individuals at a pre-Columbian cemetery in Illinois indicated that there was no appreciable reduction in genetic variation in this area following European contact.

Studies by Erika Hagelberg and Clegg on mtDNA polymorphisms in prehistoric skeletal remains from several archaeological sites in the Pacific, including bones found at Lapita sites, suggested that the people associated with the *Lapita complex might have originated in Melanesia rather than Southeast Asia. This would indicate an expansion of Melanesian people into the central Pacific and/or an extremely "fast train" to Polynesia by people not associated with Lapita, much more recently than the archaeological evidence would allow for. Work is now in progress to obtain more information on the migration patterns of the proto-Polynesians in island Melanesia and the central Pacific.

Another question that was addressed using ancient DNA techniques is that of the origins of the prehistoric inhabitants of *Easter Island. Although most archaeological evidence supports the idea that Easter Island was settled from Polynesia, some workers, most notably Thor Heyerdahl, argue that the earliest inhabitants of Easter Island came from the Tiwanaku area of South America. The evidence from genetic analyses on modern inhabitants of Eastern Island is unreliable, as most people today are the descendants of Chilean migrants. Analysis of mtDNA in prehistoric skeletal remains from Easter Island, however, revealed characteristic mtDNA markers that pointed to a Polynesian origin.

One of the most extraordinary archaeological finds of recent years was the discovery in September 1991 of the body of a Bronze Age man in the high mountains between Austria and Italy. Although radiocarbon dating of the skin gave dates between 5300 and 5100 B.P., some scientists argued that the body was an ancient Egyptian or South American mummy placed recently in the ice as an elaborate hoax. MtDNA of the Iceman fell within the range of mtDNA variation of Europeans, however, and was therefore probably not from an Amerind or Egyptian mummy. A more precise determination of the origins of the individual will need to await a much better understanding of genetic variability in modern European populations.

Although most current genetic studies concern the genetic relationships between humans in different parts of the world, research on animals is providing valuable information about farming and domestication. A group of geneticists at Trinity College Dublin have started an extensive survey of mtDNA and nuclear DNA variation in European and African cattle, which together with data generated from ancient breeds will help in understanding the processes of domestication and the complicated relationships between humans and their animals.

To conclude, despite the significant power and promise of genetics, it is important to remember that the gross misuse of genetic information in the first half of this century by the eugenics movement and the nefarious consequences of the ideology of racial hygiene in Nazi Germany have blemished the reputation of the subject, and some scholars still question the use of genetics for understanding human affairs. Nevertheless, scholars should also remember that human beings warred with each other over perceived differences in religion or ethnicity for millennia before the advent of modern genetics. The fact remains that genocide, together with famine, disease, and migration, was and is one of the most important forces in shaping the observed patterns of human genetic variation in the world. Genetics should not be imbued with some kind of malignant power, as it is basically just a collection of methods for looking at inherited traits in living beings. An informed understanding of the meaning of genetic data, coupled with information from other sources, may be able to provide invaluable insights into the development of human societies.

[See also HUMANS, MODERN: ORIGINS OF MODERN HUMANS; PACIFIC ISLANDS: INTRODUCTION.]

■ R. L. Cann, M. Stoneking, and A. C. Wilson, "Mitochondrial DNA and Human Evolution," *Nature* 325 (1987): 31–36. C. Renfrew, *Archaeology and Language: The Puzzle of Indo-European Origins* (1987). A.V.S. Hill, D. F. O'Shaughnessy, and J. B. Clegg, "Haemoglobin and Globin Gene Variants in the Pacific," in eds. A.V.S. Hill and S. W. Serjeantson, *The Colonization of the Pacific: A Genetic Trail* (1989). E. Hagelberg and J. B. Clegg, "Genetic Polymorphisms in Prehistoric Pacific Islanders Determined by Analysis of Ancient DNA," *Proceedings of the Royal Society of London, Series B* 252 (1993): 163–170. S. Jones, *The Language of the Genes* (1993). L. L. Cavalli-Sforza, A. Piazza, and P. Menozzi, *The History and Geography of Human Genes* (1994). E. Hagelberg, "Ancient DNA Studies," *Evolutionary Anthropology* 2 (1994): 199–207. E. Hagelberg et al., "DNA from Ancient Easter Islanders," *Nature* 369 (1994): 25–26. O. Handt et al., "Molecular Genetic Analyses of the Tyrolean Ice Man," *Science* 264 (1994): 1775–1778.

Erika Hagelberg

GEOGRAPHICAL INFORMATION SYSTEMS.

A geographic information system (GIS) is simply a spatially referenced database that allows for the storage, analysis, retrieval, and display of spatial data. As Kenneth Kvamme stated so clearly in his seminal article, "Geographic Information Systems in Regional Archaeological Research and Data Management," since artifacts are distributed in sites and sites are distributed in regions, there is almost nothing archaeologists do that does not have some spatial reference.

A GIS consists of a number of data layers, sometimes referred to as coverages. These thematic layers may include data such as contours, roads, soil types, hydrology, vegetation zones, and archaeological sites or features. An important feature of a GIS is the construction of new data layers from these base coverages. Aspect, slope or grade, view, or other features can be generated. Additional data types might include aerial photographs or satellite images that are either used as independent coverages or used to generate data layers such as structural geology, vegetation, soil moisture, and other features.

The most common GIS software organize data either in vector or raster formats. Vector systems are most often used in facilities management or land management and have what is termed a topological structure consisting of points, lines, and areas or polygons. The advantages of using vector systems for management of facilities such as utilities, roads, cities, and other entities where many of the data types are easily conceived of as points (traffic lights, manhole covers, stop signs, as lines (streets, pipelines, power lines), or as areas or polygons (towns, blocks, properties) are rather obvious. They are often used in archaeology to define site or survey boundaries and are useful when investigating coastal areas. Many historic preservation agencies have adopted vector GIS systems for resource management.

Raster-based GIS is somewhat more popular in archaeology. In these systems, the area under study is gridded (as a matrix) so that each grid unit has a row and column coordinate and a number of data categories might be attached to each grid square. The size of the grid should be dictated by the research question being investigated, but more often the grid size is determined by limits in the software, hardware, or the quality of the data.

In the past raster systems were more often less expensive, with a number of early raster GIS packages built for personal computers. Archaeologists also find grid-based systems more intuitive because that is exactly how archaeologists analytically view sites and landscapes. They also find it somewhat easier to extract data for quantitative analyses from grid matrices for the purposes of predictive modeling. Today most GIS systems can handle both kinds of data, but to different levels of sophistication. The goal of the archaeologist is to pick, through a careful research design, the analysis tools necessary for the research problem at hand. Unfortunately, the use of GIS in archaeology is currently dictated by technology, not by scientific inquiry.

One of the important uses of GIS in archaeology is in exploratory data analysis (EDA). EDA is simply problem driven exploration of the data. The recent proliferation in computer-based graphics, combined with modern EDA, allows archaeologists to ask "what do these data look like?" or "what are the structural relationships between these variables?" Often patterns emerge which, after further analysis, are behaviorally meaningful even though there was no preconceived hypothesis predicting the relationship. Of course it also lets the archaeologist identify absolutely meaningless relationships.

Viewshed construction is another interesting use of GIS in archaeology. Viewsheds allow the construction of data layers that are a product of the interrelationship between a point on the landscape (the viewer) and a digital representation of the landscape or digital elevation model (DEM). The result is an image or coverage of all of the possible areas of the landscape visible from any one point. Viewsheds have been used outside of archaeology for some time, especially in relation to architecture and scenic views, such as parklands.

Viewsheds have been most popular in archaeology when attempting to get at elements of cognition. In a seminal work, Lock and Harris used viewsheds to demonstrate that no long barrow (among many) in the Danebury region of England could be seen from any other. Maschner used viewshed analysis on the Northwest Coast of North America to demonstrate that in the Middle to Late Phase transition (approximately A.D. 500), villages moved to locations that had approximately three times more view than they had previously—a measure of increasing defensibility in this region.

Archaeologists have also begun to use GIS capabilities to address the issue of site-catchment analysis and boundary definition using cost surfaces and other features. Cost surfaces allow distance to be weighted by slope, vegetation, or other natural features that might act as obstacles or facilitators in travel. One of the original, and longest-lasting, critiques of site-catchment analysis as it was used in archaeology was that the concentric rings drawn around sites did little to represent, or account for, the natural landscape. It has been casually argued for some time that GIS should be able to solve this through the incorporation of friction surfaces (time/effort principle) produced from actual landscape data.

Thiessen polygons are often used in archaeology to define boundaries, and these can be constructed by most GIS software. The outcome of the construction of Thiessen polygons is a line perpendicular and equidistant to two points or centers. Some of the problems inherent in these types of analyses is that there has been little control for natural features of the landscape. There is also no control for variations in agricultural productivity, population size, political power, or time. This is because most software that will conduct a Thiessen tessellation assumes that all points are contemporaneous and are of equal weight. A good example of catchment analysis, Thiessen polygons, and other territorial analyses can be found in Gaffney and Stancic's analysis of the archaeological data from the island of Hvar.

One of the most important issues and uses for GIS in archaeological research is for the predictive modeling of archaeological site locations. The goal of predictive modeling is to identify environmental and social variables that can be used to describe known site locations, and then to use those variables to predict the locations of unknown archaeological sites. These models need not be simply locational and a number of papers have demonstrated the versatility of GIS for modeling beyond mere site prediction. These include studies of early historic trade, studies of environmental change and agricultural production, analyses of political decision making, and paleodemography.

GIS as a database tool for managing archaeological data is also important. This is seen both in the storage of raw data and in the organization and presentation of the data. Archaeological data are spatially and temporally distributed, both by site and by region, and are thus spatially referenced. A GIS will allow the storage, cataloging, and management of huge amounts of spatial information that can be easily retrieved, analyzed, cross-referenced, and correlated. The ability to associate a site description and map location, or to find all of the sites within approximately 333 feet (100 m) of a roadway through a simple buffering routine, has revolutionized some preservation agencies's management abilities.

[*See also* ARTIFACT DISTRIBUTION ANALYSIS; CULTURAL RESOURCE MANAGEMENT: SITE MANAGEMENT; ENVIRONMENTAL ARCHAEOLOGY; PALEOENVIRONMENTAL RECONSTRUCTION; SETTLEMENT ARCHAEOLOGY; SETTLEMENT-PATTERN ANALYSIS.]

■ Kenneth Kvamme, "Geographic Information Systems in Regional Archaeological Research and Data Management," in *Archaeological Method and Theory: Volume 1*, Michael Schiffer, ed. (1989): 139–204. K. S. Allen, Stanton W. Green, Ezra B. W. Zubrow, eds., *Interpreting Space: GIS and Archaeology* (1990). R. Warren, "Predictive Modelling in Archaeology 1990," in *Interpreting Space: GIS and Archaeology*, K. S. Allen, Stanton W. Green, Ezra B. W. Zubrow, eds. (1990): 90–111. V. Gaffney and Z. Stančič, *GIS Approaches to Regional Analysis: A Case Study from the Island of Hvar* (1991).

Herbert D. G. Maschner

GERMANS AND GERMANIC INVASIONS. By the second century B.C. and perhaps earlier, the Classical world had become aware of large tribal groupings in northern Europe, north and east of the Celts, extending from the Rhine to the Vistula and from southern Scandinavia to the Danube. Greek and Roman writers gave the name *Germanoi* or *Germani* to these peoples, a term obscure in origin and not used by the peoples themselves. These tribal societies were not bound together by any sense of ethnic unity and there were evident cultural differences between the various groups. Those close to the Rhine and Danube bore the influence of Celtic culture to a marked extent. Those in southeastern Europe had links with the nomadic peoples of the steppes. Although the Germanic peoples first emerge in the literary record in the first century B.C., their archaeology can be traced back to the early first millennium B.C., when stable societies were established across the north European plain and the lands around the Baltic. These peoples probably shared a language, or interrelated dialects, of Indo-European origin and of clear relation to the Celtic language. By the later first century B.C., the Germanic peoples had become the dominant power in northern Europe, displacing the *Celts in the center of Europe and compelling Rome to attempt their conquest in the reign of Augustus (12 B.C. to A.D. 9), and when that failed, convincing Rome to establish strongly manned frontiers against them.

Germanic society was geared to warfare. Kingship existed, but the power of kings was limited and deposition frequent. Some of the most successful war-leaders (e.g., Maroboduus and Arminius) had earlier seen service in the Roman army and exploited what they had learned there in developing their power among their own peoples. Around the war-leaders gathered the fighting men in retinues (*comitatus*), bound to their lords by social and military obligations. Below them in turn were the free peasantry. This social structure proved very durable, surviving down to the early Middle Ages. Economically, Germanic societies depended very heavily upon agriculture and their settlement sites reveal that fact clearly. The most fully examined sites lie in the northern coastlands (e.g., *Feddersen Wierde, Tofting, and Nørre Fjand) and the Dutch lowlands (e.g., Wijster, Rhee, and Bennekom). These were the settlements of developed peasant societies reliant upon mixed farming regimes, in which animal husbandry (especially of cattle) was prominent. A wide range of grain crops was raised, including various forms of wheat, rye, and barley. Most settlements were relatively small before the first century A.D., the hamlet or small village being the common form. Large nucleated settlements or towns were unknown and strongly defended sites were rare. In the northern coastlands and close to the Roman frontiers, there was a tendency for settlements to increase in size after about A.D. 200.

Trade and exchange were actively pursued with the Roman world from the first century B.C. onward. Roman imports of bronze and silver vessels, glassware, pottery, brooches, weapons, and coinage crossed the frontiers and reached richer Germans in quantity, in return for agricultural products, amber, and slaves. A notable concentration of imports was drawn to the western Baltic lands, where trading posts like Gudme (Fyn, Denmark) acted as centers of redistribution. These trading connections brought the Germanic peoples into close contact with the Roman world and led to a change in economic life and artistic standards, especially in metalwork. This process of acculturation was to have far-reaching effects on Germanic culture in the migration period. Another important area of association with far-reaching consequences was military service. From the early Roman Empire onward, Germans were recruited into the Roman army as Imperial guards, officers, and increasingly as infantry soldiers. By the fourth century A.D., a large proportion of the Roman forces consisted of Germans and many of the highest ranking commanders were *Franks and Alamanni. These connections contributed much to the background of migration and the wider search for settlement in the Empire.

The Period of Migration. The great migrations of peoples from the late fourth century to the seventh century framed a period of transformation in Europe, accompanying and contributing to the collapse of the western Roman Empire. The origins of the migrations lie in a major realignment of peoples which began in the late second and early third centuries, as emergent confederacies east of the Rhine and north of the Danube began to pit their strength against the Roman frontiers. East of the Rhine, the Franks and Alamanni emerged as groups of war-bands which harried the Roman provinces on the Rhine and broke through the defenses in devastating fashion between A.D. 250 and 275. The Alamanni later settled between the upper Rhine and upper Danube. The Franks began to infiltrate Roman territory on the lower Rhine from the later fourth century onward. That migration was a gradual and piecemeal process, stimulated at first by the rewards offered for service with Rome and later given impetus by the rising ambitions of Frankish leaders.

Archaeologically, the Franks are difficult to identify before the mid-fifth century. For much of the fifth century Frankish settlement was contained within a number of petty kingdoms in the Rhineland, the Moselle valley, and in western Belgium. The grave of one of the early kings, Childeric of Tournai (d. A.D. 481), found in 1653, is a vitally important fixed point in Frankish archaeology. This man's son, Clovis or Chlodovech, was later to unite the minor kingdoms in a powerful union which dominated northern Gaul and quickly expanded against the Alamanni, the Burgundians, and, eventually, the Visigoths of Aquitaine after the battle of Vouillé in 507.

The most successful and enduring of Germanic kingdoms were those of the Ostrogoths in Italy, the Visigoths in Spain, and the Franks in Gaul. The Visigoths entered the Roman Empire as suppliants, fleeing before the Huns from the steppes in the 370s. Later, under their king Alaric, they moved west to threaten Italy in the first decade of the fifth century, seizing Rome briefly in 410. Having failed to achieve a permanent settlement in Italy, they were eventually settled as allies of Rome in Aquitaine in 418, maintaining a kingdom there until the early sixth century. Under pressure from the Franks, they moved their seat of power to Spain and dominated the Spanish peninsula throughout the sixth and seventh centuries. Their kingdom exploited the surviving Roman cities, institutions, and industries and in the seventh century was culturally the most advanced of the Germanic powers. Its demise, however, was sudden in the face of the Arab invasion of Spain in 711.

The Ostrogoths, long subject to rule by the Huns, were released when the Hun Empire collapsed in the mid-fifth century. They built up a strong power base in Pannonia on the middle Danube and were led into Italy by their young and vigorous king, Theoderic, at the behest of the Byzantine emperor. The kingdom which Theoderic established in Italy preserved much from the Roman past and during the king's lifetime was a stable presence in the central Mediterranean. His capital, Ravenna, was adorned with several fine churches decorated with superb mosaics, some of which still survive (e.g., St. Vitale, St. Apollinare in Classe, and St. Apollinare Nuovo). But Ostrogothic power quickly waned after Theoderic's death and the people never regained their former dominance.

An exceptional migration of the early fifth century, involving a mass movement by sea, was that of the Vandals, a migration which carried this people from the Rhine to possession of the rich coastlands of Africa in only twenty-five years. The Vandal sweep through Gaul and Spain was accomplished in only three years (A.D. 406 to 409). Their ravages severely depleted the resources of Spain and the untouched riches of Africa beckoned. In 428, a host of Vandals crossed the Strait of Gibraltar and rapidly conquered the North African seaboard. Within the next two years most of the Roman cities had fallen to them and for the next century much of North Africa was a Vandal kingdom. Many of the leading Vandals settled in the fertile hinterland of *Carthage, others in the plain about Tipasa and Cherchel. There was no development of a distinctive Vandal culture. The incomers were absorbed within the late Roman order to a large extent and less disruption was caused to the social and economic structure than was once believed. Vandal power was eventually ended by the Byzantine reconquest of North Africa of A.D. 533.

The peoples of the northern coastlands—Frisians, Angles, Saxons, and others—began to raid the Roman provinces in the third century and by the early fifth century had begun to make lodgements on Roman territory. The Saxons settled in northern Gaul and eastern Britain, the Angles and the Frisians also in the island, possibly at first with the sanction of Romano-British communities there. The earliest arrivals seized land in East Anglia and Essex, though others quickly established themselves in Kent, Sussex, and the Thames Valley. About the middle of the fifth century, larger numbers of Angles and Saxons began to arrive in Britain. Although defeated by the Britons in battle at Mount Badon late in the fifth century, the forward movement of Germanic groups was resumed from about A.D. 500 and over the next century the foundations of a number of kingdoms were laid in southeastern Britain. The most advanced of these lay in Kent, which had cultural and diplomatic contacts with the Franks in Gaul, and it was to the ruler of Kent that Pope Gregory dispatched his Christian mission in 597.

The sixth century witnessed a second major wave of migration which was to have considerable impact on later Europe. The Slavs began their movement into the Balkans and westward to the Elbe. Meanwhile, the Lombards, threatened by the nomadic Avars, were led by their king, Alboin, into Italy in 568 and there quickly became the dominant force from their base between the Alps and the Appennines. Their leaders did not immediately create an orderly system of government; not until about 600 did the Lombard

kingdom take shape. The main area of Lombard settlement remained northern Italy, though new strongholds were founded further south, such as Castel Trosino and Nocera Umbra, both of these commanding important routes towards Rome. Culturally, these groups of settlers were influenced by warriors whose graves are found in cemeteries of the late sixth and seventh centuries, for instance, those at Cividale.

Thus, by the end of the sixth century A.D., most of western and central Europe was occupied by Germanic peoples at several levels of political organization, ranging from settled kingdoms to surviving tribalism. These were the powers which were to provide the essential basis for the civilization of medieval Europe.

[See also BRITISH ISLES: THE ANGLO-SAXONS; EUROPE: ROMAN AND POST-ROMAN EUROPE; ROMAN EMPIRE: THE ROMAN FRONTIER.]

■ E. A. Thompson, *The Early Germans* (1965). L. Musset, *The Germanic Invasions* (1975). J. Campbell, ed., *The Anglo-Saxons* (1982). H-J. Diesner, *The Great Migration* (1982). J. M. Wallace-Hadrill, *The Barbarian West* (rev. ed. 1985). Edward James, *The Franks* (1987). H. Wolfram, *History of the Goths* (1988). Peter Heather, *Goths and Romans* (1991). Malcolm Todd, *The Early Germans* (1992).

Malcolm Todd

GREAT WALL OF CHINA. The Great Wall of China, snaking its way along the mountaintops of northern China, is probably the largest construction on Earth, and is the only human product visible from the moon. It is not a continuous wall, nor is it a single wall. In places there are as many as three walls 62 miles (100 km) or more apart, and where the terrain made a wall unnecessary, there are gaps between wall segments. The wall stretches 3,700 miles (6,000 km), from Shanhaiguan on Bohai Bay in the east to Jiayuguan, at the edge of the desert in Gansu Province in the west. The wall known today is largely the Ming Wall, which was made of stone, bricks, and stamped earth, with fortresses and watchtowers erected along its length.

It is often said that the Great Wall was constructed to keep the nomads out, but this is an overly simplistic notion. In fact, peoples to the northeast of the Great Wall were settled farmers as early as any living south of the (later) wall; the nomads were mostly in the north and northwest. Some of the earliest stretches of the wall were probably from the Warring States period (500–221 B.C.), but one of the accomplishments of the Qin dynasty (221–206 B.C.) was the joining and strengthening of scattered fragments of walls erected by conquered states. Other walls were known in China from various periods, including long stretches of walls in Liaoning Province, in some places made of wooden palisades. Some smaller linear stone walls are found in the Lower Xiajiadian culture (2000–1500 B.C.) in western Liaoning, indicating the very long history of such defensive walls in China.

The walls were periodically refurbished, and the walls visible today are largely attributable to the Ming dynasty (1368–1644). The succeeding Qing, having originated in Manchuria beyond the Great Wall, had no need of a wall. In most of the places where tourists are taken to see the wall, especially outside Beijing at Badaling, the wall is of recent reconstruction by the People's Republic of China, to attract tourists, rather than for defensive purposes.

Corvée labor, army troops, and convicts constructed the walls, and many died in the process. The Qin Wall was built in about twelve years by 300,000 soldiers and 500,000 conscripted peasants. Construction of the wall under the Ming dynasty took place in sections throughout the dynasty, with uncounted millions of laborers. Although local materials were used, the task of procuring the building materials and supervising the construction was formidable. The continuously varying elevations of the wall caused special problems in construction methods. Even the Ming Wall is faced only with stone, having a rock, earth, and rubble core. Thousands of gates allowed limited passage through the wall, and battlements protected the defenders along with wider platforms found at intervals along the wall. Fortifications were located at strategic spots for defense. Beacon towers were erected on high ground so that each could be seen from the next on either side. Other buildings included barracks for soldiers, tea houses, and temples. The wall, even in its ruined state, remains one of the world's wonders.

[See also ASIA: PREHISTORY AND EARLY HISTORY OF EAST ASIA; CHINA: INTRODUCTION.]

■ Luo Zhewen et al., *The Great Wall of China* (1981). Luo Zhewen and Zhao Luo, *The Great Wall of China in History and Legend* (1986). Arthur Waldron, *The Great Wall of China* (1990).

Sarah Milledge Nelson

GREAT ZIMBABWE. The impressive Great Zimbabwe ruins are located approximately 17 miles (28 km) southeast of Masvingo, a modern town in south-central Zimbabwe. The ancient African Iron Age site lies on a steep-sided rocky hill and spreads into an adjacent valley on the southeastern edge of the Zimbabwe plateau. The ruins, which are a national monument, comprise dry-stone walls and numerous earth (daga) house remains of varying sizes, constructed over an area of approximately 1,779 acres (720 ha).

The Iron Age settlement is one of more than two hundred stone ruins scattered all over southern Africa. The word "Zimbabwe" is derived from the Shona (a variant of the Bantu language) word *dzimbabwe* meaning "houses of stone."

Archaeological Background. During the Iron Age Period, the Great Zimbabwe site was probably the largest settlement in sub-Saharan Africa. It was certainly the largest built-up area before the colonization of the region by Europeans. The pattern of this Iron Age settlement reflects the socioeconomic arrangements and cultural ethos of local African communities during this period. The settlement was constructed over several centuries, starting from A.D. 1100 to about A.D. 1500. At its peak, between twelve thousand and twenty thousand people settled around the stone buildings. The monument is what remains of an ancient capital which controlled a large emporium extended over 38,613 square miles (100,000 sq km) between the Zambezi and the Limpopo. Its wealth was based mainly on cattle husbandry, crop cultivation, and the domination of the trade routes between the gold areas in the north and the coast of the Indian Ocean in the east. The wealth enabled the rulers of Great Zimbabwe to extend their influence in the region. The trade contacts between Great Zimbabwe and the Arab-Swahili on the east coast were established by A.D. 900. By A.D. 1250 the Iron Age town had become an important trading center involving many countries around the Indian Ocean. The trade contact within the region is attested by some of the artifacts found on the sites. These include copper crosses, which were used as a form of currency. Chinese stone and glassware have also been recovered from Great Zimbabwe. Great Zimbabwe bartered raw materials such as gold, copper, and ivory in exchange for imported china, glass, cloth, and other artifacts from countries from the Indian Ocean. With this trade Zimbabwe became an integral part of a vast economic system, which connected southern Africa to a much wider world.

By the end of the fifteenth century the population of the settlement began to decline. The ecological imbalance caused by such a concentration of population and the need to control directly the alluvial gold working to the north, as well as the plateau, may have contributed to the decline of the settlement. Although largely abandoned by its inhabitants, the site continued to play an important role in the region. By the nineteenth century, there is evidence that the settlement was being used partly as a religious site and center of refuge, but most areas of the site had been abandoned and were now in a ruinous state.

Great Zimbabwe was first brought to the attention of the outside world by Portuguese writers like João de Barros during the sixteenth century. However, in 1871 the German geologist Carl Mauch visited the site and described Great Zimbabwe to the Western world in detail. Early European settlers attributed the construction of the site to the Phoenicians. However, archaeological investigation at Great Zimbabwe by David Randal-MacIver in 1905 and Gertrude *Caton-Thompson in 1929 confirmed the site's African origin.

Architectural Details. The structures at Great Zimbabwe ruins, whose architecture is one of the principal cultural identities of the African Iron Age Period, were not built to a master plan. They were constructed and altered over many centuries. The granite stone walls were built in order to screen off and divide space in this huge settlement. The houses in which people lived were built of daga. The structures were also a symbol of power and wealth of the people who built them. The site can be divided into three main areas, the Hill Complex, the Great Enclosure, and the Valley Ruins.

The Hill Complex, is constructed on a hill located north of the site. The occupation of the hill goes back to the Early Iron Age, when the community had not yet acquired the technique of stone building. The stratigraphic sequence shows that the stone-building phases started in the hill around A.D. 900. The stone-building phase coincides with the movement of the Late Iron Age communities from places like *Mapungubwe in the south. The dry-stone walls constitute the major architectural features on the hill, the western wall with its solid stone conical turrets and monolith decorations being the largest wall. With its stone-lintelled entrance, this is perhaps the finest architectural detailing on the site. Another spectacular piece of engineering is the south wall, built on the brink of a rock precipice; although its height is approximately 33 feet (10 m), the base is only 14 feet (4 m) wide. In the various enclosures on the hill natural granite boulders were incorporated into the matrix of the stone structures. Most of the dry-stone structures on the hill are free standing. Few daga structures remain as part of the Hill Complex, but when Carl Mauch visited it in the late nineteenth century the western enclosure had molded daga platforms. He also found some carved soapstone birds in one of the Hill enclosures. The birds, whose function has not yet been fully established, are unique to Great Zimbabwe.

The Great Enclosure, situated across the valley, is perhaps the most spectacular and substantial structure at Great

Zimbabwe. With its outer wall of approximately 912 feet (278 m) in length and with a maximum height of 31 feet (9.5 m), it is by far the largest single prehistoric structure in sub-Saharan Africa. Inside, it contains a number of internal stone enclosures, daga platforms, and other architectural features, including the impressive conical tower. The tower is regarded as a symbol of power and fertility by many researchers. The back of the Great Enclosure wall is decorated with stone monoliths and a chevron pattern. The entrances were originally lintelled with wood.

The Valley Ruins, located between the Hill and the Great Enclosure, contain most of the architectural features already described. They are similar to the Great Enclosure except that the Valley Ruins comprise several individual enclosures. The external entrances, although they have the semicircular buttresses, are much wider. There are a number of earth mounds, which is an indication of the previous existence of daga structures. Recent excavations of some of the mounds at Great Zimbabwe have revealed that the daga houses during this time were as impressive as the monumental stone structures. The prehistoric structures were designed to last and were more complex than the more recent single-compartment hut dwellings synonymous with daga material. They were often divided into two or more compartments, with verandas, complete interior platforms, and fittings. Some of the soapstone birds which have become a national symbol were found in the Valley Ruins.

Conclusion. With the Great Zimbabwe state declining from about the fifteenth century, new powerful Shona states were found in the north and southwest parts of the country. In the north the powerful Munhumutapa state was established, and it soon replaced Great Zimbabwe as a major trading center with the east coast. In the southwest a new capital was found at *Khami. At Khami the stone architectural styles which were initiated at Great Zimbabwe were continued and perfected. Other lesser known stone capitals were established at such sites as Danamombe, Nalatale, and Shangagwe.

[See also AFRICA: THE RISE OF KINGDOMS AND STATES IN AFRICA; TRADE, AFRICAN.]

■ G. Caton-Thompson, *The Zimbabwe Culture* (1931). E. E. Burke, *The Journals of Carl Mauch* (1969). P. S. Garlake, *Great Zimbabwe* (1973).

Webber Ndoro

GREECE

OVERVIEW

Beginning in the period of social upheaval and economic change that marked the disintegration of the Mycenaean culture on the Greek mainland—and of the reorganization of settlement in the formerly Hittite-controlled territories along the western coast of Asia Minor—disparate cultural and political elements begin to coalesce into the complex cultural constellation that would eventually become known as the civilization of classical Greece. In the sections that follow, the archaeological remains of the Submycenaean period and the so-called Greek Dark Ages will be described,

as will the emergence of a network of relatively autonomous city-states. These polities, whose culture was based on local traditions and veneration of local heroes, nonetheless embodied religious traditions and social relations that were common throughout mainland Greece and the Aegean region.

These ultimately became the nucleus of cultural and political forms that would comprise the basis of the independent polis. Together with the distinctive styles of artistic expression, architecture, language, and literature, the evolving cultural complex of the Greek city-states spread first to the Greek colonies of Magna Graecia and then, through the agency of the Macedonian kingdom, throughout much of the Near East. In its Hellenistic forms, Greek culture had enormous influence on shaping the culture of *Rome. Indeed, the classical Greek traditions would exert continuing influence in the Near East and the eastern Mediterranean throughout the Byzantine Period. Their longer-range impact would be felt in the formulation of western European culture through the Middle Ages and beyond.

[See also GREECE: BYZANTINE GREECE; GREEK ART AND ARCHITECTURE, CLASSICAL, articles on CLASSICAL GREEK POTTERY, CLASSICAL GREEK SCULPTURE, CLASSICAL GREEK ARCHITECTURE.]

Neil Asher Silberman

DARK AGE GREECE

The period between the demise of Mycenaean civilization (conventionally dated sometime after 1200 B.C.) and the rise of Archaic Greece (ca. 700 B.C.), or part of it, has attracted the name "Dark Age," which is actually a pejorative term for the Early Iron Age. The concept of a "dark age" is more of a modern scholarly construction than one based on solid archaeological evidence; Greeks of the historic era, including Herodotos and Thucydides, knew of no dark age. In modern scholarship it forms a rather unsatisfactory interlude between two comparatively well-explored cultural phases: the earlier, Mycenaean, characterized by a syllabic script (Linear B) used to record numerous, centrally administered transactions, and a later period corresponding to the adoption by the Greeks of the Phoenician alphabet sometime in the eighth century B.C. The study of the period between these two literate phases has been colored by its lying between the two scholarly traditions of *classical archaeology and Aegean prehistory. For classical archaeologists the Early Iron Age signifies the beginning of something distinctly "Hellenic," even though the decipherment of Linear B as an early form of Greek forty years ago should have revolutionized the teaching of early Greek history. For Aegean prehistorians on the other hand, the destruction of the great Bronze Age palaces and the advent of iron technology represent convenient, if artificial, stopping points. The fact that an era designated as "dark" is ushered in by a technological innovation as evidently important as the widespread use of iron in the Greek mainland is, in itself, significant. The overall length of this passage of darkness encompasses, for some scholars, the entire era of illiteracy, whereas others allocate it a shorter time span, specifically the earlier part of the period, viewing the later Early Iron Age, or Geometric Period, as a time of recovery. Many scholars agree that the eighth century heralds a virtual "renaissance" in Aegean culture.

The relative chronology of the Early Iron Age is based on that aspect of material culture most abundantly preserved and subjected to closest scrutiny: painted pottery, much of it from burial contexts. The internal chronology of the period as a whole has been closely linked to the successive pottery styles of the Aegean Early Iron Age, namely, "Final Mycenaean/Submycenaean," Protogeometric, and Geometric. Ceramic style alone, however, can sometimes be a misleading indicator of social change, and the specific stages of ceramic history should not be confused with social, political, or economic developments. The question of the absolute chronology of this period continues to generate a good deal of controversy and revision. The flattening out of the radiocarbon calibration curve between ca. 800 and 400 B.C. and the lack of substantial timber samples for dendrochronology leave the absolute chronology of the Aegean Early Iron Age dependent on contexts in which artifacts, almost invariably pottery, can be connected with recorded historical events. The only such events in the Greek world are the foundation dates, derived from the writings of Thucydides and later authors, of the Greek colonies in Sicily and south Italy. The validity of these dates has been questioned; they are limited to the closing stages of the period (mid-eighth century B.C. and later) and there is no guarantee that pottery found at particular sites coincides with the attested foundation dates for those colonies. In the east, Greek Early Iron Age pottery is more abundant in stratified contexts at various sites in north Syria, Cilicia, and Palestine (especially Al Mina, Tell Sukas, Tabbat-al-Hammam, Tarsus, Tell Abu Hawam, Megiddo, Samaria), but the historical interpretation of these contexts has led to disagreement. In addition, a number of contexts, mostly tombs, especially in Crete, the Dodecanese, and Cyprus, have yielded large groups of pottery of various Greek local styles, as well as Cypriot, that has permitted the cross-linking of Greek and Cypriot material. Although potentially significant, the quantity of Egyptian objects, particularly items inscribed with regnal dates of pharaohs, found in good contexts with Greek material is very limited. However problematic, the essential lines of this chronology are fixed with reasonable clarity. The recent challenge to the established chronology, which dates the end of the Bronze Age to ca. 950 B.C., has met with stiff resistance from both Near Eastern and Aegean archaeologists.

In all aspects of material culture such as pottery, metalwork, burial customs, and architecture, there is much regional variation within the Greek world. At the same time, cultural contact, trade, and other forms of interchange kept various settlements closely linked throughout the period, especially those situated around the Aegean Sea. In central Greece, *Athens was a thriving settlement that appears to have exerted some cultural influence over neighboring regions, such as Boeotia, as well as islands such as Aegina and Keos. Athenian pottery of the Protogeometric and Geometric styles has been found throughout the Aegean and eastern Mediterranean, and has often been used as a chronological yardstick. Athenian, or Athenian-inspired, pottery found in coastal western Asia Minor, especially at Old Smyrna and Miletus, as well as a number of islands of the central Aegean, may well provide archaeological evidence of the Ionian migrations discussed by various ancient authors.

Euboea, parts of Thessaly, and the northern Cyclades form a regional koine that is quite distinct. Euboean pottery in particular is found in some quantity in Cyprus, the coastal Levant, and in Italy, especially at Pithekoussai. The most fully explored site on Euboea, Lefkandi, has shed much light on the period, especially its numerous graves, many richly furnished (some with the earliest post-Mycenaean eastern imports to Greece), the monumental apsidal building on the Toumba Hill, and direct evidence for metalworking and other industrial activity at the site. In the Peloponnese, the Argolid, the traditional Mycenaean homeland, along with the Corinthia, appears to form a separate regional cultural unit, as does Lakonia with parts of western Greece. In Epiros, Macedonia, and Thrace, on the other hand, cultural/archaeological assemblages continue from the Bronze Age with little perceptible change, while coastal sites such as Torone and others in Chalkidike display strong links with central and southern Greece.

This pattern of regional diversity is nowhere more evident than on Crete, an island where native "Sub-Minoan" tradition met some influence from mainland Greece, particularly Athens and Euboea, and close commercial ties with the eastern Mediterranean, especially Cyprus and Phoenicia. This is clearly seen at *Knossos, a large settlement site. Direct evidence of Phoenician immigrant craftsmen has recently come to light from the excavations at Kommos and Eleutherna. Similar connections with the east are also evident in the Dodecanese, especially Rhodes and Kos. These various regional entities accord, in a general way, with the distribution of the later Greek dialects. Such a regionally defined spread of literacy helped to harden linguistic units and contributed to a more explicit definition of Archaic territorial polities.

Diachronically, the traditional view of the "dark age" in Greece has been one of decline (twelfth and earlier eleventh centuries), followed by isolation (later eleventh and tenth century), then the beginnings of recovery (late tenth to early eighth centuries), culminating in the "Greek renaissance" (mid-late eighth century). Such an overview is, however, purely descriptive; it lacks explanatory power. The reasons for the demise of a civilization as archaeologically visible as the Mycenaean have long been a matter of debate. The two most popular scenarios are an invasion(s) theory, conventionally linked with supposed Dorian invaders (and handmade burnished pottery), phenomena which are themselves loosely pinned onto the later literary tradition of the return of the Herakleidai. The other explanation is "a social uprising" (sometimes also linked with a Dorian "substratum" of Mycenaen society), or internal collapse. Certainly the twelfth century was a period of upheaval, witnessing movements of peoples not only in Greece, but throughout the entire eastern Mediterranean. Whatever the causes of the disintegration of Mycenaean civilization, there was a significant shift in the nature of occupation and in subsistence strategies in Greece in the later twelfth and eleventh centuries, largely defined by a less centralized political landscape. The intimations of poverty and the depopulation of the countryside inherent in the traditional view of the period are based on a certain reading of the archaeological record, relying on historical explanation. Yet the transition from the Bronze Age to the Iron Age should be seen as a period of fundamental social transformation. The centrally administered palace economies of the second millennium gave way to less-centralized forms of economic organization. This new Iron Age pattern did not rise suddenly out of the ashes of Mycenaean bureaucracies, but had already begun to take shape long before 1000 B.C., contributing to the processes underlying the disappearance of Bronze Age centers.

Too much was happening in Early Iron Age Greece for it

to warrant the term "dark age." The period witnessed continued contacts with the east and west, but commercial activity was no longer dominated by state-controlled exchange and the eastern Mediterranean as a whole enjoyed a new era of mercantile enterprise. The emergence of iron production represented a significant technological innovation with far-reaching effects, not only on the nature of trade. The impetus in the quest for metals, not just iron, and their exploitation, may have come from Phoenicia, and Phoenician activity on Aegean islands such as Thasos is well known from later Greek authors. Other specialized manufacturing activities in the Aegean Early Iron Age included perfumed oils, indicated by appropriate flasks of terra-cotta and faience, especially from Rhodes, and Greek textiles suggested by some of the distinctive patterns on Geometric pottery. These activities, like mining and metal-working, were labor-intensive, and their development may have altered the nature of slavery. It is also to this period that most scholars attribute the rise of the Greek city-state, one of the most remarkable social formations in history. And it is in this period that the need arose for a new form of literacy. When the Greeks adopted and adapted the Phoenician alphabet in the eighth century, writing no longer served palace administration, but preserved Homeric poetry. The fact that the earliest-known Greek inscriptions are in metered verse underlines the enduring power of the oral tradition. In the end, the only thing "dark" about Early Iron Age Greece is our knowledge of it and the traditional concepts applied to the period.

[See also GREEK ART AND ARCHITECTURE, CLASSICAL: CLASSICAL GREEK POTTERY; MEDITERRANEAN TRADE; MEDITERRANEAN WORLD: THE RISE OF AEGEAN AND MEDITERRANEAN STATES.]

■ A. M. Snodgrass, *The Dark Age of Greece: An Archaeological Survey of the Eleventh to the Eighth Centuries B.C.* (1971). V. R.d'A. Desborough, *The Greek Dark Ages* (1972). J. N. Coldstream, *Geometric Greece* (1977). R. Hägg, ed., *The Greek Renaissance of the Eighth Century B.C. Tradition and Innovation.* Proceedings of the Second International Symposium at the Swedish Institute at Athens, June 1–5, 1981 (1983). I. Morris, *Burial and Ancient Society: The Rise of the Greek City-State* (1987). J. T. Hooker, "From Mycenae to Homer," in *Studies in Honour of T.B.L. Weber*, Vol. 2, J. H. Betts, J. T. Hooker, J. R. Green, eds. (1988): 57–64. P. James et al., *Centuries of Darkness: A Challenge to the Conventional Chronology of Old World Archaeology* (1991). D. Musti et al., eds., *La transizione dal Miceneo all'Alto Arcaismo: Dal palazzo alla città.* Atti del Convegno Internazionale a Roma, Marzo 14–19, 1988 (1991). W. A. Ward and M. S. Joukowsky, eds., *The Crisis Years: The 12th Century B.C. from beyond the Danube to the Tigris* (1992). S. and A. Sherratt, "The Growth of the Mediterranean Economy in the Early First Millennium B.C.," *World Archaeology* 24 (1993): 361–378.

John K. Papadopoulos

THE RISE OF GREEK CITY-STATES

The Greek city-states (*poleis*; singular, *polis*,) of the Classical Period (480–323 B.C.) varied greatly in size, social structure, and government, but it is possible to make certain generalizations about them. The best-known example, *Athens, covered approximately 960 square miles (2,400 sq km), and at its peak, around 435 B.C., had a total resident population of perhaps 350,000. Of these, perhaps 50,000 were full citizens, men over eighteen years old, born within recognized citizen families. Within this group there were strong egalitarian tendencies, such that from 507 to 322 B.C. the Athenian citizens ruled themselves as a democracy, in which all citizens, regardless of wealth, education, or any other factor,

had an equal vote in a mass assembly. The power of ordinary citizens to resist the rich makes Athens unlike the models which archaeologists in other parts of the world construct of "the early state," and study of the rise of the Greek city-state tends to concentrate on explaining these peculiarities rather than on treating ancient Greece as one more example of a universal process of state formation.

Athens was in many ways unique within Greece. Most *poleis* were much smaller, with only a few hundred citizens; but many of the other city-states of central Greece also practiced democracy, and even in those run by a narrower oligarchy there could be a strong sense of social equality within the citizen group. Unlike medieval European city-states, few *poleis* drew legal or political boundaries between town dwellers and countrymen. The town would normally be the center of the community's rudimentary administration and a privileged cult location, but other distinctions were minimized. Many *poleis* had a large servile population, with the citizens alienating exploitation onto excluded groups of slaves and resident foreigners.

Outside the central area of Greece, there were somewhat different types of social structure. Sparta, for instance, differed radically, basing its small citizen population on serf labor, and allowing a certain degree of social mobility (especially downward) between the two groups. The city-states of Crete seem to have had much more in common with Sparta than with Athens, and in the larger, looser, federal states of northern Greece (e.g., Macedonia, Thessaly, or Epirus) central Greek notions of civic egalitarianism were still weaker. However, no hard-and-fast line can be drawn between the state forms of central Greece, with their relatively egalitarian citizen bodies, and those of other parts of the Greek world. We should probably see a spectrum of state forms rather than rigidly opposed ideal types; and consequently, we should think of state formation as an ongoing process of constant change, rather than a single episode distinguishing two stages of social evolution.

In the eighteenth century, historians tended to reconstruct the origins of the city-state from Homer, assuming that the *Iliad* and *Odyssey* were reliable guides to a "heroic society" existing in early times. But as the nineteenth century wore on, more and more scholars came to accept the implications of new techniques of philological analysis pioneered in Germany, which suggested that "Homer" was in fact the compiler of old folk lays, which told us little about an earlier phase of Greek history. Heinrich *Schliemann's excavations, beginning at Troy in 1870 and Mycenae in 1874, shattered this interpretation. By the 1880s, Schliemann's view, that Homer was a good guide to the ways of life of the heroes who had inhabited the Mycenaean palaces, was gaining wide support. In 1890, Flinders *Petrie dated the destructions of the Mycenaean palaces by Egyptian synchronisms to around 1200, and it became clear that there was roughly a five hundred-year gap between the end of this Bronze Age social order and the earliest literature giving hints of the existence of the society of the Greek city-states. By 1900, the period between 1200 and 700 was commonly thought of as a "dark age," followed by a "renaissance" in which the *poleis* took shape.

The Dark Age received little systematic study until about 1950, but since then a mass of evidence has been accumulated to suggest that there was a dramatic transformation in Greek society in the eighth century B.C., commonly thought of as a "Greek renaissance," on the somewhat misleading analogy of the changes in western Europe in the fourteenth to sixteenth centuries A.D. Since the 1970s, the end of the Dark Age has begun to be seen primarily as the process of "the rise of the *polis*," making political and economic changes, rather than those in the religious or artistic spheres, the most important factor to be explained.

The dominant model suggests that there was a very sharp population rise after 800 B.C., in some formulations reaching a rate as high as 4 percent per annum at Athens, which is as fast as human populations have ever been known to grow. This, it is suggested, led to increased competition between communities for control of vital resources. The result was political centralization (the rise of the state), more intense warfare, more advanced technologies (including the reintroduction of writing), fissioning of communities leading to a wave of colonization around the shores of the Mediterranean, and perhaps a shift toward more intensive agriculture.

The archaeological evidence suggests that these changes must be linked to a massive cultural transformation, which was most pronounced in the central areas of Greece, where egalitarian citizenship was to flourish most strongly in later times. Religious activity before the eighth century has been difficult to detect in this part of the Aegean, although recent digs at sites like Isthmia and Koukounaries on Paros suggest that small-scale open-air sacrifices accompanied by ritual eating and drinking had been going on since at least the tenth century. But around 750, practices changed. Huge numbers of cheap pots began to be given to the gods, and by 700, metal offerings became common, sometimes including gold and elaborate eastern imports. These were particularly spectacular at Panhellenic sanctuaries such as Olympia and Delphi. By 700, many sites—even small villages—had substantial stone altars and temples, and many major cities built monumental "hundred-footer" temples. Recent work at sites like *Ephesus and Yria on Naxos suggest that earlier digs may often have missed evidence for pre-750 temples, thus exaggerating the scale of the change at this time; but even if that is the case, there was, nevertheless, still a huge change between 750 and 700 in the level of energy expended on the worship of the gods.

Cemeteries point to a similar ritual revolution. Grave goods escalated sharply around 750, with a small number of super-rich graves appearing at most major sites. Late-eighth-century cemeteries were far more varied and complex than those of earlier periods. After 700, though, grave goods declined, and most central Greek *poleis* began to be characterized by large, homogeneous cemeteries along the roads leading away from settlements. Cemeteries, sanctuaries, and settlements became spatially more distinct, and were often separated by walls. At just the same time, new multiroom houses began to displace the earlier single-roomed huts of central Greece. The change is clearest at Zagora on Andros and some of the western colonial sites, such as Megara Hyblaea on *Sicily. Dark Age villages had been very open, but after 700 houses tended to be closed around courtyards, with their inner life hidden from prying eyes. The new domestic space of the late eighth century seems more strongly gendered than that of the Dark Age, which may mean that the idea that permeates the literature of the seventh through the fourth centuries, of the *polis* as a male-citizen community, with women sharply set apart, was taking form in this period. There was a total reconceptualization of space between 750 and 600, and the patterns established changed relatively little until Roman times.

The Greek evidence for population growth, centraliza-

tion, and escalating warfare can be paralleled in most parts of the Mediterranean world in the eighth century, but the outcome—the emergence of the peculiar social relationships of the *polis*—cannot. So far, archaeologists have been less successful in explaining the unique features of this male civic egalitarianism than in accounting for the more widely shared elements of Iron Age state formation. There is little agreement over whether we should continue to see the eighth century as a period of abrupt change, or whether we should instead imagine more continuous evolution; over the role of class conflict; over whether we should see the colonization movement as a symptom or a cause of the new social relationships; and over the extent of economic change. But by the early seventh century, the main material forms of the Greek city-state were strongly established in central Greece.

[*See also* GREEK ART AND ARCHITECTURE, CLASSICAL: CLASSICAL GREEK ARCHITECTURE; MEDITERRANEAN WORLD: THE RISE OF AEGEAN AND MEDITERRANEAN STATES.]

■ Anthony M. Snodgrass, *Archaeology and the Rise of the Greek State* (1977). Anthony M. Snodgrass, *Archaic Greece* (1980). Robin Hägg, ed., *The Greek Renaissance of the Eighth Century* B.C. (1983). François de Polignac, *La naissance de la cité grecque* (1984). Ian Morris, *Burial and Ancient Society* (1987). Robin Hägg, ed., *Early Greek Cult Practice* (1988). Susan Alcock and Robin Osborne, eds., *Placing the Gods* (1994). Susan Alcock and Robin Osborne, eds., *Darkness and Heroes* (1996).

Ian Morris

THE GREEK ARCHAIC PERIOD

The Greek Archaic Period stretches from the mid-eighth century B.C., the time of Homer, to the Persian invasion by Xerxes in 480 B.C. Emerging from several centuries of the Dark Age, Greek civilization entered a new phase during the eighth century B.C. with the wide diffusion of the alphabet and the return of literacy, renewed contact with the older cultures of Egypt and the Near East, the rise of the polis, or city-state, and the beginning of a colonization movement that would establish a Greek presence in every corner of the Mediterranean over the course of two centuries.

The geographical extent of Greece in this period coincides largely with the boundaries of the modern nation, with the addition of the western coast of Turkey, ancient Ionia, and Aeolis. This latter area had been settled by mainland Greeks in the earlier first millennium, the so-called Ionian Migrations, and included some of the major cultural centers of Archaic Greece, such as Miletos (home of the earliest philosophers) and *Ephesus. Bordering Ionia were the Near Eastern kingdoms of Lydia and Caria, with which the Greeks enjoyed close and fruitful cultural contacts.

Most Greek city-states, with the notable exception of Sparta, experienced a period of tyranny in the seventh and sixth centuries B.C., one-man rule usually characterized by an ambitious aristocrat who had seized power but who was seldom able to create a stable dynasty lasting more than two generations. Many tyrants tried to win popularity and prestige with lavish public buildings and dedications in sanctuaries. Of the earliest monumental stone temples, many can be associated with the patronage of the tyrants, such as Polycrates's Temple of Hera on Samos and the Temple of Olympian Zeus at Athens, begun by the sons of Peisistratus but finished seven centuries later by the emperor Hadrian. When not ruled by a tyrant, most Greek city-states had some form of oligarchy, and only toward the end of the

Archaic Period (508 B.C.) did the Athenian statesman Kleisthenes establish the first democracy.

Archaeology has enabled us to fill in the history of the overseas colonization movement that is only sketched by Thucydides and other Greek writers. Among the earliest focal points were the area around the Bay of Naples, *Sicily, and the Sea of Marmara, at the entrance to the Black Sea. The first colonists often originated from the island of Euboea, Megara and Corinth in the Peloponnese, and Miletos in Asia Minor. Excavation has confirmed an eighth-century-B.C. presence in the west, on the island of Ischia, off Naples, and at Naxos, Megara Hyblaea, Syracuse, and Leontini in Sicily. In the seventh century B.C., some of the major foundations include Thasos, off the Thracian coast in the North Aegean (founded from the island of Paros), Cyrene in Libya (from the island of Thera, modern Santorini), and Sicilian Gela (a joint foundation of Crete and Rhodes). By 600 B.C. Greeks had pushed as far west as Marseilles (ancient Massalia, founded from Phocaea in Asia Minor) and southern Spain.

The colonists usually brought with them the major cults of the mother city. Thus the sixth-century B.C. Temple of Apollo in Syracuse, a foundation of Corinth, is roughly contemporary with the Temple of Apollo at Corinth itself. Colonies tended to import goods such as pottery from the mother city and have often yielded better examples than those found in the city of manufacture.

In order to compensate for the political fragmentation into many autonomous city-states, the Greeks came together at Panhellenic sanctuaries, to worship their principal gods and to compete in athletic and other (e.g., musical and dance) competitions in their honor. Most of these sanctuaries reached the height of their prestige and architectural splendor in the Archaic Period, and three of the four Panhellenic games were established within a few years in the early sixth century B.C. (the Pythian, at Delphi, in 582 B.C.; the Isthmian also in 582 B.C.; and the Nemean in 573 B.C.). Only those at Olympia were much older, traditionally begun in 776 B.C. The competitive spirit of these games and the glory that each victor brought home to his own city is best captured in the odes of Pindar in the early fifth century B.C. But the physical setting for the games and the accompanying festivals is equally well known because of the efforts of archaeologists from several countries over several generations.

Olympia and Delphi, the two greatest Panhellenic sanctuaries, have each been excavated continuously for over a century, Olympia by German and Delphi by French archaeologists. At Olympia, dedications of bronze tripods, cauldrons, and figurines confirm the site's importance by the early eighth century B.C. The games honored Zeus, but his consort Hera was worshipped alongside him from early times, in a large temple built ca. 600 B.C. and later devoted to Hera alone when the great early Classical Temple of Zeus was constructed (ca. 470–456). In the course of the sixth century B.C., many cities built small treasuries, one beside the other, on a low terrace overlooking the sanctuary and stadium. These represent some of the cities who sent athletes to compete in the games and include several western colonies now grown rich and powerful, such as Gela, Selinus, and Metapontum.

Delphi had the oracle of Apollo, the most respected and influential in Greece, attracting pilgrims from all over the Greek world and even foreign dynasts like Croesus of Lydia. The temple that housed the oracle was of great antiquity,

supposedly built of laurel, then of bronze by Hephaestus and Athena, before the first stone temple was built in early Archaic times. That temple burned in 548 B.C. and was replaced ca. 510 B.C. by one financed in part by an Athenian noble family exiled by the tyrant Peisistratos, the Alkmeonidai (led by Kleisthenes), who thereby gained considerable influence with the oracle. The temple on the site today is a fourth-century B.C. rebuilding. Delphi, too, received rich dedications and treasuries, the most elaborate of which was put up by the otherwise obscure island of Siphnos, whose inhabitants had found rich silver mines ca. 530 B.C. Because of its central location within Greece, many visitors, and enormous prestige, Delphi was the favored location for cities to celebrate military victories with conspicuous dedications. Thus the Athenians built a treasury to commemorate turning back the Persians at Marathon in 490 B.C., and a decade later some thirty-one cities who had joined to defend Greece from the second Persian invasion put up a unique monument at Delphi, a twenty-foot-high (6 m) bronze column terminating in three intertwined snake heads supporting a gold tripod. The column itself, minus snakes and tripod, can still be seen in the Hippodrome in Istanbul.

Nemea and Isthmia, both in the northeastern Peloponnese, held games in honor of Zeus and Poseidon, respectively. At Isthmia, the early Archaic temple, discovered in 1952, proved to be one of the earliest stone temples known in Greece, of the mid-seventh century B.C. Nemea has thus far yielded mainly buildings of the Late Classical Period.

Apart from the four sanctuaries with "crown games" (so named for the wreaths given as prizes), other sanctuaries attracted worshipers from far afield, such as Dodona, in Epirus (northwestern Greece), whose oracle of Zeus was second in importance only to Apollo's at Delphi. Here small dedications and bronze tablets with oracular responses testify to activity as early as the seventh century B.C. The island of Delos was sacred to Apollo and his sister Artemis, whose mother Leto had given birth to them there, and served as a gathering place for all those Greeks who called themselves Ionian (as opposed to the Dorians of the Peloponnese). Probably controlled by the neighboring island of Naxos during most of the Archaic Period, Delos attracted some of the earliest monumental sculptural dedications, including the first life-size marble *kore* (statue), dedicated by a Naxian woman, and one of the first colossal marble *kouroi* (youths).

The unique shape of the Greek city-state, with its principal sanctuary and civic center, or agora, developed during the Archaic Period, with many regional variations. Some local sanctuaries won fame throughout Greece because of architectural innovations or sheer size and splendor. On Samos, for example, successive temples of Hera were built starting in the early eighth century B.C., the third by the famous architects Rhoikos and Theodoros and the fourth, soon after, under the patronage of the tyrant Polycrates. Rivaling this were other monumental Ionic temples to Artemis at Ephesos and Miletos and to Apollo at Didyma. Some western Greek cities outdid the mainland by erecting multiple temples in close proximity, as at Selinus in Sicily and Paestum (Poseidonia) in southern Italy.

Athena's sanctuary on the acropolis of *Athens has been perhaps more intensively studied than any other since Greek excavations of the 1880s. Yet despite this, and the secure fixed point of the Persian sack of 480 B.C., the topography of the Archaic Acropolis remains hotly debated. One plausible hypothesis posits a modest Geometric Period (eighth century B.C.) temple on the north side, known to Homer (*Odyssey* 7.81), replaced by a much larger one ca. 566 B.C., the year that the Panathenaic festival was reorganized and elaborated with games to rival the recently instituted crown games. That temple was renovated after the fall of the tyrants in 510 B.C., with a splendid marble pediment of Athena fighting the Giants, only to fall victim to Persian fire in 480 B.C. Meanwhile, to commemorate the victory at Marathon in 490 B.C., a second temple was begun on the south side but was still unfinished when the Persians came. It was finally completed, as the Parthenon, under Pericles in the 430s B.C.

The open square, called an agora, a combination of marketplace and civic/political center, often with a religious component as well, has been identified at many Archaic sites, though few actual buildings survive. Typically the features of an agora would include a *bouleuterion,* or council chamber, headquarters for magistrates, and a fountain house providing fresh water to the community. Although the Athenian agora did not escape the Persian destruction, painstaking excavation by American archaeologists since 1932 has recovered the plan of the Archaic agora and the foundations of most of its buildings. They reflect a continuous development since the time of Solon (ca. 593 B.C.) to meet the needs of a growing population. Archaeology as a mirror of political change is particularly striking here, as several structures can be correlated to the establishment of the democracy in 508 B.C.: the Old Bouleuterion, to house the new Council of 500, and the Royal Stoa, a columned portico serving as the office of a chief magistrate and repository of the laws of Solon.

[*See also* GREEK ART AND ARCHITECTURE, CLASSICAL: CLASSICAL GREEK ARCHITECTURE; MEDITERRANEAN TRADE; MEDITERRANEAN WORLD: THE RISE OF AEGEAN AND MEDITERRANEAN STATES.]

■ Gottfried Gruben and Helmut Berve, *Greek Temples, Theatres and Shrines* (1963). Brigitte Bergguist, *The Archaic Greek Temenos* (1967). Ernst Homann-Wedeking, *Archaic Greece* (1968). R. A. Tomlinson, *Greek Sanctuaries* (1976). John Boardman, *The Greeks Overseas* (1980). Anthony Snodgrass, *Archaic Greece: The Age of Experiment* (1980). John Boardman, "The Material Culture of Archaic Greece," in *The Cambridge Ancient History,* 2nd ed., vol. III (1982), pp. 442–461. John Boardman, "The Greek World," in *The Cambridge Ancient History,* 2nd ed., vol. III (1984), pp. 195–289. Jeffrey M. Hurwit, *The Art and Culture of Early Greece, 1100–480 B.C.* (1985).

H. A. Shapiro

CLASSICAL GREECE

The Classical Period begins with the Greek victories over the Persians in 490 and 480/479 B.C. and ends around the year 330 B.C. with the reign of Alexander the Great. The term itself has come to have two meanings, one designating a specific historical and cultural period, and the other more descriptive and qualitative, referring to a period of Greek culture regarded in antiquity and in modern times as an authoritative cultural standard. It is during this period that the most renowned and influential philosophers, writers, and artists of Greece were active and democracy developed.

Conceptually, the Classical Period marks not so much a radical and quick break with the preceding Archaic Period, but a series of elaborations and innovations building upon trends and patterns established earlier. Geographically, Greece and its colonies during this period extended to the same areas as during the preceding Archaic Period, encompassing southern Italy and Sicily, the western regions of

Turkey (Ionia), and the Black Sea coast. Many of the sites of the Archaic Period continued to be important in the Classical Period. An important source of materials, including timber, was Thrace in northern Greece, and control of this area was a source of dispute. Trade contacts, attested by documentary and archaeological evidence, extended to the regions north of the Black Sea—a significant source of grain—and throughout the Mediterranean and Near East.

The history of Greece during the Classical Period is dominated by its relations with the Persian Empire and by internal struggles for ascendancy. War with the Persians, waged by a shifting alliance of Greek city-states led by *Athens and Sparta, dominated the early phase of the period to about 450 B.C. Greek victories at Marathon (490), Salamis (480), and Plataea (479) turned back Persian invasions of the Greek mainland. Following these victories, Athens split from Sparta and continued the war with the purpose of taking back the territory of Ionian Greece lost to the Persians in the Archaic Period. To pursue the war, the Athenians created the Delian League, a confederation of city-states that became the basis of an Athenian Empire. The Athenians defeated the Persians in Anatolia and concluded a peace treaty in 449. During the last phase of this war, Athens had also fought a war with Sparta, Corinth, and their allies which also resulted in a peace treaty in 446.

It is during this same period that Athenian democracy was further strengthened. Reforms in 462 increased the power of the assembly and introduced jury pay to broaden the range of participation in legal questions, on which bodies of hundreds of citizens customarily sat in decision. In foreign policy, Athens frequently promoted democratic factions elsewhere in Greece, countering forces allied with Sparta or other opponents.

Following the truces in the early 440s was a short period of peace during which Pericles, leader of Athens, undertook an ambitious building project on the Acropolis of Athens that saw the creation of the Parthenon and the chryselephantine statue of Athena by Pheidias. Tensions with its subject states and with Sparta grew, escalating in 431 in the outbreak of the Peloponnesian War, a civil war between the Athenian and Spartan alliances that also extended to western colonies. The war proved disastrous for Athens, causing the destruction of an Athenian fleet at Syracuse in 413 and ending in the loss of its navy at Aegospotami in 405. The Spartans triumphed finally in 404 and imposed an oligarchic government on Athens.

The fourth century saw continued struggles among the Greek states for hegemony. Persia had supported Sparta financially during the Peloponnesian War, but following the defeat of Athens Sparta took over the leadership of the Greek conflict with the Persians. Peace was concluded in 387/386, leaving the Greek states autonomous but with Sparta as overseer of that autonomy. In the west, Sicily and southern Italy were at first dominated by the dictatorship of Dionysius, an ally of Sparta, but by the middle of the century the western colonies verged on anarchy. Spartan hegemony extended to Thrace and Thebes, but in the 370s was vigorously contested by an alliance of Athens and Thebes. Following the complete defeat of the Spartans by Thebes in 371, there was a short period of Theban hegemony contested by Athens.

Following the decline of Thebes, the end of the Classical Period saw the emerging dominance of the northern kingdom of Macedon. Philip II, who ruled from 359 to 336 formed an anti-Persian federation of Greek states, whose agenda was the conquest of the Persian empire. This goal was only carried out after his assassination, when his son Alexander, ruler from 336 through 323, solidified control of Greece and conquered an empire extending from Egypt to the Indus valley. Excavations of the Macedonian capital at Pella and of the royal tombs at Vergina provide some of the most important examples of art and architecture, especially mural painting, from the later fourth century.

Despite the turmoil of most of the Classical Period, Greek culture flourished. Greek philosophy sought to provide a rational explanation for phenomena, seeking to discover the underlying forms and order within nature and society. Philosophers such as Protagoras argued for the importance of subjective experience as a source of knowledge. Systems of rhetoric and logic developed that culminated in the fourth century with the work of Plato and Aristotle who sought to create ideal systems of government and ethics. Philosophies such as Stoicism and Epicureanism emphasized the cosmopolitan nature of humanity and sought to provide a more personal response to the troubles of the time. Drama, tragedies and comedies performed as part of religious festivals, became a major literary form during this time with the plays of Aeschylus, Sophocles, Euripides, and Aristophanes. Theater and stage design began to develop in conjunction with these literary developments. Philosophers, writers, and artists traveled widely, bringing a measure of unity to Greek culture absent from its political life.

Religion continued to be a means for unifying the Greeks as it had been during the Archaic period. Athletic and literary contests, usually part of religious festivals, brought individuals together both as larger groups and in smaller groups at communal meals. The Great Panhellenic shrines of Olympia, Delphi, Nemea, Delos, and others continued to be important, although control of the sanctuaries was frequently a sore point among rival states. The Classical Period saw the construction of many temples and subsidiary structures at these sites, including a new temple of Zeus at Olympia (470 to 457), a new temple of Apollo at Delos built by the Athenians (ca. 418), and a rebuilt temple of Apollo at Delphi in the fourth century. Other important temples were also built during this time, including that of Athena Polias at Priene. In the fourth century, new sites, such as the sanctuary of Asclepius at Epidauros, became important cult centers, and religious life began to emphasize more personal experience.

Athens, in addition to being a center of literary and philosophical work, was also the site of some of the most impressive building projects of the Classical Period. Its form has been partly preserved in situ, and has also been revealed in large part by excavations. Upon and with the debris from the Persian destruction of the city in 480, the Athenians began to rebuild their city, attending first to new city walls that incorporated debris from old structures. Beginning in 448, work began on a new sanctuary on the Acropolis, which included the Parthenon, the Propylaea, the Temple of Athena Nike, and finally the Erechtheum, in addition to numerous works of art and inscribed plaques. Below the Acropolis there was also activity in the agora, including temples, political and civic structures, and new stoas.

The excavations of the agora and some of the surrounding houses have revealed a great deal about urban life in the Classical Period. Our knowledge of this subject will increase substantially in the next few decades as emergency excavations conducted during the building of the subway in Athens reveal new material in previously unexcavated areas of the city. Archaeology has revealed a great deal about the daily life of the Classical Greeks. Paintings on vases provide glimpses of everyday activities, including images of the symposium or dinner party which often followed religious festivals and which combined food, wine, entertainment, and discussion. Excavations in the agora of Athens, in the northern city of Olynthos, and in the Anatolian city of Priene have revealed the shape of the urban house of the Classical Period, centered around an atrium. Priene and Olynthos are also laid out on a grid plan, and demonstrate principles of organized town planning traditionally associated with Hippodamus of Miletus.

Cognizance among the Classical Greeks of the importance of monuments and works for future understanding of the past can be seen in the Athenian historian Thucydides, who wrote of Athens that if it were to become desolate, still from the remains one would think that the city had been twice as great as it was.

[See also GREEK ART AND ARCHITECTURE, CLASSICAL; MEDITERRANEAN TRADE; MEDITERRANEAN WORLD: THE DOMINANCE OF GREECE AND ROME.]

■ A. R. Burn, *Persia and the Greeks* (1962). R. Mieggs, *The Athenian Empire* (1972). J. J. Pollitt, *Art and Experience in Classical Greece* (1972). J. Bury and R. Mieggs, *A History of Greece to the Death of Alexander the Great*, 4th ed. (1975). W. Biers, *The Archaeology of Greece*, 2nd ed. (1987). D. M. Lewis, J. Boardman, J. K. Davis, M. Ostwald, eds., *The Fifth Century B.C.*, in *Cambridge Ancient History*, 2nd ed., (1992). G. Crane, ed., *Perseus 1.0* (1992). J. G. Pedley, *Greek Art and Archaeology* (1993). I. Morris, ed., *Classical Greece: Ancient Histories and Modern Archaeologies* (1994).

Mark D. Stansbury-O'Donnell

THE HELLENISTIC AGE

The rise of the Macedonian kingdom as the leading power in Greece slowly put an end to the polis-centered world of the Classical Period and prepared the way for the long and complex Hellenistic Age (323–30 B.C.).

Macedonian Rulers and Successors. Guided by King Philip II (r. 359–336 B.C.), the Macedonians gained control over most of mainland Greece by 338, after which they prepared to invade the huge Achaemenid Empire. The Greek aim was to push the Persians out of the Aegean littoral and to avenge the attack on Athens that had been led by Xerxes in 480 B.C. The assassination of King Philip, whose remains may now have been excavated in a remarkable royal cemetery at Aegae (modern Vergina), left his young son Alexander the Great (r. 336–323 B.C.) in charge of the Greek coalition against *Persia. Alexander's success was phenomenal. His army of nearly 40,000 troops defeated the forces of the last Achaemenid king, Darius III (r. 336–330 B.C.), in a series of great battles that quickly gave the Greeks mastery of the entire Near East. Alexander continued eastward into central Asia and India before returning again to Babylon, where he died suddenly at the age of thirty-two in June 323 B.C. From Athens to India, the ancient world was transformed by Macedonia's aggressive leadership of the Greeks. Now the sovereign king, not the individual city-state, was the effective center of power among the Greeks, and Alexander's extraordinary use of that power broadened the horizons of Hellenic culture far beyond their Balkan homeland.

These new political and cultural patterns are the salient features of the Hellenistic Age. As Alexander's generals struggled for sovereignty in the absence of a suitable heir, monarchy proliferated. Macedonia and much of Greece fell to the new Antigonid dynasty; only a few Greek cities, some allied for the first time into true federal states (the Achaean and Aetolian leagues), managed to keep their independence from the kings. In Egypt, the Macedonian general Ptolemy proclaimed himself monarch and established a dynasty that would culminate centuries later in the remarkable reign of Queen Cleopatra VII (r. 51–30 B.C.). Vast territories from Asia Minor to India were claimed by Seleucus, whose successors struggled in vain to hold together a kingdom that gradually disintegrated into smaller states led by local monarchs. Out of the Seleucid realm, for example, there emerged independent kingdoms in Bactria, Parthia, India, Pergamon, Judea, Commagene, Characene, and Nabataea. All of these rulers maintained lavish courts and raised large armies in the Macedonian manner. Competition among them led to an arms race, manifested in the building of huge warships and the breeding of war elephants. Luxury goods from exotic places were amassed through commerce and conquest. Particularly in the eastern realms, ruler cults conferred divine status upon such Hellenistic dynasties as the Ptolemaic and Seleucid. Exalted, heroic kingship remained an inescapable inheritance from the days of Philip and Alexander.

Cultural Interaction. Royal ambition and patronage did much to promote the continued *diffusion of Hellenic culture into the distant lands of Alexander's conquests. Greek mercenaries, merchants, artists, and intellectuals were heavily recruited by the Hellenistic kings to help administer their new realms. Along with innumerable garrisons and dozens of large cities, immense royal capitals such as *Alexandria in Egypt and Antioch in Syria became notable islands of Hellenism in the Semitic Near East. These new foundations, generally governed in the Greek manner with boule (council) and agora (marketplace), transplanted Hellenic art and architecture throughout the Hellenistic East. Even as far away as Bactria (modern Afghanistan), archaeologists have found at Ai Khanoum all the essential features of Greek civic life, including a sizable theater and gymnasium. Other important Hellenistic sites have been excavated at Pergamon in Asia Minor, Failaka in the Persian Gulf, Petra in the Negev, Memphis in Egypt, and Scythopolis in Palestine. Archaeology shows, however, that the Greeks were also strongly influenced by the older cultures they conquered. Each of these excavated cities and fortresses shows important indigenous features alongside the Hellenic, and non-Greek elements may also be seen in the Hellenistic levels of the famous cities of old Greece, including *Athens, Corinth, Pella, Delos, Dion, and Delphi.

The extent to which Greeks and non-Greeks actually intermingled and willingly exchanged cultural traits as partners or equals has always been one of the foremost questions of Hellenistic history. Some Greek military colonists (kleroukoi) certainly married into the indigenous populations of the East, worshipped local deities, and raised bilingual children, but in general it seems that the Greeks held tightly to their Hellenic traditions and maintained social and cultural barriers between themselves and the peoples they ruled. The city plan of Ai Khanoum, for example, reveals segregated housing and perhaps controlled access to areas reserved for Greek citizens only. As under Alexander, most of the limited processes of cultural interaction were actually colonial and imperialist in nature. As a matter of expedience, some non-Greeks were allowed to serve in Hellenistic armies and local bureaucracies; the offi-

cial use of native languages was sometimes conceded, as attested by cuneiform archives at *Babylon and the famous *Rosetta Stone in Egypt. Yet Koine Greek became the lingua franca of the entire Near East, royal Greek coinage became the basis of most commerce, and Greeks held almost every post of importance in the camps and courts of the Hellenistic kings. Even non-Greek rulers, such as the kings of Parthia and Characene, used the Greek language and minted Greek coins in order to participate fully in a world dominated at the highest levels by Hellenism. Thus, while the Greeks never achieved—if indeed they ever attempted—the cultural conversion of the indigenous peoples, military conquest and royal patronage gave Hellenism a privileged status that assured its place in the rich cultural history of Syria, Palestine, Egypt, Mesopotamia, central Asia, and India.

Contributions of Archaeology. Our knowledge of these complex developments owes much to modern archaeology. Without the abundant literary sources so often used to reconstruct other periods of Greek history, scholars have eagerly explored the diverse material evidence available for the Hellenistic Age. In some cases, most notably the Bactrian and Indo-Greek kingdoms, whole histories have been recovered from archaeological and numismatic data alone. Such work tends to be highly innovative and multidisciplinary in scope, especially given the many ancient languages and cultures involved. This effort has made Hellenistic studies one of the pioneering branches of ancient history and archaeology. Thanks to this cooperation among specialists, scholars now see this period more clearly and confidently than ever before, and with greater appreciation for its cosmopolitan spirit and considerable achievements in the arts and sciences.

Achievements and Legacy. It was the Hellenistic Age that gave rise to the magnificent Alexandrian library and museum, one of several royal research institutions that shifted the center of the Greek intellectual world eastward away from Athens. Technical advances of all types came quickly in this milieu: an accurate measurement of the earth's circumference, experiments with steam power, rigorous medical research, new engines of war, improved hydraulics, and even complex geared mechanisms like those recovered from a shipwreck near Antikythera. The Alexandrian lighthouse itself, one of the Seven Wonders of the Ancient World, exemplifies the advanced engineering skills and gigantic scale usually associated with Hellenistic building. Ruled by kings, enriched by war, and challenged by wider cultural horizons, the Hellenistic Greeks created a cosmopolitan civilization not unlike our own—worldly, wealthy, inventive, eclectic in religious and artistic tastes, ever mindful of the individual, and obsessed with personality.

This extraordinary age, twice the duration and many times the size of the city-state world of Classical Greece, left an enduring legacy both to East and West. The major Hellenistic kingdoms along the Mediterranean shores were eventually absorbed into the expanding Roman state. Macedonia and Greece were annexed in 146 B.C. after a series of disastrous wars. Pergamon followed in 133, Seleucid Syria in 63, and finally Ptolemaic Egypt in 30. As a result, the Romans were profoundly influenced by the essential qualities of Hellenistic civilization. The Republic readily embraced Greek culture, and the Roman Empire was ruled by men seen in the East as the heirs of Hellenistic monarchy. Beyond Rome's imperial frontiers, Hellenistic civilization left a strong imprint upon the once-nomadic peoples who occupied the eastern lands of the old Seleucid monarchy. Parthia, for example, grew into a powerful Hellenized state that for centuries rivaled the might of Rome. In central Asia, archaeology now confirms that the Kushana likewise adopted Greek art and institutions from the vanquished Bactrian kingdom. Thus, the political and cultural patterns of Hellenistic life long outlived the successor states of Alexander's empire.

[See also GREECE, articles on CLASSICAL GREECE, BYZANTINE GREECE; GREEK ART AND ARCHITECTURE, CLASSICAL; MEDITERRANEAN TRADE; MEDITERRANEAN WORLD: THE DOMINANCE OF GREECE AND ROME.]

■ Alan E. Samuel, *From Athens to Alexandria: Hellenism and Social Goals in Ptolemaic Egypt* (1983). Frank Walbank, A. E. Astin, M. W. Frederiksen, and R. M. Ogilvie, eds., *The Cambridge Ancient History*, vol. 7 (2nd ed., 1984). Stanley M. Burstein, ed., *The Hellenistic Age from the Battle of Ipsus to the Death of Kleopatra VII* (1985). Amélie Kuhrt and Susan Sherwin-White, eds., *Hellenism in the East: The Interaction of Greek and Non-Greek Civilizations from Syria to Central Asia after Alexander* (1987). Alan B. Bosworth, *Conquest and Empire: The Reign of Alexander the Great* (1988). N.G.L. Hammond and Frank Walbank, *A History of Macedonia*, vol. 3 (1988). Peter Green, *Alexander to Actium: The Historical Evolution of the Hellenistic Age* (1990). Peter Green, ed., *Hellenistic History and Culture* (1993).

Frank Holt

BYZANTINE GREECE

In Greece, the period from the seventh through the ninth centuries is described as the Byzantine Dark Ages or the Early Byzantine Age and was marked by economic and social disruption, the apparent collapse of urban society, barbarian and Arab raids, and the establishment of Slavic settlements in various parts of the countryside. The period from the tenth through the twelfth centuries is usually described as the Middle Byzantine Age, and it witnessed the apparent high point of Byzantine civilization in Greece, with the efflorescence of cities, trade, and culture. The Fourth Crusade and the fall of Constantinople to the Crusaders in 1204 marked a major turning point, and from that time Greece was divided and ruled by various powers: the western Crusader states, the Italian merchant republics, and the revived Byzantine states.

In the broadest terms one may speak of Byzantine Greece as a geographical entity, since Greek culture survived (or reemerged) in these regions despite various invasions and threats. Nonetheless, there were many regional differences, and the countryside was politically divided. At the beginning of the Byzantine Period all of Greece was subject to the western Roman Empire, and the church was administratively under the Pope in Rome. The country was divided into the provinces of Thessaly, Macedonia, and Thrace in the north, Epiros in the northwest, and Achaia in the center and south; the Aegean Islands were part of a province of the islands, and Crete was administered as a province along with Cyrene in Africa. Thessalonike became the seat of the prefecture of Illyricum and one of the major administrative centers of the empire. From the seventh century onward Greece was brought into the Byzantine administrative system of "themes" (*themata*), and religiously it was placed under the authority of the patriarch of Constantinople. Central Greece became the theme of Hellas, and there were themes of the Peloponnesos, Nikopolis, Thessalonike, Macedonia, and the Kibyrrhaiotai. The theme system began to disintegrate in the twelfth century due to regionalism, and

it was swept away by the Latin conquests in the early thirteenth century. Various Frankish principalities ruled much of the countryside: the kingdom of Thessalonike (an immediate dependency of the Latin Empire in Constantinople) in the north, the duchy of Athens in central Greece, and the principality of Achaia in the Peloponnesos, but in fact semiautonomous western feudatories controlled most of the land. Greek "survivor states" existed in the despotate of Epiros and the despotate of the Morea, and the revived Byzantine Empire exerted its control against the Latin rulers until it too was ultimately displaced by the growing power of the Ottoman Turks in the fourteenth and fifteenth centuries. Byzantine culture, of course, lived on after the Ottoman conquest, and it survives in many aspects of Greek life today.

Byzantine archaeology has been relatively well developed in Greece, in part because the Byzantine heritage is considered to be of some contemporary importance. Nevertheless, excavation and study has tended to focus almost exclusively on ecclesiastical monuments, especially early Christian basilicas, frescoes, and icons, and interest has been more characteristically art historical rather than historical or archaeological. In addition, Byzantine archaeology in Greece suffers by comparison with the much higher prestige afforded to the archaeology of prehistory and the Classical Period.

From the Early Byzantine (or Late Roman) Period most work has been done on the literally hundreds of basilicas discovered throughout the country. Most of these were located in the ancient cities in the plains, or more commonly along the sea, and nearly all of these were discovered in a state of complete destruction, the result of the Byzantine Dark Ages, when many of the buildings were apparently abandoned and left to collapse. A few early Christian basilicas are still preserved and in use, but these are primarily in the north (most notably Thessalonike) and they have all undergone extensive renovation. Early excavation (prior to 1950 and not uncommonly since) has focused primarily on the uncovering of the plan of the church and the recovery and of any decorative scheme (most notably the mosaic floors), and little attention has been paid to stratigraphy or to social or liturgical considerations. A primary interest has involved the determination of architectural types and their place of origin. Thus, it has become commonplace to see early Byzantine Greece as an architectural crossroads, with influences coming from Constantinople, western Asia Minor, Syria, and Italy.

Among the most important monuments of this period are the churches of Thessalonike, especially the basilicas of St. Demetrius and the Acheiropoietos, and the "rotunda" of St. George. Nea Anchialos (Thessalian Thebes) preserves a remarkable series of early churches, and the islands of the Aegean are especially rich in the number and lavishness of the early Christian buildings, including the Panagia Hekatontapyliane in Paros and at least fifty-four churches from the island of Lesbos. Few secular monuments of the period have been excavated or studied; most important of those are from the agora in Athens.

The Byzantine Dark Ages are, not surprisingly, poorly documented archaeologically. Investigation has focused primarily on urban collapse and the effect of Slavic and other barbarian invasions in Greece. The question of the nature and extent of Slavic settlements in Greece remains problematic.

The archaeology of Middle Byzantine Greece has been

concerned almost exclusively with the documentation of standing churches and their mosaic and frescoed decoration. The work of A. K. Orlandos has been especially important in this regard. Notable buildings such as Hosios Loukas in Phokis and Daphne near Athens have received detailed treatment.

The cultural contacts in the period from the thirteenth century onward present a picture of remarkable variety. Archaeological investigations, again, focus almost exclusively on description of the many standing buildings. An important exception is the recent excavation of a large Frankish ecclesiastical complex in Corinth. The Frankish castles have been studied in detail by A. Bon, the monastic complex at Meteora by D. M. Nicol, and the well-preserved city of Mistra and its houses and churches by many scholars. Important Late Byzantine churches are found throughout the country, and regional styles of architecture and painting developed, especially in Macedonia, Thessaly, and Epiros. More detailed and intensive archaeological investigation in the future will allow important new insights into the history and social and cultural interactions characteristic of this period.

[See also BYZANTINE CULTURE, articles on BYZANTINE DECORATIVE ARTS, BYZANTINE FORTIFICATIONS.]

■ Antoine Bon, Le péloponnèse byzantin jusqu'au 1204 (1951). Antoine Bon, La Morée franque (1969). Allison Frantz, The Church of the Holy Apostles (1971). Paul Hetherington, Byzantine and Medieval Greece (1991).

Timothy E. Gregory

GREEK ART AND ARCHITECTURE, Classical

OVERVIEW

In considering the impact of classical Greek civilization on the evolving cultures of the Near East and Europe, Greece's artistic and technological achievements must be seen as no less important than its contributions to modern western political life and philosophy. Archaeology, with its unique ability to chart the development of material life and explore its subtle links to a society's economy and everyday lifeways can sometimes provide a counterpoint and often provide new understandings of written historical sources. This is certainly true in the case of classical Greece, the subject of intense research and exploration since the birth of modern antiquarian study during the Renaissance.

The following sections will explore the most well-known material facets of classical Greek culture: architecture, sculpture, and pottery. As will be seen, the study of classical Greek architecture encompasses both the aesthetics of design (the establishment of architectural orders and the development of basic engineering of colonnades and pediments) as well as an analysis of the impact of the built environment within Greek society. Greek sculpture will likewise be seen to embody both artistic styles and a wider ideological message, as conveyed in the familiar motifs of mythology and tradition and in the changing image of the human form. Ancient Greek pottery, among which painted vases were long considered the only types worthy of study, is now recognized as an invaluable tool for the examination of technology, foodways, economic change, and trading

links. Though even today the archaeology of classical Greece still retains much of the antiquarian heritage of connoisseurship, the study of material remains and artistic expressions continues to shed new light on the nature of ancient Greek society.

[See also GREECE: CLASSICAL GREECE.]

Neil Asher Silberman

CLASSICAL GREEK POTTERY

Most ancient Greek pottery forms were made primarily for local use and are found almost exclusively near where they were produced. Local coarse wares, used primarily in the household, are ubiquitous. A few fine wares, such as Corinthian and Attic, were widely distributed in the Mediterranean at different times and are exceptions. The *Etruscans, in particular, were fond of painted Attic pottery for their graves. The provenances of vases sent abroad provide valuable evidence for trade routes. Transport amphorae, the most important of the undecorated vases, are often found in shipwrecks and provide the most useful information.

Practical, sharply defined, and well-proportioned shapes are another characteristic of Greek pottery. Although the details changed over time and varied in different areas, most of the same forms were used for centuries, and some are still with us today. The more important are large containers (amphorai, hydriai, and pelikai), small containers primarily for oil and perfume (alabastra, aryballoi, and lekythoi) or for small objects (lekanides and pyxides), drinking vessels (cups, kantharoi, and skyphoi), mixing vessels (dinoi, kraters, and stamnoi), jugs (oinochoai), storage vessels (pithoi), plates (pinakes), and ritual vessels (loutrophoroi and phialai). The potting is so distinctive and fine in some cases that individual potters have been identified. Some of the shapes, and perhaps many, are derived from metal prototypes, while a few are adaptations of foreign shapes or of vessels made from other materials such as wood, stone, and leather.

Stylistic Development. Figured decoration in a central band around the pot is a characteristic of most Greek fine wares. Stick figures, first animal and later human, appear in the eighth century B.C. during the later half of the Geometric Period (ca. 900–700 B.C.), so-called after the neat and balanced rows of geometric patterns decorating parts of the vase. Although pottery in the Geometric style was produced in many regions of the mainland, islands, Italy, and the western coast of Turkey, the Athenians were the leaders in the development of figured scenes.

In the succeeding Orientalizing Period (ca. 700–600 B.C.), the stick figures flesh out, the geometric patterns disappear, and Orientalizing motifs, such as rosettes, pepper the background of the scenes that often include various Oriental beasts. A variety of drawing techniques are developed, including outline, polychrome, incision, and black figure, and mythological pictures start in earnest. Corinth is the leader, and Proto-Corinthian pottery (ca. 720–630 B.C.) with its lively animated scenes is the forerunner of full Corinthian (ca. 620–550 B.C.), which is characterized by the "animal style," that is, stacked friezes with rows of animals— lions, panthers, goats, Sphinxes, and Sirens, among others. Corinthian vases were the most widely exported ware in the seventh century B.C., and they are found throughout the Mediterranean also during the first half of the Archaic Period (600–480 B.C.).

In the sixth century B.C., Attic black-figure pottery became the predominant fabric, replacing Corinthian by mid-century. It is characterized by figures painted black on the red-orange background of Attic clay with incision and added white and purplish red for details. Early on, the Corinthian animal style is often imitated, but later it and the Orientalizing fillers disappear, and mythological and everyday life scenes are the norm. Other regions developed their own black-figure pottery, the most important being Laconian, Boeotian, and Chalcidian. The latter is now believed to have been made in southern Italy. There are also several important eastern Greek painted wares, such as Wild Goat and Fikellura.

Around 530 B.C. the red-figure technique is invented in Athens. It is the photonegative of the black-figure technique in that the figures are left in the red-orange color of the clay, having been outlined with a thick strip of black, and the background filled in with black. Relief lines help delineate many of the important features, and golden dilute gloss, the lesser features, and added white and purplish red are used, but to a lesser extent than on black-figure pottery. The more fluid, painterly lines produced with this technique quickly led to experimentation in foreshortening and depicting anatomy. By 480 B.C., Attic red figure had replaced black-figure pottery as the predominate fine ware in the Mediterranean.

White-ground pottery is another important Athenian fifth-century-B.C. technique. The decorated area of the vase was first covered with a white slip, and then the figures and ornament were added over it in black gloss, dilutions thereof, and polychrome, the latter playing an ever increasingly important role. Lekythoi, intended primarily for local funerary use, are the dominant shape.

Later in the century two southern Italian regions start producing their own red-figure pottery. Lucanian is the earliest, ca. 440 to 430 B.C., followed shortly by Apulian. At first they are highly dependent on Attic models, but later develop their own traditions, including the tendency for more elaborate decoration with a much greater use of color, floral ornamentation, and tiered compositions. Other important southern Italian red-figure pottery fabrics that developed in the fourth century B.C. are Sicilian, Campanian, and Paestan. The Italian fabrics replace Attic in Italy as the preferred, and a much larger portion of Attic is sent to the Black Sea and eastern Mediterranean than previously. Several other areas develop their own local red-figure pottery, including Boeotia and Corinth. The Etruscans also produced their own red-figure pottery, as they had black-figure earlier. All of these were primarily for local use. Attic red-figure pottery loses its popularity at the end of the Classical Period (480–323 B.C.), and red-figure ware of all types virtually disappears by the end of the fourth century B.C.

In the Hellenistic Period (ca. 323–31 B.C.) the tradition of painted figured decoration lingers on in a much reduced form, primarily as occasional minor decoration on black wares. The two most important are West Slope ware on the mainland and in the east and Gnathian in the west. Figured scenes are found on some relief bowls, mold-made vessels produced in several locales, including Athens, Boeotia, the Peloponnese, Thessaly, Asia Minor, and Macedonia.

Fine ware painted black, sometimes banded or with stamped or incised decoration, was another important and widely exported fabric made in Athens between the sixth and fourth centuries B.C. Many areas made local imitations of it, and these took the place of Attic after ca. 400 B.C. With the cessation of red-figure pottery ca. 300 B.C., black gloss became the most important fine ware. Redwares replaced

black gloss late in the Hellenistic Period, earlier in the east than in the west.

The Study of Ancient Greek Pottery. Several of the artists decorating painted vases signed them, but most did not. Sir John D. Beazley (1885–1970) was the first to use the methodology of the art critic Giovanni Morelli (1816–1891), who believed that artists had standard formulae for many of the minor elements of their drawing by which they can be recognized. By comparing the details of drawing carefully, Beazley was able to isolate the many anonymous artists who decorated Attic black-figure, red-figure, and white-ground vases and to establish their stylistic relationships. Similar work has been done for other fabrics, most notably by Arthur Dale Trendall for southern Italian red-figure pottery. In this manner the major artists and their characteristics and accomplishments have become known, and a firmer grasp on the development of Greek art has been gained.

This stylistic sequence has been coordinated with securely dated monuments and the vases found in several finds with fixed historical dates so that most fine wares can be dated securely within a quarter of a century and some even within a decade. This makes them an extremely important dating tool for excavators.

The range of subjects depicted on Greek painted pottery is remarkable. Mythological scenes have received the most attention. Not only do they provide pictures of many of the stories from Greek and Roman literature, but in some cases they provide myths or versions of myths, which are otherwise unknown. Sometimes they are our earliest source for a particular mythological character or story. The François vase in Florence, the most famous of all Greek vases, with its 270 figures, 130 inscriptions, and 8 mythological friezes, is the best example and an important early source for myth.

The study of the iconography of mythological scenes not only illuminates the changing nature over time of different stories and characters, but it also provides insights into various aspects of Greek life. Some vases are clearly connected with the theater and provide information about lost plays. Other scenes and figures are thought to reflect political or historical events. For example, many scholars believe that the sudden popularity of scenes with Theseus in Athens at the end of the sixth century B.C. is connected with the founding of the new democracy. Still other depictions appear to reflect lost monuments, such as the Niobid krater in the Louvre, which was almost certainly inspired by large-scale mural wall paintings.

After the middle of the sixth century B.C. the range in scenes of everyday life expands. Just about every aspect of Greek life is depicted, making the vases an extremely important source. The activities include religious, military, seafaring, social (such as the wedding ceremony), athletic, industrial, domestic, musical, dance, and other entertainment. Some scholars have focused their attention on the subliminal meanings and attitudes reflected in both these and mythological scenes, giving us a better understanding of the Greek mentality.

Many vases, but not a large proportion of the total, have inscriptions, a few of which are some of the earliest known examples of Greek writing. These are important documents for the history of the language and writing. The terms "egraphsen" and "epoiesen" occur most frequently on Attic pottery between 550 and 460 B.C., and although there is disagreement about the exact meaning in every case, "painter" for the first and "potter" or "workshop owner" for the second are the best and usual interpretations of the terms. The evidence from these combined with that from studies of individual shapes and painters suggests that most pottery workshops were small, family affairs. Other types of inscriptions provide useful information about prosopography and chronology: these include *kalos* names praising the beauty of young Athenian aristocrats on Athenian pottery (primarily between ca. 550 and 450 B.C.), the archons and several other officials named on fourth-century Athenian Panathenaic prize amphorae, the manufacturers and officials listed on the stamps of transport amphorae, and the prominent citizens inscribed on *ostraka*, the pot shards used in Athens for voting in the process of ostracium.

Some vases have trademarks that are painted or incised. Although they provide some information on prices and names of shapes, the meaning of many is unclear or far from certain in respect to their role in the commercial process.

[*See also* GREECE: CLASSICAL GREECE; MEDITERRANEAN TRADE.]

■ *Corpus Vasorum Antiquorum* (1923–). Paolo E. Arias, Max Hirmer, and Brian B. Shefton, *A History of Greek Vase Painting* (1962). Robert M. Cook, *Greek Painted Pottery*, 2nd ed. (1972). Erika Simon, Max Hirmer, and Albert Hirmer, *Die griechische Vasen* (1976). *Lexicon Iconographicum Mythologieae Classicae* (1981–). Ingeborg Scheibler, *Greichische Töpferkunst. Herstellung, Handel und Gebrauch der antiken Tongefässe* (1983). Brian A. Sparkes, *Greek Pottery: An Introduction* (1991).

John H. Oakley

CLASSICAL GREEK SCULPTURE

Awareness of Classical Greek sculpture (ca. 480–330 B.C.) was for many centuries based upon ancient literary texts describing works of art and statues produced during the Roman Empire that were identified as copies or originals of ancient Greek sculpture. Direct knowledge of Classical sculpture based upon examples found in Greece only began in the late eighteenth and early nineteenth centuries when works like the sculptures from the Parthenon in *Athens and the Temple of Apollo at Bassae were brought to the attention of scholars, at times overturning the picture that they had formed indirectly of Greek art. Since that time archaeological investigation has produced a more complete picture of Classical Greek sculpture, a picture that is still developing.

Sculptural works of this period have been regarded since antiquity as precise, beautiful, monumental, balanced, and perfect in their rendering of the human form. The fame of sculptors like Myron, Polyclitus, Pheidias, Alcamenes, Praxiteles, Scopas, and Lysippos is amply attested in ancient literature. These artistic personalities, who defined a naturalistic and idealized style that continued to resonate in later Roman and Renaissance art, have held an enduring interest in the period. However, focus upon the artistic personality, especially in the absence of firmly documented works from their hands, has at times overshadowed the study of the extant material, most of which is unattributed.

Context and Typology. The human figure constitutes the central form of Classical sculpture, as found in metal, stone, and terra-cotta statues and reliefs carved on temples, other civic buildings, tombs, and commemorative plaques. Subjects include narratives drawn from mythology, or more rarely from contemporary events like the Battle of Marathon. Frequently, however, myth is used metaphorically, so that a subject like the battle of the Amazons and Greeks

symbolizes the struggles of the Greeks with the Persians. Freestanding statues depicted gods and goddesses, heroes, or idealized representations of generic figures. Their purpose ranged from cult statues to votive offerings for victories and other benefices, from symbols of groups or the *polis* to honorific portraits.

Sculpture from the Classical Period has survived in large numbers, though often in a very fragmentary condition, from a wide range of areas, contexts, and quality. Much has been found in the excavations of religious sanctuaries and civic areas like the agora. The surfaces of stone buildings provided a platform for sculpture, mostly of stone. Sculpture in Doric buildings was concentrated in the pediments and metopes of the superstructure, while in Ionic and Corinthian buildings pediments, friezes, and the drums of columns were frequently used. Crowning acroterial figures standing on temple roofs were also an integral part of building decorations. In each case, the subject, composition, and pose of the figures had to fit within the confines of the architectural space. This was most problematic in triangular pedimental compositions like those on the Temple of Zeus at Olympia (470–457 B.C.), the Parthenon (437–432 B.C., and the Temple of Asclepius at Epidauros (380–370 B.C.). A progression of standing, striding, seated, and reclining figures from center to corner provided a unity of scale, but an overall unity of design and composition resulted from the ability to show emotion and reaction among the figures.

Inside the temple were freestanding statues, including cult images. The chryselephantine statues of Athena for the Parthenon and of Zeus for his temple at Olympia by Pheidias, whose workshop at Olympia was found in excavations, were two of the most elaborate made during this period. The written testimony of ancient viewers reveals the feelings of wonder and awe that such statues were meant to invoke. Unfortunately, most of these cult statues, frequently made of valuable materials, have been lost, while the architectural sculptures that do survive attracted less attention originally.

The desire to leave an enduring public testimony to an individual or accomplishment resulted in votive and honorific statues. These include single figures or groups, including chariot teams, and represent either mythological, eponymous, or generic subjects or specific individuals. During the Classical Period these statues were frequently done in bronze and have disappeared, although bases for these statues found in excavations reveal some information about their original position and purpose. Many of these statues were cast in bronze, using the more complicated and multiple-step lost-wax method that was perfected during the Classical Period. Examples of large-scale sculpture in this material are quite small due to the frequent melting of statues for their valuable metal material, but in some cases their stone bases survive. Discoveries of bronze sculpture through excavation, especially of ships lost at sea, have provided some material for the study of style and techniques in that medium.

Several other types of smaller-scale sculpture also existed. Small terra-cotta figurines and plaques are found in large numbers in sanctuaries as votive offerings, and are functionally similar to the larger-scale votive statues of bronze and stone. These works were mass produced from molds and then painted, constituting a more affordable type of dedicatory work. Although these figures are not as precise and carefully produced as larger-scale sculpture, their style and composition parallel developments in larger media and show the diffusion of the style and ideals of Classical art to a broader level of society. Relief plaques in stone were made for graves or to commemorate a specific event or document. Grave reliefs usually show the deceased in an idealized manner, sometimes surrounded by members of the household. Laws against individual extravagance occasionally suspended production of this type of work, but there are numerous examples coming from Attica in the later Classical Period. Commemorative reliefs often combine an image of heroic or mythological nature with an inscription below. These works are important because they sometimes provide a date derived from the text for their creation, giving a fixed point for the development of style in sculpture.

Style. Classical Greek sculpture is distinguished from the arts of other cultures of the ancient Mediterranean and Near East by its style. A notable feature of this style is its mimetic or naturalistic quality: The sculpted figure approximates the appearance and movements of the real human figure, rather than relying upon a series of more abstract conventions. For example, statues, rather than standing squarely on both feet as in the Archaic Period, place the weight on one leg (*contrapposto*), leaving the other leg free and introducing asymmetries into the figure. Classical sculpture is idealized, utilizing systems of proportions, balance, and expression that bring order, serenity, and completeness to the figure.

Style in Greek sculpture is less fixed than in many other periods and cultures and shows a relatively steady and rapid progression. In the Early Classical Period (ca. 480–450 B.C.), figures display a more naturalistic sense of movement than in the Archaic period, exploring the patterns of movement and adjustment in the body in the performance of an action, encapsulated in the Greek term *rhythmos* and seen in works like the Kritios Boy from the Acropolis in Athens. Sculptors also focused upon facial expression, gesture, and attitude to convey emotion, or *pathos*, giving the figure a psychological movement in addition to a physical movement. These developments allowed the artist to explore the character (*ethos*) of the figure. Some of the most important examples of this can be seen in the sculptures from the Temple of Zeus at Olympia, found in the excavations of 1876 to 1882, but still presenting problems in the reconstruction of their original placement, and in the bronze figure known as Riace Warrior A, found in a shipwreck off the coast of Italy in 1972. The figures of this phase have a solidity and simplicity of surface that has led to the term "Severe Style" for this period.

In the succeeding High Classical phase (450 to 430 B.C.), artists perfected their rendering of the anatomy and included more detailing and modeling of the modeling surface. The figures convey more effectively the impression of motion that has been frozen in time and space, and display a serene and contained expression that turns away from the earlier interest in *pathos* and is more evocative of a perfected ideal often referred to as Olympian. The transition to the High Classical style and its development can be seen in the Parthenon, dated from the inscribed building accounts to the years 447 through 432.

Late Classical sculpture between 430 and 400 B.C. develops a more ornamental and sensual style. The figures of Victory (*Nike*) on the balustrade from the Temple of Athena Nike on the Acropolis portray a new kind of sensuality and refinement through transparent draperies that reveal the figure underneath and with intimate poses and situations,

found more broadly in grave reliefs and vase paintings of the time.

Sculpture of the fourth century shows more diversity in style. An intense emotionalism, associated with Scopas, can be seen in the sculptures from the temples at Epidauros and Tegea and in some of the figures from the Mausoleum at Halikarnassos. The strong lines, sharp movement, and deep undercutting of this work forms a strong contrast to the smoother surfaces, contrasts of textures, and more languorous poses of the Hermes from Olympia, once identified as an original of Praxiteles. Praxiteles also created one of the most famous statues in antiquity, the cult statue of Aphrodite at Cnidus, known only from copies. A third tendency in the fourth century was toward a greater realism of detail and fidelity toward the appearance of real life that is associated with Lysippos, whose work is linked with the Agias from the Daochos Monument found at Delphi and the bronze Getty Athlete. The development of psychological portraiture and of a dramatic sense of composition can also be linked to Lysippos, making him a transitional figure between Classical and Hellenistic art.

The existence of fixed chronological points for some works and the developmental nature of style in Classical sculpture provide criteria for dating works and contexts without written documentation. Although this model has come under some criticism in recent years, it is generally sound. Problems with this model lie in the copies produced of classical works in the Roman Empire, which do not precisely replicate the original, and in the phenomenon of revivals of older styles which begins to appear in the fifth century and which expands from that point onward. Determining whether a work is Classical or classicizing can frequently create problems for determining the date of associated works and material from a context.

[*See also* GREECE; CLASSICAL GREECE; ROMAN DECORATIVE ARTS: ROMAN SCULPTURE.]

■ R. Lullies and M. Hirmer, *Greek Sculpture* (1960). G. Higgins, *Greek Terracottas* (1966). S. Ridgway, *The Severe Style in Greek Sculpture* (1970). J. J. Pollitt, *Art and Experience in Classical Greece* (1972). J. Boardman, *Greek Sculpture: The Classical Period* (1984). J. Boardman, *The Parthenon and Its Sculptures* (1985). B. S. Ridgway, *Fifth-Century Styles in Greek Sculpture* (1986). C. C. Mattusch, *Greek Bronze Statuary* (1988). A. S. Stewart, *Greek Sculpture: An Exploration* (1990). W. Biers, *Art, Artefacts, and Chronology in Classical Archaeology* (1992).

Mark D. Stansbury-O'Donnell

CLASSICAL GREEK ARCHITECTURE

Monumental Greek architecture has traditionally been discussed and analyzed descriptively; the arrangement of molding profiles and proportions of plan and elevation and, ultimately, the arrangement of entire buildings with chronological schemes of stylistic development have been the primary goal of its study. General syntheses and interpretations of meaning have been noticeably absent. The Periclean Parthenon of fifth-century-B.C. *Athens has always been exceptional in this respect, due primarily to the preservation of a remarkably detailed historical and cultural context. Yet it still tends to be seen as a reflection of other aspects of Greek history and culture as known through literature, rather than as a primary source for the understanding of antiquity.

In fact, as domestic architecture provides the physical context for the daily life of the ancient Greeks, so monumental architecture is an invaluable primary source for the attitudes, aesthetics, and technology of the Greeks; it is perhaps the most elaborate expression of the public life of the community, and provides a physical, as well, sometimes, as a spiritual context for that life. And as monumental architecture from the Archaic and Classical periods was created predominantly within the context of religious sanctuaries, the temple must be at the heart of any such discussion.

Greek monumental architecture was an architecture of stone, and Doric and Ionic represent its two most basic regional variations. As expressions of religion, these architectural orders were as conservative as the rituals that surrounded them, and so sometimes appear to be passed down unchanged from building to building, century to century. The propositions of Doric columns were markedly thicker than those of their Ionic counterparts, and the decorative scheme of the Doric order was "sober" in comparison to the elaborate carving of Ionic. Furthermore, at least initially, the scale of Ionic temple architecture was colossal in comparison to the Doric temples of the mainland. Yet both orders consisted of cylindrical, vertically channeled columns resting on a stepped platform and supporting the horizontal members of a multicoursed entablature. And in the standard expression of both Doric and Ionic temple architecture, continuous colonnades surrounded a solid-walled, rectangular, inner building.

The Archaic Period. It has probably always been recognized that the post-and-lintel system of Greek temple architecture is more at home in wood than in stone, and by the first century B.C. the Roman architectural historian Vitruvius explained the decorative elements of the Doric and Ionic orders as the direct translation of wooden forms into stone. Recent discoveries and studies of early mainland architecture have shown, however, that, at least in the Doric world, the Greek temple was not, as Vitruvius implies, suddenly transformed into a stone sculpture of a mud-brick and wood structure; the "petrification" of the Greek temple took over a century to accomplish. Nor, as Vitruvius also implies, were the earliest stone temples on the mainland recognizably Doric; in fact, they were simple rectangular structures with no surrounding colonnades, with no pediments (the roofs were hipped at both ends), and with few if any of the decorative elements of the later order.

Although a concern with monumentality did play a significant role in this transformation, the primary inspiration for the ever-increasing use of stone was structural necessity. In fact, the single greatest determinant of the design of the earliest monumental temples in Greece was the support of the heavy terra-cotta-tiled roofs, which began to replace traditional thatch in the early seventh century B.C. In addition to solid foundations of cut stone, the necessity of a sturdy stone course at the top of the wall as a counterbalance to the immense weight of the new roof was quickly recognized. The first stone cornice appeared in the seventh-century-B.C. Temple of Apollo in Corinth, set on a half-timbered mud-brick wall with cut-stone foundations. Shortly thereafter, in another Corinthian temple at the nearby sanctuary at Isthmia, cut stone was also employed between foundation and cornice, and Greece had its first solid stone temple with tiled roof.

The succeeding generation of Greek monumental architecture was one of decorative elaboration, and Doric crystallized as an architectural order (perhaps first in the Temple of Artemis at Corfu). Other traditions of pre-Doric monumental architecture did exist in regions outside the Corinthia, and Doric almost certainly represents the merging of various location traditions, yet almost all of the decorative features of its entablature find structural parallels in the technical details of roof support in early Corinthian architecture. Only the decoration of the Doric frieze falls outside the realm of those practical details, but as a course, the frieze may well have been intended as structural compensation when the solid-walled support of the earliest roofs was replaced with the comparatively flimsy colonnade. The continuous colonnade (peristyle), added to Greek temple architecture in the late seventh or early sixth century B.C., is perhaps the one element of developed Greek architecture that cannot be correctly understood as a logical product of the evolution of local architectural tradition; its inspiration is probably to be found in the columned halls and courts of contemporary Egypt.

The earliest temples in Greece (and the simple altars that often preceded them) were set in the landscape at points where the presence of divinity was perceived and where, for whatever reason, the Greeks felt divinity might be approached by mortals. The metaphorical resonance between these spots of spiritual transition and the temple's transformation from a modest structure of wood and mud-brick to a monumental architecture of stone is at the heart of the Greek concept of monumentality and is central to the semantics of Greek architecture.

The nature of this transition between mortal and divine was also articulated in the powerfully confrontational pedimental sculpture that often dominated the countenance of early Doric temples. Through the uncompromising frontality of their gaze, the monstrous Gorgons (at Corfu or in Sicily) bloodthirsty lions (on the Athenian Acropolis) of early pedimental groups interacted directly with the viewer rather than with the other figures in their pediment. Anyone approaching the temple was directly confronted by an aggressive emblem of the awesome power of divinity. And although the emblems themselves became increasingly human in form (as, for example, in the Temple of Apollo at Delphi), temple fronts continued to be the realm of confrontation and abstract divinity throughout the sixth century B.C., and even in the fifth, as in the Temple of Zeus at Olympia and the Parthenon at Athens. Narrative action, on the other hand, was from the beginning characteristic of back temple pediments and the pediments of little treasuries set up within the sacred boundaries of large sanctuaries.

The Classical and Hellenistic Periods. This consistent distinction in pedimental character represents the direct architectural expression of two specific elements of Greek religion: hieratic direction and sacred procession. Its clearest illustration is found on the Athenian Acropolis, whose architectural and ritual organization was closely associated with the culminating procession of the great Panathenaic festival of Athena and was meticulously passed down from the Archaic sanctuary to the rebuilt Acropolis of Pericles in the later fifth century B.C. The Panathenaic procession traversed the Acropolis from west to east—passing through successively more sacred realms—from the border with the secular world, through the realm of private dedications and treasuries, to the backs of temples and stories of gods and heroes, and finally to the altar of Athena at the east end of the temples, where more abstract conceptions of divinity, of emblem and emotional confrontation, held sway.

Doric was the architectural style native to the Greek mainland, Ionic to Asia Minor or East Greece, and it was for the architectural expression of religious procession that the

Ionic order was integrated so fully into the more naturally Doric fabric of the Periclean Acropolis. The traditional temple architecture of Ionia was colossal in scale and processional in nature: Everything about it—from its proportionately low platform and consequent horizontal emphasis, to its doubled and tripled colonnades, to its closed back wall, to the graduated spacings and axial emphasis of its front colonnades—blurred the boundary between exterior and interior and channeled the pilgrim to the front of the temple, then to its axis, and finally inside. This was in direct opposition to traditional Doric—essentially an architecture of the exterior—which presented an architecturally identical front and back and whose higher platform and decorative graduation from bottom to top emphasized the vertical instead of the horizontal and set the temple apart from its surroundings and from anyone approaching it. On the Acropolis, the Ionic processional spirit was incorporated most literally in the Propylaia, the great entrance gate. Its Doric facade employed the Ionic technique of graduated column spacings for visual channeling to the axis of the building; there, in turn, a corridor of Ionic columns led through its interior hall and into the sanctuary of Athena. The Parthenon, too, evoked a strong sense of Ionic procession through its seemingly doubled facade colonnades, its Ionic frieze (carrying, appropriately enough, the representation of a religious procession), and through the elaborately decorative nature of its interior.

Following the subjugation of Ionia by the Persians in the early fifth century B.C., Ionic rarely appeared as the primary order of Greek temples until the later fourth century B.C. with the Periclean Acropolis, however, Ionic became a regular element of Doric interiors. This new interest in decorative elaboration suggests a new accessibility of temple interiors and reflects an increasingly personal approach to Greek religion that continued throughout the final century of the Classical Period; it is well illustrated in the increasingly decorative interiors of the Temple of Apollo at Bassai, the Temple of Athena Alea at Tegea, and the Temple of Zeus at Nemea.

As a consequence of the conquests of Alexander the Great in the third quarter of the fourth century B.C. and the subsequent political elevation of the Greek East, Ionic experienced a dramatic rebirth. The colossal temples of Archaic Ionia were rebuilt (for example, the temples of Artemis at Ephesos and Apollo at Didyma), treatises were written on the innate superiority of Ionic over Doric, and Ionic (under the heavy influence of mainland Ionic and even classical Doric) became the dominant style of temple architecture in the Hellenistic world. Temples, however, no longer remained the primary expression of monumental architecture.

Perhaps the most characteristic aspect of Greek architecture in the fourth century B.C. and throughout the Hellenistic Period was the multiplication of monumental building types. The breaking of architectural taboo, that is, the radical break with strict Doric canon in the buildings of the Periclean Acropolis, coupled with the continued humanization of the gods and a growing interest in the individual and his personal experience, helped liberate monumental architecture from its overwhelmingly religious context and resulted in its increasingly frequent creation for individual mortals. By the third quarter of the fourth century B.C., Philip, king of Macedon, had constructed a colonnaded round building (tholos) within the boundary of the great Sanctuary of Zeus at Olympia to celebrate one of his military victories. Inside the tholos, in materials traditionally reserved for the cult images of the gods, he placed gold and ivory statues of himself, his father, and his son.

Hellenistic rulers were worshipped as gods, and the realm of their divine accomplishment was the state. Coincidentally, the civic centers of cities increasingly became the objects of monumental elaboration, and the stoa—the most traditional civic architectural form in Greece and almost infinitely flexible in its simplicity (a rectangular building open on one long side in a colonnade)—because the tool with which it was accomplished. Similarly, it came to be employed as the organizing principal of religious sanctuaries. Perhaps better than any other building type, the stoa typifies the architectural and spiritual character of the Hellenistic state.

[See also GREECE, articles on THE RISE OF GREEK CITY-STATES, THE GREEK ARCHAIC PERIOD, CLASSICAL GREECE, THE HELLENISTIC AGE.]

■ Vincent Scully, The Earth, the Temple and the Gods (1962). Helmut Berve and Gottfried Gruben, Greek Temples, Theaters and Shrines (1963). Bernard Ashmole, Architect and Sculptor in Classical Greece (1972). William B. Dinsmoor, The Architecture of Ancient Greece, 3rd ed. (1975). J. J. Coulton, Greek Architects at Work (1977). A. W. Lawrence, Greek Architecture, 4th ed. (1983). Gottfried Gruben, Die Tempel der Griechen, 4th ed. (1989). Robin F. Rhodes, Architecture and Meaning on the Athenian Acropolis (1995); Robin F. Rhodes, A Story of Monumental Architecture in Greece (forthcoming).

Robin Francis Rhodes

GUILÁ NAQUITZ is a small cave (elevation: 6,320 feet [1,925 m]) some 3 miles (5 km) northwest of Mitla, Oaxaca, Mexico. Its dry location in the Piedmont of the *valley of Oaxaca led to superb preservation of ancient food plants, including early cultivars. During its first stage of use (8750–6670 B.C.), the cave would have been near a deciduous thorn forest with oaks, piñon pine, prickly pear and organ cactus, and acacia. Wild runner beans (Phaseolus) and wild squash (Cucurbita) grew in the underbrush.

Guilá Naquitz was excavated in 1966 by a team of archaeologists, botanists, zoologists, geologists, and palynologists under the direction of Kent V. Flannery of the University of Michigan. Owing to its small size (230 square feet [64 sq m]), the cave was excavated in its entirety. Its six earliest living floors had been occupied by small groups of aceramic hunter-gatherers who eventually began to include runner beans and squash in their diet.

These early food collectors hunted deer with the atlatl (spearthrower), trapped rabbits, made fire with wooden drills, and collected plants using baskets and knotted net bags. Probable women's work areas yielded hearths, storage pits, concentrations of plant processing refuse, and utilized flint flakes. Probable men's work areas displayed flint knapping, tool repair, and butchering of animals. The complex of plant and animal remains suggests that the cave was repeatedly occupied between August and December, when plant resources in the Piedmont were at their peak.

While the initial occupants of Level E had left behind only wild plants, some bottle gourds (Lagenaria) and squash (Cucurbita) appeared by the time of Level C (ca. 7450–7280 B.C.). Two close relatives of other cultivars—the wild runner bean and the wild coyote melon (Apodanthera)—were also used at this time, suggesting a period of incipient cultivation.

Collaborator Robert Reynolds of Wayne State University undertook a computer simulation of incipient cultivation using data from Guilá Naquitz. His study suggests that the "mix" of wild and domestic species seen in the later aceramic living floors (such as level B1) could have resulted from gradual attempts by the local hunter-gatherers of the Mitla region to improve the efficiency of their foraging by reducing search area while maintaining an average harvest of 2,000 kilocalories and 40 grams of protein per person per day.

[*See also* MESOAMERICA: ARCHAIC PERIOD IN MESOAMERICA; MESOAMERICA, ORIGINS OF FOOD PRODUCTION IN; OAXACA, VALLEY OF.]

■ Kent V. Flannery, ed., *Guilá Naquitz: Archaic Foraging and Early Agriculture in Oaxaca, Mexico* (1985).

Kent V. Flannery

GUITARRERO CAVE. Earliest of the thoroughly substantiated sites in South America, Guitarrero Cave also is significant for its preservation of organic remains, such as wood and leather tools, basketry, fiber, bone, and gathered and cultivated plant foods. Archaeologist Thomas Lynch and his associates report the context, importance, detailed stratigraphy, and results of excavations in this dry cave, found in 1968 during an investigation of seasonal settlement patterns and agricultural beginnings in a Peruvian intermontane valley.

Paleo-Indians may have been the first to shelter at Guitarrero, as early as ca. 12,560 B.P., according to a radiocarbon date on campfire charcoal, but this would precede the generally accepted settlement of the continent. There is no doubt about a series of occupations by transhumant Early Archaic hunter-gatherers, who used Guitarrero as a base camp, around 10,100, 9,400, and 9,000 B.P. Thirteen Oxford Accelerator Mass Spectrometry (AMS) radiocarbon dates, on the wood and fiber artifacts as well as wood charcoal, together with nineteen conventional radiocarbon dates, support the essential integrity of the early layers and South America's earliest textiles and other perishables.

Remains of maize, and possibly beans *(Phaseolus)*, may be attributed to sporadic use of Guitarrero by agriculturalists during the last four millennia, as suggested by AMS determinations, but the case for Early Archaic agriculture is supported convincingly by the morphology of the cultivars themselves and their systematic association with dated charcoal, textile, wooden, and leather artifacts. The analysis of the cave sediments, contained pollen, plant macrofossils, and food bones confirms an Early Archaic broad spectrum adaptation that involved seasonal transhumance and some agriculture.

Guitarrero also provides a well-described series of stone types that have become key to the central Andean preceramic tradition. Other remarkable artifacts include wooden fire-starting drills and hearths, and wooden and bone tools used in weaving, hunting, and trapping. Finally, this strategic site became a symbolically important center for cist burials and wall paintings during the Early Horizon, Early Intermediate, and Middle Horizon periods from about 1000 B.C. to A.D. 1000.

[*See also* SOUTH AMERICA: EARLY PREHISTORY OF SOUTH AMERICA; SOUTH AMERICA, ORIGINS OF FOOD PRODUCTION IN.]

■ T. F. Lynch et al., *Guitarrero Cave* (1980). T. F. Lynch, "The Paleo-Indians," in *Ancient South Americans*, ed. J. D. Jennings (1983), pp. 87–137. T. F. Lynch et al., "Chronology of Guitarrero Cave, Peru," *Science* 229 (1985): 864–867.

Thomas F. Lynch

GUNDESTRUP CAULDRON is a masterpiece of prehistoric art. It was discovered in 1891 by peat cutters in a bog near the village of Gundestrup in the Himmerland region of Jutland, Denmark. It is a large silver vessel covered with elaborate, partially gilded, repoussé depictions of deities and ritual scenes, widely believed to represent a detailed visual record of aspects of Iron Age Celtic religion. But there are many difficulties with this belief. The cauldron was recovered incomplete, dismantled into its constituent parts; a peat core taken at the moment of the discovery demonstrated that it had been abandoned on dry ground around the time of Christ, and that the bog subsequently grew up over it. It was not a votive deposit, and may have been hastily discarded, possibly looted from a defended Iron Age settlement that lies near where the cauldron was found. It is made up of a hemispheric basal bowl, five inner plates, and seven (of a presumed original eight) outer plates, along with two short sections of tubular rim and a circular base plate— originally a horse-harness roundel (or *phalera*), which had at one time been soldered into the bottom of the bowl to patch a hole. The reconstructed vessel, now in the National Museum in Copenhagen, is 27 inches (690 mm) across and 15.6 inches (400 mm) high; the original order of the decorative plates cannot be reconstructed with any certainty.

The cauldron has frustrated all attempts to demonstrate that a sequential narrative informs its diverse scenes and images. Some of the figures depicted carry clearly identifiable *La Tène Celtic equipment—warriors blowing animal-shaped trumpets *(carnyxes),* and wearing animal-headed helmets and spurs. The equipment suggests a date of 175–150 B.C. Jutland was never culturally part of the Celtic world; the Himmerland area takes its name from the Cimbri, a Germanic tribe that moved there after their defeat in 113 B.C. by the Romans at the battle of Noreia in southern Germany. Neither Germanic nor Celtic Europe displays any tradition of repoussè silversmithing, and it has long been argued that the cauldron is a product of the Thracian toreutic tradition, which flourished in southeastern Europe between the fifth century B.C. and the second century A.D. A fragment of wall plate from another cauldron of similar dimensions, along with part of a silver carnyx, is known from a first-century B.C. hoard at Săliştea in Romanian Transylvania. Central European Celtic tribes moved into this region from the fourth century B.C. onward, pushing progressively southward; it was on the lower Danube that Alexander met the Celts prior to his campaigns in Asia. Celtic burials and hoards from the region contain La Tène equipment of like type to that depicted on the cauldron. Some of these Celts are known to have been raided by the Cimbri prior to the battle of Noreia. Thus, known historical events and archaeological evidence connect the region of the cauldron's manufacture with its place of deposition in an appropriate manner.

There have been recent advances in understanding the precise circumstances of the cauldron's manufacture and the content of its iconography. On the basis of microscopic analysis of a wide range of tool-mark "signatures," the constituent pieces can be divided into five groups, supporting a prior stylistic conclusion that four different silversmiths worked together on the cauldron, with the work of an independent fifth represented in the base plate; this *phalera* is of a type that has a wide distribution, from the Indo-Scythian and Kushan regions in the east, via the Don and Danube Valleys, to Atlantic Europe in the west— whence they were brought by Thracian cavalry auxilliaries who served in the Roman army. Alongside Celtic and Pontic Greek images, a number of motifs on the cauldron have close Indian parallels—most strikingly versions of the goddess Lakshmi being bathed by elephants, and Hariti, the protectress of children.

Some Celtic scholars have tried to explain the oft-noted similarities between the personages and myths of the Old Irish and Welsh epics on the one hand and the Indian epics on the other by reference to a shared Indo-European ancestry of great antiquity; others have argued that more recent and specific connections were responsible. The cauldron supports the latter idea, as it is clearly part of a technical *koine* that linked east and west at the end of the first millennium B.C. and which existed against a background of more general links, among both the mobile steppe tribes north of the Black Sea and those that formed in the wake of Alexander's more southerly push to the Indus—a campaign in which Celts and Thracians almost certainly served. The most famous image on the cauldron occurs on one of the inner plates and is usually identified as the Celtic god Cernunnos. The figure, surrounded by animals, is in a strange, semi-yogic levitated pose, sprouting stag antlers

and holding a torc and a ram-headed snake. It is sexually ambiguous in comparison to the clearly marked male and female figures of the cauldron's outer plates, and is but one of a number of curiously posed androgenous images from various parts of Iron Age Eurasia that suggest, in the light of textual references, that druidism, steppe shamanism, and tantric yoga may have developed as interlinked systems of ritual specialization in the Eurasian later Iron Age. There is no space here to discuss aspects of the general representational program of the cauldron in any greater detail, except to say that it was the product of a polyethnic milieu, and that it seems possible that the silversmiths were ritual experts with far-flung connections, who may not only have produced the cauldron but also presided in the rites for which it was once needed.

[*See also* CELTIC ART; CELTS; EUROPE: THE EUROPEAN IRON AGE.]

■ O. Klindt-Jensen, *Gundestrupkedelen* (1961). A. Bergquist and T. Taylor, "The Origin of the Gundestrup Cauldron," *Antiquity* 61 (1967): 10–24. T. Taylor, "The Gundestrup Cauldron," *Scientific American*.

Tim Taylor

H

HADRIAN'S WALL is the most famous, most intensively explored, and best surviving of all the artificial frontiers built by the Roman army. In A.D. 83 the governor Agricola had defeated the Caledonian tribes at the battle of Mons Graupius, but within a generation the most northerly forts in Britain lay back on the Tyne-Solway isthmus, most based on the road known as the Stanegate. In 122 the emperor Hadrian visited Britain and, according to his biographer, ordered the construction of a wall 80 miles long (73 standard miles, or about 117 kilometers) from sea to sea to divide the Romans from the barbarians.

Hadrian's Wall, as originally conceived, consisted of a stone wall, 10 Roman feet wide and about 15 feet high, from Newcastle upon Tyne for 45 Roman miles to the River Irthing and a turf wall, 20 Roman feet wide at its base, thence for 30 miles to Bowness on Solway. It is not clear whether the wall top was patrolled. The barrier was fronted by a ditch, except where rendered unnecessary by crags. At mile intervals were fortlets (milecastles)—gates protected by small enclosures—and between each pair of milecastles two towers (turrets), implying the presence of a tower over each milecastle north gate in order to complete a regular one-third mile spacing. The system of fortlets and towers continued beyond Bowness for at least twenty-six miles down the Cumberland coast. The troops to man these structures were probably supplied by the regiments based in the forts behind the wall on the Stanegate.

The purpose of the wall was to control the movement of people into and out of the empire and to counter low-intensity threats. However, the wall obstructed the mobility of the army, and during building operations, there was a change of plan—forts were built not on the Stanegate but on the line of the wall itself. Each fort, except where topography rendered it difficult, was placed astride the wall, with the equivalent of six milecastle gates opening to the north. At the same time the rear of the military zone was protected by the construction of an earthwork known as the Vallum. This consisted of a central ditch flanked north and south by a mound and could, perhaps, be regarded as the Roman equivalent of barbed wire. The stone wall was completed at a width of six to eight feet, the narrowing presumably a consequence of the additional work. The barrier was also extended four miles down the Tyne to Wallsend.

Hadrian's Wall was abandoned about 140 when the Antonine Wall was constructed, but was reoccupied about 165 (repair work also took place in 158 according to a lost inscription). In the late second century a road, the Military Way, was built alongside the wall, many turrets were abandoned, and several milecastles had their gates narrowed. Outside most, if not all, forts lay civil settlements, and immediately to the south lay the towns of Carlisle and Carbridge.

Peace on the northern frontier was disturbed in the early 180s, the late 190s (when it is clear that a treaty existed between the Romans and the Caledonians), and between 208 and 211 (when the emperors Septimius Severus and Caracalla campaigned in Scotland). After a period of quiescence the rise of the Picts (first mentioned in 297) heralded a shift in the balance of power and several military expeditions in the fourth century. Yet Hadrian's Wall was not abandoned before the end of Roman Britain, having effectively completed its task.

Antonine Wall. Hadrian's Wall was the first linear barrier known to have been constructed in Britain. Hadrian died in July 138 and was succeeded by Antoninus Pius. Within months of his succession the new emperor had reversed the policy of his predecessor and ordered an advance northward and the building of a new wall, the Antonine Wall. The reason for this may have been to provide the new emperor with military prestige, or because of warfare in north Britain and the suggestion that Hadrian's Wall was a success but built too far from the main enemy in the north, the Caledonians.

The Antonine Wall was constructed in the early 140s by soldiers of the three legions of Britain who marked their stretches of work by ornamental inscriptions. It appears to have been abandoned in the mid-160s, after major structural changes in the late 150s. The wall stretched for thirty-seven miles from Bo'ness on the Forth to Old Kilpatrick on the Clyde, following for much of its length the Central Valley of Scotland. It consisted of a turf rampart, at least ten feet high, placed on a stone base, fifteen Roman feet wide, and possibly topped by a timber breastwork. In front lay a wide and deep ditch. Forts, linked by a road, were placed at intervals of about eight miles. Fortlets have been found between some pairs of forts, probably forming part of a regular series. Three pairs of "expansions" were attached to the rear of the rampart, but their function is unknown but is thought to be connected with signaling. Before this plan was completed the number of forts was increased from an initial six to at least sixteen. Unlike the first series, most of these secondary forts were too small to hold complete regiments. The purpose of the wall was frontier control, but it was not the frontier itself, for outpost forts shielded the eastern foreground.

[*See also* BRITISH ISLES: ROMAN BRITAIN; EUROPE: ROMAN AND POST-ROMAN EUROPE; ROMAN EMPIRE: THE ROMAN FRONTIER.]

■ C. M. Daniels, ed., *J. Collingwood Bruce's Handbook to the Roman Wall* (1978); W. S. Hanson and G. S. Maxwell, *Rome's North-West Frontier, the Antonine Wall* (1986). D. J. Breeze and B. Dobson, *Hadrian's Wall* (1987); S. Johnson, *English Heritage Book of Hadrian's Wall* (1989). A. S. Robertson, *The Antonine Wall* (rev. ed. 1990).

David J. Breeze

HALLSTATT is an important late prehistoric salt-mining site in western Austria, associated with an early Iron Age cemetery, which has given its name to the first period of the Iron Age in central and western Europe (700–450 B.C.). The site is located about 31 miles (50 km) southeast of Salzburg, in a small valley high above a lake in the Salzkammergut area of the Austrian Alps, a region with major salt deposits that have been heavily exploited in prehistoric and historic as well as modern times.

Mining operations in the Medieval and later periods produced sporadic evidence of prehistoric activity, but the first systematic archaeological research was undertaken between 1846 and 1863 by Johann Georg Ramsauer, the manager of the salt mines, who excavated 980 graves of an early Iron Age cemetery. A series of subsequent excavations raised this total to well over 1,100 graves, which belong mainly to the seventh and sixth centuries B.C., though continuing into the fifth century. As well as being one of the largest Iron Age cemeteries known in Europe, it is also one of the richest, and the grave goods, including ornaments, weapons, armor, and bronze vessels, demonstrate the importance of the salt trade in later prehistory. Many of these items are not of local manufacture, and goods from Slovenia, Italy, southern Germany, and the western Alps, as well as amber from the Baltic, show the extent of the trade.

No certain evidence has been found of the settlement of the people buried in the cemetery, but it must have been substantial. Analysis of the burials supports the idea of a community of normal family units of men, women, and children, rather than a specialized work group of men, as has sometimes been suggested.

The reason for the presence of the cemetery, and its wealth, is a major deposit of rock salt, about 1.9 miles (3 km) long and up to 1,600 feet (500 m) deep, including some veins of very high purity. Salt has been extracted since A.D. 1311, and there is archaeological evidence for three main phases of earlier activity, geographically separate and using rather different mining techniques. The earliest method was probably the extraction of salt from wells and springs, but the first mining belongs to the Late Bronze Age (ca. 1000–800 B.C.). The main phase of mining was the one associated with the cemetery, from the eighth to the fifth centuries B.C.; its decline may have been due to the rise of another nearby mining center at Hallein-Dürrnberg, but there was also a catastrophic landslide that blocked many of the shafts. There was a third phase of mining activity around the first century A.D.

Shafts were dug obliquely downward from the surface to the salt deposits, and tunnels with side shafts were then dug to follow the salt veins. The rock salt was extracted in blocks, using bronze picks, and carried to the surface. The saline environment has preserved a large number of finds from the prehistoric galleries, including many of organic materials, which give a vivid picture of conditions in the mines. Tools include bronze picks with wooden handles, wooden shovels and mallets, wooden vessels, and shoring timbers; leather sacks for carrying the salt have been found, as well as leather satchels on wooden frames in the Late Bronze Age workings. Wooden splints of fir and spruce provided light for the miners. There are also many fragments of clothing, including textiles of wool and linen, as well as leather shoes and hats of leather with fur lining. Mining was dangerous, as well as potentially rewarding; in 1734, the body of a prehistoric miner was found, complete with clothes and shoes, and was reburied in the local cemetery.

[See also EUROPE, *articles on* THE EUROPEAN BRONZE AGE, THE EUROPEAN IRON AGE.]

■ P. S. Wells, *The Emergence of an Iron Age Economy: The Mecklenburg Grave Groups from Hallstatt and Stična* (1981). F. R. Hodson, *Hallstatt, the Ramsauer Graves* (1990). F. E. Barth, "The Hallstatt Salt Mines," in *The Celts*, eds. V. Kruta, O. H. Frey, B. Raftery, and M. Szabo (1991), pp. 163–166.

Timothy Champion

HARAPPA, one of the best-known cities of the Indian Bronze Age, is located in Punjab Province of Pakistan on the southern, or left bank, of the Ravi River. It is the type of Harappan or *Indus civilization site that flourished on the plains of Pakistan and western India from about 2500 to 2000 B.C. *Mohenjo-daro lies 400 miles (645 km) to the southwest. These cities were once thought of as twin capitals of a vast Harappan empire, but that is no longer a valid perspective. Recent discovery of a third Harappan city at Ganweriwala in Cholistan, midway between Harappa and Mohenjo-daro, is the most powerful reason to reject that notion. No one knows how the Harappan polity operated or the role urban centers played.

Harappa was first recognized as an archaeological site by Charles Masson, a deserter from the British army, in 1826. It came under systematic excavation in the winter field season of 1920 to 1921 by Rai Bahadur Daya Ram Sahni of the Archaeological Survey of India. Excavation continued through the 1920s and 1930s. The key report for this work is M. S. Vats (1940). Sir Mortimer *Wheeler conducted one season of work in 1946 and George F. Dales renewed work there in 1986. Work continues today under the direction of Richard Meadow.

The apparent size of Harappa, taken from the mounded area and associated artifact scatter, is approximately 250 acres (100 ha). But, archaeological deposits dating to the Mature phase of the Harappan Culture Tradition have been found under alluvium around the city, and no one is certain of its exact size, but it is perhaps as large as 495 acres (200 ha). With a population density of about 200 people per hectare, and all 250 acres (100 ha) settled at one time, total population would have been about 20,000.

Recent work at the site has defined five phases of occupation: Period V (Cemetery H, Post-urban Harappan, ca. 1900–1500 B.C.); Period IV (Transition from Mature Harappan to Post-urban, ca. 2000–1900 B.C.); Period III (Mature Harappan, ca. 2500–2000 B.C.); Period II (Transition from Early to Mature Harappan, ca. 2600–2500 B.C.); and Period I (Early Harappan, ca. 3200–2600 B.C.). Periods have been defined stratigraphically. Absolute chronology is based on calibrated radiocarbon dates.

There is an imposing high area on the west surrounded by substantial brick walls. It is generally called the A–B Mound. Wheeler labeled it a "citadel," another archaic thought about the city. A large building on Mound F at the northern end has sets of parallel walls laid precisely on either side of a central road or corridor and is thought of as a granary, although this has never been confirmed by charred grain, storage vessels, or other collateral evidence. There are, however, a series of circular threshing platforms to the south of the "granary" building. Their function has been determined through careful excavation of the wooden mortars in their centers, associated with grain husks.

Two cemeteries, one designated R-37, the largest known place of interment at that time is associated with Period III; cemetery H is a burial ground for Period V. There was diversity in the treatment of the dead, although skeletons have been found in an extended, supine position inside wooden coffins.

Artifacts from the Mature Harappan period include the usual square stamp seals, black-on-red painted pottery, and carnelian beads, some of which were etched. There is extensive use of baked brick, a distinctive feature of the Harappan civilization.

[See also ASIA: PREHISTORY AND EARLY HISTORY OF SOUTH ASIA.]

■ Mado Sarup Vats, *Excavations at Harappa,* 2 vols. (1940). R. Eric Mortimer Wheeler, "Harappa 1946: The Defenses and Cemetery R-37," *Ancient India* 3 (1947): 58–130. George L. Possehl, "Discovering Ancient India's Earliest Cities: The First Phase of Research," in *Harappan Civilization: A Contemporary Perspective,* ed. Gregory L. Possehl (1982), pp. 405–13. Jonathan Mark Kenoyer, "Urban Processes in the Indus Tradition: A Preliminary Model from Harappa," in *Harappa Excavations 1986–1990: A Multidisciplinary Approach to Third Millennium Urbanism,* ed. Richard H. Meadow (1991), pp. 29–60.

Gregory L. Possehl

HARRAPPAN CIVILIZATION. *See* INDUS CIVILIZATION.

HAWAII. The Hawaiian Islands are the most isolated major archipelago in the world. Rising from the sea floor, these immense mountains form island laboratories where scientists have witnessed the dramatic consequences of evolutionary change in natural and human history. Archaeological research has made its contribution to this understanding, documenting a rich prehistory even as many details remain unresolved.

History. Archaeological work in the Hawaiian Islands began nearly a century ago and can be closely linked to the founding of the Bernice P. Bishop Museum in 1889. John Stokes, hired by the museum in 1899, conducted the first fieldwork on petroglyphs, walled fishponds, and monumental religious structures *(heiau)*. Stokes's *heiau* survey on the Island of Hawaii in 1906 set out to test a hypothesis of stylistic change in architecture attributed to migratory intrusion. In 1913 Stokes conducted the first Hawaiian excavations at a rockshelter on the small island of Kahoolawe.

From 1920 archaeological fieldwork continued in the islands, but the focus shifted to surface surveys. The goal for archaeology, along with ethnology and physical anthropology, was to chart Polynesian origins, migrations, and external contacts—consistent with the cultural historical approach dominant in the discipline. Researchers in Hawaii neglected excavation, assuming that Polynesian settlement had little time depth and that most artifacts would not survive the tropical conditions.

Kenneth Emory (1897–1992) is Hawaii's best-known archaeologist. Emory, working for the Bishop Museum, conducted extensive field surveys on several islands in Hawaii and the South Pacific. In 1950 he taught a University of Hawaii field school with excavations at Kuli'ou'ou Rockshelter on the island of Oahu. At Kuli'ou'ou Emory discovered two things that changed archaeology in Hawaii. First, he recovered a variety of unique, well-preserved artifacts providing evidence for comparisons not available in ethnographic collections. Second, Emory submitted the first radiocarbon date from the Pacific showing a time depth of human settlement in the islands of at least 1,000 years. In the 1950s an intensive excavation program began on several islands. Emory and his colleagues Yosihiko Sinoto and William Bonk excavated at the Pu'u Ali'i site at South Point,

Hawaii Island. This, and other excavations in Hawaii, Tahiti, and the Marquesas, provided chronological and artifactual evidence for hypothesizing origins and secondary contacts within Polynesia. Under Emory's lead, prehistorians in Polynesia placed significant emphasis on historical linguistics to postulate sources and order of island colonizations.

In the 1960s and 1970s, as goals in the discipline changed, archaeologists in Hawaii shifted their attention to *settlement-pattern analysis. Peter Chapman, Stell Newman, Roger Green, and Patrick Kirch made early and significant contributions, particularly in comparative analysis of Hawaiian settlement and adaptation to dry leeward slopes and wet windward valleys.

Hawaiian Origins and Chronology. Western speculation surrounding Hawaiian origins began with European discovery of Hawaii. In 1778 Captain James Cook landed on the shores of Hawaii Island and observed similarities in language, human biology, and culture in what he called a Polynesian nation. Scholars over the two centuries following European contact would propose a variety of explanations for Polynesian origins and for the immediate origins of the Hawaiians. Most were easily discredited. Our modern understanding owes much to careful research in archaeology, human biology, and linguistics.

Using available archaeological and linguistic evidence from Tahiti and the Marquesas, Emory and Sinoto proposed a dual settlement sequence for Hawaii. In their view, the initial colonization of Hawaii came from the Marquesas, followed by a later, influential migration from Tahiti. They based their conclusions on unique language sharing and similarity in artifact forms, especially fishhooks.

Several lines of recent research raise questions about a simple two-migration sequence as the explanation for Hawaiian origins. Experimental work on voyaging reported by Ben Finney (see *Voyage of Rediscovery,* 1994) and Geoffrey Irwin (*The Prehistoric Exploration and Colonisation of the Pacific,* 1992) suggests that Polynesians were not as isolated as scholars once believed. Multiple voyages of discovery and colonization continued throughout much of the prehistoric period. This continuing contact over much of the region would make a simple A to B to C sequence of settlement false. Instead, island histories were no doubt replete with long-distance contacts, trade, and secondary waves of migrants. The evidence supports our renewed sense of a complex settlement history—and thus multiple origins of Hawaiians within Polynesia.

The archaeological evidence Emory and Sinoto once used to postulate an initial Hawaii-Marquesas link has proved to postdate the colonization of the islands. For example, fishhooks and other artifacts from the Pu'u Ali'i site date centuries later than even conservative estimates for the first settlement of Hawaii. The same is true for the artifact assemblages from the Marquesas once believed critical in such comparisons. Thus archaeologists do not presently have the needed comparative evidence in artifacts to trace the source or sources of initial Hawaiian colonization. Similarity in fishhook form from later time periods show likely connections between Hawaii, Tahiti, and the Cook Islands. Other lines of evidence support a view of multiple origins for Hawaiians within Polynesia. Linguistic data reveal strong similarities between Hawaiian and Tahitian, Rarotongan (Cook Islands), and Marquesan. Human biology shows links between Hawaii and the Marquesas (cranial evidence), and between Hawaii and the Cook Islands (genetic evidence). Finally, native Hawaiian oral traditions recount multiple voyages to and from Hawaii to the southeastern Pacific.

Archaeologists are divided on the issue of when the initial colonization of the Hawaiian Islands took place. Some support a long chronology and others a short one. The long chronologists have analyzed the radiocarbon dates from multiple sites across the archipelago and postulate that the temporal-spatial distribution attests to colonization, then gradual human expansion across the landscape beginning sometime between A.D. 200 and 600. Paleoenvironmental evidence and radiocarbon dates that seem too old may be clues to a longer chronology awaiting better evidence. Proponents of a short chronology base their view on a highly selective acceptance of radiocarbon dates and argue for Polynesian settlement of Hawaii sometime after A.D. 600–800. Additional field work and recent advances in *radiocarbon dating and age calibration will help to resolve this issue for Hawaii.

Themes in Current Research. Researchers in Hawaii over the past two decades have focused much of their attention on two prevalent themes: natural and human-induced environmental change, and the evolution of sociopolitical complexity. These themes are seen by many to be related. Research surrounding them includes paleodemography, settlement pattern and land use, and studies of monumental architecture (heiau). The collaboration of natural scientists and archaeologists focusing on environmental change has generated work in *paleobotany, geomorphology, and paleontology.

Paleoenvironmental and archaeological work has documented the dramatic transformations that occurred with human settlement and use of the islands (see Paleoenvironmental Reconstruction). Forest clearance and burning replaced native lowland forests with anthropogenic vegetation. This agricultural-economic landscape comprised highly productive irrigated pond-fields for taro (Colocasia esculenta), dryland fields of shifting cultivation, orchards (e.g., breadfruit, Artocarpus altilis), and fishponds for aquaculture. Prehistoric and historic transformations of the landscape brought massive extinction of native flora and fauna. For example, about 70 percent of Hawaii's nonmigrant birds have become extinct. Changes also occurred in shorelines as shallow embayments became filled with increased sedimentation from human activities. However, researchers have also taken account of natural factors from climate to sea level—in Hawaiian paleoenvironmental change.

Scholars have given significant attention to understanding the evolution of a highly stratified social-political hierarchy in the Hawaiian Islands. Ross Cordy, Robert Hommon, and Patrick Kirch have drawn on a well-documented archaeological record and ethnohistorical accounts to build their reconstructions of social and political change, especially for the Island of Hawaii. Their explanations view population growth, production intensification, chiefly competition, and territorial warfare as significant factors in the evolution of Hawaiian chiefdoms.

Archaeological fieldwork continues in Hawaii at a rapid pace. Much of it is driven by *cultural resource management because of the growth in development of highways, resort hotels, housing, and other infrastructure. This work generates abundant material in need of intensive analysis and synthesis. Archaeologists in Hawaii are faced with this challenge, and will likely reap significant rewards in meeting it.

[See also PACIFIC ISLANDS: SETTLEMENT OF POLYNESIA; PACIFIC ISLANDS CHIEFDOMS; PACIFIC ISLANDS NAVIGATION AND WATERCRAFT.]

■ Kenneth Emory, William Bonk, and Yosihiko Sinoto, Hawaiian Archaeology: Fishhooks (1959). Ross H. Cordy, A Study of Prehistoric Social Change: The Development of Complex Societies in the Hawaiian Islands (1981). Patrick V. Kirch, Feathered Gods and Fishhooks: An Introduction to Hawaiian Archaeology and Prehistory (1985). Robert J. Hommon, "Social Evolution in Ancient Hawaii," in Island Societies: Archaeological Approaches to Evolution and Transformation, ed. P. V. Kirch (1986), pp. 55–68. Matthew J. Spriggs and Patricia L. Tanaka, Na Mea `Imi i ka Wa Kahiko: An Annotated Bibliography of Hawaiian Archaeology (1988). Patrick V. Kirch, "The Evolution of Sociopolitical Complexity in Prehistoric Hawaii: An Assessment of the Archaeological Evidence," Journal of World Prehistory 4 (1990): 311–345. John Stokes, Heiau of the Island of Hawai`i, ed. Tom Dye (1991). J. Stephen Athens and Jerome V. Ward, "Environmental Change and Prehistoric Polynesian Settlement in Hawai`i," Asian Perspectives 32 (1993): 205–223. Michael Graves and David Addison, "The Polynesian Settlement of the Hawaiian Archipelago: Integrating Models and Methods in Archaeological Interpretation," World Archaeology 26 (1995): 380–399.]

Terry L. Hunt

HEMUDU, located in the lower Yangzi (Yangtze) Valley, south of Hangzhou Bay in Zhejiang Province, is one of the early sites of extensive rice cultivation in China. Carbon 14 dates suggest a founding date of around 5000 B.C. The excavated area is 8,719 square feet (810 sq m), with four occupation layers, of which the lower two are the most significant. Not only do layers three and four have a great deal of rice, but they also have large numbers of bone- and wood-cultivating tools and evidence of wooden architecture using mortise and tenon joints. The buildings stood on wooden pilings by a small lake. Reconstructions indicate that the buildings were about 75 by 23 feet (23 by 7 m), with a porch or corridor one and one-third meters wide along the length, raised about one meter above the ground. Garbage that had collected under the houses has provided abundant evidence of subsistence. Rice straw, grains, and husks were ubiquitous. The rice is identified as Oryza sativa indica. In addition to rice, bottle gourd, acorns, and various fruits have been identified, and the local flora was dominated by broadleaf deciduous forest, suggesting a climate warmer and moister than the present. Domesticated animals include water buffalo, dog, and pig. Wild animals were also present, such as monkeys, sheep, deer, rhinoceros, elephant, tiger, and bear. Bird, reptile, and fish bones were also identified.

The pottery, with organic temper, is characteristically black, crude, low-fired, and thick, with cordmarks on the body and incised designs or punctates near the rim. The designs are elaborate, curvilinear, and plantlike. The most common vessel was the cooking pot. Ridges around the center or upper part of jars are common, and collars and loop handles also occur. Clay figurines of pigs, sheep, and a human head have also been found.

Stone tools were few, compared to those of wood and bone. Stone axes and chisels were the most common, largely with polished edges. The bone hoes have two holes for hafting, and correspond to an implement that is depicted on oracle bone inscriptions. Wooden handles have been found, as well, allowing reconstruction of the entire tool. Other bone tools include projectile points, needles, awls, spatulae, and the earliest known weaving shuttle. A "butterfly-shaped" object made of wood, stone, or bone has been suggested to be an atlatl, or spear weight, and numerous ornaments of bone and stone were found with curvilinear and complex incised designs. Wooden artifacts are plentiful, and include spindle whorls, hoes, paddles, spears, mallets, and other objects. A red lacquered wooden bowl is the earliest lacquer ware yet known in China.

[*See also* ASIA: PREHISTORY AND EARLY HISTORY OF EAST ASIA; CHINA: INTRODUCTION.]

■ Richard Pearson, "The Ch'ing-lien-kang Culture and the Chinese Neolithic," in ed. David N. Keightley, *The Origins of Chinese Civilization* (1983). Xin Wen, "The Remains of a 7,000 Year Old Society at Hemudu Village," in *Recent Discoveries in Chinese Archaeology* (1984), pp. 8–10. K. C. Chang, *The Archaeology of Ancient China* (1986).
Sarah Milledge Nelson

HERCULANEUM AND POMPEII, located along the Bay of Naples (Campania, Italy), are in many ways where archaeology had its beginnings. Frozen in time by the eruption of Mount Vesuvius on August 24, A.D. 79, these two sites offer a glimpse into daily life under the early Roman empire in almost unparalleled detail, and they continue to serve as a laboratory for the development of techniques in *excavation and conservation and of concepts in site management and museology. While Herculaneum was a small seaside resort for nearby Neapolis (modern Naples), Pompeii was a well-known commercial center at the mouth of the Sarno River.

The city plans of both Herculaneum and Pompeii were laid out on the Roman system of *cardines* and *decumani* (large streets running respectively north-south and east-west), with smaller streets dividing them further into rectangular blocks. While little can be said of the origins of Herculaneum's city plan, the early plan of Pompeii seems to be reflected in the irregular pattern of streets enclosed by the via dei Soprastanti and the via dei Lupanare in the city's southwestern corner. Archaeological excavation has not been able to provide conclusive proof that these streets mark the line of an early city wall, but the city does seem to have grown around an original center where the forum is now located. The full extent of the city's plan was reached with the construction of a city wall, most likely as part of a single, coherent design in connection with Roman defense strategy during the Second Punic War at the end of the third century B.C. Monumental cemeteries lie along major thoroughfares leading from the four city gates, and there are many suburban villas as well as many simple and complex rural villas for both agriculture and residence.

A handful of Greek and Etruscan inscriptions date the earliest settlement at Pompeii to the sixth century B.C. By the third century B.C., the city had a mixed ethnic population with a major component from the Samnite peoples of the interior regions, who had settled along the Campanian coast some two centuries earlier. The settlement of Romans at Pompeii and the reconstitution of its government in 81 B.C. as the Colonia Cornelia Veneria Pompeianorum by the Roman dicator Lucius Cornelius Sulla brought a new and dominant component to the city's population. Inscriptions carved in honor of important patrons as well as electoral slogans, announcements, and other graffitti painted onto the walls give precious insight into the city's political structure and the lifeways of its neighborhoods.

The relatively complete excavaton of Pompeii has revealed a wide variety of public and private buildings, including the earliest preserved examples both of the basilica (the basilica in the forum constructed ca. 130–120 B.C.) and the amphitheater (80 B.C.). Inscriptions document the private sponsorship that financed the construction of the Building of Eumachia, probably a guild hall for the fullers' association, and the larger and smaller theaters, which are good examples of the evolved Hellenistic theater form in southern Italy. The forum is dominated by the Temple of Jupiter erected on its northern side, most likely with the institution of the Sullan colony. This temple appears together with the Arch of Drusus, the *castellum aquae* or main water tower, and the Vesuvius gate in relief on the *lararium* (household altar) of the House of Lucius Caecilius Iucundus, which represents the earthquake of A.D. 62. The city's earliest structure, the Doric temple dated to the sixth century B.C., in the so-called Triangular Forum, may have stood outside the original inhabited area and may have been a ruin maintained much as an archaeological park during the city's latter decades. It stood beside the temples of Jupiter, Apollo, and Isis, important religious centers in the city.

The atrium plan provides the basis for most domestic structures inhabited by the well-to-do at both Pompeii and Herculaneum; many of these dwellings are decorated with wall frescoes. Nonatrium designs characterize homes of the less wealthy. Sometimes, the buildings of an entire block were eventually incorporated into a single structure, for example, the House of Pansa in the Insula Arriana Polliana and the House of the Faun. Semiprivate eating clubs (e.g., the House of Julia Felix), and a variety of hotels and street-side eating establishments can be found both at Pompeii and Herculaneum. Significant alterations in the architectural fabric of Pompeii following the earthquake of A.D. 62 can be seen in the House of the Vettii and in the elimination of entire blocks, which were transformed into agricultural spaces within the city walls. Pioneering studies of gardens by Wilhelmina Jashemski have identified ancient ground surfaces, root cavities, plant types, and Roman methods of staking and arranging vineyards and orchards.

The eruption of Mount Vesuvius in A.D. 79 is well documented. From the careful description in a letter by Pliny the Younger (*Letters*, VI.16) and a series of exceptionally clear stratigraphic sequences, volcanologists have identified the events that occurred to the south and southeast of Vesuvius as an eighteen-hour fall of pumice followed by several violent surges of gasses and molten material, each followed by slower flows of pyroclastic lava. As a result of the sudden and complete catastrophe, the excavations of Herculaneum and Pompeii have yielded notable finds, including vessels in silver and in glass, gold jewelry, wax tablets bearing bankers' accounts, and samples of seeds and ancient pollen. Perhaps the most unique and valuable finds are the remains of the people who perished in A.D. 79. Roman skeletal material is rare in early imperial contexts because of the Roman practice of cremating the deceased. The eruption preserved a rare sample spanning individuals of all ages and socioeconomic classes, especially at Herculaneum, where the remains of over 130 individuals were found in archways along the beachfront.

The excavations of Herculaneum and Pompeii are landmarks in the history of archaeology. The exploration of Herculaneum began following the chance discovery of its theater in 1732. The excavation of tunnels beginning in 1738, eventually under the authority of the reigning Bourbon royal house of Naples and Palermo, led to the recovery of statuary now in the Farnese collection of the Naples Museum. This exploration also resulted in the creation of surprisingly accurate architectural plans, especially of the so-called Villa dei Papiri, by the engineer Karl Weber. Excavation began at Pompeii in 1748 and continued after efforts at Herculaneum were suspended because of the great difficulty in cutting through the 33–75 feet (10–23 m) of solidified volcanic material that covered the site. Among the buildings first to be explored were the smaller theater (or Odeon, 1764), the Temple of Isis (1764), the so-called Gladiators' barracks (1767), and the Villa of Diomedes outside the Herculaneum Gate (1771).

Criticism of the Bourbon excavation methods by the art historian Johann-Joachim Wincklemann (1762) led to the adoption of the following criteria for archaeological exploration: (1) excavation must concentrate on topographic unities that would eventually be joined, (2) wherever possible, buildings would not be covered over after the excavation but left for visitors to see, (3) the destruction of wall painting considered to be inferior to that desired by the Royal Museum would be halted, and greater attention would be given to architectural context. During the brief rule of Napoleon's Parthenopean Republic (1798–1799), there was further systematization of archaeological work at Pompeii, involving the discovery of the city wall and the purchase of all the land within its circuit as well as the appearance of two scientific publications (F. Mazois, *Les ruines de Pompeii* and William Gell, *Pompeiana*). The modern ground rules for work at Pompeii were laid in the 1860s by Giuseppe Fiorelli, who defined nine regions (eight laid counterclockwise around a central ninth), each with numbered blocks and entranceways; locations at Pompeii are specified in this manner today.

[See also HISTORY OF ARCHAEOLOGY BEFORE 1900: EUROPEAN ARCHAEOLOGY; ROMAN DECORATIVE ARTS, *articles on* OVERVIEW, ROMAN ARCHITECTURE; ROMAN EMPIRE, *articles on* INTRODUCTION; THE COUNTRYSIDE OF THE ROMAN EMPIRE.]

■ Wolfgang Leppmann, *Pompeii in Fact and Fiction* (1966, Eng. ed. 1968). M. Grant, *Cities of Vesuvius, Pompeii and Herculaneum* (1971). W. Jashemski, *The Gardens of Pompeii, Herculaneum and the Villas Destroyed by Vesuvius* (1979). H. Sigurdsson et al., "The Eruption of Vesuvius in A.D. 79," *National Geographic Research* 1 (1985): 332–387. S. Bisell, "'Human' Bones at Herculaneum," *Rivista di Studi Pompeiani* 1 (1987): 123–129. L. Richardson, Jr., *Pompeii, an Architectural History* (1988). *Rediscovering Pompeii*, Exhibition IBM-ITALIA, New York (12 July–15 September, 1990). R. Etienne, *Pompeii, the Day a City Died* (1987, Eng. ed. 1992).

Brian E. McConnell

HEUNEBURG. Approximately 30 miles (50 km) north of Lake Constance in southwest Germany lies the Heuneburg—nowadays a steep hill overlooking the Danube River. The plateau on top of this hill lies 197 feet (60 m) above river level and has a surface of approximately 985 by 493 feet (300 × 150 m), shaped roughly like a kite. Used from the Middle Ages to today as farmland, this formerly fortified place controlled a crossing of the Danube and the important road on the other side of the river. Regular archaeological research took place here in 1950–1958 and again in 1963–1979; altogether, 40 percent of the whole area has been excavated.

From the system of fortifications and from the objects found on the Heuneburg, we can say that the beginnings of settlement here lie in the Middle Bronze Age. Around 650 B.C., the fortification of the site was radically transformed through the adoption of methods and techniques unknown to any other place north of the Alps: The Heuneburg became the unique example of an Iron Age settlement in temperate Europe with a wall consisting of sun-dried mud

bricks. There must have been extensive trade between the Heuneburg and the Mediterranean, involving not only the import of Greek amphorae and black-figured vases but also the idea for such a wall and the method for realizing it. It had a stone foundation about 10 feet broad and 16 to 32 inches high (3 meters broad, 40 to 80 cm high) and consisted of mud bricks 16 by 16 inches (40 × 40 cm) and 3 to 4 inches (8 to 10 cm) high; the total height was about 13 feet (4 m). The wall was coated with lime plaster and the top was protected against rain by a wooden walkway. The wall survived for nearly 100 years and was finally destroyed in a great fire. After that catastrophe (in approximately 500 B.C.), a second, different kind of wall was constructed, following the widespread Celtic model: a wooden framework protected on the outside by a stone wall. This wall, too, perished in a fire, after which the inhabitants of the Heuneburg abandoned the place. During the following centuries, the Heuneburg remained unoccupied, the first traces of a new settlement dating to A.D. 700. At this time, the site was fortified again and the hill was shaped the way we see it now. The Heuneburg was finally deserted during the eleventh century A.D.

The Heuneburg is well known for its highly developed *ceramics production, and there must have been intensive trade in pottery and iron to make the Heuneburg an important center of cultural exchange and trade. In this perspective, and considering the extravagant method of fortification, one can think of it as a "Swabian Troy." Most of the objects found during the excavations are now on display in the Heuneburg Museum in Hundersingen.

[See also EUROPE: THE EUROPEAN BRONZE AGE; HILL FORTS.]

■ *Heuneburgstudien*, 9 vols., in *Römisch-Germanische Forschungen* (1962). Wolfgang Kimmig, *Die Heuneburg an der oberen Donau*, 2nd ed. (1983).

Egon Gersbach

HIEROGLYPHIC/HIEROGLYPHS. *See* WRITING: EGYPTIAN HIEROGLYPHIC.

HIGH ALTITUDE OCCUPATIONS IN THE AMERICAN WEST. There are traces of successful prehistoric human use of environments at altitudes in excess of 9,842 feet (3,000 m) in mountain ranges scattered throughout the American West. This record is generally sparser initially than that in adjacent lowlands but is nearly as ancient and becomes increasingly intensive with time. The best known alpine complexes are in the Rocky Mountains and Great Basin.

In the Rocky Mountains, high altitude base camps and hunting sites have been studied and reported in the Tetons and Absoroka Ranges of Wyoming, in the Fishlake National Forest of Utah, and at various locations in central and eastern Colorado. Most of these seem to involve residential use by complete social groups (e.g., families or bands) rather than specialized use by task groups operating from low-elevation residential camps. Perhaps the most intensive alpine research project in the Rocky Mountains has been conducted along the crest of the Colorado Front Range, west of the modern towns of Ft. Collins and Golden. It revealed extensive complexes of game drives, butchering stations, campsites, and sacred sites connected with at least two distinct patterns of prehistoric land use. Groups of the Mt. Albion complex, 5800 through 5300 B.P., wintered along foothill margins east of the high mountains but spent much of the rest of the year along the crest of the Front Range, confining most of their activities east of the Continental Divide. This pattern may have been prompted in part by low-elevation environmental deterioration resulting from mid-Holocene climatic warming and drying (i.e., the Altithermal or Hypsithermal). Groups of the Hog Back complex, 1400 through 800 B.P., were less tethered to the Front Range. They also wintered in piedmonts east of the Front Range but followed a "grand circuit" that took them northward and westward from their winter settlements to the Laramie Basin in the early spring, traveling south to the high plateaus of North and Middle Parks by summer. From there they moved east into the Front Range for animal drives in the fall, dropping afterward into winter camps in sheltered draws east of the Front Range foothills.

Great Basin alpine archaeology has focused on a spectacular series of villages at elevations between 10,000 and 12,631 feet (3,050 and 3,850 m) in the White Mountains of eastern California and the Toquima Range of central Nevada that are by far the highest residential bases reported anywhere in North America. They vary in size but always contain the remains of at least one roofed dwelling and a diverse array of chipped- and ground-stone tools. Faunal assemblages dominated by marmots (*Marmota flaviventris*) and mountain sheep (*Ovis canadensis*) and abundant projectile points indicate that hunting was important. Charred plant remains and abundant milling equipment show that alpine plants and plants imported from lower elevations were also major components of the diet. Altogether this suggests extended occupations between June and September by individual families or groups of families, who would have been unable to set aside any substantial surplus of alpine game or plants and must have relied on resources obtained at other times at lower elevations (e.g., pine nuts) for winter food.

Great Basin alpine villages appear sometime during the first millenium A.D. and substantially postdate numerous hunting blinds and lithic scatters believed to represent short-term intrusions by individual hunters or hunting parties in the White Mountains and Toquima Range beginning around 2500 B.C. The appearance of Great Basin alpine villages thus marks the termination of this specialized pattern of alpine hunting by a more intensive and generalized pattern of mixed alpine hunting and gathering. This may have occurred when regional populations first exceeded the capacity of traditional lowland plants and animals and were forced to rely seasonally on resources from more marginal settings. The White Mountain villages may be associated with the late prehistoric spread of Numic-speaking peoples (e.g., Paiute and Shoshone) into the Great Basin, which is thought to have begun at approximately A.D. 1000 from a homeland in the general vicinity of the White Mountains. A reported increase of alpine occupation in the Toquima Range after A.D. 1300 could mark the initial Numic presence there. Termination of the Great Basin alpine village pattern in very early historic times as the result of Euroamerican contact likely explains their absence in the ethnographic record.

[*See also* HUNTER-GATHERERS, NORTH AMERICAN ARCHAIC; NORTH AMERICA: THE NORTH AMERICAN WEST.]

■ Robert L. Bettinger, "Aboriginal Occupation at High-Altitude: Alpine Villages in the White Mountains of Eastern California," *American Anthropologist* 93, 3 (1991): 656–679. James B. Benedict, "Footprints in the Snow: High Altitude Cultural Ecology of the Colorado Front Range, USA," *Arctic and Alpine Research* 24: 1 (1992): 1–16.

Robert L. Bettinger

HIGH TECHNOLOGY. No single technology better characterizes the twentieth century than the digital computer. Computers revolutionized the behavioral sciences, including archaeology, in the 1960s. Archaeologists could finally manage and manipulate mass quantities of data. Analyses that took weeks or even months when computed by hand now took a matter of minutes. Over the next thirty years, computing technology advanced and miniaturized the revolutionary power of the 1960s mainframes to desktop size. The cost of access to the technology dropped to a fraction of the 1960s prices. Along with simplified operating systems, commercial software made the technology accessible to all. Miniaturization facilitated other technological advances as specialized processors were built into everything from automobiles to hand-held global positioning units.

The earliest technology to impact archaeology was remote sensing, especially aerial photography. Aerial photographs made from balloon flights over Stonehenge in 1906 evolved into satellite-based imagery, although limitations of scale and image resolution restricted most remote sensing efforts to low-level plane flights and human photointerpretation. Continuing developments in films and in digital imaging systems are expanding the usefulness of remote sensing. For example, the Corinth Computer Project combines remote sensing, electronic surveying, photographs, and digitized historical maps in a computerized drafting system to produce a qualitatively superior spatial database. Not only are their maps more accurate, but by entering different classes of information on different levels, they can rapidly create a wide variety of comparative maps for analysis.

Locating and mapping archaeological sites and features creates a rudimentary database, but digital technologies led to the development of *Geographic Information Systems (GIS). GIS techniques allow a variety of landscape, geologic, socioeconomic, environmental, and archaeological data to be combined with maps to facilitate analyses based on the retrieval and display of spatial information. While the most powerful GIS applications remain difficult to learn and master, the rapid evolution of GIS software promises to put the technology within reach of every archaeologist. Accessible technology does not guarantee productive results and GIS is one example of the problem of technology used for its own sake. Early in its development, GIS was identified with the prediction of site locations to streamline federal land management responsibilities, useful but not very interesting archaeologically. The more challenging application of GIS to develop and test anthropological theory has emerged slowly and applications are not always recognized as GIS unless they showcase the fancy technology. Jonathan Haas, for example, based his model of warfare and tribal evolution in the American Southwest on clearly defined geographic variables and site locations, but it was never identified as an application of GIS.

Other promising analytic advances never fulfilled their potential. Computer simulations allow the dynamic exploration of archaeological models when observing real events is impractical. Where it may have taken five thousand years for an archaeological record to develop, a model of the processes behind the formation of that record can generate multiple "records" in a few days. At each iteration, the archaeologist varies one or more assumptions to see how they affect the processes of interest. For example, Kent Flannery, Joyce Marcus, and Robert Reynolds used simulation to study the growth and stability of llama herds in *The*

Flocks of the Wamani (1989). They modeled herd growth under a variety of conditions over fifty-year cycles and demonstrated the adaptive advantage of ritual giving in preventing the extinction of llama herds. Unfortunately, the skills necessary to write simulations are beyond the reach of most archaeologists due to a general lack of training in computer-programming languages. Object-oriented languages may make computer simulations easier to program. But, the ease with which technology places such techniques in the hands of archaeologists can be a serious drawback to their use. Not all processes can be adapted to simulations and not all models are good models.

Many of the techniques that accompanied the digital revolution have been challenged by a shift away from the quantitative focus of the 1960s' New Archaeology. The 1980s' post-processual and 1990s' post-modern movements challenged the assumptions behind the analytic techniques used in quantitative archaeology and other behavioral sciences. To a certain extent, these challenges are valid. One cannot be assured that archaeological samples are drawn from normal distributions or even random samples of mostly unknown and buried data. Even as these challenges were developing, however, technological advances in computer graphics and statistical visualization facilitated the exploration of data for trends and possible relationships in more than two dimensions without resorting to traditional summary statistics.

Still, these new tools are only as good as the skill of the people that use them. Easy access to statistical routines was followed by the generation of enough meaningless statistics to fuel the counterrevolution. The use of graphics could suffer the same fate. A computer will produce statistical results regardless of the numbers fed into the program. Meaningful statistics depend on the accuracy of the data and the appropriateness of the data to the question at hand. Edward R. Tufte's *The Visual Display of Quantitative Information* (1983) warns against the creation of "chartjunk" and "data ducks," a reference to architectural excesses of the 1950s and the 1990s preference for three-dimensional bar charts—lest form take precedence over function.

Advances in digital recording techniques and visualization have facilitated the asking of more complex questions and they have accompanied changes in archaeological ethics as well. As archaeologists confronted the ethics of dealing with human burials, they turned to technologies such as ground penetrating radar that permit the subsurface investigation of archaeological sites before excavation. Dale Davidson and Phil Geib used the technology to identify and avoid suspected burials in their excavations of Old Man Cave in southeastern Utah as seen in the video, *The Ancients of North America* (1992).

Technological advances in *archaeometry, primarily in materials studies such as ceramics and metallurgy, expanded the range of questions that could be studied and sometimes created new fields of study. For example, archaeologists largely avoided rock art because it could not be directly dated. The technology to take microsamples, prepare thin sections, examine them using high-power microscopes, and separate microscopic layers of organic deposits with lasers, developed over the past twenty years resulting in rock-art dating technologies that helped refine and sometimes redefine the history of human artistic achievement on five continents.

While the goal of archaeology is the creation of new information about human evolution, adaptation, and cultural development, the ultimate challenge is communicating that information to other archaeologists, students, and the general public. Multimedia applications in the classroom already take students on aerial tours of ancient cities or help them design and implement survey strategies for the Valley of Mexico. Recording artifacts using high resolution digital imaging systems facilitates analysis and aids in conservation by reducing the need to handle them. Museum catalogs are beginning to incorporate digital images to supplement standard catalog data. The next step is to share images over high-speed digital networks.

Information is the commodity of the future. The growing body of archaeological books, journals, and CRM gray literature makes it difficult to stay current. Digital technology promises to help control this proliferation through on-line search and retrieval facilities, networked page imaging systems, and electronic books and journals that include sound and video segments along with traditional text and graphics.

Unfortunately, technology widens the rift between the industrial nations of the Northern Hemisphere and the Third World. Even though technology rapidly declines in price, even the cheapest technologies are beyond those who cannot afford teachers or even books for their libraries. Archaeology benefits from high technology. In return, it might contribute in some small way to helping understand and manage where technology may lead to social change.

[See also ANALYSIS, METHODS OF; ARCHAEO-PALEOMAGNETIC DATING; CULTURAL RESOURCE MANAGEMENT: INTRODUCTION; DATING THE PAST; FISSION-TRACK DATING; LUMINESCENCE DATING; OBSIDIAN HYDRATION DATING; POTASSIUM-ARGON DATING; RADIOCARBON DATING; SCIENCE IN ARCHAEOLOGY; SITE LOCATION: REMOTE SENSING; SOURCING ARCHAEOLOGICAL MATERIALS; SUBSURFACE TESTING, *articles on* INTRODUCTION, SOIL RESISTIVITY SURVEY, MAGNETOMETER SURVEY, GROUND PENETRATING RADAR.]

■ James I. Ebert, "Remote Sensing Applications in Archaeology," in *Advances in Archaeological Method and Theory*, vol. 7, ed. Michael B. Schiffer (1984). William S. Cleveland, *The Elements of Graphing Data* (1985). Prudence M. Rice, *Pottery Analysis: A Sourcebook* (1987). Kenneth L. Kvamme, "Geographic Information Systems in Regional Archaeological Research and Data Management," in *Archaeological Method and Theory*, vol. 1, ed. Michael B. Schiffer (1989). Kathleen M. S. Allen, Stanton W. Green, and Ezra B. W. Zubrow, eds., *Interpreting Space: GIS and Archaeology* (1990). Jonathan Haas, "Warfare and the Evolution of Tribal Polities in the Prehistoric Southwest," in *The Anthropology of War*, ed. Jonathan Haas (1990). Mark Aldenderfer, "The Analytical Engine: Computer Simulation and Archaeological Research," in *Archaeological Method and Theory*, vol. 3, ed. Michael B. Schiffer (1991). Ronald I. Dorn, "Paleoenvironmental Signals in Rock Varnish on Petroglyphs," in *American Indian Rock Art*, vol. 18, ed. Frank G. Bock (1992). Yuriko Fukasawa, "TRI: Three-Dimensional Imaging for Recording and Analysing Stone-Artefact Concentrations," *Antiquity* 66 (1992): 93–97. David Gilman Romano and Benjamin C. Schoenbrun, "A Computerized Architectural and Topographical Survey of Ancient Corinth," *Journal of Field Archaeology* 20 (1993): 177–190.

William D. Hyder

HILL FORTS. The term "hill fort" is used in prehistoric and early historic European archaeology to refer to sites characterized by the presence of substantial enclosing features and a hilltop location. It is most commonly used in the context of later prehistoric sites in the British Isles, but analogous sites are known in many other parts of Europe and from a wide chronological range. The term is now well established in the English language literature of archaeology, but is not a satisfactory one, and not always helpful to understanding the true function of prehistoric sites.

In the first place, the term is an apparently objective classification of sites on the basis of morphological (presence of defenses) and topographical (hilltop location) characteristics. The "fort" element of the term, however, is itself an interpretation, suggesting defensive or even military purposes; this excludes comparable sites interpreted as having other functions, and predetermines the interpretation of those of unknown function. In fact, sites may have been enclosed for many reasons other than defense, for example, to demarcate a symbolically or ritually important area, or to exclude certain categories of people. Even enclosures that could have been used defensively need not necessarily have been built for such a purpose.

Second, the term has been used to class together sites that are now known to have had a variety of different social and economic functions. It has at various times been applied to enclosed settlements of a single household, the residences of elite families or lineages, nucleated villages, and sites of an urban nature. Any term that covers such a wide range must be of limited value. In fact, other classificatory schemes may be more informative, for instance, hilltop sites, whether defended or not; enclosed sites, whether on a hilltop or not; or a classification by supposed social or economic function, regardless of location or presence of an enclosure.

Third, the term as conventionally applied excludes some sites that fall strictly within the definition. Some enclosed sites of the Neolithic, for instance, are not normally referred to as hill forts, because their function is conceived as being economic or ceremonial.

The difficulty with the use of the term is compounded by the fact that there are no exact equivalents in other European languages. The term was adopted primarily to refer to later prehistoric sites in Britain, and in other parts of Europe there are not only different histories of prehistoric settlement but also different traditions of classifying and interpreting them. Thus in France the Latin word *oppidum* is used mainly, but by no means exclusively, to refer to the urban sites of the Late Iron Age. In the German terminology, *Hohensiedlung* refers strictly to any hilltop settlement, defended or not, though most of them were, while *Burg* is used mainly in reference to sites of the early medieval period.

Modern use of the term "hill fort" is, therefore, a combination of classification, interpretation, and conventional practice, rather than a product of strict logic. If it is taken in a broad sense to refer to substantially enclosed sites in hilltop locations, but excluding domestic settlements of a single household, such sites are found widely throughout Europe at a variety of chronological horizons and with a variety of social functions.

Enclosed sites are known among the early farming communities of the Neolithic, for example, the rectangular palisaded villages in the early phases of tell sites such as Polyanitsa in Bulgaria, or the large enclosed villages of the Tavoliere in Italy, or the probably ceremonial enclosures of the Linearbandkeramik and Lengyel cultures in central Europe. Few of these, however, occupy a markedly hilltop situation. At the eastern end of the agricultural expansion, on the other hand, early farming sites in the Ukraine were regularly located in nucleated clusters on hilltops or promontories, cut off by substantial ditches. Both the clustering into villages and the topographic location were to defend the farmers against other competing groups.

Among the more developed farming communities of the late fourth millennium B.C. defended sites are common in central, western, and northern Europe. Many, but by no means all, were on hilltop sites, though they are generally referred to as "camps" or "fortified sites" rather than "hill forts." In Britain, for instance, they are called causewayed camps, after the interrupted or segmented form of their ditches, which ignores the frequently very substantial nature of their walls of stone or earth and timber. The size of such sites and the nature of their defenses varied considerably throughout Europe, and their functions may have included elite residence as well as economic and ritual centers. Some were certainly the focus of military activity and defense; in southern England, a large hilltop area was enclosed with massive defenses at Hambledon Hill, and at the promontory fort of Crickley Hill, stone arrowheads and burning show clear evidence of violent attack.

These sites were abandoned by the early third millennium B.C. and the next horizon of defended sites was not until a thousand years later, in the later early Bronze Age of central Europe. Small but heavily fortified sites were constructed, often on key communication routes such as river valleys or mountain passes, and their function was not only defense and residence of an elite, but also control of the distribution of valuable resources, especially copper and gold. These sites were defended with elaborate wall and ditch structures of stone or earth and timber, similar to those that would be common in the Iron Age, as at Nitriansky Hradok or Spišsky Štvrtok, Slovakia. At the latter site, hoards of gold and bronze hidden in some of the houses suggest the wealth and importance of these sites.

Hilltop defended sites did not become common in Europe until the first millennium B.C., but from about 1100 B.C. many regions show evidence for their construction, though they vary greatly in size, structure, function, and chronology. Defenses made use of locally available materials. Where stone was available, it was used to create walls, sometimes with internal timbers for strength; where there was no stone, timber was used in a variety of designs. Some of the earliest defenses were a simple wooden palisade; more complex structures comprised an elaborate vertical wooden face to the front and rear, infilled with earth and rubble. Later, as such structures proved difficult to repair or maintain, defenses more often comprised massive banks with smaller palisades at their crest.

Hill forts were common throughout much of central and western Europe in the Late Bronze Age and Early Iron Age, though they often appear in regional clusters, sometimes comparatively short-lived. Few areas had hill forts in use throughout the first millennium B.C., and in some areas they were never built.

One distinctive regional group are the forts of the Lausitz culture in eastern Germany and Poland. These often show regularly planned village settlements, but with no sign of internal hierarchy or differentiation. One of these defended sites, at *Biskupin in Poland, was not on a hilltop, but on low-lying marshy ground. It contained over a hundred standardized houses arranged in parallel rows along wooden streets, all built in a single brief episode. Such sites show a society capable of centralized decision making and the mobilization of considerable resources of labor and materials, but its precise social organization is debatable.

Farther west, by contrast, though fewer sites have been extensively excavated, some forts show evidence of the production of prestige goods, especially bronze, and can be attributed to an elite. This is certainly true by the sixth century B.C., when hill forts are found associated with rich aristocratic burials in eastern France and southern Germany, as at Mont Lassois and the *Heuneburg. The latter is the most extensively excavated and shows evidence of an aristocratic elite using imported goods from the Mediterranean as well as local luxury goods, some actually produced in the fort itself. These forts had mostly gone out of use by the fifth century B.C., and though a few were still occupied, they had more the character of a village.

Many sites were redefended, or new ones built, in the final period of the Iron Age, with the growth of the *oppida*, or early towns. Many of these towns started as open sites in low-lying locations, but were subsequently defended, as at *Manching in Germany, or moved to hilltop sites with defenses, as at Gergovie in central France. Excavation of such sites as Mont Beuvray, France, is beginning to reveal their economic and political role.

The British Isles contain one of the densest concentrations of hill forts, and a long tradition of research has shown the enormous regional variability. In Scotland and northern Wales the earliest forts were built in the Late Bronze Age, in southern England a major phase of construction took place in the sixth century B.C., but in the east they were rare before the third century B.C. Few show any sign of being aristocratic residences, such as prestige goods or distinctive domestic architecture; the second phase of Iron Age occupation at Crickley Hill has one large roundhouse surrounded by smaller structures, but this may perhaps be a ceremonial building. Many of the sites show nucleated domestic settlement and an involvement in agricultural activities, particularly grain storage.

The sequence in central-southern England has been particularly well explored. Many forts were constructed around the sixth century B.C., but most had a comparatively short life. Some of these forts continued in use, and were enlarged or embellished by additional defenses, as at *Maiden Castle, excavated by *Wheeler. Large-scale excavations by Cunliffe at Danebury have shown how the interior was planned, with streets and the spatial separation of different activities. Some were densely occupied, and control of the subsistence economy, especially through storage of grain in pits and granaries, was important, though the role of such forts as political or economic centers is more doubtful. In some cases, however, hill forts were built in such remote locations that it is doubtful if they were ever occupied permanently, and a ritual function may be more likely.

Some hill forts were occupied during the Roman period, especially in peripheral parts of Europe such as Ireland, but they became more common again in the centuries after the collapse of Roman power. In southern Britain several Iron Age forts were reoccupied, and in Scotland steep rocky outcrops such as Dunadd became the fortified centers of royal power. Defended sites were also built in southern Sweden and the Baltic islands, such as Eketorp in Öland, where the internal occupation was carefully planned, again suggesting a powerful political organization. Hill forts were also a common feature of early Slavic settlement in eastern Europe, as the residences of local chiefs.

[See also BRITISH ISLES: CELTIC IRELAND; CAMPS AND ENCLOSURES, CAUSEWAYED; EUROPE, *articles on* THE EUROPEAN BRONZE AGE, THE EUROPEAN IRON AGE.]

■ T. C. Champion et al., *Prehistoric Europe* (1984). B. W. Cunliffe, *Iron Age Communities in Britain,* 3rd ed. (1991).

Timothy Champion

HISTORICAL ARCHAEOLOGY is a text-aided archaeology that uses a combination of archaeological and historical methods, sources, and perspectives to study the recent past. Strictly speaking, historical archaeology was first practiced in 1855 when the Jesuit Father Félix Martin traveled to the backwoods of today's Ontario, Canada, to investigate the site of Ste. Marie I. Earlier Jesuits had built a mission there to the Huron Indians in 1639. Martin went there to map the site, and unknown to him, he created historical archaeology.

The multidisciplinary perspective and many of the methodological roots of historical archaeology share a kinship with Egyptology, Assyriology, and Mayan, Chinese, and *Classical archaeology, because of their use of written records. In spite of this illustrious geneology, historical archaeology grew slowly before the 1960s. With the independent creation in 1967 of the Society for Historical Archaeology in the United States and the Society for Post-Medieval Archaeology in Great Britain, historical archaeology was assured a place in modern science. Three years later, Australian archaeologists formed the Australian (now Australasian) Society for Historical Archaeology. Professional organizations for historical archaeology now exist in several other countries.

Historical archaeology may share a few affinities with other "historical" archaeologies, but it differs significantly in subject matter and temporal focus. The subject matter of historical archaeology begins in the fifteenth century. Many historians believe that the Portuguese capture of Ceuta in North Africa in A.D. 1415 marks the commencement of the "modern" age and Europe's search for worldwide power and wealth. Historical archaeologists thus focus on both the famous and the anonymous men and women of colonial and early modern history. European colonists, African American slaves, Native American fur traders and laborers, Chinese railroad workers, Cornish miners, German immigrant farmers, Irish tenants and their English landlords, and Australian prisoners are among the people studied by historical archaeologists.

An interest in recent history means that historical archaeology has a special ability to address issues with which we continue to wrestle today: multiculturalism, changing gender roles, internationalism, racism, class development and maintenance, and mass consumption and consumerism. The direct and indisputable tie between the present and the historical past means that historical archaeologists have a special responsibility to communicate their insights not only to their colleagues but also to the general public.

Inseparably linked to this emphasis on the modern world is a strong interest in the growth and spread of mercantile capitalism. Most of the prominent research problems in today's historical archaeology have a foundation in the capitalist transformation of the world. This interest in capitalism is sometimes used to argue that historical archaeology is Eurocentric, but the best studies are those which permit the examination of complex issues from a number of perspectives, both European and indigenous.

One of the ways in which historical archaeologists divulge their interpretations to the world at large is through historic preservation and the reconstruction of long-destroyed or abandoned buildings. The field enjoys a unique and intimate relationship with the historic preservation movement. Since the 1930s, pioneering historical archaeologists have played a significant part in the reconstruction and interpretation of some of the world's most notable historic sites, ranging from Thomas Jefferson's Monticello in Virginia, to the Portuguese colonial outpost, Fort Jesus, at Mombasa, Kenya. The reconstruction of sites associated with the eminent people of history constituted much of the focus of historical archaeology before 1967. Today, most historical archaeologists have an equal interest in the homes and properties of non-prominent men and women, and many are collaborating in the reconstruction of numerous vernacular structures around the world.

The emphasis of historical archaeology on the social and the physical landscapes of the recent past suggests that the field will become more prominent as archaeologists continue to explore the complex relationships between the past and the present. The field will mature further as its practitioners develop their methodological tools and interpretive insights for understanding our contemporary world.

[See also BATTLEFIELD ARCHAEOLOGY OF NORTH AMERICA; COMMERCIAL ARCHAEOLOGY; INDUSTRIAL ARCHAEOLOGY; LANDSCAPE ARCHAEOLOGY; MISSION ARCHAEOLOGY.]

■ Ivor Noël-Hume, *Historical Archaeology* (1972). James Deetz, *In Small Things Forgotten: The Archaeology of Early American Life* (1977). Mark P. Leone and Parker B. Potter, Jr., eds., *The Recovery of Meaning: Historical Archaeology in the Eastern United States* (1988). Barbara J. Little, ed., *Text-Aided Archaeology* (1992). Charles E. Orser and Brian Fagan, *Historical Archaeology* (1995).

Charles E. Orser

HISTORY OF ARCHAEOLOGY, Intellectual. There are many equally valid ways to write a history of how archaeologists contributed to the intellectual climate of their times. Some historians emphasize the discipline's dependency relations with history, geology, or anthropology. For others, prehistorians' priorities simply reflect evolving middle-class values. These views do not give archaeologists their due. The intellectual history of archaeology has been the search to comprehend unrecorded motivations. Were the actors upon the ancient stage much like us, such that we can recreate their motivations in our mind? Or were they playing to a script that is untranslatable to an audience from another time, another society?

Recently, these same questions have split philosophers of the social sciences into partisan camps. Beginning with their Enlightenment forbears, archaeologists anticipated many of the arguments that now set philosophers at each others' throats.

One dominant faction in the philosophy of the social sciences assumes that there must be a basis for cross-cultural understanding. They accept that there is no objective way to judge between two mutually incompatible theories about motivations for a certain action. Nevertheless, they argue for a unity of method with the natural sciences as the best way to find progressively better ways to predict future behavior. Goals of cross-cultural understanding and prediction are just too much for the competing faction. This second group believes that childhood socialization endows each neatly bounded social group with sets of inner rules, intuitive manuals of translation of appropriate behavior. This manual is closed fast to the outsider. The insightful observer might judge the internal coherence of acts guided by another group's inner rules, but will forever be a stranger to the deeper, mystical inner logic. A third minority faction asserts that all humankind shares universal ways of looking at the world. Such innate dispositions define our common humanity.

Almost every core concept—unity of method, predic-

tion, inner rules, internal coherences, innate dispositions—has surfaced repeatedly for 250 or so years as archaeologists have struggled to know how scatters of lithics or a Greek krater might provide a window onto the maker's motivations. This obsession to understand the motivations of the long dead grew partially out of contact with peoples whom Europeans could rank as progressively more primitive, and partially out of something moldering in the soil beneath their feet.

Intellectual Liberation: The Enlightenment. Europe's world expansion would not have sufficed to challenge medieval ecclesiastical doctrine that all but the Christian chosen were lesser approximations of God's image. There was far too much need for justification of conquest and genocide, such as Fray Ginés de Sepúlveda's (ca. 1560) assertion that the "savages" of the Americas were not even human. All that began to change with the realization that the rude stones and bones being unearthed in increasing numbers from the ancestral soil of Europe looked undeniably like those made by barbarous tribes far away. The best Enlightenment minds asked the archetypal archaeological question that rests the basis for all current assertions of universal human rights: are they what we were once—or are now still? It is difficult, with our late twentieth-century cynicism and ennui, to imagine the intellectual liberation that resulted.

Some historians of archaeology date the intellectual birth of the discipline to 1859. In that indisputably revolutionary year, the biblical short chronology of a 6,000-year span for humankind fell apart. However, a century earlier the inquiring minds of Europe began to invent a new authority to interpret distant savages and their own distant ancestors. The *philosophes* looked upon the face of modern savages and ancient brutes and saw there none of the revealed certainties of the senescent medieval order.

Of course, the Enlightenment was not conceived in a vacuum. Since the sixteenth century, curios from voyages of discovery and amateur diggings, together with natural science samples, found their way into *Wunderkammern*, or Cabinets of Curiosities. These were far more than proto-museums. They were the mirror of the universe, where Divine purpose was exposed to scrutiny of reason. Scholars scrutinized their *Wunderkammern* for universal, mechanical laws championed by Descartes, Kant, Buffon, and Newton. For humans, too, were forged into God's Great Chain of Being and so belonged with all things measurable—animate and inanimate, present and ancient.

God made the Great Chain according to immutable principles. The principle of plenitude asserted that each link in the Great Chain was a unique, well-differentiated "natural species." Each link was present since the creation, each unchanging. Open inquiry was soon to show that the chain was not static; extinctions and evolution of new forms had to be accounted for. Nevertheless, the plenitude principle of unique entities reemerges again and again. Of more immediate influence on Enlightenment thinking were the principles of graduation and continuity: each organism differs only slightly from its lower or higher neighbor on a Great Chain forged without gaps. Progress.

Linnaeus was ranking species according to graduation and continuity when he invented, *Homo troglodytes*, the link immediately below the rudest of living primitives. So too, Soame Jenyns, who produced a seriation of humanity from the "brutal Hottentot" to Newton in 1790. In Peter Heylyns's *Microcosmos* of 1636, we find North American aboriginals compared to Europeans three hundred years after Noah's flood. While the members of the Scottish Enlightenment (Ferguson, Stewart, Adam Smith, Millar) and their French counterparts (Turgot, de Condorcet, Buffon, Montesquieu, Voltaire) were to make God an irrelevancy to the discovery of the principles of causation, they embraced concepts of gradation and continuity as they grappled with the evidence of ancient times in their endeavors to know the workings of the minds of people very different than themselves.

The Enlightenment equation of ethnographic distance from Europe with the historical distance from ancestors was not in itself particularly revolutionary. Certainly, it would not have been considered a remarkable insight when, in 1750, Turgot stated that all stages of development leading to the European nations were represented somewhere in the world. Earlier, the Scandinavian and English nationalists had made similar uniformitarianist assumptions about their ancestors. What was pioneering were the methods of analysis and the initial presumption of a transcendent, constant human nature.

The goal of these studies was to isolate the laws of human history by pragmatic observation, classification, and experiment. The laws thus revealed were to possess the same structure as natural science laws, and, because they were lessons to reduce humanity's pain, were of even higher status. Laws were predictive. Infinite perfectibility was the law of nature. Societies develop along universal, linear stages, each developing out of the preceding. Scientific society was the highest moral end of history.

History could only be treated as an equal to natural science because of an abiding faith that all humanity was born of a common ancestor. This (monogenist) faith in global innate equality of intelligence, articulated by Buffon (1749) and Ferguson (1767), is passed on to the next generation by Prichard (1813, 1841) as the "'psychic unity" of the Social Evolutionists. But, de Condorcet, in his ten-stage, unilinear history *Esquisse d'un Tableau Historique des Progrès de l'Esprit Humain* (1793), is the most revolutionary in his use of antiquity. Modern hunters and gatherers are survivals from the original human condition. They may still be steeped in ignorance because of environment or historical accident, but not because of biological (racial) barriers to progress or because they degenerated from an earlier condition. In fact, Thomas Jefferson's 1784 excavations of Virginia burial mounds (arguably the only systematic archaeological excavation conducted as part of the Enlightenment project) were undertaken to gather data to counter the argument of the degeneration of North American animals, indigenous peoples, and their institutions. Thus, the problem of comprehending the motivations of peoples distant in customs or in time was really a non-problem: they may be us as we once were, but they are us, nonetheless.

Culture and Race Conflated. The Enlightenment remained in its armchair. As the nineteenth-century reaction against revolutionary ideas of equality and the Napoleonic betrayal set in, nascent field archaeology fell increasingly into the hands of nationalists and mystical Romantics. To be sure, Saint-Simon (1813 to 1825) and, especially, Auguste Comte greedily consumed classical antiquity and comparative prehistory as they carried the sputtering torch of progress and unity of method. In his *Système de Politiique Positive* (1824) and *Cours de Philosophie Positive* (1830 to 1842), Comte articulates a grand hierarchy of all the sciences. Social Physics (history) will be the last to mature, but will boast the profoundest laws. In the end, however, Comte's grandiose plans for history simply became irrelevant to the growing numbers of advocational field archaeologists. For them, the living prehistory represented by the diverse peoples of the new colonies overseas served as a quite adequate and uncomplicated illustration of how ancient peoples lived. If those savages had had a history, it was irrelevant. These nationalists and mystics held that each people had their own particularistic history, determined by geographical accident or race. Nationalism melded with the conceit that natural selection produced some races superior in intelligence and capacity for complex social institutions, while others, argued Lubbock in his *Prehistoric Times* (1865), were destined only for cultural stasis. Thus was plenitude elevated to doctrine and graduation and continuity abandoned to dreamers.

Much of early antiquarian archaeology was conducted to illustrate the long continuity of the sovereign character of separate European peoples at a time when middle-class nationalism competed with the internationalism of the tired aristocracy. Belief in a monogenist humanity was replaced by a devotion to unities and boundaries. As early as 1734, the Society of Dilettanti was founded on the premise that the monuments of Greece and Rome illustrated the distinct, immutable character of those civilizations. The argument was strengthened by the very alienness of ancient pharonic civilizations illustrated in Denon's *Description de l'Egypt* (1809) and of the wondrous finds revealed by the tunnelings of *Layard at Nimrud (1844), *Botta at *Ninevah (1842) or by *Schliemann at Hissarlik (*Troy, 1870 to 1879) and Mycenae (1876). Many of these finds were removed to the great European museums, where today we still see the ethos of the bounded civilization in Assyrian or Egyptian wings. In how many museums are floors devoted to global stages of social evolution?

While Boucher de *Perthes at Abbeville (1830s to 1860s) or Rigollot at St. Acheul (early 1800s) might use ethnographic examples to illustrate the uses of the stone tools they found, or Frere (1797) and MacEnery (mid 1800s) use hand axes from British caves, the underlying purpose of these excavations was to prove that sufficient time had elapsed for a deep foundation for, respectively, a distinctively French or English culture. In England this approach had its precedents in the older antiquarian publishing of ancient monuments by Thomas Leland (1533), William Camden (1586), John Aubry (1670), and especially William Stukeley (1740s). Some invented mythological ancestry for the ancient Britons derived from the Classical texts. But in Stukeley's Druids, we see the yearnings for distinguished ancestors.

Often, the search for the unique and for the universal coexisted by an uneasy truce. Ole Worm (early 1600s), C. J. *Thomsen (1819 to 1836), J.J.A. *Worsaae (1849) and S. Nilsson (1868) argued, on the one hand, for applicability of their *three-age system (Stone, Bronze, Iron) beyond Scandinavia. Yet, these same pioneers argued that the souls of modern nations are embedded in their antiquities. Arguments of separate (polygenist) creation and boundedness of peoples proliferated, as did dreamy-eyed arguments of mystical inner rules dividing Frenchmen from Germans, as they did Gaul from Teuton.

In this ethos of unique entities, the often irreconcilable divisions of archaeology were born. *Classical Archaeology and Egyptology emerged from their origins as high-class looting. What authority for interpretation could not be had directly from the texts (epigraphy) was derived by connoisseurship. Certain masterpieces allowed an empathic knowledge of the makers' intentions because they were material expressions of the genius of the makers' era. Entire critical, but text-poor periods (the Nile Pre-Dynastic, for example) were relatively ignored. In Biblical Archaeology, the Text was even more omnipresent but, unfortunately, not always the object of disinterested, objective scholarship. We see that legacy in Israel today, where much very fine field archaeology is shackled to elements of highly nationalistic ideology or to the desire to confirm Bible stories. In colonial Rhodesia, the meticulous excavation results of MacIver (1905) and *Caton-Thompson (1931) were suppressed in favor of a farcical, biblical-based interpretation of *Great Zimbabwe, a situation not officially reversed until the recent independence of the nation that now bears the name of those ruins. In North America, scholars who refused to believe indigenous peoples capable of building large earthen monuments had to invent biblical (Lost Israelites) or legendary peoples (Mound Builders).

Text-driven and art-historical interpretations are not a western monopoly. China had its own version of the Three Age system, as early as the first century B.C., based upon Yüan K'ang's study of ancient artifacts. However, *Li Chi, who found oracle bones at *Anyang (1928) that confirmed Bronze Age dynastic records, is more honored than, for example, the brilliant Shen Kua, who in the eleventh century tried to interpret ancient objects independent of Confucian tradition. Even after 1949, there has been a tendency in China to devote enormous resources to elite finds (such as the terra-cotta army of the first Ch'in emperor), rather than to investigate the lives of all segments of society. Japan devotes vast sums to an archaeology driven by official dynastic chronicles or dedicated to the identification of putative physical types, if not to the demonstration of racial purity. Little wonder that pseudo-archaeology is a major prop to the rightist movement. In India, very early civilizations, such as the Indus, are identified from the ancient texts as pre-Vedic, the destroyers as the migratory Aryans. What unites all these examples is the fundamental belief that archaeology properly is the study of unique peoples who made decisions about how to deal with the physical and social environment in ways peculiar only to themselves, understandable only to their direct descendants.

Radical nationalism is mystical. In this nineteenth-century invention that was to have horrific consequences in our own century, understanding of past peoples' motivations can only be achieved by their direct historical descendant, those sharing the same inner logic. Each age, each people has its own discrete "spirit," unchanging over vast expanses of time, but utterly impenetrable by the sciences. Knowledge comes about only by a mystical communication with human feelings of the past. Such ideas had their most influential expression in the German historicist school of Humbolt, Ranke, and Herder (with his fixed races and Germanic uniqueness), supported by the writings of the philosophers Schleiermacher, Fichte, and Dilhtey. The last, particularly, described the "internal coherences" that made peoples distinct and could allow empathic communication (Verstehen) with the spirit of their age.

Hegel's Lectures on Aesthetics (1823–1829) gave the key to a long and often shameful articulation of archaeology with historicism. Hegel argued that historical essences of nations were lodged in certain privileged aesthetics and that different peoples' destinies were of unequal historical and moral

rank. Hence his assessment of Africans as "capable of no development or culture, and as we see them at this day such have they always been." Only the direct historical descendant of the same group or the scholar who can lose him or herself in the diagnostic aesthetic can read that particular manual of translation. Historicist nationalism was a boon to field work. G. *Kossinna in his Die Deutsche Dorgeschichte (1912) encouraged "Indo-Germaic" archaeology as the way to find the objects with which to communicate with a people whose heroic moment came one thousand years before the Romans. O. Spengler (The Decline of the West, 1926) presented a vast tableau of eight nations and their defining aesthetics—stone for Egypt, the symmetrical human body for Classical Greece, and the (tragically) expansive "Faustian" space for the Germans. A horrified Spengler lived long enough to see Kossinna's and his ideas perverted into Hitler's theories of Aryan culture builders and Untermenschen culture destroyers, but not long enough to witness the extensive excavations to find artifacts of the Germanteum (racial essence) of the Germanic tribes, undertaken during the early 1940s by Himmler's archaeological corps, the SS-Ahnerebe. Similarly, Mussolini's minions excavated the Forum of Trajan to celebrate the Italian nation's rediscovered glory. These were theories of how to know the ancients that incinerated the world.

The insecurities of Germany's unification process spawned these mystical archaeologies. In prosperous and confident England and America, some Enlightenment ideas were repackaged as Social Evolutionism. The first of these was the belief that cross-cultural ethnographic and archaeological could reveal universal social laws. Herbert Spencer's Social Statistics (1850) promulgated one such law: the rise of civilization and the progress of humankind (unequal, because of racial or environmental differences) were the results of the struggle caused by population increases and insufficiency of food predicted by Malthus (1798). The vast comparative projects of L. H. *Morgan (1877) and E. B. *Tylor (1865 to 1893), following on work by Bachofen (1861) and McLennan (1865), led to elaborate schemes of unilinear social evolution with their ranked universal stages. In Ancient Society, Morgan offers seven ethical stages from Lower Savagery to Civilization, each with its characteristic artifact, way of life, social and family organization. The grand synthesizers created a new demand for quality data, cheerfully provided by evolutionist archaeologists such as *Pitt-Rivers, who pioneered principles of recording and stratigraphic excavation at Cranborne Chase (1887 to 1898). Few saw the need to question the plenitude thesis that variability in the ethnographic record mirrors humanity's past. So argued Lubbock in 1865. So Sollas still maintained in his 1911 Ancient Hunters, where he equates Tasmanians with the European Lower Paleolithic society, the Middle Paleolithic with Australian Aboriginals, and the Upper Paleolithic with the Eskimo and Kalahari San.

The Social Evolutionists revived another Enlightenment belief. In his 1851 Man and His Migrations, Latham asserted that the question of the unity or non-unity of humankind was one of the outstanding questions of prehistory. The Social Evolutionists reinvented several versions of "psychic unity." Within the same stage, ethnographic and archaeological peoples share the same emotions and same intellectual capacities. Such was Bastian's (1860) argument for his concept of Elementargedanken, "elementary ideas" and the foundation of Frazer's (1887, 1890) belief in cross-cultural survivals of primitive totems and religion. The motivations of ethnographical peoples and of the ancients, however alien, were ultimately comprehensible. One could again look to a science of culture.

Only a limited amount of field archaeology was conducted explicitly under the original Social Evolutionary rubric. An enormous amount was done under its Marxist descendant. Great irony attaches to the history of *Marxist archaeology. In Marx's 1859 *Critique of Political Economy*, history is not about mysticism or the progress of the human mind, but about changes brought about by material conditions. From his reading of Morgan, Engels developed an authoritative ideology of universal human development, a Theory of Stages, in his 1884 *Origin of the Family*.

However, the doctrinaire Marxist-Leninist social evolutionism that ossified by the 1930s proved inadequate to interpret the great diversities of societies exposed by the voluminous excavations in mainland China and the Soviet Union. In time, historical materialism yielded to determined nationalism. Increasingly, the interpretive chapters of fine technical site reports would have little to do with the excavated material. In the Soviet Union after World War II, research was increasingly devoted to defining ethnic areas or to ethnogenesis. In China, archaeology was an instrument of political education. Theoreticians, such as Xia Nai (1979), devoted their efforts to reconciling Marxist laws to a special, proudly Chinese case of social development and to a chauvinistic search for innovation centers (eg., Honan and East Shensi for Neolithic and Bronze Age origins). By the 1950s and 1960s, western archaeologists looking to these countries for a processual, materialist alternative to culture history were severely disappointed.

Stability and Discreteness: Culture History. By mid-century, Marxist archaeology more resembled one of several alternatives to Social Evolutionism, rather than its scientific refinement. The culture history alternative in the United States was the product of Boas's rejection of cross-cultural unilinearism and of reactions against the racist Mound Builder theories. Boas reacted eloquently against all forms of speculative, comparative laws of evolution, race, or progress. He argued that culture was far too complex. He and the influential two generations of archaeologists trained by him or by his students argued that discrete cultures were the appropriate units of study, but only in their geographical and temporal distribution.

North American archaeology had been developing in this direction since the early decades of the new century, after S. F. Havens (1856) and Cyrus Thomas (1885, 1898) discredited the Mound Builder thesis. Excavation was increasing apace, but the data were in a theoretical chaos. Cushing (1886) and Fewkes (1900), after experiments with evolutionism, pioneered the direct historical method. Prehistoric remains should be interpreted by analogy with practices of presumed descendant groups. Spinden's (1917) Archaic complex was a mature early example of the culture history methodology that depended closely upon time and space charts identical to those that made V. G. *Childe's *Dawn of European Civilization* (1925) so revolutionary. The cultural history method was historically particularistic. Boundaries between cultures were relatively impermeable. *Diffusion did occur (innovations coming ultimately from a Mesoamerican center of innovation), but living ethnic groups were presumed to have changed little from their prehistoric progenitors. Kroeber (1916) and Spier (1917) at Zuni, *Kidder on the Pecos (1924), and Ford in the Mississippi Valley (1936) improved excavation techniques and

pioneered the analytical tools, such as seriation and formal artifact taxonomies, that would be formalized into elaborate classifications of ethnic systems, type artifacts, and geographical boundaries, such as McKern's Midwestern Taxonomic Method (1939).

By mid-century, both Europeans and North Americans shared a fundamental skepticism that the motivations of the long dead could ever be known. C. *Hawkes provided the classic articulation of the unscalable ladder of archaeological inference. Archaeologists might understand technology and perhaps economy and subsistence, but social rules, political organization, and particularly beliefs were forever closed books (except insofar as direct historical descendant informants were available to enlighten us). Peoples of a bounded culture shared values, norms, and cultural expectations. If not born to that society, one could do no more than classify the geographical horizon styles and the time-persistent cultural traditions of the infinite variety in human culture.

As field work intensified in the early decades of the twentieth century, European archaeologists were at the disadvantage of being less certain of the presumed direct descendants for the great and chaotic proliferation of prehistoric cultures which were being identified. Archaeologists were influenced by Ratzel (1885 to 1888) and the *Kulturkreis* school of discrete folk cultures spreading from innovation centers and by the *Ex Oriente Lux*-brand of Near Eastern diffusionism of O. *Montelius (1899). There was a proliferation of historically and geographically discrete cultural entitles, each given a find spot or diagnostic-artifact name (Beaker folk, Battle Axe culture, La Tène). In all this particularistic detail, the big picture was often lost. Perhaps it is no wonder that the great archaeology-loving public turned to the hyper-diffusionist drivel of G. Elliot Smith (1928) or Lord Raglan (1939).

The great exception was V. G. *Childe. Childe made his reputation with the grand synthesis *(Dawn of European Civilization)* that extracted time and space order out of this confusion of local cultures. He used a framework of technological stages and diffusion of the big ideas of prehistory out of the Near East. Archaeological cultures were still individual entities, best classified by ethnicity rather than by technology. Diffusion was a major mechanism of change, but the circumstances were always local.

In his cross-cultural comparative interests and his view of cultures as open, adaptive systems driven by materialist processes, Childe was very much the exception for his time. There were other exceptions that prefigured major aspects of the New Archaeology: the insistent adaptive ecology of J.G.D. Clarke, the Virú Valley settlement patterns from Peru of G. Willey, and the peerless statistics of A. Spaulding. W. W. Taylor was perhaps the best publicized prophet of changes soon to sweep the field. In his 1948 *A Study of Archaeology*, he made a classic New Archaeology argument about the descriptive sterility of culture history and advocated what he called conjunctive archaeology. If culture is to be thought of in functionalist terms as all practices that allow humans to adapt to their environment, then the archaeologist must make an integrated study of food, settlement, environment, etc., as well as tools and ceramics.

The New Archaeology. However, in one significant way W. W. Taylor cannot be called the first New Archaeologist. Taylor argued that the archaeologist can never be a part of the past, so it is impossible for him or her to reconstruct a civilization. The archaeologist is cut off forever from past motivations. Contrary to that essential pessimism, nothing was impossible in the unbounded enthusiasm of New Archaeology's first flush. Archaeology as a science would transform the discipline into a true anthropology of the past. It was simply a matter of time before archaeologists would have access to all rungs of Hawkes's ladder of inference. In 1968—the publication date of Sally and Louis Binford's call to action, *New Perspectives in Archaeology*—science and computers promised a new world that could be compatible with the infant ecological and ZPG movements, revolution was in the air in politics and civil rights, and the key word was *relevance*. Archaeology would never be relevant if archaeologists ignored the person behind the pot. An examination of case studies from the American Southwest and Mousterian France, the Binfords' landmark book even purported to reveal the motivations of the long dead. Historical particularism was out. Cross-cultural analogies were in. And so, too, was a promise of a new science that would use all the statistical power, isotopic dating, and laboratory techniques and models borrowed from brethren sciences to create new laws of society that were every bit as powerful for prediction as those in the natural sciences. This was not just derivative unity of method with the sciences. Archaeology would be a science that physicists would envy (although old fogies soon quipped about "physics envy").

The New Archaeology was many things and would soon be accused of many others. It is useful to look at the debates that quickly wracked the New Archaeology, because these show us what the practitioners themselves judged to be important. The issue of how to judge itself a mature science soon divided the North American and British versions. The spokesman for the latter was David Clarke, who argued that the "undisciplined empirical discipline" needed a corpus of models. Clarke saw these as visualizing devices that functioned in the other sciences to relate observation to theoretical ideas. He saw culture as a dynamic equilibrium system, very close in concept to contemporary culture ecology. However, he had little time for formal logical proofs.

In the United States, debate raged for or against formal rules of explanation. Some like Kent Flannery argued for an organic systems theory of culture as an adaptive interaction of subsystems. Others, with Watson, LeBlanc, and Redman's *Explanation in Archaeology* (1971) as their bible, argued for nothing less than the hypothetico-deductive method of explanation by Covering Law to boost the discipline to science's elevated status.

The second debate concerned what many felt was the fastest, most reliable route to high-level inferences about what motivated behavior in the past, namely explanation by analogy. How directly historical did the sources for analogy have to be? This was a question that was to splinter the remarkably monolithic New Archaeology and that pushed one of the founders, Louis Binford, to reverse entirely his position on the question of whether ancient beliefs and intentions could ever be reconstructed. At about that time, a shrill challenge to New Archaeology's scientific optimism sounded from across the Atlantic.

Recent Reinvention of a Cognitive Archaeology. The most aggressive application of the post-modern critique of claims of objectivity and of authoritative scholarship has come principally from Cambridge and a few English redbrick universities. The majority of English-speaking archaeologists, however, have remained fundamentally skeptical of the underlying message that the Real Past may never be accessible and that even to attempt is an intolerable act of political repression. The so-called Post-processualists began first to mine the positivist breastworks of New Archaeology. They decried the determinism of the systems approach, cultural ecology, and the stadial, evolutionary schemes that had come to dominate the study of complex societies. The unofficial spokesperson of the movement, Ian Hodder, converted from a being a models-and-math student of David Clarke. Showing the influence of the Frankfurt school and, particularly, Giddens and Bourdieu, Hodder renounced all attempts to make archaeology into an anthropology aping the natural sciences. Hodder and D. Miller turned their attention to artifacts as symbols. They posited that material symbols reflect and simultaneously create the inner logic of a community, the guide to practical action for all members of that community. Behavior is negotiation between individuals and between different subgroups (classes, genders, minorities) with these symbols as currency.

The Post-processualists use many ethnographic examples (and many more from contemporary Britain) to reinvent the historicist argument that anyone not a member of a community can never know true motivations behind socially created meaning. Different cultures generate alternative forms of reality. It is only the pure hubris of western social science (and the New Archaeology in particular) that allows an archaeologist from the outside to presume to know better than anyone else what is going on. Hodder in *Reading the Past* (1986) takes the historian R. G. Collingwood as his direct bridge back to the historicist philosophers, specifically Dilhtey. He argues that demonstrable direct descendants are the only authoritative source for knowing the beliefs and meanings of a particular people in the past. Lacking those existential expects, one must use the decidedly inferior expedient of historical imagination excited by analogy and a deep intuitive feeling for the "internal coherences" of the symbolic evidence.

One of the triumphs of the New Archaeology was an explosion of field work on a number of processual issues, such as the emergence of food production or the growth of complex society (states, cities). Now Post-processualists, such as Hodder and Miller and Tilley, say all that must stop. The very act of "discovery," as conducted by western archaeologists, is political expropriation and social control. Excavation is necessarily appropriation of the past for the purpose of maintaining structures of political inequality in the present. Prehistories are only folktales. According to Hodder (1984), ". . . it is presumptuous and dangerous for an archaeologist to write the past for others."

The intention is to encourage alternative voices in archaeology, but the reaction to such statements by Third World colleagues has been swift and scathing. These critics resent the paternalism that assumes that non-western scholars will passively accept anything written about their past. They go on to argue that, since most research has been conducted in Europe, the United States, or in lands critical to the west's view of its superior cultural heritage (eastern Mediterranean and Near East), to ban future field archaeology as despised "discovery" would forever render the past of most of the globe an impoverished, derived shadow of the richer past of better-researched lands. Dirt archaeologists point to the weaknesses in the ethnographic examples used and to the lack of excavation conducted under the Post-processual banner at a time when the archaeological record is disappearing at a breathless rate.

The theoretical reaction to Post-processualism is still

vague. It does not even have a name. However, in early responses to the Post-processualist charges of excessive positivism and political repression and in the new research themes emerging during the second half of the 1990s, the reaction appears to resemble what the philosophers of the social sciences call interpretive pluralism. It can serve, therefore, to summarize the often opposing currents of claims to know the motivations of long-dead peoples that have coursed through the intellectual history of archaeology.

Post-processualists are accused of having attacked a caricature of the New Archaeology. In its place, they have elevated their own internal circle of logic, without criteria of good or bad interpretation, that leads to unverifiable just-so stories and speculations about unrecorded intentions. Reaction focuses on their unwillingness to conduct an auto-deconstruction of the post-modernist presumptions that they have mined from the humanities or from Critical Theory and applied to archaeology without regard to the consequences. Such consequences are, according to Third World colleagues, a new paternalism propped up by a tyranny of jargon and, according to mainstream archaeologists, the appearance of nihilism as the Post-processualists sever all links to the Real Past of the external world.

For a minority, reaction takes the form of retreat into narrow empiricism of ethno-archaeological, actualistic, and experimental studies to develop Middle-Range statements about how mechanical behavior translates into the statics of the archaeological record. Others import biological models of adaptive evolution to study complexity. French colleagues are pioneering Logicism, a formal logic for reducing artisan knowledge into sequence chains that can be organized algorithmically. Most contemporary archaeologists are uncommitted to formal unity of method with the natural sciences and are uncertain about what prediction might mean in archaeology. They are, however, committed to cross-cultural comparisons, to the study of processes, and to the proposition that an external world and a past exist independent of our imaginations. The duty of the archaeologist, then, is to find a new but not exclusionary empiricism that will encourage multiple ways of looking at a phenomenon by scholars bringing different values and experiences to their choice of theories. Interpretations must respect constraints imposed by the data.

One of the enduring legacies of Post-processualism is the general acceptance that archaeology is the study of the remains of past people's actions upon a world as socially constructed and perceived. The process of social construction, however, is not mystical. Behavior does not depend upon an inner logic (manual of translation) that is forever hidden from outsiders to the community. As C. Renfrew and E. Zubrow state in The Ancient Mind (1994), "one of the most troubling problems in archaeology is to determine about what or in what manner did prehistoric people think."

There is an emerging optimism that past motivations can be at least partially revealed through the investigation of how symbols and objects function as devices or insignia communicating peoples' views of themselves. The faith in the comprehensibility of motivations can be seen in just a sample of new research themes: looking for the transformations of millennia-old reservoirs of symbols and ideologies in, for example, Chinese or Mayan shamanism and cosmology or in African systems of occult knowledge; the convergence in prehistory, classical archaeology, and Egyptology in a search for representations of reality in literate ancient societies; climate, not as something passively to be responded to, but to be entered as myth or legend into the social memory as a reservoir of options for future stress. There appears to be a determination not to descend into the vituperative denigration of opponents. This is fertile ground, then, for the growth of interpretive pluralism in archaeology: for the respectful, yet skeptical interaction of multiple points of view about how to achieve cross-cultural knowledge of what motivated people's actions in the past and about how to enter data fields that, today, we do not even imagine exist.

[See also ARCHAEOLOGY AS A DISCIPLINE; CRITICAL THEORY; CULTURAL ECOLOGY THEORY; CULTURE HISTORICAL THEORY; DARWINIAN THEORY; GENDER, ARCHAEOLOGY OF; GENERAL SYSTEMS THEORY; METHOD, ARCHAEOLOGICAL; MIDDLE RANGE THEORY; NATIONALISM; POLITICAL USES OF ARCHAEOLOGY; POST-PROCESSUAL THEORY; PROCESSUAL THEORY; PSEUDO-ARCHAEOLOGY: INTRODUCTION; SCIENCE IN ARCHAEOLOGY; THEORY IN ARCHAEOLOGY.]

■ Arthur O. Lovejoy, The Great Chain of Being (1936). Glyn Daniel, The Origins and Growth of Archaeology (1967). Marvin Harris, The Rise of Anthropological Theory (1968). Gordon R. Willey and Jeremy A. Sabloff, A History of American Archaeology (1974). John D. Evans, Barry Cunliffe and Colin Renfrew, eds., Antiquity and Man (1981). Donald K. Grayson, The Establishment of Human Antiquity (1983). David J. Meltzer, "The Antiquity of Man and the Development of American Archaeology," Advances in Archaeological Method and Theory 6 (1983): 1–51. Bruce G. Trigger, A History of Archaeological Thought (1989). Pauline M. Rosenau, Post-Modernism and the Social Sciences (1992). Stephen K. Sanderson, Social Evolutionism (1993). Norman Yoffee and Andrew Sherratt, Archaeological Theory: Who Sets the Agenda? (1993). A. Bowdoin Van Riper, Men Among the Mammoths (1993). Colin Renfrew and Ezra Zubrow, The Ancient Mind: Elements of Cognitive Archaeology (1994).

Roderick J. McIntosh

HISTORY OF ARCHAEOLOGY BEFORE 1900

Overview
European Archaeology
Near Eastern Archaeology
Classical Archaeology
Archaeology of the Americas

OVERVIEW

Archaeology has roots in scholarly and philosophical curiosity about the remote past. Although the Babylonian King Nabonidus excavated in search of artifacts owned by his predecessors, and Roman emperors and scholars collected antiquities, serious archaeological inquiry began with the revival of interest in Classical studies during the Renaissance. As Leo Klejn shows, modern prehistoric archaeology began with attempts to explain finely made stone axes associated with the bones of long-extinct animals in European river gravels. These finds were controversial because of theological dogma, which held the biblical Creation was only six thousand years old. Serious archaeological excavations stemmed from wholesale diggings into ancient burial mounds. And the finds from these excavations formed a confusing jumble, which eluded classification until Danish archaeologist C. J. *Thomsen developed his famous *Three-Age System, validated stratigraphically by J.J.A. *Worsaae. The establishment of human antiquity in 1859 placed the study of the prehistoric past and of human biological and cultural evolution on a scientific footing.

These developments unfolded at a time when interest in

Classical and Near Eastern archaeology was intensifying. Morris and Schoville describe the early discoveries at *Herculaneum and Pompeii, the dramatic excavations by Paul Emile *Botta, Austen Henry *Layard, and others, which revealed Assyrian civilization, and the intense scientific efforts which led to the deciphering of cuneiform and hieroglyphs. Their articles show how the German school of excavation exercised a profound influence over both Classical and Near Eastern archaeology after the 1870s, while Flinders *Petrie's research into ancient Egyptian potsherds showed the potential for cross-dating historic and prehistoric cultures in the Mediterranean Basin.

American archaeology also began with speculations about the origins of the Native Americans. Early workers considered them descendants of long-forgotten immigrants from Europe, even members of the Ten Lost Tribes of Israel. Only a few scholars assumed the first settlers had crossed from Asia long before Europeans arrived. Givens describes the controversies which swirled around the first Americans and around the identity of the Moundbuilder peoples of North America. He also places the epic Maya discoveries of Frederick Catherwood and John Lloyd *Stephens in a broader scientific context.

[See also NEAR EASTERN ARCHAEOLOGY; CLASSICAL ARCHAEOLOGY; ARCHAEOLOGY OF THE AMERICAS.]

Brian M. Fagan

EUROPEAN ARCHAEOLOGY

European archaeology began in a long tradition of antiquarian inquiry and leisured travel to classical lands. As early as Renaissance times, Europe's nobility flocked to Italy. They collected Greek and Roman antiquities, which they displayed in their homes, often in cabinets of curiosities. A few learned men, like Cyriacus of Ancona (1391–1452), traveled widely in Greece and the Near East, studying ancient inscriptions, but most classical antiquarians were content to collect art for art's sake. Some scholars tried to explain prehistoric remains. The Vatican physician Michele Mercati (1541–1593) collected minerals and puzzled over finely made, polished stone axes from disturbed graves found in European fields. He narrowly escaped accusations of heresy when he declared them not to be the natural "thunderbolts" of popular belief, but humanly manufactured artifacts from ancient times. By the eighteenth century, the Grand Tour through Mediterranean lands was an established part of an aristocratic education. Collecting classical antiquities became fashionable among the wealthy, a major stimulus for the excavations at *Pompeii, where Johann Joachim Winckelmann (1717–1768) was the first to study changes in classical art styles through time. Throughout Europe, less affluent antiquarians studied prehistoric artifacts and Roman sites nearer home. William Camden described Britain's antiquities in his classic Britannia in 1588. By the seventeenth and eighteenth centuries, the collecting of prehistoric artifacts flourished throughout Europe. Collecting went hand in hand with field observations. John Aubrey (1626–1697) described Avebury and *Stonehenge in southern Britain, using comparisons with living non-Western peoples such as Native Americans to describe both sites as cult monuments. Nearly a century later Jesuit-missionary Joseph-François Lafitau (1670–1740) wrote a study of Native Americans, comparing them to "prehistoric times." The emerging European antiquarianism was very haphazard, the province of learned men and landowners

who excavated burial mounds and Roman fortifications, collecting antiquities for the sake of collecting them. Antiquities were perceived as being ancient, but they belonged to a human past constrained by the 6,000 years of biblical time said by theological dogma to have elapsed since the Creation and the Garden of Eden. Scholars throughout Europe were well aware of the philosophical speculations of Lucretius and other classical authors about ancient ages of stone, bronze, and iron, but it was not until Danish museum curator Christian Jurgenson *Thomsen arranged the collections according to his *Three-Age System in the early nineteenth century that some order was brought to prehistoric times. Thomsen's new system remained largely hypothetical until his pupil, J.J.A. *Worsaae, proved its stratigraphic validity with excavations in prehistoric burial mounds.

The Three-Age System soon became the framework for European prehistory, and, for many generations, for all of Old World archaeology. Its widespread adoption coincided with the establishment of the *Antiquity of Humankind in 1859, with its proof of the contemporaneity of human artifacts and the bones of extinct animals in France's Somme Valley and England. By the late nineteenth century, the general outlines of European prehistory were known. Sir John Lubbock (1834–1913) was the first to use the terms *"Palaeolithic, Old Stone Age," for a long period of prehistory when chipped stone tools were used, and "Neolithic, New Stone Age," for a later era of polished stone technology, in his book Prehistoric Times (1865). The earliest Palaeolithic cultural manifestations were very crude stone tools, the so-called eoliths, or drawn stones, then stone hand axes from the Somme River gravels, followed by the spectacular Neanderthal and Cro-Magnon rock shelters of southwestern France. The Swiss *lake dwellings, excavated by Swiss archaeologist Ferdinand Keller in the 1850s, documented Neolithic and later farmers. Bronze Age and Iron Age sites joined the prehistoric sequence to the archaeological and historical record of the Roman Empire. As the pace of excavation accelerated, Italian and Hungarian scholars divided the central European Bronze Age into both a Copper Age and a Bronze Age. The Iron Age was also split in two, following excavations in the *Hallstatt Iron Age cemetery in Austria, dug in the 1840s to 1860s, and at the *La Tène settlement in Switzerland, excavated at about the same time. Archaeologists pored over Julius Caesar's Conquest of Gaul and over the writings of Herodotus, as they began a search for the ethnic identities of Iron Age societies. Excavations at the towns of Alesia and Bibrakte, both described by Caesar, identified the La Tène people as Celts, and, in Russia, scholars used the writings of Herodotus when digging into Scythian burial mounds.

During the late nineteenth century, European archaeology had a strong evolutionary bias, partly because of the theories of the social evolutionist Herbert Spencer (see Darwinian Theory), and because of the close ties between Stone Age archaeology and stratigraphic geology. French prehistorian Gabriel de Mortillet and others thought of Stone Age cultures as succeeding one another in orderly, progressive "epochs," as if prehistory was as universal as geology. De Mortillet classified his epochs on the basis of stone tool assemblages named after "typical" sites in southwestern France, erecting a sequence of cultures ranging from the more primitive (Chelles) to the most sophisticated (Magdalenian after La Madeleine). While de Mortillet ordered the Stone Age, other archaeologists like Augustus Lane Fox *Pitt-Rivers in England and Hans Hildebrand (1842–1913) and Oscar *Montelius in Sweden developed evolutionary series of Bronze and Iron Age swords, axes, fibulas, and other artifacts in later prehistory. Montelius developed a typological method. He built sequences of artifacts on the assumption that the more similar objects were in shape, the nearer to each other they were in date, while his Danish opponent, Sophus Müller, used the same principle to link not just similar artifacts, but entire assemblages.

Evolutionists thought of prehistoric culture as developing continuously and uniformly everywhere, as a single whole. Soon, however, archaeologists began to look at artifacts not only through time but in space, at geographical distributions. They became interested in the *diffusion of artifacts, ideas, and technologies, tracing distinctive culture traits from the Balkans and the Near East into the heart of Europe. Montelius himself was interested in diffusion, despite his strong evolutionary bias. He argued that the institutions and technologies of European society spread into temperate regions from the east, a central thesis in V. Gordon *Childe's syntheses of European prehistory from the 1920s to the 1950s.

While diffusion and evolution assumed great importance in European archaeology, some central and eastern European scholars thought in more conservative terms. Rudolf Virchow (1821–1902), a German archaeologist and biological anthropologist, developed a cellular theory of prehistory, which held that heredity and autonomy were more important than progress in ancient times. Medically speaking, each cell originated in a cell, argued Virchow, and an organism was a state of cells acting autonomously. So the doctor treated a disease, not a sick person. Virchow transferred this idea to the study of prehistoric culture. Thus, he said, every people lived in their own stable culture, which was determined by a distinctive and separate cultural heritage. Virchow's researches were aimed, in part, at establishing ethnic identities from archaeological remains, identifying such entities as the Burgwall culture of Germany with the Slavs, a culture distinct from that of Urnfield peoples. In 1869 Virchow and others founded the Berlin Anthropological Society, paving the way for a new generation of scholars. One was Gustaf *Kossinna (1858–1931), who carried the research of the Virchow school to extremes. He delimited cultural provinces in ancient Europe and then gave them ethnic identities, interpreting the past in dramatic migratory patterns with strong nationalistic undertones.

[See also ANTIQUITY OF HUMANKIND: ANTIQUITY OF HUMANKIND IN THE OLD WORLD; HISTORY OF ARCHAEOLOGY, INTELLECTUAL; PALEOLITHIC; SCIENCE IN ARCHAEOLOGY.]

■ Annette Laming-Emperaire, Origines de l'archéologie préhistorique en France (1964). Glyn E. Daniel, A Short History of Archaeology (1981). Glyn E. Daniel, ed., Towards a History of Archaeology (1981). Karel Sklenář, Archaeology in Central Europe: The First 500 Years (1983). Bo Gräslund, The Birth of Prehistoric Chronology (1987). Bruce C. Trigger, A History of Archaeological Thought (1987).

Leo S. Klejn

NEAR EASTERN ARCHAEOLOGY

Near Eastern archaeology reflects Western culture rather than indigenous development. Until recently the history of the archaeology from the Mediterranean east to the borders of India was largely written by archaeologists from Europe and North America. Archaeology in the region evolved from fascination with the monumental to appreciation of the mundane. Methodologically the evolution of Near Eastern archaeology correlates with that of Europe, particularly in the nineteenth century.

Under the influence of biblical lore, Europeans have been fascinated with the Near East from the time of Constantine (ca. A.D. 325) until today. This interest, combined with the Age of Empire, brought into the Near East an extraordinary group of British, French, and German adventurers (with Americans as "johnny-come-latelies") whose explorations initiated the recovery of ancient Near Eastern history.

Mesopotamia and Iran. Mesopotamian archaeology started with the 1811 survey of *Babylon conducted by Claudius James Rich (1787–1820). Rich, while an agent of the East India Company in Baghdad, indulged his antiquarian interests. For such intelligent and educated individuals archaeology provided a diversion and an opportunity to collect museum pieces for their European homelands. They had no interest in systematic excavation. The age of scientific archaeology had not yet dawned, but Rich's Memoir on the Ruins of Babylon (1815) generated intense scholarly interest, particularly in the peculiar *cuneiform tablets he had found. Felix Jones succeeded Rich at Babylon and published his results in 1854, but Babylon lay unexcavated for another half-century.

In 1835 British army officer Henry C. *Rawlinson discovered and transcribed the Behistun Inscription of the Persian monarch Darius I. Cut into the face of a cliff in the Zagros Mountains, the cuneiform script harbored three languages: Old Persian, Elamite, and Babylonian. The discovery provided the key to comprehending cuneiform writing, although the process of deciphering the script dragged on for decades.

The earliest excavations in the Near East were those of the French physician and consular agent at Mosul, Paul Emile *Botta (1802–1870). His excavations in 1842 at ancient *Nineveh near Mosul failed to recover monumental museum pieces, so he moved fourteen miles (22 m) up the Tigris to Khorsabad. Swift success followed. He discovered the ruined palace of Sargon II, adorned with huge sculptures destined for the Louvre. Meanwhile, Austen Henry *Layard (1817–1894) began excavating Nineveh in 1842, discovering the palace of Ashurnasirpal II and thereby enriching the British Museum with treasures superior to those of Botta. Victor Place followed Botta at Khorsabad (1851–1855). At Nineveh, Layard was followed by Hormuzd Rassam (1854, 1878), and then George Smith (1872–1873).

These early excavators recovered evidence of the Assyrians, but Ernest de *Sarzec was destined to discover evidence for an earlier, previously unknown civilization, that of the Sumerians. From Telloh, the site of his discovery, between 1877 and 1901 he recovered thousands of Sumerian cuneiform tablets and a wealth of artifacts. Upon his death, his work was continued by Gaston Cros.

American involvement began with a survey by W. H. Ward in 1884. Excavations directed by John P. Peters began at Nippur in 1888 and continued sporadically under several directors through 1900, with mediocre results.

Meantime to the east Marcel-Auguste Dieulafoy with his wife, Jeanne Magre, uncovered the palace of Xerxes in Susa (1884–1896). They were succeeded by Jacques de Morgan (1897–1912). In his first season he uncovered the initial evidence of the prehistoric Úbaidian culture, but two decades elapsed before the significance of his discovery was recognized.

Asia Minor/Turkey. Turkish archaeology involves two disparate eras—the ancient Hittite period in the east and the much later Classical period in the west. Frenchman Charles Texier visited Boghazkoy in 1834 without recognizing the ruins as Hattusas, the Hittite capital. In 1872 strange hieroglyphs from the region were recovered by William Wright. He attributed them to the Hittites. In 1893–1894 Ernest Chantre found fragments of clay tablets in cuneiform script at Boghazkoy. These became the key for deciphering the language, accomplished by the Czech scholar Bedrich Hrozny in 1915. Excavations at Hattusas, however, began only in 1906.

The exploration of classical sites began with Heinrich *Schliemann at Hissarlik *(Troy) in 1870. William Dorpfeld joined him in 1882, and thereafter careful attention was paid to debris layers as well as to accurate recording. Besides improving excavation techniques, Schliemann is remembered as the first archaeologist to publish a scholarly description of his results rather than a popular report.

Syria-Palestine. The search for biblical sites largely dominated the early explorations. From 1805 to 1807 Ulrich Seetzen explored Transjordan, identifying Caesarea Philippi, Gerasa (Jerash), and Philadelphia (Amman). Johann Ludwig Burckhardt traveled in the same area (1801–1812) and discovered Petra, capital of the Nabataeans. But the premier explorer was the American Edward Robinson. In 1838 Robinson and his Arabic-speaking companion, Eli Smith, identified scores of biblical sites through careful, methodical travel while noting the affinities of modern Arabic place-names to biblical equivalents. Following Robinson but with the same interest in historical geography were the Swiss explorer Titus Tobler and the Frenchman Victor Guérin.

The region endured a period of haphazard attention following Robinson, involving such diverse groups as the Catholic and Orthodox Churches, the French government, the American military, and the social elite of Great Britain—all hampered by the arcane Turkish bureaucracy. Meantime, the establishment of the Palestine Exploration Fund (PEF) in 1865 set the stage for significant scientific study in the region. By the close of the century similar organizations were established in Germany, France, and the United States.

In Lebanon the earliest excavations were those of Ernest Renan at Aradus, Byblos, Tyre, and Sidon beginning in 1860. Earlier, Phoenician inscriptions were discovered on Cyprus and Crete. Their decipherment was published by Wilhelm Gesenius in 1837. Renan followed the trend of the times by rummaging in and around sites to recover inscriptions, statuary and the like. In Palestine, Felician de Saulcy cleared the Tombs of the Kings in northern *Jerusalem in 1850–1851, believing that these first century A.D. rock-cut tombs were those of the Davidic dynasty. But the first systematic investigation of Jerusalem, the site par excellence for the early archaeologists, was undertaken by the PEF. First Charles Wilson, then Charles Warren, systematically surveyed the city, and Warren began excavations in and around the Temple Mount in 1867. Due to the interference of local officials, he pursued his investigations clandestinely, using a method that would horrify modern archaeologists—tunneling. But the most notable achievement of the PEF was the survey and mapping of western Palestine carried out between 1872 and 1878 by Claude R. Conder and Horatio H. Kitchener.

The PEF also supported non-British investigators. The German Gottlieb Schumacher mapped much of Transjordan from 1884 onward. Later he made his mark as an excavator. Charles Clermont-Ganneau was appointed French consul in Jerusalem in 1867. He recovered the Moabite Stone in 1870. He also discovered a Greek inscription warning Gentiles against entering the inner courts of the (Herodian) temple.

The main result of these early efforts was the mapping of Palestine. The early excavators had failed to establish both a reasoned approach to excavation and a sound chronology. Nor did they recognize that tells (city mounds) contained the remains of ancient cities. The work of Schliemann and Dorpfeld at Troy, however, was instructive; British scholar A. H. Sayce made the connection between the stratified mound Schliemann was excavating and the tells dotting the terrain of Palestine, a useful step forward.

Both Schliemann and Dorpfeld were deeply interested in the chronological significance of painted vases, but unpainted potsherds were meaningless to them. It was left to British Egyptologist W. M. Flinders *Petrie to discern the value of plain potsherds for dating the past. Petrie (1853–1942) had excavated for a decade in Egypt, developing scientific techniques for the sequence dating of pottery (*see* Seriation), before he carried out the first PEF excavation in Palestine. In 1890 at Tell el-Hesy, he applied his experience, taking care to distinguish debris layers and their related artifacts. Understanding the value of unpainted potsherds as indicators of stylistic change, his publication of the excavation in 1891 introduced stratigraphic digging to Palestine and established a relative chronology on the basis of typological variations. Frederick J. Bliss succeeded Petrie at the site, after undergoing a two-week short course in archaeology with his mentor in Egypt.

Bliss excavated in Jerusalem in 1894–1897, joined by British architect A. C. Dickie. Between 1898 and 1900, he and R.A.S. Macalister explored nine sites in the lowlands looking for Philistine Gath. *Excavations in Palestine During the Years 1898–1900* noted stratification and presented a selection of pottery allocated to four sequential periods. By the close of the nineteenth century, archaeologists were turning their attention from hunting treasure to diagnosing debris. The use of photography in archaeology also began in the last quarter of the century. A new era in archaeological investigation was on the horizon as the twentieth century dawned.

[See also CLASSICAL ARCHAEOLOGY, ARCHAEOLOGY OF THE AMERICAS; HISTORY OF ARCHAEOLOGY FROM 1900 TO 1950: NEAR EASTERN ARCHAEOLOGY.]

■ George Roux, *Ancient Iraq* (1964). Y. Ben-Arieh, *The Rediscovery of the Holy Land in the Nineteenth Century* (1972). Philip J. King, *American Archaeology in the Mideast: A History of the American Schools of Oriental Research* (1975). Seton Lloyd, *The Archaeology of Mesopotamia* (1978). J. Mellaart, *The Archaeology of Ancient Turkey* (1978). Neil A. Silberman, *Digging for God and Country: Exploration, Archaeology, and the Secret Struggle for the Holy Land, 1799–1917* (1982).

Keith N. Schoville

CLASSICAL ARCHAEOLOGY

In the European Middle Ages there was little interest in Greek art or history, but the Roman past was much more compelling. Educated people saw themselves primarily as Christians, connected to the world of the New Testament by the Roman Empire. Greece was largely irrelevant to this self-image. The Renaissance of the fourteenth century on was almost exclusively a revival of the Roman past. As early as the fifteenth century several Popes tried, with little success, to control digging in Rome. By collecting Roman sculpture noblemen could associate themselves with the grandeur of the Roman Empire. Sixteenth-century French kings in particular likened their state to a "New Rome." In England, Henry VIII sent John Leland to study the ruins of Roman Bath in 1536–1542, and William Camden (1551–1623) was active in promoting English links with the Roman past.

But even the interest in Rome was mainly textual rather than artifactual. Digging began at *Herculaneum as early as 1738, but only because the new queen of Naples found old statues in her garden and wanted more. In 1748, after consultations with scholars, the nearby site of *Pompeii was identified. Digs began there, but at both sites there was merely haphazard looting of statues and frescoes.

There were major changes in the later eighteenth century. Most important was the shift among intellectuals from seeing themselves as Christians to seeing themselves as Europeans. European-ness began not with Rome but with Greece, which was reconstructed within the growing Romantic movement as a pure, young, vivacious, and spontaneous civilization, unlike the powerful but decadent civilizations of Rome and Egypt.

Johann Joachim Winckelmann (1717–1768) was the most important figure in this change. He went to Rome in 1763 to become papal antiquary, but was fully attuned to the proto-Romantic ideologies. In his *Geschichte der Kunst des Altertums* (1764) he applied to Greek sculpture the four-stage scheme devised by J. J. Scaliger for Greek poetry in 1608, seeing art as the expression of the Greek spirit. His ideas were taken up enthusiastically by German men of letters such as Goethe, Fichte, and Schiller, and later by Alexander von Humboldt, appointed as Prussian minister of education in 1806, with a brief to reconstruct national morale after crushing defeats at the hands of Napoleon.

Ancient Greece was taken over in western Europe as a symbol of liberal and bourgeois causes. Poets and painters claimed that Greek art could rejuvenate the decadent forms of the modern world. But Roman art long remained more attractive to aristocrats and kings. Pope Pius VI (1775–1799) greatly expanded excavations in Italy. Napoleon did the same in France and in Rome, during his brief control, and while in England, the discovery of a Temple of Minerva when the fashionable Pump Room at Bath was rebuilt in 1790 caused national excitement.

Between the 1770s and the 1820s there was a gradual shift from texts to artifacts as the focus of attention, and from Rome to Greece. As papal antiquary Winckelmann had had access to virtually all new finds in the 1760s, but even he had imagined the Greek spirit primarily in terms of ancient literary accounts of art. His knowledge of actual Greek sculpture was rather limited. In 1751, though, the Society of Dilettanti had sent British painter James Stuart and architect Nicholas Revett to Athens to paint pictures of the ruins, which, it was hoped, would revive English art. Throughout the 1760s, Sir William Hamilton, British ambassador to Naples, was promoting the idea that his collection of ancient pots could also revive modern art. Josiah Wedgwood's first vases, thrown at Wedgwood's new factories in 1769, were based on illustrations in Hamilton's books. Wedgwood believed that these pots were Etruscan not Greek, but by 1772 Hamilton persuaded the British Museum not only that they were Greek but also that they were paradigms for modern art, and sold them for a staggering 8,000 guineas.

There was an escalation in ideas of how much exposure to ancient art modern artists needed to be saved from decadence. In 1784 the Comte de Choiseul-Gouffier wrote to Fauvel, his agent in Athens: "Take everything you can. Do not neglect any opportunity for looting all that is lootable in Athens and the environs. Spare neither the living nor the dead." Fauvel was still there in 1798, when Lord Elgin arrived as British ambassador to Turkey. Elgin had planned to save English art by making casts of statues, only to find Fauvel trying to persuade the Turks to let him take the statues themselves off the Athenian Acropolis. When the British chased Napoleon out of Egypt in 1799, a grateful Turkish government gave Elgin permission to do what it had consistently denied to Fauvel.

Elgin seems to have planned to repeat Hamilton's windfall profits, but the British Museum was unsure whether it needed actual statues. A commission debated until 1816 before being persuaded that the statues did in fact illustrate Joshua Reynolds's theory of idealism. By this time, the need to demonstrate European-ness through possession of Greek art had largely displaced the need to demonstrate Christianness through Roman art in most western states. Each state needed its own Greek sculptural or architectural masterpieces. After a squalid dispute, Bavaria ended up with the Aegina marbles in 1812, and the French bought the Venus de Milo in 1820. France also sent a "scientific mission" of 100 men to take statues from Olympia in 1829. But once a national stake in Greece had been established through a strong museum collection of Greek statues, interest in unearthing more generally faded away.

Archaeology changed dramatically after 1850, through a combination of new forms of nationalism and new ideas of science. Both developments came together in Giuseppe Fiorelli, who looked at archaeology more as a way to experience the past than as a source of artwork for museums. In 1860 he took over work at Pompeii. He systematized the scattered pits dug since 1748, and began to record the digging. His excavations could hardly be called stratigraphic, but they were far more organized than any earlier work. He tried to clear complete buildings, and wherever possible to leave finds *in situ*, so that Italians could know what it meant to be Roman, and be inspired by it. At the same time, the expansion of the modern city of Rome constantly revealed ancient relics. In the 1880s Rodolfo Lanciani excavated and planned huge expanses of architecture. The urban expansion of London and Paris and a more assertive nationalism similarly encouraged Roman archaeology in Britain and France.

Greece had been independent since 1830, but its nationalism was a more complex matter. Its past had already been appropriated by westerners, who claimed to be the real heirs to classical Greece. Some Greek intellectuals pursued antiquity as a path to greater European-ness; others remained ambivalent.

As early as 1852 Ernst Curtius began trying to raise money for a new kind of dig at Olympia, one which would not necessarily bring home sculptures but would reveal what this foundational point in the European past had really been like. He found little support for this Fiorellian project, and it was left to Heinrich *Schliemann, relying on his own wealth, to show what could be done. Schliemann was an old-fashioned figure outside German intellectual circles. He began digging at *Troy in 1870 to prove his very eighteenth-century view that Homer was literally true. Although his digs were very destructive, he recovered more artifacts and kept more detailed records than earlier workers in the Aegean. In 1874 he moved to Mycenae. This triumph of science impressed German notables, and in 1875 Curtius finally won his funding. The Olympia excavation far surpassed Schliemann's and set the mold for Greek archaeology as a "big dig" published in a series of monographs that focused on different types of artifacts.

The Germans set up a school of archaeology in Athens in 1874, and in the 1880s the British, Americans, and Italians followed suit (France had had an artists' colony in Athens since 1846). Each school or national professional organization had its own journal, and all launched their own big digs, usually in a sanctuary, before 1900. By then, classical archaeology was firmly anchored within the field of classics, which had emerged as the major academic way to study the origins of European-ness. Archaeology was subordinate to philology, and Roman studies to Greek. The justification for archaeology within classics was that Greek (and to some extent Roman) art revealed the spirit of the ancients as clearly as did their literature. Classical archaeology thus had much stronger links to art history than to social history or anthropology.

[See also CLASSICAL ARCHAEOLOGY; HISTORY OF ARCHAEOLOGY, INTELLECTUAL.]

■ Rodolfo Lanciani, *Storia degli scavi di Roma, 1000–1605*, 4 vols. (1902–1912). Rodolfo Lanciani, *Ancient Rome in the Light of Recent Discoveries* (1888). Martin Bernal, *Black Athena* I (1987). Frank M. Turner, *The Greek Heritage in Victorian Britain* (1981). Barry Cunliffe, *Bath Rediscovered* (1978). C. P. Bracken, *Antiquities Acquired* (1975). Ian Morris, "Archaeologies of Greece," in ed. Ian Morris, *Classical Greece: Ancient Histories and Modern Archaeologies* (1994), pp. 8–47.

Ian Morris

ARCHAEOLOGY OF THE AMERICAS

Archaeological practice in the Americas before 1900 was characterized by armchair theory and speculation about the origins of peoples and their cultures throughout the Americas. Speculation about the origins of Native American populations and how the Old World may have contributed to the peopling of the Americas held force for at least three and a half centuries.

The central question to be answered during this time was "Who were the Native Americans of the New World?" Frequently, the Ten Lost Tribes of Israel were seen as ancestral to the Native American populations. This explanation was favored by Fray Diego Duran as well as by the American writer James Adair (1775). However, others saw Native American origins in Plato's Atlantis. This hypothesis was suggested by Fracastoro (1530) and by Gonzalo Fernandez de Oviedo y Valdes (1534). By the mid-seventeenth century, Dutch scholars suggested that the origins of Native American populations could be found in Scandinavia while others accepted the Scythians from Central Asia as ancestral. By 1648 Thomas Gage had suggested that the Bering Strait provided the linkage between ancestral Mongolia and the Americas. However, the intellectual climate of this period still favored a more romantic interpretation of the origins of peoples in the New World, an interpretation that fit the socially stratified class system of Europe at the time.

Foundations of North American Archaeology. Beginning about 1840, avocational archaeologists such as Thomas Jefferson and Caleb Atwater began to undertake archaeological excavations in Virginia and Ohio. The first major contribution to North American archaeology came with E. G. Squier and E. H. Davis's *Ancient Monuments of the Mississippi Valley* (1847). Squier and Davis described and partially excavated some of the mounds they studied. Many

of the mounds described are no longer extant, their description being the only record of them.

In 1839 acceptance of the "lost race" connection between extant and ancestral populations was challenged with the publication of S. G. Morton's *Crania Americana*. Morton measured cranial material taken from mounds and from recently deceased Native Americans. His evidence suggested an ancestry involving only one racial group. Later, Samuel *Haven conducted a Smithsonian Institution study of the Mound Builders. The Smithsonian published his conclusion (1856) that the "lost race" Mound Builder theory could not be proved. In addition Henry Schoolcraft also opposed the Mound Builder theory because of his examination of materials coming from Grave Creek Mound in West Virginia. He was also able to connect the Mound Builders to extant populations in the eastern United States. In 1882, Cyrus Thomas dealt the final blow to the "lost race Mound Builder" theory as head of the Smithsonian Institution's Division of Mound Exploration.

Two institutions played an important role in the development of North American archaeology prior to 1900: the Smithsonian Institution's Bureau of Ethnology directed by John Wesley Powell and the Peabody Museum of Archaeology and Ethnology (Harvard University) and its director, Jeffries Wyman. Powell arranged studies of the archaeology, ethnology, and linguistics of the Native American, and Wyman was interested in shell-mound excavations in Florida. Later the Peabody Museum's Frederic Ward Putnam conducted archaeological work on the Great Serpent Mound in the Ohio Valley and initiated a study of Late Pleistocene peoples with Charles C. Abbott in Trenton Gravels (New Jersey), from which he would later withdraw support. The Trenton work was done in the shadow of Old World discoveries by Boucher de *Perthes linking Pleistocene (Ice Age) and Paleolithic cultural materials together with Darwinian evolutionary theory, which influenced the emerging archaeological science in both Europe and America.

Some of the first archaeological investigations in the American Southwest were organized by the Smithsonian's Bureau of Ethnology and the Archaeological Institute of America. James Stevenson, Cosmo and Victor Mindeliff, Richard Wetherill, Adolph *Bandelier, J. W. Fewkes, and Byron Cummings were involved in excavating and describing various sites.

In the American Southeast, Clarence B. Moore explored a number of sites along rivers in Arkansas, and Gerald Fowke and Warren K. Moorehead worked in the American Midwest studying Ohio mounds and the largest archaeological site north of Mexico, *Cahokia (see Mounds of Eastern North America).

In the American West and Alaska, Max *Uhle, Nels Nelson, and William Dall made significant contributions, especially on the application of stratigraphic methods to create chronologies of archaeological sites. Uhle and Nelson worked on the California coastal shell mounds at Emeryville and San Francisco, and Dall worked in the Aleutian Islands.

Foundations of Middle American Archaeology. The earliest archaeological interest in Middle America is traced to chroniclers traveling with the Spanish Conquistadors and priests. Don Carlos Siguenza y Gongora's excavations at *Teotihuacán, Alexander von Humboldt's (1811) work in both Peru and Mexico, Garcilaso de la Vega's early historical accounts of the Aztecs, and Bishop Diego de Landa's Mayan inquiries set the stage for further interest.

Two of the major published works of early Middle American archaeology were by John L. *Stephens (1841) and Frederick Catherwood (1844), who traveled in Central America, Chiapas, and Yucatan. Their explorations led others such as Désiré Charnay and Augustus LePlongeon to study other Mayan sites. Later, Alfred Maudslay's *Biologia Centrali Americana* appeared (1889–1902), which contained descriptions of sites explored and mapped. Adolf Bastian (1876) was interested in Mayan sculpture, and Karl Sapper (1895) classified Mayan ruins into architectural typologies and linked them to ethnographic areas. Later, William Henry Holmes (1895–1897) in Mexico would link ceramic vessels and ceremonial architecture to attempt archaeological comparisons.

The first large-scale excavations to occur in Middle American archaeology prior to 1900 were undertaken by Harvard University's Peabody Museum and were directed by Marshall Saville, John Owens, and G. B. Gordon, respectively.

Foundations of Archaeology of South America. In early South American archaeology, P. W. Lund (1842) set the stage with his work on the Lagoa Santa Caves of Brazil. But, the more important and familiar early work in South American archaeology was that of Johann Tschudi (1869), Francis de Castelnau (1852), Charles Wiener (1880), E. W. Middendorf (1893–1895), and Ephraim Squier (1877), who began the process of site description. Before 1900, the archaeological sites of Peru and Bolivia were the center of archaeological attention.

[See also EUROPEAN ARCHAEOLOGY; HISTORY OF ARCHAEOLOGY, INTELLECTUAL; ANTIQUITY OF HUMANKIND: ANTIQUITY OF HUMANKIND IN THE AMERICAS; MESOAMERICA; NORTH AMERICA; SOUTH AMERICA.]

■ James Adair, *The History of the American Indian* (1775). Alexander Von Humbolt, *Researches Concerning the Institutions and Monuments of the Ancient Inhabitants of America* (1814). Caleb Atwater, "Description of the Antiquities Discovered in the State of Ohio and Other Western States," in *Transactions and Collections of the American Antiquarian Society*, Vol. 1 (1820), pp. 105–267. Edward Kingsborough, *Antiquities of Mexico* (1831). John L. Stephens, "Incidents of Travel in Central America, Chiapas, and Yucatan," 2 vols. (1841). P. V. Lund, "Blik poa Brasiliens Dyreverden, etc.," in *Det Kongeliege Danske Videnskabernes Selskabs Naturvidenskabelige og Mathematiske Afhandlinger, Niende Dul* (1842), pp. 195–196. Frederick Catherwood, *View of Ancient Monuments in Central America, Chiapas, and Yucatan* (1844). Ephraim G. Squier and E. H. Davis, *Ancient Monuments in the Mississippi Valley* (1848). Diego de Landa, *Relations de choses de Yucatan de Digeo de Landa* (1864). Alfred P. Maudslay, "Archaeology," in *Biologia Centrali Americana*, 4 vols. (1889–1902). Cyrus Thomas Report of the Mound Explorations of the Bureau of Ethnology (1894). Bruce Trigger, *A History of Archaeological Thought* (1989). Gordon R. Willey and Jeremy A. Sabloff, *A History of American Archaeology* (1990).

Douglas R. Givens

HISTORY OF ARCHAEOLOGY FROM 1900 TO 1950

Overview
European Archaeology
Near Eastern Archaeology
Classical Archaeology
Archaeology of the Americas
Chinese and Southeast Asian Archaeology

OVERVIEW

Archaeology came of age in the first half of the twentieth century, as both survey and excavation methods were refined beyond all recognition. New dating techniques like

*dendrochronology were developed. While digging techniques were still inferior to the fine-grained approaches used today, excavators like Flinders *Petrie in Egypt and Mortimer *Wheeler in Britain brought more discipline to all forms of archaeological excavation, paying closer attention to stratigraphic analysis and small artifacts. At the same time, the focus of Old World archaeology broadened dramatically from the narrow confines of Europe and the Near East into Africa, Asia, and the Pacific. Paul Bahn's article summarizes some of the notable advances in European archaeology during these fifty years, and describes how archaeology became important enough for Nazi propagandists to make use of spurious archaeological findings to justify doctrines of racial superiority. Archaeological researches in the Near East flourished during the period, dominated by the discovery of the *Tutankhamun's Tomb in Egypt and by Leonard *Woolley's excavations at *Ur in Iraq. As Keith Schoville points out, there were also major advances in Stone Age archaeology, notably under Dorothy Garrod at Mount Carmel, Palestine. At the same time, excavation methods and pottery analyses were refined far beyond Petrie's early efforts. *Classical archaeology became more professional in the first five decades of the twentieth century. More excavators paid careful attention to stratified layers and less spectacular artifacts. Ian Morris described John Beazley's pioneer work with Greek pottery, the growth of Aegean archaeology, and the simple theoretical explanations used to define culture change in late prehistoric times. Charles Higham summarizes the dramatic advances in Chinese and Southeast Asian archaeology, dominated by the discovery of the Shang civilization in northern China and the excavation of *Zhoukoudian Cave, where "Beijing Man" was first discovered. By 1950, a broad cultural sequence for Southeast Asian prehistory was also in place.

American archaeologists were preoccupied with chronology, stratigraphic analysis, and culture history reconstruction during these decades. Douglas Givens emphasizes the importance of the direct historical method and southwestern archaeology in the development of prehistoric sequences throughout the Americas. He also summarizes some of the classification schemes, which were developed to bring order to the myriad of prehistoric cultures in the Americas.

The early- and mid-twentieth century was a period of spectacular discoveries and solid methodological advances, which laid the foundations for today's multidisciplinary archaeology.

Brian M. Fagan

EUROPEAN ARCHAEOLOGY

The history of archaeology in Europe during the first half of this century is dominated by three major themes: first, the consolidation of nineteenth-century developments and the transition from an amateur activity to a scientific discipline; second, an enormous variety of discoveries and of technical and methodological advances; and third, the tremendous impact of political events.

The quality of excavations gradually improved but was still simplistic and underestimated the complexity involved in sediment accumulation. Excavators noted only the more obvious stratigraphic units. Only the bones of large mammals were usually collected, and little attention was paid to the vertical or horizontal distribution of objects in the layers. Much lithic and faunal material was discarded. Gradually, however, pioneers such as Denis Peyrony in France and Mortimer *Wheeler in Britain improved the planning of excavations and of the publication of site-plans and other details.

One particularly noteworthy development in European archaeology was the acceptance at the turn of the century of the existence and authenticity of Paleolithic cave art. Discoveries of decorated caves snowballed in southern France and Spain, culminating in the discovery of *Lascaux in 1940.

The outbreak of World War I (1914–1918) had a radical effect on archaeology all over Europe. One of its few positive contributions was the revelation of the potential of aerial photography, although the first archaeological air photographs (of *Stonehenge, taken from a balloon) date from 1906. The aerial view laid out the landscape rather like a map and made it possible to see features, such as buried banks and ditches, invisible to an observer on the ground. Aerial photography was soon being applied widely to the study of archaeological remains. In England, the leading protagonist of the new technique was O.G.S. Crawford, who in 1928 published a book containing aerial views of the archaeological sites of *Wessex. Aerial photography was also used by French and German archaeologists, though, given the rarity of aircraft and the cost of flying, it did not achieve its full potential as an archaeological tool until after the Second World War.

The USSR. In Russia, World War I ended with two revolutions, civil war, and famine. As field studies gradually resumed in the 1920s, they followed the familiar path of prerevolutionary archaeology. But in 1929, the Communist Party attacked archaeology as a citadel of reaction and "bourgeois science," and some archaeologists were arrested by the secret police. There was an official call to replace the dilapidated field of archaeology with a "history of material culture" based on Marxist principles. Nevertheless, scholarly contact was maintained between Russian and Western European archaeologists during the 1920s, and there was considerable similarity between approaches to archaeological scholarship in both areas.

However, by 1928 non-Marxist scholars were being purged and nonconforming institutions eliminated. A number of archaeologists were arrested and subsequently either exiled or shot. Contacts with foreign scholars and archaeological literature were prohibited, and Russian researchers became isolated from the outside world.

One positive development, a consequence of the Soviet aim of fully reconstructing a past society, was the undertaking of archaeological excavations on a hitherto unknown scale. Soviet archaeologists were the first to recover entire Paleolithic dwellings and complete Neolithic villages and to expose large percentages of urban sites.

After 1935, the term "archaeology" was formally reinstated, and no more archaeologists were arrested. The period of revolutionary change had come to a close, and the "Marxist history of material culture" evolved into Soviet archaeology.

The Second World War had drastic effects on archaeology throughout Central and Eastern Europe. Sites were damaged, collections were destroyed, and many archaeologists were killed. The defeat of Germany and its allies and the occupation of Central Europe by Soviet armies in 1945 also had significant consequences for archaeology. New territory annexed by the Soviet Union offered new opportunities for field research, while academic institutions throughout Central Europe were brought under the control of the Communist Party. Archaeological research was placed under more centralized state control, and archaeologists were trained in *Marxist theory. Nevertheless, archaeological research was generously staffed and funded by the new regimes.

Germany. The nationalism that had characterized much archaeology in Germany in the nineteenth century reappeared in the twentieth century, this time in an extreme form that was used to support claims of racial and ethnic superiority and territorial title. The most imposing figure associated with the rebirth of nationalist archaeology was Gustav *Kossinna, a German scholar who equated cultural material with ethnic identity and embedded this approach in an explicitly nationalist and racialist ideology, attacking attempts to study non-Germanic populations, such as the Celts and Romans, in Central Europe.

Kossinna died in 1931, but the rise to power of the Nazis ensured that his view of the German past was imposed on German scholarship. The rise of National Socialism and Adolf Hitler to the head of the government of Germany in 1933 began one of the most curious episodes in the history of archaeology, perhaps the closest connection ever between archaeologists and a national government and one of the most extraordinary manipulations of the past to support social and political theories. Never before had the study of the past enjoyed such official patronage. The goal was to establish the antiquity and superiority of the Germans among the European peoples.

Developments throughout Europe. Data from the "tell" of Vinca (Serbia), excavated in 1908–1911, provided the first real chronological yardstick for the Balkan Neolithic, into which could be linked both the better-known cultures of the southern Balkans and Greece on the one hand and Central Europe on the other. Connections proposed between the Vinca sequence and the Aegean Bronze Age made a strong impression on the esteemed archaeologist V. Gordon *Childe as he traveled through this area in the 1920s; he focused his major works, such as The Dawn of European Civilization (1925), on the Vinca sequence. Excavations in places such as Malta and southern Spain, together with new work in Italy and Sicily, also stimulated interest in the prehistoric archaeology of southern Europe, which slowly but surely became integrated with that of the rest of the Continent; however, the attention of many archaeologists remained focused on the Classical and Roman remains in these lands.

Postwar Developments. Arguably the most significant development in archaeology during the twentieth century was the development of radiocarbon dating. This process was truly revolutionary, for in providing an absolute age for finds, it released archaeologists from having to spend so much time on dating and organizing their data. New ideas could be pursued and more substantive questions asked. The technique was developed in 1949 by Willard Libby, an American scientist interested in cosmic radiation and its effects on the earth's environment. Archaeologists quickly realized its potential. However, since this development was a product of atomic bomb research, archaeologists in Eastern Europe and the Soviet Union had considerably less access to *radiocarbon dating than their counterparts in the United States and Western Europe.

In Western Europe, faith was quickly placed in the radiocarbon method, and science proceeded forward. In Central and Eastern Europe, however, some scholars questioned the validity of the radiocarbon method. Others simply chose to ignore it altogether. The inability to date their own samples led many archaeologists in this area to adopt a "sour grapes" attitude toward radiocarbon dating. It was not until the 1960s, when laboratories in these regions began to date numerous samples of their own, that virtually all archaeologists who worked in Central and Eastern Europe were quickly converted by the weight of the evidence to accept the new chronology.

[See also HISTORY OF ARCHAEOLOGY BEFORE 1900: EUROPEAN ARCHAEOLOGY; HISTORY OF ARCHAEOLOGY SINCE 1950: EUROPEAN ARCHAEOLOGY.]

■ P. G. Bahn, ed., The Cambridge Illustrated History of Archaeology (1996).

Paul G. Bahn

NEAR EASTERN ARCHAEOLOGY

The first half of the twentieth century witnessed a growing sophistication in Near Eastern archaeology characterized by a shift in focus from treasure to trash, as the value of the mundane became increasingly evident. The international flavor of Near Eastern archaeology increased as Americans and Europeans developed national organizations and centers focused on the region. Yet *nationalism was ameliorated by collegial interests and exchange. With varying success, excavators built on the methodological and conceptual foundations established by their predecessors. The period from 1900 to 1950 conveniently divides into three subperiods: pre–World War I; between the wars; and post–World War II.

Mesopotamia and Iran. As the new century opened, the French expedition to Susa continued under Jacques de Morgan and that at Telloh under Gaston Cros. Telloh produced the first evidence of the pre-Assyrian Sumerian civilization. German architect Robert *Koldewey and Walter Andrae began excavating *Babylon in 1899 on behalf of the Berlin Museum and the Deutsche Orient Gesellschaft. Koldewey continued there until World War I, then publishing his remarkable discoveries in The Excavation at Babylon. Koldewey developed techniques for distinguishing mudbricks from soil, an absolutely essential methodological advance for Mesopotamian archaeology, with implications for all places where ancient people had used mudbrick construction.

Andrae soon moved northward to excavate the Assyrian capital, Ashur, on the Tigris River. He mastered stratigraphic digging by uncovering a sequence of Ishtar temples reaching back to the Early Dynastic Period (ca. 2900–2250 B.C.) and confirmed by dedicatory inscriptions. Concurrent with the Babylon and Ashur excavations, Julius Jordan worked at *Uruk (Warka). Excavations resumed in 1919 and continued under a sequence of directors until 1939. The earliest forms of cuneiform writing were recovered there.

In the aftermath of World War I, archaeology in the region flourished, in part due to the elimination of a restrictive Turkish bureaucracy. R. Campbell Thomas, assisted by Max E. L. Mallowan, discovered the palace of Ashurbanipal II while excavating *Nineveh. Mallowan subsequently excavated nearby Nimrud for fourteen seasons, discovering extraordinary Assyrian palaces, temples, and exquisitely carved ivories. Further up the Tigris, Americans under Gordon Loud returned to Khorsabad, clarifying the earlier work of the French under Victor Place.

Leonard *Woolley headed a joint British and American expedition to *Ur in the 1920s. Almost immediately he discovered the Royal Cemetery, a treasure hunter's dream come true, but with exceptional scientific reserve he refrained from excavating the cemetery for four years, until his staff and workers had acquired the requisite skills and discipline that Woolley deemed necessary for the task. His patience was rewarded with rich evidence for Sumerian culture. Excavating at nearby al Úbaid, he uncovered distinctive predynastic painted pottery; thereafter, the cultural phase was named Úbaidian after the site. Such discoveries pushed the frontiers of knowledge back into prehistoric periods.

The American Schools of Oriental Research, organized in 1900, had interests throughout the Near East. George A. Barton excavated at Nuzi, a Mitannian site in the late 1920s. Nearby, in the early 1930s, Mallowan uncovered Úbaidian pottery at Arpachiyah. An American scholar, Ephraim A. Speiser, was excavating Tepe Gawra, where similar preliterate period pottery appeared and beneath it even earlier distinctive ceramics. The new style came to be known as Halafian ware, after the type site Tell Halaf, first explored by Ernst Herzfeld in 1914. An even earlier culture was discerned at Hassuna in 1943 by Seton Lloyd and Fuad Safar.

As scholars from many countries centered on the origins of civilization, Cambridge archaeologist Dorothy A. E. Garrod focused on much earlier human settlements. She identified Paleolithic remains in northern Iraq as early as 1928, but she soon shifted her research to the Mt. Carmel Caves in Palestine, where she unearthed important and varied Neanderthal remains.

After World War II, Robert J. Braidwood began work at Jarmo and continued through the 1950s to explore the origins of food production. Both Braidwood and Kathleen Kenyon (at *Jericho) pushed the frontiers of agriculture to about 8000 B.C. Since then, prehistoric anthropological archaeology has expanded across the Near East.

In Iran at the turn of the century, Ernst Herzfeld probed the ruins of Pasargadae, the early capital of ancient Persia. Actual excavation began, however, in 1949 under Ali Sami, director of the Archaeological Institute at Persepolis. The Oriental Institute of the University of Chicago began excavating Persepolis itself in 1931, directed first by Herzfeld and then by Erich F. Schmidt. The U.S. effort ended in 1939, but the Iranian Archaeological Service continued to excavate in the 1940s, and restoration work was in progress until the fall of the shah.

Turkey. As the nineteenth century closed, western scholars were increasingly aware that the Hittites had once been a powerful force in the Near East. The initial excavation of Boghazkoy, the major city of the second millennium B.C. Hittites, began in 1906, under the direction of Hugo Winckler, for the German Oriental Society. Winckler's expedition recovered some ten thousand cuneiform tablets. After a long hiatus, Kurt Bittel renewed the excavation in 1931, only to be interrupted again by the outbreak of World War II. H. H. Von der Osten established the Bronze Age pottery sequence of Hatti in his work at Alishar, while Helmut T. Bossert discovered bilingual Phoenician-Hittite inscriptions at Karatepe in the 1940s. Meanwhile, Hetty Goldman worked at Tarsus from 1935 to 1949.

Archaeology in western Turkey began with Heinrich *Schliemann at Hissarlik (Troy) in 1870. Excavations were initiated by Howard C. Butler at Sardis in 1909, but work at Smyrna under John Cook was delayed until 1947. *Ephesus was first excavated in 1904–1905 by D. G. Hogarth. Pergamum, the city in which parchment originated, came under the hands of T. Wiegand in 1928 as the pace of research picked up in the aftermath of World War I. As in Iraq, archaeological work in Turkey during this period also began to reveal prehistoric evidence.

Syria-Palestine. Following Flinders *Petrie's pioneering work, Frederick J. Bliss and R. A. Stewart Macalister improved stratigraphic excavation and the art of pottery dating. George A. Reisner, Clarence S. Fisher, and David G. Lyon at Samaria (1908–1910) established new standards of careful digging, accurate recording, employing photography as well as written records, and providing sophisticated interpretation, but others failed for decades to follow such trailblazing.

After World War I the former Turkish territories of Syria and Lebanon were mandated to the French, while the British controlled Palestine. Claude F. A. Schaeffer began making extraordinary discoveries at Ugarit in 1929, and André Parrot started at *Mari in 1935. Both sites were rich in epigraphic finds and destined for lengthy excavations. An additional significant Syrian excavation, at Alalakh (1937–1939, 1946–1949), was directed by Woolley.

William F. *Albright was a key figure in Palestine. His field work at Gibeah (1922–1923) and Tell Beit Mirsim (1926–1936) established the chronology of Palestinian pottery on a firm foundation. Noteworthy expeditions before the outbreak of World War II included John Garstang at Jericho (1929–1936), where he discovered a pottery Neolithic culture; John W. Crowfoot at Samaria (1930–1935); Clarence S. Fisher, Alan Rowe, and G. M. Fitzgerald at Bethshan (1921–1933); Fisher, Philip L. O. Guy, and Gordon Loud at Megiddo (1925–1939); and James L. Starkey at Lachish (1932–1938).

Among Albright's students in *Jerusalem were a number of Jewish students—Eliezer L. Sukenik, Benjamin Mazar, Shemuel Yeivin, M. Stekelis, Michael Avi-Yonah, Nahman Avigad, and I. Ben-dor. They were destined to become leading Israeli archaeologists, when archaeological interest rebounded after World War II with the accidental discovery of the *Dead Sea Scrolls in 1947. The end of the British Mandate and the establishment of the State of Israel in 1948 set the stage for the next phase of Near Eastern archaeology.

[See also HISTORY OF ARCHAEOLOGY BEFORE 1900: NEAR EASTERN ARCHAEOLOGY; HISTORY OF ARCHAEOLOGY SINCE 1950: NEAR EASTERN ARCHAEOLOGY.]

■ Philip J. King, *American Archaeology in the Mideast* (1975). Seaton Lloyd, *The Archaeology of Mesopotamia* (1978). J. Mellaart, *The Archaeology of Mesopotamia* (1978). Neil A. Silberman, *Digging for God and Country: Exploration, Archaeology, and the Secret Struggle for the Holy Land, 1799–1917* (1982). Joel F. Drinkard, Gerald L. Mattingly, Jr., and J. Maxwell Miller, eds., *Benchmarks in Time and Culture* (1988). P.R.S. Moorey, *A Century of Biblical Archaeology* (1991). Amnon Ben-Tor, *The Archaeology of Ancient Israel* (1992). Mary Ellen Lane, ed., *The State of Archaeology: An American Perspective* (1993). William H. Stiebing, Jr., *Uncovering the Past: A History of Archaeology* (1993).

Keith N. Schoville

CLASSICAL ARCHAEOLOGY

The framework created for classical archaeology in the nineteenth century changed relatively little before 1950. Greek archaeology continued to be seen as more prestigious than Roman and received earlier and stronger support. In Britain, for instance, the Society for the Promotion of Hel-

lenic Studies was created in 1879, whereas an equivalent Roman Society was not formed until 1910. Greek archaeology generally retained a more dilettantish and elite tone than Roman, which was dominated more by professional academics at universities and, increasingly over time, by archaeologists working for museums or national or local societies. But both Greek and Roman archaeologists tended to feel stronger ties with Classical philology than with prehistoric archaeology. In the early part of the century, this brought them higher prestige than that enjoyed by their more anthropological colleagues, but by the 1940s this was no longer the case.

The nineteenth-century research programs changed little in this period. Art history, with artifacts expressing the Classical spirit, continued to be the main focus. Information was ideally recovered through big digs in major ancient cities like Pompeii or Dura-Europos, which generated vast quantities of finds. These digs required large teams of researchers to work for decades to publish the findings, usually as a series of monographs organized around categories of artifacts.

The most significant development in the first half of this century was the steady professionalization of Classical archaeology. In both Italy and Greece the archaeological services grew rapidly, and new laws controlled fieldwork. The fascist government in Rome (1922–1944) strongly supported archaeology and tried to bring it under state control. This trend toward professionalism resulted in a general improvement in the quality of fieldwork. Stratigraphic excavation became normal, along with careful monitoring of finds. Greek and Roman sites—especially the urban centers and sanctuaries that attracted the most attention in these years—tend to be multiperiod, which meant that recording became very complex. Archaeologists like Mortimer *Wheeler in Britain carried out major excavations on Roman sites and refined stratigraphic control to heights that have rarely been surpassed. However, few Classical archaeologists showed an interest in bone or seed remains or in any kind of social or economic archaeology.

In many ways, the quintessential excavation of these years was in the agora of Athens, beginning in 1931. Unlike the situation in Italy, where Mussolini's regime kept tight control over its own past, Greek governments continued to be ambivalent toward the Western-dominated Classical periods, and some leading politicians thought that having the site excavated by the Americans, rather than by the Greeks themselves, would bring more credit to Greece. In any case, the Greek Archaeological Service and Society lacked the funds for such an ambitious project, and state support was not forthcoming. Supported by more than one million dollars from John D. Rockefeller, between 1931 and 1939 the American School of Classical Studies at Athens demolished 365 buildings in the heart of modern Athens and removed 250,000 tons of earth from 16 acres. The excavators paid scant attention to post-Roman finds and sometimes even concentrated ruthlessly on the purely Classical Period (conventionally 480–323 B.C.). But within those limits, the agora raised Classical archaeology to new levels of professionalism. It generated vast quantities of artifacts that have kept researchers busy ever since. It has played a decisive part in confirming the relative chronology of Greek pottery, and the numerous inscriptions have permanently changed our understanding of Greek political and economic history.

A second development in these years, to some extent

dependent on the growth of the big-dig programs, was the systematization of archaeological knowledge. Archaeologists had already begun assembling complete corpora of finds in the nineteenth century, most notably of Latin and Greek inscriptions, as well as identifying and dating artistic categories, most successfully in Mau's studies of Pompeian wall paintings. But in the early twentieth century this categorization was extended to "low" art such as Athenian and Italian painted pottery and Roman lamps.

By far the most impressive achievement in this area was John Beazley's series of catalogs of Athenian black- and red-figured vase painting; Beazley listed tens of thousands of pots and attributed them to individual painters, schools, or styles. Beazley published in this field from 1910 to the 1960s. Although he himself wrote little about methodology, he seems to have borrowed heavily from Giovanni Morelli's approach to Italian Renaissance painting, identifying artists by unconscious details such as the ways they rendered hair, fingernails, or floral decoration. Beazley's achievement became the dominant model for the nonfieldworking Classical archaeologist.

The third major development was the growth of Aegean prehistory. This field was as old as excavation itself, beginning with Heinrich *Schliemann's discoveries at *Troy in 1870, but its main growth came after 1900. In 1899 Arthur *Evans had discovered the Minoan civilization on Crete at *Knossos, and over the next fifty years archaeologists carried out a remarkable number of prehistoric excavations. The pottery chronologies that they established remain in use, with relatively few changes, today; and an absolute chronology was partially fixed through synchronisms with Egypt. This work was the basis for the "short chronology" of European prehistory that underlay V. Gordon *Childe's work. By 1941 Arne Furumark was able to provide a comprehensive framework for categorizing and dating Mycenaean pottery.

The main explanatory models in Mediterranean prehistory were invasion and diffusion. In Italy, some archaeologists equated different Iron Age burial customs with different races and then saw these as evolving into the patrician and plebeian orders; Greek archaeologists often tried to identify the "coming" of the Indo-European Greeks who displaced aboriginal populations. This way of looking at archaeology was very different from that in the historically documented periods, and although these frameworks have fallen out of favor since 1945, Aegean prehistory has remained one of the main ways in which new ideas and methods have entered Classical archaeology. The work of archaeologists of the 1920s and 1930s has also made more lasting contributions. In particular, the excavations at Pylos, begun in 1939, established beyond doubt that the mainland palaces, as well as at Knossos, had used Linear B tablets to keep records. This influx of new finds was crucial to Michael Ventris's 1952 discovery that the tablets were written in Greek.

[See also HISTORY OF ARCHAEOLOGY BEFORE 1900: CLASSICAL ARCHAEOLOGY; HISTORY OF ARCHAEOLOGY SINCE 1950: CLASSICAL ARCHAEOLOGY.]

■ L. E. Lord, *A History of the American School of Classical Studies at Athens, 1882–1942* (1947). Paul MacKendrick, *The Mute Stones Speak* (1969). Donna Kurtz, ed., *Beazley and Oxford* (1985). William A. McDonald and Carol G. Thomas, *Progress into the Past*, 2d ed. (1990). Ian Morris, "Archaeologies of Greece," in *Classical Greece: Ancient Histories and Modern Archaeologies*, ed. Ian Morris (1994), pp. 8–47.
Ian Morris

ARCHAEOLOGY OF THE AMERICAS

Archaeological practice in the Americas from 1900 through 1950 was characterized by the concern for dating archaeological sites by stratigraphic means, the development of a cultural and historical synthesis of the Americas, and the introduction of a multidisciplinary approach to the analysis of archaeological problems in the field and in the laboratory.

The practice of *stratigraphy (the earliest method of dating archaeological sites in the Americas) is traced to the rise of Sir Charles Lyell's (1830) scientific geology in Europe and to Sir Flinders *Petrie's stratigraphic digs in Egypt. The "stratigraphic revolution," as it has been labeled by historians of archaeology, arrived late in the Americas as compared with Europe. The delay in the acceptance of stratigraphic dating in the Americas lies in the early rejection of Darwinian and cultural evolution. Thus the years before World War I in the Americas saw little stratigraphic excavation, and "'archaeological chronology was still in its infancy" (Willey and Sabloff 1993: 84).

The application of stratigraphic dating to archaeology is based on the idea that the mantle of the earth is made up of layers and that each stratum or layer has a relationship to other strata by the principle of "superposition." This idea revolutionized the conduct of fieldwork in American archaeology from 1907 forward. One of the earliest Americanist practitioners of stratigraphy during this period was Max *Uhle, who had earlier published on his excavations in Peru (1903). Uhle later (1907) conducted excavations at the Emeryville Shellmound in the San Francisco Bay area of California. At Emeryville, Uhle excavated the mounds of shells "stratum by stratum" and delineated ten strata that he linked to cultural stages of human development. He even recognized the continuity of strata by linking the Emeryville strata to those on the West and East Coasts of the United States and also to those of Denmark. In 1909 Nelson, influenced by Uhle, published on his San Francisco shellmounds work and later (1910) on the Ellis Landing Shellmound in California. However, he did not follow the lead of Uhle's interpretations.

Manuel Gamio, who had been a student of Franz Boas at Columbia University, continued the pattern of stratigraphic excavation in the Americas. Boas, along with Alfred Marsten Tozzer and G. C. Engerrand, suggested that Gamio initiate stratigraphic excavations in the Valley of Mexico. Gamio stratigraphically excavated the Atzacapotzalco site under the auspices of Boas's ill-fated International School of American Ethnology and Archaeology (1912–1913).

Nels C. Nelson had worked under Alfred Kroeber at the University of California at Berkeley and in 1914 continued his stratigraphic work at San Cristobal Pueblo in the Galisteo Basin of New Mexico. It was Nelson's work there that led A. V. *Kidder and others in southwestern archaeology to begin thinking about the stratigraphic chronological relationships between sites. From the American Southwest, stratigraphic dating took hold in other areas of American archaeology, with a vengeance.

Kidder, greatly influenced by Nelson's work in the Galisteo Basin, raised stratigraphic dating to a grand scale through his excavations of Pecos Pueblo (1915–1924). Kidder was able to stratigraphically excavate Pecos Pueblo and establish relative chronologies based on stratigraphic depositions of pottery sherds from Pecos to that of many surrounding Pueblo archaeological sites. Kidder's stratigraphic work at Pecos Pueblo was the first large-scale use of the technique in Americanist archaeology.

From outside the American Southwest came the work of George C. Vaillant, a student assistant of Kidder's at Pecos Pueblo. Vaillant published his stratigraphic work on the Valley of Mexico (1937) while Wendell C. Bennett (1934) carried out stratigraphic tests at Tiwanaku, Bolivia. Henry B. Collins (1937, 1943) formulated an Arctic chronology of the Eskimo through stratigraphy and seriation. In the 1930s stratigraphic excavation was employed throughout southeastern archaeology in the United States, particularly under the leadership of James Ford (1935, 1936) and William S. DeJarnette and David DeJarnette (1942).

The efforts of Americanist archaeologists to create a cultural and historical synthesis of the Americas mark the second hallmark of archaeological practice during this period. Uhle had earlier (1892) written a synthesis of Tiwanaku archaeology. But, for the period under discussion, Kidder wrote the first archaeological synthesis of what was then known about the archaeology of the American Southwest (*Introduction to Southwestern Archaeology*, 1924). In 1927 the participants in the first Pecos Conference gathered at Pecos Pueblo, New Mexico. The objectives of this conference were to create a general classificatory system that would enhance the communication between southwestern archaeologists and to create an orderly arrangement of temporal and ceramically classified cultures throughout the Southwest. Later Harold Gladwin and Winifred Gladwin published *A Method for the Designation of Cultures and Their Variations* (1934). This work utilized the analogy of a tree to describe the growth of culture in the Southwest and also suggested that a standardized nomenclature is essential to a universal system of culture synthesis. In 1939 the McKern Midwestern Taxonomic Method was put forward as a means of obtaining an orderly way to describe the origins and growth of culture in the American Midwest. Its hallmarks were the descriptions of archaeological sites both in time and in space. However, the McKern system operated without much use of stratigraphy in the Midwest because of the apparent lack of deep refuse mounds within which cultural remains could be ordered. This method of reaching a cultural and historical synthesis "operated solely with the cultural forms themselves—that is, with typology" (Willey and Sabloff 1993: 106). All of these classification systems were created in the context of ongoing field archaeology throughout the United States.

Vaillant's work for his doctoral dissertation (1927) is the beginning of the effort to write a cultural synthesis of archaeological practice in Mexico. His concern for creating a synthesis of what was known in Mexican archaeology culminated in his book *Aztecs of Mexico*, which appeared in 1941.

Later, in the eastern United States, a taxonomic synthesis of eastern archaeology was published by Thorne Deuel in 1935. James A. Ford and James B. Griffin also produced a synthesis of eastern archaeology. In 1941 Gordon R. Willey and James Ford published a chronology and cultural classification system that was similar in construction to Kidder's *Pecos Classification*.

Several cultural syntheses of Arctic archaeology appeared between 1933 and 1940 (Diamond Jenness, 1933; Kaj Birket-Smith, 1936; Therkel Mathiassen, 1937). However, Henry B. Collins's (1937) work provides the best look into what was known at that time about Arctic archaeology.

To a minor degree, one other system influenced the de-velopment of method and theory of Americanist archaeology during this period: the *Kulturkrislehre* school from Austria. This school of thought suggested that cultures spread worldwide, both through diffusion and by the migration of populations. Oswald F. A. Menghin's work (1957) in Argentina examined archaeological data from the *Kulturkrislehre* model.

Aside from typology and classification systems designed to create a cultural-historical synthesis of the archaeology of the Americas, Americanist archaeologists first began applying the "direct historical approach" to their analysis of archaeological sites as early as 1938 with the work of Waldo R. Wedel. With this approach, the archaeologist works back into prehistoric periods from a documented point in historical time. With the publication of Julian Steward's paper "The Direct Historical Approach" in the Society for American Archaeology's official journal (*American Antiquity*, 1942), many archaeologists came to realize that this "new" approach was far better that the earlier systems of typology and classification. Cultural synthesis would now be able to link archaeological populations to their living descendants.

During this period, Americanist archaeology added to its fieldwork and laboratory analytical tool-kit the methods of some of the "hard sciences." It was Kidder's fourth field season (1920) at Pecos Pueblo that brought the archaeologist and the physical anthropologist together for the first time to work on in situ burial remains. Kidder recognized the need for expertise outside the realm of archaeology to resolve archaeological problems of analysis and explanation. He continued to practice his "pan-scientific" approach during his tenure as director of the Division of Historical Research at the Carnegie Institution of Washington. While with the Carnegie Institution, his multidisciplinary approach to the study of the Maya brought together geneticists, public health experts, geologists, and representatives from many of the sciences to aid the archaeological explanation of the Maya.

Americanist archaeology between 1900 and 1950 was characterized by the use of stratigraphic dating procedures, an effort to create a cultural-historical synthesis of American archaeology, and the utilization of "sciences" outside archaeology to attack archaeological problems. As opposed to the earlier period, these years went beyond armchair speculation to create methods of analysis and explanation of the archaeological record.

[*See also* HISTORY OF ARCHAEOLOGY BEFORE 1900: ARCHAEOLOGY OF THE AMERICAS; HISTORY OF ARCHAEOLOGY SINCE 1950: ARCHAEOLOGY OF THE AMERICAS.]

■ A. V. Kidder, *An Introduction to Southwestern Archaeology with a Preliminary Account of the Excavations at Pecos* (1924). Bruce G. Trigger, *A History of Archaeological Thought* (1989). Douglas R. Givens, *Alfred Vincent Kidder and the Development of Americanist Archaeology* (1992). Gordon R. Willey and Jeremy A. Sabloff, *History of American Archaeology*, 3d ed. (1993).

Douglas R. Givens

CHINESE AND SOUTHEAST ASIAN ARCHAEOLOGY

Archaeology in China and Southeast Asia was transplanted from the West in the wake of colonialism or increased mercantile or military interest. In China, initial Western fieldwork followed the foundation of the Geological Survey of China in 1916. Within five years, the Swede J. Gunnar Andersson encountered and excavated the Neolithic settlement of Yang Shao Cun, recovering a distinctive style of painted pottery. In 1923, having identified the first prehistoric culture of China, he estimated its antiquity as 3000–1500 B.C. and set a trend widely followed by his successors in tracing its origins to Western sources. This same year saw the return to his native land of *Li Chi, the founder of an indigenous Chinese tradition of archaeology. Having received his training in anthropology under Earnest Hooton and Alfred Tozzer at Harvard, he returned to undertake excavations at Xi-yin-cun, a site of the *Yangshao culture. In 1928, he was appointed dean of the newly established Department of Archaeology in the Academia Sinica and set in train the excavation at Yin-xu, capital of the *Shang civilization. Thus within less than a decade, the archaeological foundations of the ancient state of China were established and documented through excavations.

In 1921, Andersson also began excavations at the caverns at *Zhoukoudian and showed the potential of the site for documenting the initial human settlement of East Asia when two hominid teeth were found in 1926. This site was to attract many further excavations involving Wong Wen Hao and Father Teihard de Chardin. By World War II, the remains from thirty-eight individuals had been found, in association with a distinctive flaked stone tool industry.

Meanwhile, a decade of excavations at Yin-Xu under Li Chi, involving as it did numerous young Chinese scholars, laid the foundations for much progress as they began their own projects, or began the long and painstaking task of analyzing the numerous bronzes and oracle bones, graves, and human remains recovered. By 1949, Li Chi was able to achieve another first when he was appointed chairman of the pioneer department of archaeology at a Chinese university in Taipei.

The establishment of the French colonial regime in Indochina brought with it official support for archaeology through the foundation of the Ecole Française d'Extrême Orient in 1898. This institution, founded on the same principles as the schools in Cairo and Rome, involved the establishment of a library and museum, the appointment of a director, and employment of a staff of specialists. Until its foundation, archaeology in Vietnam, Laos, and Cambodia was an adjunct to investigations into natural history and geology. Its presence led to directed excavations, site recording and restoration, and through its annual bulletin, the rapid publication of new information.

Site recording and restoration, which were undertaken in association with the recovery and interpretation of a growing corpus of historic inscriptions, were mainly directed to the many great historic sites, such as Angkor, Mison, and Dong Duong. But prehistory was not overlooked. Encouragement was given to the excavation of *Dong Son, while the indefatigable Henri Parmentier contributed to the excavation at Sa Huynh. Meanwhile, Lunet de Lajonquière and Parmentier undertook extensive site surveys. The former extended his fieldwork into northeastern Thailand. Thailand, never colonized, received much encouragement from royal patronage. In 1904, a meeting held at the Oriental Hotel in Bangkok saw the foundation of the Siam Society, and an early contribution was provided by Prince Damrong, who chose as his subject the foundation of the previous capital at Ayutthaya. This society was a forum for those concerned with Thailand's past, and was followed in 1924 by the opening of the Archaeological Service of Siam by the government. The service assumed many of the responsibilities now covered by its successor, the Fine Arts Department, with particular reference to the conservation

of historic monuments. In 1926, the National Museum of Siam was opened.

Prehistoric research received less attention than the remains of the historic civilizations, both in Thailand and the French colonies. In the latter territories, significant work was undertaken by officials of the Geological Service of Indochina. Madeleine Colani and Henri Mansuy were able to define the later prehistoric hunter-gatherer groups Hoabinhian and Bacsonian. Mansuy also conducted excavations at the settlement site of Samrong Sen in Cambodia, a key site in the early history of archaeology in Southeast Asia. In consequence, by 1950 the rudiments of a prehistoric sequence were in place, the outline of the dynastic sequences of the historic kingdoms were defined, and the stage was set for the upsurge in research undertaken from the 1960s.

[See also HISTORY OF ARCHAEOLOGY SINCE 1950: CHINESE ARCHAEOLOGY.]

■ K.-C. Chang, *The Archaeology of Ancient China* (1986). C.F.W. Higham, *The Archaeology of Mainland Southeast Asia* (1989).

Charles Higham

HISTORY OF ARCHAEOLOGY SINCE 1950

OVERVIEW

Since 1950, archaeology throughout the world has become increasingly multidisciplinary in its scientific perspectives. It has also undergone a revolution in both method and theory, which began with the development and first widespread use of radiocarbon dating in the 1950s. The computer, trace element analyses of all kinds, isotopic methods, and remote sensing are among the new methodologies and techniques that have married archaeology closely to the natural and physical sciences. The same period has been a watershed in theoretical approaches to archaeology, which have become increasingly explicit and processual, with a major emphasis on environmental relationships and reconstruction, and the application of scientific method. In recent years, the so-called processual approach has given way to post-processual theories and research, which place a greater emphasis on the role of individuals and people in culture change. Archaeology has witnessed a dramatic expansion in research and the number of professional archaeologists since 1950, not only in Europe, the Near East, and North America, but throughout the world. At the same time, the development of radiocarbon and other dating methods has allowed archaeologists to examine culture change on a global basis and to study the broad issues of world prehistory for the first time. Spectacular discoveries have abounded during the past half-century, notable among them new research into human origins in Africa and Asia, the unearthing of royal tombs in China, and the accidental discovery of the Moche Lords of Sipán in coastal Peru. Recent finds include the Grotte de Chauvet with its Cro-Magnon paintings, Similaun Man (the "Ice Man") in the European Alps, the earliest human corpse known, and the Uluburun shipwreck off southern Turkey, which is a priceless archive of information on ancient Mediterranean trade. More important, perhaps, are the advances in scientific knowledge resulting from research in hitherto little-known archaeological areas such as Australia and the southwestern Pacific. For instance, we now know that humans settled on the Solomon Islands before 30,000 years ago, and lived on Tasmania during the height of the last glaciation. All these developments have unfolded during a period of unprecedented industrial expansion and destruction of the finite archaeological record, which has resulted in the loss of large parts of the world's archaeological archive. At the same time, the international antiquities market has fueled looting and pothunting in many countries in the interests of financial gain.

Brian M. Fagan

EUROPEAN ARCHAEOLOGY

The theory and practice of archaeology in Europe changed rapidly in the years after 1950. These changes embraced new theoretical orientations toward the understanding of the past, an increase in the number of archaeologists and growth in the scale of projects undertaken.

In many countries the number of archaeologists and the financial resources available to them grew dramatically. This was partly the result of an expansion in opportunities for higher education, but more importantly of a growing recognition by national and regional government of the importance of archaeology, whether for purely intellectual reasons or motives more akin to national pride or tourism.

Economic prosperity, especially in western Europe from the 1960s, resulted in an unprecedented wave of building and development projects, and the destructive effect of such works began to be fully realized. Postwar reconstruction, especially in such heavily bomb-damaged cities as London or Cologne, had already revealed the archaeological potential of historic towns, but the scale of later redevelopment was much greater. The first focus of attention was on historic cities, such as Winchester, but it was soon realized that other projects, such as roads, railways, and pipelines, or mineral extraction, as well as industrialized agricultural operations, had a similarly destructive effect. New procedures for recording and protecting archaeological remains were developed, but there was inevitably an enormous increase in emergency excavation before destruction, frequently on a very large scale. On the Aldenhoven Plateau, near Cologne in western Germany, an entire landscape was investigated in advance of open-cast coal mining, and many sites, especially Neolithic settlements, were excavated.

Another major focus of attention was the wetlands, frequently under threat from drainage for agricultural purposes, or for peat extraction. Many larger-scale projects were organized, such as those in the Somerset Levels in western England, or the exploration of prehistoric settlements submerged in the lakes of the French and Swiss Alps.

Many of the new archaeological methods were the result of the increasing application of scientific techniques to the study of the past. One of the first, and most dramatic, was *radiocarbon dating. Despite some initial doubts about the acceptability of the early dates, and some still lingering skepticism and reluctance to prefer such dates to those derived by traditional archaeological methods, the method has gained widespread acceptance and has been applied

with increasing regularity in many countries. The impact of such an independent dating method, most strongly felt in prehistory, has been twofold: first, to allow studies of material culture to concentrate on questions other than *typological analysis for chronological purposes, and second, to establish a chronology far more extended than previously imagined. This required a fundamentally new approach to the understanding of European prehistory; many of the important events in European prehistory that had previously been explained as the result of inspiration from the Mediterranean region, such as megalithic architecture, were now seen to be earlier than their alleged prototypes; European prehistory as a whole was much longer and processes of change much more extended than previously thought, thus requiring different sorts of explanation.

Other scientific methods have also contributed by opening up new possibilities for understanding the past. Physical, chemical, and petrological methods have been increasingly used since the 1960s, particularly to study pottery, stone implements, and glass and metal objects (notably gold, lead, and copper alloys), thus opening up new knowledge concerning production and distribution processes. The growth of *environmental archaeology has not only permitted a better understanding of the interaction between humans and their environment, but, with the development of new techniques for the recovery of items such as insect and parasite remains, has also given a new insight into living conditions, especially in towns.

More important than all the changes in the nature and scale of archaeological research were changes in the theoretical approach to the understanding of the past. In the early 1950s, a culture-historical approach was firmly established throughout much of Europe; major concerns were the typological development of material culture, and the tracing of interregional comparisons, mainly for chronological purposes by reference to established historical dates in the Mediterranean region and the Near East. Cultural change was attributed to external influences, within an overall concept of European innovation being derived from southern or eastern inspirations.

The explosion of new sources of evidence opened up new possibilities for research, and much attention has been paid especially to subsistence economies and the environment, to production and exchange, especially of rare and valuable materials such as stone axes or metal artifacts, and the evidence for social hierarchies. The growth of urbanism and centralized political authority in later prehistory and again in the early medieval period have also been addressed. European prehistory has been particularly affected by the new radiocarbon chronology; many correlations with the classical and New Eastern worlds have been discarded, and European innovations are not so readily attributed to external influences.

Explicitly theoretical concerns have been addressed in different ways in different parts of Europe. The ideas of the American "New Archaeology" (*see* Processual Theory) were taken up particularly in Britain, Holland, and Scandinavia, and later in other countries such as Spain. In Britain, David Clarke argued for a more rigorous and explicitly theoretical archaeology. Colin Renfrew was the main proponent of the processual approach of the "New Archaeology," seeking a new form of explanation for social change in prehistoric Europe by reference to internal developments rather than external influences. Such theoretical debates have been commonest in European prehistory; for the most part, *classical and medieval archaeology have continued to operate within a historical paradigm, though the work, for example, of Klavs Randsborg on the early medieval period shows a similar interest in general processes of social change.

Reactions to such ideas, the so-called post-processual archaeology (*see* Post-processual Theory), have also been mainly focused in Britain; Ian Hodder in particular has articulated criticisms of its generalizing approach and adaptive view of human culture. Some archaeologists have looked to the ideas of French neo-marxist anthropologists, who have stressed the conflicting interests of individuals or groups within society as a source of social change. Particular attention has been paid to control of resources, not only food and raw materials but also control of ritual and ceremonial knowledge; subsistence economies, prestige goods and ritual activities, particularly associated with graves, have therefore been much studied. Others have been more concerned with the meaning of material culture, with considerable attention paid to the use and deposition of artifacts in an attempt to discern their symbolic significance.

Elsewhere, a traditional culture historical approach still prevails; in Germany, for instance, perhaps because of the extreme *political uses of archaeology in the 1930s, there has been little attempt to move beyond typology and chronology to make inferences about past society. In eastern Europe for most of the second half of the twentieth century, communist regimes predominated and various forms of marxist interpretations (*see* Marxist Theory) of the past were officially sanctioned, though other traditions also existed.

With the collapse of the communist regimes in the 1990s and the reemergence of ethnic nationalism, archaeology has again been invoked in pursuit of modern political claims. In western Europe, too, the debate over the concept of a federal Europe has appealed to prehistory proponents on either side arguing whether the cultural achievements of prehistoric Europe were due to the unity or the fragmentation of Europe in the past.

[*See also* CULTURE HISTORICAL THEORY; HISTORY OF ARCHAEOLOGY FROM 1900 TO 1950: EUROPEAN ARCHAEOLOGY.]

■ B. Trigger, *A History of Archaeological Thought* (1989). I. Hodder, ed., *Archaeological Theory in Europe: The Last Three Decades* (1991).

Timothy Champion

NEAR EASTERN ARCHAEOLOGY

Since the 1950s, Near Eastern archaeology has undergone remarkable changes, despite a volatile political climate and occasional armed conflict.

Iraq and Iran. With the end of World War II, Iraqis focused on developing national archaeologists trained in Western practices. They excavated Hassuna, Eridu, and Hatra and worked at Sippar, *Nineveh, Harmal, Tepe Gawra, Samarra, Nippur, and Eridu. The 1958 revolution caused a brief comma in their research, but the oil boom of the 1970s provided resources for excavations, conservation, and reconstruction at Assur, *Babylon, and Hatra. This activity was interrupted by the Gulf War in the early 1990s.

International archaeologists also continued to work in Iraq. Roman Ghirshman excavated Choga-Zambil from 1952 to 1960. Americans returned to Nippur in 1948. Max E. L. Mallowan continued at Nimrud in the 1950s, followed by David Oates. Ralph S. Solecki discovered Neanderthal remains in the Zagros Mountains in 1957, and a Danish team headed by A. V. Glob excavated a Kuwaiti island in the Persian Gulf.

In Iran, a joint Iranian-American group worked at Hassanlou during the 1950s and 1960s. Concurrently, the Institute of Archaeology of the University of Teheran investigated nearby Marlik. In 1959 a joint German-Iranian-Swedish group excavated a Sassanian site, Tahki-Suliman. David Stronach dug at Pasargadae in the 1960s, the same period in which Robert J. Braidwood continued research on early domestication and village life in the north of Iran and Iraq. The overthrow of the shah of Iran and subsequent events virtually halted archaeological activity in Iran.

Turkey. Work at Boghazköy resumed in the 1950s and at Smyrna (Izmir) Beycesultan, *Ephesus, Gordion, and Sardis. *Troy too is under reexcavation. Development in Turkey in the 1980s and 1990s involved salvage operations by international teams before the construction of dams on the Tigris and Euphrates Rivers. These operations have documented evidence of the Paleolithic through Ottoman occupational periods. In the 1990s at Göltepe the first evidence was uncovered for tin mining in Turkey. *Underwater archaeology, pioneered by George F. Bass in 1960 at Cape Gelidonya, continues at the Uluburun site off southern Turkey.

Syria-Palestine. The French resumed excavations at Ras Shamra (Ugarit) and *Mari in the early 1950s. In the 1960s, with an international cadre of archaeologists, Syria began the Tabqa Dam salvage effort, similar to the project in Turkey. The Italian expedition to Tell Mardikh (*Ebla), begun in 1964, drew worldwide attention in 1974–1975 with the discovery of an EBIV deposit of cuneiform tablets. In Syria, research in the 1980s focused on the Khabur River valley with excavations at Tell Leilan, Tell Brak, and Tell Mozan. In the last decade of the twentieth century, almost 450 foreign expeditions are at work in Syria, but the area remains an archaeological frontier.

Lebanon. Political instability and armed conflict virtually eliminated archaeological work in Lebanon after 1950. However, James B. Pritchard excavated Sarafend in the late 1960s, while Pierre M. Bikai worked at Tyre. Stability in Lebanon will open an area rich in potential for archaeological research.

Israel. The establishment of the State of Israel concurrent with the discovery of the *Dead Sea Scrolls opened an era of intense archaeological activity that continues unabated. After World War II, the first American expedition began in 1956 at Shechem, serving as a field school to train a new generation of American archaeologists. This expedition also exemplified a post–World War II trend: the reexcavation of major tells. The dominant figure in post–World War II Syro-Palestinian archaeology was Kathleen Kenyon. At *Jericho in 1952 she used refined excavation techniques, which have since been adapted by all excavators in the Near East. Other sites reexcavated or under reexcavation include Gezer, Lachish, Megiddo, Ashkelon, Beth-shan, and *Jerusalem.

Israeli archaeology developed quickly after the establishment of the state in 1948. The 1967 and 1973 wars opened to Israeli archaeologists previously inaccessible areas in the Sinai, the West Bank, and the Golan Heights. In the same period, important discoveries were made in the Jewish Quarter, on the Temple Mount, and in the City of David areas of Jerusalem.

The first generation of Israeli archaeologists distinguished themselves with significant research: Shemuel Yeivin (Tell el-'Areini), Moshe Dothan (Ashdod, Akko), Ruth Amiran (Arad), Avraham Biran (Dan), Yigael Yadin (Hazor, Masada), Benjamin Mazar (Beth Shearim, Temple Mount), Nahman Avigad (Jewish Quarter), Yohanan Aharoni (Arad,

Tell Sheva). A second generation has followed in their footsteps— Trude Dothan, Moshe Kochavi, David, Ussishkin—while a third generation is on the rise. The Israeli archaeological community now dominates the research in Israel; nevertheless, competent archaeologists from other nations are welcomed, and recently a number of joint expeditions codirected by Israeli and foreign excavators have been in the field.

The use of volunteer workers—students from the United States, Canada, Europe, and Israel—rather than local labor also marks this period. Y. Yadin introduced this change at *Masada in 1963, and the innovation rapidly spread to American and other foreign expeditions.

Jordan. The Department of Antiquities of the Hashemite Kingdom of Jordan has its roots in a similar department created in 1923 under the British Mandate. After the cessation of conflict and the establishment of the State of Israel, Gerald Lankester Harding continued as director; Awni Dajani succeeded Harding as the first Jordanian director. Since 1967, Jordanian archaeology has been focused east of the Jordan River. Foreign archaeologists dominated Jordanian archaeological research in the 1950s and 1960s, but Jordanian archaeologists now teach in their universities and direct their own excavations or work cooperatively with foreign archaeologists; the royal house enthusiastically supports archaeology. Besides excavations at major tells, a number of surface surveys have been made, revealing cultural horizons from the Paleolithic to the Ottoman periods. Jordan is also rich in Neolithic culture remains.

Trends. Despite the unstable political situation that has dominated so much of the Middle East in recent decades, trends in archaeology cross national boundaries and surface in thought and practice. Several trends are evident. First, the historical scope of archaeological research has broadened to include both prebiblical and postbiblical periods. Second, archaeology has become a multidisciplinary activity, with increasing interest in the ecology of the past in all periods and with the use of modern sciences in both the excavation and the analytical processes. Third, the "New Archaeology" of anthropologists has had a marked influence on research designs, field techniques, and interpretations in Near Eastern archaeology. Fourth, national schools of archaeology have become the dominant forces in research in the region, but they are tempered by the flavor of oriental hospitality, which invites foreign participation. The possibility of peace and the development of open communications between the states of the Near East promise a future golden age for archaeology in the region.

[See also HISTORY OF ARCHAEOLOGY BEFORE 1900: NEAR EASTERN ARCHAEOLOGY; HISTORY OF ARCHAEOLOGY FROM 1900 TO 1950: NEAR EASTERN ARCHAEOLOGY.]

■ Henry O. Thompson, *Biblical Archaeology: The World, the Mediterranean, the Bible* (1978). Philip J. King, *American Archaeology in the Mideast* (1983). Joel F. Drinkard Jr., Gerald L. Mattingly, and J. Maxwell Miller, eds. *Benchmarks in Time and Culture* (1988). William G. Dever, *Recent Archaeological Discoveries and Biblical Research* (1990). P.R.S. Moorey, *A Century of Biblical Archaeology* (1991). Amnon Ben-Tor, ed., *The Archaeology of Ancient Israel*, trans. R. Greenberg (1992). Mary Ellen Lane, ed., *The State of Archaeology: An American Perspective* (1993).

Keith N. Schoville

CLASSICAL ARCHAEOLOGY

World War II was a major disruption to *Classical archaeology, particularly in Greece, where civil wars raged until 1949. However, after the war, the goals and methods of Classical archaeology changed little at first. Most of the leading archaeologists immediately set out to renew the prewar big-dig strategies. Even in war-torn Greece, the American School of Classical Studies was encouraged to start up excavations in the Agora as early as 1946, and the Germans were allowed to return to Olympia in 1952. In Italy, the fascists' propagandistic uses of the Roman past did little to damage the nationalist value of Roman archaeology, and between 1948 and 1956 a series of remarkably successful large-scale digs began at Cosa, Alba Fucens, Pithecusae, the Vatican, and numerous other sites.

The traditional style of excavation, oriented toward the recovery of spectacular works of art, continues to play a major role in Classical archaeology in the 1990s. Postwar digs have indeed produced finds comparable to the great discoveries of the nineteenth century. The "Grotto of Tiberius" at Sperlonga provided a remarkable haul of Roman statuary, and several astonishing treasures, such as the Riace bronzes and the Rogozen hoard, have broadened our knowledge of Classical art in metal. Two of the richest artistic discoveries ever made in Greece have come to light within the last generation. At Vergina, Manolis Andronikos uncovered a series of tombs that probably belonged to the Macedonian royal family, including what may well be the burial of Philip the Great. These have yielded great wealth in gold but also the most outstanding examples of Hellenistic wall painting. On Santorini, Spyridon Marinatos discovered a Minoan version of Pompeii, with beautiful frescoes.

But changes in purchasing power and in the funding of fieldwork since the 1960s have made it increasingly difficult to continue within the big-dig framework. It is not so easy now to hire huge teams of workers, and (particularly since 1973) rising fuel costs have made it hard to transport large numbers of specialists to the Mediterranean. There have been three main responses: persevere, looking to government agencies to meet the escalating costs; turn to surface survey as an end in itself rather than as a preliminary step to excavation; and choose smaller sites for excavation. These new challenges have coincided with the first major shift in research strategies in Classical archaeology since the 1870s. Neither surveys nor excavations on small rural sites are likely to produce works of art revealing the Classical spirit, and they appeal only to archaeologists interested in economic and social questions. Such archaeologists have become much more numerous since the 1970s, and in the 1990s even art history is no longer a safe haven for traditionalist scholarship. The "Paris School" introduced structuralism into the study of Greek vase painting in the 1980s, and poststructuralists, particularly in Cambridge, Paris, and Oxford, are now finding Classical art a very fertile field.

There are many possible explanations for these new directions. We could take a purely instrumentalist view, seeing the changes as necessary responses to new economic circumstances, or an internalist view, seeing them as the natural result of the success of the Beazleyan paradigm, which was left with nothing to do. The epistemological issues raised by the processual and post-processual prehistoric archaeologies in the 1960s and 1980s seem to have had only a limited impact on Classical archaeology. The main exception is Aegean prehistory, where Colin Renfrew in particular showed the value of systems theory and neoevolutionary frameworks for understanding the emergence of palatial civilization.

Changes in fieldwork priorities have followed similar

paths in both Greek and Roman archaeology. In Italy, John Ward Perkins surveyed a vast area of Etruria between 1950 and 1974, totally transforming our understanding of economic processes. This project spawned a number of more intensive surveys, particularly in the former Roman provinces. In the 1960s and 1970s many Roman archaeologists also shifted attention away from cities and toward rural sites. Some of the villas they excavated, such as Francoline and Settefinestre in Italy and Fishbourne in England, did produce the kind of artworks that earlier archaeologists had sought; but at the same time, these sites also gave us a new picture of rural life. Settefinestre has been particularly important in debates over marxist models of Roman economic history. Finally, there has been something of a shift of interest away from the late republic and empire toward the earlier period of state formation in the eighth through the sixth centuries. Funerary archaeology, often combined with evolutionary models drawn from processual theory, has become increasingly important as part of this movement.

In Greece, the first major modern survey, William McDonald's Messenia Project in the 1960s, was very much a prehistoric project, primarily aimed at reconstructing the Bronze Age environment. It also led to one of the most successful small excavations, at Nichoria. Like the survey, the excavation had the Bronze Age settlement as its main interest, but it also produced important Iron Age remains. As in Italy, extensive surveys gradually gave way to intensive work. Renfrew directed the first such survey, on Melos in the 1970s, again with a chiefly Bronze Age focus and carried on in conjunction with a major Bronze Age excavation at Phylakopi. But archaeologists and historians more interested in later periods were already recognizing the potential of these methods. Michael Jameson directed a survey in the Argolid in the 1970s, along with an excavation at the Classical site of Halieis, and Anthony Snodgrass surveyed in Boeotia in the 1980s. Greek survey work has adopted a level of intensity rarely paralleled in other parts of the world. Most parts of the Mediterranean are very artifact-rich, and the most recent surveys cover only small regions but do so at an extremely detailed level.

Although most Classical archaeologists do continue to be interested primarily in art history, the face of the field has changed dramatically since the 1960s. This needs to be seen in a broad intellectual context. Since the late eighteenth century, humanists have, to a great degree, been concerned with asserting or explaining the superiority of Western culture. Classics has understandably been at the very heart of this enterprise, analyzing Roman and particularly Greek civilization, which was felt to stand at the origin of Europeanness. But beginning in the 1960s, increasing numbers of humanists started to reject this entire way of thinking. For a century most academics had felt that Classical archaeology was all-important, since it was the study of artworks that expressed the Greek spirit, from which all else descended. But once the premise that the humanities should explain Europeanness was undermined, Classical archaeology as it was traditionally conceived began to lose its utility. One result has been a decline in its status within the academy; but another result has been that at least some of its practitioners have begun to look for new reasons why they should pursue their craft. The result is a field that combines massive amounts of evidence with sometimes highly experimental attitudes. It remains unclear whether the traditional forms of art history will continue to dominate the field or

whether the field will move toward anthropological styles of archaeology and toward cultural history.

[See also HISTORY OF ARCHAEOLOGY BEFORE 1900: CLASSICAL ARCHAEOLOGY; HISTORY OF ARCHAEOLOGY FROM 1900 TO 1950: CLASSICAL ARCHAEOLOGY.]

■ Anthony Snodgrass, *An Archaeology of Greece* (1987). Stephen L. Dyson, "Complacency and Crisis in Late Twentieth Century Classical Archaeology," in *Classics: A Discipline and Profession in Crisis?*, ed. Phyllis Culham, Lowell Edmunds, and Alden Smith (1989), pp. 211–220. Nigel Spivey and Tom Rasmussen, ed., *Looking at Greek Vases* (1991). Ian Morris, "Archaeologies of Greece," in *Classical Greece: Ancient Histories and Modern Archaeologies*, ed. Ian Morris (1994), pp. 8–47.

Ian Morris

ARCHAEOLOGY OF THE AMERICAS

Archaeological practice in the Americas since 1950 has been, and is, characterized by the development of bodies of method and theory to advance the quality of archaeological explanation of the past. The years 1900–1950 provided the foundation on which methods of archaeological explanation from 1950 on would be generated. Concern for developing better ways to explain the archaeological past was demonstrated as early 1936 with the work of William Duncan Strong and later with the work of Paul S. Martin (1938, 1939). In 1940 Clyde Kluckhohn criticized Americanist archaeology as having no clear objectives in its practice and suggested the development of a conceptual framework for carrying out its work. Later (1948), archaeologists in the United States would be shocked to read in Walter W. Taylor's *Study of Archaeology* that they were not explaining the past but promoting chronicle and historiography. With some deep-seated anger and bitterness because of Taylor's work, the Americanist archaeological community gradually grappled with the emerging need to give chronology building its proper place in archaeology and get on with the business of carrying archaeology beyond the level of chronology.

The foundations of the practice of archaeology since 1950 are seated within an earlier concern for the context and function of site features and artifacts found in archaeological excavations. Artifacts were seen as evidence of social and cultural behavior. Second, settlement pattern studies were seen as another avenue to enhance archaeological explanation because such studies delve into how human populations "arrange themselves upon the landscape, with relation to its natural features and with relation to other people" (Willey and Sabloff 1993: 153). Such studies were seen as the foundation for understanding the political and economic climate of archaeological populations. The third concern was for the linkage of culture to the environment. Here was the recognition that the environment influenced the development of culture.

In 1950 the attention to context and function in Americanist archaeology was typified by artifact typology. James Ford (1952) suggested that type distinction of artifacts was *imposed* on archaeological data by the archaeologist, whereas Albert Spaulding (1953) suggested that artifact typology was found *within* the data about the artifact. This debate continued from 1952 through 1960 and centered on the meaning of artifact type and its relation to culture change.

In 1958 the concern with context and function (especially the linkage of artifacts to behavior in archaeological explanation) was carefully discussed in *Method and Theory in*

American Archaeology, by Philip Phillips and Gordon R. Willey. Archaeological research was seen to occur at three levels: the conduct of fieldwork, the historical description of culture, and the "processual interpretation" of the archaeological past.

Settlement pattern studies were another means to study context and function in site excavations. The Virú Valley Project was one of the earliest examples of the use of settlement pattern studies in Americanist archaeology. Although most of the fieldwork for the project was done in 1946, Willey's *Prehistoric Settlement Patterns in the Virú Valley* (1953) was the first lengthy treatment of regional settlement patterns. Context and function were examined through studies of how populations in the Virú Valley distributed themselves over the landscape and how they interacted with their environment.

Cultural and environmental studies also were a means to enhance context and function analysis in archaeological explanation. Emil Haury (1950) brought together the services of geologists and other natural scientists to study the environment at Ventana Cave, while Waldo Wedel (1953) discussed subsistence technologies in the context of the environment, especially in the Great Plains.

During this period, archaeological explanation was freed from the reliance on the stratigraphic-potsherd analysis of earlier times by Willard Libby's radiocarbon (carbon 14) method of absolute dating. Although the theory and the practice of *radiocarbon dating were formulated during the late 1940s, its dramatic effects on Americanist archaeology began to be seen clearly from the 1950s onward. The technique conclusively showed that human populations reached North America more than ten thousand years ago. The technique also was able to create a more detailed picture of the Archaic time period.

Out of the concern for context and function in archaeological explanation from 1950 through 1960 came a new theoretical approach often referred to as the "New Archaeology." The New Archaeology was the hallmark of Americanist archaeology from the 1960s through the 1980s. It incorporated an evolutionary approach, studies of cultural variability, and an ecological approach to the study of culture into a new system of archaeological explanation. The New Archaeology also introduced statistical techniques for the analysis of site variables.

Lewis R. Binford best exemplifies the early New Archaeology in the Americas. Binford's influential paper "Archaeology as Anthropology" (1962) outlined the methodology of the New Archaeology. The effect of his early work on the Americanist archaeological community was immediate. Binford's New Archaeology took a systems approach to archaeological explanation. His article asked archaeologists to look at cultural subsystems that were technological, social, and ideological. He suggested that artifacts discovered in sites must be explained on those grounds. Kent V. Flannery (1968), with his "ecosystem" approach, went even further than Binford, creating a more holistic approach to the study of how humans interact with their environment.

Another important feature of the New Archaeology was its quest to become "more scientific." The use of computers to run statistical applications to analyze the significance of site variables was seen as another feature of "science" in archaeology. In addition, methods of physical and chemical analysis of archaeological remains also heralded a new attitude: that archaeology can and should be more precise in the manner in which it draws conclusions.

The push toward a "scientific archaeology" also came from other quarters of investigation. The philosophers Thomas Kuhn and Carl Hempel provided the philosophical foundations on which some Americanist archaeologists would forge newer means of explaining the archaeological record. Hempel's deductive-nomological approach to explanation stimulated Patty Jo Watson and her colleagues to write their book *Explanation in Archaeology* (1971). They argued that the construction of scientific laws and theories should guide archaeological research so that explanations could be given and predictions made about data. To a great degree, this book marked the end of the first stage of activity of the New Archaeology.

The study of residence patterns and social organization marked the opening of the second stage of the New Archaeology. The 1968 work of William Longacre in central Arizona and the work of James N. Hill at Broken K Pueblo were models of archaeological explanation involving architectural analysis of room functions. Both men conducted statistical and material analysis of ceramic and artifactual materials.

Lately, the domain of post-processualism has risen as another avenue of explanation in Americanist archaeology. Post-processualism firmly disagrees with the processualists' view that all human activities can be fully analyzed by objective or scientific methods. "Critical archaeology" is one of the features of post-processualism. Seen as somewhat polemical in its approach to the analysis of the state of archaeological interpretation, "critical archaeology" has opened the door to other avenues of explanation that the New Archaeology or processualism had not embraced. It asserts that there are modes of explanation other than those oriented toward science. The processualist–post-processualist debate continues as archaeologists continue their search for ever more sophisticated interpretations of the past.

[*See also* HISTORY OF ARCHAEOLOGY BEFORE 1900: ARCHAEOLOGY OF THE AMERICAS; HISTORY OF ARCHAEOLOGY FROM 1900 TO 1950: ARCHAEOLOGY OF THE AMERICAS.]

■ Walter W. Taylor Jr., *A Study of Archaeology* (1948). Patty Jo Watson, Steven A. LeBlanc, and Charles L. Redman, *Explanation in Archaeology: An Explicitly Scientific Approach* (1971). Valerie Pinsky and Alison Wylie, eds., *Critical Traditions in Contemporary Archaeology* (1989). Gordon R. Willey and Jeremy A. Sabloff, *History of American Archaeology*, 3d ed. (1993).

Douglas R. Givens

CHINESE ARCHAEOLOGY

Modern archaeology began in China with the discoveries of the sites of Yangshao and Longshan in the 1920s and 1930s, and the *Anyang excavation of 1928. These achievements—which established that China, contrary to what was previously believed, had passed through the Stone Age, and that the traditional historical sources were reliable—paved the way for the post-liberation investigations into the origins of Chinese civilization.

In the early 1950s, soon after the liberation, laws were issued to protect the national heritage, and the State Bureau of Cultural Relics was established within the Ministry of Culture. In addition, the Beijing-based Chinese Academy of Social Sciences (formerly the Academy of Sciences) created the Institute of Archaeology as well as some local archaeological work stations. This new system was a step forward in the modernization of the discipline, even though it brought upon the archaeologists the tight ideological and financial control of the state. Around the same time, three major archaeological journals were formally established: *Wenwu* ("Cultural Relics," originally *Wenwu Cankao Ziliao*); *Kaogu* ("Archaeology," originally *Kaogu Tongxun*); and *Kaogu Xuebao* ("Acta Archaeologica Sinica").

From the 1950s to the mid-1960s, when the Cultural Revolution (1966–1976) halted research, archaeological work concentrated on the Yellow River Valley, but by the 1970s additional excavations were conducted beyond this traditional center of Chinese civilization. In the 1980s, as a consequence of economic reforms, the Institute of Archaeology was decentralized and branches in charge of research and excavations within the provincial boundaries were established in each province. This allowed for greater independence in research strategies, which resulted in an increased interest in regional cultural phenomena, but at the same time it caused financial problems because less money for archaeological projects was received from Beijing. These financial problems are, however, turning out to be healthy stimuli, prompting archaeological institutes to require moneys for salvage excavations from private organizations and individuals that choose to build in archaeological areas, and, more importantly, causing the State Bureau of Cultural Relics in 1991 to make it legal for provincial archaeological institutes and universities to establish contacts for foreign cooperation in excavations.

Today, joint excavations and other relations with foreign institutions are bringing in new techniques and ideas and are making Chinese archaeologists and theoreticians rethink their rather obsolete Morgan- and Engels-based marxist theoretical framework originally developed in the 1940s by the social historian Guo Moruo (1892–1978). The marxist theory of social evolution, which still dominates the field, is in the majority of cases accepted uncritically without any modification and has become a routine formula employed to describe a status quo in the archaeological record.

Among the foreign theories that in recent years have gained some attention within China are the so-called New (or processual) Archaeology and some form of structuralism. The latest advances in theory and the post-processual debate are still little known. This is probably because Chinese archaeology, being heavily influenced by a long historiographic tradition, is still at the stage of documentation, more concerned with the historical rather than the philosophical aspects of the discipline.

Aside from *Li Ji (1895–1979), who supervised the excavation of Anyang but later fled to Taiwan, other prominent Chinese archaeologists of the first generation were Xia Nai, an expert on typology and the late chair of the Institute of Archaeology, and Yin Da, a specialist in Neolithic archaeology. Their work shaped Chinese archaeology for future generations of archaeologists from both the technical and theoretical point of view, and was instrumental in reinforcing national pride at a more general level. Today the field has noticeably expanded, and several archaeologists are particularly active. Among them are Su Bingqi, Zhang Zhongpei, An Zhimin, Su Bai, and Yan Wenming, a professor at Beijing University who concentrates on the problem of the origins of civilization and the state in China. Particularly interesting and groundbreaking is also the work of Wang Ningsheng in ethnoarchaeology (based on his in-depth studies of the southern minorities), and that of Chen Zhaofu on Chinese rock art.

In Paleolithic research the most important advances are the discoveries of remains of *Homo erectus* at two locations near Lantian (Shaanxi) in 1963 and 1964, at Yuanmou (Yunnan) in 1965, and in the Jinniu Mountains (Liaoning) in 1984. Dating placed Lantian Man at 800,000–650,000 B.P., Yuanmou Man at 600,000–500,000 B.P. (previously thought to date to 1,700,000 B.P.) and Jinniu Man at 280,000 B.P. Recent discoveries of earlier hominids in southern China have also opened up a debate on the possibility of a focus of human origin in east Asia, which is strongly disputed by those who believe modern humans originated in Africa. Upper Palaeolithic evidence has also been discovered within Chinese borders, in particular at the sites of Beijing Man at *Zhoukoudian and at Shiyu (Shou County, Shaanxi), where in 1963 a bone tool with carved designs was recovered, so far the earliest manifestation of art from China (carbon dated 26,995 ± 1370 B.C.). No Paleolithic cave art is known from the Chinese continent.

Great advances have been done also in the research on the origin of food production and settled life. Archaeological discoveries in Guangdong, Guangxi, and Hebei Provinces now place the first agricultural communities in China at 10,000–8,000 B.C. The excavation of several Neolithic villages in the Yellow River Valley showed that a more advanced agricultural production based on millet cultivation (*Setaria italica* and *Panicum miliaceum*) was reached in northern China by about 7000–6000 B.C. In the south, the discovery of Hemudu culture in 1973 proved that rice (*Oryza sativa*) was cultivated in the lower reaches of the Yangzi River Valley as early as 5000 B.C.

Among the most notable Late Neolithic sites (ca. 5000–3000 B.C.) are the villages of Banpo and Jiangzhai (Shaanxi), excavated in the 1950s and in the 1970s, respectively; the tomb of a high-rank individual with human sacrifices at Puyang Xishuipo (Henan) in 1987; the necropolis of Dawenkou (Shandong) discovered in 1959; and the Hongshan ceremonial site of Niuheliang (Liaoning) investigated between 1983 and 1985. These sites and others dated in the same period and found beyond the Yellow River Valley (Majiayao, Daxi, Majiabang, etc.) showed that, contrary to what was previously believed, the Chinese Neolithic had more than one focus and that the Yellow River Valley was not necessarily more advanced than the surrounding areas.

Much research has been done recently on the subject of the origin of civilization and state formation in China. This involved a thorough investigation of the predynastic Longshan era (ca. 27th–22nd centuries B.C.), associated with the so-called "Five Emperors" period that preceded the first dynasty, Xia. The most startling new discoveries since 1950 are those of seven walled cities at the northern Chinese sites of Pingliangtai, Wangchenggang, Haojiatai, and Mengzhuan in Henan Province, Bianxianwang and Dinggong in Shandong Province, and Laohushan in Inner Mongolia. At Pingliangtai evidence was found of a system of water pipes for draining purposes; at Wangchenggang early bronze remains were discovered, and in 1992 at Dinggong a potsherd with an as yet undeciphered inscription was unearthed, one of the oldest examples of writing discovered in China. In the Lower Yangzi River Valley area much effort has been put into the study of Liangzhu, a culture located in the Jiangsu-Zhejiang area and partly contemporaneous with the Longshan era. There, in 1986 the necropolis of Fanshan was discovered and in 1993 the altars of the ceremonial site of Mojiaoshan. Liangzhu, which is famous for the thousands of fine jades discovered at its sites, opened up a debate on the existence of a jade age preceding the Bronze Age.

In the early dynastic period (Bronze Age), one of the most notable discoveries was the urban site of Erlitou (Yanshi, Henan) in 1956, which, notwithstanding the skepticism of some, was proved to be the site of the last capital of the Xia dynasty (ca. 21st–17th centuries B.C.). This discovery ended the speculations on the legendary nature of this dynasty.

The period of the second dynasty (Shang, ca. 16th–11th centuries B.C.) was well known also before 1950; new archaeological discoveries have, however, led to the understanding of critical elements of the Shang period that were previously little known. For example, the 1955 excavation of the site of Erligang (Zhengzhou, Henan) shed more light on the early Shang period; the investigation in 1976 of the tomb of the so-called Lady Hao, the first grave of a member of the Shang royal family to be discovered intact, gave a glimpse into both Shang mortuary practices and the life of upper-class women; and the exploration in the 1980s of the southern cities of Panlongcheng (Hubei) and Sanxingdui (Guanghan, Sichuan) showed that the political influence of the Shang was far from limited to the Yellow River Valley. Advances have also been made in the interpretation of oracle bone and bronze inscriptions.

Archaeological research on the Zhou dynastic period (11th century–221 B.C.) has also greatly advanced. Since 1950 explorations in the homeland of the Zhou in Shaanxi Province and beyond have provided insight into both the origin of the Zhou people and on the subsequent establishment and development of the dynasty. Particularly important are the 1950s explorations of the Western Zhou (22nd century–770 B.C.) capital sites of Feng and Hao near Xi'an, and the excavations of the 1970s at Zhouyuan (Qishan-Fufeng, Shaanxi), which revealed a ceremonial center and uncovered the existence of Zhou oracle bone inscriptions. In addition, Western Zhou bronzes with historically relevant writing have been excavated in several provinces.

The excavation of city sites and cemeteries of the Eastern Zhou period (770–221 B.C.) throughout China confirmed claims from historical sources concerning the splitting of the Zhou territory into progressively independent states and the consequent formation of regional polities with cultures of their own, although related to the Zhou tradition. Worthy of note is the archaeological research in the area of influence of the ancient Chu state in the Middle Yangzi River Valley, where several well-preserved burials have been found. Among them are the tomb of the Marquis of Zeng at Leigudun (Sui County, Hubei), whose sixty-five-bronze-bell chime has opened new avenues of research on ancient Chinese music, and Mashan 1 (Jiangling, Hubei), an upper-class female burial renowned for its silks. Tombs of comparable wealth have been discovered in the north as well, but in smaller numbers, since the conditions of preservation are poorer. One of the best examples is the burial of the king of Zhongshan at Pingshan (Hebei), from whose excavation in the late 1970s were retrieved several inlaid and inscribed bronzes.

Much insight into the short-lived Qin dynasty (221–207 B.C.) was gained from the excavations between 1974 and 1976 of part of the tomb of the First Emperor at Lintong near Xi'an (Shaanxi), which uncovered the now-famous terracotta army, and from the ongoing exploration of Xianyang, the Qin capital (near Xi'an). As to the Han period (206 B.C.–A.D. 220), archaeological exploration of a number of tombs has supplemented historical knowledge, especially in the fields of mortuary practices and religious beliefs. In the early 1970s, two outstanding tombs of Han aristocrats were excavated: that of the Marquise of Dai at Mawangdui (Changsha, Hunan), where the fully preserved corpse of the deceased was unearthed as well as hundreds of lacquers, silks, books, and a silk painting; and the one of the Prince Liu Sheng of Zhongshan and his wife at Mancheng (Hebei), who were found enveloped in shrouds of jade tablets sewn together with gold threads. In addition the discoveries in the 1980s of several mummified corpses of Caucasoids in Chinese Central Asia (Xinjiang) reopened the debate on East-West contacts and on the archaeology of the Silk Route.

The restoration in 1987 of the Famen temple (Fufeng County, Shaanxi) allowed the retrieval of Buddhist relics as well as a treasure of Tang (A.D. 618–907) gold, silver, and jade objects and porcelains and marked a great advance for Buddhist and Tang studies. The opening of the Liao period (A.D. 916–1125) tomb of a Qidan princess in 1986 in Inner Mongolia, from which were retrieved over one thousand silver, gold, and other objects and a wall fresco, added precious new information on the early stages of development of Chinese painting as well as on the lives of the northern nationalities.

[See also HISTORY OF ARCHAEOLOGY FROM 1900 TO 1950: CHINESE AND SOUTHEAST ASIAN ARCHAEOLOGY.]

Paola Demattè

WORLD ARCHAEOLOGY

The advent of *radiocarbon dating and the increasing influence of science on archaeological research coincided with an explosion in the pace of archaeological research outside the narrow confines of Europe, the Mediterranean Basin, and the Americas. The 1950s were a time when many British and French colonies were establishing territorial museums and refining antiquities legislation. Many British archaeology graduates, notably from Cambridge University, took up museum and academic appointments in Africa, Australia, and New Zealand, where they built on the research of pioneers like *Louis and Mary Leakey and J. Desmond Clark in tropical Africa and John Mulvaney in Australia. Although most of these young archaeologists worked with minimal resources, the U.S. government provided much more abundant funding for overseas scientific expeditions in the late 1950s and thereafter, resulting in major American research projects in the Near East, in Africa, and in parts of the Pacific, as well as in Central and South America. Much of this research had strong multidisciplinary themes, like the University of Chicago investigations into the origins of food production in the Near East, research headed by Robert Braidwood, who took botanists, geologists, and zoologists in the field with him. After the discovery of *Zinjanthropus boisei* at Olduvai Gorge by Mary Leakey in 1959, massive National Geographic Society and U.S. government funding poured into research into human origins in East Africa, revolutionizing our knowledge of early human evolution.

As many nations gained independence in the 1960s, archaeological research in tropical Africa acquired increasing importance as a source of information on early African history. Archaeologists played a leading role in the development of multidisciplinary history using nontraditional sources such as excavated data and oral traditions, as well as documentary records. *Nationalism, and the use of history to provide precedent and context for modern-day developments, led many other governments to large-scale archaeological programs after the 1960s. The Chinese government invested heavily in archaeology under Mao Zedong's tenet that the past should inform the present. The resulting discoveries included Han royal tombs and the terra-cotta regiment guarding the tomb of Emperor Qin *Shihuangdi.

The development of radiocarbon chronologies allowed archaeologists to think in terms of a global prehistory for the first time, to compare cultural developments in different parts of the world, and to measure the rate of culture change over long periods of time. In 1961 the Cambridge archaeologist Grahame Clark published *World Prehistory*, the first modern synthesis of the human prehistoric past on a global canvas. Clark's influential book highlighted some of the glaring gaps in the world archaeological record. Since its publication, archaeological research in all corners of the world has filled many of these gaps and shown that such developments as art, agriculture, and civilization appeared at different times in widely separated areas of the world. But many controversies remain. For example, vigorous debate surrounds the dates of the first settlement of the Americas and Australia, while recent developments in AMS radiocarbon dating have resulted in drastic shortenings of the chronologies for the appearance of maize in the Americas.

As archaeological research has become more specialized, finer-grained, and more locally focused, the leap from purely regional archaeology to world prehistory has become harder to bridge, notably because few archaeologists now possess the broad comparative knowledge of early archaeologists like V. Gordon *Childe or Gordon Willey. The theoretical underpinnings of archaeology have become more complex in recent years as archaeologists grapple with the complexities of understanding human adaptations to changing environments and also move away from the simplistic notion of inevitable, if diverse, cultural progress, an idea that has dominated world prehistory in recent years. Future interpretations of world prehistory will depend on sophisticated mixes of complex environmental data that extend over many millennia, theoretical formulations that blend individual human behavior with cultural processes, and increasingly accurate chronologies that allow the trading of complex human migrations, even those of hundreds of thousands of years ago. While these theoretical developments unfold, other archaeologists are seeking to move away from what they consider unduly ethnocentric perspectives on human prehistory, perspectives that are based on European and American perceptions of the past and that underrate cultural developments elsewhere. These archaeologists are grappling with fundamental questions. To what extend to one's own cultural biases influence one's view of human prehistory? How does one reconcile a prehistory developed by multidisciplinary Western science with alternative views of the past held by Native Americans, Australian aborigines, and many other peoples? Such alternative, and often sophisticated, perspectives will play an increasingly important role in the world prehistory of the twenty-first century.

■ Grahame Clark, *World Prehistory* (1961). Glyn Daniel, *A Hundred and Fifty Years of Archaeology* (1981). Bruce Trigger, *A History of Archaeological Thought* (1989). Clive Gamble, *Timewalkers: A Prehistory of Global Colonization* (1994).

Brian M. Fagan

HITTITES. *See* ANATOLIA.

HOABINHIAN. The term "Hoabinhian" refers to archaeological assemblages found in caves and open sites on the mainland of Southeast Asia and northern Sumatra, from about thirteen thousand years ago until the spread of rice agriculture after 3000 B.C. Named after discoveries made in the 1920s in the former Hoa Binh Province of northern Vietnam, the Hoabinhian has acquired importance because of claimed associations with the origins of *agriculture in Southeast Asia. These associations still lack definite proof.

One of the most significant points about the Hoabinhian is that it seems to represent a major period of colonization of the wet Holocene rainforests of the Malay Peninsula and northern Sumatra. It also indicates a considerable increase in population density in certain more northerly zones of seasonal rainfall distribution, especially western Thailand and northern Vietnam. Demographically, therefore, it appears to represent some degree of success in the forging of new adaptations to postglacial environments, following an evidently thin human population of the region during the last glacial maximum.

Evidence for Hoabinhian occupation and burials occurs mainly in limestone caves and shelters. There are also a few coastal *shell middens dating from after eight thousand years ago in northern Sumatra, western peninsular Malaysia and northern Vietnam; any older than this would probably have been destroyed by rising sea levels. Hoabinhian tools were characteristically made on flat, oval, or elongated river pebbles flaked around their peripheries and over one or both surfaces. These pebble tools occur sporadically with other flake tools, occasional edge-ground axes, grindstones, bone points, and bone spatulae. Hoabinhian burials are mostly flexed or contracted, and often dusted with haematite; they lack grave goods apart from occasional stone pillows or stone slab covers.

In the upper levels of many Hoabinhian cave sites there are also potsherds: plain or vine/ mat impressed in Vietnam, cord-marked in most other areas. In some cases this probably reflects disturbance, but pottery does appear fairly definitely in late Hoabinhian contexts in northern Vietnam by about 5000 B.C.

It is clear from most sites that the Hoabinhians were hunters; bones of a wide range of mammal species have been found, with pig and deer predominating. Plant remains, on the other hand, are scarce, with the most important coming from early Holocene contexts in *Spirit Cave, northwest Thailand. These include parts of food plants (almond, and possibly some legumes), stimulants (betel nut), poisons (butternut kernels), and other useful plants including bamboo and gourd. No remains of cereals such as rice or millet have been found, although rice does occur in northeast Thailand by 3000 B.C. In general, none of the early Holocene Spirit Cave plant remains can be proven to be from domesticated plants, and it seems that they may belong to a stable and broad-spectrum hunter-gatherer adaptation.

[*See also* ASIA: PREHISTORY AND EARLY HISTORY OF SOUTHEAST ASIA; ASIA, ORIGINS OF FOOD PRODUCTION IN: ORIGINS OF FOOD PRODUCTION IN SOUTHEAST ASIA.]

■ P. Bellwood, *Prehistory of the Indo-Malaysian Archipelago* (1985). C.F.W. Higham, *The Archaeology of Mainland Southeast Asia* (1989).

Peter Bellwood

HOARDS AND HOARDING. "Hoards" and "hoarding" mean different things to different archaeologists. For those concerned with chronological studies, a hoard is simply a collection of artifacts which entered the archaeological record together. It is a distinctive class of deposit whose contents form a closed association. Hoarding, however, is a particular kind of human activity, and for those who are more interested in investigating past behavior it is a process that demands attention in its own right. Why were certain artifacts deposited and never recovered? They could have been concealed until their positions were lost, but they might also have been intended as offerings, in which case it would be their defining characteristic that they were never meant to be retrieved.

Deposits of this kind have a very wide distribution and are as common in the New World as they are in the Old. But the same dualities permeate their investigation. Stores of artifacts that were intended for recovery are described as "caches" in American archaeology, just as offerings are sometimes characterized as treasures. But although the same problems affect the archaeology of many different regions, at present it is only in Europe that we can follow the development of one basic tradition of "hoarding" from its inception among the last hunter-gatherers to its demise five thousand years later.

There are procedural problems to address, just as there are problems of definition. It is always difficult to prove a negative. How can we tell that particular objects were lost accidentally? Can archaeologists demonstrate that valuables were deliberately relinquished? At one level we can discuss practicalities. There are certain deposits that could have been concealed, perhaps because their position had been marked, but then again there are others, such as river finds, where recovery would have been difficult or impossible. Similarly, there are deposits of bulky but valuable raw materials which might plausibly be regarded as stores, whereas the treatment of certain objects, or their association with human or animal bones, may suggest a more structured approach to deposition. The greatest problem in resolving these questions has been the tendency to undertake minute studies of the evidence from one phase of activity and to extrapolate from those observations to the archaeological sequence as a whole. That has led to contradictory interpretations, and has obscured some of the most striking developments that took place over time.

The origins of these practices remain uncertain, although in southern Scandinavia it does seem likely that the earliest offerings in watery locations were made during the Mesolithic Period. Some of these consisted of organic material such as antler, but other items, like pots, involved a reference to the material culture of the farmers living further to the south. It was certainly around the rim of Neolithic Europe that artifacts were most often deposited in water. Such items included pottery vessels containing foodstuffs, meat joints, amber beads, and human remains, but, just as we find in Brittany, the most important item was the polished axe. In both regions the same categories of material came to be associated with newly built monuments, both *megalithic tombs and specialized earthwork enclosures. Throughout there seems to have been an emphasis on fertility and on objects associated with new forms of food production.

To some extent these deposits existed in parallel with a new range of weapons and personal ornaments which accompanied the dead to the grave. This duality was only intensified once metal artifacts were adopted, perhaps because these were more obviously of non-local origin. As a result, we can distinguish between one set of objects, exemplified by the dagger, which were primarily associated with burials in special monuments, and a second set, including the axe, which were deposited in isolation, usually in water. This distinction extends well beyond the initial distribution of votive deposits and could be illustrated in most parts of north and northwest Europe. It was only in central Europe that a more complex pattern seems to have developed during the Early Bronze Age, for in areas with an abundant supply of local raw materials this duality seems to have lost its force. Just as important, the archaeology of this area illustrates two further developments which are not recognized in other regions until later in the Bronze Age: a massive increase in the quantities of metalwork taken out of circulation in hoards, and the first archaeologically detectable attempts to accumulate scrap metal for recycling. Here it is especially difficult to distinguish between utilitarian and votive interpretations of hoarding.

Across large areas of Europe that duality broke down after 1500 B.C., when the construction of large mounds became less common and fewer burials were associated with grave goods. At that point there were major changes in the scale and character of metalwork deposits. Although we do find hoards that seem to be intimately connected with the process of bronze production—they may include unfinished artifacts or collections of raw material—the main emphasis shifts to bogs, rivers, and lakes, where increasing numbers of weapons were discarded in apparent isolation. These would seem to be the direct successors of the artifacts associated with earlier burials, and it is tempting to suggest that as the grave lost much of its importance as a place for depositing valuables, similar objects were deposited in other, natural locations. In fact this was not a wholly new development, as the deposition of metalwork in rivers seems to have been a more extravagant variant of a long-established practice. What is largely new, however, is the presence of human bones, especially skulls, in the same places.

The scale of deposition was considerable and may have increased during the later Bronze Age, as these practices took on a competitive aspect. The emphasis was still on the non-local, and it is usual to find that a significant proportion of the weapons deposited in major rivers originated in other areas. In fact, the distribution of river deposits particularly features those regions which had no metal supplies of their own. The main emphasis was on north and northwest Europe, but there are echoes of this practice as far south as Italy and as far west as the Iberian Peninsula.

For reasons that still remain obscure, the long-distance movement of bronze was severely curtailed around 800 B.C. Iron artifacts began to be used in significant numbers, but the earliest of these do not feature so prominently in votive deposits. Perhaps this was because, unlike bronze, the raw material did not evoke clear connections with remote places. Instead there was something of a reversion to the simpler practices associated with the Neolithic Period. Again we encounter structured deposits of pottery, food, agricultural equipment, and even human remains. There may be a similar link with ideas of natural fertility, for these new deposits were created at a time of agricultural intensification and are associated not just with watery locations but also with grain storage pits.

During the later years of the Pre-Roman Iron Age such deposits diversified. In addition to those offerings concerned with food production, there was a resurgence in the deposition of weapons in rivers, and once again some of these seem to have been accompanied by human skulls. Around the limits of the Roman Empire the provision of offerings changed still further. Some of the major groups of river finds focused on territorial borders, while many of the same categories of material were deposited at purpose-built shrines in Britain and Gaul. These were often the direct ancestors of Roman rural temples, where a more restricted range of offerings was still made after the Roman conquest. The main difference was that the offerings now included coins. Other votive deposits took on a more standardized character and in time the deposition of offerings became assimilated with the Roman conception of sacrifice as a payment made to the gods for services rendered. No longer did these practices afford an opportunity for competitive display; they were a truer reflection of the law of contract.

This was not the case outside the Roman frontier, where similar practices endured until the Viking Age. In northern Europe there was a renewed oscillation between the deposition of valuables in graves and their use in votive deposits, but in this case the finds from the votive hoards have one new characteristic. They contain massive collections of weaponry which has been deliberately damaged and destroyed. These do not seem to have been the personal property of the communities who offered them. Detailed analysis of their stylistic affinities, combined with the study of use damage, shows that they were most likely the property of foreign war bands who had been defeated in battle. In one instance the collection of metalwork was so lavish that it was loaded into a boat and sunk in shallow water.

Inside the frontiers of the Roman Empire the extravagant deposition of metalwork was severely truncated, and social transactions seem to have taken different forms. In the same way, the Scandinavian tradition of providing lavish offerings came to an end with the establishment of the Viking state. That comparison may be revealing, for it suggests that such episodes of conspicuous consumption may be a particular feature of societies riven by instability and conflict. They were perhaps among the ways in which status was won and maintained. If so, the development of more ordered societies in different areas of Europe may have rendered those practices obsolete.

[See also EUROPE: THE EUROPEAN BRONZE AGE; SCANDINAVIA: SCANDINAVIA IN THE BRONZE AGE.]

■ Janet Levy, *Social and Religious Organisation in Bronze Age Denmark: an Analysis of Ritual Hoard Finds* (1982). Richard Bradley, *The Passage of Arms; an Archaeological Analysis of Prehistoric Hoards and Votive Deposits* (1990). Lotte Hedeager, *Iron Age Societies* (1992).

Richard Bradley

HOHOKAM CULTURE. The Hohokam are the prehistoric farmers who inhabited approximately 45,000 square miles (120,000 sq km) in the Sonoran Desert of the south central portion of Arizona. Within this vast territory, significant axes of environmental variability are created by the related factors of elevation, climate, and hydrology. Although annual precipitation throughout is less than 15 inches (380 mm), the highest average amounts exceed the lowest by a factor of two. In the center of the Hohokam world, the broad, flat Phoenix basin experiences the lower range of precipitation at 7.5 inches (180 mm) and the hottest temperatures, with over ninety days above 100° F (56° C). An arc of somewhat higher elevation, lower temperatures, and increased rainfall surrounds the Phoenix basin to the north, east, and south.

The harsh climate of the Phoenix area is ameliorated by two perennial rivers arising in mountain watersheds outside the low desert. The Salt and Gila Rivers supplied the massive irrigation systems for which Hohokam *agriculture is noted. In the surrounding arc of less extreme climate, the rivers are intermittent. Small-scale irrigation from river segments with more permanent flow, floodwater farming from ephemeral drainages, and diversions of surface runoff supported crops. The Sonoran Desert peoples were skilled farmers who cultivated a suite of plants that are both drought tolerant and varied, including sixty-day corn, tepary beans, grain amaranth, agave, and little barley, as well as the other typical southwestern crops.

Despite considerable environmental diversity in the Hohokam region, archaeological interpretations have emphasized spatial uniformity in cultural and stylistic expression. Models characterizing this homogeneity have attributed cultural cohesiveness to the existence of a single or set of closely related ethnic groups, an underlying peasant tradition, and an interaction sphere, horizon style, or regional system grounded in religious ideology. The Hohokam are distinguished from other prehistoric peoples of the southwestern United States by a strong cultural orientation toward the Mesoamerican fringe to the south. In fact, changes in material culture and society through time have often been explained as migrations from Mexico or as religious transformations connected with ideological upheavals in Mesoamerica.

The name Hohokam is usually reserved for the pottery-making peoples who lived between A.D. 200 and 1450, although their Late Archaic predecessors had adopted a farming lifestyle in some locations by 700 B.C. The culture is distinguished from other southwest ceramic traditions by repetitious designs of small elements in red paint on buff, brown, or gray pottery during all but the initial and final segments of the ceramic sequence. Villages consist of dispersed houses and house clusters, with larger settlements more formally organized around plazas, ball courts, and platform mounds. In the Phoenix area, individual canal lines carried water distances greater than 15 miles (30 km) and economically linked multiple communities. Other distinguishing traits include a widespread trade network involving large amounts of exotic material such as shell and obsidian, a set of carved stone ritual objects, cremation burial, and an iconography emphasizing desert fauna and human forms.

Characterization of social and organizational complexity is a subject of much controversy. The Hohokam, Chaco Canyon, and *Casas Grandes are usually considered to have attained the greatest complexity and social hierarchy in the Southwest. Attributes of complexity for the Hohokam include construction of the largest prehistoric canal system in North America, dense and permanent populations, and the erection of relatively massive public architecture. The necessity for cooperation and coordination in the construction of the very large canal networks is apparent. However, conclusions concerning levels of effort, the need for centralized control, and the relationship of canal networks to polities are not matters of consensus.

Until recently, most investigations have focused on detailed examination of a few large sites in the Phoenix area, and major publications have been sporadic. This emphasis has promoted a model of Hohokam culture emanating from a strong central source, surrounded by less well-developed and colonial spheres. A core-periphery contrast is articulated in a distinction between riverine and nonriverine or desert regions, based on the implications of differential opportunities for irrigation and the related development of an integrative ideology in the Phoenix basin. Perhaps more than for any other culture area in the United States, there has been an explosion in primary data bearing on the Hohokam during the past decade as the result of development-related funding required by environmental legislation. As the resulting information is assimilated and synthesized, existing regional and holistic models formulated from only a few well-studied sites are being challenged. The strength of the core-periphery contrast is currently being modified by the increasing documentation of unanticipated levels of population and centers with public architecture outside the Phoenix basin.

[See also MESOAMERICA: CLASSIC PERIOD IN MESO-AMERICA; MOGOLLON AND MIMBRES CULTURES; NORTH AMERICA: THE NORTH AMERICAN SOUTHWEST.]

■ Emil W. Haury, The Hohokam: Desert Farmers and Craftsmen (1976). Patricia L. Crown, "The Hohokam in the American Southwest," Journal of World Prehistory 4(1990):223–255. Patricia L. Crown and W. James Judge, eds., Chaco and Hohokam: Prehistoric Regional Systems in the American Southwest (1991). George P. Gumerman, ed., Exploring the Hohokam: Prehistoric Desert Peoples of the American Southwest (1991). Paul R. Fish and Suzanne K. Fish, "Southwest and Northwest: Recent Research at the Juncture of the United States and Mexico," Journal of Archaeological Research 2(1994): 3–44.

Paul R. Fish

HOLOCENCE

INTRODUCTION

The Holocene is the most recent of the time periods into which the geological history of the earth is divided, and is the latest stage of the *Pleistocene or Quaternary system. It began 10,000 years ago, at the end of the last Ice Age, when rapid rise in temperatures caused an acceleration in the melting of the ice sheets in the northern hemisphere. The meltwaters drained into the oceans and caused a major rise in the sea level. This made more water available to evaporate and fall as rain, and resulted in moister conditions generally and the shrinking of the vast deserts found in tropical latitudes at the height of the last Ice Age. Holocene climatic improvement led directly to changes in vegetation, as trees and other plants colonized previously hostile regions.

Holocene vegetation increased the abundance of food resources but also demanded new adaptations. As dense forests spread over previously open landscapes many species of animals were displaced and several became extinct. The new vegetation favored species living alone or in small groups rather than the large herd-dwelling mammals of the tundra and the steppe. Predators, including human communities, had to adapt their hunting strategies accordingly. One adaptation may have been a greater dependence on vegetable foods in northern latitudes, which were more readily available as temperatures rose and vegetation improved. Another was the adoption of agriculture in many parts of the world as human societies grew in size and numbers.

The melting of the ice sheets had other effects. Regions that had been covered by a massive loading of ice now experienced a rebound phenomenon and experienced isostatic uplift, outstripping the rise in sea level. Most lowland coastal areas, however, were drowned out by the eustatic sea-level rise, which rendered unusable some of the fertile plains on which earlier human communities had lived. Throughout history, coastal regions have been one of the most attractive regions for human settlement, and the loss of Paleolithic coastlines to postglacial sea-level rise has undoubtedly destroyed a wealth of information about earlier human lifestyles.

These general trends of the Early Holocene were not represented everywhere to the same degree, and some regions experienced a modification or even a complete reversal of the general pattern. As climate and vegetation changed, for example, some regions became drier and others wetter than today. Thereafter they slowly declined, a deterioration which has continued into recent times. The effect of these long-term trends has, however, often been masked by shorter episodes of colder or drier conditions which have had a dramatic impact on human communities, especially those dependent on farming. The Little Ice Age—a period of cooler and wetter conditions from the sixteenth to nineteenth centuries A.D.—is but one recent example.

In geological time perspective, the Holocene is simply another interglacial period, and a return to glacial conditions may be expected at some time in the future. Against this is the fact that the Holocene is unique in one major respect: the impact of humans. The prodigious expansion in human numbers and activity has transformed the face of the globe over the last 10,000 years, equalling if not exceeding the impact of climate. The adoption of farming—itself a consequence of new opportunities offered by Holocene climate and vegetation—has led to large-scale clearance and manipulation of landscape. The extensive use of fossil fuels within the last two hundred years may be causing global warming through the "greenhouse effect." The interplay of human and natural factors is indeed one of the key features of the postglacial period. The Holocene is thus not just a climatic or environmental backdrop against which the human events of the last 10,000 years were played out; instead, it is an integral part of the story, acting in different ways and at different times as both cause and effect.

[See also DOMESTICATION OF ANIMALS; DOMESTICATION OF PLANTS; MEGAFAUNAL EXTINCTION; PALEOLITHIC, articles on LOWER AND MIDDLE PALEOLITHIC, UPPER PALEOLITHIC.]

Chris Scarre

HOLOCENE ENVIRONMENTS IN EUROPE

The environment of *Europe changed dramatically during the Holocene due to both natural and human factors, the relative importance of which varied through time. At the end of the last Ice Age, a large part of northern Europe was covered by ice sheets, while much of the area further south experienced cold conditions and supported open herb-dominated vegetation or open woodlands of birch (Betula) and pine (Pinus). Sea level was below its present height because of water held in the ice sheets, and Britain was joined to the continent by a land bridge.

The rapid temperature rise at the onset of the Holocene (10,000 B.P.) enabled trees to spread northwards, leading to the development of dense woodland over much of Europe by ca. 8000 B.P. In northwestern and central Europe this woodland was a mixture of broad-leaved trees, including hazel (Corylus avellana), oak (Quercus), elm (Ulmus), lime (Tilia), and alder (Alnus), while pine, birch, and spruce (Picea) were dominant in Scandinavia and eastern Europe. Rising sea levels separated Britain from the continent by 8000 B.P. and the coastline of Europe resembled that of today by ca. 7000 B.P.

These changes presented Mesolithic peoples with a varying resource base, as plant and animal populations changed and the extent and distribution of coastal resources shifted. For example, Franchthi cave in southern Greece today lies a few meters above sea level on a rocky coast, but at the start of the Holocene the sea was up to 2 miles (2–3 km) away, and separated from the cave by mudflats. This change in the position of the coastline is reflected in changes in the type of mollusk exploited by the inhabitants of the cave, from mudflat species to types characteristic of rocky shores at ca. 8000 B.P.

Away from the coast, Mesolithic sites clustered around lakes and rivers, enhancing mobility and providing opportunities for fishing. The Early Mesolithic (ca. 9600 B.P.) site of 'Star Carr, northern England, was on the edge of a large lake surrounded by open birch woodland. Red deer (Cervus elaphus), roe deer (Capreolus capreolus), elk (Alces alces), aurochs (Bos primigenius), and pig (Sus scrofa), were hunted by the occupants of the site; birch trees were used for timber and birch bark was collected, possibly for resin.

Hazel was the dominant tree over much of northwest Europe between ca. 9500 and 7500 B.P., and at some Mesolithic sites hazelnuts seem to have been an important part of the diet. It has been suggested that the human population may have managed hazel by using fire to suppress its competitors, although pollen and charcoal analyses do not support this. Nevertheless, fire may have been used to create small clearings or to drive game, and there is evidence from some upland areas of northern England that burning was widespread in the later Mesolithic period.

*Agriculture was first introduced into southeast Europe at ca. 9000–8000 B.P., and had spread to the northwest by 5500–5000 B.P. Cereal cultivation required clearance of woodland to create fields, and minor clearings, or "landnam" episodes, appear in pollen diagrams from this time. The overall extent of woodland was not greatly reduced, and it continued to be used as a resource. That some woodland may have been managed is suggested by the uniform poles of wood used in some of the *Somerset Levels trackways in southwest England. Trees, particularly elm and lime, also provided a source of leaf fodder for cattle, as suggested by the find of leaf hay in byres at the Early Neolithic site of Thayngen-Weier in Switzerland. This type of exploitation may have been at least partially responsible for the decline of elm in 5000 B.P., which is widely recorded in pollen diagrams from northern Europe.

From the Late Neolithic and Bronze Age, human impacts on the environment increased, as woodland was cleared to provide land for cultivation and pasture, often leading to the onset of soil erosion. In upland areas of northwest Europe, the onset of blanket peat formation seems to have resulted from changes in the water balance brought about by woodland clearance, while in areas of lower rainfall, heathland formed on nutrient-impoverished soils. The original woodland of the Mediterranean area was replaced by thorny grazing-resistant shrubs (macchia and garrigue). The last four thousand years, therefore, have witnessed a major change in the nature of European environments, from a substantially wooded landscape to one with a mosaic of vegetation types, most of which owe their character, directly or indirectly, to human activity.

[See also ELM DECLINE, EUROPEAN; MEGAFAUNAL EXTINCTION; PALEOENVIRONMENTAL RECONSTRUCTION; PLEISTOCENE.]

■ B. Huntley and H.J.B. Birks, An Atlas of Past and Present Pollen Maps for Europe: 0–13000 Years Ago (1983). B. Huntley and T. Webb III, Vegetation History (1988). Neil Roberts, The Holocene (1989).

Petra Day

HOLOCENE ENVIRONMENTS IN AFRICA

African environments, ultimately, are determined primarily by the local climates, in which there were many and profound changes during the Holocene. Climatic changes within and outside the tropics sometimes seem to have been out of phase, but this may in part result from the imprecision of the dating. Also, there were important local and regional anomalies within the overall climatic patterns.

Since most of *Africa lies at low latitudes, temperature changes have not been very marked. At the beginning of the Holocene, temperatures were still recovering from their minima during the Last Glaciation (overall, perhaps 9° F [5° C] lower than today). Southern Africa was warmer than at present between about 9000 and 4700 B.P., but was generally cooler both before and since. In eastern equatorial Africa, in contrast, modern temperatures were not reached until about 6700 B.P.; warmer temperatures are also detectable in western and northern Africa by 7000 B.P.

Rainfall is the critical determinant of African environments. Much of the continent witnessed extreme aridity until about 12,500 B.P., when the tropics became much wetter. Lakes filled closed basins throughout the region, the larger lakes reaching higher levels (sometimes more than 330 feet [100 m] higher than their modern successors, and some of them overflowing. There was a brief arid phase at about 10,500 B.P. (perhaps reflecting the glacial readvance at higher latitudes), but the lakes seem to have reached their maximal stands between 9500 and 8500 B.P. Lake Chad, which overflowed, stood 130 feet (40 m) higher than it does today and covered an area of some 135,000 square miles (350,000 sq km). The Nile, fed by increased rainfall in its headwaters, began to cut down into its floodplain at about 12,500 B.P., even though the level of the Mediterranean was rising, and continued down-cutting until about 6000 B.P.

Reflecting the higher rainfall and temperatures, the rainforests began to expand at 13–12,000 B.P., and were at their maximal extent from 7000 to 3500 B.P. At this time, they reached some 220 miles (350 km) north of their present limit, and the Dahomey Gap (the break in rainforest distribution in Togo and Benin) was closely closed.

The Early Holocene wet phase also involved a northward expansion of the monsoon belt. Rains had reached the eastern Sahara by about 11,000 B.P., and by 9500 B.P. affected most of the modern Sahara and Sahel. Rainfall was not necessarily high: in the eastern Sahara, it may not have exceeded 4 inches (100 mm) a year, but this is a region where no rain had fallen for perhaps 50,000 years and where none falls today. The Sahelian environment expanded into what is now high desert, and intensive use of some of the Sahelian plants eventually domesticated in Africa, particularly sorghum, began at this time. At 9500 B.P., the Niger breached the dune barrier and flooded the Azawad delta 190 miles (300 km) northward. By 8300 B.P., there were permanent lakes in a steppe parkland all across the Sahel and Sahara up to 24° N, supporting groups of gatherers and fishers.

The early northward expansion of the monsoon rains across the Sahara was probably not associated with a southward expansion of the Mediterranean winter rains. However, the monsoons reached as far as southern Israel, so that all of the eastern and central Sahara received rainfall. It is possible that northwestern Africa remained arid somewhat longer. The western Sahara was not populated until about 7000 B.P., when Mediterranean faunal elements indicate that the desert had finally, if temporarily, disappeared.

Rainfall was not consistently high in the tropics. Most lake levels fell at about 7500 B.P.; they had recovered by 7000 B.P. but were not so high as before, and in both eastern and western Africa, rainfall became more seasonal. Aridity had begun to increase throughout the continent by 4500 B.P. The eastern Sahara had already been long abandoned, except for the massifs and the great oases, and even the western Sahara was unoccupied after 4–3000 B.P. The retreat of the rainforests before the encroaching savanna, beginning around 3500–3000 B.P., may have been a factor in the synchronous Bantu expansion. There have been later, more humid episodes, but they have been brief, localized, and comparatively minor.

Environmental variations in southern Africa were initially the reverse of those farther north. Thus, after being more humid during the maximum cold of the Last Glaciation, southern Africa became drier at about 12,000 B.P., and the major Holocene wet phase was not established until about 9000 B.P. Thereafter, most of the southern part of the continent generally was in phase with the rest of Africa, the wet period ending by about 4000 B.P.

[See also MEGAFAUNAL EXTINCTION; PALEOENVIRONMENTAL RECONSTRUCTION; PLEISTOCENE.]

■ J. A. Allan, ed., *The Sahara. Ecological Change and Early Economic History* (1981). F. A. Street-Perrott and N. Roberts, "Fluctuations in Closed Basin Lakes as an Indicator of Past Atmospheric Circulation Patterns," in *Variations in the Global Water Budget*, ed. F. A. Street-Perrott, M. Beran, and R. Ratcliffe (1983), pp. 331–345. Richard G. Klein, ed., *Southern African Prehistory and Palaeoenvironments* (1984). P. D. Tyson, *Climatic Change and Variability in Southern Africa* (1986). A. T. Grove, "Africa's Climate in the Holocene," in *The Archaeology of Africa: Food, Metals and Towns*, ed. Thurstan Shaw, Paul Sinclair, Bassey Andah, and Alex Okpoko (1993), pp. 32–42. J. Maley, "The Climatic and Vegetational History of the Equatorial Regions of Africa during the Upper Quaternary," in *The Archaeology of Africa: Food, Metals and Towns*, ed. Thurstan Shaw, Paul Sinclair, Bassey Andah, and Alex Okpoko (1993), pp. 43–52.

Angela E. Close

HOLOCENE ENVIRONMENTS IN THE AMERICAS

About 12,000 years ago, prior to the onset of the Holocene, there was a general warming trend throughout North America. This decreased the area and thickness of the Laurentide ice sheet. By 12,000 years ago, the prevalent anticyclonic winds, which probably dominated the climates of the western United States during the glacial maximum, weakened, so that more dominant westerly winds began to blow across the United States. Reduction of the ice sheet and the accompanying warming trend reduced the spruce forests of the midwestern United States and eliminated spruce from southerly regions, such as Texas. In the western and southwestern United States, alpine woodlands that had extended their range downslope during the glacial maximum were now in full retreat and were soon restricted to higher elevations. In the same regions, shallow playa lakes

dried, and surface levels in larger lakes, such as Lake Bonneville, were dropping. In the southeastern United States, mixed deciduous forests were expanding into regions that had once been dominated by conifer forests of spruce or fir.

By the beginning of the Holocene, at 10,000 years ago, an increase in summer insolation raised temperature averages by as much as 36 to 39° F (2–4° C) in much of *North America, except in northeastern Canada, where a smaller and thinner remnant of the Laurentide ice sheet still existed. Nevertheless, the remaining ice sheet continued to influence the Early Holocene climate of North America. As the remaining ice sheet in North America and alpine glaciers in South America melted, sea levels rose, causing flooding in many low-lying coastal areas. Early Holocene precipitation levels in North America and in tropical regions of *Central and *South America were higher than present levels; however, by 9,000 years ago there was a reverse pattern in the southern temperate regions of South America, where rainfall levels decreased. A weak glacial anticyclonic wind pattern was still present in the eastern regions of North America. However, subtropical highs over the Pacific Ocean strengthened and created a dominant westerly wind pattern across the western and central portions of North America and throughout most of South America. By the Early Holocene, climates in most areas of North America were becoming similar to climates in those regions today. Exceptions were northeastern North America and continental alpine regions, where climatic conditions remained colder than they are at present due to the effects of remaining ice sheets or alpine glaciers. Southerly, warm, monsoonal winds began flowing northward from the Gulf of Mexico during the Early Holocene into adjacent regions of Central and North America. Overall, the improving climatic conditions throughout the Americas created modern biomes, similar to those of the present, by 8000 years ago. The major exceptions were in some regions of South America, where mesic forests reached their greatest expansion.

In much of North and South America, the Early Holocene climatic conditions continued until around 6,000 years ago, when precipitation levels began to drop below present-day levels. Summer temperatures continued to rise in interior North America and soon reached a maximum average 36–39° F (2–4° C) higher than temperatures in those regions today. The effects of these climatic changes led to elevational rises of traditional lowland biomes upslope in mountainous regions and led to the formation of dunes and stream erosion in areas of arid lowlands. Similar patterns occurred in South America, where lake levels dropped in response to warmer climates and higher evaporation rates. By 6,000 years ago, the southerly winds from the Gulf of Mexico strengthened, while in the west and midwest strong westerlies prevailed. The Middle Holocene rise in summer temperatures, coupled with increased evaporation caused by the hot, dry westerly winds, reduced the remaining forested and parkland areas in the central part of North America and allowed prairies to expand to their maximum size. In the southern areas of South America, warmer conditions during the Middle Holocene reduced the expanse of mesic forests and created an expansion of grasslands. In North America, the southern boundary of spruce forests receded to its northernmost latitude and treeline during the Holocene.

By the Late Holocene (ca. 3000 B.P.–present), summer temperatures and evaporation levels in the interior of North and South America gradually decreased from their Middle

Holocene highs to the levels currently found in these regions today. During this time period, the strength of the westerlies weakened in North America, but today they still blow from essentially the same direction. Along the northern border of the United States, spruce forests began moving southward to their present boundary in these regions of North America. The boundaries of the present biomes in the Western Hemisphere were in place by 1,000 years ago in almost all regions.

[*See also* MEGAFAUNAL EXTINCTION; PALEOENVIRONMENTAL RECONSTRUCTION; PLEISTOCENE.]

■ J. Rabassa, *Quaternary of South America and Antarctic Peninsula*, vol. 1 (1983). V. M. Bryant and R. G. Holloway, *Pollen Records of Late-Quaternary North American Sediments* (1985). COHMAP Members, "Climatic Changes of the Last 18,000 Years: Observations and Model Simulations," *Science* 241 (1988): 1043–1052.

Vaughn M. Bryant

HOMO ERECTUS is a species of early human that appeared approximately 1.8 million years ago and survived until at least 250,000 years ago. It was the first early human to be found not only in Africa but also in eastern Asia and arguably in Europe. *Homo erectus* differed in a number of ways from its australopithecine antecedents. It was both heavier and taller than these earlier hominids and had a more linear body form. Its legs were longer in relation to its trunk length, which suggests, as do other aspects of its anatomy, that it was more efficient in walking on two legs. There was less sexual dimorphism, or difference in size between males and females, and its brain was also larger than the australopithecine brain. The average brain size, or cranial capacity, of *Homo erectus* was 50 cubic inches (820 cc), about midway between that of the gracile australopithecines (about 27 cubic inches, or 440 cc) and that of living modern humans (about 76 cubic inches, or 1250 cc). *Homo erectus* was also the first early human to have a projecting nose. The projecting nose has been interpreted as a condenser to reclaim moisture from exhaled air. This would have been highly important in maintaining the water balance of these early humans under the relatively open, hot, and dry conditions of eastern Africa where they are assumed to have evolved.

Other *Homo erectus* features included a long, low skull with large brow ridges over the eyes and a sagittal ridge, or keel, on the top of the cranium. The face was larger than that of modern humans. It was also more projecting, and there was no chin on the mandible. Many *Homo erectus* fossils have unusually thick bone not only in their skulls but also throughout the rest of their skeletons. Although they were fully adapted to upright walking, the *Homo erectus* pelvis and thigh bone (femur) were different enough from those of modern humans to suggest a form of bipedal locomotion that was different from what we see today.

Homo erectus in the Far East. The name *Homo erectus* did not come into use until the 1940s, when Ernst Mayr revised and simplified the classification of early humans. Prior to this time, fossils that we now recognize as *Homo erectus* were included in a number of taxa among which the most important were *Pithecanthropus erectus* from Java and *Sinanthropus pekinensis* from China.

Pithecanthropus erectus was the name given to the first discovered *Homo erectus* fossils, which were found by Eugene Dubois in 1891 and 1892 at the site of Trinil on the Solo River in Java. Further Javanese discoveries were made between 1936 and 1941 by G.H.R. von Koenigswald at the sites

of Modjokerto in eastern Java and Sangiran near Trinil. Additional fossils came to light between 1952 and 1975 and have been reported by the Indonesian scientists S. Sartono and T. Jacob. These included a skull from the locality of Sambungmachan and another from Sangiran (Sangiran 17), one of the most complete *Homo erectus* skulls known. In 1993 another relatively complete skull (Skull IX), was recovered from Sangiran and reported by S. Sartono and two American anthropologists, Grover S. Krantz and Donald E. Tyler.

The age of the Javanese *Homo erectus* has always been uncertain. The material comes from two geological formations, the Kabuh Formation, which is believed to be between 0.5 and 0.7 million years old, and the Pucangan Formation, which underlies it and is older. Until recently, material from this underlying formation had been assumed to be no older than 1 million years. But recent *potassium-argon dating of deposits from the sites of Modjokerto and Sangiran suggests that some of the *Homo erectus* fossils may be 1.8 million years old. This is as old as the earliest known *Homo erectus* fossils from Africa and implies that early humans reached eastern Asia almost 1 million years earlier than previously thought.

Homo erectus may have persisted until relatively recent times in Java. The eleven Solo (or Ngandong) skulls, recovered by von Koenigswald between 1931 and 1933, come from the more recent Notopuro Formation and may be younger than 100,000 years old. If this date is correct, it suggests not only that *Homo erectus* existed for over 1.5 million years in Java but also that it was still extant when modern humans began to appear in the eastern Mediterranean (Skhul and Qafzah in Israel) and possibly also in Africa.

Homo erectus fossils are also known from China and were originally assigned to the taxon *Sinanthropus pekinensis*. The first tooth was found at the site of *Zhoukoudian (formerly spelled Choukoutien) in 1923 by Austrian palaeontologist Otto Zdansky. In 1927 Davidson Black, a Canadian anatomist at the Peking Union Medical School, organized large-scale excavations at the site, first under the field direction of Birgir Bohlin and then under W. C. Pei. By 1937 these excavations had resulted in fossils of an estimated forty individuals. Black died in 1933 and was succeeded by the German anatomist Franz Weidenreich, who produced excellent plaster casts of the specimens and detailed anatomical descriptions. This was particularly fortunate because all of the original Zhoukoudian fossils were lost during the Second World War. Locality 1, the source of the original *Homo erectus* fossils from Zhoukoudian, dates between approximately 500,000 and 240,000 years old and has produced additional fossils in more recent years.

Since 1949, additional *Homo erectus* material has also been found at other Chinese sites, including Gongwangling (850,000–750,000 years ago), Chenjiawo (formerly Chenchiawo and dating between 590,000 and 500,000), and Hexian (200,000–150,000). Based on these presently accepted dates, Hexian is the most recent of the Chinese *Homo erectus* sites and suggests that *Homo erectus* lived at a time when more modern hominids were beginning to appear in China. These more modern archaic *Homo sapiens* include Jinniu Shan (300,000–210,000), Dali (230,000–180,000) and two skulls from Yunxian that are yet to be precisely dated. The dating evidence might imply that more modern hominids entered China from elsewhere. But these dates are close enough and there is enough error in their determination to leave open the possibility that *Homo erectus* evolved into archaic *Homo sapiens* in the Far East.

***Homo erectus* in Africa.** By far the most famous *Homo erectus* sites in sub-Saharan Africa are *Olduvai Gorge, Tanzania, and *Koobi Fora and Nariokotome in the Lake Turkana region of northern Kenya. In 1960, Louis and Mary *Leakey discovered a well-preserved *Homo erectus* skull cap at Olduvai Gorge (Olduvai Hominid 9), which was followed in 1962 by a fragmentary cranium (Olduvai Hominid 12) and in 1970 by a partial pelvis and femur shaft (Olduvai Hominid 28). Olduvai Hominid 9 from Upper Bed two is approximately 1.2 million years old, while Olduvai Hominids 12 and 28 from Upper Bed IV are between 730,000 and 620,000 years old. Between 1973 and 1975, Richard Leakey and his team uncovered a partial skeleton (KNM-ER 1808), two relatively complete skulls (KNM-ER 3733 and 3883), and other cranial mandibular and limb bones at the site of Koobi Fora on the eastern shore of Lake Turkana, northern Kenya. KNM-ER 3733 and 1808 are among the oldest of this material, dating to between about 1.8 and 1.7 million years ago.

In 1984 Leakey and his team recovered a nearly complete skeleton of a *Homo erectus* youth (KNM-WT 15000) from the site of Nariokotome on the western shore of Lake Turkana. This specimen is about 1.6 million years old. Based on its dentition and stage of skeletal growth, it would have been under 15 years old at death, and more probably between about 11 and 13 years old. Its inferred stature at death would have been about 5 feet, 3 inches (160 cm) and it would have been about 6 feet (185 cm) tall if it had lived to adulthood. Juvenile and adult body mass estimates suggest that it would have had the lean body form characteristic of modern humans living in the hot and dry east African savannas.

Homo erectus fossils have also been recognized from other sites in both northern and sub-Saharan Africa. From the site of Ternifine, Algeria, in northern Africa, there are three mandibles and a skull fragment (originally called *Atlanthropus mauritanicus*) which probably date between about 730,000 and 600,000 years. There are also mandibular fragments from Sidi Abderrahman, Morocco, and a mandible and cranial fragments from Thomas Quarries, Morocco, which are more recent, at about 500,000 years. From sub-Saharan Africa there is a cranial fragment from Gomboré II (Melka Kunturé), Ethiopia, dating between 1.3 and 0.75 million years. There are also a parietal fragment and temporal fragments from Omo, Shungura Formation member K, Ethiopia (1.3–1.4 million years ago); teeth and a femoral fragment from Lainyamok, Kenya (700,000–560,000 years); and various bones from Swartkrans, South Africa (1.0–0.7 million years ago). It is perhaps significant that *Homo erectus* gives way to more advanced archaic *Homo sapiens* at least 250,000 years earlier in Africa than in the Far East.

***Homo erectus* in Europe.** There is no direct fossil evidence that *Homo erectus* ever occupied Europe. The earliest specimen that has affinity with *Homo erectus* is the mandible from Dmanisi in Georgia that was found in 1991. The Dmanisi mandible is at least 900,000 years old and could be as old as 1.6 million years. But its location in Georgia, at the far eastern periphery of Europe, says nothing about human occupation in more western areas. The earliest fossil hominids from Europe date to 780,000 years ago and are from the Gran Dolina site at Atapuerca, Spain. There are also archaeological sites, unfortunately without fossil hominids, at Le Vallonet Cave and Soleihac in France and at Isernia La

Pineta in Italy, and Kärlich in Germany that may document human occupation in Europe at the beginning of the Middle Pleistocene and possibly much earlier. These sites are controversial in themselves, and there is no way of knowing whether the makers of the stone tools recovered from these sites were *Homo erectus* or another species of hominid.

Slightly more recent in time are a fragmentary tibia from Boxgrove, England, and a mandible from Mauer, Germany. Both of these date to approximately 500,000 years. The tibia is a massive bone from a relatively tall individual with an estimated body mass of about 176 pounds (80 kg), but is undiagnostic as to species. The Mauer mandible is also large and has affinities both with *Homo erectus* and with archaic *Homo sapiens*. The remaining European fossils from the Middle Pleistocene Period come from sites that include Petralona in Greece, Arago in France, Vértesszöllös in Hungary, *Bilzingsleben and Steinheim in Germany, Swanscombe in England, and Sima de los Huesos, Atapuerca, in Spain. All of these sites are more recent in time than Mauer or Boxgrove, dating between about 400,000 and 200,000 years ago. Although some of the more fragmentary finds, such as the occipital bone from Vértesszöllös and a frontal bone from Bilzingsleben, have been claimed to be *Homo erectus* in the past, this interpretation now seems unlikely. There are over 700 specimens belonging to at least 24 individuals that are currently known from Sierra de Atapuerca. These fossils show a mixture of features, some of which are found in *Homo erectus* and others in the more recent European *Neanderthals. The degree of intrapopulation variation observed in these specimens suggests that the features found in the more fragmentary European Middle Pleistocene material can all be accounted for in one contemporaneous population that is more advanced than *Homo erectus* but still retains some *Homo erectus* features.

The Origin of *Homo erectus*. The earliest dates for *Homo erectus* are 1.8 million years ago for the material from Koobi Fora, Kenya, and Modjokerto, Java. There is a rich hominid fossil record in Africa that currently extends back to 4.4 million years (*Ardipithecus ramidus*), but there are no known earlier hominids in the Far East. Because of this, it is most probable that *Homo erectus* evolved in Africa and migrated from there to the Far East. If the 1.8 million years date for the infant's skull from Modjokerto proves to be correct, *Homo erectus* would have had to have departed Africa shortly after its first appearance. At present, its most likely precursor in Africa is *Homo habilis*, a hominid with a brain size of about 30.5 cubic inches (500 cc) and an australopithecine-like skeleton with relatively short legs in relation to arms and inferred body weight. But certain features of its skull, such as the form of its occipital region and of its brow ridges, foreshadow *Homo erectus*.

If *Homo erectus* did leave Africa sometime before 1.8 million years ago, this would explain one of the mysteries surrounding the distribution of the Acheulian, or hand-axe, tool tradition. This tool tradition is associated with *Homo erectus* in Africa and is also found throughout Europe and as far east as India, but it is not found further to the east in Asia. The Acheulian does not appear until 1.4 million years ago in Africa. If *Homo erectus* left Africa sometime prior to 1.8 million years ago, it would have been before the appearance of this distinctive tool tradition.

The fact that the *Acheulian tradition never spread to the Far East might have one of two explanations. It is possible that once the hominids reached the Far East, there was minimal communication with other hominid populations in the more western areas. Alternatively, it is also possible that tools equivalent to the distinctive Acheulian hand axe were made of other materials in the East, such as bamboo.

Questions about *Homo erectus*. There has been considerable debate in recent years over whether or not the African fossils should be included in the taxon *Homo erectus* or whether this taxon should be used to refer only to the fossil material from eastern Asia. Bernard Wood has recently suggested that the oldest African *Homo erectus* fossils from Koobi Fora and Nariokotome, Kenya, should be included in the taxon *Homo ergaster* and not *Homo erectus*. He argues that although these fossils have reached the *Homo erectus* grade of evolution, they are very primitive in relation to the Asia *Homo erectus* fossils. The African fossils lack the very thick bone throughout the skeleton that characterizes the Asian forms, and they also lack certain details of the skull, such as thick brow ridges or an angular torus, that have been considered diagnostic of *Homo erectus*. Other palaeoanthropologists, such as Chris Stringer and Peter Andrews, have also argued that there are such fundamental distinctions between Asian and African *Homo erectus* fossils that none of the African forms should be classified as *Homo erectus*. Rather, they suggest that the African forms be called archaic *Homo sapiens*. This is a minority opinion, however, and many palaeoanthropologists follow Philip Rightmire in suggesting that the type of variation in cranial form that exists between Asian and African fossils would be expected in such a species as *Homo erectus*, a species with a large temporal and geographical distribution.

[See also AFRICA: PREHISTORY OF AFRICA; AUSTRALOPITHECUS AND HOMO HABILIS; CHINA: STONE AGE CULTURES OF CHINA; EUROPE, THE FIRST COLONIZATION OF; HUMAN EVOLUTION: FOSSIL EVIDENCE FOR HUMAN EVOLUTION; HUMANS, MODERN: PEOPLING OF THE GLOBE; PALEOLITHIC: LOWER AND MIDDLE PALEOLITHIC; PLEISTOCENE.]

■ Richard G. Klein, *The Human Career: Human Biological and Cultural Origins* (1989). G. Philip Rightmire, *Homo Erectus: Comparative Anatomical Studies of an Extinct Human Species* (1990). G. Philip Rightmire, "*Homo erectus*: Ancestor or Evolutionary Side Branch?" *Evolutionary Anthropology* 1 (1992): 43–49. L. Tianyuan and D. A. Etler, "New Middle Pleistocene Hominid Crania from Yunxian in China," *Nature* 357 (1992): 404–407. B. A. Wood, "Origin and Evolution of the Genus *Homo*," *Nature* 355 (1992): 783–790. M. B. Roberts, C. B. Stringer, and S. A. Parfitt, "A Hominid Tibia from Middle Pleistocene Sediments at Boxgrove, UK," *Nature* 369 (1994): 311–313. C. C. Swisher, G. H. Curtis, T. Jacob, A. G. Getty, and A. Suprijo, "Age of the Earliest Known Hominids in Java, Indonesia," *Science* 263 (1994): 1118–1121.

Leslie C. Aiello

HOMO SAPIENS, Archaic. This term is used widely to denote a category or grade of *Homo sapiens* including fossil hominids which are anatomically more evolved than *Homo erectus* but still archaic looking and different from modern *Homo sapiens*. In most cases archaic and modern *Homo sapiens* specimens can be clearly distinguished from each other. For example, continuously running ridges above the orbits (supraorbital tori) are a characteristic of the former and are almost completely missing in the latter.

In contrast, it is more difficult to draw a line between late *Homo erectus* and early archaic *Homo sapiens*, since this transition shows a rather continuous mosaic-like pattern. Specimens from this period usually exhibit individual combinations of *erectus*-like and progressive *sapiens* features. An example of the difficulties in classifying such hominids is the Bodo cranium from Ethiopia, often considered an archaic *Homo sapiens* but most recently dated back to ca. 0.6 million years B.C.—the later *erectus* period in Africa.

The term "archaic *Homo sapiens*" designates a broad grade of human evolution which existed in Africa, Europe, and the Far East. Taxonomically it is less clear which subspecies or even species should be subsumed under this heading. Some researchers regard the Neanderthals as a separate species, whereas others include them within archaic *Homo sapiens*. The classification of the Ngandong hominids from Indonesia is also equivocal: they are either assigned to *Homo sapiens soloensis* (i.e., a subspecies of archaic *Homo sapiens*) or *Homo erectus soloensis*. These and other disagreements reveal the difficulties in defining the *erectus/sapiens* boundary and in defining the taxonomic level at which subgroups of archaic *sapiens* should be separated. The fossil record indicates that early archaic *Homo sapiens* appeared in Africa and Europe around 400,000 years ago and in East Asia between 200,000 and 300,000 years ago. These transitions probably occurred to a great extent independently in different regions, but relevant gene flow (e.g., into East Asia) might also have been involved. The assumption of several regional transitions is understandable only if the *erectus/sapiens* border does not distinguish between two different biospecies but only between morphologically defined palaeospecies, as many specialists assume. Archaic *Homo sapiens* evolved in different ways on the various continents.

In general, archaic *Homo sapiens* can be characterized by a further increase in cranial capacity reaching modern human conditions in later specimens. In contrast to *Homo erectus* there are also several changes in cranial shape. Among these are the more vertically oriented lateral walls of the skull, a less strongly angulated occipital bone with a more vertical upper part, and a tendency for reduced projection of the supraorbital and occipital tori. Besides these and other general trends there are also more specific features characteristic of the different regional lineages of archaic *Homo sapiens*.

In Europe, archaic *Homo sapiens* (ca. 400,000 to 30,000 years B.P.) shows a rather continuous evolutionary sequence which can be divided into three grades: Anteneanderthals, early Neanderthals, and late Neanderthals. The Anteneanderthals, especially known from France (Arago), Spain (Atapuerca), Greece (Petralona), England (Swanscombe), and Germany (Steinheim), date from about 400,000 to 200,000 years B.P. Besides derived (specialized) *sapiens* features, they reveal a considerable variability (e.g., in facial shape) even within a sample from one single site such as Atapuerca. Nevertheless, the Anteneanderthals exhibit various Neanderthal features and are followed by early Neanderthals, as from Biache St. Vaast (France) or Saccopastore (Italy), dating from around 200,000 to 70,000 years B.P. The early Neanderthals are clearly more similar to the subsequent late Neanderthals. This latter group is widely known from Europe and West Asia and exhibits many specialized features of the cranium and postcranium which also reflect adaptation to Ice Age conditions. Neanderthals lived up to around 32,000 years ago when they were replaced in the course of a few thousand years by anatomically modern humans.

African archaic *Homo sapiens* (ca. 400,000–130,000 years B.P.) can be subdivided into the early and late archaic grades which show an evolutionary sequence very different from that in Europe. Instead of an increase in robusticity leading to the massively built Neanderthals, a modernization of the skull shape can be observed from early to late archaics in Africa. While in Europe the evolution toward the late Neanderthals was still under way, the process in Africa had already led to the origin of anatomically modern humans about 130,000 years ago. The fossil record of archaic *Homo sapiens* in Africa has been enlarged and the dating has improved over the last two decades. Relevant early archaic specimens (ca. 400,000—200,000 years B.P.) come from South Africa (Elandsfontein), Zambia (Kabwe), Tanzania (Ndutu, Eyasi), and Morocco (Salé). Well-preserved late archaics (ca. 200,000–130,000 years B.P.) were found in South Africa (Florisbad), Tanzania (Laetoli), Kenya (Eliye Springs), Ethiopia (Omo Kibish 2), and Morocco (Jebel Irhoud). Among this latter group are specimens, such as Laetoli H. 18 or Florisbad, which can be regarded as close to the threshold of modern humans. Thus, it is both the occurrence of anatomically modern specimens around 130,000 years ago and the rather well-established archaic *Homo sapiens* sequence in Africa that document the process of an early origin of modern humans on this continent.

Although the fossil record is more sparse in the Far East, there are a number of specimens, especially from China, that clearly belong to the evolutionary grade of archaic *Homo sapiens* and date roughly between 280,000 and 100,000 years B.P. Among the better-preserved specimens are the skeleton from Jinniushan, the complete cranium from Dali, and the cranial fragment from Maba. There is little evidence from the time period after 100,000 years until the appearance of the first fully modern humans at around 30,000 years ago. As the Dali specimen dates to 150,000 or 200,000 years, and is quite robust, having strongly developed supraorbital tori, it is difficult to document any clear trends within the Chinese archaic *sapiens* material. Another problem is the *erectus/sapiens* transition in this region. As late *erectus* specimens, such as the cranium from Hexian, appear to date to only 200,000 years ago it would be remarkable if the more derived archaic *sapiens* individual from Jinniushan (probably 280,000 years old) had evolved directly from this lineage. In this context, scholars have debated whether there were relevant influences by other archaic *Homo sapiens* populations from the west or whether this transition was primarily a regional phenomenon.

From Indonesia it is the Ngandong cranial series which has been assigned by several authors to archaic *Homo sapiens*. Recent U-Series dating points to an age of only about 100,000 years for this material. Morphologically the crania show some derived *sapiens* features (e.g., in the supraorbitals). On the other hand, the total morphology exhibits similarities so close to Indonesian *Homo erectus* that some authors prefer a grouping within this species. As with China, there is a gap in the fossil record here until the first modern humans appear some 40,000 or 30,000 years ago.

Finally, there is one isolated cranium from the Narmada Valley (Hathnora) in India, which has also been classified as archaic *Homo sapiens*. It has not yet been absolutely dated but based on associated fauna it might derive from later Middle Pleistocene deposits.

Summarizing the different regional developments of archaic *Homo sapiens* it appears that only the African lineage led to anatomically modern humans. In Europe, there is a clear evolutionary sequence leading to the highly specialized Neanderthals which were relatively rapidly replaced by anatomically modern humans. In China and Indonesia, there are gaps in the fossil record between ca. 100,000 and 40,000 or 30,000 years B.P., which preclude a

reconstruction of the evolution of later archaic *Homo sapiens* in these regions. Yet the present fossil record as well as other indications (*see* Origins of Modern Humans) make it unlikely that there were regional evolutionary lineages leading up to modern Chinese and Australians, respectively.

From the archaeological point of view, the transition between *Homo erectus* and archaic *Homo sapiens* cannot be defined. Early archaic *Homo sapiens* in Europe and Africa (e.g., Elandsfontein or Swanscombe) were associated with the *Acheulan tradition as was *Homo erectus*. Nevertheless, late Acheulan hand axes were more sophisticated and symmetrical in shape, revealing greater manufacturing skills. Many flakes were struck off a cobble to give it the right shape. While the hand axes themselves slowly lost their importance (possibly owing to the invention of hafting) a new innovative technology of tool production arose based on flakes that were removed from a preshaped core (Levallois technique). This change marked the transition from Lower to Middle Palaeolithic–Middle Stone Age in Europe and Africa and began at roughly 200,000 years B.P. It also coincided with the beginnings of late archaic *Homo sapiens* in Africa and early Neanderthals in Europe. Thus it was the Middle Palaeolithic–Middle Stone Age background that characterized both the evolution from late archaic *sapiens* towards early modern humans in Africa, and the development from early to late Neanderthals in Europe and West Asia. These large-brained late archaic people developed a variety of Mousterian and Middle Stone Age cultures. It is the Neanderthals that provide most evidence for the way of life, burying their dead and taking care of old and disabled group members. There is also evidence of grave goods and the use of pigment by Neanderthals. In China, archaic *Homo sapiens* is associated with unspecialized flake-tool assemblages accompanied by choppers, similar to the tool kits found with *Homo erectus* at Zhoukoudian. To explain the persistence of this techno-complex it has been suggested that the tools of these early East Asian communities were largely made from bamboo.

[*See also* HOMO ERECTUS; HUMANS, MODERN, *articles on* ORIGINS OF MODERN HUMANS, PEOPLING OF THE GLOBE; NEANDERTHALS; PALEOLITHIC: LOWER AND MIDDLE PALEOLITHIC.]

■ Günter Bräuer and Fred H. Smith, eds., *Continuity or Replacement: Controversies in Homo sapiens Evolution* (1992). Christopher Stringer and Clive Gamble, *In Search of the Neanderthals* (1993).

Günter Bräuer

HOPEWELL CULTURE. The first archaeological ruins recognized in the eastern woodlands of North America were earthen and stone burial mounds and earthworks. Lumped as "ancient monuments" for most of the nineteenth century, by 1900 significant cultural differences had been identified among them. Excavations in 1893 on the Hopewell family farm in southern Ohio renewed interest in them and their significance. At this remarkable site, the largest of its kind, were found burial mounds containing artifacts of rare beauty made of materials from far-flung places and associated with circular and square earthworks and a 111-acre (45-ha) enclosure. Sites with these properties, from that point on, were said to be part of the Hopewell culture.

*Radiocarbon dating of Hopewell remains has placed the culture in the period from ca. 200 B.C. to A.D. 400 (the Middle Woodland Period). Burial mounds range in size from individual interments measuring 9.8 feet (3 m) in diameter and

12 inches (30 cm) in height to Hopewell Mound 25, which measured 151 by 550 feet (46 by 168 m) at the base and 29.5 feet (9 m) in height and contained dozens of graves. The enclosed area ranges from less than 2.4 acres (1 ha) for some of the small circles to 123 acres (50 ha) for the entire Hopewell site.

Excavations over the last 200 years, especially in southern Ohio, in western Illinois, and along the middle Tennessee River, illuminate knowledge of Hopewell burial practices. In the Ohio area, Hopewell people chipped ceremonial daggers from obsidian acquired in the Rockies and cold-hammered copper from Lake Superior sources to make bracelets, broaches, necklaces, headdresses, and ornamental cutouts. Mica from southern Appalachia was cut into various forms and attached to clothing (skin and woven cloth). Buscyon shells from the Gulf coast were used as containers. Pipestone from local sources was carved to form effigy platform pipes, the bowls of which often depicted the region's common birds and mammals. Special ceramic jars, some of them imports from southern Appalachia, were present in most houses and often found in graves. Burial facilities included cremation pads, shallow earth-covered graves (sometimes lined with bark, stone, or logs), log tombs, and charnel houses.

By the 1960s, twelve varieties of this pattern were known within an area extending from the Great Lakes to the Gulf coast. The most prominent are the Scioto and Havana traditions of southern Ohio and western Illinois. Of these, the Scioto tradition Hopewell sites were found to contain the largest quantity and diversity of Hopewellian artifacts and nonlocal materials, all in cemeteries associated with geometric earthworks, such as Mound City, Liberty Works (Harness Mound), Seip, Hopewell, and Hopeton. This is the classic Ohio Hopewell Area.

The Ohio Hopewell settlement pattern was one of dispersed sedentary households and hamlets clustered around a ceremonial center. Ceremonial centers commonly contained earthworks in geometric shapes such as circles, squares, semicircles, arcs, and parallel walls. The orientation of some of these figures has suggested that Hopewellians recognized the cycles of the moon, sun, and Venus. In Illinois, the Havana Hopewell centered on the Lower Illinois Valley and was distinguished by a nucleated sedentary settlement pattern with burial mound cemeteries adjacent to or on bluffs overlooking settlements.

Linking regions was the practice of burying objects of value with the dead and covering the grave with earth. Copper, mica, and shell were highly valued materials in this ritual system and occur as raw material or artifacts well away from their source, especially north of the Ohio River, where this behavior evolved out of the *Adena culture. Some Hopewellian artifacts (mica, ceramic vessels, copper) extend across many regions and represent community-to-community exchange. Others, such as obsidian, have a spotty distribution and suggest individual treks. Sites containing Hopewell artifacts are located along prominent drainages and on optimal cross-country routes. Whether organized trade, chains of intercommunity exchange, or individual effort, some form of interregional interaction prevailed.

Strong regional differences in settlement patterns discourages generalizing about Hopewell social structure. Some archaeologists argue that Hopewell must have had a chiefdom type of society in which a single lineage dominates the social order, aggregating and redistributing resources through negotiation. Others have envisioned a more egalitarian system in which leaders emerged through achievement, as among modern tribal societies, and the structure was not institutionalized. Ranking within lineages has been demonstrated for Hopewell, but not differentiation between lineages, as would be expected of a complex society. And a case has not been made for specialization of labor.

Early archaeologists considered Hopewellians to have been farmers, and recent research has confirmed this. But, the major domesticated plants evolved from native species such as sunflower, chenopodium, polygonum, erect knotweed, and maygrass, not from maize and squash as first thought.

The raptorial bird motif characterizes Hopewell *art. In stylized form, eagles, hawks, and falcons were incised on ceramic vessels, etched on shell, cut from copper and mica, hammered into plaques of copper, and carved from pipestone. Bear and deer are common as well. Pipes are a common offering and may give a clue to at least one facet of Hopewell society. Pipe smoking was an important part of council sessions among Indian tribes in the historic era and may have functioned similarly in Hopewell society.

Hopewell represents a unique cultural heritage for which no counterparts exist today, although similarities have been noted with Northwest coast fishing communities of British Columbia and the Mapuche farmers of Chile. Arising among residentially stable horticulturalists with a rich tradition of craft art, Hopewell ritual demanded that a wealthy individual's most valued possessions be interred with him or her. The grave goods often include objects such as pipes or gorgets that were the deceased's "tools" of social intercourse and identify the individual as having had a high rank within the community. The largest of the ceremonial centers represent places where this practice was maintained the longest and are a monumental testimony to the stability of some Hopewellian communities.

Over two hundred years of research has not yet produced a complete picture or explanation of Hopewell. In particular, it is not known why this distinctive pattern collapsed and became extinct. Internal social conflict, climate cooling, population pressure, invasion, and adaptive transformation have all been cited as explanations, but none is accepted completely.

[See also MOUNDS OF EASTERN NORTH AMERICA; NORTH AMERICA: THE EASTERN WOODLANDS AND THE SOUTH; NORTH AMERICA, ORIGINS OF FOOD PRODUCTION IN.]

■ D. S. Brose and N. B. Greber, eds., *Hopewell Archaeology: The Chillicothe Conference* (1979). N. B. Greber and K. C. Ruhl, *The Hopewell Site: A Contemporary Analysis Based on the Work of Charles C. Willoughby* (1989). Robert C. Mainfort, Jr., ed., *Middle Woodland Settlement and Ceremonialism in the Mid-South and Lower Mississippi Valley* (1989). M. F. Seeman, ed., *Cultural Variability in Context: Woodland Settlements of the Mid-Ohio Valley* (1992).

William S. Dancey

HORSE, Domestication of the. The impact of the earliest domestication of the horse on human society must have been as profound as that of the invention of the steam engine, and yet we know very little about when, where, or how it happened. The increased mobility provided by the horse would have enabled people to move further as well as faster and to take more with them than ever before. They could exploit larger and more diverse landscapes, maintain larger families, and increase the range of their trade contacts. They could move into previously uninhabitable regions such as the Eurasian steppe. And since a man on foot is no match for a man on horseback, the military implications of horse domestication would have been revolutionary. John C. Ewers has shown how profoundly the introduction of the horse into North America changed Blackfoot culture. We should expect no less of its early domestication in central Eurasia. And yet, until recently, very little attention has been paid to this problem.

It is important to note, first of all, that wild horses, particularly as foals, can be captured and tamed and, as such, ridden, harnessed, slaughtered, and eaten without being domesticated. Aboriginal peoples throughout the world are known to tame all kinds of wild animals to keep as pets. There is no reason to think that this would not have been the case at least from the time of the earliest anatomically modern *Homo sapiens*. And when the need arose, taming would probably have been the first step toward domestication.

Though customarily defined as the controlled breeding of plants or animals by humans, the real distinctiveness of domestication lies in the fact that it involves ownership and thus results in a completely different level of human commitment than does taming or hunting. The social and economic implications of horse taming would have been, at most, superficial and localized, and would have disappeared with the death of the animals involved, while the repercussions of domestication would have spread throughout the whole society. What this means is that we are not simply trying to identify horse riding, traction, milking, and meat eating in the archaeological record, but rather, we are looking for evidence of horse breeding, which is, as such, archaeologically invisible. It may be approached indirectly, however, through an investigation of population structure, archaeological context, and other characteristics of the data.

Paleolithic Horse Exploitation. We have no convincing evidence that horses had been either tamed or domesticated during the Paleolithic. Paul Bahn has put forward iconographic and anatomical arguments propounding such a theory, but they are not supported by the available data. On the one hand, the evidence of cave art is inescapably ambiguous. On the other hand, the tooth wear anomalies Bahn has described as arising from crib biting or from rubbing against a strap could more easily be explained by bark biting, abnormal occlusion, or accidental chipping. Moreover, the stratigraphic integrity of sites excavated as long ago as La Quina and Le Placard—that is, around the turn of the century—is not reliable.

This does not prove that horses were never ridden in the Paleolithic or that they were not domesticated, but it does mean that we have no evidence at all that they were, or even could have been. On the other hand, there is strong evidence, based upon kill-off profiles from a series of relatively recently excavated sites—including Solutré, Feldkirchen-Gönnersdorf, Combe Grenal, and Pech de l'Azé—that throughout the Middle and Upper Paleolithic in western Europe horses were, in fact, hunted.

Evidence of Early Horse Husbandry. Horses are relatively uncommon in Mesolithic and Neolithic archaeological deposits. It has therefore commonly been held that they could not have been domesticated during those periods. On the other hand, relatively large quantities of horse bones and teeth have been recovered from Chalcolithic (or Eneolithic) sites on the central Eurasian steppe. Although other information, such as tooth morphology, population structure, representation of anatomical elements, and taxonomic distinctions based upon measurements are credited as evidence for horse domestication, until recently the real evidence has been that of the increased representation of horse remains at archaeological sites. In fact, until recently, the methodologies employed for interpreting the data have been seriously flawed. This is not meant as a criticism of past scholarship, but rather recognition that the analytical techniques of *zooarchaeology have progressed quite considerably in recent years.

Dereivka, an Eneolithic habitation site, is central to the problem of horse domestication. It is situated on a tributary of the Dnepr River in the Ukraine and dated between 3380 and 4570 B.C. (Sredni Stog, Phase IIa). Excavated by D. Y. Telegin (Institute of Archaeology, Kiev) between 1960 and 1983, Dereivka has been regarded as the site with the earliest evidence for the domestication of the horse. Moreover, until recently there was a consensus that horses had been raised there first of all for meat, but also for riding, the evidence being the remains of what have been described as bridle cheek pieces.

The methodological framework used to reach these conclusions was, however, the conventional but unsound one just described. Criteria used as evidence that the horses from Dereivka were domesticated include the following: (1) the absence of old horses, (2) the presence of a high proportion of male skulls, (3) the presence of objects identified as bridle cheek pieces, (4) the results of a morphological analysis comparing the Dereivka horses with other equid material, (5) their association with other domesticates—cattle, sheep, goat, pig, and dog—and (6) the relatively high percentage of horse bones and teeth in the deposit.

In reality, on the basis of archaeological, ethnographic, and ethological comparisons, the absence of old individuals is much more likely to indicate hunting than herding. Males would outnumber females either if bachelor groups or stallions protecting their harems were targeted in the hunt. The cheek pieces might not have been cheek pieces at all. The morphological study involved very small and disparate samples and produced contradictory results. The association of horses with other assumed domesticates is not evidence of horse domestication. In any case, they were also associated with the remains of wild animals. In fact, the most important criterion is the relatively high proportion of horse bones and teeth present at the site. This apparent change could also have resulted, however, from an increase in horse hunting by comparison with earlier sites.

Levine's reassessment of the data related to population structure indicates that the vast majority of the horses from Dereivka had been killed in the hunt. Moreover, D. W. Anthony and D. R. Brown have presented strong evidence of bit wear on the teeth of an individual from a ritual deposit, indicating that it most probably had been either tamed or domesticated and ridden. It is quite possible that this individual had been used to hunt wild horses for their meat. It may well have been the case that the development of horse riding allowed the inhabitants of Dereivka, located on the steppe/forest-steppe boundary, to intensify their exploitation of steppe resources such as wild horses. This could explain the increased representation of horses in Eneolithic deposits.

The Spread of Horse Husbandry. Our understanding of the spread of early horse husbandry is as bedeviled by obsolete methodologies as is the problem of its earliest domestication. It nonetheless seems clear that the period bridging the Copper and Bronze ages was characterized by important social and economic changes. These involved increased trade, the development of social ranking, and possible changes in land tenure, which may have been associated with a less egalitarian society. All of these could have arisen in connection with the increasing importance of the domesticated horse.

After the Early Bronze Age, although horses were apparently no longer killed in very large numbers, their wide distribution throughout Europe and their association with high-prestige human burials leaves no doubt as to their importance. Then, during the first half of the second millennium B.C., a series of conquests shook the ancient world. Egypt, Mesopotamia, Syria, Asia Minor, and India were overrun respectively by the Hyksos, Kassites, Mitanni, Hittites, and Aryans, charioteers who came from the north, bringing social and economic as well as military and political change in their wake. They all belonged to aristocratic federations, usually described as feudal in character, in which horses played a crucial role.

Throughout subsequent millennia, horse-powered polities were able to increase the scope of their conquests to encompass progressively larger geographical areas. During the first millennium B.C., the horse-riding tribes of the two Scythias, Europeans and Asiatic, controlled central Eurasia from the foot of the Carpathians to Mongolia. The horse-dominated military machine reached its apogee during the thirteenth and fourteenth centuries A.D. under the Mongols, whose empire at its greatest extent reached from Hungary to Korea. It was the largest continuous land-based empire in history. The horse was the main instrument of destruction in warfare until well into the Gunpowder Age, that is, until around A.D. 1500, when it was superseded by firearms.

This pattern was echoed in the Americas, where the power conferred by the horse and the terror it inspired played a crucial role in the European conquest. Moreover, the subsequent acquisition of the horse by the indigenous inhabitants of the New World transformed their own societies in ways that remind us of the beginnings of horse husbandry in Eurasia—for example, in the development of less egalitarian and more hierarchical social structures and in the increased exploitation of previously marginal ecological zones.

New Directions. Although progress has been made in the study of the development of horse husbandry, all the big questions concerning the horse's earliest domestication and subsequent diffusion still need to be addressed.

It seems that by the period 4500 to 3400 B.C., the horse had either been tamed or domesticated for riding in the Ukraine. No other region has been studied intensively enough for us to know whether such behavior was widespread, however, or developed earlier elsewhere, or whether it developed from a single or many loci. Research is now in progress in the Volga-Ural zone and Kazakhstan, but further work also needs to be carried out in the Carpathian and Caucasus regions adjacent to the steppe, the northern Black Sea coast, and possibly further west as well. Both widespread assumptions—that horse domestication must have evolved on the steppe and that it must have arisen out of a settled agricultural community—need to be challenged.

The problem of the evolution of social ranking in Europe has been debated extensively, but without taking the horse into the equation in any serious way. Data need to be collected that will help us to understand better the links between the dispersal of horse husbandry and the development of trade, warfare, and the differential distribution of wealth and power.

[*See also* CAMEL, DOMESTICATION OF THE; DOMESTICATION OF ANIMALS; HUNTERS OF THE NORTH AMERICAN PLAINS; LAND TRANSPORTATION: USE OF ANIMALS FOR TRANSPORTATION.]

■ V. I. Bibikova, "A Study of the Earliest Domestic Horses of Eastern Europe" (1967, 1970), reprinted in *Dereivka, a Settlement and Cemetery of Copper Age Horse Keepers on the Middle Dnieper*, ed. D. Y. Telegin (1986), pp. 135–162. V. I. Bibikova, "On the History of Horse Domestication in Southeast Europe" (1969), reprinted in *Dereivka, a Settlement and Cemetery of Copper Age Horse Keepers on the Middle Dnieper*, ed. D. Y. Telegin (1986), pp. 163–182. H. B. Barclay, *The Role of the Horse in Man's Culture* (1980). Juliet Clutton-Brock, *Horse Power* (1992).

Marsha A. Levine

HUACA DEL SOL (Shrine of the Sun) is one of the very largest platform mounds ever erected in South America, and it is the biggest solid mud-brick structure in the Andean cordillera. Constructed in the Moche Valley on the northern coast of Peru between the time of Christ (Moche Phase I) and A.D. 600 (the end of Phase IV), Huaca del Sol and the adjacent mound complex of Huaca de la Luna (Shrine of the Moon) dominate the archaeological type-site and political center of the pre-Hispanic Moche kingdom or polity. The settlement area exceeds 0.4 square miles (1 sq km) and is covered with thousands of looters' pits produced by centuries of grave robbing. Cultural deposits, up to 23 feet (7 m) in depth, comprise refuse, remnants of public buildings, residential quarters, and other architectural remains that are now buried by ancient flood deposits and aolean sands.

Colonial period looters diverted the Moche River against the west side of Huaca del Sol and hydraulically mined away much of the city and more than half of the great mound. The surviving eastern remnant measures 1,115 feet (340 m) north to south by 525 feet (160 m) and stands over 130 feet (40 m) high. If the platform had symmetrical sides, then Huaca del Sol was shaped like a giant cross in plan. In profile, there are four steplike sections of different height, each supporting courts, corridors, and other summit buildings. The first or lowest section was in the north. The second section is somewhat higher; it is also wider than the rest of the platform and gives Sol its cross-shaped layout. The third section is the highest, while the fourth is lower.

Hydraulic mining of Sol left a clifflike face exposing the core of the mound and revealing how the vast structure was built. Similar to later Inca practices, constructions relied on labor taxes levied upon communities; each subject settlement was required to contribute a gang of workmen. Construction was subdivided into numerous segments or modular building units, each assigned to a particular work gang. Each gang produced its own bricks, stamped them with a distinguishing maker's mark, and then laid the bricks in the assigned section to fulfill the community's work tax. Over the course of centuries, Sol underwent at least eight major stages of construction. At each stage, new summit structures were erected; these were used for a time before being built over. Garbage accumulated in some out-of-the-way quarters, indicating that people resided on the Huaca. These were most likely the ruling elites. If they were also buried in the mound, then the recovery of royal tombs is what later prompted hydraulic mining of the monument.

Some construction phases in Huacas Sol and Luna were

rebuilding episodes triggered by El Niño events that brought destructive deluges and flooding to the otherwise rainless desert. A severe flood struck the Moche capital late in its history, around A.D. 560, eroding away much of the city. The metropolis was rebuilt. It was then encroached upon and gradually buried, however, by massive sand dunes, which also swept across adjacent farm land. This fostered abandonment of the city and its Huacas during an era of widespread changes at the end of Moche Phase IV and the beginning of Phase V.

[See also ANDEAN PRE-INCA CIVILIZATIONS, THE RISE OF, articles on INTRODUCTION, EFFECTS OF EL NIÑO ON PERUVIAN CIVILIZATION; MOCHE CULTURE; SOUTH AMERICA: THE RISE OF COMPLEX SOCIETIES IN SOUTH AMERICA.]

■ Max Uhle, "Die Ruinen von Moche," *Journal de la Societe des Americanistes,* new series, vol. X (1913): 95–117. Rafael Larco Hoyle, "La Cronica y Variedades," *Los Mochicas,* vol. 1 (1938). Rafael Larco Hoyle, "Rimac," *Las Mochicas,* vol. 2 (1939). Christopoher B. Donnal and Carol J. Mackey, *Ancient Burial Patterns of the Moche Valley, Peru* (1978). Santiago Uceda and Jose Canziani Amico, "Evidencias de Grandes Precipitaciones en Diversas Etapas Constructivas de La Huaca de La Luna, Costa Norte del Peru," *Bulletin Instituto Frances Etudes Andines,* vol. XXII (1993): 313–343.

Michael E. Moseley

HUMAN EVOLUTION

Introduction
Primate Ancestors of Humans
Fossil Evidence for Human Evolution
The Origins of Human Behavior
The Archaeology of Human Origins

INTRODUCTION

The search for evidence and an understanding of human evolution began with the publication and increasing acceptance of Darwin's theory of evolution by natural selection in 1859. The subsequent history of the study of human evolution, or paleoanthropology, as it is currently known, has been an intertwined pattern of fossil discoveries and changing ideas.

Fossil Discoveries. The first fossils of ancient hominids were discovered in the 1850s, but were only placed into a framework after the *Origin of Species* was published. These were the *Neanderthals, a closely related form to modern humans. Discoveries by Eugene Dubois in the 1890s in Java of what he referred to as *Pithecanthropus erectus* (now called *Homo erectus*) provided a more distant ancestor, while discoveries in China in the 1920s by Davidson Black showed that fossil hominids were diverse and widespread. However, the real revolution in the discovery of evidence for human evolution came in 1924 with Raymond *Dart's description of the first early African hominid (*Australopithecus africanus*), the specimen from the site of Taung in the Transvaal. Although controversial at the time, this and subsequent discoveries in South Africa by Robert Broom shifted the focus for human evolution away from Europe and Asia to Africa, and subsequent research has continued to emphasize the central role that Africa has played in human evolutionary history.

While the period prior to the Second World War was dominated by finds in southern Africa, in the 1960s it was eastern Africa that proved to be the treasure house of human evolution. The Great Rift Valley, which stretches from Zambia to the Dead Sea, is a geological structure that combines the right conditions for fossilization with the right sorts of environment for the support of hominids. Louis and Mary *Leakey, Richard Leakey, Glynn Isaac, Andrew Hill, Don Johanson, Yves Coppens, and Clark Howell, among many others, have been responsible for the explosion of fossil evidence for early hominid evolution. Although in 1925 there was only one known African fossil hominid, now there are over two thousand.

While Africa, and East Africa in particular, have been the center of most interest, other regions have had both their great discoverers and great fossils. The Mount Carmel region of Israel has yielded a range of key later hominid fossils, while Neanderthals have continued to be discovered in many parts of Europe. The fossil record for eastern Asia has expanded, and in the last few decades the antiquity of people in Australia has been extended back well into the *Pleistocene. Not all fossils, though, have necessarily helped clarify the situation. In many cases dating or provenance has been confusing or ambiguous. In the classic case of the Piltdown skull, discovered in England in 1913, not only was the fossil misleading, but it was a deliberate fraud not exposed until 1953.

Changing Concepts. Piltdown demonstrates that fossils can be misleading, but it is also the case that fossils on their own do not tell the whole story of human evolution. Any understanding is dependent upon both the scientific methods available and the conceptual frameworks employed. Two examples of the impact of scientific techniques demonstrate the point. The first is the development of radiometric dating techniques, especially, in the case of human evolution, *potassium-argon dating and, more recently, electron spin resonance. These have provided a well-established time scale for human evolution and have shifted earlier speculation to a more precise discussion of actual rates of evolution. The second is the development of techniques drawn from molecular biology and applied by people such as Allan Wilson, Vince Sarich, and Morris Goodman to problems in human evolution. These in particular have established the very close human relatedness with African apes, and hence have provided a theoretical underpinning to the abundance of early African fossil evidence. Scientific techniques are also beginning to have a major impact in terms of the structural and chemical analysis of the fossils themselves—for instance, by providing good evidence for changing rates of growth during the course of hominid evolution.

In the same way that scientific techniques have developed and the fossil record has expanded, so too has the theoretical framework altered over the past 150 years. For the most part, the changes have reflected the development of ideas in evolutionary biology as a whole, but it is also probably the case that they reflect changing attitudes within society. This may be seen most clearly in the disappearance over the last fifty years of many of the central concerns of the founding evolutionary scientists: race is no longer seen as a useful or valid category for analysis, and human evolution is not viewed as an inevitable completion of the *scala naturae* in which most Victorians believed.

For most of the time since *Darwin a number of key questions have dominated. Fossil discoveries tended to focus on two in particular: How old is the human lineage, and where did our ancestors evolve? These questions have largely been resolved, with Africa located on current evidence as the site of both hominid divergence from the apes and the origins of modern humans. The scale of the evolutionary process for hominids is between 10 and 6 million years, but within this overall process, *Homo sapiens* is present for only the last 100,000 or 200,000 years.

Questions relating to time and place have tended to be considered in the context of phylogenetic issues—or who is related to whom. For the most part, this has been explored in terms of the evolutionary relationships between humans and other animals, or "man's place in nature," in T. H. *Huxley's phrase. Anatomy and genetics have established not only that humans are closely related to the apes, but that this relationship is far closer than had previously been thought. Whereas Darwin expected the problem to be one of tracing human ancestors further and further back into the remote past, it is the recency, in geological terms, that has turned out to be the surprise.

More recently, with the richer fossil record, attention has focused more on relationships among the hominids. During the first half of the century, there was a tendency among paleoanthropologists to describe every new specimen as a new species at the very least, and more likely as a new genus. Forgettable Latin names proliferated, with endless side branches along the course of human evolution. The introduction of the modern synthesis to anthropology in the 1950s radically pruned the human tree, and for most of the 1960s and 1970s, hominid phylogeny was greatly simplified. The current view is that the hominid evolutionary tree is extremely diverse, with many species present, especially in the earlier segment. The presence of several species has meant that there has been a rich debate about which ones are ancestral to modern humans. This has focused both on the first hominids (the australopithecines) and the more recent evolution of *Homo sapiens*, and has resulted in a far more rigorous methodology for reconstructing human evolutionary history as well as greater consideration of the evolutionary processes involved. While there is no complete consensus, there is general agreement now that hominid evolution is best described as a series of adaptive radiations rather than a unilinear progression toward modern humans.

Outside paleoanthropology, the development of evolutionary biology has a rather different focus. Evolutionary analyses are concerned not just with who is related to whom, but with function and adaptation. This has led to much greater research into the ecology and behavior of the fossil hominids, including attempts to reconstruct their environments, their ecology, their lifestyles, and even their social behavior. Such work has tended to be far more interdisciplinary, bringing in many comparative perspectives from the study of the primates and other mammals. As a result, a considerable amount is now known, for example, about the diet, the patterns of growth, and the energetics of extinct and evolving hominids.

This is a new emphasis and represents a considerable shift from the approaches of the early Darwinians and the exploring fossil hunters. It has brought the focus of the subject, however, very close to its original interest—explaining why humans evolved. As a result, there is now considerable evidence concerning the significance and timing of the evolution of key human traits: bipedalism, hunting, tool making, language, and intelligence. Attempts to unravel the roles of these various features are increasingly subject to empirical testing rather than simply serving as reflections of contemporary assumptions about humanity.

Hominid Evolution. Within the broad sweep of development, hominid evolution refers to the evolution of the classificatory family to which humans belong (formally, the Hominidae). This is traditionally understood to include humans, their ancestors, and other close relatives subsequent to the evolutionary split with their closest relatives, the apes.

Accordingly, hominid evolution begins around 7 million years ago. Genetic evidence indicates that humans are most closely related to chimpanzees in particular, and the African apes more generally. The close genetic similarity and estimates of the rate of genetic evolution suggest that the first hominids occurred in Africa between 8 and 6 million years ago. These dates have not been confirmed by fossil evidence yet. The first indisputably hominid fossils occur around 5 million years ago. These are in eastern Africa (the sites of Lothagam, Tabarin, and the Middle Awash), confirming the African origin of the hominid lineage, given that there is no fossil evidence outside Africa until younger than 2 million years ago.

These first hominids and subsequent ones known from the period down to 2 million years ago provide excellent evidence for the nature of early hominid evolution and the overall pattern of the path to humans. Known generally as australopithecines (formally, *Australopithecus*, of which there are several species recognized—*A. afarensis*, *A. africanus*, *A. aethiopicus*, *A. robustus*, and *A. boisei*), these creatures show characteristics that are both humanlike and apelike. It appears that all of them are bipedal, capable of upright walking on two legs, and this is generally thought to be the key characteristic that allows us to distinguish hominids from other apes. Apart from the anatomical evidence provided by such fossils as "Lucy," a relatively complete *Australopithecus afarensis* from Ethiopia dated to 3 million years ago, confirmation also comes from a set of footprints from a site in Tanzania called Laetoli; these show a track of bipedal prints that have been preserved from over 3.5 million years ago. The precise nature of the bipedalism is not fully clear, and a case can be made that it differs significantly from that found in modern humans.

In other ways the australopithecines are quite apelike, and are often best thought of more as bipedal apes than as human beings. Their brain size was seldom significantly larger than that of an ape, there is no evidence for any stone tool making, and they were confined ecologically to the drier zones of eastern and southern Africa. Furthermore, rather than being part of a single development leading toward humans, they actually display considerable evolutionary diversity, with several species occurring and with a number of distinctive adaptive traits. Among the most distinctive of these are the "robust" australopithecines, which are found in east and south Africa from about 2.5 million years ago. These are hominids, but are not ancestors of modern humans. Instead they represent a specialized side branch that developed massive teeth and jaws for processing coarse plant foods. They went extinct around 1 million years ago.

The pattern of early hominid evolution is best thought of as an adaptive radiation of apelike creatures, adapting to the increasingly dry environments of the late Miocene and Pliocene by bipedalism and a suite of other morphological and behavioral traits. Climatic deterioration, the loss of forests, and the expansion of open environments probably underlay the initial success of hominids and led to their evolutionary diversity.

Development of the Genus *Homo*. A more specifically human trend within hominid evolution does not occur until between 2.5 and 2 million years ago. It is at this point that the genus *Homo* is first found, again in eastern Africa. The key specimens come from sites in Kenya and Tanzania (*Olduvai Gorge, *Koobi Fora, West Turkana). These specimens show the beginnings of the enlargement of the brain above that found in living apes. Their faces are smaller and flatter, with reduced tooth size and an overall more modern morphology. The earliest forms are known as *Homo habilis*, a small-bodied hominid with many australopithecine features in addition to the larger brain. There is increasing evidence that there may have been more than one species of the early types of *Homo*, and that this may be a continuation and extension of the radiation of the African hominids.

By soon after 2 million years, though, the basic morphology and evolutionary lineage of *Homo* had been established by what is generally referred to as *Homo erectus*. This is a fully upright hominid with a much larger brain; it differs from modern humans by being relatively robust and possessing distinctive features such as a very pronounced brow ridge set on a low, sloping forehead. The key evolutionary significance of *Homo erectus* lies in the fact that it was this hominid that first spread beyond the limits of eastern and southern Africa and colonized most parts of the Old World. By soon after 2 million years, hominids had reached Java in southeast Asia, and probably by 1 million years at least, they were in the colder parts of Asia and the warmer parts of Europe.

With *Homo*, and especially *H. erectus*, there is evidence for more humanlike behavior. Tool making becomes established, as does some level of meat eating and hunting. Ecologically there is evidence of a more adaptable and flexible species, and there are good reasons for thinking that in other ways these hominids were behaviorally complex. Evidence, however, that they are not behaviorally fully modern comes from the fact that they grew at faster rates than modern humans (i.e., in a more apelike manner) and from the fact that their technology is remarkably conservative over vast periods of time and geographical areas.

Homo erectus is present from close to 2 million years ago to less than half a million years ago. From around this time, there is evidence for greater evolutionary change and geographical diversification. The ultimate product of this period of evolution was the appearance of our own species (*Homo sapiens*), but this is not the whole story. With *Homo erectus* as a very widespread species, isolation and local adaptations led to the development of anatomically distinct geographical populations. Each of these shows relatively separate patterns of evolution, although there is considerable controversy concerning the links between them and their subsequent evolutionary fate. In Europe, under conditions of intense cold associated with glaciation, the Neanderthals evolved in the period from 200,000 years ago. These have all the characteristics of local and well-adapted regional populations persisting for tens of thousands of years. Less is known about their counterparts in Asia, but in Africa the regional populations show a trend toward modern humans. It is most probably here that *Homo sapiens* evolved in a small population, between 150,000 and 160,000 years ago. After 100,000 years ago, these modern humans dispersed from Africa throughout the world, for the first time colonizing Australia and the Americas. There is considerable controversy about the extent to which regional archaic hominid populations from other parts of the world have contributed to the subsequent evolution of modern humans, but it is most likely that multiple dispersals both

from Africa and elsewhere over the last 50,000 years have created the pattern of human diversity we see today.

Overall, the emerging picture of human evolution shows that modern humans are a small part of a much larger evolutionary event (that of the hominids) occurring over a period of about 7 million years. Further, it is known that the early hominids were bipedal but probably more apelike than human in their behavior. Indeed, it was only with the emergence of *Homo erectus* that hominids began to show significant changes in brain size and behavior and move from being a strictly African to a panglobal species. Even then, it is only with the appearance of *Homo sapiens* in Africa around 150,000 years ago that fully modern behavior is observable and the archaic hominids disappear from the world. Furthermore, it is clear that throughout the course of hominid evolution, Africa has remained the center of evolutionary novelty.

[See also ANTIQUITY OF HUMANKIND: ANTIQUITY OF HUMANKIND IN THE OLD WORLD; AUSTRALOPITHECUS AND HOMO HABILIS; DARWINIAN THEORY; GENETICS IN ARCHAEOLOGY; HOMO SAPIENS, ARCHAIC; HUMANS, MODERN.]

Robert Foley

PRIMATE ANCESTORS OF HUMANS

Human beings belong in the superfamily Hominoidea, and hominoid origins are generally considered to have been about 30 million years ago in Africa. Fossil apes are known in some abundance from shortly after this time until the time of human origins about 5 million years ago. The earliest putative human ancestor is *Australopithecus ramidus*, from 4.5-million-year-old deposits at Aramis, Ethiopia. Following is an account of the fossil apes that predate this find and may have some bearing on human origins.

The earliest-known fossil apes are known from eastern Africa, spanning a period from 24 to 14 million years ago. This is the family Proconsulidae, and the first specimens of *Proconsul* were found by Arthur Tyndall Hopwood of the Natural History Museum, London, in 1933. He found just nine fossils from 19-million-year-old deposits at Koru, Kenya, but subsequently Louis *Leakey, the well-known anthropologist from Kenya, found many hundreds of *Proconsul* specimens from sites such as Rusinga Island and Songhor, in western Kenya. He described these in collaboration with Wilfred Le Gros Clark of Oxford University. Leakey recognized the distinctiveness of these fossils, erecting the family Proconsulidae, but David Pilbeam, working twenty years later at Yale University, attempted to group the different *Proconsul* species into lineages leading to living apes. This conclusion was discarded soon afterward, with the description of additional material from Kenya by Peter Andrews, when he put forward the now generally accepted view that the seven or eight species from the early Miocene deposits of Kenya belong to Leakey's family, Proconsulidae. These species lack most hominoid characters, but details of the morphology of the elbow region and the probable lack of a tail indicate that they were primitive apes. The earliest fossils that can be assigned to the family have been found recently by Meave Leakey at Lothidok in northern Kenya in deposits dated to about 24–25 million years ago, and the latest comes from Fort Ternan, also in Kenya, at about 14 million years ago.

Slightly later in the early Miocene at East Africa, the recently described *Afropithecus turkanensis* comes from the site of Kalodirr in northern Kenya. It was found by Richard and Meave Leakey, and it differs from *Proconsul* by sharing more advanced hominoid characters with later apes. In particular, it had massive canines and premolars, and it had a more robustly built and longer face than was present in the earlier fossils. The closely related *Heliopithecus leakeyi* from Ad Dabtiyah, Saudi Arabia, shares many of the same characters. A small collection was made from this site by Roger Hamilton and Peter Whybrow of the Natural History Museum, London, and additional material is needed to fill in the gap between proconsulids and later fossil hominoids.

Another fossil ape very similar to the afropithecines is the genus *Kenyapithecus*, an enigmatic and poorly known group of fossils from Middle Miocene deposits on Maboko Island and Fort Ternan in southern Kenya and Nachola in northern Kenya. Many of these specimens were again found by Louis Leakey, with additional material coming from excavations at Nachola and Maboko, and all are dated at between 15 and 14 million years ago. Interpretations range from grouping them all in the same species to putting them into different tribal groupings, but it is becoming accepted that they are distinct, either at the generic level or at a still higher taxonomic level.

At this stage of the Middle Miocene, the earliest hominoids outside Africa are encountered in Turkey, at the site of Pasalar, which is dated to about 15 million years ago. The huge collection of fossil hominoids from this site (well in excess of one thousand specimens) have been collected by myself and Berna Alpagut, of the University of Ankara, and we conclude that the species *Griphopithecus alpani* is very similar to *Kenyapithecus* from Fort Ternan and that the two genera should be grouped taxonomically. After this period, fossil apes become abundant in Europe and Asia and extremely rare in Africa, although the reasons for this are not known. For instance, the later fossil record in Africa can be summarized as follows: a single tooth from 12-million-year-old deposits at Ngorora; another single tooth from Lukeino, dated at about 8 million years ago; and an upper jaw from Samburu Hills, not yet named but clearly a new genus and species probably related to the gorilla. The age of the Samburu Hills deposits is between 8 and 4 million years ago.

One of the most common groups of fossil ape in Eurasia, from about 12 to 7 million years ago, is the lineage leading to the orang utan. Abundant fossils of *Sivapithecus* have been found by many field workers from Turkey in the west to China in the east, with the most notable collection being made by David Pilbeam and his colleagues, who have made large collections ranging from over 12 to about 7 million years ago in sediments on the Potwar Plateau in Pakistan. A nearly complete face complements a partial face from similar-aged deposits in Turkey, showing many similarities shared by *Sivapithecus* and the orang utan, so this lineage appears to have arisen some time before 12 million years ago. This branching point is frequently used today in calibrating molecular clocks, as is also the divergence date for the whole hominoid group from 30 million years ago. Many other fossils from Europe and Asia are now also put into the orang utan lineage, notably the large collection of skulls, mandibles, and teeth from Lufeng in southwestern China, *Lufengpithecus*.

Two other groups have also been grouped with the orang utan by some archaeologists. The species *Dryopithecus fontani* was the first fossil ape ever described, in the publication of the first specimens, which preceded Darwin's *Origin of Species* by more than twenty years. The earliest finds came from 12-million-year-old deposits in France, but more recently better collections have been made in Spain by Miguel Crusafont and in Hungary by Miklos Kretzoi. The main Spanish site, Can Llobateres, is between 10 and 9 million years old, and it has more recently been excavated by Salvador Moya-Sola and Meike Kohler from the Crusafont Palaeontological Institute in Sabadell. They have found a skull and parts of the skeleton of a single individual of *Dryopithecus* that they claim shares characteristics with the orang utan, leading them to group the fossil ape with *Sivapithecus* in the orang utan lineage. This view is hotly contested by David Begun and Laszlo Kordos, who together are working on the new collections from Rudabanya, the Hungarian site. This is the same age as the Spanish sites, and the species of *Dryopithecus* found there has many similarities to the Spanish species, although clearly they are not the same species. A skull has also been found recently at Rudabanya, and Begun and Kordos conclude that the morphology of this shows that *Dryopithecus* is first of all a member of the great ape and human clade, and secondly that it may have some affinities with the African apes as opposed to the orang utan. In both cases, there are morphological similarities justifying these opposing claims, and it is not clear at present which of these are based on homologous similarities and which are not. More detailed analysis of character polarity is necessary to resolve this conflict.

The last fossil to be considered is in some ways the most controversial of all. This is a collection from Greece, again from similar-aged deposits to Rudabanya and Can Llobateres, and the fossils have been named *Duranopithecus macedoniensis* by Louis de Bonis of the University of Poitiers in France. They are similar to the prior-named *Graecopithecus freybergi* described by the late Ralph von Koenigswald, and there is some disagreement as to which name is correct. A skull has recently been described in addition to the abundant jaws and teeth, and this shows characters of the nasoalveolar region and the hafting of the face on the skull that are found in living forms only in the African apes and humans. The orang utan is distinct in these characters, so de Bonis's conclusion is that *Duranopithecus* is part of the African ape and human lineage. He actually goes further and claims that it is directly ancestral to humans on the basis of reduction in size of the canine, but this conclusion is not justified by the slender evidence. In particular, it contrasts with the recently discovered *Australopithecus ramidus* in characters such as enamel thickness and relative canine size.

[*See also* AUSTRALOPITHECUS AND HOMO HABILIS; GENETICS IN ARCHAEOLOGY.]

■ Frederick Szalay and Eric Delson, *Evolutionary History of the Primates* (1979). Russell Ciochon and Robert Corruccini, eds., *New Interpretations of Ape and Human Ancestry* (1983). Bernard Wood, Lawrence Martin, and Peter Andrews, *Major Topics in Primate and Human Evolution* (1986). John Fleagle, *Primate Adaptation and Evolution* (1988). Ian Tattersall, Eric Delson, and John van Couvering, *Encyclopaedia of Human Evolution and Prehistory* (1988). Peter Andrews and Christopher Stringer, *Human Evolution, an Illustrated Guide* (1989).

Peter Andrews

FOSSIL EVIDENCE FOR HUMAN EVOLUTION

Although fossil evidence is our main source of information documenting the course of human evolution, it is not the only relevant evidence. This is particularly true in determining the antiquity of the human line. Analysis of DNA similarities and differences between humans and living apes suggest that humans separated from our closest living relatives, the African apes, sometime prior to about 6 million years ago. The earliest fossils that have been assigned to the human line are two small fragments of mandible dating shortly after this time from the sites of Lothagam (approximately 5.5 million years ago) and Tabarin (approximately 5.0 million years) in Kenya. The relationship of these fossils to the newly defined basal hominid *Ardipithecus ramidus* from Aramis, Ethiopia (approximately 4.4 million years ago) is as yet unclear. After 4.5 million years, fossils become more numerous and can be divided into two major groups, the australopithecines and early members of the genus *Homo*.

Australopithecines. The first australopithecine was discovered at the site of Taung in South Africa in 1924 and was named *Australopithecus africanus* by Raymond *Dart. Subsequently, many other australopithecine fossils have been found at other sites in southern and eastern Africa. The genus *Australopithecus* lasts for over 4 million years. There are currently six species recognized in the genus: *A. anamensis, A. afarensis, A. africanus, A. aethiopicus, A. boisei,* and *A. robustus*. The first three of these species are sometimes referred to as gracile australopithecines and the last three as robust australopithecines. Some researchers emphasize the difference between these two groups by putting the robust australopithecines in their own genus, *Paranthropus*.

The oldest australopithecine taxon, *Australopithecus anamensis,* was established by Meave Leakey and her co-workers in 1995 for fossils from the Lake Turkana region of Kenya. This taxon is approximately 4.2 to 3.9 million years old and differs from the earlier *Ardipithecus ramidus* in many details of its anatomy, including the thick enamel on its teeth. Its teeth are similar in some features to those of earlier representatives of the slightly later australopithecine species, *A afarensis,* but its postcrania appears to be more modern in form.

A. afarensis, was established by Don Johanson in 1978 and now includes fossils from Hadar, the Middle Awash, and Omo in Ethiopia, Laetoli in Tanzania, and *Koobi Fora in Kenya. *A. afarensis* spanned a period of almost a million years, from 3.9 to 3.0 million years ago, and occupied a variety of habitats, from relatively forested to open country. The most well-known *A. afarensis* fossil is a partial skeleton called Lucy (AL 288-1) that was discovered at Hadar in 1974. It shows that these australopithecines had skeletons that were very different from our own, with short legs in relation to their inferred body sizes and features of the hands, arms, and chest that suggest they were adept at climbing in trees. But features of the pelvis and legs confirm that they were also capable of bipedal locomotion. The well-preserved 3.6-million-year-old footprint trail discovered by Mary Leakey at Laetoli, Tanzania, is also clear evidence that they walked on two legs when on the ground.

The reasons for the evolution of bipedalism are still unclear. It has recently been suggested by Peter Wheeler of the Liverpool John Moores University that bipedalism is a thermoregulatory device. By walking upright, the australopithecines would have absorbed 60 percent less heat from the sun during the midday hours. This would have helped them to keep down their core temperatures, allowing them to forage in open environments for longer periods of time, while other animals would have had to seek shade. Alternatively, it has also been suggested that bipedalism first evolved as a feeding adaptation in the forest.

Whereas *A. afarensis* and *A. anamensis* are found only in eastern Africa, the third gracile australopithecine, *A. africanus,* is found only in southern Africa, at the sites of Sterkfontein, Makapansgat, Taung, and, more recently, Gladysvale. It is slightly more recent in age and dates to approximately 3 to 2.5 million years. *A. africanus* differs from *A. afarensis* in details of its skull, teeth, and feet; however, in other aspects they are so similar that Phillip Tobias of the University of the Witwatersrand has suggested in the past that they should only be separated at the subspecific level.

The main difference between these gracile australopithecines and the robust australopithecines is the large size of the jaws and teeth in the robust species. Fossils that have since been assigned to *Australopithecus robustus* were discovered by Robert Broom in the 1930s at Kromdraai and Swartkrans in South Africa. In 1959, fossils of a species with even larger teeth and jaws, *Australopithecus boisei,* were discovered by Louis and Mary *Leakey at Olduvai Gorge, Tanzania, and have subsequently been found at sites such as Lake Natron (Peninj) in Tanzania and Chemeron and Koobi Fora in Kenya. Both *A. boisei* and *A. robustus* first appear about 2 million years ago.

The evolutionary relationships of the australopithecines are highly controversial. However morphological features of *A. aethiopicus,* an early robust australopithecine discovered by Richard Leakey and his team on the western shore of Lake Turkana in Kenya in 1985 and dated to about 2.5 million years, suggest to some authorities an evolutionary link between the earlier *A. afarensis* and the later *A. boisei* in eastern Africa. Some would also see a link between *A. afarensis, A. africanus,* and *A. robustus* in southern Africa. The relationship between *Ardipithecus ramidus* and *A. anamensis* and these later species is currently unknown.

Early *Homo*. Early *Homo*, with larger brains and smaller teeth than the australopithecines, first appears at about 2.5 million years ago in Africa, about the same time as the first stone tools in Ethiopia and Kenya. Elizabeth Vrba of Yale University suggests that the appearance of early *Homo* at this time correlates with a period of worldwide climatic cooling. This is called the Turnover Pulse Hypothesis. She argues that as the climate changed, hominids as well as other animals would have had to adapt to increasingly arid and open conditions. Early *Homo* would have achieved this through the evolution of tool use, a larger brain, and an arguably more complicated social structure. The australopithecines would have adapted by alternative means, primarily through larger teeth and jaws that would have allowed them to process larger quantities of food of relatively low nutritional value. Although this idea is intriguing, John Kingston of Yale University has provided evidence based on stable carbon isotope analysis that the climate in Africa has not changed substantially throughout this period.

Whatever the reasons behind the evolution of the genus *Homo* and the diversification of the australopithecines, it is important to realise that *Homo* coexisted with the australopithecines in Africa for a period of more than a million years. There are currently three recognized species of early *Homo: Homo habilis, Homo rudolfensis,* and *Homo ergaster*. *H. habilis* was the first-recognized of these species and dates between about 2 and 1.5 million years ago. This species was established for fossils at Olduvai Gorge in 1964 by Louis Leakey, John Napier, and Phillip Tobias, and is now recognized at both Olduvai Gorge and Koobi Fora. *Homo habilis* has the smallest brain size of any of the early members of the genus *Homo* and has a skeleton that resembles that of the australopithecines, with relatively short legs as well as other features suggesting it was still adept in the trees. *Homo rudolfensis* appears at about 2.5 million years. It is a larger-brained species and is currently recognized at Koobi Fora, Kenya, and Uraha, Malawi. Although it has a larger brain size than *H. habilis*, it also has larger teeth and a face that retains some australopithecine features.

The third species of early *Homo, Homo ergaster,* is the only one that is indisputably advanced in its morphology over the other Plio-Pleistocene hominids. It appears about 1.8 million years ago and combines a large brain size with a humanlike skeleton that lacks any evidence of a continued life in the trees. The best-preserved specimen of this species is a remarkably complete skeleton (KNM-ER 15000) of a ten- to eleven-year-old youth that was found in 1984 at the site of Nariokotome on the western shore of Lake Turkana by Richard Leakey and his team. It clearly shows humanlike long legs relative to its inferred body weight and had body proportions similar to those of modern people who live in hot, dry climates. *Homo ergaster* is, at present, the most probable ancestor of the hominids that left Africa and spread into Europe and Asia.

Homo erectus. The first fossils that are now recognized as *Homo erectus,* a skullcap and femur, were found in 1891 and 1892 by the Dutchman Eugene Dubois, at the site of Trinil in Java. He gave the name *Pithecanthropus erectus* to this material. The skull was thick boned, with a flat forehead and large brow ridges and a cranial capacity of about 55 cubic inches (900 cubic cm). Many more fossils have been recovered from Java in subsequent years at the sites of Mojokerto, Sangiran, and Sambungmachan. Carl Swischer has recently provided new absolute dates of 1.81 million years ago for an infant skullcap from Mojokerto and of 1.66 million years ago for two specimens from Sangiran. These dates suggest that *Homo erectus* or its ancestors first reached Java at about the same time that *Homo ergaster* appeared in Africa, almost 1 million years earlier than most scientists would have suggested. These new dates also help to put into context the controversial date of 1.4 million years for a *Homo erectus* mandible from the site of Dmanisi in Georgia, material that was previously considered to be from the oldest non-African hominid.

In the 1920s and 1930s, fossils similar to *Pithecanthropus* were found at *Zhoukoudian in China. These were originally given the name *Sinanthropus pekinensis.* Recent thermoluminescence dating has established that Zhoukoudian was occupied by hominids between about 400,000 and 250,000 years B.P. More recently, similar fossils have been found at a variety of sites throughout China, such as Chenawo, Gongwangling, Lontandong Cave, Hexian Country, and Yuanmou, Jianshi. Fossils assigned to *Homo erectus* have also been found in northern Africa *(Atlanthropus),* South Africa *(Telanthropus),* Tanzania (Chellan Man), and Germany (*Bilzingsleben). All of these fossils are highly variable, and some scientists have suggested that they are too variable to represent one interbreeding species. This interpretation argues that *Homo erectus,* defined as only those fossils from Java and China, represents a completely different species than do contemporaneous fossils known from Africa and Europe. The more common interpretation is that these fossils represent one species and their diversity can be explained by the great geographical and temporal distances separating them.

Other more recently discovered fossils from China suggest that after 250,000 B.P., *Homo erectus* in the Far East begins to change into what is known as archaic *Homo sapiens.* These fossils, from the sites of Jinnu Shan (Liaoning Province), Yuxian (Hubei Province), and Dali (Shaanxi), show various combinations of thinner bone, larger brain sizes, more rounded skulls, and smaller, more modern faces. The fossils might indicate the movement of people from elsewhere in the world into China. Alternatively, they may indicate that *Homo erectus* in Asia evolved into archaic *Homo sapiens* with relatively little genetic contact with other areas in the world.

Archaic *Homo sapiens.* Archaeological and palaeontological evidence suggests that Europe was occupied by hominids at least by the beginning of the Middle *Pleistocene (750,000 B.P.) The most informative European Middle Pleistocene site is Atapuerca in northern Spain. This site has yielded the earliest European fossils (750,000 years ago) as well as over 700 hominid fossils representing at least twenty-four individuals from later deposits dating to about 300,000 years ago. These fossils show an interesting mixture of features, some of which are found in *Homo erectus* and others in the more recent European *Neanderthals. They also show a large degree of intrapopulation variation, suggesting that the features found in other isolated European fossils from this period such as Steinheim (Germany), Swanscombe (England), Arago (France), and Petralona (Greece) can all be accounted for in one contemporaneous population. They also establish that evolution in Europe during the Middle Pleistocene was moving toward the Neanderthals. Anatomically modern *Homo sapiens* must have arisen elsewhere.

The Neanderthals lived throughout Europe and the Levant from about 130,000 B.P. until about 30,000 years ago. They had squat bodies and short distal limb segments that can be interpreted as adaptations to cold, glacial conditions. One of the most complete Neanderthal skeletons was found at the site of Kebara, Israel, and this suggests that although Neanderthals walked on two legs, their type of bipedalism might have been different from that found in modern humans. The Kebara Neanderthal also has a fully modern hyoid bone, indicating that it most probably had a larynx (voice box) that was capable of producing the full range of modern speech sounds. One of the most recent Neanderthals comes from the site of Saint Cesaire in France and dates to about 36,000 years ago. Archaeological evidence from other sites such as El Castilla and L'Arbreda Caves (Spain) suggests that modern humans appeared in Europe before the Neanderthals disappeared and may have coexisted with them for perhaps 5,000 years. The fate of the Neanderthals is unknown, although it is likely that they were either replaced by or genetically absorbed into these modern populations.

Europe is not the only place that the Neanderthals seem to have been contemporaneous with modern humans. In the Levant, anatomically modern humans first appear at about 100,000 B.P. and are known from the sites of Qafzeh and Skhul in Israel. Neanderthals are also known from this period or possibly earlier, from the site of Tabun, and are found, in addition, in more recent sites, such as Kebara and Amud in Israel and Shanidar in Iraq. There is considerable controversy over whether these fossils represent two separate and discrete, noninterbreeding species or whether they represent two populations of humans and show evidence of interbreeding.

The only other area of the world where there are such

early dates for modern humans is Africa. Here fossils from sites such as Omo in Ethiopia as well as Border Cave and *Klasies River Cave in southern Africa are about 100,000 years old and have been interpreted as modern in form. These fossils appear to be the end of a continuum of evolution that begins with *Homo erectus* in the form of Olduvai Hominid 9 (Chellan Man), which dates to about 1.2 million years ago. By about 400,000 or 300,000 years ago, the African hominids are more modern than the earlier *Homo erectus* fossils, having larger brains and more rounded skulls. This trend continues through fossils such as Florisbad from southern Africa and Ngaloba from Tanzania, which may date between 200,000 and 100,000 years ago and up to the fully modern hominids.

This sequence suggests that while Neanderthals were occupying Europe, modern humans were appearing in Africa and the Levant. The evidence seems to be clear that these modern humans ultimately spread into Europe to replace the Neanderthals. But what happened in the Far East? It is possible that modern humans also spread eastward to replace *Homo erectus* in Java and China. Genetic evidence tends to support this idea. The apparent transitional fossils such as Jinnu Shan and Dali, which date earlier than the appearance of modern humans in Africa and the Levant, however, may indicate that the story is more complicated, involving not only population movement and hybridization but also local continuity and selection throughout the later part of the Middle Pleistocene and the Late Pleistocene periods.

[See also AUSTRALOPITHECUS AND HOMO HABILIS.]

■ R. G. Klein, *The Human Career: Human Biological and Cultural Origins.* (1989). B. Wood, "Origin and Evolution of the Genus *Homo*," *Nature* 355 (1992): 783–790. L. C. Aiello, "Human Origins: The Fossil Evidence," *American Anthropologist* 95 (1993): 73–96. J.-L. Arsuaga, I. Marínez, A. Gracia, J.-M. Carretero, and E. Carbonell, "Three New Human Skulls from the Sima de los Huesos Middle Pleistocene Site in Sierra de Atapuerca, Spain," *Nature* 362 (1993): 534–536. R. Lewin, *Human Evolution: An Illustrated Introduction*, 3rd ed. (1993). M. B. Roberts, C. B. Stringer, and S. A. Parfitt, "A Hominid Tibia from Middle Pleistocene Sediments at Boxgrove, UK," *Nature* 369 (1994): 311–313. C. C. Swisher III, G. H. Curtis, T. Jacob, A. G. Getty, A. Suprijo, and Widiasmoro, "Age of the Earliest Known Hominids in Java, Indonesia," *Science* 263 (1994): 1118–1121.

Leslie C. Aiello

THE ORIGINS OF HUMAN BEHAVIOR

While humans are distinct in the animal kingdom through a number of anatomical characteristics, it is their behavior that is most distinctive and sets the species apart. To some extent there is a high degree of integration between the anatomical features and the behavioral ones. For example, bipedalism allows the hand to become a specialized and highly dextrous organ capable of very complex manipulation; the large brain allows for massive levels of information processing and a wide range of creative and logical thought processes. Furthermore, the development of biology, especially neurobiology, is increasingly showing the interactions between cognitive and psychological states and biochemical activity. Behavior, therefore, cannot be divorced from the rest of the evolutionary process.

Such developments have important implications for the study of the evolution of human behavior. It is not the case that there is a replacement of biological evolution, focusing on hard anatomy, by cultural evolution, concerned with malleable behavior. Genes play a part in behavior, and therefore the operation of natural selection on behavior can be expected. The emergence of human behavior is an essential part of evolutionary biology.

A key problem is gaining access to information about the evolution of behavior. The starting point should be the behavior of living apes and monkeys, and much insight has been gained in recent years by the study of primate behavior in the wild. The primary impact has been to close the apparent gap between human and nonhuman capacities. Whereas it was once generally held that humans were unique as tool makers, hunting primates, language users, and social animals, it is now clear that these characteristics occur in other animals. Chimpanzees are known to use tools—twigs for extracting termites from their nests, stone hammers for cracking open nuts. They also hunt, both individually and cooperatively, probably obtaining more than five percent of their food from meat. All anthropoid primates are highly social, living in a variety of social systems, often held together by bonds of kinship. Their cognitive capacities vary between species and are difficult to assess, but studies and experiments have shown that some possess rudimentary language (meaning-specific sounds, context-dependent vocalizations, and, in chimpanzees, an ability to communicate grammatically using sign language). There also appear to be considerable abilities to employ innovative behavior, and both macaques and chimpanzees have been shown to possess "cultural traditions" within particular populations.

The behavior of living primate species cannot be applied uncritically to hominids. It is probably the case that the detailed behavior of each species is particular to it, and many errors have been made in the past by applying single-species models to early hominids. Chimpanzees, on account of their close relationship to humans, and baboons, due to their assumed environmental similarity with the australopithecines, have been extensively used in this way. However, what these studies do provide is an idea of the baseline from which hominids have developed their own unique characters. The most important conclusion is that this baseline is not that of a simple, asocial, and instinctive organism but that of an already highly complex mammal. In particular, it is likely that the first hominids lived in social groups, hunted and scavenged, and used rudimentary tools. More specifically, on account of their relationships with the African apes, it is likely that they were male-kin bonded with already extensive patterns of parental care.

Such inferences drawn from the primates need to be placed against the archaeological and fossil evidence, partly to determine the timing of events and partly to understand the reasons why certain characters evolved. The particular aspects described here are bipedalism, tool making, foraging behavior, and language.

Bipedalism seems to be the fundamental characteristic of the hominids, occurring earlier than other traits. It is found in the earliest australopithecines and is probably the unifying feature of the Hominidae. A number of explanations for the evolution of bipedalism have been proposed. Freeing the hands for tool making was *Darwin's original suggestion, but this seems unlikely in view of the later development of stone tool manufacture. More probable is that bipedalism is an energetically efficient response to the spread of nonforested environments between 10 and 5 million years ago. Apart from its locomotor efficiency in terrestrial environments, it has also been convincingly argued that it provides a number of clear thermoregulatory advantages in what would have been considerably hot environments. It is thus linked to other unique human traits such as copious sweating and loss of body hair.

As described earlier, chimpanzees use and make tools in the wild, and have been shown in captivity to be capable of making stone flakes. However, the first clearly recognizable stone tools do not appear until shortly before 2 million years ago, around the time of the appearance of *Homo.* An implication is that the early australopithecines were not consistent manufacturers of stone tools. The presence of stone tools provides considerable information about the capacities of the hominids: It has been suggested that they were predominantly right handed and capable of sufficient forethought to locate, extract, and modify natural materials. It is apparent that some at least were used in animal butchery. It is also the case that stone tool practices such as the *Acheulean tradition provide evidence for some form of cultural inheritance. In contrast, though, to these inferences of more human behavior, it should be noted that until the Upper Pleistocene, stone tool traditions show very little variation and are conservative over enormous geographical areas and time periods.

Evidence for changes in foraging behavior comes primarily from the archaeological record, and is therefore dependent upon the presence of stone tools. Additional information comes also from tooth morphology and wear, and more recently from chemical analysis of hominid fossil bones. The question of early hominid foraging has been one of considerable controversy in recent years. On one side, it has been argued that stone tools, cut marks on bones, and the association of stones and bones together is evidence for well-developed hunting behavior from the origins of the genus *Homo.* This has been used to support a model for the early appearance of relatively modern behavior, with only gradual change during the course of the *Pleistocene. On the other side, it has been claimed that such evidence is misleading, that only opportunistic scavenging and hunting of small prey occurred, and that it was only with the appearance of modern humans in the last 100,000 years that strategies akin to hunting and gathering were present. This interpretation has usually been associated with a model that contrasts markedly the behavior of all archaic hominids with that of modern *humans, and proposes some form of human revolution in the Upper Pleistocene associated with cultural, symbolic, or linguistic abilities. A number of intermediate positions can be held, but it is probably the case that in the past there has been a tendency to overemphasize the humanness of the early hominids.

Closely linked to this controversy has been the problem of language origins. Evidence for language has been inferred from basi-cranial anatomy, the structure of the brain in fossil endocasts, and archaeological evidence. Again, some have proposed that language can be traced back to earliest *Homo,* while others have argued that only *Homo sapiens* was capable of language, and that the explosion of art, tool making, and other cultural characteristics of the Upper *Paleolithic are evidence for this. Drawing on genetic and modern linguistic evidence, it is probably the case that all known languages go back to a common stock around 100,000 years ago, and that this would be the origin of modern languages, but it does not follow that other hominids, such as *Neanderthals, had no language or communicative skills. The fact that these languages have become extinct is not evidence for absence. Furthermore, it is clear from the enlargement of the brain that occurred from about

2 million years ago and accelerated from 400,000 years ago that archaic hominids were intelligent, social animals. As indicated earlier, the results of studying living primates shows that the baseline for hominids was considerable.

In the past, debates about the origins and evolution of human behavior tended to focus on alternative single-factor explanations—culture, language, tool making, and so on. More recently, and with much better chronological control, there has been a much more concerted effort to look at the interaction of several factors, and this has led to further controversy over the timing of particular events. These developments have led to a more ethnological approach drawn from the study of animal behavior, with less emphasis on the anthropocentric concept of human culture.

[*See also* DARWINIAN THEORY; GENETICS IN ARCHAEOLOGY.]

Robert Foley

THE ARCHAEOLOGY OF HUMAN ORIGINS

By definition, the prehistoric archaeological record begins when the earliest artifacts (objects modified through manufacture or use) produced by humans or protohumans can be recognized. Although a range of organic materials, such as wood, bone, tooth, and horn may have served as tools by early hominids, it is difficult to identify such possible implements. Wood, for instance, rarely survives in the prehistoric record, and bone, tooth, and horn can be modified by a host of other non-hominid agencies, such as carnivore and rodent gnawing, trampling, and postdepositional breakage, making it very difficult to identify unambiguously bones that have been worked or used by early hominids in the early prehistoric record. Fortunately, hominid-modified stones are much easier to identify and tend to be fairly indestructible, and therefore serve as useful markers of early hominid behavior. At present the archaeology of human origins can be taken back to about 2.5 million years ago on the African continent.

Appearance of the First Hominids in Africa. Although the postulated time of divergence between the African apes and humans is estimated to be between six and ten million years ago, the earliest clear evidence for small-brained, bipedal hominids in the fossil record is between four and three million years ago and comes from East African localities such as Hatar and the Middle Awash in Ethiopia and Laetoli in Tanzania. These fossils are usually assigned to *Australopithecus afarensis* (although some scholars believe that the range of anatomical variation warrants at least two taxa). Although upright walkers, these creatures still exhibit apelike features such as relatively long arms and curved phalanges, interpreted by some as arboreal adaptations. Brain size is essentially that of modern African apes, around 18 to 24 cubic inches (300 to 400 cu cm). Although hand bones suggest that *Australopithecus afarensis* had a high degree of digit opposability, no recognizable stone tools are known from this period of time.

Between 3 and 2.5 million years ago, two new taxa appear to have emerged from this ancestral bipedal stock: *Australopithecus africanus* in South Africa (known especially from the cave of Sterkfontein) and *Australopithecus (Paranthropus) aethiopicus* from West Turkana, Kenya. Again, no recognizable archaeological traces are associated with these forms. The robust *Australopithecus aethiopicus* skull exhibits a strong sagittal crest and enlarged premolars and molars that characterize later robust hominids of Africa between

2.5 and 1 million years ago: *Australopithecus (Paranthropus) robustus* in South Africa, found at the cave deposits of Swartkrans and Kromdraai, and *Australopithecus (Paranthropus) boisei* in East Africa, from localities such as East and West Turkana, Kenya and *Olduvai Gorge in Tanzania. These robust austalopithecines exhibit cranial capacities of between 25 and 34 cubic inches (400 and 550 cu cm).

Between 2.5 and 1.8 million years ago, larger-brained gracile forms with cranial capacities of between 37 and 50 cubic inches (600 and 800 cu cm) are known from African localities such as East Turkana in Kenya and Olduvai Gorge in Tanzania. These forms have usually been assigned to *Homo habilis* (some anthropologists have distinguished between those with a somewhat smaller body and brain size as *Homo habilis*, and those of a larger body and brain size *Homo rudolfensis*).

Beginning about 1.8 million years ago, a larger-brained hominid emerges in Africa, *Homo erectus* (some anthropologists call the earliest African forms *Homo ergaster*). With a cranial capacity of 50 to 55 cubic inches (800 to 900 cu cm) and a larger body size similar to that of modern humans, *erectus* appears to have spread out of Africa and into Eurasia sometime between 1.8 and 1 million years ago. Recently it has been suggested that some of the Java fossils of *Homo erectus*, notably one from Modjokerto, may be as old as 1.8 million years. If true, this suggests a migration out of Africa soon after the emergence of *Homo erectus*. The robust austalopithecines of East and South Africa went extinct by one million years ago, leaving the genus *Homo* as the only hominid lineage to continue into the Middle Pleistocene.

Earliest Archaeological Sites. The earliest recognizable stone artifacts are in the form of simple flaked and battered rocks that characterize the Oldowan Industrial Tradition (named after the locality of Olduvai Gorge) or Mode 1 industries. The oldest of these sites appear to be about 2.5 million years old, and a range of sites exhibiting such a technological stage are known between 2.5 and 1.5 million years ago. Such sites include the Omo, Gona, Melka Kunture, and Gadeb in Ethiopia; West and East Turkana and Chesowanja in Kenya; Swartkrans and Sterkfontein in South Africa; and Ain Hanech in Algeria.

Technology. The majority of these early African stone assemblages were dominated by lava, quartz, quartzite, or limestone as principal raw materials, usually obtained in the form of water-worn cobbles or angular chunks. Hard-hammer percussion and sometimes bipolar technique were the principal techniques used. Oldowan core forms are traditionally classified into types such as choppers, discoids, polyhedrons, and heavy-duty scrapers; retouched artifacts ("light-duty tools") made on flakes include scrapers and awls. Artifacts showing signs of battering and pitting include hammerstones, spheroids and subspheroids, and anvils. Experiments have suggested that many of the Oldowan core or "core-tool" forms could simply be by-products of producing sharp, serviceable flakes, although some of these cores could have been used for wood chopping or shaping. At Olduvai Gorge, a number of sites in Bed II have higher proportions of light-duty tools and spheroids, and have been designated "Developed Oldowan" by Mary Leakey.

Around 1.5 million years ago, after the emergence of *Homo erectus* in the fossil record, new elements could be seen at some stone artifact assemblages: largish hand axes, picks, and cleavers often made of large flakes struck from boulder cores. These large bifacial forms were the hallmark of the *Acheulean Tradition (Mode 2 technologies). Early Acheulean sites include DK in Bed II at Olduvai Gorge and sites at Peninj, Lake Natron in Tanzania, and Konso Gardula in Ethiopia.

Besides typological classificatory studies, a range of other methodological approaches have been applied to Early Stone Age sites. Experimental replicative and functional studies have been very useful in understanding why recurrent artifact forms are found at many archaeological sites, and how the rock type, shape, and size of a raw material can affect the resultant products. Microwear analysis of fresh, fine-grained siliceous artifacts can yield valuable clues pertaining to artifact function. And refitting studies of flaked stone from early archaeological sites can help to show what stages of flaking are represented at an archaeological site, as well as giving a "blow-by-blow" sequence of flaking events for a given core or retouched form. Refitting studies can also help to assess whether a given site has been heavily disturbed by water action or vertical disturbance from such agencies as roots and burrowing animals.

Environmental Studies. *Paleoenvironmental reconstruction of early archaeological sites has been approached from a range of different methods, including evidence from fossil faunal remains, fossil plant remains (normally in the form of pollen and root casts), and geological and geochemical analysis (in particular carbon and oxygen isotope studies). Such evidence suggests that major drying/cooling phases on the African continent occurred several times, including one period about 2.5 million years ago. Some researchers have suggested that this climatic change may have led to many extinctions of animal forms as well as the emergence of new forms adapted to new conditions. The emergence of the genus *Homo* and Oldowan sites at about this time could have been a response to such changes.

Social Organization. There is little direct evidence to suggest what types of social organization characterized early hominids; patterns observed among nonhuman primates as well as modern human foragers have often served as partial models in attempts to interpret social organization and behavior. Prior to the emergence of *Homo erectus*, it would appear that early hominids were characterized by a high degree of sexual dimorphism, suggesting to many anthropologists that there was competition between males for access to females, and that some sort of nonmonogamous mating pattern existed.

Homo erectus appears to have exhibited a reduced degree of sexual dimorphism, which may suggest less antagonism among males in competing for females and dominance. *Homo erectus* also was characterized by a larger brain and body size than earlier hominids, which may imply a larger home range as well. Limb bones of this taxa suggest that these creatures were more efficient at long-range bipedal walking than were earlier hominids, which may in part explain why *Homo erectus* is the first hominid form known to have migrated out of Africa and why *Homo erectus* had a larger brain and body size than earlier hominid forms.

Theories of Archaeological Site Formation. Both hominid and nonhominid forces are involved in the formation of Early Stone Age archaeological sites. Most of these sites are buried by sediments that have been carried by river and delta floods or lake transgressions, and such water action may have affected the distribution of prehistoric materials since the time of hominid occupation. Scavenging animals may have carried away or further modified bones at these sites, and trampling and bioturbation by roots or burrowing animals may have affected the vertical and horizontal distribution of the prehistoric materials.

How did the concentrations of stone artifacts and sometimes animal bones form in this early archaeological period? Theories to explain how these archaeological sites formed have included a range of interpretations: hydrological jumbles of stone tools and animal bones swept downstream and reconcentrated, with little behavioral integrity; palimpsests of hominid and nonhominid activities at focal points on the landscape over relatively long periods of time; central foraging places (home bases / camps) where early hominids carried out many subsistence and social activities; in some models, food sharing is an important part of this adaptive strategy; secondary stone caches collected on the landscape as an energy-saving strategy during daily foraging; scavenging stations where early hominids brought animal carcasses or parts of carcasses in order to safely process them with stone tools; and favored places where hominid individuals or groups repeatedly visited and carried out tool-making and tool using activities.

It is likely that a number of these scenarios were involved in the formation of early archaeological sites. One of the principal tasks for researchers interested in the archaeology of human origins is to build testable models that examine the hominid and nonhominid agencies that formed these sites.

Diet and Subsistence. The reconstruction of patterns of early hominid diet and subsistence are paramount to our understanding of the adaptation and evolution of these creatures. Based upon what is known among modern nonhuman primates as well as modern hunter-gatherers in tropical Africa, it is likely that early hominids in Africa had a diet that was predominantly plant foods, supplemented by animal food resources. Unfortunately, plant matter rarely survives in the early archaeological record; therefore, this important aspect of early hominid diet is largely conjectural. It is likely that a range of berries, nuts, seeds, underground plant foods (roots, tubers, corms), etc., were exploited, perhaps with the assistance of technological aids such as stone hammers and anvils to crack open nuts and hard-shelled fruits, digging sticks to uncover underground foodstuffs, and simple containers (bark tray, hide, tortoise or ostrich eggshell) to carry or store such foods.

When fossil animal bones are found at early archaeological sites, they may bear patterns of modification that suggest hominids were feeding on these animals. An excellent example is the FLK Zinjanthropus site in Bed I of Olduvai Gorge (ca. 1.8 million years ago). Cut marks on bone surfaces can usually be distinguished from marks from nonhominid agencies (carnivore and rodent gnawing, root etching, etc.) and can show where hominids used stone knives for skinning, dismembering, and defleshing. Fracture patterns of long bones showing percussion flakes and scars, as well as abrasion to bone surfaces from hammerstones are typical of hominid marrow processing.

The interpretations of these patterns of animal-bone modification have varied widely, however. At one extreme, it has been argued that early hominids appear to have been efficient predators (or very efficient competitive scavengers) and able to acquire the meaty remains of large mammals before carnivores had modified the bones to any significant degree; at the other extreme, others have argued that these modified animal bones represent marginal scavenging of carnivore leftovers in which only dried, relict

meat and marrow were obtained. It is likely that a combination of strategies was employed by opportunistic early hominids, including small-scale predation and scavenging of larger mammalian taxa.

Other clues that are useful in attempting to infer dietary patterns include wear studies on fossil hominid teeth, which can indicate how hard or gritty food items that were eaten were, and chemical analysis of fossil hominid bones (such as strontium / calcium ratios and carbon isotope ratios), which can indicate the relative abundance of meat in the diet and the herb and tree / grass ratios in plant foods. Paleopathologies on bones and teeth (e.g., hypoplasia, hypervitaminosis) may also suggest nutritional stresses or an overabundance of certain types of harmful dietary items.

Conclusion. Future research into the archaeology of human origins will almost certainly focus upon behavioral and ecological issues such as cognitive capabilities, social organization, land-use patterns, biogeographical spread, behavioral site-formation processes, tool function, diet, and competition with other animal taxa. Explanatory models for the emergence of tool-using hominids, as well as technological, behavioral, and evolutionary changes in time and space will be examined in the context of regional and global environmental changes. Refined or new dating techniques should also bring a higher resolution to the chronological placement of hominid fossils, archaeological occurrences, and other evolutionary events.

[*See also* AUSTRALOPITHECUS AND HOMO HABILIS.]

■ Mary Leakey, *Olduvai Gorge, Volume 3: Excavations in Beds I and II, 1960–1963* (1971). John W. K. Harris, "Cultural Beginnings: Plio-Pleistocene Archaeological Occurrences from the Afar, Ethiopia," *The African Archaeological Review* 1 (1983): 3–31. Barbara Isaac, ed., *The Archaeology of Human Origins: Papers by Glynn Isaac* (1989). J. D. Clark, ed., *Cultural Beginnings: Approaches to Understanding Early Hominid Life-ways in the African Savanna* (1991). Kathy Schick and Nicholas Toth, *Making Silent Stones Speak: Human Evolution and the Dawn of Technology* (1993).

Nicholas Toth and Kathy Schick

HUMAN REMAINS, Analysis of. Human remains from archaeological contexts may be the single most important source of information available about prehistoric people and their lifeways. Through the data they provide on evolutionary processes, biological relatedness, diet, health, activity patterns, and levels of violence, human remains tell a story of adaptation and change not available from any other source.

The human remains found in archaeological contexts are generally those elements, such as bones and teeth, that are resistant to normal decay processes. However, there are rare cases, such as the mummified corpses of ancient *Egypt and Chile, where *mortuary practices in combination with naturally dry environments have resulted in the preservation of soft tissue elements as well. The anaerobic peat bogs of England and Denmark, and permanently frozen landscapes such as those of arctic Alaska, Greenland, and the Austro-Italian Alps have also preserved whole bodies, providing unprecedented glimpses into a mysterious, and sometimes dark, past. The slit throat of Grauballe Man, tossed into a Danish peat bog 2,000 years ago, is a case in point.

Anthropological interest in human remains can be traced back to the late eighteenth century, when scientists first set about ordering the living world around them. Anthropometry, the comparative analysis of human body measurements, was the first method used to scientifically order modern and ancient humans. Particular interest was focused on cranial measurements, as the size and shape of the skull was thought to reflect human intelligence. Not surprisingly, some early anthropometric studies were oriented toward maintaining the status quo—proving that the race of the European researchers was superior to all others. This was not a propitious start for the study of human remains, and despite its many useful applications, the science of anthropometry has never been able to shake this legacy of racism.

The history of human disease was another subject explored in early studies of human remains. Articles on diseases in antiquity began to appear in the medical literature around the turn of the century, largely written by medical professionals. The focus of this work was on identifying and diagnosing *disease conditions in archaeological specimens. Research on ancient diseases continues to this day and constitutes a major subdiscipline of physical anthropology known as paleopathology, although the case study approach has increasingly been replaced by population-level epidemiological analyses.

During the 1940s and 1950s, when major theoretical revolutions were taking place in both anthropology and biology, evolutionary theory was adopted as the guiding force behind the study of human remains. Problem-oriented research has become increasingly prevalent since the inception of the New Archaeology of the 1960s and 1970s. Modern skeletal research is focused on the complex relationship between human biology and the environment, both physical and social. The archaeological context of human remains has therefore become an important part of human skeletal research.

Today, there are two major avenues of anthropological inquiry that rely on human (or hominid) remains from archaeological contexts. The first is the study of *human evolution through the analysis of fossilized bones and teeth from ancient sites and landscapes, a subdiscipline of physical anthropology known as paleoanthropology. Lucy, the little australopithecine from the ancient fossil beds of Ethiopia, provides a good example of the way in which paleoanthropological research progresses. Prior to Lucy, it was believed by some that significant brain expansion had preceded the development of upright walking. When her 3.5-million-year-old remains were found, it was clear that the opposite was true, for Lucy's leg bones were those of a competent biped, whereas her brain case more closely resembled that of a modern chimpanzee.

The second major focus of research involving human remains is the study of prehistoric lifeways and the causes and biological consequences of lifestyle transitions. Such studies come under the heading of bioarchaeology, a relatively new discipline that stresses the human osteological component of the archaeological record. Bioarchaeologists address many of the same theoretical questions addressed by archaeologists, but attempt to answer these questions through the analysis of human biological rather than cultural remains. Mary Lucas Powell's treatment of status differentiation at Moundville, Alabama (*Status and Health in Prehistory*, 1988) is a good example of this approach.

The range of information available from human skeletal remains is limited to a large extent only by the questions people ask. For the paleoanthropologist, the questions asked of the bones are often quite basic. Is it human? What makes it human? How is it different from modern humans?

However, they must also coax from the bones answers to more complex questions about the meaning of observed differences in form. The bioarchaeologist is more likely to focus on the composition of populations, variations in heritable traits, indicators of diet and disease, and evidence of violence.

Regardless of the questions being asked, certain types of baseline data are essential to all studies of human remains. Sex and age data are foremost among these. Sex is most accurately determined from sex-specific features of the pelvic bones. These features differ between men and women because of the breadth requirements of childbirth, and become increasingly evident with sexual maturation. Features of the skull and jaw and the size of limb bones are also used to assess the sex of adult individuals, particularly when the fragile pelvic bones are not preserved. Unlike sex, age is most accurately determined for subadults. Up until about 22 years of age, teeth are erupting and long bone epiphyses are fusing at a known rate. After this age, molar tooth wear, cranial suture closure, and degenerative changes in the pelvic bones and ribs are used to estimate age, albeit less accurately.

If the sample is relatively large and well preserved, sex and age data can be used for demographic analyses. Population profiles provide information on life expectancy and differential mortality, yielding important clues about such things as the stresses of childbirth and the severity of intergroup conflict.

When research questions pertain to biological relatedness, detailed information is collected on heritable traits known to vary between individuals and populations. These include such things as extra cusps on molars and shoveling of the central incisors. This latter trait, for example, is often well developed in Native Americans, and documents an ancestral link with East Asians, who share the trait.

Diet and health are probably the most common themes in current bioarchaeological research, a significant portion of which pertains to the biological consequences of economic transitions. Much of this research has focused in particular on the economic shift from hunting and gathering to agriculture. The dietary aspect of this transition has been investigated through the chemical analysis of bones and teeth as well as through direct observations of diet-related tooth wear and dental cavities. Relative health is assessed with reference to a number of different skeletal measures, including indicators of childhood growth disruption, such as bands that form on tooth crowns and lines that form in the internal structure of long bones. Pitting of the eye orbits caused by iron-deficiency anemia and skeletal lesions caused by such infectious diseases as tuberculosis and syphilis serve to document a population's disease load. These data make it possible to accurately assess the health costs associated with different lifeways and lifestyle transitions.

These are but a few of the types of studies conducted using human skeletal remains. Workload, violent conflict, and the impacts of European contact are other issues that have only recently begun to be addressed in this way. Unfortunately, because of past abuses and a continuing lack of communication, many human skeletal collections in North American and Australian museums are being recalled for reburial by native descendants. From a scientific perspective, it is a tragedy that at the moment we are finally in the position to learn so much about past peoples, the opportunities to do so are slipping away.

[*See also* PALEOPATHOLOGY; REBURIAL AND REPATRIATION.]

■ Don Brothwell and A. T. Sandison, eds., *Diseases in Antiquity* (1967). Mark N. Cohen and George J. Armelagos, eds., *Paleopathology at the Origins of Agriculture* (1984). Robert I. Gilbert, Jr., and James H. Mielke, eds., *The Analysis of Prehistoric Diets* (1985). C. S. Larsen, "Bioarchaeological Interpretations of Subsistence Economy and Behavior from Human Skeletal Remains," *Advances in Archaeological Method and Theory* 10 (1987): 339–445. Richard G. Klein, *The Human Career* (1989). T. Douglas Price, ed., *The Chemistry of Prehistoric Human Bone* (1989). Marc A. Kelley and Clark Spencer Larsen, eds., *Advances in Dental Anthropology* (1991). Tim D. White, *Human Osteology* (1991).

Patricia M. Lambert

HUMANS, Modern

Origins of Modern Humans
Peopling of the Globe

ORIGINS OF MODERN HUMANS

In the context of the long course of human evolutionary history, the origin of modern humans is a relatively recent event. Fossils of modern humans first appear in Africa and the Levant between about 130,000 and 70,000 B.P. Important fossils are Omo I from the Omo Kibish Formation, Ethiopia (130,000 B.P.), Border Cave I from southern Africa (80,000–70,000 B.P.), the numerous fragmentary fossils from *Klasies River Cave, southern Africa (the oldest of which date to greater than 90,000 B.P.), and the skeletons from Qafzeh and Skhul, Israel (about 100,000 B.P.).

All of these fossils are controversial. Either the dating has been questioned (e.g., Border Cave, Omo I) or the fossils themselves have been interpreted as archaic rather than fully modern (e.g., Klasies River Cave, Qafzeh, Skhul). Furthermore, none of these early fossils have been found associated with the advanced stone tool traditions that occur with indisputably modern humans after about 40,000 B.P. In the Levant they are rather associated with the Mousterian tool tradition that is also found with the *Neanderthals, while in Africa they are associated with the similar Middle Stone Age tradition that occurs with premodern African hominids (archaic *Homo sapiens*). It is only the later, more advanced traditions, the Upper *Paleolithic in Europe and the Levant and the Late Stone Age in Africa, that have been interpreted to reflect fully developed modern human culture with cognition and symbolic language.

One of the main controversies surrounding the origin of modern humans is whether the earliest fossils in Africa and the Levant are fully modern and, if so, whether they indicate that modern humans first evolved in this region and then spread out from there, displacing the premodern indigenous populations in Europe and the Far East. This has come to be known as the Out-of-Africa, or African Replacement, Hypothesis, and is primarily associated with paleoanthropologist Chris Stringer and geneticists Rebecca Cann and Alan Wilson. The major alternative explanation, the Multiregional Hypothesis, denies the fully modern status of the controversial early fossils and suggests that premodern populations in Africa, as well as in Europe and Asia, evolved into modern humans in their specific geographic regions. An important corollary of this hypothesis is that hominids are not fully modern unless they are accompanied by archaeological remains that can also be interpreted as fully modern. The Multiregional Hypothesis grew out of the work of Franz Weidenreich in the 1930s and 1940s and is today associated primarily with the paleoanthropologists Milford Wolpoff and Alan Thorne. It argues that there was considerable gene flow between the major population groups in Africa, Europe, and Asia but denies that modern humans evolved earlier in any one of these areas than in the others.

These two major schools of thought use different evidence to support their opposing views of modern human evolution. The Multiregional Hypothesis is based primarily on the recognition of anatomical traits in the skulls of modern Australians and Chinese that are also found in the earlier *Homo erectus* populations of Java and China. These features, such as the form of the cheek bones or of the bridge of the nose, are interpreted to represent a direct genetic link between the fossil and modern populations. Opponents of the Multiregional Hypothesis argue that these features are inconclusive because (1) some of them are found with greater frequency in modern populations elsewhere in the world, (2) some merely reflect robusticity, and (3) early modern fossils in China, such as Upper Cave 1 from *Zhoukoudian, lack any evidence of the continuity traits, thereby confounding the inferred genetic connection.

The Out-of-Africa Hypothesis is based on the argument that the controversial fossils from Africa and the Levant are anatomically modern and that they significantly predate similar modern people elsewhere in the world. There is no doubt that the early moderns from Omo, Klasies River Cave, Qafzeh, and Skhul variably retain primitive features such as brow ridges, relatively large teeth, and a considerable degree of size and robusticity dimorphism between males and females. However, supporters of the Out-of-Africa Hypothesis argue that they have modern features in the skull and also in the postcranial skeleton that fundamentally distinguish them from contemporary archaic humans elsewhere in the world and align them with living humans.

There is also genetic support for the Out-of-Africa Hypothesis, which derives primarily from the fact that both nuclear DNA and mitochondrial DNA show a greater diversity among living Africans than among human populations elsewhere in the world. If that diversity can be equated with antiquity, it would suggest that human populations have been evolving longer on the African continent than elsewhere in the world. This implies a greater antiquity for modern humans in Africa than elsewhere.

Until recently it was also suggested that mitochondrial DNA indicated that all living humans could trace their ancestry to a single female who lived in Africa approximately 200,000 years ago. Although the analyses upon which this conclusion was based have been shown to be seriously flawed, new analyses of mtDNA diversity by Henry Harpending and his colleagues provide a model for the evolution of modern humans that is consistent with a single, localized origin. Arguing from the degree of mtDNA variation in people today, these authors suggest that the population giving rise to modern humans could not have been larger than 5,000–50,000 people (1,000–10,000 effective females). Because this number is significantly smaller than the total population size inferred for *Homo sapiens* in Africa, Europe, and Asia during the Middle Pleistocene, the magnitude of mtDNA diversity in people today would be incompatible with the Multiregional Hypothesis, which assumes that the total *Homo erectus* population was ancestral to modern humans.

Furthermore, the pattern and magnitude of mtDNA diversity within and between living populations suggests two things. First, Europeans most probably arose from African ancestors. Second, between-population diversity in mtDNA is greater than within-population diversity, suggesting an initial spread of people from a localized origin followed by a period of relative genetic isolation of the migrating people. This would allow the interpopulational variation to develop. Only later in time would there be a rapid increase in population size in the different geographical areas followed by a higher level of gene flow between populations.

This new genetic model for the origin of modern humans implies that the factors involved in the initial evolution and spread of modern human populations were not the same factors that were associated with the subsequent rapid increase in population numbers of these people. It also fits relatively well with what is known from the fossil and archaeological records. Modern human populations from Africa could have spread through the Levant and eastward into Asia sometime around 100,000 years ago, occupying these regions in relatively low density and perhaps interbreeding to some extent with the indigenous populations. At this stage their migration westward into Europe would have been blocked by the Neanderthals. The ultimate spread of modern humans into Europe correlates with the development of the Upper Paleolithic, which appears between about 45,000 and 40,000 years ago not only in Europe but also in the Levant and in Siberia. It would be fair to assume that the cultural advances represented by the Upper Paleolithic were fundamentally associated with the ability of modern humans to displace the Neanderthals and also with the rapid population increase experienced by modern humans in Europe and elsewhere.

It has been argued that some major biological change associated with the evolution of modern humans, such as the evolution of fully developed human cognition and symbolic language, underlies the development of the Upper Paleolithic in Eurasia and the Late Stone Age in Africa. However, there is minimal, if any, evidence for such a biological change. It is now accepted that Neanderthals were functionally capable of producing the full range of modern human speech sounds. Furthermore, there is also behavioral evidence suggesting that they had at least basic symbolic capacity. The important question is why Neanderthals and other premodern humans did not develop the Upper Paleolithic (or the Late Stone Age) and conversely why it took the early modern humans represented by Skhul, Qafzeh, Omo, and Klasies River Cave more than 50,000 years before they did.

The answer to this question may be simply that at this stage of evolution it was culture, rather than biological evolution involving intelligence or cognitive capability, that was the driving force of change. The factors underlying the evolution of human language, underlying the rapid and virtually simultaneous appearance of the Upper Paleolithic and the Late Stone Age in Eurasia and Africa, and underlying the apparently associated rapid expansion of human populations may better be seen to include fundamental changes in the social organization of the hominids involving economic division of labor, food sharing, greater paternal investment in the offspring, as well as ritual behavior associated with these fundamental changes.

[See also CRO-MAGNONS; GENETICS IN ARCHAEOLOGY.]

■ P. Mellars and C. Stringer, The Human Revolution: Behavioural and Biological Perspectives on the Origins of Modern Humans (1989). C. B. Stringer, "The Emergence of Modern Humans," Scientific American (December 1990): 68–74. G. Bräuer and F. H. Smith, Continuity or Replacement? Controversies in Homo sapiens Evolution (1992). A. G. Thorne and M. H. Wolpoff, "The Multiregional Evolution of Humans," Scientific American (April 1992): 28–33. A. C. Wilson and R. L. Cann, "The Recent African Genesis of Humans," Scientific America (April 1992): 22–27. H. C. Harpending et al., "The Genetic Structure of Ancient Human Populations," Current Anthropology 34 (1993): 483–496. M. Stoneking, "DNA and Recent Human Evolution," Evolutionary Anthropology 2 (1993): 60–73.

Leslie C. Aiello

PEOPLING OF THE GLOBE

The spread of Homo sapiens sapiens, anatomically modern humans, across the Old World and into the Americas is a highly controversial issue in archaeology. There are two schools of thought. One believes that all modern humans evolved in tropical Africa before 100,000 years ago, and then spread across the Sahara Desert into the Near East by 100,000 years ago. After more than 50,000 years, much later modern human groups spread into southern and eastern Asia, and into northern latitudes, crossing into the Americas either during or after the Late Ice Age, by at least 15,000 years ago. Another group of scholars argues that modern humans evolved in several parts of the Old World after 250,000 years ago, and that anatomically modern people enjoyed considerable biological diversity from their first appearance. The controversy is still unresolved, but most archaeologists currently believe Homo sapiens spread from the Near East into other parts of the Old World after 50,000 years ago. This account summarizes this remarkable series of population movements, but it should be stressed that this reconstruction is highly speculative. It is based, in large part, on radiocarbon dates, scatters of stone tools, and occasional human fossils, sparse evidence indeed for the most important biological and cultural radiation in human history.

If the Out-of-Africa Hypothesis is correct, then Homo sapiens sapiens spread from the African tropics across the Sahara Desert into the Mediterranean region before the last glaciation caused the Sahara to dry up. There is at present no archaeological evidence for this apparently rapid population movement. The earliest occurrence of modern humans in the Near East dates to about 100,000 years ago at Qafzeh Cave in Israel. But important fossil discoveries at Mount Carmel and elsewhere tell us that for 50,000 years, both anatomically modern and more archaic, Neanderthal-like humans lived alongside one another in this region, apparently still using old-fashioned, simple tool kits. It is only after about 45,000 years ago that the characteristic blade technology and more specialized artifacts associated with modern humans appear in the Near East, perhaps a response to drier conditions that required more efficient stone tool technology. No one has been able to explain the apparent contemporaneity of archaic and modern humans for such a long period of time within such a small area. Some believe modern humans may have evolved not in Africa, but in the Near East. Others argue the two groups lived in the same area, but had different lifeways and territories. Many more fossil discoveries will be needed to resolve the issue.

South and Southeast Asia. At some point during these 50,000 years, modern human groups may have spread into India and other parts of South Asia, but there is at present no archaeological evidence for them. Such population movements were probably not the result of deliberate migrations, but the consequence of the natural dynamics of hunting and gathering in tropical and arid lands where food resources were distributed over large territories. Population densities were never large, and were scattered over enormous distances, making it entirely possible for small bands of foragers to cover large areas within a few generations. Such constant movements leave but exiguous signatures in the archaeological record, and the search for them in South Asia has barely begun.

Homo sapiens appeared in Southeast Asia by at least 50,000 years ago. At the time, sea levels were much lower than today, so human settlement on the exposed continental shelf may have been concentrated in river valleys, along lake shores, and on the coasts. The sparse populations of tropical rain forests may have evolved biologically, but they continued to use much the same simple material culture as their more archaic predecessors. The Southeast Asian coastlines that faced offshore were relatively benign waters that probably offered a bounty of fish and shellfish to supplement game and wild plant foods. Perhaps coastal peoples constructed simple rafts for fishing in shallows or used rudimentary dugout canoes for bottom fishing. At some point, some of these people crossed open water, either deliberately or by accidents, to New Guinea. There are traces of human settlement on New Guinea's Huon Peninsula at least as early as 40,000 years ago. Pioneer forager populations had spread rapidly in the Solomon Islands from New Guinea by 28,000 years ago, but lacked the foods or canoe technology to move farther offshore to more distant, biologically impoverished islands. Human occupation in Australia is well documented by 35,000 years ago, but may extend back 10,000 to 15,000 years earlier—the evidence is controversial. By 31,000 years ago, human beings had crossed the low-lying strait that joined the island of Tasmania to the Australian mainland in the far south, to colonize the most southerly region of the earth settled by Ice Age people. As sea levels rose after 15,000 years ago, the Tasmanians were isolated from their relatives on the mainland until European contact in the late eighteenth century, while the Australian Aborigines continued to receive some cultural innovations from the islands of Southeast Asia to the north.

Europe and Eurasia. Forty-five thousand years ago, Europe and Eurasia were intensely cold, with long, subzero winters. These severe climatic conditions may have inhibited the spread of modern humans into northern areas and onto open plains and steppe-tundra landscapes until the development of more effective, specialized tool kits that allowed the working of bone and the making of tailored clothing for bitterly cold conditions. Whatever the cause, no anatomically modern humans appeared in Europe before about 43,000 years ago, when, apparently, they crossed the then-dry Bosporus into the Balkans.

The first fully modern Europeans are known to biological anthropologists as the *Cro-Magnons, named after a rock shelter near the village of Les Eyzies in southwestern France. They are indistinguishable from ourselves, strongly built, large-headed people whose appearance contrasts dramatically with their Neanderthal predecessors. The anatomically modern ancestors of the Cro-Magnons had settled in southeast and central Europe by at least 43,000 years ago, apparently near Neanderthal groups. Some of them had penetrated into the sheltered, deep river valleys of southwestern France by 40,000 to 35,000 B.P. There they

seem to have lived alongside the *Neanderthals, but the relationship between the two groups is still little understood, despite some borrowing of tool kits. But by 30,000 years ago, the Neanderthals had vanished and the density of Cro-Magnon settlement intensified considerably. The ancestors of the Cro-Magnons had entered Europe during a brief period of more temperate climate. Even then, climatic conditions and seasonal contrasts may have been such as to require new artifacts and much more sophisticated hunting and foraging skills. These adaptations developed rapidly, indeed spectacularly, after 30,000 years ago, when the climate grew colder. It was during these millennia that *Homo sapiens* finally mastered winter, for it was in northern latitudes that human ingenuity and endurance were tested to the full. The Cro-Magnons of western and central Europe developed elaborate and sophisticated hunting cultures during this period. They subsisted off reindeer and a wide range of big game, as well as salmon runs and a wide range of plant foods in spring and summer. Their cultures were marked not only by many technological innovations, but by a flowering of religious and social life, reflected in one of the earliest art traditions in the world. The Cro-Magnons survived in a harsh and unpredictable environment not only because they were expert hunters and foragers, but because they had effective ways of keeping warm outside in the depth of winter and the ability to store large amounts of meat and other foods to tide them over lean periods. For most of the year, the Cro-Magnons lived in small groups, subsisting off a wide range of game and stored foods. The times when they came together in larger groups may have been in spring, summer, and early fall, when reindeer and, in later times, salmon were abundant. As winter closed in, the groups would disperse through the sheltered river valleys, returning to their stored foods and the small herds of game animals that also took refuge from the bitter winds. The highly successful Cro-Magnon cultures survived from at least 32,000 years ago to the end of the Ice Age, when the glaciers finally melted and dense forest spread over the open plains and deep valleys of central and western Europe.

The open steppe-tundra plains that stretched from the Atlantic to Siberia were a far harsher environment. To live there permanently, Late Ice Age people had to find sheltered winter base camps, have the technology to make tailored, layered clothing with needle and thongs, and the ability to build substantial dwellings in a treeless environment. Only a handful of big-game hunting groups lived in the shallow valleys that dissected these plains before the glacial maximum 18,000 years ago. Thereafter, the human population rose comparatively rapidly, each group centered on a river valley where game was most plentiful, and where plant foods and fish could be found during the short summers. It was here that the most elaborate winter base camps lay, settlements like Mezhirich in Ukraine, which is famous for its finely made mammoth bone framed houses. Some of these groups traded with neighboring bands over hundreds of miles, exchanging sea shells and exotic toolmaking stone with one another.

Somewhat similar but still almost unknown Late Ice Age groups settled much of the steppe-tundra as far northeast as Lake Baikal in Siberia, not through a deliberate process of migration, but as a result of the natural dynamics of forager life in an environment where game was widely dispersed and most seasonal food resources concentrated near lakes and in river valleys. The steppe-tundra hunters lived in small, highly flexible bands. As the generations passed, one band would coalesce into another, sons and their families would move away into a neighboring, and empty, valley. And, in time, a sparse human population would occupy thousands of square miles of steppe-tundra, concentrated for the most part in river valleys, at times venturing out onto the broad plains, and always on the move. It was through these natural dynamics of constant movement, of extreme social flexibility and opportunism, that people first settled the outer reaches of Siberia and crossed into the Americas. These peoples were part of a widespread Late Ice Age cultural tradition that reflects a varied adaptation by *Homo sapiens* to an enormous area of Central Asia and southern Siberia from well west of Lake Baikal to the Pacific coast by 30,000 to 20,000 B.P. Not that many Eurasian groups seem to have penetrated far northeast of Lake Baikal, where the Late Ice Age climate was extremely severe. Some northeastern Siberian groups probably originated not in the west, but in the arid regions of Mongolia and northern China.

The Far East. Many biological anthropologists assume that *Homo sapiens sapiens*, originally a tropical and subtropical animal, settled in the warmer southern parts of China first and then radiated northward into more temperate environments. The first appearance of modern humans is still undated but may be at least 50,000 years ago. Some Chinese paleoanthropologists argue that modern humans evolved from earlier archaic people in eastern Asia itself, but the biological traits they use to support their view are considered controversial by many Western authorities. Human settlement in far-northern China and the arid landscapes of the Ordos and Mongolia was very sparse indeed throughout the last glaciation. But it was not until just before 35,000 years ago that a few signs of human settlement appeared in the arid grasslands of Mongolia. Open landscapes such as this, and the neighboring steppe-tundra, could support but the sparsest of forager populations, people who placed a high premium on mobility and portable tool kits. Some of these little-known groups may have been remotely ancestral to the first Americans, spreading northward into northeastern Siberia, where mobility and diverse foraging lifeways were highly adaptive. We do not know when northeastern Siberia was first settled, but it may have been after 20,000 years ago, soon after the coldest millennia of the last glaciation. The little-known, but widespread, D'uktai culture flourished in northeastern Asia at the end of the Ice Age, and may have been among the ancestral cultures that spread into the Americas.

First Settlement of the Americas. Everyone agrees that the Native Americans originated among Late Ice Age Siberian populations, but the date when modern humans first crossed the low-lying Bering Land Bridge (Beringia) into Alaska is much debated. Most scholars hypothesize first settlement came at the end of the Ice Age, perhaps between 15,000 and 12,000 B.P., when the Bering Land Bridge was severed and sparse human populations moved onto higher ground to the east. A small number of archaeologists argue for much earlier settlement, perhaps as early as 40,000 years ago. At present, there is no reliable evidence for Late Ice Age occupation in northeastern Siberia any earlier than about 20,000 years ago. Nor are there any widely accepted pre-15,000-year-old sites known in the Americas, so a post–Ice Age date for first settlement seems more plausible. Certainly, by 11,000 years ago, small numbers of modern humans had settled throughout the New World, adapting to every kind of arctic, temperate, and

tropical environment imaginable. The archaeological record for the Americas becomes more abundant after that date, when the so-called Clovis culture flourished over a wide area of North America and southward into Mesoamerica.

With this complex process of settlement in the Americas, the great diaspora of anatomically modern humans ended, to resume after 4000 B.C., when island Southeast Asians with domesticated animals and crops, as well as deep-water canoes, began to settle the Pacific offshore islands. By the end of the Ice Age, *Homo sapiens sapiens* had adapted not only to tropical environments, to savanna and rain forest, but to temperate landscapes, harsh deserts, and both coastal and terrestrial environments far more severe than any on Earth today. That modern humans were able to do so is a tribute to their enhanced powers of reasoning and intelligence, which allowed them to develop both technologies and foraging strategies to cope with all manner of environmental extremes. And, at the same time, they also developed the rich symbolic life and complex religious and spiritual beliefs that are the hallmark of all recent human societies.

[*See also* AMERICAS, FIRST SETTLEMENT OF THE; AUSTRALIA AND NEW GUINEA: FIRST SETTLEMENT OF SUNDA AND SAHUL; EUROPE: THE FIRST COLONIZATION OF; HOMO SAPIENS, ARCHAIC; PALEOLITHIC: UPPER PALEOLITHIC.]

■ Clive Gamble, and Chris Stringer, eds., *The Human Revolution*, 2 vols. (1989, 1990). Brian Fagan, *The Journey from Eden* (1990). Clive Gamble, *Timewalkers* (1994). Roger Lewin, *The Origins of Modern Humans* (1993).

Brian M. Fagan

HUNTER-GATHERERS, African. Hunter-gatherer communities of sub-Saharan Africa have been central to debates on the history, archaeology, and anthropology of hunter-gatherers generally. Kalahari groups are probably the most often used as ethnoarchaeological models. As recently as 3,000 years ago most people in the subcontinent made their living by hunting and gathering, whereas by the midtwentieth century hunter-gatherers lived alongside or encapsulated among people who herded or farmed for a living. This transformation took place almost wholly without documentation by literate observers and has proven a challenge to reconstruct from surviving traces—linguistic, genetic, and archaeological. The main problem has been to recognize and distinguish between the processes of replacement, transformation, acculturation, incorporation, and movement of and among population segments.

Two opposed views can be identified in recent thinking on hunter-gatherers. One would see African hunter-gatherers as relatively isolated residual populations; the other, as impoverished components of wider social and economic systems. African hunter-gatherer groups (San or Bushmen, Aka and Efe "pygmies," Hadza, Sandawe, and Ndorobo or Okiek, though there are many others) are discussed below in terms of prevailing debates on identity, aboriginality, and contact.

Symptomatic of the problem is the vexing question of names. Hunter-gatherer groups have often emerged in written records secondhand through conversations between literate colonizing observers and indigenous farming or herding groups. Hence they have often been referred to by names (Bushmen, San, Ndorobo, pygmy) not used by themselves. Self-generated names usually apply only at a local scale. Ju/'huansi, for example, is a word used by some

Kalahari groups to refer to themselves but is probably not appropriate to use with reference to broad categories of hunter-gatherers, a need perhaps felt only by anthropologists. Southern African hunter-gatherers were first called "soaqua," which became "boesjiesmans," which was later anglicized as "Bushmen," then "San"; now, in some cases, they themselves opt for "Bushmen." But all such terms have been externally imposed, and are derogatory, variously implying poverty, nonownership of domestic stock, marginal or "bush" existence, and aboriginality.

Even the apparently innocuous term "hunter-gatherer" is not without problems, as a major debate has erupted over the utility of this broad category. In many ways hunting and gathering of food is the fall-back option of many, if not most, African communities and can be opportunistically taken up or set aside as a strategy, depending on circumstances. For many anthropologists and historians participating in this debate, hunter-gatherers observed in the late nineteenth or early twentieth century were simply herders who had lost stock and shifted into hunter-gatherer mode. Had they been observed earlier or later they might have required a different name. For such researchers—termed "revisionists"—any characteristics observed had little value as models for earlier hunter-gatherer groups prior to contact with farmers or herders. For other researchers the term "hunter-gatherer" implies far more than the mere practice of hunting and gathering but refers to a set of interconnected values and practices including egalitarian sharing that is incompatible with the accumulation ethic common among herders and farmers. From this perspective, surviving hunter-gatherers provide a residual insight into the values and world view of earlier hunter-gatherers, whose behavior can thus be hypothesized.

The debate has revolved, in almost identical terms, around both the Kalahari San and the Ndorobo of the Kenyan highlands. Although reconciliation seems unlikely between such diametrically opposed positions, it may be that some populations have survived with little impact from neighboring farming or herding communities, whereas others have opportunistically manipulated their identity in a complex economic and political arena. In all cases social arrangements probably reflected both inherent and acquired characteristics. Opportunistic shifts may have been more common between hunters and herders than between hunters and farmers, whereas retention of a hunter-gatherer lifeway may have been more likely where refugia, areas unsuitable for farming or herding, were available.

It is perhaps to deal with the contextual nature of the practice of hunting and gathering that other dimensions such as language and genetics have been injected into the debate. The classic liberal African history denied any necessary connection between language, physical type, and economy, despite some obvious congruences on the ground. Of particular interest here is the phenomena of hypergyny, with the Efe and neighboring Lese illustrating well the practice of hunter-gatherer women marrying farmers. So many of these "marrying up" instances occur that Efe men apparently struggle to find wives. Mapping the frequency distributions of genetic characteristics has shown patterns that are consistent with such interactions over many hundreds, perhaps thousands, of years. Beyond this, the stature of hunter-gatherer communities has figured strongly in this debate. Hunter-gatherers of the arid south (San) and the equatorial forest (Aka and Efe) are documented as shorter than neighboring herders or farmers,

despite living in environments dramatically different from one another. The close economic relations between short Aka and Efe and taller farmers is repeated in equatorial settings in America and Asia, suggesting that something other than local histories is involved, but no clear synthesis has emerged.

Most if not all groups referred to as San in southern Africa speak a language that is not part of the Bantu group of the Niger-Congo family used by all southern African indigenous farmers. Some congruence is undeniable between those independently classified as hunter-gatherers, San and non-Bantu speakers. In central and eastern Africa, hunter-gatherers and neighboring farmers or herders speak languages that are more closely related than in the south. Exceptions to this are the Hadza and Sandawe of Tanzania, whose implosive consonants (clicks) have led some to classify them as part of the greater "Khoisan" language family. Assuming some relatedness, the question then arises as to whether Sandawe and Hadza are residual islands from a former more widespread Khoisan distribution, or vanguards of a much later Khoisan advance.

The clicks of southern African non-Bantu languages have proven a complex issue, with at least one authority denying them any classificatory significance. The lesser but prevalent use of implosive consonants in, for example, Zulu and Xhosa is for some a parallel for the spread of genetic markers between hunter-gatherers and farmers and, thus, evidence for considerable historical interaction. The Hadza and Sandawe remain enigmatic in being geographically isolated from Bushmen; they are physically different and linguistically only distantly related at best. The Dama in Namibia provide another dimension to the enigma in that they are physically very different from San hunter-gatherers, yet speak a Nama (Khoekhoe, herder) language and were historically known to emphasize hunting and gathering.

It is hard to leave the overview of sub-Saharan hunter-gatherers without referring to the Khoekhoe or Quena (Hottentots), herding people known historically from South Africa and Namibia. Linguistically, physically, and culturally more closely related to neighboring hunter-gatherers more often than to neighboring farmers, they provide a gradient of diversity to the demography of southern Africa. For many they are hunter-gatherers of San or Bushmen affinity who acquired livestock (from non-San) and developed an accumulative ethic more in keeping with farmers but retaining elements of an earlier hunter-gatherer past. In the various parts of southern Africa this development allowed for a variety of interactions, transformations, and competitive relations. Archaeologists, in particular, have struggled to recognize such identities and such interactions in the material remains of their sites and have, perhaps, imposed a false structure of inflexibility on what was a dynamic and fluid social arena.

Despite these many problems African hunter-gatherers have been taken as epitomizing the hunter-gatherer lifeway and providing a yardstick or model for prehistoric groups. Characteristics taken as archetypal are the use of the bow; short stature; honey gathering; a preference for arid, forested, or otherwise rugged landscapes; and, above all, a social ethic that emphasized food sharing.

Even here there are debates. A question has arisen over the occupation of the tropical forests by hunter-gatherers prior to the appearance of farmers. One position is that there is too little available carbohydrate for hunter-gatherers to use pristine forest on a permanent basis without the spread of secondary forest produced by slash-and-burn agriculturalists. Perhaps, it is argued, hunter-gatherers followed farmers into the forest and then positioned themselves strategically as specialists in providing forest products (fiber, skins, honey, protein) for exchange with manufactured goods or domestic carbohydrate (cereal). This would explain the geographic and ritual interconnections between hunter and farmer, but again would dispel the myth of ethnographic hunter-gatherers as survivors of an ancient prefarming way of life. The view of modern or recent African hunter-gatherers as professional hunters emphasizing their difference from farmers as they increasingly marginalized themselves and played on their image as rainmakers might also be used in the arid or mountainous regions of southern Africa. Such a scenario would require us to rethink archetypal characters and is testable only with a good and detailed archaeological record.

This, it has to be admitted, does not exist. To answer the question of whether people have lived regularly in arid or forested regions for some millennia requires a level of archaeological investigation that has not yet been possible. Some parts of eastern and southern Africa have been investigated thoroughly enough to produce answers to questions about Holocene settlement, but the Kalahari Desert and Zaire forests are not among these. It remains entirely possible that the population of sub-Saharan Africa between 10,000 and 2,000 years ago was very low and able to ebb and flow in regional landscapes in accordance with people's perceptions of attractiveness and habitability. Only during the last 2,000 years, when farming and herding became more prevalent, did population density begin to rise in particular parts of the landscape, along with options for exchange relations, clientship, assimilation, and particular forms of conflict.

A series of important issues, apparently accessible to archaeological enquiry, remain clouded. Of considerable interest is the observation that sub-Saharan African populations form two closely related but separable groups, one Negroid and the other Khoisanoid. Under what circumstances did the separation arise, and what have been the histories of the two populations? Resolution is obscured by the complete lack of human skeletal material in the region prior to the Early Holocene, with the exception of much earlier, and much more fragmentary, finds such as those from *Klasies River Mouth Caves and Border Cave. A likely scenario would see the Khoisan physical type arising in the extreme south, geographically all but isolated from populations to the north, which were genetically drifting in another direction. There is some archaeological evidence that the regions north of the present Cape Province were dry and very sparsely occupied for several tens of thousands of years in the Late *Pleistocene. With a great extension of land to the south, the result of a considerable lowering of sea level, Khoisan populations may have evolved as truly southern hunter-gatherers with little genetic exchange to the equatorial north.

The very close relationships between widely spread Bantu languages of the Niger-Congo family, the strong relationship between Bantu language use and a farming economy, and a similar one between Khoisan languages and hunting and gathering has long prompted a particular historical construction. This would see Khoisanoid hunter-gatherers speaking Bush languages gradually replaced by Negroid farmers speaking Bantu languages. Genetic and linguistic exchanges reflect intermarriages during what is presumed to be a relatively rapid process, beginning about 2,000 years ago. This is, of course, the package so frowned upon by liberal scholarship. Language affiliation is difficult to recover archaeologically, but the almost complete absence of human skeletal remains from late hunter-gatherer sites in the eastern parts of southern Africa make this model hard to challenge. It remains possible that some southern African populations of hunter-gatherers were Negroid, but no conclusive evidence yet exists.

African hunter-gatherers must therefore be seen in historical context. The patterns of behavior exhibited are the result of some constraints imposed by the hunting-gathering way of life, some environmentally determined limitations, and the consequences of particular historical trajectory. The extent to which they display behavior shared by precontact hunter-gatherers is to be determined by appropriate examination of the archaeological record. Regional archaeological trajectories must, of course, terminate in present social and political scenarios, but the former existence of subsistence and other behaviors quite unlike those of recent hunter-gatherers should be anticipated.

[See also AFRICA: PREHISTORY OF AFRICA; ETHNOARCHAEOLOGY; ROCK ART: ROCK ART OF SOUTHERN AFRICA.]

■ Eleanor Leacock and Richard Lee, eds., *Politics and History in Band Societies* (1982). Carmel Schrire, ed., *Past and Present in Hunter Gatherer Studies* (1984). Edwin N. Wilmsen, *Land Filled with Flies: A Political Economy of the Kalahari* (1989). Tim Ingold, David Riches, and James Woodburn, eds., *Hunters and Gatherers: History, Evolution and Social Change* (1991). Alan Barnard, *Hunters and Herders of Southern Africa: A Comparative Ethnography of the Khoisan Peoples* (1992).

John Parkington

HUNTER-GATHERERS, Eurasian.

The Eurasian archaeological record of hunting and gathering begins by at least 40,000 years ago, with some cultural developments perhaps arising some 15,000 years earlier. Chronologically, these dates associate this record with anatomically modern humans, but there is some evidence for both *Neanderthals and *Homo sapiens sapiens* living alongside one another during an early transition period. By 30,000 years ago, hunter-gatherers enjoying lifeways somewhat similar to known ethnographic peoples were occupying all of what is now temperate Eurasia. The archaeological record reveals a great diversity of subsistence practices, fine-turned to local environmental conditions. For example, the groups who occupied such sites as Dolni Vestonice, Pavlov, and Predmosti in Moravia (the Czech Republic) some 28,000–23,000 B.P. exploited a variety of large-sized gregarious herbivores and were seasonally quite mobile, including southern Poland and western Slovakia in their annual rounds. They aggregated seasonally into large communities, where probably a good deal of ritual behavior took place, which included the production and use of items of personal adornment and of portable art. It is these East Gravettian groups who invented the art of firing ceramics, which was used for the production of animal and female figurines, while the use of pottery had to wait another 15,000 years. Their inventories also show the use of stone polishing to produce beads and pendants, which became widespread in Eurasia during the Mesolithic. Similar features and inventories are found some 1,240 miles (2,000 km) to the east at such sites as Avdeevo and Kostenki in European Russia. These sites, which also contain elaborate inventories of worked bone and ivory and portable art, date a few thousand years younger than the ones in Moravia and indicate that demographic shifts occurred in Late Pleistocene Eurasia in response to changing environmental conditions. Evidence for rich burials, a form of ritual behavior, is extensive for this time period. The fact that some individuals, often including children, were buried with extraordinarily rich grave goods at such sites as *Sungir in European Russia, Brno II in Moravia, and at Mal'ta in Siberia, suggests that some of the Late Paleolithic hunter-gatherers living before the last glacial maximum (20,000–18,000 B.P.) were probably already living in complex social groupings that featured forms of social inequality.

A look at Eurasia some 18,000–12,000 years ago indicates a great diversity in hunter-gatherer adaptations to the unique open periglacial steppe landscapes extant at the time. By 15,000 years ago, East Gravettian groups living along the valleys of the Dnepr and its tributaries, in Belorus, Russia, and the Ukraine, practiced in-ground storage of food, lived together in larger numbers, especially during the long cold seasons (which may have lasted as long as nine months), and built elaborate dwellings made out of mammoth bones (e.g., at such sites as Mezin, Mezhirich, and Yudinovo). These groups, because they insured their food supply by storing food at the time of its peak abundance, were less mobile than their western counterparts and lived together in larger numbers on a more permanent basis. While still seasonally mobile between their more permanent cold-weather and less-permanent warm-weather camps, their settlement systems did not feature aggregation-dispersal pulsations characteristic for simpler hunter-gatherers. They maintained long-distance contacts and exchange with groups well to the south. Some scant 185 miles (300 km) to the south, the area of the Russian and Ukrainian steppe zone, saw occupation by mobile groups who some 18,000 years ago concentrated on hunting wild steppe bison at such sites as Amvrosievka. These various Late Paleolithic hunter-gatherer societies possessed the tailored clothing and long-distance kill weaponry that allowed them to colonize the cold and harsh latitudes of Eurasia. They ventured close to the Arctic Circle during the milder interstadial climate phase of some 25,000 years ago (the site of Byzovaya on the Pechora River in European Russia) and into the Arctic Circle by 12,000 to 14,000 B.P. (the site of Berelekh in Siberia). Eventually, groups with basically similar adaptations penetrated deep into northeastern Asia and across the Bering Land Bridge into the Americas.

The close of the *Pleistocene some 10,000 years ago brought profound changes to the Eurasian natural environments. The warming temperatures and the melting of the continental and mountain glaciers that covered large parts of both continents during the Late Pleistocene brought about the disappearance of the huge expanses of cold and harsh but highly productive periglacial steppe environments that were able to support large numbers of gregarious herbivores. This unique biome, which has no present-day analogues, was replaced by latitudinal environmental zones of today that had most of Eurasia covered by boreal and temperate forests. Because humans can digest little, other than fruit, that forested biomes produce, and because game animals are more solitary in habitats that contain fewer humans, it is not surprising that Eurasian Holocene groups both widened the range of resources they harvested and payed special attention to aquatic resources such as fish and shellfish. This switch in subsistence focus from terres-

trial gregarious herbivores to forest and aquatic species brought about a repositioning of Eurasian groups, who were found in greatest numbers in ecotones that permitted the exploitation of both aquatic and terrestrial foods. This new focus on water resources was accompanied by an elaboration of technologies associated with water transport and fishing. Some of these groups, such as those found in profusion in northwestern Europe, appear to have lived in small-sized settlements year-round (e.g., the site of Mt. Sandel in Ireland dating to some 7000 B.C.), while evidence from large cemeteries from such diverse regions as Denmark, Karelia, and Portugal suggest both an increase in the complexity of sociopolitical relationships of these groups as well as a substantial increase in inter- and intragroup violence. Finally, evidence from such sites as *Lepinski Vir on the Danube in Serbia, where a number of trapezoid-shaped stone dwellings have been found together with many non-utilitarian items of material culture, may attest to successful adaptations oriented to fishing and year-round village living by good-sized communities.

This way of life ended slowly and patchily in Eurasia during the Holocene. Food-producing economies, which originated in southwestern Asia some 12,000 years ago, in time profoundly affected the rest of Eurasia. In some regions, such as the most southern parts of Europe, it terminated with the advent of food producers from elsewhere some 8,000 years ago. In more northern latitudes of Eurasia the record indicates a much longer period during which farmers and herders both expanded their regions of occupation and affected nearby hunter-gatherers, some of whom took up food production. It should be noted also that some hunter-gatherer-fishers successfully persisted in these subsistence pursuits in the remoter and less hospitable parts of Siberia until very recent times.

[See also AMERICAS, FIRST SETTLEMENT OF THE; CRO-MAGNONS; HOLOCENE: HOLOCENE ENVIRONMENTS IN EUROPE; ROCK ART: PALEOLITHIC ART.]

■ Richard G. Klein, *Ice Age Hunters of the Ukraine* (1973). Olga Soffer, *The Upper Paleolithic of the Central Russian Plain* (1985). Brian M. Fagan, *People of the Earth* (1989). Brian M. Fagan, *The Journey from Eden* (1990).

Olga Soffer

HUNTER-GATHERERS, North American Archaic.

In current usage, the term "Archaic" refers to those pre-agricultural New World culture units whose subsistence derives from a mixed spectrum of resources that is not limited to large mammals and generally includes plants. The term was first used in reference to hunting and gathering economies by William A. Ritchie to designate a distinctive New York State cultural manifestation (Lamoka) based on a mixture of hunting, fishing, and gathering. Relationships subsequently noted between this and other widely separated entities across the eastern United States (e.g., in Kentucky) caused the term to be defined in broader and more general terms as part of the Midwestern Taxonomic System. In that scheme it refers to post-Paleo-Indian, pre-agricultural manifestations at least partly reliant on shellfish.

Willey and Phillips were the first to use the Archaic in an explicitly developmental sense as part of a general cultural sequence they held as applying throughout the New World. In the Willey and Phillips scheme, the Archaic stage is one of mobile hunting and gathering. It follows the Lithic stage, which is characterized by mobile groups dependent on large game (largely extinct megafauna), and precedes the Formative stage, in which total or partial reliance on agricultural products, or on unusually abundant wild resources, supports sedentary village life.

Jennings presents the most comprehensive recent treatment of New World prehistory that employs the Archaic concept as an interpretive tool. Following Caldwell, Jennings defines the Archaic as a stage of continual change over the course of which New World hunter-gatherers became increasingly efficient in their use of native plant and animal resources. This results in the development of local resource specializations, some of which permit sedentary or nearly sedentary lifeways in places where resources are relatively abundant (e.g., salmon in the northwestern United States; acorns in California). In short, the hunter-gatherers of Willey and Phillips suffer in ignorance; their Archaic stage is therefore static, technologically generalized, and culturally impoverished. The hunter-gatherers of Jennings and Caldwell are innovative and resourceful; their Archaic stage is therefore dynamic and, with time, more specialized and technically, socially, and politically advanced.

Most contemporary scholars align themselves more closely with Jennings than Willey and Phillips, but there is no generally accepted definition of the Archaic beyond the one given at the outset. This is perhaps to be expected because the Archaic takes on markedly different outward characteristics according to the native resources upon which it is dependent, and these differences increase as local Archaic economies become more specialized with time.

In the northeastern United States, the Archaic runs from 8000 B.C. to approximately 1000 B.C. and, as in most places, is divided into early, middle, and late periods. The Early Archaic (8000–6000 B.C.) and Middle Archaic (6000–4000 B.C.) are sparsely represented, possibly owing to the dominance of relatively unproductive pine-oak vegetation during those intervals. The chipped-and-ground celt is present and stemmed, and indented-base *atlatl* points are typical. By the Late Archaic (4000–1000 B.C.) the rich deciduous forests that presently characterize the area were stabilized, and human populations thrived on the nuts, game, and fish supported therein. Sites are larger and richer, and several distinctive regional patterns, termed "traditions," are evident. These are (1) the Laurentian Tradition, characterized by ground slate points and knives and stone gouges; (2) the Piedmont Tradition, characterized by narrow stemmed points; and (3) the Susquehanna Tradition, characterized by broad stemmed points. Running parallel to these is the Maritime Archaic of Labrador, which begins about 5000 B.C. and is characterized by a subsistence emphasis on marine mammals taken with a sophisticated technology that included the toggling harpoon.

The Archaic of the Southeast and Midwest is similarly divided into Early (8,000–6000 B.C.), Middle (6000–4000 B.C.), and Late (4000–1000 B.C.) periods, locally designated by different names. Throughout these areas the Early Archaic is less strongly represented as one moves north, and it is hardly present at all in the Great Lakes region. As in the Northeast, this may have to do with the southern confinement in the Early Holocene of the deciduous forest species that formed the subsistence base for the eastern Archaic. The Early Archaic projectile points series almost always begin with Dalton (which is sometimes considered a Paleo-Indian affiliate) and always include stemmed, indented

base forms (e.g., Stanly and LeCroy). Chipped stone adzes and groundstone milling equipment, presumably for plant processing, are Early Archaic innovations. The Middle and Late Archaic are notable for the increasing intensity of use of resources other than game, particularly shellfish and nuts, and in the emergence of locally elaborate ceremonial paraphernalia and finely made objects evidently connected with wealth and status.

Plains Archaic (6000 B.C.–A.D. 500) assemblages are readily distinguished by the presence of points whose hafting elements generally include side, and sometimes corner, notches in contrast to the weakly shouldered lanceolate forms typical of Paleo-Indian. The early Plains Archaic coincides with a period of drought (Altithermal or Hypsithermal) that undoubtedly limited the quantity of resources, especially bison, available to Plains folk, which may account for the scarcity of sites attributable to the period. There is evidence that the high elevations in the Colorado Front Range may have served as refugia for drought-stressed Plains dwellers. It is sometimes argued that big-game animals were completely absent from the Plains at this time; however, Early Archaic bison kills have been noted in the High Plains, as have pit houses. Both patterns are subsequently persistent through the Middle and Late Archaic. Milling equipment, also present in the Early Archaic, becomes a dominant element of the Middle and Late Plains Archaic, as does the stone circle (the so-called tipi ring), which, along with the large earth oven for meat and plant roasting, is a Middle Plains Archaic innovation. The implication is that Middle and Late Plains Archaic folk depended heavily on plants but, with improving climatic conditions and the comeback of larger herbivores, also on a variety of medium (e.g., deer) and large (e.g., bison) mammals.

The best-known Early Archaic components of the Southwest are termed *Cochise culture, a manifestation readily accommodated within what was once termed the Desert culture. Virtually the whole of the later southwestern Archaic is included in what is termed the Picosa, which is essentially the southwestern expression of the Desert Archaic. Three major areal variants of Picosa are recognized: the San Dieguito-Pinto (southern California, southern Arizona, and southern Nevada), Oshara (northern Southwest), and Cochise (southern Southwest). In all cases, there is increased use of plants over time, as evidenced by increasing quantities of milling equipment. Domed cobble scrapers and choppers used in the procurement and preparation of yucca and agave for food and fiber are distinctive elements of the southwestern Archaic. It is generally held that Oshara is antecedent to the Basketmaker/Pueblo/Anasazi sequence and, in the same way, that Cochise is antecedent to Mogollon (i.e., it is suggested that these two classic agriculture-based southwestern cultures developed indigenously).

The Archaic of California, the Great Basin, and the Northwest are continental anomalies in the sense that in these areas, as well as in the Arctic and Subarctic, nearly the whole of human occupation is best classified as "Archaic." Evidently early assemblages (probably pre-3000 B.C.) in these areas have produced basally thinned-and-ground lanceolate points that share affinities with Clovis and Plano forms, but there is little evidence that these were associated with a classic Paleo-Indian economy based primarily on large game. Subsistence may have been more specialized (consisted of few resources) than that of later times but still probably included a mixed spectrum of game and some plants, perhaps approximating the kind of diet one might have observed in ethnographic times in the Subarctic or plateau. Archaic manifestations that follow these early cultures are invariably distinguished by a shift in projectile point shape from lanceolate to (mainly) stemmed and strongly shouldered pieces that generally decrease in size over time, especially after about A.D. 500, when the bow and arrow appear. Much of the Archaic in these areas centers on resource intensification that targeted key species.

The Great Basin Archaic is still frequently termed the Desert culture, although, strictly speaking, the term "Western Archaic" is more correct. The latter is simply the western expression of the continental Archaic stage and refers to a generalized pattern of hunting and gathering that emphasizes locally abundant resources and that becomes more locally specialized with time. In the Great Basin the key resources around which specializations develop include grass seeds and piñon nuts; in California, the acorn, and shellfish on the coast; and in the Northwest, salmon, sea mammals, and shellfish. These developments are so successful that in most of California and the Northwest, and in some parts of the Great Basin, hunting-and-gathering economies supported densely settled sedentary populations that developed highly complex ritual, social, and political practices. These groups refute the traditional culture evolutionary premise that hunting and gathering is insufficiently productive to support complex sociopolitical developments. This was, of course, the basis for Caldwell's objection to the Archaic and Formative of Willey and Phillips and the consequent basis for Jennings's ideas about the Archaic.

[See also AMERICAS, FIRST SETTLEMENT OF THE AMERICAS AFTER 13,000 B.C.; DALTON CULTURE; HIGH ALTITUDE OCCUPATIONS IN THE AMERICAN WEST; HUNTERS OF THE NORTH AMERICAN PLAINS; MEGAFAUNAL EXTINCTION; NORTH AMERICA: INTRODUCTION.]

■ William A. Ritchie, *The Lamoka Lake Site* (1932). Gordon R. Willey and Phillip Phillips, *Method and Theory in American Archaeology* (1958). Jesse D. Jennings, *Prehistory of North America* (1968) Joseph R. Caldwell, *Trend and Tradition in the Prehistory of the Eastern United States* (1958).

Robert L. Bettinger

HUNTERS OF THE NORTH AMERICAN PLAINS.

The American bison (*Bison bison*) was the primary game animal for most Native American groups who inhabited the Great Plains region from 11,000 B.P. until the near extermination of bison during the 1870s and 1880s. During these millennia, however, the character of the Great Plains climate, environment, and ecology changed substantially. Likewise, the human groups who lived in the region were diverse from the earliest to latest times. Bison also changed, becoming smaller in size, more gregarious, and increasing in population.

Distinct cultural groups with different languages, cultural characteristics, and lifeways occupied the Plains area, and their dependence upon bison varied by region, year, season, and overall economy. For most, however, bison provided a truly astonishing array of technological resources and food. Food from bison included meat, fat, bone marrow, blood, organs, and rumen content. Other products included hides used to make clothing, containers, shelters, blankets, ropes, lashings, and handles; sinew used for sewing and lashing; dung used for fuel; and bones used for a wide variety of tools including hoes, awls, arrowpoints, musical rasps, handles, knives, arrowshaft straighteners,

quill flatteners, hide fleshers, digging stick tips, and paint applicators.

For most of prehistory Great Plains people lived as hunter-gatherers whose use of bison was complemented by a wide variety of other plant and animal resources. By late in the first millennium A.D., numerous groups lived in hamlets and villages along the primary rivers and tributaries of the Plains and raised domestic crops including corn, beans, squash, and sunflowers. These late prehistoric Plains villagers, who were ancestral to the historic Arikara, Mandan, Hidatsa, Pawnee, Ponca, and Wichita, all depended on seasonal bison hunting and trade with nomadic groups. The significance of bison to these part-time horticulturalists varied. Two annual bison hunts, one during summer after spring planting and one in the fall following harvest, were a common pattern. The success of these hunts was critical to the economies of Plains village societies, but there was considerable variation in annual crop and hunt productivity and in reliance on trade.

Plains villagers' processing of bison for long-distance transport and long-term storage resulted in distinctive patterns of carcass butchery and use. Nomadic hunters, however, were not tied to permanent villages and did not have to schedule hunting around planting and harvesting of crops. The early nomads lived by following and intercepting bison herds and camping as long as feasible near kill locations, perhaps much of the winter in some cases. As a result, the nomads' concerns for transport and storage, and their seasonal patterns of movement, were significantly different from those of the villagers. Historically, horse-using Plains nomadic bison hunters were represented by such groups as the Blackfeet, Sioux, Cheyenne, Arapaho, Plains Apache, Kiowa, and Comanche.

The production of pemmican, a combination of dried and pounded meat mixed with grease and fat (derived from boiling cancellous bone) and sometimes enhanced with the addition of dried fruit or berries, was a key technological development for storage and transport of bison products. Intensive processing of bison bone for extraction of grease needed in pemmican production apparently developed late in Plains prehistory. Prehistoric village groups and nomads involved in trading with Villagers, or with Pueblos to the southwest, relied heavily on pemmican, which was stored in rawhide containers called parfleches. Debate continues about the significance of bison products and intergroup trading in prehorticultural time and during the prehorse period. The corn-based high-carbohydrate, low-protein diet of late prehistoric Plains villagers and eastern Pueblos may have made bison hunting and trade with hunters extremely important for nutritional reasons. A generally symbiotic relationship developed, which was enhanced with the additional transport and interaction potential provided by the horse. In prehorse times the dog was the primary beast of burden for the Plains tribes.

The first unequivocal evidence for bison hunting by Native Americans comes from sites that date to about 11,000 B.P. These early Paleo-Indian cultural groups are recognized by distinctive projectile point types and other characteristic tools. The earliest bison-hunting cultures include people of the archaeologically recognized Clovis, Folsom, and Goshen Complexes. Some Clovis sites in the Plains region, dating from 11,200 to 10,900 B.P., have evidence of bison hunting or butchering. These include Murray Springs, Arizona; Blackwater Draw, New Mexico; and Aubrey, Texas. Most Clovis sites from Montana and Wyoming to Texas and

Oklahoma have evidence for hunting or use of mammoth in addition to or excluding bison. Other extinct species sometimes represented at Clovis sites include camel, horse, mastodon, sloth, and large turtles. Antelope and deer are represented in the early Plains diet from at least Folsom times on, and antelope drives and mountain sheep trapping are represented later in the prehistoric record.

Folsom culture sites, dating from about 10,800 to 10,200 B.P., represent the first widespread hunting groups who relied heavily on the Late Pleistocene bison subspecies *Bison bison antiquus*. The distinctive stone tools of Folsom people, including projectile points that were delicately made and usually thinned by fluting (removal of long flakes from the base to near the tip), represents what was perhaps the first cultural tradition to originate and develop in the Great Plains region. Folsom sites occur from Canada to southern Texas and through the Rockies to the eastern prairie margin. A wide variety of site types are represented including camps that sometimes have hearths and evidence of small circular shelters, bison bone beds or kill sites, hunting stations and overlooks, lithic quarries and workshops, isolated finds and limited activity sites, red ocher quarries, and combinations of these. Extensive campsites, of which Lindenmeier in northern Colorado is the best-known example, usually occur in sheltered settings, or adjacent to kill sites or lithic sources.

The number of bison in individual Folsom- and Clovis-age kills varies from a single or few animals to as many as fifty-five or sixty at the Lipscomb site in the Texas Panhandle. Bison-hunting techniques were well developed even during this early period. Trapping animals in small box canyons or steep-sided *arroyos* was a common tactic. A Folsom-age bison jump is represented at Bonfire Shelter in southern Texas, where animals were driven over the vertical wall of a deep canyon. Bison jump sites where animals are driven over such abrupt precipices (which generally are not obvious to the approaching animals) were used intensively during later prehistoric periods. The Old Women's and Head-Smashed-In bison jumps in Alberta are good examples of repeatedly used jump locations. Other hunting methods included running a herd into a deep, narrow gully, as at the 10,000 B.P. Olsen-Chubbock site in Colorado; trapping them in a deep sinkhole, as at the A.D. 1500–1800 Vore site in Wyoming; trapping in a parabolic sand dune, as at the 9800 B.P. Hell Gap–age Casper site in Wyoming; and surrounding a herd using stalking techniques, which in historic times often included use of wolfskin disguises by hunters. Also, use of brush fences or deep snow, in conjunction with snow shoes, have been suggested as possible aids at sites where the land surfaces have provided no obvious clues as to how a herd might have been trapped or contained.

Ritual activity of the 10,500-year-old Folsom culture may be evidenced by intentional abandonment of well-made stone projectile point preforms, by the occurrence of red ocher in domestic and kill site contexts such as at the Agate Basin site in Wyoming, by a possible bison skull "shrine" feature at Lake Theo in Texas, and by a red painted zigzag line on a bison skull in the lowest of three bone beds at the Cooper site in Oklahoma. The use of red ocher in treatment of the dead during burial is also evident at the few Paleo-

Indian-age burials that have been documented in the Plains region.

Possible ceremonial activity associated with early bison hunters is also evidenced at the Hell Gap–age Jones-Miller site in eastern Colorado, where a miniature Hell Gap point, a possible bone whistle, and a butchered dog skeleton were found with a posthole (which would have supported a large pole) near the center of the bone bed. These features were probably the focus of hunting-related ritual activity. Very similar evidence is found in the ethnographic literature on Plains bison hunters almost 10,000 years later. There is, then, the possibility of some elements of continuity in the Plains region from the time of the earliest bison hunters until the historic period. As indicated, however, there were some important and basic differences in the manner that these earliest hunters and late prehistoric and historic groups utilized bison resources.

The Early Holocene bison hunters from about 10,000 until 8,000 B.P., generally referred to as late Paleo-Indian, were widespread throughout the Plains region and are represented by a variety of distinctive artifact and projectile point types such as Agate Basin, Hell Gap, Alberta, Scottsbluff, Allen, Plainview, Milnesand, and others. Some late Paleo-Indian bison bone beds are quite large with up to several hundred bison carcasses represented, as at the Hudson-Meng site in northwestern Nebraska. More than one kill event is represented at several sites.

Extensive mobility of these early prehistoric hunting groups is indicated by the distinctive stone types that were used in the production of their lithic artifacts. Key sources of high-quality stone, such as the Knife River Flint quarries in western North Dakota and the Alibates quarries in the Texas Panhandle, are often well represented by artifacts in tool assemblages found from 62 to 186 miles (100 to 300 km) from the sources. Trade became important during late prehistory, when regional population had increased and permanent villages existed. During the Paleo-Indian period, however, movement of quality stone used for artifact manufacture is believed to represent the actual movements of these early nomadic hunters who might traverse an area tens of thousands of square kilometers in extent during a few seasons.

During the Middle Holocene (8,000–4,000 B.P.), there are fewer well-documented bison kill or processing sites. That bison hunting remained important in most of the Plains during the droughty climatic conditions of the Middle Holocene is evidenced by such sites as Hawken in the Wyoming Black Hills, Logan Creek in eastern Nebraska, the Cherokee site in western Iowa, and Lubbock Lake in the Texas Panhandle.

[*See also* NORTH AMERICA: THE NORTH AMERICAN PLAINS.]

■ John C. Ewers, *The Horse in Blackfoot Indian Culture* (1955). Preston Holder, *The Hoe and the Horse on the Plains* (1970). Joe Ben Wheat, *The Olsen-Chubbock Site: A Paleo-Indian Bison Kill* (1972). Leslie B. Davis and Michael Wilson, eds., *Bison Procurement and Utilization: A Symposium* (1978). John D. Speth, *Bison Kills and Bone Counts* (1983). Waldo R. Wedel, *Central Plains Prehistory* (1986). Leslie B. Davis and Brian O. K. Reeves, eds., *Hunters of the Recent Past* (1990). George C. Frison, *Prehistoric Hunters of the High Plains*, 2nd ed. (1991). Dennis J. Stanford and Jane S. Day, eds., *Ice Age Hunters of the Rockies* (1992).
Jack L. Hofman

I

ICE MAN. *See* SIMILAUN MAN.

IDEOLOGY AND ARCHAEOLOGY. Although much archaeological interpretation focuses on economic and social aspects of life in the past, some archaeologists also turn their attention to the interpretation of ideology in past societies. Until recently, most archaeologists considered ideology to be synonymous with belief system, cosmology, and *religion, and it was discussed most often in terms of burials and related ritual contexts. Thus, tombs and burial mounds were, and are, examined for evidence of the belief system of a past society. This is interpreted from iconography and other decoration on ceramic, stone, metal, and bone items interred with the dead, particularly in depictions of gods, goddesses, spirits, or heroic ancestors; from the spatial arrangement of human remains in the tomb or mound; from the treatment of the dead by cremation, mummification, or other means prior to *burial; and from evidence of secondary burial, suggesting a ritual activity for the larger kin group or community.

Other interpretations of belief systems have involved detailed analyses of art forms and glyphs. One well-known example is the Upper Paleolithic *art found in caves in France and Spain, in the form of paintings and engravings on cave walls and ceilings as well as portable sculpture and engraved objects. This cave art has been variously interpreted to represent hunting magic, calendrical and locational notation, beliefs about sexuality and gender divisions, and symbols used by age-graded groups in rituals related to the life cycle.

The analyses of glyphs in Mesoamerica provides an example of another kind of interpretation. These writing systems may be seen in stelae, monumental architecture, jade and shell objects, ceramic vessels, and folding-screen bark books. The writing system that has received the most study is that of the Maya, especially from the Classic (A.D. 200–900) and Post-Classic (A.D. 900–1541) Periods. Glyphs include depictions of specific deities, places, ancestors, and rulers as well as calendrical dates; they relate historical and mythical events (not necessarily separate things) and convey nuance, puns, and metaphor. The deciphering of the Maya writing system has had profound effects not only on our understanding of Maya belief systems but also on our understanding of other aspects of precontact *Maya civilization.

Although archaeologists traditionally have interpreted ideology as a separate sphere analogous to the economic, technological, and social spheres, more recent interpretations view ideology and belief systems as embedded in all aspects of society. These interpretations are of two kinds, although some archaeologists combine them. First, there is a structuralist or symbolic approach to understanding ideology, concerned with the underlying structures as reflected in material culture. In structuralist theory, meaning is often discussed in terms of dualistic oppositions (such as male/female, hot/cold, inside/outside, and pure/polluted), which are interpreted from the form, decoration, and distribution of material items. Second, there is a Marxist approach, most often concerned with the ways in which belief systems mask inequalities operating in a past society. For example, the ideology or belief system of a particular culture, as interpreted through material remains, appears to celebrate group cohesion and unity, masking the fact that some members of the group have greater access than others to particular goods and information.

More recently, some archaeologists have examined ideology in past societies using feminist approaches. In addition to revealing the androcentric biases of previous research, these studies have looked specifically at cultural constructions of gender. Such research has included, for example, reexamination of Upper Paleolithic art and reinterpretation of northern European Neolithic social organization, as well as new studies concerned with gender ideology in past societies.

Finally, archaeologists have used reflexive approaches, including *critical theory, to reveal the ways in which archaeological knowledge has been and is being used to support and legitimize the authority of dominant groups, especially in state-level societies. By establishing ideological ties with the society's ancestors (distant or recent), the present dominant group can seem to be that group which should be in charge, "naturally," following the path of the society's forebears. In addition, these archaeologists remind us that interpretations of past belief systems are not value neutral; archaeologists bring their own sociopolitical biases to their research and need to consciously reflect on the ways in which that affects the work they do.

[*See also* GENDER, ARCHAEOLOGY OF; HISTORY OF ARCHAEOLOGY, INTELLECTUAL; MARXIST THEORY; POST-PROCESSUAL THEORY.]

■ Ian Hodder, ed., *Symbolic and Structural Archaeology* (1982). Daniel Miller and Christopher Tilley, eds., *Ideology, Power and Prehistory* (1984). Linda Schele and Mary Ellen Miller, *The Blood of Kings: Dynasty and Ritual in Maya Art* (1986). Don D. Fowler, "Uses of the Past: Archaeology in the Service of the State," *American Antiquity* 52 (1987): 229–248. Michael Shanks and Christopher Tilley, *Social Theory and Archaeology* (1987). Joan M. Gero and Margaret W. Conkey, eds., *Engendering Archaeology* (1991).

Elizabeth M. Scott

INCA CIVILIZATION

Inca Roads
Inca Religion
Pizarro and the Conquest of the Incas

INTRODUCTION

Early in the fifteenth century, the Incas launched the formation of the largest pre-Hispanic empire in the Americas, by extending dominion over their neighbors in Peru's southern Andes Mountains. By 1532, the Inca Empire, Tawantinsuyu—Land of the Four Parts—stretched 2,485 miles (4,000 km) along western South America, from the Ancasmayo River, between modern Ecuador and Colombia, to the Maule River, near Santiago, Chile. Centered at *Cuzco, the empire encompassed over a hundred societies, who inhabited nearly 386,000 square miles (1,000,000 sq km) of the strikingly diverse Andean environment. Their domain included coastal deserts cut by lush drainages, intermontane valleys, rolling pasturelands (puna), the high Bolivian altiplano, and the semi-tropical eastern forests (montaña). Andean peoples combined maize and high-elevation tuber (primarily potato) agriculture with llama and alpaca herding for their subsistence.

Because no indigenous writing system existed in the Andes, Inca civilization is accessible through archaeology, early Spanish documents, and colonial-era native accounts. Tawantinsuyu's origins are clouded, for the narratives meld myth and history and do not fully coincide with archaeological data. Inca legends report separate creations of the Inca royalty, nobility, and commoners. In one myth, the Incas emerged from three caves at Pacariqtambo, 20 miles (30 km) south of Cuzco. In another, the deified ancestor Manco Qhapaq came from the Isle of the Sun in Lake Titicaca. The ancestors performed miraculous feats on their journey to Cuzco, where they founded their dynasty through incestuous couplings and local marriages. The codified king list continued with Sinchi Roca, Lloque Yupanki, Mayta Qhapaq, Qhapaq Yupanki, Yawar Waqaq, Viracocha Inka, Pachacutec Inka Yupanki, Thupa Inka Yupanki, Wayna Qhapaq, Wascar, and Atawallpa.

The conventional historical chronology, which draws from Cabello de Valboa's (1586) sequence of dates, reports that the Incas were embroiled in volatile local politics until the rule of Viracocha, when expeditions ventured south. About A.D. 1438, Viracocha fled Cuzco in the face of an attack by the neighboring Chankas, who were overcome by a divinely assisted defense led by Inka Yupanki. Taking the name Pachacutec, Yupanki usurped the throne and undertook conquests in southern Peru and the Titicaca basin. About 1463, Pachacutec retired to build the sacred capital of Cuzco, yielding titular command to the youth Thupa Inka, who accompanied campaigns that annexed most of Peru and highland Ecuador. About the time of Pachacutec's death in 1473, Thupa Inka incorporated lands extending through Bolivia to central Chile and northwestern Argentina. Wayna Qhapaq (r. 1493–1528) oversaw campaigns in Ecuador, but concentrated on organizing imperial rule, until he died from smallpox in an epidemic that prefaced the Spanish invasion. Civil war between two royal aspirants ended as the Spaniards arrived in Cajamarca, Peru, in November 1532. Wascar, Cuzco's leader, fell to the Ecuadorian contingent, led by his half-brother Atawallpa. Once captured by the conquistadores, Atawallpa ordered Wascar killed, providing the Spaniards a pretext for garroting him and triggering the empire's collapse.

Archaeological evidence suggests that the Cuzco region was relatively tranquil by A.D. 1200, as indicated by the widespread Killke ceramic style and a dearth of fortified sites prevalent elsewhere. Radiocarbon dates from early imperial sites, such as Pumamarca (Urubamba Valley), suggest that the expansionist polity was taking form by the mid-1300s. Other carbon dates place the major expansions twenty-five to fifty years earlier than Cabello does, raising doubts about the completeness of the royal histories.

Military tactics included pitched battle with overwhelming numbers and protracted sieges, but the Inca expansion gained as much from diplomacy as from military conquest. It was aided by mobilizing conquered groups for subsequent campaigns and offers of favorable treatment to loyal subject elites (kurakas). Armies were mobilized seasonally as a labor duty, although some campaigns lasted years. Military successes were tempered with disastrous campaigns into the eastern forests and plains, defiance in Ecuador, and invasions. Protective cordons of forts were erected at Pambamarca (Ecuador) and along the southeastern perimeter (e.g., Inkallacta, Bolivia; Pucará de Andalgalá, Argentina; Chena, Chile).

Tawantinsuyu's rule was fashioned around systematic principles tailored to local circumstances. Below the emperor were his lineage and ten royal kin groups (panacas), five each in upper (hanan) and lower (hurin) Cuzco. Each panaca also contained moieties (halves). A three-part hierarchical (qollana, payan, kayaw) intersected this structure. Because the ablest son was supposed to succeed each emperor, fratricidal infighting attended royal successions, even after co-regencies were instituted to ease the transition. The resultant political instability invited rebellions, notably by the powerful Qolla (Titicaca basin).

Tawantinsuyu comprised four parts, Chinchaysuyu (NW), Antisuyu (NE), Qollasuyu (SE), and Condesuyu (SW), each with its own governor. Each quarter contained numerous provinces, each with a governor (t'oqrikoq), normally an ethnic Inca. Provinces were divided into two or three saya, usually headed by ethnic elites. In the Peruvian heartland, the population was organized into units of 100, 500, 1,000, 5,000, and 10,000 households, the last ideally forming a saya. Because provinces and saya were created from existing etnías (ethnic groups), populations were shuffled and the administrative ideal adjusted to make the design and demographic reality coincide. The decimal hierarchy was used for census taking and corvée and military recruitment, but was not installed toward the southern and northern perimeters. In Ecuador, local chiefdoms were sometimes pooled under leaders recognized by the state. Conversely, the Chimu Empire of Peru's north coast was broken into constituent valleys, and its paramount was taken hostage to Cuzco.

A state ideology was central to Inca rule. Viracocha, the creator, was the divine ancestor of the royal lineage, linking the emperor (SapaInka) to the pantheon, thus legitimizing Inca dominion. Ancestor worship found its most elaborate form in the panacas. The mummified kings, or a surrogate stone, were kept in state by their descendants, sustained by dedicated resources. Principal gods included the sun god Inti and the thunder god Ilyap'a. The sacred calendar contained twelve lunar months, beginning with Qhapaq Raymi, which contained the winter solstice. Each month was tied to a ritual cycle, marked by public ceremonies. The Incas envisioned the landscape as populated by myriad sacred features called w'akas, among them springs, rocks, and mountains. Caches of gold and silver figurines, ceramics, and human beings were buried at the frontier and at high-elevation sites *(apacheta)*, to claim territory and venerate spirits.

Provincial rule depended on feasting and disbursing gifts to subjects, including the valued coca leaf. The state hosted festivals at its centers, dispensing copious amounts of maize beer *(chicha)*; bone chemistry suggests that males may have had preferred access to the brew. Political relations were abetted by preferential treatment of some ethnic groups. The Chincha of the central Peruvian coast held an elevated status, perhaps because of their voyages to Ecuador for *Spondylus* shell. The Chachapoyas (Peru) and Cañares (Ecuador) were favored soldiers, and the Lucanas (Peru) litter bearers.

Several policies helped stabilize state rule. A major program moved communities of internal colonists *(mitmaqkuna)* to new areas as state farmers, artisans, or garrisons. High fortified subject settlements were abandoned and the populace dispersed at lower elevations, a practice recognizable in archaeological site distributions. The Incas also insisted that all imperial business be conducted in the Quechua language and that selected sons of provincial elites be trained in Cuzco.

Although the state intruded ubiquitously into daily life, its success depended on local socioeconomic stability. Highland Andean society was based on the *ayllu*, a kin-based, endogamous, landholding corporate group. The nuclear family was the minimal economic unit. Household labor was allocated by age group and sex, and communities often pooled labor for production. Rights to resources were allotted through usufruct. Descent and inheritance were bilineal, males through the male line and females matrilaterally. The *kurakas*, who were confirmed or replaced by the Incas, served as state administrators. Depending on their status, elites were relieved from labor duty, had their lands and herds tended, and received household service and multiple wives.

Upon occupying a region, the Incas claimed ownership of all resources, including farming and grazing lands, natural biota, and raw materials. Lands were nominally divided among the state, state religion, and communities, but local societies retained many traditional resources. The Incas adopted the language of reciprocal obligations between subjects and their lords to legitimize taxation. State activities were supported mostly through a rotating labor tax assessed to each household and by labor specialists. Over forty kinds of labor were owed, including farming, military service, herding, artisanry, construction, mining, and guard duty. Native testimony, from Huánuco (Peru) and Chucuito (Bolivia), indicates that labor exactions were partially adapted to local resources and skills. Analyses of household middens and skeletal remains in the Mantaro Valley (Peru) suggest that, despite the onerous burdens, aspects of life improved as local conflict was dampened, infant mortality dropped, and people ate more maize and camelid meat.

State artisans often resided in discrete communities, making fine wool tapestries *(qompi)* and feathered textiles, metal and wooden goods, and polychrome ceramics, among other objects. The textiles and ceramics had distinctive geometric designs that provided emblems of imperial rule in the multilingual but aliterate society. Other specialists included the *yanakuna*, individuals assigned to tasks ranging from household service to administration, and *aqllakuna*, young women sequestered at state centers to weave and brew *chicha*, before being awarded in marriage.

The Incas built an infrastructure of provincial centers and more than 2,000 way stations *(tampu)*, linked by 18,640 miles (30,000 km) of roads. The grandest centers lay between Cuzco and Quito: Willkawaman, Hatun Xauxa, Pumpu, Huánuco Pampa, Cajamarca, and Tumipampa. They were hubs for administration, military encampment, religion, artisanry, and labor recruitment. Everything from food to armaments, clothing, and status goods was kept nearby in immense storage complexes; botanical remains from Huánuco Pampa and Hatun Xauxa storehouses largely match crops that could be grown locally. Storehouse contents, along with censuses, histories, and other accounts, were recorded on *khipu*, mnemonic knotted strings. The royal highway *(qhapaq ñan)* included highland and coastal routes, connected by transverse trunks. The roads, whose use required state approval, expedited travel, transport by human and llama caravan, and communication by runners *(chaski)* posted at about two-and-a-half-mile (4 km) intervals.

Inca settlement planning reflects both order and ties between society and the cosmos. Cuzco was laid out in the form of a puma, with upper and lower sectors that housed the moieties of Inca royalty. A series of forty to forty-one conceptual lines *(zeques)* radiated out from the central plaza of Haucaypata, each linking a set of w'akas to the conceptual core of the universe. Other planned settlements were laid out on orthogonal or trapezoidal grids around a large plaza containing a truncate pyramid platform.

Inca architecture is renowned for its fine cut-stone, mortarless ashlar masonry, which echoed the earlier Tiwanaku style (Lake Titicaca). Examples are found in the *Qoricancha* (Temple of the Sun) in Cuzco, in the megalithic terraces of nearby Saqsaywaman, and in buildings at Ollantaytambo and *Machu Picchu. Many Inca buildings combined fieldstone and mud-brick walls. Coastal centers, including Inkawasi, La Centinela, and Tambo Colorado, were built of adobe. Large single room structures *(kallanka)*, used for garrisons and gatherings, were important in provincial centers. Residential compounds were rectangular enclosures *(kancha)* with gabled houses facing onto patios. Distinctive architectural features include canted walls, trapezoidal niches, and double-jamb doorways. Inca engineering is preserved today in paved and buttressed roads, fitted stone foundations for suspension bridges, irrigation systems, and spectacular terraces (e.g., Pisac, Colca Valley), many of which form parts of aristocratic estates.

[*See also* SOUTH AMERICA, *articles on* THE RISE OF COMPLEX SOCIETIES IN SOUTH AMERICA, HIGHLANDS CULTURES OF SOUTH AMERICA.]

■ Cabello de Valboa, *Miscelánea Anártica* (1586/1951). Bernabé Cobo, *History of the Inca Empire* (1653/1979). Bernabé Cobo, *Inca Religion and Customs* (1653/1990). John H. Rowe, "Inca Culture at the Time of the Spanish Conquest," in *Handbook of South American Indians*, vol. 2, ed. Julian Steward (1963), pp. 183–330. Graziano Gasparini and Luise Margolies, *Inca Architecture* (1980). John V. Murra, *The Inka Economic System* (1980). John Hyslop, *The Inka Road System* (1984). Craig Morris and Donald Thompson, *Huánuco Pampa* (1985). John Hyslop, *Inka Settlement Planning* (1990). Brian Bauer, *The Formation of the Inca State* (1992). Terence N. D'Altroy, *Provincial Power in the Inka Empire* (1992). Terry Y. LeVine, ed., *Inka Storage Systems* (1992). Michael Malpass, ed., *Provincial Inca* (1993).

Terence D'Altroy

INCA RULING DYNASTIES

Tawantinsuyu, the Inca Empire, was ruled from *Cuzco by the Sapa Inca (Unique Inca). When the Spanish invaded in

1532, a succession of rulers was represented by mummified bodies kept in Cuzco and venerated as virtual deities. Officially the royal line descended from the sun, and only people descending from one of the kings were accorded the status of Inca. Cuzco Incas consisted of ten *panacas*, or descent groups, each founded by one emperor. Every *panaca* was paired with a similar but larger descent group, an *ayllu*, composed of original occupants from the Cuzco region, allied to the Incas. These *ayllus* owed periodic labor in Cuzco. While serving, they resided on the land of and were supervised by the Inca *panaca* with which each was paired. The people of these *ayllus* were Incas by privilege, while all others in the empire were known by other ethnic names.

The Incas had no writing, so they recorded no history, although there were official narrative poems commemorating the exploits of each Sapa Inca that were memorized and recited by professional courtiers. Following the Spanish conquest the viceroy, whose government had deposed the Incas, conducted an investigation of Inca rulership. An Inca dynastic history was constructed, one that showed the Incas to be recent conquerors whose legitimacy was questionable in the eyes of Spanish royalty. Modern researchers must ask whether this dynastic history represents a native understanding of Inca kingship or a European imposition. Two positions have developed. One championed by John H. Rowe assumes that the Incas dealt with the past in terms of linear history, as Europeans do. The modern researcher must sift through conflicting accounts from the sixteenth century and determine which are most likely to be true by evaluating each chronicler's knowledge and honesty. Rowe's version of the Inca past is critiqued by R. Tom Zuidema, arguing that Inca narrative poems were more like Indonesian epics, charters for social structure. Confusions and contradictions in early chronicles are not errors, but they help reveal what the Incas intended before the accounts were rendered meaningful for Spanish readers. Rowe concluded that thirteen successive Sapa Incas ruled Tawantinsuyu, the first five from the lower moiety and the rest from the upper moiety.

The kings from the lower moiety were Manco Capac, Sinchi Roca, Lloque Yupanqui, Mayta Capac, and Capac Yupanqui. The kings from the upper moiety were Inca Roca, Yahuar Huaca, Viracocha Inca, Pachacuti Inca, Topa Inca Yupanqui, Huayna Capac, Huascar, and Atahuallpa.

The early kings were little more than war chiefs who led the Inca ethnic group into the Cuzco Valley several centuries before the empire, won lands, and settled down to raiding their neighbors. Old narrative poems about these rulers were probably heavily mythologized and could not be counted on to represent historical fact. However, in the early fifteenth century, Viracocha Inca ascended the throne. He followed successful raids by imposing control and tribute, beginning imperial government.

About 1438 the ninth ruler was crowned, after successfully defeating an attack on the Cuzco Valley and executing Viracocha Inca's heir. Crowned Pachacuti Inca—cataclysm and reformer of the world—he extended Inca control widely, always imposing provincial government. Pachacuti was blessed with a militarily brilliant son, Topa Inca. Before death he turned the armies over to Topa (around 1463) and devoted himself to organizing state administration and rebuilding the capital city of Cuzco. He built impressive palaces for himself and Topa, as well as for each of his predecessors, officializing a succession of ten kings. To create a spectacular ritual life for the new capital,

he granted each former Sapa Inca an estate, to be administered by that king's descendants in ritual veneration of the ancestor mummy on specified occasions.

Huayna Capac became the eleventh Sapa Inca (about 1493) but, along with his heir, died in a devastating epidemic about 1527. Another legitimate son, Huascar was crowned in Cuzco, but his rule was contested by Atahuallpa, also a legitimate son. Atahuallpa had the loyalty of the army, and by 1532, defeated his half-brother.

According to this historiographic approach, when an Inca king founded his descent group, or *panaca*, the new king did not inherit the property of his father. It has been argued by some that this was a novel invention that produced the Inca's empire by obliging each new king to embark on conquests to accumulate enough wealth to endow his own descent group and insure his cult. They refer to the rule as "split inheritance" (one son received the throne, and the rest of the descendants got the estate), but it is unlikely that this explains Inca expansionism. Rather, there seems to have been a nearly universal Andean preference for stewardship of accumulated wealth and estate by a corporate group of descendants, real and fictive, who rendered cult to their founding ancestor. Rather than forcing younger Inca kings to acquire wealth through conquest, it was this kind of behavior that offered young men means of social ascension. By successfully embarking on accumulative exploits, and attracting a strong following of real and fictive descendants, one could become a leader and perhaps even a king.

R. Tom Zuidema offers alternatives to important points in the historiographic interpretation of Inca kingship. The total of ten kings seemingly officialized by Pachacuti Inca represented not dynastic reality of the moment but a structural imperative. Cuzco consisted of two complementary moieties, each divided into five social groups—the *panacas*. Each *panaca* required a symbolic founder, whose kinship position relative to the ruling Sapa Inca expressed the status of the *panaca*. Consequently the importance of former emperors' mummies was not genealogical succession but their *panaca*'s structural position in the social hierarchy of Cuzco, that was reconstituted with the ascension of each new Sapa Inca—representative of the sun on Earth.

The kings of lower Cuzco and upper Cuzco were actually simultaneous kings. Spanish investigators became confused because the upper moiety was superior to the lower moiety, and kin terms expressing this rank relative to the Sapa Inca (of the upper moiety) used generations of removal to indicate status. Thus the founders of the ranked *panacas* of the upper moiety were father, grandfather, great-grandfather, and so on of the living king. Founders of lower moiety *panacas* were great-great-great-great-grandfather and even more distantly removed from the king. These terms were understood as generations of history, not relative status by Spaniards. The Sapa Inca's sons also used kinship terminology to denote status. Sons by full sisters referred to the king as father, but those of lower Inca women called him grandfather, great-grandfather, and so on, depending on their mother's status. Sons by non-Inca women referred to the Sapa Inca as uncle (mother's brother), great-uncle, and so on, even though they were genealogical children of the king. They became members of a lower Cuzco *panaca* that recognized one of the former kings of lower Cuzco as its founder, not because of real genealogical origin, but because of the status ascribed them within Inca society.

The historiographical approach to Inca kingship, critiqued from a structural perspective, is beginning to reveal unexpected complexity in Inca dynastic relations. New insights will be forthcoming, but because this remarkable system was not described until it had been destroyed, and then from a European perspective, we may never achieve complete understanding.

[See also SOUTH AMERICA: THE RISE OF COMPLEX SOCIETIES IN SOUTH AMERICA.]

■ John H. Rowe, "Inca Culture at the Time of the Spanish Conquest," in Handbook of South American Indians, vol. 2: The Andean Civilizations, ed. J. Steward (1946), pp. 183–330. John H. Rowe, "An Account of the Shrines of Ancient Cuzco," Ñawpa Pacha 17: 1–80. R. Tom Zuidema, "Dynastic Structures in Andean Culture," in The Northern Dynasties: Kingship and Statecraft in Chimor, ed. M. A. Moseley and A. Cordy-Collins (1990), pp. 489–537. R. Tom Zuidema, Inca Civilization in Cuzco (1990). Franklin Pease, Los Incas: Una Introduccion (1991). Brian Bauer, The Development of the Inca State (1992).

William H. Isbell

INCA ECONOMIC ORGANIZATION

The Inca Empire represents one of the great ancient states in world history. Expanding out of its capital in highland *Cuzco, the empire conquered most of western South America in a few generations. As the Inca incorporated new provinces into their political orbit, they created an imperial economy of impressive proportions and complexity.

Economic production in the Inca state was ideally organized around the household coupled with a complex system of labor organization that was imposed upon conquered groups. One point in which most Andeanists agree is that the extraction of wealth in the Inca state was based upon a labor tax, and was not a system based upon tribute-in-kind such as that found in the Aztec Empire.

Catherine Julien and others have argued that this labor recruitment system was ideally organized around a decimal system. Each married male and his household constituted a tribute-paying unit. Units from 10 to 10,000 tribute-payers were hierarchically organized and headed by both Inca and indigenous elite. The Inca administrators would assign labor requirements for certain tasks. These tasks included bridge building, military quotas, maintaining road way-stations, weaving, pottery making, working agricultural land, and so on. Lower-level elite, in turn, would assign the specific households to fulfill these orders.

The Inca state's imperial system was built firmly within the constraints and opportunities of central Andean environment and culture. Traditional redistribution and reciprocity mechanisms were elaborated into a formal imperial system on a massive scale. As Terence D'Altroy and others have noted, these relationships between the state and the tribute-paying populations were couched in ideological terms of equality, but in reality constituted a complex and grossly unequal system of resource extraction. One of the most important features of Inca political economy was the use of transplanted colonists known as mitimaes or mitmaqkuna. Colonists were expected to maintain the dress and other ethnic markers from their home territory.

According to Thomas Patterson, mitimaes were not under the control of the local elite, although the latter had to provide for some of their subsistence for two years of their residence. Patterson distinguishes several types of mitimae ranging from resettled rebels and garrisoned peoples in frontiers to colonists in underpopulated regions. In fact, mitimae served a number of economic and strategic functions. Resettled peoples in underpopulated areas served to

increase agricultural productivity. The strategic value of placing loyal subjects among potentially rebellious ones is obvious. While most preindustrial empires have used population displacement as an imperial strategy, the mitimae institution of the Inca represents a strategy of massive population and labor control.

Darrell La Lone has demonstrated that there was no market economy in the Inca state. La Lone notes the lack of true money, the absence of marketplaces, and the lack of merchants. Even in the huge Inca imperial system, the basic exchange structure was organized around "asymmetrical reciprocity" or complex redistributive relationships woven into a vast and extremely hierarchical political economy.

Economy and ideology were intimately linked in Inca society. Origin myths legitimized the conquest of territories. Imperial ideology also sought to define the economic relationships as just in traditional Andean terms. The chief means of promoting the ideal of elite generosity was the sponsoring of feasts or the distribution of certain commodities to tribute-payers when in actuality, the tribute-payers were fulfilling their labor obligations. In these redistributive transactions, maize beer (chica), textiles, and other commodities were redistributed. The basic strategy was to collect maize, wool, and so forth from the tribute-payers and transform these raw materials also into commodities. Periodically, a small portion of these commodities and other goods were redistributed to assembled commoners in elaborate festivals. Such rituals only tangentially involved the highest Inca authorities. Instead they provided a face-to-face "reciprocal" interaction between commoners and the local elite, the latter acting as representatives of both their own authority and the Inca elite in Cuzco.

In sum, the Inca economy was based largely upon the manipulation of existing political and economic mechanisms in Andean society. The household was the basic unit of economic production. The mechanisms of reciprocity and redistribution, typical of pre-Inca Andean society, were transformed into an elaborate imperial political economy. Feast-giving was also a common facet of elite strategies in the Andes well before the advent of the Inca state. The political conquest of new provinces was legitimized by the use of religious ideology, and the unequal economic relationships between elite and commoner were portrayed as just and proper through a variety of periodic rituals.

[See also TEXTILES.]

■ Pedro Cieza de Leon, The Incas of Pedro de Cieza de León (1959). John V. Murra, "The Economic Organization of the Inka State," Research in Economic Anthropology (1980). Nathan Wachtel, ed., "Reciprocity and the Inca State: From Karl Polanyi to John V. Murra," Research in Economic Anthropology (1981). Darrell E. La Lone, "The Inca As a Nonmarket Economy: Supply on Command versus Supply and Demand," in Contexts for Prehistoric Exchange (1982). John Hyslop, Jr., The Inka Road System (1984). Catherine Julien, "How Inca Decimal Organization Worked," Ethnohistory 35 (1988): 257–279. John Hyslop, Jr., Inca Settlement Planning (1990). Charles Stanish, Ancient Andean Political Economy (1992).

Charles Stanish

INCA ROADS

Tawantinsuyu, the Inca Empire, consisted of some 6 million to 30 million inhabitants spread across thousands of kilometers of mountains, deserts, and jungles. Political unification represents a remarkable success in large part based on a marvelous highway system that included at least 25,000 miles (40,000 km) of serviced roads.

To understand Inca roads we must remember that the Incas, like other Native Americans, did not use wheeled vehicles. Traffic consisted of human pedestrians—travelers as well as professional porters who carried commercial loads but also litters and sedan chairs ridden by wealthy nobles, queens, and kings—and pack trains. The llama, a small relative of the camel, carries about 65 pounds (30 kg) and walks swiftly and sure footedly on padded feet. Caravans with hundreds and even thousands of llamas traversed Tawantinsuyu, transporting products from one climate zone to another, supplying campaigning troops with food and equipment, and carrying produce or craft goods to state storage centers.

The hallmark of Inca roads was functional solutions to environmental challenges, and there was no standard width, surfacing material, construction technique, or other technical feature. Designed for foot traffic, Inca roads could ascend as steeply as fifty degrees from horizontal by incorporating long flights of steps. In difficult places the road could narrow to as little as roughly 3 feet (1 m) across, broaden again to the more typical 13 to 16 feet (4 to 5 m) wide in easy terrain, and expand to 33 feet (10 m) or more as one approached a city or administrative center. In wet country raised, stone-paved causeways with culverts and bridges protected the road from washing out, but in dry desert the highway was often no more than natural sand defined by a row of stones at each border. In cultivated valleys the highway was usually walled on both sides to protect crops from travelers, and in steep mountains the road was defended from landslides by extensive retaining walls and drainage ditches.

The backbone of the highway system consisted of two main north–south trunks, one along the coast and the other through the Andes Mountains. The highland route began at the Ancasmayo River on the Colombian border and went south through Quito, Tomebamba (modern Cuenca), Cajamarca, Jauja, Vilcas Huaman, *Cuzco, Chuquito, Paria (near modern Oruro), and into Argentina, almost to modern Mandoza. The coast highway began in Tumbez on Peru's modern border with Ecuador, and followed the coast south, eventually turning somewhat inland to reach Arequipa and then continued south to San Pedro de Atacama, from which it went on to Chile's rich central valley. Lateral roads branched from the trunk highway, many connecting the coast and highland roads, such as spurs inland from Tumbez, another inland from Paramonga to the Callejón de Huaylas, and another from the Pachacamac to Jauja. Other lateral roads penetrated east from the highland trunk into the Amazon jungle. Secondary roads and tertiary trails connected small towns, villages, and hamlets of the empire into the main highway system.

In the mountainous terrain Inca roads sometimes employed tunnels and often used bridges. Short spans were crossed with great slabs of rock, but other bridges consisted of trunks from trees brought from the jungle. The greatest spans required suspension bridges, such as the one over the Apurimac River, which was 150 feet (45 m) across. Suspension bridges were woven of vegetable fibers, and usually three thick ropes the girth of a man's thigh formed the floor of the bridge, and two more its sides. These were tied and woven into a durable whole, but the bridges still sagged deeply in the middle, and swayed back and forth in the wind, especially as traffic was passing. Such bridges had permanent attendants, not only to service the ropes but to help travelers and caravans cross.

Inca roads were built and maintained by the local communities, as tax obligations, under the supervision of Inca engineers and administrators. Typically roads were kept in good repair, but it is worth noting that the first European invaders did comment that some roads were sorely in need of service.

The Inca road system included more than highways and bridges. There were state rest centers called *tambo*, as well as post houses, or *chaskiwasi* (*chaski*, messenger; *wasi*, house). The post houses were part of a communication system that was able to send short messages and small objects over long distances quite quickly. One or two young men, usually with wife and family, were assigned to each post house, which were little more than small huts or a pair of huts at the side of the road. Carrying a message involved quickly memorizing it and running on to the next post house. As the messenger approached he blew a shell trumpet to alert the resident runner, who came out and ran with him a short distance while memorizing the message and receiving any accompanying objects. Then the new runner set off at top speed for the neighboring post house. Descriptions vary, but there seems to have been between little more than half a mile and 5 miles (1 and 8 km) between post houses. Perhaps the distance was a function of the terrain that had to be covered by the runner—shorter for steep uphill segments, but long in flat, open land. It was claimed that the Inca king ate fresh fish in Cuzco, relayed up from the coast by the post runners, and that he received dispatches from Quito, 1,865 miles (3,000 km) away, within a week of their posting.

Tambos were separated by distances apparently intended to be about a day's march but varied from as little as 6 miles (10 km) to as much as 25 miles (40 km). They were small centers where local peoples organized for state activities, and they included storage buildings with food and other goods, rooms that could be occupied by travelers, and sometimes other facilities. Some *tambos* were virtually small administrative centers consisting of dozens of buildings, but others were little more than walled enclosures with an elongated, one-room building, some storehouses, and rotating personnel capable of meeting official travelers' needs.

The highway system of the Incas, with its *tambo* inns and its post houses with messengers, linked the Inca Empire into a single communication and administrative network. Government officials, military contingents, and citizens paying labor taxes could travel quickly and safely to designated places. They were never beyond the protection and supervision of the state, whose roads were at once the vehicle and symbol of Inca power.

[See also SOUTH AMERICA, *articles on* INTRODUCTION, HIGHLANDS CULTURES OF SOUTH AMERICA.]

■ V. W. von Hagen, *Highway of the Sun* (1955). V. M. von Hagan, *The Royal Road of the Inca* (1976). John Hyslop, *The Inka Road System* (1984). Katharina J. Schreiber, "Prehistoric Roads in the Carhuarazo Valley, Peru," in *Current Archaeological Projects in the Central Andes: Some Approaches and Results*, ed. A. Kendall (1984), pp. 75–94. Terence N. D'Altroy, *Provincial Power in the Inka Empire* (1992). Thomas F. Lynch, "The Identification of Inca Posts and Roads from Catarpe to Río Frío, Chile," in *Archaeological and Ethnohistorical Assessment of the Impact of the Inca State*, ed. M. A. Malpass (1993), pp. 117–142.

William H. Isbell

INCA RELIGION

There are two caveats that should preface an overview of Inca religion and its archaeological manifestations. First, all accounts of Inca civilization and culture that are available to us at present were written by Spaniards, or Spanish-trained natives, during the decades immediately following the Spanish invasion of the Andes, beginning in 1532. Unfortunately, many of these commentaries reflect the religious ideas and prejudices of Spaniards of the time. And second, although the Incas established their empire throughout the Andes Mountains, Inca religion should be distinguished from Andean religion. The latter refers to locality-based sets of beliefs and practices—varying to a certain extent from place to place—identifying and paying homage to local earth, mountain, and water spirits and deities that were linked to local kinship and ethnic groups, and their ancestors. Inca religion, on the other hand, encompasses the beliefs and ritual practices that were promoted by the Inca nobility—often through their priestly and political agents—for the benefit of the Inca state. Although there were numerous similarities and interconnections between the two, the focus of Andean religion was on the unity and perpetuation of each of myriad local kinship and ethnic groups, whereas the driving force behind Inca religion was the unification of all such local groups within the empire in the service, and under the hegemony, of the Incas.

The capital of the Inca state was the city of *Cuzco, in present-day south-central Peru. It was here that Inca religion reached its highest expression and assumed its most complex form. The life of the city centered around the ruling Inca, called *Intip Churin* ("Son of the Sun"), who was believed to be the descendant and earthly manifestation of the sun; the queen (*Qoya*), who was associated with the moon; and the other members of the Inca nobility, who were relatives of the living king or close descendants of past kings. There were a number of royal residences located around the central plaza in Cuzco, some of which housed the families and retainers of the ruling Incas, others the descendants of past Incas, and still others the imperial administrators and attendants of the Inca kings, such as the *Amautas* (priests) and *Aqllas* (the Virgins of the Sun). The foundations and lower portions of walls of many of these buildings are still standing today.

At the ritual and spiritual center of Cuzco was the *Coricancha* ("golden enclosure"), a building—much of which stands today—composed of several rooms of finely cut stone, each devoted to a particular deity or object of worship in Inca religion. These included *Viracocha*, the "creator god" of Inca and Andean religion, the sun, the moon, Venus, lightning, thunder, and the rainbow. Mummies, or images, of past kings were also kept here. The *Coricancha* and the plaza were the principal sites of ritual activities in the ancient city, such as the two festivals called *Inti Raymi* ("sun festival"), one around the December solstice, the other around the June solstice. The Incas built temples of the sun in the major administrative centers in the empire, such as Vilcashuaman, Huanuco Pampa, and Hatun Colla, as well as the coastal oracle of Pachacamac. Each of these sites is represented by extensive archaeological remains.

Within the valley of Cuzco were located several hundred "sacred sites," called *huacas*, which took a variety of forms, such as buildings, carved rocks, and springs. Each *huaca* was accorded special significance in Inca mythology and received sacrificial offerings—ranging from shells and coca leaves to children—on a particular day in the Inca ritual calendar. Certain of the *huacas* were important in making astronomical observations for the regulation of the ritual calendar (of 328 days) and the correlation of the ritual and annual solar calendars. The organization of *huacas* in the

valley of Cuzco sanctified the landscape and provided the liturgical framework for religious activities in and around the Inca capital.

In addition to daily sacrifices in Cuzco, there were special monthly sacrifices of llamas, whose symbolism was linked to the fertility and regeneration of crops and livestock in the empire. On certain special occasions—for example, the death of one Inca and the coronation of his successor—sacrificial victims, called *capacochas*, were sent from the provinces to be sacrificed in Cuzco. *Capacochas* were also occasionally sent from the provinces to Cuzco, where they were sanctified, and then returned to their home community for sacrifice. Such sacrifices sealed a bond of loyalty between the Inca in Cuzco and the provincial nobility. The bodies of a few such sacrificial victims, interred on high mountaintops, have been found in recent years.

Inca religion was eclectic, so as the empire expanded, local deities and objects of worship were absorbed into the state religion—but always in a subordinate position to the principal deities of the Incas (i.e., Viracocha, the sun, and the moon). This tradition of eclecticism continued into the Spanish colonial era, which resulted in the syncretism of the god and saints of Catholicism with native deities, and of pre-Hispanic rituals with those of European Christianity. Since the Spaniards themselves did not practice religious eclecticism or tolerance, most of the beliefs and practices of what constituted Inca religion were destroyed following the conquest; what remained of pre-Hispanic religion—and in some cases remains even to the present day—was a blend of Catholicism and what has been characterized above as Andean religion.

[See also INCA CIVILIZATION, *articles on* INTRODUCTION, INCA RULING DYNASTIES, INCA ECONOMIC ORGANIZATON, PIZARRO AND THE CONQUEST OF THE INCAS; SOUTH AMERICA, *articles on* THE RISE OF COMPLEX SOCIETIES IN SOUTH AMERICA, HIGHLANDS CULTURES OF SOUTH AMERICA.]

■ John H. Rowe, "Inca Culture at the Time of the Spanish Conquest," in *Handbook of South American Indians*, vol. II (1946), pp. 183–330. Irene Silverblatt, *Moon, Sun, and Witches* (1987). R. Tom Zuidema, *Inca Civilization in Cuzco* (1990). Sabine MacCormack, *Religion in the Andes* (1991). Frank Salomon and George L. Urioste, trans. and eds., *The Huarochirí Manuscript: A Testament of Ancient and Colonial Andean Religion* (1991). Michael Moseley, *The Incas and Their Ancestors* (1992).

Gary Urton

PIZARRO AND THE CONQUEST OF THE INCAS

The Inca Empire developed rapidly after 1438, when Pachacuti led the successful defense of the Inca capital, Cuzco, against the Chancas. In less than a hundred years, the Incas brought the entire Andean sedentary agriculture zone under their control. At its acme, the empire contained perhaps eight million people, but the subjugated provinces largely retained their traditional autonomy and ethnic identities. Most continued under the immediate rule of their local lords, *kurakas*, and the masses had little direct contact with imperial officials except when performing rotary draft labor service, or *mit'a*. The Incas, though, did construct several major administrative and provisioning centers along highways in the provinces.

Few of these peoples routinely contributed fighters to the Inca army. Nonetheless, the Incas could readily assemble armies in the tens of thousands and maintain them in the field for months, even moving them dependably over hundreds of miles. These troops, though, were composed of commoners delivering temporary service to the empire. Only a few elite units consisted of full-time professional warriors.

A persistent weakness in the Inca imperial framework was competition among pretenders to the throne upon the demise of the reigning emperor. This deficiency was largely built into the structure of the imperial lineage, for the emperor had multiple wives, and the sons of at least several of them had some claim on the throne. Competing descent groups proliferated within the larger royal lineage. Rival claimants rose up against the anointed emperor several times after transitions. The conflict going on between Atahuallapa and Huascar when the Spaniards arrived was not without precedent in earlier decades.

Francisco Pizarro's expedition was organized in Panama, one of the first mainland colonies. Pizarro was a seasoned commander of men and had maintained a long-term partnership with Diego de Almagro. They led largely unsuccessful voyages down the Pacific coast in the mid-1520s but did learn of a significant civilization farther to the south. Pizarro thereupon returned to Spain to gain royal license for the conquest and to assemble a body of men, for Panama contained few. He recruited several half-brothers and other close associates from his hometown of Trujillo.

Pizarro led a group of only 168 men with about thirty horses into Inca territory in 1531. Typical of such Spanish expeditions, the participants were not soldiers but rather persons of middling rank back in Spain who had migrated to the frontier to better their fortunes. This undertaking was not organized as a military enterprise but as a business company, with each person signing on for a share of any possible proceeds depending on what he brought to the venture.

By the time the Spaniards penetrated the Andes, Atahuallpa had defeated Huascar's army. Atahuallpa regarded the foreigners as coastal raiders, a recurrent problem, and intended to take them captive. He and his fellow Incas never confused the Spaniards with supernatural beings. Likewise, although smallpox had afflicted the Andes in the mid-1520s and even killed an emperor, no epidemics weakened the Inca Empire while Pizarro was directing its overthrow. Indeed, the conquest was effectively completed before the Spaniards received the allegiance of any subjugated peoples.

Pizarro's tactic of seizing the emperor as soon as possible was unexceptional. Ruling a region through a captured headman was standard practice among the Spaniards in their overseas expansion. Atahuallpa had perhaps 30,000 seasoned warriors with him when he met the Spaniards at Cajamarca. On 16 November 1532, Pizarro's men grabbed the emperor after slaughtering his honor guard, which, though armed, was not expecting an attack. The Spaniards killed perhaps six thousand Incas in two hours without suffering a casualty of their own.

With Atahuallpa captive, Pizarro ruled the empire for some months. During this time, great numbers of gold and silver sculptures and decorations were delivered to the Spaniards and melted down as ransom for the freedom of the emperor. Other members of the royal lineage began to negotiate with the Spanish commander, while the several Inca armies in the field stayed inactive, as their leaders contemplated what to do. Eventually, the Spaniards executed Atahuallpa, for his utility had diminished and he was suspected of arousing his loyal forces against them. By late 1533, Pizarro, now a kingmaker, had designated Manco

Inca, a young man from Huascar's faction, as emperor. Before the year was out, Pizarro was in *Cuzco ruling through the new Inca. The empire had fallen to him without the devastation of a major settlement or a large number of people.

An Inca army under Quizquiz still remained intact in highland Peru. Pizarro dispatched Hernando de Soto with 50 horsemen and 5,000 of Manco's men in pursuit. The Inca force proved unable even to invest the city of Jauja, where about eighty Spaniards were isolated among the Huancas, the local ethnic group. The Spaniards drove Quizquiz's army into the hills in total disarray. Another Inca army under Rumiñavi was located near Quito. In May 1534, perhaps fifty cavalry under Sebastián de Benalcázar routed this force, destroying it as an organized military unit. Rumiñavi was soon captured, and Quizquiz was killed in a dispute with his own officers. By the end of 1534, no Inca military units remained to challenge the Spaniards.

But by late 1535, the royal Inca lineage, led by Manco Inca, fully appreciated the depth and permanence of the Spaniards' domination and decided to expel them. Manco quietly organized a massive insurrection that isolated nearly two hundred Spaniards in Cuzco, controlled the mountain passes to the coast, and even attacked Lima, though unsuccessfully. The siege of Cuzco by more than one hundred thousand men began in April 1536 and endured for a full year before it was broken by a relief column from the south. Nonetheless, the Spaniards' military supremacy over the Incas because of their horses and metal weapons was such that fewer than twenty of their number were killed the entire time. Further, they were soon able to push the Inca army far back from the city and kept it largely in a defensive posture for most of the year. The defenders even sent contingents safely some miles into the countryside to collect grains and animals. With the collapse of the rebellion in early 1537 and Manco Inca's flight into the tropical region east of the Andes, Spanish political hegemony over the former empire was unalterably secured.

■ John Hemming, *The Conquest of the Incas* (1970). James Lockhart, *The Men of Cajamarca: A Social and Biographical Study of the First Conquerors of Peru* (1972). Thomas Flickema, "The Siege of Cuzco," *Revista de Historia de América* 92 (July–Dec. 1981): 17–47. Geoffrey W. Conrad and Arthur A. Demarest, *Religion and Empire: The Dynamics of Aztec and Inca Expansionism* (1984). Karen Spalding, *Huarochirí: An Andean Society Under Inca and Spanish Rule* (1984). John V. Murra, "The Expansion of the Inka State: Armies, War, and Rebellions," in John V. Murra et al., eds., *Anthropological History of Andean Polities* (1986), pp. 49–58. John F. Guilmartin Jr., "The Cutting Edge: An Analysis of the Spanish Invasion and Overthrow of the Inca Empire, 1532–1539," in Kenneth J. Andrien and Rolena Adorno, eds., *Transatlantic Encounters: Europeans and Andeans in the Sixteenth Century* (1991), pp. 40–69. Thomas C. Patterson, *The Inca Empire: The Formation and Disintegration of a Pre-Capitalist State* (1991).

John E. Kicza

INDO-EUROPEANS. The Indo-Europeans comprise the largest of the world's language families and include at least eleven language stocks that are derived from a common ancestral language known as Proto-Indo-European. These stocks, broadly speaking from west to east, include: (1) the Celtic languages (Gaulish, Irish, Welsh, Breton, etc.), historically attested in west and central Europe since the La Tène Iron Age (ca. 500–1 B.C.); (2) the Italic languages (Latin and the Romance languages, Osco-Umbrian, etc.), which have left written documents since the Iron Age; (3) the Germanic languages (Scandinavian, English, Dutch, German, Gothic, etc.), which provide some lexical evidence from the Iron Age but whose records primarily begin during the early medieval period; (4) the Baltic languages (Old Prussian, Lithuanian, Latvian, etc.) which, other than personal and place-names, do not provide written texts until the sixteenth century A.D.; (5) the Slavic languages (Polish, Czech, Slovak, Serbo-Croatian, Bulgarian, Russian, Ukrainian, etc.) that spread over large portions of eastern and central Europe after ca. A.D. 500; (6) several extinct and only marginally attested Balkan languages such as Dacian (Romania), Thracian (Bulgaria), Illyrian (Croatia, Bosnia, Albania) and one modern descendant, Albanian, first known in written records of the fifteenth century; (7) Greek, earliest known in Bronze Age Linear B documents of ca. 1300 B.C.; (8) Armenian, which has left early liturgical literature since the Middle Ages; (9) the Bronze Age (Hittite, Luwian, Palaic) and Iron Age (Lydian, Lycian, Carian, etc.) languages of Anatolia, whose earliest attested existence dates to ca. 1900 B.C.; (10) the Indo-Iranian superstock of languages, whose earliest extensively known documents are known in the Sanskrit literature of India and the Old Persian and Avestan languages of Iran; and (11) the Tocharian languages Chinese Turkestan, which is largely confined to liturgical documents that date from the seventh to tenth centuries A.D. In addition, there are poorly known Iron Age languages such as Venetic (northeastern Italy), Messapic (southeastern Italy), and the Phrygian (central Anatolia), all of which boast disputed relationships to one of the major stocks.

The derivation of these languages from a common prehistoric ancestor was first proposed in the late eighteenth century by scholars such as the English jurist Sir William Jones. By the end of the nineteenth century the study of the Indo-European languages and attempts to reconstruct their original source language had stimulated the development of comparative or historical linguistics, which is now applied to all of the language families in the world.

Indo-European Culture. The culture of the earliest Indo-Europeans is primarily known through the reconstruction of the Proto-Indo-European vocabulary. For example, the series of cognate words for "sheep" seen in Old Irish ói, Latin ovis, Old High German ouwi, Lithuanian avìs, Greek ó(w)is, Luvian haw-, and Sanskrit ávi- not only exemplifies the phonological similarities between these languages but also supports the conclusion that the protolanguage itself possessed a word *ówis or *h₂ówis that meant "sheep," and presumably, this animal was known to the speakers of Proto-Indo-European. Such lexical-cultural reconstructions do have procedural difficulties and cannot possibly yield a full picture of the cultural vocabulary, but they can still provide valuable evidence for the material culture, environment, economy, and both social and religious behavior of the earliest Indo-Europeans.

The lexical evidence suggests that the Proto-Indo-Europeans knew at least the birch, oak, willow, and ash, perhaps the yew and pine, and more controversially, the more geographically confined beech. Wild mammals include at least the otter, beaver, wolf, fox, bear, lynx, elk, red deer, hare, hedgehog, mouse, and perhaps the roe deer. Fish and bird names are not plentiful, although the salmon trout was known, as well as the duck, goose, and a number of other bird names. In general, the environmental evidence tends to be ubiquitous across much of Eurasia except for some of the periphery.

The Proto-Indo-Europeans possessed at least a Neolithic vocabulary since there are a series of terms for domesticated animals and plants as well as technology commonly ascribed to early farming communities. The animals include cattle, sheep, goat, pig, and dog; a word for "horse" is also unquestionably attested and is generally regarded to refer to the domestic rather than wild animal. Names for "grain" and designations of various cereals are also attested. Agricultural technology is indicated by reconstructed words for "plow," "sickle," and "grinding stone," and an assortment of terms for ceramic vessels. Other technological items would include the awl, knife, spear, axe, bow and arrow, and beads; copper appears to have been known and possibly gold and silver. The existence of wheeled vehicles and boats is also attested.

The social vocabulary of Indo-European institutions, particularly kinship, suggests the existence of some form of Omaha system of kin reckoning. The linguistic evidence points to a patrilineal society where women, on marriage, were literally led to the homes of their husbands. Terms for "settlement" and "clan" have crossed to suggest a residence unit above the family in which related kin dwelt. Some form of social ranking is suggested, while there also exists some terms related to military institutions, for example, "army" and "people (under arms)."

Finally, the different Indo-European stocks indicate the earlier worship of a sky god (e.g., the Indic Dyaupitár, Greek Zéus patér, and Latin Ju-piter, literally "sky father"); there are also common terms for other nature divinities such as the goddesses of the dawn and sun, as well as for "spirit," "reverence," "law," "order," some type of ritual meal, and possibly "libation" and "cattle sacrifice." The structural rather than linguistic analysis of Indo-European religion has suggested that it perceived society as a social totality comprised of priests, warriors, and commoners (herder-cultivators).

That Proto-Indo-European possessed a Neolithic vocabulary suggests that it is unlikely to have appeared anywhere in Eurasia before about 7000 B.C., while wheeled vehicles and the possible existence of a word for "silver" suggests a date not much earlier than the fourth millennium B.C. Written testimony indicates the existence of Anatolian languages already by ca. 2000 B.C. and the differences between the Anatolian stock and the other "Bronze Age stocks" of Indo-Iranian and Greek requires a date of separation no later than 2500 B.C. On these grounds, the existence of the Proto-Indo-European language is commonly ascribed by linguists to the period ca. 4000–2500 B.C. with some room for debate concerning how much earlier one may set the existence of the protolanguage.

The Homeland Problem. For more than 150 years scholars have sought to locate the homeland of the Indo-Europeans and trace their migrations across Eurasia to their historic seats. That the Proto-Indo-Europeans were once confined to a smaller area than that in which we first find them is incontestable. For example, Iron Age inscriptions in Iberia suggest the existence of earlier languages, Iberian and Tartessian, that occupied the peninsula prior to the spread of Hispano- (or Ibero-) Celtic while the Basques of northern Spain and southern France still resist assimilation by Romance speakers; Latin spread over the earlier territory of the Etruscans, generally presumed to be non-Indo-European; the earliest Hittite records indicate that they established their empire in central Anatolia in the previous state of the Hatti, a non-Indo-European people; the Armenians emerged only after the fall of the earlier non-Indo-European states of the Hurrians and Urartians in eastern

Anatolia; Iranian spread southward over the earlier territory of the Elamites; and the Indic or Indo-Aryan languages indicate a spread over earlier Dravidian languages, still dominant in the southern third of the subcontinent.

The location of the original homeland of the Indo-Europeans is one of the most contested issues of prehistoric research, and solutions have ranged from the Atlantic to the Pacific and from the North to South Poles. Originally the homeland was presumed to be in Asia in the highland regions of Iran to northern India. Then the consensus shifted to Europe, and by the late nineteenth century the earliest seat of the Indo-Europeans was often placed in northern Europe, where the Aryans, as the early Indo-Europeans were then occasionally termed, were identified as an originally tall, blond, and long-headed Nordic race, a theory that was embraced by racists in Germany and elsewhere. The most popular current solutions (and there are very many) differ not only in terms of place but also chronology. One widely accepted theory is that during the Mesolithic, populations in central Europe and on the Russian-Ukrainian steppe shared a common linguistic ancestry and by the Neolithic Period emerged as two linguistically related but culturally different zones of Indo-European speakers, those in Europe proving ancestral to the European languages, while those of the Eurasian steppe expanded southeastward to become the Indo-Europeans of Asia. The attraction of this theory is that it links two areas that appear culturally disparate in the Neolithic and later periods but which both have a strong claim to be identified with early Indo-European societies. The theory's main virtue is also its greatest liability, since there are no archaeological grounds for combining the two regions in the Mesolithic. The second theory, with a number of variations, assigns the earliest Indo-Europeans to Anatolia and identifies their expansion with the spread of agriculture in the Early Neolithic into both Europe and through Asia from about the seventh millennium B.C. The primary attraction of this theory is that it identifies a mechanism for language spread in the expanding front of agricultural communities over much of Eurasia. Criticism of this theory emphasizes that the proposed homeland territory was probably not occupied by Indo-Europeans until the Bronze Age and that the spread of agriculture into Europe from Anatolia still cannot account for the existence of the Indo-Europeans of Asia, and the beginning of the Neolithic is incongruent with the reconstructed Indo-European vocabulary (e.g., wheeled vehicles do not appear until the fourth millennium B.C.). The third theory attributes the expansions of the Indo-Europeans to movements of the so-called Kurgan culture (named for their tumulus, or *kurgan*, burials) from the Eurasian steppe that are archaeologically traced to the fourth and third millennia B.C. This theory enjoys widespread support, since the cultural zone attributed to the Proto-Indo-Europeans provides a best fit with the more diagnostic items of lexical-cultural reconstruction (domestic horse, wheeled vehicles) and the proposed expansions are both geographically and chronologically congruent with the expectations of linguists. Although this theory can show some evidence for population movements into southeastern Europe, it cannot demonstrate archaeologically the progressive movement of Indo-Europeans into the rest of Europe. It is for this reason that although the various solutions to the homeland problem may enjoy considerable popularity, none can be regarded as a wholly acceptable resolution of one of the longest-standing problems of prehistoric research.

[*See also* EUROPE, *articles on* THE EUROPEAN MESOLITHIC PERIOD, THE EUROPEAN NEOLITHIC PERIOD; POLITICAL USES OF ARCHAEOLOGY.]

■ W. B. Lockwood, *A Panorama of Indo-European Languages* (1972). Emile Benveniste, *Indo-European Language and Society* (1973). Philip Baldi, *An Introduction to the Indo-European Languages* (1983). Jaan Puhvel, *Comparative Mythology* (1987). Colin Renfrew, *Archaeology and Language: The Puzzle of Indo-European Origins* (1987). Andrew and Susan Sherratt, "The Archaeology of Indo-European: An Alternative View," *Antiquity* 62 (1988): 584–595. Marek and Karel Zvelebil, "Agricultural Transition and Indo-European Dispersals," *Antiquity* 62 (1988): 574–583. J. P. Mallory, *In Search of the Indo-Europeans* (1989). T. V. Gamkrelidze and V. V. Ivanov, *Indo-European and the Indo-Europeans* (1995).

J. P. Mallory

INDUS CIVILIZATION. The Indus, or Harappan, civilization rose on the plains of the Greater Indus Valley of Pakistan and northwestern India in the middle of the third millennium B.C. The civilization is now dated to 2500 to 2000 B.C. This period is also called the Mature Harappan. It was the time when the great cities of *Mohenjo-daro and *Harappa were functioning urban centers. They were inhabited by a population acquainted with the art of writing, and there is abundant evidence for social stratification and craft and career specialization.

Unlike the Mesopotamian civilization and Dynastic Egypt, the Indus civilization was not part of the ancient literature of the Indian subcontinent. Evidence for both of the western civilizations was preserved in the Bible and other lore known to the scholarly world. The standing monuments of Dynastic Egypt that survive to the present day were also testimony to the Bronze Age civilization of northeastern Africa. But the Vedic texts of ancient India, the earliest of the subcontinents' historical literature, contain no direct reference to the Harappan civilization. The same is true for the Brahmanas, Aryanakas, and Upanishads, which form the balance of the large body of literature that is called "Vedic." Archaeologists employed by the British colonial government of India had no hint that there was a vast civilization of the third millennium, and it was an act of pure archaeological discovery that brought it to light.

The story of discovery begins in the nineteenth century, when the distinctive square stamp seals were found at the site of Harappa on the banks of the Ravi River in the west Punjab of Pakistan. The writing on them was unknown to epigraphers of the age, which gave an importance to these objects and a constant, but low-keyed interest in the site. For this reason Sir John Marshall, the Director General of the Archaeological Survey of India, sent his colleague Rai Bahadur Daya Ram Sahni to excavate there in the winter field season of 1920 to 1921. Sahni found more seals, but still had nothing to connect them. A year earlier Rakal Das Banerji, the Superintending Archaeologist of the Western Circle of the Archaeological Survey of India, had visited Mohenjo-daro, 400 miles (644 km) to the southeast of Harappa, on the banks of the great Indus River of Sind Province. The site had been first recorded in 1911 to 1912, but its significance had not been recognized. Banerji seems to have been a man with sharp intuition and he conducted a small-scale excavation at Mohenjo-daro with his own modest field funds. His work also produced the square stamp seals with the unknown script on them and he recognized the parallels with the seals published from Harappa. The next year (1923–1924) there were teams digging at both sites, with the full blessings of the Director General's office of the Survey.

Marshall made a public announcement of the discovery of a new civilization in the same year.

Archaeology in Egypt, the Near East, and South Asia was prospering in the 1920s. It was the era during which *Tutankhamun's tomb was discovered, and the British Museum and The University Museum, Philadelphia, excavated at Ur where they discovered the famous "Royal Graves." Excavation at Mohenjo-daro continued on a very large scale until 1931, when the Great Depression forced the termination of work there.

The chronology of the Mature Harappan civilization is based on radiocarbon dates, with one reasonably good, if general, cross-tie to the Akkadian Period of Mesopotamia. There are 105 radiocarbon dates for the Mature Harappan that have a wide range but average around 2282 B.C. The best range for the Mature, Urban Harappan can be taken to be roughly 2500–2000 B.C. This correlates well with the date for the Akkadian Period in Mesopotamia. A fairly large number of Harappan artifacts, including Indus stamp seals, etched carnelian beads, and other iconography have been found in these contexts. There are also Mesopotamian texts with the personal name "Meluhha," which has been identified as the Mesopotamian name for the Indus civilization. The objects with citations to people from ancient India and Pakistan, resident in Mesopotamia, support the general dating of the Indus civilization very well.

Geography. Settlements of the Mature Harappan Period are found over a very large area, exceeding one million square kilometers. The most westerly of these settlements is a fortified site called Sutkagen-dor, near the border between Pakistan and Iran near the Arabian Sea. This was once thought to be a port, but that idea is no longer contemplated. The site of Lothal in Gujarat anchors the southwestern point of the Mature Harappan. The northeastern sites are found in the upper portion of the Ganga-Yamuna River Doab, mostly in Saharanpur District of Uttar Pradesh. There is one settlement at Manda in Jammu (India), near Ropar on the upper Sutlej River. The greatest concentration of sites is in Cholistan (Desert Country) of Bahawalpur and Rahimyar Khan Districts of Pakistan, with one hundred eighty-five closely spaced around the terminal drainage of the ancient Sarasvati, or Hakra River. The most northern of the sites is Shortughai on the Oxus River in northern Afghanistan. This was almost certainly a trading center. It is distantly removed from other Mature Harappan settlements and therefore not used in the calculation of the total area.

Urban Origins. The beginnings of the Mature Harappan are still not well understood. There was a widespread Early Harappan period with no cities, or even particularly large settlements. There is little sign of social stratification in the Early Harappan and craft specialization is not developed to a marked degree. There appears to have been a period of rapid culture change at about 2600 to 2500 B.C. during which most of the distinctly urban or complex sociocultural institutions of the Indus civilization came together.

Major Settlements. The major settlements of the Harappan civilization are Mohenjo-daro and Harappa. There is a third city, Ganweriwala, which is approximately 198 acres (80 ha) in size in Cholistan. It has not been excavated. Other major sites are Chanhu-daro, Lothal, Dholavira, and Kalibangan.

Chanhu-daro, located 70 miles (113 km) south of Mohenjo-daro, a Mature Harappan town, was important for the presence of a workshop and for understanding the strati-

graphic relationship between the Mature Harappan and succeeding cultures.

Lothal, located in Gujarat at the head of the Gulf of Khambhat (Cambay) provides an understanding of Mature Harappan trade and artisanry and the stratigraphic relationship between the Mature Harappan trade and the Post-Mature Harappan in the region. The large brick-lined enclosure at the site, which was once described as a dockyard, probably does not fit that description.

Dholavira, located in Kutch, midway between Chanhu-daro and Lothal is a 145-acre (60 ha) site under excavation. It is fortified and has a stratigraphic succession from the Early or Pre-Harappan to the Mature Harappan and succeeding cultures.

Kalibangan is very close to the present border between India and Pakistan on a now dry river, known today as the Ghaggar-Hakra and in antiquity as the Sarasvati. It is a good example of a regional center of the Indus civilization and has a well-documented stratigraphic succession from the Early to the Mature Harappan.

Writing. In spite of many claims to the contrary, the Indus script remains undeciphered.

Subsistence. The peoples of the Indus civilization were farmers and herders, with hunting, fishing, and gathering as subsidiary activities. The chief food grains were barley and wheat, in that order of importance. They also cultivated at least two forms of seed plants, the chickpea, field pea, mustard, and sesame. The evidence for the cultivation of rice during the Mature Harappan is ambiguous, but possible. The Harappans used grapes, but their status as a domesticated plant is unknown. They engaged in some gathering of wild plants, the most common of which is the Indian jujube. Surkotada, a Mature Harappan site in Kutch District of India, has produced a diverse set of wild plants that all seem to have been gathered for their seeds. Twenty-five species or genera were found, including well known plants such as *Dichanthium*, *Panicum* sp., *Carex* sp., *Amaranthus* sp., and *Euphorbia* sp. Date seeds are also part of the Mature Harappan palaeobotanical sample.

The earliest cotton in the Old World was found at Mohenjo-daro. Several examples of this material exist, all being preserved in the corrosion product of metallic objects. One patch of cloth was preserved from the bag used to hold a silver vessel hidden in a floor. A line used for fishing was preserved when it was wrapped around a copper hook. Cotton seeds may be present at the site of *Mehrgarh in Period II.

The peoples of the Indus civilization were cattle keepers on a grand scale. One of the consistent patterns in Harappan archaeology is that cattle remains are usually above 50 percent of the faunal assemblage, often much more. This observation and the cattle imagery in art make it clear that this was the premier animal in their culture, and that it is highly likely that it may have been the principal form of wealth. The Harappans also kept substantial numbers of water buffalo, sheep, goats, and pigs. They kept domesticated dogs and the figurines show that some of them wore collars, and that there were breeds: some with curved tails over the back, one that looked something like a bulldog, and a thinner, more gracile breed that resembles the modern Afghan. The chicken was domesticated from the wild Red Indian Jungle Fowl, the earliest remains of which are found at Mohenjo-daro.

These people were also fish eaters. Most river sites have the remains of the local freshwater fish, especially a variety of carp. Recent excavations at Harappa have revealed the presence of marine fish, indicating some form of commerce in dried or salted fish. The Mature Harappan occupation at Balakot, a site near the Arabian Sea just to the east of Karachi, had sufficient remains from marine animals, especially a grub, to roughly estimate that maritime food resources contributed about half of the dietary intake from all fauna, with most of this coming from fish.

Trade and Crafts. The peoples of the Mature Harappan were wide-ranging traders, within their territories of Pakistan and northwestern India, and in more distant places, including Afghanistan, Central Asia, the Iranian Plateau, and Mesopotamia.

The internal trade and commerce involved subsistence materials, such as the aforementioned fish. It extended to the following raw materials: copper (abundant resources in Baluchistan and the Ketri Belt of Rajasthan); gold (placer and dust available in the Indus River, Kashmir, and other places); silver (southern Khetri Belt, Kashmir); chert (abundant resources in the Rohri Hills of northern Sind); soft gray stone or "steatite" (widely available in Baluchistan, Northwest Frontier, and Rajasthan); chalcedony and other semiprecious stones (in Gujarat, Kutch, Western Ghats, and Baluchistan); lapis lazuli, an important rich blue stone (available in the Chagai Hills of Baluchistan as well as the better-known Afghan source in Badakhshan); shell (the species used broadly available from the maritime coast); and timber (in the Himalayas).

The roots of artisanry for the Indus civilization are historically deep, going back to Period III at Mehrgarh, which dates to the middle of the fifth millennium B.C. It is in these contexts that one sees the beginnings of copper-based metallurgy, the development of wheel-turned pottery, and the firing of hard red wares, as well as the development of the bead-making technology for which the Harappans are so famous.

The Harappan artisans took these materials and others and turned them into a wide range of products. Major craft centers have been found at the sites of Chanhu-daro, Lothal, and Mohenjo-daro.

Harappan foreign commerce is a vast topic. The trade and interaction with Central Asia is covered in works by Ahmad Hasan Dani (1990) and Henri-Paul Francfort (1992). This interaction has deep roots and began much earlier than the Mature Harappan, as demonstrated by an examination of the ceramics of the two regions, especially the so-called Quetta Ware, and female figurines with distinctive long, joined legs, stretching to the front. It seems to be rooted in the pastoral nomadism that links Central Asia with the Punjab and Indus Valley. The interaction with the Iranian Plateau is not well documented, but one of the best sources in English is Asko Parpola's piece in *South Asian Archaeology 1981* (1984).

The trade with Mesopotamia, which for the most part seems to have been maritime trade, is well documented, with book-length treatments by Shereen Ratnagar (1981) and Daniel T. Potts (1990). A hypothesis about the beginnings of this maritime trade appears in Possehl's *Kulli* (1986). The merchandise that appears most prominently in the textual references to products of Meluhha includes: carnelian, lapis lazuli, pearls, a thorn tree of Meluhha, mesu wood, fresh dates, a bird of Meluhha (5 as figurines), a dog of Meluhha, a cat of Meluhha, copper, and gold. The products traded to Meluhha are not as clearly documented, but included food products, oils, cloth, and the like.

There are many Harappan artifacts in Mesopotamia, including seals, etched carnelian beads, and ceramics. The Mesopotamian products found in Harappan contexts at Indus sites are very few and there is a considerable disparity in the archaeological record of this subject.

Religion. The best discussion of the religion of the Harappan peoples remains the essay by Sir John Marshall (1931), although the notion that there is a "Proto-Shiva" on the famous seal from Mohenjo-daro is not part of contemporary thought. The central theme of Harappan religion as it comes from the archaeological record is the combined male-female deity, symbolized by animal horns and the broad, curving plant motifs. This is a very broadly defined set of images that reflects an equally broad set of ideas about the principal Harappan deity, although there seems to be no image of this entity. What is seen is a male, horned animal god, generally associated with the water buffalo, and a female plant deity represented as either a plant motif or a human figure standing in or under a plant.

The imagery for these two gods is clearly cognate with the broad, sweeping curve of the buffalo horns found in the plant designs. This relationship was there for some purpose and it is reasonable to speculate that it was to convey the sense that what one sees as two is, in fact, a single, unseen entity or idea. It would have been an androgynous being, combining the features of both male and female and obviously not sexually neuter. This is a feature of gods in the Hindu pantheon, as exemplified by Ardhanarisvara, the manifestation of Siva, who is half man and half woman. It also carries a sense of synthesis for the dualism of what came to be called *saktism* that Sir John Marshall noted in his early essay on Harappan religion. This imagery is proposed here, but it should be considered a hypothetical extension of what is seen quite clearly—the dualism of male/female and animal/plant.

All of the plant and animal worship discussed by Marshall can be seen as specific aspects of the great duality of the Harappan Great Tradition. The multiheaded animals, "unicorns" with elephant trunks, perhaps "unicorns" themselves as in the terracotta figurines from Chanhu-daro, are all themes appropriate to zoolatry. So are the tigers with bull horns and half human–half quadrupeds seen on the seals, such as on the cylinder from Kalibangan. These are proposed here to be only an elaboration of the animal themes supremely portrayed by the Buffalo Deity on seal number 420 and earlier on the Buffalo Deity pot from Kot Diji. The abundant plant motif, especially as pictured on sealings and painted designs on pottery, is an analogous elaboration of the principal theme seen, for example, on the seal of Divine Adoration (number 430), or the painted motifs on pottery from Kalibangan or Mundigak.

The place of water in Indus ritual, or the Harappan civilization generally, seems to be prominent. There is abundant evidence that the Harappan affinity for cleanliness (household and civic drainage, bathing facilities in many if not most houses) was simply a microcosm of the Great Bath. Seen from this perspective the Great Bath was the civic-level facility for water ritual, bathing, and cleanliness, that took place in the homes of ordinary citizens on a regular basis. The importance of water for the growth of plants and the crops that sustained the Harappan peoples would suggest that the water ritual was affiliated with the female/plant side of the duality in the Harappan Great Tradition.

Fire worship, if the evidence from Kalibangan is accepted, is somewhat more difficult. It plays an important role, at times with water, in the religious life of many peoples and would not be unexpected in Harappan life. There is a temptation to see fire as the opposite of water and to place it on the male / animal side of the great Harappan duality. This should be considered a tentative suggestion, since it builds on logic that has already been qualified.

Seen from this perspective the religion of the Harappan civilization can be perceived as a single institution, with perhaps two different aspects in the personae of the male / animal deity and the female / plant goddess. The possibility that various domains, settlements, or peoples claimed to be devotees of one or the other of these gods has been suggested, along with the thought that older, diverse parts of the Early Harappan systems of belief were practiced in Mature Harappan times as well. The parallels to these observations found in later Hinduism are in some respects quite striking.

The Eclipse of the Ancient Cities of the Indus. The excavations at Mohenjo-daro between 1922 and 1931 demonstrated conclusively that this ancient city was largely abandoned at the end of the Mature Harappan. There is a very small amount of pottery associated with the so-called Jhukar Culture. The distribution of this pottery at Mohenjo-daro is not well understood, nor is its development out of the wares of Mature Harappan. It may indicate that there was a small community of people living in some probably restricted parts of Mohenjo-daro in the early second millennium. There is also a later Buddhist monastery and stupa on the Mound of the Great Bath. For all intents and purposes, it is fair to say that the city had been dead as an urban center since the opening decades of the second millennium B.C.

Similar evidence was gained through the excavations at Harappa, although the early second millennium there, called Cemetery H after the excavation area where it was first observed, is somewhat larger and more apparent than the Jhukar occupation of Mohenjo-daro. The situation at Ganweriwala is less clear since there has been no excavation there, but surface prospecting indicates that the occupation was limited to Mature Harappan times.

The evidence from the three urban centers, as well as regional surveys, indicates that Sind and the west Punjab experienced the widespread abandonment of Mature Harappan settlements at the opening of the second millennium. There was either a migration out of these areas or a shift in the system of settlement and subsistence to an area that left very little archaeological trace, since site counts drop in a precipitous way: from sixty-six Mature Harappan sites in Sind down to just nine in the Jhukar era, and from one hundred ninety Mature Harappan sites in the west Punjab down to forty-seven in Cemetery H times.

The same is not true everywhere. In Gujarat, site counts are about half the Mature Harappan in the Post-Urban Phase of the second millennium. Rojdi, an important site in central Saurashtra, underwent a major rebuilding in the opening centuries of the second millennium that expanded its total size by half. In the Indian Punjab, Haryana, northern Rajasthan, and western Uttar Pradesh, there are two hundred sixteen known Mature Harappan settlements. The opening centuries of the second millennium see this number increase to eight hundred fifty-nine, a fourfold rise. No one knows for sure the full meaning of these observations, but it does seem to indicate that the eclipse of the Mature Harappan was a regional phenomenon that did not strike all parts of the Harappan world in the same way.

Older theories which hold that the cities and civilization were destroyed by invading Aryan tribes, as depicted in the Rig Veda, make very little sense. This is in part because there is no evidence for the sacking of any of the Mature Harappan settlements, nor is there chronological agreement between the date of the Vedic texts and the changes seen so graphically at Mohenjo-daro and Harappa.

The proposition that a natural dam formed across the Indus River in Sind and flooded out the civilization has been widely critiqued and is not a viable proposition.

Conclusion. There is still much to be learned about the Indus civilization. We know of the grandeur of its cities with early grid town planning and a mastery of civic drainages, of its wide-ranging contacts and technological sophistication. But many things elude us about these people: their social and political organizations, the details of their religion, the manner in which their cities were governed, the nature of warfare (if present), and the place of writing in their culture. There is a great deal to be done to clarify and expand our knowledge of the ancient city dwellers of India and Pakistan.

[See also ANURADHAPURA; ASIA: PREHISTORY AND EARLY HISTORY OF SOUTH ASIA; NINDOWARI; VIJAYANGARA.]

■ Sir John Marshall, "Religion," in *Mohenjo-daro and the Indus Civilization*, 3 vols, ed. Sir John Marshall (1931): 48–78. Sir Mortimer Wheeler, *The Indus Civilization, 3rd ed.* (1968). B. K. Thapar, "New Traits of the Indus Civilization at Kalibangan: An Appraisal," in *South Asian Archaeology* ed. Norman Hammond (1973): 85–104. Walter A. Fairservis, Jr., *The Roots of Ancient India*, 2nd ed. (1975). Gregory L. Possehl, ed., *Ancient Cities of the Indus* (1979). Shereen Ratnagar, *Encounters: The Westerly Trade of the Harappa Civilization* (1981). Asko Parpola, "New Correspondences Between Harappan and Near Eastern Glyptic Art," in *South Asian Archaeology 1981*, ed. Bridget Alchin (1984): 176–95. Gregory L. Possehl, *Kulli: An Exploration of Ancient Civilization in South Asia* (1986). R. J. Wasson, "The Sedimentological Basis of the Mohenjo-daro Flood Hypothesis—A Further Comment," *Man and Environment* 11 (1987): 122–3. Ahmad Hasan Dani, "Central Asia and Pakistan Through the Ages," *Lahore Museum Journal* 3:1 (1990): 1–13. Gregory L. Possehl, "Revolution in the Urban Revolution: The Emergence of Indus Urbanization," *Annual Review of Anthropology* 19 (1990): 261–82. Daniel T. Potts, *The Arabian Gulf in Antiquity*, 2 vols. (1990). Henri-Paul Francfort, "New Data Illustrating the Early Contact Between Central Asia and the North-West of the Subcontinent," *South Asian Archaeology 1989*, ed. Catherine Jarrige (1992): 97–102. Gregory L. Possehl, ed. *Harappan Civilization: A Recent Perspective*, 2nd rev. ed. (1993).

Gregory L. Possehl

INDUSTRIAL ARCHAEOLOGY. The term "industrial archaeology" was almost certainly thought up in England early in the 1950s by Donald Dudley, later professor of Latin in the University of Birmingham and at that time director of the university's Extra-Mural Department. It had useful shock value in its early days—"the impossible offspring of two parents who should never have been allowed to breed." Its first appearance in print appears to have occurred in 1955, in an article written for *The Amateur Historian* by one of Donald Dudley's colleagues, Michael Rix. For Rix, and for many others since then, industrial archaeology should be concerned primarily with the surviving monuments of the Industrial Revolution, eighteenth- and nineteenth-century factories, "the steam engines and locomotives that made possible the provision of power, the first metal-framed buildings, cast-iron aqueducts and bridges, the pioneering attempts at railways, locks, and canals." All these, he believed, "represent a fascinating interlocking field of study, whole tracts of which are still virtually unexplored."

Since then, the definition has widened. Industrial archaeology is now generally considered to cover the discovery, recording, and study of the physical remains of yesterday's industries and methods of communication, irrespective of period. The early days of synthetic fibers and electric power, for instance, are obviously quite close to our own times, but this in itself does not make them any less worthy of attention than old cotton mills or coal mines. During the 1960s and 1970s, the activities of industrial archaeologists in all industrialized countries were necessarily concerned with locating and recording, since so much valuable historical evidence was being ignorantly swept away in the course of postwar modernization. Most of this urgent work was necessarily carried out by people who were, in the best sense of the word, amateurs, partly because professional industrial archaeologists hardly existed and partly because of the sheer quantity of material to be dealt with. Many of the people involved—architects, engineers, building craftsmen—were, however, experts within their own special fields.

The industrial archaeology movement coincided with a similar wave of popular enthusiasm for local history and for the more traditional kinds of archaeology. What was, and still is, common to all three types of interest and study was an emphasis on fieldwork, associated with careful recording. The chief value of industrial archaeology has been in its essentially practical nature. It has added another dimension to the writing of industrial history and caused many previously held beliefs and theories to be questioned and revised. Its basic techniques are the same as those employed in other forms of archaeology. They include excavation, photography, photogrammetry, and the preparation of accurate measured drawings. Wherever possible, the results of fieldwork are, of course, interpreted in the light of what can be discovered from written records.

No developed country has failed to show some degree of active interest in industrial archaeology, although the main centers have been the United Kingdom, the United States, Sweden, Germany, and Italy—all countries with a great abundance of material relating to manufacturing and transport from the eighteenth century onward. To select individual contributions to such a broadly based accumulation of knowledge is somewhat invidious, but one should certainly mention the important work of Marie Nisser in Sweden, Robert M. Vogel in the United States, Anders Jespersen in Denmark, Massimo Negri in Italy, and Neil Cossons and R. A. Buchanan in the United Kingdom. Kenneth Hudson's *Industrial Archaeology: An Introduction*, published in London in 1963, was the launchpad of the movement, which, from 1973 onward, has been held together and given status by the International Committee on the Conservation of the National Heritage. The committee holds regular international conferences in different countries.

The most ambitious and comprehensive recording programs involving industrial monuments are those organized in the United States by the Historic American Buildings Survey and the Historic American Engineering Record. These "reflect the Federal Government's commitment to document, understand and, in some cases, preserve architectural, engineering and industrial sites that are important to our nation's past." There is no corresponding government achievement elsewhere.

[*See also* BRITISH ISLES: THE INDUSTRIAL REVOLUTION; HISTORICAL ARCHAEOLOGY.]

■ Kenneth Hudson, *Industrial Archaeology* (1963). W.H.G. Armytage, *A Social History of Engineering* (1966). Theodore Anton Sande, *Industrial Archaeology: A New Look at the American Heritage* (1970). Arthur Raistrick, *Industrial Archaeology: An Historical Survey* (1972). Kenneth Hudson, *Industrial History from the Air* (1984).

Kenneth Hudson

INYANGA. The Inyanga District, in eastern Zimbabwe, is archaeologically well known for its extensively terraced hillsides associated with stone-lined pit structures, hill forts, and stone enclosures. These features are broadly dated to between the fifteenth and eighteenth centuries A.D. and identified with farming communities of the later Iron Age.

The remains were first reported and described by Randall-MacIver (1906), and the most detailed archaeological investigations to date are by Summers (1958).

The revetment walls between terraces are dry stone walls, which measure about 6.5 feet (2 m) high, 1.6 to 3.2 feet (.5 to 1 m) thick, and stretch for up to 328 feet (100 m). The terraces themselves measure 10 feet (3 m) to 16 feet (5 m) across, and it is now agreed that they were agricultural fields constructed mainly to conserve the soil.

The terraces and the walls are associated with pit structures, circular in shape, about 16 feet (5 m) in diameter and about 6.5 feet (2 m) deep with long narrow tunnels providing entrances. These pits are associated with house remains, indicating that they were part of a homestead. Although controversy surrounds their function, it is generally thought that they were livestock pens.

Hill forts, whose function is assumed to have been defensive, consist of dry stone walls about 6.5 feet (2 m) high, a meter thick, and about 66 feet (20 m) in diameter.

Stone wall enclosures appear in various forms, the most elaborate being the Dziwa Complex, covering a large area consisting of enclosures, passages, and pit structures.

Excavations in Inyanga have yielded pottery, glass beads, animal bone, and plant seeds, including sorghum and millet. These finds and the associated features give a picture of settled communities practicing a distinct agricultural system in southern Africa.

The work done in Inyanga thus far has permitted only a limited conception of the prehistory of the area. The University of Zimbabwe is currently engaged in research from which a clearer picture should emerge.

[*See also* GREAT ZIMBABWE; SOUTHERN AFRICA, LATER IRON AGE SOCIETIES OF.]

■ D. Randall-MacIver, *Medieval Rhodesia* (1906). R. Summers, *Inyanga* (1958).

Gilbert Pwiti

IRON AGE. *See* THREE-AGE SYSTEM.

IRONBRIDGE. The Ironbridge Gorge is a complex industrial landscape that was the location for a number of the most significant technological developments of the Industrial Revolution in Britain.

Ironbridge is a deep valley, cut by the River Severn as it flows south from northern Wales and the English Midlands to the sea beyond the port of Bristol. Coal, ironstone, clay, and limestone outcrop on the sides of the valley, and small streams drop down to the river below, providing potential sources of waterpower. The combination of easily accessible minerals, power, and transport via the River Severn certainly contributed to the development of mining, ironworking, and the manufacture of bricks, tiles, and pottery. Archaeology can cast particular light on the way in which the interaction of people with the landscape through time generated what was described by a contemporary as "the most extraordinary district in the world."

In 1708 Abraham Darby, a Bristol brass maker, took over an old charcoal blast furnace at Coalbrookdale. The area was already busy with coal mines, ironworking, and clay pipe manufacture. Medieval mill ponds were in use for waterpower, new industrial settlements had grown up on former commons and in woodland, and there was a network of wooden railways taking coal wagons down to boats waiting on the riverside. Darby's experiments were successful, and he was able to produce cast iron using locally available coal rather than charcoal.

It was not until the 1750s that ironmasters could produce iron with coke, which could successfully be converted into the more valuable wrought iron. Within ten years there were at least eight more blast furnaces in the gorge. Brickworks served the mines and the furnaces, potters made the slip-coated domestic wares found in every household, and hundreds of boats plied the river trade.

Today the most visible reminder of this period is the spectacular Iron Bridge, perhaps the first cast iron bridge in the world, built across the River Severn. Erected in 1779 by Darby's successors, the Coalbrookdale Company, and probably designed by a local architect, it demonstrated that cast iron could be used in large engineering structures. The bridge is not the only monument to survive—Darby's original furnace stands at Coalbrookdale, and there are other furnaces at Bedlam and Blists Hill. The wooded slopes of the gorge are full of tramways, limekilns, and coal shafts. At Coalport, the construction of a canal and wharfs in the 1790s to link the river with areas inland provided the focus for a group of industries including the famous Coalport China works, making decorative porcelain. An ingenuous inclined plane took tub boats from the canal at the top of the valley down 228 feet (69 m) to the riverside. Many of these monuments are in the ownership of the Ironbridge Gorge Museum Trust and are accessible to the public.

Industry did not cease in the eighteenth century. A hundred years later there were still clay industries, limeworks, ironworks, and factories producing decorative Victorian tiles. But the early advantages of the gorge became handicaps, and large industry moved away, drawn by better transport links and more abundant raw materials. Perhaps because of this, much of the physical evidence of early industrialization survives in the landscape today as a valuable resource for providing an archaeological perspective on the Industrial Revolution.

[See also BRITISH ISLES: THE INDUSTRIAL REVOLUTION; INDUSTRIAL ARCHAEOLOGY.]

■ Neil Cossons and Barrie Trinder, *The Iron Bridge: Symbol of the Industrial Revolution* (1979). Barrie Trinder, *The Industrial Revolution in Shropshire,* 2nd ed. (1981). Arthur Raistrick, *Dynasty of Ironfounders,* 2nd ed. (1989). Judith Alfrey and Catherine Clark, *The Landscape of Industry—Patterns of Change in the Ironbridge Gorge* (1993). Catherine Clark, *English Heritage Book of Ironbridge Gorge* (1993).

Catherine Clark

IROQUOIS AND ALGONQUIAN CULTURES.

The Iroquois proper were historically a confederacy of first five, and later six, independent nations called the League of the Iroquois in what is now New York State. These were the Mohawk, Oneida, Onondaga, Cayuga, Seneca, and (after 1711) Tuscarora nations. Each spoke a distinct Northern Iroquoian language. All six survive on reservations in the United States and Canada.

The Iroquois name comes down through French from a Basque word meaning "killer people." This was used by sixteenth-century Basque fishers who traded with the Iroquois and various other Iroquoians and Algonquians around the Gulf of St. Lawrence. The name the Iroquois still use to refer to their league is Hodenosaunee.

There were several additional Northern Iroquoian nations in the seventeenth century, including the Susquehannock, Wenro, Petun, Huron, Neutral, Erie, and St. Lawrence Iroquoians. The last four were sets of independent nations that at least sometimes acted as confederacies. There were altogether nearly 100,000 Northern Iroquoians living in the early seventeenth century in New York, northern Pennsylvania, and the southern portions of Ontario and Quebec. Later, colonial wars and epidemics greatly reduced their numbers.

The Northern Iroquoians are linguistically related to the Cherokee of the Southeast, and their distribution in the Northeast suggests an intrusion into what was otherwise Algonquian territory sometime in the past. Some archaeologists conclude that the intrusion was early and that Northern Iroquoians developed out of earlier cultures already present in the region 2,000 years ago. Others suggest that Northern Iroquoians intruded into the region around A.D. 900 from the central Appalachian uplands. All agree that the distinctive Northern Iroquoian culture was thriving in the Northeast from that time on.

The Northern Iroquoians are distinguished by their strongly matrilineal systems of social organization and their compact villages of large multifamily longhouses. Each household was comprised of the families of closely related women. Senior women ran household affairs, and household members other than in-marrying husbands belonged in each case to the same clan. Villages were usually palisaded and held anywhere from a few to a few dozen longhouses, each of them home to one of three or more matrilineal clans, the number depending upon the clan composition of each nation. Iroquois nations were made up of clusters of two or more such villages, each village containing up to around 2,000 people.

The Iroquoians were slash-and-burn horticulturalists that depended upon three staples, maize (Indian corn), beans, and squash. Animal protein came from deer, fish, and other game, while gathered plants added variety to the diet. The lack of fertilizer and pesticides forced the periodic abandonment of old fields and the clearing of new ones. This in turn led to the periodic relocation of villages every decade or two. Normal moves were of only a few kilometers at most, but when dislodged by warfare, villages sometimes relocated to new sites at much greater distances.

While women ran household affairs and were primarily responsible for the fields and crops, men were responsible for political and diplomatic matters within the village, the confederacy, and the world at large. Men were appointed to their positions as chiefs by the women of designated leading households. The confederacy of the Iroquois proper (the League of the Iroquois) was governed by fifty chiefs so appointed by specific households of the founding five nations. The league was often thought of as a large metaphorical longhouse stretched across upstate New York.

Because of their periodic relocation, Iroquoian villages each produced many archaeological sites. Over a thousand Northern Iroquoian village sites are known in the Northeast, and many have been systematically excavated by archaeologists. A few have been preserved and are open as public exhibit sites in New York and Ontario.

Recent Iroquoian History. The St. Lawrence Iroquoians disappeared after their contact with Jacques Cartier early in the sixteenth century. They were probably dispersed by other Iroquoians and absorbed by Hurons and Mohawks. The nations of the League of the Iroquois were principally responsible for the destruction of the Huron, Petun, Erie, Neutral, Wenro, and Susquehannock nations in the seventeenth century. Some of these were dispersed westward, where they came together later as the Wyandot nation. Others took refuge with French colonists in Quebec. However, most survivors were absorbed by the league nations, who needed them to replace their own declining numbers.

The six nations of the League of the Iroquois thus survived through later centuries. They were major players in the colonial wars of the eighteenth century, during which some pro-French Iroquois relocated to Quebec. The divisions of the American Revolution tore apart the longhouse of the league. Pro-British Iroquois relocated to reserves in Ontario, while pro-American and neutral Iroquois remained on shrinking reservations in the United States, mainly in New York. Eventually two separate leagues were revived in New York and Ontario, where they still continue some political activities. Some Iroquois relocated to Oklahoma and Wisconsin, while those remaining in New York survived by selling much of their remaining land, their only major resource. Today the Iroquois are nearly as numerous as they were five centuries ago.

Algonquian Cultures. Algonquian tribes were once distributed widely through the central and eastern subarctic parts of Canada and the Great Lakes basin. Their adaptive radiation throughout this area is probably represented by what is referred to by archaeologists as Point Peninsula culture. The spread took place during the first millennium A.D. and was probably made possible by their acquisition of the bow and arrow, perhaps along with other innovations.

Subsequent to their main spread throughout what is now eastern Canada and the northeastern United States, Eastern Algonquian tribes spread southward along the east coast from New England to as far as North Carolina. This might have been made possible by their acquisition of crops from more interior peoples, along with their talents for exploiting the natural resources of coastal and estuary environments. At first contact with Europeans, the Massachusetts, Mohegan-Pequots, Mahicans, Delawares, and other fragmentary Eastern Algonquians, such as those known as the Powhatans, were living in villages of domed wigwams and subsisting on mixed economies of hunting, gathering, fishing, and cultivating. Elongated wigwams containing two or more families were sometimes used, but the Eastern Algonquians never had the large longhouses and strong matrilineal social systems of their Iroquoian neighbors farther inland.

The northern Algonquians, who lived from the Great Lakes basin and northern New England northward, lived almost exclusively by hunting, gathering, and fishing. A few traded hides and game for maize and other crops supplied by nearby cultivators, mainly Iroquoians. Northern Algonquian groups included the Algonquin proper (from whom the language family name has been borrowed), Cree, Montagnais, Naskapi, Ojibwa (Chippewa), Saulteaux, Ottawa (Odawa), Nipissing, and Attikamek. The Micmac, Malecite, Passamaquoddy, and Abenaki (includ-

ing Penobscot) tribes of northern New England were similar. Central Algonquians living just south of the Great Lakes are well known, but have histories that were confused by the disruptions of European contact and colonization. These include the Menominee, Potawatomi, Sauk, Fox, Kickapoo, Mascouten, Shawnee, Miami, and Illinois peoples.

The arrival of the horse from Spanish settlements in the Southwest drew some Algonquian groups on to the Great Plains, where they participated with other Native American nations in the creation of classic Plains Indian cultures. The Blackfeet, Gros Ventre, Plains Cree, and Plains Ojibwa moved on to the northern Great Plains. The Cheyenne and Arapaho people, also Algonquians, moved to the central Great Plains.

Even more distantly related Algonquian groups had earlier made their way as far west as northern California. The Yurok and Wiyot tribes are known to speak languages related to Algonquian languages, but the circumstances of their ancient migration to California are poorly understood.

Most Algonquian societies were traditionally bilateral in their organization. In some cases patrilineal principles predominated. The more northern groups lived most of the year in small dispersed bands. These might be as small as one or two nuclear families in the winter, or grow to dozens of people when the abundance of fish or some other resource allowed them to congregate. Central and Eastern Algonquian people often maintained large central villages at key points such as river junctions. In some cases they lived in these central places for much of the year, dispersing to interior hunting camps, coastal camps, or fishing stations as needed.

Most Algonquian peoples traditionally traveled by birchbark canoes. Other specialized equipment for which they are well known include snowshoes and toboggans. Tailored clothing of deer and other hides was essential in their cold environment.

Several Eastern Algonquian groups became extinct in the face of European colonization, while others survive on small reservations. The Central Algonquians and those who moved on to the Great Plains were first displaced and later settled on reservations, often far from their homelands. Northern Algonquians, always the most dispersed, survive largely as small communities in their native northern forests, protected to some degree from encroachment by the hostility of their environment.

The dress of both Iroquoians and Algonquians changed quickly after first European contact. Few contemporary images survive from the early years of contact, and native clothing styles are not easy to reconstruct. European broadcloth quickly replaced hides as preferred material for clothing. Glass beads quickly replaced porcupine quill decorations. Breechcloths, leggings, and long shirts were probably standard for men both before and after the arrival of broadcloth. Women generally wore long skirts, leggings, and long overblouses. Both men and women wore leather moccasins, and both wore fur capes in cold weather. Children were swaddled on cradleboards as infants.

As broadcloth reduced the need to hunt for hides, European demand for beaver and other pelts caused Iroquoian and Algonquian men to shift their attention to the hunting of fur-bearing animals. The fur trade gave them access to guns, copper kettles, iron tools, and other foreign manufactured goods, which gradually replaced some traditional artifacts. Later the passing of the fur trade left many without cash for these goods, prompting them to sell land as a way to stay in the world economic system. Today many Iroquoians and Algonquians still live on small reservations but carry on successful careers in the surrounding American and Canadian economies.

[*See also* EUROPEAN COLONIES IN THE NEW WORLD; NORTH AMERICA, *articles on* THE EASTERN WOODLANDS AND THE SOUTH, THE NORTH AMERICAN PLAINS.]

■ Lewis Morgan, *League of the Iroquois* (1851). Bruce Trigger, *Northeast: Handbook of North American Indians,* Vol. 15 (1978). Bruce Trigger, *Natives and Newcomers* (1986). Dean Snow, *The Iroquois* (1994).

Dean R. Snow

ISLAMIC CIVILIZATION

Introduction
Mosques

INTRODUCTION

Islamic civilization encompasses a vast array of urban and rural cultures, stretching from the North African shores of the Atlantic to the western periphery of the Pacific and from Central Asia to sub-Saharan Africa, all sharing the heritage of Islam and its associated intellectual traditions. Its point of inspiration lies in the religion of Islam, which was born in the urban milieus of Mecca and Medina, prominent cities of western Arabia, and grew out of an early state founded around these cities, which by the turn of the eighth century A.D. had become an absolutist empire. By the tenth century, the state had lost its imperial authority, leaving in its stead an array of regional polities within a cultural commonwealth, which lasted until the return of imperial absolutism at the beginning of the sixteenth century. Thus, initially by conquest and later through commerce, Islam and the civilization it engendered came to include peoples of various religious and cultural traditions; consequently, the archaeology of Islamic civilization necessarily entails a tremendous variety of regional assemblages, aesthetic traditions, and social practices.

Islamic history, as recorded by Muslims, dates from the year 1 A.H. (Anno Hegirae) / A.D. 622 when Muhammad, a long-distance trader and minor member of the commercially prosperous Quraysh tribe who by that time had received God's (Arabic: Allah) revelation over a period of some years, was compelled by the powerful Banu Umayya clan of the Quraysh to break his ties of kinship and emigrate along with a small group of believers from the commercial hub and pagan shrine of Mecca to the largely agricultural community of Yathrib, some 124 miles (200 km) to the north. Within the first few years of residence in Yathrib, subsequently called al-Madinah (Arabic: "the place of jurisdiction"; modern Arabic, "the city") or more completely Madinat al-Nabi (referring to the place of the Prophet), the Muslim community established itself as a self-sufficient polity, in large measure because Muhammad had succeeded in obtaining the allegiance of tribes elsewhere in Arabia. The community's last major victory under the leadership of the Prophet was the surrender of the Banu Umayya in Mecca, whereupon that city's pagan shrine was transformed into the ritual center of Islam. With the death of Muhammad two years later in 632, political and religious (no longer divinely inspired) leadership of the Muslim community passed to the elected "caliph," the successor to the Prophet, the first four of whom tradition calls the "Rightly-Guided" in distinction to subsequent holders of the office who followed dynastic rules of succession. Many of the tribes of Arabia allied to the Muslims then renounced their submission, and Abu Bakr, the first caliph of Islam, successfully led the Muslims in the Ridda (apostasy) wars (632 to 634). Under the second caliph, Umar, the Muslim armies extended their attacks against the Byzantine and Sasanian Empires, and by 661, the end of the era of the Rightly-Guided caliphs, the Muslim armies had advanced to the Cilician Gates in Anatolia, penetrated North Africa, and occupied the entire Iranian plateau and southern Caucasus.

Subsequent Muslim historians recorded that the conquests were accompanied by the foundation of settlements (sing.: *misr;* pl.: *amsar*) in Central Asia, Mesopotamia, Syria, Egypt, and North Africa, which rapidly transformed into principal cities of the new empire. Of these, Fustat (Egypt) and Kufa (Iraq) have been partially excavated, although their full plans remain unknown; only later occupation at Marv (Turkmenistan) has been located. Such early Islamic planned cities as Aqaba (Jordan) and Istakhr (Iran) suggest the hypothesis that the establishment of urban foundations was an even more widespread policy of the state in the earliest phases of conquest. The last years of the rule of the Rightly-Guided caliphs were marred by dissension over the process of caliphal succession, ultimately resulting in the splintering of the Muslims into what came to be the Sunni, Shi'i, and Khariji communities. The caliphate was eventually won by a scion of the Banu Umayya, initiating the Umayyad dynasty (661 to 750).

In the 690s, the Umayyad caliph 'Abd al-Malik (reign 685 to 705) transformed the state into a distinctly Islamic entity. Within the space of a few years, the Byzantine and Sasanian currency in circulation was supplanted by an Islamic precious-metal coinage of exclusively epigraphic types. Arabic, replacing Byzantine Greek and Sasanian Persian, was introduced as the state bureaucracy's official language, extant in papyrus documents found at sites in Egypt and southern Palestine. Noteworthy among the sites of this period are the "desert castles" of geographical Syria, most of which are dressed-stone structures, frequently with high, tower-supported walls and crenellated parapets, although scholars have come to recognize that these monuments should not be taken as a kind and may in some cases antedate the Islamic period. The lavish mosaics and figural paintings of sites such as Khirbat al-Mafjar (Palestine) and Qusayr 'Amra (Jordan) have long attracted the attention of art historians; archaeologists have emphasized other aspects of these sites, suggesting commercial, agricultural, or political functions. More recent discussion centers on the socio-political organization of elements of early Islamic society, interpreting their site plans as evidence of hierarchically apportioned accommodations for political-military leaders and their retainers and clients.

By the first decades of the eighth century, the state's armies had advanced in the West to southern France, where they were stopped near Poitiers, and had secured an eastern frontier with settlements at Qandahar (Afghanistan) and Multan and Mansoura (Pakistan) on the Indus River. The Umayyad state was overthrown in 750 by supporters of the Abbasid family of the Quraysh clan of Hashim, related to the Prophet through his uncle Abbas, thus boosting their political legitimacy. The revolutionary forces first struck in northeast Iran, although the historical tradition has recorded that their early seventh-century homestead was at Humayma (Jordan), a site currently being excavated. The second Abbasid caliph, al-Mansur, established a new capital at Baghdad on the Tigris River, circular in plan according to historical sources, although this configuration has never been verified archaeologically. The grandeur of Abbasid Baghdad might be extrapolated from such massive, walled sites as Rafiqa (Syria), a complex of palaces enclosed by a 5,470 yards (5,000 m), horseshoe-shaped, perimeter wall; Heraqlah (Syria), circular in plan, 547 yards (500 m) in diameter; and Husn al-Qadisiya (Iraq), an octagonal enclosure 1,640 yards (1,500 m) across founded by Abbasid caliphs of the second half of the eighth century. In the 830s, the Abbasid capital was moved to Samarra, upstream from Baghdad. Surface survey there has detected three major phases of building, including two horse-race tracks, six palace complexes, each more than 547 yards (500 m) in length, one hundred twenty-five other major buildings, and hundreds of other residences configured in a series of gridded street patterns, the remains of which stretch for about 25 miles (40 km) along the Tigris.

During these years the Abbasid caliphs fostered a scholarly environment in which the early Islamic juridico-religious and literary-historical canons were assembled, and which encouraged the translation of Sanskrit, Pahlavi Persian, Syriac, and Greek scientific and philosophical works into Arabic. The caliphs recruited a soldier mainly of enslaved non-Muslim Turks who converted to Islam in the course of their training, accommodations for whom would have been furnished in the extensive residential areas of Samarra in accord with patron-client obligations. As early as the late eighth century, the political centralization of the empire began to deteriorate, with governors asserting their political independence of the caliphate by various means of legitimation: minting of coinage, pronouncement of their names prior to the Friday sermon, refusal to send tax revenues to the caliph, and monumental building. The Spanish Umayyads built the Great Mosque of Cordova (Spain) in 785–6; the Idrisids founded their capital at Fez and the provincial city of al-Basra (both in Morocco) in the early ninth century; the Aghlabids built the Mosque of Qayrawan (Tunisia) in 836; and the Tulunids established a capital at al-Qata'i' (the mosque of which still stands) in 870 just north of al-Fustat. Abbasid religious authority was challenged by the rise to power of the Shi'ite Fatimid imams in North Africa, who, upon their occupation of Egypt in 969, established themselves as the principal ideological rivals of the Abbasids, and built their capital, al-Qahirah (Cairo), north of that of their Tulunid predecessors. Abbasid political weakness had dissolved to political impotence when in 945 Shi'ite Buyid generals from western Iran marched into Baghdad and instituted military rule, without removing the Sunni 'Abbasid caliphs from office.

The political fragmentation of the Abbasid Empire resulted in the elaboration of a social system founded on an array of regional polities in which local notables became relatively more powerful and rulers resorted to various forms of legitimizing acts to secure their positions, which included patronage of art and scholarship. Most of these regional rulers came from a servile, military background; significant exceptions were the Abbasid caliphs at the turn of the thirteenth century, who reinstated the caliphate's political control in lower Mesopotamia and declaimed their leadership of an integrated Sunni Islam through the foundation of the Mustansiriya college in Baghdad (1233), the first such institution to accommodate all four schools of Sunni jurisprudence. These centuries also witnessed a broadening of the patronage of monumental architecture, no longer the exclusive domain of political leaders. The overall consequence was the development of a cosmopolitan, urban civilization bound together chiefly by a class of scholarly elite transcending political borders, in which urban institutions (hospitals, colleges of law, and convents for ascetics) rather than complete urban foundations became the principal expressions of power and patronage.

By the eleventh century, when a number of formerly marginal ethnic groups attained power, a diffuse urban-based social system was firmly rooted. In the west, reformist Berber dynasties (the Almoravids and the Almohads) took control of North Africa and Andalusia, where trans-Saharan trade prospered at such sites as Sijilmassa (Morocco). In the east, the Ghurids established one of the last planned urban foundations at Lashkari Bazar, revived Qandahar (both in Afghanistan), and secured an empire that extended to northern India. In the Near East, large-scale migration of Turkic pastoralists dominated by the Seljuk family established a sultanate associated explicitly with the Sunni cause, freed the Abbasid caliphs from their Buyid overlords, and challenged the Fatimid imamate. Seljuk success against the Byzantines in Anatolia provoked the fears of western Christendom, resulting ultimately in the Europeans' holy war and a two-century Crusader occupation of largely fortified sites in the Levant such as the Red Tower (Israel). The Seljuks, like the Buyid generalissimos before them, kept the religious apparatus of the state headed by the Abbasid caliph, retained the Persian bureaucracy, and relied on a predominantly Turkic army recruited from outside the lands of Islam.

The Seljuks' appanage (grants) system of succession, common among the steppe pastoralists of Central Asia, soon resulted in a centrally weakened state and a resurgence of local rulers. Among these were the Seljuks of Rum, who left an extensive record of architectural monuments in Konya (Turkey) and elsewhere in Anatolia. The Zangids, Turkic military rulers in Syria, realized the legitimizing power of the war against the Crusaders and championed the cause of Islam against the foreign invaders. From these circumstances came Salah al-Din al-Ayyubi (Saladin), a Kurdish general who managed to take control of the by then crumbling Fatimid state in Cairo in 1171, and after the death of his Zangid military patron in north Syria, secured for himself the role of principal Muslim leader there as well. In 1258, the Mongols sacked Baghdad and executed the Abbasid caliph, who had not submitted to the authority of the Mongol world empire. The tendency to militarist rule culminated in a coup in Cairo in 1250 in which the Mamluk dynasty was established; after their victory over the non-Muslim Mongol army in 1260 in Palestine and their reinstitution of the Abbasid caliphate in Cairo, the Mamluks fashioned themselves as the protectors of Islam.

During the middle and later centuries, Islam expanded by commerce and proselytization into the Indian Ocean (sites in Ceylon, the Comoros Islands, and Madagascar), Southeast Asia (Thailand, Indonesia, and the Philippines), as well as into coastal East Africa (Somalia, Kenya, and Tanzania). In the west, while Islam was carried across the Sahara into West Africa (Nigeria and Mali), Muslim territory retracted before the advance of the *reconquista*, well documented in the historical record and supplemented by survey and excavation in the Sierra de Espadan (Spain) and Qsar es-Seghir (Morocco). By the mid-thirteenth century the Islamic world consisted of an array of regional empires whose capitals and countryside were filled with the declamatory monuments of their rulers. The Nasrids in Andalusia built the citadel known as al-Hamra' (Alhambra). Dominating North Africa were the Marinids and Hafsids, the latter of whom introduced the first colleges to North Africa. The Mongol successor state of the Ilkhans in Mesopotamia and the Iranian plateau, eventually adopting Islam and Persian culture, founded an observatory at Maragha and a summer capital at Sultaniyah (both in northwest Iran), more likely reflecting a tradition of transhumance rather than that of the early Islamic cities. The Mamluks and Timurids filled the cities of their respective domains with a remarkable array of religious, scholarly, and commercial institutions. In the wake of the Ghurids, and particularly from the time of the Mongol conquests, the Indian Muslim dynasties fostered Persianate Muslim culture at such sites as Daulatabad, Delhi, Chapaner, and Golconda (India).

Early in the sixteenth century, highly centralized imperial absolutism returned to Islamic civilization for the first time since the heyday of the Abbasid caliphate: The Ottoman Turks built an empire that extended from Mesopotamia to Morocco; the Mughals, a dynasty descended from Timur, established an empire in the Asian subcontinent; and the Safavids secured for themselves the Iranian plateau.

■ M.G.S. Hodgson, *The Venture of Islam*, 3 vols. (1974). *World Archaeology*, vol. 14, no. 3 (1983), *passim*. R. Ettinghausen and O. Grabar, *The Art and Architecture of Islam 650–1250* (1987). K.A.C. Creswell and J. W. Allan, *A Short Account of Early Muslim Architecture* (1989). U. Rebstock, "Das islamische Reich unter den vier ersten Kalifen," in *Tübinger Atlas des Vorderen Orients*, BVII 2 (1989). A. Northdege, "Beispiele islamischer Städte: Samarra," in *Tübinger Atlas des Vorderen Orients*, BVII 14.4 (1990). *Archéologie islamique*, vols. 1–3 (1990–1992), *passim*. S. Blair and J. Bloom, *The Art and Architecture of Islam 1250–1800* (1994).

John L. Mcloy

MOSQUES

The mosque, or *masjid*, is a general term for a Muslim religious structure in which prayer is generally, but not exclusively, conducted. Within the general debate of whether there has ever been an urban type that may be described as an "Islamic city," the presence of a mosque, particularly a large, congregational mosque (*masjid jami'* or *jami'*) may be taken as the crucial (and for some the only) institution allowing an Islamic characterization to be made.

The original model for the mosque appears to have been the house of the Prophet Muhammad at Medina. This mosque was continually enlarged and embellished until very little detail may be reconstructed except from documentary sources. The essential element was a large, rectangular, open yard delimited by simple walls in which the Muslim community gathered for prayer. The addition of a shaded portion, apparently simple thatching supported on palm logs, may represent the origin of the hypostyle style of many mosques; such structures are often characterized as the Arab mosque. The living apartments or rooms of the Prophet were attached to the southeast side of the mosque, a pattern apparently duplicated in the residence of the first governors of Islamic cities.

The crucial architectural element was the *mihrab*, a point or sector of the *qibla* wall (the wall nearest to Mecca and hence the direction of prayer). While it is generally agreed that the earliest *mihrabs* may not have been structural elements, this most diagnostic feature of the mosque evolved into a niche, either rectangular or more often semicircular, with varying decoration. The *mihrab* often produced a protruding element on the exterior of the building, allowing identification from the outside. Many later buildings have been excavated and identified as mosques solely on the strength of a *mihrab*. In the desert, any line of stones with a central semicircle (or even prominent stone) also has been labeled a mosque; their dates have been estimated from the earliest years of Islam (in the Negev) to evidence of Wahhabi fundamentalism in the eighteenth and nineteenth centuries.

One of the most problematic elements of mosques is the orientation of the *qibla* wall. In theory, this wall should be oriented perpendicular to the axis leading toward Mecca; worshipers lined in rows with this wall should all be facing the correct direction of prayer. Determination of this direction has not been an easy matter and a number of mosques show radical changes in orientation as corrections have been made. King (1992) has shown that the situation is even more complex as local geodesic traditions became important based on winds and astral signs. There is increasing evidence that a common southeast or southwest orientation may have been an early norm, no matter what the true direction to Mecca. Hypotheses on early orientations to the east or toward Jerusalem remain unsupported by archaeological evidence.

Studies on activities in the mosque of Medina and other early mosques make it clear that the earliest usage incorporated religious, administrative, and commercial functions within its precinct. The sacralization of this space came about gradually, mainly due to growth in the complexity of administrative state functions. The mosque also retained (and often still holds) juridical, political, and educational functions. The image of scholarly discourse among the colonnades need not be confined to classical times but recurred as a prime element in Islamic civilization. The claim of al-Azhar mosque in Cairo as the oldest college in the world is an outgrowth of this function.

A number of mosques revealed through archaeological excavations point to architectural developments characteristic of the late eighth and early ninth centuries. These mosques are in Istakhr, Isfahan, and Susa in Iran, Banbhore in Pakistan, al-Balad in southern Oman, Qal'at 'Ana in Iraq, al-Rabadha in Arabia, and Aqaba in Jordan. They were constructed on platforms with periodically renewed gravel floors and often had stairways giving access to multiple doorways. The hypostyle hall was often embellished with arches and occasionally a small dome before the *mihrab*. These mosques often began with only two or three rows of columns (*riwaq*) in the sanctuary and a single row around the courtyard (*sahn*). Many of them demonstrate a pattern of near continual growth through demolition and reconstruction.

One of the longest stratigraphic sequences has been revealed in the Congregational Mosque at Siraf on the gulf coast of Iran. Whitehouse has excavated a structure of the fifteenth century overlying a progression of smaller structures, the earliest of which dates to the early ninth century. While the port city of Siraf stretches naturally along the shore, its congregational mosque is not centrally located. In other cities, the mosque is usually in one quadrant (often southwest) and not the absolute center of the idealized city type. The administrative complex (and ruler's residence, *dar al-imara*) is usually positioned on an axial alignment next to the *qibla* wall. Very often, a large *maydan* or plaza leaves the other three sides open for open markets *(suqs)*. Thus the congregational mosque often comes to focus upon the three functional elements (religious, administrative, commercial) necessary for an urban settlement, in this case an Islamic city.

This same site of Siraf has revealed a possibly more significant series of small mosques, neighborhood religious locations possibly analogous to the plethora of chapels which tended to develop in Byzantine towns. Small mosques featured as ancillary entry elements, at Qasr al-Hayr al-Gharbi, in "palaces" of Raqqa, or even more frequently in stations along the Darb Zubayda. The tendency is to describe any single room structure with a niche in the appropriate wall as a mosque; such an oratory may be described as the *bayt al-salat,* known from Khirbat al-Mafjar and other early complexes. Such rooms later become funerary chapels with the addition of a central tomb (or tombs) as at Aswan and many other places. The *Wali* or *Pir,* as they are popularly known, may stand as an isolated feature in the town or countryside or as a structural element of cemeteries.

Later congregational mosques, particularly after the tenth century, tended to depart from the hypostyle mosque type; new types combined multiple *iwans* (vaulted halls open at one end), often in cruciform arrangement, around a yard or completely covered central room. Such mosques have usually been found still standing or in use; they have been studied by Creswell and have been considered the proper research of art historians more than archaeologists. This is also generally true of decorative embellishments and epigraphy; whether stucco, mosaic, or carved wood, no style or medium may be seen as specific to mosques. Indeed, the very lack of decoration may be a signal feature in many regions. Other glorious mosques such as that in Cordoba belie this tendency and may be studied for their aesthetic accomplishments. The manifold meaning which mosques held in various regions and periods is a current subject of archaeological fieldwork and synthesis.

[*See also* NEAR EAST: MIDDLE AGES IN THE NEAR EAST.]

■ D. Whitehouse, *Siraf III: The Congregational Mosque.* K.A.C. Creswell, *Early Muslim Architecture* (1952). G. Bisheh, *The Mosque of the Prophet at Madinah* (1979). R. Hillenbrand, "Masjid, the Architecture of the Mosque," *Encyclopedia of Islam* 2nd ed. (1989), pp. 677–88. D. A. King, "Qibla Charts, Qibla Maps and Related Instruments," *The History of Cartography* Vol. 2 (1992), pp. 189–205. G. Avni, "Early Mosques in the Negev Highlands," *BASOR* 294 (1994): 83–100. B. Finster, *Fruhe iranische moscheen* (1994).

Donald Whitcomb

J

JAPAN AND KOREA

Introduction
Early States of Japan and Korea

INTRODUCTION

During the final phases of the Old Stone Age, the prehistoric inhabitants of the Korean peninsula and the Japanese islands embarked on a new cultural path, pursuing new lifeways, new economic systems, and technology. For the first time, the moving bands of hunters and gatherers settled down in permanent villages, made potteries, and produced new kinds of stone implements. For food sources, they exploited not only wooded forests but also rivers, bays, and coasts.

Korea: The Chulmun Period (6000 B.C. to 1300 B.C.). In the Korean peninsula, the earliest pottery, found at Osan-ni on the east-central coast, was of the applique-ware tradition and dated to ca. 6000 B.C. This initial *ceramic was soon replaced by a new pottery tradition employing a variety of impressed, incised, or pinched surface decorations of comb-tooth, wave-dots, way lines, punctate, herring-bone, tiny circles, arcs, and short parallel lines, similar to the *kam keramik* traditions of Neolithic Eurasia. Because of the predominance of surface impressions similar to those made by comb-tooth, these ceramics are called *chulmun* pottery, meaning "comb-tooth pattern" in Korean.

By 5000 B.C. Chulmun pottery was a distinct tradition with regional variations. Differences were particularly marked between the northwestern and the northeastern Chulmun, whose tradition was characterized by flat bases and straight bodies, in contrast to the pointed bases and spherical- or globular-shaped bodies of the northwest and other regions. Late Chulmun pottery of the northwest also tended to be more flat-based and lose surface decorations. In the late Chulmun horizon at Namkyong and Kumt'al-li, both decorated Chulman and plain vessels occurred together, with the latter eventually predominating.

Archaeological data from various Chulmun sites (Chit'ap-ni, Kungsan-ni, Namkyong, Sejuk-ni, Sinam-ni, and Kumt'al-li in the northwest; Nongp'o-dong, Sop'o-hang, Kulp'o, and Hogok in the northeast; Amsa-ri and Misa-ri in the west-central region; and Tongsam-dong on the southeast coast) reveal that the people lived in villages of semisubterranean pit houses, close to the riverbanks or the seashore. They engaged in hunting, fishing, and gathering nuts, berries, and shellfish. Their tools were made of stone, bone, and antler. Stone tools included ground adzes, picks, polished stone arrowheads, saddle querns, net sinkers, and compound fishhooks. Bone and antler implements included digging sticks, fishhooks, barbed harpoons, spearheads, awls, and needles.

By around 1500 B.C., the Chulmun people were growing millet, which had been established in southern Manchuria by 5000 B.C. Finds of Chulmun cultigens include carbonized millet from a late horizon at Namkyong and also from a late horizon at Chit'ap-ni. Other evidence for agriculture comprises increasing numbers of stone tools closely associated with productive activities: shovels, hoes, picks, saddle querns, and axes.

During their long, successful adaptation to their natural environment and settled village life, the late Chulmun people also increased in societal complexity, as suggested by the presence of differentiated architecture in the late Chulmun horizon at Namkyong in the northwest. The successful adaptation to the ecosystem and the established sedentism in time led to the emerging of influential elites, who in turn spurred agricultural experimentation. The marked sociocultural changes in the succeeding Mumun Period were a consequence of the late Chulmun dynamism.

Japanese Islands: The Jomon Period (10,000 B.C. to 300 B.C.). Technological as well as sociocultural developments on the Japanese islands during the final phases of the Old Stone Age and afterward were remarkably similar to those of the Korean peninsula. As in Korea, the earliest ceramic remains found in Japan (at Ishigoya Cave in central Japan and Fukui Rock Shelter in Kyushu, dated to ca. 10,000 B.C.) were of applique-ware tradition. These first appeared in the south and in time spread to the northern and eastern regions of the islands.

Also, as in Korea, the applique ware were soon replaced by a new pottery tradition characterized by complex surface designs. First, there appeared cord-marked or *jomon* ware of Igusa and Natsushima types in the Kanto district of central Japan ca. 7500 B.C. (Early Jomon Period). Almost at the same time, there appeared in the Aomori region of northern Japan, most likely from northeastern Asia, pottery with comb-pattern designs and a conical base (Shirahama or Kominatotai types) similar to the Chulmun pottery of Korea. In time, however, the cord-marked or *jomon* pottery became predominant throughout Japan.

As Jomon pottery (handmade) evolved, it took on new forms in shape and design. By Middle Jomon, around 3000 B.C., there appeared vessels with a deep body and elaborate sculptured designs; by Late Jomon, ca. 2000 B.C., a variety of small vessels such as bowls and pots often with zoned cord-marked decorations appeared; and by Final Jomon, ca. 1000 B.C., Jomon pottery manifested multi-decorative forms including broad-line impressions, zoned cord-marks, and polished plain surfaces.

Jomon sites, many of which are concentrated on resource-rich coastal and bay areas, are numerous and scattered throughout Japan: Natsushima Shell Mound, Kamo, Torihama Shell Mound, Togariishi, Idojiri, Kasori Shell

Mound, Kaido, Shijimizuka, Fudodo, Mizukamidani, Kamegaoka in central Honshu; Sozudai and Todori Shell Mound in Kyushu; and Tosamporo and Tokoro Shell Mound in Hokkaido. From these sites have come mountains of archaeological data that clearly suggest that as early as 8000 B.C. the Jomon people had become highly efficient in their adaptation to the natural-biotic environment and that a stable economic and social system had emerged, lasting for nearly eight thousand years. Their successful adaptation resulted in permanent villages consisting of semisubterranean pithouses.

The presence at Jomon sites of grinding stones, digging sticks, hoes, and large storage pits suggests that the Jomon economic system was based on skillful seasonal exploitation of vegetation that included edible roots, tubers, greens, berries, and nuts. Equally important was their efficient exploitation of shellfish and seasonally migrating marine resources as evidenced by thousands of Jomon shell mounds, bone fishhooks and harpoons, and net sinkers.

Archaeological remains of large architectural features in the center of settlements from Middle Jomon sites such as Fudodo and Mizukamidani in central Japan suggest that by that time there was also emerging a social organization reflecting differentiated social groups as well as societal centralization.

Korea: From Agriculture to Three Kingdoms (ca. 1300 B.C. to A.D. 300). The long sedentary village life based on the hunting-fishing-gathering economy of Chulmun and Jomon peoples came to an end with the emergence of agriculture in Korea ca. 1300 B.C. and in Japan ca. 300 B.C., about a thousand years later. With an agricultural economy there arose new cultural innovations as well as increasing societal complexity, including new forms of pottery, tools, and burial systems, and a hierarchical society.

In the Korean peninsula, the incipient agriculture of the Late Chulmun Period continued to expand, and according to archaeological remains from Hokok (Musan) and Odong (Hoeryong), by 1500 B.C. Chinese millet, foxtail millet, sorghum, beans, and peas were grown in northern regions of Korea. By 1000 B.C., rice (*Oriza sativa japonica* type) and barley were being cultivated at Namkyong in northwest Korea as well as at Hunam-ni in the west-central region. Soon, these cultigens spread southward to other parts of the peninsula, as shown in the archaeological remains of Songguk-ni in the southwest.

In association with food cultivation, farming implements such as hoes, picks, shovels, axes, sickles, and reaping knives appeared. Initially the agricultural implements were made of stone and wood; stone tools have survived in abundance but the remains of wooden implements are rare in Korea. Settlements exploded and expanded, springing up in nearly all parts of the peninsula, including many inland hilly zones. They were not only more numerous but also much larger in size than in Chulmun times.

Artifacts clearly intended for ceremonial or symbolic use arose as well. They first included polished stone daggers and arrowheads of great beauty and craftsmanship. Around 800 B.C. bronze daggers and mirrors were imported from the Lioning region in southern Manchuria. These were owned by elites and were buried with them.

The type of pottery of this early agricultural period was the so-called plain, or *mumun* ("no decoration"), ware tradition. First appearing in the Late Chulmun Period, ca. 1500 B.C., the Mumun pottery gradually replaced the Chulmun pottery and became the predominant ceramic ware of Korea until about 100 B.C., manifesting a variety of local forms and styles.

Around 300 B.C. or shortly before, local bronze industries emerged in the northwest, and by 200 B.C., they spread southward to the Kum River, the Youngsan River, and the Naktong River Basins. Locally manufactured bronze artifacts include spears, adzes, daggers, halberds, chisels, mirrors, needles, fishhooks, chariot fittings, horse trappings, bells, and various ornaments. The most impressive bronze objects come from burials of 300–100 B.C. In the Kim River Basin alone, twenty burials within a 31 mile (50 km) radius yielded two hundred bronze objects.

Almost at the same time, local iron technology arose under Chinese influence. By around 200 B.C. standardized iron items were being produced in the north, and shortly thereafter, iron tools became abundant in central and southern Korea, as shown by iron remains from Majang-ni (Kap'yong), Namyang-ni (Changsu), Hapsong-ni (Puyo), and Tahori (Uichang). The Lower Naktong River Basin, in particular, was a major iron production center for northeastern Asia ca. 100 B.C. to A.D. 300. Locally made iron implements included axes, knives, sickles, hoes, chisels, fishhooks, spears, arrowheads, daggers, halberds, and long swords. Korean iron products were sought after by the Chinese as well as by elites in Japan.

Coinciding with the development of agriculture and metallurgy was the rise of increasingly differentiated burials. Initially, such burials appeared in the form of megalithic structures or dolmens in varying sizes and forms. First appearing in the northwest around 1300 B.C., the megaliths spread to all parts of the peninsula. Around 800 B.C., cist burials containing valued goods also appeared in the north, gradually replacing dolmens as they spread southward. In the second century B.C., jar-burials became popular in the southwest.

By the third century B.C., burials were differentiated not so much by their external shapes as by their valuable contents. Generally in the form of pit graves lined with natural or cut stones, the burials contained bronze and iron artifacts of great value in varying amounts. Grave Number One of Tahori in the Lower Naktong River Basin (ca. 50 B.C. to A.D. 100), for example, though robbed, contained three times as many goods as unrobbed graves nearby. The latter were also smaller in size than the former. The quantitative and qualitative differences among the burials suggest clearly defined, vertical differentiation and a hierarchically ordered society. Presumably, the person who controlled the bronze and iron also had the most and best productive land and, accordingly, occupied the highest sociopolitical position in the region or subregion within each major river valley.

Thus the differentiated society which had emerged in association with megalithic architecture and cist burials ca. 1000 B.C. to 500 B.C. was witnessing, in the second century B.C., the rise of numerous independent polities or complex chiefdoms in major river valleys throughout the peninsula.

During the first three centuries of the Christian era, called the Protohistoric Period in Korean history, the complex chiefdoms, through rivalry, warfare, and alliances, were being transformed into kingdoms of Kokuryo in the north, Paikche in the southwest, and Shilla in the southeast as well as into various Kaya states in the lower reaches of the Naktong River. As a distinguishing mark of full-fledged status, the ruling aristocracy of Korea's early states built mounded tombs in the manner of Chinese practice on the mainland.

Critically important to the momentous socio-cultural developments in the Korean peninsula resulting in the emergence of a highly stratified society and the three kingdoms was the steady flow of Chinese influence, first with the expansion of the Yan state into Manchuria in the third century B.C. and next with Chinese invasion of northwest Korea in 108 B.C. For over four hundred years, Chinese commanderies at Lelang (modern Pyongyang) functioned as the political and military arm of Chinese dynasties, beginning with Han, as well as the major contact point between the advanced Chinese civilization and the local population. Even as local chieftains disdained the Chinese occupation, their conflicts with the Chinese commanderies served as a catalyst for useful political alliances. They also acquired from the Chinese residents advanced technologies including wet-rice cultivation, iron technology, and high-fired ceramic technology.

Japanese Islands: Yayoi, Kofun, and Early States (300 B.C. to A.D. 700). While the Korean peninsula was undergoing sociocultural revolution under the emerging agricultural economy, Jomon hunting-fishing-gathering lifeways largely continued on the Japanese islands, enhanced by the abundance of their natural resources. Beginning around 300 B.C., however, the eight-thousand-year-old Jomon lifeways rapidly came to an end with the introduction of wet-rice agriculture and metallurgy from the continent, by immigrants from the southern regions of the Korean peninsula. After their initial appearance at Itatsuke area in northwestern Kyushu, closet to Korea, the new technologies spread rapidly eastward to the Kyoto-Osaka region, where they flourished. By A.D. 200 they became firmly established throughout all Japanese islands except the northernmost Hokkaido region.

The type of pottery closely associated with the emerging rice agriculture in Japan is called *yayoi*, pottery named after the Yoyoi district in Tokyo where it was identified. Accordingly, the period between 300 B.C. and A.D. 300 is referred to in Japanese history as the Yayoi Period.

Even though some Jomon decorative elements persisted through the Early and Middle Yayoi Periods, Yayoi pottery as a whole took up its own tradition, under a strong continental influence. This was specially so during the Late Yayoi Period, ca. A.D. 100 to A.D. 300. Globular jars, deep pots, and pedestaled bowls of the Early Yayoi Period of 300 B.C. to 100 B.C. as well as the double-jar burial urns of the Middle Yayoi of 100 B.C. to A.D. 100 and the long- and short-necked plain jars of the Late Yayoi Period of A.D. 100 to A.D. 300 were strikingly similar to the Korean *mumun* pottery and its successors.

The arrival of immigrants as well as elements of advanced culture from Korea (wet-rice cultivation, farming implements, bronze and iron technology, loom weaving, and megalithic burials, among others) had revolutionary effects on Japan's indigenous Jomon society, transforming it into an ever increasingly complex society during the Yayoi Period.

Archaeological remains from numerous Yayoi sites (Itatsuke, Mikumo, Ankokuji in northern Kyushu; Ama, Tenjinyama, and Uriyudo in the Kyoto-Osaka region in west-central Honshu; and Toro in central Honshu) suggest that cultural imports from the continent were fully indigenized on the Japanese islands within a few centuries. For example, the Toro site (from the Middle to Late Yayoi Period) has yielded well-developed paddy-fields and an abundance of wooden implements associated with wet-rice cultivation.

Bronze and iron industries flourished at Kasuga in the Kyushu region, where bronze spears and iron axes were locally manufactured. Likewise, local bronze industry developed in the Kyoto-Osaka region, producing hundreds of impressive-looking ceremonial copper bells known as *dotaku*.

Middle Yayoi village sites of Yoshinogari in northern Kyushu and Otsuka in central Honshu were surrounded by moats and palisades, suggesting that warfare was common by ca. 100 B.C. Discovery of iron arrowheads in village defensive installations as well as stone arrowheads in human skeletal remains at Yoshinogari is clear evidence of warfare.

As in the Korean peninsula, highly differentiated burials emerged during the Yayoi Period, as suggested by the presence of burials containing bronze daggers, mirrors (the local type as well as Han Chinese), and glass beads. By the end of the Yayoi Period, ca. A.D. 300, Japanese society had reached the level of a highly stratified society of numerous chiefdoms based on stable farming villages, intensive wet-rice cultivation, and craft specializations.

During the following four centuries, from A.D. 300 to A.D 700, mounded tombs *(kofun)* began to appear, first in the Kyoto-Osaka region and then moving outward. The rise of mounded tombs was closely associated with the new level of cultural and sociopolitical sophistication that Japanese society had reached.

Particularly significant was the process of political centralization taking place in the Kyoto-Nara-Osaka region, the traditional home of Japan's first (Yamato) state and its imperial power. The initial emergence of the distinctive keyhole shaped tumuli in the region and their growing size in time, as well as their gradual expansion westward, appear to have coincided with that of centralizing political power. Along with the mounded burials the emerging early states employed differentiated *haniwa* funerary sculptures to symbolize their ranks in relation to one another. In order to strengthen their political linkage they also exchanged bronze mirrors.

Discovery of weapons including iron arrowheads, metal spearpoints, and halberds in great numbers as well as horse trappings and iron armours at Kofun sites suggest that since the Yayoi times warfare had been frequent, galvanizing formerly independent chieftains into major political alliances and eventually into a centralized state under the Yamato hegemony in the Nara Basin.

Greatly enhancing the Kofun Period sociopolitical and cultural developments was again the ongoing impact of advanced civilization of the continent, particularly from the Korean peninsula. Incessant warfare among three kingdoms of Koguryo, Paikche, and Shilla, as well as among dozens of smaller Kaya states between Paikche and Shilla, resulted in the movement of Korea's warrior aristocratic elites as well as their artisans and craftsmen across the sea to Japanese islands, where they established new homes or joined emerging local chieftains. The Korean immigrants helped develop the high-fired Sue ware, the type of pottery of the Kofun Period, as well as aristocratic tombs with side-passage chambers, and sophisticated iron technology producing iron weapons and iron armors.

The civilization path that Korea and Japan took from early times was remarkably similar. It was essentially one of secondary formation in which indigenously evolving societies reached a high level of cultural and sociopolitical maturity under the influence of a more advanced civilization.

In Korea, the Chulmun society of hunting-gathering-fishing lifeways began to undergo increasingly rapid changes toward civilization under the influence of China. China's impact became increasingly pronounced beginning with its northeasterly expansion in the third century B.C. and particularly following Han China's invasion of northwest Korea in the second century B.C. In Japan, the Jomon society underwent rapid and even revolutionary changes under the influence of Korea—Korean immigrants and such crucial technologies as wet-rice cultivation and metallurgy. Once full-fledged centralized states became established in Korea by the fourth century A.D. and in Japan by the seventh century A.D., Korea and Japan actively pursued the incorporation of Chinese elements into their culture and society through direct contacts with succeeding Chinese dynasties, in art and architecture, religion and philosophy, administration, urban planning, and various areas of material technology.

[See also ASIA; CHINA; JOMON TRADITION; KOFUN (MOUNDED TOMBS OF JAPAN AND KOREA).]

Song Nai Rhee

EARLY STATES OF JAPAN AND KOREA

Between the third and seventh centuries A.D. a number of state-level polities arose in the East Asian Pen/Insular region (the Korean Peninsula and Japanese archipelago). These included Koguryo, Paekche, and Shilla on the peninsula and Yamato in the islands. The rise of these states can be seen as a response to the vacuum created by the demise of China's Han dynasty (206 B.C.–A.D. 220). The process itself can be likened to the fall of the Roman Empire and the rise of the Anglo-Saxon kingdoms in Britain, which occurred roughly on the same time scale.

The early states of East Asia are secondary states, having had models of elite hierarchy and strong central organization provided by the Han. The Chinese had reached out and actually incorporated the northern part of the Korean Peninsula into their empire by establishing, in 108 B.C., the military commandery of Lelang, now the T'osongni site near modern P'yongyang: from there, they brought the southern peninsula and the Japanese archipelago into their political sphere by economic means. It is interesting to note that the chiefdoms of the Yayoi Period (ca. 300 B.C.–A.D. 300), including Yamatai, in the western archipelago flourished during contact with the Han Court, but they did not proceed on to early state status. Instead, the focus of development shifted inland to the Kansai region, which had no direct economic ties with China during Yayoi times. It thus appears that the areas which came under direct Chinese influence (the southern peninsula and Kyushu Island) were politically retarded by the experience, while those areas most socially isolated from the Han spawned strong states (Koguryo, Shilla, Yamato). One group of chiefdoms in the Naktong River Basin of the southeastern peninsula, termed the Kaya confederacy, never quite coalesced into statehood before succumbing to Shilla in the sixth century.

The periods of state formation in the Pen/Insular region are the Three Kingdoms Period of Korea (A.D. 300–668) and the Kofun Period of Japan (A.D. 300–710). Both are marked by monumental burial architecture as a function of elite ranking [see Kofun (Mounded Tombs of Korea and Japan)]. Curiously, the Korean Peninsula hosted three protohistoric states (Koguryo in the north, Paekche in the central west, and Shilla in the southeast), while the Japanese Islands, with

more land area, produced only one (Yamato in the Kansai region). The Yamato state began the process of administrative integration of the archipelago in the sixth century, incorporating many smaller, competing chiefdoms by giving their leaders central court status. Shilla, on the other hand, used military force to conquer Koguryo and Paekche and unify the Korean Peninsula in the seventh century. Shilla and Yamato then adopted many administrative techniques from the resurgent Chinese court of the Tang Period (618–907), thus ensuring their survival into the United Shilla (668–935) and Nara-Heian (710–1185) Periods, respectively. These early states are looked upon as the direct ancestors of the modern nation-states of Korea and Japan, giving them the aura, together with China, of being the longest-lived bureaucracies and/or imperial lines in the world today.

The East Asian Pen/Insular states are protohistoric: Chinese dynastic histories contain references to them at times when they did not yet have writing, and their own earliest written histories date from periods later than the material covered in them. The earliest extant Korean histories are the *Samguk Sagi* and *Samguk Yusa*, produced in the twelfth and thirteenth centuries, respectively, while the earliest Japanese histories, the *Nihon Shoki* and *Kojiki*, date from the eighth century. Writing might have been introduced into the Pen/Insular societies by proselytizing Chinese Buddhist monks from the late fourth century onward, and it is known that scribes from Paekche performed duties at the Yamato court.

The relations among the East Asian Pen/Insular states comprised constantly shifting alliances and hostilities. The enmity between Koguryo and Paekche caused Paekche in the fourth century to call on Yamato for assistance in the form of troops and supplies. Koguryo shifted its capital southward from the Yalu River Basin (at modern Ji'an, China) to the old commandery headquarters at P'yongyang. In Koguryo's push south, Paekche was successively banished from its Han River base (maybe at the site of Mongch'on T'osong near Seoul) to Ungjin (modern Kongju) and Sabi (modern Puyo) in the southwest; much of mature Paekche material culture is present at these sites. Yamato was also heavily involved in the Kaya region of the southern peninsular coast, which was a major production area for iron and stoneware. Stoneware potters from Kaya were resettled in the Yamato region in the early fifth century to produce vessels for the regional elite, and later that century, large groups of craftspeople from Paekche became the specialist gold workers, saddlers, weavers, and others for the Yamato court. Yamato received its entire iron supply from Kaya until local smelting of iron sand began in the sixth century. In that century Shilla conquered the Kaya chiefdoms and began to extend its military threat overseas to Yamato.

There are two outstanding problems in understanding the protohistoric relations among the East Asian Pen/Insular states. The first is Egami Namio's theory of the conquest of Yamato in the early fifth century by a continental horse-riding elite, identified as Paekche by Gari Ledyard. The idea of conquest was stimulated by similarities in material culture, especially horse trappings. However, no doubt there were other kinds of close connections between Paekche and Yamato operating in the fourth and fifth centuries—elite gifts, trade, migration by political refugees, maybe even marriage alliances—so that other social processes can account for such similarities. The second is the implication in the *Nihon Shoki* that Yamato once maintained a colony, called Mimana, on the southern Korean coast. Since Kaya was Yamato's sole source of iron, it would not be surprising if the court had some means of ensuring its supply; however, a military colony or annexation was not necessary in achieving economic access. Discussion of these problems is exacerbated by the more recent history of Japan's colonization of Korea between 1910 and 1945; delicate national sensitivities color research into these questions.

The sharing of an elite material culture among the Pen/Insular states was facilitated by transfer of technologies and later by the adoption of Buddhism. However, urban forms were markedly different until the adoption of the gridded city plan from China in the seventh century. On the Korean Peninsula, walled enclosures constructed of earthen ramparts or stone masonry functioned as administrative centers, fortresses, and military headquarters. The peninsula is littered with hundreds, even thousands, of these remains, which are visible parts of today's landscape—as at P'anwolsong, the Old Shilla capital in Kyongju. In the western Japanese islands, a few such defensive walls were built in response to Shilla's military threats, but the indigenous settlement forms during state formation consisted of elite housesteads—pillared buildings surrounded by and sometimes divided into clusters by moats and/or palisades, as at the Ozono site in Osaka—that were spatially separate from commoner villages with pit-building architecture. It appears that early capital areas in Japan consisted of dispersed craft production sites and elite housesteads rather than highly nucleated cities.

Data on protohistoric administrative practices have been gleaned not from archaeology but from the existing textual records. The peninsular Three Kingdoms apparently divided their capital territories into five or six administrative areas called *bu* to be ruled directly, while leaving the outer regions under the control of local elites. The *bu* terminology was later adopted and modified by Yamato to provide a system of resource procurement for the court (the *be* system). Shilla's elite depended on kinship ranking as determined by "hallowed bone" (royal blood) descent prerogatives; Yamato also imported this system as a method of assigning rank within the court.

These indigenous practices were superseded in the seventh century by the adoption by all states of elements of the Tang administrative structure. Most importantly, this provided the centers with the means for provincial administration, financing of the court economies, and routinizing the raising of armed forces. Buddhism became the state religion in Shilla and Yamato, and in Nara-Period Japan a Buddhist administrative hierarchy—of main headquarters (at Todaiji in Nara) and provincial monasteries and nunneries—paralleled the bureaucratic system of territorial control. The gridded-city capitals of these mature states were Shilla's Kumsong (outside modern Kyongju city) and Nara's Heijo (outside modern Nara city). Both are undergoing constant excavation, with on-site museums and reconstructed buildings.

An important artifact category found mainly at these administrative sites (provincial capitals included) is the wooden tablet on which provisioning orders, tax records, bureaucratic hour-keeping, staff evaluations, and so on, were written in ink. The corpus has increased enormously, especially in Japan, since their initial discovery in 1961. The inscriptions form written documentation of a functioning bureaucracy that can be compared to the more politically oriented court histories such as the *Nihon Shoki* and *Shoku Nihongi*. Much has already been clarified about the palace provisioning system operating through taxes in kind. For example, in Japan it was the county office rather than the provincial office that was responsible for collecting taxes and delivering them to the capital each year. Continuing analysis should add immensely to our understanding of these early state systems.

[*See also* ASIA: PREHISTORY AND EARLY HISTORY OF EAST ASIA; CHINA: HAN EMPIRE.]

■ W. G. Aston, trans, *Nihongi: Chronicles of Japan from the Earliest Times to A.D. 697* (1972). Gari Ledyard, "Galloping Along with the Horseriders: Looking for the Founders of Japan," *Journal of Japanese Studies* 1, 2 (1975): 217–54. Jon Carter Covell and Alan Covell, *Japan's Hidden History: Korean Impact on Japanese Culture* (1984). Gina L. Barnes, *Protohistoric Yamato: Archaeology of the First Japanese State* (1988). Gina L. Barnes, "Early Korean States: A Review of Historical Interpretation," in *Bibliographic Reviews of Far Eastern Archaeology 1990*, ed. G. L. Barnes (1990). Edward B. Adams, *Korea's Golden Age: Cultural Spirit of Silla in Kyongju* (1991). K. Tsuboi and M. Tanaka, *The Historic City of Nara: An Archaeological Approach* (1991). Gina L. Barnes, *China, Korea and Japan: The Rise of Civilisation in East Asia* (1993).

Gina L. Barnes

JERICHO. Tell el-Sultan, better known as the ancient site of Jericho, is situated north of Wadi el-Mafjar on a moderately sloping plain formed by the Late Pleistocene Lisan Lake. Rising as a mound some 26 to 39 feet (8–12 m) above the current landscape, the site of Jericho covers an area of at least 30,000 square yards (25,000 sq m) and is oval shaped, with its long axis oriented along a north-south line. Originally intrigued by the biblical tale of the walls of Jericho, many archaeologists have undertaken prehistoric and biblically oriented excavations at Jericho. The earliest of these archaeologists was C. Warren, who excavated a series of deep shafts into the mound in 1873. Following this, E. Sellin and C. Watzinger (1907–1908) opened up a series of trenches, and were followed by the extensive excavations of J. Garstang (1930–1936). Focusing on the Early and Middle Bronze Age occupation, these researchers demonstrated that in the Bronze Age Jericho was surrounded by extensive defensive wall systems with a number of elongated rectangular towers between 49 to 70 feet (15–20 m) in length and 20 to 26 feet (6–8 m) in width. Jericho appears to have been continually occupied into the Middle Bronze Age, indicated by the extensive cemetery, with vertical shaft tombs and underground burial chambers. In the Middle Bronze Age, the town was expanded with the construction of glacis defensive fortifications. The elaborate burial offerings placed in some of the tombs of this period may reflect the emergence of local rulers. After destruction in the Late Bronze Age, Tell el-Sultan no longer served as an urban center.

While excavating Bronze Age Jericho, Sellin and Watzinger and Garstang uncovered remains of an earlier Neolithic occupation. Intrigued by these materials, Dame K. M. Kenyon (1952–1958) undertook large-scale excavations of the pre-pottery Neolithic occupation at Jericho. Kenyon's excavations demonstrated that Jericho was originally founded by sedentary foragers/collectors in the Natufian Period (12,800–10,500 B.P.), living in large semisubterranean oval stone structures, although it is unclear how extensive this occupation was. With the introduction of domesticated plants in the Pre-Pottery Neolithic A period (PPNA) (ca. 10,500/10,300–9300 B.P.), Jericho mushroomed into a large regional agricultural community covering an area of some 300 square yards (25,000 sq m). Villagers, like those of the nearby sites of Netiv Hagdud and Gilgal I, lived year-round in roofed, oval semisubterranean dwellings, and engaged in long-distance trading of Anatolian obsidian and shells from the Mediterranean and Red Sea. Living on domesticated and wild plant crops as well as hunting of wild game, adult individuals were buried in single graves, almost always with their cranium later removed to secondary locations. Kenyon's excavations also uncovered a spectacular large circular tower situated just inside of a 12-foot-high (3.6-meter-high) perimeter wall. Made of field stones, the tower was 28 feet (8.5 m) in diameter, preserved to a height of 26.5 feet (8 m), and had an internal staircase. Kenyon argued that the tower and walls comprised an early defensive system. O. Bar-Yosef has questioned this view, arguing that the tower and perimeter wall served as a water diversion system to protect the PPNA occupants from winter floods. It is also possible that the western wall, which does not totally surround Jericho, facilitated the ponding of water so as to support agricultural and a waterfowl habitat.

With the appearance of domesticated goat and sheep in the Pre-Pottery Neolithic B period (PPNB) (9300–8000 B.P.), significant changes occurred at Jericho. The tower and perimeter walls of the earlier period were abandoned and villagers lived in rectangular thirteen-by-twenty-six-foot (4 by 8 m) houses with painted red and white lime plaster floors. While displaying continuity with earlier burial practices, PPNB villagers often cached multiple human skulls, up to nine at one time, beneath house floors. Evidence of these plastered human skulls, often with inset saltwater shells for eyes, and painted representations of hair and other facial features, clearly indicates the practice of a complex form of ancestor worship and the emergence of more complex social and ritual organizations.

Kenyon's excavations of the Neolithic deposits have clearly demonstrated that, as one of the earliest and most important agricultural villages in the Jordan Valley, Jericho existed as a regional focus for the trade of exotic goods and agricultural products. As the most extensively reported of Neolithic sites in the southern Levant, our archaeological knowledge of Jericho serves as the foundation for understanding Neolithic cultural chronology, the emergence of agriculture, and the development of complex social organizations in the Levantine Neolithic Period. Its continued cultural and economic development through the Bronze Age is testimony to its importance as a regional center.

[See also NATUFIAN CULTURE; NEAR EAST, articles on THE BRONZE AGE IN THE NEAR EAST, THE NEOLITHIC AND CHALCOLITHIC (PRE-BRONZE-AGE) PERIODS IN THE NEAR EAST.]

■ K. M. Kenyon, Digging Up Jericho (1957). J. Mellaart, The Neolithic of the Near East (1975). P. Dorrell, "The Uniqueness of Jericho," in ed. R. Moorey and P. Parr, Archaeology in the Levant: Essays for Kathleen Kenyon (1978). K. M. Kenyon, Excavations at Jericho, Vol. III (1981). O. Bar-Yosef and M. E. Kislev, "Early Farming Communities in the Jordan Valley," in ed. D. Harris and G. Hillman, Foraging and Farming: The Evolution of Plant Domestication (1989), pp. 632–642.

Ian Kuijt

JERUSALEM is located in the central part of Israel on the Judean Mountains on an average level of 810 yards (740 m) above sea level. The earliest evidence of settlement is found on the southeastern hill of the city of David. Excavations there uncovered remains dating from the fourth millennium B.C. Tombs of this era were found by the only perennial spring—the Gihon—which suggests the reason for the original location of the city. The first fortifications of the city are dated from the eighteenth century B.C.—a dating that also agrees with the earlier mention of Jerusalem in Egyptian sources. In the fourteenth century B.C. Jerusalem was a prosperous city-state, as reflected in the archaeological finds of local and imported pottery and in the biblical accounts of the later Jebusite rule (esp. 2 Samuel). According to the biblical sources, King David conquered the city around 1000 B.C. and made it his capital. The most conspicuous of the Davidic remains is an 60-foot-high (18-meter-high) stepped structure originally built in the fourteenth century B.C. but considerably reinforced by the Judaean king. It apparently served as a podium for the royal palace or the city's acropolis. In the times of Solomon, David's successor, Jerusalem expanded northward. Although there is no direct archaeological evidence for the Solomonic Temple and all the information about it is drawn exclusively from the Bible (1 Kings and 2 Chronicles), it is highly probable that the Temple Mount (Mount Moriah) was surrounded by a wall by around 960 B.C. In the eighth century B.C., probably under the kings Uzziah and Hezekiah, the city expanded westward to the hill hitherto known as Mount Zion, which was surrounded by a fortification wall. Extensive building works also took place on the hill of the city of David itself. The famous subterranean tunnel commissioned by King Hezekiah in order to prepare the city for the Assyrian siege of 701 B.C. by securing the water supply even under siege is among the most impressive remains of this period. The many burial caves dated from the eighth to the seventh centuries B.C. found in a wide band around the city mark its approximate extent. The Babylonian destruction of 586 B.C., however, put a temporary halt to urban life in Jerusalem.

Although the archaeological evidence is scant for the history of Jerusalem in the Persian Period (538–332 B.C.), it seems that settlement was restricted to the city of David. During the subsequent Hellenistic Period, the city gradually expanded westward again to Mount Zion. Some of the earlier remains there, such as the eighth-century B.C. city wall, were still visible and were incorporated into new fortifications. Archaeological evidence indicates that by the beginning of the first century B.C., during the rule of the Maccabean rulers, the city enjoyed great prosperity. It is highly probable that by that time the Temple and its precinct were rebuilt in a squarish plan that would later be replaced by Herod the Great (37–4 B.C.) with the massive Temple Mount platform still visible today. The excavations around the Temple Mount precinct have revealed broad, beautifully paved streets and entrances to the Temple Mount including spacious staircases on the south and southwest and a gate on the west with its original sill and the southern gate jamb. All the four retaining walls of the Temple Mount were surveyed in the nineteenth century, but recent excavations have revealed a "Master Course" composed of four gigantic stones, the largest of which weighs 590 tons (600 metric tons). On the western hill excavations have revealed a wealthy residential quarter that was founded in the Maccabean period and was extensively rebuilt during the early eighteenth century A.D. The remains comprise a neighborhood built in an insulae pattern of streets. The individual houses were decorated with frescoes and mosaic floors, which in accordance with Jewish law included no human or animal images. Evidence of the conflagration of A.D. 70, when the city was stormed and destroyed by the Romans, is ubiquitous in this quarter and it marks a major turning point in the history of the city. Other important archaeological remains from the pre–A.D. 70 period include sections of the northern "Third Wall" of the city built by King Agrippa (A.D. 41–44); cemeteries of the city, which have been found surrounding the built-up area, especially northeast and east; and the main aqueducts conveying water to the temple from springs south of Bethlehem.

The Roman city known as Aelia Capitolina (A.D. 130–330), built initially by the emperor Hadrian on the ruins of Jerusalem, consisted of streets built on a new criss-cross pattern, excavated especially in the northern half of today's Old City. A number of Latin inscriptions found in secondary use have been connected with the activities belonging to legionnaires of the Tenth Legion, which was stationed in a camp on the western hill. From the coins struck in the city, the worship of the various deities in the city is deduced, although the remains of only two temples have been found—that of Asclepius in the eastern part of the city and a temple to Aphrodite constructed at the site where the Church of the Holy Sepulchre would later be built. A temple to Jupiter on the site of the Jewish Temple is known only from literary sources. Four triumphal arches are attributed to Hadrian. One was outside the city on the main highway to Caesarea. Another was under Damascus Gate (and was incorporated into that gate in the third century when the city's fortifications were installed). The third served as an entry to the western forum of the city and was located south of the Temple of Aphrodite, and the fourth, known today as the "Ecce Homo" arch, was built to serve as the entry to the eastern forum of Jerusalem. In A.D. 289 the Tenth Roman Legion was moved to Aila on the Red Sea, and it was probably then that the city was fortified. The city walls were built on a new alignment, which has remained essentially the same ever since that time. Among the most conspicuous phenomena of Jerusalem's transformation to a Christian city during the Byzantine Period (A.D. 330–638) was extensive church building. Excavations have revealed the remains from the time of Constantine the Great of the Church of the Holy Sepulchre, the Eleona Church, and the Church of the Ascension on the Mount of Olives. Church construction continued throughout the period and reached its culmination in the days of Emperor Justinian, who built the massive "Nea" church in the south of the city in A.D. 549. Considerable information has recently been obtained regarding the city plan of the Byzantine period. Excavations have uncovered the remains of Jerusalem's Cardo, or main north-south street, and sections of its fortification walls. While these were based, in the north, on the earlier Roman walls by the fifth century A.D., in the days of Empress Eudoxia, all the southern section of the city including Mount Zion and the city of David were once again included within the circuit of the city's walls. The Empress Eudoxia also sponsored the construction of additional churches in Jerusalem, including the Church of Siloam, the Church of St. Stephen, St. Peter in Galicantu, and an addition of an aisle to the Church of Zion. Outside the city walls, the church of the Tomb of the Virgin, the Church of Gethsemane, burial chapels north and west of the city have also been identified and excavated. The latest structure built by the Byzantine rulers was the Golden Gate constructed in Jerusalem's eastern wall to commemorate the return of the True Cross from the Persian captivity in the early seventh century A.D.

In the wake of the Arab conquest of the city (A.D. 638), Jerusalem did not undergo many major changes. The "Nea" church was the only significant Christian monument to be destroyed. Archaeological excavations have, however, revealed a unique administrative quarter built south of the Temple Mount. Such quarters are known to have existed in all the important cities of ancient Islam, but it is only in Jerusalem that extensive archaeological remains have been studied. The early caliphs also took care to restore the Temple Mount: They rebuilt its retaining walls and constructed the two mosques—al-Aqsa and the Dome of the Rock. They also rebuilt the bridge and road leading to the Temple Mount from the west. The city underwent very slow modifications, which are difficult to follow because of the extensive works in the following period. Hence the dearth of contemporary remains. In 1033 an earthquake shook the city and practically destroyed it. The subsequent reconstruction of the city walls is well documented in historical sources and is further shown by excavations along the present western city wall, where an eleventh-century wall was recently uncovered. It seems that the Temple Mount suffered great damage in the earthquake, as the Aqsa mosque, the subterranean halls known as "Solomon's Stables," the gates leading into them, the single and triple gates, and the gate in the western Temple Mount wall were all reconstructed at this time.

Crusader Jerusalem (A.D. 1099–1187) enjoyed great prosperity. The Church of the Holy Sepulchre, which was destroyed in 1009 and repaired in a poor manner, was rebuilt by the Crusaders in 1149, and assumed the basic form it still possesses today. Other crusader churches still in use include St. Mark and St. Agnes. Others such as St. Julian, St. Thomas Almanorum, and St. Peter in Chains were discovered in excavations in recent years. Excavations have also uncovered the remains of the royal palace near the citadel. The only section of the city wall that was built during this period (a section constructed by the Templar knights south of the Temple Mount) has been shown by excavations to have protected the southern approach to the Temple Mount.

Following the expulsion of the Crusaders, Saladin and his descendants ruled over Jerusalem for sixty-three years (1187–1250). During this time (known as the Ayyubid Period), they reconstructed the city walls, adding a new tower at the northwest corner, six towers in the southern wall, and walls bordering Mount Zion from the east. From inscriptions found in Jerusalem, the building of even more structures can be deduced. Due to a change in the policy of the defense of the Ayyubid realm, however, the fortifications of the city were demolished in 1219, not to be restored till the days of Ottoman sultan Suleiman the Magnificent in the sixteenth century.

[See also CHRISTIANITY, EARLY; ISLAMIC CIVILIZATION: INTRODUCTION; NEAR EAST; NEAR EASTERN ARCHAEOLOGY.]

■ Louis H. Vincent and Felix M. Abel, *Jerusalem Nouvelle* (1914–1926). J. Simons, *Jerusalem in the Old Testament* (1952). Kathleen M. Kenyon, *Digging Up Jerusalem* (1974). Benjamin Mazar, *The Mountain of the Lord* (1975). Yigael Yadin, ed., *Jerusalem Revealed* (1975). Virgilio C. Corbo, *Il Santo Sepolcro di Gerusalemme* (1982). Nahman Avigad, *Discovering Jerusalem* (1983). Yigal Shiloh, "Excavations at the City of David," *QEDEM* (1984).

Dan Bahat

JOMON TRADITION. The cultures that arose in Early Holocene Japan after 13,000 B.P. are collectively known as the Jomon. Its various regional manifestations saw over ten millennia of development in relative isolation from mainland Asia. The Jomon variants shared a technology based on stone, wood and other plant materials, pottery, and no metal. Populations lived in hamlets or villages or pit houses, that is, houses with floors excavated to depths up to a meter or more below the surface. The Jomon economy was essentially a foraging one based on hunting, fishing, and collecting resources from rich temperate to subtropical ecosystems. Many archaeologists argue that by the Middle Holocene a few plants had come to be gardened, but by no means is there a consensus on this issue.

The Paleolithic occupants of sites such as Fukui in southwestern Japan adopted pottery by about 12,500 B.P. Debate centers on whether pottery was a local innovation or an imported technology, but, so far, no antecedents are known from mainland Asia. The earliest decorations include linear relief and fingernail impressions. At a few cave sites (e.g., Kibakoiwa, Murya) and the open Natsushima site dating to about 10,000 B.P., pottery motifs began to include exterior cord impressions usually made by rolling or impressing single strings into the clay. "Jomon" is the Japanese word for "rope, or cord, pattern," thus the pottery style is viewed as the hallmark of Jomon cultures. Jomon pottery is found throughout Japan by 9500 B.P.

Five Jomon phases are recognized throughout Japan, and two others are less widespread. The pan-Japan Jomon periods are, from oldest to youngest: Initial, Early, Middle, Late, and Final. The Incipient Jomon, with the earliest pottery, is restricted to southwestern Japan while the Epi- or Zoku-Jomon is unique to the northeast and reflects the continued presence of the Jomon there after it ceased to exist elsewhere. Temporal trends include increasing formal complexity of pottery and increasing complexity of social and economic arrangements along with a growing population. Specific combinations of cords and the patterns they form on the pottery in association with specific vessel forms define local Jomon traditions. Sometimes forms of stone tools help delineate these local traditions, but they are far less useful than pottery for the purpose of defining temporal and spatial boundaries within the Jomon.

Population densities during the Incipient and Initial Jomon were low. Vegetation was adjusting to the warmer Early Holocene. Steppe ecosystems as well as some oak woodlands are evidenced by a number of pollen profiles in southwestern Japan. Mixed forests were forming in the northeast; however, woodlands were still dominated by fir, spruce, and pine. Incipient Jomon settlements were small and transitory, but by the Initial Jomon, sites such as Nakano in Hokkaido indicate that small hamlets of a few pit houses were the preferred settlement type. Shell mounds such as Natsushima appear as well, indicating a coastal focus for some populations. The scant evidence for food-getting suggests that riverine and ocean fishing, shellfish harvesting, hunting, and nut collecting were important. Pottery during the Initial Jomon was normally conical based.

Several co-traditions such as the Ento and Daigi are discernible in the archaeological record in the Early and Middle Jomon periods. These were presaged by an Initial Jomon southwest-northeast distinction of cord-marking versus roller-stamping on pottery. The Ento, or Cylindrical Pottery, tradition is named after the characteristic tall, flat-based, cylindrical pottery found at Early and Middle Jomon sites in the northeast. The principal difference between the Early and Middle Jomon Ento pottery is the presence of

appliqué and the construction of elaborately ornamented rims that often included castellations on Middle Jomon Ento pottery. The Hamanasuno site is an Early Ento site in Hokkaido. Houses there are often 33 feet (10 m) in diameter and number over a hundred. The nearby Usujiri site is a Middle Jomon Ento village. The houses are smaller than at Hamanasuno. The relatively undifferentiated nature of the Early Ento sites contrasts the Middle Ento, which exhibits greater socioeconomic complexity. Pottery at Usujiri, in Hokkaido, is spatially separated into two groups suggesting contemporary social differentiation of some sort. Tominosawa in Aomori has at least one large, presumably communal building and a small, stone-encircled cemetery. Katsusaka pottery in central Honshu is more elaborate than its northeastern counterparts. Zoomorphic forms and external painting are common, as are pots so elaborate that their functions must have transcended simple utilitarian purposes.

During the fourth millennium B.P. the climate cooled to more modern levels. Sea levels lowered and, along with tectonic uplift, exposed expanses of coastal lowland. Late and Final Jomon peoples moved into these new territories. Spurred by the availability of new land and further economic developments that appear to have included some gardening, populations increased further. In northeastern Japan the cylindrical pottery styles gave way to a variety of bowls, jars, and pots. Throughout Japan, cord markings came to be arranged in zones separated by blank areas later forming what are known as cloud patterns. By the end of the Late Jomon, particularly in Tohoku and Hokkaido, stone circles such as Ohyu surrounded cemeteries sometimes more than 330 feet (100 m) in diameter. They are often, but not always, isolated in hills overlooking lowlands and the sea. The Late Jomon stone circles appear to be a development of a low-scale Middle Jomon phenomenon. In some locations, particularly on the Ishikari plain in Hokkaido, Late Jomon peoples enclosed circular spaces with earthworks several meters high and over 33 feet (10 m) thick at the base. In Chitose, at least six of these circles are arranged in one location. Some of the burials are layered with red ochre and are accompanied by polished stone staffs considered symbols of rank.

Efforts expended to create sacred spaces for cemeteries were lessened in the Final Jomon. Burials were carefully constructed with individuals often interred in large jars. The familiar cloud pattern motif was refined, but distinct sets of pottery, part of the Ohbora tradition, appear at such sites as Kamegaoka in Aomori. One set is plain and utilitarian. The other consists of elaborately designed ware that includes oil lamps or incense burners in addition to teapot forms. Clay masks with twisted mouths and clay anthropomorphic figurines are part of the northeastern assemblages. Figurines from Initial through Middle Jomon are usually flat, small, and triangular in outline. The Final Jomon figurines are more anthropomorphic and much larger with elaborate adornments. Many have "goggle eyes" suggesting snow goggles.

The Final Jomon ended first in the southwest upon meeting significant numbers of newcomers from mainland Asia during the second half of the third millennium B.P. This marked the initiation of the Yayoi period. There was no impact on the northeast by this development until two or three centuries later. The Final Jomon, with a mixed economy, continued in the northeast while the Early Yayoi frontier pushed northward. Cultures in northern Honshu eventually took on agriculture, but rather than through a process of replacement of local populations by newcomers, the dense populations of northern Honshu adopted many of the Yayoi lifeways, perhaps in order to maintain their existence in the face of the rapid changes taking place in the south.

The changes that transformed the southwest were affecting northeastern Honshu by the end of the third millennium B.P. Northeastern Yayoi pottery appears Jomon-like with its cord markings. Conversely, late Final Jomon pottery had adopted Yayoi traits such as pedestaled bases. Rice paddies appear in the latest Final Jomon phase at Tareyanagi as well. In fact, the identification of a northeastern Yayoi as distinct from the Final Jomon is debated. If it were not for clear evidence of intensive food production and its related technology, for example, the northern cultures would still appear to be Final Jomon. Despite the difficulties of rice production in northern Honshu, millet, barley, wheat, beans, and other dry crops allowed an agricultural economy to flourish. In fact, evidence suggests that rice production failed and dry crops developed nearly complete dominance in northern fields. This signaled the rise of cultures that are ancestral to the Ainu, or Utari, of northeastern Japan.

While the northeastern Honshu Yayoi developed as a tradition distinct from its southwestern counterparts, the Jomon continued on Hokkaido. The Epi-Jomon lasted until about 1500 B.P. Gone were the elaborate material trappings of a complex sociopolitical system characteristic of the Late and Final Jomon. Cave sites such as Fugoppe Dokutsu are filled with rock art depicting a strength of spirituality reminiscent of the preceding Jomon. Occupations are poorly known, however, probably because their settlements were no longer predominantly composed of arrangements of pit houses. Besides Fugoppe Dokutsu, the best-documented sites include Sappopro Station and Mochiyazawa, both of which appear to be short-term encampments associated with cemeteries.

Eventually the Zoku-Jomon met its demise in the face of events to the south. Conflicts between the developing Japanese state headquartered in the Kyoto region (Yamato) and the ancestors of the Ainu (Emishi) forced the Emishi into Zoku-Jomon territory. With this move the Jomon ended.

[*See also* ASIA: PREHISTORY AND EARLY HISTORY OF EAST ASIA; JAPAN AND KOREA, *articles on* INTRODUCTION, EARLY STATES OF JAPAN AND KOREA.]

■ J. Edward Kidder, *Prehistoric Japanese Arts: Jomon Pottery* (1968). Fumiko Ikawa-Smith, "Current Issues in Japanese Archaeology," *American Scientist* 68 (1980): 134–145. Melvin C. Aikens and Takayasu Higuchi, *The Prehistory of Japan* (1982). Takeru Akazawa, "Hunter-Gatherer Adaptations and the Transition to Food Production in Japan," *Journal of World Archaeology* (1986): 151–165. Richard J. Pearson, ed., *Windows on the Japanese Past: Studies in Archaeology and Prehistory* (1986). Gary W. Crawford and M. Yoshizaki, "Ainu Ancestors and Early Asian Agriculture," *Journal of Archaeological Science* 14 (1987): 201–213. Gary W. Crawford and H. Takamiya, "The Origins and Implications of Late Prehistoric Plant Husbandry in Northern Japan." *Antiquity* 64 (1990): 889–911.

Gary Crawford

K

KALAMBO FALLS. This spectacular 722 foot (220 m) single-drop waterfall lies on the frontier between Zambia and Tanzania, near the southeastern corner of Lake Tanganyika. It has been formed by the Kalambo River flowing over the eastern scarp of the Western Rift Valley into a deep rocky gorge. A small lake basin behind the lip of the falls was for long a focus of prehistoric occupation: It now contains extensive archaeological deposits ranging in date from the Late Acheulean into recent times. Discovered in 1953 by J. Desmond Clark, the site has since been intensively investigated by him and his collaborators.

Archaeologically, Kalambo Falls is of great importance for several reasons. It is one of comparatively few places anywhere in the world where traces of Acheulean occupation have survived *in situ*, without having suffered postdepositional disturbance. Furthermore, it displays a long sequence of stratified deposits that preserve prehistoric artifacts together with evidence for past environmental conditions. Last, it provides detailed insight into the prehistory of a region and a period that have so far received comparatively little archaeological attention. Two volumes of the site report were published in 1969 and 1974. The third, which will be devoted to the Acheulean and its immediate successor industries, is eagerly awaited.

The lowest horizons investigated lie close to the modern water level: They contain Acheulean artifacts in apparently undisturbed contexts, probably representing dry-season encampments on the riverbanks. Bone is not preserved, but wood and other plant remains have survived, including pollen, which indicates that the site's Acheulean inhabitants initially enjoyed a climate somewhat warmer and drier than that of today, but becoming progressively cooler and damper. It is uncertain whether any of the wooden objects show signs of human craftsmanship, or whether any of the burned pieces attest controlled use of fire. An arc of stones has been interpreted as the base of a windbreak, and two grass-filled hollows as sleeping places. Radiocarbon dates of ca. 55,000–50,000 B.P. for the Acheulean occupation at Kalambo Falls are now interpreted as representing only a minimum age, its true antiquity probably being in the order of 200,000 years.

Later deposits at Kalambo Falls contain a large series of Sangoan artifacts, provisionally dated ca. 100,000–80,000 B.P., which have not yet been recovered from an undisturbed context. The same is true of the subsequent Lupemban industry, which demonstrates links between the Kalambo Falls area and the equatorial forest zones farther west.

After the Lupemban occupation the prehistory of the Kalambo basin for several tens of thousands of years remains unknown. There is evidence that microlithic technology was practiced at least 10,000 years ago. By about the third century A.D. the area was inhabited by metal-using farming peoples. Several successive village sites of this period have been recognized at Kalambo Falls, some of which were marked by deep cylindrical pits of unknown use. Their pottery shows strong typological connections with the broadly contemporary Urewe ware in the East African interlacustrine region.

[*See also* ACHEULEAN TRADITION; AFRICA: PREHISTORY OF AFRICA; HOMO ERECTUS; HUMAN EVOLUTION: THE ARCHAEOLOGY OF HUMAN ORIGINS.]

■ J. Desmond Clark, *Kalambo Falls Prehistoric Site,* Vols. 1 and 2 (1969 and 1974). J. Desmond Clark, "The Middle Stone Age of East Africa and the Beginnings of Regional Identities," *Journal of World Prehistory* 2 (1988): 235–305.

David W. Phillipson

KAPOVA. The cave of Kapova in Bashkortostan, in the southern Ural Mountains of Russia, is, together with the nearby cave of Ignatiev, the easternmost example of Paleolithic cave art known in Europe. Also known as Shulgan-Tash, Kapova has an imposing entrance facing southeast on the right bank of the Belaya River. It lies 492 feet (150 m) from the river and 25 feet (7.5 m) above it.

The cave was first described in 1760, but its paintings were discovered only in 1959 by A. V. Ryumin, a zoologist, and were subsequently studied by O. Bader in the 1960s and 1970s. About forty figures are known at present, though many more may remain hidden beneath calcite that covers the very damp walls. All are done in red ocher, though some also have black pigment, and they comprise both fairly naturalistic and stylized animal figures as well as many apparently abstract signs—grids, triangles, and especially large trapezoids or truncated cones with internal stripes and a kind of loop at each upper corner. This last is a motif that is unknown in the caves of western Europe.

Kapova contains about one mile (2 km) of galleries, divided into a lower and an upper network. These probably constituted separate caves, since it is highly unlikely that Paleolithic people could have made the sheer 46-foot (14 m) climb into the upper galleries, which therefore must have had a different entrance that has not yet been found. The lower system is about 985 feet (300 m) long, and contains a series of large chambers and galleries. Its walls feature primarily signs, but there are also two fine horses, a possible mammoth, and a bending anthropomorph.

About 328 feet (100 m) into the lower gallery are the modern ladders leading to the upper system, where two major painted panels are located on opposite sides of one large chamber. The first has an impressive array of four mammoths, two horses, and a rhinoceros, as well as a large trapezoid. The other has a line of three mammoths and a bison. All the animals in the cave face left except for one mammoth.

For decades, the art of Kapova Cave was attributed to the upper *Paleolithic only on the basis of comparison with the cave art of western Europe, although its style is somewhat distinctive. In the 1980s, however, excavation by V. Shchelinsky of an area of about 59 square yards (50 sq. m) in the lower gallery, 525 feet (160 m) from the entrance, exposed a cultural layer. It yielded a few blade tools and two bone implements, as well as evidence of several large fires, the remains of a mammoth tusk, and bones of cave bear, hare, fox, and microfauna. Charcoal produced two radiocarbon dates of 14,680 and 13,930 B.P. There were also a few remarkable finds, such as stone beads of green and brown serpentine, a beautifully carved cup of the same green serpentine, and the base of a fired-clay cup. This last may have served as a lamp or, more likely, as a bowl for mixing pigments, traces of which survive in it. The cultural layer also produced lumps of ocher, but the best evidence for an association between this upper Paleolithic occupation and the art on the cave walls was a fragment of fallen limestone wall on which can be seen the lower part of a red painted figure (probably a mammoth).

[See also EUROPE: THE EUROPEAN PALEOLITHIC PERIOD; ROCK ART: PALEOLITHIC ART.]

■ O. N. Bader, La Caverne Kapovaïa. Peinture Paléolithique (1965).
Paul G. Bahn

KARNAK AND LUXOR. The Temples of Karnak and Luxor were the key sanctuaries of the ancient city of Thebes (Egyptian Waset), in Upper Egypt, Karnak becoming one of the largest religious complexes of all time. The principal deity worshiped was the local god Amun, who became a supreme national deity as Amun-Re, King of the Gods. However, a number of subsidiary temples and chapels were dedicated to such other divinities as Amun's wife and son, Mut and Khonsu, the war god, Montju, and various other significant deities.

The earliest certain elements of the Karnak temple date to the early Middle Kingdom, in particular, the reign of Senwosret I, with additions constructed into the Second Intermediate Period. Major expansion began in the Eighteenth Dynasty, particularly under Thutmose I, Hatshepsut, and Thutmose III, who added pylon gateways, obelisks, chapels, sanctuaries, and halls around the ancient core. Steady development continued until the death of Amunhotpe III, when there was a hiatus caused by the abolition of the polytheistic religion by his son, Akhenaten. The latter built a temple to his sole god, the Aten, or solardisc, to the east of Amun's sanctuary. This was demolished following the restoration of the old cults under Tutankhamun. The building blocks from its walls were used as the filling of the new pylons erected by Horemheb and the first kings of the Nineteenth Dynasty. The Nineteenth Dynasty kings also constructed a great hypostyle hall in front of the temple, comprising no fewer than 134 columns, fronted by the Second Pylon.

Amunhotpe III, as well as building elements of the main Karnak Complex, was also responsible for the temples of Montju and Mut, which lie to the north and south, together with the Temple of Luxor, lying some distance farther south, and connected to the Karnak Complex by an avenue. Closely connected with the cult of the royal divinity, Luxor played a key part in the annual Festival of Opet, when the image of Amun traveled from Karnak to the southern sanctuary. Unfinished on Amunhotpe III's death, work was continued by Tutankhamun and Horemheb, with a forecourt, pylon, and obelisks added by Rameses II.

In the Twentieth Dynasty, some additions were made to the main Karnak temple, and the Temple of Khonsu was built in the southwest part of its enclosure. Subsequent work was far less extensive, essentially restricted to some construction in the earlier Twenty-second Dynasty, a large colonnade erected in front of the existing front, together with other works, in the Twenty-fifth, and a final pylon in the Thirtieth or later. Some restoration was carried out under the Ptolemies, who also added a number of gateways, but the temples gradually fell into disuse, suffering damage in the Upper Egyptian revolts of Roman times. A number of obelisks were subsequently removed to Rome.

By the nineteenth century, the Karnak and Luxor temples were filled to a considerable depth with debris and houses. These were later removed by the Egyptian Antiquities Service, and work on excavation, restoration, and copying has continued to the present day, particularly by the Epigraphic Survey of the University of Chicago and the Centre Franco-Egyptien and its predecessors. Huge quantities of statues have been recovered, any from the Karnak cachette in which they had been placed in the Late Period. The Luxor temple is presently badly threatened by the rising water table, making its preservation and careful recording a matter of priority; during 1995, the columns in its second courtyard were dismantled to allow the investigation and consolidation of their foundations.

[See also EGYPT, articles on OVERVIEW, MIDDLE KINGDOM EGYPT, NEW KINGDOM EGYPT.]

■ B. Porter and R. B. Moss, Topographical Bibliography of Ancient Egyptian Hieroglyphic Texts, Reliefs, and Paintings, 2nd ed. (1972). P. Barguet, "Karnak," Lexikon der Ägyptologie, Vol. III (1980), pp. 341–352. P. Barguet, "Luxor," Lexikon der Ägyptologie, Vol. III (1980), pp. 1103–1107.
Aidan Dodson

KHAMI. Khami ruins, 14 miles (22 km) west of Bulawayo, is the second-largest archaeologic site in Zimbabwe. It consists of stone-walled house platform and hut sites in the surrounding hills and open areas. The central settlement was along the Khami River and includes the Hill complex believed to have been the King's residence.

Considerable digging was carried out by treasure hunters and amateur archaeologists between 1897 and 1910. During the same period the Rhodesia Scientific Association produced several plans and papers on Khami. In 1905 British archaeologist Dr. Randall MacIver briefly surveyed the ruins. In 1947 the Historical Monuments Commission of Rhodesia sponsored research which resulted in Keith Robinson's book Khami Ruins (1959). The research concluded that Khami was built and occupied by Bantu farmers from about the fifteenth century A.D. The stone and daga (clay) architecture, pottery, and settlement layout show similarities with *Great Zimbabwe. Hunting was a major activity at Khami. With the exception of glass beads, very few imports were recovered and these were from later layers.

Khami is associated with the historical state of Torwa during the period from the fifteenth to seventeenth century A.D. Later Khami sites like Dlo Dlo and Ntaba zaka Mambo are linked to the Rozvi Mambos (Kings) who lasted up to the nineteenth century.

Religion, as evidenced by religious objects found during excavations, played a central role in the Khami political organization.

Current work at Khami is divided between conservation of the site and research into Khami's outlying settlements. Most Khami sites are concentrated within a 3-mile (5-km) radius of the Hill complex. The commoner sites lack stone walling and solid daga houses found in the elite areas. Khami was not densely occupied and might not have had a population of more than 5,000 people.

[*See also* SOUTHERN AFRICA, LATER IRON AGE SOCIETIES OF.]

■ K. R. Robinson, *Khami Ruins* (1959).

Ivan Murhamu Murambiwa

KHMER CIVILIZATION AND THE EMPIRE OF ANGKOR.

When Simon de la Loubère visited the court of King Narai at Ayutthaya in 1687, he encountered a royal tradition steeped in the beliefs and structures of the Khmer civilization. Only two centuries had elapsed since the Thais had invested and destroyed Angkor. Prior to that, the Thais had served as mercaneries in the Khmer army. De la Loubère noted that two languages were employed at Ayutthaya. When speculating on the origins of the Siamese, he noted, in his own words, that

. . . the Siameses understanding of two languages, viz the vulgar, which is a simple tongue consisting almost wholly of monosyllables, without conjugation or declension, and another language, which . . . is a dead tongue known only by the learned, which is called the Balie tongue, and which is enrich't with the inflections of words, like the language we have in Europe. (de la Loubère, 1693:14)

This distinction represents an appreciation of the similarities between Pali and European languages a century before Sir William Jones's famous recognition of Indo-European. It also helps us to understand the origins and development of the Khmer civilization.

The Khmer language belongs to the eastern branch of Mon-Khmer, which in turn comprises part of the Austroasiatic language family. Until recently, the relationships between Austroasiatic and other language families in Southeast Asia and southern China were not known, but we now have good evidence that we can link it with Austronesian languages within the Austric phylum. Austric might be compared, in terms of the area of distribution and variety, with Indo-European. It lies at the origins of the early development and then the spread of rice cultivation from the Yangzi Valley.

A southward expansion of rice cultivators brought small village communities down the Mekong into Cambodia by the third millennium B.C. We can trace their development over the millennia: by 1500–1000 B.C., they were adept at bronze casting. From 500 B.C., iron was added to the repertoire, and during the later first millennium B.C., population numbers grew, chiefdoms developed, and steps were taken to cope with problems posed by the environment. The Khmer civilization developed in an area exposed to the vagaries of the monsoon. In its heartland on the northern shore of the Tonle Sap, the Great Lake of Central Cambodia, the rainy season lasts from May until November, to be followed by the long and difficult dry season. Even during the former, rainfall is unpredictable and there can be weeks of dry weather highly injurious to rice cultivation. As the population in chiefly centers grew, so steps had to be taken to conserve and reticulate water. This was achieved by digging circular moats around settlements and allowing water to flow into the rice fields beyond. It is likely that such

a system was used only to maintain the rice in the absence of wet season rains, and the moats would have also supplied the populace with water, defense, and aquatic food. Roughly circular-moated sites are abundant in the Siem Reap Plain, seat of Angkor from the ninth century.

How and why did the civilization of this area incorporate Pali and Sanskrit into its court rituals? These are the sacerdotal languages of Buddhism and Hinduism, and the answer to this question lies in the increased mercantile contacts established between Rome, India, and China during the last few centuries B.C. Southeast Asia benefited from this international exchange system, and the local chiefs, particularly those in favored coastal areas, were quick to perceive that esoteric knowledge and a novel religion, quite apart from the control of the flow of goods, could serve to augment their status and prestige. Indian notions of kingship, which included the erection of commemorative stelae, architectural and art styles, the legal code, the use of a script, and the Hindu religion were selectively and skillfully woven into the emerging statelike polities of Cambodia. The stelae, which date from the fifth century A.D., employed Sanskrit. But they also included secondary texts in archaic Khmer. We find that rulers adopted Sanskrit names, such as Jayavarman, "protege of victory," Īśānavarman, and Mahendravarman, meaning respectively the protégé of Śiva and of the Great Indra.

An appreciation of the Khmer civilization must take into account the beliefs which came with the Hindu religion. In particular, it recognized that supreme ascetic devotion to Śiva could imbue the overlord with divine qualities. Worship involved the construction of temples in stone, and these, initially unicameral structures, were surrounded by sacred, walled precincts. From the early days in the fifth to the eighth centuries A.D., the Khmer paid particular attention to geometric order, and their temples were laid out within rectangular enceintes. The interior of these temples would normally contain, within the darkened chamber, a stone *linga*, or phallus, named after the ruler and symbol of his potency. It was also the ruler's duty to construct moats and *barays*, or reservoirs, as part of his court center. These fulfilled several objectives. Mt. Meru, home of the Hindu gods, was ringed by the oceans. The *barays* projected a powerful symbolic statement in that the court center represented the sacred mount. It is also likely that the trend established in late prehistory accelerated, for the ruler could hardly maintain followers without providing them with food and water. Many titles of rank during this period related to those charged with maintaining the water supply.

A glimpse of such a center is seen in a Chinese account, quite possibly of Īśānapura, seat of the overlord Īśānavarman who ruled in the early seventh century. It describes a great hall in the middle of a settlement housing over twenty thousand families. The overlord gave an audience every third day. He wore a cap of gold encrusted with precious stones, and reclined on a couch made of aromatic wood. He was accompanied by five great officials and many other functionaries, and his palace was protected by armed guards.

The last point stresses the endemic conflict between competing polities, the flavor of which is clearly found in the inscriptions. These describe military expeditions and the conquest of rivals. But the inscriptions from this period also refer to rice fields, herdsmen, water tanks, orchards, and temples, scenes and actors to be found in rural Southeast Asia to this day. It must be appreciated that donations of goods and services to the temple, and by inference to the overlord, were rewarded with merit. It was and remains a powerful bonding mechanism between the ruling elite and the sustaining populace.

There was a distinct watershed, dated to the year 802, whereby a series of competing polities were joined into one enduring and powerful central state. This transition involved a process of centralization instituted by the overlord Jayavarman II (ruled 802 to 834). Jayavarman seems to have identified a means of unifying formerly competing overlords which was rooted first in military conquest, then by placing his followers in positions of authority. This had the effect of establishing a central rule through replacing independent polities by provinces. He also must have appreciated the importance of stressing the mystical properties of kingship by instituting the cult of the *kamraten jagat ta rāja*, meaning "the god who is king." Deification of the ruler, linked with vesting the rights to consecrate a new god-king in successive members of a given family, meant that the succession should be assured.

Remarkably, the ensuing five centuries witnessed a considerable degree of legitimacy in the succession, being largely confined to members of the aristocratic lineage of Aninditapura. Vickery's perceptive analysis of relevant inscriptions has shown that succession revolved around the degree of seniority between the new overlord and the ancestors, with particular reference to the mythical founder, Kambu. This, Vickery suggests, denotes the possible operation of a conical clan. Certainly, there was no imperative for a son to follow a father. Jayavarman was succeeded by his son, it is true, but he was followed in turn by a cousin, Indravarman I. This concern with the ancestors is a characteristic which might very well have been rooted deep in the prehistoric past, where kin-structured cemeteries were ubiquitous.

Jayavarman chose the gently sloping land between the Kulen Hills and the Tonle Sap as the location for his early court and cult centers. This area is crossed by a series of streams which flow south from the hills, and which provide an assured source of water. The lake remains one of the richest sources of fish in Southeast Asia, and transport by boat was possible across the lake, down the Tonle Sap River to the Mekong, and ultimately to the sea. He moved his court at least five times within this region, finally choosing a location on the edge of the lacustrine floodplain known as Hariharālaya. Indravarman I (877 to 889) established here a building tradition, which continued to the final sack of Angkor, and which in some respects continues today in the royal court of the Chakri dynasty in Thailand. Indravarman first had constructed a mighty reservoir called the Indratataka after himself. It covers a far larger area than any early example, measuring 2.1 by .4 miles (3.3 by 0.7 km). He also set in train the construction of the Bakong, his temple mausoleum. This again dwarfed its predecessors, its outer limits measuring 2,625 by 2,133 feet (800 by 650 m). The new scale, made possible not only by personal ambition, but a larger source of labor, is best illustrated by noting that the reservoir was 150 times the area of any earlier *baray,* and the temple volume exceeded by a hundredfold that of any previous construction.

Yaśovarman succeeded his father in 889, and moved his center about 9 miles (15 km) to the northwest. A small hill known as the Bakheng (Mount Mighty Ancestor) attracted his interest. On top, he constructed his temple mausoleum, and ringed it with a walled precinct enclosing 3,955 acres

(1600 ha). It is with the Bakheng that we can acquire an initial feel for the symbolism associated with such monuments, which reached its apogee with Angkor Wat and the Bayon. The Bakheng is so constructed that, from a central position on any of the four sides, one can see only thirty-three of the towers, which is the number of gods in Indra's heaven. The seven levels represent the seven heavens. There are 108 towers which, when divided by four, result in a figure of twenty-seven, each representing phases of the lunar cycle. Each terrace bears twelve towers representing the twelve-year cycle of the planet Jupiter. Wheatley sees the monument as a representation of Mount Meru, and an astronomical calendar in stone. Yaśovarman was also responsible for the Eastern Baray, a reservoir fed from the diverted Siem Reap River, which had a capacity, within its area of 4.4 by 1.1 miles (7.1 by 1.7 km), of 2,119 cubic feet (60,000,000 cu m) of water. Although the name of this new complex was Yaśódharapura, it is now better known as Angkor, the Sanskrit word for "Holy City."

Space forbids consideration of each overlord, but Angkor was particularly influenced by two, Sūryavarman II, who ruled from 1113 to 1150, and Jayavarman VII, who ruled from 1181 to 1219. Hinduism involved a pantheon of gods, and the former was particularly devoted to Viṣṇu. His temple pyramid, known today as Angkor Wat, is arguably the largest religious monument built, the surrounding moat alone being 655 feet (200 m) wide. But again, it is in the symbolism that we can penetrate the mind of its builders. Measuring the principal dimensions has allowed the reconstruction of the lowest common denominator, the Khmer *hut* 1.43 feet [0.435 m]). The length and breadth of the central structure adds up to 365.37 *hat*, while the axial distances of the great causeway correspond with the four great eras in the Hindu conception of time. It was possible through the structure's layout to predict lunar eclipses, and a person standing in front of the western entrance on the spring equinox was able to see the sun rising directly over the central lotus tower. The name Sūryavarman means "Sun King."

The Bayon is a fantastical structure built by Jayavarman VII, a ruler who suffered from a building frenzy, and saw himself as the apotheosis of the Buddha. Each of the fifty towers on the Bayon, his temple mausoleum, bears an image of the Buddha looking out over his domain. This home of gods bears fish, carved in stone around the exterior, representing the netherworld below the oceans. The Angkor seen today by visitors is very much that bequeathed by Jayavarman. It was he who saw to the construction of many other buildings across his empire, including roads with guest houses every 9.3 miles (15 km) which linked Angkor with vice regal centers such as Phimai. He built bridges, hospitals, and mausolea for his parents and son. The latter is commemorated at the remote site of Banteay Chmar, the former at Ta Prohm and Preah Khan.

The roads linked provinces and villages with Angkor, and it is important to recall that life in the countryside probably differed little from that found before the Khmer Rouge. Overlords called on the villages for the surpluses required to maintain the court, the army, and the offices of state. Some idea of the scale of this appropriation can be gained by reference to the foundation stela of the Ta Phrom temple mausoleum: 3,140 villages were called on to supply the daily needs of the officiants. The precise statistics set in stone also record the provision of 11,192 tons of rice from 81,640 people living in 838 villages to the 102 hospitals maintained under Jayavarman. This represents half the requirements of the villagers themselves. The Khmer Empire had no currency; therefore, the goods needed to sustain the elite had to be brought physically to the center, and recompense came in the provision of merit for services dedicated to the deified ruler. Rice was not the only item required: we also read of honey, sugar, wax, spices, salt, livestock, feathers, rhino horn, and aromatic woods, not to mention cloth and gold. Some idea of the splendor of Angkor as late as 1297 can be obtained through the eyes of Zhou Daguan, a Chinese visitor who described a court procession under Indravarman III. Following numerous court women and functionaries, the king was seen standing on an elephant whose tusks were encased in gold.

The symbiosis between the sustaining villages and the center depended, in the final analysis, on the perceptions of the sustaining peasantry. Despite the control of the means of destruction by the overlord through his army and war elephants, a steady flow of goods from the countryside was essential. It is possible that the excessive demands of Jayavarman VII, and the spread of Hināyāna Buddhism, which stresses the importance of the individual, undermined this relationship. Certainly, building activity declined after the death of Jayavarman, and the central grip on provinces which formerly deferred to Angkor, slackened. But Angkor was not alone: the Chams to the east represented a potent force, as did the vibrant Thai state centered at Ayutthaya. When the latter invested and sacked Angkor, they removed a competitor, but maintained the traditions of kingship expressed in the rituals and esoteric language which de la Loubère was to encounter at the court of King Narai.

[See also ASIA: PREHISTORY AND EARLY HISTORY OF SOUTHEAST ASIA.]

■ S. de la Loubère, *A New Historical Relation of the Kingdom of Siam* (1693). R. B. Smith and W. Watson, eds., *Early South East Asia* (1979). M. Vickery, "Some Remarks on Early State Formation in Cambodia," in *Southeast Asia in the 9th to 14th Centuries*, eds. J. G. Marr and A. C. Milner (1986), pp. 95–115.

Charles Higham

KHOK PHANOM DI. The mound of Khok Phanom Di, which covers approximately 12 acres (5 ha) and rises 40 feet (12 m) above the surrounding plain, is located in the lower floodplain of the Bang Pakong River in central Thailand. Discovered in 1976 when building operations revealed prehistoric pottery and marine shellfish, it has been excavated on three occasions, the largest involving the examination of 1075 square feet (100 sq m) in 1985.

These excavations revealed a complex stratigraphic sequence, dated between 2000 and 1500 B.C. The survival of organic material, including wood, rice, leaves, nuts, partially-digested food, and feces has permitted a clear reconstruction of the site's environment. It was initially located on or near the estuary of a major river, but sedimentation and probably the relocation of the river channel meant that, with time, the inhabitants were cut off from easy access to the estuary.

After an initial and probably brief period, when the area excavated was used for occupation and the making and firing of pottery vessels, the inhabitants established a cemetery. Such was the pace of accumulation of the ash lenses and shell middens that the dead were progressively interred over their ancestors. Graves were found in discrete clusters on a checkerboard pattern, each cluster comprising

the remains of men, women, children, and infants. The dead were interred in a ritual which changed little with time: the grave was oriented with the head to the rising sun, and the body was interred on a wooden bier, with a range of grave goods and usually covered with a shroud of asbestos fiber or beaten bark cloth.

Grave offerings included pottery vessels which bore incised designs of great beauty, shell jewelry, stone adzeheads, turtle carapace ornaments, clay anvils for making pots, and the stones used to burnish them. The detailed analysis of these associations indicates that for the first ten or so generations, no clusters were regularly richer than any other. However, with a major change in the habitat which involved relocation of the river, some individuals acquired much wealth, and it is suggested personal prestige, during their lifetimes. At the same juncture, women and children only were found buried with clay anvils, and one route to acquiring status may well have been in the making of superb pots for exchange.

Subsistence involved fishing, collecting marine resources such as crabs and shellfish, and the cultivation of rice. Hoes and shell-harvesting knives have been found, together with rice remains. The wide-ranging exchange network and achievement of personal prestige through individual skill reveal the cultural complexity which was present in Southeast Asia prior to the first evidence for smelting copper or tin ores.

[See also ASIA: PREHISTORY AND EARLY HISTORY OF SOUTHEAST ASIA; ASIA, ORIGINS OF FOOD PRODUCTION IN, ORIGINS OF FOOD PRODUCTION IN SOUTHEAST ASIA.]

Charles Higham

KIDDER, Alfred. Alfred Vincent Kidder (1885–1963) received his Ph.D. in Anthropology from Harvard University in 1914. His field career began in the Southwest in 1907 with the School of American Research and continued for several years with the Peabody Museum at Harvard. He then turned to Pecos Pueblo (1915–1929) with the support of the Phillips Academy. The Pecos excavations were the largest of their time in North America. Kidder's synthetic skills created the first great regional synthesis in North American archaeology, *An Introduction to the Study of Southwestern Archaeology* (1924).

Kidder then turned his attentions to the Maya region. In 1929, he became the chairman of the Carnegie Institution of Washington's new Division of Historical Research, and administered excavations at *Chichén Itzá, Uaxactun, and Kaminaljuyu (among many other projects). He called for a "pan-scientific" approach to Maya studies, one of the first explicit multidisciplinary programs in American archaeology. He retired in 1950.

Kidder's leadership in professional organizations, in scholarly conferences, and in institution building left a lasting imprint on American archaeology. His scholarly contributions exemplified American archaeology in the second quarter of the twentieth century.

[See also HISTORY OF ARCHAEOLOGY FROM 1900 TO 1950: ARCHAEOLOGY OF THE AMERICAS.]

■ Walter W. Taylor, "A Study of Archaeology," *American Anthropologist* 50:3 (1948). Richard B. Woodbury, *Alfred V. Kidder* (1973). Gordon Randolph Willey, "Alfred Vincent Kidder," in *Portraits in American Archaeology*, ed. G. R. Willey (1988), pp. 293–314. Douglas R. Givens, *Alfred Vincent Kidder and the Development of Americanist Archaeology* (1992).

Stephen H. Lekson

KILWA was one of the principal ports serving the Indian Ocean trade in which African commodities, particularly ivory and minerals from southern Africa, were exchanged for manufactured items from the Near East, India, and China. The ruins, among the best preserved on the coast, are located on the island of Kilwa Kisiwani on the southern coast of Tanzania. The site received initial interest from archaeologists and historians because of the survival of two sixteenth-century histories of Kilwa and the discovery of numerous coins, minted by the rulers of Kilwa, which were widely used along the coast from A.D. 1000 to 1520. Kilwa (and the nearby town of Songo Mnara) has been designated a UNESCO World Heritage Site.

Modern archaeological work began at Kilwa in 1955, when Dr. James Kirkman placed a trench across a seawall. Large scale excavations were undertaken from 1961 to 1966, under the direction of Neville Chittick from the British Institute in Eastern Africa, and published as a monograph in 1974. The architecture of the site was studied by Peter Garlake, while G.S.P. Freeman-Grenville correlated the numismatic evidence with the historical sources, often at considerable variance to Chittick's own archaeological conclusions. Since the middle of the 1970s the Kilwa sequence has been reexamined in the light of new discoveries in the Lamu archipelago and Zanzibar with small scale excavations undertaken from 1990 through 1992 by E. S. Matteru of the Tanzanian Antiquities Unit.

While a small Late Stone Age site has been found on the island, the main occupation dates from ca. A.D. 800—with scattered pits and postholes, but no evidence for stone buildings, an architectural technique introduced around A.D. 1000. A "Shirazi" phase associated with the arrival of Islam, the construction of the Great Mosque, and the production of copper coins was dated by Chittick to around 1150 through 1200, but this phase is now placed in the eleventh century. Kilwa's period of greatest prosperity was ca. 1300 to 1350, under the Mahdali rulers of which the most notable was al-Hasan ibn Sulaiman Abu'l-Mawahib, who ruled ca. 1310 to 1333. His court was described by Ibn Battutu, who stayed at Kilwa in 1331. To this dynasty (and probably to this ruler) can be attributed major building works, including the annex to the Great Mosque, a structure with domes and barrel vaults supported on twenty columns, and the construction of innovatory palace and market complexes, Husuni Kubwa and Husuni Ndogo, 1640 yards (1500 m) east of the main town. A coin of Hasan ibn Sulaiman has been found at Great Zimbabwe, which has led some to speculate that the two sites were linked by the gold trade. The only known gold coins were also issued from Kilwa at this time.

In the late fourteenth century, the prosperity of Kilwa declined and the mosque partly fell down. There was still gold in the town for Vasco da Gama to obtain sufficient tribute in 1502, which the King of Portugal later gave to construct a *custódia* at the monastery at Belém. The Portuguese sacked Kilwa in 1505, and built a fort, fragments of which survive, but the fortunes of the town declined, with a brief revival in the 1770s through slave trading during which the Sultan was able to build himself a new palace at Makutani. The establishment of Kilwa Kivinji, ca. 1820, on the mainland led to the diversion of trade, now largely in Indian hands, and the last Sultan was deported to Muscat ca. 1843, although a village still remains on the site to this day.

[*See also* EAST AFRICA: COASTAL TOWNS OF EAST AFRICA.]

■ P. S. Garlake, *The Early Islamic Architecture of the East African Coast* (1966). G.S.P. Freeman-Grenville, "Coin Finds and Their Significance for Eastern African Chronology," *Numismatic Chronicle* 9 (1971): 283–301. H. N. Chittick, *Kilwa: An Islamic Trading City on the East African Coast* (1974). Helen Brown, "Three Kilwa Gold Coins," *Azania* (1991): 1–4.

Mark Horton

KLASIES RIVER CAVE, the main site on the south coast of South Africa (30°06'S, 24°24'E), is a complex of tunnel-like openings and overhangs, forming a large single depository. The well-stratified sediments have a total thickness of some 66 feet (20 m). These comprise multiple occupation horizons with hearths, shell and bone food waste, and stone artifacts that are separated by interbedded sands. The use of dating techniques such as uranium disequilibrium dating, electron spin resonance dating, and amino acid dating as well as biostratigraphy show that the bulk of the deposits accumulated between 130,000 and 60,000 years ago. Middle Stone Age people were episodic occupants during this time range. *Radiocarbon dating establishes that the deposits were partly eroded by the rise of sea level 6,000 years ago and that the site was reoccupied by Later Stone Age people thereafter.

The site was excavated by Ronald Singer and John Wymer in 1967–1968 and by H. J. Deacon from 1984 to the present. Noteworthy among the finds of food waste are large quantities of shellfish and seal and penguin bones, showing the systematic use of marine resources as early as the Last Interglacial (118–130,000 years ago). This is among the oldest evidence available for shellfish gathering. The Middle Stone Age artifacts are made mostly in local raw materials. The exception is in the Howieson's Poort layers, dated in the range of 80,000 years ago, when there occurred selection of nonlocal materials for making tools like standardized blunt-backed segments and trapezes. These are the type of tools that occur almost universally much later in time as inserts into the hafts of composite tools. Tools made of such costly materials would have more than functional value, and this suggests that the occupants may have been involved in behaviors normally associated with modern people, for example, cementing alliances by trading gifts.

Fragmentary human remains were found at the site. Most of these came from two layers dated to 90,000 and 120,000 B.P. The human bones show cut marks and burning and occur with other food waste. They are not from conscious burials. Although the evidence is consistent with the practice of cannibalism, dietary cannibalism is not necessarily implied. In South Africa, medicine murders, which are ritualized cannibalism, still occur and may have a long history. The human bones are mostly cranial pieces of very dimorphic robust male and gracile female individuals. A number of features in the dentition and the face show that the people were different from the *Neanderthals, their contemporaries in Europe, and were anatomically like modern people. The existence of Middle Stone Age people with complex behavior and robust but modern anatomy 120,000 years ago at the southern tip of Africa is support for a high antiquity of modern people in Africa versus Europe. These people may represent early ancestors of the Bushman or Saan, an African population that is genetically distinct and has been long isolated in this most remote part of the Old World.

Ongoing research is studying the taphonomy of the human remains and investigating the similarities and differences between the behavior of the Middle Stone Age occupants at the Klasies River main site and their Later Stone Age successors.

[See also AFRICA: PREHISTORY OF AFRICA; HUMANS, MODERN: ORIGINS OF MODERN HUMANS.]

■ R. Singer and J. Wymer, *The Middle Stone Age at Klaises River Mouth in South Africa* (1982). H. J. Deacon, "Southern Africa and Modern Human Origins," *Philosophical Transactions of the Royal Society London* B 337 (1992): 177–183.

H. T. Deacon

KNOSSOS was famed in antiquity as the home of the mythical king Minos, and the location of the Labyrinth, which imprisoned the monstrous, bull-headed Minotaur. By the nineteenth century the site was known to scholarship, and leading archaeologists, including *Schliemann, the excavator of *Troy and Mycenae, were keen to dig there. It was the English archaeologist Arthur *Evans who was successful; he started investigations in 1900, completing the work of excavation and conservation in 1929. Equally important was his monumental multivolume analysis of Minoan civilization, *The Palace of Minos at Knossos*.

Knossos is in north central Crete, 3 miles (5 km) from the coast. The site is located on a low hill, Kephala, within a small, high-walled valley. The valley is fertile and well-watered, and controls one of the main routes southward from the coast. This strategic location clearly accounts for the continuity of settlement at Knossos, going back to the Aceramic Neolithic Period around 6000 B.C. By 1900 B.C. (Middle Minoan Ib), the conventional date for the founding of the palace, the settlement extended up the west and north slopes of the valley. This indicates that the palace developed out of the preexisting settlement: indeed, recently trial excavations suggest that as early as ca. 2400 B.C. an urban "mega-structure" was beginning to evolve, though its internal arrangement and function are unknown.

The palace had certainly achieved its canonical form by ca. 1900 B.C.: a single structure centered around a Central Court and flanked on the west by another court. The internal arrangement of this First Palace phase is obscured by later destructions and rebuilding, but finds reveal that its economic functions were fully developed. Near the West Wing store-rooms (magazines) are clay sealings stamped with pictorial designs and groups of hieroglyphic symbols, suggestive of a centralized administrative system. Fine polychrome decorated vases reveal that the palace was supporting specialist crafts, and precious artifacts made from faience and gold indicate foreign trade contacts with Egypt and the Near East.

In around 1700 B.C., Crete was devastated by a massive earthquake. The destruction of Knossos was so extensive that the rebuilders levelled off the palace platform, removing many earlier layers. Consequently much of the Second Palace is built directly on Neolithic remains. During this Second Palace Period (c. 1700–1450), Knossos and Crete reached the zenith of cultural sophistication and power.

The complexity of the internal arrangement of the palace is clearly the origin of the labyrinth myth, but far from confusing, there is a coherent, functional order, revealed by the finds and supported at significant points by Knossos's most striking decorative feature, the fresco wall-paintings. The prime functions were economic and religious, providing respectively the wealth and ideology by which Knossos

maintained its status at the top of the Minoan political hierarchy.

The 18 West Wing storage magazines contained large jars for foodstuffs (oil, wine, olives, cereals) and stone-lined pits for precious artifacts (stone, gold, ivory). The production and redistribution of this wealth was administered here, as is revealed again by clay sealings and tablets inscribed with the Linear A and, later, Linear B, writing systems. Prestige crafts such as pottery, weaving, and metal-working were located in the north part of the East Wing.

Cult equipment of all sorts (figurines, idols, libation vessels, double-axes, and other symbols) identifies many shrines within the palace. It is the frescoes, however, that give the most coherent "picture" of cult activity. Though fragmentary, the frescoes seem to present a thematic unity associated with the worship of the Minoan Goddess. A fertility goddess, normally linked with nature, her worship seems to have been channeled through the palace as the ideological component of elite dominance. An example is the Knossos throne-room where the throne, flanked by griffin wall paintings, dynamically recreates an emblem of divine power.

Around 1450 B.C. (Late Minoan Ib) the major Minoan sites suffered a series of fire destructions, probably from warfare. The Knossos palace, though not the town, escaped this disaster, but with a changed character. The evidence of pottery, nearby "Warrior" tombs, and more conclusively the decipherment of Linear B as Mycenaean Greek, suggest the presence of Mycenaeans as a dominant element among the Knossian elite. The final destruction of Knossos, conventionally dated to 1375 B.C., has been interpreted as a Minoan rebellion against Mycenaean Knossian overlordship. Postpalatial Crete enjoyed several centuries of cultural "Indian Summer" before the final collapse of the Bronze Age, but Knossos was never reoccupied.

[See also AEGEAN CULTURES, *articles on* MINOAN CULTURE, HELLADIC (MYCENAEAN) CULTURE, MYCENAE; MEDITERRANEAN WORLD, *articles on* THE MEDITERRANEAN PRE-BRONZE AGE, THE RISE OF AEGEAN AND MEDITERRANEAN STATES.]

Alan A. D. Peatfield

KOFUN (Mounded Tombs of Japan and Korea). The tradition of mounded-tomb building in Japan and Korea derived mainly from that of China, where large mounds began to be added to Shang-type shaft graves during the first millennium B.C. By the Han Period (206 B.C.–A.D. 220), mounded-tomb architecture was typical of elite burial in China and this tradition was implanted on the Korean Peninsula during the expansion of the Han Empire. The appearance of indigenous types of monumental tombs from the third century onward signified the rapid stratification of Korean and Japanese society after the fall of the Han.

Among the early states of Korea, Koguryo in the north and Paekche in the west-center shared a mature form of stone pyramid tomb construction, which had developed from earlier cairn burials in the Koguryo region. Outstanding examples include the "General's Tomb," one of thousands in the Ji'an region of northeastern China (the Koguryo capital until 427), and the Sokch'on-dong tomb cluster in the Han River basin near Seoul (Paekche's capital until 475). The transfer of pyramid burial architecture from Koguryo to Paekche might have been the material result of a splitting of the Koguryo ruling line, as suggested by Paekche claims to Koguryo descent. As animosity developed between these two states in the fifth and sixth centuries, however, each adopted different Chinese-style earth-mounded stone-chamber tomb architecture, from the northern mainland in the case of Koguryo (the Anak tomb clusters near P'yongyang), and from the southern mainland for Paekche (the tomb clusters in Kyongju and Puyo, especially the Murong Tomb).

The southeastern part of the Korean peninsula began its monumental tomb tradition with multiple stone-lined-pit burials covered by a single earthen mound. This type of tomb was distributed through Kaya (at Koryong) and what later became Shilla territory (in Kyongju) in the fourth century A.D. With the emergence of the Shilla state in the fifth century, a unique tomb architecture was adopted, combining a Han-style wooden-chamber burial with a cairn covering echoing Koguryo and finished with an earthen mound. Such tombs make up Tumuli Park in modern Kyongju, where the Tomb of the Heavenly Horse is open as a site museum. The Shilla elite thus sought to create a separate identify from Kaya, which it later conquered.

The monumental tomb tradition of the Japanese archipelago followed on from the Yayoi Period (300 B.C.–A.D. 300) tradition of regionally diverse, chiefly mound burials. Tombs of the Early Kofun Period (300–710) had a stone-lined-pit chamber sunk into the summit, but from the late fifth century, the continental-style stone-chamber tomb with corridor entrance was introduced from Korea. A distinctive aspect of the Early Kofun Period mounded tombs is their homogeneity in structure and contents throughout western Japan; the different tomb shapes (round, square, and keyhole) are not regionally distributed but are thought to relate to social status. The tomb tradition affected the stratification of society and drew the newly coalesced elite of the previous Yayoi chiefdoms into a widespread Kofun Period interaction sphere. This situation is in sharp contrast to the Korean peninsula, where differences between the regional elites were maintained through contrasts in material culture.

One such Korean regional tradition was the painted tomb complex of Koguryo. The fifth- to sixth-century chamber tombs often had sophisticated internal architecture employing antechambers and pillars, and several of the walls and ceilings bear painted pictures and motifs. Some paintings were brushed onto bare stone walls, while others used a plaster base. An evolution in motif and composition accords with mainland Chinese influences: the earliest paintings appear to be formal portraits of the deceased, but later these yield to genre paintings illustrating aspects of Koguryo elite lifestyle. Contrasting cosmological systems are represented in later tombs: Buddhist motifs such as lotus flowers are used for spatial fillers, whereas the Chinese Directional Deities might appear on the relevant walls: the White Tiger of the West, Green Dragon of the East, Red Bird of the South, and Black Warrior (snake and turtle intertwined) of the North. Despite their obvious attraction and importance, such painted tombs make up less than one percent of all known Koguryo tombs.

The sizes of the elite tombs of the Japan and Korea pen/insulae give them monumentality, and indicate great command of labor and materials for their construction. The stone pyramids of Koguryo and Paekche commonly reach 150 to 165 feet (45–50 m) on a side and might stand 13 to 16 feet (4–5 m) high; the largest square tomb in the Japanese Islands (Masuyama Tomb in Nara) measures 280 feet (85 m) on a side. The largest Kaya multiple-cist tombs measure 82 feet (25 m) in diameter and 20 feet (6 m) in height; in addition, they were positioned on high mountain ridges, in order to isolate the elite spatially and conceptually as a class separate from commoners. Shilla tombs were also roughly 82 feet (25 m) in diameter but reached 40 to 43 feet (12–13 m) in height. In the Japanese Islands, large round mounds measured 148 to 164 feet (45–50 m) in diameter and 26 to 33 feet (8–10 m) in height, whereas the largest keyhole-shaped tomb compound, the Nintoku Mausoleum on the Osaka Plain consisting of two moats and three greenbelts, covers thirty-two hectares; the keyhole tomb itself is 1,595 feet (486 m) long. In central Yamato (Nara), keyhole tomb sizes fall into two groups, averaging 330 feet (100 m) and 740 feet (225 m) in length; members of the groups cluster differently across the landscape in what can be interpreted as two or three primary (large-sized tombs) and five to six secondary (medium-sized tombs) centers, which might correspond to a territorial administrative hierarchy of chiefly and sub-chiefly centers.

The objects buried in all these tombs were products of a prestige goods system of production in which valuable materials and skilled personnel were co-opted for elite purposes. Among the more notable products are the gold crowns of Shilla; the jasper beads and bracelets and the earthenware funerary sculptures called *haniwa* of Yamato; Paekche-style gilt-bronze horse trappings; and the ubiquitous gray stoneware called Kyongjil in Korea and Suē in Japan. Bronze mirrors were imported from China before local production of large-sized mirrors was instituted in Yamato; glass objects from the *Silk Route running through Afghanistan to the West made their way into Shilla and Yamato tombs. Finally, various forms of iron armor and weaponry—swords, arrowheads, helmets, lamellar body armor, cuirasses, tassets, and horse armor— in Yamato had their counterparts in the Kaya graves.

Because of their monumentality and wealth of contents, mounded tombs have served as the major informant on the rise of the small states in Japan and Korea pen/insular region. As tombs of the political elite, they embody the social hierarchy and the spatial distribution of ranked persons across the landscape. But care must be taken not to equate the elite subculture that they represent directly with administrative practices, since cultural similarities often mask political hostilities. Shifts in cultural preferences also contributed to the decline in tomb building after the seventh century A.D. With the adoption of Buddhism, cremation was increasingly an option for elite burial, whereas resources for elite aggrandizement were poured into temple building.

[See also ASIA: PREHISTORY AND EARLY HISTORY OF EAST ASIA; CHINA: HAN EMPIRE.]

Gina L. Barnes

KOOBI FORA. The area of Koobi Fora lies to the east of Lake Turkana (formerly Lake Rudolph) in northern Kenya. It was discovered by Richard Leakey in 1968 while he was involved in research at Omo at the northern tip of the lake. Investigations in this area have identified a large number of localities which yield hominid fossils and artifacts, generally not in association. The badland landscape provides a total section depth of 1,166 feet (350 m) and comprises deposits derived from channel, delta, and floodplain contexts which are interleaved between a series of volcanic tuffs.

There are two cultural traditions identified at Koobi Fora, the KBS and Karari industries. The former is the earliest and comes from the KBS tuff of the Lower Member of the Koobi Fora Formation. Dating this tuff has been controversial. It may be as old as 2.1 to 2.3 million years ago and so predate the sequence at Olduvai Gorge, but it is generally thought to be contemporary with the basal part of the Olduvai sequence at 1.8 million years ago. The cultural material from the KBS industry resembles the Oldowan of Bed I, Olduvai, but differs in lacking spheroids, subspheroids, and small scrapers. The tools are also generally smaller. The type locality for the KBS industry is FxJj 1 KBS.

The Karari industry derives from the Okate Tuff beds at the base of the Upper Member of the Koobi Fora Formation. The Karari industry resembles the Developed Oldowan of Bed II, Olduvai. It has choppers, polyhedrons, and discoids, hand axes and cleavers are rare but present. Most significant, however, is a unique series of core scrapers and massive flake scrapers. The type locality is FxJj 18. The Karari is dated to 1.5 million years ago, which makes it contemporary with middle Bed II, Olduvai.

In addition to the stone tools, more than 150 individuals are represented in the hominid fossil collection. Four species are represented, *Australopithecus boisei, Australopithecus africanus, Homo habilis,* and *Homo erectus.* The size of the hominid collection makes Koobi Fora especially important for the study of fossil variability.

The Koobi Fora sites are important as both confirming, and adding to, the evidence from Olduvai Gorge. Specialized sites for butchery are represented, home bases have been defined, and the model of hominids with structured settlement patterns and division of labor have been derived from the evidence of Koobi Fora.

Also important at Koobi Fora was the integration of the archaeology with broader studies of taphonomy and ethnoarchaeology. These latter disciplines both stimulated the basic model and then provided testing for questions about site formation. The Koobi Fora sites are a mixture of accumulations deriving from both human and natural causes and the home-base model is suspect. As at Olduvai, a limited range of environments are represented by the individual localities. They are mostly associated with either lake shores, flood plains, or water courses. Such environments provide access to water, stone raw materials, and diverse vegetation cover. These environments are also frequented by a variety of game although the threat of carnivores must have been a limiting factor. Work continues at the site through training schools and investigations have moved to the west of Lake Turkana itself.

[See also: AFRICA: PREHISTORY OF AFRICA; HUMAN EVOLUTION, *articles on* FOSSIL EVIDENCE FOR HUMAN EVOLUTION, THE ARCHAEOLOGY OF HUMAN ORIGINS; OLDUVAI GORGE.]

■ M. G. and R. E. Leakey, *The Fossil Hominids and an Introduction to their Context, 1968–1974* (1978). R. H. Tuttle, "What's New in African Paleoanthropology?" *Annual Review of Anthropology* 17 (1988): 391–426.

Tim Reynolds

KOREA. See JAPAN AND KOREA.

KOSSINNA, Gustaf (1858–1931) has often been portrayed as the evil mind behind the Nazi exploitation of prehistoric archaeology in Germany. This, however, is an oversimplification in retrospect that misses the key point and varies sharply from his assessment by contemporaries. Despite the strong nationalistic, indeed racist, prejudices in his thinking, Kossinna occupies a key position in the emergence of prehistory as an academic discipline.

Kossinna was born in 1858 in Tilsit, East Prussia, the son of a school teacher. He started his university studies, (which led him to Göttingen, Leipzig, Berlin, and Strassburg) in 1876, attending lectures in the field of classical philology, though later shifting his interests to Germanic philology, German antiquity, local history, and art history.

On leaving the University, Kossinna's continued attempts to find a job at various archaeological museums brought no success until, in 1902, an extraordinary chair was established for him at Berlin university. Here he began systematically to build up a university institute devoted to the study and teaching of prehistoric archaeology.

By this time, Kossinna had already sketched out the principles of his so-called siedlungsarchäologische Methode in a paper presented at a meeting of the Anthropological Society in 1895. The aim of this method was the delimitation of the settlement areas of past peoples by analyzing the spatial distribution of significant artifact types. He continued to develop these ideas in the following decades, and tried to apply them on a large scale to European prehistory. An extended presentation of his methodological principles appeared in 1911 under the title *The Origin of the Germani: On the Settlement Archaeological Method.* In this book Kossinna made his famous statement: "Sharply defined archaeological culture areas correspond unquestionably with the areas of particular peoples or tribes." This guiding principle is linked with a second, the retrospective method, which involves using the ethnic conditions of the present (or the historically documented past) to infer the situation in prehistory. Working backward from early historical times, Kossinna tried to shed light on the prehistoric development of historically known peoples by tracing continuities within particular settlement areas.

Kossinna's scientific reputation suffered severely in later years due to his inadmissible equation of people and race and the way this notion slipped into the ideology of the Germanic master race. In his concept of an Aryan, Nordic ideal race, superior to all other people—his Germani (and their supposed predecessors, the Indo-Europeans)—he saw the key to an unwritten history, as it lay hidden in his prehistoric culture provinces. In the light of these ideas it comes as no surprise that Kossinna finally attempted to derive political demands from the results of his ethnohistoric research. Kossinna died in 1931 and therefore had no chance to comment on the use or misuse of his theories by the Nazis. There can be little doubt however, that he would have looked on with considerable satisfaction even if the new propagandists did not do adequate justice to his work.

It is no surprise that these political aspects have in recent years given rise to a new interest in Kossinna and Nazi Archaeology within Anglo-American archaeology with its strong emphasis on the social production of archaeological knowledge. On the other hand an interest in Kossinna's methodological concepts is generally regarded as old-fashioned. His methodology nonetheless formed an essential step in the process of transformation from an evolutionary into a culture-historical paradigm, which through the work of *Childe and others dominated archaeology until long after World War II.

[See also HISTORY OF ARCHAEOLOGY BEFORE 1900: EUROPEAN ARCHAEOLOGY; HISTORY OF ARCHAEOLOGY FROM 1900 TO 1950: EUROPEAN ARCHAEOLOGY; IDEOLOGY AND ARCHAEOLOGY; NATIONALISM; POLITICAL USES OF ARCHAEOLOGY.]

■ Günter Smolla, "Das Kossinna-Sydrom." *Fundberichte aus Hessen* 19/20 (1979–1980): 1–9. Hildegard Schwerin von Krosigk, *Gustaf Kossinna, Der Nachlaß-Versuch einer Analyse*, Offa-Ergänzungsreihe, Bd. 6 (1982). Günter Smolla, "Gustaf Kossinna nach 50 Jahren." *Acta Praehistorica et Archaeologica* 16/17 (1984–1985): 9–14. Ulrich Veit, "Gustaf Kossinna and His Concept of a National Archaeology," in H. Härke ed., *Archaeology, Ideology and Society: The German Experience* (forthcoming).

Ulrich Veit

KOSTER SITE. The Koster site is a deeply stratified site located adjacent to the eastern bluffline of the lower Illinois River valley in Greene County, Illinois. The small, southeast-facing valley in which the site is located has been partially filled with colluvial and alluvial deposits within which twenty-five different cultural horizons have been recognized. The cultural deposits at Koster span the majority of the Holocene, beginning at approximately 9000 B.P. and extending into the Historic Period. The Archaic Period sequence, however, is the most significant and is subdivided as follows: Early Archaic I (ca. 9000 B.P., Horizon 13), Early Archaic II (8700–8450 B.P., Horizons 12 and 11), Middle Archaic I (8300–7600 B.P., Horizons 10B–8E), Middle Archaic II (7300–6850 B.P. Horizons 8D–8B), Middle Archaic III (5800–4900 B.P., Horizons 7B–6A) and Late Archaic (3950–2950 B.P., Horizon 4).

A wide variety of projectile points, other chipped stone tools, debitage, ground stone implements, bone artifacts, faunal remains, and floral remains have been recovered from the Koster site. Flotation, pollen, and other soil samples supplement the assemblage. Human burials were recovered from several of the horizons, most notably from Horizon 11 and from two distinct burial areas in Horizon 6A. Five dog burials were recovered from Horizon 11. However, the most significant features are the structure platforms found in Horizon 8C, the principal component of Middle Archaic II.

Whereas the Early Archaic and Middle Archaic I horizons are interpreted as representing multiple residential encampments of short-term duration, the later components are believed to represent multiseasonal base camps, from which extractive activities were staged. This change is associated with increased selection of key food resources such as freshwater mussels, fish, hickory nuts, and deer beginning with Middle Archaic II. Thus, the Koster record suggests that the first steps toward a more sedentary lifestyle were taking place during the Middle Archaic.

Credit for the realization of Koster's significance belongs to Stuart Struever, an archaeologist from Northwestern University, who in 1969, conducted test excavations at Koster because the site appeared to be an unusually large Late Woodland village. He found that the Late Woodland and Mississippian materials at Koster were far less significant than the presence of stratified Archaic deposits.

Recognizing the uniqueness of a stratified open-air Archaic Period site, Struever expanded the Koster site excavations. With the assistance of James A. Brown, and a number of other midwestern archaeologists, major excavations were undertaken at the Koster site between 1969 and 1978. Interdisciplinary analyses were conducted during the 1970s and the early 1980s. Nevertheless, there is still considerable potential for research utilizing data collected from the Koster site particularly with respect to the Early Archaic materials which have yet to be fully studied.

During the 1970s, Koster was a major attraction for the public education programs (*see* Education in Archaeology: Popular Education) of the Foundation for Illinois Archaeology (now the Center for American Archaeology) based in Kampsville, Illinois. Thousands of individuals discovered midwestern archaeology by watching the excavations at the Koster site. However, the popular significance of the Koster site should not overshadow its contributions to research on the Archaic. The Koster sequence provides important insight into Archaic Period subsistence and settlement change. It suggests that the Middle Archaic, rather than the Late Archaic, is the crucial time frame for understanding the first steps toward sedentism and associated subsistence change in the Midwest. It is most probable that there was considerable temporal and spatial variability in the process of increasing sedentism, but Koster provides one important perspective. In any event, the Koster record has been instrumental in stimulating a reassessment of early simplistic models of Archaic subsistence and settlement.

[*See also* HUNTER-GATHERERS, NORTH AMERICAN ARCHAIC; NORTH AMERICA: THE EASTERN WOODLANDS AND THE SOUTH.]

■ Gail L. Houart, *Koster: A Stratified Archaic Site in the Illinois Valley* (1971). Nancy B. Asch, Richard I. Ford, and David L. Asch, *Paleoethnobotany of the Koster Site* (1972). Thomas Genn Cook, *Koster: An Artifact Analysis of Two Archaic Phases in Westcentral Illinois* (1976). Stuart Struever and Felicia Antonelli Holton, *Koster: Americans in Search of Their Prehistoric Past* (1979). James A. Brown and Robert K. Vierra, "What Happened in the Middle Archaic?" in *Archaic Hunters and Gatherers in the American Midwest*, eds. James L. Phillips and James A. Brown (1983), pp. 165–195. Michael D. Wiant, Edwin R. Hajic, and Thomas R. Styles, "Napoleon Hollow and Koster Site Stratigraphy," in *Archaic Hunters and Gatherers in the American Midwest*, eds. James L. Phillips and James A. Brown (1983), pp. 147–164. Sarah W. Neusius, "Generalized and Specialized Resource Utilization During the Archaic Period: Implications of the Koster Site Faunal Record," in *Foraging, Collecting and Harvesting: Archaic Period Subsistence and Settlement in the Eastern Woodlands*, ed. Sarah W. Neusius (1986), pp. 117–137.

Sarah W. Neusius

KOT DIJI is an imposing site on the eastern side of the Indus River in Sind Province of Pakistan. It is about 250 miles (400 km) from the Arabian Sea and just across the Indus River from the great urban site of *Mohenjo-daro, one of the principal centers of the Harappan civilization. The main mound of Kot Diji is 40 feet (12 m) high and is an unmistakable feature of the old Indus Plain. Spread below it is a lower habitation area, with a surface rich in pottery and stone tools.

Kot Diji was first recorded as an archaeological site by G. S. Ghurye (1936) in the course of his assessment of the antiquarian remains of Sind. The Pakistan Department of Archaeology under the direction of Dr. F. A. Khan assessed the potentials of Kot Diji in 1955 during the first season of excavation there. Work was resumed in 1957.

Both excavated areas, one on the mound itself and the other in the lower habitation area, have a stratigraphic succession from an Early Harappan (3200–2500 B.C.) to a Mature Harappan occupation (2500–2000 B.C.). The Early Harappan is the distinctive Kot Dijian type, defined through these excavations.

The Mature Harappan occupation provides evidence for copper/bronze objects including a fine example of a Harappan flat axe, bangles, arrowheads, and two chisels. Numerous terra-cotta antiquities including bangles, cart frames and wheels, styli, beads of several types, large and small balls, cones, and triangular cakes were recovered.

Figurines recovered include bulls, humped and unhumped, birds, painted and plain, and human figures, which seem to conform to other examples from Mohenjo-daro and Chanhu-daro. The absence of lapis lazuli, turquoise, and other luxury raw materials is noteworthy although an etched carnelian bead and faience disk beads were recovered. There is no report on either plant or animal remains.

Kot Diji is an extraordinary site for three reasons. It occupies a strategic position on the Indus Plains, on the more lightly settled eastern side of the valley. It superbly documents the Kot Dijian Phase in upper Sind, and was important in the definition of the Early Harappan. Further work at the site should offer an opportunity to gain important information on the subsistence regime.

[See also ASIA: PREHISTORY AND EARLY HISTORY OF SOUTH ASIA; HARAPPA; INDUS CIVILIZATION.]

■ Govind Sadashiv Ghurye, "An Account of an Exploratory Tour in Certain Parts of Sind in Search of Pre-Historic Culture," *Journal of the University of Bombay, Arts and Law* 8:6 (1936): 1–18. Fazal Ahmed Khan, "Excavations at Kot Diji," *Pakistan Archaeology* 2 (1965): 11–85. M. Rafique Mughal, *The Early Harappan Period in the Greater Indus Valley and Baluchistan*. Ph.D. Dissertation, University of Pennsylvania (1970).

Gregory L. Possehl

KUK. Kuk Swamp, at an altitude of approx. 1 mile (1.6 km) in the Wahgi Valley of the Papua New Guinea Highlands is the subject of archaeological investigation begun in 1922 under the direction of Jack Golson. The site has been interpreted as yielding a sequence of six periods of drainage channels and chronologically varying patterns of associated garden ditches defining planting areas. Back to 6000 B.P., the beginning of Phase 2, this interpretation is secure.

Its extension back to 9000 B.P. and the claim for the beginnings of dryland cultivation at the same date depend mainly on geomorphological evidence, but some support is lent by palynological (*see* Paleobotany) results elsewhere indicating early forest clearances. All this has been used in support of a thesis of independent origins for agriculture in New Guinea proposed on other grounds.

The sequence in the swamp is seen as reflecting, on the one hand, the adjustment of the subsistence system to an ecological transformation from forest to regrowth and grassland under sustained agricultural clearance, and on the other, increasingly more intensive use of swampland for cultivation to provide for the upkeep of pigs as wealth items in a developing system of competitive exchange. The decisive change comes around 2000 B.P.: earlier gardening systems (Phases 1 to 3) are thought to represent mixed plantings of wetland (e.g., *Colocasia* taro) and dryland (e.g., yam, banana, sugarcane) crops, later ones monocropping, of taro in Phases 4 and 5 and, in Phase 6, beginning about 250 B.P., of sweet potato, a post-Magellanic introduction from the Americas, which today is the Highlands staple.

[See also AUSTRALIA AND NEW GUINEA; NEW GUINEA, ORIGINS OF FOOD PRODUCTION IN.]

■ Jack Golson, "No Room at the Top: Agricultural Intensification in the New Guinea Highlands," in *Sunda and Sahul: Prehistoric Studies in Southeast Asia, Melanesia and Australia*, ed. J. Allen, J. Golson, and R. Jones (1977), pp. 601–638. J. Golson and D. S. Gardner, "Agriculture and Sociopolitical Organizations in New Guinea Highlands Prehistory," *Annual Review of Anthropology* 19 (1990): 395–417.

Jack Golson

KUSH. *See* NUBIA.

L

LA TÈNE is an important site in the later prehistory of Europe, which has given its name to the second period of the Iron Age in central and western Europe (450–50 B.C.).

The site is located at the northeastern end of Lake Neuchâtel in western Switzerland, near the point where the River Thielle flows out of the lake. It was first discovered in 1857, when unusually low water levels revealed a series of wooden piles. Iron objects were dredged up from the bottom of the lake, and the collection of antiquities grew rapidly, consisting mainly of weapons. In 1876 the lake level was lowered and the rivers canalized, draining the site of the archaeological finds, which were located along a former course of the Thielle. Excavations carried out from 1880 to 1885 by Emile Vouga produced more finds and human skeletons, as well as evidence for timber structures interpreted as buildings along the banks of the river and two bridges or causeways across it about 361 feet (110 m) apart. A much more systematic campaign of excavations was carried out from 1907 to 1917 by William Wavre and Paul Vouga.

There has been no archaeological investigation of the site since 1917, and no systematic reconsideration of the evidence. The precise physical setting of the site, and in particular the water level in the Iron Age, is unknown. This makes it very difficult to judge the function of the wooden structures, both the buildings, and the linear features interpreted as bridges or causeways. The site appears to have been defended or delimited on its northern side by a wooden palisade.

Although the objects found at La Tène constitute one of the most important collections of material from later prehistoric Europe, only a few categories of the finds, which are now dispersed among many museums, have been reassessed. The greater part of them date from the third and second centuries B.C., but there are also significant quantities from the first century B.C., as well as some later finds. The vast majority are of iron, though there are also bronze, wooden, and bone items, wickerwork, textile fragments, leather, and pottery, as well as human and animal bones.

A complete inventory is impossible, but the most impressive items are the weapons. These include at least 166 swords, many with their scabbards, 269 spearheads, and 29 shields. There are also personal ornaments, for example, 382 brooches and 158 belt clasps, in addition to many other objects, including bronze cauldrons, cart wheels, wooden buckets, and craft tools for working metal, wood, and leather. Many of the objects were of high quality and in a new condition, some of them wrapped in textiles.

The assemblage is a highly unusual one, unlike those known from settlement or cemetery sites. It is marked by a high proportion of metalwork, especially weapons, a low proportion of domestic material such as pottery, and an almost total lack of specifically female items. Even the animal bones are unusual, being dominated by the skulls and hooves of cattle and horses.

Interpretations of the function of the site have been many and varied. The earliest ideas followed the nineteenth-century enthusiasm for *lake dwellings, but subsequent theories have varied between military functions, such as arms depot or fortified stronghold, and commercial ones, such as a trading or manufacturing center, or a customs post. These explanations have paid little attention to the problem of the disposition of the finds along the river, though it has been suggested that the site was overwhelmed by a sudden rise in water level. Modern ideas would favor its interpretation as a place of deliberate votive deposit, a practice well documented elsewhere in the European Iron Age.

[See also ARMS AND ARMOR; CELTIC ART; EUROPE: THE EUROPEAN IRON AGE.]

■ Paul Vouga, La Tène (1923). J. M. de Navarro, The Finds from the Site of La Tène, Vol. I, Scabbards and the Swords Found in Them (1972). Cynthia Dunning, "La Tène," in eds V. Kruta, O.-H. Frey, B. Raftery, and M. Szabo, The Celts (1991), pp. 366–368. Michel Egloff, "Celtic Craftwork at La Tène," in eds V. Kruta, O.-H. Frey, B. Raftery, and M. Szabo, The Celts (1991), pp. 369–371.

Timothy Champion

LA VENTA. Archaeological knowledge of the *Olmec civilization, until quite recently, came almost exclusively from the site of La Venta, located on an old channel of the Río Tonalá in the state of Tabasco along Mexico's hot and humid southern Gulf coast. The site, located atop a geological "salt dome," or low plateau known to overlie extensive petroleum reserves, rises like an island above seasonally inundated floodplains and coastal estuaries. At its climax during the Middle Formative Period (900–400 B.C.), La Venta may have been one of the largest towns anywhere in Mesoamerica. It was the center of a regional settlement system of perhaps as many as twenty thousand persons, with exchange contacts for procuring exotic resources extending to distant locations all over lowland and highland Mesoamerica. The town and its hinterland may have been controlled by a paramount ruler and his royal kinfolk who resided at the ceremonial, political, and economic center of the region. La Venta is best known for its 108-foot (3 m)-tall fluted-cone pyramid, rising high above the surrounding plain, and the impressive mortuary features and exotic dedicatory deposits buried deep below its surface.

The site, known to early-twentieth-century travelers and explorers of southern Mexico for its colossal stone heads, carved stelae, and massive basalt altars, was first opened to serious archaeological research by Matthew Sterling of the Smithsonian Institution in the early 1940s. Sterling's excavations in a small section of the site north of the principal pyramid uncovered a treasure trove of riches unparalleled in the history of Mesoamerican archaeology, including colored clay floors, polished jade celts, a carved stone sarcophagus in the form of a snarling jaguar, and a "log" tomb of columnar basalt filled with exotic burial offerings. Below this were serpentine mosaics resting on an enormous deposit of serpentine blocks totaling several hundred tons in weight.

Most of the site remains essentially unknown, but renewed research at La Venta by Mexican archaeologists in the 1990s has preserved it from further petroleum development and destruction and promises to enhance our understanding of the Middle Formative Period Olmec. Research in La Venta's nearby hinterland has documented village settlement in this area dating back to the beginning of the second millennium B.C. These early Olmec or pre-Olmec peoples settled along now-extinct river levees and subsisted on fish, shellfish, estuarine wildlife, wild plant collection, and a tiny form of early maize. From these humble beginnings Olmec society continued to grow around the town of La Venta, persisting for almost a thousand years to become one of the most important centers of economic power and complex sociopolitical development anywhere in Formative Mesoamerica.

[See also MESOAMERICA: FORMATIVE PERIOD IN MESO-AMERICA.]

■ Phillip Drucker, Robert F. Heizer, and Robert J. Squier, *Excavations at La Venta*, Bureau of American Ethnology Bulletin 170 (1955). Rebecca González Lauck, "Proyecto Arquelógico La Venta," *Arqueológia* 4 (1988): 121–165. William F. Rust and Robert J. Sharer, "Olmec Settlement Data from La Venta, Tabasco," *Science* 242 (1988): 102–104.

Thomas W. Killion

LAKE DWELLINGS, European. During the winter of 1853–1854, an exciting discovery was made in the waters of Lake Zurich, near Obermeilen: several thousand wooden piles associated with abundant remains of pottery, worked bone and antler, and polished stonework were found. Ferdinand Keller, president of the Antiquarian Society of Zurich, immediately realized the importance of the discovery, and during the years that followed, a growing number of similar discoveries came to light in Biel, Neuchâtel, and Morat Lakes. As early as 1854, Keller published an account of his researches, drawing also on the ethnographic work of Dumont d'Urville in New Guinea. He imagined the Swiss sites as ancient villages built on platforms raised above the waters of the lakes. This remained the accepted interpretation of these sites for over a century.

The late nineteenth century was marked by the continuing hunt for lake villages. Similar sites soon came to light in eastern France, Italy, and southern Germany, not to mention the Glastonbury lake villages and Iron Age crannogs of the British Isles. A key issue that dominated much early research in the Alpine region was the question as to whether these villages had stood on piles above the lake waters, were raised up on platforms at the lake edges, or rested on the lake shore itself. In the 1950s, specialists emphasized that the principal characteristic of sites of this kind was the excellent preservation of the organic material (piles, seeds, etc.), which set them apart from terrestrial sites where upright house timbers were reduced to postholes.

Modern Research on the Lake Settlements. New resources became available for the excavation and study of Alpine lake villages in the 1970s. In Switzerland, a program of road building led to a series of well-funded excavations making use where necessary of expensive specialized equipment such as watertight coffer dams and underwater gear. At the same time, there was a development of dating techniques, notably the use of *dendrochronology. The average Alpine lake village has between 2,500 and 5,000 piles, a rich assemblage of dendrochronological analysis. The development of a reliable dendrochronological time scale made it possible to follow the year-by-year development of the timber structures of a settlement up to 6,000 years old.

The massive quantity of finds produced by these excavations in itself poses special problems of analysis. The Late Neolithic settlement of Saint-Blaise / Bain des Dames, for example, yielded no less than 360 tons of stone, 400,000 animal bones, 22,000 pieces of worked greenstone, 18,000 flints, 8,500 flakes of wood, and more than 3 tons of pottery.

Alongside the major state-funded excavations in Switzerland, as at Auvernier and Hauterive-Champréveyres, there have been many other important excavations in advance of building works (Zurich-Mozartstrasse) or following underwater erosions (Cortaillod-Est). In a few cases (Clairvaux in the French Jura, for example, or Fiavé-Carera in Italian Trentino or Hornstaad-Hörnle in Baden-Württemberg, Germany), long-running research excavations have been mounted, with fieldwork continuing year after year. In these circumstances it is possible to redefine excavation strategies at regular intervals and to redirect attentions to obtain new kinds of information. The final result is the same, however: a colossal mass of information that has to be sorted, studied, and published.

The earliest of the known Alpine lake villages date to the Middle Neolithic Period, although lake-edge settlements of Upper Paleolithic date (such as the Magdalenian site of Neuchâtel-Monruz) have also been discovered. They are a particular feature of the Neolithic and Bronze Age (fourth to early first millennium B.C.), but well-preserved lake settlements of later date are also known in other regions of Europe, such as *Biskupin in Poland and Flag Fien which date to the Iron Age (mid–late first millennium B.C.).

The Late Bronze Age Village of Cortaillod-Est. One of the best examples of a recently excavated Alpine lake settlement is Cortaillod-Est. This is a late Bronze Age village photographed from the air in 1927. Beneath the waters of the lake could be made out the parallel light marks of the houses, the dark lines of the streets, and on the shoreward side a palisade.

A little over a century ago the lake level here was lowered by 9 feet (2.7 m), causing erosion of the lake bed sediments and loss of over 4 feet (1.2 m) of deposits. It was for this reason that a total excavation of Cortaillod-Est was carried out by divers between 1981 and 1984. An area of 8,600 square yards (7,200 sq m) was systematically explored, and 150,000 potsherds were recovered, to which must be added 1,000 bronze artifacts, 9,000 bone fragments, 95,000 pebbles, and 2,200 wooden piles.

*Dendrochronology has enabled the foundation of the village to be dated to 1009 B.C., the buildings being constructed of posts cut from oak trees felled during the winter of 1010–1009 B.C. Three houses were built in 1009, nine more added in 1007, and five further houses between 1005 and 1001. The grid-plan layout of the village must certainly be the result of a central direction that the excavators called "early town-planning." It lasted only fifteen years, however, since the terrace on which the village was built was soon found to be too small. Later buildings departed from the original grid plan to follow the contours of the sloping ground. It was also after about fifteen years that the foundations of several houses were repaired.

In the spring of 1005 B.C. a palisade was erected on the shoreward edge to block a small valley emerging in the middle of the village, and to divert the water that sometimes flowed along it. When the village was enlarged once again, in 992–991 B.C. (perhaps to make space for a new generation of adults), the palisade was also extended at both ends.

The final repairs date to 964–955 B.C., a period during which the settlement shifted some tens of yards to the north. During the whole half-century of its use, there had not been a single major fire. It should also be noted that at each stage of the village's expansion a loose fence can be identified, based on a series of posts some 26 to 32 feet (8 to 10 m) apart defining the lakeward limit of the settlement.

Although it is impossible to excavate all the other settlements of this period with the same thoroughness, comparisons can be drawn between them, based in particular on aerial photographs taken during winter when the lake waters are especially transparent. These comparisons show that all the Late Bronze Age settlements were built in the same compact manner and surrounded by a palisade. They were spread out along the lakeshore at intervals of 1.2 to 1.9 miles (2 to 3 km).

Conclusion. The example of Cortaillod-Est, though belonging to the latest phases of the Alpine lake-edge settlements, illustrates recent research on these sites. Their principal characteristic is more the exceptional preservation of the organic remains than the nature of the construction, whether they rested on piles or low sand banks, or whether they were built on the shoreline, on a lake-edge platform, or directly over the waters of the lake (as at Fiavé-Carera). Every such excavation does, however, leave an essential feeling of unfinished work, by reason of the very richness in information of the waterlogged sediments, only a fraction of which can be recovered. Within current limitations of time and money, however, it is difficult to see what more could be done, save perhaps to abandon the excavation of these sites and strive only to preserve and protect as many of them as possible for the future.

[See also EUROPE, *articles on* THE EUROPEAN BRONZE AGE, THE EUROPEAN NEOLITHIC PERIOD.]

■ B. Coles and J. M. Coles, *People of the Wetlands: Bogs, Bodies and Lake-dwellers* (1989). B. Arnold, *Cortaillod-Est et les villages du lac de Neuchâtel au Bronze Final. Structure de l'habitat et proto-urbanisme* (1990).

Béat Arnold

LAND TRANSPORTATION

Roads and Tracks
Use of Animals for Transportation
Vehicles

ROADS AND TRACKS

The archaeological study of land transport can be divided into two halves: the study of the vehicles and animals used for carrying or pulling loads or for riding, and the study of the roads and tracks which formed the principal routes of communication.

Roads and tracks are one of the more difficult subjects for archaeology to document, especially in the most distant of time periods. The earliest hominids must have had trackways between favored eating or sleeping places, and between water sources, hunting grounds, and stone supplies, but these have left no recoverable traces. We are on firm ground only when communities began to build or mark trackways during the Neolithic and later in Europe and elsewhere. Some of the earliest known trackways are those which have been preserved in the peatbogs of northern Europe. The oldest of all is the Sweet Track in the *Somerset Levels of southwest England. This was an ingenious raised-plank walkway running for approximately 6,000 feet (1,800 m) across wet reed swamp from the southern end of the Levels to Westhay Island. *Dendrochronology has dated the construction precisely to the winter of 3807 / 3806 B.C., making it Europe's oldest road. It was followed by a whole series of further trackways built across the Somerset Levels to give access from island to island. Later European trackways, such as the Neolithic Bourtranger Moor roadway on the Dutch / German border and the Iron Age Corlea trackway in Ireland, consisted of split-oak planks laid side to side and laid out wide enough to take wheeled vehicles.

The effort which went into the making of these timber trackways shows the importance placed on communications even by early farming communities. It comes as no surprise, then, to find that state societies were prepared to invest even greater amounts of labor in the construction of extensive road networks. Among the most impressive are the Roman road system of Europe and the Inca road system of South America. These were sophisticated all-weather roads incorporating stone paving and elaborate bridges where necessary. Both were the creation of empires which placed a high priority on the rapid movement of troops and messengers, and in neither case was the road system designed for merchants or traders. Furthermore, these systems were exceptional in their extent and sophistication, far surpassing what was available for example in post–Roman Empire Europe before the Industrial Revolution.

The evidence of roads must be put alongside that of the transport itself. Here there emerges a sharp contrast between the Old World, where domestic animals came to be used as a source of traction for pulling carts and wagons, and the New World, where such roads were built for the use of foot travelers or pack animals. The story of land vehicles in early times (as opposed to that of roads) is therefore very much an Old World story, and follows from the invention of wheeled vehicles in the Near East or the Caucasus/Ukraine region in the fourth millennium B.C. The four-wheeled wagon, pulled by oxen or equids, gave rise in due course to the light two-wheeled chariot for warfare or hunting, and such was the vogue for chariots among the Bronze Age elites that they are found as far east as Shang China. How effective they really were, in the absence of well-made roads or on uneven terrain, may well be questioned, and it is not surprising to find that the chariot was abandoned in most areas in favor of the ridden horse in around 1000 B.C. (*see* Horse, Domestication of the). The mounted horseman, aided by the introduction of stirrups in the early Middle Ages, remained a major element in the Old World armies until replaced by the petrol engine in the twentieth century.

The use of animals for riding or traction represents only one aspect of their role in land transport, for they also fulfilled a vital function in carrying loads as pack animals. The rarity of well-made roads limited the effectiveness of wheeled vehicles and where terrain was rough or thickly forested, pack animals (horses, asses, mules, or camels, or llamas in the New World) represented a much more practical option. The extensive trade routes of the ancient Near East depended almost entirely on merchandise carried by pack animals, especially when traveling in an upstream direction where river transport, against the current, was less efficient. For the bulk transfer of goods, however, land transport could never until recent times compete with water transport, and even in the Roman Empire it was cheaper to ship grain from Spain to Syria than to move it a relatively short distance inland. This does not mean that land transport was less important, however, since many places are inaccessible by sea or river; but it was only with the invention of railways—a felicitous combination of trackway and vehicles—that these constraints began to be overcome, a process completed by the metalled roads and petrol-engined vehicles of the twentieth century.

[See also INCA CIVILIZATION: INCA ROADS; ROMAN EMPIRE: ROMAN ROADS; WHEEL, THE.]

■ S. Piggott, *The Earliest Wheeled Transport* (1983). J. Hyslop, *The Inka Road System* (1984). B. Coles and J. Coles, *People of the Wetlands* (1989).
Chris Scarre

USE OF ANIMALS FOR TRANSPORTATION

For the hunter, the main burden to be transported is meat. The domestication of livestock solved this problem for the farmer and at the same time provided a means of transporting other materials. Livestock might be used to drag heavy loads, to pull vehicles, to carry human passengers, or to act as pack animals; even domesticated birds might be used to carry messages or to hunt and retrieve game. While certain species are preeminently suited to certain of these roles, there has been considerable flexibility in the way that different species have been used by human populations. Sheep, for instance, seem unlikely pack animals, but they have nevertheless been employed as carriers of small loads when their transhumant movements have coincided with the need to move other goods (as shown, for instance, in Hellenistic figurines of a sheep carrying a pack). Deer, goats, and dogs have been used as draught animals, while a plow pulled by a camel and a donkey is not an unusual sight in North Africa or the Near East. In Tibet, the yak serves all purposes. Specialized transport animals have usually been valuable and have themselves been an important commodity of trade.

Animals were first domesticated for meat, and the specialized transport animals of the Old World belong to a second round of domestication (see Secondary Products Revolution) that occurred some two or three millennia later. Some of the primary domesticates found new uses: Cattle became the first traction animals and served as a model for others. In western Eurasia *Bos* was the primary traction bovid; in East Asia the water buffalo (*Bubalus*) and the gaur and banteng (*Bibos*) also came to perform similar roles, with the yak (*Poephagus*) in mountainous areas from the first millennium B.C. The use of bovids for traction initiated the series of technological experiments with harnessing and vehicles that led to the development of the *wheel and a variety of economic, social, and military applications. In most areas such animal-drawn vehicles were important only for short-distance transport, either for social purposes or for agricultural use. In the absence of a well-maintained road network, however, and of specialized types of horse-drawn vehicles, which did not appear until recent times, they were of little use for transporting goods over long distances. Most early overland trade was concerned with valuable rather than bulky goods, as the latter could be moved only by sea or river. In steppe and semidesert areas animal-drawn wagons and carts achieved a further significance; in pastoral (and especially nomadic) populations, they were used to transport equipment or served at certain times as mobile houses. Clay models of large covered wagons with arched tilts have been found in Syria and on the Pontic steppes dating to the third and second millennia B.C.; a complete example has been recovered from a water-logged grave at Lchashen in the Caucasus; and models of a variety of covered carts and wagons are known from Scythian contexts in the first millennium B.C. All such large and heavy vehicles could have been drawn only by oxen.

Cattle probably began to be used for traction purposes in the seventh or sixth millennium B.C. in Greater Mesopotamia, and no doubt they were also used (if only occasionally or in sport) for riding, as is known ethnographically. But the usefulness of cattle for purposes other than meat was limited, and other animals were found to be worth domesticating as specialized transport animals. In the dryer areas that surrounded the oases and river valleys where farming and urbanism began, the camelids and equids were domesticated as specialized beasts of burden.

The Bactrian camel was apparently used in Turkmenistan in the third millennium B.C. as a traction animal (if a camel-headed clay model of a wagon from Altyn Depe is meant to indicate its motive power), and this usage may have preceded its employment for riding and pack transport. Its application to longer distance transport, however, soon became invaluable in linking Turkmenistan with Seistan and the Indus Valley, as trade and urbanization developed during the third millennium B.C. on the Indo-Iranian plateau. The camel also had an essential role in making possible the *Silk Route, the main artery of overland trade linking the eastern and western ends of Eurasia, from Persia to China, from the second millennium B.C. onward. The Arabian dromedary (camel) may also have been domesticated, in the third millennium B.C., in the part of Arabia facing the Persian Gulf, but became important as a transport animal only from the late second millennium B.C. onward, in the trans-desert trade along the Incense Route between western and southern Arabia and the Levant. Specialized Semitic nomad tribes used the animal for transport, work, and warfare. Because of its greater capacity for endurance (being more highly adapted to desert conditions), the dromedary spread more widely than the Bactrian, for instance, into North Africa during the first millennium B.C. onward, and tended to replace the Bactrian on the Silk Route. It was a vital element both in the penetration of Berber-speaking populations into the Sahara and in the spread of Islam.

Among the equids, three species have contributed, in different ways, to transportation: the ass (donkey) for riding and as a pack animal, the onager (or its hybrids) as a traction animal, and the horse in all three capacities. Since these species are interfertile in the first generation, their hybrids have also been important, most notably the mule and, when horses were rare in the Near East, perhaps the horse-onager cross, which may be the equid shown pulling Sumerian battle cars. Although the history of the horse, as a draught animal for the chariot and as a mount, has been more spectacular and was certainly important in warfare, the role of the pack ass has been more crucial in economic development. The first evidence for this usage is a series of later fourth millennium B.C. clay figurines from the southern Levant showing donkeys with panniers. It was perhaps first used to move copper supplies from desert sources. The horse was domesticated a millennium earlier on the Pontic steppes by groups already familiar with domestic livestock, apparently as an aid to hunting the herds of wild horses themselves. The onager, hunted for food, is likely to have been employed principally to supplement the numbers of the other two species by interbreeding, during the time that these valuable animals were being introduced into Mesopotamia. Horses remained the prerogative of the elite in the Near East, and their uses were principally military and ceremonial. Pack donkeys, however, soon became integral to the system of economic distribution, for instance, making possible the early second millennium B.C. textile and metal trade between Aššur (in Iraq) and Kanish (in Arabia) recorded in the Kültepe tablets. They also formed part of integrated transport systems: Herodotus records how in his day skin boats (like modern Tigris *quffas*) were built on the Upper Euphrates and used to carry wine down to *Babylon, and then the donkey was used to carry the valuable hide covering back again, since the light boats could not be paddled upstream. Many of the main urban centers of northern Mesopotamia are situated at the intersection of overland pack routes and river routes.

[*See also* CAMEL, DOMESTICATION OF THE; HORSE, DOMESTICATION OF THE.]

■ R. W. Bulliet, *The Camel and the Wheel* (1975). Mary A. Littauer and Joost Crouwel, *Wheeled Vehicles and Ridden Animals in the Ancient Near East* (1979). Stuart Piggott, *The Earliest Wheeled Transport* (1983). Juris Zarins, "Pastoralism in Southwest Asia: The Second Millennium B.C." in ed. Juliet Clutton-Brock, *The Walking Larder* (1989). Stuart Piggott, *Wagon, Chariot and Carriage: Symbol and Status in the History of Transport* (1992). Michal Artzy, "Incense, Camels and Collared Rim Jars: Desert Trade Routes and Maritime Outlets in the Second Millennium," *Oxford Journal of Archaeology* 13 (1994): 121–147.

Andrew Sherratt

VEHICLES

Human communities that transport their food to living sites rather than consuming it on the spot have a continuing need for a means of conveying loads—even if it is only a pole carried by two hunters with game slung beneath. To create a vehicle, a device for taking the weight of a load during transport, requires some means of reducing friction and a connection to the person or animal pulling it. Friction can be reduced by concentrating the load on two rods, or runners, parallel to the direction of travel. The resulting sledge can be pulled by rope or (in earlier times) by leather or rawhide thongs. The principle was probably familiar from use on snow-covered ground; remains of skis and sledge runners have been recovered from early Holocene peat bogs at sites like Vychegda and Gorbunovo in Russia, and were probably familiar in the Upper Paleolithic of that region. The full significance of such vehicles became apparent, however, only when a nonhuman motive power was discovered, through the harnessing of domestic livestock. The use of dog teams to pull sleds was not the prototype of such employment of animal traction but an application derived from millennia of experience with harnessing first oxen and then horses.

In the absence of snow, sledges pulled by people are of limited use; the power of four-footed animals is required to move a reasonable load. Domesticated livestock became available in the Near East from early in the Holocene, but it was only with cattle domestication and the use of castrates (oxen), probably from the seventh or sixth millennium B.C., that suitable draught animals became available. It seems likely that the primary motive for harnessing oxen was to pull a simple plow, but the same harnessing system and training for draught could also be used for pulling a sledge. Such usage may be inferred for northern Mesopotamia in the sixth millennium B.C., and receives confirmation in the fifth or fourth millennium B.C. from clay models, apparently representing sledges, from domestic sites of the Cucuteni-Tripole culture in Romania and the Ukraine. These show a roughly rectangular, apparently flexible structure on two runners, although no means of harnessing is shown. Two possibilities exist: a rope or plaited thong connection, or a draught pole and yoke, as with a cart. The yoke implies paired draught; the ropes could be used with a single animal. The yoke or ropes could be secured either to the base of the animals' horns or by means of a wooden neck halter. A sledge with attached draught pole was recovered from the ED III tomb of Pu-Abi at Ur, dating to the mid-third millennium B.C. Such ox-drawn sledges might be used to transport harvested crops or manure, or (as known from early historical Mesopotamia) for threshing—a usage that continued in the Roman *tribulum* (threshing sledge), probably equipped as now in the Near East, with rows of robust flint teeth set into a flat baseboard. Perhaps the most compelling use, however, was simply as a symbol of prestige and authority when used as a means of personal (perhaps ceremonial) transport, in societies where draught oxen must have been a luxury, and perhaps held in common by the community. This would have provided the incentive for the development of a device to reduce friction still further, by the use of a captive roller or, by the fourth millennium B.C., a simple disc wheel. The Mesopotamian Protoliterate pictographs suggest that this transition took place in the vicinity of the first cities, probably on the northern plains (where land vehicles were more important than in the canal-crossed, boat-going south); but the evidence of clay representations of four-wheeled wagons and yoked oxen from central Europe in the mid-fourth millennium B.C. (contemporary with the first well-dated plow marks) shows how rapidly the traction complex dispersed.

The occurrence of model wagons in the form of drinking cups in Baden culture graves, as at Budakalász and Szigetszentmárton in Hungary, is indicative of the prestige that was attached to these primitive vehicles. These two clay models show two pairs of disc wheels (indications of a circular nave on the Budakalász example suggest that the wheels rotated independently on a fixed axle) on axles passing under each end of the base of a roughly square vehicle body constructed of longitudinal planks (presumably pegged with treenails). They have an open, outward-sloping superstructure rising to the four corners, which would indicate a flexible material such as matting or hide, lashed (as indicated by the zigzag incised decoration) to four diverging uprights. Similar representations continue in this area for another two millennia. The distribution of clay figurines of yoked oxen indicate the use of draught-animals in the TRB (Funnel Beaker) culture in southern Poland (Bronocice, Krężnica Jara) and the Early Helladic II period in central Greece (Tsungiza); at Bronocice there is a fine drawing of a wagon on a pot. By the later fourth and early third millennium B.C., such solid-wheeled vehicles are known from large numbers of burials on the Pontic steppes, associated with the Pit-Grave culture. Individual wheels from this period have also been found in bogs in northwestern Europe, associated with the Corded Ware culture. By the end of the third millennium B.C., there is also evidence of the use of solid-wheeled vehicles (and traction plows) in the Harappan civilization of the Indus Valley.

Greater diversity of vehicle types is evident during the third millennium B.C. in Mesopotamia and surrounding areas (including Syria). It is evident that a primary motivation for such differentiation was the employment of vehicles in military contexts, where they were pulled by teams of two or four equids (probably donkey- or horse-onager hybrids). Such vehicles included four-wheeled battle wagons, like the one shown on the "Standard of Ur," an inlaid box with scenes of warfare from the Royal cemetery of Ur, mid-third millennium B.C., or two-wheeled platform cars and straddle cars, on which the driver stood and sat, respectively. All of these had solid or crossbar wheels, independently rotating. It was these experiments that led to the development, in the early second millennium B.C., of the chariot—a much lighter vehicle, capable of being pulled by a pair of the small breeds of Bronze Age horses. The evidence for the location of this development is ambiguous; calibrated radiocarbon dates from the southern Urals suggest a date around 2000 B.C., while the appearance of spoked-wheel vehicles in models and representations at Acemhüyük and Kültepe (Kanish) in east-central Anatolia date to between 2000 and 1850 B.C. Southeast European models belong to the same period. Anatolia—opened up by Old Assyrian merchant colonies—had the incentive and background in light vehicle building; the Pontic steppes, from the Danube to the Urals, had the expertise in horsemanship and perhaps the bentwood technology (e.g., for bows); the mouth of the Danube and the Carpathian margins might have provided a meeting ground between the two, as part of the quest for rarer metals (tin, silver, gold) at this time. This creative synthesis produced a vehicle that by the middle of the second millennium B.C. was in use over an area from Scandinavia via Greece to Egypt and from central Europe across the steppes to the Altai. In China, as in Egypt, the spoked-wheel chariot intruded into an area where solid-wheeled vehicles had not been used, and it was rapidly adopted as a weapon of war. Chariots form a prominent feature of the royal burials at *Anyang in the Shang Period, and they continued in the Zhou Period to be a focus for elaborate decorative bronze attachments. Thereafter, as in the rest of the chariot-using world, it tended to lose its military importance and become a prestige and pleasure carriage.

In many of the rural areas of the Old World, solid-wheeled vehicles persisted for basic agricultural use and perhaps even the sledge, judging from the extensive rut tracks of Malta, which may have been created in the Bronze Age in shifting soil to keep the island cultivable after earlier deforestation. Spoke-wheeled vehicles were for moving people rather than goods, and overland transport was prohibitively expensive. Roman roads were for military rather than distributive purposes, and most goods were moved by river and sea, with pack animals for overland stretches. Vehicles became important only in the transportation of traded materials after the Industrial Revolution, with the development of the railways. Before that time, they were for agricultural or miltary use, or simply "transports of delight."

[See also HORSE, DOMESTICATION OF THE; WHEEL, THE.]

■ Richard W. Bulliet, *The Camel and the Wheel* (1975). Mary A. Littauer and Joost Crouwel, *Wheeled Vehicles and Ridden Animals in the Ancient Near East* (1979). Stuart Piggott, *The Earliest Wheeled Transport* (1983). P. Roger S. M. Moorey, "The Emergence of the Light, Horse-Drawn Chariot in the Near East, c. 2000–1500 B.C.," *World Archaeology* 18 (1986):196–215. Stuart Piggott, *Wagon, Chariot and Carriage: Symbol and Status in the History of Transport* (1992).
Andrew Sherratt

LANDSCAPE ARCHAEOLOGY is concerned with both the conscious and the unconscious shaping of the land: with the processes of organizing space or altering the land for a particular purpose, be it religious, economic, social, political, cultural, or symbolic; with the unintended consequences of land use and alteration; with the role and symbolic content of landscape in its various contexts and its role in the construction of myth and history; and with the enactment and shaping of human behavior within the landscape.

Within North American historical archaeology, the study of the landscape has coalesced into a distinct specialization. Landscape archaeologists endeavor to reconstruct and interpret the historical and cultural meaning of past landscapes from the time of contact between Europeans and Native Americans to the present day. Although this article summarizes advances in the archaeology of historical landscapes in North America, landscape studies are not limited by geographic location or by the presence of written records and oral tradition. Recent works on the historical landscape are based on data from Italy, Greece, Britain, and South Africa, for example, while prehistorians have long been concerned with environmental studies, settlement patterns, and more recently, interpretive approaches to the landscape.

Historical sites have always been part of the "landscape," but the significance of landscape as culturally constructed artifact was not addressed in *historical archaeology until recently. Gardens have been excavated for the purpose of restoration since the 1930s (for example, the Governor's Palace in Williamsburg, Virginia, and the William Paca garden in Annapolis, Maryland), but the work of William Kelso in the early 1970s was notable for demonstrating the potential of a landscape archaeology. His investigations at Jefferson's Monticello and Carter's Grove in Virginia led to a reexamination of the landscape within historical archaeology, followed in the mid-1980s by the first conference sessions and publications to explore directly the recovery and interpretation of past historical landscapes. While the formal gardens of the elite initially were the focus of study, landscape archaeologists have broadened their scope of research to consider the urban landscape, the agricultural or rural landscape, the industrial landscape, the battlefield, and the landscape at the point of contact between Native Americans and Europeans.

To recover the widest possible range of information, archaeologists use a multidisciplinary framework for data recovery and analysis. Field excavations are augmented with techniques borrowed from the physical sciences. Because the evidence of past landscapes is also preserved above-ground in historical documents, material objects, topographic features, living plants, and oral tradition, historical archaeologists employ methods and analytical techniques from anthropology, history, cultural geography, material culture studies, oral history, folklore, architectural history, landscape architecture, ethnobotany, and garden history. Many projects are interdisciplinary both in design and implementation.

What do landscape archaeologists look for? Significant features include physical evidence of earthmoving activity such as terracing or landfill practices; vegetation patterns, *field systems, evidence of manuring practices; drainage ditches and fence lines; tree and planting holes or garden beds that appear as stains in the soil; walkways, allées, and roads; evidence of deforestation, changes in yard surfaces, or changes in land-use practices over time; and archaeobotanical remains. The types of evidence sought vary according to the scale and focus of the analysis.

As landscape analysis has become increasingly sophisticated, archaeologists have utilized a wide array of techniques and strategies for investigating past landscapes. These may be precise enough to distinguish between individual planting holes or broad enough to observe large-scale patterns embedded in the landscape. Nondestructive methods of exploration include remote sensing techniques such as ground-penetrating radar, soil resistivity, magnetometer survey, aerial and infrared photography, and topographical survey. Soil coring or augering and subsurface testing are used to preview archaeological soils. Excavation strategies for large expanses may involve areal, or horizontal, excavation, and mechanical and hand-dug trenches, or they may focus on smaller areas using the traditional 5-by-5-foot (1.5 x 1.5 m) excavation unit.

Landscape archaeologists work with paleoethnobotanists to recover and interpret the remains of long-vanished plants and trees. Pollen analysis may offer clues about earlier environments, while phytoliths, pollen, and macrofloral remains may reveal what plants were grown or used on a site. For this reason, flotation and soil *sampling are standard practices in landscape projects. Tree coring and modern vegetation surveys frequently are used to discover modern survivals of historical plants, while casts of root cavities are used to identify tree species. Chemical analysis of archaeological soils, such as phosphate and pH testing, are used to reconstruct earlier soil conditions. *Geographical Information Systems and other computer simulations have the potential to help archaeologists recreate and visualize historical landscapes over time and space.

Written records, visual representations, and oral tradition are used to establish the historical and cultural context of earlier landscapes, contemporary gardening and land-use practices, and the symbolic content of historical plants and landscapes. This information is meshed with archaeological and above-ground data to reconstruct and interpret past landscapes. Archaeologists draw from a number of theoretical perspectives to interpret the data. Many fall under the heading of *post-processual theory: *cognitive archaeology, contextual and symbolic approaches, *gender theory, *Marxist theory, and *critical theory, for example.

Landscape archaeology is significant for several reasons. First, archaeology provides morphological and environmental data on earlier landscapes that are available nowhere else. In developing an appropriate methodology, landscape projects have served as a testing ground, leading to the refinement of techniques used by other archaeologists, while the multidisciplinary and interdisciplinary frameworks used to study landscapes have stimulated research among scholars in many fields. Landscape studies touch on many concerns of contemporary archaeology, including issues of gender, ethnicity, multiculturalism, and the construction of the past. Historical landscapes are of interest to many individuals today; thus landscape archaeology is often closely linked to the interests of preservation

groups and historical societies. Landscape is a primary context for human behavior, and the recognition of its importance as cultural artifact speaks to the importance of landscape to our understanding of both the past and the present.

[See also BATTLEFIELD ARCHAEOLOGY OF NORTH AMERICA; EUROPEAN COLONIES IN THE NEW WORLD; NORTH AMERICA: HISTORICAL ARCHAEOLOGY OF NORTH AMERICA; SITE LOCATION; SUBSURFACE TESTING; URBAN ARCHAEOLOGY.]

■ William M. Kelso, "Landscape Archaeology: A Key to Virginia's Cultivated Past," in British and American Gardens in the Eighteenth Century, ed. Robert P. Maccubbin and Peter Martin (1984), pp. 159–169. J. M. Wagstaff, ed., Landscape and Culture: Geographical and Archaeological Perspectives (1987). William M. Kelso and Rachel Most, eds., Earth Patterns: Essays in Landscape Archaeology (1990). Barbara Bender, ed., Landscape: Politics and Perspectives (1993). Naomi F. Miller and Kathryn L. Gleason, eds., The Archaeology of Garden and Field (1994). Rebecca Yamin and Karen Bescherer Metheny, eds., Landscape Archaeology: Reading and Interpreting the American Historical Landscape (1996).

Karen Bescherer Metheny

LANGUAGE. See SPEECH AND LANGUAGE

LAPITA COMPLEX. Lapita has at different times been employed in the archaeological literature on the Pacific Islands as a designation for a distinctive ceramic series, a culturally very extensive horizon or a long enduring tradition and as a major intrusive culture within western island Melanesia from Southeast Asia. The term "Lapita" also refers to a people, or to them constituting an ethnic group responsible for the initial spread of the Oceanic Austronesian languages. Most common, however, is the treatment of Lapita as a widespread cultural complex represented by sites extending from the Bismarck Archipelago part of an already long-occupied Near Oceania out into the western portion of a much more recently settled Remote Oceania (eastern island Melanesia and Western Polynesia), where they formed its founding populations.

Temporally this cultural complex first appears in various localities (frequently off-shore islands) of the Bismarcks at ca. 1500 B.C. By 1300–1200 B.C., assemblages assigned to the complex are found in the zone from the Reef/Santa Cruz Islands to New Caledonia and Fiji, and by 1100 B.C., they appear throughout the high islands of Western Polynesia. It is this rapid distribution over long distances, based on sophisticated navigation skills, an upwind voyaging strategy, and an oceangoing, sail-powered double-canoe technology, that has led to Lapita's designation as a horizon.

The hallmark of this horizon has been the elaborate decorated pottery, especially characteristic of the early assemblages in each region. Historically, the pottery is best described as comprising a ceramic series, which begins with complex vessel shapes decorated by dentate stamping, incising, and appliqué techniques that everywhere form an easily recognizable design style, whose common geometric motifs can be analyzed and coded according to a limited set of rules. Over time the ceramic assemblages within the various island sequences change, usually independently of one another. Frequently this is by the loss of the more complex vessel shapes bearing the most elaborate decorations, until simpler vessels of largely plain ware predominate. These ceramic changes, traceable over spans of up to a thousand and more years, have caused some to speak of a Lapita tradition, as they provide a deep but variable set of time depths to the horizon concept. Thus terminal Lapita assemblages in the ceramic series end in different regions at various intervals from 500 B.C. to A.D. 200 or 300.

The characterization of Lapita as a cultural complex has resulted from the association of the pottery with a wide variety of evidence derived from more than thirty excavated sites. Most restricted have been human remains, described from only four localities (Mussau, Watom, Fiji, and Tonga) and amounting to less than a dozen individuals. As a consequence, it is still difficult to describe Lapita as a people.

What can be described more fully is the economy, with its maritime, arboricultural, and domestic plant and animal components. Because at times, and especially during the settlement of newly inhabited landscapes, the populations associated with the spread of Lapita ceramics had initially to depend on the resources of the sea, midden remains yield varying quantities of shellfish and fish bones that reflect sustained exploitation of tropical inshore, lagoon, and reef zones. Turtle bone is also important, especially in earlier sites. Use of a range of economically valuable trees indigenous to the Pacific Islands, particularly the carnarium and coconut, is now well attested from waterlogged deposits. Some of the bones recovered indicate the hunting of a few terrestrial fauna (including the commensal Polynesian rat), some birds, and occasional marine species. More significant, however, are bones of the domestic chicken, pig, and dog. The presence of the Oceanic root and tree crops (yams, taro, breadfruit, bananas, etc.) is not directly attested, but is indirectly indicated by tools for their preparation, earth ovens with heated stones, and pots for their cooking, plus pits for storage, along with linguistic evidence suggesting their presence at this time. The distributional evidence is supported by the increasing need for populations settling Remote Oceania to bring with them the domestic plants and animals on which the permanent habitation of those islands depends.

Finally, the Lapita economy is generally associated with data reflecting an extensive exchange network documented by imported hard goods such as pots, obsidian, chert, adzes, shell ornaments, oven stones, and a range of lesser items. Most networks operated as regional systems involving sea travel of between 62 and 373 miles (100 and 600 km), but in particular regions such as the Reef / Santa Cruz Island group and with certain items like obsidian, interregional distances of up to 1367 feet (2,200 km) were involved. It is this information that strongly underpins inferences attributing sophisticated voyaging abilities to Lapita, which allowed them or their descendants, such as the Polynesians or eastern Micronesians, to colonize most of Remote Oceania.

Portable artifacts usually associated with Lapita ceramics constitute further evidence for the complex, although they exhibit a polythetic pattern with respect to occurrence in individual sites. Based on some twenty-two excavated sites, more than fifty different types of artifacts have been recovered. Those most consistently encountered include stone adzes with rectangular, oval, and plano-lateral cross sections plus tridacna clam shell adzes with thick bodies and those made from the dorsal margin, one-piece shell fishhooks, net sinkers of several kinds, bone awls, and a range of shell ornament forms. The last, often seen as exchange valuables, consist of broad and narrow bracelets, rings, long bead units, pendants, and beads. Sling stones, nut-cracking anvils, tattooing chisels, and perforated shark teeth occur less frequently.

Settlement sizes, based on surface pottery distributions

for thirty-six Lapita sites, correlate well with ethnographic hamlet and small village areas in Oceania. In addition to a few rock shelters, hamlet-sized Lapita settlements ranged from 598 to 5,382 square yards (500 to 4,500 sq m), and those of village size ranged from 11,362 to 16,744 square yards (9,500 to 14,000 sq m). A few examples of larger multicomponent sites are also known. Major investigations involving areal excavation have been carried out at only a dozen sites, the three best-known examples being Talepakemalai in the Mussau group of the Bismarck Archipelago, the Nenumbo site in the Main Reef Islands of the southeastern Solomons, and the basal levels of the Sigatoka dune site in Fiji. At the first of these, part of a dwelling built on stilts in the shallow lagoon has been identified; at the second, a substantial ground-level central domestic building, with cooking sheds to the south of it, was uncovered.

In sum, Lapita as a complex reflects in most aspects a typical Neolithic Oceanic culture, one that quite adequately serves as a base from which many later societies in that region could derive.

[See also AUSTRALIA AND NEW GUINEA: FIRST SETTLEMENT OF SUNDA AND SAHUL; PACIFIC ISLANDS: SETTLEMENT OF MELANESIA AND MICRONESIA; PACIFIC ISLANDS, ORIGINS OF FOOD PRODUCTION IN THE; PACIFIC ISLANDS NAVIGATION AND WATERCRAFT.]

■ Roger Curtis Green, *Lapita*, in Jesse D. Jennings, ed., *The Prehistory of Polynesia* (1979): 27–60. Jim Allen and Chris Gosden, eds., *Report of the Lapita Homeland Project*, Department of Prehistory, Research School of Pacific Studies, Australian National University, Occasional Papers in Prehistory No. 20 (1991). Jean Christophe Galipaud, ed., *Poterie Lapita et Peuplement, Actes du Colloque Lapita, Nouméa, Janvier 1992* (1992).

Roger C. Green

LASCAUX. The cave of Lascaux, situated on a hill above the town of Montignac (Dordogne, France) is still, alongside *Altamira, the most famous and most spectacular Paleolithic decorated cave ever found. It was discovered on September 12, 1940, by four teenage boys, and opened to the public in 1948; but it had to be closed again in 1963 when authorities recognized that the excessive numbers of visitors (which eventually reached 100,000 per year, and two thousand per day in summer) were having a radical effect on the cave's microenvironment, causing the proliferation of algae and bacteria. These problems have now been overcome, and although the general public is no longer admitted, a fine facsimile of the cave and its paintings, Lascaux II, has been constructed nearby. This was opened in 1983, and receives about 300,000 visitors per year.

Unfortunately, no proper excavation was ever done of the main parts of Lascaux, and much of the archaeological layer was lost when the floor was lowered and the cave adapted for tourism. Nevertheless, it is possible to be fairly sure that this was never a habitation site, and that people merely made brief visits periodically for artistic activity or ritual. Charcoal fragments have provided radiocarbon dates around 15,000 B.C.

Lascaux is best known for its magnificent paintings, but in fact it is far richer in engravings, housing one of the biggest collections of Paleolithic parietal engraved figures, for whereas there are about six hundred painted animals and abstract "signs," there are almost fifteen hundred engravings.

The Paleolithic entrance of the cave has never been found, but it may have been close to the modern artificial entry. The first space is the great "Hall of the Bulls," about 66 feet (20 m) across and 16 feet (5 m) high, the walls of which are covered in painted figures. The main frieze is dominated by a series of four enormous black auroch bulls, over 16 feet (5 m) in length (and all probably by the same artist), as well as smaller horses and tiny deer, and it begins at the left with an enigmatic "imaginary" animal, with two straight horns, known oddly as the "Unicorn."

The hall is prolonged by the "Axial Gallery," 66 feet (20 m) in length and 5 feet (1.5 m) wide at the bottom, but 11 feet (3.5 m) wide above. Hence it has a "keyhole shape" in cross-section, and it is the upper walls and ceiling which were decorated with paintings of cattle, deer, and horses, as well as with dots and quadrilateral "signs."

Leading off to the right from the Hall of Bulls is the Passage, 49 feet (15 m) long and 6.5 to 13 feet (2 to 4 m) wide. This space forms the transition from painting to engraving, since there are a few fragments of painted figures here (the rest weathered away) but almost four hundred engravings, dominated numerically (like all of the cave's art) by horses. To one side is the great apse, which contains over one thousand often superimposed engraved "graphic units" (including 125 horses, 70 deer, and at least 377 "signs"). Within the apse is the entrance to the shaft, 5 meters deep, containing the famous scene (one of the very few recognizable scenes in Paleolithic art) of a birdheaded man (the cave's only human figure) who has an erect phallus and is falling back in front of an apparently speared bison with its entrails spilling out. A bird on a stick stands nearby, and a rhinoceros painted in a different style walks off to the left. There are many interpretations of this scene, many of which involve shamanism.

Beyond the apse is the "Nave," 16 feet (5 m) wide and high, with its celebrated frieze of five black deer heads, each about 3 feet (1 m) high, and usually described as swimming. The Nave also has two painted male bison, facing in different directions and with overlapping rumps. Finally, the cave ends with the narrow (3 foot [1 m]) "Gallery of the Felines," 82 feet (25 m) long, into which one has to crawl. It is covered in engravings, including six felines.

Lascaux gives important evidence of the techniques of Paleolithic cave art. Stone tools suitable for engraving were found only in the engraved zones. Many lamps were recovered. No fewer than 158 mineral fragments were found in the cave, many with scratches and use-wear, together with crude "mortars" and "pestles" stained with pigment and naturally hollowed stones still containing powdered pigment. Black dominates heavily (105 fragments), followed by yellows, reds, and white. There are sources of ocher and manganese dioxide within .3 miles (.5 km) and 3 miles (5 km) of the cave, respectively. Chemical analysis has revealed sophisticated heating and mixing of different minerals to produce a variety of hues.

It is clear that ladders or scaffolding must have been used at Lascaux, and remains of wood in the cave may come from these constructions (some are from large oaks). In the Axial Gallery some twenty sockets are cut into the rock on both sides, about 66 feet (20 m) from the floor. These were packed with clay, and holes about 4 inches (10 cm) deep in the clay suggest that branches long enough to span the gallery were fitted into the sockets and cemented into place with the clay. These solid joists could then have supported a platform providing easy access to the upper walls and ceiling.

[See also EUROPE: THE EUROPEAN PALEOLITHIC PERIOD; ROCK ART: PALEOLITHIC ART.]

▪ Fernand Windels and Annette Laming, The Lascaux Cave Paintings (1949). Annette Laming, Lascaux: Paintings and Engravings (1959). Georges Bataille, Prehistoric Painting: Lascaux or the Birth of Art (1955). Arlette Leroi-Gourhan and Jacques Allain, eds., Lascaux Inconnu (1979). Brigitte and Gilles Delluc, Lascaux: Art & Archéologie (1984). Mario Ruspoli, The Cave of Lascaux, the Final Photographic Record (1987).

Paul G. Bahn

LAYARD, Austen Henry.

Austen Henry Layard (1817–1894) was born in London and trained as a lawyer. In 1839, he and a fellow lawyer, Edward Mitford, set out to ride from England to Ceylon. Layard became fascinated with archaeology during a visit to Petra and *Nineveh, then spent a year wandering with the Bakhtiari nomads of Iraq before becoming an unpaid diplomatic attaché in Constantinople. He excavated at Nimrud, biblical Calah, from 1845 to 1847. He discovered the palaces of Kings Assurnasirpal and Esarhaddon within a few weeks. Layard's excavation methods were brutal by modern standards. He tunneled into the Nimrud mounds, following room walls, removing as many decorated panels and spectacular finds as possible. In 1847, Layard moved to Kuyunjik, ancient Nineveh, finding another Assyrian palace under deep overburden, which had thwarted Emil Botta.

Layard returned to England in 1847 to find himself a popular hero. His Nineveh and Its Remains appeared in 1849 and became an immediate bestseller, remarkable for its lively prose and attempts to use cuneiform inscriptions to interpret Assyrian civilization. He resumed excavations at Nimrud and Nineveh in 1849. This time, he had the benefit of much more accurate cuneiform translations by Henry *Rawlinson and other scholars, which enabled him to identify the palace of Sennacherib at Nineveh and his siege of biblical Lachish, described in II Kings. He also recovered the royal library of King Assurbanipal at Kuyunjik.

Layard's crude digging methods were ineffective in southern Mesopotamia, so he returned to England in 1851. His second book, Discoveries in the Ruins of Nineveh and Babylon (1853), included a provisional chronology for the Assyrian kings and description of their state. Subsequently, Layard became a politician before becoming British Ambassador in Madrid and then Constantinople. Self-taught and energetic, Layard ranks as one of the immortals of early archaeology.

[See also HISTORY OF ARCHAEOLOGY BEFORE 1900: NEAR EASTERN ARCHAEOLOGY.]

▪ C. J. Gadd, Stones of Assyria (1936). Gordon Waterfield, Layard of Nineveh (1963). Brian Fagan, Return to Babylon (1977).

Brian M. Fagan

LEAKEY, Louis (1903–1972) and Mary (b. 1913),

pioneered archaeological and human evolutionary research in East Africa, most notably in Kenya and Tanzania. They demonstrated that East Africa was a major "cradle of humankind" that yielded much important evidence of human origins.

Louis began archaeological fieldwork at *Olduvai Gorge in northern Tanzania in 1931 (Mary joined Louis starting in 1935). This gorge has yielded an unsurpassed sequence of prehistory from about two million years ago to recent times, documenting major evolutionary, technological, and paleoenvironmental changes. Some of the earliest work with potassium-argon dating and fission-track dating was conducted by geochronologists at Olduvai. Famous hominid fossils found by Louis and Mary Leakey include the megadont "Zinjanthropus" (now called *Australopithecus or

Paranthropus boisei), found in 1959, and the larger-brained *Homo habilis* (see *Australopithecus* and *Homo habilis*) found in 1960, both dated to about 1.8 million years ago. In addition they are credited with the first-known African example of **Homo erectus* ("Chellean Man"), found in 1960 and dated to about 1.4 million years ago.

The Leakeys also carried out fieldwork at Early and Middle Miocene localities in western Kenya, which yielded hominoid remains of *Proconsul* from Rusinga Island and *Kenyapithecus* from Forth Ternan. *Proconsul*, dating to about 20 million years ago, is believed by some paleontologists to be near the common stem for all modern apes.

Other archaeological sites worked by the Leakeys included the Acheulean occurrences at **Olorgesaillie* and Kariandusi, as well as the later prehistoric sites of Gamble's Cave, Njoro River Cave, and Hyrax Hill, all in Kenya. Mary is also well known for her studies of the prehistoric rock art from East African sites.

Mary Leakey's careful and well-documented excavations at Olorgesaillie and **Olduvai Gorge* were the first large horizontal excavations attempting to establish the spatial patterning of early Stone Age "living floors" in East Africa. Mary developed a typological classification system for the artifactual remains from Olduvai, one that is still widely in use on the African continent today. Based on the characteristics of different assemblages, she assigned artifacts at Olduvai Gorge sites either to the Oldowan (simple chopper, discoid, and polyhedron core forms, casually retouched flakes, etc.), to the Developed Oldowan (with the addition of more spheroids, light-duty tools, etc.), or to the **Acheulean* (hand axes, cleavers) tradition.

Following Louis Leakey's death in 1972, Mary continued work at Olduvai Gorge and the nearby Pliocene site of Laetoli. At Laetoli her team discovered a number of hominid fossils usually attributed to *Australopithecus afarensis* as well as fossil hominid footprints in a 3.6 million-year-old volcanic ash deposit. These footprints represent tracks made by three bipedal hominids, all walking in the same direction.

The Leakeys' contributions to African prehistory and human evolutionary studies cannot be overestimated. At a time when many paleoanthropologists were searching in Europe and Asia to find humankind's oldest ancestors, the Leakeys' discoveries demonstrated that the East African Rift Valley was an incredibly rich area for research and, along with the australopithecine cave sites in South Africa, contained fossil hominids that were substantially older than those known in the rest of the world. Louis organized the First Pan-African Congress in Nairobi in 1947. Both Louis and Mary felt that the antiquity of the genus *Homo* went far beyond three million years ago, an idea carried on by their notable son Richard as well. Media coverage, especially that provided by *National Geographic* magazine and television shows, catapulted Louis and Mary Leakey to a celebrity status and inspired a whole generation of young anthropology and primatology students who became involved in similar studies in Africa and elsewhere.

[*See also* HISTORY OF ARCHAEOLOGY SINCE 1950: WORLD ARCHAEOLOGY; HUMAN EVOLUTION: THE ARCHAEOLOGY OF HUMAN ORIGINS.]

Nicholas Toth and Kathy Schick

LEPENSKI VIR lies on the Serbian bank of the dramatic Iron Gates Gorge of the Danube, on a sandy ledge facing a whirlpool. The site was discovered in 1967 during rescue operations in advance of hydro-electric dam construction. Excavations over five seasons by Professor Dragoslav Srejovic revealed a three-level site, with complex foraging villages in Phases I and II (6000 to 5100 B.C.) and less complex farming occupations in Phase III (5100 to 4900 B.C.). The structures and finds from Phases I and II indicate that this was the central site of the most sophisticated social network yet known from Mesolithic Europe, with the world's first monumental sculpture, set in trapezoidal houses.

Six foraging villages lie superimposed at the site, Phases 1a through 1e and Phase II. Each village is laid out around a central space facing the Danube. The trapezoidal house plan exhibits remarkable dimensional stability, based on a Fibonacci series, throughout the eight hundred-year occupation. The house floors are made of Europe's first sandstone mortar with stone hearths set axially, surrounded by paving slabs. Fish-roasting spit supports were found around the hearths, which were often full of bones of carp, catfish, and sturgeon. The erection of sculptures and altars, carved out of sandstone boulders, at the rear and sides of houses in Phase I indicates an association with hearths, warmth, and fertility within a household context of privacy. The most striking sculptures, however, involving fish-human representations, are those which occur in front of several houses in Phase II, indicating a change both in social relations and in the use of the sculptures. Many other artifacts were highly decorated, including antler batons, stone fish-stunners, and polished bone pins. Smaller-scale stone carving included images of vulvae and motifs adopted from the canon of contemporary farmers. The final act of occupation in many houses was the burial of an individual, often with antler and fishbone offerings. A total of eighty-five burials is known, from inside or between the houses.

Contemporary with the foraging occupation at Lepenski Vir, early farmers of the Starcevo-Cris group settled on the margins of the gorge on fertile terrace soils. These farming groups exchanged pottery and foodstuffs, including joints of beef, with the foragers, as well as shells, flint, and obsidian from up to approximately 315 miles (500 km) away. Although Lepenski Vir and similar Iron Gates sites show evidence for intensification of fishing and hunting, as well as wolf domestication, the topographical constraints of the gorge made farming impossible. Hence the contacts between Lepenski Vir and the nearby farmers put pressure on the social relations of the foragers, resulting in the overt display of ancestral sculptures in Phase II and, eventually, in the abandonment of their hitherto successful foraging way of life. The Phase III occupation represented a devolution from foraging complexity into an occupation where the main farming symbol—of painted pottery—replaced the trapezoidal houses and monumental sculptures of the foraging community.

[*See also* EUROPE: THE EUROPEAN MESOLITHIC PERIOD.]

■ Dragoslav Srejovic, *Europe's First Monumental Sculptures: New Discoveries at Lepenski Vir* (1972). Dragoslav Srejovic and Ljubinka Babovic, *Lepenski Vir. Menschenbilder einer fruher europaischer Kultur* (1981). Dragoslav Srejovic and Ljubinka Babovic, *Art of Lepenski Vir* (1983). John Chapman, "Demographic Trends in Neothermal South-East Europe," in *The Mesolithic in Europe*, Clive Bonsall, ed. (1989).

John Chapman

LI CHI (1895–1979) was born in Zhongxiang, Hubei Province in southern China. Li Chi (Li Ji in *pinyin*) grew up to become "the father of modern Chinese archaeology." His life was a succession of firsts: After receiving a traditional education in the Chinese classics, he entered the first modern school established in his home region and then graduated, in 1909, into the first Western-style preparatory school established in China, the Chinghua (Tsinghua) Academy in Beijing. In 1918 he left China to study abroad in the United States, entering Clark University in Worcester, Massachusetts. There he studied psychology and sociology, receiving a B.A. and an M.A. in these subjects respectively. Continuing at Harvard University, he received a Ph.D. in anthropology in 1923. Though he studied some archaeology under Tozzer, his main research interests were in ethnology and physical anthropology. His dissertation was published by Harvard University Press as *The Formation of the Chinese People: An Anthropological Enquiry* (1928).

Upon graduating from Harvard, Li returned to China for work at Xiyincun, a Yangshao (*see* Yangshao culture) site in Shanxi, becoming the first native scholar to conduct an archaeological excavation. In 1926, having returned as a professor to his *alma mater* the Chinghua Academy back in Beijing, he participated in the Freer Gallery of Art expedition to China. The results of his fieldwork were published as an "Archaeological Survey of the Fen River Valley, Southern Shansi, China" in the *Smithsonian Miscellaneous Collections* 78.7: 123–37. It was perhaps from this time that Li recognized the absolute importance of fieldwork to the discipline of archaeology, and his report stands as a rare—if not the only—systematic field survey published for China.

In 1928 Li Chi was appointed head of the newly established Department of Archaeology in the Academia Sinica. Lodged in the Institute of History and Philology, this department was established for the excavation of Yinxu, the Late Shang (*see* China: Shang Civilization) capital at Anyang, which continued until disbanded in the face of war in 1937. Work at the site was stimulated by the tracing of oracle bones for sale by Chinese druggists to the area northwest of Anyang. Chang Kwang-chih has pointed out that because of this coincidence of inscriptional material and new archaeological methods, standard Chinese archaeology has very much developed as a protohistorical discipline with great emphasis on inscriptional data, thus continuing the historiographical bent of traditional research. At Yinxu, Li was responsible for training the future generation of great Chinese archaeologists, and his account of the excavations is forever accessible to Westerners as *Anyang* (1977). During this time, he also published *Manchuria in History: A Summary* (1932)—no doubt stimulated by increasing Japanese military interest in the area—and the site report for the Longshan site of Chengziyai (1934), translated as *Ch'eng-tzu-yai* (1956).

His post-war appointment as Director of the new Central Historical Museum in Beijing was short-lived: Upon the Communist takeover of China in 1949, Li moved to Taiwan. There he established the Department of Archaeology and Anthropology at the National Taiwan University in Taipei and became Director of the relocated Institute of History and Philology, Academia Sinica. During the last thirty years of his life in Taiwan, Li Chi continued to write on Anyang in both Chinese and English (*The Beginnings of Chinese Civilization*, 1957) and to contribute to international scholarship ("Archaeological Studies in China" in *Essays on the Sources for Chinese History*, 1973). Unfortunately, the prewar Anyang excavations have never been fully published.

[*See also* HISTORY OF ARCHAEOLOGY FROM 1900 TO 1950: CHINESE AND SOUTHEAST ASIAN ARCHAEOLOGY; HISTORY OF ARCHAEOLOGY SINCE 1950: CHINESE ARCHAEOLOGY.]

Gina L. Barnes

LITHICS

Introduction
Technological Analysis of Lithics
Microwear Analysis of Lithics

INTRODUCTION

Stone tools provide archaeologists with the earliest evidence of human craftsmanship. Indeed, they played a major role in establishing the antiquity of humans in the eighteenth and nineteenth centuries. Early discoveries included a hand axe associated with Pleistocene elephant remains in England, reported by John Frere in 1797, and the persistence of Boucher de *Perthes in France, from the 1830s to the 1850s, in demonstrating the relationship of chipped-stone artifacts to fossil animal remains. The history of lithic research began in Scandinavia in the 1830s, while the first broad synthesis of stone tools was published in 1872 in England by John Evans. In the United States, early studies of lithic quarries and manufacturing sequences were done by W. H. Holmes.

Stone tool research, or "lithic technology," is critical, for such specimens are, in some parts of the world, the only major artifact category preserved for archaeological analysis. Raw materials used in stoneworking include flint, chert, chalcedony, obsidian, basalt, quartzite, and a variety of other cryptocrystalline materials that can be fractured in a controlled fashion. Lithics can often be used to date associated cultural remains through typology, to identify sources of raw material (especially obsidian) that reflect ancient trade, to examine wear patterns and residues indicative of tool function, and to recognize the emergence of craft specialization. While lithics were among the first materials to be worked by human hands, and were extensively used by hunting and gathering peoples, they also had important roles in some early civilizations.

Lithic artifacts were produced by a variety of methods. There are many archaeologists who are skilled at replicating stone tools using ancient techniques. These "flintknappers" have provided tremendous insights into the technology of manufacture. For example, there are breakage patterns that represent different stages in the process of lithic reduction, as well as types of waste flakes (debitage) that reflect this process. The flintknappers have helped archaeologists to recognize these data in site deposits, providing clues to site function.

The basic techniques of manufacture include: anvil percussion (striking the raw material nodule [core] against another stone resting on the ground); direct percussion (striking the core, to remove flakes, with either a hand-held hammerstone or a billet made of heavy antler); bipolar percussion (placing a nodule on a hard surface, usually a flat stone, and then smashing it with direct percussion); indirect percussion (precise removal of flakes using a "punch" made of pointed antler or bone as an intermediary, placing the tip on the core edge and then striking the end of the punch with a hammerstone); and pressure (the final stage in shaping an artifact, utilizing a pointed deer antler to press off small flakes along the tool edge).

Raw material was sometimes altered by heat prior to tool making, especially tough or flawed nodules of flint or chert.

Such "heat treatment" can be traced back to the Upper Paleolithic in Europe and is widespread in North America, known both archaeologically and ethnographically. Such intentional alteration (at temperatures of 600°F [316°C] to 750°F [399°C]) affected the structure of the stone and made the raw material more brittle and easier to flake.

One problem that has plagued lithic studies is distinguishing between humanly and naturally fractured stone. In the early twentieth century, British scholars debated the origins of "eoliths." Were these early human artifacts or cobbles modified by wave action on a beach? Similarly, archaeologists working at the Calico Hills locality in southern California have made claims for the great antiquity of chipped-stone objects, which other scientists dismiss as "geofacts"—in this case, pebbles shaped by nature in a vast gravel deposit. Recognizing humanly made tools depends on the context in which they are found, along with the angle at which flakes are removed from a nodule's edge.

The antiquity of lithics clearly modified by humans has now been established at 2 to 2.5 million years ago. The sequence of early stone tools is chronicled in detail by Kathy Schick and Nicholas Toth in their book, *The Silent Stones Speak* (1993). The first distinctive tools were choppers, scrapers, and hammers of the Oldowan technology of ca. 2.5 to 1.5 million years ago. Schick and Toth suggest these were made by the earliest human species, *Homo habilis*, although the role of other early African hominids, the Australopithecines, cannot be ruled out.

Around 1.7 million years ago, a separate human species, *Homo erectus*, had emerged and in contrast to the simple Oldowan tools, they produced hand axes and cleavers with preconceived, repeated shapes (mental templates). These tools, known as Acheulean, are largely bifacial (flaked on both sides), though some are unifacial. They were used for butchering animals, for digging up plants, and—as cores for the production of flakes—used for cutting and scraping tools.

It is not until about one hundred thousand years ago that this long-lived tradition, found throughout the Old World and usually called the "Lower Paleolithic" (Old Stone Age) was replaced by the stone tools of *Homo sapiens*. In the Middle Paleolithic, finely made hand axes continued, but the focus was on the shaping of a specific type of core, known as Levallois, from which a pointed flake could be produced. These flakes were likely hafted to be used as knives or spear points. By forty thousand years ago, modern species of *Homo sapiens* were widespread and lithics had become much more complex. Blade-core technology predominated, designed to produce regular, rectangular flakes ("blades") that could be made into a variety of tools, such as knives, scrapers, burins, and projectile points. Finely made bifacial points appeared, and by at least eleven thousand years ago, humans spread into the New World, again with distinctive, fluted, bifacial Clovis points, sometimes found associated with mammoth kills.

The New World hunters and gatherers made a variety of stone tools, often emphasizing formal shapes, such as temporally and spatially distinct projectile-point types. Among some of these Native American groups, lithics continued to be used well into the Historic era. One example of such persistence is among the Yurok of the northwest California coast, where stone knives were preferred over steel ones for processing salmon.

The Australian aborigines also used stone tools into modern times; ethnoarchaeological studies have provided insights on the cognitive aspects of stone tools in this culture. In contrast with North American hunters and gatherers, the Australians did not develop formally shaped lithics, and often designated tools of certain function by the location of a working edge, and not by their configuration.

The ancient Egyptians continued to use stone tools into the Old and New Kingdoms, although copper had taken the place of stone for cutting and sawing. In large part, this appears to have had ritual importance, with Old Kingdom tomb scenes of butchers using (and resharpening) stone knives to cut up oxen as part of the entombment process. At the Middle Kingdom site of Beni Hasan, tomb paintings depict the flaking of large stone knives.

The Maya civilization of Central America was literally built and maintained with stone tools. Standard forms were in place by 300 B.C. and the long-distance exchange of chert tools can be documented in the Maya lowlands. This is related to the development of craft specialization at sites like Colha, Belize, with their mass production of stone tools and their distribution to farmers and villagers in areas where chert did not occur naturally. In addition to utilitarian tools, such as axes, adzes, and hoes, there were symbolic artifacts, including oddly shaped "eccentrics" and large, stemmed blade daggers and points, widely traded among the elite. Eccentrics often occur in tombs and offertory caches, where they doubtless had both cognitive and ceremonial significance.

Lithics are important worldwide in providing a variety of perspectives on human behavior. They are increasingly used by archaeologists to document many facets of prehistoric activity. Among the most exciting developments is the study of tool function through microscopic use-wear patterns, coupled with the identification of organic residues, including lipids, blood, and plant residues, which promise to give the archaeologist better information on the role of lithics in human cultures.

■ Don E. Crabtree, *An Introduction to Flintworking* (1972). Brian Hayden, ed., *Lithic Use-Wear Analysis* (1979). Lawrence H. Keeley, *Experimental Determination of Stone Tool Uses* (1980). Kenneth Honea, *Lithic Technology: An International Annotated Bibliography 1725–1980* (1983). Lucile R. Adington, *Lithic Illustration* (1986). Robin Torrence, *Production and Exchange of Stone Tools* (1986). Thomas R. Hester and Harry J. Shafer, eds., *Maya Stone Tools* (1991). Barbara E. Luedtke, *An Archaeologist's Guide to Chert and Flint* (1992). John C. Whittaker, *Flintknapping, Making and Understanding Stone Tools* (1994).

Thomas R. Hester

TECHNOLOGICAL ANALYSIS OF LITHICS

Analyses of technical properties of stone tools address two primordial questions asked of most ancient artifacts: How was the tool made? And how was it used? Evaluations of a tool's practical physical properties and shape design are considered to be "functional" analyses. As the term is currently used, "technological" analysis concerns only manufacturing techniques and does not refer to technical observations made by modern analysts per se. Technological analyses are most commonly undertaken for chipped stone artifacts, but all stone artifacts, including everything from polished axes to carved beads, can be so analyzed.

Technological analysis consists of four necessary steps designed to resolve the following philosophical problem presented by prehistory: How can one translate observations of ancient tools into meaningful statements of past tool manufacture? Anthropologists observe fabrication of implements among traditional peoples and can ask native artisans how particular tools were made, but neither avenue of inquiry is open to prehistorians. One can only justifiably infer how stone tools from extinct cultures were made by comparing observations of ancient artifacts to tools of known manufacture. Although some traditional peoples continue to make tools similar to some recovered archaeologically, study of their stone tools and techniques provides only a limited base for wider inference because many artifacts found archaeologically are much more complex than those made currently, or in the recorded past. To extend the inferential base beyond that provided by anthropological observations of modern stone tool manufacture, analysts rely on replication experiments. These are designed to replicate ancient artifacts and to provide reference collections of tools made under controlled conditions that can be compared to tools of unknown manufacture. A thorough technological analysis thus involves four critical steps: (1) creation of modern replicas under controlled conditions, (2) determination of specific manufacturing traces characteristic of particular techniques and fabricating tools, (3) analysis of artifacts for manufacturing traces, and (4) interpretation of the manufacturing marks on artifacts in light of the experimentally derived reference collection. Clearly, a technological analysis can never be better than the quality and comprehensiveness of the original experiments nor the level of detail observed in studying the finished replicated tools or in comparing them to archaeological specimens.

Two approaches to experimentation are popular, and each has advantages and limitations. The traditional approach stresses actual manufacture, under realistic conditions, of special artifact forms. The second, more analytic approach focuses on physics, fracture mechanics, and the physical properties of various classes of raw materials. Experiments undertaken in Europe at the turn of the century to distinguish "man-made" handaxes from "eoliths" (pseudoartifacts from nature) exemplify the first approach. In contrast, a standard analytic experiment consists of dropping small steel balls of known mass, from various heights and angles, on glass prisms to determine the relationships among force, striking angles, and resultant flake sizes and shapes. Laboratory conditions allow control of individual variables and duplication of results, but they suffer an insuperable limitation. Such experiments do not adequately model the complexity of actual knapping nor are they designed to replicate complex tools similar to those found archaeologically. Replication experiments, in turn, are realistically complex but suffer from an inability to consider variables individually or to duplicate results satisfactorily between different experimenters. Thus, results from such experiments are inherently indeterminate and open to other interpretations.

Technological analysis attempts to reconstruct entire production sequences. Chipped stone technologies are ideal for such studies because stone preserves well and each fragment removed during manufacture of a finished tool can be analyzed. The principal limitation of early experiments was their narrow focus on finished tools and failure to consider the waste by-products generated during production. To appreciate the entire manufacturing process of a tool, one must identify all chips, flakes, and fragments generated during its production and relate each to procedures at various stages of the process. Adequate replication experiments, therefore, are comprehensive and replicate entire assemblages (finished forms and all their by-products)

as well as the tools used during production. This ideal is rarely achieved.

The end results of a technological analysis are a typology of stone tool types and a "reduction" sequence, or flow chart, showing where each type fits in the overall manufacturing sequence. "Reduction" refers to the continual diminution of the original stone as it is chipped into final form. The principal advantages of classifying stone artifacts by technological types are threefold: (1) the artifact types are inherently meaningful in terms of past behavior in a way perhaps recognizable by the ancient artisans themselves, (2) the diagram of the manufacturing process shows the relationships among all the types and their manufacturing techniques, and (3) the typology and reduction sequence provide a ready framework for behavioral inferences as each is keyed to replication experiments. On the other hand, there are serious limitations related to the unavoidably subjective nature of technological analysis. These relate to (1) incomplete or sloppily executed experimental programs, (2) insufficient analysis of experimental results, (3) inadequate levels of observation of the experimental replicas or archaeological artifacts, and (4) inability to "see" subtle, technological characteristics. These difficulties are compounded when analysts lack the ability to carry out replication experiments and must rely on written descriptions of the critical attributes. Technological analysis is necessarily subjective and only works when analysts train themselves through the actual process of producing stone tools. In short, not every lithic analyst can, or should, attempt technological analysis. For those sufficiently trained in the technique, however, it provides a powerful instrument for interpreting the past.

[See also ANALYSIS, METHODS OF.]

■ Don E. Crabtree, "A Stone Worker's Approach to Analyzing and Replicating the Lindenmeier Folsom," *Tebiwa* (1966): 3–39. Payson D. Sheets, "Behavioral Analysis and the Structure of a Prehistoric Industry," *Current Anthropology* (1975): 369–391. K. Lewis Johnson, "A History of Flint-knapping Experimentation, 1838–1976," *Current Anthropology* (1978): 337–372. John M. Coles, *Experimental Archaeology* (1979). J. Jeffrey Flenniken, "The Past, Present, and Future of Flintknapping: An Anthropological Perspective," *Annual Review of Anthropology* (1984): 187–274.

John Clark

MICROWEAR ANALYSIS OF LITHICS

"Microwear analysis" refers to the examination, usually with the aid of a microscope, of the ways in which a tool's edges are modified during use, in an attempt to infer the way in which that tool was used in the past. Although archaeologists have noted use modifications on stone tools since the nineteenth century, systematic microwear studies have developed only since the early 1960s. Technical trends since that time have generally been toward the use of more and more powerful microscopes and toward documenting the effects on tool edges of a wider and wider range of human and non-human processes.

Microwear analysts generally identify three classes of use modification: edge damage, or small flakes removed from the working edge; striae, or scratches immediately adjacent to the edge; and polishes, or alterations in the brightness and surface texture of the edge. Physical residues of the material on which a tool was used comprise a fourth class of use traces whose analysis requires a distinct set of knowledge and techniques. Of the first three kinds of modifications, edge damage can usually be studied with a stereomicroscope at magnifications from 10x to 75x, while striae and polishes are often invisible without the aid of an incident-light microscope, which can attain magnifications of 100x to 400x, or an even more powerful scanning electron microscope (SEM). In practice, few analysts use the SEM, and most of those who examine striae and polishes work at magnifications below 400x. Archaeologists who specialize in microwear analysis can generally be divided into "low-magnification" analysts, who look primarily at edge damage and secondarily at striae (when these are visible at low magnifications), and "high-magnification" analysts, who look at all three classes of use traces.

Accurate interpretation of the traces observed under a microscope depends on comparisons between traces produced experimentally and those observed on archaeological material, and microwear analysts must therefore conduct a wide range of controlled experiments in stone-tool use. The accuracy of the high- and low-magnification approaches to microwear analysis can be assessed by the use of "blind tests," in which analysts who have conducted such a range of experiments attempt to interpret use traces on experimental tools made and used by other people.

Blind tests to date suggest that all three classes of use traces, and, therefore, both the high- and low-magnification approaches, can provide information on whether or not an edge was used and on the manner of tool use (whether an edge was used, for example, to cut, to scrape, or to drill). Studies of edge damage seem also to provide valuable information on the general hardness of the material on which a tool was used, but do not by themselves seem to reveal the specific nature of this material. Differences among the polishes observed on tool edges appear to be the most accurate and widely available source of information on specific worked materials; blind tests indicate that analysts who examine polishes along with other use traces can distinguish among tools used on meat, fresh hide, dry hide, bone/antler/ivory, wood, plants, and shells. Less certain distinctions may also exist among the polishes produced by use on stone, ceramics, and fish, and there is some evidence of variation among polishes produced by different kinds of plants.

Several important factors limit the applicability of even the high-power approach. Most polishes form only on microcrystalline silicates: non-silicious stone and silicates with an amorphous structure (such as obsidian) or very large grain size (such as many quartzites) are poor candidates for high-magnification study, although they remain suitable for low-magnification analysis. However, the structure and chemistry of these different materials also affects the way they flake and scratch, and some uses may leave few or no traces visible at any magnification on very durable kinds of stone. Use traces also take some time to form, and very brief periods of use on any kind of stone usually produce generic rather than specific wear patterns; the use of a single tool for more than one purpose also complicates analysis. Exposure of a tool to physical and chemical processes prior to recovery by an archaeologist can also obscure or destroy both high- and low-magnification traces.

In addition to physical alterations of tool edges, archaeologists have identified a variety of residues on flaked stone tools, including blood, hairs, and phytoliths and other plant parts. When residues can be identified, they provide important information on worked materials. Some residues, particularly hairs and substantial fragments of plants, occur only under exceptional preservation conditions, as in dry caves. Other residues, particularly phytoliths and blood, have been identified more widely. Phytoliths and other microscopic silicious plant parts, which can often identify the genus and, sometimes, the species of plants, can be seen at very high magnifications under an SEM adhering to the surface of polished areas of tool edges, and the dissolution of the silica in these structures seems to play an important role in the formation of plant polishes. Most recently, researchers relying on a variety of chemical techniques have identified blood on stone tools as much as 10,000 years old, and have claimed to be able to identify the genus and, sometimes, the species of animal producing that blood. However, comparative tests carried out by different workers on a single set of tools indicate that, although current techniques can show that blood is present, more specific inferences may be problematic.

■ Lawrence Keeley, *Experimental Determination of Stone Tool Functions* (1980). Patrick Vaughan, *Use-Wear Analysis of Flaked Stone Tools* (1985). Linda Owen and Guenther Unrath, "Technical Aspects of Microwear Studies on Stone Tools," *Early Man News* (1986). Douglas Bamforth, "Investigating Microwear Traces with Blind Tests: The Institute Results in Context," *Journal of Archaeological Science* 15 (1988): 11–23. Douglas Bamforth, George Burns, and Craig Woodman, "Ambiguous Use Traces and Blind Test Results: New Data," *Journal of Archaeological Science* 17 (1990): 413–430. Jerold Lowenstein, "Prehistoric Bloodstains," *Pacific Discovery* (1992): 46–47.

Douglas B. Bamforth

LONDON is situated close to where in the pre-Roman Iron Age would have been the tidal head of the River Thames. Prehistoric trackways probably crossed the Thames slightly to the west of the Roman town, with a probable ferry point between Westminster and Lambeth. Nevertheless, by ca. A.D. 50 a Roman settlement existed on the site of the later city, even though access to the south bank of the Thames at Southward could be achieved only by linking together a number of gravel islands surrounded by low-lying ground which was susceptible to flooding. Settlement took place on both sides of the river, but the main focus seems to have always been the north bank. This area was naturally divided by small tributaries of the Thames of which the Fleet marked the eastern limit of the Roman city whilst the Walbrook divided the city into two approximately equal parts.

In A.D. 66 the fledgling Roman town was sacked in the Boudiccan rebellion. Traces of destruction from this event show that settlement was concentrated to the east of the Walbrook, but had already spread to the west, along the western approach road, Watling Street.

By ca. A.D. 70 a timber bridge existed across the Thames. To its north lay a grid of streets arranged around a forum. The early town grew quickly, and a commercial and industrial suburb developed west of the Walbrook, where excavations at the GPO site in Newgate Street revealed buildings which were rebuilt several times in the later first and early second centuries. North of the suburb stood the Cripplegate Fort, also built in the early second century, and to its southeast, the amphitheater. East of the Walbrook, the forum itself was rebuilt on a larger scale in the early second century, as was the basilica to the north.

The town itself was not walled until the later second century, and then only on its landward side. The pace of development in the town seems to have slowed dramatically around this time, and parts of the city apparently reverted to a horticultural or agricultural land use in the late second or third centuries. Quantities of dark earth were dumped over the remains of demolished buildings, although the road system itself was mostly retained.

In the southwest quarter of the city a series of high-status and monumental structures were built. These include a probable temple, erected in A.D. 294 to 295, a large bath complex, excavated at Huggin Hill, and a series of structures identified as the Governor's Palace. At the northern limit of this complex stood the temple of Mithras, built on the west side of the Walbrook valley. During the fourth century the circuit of city walls was completed along the Thames riverfront while on the eastern part of the landward circuit bastions were added to the walls.

Outside of the walled city were extensive cemeteries, established in the first century and continuing in use to the beginning of the fifth century. Within the walls, the latest evidence for occupation comes from the strip of land immediately north of the river and east of the bridge, notably at the Tower of London, where a defensive work which may be attributed to Stilicho was excavated. In Southward, too, there is evidence for continued occupation through the fourth century.

The fifth and sixth centuries are sparsely represented by archaeology in London. The only secure evidence of activity within the city walls is a brooch from the middle of the fifth century found in the collapsed roof of a bathhouse at Billingsgate. In 604, however, the city was chosen as the seat of the first Anglo-Saxon bishop of the East Saxons. It is presumed therefore that the cathedral of St. Paul was founded at that time, although there is a long period in the middle of the seventh century when Christianity seems to have had a weak grip on the kingdom and when consequently the cathedral site may have been unoccupied.

By the middle of the seventh century there was also a port at London. Although lost from history until the middle of the 1980s, this port is now known to have been situated outside, to the west of the walled city, between Fleet Street and Trafalgar Square. From its small beginnings, around Charing Cross, the settlement expanded to the north, west, and east, but was probably severely affected by the Viking attacks of the mid-ninth century.

A royal palace may have existed within the walled city, on the side of the Cripplegate Fort, but the main reoccupation of the city took place in the late ninth century with the active encouragement of Alfred of Wessex, who is thought to have provided the city with a grid of streets to the west of the Walbrook.

By ca. 1050, the walled city was extensively occupied, reflected by the large number of churches then in existence. Along the riverside there is evidence for the use of the waterfront, in some areas dated by *dendrochronology to the middle of the eleventh century onward. The main consequence of the conquest for London was the construction of the White Tower in the southeast corner and of Baynard's Castle and Montfichet Tower in the southwest. To the west of the walled city, the Abbey of Westminster, which had existed from at least the eighth century, was completely remodeled by Edward the Confessor while the palace of Westminster was constructed in the reign of William Rufus. Extramural ribbon development along the major approach roads to the city also took place at this time, while inside the city walls the riverside wall was demolished and Thames Street was laid out on its line.

Early in the following century several religious houses were founded on the fringes of the city. The timber domestic houses characteristic of London until this time were mainly rebuilt in stone, often with stone cellars or undercrofts. From the middle of the twelfth century until the early fifteenth century reclamation took place to the south of Thames Street, organized on a property-by-property basis. The made ground associated with this reclamation is a rich source of artifacts, many of which can be closely dated by dendrochronology.

Both along the Thames waterfront in the western half of the walled city and outside the city walls along Holborn and the Strand a number of residences were built to house both lay and ecclesiastical lords. Their construction started in the thirteenth century and continued throughout the medieval period. Notable in the later period was the late fifteenth-century royal palace of Bridewell, on the west bank of the Fleet. The Tower of London too was retained as a royal residence, although it was used increasingly for the housing of high-status prisoners.

Following the dissolution of religious houses in the 1530s, many of their precincts were used as workshops, especially for immigrant craftsmen such as those at Holy Trinity Priory, which produced tin-glazed pottery. Later in the century the London clay-pipe industry was much in evidence—the city seems to have held a monopoly on pipe production in England for a generation and was an important pipe production center for the New World until the end of the seventeenth century. The pottery industry also flourished, notably at Dwight's Fulham pottery, established in the 1670s.

The civil war of the 1640s did not seem to affect London unduly, although soon afterward the city ditches were finally backfilled and housing built on their site. In the main, however, the walls survive to the present day. The Great Fire of 1666 had a much more devastating effect on the city and over a third of the walled area was razed to the ground. Post-fire rebuilding took place over a period of years, and among the main achievements of this period were the building of St. Paul's Cathedral and many of the city churches by Christopher Wren and others, and the straightening and the widening of several of the streets.

[See also BRITISH ISLES, *articles on* PREHISTORY OF THE BRITISH ISLES, ROMAN BRITAIN, THE ANGLO-SAXONS, MEDIEVAL BRITAIN, THE INDUSTRIAL REVOLUTION.]

Alan G. Vince

LONGSHAN. The Longshan Period refers to late prehistoric sites in the Yellow River Valley of northern China dating from ca. 2500 to 1900 B.C. Archaeologists have identified seven major regional types of Longshan culture. One important topic of research is identifying the cultural antecedents of the Xia, Shang, and Zhou dynasties. Another important topic is the development of sociopolitical complexity. Much work has been devoted to documenting the emergence of key features of early Chinese civilization. There are debates about the degree of complexity represented by the Longshan Period (such as chiefdom or state) and the process by which changes over time in sociopolitical organization took place.

There are many similarities in the kinds of remains found at sites throughout this wide area, suggesting extensive inter-regional interaction. One of the most distinguishing features of the period is the presence of relatively large (from about 2.5 acres [1 ha] to 49 acres [20 ha]) sites with surrounding walls of rammed earth (*hangtu*) such as Wangchenggang, Pingliangtai, and Chengziyai. Over ten walled sites have been found in five of the areas mentioned above. There are debates about the kinds of activities that took place at these sites and the significance of variation in size, architectural features, and remains of craft production. It is likely that elites lived at these protected settlements and sponsored the production of prestige goods such as metal items and labor-intensive pottery vessels.

There is evidence for craft production at sites without walled enclosures as well. Traces of metallurgy have been found at a few sites. There are debates about chemical composition, dating, and kinds of artifacts represented. It appears that the earliest evidence for cast bronze vessels dates to the late Longshan Period at the walled site of Wangchenggang in Henan. Thin-walled and other labor-intensive pottery vessels are more common. Tall, polished black beakers have been found at settlements in Henan and "eggshell-thin," tall-stemmed black cups at cemeteries such as Sanlihe in Shandong. Jade artifacts are more numerous in mortuary contexts. In each area, there is a wide variety of utilitarian pottery vessels. Some scholars propose that household specialization characterizes pottery production.

Finally, cemeteries in Shanxi such as Taosi and in Shandong provide evidence for social status differentiation. There is a marked variation in the size and the construction method of graves as well as the quality and quantity of artifacts. Similarly, there are differences in size and construction material for housing at habitation sites.

[See also ASIA: PREHISTORY AND EARLY HISTORY OF EAST ASIA; CHINA, articles on EARLY CIVILIZATIONS OF CHINA, SHANG CIVILIZATION.]

■ Kwang-chih Chang, The Archaeology of Ancient China, 4th Edition, (1986). Anne P. Underhill, "Pottery Production in Chiefdoms: The Longshan Period in Northern China," World Archaeology 23:1 (1991): 12–27. Anne P. Underhill, "Variation in Settlements During the Longshan Period of Northern China," Asian Perspectives 33:2 (1994): 197–228.

Anne P. Underhill

LOS MILLARES

LOS MILLARES was a fortified Copper Age (ca. 3000 to 2200 B.C.) settlement and cemetery of megalithic tombs, defended by thirteen outpost forts, and located on a promontory in the Middle Andarax Valley, Almeria Province, southeast Spain. Excavations have been undertaken by Louis Siret (1892), Martin Almagro and Antonio Arribas (1953 to 1957), and Arribas and Fernando Molina (from 1978). Los Millares is the type-site for the local Copper Age culture (the Millaran). Its domestic and funerary architecture (concentric dry-stone walls with bastions and towers, dry-stone walled passage graves with corbelled vaults), as well as associated cultural materials (metal artifacts, decorated pottery, fine bifacial flintwork, imported items of ivory and ostrich-egg shell) have formed the basis for debates over the local or external origins of this culture as well as for reconstructions of the local social organization.

The settlement occupies 12 acres (5 ha) and is the largest in the region. The "citadel" on the tip of the promontory is defended by three walls, the outermost located ca. 1,490 feet (450 m) from the "citadel," and cutting off access to the promontory. All walls were subject to multiple phases of building and the outer wall (the most recently constructed) had a "barbican" entrance at its center. Excavations have been confined mainly to the defenses, but areas of metalworking activity have been found. Of the associated outpost forts, the largest-scale excavations have concentrated on Fort 1, a multiphased construction of a central tower, two concentric stone walls with bastions, and two external ditches, the whole occupying a diameter of ca. 182 feet (55 m). Areas devoted to metalworking, the production of flint

arrowheads, and the processing and storage of cereals have been located here.

Over eighty megalithic tombs are visible outside the settlement. The majority are of the type mentioned above, but tombs without corbelled roofs also exist. The chronology of tomb construction and use is unclear, but analysis of tomb forms, sizes, numbers of burials, contents, and distributions suggests that the dead were selected for interment and that social ranking had emerged, with higher-ranked groups being buried in tombs located close to the settlement.

Survey in the Middle Andarax Valley has located a hinterland of smaller settlements and cemeteries contemporary with, and subordinate to, Los Millares. The network of forts enabled visual control of this hinterland, which had better water and agricultural resources than Los Millares. For the first time, this site can now be studied in a regional context.

[See also EUROPE: THE EUROPEAN COPPER AGE; MEGALITHIC TOMBS.]

■ A. Arribas et al., "Informe preliminar de los resultados obtenidos durante la VI campaña de excavaciones en el poblado de Los Millares, 1985," Anuario Arqueologico de Andalucia 1985 (1987): 245–262. R. W. Chapman, Emerging Complexity: The Later Prehistory of Southeast Spain, Iberia and the West Mediterranean (1990).

Robert Chapman

LUMINESCENCE DATING

LUMINESCENCE DATING. There are many varieties of luminescence. Artificial heating of some minerals produces thermoluminescence (TL). TL dating of fired *ceramics was first successfully developed at the University of Oxford (England) during the 1960s and 1970s, following some pioneering work in North America during the 1950s and 1960s using TL from rock minerals. The potential for TL dating of the last exposure of unheated sediments to sunlight was first recognized by Morozov and Shelkoplyas (1968–1971) at the Institute of Geology of the Ukrainian Academy of Sciences in Kiev. TL sediment dating was then developed into practical, accurate procedures at Simon Fraser University (Canada) in the late 1970s and early 1980s. Dating sediments using laser-light (or optically) stimulated luminescence (OSL) also originated at Simon Fraser University, in 1985. Such luminescence geochronometric methods supplement, and surpass, *radiocarbon dating because they can directly date the sediment grains or artifacts (pot shards) of interest and because they are applicable over the time range from a few hundred years to several hundred thousand years, well beyond the limit of standard radiocarbon dating, 30 to 40 thousand years.

Some mineral grains (e.g., quartz, feldspars, flint, pyroclastic glass) behave as natural radiation dosimeters when buried, storing as trapped electrons (at grain-defect sites) a portion of the energy deposited by background nuclear and cosmic radiations. Both the last exposure to daylight and the last heating event can be dated (but not for the same sample). Daylight empties light-sensitive electron traps; heating empties all electron traps. After burial, ionizing radiations repopulate emptied traps at a nearly constant rate. In the laboratory, traps are again emptied by either heating or intense illumination. The resulting electron-hole recombination (e.g., at grain impurity ions) produces luminescence (TL or OSL).

The longer the burial time (the sample's "age"), the larger the number of trapped electrons and the greater the intensity of luminescence. To translate this luminescence into an age in calendar years, two independent tasks are performed: known artificial doses of nuclear radiation (from calibrated radiation sources) are applied to subsamples to scale the signal, yielding an "equivalent dose" or D_E value (having units of grays or Gy); and the burial dose rate D_R (GY/year) is derived from measured radioactivity in portions of the sample grains and the surrounding sediments. Then the age $A = D_E/D_R$, independent of any other chronometric technique.

There are advantages and disadvantages to using TL or OSL. TL works best for heated grains (pot shards, volcanic glass shards, burnt flint, burnt sediment), where all the signal was acquired since burial. Unheated sediments retain at least a light-insensitive signal at burial. This relict signal must be subtracted from the measured TL signal to give a D_E value. However, recent research, using tests with known-age unheated sediments, has shown which subtraction and D_E-measuring procedures are accurate. Loess and beach sands up to 800,000 years old can now be dated. For lake and floodplain sediments, subtracting a relict signal is more difficult, but such waterlain sediments as old as approximately 300,000 years can now be dated accurately. An inherent advantage of TL is that luminescence from successively more retentive traps is released during the slow heating. The resulting internal stability test (plateau test) permits the longer-lived signal components to be isolated in a single experiment. In contrast, OSL lacks an internal plateau test, so additional (heating) experiments are needed to isolate the longer-lived components.

The consummate advantage of OSL is that, in principle, only a small or negligible correction is needed for relict OSL with unheated sediments, because only light-sensitive traps are emptied in the laboratory. This benefit produces a greater precision in OSL ages of unheated sediments, and a lower age limit (decades, rather than hundreds or thousands of years) than does TL. In practice, in some sediments that are deposited relatively quickly (e.g., fluvial, slope wash), individual grains inside clumps and slurries, for example, may be shielded from much daylight, thus carrying a large relict OSL signal when buried. Hence, geological processes need to be considered whenever OSL (and even TL) techniques are to be applied to unburnt sediments at archaeological sites. However, as unheated sediments are much more common than adequately heated materials at most archaeological sites, the sediment-dating capabilities of the TL and OSL clocks vastly extend the scope of luminescence dating for archaeological and paleoanthropological sites.

TL dating is well established for dating burnt pot shards, flint, and sediments at archaeological sites. An important recent example is the careful dating of burnt flints from two caves in Israel (Kebara and Qafzeh) at approximately 60,000 years B.P. and from Biache-Saint-Vaast in northern France at approximately 175,000 years B.P. Both results have dramatic implications for the history of *Neanderthals. The application of TL dating to relevant unheated sediments is less common, and OSL dating applications for such sites are still in their infancy. However, tests of OSL dating at controlled geological sites indicate the enormous potential utility of OSL dating techniques for archaeological sites.

[See also ARCHAEO-PALEOMAGNETIC DATING; DATING THE PAST; DENDROCHRONOLOGY; FISSION-TRACK DATING; OBSIDIAN HYDRATION DATING; POTASSIUM-ARGON DATING; STRAIGRAPHY.]

■ Martin J. Aitken, *Thermoluminescence Dating* (1985). David J. Huntley, Dorothy I. Godfrey-Smith, and Michael L. W. Thewalt, "Optical Dating of Sediments," *Nature* 313 (1985): 105–107. David J. Huntley, John T. Hutton, and John R. Prescott, "Optical Dating Using Inclusions within Quartz Grains," *Geology* 21 (1993): 1087–1090. Jeff Ollerhead, David J. Huntley, and Glenn W. Berger, "Luminescence Dating of the Buctouche Spit, New Brunswick," *Canadian Journal of Earth Sciences* 31 (1994): 523–531. Martin J. Aitken, "Optical Dating: A Review for Non-specialists," *Quaternary Science Reviews* (in press). Glenn W. Berger, "Thermoluminescence Dating of Sediments Older than ~100 ka," *Quaternary Science Reviews* 12 (in press).

Glenn W. Berger

M

MACHU PICCHU. Located in the forested lower Urubamba Valley of Peru, northwest of the ancient Inca capital
of *Cuzco, few archaeological sites have inspired the
imagination—of visitors as well as of archaeologists—as
much as Machu Picchu. The site lies on the cloud-covered
ridge between two mountains, Machu Picchu (in Quechua, "old Picchu") and Huayna Picchu ("young Picchu"),
which rise over three thousand feet (915 m) from the valley floor. Buildings are constructed of local white granite;
some have the finely fitted masonry seen in Cuzco. The
layout includes discrete groups, separated by walls,
streets, plazas, and terraces. Most buildings are single-
room rectangular structures which originally had steeply
pitched thatch roofs, appropriate for this tropical region.
In form and scale, these groupings are typical of planned
Inca residential structures. Several architectural groups
must have served less mundane ends. In these, finely fitted stonework merges with carved bedrock to sculpt out
eccentric spaces that shelter, or are oriented to face, carved
rock outcrops.

Machu Picchu first came to public attention when it was
"discovered" by the American explorer, Hiram Bingham, in
1911. Following directions given to him by colleagues in
Cuzco, Bingham entered the ruins on July 24. He cleared
away vegetation and mapped and photographed the site. In
1912 he returned to do more mapping and excavations
sponsored by Yale University and the National Geographic
Society. Based in part on the different styles of stonework he
observed at the site (finely fitted masonry and less well-
fitted coursed masonry) Bingham concluded that there
were two construction phases for Machu Picchu. The earlier
he attributed to the ancestors of the Inca kings, equating the
site with Tambo-Toqo, the mythical original caves of the
Incas mentioned by Spanish chroniclers. The later construction he attributed to Manco Inca, the post-Conquest Inca
leader who fled to the jungle and maintained an Inca
government-in-exile at a place called Vilcabamba, which
Bingham identified as Machu Picchu. Neither of these identifications is now accepted by experts, nor is Bingham's
claim that the site was entirely unknown to the Spaniards
after the fall of the Incas.

Machu Picchu is now considered to be part of the royal
estate developed by the Inca king Pachacuti, who reigned
from about A.D. 1438 to 1471. Both the style and the layout of
the architecture of this site are typical of Inca royal estates,
which generally provided housing and farmland for resident workers, housing for the owner and his relatives, and
places for the devotional activities required of the king and
the descendants who cared for his mummy. Stylistically,
Machu Picchu is consistent with other complexes built by
Pachacuti. Its identification is confirmed in a legal document from 1568 that notes his ownership of the lands
around Machu Picchu. His military conquest of this area is
confirmed in several Spanish chronicles.

[*See also* INCA CIVILIZATION, *articles on* INCA RULING DY-
NASTIES, INCA ECONOMIC ORGANIZATION, INCA RELIGION,
PIZARRO AND THE CONQUEST OF THE INCAS.]

■ Hiram Bingham, *Inca Land* (1922). Hiram Bingham, *Machu Picchu:
A Citadel of the Incas* (1930). Hiram Bingham, *Lost City of the Incas: The
Story of Machu Picchu and Its Builders* (1948). Alfred M. Bingham,
Portrait of an Explorer: Hiram Bingham, Discoverer of Machu Picchu
(1989). John H. Rowe, "Machu Picchu a la luz dedocumentos de
siglo XVI," *Histórica* 14(1)(1990): 139–154.

Susan A. Niles

MADAGASCAR is large subtropical island lying off the
coast of southern Africa; it has a highly variable ecology and
climate, with rainfall ranging from 2 to 14 inches (50 to 350
mm). It is of great biological interest through its unique
Miocene fauna, which survived through separation from
continental Africa, 35 million years ago. The island also
presents a case study of humanity's impact upon this fragile
environment during the last two thousand years, with the
rapid extinction of surviving megafauna, such as the elephant bird, giant tortoises, and hippos, as well as species of
primate and carnivore.

The settlement history of Madagascar remains unresolved in detail. An Austronesian language, Malagasy, is
spoken over the whole island, with the exception of a few
ki-Swahili speakers on the north coast. Malagasy has been
closely compared to Maanyan, spoken in the Barito valley
of Borneo, although a general origin within insular Southeast Asia is now thought most likely. Attempts to use glottochronology and linguistic predictions, based on the general absence of Sanskrit words in Malagasy, have indicated
settlement from Southeast Asia between 1000 and 2000 B.P.
Ethnographic evidence also supports theories of Austronesian settlement on Madagascar, with material culture indicators such as looms, smelting techniques and outrigger
canoes, architecture, and introduced food crops and cultivation techniques.

A "Bantu substratum" has also been recognized linguistically and culturally. This could have been due to
earlier African settlement of the island, or because the
Austronesian settlers arrived via the East African coast, or
through later-settlement East African coastal groups. It is
generally thought that the widespread cattle pastoralism
practiced in the central highlands is of East African origin,
while the coastal communities in the north were clearly
linked into the Swahili trading complex.

Archaeological evidence for settlement prior to A.D. 1000
is scant. In the southwest, subfossil remains of extinct large
animals have been studied; a few, excavated at the turn of
the century, show evidence of butchery marks. Radiocar-

bon dates on bones from Ambolisatra and Lanboharana range from A.D. 80 to 380, but these isolated dates are unreliable. Pollen core analysis suggests that the clearance of woodland and the development of grasslands, linked to human impact, dates to A.D. 150 through 190. The southwest end of the island does seem to be an unlikely location for primary Austronesian colonization; settlement at this date from continental Africa is a possibility in view of the recent discovery of early Iron Age coastal sites in Mozambique.

In the far north, a rock shelter has been excavated at Lakaton'i Anja, in which early deposits were found sealed below imported Near Eastern sgraffiato pottery from the eleventh to the thirteenth centuries. Earthenware pottery was associated with animal and fish bone, and associated carbon dated from A.D. 250 to 970; there is nothing distinctively "Austronesian" about this occupation, and it may be linked to coastal groups involved in Indian Ocean trade, exploiting the forests for their natural products, such as copal and honey.

One of the exports of Madagascar was chlorite schist, traded from around A.D. 900, when it first appears on Swahili sites of the East African coast. On Madagascar, the island site of Nosy Mangabe, with a radiocarbon date of A.D. 670 to 980, contains chlorite schist, as well as local pottery and imported Near Eastern white-glazed wares of ca. 800 to 1000. The earliest proto-urban site is Mahilaka, on the northwest coast, with stone buildings as well as mosques, dating from the eleventh to the fourteenth centuries. Scattered villages, including Nosy Be and Irodo, are known from the northeast and northwest coasts but with little direct evidence for Islam. The large cemetery of Vohémar contained numerous graves oriented in the correct Muslim position but furnished with schist vessels and Chinese ceramics. A coastal population may have been heavily influenced by Islam and the Swahili world, but retained its local identity. After European contact in the sixteenth century and the introduction of firearms, two independent trading polities, Betsimisaraka and Sakalava, developed on the north coast.

Evidence for settlement away from the coast in the central highlands dates from the thirteenth century. The sites of Fiekena and Ankadivory seem to be associated with a largely cattle-keeping economy. Settlements increased in size and complexity, although a change occurred in the fifteenth century, with the presence of rice at Fanongoavana. During the next two hundred years, the Merina state developed in the central highlands, based on irrigated rice cultivation. Large polygonal fortresses were built as central places controlling smaller forts and villages.

[See also AFRICA: EARLY IRON AGE SETTLEMENTS OF SUB-SAHARAN AFRICA; EAST AFRICA: COASTAL TOWNS OF EAST AFRICA; TRADE, AFRICAN.]

■ J. Mack, Island of Ancestors (1986). P. Vérin, The History of Civilisation in North Madagascar (1986). R. Dewar and H. T. Wright, "The Culture History of Madagascar," Journal of World Prehistory 7(4)(1993): 417–466.

Mark Horton

MAIDEN CASTLE is one of the most famous and impressive monuments of the chalk downs of southern England. Two major excavation campaigns have been undertaken. The first, in the late 1930s, was directed by Sir Mortimer *Wheeler, and was of considerable importance in establishing a scientific approach to archaeological excavation. In particular, it provided a detailed exposition of the importance of *stratigraphy. The second was in the mid-1980s,

conducted by the author. This built on Wheeler's work by recovering a suite of environmental and ecological data. These excavations have provided a clear picture of a long history of occupation on the hilltop, and have made a valuable contribution to understanding the Neolithic and Iron Age of southern England.

The principal feature of the Neolithic occupation was an enclosure (or causewayed camp) dating to about 4000 B.C., defined by two concentric ditches. Enclosures such as these are a common feature of the Neolithic occupation of southern England; the Maiden Castle enclosure is a particularly large one (15.8 acres [6.4 ha]) but like the others there is very little evidence for buildings in the interior. There was a large quantity of occupation debris in its inner ditch, however, which indicates that this enclosure was an important center, and was probably inhabited for at least part of the year. The material included large quantities of animal bone and crop remains which show that the occupants had a mixed agricultural economy specializing in cattle herding and the production of emmer wheat. Wild plants were harvested, but there is very little evidence for the hunting of wild animals. Large quantities of flint tools and debris, fine quality ceramics, and stone axes were also found. The axes and ceramics were imported from Cornwall and it seems likely that the occupants of the enclosure were producing flint axes to exchange for these prestigious goods. The abandonment of the Neolithic enclosure occurred about 3500 B.C. and appears to have been quite sudden. Soon after, a long barrow, which lay adjacent to the western edge of the enclosure, was extended to create a "bank barrow" over 1,791 feet (546 m) long, reaching across the ditches and into its interior. The "bank barrow" may have marked a boundary between two quite separate economic territories. After the construction of this unique monument the hilltop appears to have been abandoned for several hundred years.

At the beginning of the Iron Age (ca. 500 B.C.) another enclosure, consisting of a large single bank and ditch, was constructed over the original Neolithic ditches. From the establishment of this hill fort to the Roman invasion, occupation inside the enclosure was continuous and permanent, but the form and significance of the hill fort changed considerably. One of the principal activities in the first three hundred years of the hill fort was the construction, modification, and reconstruction of the enclosing banks and ditches. After a refurbishment of the original defenses, the enclosure was extended to the west to enclose a further 31 acres (12.6 ha). Further external ramparts and ditches were then constructed and the original inner rampart was heightened. By the second century B.C. the hilltop was enclosed by three to four lines of ramparts and ditches and the inner rampart stood over 18 feet (5.5 m) high. The exceptional double-portaled gateways to the east and west are a maze of overlapping banks and ditches which form an imposing entrance even to present-day visitors. The original hill fort was similar to many others found in southern England at this time, but hill forts similar to the later "developed" one are less common. Maiden Castle is in fact one of the largest and most elaborately enclosed hill forts in Europe.

At the beginning of the Iron Age occupation, the interior of the fort was only sparsely used. Dispersed groups of small circular houses, silos for grain storage, and ancillary structures are found scattered across the hilltop. Gradually houses and, presumably, their inhabitants increased in numbers. This coincided with the abandonment of neighboring settlements. Around 250 B.C., at the end of the principal period of rampart building, a major reorganization of this settlement appears to have occurred, so that rows of houses straddled the hilltop forming streets running between the east and west entrances. At this time, the settlement, though nucleated, was dominated by agricultural activities. Very large quantities of grain were brought to the site for processing, storage, and consumption. Numerically, sheep dominated the pastoral economy, but cattle were probably economically more important. There was a rich and varied material culture with large quantities of ceramics, stone, bone, and metal tools used and discarded on the settlement. Most of these items were produced by individual households with little sign of any specialized industries. If specialist products were required (for example, iron and bronze tools), these were obtained from settlements at some considerable distance from the fort where craft production was concentrated.

In the first century B.C. there was a further dramatic reorganization of the settlement. Much of the enclosed area was abandoned, the inhabitants apparently moving to settlements in the surrounding landscape. The remaining occupants were concentrated in the primary hill fort. In contrast to the period when the hill fort was densely occupied, large quantities of the objects in everyday use, including most of the ceramics used by the inhabitants, were produced by specialists. Most of these were imported from other settlements but just outside the eastern gateway there was a smith's workshop indicating that specialists now also worked at Maiden Castle itself. Further out among the earthworks of the gateway was a large cemetery with individuals placed in graves in a characteristically crouched position. Cemeteries similar to this developed in Dorset at the beginning of the Late Iron Age and formed one of the defining cultural characteristics of the tribe known by the Romans as the Durotriges. The Maiden Castle cemetery, however, has various peculiarities: paired burials, extended burials, and burials of individuals who have suffered mortal injuries. These peculiarities and other features were used by Wheeler to suggest that the hillfort was stormed by the Roman army during the conquest of southern England, and the historical re-creation he imagined has proved very popular and enduring among the general public.

Detailed and extensive excavations of the developed hill forts of southern England will always be exceptional, as these proto-urban settlements are some of the most complex and productive prehistoric settlements in the British Isles. The sequence at Maiden Castle will always remain crucial to the interpretation of this period as it demonstrates the complex transformation in material culture and settlement form that preceded the Roman conquest of southern England. The site will also retain an enduring academic importance as one of the test beds for scientific archaeology in the twentieth century.

[See also BRITISH ISLES: PREHISTORY OF THE BRITISH ISLES; EUROPE, articles on THE EUROPEAN NEOLITHIC PERIOD, THE EUROPEAN IRON AGE.]

■ R.E.M. Wheeler, Maiden Castle (1943). N. M. Sharples, Maiden Castle: Excavation and Field Survey 1985–86 (1991). N. M. Sharples, The English Heritage Book of Maiden Castle (1991).

Niall M. Sharples

MAIKOP. At Maikop (also spelled "Maykop" in some English-language literature), on the Belaya River in the Kuban region of Russia, north of the Caucasus Mountains and east of the Black Sea, a large burial tumulus was opened in 1897. The "Maikop Kurgan" was about 33 feet (10 m) high, about 656 feet (200 m) in circumference, and contained two graves, a rather impoverished one lying on the prehistoric ground surface under the mound, and a spectacularly rich one in a sunken chamber. The rich burial contained a tripartite wooden mortuary structure with a stone pavement, 18 by 12 feet (5.5 by 3.75 m), each part with a single skeleton. In the two smaller chambers were the skeletons of females, while the larger chamber contained a male. The skeletons were lightly flexed and accompanied by red ocher.

The finds in the Maikop mortuary chamber, particularly those associated with the male burial, are extraordinary. Four silver and gold posts with cast golden finials in the shape of three-dimensional bulls supported a canopy with 135 figures of bulls and lions as frontal ornaments. The burial itself featured a gold diadem with rosettes, carnelian, turquoise, and gold beads and earrings, six rings of gold and silver, and seventeen vessels of gold, silver, and stone. Two of the bowls were decorated with engraved figures of mountains, streams, and animals (again, lions and bulls). Nearby were tools and weapons of copper and bronze, flint arrowheads, and a number of ceramic vessels.

The various artifacts in the Maikop tumulus are interpreted as emblems of royalty or divinity. They have parallels to materials from Early Dynastic III contexts in Mesopotamia and from Alaça Hoyuk in *Anatolia, making it probable that the Maikop grave dates between 2500 and 2200 B.C. Although arguments have been advanced for an earlier dating for Maikop, contemporaneous with the Copper Age cultures of the Black Sea region in the late fourth millennium B.C., such a dating is difficult to support at the moment in light of the strong parallels to the finds in Mesopotamia and Anatolia.

Over the last century, other rich burials have been found at Tsarskaya (now Novosvobodnaya—with a "dolmen"-like stone cist), Nalchik (a collective tomb with 120 burials), and Stavropol, all in the Kuban region. These burials, along with a number of settlements such as the large site at Meshoko, make up what is known as the "Maikop Culture" of the Early Bronze Age in the Kuban region. The settlements are distinguished by stone defensive walls which enclose up to ten houses.

[See also EUROPE: THE EUROPEAN BRONZE AGE.]

■ A. M. Tallgren, "Maikop" in Reallexikon der Vorgeschichte, ed. Max Ebert (1927), pp. 347–348. A. M. Tallgren, "The Dolmens of North Caucasia," Antiquity 7 (1933): 190–202. V. Gordon Childe, "The Axes from Maikop and Caucasian Metallurgy," Annals of Archaeology and Anthropology 23 (1936): 113–119. Tadeusz Sulimirski, Prehistoric Russia, an Outline (1970). Peter Glumac and David Anthony, "Culture and Environment in the Prehistory Caucasus: the Neolithic through the Early Bronze Age," in Chronologies in Old World Archaeology, third edition, ed. Robert W. Ehrich (1992), pp. 196–206.

Peter Bogucki

MALTA. The Maltese Archipelago consists of small rocky islands approximately 62 miles (100 km) south of Sicily forming a land bridge between Africa and Sicily and centrally situated between the western and the eastern basins of the Mediterranean Sea. Two islands are inhabited, Malta, with 95 square miles (246 sq km), and Gozo with 26 square miles (67 sq km). In addition, there are some very small islands which are now uninhabited, such as Comino between Malta and Gozo, and Filfila to the southeast of Malta.

Functionally, the islands are miniature continents, each

self-contained and culturally independent. Malta has seen two eras of great splendor, the Neolithic Period (fifth through third millennium B.C.) and the time of the Knights of St. John (sixteenth to eighteenth century A.D.).

The Neolithic Period. The first people settling on Malta found the islands very different from the stony and barren appearance of today. They were covered by low forest and brush land and as the sea level was much lower, the islands were larger, making them closer to Sicily than today. The impressed decorations on the pottery from the Ghar Dalam Cave, where the earliest evidence of human activity was found, point to connections with the Stentinello Culture on *Sicily and date to the late fifth or early fourth millennium B.C. Flint also was imported from Sicily, while obsidian came from the Aeolian Islands. Evidence of the earliest period, called *Ghar Dalam Phase* after the first site of its discovery, is apparent at Skorba, with some primitive architecture of daub with wattle on stone foundations.

The following periods, the Grey Skorba Phase and the Red Skorba Phase, cover the fifth millennium B.C. Little is known about these and the next two periods of the early fourth millennium, the Zebbug and Mgarr Phases. The pottery, the flint and obsidian tools, as well as the few pieces of artworks, such as terra-cotta figurines of standing females with stylized heads, show a continued contact with Sicily. The tombs initially consisted of shallow oval pits which were made deeper and more elaborate in later periods.

During the Mgarr Phase, ca. 3600 to 3500 B.C., the tomb architecture developed into the complex rock-cut tombs at Xemxija. This was the period when contacts with Sicily became rare as the sea level reached its present height. We now witness the beginning of an insular personality in the material culture and, in particular, in the realm of spiritual and ritual life. The emphasis appears to have been on the cult of the Mediterranean Great Mother engendering the construction of unique cult centers.

The next three periods, the Ggantija Phase of the second half of the fourth millennium, the Saflieni Phase around 3000 B.C., and the Tarxien Phase of the early third millennium B.C. saw an unprecedented and unparalleled development of a society which erected some of the most impressive monuments of the entire Old World, one thousand years earlier than the monuments of Egypt. With the exception of some of the megalithic monuments of the Iberian Peninsula or of Brittany, it is the oldest monumental architecture still surviving to date. There are enigmatic indications of close contacts with the megalithic Chassey culture of France, such as lightly scratched lines on pottery to hold crested decorations and handles with V-shaped holes.

The earliest evidence of the characteristic trefoil temples is found at Ta Hagrat, Skorba, and Kordin III. They probably developed out of the layout of oval houses with a sunken floor, entered on the long side and combined with conceptions of rock-cut tombs to create artificial caves as symbols of the entrance to the netherworld or the womb of mother earth. A central apse opposite the entrance was added to the original simple oval structure, or two ovals were joined, one behind the other, resulting in the classic design of the temples of Ggantija South and Hagar Qim. This was the beginning of the true megalithic tradition of temple building on Malta and Gozo. Massive boulders of coralline limestone, some up to 20 feet (6 m) long and weighing 50 tons, form the outer wall of the Ggantija. They are arranged in a rhythm of headers and stretchers, with 13-foot-high (4 m) monoliths used as doorjambs of the monumental entrance. The facades of the temples, normally facing southeast, form a concave curve creating a ceremonial space for public rituals which was on a raised platform and probably enclosed.

The space between the outer and the inner walls was filled with rubble. These walls had no relationship with one another, as the outer walls were generally circular, whereas the interior walls formed three or more apses. These interior walls, stuccoed and painted, were erected over a dado of large orthostats with each row of stones slightly projecting inward.

According to small contemporary models and a carving on the entrance of the temple at Mnajdra, the roofing appears to have consisted of wooden beams and packed earth. The various apses of the interior were furnished with altars, offering tables or other ritual objects. The floors consisted of large flagstones and of torba, a hard cement made with crushed globigerina and water.

Rock-cut tombs of the Ggantija Phase were found at Xemxija, Borg en-Nadur, and the earliest phase of the Hypogeum of Hal Saflieni at Paola near Valetta.

In the course of time, the design of the temples became more complicated by adding more and more rooms into an intricate labyrinth, such as at Hagar Qim, or by duplicating the same basic design beside the old structure, such as at the Ggantija and Mnajdra, resulting in twin temples. The younger structures show increasingly regularly squared and dressed stonework. The outer room increased in size, and probably in ritual importance, whereas the inner central apse was made smaller and became a mere niche. Small openings, called oracle holes, led to tiny spaces behind the inner walls. Many blocks of the interior were now decorated with a pecked design to hold a pigment or reliefs of spirals and other plant motives. The temples were filled with human statues of corpulent figures, apparently mostly females but also many without any indication of gender. The peak of this late and highly artistic phase is found at Hal Tarxien, with its profusely decorated stone slabs, altars, animal reliefs, and human figures, including the lower part of a huge statue of a female deity whose height must have reached 10 to 13 feet (3 to 4 m).

Twenty-four temples are known today, some in pairs, resulting in fourteen sanctuaries evenly spaced out over the two main islands. It has been suggested that this distribution pattern offers a territorial division comparable to the modern parishes. The most important remaining temples today are Ggantija on Gozo, Skorba, Kordin, Hagar Qim/Mnajdra, and Hal Tarxien on Malta.

The Hypogeum was enlarged during the Tarxien Phase and a series of rooms on three levels were carved out of the soft rock. An impressive facade of a temple was created underground. The rooms were painted with spiral or geometric designs in red ocher. Some of the most beautiful pieces of Maltese art, such as the "Sleeping Ladies" and a plate decorated with representations of animals, were found here. There is little doubt that a variety of ritual functions took place in the Hypogeum, perhaps as a place of healing or meditation, besides its funerary function, which could be a late phenomenon. It has been estimated that some seven thousand burials took place in the Hypogeum. There is evidence that a temple stood on the surface above it.

We know nothing about the events leading to the end of this culture. As long as we are ignorant about Malta's prehistoric peoples' daily life, social order, economy, diet, domestic architecture, settlement pattern, or even their everyday pottery (most of the pottery we know was found in or near temple complexes or in tombs), we cannot even attempt to guess the causes of the decline of this magnificent culture. It may have been a combination of overexploration of an already fragile environment and its resources leading to famine and disease, or invasions which might have led to collapse. Or was it simply that this archaic and isolated culture had run its course and died a natural death?

Chalcolithic Period, Bronze and Iron Ages, and Historical Periods. The question of a gap in occupation after the end of the Neolithic culture was often raised but appears to be quite unlikely. Most probably, life simply returned to the level of a primitive subsistence economy of fishermen and horticulturists of the earlier periods. Based on his estimate that monumental building had ended by the middle of the third millennium B.C., Mattanyah Zohar suggests that the general ecological and economical crises which affected the central and eastern Mediterranean countries and northern Africa at the end of the Levantine Early Bronze Age and the end of the Old Kingdom in Egypt also took their toll on Malta.

The Chalcolithic Tarxien Cemetery Phase of the end of the third millennium B.C. was found embedded into the ruins of the Hal Tarxien temple, which was abandoned for several centuries and covered by a layer of sedimentary soil. This gave rise to the previously mentioned theory of a gap of occupation between the Tarxien and the Tarxien Cemetery Phases. There is, however, no other corroborative evidence from other sites on the island or on Gozo to confirm this and it appears that some of the temples were in continuous use. The introduction of cremation with urns covered by dolmens and cairns and the first appearance of metal make it clear that a new people had arrived and that an entirely new culture had begun. The pottery of this phase is related to the pebble-burnished pottery of Capo Graziano of Lipari. There is, however, no hard evidence supporting the hypothesis that these newcomers were directly responsible for the end of the preceding culture.

The next period, the Bronze Age Borġ-en-Nadur-Phase, was probably introduced by another immigration from Sicily around 1500 B.C. or slightly earlier. Fortified settlements were erected on promontories or on defendable hilltops similar to those found on contemporary Sicily and in Apulia. The mysterious so-called cart tracks often found in the vicinity of these settlements are probably the remains of some sort of water-catching devices for irrigation and/or against soil erosion. Bronze or copper weapons and ornaments indicate a warlike aristocracy who probably engaged in piracy or other lucrative seagoing activities and possibly were even drawn into the maelstrom of the famous "Sea People Invasion" of the eastern Mediterranean during the thirteenth and twelfth centuries B.C.

After an evasive Late Bronze Age Bahrija Phase at the beginning of the first millennium B.C., the Phoenicians and Cartheginians began to dominate the region around 850 B.C. Little is known from that period, and apart from a relatively large number of rock-cut tombs and their contents, no architectural remains have survived. The end of the Second Punic War and the defeat of *Carthage in 218 B.C. brought the Romans, who also left hardly any material traces except the remains of a Roman villa in Rabat and a few early Christian catacombs. The islands shifted hands at various times. The Byzantines lost Malta in A.D. 869 to the Arabs who Islamized and Arabized the inhabitants. Their princi-

pal legacy is the Maltese language, an Arab dialect mixed with a large amount of Italian words and written in Latin script. The legacy of the Normans, who ruled Malta from 1090 on, is mainly preserved in Victoria on Gozo. The Spaniards ruled Malta from 1284 on, and in 1530, Charles V handed the islands over to the Order of the Knights of St. John, who built the beautiful Barock architecture to be seen in Valetta and Medina. They were expelled by Napoleon in 1798, and in 1800 the rule of Britain began. In 1964, Malta became an independent republic.

[*See also* MEDITERRANEAN TRADE; MEDITERRANEAN WORLD: THE MEDITERRANEAN PRE-BRONZE AGE.]

■ H.P.T. Hyde, *The Geology of the Maltese Islands* (1955). J. D. Evans, *Malta* (1959). D. H. Trump, *Skorba. Excavations Carried Out on Behalf of the National Museum of Malta 1961–1963* (1966). J. D. Evans, *Prehistoric Antiquities of the Maltese Islands* (1971). D. H. Trump, *Malta: An Archaeological Guide* (1972). M. Ridley, *The Megalithic Art of the Maltese Islands* (1976). H. Lewis, *Ancient Malta. A Study of Its Antiquities* (1977). D. H. Trump, "Megalithic Architecture in Malta," in *The Megalithic Monuments of Western Europe*, C. Renfrew, ed. (1983). A. Bonanno, "A Socio-Economic Approach to Maltese Prehistory: The Temple Builders," in *Malta—Studies of Its Heritage and History* (1986).

Mattanyah Zohar

MANCHING. The most extensively excavated Iron Age oppidum (an urban site) in Europe is at Manching, near Ingolstadt in Bavaria. It controls the major east–west route running along the Danube, and sits astride the gravel terrace south of the river, at a point where the easily traversed land narrows to a few hundred meters; it also controls the crossing of the River Paar, a tributary of the Danube. With *murus gallicus* rampart constructed perhaps as early as 120 B.C., and pincer gate entrances, its early defenses are typical of the western European oppida. These ramparts, enclosing a roughly circular area of 865 acres (350 ha), were subsequently twice reconstructed in the style of central European oppida, with a dump rampart revetted in front with a wall of vertical posts and drystone walling.

In other respects Manching is a very atypical oppidum. Lying on the gravel terrace just above the river floodplain, it is not in a naturally defensive position. This is due to its origin as an open, undefended settlement; the defenses were constructed late in its history. The earliest phase of settlement, presumably a small agricultural village, has not yet been excavated, but its existence is demonstrated by a small inhumation cemetery at Hundsrucken in the center of the later oppidum and dating to the third or second century B.C. As is characteristic for the period, the men are generally buried with weapons—sword, spear, and shield—and the women with their bronze ornaments. The subsequent gradual expansion of the settlement is documented by the wider and wider distribution of brooches and other datable objects; the early ones are found only near the center of the oppidum, and the later throughout the enclosed area. This gradual development from village to urban settlement is unique among the Iron Age oppida.

The extensive excavations initiated by Werner Krämer in the 1950s, and still continuing, have shown a dense clustering of small workshops along the main east–west road, in the area excavated, apparently occupied by specialists in textile production. Other areas produced slag and other debris from metalworking; one of the palisaded enclosures, for instance, contained a dense concentration of fragments of coin molds for gold and silver coins. Different quarters of the site may have had their own specialties. Slag from smithing iron is fairly widely scattered over the settlement, some of the iron being smelted from bog iron deposits a few hundred meters south of the oppidum; other iron was probably imported from the oppidum of Kelheim 31 miles (50 km) down the Danube. The extensive finds of iron objects at Manching and other contemporary sites are testimony of an enormous upsurge in iron production at this period, including items such as keys, personal ornaments, swords, spears, and shield bosses, as well as a wide range of specialist tools, including various types of hammer, files, compasses, drills, plowshares, wagon fittings, and sickles.

Though kilns have not been located, Manching was certainly a center of pottery production. For the high-quality *Graphittonkeramik* cooking pots, special clay containing graphite had to be imported from Passau 124 miles (200 km) downstream; the products were traded widely in central and southern Germany, even reaching central France. Fine painted wares and wheel-turned and handmade domestic and storage vessels were also mass produced. From outside, Italian wine amphorae and fine table wares reached the site in small quantities.

The demise of Manching is still a matter of controversy. Few scholars would not suggest that it survived until the time of the Roman conquest in 15 B.C., as it seems to have been abandoned around the middle of the first century B.C. Destruction by Germanic invaders from the north is one suggestion, but the recent excavation in the north of the *oppidum* indicates that occupation there continued later than elsewhere, suggesting a more gradual decline and abandonment.

[*See also* EUROPE: THE EUROPEAN IRON AGE; HILL FORTS.]

■ *Ausgrabungen in Manching* (series). *Germania* (periodical). H. Dannheimer and R. Gebhard, eds. *Das Keltische Jahrtausend* (1993).

John Collis

MAPUNGUBWE AND TOUTSWEMOGALA.

Mapungubwe (on the borders of South Africa) and Toutswemogala (in Botswana) are the sites of two of the earliest towns in southern Africa. Standing at the threshold between the small, dispersed farming villages of the southern African Early Iron Age and the complex, centralized state formed around *Great Zimbabwe, Mapungubwe and Toutswemogala are crucial to understanding the second millennium south of the Zambezi River.

Mapungubwe, named after a stark, sandstone outcrop that rises abruptly from the arid valley of the Limpopo River, was first discovered by a local farmer who chanced on gold grave goods that had eroded out of their context. Seen as South Africa's equivalent to Great Zimbabwe, the land was purchased by the South African government and an ambitious excavation program initiated. However, the site had a checkered history, with bizarre interpretations of some of the finds, long delays in publication, and stratigraphic sequences that have made little sense. Mapungubwe was initially believed to be an offshoot of Great Zimbabwe, but radiocarbon date series have shown convincingly that it entirely predated the stone-walled buildings on the edge of the plateau to the north of the river. The most recent excavations, now completed some years ago, were carried out by the University of Pretoria, but the full results have not been made available.

In order to understand developments at Mapungubwe, it is necessary to consider earlier Iron Age settlement in its immediate hinterland. Southern Africa's first farmers eschewed this area—not surprisingly, given its arid conditions—but after about A.D. 800 a number of villages were built close to the Limpopo. Excavation of sites such as Pont Drift and Schroda have revealed an economy in which cattle, sheep, and goats were overwhelmingly important. But excavation has also shown that villagers had obtained cowrie shells from the Indian Ocean coast as well as glass trade beads, not made in Africa but ubiquitous stock for Arab traders who, by this time, were regularly mounting expeditions south of the Limpopo River mouth. Copper and iron were probably also traded, while the unusual number of carnivore bones in Schroda's rubbish middens, as well as slivers of elephant ivory, suggest that villagers were obtaining exotic goods in return for animal pelts and tusks.

A further village to benefit from trade connections with the faraway coast was K2 (so named by an excavator because the massive rubbish middens reminded him of settlement mounds, or *koms*, in North Africa). K2, occupied in the tenth and eleventh centuries, was in the shadow of Mapungubwe Hill. It has been suggested that the village grew to become too big for itself; long-established methods of marking out high status by residence at the head of an elliptical arrangement of huts became impractical as the population grew, and a more pronounced way of underlining authority through settlement design became essential. The solution, according to this interpretation, was to take full advantage of the topography of Mapungubwe Hill, building an enclave for those in power high on its summit.

The first buildings were erected on the top of Mapungubwe Hill early in the twelfth century. The remnants of successive houses have been unearthed, as have richly adorned burials. More closely packed houses clustered around the foot of the hill, rebuilt repeatedly as their mudand-thatch construction yielded to the harsh climate. Apart from continuing to make use of the now long-established trade links with the coast, the people of Mapungubwe also seem to have specialized in crafts such as ivory working (particularly bracelets), manufacturing bone points, and weaving—the latter indicating indirectly that exotic cotton plants were by this stage being cultivated.

As with complex societies in other parts of the world, it is probable that Mapungubwe was at the head of a hierarchy of lesser settlements. Contemporary, somewhat smaller sites with similar planning arrangements have been described from within a 62-mile (100-km) radius of Mapungubwe. However, little research has been conducted on the nature of the connections between such places, or on the small villages in which ordinary people must have continued to live, as they had since the earliest farming settlement.

In contrast, a considerable amount is known about Toutswemogala's allied settlements and hinterland. These sites are grouped together as the Toutswe Tradition, which is dated to between about A.D. 700 and 1300. They are found where the upper catchment of the Limpopo River meets the eastern edge of the Kalahari Desert, and have a distinct hierarchy in their size. The smallest sites in a variety of topographical locations have shallow deposits with little evidence for successive reoccupation. Settlements in the second category are significantly larger, have hilltop locations, and were occupied for periods of up to three hundred years. The largest Toutswe sites—Bosutswe, Shoshong, and Toutswemogala itself—are about 100 kilometers from one another and were built on well-protected hill summits. They have massive midden accumulations, indicating that they were towns ten times larger than the middle category of Toutswe "'regional centres."

Toutswemogala was initially believed to be an isolated ironworking site, but its massive accumulations of vitrified deposit were later identified as burnt animal dung. Many Toutswe sites have proved to have this distinctive feature, resulting in dense stands of buffalo grass, which are conspicuous on air photographs. Excavation has revealed a long series of stratified house floors and stone enclosures that, by ethnographic analogy, have been interpreted as men's assembly areas. The radical differences in the sizes of Toutswe Tradition settlements is strong circumstantial evidence for the accumulation of wealth at Toutswemogala, presumably in the form of livestock. But in contrast to contemporary Mapungubwe and other settlements farther down the Limpopo, there is little evidence for trade in exotic imports originating from the East African coast. At present, then, the nature of the relationship between Toutswemogala and Mapungubwe remains unknown.

Both Mapungubwe and Toutswemogala went into decline in the twelfth and thirteenth centuries, and were eventually completely abandoned. Warfare, bubonic plague, and environmental deterioration are suspected as culprits, perhaps because of the rise of Great Zimbabwe to the north. It is probable that the early Zimbabwe state cut off the Limpopo Valley routes with the coast, taking for itself the lucrative trade that must have been essential to the survival of the elite inhabitants of hilltop enclaves.

[See also KHAMI; SOUTHERN AFRICA, LATER IRON AGE SOCIETIES OF; TRADE, AFRICAN.]

■ L. Lepionka, "Excavations at Toutswemogala," *Botswana Notes and Records* 9 (1978): 1–16. James Denbow, "Cows and Kings: A Spatial and Economic Analysis of a Hierarchical Early Iron Age Settlement System in Eastern Botswana," in *Frontiers: Southern African Archaeology Today*, ed. M. Hall et al. (1984). Thomas Huffman, "Iron Age Settlement Patterns and the Origins of Class Distinction in Southern Africa," *Advances in World Archaeology* 5 (1986): 291–338. Martin Hall, *Farmers, Kings and Traders: The People of Southern Africa, 200–1860* (1990).

Martin Hall

MARI, the modern Tell Hariri, is located along the middle reaches of the Euphrates River in Syria, about 31 miles (50 km) upstream from the Iraqi border. The site, somewhat more than 124 acres (50 ha) in size, sits in the river valley, with the desert plateau rising behind to the west and the present-day course of the river flowing some 1.2 miles (2 km) to the east. French archaeologists, led first by André Parrot and after 1979 by Jean-Claude Margueron, have been working at the site since its discovery in 1933.

Founded at the beginning of the Early Dynastic Period (ca. 3000–2334 B.C.), Mari was on the northwestern periphery of the Mesopotamian heartland, well situated to benefit from the traffic and trade that moved along the Euphrates between southern Mesopotamia's urban centers and the resource-rich regions of Syria and Anatolia to the west and north. Its importance is confirmed by the Sumerian King-List, compiled at the beginning of the second millennium B.C., which lists Mari as one of several cities upon which the gods in turn bestowed the kingship over all Sumer and Akkad (southern Mesopotamia). Most of the early material from Mari is from the third quarter of the third millennium B.C. Several dozen tablets show that at that time Mari's Semitic-speaking scribes wrote in Sumerian. Palaces and temples of that period have been uncovered; from the latter have come some of the finest votive statuettes in the Sumerian style ever found. The liveliness and personality displayed by these statuettes contrasts sharply with the simple, severe style characteristic of sculpture at Mari during the following centuries and typified by the statue of the ruler Ishtup-Ilum (ca. 2100 B.C.), which was found in the ruins of Mari's celebrated royal palace.

That palace was constructed over a span of some 300 years and contained more than 250 rooms on its ground floor alone. During the palace's long life Mari was fought over by contending Amorite dynasties. Shamshi-Adad, ruler of all northern Mesopotamia at the beginning of the eighteenth century B.C., seized the city and installed his son Yasmah-Adad as its ruler. In 1779, however, Zimri-Lim, son of an earlier ruler, took back the throne and ruled until he was defeated by Hammurabi of Babylon around 1760. In 1757 Hammurabi burned and demolished the great palace along with the other major buildings of Mari. Some 15,000 cuneiform tablets, mostly administrative texts and letters from Zimri-Lim's time, were sealed in the destruction. These texts have shed extraordinary light on the history, political structure, and social organization of the kingdom of Mari. Moreover, because of Mari's central position among the other kingdoms of Mesopotamia and Syria, they have also proved to be essential for understanding the history of the entire Near East during the early second millennium B.C.

[See also MESOPOTAMIA, articles on THE RISE OF URBAN CULTURE, SUMER AND AKKAD; NEAR EAST: THE BRONZE AGE IN THE NEAR EAST.]

■ Kay Kohlmeyer, "Mari (Tell Hariri)," in ed. Harvey Weiss, *Ebla to Damascus* (1985), pp. 134–148, 194–197.

James A. Armstrong

MARTIN'S HUNDRED, a British colonial site in Virginia, extensively excavated beginning in the 1970s. The history of Martin's Hundred began with the consortium of London merchant adventurers who formed the Society of Martin's Hundred; their first colonists were sent to Virginia in the autumn of 1618. After a year's delay they settled a 20,000-acre tract on the James River seven miles below the colony's capital at Jamestown. On 22 March 1622, Martin's Hundred was largely destroyed in one of many Native American attacks on the English plantations that came close to terminating Britain's foothold in Virginia. Among the Martin's Hundred losses were about 56 of its approximately 114 inhabitants and most of its core settlement of Wolstenholme Towne, this last named for shareholder Sir John Wolstenholme.

Partially repopulated after the attack, Martin's Hundred suffered further depredation after the new arrival's relief ship *Abigail* landed disease rather than relief, bringing an epidemic that killed more in the winter of 1623 than the natives had in the previous spring. By the end of 1623 the Hundred's population had stabilized at around thirty, continuing at that level until the 1640s when, for reasons yet to be determined, all but one of the known dwelling sites were abandoned.

In the eighteenth century the heart of the Martin's Hundred tract became part of Carter's Grove Plantation, whose 1755 mansion and diminished acreage survives today as a living museum within the framework of the Colonial Williamsburg Foundation. The latter's Department of Archaeology undertook an archaeological survey of the Carter's Grove acres in 1970 with a view to locating and reconstructing support buildings associated with the eighteenth-century mansion. While doing so, seventeenth-century postholes, pits, ditches, and graves were encountered, but not being of interest to the restorers, they were mapped and left unexcavated. Six years later, when a field overlying several then-undated graves was needed to erect eighteenth-century craft exhibits, the archaeologists were instructed to return and determine the cemetery's dimensions.

The ensuing excavations determined that the burials dated to the first half of the seventeenth century, and at the same time exposed the posthole-defined remains of a post-in-the-ground complex that included three houses, sheds of various sizes, several fenced yards, and a cellared barn whose fill included H-shaped lead containing within its channel the embossed inscription "Iohn Byshopp of Exceter Gonner 1625." Glaziers' visemaker Bishop later moved to London and became gunmaker to Charles I.

The exposed complex dated between ca. 1622 and 1645 and represented the earliest complete farmstead layout discovered in British America. Among the recovered artifacts was a virtually complete alembic that was spectrographically determined to be of the local clay, and with it a tile and other sherds indicating that the kiln source was nearby. Although these discoveries were not in the mainstream of Colonial Williamsburg's eighteenth-century-oriented interests, support from the National Geographic Society's chairman emeritus Melville Bell Grosvenor enabled excavations to resume in 1977. The kiln was not found, but sustaining National Geographic Society funding continued until 1981. During that time several more Martin's Hundred sites were excavated, the most important being that of Wolstenholme Towne.

Although about half the settlement had been lost to river erosion, the landward end of a town plan comparable to those of contemporary villages protected by adjacent fortified enclosures (bawns) in Ulster survived. Buildings included a tent-shaped barn, longhouse, store, cottage, and a palisaded fort. All these structures were either destroyed or abandoned at the time of the native attack, and therefore provide depositional dating brackets of 1620–1622. Among the finds were two virtually intact close helmets of a transitional type unparalleled in English collections but fairly closely matched in the Landeszeughaus Armory at Graz. Also recovered were wasters and other pottery from a kiln site of the same date. From another site datable to ca. 1625–1640 came a locally made slipware dish dated 1631 that, being at the bottom of an artifact laden pit, provided an invaluable *terminus post quem*.

As closely datable examples of impermanent building construction in seventeenth-century Virginia, the Martin's Hundred sites are important to architectural historians; however, their greatest value rests in their ability to provide very close dating for a wide range of domestic and military artifacts.

The sites and their artifacts have been published in part in a book, *Martin's Hundred* (1981); a 1983 Colonial Williamsburg booklet, *Discoveries in Martin's Hundred;* in two articles in *National Geographic* (June 1979 and January 1981); as well as in a prize-winning television documentary, *Search for a Century.*

Carter's Grove Plantation is part of the Colonial Williamsburg Foundation's museum complex. Its Wolstenholme Towne site has been skeletally reconstructed, and visitors to it first pass through a subterranean museum that exposes them to archaeological techniques and reasoning, and puts key artifacts into their historical and cultural contexts.

[*See also* EUROPEAN COLONIES IN THE NEW WORLD; NORTH AMERICA: HISTORICAL ARCHAEOLOGY OF NORTH AMERICA.]

■ Ivor Noël Hume, "First Look at a Lost Virginia Settlement," *National Geographic* 155 (June 1979): 735–767. Ivor Noël Hume, *Martin's Hundred* (1979). Ivor Noël Hume, "New Clues to an Old Mystery," *National Geographic* 161 (January 1981): 52–77. Ivor Noël Hume, "Excavations at Carter's Grove Plantation, Virginia, 1976–1979," *National Geographic Society Research Reports* 17 (1984): 653–675.

Ivor Noël Hume

MARXIST THEORY. Contemporary marxism is a philosophy, a hundred-year-old tradition of thought, and a mode of theoretical production that has many strands and variations. Marxist archaeologies have been developed in many parts of the world including the former Soviet Union, Europe, China, Latin America, and Japan. Only recently have British and American archaeologists explicitly used marxist theory. Marxism provides British and American archaeology with methods and theories to understand cultural change, to critically examine the role of archaeology in the modern capitalist world, and to guide action in that world.

History. The history of marxism in British and American archaeology is a hidden one. For most of the twentieth century marxist perspectives have been discriminated against in the United States and Great Britain, and it is only since the 1960s that marxist ideas could be openly discussed in the academy.

V. Gordon *Childe's interest in marxism predated a more general interest among English-speaking archaeologists. In 1935 he turned to the theory of Soviet archaeology, especially its antifascism. In four books he laid out his own marxist view of European prehistory to challenge fascist German prehistory. In the 1950s Childe rejected the dogmatic archaeology done under Stalin, and he published critical theoretical works.

Many bits and pieces of marxist theory entered archaeology in the postwar period. Theoretically oriented archaeologists drew on marxist concepts filtered through evolutionary and ecological theories in anthropology. Robert Adams turned to Childe's work, especially *Man Makes Himself* (1951), and to the research of Julian Steward. The "New Archaeology" of the 1960s built theories of culture change on Leslie White's marxist-influenced evolutionism.

Some U.S. and British archaeologists rejected processual archaeology and instead employed explicit marxism. In the 1960s, Bruce Trigger read the works of Childe for a marxist theory of archaeology. Thomas Patterson encountered marxist politics in Peru and began a lifelong engagement with Latin American marxist archaeologists. In the 1970s Antonio Gilman and Philip Kohl joined these two innovators. Also in the mid-1970s Mark Leone, in the United States, and Michael Rowlands, Barbara Bender, and Kristian Kristiansen, in Europe, applied structural marxist theory to archaeological problems.

In the 1980s, even as U.S. and British society became more conservative, radical thought flowered in the universities. Many archaeologists who had been radicalized by the New Left of the 1960s and 1970s, rejected processual archaeology and turned to marxism instead. Prominent among these were Robert Paynter, Carol Crumley, William Marquart, and Russell Handsman in the United States and Thomas Williamson, Matthew Spriggs, Liz Bellamy, and Thomas Saunders in Great Britain. Despite a growing interest in marxism, it remains a minority position in British and American archaeology in the 1990s.

Marxism and Other Theories. Marxist archaeologists share several themes. Each recognizes Karl Marx as an important intellectual ancestor. All view society as being made up of contradictory and conflicting social relations, and all locate the motor of cultural change in these relations. Each seeks to break down theoretical oppositions such as mentalist versus materialist, history versus evolution, and relativism versus determinism. All take a human-centered view of history that acknowledges that intentional, knowledgeable human beings produce cultural change. Finally, each acknowledges that archaeologists create knowledge of the past in a social context and that such knowledge is a complex mix of the reality of that past and that social context.

Processual archaeology shares many empirical concerns with marxism, specifically questions about subsistence and social organization. Marxists, however, dismiss the functionalist systems logic and strong materialist cant of processual theory. They also reject the processualists' belief that cultural change can be explained by abstract laws.

Commentators often lump marxism with post-processual and feminist theory in the radical left of archaeological theory. All three of these approaches reject the idea of value-free science, and stress the role of humans as active agents in cultural change. Most Marxists, however, find post-processual archaeology too subjective, overly intellectualized, and too eclectic. Marxism places economic relations (class) at the center of the study of the past, while feminism puts gender relations in this position. These positions are complementary as long as archaeologists recognize the interaction of class and gender and do not reduce process of cultural change to one or the other.

Contributions. Marxism reintroduced history into British and American archaeology in a more complex way than the empiricism of cultural historical theory. Marxists argue that general developmental processes operate in cultural change but that these processes exist only in the lived experience of people in real historical sequences. For example, this means that we can make generalizations about the rise of specific states, but we can never come up with an explanation for the rise of the state as an abstract entity.

Both marxist and nonmarxist archaeologists have applied marxist concepts and models to the study of specific cases of cultural change. Susan Kus's use of the idea of objectification to study the Imerina kingdom of Madagascar, Dean Sattia's notion of subsumed classes in the prehistoric American Southwest, and LouAnn Wurst's study of class and ideology in rural nineteenth-century New York are examples of such concepts. Archaeologists have used the models of world systems theory, the lineage mode of production, and prestige goods economies to dispute functionalist, ecological explanations in many parts of the world.

Finally, marxism allows us to examine critically the role of archaeology in the making of modern ideologies, and in the domination of subordinate groups, such as Native Americans. Leone and Parker Potter have critically examined how archaeology reinforces capitalist ideology, and Patterson and Trigger have written critical social histories of archaeology.

[See also CULTURE HISTORICAL THEORY; GENDER, ARCHAEOLOGY OF; HISTORY OF ARCHAEOLOGY, INTELLECTUAL; POST-PROCESSUAL THEORY; PROCESSUAL THEORY; STRUCTURALISM; THEORY IN ARCHAEOLOGY.]

■ Matthew Spriggs, ed., *Marxist Perspectives in Archaeology* (1984). Thomas C. Patterson and C. W. Gailey, eds., *Power Relations and State Formation* (1987). Carol L. Crumley and William Marquart, *Regional Dynamics: Burgundian Landscapes in Historical Perspective* (1987). Robert Paynter, "The Archaeology of Inequality," *Annual Review of Anthropology* 18 (1989): 369–399. Randall H. McGuire, *A Marxist Archaeology* (1992). Thomas Patterson, *Archaeology: The Historical Development of Civilizations* (1993).

Randall H. McGuire

MASADA. Located on an isolated plateau near the southwestern coast of the Dead Sea, the fortress-palace complex of Masada provides vivid and important evidence of Roman cultural penetration into the Near East and of the sophisticated nature of Roman siege craft. Masada is described in detail by the first-century-A.D. historian Josephus Flavius as a royal fortress founded by one of the Hasmonean kings of Judea in the late second century B.C., lavishly embellished by King Herod a century later, and defended to the death by Jewish rebels against an ultimately successful Roman siege during the war of A.D. 66 to 74. In excavations conducted from 1963 to 1965, Professor Yigael Yadin of the Hebrew University of Jerusalem cleared much of the upper surface of the plateau and its steep sides, and conducted trial probes in several of the Roman siege camps below. Because of the extreme aridity of this region, the finds from the Masada excavations included remains of food, textiles, leather, basketry, and fragments of parchment scrolls.

Despite the testimony of Josephus, no hard evidence has been uncovered to verify the initial Hasmonean occupation of the site. The earliest building activities distinguished in the excavations were also the most extensive, that is, King Herod's self-supporting palace-fortress complex, which included royal residences, bathhouses, extensive storehouses, and administrative buildings. A sophisticated water system channeled the brief, surging torrents of winter floodwaters into gigantic rock-hewn cisterns, permitting year-round occupation at the site. Most notable among the many royal buildings at Masada are the Western Palace, decorated with elaborate geometric-patterned mosaic floors, and the Northern Palace, built on three colonnaded platforms on the narrow, prowlike northern end of the plateau.

Following the death of Herod in 4 B.C., the site was apparently maintained for decades by a small military garrison. With the outbreak of the Jewish Revolt in A.D. 66, however, a rebel group identified by Josephus as the *sicarioi*, or "knifemen," captured Masada and used it both as a refuge from the main Roman forces and as a base for guerilla raids on neighboring settlements. The evidence of this rebel occupation is clear in the rough partitioning of the rooms of the former royal palaces and even of the chambers in the casemate fortification walls. These small chambers were apparently used for the habitations of small family groups, as indicated by the presence of simple clay ovens and personal possessions in many of them. Hundreds of ostraca—or inscribed pottery shards—bearing cryptic symbols or Greek and Hebrew letters were also found on this level and seem to have been used as tokens for the distribution of provisions. Religious observance is indicated by the discovery of a synagogue and fragments of biblical and apocryphal scrolls.

The mass suicide of the 960 rebels of Masada as reported by Josephus remains unverified archaeologically. The remains of fewer than thirty individuals were recovered in the excavations and the precise cause of death is unclear. It seems evident, however, that the majority of the Masada rebels were either killed or captured in the Roman siege operation, which has been fully documented by the archaeological evidence. Surveys and limited excavations have been conducted at the main siege camp, along the circumvallation or siege wall, and in several of the smaller camps located in intervals around its circuit. The Masada expedition also examined the construction of the massive earthen siege ramp on the western side of the plateau, up which the Roman forces brought a battering ram in order to breach Masada's outer fortification walls.

The Masada excavations also uncovered evidence of the site's settlement history after the Roman conquest in A.D. 74. Pottery, coins, and papyruses indicate that the Roman forces maintained a garrison at the site until the early second century A.D. After a brief reoccupation of the site in the fifth and sixth centuries A.D. by Christian monks who constructed living quarters and a small chapel from the ruins of the earlier structures, the history of the site of Masada was forgotten until its re-identification by western scholars in the early nineteenth century. As an impressive ancient monument and powerful modern symbol for political independence, Masada has become one of the most celebrated archaeological sites in Israel.

[See also ROMAN EMPIRE: THE EASTERN PROVINCES OF THE ROMAN EMPIRE.]

■ Yigael Yadin, *Masada: Herod's Fortress and the Zealots' Last Stand* (1966). Israel Exploration Society, *Masada: The Yigael Yadin Excavations, 1963–1965. Final Reports.* (1989).

Neil Asher Silberman

MATERIALS, Analysis of. The recovery of artifacts and the uncovering of features long buried in archaeological sites is one exciting and rewarding aspect of archaeology. Recovery is not the ultimate goal of modern archaeology, however, and following recovery comes the long, painstaking, and ultimately rewarding job of conserving, analyzing, and curating the products of excavation. This article provides a brief overview of the various types of materials recovered from archaeological sites and the types of analyses that those materials typically undergo. The interested reader is directed to more complete descriptions of these materials and their analysis in the longer pieces on each material type in this volume.

The types of materials archaeologists may recover from any given site will depend on the types of materials that were used by the original occupants of the site and the conditions of preservation at the site after its abandonment. Stone is the most durable material used by humans, and hence stone artifacts (lithics) have the greatest chance of preservation over the longest period of time. Following stone in order of likelihood of preservation are: ceramics, shell, bone, metals, wood, plant remains, and textiles. Ceramics and shell tend to preserve well because they are both composed of generally stable, mineral rich, materials. Bone may be preserved if the conditions of deposition are relatively stable with little variation in temperature or moisture. The same is true for metals, with the added provision that the chemistry of the deposition environment must not be overly reactive with the type of metal, hence preventing corrosion. Wood, textiles, and plant remains are least likely to be preserved except when the conditions of deposition are stable, as with bone, and either extremely dry, or cold, or

constituting a sealed, anaerobic environment such as a peat bog or lake bottom. The latter three conditions are necessary to avoid natural decomposition of the materials due to the actions of bacteria, insects, and the like. These last three types of materials can also be preserved if they have been reduced to charcoal by intentional or unintentional slow burning.

The analysis of these general material categories can be broken down into roughly three types: morphological / typological analysis, material analysis, and technological analysis. Morphological / typological analysis refers to studies that seek to categorize materials according to their form or presumed function. This type of analysis can be conducted for any of the materials listed above, and is the most common type of analysis. Material analysis refers to studies of the actual composition of the artifacts. The chemical analysis of metal or stone artifacts, or the petrographic analysis of ceramics, are examples of material analyses. Technological analyses are conducted in order to understand the way in which artifacts were made or processed. As each of the detailed articles in this volume on the analysis of animal remains, ceramics, human remains, lithics, metals, plant remains, textiles, and wood indicates, each of the three categories of analysis plays a different role and is conducted in a different way for each of the general material types.

[See also CERAMICS, TECHNOLOGICAL ANALYSIS OF CERAMICS; METALS, ANALYSIS OF METALS; PLANT REMAINS, ANALYSIS OF; WOOD, ANALYSIS OF WOOD.]

George Michaels

MAWANGDUI is a group of three tombs from the Western Han dynasty (206 B.C. to A.D. 24), located approximately 1.86 miles (3 km) east of the city of Changsha, Hunan Province. One tomb is notable for the preservation of perishable artifacts, including clothing, lacquerwares, bamboo books, musical instruments, wooden figurines, and even food. The body in the tomb, that of a woman in her fifties, was so well preserved that an autopsy could be performed, revealing that she had eaten melons shortly before her death.

The three tombs housed a husband and wife and their adult son. Clay seals announce the tomb occupants as the family of Marquis Da, known from the historical records of the Western Han. Tomb 1 is that of the wife, Tomb 2 belongs to the Marquis, and Tomb 3 to the son, who died around the age of thirty. Tomb 2 had been plundered, but the other two were extraordinarily rich in material goods and information about the time period.

Tomb 1 was under a mound 56 feet (17 m) high, with a vertical shaft down to a burial chamber constructed of wood. Inside the chamber were grave goods and a set of three nested, painted coffins, each protected by layers of charcoal and white clay. The body was dressed in multiple layers of silk robes and covered with twenty quilts, neatly wrapped and tied with nine ribbons. Altogether fifty-eight items of silk clothing and forty-six rolls of silk cloth were found in good condition. Dresses and skirts were either lined or unlined, and silk pillow cases, gloves, shoes, and socks were also found. The fabric was woven in various degrees of fineness and in several colors. One-color damasks were woven with complex patterns, and other garments were edged with multi-color brocades. Embroidery with twenty colors of silk thread was done on forty of the articles of clothing.

Tombs 1 and 3 each had a T-shaped painted silk cloth, more than 6.5 feet (2 m) long, covering the coffin. Each has allegorical paintings, representing the last journey of the soul. Other paintings include two maps and a scroll illustrating the practice of *gi gong*, or breathing exercises, accompanying a book on the topic.

The lacquerware included mugs with handles, oval cups, ladles, large tripods, jars with lids, and various pieces of furniture such as tables and screens. Most were black lacquer painted with intricate geometric and floral designs, as well as dragons, phoenixes, and other birds, cats, and turtles. Wooden figures of servants and a small orchestra were also placed in the tomb.

The books recovered from the site were written on strips of bamboo and silk, and contain more than 120,000 characters. These books have inestimable value for scholars, since some were previously known only as titles, and others thought to be forgeries are clearly genuine.

[*See also* CHINA, *articles on* INTRODUCTION, HAN EMPIRE.]

■ Qian Hao, "The Han Tombs at Mawangdui, Changsha: Underground Home of an Aristocratic Family," in *Out of China's Earth*, ed. Qian Hao (1981): 87–125.

Sarah Milledge Nelson

MAYA CIVILIZATION

INTRODUCTION

On his fourth voyage to the Americas in 1502, Christopher Columbus spotted a large oceangoing canoe in the Bay of Honduras. Traveling in the canoe were Mayan men, women, and children who were seated among a hefty cargo of cotton mantles, chocolate (*cacao*) beans, razor-sharp stone blades made of obsidian (volcanic glass) and chert, and containers of sweet honey produced by the stingless bee of the Yucatán Peninsula. This long-distance trading venture —so characteristic of the Postclassic Period (A.D. 900/1000 to 1500)—took place along the eastern Caribbean border of the Maya world. During the first and second millennia A.D., the region occupied by Mayan-speaking peoples included the southern states of Mexico (Chiapas, Campeche, Yucatán, and Quintana Roo) and the Central American countries of Belize, Guatemala, El Salvador, and the western portion of Honduras. Located well within tropical latitudes, the Maya region, nevertheless, contained a variety of habitats including steamy lowland rain forests and cooler highland conifer forests.

Strictly speaking, Maya civilization developed in the lowland zone of the Yucatán Peninsula and extended down the eastern side of the peninsula as far as the Bay of Honduras. The following major characteristics of the elite segment of Classic Maya society were restricted to this region: a hieroglyphic script (written in media as diverse as stone, wood, plaster, polychrome ceramics, and paper-bark books); complex calendrical reckoning and a developed system of astronomy/astrology; stone sculpture that com-bined pictorial representation with hieroglyphic texts (generally recounting life histories of rulers and important royalty); and a distinctive architectural style incorporating features such as corbel arches (freestanding or as roofing), masonry buildings, and core-veneer facades.

Classic Maya society of the first millennium A.D. developed from an earlier tradition of small, agrarian villages. The Middle Formative Period (1000 through 400 B.C.) is really the first well-documented era in the Maya lowlands. During this early time period, scattered agricultural villages were established in the rain forests and along the major river courses of the Petén region of Guatemala and the northern portion of Belize. Relying on a suite of cultigens which included maize, root crops, and tropical orchard species such as *avocado, chico-zapote, mamey,* and *cacao,* villagers supplemented their plant foods with locally available protein from fish, turtle, deer, peccary, armadillo, and other tropical species. Available archaeological evidence indicates that most Middle Formative villages lacked ostentatious architecture, suggesting an absence of social classes or political centralization.

During the succeeding Late Formative Period (400 B.C. to A.D. 250), however, life changed dramatically in many parts of the Maya lowlands, as the building of monumental structures (pyramids, ball courts, and large building platforms) as well as sprawling residential compounds commenced. During this time, monumental architectural complexes were built in Mexico at Calakmul and Dzibilchaltún, in the Petén forests of Guatemala at El Mirador, Uaxactun, *Tikal, Nakbe, and Tintal; in Belize at Cerros, Cuello, Lamanai, and Nohmul; and in El Salvador at Chalchuapa. Smaller villages such as K'axob in northern Belize also saw explosive growth during this time as well as significant changes in the treatment of the dead, the latter indicative of the genesis of ancestor veneration. During the latter part of the Late Formative, long-distance trade in valuables such as jadeite, marine shell, quetzal feathers, and obsidian appear to have become linked, as status goods, to an emergent elite sector of society. Stone implements called *eccentrics* which were used exclusively for ritual purposes first appeared at this time, as well as the practice of dedicating structures through the "caching" of vessels and other offerings within the construction core of buildings.

In the following Early Classic Period (A.D. 250 through 600), the political structure of the Maya lowlands crystallized into a system of multiple competing kingdoms that were linked, on an elite level, by a shared cosmology or world view, a written hieroglyphic script, the use of a calendrical long count, and, most importantly, the political institution of divine kingship. The initiation date for the Early Classic is roughly coincident with one of the oldest long-count dates from the Maya region: Stela 29 of Tikal, which shows, in profile, an early ruler; on the back of the stela is a long-count date of A.D. 292 or 8.12.14.8.5. The initiation of the long count is often linked to the emergence of the institution of divine kingship because the two are temporally coincident. In Classic Maya society there was a great emphasis on recounting one's genealogy far back into the dim recesses of time, and the long count facilitated the recording of august family histories—a necessary prerequisite for the legitimate rule of a divine king.

The political units over which divine kings reigned, on average, covered about 965 square miles (2500 sq km) with the exception of cities such as Tikal or Calakmul which seem to have exercised hegemony over a larger area. The political heart of each kingdom contained a zone of monumental construction built in a local expression of Maya architectural canons. Buildings were arranged around large, central plazas often capable of accommodating thousands of people for events of ritual pageantry. The exterior of buildings might be adorned with large stucco or stone mosaic masks of important deities such as have been uncovered by archaeological field work at Lamanai, Tikal, and Kohunlich. Inside these buildings, the walls of the long, narrow rooms were often covered with murals depicting scenes of ritual, festivities, or warfare as have been discovered at Bonampak in Chiapas, Mexico. On lintels, doorjambs, stairways of palaces, and freestanding stelae there were inscribed hieroglyphic texts recounting important events in the lives of royal personages. Often these texts were accompanied by portraiture as on Lintel 26 of Yaxchilan, in which "Lady Xoc" assists her husband, ruler "Shield Jaguar," in donning his regalia for warfare. These vivid images evoke a very personalized style of leadership.

The political epicenters of Maya capitals invariably contained several pyramidal structures in excess of 49 feet (15 m) in height capped by summit temples. Within these artificial "mountains," revered ancestors were interred and a commemoration of them and rituals designed to communicate with them were enacted by rulers and priestly scribes on the front staircases and summit sanctuaries of these structures. The burial of Pakal—the great ruler of *Palenque —inside of the Temple of the Inscriptions is particularly illustrative of this practice. The text and long-count dates inscribed on the lid of the sarcophagus of Pakal proclaim that he was born in A.D. 603 and, after living for 80 years, died in A.D. 683.

The descendants and close relatives of venerated rulers such as Pakal resided in the core area—inhabiting palatial structures often built of stone with a corbel-arch roof such as the Palace complex of Palenque or the Central Acropolis of Tikal. Surrounded by a multitude of servants and retainers, Classic Maya royalty engaged in affairs of the state: organizing and leading military campaigns against neighboring kingdoms, performing impressive ritual pageantry (which sometimes included self-sacrifice as well as the sacrifice of captives), acting as mediator between the supernaturals and the populace, and sponsoring lavish feasts. Other members of royal and minor elite families became scribes, priests, seers, painters, sculptors, and architects, as archaeological research at the scribal "House of the Bacabs" at Copán has shown. Outside of the political center of each kingdom there was an expansive population living in dispersed, often extended-family compounds. Orchards, fields, and gardens enveloped these family residences, the majority of which were constructed of perishable pole-and-thatch materials. Often, several houses were grouped around a central patio or communal work area. The ritual focus of the larger compounds might be a small pyramid or shrine at which ancestors of the household group were venerated. These large residential compounds indicate the continued importance of macrofamily kin groupings in Classic Maya society and also suggest that multifamily cooperatives organized agricultural labor and landholdings. Available textual evidence does not indicate active involvement of Maya divine kings in the everyday farming and trading affairs of nonelite Maya. In fact, the production and exchange of well-crafted stone tools (large bifaces, celts, and macroblades, among other forms) from the ancient workshops of Colha, Belize, predates the emergence of the

political institution of kingship and continues, essentially unchanged, through the Classic Period.

By the Late and Terminal Classic Period (A.D. 600 through 900/1000), there were profound changes in the economic fabric of Maya society. Archaeological surveys of settlement throughout the lowland area indicate a steep rate of population growth through the Late Classic with population estimates for the central lowlands in excess of three million. Evidence of efforts to intensify agricultural production by reclaiming wetlands at places such as Pulltrouser Swamp and along the Rio Hondo or by terracing hill slopes in the Río Bec region and along the Belize River Valley further indicate that the Classic Maya population had effectively filled its habitat.

The political geometry of the Classic Period kingdoms indicates a factionalization of political realms during the Late Classic. Places such as Jimbal that were subsidiary to Tikal during earlier times began to erect their own inscribed monuments using a particular hieroglyphic compound (called an emblem glyph), which seems to connote political autonomy. Moreover, the topical content of carved monuments changed during the Late Classic. Topics such as royal marriage, birth, death, and accession to the throne were partially supplanted by an increased emphasis on warfare, conquest, and sacrifice of captives. During the Late Classic, the greatest elaboration of the hieroglyphic writing system occurred. Combining and substituting semantic glyphs with phonetic ones, the Maya writing system is characterized as logosyllabic; and not only could words be written phonetically but texts were arranged according to principles of grammar and syntax. In this regard, Maya script was the most highly developed writing system in pre-Columbian America.

By A.D. 850 the core areas of the well-built southern lowland Maya cities seem to have been abandoned. No further royal constructions were undertaken at the once great capitals of Palenque, Tikal, or Copán. For a brief time, newer cities flourished in the north at places like Uxmal, Sayil, Kabah, Labna, and *Chichén Itzá. Utilizing all of the traditional canons of Maya architecture, these northern capitals surpassed the architectural splendor of the older cities of the south with higher and wider corbel arches, complex and repetitive stone-mosaic friezes, multistoried palaces, and—at Chichén Itzá—the largest ball court ever constructed in the Maya region. Most of these northern cities thrived for less than three hundred years and only Chichén Itzá survived into the thirteenth century. Because of its architectural similarity with the small highland capital of Tula, Chichén Itzá was once thought to have been an outpost of the militaristic *Toltec Empire. More recent dating of the two sites, however, casts doubt on this interpretation due to the chronological precedence and greater size of Chichén Itzá. In fact, of all the great capitals that existed in the course of Maya civilization, only Chichén Itzá is believed to have held political hegemony over an area large enough to have been called an empire.

After the fall of Chichén Itzá in the thirteenth century, a period termed the Late Postclassic persisted until the first landfall of Spaniards in 1517 off the coast of the Yucatán Peninsula just north of Cozumel Island. During this final epoch of autochthonous Maya society, a series of small capitals such as the walled city of Mayapan were established. Increasing involvement in long-distance maritime trade is indicated by the establishment of a series of ports along the shoreline of the Yucatán Peninsula at places such as Tulum and on Cozumel Island. The abandoned area to the south was reoccupied and a new capital established in the middle of Laguna Petén Itzá at Tayasal. This kingdom was to stay independent of Spanish control until 1697. During the Late Postclassic, the lowland Maya increasingly were involved in trade relations with emissaries of the highland empire of the Aztecs, who were highly desirous of lowland products such as *cacao*, cotton, bird feathers, and generally of slaves.

[*See also* MESOAMERICA, *articles on* INTRODUCTION, FORMATIVE PERIOD IN MESOAMERICA, CLASSIC PERIOD IN MESOAMERICA, POST-CLASSIC PERIOD IN MESOAMERICA; MESOAMERICA, ORIGINS OF FOOD PRODUCTION IN.]

■ B. L. Turner II, *Once Beneath the Forest: Prehistoric Terracing in the Rio Bec Region of the Maya Lowlands* (1983). B. L. Turner II, *Pulltrouser Swamp: Ancient Maya Habitat, Agriculture, and Settlement in Northern Belize* (1983). T. Patrick Culbert, "The Collapse of Classic Maya Civilization," in *The Collapse of Ancient States and Civilizations,* N. Yoffee and G. L. Cowgill, eds. (1988). Stephen D. Houston, *Maya Glyphs* (1989). David Webster, *The House of the Bacabs* (1989). Mary D. Pohl, *Ancient Maya Wetland Agriculture* (1990). B. L. Turner II, "Population Reconstruction for the Central Maya Lowlands: 1000 B.C. to A.D. 1500," in *Precolumbian Population in the Maya Lowlands,* T. P. Culbert and D. S. Rice, eds. (1990). William L. Fash, *Scribes, Warriors and Kings* (1991). Harry J. Shafer and Thomas R. Hester, "Lithic Craft Specialization and Product Distribution at the Maya Site of Colha, Belize," *World Archaeology* 23 (1991): 79–97. William J. Folan, "Calakmul, Campeche: A Centralized Urban Administrative Center in the Northern Petén," *World Archaeology* 24 (1992): 158–168. Scott L. Fedick, "Ancient Maya Agricultural Terracing in the Upper Belize River Area: Computer Aided Modeling and the Results of Initial Field Investigations," *Ancient Mesoamerica* 5 (1994): 107–127. Patricia A. McAnany, *Living with the Ancestors: Kinship and Kingship in Ancient Maya Society* (1995).

Patricia A. McAnany

THE MAYA CALENDAR

There are three major structural characteristics of the Maya calendar, a 365-day "year," a 260-day sequence analogous to our week, and a count from an era base. The year is composed of eighteen named periods of twenty days each (in Yucatec: Pop, Uo, Zip, Zotz, Zec, Xul, Yarkin, Mol, Ch'en, Yax, Zac, Ceh, Mac, Kankin, Muan, Pax, Kayab, Cumku) plus a nameless and unlucky period of five days referred to as *uayeb*.

The twenty-day periods are generally called "months" by modern scholars. Each of these periods had a presiding deity or deities, and festivals for them were held during the appropriate month. In highland Mexico, probably among the Maya, these rituals accompanied markets. Different ethnic groups had different patron gods and used calendars beginning with different months, perhaps emphasizing their own deity. The Maya held major ceremonies accompanying the change of presiding deities at the New Year.

The twenty day names (Imix, Ik, Akbal, Kan, Chicchan, Cimi, Manik, Lamat, Muluc, Oc, Chuen, Eb, Ben, Ix, Men, Cib, Caban, Etz'nab, Cauac, Ahau) are an endlessly repeating sequence combined with numbers from 1 to 13, starting with 1 Imix, 2 Ik . . . 13 Ix, 1 Men . . . 7 Ahau (ending the first sequence of 20), and proceeding to 8 Imix . . . 13 Ahau, when the sequence started again with 1 Imix.

The 260 days are integrated with the 365-day year so that each day can fall in only seventy-three places in the year and must occur in each of them before it will again return to its first position after 18,980 days (73 × 260 = 52 × 365). This cycle is known as the calendar round. During this period,

the months shifted thirteen days in their tropical year (seasonal) positions, but no correction was ever made. The Maya knew that the months would be back in step with the seasons after twenty-nine calendar rounds (1,508 Maya years = 1,507 tropical years without a sensible error). The Maya days that could begin the year were Akbal, Lamat, Ben, and Etz'nab; after a calendar reform, these became Kan, Muluc, Ix, and Cauac. The beginning days named the year and followed in mathematically determined regular sequence: 1 Akbal, 2 Lamat, 3 Ben, 4 Etz'nab, 5 Akbal . . . ; 1 Imix, which began the 260-day period, could fall only on the fourth, ninth, fourteenth, and nineteenth days of the month and hence could never begin the year. Day names were associated with many other phenomena. Those most emphasized by the Maya were colors and directions.

The most commonly used era base was a day 13.0.0.0.0 4 Ahau 8 Cumku, 3,000 years before the earliest known dated monuments were erected. The recorded date was given in days (*kins*), twenty-day periods (*uinals*), 360-day "counting years" (*tuns*), twenty-tun intervals (*katuns*), and twenty-katun intervals (*baktuns*), which had elapsed since the base. These are normally transcribed in order from the largest unit to the smallest, followed by the resultant calendar round date. Thus 9.16.4.10.8 12 Lamat 1 Muan means that (9 × 144,000) + (16 × 7,200) + (4 × 360) + (10 × 20) + 8 days, a total of 1,412,848 days, had elapsed from 13.0.0.0.0 4 Ahau 8 Cumku to this particular repetition of the calendar round date 12 Lamat 1 Muan.

Era dates are found on monuments and pottery, and in one of the surviving Maya books. The monuments depict rulers in accession scenes, conquests, and ritual acts, including ball games. Some art works are signed by sculptors or painters, who were sometimes members of the ruling families. The importance of the date is frequently emphasized because it may make up over half of the text of a monument.

Another era base is found in the *Dresden* Maya codex, where a series of ten dates are counted from a base 9 Kan 12 Kayab. The earliest date of this series was more than 33,000 years after the base date.

While the calendar round dates are common to all the Mesoamerican calendars, the era bases are restricted to Mayan and Olmec inscriptions. The earliest contemporary date is 7.16.3.2.13 6 Ben, but too little of the monument is preserved to be certain whether it is Mayan or Olmec. Which of the two invented the calendar is uncertain.

[*See also* MESOAMERICA, *articles on* INTRODUCTION, CLASSICAL PERIOD IN MESOAMERICA.]

■ David Humiston Kelley, "The Maya Calendar Correlation Problem," in *Civilization in the Ancient Americas: Essays in Honor of Gordon R. Willey,* eds. Richard Leventhal and Alan Kolata (1983), pp. 157–208.

David Humiston Kelley

MAYA WRITING

In all of the pre-Columbian New World, only the Maya can be said to have possessed true writing, if we define that as human speech made visible: the Maya script was capable of recording anything that could be expressed in everyday utterances. Until the middle part of this century, it was believed that little more than calendrical and astronomical matters were contained in the extant Maya texts, but the rapid pace of decipherment since then has shown the full extent of subjects treated by the ancient Maya scribes, as well as the close fit between the writing system and the spoken language. Although there are about thirty-one languages within the Mayan linguistic family, all known texts are either in Cholan (languages spoken in the southern lowlands) or in Yucatec (spoken in the northern lowlands), but there are some Classic inscriptions sharing the features of both.

The first part of the script to be deciphered was that dealing with mathematics and calendrics. Maya numeration is remarkably parsimonious, using only three symbols: a dot for one, a bar for five, and a stylized shell for nought. Very large numbers were written using a vigesimal or base-twenty positional numeration. Like other Mesoamericans, the Maya employed the fifty-two-year Calendar Round, based on the permutation of a sacred 260-day count with a 365-day approximate solar year. However, the Classic Maya also expressed dates in the Long Count; this is a day-to-day sequence of elapsed days beginning at some point in the year 3114 B.C. In addition, the Maya kept careful track of lunations, and constructed eclipse warning tables. It is now apparent that they also made accurate calculations for the movements of the visible planets, not only against the horizon, but against the background of fixed stars.

Thanks to the pioneering research of the Russian epigrapher Y. V. Knorosov, a great deal is known about the noncalendrical part of the script, which in structure bears a notable resemblance to some Old World writing systems, such as Egyptian, Sumerian, Hieroglyphic Hittite, and Japanese. The total number of signs or "glyphs" is more than eight hundred, but at any one time only about two to three hundred were in general use. Maya glyphs are oblong or pebblelike in outline, and the preferred direction of writing is from left to right and top to bottom, often in paired columns. In general, the script can be classified as "logosyllabic," that is, made up of logograms (semantic signs standing for morphemes or whole words) and syllabic-phonetic signs. There are more than one hundred of the latter, but some of these are allograms—mere scribal variations. Each syllabic sign represents either a consonant (C) and its following vowel (V), or a "pure" vowel. Because most Maya words are of the CVC type, the scribes perforce wrote them with two syllabic signs as CV-C(V), the sound of the second vowel being suppressed. Nevertheless, Knorosov discovered that the second sign was usually chosen so that its silent vowel would be in harmony with the first. Thus, to write phonetically the word *k'uk'* ("quetzal"), the scribe merely reduplicated the syllabic sign for *k'u*.

It is clear from this that the scribes could have written everything with syllabic glyphs only, yet they did not—the logograms had too much prestige. To make the latter easier to read, they prefixed or postfixed syllabic signs to them as phonetic indicators. Also available in the script's repertoire was *polyvalence*: a single sign could have more than one reading, and, conversely, the same sound or word could be expressed by any one of several glyphs (i.e., the word *caan* could be written with the number four, or a snake, or the sign for "sky," all of which are *caan* in Yucatec Maya). The scribe could play with these alternatives to achieve desired aesthetic effects.

During the Classic Period (ca. A.D. 250 to 900), monumental carved-stone texts are found throughout much of the Maya lowlands; these are largely freestanding stelae and architecturally bound lintels and panels. The subject matter of these public texts, and of the pictures which accompany them, is almost entirely historical, comprising the dynastic records of the elite who ran the Classic city-states: royal births, accessions, marriages, war exploits and captive taking, calendrical rituals, and even deaths. Such statements tend to be somewhat terse, third-person accounts placed in the context of their complex calendar. Personal names, titles (including references to enemies taken in battle), and "Emblem Glyphs" are given in nominal phrases. Emblem Glyphs, to be read as "holy king (*ahau*) of such-and-such a polity," may have originated as place-names, but by the Late Classic Period could include more than one city-state under one rubric. In a few cities, such as *Palenque, there are very long texts which take these dynasties far back into the mythological past, to the very moment of the creation of the cosmos.

Only four screenfold books or codices have survived until today. These have been written on bark paper coated with a layer of white gesso, and are entirely of ritual-astronomical character. Although all belong to the Post-Classic Period, there were probably many thousands of such books in the Classic Maya cities. Representations on Classic ceramics often depict gods and scribes writing in screenfolds fitted with jaguar-skin covers. Although traces of such codices have been found in tombs, not one has outlived the Classic Collapse.

Epigraphers have until recently ignored the texts on Classic pictorial (carved or painted) ceramics, even though many of these are as long or longer than the average monumental inscription. Ubiquitous on these vessels is the Primary Standard Sequence (PSS), a formulaic text that usually ends with the name and titles of the patron (or patronness) for whom the object was made. Much of the PSS is dedicatory, and includes a description of the vessel's shape, a statement of whether it is painted or carved, and often a naming of the liquid contained in it (chocolate in the case of cylindrical jars). The Secondary texts on ceramics refer specifically to the scenes depicted, and the actors, whether gods, humans, or animal-companion spirits; such texts might include first-person statements.

The PSS is part of a larger phenomenon known to epigraphers as "name tagging": an object, such as a jade ear spool, might be inscribed with the formula "his ear spool, X (name and titles of owner)." Name tagging is widely applied in the Classic Maya cities, not only to portable objects, but also to stelae, altars, lintels, buildings and parts of buildings, plazas, and ball courts.

The Spanish missionaries of the early Colonial Period, such as Bishop Landa, savagely repressed all knowledge of Maya writing, burning books whenever they could find them, and persecuting scribes and priests. By the eighteenth century, it is doubtful whether one Maya was left who could read the script of his ancestors.

[See also WRITING: MANUSCRIPTS AND CODICES.]

■ Linda Schele and Mary E. Miller, *The Blood of Kings* (1986). Steven D. Houston, *Maya Glyphs* (1989). Michael D. Coe, *Breaking the Maya Code* (1992).

Michael D. Coe

MAYA RULERS AND WARFARE

The recent decipherment of Maya hieroglyphic writing has demonstrated that a substantial proportion of the inscriptions and pictures carved in stone during the Classic Period (A.D. 250–900) were devoted to historical records of the kings of Maya sites. The political fortunes of these polities waxed and waned as a result of a never-ending series of wars and alliances. The rulers of individual sites were tied into a web of great royal families interrelated through marriages, royal visits, and ceremonial interaction.

Some of the rules that governed kingship can be elicited from the information about the reigns of individual kings. The concept of rulership of sites was very important, and most sites traced kingship from an original founder by giving each ruler a successor number. *Copán, for example, had sixteen rulers in a period of four centuries, while *Tikal notes twenty-nine kings in somewhat more than six hundred years. Although only about twenty percent of Maya rulers name their parents, the examples available indicate that descent from father to son was common, although sometimes succession passed through a set of brothers before returning to the son of the first-ruling brother.

The great majority of Maya rulers were men, although a few women bore the full titles and insignia that indicate rulership. In addition, a number of women who did not rule seem from their inscriptions to have been very influential, either as regents for young royal sons or as politically powerful individuals in their own right.

During their lifetimes, kings lived in royal compounds of multiroomed stone buildings located adjacent to the main ceremonial precincts of their sites. These compounds must have housed the most important members of the royal family and were probably also used for storage of valuables and perhaps some administrative functions. After death, Maya rulers were buried in lavishly stocked tombs, usually deep underneath the largest temples at their sites. Now that inscriptions can be read, tombs can sometimes be identified as those of specific kings. The most famous example is the ruler Pacal (A.D. 603–683) of *Palenque, whose tomb and great stone sarcophagus were discovered underneath the Temple of the Inscriptions.

The duties of Maya kings in ritual and warfare stand out clearly in the epigraphic and artistic record. The ruler held special ties to the gods, and his ceremonies opened the mundane world to contact with the divinities. In his ceremonial role, the king is frequently depicted as performing offerings, either by self-bloodletting or by conducting the sacrifice of others. In addition, he dedicated temples and honored his subordinates by ceremonial visits. The inscriptions also emphasize the king's role in warfare, stressing the important prisoners he captured, although the rites in which such prisoners were subsequently sacrificed receive greater attention than the acts of capture. Far less clear are the king's economic and administrative duties, although the scale of Maya society by the Classic Period makes it evident that they must have been substantial.

Tombs and fragmentary murals showing the insignia associated with royalty go back at least as far as 100 B.C., so the institution of Maya kingship must already have been established by that date. At the end of the Classic Period there may have been a change in the system of governance to one that was more broadly based, with a ruling council rather than an authority so strongly vested in a single ruler. Hints from inscriptions and art at the Post-Classic site of *Chichén Itzá (A.D. 1000–1250) point to this broader authority, as do descriptions of the even later state centered at Mayapán (A.D. 1250–1441).

Although the Classic Maya were once pictured as a gentle, peaceful people, the frequency with which war and captives are noted in the art and inscriptions now makes it clear that they were, in fact, obsessed with war. Nevertheless, we know little about the nature of Maya warfare. Classic murals at the site of Bonampak and Post-Classic ones at Chichén Itzá show battle scenes that are melees of hand-to-hand combat rather than confrontations of troops arrayed in formations. This is slim evidence, however, upon which to base far-reaching conclusions. Fortifications appear at some Classic and Post-Classic sites, but they are more often absent, and site locations usually offer few defensive possibilities.

The weapon most commonly depicted in Maya art is a spear tipped with a stone point. Clubs are also depicted, and stone knives, although usually shown as implements for sacrifice, were surely used in hostilities as well. The spearthrower, borrowed from Mexican neighbors, was known during the Classic Period but may not have been much used until later. The bow and arrow were added to the list of weapons during the Post-Classic period. Maya warriors defended themselves with small, hand-held shields and dressed themselves in waist-length armor of quilted cotton. Warriors are also shown wearing great headdresses that would have been a severe detriment in combat, so it seems likely that these were part of ceremonial costumes to be worn during pre- or postwar ritual.

Neither the size nor the organization of Maya military forces is clear. All male nobles probably served as warriors and derived prestige from the activity. A professional army, however, seems unlikely. At the time of the Spanish Conquest, sizable armies were fielded by conscripting commoners for the length of a campaign, a system that might also have been used in earlier days.

That warfare had both ceremonial and secular dimensions is clear. A king's prestige rested upon capturing and sacrificing prisoners and, best of all, rulers of opposing sites. But victories also must have brought such material rewards as land, booty, and tribute. There is sharp disagreement, however, about whether ceremonial or material objectives were the primary motives for war.

Evidence from Late Classic inscriptions indicates that the lowlands were divided into two great power blocks centered at the sites of Tikal and Calakmul. The two major powers contested each other with strategies that involved enlisting allied and vassal sites to attack their rival. Calakmul seems to have had the upper hand between A.D. 550 and around 700, when a series of its allies attacked Tikal. Tikal, however, bounced back as its ruler captured and sacrificed the king of Calakmul in A.D. 695 and then engaged in a series of victories over the allies of Calakmul.

It is possible that both the size of political units and the scale of warfare may have increased further in the Post-Classic Period (A.D. 1000–1540). Chichén Itzá seems to have had tight control of Yucatán for about two hundred years. Following this, Mayapán became the leading site and is credited in native histories with a comparable span of political dominance. At Chichén Itzá particularly, the art depicts hundreds of warriors, while murals show battle scenes in which towns and villages are overrun and burned. This might indicate a grander scale of war. It might also be a reflection of the more equal division of power suggested above that made it imperative to glorify larger numbers of individuals than just the ruler. By the time the Spanish arrived, however, Yucatán had fallen into political chaos and was divided into sixteen provinces that continually fought each other for power and territory.

[See also MESOAMERICA, articles on INTRODUCTION, CLASSIC PERIOD IN MESOAMERICA.]

■ Linda Schele and Mary Ellen Miller, The Blood of Kings: Dynasty and Ritual in Maya Art (1986). Linda Schele and David Freidel, A Forest of Kings: The Untold Story of the Ancient Maya (1990). T. Patrick Culbert, ed., Classic Maya Political History (1991). William L. Fash,

Scribes, Warriors and Kings: The City of Copan and the Ancient Maya (1991). Ross Hassig, War and Society in Ancient Mesoamerica (1992).

T. Patrick Culbert

MAYA VILLAGE LIFE

Maya village life has existed for at least three thousand years. Since villages were first established, before 1000 B.C., they have been the most persistent form of Maya settlement, in contrast to the larger types of Maya settlements, towns and cities. Towns or cities rarely lasted for more than a few centuries. Maya civilization has come and gone during the Classic Period, but village life continues. It is within the Maya village and household that Maya culture and language have been transmitted from generation to generation.

The earliest Maya villages, composed of a dozen or more households, were largely self-sufficient. Food was grown locally, and nearby sources of stone for cutting, scraping, and grinding purposes were exploited. Clays were obtained locally and used for making pottery and in-house construction. Decision-making was by consensus, and the early villages were not dominated by outside authority. The housing and possessions of the individual households in egalitarian villages were very similar to each other, since wealth, power, and status differences were avoided.

Most villages had at least three functional zones: domestic, agrarian, and communal. The domestic zone of villages was where household members lived, slept, stored food, ate, shared commodities and labor tasks, stored artifacts and food, and engaged in crafts and various family activities. Villages had agrarian zones, often infields (kitchen gardens) and outfields where food was produced. Many Maya villages produced seed crops (e.g., maize, beans) and root crops (e.g., manioc, xanthosoma), and they exploited various wild foods such as nuts and fruits. Most villages had a public communal area, at least a plaza for community activities. In larger villages, such as *Ceren, a civic building or buildings were built around the plaza. Many villages also had religious shrines, and village religious activities took place within the household and under the guidance of shamans ("seers" or curers). Shamans are religious specialists who are particularly effective in curing villagers, predicting the future, and contacting the supernatural realm.

Most of the research on the ancient Maya conducted during the nineteenth and twentieth centuries has focused on the elite in the big centers during the Classic Period, especially on their elegant temples, pyramids, palaces, and monumental plazas. It was not until archaeologists began conducting settlement-pattern studies after World War II that the dwellings of commoners, who compose eighty to ninety percent of the population, became a principal objective of research. Gordon Willey found abundant household remains in the Belize Valley, and William Coe discovered that vast areas surrounding the elite center of *Tikal were occupied by house mounds. William Sanders and Joseph Michels found numerous Maya villages in the highland landscape around Kaminaljuyu. A survey of the Zapotitan Valley of El Salvador revealed a landscape dotted with villages and an estimated population density of forty to seventy people per square kilometer. One result of research on commoner villages and households is the realization that the Maya landscape was densely occupied and intensively utilized, particularly during the Classic Period. For most of the pre-Columbian era, the adaptation was successful, and only during the last few centuries of the Classic Period did the Maya cross the threshold from sustainability.

Ongoing research at *Copán and Ceren has shown that agrarian villagers constructed multiple structures per household, focused on a common plaza. Villages with even modest degrees of self-sufficiency are characterized by high material standards of living (e.g., Ceren), with ample housing and a wide variety of foods stored for household use. Individual households had over seventy ceramic vessels for storage, cooking, and food serving. In contrast, commoners within a hierarchical society under demographic and ecologic stress, such as Tikal in the eighth and ninth centuries, had difficulty meeting basic nutritional needs.

The key functional unit within the village is the household, the coresidential adaptive unit that is often kin-based. The household shares functions of production and reproduction, distribution, transmission, and sharing-pooling. It is a social, cultural, religious, linguistic, and economic unit. Because education and enculturation occur within the unit, it is able to replicate itself and maintain a long-term tradition. Village culture is transmitted from generation to generation largely by intrahousehold activities.

An issue in Maya village studies is the relationship between elites and commoners. Compared with the commoners in relatively independent, self-sufficient villages, are the commoners in villages that are part of a hierarchical society exploited by the power centers? Are the commoners in a complex society impoverished by their subservient relationship to the elites? William Rathje and Randall McGuire concluded that the Maya commoners in hierarchical villages were indeed impoverished by the elites. However, they also suggested that the elites provided intangibles, such as ritual and ceremony, for the impoverished villagers.

During the past few decades ethnographers, such as Evon Vogt in Zinacantan, Chiapas, Mexico have studied many functioning Maya villages in southern Mexico and northern Central America. A few archaeologists, such as Brian Hayden in the Coxoh area of southern Mexico, have studied Maya villages, with an emphasis on recording and interpreting material cultural items that archaeologists, given good preservation, could find in ancient sites.

Maya villages have demonstrated their success in resisting outside influences, pressures, and conquest. They have effectively maintained their language and culture in the face of pressure from *Teotihuacán, the Aztecs, other Central Mexican ancient societies, and the Spanish and more recently against Western culture, militarized governments, and missionaries of various persuasions.

[See also MESOAMERICA, articles on FORMATIVE PERIOD IN MESOAMERICA, CLASSIC PERIOD IN MESOAMERICA.]

■ Gordon Willey, Prehistoric Maya Settlements in the Belize Valley (1965). William Coe, Tikal (1967). Joseph Michels, Settlement Pattern Excavations at Kaminaljuyu, Guatemala (1979). Payson Sheets, ed., Archeology and Volcanism in Central America: The Zapotitan Valley of El Salvador (1983). Brian Hayden, ed., Lithic Studies among the Contemporary Highland Maya (1987). Richard Wilk and Wendy Ashmore, eds., Household and Community in the Mesoamerican Past (1988). Evon Vogt, The Zinacantecos of Mexico (1990). Payson Sheets, The Ceren Site: A Prehistoric Village Buried by Volcanic Ash in Central America (1992).
Payson D. Sheets

MAYA PYRAMIDS AND TEMPLES

If one had to choose a single image to represent ancient Maya civilization, an obvious choice would be a temple soaring skyward atop a dizzyingly steep pyramid. It is, in fact, the "temple-pyramid" combination—the location of the temple building atop a flat-topped pyramid—that is so characteristically Maya.

The pyramid, consisting of a number of tiers of decreasing size, functions primarily to thrust the temple upward. It is a solid mass of construction that contains no rooms or passageways. Buried within its mass, however, are almost always the remains of earlier temple-pyramids. This constant burial of old structures within new ones can be attributed to the self-glorification of Maya rulers, all of whom dreamed of outdoing their predecessors with bigger and more imposing structures. These same rulers were usually buried deep beneath their temples in tombs that cut through earlier structures and often into bedrock below.

The temple building was a structure with an uneven number of doorways (one, three, and five were the most common) facing down the single stairway of the pyramid. The rooms within were surprisingly cramped because the unsteady corbeled arch used by the Maya for construction was capable of spanning only very narrow spaces. Above the temple rose a large crest, called a roof comb, a great additional mass of masonry that served to increase the height and provide more space for decoration.

This entire architectural assemblage, built from the easily worked limestone that underlies the shallow soil throughout much of the Maya lowlands, gives the impression of towering verticality. The staggeringly steep stairway of the pyramid (with treads too small for more than the front part of a foot) draws the eye of the viewer upward to the temple, while the roof comb extends the vision skyward. The visual image was enhanced by such architectural tricks as inset corners and overhanging moldings that break the effect of sheer mass and create an interplay of light and shadow in the tropical sunlight. The architectural sophistication was not accompanied by engineering precision, however. Corners were rarely precise right angles, and two temples facing each other were often slightly out of line.

The earliest large temples discovered to date are at the site of Nakbe, in far northern Guatemala. There, temple-pyramid construction began in the Middle Pre-Classic soon after 600 B.C., and by 300 B.C. the largest temple had reached a height of 150 feet (46 m). In the Late Pre-Classic (300 B.C.–A.D. 250), a number of sites had very large temple-pyramids, especially El Mirador, only eight miles from Nakbe. The Danta temple complex at El Mirador covers an area equivalent to four city blocks and reaches a height of 230 feet (70 m), exceeding in both height and volume any later temple complexes.

But it was in the Classic Period (A.D. 250–900) that temples reached their most characteristic form. At *Tikal in north-central Guatemala, five great temples of the Late Classic (A.D. 600–850) stand more than 150 feet (46 m) tall, and dozens of other sites are filled with comparable, if not quite so large, structures. Although all temple-pyramids share the basic features described above, there was great variety in regional architectural expression and decorative embellishment.

In the Post-Classic period (A.D. 900–1540), most large Maya sites were located in the Mexican part of the Yucatan Peninsula. By the Early Post-Classic (A.D. 900–1250) at *Chichén Itzá, temples were less common than before and multiroomed "palaces" more common. The Castillo, the only large temple-pyramid at the site, had four stairways and a flat roof without a roof comb. Other temples at the site, although still elevated, do not have the very large pyramids of the Classic Period. In the Late Postclassic (A.D. 1250–

1540), temples had become even smaller and less significant parts of the sites.

Maya temple-pyramids occurred in a variety of surroundings. Sometimes they were isolated from other structures and commanded attention from afar. More often, they were positioned in groups surrounding ceremonial plazas. Some temples were placed on the top of large, raised building complexes, called acropolises, where they shared space with other types of structures. There were also characteristic arrangements of multiple-temple units. A unit known as an "E Group" consists of three temples in a row facing a single temple. E Groups seem to have functioned as astronomical markers, because when the group is viewed from the fronting temple, the sun rises behind one or another of the three temples on the solstices and equinoxes.

At the outskirts of Maya sites, smaller temple-pyramids appear, which one can easily imagine to have served neighborhood populations. Many of these outlying "temples" now consist of only pyramids without stone structures on top and were probably once crowned with wooden temple buildings.

Many types of decoration, varying temporally and regionally, were used on pyramid-temples. The stairways of pyramids were often flanked by stucco masks of deities. The facades of temples were also decorated in either stucco or cut stone, while the space provided by the roof comb was often the location for large modeled figures. The decorations depicted supernatural beings and sometimes human figures. Often, they consisted of geometric designs that were full of symbolic meaning to the ancient Maya.

Temples were associated with mountains, for they sometimes showed a Witz (the Maya word for "mountain") Monster. The temple buildings, then, may have represented sacred caves, considered by modern Maya as the entrances to the supernatural world and the abode of ancestors. The doors of temples represented the mouths of supernatural beings, an image made explicit in *Copán Temple 22 and many Yucatecan sites where the front facade is carved with the image of a serpent, the open mouth of which is the temple doorway.

That temples actually served for religious ceremonies is clear because structures of the same temple-pyramid form were seen in use by the first Spanish visitors, who described with horror the sacrificial rites and blood-splattered priests. Exactly what ceremonies took place in earlier temples is not known, but given the Maya obsession with self-sacrificial bloodletting and the sacrifice of prisoners, it is likely that the rites were similar to those described by the Spanish conquistadores. Because the platforms on top of the pyramids were small and the temple rooms limited in space, only a select few could have been admitted to these holy spaces, but most temples were fronted by large plazas in which thousands of visitors might have watched what happened on the temple platforms far above them.

[See also ASTRONOMY: ASTRONOMY IN THE AMERICAS; MESOAMERICA, articles on INTRODUCTION, CLASSIC PERIOD IN MESOAMERICA.]

■ Tatiana Proskouriakoff, *An Album of Maya Architecture*, 2nd ed. (1963). George F. Andrews, *Maya Cities* (1975). George Kubler, *The Art and Architecture of Ancient America*, 3rd ed. (1984). Linda Schele and David Freidel, *A Forest of Kings: The Untold Story of the Ancient Maya* (1990).

T. Patrick Culbert

MAYA CRAFT SPECIALIZATION

In a seminal article published in 1970, R.E.W. Adams raised the issue of the true nature of Maya civilization. Chief among the points he raised about the nature of Maya society was whether or not there was evidence for true craft specialization as a regularly practiced economic activity among the ancient Maya. In the intervening twenty-five years, quite a number of archaeologists have spent considerable effort investigating this aspect of ancient Maya life. While significant effort has been expended and quite a number of interesting results have ensued, there is still significant disagreement about both the presence and the nature of craft specialization among the ancient Maya.

Simply put, craft specialization is one form of occupational specialization wherein its practitioners obtain some part of their income from the manufacture and exchange of material goods: stone tools, pottery, grinding stones, and the like. There are two general types of craft specialization that are recognized. The first type, independent specialization, is the manufacture of goods for trade on an open market for general consumption. The second type, attached specialization, is the manufacture of goods for a patron or sponsor. What is currently unclear about craft specialization among the ancient Maya is which form of specialization was predominant or most typical and why.

Since 1979, substantial research at the remarkable site of Colha in northern Belize has revealed a tradition of nearly industrial-level production of stone agricultural implements from the Middle Pre-Classic (1000 B.C.–400 B.C.) through the Late Classic Periods (A.D. 700–900), with a lower-volume tradition continuing into the Early Post-Classic Period (A.D. 900–1250). The tools produced at Colha, numbering literally in the millions, were traded throughout northern Belize over this entire time period. Production seems to have been organized by corporate family units, with workshops generally located in the center of relatively large plaza groups. The organization of the distribution of these tools is still unclear, and may never be known. Thus we do not know if each corporate family unit was also responsible for distributing their own wares to other sites, or if some higher authority at Colha collected the production of the various corporate groups and then acted as a middleman to handle distribution of the goods throughout the region. The argument has been made that Colha represents some form of true independent specialization, although as indicated, until we know more about the organization of distribution, this will remain an arguable point. What is quite clear is that the quantity of stone tool production at Colha was extraordinary, not just for the ancient Maya but for almost any other region of the world during the same time period, and the skill of the craftsmen working at Colha was truly remarkable.

The second site where the most fruitful research on Maya craft specialization has been conducted is *Copán in Honduras. Here evidence for specialist production of *ceramics, shell ornaments, jewelry made of lapis lazuli, and rhyolite grinding stones (manos and metates) has been investigated. As opposed to Colha, the level of production in most of these material categories appears to have been constant but fairly limited. In addition, most evidence for workshop space at Copán is in association with the residences of elite families. This last point has led researchers at Copán to conclude that craft specialization at Copán was typically attached specialization, or production under the patronage of the elites. A similar pattern of evidence for craft specialization has also been sketched in for the highland Maya site of Kaminaljuyu in Guatemala.

While Colha, Copán, and Kaminaljuyu have received the most concerted research efforts aimed at understanding the nature of Maya craft specialization, they are not the only locales where this question has been investigated. For example, recent research in the upper Belize River valley has indicated tantalizing evidence for attached specialists with a highly refined stone tool kit, consisting of both chert and obsidian tools, probably engaged in fine woodworking. Unfortunately, only the tools remain and none of the products or manufacturing debris. Similarly, notable Belizean coastal sites such as Moho Cay have revealed evidence of specialized salt production stations and possible obsidian transhipment points joining coastal and riverine trade routes.

On the basis of the current evidence, it is quite clear that some portion of the ancient Maya population was regularly engaged in specialized craft production activities. In most cases, those activities were probably under the patronage of the local ruling elites rather than independent economic activities. The one clear exception to this reconstruction is the site of Colha in northern Belize, where restricted chert resources in the region were masterfully exploited by the residents of Colha to serve the demand for stone implements in the rest of northern Belize, where appropriate stone resources are not generally available. The continuing trend in Maya archaeology of focusing on the houses of commoners rather than the houses of elites and monumental architecture will undoubtedly modify and enhance the currently sketchy picture of the nature and extent of craft specialization among the ancient Maya.

[See also LITHICS: INTRODUCTION.]

■ William T. Sanders and Joseph W. Michels, *Teotihuacan and Kaminaljuyu: A Study in Prehistoric Culture Contact* (1977). William Leonard Fash, *Scribes, Warriors, and Kings: The City of Copán and the Ancient Maya* (1991). Thomas R. Hester, Harry J. Shafer, and Jack D. Eaton, *Continuing Archeology at Colha, Belize*, Studies in Archaeology 16 (1994).

George Michaels

MAYA BALL COURTS

The game of soccer is arguably the modern derivative of ancient Mesoamerican ball game, which was played throughout Mesoamerica in what now constitutes Mexico, Belize, Guatemala, El Salvador, and western Honduras. Ball-game paraphernalia (stone yokes) have also been found in the Caribbean archipelago and a version of the ball game was played by the ancient Hohokam in North America and by Amazonian groups of South America. In the sixteenth century, the game was very popular throughout the highland Aztec Empire. Spanish chroniclers, particularly the friar Diego Durán, collected eyewitness descriptions of the ball game and of the high stakes, often life or death, over which the "game" was played. During the first millennium A.D., the ball game was extremely popular along the southern Gulf Coast of Mexico. At the site of El Tajín, for example, over a dozen ball courts have been uncovered by archaeological research in the central portion of the site. At Tajín and elsewhere, ball courts are recognizable by virtue of a long, thin playing alley or court (generally between 49 and 115 feet (15 and 35 m) in length and 10 to 39 feet (3 to 12 m) in width) which is demarcated by two parallel platforms. Sometimes the platforms are banked as if to accommodate bleacher seats and at other times the playing field is bounded by sharply vertical walls. Often a stone ring is anchored to the side wall about 6.5 to 10 feet (2 to 3 m) off the ground. The interior diameter of the ring (between 8 and 16 inches (20 and 40 cm)) gives a maximum diameter for the rubber ball. Apparently, shooting the ball through the ring—no easy feat—translated into an instant win.

Although the rules of the "game" are not completely clear and may have varied from place to place, players apparently faced off on either side of a line that ran parallel to the long axis of the court rather than perpendicular to it. Ancient ball players could use only their head, shoulders, and hips.

The earliest ball courts in the Maya lowlands—which occur in Belize at Cerros and Colha—were constructed after 400 B.C. By A.D. 250, the ball game occupied a central place in elite society. Often a political contest and always imbued with ritual significance, the ball game of Classic Period elites (A.D. 250 to 1000) was played on a masonry construction. A stone-lined court flanked by platforms was not a necessary prerequisite for playing the game, however, and we can surmise that the ball game was played by individuals from all walks of life anywhere there was a flat, compact surface. The elite masonry ball courts, on the other hand, are always located proximate to the central core of monumental architecture at lowland Maya sites, and almost all large Classic Period sites have at least one court. The size of the courts, paradoxically, does not seem to be indicative of the political importance of a place, since the large and powerful capital of *Tikal in the Petén of Guatemala has relatively small ball courts. One of the largest and most elaborate courts known from the Maya lowlands occurs at the late, northern site of *Chichén Itzá where there exists a playing alley 551 feet (168 m) long and 229 feet (70 m) wide. Scenes carved in stone on the side walls of the playing field reveal to us the deadly seriousness of this game. Two players are shown facing off with a large rubber ball situated between them. One is standing upright while the other, unfortunate player has been brought to his knees. He has been decapitated and the opposing player holds his severed head in his hand by a shank of hair. Images of sacrifice and decapitation, in fact, are often associated with Classic Maya ball playing, and frequently the sacrificed individual appears to have been a captive taken in a skirmish with a neighboring kingdom. Such images go back to the exploits of the epic Maya hero twins, Hunahpu and Xbalanque, who played a deadly ball game with the lords of the underworld and finally emerged victorious. Such themes of death and regeneration permeated the Maya ball game.

[See also MESOAMERICA: INTRODUCTION.]

■ Vernon L. Scarborough and David R. Wilcox, *The Mesoamerican Ballgame* (1991).

Patricia A. McAnany

CLASSIC MAYA COLLAPSE

Complex urban civilization thrived in the southern Maya lowlands for over a millennium from 300 B.C., if not earlier, to A.D. 800 during the Late Pre-Classic and Classic Periods. After reaching its zenith in the eighth century, this civilization collapsed in the ninth century, as major architectural construction ceased at a large number of sites and many urban centers were depopulated and abandoned. The relatively rapid disappearance of Classic Maya civilization in the southern lowlands, at a time when it seemingly was at its height, and the lack of recovery after the collapse have attracted considerable archaeological, as well as popular, attention for many years. Although numerous explanations have been offered, an air of scientific mystery has hung over the question of the collapse. However, in recent years, new research results and reexaminations of existing data from new perspectives have led to clearer understandings of the causes of the cultural changes in eighth-century Maya civilization.

During the eighth century A.D., Classic Maya civilization reached its demographic height. Population in the southern lowlands is thought to have been in the millions, although estimates vary widely. Population increased at long-established cities and new centers were founded as the overall landscape filled up with people. Construction boomed, as many new temples, palaces, and houses were built. Trade, including long distance, regional, and local, also flourished, as did the ruling elite. Evidence for the latter can be found in their increasing wealth and power, which were chronicled in the inscriptions on the large number of carved stelae that were erected in the eighth century.

During the period between 9.17.0.0.0 and 10.0.0.0.0 in the Maya calendar, or A.D. 771 to 830, many of these activities had ceased at a large number of cities and towns. Not only did construction halt, but most centers and their sustaining areas appear to have been either partially or totally abandoned. At a few sites on the Rio Pasion, such as Seibal and Altar de Sacrificios, there was a brief late florescence, but by the end of the ninth century these sites, too, declined. There also was continued occupation around the lakes of the central Petén, although on a diminished scale, and a limited number of cities situated along rivers in northern and central Belize maintained their vitality. In addition, recent research at *Copán indicates that while the urban core was abandoned, there was continued occupation of the city's hinterlands for a few more centuries.

Past explanations for the disappearance of Classic Maya civilization have run the gamut from single-factor natural disasters, such as earthquakes, hurricanes, climatic change, and insect plagues, to more complex formulations centering on soil exhaustion, warfare, and peasant revolt. None of these explanations have found general acceptance.

In the 1970s, important strides in understanding the collapse were taken as attention shifted to explanations centering on a multiplicity of interacting causes. These formulations also focused on the disappearance of the Classic civilization not as a short-term phenomenon but as a long-term process, the roots of which could be found much earlier in the Classic Period. Moreover, they attempted to robustly explain not only the collapse but the lack of recovery in the southern lowlands after the fall.

This new generation of hypotheses frequently had as their central theme the pressures that population growth and territorial expansion had on the agricultural, economic, and sociopolitical systems and, in turn, on the environment and interpolity competition and warfare. The reinforcing role of ideology on this cycle was also considered. This general theme was bolstered by new research data that pointed to the possibilities of environmental stress and deterioration in the Late Classic Period (A.D. 600 to 800). Large-scale forest clearing and the intensification of agriculture were seen as exacerbating factors. As the environmental deterioration, territorial expansion, and competition lowered the per capita food supply and imperiled intersite exchange, it was hypothesized that the Maya elite reacted by intensifying the pressures that already were stressing the system. Although the specific trigger for the ninth-century collapse was not identified, general agreement among scholars about the underlying causes began to emerge. By the ninth century, ecological disasters coupled with political breakdowns, further reinforced by military and economic pressures on the frontiers of the southern lowlands, led to widespread population loss due to increased mortality and emigration. Recovery was forestalled by the severity of the environmental destruction and the changing economic scene in Mesoamerica that favored areas with direct access to desired raw materials and waterborne trade routes.

Further studies in the 1980s have helped refine these new systemic understandings. New research in the northern lowlands and the reconsideration of older chronologies have shown that just as sites in the south were collapsing, major centers in the north, such as the Puuc Region cities (including Uxmal, Sayil, and Labna) and *Chichén Itzá, were beginning a major florescence. Moreover, cultural links were found between the newly arising northern sites and the southern centers on the Pasion and in Belize that continued to thrive in the ninth century, as were connections to the Chontal Maya (or Putun) of the Gulf Coast lowlands, who came to dominate long-distance trade around the Yucatan Peninsula at this time. In other words, scholars found that there was a significant demographic shift from south to north around A.D. 800 and that the Classic civilization did not totally collapse but continued to develop during Terminal Classic (A.D. 800 to 1000) times in the northern lowlands. Thus, the Classic "collapse" has recently begun to be seen by many archaeologists as a southern phenomenon and part of a larger picture of ancient Maya development that sees the fall of Chichén Itzá around A.D. 1200 as marking the end of the Classic tradition rather than the ninth-century demise of many Classic centers in the southern lowlands.

Scholars also have begun to recognize that even in the southern lowlands it is difficult to talk of a monolithic collapse, since there was significant regional and local variation in terms of environmental stress, economic change, and urban and rural abandonment. Varying proximity to waterborne trade routes that linked certain southern centers to new markets in the Maya lowlands and throughout Mesoamerica appears to have been particularly important to the onset and severity of cultural collapse in the southern lowlands.

[See also MESOAMERICA, articles on INTRODUCTION, CLASSIC PERIOD IN MESOAMERICA, POST-CLASSIC PERIOD IN MESOAMERICA; STATES: THEORIES OF THE COLLAPSE OF STATES.]

■ T. Patrick Culbert, ed., The Classic Maya Collapse (1973). Don S. Rice and Prudence M. Rice, "Lessons from the Maya," Latin American Research Review 19 (1984): 7–34. John W. G. Lowe, The Dynamics of Apocalypse: A Systems Simulation of the Classic Maya Collapse (1985). Jeremy A. Sabloff and E. Wyllys Andrews V, eds., Late Lowland Maya Civilization (1986). Joseph A. Tainter, The Collapse of Complex Societies (1988). Jeremy A. Sabloff, The New Archaeology and the Ancient Maya (1990). David Webster and AnnCorrine Freter, "Settlement History and the Classic Collapse at Copan: A Redefined Chronological Perspective," Latin American Antiquity (1990): 66–85. Jeremy A. Sabloff, "Interpreting the Collapse of Classic Maya Civilization: A Case Study of Changing Archaeological Perspectives," in Metaarchaeology, ed. Lester Embree (1992), pp. 99–119. Jeremy A. Sabloff and John S. Henderson, eds., Lowland Maya Civilization in the Eighth Century A.D. (1993).

Jeremy A. Sabloff

MEADOWCROFT ROCKSHELTER is a deeply stratified, multicomponent site located about 30 miles (48 km) southwest of Pittsburgh, Pennsylvania. It is situated on the north bank of Cross Creek, a small tributary of the Ohio River, some 7.5 miles (12 km) west of that river.

Meadowcroft Rockshelter was originally discovered (and subsequently protected) by Albert Miller, whose family has owned the property continuously since 1795. The site was brought to the attention of J. M. Adovasio, and became the focal point of a long-term multidisciplinary project, the field phase of which began in 1973 and terminated in 1978. The analysis and publication phase is ongoing.

There are eleven strata at Meadowcroft, representing the longest occupational sequence in the New World. A remarkable corpus of artifactual, floral, and faunal data is anchored by some fifty-two stratigraphically consistent *radiocarbon dates which indicate that intermittent seasonal occupation/utilization of this locality minimally extends from ca. 14,000–14,500 B.P. to A.D. 1776. Though contamination of the earliest carbon 14 dates from the site has been suggested (Haynes 1980, Tankersley et al. 1987), repeated laboratory analysis including accelerator mass spectrometry (AMS) determinations has consistently failed to detect the presence of particulate or nonparticulate contaminants (Adovasio et al. 1990, 1992).

The earliest occupants at Meadowcroft are ascribable to the Miller Complex, a pioneer population of generalized hunter-gatherers with a sophisticated lithic technology based on the production of blade tools produced from polyhedral blade cores and also characterized by the manufacture of distinctive unfluted bifacial projectile points called Miller lanceolates (Adovasio et al. 1988). Significantly, the extant paleoenvironmental data indicate that the site's earliest inhabitants operated in an environment not radically different from that of present times (Adovasio et al. 1984, 1985). Later occupations at the site include local representatives of all major cultural periods/stages now recognized in eastern North America. Throughout its history, the site served as a temporary locus for hunting, collecting, and food-processing activities focused on Cross Creek and the immediately contiguous uplands.

In a culture-historical perspective, many believe that Meadowcroft and *Monte Verde provide the best evidence for a pre-Clovis human presence in North and South America, respectively.

[See also AMERICAS, FIRST SETTLEMENT OF THE: SETTLEMENT OF THE AMERICAS BEFORE 12,500 B.C.; ANTIQUITY OF HUMANKIND: ANTIQUITY OF HUMANKIND IN THE AMERICAS; HUNTER-GATHERERS, NORTH AMERICAN ARCHAIC; NORTH AMERICA: THE EASTERN WOODLANDS AND THE SOUTH.]

■ C. V. Haynes, "Paleoindian Charcoal from Meadowcroft Rockshelter: Is Contamination a Problem?" American Antiquity 45 (1980): 582–587. J. M. Adovasio et al., "Meadowcroft Rockshelter and the Pleistocene/Holocene Transition in Southwestern Pennsylvania," in Contributions in Quaternary Vertebrate Paleontology: A Volume in Memorial to John E. Guilday, ed. H. H. Genoways and M. R. Dawson (1984), pp. 347–369. J. M. Adovasio et al., "Paleoenvironmental Reconstruction at Meadowcroft Rockshelter, Washington County, Pennsylvania," in Environments and Extinctions: Man in Glacial North America, ed. J. I. Mead and D. J. Meltzer (1985), pp. 73–110. K. B. Tankersley, C. A. Munson, and D. Smith, "Recognition of Bituminous Coal Contaminants in Radiocarbon Samples," American Antiquity 52 (1987): 318–329. J. M. Adovasio, A. T. Boldurian, and R. C. Carlisle, "Who Are Those Guys? Some Biased Thoughts on the Initial Peopling of the New World," in Americans before Columbus: Ice

Age Origins, comp. and ed. R. C. Carlisle (1988), pp. 45–61. J. M. Adovasio, J. Donahue, and R. Stuckenrath, "The Meadowcroft Rockshelter Radiocarbon Chronology, 1975–1990," *American Antiquity* 55 (1990): 348–354. B. F. Fagan, "Tracking the First Americans," *Archaeology* Nov./Dec. (1990): 14–20. J. M. Adovasio, J. Donahue, and R. Stuckenrath, "Never Say Never Again: Some Thoughts on Could Haves and Might Have Beens," *American Antiquity* 57 (1992): 327–331.

J. M. Adovasio

MEDIEVAL EUROPE

OVERVIEW

The Medieval Period, or Middle Ages, in Europe falls between the fifth and fifteenth centuries A.D., a span of around one thousand years. Neither its beginning nor its end is firmly agreed upon, however, and in some regions an intervening period is inserted between the end of the Roman Empire and the Middle Ages proper. In England, for example, the Roman Period is followed by the Anglo-Saxon period and the Middle Ages are usually considered to begin only in the eleventh century at the Norman Conquest.

The categories of evidence available for Medieval Europe are rich and varied, and include standing buildings (many of them still in use) and contemporary written records, as well as the more customary archaeological fare of sites and artifacts. In the early Middle Ages, documentary evidence is sparse and most of the information comes from archaeology alone. The Germanic invasions of the Roman Empire (with which the period begins) are difficult to document in detail, however, and it is only with the foundation of the kingdoms of Franks, Goths, and Anglo-Saxons that a broad archaeological pattern becomes visible. Investigation of Germanic cemeteries such as *Frénouville in northern France and the royal ship burial of *Sutton Hoo in eastern England illustrate the information available from this kind of work. Future DNA studies of cemetery remains may help to determine the extent to which the existing populations were replaced by newcomers.

The eighth to eleventh centuries were marked by an upsurge in church building and by the expansion of Viking trade. Dublin was one of the trading towns founded by the Vikings, who also injected new life into existing centers such as *York. They also sailed down the great Russian rivers, founding the city of Novgorod and stimulating the development of the Russian state of Kiev. This eastern trade brought the Vikings into contact not only with the Slavs but also with the Byzantine Empire (the remnant of Roman rule in Asia Minor and the Balkans) and with the Islamic kingdoms of the Near East. At the opposite geographical extreme, the Vikings used their oceangoing vessels (well represented by the *Oseberg ship burial) to explore the coast of North America and to found a Viking settlement on L'Anse aux Meadows on Newfoundland.

The twelfth and thirteenth centuries were a period of sustained economic growth in much of Europe. Splendid churches and cathedrals in Romanesque and Gothic styles were built in the major centers of western Europe, and cities grew in size and importance. Kings and local lords built increasingly elaborate castles to protect themselves and their estates. Growth and population increases continued into the fourteenth century, but had already begun to decline when the plague known as the *Black Death struck in 1347. As much as one-third of the European population may have died in the epidemic. Calamitous though it was, this helped to release the pressure on land and in England allowed the expansion of sheep farming and the lucrative export of wool. Deserted villages such as *Wharram Percy testify to these economic changes, though it is clear that the depopulation following the Black Death was far from being the only factor behind their abandonment.

Despite the Black Death, Europe recovered economically during the fifteenth century and witnessed a new interest in Classical learning, a classicizing tendency in the arts, and a number of major technological innovations such as printing. By the middle of the century the European Renaissance was in full swing in Italy and the Low Countries, and Portuguese navigators had embarked on the first of those voyages of exploration which were to lead to the discovery of the New World in 1492.

[*See also* BRITISH ISLES: MEDIEVAL BRITAIN; GERMANS AND GERMANIC INVASIONS.]

Chris Scarre

CASTLES OF MEDIEVAL EUROPE

Sites enclosed by an artificial defensive work go back to Bronze Age or Neolithic times in western Europe, and adopted a more disciplined form in the European parts of the Roman Empire. Earthwork defenses are not a marked feature of the migration period, but became increasingly common as the first millennium advanced. They are especially associated with the Vikings. The circular earthworks of Denmark and Germany of around the year 1000 A.D., however, are not castles, since the latter owe their existence to the particular form of society they served, further to the south.

Initial Functions. Feudalism, a social and political system in which a vassal did homage to his lord in return for his land, and supplied armed knights as part of the tenure of land, developed in western Europe late in the first millennium A.D. With it developed the castle, the title deed, so to speak, of the lord who controlled the territory surrounding it. Unlike earlier fortifications, it was not a tribal, communal, or military (in the Roman sense) work but a highly personal structure displaying the claims of an individual to the loyalty and subservience of the population in the (usually large) territory surrounding it. The lord's position was clearly reflected in the division of the early castle into two parts: the *donjon* (derived from Latin *dominium*, lordship), and the *basse-cour*, or bailey below, where the household and retainers lived. The donjon could consist of a stone tower, or *keep*, though in the great majority of cases it was a wooden structure (that no longer survives) set on an earthen pedestal or mound, the *motte*. Such superstructures are depicted on the Bayeux tapestry (ca. 1070) although the interpretation of the images is controversial.

Feudalism, and so castles, first emerged in France, although the precise location of the origin of castles is not known. The practice of building these structures spread eastward by acculturation into Germany, westward by conquest into England (1066), and southward into Spain, Sicily, and Italy, and from the time of the First Crusade (1098), into the eastern Mediterranean region. Influenced perhaps by the indigenous forms of fortification in the eastern Mediterranean area, the shape of European castles changed in the later twelfth century, coming to rely on a strong perimeter studded with flanking towers. The design became more geometrical and workmanship more refined in the later Middle Ages, so that a fourteenth- or fifteenth-century castle is quite a different structure from one of the eleventh or twelfth century.

There is no rule about situation: The choice was to take advantage of gravity at the top of a hill or of water in the valley. As the undermining of walls and towers became something of a menace, the tendency was to move down into the valley, as at Old Bolingbroke, Lincolnshire. Often the choice was constrained by a preexisting village or town. The *Domesday Book* (1086) refers several times to houses being cleared to construct a castle. A common solution was to build the castle in the inner angle of the earlier Roman wall, as in the case of the Tower of London.

A castle was essentially a fortified residence with permanent officials running a large farm: It lay at the center of an organization whose purpose was to make money, not spend it. The surrounding community owed labor or other services to the lord and the manorial, and higher courts were held in the castle, which was very much the hub of local administration. The lord himself was resident from time to time, with a household that might run into hundreds. The party typically brought its own furniture and had its own administrative organization and staff. The lord himself was primarily interested in hunting and hawking in the park and forest associated with the castle. Some castles had special pleasure gardens, like the Pleasance at Kenilworth Castle, Warwickshire, constructed by Henry V (1413–1422).

From an archaeological point of view, the most conspicuous remains at a castle are the fortifications: ditches, towers, and gatehouse. These were not ornamental but intended to be used, and in the eleventh and twelfth centuries probably were. Their construction and maintenance were major outlays for the lord. The domestic buildings within the castle were usually disposed against the curtain wall, which conveniently created a long side for a rectangular building. Medieval aristocratic culture had been, since the migration period, a hall culture; the whole complex of buildings within any domestic assembly was dominated by a great hall. In continental Europe, the hall was normally on the first floor, but in England from the late twelfth century the preference was for a ground floor hall, often with aisle arcades (like a church), central hearth below an open roof, and a louver to let out smoke. At one end was a passage between doors on the opposed walls, and beyond that an external kitchen, while at the other end there was direct access to the lord's chamber. The primary function of the hall was to serve as a communal dining room for the two main meals of the day, but as the trestle tables on which these were served could be taken down, the hall could become a courthouse, a theater for ceremonies and recitals, or a dormitory for use at night. It was a multifunctional building, central to the whole life of the community.

Strung along the curtain wall from the lower end of the hall were the kitchen, bread ovens, and other services, and from the upper end, the lord's quarters and the chapel. In a large castle, there might be several chapels and certainly several private oratories. In continental Europe, a chapel over the gateway allowed the outgoing or incoming traveler to celebrate the Eucharist. In most castles the mural towers were put to use for accommodation; a peculiar development in England was the construction of a large residential gatehouse. As with unfortified houses, a distinctive feature of late medieval castles was the provision of ranges of cellular lodgings, separate accommodations for individuals, a good example being the ranges on the east and south sides of the upper ward of Windsor Castle.

Varied Castle Features. The earliest castles in England, such as Chepstow (Gwent), had a hall-like structure as their primary element. It is likely that the great keeps of the end of the eleventh century, the White Tower at the Tower of London and the even bigger royal keep at Colchester, were built by the Norman invaders in response to the need for protected accommodation in a land where the natives were not always friendly. It has been suggested that keeps are of two kinds: (1) smaller ones for the personal use of the lord, affiliated to the structures on motte tops, and (2) large hall-keeps intended to accommodate most if not all of the household. Large keeps virtually disappeared in England around 1200, but they continued to be built in continental Europe, where the most famous was the huge cylinder at Coucy built in the thirteenth century (sadly, destroyed in the First World War). In Germany, the uninhabited *Bergfriede*, massive keeplike towers, seem to have had a primarily symbolic significance.

Probably the most famous of European castles, Château Gaillard (Eure, France) was erected by Richard I of England in 1197–1198 to protect his duchy of Normandy against his nominal feudal overlord, the king of France. It was a major undertaking to build the castle and associated town. Richard, the hero of the Third Crusade, was likely to have been influenced by fortifications he had seen in the Middle East, and some features, notably the strange form of machicolation, are said to point to this. If construction of the castle was spectacular, hardly less so was its successful siege and capture in 1204 by Philip Augustus, king of France (1180–1223), who subsequently retook the whole duchy.

Oriental influences are clearer at Castel del Monte (Apulia, Italy). This castle was built by the German emperor Frederick II (1212–1250), a cosmopolitan figure, more Italian than German. It is two-storied and octagonal in plan, with towers at the angles—and an altogether more sophisticated structure than we might expect to encounter in feudal Europe. The octagonal castle at Boulogne-sur-mer or the cruder hexagonal one at Bolingbroke, Lincolnshire, appear to be slightly earlier in date but owe something to the same source as Castel del Monte.

The great castle-building campaigns of Edward I (1272–1307) in north Wales in 1277 and 1283 must also be mentioned. The wealth of surviving royal records on the costs of the construction of these castles can be closely tied to the splendid ruins at Caernarfon, Harlech, Conwy, and Beaumaris, so the year-by-year progress of work, the place of origin, the numbers of craftsmen and laborers, and even their rates of pay can be studied. Indeed, these records provide our main body of evidence on medieval castle building. The fact that the mason in overall charge (in effect, the architect), James of St. Georges d'Esperanches, came from Savoy in southeastern France gave the operation a European dimension.

From the mid-fourteenth century, there was a change in the character of castles; they became a cult, a source of pleasure in their own right, although castles like Vincennes still remained formidable defensive works. The exquisite pictures of castles in the calendar in the *Très Riches Heures* of the Duc de Berry in the early fifteenth century make the point well. It was but a short step from this self-conscious attitude to the Renaissance châteaux of the Loire. This step was hastened by the invention of firearms in the fourteenth century and the discovery of the angle bastion in the early sixteenth century, which really made a fortified private residence no longer feasible.

Recent Research. Castles have been the subject of a growing amount of recent research. The wealth of English royal records has been referred to in relation to Edward I's Welsh castles, and this royal archive, the most extensive in Europe, has been the basis for the first two volumes of the great six-volume *History of the King's Works* (1963). By associating the written sources with the physical remains, an incomparable work of reference was created for the royal castles—or those at some point in royal hands—and the king owned by far the greatest number of castles.

Archaeology has had most to contribute to castle studies in the eleventh and twelfth centuries, for it is in this period that the written sources are of least help. It is sufficient to comment that it was not grasped until the early years of the twentieth century that the majority of the castles of the eleventh century were built of timber. The reconstruction we make in our mind's eye of the landscape of the period now has carved and painted wooden structures that more closely resemble the villages of the Native peoples of the northwest coast of North America than stone castles of later times.

Brian Hope-Taylor was able to identify traces of a square structure on the motte top at Abinger, Surrey, although they were perhaps interpreted too closely in terms of the Bayeux tapestry. At Farnham in 1958, Michael Thompson revealed a huge square masonry structure built on the original ground surface and enlarged at the top, against which the mound had been thrown up step by step, consolidating the chalk marl as the work proceeded. This raised the question whether mottes generally were built up around a preexisting structure and whether supports for a superstructure were to be found in all motte mounds. The questions remain unanswered, mainly because of the practical difficulties of motte dissection.

The most comprehensive investigation of a motte and bailey has been carried out over nearly thirty years by Robert Higham and Phillip Barker at Hen Domen on the Welsh border. Not only were there traces of a nearly 20-foot (6 m) square structure on top of the motte, but detailed excavation revealed evidence for elaborate timber defenses. More surprising, the excavations showed that there had been timber buildings all through the interior of the bailey, with the hall beside the motte ditch and directly linked by a bridge to its summit. There were several periods of reconstruction of the wooden buildings. Perhaps the most interesting general question that arises from these excavations is whether the lord at Hen Domen lived permanently on top of the motte.

In France the most suggestive excavations have been those carried out by Michel de Bouard at Doué-la-Fontaine (Maine-et-Loire) from 1967 to 1970. Here there was a sequence of three periods: a stone building 21 by 77 feet (16 by 23.5 m) of the ninth century, raised by the addition of a first floor in the tenth century so as to transform what had originally been a hall into a keep. The third stage was the addition of a mound, or motte, in the eleventh century, burying the ground floor. There is no doubt that the mound

was an afterthought in this case, and its late position in the sequence is of interest. The excavation at Doué-la-Fontaine is indeed pregnant with matter for anyone concerned with the genesis of the European castle.

[*See also* ARMS AND ARMOR; BRITISH ISLES: MEDIEVAL BRITAIN.]

■ Ella Armitage, *Early Norman Castles of the British Isles* (1912). A. H. Thompson, *Military Architecture in England during the Middle Ages* (1912). Howard Colvin, Arnold Taylor, and Allen Brown, *A History of the King's Works*, vols. 1–2 (1963). Jean Longnon and Raymond Cazelles, *Les très riches heures in Duc de Berry* (1969). Michael Thompson, *The Decline of the Castle* (1987). John Kenyon, *Medieval Fortifications* (1990). Jean Mesqui, *Châteaux et enceintes de la France medievale: de la defense à la residence*, 2 vols. (1991). Michael Thompson, *The Rise of the Castle* (1991). Phillip Barker and Robert Higham, *Timber Castles* (1992).

Michael W. Thompson

CHURCHES AND CATHEDRALS OF MEDIEVAL EUROPE

The form of the early Christian church was based on the architecture of the Roman basilica, and the earliest purpose-built church buildings of the post-Roman period were aisled rectangles built of stone, usually with tiled roofs. At the eastern end there was an apse, at the west an entrance door. This basilican plan is found, with local variations, throughout the Roman Empire and the barbarian successor states in western Europe from the fourth century onward.

Early Structures. At old St. Peter's in *Rome and in other structures, the simple rectangle of the basilica could be elaborated by adding side rooms (transepts) at the eastern end to give a cross-like shape to the plan. At the west, there was a colonnaded courtyard with an entrance opposite that in the west wall of the church. St. Peter's was paralleled by smaller churches of Late Roman and immediately post-Roman date throughout Europe. In these churches, the altar was usually located in the eastern apse, and the congregation would sit in the main rectangular area (the nave).

From the Late Roman period onward, it is also possible to recognize an architectural division between those churches designed for the use of specific families or local populations and those connected with a bishop. The latter (episcopal) churches were usually larger in size and of more complex plan than those in the former group. Around episcopal churches (cathedrals), there were often groups of domestic and other buildings connected with the bishop and his entourage. Such buildings were essential to the administrative and residential functions of the cathedral complex, while the ritual of baptism by bishops meant that a baptistry was also part of the assemblage of buildings. All these aspects can be seen in the fifth-century and later cathedral of St. Pierre at Geneva. There, a large basilican church stands adjacent to a second smaller church of similar plan, across a courtyard bounded on its eastern side by a baptistry. The bishop's residence, with its own smaller chapel and mosaics in Late Roman tradition, was part of the same group of structures. Such episcopal building groups have been found throughout fourth-century Gaul, and form the basis for medieval cathedral closes.

During the course of the fourth to seventh centuries, church plans, especially cathedral plans, became more elaborate and larger in scale, the cruciform plan (either Latin cross or equal-armed cross) becoming widespread. Side chapels and porches were frequently added, and towers as well as internal and external balconies were occasionally provided. Round and polygonal churches were also built, some with apses. In short, by A.D. 800, a very wide repertoire of plans and elevations had been established. Contacts throughout Europe meant that new designs were rapidly adopted in areas distant from each other, and architectural innovation was taking place in many different centers.

By the ninth century, this process had resulted in the development of monumental cathedrals in many European towns, paralleled by churches of equivalent architectural magnitude at monastic sites. The most widely known church of this period is in fact the palace chapel at Aachen (Germany), built in the late eighth century for Charlemagne's court. The eleventh century saw buildings of even greater size and elaboration, as, for example, at Durham (England) and Speyer (Germany). These cathedrals, built in the Romanesque style, were to be found in every great city of medieval Europe.

The Gothic Style. Romanesque architecture, with its heavy forms, round-headed arches, and thick columns, was succeeded by the great age of medieval cathedral architecture in the so-called Gothic style, originating in the twelfth century. This style employed more window openings, more finely defined traceries, and pointed rather than round-headed arches, and lasted until the latter part of the fourteenth century. An early example is Laon Cathedral in France, built from about 1165 onward in this style.

By the end of the twelfth century, similar buildings had been initiated at Chartres, Bourges, and Canterbury. The Gothic style incorporated much more internal and external decoration than Romanesque, for example, in the elaborately carved tower at Freiburg-im-Breisgau and at Cologne and Strasbourg cathedrals.

Elsewhere, the transition from Romanesque to Gothic architecture was less abrupt. At Monreale and Cefalu in Sicily, churches continued to be built in the Romanesque style, with influences from Mediterranean rather than north European architecture. Another example of Italian late Romanesque architecture is the tower of Pisa Cathedral, now known as the Leaning Tower of Pisa (built in 1174).

The Gothic style remained the predominant architectural mode for west European cathedrals during the thirteenth century, while Italy continued to build in Romanesque style. In Germany, however, a new form of church design developed, the hall church, with nave and aisles of equal height.

Regionalism. The cathedral architecture of the following century lacked the uniformity of the thirteenth-century Gothic. Regionalism, however, does not mean a decline in architectural achievement. Antwerp and Milan cathedrals were started at this time, while the Perpendicular style was introduced in Britain, resulting in a number of fine churches, such as Gloucester Cathedral. Regionalism continued in the fifteenth-century, when the earliest Renaissance buildings may be found in Italy. In Germany the Gothic hall church tradition continued, while in England, the Perpendicular chapel of Kings College, Cambridge, and central tower of Canterbury Cathedral show the continuation of this style. On the brink of the Renaissance and the Reformation, medieval church architecture remained vigorous but diverse.

The architecture of smaller churches, whether parish church or private chapel, was closely related to that of the great cathedral and abbey churches. Smaller churches showed the same architectural trends at later dates and in more muted form, while attempting to emulate the leading architectural monuments of their day.

Functions of Cathedrals and Churches. Yet none of these buildings was simply either a monumental structure or a vehicle for display. Each was also a functioning place of religious worship, designed and decorated to facilitate this purpose. At the eastern end or in the center of the church was the altar. In the nave, the congregation would sit either on the floor or, less usually, on wooden benches. The walls, today usually undecorated, bore colorful painted designs, some showing religious scenes, with or without identifying texts, others containing references to local aristocrats or leading events.

*Burial took place within and around each church. Where a person was buried and with what form of monument (if any) was an indication of social and religious status. An aristocrat might be buried within the church beneath a stone tomb topped with a carved effigy. Such effigies, along with elaborately engraved metal plaques set into stone, formed characteristic memorials to the secular and religious elite of medieval Europe, and survive in large numbers, as do simpler rectangular tombstones, often tapering at one end. The latter usually bear a carved cross, sometimes elaborate in design and occasionally also showing the "tools of the trade" of the individual buried beneath. A knight might be indicated by a sword, a priest by chalice and paten (the goblet and plate used for Communion). Still more elaborate royal tombs are known, and the physical remains of saints (relics) were venerated and accorded both portable and monumental shrines.

The shrines of saints were a focus of religious devotion in the Middle Ages. They were often the goal of pilgrimages, frequently involving travel over great distances. St. James at Compostela (Spain) attracted pilgrimages from all over Europe. Metal badges (pilgrim badges) bought at these shrines enable us to trace returned pilgrims, since each shrine had its own distinctive pilgrim badge and symbols. An excellent example is the discovery of symbols of pilgrimage in a medieval grave at Worcester Cathedral (England), enabling us to identify this as the tomb of a pilgrim who had been to Compostela.

For the majority of the population, however, burial was in a simple grave in the churchyard. Tombstones were not in general use for the lower classes, although wooden crosses or other markers may have been erected. A wall (usually of stone) separated the churchyard from its surroundings. In the case of cathedrals, these surroundings were the buildings of the close, with its own enclosure wall and gate, but the majority of medieval churches stood in or near settlements, whether towns or villages. Cathedrals and churches stand today as the most widespread of surviving medieval buildings, although later modifications and damage have often altered their appearance.

Church Archaeology. The close involvement of medieval populations with their churches and the burial of the majority of local people in their church or its yard makes church archaeology a valuable resource for understanding medieval communities. The size and splendor of churches can give an indication of local wealth and patronage; the architecture and decoration can show external contacts and artistic tastes. Local craftsmanship and technology appear in building techniques, the sources of materials, and in fittings such as tiles and wall paintings. The evidence of cemeteries may elucidate both social structure and the health and composition of the local population. When historical sources survive for a specific church, more detailed studies can produce links between historical and archaeological evidence. The combination of this information with the excellent evidence of sequence and chronology provided by archaeological excavations can place church archaeology at the heart of the study of medieval Europe. Given the importance of the church in both the Middle Ages and today, this seems only fitting.

■ Richard Krautheimer, *Early Christian and Byzantine Architecture* (1965). Andrew Martindale, *Gothic Art* (1967). John Beckwith, *Early Medieval Art*, 2nd ed. (1969). Colin Platt, *The Atlas of Medieval Man*, 2nd ed. (1985).

Ken Dark

TOWNS AND CITIES OF MEDIEVAL EUROPE

The origins of the medieval European town are twofold: Roman and indigenous. The Romans had established a network of towns throughout Europe and, after the fall of the Roman Empire, urban life continued in many of these. In such centers, medieval town life emerged within an urban landscape, the framework of which was formed by the Roman street pattern and the location of major Roman stone buildings, gates, and walls. Such towns are common in Italy, Spain, and France and the survival of Roman streets and public buildings is often detectable in the modern urban landscape, examples being Nimes and Arles in France, or Pavia and Verona in Italy.

Other features of the Roman urban landscape also played a central role in shaping the medieval town. At Tours (France), for example, the location of graves of Christian martyrs outside the Roman center (Roman law having forbidden burial within the settlement) led to a shift in focus in the fourth, fifth, and sixth centuries from the Roman walled town to the extramural cemetery. Such a process could often result in the growth of new, post-Roman towns on Roman cemeteries rather than on the Roman town-sites themselves. Where medieval towns did emerge from continuity of occupation within the walls of their Roman predecessors, this frequently involved the reuse of Roman stone buildings for new purposes. Amphitheaters and gateway towers could become aristocratic fortresses, while public buildings such as basilicas and temples might be reused as churches. Classically seen at Trier (Germany), this was a widespread trend throughout continental Europe in the fifth and sixth centuries within what had been, in A.D. 400, the Roman Empire.

In Britain, there is no convincing evidence of continuous urban occupation at any Roman town site, but several— such as Lincoln and *York—show evidence of continued occupation in a non-urban fashion into the fifth and sixth centuries. Continuity of occupation seems to have been more widespread in those areas which remained under British (or "sub-Roman") control in the fifth and sixth centuries, than in those which passed into the hands of the Anglo-Saxons. The early Anglo-Saxons, unlike many of the other Germanic peoples who invaded the Roman Empire, did not attempt to maintain urban life in its Roman form, nor did towns survive long in areas under their political control. An especially interesting case is the town of St. Albans, where there are hints of a similar situation to that more fully evidenced at Tours. An extramural martyr's shrine was probably established here in the Late Roman period, but seems to have been continuously respected through the fifth, sixth, and seventh centuries, and is well attested as an Anglo-Saxon church site. Today this has been replaced by St. Albans Cathedral, one of England's principal medieval churches. The adjacent Roman town also

shows evidence of occupation in the fifth and sixth centuries, but not continuity of use as an urban center. Interestingly, unlike much of the surrounding area, St. Albans probably remained within a sub-Roman British Christian enclave in pagan early Anglo-Saxon England until the eve of (or even after) the conversion of the surrounding Anglo-Saxons. This fact may have assisted its survival as an important religious center.

The second source of origin for the medieval European town is the emergence in the seventh century A.D. of trading places and markets associated with the long-distance exchange of luxury artifacts and raw materials. Such towns *(emporia)* owed little to the Roman heritage but arose as nodes in a Europe-wide maritime trading network. Seldom on Roman sites, they consisted of timber buildings, usually rectangular in plan with thatched roofs, set along gravel streets. Although sometimes enclosed by an earthen bank or ditch, these settlements were not defended by stone walls. A few of the major buildings, notably churches in Christian lands, might be built of stone, but only seldom did the many buildings in these emporia achieve a high level of architectural magnificence prior to the ninth century.

These trading towns may be exemplified by the sites of Hamwic and Ipswich in England and Quentovic in France. The role of craftworking and trade is extensively evidenced by archaeological discoveries, especially of imported pottery from geographically distant areas. Some emporia, such as *London and York, did grow up close to what had been Roman walled cities, but the sites on which they developed reflect the different priorities of their founders. Characteristically, they were outside the Roman walls on the shores of major rivers, for these were not fortresses but centers of production and exchange.

By the start of the Viking Age, this second type of town had become the basis of a trading network extending from Scandinavia to France. It linked together the kingdoms of Viking Age Europe and was associated with the growing use of coinage for trading purposes. Emporia were frequently the site of mints and were often under royal control.

The Vikings engaged in intense commercial activity within this North Sea trading network. Towns such as York and Lincoln in England, and Dublin in Ireland rose to both economic and political importance in the Viking kingdoms. Ireland, indeed, owes its very oldest towns to the Vikings. In Scandinavia, too, trading centers such as Hedeby (Germany) and Birka (Sweden) played a central role in the Viking Age economy. These towns adhered closely to the form which we have already seen at Hamwic as early as the seventh century and have yielded much valuable archaeological information concerning the Scandinavian economy during this period.

The foundations laid in the pre-Viking period also formed the basis for the development of medieval towns within the non-Viking kingdoms of Europe. Both towns surviving from the Roman period and those founded as post-Roman trading places, saw consolidation and development of urban functions and the organization of the urban landscape during the Viking Age. Defenses were constructed, internal spaces replanned and adorned with major new buildings constructed in stone, of much greater magnificence and technical accomplishment than before. This is perhaps most clearly seen at Winchester (England), where rescue excavation and other studies have shown that the Late Saxon town was not merely a thriving urban center but, by the tenth century, contained large and architecturally sophisticated stone buildings such as the Old Minster, a cathedral built on an impressive scale.

The expansion in the geographical distribution, number, scale, and sophistication of European towns during the Viking Age provides the immediate background for the medieval European town of the eleventh to sixteenth centuries throughout most of Europe. Regional variations can be found, however, notably the hilltop towns of southern Europe—especially in Italy—which originated as administrative centers and fortresses at the end of the Roman Empire.

Medieval European towns of the post-Viking era show many common characteristics, especially in the case of the larger and more important towns. Great trading centers, with populations in the many thousands, now had planned networks of internal streets as well as less-formal lanes and passages between timber-built houses and workshops. Grander buildings might be constructed in either timber or stone, but most churches and residences of the urban elite were now built with stone. The major buildings frequently reflected the latest architectural styles and increased in scale and complexity through the later Middle Ages. Also stone built were the defensive walls, furnished with turrets and towered gates, which enclosed these towns. Along riverfronts, wooden quays and warehouses were to be found, and docks crowded with trading ships.

Towns thus became important political and economic centers during the Middle Ages. The kings of England and France, for example, ruled from great cities adorned with palaces and castles, while maintaining other castles as fortresses and residences in rural locations. Aristocracies, too, had their residences and castles in towns as well as in the countryside, making rich households a characteristic of urban life and towns important strategic centers during wars.

The medieval town was, therefore, more than a trading and population center: It was also a place of administration and a place for the dispensation of justice through courts. Not only kings and aristocrats but bishops too had their administrative centers in towns, and cathedrals dominated the landscape of the cities in which they were located. Nowhere was this more true, of course, than in medieval Rome.

Aristocrats, kings, and bishops also provided patronage to arts, music, drama, and intellectual life. It was in the medieval town that, for example, the great universities of Europe were founded, Oxford and Cambridge in England, Paris in France. Towns were centers of religious life, with many churches and charitable institutions. They also contained monasteries, and these, too, could be centers of cultural activity.

Town life offered greater personal freedom to the urban population than the strict feudalism of the medieval countryside. It offered, too, the economic freedom to seek social advancement and wealth through commerce. As such, artisans, merchants, and intellectuals formed a class unparalleled in rural society. This class had its own institutions, notably "guilds," or trade associations.

Despite its many advantages and relatively high standards of living, however, medieval town life had its dangerous side. Crime was prevalent and no formal police or fire service existed. Fires in largely wooden-built towns could prove disastrous both for safety and property; once started, they spread rapidly, devouring large areas of the urban landscape. Even more dangerous, perhaps, was the poor hygiene and the rapid spread of disease, especially

since urban trading communities were constantly in contact with other populations in distant lands. A major outbreak of infectious disease, such as the *Black Death, could have catastrophic effects on the urban population. For this reason alone, the flow of people from the countryside to towns, attracted by the advantages of urban life, was crucial to the survival of the towns as population centers. Nor were "natural" hazards, such as fire or plague, the only risks. In cosmopolitan communities, such as the major trading centers, ethnic tensions could be fraught. This was especially a problem for the principal European city-based ethnic minority: the Jews. Jewish communities were present in most medieval trading centers by the eleventh century, and were often among the wealthiest inhabitants of such towns. Occasional massacres are recorded throughout the Middle Ages, especially during the period of the Crusades.

Nor were feudal social tensions completely absent from towns. The construction of castles by the nobility could cause major upheavals for local people. Houses, even complete streets or neighborhoods, were sometimes demolished in order to make way for castles.

Since many medieval towns, such as London and *Paris, are still major urban centers today. It also demonstrates the medieval heritage of modern Europe. Modern redevelopment is continually providing opportunities for new archaeological discoveries, and medieval urban studies have become one of the growth areas of European archaeology in recent years.

[See also BRITISH ISLES: MEDIEVAL BRITAIN; EUROPE: ROMAN AND POST-ROMAN EUROPE.]

■ R. Hodges, *Dark Age Economics* (1982). R. Hodges and B. Hobley, *The Rebirth of Towns in the West* (1988).

Ken Dark

DESERTED VILLAGES OF MEDIEVAL EUROPE

The village was the characteristic settlement of rural Europe during the Middle Ages, though villages varied considerably in size, and isolated farms were more numerous in certain areas. Two main village forms may be distinguished: the fortified hilltop villages of the Mediterranean region, and the unenclosed villages of northern Europe.

Northern European villages consisted of rectangular houses and other structures of wooden or stone-built construction, often with animals stalled alongside the human inhabitants. Characteristic buildings of most villages included not only peasant houses but also a church and the residence of a feudal overlord. Within this broad regional grouping, there are many similarities. The twelfth/thirteenth-century village of Pen er Malo in Brittany, with drystone and timber buildings of subrectangular form, may be compared with similar buildings of contemporary villages in England, such as Goltho and Hound Tor. Lordly dwellings, too, show strong similarities, usually organized as a rectangle of buildings within an enclosure, centered on the dwelling house of the landowner or his local steward. Lordly residences were often enclosed by moats, as at Weoley and Writtle in England.

The hilltop villages of the Mediterranean zone are well illustrated by the site of Rougiers, a walled hilltop village in southern France occupied from the twelfth century. Here rows of conjoined rectangular houses with stone walls and an upper story stood adjacent to a castle. The Mediterranean walled village stands in sharp contrast to the unenclosed medieval villages of northern Europe.

Reasons for Desertion. Many medieval villages have remained in occupation down to the present day, but where abandonment has occurred, they have taken their place as part of the archaeological landscape of medieval Europe. The systematic study of deserted medieval villages began in Britain and Scandinavia in the 1940s and 1950s, and several have been the subject of excavations, most famously the site of *Wharram Percy in England. The reason for the desertion of these villages has, however, remained controversial. Some have attributed desertion to plague, others to demographic factors or to changes in land ownership or in land-owner attitudes toward tenants. Yet it is still difficult to generalize about the causes of village desertion.

In specific cases, historical and archaeological evidence can be used together to recognize local explanations for population changes. In Alsace, for example, 250 sites were deserted by migrants going to the towns for safety, while in England during the late Middle Ages, reorganization of the landscape (enclosure) may have resulted in the desertion of over a thousand villages.

High figures such as these can be paralleled in other areas, such as parts of Germany, and though a much lower percentage of villages was deserted in France, desertion was a European-wide phenomenon. A key problem in using these sites as a model for medieval villages in general is that we do not know for sure how typical were those sites that became deserted. It might be claimed, for example, that only sites with specific types of history or in unfavorable ecological settings failed to survive through the Middle Ages.

Several strands of evidence enable us to refute this proposition. There are strong similarities between sites that were deserted across a range of ecological settings and between sites that were deserted and those beneath modern villages. There is nothing to suggest that deserted sites differ from those that survived into the postmedieval period. Similar structures and finds occur at each, and similar economies and social structures are evidenced by them.

Historical evidence also enables us to argue for the typicality of all but the penultimate phases of deserted villages. Written sources show that the reasons for desertion were often short-term or regional processes affecting both deserted and surviving sites. Deserted villages might be only those sites that were more severely affected by common processes, such as demographic change. The realization that deserted medieval villages are not atypical renders their study an extremely valuable source for reconstructing medieval rural life.

Deserted Villages as Evidence. The archaeological study of deserted medieval villages has helped to confirm many hypotheses derived from written evidence and has played an important role in supplementing this evidence at well-documented sites. Important new evidence has also been gained through excavation. This work has enabled archaeologists to reconstruct standards of living through the Middle Ages across wide areas of Europe and to gain evidence of surprisingly high levels of material prosperity, nutrition, and health.

The image of dirty hovels inhabited by squat and sickly peasants has been swept away in favor of relatively spacious and well-built houses occupied by villagers of similar stature and health to those of the Early Modern Period. This is not to say that feudal society could not be oppressive, merely that the material standards of living of the medieval population were higher than those assumed on the grounds of textual evidence alone. Even the stalling of animals in the houses has been shown to have its advantages, as the heat they generated provided warmth for the domestic areas in winter. The partitioning of domestic areas from animal stalls provided separation of animal and human habitation within the same building.

Excavation of deserted settlements has also played an important part in elucidating the development of medieval architecture. While much of the medieval European architecture surviving above ground is stone built, the excavation of deserted villages has provided a wealth of evidence about building in timber.

Domestic structures were often built of posts set in—or beams laid on—the ground, with panels of wattle and daub between upright timbers. Earthen walls without timber support (known as cob) were also common, and stone (whether with or without mortar bonding) was used in some areas, although mortared stone walls were a characteristic of Mediterranean rather than northern Europe. Turf walling is found in Germany and Denmark, as shown by the well-preserved fourteenth-century turf-walled site of Solvig. In Germany, jointed planks were also used, as at Buderich. Roofs varied, both in the way they were covered (turf, stone or ceramic tiles, thatch, or wooden shingles), and in the way they were supported. Roof supports ranged from internal posts to inwardly curved posts, known as crucks. During the later Middle Ages, rapid architectural development in both timber and stone building led to increasingly more sophisticated and architecturally more efficient timber and stone buildings, and it is these that form the majority of surviving examples of medieval domestic architecture.

■ Maurice Beresford and John Hurst, *Deserted Medieval Villages* (1971). Jean Chapelot and Robert Fossier, *The Village and House in the Middle Ages*, trans. Henry Cleere (1985). Maurice Beresford and John Hurst, *Wharram Percy: Deserted Medieval Village* (1990).

Ken Dark

INDUSTRY AND COMMERCE IN MEDIEVAL EUROPE

Medieval industry was by and large established on a technological base which was familiar to the ancient world. Examination of medieval artifacts shows that few of the techniques used to produce pottery, metals, or textiles were unavailable in the fourth century A.D. and yet there are great differences in the way in which industries were organized at the beginning of the Medieval Period and at its end.

An example of these developments is the milling of grain. In the Roman world rotary querns were common finds but they were rare from the eleventh century onward, and after this date were probably used only for specialized purposes. By contrast, *Domesday Book* reveals that in England in the later eleventh century few streams or rivers were not harnessed for at least one water mill. During the following century, under the influence of the Cistercian order, the uses of waterpower were extended from grinding corn to fulling cloth and crushing ore. Yet during the Roman Period, though the water mill was known, it had only a limited use.

Pottery manufacture too illustrates this contrast. The potter's wheel, the use of a kiln and the application of lead glaze were all well-established techniques by the first century A.D. and yet over much of northwest Europe the techniques were lost, or ignored, from the end of the fourth century for a period of at least half a millennium. Glaze was used sparingly on pottery in the Roman world and glazed pottery appears to have been a luxury item. By contrast, in the eleventh century the market for glazed pottery suddenly expanded, mirroring the growth of sea-borne trade, and by the later twelfth century potteries making glazed jugs were present throughout the western seaboard of Europe and their products were available to all levels of society.

This is almost the mirror image of the situation with glassware. In the Roman Empire glass had been used both for luxury items, mainly for use in drinking and dining, and for everyday utensils, such as bottles and other containers. Both fine and utilitarian glass fragments are common finds on Roman sites, but the relative quantity of glass in use must have fallen sharply in the fifth century. It appears to have become even more rare in the eleventh century, following the replacement of soda by potash "forest" glass. By the thirteenth and fourteenth centuries glass was a rare and high-status commodity. It was in fact not until the later sixteenth century that vessel glass began to approach the levels of use found in the fourth century.

A very few medieval techniques or technologies were not present, however, in Europe during the Roman Period. The most notable of these were the windmill, introduced to Europe during the twelfth century, and gunpowder, introduced in the fourteenth century. Significantly, neither were medieval European inventions, but like many advances in West European culture they arrived in Europe via the Arabic world.

Explanations for the differences between industry in the ancient and medieval worlds have been sought by several writers and in most cases are attributed to differences in the social ties which bound the elite to the peasantry. Clearly, if an estate was run by slaves there was little incentive to adopt a technology which would create unemployment and require investment in machinery. In a feudal society, on the other hand, the lord had no responsibility for the welfare of his serfs, merely the right to collect dues and services from them. In such circumstances the stimulus to produce goods by the most economical means available may come from the peasantry itself. There could, however, be no stimulus without a market for the goods. The development of industry in medieval Europe was therefore intimately linked to the development of commerce.

Commerce in the ancient world played an important part in the economy, although the power of the state and the extreme wealth of the senatorial class meant that goods were often produced and distributed in ways that fell outside the usual logic of the market economy. The huge population of Rome, for example, was supported by state-supplied grain while the marble used in imperial building projects was shipped throughout the empire with little apparent concern for the distances involved.

In northwest Europe, especially outside the limits of the Roman Empire, the development of commerce in the medieval period is thought to have involved a change from embedded to market-oriented exchange. The discussion here centers on the degree to which societies were self-sufficient. Archaeologically, this is best studied by determining the origin of goods found in graves and settlement sites and by studying the development of systems which aid exchange, such as coinage and the standardization of weights and measures. Archaeology is, however, unable to study directly such matters as barter or credit and many of the details in the development of commerce are consequently lost.

Much has been made of the importance of the core–periphery relationship between northwest Europe and Scandinavia on the one hand, and the eastern Roman Empire and the Arabic world on the other, to explain the development of commerce. Pirenne, for example, identified a major break in contact between the European and Mediterranean worlds in the seventh century, following the collapse of trade routes across the western Mediterranean. One example of the effect of this break was the replacement of papyrus by parchment in European monastic scriptoria. More recently, Hodges and Whitehouse have accepted the existence and importance of the seventh century break but have gone on to look at the effect of alternative riverine trade routes between Byzantium and the Baltic as a stimulus to Scandinavian commerce. This is reflected archaeologically in the development of beach markets and permanent trading centers along the Baltic coast.

Opinion is divided as to the status of these centers but there would seem to be a shift from an initial period in the early first millennium to a later period ending perhaps in the late tenth century. The early centers, such as Luneborg on the east coast of Fyn, are thought to have been closely controlled by local aristocracies and access to the imported goods would have been used to enhance the power and prestige of the controlling elite. The later centers, such as Birka on the island of Bjorko in Lake Malaren or Hedeby / Haithabu (which supported a mint), had larger, more permanent populations less closely controlled by the elite.

Between these two extremes were a series of coastal trading sites flourishing in the later seventh and early eighth centuries in which a wide variety of crafts were practiced and which seem mainly to have had their own mints. Archaeologically the best known of these is Dorestad, in the Lek in the Rhine-Maas delta. Some consider these sites at least proto-urban, having an ancestral relationship to later medieval towns, but others place them on a separate branch of settlement development, since elite control was so strong. There is much discussion as to the level and degree of trade through these "wics" or "emporia" as they are known. The role of coinage in trade (as opposed to the collection and distribution of taxation) is still a matter of debate, although here too it seems that there is a gradual shift from the sixth and seventh centuries, when coinage in northwest Europe was used primarily for noncommercial purposes, to the later seventh and early eighth centuries, by which time estimates of coin production suggest that they had a commercial function. Clearly, at least until the later eleventh century, European society included a heterogeneous mixture of commercial and embedded economies all to some extent in contact with and reacting to their fellows.

The later eleventh century seems by most accounts to have been a period of rapid urban growth. Closely related to this was the development of commerce and industry. Studies of pottery distribution show that urban production centers were by this time supplying the hinterlands. Unlike previous proto-urban centers these towns were often situated inland and were clearly linked to the countryside by a network of overland routeways. In parts of northwest Europe, market-oriented production and exchange probably existed in the ninth century while for the majority of the continent, and especially at its periphery, it was not until the middle of the twelfth century that the commercial infrastructure was complete. While many of the larger towns and cities have earlier, often Roman, origins, these form only a small minority. Almost all European towns of the Present day, however, were in existence by the late twelfth or early thirteenth century.

Studies of loose coin finds, both those recovered from within urban centers through archaeological work and those found in the countryside (often as a result of metal detection), suggest a rapid growth in the use of coins in the late twelfth century. Alongside this change was the increased use of smaller denomination coinage (produced at first by physically cutting coins into halves and quarters) and of tokens made of lead or pewter. It was also in this period that trade guilds first appeared in many towns, controlling and regulating a wide variety of crafts. Settlements, whether in town or country, demonstrated the wide catchment area now accessible through this market system. Peasants in the village of Wharram Percy, for example, situated in a remote area of rural Yorkshire, were able to obtain fish from the North Sea and pottery from sources up to 30 miles (48 km) away.

The trauma of the Black Death in the second quarter of the fourteenth century seems to have affected commerce and industry throughout northwest Europe. The results, however, were complex. First, the removal of over a third of the population decreased pressure on land and at the same time gave a boost to the labor market. Peasants tied to the land by feudal dues were able to commute these to a monetary rent (in fact a change which had already begun to take effect well before the mid-fourteenth century). Crafts such as house building, which before the Black Death seemed to have been communally shared, became universally the prerogative of professional craftsmen. The production and supply of pottery shows the changes of this period particularly clearly. Centers were fewer in number and were normally the most successful of those which had been producing pottery in the early fourteenth century. Concentration of industries in particular regions became even more pronounced than before. This is reflected both in an increased standardization of products and a wider distribution area, one of the best examples being the Coarse Border Ware industry of the Surrey-Hampshire border. The Rhenish stoneware industry, concentrated at this period around Siegburg, was now operating on a vast scale. Metal wares showed similar patterns of production and trade although the needs of agriculture (mainly horseshoes and plowshares) meant that smithing remained a widely practiced craft throughout the later Middle Ages.

The development of commerce and industry in the medieval period makes a sharp and interesting contrast with their perceived relationship today. In technological terms, virtually none of the goods produced at the end of the Middle Ages could not have been produced at their start. Some later Roman pottery, for example, was being fired at temperatures comparable to those required for medieval stonewares. Despite this conservatism of technological knowledge there were, however, tremendous changes in the actual mode of production. These were brought into effect almost entirely by commercial developments and the loosening of the ties between craftsmen and patrons.

Alan G. Vince

MEDITERRANEAN, Historical Archaeology and Ethnoarchaeology of.

While the majority of archaeological research in the Near East and the Mediterranean has focused on those regions' ancient civilizations, an ethnographic search for modern analogies of the technologies and customs of those lost cultures has long been interwoven with the excavation of ancient sites. Modern anthropological analogies to ancient practices have been gathered both from distant cultures and from peoples living in the immediate vicinity of the archaeological sites under investigation.

While the ethnography of modern populations has provided some useful models for understanding the past, until recently only minor interest has existed for archaeological exploration of the cultural juncture between antiquity and the modern world. Since the mid-1980s, that gap in the archaeological sequence between the distant past and the present has begun to be filled by the study of the material culture of the last several centuries. Thus, in terms of disciplinary boundaries, the study of the material culture of the present for use as a source of illustration of ancient lifeways is known as ethnoarchaeology; the excavation of material remains of the last several centuries is known as postmedieval, or historical, archaeology.

Ethnoarchaeology. Ethnoarchaeology grew out of attempts to understand the behaviors or customs that lay behind artifacts uncovered in excavations. Struggling with the material remains extracted from the earth, archaeologists turned to the ethnographic study of local villagers and nomads. For example, during the nineteenth and early twentieth centuries, the *Palestine Exploration Quarterly* contained numerous articles on peasant agriculture, pottery making, the habits of nomads, among other topics conceived as useful for understanding the past landscape. Ethnoarchaeology has more closely linked modern material culture with the archaeological record by focusing on highly specific correspondences between modern behavior and the form or distribution of elements of material culture of the distant past.

The main foci of ethnoarchaeology in the Mediterranean and Near East are studies of ceramic production, architectural styles and building techniques, settlement patterns, and agricultural practices. The goals are typically to develop a more complex understanding of the uses of objects, places, and spaces in the distant past. Insights on broader social interactions, gender relations, and the processes of production and consumption have also come from ethnoarchaeological studies.

Among the recent, innovative uses of ethnoarchaeology is the seminal work of Wobst (1977) on archaeological style as it may be understood through the use of distinctive forms of headdress by modern populations of what was then Yugoslavia. Wobst scrutinized the context and style of this material culture and concluded that the diversity of styles served to facilitate information exchange about the wearer's ethnic affiliation and social status at a distance. This understanding is particularly significant for recognizing expressions of ethnicity and social identity in the styles of artifacts.

Another important branch of ethnoarchaeology focuses on the survival of material culture elements over centuries. One category of ethnoarchaeological research compares architecture from the present-day villages to the excavated remains of ancient settlements. Its primary goal is to utilize observations on the reasons for modern variation in land use, variation within and among houses, and the relationship between built space and population density, to deepen our understanding of the inner workings of ancient communities.

Since ceramics are the most common archaeological finds, a large corpus of studies has concentrated on the mechanisms of pottery production and distribution. Peacock (1982) focused on pottery production in the present complex market economies of the Mediterranean in an attempt to uncover the processes of pottery production within the Roman Empire. In this and other ethnoarchaeological studies, modern evidence is used to assess the relative probabilities of various explanations of the archaeological record. The success of such studies, of course, is determined by the explanatory power of the modern evidence.

One of the main premises of ethnoarchaeology is that modern, nonindustrialized cultures bear important similarities to cultures of the distant past. The historical development of those nonindustrialized cultures is usually left to the historian. Historical archaeology, in contrast, has begun to address the genesis of all modern material cultures—industrialized and nonindustrialized—in the centuries after the end of antiquity.

Historical Archaeology. The term *"historical archaeology" has several meanings. One approach comes from differentiating all archaeology into either the study of nonliterate peoples deep in the past (*prehistoric archaeology) or the study of literate or documented peoples (historical archaeology). Since documentation ranges widely across time and space in the broad Mediterranean region (starting with the Sumerians nearly 5,000 years ago), an inclusive archaeology of all literate peoples in the region is possible but not the intent of the formulation "historical archaeology." It is actually closer to the discipline of historical archaeology as practiced in North America, with its goal of documenting the character of European settlement and influence in the New World. The aim of post-sixteenth-century research in the Mediterranean is likewise an interpretation of the development of the modern world, or, in other words, a search for the material roots of the present. In recent years, this type of historical archaeology has moved along several avenues: landscape analysis, the archaeology of architecture, and the archaeology of commodities.

For the eastern side of the Mediterranean the research on the last several centuries is considered Late Islamic archaeology. Since a major focus of archaeology in the Near East has been on the excavation of tells, information for historical archaeology has come from the study of finds from the uppermost stratigraphic levels. Archaeologists have uncovered artifacts from the last several centuries and occasionally included examples in reports. For example, Toombs (1985) excavated and analyzed a Muslim cemetery on the top of Tell el-Hesi in Israel. In Turkey, Foss (1976) employed historical accounts and archaeological finds for discussion of the history of Sardis from the Byzantine through the Ottoman periods.

Historical archaeology is not limited to excavations; in the western Mediterranean, the research is carried out in the context of postmedieval studies. Archaeologists, such as Mangan (1994), have analyzed standing architecture. Her regional analysis in Catalonia focuses on the aspects of and the mechanisms for the transition from feudalism to capitalism in an urban setting. The nature of this transition is the unifying issue for the post-sixteenth-century period throughout the Mediterranean region.

Going beyond the study of specific sites, productive lines of research have come from rural surveys. Surveys of past landscapes often explain the apparent lack of historical evidence from the sixteenth through nineteenth centuries. A comprehensive analysis of this problem comes from the survey research of Davis (1991) among the Cycladic Islands of the Aegean. In combination with analysis of Ottoman taxation records Davis has accounted for apparent gaps in the material record as the result of transformations in the intensity of productivity rather than in changes in population density. This study fulfills an ethnoarchaeological function by constructing a diachronic model for agricultural practices and their material correlates in the Aegean. It also fills a gap of knowledge regarding rural life in the early modern period.

Another historical theme to which historical archaeology responds is the transformation of everyday life. The dramatic transition in common eating and drinking habits that occurred over the last several centuries can be seen through the spread of certain commodities indicative of the global transformations associated with capitalism. For the Mediterranean, three stimulants are particularly significant: tobacco (which entered the Old World in the aftermath of the Columbian voyages to the Americas); coffee (trade in which provided the merchants of Egypt with a replacement for the spice trade that Portuguese merchants appropriated via new trade links to eastern Asia); and sugar (whose production shifted from Cyprus and North Africa to the plantations of the Caribbean in the sixteenth century).

Of these commodities, tobacco is the most visible and can be traced archaeologically through the appearance of clay tobacco pipes. Robinson (1983) produced the seminal research for organizing these ubiquitous artifacts. Her chronological typologies are proving useful in the study of sites across the eastern Mediterranean. As these and other archaeological tools are being developed, more robust use of material resources is contributing to understanding change in the region across time.

In sum, both ethnoarchaeology and historical archaeology are innovative examinations of material culture within social context. As such, both are broadening anthropological understandings of the Mediterranean region.

[See also AEGEAN CULTURES: OVERVIEW; GREECE: OVERVIEW; MEDITERRANEAN TRADE; MEDITERRANEAN WORLD: INTRODUCTION; ROMAN EMPIRE: INTRODUCTION.]

■ Clive Foss, *Byzantine and Turkish Sardis* (1976). H. Martin Wobst, "Stylistic Behavior and Information Sharing," in *For the Director: Research Essays in Honor of James B. Griffin*, Anthropological Papers, No. 61, Museum of Anthropology, University of Michigan, Ann Arbor (1977), pp. 317–342. D.P.S. Peacock, *Pottery in the Roman World: An Ethnoarchaeological Approach* (1982). Rebecca C. Robinson, "Clay Tobacco Pipes from the Kerameikos," *Mitteilungen* 98 (1983): 265–285. Lawrence E. Toombs, *Tell el Hesi: Modern Military Trenching and Muslim Cemetery in Field I, Strata I and II. The Joint Archaeological Expedition to Tell el Hesi*, vol. two (1985). Jack L. Davis, "Contributions to a Mediterranean Rural Archaeology: Historical Case Studies from the Ottoman Cyclades," *Journal of Mediterranean Archaeology* 4 (1991): 131–215. Patricia Hart Mangan, "Changes in the Landscape During the Transition from Feudalism to Capitalism: A Case Study of Montblanc, Catalonia, Spain," Ph.D. Dissertation, University of Massachusetts at Amherst (1994).

Uzi Baram

MEDITERRANEAN TRADE. The early development of seafaring on the Mediterranean Sea facilitated extensive trade relations among peoples separated by great distances. Trade in the Mediterranean became one of the chief factors in the formation of cultures and in the interaction between cultures, creating cultural change throughout ancient times.

Sources of Information. A wide variety of sources teach us about ancient Mediterranean trade. Written history by peoples surrounding the Mediterranean Sea go back to the third millennium B.C. We hear about trade relations from Mesopotamian monarchs, Egyptian pharaohs, biblical kings, Greek adventurers and historians, Roman bureaucrats, and Phoenician sailors. For example, the wisdom literature of Egypt contains the eleventh-century B.C. tale of the woeful Wen Amun, who suffers many misadventures when sent by his pharaoh to procure timber from the Levantine coast. The biblical Book of Kings provides documentary evidence of the trade of tenth-century B.C. King Solomon, who exchanged Israelite grain for the Phoenician lumber of King Hiram of Tyre. Among the stories of the Greek historian Herodotus is the tale of the Samian Colaeus, the first Greek to trade with the Tarsessos colonies in Spain, a man who was greatly honored for his feat upon his return to Samos. Unfortunately, little documentary evidence comes from the traders themselves. This is largely due to the nature of the written record—most trading documents in ancient times were on perishable materials that have not been preserved. Equally useful are pictorial records of trading parties. Some, like the fifteenth-century B.C. Kenaumun tomb from Thebes, Egypt, carefully depict the unloading of the cargo of slaves and wine from a ship from distant Canaan.

Several types of archaeological information fill in the bulk of the picture. Traditionally, archaeologists have identified trade patterns through the discovery of foreign goods, items from one locale found at a distant site. Recent work shows the picture to be much more complicated, in that the source of trade goods and the party transporting them were not necessarily the same. It is likely, for example, that Greek goods found in southern Spain in the seventh and sixth centuries B.C. were actually brought there by the Phoenician traders who controlled this trade route. Similarly, the fourteenth-century B.C. ship that was wrecked off Uluburun, Turkey, was en route to a Mycenaean port in the Aegean carrying, in addition to cargo from Canaan and *Cyprus, numerous ceramic vessels made in the Aegean, certainly not intended as exports.

Shipwrecks, then, are another important source of our information on Mediterranean trade, providing us with a snapshot of a single cargo at a single point in time, in addition to important information on shipbuilding techniques, economic patterns and products, and lifeways of sailors and merchants. Over one thousand ancient and medieval shipwrecks have been found to date in the Mediterranean.

Survey and excavation at coastal sites add another important component to our base of knowledge. Large-scale excavations of harbors, such as Ostia in Italy and Caesarea in Israel, have substantially increased our knowledge of Roman shipping and port activities. Technological improvements and changes in harbor construction technology help us understand how trade was facilitated in the ancient world. Excavations at such notable coastal sites as *Carthage in Libya, Ugarit in Syria, or Ashkelon in Israel, all cities economically dependent on trade, have helped us identify trade patterns through the patterns of urban settlement and development, modes of economic production, and cultural influences shown in the preserved material culture of these coastal sites.

Finally, *ethnoarchaeology and *experimental archaeology add yet another dimension to our body of knowledge. Studies of Portuguese fishermen, Italian potters, or Cypriote smiths provide us with ways to gauge the activities of their predecessors. Reconstructions of ancient vessels, such as the seaworthy replica of the third-century B.C. merchantman found at Kyrenia, Cyprus, help us confirm our assumptions about the practices of ancient sailors.

Patterns of Trade. Trade through the Mediterranean Sea was of two varieties: local and long distance. The former must have begun at a very early date based upon the existence of imported obsidian dating to the eleventh millennium B.C. Seaborne trade was obviously necessary for island populations such as the inhabitants of Crete, Cyprus, and the Aegean Islands. But local trade in rough coastal areas such as the Levantine coast or the Greek mainland was also best conducted by sea because of the absence of easy land routes over the terrain.

Long-distance trade brought distant peoples into contact in a variety of ways. Much early trade was carried on in down-the-line fashion, where external trade goods were handed along from port to port through a series of local trading arrangements. Mediterranean ports also served as transmission points for goods coming from farther away. *Egypt, for example, provided ivory, ebony, gold, spices, and other southern Arabian and eastern African goods not found in the Mediterranean trading system.

Colonies were also a common method of fostering trade in the Mediterranean. Best known are the Greek settlements in Italy and Sicily. The Greeks also established eastern entrepots at such places as Al Mina in Syria, Mesad Hashavyahu in Israel, and Naucratis in Egypt. Even more adept in the art of colonization were the Phoenicians. They deposited settlers wherever they traveled, founding Carthage in North Africa, Utica in Italy, and Cadiz in Spain, among many other cities. Smaller colonies of Phoenician traders and craftsworkers were found among native peoples throughout the Mediterranean, such as at Teke on Crete or Lefkandi in *Greece.

The labor and resource investment necessary to carry on long-distance trade across the sea requires considerable social organization and is generally the task of more complex societies. It is no coincidence, then, that the beginnings of Egyptian seaborne trade with western Asia coincides with state development in Egypt in the late fourth millennium. This, and much of the rest of Mediterranean trade, was likely state controlled and driven. This has led to the long-standing scholarly debate over the nature of ancient Mediterranean trade. Did it possess the "modern" features of capitalist trade—price-setting markets, investment risk, capital accumulation, and price fluctuations? If so, how important was it in the functioning of the ancient economy? No scholarly consensus can be expected on either question. But comparative studies of Mesopotamian and Persian Gulf trade in the third and second millennia B.C. indicate that the beginning of entrepreneurial trading is extremely early. The relationship between trader and state was complex and changed over time, though entrepreneurs usually had some form of state control and support, and the state often used private parties to do its work. A third element was added in later empires, where the trading system intersected the system of tribute and taxation of the dominant powers in the region. Thus the chief impetus for the rapid Phoenician expansion to the far west was the need to procure silver to pay tribute to Assyria. Similarly, trade goods often piggybacked on ships bringing tributary grain to Rome from Egypt and North Africa.

Objects of Trade. Our knowledge of trade objects is best known from ceramics discovered at ports and in shipwrecks, but it is rare that pots themselves were traded objects. More often, it was the contents of the pots that mattered. These can be generally divided into three categories: bulk agricultural goods, prestige or status items, and precious metals and currency.

Grain imports to Italy from North Africa were crucial to feed an overurbanized Roman population. Maritime Levantine cities with no rural hinterland, such as Tyre, Sidon, and Ashkelon, were also likely to have been regularly supplied with agricultural products by sea as early as the Bronze Age. Wine and olive oil, major regional products of the Mediterranean, were regularly shipped from one area to another. Amphorae containing these two products are ubiquitous feature of excavated shipwrecks from all periods. Their distinctive shapes and occasional inscription help us identify the source, ownership, contents, and destination of the products. Roman-period Italian and Spanish amphorae are found as far afield as England and the Black Sea.

Precious objects sent in trade, tribute, or gifts to the elite strata of trading partners were also a regular feature of Mediterranean trade. Finds from the Uluburun shipwreck, for example, included unworked ivory, jewelry of gold, silver, faience, and Baltic amber, glass ingots, a gold chalice, seals, finger cymbals, and Arabian spices. Perishable goods such as exotic foods, wild animals, and fine textiles were probably also common trade commodities, although few are preserved.

Precious metals were extremely common trade goods. Bronze Age Egypt had ample quantities of gold but little silver, *Mesopotamia the reverse. Trade between the two for these ores predate historical records. The Laurion silver mines provided Athens with a key export in the development of its trade. Oxhide-shaped ingots of copper and tin are regularly found in Bronze Age shipwreck sites and are depicted on Egyptian frescoes concerning seaborne trade. Cypriote trade was dependent on its extraction and export of copper and iron. In Greco-Roman times, trade cargo often took the form of scrap metal being returned for recycling, such as the recent discovery of a hoard of bronze statue fragments in Brindisi harbor.

A Brief History of Mediterranean Trade. Our earliest evidence of long-distance Mediterranean trade, between Egypt and Mesopotamia probably through the Levantine port of Byblos, can be traced back to the fourth millennium B.C. Regular trade between these two centers through intermediary sites along the Levantine coast continued throughout the span of the ancient world. The system grew to include the southern Syro-Palestinian coast, Cyprus, Crete, and the Aegean. By the fifteenth century B.C., products from these areas were regularly intermixed through continuous contact between the cultures. The end of the Late Bronze Age and the movement of the Sea Peoples in the twelfth and eleventh centuries disrupted this system.

By the tenth century B.C., Phoenicians had begun to reestablish trade relations throughout the eastern Mediterranean, establishing colonies in North Africa, Cyprus, *Sicily, Sardinia, and as far away as southern Spain. Their goal was largely a search for precious metals, which were extracted from a variety of colonies. Much of their cargo ended up as tributary goods to the Assyrian empire that dominated the Levant in the eighth and seventh centuries

B.C. The Phoenician Cadiz colony exploited Spanish silver mines to the extent that it left 20 million tons of silver slag on the Spanish landscape along Rio Tinto. A document attributed to Aristotle describes how Phoenician traders loaded so much silver on their ships that they even forged anchors made of silver. Exquisitely crafted Phoenician goods are found throughout the Mediterranean and in the Aegean from this period. Alphabetic writing probably also accompanied the Phoenician expansion.

The beginnings of Greek Mediterranean trade followed the Phoenicians by about a century and tended to operate in the shadow of the far more effective Phoenicians. It was only with the collapse of the Assyrian empire and the subsequent difficulties faced by Phoenician city-states with the Egyptians and Babylonians in the late seventh and sixth centuries B.C. that Greek traders first began to make a major impact. According to Herodotus, the earliest Greek trade was conducted by the Phocaeans, later replaced by the Corinthians and Athenians.

The Greek expansion beyond its Ionian and Italian colonies was stymied by the Persian empire in the east and by the Carthaginians in the west. The latter replaced the Phoenicians and dominated the routes along Africa to Spain. This forced Greek trade through Sardinia and the Baeleric Islands, through the port of Ibiza, to the French coast and the eastern coast of Spain. Carthaginian hegemony over long-distance trade can be demonstrated by the shipwreck at El Sec, Majorca, from the fourth century B.C., of a Punic ship bound for Spain containing Attic red figure vessels and vine stalks for planting grapes.

With the downfall of Carthage at the hands of the Romans, trade patterns switched dramatically. Amphorae found at various sites and in wrecks show a pattern of wine export from Italy in the first centuries B.C. and A.D., later replaced by Spanish wine and fish sauce exports. Slightly later in Roman times, North African products appear in great abundance at many European and Near Eastern sites, probably related to tributary grain shipments to Rome. When the center of the empire moved farther east, so did the locus of trade, centering on the highly urbanized cities of Syria and Palestine. Gaza became the port receiving large groups of religious pilgrims and exported large quantities of wine to be used in Christian sacraments throughout the empire.

Neither the Arab conquest in the east nor the accession of Germanic tribes in the west caused the collapse of the ancient Mediterranean trading system, though the fragmentation of the system progressively narrowed its scope in early medieval times.

[See also MEDITERRANEAN WORLD: THE MEDITERRANEAN PRE-BRONZE AGE; MESOPOTAMIA: ASSYRIA; NEAR EAST: THE NEOLITHIC AND CHALCOLITHIC (PRE-BRONZE AGE) IN THE NEAR EAST; SHIPS AND SEAFARING; UNDERWATER ARCHAEOLOGY.]

■ A. G. Woodhead, *The Greeks in the West* (1962). William Culican, *The First Merchant Venturers: The Ancient Levant in History and Commerce* (1966). John Boardman, *The Greek Overseas*, 2nd ed. (1980). Peter Garnsey, Keith Hopkins, and C. R. Whittaker, eds., *Trade in the Ancient Economy* (1983). Peter Throckmorton, ed., *History from the Sea: Shipwrecks and Archaeology* (1983). D.P.S. Peacock and D. F. Williams, *Amphorae and the Roman Economy* (1986). Sabatino Moscati, ed., *The Phoenicians* (1988). Maria Aubet, *Phoenicians in the West* (1993). Lionel Casson, *Ships and Seafaring in Ancient Times* (1994).
Mitchell Allen

MEDITERRANEAN WORLD

INTRODUCTION

The Mediterranean Sea, lying between Europe, Africa, and Asia, has played a role in human history as both a barrier and a bond between the communities clustered around its shores. It has also been the focus of a series of major urban civilizations: Egypt, the Near East, Crete, and Mycenae; Assyrians and Persians; Classical Greece and the Roman Empire; the Islamic world and medieval Christendom.

In geographical terms the lands around the Mediterranean are widely varied in character and arable potential. The southern shore—North Africa—is generally arid apart from a narrow coastal strip that is backed by desert and mountains, with only a single major river, the Nile. The northern shore of the Mediterranean stands in complete contrast to this; less arid and more agriculturally productive, it is punctuated by rivers and peninsulae, and gives direct access northward to the hinterland of the European continent.

The importance of the Mediterranean Sea can be traced back to at least the end of the last Ice Age. As the ice sheets melted, sea levels rose and large areas of productive lowland were flooded in the Adriatic basin, off the southern coast of France, around the shores of the Aegean, and in the Gulf of Sirte off the Libyan coast. An equally crucial change was the use of seagoing ships. Direct evidence comes from obsidian found in levels dated approximately 9500 B.C. at the Franchthi Cave in southern Greece. The obsidian had been collected from the Aegean island of Melos and brought by boat to the mainland, a journey which (even with the lowered sea levels of the tenth millennium B.C.) would have required the crossing of over 62 miles (100 km) of open sea. It is possible that coastal communities dependent on fishing from boats had already become established by this period.

In the seventh and sixth millennia B.C., Mediterranean communities underwent a major transformation, adopting cereal agriculture and domestic livestock from their Near Eastern neighbors. This led to the growth of a village farming lifestyle, and ultimately helped stimulate the development of new kinds of society in the third and second millennia: the cities and states of Egypt, the Levant, and the Aegean region (Minoans and Mycenaeans). The eastern Mediterranean became a major nexus of trade between these prosperous communities, carrying both manufactures and raw materials such as metals. This is shown especially clearly by the shipwreck sites of the fourteenth and thirteenth centuries B.C. at Kas and Cape Gelidonya off the southern coast of Turkey.

The western Mediterranean meanwhile followed a separate course of development. Iberia saw the formation of stratified societies during the fourth and third millennia B.C., with walled centers such as Los Millares, and richly furnished tombs. Distinctive styles of architecture developed on the western Mediterranean islands, notably the megalithic temples of Malta and Gozo, and the fortified nuraghi of Sardinia. Nowhere in the western Mediterranean did unified states develop at this time, however, nor did cities make their appearance until the first millennium

B.C., and then only in response to colonization by Greeks and Phoenicians.

The foundations of colonies by Greeks and Phoenicians around the shores of North Africa, southern France, southern Italy, and *Sicily in the early first millennium B.C. brought the Mediterranean closer to being a single sphere of cultural interaction. The purpose of the colonies was twofold: to find new land for the growing populations of the mother cities, and to provide centers for trade and commerce with the hinterlands of Africa and Europe. The Phoenician (later Carthaginian) colonies of North Africa established links across the Sahara with peoples of tropical Africa, while items of Greek manufacture are found at early Celtic centers on the Danube. The period of colonization also coincided with an urban and cultural fluorescence in both Greece and northern Italy, and the rise of prosperous city-states (respectively Greek and Etruscan) in these areas.

The fifth century was the great age of Classical Greece. The Greek city-states together repelled the invasion of their powerful eastern neighbor, the Persian Empire, but then continued to fight among themselves, notably in the Peloponnesian War (431–404 B.C.). Athens emerged as the leading cultural center, and until its defeat in the war controlled an extensive Aegean empire by means of its powerful fleet. During the fourth century, however, Greece was politically overshadowed by the kingdom of Macedon to the north, and it was under the Macedonian leadership of Alexander the Great that Greek culture was carried across Asia in the wake of his conquests, as far as the borders of India.

In the west, the city of *Rome grew to dominate Italy in the third century B.C. and rose to mastery of the western Mediterranean with its defeat of the Carthaginians in the Punic Wars. Rome went on to conquer the eastern Mediterranean, including Egypt, until the Mediterranean itself became known to the Romans as "Mare Nostrum." By the first century A.D. all the lands directly bordering on the Mediterranean had been incorporated into the Roman Empire, and trading ships crisscrossed it carrying grain and other commodities to feed the urban population of Rome and other cities. Having linked east and west under a single government, the Romans succeeded in imposing a degree of cultural uniformity on these disparate lands, but there were still crucial differences, and during the fifth century A.D. the empire broke decisively into two halves. The east survived as the Byzantine Empire, but the west came under the control of Germanic elites: Ostrogoths in Italy, Franks and Visigoths in Spain and France. It was these groupings that went to form the basis of the modern countries of western Europe. The Mediterranean, however, came near to recovering a degree of cultural uniformity with the expansion of Islam over the Near East and North Africa in the seventh century, later spreading into Spain, Sicily, and (under the Ottoman Turks) the Balkans. It was only with the decline of Ottoman power in the nineteenth and early twentieth centuries that the present-day political geography of the lands bordering the eastern Mediterranean became established.

[See also AEGEAN CULTURES: OVERVIEW; GREECE: OVERVIEW; MEDITERRANEAN TRADE; MEDITERRANEAN, HISTORICAL ARCHAEOLOGY AND ETHNOARCHAEOLOGY OF THE; ROMAN EMPIRE: INTRODUCTION.]

■ R. Hodges and D. Whitehouse, *Mohammed, Charlemagne and the Origins of Europe* (1983). S. Arenson, *The Encircled Sea* (1990). K. Randsborg, *The First Millennium AD in Europe and the Mediterra-*

nean (1991). B. Cunliffe, ed., *The Oxford Illustrated Prehistory of Europe* (1994).

Chris Scarre

THE MEDITERRANEAN PRE-BRONZE AGE

Human settlement of the Mediterranean region has a long history. At Ubiediya in Israel, early stone tools attest to the presence of humans by 1.4 million B.P. and provide evidence of early human migration from Africa to the Mediterranean zone. From one million B.P., sites are found in North Africa, the Near East, Turkey, and Europe, documenting the widespread settlement of human groups. Early sites are rare, however, because of erosion, tectonic and seismic activity, and modern development.

Mediterranean prehistory falls into two great epochs. In the Pleistocene, small bands of humans, no more than twenty-five to fifty strong, subsisted by foraging wild plant and animal foods. With the onset of modern climate in the Holocene, people began to live in permanent villages with an economy based on food production utilizing domesticated species of plants and animals. Within a few millennia, these villages grew to become towns or small cities with hundreds or thousands of inhabitants. The existence of the economic transition from foraging to farming is the most important discovery of archaeology in this century, and explaining it is one of the key goals of modern research.

Mediterranean prehistory is divided into archaeological periods for convenience. The first of these, the *Paleolithic, dates from 1.4 million to 11,000 B.P., and corresponds to the period of Pleistocene foragers. The Mesolithic (also called the Epipaleolithic) comprises foragers who lived in the Early Holocene from 11,000 to 9000 B.P. The Neolithic is the period of village farming from 9000 to 5000 B.P.

The Paleolithic is subdivided into Lower, Middle, and Upper Paleolithic. These divisions reflect changes in the techniques used to flake flint tools and also correspond to grades of human evolution, though less neatly than was once thought. *Homo erectus* was once associated with the Lower Paleolithic, *Neanderthals with the Middle Paleolithic, and anatomically modern *Homo sapiens* with the Upper Paleolithic. *Homo erectus* fossils are elusive in the Mediterranean outside North Africa, however, and classification of existing fossils is debated. Some authorities identify fossil skulls from Greece, Germany, England, and France as *Homo erectus*, but others see in them characteristics of early *Homo sapiens*, perhaps ancestral to both the later Neanderthals and anatomically modern humans. The fossils date to between 400,000 and 200,000 B.P., and are only rarely associated with the stone tool sites of the Lower Paleolithic.

At around 200,000 B.P., smaller flake tools began to replace those of the Lower Paleolithic. This marks the beginning of the Middle Paleolithic, the period when Neanderthals were present in Europe and the Near East as distinct regional populations. Archaeologists for a long time assumed that Neanderthals alone made the flaketools called "Mousterian," but remains of anatomically modern humans are also associated with Mousterian artifacts in Israel (e.g., at Qafzeh and Skhul) as early as 100,000 B.P. Neanderthals in the same region are dated later, to 60,000 B.P. This shows that moderns and Neanderthals overlapped in time and shared fundamentals such as stone tools and territory. Neanderthals have been discovered in Europe (e.g., at Saint Cesaire, France) in association with Upper Paleolithic tools once thought to be the work of later humans.

The earliest modern humans in the Mediterranean area lived in the Near East. From there they spread westward through the Balkans (42,000 B.P.) to western Europe (35,000 B.P.). The last Neanderthals disappeared by 32,000 B.P., and their fate is unexplained. It is possible that they evolved into modern humans through local evolution, but one theory places the origin of modern humans in Africa, whence they migrated and replaced the Neanderthals throughout their range. The east-to-west movement of Upper Paleolithic stone tool industries supports the replacement hypothesis, but it remains unproven.

During the Last Glacial Maximum, modern humans were found throughout the Mediterranean region. Upper Paleolithic stone tool industries show marked regional differences, which continue in later Bronze Age and Iron Age cultures. Mediterranean climate in the Pleistocene was relatively mild, favoring human settlement. Summers were cool and winters were cold and dry. Higher elevations were dominated by shrub vegetation, and richer habitats were found on large coastal plains exposed by the low sea levels. Coastal plains existed in the Adriatic, along the North African coast, and between Greece and Turkey, and were well watered, sheltered from the cold winters, and rich in plants and animals. The plains were unlike habitats that exist today, but were a unique ecological niche. Rising sea levels in the Holocene submerged the coastal plains under as much as 492 feet (150 m) of water, radically altering the Mediterranean landscape.

Upper Paleolithic foragers preferred habitation in rock shelters and caves, and the excavated remains from most sites are dominated by stone tools, typically scrapers and points for weapons; animal bones, often of preferred species such as horse, elk, or reindeer; and rare objects of personal adornment such as beads and pendants. There is little evidence for Paleolithic art in the Mediterranean region. Known occupation sites are commonly interpreted as seasonal hunting camps or activity areas used by small groups of foragers who had their base camps on the coastal plains.

In the Early Holocene, Mesolithic foragers moved to higher elevations not inundated by the rising sea, and their economy shifted to the exploitation of aquatic resources, especially fish and shellfish. Foragers persisted in some areas for one or two millennia, but they were rapidly replaced by farmers who dwelt in villages. The earliest Neolithic settlements associated with *domestication of plant or animal species are found by 10,000 B.P. in the eastern Mediterranean in a band stretching from the Levant through Lebanon, Syria, and Turkey down into Iraq and Iran. Explanations for the origins of *agriculture remain elusive. The timing of the change, at the end of the Pleistocene, suggests that climate played some role. Growing populations and the new sedentary life of the villages gave an impetus to farming to increase the food supply, and economic interdependence, seen in expanding trade routes among sites in different physical settings, has been invoked as a contributing factor. Recent studies of plant genetics show that the transition from wild to fully domesticated plants can occur in short periods of time, between twenty and two hundred years. The transition to the Neolithic may have taken place relatively quickly.

The Mediterranean basin was settled by Neolithic agriculturalists in less than five millennia. In southern Greece the transition from foraging to farming can be seen at Franchthi cave, which has a stratified sequence from the Upper

Paleolithic to the Neolithic. Excavators see continuity from the Paleolithic to the Mesolithic, but the transition to the Neolithic is rapid and abrupt. The movement of farmers from the Near East to Greece and southern Europe, documented by the presence of animal and plant species domesticated originally in the Near East, suggests that agriculture was spread by migrants. Mesolithic sites in some regions overlap the transition to the Neolithic, particularly in France and Spain, suggesting that the domesticated plants and animals needed for farming were acquired by local inhabitants from neighboring farmers, perhaps by trade. The present consensus is that immigration and adoption of farming by locals both played a part in spreading the new economy.

Once the Neolithic began, there was no turning back, and the village farming way of life persisted for thousands of years. The success of the new economy was accompanied by population increases and the development of villages into towns and small cities. These irreversible changes provided the foundations for the emergence in the Bronze Age of historic urban civilizations.

■ Clive Gamble, *The Palaeolithic Settlement of Europe* (1986). Alasdair Whittle, *Neolithic Europe: A Survey* (reprinted 1988). Paul Mellars, ed., *The Emergence of Modern Humans* (1990).

Curtis Runnels

THE RISE OF THE AEGEAN AND MEDITERRANEAN STATES

Early in the second millennium B.C. a complex, state-organized society first developed in the Aegean on the island of Crete. The focus of this civilization was the Minoan palaces, the best known of which is the palace of *Knossos in north-central Crete.

Two major chronological phases of Minoan palatial society have been recognized archaeologically: the Protopalatial, or First Palace Period (ca. 1900–1700 B.C.), succeeded by the Neopalatial, or Second Palace, Period (ca. 1700–1450 B.C.) in the wake of widespread destruction.

All the major functions that are considered characteristic of a state society were organized through these palaces. They operated as the seat of a centralized political administration, which controlled and utilized the surrounding region. Palatial control of the economy is clearly documented through the role of the palace as storer, consumer, producer, and regulator of goods. Specialized storage areas held substantial quantities of food produce, such as oil, olives, grain, pulses, and wine, in large clay jars *(pithoi)* as well as valuable artifacts. Precious and exotic material (e.g., metals, ivory, imported stone) were acquired and made into objects in workshops in and around the palace. The palace's bureaucratic role in recording and regulating goods is indicated by two classes of finds: carved seals made from stone, bone, and ivory, with their impressions in clay, and the first use of a writing system inscribed on clay tablets. There is also abundant evidence for religious and ceremonial activity within the palaces. The elaboration of cult equipment and shrines, and palatial involvement in the essentially rural "peak sanctuary" cult are especially characteristic of the Second Palace Period, and are collectively suggestive of the use of religious imperatives to validate political authority.

How and why palatial civilization arose on Crete at this time is one of the most challenging problems in Aegean prehistory, and one to which there is no simple answer. Early discussions of the problem focused heavily on the role of the eastern Mediterranean; by this scenario the development of Minoan trading contacts with the East in the Prepalatial Period led to the emergence of Minoan palatial society, which copied or was inspired by the older palatial states of Egypt and the Near East, established toward the end of the third millennium B.C.

Subsequently, explanations that regard indigenous developments as the fundamental factor in Minoan state formation have been favored over the idea of external, diffusionist influence from the Near East. The first detailed model for indigenous development was put forward by Colin Renfrew. He emphasized the interaction of agriculture, craft specialization, and trade in the creation of wealth and surpluses, and drew attention to the importance of the palace as a center for the collection and redistribution of agricultural staples.

More recent studies have widened the scope of the debate beyond this question of indigenous development versus foreign influence. Two points are particularly significant. First, Minoan palatial civilization cannot be understood as emerging inevitably and stage by stage, like a flower blooming from a bud, out of the achievements of early Minoan culture. Many features of palatial society, for example, architectural elements of the palaces, can be traced back to the Prepalatial Period, but that does not in itself provide an explanation of why state-organized society developed when it did. In this context John Cherry has proposed the possibility that state formation could have happened in one or more sudden bursts as opposed to gradual stages; in other words revolution not evolution. In order to make an informed choice between these alternative scenarios we need both a more detailed understanding of the early development of the major palatial sites within their respective regions, and a more precise chronological framework in which to place those developments.

Secondly, the problem of Minoan state formation has also benefited from being viewed in a wide, Mediterranean context. Why did state society emerge at this time only on Crete, but not elsewhere within the Aegean or in Mediterranean Europe? The absence of other state societies throughout this area indicates that the rich agricultural potential of the Mediterranean environment, while conducive to the development of complex society, cannot be considered the determining factor in the emergence of the Minoan state. Indeed it is striking that palatial civilization did not develop on other Mediterranean islands with closely comparable environments, such as Corsica, Sardinia, *Sicily, and especially *Cyprus, which is so geographically close to the older states of the eastern Mediterranean.

Several factors my be suggested then as being collectively unique to Crete and therefore important in the emergence of the Minoan state. The Early Bronze Age cultures of Crete, the Greek mainland, and the Cycladic islands flourished in an atmosphere of strong cultural diversity and lively inter-Aegean trade and interaction. Minoan cultural development is unbroken from the Early into the Middle Bronze Age; this factor separates Crete from its Aegean neighbors, since both the Cyclades and parts of the mainland suffered destructions and disruptions in the latter part of the Early Bronze Age, after which time their societies are markedly less complex and more inward looking. Crete benefited through its physical location from direct contacts with Egypt and the Near East. The archaeological evidence of exchanged objects and raw materials shows that these contacts were intensified toward the end of the Early Bronze Age.

One aspect of Minoan palatial society which separates it from the states of the eastern Mediterranean, and indeed is unusual for any state society, is the lack of overly militaristic features. The popular view of Minoan society as peace loving is misplaced, for the Minoans did build defenses and develop effective weaponry. Yet it is striking that powerful-ruler iconography—such as the Egyptian pharaoh tramping over his Lilliputian enemies—and militaristic display are absent from Minoan society.

Mycenaean state-organized society, which arose in southern Greece (ca. 1600–1200 B.C.), was from the military viewpoint a more conventional state. Mycenaean palaces at Mycenae and Tiryns in the Argolid were heavily defended citadels encircled by massive fortification walls, and weaponry and combative scenes of battle and hunting are prominent features of Mycenaean culture. Mycenaean palatial society is understood as an example of secondary state formation within the Aegean; it emerged as a result of contact with the Minoan palaces. Though physically very different from a Minoan palace, the Mycenaean palaces fulfilled broadly similar functions, operating as centers of political, economic, and religious activity. Among the specifically Mycenaean contributions to the history of the early state in the Aegean we may note their extensive trading networks, evidenced by the widespread distribution of Mycenaean pottery throughout the Mediterranean, and the development of a highly bureaucratic system of recording and redistributing goods using the Linear B script (an early form of Greek). This writing system was, ironically, adapted from the Linear A script of the Minoans, whom the Mycenaeans replaced as the major state society in the Aegean.

[See also AEGEAN CULTURES: OVERVIEW; GREECE: THE RISE OF GREEK CITY-STATES.]

■ J. Lewthwaite, "Why Did Civilisation Not Emerge More Often? A Comparative Approach to the Development of Minoan Crete," in Minoan Society, eds. O. Krzyszkowska and L. Nixon (1983), pp. 171-183. J. F. Cherry, "The Emergence of the State in the Prehistoric Aegean," Proceedings of the Cambridge Philological Society 30 (1984): 18-48. J. F. Cherry, "Polities and Palaces: Some Problems in Minoan State Formation," in Peer Polity Interaction and Socio-political Change, eds. C. Renfrew and J. F. Cherry (1986), pp. 19-45. R. Hägg and N. Marinatos, eds., The Function of the Minoan Palaces (1987). P. Halstead, "On Redistribution and the Origin of Minoan-Mycenaean Palatial Economies," in Problems in Greek Prehistory, eds. E. B. French and K. A. Wardle (1988), pp. 519-530. M. Dabney and J. C. Wright, "Mortuary Customs, Palatial Society and State Formation in the Aegean Area: A Comparative Study," in Celebrations of Death and Divinity in the Bronze Age Argolid, eds. R. Hägg and G. C. Nordquist (1990), pp. 185-97.

Christine E. Morris

THE DOMINANCE OF GREECE AND ROME

By the end of the second millennium B.C. life in Greece was at a low ebb: poor living conditions, depopulation, lack of centralized political authority, loss of writing, and little contact beyond the immediate Aegean area. By the eighth century major strides forward had been made: Greek speakers had begun to gather at the sanctuary at Olympia to express their common identity in worship and athletic competition, overseas contact had been reestablished, alphabetic writing had been learned from the seafaring Phoenicians, and small groups had begun to search for metals and for land outside Greece, mainly westward in Italy and *Sicily. These external contacts affected Greece itself and influenced the areas where Greeks settled and traded.

A new political and social organization, different from those of the contemporary Near East and from the earlier Bronze Age cultures of Greece itself, also began to be formed: the independent polis, or city-state. This system was based on an expanse of territory (chora) including a single settlement (usually with defensive acropolis and agora, or gathering ground, and with cemeteries outside the living area). Agriculture was the essence of their livelihood, based on the Mediterranean triad of cereal, vines, and olives. Ownership of land gave social prestige and brought political power. The whole structure was buttressed by slaves, acquired either from war or through slave trading. War was endemic and slavery a fact of life throughout classical antiquity.

The Archaic Period (ca. 620–480 B.C.) was one of increasing prosperity, growth, and diversity. Each polis had its citizen army of aristocratic cavalrymen and simple foot-soldiers formed to fight in hoplite ranks that expressed the solidarity of the community. "Greece" existed wherever Greeks were settled, whether in southern Italy, North Africa, or round the Black Sea. In such a volatile small-scale milieu, political changes were inevitable: In some cases dictators took over for a short or long period and initiated architectural developments on a grand scale; in others the franchise was made more widely available, as at *Athens. While the city-states were quarreling and fighting, power, especially in the kingdoms of the Near East, was still vested in single monarchs, and unified military action on a large scale was possible. *Persia was the largest and most troublesome to the Greeks, at first in Asia Minor, and then in Greece itself. Panhellenic unity of action was achieved only at the last moment in 480 B.C., and the Persians were expelled from Greece.

Classical Greece (480–323 B.C.) was dominated initially by the Athenians, who developed their navy and established ascendancy over their tribute-paying allies in what became an Athenian empire. The Athenian navy of triremes patrolled the merchant routes that brought food and supplies from the edges of the Greek world, while in Athens itself buildings were erected to underline the prestige of a successful and powerful city-state. The prolonged war between Athens and Sparta (431–404 B.C.), the defeat of Athens, and the inability of any individual state to maintain control over others led to the encroachment into Greece of the Macedonian army under Philip II and the eventual loss of Greek independence in 338 B.C.

As a consequence of the eastern military successes of Philip's son, Alexander the Great, the Hellenistic age (323–31 B.C.) presents an entirely new map of the eastern Mediterranean and beyond. Massive kingdoms were formed by his successors, and Greeks with their language, administration, ideas, and values now overran the Near East and beyond. Cities were established where urban living was a novelty, and gymnasia and theaters were constructed to feed Greek social demands. Later, the farther eastern reaches of the Hellenistic kingdoms were lost, and by the first century B.C. what remained, including Greece itself, had fallen to the power of *Rome.

In the north of the Italian peninsula, the major culture at the beginning of the first millennium was the Villanovan. From the eighth century B.C., with influence from the Greek traders and settlers in the south, this culture had developed into the Etruscan and spread both north and south. At this time Rome was a small but expanding Latin settlement by the side of the River Tiber, one of a number of similar agricultural communities. The rise of Rome to a position when she was able to take over the Hellenistic kingdoms (second and first centuries B.C.) was marked first by her conquest of central Italy, her involvement with the Greeks in the south, and her major and successful struggle against *Carthage in North Africa. As a consequence, Rome found herself in control of much of the western Mediterranean. The need to maintain a balance between security and conquest took her into the eastern Mediterranean of the Hellenistic kingdoms, which she brought under her command. Organization of this vast empire fell to the senate, consuls, and executive officers, with wealth to be made both for Rome and for the individuals themselves. Huge agricultural estates (latifundia) were worked by gangs of slaves. Engineering and technology improved: Aqueducts supplied the necessary water to the large urban centers, concrete enabled more massive buildings (basilicas, baths, etc.) to be erected, roads initially constructed for military and political communications enhanced economic trade.

By the first century B.C. the Roman Republican system was collapsing, dictators and military leaders fought for supremacy, and out of civil strife the Roman Empire was created. The emperors gained sole power for life. Little was added territorially to what Rome already held, but the administration changed. Some provinces were administered by representatives of the senate, some came under the direct control of the emperor, and the dangerous frontiers were patrolled by standing armies. The hand of Rome is visible in the remains that still exist wherever she ruled: Italy, North Africa, Celtic Europe, and the Greek East. Such a vast empire inevitably crumbled through internal mismanagement, economic difficulties, and external pressures, and by the third century A.D. the Roman Empire was in disarray. The transfer of the capital from Rome to *Constantinople in the early fourth century spelled the collapse of the Western Empire; the Eastern Empire survived for another thousand years.

The amount of archaeological material of Classical Greece and Rome that endures is enormous. Besides the actual remains of buildings and of clay, stone, and metal objects, the contexts of deposition are varied: settlement, sanctuary, cemetery, with increasing attention now focused on the countryside and the seabed. Added to this material is the documentary and literary evidence, derived from literary manuscripts, administrative papyri, and public and private inscriptions, all of which, like archaeological data, must be interpreted as artifacts. Besides investigating the relationship between written sources and archaeological evidence, major themes that interest the classical archaeologist are the varying nature of the contact between Greeks and Romans and their barbarian neighbors, the mutual effects of that contact, the pattern of settlements and the growth of urbanism, and finally the slow economic development behind the rapidly changing face of history, whether expressed in land use, trade and transactions, routes taken or goods exchanged. More traditional concerns center on such matters as techniques of manufacture, architectural developments, burial rituals, and chronology.

[See also GREECE, articles on CLASSICAL GREECE, THE HELLENISTIC AGE; ROMAN EMPIRE, articles on INTRODUCTION, THE ROMAN FRONTIER, THE EASTERN PROVINCES OF THE ROMAN EMPIRE.]

■ Tim Cornell and John Matthews, eds., Atlas of the Roman World (1982). John Boardman, Jasper Griffin, and Oswyn Murray, eds., The Oxford History of the Classical World (1986). Kevin Greene, The Archaeology of the Roman Economy (1986). Peter Garnsey and Richard Saller, The Roman Empire: Economy, Society and Culture (1987). Robin Osborne, Classical Landscape with Figures: The Ancient Greek City and Its Countryside (1987). Michael Grant, The Visible Past: Greek and Roman History from Archaeology, 1960–1990 (1990). Massimo Pallottino, A History of Earliest Italy (1991). John Rich and Andrew Wallace-Hadrill, eds., City and Country in the Ancient World (1991).

Brian A. Sparkes

MEGAFAUNAL EXTINCTION. Toward the end of the Quaternary, during the last 40,000 years, the continents of the world lost 85 genera of large mammals, over half of the number still living. The extinct megafauna (mammals above 100 pounds [45 kg] adult body weight) include Eurasian woolly rhinoceros and giant deer, North American and Eurasian mammoths, North American mastodons, sabertooth cats, ground sloths, horses, camels and glyptodons, South American mastodons, toxodons and ground sloths, Australian giant kangaroos and diprotodonts, and a few African bovids. On the larger oceanic islands giant birds, the moas, vanished from New Zealand; elephant birds and giant lemurs from Madagascar; pygmy hippo, pygmy elephants, and goat-antelopes from islands of the Mediterranean; dwarf ground sloths from the West Indies; and flightless geese, flightless ibis, and seabird colonies from Hawaii. Oceanic islands of the Pacific lost as many as 2,000 species of birds, dominated by flightless rails.

Late Quaternary extinctions were neither universal nor synchronous. Sparing aquatic life, they struck at different times and with different intensities in different parts of the globe. Prehistoric artifacts may or may not be found associated with the extinct faunas. In Eurasia, some upper *Paleolithic sites yield bones of mammoths and other extinct megafauna, especially in central Europe and the Russian plain. In North America, the Clovis culture appeared suddenly around or after 11,500 B.P. equipped with well-designed weapons and a well-developed knowledge of large-animal hunting. Clovis points are found mainly with bones of mammoth in a dozen sites. In Australia, occasional and uncertain cultural associations with extinct giant marsupials are yet to be confirmed. In Madagascar, extinction 1,000–2,000 years ago evidently coincided with human invasion, although kill sites or processing of extinct giant lemurs and other extinct Malagasy species are as yet unknown. In New Zealand, the bones of extinct moas are abundantly associated with Polynesian artifacts.

Recent improvements in geochemical dating, in particular radiocarbon assay, have vastly improved methods of estimating age of the extinct fauna. Refined methods of sample pretreatment and the capability of accelerators to date minute samples have illuminated important features of the tempo and mode of prehistoric extinction.

For example, large mammal losses in both Europe and North America can now be compared with profit. In Eurasia, a warm (interglacial) fauna of hippo (Hippopotomus), straight-tusked elephants (Paleoloxodon antiquus), and extinct rhino (Dicerorhinus) preceded the extinction of a cold fauna of woolly mammoth (Mammuthus primigenius), woolly rhinoceros (Coelodontia), giant deer (Megaceros), and cave bear (Ursus spelaeus). Climatic changes accompanied faunal extinction, and it had long been assumed that they were its main cause.

The warm fauna contracted enormously at the end of the last (Eemian or Ipswichian) interglacial 113,000 B.P., surviving into the last cold stage in the Mousterian of Italy and southern Spain. The cold fauna of Europe's Quaternary flourished through the last cold stage, although shrinking ranges and declining populations are increasingly apparent since the last glacial maximum around 18,000 B.P. Woolly mammoth ranged farther south before then, during the height of the last glaciation about 18,000 B.P. Scattered fossils of woolly mammoth are known from England, Scandinavia, France, Switzerland, and Germany during the late glacial (14,000–12,000 B.P.) and in northernmost parts of Siberia until 10,000 B.P. While the last mammoths, recently discovered on Wrangel Island in the Arctic Ocean, lived until only 4000 B.P., the reduction of Eurasian proboscideans began with the extinction of straight-tusked elephants roughly 70,000 years earlier, long before any hint of megafaunal decline in the New World.

In the New World, various summaries of the extinction chronology based on radiocarbon dating indicate a punctuated, not a gradual, extinction of megafauna, centering around 11,000 B.P. Although some North American extinct genera lived in cold climates (woolly mammoth, bonnet headed musk ox, stag moose) while others inhabited temperate or tropical regions (glyptodons, ground sloths, giant armadillos, tapir), there are no stratigraphic or geochronological data to support the extinction of one in advance of the other, as in western Europe. Furthermore, over many thousands of years prior to extinction there is no apparent shrinkage in range or decrease in numbers of American as compared with Eurasian mammoths. The difference in the extinction chronologies is compatible with a gradually intensifying human predation slowly reducing the Eurasian megafauna. In contrast, in the New World, human invaders explosively eliminated naïve prey. Whatever the cause, the extinction chronologies appear independent of major climatic changes, which are essentially synchronous in the two continents.

Dry caves of the Grand Canyon of the Colorado River have proved especially rich in perishable organic remains of extinct species, providing an unusual opportunity to test the New World extinction rate. Dung, keratin, and body tissues are ideally suited not only for radiocarbon assay but also for determining diet and the local environment in which the animals lived. The region includes three ground sloth caves, at least a dozen extinct mountain goat caves, and more than ten caves yielding perishable remains of the California condor, one with its food remains. Immediately upstream of the Grand Canyon are large caves harboring mammoth dung.

The Shasta ground sloth (*Nothrotheriops shastensis*), known from the western end of the Grand Canyon, consumed globe mallow, prickly pear cactus, Indian tea, and yucca. The extinct mountain goats (*Oreamnos harringtoni*) and mammoth (*Mammuthus columbi*) were mainly grass eaters. Food scraps from condor nests include identifiable remains of bison, camel, extinct mountain goat, and part of a tooth plate of a mammoth. Suites of radiocarbon dates on ground sloths, extinct goats, and condors terminate in each case around 11,000 B.P. with a few animals possibly lingering to 10,000 B.P. Associations of mammoth bones in Clovis sites as well as direct carbon-14 dating on suitably preserved mammoth bone demonstrate survival until 11,000 B.P. Few visitors to Grand Canyon National Park appreciate the magnitude and rate of loss of native fauna 11,000 years ago.

Cause or causes of extinctions near the end of the Quaternary have become the subject of much interest and debate. With no extinctions of marine organisms beyond a very low background level and with terrestrial extinctions on the continents restricted mainly, if not entirely, to large vertebrates (those in excess of 97 pounds [44 kg] adult body weight) and bird extinctions concentrated on oceanic islands, the late Quaternary event is quite unlike mass extinctions earlier in the Phanerozoic, which involved many kinds of organisms in different phyla, many confined to salt water. Given that extinctions in Eurasia and Australia preceded those in America, whose losses preceded extinction on oceanic islands by thousands of years, the prospect for a meteor impact or some other extraterrestrial accident simultaneously driving all extinctions in the late Quaternary, as is proposed for the late Cretaceous, seems unlikely.

On oceanic islands in the warmer waters of the globe, human invasion inevitably precedes severe reduction of birds, reptiles, mammals, and even minute species of land snails. Recent archaeofaunal studies in Tonga, the Line Islands, the Marquesas, the Cook Islands, and the Rapanui (Easter) Islands have yielded far more extinctions and associations of locally extinct land and sea birds from cultural deposits than were known or suspected until quite recently. While climate-driven extinctions may be expected in parts of the Pacific where rainfall varies considerably, background extinction rates appear to be very low, two orders of magnitude below the extinction rate accompanying human colonization.

Pacific colonization began in Meganesia (Australia and New Guinea) about 30,000 B.P. and did not spread into the Pacific archipelagos until the Lapita culture some 4,000 years ago, with human colonists reaching Hawaii and New Zealand roughly 1,000 years ago. The destructive side effects included a variety of domestic species such as dogs, pigs, chickens, rats, continental species of land snails and soil microorganisms, and such pathogens as avian malaria. Burning of native forest for cultivation also contributed to loss of island endemic biota. Human colonizers may have increased beyond human carrying capacity, as in the case of the Rapanui, Henderson, and Pitcairn Islands and other "islands of doom" in which abandonment followed bird extinctions.

On continents, especially North America, some vertebrate paleontologists account for extinction of larger mammals by proposing a loss of equability based on the changing ranges of small mammals. In Beringia, an increase in snow depth and reduction in forage quality is held responsible for extinctions of mammoths and other large mammals. Late Quaternary drought may have forced extinction of giant marsupials in Australia and of mammoth, horse, and camel in arid America. One problem with these and other climatic models is that they require a unique climatic pulse, an extreme event not seen earlier in the Quaternary to account for the unusual magnitude of large mammal loss. The proxy data commonly used to estimate Quaternary climates, that is, oxygen isotopes, ice core resistivity, and fossil pollen records, do not disclose extraordinary climatic conditions accompanying the extraordinary extinctions.

Given the scarcity of kill or processing sites or other field evidence, some archaeologists discount human colonization as a driving force in extinction of large animals. Furthermore, some archaeologists report archaeological sites predating Clovis. An abundance of kill or processing sites need not be expected if extinction was rapid, a "blitzkrieg" driven by first contact with a potent new predator, as one may assume in Australia and the New World following colonization by anatomically modern representatives of

Homo sapiens. With populations of the new colonizers increasing by two percent to four percent annually, a continent could be overrun in a few hundred years and any local region in only a few years, a far more intense and rapid rate of change than is seen in the Old World.

One effective test of these and other models turns on careful radiocarbon dating of faunal extinction, environmental change, and human colonization. Finally, it should be noted that nowhere in the fossil record do remains of the extinct animals themselves yield unambiguous evidence of the immediate cause of their extinction. The most one may hope for is circumstantial evidence of a related event potentially sufficient to drive the extinctions and to account for the pattern of loss. In the late Quaternary that event appears to be human activity following human colonization.

[*See also* AMERICAS, FIRST SETTLEMENT OF THE.]

■ Paul S. Martin and Richard G. Klein, eds., *Quaternary Extinctions: A Prehistoric Revolution* (1984). Richard G. Klein, *The Human Career: Human Biological and Cultural Origins* (1989). Paul S. Martin, "40,000 Years of Extinctions on the 'Planet of Doom,'" *Palaeography, Palaeoclimatology, Palaeoecology* 82 (1990): 187–201. Anthony J. Stuart, "Mammalian Extinctions in the Late Pleistocene of Northern Eurasia and North America," *Biological Reviews* 66 (1991): 453–562. David A. Burney, "Recent Animal Extinctions: Recipes for Disaster," *American Scientist* 81 (1993): 531–541. Donald K. Grayson, *The Desert's Past* (1993). Olga Soffer and N. D. Praslov, *From Kostenki to Clovis: Upper Paleolithic—Paleo-Indian Adaptations* (1993). David W. Steadman, "Prehistoric Extinctions of Pacific Island Birds: Biodiversity Meets Zooarchaeology," *Science* 267 (1995): 1123–1131.

Paul S. Martin

MEGALITHIC TOMBS are one of the most widespread and conspicuous landscape monuments of the western European Neolithic. The term "megalithic" itself is derived from the Greek words "lithos" meaning stone and "megas" or "large." They are thus in essence large stone monuments, but by extension "megalithic tomb" is often used to refer to all Neolithic chambered tombs of western Europe, including those where construction was in dry-stone walling or timber. Recent excavations at Haddenham in Cambridgeshire showed that the timber elements in nonstone chambered tombs could themselves be of great size, and the term "megaxylic" ("large timber") was proposed to refer to these, but so far this has not found general acceptance in the archaeological literature.

The variety of monuments comprised within the category of megalithic tombs is enormous, ranging from simple box-like burial chambers beneath small circular mounds to enormous mounds with multiple passages and chambers such as Knowth in Ireland or Barnenez in Brittany. Furthermore, the tombs form part of a larger tradition of western European prehistoric monuments, which also includes standing stones, stone circles, and in Britain, henges and cursus monuments. This monumentalism is a key feature of the western European Neolithic and suggests some conscious attempt on the part of these early societies to create a cultural landscape of conspicuously visible humanly made structures.

Among the immense variability of megalithic tombs a number of key types have been identified. One of the earliest and most widespread is the passage grave, where the burial chamber under its covering mound of earth or stones is reached by a passage starting from the edge of the mound. This design allowed continued access to the chamber long after the mound was completed, although in many cases the passage was low and narrow and could be negoti-

ated only by crawling through it. Examples of the passage grave type are found in most of the regions where megalithic tombs were built, including Iberia, France, the British Isles, and southern Scandinavia, but in addition to the passage graves each region possesses other types of megalithic tomb. In France, there are the *allées couvertes,* or gallery graves, consisting of an elongated burial chamber reached by a short vestibule. In Ireland, there are court cairns, where long curved arms extend from one end of the mound to enclose an unroofed courtyard. In northern Europe, there are the *dysser,* in which the chamber is a simple stone compartment beneath the mound, without any means of entry from the outside. In most regions there are additionally other kinds of Neolithic mounded tomb such as the unchambered long mound or round mound; these unchambered monuments, properly speaking, fall outside the category of megalithic tombs, although it is clear they are a related phenomenon.

One of the most interesting findings from work on megalithic tombs over the past fifty years has been the realization that most are not single-phase structures of unitary design but the result of many separate episodes of building, modification, and addition. The form of the monument as it appears today is often the final outcome of a process extending over several centuries. A good example of this is the tomb known as Wayland's Smithy in southern Britain. This is a megalithic tomb with a burial chamber of cruciform plan at one end of an elongated mound. The entrance to the passage leading to the burial chamber is in the center of one end of the mound, flanked by large upright stones that create a ceremonial facade. This associated facade is the most conspicuous of the surviving structures but represents only the latest phase of the monument. The original structure consisted of a timber mortuary house containing the bones of fourteen to seventeen individuals. Subsequently, the mortuary house was allowed to decay and the remains covered by an oval mound. At a later stage this was incorporated in the monument that we see today, the oval mound being entirely hidden within the long mound and a separate megalithic passage grave built at one end.

Origins and Chronology. Until the advent of radiocarbon dating in the 1950s conventional wisdom placed most megalithic tombs in the late third or early second millennium B.C., or in some cases even later; in the 1920s, the *allée couverte* of Tressé in Normandy was attributed by its excavator to the Iron Age (first millennium B.C.). At that time, many prehistorians considered megalithic tombs to be derived from the eastern Mediterranean or Aegean region, and the corbel vaults of Newgrange in Ireland and Maes Howe in Scotland were traced back to Mycenaean forebears such as the famous Treasury of Atreus at Mycenae itself.

The first radiocarbon dates quickly demonstrated that the western European megalithic tombs were much older than their supposed Aegean antecedents, and the hypothesis of an eastern Mediterranean origin was replaced by theories of independent development. These new dates placed the earliest megalithic tombs in the fourth millennium B.C., and with the calibration of the radiocarbon chronology the oldest dates have been pushed back to around 4800 B.C. in calendar years. This makes them the oldest monumental architecture in the world. Radiocarbon dates have also enabled the chronology of the different varieties of megalithic tomb to be fixed, and have shown that megalithic tombs were still being built and used around 2500 B.C. in Ireland and certain regions of France. The use of megalithic tombs has thus been shown to extend over a period of more than 2,000 years.

The earliest reliably dated tombs are the passage graves of northwestern France, although it is likely that megalithic tombs in certain regions of Portugal belong to approximately the same period. Most theories of origin place particular emphasis on the geographical distribution of the tombs, especially that of apparently early types such as passage graves. Their distribution along the Atlantic margin of Europe suggests that maritime contacts, perhaps between sea-fishing communities, may have played a part in the genesis and dissemination of the concept. This idea gains support from the discovery of collective graves containing the skeletons of up to six individuals in the mesolithic shell middens of Téviec and Hoëdic off the southern coast of Brittany. The practice of collective burial, which is such a widespread feature of western European chambered tombs, could well have arisen from such modest mesolithic origins.

The concept of the mound may have been a response to the social changes connected with the adoption of a new economy or ideology at the beginning of the Neolithic Period. It has been argued that pressure from farming groups spreading across northern France from the east could, in turn, have led to pressure on land and resources in Brittany, stimulating the construction of monumental tombs that acted as territorial markers. Other arguments place the emphasis not on economic change but on the ideology of the longhouse. Longhouses of massive timber construction were a key feature of early framing communities in central Europe, and are thought to have been translated into long mounds for burials by the early farming communities of northern and northwestern Europe. Long mounds are found in northern France as far west as Brittany, and some have argued that it was from these long mounds that all other varieties of mounded tomb, including the passage graves, were derived. This hypothesis fails to account for the early development of megalithic tombs in Iberia, however, where neither long mounds nor longhouses were present. For this reason it remains probably that megalithic tombs derived their origin, in part at least, from local Mesolithic burial traditions.

Usage and Meaning. Megalithic tombs consist of two principal components: the burial chamber and the covering mound, or barrow. A third element sometimes found is a court or forecourt. There is some evidence to suggest how these elements were used, although usage must have varied considerably from generation to generation and from one region to another.

The principal burial place was the chamber, although burials sometimes were also placed in the passage. At the Hazleton long mound in southern Britain burials had been placed in the passage only after access to the chamber beyond had been blocked by collapse, so in this case the passage appears to have served as an overflow. The predominant practice in megalithic tombs was that of collective burial, in which remains of up to 350 individuals were placed together in the same tomb. Grave goods were usually few, and most of the bones had become disarticulated. In some tombs there was evidence that the bodies had first been buried or exposed elsewhere, and it was only the cleaned and disarticulated bones that were placed in the chamber; in other cases, entire bodies were introduced, and any disarticulation was the result of later disturbance after they had decomposed.

The presence of an entrance or passage was clearly designed to allow repeated access to the burial chamber over a period of decades or centuries, and evidence shows that earlier burials were sometimes displayed to make way for new interments. There are also indications that in some tombs the bones had been sorted into categories, such as long bones or skulls, which were grouped together in particular areas of the chamber. This suggests that not only may new burials have been introduced via the passage, but selected bones from existing interments may have been extracted for use in cults or ceremonies. Such ceremonies, perhaps involving offerings to the dead, may have taken place in the courts or forecourts.

The monumentality of the tombs suggests that the bodies placed in them were of great importance to the communities that built the tombs. A suggestion that has gained broad acceptance is that the tombs drew their significance from being the resting place of the ancestors. In many small-scale societies an individual derives the right to use of the land from his or her lineal descent from the ancestors. The burial mounds may therefore have symbolized ancestral right to land, and this line of reasoning can help to explain why the burial mound is often much larger than would be needed simply to cover the burial chamber itself.

Social Context. A number of exercises, both paper and practical, have attempted to calculate the work effort involved in the construction of a megalithic tomb. This includes quarrying and transport of the stone, construction of the chamber and other structures on site, and completion of the mound. These exercises have shown that it would have been within the capability of a small-scale community of some few dozen persons to build one of the smaller tombs, but that construction of a large tomb such as Knowth, in Ireland, where there are two long and heavily decorated passage graves beneath a mound over 200 feet (60 m) in diameter, would have required the cooperation of a large number of individuals, from several different communities. The fact that, in general, the larger tombs belong to the later stages of megalithic tombs could be related to the development of increasingly hierarchical societies, where power was concentrated more and more in the hands of a ruling elite. Thus what we may be witnessing is a transition from a landscape of relatively egalitarian communities, each with their ancestral monument, to a more hierarchical organization where burial mounds are fewer, larger, and concentrated in emerging centers of power, such as the *Boyne Valley or Orkney mainland.

Not all regions exhibit such a hierarchical progression, however, and there is evidence that even in the third millennium B.C. some of the tombs were still being shared by a small number of families who chose to bury their dead in a communal burial place. The *allée couverte* of La Chaussée-Tirancourt in northeastern France contains two distinct layers of burial separated by an intentional deposit of chalk. Genetic abnormalities in the bones show that the same families were burying in particular areas within the tomb in both layers. This suggests that these families retained rights to their own specific part of the chamber throughout the life of the tomb.

Megalithic Art. An intriguing feature of some megalithic tombs is the presence of designs carved into the surface of the stones. These designs, known as "Megalithic art," are found in tombs along the Atlantic margin of Europe from Iberia to the Orkney Islands but are especially common in Ireland. In the great Boyne Valley tombs such as Knowth and Newgrange, decorated stones occur both in the slab-built curbs that encircle the base of the burial mounds and on the stones of the passage and chamber. In addition to pecked designs, traces of painted decoration have been found on certain Portuguese tombs. It is unclear whether this kind of decoration is a local Portuguese phenomenon, or whether it was originally much more widespread and survived only in the warmer Portuguese climate.

A wide variety of motifs, both representational and abstract, are present in Megalithic art. They may be divided chronologically into three principal phases. In the first phase (ca. 4800–4000 B.C.), the art appears to be restricted to Brittany and consists of motifs that are schematic but representational rather than purely abstract, as in later phases. Motifs include axes, hafted axes, crooks, and crosses. They are found on menhirs and on simple passages graves. (See Statue-Menhirs.)

The second phase coincides with the period when the classic passage graves were being built (4000–3500 B.C. or possibly as late as 3200 B.C.). The art is now more widespread, being found in Iberia, France, and the British Isles, and in contrast to the preceding period the principal art motifs are nonrepresentational, consisting of abstract curves, circles, spirals, and meanders, often in closely spaced concentric patterns. This kind of art is represented most spectacularly at Gavrinis, a passage grave on a small island in the Gulf of Morbihan in southern Brittany, but by far the greatest number is found in the passage graves of the Boyne Valley.

Finally, the third phase is marked by a return to a greater regional variation in Megalithic art. The best-known examples are from northern France, where representational elements become dominant once more. Certain of the motifs seem to be anthropomorphic: necklaces and paired breasts in Brittany and anthropomorphic outlines on the walls of rock-cut tombs in the Marne region. These might be the first representations of spirits or supernatural beings in northwestern Europe since the end of the last Ice Age.

The presence of Megalithic art in different regions suggests some measure of interregional contact and cultural sharing. Under certain circumstances, however, identical artistic motifs may be developed by different societies entirely in isolation. This is the alternative possibility presented by recent writers seeking to demonstrate the entoptic nature of the designs involved. Entoptic motifs are a universal product of the human psyche in certain altered states of consciousness, such as trances induced by narcotics or other intoxicants. The abstract patterns that are seen in these circumstances are the same irrespective of cultural or social background. If it is accepted that some megalithic art consists of entoptic motifs, then we need not expect to find direct cultural contacts between the regions using this art. Any specific parallels would be indicative not of cultural contact between these regions, but would stem instead from the origin of these motifs in universal characteristics of the human psyche.

The possibility that trance-inducing substances were used in these societies is strengthened by the discovery in a number of French Neolithic burial chambers of fragments of ceramic incense burners. These may have been designed for the inhalation of a narcotic such as opium. Together with the evidence of sorting and manipulation of the bones this provides tantalizing indications of the kinds of ritual practiced in and around megalithic tombs.

Megaliths Worldwide. Although the best-known Mega-lithic tombs are those in Europe, it should be noted that monuments of a similar character and construction are found in other parts of the world, including southern India, the Caucasus, Madagascar, and parts of South America. The use of large stone blocks to create a tomb chamber appears thus to have been adopted independently by a number of human societies at different times in the past.

[See also BRITISH ISLES: PREHISTORY OF THE BRITISH ISLES; BURIAL AND TOMBS; EUROPE: THE EUROPEAN NEOLITHIC PERIOD; STONE CIRCLES AND ALIGNMENTS.]

■ J. D. Lewis-Williams and T. A. Dowson, "On Vision and Power in the Neolithic: Evidence from the Decorated Monuments," *Current Anthropology* 34 (1993): 55–65. J.-P. Mohen, *The World of Megaliths* (1989). C. Renfrew, ed., *The Megalithic Builders of Western Europe* (1983). E. Shee Twohig, *The Megalithic Art of Western Europe* (1981).

Chris Scarre

MEHRGARH. The site of Mehrgarh, on the Kachi Plain of the Indus Valley in Pakistan (29°25′ N, 67°35′ E), is a major archaeological discovery. It is an area of over 495 acres (200 ha). Excavations have shown that the area was never totally settled at any one time, and there is a great deal of lateral stratigraphy. The site was discovered and developed by a team of French archaeologists headed by Jean-Francois Jarrige and his counterparts in the Pakistan Department of Archaeology. Excavation began in 1974–1975 and continued through the 1985–1986 field season without interruption. The focus of research then shifted to the nearby Early and Mature Harappan site of Naushari. There is no final report on the Mehrgarh excavations, but there are privately circulated yearly reports, and Jarrige and his team published on the site widely.

Mehrgarh is on the Bolan River, a perennial stream that drains out of the highlands of Baluchistan into Kachi. It is a rich alluvial area, with adequate water resources for agriculture. The river has greatly damaged the site over the millennia, and a substantial portion of the midden has been removed by erosion.

There are seven periods within the confines of the site, dated by a series of radiocarbon dates. The estimated chronology is as follows: Period VII: Damb Sadaat (3200–2600 B.C.); Period VI: Kechi Beg / Damb Sadaat (3500–3200 B.C.); Period V: Kechi Beg (3800–3500 B.C.); Period IV: Togau / Kechi Beg (4000–3800 B.C.); Period III: Togau (4500–4000 B.C.); Period II: Burj Basket Marked (5500–4500 B.C.); and Period I: Neolithic (7000–5500 B.C.).

Period I. Occupation begins with an aceramic Neolithic in Period IA in an area called MR.3, in the northeastern corner of the site. Mehrgarh I, a small village of farmers and herders, was 7 to 10 acres (3 to 4 ha). Dwellings and compartmented buildings, apparently granaries, were found. Storage facilities of this type began in Period I, and as agricultural production increased, so did their number and sophistication. The dwellings were simple mud-brick structures, 16 by 13 feet (5 by 4 m) on the average, frequently subdivided into four to six rooms. The floors occasionally had reed impressions. Ovens and hearths were usually found in the corners of rooms, and signs of their use are reflected in traces of smoke on the plastered walls. One circular oven lined with bricks had a dome, which was traced in its collapsed condition.

The technology of Mehrgarh I was simple. The small amount of copper is thought to be of the native variety, not smelted. The bed of the Bolan River carries cobbles of light brown flint from which tools were fashioned; some were sickle blades that occasionally carried sheen. Ground-stone food processing tools were found: quern and grinding-stone fragments, two small limestone chisels, a small bowl, and a small mortar.

There were basket containers, some lined with bitumen to strengthen and waterproof them. Slabs of bitumen with basket impressions are known. A small amount of pottery and unbaked, clay figurines appear toward the end of Period I (called Period IB).

There is a rich bone industry. Awls, spatulas, a bone needle, and two highly polished bone pendants with round perforations were found.

Palaeobotanical material from Period I is rich and complex. Most of the evidence came from thousands of impressions in the abundant mud bricks of the period. The dominant plant is naked six-row barley (*Hordeum vulgare*, subspecies *vulgare,* variety *nudum*). More than 90 percent of the seeds and imprints were identified as this plant. There is hulled six-row barley (*H. vulgare,* subspecies *vulgare*), two-row barley (*H. vulgare,* subspecies *spontaneum,* and *H. vulgare, subspecies distichum*), einkorn (*Triticum monococcum*), emmer (*T. turgidum,* subspecies *dicoccum*), and hard wheat (*T. turgidum,* cf. conv. *durum*) present in greatly reduced amounts. The only unidentified noncereals include the Indian jujube (*Zizyphus* sp.) and dates (*Phoenix dactylifera*), represented by stones in an upper level of Period IB as well as Period IIB. Einkorn and emmer disappear from use in the region, but bread wheat and shot wheat continue on as the eastern species of *Triticum*.

In Period IA, the animal economy is dominated by twelve species of large game animals. Richard Meadow takes this to indicate that the first inhabitants of aceramic Mehrgarh I exploited not only the surrounding hills but the Kachi Plain itself. Fish and birds are lacking in any quantity, which seems to signify that the Bolan River and the wet environments around it were not important to the inhabitants of Mehrgarh.

By the end of the aceramic period the faunal assemblage is different: "Almost all of the faunal remains that can be identified come from sheep, goat or cattle, three of the domestic animals of principal importance in the Middle East and South Asia today. The very fact of their overwhelming importance in the faunal assemblage is good evidence of the keeping of these animals by the peoples of later Period I" (Meadow 1984: 335).

The appearance of chaff-tempered pottery in Period IB appears on the scene between about 6000 and 5500 B.C. and helps in interpreting these dates.

Continuity and change are marked with the introduction of soft, buff, chaff-tempered pottery in Period IIA. This ceramic seems to have broad similarities on the Iranian Plateau (e.g., Yahya Periods VII–V, Tepe Sialk, Belt and Hotu Caves), perhaps as far west as the Zagros (Jarmo), but has not yet been described in detail at Mehrgarh.

Period II. Period II occupies a part of the site called MR.4. The remains form a broad band of deposits that encircles the deposits of Period IB. There is growth and continuity out of Period I and some justification for considering the two periods a single unit. Rectangular houses subdivided into rooms, contemporary with the compartmented buildings of Period II, are important to our knowledge of the South Asian village farming community. Craft activity, which included flint knapping, tanning, and bead making, is of consequence because of its diversity. Pottery was probably made at the site or close by. Cotton is present, although

identification is from seeds and the exact use of this plant at Mehrgarh has not yet been determined. A fireplace contained several hundred charred seeds, some of which have been identified as grains of cotton (*Gossypium*).

Period III. The remains of Period III are found in sector MR.2, south of the original settlement. Three features of Mehrgarh III seem to characterize this period. The first of these is the size of the settlement. Period III remains cover an estimated 170 acres (70 ha), slightly smaller than *Mohenjo-daro. The area is not likely ever to have been fully settled at any one time, but it must have been a very large settlement for its day. The second distinguishing feature is further development of craft activities. The creation of new industries is not always involved, but evidence for metallurgy first appears at this time, and there is marked quantitative growth. The third feature is the evolution of the ceramic industry in Mehrgarh. It is dominated by fine red ware and wheel-made vessels, characterized by a style of painting that has come to be called "Togau."

The expansion of crafts, including the development of Togau ware, is linear. Two kinds of architecture persist, with continued construction of compartmented buildings and domestic structures, but with some changes.

Craft Production in Early Periods. Much of the craft production of Period II took place among the interdigitated buildings of MR.4. There is some difference during Period III. Before excavating, a careful study was made of the surface of MR.2. Evidence was found for manufacturing processes involving lapis lazuli, carnelian, calcite, garnet, turquoise, shell, and bitumen. Fragments of these were clearly waste products of workshops in the area. In one area, a microdrill in phanite, wasters, and fragments of lapis lazuli, carnelian, and steatite were found together with ornaments in shell, two fragments of rattlelike objects, and a few bone awls. Several stone objects such as grinding stones, pestles, and flint tools also were recorded. One other exceptional find is a polished stone axe. The phanite drills are of a type found at Shahr-i Sokhta Mundigak and Ghazi Shah, a clear indication that these sites shared a common bead-drilling technology that linked distant places. Unfinished phanite drills were found in the debris associated with the flaking of semiprecious stone.

Steatite was used for bead making. It was heated to make it more malleable, then squeezed through a thin metal tube. As the soft material emerged, it was cut, creating a thin wafer bead. The process was used at Mehrgarh from Period III on. A similar process for microbeads was reconstructed from materials at Zekhada, a Sorath Harappan site in North Gujarat.

A shell industry using conch shells (*Fascolaria trapezium* and *Turbinella pyrum*) continues from Period II contexts. Fragments of *Turbinella pyrum,* some incised, have been found. A bangle fragment was decorated with incised parallel lines.

Perhaps the most significant craft was *metallurgy. A small amount of metal was found in Periods I and II. Notable is a pin with a double spiral head, an early example of the type; three compartmented seals; and some unidentifiable fragments. A tubular gold bead represents the earliest example of that metal found at the site. In Period III evidence for melting, refining, and possibly smelting copper came from a domestic structure. Its floor and walls were heavily burnt, and it is likely that it was used as a firing structure. The walls are made of bricks about $16 \times 4 \times 4$ inches ($40 \times 10 \times 10$ cm). The structure was bordered by an open space filled with animal bones, among which were found one complete and thirteen broken crucibles containing copper deposits and stains.

*Ceramics are the most ubiquitous evidence for craft production at Mehrgarh. A series of kilns associated with Period III ceramics was found, indicating that pottery used at the site was manufactured there. The kilns, of which only bases are preserved, are circular or oval in shape, with an average circumference of 8 feet (2.5 m), and built of mud bricks. Testing in the kiln area showed that the deposit there is 19 feet (6 m) deep, with loosely stratified ash, kiln debris, and wasters.

Period III at Mehrgarh was a time in which craft production expanded significantly. There is both continuity and change, but the unmistakable development of copper and possibly gold metallurgy is very important, as is the invention of the basic bead-drilling technology that would be employed for several millennia. Some of this is a kind of settling in of technological processes already well established, such as pyrotechnics and pottery production. It could be said that by the end of Mehrgarh III, the technology used by the Harappan civilization was already in place on the plains of the Indus River. So too, was long-distance trade.

Periods IV–VII. Periods IV through VII are located on the MR.1 mound at the southern end of the site. It is an area with more stratification than other places, which permits some control in determining the relative chronology. MR.1 is also an area that was until recently under intensive cultivation, abandoned because of salinization. There are clear signs that farmers cleared and leveled, that is, pared away at the site to enhance their fields. Thus the 15 acres (6 ha) of area that are known today may have little or no relationship to the actual size of the settlements involved.

Some time during the Period VII occupation another major settlement was established at Nausharo, next door to Mehrgarh. The emphasis on settlement seems to have shifted at this time. Mehrgarh was eventually abandoned, and Naushero was occupied into the Mature, Urban Phase Harappan, preserving important levels of the somewhat elusive transitional phase between the Early and Mature Harappan.

[*See also* ASIA: PREHISTORY AND EARLY HISTORY OF SOUTH ASIA; INDUS CIVILIZATION.]

■ Jean-Francois Jarrige and Richard H. Meadow, "The Antecedents of Civilization in the Indus Valley," *Scientific American* 243 (2) (1980): 122–133. K.T.M. Hegde, R. V. Karanth, and S. P. Sychanthavong, "On the Composition and Technology of Harappan Microbeads," in *Harappan Civilization: A Contemporary Perspective*, ed. Gregory L. Possehl (1982): 239–244. Lorenzo Costantini, "The Beginnings of Agriculture in the Kachi Plain: The Evidence from Mehrgarh," in *South Asian Archaeology 1981*, ed. Bridget Allchin (1984): 29–33. Jean-Francois Jarrige, "Chronology of the Earlier Periods of the Greater Indus as Seen from Mehrgarh, Pakistan," in *South Asian Archaeology 1981*, ed. Bridget Allchin (1984): 21–29. Jean-Francois Jarrige, "Towns and Villages of Hill and Plain," in *Frontiers of the Indus Civilization*, ed. B. B. Lal and S. P. Gupta (1984): 289–300. Richard H. Meadow, "Animal Domestication in the Middle East: A View from the Eastern Margin," in *Animals and Archaeology: Three Early Herders and Their Flocks*, ed. Juliet Clutton-Brock and Cardine Grigson (1984): 309–337. Anonymous, *Civilizations Anciennes du Pakistan* (1989). Anonymous, *Les Cites Oubliees de Indus: Archaeologie du Pakistan* (1989). Michael Jansen, Maire Mulloy, and Gunter Urban, eds., *Forgotten Cities on the Indus: Early Civilization in Pakistan from the 8th to the 2nd Millennium* B.C. (1991). Gonzaque Quivron, "The Neolithic Settlement at Mehrgarh: Architecture from the Beginning of the 7th to the first half of the 6th Millennium B.C.," in *Forgotten Cities on the Indus: Early Civilization in Pakistan from the 8th to the 2nd Millennium* B.C. (1991): 59–65. Anaick Samzun, "The Early Chalcolithic: Mehrgarh Period III," in *Forgotten Cities on the Indus: Early Civilization in Pakistan from the 8th to the 2nd Millennium* B.C. (1991), 66–72.

Gregory L. Possehl

MEROE. The ruins of the ancient town of Meroe lie on the east bank of the Nile about 124 miles (200 km) north of Khartoum in the present-day Republic of the Sudan. It was occupied from about 750 B.C. to about A.D. 350, and from perhaps 590 B.C. it was a royal residence and administrative capital of the state of Kush. It consists of the remains of royal palaces, temples, and domestic and manufacturing areas. Close by are royal cemeteries where the rulers from about 300 B.C. were buried under small pyramids.

Mentioned by several Greek and Roman writers, Meroe was first tentatively identified by the Scottish traveler James Bruce in 1772 on returning from a journey to Ethiopia. It was positively identified to be the site of ancient Meroe with the excavations of (John) Garstang in 1910–1914. Excavations after those of 1910–1914 were continued from 1965 to 1984 by a joint expedition of the Universities of Calgary and Khartoum and are now being continued by the Humboldt University of Berlin from 1991.

As the main town of a state that controlled the Nile Valley from a short distance south of the first Nile cataract in Egypt to at least as far as Sennar on the Blue Nile, Meroe is of importance as containing both royal and religious monuments and large areas of domestic occupation known from two large occupation mounds lying on the eastern side of the site.

The cultural remains consist of a large walled enclosure containing what are reasonably assumed to be the remains of the royal residence—built mainly of stone but with both fired and unfired bricks. To the east of this wall lies the largest Kushite temple known, similar in layout to a traditional Pharaonic Egyptian temple and known to be dedicated to the god Amun, state god of Egypt and of Kush. Several smaller temples lie to the east flanking a ceremonial way leading east and away from the river.

The domestic part of the site consists of many small, tightly packed houses of sun-dried brick in areas that show stratigraphically the development of the town. There are also areas of ironworking, where smelting furnaces and large mounds of iron slag have been found, some of which date to the fifth century B.C.

The culture of Kush shows strong Egyptian influence mainly in religious architecture and iconography arising from the close relationship with Egypt during the Twenty-fifth Dynasty, when Kushite kings, coming from Napata farther north, ruled Egypt for nearly one hundred years. As time went on, more indigenous features are seen in the art, several pieces of sculpture having been found at the site, and particularly in the distinctive painted pottery.

The later Kushites (often known as Meroites) developed their own syllabic writing system, derived from a selection of twenty-three Egyptian hieroglyphs. Although the phonetic values of the signs are known, texts in Meroitic cannot be translated.

Research at Meroe has not as yet shown a great deal about the society of the time, although there was a clear-cut class division between royalty living in stone palaces and those who did the iron smelting, pot making, and other manufacturing activities. It was certainly a society with a powerful ruling class shown not only by the palatial buildings but also by the elaborate royal tombs.

[See also AFRICA: THE RISE OF KINGDOMS AND STATES IN AFRICA; EAST AFRICA: NORTHEASTERN MEDIEVAL STATES OF EAST AFRICA; EGYPT AND AFRICA; NUBIA.]

■ P. L. Shinnie, *Meroe: A Civilization of the Sudan* (1967). W. Y. Adams, *Nubia: Corridor to Africa* 1977).

Peter Shinnie

MESA VERDE. Every year thousands of visitors to Mesa Verde National Park in southwestern Colorado stop at a lookout point at the north edge of the mesa. Below, they can see much of the Anasazi world. To the east lie the La Plata Mountains, and below, the rich Montezuma Valley. To the west lies Sleeping Ute Mountain, and farther, the Comb Ridge. Much of this area is deep green, indicating a well-watered landscape. To the south, the view turns from greens to browns and grays, as Shiprock and the San Juan River basin dominate the landscape. This is a panorama of contrasts, one in which the prehistoric Anasazi of the North American Southwest were able to carve out a unique existence in an unforgiving environment. Part of the reason for the success of the Anasazi was their recognition of the varied productivity of their immediate environment as it, and subsequently they, responded to climatic change.

The area surrounding Mesa Verde was one of the most productive environments the Anasazi exploited during prehistoric times, and the archeological record of the region reflects this productivity by the sheer abundance and the extremely large size of many of the sites in the region. Over 10,000 sites of various types have been recorded in the region, and estimates of population numbers at their highest exceed 30,000 people. In addition, the cliff dwellings of Mesa Verde are some of the most unusual and spectacular sites found anywhere in the Americas. While cliff dwellings are common from southern Utah and Colorado south into Mexico, the cliff dwellings of Mesa Verde are unsurpassed in terms of size and complexity.

Yet, the multistoried masonry cliff dwellings that Mesa Verde is famous for are only part of the record. People have been in the area since Paleo-Indian times at the end of the geological period known as the Pleistocene. The Anasazi record begins with Basketmaker occupations probably around A.D. 500, but evidence is scarce. Basketmakers were the first agriculturalists in the area, and they likely lived seasonally in small groups of villages of six to ten pit structures. Hunting and gathering were still very important, and agriculture was likely adopted as a means of broadening their subsistence base. Pottery was also introduced by Basketmaker peoples into the area, and by A.D. 900 a distinctive local black-on-white ceramic tradition had developed. It was not until the early 800s that people began to build above-ground masonry structures, preferring until that time pit structures, or above-ground wattle-and-daub construction. Population growth was fairly steady, and by A.D. 1100 a number of large sites were occupied, including Yellow Jacket, Lowry Ruins, and Goodman Point Ruin. These villages were multistoried masonry pueblos that housed over 1,000 people, with habitation rooms, storage rooms, plazas, and subterranean ceremonial rooms called kivas. Yellow Jacket was probably the largest, with approximately 1,800 rooms that probably housed a population of over 2,500 people. Many of these larger ruins had public architecture that took the form of either "great kivas" or rare tri-walled structures of unknown function.

Between A.D. 1100 and 1200 people began to build cliff dwellings, and constructed on Chapin and Wetherill Mesas of Mesa Verde the spectacular ruins of Cliff Palace, Oak Tree House, Sunset House, New Fire House, Mummy House, Spruce Tree House, Square Tower House, and dozens of other cliff dwellings. Many other cliff dwellings are located nearby, and are open-air sites. Fields were necessarily located above the sites on the mesa top, with few trails connecting the dwellings to the fields. The cliff dwellings are located in natural alcoves along major drainages of the mesa, and offer protection from the elements, and possibly from enemies as well. Many archaeologists believe that these cliff dwellings were built for defensive purposes.

By A.D. 1300, people had abandoned the area, possibly migrating to the Rio Grande Valley, or to Hopi or Zuñi. The reasons for abandonment are unclear, but disease, warfare, internal factionalism, and environmental problems have been considered as causes. Regardless, the prehistoric inhabitants of the area left clear evidence of their remarkable adaptation for the visitors to Mesa Verde National Park and surrounding areas to appreciate.

[See also ANASAZI CULTURE; CHACOAN PHENOMENON; MOGOLLON AND MIMBRES CULTURES; NORTH AMERICA: THE NORTH AMERICAN SOUTHWEST.

Robert D. Leonard

MESOAMERICA

OVERVIEW

Early Mesoamerican peoples were highly mobile hunter-gatherers who manipulated their environment in ways that eventually changed the distribution, production, and genetic structure of many of the plants they utilized. By 7000 B.C. domestic varieties of corn, beans, and squash had developed. As a complex these three plants figured prominently in the prehistory of populations throughout the Americas.

By 1800 B.C., the beginning of the period known as the Formative, people were living in small horticulturally based villages. Over the next several hundred years, social complexity evolved rapidly and population increased significantly. By the Middle Formative there is evidence of the construction of public ritual architecture in many regions. Most well known among mid-Formative cultures are the Olmec, noted for the large stone heads they left behind.

By the Early Classic Period a number of large population centers had appeared in central Mesoamerica. The largest was *Teotihuacán, well known for its Pyramids of the Sun and Moon. At Teotihuacán's height, another state—that of the Maya—was on the rise to the south. The Maya expanded throughout southern Mesoamerica, building large cities such as *Tikal in Guatemala, *Copán in Honduras, and *Chichén Itzá in Mexico. The Maya developed hieroglyphic writing as well as a calendrical system possibly more accurate than that used today.

By the end of the Classic Period there is evidence of

considerable contact throughout Mesoamerica, in the form of both trade and warfare. At the beginning of the Postclassic Period Maya control to the south was declining, and Teotihuacán had completely collapsed. The void left by Teotihuacán was quickly filled by the Toltecs, who gained control of large sections of central Mexico. The *Toltec Empire, however, was short-lived, but their territory was soon absorbed by the *Aztec Empire, the center of which was *Tenochtitlán. In 1521 Cortez laid siege to Tenochtitlán, and aided by the effects of smallpox, inadvertently introduced by a Spanish soldier, Cortez and his men brought down the powerful Aztecs.

Charlotte Beck

INTRODUCTION

Mesoamerica is the term proposed by anthropologist Paul Kirchoff to describe the area of Mexico and adjacent Central America inhabited by Native American civilizations before the Spanish conquest in the late fifteenth century. At European contact, this area, which covered more than 386,000 square miles (1,000,000 sq km), sustained as many as 25 to 30 million people speaking more than 200 distinct languages. The complex societies of pre-Hispanic Mesoamerica shared a number of cultural traits that set them apart from their New World neighbors in northern Mexico, lower Central America, and Andean South America. Mesoamericans lived in cities and towns, centered on monumental precincts consisting of plazas, pyramids, temple structures, public buildings, and palaces. Within the monumental core of the city, a hereditary ruling class governed and legitimized political and economic power through ritual displays including human sacrifice, ritual blood-letting, the worship of supernatural beings and gods, and the ball game. Their authority was further enhanced and formalized through public observance of a complex sacred calendar that governed decisions concerning agriculture and warfare. Through the production of pictographic and hieroglyphic texts on stone, paper, and other media, elite scribes blended actual and legendary events of the past that preserved cosmological traditions and aligned history with the political needs of the ruling nobility.

Governance, trade, and ceremonial activities undertaken by the elite strata of Mesoamerican society were supported by an agricultural sector that, in most cases, constituted more than eighty percent of the total population. Around the monumental core of the city spread suburban residential areas that, in turn, were bordered by agricultural fields. In many areas of lowland Mesoamerica suburban and cultivated areas coalesced in a kind of "garden city" relatively unique among urban forms in the ancient world. This adaptation was primarily the result of transport and labor constraints, for ancient Mesoamerica lacked the larger beasts of burden so instrumental to the rise of complex society and intensive agriculture in the Old World. Agriculture featured a unique set of crops including maize, beans, squash, and other cultigens, all of which were originally domesticated in Mesoamerica. Crop production was based on a distinctive and sustainable mix of farming techniques including shifting cultivation, residential gardening, and more intensive practices such as irrigation, terraces for steep slopes, and raised fields, such as the *chinampas* of Aztec central Mexico, for the agricultural reclamation of wetlands.

While many differences existed among the widely separated cultures of Mesoamerica, basic similarities persisted during the many millennia preceding the arrival of Europeans. Interregional communication and commerce among nations helped to establish a Mesoamerican world system within which calendrics, knowledge of writing, styles of dress and display, religious beliefs, and valued material commodities were exchanged. Raw and worked items of obsidian, jade, crystal, metal, and feathers were universally valued. Finished products, such as cotton cloth, were traded, offered as tribute, and consumed in great quantity as a central element of public display by the ruling class. Jaguar skins, cotton, cacao, and fine pottery were also traded widely, representing a kind of pan-Mesoamerican common currency. The political economy that tied together the nations of Mesoamerica was reinforced by a set of related iconographic conventions based on shared ideologies that drew images from the natural and supernatural worlds and featured feathered serpents, lords of the underworld, rain and lightning deities, and the veneration of ancestors. Across the barriers of language, ethnicity, and geography there existed a fundamental cultural unity among the indigenous cultures of ancient Mesoamerica, which persists to the present day.

Mesoamerican Environment. The natural world of Mesoamerica lies within the northern portion of the American tropics. Within this area are a variety of environments that posed different challenges to regional cultures but also encouraged economic symbiosis among regions. The essential environmental contrast of Mesoamerica, the wet and the dry, produces marked seasonal variation in temperature and precipitation in both highland and lowland environments. Dominating much of northern Mesoamerica are the Sierra Madres, a large wedge-shaped mass of mountains and deserts where agriculture requires irrigation. Vegetation is sparse and adapted to frequent drought throughout much of the highlands, although pine and oak forests occur at higher, wetter elevations. Volcanic soils in the southern highlands of Mesoamerica combine with warmer temperatures and greater rainfall to greatly extend the growing season and make irrigation unnecessary. Mesoamerica's highland regions provided the greatest potential for the growth of human populations following the establishment of fully agricultural economies in later prehistoric times.

Mesoamerica's lowlands begin in the north as thin coastal strips along the Atlantic and Pacific littorals. The coastal plain broadens to the south and opens, finally, onto the flat limestone plains of peninsular Yucatán. Below the Isthmus of Tehuantepec, where the continental landmass constricts, rain forests predominate in both the highlands and the lowlands with the exception of the drier portions of northern Yucatán. These areas provided a rich and varied resource base for human groups dependent on wild-food collection and early forms of cultivation. The coastal and riverine environments of the lowlands fostered demographic growth and complex social development during the early stages of civilization in ancient Mesoamerica.

Archaic Period. The roots of Mesoamerican civilization stretch back to the end of the Pleistocene, and conservative estimates date the entry of humans into this area about 15,000 years ago. Before about 10,000 B.C. nomadic groups, hunting mammoth, mastodon, and horse, traversed large territories extending from the dry highlands of central Mexico south to the warm and forested highlands of Guatemala. Climate became considerably warmer and drier by about 8000 B.C. and populations shifted to the exploitation of a wider range of animals and plants found within smaller foraging territories.

During the early Archaic Period, beginning by about 7000 B.C., mobile hunters and gatherers lived in widely dispersed extended-family groups of fewer than thirty individuals and exploited seasonally available faunal and floral resources within single valley systems. By the end of this period, around 2000 B.C., people began producing groundstone tools for food processing and pottery for feasting and cooking. Larger social groups began living in open-air villages and buried their dead within residential areas, according special treatment to important ancestors.

The domestication of a variety of Mesoamerican crops was also achieved during the Archaic Period. Bottle gourds and squash were the first crops to be cultivated and may have been used as containers before the invention of pottery. Beans and maize now appear to have been domesticated no earlier than the fourth millennium B.C. Early maize, a mutation of the wild grass *teosinte*, remained a small-sized cultigen through the end of the Archaic and well into the subsequent Formative Period.

Formative Period. The Formative Period in Mesoamerica (2000 B.C.–A.D. 200), also known as the Preclassic Period, witnessed the appearance of pottery, fully sedentary village life, steady increases in population, the beginning of political complexity, and the rise of social stratification and formalized inequality. The Formative Period is also marked by the intensification of interregional exchanges that produced broad zones of similarity in material culture. The earliest centers of population and settlement growth are found along the Pacific and Gulf coasts of Guatemala and Mexico from 1600 to 1200 B.C. After 1200 B.C. socially complex village cultures also take hold in the southern highlands of Guatemala and Chiapas, the valley of *Oaxaca, and the basin of Mexico. All show the strong influence of earlier cultural developments on the Gulf coast.

The Olmec. One of Mesoamerica's most important Formative Period cultures, the *Olmec civilization, arose along Mexico's Gulf coast between 1200 and 400 B.C. At *San Lorenzo, a major riverine center of the early Olmec, craftsmen sculpted colossal basalt heads to honor their kings, and master builders constructed large earthworks for elite residence and ceremonial activity. Public ritual was conducted on a grand scale, and exotic resources such as jade, serpentine, and magnetite were procured from distant locations in the highlands for elite burial offerings. Olmec art depicted a world of heroic ancestors, supernaturals, and gods imbued with the appearance of jaguars, crocodiles, eagles, serpents, and sharks. The later Olmec center of *La Venta grew to be a large town and was centered on an enormous pyramid that may have been the largest structure of its time in all of Mesoamerica. Olmec influence spread well beyond the Gulf coast heartland with well-documented examples in the valley of Oaxaca, at Chalcatzingo in highland Guererro, and at Tlatilco in the basin of Mexico.

Late Formative Period. By Late Formative times (400 B.C.–A.D. 1) complex, urban-dwelling societies, supported by highly productive maize agriculture, had taken hold all over Mesoamerica. The Izapa culture of Pacific Guatemala, noted for the elaborate iconography of its carved stone monuments, developed the long-count calendrical system and stimulated developments in the southern highlands at the major center of Kaminaljuyu in Guatemala. These advances had an influence on the Late Preclassic (Late Formative) Maya who subsequently began a long tradition of writing and city building at sites such as El Mirador in the central Petén lowlands and at Dzibilchaltun on the plains of northern Yucatán. In the valley of Oaxaca, the Late Formative *Zapotec civilization developed the first Mesoamerican writing system, the 260-day calendar cycle, and a confederated form of regional government at the hilltop center of *Monte Albán.

Teotihuacán and the Formative to Classic Period Transition. *Teotihuacán, the largest city ever to develop in ancient Mesoamerica, arose during the Late Formative and expanded during the Early Classic Period (200 B.C.–A.D. 400) in the highlands of central Mexico. Arrayed on an enormous grid plan and centered on the largest pyramidal structure ever to be constructed in pre-Columbian America, this urban giant was the center of a powerful state that dominated the politics and economy of the basin of Mexico and had long-distance commercial and political ties throughout Mesoamerica. The city may have housed as many as 150,000 persons supported by a system of intensive agriculture including terraces and irrigation canals. The population of Teotihuacán was housed in large apartment complexes that covered a densely built-up area of more than 7.5 square miles (20 sq km). Craft workshops dispersed across the city fashioned obsidian blades and pottery traded by Teotihuacán merchants to the far reaches of Mesoamerica.

Classic Maya. Teotihuacán's political and economic might was felt at the early centers of Maya civilization that flourished during the Classic Period from A.D. 300 to 900 in the eastern lowlands of Mexico and Guatemala. The early rulers of *Tikal, the Maya region's largest city, may have been Teotihuacán-affiliated royalty from Kaminaljuyu, a Teotihuacán trading center in highland Guatemala. The Classic Period Maya went on to develop one of the most sophisticated civilizations of Mesoamerica with unparalleled accomplishments in art, architecture, and writing. By about A.D. 500 highly competitive ruling dynasties controlled hundreds of city-states distributed across the Maya lowlands including the major centers of Coba, Tikal, *Palenque, Calakmul, and *Copán. Maya rulers, residing at these and other urban centers in the lowlands, engaged in elite innercity marriages, political intrigue, and warfare. They recorded their exploits as historical texts on limestone stelae, lintels, and altars erected within the monumental plazas, pyramids, and palaces located at the core of a dispersed urban landscape that expanded to sprawl across their lowland rainforest environment. Intensive agriculture, including terraces, raised fields, residential gardens, and orchards, supported a dense peripheral population of farmers and lesser nobility that in some areas reached levels in excess of 500 persons per square kilometer. During the eighth century A.D. the Maya society of the Petén and surrounding eastern lowlands experienced a rapid collapse, and many of the Classic Period cities were abandoned. The cause of the collapse is still not well understood, but environmental degradation, agricultural failure, political turmoil, and accelerated warfare appear to have acted in concert to undermine political centrality, exchange systems, and the shared ideologies that sustained Maya advances throughout the Classic Period. In the coastal areas of Belize and in the Puuc region of northern Yucatán, Classic Period Maya civilization persisted through the end of the first millennium A.D.

Post-Classic Mesoamerica. Following the collapse of Maya civilization in the eastern lowlands, Mesoamerica entered into half a millennium characterized by the rise and fall of empires and cities, intervening periods of intense regionalization and warfare, and increased trade and exchange. This period, known as the Post-Classic, begins at about A.D. 1000 and ends with the conquest of *Tenochtitlán, capital of the Aztec Empire, by the Spanish in 1521. Archaeological knowledge of the period is greatly enhanced by written accounts, or codicies, the folding books of Mesoamerican history and religious knowledge, recorded during the sixteenth century and earlier. These books chronicle the early rise of the Toltecs at the city of *Tula in central Mexico and related developments at the Postclassic Maya center of *Chichén Itzá in northern Yucatán. Other accounts detail the later Mixtec kingdoms of Oaxaca, the Tarascan state in Michoacán, and finally the rise of the Aztecs, or Mexica, in the centuries just before the conquest.

The Toltecs of central Mexico, like the Aztecs that followed them, spoke a variety of Nahua, the language still spoken by many native peoples inhabiting the highlands of Mexico today. From about A.D. 900 to 1200, the Toltec capital at Tula, Hidalgo, represented the largest urban center in western Mesoamerica with perhaps as many as 60,000 inhabitants. While the actual *Toltec empire was limited to the central highlands, their trading and military influences spread to the highlands of Guatemala and to the Yucatán Peninsula, where the art and architecture of the large urban center of Chichén Itzá implies significant contact if not outright colonization of Toltecs from central Mexico.

The rise and subsequent expansion of the Aztecs fills the void left by the fall of Tula in A.D. 1200. The imperial Aztecs, who rose from humble beginnings in the basin of Mexico, eventually came to dominate the largest tribute empire ever to develop in ancient Mesoamerica, stretching from the central highlands south to the borders of present-day Honduras. Their capital at Tenochtitlán, the site of present-day Mexico City, may have housed as many as 200,000 persons, arguably one of the largest cities in the world during the fifteenth century. The Aztec capital, first beheld by Hernando Cortez and his small band of Spanish conquistadores in 1519, was the center of the last great Native American state and international empire of ancient Mesoamerica.

[See also AZTEC CIVILIZATION: INTRODUCTION; CENTRAL AMERICA, ARCHAEOLOGY OF; CEREN; GUILÁ NAQUITZ; MAYA CIVILIZATION: INTRODUCTION; MESOAMERICA, articles on ARCHAIC PERIOD IN MESOAMERICA, FORMATIVE PERIOD IN MESOAMERICA, CLASSIC PERIOD IN MESOAMERICA, POSTCLASSIC PERIOD IN MESOAMERICA, SPANISH SETTLEMENT IN MESOAMERICA, HISTORICAL ARCHAEOLOGY OF MESOAMERICA; MESOAMERICA, ORIGINS OF FOOD PRODUCTION IN; TEMPLO MAYOR.]

■ Paul Kirchoff, "Mesoamérica, sus límites geográficos, composición étnica, y carácteres culturales," Acta Americana 1 (1943): 92–107. Richard E. Blanton, Ancient Mesoamerica: A Comparison of Change in Three Regions (1981). Jeremy A. Sabloff, Archaeology, vol. 1, Supplement to the Handbook of Middle American Indians, ed. Victoria Bricker (1981). Richard E. W. Adams, Prehistoric Mesoamerica, 2nd ed. (1991). Michael D. Coe, Breaking the Maya Code (1992). Joyce Marcus, Mesoamerican Writing Systems: Propoganda, Myth, and History in Four Ancient Civilizations (1992). Murial Porter Weaver, The Aztecs, the Maya, and Their Predecessors, 3rd ed. (1993).

Thomas W. Killion

ARCHAIC PERIOD IN MESOAMERICA

The Archaic Period (7000 to 1500 B.C.) in the general Mesoamerican chronology refers to the time interval between when prehistoric people relied completely upon wild plants and animals in the preceding Paleoindian Period, to when farming was of utmost importance, beginning in the subsequent Formative Period. It was a time of profound social change, involving not only transformations in subsistence, but also in every aspect of social life. The period starts during the Holocene Epoch, a time interval in the geologic time scale when modern flora and fauna had replaced those of the earlier Pleistocene Epoch. Its end date is variously placed between 2000 and 1500 B.C., depending on the perspective of the individual prehistorian.

Uplands. The foremost landmark study of the Archaic Period took place in the 1960s at Tehuacán Valley, Puebla, Mexico. This well-funded, interdisciplinary project, directed by Richard S. MacNeish, was launched in order to investigate the botanical origins of maize (Zea mays), the staple crop of much of the Americas. The evolution of this cultigen was one of the major puzzles of New World archaeology and *paleobotany since no wild progenitors were known, in contrast to the situation of most Old World cereals. The Tehuacán Archaeological-Botanical Project was the first comprehensive regional study with an ecological focus in Mesoamerica and it broke new methodological ground, in addition to providing the first overview of human lifeways during the Archaic Period. Investigators studied a total of 456 sites in the valley, with specialists analyzing approximately 105,000 plant remains, 36,000 animal remains, 263,000 artifacts, 70 human burials, and 237 human and animal feces dating to all periods of the past.

Archaic Period cave and open-area sites in different locations in the valley were studied, thus allowing the reconstruction of both the settlement patterns and subsistence patterns over time. At the beginning of the period (El Riego Phase 6500 to 5000 B.C.), ancient inhabitants of the valley were living in small groups that apparently moved from one resource area to another in synchrony with the availability of seasonal resources. At that time, game contributed 65 percent of the total diet and wild plants contributed 35 percent. Domesticated plants were just appearing but there were no domesticated animals. This is a typical foraging pattern as defined by Lewis Binford, who discovered that it tends to be manifest by nomadic hunter-gatherers, living in small groups, and displaying relatively simple social organizations.

By the close of the Archaic Period (Purrón Phase at 1500 B.C.) the contribution of game had dropped to approximately 27 percent. Plant foods had gained dietary ascendancy, with wild plants contributing approximately 31 percent and cultigens 37 percent of the total diet. Domesticated animals were present but contributed very little to the diet. The subsistence change was paralleled by changes in the settlement system: Villages that were occupied year-round had emerged, as had locations for the exploitation of specific types of resources that were used by specialized work groups. This is what Binford refers to as a collector pattern, usually associated with hunter-gatherer people with relatively complex forms of social organization.

The substantial reorganization of human lifeways in the Tehuacán Valley was made possible by genetic changes in some plants that were transformed from wild species to cultigens. Especially significant for the diet of later Mesoamericans were maize, beans, and squash, all of which were documented by the project as having evolved during the Archaic Period.

A second comprehensive regional study, directed by

Kent V. Flannery, focused on the Valley of *Oaxaca, another dry upland valley. Archaic Period deposits were discovered and studied in various sites, including *Guilá Naquitz, a dry cave with abundant, well-preserved organic remains: 21,705 plants and more than 360 identifiable animal bones. Here, the specifics of plant and animal use through time varied somewhat from those of the Tehuacán Valley, but the overall pattern of increasing dependency upon plants and increasing sedentism from the Early to Late Archaic Period is similar to the pattern in the Tehuacán Valley study. Firm evidence for cultivation as early as 7000 B.C. was discovered in the form of squash and bottle-gourd remains in the cave, which tends to reinforce more tentative evidence from the Tehuacán Valley and elsewhere. Bottle gourds were widely used as containers during this time before the invention of pottery. No further insights into the origins of maize resulted from this study, presumably because its preceramic deposits are too early.

Other studies in the uplands are less regionally comprehensive but amplify the reconstructions in the Tehuacán and Oaxaca valleys: at the Zoapilco site, in the Valley of Mexico; Santa Marta cave and the Aguacatenango Basin in Chiapas; caves in the Sierra de Tamaulipas, Tamaulipas; and sites in the Quiché Basin of highland Guatemala.

Lowlands. Research on the Archaic Period has lagged in the Mesoamerican lowlands primarily because of difficulties in locating early sites, which tend to be underwater or buried by sediments, and poor preservation of organic remains, which decompose rapidly in most archaeological contexts on the coast. Investigators would like to determine whether the tempo and pattern of the shift from foraging to farming was similar to or different from the pattern in the uplands. For example, when did agriculture take hold in the lowlands and was it based on maize, beans, and squash or were other crops, possibly root crops, more important in early times? Although these questions cannot be fully answered, some progress is being made.

The only truly regional project that has focused on establishing the settlement and subsistence systems for preceramic peoples of the Mesoamerican lowlands was the Belize Archaic Archeological Reconnaissance (BAAR) project, conducted in the early 1980s under the direction of Richard S. MacNeish. After four seasons, approximately one hundred possible preceramic sites had been recorded and over 500,000 stone tools and flakes were analyzed. The Archaic record begins around 7500 B.C., when people of the Sand Hill complex were depending upon modern flora and fauna, in contrast to the reliance upon Pleistocene biota in earlier times. Diversification in habitat use is indicated by the location of sites within different resource zones. Site use may have been seasonal, which suggests that these people may have been foragers. Investigators have been cautious about making settlement-pattern reconstructions because the data are weak. By the close of the Archaic Period (Melinda complex; 4200 to 3000 B.C.) the tool kit had expanded and apparently long-term occupation sites, such as villages, had emerged. Thus there are hints that a collecting settlement and subsistence pattern had developed by late Archaic Period times in the Belizean lowlands.

In northern Belize a coring program has produced a complete stratigraphic record of radiocarbon dates, pollen, and artifacts from 5000 B.C. to the present. Maize and manioc (*Manihot esculenta*) pollen is detected as early as 3000 B.C., with indicators of substantial forest disturbance appearing ca. 2500 B.C. This suggests to Mary Pohl, Kevin Pope, and their collaborators that dry farming was expanding rapidly about that time.

Excepting the Belizean data, no other studies have produced information about lowland people during the early portion of the Archaic Period, but additional information is available for the late span of this time interval. Jeffrey Wilkerson reported two sites dated between approximately 3000 to 2650 B.C. (Palo Hueco Phase) in southern Veracruz. At Santa Luisa, a multicomponent site, Wilkerson discovered an initial occupation surface with lithic artifacts and shell ecofacts. The artifact assemblage is sufficiently diverse to suggest a wide range of activities, and the site has been interpreted by the excavator as a settled village. Nearby, a contemporaneous site, La Conchita, may have been used as a hunting camp. These data are compatible with a collector-pattern model, as suggested by the Belizean data.

On the Pacific seaboard, late Archaic Period deposits have been identified in Nayarit, Guerrero, and Chiapas, Mexico. Joseph Mountjoy recorded the destruction of a mound at San Blas, Nayarit where Late Archaic Period deposits, dating to the Matachén Phase (2000 to 1500 B.C.) were exposed by road crews mining the mound for construction material. Mountjoy inventoried the artifacts and ecofacts from these deposits. He interpreted the site as a food-extraction station, rather than a general habitation site.

Charles Brush, working near Acapulco in Guerrero, found aceramic deposits at the bottom of a test pit. Only a small volume of material was recovered but it was used to define the Ostiones Phase (2950 to 2450 B.C.). Brush considered this to be a trash midden, the presence of which suggests a fairly settled occupation, but the small volume of excavated material makes interpretations very tenuous.

On the south coast of Chiapas, six sizable shell mounds have produced information about the Chantuto Phase (4000 to 1500 B.C.) occupation, with the greatest amount of data from the Tlacuachero site. These sites consist overwhelmingly of marsh clam shells, and have a low diversity of tool types, suggesting a narrow procurement focus that Barbara Voorhies thinks included shrimp and fish, as well as clams. These products were collected from the lagoons and canals, sun-dried at the sites, and taken inland to supplement a heavily vegetarian diet. Bone chemistry on skeletal remains of two individuals from Tlacuachero supports the reconstruction that these people were depending heavily on plant foods. Voorhies thus interprets these sites as specialized locations for the procurement and the processing of wetland resources, which implies that the settlement system of the Chantuto people would have included other site types as well.

A contemporaneous inland site, situated upriver from one of the shell mounds, may be the remains of a village. The excavated portion of the Vuelta Limón site revealed a trash disposal area that perhaps served a village or hamlet, but no features such as hearths or house remains were uncovered. The diversity of artifacts suggests a wider range of activities than at the wetland sites. Analysis of phytoliths indicates that the site was located in a forest, but whether the inhabitants were farming has not yet been determined.

In summary, the data for human lifeways in the Mesoamerican lowlands during the Archaic Period are especially inadequate for the early part of the record where the paucity of sites prevents reconstruction of the settlement system, but sediment core data suggests that genetic changes in key plants were underway. The data for the Late Archaic Period indicates that some lowlanders manifested a collector settlement pattern, broadly similar to that manifested by contemporary peoples in the uplands, but the data do not as yet permit a detailed reconstruction of the subsistence economies of these people.

[*See also* MESOAMERICA: FORMATIVE PERIOD IN MESOAMERICA; MESOAMERICA, ORIGINS OF FOOD PRODUCTION IN.]

■ Richard S. MacNeish, "A Summary of the Subsistence," in *The Prehistory of the Tehuacán Valley*. Volume One: *Environment and Subsistence*, Douglas S. Byers, ed. (1967): 290–309. Richard S. MacNeish, Frederick A. Peterson, and James A. Neely, "The Archaeological Reconnaissance," in *The Prehistory of the Tehuacán Valley*. Volume Five: *Excavations and Reconnaissance*, Richard S. MacNeish et al., eds. (1972): 341–495. Lewis R. Binford, "Willow Smoke and Dogs' Tails: Hunter-Gatherer Settlement Systems and Archaeological Site Formation," *American Antiquity* 45 (1980): 5–20. Kent V. Flannery, "Settlement, Subsistence and Social Organization of the Proto-Otomangueans," in *The Cloud People: Divergent Evolution of the Zapotec and Mixtec Civilizations*, Kent V. Flannery and Joyce Marcus, eds. (1983): 32–36. Kent V. Flannery, *Guilá Naquitz: Archaic Foraging and Early Architecture in Oaxaca, Mexico* (1986). Richard S. MacNeish, "The Preceramic of Middle America," in *Advances in World Archaeology*, vol. 5, Fred Wendorf and A. E. Close, eds. (1986): 93–129. Judith Francis Zeitlin, Robert N. Zeitlin, and Richard S. MacNeish, *Investigating the Maya Archaic: A View from Belize* (1991). Barbara Voorhies, "The Transformation from Foraging to Farming in the Lowlands of Mesoamerica," in *The Managed Mosaic: Ancient Maya Agriculture and Resource Use*, Scott L. Zedick, ed. (1995).

Barbara Voorhies

FORMATIVE PERIOD IN MESOAMERICA

The Formative Period began quite modestly about 1800 B.C., marked by the first appearance of pottery in the archaeological records of the simple horticultural societies that populated both the highlands and lowlands of the geographically diverse region defined as Mesoamerica. By the time the Formative Period ended 2,000 years later, ca. A.D. 200, spectacular social transformations had taken place, and societies across that diverse landscape had evolved to the point of state-level complexity. The cultural achievements that unfolded during the Formative (or Pre-Classic) Period are significant, since they became the crucial building blocks leading to Mesoamerica's great Classic and Post-Classic Period urban civilizations. Because of the extensive time span encompassed by the Formative Period and the significant developments therein, scholars customarily subdivide it into Early (1800–900 B.C.), Middle (900–500 B.C.), and Late (500 B.C.–A.D. 200) Formative subperiods.

Social complexity seems to have evolved rapidly during the Early Formative Period. Although at 1800 B.C. some societies may have been egalitarian, within 300 years there is evidence of social "ranking" and incipient chiefdom-level societies in Mesoamerica. About 1500 B.C., the construction of public/ritual architecture began at sites in many regions, taking the form of elaborate houselike structures in some areas and raised platform mounds in others. By 1150 B.C., some religious concepts become discernible, as different peoples across a large area of western (non-Maya) Mesoamerica started decorating their pottery vessels with a nearly identical set of abstract motifs. Those motifs apparently represent several supernatural creatures important in Formative Period cosmological beliefs. Solid and hollow pottery figurines also occur in significant quantities at this time. One culture, the *Olmec communicated their ideological beliefs through an additional medium as well: stone monuments.

The Middle Formative Period is marked by further social complexity. Settlements became both more abundant and larger in size, providing archaeologists today with evidence of population increase over time; multilevel regional site hierarchies are also more common. Public/ritual mound architecture occurred more frequently, with the mounds at some sites classifiable as "pyramids." In addition, the pattern of placing public/ritual architecture around a rectangular plaza took firm root during this period. Exotic objects found in some Middle Formative Period graves provide evidence of an emerging elite who marked their special social rank with jade ear ornaments and jewelry, and iron ore mirrors. Many of the iconographic motifs common to pottery in the Early Formative now appeared across Mesoamerica on elite objects. Monumental art continued to be a prominent feature of Gulf coast Olmec centers, and was also adopted briefly at several sites in west-central Mexico (Chalcatzingo, Teopantecuanitlan) and on the Pacific coast of southern Mesoamerica (e.g., Abaj Takalik, Chalchuapa, Pijijiapan).

About 500 B.C. another marked change is visible in the archaeological record throughout much of Mesoamerica. In each region, local populations began to nucleate in and around one large center, for example, *Monte Albán in the valley of *Oaxaca and Cuicuilco in the basin of Mexico. At Cuicuilco, there is also archaeological evidence of canals utilized for intensive irrigation. With nucleation and intensive agriculture, Mesoamerica began its urban revolution. Writing and calendrical systems, often considered by archaeologists to be characteristics of civilization, appeared for the first time on Late Formative monuments and inscriptions in several regions of southern Mesoamerica. During the Late Formative Period, Mesoamerica reached the threshold of state-level society and civilization.

This brief synthesis has focused primarily on non-Maya Mesoamerica, and although the general evolutionary trends in the Maya area are similar, the data on the Early Formative Period there are presently far more scarce. In considering the Formative Period in general, however, it is important for readers to realize that two strongly conflicting viewpoints exist today over how the Formative Period archaeological record should be interpreted. The major disagreement revolves around the Olmec, and the role they may have played in Formative Period developments; they are summarized below.

The archaeological culture that is called Olmec was dominant in the tropical Gulf coast region of southern Mexico from about 1150 to 500 B.C., that is, during the Early and Middle Formative Period. The Olmec stand out as the first society in Mesoamerica to create stone monuments, and those impressive creations are the distinguishing trait setting the Olmec apart from other Mesoamerican societies at that time. The Gulf coast sites of *La Venta, *San Lorenzo, and Laguna de los Cerros are prominent for their size, mound architecture, and abundant monuments, and are recognized as the major Olmec centers. In the first serious investigation of any Olmec center, Matthew Stirling's 1942–1943 research at La Venta recorded many impressive stone monuments and unearthed fabulous offerings of jade objects in Complex A, an area of royal tombs. Stirling's remarkable discoveries came at a time when very little was known about Formative Period societies anywhere in Mesoamerica, and in that light, those other societies appeared less advanced than the Olmec.

Even as Stirling was conducting his explorations at La Venta, scholars investigating sites in central Mexico recognized that the decorated pottery vessels, clay figurines, and jade objects used by the early societies (that we now identify as Formative Period) in those areas exhibited many similarities to those being found on the Gulf coast (i.e., the widespread common set of iconographic motifs mentioned earlier for Early Formative ceramics and Middle Formative jades). More recently, as archaeologists have investigated sites in other areas of Mesoamerica, the immense extent of the shared symbol system of the Early and Middle Formative has become increasingly apparent. However, because the motifs and objects are similar to those found in the Olmec area, scholars years ago applied the term "Olmec art style" to the phenomenon, and that terminology is still common today. Thus the term "Olmec" presently refers to both the archaeological culture of the Gulf coast and a more widely distributed set of motifs and objects utilized by various societies in other regions of Mesoamerica. The continuing disagreement among scholars is whether a significant causal or historical relationship existed between the archaeological Olmec and the far more widespread art style.

The dominant scholarly viewpoint for five decades has been that the Olmec were culturally more advanced than other Early/Middle Formative Period societies (Olmec civilization), and that the widespread art style is attributable to Olmec influences, that is, the desire for Olmec ideas and objects by less advanced peoples in other regions. From that perspective, the significant Early/Middle Formative Period developments underlying Mesoamerica's later civilizations are believed to have originated with the Olmec, who can therefore be viewed as "Mesoamerica's mother culture."

The second interpretive viewpoint has been emerging over the past two decades. Many proponents esteem the Gulf coast Olmec achievements, but believe that the overall role played by the Olmec in Formative developments has been misunderstood to the point of obscuring significant contributions by other Formative Period Mesoamerican societies. To some, the Olmec's magnificent monuments are not evidence of their advanced status (or civilization), but instead evince an ideology different from that of neighboring societies, their peers. That viewpoint also lends a different perspective to the art style, which on close inspection exhibits significant variations from region to region, as societies manipulated it in their own way. The style's importance lies precisely in how its various elements functioned in the rituals and daily life of every different society, and not in its obscure origins. There is no archaeological evidence to date that any of the style's motifs or objects appear earliest on the Gulf coast.

During the Early and Middle Formative Period many regions of Mesoamerica manifested important developments in architecture and social complexity that were apparently endemic to them. In studying the Formative Period it would be a mistake to ignore those regional developments, or to attribute them to Olmec influences that are unproven at this time. In fact, a knowledge of the distinctive regional differences that existed during the Formative Period may eventually help scholars to understand the diverse evolutionary trajectories taken by Mesoamerica's later civilizations. However, at the present time, our understanding of the Formative Period pathways that led to those civilizations is still rudimentary.

[See also CENTRAL AMERICA, ARCHAEOLOGY OF; MAYA CIVILIZATION: INTRODUCTION; MESOAMERICA, articles on INTRODUCTION, ARCHAIC PERIOD IN MESOAMERICA, CLASSIC PERIOD IN MESOAMERICA.]

■ Michael Coe, "The Olmec Style and Its Distribution," in The Handbook of Middle American Indians, vol. 3, ed. Robert Wauchope (1965), pp. 739–775. Michael Coe, America's First Civilization: Discovering the Olmec (1968). Elizabeth Benson, ed., The Olmec and Their Neighbors (1981). David Grove, "The Formative Period and the Evolution of Complex Culture," in The Handbook of Middle American Indians, Supplement 1, Archaeology, ed. Jeremy Sabloff (1981), pp. 373–391. Roman Piña Chan, The Olmec: Mother Culture of Mesoamerica (1989). David Grove and Susan Gillespie, "Ideology and Evolution at the Pre-State Level: Formative Period Mesoamerica," in Ideology and Pre-Columbian Civilizations ed. Arthur Demarest and Geoffrey Conrad (1992), pp. 15–36.

D. C. Grove

CLASSIC PERIOD IN MESOAMERICA

The part of Central America referred to as Mesoamerica (located in the present-day countries of Guatemala, Belize, most of Mexico, and parts of El Salvador and Honduras) constitutes one of the world's heartlands for the development of complex political systems. These complex systems —sometimes referred to as "state" societies—were in place throughout Mesoamerica by the Classic Period. The term "Classic Period" is used today to imply a temporal period (A.D. 100 to 750 for central Mexico and Oaxaca; A.D. 250 to 950 for the Maya area); however, historically the term had developmental overtones. These developmental overtones have been superseded by newer archaeological data which indicate that the Classic Period may not have represented the apex of a particular Mesoamerican culture or site and that many of the changes once thought to be equated with the Classic Period are now known to occur either earlier or later. For example, monumental architecture of a massive scale—thought by some to represent a true state-level society—existed in the Maya lowlands by at least 300 B.C.

Three culture areas within Mesoamerica form the primary focus of any consideration of this region's Classic Period: central Mexico, central Oaxaca, and the Maya lowlands. Mesoamerican prehistory has long been cast as a series of precocious developments in its drier highland areas, which are seen as having impacted on its wetter lowland neighbors. Under this widely held scenario, broadly articulated by William Sanders and Barbara Price (Mesoamerica, 1968), the development of Classic era *Teotihuacán in the Valley of Mexico has been viewed as the dominating and driving influence for all of Classic Period Mesoamerica. A partially independent, and potentially competing, highland domain is seen as having arisen in the Valley of *Oaxaca, directly reflected in the site of *Monte Albán. Under this same paradigm, Maya civilization has traditionally been cast as a reactionary development to primary forces emanating from highland Mexico. However, recent archaeological data dealing with the earlier Late Preclassic era (300 B.C. to A.D. 250) of the Maya lowlands calls this paradigm into serious question by suggesting that the first true Mesoamerican "states" may have arisen in the lowland Maya area rather than in the Mexican highlands.

Regardless of where complex political systems first arose, the site of Teotihuacán is undoubtedly one of the most important Mesoamerican centers known. It is located 24 miles (39 km) northeast of the center of present-day Mexico City. Its areal extent is estimated to have covered some 21 square miles (55 sq km) and to have held a population of over 147,000 people at its height. Unlike most other Mesoamerican sites of the Classic Period, Teotihuacán is laid out in a broad gridlike pattern with two major perpendicular and linear roadways bisecting each other in the center of this city. Public architecture lines the full distance of the road running north–south; two of the largest pyramids in Mesoamerica, Teotihuacán's Pyramids of the Sun and Moon, are situated on this roadway. The site also contains architectural complexes that have been interpreted to be a massive regal residence and a specialized market area. Square or rectangular apartment compounds (measuring approximately 330 feet [100 m] per side) dominated Teotihuacán and formed the living quarters for the majority of the city's population. The greatest expansion of Teotihuacán is believed to have occurred after A.D. 100; by about A.D. 600 some 63 percent of the total population of the Basin of Mexico (147,000 out of 234,000 people in an area of about 1,930 square miles (5,000 sq km) resided in the city. Widespread abandonment of Teotihuacán is presumed to have been intentional and involved extensive burning (either destructive or ritual); it is believed to have occurred about A.D. 750, although scattered remnants of the population still remained for centuries in some of the city's compounds.

Like its northern neighbor, Monte Albán also came to dominate its environs, in this case the Oaxaca Valley, reaching a total "urban" population estimated at some 24,000 individuals at about A.D. 650 (out of a valleywide population of 55,000). The site itself covers approximately 5.8 square miles (15 sq km) and consists of a massive ridgetop plaza bracketed by public architecture with acropolis groups at its northern and southern ends; much of the population is thought to have lived on the surrounding terraces that cascade down the slopes of a raised upland area central to the Oaxaca Valley. Various models have been posited for Monte Albán's origin and development; it is clear, however, that extensive warfare played a part in both its rise and its expansion. Although Monte Albán is viewed as being an independent political development, apart from Teotihuacán, the two sites maintained a close relationship, as is evinced in the art of Monte Albán and in the existence of an "Oaxaca barrio" at Teotihuacán. Even though spatially more proximate, any extant relationships between Monte Albán and the Maya area are largely unknown and unexplored.

Interpretations concerning the Maya have long been colored both by theoretical perceptions concerning the suitability of a jungle environment for the evolution and maintenance of a state society and by modern-day practical difficulties in carrying out work within a tropical rain forest. While the Maya are archaeologically identifiable back to at least 1200 B.C., the well-known trappings of their civilization—temples, tombs, carved artworks, and polychrome pottery— date primarily to the Classic Period and to some extent have been used to define this era. The Classic Period Maya are also characterized by extensive hieroglyphic texts which provide many insights into their past political relationships and cosmological beliefs. These texts bracket the entire Classic era, dating from A.D. 120 to A.D. 909, and provide politicized histories of various Maya dynasties and their associated cities.

An estimated twelve million Maya occupied hundreds of cities and towns at the height of the Classic Period. Many of these centers have been investigated archaeologically. Yet, the plentiful information that exists for the Classic Period Maya has not resolved some of the most basic questions about them. How much external influence was there on Maya political systems and their rise to complexity? How complex and bureaucratic was Maya society? And, how many people actually occupied Maya centers and polities? In spite of almost two centuries of archaeological work on the Maya, debate still rages on almost all aspects of their society.

Largely because of the lack of consensus in Maya studies, the role of the lowland Maya sites in the development of Mesoamerican civilization has been underplayed in comparison to its two highland neighbors of the Classic Period. Whereas only two urban areas and polities of moderate size would appear to dominate theoretical debate over complexity and development in highland Mesoamerica, a larger number of polities of equal size and importance must be considered in the Maya area. Classic-era population estimates are particularly difficult to derive in the jungles of the Maya lowlands. However, some 425,000 people are presently believed to have occupied the Guatemalan polity of *Tikal (766 square miles [1,963 sq km]); and, other Maya polities were at least equivalent in terms of population and some were certainly larger in terms of territory. Urban populations for some of the larger Classic Period Maya sites are estimated at: 62,000 for Coba, Mexico; 65,000 for Calakmul, Mexico; between 62,000 (46 square miles [120 sq km]) and 92,000 (121 square miles [314 sq km]) for Tikal, Guatemala; and, at a minimum, 115,000 (68 square miles [177 sq km]) for Caracol, Belize. Although no population counts have been extrapolated, the Mexican sites of Uxmal and *Chichén Itzá can likely be placed within the upper echelon of well-populated Maya sites as well. Smaller Maya polities (similar in size to Monte Albán) were also centered at such sites as Dzibilchaltun (Mexico), Edzna (Mexico), *Palenque (Mexico), Tonina (Mexico), Dos Pilas (Guatemala), Altun Ha (Belize), and *Copán (Honduras); they certainly played influential roles in Classic Maya prehistory. Whereas the Classic Period of highland Mesoamerica has been cast in terms of two (or three, if Cholula is included) primary sites, the political landscape of the lowland Maya area of the Classic era is populated by a larger number of sites and polities; however, these matched the size and scale of the northern, Mexican highland neighbors.

Mesoamerican cities of the Classic Period were, thus, numerous, and centers that were characterized by large populations were found in all regions. There was also substantial contact throughout Mesoamerica—contact that increased in frequency through the Classic Period. And it is in the interactions between these Mesoamerican sites and regions that the seeds for the transformation of "Classic" societies to "Postclassic" societies are to be found. This transformation surely involved warfare; however, the subsequent changes were not entirely uniform throughout the area. In the highlands of Mexico, smaller sites such as Tajin, Xochicalco, and Cacaxtla—all of which celebrate and demonstrate warfare in their art—replaced the more massive Teotihuacán in prominence after A.D. 750; they, in turn, were replaced by *Tula two hundred years later. In the Maya area, warfare both decimated and consolidated polities. Some important centers in the Maya lowlands, such as Dos Pilas, were abandoned during the height of the Classic Period, at a time when other Maya centers are seen as reaching their zenith; other Maya polities—such as Seibal, Caracol, Uxmal, and Chichén Itzá—exhibit signs of expansion and prosperity after A.D. 800, or almost at the very end of the Classic era. Thus, the Classic Maya "collapse" may be viewed as resulting from long-standing patterns of internecine warfare, which grew more intense, violent, and destructive over time and which severely and irreparably ravaged large parts of the Southern lowlands. This same "collapse" may also be cast in terms of larger Mesoamerican patterns which show the transformation of complex "state" systems into even more complex alliance patterns, sometimes called "empires."

In summary, the Classic Period of Mesoamerica reveals a series of initially geographically diverse and complex civilizations whose histories became increasingly more intertwined over time. Different regions came to be dominated by single centers which then attempted to dominate other centers and regions; such patterns are clearly mirrored in Maya hieroglyphic texts. It is likely that Mesoamerican warfare at the end of the Classic Period was truly "international," with Maya(nized) groups operating in the Mexican highlands and Mexican(ized) groups ranging throughout the Maya lowlands. The complicated interactions between these diverse cities and regions provided impetus and direction to Mesoamerican prehistory during the Classic Period, first within similar ethnic groups and then between different ethnic groups. These final Classic Period interactions also represent the initial attempts at Mesoamerican "empire" building, which was continued by both the Maya and the Aztec of the Post-Classic era.

[See also CENTRAL AMERICA, ARCHAEOLOGY OF; CEREN; MAYA CIVILIZATION: CLASSIC MAYA COLLAPSE; STATES: THEORIES OF THE COLLAPSE OF STATES; ZAPOTEC CIVILIZATION.]

■ W. T. Sanders, J. Parsons, and R. Santley, *The Basin of Mexico* (1979). R. E. Blanton, S. A. Kowalewski, G. Feinman, and J. Appel, *Ancient Mesoamerica* (1981). K. V. Flannery and J. Marcus, eds., *The Cloud People* (1983). T. P. Culbert and D. S. Rice, eds., *Precolumbian Population History in the Maya Lowlands* (1990). L. Schele and D. A. Freidel, *A Forest of Kings* (1990). J. C. Berlo, ed., *Art, Ideology, and the City of Teotihuacan* (1992). D. Z. Chase and A. F. Chase, eds., *Mesoamerican Elites* (1992). N. Grube, ed., *From Preclassic to Early Classic: The Emergence of Maya Civilization* (1994).

Arlen F. Chase

POST-CLASSIC PERIOD IN MESOAMERICA

The Post-Classic Period in Mesoamerica has conventionally been defined as beginning in A.D. 900 and ending with the Spanish conquest of the Aztec Empire, which took place between 1519 and 1521. This 600-year time span has been treated by archaeologists as both a developmental stage and a chronological period. When it was initially proposed as a developmental stage archaeologists characterized the Post-Classic Period as a time of increasing militarism associated with the formation of empires, urbanism, greater secularization, and a decline in the quality of art and architecture, which they contrasted with the peaceful theocratic civilizations of the Classic Period.

Research during the last half-century has shown, however, that militarism involving human sacrifice and territorial expansion, urbanism, and commerce occurred to varying degrees in all the Classic Period civilizations whose societies were ruled by kings. Archaeologists have also learned that the breakup of the Classic Period civilizations that traditionally marked the beginning of the Post-Classic Period was not synchronous; neither was the process uniform. *Teotihuacán, the largest Classic Period city, located northeast of present-day Mexico City in the central highlands of Mexico, and *Monte Albán, the capital of the *Zapotec civilization, centered in the valley of *Oaxaca in the southern highlands, both began to decline about A.D. 750. In the southern Maya lowlands of Yucatán, the collapse of most cities and elite culture, along with depopulation of

the countryside, was underway by the ninth century; however, Classic lowland Maya civilization continued in the north for at least another two centuries, from A.D. 800 to 1000, or the Terminal Classic Period. Some archaeologists now favor extending the Terminal Classic period to A.D. 1250 when the city of *Chichén Itzá's dominance over the northern Yucatán ended. Thus the Post-Classic Period is most appropriately understood as a chronological period, and while important changes took place during this time span, these changes were not uniform, and there was significant continuity with earlier periods.

The city-state formed the basic political unit in Mesoamerica during the Post-Classic Period. In the wake of Teotihuacán's declining influence, a period of political fragmentation ensued in central Mexico, and the basin of Mexico was divided into a series of small city-states. New centers of political power emerged outside the basin—for example, Xochicalco in western Morelos grew rapidly after Teotihuacán's decline, reached its maximum size about A.D. 800, and was largely abandoned by A.D. 900.

Xochicalco covers 1.5 square miles (4 sq km) and is situated on a hilltop that was flattened for the construction of temples, administrative buildings, and elite residences; a complex of moats and walls fortified the site. Residential terraces were located on the sides of the hill. Xochicalco dominated western Morelos and adjoining parts of the modern state of Guerrero. Conquest slabs on stelae and scenes of human sacrifice at the site indicate that Xochicalco expanded its control through military conquest to extract tribute and control important trade routes.

The growth of Cholula in Puebla during the Post-Classic Period also seems related in part to trade. The site lies in an area of rich agricultural productivity, but it is also situated on a major trade route that links the basin of Mexico with areas to the east. Cholula was a regional center during the Classic Period. While little of this city has been excavated and its chronology is still debated, an older temple pyramid was enlarged four times eventually to cover 40 acres (16 ha) and stand 180 feet (55 m) high—the largest building in pre-Hispanic Mesoamerica. Cholula might have controlled the southern basin of Mexico between A.D. 950 and 1150. It was a major city of 20,000–40,000 people and was an important political and pilgrimage center throughout the Post-Classic Period that allied with the Aztec Empire in the fifteenth century.

*Tula, located on the northwestern edge of the basin of Mexico, is generally accepted as the site of Tollan, the capital of the *Toltec Empire, which reached its maximum extent between A.D. 900 and 1150. Although the Spanish burned most native books, some native histories were recorded after the conquest, and Tula (Tollan) figures prominently in these accounts, as later rulers sought to legitimize their position by claiming descent from the Toltecs. Archaeological surveys indicate that Tula covered 5 square miles (13 sq km) and had an estimated population of 30,000–60,000; another 60,000 people lived on the surrounding plain. The city's economy was based on irrigation agriculture and the production of a variety of goods for local and foreign markets.

Although the extent of Tula's domain is not altogether clear, its control encompassed areas to the north in the modern state of Hidalgo, the valley of Toluca, the northern basin of Mexico, and portions of Morelos and the Bajio. Trade goods and architectural affinities suggest that Tula's contacts extended to other parts of Mesoamerica as well.

The nature of Toltec interactions with the northern Maya lowlands is especially intriguing because the city of *Chichén Itzá, located 77 miles (124 km) east of the modern city of Merida, contains both "Toltec"-influenced architecture and iconography similar to that found at Tula and buildings in the typical Terminal Classic (Puuc) style of the northern Maya lowlands. The Toltec or central Mexican structures were once thought to have been constructed in a part of the city separate from the older Puuc buildings. Recent excavations, however, suggest that the Puuc and central Mexican styles overlap and that some of the Mexican attributes may even predate the tenth century. These findings call into question the conventional view that Toltec invaders took over Chichén Itzá. Some archaeologists now think that the "Toltec" influence was mediated by Mexicanized Maya from the Gulf coast.

Chichén Itzá dominated the northern Maya lowlands (or at least the western half) for 200 years. For reasons that are not well understood, its power, which was partly based on control of coastal trading networks, began to decline at the end of the twelfth century, and by A.D. 1250, the city of Mayapan, south of Chichén Itzá, that had been founded ca. A.D. 1100, became the dominant political power in the northern Maya lowlands.

In its physical configuration, Mayapan is quite distinct from earlier lowland Maya cities. This was a tightly nucleated city of approximately 12,000 people who lived within a four-square-kilometer area fortified by a stone wall. Mayapan headed a league of provinces, each with its own ruling dynasty. Politically independent centers, such as Tulum and Cozumel, developed during this time along the east coast and were actively engaged in circum-peninsular trading networks reflecting an intensification of coastal trade and commerce in the lowlands. Warfare and internal power struggles led to the destruction of Mayapan in A.D. 1441, and from then until the Spanish conquest the northern lowlands were divided into a series of sixteen independent city-states or provinces.

The central highlands of Mexico also entered into a period of political fragmentation following the breakup of the Toltec macrostate by A.D. 1175. The reduction in Toltec power and the abandonment of Tula have been attributed to a combination of internal and external factors, including strains on agricultural production as a result of population growth, pressure from northern groups moving southward as the boundary for farming retracted, disruption of trade networks, and growing ethnic conflict within the city of Tula and its immediate environs.

Much of Tula's population gradually moved elsewhere, including into the basin of Mexico, which by the thirteenth century was divided into fifteen city-states. Each city-state consisted of rural dependencies organized around a major town or city that contained the ruler's palace, major temples, craft specialists, and a marketplace. Recent archaeological investigations have revealed significant differences in the economic organization of these city-states, especially in the degree of centralization of craft specialization and exchange.

These city-states fought and allied with one another until A.D. 1350, when the Alcolhua of Texcoco, plus their allies on the east side of the basin and the Tepaneca of Azcapotzalco on the west side of the basin and their tributaries, began to expand their control to areas outside of the basin. The Tepaneca and their allies defeated the Alcolhua in A.D. 1418. At that time the Tepanec tributaries included the Mexica of *Tenochtitlán, who, according to native histories, were one of the last immigrant groups to settle in the basin after the breakup of Tula. The Mexica broke away from the Tepaneca and in 1428 allied with Tlacopan (another Tepanec tributary) and the Alcolhua to form the Triple Alliance. The Triple Alliance defeated the Tepaneca in 1430, and after consolidating their control, they embarked upon an ambitious campaign of military conquest outside the basin.

By the early sixteenth century the Triple Alliance, or Aztec Empire, had become the largest state and civilization in pre-Columbian Mesoamerica. The basin of Mexico, the core of the Aztec Empire, was heavily urbanized and densely populated. Some 1–1.25 million people resided in the basin; the population of Tenochtitlán had grown to 150,000–200,000, and its sister city, Tlatelolco, was the site of an enormous market that served 20,000–25,000 people daily. The fifteen previously autonomous city-states, along with thirty-five new centers, became semiautonomous administrative units within the empire.

The Aztec Empire encompassed about 77,200 square miles (200,000 sq km), with Nahuatl (Aztec language) colonies located as far away as present-day Panama. Outside its core, the Triple Alliance relied more on a strategy of subjugation than incorporation; they exacted tribute from conquered areas but left internal affairs largely in the hands of local rulers, although they sometimes established garrisons and fortresses along the empire's boundaries. Unlike the Inca Empire of South America, the Aztecs did not conquer all state-level societies in Mesoamerica; their western boundary abutted the Tarascan Empire of Michoacan, which governed an area of 28,950 square miles (75,000 sq km). Other independent kingdoms included Tlaxcala, southwest of the basin, Meztitlan, north of Tlaxcala, and the Mixtec kingdoms of southern Oaxaca.

In 1519 Hernando Cortés and his troops landed on the coast of Veracruz, and within two years—aided by superior military technology and strategy, factionalism within the Aztec Empire, cultural and religious differences, and epidemic diseases that decimated indigenous populations—the Spaniards conquered Tenochtitlán and defeated the Triple Alliance. The legacy of the Aztec Empire remains today, proudly represented on the national emblem of the modern nation-state of Mexico by the eagle on the cactus, the Mexica symbol of the founding of Tenochtitlán.

[See also AZTEC CIVILIZATION: INTRODUCTION.]

■ William T. Sanders, Jeffrey R. Parsons, and Robert S. Santley, *The Basin of Mexico* (1979). Frances E. Berdan, *The Aztecs of Central Mexico* (1982). Richard A. Diehl, *Tula, The Toltec Capital of Ancient Mexico* (1983). Kent V. Flannery and Joyce Marcus, *The Cloud People* (1983). Jeremy Sabloff and E. Wyllys Andrews V, eds., *Late Lowland Maya Civilization* (1986). Eduardo Matos Moctezuma, *The Great Temple of the Aztecs* (1988). Richard A. Diehl and Janet Catherine Berlo, eds., *Mesoamerica after the Decline of Teotihuacan* (1989). Dan M. Healan, ed., *Tula of the Toltecs* (1989). Jeremy A. Sabloff, *The New Archaeology and the Ancient Maya* (1990). Helen Perlstein Pollard, *Taríacuri's Legacy: The Prehispanic Tarascan State* (1993).

Deborah L. Nichols

SPANISH SETTLEMENT IN MESOAMERICA

In 1517, a quarter of a century after Columbus first made landfall in the Bahamas, Hispanic populations, expanding from their initial settlements on the Caribbean islands, began what subsequently became continuing contact with the Maya city-states of the Yucatán Peninsula and with other indigenous civilizations of most regions of Mesoamerica.

During the next three decades Spanish conquistadores, followed by friars, settlers, and the inevitable government administrators, brought under Spain's control to some extent Maya, Aztec, Tarascan, Mixtec, Zapotec, and other regional variants of Late Post-Classic (A.D. 1200–1521) civilizations. Spain incorporated these Mesoamerican civilizations politically and economically into the developing worldwide Hispanic empire.

Although regionally distinct, the Mesoamerican civilizations shared many characteristics. All were at a state level of political organization, with large populations divided into at least two hereditary classes, an elite ruling class and a lower class of commoners. The basic unit of political and economic organization throughout Mesoamerica was the city-state. In some instances city-states had been integrated through conquest into larger political units, such as indirectly ruled tributary empires (e.g., the Aztecs), or were voluntarily incorporated into loose confederacies or alliances (e.g., Tlaxcala, Cholula, Huejotzingo, and Atlixco). There was only limited development of more permanent administrative and integrative political structures.

Economically all states were agrarian-based. Most people, the commoners, engaged in agricultural production. Craftspeople, full- or part-time, produced items for the elite (e.g., earspools by lapidaries) or for mass consumption (e.g., ceramics and figurines by clay workers, obsidian prismatic blades by blade makers). Most goods were distributed through market and tribute systems. Although regionally varied, basic religious, cosmological, and scientific concepts, including writing, were shared throughout Mesoamerica. Settlement patterns ranged from low density, widely dispersed settlements to nucleated rural and urban centers.

There is rich and abundant written documentation for the Late Post-Classic Period and the Early Colonial Period (A.D. 1521–1620). These data have formed the bases for historical and ethnohistoric syntheses of the contact and postconquest periods in many regions. More archaeological data are available for the preconquest period than for the Early Colonial Period and more for the Early Colonial Period than for any later postconquest period. Information from studies in two regions, central Mexico and southern Mesoamerica, illustrate some topics central to an understanding of the Early Colonial Period.

Demographic Disaster: Context for Change. It is generally agreed that throughout Mesoamerica during the sixteenth century, a rapid and devastating decline in indigenous population provided the contexts for ideological, political, and economic changes then and later. This decline resulted from inadvertently introduced European epidemic diseases against which the indigenous populations possessed little or no immunity. There is no consensus on the precise size of the pre-Hispanic Mesoamerican population as a whole or by region. Nor is there agreement on the sequence, scale, and velocity of decline, the duration of the period of depressed population, and, in those regions where it occurred, the timing and rate of recovery.

In central Mexico and southern Mesoamerica archaeological data, consisting of settlement patterns and paleodemographic reconstructions based on skeletal populations, when combined with detailed baptismal, marriage, and death records, and with other population records, by community or by region, present a profile of populations in rapid decline during the Early Colonial Period.

Archaeological Record of the Early Colonial Period.

Archaeological studies of this period have focused on the social and economic position of indigenous peoples. Hispanic presence at this time is most dramatic in urban areas, where most of the Spaniards lived. Structures, archaeological and extant, and city plans are obvious markers of this presence. In urban centers such as Mexico City, Cuernavaca, and Merida, relatively high frequencies of archaeologically recovered imported or locally made ceramics of European origin, (e.g., majolicas and glazed earthenwares), and after 1576, imported oriental porcelains, along with glass and metal items, reflect the social and economic dominance of the Hispanic population. On the other hand the inferior position of the indigenous urban population of Tlatelolco in central Mexico is marked by changes in the forms and designs of selected local indigenous ceramics and the adoption of a limited number of Hispanic ceramic forms, designs, and technology (glazing). Most items of European and oriental origins were absent.

In rural indigenous communities of the same period archaeological evidence for Hispanic influence is limited. In central Mexico and southern Mesoamerica such influence is restricted to the introduction of churches or chapels with atrios and residences, European-style cemeteries, and small numbers of nonindigenous items including glazed pottery, glass, jewelry, coins, and metal implements. More of the last three categories are reported from sites in Belize, the Chiapas highlands, and the Chiapas Pacific coast than from central Mexico. In all areas pre-Hispanic ceramics continue with modifications. Indigenous lithic technology continues in central Mexico, Belize, and the Chiapas highlands but is replaced on the Chiapas Pacific coast by metal tools. Where it continued, there is an increasing emphasis on local sources of materials and a reworking of previously discarded tools. Residential structures in central Mexico, the Chiapas highlands, and the Pacific coast follow preconquest architectural patterns, but those in Belize are marked by a break in architectural style. European animals and crops were introduced during the sixteenth century, but virtually no archaeological evidence of their use by indigenous peoples has been found in rural sites. This contrasts strongly with the urban Spanish occupations.

Archaeological evidence for Spanish occupation in rural areas begins late in the sixteenth century. In rural areas the population decline was met with the *Congegación* policy, which consolidated remnant populations into a few towns, leaving many towns and lands abandoned. At this time (1580–1620) small ranches appear in many areas, operated either by Spaniards or members of the local indigenous elite, and utilizing through rental, purchase, or land grant the unused native lands. Excavated ranch structures (all from central Mexico) incorporate indigenous and Hispanic architectural technology and style. The associated ceramics and artifacts include high frequencies of items of European origin produced in Mexico, and similar items imported from Europe and the Far East. These are found in association with indigenous and modified-indigenous ceramics. This complex suggests that rural Spaniards and indigenous elites held socioeconomic positions between urban Spaniards and rural natives, an interpretation supported by data from other areas. Similar artifactual complexes occur in the Chiapas Pacific coast town of Ocelocalco (1572–1767), an indigenous community whose inhabitants retained control over town lands and the lucrative production of cacao. From the earliest occupation there were abundant Spanish ceramics, metal, and glass artifacts associated with an indigenous and modified-indigenous ceramic tradition. In another case sixteenth-century Spanish-style houses in the town of Tecoh, Izamal, Yucatán, have been associated with elite indigenous occupants.

Archaeological investigations of the Early Colonial Period show that some of the factors involved in the variable socioeconomic impact of conquest on indigenous civilizations include the degree of urbanism and proximity to Hispanic settlers, the degree to which local indigenous elites retained their positions and support, and the extent to which indigenous people were able to retain economic independence.

[See also AMERICAS, INTRODUCTION OF DISEASES INTO THE; AZTEC CIVILIZATION: THE SPANISH CONQUEST OF THE AZTECS; EUROPEAN COLONIES IN THE NEW WORLD; MESOAMERICA, articles on POST-CLASSIC PERIOD IN MESOAMERICA, HISTORICAL ARCHAEOLOGY OF MESOAMERICA; TENOCHTITLÁN.]

■ Thomas H. Charlton, *Post-Conquest Developments in the Teotihuacan Valley, Mexico* (1973). J. H. Parry, *The Spanish Seaborne Empire* (1973). Gonzalo Lopez Cervantes, *Cerámica Colonial en la Ciudad de México* (1976). Norman Hammond and Gordon R. Willey, eds., *Maya Archaeology and Ethnohistory* (1979). Nancy M. Farriss, *Maya Society under Colonial Rule* (1984). Arlen F. Chase and Prudence M. Rice, eds., *The Lowland Maya Post-Classic* (1985). Ross Hassig, *Aztec Warfare* (1988). David Hurst Thomas, ed., *Columbian Consequences*, vol. 3, *The Spanish Borderlands in Pan-American Perspective* (1991). William M. Denevan, ed., *The Native Population of the Americas in 1492*, 2nd ed. (1992). Paul Farnsworth and Jack S. Williams, eds., *The Archaeology of Spanish Colonial and Mexican Republican Periods* (1992). James Lockhart, *The Nahuas after the Conquest* (1992). J. Daniel Rogers and Samuel M. Wilson, *Ethnohistory and Archaeology* (1993).

Thomas H. Charlton

HISTORICAL ARCHAEOLOGY OF MESOAMERICA

The development of *historical archaeology as a social science in Mesoamerica is a relatively recent phenomenon. Traditionally, Mesoamerican archaeologists have focused their attention on the region's rich prehistoric past; as a result, the archaeology of the Colonial Period (ca. 1521–1821) and the post-Independence periods (1821–the present) has been limited almost exclusively to the recovery of materials associated with the architectural conservation, consolidation, and restoration of important buildings (e.g., religious structures, forts, and the homes of important historical figures). In some cases, entire towns that were once important colonial centers have been partially restored and are preserved as colonial monuments (e.g., Taxco, San Miguel de Allende, Guanajuato in Mexico, and Antigua in Guatemala). Exceptions to this general trend are the numerous salvage archaeology projects sponsored by Mexico's Instituto Nacional de Antropología e Historia (INAH).

Many architectural restoration and salvage projects have been carried out within the Mexico City metropolitan area. Excavations associated with architectural restoration projects include the convent of San Jeronimo, the Church of Santa Teresa La Antigua, the convent of Capuchinas, the archbishop's palace, and the College of Tepotzotlan. Important salvage projects include excavations associated with the construction of the Metro (subway) and the stabilization of the Metropolitan cathedral and the Complejo Hidalgo. In the Yucatán Peninsula a number of buildings have been consolidated or partially restored including the House of Montejo, Merida, the convent at Mani, and the forts at Bacalar and Campeche, as well as other colonial buildings in Merida, Campeche, Izamal, and Valladolid. Elsewhere in Mexico archaeological investigations associated with the

restoration of historic buildings include the Palacio de Cortes in Cuernavaca, the colonial buildings at Mitla, Oaxaca, the convent of San Agustin, Veracruz, and the convent of Tecamachalco, Puebla. Salvage projects also have been conducted in Campeche. In Chiapas a large salvage project was carried out prior to the building of the Chicoasen Dam that flooded a large area of the Grijalva Valley, and the project included excavations in a colonial church of the town of Osumacinta.

In Guatemala, archaeological investigations have been carried out in several important buildings in Antigua, Guatemala, including the Dominican convent, the Jesuit convent, and several other churches. Antigua, for over two hundred years the capital of Spanish colonial Central America, has been declared a national monument by the Guatemalan government, and an international monument by UNESCO. As a result, a large number of historical structures have been preserved, and the potential for more problem-oriented archaeology is great in this area.

The archaeological aspects of both architectural restoration and salvage archaeology projects have produced valuable studies of historic period architecture and artifacts, particularly technological and stylistic analyses of ceramics. But most of these studies have been limited to descriptive reports, with little attention paid to the social context of material culture. In recent years, however, a growing number of archaeologists working on the historic period in Mesoamerica have begun to formulate research designs that move beyond artifact description and architectural restoration. Increasingly, historical archaeologists working in Mesoamerica are addressing issues such as acculturation, ethnicity, economic exploitation, exchange systems, and changing patterns of socioeconomic stratification. For the most part, these studies focus on the native populations of Mesoamerica and on indigenous communities rather than on the elite and institutional buildings of the Spanish conquistadores.

Since the 1970s, there has been a small but steadily growing number of archaeologists who have approached Mesoamerican historical archaeology in new ways. Influenced by the "New Archaeology" (or so-called processual archaeology) that had come to dominate the field of archaeology as a whole in North America and by intellectual trends in Latin America that tended to take a marxist or historical materialist perspective, these archaeologists have sought to explain social and historical processes. More recently, the influence of the so-called post-processual archaeology (or archaeologies) has begun to be felt in a few studies, and it is clear that these approaches will be utilized more in the future.

Historical archaeological research projects, whose objectives extend beyond architectural restoration to a wide range of social issues, have been conducted in several areas of Mesoamerica. These areas include central Mexico—primarily the basin of Mexico, the Nochixtlan Valley, Oaxaca, the Isthmus of Tehuantepec, the highlands and Pacific coastal plain of Chiapas, the central highlands and southeastern lowlands of Guatemala, the Yucatán Peninsula (including Belize), and western and Caribbean Honduras. This research has provided new and sometimes unexpected information about the response of a wide range of indigenous groups (e.g., the Aztecs, Otomi, Mixtecs, Zapotecs, Zoques, several Maya groups, and Lenca) to Spanish colonial rule.

In the basin of Mexico, research in the late 1960s in the Teotihuacán Valley involved the systematic survey and excavations of Colonial and Republican period settlements.

subsequently, research conducted within the Aztec city-state of Otumba in the eastern part of the valley has yielded important data on the late Pre-Hispanic and Colonial periods. In these studies, which assess the impact of the colonization process upon the native population, important differences between rural and urban populations and between elite and nonelite indigenous peoples have been identified, with rural, nonelite populations experiencing the fewest changes in the Early Colonial Period.

Elsewhere in central Mexico, a large-scale archaeological survey project in the Mezquital Valley, located 95 miles (150 km) north of the valley of Mexico, was begun in 1985 under the auspices of the Escuela Nacional de Antropología e Historia. Over 450 sites have been located that date to the postconquest period. Objectives of this project have been to examine changing patterns of ethnicity, lifeways, and political and economic relations with other portions of central Mexico in prehistoric and historic times.

Farther south, in the Mixteca Alta region of Oaxaca, archaeological investigations in the Nochixtlan Valley provide architectural data comparing Late Post-Classic and Colonial Period houses. Elsewhere in Oaxaca, survey and excavations at historic sites on the Isthmus of Tehuantepec have provided information regarding colonial consumption patterns in rural native villages.

In the highlands of Chiapas, the colonial townsites of Coneta and Coapa have been excavated, and archaeological data have been used to examine issues such as acculturation and syncretism. On the Pacific coastal plain of Chiapas, in the region known as the Soconusco, the colonial townsite of Ocelocalco, a town occupied from the late sixteenth to late eighteenth centuries mostly by indigenous peoples, was excavated and a regional survey was conducted subsequently to locate other colonial sites. This research has examined how the cacao (cocoa) trade affected economic organization within the local indigenous communities.

In the highlands of Guatemala, a survey of colonial structures in the Panchoy Valley, site of Antigua, has focused on industrial and vernacular architecture (e.g., soap factories, potteries, mills, tile and brick kilns, water systems, and tanneries). Elsewhere in Guatemala, the colonial towns of Antiquipaque, Department of Escuintla, and Tacuilula, Department of Santa Rosa, have been investigated, and maps and artifact inventories have been published.

The Yucatán Peninsula is increasingly attracting historical archaeologists who are interested in a wide range of sociocultural issues. Excavations in and around colonial churches and chapels at the sites of Tancah, Tamalcab, Oxtankah, Xcaret, all in Quintana Roo, and Lamanai and Tipu, in Belize, have enabled investigators to examine issues of acculturation and religious syncretism, identifying ways in which the Maya both accepted and resisted the imposition of Christianity. In addition, the recovery of a large number of burials at some of these sites has provided valuable information on diet, disease, miscegenation, and burial practices. Also, a small number of eighteenth- or nineteenth-century haciendas and townsites have been studied, allowing archaeologists to explore changing economic relationships in the latter part of the Colonial period.

In western Honduras archaeological investigations have been carried out in Colonial period Lenca settlements in the Tencoa District enabling researchers to study the colonization process in a remote frontier setting. Along the Caribbean coast of Honduras, research has been carried out in Black Carib or Garifuna communities, revealing how their material culture was used to create a new ethnic identity.

In spite of its slow beginnings, historical archaeology now has a promising future in Mesoamerica; there are more research projects underway than ever before; the volume of papers, articles, symposia, and conferences devoted to the field has increased markedly in recent years; and student training programs have been initiated in Mexico.

[See also AZTEC CIVILIZATION: THE SPANISH CONQUEST OF THE AZTECS; MAYA CIVILIZATION: INTRODUCTION.]

■ Patricia Fournier-García and Fernando A. Miranda-Flores, "Historic Sites Archaeology in Mexico," *Historical Archaeology* 26 (1992): 75–83. Janine Gasco, Greg Charles Smith, and Patricia Fournier-García, *Approaches to the Historical Archaeology of Middle and South America* (1996).

Janine Gasco

MESOAMERICA, Origins of Food Production in. Mesoamerica was one of several independent centers of prehistoric plant cultivation and eventual domestication, leading ultimately to the development of agriculturally based societies. Food production focused on several important plant species (for example, *Zea mays*, maize; *Phaseolus*, beans; *Cucurbita*, squash; *Capsicum*, chili peppers; *Physalis*, ground cherry; *Persea americana*, avocado) together with a large number of peripheral species that were cultivated with different intensities according to regional availability as well as cultural preferences.

In contrast with developments in other regions of the prehistoric world, the domestication of animal species did not proceed hand-in-hand with plant cultivation in Mesoamerica. Principal domesticates included indigenous dogs, turkeys, and, possibly, cotton-tail rabbits. Although these provided animal protein for the Mesoamerican diet as well as some raw materials for other products, they were unsuitable for the labor-intensive activities carried out by larger bovine or camelid species elsewhere.

Paleoethnobotanical data relevant to the study of the beginnings of food production have been recovered from the following archaeological sites (summarized by Flannery 1973): caves excavated by Richard S. MacNeish in the Sierra de Tamaulipas (1958) and the Sierra Madre regions (Mangelsdorf, MacNeish, and Willey 1964), both of which are located in the state of Tamaulipas, Mexico; the Tehuacán Valley in the state of Puebla, Mexico, also studied by MacNeish; the open-air site of Zohapilco, near Tlapacoya, state of Mexico, Mexico (Niederberger 1976, 1979); and caves excavated in the valley of Oaxaca, especially Guilá Naquitz (Flannery 1973, 1986). Although these investigations are well known and have been amply cited, little additional research on the problem of early food production has been carried out since. In particular, few data are available from the northern part of Central America that pertain culturally to Mesoamerica, and these correspond to much later time periods, when agriculture is clearly the dominant subsistence activity in the area as a whole.

The origin of agriculture represents the culmination of a number of interrelated processes, socioeconomic as well as biological and ecological. For instance, some plants such as maize or certain species of beans underwent mutations, altering their genetic composition and rendering them more amenable to harvesting, subsequent storage, and, finally, human consumption. Other plants were simply tolerated to varying degrees, responding with higher yields depending upon the degree of attention they received as well as their own inherent plasticity, which allowed them to adapt to variable environmental conditions. Early plant collectors observed the developmental cycles of the species they utilized, for medicinal and ritual purposes as well as food, harvesting before seeds matured sufficiently to foster their dispersal mechanisms. In addition, hunter-gatherers undoubtedly programmed their subsistence activities according to seasonal and regional availability of preferred edible resources.

The origin of agriculture has been regarded by some authors as a revolutionary moment in human prehistory. Because of its enormous consequences for the evolution of increased complexity in socioeconomic organization, a more realistic view would be to visualize a gradual process taking place over millennia, with localized regional manifestations based on different degrees of emphasis on the basic domesticated plants complemented with other locally available species as suggested previously. The chronology of the domestication of food plants in the regions cited above indicates that the incorporation of particular species varied, possibly related to the distance from the original domestication center (as in the case of maize) or to the local availability of potential domesticates (as in the case of squash). Certainly the rate of diffusion of domesticated plants varied with distance to some extent. However, it must be pointed out that the apparent sequence of adoption of domesticated plants in Mesoamerican sites may be more a product of the limited available data than representative of the true sequence of adoption in different areas.

A word on terminology appropriate to the topic of early Mesoamerican food production is "domestication." With reference to plants, "domestication" implies a series of genetic changes, generally affecting dispersal and fertilization mechanisms, which cause the plant to become dependent upon human intervention in order to complete its reproductive cycle. Such changes normally increase the plant's productivity, although other desirable characteristics may be emphasized as well. Plant cultivation does not necessarily imply domestication; plants may be cared for and exploited without selecting for favorable mutations and consequent genetic change. Finally the term *"agriculture" implies the establishment of a subsistence system dominated by the production and consumption of cultivated plants, domesticated or not.

Another aspect to consider is that the cultivation and domestication of plants do not necessarily promote rapid changes in the social organization of the groups that adopt them. Paleoethnobotanical evidence from Mesoamerica suggests that hunter-gatherers gradually incorporated some wild plants and later cultivated plants into their diet, substituting the animal component for a larger proportion of vegetal products. Data from Tehuacán Valley cave sites indicate that nomadic microbands during the Early Holocene gradually changed from a subsistence system that was predominately hunting-based and dependent on Pleistocene megafauna to one more reliant upon wild plants and smaller animal species. Population growth in the region is indicated by an increase in the size and number of seasonal camps situated in certain zones associated with seasonally available resources. Greater seasonal abundance of certain preferred foods permitted increased demographic concentrations, referred to as macrobands. The transition to increased dependence upon cultivated food plants goes hand-in-hand with an increase in the region's population together with increases in the duration of occupation of

campsites. This pattern of semisedentary camps was slowly transformed as permanent agricultural villages, dependent primarily upon agricultural produce for their subsistence, were established, about 2500 B.C. Nonetheless, hunting and wild plant collecting did not disappear, although their importance diminished as agricultural plants comprised a higher proportion of the diet.

The earliest appearances in the archaeological record of the plants that would later comprise the more important cultigens in Mesoamerica are quite variable. Not only is the area where cultivation and/or domestication of specific plants first occurred unknown, but the geographical distribution of their wild progenitors is not well documented. In some cases, however, it is possible to suggest potential areas based on the modern distribution of closely related wild relatives. Such is the case of maize, largely accepted to have evolved from teosinte (*Zea mexicana*), whose nearest relatives have been detected in the Balsas basin in the state of Jalisco, Mexico.

Pollen from teosinte is reported from the valley of *Oaxaca about 7400 B.C.; kernels from Zohapilco are dated to about 5000 B.C. Domesticated maize appears first in the Tehuacán Valley around 5000 B.C., although recent research has called the dating of the early Tehuacan sequence into question (Long et al. 1989). Domesticated runner beans (*Phaseolus coccineus*) appear quite late in Tehuacan (ca. 200 B.C., although wild species have been found in Oaxacan sites as early as about 8700 B.C. and in Tamaulipas about 7000 B.C. The earliest remains of squash (*Cucurbita pepo*) have been identified in Oaxaca, about 8000 B.C., in Tamaulipas about 7000 B.C., and in Tehuacán about 5000 B.C. The earliest dated remains of chili peppers (*Capsicum*) pertain to the Tehuacán Valley (ca. 6500 B.C., wild; ca. 4000 B.C., domesticated). Avocado (*Persea americana*) first appears in Tehuacán around 7200 B.C. Amaranth appeared in both Zohapilco and Tehuacán around 5000 B.C., but the dating in the latter region of clearly domesticated specimens (*Amaranthus cruentus*) is problematic. Other plants of variable importance include goosefoot (*Chenopodium*) and purslane (*Portulaca oleraceae*). *Agave* (century plant) may have been one of the earliest cultivars, and is outstanding in that it has multiple uses including food, fiber, and fuel, among others. *Opuntia* (prickly pear) was another important food source, exploited for its fruit as well as edible leaves. Both genera are characteristic of arid zones, and their adaptation to vegetative propagation facilitated their manipulation by human groups. Paleoethnobotanical remains pertaining to these genera are among the earliest in the Mesoamerican sequence. Finally, root crops were probably of considerable importance, especially in tropical zones; however, archaeological evidence for their use is largely absent due to poor preservation.

The transition from small microbands of hunter-gatherers to sedentary agricultural villagers associated with the introduction of cultivation and domestication as documented from the Tehuacán Valley is also evident from the Sierra de Tamaulipas and Sierra Madre zones of Tamaulipas as well as the valley of Oaxaca. All of these areas are represented by occupations in dry caves in arid to semiarid zones, where preservation conditions are excellent. The only exception is Zohapilco, where a semisedentary community is interpreted as being associated with a non-agricultural subsistence base, made possible by abundant nearby lacustrine resources, together with wild plant and animal resources available from surrounding ecological zones. Thus, while the Tehuacán Valley is an important source of archaeological data reflecting sociocultural and economic change associated with the introduction of agriculture in one particular area, there are no indications that the origin of food production took place there. One must ask to what extent the general pattern suggested by most of the currently available data is representative of Mesoamerican phenomena or whether it is restricted to arid zones where climatic conditions favor preservation.

[See also DOMESTICATION OF ANIMALS; DOMESTICATION OF PLANTS; HOLOCENE: HOLOCENE ENVIRONMENTS IN THE AMERICAS; NORTH AMERICA, ORIGINS OF FOOD PRODUCTION IN; SOUTH AMERICA, ORIGINS OF FOOD PRODUCTION IN.]

■ Richard S. MacNeish, "Preliminary Archaeological Investigations in the Sierra de Tamaulipas," *Transactions of the American Philosophical Society* 48 (1958). Paul C. Mangelsdorf, Richard S. MacNeish, and Gordon R. Willey, "Origins of Agriculture in Middle America," *Handbook of Middle American Indians*, Vol. 1 (1964), pp. 427–445. Douglas Byers, ed., *The Prehistory of the Tehuacan Valley*, Vol. I (1967). Kent V. Flannery, "The Origins of Agriculture," *Annual Review of Anthropology* 2 (1973); 271–310. Christine Niederberger, *Zohapilco: cinco milenios de ocupacion humana en un sitio lacustre de la Cuenca de Mexico* (1976). Christine Niederberger, "Early Sedentary Economy in the Basin of Mexico," *Science* 203 (1979): 131–142. Kent V. Flannery, ed., *Guila Naquitz: Archaic Foraging and Early Agriculture in Oaxaca, Mexico* (1986). C. Earle Smith Jr., "Current Archaeological Evidence for the Beginning of American Agriculture," *Studies in the Neolithic Revolution and the Urban Revolution. The V. Gordon Colloquium*, Oxford, BAR International series 349 (1987): 81–102. A. Long et al., "First Direct AMS Dates on Early Maize from Tehuacan, Mexico," *Radiocarbon* 31 (1989): 1035–1040.

Emily McClung de Tapia

MESOPOTAMIA

The Rise of Urban Culture
Assyria
Sumer and Akkad
Babylonia

THE RISE OF URBAN CULTURE

The following chronology of Mesopotamia and its environmental setting pertain to the dates cited for events and reigns after the accession of Sargon of Agade as proposed by John A. Brinkman in A. L. Oppenheim's *Ancient Mesopotamia* (rev. ed., 1977). They fall into two groups, which have been arrived at by different means and have different levels of accuracy. The first group comprises dates after 1500 B.C. These are based ultimately on ancient Assyrian records and are likely to have a margin of error of less than a decade, with dates before 900 B.C. having a somewhat greater margin of error than those after 900. The second group of dates extends from Sargon's accession to the fall of Babylon at the end of the Old Babylonian Period and are based on movements of the planet Venus recorded during the reign of the Old Babylonian king Ammisaduqa. These movements follow a cycle of fifty-six or sixty-four years, giving rise to several possible series of dates: high, middle, and low. Because they appear most frequently in the scholarly literature, the dates used here are those of the middle chronology, which places the fall of Babylon in 1595. Nevertheless, strong arguments have been put forward in support of both the high and the low chronologies.

Dates before the accession of Sargon, generally expressed here in terms of centuries or millennia, are based on a combination of archaeological evidence, conventional

wisdom, and radiocarbon dates that are still too frequently inconsistent with one another. These dates have the least claim to accuracy and are likely to undergo considerable revision and refinement in the future.

Environment. Bounded by mountains to the north and east and by deserts to the south and west, ancient Mesopotamia had roughly the same borders as has the modern republic of Iraq. In the north were the rolling plains of Assyria, where rainfall was adequate for agriculture without irrigation. The south, heartland of the world's first civilization, was a substantially different environment: a hot, dry, resource-poor alluvial plain formed by the lower reaches of the Tigris and Euphrates Rivers. Here, due to the insufficient rainfall, agriculture was possible only with the aid of irrigation. In the far south the rivers formed a broad region of marshes at the head of the Persian Gulf.

Of the two rivers that shaped the landscape of southern Mesopotamia, the Euphrates was by far the more important during antiquity because its slower-moving waters could be more easily tapped for irrigation. In ancient times the river split up into several branches after entering the alluvial plain. The most important of the branches ran down the center of the plain, east of the river's modern course. It was along these central branches that the earliest cities developed.

The alluvial plain was capable, when irrigated, of producing the agricultural surpluses necessary to support the large, concentrated populations of the first cities. Yet it was also a risky environment for human endeavor, characterized by frequent destructive floods, changeable river channels, and the danger of rising soil salinity adversely affecting crop yields.

Rise of Cities. On the basis of excavations at Tell el-Oueili near Larsa (Senkerah), it seems that the alluvial plain was settled no later than the early part of the sixth millennium B.C., corresponding to the archaeological period termed "Ubaid 0" and contemporary with the latter part of the Samarran period in northern Iraq. Earlier levels at Oueili remain to be excavated, so the early sixth-millennium date almost certainly will be pushed back further.

In the Ubaid 0 Period, Oueili was a settled agricultural village made up of large, architecturally sophisticated houses, whose inhabitants subsisted on what would thereafter remain the basic Mesopotamian diet: domesticated grains (barley and wheat) and domesticated animals (cow, pig, sheep, and goat). Remains of wild fauna were rare, indicating that hunting was not a major factor in the economy.

Since the lowest levels at Oueili remain to be excavated, we should not attempt to characterize the nature of the earliest settlements in the alluvium. We can say, however, that from Ubaid 0 on, there is a demonstrable continuity of material culture, particularly evident in the architectural and ceramic remains, into historical times.

The evolution of monumental architecture over a period of perhaps 3,000 years is attested at Eridu (Abu Shahrein), where a superimposed series of temples were found dating from the Ubaid (sixth millennium B.C.) through the Ur III (twenty-first century B.C.) periods. In a level dated to Ubaid 1, a small room founded on clean sand and containing a possible cult niche and offering table appears to represent the earliest temple in the sequence. Identifiably religious buildings were absent from the levels immediately above, but they may have been situated beyond the limits of the small excavation trench. Beginning in the Ubaid 3 levels, however, there was an unbroken sequence of temples that became larger and more substantial over time. These were erected on a platform that grew taller with each renovation. The buildings display the characteristic features of early Mesopotamian temples: a tripartite plan, a buttressed facade, and a long central room containing an offering table and an altar. Considerable community resources must have gone into its repeated renovations and embellishments, and by the end of the Ubaid Period the elevated temple at Eridu was the most prominent building in the settlement. However, we can say little about the nature of the temple institution itself. We know nothing about any other temple holdings, nor can we speculate intelligently about the relationship that existed between the temple and the people of Eridu.

The settlement at Eridu, of course, consisted of more than just a temple building. Clustered at the foot of the temple platform was a settlement that by the Late Ubaid Period (Ubaid 4) was about 30 acres (12 ha) in area. The contemporary settlements at Oueili, Ur (Tell al-Muqayyar), and Uruk (Warka) were all of similar size, which represents the maximum for Ubaid settlements. Eridu's cemetery contained around a thousand burials, nearly 200 of which have been excavated. The similar nature of the grave goods found in each burial suggests that there was little social differentiation among the people buried there. If this cemetery represents a cross section of Ubaid society at the end of the period, then we can conclude there was still little social stratification in lower Mesopotamia at that time.

The date of the transition from Ubaid 4 to the Early Uruk Period is a matter of dispute. Calibrated radiocarbon dates from Oueili indicate that it occurred around 4500 B.C., while scholars have generally placed it early in the fourth millennium, around 3750 B.C., a difference of around three-quarters of a millennium. In any case, the succeeding Early and Middle Uruk Periods are poorly known, except as assemblages of chronologically diagnostic pottery that have been identified in archaeological surface surveys. This lack of information is regrettable, for, based on those same surface surveys, these are the periods that mark the transition from a social and political landscape made up of independent, egalitarian villages to one organized around large, socially stratified urban polities. In other words, the Early and Middle Uruk periods saw the development of the world's first cities.

This development culminated in the full-blown urban society of the Late Uruk, best attested archaeologically at the type-site of Uruk, where the size and scope of the architectural remains give some impression of this civilization's achievements. Uruk, which had occupied approximately 173 acres (70 ha) during the early and middle Uruk, grew to around 247 acres (100 ha) in the Late Uruk Period, and at that time was almost certainly the largest and most important city in southern Mesopotamia.

Two areas of the Late Uruk city have been excavated. In the first, a forty-three-foot (13 m) high platform crowned by a whitewashed tripartite temple, the so-called White Temple, was the culmination of a series of such temples extending back into the Ubaid. About a third of a mile (.5 km) east of the White Temple, the stratified remains of a group of major buildings were uncovered. Several of them were decorated with characteristic Late Uruk cone mosaics, and some may be temples, based on their tripartite plans. Little else can be said about these buildings because of their extremely fragmentary condition, but their large size and the frequency with which they were replaced attest to the human and material resources under the control of Uruk's rulers.

In addition to the buildings at Uruk and the temple sequence at Eridu, which continued through the Uruk Period, archaeologists have also uncovered a Late Uruk temple at Tell Uqair in the northern part of the alluvial plain, whose painted walls included figures of a leopard and a bull.

Given the paucity of excavated sites, archaeologists have relied on data from surface surveys to trace developments during the Uruk Period; as a result of this, most of the evidence at our disposal has to do primarily with changes in settlement size. The evolution of urban society, however, clearly involved much more than just a decision by large numbers of people to live in close proximity to one another. During the fourth millennium the social structure of southern Mesopotamia must have been altered in fundamental ways. The strength and importance of kinship ties diminished in the face of new relationships based on territoriality: Where a person lived became a more important factor in his or her life than to whom he or she was related. Social classes began to emerge based on increasingly entrenched differences in wealth, power, and access to resources; the more stratified society became, the greater the coercive power its rulers could exercise over those beneath them in the social hierarchy. In this way, people, in numbers larger than had ever before been possible, could be marshaled and deployed to build their city's infrastructure—monumental buildings, defensive walls, and irrigation systems; to produce the economic surpluses necessary to support their rulers and others, including artists and artisans, who were not directly engaged in subsistence activities; and, when necessary, to fight in their city's army.

The consequences of the so-called urban revolution were not limited to the inhabitants of the cities. The lives of village cultivators changed immeasurably as well. They, too, now belonged to a city, and the courses of their lives were likewise now shaped by the decisions of others, people they almost certainly never met.

Over the span of the Uruk Period there were notable changes in the material culture. The painted, handmade pottery of the Ubaid was replaced by largely undecorated, mass-produced, wheel-made vessels in the Uruk. One especially diagnostic form, the crudely finished, mold-made beveled-rim bowl, is represented by tens of thousands of excavated examples. The presence of these bowls on sites stretching from southern Anatolia to southeastern Iran attest to the extended reach of Early Mesopotamian civilization during the fourth millennium. Although the potter's craft may have languished, artisans who worked in stone during the Late Uruk produced cylinder seals, statuary and relief carvings, for the major institutions and members of the elite classes, that manifest an astonishing level of skill and artistic accomplishment.

Cylinder seals first appeared in the Middle Uruk. Stamp seals had already been in use for centuries, but the new cylindrical shape made it easy to cover a clay sealing with a continuous impression, making any subsequent tampering with the sealing obvious. The unique scenes carved on a seal served to identify its owner, so that it effectively functioned as a modern signature. Such devices became essential to the successful operation of the increasingly impersonal and bureaucratic social and economic structure that developed during the Uruk Period.

The burgeoning complexity of the economic order and the urgent need to keep track of innumerable transactions in Late Uruk times resulted in the young civilization's most important invention, writing. The earliest script consisted of about 1,200 pictographic signs that were drawn on clay tablets. Though in theory these signs could be used to express any language, there is good reason to believe that the language being written was Sumerian, as was definitely the case during the following Jamdat Nasr Period. Besides economic texts, there were also lists of words, used to train members of the new scribal profession. A list of titles and professions, which continued to be copied a millennium later, hints at the already mature social hierarchy that characterized urban life at the end of the fourth millennium.

During the Late Uruk Period, Susa and the surrounding Susiana plain in southwestern Iran were clearly within the orbit of southern Mesopotamian civilization. Additionally, the southern cities established trading colonies in Iran, northern Mesopotamia, Syria, Anatolia, and possibly even Egypt. The largest and best-known of these is Habuba-Kabira South, which, with its temple acropolis on Tell Qannas, stretched for about a kilometer along the west bank of the Euphrates in northern Syria. In its architecture and material culture, Habuba was almost indistinguishable from contemporary southern Mesopotamian sites.

The very end of the fourth millennium in southern Mesopotamia is called the Jamdat Nasr Period, a transition to the Early Dynastic Period that followed. The use of writing continued to spread across the alluvial plain as the writing system itself evolved. The number of signs in use decreased, and instead of being drawn into the surface of the clay tablet, they began to be composed of several short, impressed strokes of a reed stylus, thus giving rise to the cuneiform script. Though the Jamdat Nasr Period is marked by a discernable withdrawal from the Late Uruk network of interregional connections, the cities of southern Mesopotamia nevertheless prospered and continued to grow.

[See also NEAR EAST: THE NEOLITHIC AND CHALCOLITHIC (PRE-BRONZE-AGE) PERIODS IN THE NEAR EAST; UR; URUK; WRITING: CUNEIFORM]

■ Seton Lloyd, *The Archaeology of Mesopotamia* (rev. ed., 1984). Hans J. Nissen, *The Early History of the Ancient Near East, 9000–2000 B.C.* (1988). Michael Roaf, *Cultural Atlas of Mesopotamia and the Ancient Near East* (1990). Jean-Louis Huot, "The First Farmers at Oueili," *Biblical Archaeologist* 55 (1992): 188–195.

James A. Armstrong

ASSYRIA

The Assyrian heartland occupied a triangular region bounded by the Tigris and Lesser Zab Rivers to the west and southeast respectively, and by the lower elevations of the Zagros Mountains to the north. From the middle of fourteenth century B.C. to the end of the seventh century B.C., this area, encompassing the cities of Ashur (Qal'at Sherqat), Arbela (Erbil), and Nineveh, formed the irreducible core of the Assyrian state, from which it grew during expansionist periods and to which it retreated in times of weakness. The impetus to unify the Assyrian heartland came from Ashur, where a series of energetic kings, starting with Ashur-uballit I (ca. 1363 to 1328 B.C.), launched Assyria on its imperial career.

Before the fourteenth century, Ashur had pursued a more modest path. In the late third millennium the city had been controlled by the southern Mesopotamian kingdoms. During the Old Assyrian Period (ca. 2000 to 1750 B.C.),

Ashur prospered as a commercial center, selling tin and textiles in Anatolia in exchange for silver and gold. Commercial success, however, did not lead to political expansion, for at the end of the nineteenth century the city came under the control of the Amorite Shamshi-Adad I (1813 to 1781 B.C.), who styled himself "king of Ashur." He ruled a domain stretching from the middle Euphrates eastward across northern Mesopotamia to the Zagros Mountains, an empire, however, that did not long outlast its founder. Little of Ashur's history during the succeeding centuries is known, but from the fifteenth century the city seems to have been under the control of the kingdom of Mitanni, which ruled much of northern Mesopotamia and northern Syria.

Beset by the Hittites to its west in the fourteenth century, Mitanni could not resist the expansion of Assyria on its eastern flank. After the disintegration of Mitanni, Assyria under Shalmaneser I (1273 to 1244 B.C.) and Tukulti-Ninurta I (1243 to 1207 B.C.) pushed west across northern Syria, extending its control as far as the Euphrates. Tukulti-Ninurta I also conquered Babylonia, carrying off Marduk, the god of Babylon. The first Assyrian king to establish a new city as his capital, he constructed Kar-Tukulti-Ninurta (Tulul al-Aqr) a few kilometers up the Tigris from Ashur. The new strength of Assyria was reflected in the Middle Assyrian cylinder seals, with their well-composed and beautifully engraved naturalistic scenes, frequently portraying animals, both real and imaginary, and low trees or bushes.

After decades of weakness following Tukulti-Ninurta I's assassination, Assyria regained something of its earlier greatness under Tiglathpileser I (1114 to 1076 B.C.). Tiglathpileser I reported hostile encounters with Aramaean tribes in his western campaigns. Although he was able to keep them at bay during his reign, after his death the Assyrian state nearly collapsed under their intrusive pressure.

Only in the late tenth century was Assyria again able to stir from its enclave east of the Tigris. This reassertion of Assyrian military and political strength culminated in the reigns of the first two great Neo-Assyrian kings, Ashurnasirpal II (883 to 859 B.C.) and his son Shalmaneser III (858 to 824 B.C.). By means of annual military campaigns Ashurnasirpal II was able to extend Assyrian power deep into the mountains to the north and east, as well as west to the Euphrates and even beyond, to the Mediterranean Sea.

Taking advantage of the considerable wealth flowing into his kingdom, Ashurnasirpal II built a new capital at Kalhu (Nimrud) south of Nineveh. He lined the walls of his palace with 6-feet- (2 m) high, exquisitely carved stone slabs that showed the ruthless invincibility of the king and his army, his personal prowess as a hunter, and his sanctity as divinely favored ruler. Nimrud was first excavated in the mid-nineteenth century by British adventurer Austen Henry *Layard, whose explorations there, together with his excavations at Nineveh and those of the French at Khorsabad, mark the birth of Mesopotamian archaeology. Led by M.E.L. Mallowan, the British returned to continue excavating Nimrud a century later. More recently the Iraqis have discovered royal tombs containing a treasure of golden jewelry.

Shalmaneser III asserted the power of Assyria against its northern enemy Urartu and fought against coalitions of small western states, including Israel. He also campaigned in Babylonia, helping quell a revolt against the Babylonian king, whom he seems to have regarded as an equal. The most important of Shalmaneser III's building projects was the great military arsenal at Kalhu, Fort Shalmaneser.

Shalmaneser III's successors were thrown onto the defensive by the growing power of *Urartu, as well as by the increasing independence of provincial Assyrian officials. Only with Tiglathpileser III's (744 to 727 B.C.) accession, probably through usurpation, was Assyria able to reverse the resulting decline. This able monarch recovered the territory lost during the preceding reigns. He then projected Assyrian power down to the border of Egypt, and at the opposite end of his empire he personally took the throne in Babylonia. In order to strengthen royal power and to reduce the likelihood of rebellion, he reorganized the army, reduced the size of Assyrian provinces, and instituted a policy of mass deportation for conquered peoples. These reforms provided the foundation for the final century of Assyrian greatness.

Sargon II (721 to 705 B.C.) decisively broke the power of Urartu in the northwest, but had to deal with an independent Babylonia throughout much of his reign. For his capital he founded a new city, Dur-Sharrukin (Khorsabad), excavated for the French by Paul Emile *Botta and Victor Place in the nineteenth century and again by the University of Chicago in the early twentieth century.

After Sargon II's death Sennacherib (704 to 681 B.C.) abandoned his father's capital and established his own at Nineveh. He surrounded the ancient city with a 7.4-mile (twelve-kilometer) wall and constructed major canals and aqueducts to supply new farmland in the vicinity of the capital. Assyrian artists achieved new levels of dramatic power in the large, detailed battle reliefs that adorned his palace, the most famous of which was the depiction of the siege of Lachish in Judah. In 689 B.C., Sennacherib utterly destroyed Babylon after a protracted series of campaigns against rebellious Babylonia.

A civil war triggered by Sennacherib's assassination was won by his son Esarhaddon (680 to 669 B.C.). The most significant military accomplishment of Esarhaddon's reign was the incorporation of Egypt into the empire. He also restored Babylon and appointed his son Shamash-shuma-ukin (667 to 648 B.C.) as its crown prince. At the same time he designated his son Ashurbanipal (668 to 627 B.C.) as crown prince of Assyria and made his vassals swear oaths to support the succession.

Ashurbanipal was something of a scholar, and the library he assembled at Nineveh is a primary resource for the modern understanding of Mesopotamian culture and history. His palace reliefs, particularly the hunting scenes, represent a high point of Assyrian artistic accomplishment.

In 652 Shamash-shuma-ukin rebelled against his brother, and though Ashurbanipal triumphed, the war seems to have sapped Assyria's strength irremediably. Little is known of Ashurbanipal's last years or of his successors' reigns. Assyria was finally brought down by a coalition of Medes and Babylonians. Though the last Assyrian king, Ashur-uballit II (611 to 609 B.C.), held out at Harran until 609, the true end of Assyria came three years earlier, in 612, when Nineveh's walls were breached and its palaces burned to the ground.

[See also BABYLON; NEAR EAST: IRON AGE CIVILIZATIONS IN THE NEAR EAST; NINEVEH; WRITING: CUNEIFORM.]

■ Seton Lloyd, The Archaeology of Mesopotamia, rev. ed., (1984). H.W.F. Saggs, The Might that Was Assyria (1984). Michael Roaf, Cultural Atlas of Mesopotamia and the Ancient Near East (1989). John M. Russell, Sennacherib's Palace Without Rival at Nineveh (1991).

James A. Armstrong

SUMER AND AKKAD

The period extending from around 3000 to around 2300 B.C. is referred to in Mesopotamia as the Early Dynastic Period. Until the end of the twenty-fifth century B.C., this period is essentially prehistoric, known only from its archaeological remains. From the end of the Early Dynastic, however, southern Mesopotamian history can begin to be reconstructed. Texts from that time reveal that the inhabitants of southern Mesopotamia divided their country into southern and northern regions, which they referred to as Sumer and Akkad respectively, with the dividing line at the city of Nippur (Nuffar). Akkad was also the name of the as-yet undiscovered capital of the late-third-millennium empire of Sargon and his descendants. To minimize confusion, the city's name will be rendered here as Agade.

Early Dynastic Period. During the third millennium, most of the inhabitants of Sumer, the southern region, spoke Sumerian, a language that is related to no known language, living or dead; in Akkad a significant proportion, if not a majority, of the population spoke Akkadian, a Semitic language related to Arabic, Hebrew, and a host of other languages. The Sumerians were present in the land at least from the late fourth millennium, and were almost certainly there much earlier. The presence of the Akkadians is first attested—by means of their names and their language—in mid-third-millennium texts. At that time they were fully integrated into urban society, which indicates that they had probably already been living in the plain for centuries, at least from the beginning of the millennium.

The earliest Akkadians have proved difficult to identify for two principal reasons. First, they adopted the writing system of the Sumerians to express their own language, a system that was to a great extent logographic, so many signs could be used without alteration to express either language. Furthermore, there was no distinctively northern (or Akkadian) material culture until the period of the empire of Sargon in the late third millennium.

It is abundantly clear that the division between Sumer and Akkad never represented a firm political or cultural boundary. Indeed, the city that sat astride that division, Nippur, was the seat of the head of the pantheon, Enlil, and was therefore one of the most important cities in the country. Nippur never had significant political or military power itself, but it came to be closely identified with the ideal of a unified state, comprising both Sumer and Akkad. Certainly by the twenty-fourth century B.C., if not before, any ruler who claimed dominion over the whole land had to possess Nippur, the religious capital. The Sumerian King List gives expression to this ideal of unification. According to this document, which was compiled in Isin (Ishan Bahriyat) at the beginning of the second millennium in order to buttress that city's claim to hegemony, the gods had throughout history chosen different cities in turn to rule over all of Sumer and Akkad.

Whatever the ideal, any unification of the country was in practice difficult and was rarely achieved. The norm was of individual, independent city-states, each with its own ruler, who was able when necessary to muster an army to fight on the city's behalf against its neighbors. Each city was the property of a god; for example, Uruk belonged to Inanna, goddess of love and war, while Ur served Nanna, the moon god. There were, of course, temples to other gods in each city as well. The temples, particularly in Sumer, owned much of the agricultural land—in some cases, most of it—

and thus played a major economic role in the lives of the cities and their citizens.

Uruk, probably the most important city of the fourth millennium, continued to take the developmental lead at the beginning of the third, when it grew to cover 1,000 acres (400 ha) and was enclosed by a great defensive rampart 6 miles (10 km) in circumference. Dense urban settlement actually spread well beyond the limits of the city's walls. At midmillennium, wealthy and powerful Lagash (al-Hiba), whose state atypically included the other cities of Girsu (Telloh) and Nina (Surghul), occupied more than 1,500 acres (600 ha). Uruk and Lagash were among the largest of the twenty or so cities strung out along the branches of the lower Euphrates, usually situated between 18 and 30 miles (30 and 50 km) apart. In several cases major centers grew up within sight of each other, Uruk and Larsa, for instance, or Eridu and Ur. Though wars between cities were not infrequent, cooperation was also known. At the very beginning of the third millennium, seal impressions appear that bear the symbols of groups of cities located in both Sumer and Akkad; these have been interpreted as evidence for the early existence of urban alliances.

Agricultural surpluses made the cities and their rulers quite wealthy, and they imported raw materials from Turkey, Syria, Arabia, Iran, Afghanistan, and even the Indus valley. The most spectacular testimony to this wealth was excavated in the so-called Royal Cemetery of Ur, dated to the twenty-sixth century B.C., where the richest burials, apparently those of the city's rulers, included vessels of gold along with jewelry and other items made of gold, silver, shell inlay, lapis lazuli, and other imported stones. These burials also attest to the practice, hitherto identified only at Ur, of sacrificing human victims, as many as eighty at one time, to accompany the wealthiest members of the community into the afterlife.

From a little before 2400 B.C., scholars can begin to sketch out something of the history of time. The largest collection of early historical texts comes from the city of Girsu in Lagash. These texts record the history of a border dispute with the neighboring city-state of Umma (Tell Jokha) that lasted several generations. Of particular interest is the fact that the border between the two states was established by an earlier ruler named Mesalim, who bore the title "king of Kish" and is known to have exercised suzerainty over Adab (Bismaya) and Lagash. Later in the third millennium, "king of Kish" was a symbolic title denoting lordship over the entire country, and the rulers who bore it did not actually come from Kish (Tell al-Uhaimer). This may indicate that early in the third millennium kings of Kish in fact ruled the whole country, a hegemony about which we otherwise know nothing. The significance of the title in the case of Mesalim, who otherwise is not known to have ruled at Kish, is uncertain.

City-states were not confined to the alluvial plain. In fact, the basic archaeological sequence for the entire third millennium was worked out from excavations at cities in the Diyala River basin, northeast of the plain. By midmillennium, urban-based polities dotted the landscape of northern Mesopotamia and northern Syria, and the influence of southern Mesopotamian culture was felt across a broad area. At *Mari (Tell Hariri) on the Euphrates, Semitic-speaking scribes were writing in Sumerian. Mari's material culture was in most respects virtually indistinguishable from that of the Sumerian heartland; among the votive statues found there are some of the finest known examples of Sumerian art. Farther to the north and west, the impact of Sumerian material culture was more attenuated. Nevertheless, at the north Syrian site of Tell Chuera, local artisans were carving statues in Sumerian style, while at *Ebla, modern Tell Mardikh, south of Aleppo, royal scribes during the twenty-fourth century were writing in Sumerian as well as utilizing cuneiform to express their own Semitic language.

Akkadian Period. Whatever the import of the earlier title "king of Kish," the unification of all the cities of Sumer and Akkad under one ruler was accomplished during the twenty-fourth century by Sargon of Agade (2334–2279 B.C.). In an act that would be repeated by Mesopotamian rulers for the next five centuries, the Akkadian Sargon then installed his daughter En-heduanna in Sumerian Ur as high priestess of the moon god Nanna, a symbolic expression of the country's unification.

Sargon's political ambitions were not limited to Sumer and Akkad. By the end of his reign, he had created an empire, extending its limits to include most of northern Mesopotamia and northern Syria and parts of western Iran. Sargon maintained a standing army, with 5,400 soldiers eating at his table daily. His empire, however, was brittle, and rebellions were frequent, climaxing with the near total revolt that greeted the accession of Naram-Sin (2254–2218 B.C.), his grandson.

To strengthen the imperial structure, Naram-Sin created a provincial system ruled by members of the royal family or close allies and made Akkadian the language of his new unified administration. On the ideological level, he claimed divinity, thereby placing himself on a plane higher than that occupied by his subject kings.

The Akkadian Period, especially the reign of Naram-Sin, represents a high point in the history of Mesopotamian *art. Cylinder seals, stone reliefs, and statues in cast copper—all are set apart by their accomplished naturalistic rendering and unrivalled sense of design and composition. The best pieces share in the restless energy and drive that characterized the period as a whole.

Naram-Sin's reforms notwithstanding, the empire began to fall apart during the reign of his son Shar-kali-sharri (2217–2193 B.C.). Gutian tribes from the Zagros Mountains played a major role in the Akkadian collapse, and in the chaotic aftermath they seized control of the northern part of the alluvial plain.

Period of Gudea and the Ur III Kings. For much of the twenty-second century B.C., Akkad endured the depredations both of the Gutians and of the Elamites of southwestern Iran. In much of Sumer, though, there seems to have been relative calm, security, and even prosperity. Certainly Lagash took advantage of its newly recovered independence, flourishing during this interlude. Gudea (ca. 2100 B.C.), Lagash's most famous ruler, erected a number of votive statues of himself at Girsu. While displaying the same high level of technical skill as the Akkadian works, they manifest an entirely different spirit. Missing here is the energy that infuses the earlier pieces. In its place is an almost tangible feeling of serenity, power, and satisfaction. Carved from diorite, a very hard black stone imported from India, the statues attest to Sumer's continuing wealth as well as the cosmopolitan nature of its commercial connections.

While Gudea ruled in Lagash, Utu-Hegal (2119–2113 B.C.) of Uruk took the first steps toward the reunification of the country by driving the Gutians out of Sumer and seizing the nearby city of Ur. He was succeeded by his governor at Ur, Ur-Nammu (2112–2095 B.C.). Founder of the Third Dynasty of Ur, Ur-Nammu completed the reunification of Sumer and Akkad by forcing the Elamites out of the northern region. The Ur III kings devoted considerable state resources to construction projects. In the cities of Ur, Nippur, Uruk, and Eridu, Ur-Nammu and Shulgi (2094–2047 B.C.), his successor, erected the first ziggurats, multi-stage temple platforms, and established overall plans for their religious precincts that survived at Ur, Nippur, and Uruk for more than 1,500 years.

Either Ur-Nammu or Shulgi promulgated the first known collection of laws. These laws differed from the later, more famous collection of Hammurabi in that *lex talionis*, the law of retaliation, was unknown. Bodily injury was compensated for financially instead of by mutilation or even death.

Shulgi was responsible for converting the kingdom into a centralized bureaucratic state. He divided his domain into provinces that were ruled by governors drawn usually from the local ruling families. Alongside these governors, however, he placed military commanders, outsiders to the local power structure who were personally loyal to him. In this fashion local sensitivities were appeased, yet local power was kept in check.

Shulgi instituted regional specialization for agricultural products and other goods. Such specialization necessitated a massive governmental redistribution system, which in turn meant that every item that passed through government hands, no matter how small, had to be recorded, giving rise to the thousands upon thousands of Ur III economic texts that have survived. Finally, like the kings of Agade before him, Shulgi made himself a god.

Expanding his domain to the north and east, Shulgi created new peripheral provinces, whose main purpose was to protect the heart of the kingdom. To the northwest and northeast were the tribal Amorites, whose encroachments Shu-Sin (2037–2029 B.C.) attempted to forestall by the construction of his Wall of Mardu, or Amorite Wall. By the reign of Ibbi-Sin (2028–2004 B.C.), one-time Iranian vassals were poised to attack from the east. Though Ibbi-Sin reigned twenty-four years, he controlled little more than Ur itself after his fifth year. Ishbi-Erra, his one-time subordinate, took power in Isin in 2017. Though he was nominally Ibbi-Sin's ally, Ishbi-Erra was clearly just waiting for the inevitable. The blow fell in 2004, when Kindattu of Anshan and Elam sacked Ur and took Ibbi-Sin into captivity.

[See also NEAR EAST: THE BRONZE AGE IN THE NEAR EAST; UR; URUK; WRITING: CUNEIFORM.]

■ Seton Lloyd, *The Archaeology of Mesopotamia* (rev. ed., 1984). Hans J. Nissen, *The Early History of the Ancient Near East, 9000–2000 B.C.* (1988). Michael Roaf, *Cultural Atlas of Mesopotamia and the Ancient Near East* (1990). Harriet Crawford, *Sumer and the Sumerians* (1991). J. N. Postgate, *Ancient Mesopotamia* (1992). Georges Roux, *Ancient Iraq* (3rd ed., 1992).

James A. Armstrong

BABYLONIA

The destruction of Ur was soon avenged by Ishbi-Erra of Isin, who drove the Elamites out and assumed the mantle of suzerainty over all Sumer and Akkad. After the expulsion of the Elamites, Isin's rule over the southern alluvial plain remained unchallenged for nearly a century, marking the first phase of the Isin-Larsa Period. During the twentieth century B.C., the Amorites, however, continued to infiltrate

from the northwest, and some cities came under their control.

By the nineteenth century B.C. the plain was a mosaic of small city-states, chief among them Isin, Larsa, *Uruk, and *Babylon. Despite the fact that most of the kings of these cities were Amorite, they still followed older Mesopotamian traditions. Thus, the rulers of the two most powerful states, Isin and Larsa, contended for Nippur, because its possession conferred the right to bear the old hegemonic title "king of Sumer and Akkad." Likewise, the possessor of the city of Ur exercised the centuries-old right to place his daughter as high priestess of Nanna. Amorite houses also ruled at Eshnunna (Tell Asmar) on the lower Diyala River and at Mari.

By the beginning of the eighteenth century, the political picture in southern Mesopotamia had become much simpler. After the conquest of Isin in 1794 by Rim-Sin I (1822–1763 B.C.) of Larsa, only two powers contended for power in the alluvial plain, Larsa in the south and Babylon in the north. At the same time, Shamshi-Adad I (1813–1781 B.C.), an Amorite, held sway in northern Mesopotamia from the Euphrates River to the Zagros Mountains.

Old Babylonian Period. The first half of the eighteenth century was marked by the collapse of Shamshi-Adad's kingdom after his death and the incorporation of all of southern Mesopotamia into the kingdom of Babylon by its strongest and most able ruler, Hammurabi (1792–1750 B.C.). This unification, which marks the beginning of the Old Babylonian Period, was accomplished late in Hammurabi's reign, after the defeat of an alliance of eastern states, including Elam, in 1764, and the conquest of rival power centers at Larsa (1763), Mari (1760 and 1757), and Eshnunna (1755). A large cuneiform archive—some 15,000 tablets—recovered from the ruins of the Mari palace, which was burned by Hammurabi in 1757, serve as our primary resource for the history of this period.

Almost nothing, however, is known of Hammurabi's Babylon, because its levels lie beneath the water table at the site. The diorite stele bearing Hammurabi's laws, perhaps the best known of all Mesopotamian antiquities, was found in the ruins of Susa in Iran, where it had been taken as a trophy of war in the twelfth century B.C. The 7.5-foot-high (2.3-m-high) stele was originally erected—perhaps at Babylon or Sippar (Abu Habbah)—shortly after the unification of the country. Though the laws themselves were almost certainly compiled at the beginning of Hammurabi's reign, the stele's prologue provides a glimpse of his kingdom at its height, with the king claiming suzerainty as far up the Tigris as Nineveh and as far up the Euphrates as Tuttul, at the junction of the Balikh and Euphrates rivers. The prologue also offers a theological explanation for Babylon's supremacy: the great gods Anu and Enlil had given to Marduk, Babylon's chief god, the functions of Enlil with respect to humanity.

Earlier collections of laws are known from the kingdoms of Ur, Isin, and Eshnunna. Such collections seem to have served more as an expression of an ideal society than as a true law code for the day-to-day administration of justice. Copies of Hammurabi's laws were placed in the kingdom's major cities, but of the numerous court cases known from the Old Babylonian Period, only one was adjudicated in accordance with their provisions.

Hammurabi's accomplishment did not survive the reign of his son Samsuiluna (1749–1712 B.C.), but it nevertheless represented a watershed in Mesopotamian history. Before

Hammurabi, the normal political order was of rival city-states contending with one another for preeminence and hegemony, the ideal envisioned in the Sumerian King List, where the mantle of rulership was assumed in turn by different cities. After Hammurabi the ideal was a territorial state, which can properly be referred to as Babylonia, whose political and cultural center would remain at Babylon.

This shift in political orientation was apparently reinforced by shifts in the flow of the Euphrates that weakened the old southern cities. During Samsuiluna's reign it appears that the bulk of the water in the Euphrates system shifted farther west, abandoning the cities along its courses in the central and southern plain. It is not certain what factors brought about such a change, but a combination of any or all of the following seem likely: an irreversible channel shift during a period of high stream flow, the diversion of water to support expanded irrigation *agriculture in the northwestern region around Babylon, or the diversion of the river as a tactic of war. This last suggestion is attractive because the crisis that hit the cities of the central and southern alluvial plain, a crisis so devastating that the cities of the far south were abandoned and all dated documents ceased for several centuries, occurred in 1739, a few years after the south broke away from Samsuiluna's rule and during the period when he was engaged in putting down the rebellion.

By 1720 the cities of the central plain, including Nippur and Isin, had been abandoned as well, and literate, urban Babylonia consisted of little more than the northwest corner of the alluvial plain and a stretch of land upstream along the Euphrates. In succeeding years, dune fields, traces of which have been found in excavations at Nippur and Larsa, blew through the ruins of the old cities of the Sumerian heartland. If the southern cities' collapse was due in part to environmental sabotage by Samsuiluna, then his victory was ultimately a bitter one, for in fighting to hold his kingdom together, he had helped eviscerate it.

The Old Babylonian kingdom continued to exist through the seventeenth century, growing progressively weaker, until Babylon was raided and sacked in 1595 by the Hittite king Mursilis I. In the far south a line of kings, called the Sealand Dynasty after the marshes from which they hailed, had arisen in the late eighteenth century, and for an indeterminate period controlled land as far north as Nippur. Some of the Sealand kings bore unusual Sumerian names, and they appear to have ruled at Babylon, perhaps only briefly, in the aftermath of the Hittite raid. Otherwise nothing is known of their kingdom. Indeed almost nothing is known of Babylonia for a century and a half after the Hittite sack.

Kassite Period. Sometime during this interval a dynasty of non-Mesopotamian origin, the Kassites, took power in Babylon. The Kassites are thought to have hailed originally from the mountainous region northeast of Babylonia, but in Mesopotamia they were first encountered along the middle Euphrates to the northwest. Like the Amorites before them, they seem to have infiltrated Babylonia during a period of upheaval, and at an opportune moment seized political control in Babylon. Sometime around the middle of the fifteenth century B.C., they reestablished Babylonian hegemony over the far south and, except for a short period during the late thirteenth century, the country remained united under their rule for about three hundred years.

On the domestic front the Kassites adopted and promoted the culture of their new domain. They seem to have encouraged the preservation of older Mesopotamian literary traditions. Shrines in the old Sumerian cities were repaired and renovated for the first time in several centuries. They also invested considerable resources in the canal systems, apparently in an attempt to bring water back to the center of the alluvial plain from the west. The lines of several such networks have been identified through archaeological surface surveys in the vicinity of Nippur in the central alluvial plain and farther south at Uruk. Such undertakings could not have been accomplished overnight and must have taken decades to bring to completion. For example, even though the Kassites had reestablished political control over all of Babylonia by the midfifteenth century, it took another hundred years for signs of new life to appear at the venerable city of Nippur. A principal beneficiary of royal largesse, Nippur thereafter grew to become one of the major cities of the kingdom during the Kassite Period.

Although much effort was devoted to the reconstruction of older Mesopotamian centers, the Kassites did found at least one new city. Dur-Kurigalzu (Aqar Quf), the Fortress of Kurigalzu, which sits today along the western outskirts of Baghdad, was erected by Kurigalzu I (early fourteenth century B.C.) on the narrow neck of land between the Tigris and Euphrates rivers at their closest approach to one another. Excavators have explored the city's ziggurat complex and a large palace that was rebuilt several times during the Kassite Period. Though some questions having to do with its internal chronology remain unanswered, its overall function seems clear: like Shu-Sin's Wall of Mardu in the third millennium and Nebuchadrezzar II's defensive walls of the sixth century, Dur-Kurigalzu was built to control the northern approaches to Babylonia and to defend it against invaders.

One of the most characteristic of Kassite artifacts is the *kudurru*, typically a stone stele or tablet bearing the text of a royal land grant together with the remission of specific taxes and corvée obligations. Divine symbols, which apparently served for protection, were also carved on the stone's surfaces. Excavated examples have been found in temples where they were erected. A few early *kudurrus* can be dated to the fourteenth century B.C.; they are more commonly found in the latter part of the Kassite Period and during the post-Kassite centuries.

In the realm of foreign affairs, the Kassites were operating in a world much larger than that of their predecessors. At the beginning of the fourteenth century, Babylonia was one of several major powers—the others were *Egypt, Mitanni, and the Hittite kingdom—who among them controlled most of the Near East. The kings regarded one another as equals and for several decades carried on a lively correspondence in Babylonian, the language of international diplomacy. Traces of this correspondence have been found at several Middle Eastern sites, but the greatest part, some 350 tablets, was discovered in A.D. 1887 at el-Amarna, ancient Akhetaten, the capital of the Egyptian king Akhenaten. From their letters we learn that these kings exchanged ambassadors, sent one another costly presents, and arranged diplomatic marriages among their families.

The relationship between Babylonia and Egypt seems to have grown more distant during the latter half of the fourteenth century. At about the same time, Assyria, newly emergent under Ashur-uballit I (1363–1328 B.C.), was recognized as a major power in the region, though not without some grumbling on the part of Burna-buriash II (1359–1333 B.C.) of Babylonia, who seems to have regarded the Assyrians as his subjects. Whatever the nature of the Babylonians' reservations, Assyria was soon acting like a major power. For example, when Kara-hardash (1333 B.C.), Burna-buriash II's successor and son from his marriage to Ashur-uballit I's daughter, was deposed, Ashur-uballit I descended on Babylon and installed Kurigalzu II (1332–1308 B.C.), his own nominee from the Kassite royal house, on the throne. Babylonia continued to maintain close but frequently tense relations with Assyria as the balance of power between them shifted back and forth.

A century later, in the 1220s, Tukulti-Ninurta I (1243–1207 B.C.), the most energetic of the Middle Assyrian monarchs, attacked Babylonia, claiming that the Kassite Kashtiliashu IV (1232–1225 B.C.) had attacked first. Tukulti-Ninurta I deposed the Babylonian king and took the Babylonian throne himself in 1224 B.C. He then appointed a series of local nominees to rule the country for him. Although the Kassites finally dislodged the Assyrians and extended their rule for another half-century, the countryside had suffered from the depredations of the Elamites during the interim, and much of the system that carried irrigation water to the center of the country seems to have broken down. The Elamites and the Assyrians attacked Babylonia again in the middle of the twelfth century. Shutruk-Nahhunte of Elam invaded around 1160 and carried off numerous monuments as booty, including Hammurabi's laws and Naram-Sin's victory stele. Several years later, his son Kutir-Nahhunte brought the Kassite dynasty to an ignominious end with his capture of Enlil-nadin-ahi (1157–1155 B.C.), its last king, and his seizure of the statue of Marduk, which he carried off to Susa.

Unstable Conditions. The most celebrated of the successors of the Kassites in Babylonia was Nebuchadrezzar I (1125–1104 B.C.), who attacked Susa in a daring summer raid and recaptured the Marduk's statue. Nebuchadrezzar I's victory notwithstanding, Babylonia at the end of the twelfth century was in fact entering an extended period of military weakness and political instability. The Assyrians under Tiglathpileser I (1114–1076 B.C.) sacked Babylon at the beginning of the eleventh century. However, the greater threat to Babylonia's existence came from another direction. Between the eleventh and ninth centuries, Babylonia endured the migration of Aramaean and Chaldaean tribes into the alluvial plain and their settlement throughout the country. During the darkest years of the tenth century, conditions in the countryside around Babylon were so unsettled that the New Year's festival, which necessitated a journey by Marduk outside the city walls, was repeatedly cancelled. In later years, leaders of these tribes would themselves sit on the Babylonian throne.

From the middle of the ninth century until the end of the seventh, the Babylonians had to deal with the expansionist aims of their northern neighbor, Assyria. Assyria overshadowed and dominated Babylonia, indirectly or directly, throughout this period. Over time, the Assyrians became more intimately involved in running Babylonian affairs, with several of the later Assyrian kings actually taking the Babylonian throne or installing their sons there to rule on their behalf. Rebellions repeatedly broke out, however, and finally the Assyrian Sennacherib (704–681 B.C.) was moved to destroy Babylon completely. But Assyrian feelings toward Babylonia were always ambivalent. The reality of having to deal with an incessantly fractious and rebellious Babylonia inspired rage in the Assyrians, but at the same time they had the deepest respect for the ancient civilization of southern Mesopotamia and for its gods. Thus Sennacherib's son Esarhaddon (680–669 B.C.) rebuilt Babylon after his father's death. With the accession of Esarhaddon's son, Shamash-shuma-ukin (667–648 B.C.), to the Babylonian throne, the country entered some four decades of relative stability, punctuated, nevertheless, by Shamash-shuma-ukin's own rebellion against his brother Ashurbanipal (668–627 B.C.) in 652. The stability that the Assyrians finally achieved in Babylonia had an unintended consequence in providing a foundation for the consolidation of Babylonian political, economic, and military power. Thus, when Assyria faltered in the late seventh century, Nabopolassar (625–605 B.C.) successfully threw off the Assyrian yoke. Babylonia then went on the offensive in coalition with the Medes of northwestern Iran, destroying Assyria completely in a series of campaigns that took place between 615 and 609.

Neo-Babylonian Empire. The Babylonians under Nabopolassar and his son Nebuchadrezzar II (604–562 B.C.) inherited rule over the western portions of the Assyrian Empire. After taking the throne, Nebuchadrezzar II continued to campaign in the west. He first conquered *Jerusalem in 597, and returned to destroy the rebellious city in 586. The course of his campaigns in other parts of the Neo-Babylonian empire is less certain.

With the wealth that was now theirs to command, the Babylonians completely renovated Babylon to fit its new role as imperial capital. Some 3 square miles (8 sq km) were enclosed by new city walls. The palaces and temples of the city were enlarged and embellished, frequently utilizing expensive baked bricks instead of the customary sun-dried variety. Stones were even imported to pave the Processional Way. Multicolored, glazed bricks depicting lions in relief formed a frieze on either side of this street, while the Ishtar Gate through which it passed was similarly decorated with bulls and dragons. The as-yet undiscovered Hanging Gardens, Nebuchadrezzar II's most famous construction, were built as an antidote to homesickness for his Median wife. Nebuchadrezzar II also built two walls to defend against attacks from the north, one between Babylon and Kish immediately to the north of those two cities, the other between the Euphrates and the Tigris just north of Sippar.

The years immediately following Nebuchadnezzar's death were a confused time, with his son, son-in-law, and young grandson taking the throne in quick succession. After the last of these was murdered, the assassins gave the throne to Nabonidus (555–539 B.C.), son of the governor of Harran. Nabonidus was an ardent follower of the cult of Sin, the moon god, and he seems to have neglected and offended the Babylonian religious establishment. Furthermore he abandoned Babylonia for ten years to dwell at Taima in northern Arabia, and because of his absence the New Year's festival could not be observed at Babylon, further increasing popular resentment.

Soon after Nabonidus's return from Arabia, he faced a new threat in the form of Cyrus II (559–530 B.C.) of Persia. Over the course of two decades, Cyrus II had conquered an empire stretching from the Indus to the Aegean, and in 539 he turned his attention toward Babylonia, whose capitulation was almost immediate. In quick succession, the Persians defeated the Babylonian army at Opis on the Tigris, took Sippar without a fight, and entered Babylon unopposed. The Persian king seems to have been greeted by the citizens less as a conquerer than as a restorer of ancient Babylonian traditions.

In fact, however, everything had changed. While the advent of Persian rule at Babylon was not the end of Babylonian history, the country had nevertheless irretrievably lost its independence and would henceforward be ruled by others.

[*See also* MARI; NEAR EAST, *articles on* THE NEOLITHIC AND CHALCOLITHIC (PRE-BRONZE-AGE) PERIODS IN THE NEAR EAST, THE BRONZE AGE IN THE NEAR EAST, IRON AGE CIVILIZATIONS IN THE NEAR EAST; NINEVEH; UR; WRITING: CUNEIFORM.]

■ Seton Lloyd, *The Archaeology of Mesopotamia* (rev. ed., 1984). Joan Oates, *Babylon* (rev. ed., 1986). Michael Roaf, *Cultural Atlas of Mesopotamia and the Ancient Near East* (1990). Georges Roux, *Ancient Iraq* (3rd ed., 1992).

James A. Armstrong

METALLURGY

Metallurgy in the Old World
Metallurgy in the Americas

METALLURGY IN THE OLD WORLD

Metals, together with *ceramics, were the first synthetic materials, and their production was at the forefront of human technical development. The ever-increasing reliance on tools and weapons impinges on many other areas beyond the purely technical, including the very organization of society itself.

Ancient mines and smelting places are now being recognized and investigated in increasing numbers around the world. The debris of production, the slags, fragments of furnaces, crucibles, tuyeres, and other refractories survive in quantity, together sometimes with intact furnaces themselves. Their careful excavation and detailed scientific study can reveal many of the operating parameters of the ancient processes. These can be checked and amplified by experimental simulations. In general, early written sources are often confused and sparing in detail and serious practical sourcebooks only begin in the Medieval Period with texts such as Theophilus on metalworking, culminating in Agricola's *De re Metallica*, whose publication in 1553 may be said to end the prehistory of metallurgy.

Neolithic cultures used native copper from the eighth millennium B.C. on. This was part of a general interest in exotic materials such as obsidian and bitumen but included purely decorative prestige materials such as lapis lazuli. The first metal was collected from surface outcrops, such as those at Caonüyü Tepe in southern *Anatolia and distributed over very wide areas. It was fashioned into small decorative pins and pendants, a phase that has aptly been called trinket metallurgy.

The metal was initially shaped solely by successive hammering and annealing. Once copper had been heated enough to melt and cast it (over 1,981.4° F or 1,083° C), there was no great barrier to smelting the metal from its ores. Native copper is found in association with copper ores, and smelting the native metal with mineral attached would inevitably have led to smelting. Evidence for the melting and smelting of copper in the form of crucibles and primitive slags have been found at sites such as *Catal Hüyük dating from the sixth millennium B.C. It is perhaps significant that the first artifacts of lead, which does not occur as a native metal, are also known from this period. From the fifth and fourth millennia B.C. comes the first evidence for mines and smelting places. The first mines were generally simple quarries, trenches, or small pits, where the ore outcropped at the surface and was followed down until work was halted by drainage or ventilation problems. The most common surviving mining tools are stone hammers. These are cobbles of locally available hard rock, typically weighing between two and seven pounds (1 and 3 kg). They usually have a meridional groove or some indentation to aid hafting. Antler picks and other tools of bone or wood were also widely used but less often survive. The host rock was normally too hard to be attacked directly with such tools, but first had to be weakened by fire setting, which has left characteristic smooth, continuous workings with rounded profiles.

The ore would have been coarsely crushed and the mineral carefully sorted out by hand picking or washing (known as *beneficiation*). The earliest smelting processes, as evidenced at such sites as Feinan in Jordan or Los Millares in Spain, operated at relatively low temperatures and in poor reducing conditions, apparently often in simple hearths or crucibles with air supplied through blowpipes rather than in true furnaces. One consequence is that little or no slag or other permanent debris was formed, and so there is now little tangible evidence of the processes. During the third millennium B.C. there were major developments; metal was smelted in small furnaces blown by bellows. The more rigorous smelting conditions meant that it was now possible to melt out the waste material in the ore (known as the *gangue*) as a liquid slag that could be periodically tapped out of the furnace, enabling the process to continue for many hours and a considerable body of metal to build up in the bottom of the furnace. The long-term excavation and scientific study of the mines and smelters at Feinan, and also at Timna in Israel, have greatly increased our knowledge of the development of nonferrous smelting technologies in the Bronze Age. These processes continued without great change until the Medieval Period and the application of waterpower to the bellows, which enabled much bigger furnaces to be used.

Copper and lead were joined by gold, the earliest use of which seems to have been at *Varna in Bulgaria in the fifth millennium B.C. Throughout antiquity, native gold was obtained from secondary alluvial deposits by panning or other forms of washing.

Silver was also known from the fifth millennium B.C., probably from native silver and some very rich ores. Most silver, however, was and is obtained from very low-grade ores, usually contained within lead ores. By the third millennium B.C., silver was being recovered from lead by cupellation. In this process, air was blown across the molten argentiferous lead in an open hearth or crucible (the *cupel*) at temperatures of approximately 1,832° F (1,000° C), causing the lead to oxidize to litharge, adsorbing all other impurities, and leaving the pure molten silver "floating like oil on water," to quote Pliny's memorable phrase from *Natural History*.

Copper ores often contain some arsenic, and when smelted these would have produced a natural alloy. Arsenical coppers are common in Bronze Age cultures across the world, but the extent to which they should be regarded as deliberate alloys, or even whether their potential metallurgical properties were appreciated or realized, is still very uncertain.

Tin ores are of rather limited occurrence, but the metal was known and used to make the alloy bronze from the early third millennium B.C. The sources of tin used in the eastern Mediterranean and Middle East in antiquity have long been a subject of debate, but the discovery of major tin mines at Kestel in the Taurus mountains of southern Anatolia have gone some way to resolving this question. At the same time, the discovery suggests that there are many more sources that would now be regarded as insignificant, waiting to be rediscovered.

The question of long-distance trade in metals such as tin raises the problem of the dissemination of metallurgy itself. It seems certain that metal was first smelted within the Middle East, but it is still not certain to what degree metallurgy spread to other parts of the Old World or was developed independently. This is of course another aspect of the *diffusion versus independent discovery argument. Extractive metallurgy, by its very nature, could not develop continuously, but only where the ore bodies occurred, often hundreds of miles apart, and more recent studies have tended to support independent discovery.

Iron is a very different and fascinating metal, being commonplace yet requiring the highest technology to realize its full potential. Meteoric iron was used on a very minor scale from the inception of metallurgy, and was known as "metal from heaven" in many early cultures. The smelting of iron probably began in the later third millennium B.C., but only began to gain in popularity a thousand years later. Because of its high melting point (2,786° F or 1,530° C) iron was produced as a solid lump (the bloom) in the West and hammered to shape (forged). When combined with a little carbon (steel) the properties can be dramatically improved by the correct heat treatment (quenching and tempering), and this seems to have been known from the late second millennium B.C. The superiority of the metal coupled with the ubiquity of the ores ensured the rapid spread of iron working throughout the Old World in the early first millennium B.C. This must have had a major impact on existing trade networks and increased enormously the availability of metal for tools and weapons. In China technical developments were very different. From the middle of the first millennium B.C., liquid iron was being used on a large scale, with modifications to produce good-quality castings for everyday items.

In the latter part of the first millennium B.C., brass began to be made by reacting copper with calcined zinc ore and charcoal in a closed crucible at temperatures of approximately 1,832° F (1,000° C). During the first millennium A.D., it largely replaced bronze as the usual copper alloy everywhere except in China. Zinc itself is a very volatile metal and could only be isolated and collected by distillation. This was achieved in India about 1,000 years ago, and in China somewhat later. These advanced technologies, together with the blast furnace for producing cast iron, brought metallurgy into the modern world.

[See also MINES AND QUARRIES, articles on INTRODUCTION, CENTRAL AND EASTERN EUROPEAN COPPER MINES, GREEK AND ROMAN MINES.]

■ John Percy, Metallurgy: Fuel, Fireclay, Copper, Zinc and Brass (1860); Iron (1864); Lead (1870); Gold and Silver, Pt. 1: Silver (1880). Georg Bauer (Agricola), De re Metallica, trans. and ed. H. C. and H. L. Hoover (1912, reissued 1950). John G. Hawthorne and Cyril Stanley Smith, eds. and trans., On Divers Arts: The Treatise of Theophilus, (1963). R. Maddin, The Beginning of the Use of Metals and Alloys (1988). W. Rostoker and B. Bronson, Pre-Industrial Iron (1990). R. F. Tylecote, A History of Metallurgy, 2nd ed. (1991). P. T. Craddock, Early Mining and Metal Production (1995).

Paul T. Craddock

METALLURGY IN THE AMERICAS

American metallurgy developed in two primary zones, in the mineral-rich regions of Peru, Bolivia, and Ecuador, where the first evidence appears around 1500 B.C., and in lower Central America and Colombia, where the technology emerged at around A.D. 100. We do not know whether these two technologies developed independently or from a common source. The later metallurgy of *Mesoamerica, which appeared at about A.D. 650 in the western region, was rooted in these two technologies, but West Mexican artisans reconfigured certain elements, creating a local metallurgy that constituted a unique expression of them. Several major metallurgical traditions are associated with these three primary technologies but have not been as extensively studied: that of the southern Andean highlands; the elite and sumptuary component of the metallurgy of Ecuador, and Oaxaca's complex technology. However, even in the case of the three best-known technologies—those of the Central Andes, lower Central America and Colombia, and West Mexico—our evidence is preponderantly technical and stylistic. While we can use documentary and other sources to reconstruct aspects of the social milieu in which they developed, we have relatively little archaeological evidence from mining, smelting, and production sites and consequently, chronologies are tentative.

These three metallurgies differ in the metals and alloys used, in fabrication methods, and in the kinds of objects crafted. The differences arise from the range of native metals and ore minerals present in each zone and their physical and mechanical properties. They also reflect the particulars of the historical circumstances in which the technologies developed, factors that shaped the choices these artisans made among various technical alternatives.

Central Andean smiths worked metal as a solid, hammering tools to shape and fashioning ornaments and ritual items from sheet metal. They were principally interested in metallic color, especially the colors of gold and silver which, in this and other regions of the Americas, were associated with divinities. By the Early Intermediate Period (ca. 200 B.C.–A.D. 600), artisans in highland Andean and coastal zones were making ritual and ornamental sheet metal objects from gold and/or silver or copper-gold (tumbaga), copper-silver, and copper-silver-gold alloys. The lamellar microstructure of copper-silver alloys allowed smiths to fashion thin, flexible, silvery-looking metallic sheet even when the silver concentration was relatively low. Copper-silver alloy objects first appeared around A.D. 300, and by 900 to 1100 became abundant, as at the coastal site of La Compania in southern Ecuador; copper-gold first appeared at about A.D. 400. Central Andean smiths altered the surface color of objects made from copper-gold and copper-silver alloys by processes of depletion gilding and silvering. They also used electrochemical plating methods to gild copper objects. These Andean metalworkers also developed the two bronze alloys. Copper-tin bronze objects occured first in the southern Andean highlands, where tin deposits are plentiful. The use of this alloy became widespread after about A.D. 900 for tools and occasional sumptuary items; tin bronze was restricted to that region and to the adjacent coastal zone until the Inca expansion in 1438. Copper-arsenic alloys became a kind of all-purpose material for tools, axe monies, and other items in northern Peru and southern Ecuador by about A.D. 900 although examples of objects made from the alloy occur on the Santa Elena Peninsula by about A.D. 500. Batan Grande on the north coast of Peru emerged as a center of production for copper-arsenic bronze at about A.D. 900.

Lower Central American and Colombian smiths treated

metal as a liquid, casting it to shape using the lost-wax method or one- or two-piece molds. Most objects were made from gold or tumbaga, and were ritual and status items: pins, nose rings and earrings, zoomorphic and anthropomorphic figurines, and vessels. A smaller number were made from silver or from copper. These smiths, were also interested in metallic colors, particularly the range of golden hues achieved by varying alloy concentrations. The proportion of tools to these sumptuary items is extremely low, and results in part from the dearth of arsenic-bearing ore minerals or tin deposits that would allow a bronze tool technology. Researchers have identified distinct stylistic traditions for various regions of Colombia as well as Panama and Costa Rica. A unique gold-platinum metallurgy developed in Esmeraldas, the northernmost province of Ecuador. Objects made from this alloy tend to be small and are predominantly of sheet metal.

West Mexican metallurgy developed from these two traditions. West Mexican smiths were particularly interested in metallic sound, manifest in the production of large numbers of bells, the single most abundant class of metal objects in this region. Bell sounds protected, and were associated with, particular West and Central Mexican deities that represented fertility and regeneration. During Period 1 (A.D. 600–1200/1300), smiths used copper to cast bells but also to fashion tweezers, needles, and rings which they cold-worked to shape. These objects appeared by at least 800 and possibly earlier at West Mexican sites such as Amapa, Tomatlan, and Infiernillo. Metal was virtually absent in all other regions of Mesoamerica during this time apart from a handful of trade items found in southeastern Mesoamerica, probably imported from lower Central America.

Technical studies show that these technical complexes—fabrication methods, object types, and knowledge of certain ore minerals or native metals—derive from the lower Central American and Colombian casting tradition and the cold-working technology of southern Ecuador and northern Peru. They were introduced during Period 1 to West Mexico via a maritime route by the seagoing peoples of coastal Ecuador. These maritime traders primarily transmitted technical knowledge, although they sometimes traded artifacts, which were then copied using local materials.

During Period 2 (A.D. 1200/1300–1521), West Mexican artisans incorporated copper-arsenic and copper-silver alloys, introduced from Ecuador and northern Peru, and copper-tin bronze, transmitted from the southern Andean area. In most cases West Mexican smiths used the alloys to optimize the design or function of objects or to alter the color of items they had previously made in copper. The alloying element, either tin or arsenic, is present in low concentrations (2–5%) in tools, sufficient to allow hardening without brittleness. In status items (bells, tweezers, rings, etc.), these elements appear in higher concentrations; in some lost-wax castings up to 20 percent. The design of these items requires the increased fluidity and strength of the alloys. High concentrations of the alloying element also alter metallic color from a coppery to a golden hue in tin bronzes and from pink to a silvery color in arsenic bronzes. To achieve a silvery color in sheet metal items, smiths used copper-silver alloys. These artisans also fashioned sheet metal objects from copper-silver-gold and copper-gold alloys, but we currently lack comprehensive technical studies of them.

During this same time (after A.D. 1200) the little-known metallurgy of Oaxaca began to flourish, and a southeastern Mesoamerican metalworking technology took shape. Both were strongly influenced by the casting traditions of lower Central America and Colombia. In the Huastec region of eastern Mexico a local bronze-working technology developed during the century before the Spanish invasion. Documentary sources indicate that the Aztec supported a variety of metalworking industries, but we have very little archaeological or technical evidence concerning them.

The striking characteristic of these ancient American technologies is that metalworkers elected to emphasize the sumptuary and symbolic possibilities of metal, even though in West Mexico, as well as the Central Andean region, bronze alloys were fully developed and used for tools. They did so by focusing on two properties that communicated elite status and associations with divinities: on color in the Central Andes, lower Central America, and Colombia, and on color and sound in West Mexico.

[See also CENTRAL AMERICA, ARCHAEOLOGY OF; METALS; SOUTH AMERICA: LOWLANDS CULTURES OF SOUTH AMERICA.]

■ Dorothy Hosler and Guy Stresser-Paen "The Huastec Region: A Second Locus for the Production of Bronze Alloys in Ancient Mesoamerica," *Science* 257 (1992): 1215–1220. Dorothy Hosler, *The Sounds and Colors of Power: The Sacred Metallurgical Technology of Ancient West Mexico* (1994). Heather Lechtman, "The Central Andes: Metallurgy without Iron," in *The Coming of the Age of Iron*, ed. T. A. Wertime and J. D. Muhly, pp. 267–334. Joseph J. Mountjoy, "On the Origin of West Mexican Metallurgy," *Mesoamerican Studies* 4 (1969):26–42.

Dorothy Hosler

METALS

Introduction
Analysis of Metals
Conservation of Metals

INTRODUCTION

Metals constitute one of the most important groups of materials utilized by humans from prehistory to modern times. The commonly available metals included: copper, lead, silver, gold, iron, tin, and arsenic. Of these, copper, silver, and gold can occur in the native state. Tin and arsenic found their primary use in making alloys with copper in the manufacture of tin bronze and arsenical coppers. Evidence for the use of metals begins to appear in the archaeological record from the Old World, particularly from Iran and *Anatolia, from about the eighth millennium B.C. Native copper was being exploited by this time to make simple knives or cutting edges which could be hafted or inset into wood and bone, or fashioned into jewelry. Metallic salts were essential ingredients of many pottery glazes, and it is possible that early production of copper by smelting copper oxide or copper carbonate ores evolved from earlier ceramic processes.

Meteoric iron could be chipped and hammered to produce crude but useful tools and implements such as small blades. The restricted availability of copper changed during the fourth to third millennium B.C. in the Old World, and the early centuries A.D. in the New World, when copper was being smelted from oxide or sulphide ores, often containing arsenic as an impurity. These arsenical copper alloys, often with 1 percent to 3 percent arsenic content, were used for tools, weapons, decorative metalwork, and jewelry. In both the New and Old Worlds, perhaps for reasons related to the geological nature of copper deposits or for cultural reasons, arsenical copper was replaced by bronze, the alloy of copper and tin, usually with 3 percent to 13 percent of tin, although higher tin bronzes were used in antiquity. Both the Roman and Inca Empires made extensive use of bronze for the manufacture of implements and jewelry.

Brass, the alloy of copper and zinc, was restricted in early usage, since, in order to smelt zinc, a temperature has to be reached in excess of the boiling point of the metal, with the result that zinc is lost as a vapor. By the co-smelting of zinc and copper ores, brass did become important in the early centuries A.D. during the Roman period, since the zinc vapor could be absorbed by the copper to make a brass in situ, a process that is called cementation. Zinc metal was not produced in quantity before the thirteenth century A.D., but once discovered, the use of brass became common and by the time of the Renaissance, many Renaissance bronzes were, in fact, cast from leaded brass alloys. Lead found considerable use as an additive to both bronze and brass castings, since these leaded alloys melt at a lower temperature and have good fluidity. Lead was easy to extract, and could be used for tokens, drainpipes, seals, and solders, and one of its principal uses in antiquity was as a source of silver. Lead ores contain silver, and by the second millennium B.C., silver was being extracted by the cupellation of lead. In this process, lead is oxidized in a porous crucible or cup, leaving a button of silver behind. The oxidized lead can be recovered by smelting the broken crucible. In early periods, for example during the second millennium B.C., it is possible that some silver was smelted directly from silver ores. In the New World, by Incan times, silver ores were being mixed with lead and co-smelted to extract silver. Silver found extensive use in the manufacture of coinage, utensils, bowls, plaques, and decorative metalwork, often alloyed with some copper to harden the alloy, since pure silver is too soft to withstand daily use and wear.

Gold was obtained from both placer and mine deposits, and since it is a soft metal, was easily shaped into jewelry from an early period. Native gold is usually an alloy of gold with between 1 percent to 40 percent of silver, the higher-silver-content alloys being called electrum. Gold could be refined by parting, a process in which minerals, such as salt, can combine with some of the silver, enriching the natural alloy in gold. The purification of gold is potentially important for the manufacture of gold leaf or foil, since relatively pure gold is required to produce very thin sheets for the gilding of metallic or other substrates, such as wood or plaster.

Rich burial tombs often reveal elaborately made gold jewelry buried with the body, often with rich adornments and other metallic objects. Particularly in the New World, gold-copper alloys, called tumbaga, were used extensively, shaped either by hammering and annealing or by casting to produce crowns, pectorals, diadems, bracelets, plaques, and necklaces, primarily for religious or shamanistic purposes.

The use of meteoric iron was limited in both geography and extent, and by the first millennium B.C., weapons such as daggers, swords, and knives were beginning to be made of smelted iron in some quantity. Iron working appeared early in Africa, where evidence for the smelting of iron occurs from about 400 B.C. without an intervening bronze age. In the New World, by contrast, iron remained unknown until the Spanish Conquest.

The Chinese metalsmiths had always excelled at producing cast bronze objects, and their expertise in casting was to continue with iron. Cast iron was produced in China in the early centuries B.C., over a thousand years earlier than in the West. Wrought iron, produced in Europe and Africa, is iron with slag inclusions containing no or very little carbon. Steel is iron containing from 0.1 percent to 1.0 percent of carbon, while cast iron contains from 2 percent to 4 percent carbon. Wrought iron was produced by the bloomery process in which a pasty mass of iron mixed with charcoal and slag had to be consolidated and worked by the smith to produce an ingot for making iron objects. In China, cast iron which is hard but brittle was used for agricultural implements and, by reducing the carbon content, used for steel weapons and tools. By about 500 B.C., iron was in use throughout Europe and the manufacture of steel gradually became important. Low-carbon steels, with 0.2 percent to 0.8 percent carbon characterized European products, while in India, crucible steels were made by the Wootz process which could have about 1 percent of carbon. Iron and plant material were sealed in luted ceramic crucibles and heated in a strong fire: The absorption of carbon into the iron produced a steel cake which could be wrought into swords and other weapons. During the Industrial Revolution, the manufacture of iron and cast iron became paramount, and many industrial archaeological sites and mechanical engines have been preserved from this period.

Archaeological evidence for metalworking may be associated with regions of burnt or discolored clay and with the remains of furnace structures and metalworking debris. The by-products of metalworking may include crushed ore, charcoal, crucible debris, tuyeres, bellows, and slag. In the extraction of metals from their ores, a flux was usually added to remove the unwanted silica or iron. These slags are usually iron silicates which could be tapped from the furnace and which flowed like lava, hardening into opaque glasses. Or, they may be broken fragments of slag which have been crushed to remove entrapped metal. The tuyeres were often made of cane tubes with ceramic tips in order to provide a forced draft of air. It is these ceramic cones or tips that survive in burial. Recognition of the function of furnace structures may be difficult if only the structure below ground has been preserved. Evidence for metalworking in major centers of production is often associated with large accumulations of slag, and scientific examination of this metalworking debris can be used to reconstruct the processes employed for extraction and working and to identify the metals being made or worked.

Since metals were used for so many purposes they may be associated with a wide array of other materials. The most common utilitarian association is with wood and bone as hafting materials or handles. Gold and silver jewelry is often inlaid with precious or semiprecious stones, or with synthetic substances such as glass and enamel. Apart from gold, the other metals may be covered with corrosion products due to corrosion in burial. This patina or corrosion crust may preserve the shape of the object or associated organic materials such as textiles, leather, feathers, etc., by preventing biodeterioration. Corroded metals may be unstable after excavation and require conservation, either on site, or in the laboratory. It is now possible to identify traces of organic residues, such as blood, food, fats, and oils associated with metallic artifacts, and as a result the preservation of associated burial residues is increasingly important.

[See also METALLURGY, articles on METALLURGY IN THE OLD WORLD, METALLURGY IN THE AMERICAS.]

■ Sir Joseph Needham, *Science and Civilisation in China*, vol. 5, part II (1954). Ronald F. Tylecote, *A History of Metallurgy* (1976). Bob F. Brown, Harry C. Burnett, W. Thomas Chase, Martha Goodway, Jerome Kruger, and Marcel Pourbaix, eds., *Corrosion and Metal Artifacts* (1977). Theodore Wertime and James Muhly, eds., *The Coming of the Age of Iron* (1980). Cyril Stanley Smith, *A Search for Structure: Selected Essays on Science, Art and History* (1981). Ronald F. Tylecote, *The Prehistory of Metallurgy in the British Isles* (1986). Robert Maddin, ed., *The Beginning of the Use of Metals and Alloys* (1988). David A. Scott and Pieter Meyers, eds., *Archaeometry of Pre-Columbian Sites and Artefacts* (1992).

David A. Scott

ANALYSIS OF METALS

Various analyses of metal artifacts are performed to help archaeologists answer any number of questions, but most often the questions revolve around sources of ores to produce artifacts, to identify trade patterns, to determine manufacturing technology, and to authenticate an object. There are a number of chemical analytical techniques that can answer these and other questions. In recent years the four most often used analytical techniques for metal analysis are X-ray fluorescence spectrometry, atomic absorption spectrometry, neutron activation analysis, and lead isotope analysis.

In X-ray fluorescence spectrometry, a sample is irradiated with a beam of X rays, which excites the electrons on the surface of the material, which, when the X-ray beam is switched off, produces secondary X rays that fluoresce in wavelengths characteristic of different elements and with energies proportional to the concentration of the elements in the metal. A radioisotope source such as cadmium-109 is usually used as the source for the X rays. This technique is good for determining elemental composition. It is quick, inexpensive, and nondestructive; however, if there is a corroded surface, more reliable results will be obtained with a small sample taken from the interior of the artifact. Even when samples are taken, damage to the artifact is minimal, and the test still reacts only to the exposed surfaces. Level of accuracy is in the 2 percent to 5 percent range.

This technique has been used to answer a number of questions concerning technologies. In the analysis of the silver coins and discs from the 1554 Spanish Plate Fleet, these tests showed that the silver discs underwent further processing before they were made into coinage, for the discs contained more gold and lead and less copper than did the coins. The same test showed that one silver disc contained a trace of mercury, which may indicate that the patio process of mercury amalgamation had been introduced into the processing of the silver ore by this date.

Atomic absorption spectrometry is performed by dissolving a small sample of the metal in diluted acid and then spraying the acid onto a flame, where a single element of interest can be measured. This technique is one of the most accurate methods for determining elemental composition and has an accuracy of 2 percent. It is insensitive to certain elements, and each element must be determined separately. Since the test is performed on a small sample dissolved in acid, the procedure records the constituents of the interior of the sample as well as the surface, depending on where the sample is taken.

In a recent analysis of the bronze ingots from the Late Bronze Age shipwreck at Uluburun, Turkey, atomic absorption spectrometry was used to determine the elemental constituents of the ingots in an attempt to identify the source of the ore. A weakness of this technique is that it determines elemental constituents, but it is not the most reliable technique for determining the derivation of artifacts from particular ore sources.

Neutron activation is a more involved and expensive technique of determining elemental constituents. It involves sending a sample into a nuclear reactor, where the sample is bombarded with neutrons transforming the atomic nuclei of the elements in the sample into unstable radioactive isotopes. These isotopes release gamma rays characteristic of each element present, and the intensity of the gamma radiation indicates the quantity of each element. The test is often chosen because of its speed, accuracy, and sensitivity to multielement determinations. In addition, the test is nondestructive, at least to artifacts small enough to be sent into the reactor in the available containers; otherwise samples have to be taken. It can measure the presence of a wider array of elements than either X-ray fluorescence or atomic absorption and has an accuracy of 2 percent to 5 percent. The drawback to the test is the unavailability of centers capable of conducting the test. There is also a danger of making lead- and gold-bearing samples radioactive for long periods of time and, thus, unsafe until the radioactivity drops to a safe level.

Neutron activation, as well as the other tests discussed above, accurately determines elemental concentrations, but the smelting of ores to produce metal artifacts often changes the concentration of trace elements. Impurities in the ore, mixing different metals together to form alloys, and the reuse of metal can alter the element composition for given artifacts. For this and other reasons, elemental measurements are not a reliable indicator of ore source.

Lead isotope analysis has become the test choice for those interested in determining ore sources of objects made of lead as well as those made of copper, silver, and tin, all of which invariably contain trace amounts of lead. This test is free from the limitations of tests that just determine elemental concentration. Naturally occurring lead and alloys containing trace amounts of lead have four naturally occurring isotopes (Pb^{204}, Pb^{206}, Pb^{207}, Pb^{208}) that can be measured in a thermal ionization spectrometer. The lead isotopes, especially the 206, 207, and 208 forms that result from the radioactive decay of uranium and thorium, vary in proportion according to the geological formation age of the ore. More important, the isotopic composition of lead varies in very narrow ranges within any ore source, and the composition of the ore remains unchanged through the smelting, refining, working, casting, or even corrosion of any artifact made with the ore. Thus, it is ideal for determining the source of ores and determining which metal artifacts containing traces of lead are derived from the same ore source.

Recent tests on ox-hide copper ingots from the Uluburun and Cape Gelidonya wrecks indicate that they are derived from Cypriot ores. Interestingly, when atomic absorption analyses were run on copper ingot samples from Uluburun, it was concluded that they were different enough from the elemental composition of the ingots from Cape Gelidonya to suggest a different ore source, pointing out the weakness of elemental studies for determining ore sources, and hence trade patterns. However, two of the bun-shaped copper ingots from the Uluburun wreck have significantly different lead isotopic ratios, indicating a different unknown ore source. Lead isotope analysis of some tin ingot samples from Uluburun indicate an ore source in the Taurus mining region of south-central Anatolia, as do two samples of lead fishing weights.

Analytical tests run on metal artifacts have the potential to provide answers to any number of questions concerning economics, trade patterns, technology, and cultural history of any archaeological time period. The tests discussed above are just four of many available tests.

■ J. H. Carlson, "Analysis of British and American Pewter by X-ray Fluorescence Spectroscopy," *Winterthur Portfolio* (1977): 65–85. Nöel H. Gale and Sofia A. Stos-Gale, "Bronze Age Archaeometallurgy of the Mediterranean: The Impact of Lead Isotope Studies," in *Archaeological Chemistry*, IV, ed. Ralph O. Allen (1989), pp. 159–198. Cemal Pulak, "The Late Bronze Age Shipwreck at Ulu Burun, Turkey: 1989 Excavation Campaign," in *Underwater Archaeology Proceedings for the Society for Historical Archaeology Conference, Tucson, 1990*, ed. Toni Carrell (1990), 523–557. Robert Maddin, "The Copper and Tin Ingots from the Kaş Shipwreck," in *Old World Archaeometallurgy* (1989), pp. 99–105.

Donny L. Hamilton

CONSERVATION OF METALS

From the first appearance of copper artifacts ca. 7000 B.C. and the common use of iron artifacts by 1000 B.C., metal artifacts appear ever increasingly in the archaeological record. Except for a few nonferrous metals such as gold, silver, and copper, metals do not occur in a metallic state in nature; thus, most metals are produced by smelting various ores. Every metal object, depending on the activity of the metal and its burial environment, undergoes various corrosion processes and reverts back to more stable oxides, carbonates, chlorides, sulfides, etc. Prior to excavation, artifacts may have been extensively converted to corrosion products, and once removed, the corrosive attack on any remaining metal is often accelerated. Thus, the skills of a conservator are required from the moment metal artifacts are discovered. Often the initial treatment and storage determines whether or not the original form and surface of the artifact can be successfully preserved. The ability of the conservator to preserve the attributes of the artifacts contributes significant data to archaeological research.

Once excavated, the artifact is exposed to oxygen, humidity, and other factors that accelerate the corrosion processes. For example, chlorides are incorporated in the corrosion products of iron, copper, bronze, and brass when they are recovered from environments containing chlorides. Iron chlorides and cuprous chlorides react with atmospheric oxygen and moisture to oxidize and produce hydrochloric acid which re-attacks any remaining metal. The process continues until no metal remains. For these two metals it is imperative that the chlorides be removed or inactivated. While other metals undergo various damaging corrosion processes, iron is the most difficult metal to conserve due to the ease and variability of corrosion processes.

Nonferrous metals usually survive in archaeological sites much better than iron artifacts, but even these can completely convert to corrosion products when exposed to adverse conditions. For example, silver readily reacts with sulfides to convert to silver sulfides in marine sites; lead converts readily to lead carbonate. However, the corrosion products of nonferrous metals often can be converted back to a metallic state.

Depending upon the artifact, its metal composition and burial environment, conservation usually involves one or more of the following five procedures: mechanical cleaning, chemical cleaning, chemical reduction, electrolytic reduction, and casting.

Mechanical cleaning is usually a part of any of the treatments accorded all artifacts, and in many instances, it is the only treatment for artifacts that are too fragile and corroded to be processed in any other way. In these cases the metal is mechanically cleaned as much as possible and then consolidated with a synthetic resin to consolidate the remains. Extensive mechanical cleaning with pneumatic chisels is required for iron artifacts recovered from marine sites and, as in other cases, is a prelude to other treatments.

Chemical cleaning might be as simple as rinsing in water to remove soluble salts, soaking in alkaline solutions to remove water-insoluble salts, or using various acids and chemicals to remove superficial corrosion products. Chemical treatments are most commonly used on nonferrous metals or iron artifacts with low-level chloride content excavated from terrestrial sites.

An example of chemical reduction is the treatment of silver and copper/copper alloy artifacts which are placed in an airtight container containing a mixture of sodium hydroxide and sodium hydrosulfite. The strong reducing solution converts the silver and copper corrosion products to a metallic state, often preserving the details found in the fragile corrosion layer of the original surface. A similar treatment for iron, using sodium hydroxide and sodium sulfite, converts the iron corrosion products to magnetite, making it more stable. During both treatments the potentially damaging chlorides are removed.

Electrolytic reduction is used most often by conservators on metal artifacts, especially large iron objects recovered from marine sites. This process is the most effective way of removing chlorides from the metals and during the process various metal ions are reduced back to a metallic state. In this treatment the artifact is connected by a wire to the negative terminal of a regulated DC power supply and placed in a container filled with an electrolyte of (2–5%) sodium hydroxide or sodium carbonate. Surrounding the artifact is a metal screen that is attached to the positive terminal of the same power supply. During the treatment, electrons flow to the artifacts which are picked up by the metal cations (lead, copper, silver) in the corrosion products and are converted to metal. The negatively charged anions, especially the chlorides, are drawn out of the metal, concentrated in the electrolyte and disposed of when the solution is changed.

When iron is conserved by electrolysis, it depends upon the oxidation state of the iron corrosion products as to whether or not they can be reduced. If the corrosion products are in a ferric state (the highest oxidation state of iron) the most one can expect is mechanical cleaning of the corrosion layers by the evolution of hydrogen gas bubbles. If the iron corrosion products are in a ferrous state, it is often possible to convert them to magnetite—and possibly some to metal—which preserves the original surface details contained in the corrosion layers. During the reduction process, the chlorides are removed from the artifact. Electrolytic reduction is one of the most valuable and misunderstood tools of the science of conservation. Although used extensively by conservators treating artifacts from marine sites, many conservators consider it only a mechanical cleaning treatment.

Following any conservation treatment, it is usually necessary to make the conserved metal surfaces more corrosion resistant and to seal the surfaces off from the atmosphere. Iron is often treated with several coats of dilute tannic acid to color the iron black and the ferric tannate that is formed makes the iron more resistant to corrosion. A sealant of microcrystalline wax or various paints is applied as a final step. Soaking copper / copper alloys in 1 to 2 percent benzotriazole following treatment lessens the tendency of the metal to corrode and a final sealant of wax or resin completes the conservation. All conserved materials must then be properly stored.

Casting is another valuable tool often overlooked in conservation. During conservation it is often necessary to cast an epoxy replica of an artifact that is so badly deteriorated that it cannot be preserved in any other way. For instance, it is normal to find small, encrusted iron artifacts from marine sites that have completely corroded. The encrustation surrounding these artifacts forms a perfect mold of the original object. This mold can be filled with epoxy and the encrusted material chiseled away to reveal a near-perfect cast of the original object. In nautical archaeology the study of the artifacts cast from natural molds left by corroded iron artifacts is a significant part of the research.

There is a vast array of literature documenting the intricate details of archaeological conservation. This is a brief description of some of the conservation procedures used to treat metal artifacts and some of their derived benefits.

■ D. L. Hamilton, *Conservation of Metal Objects from Underwater Sites: A Study in Methods* (1975). H. J. Plenderleith and A.E.A. Werner, *The Conservation of Antiquities and Works of Art* (1977). Colin Pearson, ed., *Conservation of Marine Archaeological Objects* (1987). J. M. Cronyn, *The Elements of Archaeological Conservation* (1990).

Donny L. Hamilton

METHOD, Archaeological. Method in archaeology refers to a wide range of activities and processes engaged in at all levels of the practice of the discipline. Some archaeological methods are intimately linked to archaeological theory, while others are not. Typically, method and theory are taught together because of the often tight linkage between them. While theory serves to shape research and interpretation at the highest levels of the archaeological process, methods guide the practice of archaeology at the lowest and intermediate levels of the process.

Archaeological methods can be conveniently divided into four categories. These categories consist of general research methods, field methods, analytical methods, and quantitative methods.

General research methods consist of guidelines for conducting archaeological research defined in such terms as the deductive method, the inductive method, the hypothetico-deductive method, and so on, usually in conformance with a general acceptance of the application of the scientific method of inquiry to archaeology. At a lower level of practice, general research methods guide such activities as survey strategies for locating sites and sampling strategies for conducting regional or site surface surveys. General research methods tend to be the most intimately linked to particular theoretical perspectives, and in turn often guide or dictate the field or analytical methods employed in a given project.

Field methods are those guidelines and techniques developed for conducting efficient, effective field research. Excavation strategies, post-hole testing strategies, recording techniques, artifact collection strategies and techniques, and sample collection techniques, among many other practices, are considered field methods. The rigor with which archaeologists maintain high standards of field methods is one significant area where archaeology as a discipline differentiates itself from pot hunting or looting, and is the primary determinant in the quality of the data collected for a region or from a site.

Analytical methods refer to specialized techniques or approaches to analyzing different categories of artifacts and features, such as ceramics, lithics, burials, and so forth. In general, the analytical methods used by archaeologists, and the various specialized scientists and technicians upon which archaeologists rely, are determined less by general research methods or theory than by the type of material under analysis and the kinds of information that the archaeologist wants to extract from that material.

Quantitative methods refer to various techniques for discerning and demonstrating patterns in the data made available through analysis. The quantitative methods that archaeologists choose to employ in their analysis of archaeological data can be determined simply on the basis of the kinds of data they have generated or can be guided by more general theoretical principles or the general research methods they have chosen to use. Quantitative methods can run the gamut from simple tabulations of artifact or attribute counts to complex simulation models used in the process of either generating hypotheses to test or in testing hypotheses previously proposed.

At each step of a project, archaeologists must be aware of the methods available to them, the appropriateness of various method to different situations, and the effects that the application of different methods will have on later stages of the research. Finally, archaeologists must always clearly document the methods that were employed in their research and be explicit in explaining their choice of methods so that future archaeologists can understand both the final interpretation and the whole process that led to that interpretation. Thus, method is one pillar of the rigorous scientific discipline of archaeology, while theory is the other pillar. Good archaeology cannot be conducted without careful attention to both theory and method, principle and practice.

[See also ANALYSIS, METHODS OF; ARTIFACT DISTRIBUTION ANALYSIS; CERAMICS: INTRODUCTION; DATING THE PAST; EXCAVATION: INTRODUCTION; LITHICS: INTRODUCTION; MATERIALS, ANALYSIS OF; METALS: INTRODUCTION; MORTUARY ANALYSIS; PALEOENVIRONMENTAL RECONSTRUCTION; SAMPLING; SCIENCE IN ARCHAEOLOGY; SCIENTIFIC METHOD; SERIATION; SETTLEMENT PATTERN ANALYSIS; SITE LOCATION; STATISTICAL ANALYSIS; STRATIGRAPHY; SUBSURFACE TESTING; THEORY IN ARCHAEOLOGY; TYPOLOGICAL ANALYSIS; WOOD: INTRODUCTION.]

■ Colin Renfrew and Paul Bahn, *Archaeology: Theories, Methods and Practice* (1991). Brian M. Fagan, *People of the Earth* (8th ed., 1994).

George Michaels

MICROLITHS. The term "microliths" is applied to small, chipped stone artifacts generally, but is better restricted to Later Paleolithic and Mesolithic implements below an arbitrary size of 2 inches (5 cm). Such pieces were usually hafted and used as elements in composite tools. Occasional microlithic pieces can occur at any time and in any industry but they are most characteristic of the period from the Last Glacial Maximum (LGM) at 18,000 B.P. to the beginnings of agricultural societies between the eighth and third millennia B.C. This period is variously known as Late Paleolithic, Epi-Paleolithic, Late Stone Age, and Mesolithic. There were microlithic industries before the LGM, such as the Micromousterian of Eastern Europe (dated as older than 40,000 B.P.), but in most cases formally retouched microliths are rare and small stone tools were not systematically produced. Indeed, some quartz-based Micromousterian industries may owe their size to the nature of the raw material available.

Microlithic elements appear in the Howieson's Poort stage of the Southern African Middle Stone Age, which dates between 80,000 and 70,000 B.P. Occasional microliths occur including formal microlith types such as trapezes, crescents, triangles, and obliquely backed points, all made on flake blades. Archaeologists are still debating the significance of this industry which is succeeded by more typical Middle Stone Age materials.

Prior to the LGM, in the Aurignacian of Eurasia, backed bladelets are found, notably *lamelles Dufour*. Indeed, other Aurignacian type-fossils, the nosed and carinated scrapers, may be seen as cores for systematically producing these small bladelets.

The Aurignacian is the first widely distributed Upper *Paleolithic industry, occurring in Eurasia and North African from ca. 40,000 B.P. The later Gravettian Upper Paleolithic complex is equally widespread and shows progressive trends toward the LGM and the subsequent microlith-rich industries. The Gravettian complex gives way after the LGM to blade and bladelet assemblages known as the Epi-Gravettian. In these industries true microliths came to have increasing importance, so that by the end of the *Pleistocene they are seen as the characteristic tool of the period known as the Mesolithic.

The Mesolithic was once regarded as a degraded period when compared with the art and other achievements of the Upper Paleolithic and the pottery and groundstone technology of the Neolithic. Recent work, however, has shown it to be highly significant for the development of more complex societies and economies. Microliths are the only evidence surviving from this period in large areas of the world. Pottery and groundstone tools are now also recognized as developing within Mesolithic contexts. The term Epi-Paleolithic might be more appropriate and has been used to describe certain "Mesolithic" industries to emphasize the continuity with preceding Paleolithic cultures and their economies.

Microlithic industries are found distributed all over the globe, from the Late Paleolithic, Epi-Paleolithic, and Mesolithic industries of Eurasia to the Late Stone Age of sub-Saharan Africa and various small tool traditions in Northeast Asia and the Arctic. In Australia, microlithic tools appear late in the cultural sequence. Similar tools, such as hollow-based points, crescents, and trapezes, are found in the Toalean industry of Sulawesi. Formal microliths appear to be lacking in mainland Southeast Asia and Oceania. There are microliths in North America, within the Arctic Small Tool Tradition, and sporadic occurrences in assemblages from South America.

Most of these assemblages date to the period from the Late Paleolithic until the development of farming communities and it seems that microlithic technology was a core component in the adaptations of Late Pleistocene hunter-gatherer populations to their changing environments as temperatures increased and sea levels rose at the end of the Ice Age. It is not perhaps surprising, therefore, that microliths are generally interpreted as elements of hunting equipment: the most common forms of microliths are believed to be projectile points and barbs for arrowheads and harpoons. These interpretations have been strengthened by finds of microliths hafted to arrowshafts and the occasional

microlith actually embedded in an animal bone. Experimental replication of arrows and their use has further enhanced our understanding of the role of microliths in hunting: impact damage patterns have been studied and have enabled archaeologists to identify hunting stands where used arrowheads were mended or replaced even when stone tools are the only evidence present.

There is a clear chronological trend for geometric microliths such as trapezes, triangles, crescents, and rods to replace non-geometric forms such as backed pieces, truncations, and obliquely retouched pieces. There is also a trend for arrowheads to change from triangular points to broad transversely edged tips. Both trends indicate increasing specialization in hunting equipment and reflect an intensification of hunting, which was coupled with a diversification in the number of species exploited.

Not all microliths were used in hunting, however, and other composite tools with microlithic elements include knives, reapers, and sickles. The latter are especially interesting since they may show a wear polish (sickle gloss) which forms when silica-rich plant stems, such as cereals, are cut. This provides direct evidence for a move toward cereal harvesting which is itself part of the great change from a dependency upon hunting and gatherering to farming.

Microliths hafted in sickles and reapers have been found in early agricultural sites in the Near East and Africa. There are also microlithic scrapers, which were hafted for working hides, while another microlithic tool type is the microdenticulate, used for cutting and sawing. Hafted in series, a row of notched microliths would provide effective saw teeth, and experiments in use-wear have confirmed this function.

Microliths can occur on many different types of raw material, and while fine-grained rocks such as flint, chert, and obsidian are commonly exploited, particularly by technologies using bladelets, quartzite and quartz are also used. Quartz microliths are particularly common in the Late Stone Age of East Africa.

Microliths produced on bladelets often produce a by-product known as the microburin which results from the deliberate notching of a blade or bladelet to weaken it so that it can be snapped. This produces a useful microlithic bladelet and also a waste stub which has a twist facet caused by the snapping.

Technologically, microliths are often, but not always, made on bladelets systematically prepared from special core types. This reflects the origin of this technology in the blade-based industries of the Upper Paleolithic, and prismatic bladelet cores resembling the larger blade-producing versions are common. Also significant, however, is a tradition of elaborate core preparation for making bladelets found in Siberia, North China, Korea, Japan, and Alaska where bifacially worked wedge-shaped cores are used. These stylized technologies show clear spatial patterning which seems to indicate cultural areas. Indeed, it is a fact that microlithic industries show far greater spatial patterning than preceding Upper Paleolithic traditions throughout Eurasia—probably reflecting the significant social changes occurring at the time in response to major environmental change. These social changes included increased sedentism, larger group size, smaller territories, and a greater intensity of food getting, with an associated increase in the numbers of different game species exploited. As part of this emerging pattern of territoriality, cemeteries appear and in them are signs of intercommunity violence—microliths embedded in human skeletons.

[*See also* LITHICS: INTRODUCTION, STONE TECHNOLOGY.]

■ Francois Bordes, *The Old Stone Age* (1968). Jacques Bordaz, *Tools of the Old and New Stone Age* (1970). David Phillipson, *The Later Prehistory of Eastern and Southern Africa* (1977). Grahame Clark, *Mesolithic Prelude* (1980). Wu Rukang and John Olsen, eds., *Palaeoanthropology and Palaeolithic Anthropology in the People's Republic of China* (1985).

Tim Reynolds

MIDDLE RANGE THEORY is, at its most basic level, a set of theories or propositions that bridge the gap between the empirical observation and broad, often abstract and untestable, general or high-level theories. Unfortunately, as Raab and Goodyear point out there has been substantial confusion as to the goal, as well as the meaning, of middle range theory in archaeology. This confusion largely results from the broad acceptance of an ill-defined concept.

Middle range theory was first developed in sociology by R. K. Merton in the late 1940s as a means of dealing with problems inherent in the new sociological emphasis on abstraction. There was an increasing desire among sociologists of the time for a unified sociological theory that ultimately became so broad as to render it empirically untestable. Merton argued that middle range theories could be developed to test subsections of these high-level, abstract theories. Thus, middle range theory was developed to guide the empirical investigation of higher-order theories. The goal of this new level of theorizing was to generate the theories that were sufficiently abstract to allow behavioral generalization, and yet were satisfactorily grounded in reality, so that they could be empirically verified.

In archaeology, the concept of middle range theory has been applied haphazardly and often without reference to formal definition or knowledge of its sociological foundations. Perhaps two of the most substantial archaeological investigations oriented toward developing middle range theory are Lewis Binford's *Nunamiut Ethnoarchaeology* (1978) and *Bones: Ancient Men and Modern Myths* (1981). In the first of these two works, Binford documents the relationship between modern Alaska native hunting activities and the different types of bone assemblages that result from different site functions, hunting conditions, and meat processing. In the later work, he documents many natural processes that influence the character and condition of faunal assemblages and applies these inferences to the interpretation of the Plio-Pleistocene archaeological record. Both are successful at making bridging arguments that relate the empirical archaeological record to culture theory.

Unlike most similar studies, Binford makes it very clear that, although the building of middle range theories is necessary for obtaining a clear understanding of the dynamic processes that created the archaeological record, the ultimate goal of these studies is still the elucidation of prehistoric human cultural behavior. This conception of middle range theory in archaeology is thus very similar to Merton's calls for bridging arguments in sociology. Unfortunately, many archaeologists have seen Binford's methods of studying *site-formation processes as an end in themselves. In many cases, the development of middle range theory has become the research goal rather than the means to connect archaeological data with high-level, abstract explanations.

A concrete example of an appropriate development and use of middle range theory along the lines of the original

sociological foundation may serve to better define its usefulness. We can envision a theory of the origins of sedentary communities or villages that purports a relationship between sedentism and warfare. The theory states that "people will become more sedentary as a result of increasing violence and warfare." As such, this theory is not testable archaeologically. However, a number of middle range theories might be developed that are testable and that will allow us to evaluate the original theory. These include statements about the relationship between settlement strategies and defense, the relationship between economy and sedentism, the relationship between population size and social stress, and so on. Hypotheses are then derived from each of these middle range theories that are testable archaeologically. Thus, we are able to evaluate an untestable, high-level theory by reducing that theory to a number of middle range, testable propositions.

As indicated previously, a considerable amount of middle-range theorizing in archaeology is done without reference to the concept itself, mostly in the form of studies of site formation processes. Although such studies increase our interpretive abilities, they contribute little to the advancement of our understanding of human behavior. What is needed are not more such investigations, but a reinvestment in the desires and early expectations of the "New Archaeology" of the 1960s and 1970s. Archaeologists today spend the majority of their research efforts on the specific rather than the general, on the empirical rather than the theoretical, on the interpretation rather than the behavior—this must end. Middle range theory has an important role to play in the future of archaeology as we return to the "big-picture" issues of human history. Broad theories of the rise of social inequality, agriculture, warfare, and early empires will not, in and of themselves, be testable. But a proper understanding and use of middle range theory will allow the development of testable propositions and hypotheses that will bridge the inevitable chasm between what we believe is the explanation, and what we actually observe in the archaeological record.

[*See also* CRITICAL THEORY; CULTURAL ECOLOGY THEORY; CULTURE HISTORICAL THEORY; ETHNOARCHAEOLOGY; HISTORY OF ARCHAEOLOGY, INTELLECTUAL; MARXIST THEORY; POST-PROCESSUAL THEORY; PROCESSUAL THEORY; SCIENCE IN ARCHAEOLOGY; THEORY IN ARCHAEOLOGY.]

■ R. K. Merton, *Social Theory and Social Structure* (1949). L. M. Raab and A. C. Goodyear, "Middle Range Theory in Archaeology: A Critical Review of Origins and Application," *American Antiquity* 49 (1984): 255–258.

Herbert D. G. Maschner

MINES AND QUARRIES

INTRODUCTION

The extraction of materials from mines and quarries has a very long history and is attested as early as 40,000 years ago in the red ocher mines of southern Africa, and 20,000 years ago in the flint quarry of Koonalda Cave in Australia. Far from being restricted to recent industrial economies, therefore, mining and quarrying is a widespread human activity which has been practiced by hunters and gatherers and simple agriculturalists as well as more complex societies.

The distinction between mines and quarries is that the former use shafts and galleries to burrow deep below the surface, while the latter are open-air workings at a cliff face or in a pit. Quarries have been used to extract a wide variety of minerals including flint and obsidian, marble, granite, and other building materials. Metals such as gold, silver, copper, tin, lead, and iron, on the other hand, have usually been mined by shafts which follow the veins of material within the ground. Flint, too, has been mined as well as quarried, and European flint mines such as Grimes Graves in Britain or Rijckhold–St. Geertruid in the Netherlands provide some of our best evidence for early mining technology.

For each material we may imagine that mining or quarrying began when surface deposits were exhausted. In early prehistoric times, for example, gold and copper-bearing minerals may have been readily available as surface finds in many parts of the world, but once they became valuable any surface occurrences would quickly have been used up, so that quarrying or mining became necessary to exploit buried deposits. Few metals, however, are found naturally in pure form—most occur as ore materials—and hence mining or quarrying is only one part of a larger technical-industrial process which involves recognizing the ore, extracting it from the seams, and converting it into metal by smelting.

The known extent of ancient mines and quarries represents only a small proportion of what there must once have been, since in many cases—especially where metals or other valuable materials are involved—deposits have continued to be exploited down to the present day, and early workings have often been destroyed by later larger-scale operations. This has not prevented a number of ancient mine workings from being discovered and studied, especially where seams have either been entirely worked out or survive in quantities considered uneconomic by modern industry. Particular mention might be made of prehistoric copper mines in southern Europe, Wales, and Argentina, Roman lead mines in Spain (with sophisticated pumping machinery), the Zhou period copper mines of Tonglushan in China, and the famous Athenian silver mines at Laurion in Greece. Ancient quarries are still more widespread, and range from prehistoric examples such as the axe factories of Great Langdale in the British Lake District and the obsidian quarries on the Aegean island of Melos, to the marble quarries such as those of Carrara in Italy, which supplied the Renaissance artist Michelangelo with the material for some of his most famous sculptures. The industrial age has placed still further emphasis on mines and quarries as a means of obtaining vital raw materials and fossil fuels, notably coal. It has also stimulated the development of a new but related technology, that of drilling for gas and petroleum. Sophisticated though they are, however, these modern methods are but the latest stage in a continuous story of digging for buried resources which stretches well back into the Paleolithic.

Chris Scarre

EUROPEAN FLINT AND STONE MINES

Like the axes with which they are often closely associated, flint mines and stone quarries are categories of sites that rose to prominence during the Neolithic Period in Europe.

A small number of open-cast mines and quarries are known from Mesolithic contexts on the northern European plain, in Norway, and on islands of the western coast of Scotland. It is generally with the onset of the Neolithic, however, that we begin to find evidence for the systematic extraction of raw material from large, open-cast quarries and deep, galleried mines. Sites dating to this period have been recognized in a number of countries, including Belgium, Britain, Germany, Poland, France, Sweden, and Holland.

Mines and quarries take a variety of forms, reflecting the character and geological context of the raw materials that were exploited. Some are no more than small working hollows that were cut into seams of flint or stone that lay close to the surface. Others occur as large, vertical quarry faces that follow outcrops of workable stone around the face of a mountain: a pattern that can be seen at the appanite axe quarries of the Jura Mountains and at the volcanic tuff sources of the Lake District in England. Larger mine complexes, such as Grimes Graves in England, Spiennes in Belgium, or Maastricht in Holland, provide evidence for the sinking of deep shafts and the cutting of underground galleries to obtain large nodules of high-quality flint. Excavations suggest that many of these sites were worked with picks of antler and stone, wooden levers and shovels made from the scapulae (shoulder blades) of cattle. Evidence from a number of sites also indicates that fire was sometimes used to fracture rock faces prior to stone extraction.

Although the largest mine complexes can contain over a thousand shafts and galleries, it is unlikely that even these reflect the operation of a full-time, industrial work force. Many sources were probably exploited on a seasonal basis by relatively small groups of people, and the scale of the sites that we see today results from a pattern of episodic use which may have extended for as much as a millennium. It is also unlikely that particular sources were owned or monopolized by individual groups. Access may have been a privilege of kinship and group affiliation, and it is probable that many sites were visited by people drawn from a number of different communities.

Analyses of waste flakes and rejects show that many mines and quarries witnessed the extraction of stone for the production of a variety of tools. Large blades and blade cores have been found at a number of mines, together with a wide array of smaller tools, but the artifact that frequently dominates the assemblages is the flaked, or "roughed out," axe. Flaked or pecked into shape at the source, roughed-out axes were generally taken back to settlements where the final stages of grinding and polishing were undertaken.

The consistent emphasis upon axe production at many mines and quarries is difficult to understand in practical terms alone. The raw materials recovered from these sites would have been particularly well suited to the production of large bifacial tools. This may not in itself, however, provide us with a full understanding of the significance that was accorded to these places and their products., Flint and stone axes are found in many later Mesolithic contexts, but there is little evidence to suggest that their production involved the systematic exploitation of mines or quarries. This suggests that mining and quarrying were activities that took on a new significance with the onset of the Neolithic.

Clues as to the significance of these changes can be found in the treatment that was given to many of the axes produced at mines and quarries. Several lines of evidence suggest that these practical tools were also accorded some symbolic importance, not least as media for social exchanges within and between communities. Although practical demand probably increased with the onset of farming, the social dimensions of axes and other artifacts may have played a part in shaping the patterns of procurement and production that we see today. Mines and quarries may have been places to which people traveled to make tools that were also important tokens of identity and value. Used by members of different communities, they may have also provided a context in which people came together and at which a variety of transactions were undertaken.

[*See also* EUROPE: THE EUROPEAN NEOLITHIC PERIOD; TRADE, PREHISTORIC: PREHISTORIC AXE TRADE.]

■ G. de G. Sievering and M. Newcomer, *The Human Uses of Flint and Chert* (1987). F. Bostyn and Y. Lanchon, *Jablines Le Haut Château.* (1992). R. Bradley and M. Edmonds, *Interpreting the Axe Trade* (1993).

Mark Edmonds

CENTRAL AND EASTERN EUROPEAN COPPER MINES

Copper was used by groups in Balkan Europe from the early fifth millennium onward, with a major increase in scale after 4500 B.C. that conventionally marks the beginning of the southeast European Copper Age. This copper came from deep-mined sources. It continued to be used as the primary metal during the Bronze Age, from 2500 to 750 B.C., and it is still worked commercially in certain locations today. During the first millennium B.C., the deep-mining techniques were applied to salt working in the north Alpine area, and the excellent conditions of preservation of prehistoric objects (including organic materials) in these ancient salt mines led to their recognition in the nineteenth century in the *Hallstatt area of Austria, associated with the wealthy Late Bronze Age and Early Iron Age cemetery there. Exploration of the abundant traces of Bronze Age mining and smelting activity in this area around Salzburg (the *Salzkammergut*) has provided a detailed picture of the sophistication of Late Bronze Age (Urnfield culture) extraction procedures and their earlier Bronze Age antecedents back to ca. 2000 B.C.

Although extraction shafts for flint and chert dating to the fourth millennium were known from several parts of central Europe (e.g., Sümeg, western Hungary, or the famous examples from Poland like Krzemionki), no Copper Age mine workings were recognized in central Europe until the later 1960s. It was nevertheless clear from the conspicuous concentrations of early copper artifacts (such as the heavy shafthole axe-adzes) that their raw material came from sources in the Balkans and Carpathians. Indeed, the distribution patterns and cultural associations of successive types of these objects indicated a sequence of fluorescences of metallurgical activity which began in Bulgaria with the Marica and Gumelnitsa cultures, moved northward to Transylvania and the south Carpathian ring (Serbia, Romania) with the later Vinča, Tiszapolgár, and Bodrogkeresztúr cultures, and finally shifted by the later fourth millennium to the north Carpathians in Slovakia with the Lengyel and Baden cultures. This was then succeeded by the Bronze Age pattern, associated with exploitations of the east Alpine sources of the *Salzkammergut* (producing huge quantities of the Early Bronze Age neck-ring ingots or *Ösenringe*, deposited in hoards in the adjacent lowlands) and the high-mountain sources of northern Transylvania, also associated with a scatter of adjacent hoards like that of Hajdúsámson. Sources of copper occur at accessible altitudes (below 1,640 feet, 500 m), as opposed to the Bronze Age sources over 3,280 feet (1000 m) over much of the sickle-shaped curve of the Carpathians and Sredna Gora, their southerly extension beyond the Iron Gates where the Danube cuts through this chain of Tertiary fold mountains.

It was in the course of extensive open-cast mining at Majdanpek near Bor in northern Serbia (not far from the Iron Gates) that old shafts associated with Vinča pottery were first recognized at Rudna Glava ("ore head"), and led to the widespread identification of such sites. Shafts could be traced for over 82 feet (25 m), exploiting in particular the well-developed secondary (carbonate) copper ores such as malachite, which were generally preferred by early miners (e.g., in the southern Levant) as a rich and easily smelted source of metal. These secondary ores (sometimes also including arsenic) are well developed as a result of weathering in southern Europe and the Mediterranean, but tend to have been removed by glacial action farther north. Among the associated pottery, dating to the Vinča-Pločnik phase (ca. 4500 B.C.), were highly decorated finewares, including an "altar" (probably a lamp or censer for burning aromatics), which are not just the remains of a miner's lunchbox but suggest that propitiatory rituals were an integral part of the mining process. Comparable shafts were soon noticed in the hills behind the classic Neolithic and Copper Age tell site of Karanovo in central Bulgaria at sites such as Ai Bunar and Hrištene, associated with Gumelnitsa pottery and presumably supplying the adjacent domestic sites, some 3 miles (5 km) away. Many more such sites must remain to be found, but heavy stone mauls such as those found at Spanja Dolina in Slovakia, typical of early mining sites, hint at the locations of further examples. Third-millennium mines are now known in Greece, Turkey, and the Caucasus, as well as Iran, Oman, and the Levant. By the Late Bronze Age, mining techniques in the Alps (e.g., at the Mitterberg, Mühlbach-Bischofshofen) had become very sophisticated, with shafts over 328 feet (100 m) long and complex systems of ventilation for fire-setting chalcopyrite deposits.

[*See also* EUROPE: THE EUROPEAN COPPER AGE.]

■ Andrew Sherratt, "Resources, Technology and Trade: Early European Metallurgy," in *Problems in Economic and Social Archaeology,* eds. Gale Sieveking, Ian Longworth, and Kay Wilson (1976). E. N. Chernykh, *Gornoe Delo i Metallurgiya drevneishei Bolgarii* [Mining and Metallurgy in Early Bulgaria] (1978). Boris Jovanović, *Rudna Glava: najstarija rudarstvo bakra na centralnom Balkanu* [Rudna Glava: An Early Copper Mine in the Central Balkans] (1982). E. N. Chernykh, *Early Metallurgy in the USSR: The Early Metal Age* (1992).

Andrew Sherratt

GREEK AND ROMAN MINES

Mines were the main source of the gold and silver used by Greeks and Romans for luxury goods and coinage, and of the copper, iron, lead, and tin used for everyday artifacts. Deposits within their direct control were extensively mined, and supplemented by imports. Gold, scarce in Greece, was mined on Siphnos, Thasos, in Macedonia and around Mt. Pangaeus in Thrace, there producing 1,000 talents annually for Philip II of Macedon. It was imported also from Asia Minor, where panning in the rivers Pactolus and Hermus produced white gold, a natural gold-silver alloy, and from Colchis at the eastern end of the Black Sea, where native techniques perhaps accounted for the legend of the Golden Fleece. Silver mines producing argentiferous lead ores (mixed with iron, copper, and zinc) were worked on

Siphnos, in the Laurion district of Attica, on Thasos, and in Thrace. Their success was reflected in the prosperity of Siphnos in the sixth century B.C. and of Athens in the fifth century; their failure, in their subsequent decline.

Copper was mined near Chalcis on Euboea and in quantity on Cyprus. Trace elements perhaps accounted for early alloys (arsenical bronzes), but large-scale production of bronze depended on imported tin (from Asia, Spain, Gaul, and Cornwall). Greeks mined iron locally, obtaining more from Elba and Asia Minor. Italy was not rich in ores, but Etruscans and others mined some gold, copper, and iron, notably on Elba. Rome's expansion gave her control of rich mines of gold, silver, and base metals in Spain and in other provinces, including Britain (gold, lead, and iron). Lead and zinc, neglected by Greeks, were mined extensively by Romans.

Ancient miners used, at need, placer mining of river and alluvial deposits, open-cast workings for ores close to the surface, adits and galleries, sloping or horizontal, for ores farther in, and vertical pits with gallery extensions for deeper lodes. Prospectors often located mineral deposits from the discoloration of surface rocks, such as the rusty or dark staining caused by iron and manganese trace elements. Oxide and carbonate ores were mined nearer the surface, sulphides deeper down. Miners followed veins of ore, hollowing out pits or underground chambers where the lode was rich, economizing on labor and pit props elsewhere by cutting low (3 feet [1 m] or less), narrow galleries of rectangular or trapezoidal section. Hand tools, earlier of stone or bone, later of iron, included spiked hammers, mauls, chisels, single- and double-pointed picks, mattocks, shovels, rakes, baskets and leather bags for carrying ore, ropes, ladders, buckets, and windlasses for hauling it up pit shafts. Ore was selected at the workface and again at the surface, waste being packed into abandoned chambers or dumped outside. Miners exploited both fire and water: they lit fires and quenched them with water (or vinegar) to split rock (fire-setting). Elsewhere they directed water from streams and reservoirs to remove surface cover (hushing). They faced problems of light, ventilation, heat, and drainage. Torches and oil lamps provided a smoky light. Air circulation was improved by using cloth fans, twin shafts, parallel galleries, and ventilation shafts, often with fires lit to create up-and-down drafts. To improve drainage the Romans used channels, baling, Archimedean screws, and waterwheels (preserved fragments found at Rio Tinto, Spain, and Dolaucothi, Wales). Even so, conditions were generally appalling, and Greeks used slaves for both underground and surface operations. The Romans made use also of criminals, forced labor, and sometimes soldiers, keeping some workers permanently underground. Technicians and overseers too were often slaves.

Mining rights were usually a state monopoly, but exploitation was mostly indirect. Athens leased concessions at Laurion to citizens for fixed terms; surface works were built, operated, and sold by individuals. In Ptolemaic Egypt, mines were state-owned and state-run. In Republican Rome, mines were leased to contractors (*conductores*) and companies (*publicani*); under the Principate there was stricter control through imperial procurators.

Science and archaeology have supplemented the evidence of ancient authors and inscriptions (such as Athenian mine leases and Roman mine regulations from Portugal). Lead-isotope analysis has distinguished the characteristics of argentiferous lead ores from Siphnos and Laurion and

silver artifacts made from them. Exploration on Siphnos has revealed silver mining there in the Early Bronze Age (third millennium B.C.) and the deliberate refilling of galleries and shafts with rubble, perhaps for religious reasons. In Attica, silver mining at Thorikos has been dated back to the same early period, and elsewhere in the Laurium area, excavation has uncovered many adjuncts of the mines of the Classical period: rainwater reservoirs for ore-treatment, grinderies with blocks and handmills for ore-crushing, cemented washing tables for concentrating ore and recycling precious water, workshops, slave "barracks," and smelting furnaces.

■ Oliver Davies, *Roman Mines in Europe* (1935). R. J. Forbes, *Studies in Ancient Technology*, Vols. VII, VIII–IX (1963, 1964). John F. Healy, *Mining and Metallurgy in the Greek and Roman World* (1978). Constantin E. Conophagos, *Le Larium antique* (1980). Robert Shepherd, *Ancient Mining* (1993).

John Ellis Jones

AUSTRALIAN MINES

Throughout Australia raw material for the manufacture of stone artifacts was often procured simply by collecting rock from creek beds, gibber plains, or rock outcrops. Approximately two-thirds of recorded quarries show no signs of prehistoric digging, and procurement was limited to exploitation of naturally fractured rubble mantling the ground surface. This surficial exploitation is typical of the numerous silcrete, quartzite, and chert quarries. Artifact manufacture at these quarries generally produced a range of retouched and unretouched flakes. Such sites have proved difficult to date, although there are indications of antiquity. At Northcliffe in western Australia, for example, silcrete was obtained during the Early to Middle Holocene.

More spectacular are the quarries where rock has been dug from the ground. Archaeological manifestations of the excavations are either semicircular depressions that indicate the position of pits dug to obtain subsurface rock, or trenches that indicate excavation along a seam of rock. The oldest securely dated stone quarry is Koonalda Cave, where flint was extracted more than 20,000 years ago. Many of these excavated quarries were used to produce artifacts for exchange. Ground-edge axes were manufactured at other excavated quarries and traded widely. Important quarries for trade-related axe production include Mount William in Victoria, Lake Moondarra Quarry 1 in northwest Queensland, and the Moore Creek Quarry in New South Wales. The antiquity of these axe quarries is attested only at the Bendemeer I rock shelter, where an axe from Moore Creek was dated to more than 1300 B.P. However, the presence of axes in northern Australia during the Pleistocene may indicate that similar quarries have far greater antiquity. Other quarries, such as Ngilipitji in the Northern Territory, produced large quartzite flakes for recent exchange systems.

True mines, forming artificial subterranean passages, are rare in Australia. Horizontal shafts are known only from ocher mines. At such sites, tunnels were dug into seams of high-quality ocher, often with the use of stone or wooden wedges and stone hammers. Evidence for wooden scaffolding has also been found. The best known ocher mines are Wilgie Mia in western Australia and Campbell Ranges in the Northern Territory. At Wilgie Mia, a large open-cut pit terminates in a series of tunnels that follow seams of red and yellow ocher. Radiocarbon dates indicate that mining at Wilgie Mia has occurred for more than 1,000 years, and in 1952 D. S. Davidson estimated an antiquity of several thousand years based on the volume of rock extracted. Indications of age are also available for the ocher mine in the Campbell Ranges, where 300 tons of red ocher have been removed. Historic and modern extraction at this site averaged 110–132 pounds (50–60 kg) per annum, permitting an estimate of 5,000 to 6,000 years for mining activities at the site.

While ocher mines are renowned, much ocher was obtained by open-cut quarrying. Ocher quarries are found in all regions of Australia, but are dated only in Tasmania, where a radiocarbon date at Gog Range suggests an antiquity of 400 years. Since red ocher has been used in rock art and burial rituals for at least 20,000 to 30,000 years, ocher mining and quarrying may have a similar antiquity. Ocher was highly prized for decorative purposes, and was traded widely.

In the recent past access to major quarries central to trade networks was restricted. Restrictions came in a range of forms, and quarrying was not limited to males. For example, quarrying at the Mount William Quarry was the prerogative of a single man. At the Campbell Range site, access to ocher was controlled by an extended family, and ocher was mined by both males and females. Axe quarries near Lake Moondarra Quarry were worked by many members of the Kalkadoon group, and W. E. Roth reports a sexual division of labor, with males undertaking initial mining and females the final grinding.

■ W. E. Roth, "Domestic Implements, Arts and Manufactures," *North Queensland Ethnography Bulletin* 7 (1904). D. F. Thomson, *Economic Structure and the Ceremonial Exchange Cycle in Arnhem Land* (1949). D. S. Davidson, "Notes on the Pictographs and Petroglyphs of Western Australia and a Discussion of Their Affinities with Appearances Elsewhere on the Continent," *Proceedings of the American Philosophical Society* 96 (1952): 76–117. R.V.S. Wright, *Archaeology of the Gallus Site, Koonalda Cave* (1971). N. Peterson and R. Lampert, "A Central Australian Ochre Mine," *Records of the South Australian Museum* 37 (1985): 1–9. P. Hiscock and S. Mitchell, *Stone Artifact Quarries and Reduction Sites in Australia: Towards a Type Profile* (1993).
Peter Hiscock

MISSION ARCHAEOLOGY is a complex undertaking that amounts to no less than studying a microcosm of the colonial experience itself. Missions were among the most powerful institutions of the Spanish Crown for converting and "civilizing" the native populations, commandeering labor and provisions, and establishing a presence in the vast frontier territories of Spanish America. Friars were often the first representatives of European culture to interact with Native American groups, and their contact was frequently sustained over a considerable period of time. Consequently, the study of these unique settlements stands to make valuable contributions to our understanding of acculturation processes and to contact period studies as a whole. Mission archaeology also underscores the unique advantages of *historical archaeology, since Spaniards were fastidious in keeping both religious and civil records of events at many of the missions. Bearing in mind that they usually represent only the Spanish perspective, these documents provide an invaluable backdrop against which mission archaeologists can develop hypotheses and evaluate their findings.

The earliest Spanish mission efforts in North America began in the sixteenth century; however, their florescence did not occur until the seventeenth and eighteenth centuries. Missions were concentrated in an area referred to by researchers as the Spanish Borderlands—a broad, roughly defined territory along the northern rim of New Spain. The Spanish Borderlands encompass parts of Mexico and the present-day southern United States from Florida to California. Most people immediately associate Spanish missions almost exclusively with California and the Southwest, since the mission buildings were constructed of permanent materials and are often still marked by standing ruins. More importantly, many of the southwestern native populations have living descendants who keep their ancestors' cultural heritage alive. By contrast, there are no visible remains of any missions in the Southeast, and none of the indigenous tribes who occupied the missions of Spanish Florida survived as a people (the Seminole and Miccosukee Indians associated with Florida today are eighteenth-century immigrants). As a consequence, mission researchers in the Southeast are facing distinctive challenges. Not only must the mission settlements themselves be found through archaeological techniques, but the direct historical approach to understanding the native cultures is not an option. Therefore, while all mission archaeologists are examining cultures in transition, southeastern mission archaeologists are documenting the final episode in the lives of the early native inhabitants of Spanish Florida prior to their virtual annihilation.

In large part due to the high visibility of the ruins, mission archaeology began in the American Southwest and California long before any attempts were made at studying the missions of Spanish Florida. While there were numerous mission excavations conducted during the first half of the twentieth century in the western borderlands, full-time efforts at mission archaeology were not undertaken in the Southeast until the 1970s. As a result, data from various missions throughout the Spanish Borderlands are not always comparable, since research goals, field methods, and data bases (particularly remains necessary for environmental and subsistence studies) have changed dramatically over the decades.

Archaeologists have found that Spanish missions were as varied as the natural and cultural landscapes on which they were imposed. In parts of northern Mexico, Texas, and California, where the native populations were dispersed and semisedentary, missionization called for dramatic changes in indigenous settlement patterns and seasonal rounds. Since living in permanent communities was an essential element of being civilized by European standards, friars removed natives from their traditional house sites and forced them to live in mission compounds (*reducciones*) year-round. Archaeologists in California frequently identify the remains of Indian barracks or dormitories associated with mission complexes (for example, La Purisima Concepción among the Chumash and Mission San Antonio among the Salinans). By contrast, many of the missionaries who worked among sedentary farming societies, such as the Pueblo Indians of New Mexico and the natives of Spanish Florida, were able to establish missions at extant major villages and impose their authority through the conversion of chiefs and other tribal leaders.

Despite the fact that natives provided the labor responsible for constructing the European-style buildings at missions (including church complexes, residences, and even military fortifications), exposure to Spanish building designs, techniques, and hardware appear to have had little influence on indigenous architectural traditions. One of the best examples of this phenomenon is found at Mission San Luis de Talimali, in present-day Tallahassee, Florida. The site had no premission occupation but rather was selected by the Spaniards for its strategic location. Subsequently, a principal Apalachee chief moved his village to San Luis to be near the Spaniards. All of the buildings used by Spaniards at San Luis were rectangular, divided into rooms, and constructed with hewn support posts and iron hardware. By contrast, the Apalachee council house and domestic residences at the site were thatched, circular buildings and had changed little from prehistoric times. Furthermore, the Franciscan Church and the Apalachee council house were situated at opposite ends of the mission's central plaza, implying that both cultures' major ceremonial centers maintained equal importance. San Luis represents one example of Spanish-Indian mission cohabitation that is largely characterized by mutual accommodation, and stands in sharp contrast to other missions where directed change prevailed. At Mission Awatovi among the Hopi Indians of northeastern Arizona, for example, archaeologists found that the Franciscan Church had been deliberately built on top of a native ceremonial structure, or kiva.

Mission archaeology from California to Florida has revealed that technology and subsistence were areas of native life that sustained contact with Europeans altered irrevocably. Iron hoes, adzes, and other farming implements quickly replaced their shell and stone counterparts. And although the distribution of firearms among indigenous peoples was usually restricted, they too were preferred over bows, arrows, and hatchets. Indigenous staples (corn, beans, squash, aquatic resources, etc.) continued to be mainstays during the mission period, but European plants and animals (particularly livestock) had a significant impact at certain missions. Meat and animal by-products stored "on the hoof" proved to be the economic backbone of some mission communities, and faunal assemblages from these sites often differ strikingly from those recovered from nearby prehistoric sites by virtue of the prominence of domestic mammal remains. However, the distribution of domestic animals is very uneven across the Spanish Borderlands depending on specific environmental conditions. For example, open range areas lent themselves to raising cattle, while sheep and goats tended to thrive in rugged terrain. In general, few introduced domestic species did well along the coastal strands where endemic fauna prevailed through mission times.

We are still far from understanding how missionization changed other aspects of daily life for natives. Because the Spanish Crown encouraged intermarriage, native women residing at missions where soldiers and civilians lived often married Spaniards. Since such native women rapidly became Hispanicized, it has been virtually impossible thus far to distinguish archaeologically a Spanish residence at a mission with a Spanish wife (who undoubtedly had native servants) from one with a native or mestiza wife. Based on excavations in the Spanish colonial town of St. Augustine, we expect to find that the materials from residences with native or mestiza wives will contain relatively few items of Hispanic origin, particularly in the realm of women's activities such as cooking.

Perhaps the most controversial aspect of missionization with which archaeology has had some success is that of religious conversion. This was clearly the primary goal of friars, many of whom were martyred throughout the Spanish Borderlands attempting to do God's work. The success of their efforts is borne out archaeologically in neophyte burial practices. Distinct from prehistoric burial patterns, Christianized native burials are usually extended, with their hands folded across their chest. And while status and rank continue to be reflected in mortuary patterning, that accords with Christian tradition as well. That is, the highest-ranking individuals appear to be buried closest to the altar. In at least some areas of the Spanish Borderlands, proximity to the altar was dependent on economic standing, since we know from documentary sources that burial close to the altar was considerably more expensive than burial at the back of the church. Oftentimes the individuals buried near the altar also have the most elaborate funerary objects such as beads (possibly from rosaries), ceramics, and other personal items. At two seventeenth-century mission cemeteries in Spanish Florida, Santa Catalina de Guale on St. Catherines Island in Georgia and San Luis de Talimali in Florida, individuals were also buried in European-style coffins. The poignant remains of these individuals provide testimony to the earnest religious conversion of natives who believed that their passage to the afterlife depended on proper interment in a consecrated Christian burial ground.

Mission archaeology offers unparalleled opportunities to explore a range of responses and adaptations to a new social order imposed on the indigenous inhabitants of Spanish America. Mission research has also contributed considerable insight into Hispanic colonization strategies in the New World and has illuminated those aspects of Spanish culture that were flexible, as well as those that were conservative and resistant to change. Furthermore, at long-lived missions, we are able to investigate the emergence of a new *criollo* culture that blends elements of both Spanish and Native American traditions. The results of mission archaeology to date have been enlightening, and there is little doubt that it will continue to produce intriguing examples of human adaptation and resourcefulness under extraordinary conditions.

[See also EUROPEAN COLONIES IN THE NEW WORLD; MESOAMERICA, articles on HISTORICAL ARCHAEOLOGY OF MESOAMERICA, SPANISH SETTLEMENT IN MESOAMERICA; NORTH AMERICA: HISTORICAL ARCHAEOLOGY OF NORTH AMERICA.]

■ Mark F. Boyd, Hale G. Smith, and John W. Griffin, *Here They Once Stood: The Tragic End of the Apalachee Missions* (1951). John H. Hann, *Apalachee: The Land Between the Rivers* (1988). John H. Hann, *Missions to the Calusa* (1991). Bonnie G. McEwan, *The Spanish Missions of La Florida* (1993). David Hurst Thomas, ed., *Columbian Consequences, Volume 1: Archaeological and Historical Perspectives on the Spanish Borderlands West* (1989). David Hurst Thomas, ed., *Columbian Consequences, Volume 2: Archaeological and Historical Perspectives on the Spanish Borderlands East* (1990). David J. Weber, *The Spanish Frontier in North America* (1992).

Bonnie G. McEwan

MISSISSIPPIAN CULTURE. In its broadest sense, the term "Mississippian culture" refers to sedentary farmers of the interior riverine region in eastern North America during late prehistoric times (ca. A.D. 1000–1540). This is a large culture area that incorporates a lot of internal variation. Most features associated with the Mississippian were initially identified in the central Mississippi River Valley, where they reached their classic expression. These include subsistence based on maize agriculture, high population densities associated with earthwork complexes, ranked social structure, elaborate artifact industries, and the ubiquitous pottery tempered with crushed shell (added to prevent shrinkage and cracking when the pottery is dried and fired). This region includes the largest archaeological sites in North America and represents some of the most socially complex groups north of Mexico.

Between A.D. 800 and 1000, prehistoric populations in the

Mississippi Valley became increasingly reliant on maize agriculture. The timing and complexion of specific changes varied widely, but by A.D. 1000 several local expressions began to flourish. The scale and duration of these expressions were equally variable, but Mississippian culture dominated the late prehistory of the Southeast until European contact in the mid-sixteenth century.

The increased dependence on maize agriculture had far-reaching implications. When maize was first introduced (by A.D. 400), many subsistence economies already included cultivation of indigenous seed-bearing plants (goosefoot, maygrass, knotweed, sunflower, and sumpweed), which remained important throughout the Mississippi Period. Maize, however, was more productive; it had greater storage capabilities and the ability to support higher population densities.

Mississippian settlements concentrated along wide floodplains of the Mississippi River and its major tributaries. These are low-lying areas where minor changes in elevation mark significant differences in hydrology, soils, and vegetation, creating a complex mosaic of permanently and seasonally inundated swamps, floodplain forests, and prairies. Beyond easily cultivated soils and a mild climate of at least 200 frost-free days per year, these conditions supported abundant resources (seed plants, nuts, fleshy fruits, terrestrial and aquatic animals, birds, and migratory fowl) to supplement an agricultural diet.

The extent to which these floodplain environments could support higher population densities through times of lower crop yields may have been limited. Clearly, a variety of behaviors (storage, trade, redistribution networks) also mitigated uneven crop yields, and some of these required relatively complex social organizations. Nevertheless, higher population densities would be increasingly vulnerable to crop failure over sustained periods of time. Indeed, a broader history of the Mississippian culture suggests that maize agriculture created a fundamentally unstable situation.

One of the earliest and by all accounts the largest and most complex local Mississippian expression emerged in the American Bottom of west-central Illinois, across the Mississippi River from St. Louis, Missouri. By A.D. 800, agricultural groups occupied the region in relatively small villages and hamlets. Over the next 200 years, several large population centers with associated earthworks emerged. By A.D. 1000, *Cahokia became the largest, and would dominate the region for the next 200 years.

At its peak, Cahokia formed a dispersed town covering about 5 square miles (14 sq. km) and incorporating over 100 earthen mounds with associated residential areas. A palisade enclosed some 198 acres (80 ha) at the center of the site. Regularly spaced bastionlike structures suggest a defensive function, although it may have simply partitioned the central mound group from the remainder of the community. Monks Mound, the largest of that group (indeed, the largest in North America), was built in fourteen stages between A.D. 1000 and A.D. 1250. It has four terraces reaching a height of 98 feet (30 m) and covers an area of about 16 acres (6.5 ha) at the base. Structures on the terraces (common to many Mississippian temple mounds) were used for ceremonial purposes or elite residences.

Population estimates for Cahokia vary widely. Determining how much of the site was occupied at a given time is made difficult by at least two major episodes of internal reorganization occurring about A.D. 1000 and 1250. Furthermore, estimates vary according to assumptions about the

level of social complexity represented in the larger Cahokia system. Some estimates, where Cahokia is viewed as the center of a highly centralized regional polity, are as high as 50,000. Recent estimates, in which the region is seen as a less centralized entity, place population levels in the low thousands.

Variation among residential structures and burial practices, at Cahokia and other Mississippian sites, indicate clear differences in social status. Elite burials, sometimes found in separate cemeteries, are associated with large quantities of elaborate artifacts (sheets of mica, copper ornaments, and drilled marine shell beads), many of which were manufactured from materials acquired through long-distance trade.

Some archaeologists argue that these materials were traded through an elite network and provided a means to legitimize power and authority. The extent to which this was the case is unclear, since such items are also found in nonelite contexts, albeit in lower quantities. Long-distance trade for materials associated with ritual contexts has a long history in eastern North America, but it is possible that such trade was broadened during Mississippian times. For example, large bifacially chipped hoes from two well-known chert sources in southern Illinois and western Tennessee were traded extensively throughout the Mississippi Valley. These artifacts, used for subsistence rather than ritual activities, were intensively resharpened and recycled. They were so widely distributed that their resharpening flakes are a diagnostic Mississippian artifact at even the smallest sites.

Though impressive, developments in the American Bottom did not persist for very long. Population levels reached their maximum ca. A.D. 1150, and while mound construction and a strongly ranked social structure continued, populations gradually declined over the next two centuries. By A.D. 1250, residential activities in areas that previously functioned as plazas within mound groups suggest a secularization of space previously maintained for ritual activities and a breakdown between elite and nonelite segments of society. The American Bottom continued to be occupied at lower population levels, but the influence of Cahokia was replaced by more locally autonomous communities.

The developments at Cahokia were unique in size, but a similar sequence of events was played out across the Southeast at various times and places. Local areas experienced rapid population increases, encouraging formation of increasingly complex social organizations. Relatively large population centers emerged, usually associated with earthworks that provided a focus of community integration. The nature of these developments were highly variable. Between A.D. 1250 and A.D. 1500, *Moundville grew to dominate a number of centers along the Black Warrior River in west-central Alabama. In the lowlands of southeastern Missouri, many centers emerged, most likely at slightly different times and for varying lengths of time, but no single center appears to have dominated this region. In still other areas, one finds mound groups without large towns. These may have been focal points in regions that could not support high population densities.

Generally, most areas could not sustain high populations for long. In some regions, such as the American Bottom, the process of population decline was gradual. In the vicinity of Powers Fort at the base of the Ozark escarpment in southeastern Missouri, this process occurred abruptly ca. A.D. 1350.

In the mid-sixteenth century, when Hernando de Soto

first entered the Mississippi Valley, his chroniclers described highly populated centers. These descriptions appear consistent with the archaeological record for some but not all areas. Like all Native Americans, Mississippian people had no immunity to European infectious diseases. Because they were living in such high population densities, they were particularly vulnerable to recurring epidemics. When the French explorers entered the Mississippi Valley some 100 years later, the region was virtually vacant.

[See also MOUNDS OF EASTERN NORTH AMERICA; NORTH AMERICA: THE EASTERN WOODLANDS AND THE SOUTH.]

■ Bruce D. Smith, ed., *Mississippian Settlement Patterns* (1978). Dan F. Morse and Phyllis A. Morse, *Archaeology of the Central Mississippi Valley* (1983). Charles J. Baeris and James W. Porter, eds., *American Bottom Archaeology* (1984). Jon Muller, *Archaeology of the Lower Ohio River Valley* (1986). David H. Dye and Cheryl A. Cox, eds., *Towns and Temples along the Mississippi* (1990). George R. Milner, "The Late Prehistoric Cahokia Cultural Systems of the Mississippi River Valley: Foundations, Florescence, and Fragmentation," *Journal of World Prehistory* 4 (1990): 1–43.

Patrice Teltser

MOCHE CULTURE is one of the best-known pre-Inca cultures of Peru. It existed from about the first through the seventh centuries A.D., primarily falling within the Early Intermediate Period. Its heartland was the north coast, and its name derives from the Moche Valley, where the culture was first identified and where its largest architecture is located. Moche's fame derives from outstanding craftsmanship, especially in ceramics and metalwork, as well as impressive, flat-topped adobe pyramids arranged in groups with ramps, plazas, and other features.

The origins of Moche culture are uncertain, but they seem to have drawn upon Chavín traditions filtered through the Vicús, Salinar, and Gallinazo cultures. Moche was contemporaneous with the Recuay culture, in the highlands to the east, and with Nasca, on the south coast.

The history of Moche culture is traced through a five-phase ceramic sequence. By about A.D. 400 Moche pottery was present from the Piura to the Huarmey Valleys, covering close to 400 miles (250 km). Coastal valleys provided water for irrigation canals to maximize the cultivation of the crops that included maize, beans, peanuts, fruits, and cotton. Fields were fertilized with guano gathered from islands off the south coast. Fish were taken from the ocean by use of reed boats and nets. Deer were hunted in the valleys and hills. Muscovy ducks were domesticated, and although llamas were present, they were more valued as pack animals and for wool than as food.

The valleys in the core region of Moche culture each have a pyramid complex, and the Moche Valley itself boasts one of the largest structures built in the Americas, the Pyramid of the Sun (*Huaca del Sol), associated with a smaller structure, the Pyramid of the Moon. This has led to various interpretations of Moche political organization with possibilities ranging from a centralized state to two separate kingdoms to numerous independent principalities sharing common cultural traditions.

While the nature of Moche political structure is uncertain, there is ample evidence of the labor and resources its rulers were able to control. These included exchange systems that brought lapis lazuli from Chile, *Spondylus* shells from Ecuador, and other exotic items from distant regions. Specialists crafted objects in copper, silver, and gold for use by elites, particularly, articles of personal adornment and

ritual use. Distinctive marks on adobe bricks may indicate that a form of labor tax required communities to participate in pyramid construction.

The distinctive Moche pottery was commonly decorated by red-orange paint on a cream slip. Modeled vessels include figures of animals, plants, and human heads, the latter sometimes portraits. Painted scenes depict a host of activities that reflect human actions transmogrified into supernatural realms. Changes through time include a shift from modeling and simple painting to crowded, intricately painted scenes. Vessel shapes also change through time with variations especially noted in the form of the popular "stirrup" spouts.

Study of Moche ceramics has revealed much regarding Moche life, thought, and ceremonialism. Depictions of noninseminating sexual practices may represent ritual activities. Scenes of hunting, weaving, and metalworking also have supernatural references but likely depict quotidian activities as well. Painted scenes of warfare and sacrifice are especially common during late Moche times. Recent excavations at *Sipan and San José de Moro have uncovered the burials of personages of high rank in costumes of gods shown in sacrifice scenes on pottery.

Research indicates that the deities depicted in ritual sacrifice included the Rayed deity (warrior priest), a goddess who wore a jesterlike headdress, and a bird god. The Moche priests who enacted the roles of gods sacrificed prisoners probably taken in battle. The central ritual act was the drinking of blood taken from the sacrificed victims. This ceremony was first identified through interpretation of the "Presentation Theme" (now called "The Sacrifice Ceremony") in which the goddess, bird god, and sometimes others are commonly shown presenting chalices to the Rayed deity. In life, blood was prevented from coagulating through use of the juice of the *ulluchu* fruit, and representations of the *ulluchu* in art suggest that it was imbued with religious symbolism.

Other themes found repeatedly in late Moche art include the Burial theme, the Boat theme, and the Revolt of the Objects theme. These likely were linked in a mythic narrative, which was represented as separate scenes in art, much as events of the life of Christ were depicted in the art of medieval Europe.

The high-status tombs that have revealed information on ritual also suggest that Moche priests took most of their paraphernalia with them to the tomb, creating demand for the production of new regalia for their successors in office. Whether Moche culture was a theocracy, ruled by such priests, or whether there were higher-ranking, more secular authorities remains to be investigated.

In the early seventh century the great pyramid complex in the Moche Valley was abandoned, and the site of Galindo was established up the valley. This site lacked large-scale pyramids but foreshadowed the urbanlike qualities of sites of the later *Chimu state. Farther north, in the Lambayeque Valley, a huge pyramid was constructed at the site of Pampa Grande, which appears to have played an important role in late Moche times. A decrease in the distribution of Moche ceramics along the coast suggests that the extent of its influence contracted.

These changes occurred at about the same time as or shortly after environmental crises that included severe droughts and devastating rains related to changes in the El Niño current and resulting effects on weather patterns. Whether internal social factors contributed to the cultural crisis of late Moche times is uncertain, but external pressure from the expanding Huari state may have played a role. Whatever the specific causes, Moche society was radically transformed, ending its distinct archaeological manifestation though contributing many traditions to subsequent cultures. The Lambayeque, Sicán, and Chimu cultures drew upon Moche traditions, the latter becoming the most powerful kingdom conquered by the Incas, which, in turn, fell to the Spanish.

[See also ANDEAN PRE-INCA CIVILIZATIONS, THE RISE OF; SOUTH AMERICA: THE RISE OF COMPLEX SOCIETIES IN SOUTH AMERICA.]

■ Elizabeth P. Benson, *The Mochica* (1972). Christopher B. Donnan, *Moche Art and Iconography* (1976). Christopher B. Donnan, *Moche Art of Peru* (1978). Walter Alva and Christopher B. Donnan, *Royal Tombs of Sipán* (1993). Santiago Uceda and Elías Mujica, eds., *Moche, Propuestas y Perspectivas* (1994).

Jeffrey Quilter

MOGOLLON AND MIMBRES CULTURES.

Along with Hohokam and Anasazi, Mogollon is one of the three major archaeological traditions in the North American Southwest. The Mogollon heartland centers on the highlands of southwestern New Mexico and east-central Arizona, especially around several major rivers, such as Gila, Mimbres, and Rio Grande. The boundaries of the Mogollon are inexact, with more peripheral Mogollon remains being present in the Chihuahuan Desert to the south in Arizona, New Mexico, extreme western Texas, and Chihuahua. The Mogollon area is best known for the Mimbres culture, which produced artistically superb black-on-white ceramics, for large villages such as Grasshopper Pueblo, and for important research on the origin of agriculture.

The term "Mogollon" was first used by Dr. Emil Haury in 1936. On the basis of excavations at Mogollon Village and Harris Village, two sites in southwestern New Mexico, Haury defined Mogollon as an archaeological culture dating from A.D. 200 to 1000 with pit houses and brown pottery. He did not include the post–A.D. 1000 surface pueblo remains as Mogollon, which were thought to represent either the in-migration of Anasazi from the north or enculturation of local groups into the Anasazi tradition. Since post-A.D. 1000 puebloan groups are now considered a continuation of the Mogollon cultural tradition from their pit-house-dwelling, brownware-using ancestors, Mogollon has come to signify as much a region as a set of related cultural traditions.

Despite cultural variability among the Mogollon, there is a general sequence of historical change. Around 1500 B.C., during the Late Archaic, Mesoamerican crops (e.g., maize and squash) were introduced into the region. Scholars do not agree on the immediate impact of the introduction of crops, but it is clear that it did not lead directly to the development of sedentary farming villages. *Bat Cave, in Central New Mexico, has been one of the most important sites for analyzing the introduction of crops into the prehistoric North American Southwest.

The first Mogollon sites occur by A.D. 200 with the presence of multifamily villages with brown pottery and deep pit houses; many occur on hilltops above river valleys. Early Mogollon sites rarely have more than fifty pit houses, and not all pit houses were contemporary. While the inhabitants of these villages were farmers, the relative importance of agriculture compared to hunting and gathering is not known.

Later pit house villages, A.D. 550–1000, often were larger, more frequent, and located next to rivers. These changes seem to signify an expanding farming population aggregated into larger villages. Ceramic decoration becomes more diverse; textured (often corrugated) surfaces are developed and simple red geometric designs on a brown background are replaced by more complex red-on-white and then black-on-white designs.

Surface pueblo communities replace most pit houses in the Mogollon region around A.D. 1000. This change, along with other changes in the archaeological record, mark alterations in the organization of Mogollon societies. The nature of the changes and character of puebloan Mogollon cultures are a source of major debate.

The best-known southern Mogollon remains are the Classic Mimbres, puebloan Mogollon centered along the Mimbres and Gila Rivers of southwestern New Mexico, dating from A.D. 1000 to 1150. Because of the often stunningly executed geometric, zoomorphic, and anthropomorphic designs on Classic Mimbres black-on-white pottery, Mimbres sites are perhaps the most extensively looted in North America. Most intact vessels are found in graves placed under pueblo rooms; therefore, looters destroy the pueblo remains in search of pottery. Only a handful of large and medium Classic Mimbres sites have escaped destruction. Fortunately, several important excavations prior to 1940 (e.g., Cameron Creek, Swarts Ruin, and Galaz Site) have been reported, and several major projects since the 1970s, especially by the Mimbres Foundation and Texas A & M University, ingeniously acquired data from badly looted sites.

The Classic Mimbres lived in autonomous villages of up to 200 rooms and farmed extensively in the region. While there may have been occasional wealth and status differences between individuals and families, such differences were limited. The meaning of designs on the black-on-white pottery is not known. Limited studies suggest that some fish designs represent species found in the Gulf of California, hundreds of miles from the Mimbres homeland, and that some designs may have been emblems of social significance.

There are two current explanations for the end of the Classic Mimbres system around A.D. 1150. The first suggests that with the return of a more normal climatic regime during the end of the Classic Mimbres period, the dramatically expanded human population was not able to support itself with the farming techniques developed during the unusually favorable precipitation conditions in effect during most of the Classic Mimbres occupation. The system of social and economic relationships then collapsed under the resulting stresses, even though some Mimbreños continued to reside in the region. The second explanation argues that many Mimbreños were absorbed into the *Casas Grandes network centered in northwestern Chihuahua, which was gaining prominence and was expanding toward the end of the Classic Mimbres period, and that these changing regional relationships disrupted the Classic Mimbres cultural system.

Several Post-Classic Mimbres traditions (such as Animas and Salado) occur in the southern Mogollon areas. These clearly reflect changing regional relationships and ideologies involving Casas Grandes and the Hohokam, among others. Since it is not clear if these later traditions represent a continuation of the indigenous Mogollon cultures, most scholars would not classify them as Mogollon.

Large and late northern puebloan Mogollon communities have been extensively studied. Best known of these is Grasshopper Pueblo, a 500-room pueblo occupied from A.D. 1260 to 1380.

One of the major debates in northern Mogollon archaeology is the degree of vertical complexity, that is, the presence of elites and differences between community members. Most interpretations of Grasshopper emphasize its largely egalitarian nature, with the community integrated by a rich ritual life and multilayered but horizontal social organization. In contrast, researchers working at another large late pueblo, Chavez Pass, or Nuvakwewtaqa, argue that there were regional networks and the presence of elites. There has been no clear resolution of this discussion, but it has had two positive results: (1) Archaeologists recognize the difficulty in studying complexity in intermediate societies, those between states and clearly egalitarian villagers, and (2) it has allowed southwestern archaeologists to recognize complexity elsewhere, for example, among the Hohokam.

The prehistoric cultures of the Mogollon area interacted with other southwestern peoples and shared similar historical developments. In paths not yet fully understood, Mogollon peoples were ancestral to modern Puebloans, such as the Zuñi, Hopis, and Rio Grande Pueblos.

[See also ANASAZI CULTURE; HOHOKAM CULTURE; NORTH AMERICA: THE NORTH AMERICAN SOUTHWEST.]

■ Emil W. Haury, The Mogollon Culture of Southwestern New Mexico. *Medallion Papers* 20 (1936). J. J. Brody, *Mimbres Painted Pottery* (1977). William A. Longacre, Sally J. Holbrook, and Michael W. Graves, Multidisciplinary Research at Grasshopper Pueblo, Arizona. *Anthropological Papers of the University of Arizona* 40 (1982). Steven A. LeBlanc, *The Mimbres People: Ancient Pueblo Painters of the American Southwest* (1983). Linda S. Cordell, *Prehistory of the Southwest* (1984).

Paul E. Minnis

MOHENJO-DARO, "Mound of the Dead Men," is one of the most famous Bronze Age cities of the world. It is located in Sind Province of Pakistan on the western, or right bank of the Indus River at 27°18' north latitude, 67°07' east longitude. Mohenjo-daro and *Harappa, 400 miles (643 km) to the northeast, are the two principal excavated cities of the Indus or Harappan civilization. They prospered on the plains of Pakistan and western India from around 2500 to 2000 B.C. Stuart Piggott (1950) proposed that they were twin capitals of a vast Harappan empire, but this is not part of current theory. The discovery of a Harappan city at Ganweriwala in Cholistan, midway between Harappa and Mohenjo-daro, is a strong reason to dismiss Piggott's twin capitals notion. It is not known how Harappan polity operated or the role played by large urban places.

Mohenjo-daro was first visited by an archaeologist, D. R. Bhandarkar, in 1911 to 1912. Excavation began in the winter field season of 1922 to 1923, just after excavation had taken place at Harappa. The similarity between the remains from these sites led archaeologists to continue to excavate but the discovery of the *Indus civilization was not announced until 1924. Intensive excavation continued at Mohenjo-daro until 1931, when the Great Depression forced the end of the large-scale work which was published in two substantial reports (Marshall 1931 and Mackay 1937–38). Smaller excavations continued through the 1930s but not on a yearly basis. Sir Mortimer *Wheeler undertook one season of work there in 1950 and George F. Dales did the same in 1964. A team of architects and archaeologists headed by Dr. Michael

Jansen has been working at the site since 1979, mapping the remains, conducting intensive surface surveys, and producing general documentation.

Mohenjo-daro appears to have been occupied during the Mature, Urban Phase Harappan of the Harappan Cultural Tradition (2500–2000 B.C.). There is a later Buddhist stupa and associated monastery of the early centuries A.D., but it is small. The lowest levels of the site have never been revealed in a substantial way because of the high groundwater table of the Indus Valley, and the beginnings of the city are obscure. There is no evidence for an Early Harappan or pre-Urban Phase occupation. Michael Jansen has proposed that it may be a "founder's city" planned in the Mature, Urban Phase Harappan prior to its construction, like the Alexandrias that were built by Alexander the Great.

There are two parts to the city. A high mound to the west, with the so-called Great Bath, is separated from the Lower Town to the east by an empty space that has been shown, through excavation, never to have been settled. The Mound of the Great Bath is the site of specialized architecture. The Great Bath itself is an open quadrangle with verandas on four sides. There is architectural evidence for a second floor. A long gallery on the south has a small room in each corner; on the east, a single range of small chambers, including one with a well. In the center of the enclosed quadrangle is a large bath approximately thirty-nine feet long by twenty-three feet (12 m by 7 m) wide and sunken eight feet (2.5 m) below the surrounding paving of the court. It has a flight of steps at either end. The bath was waterproofed with a lining of bitumen below the outer courses of baked brick. Its function, insofar as it contained water, is not in doubt. Directly adjacent to the bath is a series of brick foundations that Sir Mortimer Wheeler suggested was a granary. But, just as at Harappa, there is no collateral evidence for this function, making it doubtful. The so-called Assembly Hall and College of Priests are also areas of the Mound of the Great Bath that may not as such be truly functional. The Mound of the Great Bath as a whole is elevated and separated from the living area of the city of Mohenjo-daro and because of this, seems likely to have been the abode of an elite segment of the population.

Mohenjo-daro is famous for many things. The two most prominent are its grid plan and the extensive internal drainage system that was integrated into the town plan. The grid town plan has been proved through excavation with two north–south streets (First and Second Streets) and two east–west thoroughfares (Central and East Streets). These divide the Lower Town into at least nine blocks, the internal structure of which does not necessarily conform to the grid town plan. Most houses were provided with trash chutes, sumps, and/or refuse collection bins. Some of these are integrated into a system of street drains, with sumps, manholes, and the like. These are not large-scale sewers, but functioned more like the *jube*, features of streets in Iran, Afghanistan, and parts of Pakistan. The rainfall around Mohenjo-daro is less than 4 inches (100 mm). Since rainfall in the area is thought to be about the same today as in the third millennium, contrary to some opinion, the drainage system would not have been justified by the rainfall.

The combined size of the mounds at Mohenjo-daro is approximately 250 acres (100 ha), about the same as for Harappa. But, extensive remains have been found under the alluvium to the north and east of the mounds at Mohenjo-daro and the city might have been much larger, perhaps 990 or even 1230 acres (400 or 500 ha). If all 250 acres

(100 ha) of Mohenjo-daro were settled at one time, with a population density of approximately 200 people per 2.5 acres (1 ha), the population of the city would have been about 20,000.

The people of Mohenjo-daro seem to have been engaged in craft production: copper/bronze metallurgy, stone tool manufacture, faience production, shell working, bead manufacturing, seal production, and the like. They were also farmers (barley, some wheat, cotton, and a wide range of other plants) and herders. Cattle are especially prominent in the archaeological record, both as faunal remains and artifacts, and it is clear that the ownership of these animals was almost certainly a principal way in which wealth was expressed. There is abundant evidence for long-distance trade, with contacts reaching Mesopotamia via the sea lanes through the Arabian Gulf, as well as overland to northern Afghanistan, central Asia to the north, and peninsular India to the south and east.

Mohenjo-daro was abandoned at about 2000 B.C. The reasons for this are not yet known; however, it was not invading Aryans. Many other settlements in the area surrounding Mohenjo-daro in Sind were also abandoned at this time and something similar took place at Harappa and in its hinterland. The other domains of the Indus civilization seem to have been unaffected, and there is abundant evidence for cultural continuity into the second millennium. In Gujarat and the Indian Punjab and Haryana there is even an increase in the number of settlements, some of which underwent extensive rebuilding at the point when Mohenjo-daro was being abandoned. There seems to be good reason to revise the notion of an eclipse or collapse of the Indus civilization other than in Sind and the west Punjab. There was certainly no discontinuity in the cultural tradition. Recent work by Jagat Pati Joshi of the Archaeological Survey of India has documented continuity from the Mature, Urban Phase Harappan into the Early Iron Age in Punjab and Haryana (Joshi 1978).

[See also ASIA: PREHISTORY AND EARLY HISTORY OF SOUTH ASIA.]

■ Sir John Marshall, ed., Mohenjo-Daro and the Indus Civilization, 3 vols. (1931). Ernest J. H. Mackay, Further Excavations at Mohenjo-daro, 2 vols. (1937–1938). Dan Stanislawski, "The Origin and Spread of the Grid-pattern Town," Geographical Review 36: 105–20. Stuart Piggott, Prehistoric India to 1000 B.C. (1950). Sir Mortimer Wheeler, The Indus Civilization, 3rd ed. (1968). Jagat Pati Joshi, "Interlocking of Late Harappa Culture and Painted Grey War Culture in the Light of Recent Excavations," Man and Environment 2 (1978): 98–101. Gregory L. Possehl, "Discovering Ancient India's Earliest Cities: The First Phase of Research," in Harappan Civilization: A Contemporary Perspective, ed. Gregory L. Possehl (1982): 405–413. Michael Jansen and Gunter Urban, eds., Reports on Field Work Carried Out at Mohenjo-Daro, Pakistan, 1982–86 by the Ismeo-Aachen University Mission: Interim Reports, vols. 1, 2, (1983, 1987). George F. Dales, and J. Mark Kenoyer, Excavations at Mohenjo Daro, Pakistan: The Pottery (1986). Michael Jansen and Maurizio Tosi, eds., Reports on Field Work Carried Out at Mohenjo-Daro, Pakistan, 1983–86 by the Ismeo-Aachen University Mission: Interim Reports, vol. 3 (1988).

Gregory L. Possehl

MONTE ALBÁN is an archaeological site that was the political capital of the earliest state developed by the Zapotec speakers of the valley of *Oaxaca, Mexico. It was founded at the end of the Mesoamerican Middle Formative Period, at about 500 B.C. and continued as the major Zapotec political center until its near abandonment about A.D. 700. Monte Albán's archaeological remains inform us about the growth of one of the earliest and most important Native American states, and its collapse is symptomatic of the decline of the large-scale polities of the western Mesoamerican Classic Period (A.D. 300–700). Given Monte Albán's role in these important social changes, it has been a focus of major research efforts, including long-term excavation projects by Mexican archaeologists Alfonso Caso (1896–1971) and Ignacio Bernal (1910–1992) and, more recently, a systematic archaeological survey of the urban zone (Blanton 1978; the results of these and other projects are summarized in Flannery and Marcus 1983).

Monte Albán attained its maximum population size and architectural elaboration during the Late Classic Period (A.D. 500–700). By this time, it had a population estimated at about 25,000 persons residing on some 2,000 terraces on the ridgetops and slopes of a series of low hills near the center of the valley of Oaxaca. Within the city, fifteen residential neighborhoods have been found, each consisting of a cluster of residential terraces surrounding a zone of elite residences, temples, and open plazas. The center of government, and the residence of the ruling family, was in the main plaza complex, the most massive and architecturally coherent space ever built in pre-Hispanic Oaxaca. Here, twenty pyramid platforms face onto an open plaza some 985 feet by 656 feet (300 by 200 m); among the structures are massive platforms, defining the plaza's north and south edges, that are among the largest pre-Hispanic buildings anywhere in Mesoamerica. Also found in the main plaza complex is the largest and most important corpus of Zapotec carved-stone monuments; these announce military victories and describe the activities of rulers (e.g., Marcus 1992).

[See also MESOAMERICA, articles on CLASSIC PERIOD IN MESOAMERICA, FORMATIVE PERIOD IN MESOAMERICA; ZAPOTEC CIVILIZATION.]

■ Richard E. Blanton, Monte Albán: Settlement Patterns at the Ancient Zapotec Capital (1978). Kent V. Flannery and Joyce Marcus, eds., The Cloud People: Divergent Evolution of the Zapotec and Mixtec Civilizations (1983). Joyce Marcus, Mesoamerican Writing Systems: Propaganda, Myth, and History in Four Ancient Civilizations (1992).

Richard E. Blanton

MONTE VERDE. A few centuries before the twelfth millennium B.P. a small group of humans camped at Monte Verde on the sandy banks of Chinchihuapi Creek, located in a cool temperate rain forest of southern Chile. Since 1977, interdisciplinary archaeological studies at this site have produced a phenomenal record of some of the first people in South America. In addition to the usual stone and bone artifacts, Monte Verde contains a wealth of perishable materials made of wood, bone, and plant remains, which were preserved and sealed by a water-saturated peat bog.

Perhaps the most revealing discovery at Monte Verde is the wooden foundations of twelve domestic structures and one isolated hut. Resting on the living floors inside the huts and attached to the foundation timbers were numerous pieces of animal skin, suggesting that the wooden architectural frames were hide-draped. The layout of the foundation timbers indicates that they were arranged as rows of rectangular huts agglutinated to form an elongated tent with internally separated spaces. A small clay-lined fire pit, food stains, plant remains, stone tools, and other debris were found on the floor inside each hut. Two large cooking pits, several wooden mortars and grinding stones, numerous modified stones and pieces of wood, and other miscellaneous features indicate a wide range of domestic tasks.

The isolated hut was characterized by a wishbone-shaped foundation made of gravel and hardened sand. Recovered from inside the hut were masticated leaves of *boldo*, juncus, and seaweed, all having medicinal properties. Scattered around the hut were wood, wooden artifacts, stone tools, bones of seven mastodons, and other varieties of possibly used medicinal plants, all associated with fire hearths and food pits. This evidence suggests that the wishbone structure was the place of specialized activities, such as hide and meat processing, tool manufacture, and possibly medicinal practices.

Macroscopic and microscopic analyses of floor, hearth, and stain fills have yielded the remains of various plant and animal foods, many of which were imported to the site from distant highland and coastal habitats. The Monte Verdeans had a generalized hunting-and-gathering economy throughout most of the year.

Also found at Monte Verde are the traces of an older possible campsite nearby on a buried promontory of an old lagoon. The evidence from this area consists of twenty-six stones, some of which are clearly worked by the human hand, and three hearthlike features that are radiocarbon dated to approximately 33,000 B.P. Until the final analyses are complete, however, no conclusions can be drawn about these materials.

[*See also* AMERICAS, FIRST SETTLEMENT OF THE: SETTLEMENT OF THE AMERICAS BEFORE 12,500 B.C.; SOUTH AMERICA: EARLY PREHISTORY OF SOUTH AMERICA.]

■ T. D. Dillehay, "A Late Ice-Age Settlement in Southern Chile, *Scientific American* 251 (1984): 100–109. T. D. Dillehay, *Monte Verde: A Late Pleistocene Settlement*, vol. I: *Paleoenvironmental and Site Context* (1989).

Tom D. Dillehay

MORGAN, Lewis Henry (1818–1881), nineteenth-century American anthropologist. Born and raised in western New York State, Morgan was sufficiently successful as a lawyer in Rochester, New York, that he was able to devote much of his life to scholarship. As a young adult Morgan became interested in the Iroquois Indians, and he set out to collect information on these people. His *League of the Iroquois* (1851), one of the first modern ethnographic monographs, was based on this work. In the 1850s Morgan made a striking discovery, which was that the Iroquoian pattern of kinship and descent occurred among other North American Indians as well. This suggested a common historical origin for these societies. Morgan speculated that the same system would be found in still other parts of the world, and he reasoned that this would demonstrate that all peoples were historically related, or that all human races represented a single stock, not separate species. This was an issue of considerable importance, particularly in view of the controversy over slavery. Morgan devised a questionnaire that would elicit the information he needed, and it was mailed to official outposts throughout the world. The results were as he expected. His findings also revealed the widespread existence of several other types of kinship system besides the Iroquoian. He reported his findings in the monumental *Systems of Consanguinity and Affinity of the Human Family* (1870), which forms the basis of modern kinship studies. Morgan is probably best known as a cultural evolutionist, and his *Ancient Society* (1877) offered an account of the evolution of culture from savagery to civilization. His analysis assumed that all peoples are endowed with a capacity for progress but that some advanced more quickly than others. Morgan further assumed that intelligence was a key factor in this process, and that a people's brain size correlated with their position on the scale.

[*See also* HISTORY OF ARCHAEOLOGY BEFORE 1900: ARCHAEOLOGY OF THE AMERICAS; HISTORY OF ARCHAEOLOGY, INTELLECTUAL.]

■ Carl Resek, *Lewis Henry Morgan, American Scholar* (1960). Thomas R. Trautmann, *Lewis Henry Morgan and the Invention of Kinship* (1987).

Elvin Hatch

MORTUARY ANALYSIS. Graves and deposits containing human remains are important sources for archaeologists. The bones and other surviving tissues can be analyzed to determine the age and sex of the deceased and sometimes diet, diseases, and cause of death. These methods of osteology and palaeopathology are combined with mortuary analysis to understand the organization of past societies. Mortuary analysis is the study of the deposition of the dead: how the body was treated (whether buried, burnt, or exposed), how the remains were deposited (the layout of corpse and grave goods, provision of a monument, and reuse of the bones in secondary rites), and how the variations in treatment and accompanying grave goods might reveal how societies were organized.

Modern humans were the first to bury their dead (Qafzeh, Israel, ca. 100,000 years ago), followed by Neanderthals (70,000–40,000 years ago). There is a debate about whether they provided grave goods, which are known from Upper Paleolithic burials. The burials of a man in a fine shell-embroidered costume and two children with artificially straightened mammoth ivory lances at *Sunghir in the CIS around 23,000 B.P. show that these were no skin-wrapped, club-wielding cavemen.

The burials of ancient rulers are well known for their riches (such as the tomb of Queen Shub-Ad at Ur around 2500 B.C.) and their monumental construction (like the *pyramids at Giza). Most burials excavated by archaeologists are not so spectacular but they still provide important evidence about past societies. By studying the age and sex structures of Early Bronze Age cemeteries in Hungary (ca. 2000 B.C.), Susan Shennan established that sex was marked by body position and grave orientation and that certain grave goods reflected the age and sex of the deceased. She then found that particular types of rings, pins, and necklaces were restricted to a few individuals and concluded that this was a stratified, unequal society where wealth was ascribed by heredity since some children had these elaborate costumes. Since "rich" females survived infancy better than others, she suggested that girls were cared for because descent was matrilineal. Alternatively, the small number of "rich" males might signify a polygamous and patrilineal society.

Studies of social status have analyzed how different societies have changed through time. John O'Shea's statistical analysis of cemeteries of three Plains Indian tribes between ca. A.D. 1700 and 1850 has demonstrated how fast and episodic were changes in burial rites, caused by changing conditions and perceptions in the living society.

Archaeologists' interpretations of grave goods and treatment of the body as a mirror of status and role are complicated by anthropologists' observations that death rituals embellish, conceal, and misrepresent social relationships among the living. The dead do not bury themselves and funerals are often contested political events in which inheritance, property, and power are transferred and negotiated.

The ancient rulers of Mesopotamia, China, Egypt, Greece, and Rome were sometimes buried with pomp and splendor, yet many royal funerals have left little or no trace. Sometimes rulers are buried in a fashion similar to their subjects. Religious or political ideologies may be strong influences. Much also depends on whether the power of the leadership is threatened. Lavish ritual performances have often been staged to establish or reassert political stability.

Fashions of funerary ostentation or simplicity can be traced in archaeological evidence. The adoption of Christianity in northern Europe was linked to a brief flourishing of elaborate pagan burials (such as the ship burials at *Sutton Hoo, England) and a subsequent change toward simple burial. Often the innovative funeral fashions of a ruling group have been emulated by lower social groups. Within 200 years of Emperor Nero's decision to bury his wife rather than to cremate her, inhumation was common throughout the Roman Empire.

Mortuary analysis also attempts to relate the dead to the living through the placing of the dead. The change from burial under house floors to cemeteries away from settlements in the southeastern European Late Neolithic–Copper Age (4th millennium B.C.) has been interpreted as a power shift from community identity to individual prestige in the exterior domain of hunting and warfare. The places of the dead may also mark political centers or boundaries, thereby demonstrating claims to ancestral land.

In recent years there has been a conflict over *reburial and repatriation of human remains. In many postcolonial countries, particularly North America and Australasia, where living traditions link indigenous communities to distant dead, archaeologists have been asked to rebury or to return collections of human remains. In Australia, 15,000–9,000-year-old bones from Kow Swamp were reburied by Aborigines, preventing further study. Reconciliation is sometimes possible, however, for example by the provision of "keeping places" where bones are curated by indigenous representatives.

[See also BURIAL AND TOMBS; PALEOPATHOLOGY; RANKING AND SOCIAL INEQUALITY, THEORIES OF]

■ James Brown, ed., *Approaches to the Social Dimensions of Mortuary Practices* (1971). Richard Huntington and Peter Metcalf, *Celebrations of Death: The Anthropology of Mortuary Ritual* (1979). Robert Chapman, Ian Kinnes, and Klaus Randsborg, eds., *The Archaeology of Death* (1981). Ellen-Jane Pader, *Symbolism, Social Relations and the Interpretation of Mortuary Remains* (1982). Robert Layton, ed., *Conflict in the Archaeology of Living Traditions* (1989). Ian Morris, *Death-ritual and Social Structure in Classical Antiquity* (1992).

Michael Parker Pearson

MOUNDS OF EASTERN NORTH AMERICA. Earthen mounds built by ancient Native American peoples are nowadays found throughout the Eastern Woodlands of North America, from the Gulf coast in the South to the Great Lakes in the North. Particularly large concentrations of these earthworks occur in the Midwest and South, often in or near the valleys of major rivers such as the Mississippi, the Illinois, the Ohio, and the Tennessee. The mounds themselves were made in a variety of forms, usually round or rectangular. In some cases they attained monumental proportions: The largest such earthwork built in pre-Columbian times, the so-called Monks Mound at the *Cahokia site near St. Louis, is some 98.5 feet (30 m) high and 985 feet (300 m) long.

Not surprisingly, these mounds have been the subject of archaeological interest for quite some time. Through most of the nineteenth century, the prevailing opinion among Euro-American antiquarians was that the local natives were too uncivilized to have built such grand earthworks; instead, the mounds were attributed to a vanished race of Mound Builders. There was much speculation as to the identity of these mysterious people: Phoenicians, Egyptians, and Toltecs were all mentioned as possibilities. It was not until the end of the century that this myth was finally demolished. In 1894, Cyrus Thomas, a scholar at the Smithsonian Institution, published the results of his extensive research, which proved beyond reasonable doubt that the mounds had indeed been built by indigenous peoples, ancestors of the historic Native American tribes. Thomas's work was extremely important, for it ended the rampant (and often racist) speculation, and marked the emergence of archaeology as a scientific discipline in North America.

By the middle of the twentieth century, archaeological attention had turned to questions of culture history. Many were struck by the general similarities between mound-building practices in North America and those in Mexico, particularly after A.D. 1000. Some proposed that eastern North Americans had been strongly influenced by Mexicans in pre-Columbian times, and that mound-building traditions had been adopted by the former from the latter. While this theory was popular for a time, it has, over the past thirty years, fallen out of favor, largely for lack of evidence. Not one Mexican artifact has ever been found in eastern North America (or vice versa), a strong indication that sustained contact never occurred between the two areas. Moreover, we now know that mound building in the Eastern Woodlands goes back thousands of years, long before the alleged Mexican similarities appeared. Hence, this tradition is best understood as an indigenous development, which, at various times, incorporated ideas that were widely distributed among the native people of the Americas. The broad similarities that exist between eastern North American and Mexican mounds (and indeed among mounds throughout the New World) seem now to be more the result of shared heritage than direct contact.

Archaic Period Mounds (5500–500 B.C.). The Archaic Period inhabitants of eastern North America were hunters, fishers, and gatherers who followed many different lifeways adapted to local conditions. Over time, certain regions showed signs of increases in population, sedentism, and territoriality. Such factors may have played a role in the building of the earliest mounds.

The oldest mound yet discovered dates to about 5500 B.C. and was located at L'Anse Amour on the Labrador coast. It was a low circular pile of boulders, just over 1.6 feet (.5 m) high and 29.5 feet (9 m) in diameter, that covered the grave of a child.

Somewhat later, during the third millennium B.C., burial mounds started to appear in the central Mississippi Valley and neighboring drainages, mostly in Missouri and Illinois. Generally located on hilltops, these low earthen mounds typically contained the graves of one or more individuals.

Farther south, in the Lower Mississippi Valley, considerably larger mounds, sometimes in groups, were being built at around the same time. These earthworks were generally conical or loaf-shaped, generally 6.5 to 23 feet (2 to 7 m) high. Limited excavations have not revealed any burials, so the function of these early mounds is still unknown.

This southernmost tradition eventually produced the largest Archaic Period earthworks ever built: the *Poverty

Point site in northeastern Louisiana, which was used between 1800 B.C. and 500 B.C. The site is today marked by a large pear-shaped mound some 69 feet (21 m) high, a smaller conical mound 20 feet (6 m) high, and six concentric ridges that form a semicircle slightly more than .6 mile (1 km) in diameter. The function of the bigger mound is a mystery. The smaller mound may have been a funerary structure in that it was built over a burned layer that contained human bone. The ridges were used for habitation, as evidenced by postholes, pits, and associated middens. Some archaeologists believe that Poverty Point was a large, permanently occupied town; others believe it was a sacred site where people who lived in the surrounding region would sometimes congregate. Whatever the case, these Archaic mounds bespeak a growing level of social complexity among the hunting and gathering peoples who built them.

Woodland Period Mounds (500 B.C.–A.D. 1000). The Woodland Period was marked by several trends. One was the spread of agricultural economies, largely based on the indigenous plants of the Eastern Agricultural Complex. A second was the emergence in some regions of pronounced social inequality, marked archaeologically by the elaboration of graves. And a third was the appearance of large-scale interaction spheres (such as Adena and Hopewell), which facilitated not only the exchange of material goods but also the spread of rituals, symbols, and beliefs. It was in this context that mound building became commonplace across much of eastern North America.

The most typical Woodland Period earthwork was the dome-shaped or conical burial mound. Sometimes such mounds had a relatively simple internal structure, containing little more than earthen fill with one or more burials interspersed. More often, however, they consisted of a ritual facility that had been used for some time and then sealed under a cap of earth. The nature of the facility itself was variable: Some were wooden buildings that were dismantled prior to being capped; others were cryptlike enclosures built of earth and logs; yet others were low earthen platforms usually less than 3 feet (1 m) high; and many were specially prepared surfaces that had been stripped of topsoil, burned, floored with clay, or enclosed by screens or embankments. Whatever form they took, all these facilities were connected in some way with rituals involving the dead, used either as places where corpses were cremated or defleshed, or as mortuaries where human remains were stored. Before the facility was sealed, remains of the dead were typically placed on the floor or buried beneath it. Burials were also commonly placed in the overlying earthen cap. Some mounds contained only one facility and cap, while others grew larger through many such cycles of use. The largest examples were more than 66 feet (20 m) high. Overall, the mounds shared many characteristics, but these characteristics were combined in myriad ways, as though a common pool of symbols and ritual practices were drawn upon to create a wide range of local manifestations.

In some areas, burial mounds were accompanied by large earthen embankments. By far the most elaborate expression is attributed to the *Hopewell culture of southern Ohio (ca. A.D. 1–500), who used embankments to build huge geometric enclosures—often square or circular in shape—that were grouped with mounds in a variety of ways and typically encompassed dozens of hectares.

Square or rectangular platform mounds were also constructed during this period, mostly in the southern states. In some cases these seem to have been used as ritual plat-

forms, similar to the platforms found inside some burial mounds except that they were never capped. In other cases, however, the platforms were surmounted by buildings, either temples or elite residences. By A.D. 800, this pattern was common in the Coles Creek cultures of the Lower Mississippi Valley, where it presaged later Mississippian developments.

The western Great Lakes area saw the appearance of a distinctive Effigy Mound culture after A.D. 300. Burial mounds of this culture were shaped like birds, mammals, turtles, and other creatures. Such earthworks were generally less than 3 feet (1 m) high, but often more than 328 feet (100 m) across.

Mississippian Mounds (A.D. 1000–1700). The end of the first millennium A.D. was a time of profound change, as people throughout the Eastern Woodlands turned to maize agriculture for sustenance. Sedentary hamlets and villages became the typical settlements. In the North, communities remained largely egalitarian. In the South, however, the social inequality seen in Woodland times grew more pronounced, as centralized hierarchical polities became the norm. These southern cultures, collectively called Mississippian, elaborated the practices of mound building that had pervaded the area for centuries.

Although burial mounds continued to be made in many places, the dominant form of monumental earthwork was now the rectangular platform mound with a wooden building on its summit. This building was usually a temple or the residence of a chief. Most Mississippian mounds were not constructed in a single episode but rather in multiple stages: After a mound had been used for a time, the building on its summit would be dismantled and another layer of earth would be added; a new building would then be erected on top. As this cycle was repeated, the mound's dimensions would grow. Mounds 10 to 39 feet (3 to 12 m) high were common; occasionally they reached heights of 66 feet (20 m) or more.

Mississippian mounds sometimes occurred singly but were often grouped around a plaza that served as a venue for ceremonies and other public events. A large civic-ceremonial center could have well over a dozen mounds and cover dozens of hectares.

Building such mounds and mound centers required considerable labor, which was mobilized by chiefs through tributary and other obligations. Indeed, the mounds themselves were powerful religious symbols; not only were community rituals held there, but constructing a mound was a ritual act accompanied by appropriate ceremonies and offerings. While it is impossible to reconstruct fully the nexus of meanings associated with mounds, it is a reasonable guess that the placement of residences atop such powerful icons legitimated the authority of the chiefs who lived there.

[See also ADENA CULTURE; MISSISSIPPIAN CULTURE; MOUNDVILLE; NORTH AMERICA: THE EASTERN WOODLANDS AND THE SOUTH; SOUTHERN CULT.]

■ Cyrus Thomas, *Report on the Mound Explorations of the Bureau of Ethnology* (1894, reprinted 1985). Don W. Dragoo, *Mounds for the Dead* (1963). William M. Hurley, *An Analysis of Effigy Mound Complexes in Wisconsin* (1975). William N. Morgan, *Prehistoric Architecture in the Eastern United States* (1980). Frank T. Schnell, Vernon J. Knight Jr., and Gail S. Schnell, *Cemochechobee: Archaeology of a Mississippian Ceremonial Center on the Chattahoochee River* (1981). James L. Phillips and James A. Brown, eds., *Archaic Hunters and Gatherers in the American Midwest* (1983). Jerald T. Milanich et al., *McKeithen Weeden Island: The Culture of Northern Florida, A.D. 200–900* (1984). Jon L. Gibson and J. Richard Schenkel, "Louisiana Earthworks:

Middle Woodland and Predecessors," in ed. Robert C. Mainfort Jr., *Middle Woodland Settlement and Ceremonialism in the Mid-South and Lower Mississippi Valley* (1988), pp. 7–18. Brian M. Fagan, *Ancient North America* (1991).

Vincas P. Steponaitis

MOUNDS OF THE AMAZON. Five types of archaeological mounds have been noted in the Amazon region: shell refuse mounds, artificial earth platforms for villages, earth mounds and ridges for cultivation, causeways and canals, and figurative mounds.

The shell mounds of the Amazon region are found on both flooded and unflooded land at rivers and estuaries in the Guianas, mouth of the Amazon in Brazil, mainstream of the Amazon in Brazil, along tributaries in the Bolivian Amazon, and at the mouth of the Orinoco. The mounds are piles of human refuse that accrued mainly between 7500 and 4000 B.P., although later cultures are known to have established dwellings and/or cemeteries on top of the earlier shell mounds. Nine early shell mounds in the eastern Amazon have been dated, and all share the same general chronological range. All of these are of pottery-age cultures. So far, no preceramic shell mounds have been documented. This has been a great surprise to archaeologists, who expected the tropical forest habitat to have limited sedentary settlement in the Amazon. The shell mounds appear to have been created by the activities of aquatic foragers who did not use agriculture to any great extent. Plant remains and plant organic matter are very scarce in the mounds, although abundant in both earlier and later sites. The mounds are primarily composed of fishbones, turtle shells and bones, and freshwater pearly mollusks. Traces of postholes, hearths, and wall trenches indicate simple habitations, and there are unaccompanied burials. Other cultural remains are useworn rock grinders, hearth rocks, simple stone flakes, shell and bone tools and ornaments, and sherds of simple bowls. The rare decorated pottery is incised and punctated on the rim, a tradition that has continued in use in Amazonia up to today. The earliest pottery tends to be sand tempered. In some areas shell tempering is also used.

The next type of mounds are the large earth platforms best known for the polychrome culture of Marajo Island at the mouth of the Amazon in Brazil. Several hundred have been discovered, but only two have been mapped: Teso dos Bichos and Guajara. The average mound appears to be 16 to 32 feet (5 to 10 m) high, and covers roughly 7.4 acres (3 ha). All are in the seasonally flooding savanna and gallery forest of eastern Marajo, an area of about 7,700 square miles (20,000 sq km).

Because the mounds were repositories of cemeteries and because it was assumed that large, sedentary populations could not live in Amazonia, archaeologists in the mid-twentieth century assumed that the mounds were purely ceremonial, but recent excavations have encountered many superimposed levels of house-floors, domestic hearths, and garbage heaps in the mounds. The mounds, thus, were essentially platforms built to raise villages up out of the reach of flooding. Defense may also have been a concern since the mounds are much higher than flood levels. Early research suggested that the subsistence of the society must have been based on maize and manioc agriculture, due to the elaboration of its culture. Paleodietary studies, however, have revealed a broad-spectrum mixed subsistence of fishing, collecting, and part-time cultivation. Carbonized maize was present but in very small quantities, and manioc

griddles were rare. The most common seeds in the sites were from cultivated trees and unidentified herbs.

The material culture in the mounds includes elaborate and sometimes large art objects: white, red, and/or black-brown, painted and incised and modeled pottery wares, large and small human figures, stools, spindle whorls, and finely ground axes and other cutting tools. The practices of mound building and making of fine art were thought at first to be limited to state-organized societies with social stratification and occupational specialization; such societies were not expected in the Amazon, where most soils are poor, and modern Indian societies are small and simply organized. Consequently, archaeologists hypothesized that the culture was an Andean offshoot that must have decayed rapidly in the hostile environment. However, this was before radiocarbon dating, which subsequently showed that the Marajoara culture existed many hundreds of years earlier than related cultures from the Andean foothills. The thirty radiocarbon dates from the mounds show the culture to have flourished between about A.D. 400 and 1300. In addition, no related cultures have ever turned up in the Andes, and the genetic features of the Mound Builders' skulls are affiliated much more with Amazonian Indians than Andeans. Thus, the culture must be interpreted as a native development.

In addition, the Polychrome Horizon mound builders do not seem to have been highly stratified or centralized polities. Their lack of central places and political art suggests that they were "complex tribes." Ethnohistoric studies of nonstratified societies in Africa and Asia suggest that constructing large earthworks and making fine art are activities well within the powers of such societies.

The Polychrome Horizon is found from Marajo in Brazil to the Andean foothills in Bolivia, Peru, Ecuador, and Colombia. Its place of origin in the Amazon is as yet unknown, although the earliest dates so far come from Marajo. Mounds similar to those of Marajo are found in the floodplains of the Bolivian Amazon, Middle Orinoco, and Guianas, but elsewhere, most polychrome sites are nonmound sites. Several mounds on Marajo Island and several in Bolivia have yielded radiocarbon dates as early as 500 B.C., suggesting that the first mounds were built at the end of the Formative, the period when horticulture appears to become widespread for the first time.

The remaining three types of mounds, figurative mounds, agricultural mounds, and canals and causeways, as well as house-platforms were built by the late prehistoric chiefdoms of Amazonia around 1500 to 1000 B.P. These mound-building cultures belong to the Incised and Punctate Horizon, which is also found at nonmound sites. The house platforms are low mounds of 2.5 acres (1 ha) or less. They appear to be the remains of platforms of large, multifamily houses. They have been noted at sites in many areas of the terra firme (dry land), from the Guianas and Marajo Island, the mainstream Amazon banks, the Altamira region on the Xingu River in Brazil, and in the Ecuadorian Amazon. The figurative mounds have been found only in the Ecuadorian Amazon in the terra firme Faldas de Sangay site. Shapes discerned in the mound sculptures include men, women, and a feline. These images occur at the center of a large field of mounds, most of which appear to be residential. The area of the Ecuadorian mound fields is considerable; fully 4.6 square miles (12 sq km) near Sangay are covered with mounds.

Agricultural mounds occur in several areas of Amazonia: the Guianas, the Middle Orinoco, and the Bolivian Amazon. They consist of large, low-lying fields of grouped ridges and small mounds, often in the vicinity of larger village platform mounds. So far no paleodietary studies have been conducted on materials from the agricultural mounds, although the period is one during which maize became very important in some regions judging from human bone chemistry and archaeobotanical remains from habitation sites.

Earth causeways that run between habitation mounds have been noted in the floodplains of both the Middle Orinoco and the Bolivian Amazon. Canals have been identified only in the Bolivian Amazon, and the known examples tend to be associated spatially with causeways, as if people made use of the causeway barrow pits for canoe travel and perhaps for fishing.

[See also SOUTH AMERICA, articles on INTRODUCTION, THE AMAZON, LOWLANDS CULTURES OF SOUTH AMERICA.]

■ Betty Jane Meggers and Clifford Evans, "Archaeological Investigations at the Mouth of the Amazon," U.S. Bureau of American Ethnology Bulletin 167 (1957). Anna C. Roosevelt et al., The Ancestors: Native Artisans of the Americas (1979). Anne C. Roosevelt, Moundbuilders of the Amazon: Geophysical Archaeology on Marajo Island, Brazil (1991). Anne C. Roosevelt, Amazonian Indians from Prehistory to the Present: Anthropological Perspectives (1994).

Anna C. Roosevelt

MOUNDVILLE, located on the Black Warrior River in west-central Alabama, is among the largest Mississippian civic-ceremonial centers ever built. Today, its most visible features are twenty large, pyramidal earthen mounds arranged around a rectangular plaza. These mounds served as platforms for important buildings, such as temples and the houses of chiefs. The largest earthwork is 56 feet (17 m) high. At one time, the site was fortified with a stockade that enclosed an area of some 200 acres (80 ha).

Because of its impressive size, Moundville has long attracted archaeological interest. In 1869 and 1883 the site was visited and mapped by agents of the Smithsonian Institution. Later, in 1905 and 1906, the site was excavated by Clarence B. Moore, who placed "test holes" in virtually every one of the mounds; he found a spectacular collection of copper and shell ornaments, stone implements, and pottery vessels—many bearing an elaborate iconography. Later still, from 1927 through 1941, large-scale excavations were carried out by the Alabama Museum of Natural History and the Civilian Conservation Corps; these excavations uncovered dozens of house patterns, thousands of burials, and innumerable artifacts. Since the 1940s, archaeologists have focused on interpreting the collections from these early excavations and have carried out a number of smaller digs to recover stratigraphic and dietary information that was missed in the earlier work.

Based on this research, the broad outlines of the site's history can be sketched. Starting at about A.D. 1050, Moundville comprised an aggregation of farmsteads with at least one mound of modest size. It was, at most, a local center. At about A.D. 1150, this community became the region's paramount center. The plaza was laid out and its surrounding mounds were built; Moundville was turned into a thriving fortified town with perhaps as many as 1,000 residents. At around A.D. 1300, many of its inhabitants were moved to outlying settlements, leaving only an elite contingent of chiefs, priests, and their retainers. Even so, Moundville's importance remained intact, as people throughout the region were buried in its cemeteries. The center declined after A.D. 1450 and was virtually abandoned by 1550. At its height, Moundville was the political and religious capital of a large chiefdom, supported by an economy based on agriculture, trade, and tribute; although the mechanisms are not fully understood, Moundville's rise and fall were clearly linked to this chiefdom's political fortunes.

Today, the site is well preserved and maintained as a public park by the Alabama Museum of Natural History.

[See also MISSISSIPPIAN CULTURE; MOUNDS OF EASTERN NORTH AMERICA; NORTH AMERICA: THE EASTERN WOODLANDS AND THE SOUTH.]

■ Clarence B. Moore, "Certain Aboriginal Remains of the Black Warrior River," Journal of the Academy of Natural Sciences of Philadelphia 13 (1905): 125–244. John A. Walthall, Prehistoric Indians of the Southeast: Archaeology of Alabama and the Middle South (1980). Vincas P. Steponaitis, "Contrasting Patterns of Mississippian Development," in ed. Timothy K. Earle, Chiefdoms: Power, Economy, and Ideology (1991), pp. 193–228.

Vincas P. Steponaitis

MUSEUMS AND COLLECTING. As repositories of human knowledge, culture, and artistic achievement, museums have played an important role in both scholarly research and public education. The means by which such institutions have built their collections, however, are undergoing dramatic change, brought about by recent legislation drafted to protect the cultural patrimony of signatory nations and the heritage of indigenous people. As a result, museums in the United States and abroad are being forced to reconsider their acquisitions policies.

Most of the world's great museums built their collections of ancient art and ethnographic material by launching massive campaigns to antiquities-rich countries such as Greece and Egypt, believing that they were better equipped to preserve humankind's heritage than the countries from which materials were taken. In addition to foreign nations, this practice has affected the indigenous cultures of North America, whose cultural material and human remains have been gathered by collectors and scientists alike for more than a century. By literally mining such cultural resources, museums have often placed in jeopardy the very cultures they mean to preserve.

To combat this wholesale destruction of cultural patrimony, seventy-eight countries have adopted the 1970 UNESCO Convention on the Means of Prohibiting and Preventing the Illicit Import, Export, and Transfer of Ownership of Cultural Property. And, in countries where the UNESCO Convention has proved inadequate, numerous national antiquities policies have been developed to prohibit or limit the export of artifacts and ethnographic material. In addition, a new body of international legislation, known as the UNIDROIT Convention, has been drafted by the International Institute for the Unification of Private Law in order to further strengthen a country's ability to reclaim stolen material.

Although museums alone are not responsible for the destruction of cultural patrimony, they have often become the holder of artifacts acquired under what can only be termed auspicious circumstances. In response to this, the International Council of Museums (ICOM), an international organization of museums and museum workers, adopted a Code of Professional Ethics, within which are guidelines that specifically address the acquisition of illicit material. These guidelines, adopted in November 1986, state in part that museums must recognize the connection between the acquisition of illicit material and the often destructive means used to obtain it, and that for a museum to acquire any object, whether by purchase, gift, bequest, or exchange, the institution's governing body must be able to obtain valid title to the object, ensuring that it has not been acquired in or exported from any country in violation of that country's cultural property laws, that recently excavated material is not the product of unscientific investigation or destruction to an ancient monument or site, and that finds were not removed from a site without the knowledge of the landowner or governing authority. Although the ICOM *Code of Professional Ethics* was adopted by the American Association of Museums in 1991, the date by which affiliated museums must comply with it has not yet been established. However, many museums in the United States and abroad have established their own acquisition guidelines. And, on 10 September 1993, the International Congress of Maritime Museums adopted a set of standards that follows ICOM *Code* and provides guidelines for the treatment of underwater cultural resources.

Perhaps the greatest challenge facing federally funded museums with substantial Native American holdings will be compliance with guidelines set forth in the Native American Graves Protection and Repatriation Act (Public Law 101-106), adopted by the United States in 1986. These guidelines not only address any further acquisition of Native American material but mandate the return of all human remains and associated funerary objects to lineal descendants of the tribe from which the objects were collected. For objects whose cultural origin cannot be determined, museums must prepare inventories complete with descriptions, dates collected, and geographical areas that will be made available to all Native American tribes and native Hawaiian organizations.

Legislation, both existing and proposed, will no doubt continue to have an impact on museum collection policies, forcing the development of new ways to present ancient and exotic materials. Already, many museums that once relied primarily on purchase and bequest to enhance their holdings are beginning to forge lending relationships with other institutions and cultural groups, thus providing an alternative for the exchange of cultural patrimony.

[*See also* ETHICS OF ARCHAEOLOGY AND COLLECTING; TRAFFICKING IN ANTIQUITIES.]

■ Paul M. Bator, *The International Trade in Art* (1983). Phyllis Mauch Messenger, ed., *The Ethics of Collecting Cultural Property: Whose Culture? Whose Property?* (1989). United States Information Agency, *Preserving Mankind's Heritage: U.S. Efforts to Prevent the Illicit Trade in Cultural Property* (1991). American Association of Museums, *Technical Information Services Forum. Native American Collections and Repatriation* (1993).

Angela M. H. Schuster

MUSLIMS. *See* ISLAMIC CIVILIZATION.

N

NASCA CIVILIZATION. The Nasca civilization flourished on the south coast of Peru during the Early Intermediate Period, roughly A.D. 1 to A.D. 750. No measurable precipitation falls in this region, and life depends on the small amounts of water flowing out of the Andes Mountains to the Pacific Ocean. The culture was centered in the Nasca Valley, which gives its name to the culture, and its associated art style extended north to the Pisco Valley and south to the Acari Valley, a total range of some 155 miles (250 km).

The Nasca culture produced some of the most elaborate ceramic and textile *art of any prehistoric civilization. The Nasca art style developed out of the earlier Paracas textile tradition, located just to the north of the Nasca region. For present purposes it will be most useful to divide this period into three phases: Early Nasca (also called Nasca phases 2, 3, and 4), Transitional (also called Nasca phase 5), and Late Nasca (also called Nasca phases 6 and 7).

During the Early Nasca phase, people in the Nasca Valley lived in small scattered villages, mostly located in the foothills of the Andes Mountains. Their houses were round, about 10 to 13 feet (3 or 4 m) in diameter; the walls had stone bases and were built of mud-coated brush. A single doorway provided access into each house, and a firepit was located in the center of the floor.

Some 15.5 miles (25 km) downstream, as the river valley crosses the broad coastal desert plain, a major ceremonial center, Cahuachi was located. At Cahuachi are found more than forty artificial mounds and pyramids, and the site is surrounded by enormous cemeteries. The dead were buried in stone-lined cysts, in a seated position, wrapped in cloth; sometimes several ceramic vessels were buried with an individual. There is no evidence that people lived year-round at Cahuachi; rather, it was a pilgrimage center that was only occupied during times of ceremonies. Indeed, the high temperatures and fierce winds of the desert plain make it a most inhospitable location for permanent settlement. Smaller ceremonial centers and cemetery complexes similar to Cahuachi exist elsewhere in the region of Nasca influence, indicating a widespread religious tradition at this time.

The textile and ceramic art of this phase is sometimes referred to as monumental in style. Many naturalistic themes were depicted, including birds, fish, animals, and plants; a number of supernatural beings were also depicted. One theme depicts an anthropomorphized killer whale whose teeth are spotted with drops of blood. It has human hands that hold either a small knife or a severed human head. The taking of trophy heads seems to be a characteristic of Nasca culture in all phases; heads were severed, the eyes and mouth were pinned shut, the brain was removed, and a carrying rope was inserted through a hole in the forehead, held in place by a knot inside the cranium.

During the Transitional phase, people ceased to build religious structures at Cahuachi, although they continued to make pilgrimages to the site to bury their dead and to use the site for ceremonies. Villages began to grow larger, and new ones were established in new locations. The shifts in settlement locations indicate that a major drought probably occurred at this time and that the people of Nasca developed a system of underground aqueducts to provide them with access to subsurface water. These *puquios*, as they are called today, are horizontal wells into which groundwater filters and is carried along a tunnel or open trench to a reservoir at the surface of the ground.

A series of changes in art style began during this Transitional phase, resulting in the "proliferous" styles of Late Nasca. Abstract elements were added to the earlier naturalistic designs, and the designs became more intricate. For example, in the case of the killer whale motif, the body of the whale was eliminated, and the design became a three-sided figure of a mouth with vestigial teeth, out of which a large quantity of blood flowed.

By Late Nasca times, most of the small villages had been abandoned and all of the people had moved into a small number of very large towns. Cahuachi probably continued to be used as a ceremonial center, although no new construction occurred there. This appears to be a period of increased warfare, and warriors are depicted on ceramics in greater numbers. The "proliferous" art style became very elaborate and abstract. It was during the Late Nasca phase that Nasca civilization reached its highest level of political complexity. It is not clear whether the region was divided into several small polities or was unified into a single centralized polity. Nasca society collapsed when the region was invaded by the *Wari Empire, expanding from its base in the Andean highlands.

The Nasca civilization is perhaps best known for the lines and figures etched into the desert plain. The German mathematician Maria Reiche has devoted her life to the study of the geoglyphs (or Nasca Lines as they are more popularly known). The lines were formed by clearing the surface of small red-brown stones and exposing the lighter soil beneath. Many of the straight lines radiate outward from central points, often at small hills or the ends of Andean ridges; at these centers are sometimes found small shrines and broken pottery, perhaps representing offerings. These elements suggest that the lines had a ceremonial function, perhaps serving as pathways linking sacred places. Some lines form figures of animals or plants, or geometric figures; these figures are always composed of a single line, again suggesting that the lines served as pathways. The similarity in style of some of the figures, such as the monkey, spider, and killer whale, to ceramic designs suggests that they were constructed in Early Nasca times. The straight lines, which form the vast majority of the geoglyphs, seem to date from several centuries B.C. to the Spanish colonial period of the sixteenth century A.D.

[*See also* SOUTH AMERICA; *articles on* THE RISE OF COMPLEX SOCIETIES IN SOUTH AMERICA; HIGHLANDS CULTURES OF SOUTH AMERICA.]

■ Anthony Aveni, ed., *The Lines of Nazca* (1990). Helaine Silverman, *Cahuachi in the Ancient Nasca World* (1993).

Katharina J. Schreiber

NASCA LINES. The Nasca (also "Nazca") lines (ground drawings, or geoglyphs) consist of two dozen or more zoomorphic and phytomorphic figures of decametric dimensions and several hundred straight linear features of triangular and trapezoidal shapes up to kilometric lengths. These appear on the Nasca pampa, the elevated tableland between the Nasca and Ingenio River Valleys on the south coast of Peru. They are made by removing the broken angled pieces of stone layered with desert varnish that coat the pampa, thus revealing the underlying lighter soil of the pampa within the darker boundary.

Most of the geolyphs can be dated *termino post quem* to the early Nasca epochs of the Early Intermediate Period (ca. 200 B.C.–A.D. 200) from broken ceramics that consist mostly of ceremonial ware found scattered over the surface. A number of prehistoric artifact surveys undertaken in the river valleys indicate that a considerable population thrived in the region during this period. More recently, accelerator radiocarbon dates in the range of 100 B.C. to A.D. 600 have been obtained on the underlying organic inclusions on desert-varnished fragments overturned in the building process; therefore, chronological evidence points to the same culture that created the famous colorful Nasca ceramic ware having been responsible for etching the figures on the pampa.

Why were the lines built? The astronomical theory argues that long lines were intended to point to astronomical events at the horizon and that the bird, fish, and other effigies were templates of constellations that appeared over the pampa at various times in the seasonal year. Aside from the fact that the horizon is enveloped in a perpetual haze, thus making sky observations difficult, statistical studies of the distribution of alignments of Nasca geoglyphs has provided no convincing evidence that this was ever the intention. Nor is the theory that the lines are an expression of precise Pythagorean geometry very satisfying. It has been demonstrated that a typical line can be sketched out and cleared in short order with a minimum of technology and no map or instructional plan. There is no reason to believe the figures were intended to be seen from above, other than the fact that this is how they were rediscovered by the modern world.

Theories that combine civic and practical motives with the religious and esoteric needs of ancient societies seem more realistic. One plausible hypothesis is that the straight lines were sacred pathways intended to be walked upon, perhaps in connection with some sort of ritual that dealt with the conveyance of water, a precious commodity in this extremely arid region. There are numerous examples of straight pathways walked by indigenous worshipers even in modern times. All the straight lines on the pampa are physically linked to one or more of several dozen radial centers. This makes it possible to walk across the pampa via an immense variety of interconnected routes. Furthermore, these centers are located adjacent to dry tributaries and on large dunes that flank the two major rivers.

Spanish chroniclers tell of the fifteenth-century Inca dedication to creating linear hierarchical mnemonic schemes such as the *quipu,* or knotted string device for keeping records, and the *ceque* system, a radial array of invisible sight lines that divided the capital city of Cuzco into irrigation and kin-related zones. Ethnographic analogy offers the possibility that the lines were part of a dynamic, negotiable scheme associated with setting up shared communal tasks, such as preparing for a fiesta or working on an irrigation project.

Clusters of lines appear to be especially numerous in the vicinity of the pyramids of Cahuachi (Kawachi) on the south bank of the Nasca River. This major ceremonial center is the only excavated site in the vicinity, and its chronology allows the possibility that the lines were associated with pilgrimages conducted there.

[*See also* NASCA CIVILIZATION.]

■ P. Kosok, *Life, Land and Water in Ancient Peru* (1961). A. Aveni, "The Nazca Lines: Patterns in the Desert," *Archaeology* 39:4 (1986): 32–39. A. Aveni, *The Lines of Nazca* (1990). A. Aveni and H. Silverman, "Between the Lines," *The Sciences* 31:4 (1991): 36–42. R. Dorn, P. Clarkson, M. Nobbs, L. Loendorf, and D. Whitley, "New Approach to the Radiocarbon Dating of Rock Varnish, with Examples for Drylands" *Annals of the Association of American Geographers* 82:1 (1992): 136–51.

Anthony F. Aveni

NATIONALISM. The development of nationalism in Europe from the end of the eighteenth century and the ethnic-based responses to the Napoleonic monarchy changed the attitude of Europeans toward the outside world. In line with a definition of national identity based upon imposed commonalities in culture, language, and geographical area, the concept of "other" became a necessary part of the worldview of emerging nation-states. The nineteenth century saw the expansion of imperialism and its often simplistic and racist classifications of the world's population. This entailed a downgrading of the "other" in terms of class or nationality into a necessary but subservient role legitimized by evolutionary schema derived from the natural sciences and the humanities. Archaeologists were not immune to the spread of these ideas and have often been active proponents of them, especially through the concept of the archaeological culture. The culture historical school of archaeology is closely associated with nationalist sentiments. In nineteenth-century Scandinavia, for instance, nationalist trends resulted in the assertion of a Nordic identity with an archaeological emphasis upon technological and cultural continuity and, at least in the case of Sweden, of an assertion of original populations not of black but of blond, white-skinned inhabitants.

Later, in central Europe, the impact of nationalism and its accompanying focus upon ethnicity reached its extreme formulation in the work of *Kossinna on Germany in the early twentieth century, which became, after his death, one of the ideological foundations of the Third Reich. Strong nationalist tendencies were also present in the work of Polish archaeologists attempting to demonstrate the Slav nature of archaeological remains in Poland and the Celtic basis of French culture. In the Soviet Union, Stalinist totalitarian orthodoxy imposed at home, but also exported (e.g., to China and Vietnam), induced at first a high degree of forced conformity and later a reaction involving multilineal challenges to the Stalinist "single train of history" and social evolution. Recently, with the disintegration of the Soviet

Union, more explicit nationalist accounts and in some cases a return to Tsarist concepts of ethnic correlations with archaeological cultures have appeared.

The mosaic of evolutionist, racist, and nationalist ideas has deeply affected the production of archaeological knowledge in parts of the world outside Europe. North American archaeology is faced with the need to develop a dialogue with surviving representatives of the Amerindian nations, and in Australia, concerns with Aboriginal material culture and archaeologically excavated human remains underline a global problem with strong national and ethnic overtones: "who owns the past?" What rights do present descendants of original occupants have over ancestral territories?

In Africa, nationalist movements have challenged colonial hegemony in economic, political, and cultural terms. The colonial paradigm of Africanist archaeology had used imported terminology to emphasize the classification of artifacts, particularly of the early stone-tool-using communities. More recent periods were characterized by ceramic units and the widespread application of the formula "pots = people." Interpretive schema were cast in a "tribal" mold and migrations and external diffusion were used to account for innovations and traits of cultural complexity. Towns and state systems were studied from the perspective of visible remains of stone architecture and imported finds. More extreme abuses of archaeology occurred in the attempt by the Smith regime in Rhodesia to censor results of research on *Great Zimbabwe, and further, in an attempt to reinforce the ideological basis of the white settler regime by emphasizing interpretations in which a light-skinned elite was responsible for civilization in ancient Zimbabwe.

Throughout Africa, the nationalist response to such excesses was to focus upon the achievements of black Africans of the recent past, ironically within the present national boundaries imposed by colonialism. The nationalist archaeologies stressed the validity of oral tradition and distrusted migrationist and even diffusionist interpretations of innovations such as agriculture and iron smelting. Some attempts on a regional scale have been made to understand social developments such as urbanism from a position that includes both internal and external mechanisms, rather than emphasizing only external stimuli such as trade. In general, national archaeology, in responding to the colonial paradigm, has resulted in forms of archaeology strongly linked to state bureaucracies, limited in scope to national boundaries and lacking in significant theoretical development. It is practiced by and for urban elites and only in certain limited circumstances (e.g. adult-education programs in Tanzania, traveling museum exhibitions in Botswana, and community-based archaeological research in Mozambique), has it been possible to begin the construction of a popularly based form of archaeological practice within national frameworks.

In Asia, similar trends in the development of national archaeologies can be exemplified in the emphasis upon local genius in the archaeology of immediate post-colonial Indonesia, while in Japan an elaborate bureaucratic structure for the practice of rescue archaeology has been built up, at least in part, as a nationalist response to the military defeats of the Second World War. This has resulted in a tight focus upon a concept of Japanese ethnic uniformity. Minority groups and cultures, as in so many other parts of the world, are downgraded even to the extent of denial of their existence.

The influence of nationalism upon the practice of archaeology can be seen as a response to higher-level pressure, whether of Napoleonic armies or colonial and imperial expansion, but also as a means of expression of dominance by ethnic and political groupings. Nationalist archaeology is characterized by a limited geographical scope and has a strong tendency to focus upon, and in some cases to impose, racial and cultural uniformity. The nationalist sentiment in archaeology is often diluted through international contact but it can, as happened in Germany, become transformed in combination with xenophobic ideology into a mechanism for the justification of genocide. It is the nationalist assertion of cultural uniformity that poses the greatest danger to the global understanding of multicultural reality which we face today.

[*See also* NON-WESTERN SOCIETIES, ARCHAEOLOGY AND; POLITICAL USES OF ARCHAEOLOGY.]

■ O. Montelius, *Vår forntid* (1919). P. Garlake, *Great Zimbabwe* (1973). B. G. Trigger, *A History of Archaeological Thought* (1989). J. Hubert, "After the Vermillion Accord: Developments in the 'Reburial Issue,'" *World Archaeological Bulletin* 5: 113–18. P. M. Dolukhanov, Archaeology in Russia and Its Impact on Archaeological Theory. Paper presented in the 1992 TAG conference. H. Härke, The German Tradition of Pre- and Proto-history: Reflections on Intellectual, Structural and Historical Aspects. Paper presented in the 1992 TAG conference. D. Tanudjiro, Theoretical Trends in Indonesian Archaeology. Paper presented in the 1992 TAG conference. I. Tsude, Theoretical Trends in Japanese Archaeology. Paper presented in the 1992 TAG conference. E. W. Said, *Culture and Imperialism* (1993). T. Shaw, P.J.J. Sinclair, B. Andah, and A. Okpoko, eds., *The Archaeology of Africa* (1993). S. Welinder, "Svensk arkeologis protorasistiska föreställningssediment," *Tor* 26 (1994): 193–215.

Paul J. J. Sinclair

NATUFIAN CULTURE. The Natufian culture flourished throughout the Levant region of the Near East between about 9000 and 8500 B.C. Before 9000 B.C., the Near East was populated by small groups of highly mobile hunter-gatherers, subsumed under the generic label "Kebaran." About 9000 B.C., warming temperatures throughout the Near East brought significant environmental and vegetational changes. As Early Holocene temperatures rose, plants like wild emmer wheat and barley and oak, almond, and pistachio trees colonized more fertile, higher country. These abundant cereal and nut resources within the Levant hill zone stimulated the development of more intensive foraging strategies and sedentary settlement, reflected in the emergence of the Natufian culture from the earlier Kebaran. The Natufians exploited wild emmer and barley stands and nut harvests intensively, all predictable, highly productive, and easily stored seasonal foods. The new subsistence strategies permitted more sedentary lifeways and larger village settlements. Many Natufian villages contained circular, semisubterranean houses, storage pits, and stone pavements. Natufian tool kits reflect specialized food procurement activities, especially cereal grass harvesting and hunting activity. Stone-bladed bone sickles were used in the harvest, and some of the stone blades display the characteristic silica gloss caused by friction against cereal grass stalks. In many respects, Natufian subsistence strategies bear a close similarity to those of other Holocene hunter-gatherers in Mediterranean climates, such as the Chumash Indians of southern California.

The larger Natufian sites lie in the hill zones, where cereal grass stands and fruit-bearing trees were most abundant. They lie close to boundaries between the coastal plains and grassland valleys and the hill zone. Such locations allowed the Natufians to exploit spring cereal crops, fall nut harvests, and the game that flourished on the lowlands and on the rich nut mast on the forest floor in the hills above. Unlike their more mobile ancestors, the Natufians enjoyed many months of plentiful food by exploiting first spring cereals and then fall nut harvests as they ripened at progressively higher elevations. Gazelle hunting assumed great importance at certain seasons of the year, with neighboring communities cooperating in game drives, ambushes, and other mass hunting enterprises.

By about 8500 B.C., local populations were considerably higher than in earlier times, leading to the emergence of a more complex social order. The Natufians buried their dead in cemeteries, which have yielded a wealth of information on their society. There are clear signs of social ranking, reflected in the *dentalium* sea shell, found only with a few burials. Elaborate grave furniture such as stone bowls occur with some individuals, including children, a hint of some form of inherited social status in some communities. Some archaeologists believe this emergent social ranking was the result of a need to redistribute food surpluses, and to maintain order within now larger, sedentary communities. Also the stone slab grave covers and mortar markers associated with many Natufian cemeteries may have served as ritual markers of territorial boundaries, perhaps of lands vested in revered ancestors.

After 9000 B.C., the climate of the Levant became progressively drier, just as Natufian populations were expanding. The effect of the new drought cycle was to shrink the cereal habitats in the Mediterranean climatic zone, causing the most productive stands to be found at the highest altitudes. At the same time, the Natufians were forced to spend longer periods of time in sedentary settlements close to permanent water supplies. This made the cost of harvesting cereals and nuts at remote locations much higher. With their plant staples declining, the Natufians turned to new subsistence strategies to expand existing food supplies. By deliberately planting wild wheat and barley, they augmented natural stands, a strategy that was logical for people with centuries of involvement and familiarity with plant foods. As we know from the Abu Hureyra site in Syria, and from the lowest levels of the Jericho mound in the Jordan Valley, it was only a short time before full-fledged farming societies were flourishing over a wide area of the Near East.

The Natufian culture, with its heavy dependence on intensive foraging of plant foods, was, in many senses, preadapted for food production. As such, it provides a case study in the complex developments that took hold in many hunter-gatherer societies at the end of the Ice Age, as humanity adapted to constant, and often unpredictable, climatic change in the Old and New Worlds.

[See also NEAR EAST: THE NEOLITHIC AND CHALCOLITHIC (PRE-BRONZE-AGE) PERIODS IN THE NEAR EAST.]

■ Donald O. Henry, *From Foraging to Agriculture* (1989). Andrew T. Moore, "The Development of Neolithic Societies in the Near East," *Advances in World Archaeology* 4 (1985): 1–70. Ofer Bar-Yosef and François R. Valla, eds., *The Natufian Culture in the Levant* (1991).
Brian M. Fagan

NEANDERTHALS. The Neanderthals of the northwestern Old World are the best-known Archaic human group from the *Pleistocene. They are represented by the remains of hundreds of individuals and several dozen partial associated skeletons from the last interglacial (ca. 100,000 B.P.) to the middle of the last glacial (ca. 30,000 B.P.).

They immediately preceded, or may have coexisted with, early modern humans across their range. As a result, they provide us with a glimpse into both the biology and the behavior of Late Archaic humans and the evolutionary processes associated with the emergence of modern humans.

Fossil human remains referable to the Neanderthals are currently known from across Europe and western Asia from Gibraltar, southern Italy, and Israel in the south to Belgium and the Crimea in the north, and from the Atlantic littoral in the west to Uzbekistan in the east. They appear to have occupied most of the ecozones across this region, with the exception of deserts in the southeast and periglacial tundra to the north.

It is difficult to specify the age of the "oldest" Neanderthals, since they evolved gradually out of their predecessors across their geographical range. Their origin was therefore one of subtle shifts in the frequencies of traits we recognize as "Neanderthal," most of which appeared during the later Middle Pleistocene (> 130,000 B.P.). It was only toward the end of the last interglacial, between approximately 100,000 and 75,000 B.P., that these features reached sufficient frequency and coalesced into the anatomical pattern of the Neanderthals. Their disappearances were more rapid, occurring between roughly 50,000 B.P. in the Near East and 30,000 B.P. in Atlantic Europe.

Even though the term *Neanderthal*, or *Neandertaloid*, has been applied generally to Late Archaic humans, the term is now restricted to the populations of Late Archaic humans from this geographical region of the northwestern Old World. Their Late Archaic relatives in Africa, eastern Asia, and Australasia represent a similar grade of human evolution, but they differ from the Neanderthals in the shape of the face, features of the braincase, and (apparently) bodily proportions.

Neanderthal Phylogenetic Status. Considerable attention continues to be devoted to sorting out the phylogenetic origins of early modern humans and the role of the Neanderthals in modern human ancestry. Indeed, the discussion has become inappropriately polarized into extreme "Replacement" versus "Regional Continuity" scenarios. In the former, the Neanderthals would have had little or no role in modern human ancestry, whereas in the latter would have contributed to later human gene pools. From current paleontological data indicating the degree of anatomical change between various regional late archaic and early modern human groups and the time frame available for the changes, combined with the geographical patterns of variation of early and recent humans, a most probable scenario has emerged. It appears that early modern humans (robust versions of modern humanity) emerged from local late archaic humans somewhere outside of the Neanderthal range, possibly in sub-Saharan Africa. Those early modern humans then spread geographically, mating with, absorbing, and occasionally displacing local populations of late archaic humans like the Neanderthals. It is possible that, in areas such as the Levant and western Europe, the local Neanderthals died out largely without issue. In other regions, such as central Europe, they appear to have contributed significantly to the ancestry of early modern humans. Such a complex scenario would explain both the relatively rapid spread of early modern human anatomy across this range (within 15–20,000 years), as well as the current patterns of regional ("racial") features that are known to take long periods of geological time to become established. In other words, not all Neanderthal populations were ancestral to early modern humans across the northwestern Old World, but most modern people from that region have Neanderthals among their ancestors.

Neanderthal Biology and Behavior. The behavior and biology of the Neanderthals can be inferred from their fossil remains, combined with the associated Paleolithic archaeological remains. For most of their distribution in time and space, the Neanderthals were associated with a Middle Paleolithic (or Mousterian) technology and related archaeological materials. The most recent Neanderthals in western Europe, however, are found with early Upper Paleolithic (Châtelperronian) tools, and in the Near East the earliest modern humans were also associated with Middle Paleolithic technology. As a result, the comments here are based on current knowledge of their biology and its behavioral implications, combined mostly with our knowledge of the usually associated Middle Paleolithic.

Although the Neanderthals represent in many ways the most recent part of an archaic *Homo* lineage, leading from *Homo habilis* through *Homo erectus* to groups like the Neanderthals, they nonetheless had a number of important similarities to modern humans. First and foremost, the configurations of their trunks and limbs, and especially their hands and feet, indicate that they stood, walked, and manipulated objects in much the same way that we do. There is indeed nothing in their vertebrae, joint structures, or feet to indicate anything but a fully upright, striding bipedal gait among them. And their hand joints, especially of the wrist and thumb, imply ranges of movement, and hence grip positions, comparable to ours.

In addition, although we cannot determine the internal structures of their brains, the size and proportions of their endocranial cavities, as well as their vertebral spinal canals, indicate the full range of cognitive and neuromuscular abilities known for recent humans. Indeed, it is with the Neanderthals that we see the full achievement, for the first time, of the degree of encephalization (brain : body size ratio) that characterizes modern humans. Given the developmental and energetic costs of such a relatively large brain, they must have been using those brains in such a way as to make them selectively advantageous.

Related to their large brains were the first signs of a more complex social network. Some of the earliest intentional human burials are of Neanderthals, even though most are little more than a body placed in a shallow grave. This indicates a social need for formal disposal of the dead. Although extremely rare, personal ornamentation indicating intentional modification of one's social persona appears in their sites. And even though we cannot prove its existence, these reflections of social behavior strongly imply the presence of human language, even if it was relatively rudimentary. There is certainly nothing in what can be discerned of their vocal tract anatomy that would preclude fully modern human language. This is especially likely since what is most important for language is cognitive associational skills and fine neurological control of the vocal tract, both of which were apparently present, given their modern-human level of encephalization.

These apparent mental abilities are reflected as well in their Middle Paleolithic technology. Although mechanically less efficient than the composite material tools of the Upper Paleolithic, Middle Paleolithic flint-knapping reduction sequences clearly illustrate the need for (and hence presence of) complex multistep anticipation and planning.

The Neanderthals were also the first humans to permanently occupy mid-latitude regions through full glacial cold, indicating their ability to deal with the stresses of cold and with major seasonal fluctuations in resource availability.

Nonetheless, there were a number of biological and behavioral contrasts between these late archaic humans and their early modern human successors. Many of these are evident in the multiple contrasts between the Middle and Upper Paleolithic archaeological records (bearing in mind that the earliest modern humans were associated with Middle Paleolithic tools and that the latest Neanderthals made early Upper Paleolithic toolkits). There was a technological shift, in which there was a major increase in standardized stone-tool blank forms (usually prismatic blades), which in turn permitted elaboration of tools using composite materials. Bone and antler became standard raw materials for the first time, exploited for their particular mechanical attributes. All of this contributed to a tool kit that was mechanically more effective than the Middle Paleolithic one, with greater leverage, more task specificity, hence job effectiveness, and the appearance of effective throwing projectiles (rather than just thrusting spears).

There was little change in diet and the range of animals eaten. Yet early modern humans appear to have been able to take game animals more effectively, with less risk of personal injury. This is reflected in part in a major drop in the frequency of traumatic injuries to the arms and head, injuries that would occur especially in close-quarter hunting with thrusting (rather than throwing) spears. Early modern humans also were more effective at competing with large carnivores for space and resources.

These technological and subsistence changes were associated with an explosion of social-role complexity. Personal ornamentation becomes ubiquitous. Burials become more complex, with frequent grave goods and some indication of differential social status. Art, consisting of representational forms and clear symbolic forms, combined with numerous notations on bone, indicates a major increase in the amount of information being exchanged socially. This is combined with the exchange of raw and exotic materials over hundreds of miles (km), probably between sequences of neighboring groups. Clear differential site sizes combine with this to indicate division of labor according to season or task. It is at this time, with early modern humans, that the full complement of modern human social and organizational patterns appears to have emerged.

The contrasts reflected in the archaeological record have their parallels in human biology. The Neanderthals, like all Archaic members of the genus *Homo,* were powerfully built. This is reflected in pronounced muscular markings from their necks to shoulders and hands, and to hips and knees and feet. Their legs in particular show great strength and endurance, implying frequent and prolonged movement across the landscape carrying large burdens. Their arms and hands also had greater mechanical advantages for important muscles, with an emphasis on power. Their teeth, which were otherwise very similar to those of modern humans, show exceptionally rapid wear of the front teeth down to their roots by the late thirties or early forties; they were accomplishing many holding and stripping tasks with their teeth and jaws rather than with their hands and associated tools. These patterns correspond well with the dearth of mechanically effective implements in their tool kits and the apparent rarity of organizational solutions to exploiting diverse resources in the landscape.

Early modern human limb bones were still, by standards of living humans, exceptionally strong. Yet they had lost the domination of strength and mechanical advantage that influenced the skeletons of Archaic humans like the Neanderthals. Still very active and strong, these early modern humans were nonetheless able to accomplish many more everyday tasks through technology and social organization than through brute strength and endurance.

These behavioral contrasts are reflected in the different levels of wear and tear on the bodies of these two groups of humans. Among the Neanderthals, over seventy-five percent had experienced periods of severe stress during development, and all who had lived to forty years had the scars of at least one physically traumatic experience. Indeed, few of them had lived past the fourth decade of life. Their lifestyle and level of cultural elaboration clearly had its costs, in terms of stress and life expectancy. But the reason we know so much about them and their stress levels is that they survived many of their injuries, even severely debilitating ones, sometimes for several decades. Early modern humans experienced many of the same forms of stress, but the overall incidence of lesions was lower and life expectancy appears to have increased markedly.

The Neanderthals therefore represent one regional group of Late Archaic humans. They carried on the pattern of strength and endurance established early in the genus *Homo*, adding to it more sophisticated tools, increased intelligence (and probably language), further social cohesion and role definition, and the exploitation of glacial ecozones. Yet there were a number of social, technological, and organizational changes that allowed the pattern we associate with early modern humans and the Upper Paleolithic to become the dominant one in a relatively short period of time. Independent of the actual phylogenetic events responsible for the emergence and spread of early modern humans, their behavioral system and associated biological changes clearly contained a definite, if subtle, advantage over that of late archaic humans such as the Neanderthals.

[*See also* HOMO SAPIENS, ARCHAIC; PALEOLITHIC, *articles on* LOWER AND MIDDLE PALEOLITHIC, UPPER PALEOLITHIC.]

■ Paul Mellars and Chris Stringer, eds., *The Human Revolution* (1989). Erik Trinkaus, ed., *The Emergence of Modern Humans* (1989). Chris Stringer and Clive Gamble, *In Search of the Neanderthals* (1993). Erik Trinkaus and Pat Shipment, *The Neandertals: Changing the Image of Mankind* (1993).

Erik Trinkaus

NEAR EAST

Overview
The Neolithic and Chalcolithic (Pre-Bronze-Age)
  Periods in the Near East
The Bronze Age in the Near East
Iron Age Civilizations in the Near East
The Middle Ages in the Near East

OVERVIEW

In tracing the development of settlement patterns, economic systems, and material culture from the Stone Age to the Ottoman period, archaeologists working throughout the Near East have pioneered many of the excavation techniques and research methodologies utilized at archaeological sites all over the world. The Near East, roughly defined as the region bounded on the southwest by *Egypt and *Nubia, on the south by the Arabian Peninsula (*see* Arabia and the Persian / Arabian Gulf), on the east by Iran, and on the northwest by Asia Minor, has been the scene of extensive exploration over the last 150 years. It is now recognized as one of the world's first centers of complex society, where early domestication of plants and animals as well as urban settlement evolved. As will be seen in the following sections, archaeologists working in the Near East have uncovered evidence of sedentary Neolithic cultures emerging around 10,000 B.C., gradually expanding northward into Asia Minor and southward toward Egypt.

In the Bronze and Iron Ages, distinctive regional civilizations arose in Egypt, *Mesopotamia, *Persia, *Anatolia, and Syria-Palestine. Yet beginning in the second millennium B.C., the cultural and economic connections between these regions multiplied and were supplemented by intensifying links to the emerging cultures of the Aegean world. Though the lands and peoples west of the Euphrates gradually came under the political and cultural domination of Hellenistic *Greece and *Rome (from the late fourth century B.C. to the seventh century A.D.), the earlier cultural influences survived and were expressed in the regional expressions within Eastern Christianity. Later, following the expansion of Islam from the seventh century A.D. onward, the new cultural expressions and architectural forms arose. As the following sections will demonstrate, ongoing excavations and research in the Near East have made it one of the most productive archaeological regions in the world.

[*See also* HISTORY OF ARCHAEOLOGY BEFORE 1900: NEAR EASTERN ARCHAEOLOGY; HISTORY OF ARCHAEOLOGY FROM 1900 TO 1950: NEAR EASTERN ARCHAEOLOGY; HISTORY OF ARCHAEOLOGY SINCE 1950: NEAR EASTERN ARCHAEOLOGY.]

Neil Asher Silberman

THE NEOLITHIC AND CHALCOLITHIC (PRE-BRONZE-AGE) PERIODS IN THE NEAR EAST

The bulk of the Near Eastern archaeological record consists of the remains of foraging societies who first made their appearance in the region from Africa, more than 1.5 million years ago. Sometime around 10,300–10,000 B.P., the economy of peoples in different parts of the Near East changed radically from that of hunting and gathering to one based on food production. The eminent Australian prehistorian V. Gordon *Childe in his book *New Light on the Most Ancient East* (1934) referred to the transition from food collecting to food producing as the "Neolithic revolution." Even today, many decades after Childe introduced the term and after hundreds of new sites have been discovered and excavated, the profound shift from foragers to food producers does indeed warrant the descriptive term of "revolution." By becoming food producers no longer dependent on the distribution of wild plant and animal resources for subsistence, Neolithic and later Chalcolithic societies in the Near East laid the foundations for the emergence of hierarchical societies, the beginning of metallurgy, specialized pastoral economies, and the *"secondary products revolution." Taken together, this "package" of innovations helped to promote and solidify the growth of urban centers in the Early Bronze Age.

Chronology and Stratigraphy. The discussion here focuses on developments in the Levant, one of the "hearth areas" of both Neolithic and Chalcolithic research in the Near East. There are many chrono-cultural schemes used by archaeologists to analyze the developments of the Neolithic Period, but for simplicity, we follow the basic scheme established in Kenyon's deeply stratified excavations at Jericho, where she divided the Early Neolithic into two successive phases: Pre-Pottery A and B (PPNA, PPNB). Some of the key PPNA sites include Jericho, Netiv Hagdud, Nahal Oren, Gesher, Gilgal, and Tel Aswad. Following recent excavations at Ain Ghazal in Jordan, Rollefson identified a terminal Early Neolithic phase that he labeled PPNC. The Early Neolithic Period extends from ca. 10,300/10,000 to 5700/5500 B.P. Some of the best-known excavated PPNB sites include Abu Hureira, Ain Ghazal, Aswad, Beisamoun, Bougras, Cayonu, *Catal Hüyük, Ghoraife, Jericho, and Munhatta. With the following Late, or Pottery, Neolithic Period, it is possible to calibrate radiocarbon dates with a reasonable degree of confidence. Thus, the Pottery Neolithic, extends from ca. 5500 B.C. to 4500 B.C. Recently, Gopher described the sequence of pottery-bearing Neolithic cultures as composed of three primary diachronic regional cultures, which include the early Yarmukian, followed by the Lodian (Jericho IX), and the latest Wadi Raba culture. Among the most significant Pottery Neolithic sites, mention should be made of Teluliot Batashi, Wadi Raba, Munhatta, Nizzanim, Qatif, Jericho, Newe Yam, Tel Dan, and others. The Pottery Neolithic is followed by the Chalcolithic Period, which falls between 4500 and 3500 B.C. Some of the most important sites for this period include Abu Matar, Abu Hamid, Bir es-Safadi, Ein Gedi, Gilat, Horvat Beter, Shiqmim, Tel el-Far'ah (north), and Tuleilat Ghassul. There is still no scholarly consensus concerning the internal division of the Chalcolithic.

The Beginnings of Plant Domestication. Whereas the early pristine civilizations of the Early Bronze Age emerged in the river valleys of the Nile and the alluvial plains of Mesopotamia, the beginnings of plant domestication occurred far away from these areas in the rain-fed Mediterranean zone of the "Fertile Crescent." This area extends from the northern Negev and Jordan Valley in Israel, northward along the Mediterranean littoral, eastward through Anatolia, the Taurus Mountains, and south to the alluvial plains of Iraq and Iran, to the Persian Gulf. Following the emergence of intensive food collecting and the establishment of sedentary *Natufian culture around 12,500–10,200 B.P., the beginnings of cereal cultivation seems to arise in the Pre-Pottery Neolithic A. The shift from intensive gathering to cultivation is a highly debated topic, and until recently, scholars believed that it took place at a number of different locales in the Fertile Crescent. Lately, Zohary has argued that this process happened in one small area—the Mediterranean zone in Israel and Jordan. It seems that the earliest evidence for the cultivation of domestic grain comes from Netiv Hagdud, Gilgal, and Jericho, where carbonized grains of two-rowed barley have been recovered. Some of the still unresolved questions concerning early plant domestication in the Levant are: whether there was one or several independent locations where different species were domesticated; whether it is realistic for archaeobotanists to identify transitional plant forms "on the road" to domestication; and do changes in the frequency of ground stone tool types indicate changes in food-processing activities and, hence, intensified food production? By the PPNB, it seems that all the domesticated crop plants were being cultivated and played a central role in these economies. According to Bar-Yosef, full-fledged farming communities existed during the PPNB in the Levant and expanded during the ninth millennium B.P. into Anatolia and the Zagros region.

Animal Domestication. While Early Neolithic (PPNA) settlers in the Levant were farming or intensively collecting grain crops, there is no doubt that hunting remained an important component of their subsistence activities. Animal bone assemblages from sites in central Palestine indicate that gazelle (*Gazella gazella*) was the preferred game, which was supplemented with wild boar, fallow deer, ibex, fox, and birds. In the northern Levant in the Damascus basin, cattle and caprovines were heavily exploited. According to Davis, it seems that a major shift in animal exploitation occurred during the PPNB, when a dramatic increase in the frequency of sheep and goat occurs in the archaeozoological record of sites in the central and southern Levant. This is when there is a distinct drop in the frequencies of wild game such as gazelle, wild boar, and other species. Unlike crop plants, it seems that caprovines were not domesticated in the Levant. Hesse's work with eighth millennium B.C. faunal collections from west-central Iran has shown how domestication of the goat was a two-part process, based on taming and herding animals. Three factors apparently contributed to the domestication process: climatic conditions that encouraged a shift to intensive gathering and more sedentism; the presence of tame goats controlled by different Early Neolithic Zagros populations that "pre-adapted" these animals into becoming a pastoral flock; and climatic uncertainty and the resultant fluctuations in available game put a new value on tamed animals that could be exploited at will, regardless of environmental conditions. Taken together, it seems that by around 9500/9000 B.P. domesticated caprovines were brought into the Levant, probably from the highlands of Anatolia and the Zagros Mountain region. With the full complement of domestic plants and animals, the "Neolithic Revolution" was a reality, and by the end of the PPNB, true food-producing societies were in place in the Near East.

Rise of Large PPN Settlements. One of the most remarkable features concerning the PPNB is the emergence of large settlement sites, on a scale unknown in the previous prehistoric periods. The largest sites are Ain Ghazal and Basta, which are over 30 acres (12 ha) in size, followed by Beisamoun (25 to 30 acres [10 to 12 ha]), and Wadi Shueib (25 acres [10 ha]). It is not clear whether these sites represent real settlement centers that coordinated regional patterns of socioeconomic exchange. However, the discovery of a cache of fine painted plaster statues from Ain Ghazal may point to the earliest presence of a true settlement center that facilitated social, economic, and religious activities in the region around present-day Amman. By the end of the seventh millennium B.C. there is a collapse in the Pre-Pottery Neolithic (PPN) system and the mega-village site ceases to exist. There are conflicting views as to the cause of the PPN collapse. One school of thought suggests that climatic deterioration initiated at the end of the seventh millennium B.C. was the cause. Others indicate that human overexploitation of the environment based on the cutting down of trees to produce the vast quantities of plaster used in PPNB architecture was the culprit. Whatever the cause, by 6500 B.C., the large settlement types of the PPNB disappear and PN settlement organization can best be characterized as small (less than 2.5 acres [1 ha]) autonomous village sites. The Pottery Neolithic can best be described as a late Neolithic "interlude" before the emergence of vibrant metal-producing chiefdom organizations of the Chalcolithic Period.

Pottery Neolithic. The Pottery Neolithic cultures are distinct from those of the preceding PPNB in terms of both scale and socioeconomy. By ca. 6500 B.C., PN communities are best characterized as small autonomous agricultural-based villages where hunting and foraging activities were mostly abandoned. While long-range trade and exchange in materials such as obsidian were widespread during the PPNB, during the PN, societies were more inwardly oriented. By the end of the Pottery Neolithic sequence, there is a possibility that there were external influences on Palestine from Mesopotamia and the Syro-Anatolian pottery Neolithic cultures. The PN seems to reflect a stage in the reestablishment of population in the Levant, which had suffered a severe crisis at the end of the PPNB and was only slowly readapting to a level of stability during the mid-sixth through mid-fifth millennia B.C.

The earliest pottery-bearing culture of the southern Levant is called the Yarmukian, first defined by M. Stekelis following his early 1950 excavations at Shaar Hagolan near the Yarmuk River. Whether a local or "foreign" development, the manufacture and firing of pottery indicates greater control over pyrotechnology and served as a "pre-adaptation" for early furnace-based metallurgy in the following Chalcolithic Period. Yarmukian pottery consists mostly of bowls and jars with herringbone decorative motifs. Yarmukian sites are characterized by both rounded and rectangular structures. Only a small proportion of animals were hunted during the Yarmukian. The bulk of the animals represented in faunal assemblages are sheep/goat, cattle, and pigs. Cultivation was based mostly on cereals, some legumes, and flax. At a number of underwater sites near Atlit off the Carmel coast, significant quantities of olive stones have been found. However, it is not clear if these represent domestic or wild olives. Over a hundred distinctive clay and stone figurines have been found associated with Yarmukian layers at a relatively small number of sites such as Shaar Hagolan and Munhatta. Both the clay figures, primarily of women with incised-pebble "coffee bean" eyes, have been variously linked to fertility and sexuality.

The "Jericho IX" culture has recently been labeled the "Lodian" by Gopher, and while it may represent a variant of the earlier Yarmukian culture, its distinctive ceramic repertoire helps delineate it as a separate cultural variant. The pottery is characterized by painted and burnished geometric motifs usually applied on a plain background. There is very little evidence of architecture from "Lodian" sites; however, the numerous pit features have been variously interpreted as "dwelling pits" or quarries for mud-brick material.

The Wadi Raba is the last of the well-defined Pottery Neolithic cultures in Palestine. Architecture is primarily rectilinear and appears in single- and multicelled units. It seems that no circular habitation structures are associated with this cultural entity. Like the other PN cultures, sheep/goat, cattle, and pigs were exploited, with little evidence of hunting. Mellaart suggests the origin of the Wadi Raba culture is in the Beqqa Valley in Lebanon. In recent years, a number of Wadi Raba cultural variants have been proposed such as the Qatifian in southern Palestine. At Tel Tsaf in the northern Jordan Valley, Gophna identified a unique assemblage of Halaf-inspired pottery that seems to indicate Mesopotamian influence at the very end of the PN in this part of Palestine. How exactly these very late PN cultural assemblages relate to the beginning of the following Chalcolithic Period, however, remains to be studied.

The Chalcolithic Period. The Chalcolithic Period (ca. 4500–3500 B.C.) was first identified at the type-site of Tu-

leilat Ghassul by A. Mallon in the late 1920s, and represents a radical social transformation from the preceding PN Period. While some scholars suggest that all Chalcolithic societies were egalitarian in social structure, the overwhelming material evidence points to the emergence of the first clearly definable complex societies or chiefdom organizations. Chiefdoms are characterized by, among other things, a two-tier settlement hierarchy, whereas state organizations, such as those of the later Early Bronze Age, show three- and four-tier settlement patterns. During the late fifth and early fourth millennia, Palestine was first characterized by a large number of regionally distinct archaeological cultures that were uniquely adapted to the local environmental conditions. These regional cultures have been found in the Golan Heights, Samaria, the Lower Jordan Valley, the northern Negev, and other areas. The Beersheva Valley in the northern Negev is perhaps the most intensely investigated area. Systematic survey work in this area has demonstrated the presence of a two-tier settlement hierarchy with permanent centers over 25 acres (10 ha) in size surrounded by smaller satellite sites. These centers presumably coordinated social, economic, and religious activities.

The Chalcolithic also provides the first evidence for the placement of cemetery sites outside of settlements, which can be seen as an indication of concern over territoriality on a scale not seen in earlier periods. Cemeteries have been found at Hadera, Bene Braq, Azor, Nahal Qanah, and other locales. At Shiqmim, the first Negev Chalcolithic cemetery was discovered by Levy and Alon in the 1970s. Since then, Chalcolithic cemeteries have been found along Nahal Kissufim and Eilat. Mortuary analyses of the Shiqmim cemetery indicate a level of social ranking or hierarchy among the buried population.

New levels of craft specialization in metal, ivory, pottery, and other materials were also achieved during the Chalcolithic Period. Metalworking is perhaps the most outstanding example in craft work. In the 1960s, the discovery of over 400 exquisite Chalcolithic metal finds made with high arsenical copper in the "Cave of the Treasure" Nahal Mishmar in the Judean Desert led to the suggestion that these items originated from Anatolia or Azerbaijan. More recent research shows that these items were manufactured locally in the southern Levant. Shalev and Northover have defined two metalworking industries: one based on the casting of "utilitarian tools" such as axes, adzes, chisels, and awls using pure copper; and another that used "lost-wax" casting techniques and high arsenical copper to create elaborate prestige/cult metalwork such as scepters, crowns, mace heads, and other objects. The distribution pattern of sites that show evidence of metalworking focuses almost entirely on the Beersheva Valley. This has led to the suggestion that the Beersheva Chalcolithic culture had a "monopoly" on the knowledge needed to mine, smelt, cast, and finish the manufacture of metal objects. Investigations at the main Chalcolithic ore sources in the Wadi Feinan of Jordan by Hauptmann show that unlike the following Early Bronze Age when metal production was carried out on an industrial scale, during the Chalcolithic it was relatively small scale. It seems that the distribution of metal objects, especially the prestige/cult items, was used to cement social relations among Chalcolithic elites in the Beersheva Valley. Recently, geologists identified an arsenic-rich copper ore at Wadi Tar in southern Sinai. This represents the first Levantine source for arsenic-rich copper and adds to the growing evidence that it was the local Chalcolithic cultures in Palestine that developed the earliest and most spectacular metalworking industry in the ancient Near East.

Taken together, the domestication of plants and animals during the Neolithic, and the subsequent intensification of agricultural production and craft specialization in the following Chalcolithic Period, helped to establish the socio-economic foundation for the subsequent rise of urbanism in the following Early Bronze Age. This process crystallized in the Chalcolithic Period, with what Andrew Sherratt has referred to as the "secondary products revolution." This was when societies began to exploit intensively the milk, wool, hair, and traction of herd animals. By achieving more sophisticated animal herding strategies, the full-time pastoral economies of the Near East laid the foundations for the urban-rural relationship that was essential to support the later Early Bronze Age civilizations of the region.

[See also DOMESTICATION OF ANIMALS; DOMESTICATION OF PLANTS; METALLURGY: METALLURGY IN THE OLD WORLD; PASTORALISM; RANKING AND SOCIAL INEQUALITY, THEORIES OF.]

■ K. Kenyon, *Digging Up Jericho* (1957). J. Mellaart, *The Neolithic of the Near East* (1975). C. Epstein, "The Chalcolithic Culture of the Golan," *Biblical Archaeologist* 40 (1977): 57–62. A. Sherratt, "Plough and Pastoralism: Aspects of the Secondary Products Revolution," in eds. I. Hodder, G. Isaac, and N. Hammond, *Patterns of the Past: Studies in Honour of David Clarke* (1981). S. Davis, "Climatic Change and the Advent of Domestication or Ruminant Artiodactyls in the Late Pleistocene-Holocene Period in the Israel Region," *Paleorient* 8 (1982): 5–16. B. Hesse, "These Are Our Goats: The Origins of Herding in West Central Iran," in eds. J. Clutton-Brock and C. Grigson, *Animals and Archaeology*, Vol. 3, *Early Herders and Their Flocks* (1984). A. Moore, "The Development in Neolithic Societies in the Near East," in eds. F. Wendorf and A. E. Close, *Advances in World Archaeology* (1985). T. E. Levy, ed., *Shiqmim I: Studies Concerning Fourth Millennium Societies in the Northern Negev Desert, Israel (1982–1984)* (1987). O. Bar-Yosef and A. Belfer-Cohen, "The PPNB Interaction Sphere," in ed. I. Hershkovitz, *People and Cultures in Change* (1989), pp. 59–72. R. Gophna and S. Sadeh, "Excavations at Tel Tsaf: An Early Chalcolithic Site in the Jordan Valley," *Tel Aviv* 15–16 (1989): 3–36. A. Hauptmann, "The Earliest Periods of Copper Metallurgy in Feinan/Jordan," in eds. A. Hauptmann, E. Pernicka, and G. A. Wagner, *Old World Metallurgy* (1989). D. Zohary, "Domestication of the Southwest Asian Crop Assemblage of Cereals, Pulses and Flax: The Evidence from Living Plants," in eds. D. R. Harris and G. Hillman, *Foraging and Farming: The Evolution of Plant Domestication* (1989). D. Zohary, "Domestication of the Neolithic Near East Crop Assemblage," in ed. P. C. Anderson, *Prehistoire de l'Agriculture* (1992). A. Gopher and R. Gophna, "The Cultures of the Eighth and Seventh Millennia B.P. in the Southern Levant—A Review for the 1990s," *Journal of World Prehistory* 7 (1993): 297–353. A. Gopher, "Early Pottery-Bearing Groups in Israel—The Pottery Neolithic Period," in ed. T. E. Levy, *The Archaeology of Society in the Holy Land* (1995), pp. 205–225. T. E. Levy, "Cult, Metallurgy and Rank Societies—Chalcolithic Period (ca. 4500–3500 B.C.E.)," in ed. T. E. Levy, *The Archaeology of Society in the Holy Land* (1995).

Thomas E. Levy

THE BRONZE AGE IN THE NEAR EAST

The Bronze Age of the Near East refers to cultural developments in the territories of the Mediterranean from approximately 3400 to 1200 B.C. Extending from Egypt in the south to Mesopotamia in the northeast, it includes the Afro-Asiatic land bridge commonly called Syria-Palestine in the archaeological literature. Like the term "Near East," "Bronze Age" is inherited from traditional European archaeology. Retained for convenience, it is a misnomer, because bronze did not appear in Syria or Mesopotamia until the last quarter of the third millennium, and did not become common in Syria-Palestine until the beginning of the

second millennium. The time period is characterized more accurately as one of the development of urbanism.

Early Bronze Age. The Early Bronze Age (EB) is roughly correlated with the Protoliterate and Early Dynastic Periods in Mesopotamia, and the Predynastic, Old Kingdom, and First Intermediate Periods in Egypt. Scholars agree that the period began with a transitional, proto-urban stage, commonly called EBI (3400–3100 B.C.), followed by the first fully urban stages, EBII–III (3100–2700 and 2700–2350/2300 B.C.). There is likewise agreement that the period ended with a transitional stage of urban collapse in western Palestine. The tendency of some recent scholarship is to call this latter stage EBIV (2350/2300–2000 B.C.). Other scholars continue to follow earlier terminologies linking it to the beginning of the Middle Bronze Age (MBI, EBIV–MBI, or Intermediate Bronze). Absolute chronology is approximate, relying on radiocarbon dates and correlations with Mesopotamian and Egyptian chronologies.

In EBI Palestine, a proto-urban stage was set with the establishment of a Mediterranean mixed economy, that is, horticulture (especially of grape, olive, and date), grain agriculture, and herding of sheep and goats. This economic stabilization coincided with a population shift to highly arable lands, above the 1 foot (300 mm) isohyet, which were close to water sources and defensible. Sedentary population growth ensued, as evidenced by larger, open-walled towns, enabling the production of surplus. Currently, scholars tend to emphasize the continuity of indigenous culture from the Late Chalcolithic Period, as evident in pottery decoration, burial traditions, and architecture.

Increasing social complexity culminated in multiple city-states, the first ever seen in Palestine, in EBII–III. Municipal administrations are indicated by fortifications, elaborate temple precincts, town planning, and regional trade networks, as at Arad in the south. Craft specialization is also apparent, as in the excavated ceramic kiln and workshops of Tell el Far/x6ah North, though manufacture had not advanced beyond a slow wheel. Syrian cities were even more prosperous and continued to the end of EBIV. In the Ebla Archives, we find the earliest evidence of an indigenous Semitic language, Eblaite/Eblaic. Written in cuneiform, using Sumerian logograms, it shows affinities with various Near Eastern dialects. In contrast to Palestinian city-states, *Ebla seems to have dominated a relatively large area. Its nearest rival was *Mari, adjoining Mesopotamia.

Although permanent settlements endured in eastern Palestine, all major sites were abandoned in the west by the beginning of EBIV. There was an increased number of small settlements in the southern deserts and the east. Continuity in ceramics and metals, with a stronger Syrian influence, is increasingly attributed to an indigenous population that relied more heavily on the pastoral-nomadic strategies previously existing alongside urbanism. This shift may be in response to greater drought, as well as internal social factors. Older models, however, attributed both the rise and collapse of urbanism to an influx of newcomers from the northeast.

The primary foreign influence on EB Syria-Palestine was Egypt. An ongoing controversy for EBI–II is whether the relationship was one of reciprocal exchange or forced tribute. Egyptians apparently lived at the southern sites of Tel Erani and /x6En Besor, and Egyptian luxury goods are found in the north and in Syria, suggesting that overland travel took place along the *Via Maris*, the coastal route. Syria-Palestine probably supplied agricultural surplus and natural resources. In EBIII, however, Egypt's relationship with Palestine was abandoned in favor of maritime trade with Syria, especially at the port city of Byblos. Even there, Egyptian influence waned in EBIV as its own government weakened. Thus, both the rise of urbanism, and its collapse in western Palestine, may have been, in part, stimulated by the economic relationship with Egypt.

Middle Bronze Age. The Middle Bronze Age is roughly contemporaneous with the Amorite dynasties in Mesopotamia and the Middle Kingdom and Second Intermediate Periods in Egypt. It is internally divided into three phases: MBI (2000–1800 B.C.), MBII (1800–1650 B.C.), and MBIII (1650–1500 B.C.). An older system of chronological division includes MBI (2200–2000 B.C., equivalent to EBIV), MBIIA (2000–1800 B.C.), MBIIB (1800–1650 B.C.), and MBIIC (1650–1550 B.C.). Absolute chronology is fixed, for the first time, by Egyptian correlation of an observed solar eclipse with accession dates in dynastic king lists, placing the beginning of the reign of Amenemhet I in 1991 B.C.

Urbanism was reestablished throughout Palestine in MBI. Most EB cities were reoccupied, and many small EBIV sites were abandoned. Cities were larger than ever before, reaching up to about 170 acres (69 ha), probably housing a majority of the population. Fortifications were more massive, typically consisting of an outer walled dry moat (fosse), outer retaining wall, earthen and plaster embankments (glaçis), and inner wall with a chambered gate. Similar to those in Syria, they are so impressive that, in earlier literature, they were used as the primary marker of urbanism. Other indicators of social complexity, however, include sophisticated civic water systems and cultic installations, as at Gezer, and the presence of an elite class, evident in the Jericho burials. Cities probably served as market redistribution centers to the more numerous smaller settlements. In this period, Bronze Age urbanism in Palestine had reached its zenith.

For the first time, Syria-Palestine was culturally homogeneous, as the center of a distinctive Canaanite culture. Architectural plans, though built on a far grander scale in Syria, and influenced by Mesopotamia, were paralleled in Palestine. Ceramics were formed on a fast wheel, occasionally resembling known Syrian analogues in precious metals. The manufacture of tin-bronze had diffused into Palestine from Syria, enabling the production of superior weapons and tools. According to letters in the Mari archives, tin was shipped via donkey caravan to northern Palestine. Mari was one of the Amorite city-states responsible for the conquest of Syrian cities around 2000 B.C. Before the establishment of their urban dynasties throughout Mesopotamia, Amorites apparently were a primarily Syrian village or pastoral population. The EB texts of Ebla contain a reference to Amorites, as well as the earliest use of the designation "Canaanite." By the Middle Bronze Age, therefore, the cultural identity of Canaan is well established.

Canaan's most lasting legacy is probably the acrophonic alphabet, in which each of a limited set of characters represents a sound. The first such script, proto-Canaanite/Sinaitic, was used by Asiatic slaves in Egyptian turquoise mines, as early as 1650 B.C. Progenitor of our own alphabet, its development was influenced by a shorthand form of Egyptian hieroglyphics, used to spell non-Egyptian words. Easier to learn and use than sets of pictographic or cuneiform symbols, it enabled the spread of literacy.

Canaan's political power was strongest in MBIII, Egypt's Second Intermediate Period. Since MBI, a colony of Canaanites had been settled at Avaris (modern Tell ed-Dab 'a) in the eastern Nile Delta. In MBIII, during the political chaos of the feuding Egyptian Sixteenth and Seventeenth Dynasties, the Fifteenth (Hyksos) Dynasty, centered at Avaris, ruled much of Egypt. A recent interpretation of the reason for the contemporary fortifications of the cities of southern Canaan suggests they were intended as a defense against possible Egyptian retaliation, rather than being the result of mere local rivalry. Indeed, virtually every excavated city in Palestine, as well as Tell ed-Dab 'a itself, was violently destroyed at the end of the Middle Bronze Age, the time of the Egyptian expulsion of the Hyksos.

Late Bronze Age. The Late Bronze Age dates approximately 1550–1200 B.C. LBI (A–B) is roughly correlated with Egypt's Eighteenth Dynasty up to the start of the Amarna period. LBIIA roughly corresponds to the fourteenth century B.C. LBIIB, contemporary with the Nineteenth Dynasty, continues to the end of the thirteenth century.

Egyptian military campaigns against Canaan continued throughout LBI, advancing as far as northern Syria. Many destroyed Canaanite sites show an apparent occupation gap in this period. Thutmose III's victory over a Syrian confederation gathered at the Canaanite city-state of Megiddo is especially noteworthy. This pharaoh established three administrative districts in Canaan to ease the collection of tribute: southern Canaan, the Levantine coast, and inland Syria. Canaanite cooperation was ensured through brutal treatment of captured rebels and taking hostages from ruling families to Egypt. Egyptian power was checked in northern Syria only by the kingdom of Mitanni with its Hurrian population (present in Canaan since the MB) and *Indo-European rulers.

In LBIIA, Egyptian ties to foreign powers were sealed by pharaonic marriages to daughters of Mitannian and Babylonian Kassite royalties. At home, Akhenaten changed his religious affiliation, built a new capital city called Akhentoten (modern Tell el-Amarna), and softened imperial rule over Canaan, though Egyptian garrisons were still present. The most important documentary source for this period are the Amarna Letters, cuneiform tablets discovered at Tell el-Amarna in 1888, which include correspondence from Canaanite rulers to the pharaoh, documenting strife between city-states and disorder caused by a group known as the 'Apiru, who were apparently disenfranchised troublemakers (sometimes identified with the biblical Hebrews). Whether the ardent pleas of the Canaanite rulers for Egyptian intervention were reflective of serious upheaval, or merely hyperbolic, is open to question, as is the motivation of Egypt's passive response. Possibilities range from Egyptian disinterest in Canaan due to religious preoccupation, to a deliberate policy of maintaining control by encouraging internal conflict.

It is indisputable, however, that Egypt began to lose control over Canaanite territory to the Hittite kingdom in *Anatolia by the thirteenth century B.C. Cuneiform tablets, written in a Canaanite dialect, and found in a destroyed LBIIB stratum of the city of Ugarit, by then a Hittite vassal, note Cypriot and Hittite famines and accurately foretell impending doom. Campaigns by successive pharaohs to offset losses to the Hittites were of limited success. In addition, valuable military resources had to be diverted to fight the incoming Sea Peoples, of whom the biblical Philistines were one group. These newcomers, who may have been responsible for the destruction of coastal Canaanite cities, finally settled in Palestine at the close of the Late Bronze

Age, by which time Egyptian hegemony over Canaan had ended.

Late Bronze Age Canaan was the most cosmopolitan age yet seen in the region, offering an innovative synthesis of local and foreign elements. Local material culture tended to show continuity in ceramic styles, town plans, and architecture, albeit with strong foreign influences. An increased number of Cypriot ceramics (white slip and base ring) were imported, especially in LBIIA, along with the first Mycenean ceramics from the late Helladic Aegean. All these vessels probably contained precious cosmetic and medicinal preparations. Painted decorations included stylized representations of birds and fish, in MBIIC–LBIA bichrome ware, and typically Near Eastern tree-with-ibex motifs. Religious architecture often continued to be rebuilt in the same location, though in a variety of forms. Indeed, most of our archaeological evidence for Canaanite cult practices comes from this period.

By the end of the period, urban prosperity was in decline. Although the first known use of the term "Israel" is on the LBIIB Stele of Merneptah, the nature of its namesake's subsequent emergence in Canaan, as a political entity, remains in dispute. Archaeological data for Bronze Age Canaan have been interpreted from an increasingly anthropological perspective, noting the cyclical nature of its urbanism, while the wealth of relevant cuneiform, Egyptian, and biblical texts continues to inform a fertile historical legacy.

[See also AEGEAN CULTURES: OVERVIEW; EGYPT, articles on OLD KINGDOM EGYPT, MIDDLE KINGDOM EGYPT, NEW KINGDOM EGYPT; MESOPOTAMIA: BABYLONIA.]

■ Paolo Matthiae, Ebla, trans. Christopher Holme (1980). Gordon D. Young, ed., Ugarit in Retrospect (1981). William G. Dever, "The Middle Bronze Age," Biblical Archaeologist 50 (1987): 148–177. Suzanne Richard, "The Early Bronze Age," Biblical Archaeologist 50 (1987): 22–43. Al Leonard Jr., "The Late Bronze Age," Biblical Archaeologist 52 (1989): 4–39. Amihai Mazar, Archaeology of the Land of the Bible, 10,000–586 B.C.E. (1990). Amnon Ben-Tor, ed., The Archaeology of Ancient Israel, trans. R. Greenberg (1992). Donald B. Redford, Egypt, Canaan, and Israel in Ancient Times (1992). Gordon D. Young, ed., Mari in Retrospect (1992).

Bonnie L. Wisthoff

IRON AGE CIVILIZATIONS IN THE NEAR EAST

The Iron Age spanned a period of roughly six centuries, beginning around 1200 B.C. and continuing to the fall of Jerusalem in 587/586 B.C. Though scholars have generally agreed to divide this time into two broad phases called Iron Age I and Iron Age II, they have disagreed on where the former stage ends and the latter one begins, and on how to subdivide each era with greater precision. Building upon the work of William Foxwell Albright, George Ernest Wright proposed a tripartite division for Iron Age I that included the Israelite settlement of Canaan (Iron IA, 1200–1150 B.C.), the period of the Israelite judges (Iron IB, 1150–1000 B.C.), and the United Monarchy under David and Solomon (Iron IC, 1000–918 B.C.). More recently, however, many archaeologists suggest terminating Iron I at ca. 1000 B.C., thereby shifting Israel's United Monarchy to the Iron II period. Both systems rely more on historical dates and events relating specifically to the development of ancient Israel (i.e., the rise of the monarchy around 1000 B.C. or the invasion of Israel by Pharaoh Shishak around 925 B.C.) than on widespread, unequivocal changes in the archaeological record. Similar, the subphasing of Iron Age II follows other comparable historical parameters. If one accepts the more recent chronology given above for Iron I, then Iron IIA extends from the rise of Israelite kingship to the invasion by Shishak (1000–925 B.C.), Iron IIB continues from Shishak to the fall of Samaria at the hand of Assyria (925–722/721 B.C.), and Iron IIC proceeds to the Babylonian sacking of Jerusalem (722–587/586 B.C.). Some scholars have even included the subsequent period of Babylonian hegemony over Palestine (587–539 B.C.) in the Iron Age proper.

Transition from Bronze to Iron Age. During the last half of the second millennium B.C. (Late Bronze Age), a number of great powers emerged in the ancient Near East, including New Kingdom Egypt in the south, the Hittite Empire to the north, and the Hurrian Empire (Mitanni) centered at Waššukkanni (known only from textual references). Near the close of the thirteenth century B.C., however, these kingdoms and most of the city-states they had spawned declined or crumbled in the wake of a dramatic upheaval that spread across both the Aegean and eastern Mediterranean worlds. Mycenaeans abandoned their urban centers in the wake of violent conflagrations. East in Anatolia, the once-powerful Hittite Empire collapsed, and its language passed out of use in written form. Farther south, the destruction spread to Bronze Age Canaanite city-states along the eastern Mediterranean littoral and, to a lesser extent, into the hinterland. The destruction of Ugarit (Ras Shamra), a former hub of Canaanite activity, also closed a prolific literary period in that culture. While Egypt managed to withstand these changes longer than most other Mediterranean cultures, its sphere of influence shrank considerably following a relatively short but stable period under Rameses III (1182–1151 B.C.).

Although the catalyst behind this upheaval remains uncertain (suggestions include invasions by oftentimes unidentified northern peoples, failure of certain key economic systems, climatic events such as widespread drought resulting in severe famine and displaced populations, or perhaps some combination of such factors), the effects proved disastrous. The lucrative international trade network that had connected the Aegean and the Levant collapsed. Greece now entered the so-called Dark Age, and the imported Mycenaean and Cypriot wares that had characterized Bronze Age trade ceased to enter the Levant. Archaeologists have recovered the latest securely datable examples of Late Bronze Age bichrome imports, called Mycenaean IIIB, from Deir 'Allā (biblical Succoth) in Transjordan, where they appeared alongside a faience bottle bearing the name of Queen Tewosret (1193–1185 B.C.), the last ruler of the Nineteenth Dynasty in Egypt. By correlating this change in the material record with the historical dates of Tewosret's reign, we may place the onset of the Iron Age, with its dominance of locally made pottery, at approximately 1185 B.C.

The Rise of Iron Age Cultures. The widespread decline of the literate Bronze Age civilizations resulted in a poorly documented transition to the Iron Age, particularly in Syria-Palestine. Extant Egyptian sources and the archaeological record, however, show that the emergent Iron Age cultures comprised regional principalities with limited international influence. Because of their inability to establish far-reaching areas of political influence, the disparate social and ethnic groups formed a veritable cultural mosaic in the southern Levant, which the Egyptians commonly referred to as Hurru (also sometimes Retenu, Djahi, and Kinanu ["Canaan"]), a name reflecting an earlier prominence (confirmed in the Amarna Letters) of individuals from the Hurrian ruling aristocracy throughout the Lebanese Beqa',

Damascus, Bashan, Jezreel Valley, and Acco plain areas. Because of this mixed population, proposals to use specific ethnic titles to identify these periods (Bronze Age = "Canaanite Period," Iron Age = "Israelite Period") have met with little acceptance.

Commemorating military campaigns undertaken during Merneptah's fifth regnal year (1207 B.C.), the Merneptah stela provides valuable information pertaining to the political and cultural organization of Anatolia/northern Syria and southern Syria/Palestine during the Late Bronze-Early Iron Age transition. The brief victory poem that concludes the text identifies these areas as Hatti and Hurru, respectively.

During the Bronze Age, the Indo-European Hittites ruled over Hatti Land from their capital at Hattusha (modern Boğazköy). Though they had established themselves there already in the early second millennium B.C., when they campaigned far to the east and terminated the once-powerful First Dynasty of Babylon, the period of their greatest foreign expansion occurred under Shuppiluliuma I and his son Hattushili III (1344–1239 B.C.). Together these rulers extended their hegemony as far south as Damascus. Certain biblical texts from the Iron Age reflect a historical memory of this pressure (1 Kings 9:20; 10:29; 11:1; *et passim*) while others (particularly in the Pentateuch) seem to apply the term "Hittites" to indigenous peoples within Palestine who actually had western Semitic names and customs. Many scholars have noted the close similarity in form between Hittite suzerain treaties and later, Israelite institutions and covenantal and legal material. Though others have credited the Hittites with introducing iron technologies to the ancient Near East, archaeology has shown that, either by choice or necessity, they made the bulk of their weapons and armor from bronze.

Despite their once-strong position, the Hittites succumbed to the general upheaval that was spreading through the Mediterranean world and to escalating pressures from kingdoms both nearby (Tarhuntashsha to their south) and from farther east (an aggressive Assyria led by Shalmaneser I and Tukulti Ninurta I). Hattusha, the core of the empire, collapsed near the onset of the Iron Age (1180 B.C.), leaving only scattered neo-Hittite enclaves at centers such as Carchemish, Tarhuntashsha, and Karatepe. While these and other neo-Hittite states maintained their autonomy from one another (see notices regarding multiple Hittite kings in 1 Kings 10:29 and 2 Kings 7:6), a certain degree of acculturation seems to have developed between various kingdoms in Anatolia and Syria during the Iron II Period. A lengthy, bilingual inscription from Karatepe, written in Old Phoenician and the Hieroglyphic Hittite employed for their Luwian dialect, reflects these cross-cultural connections. Though engraved on reliefs reused from the late ninth century, the inscription itself dates to the mid- to late eighth century B.C.

Merneptah's stela text highlights the organization of Hurru, the area directly affected by his campaign, in greater detail. Here the Canaanite city-states lay mainly in the coastal-lowland areas (Ashkelon, Gezer) and in the northern valleys (Yanoam), while a cultural group of rural pastoralists known as Israel occupied the wooded highlands. Together, then, Canaan and Israel seem roughly synonymous with Hurru. Because this reference comprises the only direct mention of Israel in the extant corpus of ancient Egyptian literature, some scholars have called this artifact the Israel stela.

In the Early Iron Age, only a few remaining city-states ruled over the various sectors of Canaan. A biblical text from the Iron I Period states that the Israelites met a coalition of Canaanite kings in battle at Ta'anach, near Megiddo at the strategic southwest entrance to the Jezreel Valley (Judges 5:19). A later narrative account of that encounter remembered a particular Canaanite ruler, Jabin of Hazor, as king over all Canaan (Judges 4:2, 23–24), and another Iron II text (Joshua 11:10) says that Hazor had formerly served as "the head of all those [Canaanite] kingdoms." Egyptian texts from the Iron I Period (Papyrus Anastasi I and Papyrus Anastasi III, both contemporary with Merneptah's father, Rameses II) and biblical texts from Iron II (Numbers 34:1–12; Joshua 15:1–4; Ezekiel 47:13–20, 48:1, 28) help us draw the parameters of Canaan from the Brook of Egypt northward along the Levantine coast to the mountains of Lebanon and Sirion, eastward past Kadesh (where the Hittite Hattushili I and Rameses II had earlier given treaty status to this political boundary) to Damascus (Upi), and then south and west to the Yarmuk Valley south of the Sea of Galilee. From there, it simply followed the natural boundary of the Jordan River southward to the southern tip of the Dead Sea, where it assumed a southwesterly direction, taking in Kadeshbarnea before returning to the Mediterranean coast at the Brook of Egypt. With the incursion and consolidation of multiple groups such as the Israelites, Aramaeans, and various segments of Sea Peoples in this area during Iron Age I, the Canaanite cultural and economic center shifted to the northern coastal area later known as Phoenicia. The Egyptian "Tale of Wen Amun" and Assyrian tribute lists of Tiglath-pileser I of the eleventh century B.C. identify Tyre, Sidon, Byblos, and Arvad as the foci of Phoenician maritime trade during Iron Age I and it appears from Judges 5:17 and 1 Kings 7:13–4 that various Israelite tribes that settled in northern Hurru country (Danites, Asherites) quickly based their local economies on the shipping industry and associated metallurgical trades that now thrived at these sites. During Israel's monarchic period, Solomon continued to draw upon the valuable resources (timber) and skilled craftsmen from Phoenicia (1 Kings 5) and to connect Israel's long-distance trade to that of Phoenicia (1 Kings 9:26–28; 10:11, 22).

Farther south along the coast, settlements were established by various contingents of Sea Peoples, apparent migrants from the Aegean world. Early in Merneptah's reign, the Sherden (who had earlier served as mercenaries in the Egyptian army), Sheklesh, Lukka, Tursha, and Akawasha joined Libya in an attack against Egypt. In the eighth year of Rameses III, the Peleset (Philistines), Tjekker, Shekelesh, Denyen, and Weshesh reportedly destroyed cities throughout Cicilia, Hatti, and down the Syro-Palestinian coast as they made their way toward Egypt. Reliefs and texts from the mortuary temple of Rameses III at Medinet Habu in Thebes preserve details of the resultant land and sea battles. Though Egypt succeeded in averting the incursion of these groups into Egypt, some of them subdued and settled coastal Canaan, apparently with tacit Egyptian sanction. A Philistine Pentapolis dominated the coastal plain from the Yarkon River south to Gaza, with Ashkelon apparently serving as the main seaport. This region subsequently became known as Philistia. The Pentapolis sites thus far excavated (Ashdod, Ashkelon, and Ekron) exhibit identical patterns in the development of Philistine ceramic traditions—an initial phase of locally made, monochrome vessels of the Mycenaean IIIC:1b style, followed by the classic Philistine bichrome ware. This latter ceramic class bespeaks the rapid acculturation of the Philistines into the local cultural milieu inasmuch as it reveals an eclectic mix of Canaanite and Egyptian forms with Mycenaean decorative motifs. North of Philistia, the Tjekker occupied the Sharon plain and maintained maritime trade from the port of Dor. Though the Philistines spread their political control eastward through the Jezreel and Jordan Valleys and into Transjordan, making them the archrivals of the Israelites during the Iron I Period, their material culture and that of the Tjekker became largely indistinguishable from that of the surrounding peoples by the late tenth century.

The nature of the Israelite and Aramaean settlement in Hurru/Canaan remains much less clear and a matter of ongoing research both in biblical studies and in archaeology. The Merneptah stela confirms an Israelite presence there by the fifth year of Merneptah's rule, or 1207 B.C. But the archaeological record has not supported the traditional model, based primarily on the biblical account in Joshua 1–12, for explaining the Israelite occupation as a quick, unified military conquest of the land of Canaan. Some see transhumance (seasonal migrations) as part of the process, in which originally disparate tribal elements gradually infiltrated and claimed the areas of Canaan lying between the large city-states. Still others prefer to view the process as an internal peasant revolt, in which the lower socioeconomic classes rebelled against their Canaanite overlords. Scholars have debated whether the peasants' common religion (Yahwism) provided the initial cohesion necessary to such a revolt or grew out of the cohesion that a successful revolution nurtured. More recently, some have suggested that the opening of the highland frontier for more extensive settlement resulted from a deurbanization process underway in the lowland Canaanite culture. In any event, the process was complex and likely included components of all these views. During the proto-monarchic period (1200–1000 B.C.), Israel existed as a loosely organized league of tribes whose social system was based on kinship ties, established mainly at the local level, and who might oppose as well as assist one another. This fluid social organization helps distinguish this confederation of tribes from the later amphictyonic leagues that arose in Greece.

Within the cultural mix that evolved in Syria-Palestine during the Iron Age, the Canaanite tradition continued to exert a significant impact on the many facets of Israelite life, including material culture, literature, and religion (at least as practiced at the popular or local level). Studies have cited many parallels between the great archive of Canaanite mythic texts discovered at Ugarit (Ras Shamra) in 1929 and the literature of the Hebrew Bible, particularly with regard to the more archaic biblical poetry. Further, the many (over forty) appearances in the Hebrew Bible of the Canaanite Mother Goddess Asherah, or of one of her symbols (usually the sacred tree), and the variously interpreted eighth-century Hebrew inscriptions from Khirbet el-Qôm and Kuntillet Ajrud attest to her prominence in the Israelite cult at a family or local, if not national, level. The Canaanite storm deity and male fertility god, Baal, seems to have gained even greater prominence within Israel.

Iron Age Politics and Polities. The consolidation of the Israelite monarchy marked a change in regional politics and is evident in the archaeological record in the growth of urban centers and uniform planning of fortifications and public building at sites such as Gezer, Megiddo,

Hazor, Dan, and Beersheba. Israel's former tribal (Amalekite) and urban (Philistine) rivalries faded somewhat into the background as the new nation now confronted the Aramaeans of Damascus. The Aramaeans derived from a western Semitic-speaking group that had occupied areas of northern Syria and Mesopotamia over the course of the second millennium B.C. Assyrian sources continued to locate them here during the Iron I Period, when a series of Aramaean city-states (Bit-Zamani, Bit-Bahiani, Bit-Halupe, and Laqu) stretched from the Upper Tigris River south through the Habur River area to the Euphrates River. By the tenth century B.C., Aramaean control had spread into southern Syria, with centers at Aram-Zobah and Aram-Damascus.

Biblical and archaeological evidence readily attests to the political struggles between Israel, Judah, and the Aramaeans of Damascus, as these regional powers aligned and realigned themselves to suit their own purposes. Among the most important documentary sources are the biblical books of Kings; the ninth century B.C. basalt stela fragments with old Aramaic inscription from Tel Dan, which describe early Aramaean wars against both the "king of Israel" and "the king of the House of David"; the ninth century B.C. Mesha stela from Dibar in Jordan, which describes Israel's wars with the kingdom of Moab; and the records of Assyrian king Shalmaneser III, which describe the participation of Damascus, Israel, and Hamath in an anti-Assyrian coalition in the battle of Qarqar. Eventually Assyria achieved direct imperial rule over much of the region. Damascus and the countryside of Israel fell to Tiglath-pileser III in 733/732 B.C.; a decade later, the Israelite capital city of Samaria also fell. By the end of the eighth century, Assyria controlled not only these regional powers but virtually all the Aramaean states of northern Syria named above as well as the remaining neo-Hittite centers in Anatolia, such as Patina, Hamath, Que, Gurgum, Carchemish, and Kummuhu. Both the neo-Assyrian and the later neo-Babylonian historical records consider Phoenicia, Philistia, and Syria-Palestine as part of Hatti, the regional name formerly used to denote only Anatolia and northern Syria.

[See also MEDITERRANEAN WORLD, *articles on* THE MEDITERRANEAN PRE-BRONZE AGE, THE RISE OF AEGEAN AND MEDITERRANEAN STATES; NEAR EAST, *articles on* THE NEOLITHIC AND CHALCOLITHIC (PRE-BRONZE AGE) PERIODS IN THE NEAR EAST, THE BRONZE AGE IN THE NEAR EAST.]

■ George Ernest Wright, "The Archaeology of Palestine," in *The Bible and the Ancient Near East: Essays in Honor of W. F. Albright* (1961), pp. 73–112. James B. Pritchard, *Ancient Near Eastern Texts Relating to the Old Testament* (1969). Frank M. Cross, *Canaanite Myth and Hebrew Epic* (1973). Roland de Vaux, *The Early History of Israel* (1978). Yohanan Aharoni, *The Land of the Bible: A Historical Geography*, rev. ed. (1979). Gregory McMahon, "The History of the Hittites," *Biblical Archaeologist* 52 (1989): 62–77. Gösta W. Ahlström, *The History of Ancient Palestine* (1993). Avraham Biran and Joseph Naveh, "An Aramaic State Fragment from Tel Dan," *Israel Exploration Journal* 43 (1993): 81–98. Harry A. Hoffner Jr., "Hittites," in *Peoples of the Old Testament World*, eds. Alfred J. Hoerth, Gerald L. Mattingly, and Edwin M. Yamauchi, (1994), pp. 127–155. Keith N. Schoville, "Canaanites and Amorites," in *Peoples of the Old Testament World*, eds. Alfred J. Hoerth et al. (1994), pp. 157–182. Avraham Biran, "The Tel-Dan Inscription—A New Fragment," *Israel Exploration Journal* 45 (1995): 1–18. Lawrence E. Stager, "The Impact of the Sea Peoples in Canaan (1185–1050 B.C.E.)," in ed. Thomas E. Levy, *The Archaeology of Society in the Holy Land* (1995), pp. 332–348.

Ron E. Tappy

THE MIDDLE AGES IN THE NEAR EAST

The archaeology of the Near East in the Middle Ages has the fortune of being able to draw on the wealth of textual information that accompanies the history of *Islamic civilization, although the field has been burdened methodologically by the tendency to conform archaeologically derived categories to a historically determined paradigm. Archaeological interest in the Nile-to-Oxus region, a local perspective of the area known to the European West as the Near East, has been directed predominantly toward the region's ancient societies and to a lesser extent on Crusader activity in the Levant, with somewhat haphazard results for the study of the post-Antique Near East. Early twentieth-century scholarship focused on the monuments, city plans, and luxury goods of the Islamic political centers, emphasizing a politically based periodization, a pattern that subsequent archaeologists adopted as well. The result has been that cultural assemblages have often been associated with, at best, political dynasties, or, at worst, crude ethnic categories, the unspoken premise being that material transformations are necessarily explained by political or ethnic changes. In recent years, some progress has been made toward the establishment of an archaeologically based periodization, beginning with the recognition that early Islamic society and culture may be considered more accurately a phenomenon of the late Antique rather than the Medieval world. The categories reflect common usage and convenience, although archaeologists of "the medieval Near East" often adopt the descriptor "Islamic," which, even in this region alone, covers a tremendous range of local assemblages, united by long-distance trade in luxury goods, shared cultural institutions, and a recognized, common history.

The archaeology of the Near East in the Middle Ages may broadly be measured by the influx of new peoples into the central lands of this region from its demographic hinterlands (the steppes of Arabia and Central Asia). While such events may account for the widespread introduction of Arabic and Turkish into the area, the effect of such population movements on the material record has yet to be fully determined; in a region so economically and culturally diverse, the association of material assemblages with ethnocultural categories generally proves to be simplistic. If anything, the archaeology of the medieval Near East highlights the region's capacity to absorb populations and their cultural traditions, as well as the relationship between material transformations and levels of economic integration; the region in this period would be more accurately suited to a paradigm based on a diachronic geography rather than a single chronology. Such an elaborate map remains a distant goal of Islamic archaeologists, notwithstanding advances of the recent years.

The deterioration of the formally planned classical city, and indeed the transformation of the Mediterranean world, occurred well before the arrival of Islam (the orientalist construct of the eastern city of labyrinthine alleyways is largely an extrapolation of very long-lived late medieval and early modern cities); the Muslim conquest re-invigorated the notion of planned cities in the Near East, consequently reviving the urban-rural networks that such investments depend on. As the act of emigration (*hijra*) serves as the inceptive theme of Islam and its history, the foundation of a *madina* (Arabic: "place of jurisdiction"; modern Arabic: "city"), whether an explicit result of *hijra* or not, may be taken as the quintessential artifact of the first centuries of Islam. The principal artifacts of Islam are the sacred centers of Mecca and Medina, although over the centuries these have been much changed through acts of restoration and conservation. This view of a highly complex society, however, must be tempered by the coeval archaeology of marginal areas (sites in Oman and the Negev), only recently investigated, revealing the patterns of transhumant pastoralists. Varying levels of economic integration and the symbiosis of urbanized and pastoral populations are constant themes in a comprehensive view of the Near East.

Early Cities. The earliest urban remains of this period date to the years of the conquest, accompanied by the establishment of settlements (sing: *misr*; pl: *amsar*), probably founded with a politico-military function, but which in a matter of years grew into cities. The full range of characteristics of these earliest urban foundations is not known: Of the *amsar* in the Near East, portions of Fustat (Egypt), and its southern suburb, Istabl 'Antar, have been excavated, although largely to levels dating to the eighth through tenth centuries; at Kufa (Iraq), a structure 490 feet (150 m) square was uncovered, with square-planned walls supported by half circular towers, and an early seventh century A.D. date is assumed. What is more telling about these early sites is that they were consistently located near preexisting, conquered settlements. To what extent other sites, not explicitly recognized by the historical sources as *amsar* but similarly built near older cities, such as Aqaba (Jordan) and Istakhr (Iran), represent a more general policy aimed at the foundation of settlements is not fully certain; the growing evidence, however, indicates that the significance of the conquests is as much to be found in the Muslims' building campaigns as their military achievements. These constructions resemble architecturally numerous monuments in the Levant (known as the "desert castles"), such as Anjar (Lebanon), Qasr al-Hayr al-Sharqi (Syria), and Mashatta (Jordan), which may represent another aspect of the tradition of building urban foundations. This Levantine tradition has roots in the Late Byzantine Period, and some of the desert castles may be pre-Islamic in date. Recent discussion has focused on the function of these settlements, as determined from their localities, plans, and the tradition of city-building. What has become increasingly clear is that from the advent of Islam in the Near East through the Abbasid period (when Baghdad, Raqqa, Heraqla, Husn al-Qadisiya, and Samarra were built) until as late as the tenth century (when Lashkari Bazar was built), Muslim political leaders at a variety of levels displayed a concern with the establishment of such urban foundations.

Centralized Political Power. The most dramatic change in the material record of the early medieval Near East appears in the 690s when, as part of a larger effort to centralize the state, the caliph 'Abd al-Malik issued a new, explicitly Islamic coinage, replacing the Byzantine and Sasanian currencies in circulation. Excavations in Alexandria (Egypt) show that at the end of the seventh century the site's ceramic assemblage changes, favoring locally produced Egyptian wares to imported ones, indicating an alteration of trade routes. Excavation of a kiln at the early Islamic site in Aqaba (Jordan) shows the production of a new amphora type, derived from types of the Mediterranean basin. Late seventh-century changes in the material record do not signal the introduction of a new cultural tradition as much as the reinvigoration of indigenous traditions, either by means of innovation or simply through continuous maintenance. Useful tools and practices need not to have been changed:

Dam sites at Khaybar and Ta'if (western Arabia) show a continuity with a long pre-Islamic tradition of hydraulic projects in the south Arabian highlands. Various artifact types—the Egyptian textile and glass, and pottery industries, for example—also argue for material continuity from the pre-Islamic through Islamic period.

Some elements of eighth-century assemblages of Near Eastern sites are clearly discernible from those dated to the Late Byzantine or Sasanian Periods. New utilitarian wares, also mass-produced and centrally distributed, are evident in southern Levantine sites. Glazed ceramic wares, developed from local pottery traditions, exported from Iraq (blue-green storage jars), Egypt (Coptic-glazed wares), and, perhaps somewhat later, western Arabia (Hijazi wares), are evident at sites across the southern Near East. Artifact assemblages of early Islamic sites in Arabia (al-Ma'biyat, al-Rabadhah, and other Darb al-Zubaydah trade route sites between Iraq and western Arabia) indicate regular trade links with the Mediterranean and the Persian Gulf, in the form of ceramic storage vessels, and south Arabia, in the form of stone vessels. In the eighth century, commercial links with the east became as strong as those with the west had ever been, and a number of port sites on the Persian Gulf (Basra, Siraf, and Suhar) and the Arabian littorals of the Indian Ocean and the Red Sea (Dhofar, Aden, and Aqaba) served as emporia for the eastern trade, yielding such distinct evidence as Chinese stonewares and porcelains. The capitals of the Abbasid caliphate, Baghdad and Samarra, would have been the focal points of the empire for the trade in luxury goods; by the late ninth century, however, the political fragmentation of the empire was well underway, provincial capitals growing rapidly into cosmopolitan metropolises in their own right, so that such exotica are found in abundance not only at Samarra but also at Fustat and Nishapur (northeast Iran). Textual evidence indicates that commercial activity across the southern edge of the Mediterranean thrived as much as the eastern trade, although the evidence is much more difficult to assess prior to the tenth century. As for commerce with the northern lands of the Mediterranean, shipwreck sites have provided rich evidence of trade links between the Fatimid and Byzantine states (Serçe Limani, Turkey), although the frequency of such contacts is not known. At the same time, however, and in spite of the strength of long-distance trade networks, the level of economic integration in some regions lessened; for example, starting in the tenth century in the southern Levant, hand-made utilitarian wares supersede mass-produced ones, frequently found in the same contexts as mass-produced, glazed, imported wares.

After the caliphate's loss of centralized political power in 945, the Near East had become a region within a much broader, politically decentralized, cultural commonwealth in which the power of long-distance trade continued to thrive, and in which local notables and local military commanders came to wield a relatively large amount of political and economic power. This state of affairs was reinforced when, in the mid-eleventh century, Turkish-speaking pastoralists moved into the Near East from the Central Asian steppes and established for some decades an empire ruling over the Iranian plateau, Iraq, Syria, and eastern Anatolia. A lasting impact of the Turkic conquest, however, was the institutionalization of economic decentralization in the form of non-hereditary land grants (iqta') to regional military commanders, strengthening local political autonomy and encouraging the development of cosmopolitan culture within regional cities based on a highly mobile, educated elite and patronized by local political elite.

Later Middle Ages. The archaeology of the first centuries of the medieval Near East has focused primarily on the centers of political power, and to a lesser extent on locations which served as commercial emporia. In the later Middle Ages, political power in the Near East was materially expressed in the construction of monuments, generally urban institutions. Excavations of village sites, industrial installations, port sites, and regional political centers demonstrate the diversity of the region's social and economic life during the last centuries of the medieval Near East. The site of Zabid (Yemen) illustrates that city's role in both the regional economy connecting the coastal plain and the highlands, as well as Yemen's role in long-distance trade, part of a complex system including Persian Gulf (Qal'at Bahrain, Julfar, Siraf, Kish, and Hormuz) and Red Sea ports (Tur and Aydhab). Archaeological survey in the southern Jordan River Valley has produced evidence of extensive sugarcane processing plants (Tell Abu Sarbut, Jordan). Excavations of provincial towns and villages of Samsat, Tille, and Gritille in the Euphrates River Valley (southeastern Turkey) provided a picture of holdings that would have been included within a typical 'iqta assignment, as well as the sometimes dramatic events that such settlements had to endure as armies fought over the area. Similarly, the Red Tower (Palestine) serves as an excellent example of a protected, agricultural Crusader period community, and, as an excavation, it serves as an example of the melding of archaeological and textual sources; across the Jordan River, excavation of the village site of Khirbat Faris is filling gaps in the local-level archaeological record of the Jordanian highlands.

Again in the mid-thirteenth century, the Near East was subjected to an influx of pastoralists when the armies of the Mongol advanced from the steppes of Central Asia to as far as Palestine. Aspirations to world empire were abandoned with the dissolution of the Mongol state into appanages (land grants), the Mongol area of the Near East falling to the successor state of the Il-khans, who for some decades successfully retained their identity as foreign conquerors but eventually adopted Persian culture and Islam. In spite of the rivalry and frequent enmity between the regional empires of the Near East, interstate commerce in luxury goods shows that trade was not interdicted but rather more often encouraged by state authorities. Caravanserais (caravan inns) and commercial settlements are to be found throughout the Near East, from Iran to Egypt. Frequently located in hostile environments, these sites (e.g., Quseir al-Qadim and Egypt) are testimony to the degree of external investment required to sustain long-distance commerce. Nevertheless, the fragility of sustaining economic integration in marginal environments is amply evident. Excavation and survey in the Kerak plateau (Jordan) provides ceramic evidence for a vital regional economic system during the last medieval centuries, a pattern that changed profoundly in the sixteenth century with a contraction of the trade in mass-produced pottery and the concomitant increase in handmade wares.

This particular phenomenon may well be the local manifestation of much more widespread transformations in the Near East. At the beginning of the sixteenth century, the Near East, as well as the broader Islamic world, underwent a radical realignment with the establishment of three world empires. These states imposed in the region a highly centralized political system not seen since the ninth century, realigning patterns of economic integration and effectively blocking the frontiers of the Near East until the age of European colonialism.

[See also ISLAMIC CIVILIZATION: INTRODUCTION.]

■ S. D. Goitein, A Mediterranean Society, 5 vols. (1967–1993). M.G.S. Hodgson, The Venture of Islam, 3 vols. (1974). R. Hodges and D. White-house, Mohammed, Charlemagne and the Origins of Europe (1983). P. M. Holt, The Age of the Crusades (1986). H. Kennedy, The Prophet and the Age of the Caliphates (1986). D. Morgan, Medieval Persia, 1040–1797 (1988). C. L. Redman, ed., Medieval Archaeology (1989). A. Cameron and L. I. Conrad, eds., The Byzantine and Early Islamic Near East, Vol. 2: Land Use and Settlement Patterns (1992). G. Fowden, Empire to Commonwealth (1993).

John L. Meloy

NEAR EASTERN ARCHAEOLOGY. Though comprised of many specialized disciplines and spanning a vast area from Iran on the east to Asia Minor, Cyprus, and Egypt on the west, Near Eastern archaeology retains an overall coherence in its continuing attempts to understand the origins, internal development, and external connections of a mosaic of complex cultures that first arose in the Neolithic Period. The discipline's origins can be traced to a confluence of medieval European pilgrimage traditions (that brought a continuing flow of travelers to the biblical sites of the region) and the commercial and scientific expansion of Renaissance Europe (that encouraged the search for knowledge through empirical evidence rather than legends or faith). Until the early nineteenth century, however, the study of Near Eastern antiquity was restricted to geographical exploration and the haphazard collection of relics. It was only with the beginnings of large-scale excavations in Egypt in the 1820s and in Mesopotamia in the 1830s that the systematic recovery of the region's ancient architecture and artifacts became an important tool for the reconstruction of ancient Near Eastern history.

Because of the abundance of written records from the ancient cultures of Mesopotamia, *Anatolia, Syro-Palestine, and Egypt (both those derived from classical and biblical sources and those recovered from excavations), the role of the archaeologist in this region has often been subsidiary to that of the historian. Excavated cities, temples, and monuments have often been used as tangible illustrations of traditional historical understandings—rather than being seen as the raw material for independent analyses of ancient Near Eastern history. The excavation of inscriptions and written documents has always been of primary importance. The achievement of Jean Francois Champollion in his initial decipherment of Egyptian hieroglyphics on the basis of the bilingual *Rosetta Stone, and of Henry *Rawlinson and others in the decipherment of the cuneiform scripts of Mesopotamia provided modern scholars with abundant new written material on the civilizations of the second and first millennia B.C.

During the nineteenth century, modern European evolutionary and racial theories exerted a profound effect on archaeological interpretation in the Near East. The excavations of W.M.F. *Petrie and George Andrew Reisner in Egypt, in particular, imparted an implicit developmentalist scheme to archaeological interpretations of ancient Near Eastern history. By stressing the sequence of superimposed strata within individual sites, these two scholars and their intellectual heirs began to move beyond mere illustration of traditional histories toward the illustration of the rise of social complexity in the regions—from prehistory to the Greco-Roman period. Elsewhere in the region, racial deter-minism provided the subtext of archaeological interpretation, especially in Mesopotamia and Asia Minor, where the supposed cultural superiority of the Indo-European Sumerians, Hurrians, and Hittites was seen as the motive force in the history of the Fertile Crescent and indeed of the entire Western world.

In the early twentieth century, much of the modern Near East fell under European colonial control, and conditions improved for the pursuit of Western-style archaeology. Large-scale excavations throughout the region established a detailed cultural history for the region by defining long sequences of sedentary occupation at sites such as *Jericho, Megiddo, Carchemish, Bogozkoy, and Sumer, through stratigraphically established pottery sequences and architectural styles. It was only in the post–World War II era, however, that the influence of anthropology began to be felt in Near Eastern archaeology. Beginning with the pioneering surveys and excavations of Robert Adams near Baghdad, and with the proliferation of ethnoarchaeological studies, Near Eastern archaeologists began to see the rise of complex civilization there as a regional elaboration of universal social behaviors rather than as mere illustrations of unique biblical or ancient history.

The rise of independent nation-states throughout the region after World War II also had far-reaching effects on the conduct of Near Eastern archaeology. Though the European and American expeditions to the region continued, the control of archaeological sites was now placed in the hands of local universities and departments of antiquities. The interpretive orientation of these new national archaeologies was often connected with modern political symbolism: finding in the remains of certain ancient peoples and golden ages metaphorical legitimation for modern *nationalism. In recent years, this tendency has been tempered by the adoption by local archaeologists of an increasingly internationalist, anthropological perspective—which, in its own way, embodies a powerful modern ideology.

The chronological boundaries of Near Eastern archaeology are constantly expanding. The study of human evolution, long restricted mainly to Africa and Europe, has become a particularly important field of research owing to important human fossil finds in Iran and Israel. At the other end of the chronological scale, new interest has arisen in the archaeology of the medieval and post-medieval periods, illuminating through material culture far-reaching effects of the rise of the modern world system. Indeed, the study of the archaeological record in the Near East can no longer be neatly divided into the specialized realms of Egyptology, Mesopotamian, Anatolian, and biblical archaeology. Near Eastern archaeology is being ever more closely integrated to the archaeological record of other parts of the world.

[See also CLASSICAL ARCHAEOLOGY; ETHNOARCHAEOLOGY; HISTORICAL ARCHAEOLOGY; HISTORY OF ARCHAEOLOGY BEFORE 1900: NEAR EASTERN ARCHAEOLOGY; HISTORY OF ARCHAEOLOGY FROM 1900 TO 1950: NEAR EASTERN ARCHAEOLOGY; HISTORY OF ARCHAEOLOGY SINCE 1950: NEAR EASTERN ARCHAEOLOGY; PREHISTORIC ARCHAEOLOGY.]

■ D. H. Trump, The Prehistory of the Mediterranean (1980). Bruce G. Trigger, B. J. Kemp, D. O'Connor, and A. B. Lloyd, Ancient Egypt: A Social History (1983). H. J. Nissen, The Early History of the Ancient Near East, 9000–2000 B.C. (1988). Amihai Mazar, Archaeology of the Land of the Bible (1990). Michael Roaf, Cultural Atlas of Mesopotamia and the Ancient Near East (1990). Thomas E. Levy, ed., The Archaeology of Society in the Holy Land (1995).

Neil Asher Silberman

NEOLITHIC. *See* THREE-AGE SYSTEM.

NEW GUINEA. *See* AUSTRALIA AND NEW GUINEA.

NEW GUINEA, Origins of Food Production in. The complexity of food production systems in New Guinea was fully exposed as late as 1933 when Australian explorers discovered a population of over one million people still in a stone age settled in the high valleys of the rugged central mountain ranges. These societies were particularly remarkable with their well-kept gardens, which demonstrated skillful knowledge of techniques as diverse as large-scale swamp management, hill-slope terracing, and irrigation. An intriguing aspect of the discovery was that the dominant crop cultivated, and at times as a virtual monoculture, was the sweet potato *(Ipomoea batatas)*, a plant of American origin.

The island of New Guinea still supports an enormous range of food production systems: from hunter-gatherer communities to others whose subsistence is based on swidden cultivation in the rain forest, or on intensive swampland cultivation. There are various staples according to regions, altitudes, environments, and cultural choices. Major ones include banana, breadfruit, taro, yam, sago, sugarcane, sweet potato, and cassava (another American cultivar). Some crops are endemic to New Guinea or other islands of Melanesia, others are found in Southeast Asia as well, and few have clearly been introduced from the Americas sometime in the remote past. Food production has a New Guinea origin and seems to have followed a number of internal evolutions rather than a simple monolithic change with time.

Since the early 1970s, the contributions of Jack Golson and Douglas Yen have been paramount in our investigations on the origins of food production in New Guinea. Evidence of swamp manipulation for horticulture is found at *Kuk, in a high valley of the central highlands, dating to 9,000 years ago. The Kuk swamp shows evidence of increased management over the last 6,000 years, with elaboration of drainage channels from that time on (Gorecki 1985, Golson 1989). These complex *field systems have deep sociopolitical implications, including the rise of major centers of food production (swamplands), an increase in ceremonial exchange, and the development of a long-distance trading network in which marine shells play an important role (Golson and Gardner 1990).

Given the location of Kuk (in a cold valley at high altitude) and the timing of the first evidence of swamp management (right at the end of the last glaciation), it is likely that the true beginnings of food production will be found at lower altitudes and at a time earlier than 9,000 years ago. It has been proposed by Les Groube (1989) that the earliest colonists who arrived from Southeast Asia more than 40,000 years ago were rain-forest foragers. They would have found no difficulty adapting to very similar environments in the New Guinea lowlands. He suggested that the large waisted stone blades found at a number of Pleistocene sites, particularly for the period 40,000 to 9,000 years ago, were hafted and used in a dense forest environment so as to promote the growth of trees that were of economic importance as well as other plants with edible fruits, leaves, tubers, and numerous green vegetables.

In some areas, this close relationship between people and plants eventually led to a food production system similar to the one termed "arboriculture" and still observed in parts of the Solomon Islands (Yen 1974). Wetland margins, especially those found in the lowlands, were particularly crucial in this plant husbandry, having the advantage of supporting a rich mosaic of wet and dry plants. It is the outcome of this growing reliance on a range of plant resources that has been uncovered at Kuk and dated to some 9,000 years ago.

By 6,000 years ago, massive forest clearance had occurred throughout the New Guinea highlands, indicating that dryland and wetland horticulture was widespread. At this time, major cultural changes are noted in Melanesia, indicating increased trading contact and exchange with communities from Southeast Asia. Two major outcomes of this are the introduction into New Guinea of domesticated pigs and most probably new crops, including some tubers. The impact of pigs on Melanesian societies was immense, becoming for many a source of wealth and the yardstick in social transactions. The total absence of grain crops, including the all-important rice, indicates that for the last 6,000 years Melanesian societies had a solid socioeconomic base.

What is needed now in New Guinea is a shift in research from the high valleys to the lowlands, where investigations on the origin of food production have been rather limited. Yet we do know that when the remainder of the Pacific region was settled between 3,500 and 2,000 years ago, it was by people with a New Guinea, not a Southeast Asian, agricultural system (Yen 1991). It is only after the conquest of the Pacific is achieved that the sweet potato first appears in Polynesian gardens to eventually become a most important staple in New Guinea perhaps as early as 1,200 years ago and certainly by 400 years ago.

[*See also* LAPITA COMPLEX; PACIFIC ISLANDS, *articles on* INTRODUCTION, SETTLEMENT OF MELANESIA AND MICRONESIA; PACIFIC ISLANDS, ORIGINS OF FOOD PRODUCTION IN THE.]

■ Douglas Yen, "Arboriculture in the Subsistence of Santa Cruz, Solomon Islands," *Economic Botany* 28 (1974): 247–284. Paul Gorecki, "Human Occupation and Agricultural Developments in the Papua New Guinea Highlands," *Mountain Research and Development* 6 (1986): 159–166. Jack Golson, "The Origins and Development of New Guinea Agriculture," in eds. David Harris and Gordon Hillman, *Foraging and Farming: The Evolution of Plant Exploitation* (1989), pp. 678–687. Les Groube, "The Taming of the Rain Forests: A Model for Late Pleistocene Forest Exploitation in New Guinea," in eds. David Harris and Gordon Hillman, *Foraging and Farming: The Evolution of Plant Exploitation* (1989), pp. 292–304. Jack Golson and Don Gardner, "Agriculture and Sociopolitical Organization in New Guinea Highlands Prehistory," *Annual Review in Anthropology* 19 (1990): 395–417. Douglas Yen, "Polynesian Cultigens and Cultivars: The Questions of Origin," in eds. Paul Cox and Sandra Banack, *Islands, Plants, and Polynesians* (1991), pp. 67–95.

Paul Gorecki

NEW ZEALAND was the last substantial landmass to be colonized by humans. Polynesian voyagers introduced an eastern Polynesian culture, which developed into the Maori culture described by European explorers. The eighteenth-century Maori were recognizably Polynesian in language and appearance, but many features of their culture were different from anything in tropical Polynesia. Although they shared a single language and social organization, there was considerable regional diversity in settlement and economy, from horticultural groups in the warmer northern regions to more mobile hunter-gatherers in the sparsely populated, colder south.

The date of first settlement is uncertain. In recent years, debate about the antiquity of settlement elsewhere in eastern Polynesia has led some archaeologists to argue for settlement of New Zealand as early as A.D. 500; however, critical review of radiocarbon dates has shown no clear evidence for occupation before about A.D. 1200. Certainly by A.D. 1300, settlements were established at favorable locations throughout the country, particularly on the more hospitable east coast.

Despite a large body of Maori oral tradition describing the arrival in New Zealand of numerous immigrant canoes, there is no firm archaeological evidence of multiple settlement, nor of return voyages to the putative homeland area. However, New Zealand obsidian has been found on the Kermadec Islands, more than 466 miles (750 km) northeast of New Zealand, which were uninhabited at European contact.

Artifacts in early New Zealand sites include stone adze blades, fishhooks, and personal ornaments very similar to those of broadly similar age from the Cook, Society, and Marquesas Islands, supporting the long-established view that New Zealand was settled from that area.

Artifact studies have documented changes in stone technology and in the styles of other durable artifacts, particularly fishhooks and ornaments. Eastern Polynesian styles were largely superseded by about A.D. 1500. Investigation of the processes of adze manufacture and replication studies have contributed to the understanding of stone technology.

Little is known of the development of the distinctive Maori wood-carving styles or the techniques and patterns of weaving with New Zealand flax. Rare examples have been preserved in waterlogged deposits or dry caves. Rock art sites of various ages are found in many areas, with major concentrations of relatively early sites in the South Island.

The subsistence economy of the Polynesian settlers has been a focus of investigation since the mid-nineteenth century, when the remains of moa (Dinornithiformes) and other extinct birds were first recognized in midden deposits. The term "moa-hunter," was often applied to the first Polynesian inhabitants, but has largely fallen into disuse following recognition of the diversity of regional economies and the range of big game available. Food remains from early sites reflect the importance of marine mammals such as fur seals, dolphins, and pilot whales, as well as moa. Fur seals and sea lions were widely distributed around the New Zealand coast at first settlement and suffered severe reduction in range as a result of Polynesian settlement.

Throughout New Zealand prehistory, subsistence activities included gathering of plant foods, fishing, hunting, and, where climate permitted, horticulture. There was a strong seasonal round in all regions, with an emphasis on preservation of seasonally abundant foods. Even during the initial settlement period, moa hunting was far more important in some areas than others. In all regions, however, there was a decline in hunting through time and an increased reliance on other activities such as fishing. Archaeozoological studies have made an important contribution to the understanding of Maori subsistence.

The role of horticulture in early New Zealand has been the subject of debate. Polynesian settlers successfully introduced some of the cultigens from their tropical homeland, including taro, yam, gourd, and kumara, or sweet potato. Earlier workers argued that even in the north, the early settlers were hunter-gatherers who turned to horticulture only later, as moa and seal hunting declined, and following a later introduction of cultivated plants. It is now generally accepted that horticulture was introduced by the first settlers, who quickly adapted the kumara, particularly, to a seasonal regime. Opinion remains divided as to the importance of horticulture during the early period when big game was abundant in most regions. In recent years, studies of trace elements and isotopes in human bone have begun to address the issue of relative dietary importance of different foods. Actual plant remains are seldom found; archaeological evidence of horticulture includes field systems, altered soils, and pits interpreted as crop stores.

The impact of Maori on the environment and the ability of the land to sustain settlement varied regionally. Large areas of forest were cleared, both deliberately for horticulture and accidentally as a result of fire. Changes in habitat and predation by introduced dogs and rats as well as people brought some indigenous species to extinction and drastically reduced the numbers and range of others. The effects on birds are well documented; the effects on lizards and invertebrates are only now being established. In some northern areas, forest clearance opened up large areas for horticulture without serious side effects; in others, such as Palliser Bay at the southern tip of North Island, forest clearance began processes of erosion that reduced the region's ability to support permanent Maori settlement.

Maori society did not develop the level of complexity found in some Polynesian societies such as Hawaii or Tonga. Nor did the Maori construct the massive religious edifices typical of most other eastern Polynesian societies and seen in an extreme form in Easter Island. Eighteenth-century Maori settlement pattern was dominated by pā, or hillforts. More than six thousand pā, varying greatly in size and complexity, have been recorded. The reason for their development is a major issue. All Polynesian societies were warlike, and there is some slight evidence of violence to individuals in the early period of settlement in New Zealand. However, earthwork fortifications seem to have appeared quite suddenly in most regions about A.D. 1500. There is as yet no evidence of primacy in a particular place, nor of progressive evolution of more complex forms of defense. Both population pressure in general and pressure on good horticultural land have been proposed as the cause of the development of pā. However, in the eighteenth century, pā were found in nonhorticultural and horticultural regions alike. The reasons for their development were probably more complex and involved the prestige of chiefs and tribal groups, as well as the need to protect people and resources.

Traditionally and historically, episodes of war were interspersed with episodes of peace. Peacemaking involved gift exchange. Throughout New Zealand prehistory, extensive communication networks ensured a flow of resources throughout the country. Sourcing of stone tools has revealed the extent of movement of valuable raw materials such as obsidian and the prized New Zealand jade.

Archaeology has revealed little of Maori religious practice apart from burial customs. Rare instances of ritual disposal of items in swamps and deliberate burial of items beneath house posts have been documented. Although there was diversity of mortuary practice at all periods, earlier communities tended to favor interment on the edges of settlements, whereas in later periods there was more emphasis on the hiding of bones in caves. Studies of human remains have built up a vivid picture of a healthy, active population who nevertheless, like other preindustrial people, died relatively young.

Maori society was little affected by the brief visit of the Dutch explorer Abel Tasman in 1642. However, the arrival of British and French explorers from 1769 onward began a process of increasing contact with the outside world that led to far-reaching changes in Maori culture and society.

[*See also* PACIFIC ISLANDS, *articles on* INTRODUCTION, EUROPEAN VOYAGERS AND THE END OF PREHISTORY IN THE PACIFIC ISLANDS, SETTLEMENT OF POLYNESIA; PACIFIC ISLANDS CHIEFDOMS.]

■ Roger Duff, *The Moa-Hunter Period of Maori Culture*, 3rd ed. (1977). Philip Houghton, *The First New Zealanders* (1980). Michael M. Trotter and Beverley McCulloch, *Prehistoric Rock Art of New Zealand*, 2nd ed. (1981). Janet Davidson, *The Prehistory of New Zealand* (1984). Atholl Anderson, *Prodigious Birds: Moas and Moa-Hunting in Prehistoric New Zealand* (1989). Atholl Anderson, "The Chronology of Colonization in New Zealand," *Antiquity* 65 (1991): 767–795.

Janet Davidson

NINDOWARI was discovered in 1957 during Beatrice deCardi's survey of Kalat. It is located on a tributary of the Porali River in the Ornach Valley of southern Baluchistan, Pakistan. Nindowari, or Nindo Damb, is now an oval ca. 3280 by 1640 feet (1000 by 500 m), or 124 acres (50 ha) in extent and 75 feet (23 m) high. It is the largest of the sites of the Kulli Complex so far reported. The Kulli Complex has been proposed to have been the highland manifestation of the Harappan civilization (2500–2000 B.C.). Size and the remarkable architecture found there make it an extraordinary place. Jean-Marie Casal conducted three seasons of fieldwork there in collaboration with the Pakistan Department of Archaeology (1962–1965). He found that Nindowari was built of both river-washed and flat slabs of schist, some of which were set vertically, fence-like. The main mound gradually rises from the river to a central prominence sitting on a rectangular platform that is bordered with remains of large structures. The central mound, which rises 82 feet (25 m) above the river is composed of large, raw stones, some of them being 5 to 8 feet (1.5 to 2.5 m) long and weighing more than a ton. At the summit is a circular depression ringed with stone. Around that central prominence are the remains of stone walls suggesting a succession of terraces that rise step-wise from the river bank. Staircases of significant scale lead from the platform base to the summit of the mound, suggesting that this was conceived as a single monument.

Excavation was conducted in five areas: Area A, buildings bordering the eastern side of the quadrangular platform; Area B, the quadrangular platform; Area R, an exploratory trench cut on the outer enclosure running parallel to the river; Area T, a large stone box in the northern sector; and Area KD, a separate mound ca. 590 feet (180 m) south of the main mound, deriving its name from Kulliki-an Damb, "Mound of Potteries." Area T was found to probably be Iron Age or later. Area KD, with an impressive fortification, contained Londo Ware, associated with Partho-Sassanian times in the region.

Area B was made up of a series of cells, paved with schist flags, separated by broad passages. According to Jean-Francois Jarrige, "The presence of hundreds of grinding stones in the cells and on the stone platforms would indicate that these small square cells are part of a granary" (1983). Casal noticed that there were also a number of broken vessels here, with deposits in the bottom that looked like plant remains. Evidence for what might be a pre-Kulli occupation came from this area in the form of Nal pottery.

Three seals were found in the granary area. Two of them were typical Harappan unicorn stamp seals. The third had a pattern of circles.

The material from Nindowari has not been fully published, but includes the distinctive Kulli-Harappan ware of the second half of the third millennium B.C., along with distinctive figurines (C. Jarrige 1984). Nal ware, both monochrome and polychrome, was found and suggests an Early Harappan occupation (ca. 3200–2500 B.C.) as well.

[*See also* ASIA: PREHISTORY AND EARLY HISTORY OF SOUTH ASIA; HARAPPA.]

■ Beatrice deCardi, *Archaeological Surveys in Baluchistan* 8 (1957). Jean-Marie Casal, "Nindowari—a Chalcolithic Site in South Baluchistan," *Pakistan Archaeology* 3 (1966): 10–21. Jean-Marie Casal, "Nindo Damb," *Pakistan Archaeology* 5 (1968): 51–5. Catherine Jarrige, "Terracotta Human Figurines from Nindowari," in *South Asian Archaeology 1981* ed. Bridget Allchin (1984), pp. 129–34. Jean-Francois Jarrige, "Nindowari, A 3rd Millennium Site in Southern Baluchistan," *Newsletter of Baluchistan Studies* 1 (1983): 47–50. Gregory L. Possehl, *Kulli: An Exploration of Ancient Civilization in South Asia* (1986).

Gregory L. Possehl

NINEVEH, site of the last and greatest capital of the Assyrian Empire, lies just east of the Tigris River within the modern Iraqi city of Mosul. Nineveh's ancient wall, 7.5 miles (12 km) in circumference, encloses an area of 1,853 acres (750 ha). There are two prominent mounds on the ancient city's western side: Kuyunjik, the palace mound, and Nebi Yunus, site of the royal armory and, since medieval times, the location of a shrine of the prophet Jonah.

Nineveh was favored with an agriculturally rich hinterland and controlled a major crossing-point of the Tigris. The earliest settlement was established in the seventh millennium B.C. During periods when southern Mesopotamia was expanding economically and/or politically—for example, during the fourth millennium and again in the late third—Nineveh had close connections with the south. Second-millennium Nineveh was a prominent center, being incorporated into the nascent Assyrian state during the fourteenth century B.C. Around 700 B.C., the neo-Assyrian king Sennacherib (704–681 B.C.) moved his capital to Nineveh, rebuilding, enlarging, and fortifying the city in the process. Despite its massive defenses it was sacked and burned by the Medes and Babylonians in 612 B.C. There are significant remains of a subsequent Hellenistic-Parthian settlement and traces of still later Islamic occupation. Today Nineveh is under threat by the expansion of Mosul, which has grown to cover approximately one-third of the ancient site.

The exploration of Nineveh was closely tied to the birth of modern Assyriology and Mesopotamian archaeology. After an initial attempt at exploration by French consul Paul Emile *Botta in 1842, Austen Henry *Layard, the pioneer British archaeologist, began excavating the so-called Southwest Palace, Sennacherib's "Palace Without Rival," with its spectacular sculptured stone-wall reliefs in 1846. He was succeeded by his onetime assistant, Hormuzd Rassam, who discovered still more reliefs, including the famous scenes of the royal lion hunt, in the North Palace of Ashurbanipal (668–ca. 627 B.C.). These discoveries, together with those of Botta and Victor Place at Khorsabad and Layard's finds at Nimrud, captured the imagination of Europe in the mid-nineteenth century. Less immediately fascinating at that time were the thousands of cuneiform tablets recovered from the Kuyunjik palaces. These tablets, which represented the archives of the Assyrian state in the seventh century B.C., began to receive their due attention a generation later, when George Smith identified a portion of a Mesopotamian flood story among the tablets from Nineveh in the British Museum. He returned to the site in the 1870s to recover more texts.

Since then Nineveh has been the object of numerous investigations. British archaeologist R. Campbell Thompson explored the Temples of Ishtar and Nabu on Kuyunjik and M.E.L. Mallowan, Campbell Thompson's associate in 1931–1932, excavated a deep sounding through the mound that established the basic stratigraphical sequence for the prehistoric cultures of northern Mesopotamia back to the Hassuna Period (ca. seventh millennium B.C.).

Since World War II, the work at Nineveh has largely been in the hands of Iraqi archaeologists, among them Mohammed Ali Mustafa, Tariq Madhloom, and Manhal Jabr, who have focused their energies on the mound Nebi Yunus and the city's gates. Several of the latter, including the Nergal, Adad, Shamash, and Mashqi Gates, have been excavated and restored or reconstructed. On Nebi Yunus an entrance to the royal armory was excavated in the 1950s, and, more recently, stone relief sculptures have been uncovered near the top of the mound.

Between 1987 and 1990, a team from the University of California at Berkeley under the direction of David Stronach began a broad-scale investigation involving much of the site. On Kuyunjik they continued the investigation of Sennacherib's palace and the Akkadian (ca. 2334–2154 B.C.) levels of the mound. They also began work on the old city mound north of Kuyunjik, where they exposed part of an elite quarter as well as a much less substantially built area for metalworkers and potters. At the Halzi Gate they found evidence of last-minute attempts to strengthen Nineveh's defenses before the assault of 612 B.C. and uncovered the remains of victims caught in the gate during the last days of the great city.

[See also BABYLON; MESOPOTAMIA: ASSYRIA; NEAR EAST: IRON AGE CIVILIZATIONS OF THE NEAR EAST.]

■ M. Louise Scott and John MacGinnis, "Notes on Nineveh," *Iraq* 52 (1990): 63–73. John M. Russell, *Sennacherib's Palace Without Rival at Nineveh* (1991). David Stronach and Stephen Lumsden, "UC Berkeley's Excavations at Nineveh," *Biblical Archaeologist* 55 (1992): 227–233.

James A. Armstrong

NON NOK THA was discovered during a site survey in 1964 by Chester Gorman. It is located in the upper catchment of the Nam Phong river in Khok Kaen province, northeast Thailand. Test excavations the following year revealed inhumation graves associated with pottery vessels and bronze artifacts, which led to the excavation of 3,660 square feet (340 sq m) of the site in 1966 and 1968 under the direction of Donn Bayard.

It is a small site, covering little over 2.4 acres (1 ha), and cultural material averages 4.6 feet (1.4 m) in depth. But it contains many burials which intercut and overlie each other, and thus make seriation possible. Bayard has recognized eleven phases, divided into an Early Period with three phases and a Middle Period with eight. The earliest bronze artifacts are found in EP 3.

Dating this sequence has proved to be extremely difficult. The problem lies in the rarity with which charcoal is found in sufficient quantity and security of provenance to provide a radiocarbon date related to an event in the site's history. This has led to radically different interpretations based on alternative chronological frameworks. Initially, it was proposed that the earliest bronzes dated to the early third or even the fourth millennium B.C., while others opted for far later dates in the second millennium B.C. The longer chronology would also involve great durability and cultural conservatism at Non Nok Tha, since the cemetery would have covered at least 1,500 to 2,000 years.

This uncertainty has now been resolved with the dating of rice chaff from provenanced pottery. The cemetery dates within the period from 1500 to 1000 B.C., and was not of long duration. The mortuary remains reveal inhumation of the dead in individual graves, associated with a range of grave goods. There are many complete pottery vessels, shell jewelry, stone adze heads, and bronze in the form of bracelets and socketed axe heads. The presence of a number of bivalve sandstone molds indicates local casting, probably of imported ingots. The site is located about 143 miles (230 km) south of the Phu Lon copper mines, which are known to have been worked during the second millennium B.C.

While some individuals at Non Nok Tha were buried with relatively many grave goods, there is no evidence for a dominant elite at the site, and status seems more likely to have been attained through personal achievement. Bayard has noted a rise in wealth differentials after the first bronzes became available.

The mortuary vessels often contain fish bones, and rice was used as a tempering agent in potting clay. The establishment of small communities of rice agriculturalists as evidenced at Non Nok Tha seems increasingly to have been a phenomenon with origins in the third millennium B.C., and probably reflects the expansion of rice cultivators into the network of small streams where wet season flooding would have provided an acceptable environment.

[See also ASIA: PREHISTORY AND EARLY HISTORY OF SOUTHEAST ASIA.]

■ D. T. Bayard, Non Nok Tha. The 1968 Excavations: Procedure, Stratigraphy and a Summary of the Evidence. *Otago University Monographs in Prehistoric Anthropology 4 (1971)*. C.F.W. Higham, *The Bronze Age of Southeast Asia* (1996)

Charles Higham

NON-WESTERN SOCIETIES, Archaeology and

Introduction
Archaeology and Native Americans
Archaeology and Australian Aborigines
Archaeology and African Societies

INTRODUCTION

Scientific archaeology is a creation of Western civilization. Archaeology and the study of human evolution finally cast off the shackles of Christian religious dogma with the establishment of the antiquity of humankind in 1859. Victorian archaeology had a strong evolutionary slant and was firmly rooted in racist doctrines of linear human progress, which had all humankind aspiring to the ultimate cultural achievement—industrial civilization. Such simplistic and biased explanations of the past have long given way to more sophisticated formulations based on multilinear biological and cultural evolution, and on complex interactions between humans and their environments over many millennia. Western science espouses a linear view of time, with the human past extending back over at least 2.5 million years, to the beginnings of the Ice Age and even earlier. Such a linear explanation contrasts dramatically with perspectives on the past held by many non-Western societies, which have close ties to the environment, and to their ancestors. For example, many Native American societies have a cyclical, not linear, view of history and time; beliefs based on the continuity of the world and the repetitive cycles of the seasons; the movements of the heavenly bodies; and the eternal verities of fertility, birth, life, and death. As Frankel and Zimmerman point out, many Australian Aborigines and Native Americans consider archaeology an irrelevance and an intrusion into their lives. They object to the excavation of sacred places, some of which still have important spiritual significance. Above all, they violently oppose the excavation and study of skeletal remains, not only those with links to living groups, but those of much higher antiquity as well. Until recently, archaeologists tended to disregard such objections, but legislation in Australia, Canada, the United States, and other countries now places severe restrictions on the excavation of skeletal remains, and requires their *reburial and repatriation under many circumstances. Many archaeologists oppose such legislation on the grounds that priceless biological and pathological information will be lost forever, but a common middle ground permits some scientific study of excavated remains before their reburial.

More fundamental are differences in world views. Many non-Western societies believe that the dead have an impact on the world of the living, for they tend to emphasize the world of the present, bolstered by oral history and myth time. Their world view is based on an essential continuity among past, present, and future, a continuity preserved by the ancestors and the living, and passed on to the yet-to-be-born. The remains of the past must be subject to the laws of natural decay, whereas archaeologists believe they should be preserved for all time.

For many years, Western archaeologists have argued that the past as reconstructed by archaeology has a powerful role to play in the process of nation-building, in restoring long vanished history to newly independent countries. In theory, this is a laudable goal, but one fraught with controversy for countries, like Kenya and Zambia for example, where tribalism is a major political concern. Francis Musonda argues that some of the early research carried out on tribal origins in central Africa may contribute to intertribal tensions in modern society. Far better, he argues, to concentrate on regional surveys and investigations that examine the broader picture of cultural change.

Archaeologists are caught on the horns of a powerful ethical dilemma. On the one hand, they see the archaeological record being looted and destroyed on every side. On the other, many non-Western societies argue passionately that ancient human remains and the archaeological record should be left alone to decay into historical oblivion. Fortunately for science, both sides to this important ethical debate have an interest in stopping destruction of sacred places and remains of ancestors. In North America, for example, many local constituencies of archaeologists and Native Americans are establishing levels of trust that allow cooperation within a context of respect for the past and others' cultural values and spiritual beliefs. Native Americans monitor many excavations and advise on the treatment of skeletal remains. The Zuñi tribe in the Southwest maintains its own archaeological research unit, while the Smithsonian Institution's Museum of the American Indian, to be opened after the year 2000, will offer new perspectives on Native American culture and the past.

In many parts of the world, archaeology is moving into a new era, where serious account will be taken of alternative perspectives on the past. Archaeologists can no longer go about their work without considering the interests of others involved.

[See also ARCHAEOLOGY IN THE CONTEMPORARY WORLD; NATIONALISM.]

■ Richard Lowenthal, *The Past Is a Foreign Country* (1991). Gordon Brotherston, *Book of the Fourth World: Reading the Native Americans Through Their Literature* (1992).

Brian M. Fagan

ARCHAEOLOGY AND NATIVE AMERICANS

As an outgrowth of the civil rights movement of the 1960s, Native Americans launched a multifaceted campaign to correct real and perceived injustices ranging from violations of treaty rights to stereotyping in Hollywood movies. One aspect of these protests focused on inaccurate historical views of Native Americans as extinct or savage. Because of its direct involvement in producing such views, archaeology became a convenient target.

By 1971 American Indian Movement members had disrupted a village site excavation in Minnesota and nationwide had protested treatment of human remains and funerary remains from individuals they considered to be their ancestors. Vietnam War protests eventually eclipsed the movement. Archaeology escaped notice until the end of the decade, when a renewed focus became repatriation and reburial of human remains and grave goods under a broader agenda of intellectual property rights. The so-called reburial issue has continued to be extremely contentious since that time.

The initial response of professional organizations such as the American Association of Physical Anthropologists and the Society for American Archaeology was to pass resolutions against reburial, citing the importance of long-term curation of remains and academic freedom as key concerns. Dialogue between Native Americans and archaeologists produced frank exchanges of differences, including those of world view. Intense media coverage portrayed the issue as two-sided, but a range of opinion was apparent among both Native Americans and archaeologists.

After considerable acrimony, compromise appeared in the form of state laws governing the treatment of remains and two federal statutes, the National Museum of the American Indian Act (Public Law 101-185) of 1989 and the Native American Graves Protection and Repatriation Act (Public Law 101-106) of 1986. The former set a precedent requiring that the Smithsonian Institution inventory and return remains. The latter requires that inventory for human remains in all federal or federally funded agencies be done and that remains be returned. Regular consultation with tribes is to be part of the process. Implementation of the laws has been accompanied by problems especially where genetic or cultural affiliation of remains is uncertain. Among archaeologists, the issue continues to be debated as a question of ethics, but some groups such as the Society of Professional Archaeologists and the World Archaeological Congress have developed codes of ethics giving highest priority to the wishes and involvement of those whose past is being studied.

The primary concerns of archaeology surround the loss of data. There is incontrovertible evidence that new technologies and research questions allow new data to be gathered that may answer, among others, many important questions related to demography, nutrition, disease patterns, and social organization. Worries about restrictions on the practice of science are also important. Some liken reburial to book burning. Archaeologists express concern that remains from the past are a world heritage and that reburial may actually cause harm to future generations of Native Americans who may want or need more information about their people's past.

The primary concerns of Native Americans revolve around the sacred, where protection of the rights of the dead are important. Some see the dead as having an impact on the world of the living, their poor treatment causing an imbalance in the world from which many problems for the living are derived. Other key questions relate to the validity of archaeological interpretation and its impact on contemporary Native American people. Some see little value in archaeology for contemporary Native Americans, reject its conclusions outright, and demand total control of their past as intellectual and cultural property.

Native Americans have different perspectives on time, the past, interpretation of the law, and curation of artifacts. Archaeologists tend to emphasize the past and future, while Native Americans emphasize a present that is bolstered by oral history and mythic time. Law for archaeologists is an adjudicative process, while for traditional Native Americans it may be God-given or natural law that takes precedence over human rules. Curation for archaeologists may be a process of saving remains for future use, while for Native Americans remains must be subject to natural processes of decay.

Both groups have an interest in solving the dilemmas posed by reburial. Recent laws are the result of compromise. In many local situations trust has developed to the level where archaeologists have access to remains and Native Americans have confidence that archaeologists will act respectfully. Many believe that archaeologists and Native Americans can be powerful allies for the protection of archaeological sites if they can resolve conflicts.

[See also NATIONALISM; REBURIAL AND REPATRIATION.]

■ Polly McW. Quick, Proceedings: Conference on Reburial Issues, Newberry Library, Chicago, June 14–15, 1985 (1986), Larry J. Zimmerman, "Human Bones as Symbols of Power: Native American Views of 'Grave-robbing' Archaeologists," in ed. Robert Layton, Conflict in the Archaeology of Living Traditions (1989), pp. 211–216. Randall H. McGuire, "Archaeology and the First Americans," American Anthropologist 94 (1992): 816–836. Clement W. Meighan, "Some Scholars' Views on Reburial," American Antiquity 57 (1992): 704–710. H. Marcus Price III, Disputing the Dead: U.S. Law on Aboriginal Remains and Grave Goods (1992). Anthony L. and Shirley Powell, "A Perspective on Ethics and the Reburial Controversy," American Antiquity 58 (1993): 348–354.

Larry J. Zimmerman

ARCHAEOLOGY AND AUSTRALIAN ABORIGINES

Prehistoric archaeology in Australia has always been undertaken with an awareness of an Aboriginal presence. Earlier researchers saw Aborigines as a source of data to illustrate the past. With the recent growth in Aboriginal consciousness, self-confidence, and power this role has changed from convenient object to manager. This transition has been swift and at times traumatic for archaeologists.

Australia is a federation of six states and two territories. The status of Aboriginal and Torres Strait Islanders varies considerably. In some regions (especially the Northern Territory, Western Australia, and South Australia) many Aboriginal communities maintain a cohesion and strong traditional identity, with well-established entitlement to land. Elsewhere, especially in the southeastern states, the situation is different. The pervasive image of the remote Aborigine militates against urban Aboriginal aspirations. In Tasmania the Aboriginal community has a continuing problem in demonstrating its existence. Differences in social context, and in heritage legislation, affect relationships between Aboriginal communities and researchers.

The year 1967 was critical for the Aboriginal people of Australia. By voting in a referendum to accord them full rights as citizens, Australians signaled a new attitude toward the indigenous population. The legal recognition of prior ownership of land in the Mabo case before the High Court in 1992 has led to a fundamental reappraisal of all Aboriginal issues. From the initial European settlement in southeastern Australia in 1788, Aboriginal people had been progressively dispossessed of land and rights across the entire continent. Now, Aboriginal concerns began to be addressed in a different way. Although, as highlighted by the Royal Commission on Aboriginal Deaths in Custody (1991), Aboriginal people remain severely disadvantaged, they have achieved some political power. The major thrust in Aboriginal politics has been toward land rights. From about 1980 a subsidiary concern for heritage rights has had a growing impact on archaeology, especially in the southern states.

The most obvious conflict has been over skeletal remains, clearly exposed in arguments about reburial of the Murray Black Collection. Hundreds of skeletons from along the Murray River had been collected in the 1940s. Changes in legislation in the state of Victoria in 1984 allowed Aboriginal legal action to obtain control of them. As an Aboriginal consensus moved toward a policy of reburial, academic fears for this major scientific resource were expressed. While there was no opposition to the reburial of the remains of known individuals or the less significant fragments, the reburial/destruction of older remains of undeniable scientific importance was strongly opposed. Apart from justifications based on their exceptional information value, a key debating point was their antiquity. The Western scientific denial of any legitimate personal relationships with very ancient human remains was opposed by an Aboriginal claim that time does not diminish affiliation and the need for respect. The vigorous—at times acrimonious—debate became irrelevant as new legislation placed control over all archaeological material in Aboriginal hands; by 1990 all the Murray Black Collection had been returned to local communities. So, too, had the archaeologically excavated Late Pleistocene remains from Kow Swamp, which are of global significance.

Equivalent changes have taken place in other aspects of archaeological practice in Australia. In several states, as in Victoria, Aboriginal communities now have legal authority over sites and artifacts, but even where this is not the case, heritage managers generally require researchers to obtain permission before undertaking fieldwork. While some archaeologists reluctantly accept what they see as an impediment to field research, others are fervent supporters of Aboriginal aspirations. Fears of discrimination against researchers who espouse unpopular theories have not been realized, and there is a widespread acceptance of Aboriginal control over archaeological material. Although this conditions access to some areas, sites, and collections, Aboriginal attitudes have not affected the type of problems addressed in academic research. There is a greater impact in public archaeology, where museum and management priorities are more directly affected by policy decisions and funding allocation.

There is no single Aboriginal view on any issue, including archaeology. Some resent nonAboriginal scientific views of the past and regard all archaeological research as irrelevant, preferring concepts of an indigenous creation and long cultural continuity. Associated romanticized images of traditional lifestyles are promoted and eagerly accepted by the general public. Nevertheless there is also genuine interest in research, especially of local relevance. Archaeology is also used for immediate advantage (as in support for land claims) and to emphasize prior occupation in political debate. While there are few Aboriginal people engaged in academic research, increasing numbers are employed in public archaeology, mainly at the more practical level.

[See also NATIONALISM; REBURIAL AND REPATRIATION.]

■ Rosalind F. Langford, "Our Heritage—Your Playground," *Australian Archaeology* 16 (1983): 1–6. David Frankel, "Who Owns the Past?" *Australian Society* 3.9 (1984): 14–15. Jim Allen, *The Politics of the Past* (1987). Jim Birkhead, Terry de Lacy, and Laurajane Smith, eds., *Aboriginal Involvement in Parks and Protected Areas* (1992).

David Frankel

ARCHAEOLOGY AND AFRICAN SOCIETIES

The colonial period in Africa began about 1850 and marked the beginning of archaeology on the continent. African societies could now be studied through the use of archaeological methods and interpretative approaches developed in Europe. This kind of archaeology helped enforce colonial domination and made Africans view archaeology as a Western concept that was irrelevant to them.

One hundred years later, the only role indigenous peoples played was that of informant in the interpretation of archaeological finds. Africans never controlled data analysis and interpretation of the archaeological record. For example, J. Desmond Clark interpreted stone flaking techniques at the *Kalambo Falls prehistoric site in northern Zambia relying on observations of the manufacture of gunflints in Angola. European terms such as "neolithic" continued to dominate African archaeology. Such terminologies created evolutionary stages in ancient African societies that bore no resemblance to historical reality.

The reconstruction of African prehistory has often been based on Western comparative paradigms, which employ such terms as "complex and simple," "literate and illiterate," "civilized and savage." Such evolutionary terms resulted in part from a scholarly preoccupation with the Stone Age, a field of archaeology with strong roots not only in European prehistory and evolutionary theory, but in cultural anthropology, geology, and paleontology.

During the process of decolonization in the 1960s and 1970s, increasing attention was paid to the later African prehistory, as part of the development of a truly multidisciplinary African history. At the same time, Africans began to demand access to their own past and insisted on the preservation of their cultural heritage and the strengthening of their cultural identity. As a result, historical linguistics and oral traditions gained significant recognition in the reconstruction of their past. Western concepts that had guided the study of ancient African societies now became less important in the development of African archaeology. *Great Zimbabwe offers the classic example, for early European investigators insisted the site was built not by indigenous Shona-speaking peoples but by Mediterranean colonists. The controversy continued even after Gertrude *Caton-Thompson proved beyond all doubt in 1929 that the structures were of African origin. As late as the 1970s, the settler government of what was then Rhodesia insisted that the discredited theories of foreign origin be included in official guidebooks.

The interpretation of the African past is now based on an assumption of cultural continuity between past and present, for both archaeologists and historians now realize that forces of indigenous culture shaped African history from the earliest times. In coming decades, Africans themselves will develop archaeological concepts that are relevant to their own research, whose formal training of future archaeologists will focus on interpretations of the African past based not on biased interpretations but on real historical issues. Much research into more recent societies of the past will establish close links between ancient and modern societies and culture. Such research will reflect contemporary interest in such activities as metalworking, agricultural food production, and interaction between African societies and their environments.

The development of archaeology in Africa faces formidable problems. Few African countries offer official support for archaeological research. Most argue that archaeology promotes ethnicity at the expense of fostering national identity. Archaeological studies in countries where tribalism is rife fail to emphasize regional traditions and customs for fear of reinforcing tribal feelings and regionalism, which are threats to national unity. African countries have become wary of archaeological researches that could potentially be a threat to national unity. For example, archaeological researches conducted by Brian Fagan and others in southern Zambia in the 1960s focused on building a regional cultural history. These digs revealed a long sequence of occupation beginning in the fifth century A.D., which ended in nineteenth-century plateau Tonga settlements. Politicians used this research to argue that Tonga-speaking peoples of southern Zambia were the earliest to inhabit the country. Their claims caused considerable political tension, although those archaeologists had no intention of fostering ethnicity in their excavations. Research in the region has stopped on the grounds it might be detrimental to nation building.

One outcome of these concerns has been a new emphasis on regional studies. The Swedish Agency for Research Cooperation with Developing Countries (SAREC) has supported an archaeological research program on urban origins in eastern and southern Africa, addressing the problem of how and when urbanism originated and the role played by indigenous societies in urban development. This kind of archaeology operates on a regional level rather than focusing on specific sites, thereby neutralizing tensions between ethnicity and archaeological researches.

Through the SAREC archaeological program, African archaeologists have developed a strong sense for indigenous archaeology. There is an increasing use of historical data to refine archaeological interpretations, a significant methodological approach in the study of African societies. In the absence of chronometric dating facilities and a demand for better control of the dating of materials from archaeological sites, African archaeologists have to rely on historical and ethnographic evidence for data to decode the meaning of the archaeological record. Tanzanian archaeologist N. J. Karoma and American Peter Schmidt have employed this approach to study iron smelting and technological practices in western Tanzania. The purpose has been to reveal past developments that have roots in indigenous effort instead of attributing them to outside influences. Others such as Kenyan archaeologist Osoga Odak are arguing for more emphasis on the study of later archaeological periods such as the Iron Age whose research findings are more in tune with the sociocultural development efforts of their countries. Bassey Andah urges his fellow African archaeologists to refine research goals and data-collecting strategies and to use traditions relevant to the self- and national identity of the people. Andah's emphasis on cultural identity represents the major interest Africans have in archaeology today, for to be meaningful and useful, it has to be relevant to the concerns of its audience.

It is difficult to predict the future direction of African archaeology in the twenty-first century. Judging from current trends, however, increasing emphasis will be placed on the use of ethnographic and historical evidence in the interpretation of archaeological data.

[See also NATIONALISM.]

■ R. N. Hall, Great Zimbabwe (1905). G. Caton-Thompson, The Zimbabwe Culture (1931). B. M. Fagan and D. W. Phillipson, "Sebanzi, the Iron Age Sequence at Lochinvar, and the Tonga," Journal of the Royal Anthropological Institute 95 (1965): 253–294. J. D. Clark, Kalambo Falls Prehistoric Site (1974). O. Odak, "Comments on 'Archaeology and Development' by D. Miller," Current Anthropology 21 (1980): 721. P. Garlake, "Prehistory and Ideology in Zimbabwe," Africa 52 (1982): 1–19. R. N. Hall, "Pots and Politics: Ceramic Interpretations in Southern Africa," World Archaeology 15 (1984): 262–273. P.J.J. Sinclair, "Urban Origins in Eastern Africa: A Regional Cooperation Project," World Archaeological Bulletin 3 (1989): 33–51. B. Andah, "Prologue to Cultural Resource Management: An African Dimension," West African Journal of Archaeology 20 (1990): 2–8. P. Robertshaw, ed., A History of African Archaeology (1990).

Francis B. Musonda

NORSE IN NORTH AMERICA. The ninth and tenth centuries A.D. saw a major expansion of Scandinavian peoples. Viking warriors and merchants traversed the coasts of Europe and the Russian rivers, and explored the islands of the North Atlantic. Most of these islands were already known to the Celtic peoples of the British Isles, and lands as far west as Iceland had been visited or were occupied by Irish monks. Irish tales of arable islands must have stimulated Norse interest in the North Atlantic.

Norse explorers reached Iceland about the mid-ninth century A.D., and their reports of good agricultural land produced a massive immigration from Norway. Icelandic history knows the decades between A.D. 870 and 930 as the Settlement period; by its end, the Norse population of Iceland had grown to approximately 30,000 people and all of the productive land had been occupied. The settling of Iceland resulted in the accidental discovery of land farther to the west, and by approximately A.D. 980 Norse explorers had reached Greenland and established colonies on its southwestern coast. These colonies grew to 3,000 or more people, and survived for approximately 500 years as a small European country on the edge of the North American continent.

The Norse settlements on Greenland were located within three or four days' sail of the Labrador coast and were even closer to the islands of the North American Arctic. Accidental discovery of these lands was inevitable, and their exploration was encouraged by the Greenlanders' needs for construction timber, commodities for trade with Europe, and

agricultural land. The discovery probably occurred shortly after the settling of Greenland, and attempts to explore and colonize the northeastern coasts of North America began around A.D. 1000.

The American adventures of the Norse were recorded in two Icelandic sagas, telling different versions of a story of exploration, attempted settlement, and eventual abandonment of a territory called Vinland. Vinland is also mentioned in a few European historical records of the time, but the references are too vague to add significant detail to the literary accounts. Early attempts to provide archaeological substantiation for these accounts led to a series of frauds and misidentifications, which attempted to demonstrate Norse occupation of much of the Western Hemisphere. All were rejected by archaeologists and historians, and by the mid-twentieth century no archaeological evidence had been accepted as relating to Norse exploration or settlement of the Americas.

The first find to achieve general acceptance was made in 1960, when the Norwegian writer Helge Ingstad discovered the remains of a small settlement near the fishing village of L'Anse aux Meadows, at the northern tip of the island of Newfoundland. Excavation revealed evidence of three multiroomed houses up to 82 feet (25 m) in length, built with timber frames and piled-turf walls. The construction techniques were identical to those used by the Norse in Iceland and Greenland. Rooms used for living and sleeping had elongated central hearths, while smaller rooms appear to have been used as workshops or for storage. One or two small outbuildings were associated with each house and seem to have served a number of functions. The remains of a small forge structure, littered with fragments of iron slag, was located at a distance from the other buildings.

Almost all of the artifacts recovered by excavation are remnants of forging, woodworking, and boat repair. Most characteristic are iron rivets of the type used in joining the planks of Norse boats. The slag recovered represents the smelting of a small quantity of iron, probably from limonite deposits in nearby bogs. Carpentry is represented by wood chips, treenails, a coil of spruce root, a boat rib and a possible floorboard, and a few fragmentary objects of unknown use. The presence of women at the site is suggested by a soapstone spindle whorl, a bone needle, and a stone needle hone. A small stone lamp would have been used in lighting one of the houses, while a bronze ring-headed pin and a single glass bead would have adorned the occupants of the settlement. All of these artifacts indicate a European rather than aboriginal American technology, and the most reliable radiocarbon dates, from a large and confusing series, are consistent with an occupation during the Viking period.

Excavations outside the houses and in an adjacent bog revealed no deep middens of refuse, such as would have indicated lengthy use of the site. The absence of deep middens, as well as the lack of evidence indicating repair or rebuilding of the houses, and the fact that no cemetery has been located despite intensive searching, suggests that the site was occupied for a few years at most. The maximum size of the settlement must have been less than 100 people, even if all buildings were occupied simultaneously. There is no evidence of farming activities, and it seems most probable that the L'Anse aux Meadows site was used as a winter base for exploration and commercial activities that were carried out in the Gulf of St. Lawrence area to the south. Its location at the northern entrance to the narrow Strait of Belle Isle, separating Newfoundland from the North American mainland, would have been well suited to such a function.

This location may also have been chosen because of a relatively low density of aboriginal occupation, in comparison with coastal regions to the north and south. The Icelandic sagas suggest that the Norse abandoned their Vinland activities because of conflict with the natives of the region. Archaeology indicates that, at the time of the Vinland voyages, most of the forested coasts of northeastern North America were occupied by native populations who could easily have repelled Norse attempts at settlement. The small oceangoing Norse ships could not carry large numbers of fighting men, and Norse weapons were little better than those of natives for small-scale skirmishing. Most important, the Greenland Norse did not carry the Old World diseases that cleared the way for later European conquest of the Americas. Extensive settlement, or even exploration of the New World, was not a project that could have been carried out by the small farming population of Norse Greenland.

The evidence of short-term settlement at L'Anse aux Meadows is consistent with the saga accounts, which state that Vinland was abandoned shortly after A.D. 1000. There is, however, limited evidence of later Norse contact with North America. A Norse penny, recovered from a Native American occupation site on the coast of Maine, was minted between A.D. 1065 and 1080, at least half a century after the Vinland voyages. The same site produced a number of stone tools made from rock derived from a quarry on the tundra coast of northern Labrador, as well as a distinctive stone artifact of a type made by the Paleo-Inuit peoples who occupied that region. The penny is probably evidence of a Norse visit to Labrador, from where it later reached the northeastern United States through aboriginal trade routes. Continued Norse visits to Labrador, probably in order to obtain timber from the northern forests, are suggested by a 1347 Icelandic account of a Greenland ship arriving from Markland, the Norse name for the Labrador coast.

Fragments of smelted iron, copper, and bronze, as well as other objects of Norse manufacture, are occasionally found in Inuit occupation sites dated between the twelfth and sixteenth centuries A.D. The heaviest concentration of such material has come from excavated sites on the east coast of Ellesmere Island and in the adjacent Thule district of northwestern Greenland, but objects were distributed through native trade as far as the western coast of Hudson Bay. Although all of these items might have been salvaged from a single wrecked ship, their distribution is suggestive of sporadic contact between Norse and Inuits in the eastern Arctic. One such contact episode is suggested by a small wooden figurine representing a person in European clothing, carved in Inuit style and recovered from a thirteenth-century Inuit house on Baffin Island. Norse ships bound for the forests of Labrador may have occasionally coasted the eastern Arctic, and their crews may have skirmished or traded with the occupants of the region.

The archaeological evidence accumulated over the past few decades indicates that the Norse did reach North America, and tried to establish at least one settlement there. In contrast to earlier speculation, however, it now appears that they made only brief forays into the part of the continent closest to, and most closely resembling, their North Atlantic homelands.

[See also BRITISH ISLES: VIKING RAIDS AND SETTLEMENT IN BRITAIN AND IRELAND; SCANDINAVIA: SCANDINAVIA AND THE VIKING AGE.]

■ Robert McGhee, "Contact Between Native North Americans and the Mediaeval Norse: A Review of the Evidence," *American Antiquity* 49 (1984): 4–26. Anne Stine Ingstad, *The Norse Discovery of America, Excavations of a Norse Settlement at L'Anse aux Meadows, Newfoundland, 1961–1968*, vol. 1 (1985). Helge Ingstad, *The Norse Discovery of America: The Historical Background and the Evidence of the Norse Settlement Discovered in Newfoundland*, vol. 2 (1985). Gwyn Jones, *The Norse Atlantic Saga*, 2nd ed. (1986). Birgitta Linderoth Wallace, "The L'Anse aux Meadows Site," in *The Norse Atlantic Saga*, ed. Gwyn Jones, 2nd ed. (1986), pp. 285–304. Robert McGhee, *Canada Rediscovered* (1991).

Robert McGhee

NORTH AMERICA

OVERVIEW

The prehistory of North America dates back at least 12,000 years. The articles that follow describe the events that contributed to many of the cultural developments on this continent before European contact. Evidence of pre-12,000 B.P. occupation is scanty and much debated, but after this time evidence abounds. People are believed to have entered North America across the Bering Strait, most of which was exposed in the form of a "land bridge" during the latter part of the Pleistocene. They then moved southward and eastward, expanding into most areas of the continent by 10,000 B.P.

As environments changed during the early Holocene, so did human adaptation. As people in different areas became more familiar with their surroundings, they began to focus their lifeways on local resources. After about 4000 B.P. population had increased considerably and in some areas sedentary villages began to develop. The arrival of the three major New World domesticates, corn, beans, and squash, from Mesoamerica had a major impact on many peoples of North America. In the southwest, corn may have appeared as early as 3500 B.P., but played no significant role until 2200 B.P. By this time there were sedentary villages throughout the southwest, the precursors of the agricultural populations encountered by the Spanish in the sixteenth century.

In eastern North America large sedentary settlements appeared long before significant reliance on domesticated plants. Between 2500 and 1100 B.P., peoples of the area built large burial mounds and other earthworks and participated in a wide-ranging trade network. Events culminated with the Mississippians, agricultural peoples who built large towns and mound centers throughout much of the east.

Elsewhere in North America, such as areas of the Great Plains, the Great Basin, Canada, and Alaska, peoples continued their hunter-gatherer way of life until European contact. Contact with Europeans had a devastating effect on all of the peoples of North America. Diseases introduced by the new arrivals are believed to have reduced the population by as much as 80 percent, dramatically altering the delicate balance that had developed between humans and their environment over the preceding 12,000 years.

Charlotte Beck

INTRODUCTION

Although North America may have been inhabited by humans for as little as 11,500 years, when the Spanish arrived they encountered great diversity in language and culture among the peoples of North America. It is estimated that when the Spanish first arrived in Florida during the early sixteenth century there were as many as 18 million people in North America, speaking over 300 different languages. This linguistic and cultural diversity, which was severely reduced over the next 150 years, is not disputed; however, the length of time over which this diversity developed, that is, since the time of arrival of people in North America, remains unresolved.

Paleo-Indian Occupation. The first American settlers entered North America from Asia, by way of Beringia, a large landmass that connected Siberia with Alaska during the glacial periods of the Late Pleistocene. It is believed that these early settlers came from Siberia, following game across Beringia into Alaska sometime during the Late Pleistocene, and then found their way down into the interior of the continent following a corridor that was free of glacial ice. Evidence indicates that people were in North America by 11,500 B.P., but a number of archaeologists believe that people arrived possibly as early as 25,000 to 30,000 B.P. The evidence for such an early arrival, however, is scanty and highly debated. The best candidates for a pre-11,500 B.P. occupation in the Americas are *Meadowcroft Rockshelter in Pennsylvania, from which dates as early as 17,000 B.P. have been obtained, and the site of *Monte Verde in Chile, which has yielded a date of 33,000 B.P. These and other pre-12,000 B.P. dates, however, are challenged by skeptics, and thus the issue continues to be debated.

There is little question, however, that people were in North America by 11,500 B.P., for the evidence is abundant. The first recognized culture at that time is called Clovis, after the diagnostic projectile point of the same name. Clovis points are fluted, which means they are basally thinned, creating a channel (flute) for attaching the point to the spear shaft. These points and their associated tools are found across much of North America in many different environments, desert to forest, suggesting a similar lifeway across the entire continent. These early inhabitants are believed to have been hunter-gatherers, hunting large animals, such as bison, deer, elk, and occasionally mammoth and mastodon, while gathering a variety of plants.

By ca. 11,000 to 10,500 B.P., Clovis gave way to more regional variants, the Great Basin Stemmed Tradition in the western desert, Folsom and later Paleo-Indian on the Great Plains, and *Dalton culture in the East. Except on the Plains, the subsistence base appears to have become more diversified, with small mammals, waterfowl, and additional plant foods being added to the diet. On the Plains during this early period, people continued to focus on hunting, the primary prey being the modern bison. The Paleo-Indian hunting tradition continued until about 8000 B.P. on the Plains, but in the East and Far West, the beginnings of a different lifeway were emerging by 10,000 B.P.

Archaic Occupations. The lifeway that began around 10,000 B.P. in most areas of North America is known as the Archaic, one that involved increasing generalization of eco-

nomic activities. Although most populations at this time were highly mobile hunter-gatherers, each focused on the suite of resources available to them locally; thus with the passage of time there is also a pattern of increasing regional generalization. Both of these trends are likely, in large part, responses to the changing environments of the Holocene, during which most areas experienced a warming and drying trend.

Although archaeological evidence of this period is scarce, we do know that several new technologies made their appearance during the early part of the Archaic: the *atlatl* and dart projectile technology for hunting, the grinding stone for processing seeds and grasses, and in the forested East, the ground-stone celt and adze for working wood.

The Archaic lifeway gave way in many areas, such as most parts of eastern North America, the Southwest, and the Northwest Coast, to more sedentary, less generalized strategies in which people depended upon agriculture or intensive fishing and hunting for their livelihood. In other areas, however, such as the Arctic and Subarctic, the Great Basin, much of California, parts of the Columbia and Colorado plateaus, and the western Great Plains, the Archaic lifeway continued until contact with Europeans.

In the Arctic, although there are a few sites that date as early as 12,000 B.P., evidence is more plentiful after 11,000 B.P. From this time until ca. 7000 B.P. the people of the Paleo-Arctic Tradition roamed Alaska, hunting caribou and now-extinct bison. They are known primarily from their distinctive stone tools, specifically microblades, burins, and graving tools, and are believed by many to have been related to the Dyukhtai (Divktai) culture of Siberia.

By 6000 B.P. technology had expanded, as had the resource base. Tools were being made from antler, bone, and wood, as well as stone, and sea mammals and fish had been added to the diet. About this time people began to move eastward, and by 4000 B.P., the entire Arctic, from Alaska to Greenland, was inhabited. People practiced a variety of strategies, from terrestrial hunting in the interior to whaling, winter seal hunting, and fishing along the coasts. Diet was expanded in many areas to include seabirds, urchins, and shellfish, as well as a number of plant foods when available. Harpoons and other hunting and fishing tools were often elaborately carved by their makers. The bow and arrow were introduced about 4000 B.P., and as early as 2000 B.P. people along the coasts hunted in kayaks, a practice that continued well into the historic period.

The earliest sites along the Northwest Coast date to ca. 10,000 B.P. To the north, tool assemblages of this early period are similar to those of the Paleo-Arctic Tradition, focusing on microblades, but to the south tools are in the form of large leaf-shaped bifaces and flaked cobbles. By about 8000 B.P., Archaic peoples utilized a broad array of resources from different environments: land, river, lake, and sea. After ca. 5500 B.P. there was increased exploitation of mollusks, as evidenced by the appearance of large *shell middens and, after 3500 B.P., widespread dependence on fresh and stored salmon; in some areas there was also an increased reliance on sea mammals. Burials dating to between 4000 and 3500 B.P. suggest the beginnings of differential treatment of the dead, and it is believed that by 2500 B.P. an elite class had emerged along the coast. It is also believed that by this time populations had become more sedentary. At the time of European contact, the people of the Northwest Coast had developed complex social systems but continued to rely on a wide variety of resources, both animal and plant.

The lifestyle was similar along the California coast, where a wide variety of resources were utilized, including sea mammals, fish, mollusks, and many plant foods. Along the southern California coast acorns became a staple food as early as 7000 to 5000 B.P. People used stone, bone, and antler tools, as well as basketry and woven garments. Beads were made from both bone and shell and were found throughout much of California. By ca. 1500 B.P. huge shell mounds had accumulated all along the coast, which often served as cemeteries.

In the western desert, people followed a flexible lifeway that varied greatly depending upon the abundance and availability of resources. Clovis in this area was followed by the Western Stemmed Tradition, so named for the large, often crudely made stemmed points in their tool kit. The people of the Western Stemmed Tradition practiced a subsistence strategy focused on lake, marsh, and riverine resources. It is not known how long this tradition lasted, but the large stemmed points seem to have disappeared between 8000 and 7500 B.P., when they were replaced by *atlatl* dart points. Accompanying this new technology was a warming and drying environmental trend, which substantially affected the abundance and distribution of resources. Evidence of human activity becomes scanty until about 5000 B.P., but after this time a variety of subsistence and settlement strategies appeared, from highly mobile foragers in the dryer areas to less mobile collectors in more resource-rich areas, although most utilized the highly valued piñon nut. The bow and arrow were introduced between 3000 and 2500 B.P., representing another major technological change. These strategies continued until European contact in much of the West, but changed with the adoption of domesticates, including corn, beans, and squash, in the Southwest (ca. 3500–2500 B.P.) and in parts of the eastern Great Basin and northern Colorado plateau (ca. 2200 B.P.).

On the Great Plains the Archaic lifestyle was quite similar to that of the western desert, except that there was heavy dependence on large herbivores such as bison, elk, and deer. During the Middle Holocene, different patterns developed between the eastern tall-grass prairies and the western short-grass steppe. In the West, bison hunting persisted as an important economic focus, while in the East, although bison were hunted, woodland resources such as deer, nuts, and fish were also important. In the West this way of life continued until European contact, but in the East the Archaic ended with influences from the East around 1500 to 2000 B.P., including the introduction of pottery, the burial mound complex, and, eventually, domesticated plants. In the East, Clovis was followed by the Dalton culture, which appeared between 10,500 and 10,000 B.P. Little is known about this culture except in it the beginnings of the eastern Archaic can be seen. As in other areas, the eastern Archaic brought with it increasing dietary diversity and regionalization. In the Early Archaic, all areas south of the coniferous forest appear fairly similar in their economic activities as well as in technology and style. But during the Late Archaic (ca. 5000–3000 B.P.), regional differences appeared. Along the coasts and in the interior riverine environments shellfish became an important resource. In the Great Lakes area as well as the Northeast, fishing technology was developed and fish became a staple. In deciduous wooded areas, nuts, especially acorns, and white-tailed deer were heavily utilized.

It is during the Late Archaic in the East that we see the first use of domesticated plants. Several local plants, such as sumpweed, sunflower, and several types of gourds and squash, were collected intensively beginning about 6000 to 5000 B.P. and began to show morphological changes by 4000 B.P. These and several other plants form what is known as the Eastern Agricultural Complex and were utilized as domesticates during later periods.

The Late Archaic witnessed considerable population growth in eastern North America. Along with this growth came more sedentary lifeways in many areas, as well as increased diversification in technology and style. Pottery was first introduced about 4500 B.P., and its use spread throughout the East over the next 1,000 years. Trade networks developed, focusing on materials such as shells from the Gulf and Atlantic coasts and native copper from the Great Lakes region. Artifacts of these exotic materials are found in Late Archaic burials, suggesting an increasing preoccupation with the treatment of the dead. Over the next several thousand years, the inhabitants of the East developed very elaborate burial customs and ceremonialism, while at the same time, differences in social class began to develop. In the extreme Northeast and Canada, however, the hunter-gatherer Archaic tradition continued until contact with Europeans.

Sedentism and Farming. Following the mobile Archaic hunter-gatherer lifestyle in many areas came sedentary villages in which people lived, at least partially, on cultivated crops. Farming developed in two general areas of North America, the Southwest, extending for a short period up into the eastern Great Basin and the northern Colorado plateau, and eastern North America, extending westward into the tall-grass prairies of the Great Plains. In the Southwest, gathering and growing of small-seeded annuals such as Indian rice grass, devil's claw, and maygrass, among others, was practiced for several thousand years before corn was introduced about 3500 B.P., followed in the next thousand years by squash and beans. After about 2200 B.P. the cultivation of these three crops was fairly widespread throughout the Southwest and people had become more sedentary. Because of the very dry conditions southwestern farmers planted on floodplains and at the mouths of canyons, where the soil was naturally irrigated. They also diverted water from seasonal streams and rainfall for further irrigation.

By ca. 2000 B.P. three different cultural traditions were beginning to emerge, all dependent upon farming: Hohokam, Mogollon, and Anasazi. The *Hohokam culture developed in the Sonoran desert of south-central Arizona. Their large settlements were organized around plazas, platform mounds, and ball courts similar to those found in Mexico. They participated in a widespread trade network in which exotic materials such as shell and obsidian were exchanged, and manufactured a distinctive red-on-gray or red-on-buff style of ceramics in the form of bowls, wide-mouthed ollas, and jars. The Hohokam are also known for the construction of an extensive canal system, the largest north of Mexico, for irrigation of their fields. The descendants of the Hohokam are believed to be the Pima and Papago, who live in the area today.

In the highlands of southwestern New Mexico and east-central Arizona, the Mogollon culture developed between 2000 and 1800 B.P. While farming was important, the Mogollon also remained dependent upon hunting and gathering, utilizing foods such as yucca, cactus, and sunflower.

The earlier Mogollon people lived in multifamily pit-house villages, but about 1000 B.P. pit houses gave way to above-ground pueblo architecture. One of the best-known Mogollon peoples are the Classic Mimbres, located in southwestern New Mexico, who manufactured black-on-white pottery exhibiting geomorphic, zoomorphic, and anthropomorphic designs. Although the historical developments are not completely understood, the Mogollon are believed to be in part ancestral to modern Puebloans, such as the Zuñi, Hopi, and the Rio Grande Pueblos.

In the four-corners region of Utah, Colorado, New Mexico, and Arizona, the best known of the Southwest farming traditions, the *Anasazi culture emerged sometime after 2000 B.P. The early Anasazi lived in villages consisting of a combination of pit houses and above-ground structures made of sandstone and adobe. By the period known as Pueblo II (ca. 1100–900 B.P.), however, pueblo-style architecture was dominant. During this period developments are believed to have been centered on Chaco Canyon, in which there are ten pueblos, or "great houses," that, at the time, had the capacity for housing over 5000 people. The room complexes of each pueblo opened onto a plaza, within which lay kivas, or subterranean ceremonial rooms. Chaco appears to have been a regional center, possibly an economic center for the redistribution of agricultural foods, and had far-reaching relationships at its height, but sometime between about 850 and 800 B.P., the system seems to have collapsed, which is attributed by many to five decades of severe drought.

Coeval with the early development of the Anasazi in the four-corners area was the beginning of farming to the north in the eastern Great Basin and northern Colorado plateau. Corn was adopted in central Utah by 2200 B.P., leading to the development of the Fremont culture from about 1600 to 650 B.P. The *Fremont farmers lived in sedentary communities and cultivated corn, beans, and squash, but supplemented their diet by hunting and gathering.

After about 800 B.P., when Chaco faded as a regional center, there was a period of reorganization, again attributed to the severe drought. Over the next hundred years many areas were abandoned, while other areas such as *Mesa Verde saw an aggregation of population into large, multistoried pueblos. By 700 B.P. settlement by the Anasazi was restricted primarily to the Rio Grande Valley and to the areas in the vicinity of Hopi, Zuñi, and Acoma.

In eastern North America the beginnings of sedentary life are seen in the Late Archaic, as the use of local cultigens gained hold. At this time, especially in the Great Lakes area and Upper Ohio River Valley, there was increasing care taken with burial of the dead and the inclusion in graves of artifacts made from exotic materials obtained through trade. About 2500 B.P. in the Ohio River Valley, out of late Archaic beginnings, a burial ceremonial complex emerged known as Adena. During the next 700 years there was a proliferation of specialized items that found their way into burials, such as tubular pipes supporting elaborately carved figures, thin cult figures from mica or native copper, incised tablets, and copper bracelets. Burial customs became more elaborate, culminating with mounds in which several people were interred. Burial within the mounds was in log-lined tombs or simply in clay-lined basins, but often the body was cremated. The populations are believed to have been semisedentary, utilizing the locally domesticated plants of the Eastern Agricultural Complex and continuing to hunt and gather.

About 2200 B.P. in the Illinois River Valley another culture, known as Hopewell, emerged. In many ways, Hopewell was a continuation and elaboration of *Adena culture, although Adena continued for some time in southern Ohio and northern Kentucky. The *Hopewell culture had wide-ranging influence, with an exchange network bringing copper and gypsum from the Great Lakes region, hematite and mica from the Appalachian Mountains, and obsidian from Yellowstone. The Hopewell are believed to have influenced and interacted with cultures in New York (Point Peninsula), the Lower Mississippi Valley (Marksville), and other areas in the Southeast (South Appalachian, Sant Rosa-Swift Creek, Miller-Porter).

It was during this period that the burial ceremonial complex became the most elaborate. Burial mounds became larger, some containing well over one hundred interments. Mounds often contained elaborately carved stone artifacts, such as platform effigy pipes and *atlatl* weights, rich caches of items made from copper, such as ear spools, headdresses, masks, and jewelry, and a host of other artifacts made from shell, mica, and stone. River pearls were used for armlets and anklets or were sewn onto garments. Some differences in status and wealth are indicated by the contents of these burials, some containing many elaborate artifacts made of exotic materials and others containing little or nothing. Although corn was utilized and settlement became more sedentary, subsistence was still heavily dependent upon hunting and gathering.

The burial mound complex spread westward at this time to the tall-grass prairies of the Great Plains. The elaborate artifacts and mounds found near Kansas City have led some to refer to this culture as "Kansas City Hopewell." At this time as well, populations of the eastern Plains appear to have become more sedentary and evidence of cultigens has been found.

The elaboration in material goods and burial fell off about 1600 B.P., which has led some to call the next several hundred years the "Hopewell decline." Others believe, however, that this period saw major changes in the economic system. As corn and other crops became more important, settlement strategies changed, with people moving to fertile floodplains. Also, increased reliance on cultivated crops allowed populations to grow while tying them to one place, and thus settlement became more sedentary. With the changes in economic strategy, population density, and degree of mobility, more complex social and political organization emerged.

By 1100 B.P. a completely new system, called the *Mississippian culture, was in place, one that was sedentary and that relied heavily on agriculture, although crops were still supplemented by hunting (deer, racoon, turkey, waterfowl), fishing, and gathering (nuts, fruits, berries). Styles changed considerably and new technologies were introduced. For instance, the introduction of shell-tempering allowed for the production of pottery vessels with much thinner walls that could be fired at lower temperatures. By 1000 B.P. towns emerged that were often surrounded by pallisades. Within the towns were large platform mounds on which ceremonial or other structures were built. Burial mounds were also constructed, but most burial took place in cemeteries adjacent to the towns. These burials suggest, in some cases, great differences in status and wealth.

The largest of the Mississippian towns was *Cahokia, located where St. Louis is situated today. Cahokia covered over 5 square miles (13 sq km) and contained over one hundred earthen mounds. Large mound centers such as Cahokia were placed strategically along rivers and controlled traffic and trade along those water routes. Mississippian towns and villages occurred throughout the mid-South and Southeast, but influenced and interacted with areas to the east, north, and west. At this time semisedentary horticultural villages existed throughout most of the Great Plains as well as in the Northeast.

At this same time, in the Arkansas River Valley and to the southwest, a development similar to the Mississippian took place, known as Caddoan. Caddoan peoples interacted with Mississippian peoples in trade and possibly in religious beliefs. Between 1000 and 400 B.P., a variety of styles appeared across the Southeast and into Arkansas and Texas, known collectively as the Southeastern Ceremonial Complex. Most of the content of these styles centers on warfare and/or supernatural beings, suggesting a belief in supernatural control over military conflict. It is now believed that the artifacts bearing these styles derived from several different social institutions within Mississippian and Caddoan societies, including the priesthood, the military, and the elite. The Southeastern Ceremonial Complex is viewed as a representation of a common world view attributed to Mississippian and Caddoan religion.

By the time of European contact, many of the large Mississippian and Caddoan towns were abandoned. Hernando de Soto, however, on his march through the Southeast between 1540 and 1542 came into contact with many different polities, a number of whom were warring with one another. Unfortunately, by the time the French arrived in the Southeast 150 years later, the native population had been so decimated by diseases introduced by Europeans, cultures had changed substantially from those de Soto had encountered. It has been suggested that within the first 150 years after European contact, native population declined as much as eighty percent, and thus it is difficult to make connections between prehistoric societies and those living in the area during the eighteenth century.

[See also AMERICAS, FIRST SETTLEMENT OF THE; AMERICAS, INTRODUCTION OF DISEASES INTO THE; ANTIQUITY OF HUMANKIND: ANTIQUITY OF HUMANKIND IN THE AMERICAS; ATHABASKAN CULTURES OF THE AMERICAN SOUTHWEST; BAT CAVE; BATTLEFIELD ARCHAEOLOGY OF NORTH AMERICA; CASAS GRANDES; CHACOAN PHENOMENON; COCHISE CULTURE; FRONTIER SITES OF THE AMERICAN WEST; GATECLIFF SHELTER; HUNTER-GATHERERS, NORTH AMERICAN ARCHAIC; HUNTERS OF THE NORTH AMERICAN PLAINS; MARTIN'S HUNDRED; MISSION ARCHAEOLOGY; MOGOLLON AND MIMBRES CULTURES; MOUNDS OF EASTERN NORTH AMERICA; MOUNDVILLE; NON-WESTERN SOCIETIES, ARCHAEOLOGY AND: ARCHAEOLOGY AND NATIVE AMERICANS; NORSE IN NORTH AMERICA; NORTH AMERICA, ORIGINS OF FOOD PRODUCTION IN; PLANTATION LIFE IN THE SOUTHERN UNITED STATES; POVERTY POINT; ROCK ART: NORTH AMERICAN ROCK ART; SERPENT MOUND; SOUTHERN CULT.]

■ William C. Sturtevant, ed., Handbook of North American Indians, 9 vols. (1978–1990). Robert McGhee, Canadian Arctic Prehistory (1978). Dean Snow, The Archaeology of New England (1980). Dan F. Morse and Phyllis A. Morse, Archaeology of the Central Mississippi Valley (1983). James L. Phillips and James A. Brown, eds., Archaic Hunters and Gatherers in the American Midwest (1983). Linda S. Cordell, The Southwest (1984). Michael J. Moratto, California Archaeology (1984). Richard I. Ford, ed., Food Production in North America (1985). Bruce D. Smith, "The Archaeology of the Southeastern United States, from Dalton to DeSoto (10,500 B.P. to 500 B.P.)," in eds. Fred Wendorf and Angela E. Close, Advances in World Archaeology, vol. 5 (1986): pp. 1–

92. Waldo Wedel, Central Plains Archaeology (1986). Don E. Dumond, The Eskimos and Aleuts (1987). George Frison, Prehistoric Hunters of the High Plains, 2nd ed. (1992). Donald K. Grayson, The Desert's Past: A Natural Prehistory of the Great Basin (1993). David J. Meltzer, Search for the First Americans (1993).

Charlotte Beck

THE NORTH AMERICAN ARCTIC

The North American Arctic is inhabited by people who aboriginally spoke one of the related Eskimo or Aleut languages. On the west, the area includes the Alaskan coast south to the Aleutian Islands, the Alaska Peninsula, Kodiak Island, and Prince William Sound, and touches the tip of the Chukchi Peninsula of Siberia. On the east it reaches Greenland.

Here, native lifeways lasted to modern times. Here also, in the west, is thought to have been the gateway by which the first humans entered the Western Hemisphere. But although various claims have been made for evidence of humans in Alaska long before 12,000 B.P., none has been confirmed. Indeed, it is still impossible to identify northern ancestors of the well-known North American Clovis culture.

In the Nenana Valley of central Alaska, a region unglaciated in the Late Pleistocene, a few sites dated between 12,000 and 11,000 B.P. have yielded assemblages that include large blades, scrapers, and thin, tear-drop-shaped "Chindadn points." A few analysts suggest this Nenana Complex was ancestral to the Clovis culture of North America, its bearers adding the specialized Clovis fluted projectile points after moving south of Alaska. A second set of finds, from the game-lookout Mesa site of the Arctic slope of the Brooks Range of north-central Alaska, in 1993 was dated to the same period, but includes only lanceolate projectile points and gravers. The relationship to the Nenana Complex as well as to early Americans south of Alaska is not yet clear.

After 11,000 B.P. the picture becomes sharper. From then until about 7000 B.P. Alaska was home to people of the Paleo-Arctic or Beringian cultural tradition, makers of microblades pressed from small wedge-shaped cores, of burins and scrapers, as well as of blades struck from larger cores, but these people did not penetrate eastward into what is today Canada. Faunal remains indicate chiefly terrestrial hunting, of caribou and now-extinct bison. Similar people reached the north Pacific coast by 10,000 B.P., exploiting shellfish and coastal mammals. Culturally, these were related to folk of eastern Siberia, of a culture referred to by some Russian scholars as Diuktai.

After about 6000 B.P. indications are that the relationship with Siberia ended. On the Pacific coast of south Alaska microblades were given up by makers of bone harpoon heads and chipped basalt knives and projectile points, who for subsistence concentrated on seals, sea lions, and near-shore fishes. Within a millennium these coastal dwellers were split into two separate spheres. People of the eastern Aleutian Islands still chipped artifacts in the old way, continuing a tradition that would endure in relative isolation until the arrival of Russian fur hunters in the eighteenth century. Those of the Kodiak Island region and eastward, however, began to grind major stone artifacts from slate in a systematic technological change. The open stone oil-burning lamp became common. Labrets, or lip plugs, began to be used.

In the north interior of Alaska at this time, the heavy

notched projectile points and scrapers of the Northern Archaic tradition suggest a northwestward expansion of interior-dwelling hunting peoples such as those of the Subarctic forests of Canada. These in turn appear to have descended from southerners who moved northward after the recession of Pleistocene glaciers, the movement finally stopping on the tundra short of the north Canadian coast.

The true Arctic coast was not colonized until after about 4500 B.P. with the sudden appearance of the Arctic Small Tool tradition. Discovered in Alaska in 1948 as the Denbigh Flint Complex, makers of diminutive bipointed arrow points, of delicate bifacial implements for sidehafting in projectiles or knife handles, and of burins and microblades, by 4500 B.P. had covered the Arctic from Alaska to Greenland; in the east the Denbigh relatives were known as Pre-Dorset. For long, the earliest well-dated assemblage in Alaska, the Proto-Denbigh Complex at Onion Portage on the Kobuk River, was placed only at about 4100 B.P. Recently, Denbigh-related materials have been dated on the Seward Peninsula at about 4700 B.P., strengthening an argument that the Arctic Small Tool tradition was carried to North America in direct migration by peoples of the Siberian Neolithic, giving up pottery in the rapid movement to new country. This is a second period of resemblance between Alaska and Siberia.

In the east, Pre-Dorset people evolved into Dorset sometime between about 2800 and 2500 B.P., developing further the ability to subsist on the Arctic coast, including means of winter sealing at breathing holes in the ice. Dorset folk built semisubterranean or stone houses, but they also probably developed the snow hut, so well known among later Eskimos of the central Arctic.

In the west, the Denbigh Flint Complex of northern Alaska gave way by 3400 B.P. to a sequence of cultures betraying regional ferment. The Choris culture, in a limited area north of the Bering Strait, exhibited the first use of pottery, clearly Siberian, but preserved some Denbigh-like stone implements, as well as adopting oil-burning lamps of stone, labrets, and other artifacts suggestive of the Pacific coast. By 2400 B.P. quick expansion of a related Norton culture brought homogeneity throughout the coast from the Alaska Peninsula in the south to about what is now the Alaska-Canada border in the north. These people also used pottery, some ground slate, and open oil lamps, and wore labrets, while retaining some stone artifacts reminiscent of the early Arctic Small Tool tradition. Until around A.D. 1000 they persisted south of the Bering Strait, their culture changing slowly, their occupation including both coast and salmon-rich tundra rivers.

North of the Bering Strait, however, Norton did not endure, for in the early centuries A.D. it was replaced by Ipiutak, a culture similar in many ways but without pottery, oil lamps, ground slate, or labrets, and renowned for carved ivory. Some scholars suggest that the Ipiutak people were Denbigh Flint descendants from the interior of northern Alaska who moved seaward in the early centuries A.D. to displace their Norton relatives.

Meanwhile, after 2000 B.P. on islands of the Bering Strait region, people of the Old Bering Sea culture focused strongly on sea mammals, especially walrus. Before A.D. 1000 this developed into Punuk culture, in which whaling was emphasized, and elaborate graves of whalers were set in cemeteries on the Siberian coast. Seal hunters of northwestern Alaska also were increasing their use of coastal resources, with oil lamps and many polished slate artifacts. By about A.D. 1000, the area around the Chukchi Sea was home to Western Thule culture, of people who built large, square semisubterranean houses, some hunting whales, some adapted more to life on coastal rivers.

The resulting lifeway, the most successful to occur in the North American Arctic, led in the north to a movement of Thule people across north-coastal Canada to Greenland, following the path of the Arctic Small Tool predecessors to absorb or eliminate Dorset inhabitants by A.D. 1100 or shortly thereafter; and in the south, a contemporary expansion of Thule culture led to the Alaska Peninsula and the north Pacific. These occurrences appear to have spread those Eskimo languages spoken throughout the Arctic when outsiders arrived.

Since then, except for contact with Europeans the major change was probably the response to worsening climate along the central Canadian coast after A.D. 1400, when Thule descendants gave up their constructed winter houses to adopt snow huts for all winter living as they moved onto the ice to live near breathing-hole seal-hunting areas. This is the lifeway famous for the Eskimo, although practiced by only a small percentage of those peoples, many of whose descendants now prefer to be called Inuit.

Europeans also brought change. Before A.D. 1000 the Norse settled southern Greenland. Although their impact on Dorset natives is not known, by A.D. 1500 the Norse remnants both had met early Greenland Thule people and had perished. By then, however, the English and others were exploring, and within two centuries had met Native Americans from Newfoundland north into Hudson Bay and beyond, while establishing fur-trading outposts.

In the west, contact came only after Bering's discoveries of 1741–1742. Russian fur hunters soon were sailing regularly from Kamchatka Peninsula to the Aleutians after sea otter, and in 1783 they settled on Kodiak Island.

From the westernmost Aleutians to the lower Alaska Peninsula, Russians found natives speaking dialects of the Aleut language. Beyond that point they met people speaking the distantly related but totally distinct language of the western or Yupik Eskimo group.

Both Aleuts and Yupik-speaking natives of the Pacific were open-water hunters of sea mammals, seeking also coastal fishes and salmon where available. Eskimo-speaking peoples north of the Alaska Peninsula lived on coastlines that freeze in winter. Although Russian impact was less strong there, in the nineteenth century foreign whalers brought dissolution and disease to settlements as far north as Point Barrow.

Well after the beginning of the twentieth century, Canadians and others finally contacted all native groups of the remote Arctic coast and recorded a viable lifeway in one of the most inhospitable regions known to humankind.

[See also AMERICAS, FIRST SETTLEMENT OF THE, articles on SETTLEMENT OF THE AMERICAS BEFORE 12,500 B.C., SETTLEMENT OF THE AMERICAS AFTER 12,000 B.C.; SIBERIA, PREHISTORIC.]

■ J. Louis Giddings, Ancient Men of the Arctic (1967). Robert McGhee, Canadian Arctic Prehistory (1978). Michael L. Kunz, "The Mesa Site," Anthropological Papers of the University of Alaska 20 (1982): 113–122. David Damas, ed., Arctic, vol. 5 in ed. William C. Sturtevant, Handbook of North American Indians (1984). Moreau S. Maxwell, Prehistory of the Eastern Arctic (1985). Don E. Dumond, The Eskimos and Aleuts, rev. ed. (1987). Ted Goebel, Roger Powers, and Nancy Bigelow, "The Nenana Complex of Alaska and Clovis Origins," in eds. Robson

Bonnichsen and K. L. Turnmire, *Clovis: Origins and Adaptations* (1992).

Don E. Dumond

THE NORTH AMERICAN SUBARCTIC

The North American Subarctic comprises a vast biotic province stretching across the continent, anchored in both the Pacific and Atlantic Oceans. The often harsh climatic conditions of this region have shaped its past and affected the manner by which investigations into its prehistory and history could take place. Archaeological research in many parts of the Subarctic has lagged far behind neighboring areas. Field seasons are short, characterized by temperature extremes between freezing and 38 degrees Celsius, and punctuated by constant swarms of blood-seeking insects. Travel is difficult, costly, and invariably involves small floatplanes and watercraft; subsistence costs are prohibitively expensive. Site preservation is radically affected by cyclical forest fires, frost action and permafrost, and acidic soils or a virtual lack of soil development. As a result we possess but small quantities of facts that must be extrapolated over vast areas.

As deglaciation proceeded differentially across the top of the continent, so too did the penetration of people into the landmass being freed from the clutches of the great Laurentide and Cordilleran ice sheets. Many points of entry became available to the earliest peoples to live in the North American Subarctic.

Western Subarctic (Alaska, Yukon, westernmost Northwest Territories, British Columbia). During Late Pleistocene times, human groups lived within a vast grassland in the interior of Alaska and the northern Yukon that was really a part of Asia (this eastern extension is known as Beringia). The remaining landmass of what is today Canada was covered by glacial ice. Early traces of occupation—25,000 to 40,000 B.P. old—are controversial, as they are almost uniquely constituted of secondary deposits of animal bones, many species of which are now extinct, broken by percussion and of bone fragments apparently used as implements with little or no subsequent modification.

Indisputable evidence of human occupation occurs between 10,000 and 15,000 B.P. Two distinct technological traditions have been identified; the microblade and burin-using Paleo-Arctic tradition and a nonmicroblade, biface-using group exemplified by the Nenana Complex. While origins of the former clearly lie in Siberia, it has been suggested that those of the latter are to be found in the northern maritime regions of the Far East. Slightly later, fluted point makers in the northwest (Northern Paleo-Indians) may represent an evolution from Nenana, although they may attest to a northward movement of Clovis hunters.

Until about 6000 B.P., much of the interior of the newly forested western Subarctic was occupied by groups who used lanceolate points not unlike some Late Paleo-Indian Plano projectiles. Beginning about 6000 B.P., the Northern Archaic is hypothesized to have resulted from influences emanating from the northern Great Plains. Initially, the Northern Archaic was characterized by notched spear points and by the absence of a microblade industry. At the same time, derivatives of the earlier Paleo-Arctic tradition continued on in peripheral areas and eventually became amalgamated with Northern Archaic traits, spreading east and south into northern British Columbia, Alberta, and the District of Mackenzie (the Northwest Microblade tradition).

The situation was far from simple; microblades seemed to be adopted in some cases and neglected in others. A serious problem with our ability to understand the significance of the presence or absence of microblades lies in a poor understanding of their real function. Invariably, local sequences suggest that the manufacture of microblades had ceased everywhere in the western Subarctic by 2000 to 1500 B.P., at which time the ancestors of the Athapaskan-speakers of historic times become manifest in the archaeological record.

Central Subarctic (Northwest Territories, Alberta, Saskatchewan, Manitoba). Late Paleo-Indian Plano groups using Agate Basin Plano points pushed out of the northern Great Plains into the Subarctic forests about 8000 B.P. Caribou, which calved and summered on the vast Barrenlands of Canada's Northwest Territories and wintered within the boreal forest, drew these groups to the edge of the treeless tundra. They are believed to have modified their tool kits into a more generalized assemblage of implements, which included notched projectile points, giving rise to the long-lived Shield Archaic tradition around 6000 B.P. The Shield Archaic adapted to the diverse nature of the Subarctic and then rapidly spread throughout much of the central and eastern Subarctic.

Along the northern edge of the central Subarctic, Paleo-Eskimos of the Arctic Small Tool tradition replaced the Shield Archaic tradition beginning about 3500 B.P. until roughly 2500 B.P. Eventually, these groups in their turn vacated the region and Indian-related groups (Taltheilei Shale tradition) once again occupied the northern central Subarctic. The origins of this tradition are not known, but following its appearance at the edge of the forest, it evolved through a number of phases and clearly became ancestral to the historic occupants of the region including the Chipewyan, Yellowknives, and Slavey.

The southern reaches of the central Subarctic exhibit a continuous development of Shield Archaic–related occupations until approximately 2000–1500 B.P. At this time, Initial Woodland ceramics spread into the boreal forest of Manitoba and Saskatchewan from neighboring Ontario. Further Ontarian influences a few centuries later resulted in the distinctive Selkirk ceramics, which are thought to have been produced by the ancestors of the historic Cree of the region.

Eastern Subarctic (Ontario, Quebec, Labrador). In the Upper Great Lakes, late Paleo-Indian Plano groups (Interlakes Composite) settled along former shorelines of Lake Superior and glacial Lake Agassiz about 9500 B.P. These distinctive lanceolate point makers were occupying areas only recently freed from ice. Their principal economic orientation is thought to have been the hunting of barrenland caribou, but fishing no doubt also was important. The fate of these early occupants is unknown. Was there discontinuity or population replacement at the end of the Paleo-Indian period? Research on the transitional time interval (8000–6500 B.P.) has been too spotty to tell. However, Shield Archaic groups, thought to have originated in the central Subarctic, came to occupy most of the region during the interval of 6500 to 2000 B.P.

So suited to the central and eastern Subarctic was the Shield Archaic way of life that it remained relatively unchanged until European contact throughout much of its range. While trends have been noted in artifact frequencies, styles, and sizes, the general character of assemblages, and the lifestyle they mirror, were maintained.

Beginning before 2000 B.P., ceramics made their appearance along the Rainy River in the southern fringes of the central Subarctic. Accompanied by burial mound ceremonialism and possibly the gathering of wild rice, ceramics were eventually incorporated into the material culture of Subarctic groups in Ontario, Manitoba, Saskatchewan, and westernmost Quebec. The Initial Woodland cultures persisted in some areas until the twelfth century A.D. and appear to have overlapped with succeeding Late or Terminal Woodland people, who were characterized by different ceramic and lithic assemblages. Early sites of the Blackduck ceramic tradition (probably ancestral Ojibway) date to the eighth or ninth century A.D., while Selkirk ceramics (probably manufactured by the ancestors of some Cree groups) are two or three centuries younger.

Glacial ice within the interior of Quebec persisted longer than elsewhere and delayed human occupation. However, fluted point-making Paleo-Indians in Nova Scotia and Prince Edward Island appear to have evolved, in the outer St. Lawrence estuary, into the Maritime Archaic tradition between 8000 and 9000 B.P. Equally at home in interior or coastal environments, the Maritime Archaic tradition eventually occupied the whole Labrador coast and adjacent portions of the Quebec-Labrador peninsula. A long Maritime Archaic sequence, including a rich burial complex, lasted in northern Labrador until about 3500 B.P., at which time Paleo-Eskimos replaced them.

Although it is suspected that central Quebec was first occupied by about 8000 to 9000 B.P. by late Paleo-Indian lanceolate point makers, the earliest human presence documented for the well-studied James Bay hinterland dates to only 3500 B.P. Remains there seem to relate to the widespread Shield Archaic tradition, which also appeared about the same time in southern Labrador. Subsequent developments there lead to the emergence of the historically documented Innu (Naskapi).

In much of Subarctic Quebec, changes in lithic technology and lithic trade patterns point to a marked population change beginning about 1500 B.P. Ceramics continued to be shunned in spite of occasional exchanges for ceramic containers (or perhaps, more important, their contents). Linguists believe that this wave of migrants were ancestors of the Cree-Montagnais-Naskapi. In more southern and eastern parts of Quebec, connections with native groups (Naskapi) occupying the Labrador coast and the St. Lawrence estuary (Point Revenge Complex) are evident.

Early Contacts with Europeans. The early historic period, defined on the basis of the beginning of sustained contact with non–North Americans, starts in the late sixteenth century in the Gulf of St. Lawrence. There, it was marked by seasonal trading expeditions or the summer activities of European fishers and whalers. This pattern changed once the French established colonies along the banks of the St. Lawrence River in the early and middle seventeenth century. Inland posts were soon built along complicated networks of canoe routes reaching far into the interior of the eastern and central Subarctic. Intermediary trade relationships further extended their influence.

In the late seventeenth century, the Hudson's Bay Company established a series of permanent trading establishments along the shores of Hudson and James Bays. Their initial approach was to encourage the hunters or intermediaries to come to them. Later, with growing competition from French traders established inland, the Hudson's Bay Company created a string of inland posts from which they brought the trade directly to a larger number of groups in the eastern and central Subarctic.

By the middle of the eighteenth century, the web of both English and French posts continued to spread westward into the central Subarctic. The late eighteenth century saw the first recorded foray by Euro-Canadian traders into the vast Mackenzie River Valley, although it was not until the early nineteenth century that a permanent post (Northwest Company) was established in the lower part of the valley.

In the later part of the eighteenth century, Russian traders were setting up posts along the coast of south-central Alaska and initiating contacts with Athapaskans (Tanaina, Ahtna) there. At first there was marked resistance to allowing these newcomers to access the interior. But as sea otters declined, more vigorous attempts by the Russian-American Company were made to penetrate the interior. By the middle of the nineteenth century, Europeans from the Alaskan or Mackenzie Valley trading centers were traveling inland and establishing commercial relationships with previously isolated groups throughout the western Subarctic. By the end of the century, the process was complete.

■ Walter M. Hlady, ed., *Ten Thousand Years of Archaeology in Manitoba* (1970). James V. Wright, *The Shield Archaic* (1972). Claude Chapdelaine, ed., *Images de la Préhistoire du Québec* (1978). June Helm, ed., *Subarctic* (1981). Claude Chapdelaine, ed., *Des Éléphants, des Caribous . . . et des Hommes* (1985). Jacques Cinq-Mars, "La Place des Grottes du Poisson-Bleu dans la Préhistoire Béringienne," *Revista de Arqueologia Americana* 1 (1990): 9–32. John W. Ives, *A Theory of Northern Athapaskan Prehistory* (1990). Donald W. Clark, *Western Subarctic Prehistory* (1991). William Ross, "The Interlakes Composite: A Re-Definition of the Initial Settlement of the Agassiz-Minong Peninsula," *Wisconsin Archaeologist* 72 (1991): 1–30.

Jean-Luc Pilon

THE EASTERN WOODLANDS AND THE SOUTH

Human colonization of the Eastern Woodlands occurred in the Late Pleistocene, although the timing of initial entry is unknown. Radiocarbon dates at or exceeding 12,000 B.P. have been reported at several localities, although these remain controversial. The first widespread evidence for human presence are Paleo-Indian (i.e., pre-10,000 B.P.) assemblages characterized by a range of well-made stone tools, including lanceolate Clovis fluted points, an artifact that occurs in large numbers across the East, south of the ice sheets. While few sites with these points have been reliably dated, approximate contemporaneity with western forms is assumed, at ca. 11,200–10,900 B.P. Dense site concentrations occur along major rivers such as the Tennessee, Cumberland, and Ohio, and along portions of the Atlantic Seaboard, typically near high-quality stone sources. These localities are thought to reflect areas of initial extended settlement, staging areas from which the colonization of the larger region proceeded. Paleo-Indian groups near the ice sheets targeted large game, particularly caribou, while groups in the Woodlands to the south were more generalized foragers, exploiting a wide range of animal and plant species. The extent to which Pleistocene megafauna were hunted is unclear, although indisputable associations have been found in some areas between humans and extinct species such as mastodon, bison, and giant tortoise.

Major population growth coupled with decreasing group movement characterizes the later Paleo-Indian era. A diversity of post-Clovis fluted and unfluted point forms appear after ca. 10,900 B.P., marking the emergence of distinct subregional cultural traditions. This occurred more or less contemporaneously with the demise of the Pleistocene megafauna, and likely reflects the end of the free-wandering big-game hunting adaptation inferred for the initial colonists. In the central Mississippi Valley the *Dalton culture flourished and has yielded identifiable base camps, quarries, hunting stations, and cemetery sites in clusters interpreted as the ranges of individual band-level groups. Dalton artifacts occur widely across the Eastern Woodlands, although stylistic variants are evident in different areas. All of these cultures were adopted to an essentially modern fauna, with white-tailed deer the primary game animal exploited. Near the retreating glacial margins, in contrast, tundra caribou hunters continued to use fluted points with deeply indented bases until after 10,500 B.P., and left behind dense hunting-station and base-camp remains.

By the onset of the Archaic stage at 10,000 B.P. (by convention, the Pleistocene/Holocene boundary worldwide), a variety of side- and corner-notched projectile points are recognized across the region. During the Early Archaic, spanning the first two millennia of the Holocene, assemblages continued to be characterized by formal chipped stone tools on high-quality stone, although over time these were replaced by more casually made tools on locally available materials. The presence of ground and pecked stone plant processing tools indicate subsistence was becoming increasingly diversified. Over time, annual ranges grew progressively smaller, and at the end of the subperiod were likely restricted to within portions of river systems. Periodic meetings between bands occurred in favored settings, tying together people over large areas and in several river systems, and facilitating the spread of information, mates, and materials.

The Middle Archaic, from about 8000 to 5000 B.P., corresponds to the mid-Holocene warming interval, or Hypsithermal. The expansion of pine forests and cypress swamps across the southeastern coastal plain led to a consolidation of peoples in areas where hardwood forests were maintained, like the river valleys of the mid-South and lower Midwest. Regional populations appear to have stabilized or possibly even decreased somewhat. Large earth and *shell midden sites with dense occupational debris and numerous burials appear along some of the major drainages of the midcontinent. These sites, occupied at least part of the year, served as aggregation loci and special burial areas. Burials with embedded projectile points are common, indicating conflict was occurring. While widely ranging foragers were still present, these most typically occur in geographically marginal areas.

Long-distance exchange networks spanning appreciable portions of the East emerged during the Middle Archaic, with goods in circulation including shell from the southern coasts and copper from the Great Lakes. Some materials like bone pins or elaborate bifaces were circulating over lesser areas, indicating more localized exchange networks were also operating. Interaction and exchange enhanced the status of network participants and also helped reduce or avoid conflict and overcome subsistence uncertainty by creating ties between neighboring and more distant groups. The construction of ceremonial earthen mound complexes began in several areas, including in the maritime provinces of the Northeast, in the Lower Mississippi Valley, and in coastal Florida.

Mound construction, long-distance prestige-goods exchange, and evidence for warfare continued in the ensuing Late Archaic Period (5000–3000 B.P.), culminating in dramatic cultural expressions like *Poverty Point, Stallings Island, Green River/Indian Knoll, and Old Copper. During

this interval essentially modern climatic conditions, sea levels, and vegetational communities emerged. A major increase in regional population levels is indicated, with sites found in almost all parts of the landscape. Wild plant foods were collected in increasing quantity throughout the Archaic, and by the end of the period, between 4000 and 3000 B.P., morphological changes indicative of domestication are evident in a number of local species such as goosefoot, sumpweed, sunflower, and gourds (Cucurbita). Domestication appears to have occurred in disturbed floodplain habitats near major earth and shell midden sites, or in adjoining upland areas where populations ranged to collect various plant foods. Shellfish use in the interior continued, and for the first time evidence for the use of coastal resources becomes widespread. Pottery appears in the Stallings culture in the Georgia and South Carolina coastal plain about 4500 B.P. and soon thereafter in the Orange culture of Florida. The mounds and earthworks of the terminal Archaic Poverty Point culture, a vast exchange network centered on the Lower Mississippi Valley and Gulf coast, are among the largest ever built in the East.

During the Early Woodland Period (3000–2300 B.P.) pottery use became widespread, although a marked decline in long-distance exchange and interaction occurred. People were living in more-or-less egalitarian groups loosely tied together by collective burial ritual. Most communities were small, on the order of a half a dozen structures and about fifty to sixty people. Intensive cultivation of local domesticates occurred in parts of the Midwest and mid-South, although in areas rich in natural food resources evidence for agriculture remains minimal. Charnel house and burial mound mortuary facilities located away from settlements near territorial margins occur in many areas, suggesting they served to bring differing groups together for collective ceremony. Over time mound burial came to be reserved for smaller segments of the population, a trend exemplified in the *Adena cultures of the mid-South, where circular mortuary structures and low accretional burial mounds appear around 2500 B.P.

During the Middle Woodland period (ca. 2300–1600 B.P.), societies across much of the East were tied together in exchange and religious activity, behavior that has come to be called Hopewellian interaction, after the type site and culture in southern Ohio, where spectacular earthworks and burial assemblages have been found. Many diverse cultures were actually present, onto which a thin veneer of Hopewellian exchange, iconography, and ritual was overlain in some, but not all, parts of the region. While most people were treated simply, in some societies high-status individuals were buried in elaborately constructed and furnished log-lined tombs, sometimes under massive mound deposits. While hereditary leadership positions are not apparent, there is clear evidence that some individuals or lineages were wealthier and more powerful than others, exercising considerable control over long-distance trade, public ceremony, and monumental construction. Some ceremonial complexes were enormous in scope, covering dozens of hectares, with elaborate mound, earthwork, and burial precincts. Platform mounds were built in several parts of the Southeast, and saw use in mortuary ritual and public feasting. A tribal form of social organization, consisting of a number of interacting clans, is assumed to have been present, with most people continuing to live in small communities. Native domesticates were an important source of food in parts of the region, although maize, which was present by at least 1800 B.P., did not become a major constituent of the diet until much later. Tobacco also entered the region about the same time and was soon widely used.

During the late Woodland period (1600–1000 B.P.) pan-regional exchange and religious ceremony declined markedly and mound construction and elaborate mortuary behavior ceased in many areas. Major population growth is evident. The bow and arrow appeared and spread rapidly, which may explain the increase in warfare that happens at this time. Organizational decline did not, however, occur throughout the region. Formal civic-ceremonial complexes, arrangements of residential and temple mounds around plazas and occupied by hereditary elites, occurred in the Coles Creek culture in the Lower Mississippi Valley about 1200 B.P. and elsewhere soon thereafter. By the end of the period intensive maize agriculture was present in many areas, largely replacing indigenous domesticates.

Chiefdoms ruled by hereditary elites living in densely populated civic-ceremonial centers were present in many parts of the Southeast and Lower Midwest during the Mississippian Period (1000–450 B.P.). Most of these societies were heavily dependent on intensive agriculture, with crop surpluses used to fuel elite agendas, typically the accumulation of power and status at the expense of other elites. Warfare was endemic and celebrated in a rich iconography. Ceremonial centers were typically occupied year-round and were the geographic as well as religious centers of society. Long-distance prestige-goods exchange and interaction became widespread early in the period and peaked about 800 B.P., with the regionwide expression known as the Southeastern Ceremonial Complex. During the latter half of the Mississippian period evidence for warfare increased, mound building declined, and long-distance exchange dropped off markedly. Along the middle Atlantic Seaboard, around the Great Lakes, and in the Northeast, more egalitarian yet organizationally still fairly complex agricultural and hunting-gathering populations were also present, whose interaction with the Mississippian cultures to the south and west was fairly minimal. Following contact many native societies collapsed under the impacts of disease and conquest.

[See also CAHOKIA; HOPEWELL CULTURE; IROQUOIS AND ALGONQUIAN CULTURES; MISSISSIPPIAN CULTURE; MOUNDS OF EASTERN NORTH AMERICA; MOUNDVILLE; NORTH AMERICA, ORIGINS OF FOOD PRODUCTION IN; SERPENT MOUND; SPIRO MOUNDS.]

■ James B. Griffin, "Eastern North American Archaeology: A Summary," *Science* 156 (1967): 175–191. Bruce D. Smith, "The Archaeology of the Southeastern United States: From Dalton to deSoto, 10,500–500 B.P.," in eds. Fred Wendorf and Angela E. Close, *Advances in World Archaeology* 5 (1986): 1–92; Bruce D. Smith, *Rivers of Change: Essays on Early Agriculture in Eastern North America* (1992). Judith A. Bense, *Archaeology of the Southeastern United States: Paleoindian to World War I* (1994). David G. Anderson and Kenneth E. Sassaman, *The Paleoindian and Early Archaic Southeast* (1996). Kenneth E. Sassaman and David G. Anderson, *The Archaeology of the Mid-Holocene Southeast* (1996).

David G. Anderson

THE NORTH AMERICAN PLAINS

The North American Plains include the area from the Canadian boreal forest in the north to central Texas in the south, and from the Rocky Mountains in the west to the Missouri River and the eastern boundaries of the states of Nebraska, Kansas, and Oklahoma in the east. Prior to white settlement, this region was almost continuous open grassland, interrupted by more forested locales along the major river valleys and in those areas, such as the Black Hills of eastern Wyoming and western South Dakota, where the expanse of open plains was interrupted by isolated mountainous areas. The Plains climate is extremely unpredictable, but is generally characterized by summer-dominant rainfall, a steep east to west decrease in precipitation, and cold winters. The region's fauna were dominated by the North American bison, but other species, such as deer and elk, could be found in more wooded areas.

Although early cultural anthropologists suggested that the Great Plains were unsuitable for human occupation prior to the introduction of the horse by the Spanish, archaeological research on the Great Plains since the 1920s has revealed at least 12,000 years of Native American occupation, which can be divided into five general chronological periods: a tentative "Pre-Clovis" period (prior to 10,000 B.C.), followed by the Paleo-Indian (10,000 to 6000 B.C.), Archaic (6000 B.C. to A.D. 1), Woodland (A.D. 1 to 1000), and Plains Village (A.D. 900 to 1850) periods.

As is true in other areas of North America, relatively few archaeologists believe that human beings occupied the Great Plains prior to 12,000 years ago. Sites that have been claimed to be older than this have one of two problems: Either these sites contain undoubted cultural material but have problematic dates (i.e., the Lewisville site in Texas) or they have problematic material and good dates (i.e., the Dutton and Selby sites in Colorado or the La Sena site in Nebraska). Sites in this latter category commonly produce bones of extinct animals, particularly elephants, which show patterns of breakage and other damage that are difficult to account for naturally and that resemble patterns produced by humans. The complete absence of stone tools in these sites is the principal reason for most archaeologists' skepticism about them.

Definite evidence of human occupation of the Plains first appears between 10,000 and 9500 B.C., at the beginning of the Paleo-Indian period. The Paleo-Indian period is often broken into three segments: Clovis (10,000 to 9000 B.C.), Folsom (9000 to 8500 B.C.), and Late Paleo-Indian (8500 to 6000 B.C.); this segment subsumes a variety of culture-historical constructs, including Agate Basin, Hell Gap, Cody, Firstview, and others. Human beings throughout the Plains during these periods were exclusively hunter-gatherers, and the majority of the available information indicates that they focused their attention particularly on big game: Clovis hunters took a relatively wide range of now-extinct species (including elephants, camels, and horses), while Folsom and later groups seem to have specialized in hunting bison. The Paleo-Indian period on the Plains is also well-known for the sophistication of its stoneworking: Projectile points in particular are extremely well crafted, aesthetically pleasing, and difficult to produce, and Paleo-Indian flint knappers tended to manufacture them from very high-quality stone.

Although archaeological sites from the early portions of the Archaic period are rare, those that are known indicate major changes in human lifeways; regional differences in lifeways also seem to have become more prominent. These changes were probably in response to a great increase in aridity in the region (the "Altithermal" climatic interval). The Paleo-Indian emphasis on big-game hunting may have persisted on the northwestern Plains, but humans elsewhere seem to have broken up into smaller, more mobile social groups and diversified their subsistence base: Sites on the southern Plains suggest an increased emphasis on plant foods, for example, while the more eastern Plains show a reliance on a very wide range of large and small animals and on plant foods.

The Altithermal ended by 2500 B.C., with the development of essentially modern climate. An important pattern that persists through the remainder of the Archaic and into later periods is a substantial difference between the eastern tall-grass prairies and western short-grass steppe. In the west, bison hunting persists as a key activity, although there is debate over the importance of other resources in the diet, particularly plant resources, in at least some areas. Bison hunting may actually have intensified during the Archaic in the west: Middle Archaic hunters on the northern and northwestern Plains for the first time constructed such facilities as drive lines and corrals to assist them in taking large numbers of bison in a single drive. In the east, in contrast, although bison were certainly part of the diet, woodland resources like deer, fish, and nuts were also important. Particularly during the Late Archaic, the eastern groups seem to have been substantially more sedentary than their western counterparts: For example, structures and dense concentrations of habitation debris have been identified in some sites in the east.

This eastern Plains/western Plains distinction became increasingly important during the Woodland and Plains Village patterns, as the more eastern groups became increasingly involved with cultural developments in adjacent areas of the North American Midwest. This involvement is marked at the beginning of the Woodland Period by the appearance of pottery similar to that manufactured throughout much of eastern North America over most of the Plains. In addition, people on the eastern and central Plains began to construct communal burial mounds similar to those found to the east. The most elaborate pottery and mounds are found in the vicinity of Kansas City and appear to represent a migration of people out of the Midwest; this occupation is referred to as "Kansas City Hopewell." Elsewhere on the Plains, pottery and mound construction were probably adopted by indigenous populations.

The Woodland Period introduction of ceramics and mounds (and, presumably, the religious beliefs associated with mound construction) seems to have had two distinct effects on these indigenous populations. First, on the eastern and central Plains, particularly in Kansas and Nebraska, where most research on this period has been carried out, local populations seem to have become increasingly sedentary; houses are common, sometimes grouped in communities of as many as twenty structures. Second, during later Woodland times, groups in these areas seem to have integrated a small portion of horticulture into their diet, as evidenced by the recovery of small amounts of corn, squash, and other cultigens along with a few horticultural implements. Elsewhere, particularly in more northern and northwestern areas, bison hunting persisted as the primary economic activity; along the Missouri River in South Dakota, burial mounds of the Sonota Complex have produced not only human remains but also complete, articulated bison, and the number of large bison kills seems to increase in many areas, as does evidence for frequent reuse of bison drive sites.

By A.D. 900, then, the Plains were populated by nomadic bison hunters in the north and west and at least semisedentary, incipient horticulturalists in most other areas. At this date, settled horticultural villages appear throughout most of the Plains. This latest occupation, the Plains Village Period, is best discussed in two sections: early (A.D. 900 to 1250) and late (A.D. 1250 to 1850).

During the early period, settled communities appear in the Dakotas, Nebraska, Kansas, and Oklahoma. These can be broadly divided into two occupations on the basis of architecture and other remains. On the central and southern Plains of Nebraska, Kansas, and Oklahoma, communities were generally small (averaging roughly five houses); these houses were square with rounded corners, averaged seven to nine meters on a side, and were constructed from wattle and daub. In Kansas and Nebraska, these communities are subsumed within the Central Plains Tradition, and may represent a migration of farmers out of the Kansas City area; in Oklahoma, continuities between Woodland and Plains Village ceramics and other artifacts suggest that they probably represent an indigenous development. These more southern groups probably represent the ancestors of such postcontact Caddoan-speaking groups as the Wichita, Pawnee, and Arikara.

Farther to the north, in North and South Dakota, a second occupation is evident, which archaeologists refer to as the Middle Missouri Tradition. Middle Missouri houses average about 25 feet (7.5 m) wide by 35 feet (10.5 m) long and are excavated about a meter into the earth. The superstructure of the lodge was supported by central posts and a ridge pole running the length of the structure's long axis, and the roofs were covered with earth. Generally, these lodges were arranged in fairly orderly rows, sometimes with a central plaza; typical community sizes ranged from a dozen to as many as thirty lodges, although towns including as many as ninety houses or more are known, particularly from later periods. The Middle Missouri Tradition is fairly clearly the result of a migration of farmers out of northern Iowa and southern Minnesota, and probably represents the ancestors of the modern Mandan and Hidatsa.

Both of these village-dwelling occupations relied extensively on cultivating corn, beans, squash, and sunflower, as well as on exploiting wild resources, including the bison. The development of settled ways of life at this time corresponds to a period of favorable climatic conditions for horticulture. However, between A.D. 1200 and 1250, the climate became cooler and drier, and many of the western Central Plains Tradition communities were abandoned. During the later part of the Plains Village Period, sedentary populations expanded into the Texas Panhandle (the Antelope Creek focus) and Central Plains Tradition populations moved north into South Dakota, where they began to interact intensively with Middle Missouri groups. These interactions were not always friendly: Many sites in the Dakotas dating to this period are fortified, and osteological evidence for violence is well known.

Once again, these developments are related, at least in part, to processes at work to the east, in this case the rise of Mississippian society at sites like *Cahokia and elsewhere. This is evident both in the probable migration of eastern peoples onto the Plains and in similarities in pottery styles and elements of iconography on other artifacts between the Plains and the Eastern Woodlands. Economic relations were probably important in tying the Plains to other areas at this time: For example, Antelope Creek sites concentrate near major quarry areas and are located along a network that linked eastern groups as far away as Louisiana with Puebloan groups in New Mexico.

To the west and north of the horticultural groups, nomadic bison hunters continued their ways of life with little discernable change throughout the Plains Village Period. However, the centuries just before and following European contact in the mid- to late 1500s saw substantial population shifts that are at least partly documented archaeologically. For example, Apachean groups probably moved through the Plains and settled there for some time, producing an archaeological manifestation referred to as Dismal River. Shoshonean groups also moved out of the Rocky Mountains as far north as Canada either just before or just after contact, a movement that is possibly marked by distinctive rock art at Writing-on-Stone on the Milk River in Alberta.

However, most of the archaeology of native groups on the Plains during the postcontact period pertains to the settled groups of the eastern and central Plains. Excavations in postcontact sites in these areas reveal the heavy impact of Euro-American technology, disease, depopulation, population replacement, and violence, supporting evidence in the historical record for similar processes. Archaeological remains attributable to such well-known postcontact hunting tribes as the Cheyenne or the Lakota are almost nonexistent, in part because these groups were eighteenth-century migrants to the Plains and in part because their highly mobile lifestyle produced few remains for archaeologists to examine.

Finally, the Euro-American presence on the Plains has also been documented archaeologically. Much of the work on this presence has emphasized sites linked to the fur trade on the more northern Plains, but important work has also been carried out on Spanish trade sites in the south and on the site of the Custer fight on the Little Bighorn in Montana.

[See also HUNTER-GATHERERS, NORTH AMERICAN ARCHAIC; HUNTERS OF THE NORTH AMERICAN PLAINS.]

■ Waldo Wedel, *Prehistoric Man on the Great Plains* (1961). Donald Lehmer, *An Introduction to Middle Missouri Archaeology* (1971). Henry Epp and Ian Dyck, *Tracking Ancient Hunters: Prehistoric Archaeology in Saskatchewan* (1983). Robert Bell, *The Prehistory of Oklahoma* (1984). Steven Cassells, *The Archaeology of Colorado* (1986). Waldo Wedel, *Central Plains Archaeology* (1986). George Frison, *Prehistoric Hunters of the High Plains* (1992).

Douglas B. Bamforth

THE NORTH AMERICAN SOUTHWEST

Archaeologists have defined the North American Southwest by the presence of three features: maize agriculture, pottery, and a mud-, wood-, and stone-based, pueblo-style architecture. These separate the region from neighboring areas on the north, west, and east, where the predominant prehistoric adaptations were highly mobile and focused on wild resources. To the south, however, there is no distinct boundary between the prehistoric Southwest and the northern reaches of prehistoric Mesoamerica. The maize and ceramic technology are well-known introductions from Mesoamerica; the southwestern architectural forms may have originated there, as well. Although only those three prehistoric cultures that lie north of the current international border are discussed here, an additional half-dozen lie to the south.

The Southwest differs markedly from other regions in several critical areas. The first concerns connections between today's indigenous peoples and the archaeological record. When the Spanish followed the ancient trade trails between Mesoamerica and the North American Southwest in the mid-sixteenth century, they expected to find cities of gold. Instead they found stone and mud pueblos and scattered communities of Hopi, Zuñi, Pima, and Papago, Yuman-, Keresen-, and Tanoan-speaking peoples. Between villages the Spanish caught fleeting glimpses of nomads. These nomads—today's Navajo, Apache, and Ute—were Athapaskan speakers, far from their linguistic relatives in the North American boreal forests, and Utes, related by language to the Hopi agriculturalists and the Numic hunter-gatherers of the Great Basin. The descendants of the native Southwest peoples maintain traditional practices and lifeways today, many in settlements established centuries before the Spanish *entrada*.

Another crucial feature is the Southwest's position as a frontier. Throughout prehistory, the region was crisscrossed by mobile populations, by trade routes, and by intellectual commerce binding the region to its neighbors. Movement and migration, strong themes in indigenous oral traditions, are clearly expressed in the regional archaeology. Although some settlements were occupied for centuries, most were abandoned after less than one hundred years.

Finally, the Southwest is an arid landscape, with well-preserved, abundant, and evocative ruins. These ample archaeological resources have supported over a century of research on the connections between the Southwest and neighboring regions, cultural adaptations to frontiers and arid environments, and the development of Southwest cultural patterns.

The North American Southwest stretches from the Pecos to the Colorado River, and from the southern Rockies to the Sierra Madre Occidental. It includes portions of the modern Mexican states of Sonora, Chihuahua, and Coahuila and Arizona, Nevada, Utah, Colorado, and New Mexico in the United States.

The region includes low deserts, deep canyons, and mountains that rise up past tree line. Coupled with chronically low rainfall, this considerable geographic relief gives rise to significant differences in the distribution of natural resources and agricultural potential. In the east and south, rainfall tends to occur as summer thunderstorms. In the west and north, rainfall is distributed more evenly between summer storms and winter snows. Good summer rainfall can support the Southwest staples of maize, beans, and squash in floodplain settings or on mesa tops with runoff rainwater. When summer rainfall is low, crops must be irrigated or hand watered.

Human occupation of the Southwest is now known to encompass nearly 12,000 years. The first 10,000 years include two distinct periods, the Paleo-Indian, focused on big-game hunting, and the Archaic, when economies included a wider variety of wild resources. The last 2,000 years record the evolution of farming communities and the arrival of the Athapaskans and the Europeans.

Paleo-Indian, ca. 10,000 B.C.–6000 B.C. Two small southwestern towns gave their names to the most widespread early hunting complexes in the Americas—the Clovis Spear Point Complex, used in taking extinct species of elephant, and the Folsom Complex, associated with extinct species of North American bison. In the west, along the Colorado River, Clovis is succeeded by the San Dieguito Complex, focused on plant resources and smaller animals. In the east, Clovis is succeeded by Folsom, and then by a series of other big-game hunting complexes, including Plainview, Agate Basin, Firstview, Cody, and Jay. Perhaps because the region's woodlands were not rich environments for Pleistocene fauna, the North American Southwest was only lightly occupied in this period.

Archaic, ca. 6000 B.C.–A.D. 200. Around 8,000 years ago, new regional differences developed in tool kits and in adaptive strategies. These Archaic technologies were responses to the postglacial landscape of highly seasonal productivity and considerably smaller prey species. Whether Archaic adaptations developed *in situ* from the Paleo-Indian occupation, or whether Paleo-Indian populations followed the large bison herds out of the area before 6000 B.C., is still an open question. Open as well is the nature of the relationship between regional Archaic patterns and the succeeding agriculturally based occupations. In terms of regional coverage, the Oshara tradition of the northern portions of the Southwest overlaps with the succeeding Anasazi tradition, the Cochise with the Hohokam and the western margins of the Mogollon, the San Dieguito and Pinto with the cultures of the lower Colorado River, and the Hueco and Coahuila with the eastern Mogollon.

The Late Archaic, ca. 2000 B.C.–A.D. 200, is marked by the introduction of three important domesticates: maize, beans, and squash. Maize becomes a significant part of the diet and a controlling factor in settlement organization first in the southwest part of the region. Here, ca. 500 B.C., sedentary but not pottery-using agriculturalists used pit-house architecture, storage features, trash mounds, cemeteries, and imported shell ornaments. Elsewhere, domestic crops seem to have been only slowly incorporated into diversified hunting and gathering economies. The pit house, a wood-framed room with an earthen pit foundation and an earth-covered exterior, remained the basic domestic architecture for the next twelve centuries across the North American Southwest.

Early Agriculturally-Based Communities, ca. A.D. 200–A.D. 750. The period from about A.D. 200 to A.D. 750 saw the introduction of ceramic technologies, small dispersed settlements, economies organized around farming, and the development of the three major prehistoric traditions of the agricultural Southwest: Hohokam, Anasazi, and Mogollon. The *Hohokam culture was centered on the irrigated lands of the middle Gila and Salt Rivers in what is now southern Arizona; the Mogollon culture on the eastern Arizona and western New Mexico highlands and the southern Rio Grande drainage; and the *Anasazi culture on the southern Colorado plateaus.

Pottery appears in the Hohokam area between A.D. 200 and A.D. 500 along with a settlement style of scattered, free-standing houses organized around a central plaza that carries through the next five centuries. The spatial relationships between structures in early Mogollon and Anasazi settlements are less clear. Some of these communities contain a large pit structure known as a "great kiva," so called because they share certain features with the ceremonial structures, or kivas, found in historic pueblos. They are large enough to allow a small community to gather inside or to use as staging areas for communal ceremony. In each area, these small farming communities arise from local, Archaic bases.

Although the Hohokam settlements are year-round sedentary occupations, the early settlements of the Mogollon and Anasazi were occupied only periodically. Shabik'eschee, an early Anasazi habitation, may have been occupied in response to natural production cycles in wild pinyon nuts, while the early Mogollon SU site appears to have been more dependent on agricultural crops. Agricultural dependence varied widely between these early settlements. In general, however, Anasazi settlements appear more agri-

culturally focused, and Mogollon economies were evenly balanced between hunting, gathering, and farming.

Village Development and Organization, ca. A.D. 750–A.D. 900. Regional population increases and increasingly sedentary occupations changed the nature of southwestern occupations toward the end of the first millennium A.D. In the Hohokam area, ca. A.D. 700, and the Anasazi area after A.D. 750, sedentary villages of more than 100 inhabitants form in those areas previously characterized by smaller settlements. Some Hohokam hamlets seem to grow into villages, while others are occupied contemporaneously with the larger sites. Hohokam households shared courtyard spaces, cemeteries, and possibly some economic tasks.

In the Anasazi Southwest, these new villages are aggregates of once-dispersed, smaller hamlets. They are composed of long rows of single-story "apartment" houses, each with a front living room and two or more storerooms accessible only through the front. Households shared community areas, including plazas and small pit structures that contain both domestic and ceremonial features. Great kivas may have served the entire community. Unlike the Hohokam, the Anasazi did not inter their dead in formal cemeteries.

Pit house–based settlements, some containing over fifty structures, continue to characterize the Mogollon area at this time. These may be seasonally occupied or year-round settlements; great kiva structures served the entire community. Interestingly, although individual settlements in each area appear to be forming unique identities at this time, pottery decoration links the entire region: Identical patterns may be found on Hohokam buff ceramics, Mogollon brown wares, and Anasazi white wares.

Hohokam, Mimbres, and Chaco Regional Systems, ca A.D. 900–A.D. 1150. At the end of the first millennium A.D., markedly different regional systems developed in the Hohokam, Mogollon, and Anasazi areas. Hohokam villages reached their peak in size and in numbers as irrigation-supported settlements expanded into the river drainages surrounding the Salt and Gila River basins. In the larger villages, craft specialists were making pottery and shell ornaments for local markets and export.

Hohokam settlements of this period were laid out along formal lines, with mud-plastered, formally shaped trash mounds oriented to platforms, central plazas, crematoriums, cemeteries that served various segments of the community, and ball courts. These last are large, open ovals outlined by earthen embankments where local versions of a Mesoamerican-derived ball game were played.

Along the Mimbres and other drainages in the southwestern Mogollon area, pit-house communities of the last half of the first millennium A.D. were transformed in place into rambling, single-story pueblo complexes that may have housed several hundred residents. A dozen of these new, irrigation-supported villages formed the core of the Mimbres Mogollon occupation, well known for its strikingly painted black-and-white bowls that show scenes from ceremonial and domestic contexts. This pottery style evolved locally from a red-on-brown Mogollon tradition.

While the architecture of the Mimbres villages suggests a sedentary occupation, numerous small sites—some with pit houses and some with only surface rooms—share the ceramics of the large villages, suggesting that the Mogollon moved between settlement types in an annual round. Painted pottery scenes suggest the presence of religious specialists among the Mimbres and hint at long-distance expeditions to the Gulf of California and the western Mexico coast.

The late first millennium A.D. sees the development of a regional pattern of small pueblos clustered around multistory, communal "great houses" in the Anasazi area. These "great houses" are carefully planned buildings that include kivas, multistory pueblo rooms, and plazas; individual rooms are large and have massive walls and roofs. The associated small pueblos were constructed as habitations and work spaces on an *ad hoc* basis. The great house/small house system appears to have originated in Chaco Canyon. "Outlier" settlements occur across the San Juan basin and beyond, in what is now northern New Mexico, eastern Arizona, southeastern Utah, and southwestern Colorado. Elsewhere in the Anasazi Southwest, this period is marked by the establishment of numerous small settlements.

Regional Reorganizations, ca. A.D. 1150–A.D. 1300. In each of the three regions, the A.D. 1100s and 1200s are a period of reorganization. Drought in the A.D. 1130s and 1140s probably initiated changes in the Mimbres area and in the Chacoan communities of the San Juan basin; the Hohokam area may have been affected indirectly through change on its northern and eastern borders.

For the Hohokam, this is a time of retrenchment along the main Salt and Gila drainages. Walled compounds and multistory adobe buildings replaced the dispersed houses of the earlier villages; ball courts ceased to be built, and platform mounds became increasingly common. Some mounds supported what appear to be elite residences. These elites, possibly a managerial class, may have developed in response to the collapse of the larger regional system.

The northern portions of what had been the Mogollon area are now incorporated into the Anasazi tradition. In the southern Mogollon area, rambling pueblos were replaced by walled compounds and adobe architecture, and the region became tied to the emerging northern Mexico center of Paquime, or *Casas Grandes. Paquime, which reached its peak population of some 4,700 in the mid-fourteenth century, apparently served as a distribution point for ornaments and other valuables and for a distinctive polychrome pottery industry that included numerous effigy pot forms. A new polychrome pottery was also locally produced and widely traded at this time in the Hohokam region and the immediately adjacent areas to the east.

This is a period of abandonment of the northwestern reaches of the Anasazi region, and the development of large, masonry pueblos elsewhere where multihousehold groups shared courtyards, kivas, grinding rooms, and storage space. Water-control features are associated with almost every twelfth- and thirteenth-century village, suggesting intensified agricultural production. Close to the Rio Grande, and in the far-western Anasazi region, settlement continued in small, dispersed pueblos.

Regional Abandonments and Pan-Southwest Reorganizations, after 1300. The end of the thirteenth century brings with it the Great Drought of 1276–1299, the consequent abandonment of the northern stretches of the North American Southwest, and the establishment of very large settlements elsewhere, including those portions of the Southwest occupied at the time of Spanish contact. As the northern farmlands were abandoned, population concentrated in widely separated areas in the eastern and southwestern sections. Throughout the fourteenth and fifteenth centuries, large villages were founded and abandoned in the vicinity of the Hopi mesas, in the Cibola region that is the core of ancestral Zuñi and Acoma territory, along the northern Rio Grande, and in what is now southern Arizona.

The 1300s also saw the rise of a widespread religious ideology that involved *kachinas,* the ancestor spirit beings who bring rain and well-being to the villages of the Southwest. Today, kachinas are represented by masked dancers in Pueblo village ceremonies, and the kachina concept is one of the unifying features of Pueblo religion. Two different areas are implicated in the origin of the modern kachina dances: the southern Mogollon area, where some masked dancers are shown on some Mimbres vessels from the early 1100s and individual masks occur as rock art around 1200 or 1300, and the far-western Anasazi area ca. 1300, where kachina figures are depicted in pottery in sites identified as ancestral Hopi villages.

Many of the fourteenth- and fifteenth-century villages were abandoned before the arrival of the Spanish. Some may have been lost to European diseases in advance of actual European contact. Raids and harassment from nomadic peoples probably played a role as well. Although the Athapaskan (Navajo, Apache, and Ute) peoples were present in the Southwest at European contact, the exact timing of their arrival in the region remains unknown. Archaeological evidence from the southern Great Plains identifies Athapaskan peoples hunting and foraging on the western margins of the southern Great Plains in the fifteenth century. Two centuries later, their role as trade partners to Pueblo and other aggregated communities is well documented in historic accounts. By this time, too, the Utes have begun to raid both the villagers and the Navajos. Oral histories place the Utes and Navajos in the North American Southwest as early as the twelfth century. At any rate, the interactions between the nomads and the long-resident Pueblo peoples have altered and shaped the region's cultures for over five centuries. For the past four and a half centuries, these cultures have shared the Southwest with the most recent arrivals, the Europeans.

[See also ATHABASKAN CULTURES OF THE AMERICAN SOUTHWEST; CHACOAN PHENOMENA; COCHISE CULTURE; MESA VERDE; MOGOLLON AND MIMBRES CULTURES; ROCK ART: NORTH AMERICAN ROCK ART]

■ Alfred V. Kidder, *An Introduction to the Study of Southwestern Archaeology* (1924). Alfred V. Kidder, "Southwestern Archaeological Conference," *Science* 68 (1927): 489–491. Charles C. DiPeso, *Casas Grandes: A Fallen Trading Center of the Gran Chichimeca* (vols. 1–4) (1974). David R. Wilcox and W. Bruce Masse, eds., *The Protohistoric Period in the North American Southwest, A.D. 1450–1700* (1981). J. Jefferson Reid and David E. Doyel, eds., *Emil W. Haury's Prehistory of the American Southwest* (1986). George J. Gumerman, ed., *The Anasazi in a Changing Environment* (1988). Patricia L. Crown and W. James Judge, eds., *Chaco and Hohokam: Prehistoric Regional Systems in the American Southwest* (1991). R. G. Matson, *The Origins of Southwestern Agriculture* (1991). George J. Gumerman, ed., *Themes in Southwest Prehistory* (1994).

Sarah H. Schlanger

THE NORTH AMERICAN WEST

The Paleo-Indian, or Pre-Archaic, Period marks the initial colonization by 11,500 B.P. of the Great Basin, the Columbia plateau, the Snake River Plain, the northern Colorado Plateau, interior California, and the mountains associated with these regions. Claims for earlier presence exist, and are reasonable on some grounds, but remain to be demonstrated. The concept "Paleo-Indian" highlights the notion of an advancing wave of colonists moving through an uninhabited landscape. This circumstance shaped human behavioral patterns and is an adaptive situation for which there is no modern analogy.

A technology featuring fluted projectile points (e.g., Clovis and Folsom) is often associated with the period, although large bifaces termed "Western Stemmed" are also present. Nearly all fluted points found in the region are from undated surface sites, and their ages are based on cross-dating with North American Great Plains occurrences. They are found widely in the region, but are strongly biased toward valley settings, and especially those reflecting lake-edge and wetland ecosystems of the Pleistocene/Holocene transition. Western Stemmed bifaces are known from some of the earliest dated sites in the region, but they persist into later periods, making it difficult to rely on surface occurrences to demonstrate antiquity.

Paleo-Indian lifeways are poorly documented in the west and suffer from stereotypes of big-game hunting lifeways applied uncritically from the Plains. It is clear that human presence in the western plateaus, deserts, and mountains temporally overlapped with that of various extinct mammals, but the associations are generally weak. Rather, the typical pattern is human presence beginning in levels above those containing extinct mammals and in association with Holocene taxa, especially bighorn sheep. Lifeways for the Paleo-Indian were likely variable given the ecological diversity of the region. This theme exemplifies the subsequent Archaic Period or stage, and some continuity or overlap in lifeways between the two periods is realistic. On the other hand, the fact that the first colonists encountered an open ecological niche would have favored a focus on the least expensive resources (large and medium mammals), a mobile settlement pattern, and little reliance on food storage. The paucity of grinding stones for the earliest occupations in the region is consistent with little emphasis on storage. Furthermore, some of the strategies of stone tool manufacture and raw material use are consistent with higher mobility than in later periods. In a metaphorical sense, the concept of Paleo-Indian may best be restricted to the advancing (and perhaps temporally narrow) wave of human colonization, with subsequent in-filling behind this wave described as Archaic.

The Archaic is a concept applied continentwide in North America to identify a stage of cultural evolution after initial colonization and persisting until the adoption of farming in some parts of the region. In the West, this encompasses over 8,000 years. Two somewhat contrasting interpretations of the Western Archaic are found. One emphasizes the variability in foraging lifeways incorporated in this concept, ranging from tethered foragers employing logistic systems shifting resources to central bases, to frequently nomadic adaptations, and all possibilities in between. The other view emphasizes a specific pattern for the Western Archaic, that of a flexible lifeway, geared to ecological diversity and to the changing circumstances typical of a foraging life in the region.

A trend of expanding diet breadth to include high- as well as low-cost resources is evident across space and through time in the Western Archaic as new ecological niches were exploited. The costs of procuring and processing resources is lowest with large mammals, and with decreases in the abundance of less-expensive resources, diet broadens to incorporate higher-cost foods. As general groups, these are, respectively, medium to small mammals, waterfowl, and fish; large nuts, roots, and seeds; and finally

a broad suite of expensive small seeds. Grinding stones are used for various tasks, but their routine use signals the increased processing of vegetal resources, especially hard nuts and seeds, for storage. This pattern appears first in the north and eastern Great Basin and Snake River Plain (10,000 B.P.); followed by the western and central Great Basin, and northern Colorado Plateau (between 6000 and 7000 B.P.); and the deserts of the southern Great Basin, and interior California (after 5000 B.P.). The process reflected in the time- and space-transgressive expansion of diet traces the increasingly intense human use of the region.

The relatively expensive seeds added to the diet are storable, reducing risk from fluctuations in food availability during the winter and between harvests. Storage in turn promotes tethering to local resources. Tethering is not synonymous with sedentism, and can encompass wide variance in the tempo and character of mobility as well as variance in the size of foraging ranges. Some regions, such as interior California, developed greater compartmentalization during the Archaic, while others, such as the central Great Basin, exhibited large foraging ranges. The process of diet expansion, storage, and tethering to local landscapes reflects the development of social organization defining increasingly bounded entities exhibiting local and subregional patterns. This is a feature of Archaic social patterns and is evident in the regional differentiation of material culture.

Archaic lifeways in the West can be generalized, acknowledging variation across space and change through time. A distinction between desert/mountain foraging systems versus those featuring settlement tethered to wetland environments is useful. Rather than fully nomadic, foragers of the desert/mountain Archaic moved intermittently in response to a patchy distribution of food and nonfood resources and were tethered by these resources as well as the locations of stored winter foods. Due to transportation costs, storage is likely to be close to the place of acquisition, but where environments exhibit concentrations of different resources the use of multiple central bases is promoted. Reflecting these options, camps occupied from a few days to well over a month are found in all ecosystems except the highest altitudes, which were occupied at varying intensities through the Archaic and later periods. Winter residential camps require a wood supply (a significant problem in large portions of the region with cold winters and little timber), proximity to stored foods, and may be occupied from a few weeks to several months, flagging the possibility of multiple winter camps. In all but the southern Great Basin deserts, potable water is not a primary determinant of settlement. Subsistence includes large and small mammals, birds, reptiles, insects, and a wide variety of roots and seeds. Variety in staple, storable vegetal foods requiring processing includes camas roots on the Columbia Plateau/Snake River Plain beginning by at least 4000–5000 B.P., piñon nuts in the Great Basin and northern Colorado Plateau by 5000–6000 B.P., and yucca hearts and mesquite pods in the southern deserts by perhaps 5000 B.P. Housing consists of natural shelters, brush windbreaks, and, most commonly, wickiups of brush, woven mats, logs covered with earth, and perhaps hides in some cases.

The distinction of a wetland lifeway focus has long been recognized in the region as a settlement-resource system with increased residential stability and, in some cases, logistic systems linked to central bases in wetlands. However, Archaic wetland systems are not categorically sedentary.

Wetlands supported higher population densities for at least portions of the year, and recurrently occupied camps indicate greater settlement stability than in most desert/ mountain areas. Resources include waterfowl, fish, large and small mammals, roots, and seeds, which can occur in relatively high densities in wetlands, and in closely spaced patches, lessening transport costs. Housing includes all forms mentioned for the desert/mountain systems with the addition of pit houses featuring relatively substantial pole/ log/earth superstructures, and reflecting greater investment in a stable, or at least a highly redundant, settlement pattern. Archaic pit houses appear by 5000 B.P. on the Columbia Plateau and western Snake River Plain, and mid–Late Archaic pit houses are known in rarer instances in the Great Basin and on the northern Colorado Plateau.

Wetland habitats are found in a patchy distribution, and through time decrease first in the southern portions of the region, with the clearest examples persisting in the northwestern and northeastern Great Basin. Portions of the Snake River and its tributaries exhibit riverine habitats tethering settlement through salmon fishing, although increasing distance from the ocean decreases the duration, size, and species diversity of salmon runs. Thus, interior systems exploiting salmon contrast with those on the Pacific coast in being less intensive, less specialized, and less politically complex. Wetland adaptive strategies are not known on the northern Colorado Plateau, even during moist climatic intervals within the Archaic, although wetland resources on a local scale were incorporated into the desert/mountain forager systems in that region.

Variability in Archaic lifeways also occurs through time. An example is the expansion of the piñon pine tree from Pleistocene homelands in the Southwest, north into the Great Basin and Colorado Plateau, reaching its northern limits around 7000–6000 B.P. The addition of piñon nuts, an abundant, storable resource less expensive to exploit than the small seeds already in use, stimulated a settlement system featuring the storage of large quantities of piñon nuts. This lifeway persisted into the historic period.

While the region exhibits a long history of in-place development, interaction among areas and with other regions is apparent. The Snake and Salmon Rivers formed corridors to the Plains, although links to the Great Basin are also evident. In the southern Great Basin, links with California and the Southwest become more apparent by about 3000 B.P. The northeastern Great Basin and northern fringe of the Colorado Plateau show Plains interaction, with southwestern affiliation increasing to the south, especially after 2000 B.P. In California, interaction between the interior and coastal populations is evident.

The Archaic ends with the adoption of domesticated corn, beans, and squash in the eastern Great Basin, the northern Colorado Plateau, and perhaps the eastern Snake River Plain. The Archaic continues in the mountains, the higher latitudes, interior California, and the dry areas of the Great Basin. The adoption of domesticates indicates interaction with southwestern peoples, but it was local populations that incorporated the domesticates. Corn is adopted in central Utah by 2200 B.P., followed a few centuries later by the bow and arrow, and a few centuries after that by ceramics. This time-transgressive pattern directs attention away from the migration of entire peoples to account for agricultural adoption. Rather, farming was a process resulting from trends in the Archaic coupled with the availability of domesticates. Their adoption required systems where

diet was broad, settlement was stable, or redundant, and systems possibly experiencing local population growth from reductions in mobility. Domesticates require greater expenditure of effort but set a trajectory toward intensification, resulting in higher productivity and reduced risk. These further stimulated population growth, ensuring spread of the farming strategy and consequent embellishment/intensification. Known as the Fremont culture, it is a local development with clear distinctions in material culture (e.g., basketry) and cultigens (unique form of corn, "Dent") from the Anasazi of the Southwest and spanning the period from about 1600 to 650 B.P. Fremont adaptive strategies ranged from people fully reliant on farming, to a variable reliance during the lives of individuals, to co-resident foragers/farmers. During this time ceramics were available to any group whose settlement system fostered their incorporation, and while farming diminished by 600 B.P., ceramic use continued in parts of the desert West until historic times—including parts of the region that never adopted farming.

The millennium spanning the spread and contraction of farming surely was a time of large-scale demographic fluidity due to the migration of individuals and small groups. During this time and the subsequent Late Prehistoric Period, many historically known language groups (Shoshoni, Ute, and Southern Paiute), known as the Numic, achieved their present distributions. The details and the timing of this process are debated among archaeologists and to a lesser extent among linguists. The variability known for the Archaic period also describes lifeways immediately prior to the protohistoric and historic periods, marked by the adoption of the horse and other material culture, and by European/Euro-American exploration.

[See also FREMONT FARMERS; HIGH ALTITUDE OCCUPATIONS IN THE AMERICAN WEST; HUNTER-GATHERERS, NORTH AMERICAN ARCHAIC.]

■ Robert L. Heizer ed., *The Handbook of North American Indians*, vol. 8, *California* (1978). David B. Madsen and James F. O'Connell, eds., *Man and Environment in the Great Basin* (1982). David H. Thomas, "The Archaeology of Monitor Valley I: Epistemology," American Museum of Natural History Anthropological Papers 58:1 (1983). Michael J. Moratto, *California Archaeology* (1984). Warren L. d'Azevedo, ed., *The Handbook of North American Indians*, vol. 11, *The Great Basin* (1986). David B. Madsen, *Exploring the Fremont* (1989). Donald K. Grayson, *The Desert's Past: A Natural Prehistory of the Great Basin* (1993).

Steven R. Simms

THE NORTHWEST COAST OF NORTH AMERICA

The Northwest Coast extends south some 1,120 miles (1,800 km) along the Pacific coast of North America from Icy Strait, Alaska, to Cape Mendoceno, California. Researchers commonly divide the culture area into three subareas: the northern coast (the northern British Columbia mainland, the Queen Charlotte Islands, and southeastern Alaska), the central coast (most of Vancouver Island and the adjacent mainland), and the southern coast (southern British Columbia mainland, southern Vancouver Island, western Washington and Oregon, and the northern California coast). When Europeans first entered the northeastern Pacific Ocean in large numbers during the middle and late eighteenth century, the native societies they encountered were among the most populous and socially complex hunter-gatherer societies known in human history. These societies shared several key traits: The basic economic unit was the extended house hold; households lived together in large, semi- to fully sedentary villages and towns of large, rectangular, well-made wooden houses; the subsistence economy relied on a wide range of resources, but focused on salmon, particularly stored salmon; household members were ranked by ascribed statuses; the highest-ranking household members formed an elite; slaves formed the lowest stratum of society.

Archaeological research on the coast emphasizes reconstructing and explaining the developmental history of these cultures, including when people on the coast began to rely heavily on stored salmon, when they began living in permanent villages, and when the coast's chiefly elite developed. They have also been concerned with tracing the history of the Northwest Coast's famous art style. Other important archaeological research issues involve the coast's role in the early peopling of the Americas and the development of maritime economies along the West Coast of North America and in the northern Pacific generally.

The coast's culture history is divisible into two major periods, an early one spanning the time between ca. 11,000 B.P. and 5500 B.P. and a later period between 5500 B.P. and contact with Europeans.

Early Period (11,000–5500 B.P.). The earliest firmly dated archaeological sites on the coast tend to date to ca. 10,000 B.P. These sites include Glacier Bay and Hidden Falls in southeastern Alaska and Namu on the central British Columbia coast. One possible site—the Manis Mastodon site on northwestern Washington State—produced three dates spanning the period between 11,000 and 10,000 B.P. That Manis is an archaeological site is not, however, firmly established. It is likely that the coast was occupied at least by 11,500 to 11,000 B.P. This presumption is supported by the presence of Clovis materials east of the south coast, and by recent geological research showing that extensive portions of the presently drowned continental shelf were exposed and ice-free more than 10,000 years ago. Knut Fladmark has even suggested that the Northwest Coast was the primary route by which America's first inhabitants entered the continent. At present this hypothesis is neither supported nor refuted by archaeological evidence, as there is no data that bears directly on the question. The number of excavated sites increases after 8000 B.P. Namu and Glen Rose Cannery, located near Vancouver British Columbia, are the major deeply stratified sites for the latter portions of the early period.

Early period archaeological assemblages on the northern and central coast differ from those found on the southern coast. Northern and some central coastal sites (such as Namu) contain microblades and microblade cores similar to those found in Alaska and northeast Asia, while southern coastal assemblages are dominated by an array of chipped stone tools, including laurel-leaf-shaped bifaces and cobble tools. These assemblages are similar to assemblages found east of the Cascade Mountain Range on the Columbia plateau at this time. Available subsistence data, including faunal remains, artifact assemblages, and site locations, indicate that at least after 8000 B.P. a broad array of resources were taken from an equally broad array of environments, including terrestrial ones as well as riverine, littoral, and pelagic waters. Features such as hearths or postholes that might indicate residential patterns are rare.

Late, or Pacific, Period (5500 B.P. to Contact). The Pacific Period is marked by the evolution of Northwest Coast culture as encountered in the eighteenth century. The period is known by a variety of names (Developmental, Late, Pacific),

depending on the author, and is always subdivided into three subperiods.

Early Pacific (5500–3500 B.P.). The beginning of the Pacific Period is marked by the disappearance of microblade technology in the north, and by the appearance of large *shell middens all along the coast between 5500 and 4500 B.P. (Shell middens are accumulations of shells of mollusks such as clams and mussels mixed with other organic and nonorganic debris produced by human activity. Shell middens are excellent environments for the preservation of bone, so Northwest Coast archaeologists have much more data about technology and subsistence for the Late period than for the Early period. Large shell middens do not appear on the Washington and Oregon coasts until after 3500 B.P.) The appearance of shell middens heralds significant changes in settlement, residential, and subsistence patterns, including increased exploitation of mollusks. These changes may in part be the result of the stabilization of sea levels along portions of the coast, to population growth, and to coastwide changes in salmon productivity or other, unknown factors. It is clear that during this subperiod, the basic structure of the ethnographically documented Northwest Coast subsistence economy and technology developed. There is presently debate about whether salmon storage began playing a significant economic role during this or the next subperiod. There is also debate over whether permanent elites were present on the coast before the end of this subperiod. There is evidence for relatively elaborate funeral rituals by 4000–3500 B.P., and some individuals during that time received special treatment when they were buried. Ethnographic status markers, including lip plugs (labrets) are present by 3500 B.P. The earliest examples of motifs related to the Northwest Coast art style date between 4000 and 3500 B.P. There is very little evidence about residences or other aspects of life.

Middle Pacific (3500–1500 B.P.). The Middle Pacific Period is one of profound economic, social, and cultural developments. The weight of available evidence indicates that widespread, heavy reliance on stored salmon developed between ca. 3500 and 3000 B.P. The earliest villages and rectangular surface houses date between 3200 and 2600 B.P. The Paul Mason site in northern British Columbia is the coast's best-preserved early village, with evidence for twelve houses dating between 3200 and 2800 B.P. Large samples of excavated burials from Prince Rupert Harbor in northern British Columbia and the Gulf of Georgia in southern British Columbia clearly indicate the coastwide presence of an elite by 2500 B.P. Grave goods include such wealth and prestige items as copper ornaments, shell (including dentalium) and stone beads, whale bone clubs, and stone labrets. The acquisition and making of some of these items required long-distance trade and specialized artisans. The burial and artifactual data also indicate widespread warfare. Sites are much more numerous and generally much larger than previously, suggesting more intensive occupation and larger populations. The art style was well developed by 2200 B.P. Subsistence evidence, beyond indicating salmon storage, suggests that people continued to expand food production throughout the period and in some areas developed heavy reliance on sea mammals.

Late Pacific (1500 B.P. to ca. A.D. 1750). It is generally thought that the ethnographically documented societies and cultures of the coast were present by the beginning of the Late Pacific Period. The beginning of the period is marked by a profound change in funerary ritual. During the previous two subperiods, a portion of the population was buried in the shell middens, in both residential and nonresidential sites. In some instances at least, these interments appear to have been immediately behind the dead's household. These graves are the major source of evidence about social changes, and include other important data about health and diet. This practice ceases almost completely along the coast by 1200 B.P., though younger midden burials are known. This shift probably indicates the beginnings of the burial practices of the late eighteenth and early nineteenth centuries. The reasons for the shift are unknown. On the southern coast, the Late Pacific Period is also marked by shifts in technology, probably related to fishing equipment and to the development of new fishing techniques. There are indications all along the coast of increased levels of warfare. In the north, there may have been parallel changes in social and household organization. The Northwest Coast art style appears to have taken on its historic form by ca. 900 B.P. in the north. In the south, there are tantalizing suggestions that the roles of decoration and art motifs may have changed, relative to their roles both in the north and during previous subperiods in the north and south.

European explorers and traders entering Northwest Coast waters in the eighteenth century may have been preceded by Old World epidemic diseases, particularly small pox, and by trade goods. Despite the profound impact of the last two centuries, Northwest Coast native history is preserved not only in archaeology but in the oral traditions of the coast's people.

■ Wayne Suttles, *Handbook of North American Indians*, vol. 7, *The Northwest Coast* (1991).

Kenneth M. Ames

HISTORICAL ARCHAEOLOGY OF NORTH AMERICA

Although its period of recorded history is relatively brief, the archaeological record of North America over the last 1,000 years is rich. From Viking settlements on Canada's Atlantic coast to the camps of California's gold seeking "forty-niners," archaeological techniques have been used since the nineteenth century to explore North American history. In contrast to Europe, where the term "post-medieval" archaeology is mainly applied to industrial sites, historical archaeology in North America has always been oriented toward documenting the experience of the people who colonized and lived upon this "new" land.

*Historical archaeology is based upon the principle that the written and the archaeological records are complementary. While prehistorians must be content with analogy and experimentation to guide their studies, historical archaeologists often work with written accounts that speak directly of the meaning of artifacts and sites to the people who created them. Yet historical archaeology is not validated only when it makes entirely new discoveries in the field. Rather, its method is to combine archaeological and historical information to create insights that are greater than either source could have contributed independently. To paraphrase Kathleen Deagan, historical archaeology is the archaeological study of human behavior, in which interpretations are influenced by historical sources.

Deagan's emphasis on historical archaeology as an approach to the study of human behavior, as distinct from history, is typical of the post–World War II generation of anthropological archaeologists. James Deetz's dictum that archaeology is "anthropology or nothing," is in keeping with the historical ties between Americanist archaeology and anthropology. Until as late as the 1960s, however, historical archaeology was largely the domain of practitioners who looked toward the discipline of history for their direction and goals.

The first archaeologists in North America to take seriously the excavation of historic period remains were motivated by the desire to honor their forebears by reconstructing their homes and workplaces. For example in 1856, the house of seventeenth-century settler Myles Standish was investigated with great care by an ancestor. Later, in the 1920s, architects began to use archaeology to help reconstruct eighteenth-century buildings in the colonial capital of Williamsburg, Virginia.

Although by the 1950s, organizations such as the U. S. National Park Service and Colonial Williamsburg employed specialists in historical archaeology, it was not until 1960 that the first university course devoted to the subject was taught. The potential of this field was recognized by the "New Archaeology" of the 1960s, and it was soon dominated by anthropologically trained archaeologists. With the founding of the journal *Historical Archeology* in 1967, the field finally had its own national forum.

A Laboratory for Archaeological Principles. Historical archaeologists have an independent source, the written record, against which to test their interpretations of excavated artifacts. By examining historic period remains, archaeologists have been able to examine critically several analytical methods widely used by archaeologists working in prehistoric periods.

In their classic study of individually dated eighteenth- and nineteenth-century New England gravestones, Edwin Dethlefsen and James Deetz confirmed the assumptions behind both stylistic and frequency seriation. The researchers found that the sequential changes in popularity of three decorative motifs—death's-head, cherub, and urn-and-willow—were indeed described by unimodal "battleship-shaped" statistical curves. Further, Dethlefsen and Deetz showed that the death's-head motif went through a series of subtle changes that converted a naturalistic winged skull to a barely recognizable, abstract form.

Although ethnographic analogy suggested that archaeologists can detect status differences within a population by examining food residues, a study by Peter Schulz and Sherri Gust of four mid-nineteenth-century archaeological sites graphically confirmed the reliability of this type of analysis. On the basis of historic documents, the researchers were able to calculate the relative cost of each meat cut distinguished in the faunal remains in each of the sites they excavated: a city jail, two modest restaurants, and a first-class hotel. Next, the sites were ranked in order of the social status of their clientele by examining contemporary newspapers and other documents. When Schulz and Gust plotted the faunal data from each site as frequency curves, they found clear distinctions between the four establishments that reflected their historically documented statuses.

Analytic and Interpretive Tools in Historical Archaeology. The distinctive feature of historical archaeology, the ability to call upon written records, has lead to the development of several analytic tools. These include Stanley South's mean ceramic date formula, which is widely used to determine ranges of occupation for sites where the written record is incomplete or entirely absent. To calculate the mean ceramic date, one determines the median manufacture date of each ceramic type represented on the site (as determined by contemporary records), multiplies this by the number of sherds of each type, and divides the product by the total number of sherds. The resulting date is often within a few years of the historically documented occupation date and, some feel, a better indicator of a site's occupation than conventionally derived ceramic *terminus post quem* dates.

The mean date formula is often used in association with South's analytical approach known as pattern analysis. The approach is based on the premise that the shared behavioral pattern of every culture results in a uniform, archaeologically discernable pattern of artifact groups; South's groups include kitchen-related artifacts, clothing, architectural artifacts, arms, and so on. The pattern is manifested in the ratios of artifacts of each group recovered from a site. At the simplest level, for example, sites conforming to the "frontier pattern" show a high proportion of artifacts in the architectural field, such as nails, reflecting the limited artifactual array at sites on the Atlantic frontier.

George Miller's research on the cost of several types of English eighteenth- and nineteenth-century ceramics has made it possible to determine the relative investment made by sites' occupants in these wares. Even though ceramics were not a major item in the budget of most early North Americans, expensive ceramics have been found to correlate with high social status.

The practice of historical archaeology has, for obvious reasons, taken the practice of ethnographic analogy to new levels. In his work with the archaeology of blacksmith shops on the Canadian frontier, John Light used his knowledge of contemporary smithies to model the archaeological remains that are likely to be left by blacksmiths. He then successfully used this information to devise a field method to identify blacksmithing remains in the absence of slag, the distinctive by-product of forging.

Major Research Topics of Historical Archaeology. The tools of historical archaeology have been applied to a wide range of sites and research problems. From the frontier outposts of colonial Spain to late twentieth century municipal garbage dumps, historical archaeologists have challenged cherished beliefs about how Americans lived in the past as well as assumptions about modern society's patterns of behavior.

Exploration and Settlement. The Viking settlements of the Canadian coast, Martin Frobisher's short-lived gold mine on Baffin Island, and Sir Francis Drake's landfall on the coast of California have all been investigated by archaeologists seeking some of the earliest sites of European contact. Jamestown is important as both the site of the first permanent English settlement and as the scene of extensive archaeological investigations in the mid-1950s that led to the creation of a successful seventeenth-century living history village. Parks Canada, a government agency responsible for most historical archaeology on Canadian sites, has excavated numerous frontier forts and outposts of the Hudson's Bay Company. Although historical reconstruction has been the ostensible reason for much of this work, Canada's strongly bicultural character has made it important that the contributions of all segments of the country's population be represented in historical interpretations. Archaeologists have also investigated the American Far West boomtowns created by gold and silver miners of the 1850s and 1860s, as well as the rough camps of those who struggled over the Chilkoot Pass in the northern Rockies in the 1890s.

Race and Ethnicity. The development of a culturally pluralistic society is one of the key themes in the history of North America. Following the lead of the "New Social Historians" of the 1960s, historical archaeologists embraced this theme with studies of individual ethnic groups, and their interactions with each other and with Euro-American culture. Native Americans, African Americans, and ethnic Chinese have all been studied with the goal of documenting ethnic populations that have largely been excluded from conventional history.

David Hurst Thomas's massive series *Columbian Consequences* (1989, 1990, 1991) deals with the often-devastating effect on Native Americans of Spanish and Mexican settlement from Florida to California. On the Atlantic coast, the lifeways and development of a distinctly African-American culture, marked by the presence of a pottery type known as Colono Ware, have been documented from as early as the mid-seventeenth century. In the Far West, archaeologists have examined the work camps and urban settlements of late nineteenth-century Chinese immigrants to examine the lifeway of this poorly documented group and the validity of conventional notions of Chinese cultural conservatism.

Plantations and Slavery. Although late nineteenth-century black settlements have been studied from California to South Carolina, most research has focused on the archaeology of antebellum plantations in the southern United States. The goal of much work has been to emphasize the lives of black slaves who, although they outnumbered whites on plantations, were given short shrift in both the historic record and in historic house reconstructions. The ability of enslaved Africans and their descendants to maintain familiar lifeways while adapting to their new circumstances is well represented in traditional foodways, personal decoration, and architecture.

Industrial Workers and Industrial Archaeology. In contrast to the situation in Europe where the domain of the industrial archaeologist is generally limited to technological history, in North America the field is taken to include the social and cultural aspects of industrialism. The lives of workers in North American cities—from prostitutes to factory hands—have been studied archaeologically. Mary Beaudry and Steve Mrozowski's interdisciplinary study of the Lowell, Massachusetts, Boott Mill shows how the company used architecture, artifacts, and paternalistic policies to attempt to control the after-work lives of its largely female work force during the early nineteenth century.

Consumer Goods and Social Status. The range of material goods available to nineteenth-century North Americans was enormous compared with the previous century. Historical archaeologists have examined the effectiveness of the trade networks that brought goods to the most remote locations and the relative cost and availability factors that led to some artifacts becoming symbols of their owner's social standing. The significance of tea drinking, for example, gives tea paraphernalia (such as tea sets) in an archaeological collection of this period great interpretive potential, since it is evidence of household participation in this aspect of eighteenth-century colonial British culture.

The Archaeology of Trash. Historical archaeology extends even to the present day with William Rathje's Garbage Project. Since 1973, Rathje has sampled several modern regional garbage dumps to explode myths such as the perception of landfills as massive compost piles; in fact, as little as twenty percent of food waste decomposes in fifteen years of burial.

Theoretical Trends and Future Directions. Modern historical archaeology is more than merely the "handmaiden to history" or an exercise by which prehistorians may test their methods. The field is an eclectic mixture of anthropology, history, and folklore, employing a wide range of interpretative models. This diversity reflects the general emergence of Americanist archaeology from the orthodoxy of the "New Archaeology" into a wealth of post-processual orientations from *structuralism to marxist-influenced *critical theory.

Although much historical archaeology is still undertaken to reconstruct historic buildings, its practitioners are increasingly influenced by postmodern philosophers who see the archaeological record as a text to be interpreted rather than as an objective series of facts to be deduced in an investigative fashion. An outgrowth of this trend, and one that crosses the spectrum of theoretical orientations, is contextualism. This approach emphasizes intensive historical research to construct the context for interpretation and often focuses upon small-scale humanistic research issues.

The diverse approaches of North American historical archaeologists have tended to converge on a single theme—the influence and effects of mercantile and industrial capitalism on the peoples and cultures of the New World. This theme is emerging as the basis of a historical anthropology that links scholarship in a variety of fields in the study of the most significant process in North American history.

[See also BATTLEFIELD ARCHAEOLOGY OF NORTH AMERICA; EUROPEAN COLONIES IN THE NEW WORLD; FRONTIER SITES OF THE AMERICAN WEST; INDUSTRIAL ARCHAEOLOGY; MARTIN'S HUNDRED; MISSION ARCHAEOLOGY; NORSE IN NORTH AMERICA; PLANTATION LIFE IN THE SOUTHERN UNITED STATES; URBAN ARCHAEOLOGY.]

■ Ivor Noël-Hume, *Historical Archaeology* (1968). James Deetz, *In Small Things Forgotten: The Archaeology of Early American Life* (1977). Stanley South, *Method and Theory in Historical Archaeology* (1977). Mary Beaudry, ed., *Documentary Archaeology in the New World* (1988). Kathleen Deagan, "Neither History nor Prehistory: The Questions that Count in Historical Archaeology," *Historical Archaeology* 22, 1 (1988): 7–12. Mark Leone and Parker Potter, eds., *The Recovery of Meaning in Historical Archaeology in the Eastern United States* (1988). Douglas Scott et al., *Archaeological Perspectives on the Battle of the Little Big Horn* (1989). Randall McGuire and Robert Paynter, eds., *The Archaeology of Inequality* (1991). John Cotter, Daniel Roberto, and Michael Parrington, *The Buried Past: An Archaeological History of Philadelphia* (1992). Anne Yentsch, *A Chesapeake Family and Their Slaves* (1994).

Adrian Praetzellis

NORTH AMERICA, Origins of Food Production in.

At the time of the Columbian landfall, many Native American societies north of Mexico were dependent upon food produced in agricultural settings. There were two major regions where agricultural systems seem to have evolved—eastern and southwestern North America. The history of agricultural developments in these two areas has become increasingly well known in the past three decades, but is still colored by differential investigations and quality of data. Processes of development in the East are better understood than those of the Southwest.

History of Agricultural Thought. As recently as the early 1970s, the development of agriculture in the East and Southwest was thought to be largely derived from Mexico. The Tehuacan Project of Richard S. MacNeish of the R. S. Peabody Foundation for Archaeology (1964, 1967) and the Oaxaca Valley work of Kent Flannery of the University of Michigan Museum of Anthropology (1986) established a long sequence of Mesoamerican agricultural developments

beginning as early as 10,000 years ago. It was the work of these two scholars that established the presumed Mexican primacy of agriculture in North America.

Recent research, however, has challenged and even overturned the long-held belief that agricultural developments north of Mexico were nothing more than the simple diffusion of plant production from cultures to the south. While there is little doubt that many important cultigens traveled from the south to the north, there is ample evidence that at least in eastern North America, Mesoamerican domesticates were comparative latecomers in an agricultural tradition that stretches back at least four millennia. As more information is accumulated from the Southwest, it is likely that a similar lengthy horticultural tradition will emerge.

Agricultural Origins in Eastern North America. Building upon both his own original research and the work of many others, Bruce D. Smith, curator of North American Archaeology at the Smithsonian Institution, has provided excellent technical and popular summaries discussing origins of food production in eastern North America. Smith points out that food production developed independently in the East, and was not derived from Mexico. Although two of the best-known crop plants—corn (*Zea mays*) and the common bean (*Phaseolus vulgaris*)—were introduced from Mexico, they were latecomers to a process that had been initiated thousands of years earlier.

Indigenous agricultural developments in the East took place within a broad mid-latitudinal belt between about 34 to 40 degrees north, extending from the western edge of the Appalachians to the eastern prairies. Within this broad belt, Native Americans domesticated a number of indigenous annual plants. These include those with oily seeds or kernels—sumpweed (*Iva annua*, var. *macrocarpa*), sunflower (*Helianthus annuus*), and several types of gourd / squash of the genus *Cucurbita*—and those with starchy seeds—goosefoot (*Chenopodium berlandieri*, ssp. *jonesianum*).

Each of these annuals share several characteristics that make them pre-adapted for use by humans—all thrive in the disturbed habitats of annually reworked floodplain levees and sand and gravel banks of major rivers and streams, all produce hundreds and even thousands of individual seeds per plant, and all produce their seeds in convenient collecting "packages," which make them attractive to harvest.

Several of these plants began to be collected during the Middle Archaic period (ca. 6000–5000 B.P.), but evidence of morphological changes associated with domestication does not appear until almost two thousand years later (ca. 4000 B.P.) near the end of the Late Archaic Period. A wild *Cucurbita* gourd may have been domesticated by around 3500 B.P. Two of the small-seeded annuals, goosefoot and sumpweed, were apparently domesticated about the same time.

By the beginning of the Early Woodland Period (ca. 3000 B.P.) there is ample evidence for the widespread use of domesticated annuals across the Midwest. In addition to those plants evincing morphological differences that imply domestication, there are also a group of plants that were apparently intensively cultivated, but the selective pressures of gardening were not great enough to bring about morphological change. These include maygrass (*Phalaris caroliniana*), little barley (*Hordeum pusillum*), erect knotweed (*Polygonum erectum*), and, possibly, giant ragweed (*Ambrosia trifida*).

The so-called Eastern Agricultural Complex filled the dietary needs of foragers who were dependent on the interannual variability in the production of nuts from canopy-level trees.

Emergence of Maize Agriculture in the East. Fragments of maize kernels and cobs have been found in several eastern North American sites dating between 1700 and 1200 B.P., but maize does not become an important component of archaeological plant assemblages until after about 900–800 B.P.

The processes that led to the development of highly productive maize varieties is imperfectly understood, but most archaeobotanists feel that productive varieties emerged from a diverse early gene pool by around 900–800 B.P. One of these, the so-called Eastern Complex, or Northern Flint, corns became the dominant variety grown from the Ohio River northward into Canada. In the Southeast and the central Mississippi Valley, softer-kernelled ten- and twelve-row varieties were grown.

Agricultural Origins in the Desert Borderlands. The area referred to as the desert borderlands includes Arizona, New Mexico, southern Utah, and Colorado. The development of agricultural economies is not as well understood here as in eastern North America, but a spate of work in the past fifteen years has begun to provide new and exciting information about this process.

Archaeological sites in the desert borderlands have yet to yield a record similar to eastern North America, where gathering and, ultimately, growing small-seeded annuals was practiced for thousands of years before maize was introduced. In part, this may be a product of years of archaeological neglect of sites occupied by premaize, Archaic-aged foragers. As more Archaic sites are excavated, it can probably be safely predicted that evidence will accumulate to validate local histories of intensive small-seed use, and provide a better understanding of the role of indigenous, premaize crop plants in the Southwest.

Potential candidates for a "Southwestern Agricultural Complex" include various edible grasses: little barley (*Hordeum pusillum*), Sonoran panic grass (*Panicum sonorum*), maygrass (*Phalaris caroliniana*), Indian rice grass (*Oryzopsis hymenoides*), dye (beeweed, *Cleome serrulata*), and fiber (devil's claw, *Proboscidean parviflora*) plants.

While widespread evidence for the use of small seeds is not yet available, Mesoamerican domesticates were likely additions to an ancient system of plant collecting and probably cultivation. At the few Middle Archaic, premaize sites that have been excavated, it is apparent that seeds and mast from annual plants were intensively collected. Among these, seeds of piñon pine and walnut were particularly important autumn staples, with small-seeded annuals important seasonal components of the diet.

Initial Use of Maize. Archaeological excavations in the Mogollon Highlands of west-central New Mexico in the 1940s produced evidence of early maize cultivation at Bat and Tularosa Caves. In the absence of dated maize remains from areas outside of this region, until recently it was almost universally accepted that agriculture first entered the desert borderlands from northern Mexico via this highland route. From the highlands, with its cooler and moister environment, maize was assumed to have spread into drier lowland settings.

Based upon recent excavations and associated radiocarbon dates, maize was first introduced into the desert borderlands by the Late Archaic, as early as 3500 B.P., followed shortly thereafter by squash (2900 B.P.) and beans (2100 B.P.). There is little evidence for any sort of lag, however, in the distribution of agriculture. By 2900 B.P., Wills argues that maize was an important component of regional economies of the desert borderlands in both highland and lowland settings.

Wills has articulated two distinct models of early maize cultivation in the desert borderlands. One applies to the Colorado Plateau and associated Mogollon Mountains, and the other to the lower elevation Southern Basin and Range. In Wills's model, during this initial period (3500–2200 B.P.), maize cultivation is seen as a response by foragers to even out the interannual variability in fall-producing piñon, walnuts, and other seed bearers. In this scenario, maize was planted near areas where more desirable wild resources could be expected to be available for a fall harvest; location of fields in prime agricultural settings was not of importance. Rather than an attempt by foragers to increase productivity, early cultivation might more properly be viewed as "insurance" against the potential failure of more desirable nut crops.

To the south of the Mogollon Mountains, there is also evidence for early maize cultivation in the Southern Basin and Range by the Late Archaic Period. Unlike the highlands, where maize is primarily found in caves or rock shelters, maize in the Basin and Range is found in sites situated in alluvial settings. Several contain dense, deep middens with small pit houses, large storage pits, and multiple burials.

Here, Wills argues that maize was cultivated to improve the productivity of the local environment, not necessarily to reduce subsistence risk brought about by interannual variability in mast production. On the northern margins of the Basin and Range, one of the hypothesized benefits of maize production was to enable men to pursue extended hunting trips for desirable and prestigious game that occurred in the adjacent Colorado Plateau.

Later Agriculture in the Desert Borderlands. After 2200 B.P., the cultivation of maize, beans, and squash was fairly widespread in both upland and desert environments. The familiar Anasazi cultures of the four-corners area by and large practiced floodplain farming, while the Hohokam of the Southern Basin and Range made effective use of sophisticated irrigation canals to open desert areas for cultivation. Crop plants from Mexico continued to be introduced into the desert borderlands. One of the most important was cotton (*Gossypium hirsutum*), which arrived in the Hohokam area by around 1400 B.P. While woven cotton textiles are present in the Anasazi area of northern Arizona by around 1150 B.P., there is no evidence that the plant was actually cultivated outside of the Hohokam area until about 450 B.P. Because of its practical and ritual use, Ford concludes that cotton was probably the most widely distributed southwestern cultigen.

Other later crop plants include the drought-resistant tepary bean (*Phaseolus acutifolius*); lima, or sieva, bean (*Phaseolus lunatus*); jack bean (*Canavalia ensiformis*); the green striped cushaw (*Cucurbita argyrosperma*); and the butternut squash (*Cucurbita moschata*). Each of these species was introduced from Mexico prior to the Spanish *entrada* into the Southwest.

[See also MESOAMERICA, ORIGINS OF FOOD PRODUCTION IN; NORTH AMERICA, *articles on* THE EASTERN WOODLANDS AND THE SOUTH, THE NORTH AMERICAN SOUTHWEST.]

■ Michael S. Berry, *Space, Time, and the Anasazi Tradition* (1982). Richard I. Ford, ed., *Prehistoric Food Production in North America* (1985). Richard G. Matson, *The Origins of Southwestern Agriculture*

(1991). Bruce B. Huckell, "Maize Models: Review of the Origins of Southwestern Agriculture," *Science* 257 (1992): 1571–1572. Emily McClung de Tapia, "The Origins of Agriculture in Mesoamerica and Central America," in *The Origins of Agriculture: An International Perspective,* eds. C. Wesley Cowan and Patty Jo Watson (1992), pp. 143–172. Paul E. Minnis, "Earliest Plant Cultivation in the Desert Borderlands of North America," in *The Origins of Agriculture: An International Perspective,* eds. C. Wesley Cowan and Patty Jo Watson (1992), pp. 121–142. Bruce D. Smith, *Rivers of Change: Essays on Early Agriculture in Eastern North America* (1992). Wirt H. Wills, "Archaic Foraging and the Beginning of Food Production in the American Southwest," in *Last Hunters—First Farmers: New Perspectives on the Prehistoric Transition to Agriculture,* eds. T. D. Price and A. B. Gebaver (in press).

C. Wesley Cowan

NOTATION, Paleolithic.

As with language, the ability to manipulate numbers and to systematically record sequences of events is thought to be a uniquely human capacity. Indeed, Noam Chomsky has suggested that the human number faculty developed as a by-product of the language faculty. Archaeologists attempting to trace the emergence of the ability to use numbers and to create notations face numerous difficulties. First is the problem of preservation. The notational systems used by traditional, non-Western societies are normally marked on organic materials which have a notoriously poor preservation in the Early Paleolithic record. Second is a problem of interpretation: how can a series of marks on a Paleolithic artifact be recognized as an intentionally made sequence of symbolic significance—that is, as a notation—and distinguished from a decorative design or an unintended by-product of activities such as cutting plants on a bone support? A third problem relates to the expression of the ability to create notations. The presence of such ability does not necessarily mean it would have been expressed in such a way as to leave a material trace. This raises the important issue of the social and economic contexts in which we should expect to find notations.

The first irrefutable evidence for notation comes from the early civilization of the Near East, ca. 7,000 years ago. But notation may have arisen 10,000 years prior to this during the later Upper *Paleolithic in the form of engraved artifacts within the corpus of mobiliary art. Soon after the first examples of engraved bone and antler artifacts were discovered, interpretations involving counting and notation were made. In 1860, Eduard Lartet suggested that a series of tiny parallel lines on a bone artifact were *marques de chasse.* The interpretation of such marks as hunting tallies, or the number of people attending a ceremony, soon became widespread. The study of Paleolithic mobiliary art, and the possibility of early notation, was dramatically developed in 1972 when Alexander Marshack published a provocative volume entitled *The Roots of Civilization.* This introduced the use of microscopy for the analysis of engraved marks on Paleolithic artifacts. Marshack claimed that by employing a microscopic analysis he could infer that many of the engraved objects had not simply been tallies, but complex notational representations of lunar cycles.

This inference rests on the claimed existence of distinct repeated sets marks, the correlation between these and lunar cycles, and the use of different engraving tools. Such artifacts come predominantly from the Middle and Late Magdalenian. Most notable are an engraved fragment of an eagle bone from Le Placard and the Taï plaque. The eagle bone fragment is no more than 4.5 inches (11 cm) long with more than 150 inverted "Y's," engraved at regular intervals

on two faces, and some large triangular designs on a third face. Marshack suggested that the subtle differences between the "Y's" could be used to classify them into distinct sets, which could then be correlated with the phases of the moon. The Taï plaque has a far more complicated series of engraved lines. This artifact is approximately 3.5 inches (9 cm) long by 1 inch (3 cm) wide and one of its faces is almost entirely covered by six rows of tiny parallel incisions, each less than one inch high. Marshack employed his microscopic method of examining each mark in turn to conclude that they recorded not only lunar observations, but also solar solstitial events. He concluded that the Le Placard bone, the Taï plaque, and similar artifacts reflect a nonarithmetic observational astronomical skill and lore which lasted for 20,000 years between the Aurignacian and the Magdalenian, and which also formed the basis for the calendars thought to have been used by western European communities of the third millennium B.C. and reflected in the layout of their stone circles and alignments. Moreover, he suggested that there were elite record keepers in Upper Paleolithic society.

While the details of Marshack's interpretations and some of his more extravagant claims may be questioned, the notion that such objects are Paleolithic notations is appealing. There are some well-documented ethnographic examples of calendar sticks used by hunters and herders of Siberia and North America. The most interesting of these is the calendar stick that was owned by Chief Tshi-zun-hau-kau of the Winnebago Indians of North America, which shows considerable similarities to certain Upper Paleolithic engraved items. The Upper Paleolithic of southwestern Europe is also a context in which we might expect the recording of temporal events to have occurred. We know this to have been a highly seasonal environment which was exploited intensively. Hunters would have been keenly aware of the changing seasons, and watched for the movements of animals especially in the days surrounding the freeze or the thaw. It is most likely that Upper Paleolithic hunters were keen observers of the phases of the moon. Upper Paleolithic social and economic behavior would have been dependent upon the storage and transmission of this information.

There are, however, some very substantial problems with Marshack's inference of Paleolithic notation. The most serious of these has been highlighted by Francesco d'Errico and concerns the criteria which are used to identify the changes in tools which are critical to Marshack's interpretation. D'Errico made a large series of experimentally engraved stone artifacts and found that it was possible to identify the direction in which incised lines were made, the order in which they were superimposed, and whether the marks were made by the same tool. But when this knowledge was applied to the analysis of a series of Azilian engraved stones, which had also been claimed to be lunar calendars, d'Errico found that all marks had been made in quick succession and there were no grounds for inferring a notational sequence made over a long period of time. Such comparative work with experimentally engraved bone objects is essential to verify Marshack's interpretation of the Le Placard bone and Taï plaque.

Judith Robinson has also questioned Marshack's conclusions. She suggests that Marshack has no warranty for claiming that elite record keepers existed in the Upper Paleolithic, for this derives from a poor use of ethnographic analogy. More seriously, she points out that Marshack appears able to fit almost any sequence of marks to a lunar cycle; no two artifacts "fit" the lunar month in the same way. This would suggest that each artifact was created without a prior representational scheme for the lunar cycle, which then questions Marshack's idea of a long tradition of such notation. Robinson quite rightly argues that we need to develop strict criteria for the identification of lunar cycles in engraved Paleolithic artifacts.

At present, therefore, there are very limited grounds for believing that the complex engraved objects from the Paleolithic are representations of lunar cycles. This does not invalidate them as notations, for they may be representations of other events or numbers, such as hunting tallies, as originally suggested by Eduard Lartet. But even this remains problematic. As Franceso d'Errico and Judith Robinson have argued, we need to apply strict criteria for interpreting marks as symbols and interpreting a series of such marks as notation. Until this is achieved, it remains unclear whether notation originated in the Upper Paleolithic or was first developed only in the early civilizations of the Near East.

[See also ROCK ART: PALEOLITHIC ART; WRITING: PETRO-GLYPHS.]

■ Alexander Marshack, "A Lunar Calender Stick from North America," *American Antiquity* 50 (1985): 27–51. Franceso d'Errico, "Palaeolithic Lunar Calenders: A Case of Wishful Thinking," *Current Anthropology* 30 (1989): 117–118. Alexander Marshack, "The Taï Plaque and Calendrical Notation in the Upper Palaeolithic," *Cambridge Archaeology Journal* 1 (1991): 25–61. Judith Robinson, "Not Counting on Marshack: A Reassessment of the Work of Alexander Marshack on Notation in the Upper Palaeolithic," *Journal of Mediterranean Studies* 2 (1992): 1–16.

Steven Mithen

NUBIA. Thanks to worldwide interest in Nubia, our knowledge of its ancient cultures has increased greatly in the last few decades. But it is actually the Aswan Dam, first completed in 1902, which was originally responsible for spawning international interest in Nubia. For, with each of its rebuilding and enlargement phases (1907–1911, 1929–1934, and 1956–1969), the archaeological surveying and exploration of sites was expanded to document the regions of Nubia that would be submerged under the rising waters of the Nile.

The northern border of ancient Nubia began approximately at the town of Aswan, in Egypt, and extended south to Khartoum, in the Sudan. Ancient Nubia was divided into Lower Nubia in the north (from the First to the Second Cataract of the Nile) and Upper Nubia in the south (from the Second Cataract to Khartoum). Nubia is today an ethnic and cultural area in which the Nubian languages are spoken, extending roughly from Aswan, Egypt, to Debba, Sudan.

In antiquity, this area had several names. In the Old Testament, it was called Kush; in Greek literature, it was known as Aethiopia. The Latin term "Nubia," used for the first time in the Roman period, may have been derived from the ancient Egyptian word for gold, *nebew*, as this area was a rich source of the mineral throughout pharaonic history.

From Aswan southward, the Nile's flow is broken by six large clusters of granite outcroppings called cataracts, which make river navigation difficult or impossible. One sixty-mile (96 km) stretch of rapids between the Second and Third Cataracts is called the Batn el Hagar, or the "Belly of Rocks." The climate in this area is varied and extreme. There is virtually no rainfall in northern Nubia, but as one moves south the annual rainfall gradually increases until in the vicinity of Khartoum there is up to 8 inches (20 cm) of rain annually. In antiquity and even today, exotic animals, skins, ostrich eggs and feathers, ivory, ebony, as well as gold were brought from Nubia and other places farther south in Africa to Egypt and the Near East. The Nubians exported some of these goods themselves or acted as commercial middlemen for the Egyptians.

The Paleolithic and Mesolithic Periods. About 27,000 B.P. Nubia was inhabited by nomadic bands who lived in small temporary camps close to the Nile and who depended for their survival on hunting and fishing. Little archaeological evidence of their encampments remains except for stone tools and rock drawings of the animals they hunted, such as giraffe, antelope, elephant, and gazelle.

Remains of the earliest known sedentary culture of Nubia have been found near Khartoum. This ancient culture, known as the Khartoum Mesolithic, existed approximately 8,000 years ago and was closely related to other ancient cultures of northern and central Africa. The Khartoum Mesolithic people subsisted primarily by hunting, fishing, and raising cattle. The handmade pottery of the Khartoum Mesolithic culture, produced even before the adoption of agriculture, is characterized by decoration with impressed dotted and wavy line patterns.

The Early Farming Cultures. By 4000 to 3500 B.C., Neolithic civilizations in Nubia were domesticating cattle, cultivating cereal, and creating human figurines, stone tools such as adzes, celt and mace heads, slate palettes for grinding cosmetics, and black-topped red pottery. By the beginning of the historic period, when the use of writing first appears in Egypt (about 3100 B.C.), the Nubian state was centered in Lower, or northern, Nubia. The Egyptians called it Ta-Sety, the "Land of the Bow," a reference to the famed Nubian archers. The designation A-Group was given to the material culture of this period.

Cemeteries of tumulus graves at Sayala and Qustul yielded rich A-Group graves that contained gold jewelry, decorated pottery, and stone vessels rivaling those of the Egyptian kings. Sophisticated early trade is evidenced by the presence of luxury objects imported from the Near East and Egypt. The A-Group artifacts are known for their distinctive cone-shaped pottery vessels, decorated with a variety of reddish lines imitating basketwork.

The A-Group was believed to be followed by the B-Group. However, currently there is scholarly disagreement as to whether the B-Group has enough differences from the A-Group and subsequent C-Group to be identified as a separate culture.

The C-Group culture also flourished in Lower Nubia, from about 2000 to 1700 B.C. Its people farmed along the Nile floodplain, raised cattle and sheep, traded with the Egyptians, and produced fine pottery. Since the powerful Kushite polity evolving in the area of Kerma at the Third Cataract was apparently a threat to Egypt, the Egyptian king Sesostris I began building a string of heavy fortresses farther north along the Nile in the area of the Second Cataract around 1900 B.C. The massive forts, which could accommodate up to 1,000 troops and were surrounded by enclosure walls and fortified gates with drawbridges, controlled the river trade and served as collecting stations for the gold mined in the Nubian desert.

Another Nubian group that existed at about the same time as the C-Group was the Pan-Grave culture. These people were named after their shallow, round graves, which resembled frying pans to the archaeologists and which are found throughout Egypt and Lower Nubia. These people were nomads of the eastern desert, who some scholars identify with the Medjay tribes. Famed as skilled warriors and bowmen, many of the Medjay sold their services as mercenaries in Egypt.

The Kerma Culture. By about 1700 B.C., the great Nubian kingdom of Kush, centered south of the Third Cataract, at the modern Sudanese town of Kerma, expanded its influence. Their kings ruled much of what is now the northern Sudan as well as parts of southern Egypt. The Kerma kingdom became one of the most powerful states in the history of Nubia, and the wealth of the classic phase of the Kerma kingdom is reflected in the extravagant royal burials of their kings. They were buried in splendor inside special tomb chambers at the center of huge funerary mounds. The kings' bodies were usually placed unmummified on gold-covered funerary beds, surrounded by treasures of gold, ivory, and jewelry. The bodies of many finely dressed sacrificed servants, sometimes numbering in the hundreds, were found in the corridors of the tomb. Often, a whole herd of cattle was sacrificed at each royal burial, and the skulls arranged around the rim of the earthen tomb. The ram god played an important role in early Nubian mythology and statues of a ram-headed sphinx have been found at Kerma, as well as burials containing elaborately decorated rams.

During the Second Intermediate period in Egypt, the kings of Kerma formed an alliance with a group from the eastern Mediterranean region known in Egyptian sources as the Hyksos, who ruled northern Egypt. By 1600 B.C. Kerma had become a regional power, and, together with the Hyksos, controlled most of southern and northern Egypt and its trade.

Egypt in Nubia. Kerma's power was to be short-lived. Around 1550 B.C., the Egyptian kings from Thebes fought the Hyksos and forced them out of northern Egypt. They then turned their armies south and began a war against Kush, which lasted approximately fifty years. They destroyed the capital city of Kerma and then gained control over Nubia as far south as the Fourth Cataract, ruling it as part of Egypt. A special office was created for governing this area, filled by high-ranking Egyptian officials with the title "The King's Son" and later "The King's Son of Kush." During the New Kingdom (1550–1070 B.C.) Egyptian kings built colossal temples in Nubia, some of which functioned as administrative centers. These temples became familiar features of the Nubian landscape, and the Nubians gradually incorporated Egyptian gods into their own pantheon, with special prominence given to Amun. One of the most important religious centers in Nubia was the temple of Amun at Gebel Barkal, established in the town of Napata by Thutmose III around 1500 B.C. to mark Egypt's southern frontier. Also, Rameses II erected his famous temple at Abu Simbel in the thirteenth century B.C.

The Napatan Period. In the eighth century B.C., the rulers of Kush took advantage of a period of Egyptian weakness. In 750 B.C., the Kushite king Piye (or Pi-ankhy), who ruled from the town of Napata near the Fourth Cataract, moved north and conquered Egypt. He declared himself pharaoh of all of Egypt and Nubia, and moved his capital to Thebes to begin Egypt's Twenty-fifth Dynasty. This Nubian dynasty successfully governed Egypt for about ninety years. They encouraged a revival in both literature and the arts, and rebuilt and constructed many new monuments in Egypt.

The Gebel Barkal temple complex, dedicated to Amun of Napata, was maintained as the most important shrine for the Kushite rulers. At this time, many traditional Egyptian burial practices were apparently adopted in Nubia. Pyramids were built for their kings initially at the site of El-Kurru and later at Nuri. Shawabtis, or servant statuettes, were deposited in the royal burial chamber; mummification is suggested by the presence of canopic jars. At the same time certain Nubian practices were discontinued, such as the human sacrifices and the tumulus-shaped burials. The chief remaining connection to the earlier Nubian burial style was the funerary bed.

The Kushite rule over Egypt came to an end about 660 B.C., when Egypt was invaded by the Assyrians. They destroyed the combined Kushite and Egyptian armies, and then forced the Kushite kings to flee to their homeland in Nubia. Here, far south in Nubia, the Kushites established a royal court in Meroe, which flourished for the next thousand years.

The Meroitic Period. Nubia underwent a cultural flowering in the Meroitic Period (ca. 270 B.C.–A.D. 350). The city of *Meroe, between the Fifth and Sixth Cataracts, became the center of an empire that included not only much of Nubia but also regions far south of Khartoum. Like the other great Nubian cities, Meroe contained royal palaces, government buildings, temples, and large royal cemeteries. Other centers of Meroitic culture have also been found at the sites of Karanoq, Qasr, Ibrim, and Faras.

The supreme position of the god Amun at Gebel Barkal was eclipsed at the close of the third century B.C. At this time, temples began to be built for the local gods of Meroe. The most impressive and monumental temple complexes are those found at Naga and Musawwarat es Sufra dedicated to the Nubian lion god Apedemak. During this period, Meroitic culture was the result of a blend of cultural influences, incorporating central African traditions with Egyptian and Greco-Roman stylistic elements.

The Meroites, likely for the first time in Nubian history, created their own written language in a hieroglyphic and cursive script composed of twenty-three alphabetic signs. Although it has been studied by Meroitic scholars for nearly a century, it is still undeciphered.

Christian and Medieval Nubia. Meroe had reached its peak in the first century A.D. and declined slowly over the next three centuries. By the fourth century A.D., Meroitic culture, including its class-structured society, monumental art and architecture, religion, and even literacy, had disappeared. In Lower Egypt, the Ballana culture gradually became dominant. Some of the larger Ballana sites are Qasr Ibrim, Gemai, Ferka, and Kosha. In the sixth century A.D., missionaries from Egypt and Byzantium began converting the various Nubian peoples to Christianity. Numerous churches and monasteries were built in the later Christian period, the most noteworthy being the cathedral and bishop's palace at Faras. Christianity remained the dominant religion until the fourteenth century A.D., when Islam finally came to Nubia.

[See also AFRICA: THE RISE OF KINGDOMS AND STATES IN AFRICA; EGYPT: NEW KINGDOM EGYPT; EGYPT AND AFRICA.]

■ G. A. Reisner, *Kerma Parts I–V*, Harvard African Studies, Vols. I, II, III, VI (1923). Dows Dunham, *The Royal Cemeteries of Kush*, Vols. I, II, IV, V (1950, 1955, 1957, 1963). William Y. Adams, *Nubia, Corridor to Africa* (1977). Brooklyn Museum, *Africa in Antiquity: The Arts of Ancient Nubia and the Sudan*, Vols. I, II (1978). B. G. Trigger, *Nubia under the Pharaohs* (1987). C. Bonnet, ed., *Kerma, royaume de Nubie*

(1990). T. Kendall, "Sudan's Kingdom of Kush," *National Geographic* 178 (1990). W. V. Davies, ed., *Egypt and Africa. Nubia from Prehistory to Islam* (1991). J. H. Taylor, *Egypt and Nubia* (1991). J. L. Haynes, *Nubia Ancient Kingdoms of Africa* (1992). D. O'Connor, *Ancient Nubia: Egypt's Rival in Africa* (1993).

Joyce L. Haynes

NURAGIC CULTURE. The name given to the Nuragic culture of Sardinia is derived from large towers, usually in the shape of truncated cones, constructed in Cyclopean masonry technique. About 7,000 of these nuraghi were distributed throughout the island, and were standing when goods from *Cyprus, Crete, and Mycenaean Greece arrived in the fourteenth, thirteenth, and twelfth centuries B.C.; when an Iberian weapon from the Atlantic coast of a type already known from a Nuragic hoard was found in a hoard buried in Cyprus in the tenth century B.C.; when the Phoenicians from Tyre and then from Cyprus prospected before 1000 B.C. and began to colonize in the ninth century; when Carthaginians arrived to destroy and to build, from the sixth century B.C. on; and when the Romans came to conquer and to colonize in 238 B.C.

The island of Sardinia is about 29 by 58 miles (47 by 93 km) in area, located in the Tyrrhenian Sea off the western coast of Italy, just south of Corsica, north-northwest of *Sicily, and east of the Balearic Islands. Extensive volcanic activity created the rocky and mountainous terrain and left the island rich in metals and minerals. There are only two substantial areas capable of cultivation: the Campidano, extending from the Bay of Cagliari on the southeast to the Bay of Oristano in the west-central part, and the Nurra in the coastal northwest.

The current acceleration in excavation and research has pushed back the date of the first consecutive habitation of the island to an early Neolithic phase in the seventh millennium B.C. Ongoing investigation is adding to and redefining the succession of cultures that preceded the Bronze Ages. The Early Bronze Age in Sardinia, extending from about 1800 to 1500 B.C., is now seen as the formative stage of the diverse and complex islandwide Nuragic culture that followed. During that period, the number of settlements increased, numerous large stone structures began to be built, and metalworking intensified. The specific dates of the Middle and Late Bronze Ages when most of the nuraghi were built are still in the process of refinement. Current research is also clarifying such aspects as the economy, technology, religion, and trade of the Nuragic society.

Social organization is interpreted from excavated material, the nature and spatial arrangement of the architecture, and the subject matter of several hundred bronze figurines. These suggest a stratified society, gathered in small groups, with a ruler or chief of some kind and with assemblies that were political or social. Priests, warriors, and performing athletes are represented, and specialists engaged in such crafts as pottery making and bronze casting, hunting, fishing, farming, stock raising, and cooking can be inferred.

Although wide trade contacts are suggested by the few Nuragic vases found outside the island, production of pottery appears largely to have been for domestic use. The shapes and decorations are much simplified when compared to earlier ceramics of the Neolithic Period. Metallurgy, in contrast, shows increasing technological skills, perhaps stimulated by imports. Tools and weapons were part of the metalworking manufacture, but the most noteworthy product was the bronze figurines, of which a few

hundred survive. Their presence at wells that have been made into sacred areas show that many were treated as votive offerings. Their subject matter includes warriors, shepherds, animals, and boats, the last embellished with animal decorations and perhaps used as lamps.

Nuraghi are frequently, but not always, surrounded by villages, mostly of round huts of varying function: dwellings, storage, or workshops for such crafts as pottery making or metalworking; and larger huts, considered to be council chambers, with benches around the inner wall.

The best-known Nuragic complex is at Barumini, in the south-central part of the island. It has been worked on by Giovanni Lilliu for the past fifty years, yielding information on the spectrum and sequence of Nuragic pottery, and the additions to the original central tower. The shifts required in its relative chronology have served to indicate the extent to which new techniques of dating plus changing concepts of architectural development have modified the original dating.

Nuraghe Santu Antine at Torralba in the north-central part of the island clearly illustrates Nuragic architectural techniques. The superimposed, vaulted chambers rise within what is perhaps the highest standing tower, originally almost 59 feet (18 m).

Unlike similar structures elsewhere in the Mediterranean and in the Aegean, however, the towers are not funerary in function, but were designed to be used as combined fortress, vantage point for reconnaissance and territorial control, meeting place, and residence for a chief. Another interpretation adds the desire for prestige, suggesting that they were stronger and higher than required, for the purpose of impressing others.

Although the towered nuraghe is the most common, there are several hundred of another type called corridor-nuraghe or pseudo-nuraghe. This style is characterized by low-lying, flat-roofed, single-story construction with a corridor leading to side chambers. The difference between the two types may have been determined by topography that did not favor the construction of towers, or perhaps by the desire to appear less conspicuous. The best-known corridor-nuraghe is Brunku Madugui, located near Barumini on the high plain of Gesturi. It is presently being restudied in light of the new developments since its excavation in the mid-1960s.

Inhabitants of the nuraghi were usually buried in large, communal shafts, some more than 49 feet (15 m) long, lined with slabs, and known today as "giants' tombs." At one end, a facade was constructed of standing stones in a semicircle, thus creating a space that could be used for funerary ritual. One late variation has tombs surmounted by sandstone statues of warriors and athletes.

Numerous "sacred wells," or well-temples, some within Nuragic complexes, others apparently standing alone, were designed to respect, protect, and preserve sources of water in a dry, windy climate. This was done by enclosing a well, with stairs descending to the water, a vault above it, and a walled, paved courtyard at the top of the stairs. Hoards of bronze offerings have been found at these wells, attesting to the sacred implications of water.

Megaron-shaped buildings, built in Nuragic techniques, have provided find spots for hoards of bronzes as well. The shape of the megaron as well as the vaulting in the nuraghi and "sacred wells" have prompted considerations of Aegean influence on the architecture of the Nuragic culture. Recent finds of material from Bronze Age Greece, Crete,

Cyprus, and Spain have enlivened the ongoing discussion about the relationship of Nuragic Sardinia to other areas in the Mediterranean, but more is being found to illuminate further the interaction among the various peoples and cultures.

[*See also* MEDITERRANEAN TRADE; MEDITERRANEAN WORLD, *articles on* INTRODUCTION, THE RISE OF AEGEAN AND MEDITERRANEAN STATES.]

■ Miriam S. Balmuth, "The Nuraghi of Sardinia: An Introduction," in *Studies in Sardinian Archaeology,* ed. M. S. Balmuth and R. J. Rowland, Jr. (1984), pp. 23–52. Miriam S. Balmuth, ed., *Studies in Sardinian Archaeology 2: Sardinia in the Mediterranean* (1986). Miriam S. Balmuth, ed., *Studies in Sardinian Archaeology 3: Nuragic Sardinia and the Mycenaean World, British Archaeological Reports,* International Series S387 (1987). J. W. Michels and G. S. Webster, eds., *Studies in Nuragic Archaeology: Village Excavations at Nuraghe Urpes and Nuraghe Toscono in West-Central Sardinia, British Archaeological Reports,* International Series 373 (1987). Fulvia Lo Schiavo, "Nuragic Civilization," in *A Short History of Sardinia,* in *International Conference: Early Man in Island Environments, Oliena (Sardinia), 25 September–2 October 1988,* ed. Mario Sanges (1988), pp. 19–29. F. Lo Schiavo et al., *Metallographic and Statistical Analyses of Copper Ingots from Sardinia = Quaderni (Sassari)* 17 (1990). D. Trump, *Nuraghe Noeddos and the Bonu Ighinu Valley: Excavation and Survey in Sardinia* (1990). B. S. Frizell, ed., *Nuragic Architecture in Its Military, Territorial and Socio-Economic Context. Proceedings of the First International Colloquium on Nuragic Architecture at the Swedish Institute in Rome, 7–9 December, 1989, Acta Instituti Romani Regni Sueciae,* ser. 4, 48 (1991).

Miriam S. Balmuth

OAXACA, Valley of. Amidst the rugged mountains of Mexico's southern highlands lies the flat valley of Oaxaca. At 1,500 meters above sea level, this large Y-shaped valley is relatively frost free, and compared to the steep surrounds, it is a fertile area for farming maize. Today, the most visible skyline in the valley of Oaxaca is not modern but ancient. Across the region, silhouettes of pre-Hispanic ruins sculpt the majestic mountains. The most famous ruins are the archaeological remains of *Monte Albán, the capital of the valley from 500 B.C. until A.D. 700, which sits at the hub of the three valley arms. Yet from any point in the region, it is practically impossible to walk far without encountering broken pottery, stone tools, earthen platforms, and other signs of pre-Hispanic occupation. In fact, the late Ignacio Bernal, a Mexican archaeologist with decades of field experience in Oaxaca, once wrote that the whole region might be considered an archaeological site.

Since the 1920s, archaeological studies in the valley of Oaxaca have provided some of the earliest evidence for sedentary villages (ca. 1600–1400 B.C.), writing on carved stones (ca. 500–200 B.C.), and early states (ca. 300–200 B.C.) in the highlands of Mesoamerica. Excavations conducted by Kent V. Flannery and colleagues in rock shelters and open-air sites have traced the ancestors of the region's Otomanguean (Zapotec and Mixtec) inhabitants back roughly 11,000 years, studying the beginnings of plant cultivation, the eventual rise of year-round settlements, and the emergence of institutionalized inequality. Major excavations, led by Mexican archaeologists, uncovered the monumental Main Plaza at the core of hilltop Monte Albán, while a regional perspective on pre-Hispanic occupation has been generated by a systematic, full-coverage archaeological survey of the entire valley.

From initial occupation to 1600 B.C., settlement of the southern highlands was sparse. Although domesticated plants were incorporated into a diet of wild foods prior to 5000 B.C., the valley's inhabitants remained mobile, moving seasonally. After 1600 B.C., the first Oaxacan villages were established, composed of single-room houses that were constructed of cane and mud. At the earliest of these communities (San José Mogote, located in the valley's northern arm), small lime-plastered public or ritual structures were erected. For roughly 1,000 years, until the foundation of Monte Albán (ca. 500 B.C.), San José Mogote remained a nodal site, larger and more architecturally monumental than contemporaneous communities. Nevertheless, it was not until the founding of hilltop Monte Albán that much of the valley appears to have been integrated under the hegemony of a single center.

Monte Albán grew rapidly in power and population. The establishment of a multitiered network of centers below Monte Albán suggests that the Oaxacan state was formed during the last centuries B.C. While no one factor can account for this development, Monte Albán had a central role in military matters. The era of initial state formation was marked by changes in house construction (cane to adobe brick) and burial custom (the construction of more formal household tombs), as well as agricultural intensification, the specialized manufacture of utilitarian craft goods, and increasing intravalley exchange. Although Monte Albán's farthest conquests may have occurred prior to A.D. 200, the center most fully consolidated and integrated its immediate hinterland, the valley of Oaxaca, during the Classic Period (A.D. 200–700). At this time, the mountain capital reached its apogee, encompassing roughly 25,000 people.

The decline of Monte Albán began around A.D. 700 and coincided with major political upheavals across Mesoamerica. During this period, the valley of Oaxaca was subdivided into a series of spatially separated population clusters. The largest of these concentrations surrounded the high ridge-top center of Jalieza in the valley's southern arm. As at Monte Albán, most of Jalieza's inhabitants built houses on residential terraces, which were carved out of steep piedmont slopes.

The political fragmentation that followed the fall of Monte Albán continued through the last centuries preceding Spanish conquest (A.D. 1519), at which time the valley of Oaxaca was divided into fifteen to twenty semiautonomous petty states. These polities were interconnected through exchange and marriage alliances between their ruling lords. Although the largest late pre-Hispanic centers were less than half the size of earlier Monte Albán, the regional population of the valley of Oaxaca greatly eclipsed that of the Classic Period. With the upheavals of the Spanish conquest and the introduction of Eurasian diseases, the population of the valley crashed precipitously during the sixteenth century. Precontact demographic levels were not achieved again for roughly 400 years, until early in the twentieth century.

[See also MESOAMERICA, *articles on* INTRODUCTION, CLASSIC PERIOD IN MESOAMERICA, FORMATIVE PERIOD IN MESOAMERICA; ZAPOTEC CIVILIZATION.]

■ Alfonso Caso, Ignacio Bernal, and Jorge Acosta, *La Cerámica de Monte Albán* (1967). Richard E. Blanton, *Monte Albán: Settlement Patterns at the Ancient Zapotec Capital* (1978). Kent V. Flannery and Joyce Marcus, eds., *The Cloud People: Divergent Evolution of the Zapotec and Mixtec Civilizations* (1983). Kent V. Flannery, ed., *Guilá Naquitz: Archaic Foraging and Early Agriculture in Oaxaca, Mexico* (1986). Stephen A. Kowalewski et al., *Monte Albán's Hinterland*, Part II: *Prehispanic Settlement Patterns in Tlacolula, Etla, and Ocotlán, the Valley of Oaxaca, Mexico* (1989). Richard E. Blanton et al., *Ancient Mesoamerica: A Comparison of Change in Three Regions*, 2nd ed. (1993).

Gary M. Feinman

OBSIDIAN HYDRATION DATING. In many regions of the ancient world, obsidian, a volcanic glass, was the preferred material for stone-tool production. Fracturing obsidian exposes fresh surfaces, on which hydration rinds may form. The thickness of a rind increases with the age of the artifact. Rind thicknesses, measured using powerful microscopes, can be used to date the production of artifacts.

The reactions involved in the production of a rind are complex. Recent studies indicate that four processes are involved: the leaching of alkali ions from the glass into solution, the replacement of these ions by H^+ or H_3O^+, the surface dissolution of the silica network of the glass, and the precipitation of reaction products. Factors related to these reactions affect the rate at which rinds form on obsidian artifacts. These include the chemical composition of the glass and solution, effective hydration temperature (EHT), pH, relative humidity, artifact shape, solution-flow rate, and exposure time.

Hydration measurements can be used for relative or absolute dating, with an accuracy dependent on control of these variables. Theoretically, hydration dating has no absolute temporal limitations, but rinds tend to crumble when they reach a thickness of 50 microns, making it difficult to date artifacts of great antiquity. Furthermore, several centuries must pass before a measurable rind forms. Although radiocarbon, thermoluminescence, and archaeomagnetic dating can be used to date Holocene sites, hydration dating is inexpensive and requires only rudimentary microscopy skills.

Hydration measurements are used in two fundamentally different ways to calculate the age of artifacts. The first method calibrates rind measurements with other temporal data, such as radiocarbon dates or even ceramic phases. Once a calibration curve is established, rind measurements from other contexts can be compared to the curve and absolute or relative dates can be determined. The advantage of this technique is that it is based on empirical in vivo measurements and does not require in vitro experiments under unnatural conditions. A disadvantage is that variation in local environmental conditions is not taken into account, increasing error.

Unlike the calibration approach, the induction method relies on laboratory experiments. Hydration is induced by exposing fresh obsidian to water vapor or liquid water. In order to increase the reaction rate, high temperatures and pressures are used. Under these artificial conditions, rind formation can be accurately modelled as a diffusion process, allowing the calculation of EHT-dependent hydration rates. In order to calculate absolute dates from obsidian artifacts, paleo-EHTs must be estimated. Contemporary EHTs can be measured using thermal cells or estimated using weather station data and extrapolated to the past. Although the experimental induction method is quite promising, it has serious flaws. First, in vivo rind formation is far more complex than laboratory-induced diffusion. Second, the equations used to model diffusion depend only on time and EHT, although field studies and induction experiments have demonstrated that relative humidity, pH, and other variables also affect rind-formation rates.

The earliest attempts to use hydration measurements to date artifacts were made by Irving Friedman and Robert Smith ("A New Method Using Obsidian Dating: Part I," *American Antiquity* 25 (1960): 476–522). Since then, hydration dating has been used widely, with particular success in California and the Great Basin of the United States. In this area, numerous regional chronologies have been constructed using the calibration method.

In *Mesoamerica, obsidian hydration dating has usually been used to supplement more traditional chronological data. Two important projects, however, have used hydration dating to form the backbone of the chronology. At Kaminaljuyu, Guatemala, Joseph Michels (*The Pennsylvania State University Kaminaljuyu Project—1969–1970 Seasons, Part I: Mound Excavations,* University Park, 1973) used the calibration method to produce 3,000 obsidian hydration dates that proved to be inaccurate. An unfortunate result has been that Maya archaeologists are now reluctant to use hydration dating. More recently, the experimental induction technique has been used in an attempt to fine-tune the chronology of *Copán, a Classic Maya site in Honduras. Although most of the 2,200 dates are consistent with other temporal data, several hundred are very late. David Webster and AnnCorinne Freter ("Settlement History and the Classic Collapse at Copan: A Redefined Chronological Perspective," *Latin American Antiquity* 1 (1990): 66–85) have used these dates to argue that a substantial population continued to occupy Copán until A.D. 1150. Other archaeologists question this conclusion, because very few Postclassic ceramics have been found at the site. Furthermore, there are no radiocarbon or archaeomagnetic dates later than A.D. 950. Until independent chronological evidence is found, it seems unlikely that a substantial Postclassic occupation will be accepted.

The Copán dates demonstrate that estimating error is a serious problem with the technique. Although current environmental conditions can be measured, an unmeasurable error is introduced when these conditions are extrapolated to the past. A shift in EHT of just 1 K, for example, can lead to dates that err by centuries. For this reason, hydration dating must still be considered a relatively inaccurate independent chronometric technique.

[See also ARCHAEO-PALEOMAGNETIC DATING; DATING THE PAST; DENDROCHRONOLOGY; FISSION-TRACK DATING; LUMINESCENCE DATING; POTASSIUM-ARGON DATING; RADIOCARBON DATING; SERIATION; STRATIGRAPHY.]

■ R. E. Taylor, ed., *Advances in Obsidian Glass Studies* (1976). Clement W. Meighan and Janet L. Scalise, *Obsidian Dates IV* (1988). E. V. Sayre, P. Vandiver, J. Druzik, and C. Stevenson, eds., *Materials Issues in Art and Archaeology* (1988). J. J. Mazer, C. M. Stevenson, W. L. Ebert, and J. K. Bates, "The Experimental Hydration of Obsidian as a Function of Relative Humidity and Temperature," *American Antiquity* 56 (1991): 504–513. Rosanna Ridings, "Obsidian Hydration Dating: The Effects of Mean Exponential Ground Temperature and Depth of Artifact Recovery," *Journal of Field Archaeology* 18 (1991): 77–85. Geoffrey E. Braswell, "Obsidian-Hydration Dating, the Coner Phase, and Revisionist Chronology at Copán, Honduras," *Latin American Antiquity* 3 (1992): 130–147.

Geoffrey E. Braswell

OLDUVAI GORGE is located in northern Tanzania close to the Great Rift Valley. It was discovered by Reck in 1913, although it was the work of Louis and Mary Leakey especially during the 1950s and 1960s that realized its archaeological potential. The gorge at Olduvai is ca. 9 miles (15 km) long and 330 feet (100 m) deep, presenting a series of deposits deriving from lake basin sedimentation, which span a period of almost 2 million years. Olduvai provides the most complete sequence of *Pleistocene materials in Africa and was responsible, through intensive dating studies, for the establishment of an African origin for humankind. The deposits at Olduvai represent a range of lakeside and streamside localities where hominids were living in the shadow of a volcano. This volcano erupted periodically and provided the materials for dating the Olduvai sequence. Olduvai was the first site to be dated using the potassium-argon technique. Although referred to as a site, it does in fact comprise a large number of localities, each of which might be termed a site elsewhere. There are over seventy such localities in Beds I and II alone.

The sequence begins with Bed I at the base, dated to 1.8 million years ago. The archaeological evidence from this bed shows Oldowan tools, made of cobbles and flakes, were in use, and importantly, at DK locality a stone-hut structure was present. This evidence for human alteration of the environment is confirmed at FLK where the distribution of tools and bones suggests the presence of a structure such as a windbreak.

The Oldowan tool-making tradition was defined on the basis of finds at Olduvai. Four forms are known: Oldowan, Developed Oldowan A, Developed Oldowan B, and Developed Oldowan C, with some intermediate assemblages reported. The tradition is based on direct knapping of river cobbles to form a variety of relatively undifferentiated pebble and flake tools. The different variants show an increase in tool types and their more regular flaking with time. The importance of stone tools can be gauged by the fact that some materials were occasionally transported from sources approximately 6.2 miles (10 km) away. The Oldowan tradition was replaced by Acheulean industries prior to 1.4 million years ago, in upper Bed II, but was contemporary with it until ca. 0.8 million years ago in Bed III.

The fossils found at Olduvai have also been important, the first hominid found being *Zinjanthropus boisei* (later renamed *Australopithecus boisei*), discovered by Mary Leakey in 1959 in Bed I at FLK. Since that discovery representatives of *Homo habilis* and *Homo erectus* have been discovered. The Oldowan is generally associated with *Homo habilis* and the Acheulean with *Homo erectus*.

The Olduvai localities have been reconstructed as showing complex organization of hominid behavior across the landscape, with home bases being set up along river edges and lake shores and specialist camps for butchery, tool making, caches of materials, etc. being placed elsewhere. This pattern was then used to argue for an early date for the sexual division of labor, with male provisioning of the home bases.

Since its excavation and interpretation, debate has arisen as to the reconstructions made of hominid behavior at Olduvai. It has been questioned how far the associations of tools and bones are a product of hominid behavior as opposed to natural processes such as washing together in flash floods and carnivores accumulating bones from their kills. The debate still continues as to whether hominids were hunting game or whether they were scavenging the leftovers from carnivore kills. Certainly, the role of meat in hominid diet and behavior is one factor that needs further work.

There is little research activity at Olduvai at present and attention has shifted to earlier sites elsewhere in East Africa.

[See also ACHEULEAN TRADITION; AFRICA: PREHISTORY OF AFRICA; HUMAN EVOLUTION, *articles on* FOSSIL EVIDENCE FOR HUMAN EVOLUTION, THE ARCHAEOLOGY OF HUMAN ORIGINS; KOOBI FORA.]

■ M. D. Leakey, *Olduvai Gorge, Excavations in Beds I and II, 1960–1963* (1971). R. H. Tuttle, "What's New in African Paleoanthropology," *Annual Review of Anthropology* 17 (1988): 391–426.

Tim Reynolds

OLMEC CIVILIZATION. Aztec legends, recorded in the sixteenth century, describe the inhabitants of Mexico's southern Gulf Coast as *Olmeca*, "people of the rubber country." Bernardino de Sahagún, a Spanish friar and chronicler of the time, depicted the Olmeca as a civilized nation of accomplished traders, potters, and cultivators of cacao. They occupied the Gulf Coast as well as the plateau of Puebla and fought the Toltecs in the centuries before the Spanish conquest. These historic Olmeca, however, are very different from the *Olmec* of archaeology, a much earlier culture which developed in the hot and humid lowlands of southern Veracruz and western Tabasco more than 2,500 years ago. The real name by which these more ancient Olmec knew themselves is now long forgotten. They are recognized today by images of rulers and supernaturals carved on massive basalt monuments; in renditions of powerful lowland fauna incorporated into their fine art and craft work in jade, pottery, and wood; and by massive earthen architectural mounds that still mark the centers of their ancient settlements. All bear intriguing, if enigmatic, testament to Olmec civilization, which flourished along the Gulf Coast of Mexico from approximately 1200 to 400 B.C.

During this time, comprising Mesoamerica's Early and Middle Formative Periods, village cultures throughout Mesoamerica began the transition from small-scale, egalitarian societies to complex, stratified polities settled in towns and cities. The Olmec, among the first and most distinctive of the early complex societies to arise in Mesoamerica, began as a dispersed society of hunters, fishers, and planters, but eventually established a politically precocious society that also included paramount rulers, warriors, long-distance traders, inspired stone carvers and craftsmen, and master town planners in addition to common folk. Their stylistic and iconographic legacy, rooted in the tropical lowlands and expressing the natural elements of water, earth, and sky, persisted to inspire the later civilizations of Mesoamerica such as the Late Preclassic people of Izapa and the Classic Period Maya. Until quite recently, scholars considered the Olmec to be the progenitors of all succeeding Mesoamerican civilizations. Now, based on well-documented early social and political complexity in other areas of Mesoamerica, the "mother-culture" status of Olmec society is generally rejected. In its place is a more sophisticated notion, one that measures Olmec accomplishments in light of equally complex social developments in other parts of Mesoamerica. "Olmequista" archaeology today focuses on understanding the depth of social and political diversity within the core Olmec region itself and the range of technological and ecological relationships extant within the Gulf Coastal lowlands during this important period of Mesoamerican prehistory.

Formative. The Formative Period Olmec are commonly recognized for their basalt sculpture, their buried jade and serpentine mortuary offerings procured through long-distance exchange, and distinctively decorated ceramic vessels and figurines. Upon these objects they depicted a suite of stylistic motifs referring to jaguars, serpents, crocodiles, and sharks, powerful denizens of sea, swamp, and forest with whom they shared the Gulf Coast littoral. Their monumental structures, consisting of pyramids and large building platforms of mounded earth, mark the location of major sites within the Olmec "heartland," an arc of territory encompassing the Tuxtlas Mountains of southern Veracruz, Mexico, and stretching south across the broad and relatively flat coastal plain of the Isthmus of Tehuantepec from the Río Papaloapan in the west to the Río Tonalá in the east.

The earliest Olmec are recognized at the site of San Lorenzo Tenochtitlán, an Early Formative (1200–900 B.C.) center of Olmec society located on a tributary of the Río Coatzacoalcos in the seasonally inundated floodplains of southern Veracruz. Numerous colossal basalt heads, altars, and other carved monuments uncovered at *San Lorenzo were positioned on a slight rise of the land along a bend in the Río Chiquito. This low plateau was leveled artificially— a massive construction effort for this time period—and small mounds were constructed to support stone buildings. Many of these structures were connected by an ingenious system of stone water drains, the fragmented remnants of which still litter the surface of the site. Surrounding this principal town of perhaps a thousand persons was a system of secondary centers and shrines located on or near other elevated points of land on the wide expanse of the floodplain. From a spring at the base of nearby Cerro Manatí (Manatee Hill) Mexican archaeologists have recovered the portrait busts of numerous individuals carved in tropical cedar. The busts were deposited in the spring as shrine offerings about 1000 B.C. along with woodworking tools, ceremonial axes, and large natural rubber balls, which may represent the earliest evidence of the ball game anywhere in ancient Mesoamerica.

Middle Formative. During the next phase of development, the Middle Formative Period (900–400 B.C.), the focus of Olmec political power shifted to the coastal estuary of nearby western Tabasco. Here the greatest Olmec town of all time, *La Venta, was constructed on a rise of dry land near the Río Tonalá. Massive earthen mounds occupy the top of this low plateau and surround a 100 foot (approximately 30 m) tall pyramid that represented one of the largest earthworks of its day anywhere in Mesoamerica. At this site archaeologists have uncovered many hundreds of tons of serpentine mortuary offerings attesting to the elaborate ceremonial life and long-distance trade connections of the rulership and elite strata of Middle Formative Olmec society. Little is known of the economic base of the Formative Gulf Coast Olmec, but recent findings in the environs of La Venta suggest a mixed subsistence pattern of wild food collection, hunting, and small-scale maize horticulture. Settlement pattern studies indicate a two-tiered settlement system of towns surrounded by dispersed villages and hamlets and a hinterland population of perhaps as many as 20,000 persons. This largely egalitarian, kin-based society residing in La Venta's countryside may have supported a ruling theocratic stratum occupying the large town and directing the activities of elite households, which were composed of the rulers and their close kin, warriors, ceremonial specialists, craftspersons, and common folk.

Other less-studied centers of the Olmec heartland include Laguna de Los Cerros, an upland Olmec town on the southern flanks of the Tuxtlas Mountains and a possible center of basalt monument production. Farther afield, on the western flank of the Tuxtlas range, sits the later Olmec center of Tres Zapotes, where Late Formative (400 B.C.–A.D. 200) sculptural styles and calendrical monuments mark the disappearance of the Early and Middle Formative Olmec and the rise of new societies affiliated with the proto–Maya Izapa culture of the Pacific coasts of Chiapas, Mexico, and Guatemala.

Sculpture and Other Remains. The material remains of Olmec civilization are recognized as some of the finest "high art styles" to be found anywhere in pre-Columbian America. Olmec iconographic themes, carved into basalt, serpentine, high-quality jade, and wood, and molded in clay, adhere to a distinctive set of canons that celebrate Olmec history and myth. One of the principal themes, that of rulership, is portrayed in colossal basalt heads found at three of the principal Olmec centers (San Lorenzo, La Venta, and Tres Zapotes). Seventeen of the heads, some weighing more than 20 tons, have been excavated at these sites, located up to 90 miles (approximately 150 km) away from their original basalt sources on the flanks of the Tuxtlas Mountains. Quarrying and transport of stone for the heads required the organization of many individuals probably under the direction of a ruler or elite manager. Each head appears to be the individualized portrait of such a ruler, perhaps commemorating his reign at death. The heads are carved from a single block of basalt and show physically similar individuals—heavy-featured and thick-lipped— wearing round helmets of varying designs. The heads have been likened to African physical types and the possibility of transatlantic contacts has been hotly debated. To date, however, there appears to be no compelling evidence to look beyond lowland Mesoamerica for the origins of the Olmec. The physical features portrayed in the colossal heads and other media are well within the range of variability found among the Native peoples of Mexico and Central America.

Rulership and the spatial order of the Olmec cosmos are expressed in the massive basalt "altars" or tabletop "thrones" found at the larger centers of San Lorenzo, Laguna de los Cerros, and La Venta. On the front face of the altar's base, below its flat tabletop, there is usually a central seated figure who emerges from a niche, a cave, or the maw of a reptilian monster, perhaps the Olmec equivalent of a portal to the world of the supernaturals. Above this individual is a bifurcated serpent marking what some scholars believe to be the "sky band," a cosmological design element that figures so prominently in later Classic Period Maya art. Researchers also now believe that the tabletop was a throne for the rulers depicted in the colossal heads. The thrones themselves, in fact, may have provided the raw material for the carved colossal heads representing an early form of royal "recycling" in a landscape bereft of stone resources for large-scale sculpture. Sculpted relief on the thrones and associated stelae depict rulers in fantastic regalia surrounded by ancestral supernaturals and bound captives, presumably taken in war. Olmec sculpture also shows chubby, naked babies, perhaps infant "were-jaguars" or "were-crocodiles," shown in the arms or under the restraint of a more regal seated figure. These ubiquitous Olmec "were-babies" display fangs, claws, a cleft at the top of the head, and a snarling expression framed by a turned-down mouth, physical attributes that also characterize a number of supernatural beings that inhabited the Olmec cosmos. The collection of fierce beings that dominate Olmec iconography may have represented ancestral totems, wild animals of the coastal estuary and rain forest including the harpy eagle, the jaguar, the alligatorlike caiman, the serpent, and the shark.

Range of Influence. The influence of the Formative Period Olmec is well documented outside of their Gulf Coast heartland. At Taltilco, near modern-day Mexico City in the central highlands, hollow white-ware ceramic figurines depicting the chubby Olmec infant show clear stylistic links to Early Formative San Lorenzo. At Chalcatzingo, in the highland Mexican state of Morelos, ceramics, figurines, and rock carvings show remarkable similarities to the sculptural traditions of Middle Formative La Venta. At Juxtlahuaca and Oxtotitlan in Guerrero, Olmec-like rulers and animal motifs are depicted in cave paintings. Obsidian from highland Mexico and jade, serpentine, and magnetite from Oaxaca and Guatemala attest to the fact that Olmec trade and influence outside of the Gulf Coast had reciprocal implications for the economy of the lowlands. This exchange was probably generated by the Olmec's desire for exotic wealth, which was consumed as a core element of elite ceremonial activity and display within the heartland. Exchange undoubtedly stimulated the development of complex society across most of Formative Period Mesoamerica. The symbols of Olmec rulership and political power depicted in these exotic media acted to legitimate elite authority within Formative lowland society and foreshadowed the subsequent elaboration of political economies that characterized all succeeding civilizations of ancient Mesoamerica.

[See also MESOAMERICA: FORMATIVE PERIOD IN MESO-AMERICA.]

■ Matthew W. Stirling, "Early History of the Olmec Problem," in *Dumbarton Oaks Conference on the Olmec*, ed. Elizabeth Benson (1968), pp. 1–8. Ignacio Bernal, *The Olmec World* (1969). Peter D. Joralemon, "A Study of Olmec Iconography," *Studies in Pre-Columbian Art and Archaeology* 7 (1971). Michael D. Coe and Richard R. Diehl, *In the Land of the Olmec* (1980). Phillip Drucker, "On the Nature of the Olmec Polity," in *The Olmec and Their Neighbors*, ed. Elizabeth Benson (1981), pp. 29–47. Robert J. Sharer and David C. Grove, eds., *Regional Perspectives on the Olmec* (1989).

Thomas W. Killion

OLORGESAILLIE is an Acheulian hand-axe site in southern Kenya, about 34 miles (55 km) southwest of Nairobi, which dates to about half a million years ago. The artifact-rich location was discovered by Louis and Mary *Leakey during World War II. Glyn Isaac carried out further excavations at Olorgesaillie in the 1960s and early 1970s. He established that the occupants camped in dry water courses. Here the visitors would find shade, less-saline water by digging in the sand of the streambeds, and less grass cover. They also stayed on a low, rocky promontory overlooking the lake, presumably during the rains, when mosquitoes were abundant. Dense concentrations of hand axes, cleavers, and other stone artifacts lie in an area that once lay on the shores of a small lake. Unfortunately, many of the artifacts come from sites disturbed by water action, but Isaac estimated that most camp areas were between 16 and 66 feet (5 and 20 m) across. Almost no bone was preserved at Olorgesaillie, and no human fossils have been recovered. One location yielded large quantities of baboon bones, perhaps the remains of a troop killed while sleeping in trees overhead. Many stone artifacts were made from stone brought from some distance away. They consisted for the most part of sharp-edged axes and cleavers, as well as flake tools used for butchering and processing meat and other foods. The range of variation in the tools is remarkable, and they may have been fabricated over a long period of sporadic visits to the Olorgesaillie location. Olorgesaillie is one of several locations in eastern Africa where traces of animal butchery are well preserved in the archaeological records. Unfortunately, it has not been possible to potassium-argon-date the site, but it is broadly contemporary with other butchery locations in tropical Africa.

[See also ACHEULEAN TRADITION; AFRICA: PREHISTORY OF AFRICA; HOMO ERECTUS; OLDUVAI GORGE.]

■ Glyn Isaac, *Olorgesaillie* (1977). David Phillipson, *African Archaeology*, 2nd ed. (1993).

Brian M. Fagan

OPPIDA. During his conquest of Gaul in 58–51 B.C., Julius Caesar encountered a number of settlements for which he employed the Latin word *oppidum*, meaning a town or defended place. Some of the sites named by Caesar can be identified on the ground—for instance, Alesia (Alise-Sainte-Reine), and Bibracte (Mont Beuvray, near Autun). Characteristically, they are in defensive situations, on hilltops, promontories, or islands with massive ramparts enclosing areas of 75 to 495 acres (30–200 ha). Such sites can be identified in a broad strip across Europe from Brittany to Moravia, and from Switzerland to central Germany, and Caesar's term *oppidum* has been generally applied to them by archaeologists.

According to Caesar, Bibracte was the meeting place of the *senatus* (representative assembly) of the local tribe, the Aedui, and it was also chosen for an assembly of all the Gallic tribes to coordinate their resistance to Rome. At other oppida he mentions marketplaces and merchants, especially Italian traders. From his description some of these sites were clearly capitals of tribal states and centers of government, resource storage, and trade and industry.

Caesar's description accords well with the archaeological record. Though some sites such as the Camp d'Artus at Huelgoat in Brittany contain few traces of occupation, many were intensively occupied, sometimes with a planned rectilinear layout of streets. House types are quite varied, ranging from small rectangular buildings often fronting the streets (presumably the homes and workshops of an artisan class) to large palisaded enclosures up to half a hectare or more in size and containing large timber houses, stables, workshops, and granaries. These are presumably the residences of the social elite encountered by Caesar; they are perhaps the equivalent of the courtyard houses of the classical Mediterranean towns. Public buildings have generally not been identified, other than a small number of religious shrines. In temperate Europe, construction was in timber, clay, and thatch, occasionally with some dry-stone walling; masonry buildings appear only after the Roman conquest.

Defense was a major factor in the siting of many oppida. In western Europe, especially in France, ramparts were constructed using an interlace of horizontal beams jointed where they crossed with large iron spikes; they have dry-stone walls on the front and back, the space between was filled with soil, and there was a ramp of soil against the inner face to give access to the rampart walk. This is the classic *murus gallicus* described by Caesar. These ramparts were later replaced by massive earthen banks without timber lacing, fronted by wide ditches, what Sir Mortimer *Wheeler termed the "Fécamp" construction. In central Europe an earthen bank revetted in front by vertical timber posts and dry-stone walling was more normal. Gateways were formed by turning the two ends of the rampart inward 90 degrees—the so-called pincers gateway—making a narrow passageway, at the end of which stood a timber gateway.

A few oppida functioned as specialist production sites; Kelheim in Bavaria and the Titelberg in Luxembourg exploited their local iron resources, and Bad Nauheim and *Hallstatt specialized in salt production, though these last two sites were not defended, and so strictly speaking are not oppida. Normally, oppida produce evidence for a range of industries, especially iron smelting and smithing. Crucibles indicate working of gold, silver, and copper alloys for, among other items, coins. Glass was imported to manufacture beads and bracelets; dice, buttons, and other items were made of bone. Painted pottery, cooking pots, and storage vessels were manufactured and traded, sometimes, as at *Manching, using special imported clays. Iron tools indicate a wide range of other industries—wheelwrights, wainwrights, saddlers, and other specialist carpenters, jewelers, and sword smiths—all producing a range of high-quality vehicles and weapons, as well as mass-produced trinkets.

The second and first centuries B.C. saw a massive upsurge in trade in Europe. Occasional coins and pots found far from their sources indicate the internal trade among the oppida, but exotic items are more easily identified. Amber was imported from the Baltic, and the oppidum of Staré Hradisko in Moravia specialized in manufacturing amber beads. Much more widespread are the products of the Mediterranean world, primarily from Tuscany and Campania in central Italy. Wine amphorae were reaching sites in central France by the tens of thousands, and were traded as far as southern Britain, Belgium, Bavaria, and Bohemia. The bronze vessels associated with wine drinking traveled even farther, to Scandinavia and the Baltic; on the other hand, fine Campanian tableware rarely went farther than central France and southern Germany. Rarer still are luxury items like silver drinking vessels and finger rings with engraved intaglios. The trade was seemingly organized by Italian traders. Both Caesar and Posidonius mention that they included some permanently resident on major oppida: at the Magdalensberg in Austria, perhaps the ancient Noreia. Italian traders occupied their own quarter in the town, and specialized in the export of the highly prized Norican iron. Slaves, cereals, and raw materials are also referred to by ancient authors.

The status of native traders is unknown; Caesar does not specifically mention Gallic merchants, and it is possible that their status was low, especially given the importance of the Italians. Internal exchange was encouraged from the late second century B.C. by the production of relatively low-value silver and struck and cast bronze coins, but the distribution of these was strictly local, sometimes almost confined to individual oppida. The quantities that are found on certain oppida suggest a more advanced use of coinage than in the subsequent Roman period. Gold coins, too, seem largely to have been for local consumption, though merchants on the Magdalensberg were using gold for international transactions.

Similar large defended sites, also termed oppida by archaeologists, are found in central Spain, dating from at least the third century B.C.—sites such as Las Cogatas near Ávila, or Numancia, scene of a major Roman siege in 133 B.C. In central Europe, especially Slovakia and Hungary, settlements take on a different format, with a small defended area surrounded by a large open settlement. In terms of their material culture (styles of pottery, coinage, etc.), these sites, such as Zemplín in eastern Slovakia, Liptovska Mára in northern Slovakia, and Tabán-Gellerthegy at Budapest, closely resemble their western European counterparts.

In Britain, continental-style oppida are unknown, but the trading port of Hengistbury Head in Dorset is one possible exception. The term *oppidum* is used rather to denote low-lying sites in river valleys, enclosed by intermittent linear dikes whose function seems more for display than for defense. Even a small British example such as Stanwick in northern Yorkshire, enclosing 865 acres (350 ha), is large by continental standards. The larger sites such as Camulodunum (Colchester) and Verulamium (St. Albans) enclose several square kilometers. These sites seem to be royal residences or estates, and only small parts of them were occupied by settlements of artisans and traders.

The continental oppida have been claimed as the earliest urban settlements in temperate Europe. In western Europe, dendrochronological dates from oppida such as Besançon date their foundation to around 120 B.C. Sites in central Germany and Czechoslovakia are somewhat earlier, founded probably in the first half of the second century B.C. Oppida that lie outside the subsequent Roman Empire were generally abandoned in the second half of the first century B.C., and urbanization did not reappear in these areas until the Medieval Period. By contrast, in France, Switzerland, Spain, and Britain many sites developed into Roman towns, and many still continue today. Paris, Reims, Orléans, Chartres, Bourges, Geneva, Ávila, Colchester, and St. Albans are all sites whose origins lie in the oppidum period.

[See also CELTS; EUROPE, *articles on* THE EUROPEAN IRON AGE, ROMAN AND POST-ROMAN EUROPE; HILL FORTS.]

■ F. Audouze and O. Buchsenschutz, *Towns, Villages and Countryside of Celtic Europe* (1991). J. R. Collis, *Oppida: Earliest Towns North of the Alps* (1991).

John Collis

OSEBERG. Along the margins of the Oslo Fjord, Norway, a series of impressive Viking Age boat graves was discovered in the nineteenth century; at Oseberg, 43 miles (70 km) from Oslo, on the west side of the fjord in Vestfold County, the richest boat grave known from Viking Age Scandinavia was excavated in 1904. The burial was covered by a large mound of peat overlying a blue clay subsoil; together, these soils preserved the ship's timbers, as well as other wooden objects and textiles. The grave had been disturbed in antiquity, however, and presumably robbed of items of precious metalwork, which are conspicuously absent.

The ship, built almost entirely of oak, in clinker construction, was 70.5 feet (21.5 m) long, 17 feet (5.1 m) broad, and 4.9 feet (1.5 m) deep. It had thirty oars, and a side rudder, with a mast estimated at 43 feet (13 m) tall. Other fittings included an iron anchor, a gangplank, and a bailer. Several characteristics of the ship—its size, the elaborately carved decoration at the stem and stern, its relative frailty—suggest that it was used by aristocrats or royalty for coastal voyages.

Skeletal remains of two women were found in the ship. One, aged sixty to seventy, suffered badly from arthritis and other maladies; the second was aged twenty-five to thirty. It is not clear which was the more important in life, or whether one was ritually sacrificed to accompany the other in death. Both the opulence of the burial rite and the quantity of the items interred point to this being a burial of very high status. Dendrochronological analysis of timbers from the grave chamber erected within the ship dates the burial to 834. Suggestions that the name Oseberg means "Aasa's burial mound," and that this is the burial of Queen Aasa mentioned in *Ynglingatal*, a poem praising the Vestfold kings, are speculative.

The robbers had left in place items of little value to them, which are nonetheless of exceptional rarity and interest. They include elaborately decorated wooden sledges, a cart or carriage, and five finely carved posts from some item of furniture. These are important representations of contemporary art styles, and have figured largely in discussions of Viking artistic development. There are also more mundane but still high-quality wooden items such as a chest and a range of kitchen equipment. A series of textiles includes woollen garments and imported silks as well as fragments of narrow woollen tapestries decorated with human and animal figures. All this testifies to the considerable power and prestige accruing to regional rulers and their entourages in the early Viking age. The ship and its contents are displayed at the Viking Ship Museum in Oslo.

[*See also* SCANDINAVIA: SCANDINAVIA AND THE VIKING AGE.]

■ A. W. Brøgger, H. Falk, and H. Shetelig, *Osebergfunnet Utgitt av Den norske stat*, 4 vols. (1917–1928). A. W. Brøgger and H. Shetelig, *The Viking Ships* (1971).

Richard A. Hall

P

PACIFIC ISLANDS

OVERVIEW

The settlement of the Pacific Islands began in the Late Ice Age, when world sea levels were as much as 300 feet (91 m) lower than today. Mainland Southeast Asia extended far offshore, with short straits separating the mainland from Sunda and Sahul. The first settlement of New Guinea occurred at least 40,000 years ago, that of Australia not much later (the date is disputed). By 30,000 years ago, people had settled in the Solomon Islands and in the Bismarck Archipelago. For many centuries, the Lapita Complex flourished in Melanesia, a widely flung culture of island communities joined by maritime trade networks. As contributors Michael Graves and Terry Hunt point out in other sections of this article, easily stored root crops, offshore navigation techniques, and the double-hulled outrigger canoe made more offshore settlement in Polynesia and Micronesia possible after 4,000 years ago. They also describe excavations on many islands, which are allowing archaeologists to date first settlement throughout the Pacific much more precisely. At the same time, long-term experiments at ocean voyaging in replica canoes, using traditional navigational techniques, have provided indisputable proof that the settlement of the Pacific Islands was the result of deliberate voyaging, not accidental strandings far offshore. The first European crossing of the Pacific by Ferdinand Magellan in 1520 was followed by the development of Spanish galleon sailing routes, which took treasure ships from Acapulco to the Philippines, then far northward across to California, far out of sight of land. Sustained European contact with the Pacific Islands came in the eighteenth century.

Brian M. Fagan

INTRODUCTION

The developments that led to the settlement of the Pacific Islands began during the Late Ice Age. Fifty thousand years ago, enormous ice sheets on land locked up so much water that world sea levels fell by as much as 300 feet (91 m). An extensive continental shelf extended out from mainland Southeast Asia incorporating the island of Borneo. Offshore, across two open straits no more than 62 miles (100 km) wide, lay a vast continent the geologists call Sahul, comprising New Guinea, Australia, and the present-day Arafura Sea. New Zealander Geoffrey Irwin, one of the few archaeologists who is also an open-water sailor, theorizes that ancient settlers paddled, sailed, and drifted downwind from the southeastern Asian mainland to uninhabited Sahul sometime when sea levels were far lower than today. A few scattered stone artifacts from New Guinea's Huon Peninsula document human settlement on Sahul by at least 40,000 years ago. The earliest well-documented occupation of Australia dates to about 35,000 B.P., although earlier sites are claimed.

By 30,000 years ago, small communities had settled on the Solomon Islands and on the archipelagos of the Bismarck Strait west of New Guinea, chains of islands in sight of one another and the mainland. From the very beginning, these fisherfolk and foragers cooperated in far-flung exchange networks, which took ceremonial shells from one island to the next, fine-grained obsidian for toolmaking from there to another group a few sea miles away, and so on. Every island depended on its neighbors for essential commodities. As the centuries passed, island communities throughout the southwestern Pacific were linked to one another and to communities on New Guinea and even on Borneo by local trade routes carrying obsidian and other materials. In archaeological terms, these diverse populations are still little known, but they manufactured a highly distinctive form of stamp-decorated pottery named Lapita Ware after a site of that name on New Caledonia Island. This Lapita Cultural Complex lasted from before 3000 B.C. until about A.D. 200, and represents the remains of a vast exchange system that linked island after island through reciprocal trading between kinspeople. A complex pattern of interisland movements, trade, and occasionally deliberate migration caused the Lapita Cultural Complex to spread far out into the Pacific. But, until about 1500 B.C., Lapita navigators did not venture far out of sight of land. Beyond the horizon lay open water passage of over 300 miles (480 km) to biologically impoverished and isolated islands. Only people with seaworthy, offshore double-hulled canoes, viable open-water navigational techniques, and easily stored domesticated root crops and animals could voyage to such islands, colonize them, and then return.

The colonization of Micronesia and Polynesia is closely associated with the spread of taro and yam cultivation, both roots crops that can be carried in canoes. From Melanesia in the west, Lapita canoes traveled through western Polynesia taking the plants and domesticated animals of their homelands with them. After many centuries of local voyaging, these Stone Age sailors suddenly ventured far offshore. Between 1600 and 100 B.C., their double-hulled canoes sailed westward, to Vanuatu, Fiji, Tonga, and Samoa. Six centuries of adjustment in western Polynesia ensued. The colonization of Micronesia and eastern Polynesia took place within the last 2,000 years, some 1,300 to 1,600 years after the first settlement of western Polynesia. The sudden, and apparently rapid, expansion may have resulted from population growth in already settled islands that sent voyagers farther eastward looking for new, uninhabited lands. It is thought that the Polynesians originated in the Fiji area before the great elaboration of Melanesian culture after A.D. 1. After some centuries of adjustment, population growth and food shortages sent canoes far eastward, to the Marquesas and Society Islands by A.D. 500, north to Hawaii in about A.D. 600, and down to Easter Island a century later. From the heart of Polynesia, canoes voyaged southwestward to New Zealand between A.D. 1000 and 1200. Centuries before Christopher Columbus sailed to the Americas, the Polynesians had colonized every habitable island over 11½ million square miles (29.8 million sq km) of the Pacific Ocean.

[See also PACIFIC ISLANDS NAVIGATION AND WATERCRAFT.]

■ P. V. Kirch, *The Evolution of the Pacific Chiefdoms* (1984). Peter Bellwood, *The Polynesians* (1987). Geoffrey Irwin, *The Prehistoric Exploration and Colonization of the Pacific* (1992). Ben Finney, *Voyage of Rediscovery* (1994).

Brian M. Fagan

SETTLEMENT OF MELANESIA AND MICRONESIA

Of all the questions involving Pacific Islands prehistory, those involving the origins and timing of human settlement in this vast area have most intrigued researchers. Initially, research on this topic emphasized comparisons of modern traits from languages, human biology, and culture as a means to reconstruct history. Today, it is to archaeology that we look for evidence pertaining to prehistoric human settlement.

Beginning in the 1950s with the advent of *radiocarbon dating, archaeologists have successively pushed back in time the settlement of the Pacific, and as more excavations have been completed, we know considerably more about the directions in which prehistoric settlers are likely to have moved and the conditions they faced. This work has been particularly successful in refuting the hypothesis first put forward by Peter Buck (1938) that the islands of Micronesia were used as stepping-stones in the colonization of the eastern Pacific, including much of Polynesia. It has also demonstrated the inadequacies of Heyerdahl's popularized notion that Polynesians originated in South America. Virtually all archaeologists acknowledge the role of Melanesia—the island region lying north of Australia and east of island Southeast Asia in the trajectory of human settlement of the Pacific.

Melanesia. Melanesia includes the large island of New Guinea, which during most of the *Pleistocene was part of an enormous land mass known as Sahul, a region encompassing Australia and Tasmania as well. With the discovery of Pleistocene archaeological sites in Australia, comparably aged sites were expected on New Guinea. These have now been archaeologically documented, and one site on the north coast of the island has been dated to approximately 40,000 B.P. Additional sites dated to between 25,000 and 30,000 B.P. have been identified on several other islands in Melanesia that could not have been connected by land to Sahul (or New Guinea) during the Pleistocene. These include the islands of New Ireland and New Britain in the Bismarck Archipelago (north of New Guinea) and the island of Buka in the northern Solomon Islands.

The human settlement of Sahul and its nearby islands during the Late Pleistocene represents the earliest evidence for transport capabilities over considerable distances of ocean. Irwin (1992) suggests that the most likely routes into Sahul involved a series of moves through intervisible islands in eastern Indonesia. The geographic extent of Pleistocene settlement in the western Pacific corresponds to those islands that lie within 155 miles (250 km) of each other and are intervisible. Archaeological sites from the terminal Pleistocene and the Early and Middle *Holocene have also been discovered throughout much of this same area. In the highlands of New Guinea there are agricultural features, most likely for growing taro, dated to ca. 9000 B.P. Throughout Melanesia, the archaeological evidence suggests intermittent (and in some cases, diminishing) use of sites through the Middle Holocene, with interisland voyaging and exchange as well as the purposeful introduction of animals and plants to islands lacking them.

Archaeological research has disclosed a distinctive ceramic complex geographically distributed across Melanesia (although excluding much of New Guinea) and portions of Polynesia. This complex, known as *Lapita, is now dated to 3500–3000 B.P., and for west Polynesia represents the first colonization of these islands by humans. For island Melanesia, the situation is more complex, given the earlier occupation of several islands. Unfortunately, only a few Melanesian sites are known in which preceramic archaeological deposits dating to 4000–5000 B.P. underlay or occur in the same locality as deposits containing Lapita materials. Thus archaeologists continue to debate the historical relationship between Lapita and these earlier groups in Melanesia.

Research in the 1980s by the Lapita Homeland Project (Allen and Gosden 1991) to resolve this issue has now resulted in a number of new findings. First, there is some overlap in settlement and in the subsistence and technological practices between the Preceramic and Lapita Periods. Nonetheless, Lapita is distinguished by the introduction of pottery technology into the region and is associated with more readily identifiable horticultural practices and animal domesticates, and its settlements are located on smaller offshore islands or nearby reef flats. Second, the geographic distribution of Lapita (as defined by the presence of a calcareous sand–tempered, red-slipped, and occasionally dentate-stamped pottery) was extremely widespread over a relatively short period of time. Sites with early Lapita pottery occur in the interval from ca. 3500 to 3200 B.P. from the Bismarck Archipelago to Fiji, Samoa, and Tonga in the east, a distance of over 2,170 miles (3,500 km). These latter three island groups are separated from the easternmost islands of Melanesia by a water gap of more than 310 miles (500 km), and Lapita provides the earliest evidence for this colonization. Third, the geographic distribution suggests that the groups producing this pottery had effective strategies for successful voyaging and for establishing new settlements. Perhaps one of these strategies was linked to the transport and exchange of resources (e.g., obsidian) and commodities (e.g., pottery) for which Lapita is well known. Such a strategy would have benefited the relatively isolated colonizers in west Polynesia, and may have served also to link dispersed and possibly distinct groups farther west. There is evidence of continuity between Lapita and subsequent archaeological complexes, suggesting historical relatedness.

Micronesia. Traditionally, the settlement of Melanesia

and of Micronesia have been treated separately. Recent research in the two areas suggests that their settlement may be linked in at least two respects.

First, the distinctive ceramic complex associated with Lapita is mirrored in the Mariana Islands of Micronesia by a similar form of pottery first defined by Spoehr (1957). This pottery is calcareous sand–tempered, red-slipped, or well-polished, and occasionally decorated with a series of lime-filled impressions. It is associated with the earliest period of human occupation of the Marianas, dating to approximately 3500 to 3000 B.P., but is sufficiently distinguishable from Lapita pottery. However, both pottery complexes may be derived from a common ancestral pottery-making group and / or they may reflect rapid geographic differentiation of pottery production among what were otherwise contemporary settlements. Other than the similar forms of pottery, there is as yet little else about the early prehistory of the Mariana Islands that would link it to Lapita in Melanesia. Further, there is as yet no well-accepted evidence for an equivalently early colonization of the other island groups of western Micronesia, such as Yap or Palau. These islands are located closer to Melanesia and are more centrally located with respect to insular Southeast Asia than the Mariana Islands. Thus the early settlement of the Mariana Islands does not appear to have been followed by geographically extensive movement into the other unoccupied islands of Micronesia (or alternatively, evidence for this early period has been missed). Linguistic analyses suggest that Yap and Palau could have been settled separately and from either the south (Melanesia) or the west (Southeast Asia).

The second link between Melanesia and Micronesia has emerged from more recent archaeological and comparative linguistic research. The languages of eastern Micronesia (Caroline Islands, Marshall Islands, and Kiribati) are most similar to languages spoken in Vanuatu and the southeastern Solomon Islands (located in eastern Melanesia), and both linguists and archaeologists have suggested that the latter area is the source region for the prehistoric settlement of eastern Micronesia. Computer simulations of potential voyaging conditions by Irwin (1992) support a model of eastern Micronesian settlement from this area of Melanesia or possibly farther east, from Fiji. The archaeological evidence pertaining to prehistoric settlement is meager. However, the early prehistoric pottery of the eastern Carolines is similar in form and surface treatment to that associated with Late Lapita (ca. 2500–2300 B.P.). Confounding the archaeological case, the timing of the initial human occupation of eastern Micronesia remains unclear, and there is no east to west trend in the earliest radiocarbon dates from the region. Although a few archaeologists have inferred settlement of eastern Micronesia well before 2500–2300 B.P., there are no securely dated sites until ca. 2000 B.P.

Micronesia is known for its extensive series of atoll island groups, and many anthropologists have assumed that these land forms would have been settled after the larger high islands. Yet, as Irwin (1992) documents, the atolls would have provided a larger target area for discovery, but they may not have been above sea level until after 3000 B.P. Although the high islands of the Carolines are generally assigned earlier colonization dates than the atolls, more archaeological work has been completed on these islands. However, there are early dates from the Marshall Islands that are nearly equivalent to those from the higher islands such as Kosrae and Pohnpei, suggesting the nearly contemporaneous settlement of much of eastern Micronesia.

The prehistoric settlement of Melanesia and Micronesia appears to involve some common or shared ancestry, especially for the last 3,000 years. Yet the two regions are highly distinctive in other ways. According to current evidence, the Middle Holocene settlement of Micronesia was much more variable with respect to time and space than is the case for Melanesia and west Polynesia. This probably reflects not only differences in terms of interisland distances and resource distributions between the two regions, but also the extent of archaeological work completed in each area.

[*See also* AUSTRALIA AND NEW GUINEA: FIRST SETTLEMENT OF SUNDA AND SAHUL; PACIFIC ISLANDS NAVIGATION AND WATERCRAFT; PACIFIC ISLANDS, ORIGINS OF FOOD PRODUCTION IN THE.]

■ P. H. Buck, *Vikings of the Sunrise* (1938). A. Spoehr, *Marianas Prehistory: Archaeological Survey and Excavations on Saipan, Tinian, and Rota* (1957). P. Bellwood, *Man's Conquest of the Pacific* (1979). J. L. Craib, "Micronesian Prehistory: An Archaeological Overview," *Science* 219 (1983): 922–927. P. V. Kirch and T. L. Hunt, eds., *Archaeology of the Lapita Cultural Complex: A Critical Review* (1988). J. Allen and C. Gosden, eds., *Report of the Lapita Homeland Project* (1991). G. Irwin, *The Prehistoric Exploration and Colonisation of the Pacific* (1992).
Michael W. Graves

SETTLEMENT OF POLYNESIA

The great British navigator Captain James Cook was the first Westerner to ponder the origins of the Polynesians. During a prolonged stay on Tahiti in 1769, he put his finger on the fundamental historical questions that have puzzled scholars since the eighteenth century: How did the Polynesians colonize their idyllic homeland? How had humans with only simple canoes and no metals sailed across vast tracts of open ocean and settled on the remotest islands of the Pacific? Cook talked to the Tahitian navigator named Tupaia, who carried a mental map of Polynesia, which Cook made up into a rough sketch map. Modern scholars believe he could define an area bounded by the Marquesas in the northeast, the Tuamotus to the east, the Australs to the south, and the Cook Islands to the southwest. Even Fiji and Samoa to the west lay within his consciousness, an area as large as Australia or the United States. James Cook had no doubts about Polynesian navigational abilities. "When this comes to be prov'd we Shall be no longer at a loss to know how the Islands lying in those seas came to be people'd . . . so we may trace them from Island to Island quite to the East Indies" (Beaglehole, 1955: 154). When he marveled at the Polynesians' ability to sail against the wind for hundreds of miles, Tupaia pointed out that westerlies blew from November to January, and that these were months when canoes could make good progress to windward.

Cook's shipmate, the scientist Joseph Banks, had some training in philology and collected vocabularies wherever he went. He soon showed that many Polynesian words originated in Southeast Asia. Nineteenth-century linguistic researchers proved Banks correct. They defined an enormous family of what are now called the Austronesian ("Southern Island") languages, which extended from Polynesia in the east through Southeast Asia all the way across the Indian Ocean to Madagascar. Until the European Age of Discovery in the eighteenth century, Australonesian was the most widely distributed language family on Earth, carried over two oceans by people sailing outrigger canoes.

Cook's theory of Polynesian origins has stood the test of time. But some questions remain. How and when did the great voyages begin, and when did human beings first settle throughout Polynesia? Until the 1950s, many influential scholars assumed the Pacific Islands were colonized by canoes blown accidentally far offshore. But in 1965 English cruising sailor David Lewis encountered aged canoe navigators in the Carolina Islands of Micronesia. He promptly sailed his oceangoing, European-designed catamaran from Rarotonga in the Cook Islands to *New Zealand using only a star map. In the 1970s, Lewis apprenticed himself to the Carolinian navigators, learning how they made passages with the aid of sun, moon, stars, and cloud and swell formations, even by watching passing birds. His famous book *We the Navigators*, published in 1972, vindicated the ancient Polynesians. Then anthropologist and sailor Stephen Thomas (1987) studied with navigator Mau Piailug from Satawal Island in the 1980s, acquiring the vanishing lore of a *palau*, an initiated navigator. "The knowledge of navigation brings . . . fierceness, strength, and wisdom," Piailug told Thomas during a stressful and demanding research project. Since the 1960s, sustained experiments with replicas of ancient canoes have validated the navigational skills of prehistoric voyagers and documented the ease with which double-outrigger canoes can make open-water passages to remote landmasses and return safely.

Despite Norwegian anthropologist Thor Heyerdahl's attempt to prove with the *Kon Tiki* voyage that Polynesia was settled by balsa rafts from ancient Peru, no traces of ancient American artifacts have been found anywhere in the South Pacific. The cultural roots of the first Polynesians lie far to the west, notably in the Lapita tradition of the southwestern Pacific. The ancestry of the *Lapita Complex goes back deep into the Late Ice Age, to Stone Age cultures that had settled on the Solomon Islands and on the archipelagos of the Bismarck Strait west of New Guinea, chains of islands in sight of one another and the mainland, by about 30,000 years ago. From the very beginning, these Stone Age fisherfolk and foragers cooperated in far-flung exchange networks, which took ceremonial shells from one island to the next, fine-grained obsidian for toolmaking from there to another group a few sea miles away, and so on. Every island depended on its neighbors for essential commodities. But early colonization stopped when no islands could be seen in the distance. Beyond the Solomons lay an open-water passage of over 300 miles (482 km) to biologically impoverished and isolated islands. Only people with seaworthy offshore canoes, viable open-water navigational techniques, and easily stored domesticated root crops and animals could voyage to such islands, colonize them, and then return.

The catalysts for the first settlement of Polynesia were the development of the oceangoing, double-hulled canoe and navigational techniques using the heavenly bodies. Such methods must have evolved out of simpler, line-of-sight techniques, which had been used among the islands of the southwestern Pacific for millennia. With appropriate agricultural products, it was now possible for small groups of voyagers to colonize biologically impoverished, off-lying islands and then return to their original point of departure.

After many centuries of local voyaging, Lapita navigators suddenly ventured far offshore. Between 1600 and 100 B.C., their double-hulled canoes had sailed westward to Vanuatu, Fiji, Tonga, and Samoa, where Lapita ware occurs. It is thought that ancestral Polynesian culture originated in the Fiji area before the great elaboration of Melanesian culture after A.D. 1. Six centuries of adjustment in western Polynesia may have ensued, although some authorities believe the migrations were a gradual, and continuous, process. There is evidence for environmental disturbance resulting from agriculture in the southern Cook Islands around 500 B.C., and around 200 B.C., for the northern Marquesas and northern Cooks. Eventually, population growth and food shortages sent canoes far eastward, to the *Society Islands by A.D. 500, north to *Hawaii in about A.D. 600, and down to *Easter Island (Rapa Nui) a century later. From the heart of Polynesia, canoes voyaged southwestward to New Zealand (Aotearoa) between A.D. 1000 and 1200.

Little is known of the technology and lifeway of the first settlers. The crops the people planted varied from island to island, but breadfruit, taro, coconut, yams, and bananas were the staples. Sweet potato, a South American cultigen, was a staple when Westerners first arrived. No one knows how this American crop reached eastern Polynesia, but it may have been the result of as yet unidentified Polynesian voyaging to the South American mainland. The basic technology was simple, relying heavily on polished stone axes and adzes for forest clearance and woodworking. An elaborate array of bone and shell fishhooks, along with spears and nets, were used in lagoon and offshore fishing. Once settlement took hold, the food surpluses generated from agriculture and fishing became a form of wealth with powerful social uses.

Centuries before Christopher Columbus sailed to the Americas, the Polynesians had colonized every habitable island over 11.5 million square miles (29.8 million sq km) of the Pacific Ocean. The human settlement of Polynesia seems to have taken approximately 2,500 years from its beginnings by people who were still, technologically speaking, in the Stone Age.

[*See also* PACIFIC ISLANDS NAVIGATION AND WATERCRAFT; PACIFIC ISLANDS, ORIGINS OF FOOD PRODUCTION IN THE.]

■ J. C. Beaglehole, *The Journals of Captain James Cook on His Voyages of Discovery*, 3 vols. (1955–67). David Lewis, *We the Navigators* (1972). Patrick V. Kirch, "Advances in Polynesian Prehistory: Three Decades in Review," *Advances in World Archaeology* 2 (1982): 52–102. Patrick V. Kirch, *The Evolution of the Polynesian Chiefdoms* (1984). Patrick V. Kirch, ed., *Island Societies* (1986). Peter Bellwood, *The Polynesians* (1987). Stephen Thomas, *The Last Navigator* (1987). Ben Finney, *Voyage of Rediscovery: A Cultural Odyssey through Polynesia* (1994).

Brian M. Fagan

EUROPEAN VOYAGERS AND THE END OF PREHISTORY IN THE PACIFIC ISLANDS

The European discovery of the Pacific Islands began in 1521 when Magellan sighted a low island fringed with trees, probably an atoll in the Tuamotu Archipelago in the southeastern Pacific. The last European discovery was Midway Island in the north-central Pacific made by Captain N. C. Brooks in 1859. The period of European discovery lasted 338 years and brought radical change to the populations of the region. Europeans entered the Pacific from a crowded, diseased continent with colonial aspirations. The nature, intensity, and consequences changed with later contact that came with Christian missionaries.

At the time of European contact the world of Oceania—in Polynesia, Melanesia, and Micronesia—had been fully explored, settled, populated, and had evolved into diverse island civilizations. By a few centuries prior to Europeans arriving in the Pacific, island voyagers had discovered nearly every speck of land and founded successful populations on most. Perhaps because so much of the Pacific had been discovered and settled, long-distance voyages of exploration and colonization began to decline. The high costs of overseas voyaging would not yield the same returns they once had. Pacific populations ranged from less than a hundred on small islands and atolls to hundreds of thousands on the large high islands such as those of *Hawaii, *New Zealand, and Fiji. Sociopolitical systems ranged from simple egalitarian to complex hierarchies. This range of sociopolitical organization has been the focus of much anthropological study (e.g., M. Sahlins's classic *Social Stratification in Polynesia,* 1958).

European contact brought the first written histories to the Pacific. The logs of explorers and naturalists offer observations and descriptions that provide a glimpse, although biased or Eurocentric, into the traditional societies of the Pacific. These early, primary sources are the foundations of historical anthropology for the region. Among the early explorers, Captain James Cook is probably best known for the valuable detailed record his expedition produced.

Archaeological research specifically focused on early European contact in the Pacific is still in its infancy. Historians and anthropologists have debated issues probably best resolved with the weight of archaeological evidence. The first, and most significant, is the question of demographic collapse with the introduction of disease to populations with no evolutionary history of immunity. The debate raged in American circles and has recently entered the Pacific.

Based on analysis of early historical sources, David Stannard (e.g., *Before the Horror,* 1989) argues that the Hawaiian Islands suffered early drastic population collapse. He suggests that this historically invisible collapse took a greater toll than ever imagined. Instead of Hawaiians ranging somewhere from 200,000 to 400,000 before contact, Stannard argues the real number is closer to 800,000 to one million. His global comparative analysis of collapse in non-immune populations suggests approximately 80 percent decline with the first fifty years of contact. If correct, Stannard's work has implications for other Pacific Islands. If population loss was early and severe, then precensual population estimates for Oceanic populations are flawed. If catastrophic collapse occurred as Stannard suggests, then a significant degree of social, cultural, and biological discontinuity exists in early contact histories of the region.

A second major issue surrounds the role of contact in social and political change. In Hawaii and Fiji, for example, the use of firearms and European ships appear to have tipped the balance in native warfare. This change resulted in polity formation at a scale previously unknown.

Archaeologists have begun research in the region specifically focused on these problems. Documenting the regional record of prehistoric settlement pattern and its transformation with contact will be critical to understanding the degree and chronology of demographic collapse in island settings. Archaeological research can also address related issues in the consequences of early European contact and offer an independent source of evidence in historical reconstructions.

[*See also* HAWAII; NEW ZEALAND; PACIFIC ISLAND CHIEFDOMS; SOCIETY ISLANDS.]

■ O. A. Bushnell, *The Gifts of Civilization: Germs and Genocide in Hawai'i* (1993). Patrick Kirch and Marshall Sahlins, *Anahulu: The Anthropology of History in the Kingdom of Hawaii,* 2 vols. (1992). Anne Salmond, *Two Worlds: First Meetings between Maori and Europeans, 1642–1772* (1991). David Stannard, *Before the Horror: The Population of Hawai'i on the Eve of Western Contact* (1989). Melissa Kirkendall,

"Differential Demographic and Cultural Effects of Infectious Disease in the Pacific at European Contact," *Human Ecology* (1996).

Terry L. Hunt

PACIFIC ISLANDS CHIEFDOMS. Since the European discovery of Polynesia in the eighteenth century, explorers and researchers have been fascinated with these societies of the eastern Pacific. One part of that fascination has focused on the development and operation of chiefly systems of organization, a widespread occurrence throughout Polynesia. The first sustained, systematic efforts to describe and interpret Polynesian chiefdoms were produced by cultural anthropologists earlier this century. In a series of books, the British ethnographer Raymond Firth (1936, 1939, 1959) described the organization of a Polynesian chiefdom and how it changed on the relatively small, isolated island of Tikopia in western Polynesia. Later, American anthropologists, most notably Marshall Sahlins (1958) and Irving Goldman (1970), engaged in generalizing research and identified different kinds of chiefdoms in Polynesia in an effort to show how these differences could be interpreted from a cultural evolutionary perspective. In the case of Sahlins, differences in the environmental potential of island groups provided the basis for understanding differences in the degree of social stratification among the Polynesian societies inhabiting these islands at the time of European contact. Anthropological descriptions and interpretations of Polynesian chiefdoms have often served as analogic models for neo-evolutionary archaeologists working elsewhere in the world as they have attempted to characterize prehistoric societies and trace their changes in organizational form.

Among archaeologists working in Oceania, both Robert Suggs (1961) and Roger Green (1963, Green et al. 1967) are notable for their early efforts to infer the development and function of chiefly societies in the Marquesas, French Polynesia, and *New Zealand. It is only relatively recently, however, that archaeologists working in Polynesia have made a sustained effort to identify the long-term history of Polynesian chiefdoms. Patrick Kirch (1984), Timothy Earle (1978), and Ross Cordy (1981) have advanced our understanding of when and how Polynesian chiefdoms became established or underwent elaboration.

Historical Evidence for Chiefdoms in Polynesia. Although the archaeological evidence is still equivocal, many archaeologists believe historical linguistic reconstructions confirm that the earliest settlers to Polynesia arrived with the concept of a chief and with moderate differences in rank (and associated distinctions) between chiefs and commoners. Sahlins (1958) has suggested that these societies were most likely organized along ramage lines, wherein one's rank was a function of primogeniture. Out of this common ancestral form, a considerable diversity of chiefdoms emerged in Polynesia prior to their discovery by Europeans.

Archaeological investigations since the mid-1970s have examined the trajectory of change that produced this diversity, the mechanisms or processes responsible for this diversification, and how these chiefdoms were organized. For the most part they draw from an evolutionary perspective, now often informed by political economy theory or the principles of Darwinian evolution. The former interprets change in kind, usually at the scale of entire island groups invoking the motivations and strategies of elites. The latter identifies selective mechanisms that would account for the differential persistence of either archaeological traits or their inferred organizational forms (e.g., territoriality and competition) in time and space. Both perspectives find some common ground among the processes invoked to account for the evolution of Polynesian chiefdoms.

On all islands of sufficient size to be permanently settled by Polynesians, the populations expanded to virtually all areas, including in some cases, locations at some distance from the coastline. Research throughout Polynesia has now demonstrated that the colonization of less optimal locations for agriculture and the establishment of more permanent settlements in these locations occurred relatively late in time (after ca. A.D. 1000). At about this time the first archaeological evidence for social differentiation is found in Polynesia, and includes the construction of religious and ceremonial architecture, the expression of status differences through the construction of burial monuments and offerings associated with human burials, and the establishment of inland to coastal land divisions. Agricultural expansion and intensification occurred in many islands by the thirteenth and fourteenth centuries.

Diversity among Polynesian Chiefdoms. Despite this relatively common historical pattern of chiefly development across Polynesia, there were important differences. Perhaps the most important occurred when the geographic and numerical expansion of Polynesian populations within island groups was constrained by land availability, that is, because of the size and isolation of the tracts. The chiefly elite occupied less marked positions where islands were small and isolated (e.g., Tikopia), and if larger islands were nearby, smaller island polities were often incorporated into their chiefly organizational structure (e.g., Lanai and Maui in the Hawaiian archipelago) in late prehistory.

Where larger islands occurred, chiefs could choose among several (not necessarily exclusive) strategies, and these included intragroup and intergroup competition to demarcate their territories, efforts to develop agriculturally productive lands, and sometimes attempts to vie for the resources or lands of others. The first appears to be the strategy employed where environmental contrasts within an island or group of islands was relatively small and the island's productivity fairly high (e.g., Samoa). There was substantial competition within chiefly lineages, and this was maintained by the territories each polity claimed. Chiefly prerogatives were substantial within groups and included the construction of features devoted to ritual and ceremonial activities.

Elsewhere, marked (but not severe) environmental variability provided the context for more intense intergroup competition. In most of these cases, geographic variation in agricultural production was a key variable in the evolution of several dimensions of Polynesian chiefdoms. One aspect of geography involved the distance of certain Polynesian islands from the tropics, where most of their cultigens derived, and the distance between island groups. Islands such as New Zealand and *Easter Island were both relatively isolated and marginal for tropical agricultural development. In the case of Easter Island, where a relatively small landmass is represented, in place of agricultural intensification there was an increased emphasis on the construction of monumental architecture for ceremonial purposes during late prehistory.

Environmental zones on many islands in Polynesia reflect prevailing winds and rainfall patterns. Typically, the windward sides of most islands, which receive more regular and larger increments of rainfall, provided optimal environmental contexts for early prehistoric agricultural growth and supported greater population densities, and these localities appeared to emerge early as seats of chiefly power and authority. In Hawaii, for instance, pond fields for the production of taro occurred along the windward valleys and coasts of most major islands, and these have produced some of the best evidence for early prehistoric occupations (prior to A.D. 1000). Leeward locations, where rainfall was lower and less predictable, were often occupied on a permanent basis later in time, were much more dependent upon dry land agriculture, and had lower population densities, but larger territories. Both oral histories and archaeological evidence suggest that on many islands in Polynesia, intergroup competition was structured along the windward–leeward axis.

Patterns of Chiefly Development. Endemic competition, including intergroup aggression, appears to have been one pattern of chiefly development throughout much of Polynesia. On theoretical grounds it was probably widespread on islands with marked windward–leeward environmental differences during the period in which populations expanded to more marginal localities. In some parts of Polynesia (e.g., the Marquesas), this pattern of development continued into the historic period and was observed by European voyagers. It may be the evolutionary outcome of recurrent but unpredictable droughts and the limited potential for agricultural intensification, especially on islands where territorial expansion was limited by topography (e.g., the narrow and steep-sided valleys throughout much of the Marquesas). Consequently, although there was great competition among groups for access to resources, it was difficult for polities to expand geographically to incorporate neighboring groups.

However, there is archaeological and ethnohistorical evidence that competition between polities in Polynesia was replaced in some cases by integration into larger territorial and political units. Ladefoged (in Graves and Green, eds., 1993) has explored this on the island of Rotuma in western Polynesia, and archaeologists have identified similar patterns of development in Hawaii and the Society Islands. These are islands in which there is greater potential for agricultural intensification (or there is substantial agricultural productivity), along with marked environmental differences within relatively close proximity. The topography of these islands is such that intergroup integration and territorial expansion could be effectively achieved. However, although integration occurred, it was not always permanent. In Hawaii, for instance, intergroup integration, especially when it involved more than one island, was relatively unstable during late prehistory, and archaeologists have suggested cycles of integration and disintegration of polities.

Intergroup integration was stabilized in a few instances through hegemonic strategies. This occurred prehistorically in one part of western Polynesia, centered in Tonga, where a paramount chiefly lineage extended its geographic reach to include other islands in the archipelago, and at times more remotely located islands near Fiji and elsewhere in the region. In historic times (i.e., after European contact) in *Hawaii and the Society Islands, similar hegemonic chiefdoms developed. Given the geographic scale and the institutional permanence of these Polynesian polities, they are often identified as state-level in terms of their complexity. In all three cases, the hegemonic polity was maintained by force, through control of trade (especially foreign trade), and by strategic marital and social alliances.

Archaeological contributions to understanding the evolution of Polynesian chiefdoms is increasing both in detail and in scope. We recognize greater variation among and within chiefdoms than was previously documented and their historical depth is much better known. At the same time, an evolutionary perspective offers a general framework for the interpretation of this fascinating social form in Polynesia.

[See also HAWAII; NEW ZEALAND; PACIFIC ISLANDS, articles on SETTLEMENT OF MELANESIA AND MICRONESIA, SETTLEMENT OF POLYNESIA; PACIFIC ISLANDS NAVIGATION AND WATERCRAFT; PACIFIC ISLANDS, ORIGINS OF FOOD PRODUCTION IN THE.]

■ R. Firth, We, the Tikopia (1936). R. Firth, Primitive Polynesian Economy (1939). M. D. Sahlins, Social Stratification in Polynesia (1958). R. Firth, Social Change on Tikopia (1959). R. C. Green and R. C. Suggs, The Archeology of Nuku Hiva, Marquesas Islands, French Polynesia (1961). R. C. Green et al., Archeology on the Island of Mo'orea, French Polynesia (1967). I. Goldman, Ancient Polynesian Society (1970). T. Earle, Economic and Social Organization of a Complex Chiefdom: The Halelea District, Kaua'i, Hawaii (1978). R. Cordy, A Study of Prehistoric Social Change: The Development of Complex Societies in the Hawaiian Islands (1981). P. V. Kirch, The Evolution of the Polynesian Chiefdoms (1984). M. W. Graves and R. C. Green, eds., The Evolution and Organisation of Prehistoric Society in Polynesia (1993).

Michael W. Graves

PACIFIC ISLANDS NAVIGATION AND WATERCRAFT.

The settlement of the hundreds of remote islands of the vast Pacific Ocean between 3000 and 1000 B.P. virtually completed the human settlement of the world apart from its ice caps. This was achieved without navigational instruments, and earlier theories of how it was done range from the use of skilled navigation to uncontrolled drifts.

Early European explorers observed that Pacific navigators had expert knowledge of *astronomy, weather, and island locations. Voyaging canoes were large, fast, and safe, with double hulls like catamarans, or with single hulls and outriggers. Built of planks sewn together, with keels carved from solid logs, they could average 100 sea miles in 24 hours. Practical navigational skills widespread in the Pacific were steering by stars at night and by the direction of swells by day. Estimates of position were made by dead reckoning from speed, direction, and time. Modern experiments indicate that although mistakes in position fixing occurred, they did so at random and tended to cancel each other out as voyages proceeded. Destination islands were detected from beyond sighting range by sea signs like clouds, birds, and changes in swell; island groups constituted broad, overlapping island target screens.

Esoteric skills included estimating a conceptual equivalent of latitude from the night sky by sighting the angle of stars up the mast or a weighted line, or by calibrating the hand. The position of new islands was fixed by a combination of astronomy and dead reckoning, and mental maps allowed settlement to spread across the Pacific.

Colonization was obviously deliberate because canoes carried the people and domesticated plants and animals needed for settlement. Moreover, computer simulations that considered real winds and currents have proved that major voyages did not occur by chance but were the result of directed navigation. *Radiocarbon dating supports the view that colonists went first against the prevailing winds and only then across and down them. They overcame the force of the trade winds by making strategic use of seasonal interruptions in normal weather patterns. Without a doubt it was safest to explore in a normally upwind direction because it ensured a safe return. Settlement followed the order of safety, not the order of interisland distance or accessibility. Upwind exploration also provided a simple means of finding the way home by returning to the latitude of a starting island while still upwind of it, then running with the wind along the latitude.

Sailing with safety across the prevailing winds could be done with acquired knowledge of islands to leeward of the starting island, but sailing downwind usually required returning by a different route. It is no surprise that islands requiring this strategy, like *New Zealand, were last settled. Evidently, navigational skills improved as Pacific settlement continued. Eventually, long exploratory probes were made into the more difficult weather systems of the higher latitude extremities of Polynesia and to South America. Both archaeology and computer simulation suggest that Pacific settlement was systematic and purposeful and took place with less loss of life than conventionally supposed.

[See also EASTER ISLAND; HAWAII; TAPITA COMPLEX; PACIFIC ISLANDS, articles on INTRODUCTION, SETTLEMENT OF MELANESIA AND MICRONESIA, SETTLEMENT OF POLYNESIA; SHIPS AND SEAFARING.]

■ A. C. Haddon and James Hornell, eds., Canoes of Oceania (1936). David Lewis, We, the Navigators (1972). Ben R. Finney, Hokule'a: The Way to Tahiti (1979). Geoffrey Irwin, The Prehistoric Exploration and Colonisation of the Pacific (1992).

Geoffrey Irwin

PACIFIC ISLANDS, Origins of Food Production in the.

The oldest evidence for food production in the Pacific Islands (New Guinea eastward to Polynesia, including Micronesia) comes from the New Guinea highlands, where swamp drainage for the cultivation of unknown crops (perhaps taro, sugarcane, and Australimusa bananas) was practiced at *Kuk in the Wahgi Valley from 7000 B.C. onward. So far this evidence has not been paralleled elsewhere, but pollen evidence for forest clearance and signs of increasing soil erosion occur in many other highland regions by about 5000 B.C. Exact reasons for these early and independent New Guinea developments toward *agriculture are uncertain, but climatic warming in the unique New Guinea highland environments, which have many large basins between 4,270 and 7,550 feet (1,300 and 2,300 m) above sea level, presumably played some role. It is unclear, however, whether this early food production developed first in the New Guinea lowlands or in the highlands, although none of the large southeast islands to the west, all of which lack such large contiguous highland regions, have yet produced similarly early evidence.

At about the same time as the highland developments, New Guinea lowland populations in the Sepik basin were utilizing a number of tree food products by about 4000 B.C., including candlenut, canarium nut, coconut, and pandanus and possibly sago for starch. All these plants are native to the western Melanesian lowlands. Canarium had been transported by humans from New Guinea, together with a number of wild animal species, to the Bismarck and Solomon Islands by at least 6000 B.C. However, it must be made clear that the degree of conscious cultivation and propagation occurring at this time is unknown, and the only direct evidence for agricultural management remains that from the New Guinea highlands. Melanesian lowland agricultural populations might have been kept quite small by endemic malaria.

After 2,000 years ago in the New Guinea highlands, there is evidence for an increasing spread of grassland as a result of forest clearance, with a concomitant reduction of wild fauna for hunting. By this time the Kuk farmers were developing techniques for land fallowing, including the planting of nitrogen-fixing casuarina. Increasingly formalized drained swamp *field systems are believed to be associated with more intensive production (perhaps of taro and sugarcane) to support both humans and also much larger tame pig populations. The latter provided one of the main supports, as cumulative wealth, for the competitive New Guinea highland social systems of the recent past. Pigs are not native to any of the Pacific Islands and were introduced from Indonesia about 1500 B.C.

Finally, about 400 years ago the American sweet potato was introduced into the New Guinea highlands and food production was intensified yet again, especially at high altitudes.

By 1500 B.C., therefore, archaeological and botanical evidence indicates that fairly widespread regions of swamp and shifting agriculture existed throughout the New Guinea highlands, with lowland western Melanesian populations dependent more on the orcharding of nuts, fruits, and sago palms. Population densities and settlement patterns at this time remain very poorly understood. The whole structure of Pacific prehistory outside New Guinea was changed, however, by the arrival of Austronesian-speaking populations from Southeast Asia, starting around 1500 B.C., ultimately to settle the whole of Oceania including *New Zealand by A.D. 1000. Austronesians appear to have been the first colonists to reach any of the islands beyond New Guinea, the Bismarcks, and the Solomons.

These populations doubtless adopted many western Oceanic cultivated plants, including all of those previously listed, but also brought in other Southeast Asian food plants such as the greater yam, new kinds of banana, sugarcane, and aroids (tarolike plants), and the first domesticated animals—pigs, dogs, and fowl. Earlier Austronesian populations in Southeast Asia doubtless cultivated the cereals rice and foxtail millet, but the equatorial climatic passage to the north of New Guinea and into Oceania did not favor these subtropical crops, and they were dropped from cultivation.

The subsequent 3,500 years of agricultural development in the Pacific Islands have witnessed the regional growth of a very varied universe of agricultural systems, including lowland sago management in New Guinea, raised bed cultivation of sweet potato in the swamps of the Baliem Valley in Irian Jaya, systems of intensive dry cultivation of yams in Tonga and Ponape, sunken fields dug to tap subsurface water for taro cultivation on atolls, and the remarkable landscapes of irrigated and bunded pond-fields for growing taro in New Caledonia, Fiji, Mangaia, and the Hawaiian Islands. The Maoris of New Zealand were obliged by their cooler climate to depend heavily on the Andean sweet potato, and in the cool temperate South Island and the Chatham Islands switched to maritime hunting and gathering. Other populations on islands with delicate and marginal environments, such as *Easter Island and many small and isolated Polynesian islands, underwent processes of population decline and increasing warfare, or even total abandonment, in late prehistory. The overall picture is perhaps one of the most interesting and varied in the archaeological and ethnographic records.

[See also HAWAII; LAPITA COMPLEX; NEW GUINEA, ORIGINS OF FOOD PRODUCTION IN; PACIFIC ISLANDS, articles on INTRODUCTION, SETTLEMENT OF MELANESIA AND MICRONESIA, SETTLEMENT OF POLYNESIA; PACIFIC ISLANDS CHIEFDOMS.]

■ P. Bellwood, "The Colonization of the Pacific," in The Colonization of the Pacific: A Genetic Trail, ed. A.V.S. Hill and S. Serjeantson (1989), pp. 1–59. P. V. Kirch, "Second-Millennium B.C. Arboriculture in the Mussau Islands," Economic Botany 43 (1989): 225–240. J. Golson and D. Gardner, "Agriculture and Sociopolitical Organization in New Guinea Highlands Prehistory," Annual Review of Anthropology 19 (1990): 395–417. P. Swadling, N. Araho, and B. Ivuyo, "Settlements Associated with the Inland Sepik-Ramu Sea," Bulletin of the Indo-Pacific Prehistory Association 12 (1990): 92–112. D. E. Yen, "Environment, Agriculture and the Colonization of the Pacific," in Pacific Production Systems, ed. D. E. Yen and J.M.J. Mummery (1990), pp. 258–277. P. V. Kirch, The Wet and the Dry (1994).

Peter Bellwood

PALENQUE. The ancient capital of Palenque is situated along the western edge of the tropical lowland Maya region on the foothills of the Chiapas Mountains of southern Mexico with a panoramic view of the Gulf coastal plain. Palenque is primarily a Late Classic site, its political fortunes rising during the seventh and eighth centuries under the leadership of a very strong royal lineage. Best known for its exquisite stone and stucco sculpture, extensive hieroglyphic texts, mansard-roof buildings, and the funerary pyramid of Pakal the Great, Palenque was the capital of one of the important, if not one of the largest, kingdoms in the Classic Maya world.

In 1949 Mexican archaeologist Alberto Ruz Lluillier, while working on the restoration of Palenque, uncovered a staircase that plunged into the middle of a large pyramid called the Temple of the Inscriptions, so named for the lengthy texts on its summit temple. The now legendary tomb of Palenque ruler Pakal the Great lay at the bottom of the staircase. Bedecked in jadeite beads and ear spools and covered with a mask of jadeite, shell, and obsidian, Pakal was entombed within a stone sarcophagus around which were inscribed his birth and death dates (A.D. 603–683) and the names and portraits of his significant progenitors. We now know that the hieroglyphic texts on the summit of the Temple of the Inscriptions refer to the accession of Chan Bahlum, the older son and royal heir of Pakal the Great.

Many of the significant breakthroughs in Maya hieroglyphic decipherment started with the study of the hieroglyphic texts of Palenque, which chronicle the dynastic history of the ruling families and emphasize the divinity of the royal lineage. The discovery of the tomb of Pakal was of great archaeological significance because, up until that time, pyramids in the Maya region were thought to have been simply bases for temples and not funerary structures. They are now known to have been both. Other prominent architectural features of Palenque include a group of three smaller temple pyramids called the Group of the Cross, which was constructed by Chan Bahlum, and a large palace complex with a four-story tower. For the newly expanded palace, a younger son of Pakal, Kan Xul, commissioned the inscription of a beautifully inscribed hieroglyphic text. The palace tablet details the genealogy and accession of Kan Xul, who was later captured by the lords of Toniná.

[See also MAYA CIVILIZATION, articles on INTRODUCTION, MAYA RULERS AND WARFARE, MAYA PYRAMIDS AND TEMPLES.]

■ Robert J. Sharer, The Ancient Maya, 5th ed. (1994).

Patricia A. McAnany

PALEOBOTANY is the study of plant remains recovered from prehistoric soil deposits. Although these plant remains are most often recovered from archaeological sites, they need not be. Useful samples have been collected from ancient woodrat and packrat nests, cores in dry lake beds, any place where plant remains are likely to have accumulated and been preserved.

Plant remains fall into three categories: macrobotanical, microbotanical, and pollen remains. Macrobotanical remains consist of large fragments of whole plant parts such as stems, leaves, flowers, and so on. Microbotanical remains consist of smaller plant parts, fragments, and seeds. Pollen refers to actual pollen that has been preserved due to its extremely small size and the tough silica shells that encase most pollens.

The principles of analysis are generally the same whatever the category of plant remains. Paleobotanists must have access to complete reference collections of known plants representing all major physical structures during all stages of each species' life cycle for comparison. The prehistoric plant remains are painstakingly separated from their soil matrix and other artifacts. The separated remains are sorted into species categories, making note of the proportions of plant parts represented.

A statistical or graphical analysis of these data can indicate the species of plants present, the parts that were most often collected, the season of collection, and genetic information on changes in plant species over time. The results of paleobotanical analysis have provided archaeologists with valuable reconstructions of prehistoric climate, plant resource exploitation patterns, seasonal occupation of sites, the vegetal component of prehistoric diet, and the transition from collecting wild plants to cultivating domesticated plants.

[See also DIET, RECONSTRUCTION OF; DOMESTICATION OF PLANTS; PALEOENVIRONMENTAL RECONSTRUCTION; PLANT REMAINS, ANALYSIS OF; WOOD, articles on INTRODUCTION, ANALYSIS OF WOOD.]

George Michaels

PALEOENVIRONMENTAL RECONSTRUCTION

plays an important role in the interpretation of archaeological data. It chronicles past changes in climate and vegetation and can be used to predict potential human subsistence patterns, to date sites, and to speculate on what types of cultural modifications were needed to survive during times of climatic extremes. Reconstructing paleoenvironmental sequences depends on finding adequate remains and records of plants, animals, or geologic events that were influenced by climatic changes.

Plant remains (i.e., pollen, phytoliths, seeds, wood, leaves, charcoal) can provide excellent clues about past vegetation because they reflect the presence and abundance of individual species of plants. Because the growth of specific plant types is limited by physical conditions such as moisture, temperature, elevation, and soil conditions, their remains can be used to infer past climatic conditions.

As early as the mid-1800s, some archaeologists were recording the presence of seeds and other plant remains found in the sediments of sites. Prior to the 1900s, however, there existed no systematic approach to the recovery of archaeological plant materials and no understanding of the full potential of plant remains as guides to interpreting past climatic conditions. Intensive human plant-use research, the development of new and refined sampling techniques,

the application of sophisticated analytical methods, and the creation of a new discipline devoted to the study of archaeological plant materials—archaeobotany—are all quite recent (see Paleobotany).

J. Iversen was one of the first scientists to demonstrate how paleoenvironmental data derived from plant remains could affect the interpretation of archaeological data. In his study during the 1930s, he discovered that a Danish archaeological site was first occupied by people around 4,000 years ago when the region was an island surrounded by a shallow lake. As the land rose and the water table dropped, the lake filled in and became a bog. Iversen used statistical data created from the records of fossil pollen extracted from core samples of the bog and the site to reconstruct a paleoenvironmental chronology. He noticed that around 4,000 years ago there was a sudden decline in deposited pollen from elm and other hardwood trees, indicating that the surrounding forest had disappeared. However, contemporary fossil pollen records from other nearby locales revealed that their forests had not disappeared. Based on these data, Iversen concluded that the people who occupied the site under study must have cleared the forests to plant crops and that the demise of the forest was not linked to climatic changes. Iversen was also able to date the precise time of the forest clearing by correlating similarities in his fossil pollen record with pollen sequences from other locations where dated chronologies had already been established.

The analysis of seeds and other plant remains recovered from sediments at the Lindow site near Manchester, England, proved to yield useful clues to past paleoenvironmental conditions. Using preserved *wood and seed remains, K. Barber of the University of Southampton was able to predict that when the site was occupied, 2,000 years ago, the regional summer climate was 10 percent wetter and about one degree Celsius cooler than it is today.

In another type of study, R. Ciochon and D. Piperno used silica phytoliths bonded to the enamel surface of fossil ape teeth of *Gigantopithecus blacki* to predict that those apes lived and foraged in subtropical and tropical forested regions of China. The attached phytoliths came from the leaves and fruits of plant foods the animals had eaten.

Like plants, animals also respond to environmental conditions and tend to reach optimal population levels in regions that best fulfill their needs. Animal bones were found to be associated with the cultural remains of humans at some of the first archaeological sites excavated during the middle to late 1800s. Today, the study of animal remains found in association with cultural remains is the foundation for the discipline of *zooarchaeology. Current emphasis in this discipline is centered on developing adequate sampling techniques, determining the precise ecological limits and subsistence needs of past and present faunal species, and interpreting recovered faunal remains. One example of the importance of faunal data from archaeological sites is illustrated by the discovery of both forest-dwelling animal species, such as duikers, and plains-dwelling animal species, such as gazelles, in the million-year-old deposits of Sterkfontein cave in South Africa. The mix of both types of faunal bones and their association with the remains of ancient hominids suggests that the region near Sterkfontein cave was a parkland when the site was occupied.

Natural climatic events often determine the growth or demise of glaciers, rivers, floods, winds, fires, freeze–thaw cycles, and temperature variations as well as the formation of travertine. Each of these events can potentially affect the geological deposits in which archaeological sites are formed; when present, the evidence of these events offers clues about past climatic conditions. This field of study, which combines geology and archaeology, is called geoarchaeology, and has emerged as a separate discipline only during the last several decades. Examples of commonly used geologic features that can reflect past climatic processes include: (1) the location of raised river terraces and lakeshore beaches, which suggest earlier times when water levels were higher; (2) buried glacial till and moraine deposits, which represent periods when a region may have had much colder climates; (3) cave deposits where the lower strata are filled with roof spalls from a period when severe cold froze water in rock cracks and broke the spalls from the ceiling; and (4) buried and cross-bedded strata, which reflect brief climatic periods of severe wind or water erosion and/or deposition.

[See also ENVIRONMENTAL ARCHAEOLOGY; PLANT REMAINS, ANALYSIS OF; SEASONALITY STUDIES; SUBSISTENCE.]

■ G. W. Dimbleby, *The Palynology of Archaeological Sites* (1985). D. F. Dincauze, "Strategies for Paleoenvironmental Reconstruction in Archaeology," in *Advances in Archaeological Method and Theory*, ed. M. Schiffer (1987), pp. 255–336. D. R. Piperno, *Phytolith Analysis: An Archaeological and Geological Perspective* (1988). M. R. Waters, *Principles of Geoarchaeology: A North American Perspective* (1992).

Vaughn M. Bryant

PALEOLITHIC

Lower and Middle Paleolithic
Upper Paleolithic

LOWER AND MIDDLE PALEOLITHIC

The immensely long Old Stone Age (Paleolithic Period) has from the early days of Prehistoric Archaeology been divided into Lower, Middle, and Upper sections. Most of the early discoveries were made in western Europe, from the mid-nineteenth century onward, and these classic divisions naturally reflected the situation there, though they were tacitly assumed to be of worldwide validity. The Lower Paleolithic, accordingly, was characterized by the bifacially worked hand axes and other archaic stone tools found mainly in river gravels associated with Early or Middle Pleistocene fauna. "Middle Paleolithic" referred to the elegant flake tool industries found mostly in caves and rock shelters, with Upper Pleistocene fauna and Neanderthal hominid remains. The Upper Paleolithic had fine tools made on blades, bone and ivory implements, decorative items, and anatomically modern humans.

While the terms continue in use, their meaning has expanded and changed. The Paleolithic in Western Europe is now perceived as merely one incomplete local sequence within the global Paleolithic succession, and scholars' interests have broadened considerably beyond the mere classification of artifacts, on which the divisions were originally largely based. Today, many archaeologists prefer to see the Lower and Middle Paleolithic as a single continuous stage of human development, that is, as an "Earlier Paleolithic" that started with the first traces of human activity, at least 2.5 million years ago, and ended only with the rapid spread over the Old World of anatomically modern humans, some 50,000 to 30,000 years ago. That spread of "Advanced Paleolithic" people coincided with striking technological and social advances, and with the final disappearance of all archaic human types that had hitherto survived. Some prehistorians, however, continue to find the separate terms Lower and Middle Paleolithic useful in certain respects. Insofar as they denote periods or stages, it must be remembered that these terms include not only technological and cultural developments, but also much human physical evolution and a gradual expansion of human territory to cover much of the Old World.

Lower Paleolithic. By literal definition, the Lower Paleolithic begins with the earliest known traces of stone tool manufacture, currently about 2.7 million years ago at Kada Gona, northern Ethiopia. Other traces of human activity, such as upright walking, go back about a million years further, as dramatically evidenced by the famous human footprint trails at Laetoli, Tanzania (ca. 3.68 million years ago). The hominids of this opening stage belong to the Australopithecine group, known only in sub-Saharan Africa. Though late Australopithecines survived until about one million years ago, the earliest examples of *Homo*, including *H. habilis*, appeared in East Africa between 2.5 and 2.0 million years ago, perhaps descended from the gracile Australopithecine *Australopithecus afarensis*. With the emergence of the *Homo* line, simple stone tool manufacture became a regular occurrence from ca. 1.8 million years ago (the Oldowan Tradition). Animal bones are frequently found together with stone artifacts at the early sites: the most important locations include *Olduvai Gorge (Tanzania), the Turkana Basin (mainly Kenya), and several parts of Ethiopia. The FLK sites at Olduvai and FxJj 50, East Turkana, are important excavated examples. The early humans probably depended more on scavenging than on hunting for themselves. Evidence for human control of fire at this stage is uncertain. By 2 to 1.8 million years ago, somewhat more advanced human types had appeared, of which *Homo erectus* is the best known, and by 1.8 million years ago these new people had begun a migration out of sub-Saharan Africa that was eventually to reach India, the Far East, the Near East, North Africa, and Europe.

Soon after the emergence of *H. erectus* in East Africa, important new stone tool types appear there: the hand axes and cleavers (large shaped cutting tools) of the *Acheulean Tradition. Acheulean industries subsequently spread widely over the Old World during the Early and Middle Pleistocene, though not to the Far East. Lower Paleolithic artifacts and fossil remains of *H. erectus* certainly occur in Southeast Asia and at numerous sites in China—from about one million years ago—*Zhoukoudian near Beijing being the most famous, though a few dates as old as 2 to 1.8 million years are also claimed. The artifacts often have a rather crude appearance, however, perhaps because of the nature of the local rocks.

Human Types. By early in the Middle Pleistocene, human evolution was passing from the *Homo erectus* stage to one that we designate Early *Homo sapiens*. Adaptation to so many new geographical and climatic situations created much local variability within this taxon. The European Early *Homo sapiens* population for instance, progressed to *H. sapiens neanderthalensis*, the *Neanderthals, present there in a fully developed form well before 100,000 B.P. In sub-Saharan Africa, however, evolution had by then produced the first examples of anatomically modern humans (*H. sapiens sapiens*); examples include finds from *Klasies River Mouth (South Africa), and the Omo Kibish I individual from southern Ethiopia. These new people had spread to the Near East by ca. 100,000–90,000 B.P. (Qafzeh Cave and Skhul Cave in Israel), and this becomes a crucial area, because Neanderthal hominids also reached it, doubtless from eastern Europe: examples include finds from Kebara Cave and Amud Cave (Israel) and Shanidar Cave (Iraq). The two human types may have shared the region for up to 40,000 years.

Middle Paleolithic. At the generalized Early *Homo sapiens* stage, humans made various Lower Paleolithic industries in different parts of the Old World, the later stages of the Acheulean Tradition being merely the best known. In Europe, early forms of Neanderthals are also associated with such industries, for example at Atapuerca (Spain) or Pontnewydd Cave (North Wales). What characterized the subsequent Middle Paleolithic industries was the virtual disappearance of hand axes and a new emphasis on finely made flake tools, fashioned on specially struck blanks ("prepared core technology"), featuring carefully designed scraper and projectile-point types. Many of these European Middle Paleolithic industries are called "Mousterian," after the French site of Le Moustier. In other parts of the world, notably southern Africa, the term "Middle Stone Age" is used for the wide range of industries broadly equivalent in age and technology to the European ones just described.

The basis of all Middle Paleolithic economies was hunting, gathering, and scavenging. Human geographical distribution expanded, for example, into the cold steppes of central Russia. Open sites occur with dwelling structures partly made from mammoth bones, with internal hearths, as at Molodova V (Ukraine). Humans had also reached Australia by at least 55,000 B.P., arguably a Middle Paleolithic event. The Neanderthals have left some evidence of ritual practices, notably deliberate burial of the dead, at caves and rock shelters from La Ferrassie (southwest France) to Teshik Tash (Uzbekistan) and Shanidar (Iraq), though at some of their sites human bones occur as fragments amongst animal bones and occupation debris, as at Krapina (Croatia) or L'Hortus (southern France).

During the early and middle sections of the Last Glaciation, adaptation to cold conditions made the European Neanderthals a somewhat specialized population, continuing to manufacture their Mousterian industries in habitable parts of the continent, in some cases as late as the mid-30,000s B.P. Late developments, such as the Chatelperronian industry in southwest France, with some more bladelike tools, are still associated with Neanderthal hominids, as at the St. Césaire rock shelter. The same is likely to be true of the Szeletian industries of the late Middle Paleolithic in Central Europe. In the Near East, a clear transition can be seen at ca. 45,000–40,000 B.P. from Middle Paleolithic prepared-core technology to the regular manufacture of blades as tool blanks, notably at Ksar Akil (Lebanon) and Boker Tachtit (Israel). In Europe, the end of the Middle Paleolithic was abrupt: the Neanderthal population seems to have been swept away between ca. 42,000–35,000 B.P. by a rapid incursion of anatomically modern humans making Upper Paleolithic blade tool industries.

[*See also* AFAR; AFRICA: PREHISTORY OF AFRICA; AUSTRALOPITHECUS AND HOMO HABILIS; CHINA: STONE AGE CULTURES OF CHINA; EUROPE, THE FIRST COLONIZATION OF; HOMO SAPIENS, ARCHAIC; KOOBI FORA; OLORGESAILLIE; PLEISTOCENE; TORRALBA/AMBRONA.]

■ John A. J. Gowlett, *Ascent to Civilization: The Archaeology of Early Man* (1984). Clive Gamble, *The Palaeolithic Settlement of Europe* (1986). Richard G. Klein, *The Human Career: Human Biological and Cultural Origins* (1989). A. Barbara Isaac, ed., *The Archaeology of Human Origins: Papers by Glynn Isaac* (1990). Christopher B. Stringer and Clive Gamble, *In Search of the Neanderthals: Solving the Puzzle of Human Origins* (1993).

Derek A. Roe

UPPER PALEOLITHIC

The Upper Paleolithic is the last of the three divisions of the Old Stone Age. It is a period of approximately 30,000 years duration, from the final development of the last glacial cycle 40,000 years ago, through the last glacial maximum and ending with the improved climatic conditions of the Holocene approximately 10,000 years ago. The archaeological record of the Upper Paleolithic is characterized by a number of features that clearly separate it from the Lower and Middle Paleolithic. These include new techniques of stone working, the use of bone and other nonlithic materials, the appearance of art, larger and more numerous sites, the presence of sites with a distinct structure, and specialized animal hunting strategies. These new features, together with skeletal evidence of anatomically modern humans, *Homo sapiens sapiens,* has led to the suggestion that the archaeological record of the Upper Paleolithic represents the first appearance of what has been thought to be fully modern behavior. It is the analysis of the specific nature of this behavior and its relationship to the evolution of *Homo sapiens sapiens* that forms one of the major interpretive problems of the Upper Paleolithic.

Technological Developments. A new type of stone tool technology appears with the beginning of the Upper Paleolithic. This is called blade technology and involves the production of blades, which are struck stone pieces twice as long as they are broad and often with parallel sides. These blades are then used as the raw material for the production of other tools of a definite and clear form, such as endscrapers, borers, gravers, projectile points, and much smaller pieces called *microliths. Detailed examination of these pieces indicates that they were often hafted onto wooden, bone, or ivory shafts. Microliths may have been hafted in groups onto a single shaft, resulting in a composite tool. It would then have been straightforward to replace the broken stone components of these tools while preserving the more valuable shafts. Analysis of the raw materials used for the production of these stone tools (flint in Poland or obsidian in Japan) have indicated that groups of hunters and gatherers collected raw materials from a very wide catchment area, either in the course of a generally nomadic lifestyle or by means of special purpose trips. Studies of tool design have revealed distinct assemblages of stone tools defined on the basis of the appearance (and disappearance) of distinct tool types, such as scrapers and projectile points. In Europe, these assemblages have been called Chatelperronian, Aurignacian, Gravettian, Solutrean, and Magdalenian. They were at one time thought to represent the material residues from distinct, culturally differentiated societies of hunters and gatherers, although such a social interpretation is now much questioned. In addition to these stone tool assemblages, even broader groups of stone technologies can be identified. For example, it is possible to observe a group of stone tool industries based on the production of microblades from special cores that appears at around 18,000 B.P. and covers an area stretching from the Near East across Central Asia through China, Japan, and into North America, with numerous smaller regional variations.

In addition to stone, there are marked developments in the technological use of other raw materials as well as the manufacture of new forms. Bone, antler, and ivory appear to have been used for the first time for making tools and other items. These materials were first used for the manufacture of projectile points, where their less brittle nature would have been ideal. At a later date (ca. 21,000 years B.P.), bone was used for the manufacture of the first eyed needle, possibly indicating a more elaborate clothing technology, and also for the manufacture of the first identifiable musical instruments, which take the form of flutes made from hollow bird bones.

Artistic Expression. From the beginning of the Upper Paleolithic, there also appears examples of recognizable artistic expression in the form of wall paintings and engravings and also mobiliary carvings. The wall (parietal) art includes both abstract art (lines, squares, net shapes) and representational art depicting animals in both single and multiple colors. The best known locations are the cave sites of *Lascaux in southern France and *Altamira in northern Spain. There are also clay sculptures of bison at the site of Le Tuc d'Audoubert in France. Over the years, interpretations of the meaning of the parietal art have varied enormously from hunting magic to structuralist interpretations of the relationship between men and women. More recent interpretations stress the importance of these representations in the communication of important information for successful hunting in the light of the unpredictable environmental circumstances of the time.

The mobiliary art includes bone and antler batons with carved animals such as deer and birds as well as a number of female figurines with seemingly exaggerated sexual organs. The similarity in the form of these figurines over an area that encompasses all of Europe from east to west has been interpreted as an indication of a wide exchange network of "marriage" partners that would have existed at this time of low population density to ensure a viable breeding population. Another possibility is that these figurines are self-sculptures by women not brought up within Renaissance traditions of perspective and artistic distance. An examination of the engravings on pieces of bone by Alexander Marshack has suggested that some of them may be notations, providing Upper Paleolithic people with some form of calendrical record. There is also much archaeological evidence for the manufacture of bodily ornamentation. Where preservation allows, beads are frequently found, made from bone, ivory, or seashell. The species of seashell used indicate contacts over very great distances of hundreds of miles. As is the case with the use of stone, it is not yet known whether these seashells were collected personally or acquired through contact with other groups either by direct contact or longer networks of exchange.

There are also a number of sites, such as Gönnersdorf in Germany and Parpalló in Spain, where large numbers of engraved plaques have been found. Examination of these sites in the broader context of the settlement patterns, as well as the diversity of stylistic elements within individual sites, has resulted in some being interpreted as aggregation sites, where a number of smaller bands may have met on a periodic basis, possibly for the exchange of marriage partners. Evidence from other sites, such as footprints at the cave of Niaux in France, and the isolated location of the art within cave systems, suggests that these paintings and engravings might not have been viewed like paintings hanging on the walls of modern art galleries. Rather, they were viewed in the context of structured occasions in which access to the cave might have been limited for some reason. A ritualistic viewing is a possibility.

Organized Living Space. From certain sites there is clear evidence for a structured demarcation of the living space. The finest example of this is the discovery of dwellings made from mammoth bones on the central Russian plain at sites such as Mezhirich and Kostenki. Although such dramatic evidence is exceptional, the evidence from many sites points to the existence of structures that have either decayed or been carried away. At Pincevent, for example, the refitting of stone tool manufacturing debris and the general spatial arrangement of hearths and discarded materials has pointed to the existence of three huts. Similar interpretations have been offered for Sunagawa in central Japan. On the island of Kamchatka a number of locations around the Ushki Lake have revealed evidence of sunken floor dwellings with pronounced entrance passageways and stone-lined hearths. It is possible on a broad level to interpret the spatial arrangements in these dwellings as hearth areas, discard areas, and possibly activity areas. At the site of Etiolles, close to Paris, studies of the technical abilities exhibited by the flint knappers at the site, based on their discarded debris, have even suggested that one part of the site was used by inexperienced, possibly apprentice, flint knappers, while other areas were used by more experienced craft workers.

Subsistence Organization. Examination of the animal bones at these sites has revealed complex patterns of decision making in terms of the animals to be hunted, the season of hunting, and butchery decisions once animals have been killed. It is in the Upper Paleolithic that we first have evidence to suggest that individual animal species were being preferentially exploited by human groups. There are sites in southwestern France, Spain, Germany, and South Africa where the bones of a single species constitute as much as 80 percent or more of the complete faunal assemblage. A reconstruction of the ages of the animals at the time when they were killed indicates that herds or small groups of animals may have been killed on single occasions. Evidence for the season of hunting suggests that they were killed at the time of their annual migrations or their gathering together for the breeding season. The killing of such large numbers of animals and the production of large quantities of meat perhaps indicate that techniques of efficient storage had already been developed, and stored meat allowed people to live in groups in otherwise uninhabitable environments.

In addition to specialization in the targeting of individual species, particular upland sites and site settlement patterns in areas such as northern Spain indicate that hunting may have been carried out by small task groups who would then have brought back the spoils of the hunt to a more residential site located elsewhere. Both this evidence and that of species specialization points to the existence of planning and organization.

Aspects of Modern Human Behavior. Such evidence of the ability to live in difficult environments is provided by the last major characteristic of Upper Paleolithic archaeology, the colonization of hitherto unexploited environments such as the northern plains of Europe, the desert and arid lands of the Near East and Africa, tropical and coniferous forest regions, and the American continents and Australasia. The evidence for the colonization of all of these areas postdates the appearance of anatomically modern humans.

The colonization of Australasia provides a fine example of the abilities of modern humans. Although Australia, Papua New Guinea, and Tasmania would have been linked together at times of low sea level to form the larger continent of Sahul, there would have always been water between Sahul and Indonesia with a channel at least 40 miles (65 km) wide. A mastery of water travel would have been the first necessity for colonization. The earliest radiocarbon dates for this colonization date to 40,000 years B.P. and come from the Huon Peninsula in Papua New Guinea and Swan River near Perth in southwestern Australia. There are also dates of 32,000 years B.P. for burials of anatomically modern humans from the Willandra lakes site of Lake Mungo in southern Australia. Following their arrival in the continent, we also have evidence of human colonization of the arid lands of central Australia and the rain forests of Tasmania. The colonization of Australasia was indeed rapid, and took place in a continent that was completely alien to modern humans in terms of both the plant and animal communities that they encountered.

The ability to rapidly recolonize areas rendered uninhabitable by the advance of glacial conditions at the time of the last glacial maximum, clearly evident in the archaeological record from northern Europe, is further testimony to the ability of human groups at this time to exploit new areas.

Although the Upper Paleolithic was originally defined on the basis of stone tool technology alone, such a simple technological definition is increasingly problematic and irrelevant. The variety and characteristics of the evidence from Upper Paleolithic sites reveal a clearly organized and diverse range of behavior. The key characteristic of the Upper Paleolithic is now thought to be the appearance of modern human behavior throughout the world, associated with the arrival of anatomically modern humans, although the two do not necessarily appear simultaneously in all places. The principal characteristics of this behavior can perhaps best be defined as symbolism and symbolic expression (perhaps including language) and organizational planning. Symbolism appears in a number of material forms including art, body ornamentation, styles of material goods, and possibly burial practices. Organizational planning is evident in the development of specialized subsistence practices focusing on the exploitation of a single species, the appearance of specialized task groups, the ability to exploit new environments such as the highlands, and to colonize new lands such as the Americas. This is a pattern of behavior that appears very close to that of contemporary groups of hunters and gatherers. Indeed, the evidence has frequently been interpreted in the light of archaeologists' own experiences with such groups, such as the studies of Lewis Binford among the Nunamiut. It is for this reason that it has been considered fully modern behavior.

The appearance of anatomically modern humans and of different aspects of modern behavior are crucial to any discussion of the early Upper Paleolithic, and in particular, the timing of the beginning of the Upper Paleolithic. Genetic studies of modern human populations have been used to argue that anatomically modern humans evolved in Africa and then radiated outward to other parts of the world. In so doing they replaced populations of anatomically pre-modern humans. This corresponds with the archaeological evidence from areas such as Europe where there are indications of sharp discontinuity between the Middle and Upper Paleolithic records. There are those who argue, however, that in certain parts of the world, especially the Far East, sufficient skeletal similarities exist between anatomically pre-modern and anatomically modern humans to suggest that *Homo sapiens sapiens* evolved *in situ* from the local

populations. While most scholars would not agree with this interpretation, such similarities raise the important question of the nature of the relationship between incoming modern populations and existing local populations. Was there rapid replacement in all areas, or were there periods of coexistence of varying duration?

Within Africa, examples of anatomically modern humans have been dated to 130,000 years B.P. at the site of Omo in East Africa. In the Near East anatomically modern humans have been found at the sites of Skhul and Qafzeh dating to 92,000 years B.P., but pre-modern humans (*Neanderthals) continued living in this region certainly until 60,000 years B.P. according to dates from the Kebara cave at Mt. Carmel. These early finds of anatomically modern humans have all been associated with a material culture that is no different than that of the "contemporary" pre-modern humans. Within Europe itself, the earliest archaeological evidence associated with incoming modern humans, the so-called "Aurignacian," has been dated to 42,000 years B.P. in Bulgaria and to 40,000 years B.P. in Spain. The latest evidence for pre-modern humans (Neanderthals) dates to 36,000 years B.P. and is from the site of St. Césaire in France. Interestingly, the St. Césaire Neanderthal is associated with a material culture (the Chatelperronian) that has been described as fully Upper Paleolithic, including blade stone tools and ornaments: in other words, modern. There is, therefore, good evidence for the overlap of these populations and for abandoning the simple association between modern human behavior and anatomically modern humans.

Another apparent feature of modern human behavior is the specialized animal hunting strategy. There are a number of sites where an analysis of the faunal remains suggests that a single animal species was hunted almost exclusively, and there are also sites that suggest the presence of small task groups, such as hunting parties exploiting the upland areas for the hunting of mountain goats. In Europe, this evidence appears not with the first anatomically modern humans but at the time of the last glacial maximum (21,000–17,000 years B.P.) and provides a further indication of the gradual development of modern human behavior and not the appearance of a complete package.

The appearance of aspects of fully modern behavior and of anatomically modern humans at different times in different parts of the world must inevitably force a reassessment of the timing for the beginning of the Upper Paleolithic and its redefinition in terms of the appearance of anatomically modern humans rather than aspects of recognizably modern human behavior. Within Western Europe the current date of 40,000 years B.P. would therefore continue as it ties in with both the appearance of anatomically modern humans and modern human behavior. In Australia, however, an earlier date of perhaps 60,000 years B.P. would be more appropriate as it seems likely that the first colonizers of the continent were anatomically modern humans.

Perhaps the most interesting consequence of the appearance of anatomically modern humans is that the Upper Paleolithic becomes the first period in human history when we can recognize ourselves, modern humans, in the archaeological record. We can apply direct knowledge of our modern abilities. Our own survival and the demise of our nearest relatives is the ever-present context for the interpretation of the archaeology of the Upper Paleolithic.

[See also AFRICA: PREHISTORY OF AFRICA; ART; AUSTRALIA AND NEW GUINEA: FIRST SETTLEMENT OF SUNDA AND SAHUL;

CHINA: STONE AGE CULTURES OF CHINA; CRO-MAGNONS; EUROPE: THE EUROPEAN PALEOLITHIC PERIOD; HOLOCENE: INTRODUCTION; HOMO SAPIENS, ARCHAIC; HUMANS, MODERN; NOTATION, PALEOLITHIC; ROCK ART: PALEOLITHIC ART; VENUS FIGURINES.]

■ Peter Ucko and Andre Rosenfeld, *Palaeolithic Cave Art* (1968). Alexander Marshack, *The Roots of Civilisation* (1972). Lewis R. Binford, *Nunamiut Ethnoarchaeology* (1978). Douglas Price and James Brown, *Complex Hunter Gatherers: The Emergence of Social Complexity* (1985). Olga Soffer, *The Upper Paleolithic of the Central Russian Plain* (1985). Clive Gamble, *The Palaeolithic Settlement of Europe* (1986). Paul Bahn and Jean Vertut, *Images of the Ice Age* (1988). Clive Gamble, *Timewalkers: The Prehistory of Global Colonisation* (1993).

Anthony Sinclair

PALEOPATHOLOGY is the study of *disease in historic and prehistoric populations. By examining cultural remains such as artifacts and art, documentary evidence, the biological remains such as skeletons, mummies, and even coprolites (fossilized feces), patterns of disease in a population can be discerned. This knowledge is the basis for developing a history of specific diseases. Since the prevalence and patterns of disease are a reflection of the lifeways of a society, these studies shed light on a population's biocultural adaptation (adjustments made to the environment).

Establishing the existence of disease in time and space from a biomedical focus and reconstructing the lifeways of a society from an anthropological focus are the divergent objectives of paleopathology. Most of the earliest paleopathologists were physicians and paleopathology clearly had its beginning in medicine. A recent synthesis (Donald J. Ortner and Arthur C. Aufterheide, *Human Paleopathology: Current Syntheses and Future Options*, 1991) allies paleopathology with biomedicine rather than with anthropology. However, in the last quarter of the century, anthropology, with its links between biology and culture, has had a major impact and has given paleopathology a unique identity.

While publications span the last two centuries, paleopathology is only beginning to have an impact on other sciences. Early bibliographies (G. Armelagos, J. Mielke, and J. Winter, *Bibliography of Human Paleopathology*, 1971) provide an index of this renewed interest. This bibliography was the most extensive at the time and had nearly 1,800 references. The most recent effort to list publications in human paleopathology (tentatively titled *The International Bibliography of Human Paleopathology and Related Subjects*) has reached 20,000 items. Approximately 40% of the entries are publications that date from the last decade.

The birth of paleopathology could be marked by Esper's publication in late 1774, of a sarcoma in the bones of a cave bear (probably a misdiagnosed callus of a healed fracture). In the century from the 1770s until the 1890s, the publications were largely single case studies of skeletal pathology found in human and nonhuman remains. Early paleopathologists showed remarkable diagnostic skills in identifying pathological conditions on dried bones and mummified remains. Researchers performed autopsies on mummies as early as 1825 and, by 1852, used histological techniques to reveal arteriosclerosis in a mummy. Diagnosis became an end in itself and paleopathology remained descriptive.

From 1890 to 1930, the focus of paleopathology sharpened. Unraveling the history of specific diseases such as syphilis, poliomyelitis, tuberculosis, and leprosy and uncovering evidence of medical practices was well established. The concern for infectious disease is not surprising since it represented one of the most significant medical problems of the time.

The 1890 to 1930 period was also the beginning of applications of new medical technologies to paleopathology. Soon after Wilhelm Roentgen discovered the X ray in 1895, mummies were being radiographed. Two themes emerge from this period. First, the only objective was to show diagnostic skills and write the geohistory of specific diseases. Second, the application of advanced medical technology to paleopathology became an end in itself. New technology-based descriptions, without a concern for solving specific problems, was standard practice.

It was during this same period that some of the most impressive research in paleopathology was undertaken. M. A. Ruffer, who played a key role in defining and developing paleopathology, undertook histological analysis of mummified tissue. Ruffer and coworkers found evidence of schistosomiasis, tuberculosis, pneumonia, arteriosclerosis, and variola.

Differential diagnosis of infectious disease is a difficult task since some pathogens such as viruses often do not leave distinctive lesions on the skin or bones. Fortunately, many pathogens do leave a characteristic "signature" that is diagnostic.

Even in those instances of infection (such as staphylococcus) that cause a non-distinctive change on the periosteum (the outer layer of bone), the lesion can be used as a general indicator of inflammation and infection and is very useful in population comparisons.

The 1930s are usually heralded as the modern era of paleopathology. E. A. Hooton introduced a paleoepidemiological approach that considered the relationship between the host, the pathogen, and the environment. Unfortunately, Hooton's work had little impact during the 1930s, 1940s, and 1950s. Hooton's major contribution was his use of simple frequency statistics in presenting his data. Few publications at the time provided this information. For example, an archaeological survey of Nubia with over 10,000 burials seldom provided information on the frequency of pathology found in the population.

In actuality, the modern era of paleopathology began in the 1960s. A symposium on human paleopathology organized by Saul Jarcho (*Human Paleopathology*, 1966), the publication of a popular book on paleopathology (Calvin Wells, *Bones, Bodies and Disease*, 1964), and a compendium by Don Brothwell and A. T. Sandison (*Disease in Antiquity*, 1967) were the most influential factors in the resurrection of paleopathology. In 1973, one of the strongest forces in the rejuvenation of paleopathology was the organization of the Paleopathology Association spearheaded by Aiden Cockburn.

In addition to the objectives of uncovering the historical and geographical roots of disease and determining the role that biocultural interactions has in cultural development, a third objective has emerged. Understanding the processes involved in prehistoric disease has become a major concern. In living organisms, process can be studied as the biological system undergoes a transformation. In extinct populations, the factors which bring about change are deduced from the examination of many individuals in various stages of transformation.

The development of modern paleopathology has been enhanced by the use of multiple indicators of pathology. Rather than focusing on single pathologies, a number of pathological conditions are examined in a systematic fashion. For example, periosteal lesions (an indication of systemic infection), porotic hyperostosis (an indication of iron deficiency anemia), long bone lengths and widths, evidence of trace mineral deficiencies, and enamel hypoplasia may all be used to interpret diet and disease in the population. Modern paleopathology dispels an old adage since "dead men (and dead women) *do tell* tales." They provide information on how our ancestors lived and died and provide lessons for our future.

[*See also* AMERICAS, INTRODUCTION OF DISEASE INTO THE; HUMAN REMAINS, ANALYSIS OF; REBURIAL AND REPATRIATION.]

■ R. T. Steinbock, *Pathological Diagnosis and Interpretation: Bone Disease in Ancient Human Populations* (1976). Jane Buikstra and C. C. Cook, "Paleopathology: An American Account," *Yearbook of Physical Anthropology* 9 (1980): 433–470. D. H. Ubelaker, "The Development of American Paleopathology," in *A History of Physical Anthropology, 1930–1980*, ed. F. Spencer (1982): 337–356. C. S. Larsen, "Bioarchaeological Interpretation of Subsistence Economy and Behavior from Human Skeletal Remains," *Advances in Archaeological Method and Theory* 10 (1987): 27–56.

George Armelagos

PARIS. The site of Paris has shown itself to be, both topographically and geographically, very favorable to human activity. The banks of the Seine have revealed the remains of stone tools from the Lower and Middle *Paleolithic (beginning around 400,000 B.P.). More recent periods are less well attested, and it is necessary to wait until the Neolithic to find the material traces of an extended occupation. The recent Grand Louvre excavations (1983 through 1991) and above all those at the Bercy site (1992 to 1993) have brought to light remains of early settlements along the borders of the Seine. The Bercy excavations have revealed several Neolithic dugout canoes as well as abundant remains of hunter-gatherer occupations.

Paris, as a city, originated in the Gaulish (pre-Roman Iron Age) period, but the settlement of that time is not as yet archaeologically well known. Relatively abundant discoveries in the Paris suburbs (Rungis, St. Maur-des-Fossés) and many coin finds, indicate the importance of the *pagus* of the *Parisii*, but inside the city, finds have been rare. The excavations in the Place Notre-Dame have yielded some Gaulish remains, and at the Grand Louvre site agricultural evidence of Tène III date illustrates the rural surroundings of the city. Lastly, remains of buildings and traces of fire found in excavations at the Rue de Lutèce (1986 to 1987), may be evidence of the conquest of the city by the Romans after the battle between Camulogenus and Labienus, Julius Caesar's lieutenant.

After the conquest, Lutetia expanded along the classical lines of a typical Roman city. Centered around the Ile de la Cité, it developed almost exclusively along the Left Bank (fifth and sixth districts) with much less occupation on the Right Bank. Thanks both to older and more recent archaeological discoveries, we have good knowledge of both the monumental and the everyday environment of the city. In addition to the still visible and recently re-excavated *thermae* or baths of Cluny, and the amphitheater, cleared and excavated during the nineteenth century, mention may be made of the identification of the forum at the Rue Soufflot, the theatre at the Rue de l'Ecole de Medecine, and the great *thermae* within the grounds of the Collège de France.

Recent excavations have brought to light part of the walls of the late Roman city (Place Notre-Dame) and numerous vestiges from the Early and Late Empire found on the Ile de la Cité and on the Left Bank (excavations in Rue de Lutèce, Rue Gay-Lussac, Rue de l'Abbé de l'Epée, among others), along with some scarce traces on the Right Bank (excavations in Rue Saint Martin).

Evidence for the Early Middle Ages was until recently limited to suburban cemeteries together with the remains of the church of Saint Etienne beneath Notre Dame cathedral. But in the last ten years many roads and vestiges of the Merovingian and Carolingian periods have been found, in particular on the Ile de la Cité and its immediate surroundings, which have provided new insights into these periods.

Medieval and post-medieval Paris had for a long time been totally neglected and early discoveries were limited to badly provenanced objects and much carved stonework. Around 1970, excavations in the Place Notre-Dame and at Les Halles, though incomplete and technically inadequate, revealed burials and building remains. It is only in the 1980s that real archaeological research has been undertaken into these periods. The excavation of the Grand Louvre has allowed the discovery of several important monuments: the castle of Philip Augustus, the walls of Charles V, and the tile kilns and workshops of Bernard Palissy. This work has been accompanied by the scientific study of the urban development of this part of the city.

The vestiges at present visible in Paris are the baths of Cluny (inside the Musée National du Moyen-Age de l'Hotel de Cluny), the Roman amphitheater (at the Rue Monge), the Roman walls and other vestiges at the archaeological crypt under the Place Notre-Dame, the Louvre of Philip Augustus and Charles V, and lastly the remains of the walls of Charles V (constructed around 1360) in the entrance gallery to the Louvre Museum. Finally, we should note that the Musée d'Histoire de la Ville de Paris (Musée Carnavalet, Rue de Sévigné) has recently opened new rooms dedicated to archaeology, where the remains of many objects, both from older and more recent excavations, can be seen.

[*See also* EUROPE: ROMAN AND POST-ROMAN EUROPE; FRANKS AND THE FRANKISH EMPIRE.]

■ Michel Roblin, *Le terroir de Paris aux époques gallo-romaines et franques* (1951). Paul-Marie Duval, *Paris antique, des origines au III ème siècle* (1961). Michel Fleury, "Paris du Bas-Empire au milieu du XIII ème siècle," in *Paris, croissance d'une capitale* (actes du colloque) (1961): 73–96. "Dans le sol de Paris," *Les dossiers de l'archéologie* 7 (1974). "Catalogue of the exhibition: Paris Mérouingien," *Bulletin du Musée Carnavalet* 1980 n° 1 and 2 (1982). "Catalogue of the exhibition: Lutece," *Paris de Cesar à Clovis* (1984). "Catalogue of the exhibition," *La Seine aux temps glaciaires* (1987). Pierre-Jean Trombetta, *Sous la pyramide du Louvre, 20 siècles retrouvés* (1987). "Catalogue of the exhibition: De Lascaux au Grand Louvre," *Archéologie et Histoire de la France* (1989). "Paris de la Préhistoire au Moyen Age," *Bulletin du Musée Carnavalet*, n° 1 and 2 (1990).

Pierre-Jean Trombetta

PASTORALISM. In the evolutionary schemes of Enlightenment thinkers like Adam Smith, pastoralism formed an intermediate stage between hunting and farming; and the difficulty of finding traces of substantial Neolithic and Bronze Age domestic structures in northern Europe has often led to such cultures being described as "pastoralist." The term can only be applied precisely, however, to the specialized animal-herding societies recorded historically and ethnographically. Since these represent adaptations to extreme conditions of aridity or altitude, and often to a pattern of complementary diversification in a regional economy (both of which may be relatively recent developments), the term should be applied with circumspection to prehistoric societies. It is nevertheless a useful way to describe communities characterized by a reliance on livestock and with a consequent emphasis on mobility—though not necessarily to the degree represented by recent ethnographic examples. The more specialized forms of pastoralism can be described as nomadic, a feature they share with certain other specialized mobile groups such as maritime traders or gypsies, and with certain types of hunters.

Varieties of Pastoralism. Since pastoralism is by definition associated with the importance of domestic ungulates, it is primarily (though not exclusively) an Old World phenomenon. The classic areas of pastoralism are the central Eurasian steppes and semideserts, the Near and Middle Eastern intermontane valleys and dry plains (from Anatolia to Afghanistan), with the pendant peninsulas of India and Arabia, the latter acting as a bridge to the Sahara and its margins. These areas—and notably the Sahara—were much better watered in the early Holocene, before ca. 4000 B.C., and took on their present character only in the third millennium. Besides these arid plains, pastoral ways of life are also characteristic of mountain regions like the Himalayas and other great ranges of eastern Asia—echoed on a smaller scale in the transhumant pastoralism of the smaller mountain systems of Asia and Europe. These montane pastoral systems have their New World equivalent in the Andean vertical economies and extensive grazing systems of the altiplano. On the northern edge of the Eurasian farming zone, where cultivation is inhibited by cold and sometimes wet conditions, livestock again becomes predominant; and in the more open conditions on the northern forest margins, mobile herding gains in importance—though here with reindeer rather than the more southerly species of domestic ungulates. All these specialized patterns of animal husbandry are the result of a long historical process of differentiation and specialization since the initial *domestication of plants and animals in southwest and southeast Asia, and the development of secondary uses and domesticates. They typically include not just domesticate species of livestock but also specialized transport animals (equids or camelids) and sometimes vehicles.

Besides these specialized examples, there are other economies that might loosely be classed as "pastoralist." These include early examples, where sub-Neolithic groups used livestock (as well as pottery and polished axes, but did not cultivate cereals) acquired from Neolithic farming neighbors, but did not themselves adopt farming, so that animals either domestic or wild formed the mainstay of their subsistence; or later examples (in later prehistoric and early historic times) where communities in areas like Ireland came increasingly to specialize in dairying, in a landscape deforested initially for agriculture but providing plentiful grassy pastures. These two cases, however, lack the characteristic emphasis on mobility. Yet all these different types intergrade, from the arid steppes through montane transhumance systems to lowland dairying—so that even as a description of subsistence practices the term is a relative rather than an absolute one: some groups are simply more pastoral than others. Even beyond this degree of relativism, however, pastoralism must be considered as culturally constructed and not simply a set of subsistence practices that passively reflect environmental constraints. Thus two different groups, even when a similar proportion of their diet comes from animal products rather than plant products,

may choose to emphasize either possession of animals or direct control of land as the basis of their social organization, thus giving a cultural prominence to "pastoral" or "agricultural" pursuits. This prestige of animal-keeping at certain times—"pastoralism in the mind"—may help to explain cultural changes involving the adoption of steppe or desert habits, like the spread of tumulus burial and Corded Ware in third millennium Europe, or the expansion of Islam and Arab culture in the historical Near East—and it is even distantly echoed in the contemporary popularity of blue jeans and cowboy culture.

History of Specialized Animal Husbandry. It is now generally agreed that the domestication of livestock was secondary to the domestication of crops. Pastoralism in any sense was thus an offshoot from an original pattern of mixed farming. Even the domestitation of animals such as reindeer can now be seen as a late feature, consequent on the emergence of specialized forms of steppe pastoralism: the idea of an initial phase of domestication in the Upper Paleolithic, characterized by "close herding" has now been discredited. So has the idea of continuity between the seasonal movements of glacial hunters and transhumant shepherds in Mediterranean montane areas; the two reflect quite different causes, including urban markets in the latter case. Even where the same animal was the object of both hunting and pastoral exploitation in successive phases (as with reindeer in northwest Eurasia), the crucial changes concern social relations such as ownership which do not arise indigenously within hunting communities dependent on their animals. It is clear, therefore, that the development of pastoralism cannot be separated from the general history of agricultural populations in the postglacial.

On the other hand, the development of hunting populations toward the forms represented in the ethnographic record cannot be separated from this wider context. Many recent hunters depend on domestic animals for transport (e.g., the horse in the case of Plains Indian buffalo hunters or the dog in the case of Inuit seal hunters), and hunting systems involving very extensive mobility may therefore be a development of the later postglacial. In this case they would to some extent parallel (and indeed interact with) the development of pastoral societies, as comparable extensions of animal-based economies into extreme and marginal areas of the earth's surface, where crop growing presents only limited possibilities. Both developments depended to some degree on technologies developed by more central and sedentary populations. This suggests that Pleistocene hunters may in general have been less mobile than often imagined, and that pastoralism—far from representing continuity from earlier modes of existence, or an anomalous departure from a general postglacial trend toward sedentism—may have been part of an overall pattern of increasing differentiation (into both more mobile and more sedentary ways of life) in the Holocene.

In this sense, pastoralism is part of a historical process, rather than constituting a unitary analytical category; and its specific importance is closely related to the manufacturing potential of secondary products. It is useful, therefore, to distinguish two fundamental types of pastoralism, depending on the intimacy with which they relate to adjacent agriculturalists and especially urban consumers and suppliers. These may be called *interstitial* and *extensive* types: the former characteristic of areas such as greater Mesopotamia, and the latter of the Pontic steppes and Siberia. (An intermediate—and probably historically later—type is *mon-*

tane pastoralism, which may develop from either of the others, or from local mixed farming, in appropriate environments.)

The interstitial type was closely connected with the development of the western Old World civilizations. Already in the fifth and fourth millennia, south Levantine sedentary communities were using donkeys for expeditions to procure metal supplies from adjacent desert sources. The more radical development in the fourth and third millennia is likely to have been the growth of autonomous pastoralist groups, producing wool, meat, milk products, and live animals for urban consumers, and grazing their herds on the extensive fallow of Mesopotamian irrigation systems, as well as acting as suppliers and intermediaries in the transfer of commodities acquired over long distances. Such systems depended on winter grazing on the steppes, rather than on vertical movements of stock. Steppe pastoralists of this type were a continuing component of the growth of Near Eastern (and, by extension, Indian and central Asian) civilizations, on which they were economically dependent; and this development led in the late second millennium to the emergence of specialized camel-based desert communities that were especially important in the incense trade with Arabia. Pastoralism thus expanded in parallel to the economic prosperity of urban civilization. Such pastoralist groups could usually adopt more sedentary lifestyles on marginal farming land when trade declined; and they were also capable of interfering militarily and politically in the affairs of their sedentary neighbors. The Arab expansion in the seventh and eighth centuries A.D. was the latest and most permanent of these interventions from the desert. Montane systems, with vertical seasonal movements, probably came into importance from the late second millennium B.C. onward, during the Late Bronze and Iron Ages; and they too benefited from the growth of inter-regional trade that increasingly passed through such areas.

The dry areas of central Eurasia followed a different and initially largely independent pattern. Cattle keeping spread into the Pontic steppes from east European farming groups in the sixth and fifth millennia B.C. These communities, otherwise living by fishing and hunting, lived along the rivers. During the later fifth and fourth millennia, in the Copper Age (e.g., at Dereivka near Kiev), they began to exploit the large herds of wild horses that roamed the steppes, apparently by domesticating and riding small numbers of horses, transferring their knowledge of cattle keeping to the new species. This system persisted in northern Kazakhstan (e.g., at Botai) into the early third millennium, at a time when the Pontic steppe cultures had been profoundly influenced by Caucasian and ultimately Near Eastern cultures, for instance in the transmission of wheeled vehicles (and perhaps domestic sheep and the plow) to the steppes. The resulting pit-grave culture was the beginning of a continuous steppe tradition, characterized by tumulus (kurgan) burial, that was to spread eastward across the steppe belt as far as the Altai. While later-fourth- and third-millennium burials sometimes contain carts, early second-millennium ones include chariots and horses. These Timber-Grave and Andronovo groups, which extended over much of the steppe and adjacent semidesert areas during the second millennium (and probably carried Indo-Iranian languages there), occupied substantial villages and were not nomadic, but nevertheless were critically dependent on their herds (especially sheep). Nomadic

steppe pastoralism seems to have emerged in the early first millennium at the eastern end of the steppe corridor, and was marked by the westward spread of the eastern "animal style" of art associated with the Scythians. Other groups, now speaking Turco-Tatar rather than Indo-European languages, followed in the subsequent two millennia: Huns, Turks, and Mongols. These classic steppe pastoralists, with their own states, empires, and political systems, achieved their importance because of the *Silk Route (which ran along the southern margin of the desert and the mountains) and their position on this main artery linking eastern and western Eurasia.

Domestic cattle spread early into North Africa from the Near East, via Egypt and the then well watered Sahara; hunting and fishing populations in the central and southern Sahara were using pottery by 7000 B.C. and had adopted cattle keeping by perhaps 6000 or a little later. Rock paintings from Tassili indicate the ritual importance of these animals. The desiccation of this area after 4000 caused a greater reliance on livestock and accelerated the domestication of indigenous plants on its southern margins. In East Africa pottery use and cattle and goat keeping spread among indigenous hunting and fishing groups in the third millennium, though further influences from western Asia (including the introduction of zebu cattle and perhaps the spread of donkeys and camels) took place in the later second millennium, and farming or herding was only widely dispersed with the spread of iron in the first millennium B.C. Many of these populations might be described as pastoralist, but only in the most general sense; and specialized pastoral groups such as the Fulani and the Maasai (relying entirely on their herds, rather than hunting) must be related to the ethnic differentiation and economic and ecological niching that emerged during the last two millennia, at the time of Mediterranean and Indian Ocean contacts. African pastoralism thus resembles the Near Eastern in the diversity of its adjacent peoples and lifestyles, though it differs in that cattle were not used for traction nor sheep for wool production: blood and milk were the principal secondary products of livestock.

What emerges from all these examples is the relatively late date at which the full characteristics of "pastoralism" as known ethnographically made their appearance; and the importance of adaptation, not just to environmental conditions but to human neighbors and the economic opportunities they provide.

[*See also* AGRICULTURE; CAMEL, DOMESTICATION OF THE; HORSE, DOMESTICATION OF THE; PASTORALISTS, AFRICAN; SECONDARY PRODUCTS REVOLUTION.]

■ Susan H. Lees and D. G. Bates, "The Origins of Specialised Nomadic Pastoralism: A Systemic Model," *American Antiquity* 39 (1974): 187–193. Michael B. Rowton, "Enclosed Nomadism," *Journal of the Economic and Social History of the Orient* 17 (1974): 1–30. Richard W. Bulliet, *The Camel and the Wheel* (1975). Tim Ingold, *Hunters, Pastoralists and Ranchers* (1980). Andrew Sherratt, "Plough and Pastoralism: Aspects of the Secondary Products Revolution" in *Pattern of the Past: Studies in Honour of David Clarke*, eds. Ian Hodder, Glyn Isaac, and Norman Hammond (1981), pp. 261–305. *World Archaeology* 15:1 (1983), special issue on transhumance and pastoralism. Anatoly M. Khazanov, *Nomads and the Outside World* (1984). Juliet Clutton-Brock, ed., *The Walking Larder: Patterns of Domestication, Pastoralism and Predation* (1989). Andrew Sherratt, "Sedentary Agriculturalists and Nomadic Pastoralists, 3000–700 B.C." in *UNESCO History of Humanity* (in press).

Andrew Sherratt

PASTORALISTS, African

Introduction
Saharan Pastoralists
East African Pastoralists
The Khoi Khoi of Southern Africa

INTRODUCTION

Domesticated cattle, goats, and sheep were either introduced into the Nile Valley from the Near East, or tamed in Egypt or the Sahara Desert before 6000 B.C. Pastoralism, in the sense of a major, but never totally exclusive, dependence on herding, was the basis of early Nubian village cultures along the Nile and developed early on the better watered plains of the Sahara Desert. South African archaeologist Andrew Smith has argued that the aurochs, *Bos primigenius,* was domesticated by Saharan hunter-gatherer groups before 5000 B.C. He points out that African buffalo herds are better disciplined and migrate in more predictable ways in semiarid environments. In the Sahara, humans and wild cattle existed in close association, making it easier to domesticate a large and unpredictable beast. Cattle herding became an important feature of Saharan life for many centuries. The gradual drying up of the desert after 3500 B.C. caused cattle-herding groups to move toward the fringes of the Sahara, and southward into the Sahel regions of central and western Africa, where they were well established by 2000 B.C. The same groups may have brought cereal crops like sorghum and millet with them.

African pastoralists operated in difficult environments, where cattle diseases like rinderpest were endemic, grazing grasses generally of poor to moderate fertility, and large tracts of land off-limits because of tsetse fly infestations. Despite these limitations, cattle herders were widespread on the East African highlands and in northeastern Africa by 1000 B.C., where they were to flourish until modern times. The ancestry of such groups as the Masai or Kenya and Tanzania go back at least 1,000 years. The relationships between these pastoral groups and their farming neighbors were always complex.

The spread of cattle herding into southern Africa may have taken place after 1000 B.C., but the route of such a migration and its dating is much disputed. The ancestors of the Khoi Khoi peoples of the Cape of Good Hope possessed domesticated animals by about 2,000 years ago, but whether they acquired them from farmers or by direct migration through south-central Africa and Namibia is still uncertain. The Iron Age farmers who spread throughout southern Africa about 2,000 years ago prized cattle in their mixed farming economies. In later centuries, cattle ownership played an important role in the acquisition of wealth and political power in states like Zimbabwe.

[See also AFRICA, *articles on* EARLY IRON-AGE SETTLEMENT OF SUB-SAHARAN AFRICA, THE RISE OF KINGDOMS AND STATES IN AFRICA.]

Brian M. Fagan

SAHARAN PASTORALISTS

*Pastoralism in Africa is a grassland adaptation where rainfall is inadequate to support agriculture. Most of Africa's grasslands are subject to severe drought, although this is often forgotten or ignored during the good years. In North Africa and the Sahara climatic conditions varied dramatically during the Holocene, with periods of amelioration that permitted the area to be occupied by herders. This can be seen in the detailed rock paintings of cattle in the Tassilin-Ajjer and Acacus Mountains, areas today of little or no vegetation.

The question of when pastoralism began in the Sahara is fraught with problems of definition. What constitutes a domestic animal, and how can it be recognized archaeologically? Fred Wendorf and Romuald Schild in *Cattle-Keepers of the Eastern Sahara* (1984) would have it that cattle from Bir Kiseiba and Nabta Playa in the Western Desert of southern Egypt around 8000 to 9000 B.P. were domesticated. The argument is an ecological one. The analyzed fauna consist primarily of small gazelles and hares, as well as the bones of a few large bovids identified as cattle. An environment that could only support small packages like hares and gazelles, they contend, would be incapable of maintaining large bovids without human intervention.

The counter argument is twofold. First, given that nowhere in Africa is there presently such an environment supporting hares and gazelles without there also being medium–large bovids like oryx or hartebeest, the faunal list is probably selective, therefore incomplete. Indeed, hartebeest are certainly known from rock engravings of the Central Sahara. If these larger bovids existed without human intervention, why should cattle have required human help? Second, conditions elsewhere in the Sahara at this time show evidence of more rainfall and/or lower evaporation rates than today in the form of lakes no longer in existence. If we remove the ecological constraints, what would have been the precedents or catalysts of a closer human/animal relationship?

By contrast, the period around 7700 to 7000 B.P. was one of severe aridity, and it was only after this that the first ovicaprids appeared in sites of the Eastern Sahara and elsewhere. Since the ovicaprids of Africa are derived from wild stock of the Near East perhaps it is there we should look for a pastoral connection. The arid period of the eighth millenium B.P. would have put pressure on the herders of the Sahara, possibly making them ready for innovative ideas. When conditions rebounded around 7000 B.P. the environment opened up a grassland niche across the Sahara that could be filled by hunters, or people who had already accepted a closer human/animal relationship when times were hard.

This is the period of the rock paintings of cattle in the Central Sahara, as well as the widespread appearance of cattle remains. At one site, Uan Muhuggiag in southwestern Libya, a block with two oxen painted on it was buried in the deposit; the level above was dated to 4730 B.P. Elsewhere in the site a shorthorn cow skull was dated to 5952 B.P., and from Adrar Bous, Niger, a complete skeleton of a shorthorn cow was dated to 5780 B.P. These sites are further south and west of the earlier ones in Egypt mentioned above, and may indicate the gradual spread of pastoralism across the Sahara.

The paintings of pastoral life are full of social detail. It would appear that two quite distinct human physical types involved in pastoralism are represented in the Central Sahara: one was of a black group, whose cultural attributes portrayed are very similar to modern Wodaabe Fulani. The second group shows fair-skinned, long-haired Mediterranean types, with completely different cultural material. Of interest is one panel showing dramatic use of fire (Rudolf Kuper, ed., *Sahara: 10,000 Jahre zwischen Weide und Wüste* (1978): 426–7). This may indicate pre-Islamic Berber rituals of people described as "fire worshipers."

The lithic artifacts from the period 6500 to 4500 B.P. across the Central Sahara allow stylistic boundaries to be roughly demarcated, although the economy and material culture were in general very similar. We might suggest a distribution of prehistoric pastoral groups analogous to the Tuareg today.

Around 4500 B.P. environmental conditions once more deteriorated until the Sahara was similar to today. It was at this time that the Sahelian site of Karkarichinkat and East African sites around Lake Turkana were first occupied by cattle herders. This was probably a function of a retreat of the twenty-inch (500 mm) rainfall isohyet necessary for tsetse breeding. Once tsetse corridors opened up to the south, herders could spread into the rest of Africa.

■ Jean-Dominique Lajoux, *The Rock Paintings of Tassili* (1963). Martin Williams and Hugues Faure, *The Sahara and the Nile* (1980). Fred Wendorf and Romuald Schild, *Prehistory of the Eastern Sahara* (1980). Andrew B. Smith, *Pastoralism in Africa* (1992).

Andrew B. Smith

EAST AFRICAN PASTORALISTS

The archaeological and linguistic evidence for the origins and evolution of pastoralism in eastern African remains incomplete, but available data suggest that stone tool and pottery-using nomadic pastoralists dependent upon humpless cattle (*Bos taurus*), goats, and sheep migrated from the Sudan into the Horn of Africa (Eritrea, Ethiopia, Djibouti, and Somalia) by ca. 5000–4000 B.P. The stimulus for this migration may have been the mid-Holocene period of widespread aridity that affected much of the Sahara and Sahel regions of northeastern Africa. But socioeconomic and ideological factors, as yet poorly documented, must also have contributed to the spread of pastoralism. The stylistically similar rock art of the Horn depicting herds and herders of domestic stock attest to the widespread distribution of and communication between these early pastoral communities. The extent to which these pastoral systems interacted with already established (according to linguistic evidence) farming communities in the Eritrean/Ethiopian highlands and/or local hunter-gatherer-fisher folk, remains essentially unknown.

The earliest securely dated archaeological evidence for domestic stock comes from the site of Dongodien on the eastern shore of Kenya's Lake Turkana. Dating to ca. 4000 B.P., this and other East African (Kenya, Tanzania, and Uganda) sites of this time range provide the earliest evidence for the establishment of a Pastoral Neolithic way of life characterized by nomadic peoples having a microlithic-based Later Stone Age technology, distinctively decorated handmade pottery, and an economy and settlement pattern dependent upon the hunting, fishing, and gathering of wild foods supplemented by the herding of domestic stock (cattle, goats, and/or sheep). Some of these early Pastoral Neolithic sites in northern Kenya are associated with large stone monoliths similar to those still being made in Ethiopia, prompting some archaeologists and historical linguists to speculate that the first East African pastoralists were Cushitic-speaking immigrants from Ethiopia.

By 3000 B.P., and for at least 1,000 years after, there is significant increase in the frequency of Pastoral Neolithic sites, particularly in the open woodlands and grasslands stretching from central Kenya to northern Tanzania. Sites tend to be much larger in extent and display a remarkable degree of material, economic, and spacial variability. Some scholars have interpreted this variability as evidence for ethnically and linguistically distinct populations, such as Savanna Pastoral Neolithic peoples who may have spoken a Cushitic language, and an "Elmenteitan Pastoral Neolithic comprised of Nilo-Saharan speakers. However, given the generally poor data base, other archaeologists have argued strongly against any kind of correlation between the archaeological record and ethnolinguistic groups. Also under contention is the extent to which East African pastoral groups were nomadic versus semisedentary, socially stratified, or whether they cultivated domestic crops in addition to herding. Some archaeologists suggest it was not until the coming of Iron Age populations ca. 1500–1000 B.P. that farming (and metallurgy) were introduced to East African pastoralists.

Site variability has also been explained as reflecting differing degrees of dependence upon domestic herds, ranging from a generalized pattern of hunting, fishing, gathering, and herding to specialized production where in some regions pastoralists took advantage of rich rangelands and an amicable climatic regime to establish a subsistence pattern dependent almost exclusively upon domestic stock. The potential for specialized pastoral production was also enhanced by the introduction of more drought- and disease-resistant humped cattle (*Bos indicus*) ca. 1,500 years ago, and dromedary camels sometime later.

[*See also* AFRICA: ORIGINS OF FOOD PRODUCTION IN.]

■ Stanley H. Ambrose, "The Introduction of Pastoral Adaptations to the Highlands of East Africa," in eds. J. Desmond Clark and Steven A. Brandt, *From Hunters to Farmers* (1984), pp. 212–239. Steven A. Brandt and Nanny Carder, "Pastoral Rock Art in the Horn of Africa: Making Sense of Udder Chaos," *World Archaeology* 19 (1987): 194–213. Peter Robertshaw, ed., *Early Pastoralists of South-Western Kenya* (1990). John Bower, "The Pastoral Neolithic of East Africa," *Journal of World Prehistory* 5 (1991): 49–82. Fiona Marshall, "Archaeological Perspectives on East African Pastoralism," in eds. Elliot Fratkin, Kathleen A. Galvin, and Eric Abella Roth, *African Pastoralist Systems: An Integrated Approach* (1994), pp. 17–43.

Steven A. Brandt

THE KHOI KHOI OF SOUTHERN AFRICA

The Khoi Khoi (name: *Khoekhoe*—from *khoii-khoin,* meaning "men of men") were called "Hottentots" by the early travelers and settlers at the Cape of Good Hope in the seventeenth century. Divided into clan groupings under a leader chosen by the people, they were mostly to be found in the winter rainfall area of the Cape, with the exception of the Groot Namaqua who lived north of the Orange River in Namibia.

Where the Khoi originated is as yet unknown. Linguistic similarity between the Cape Khoi and Khoe-speaking bushmen of Botswana suggests a historical connection. There is little disagreement that the Khoi were genetically linked to the aboriginal San hunters of southern Africa. The transition to herding appears coincident with the arrival of Iron Age farmers into the subcontinent around 2000 B.P., with hunters possibly being incorporated into the society of the farmers as lower-class members. Under these conditions they could have obtained sheep for services rendered, becoming herders in the process. If this scenario is correct, why they separated from the farmers and went their own way has yet to be understood. One possible route of dispersal was down the Atlantic coast of Namibia and the Cape. Archaeological evidence for early sheep and ceramics occurs at Geduld in northern Namibia by at least 1790 B.P. Similarly dates of between 2000 and 1900 B.P. have come from dating sheep bones obtained from the bottom of the Spoegrivier sequence on the Namaqualand coast. Other dates of sheep bones from Kasteelberg, Die Kelders, and Byneskranskop in the Cape are all 1630 B.P. or younger. There are dates of around 1900 B.P. from these sites that might indicate a slightly earlier appearance of ceramics.

One of the major controversies that surrounds the study of precolonial Khoi is how distinct they were from hunters or *soaqua*. Richard Elphick, in his *Kraal and Castle* (1977) sees the distinction in the historical record as one of fortune. When an individual or family had stock they were herders on an up-cycle. Loss of stock reduced them to hunting and foraging on the down-cycle. Indigenous artifacts that, from historical records, had Khoi interacting with the Dutch, were found at the seventeenth-century Dutch redoubt of Oudepost. Because no difference could be seen between the artifacts and those found on the majority of Later Stone Age hunter sites in the Cape, the excavator, Carmel Schrire, says there can be no separate archaeological signatures between hunters and herders.

The alternative view, supporting an economic and cultural distinction, sees Kasteelberg as a herder campsite where the fauna remains consist of large quantities of sheep and seal bones, few formal stone tools (0.2 percent), and large quantities of pottery. This is quite distinct from the smaller but contemporaneous rock shelter of Witklip, which shows a preponderence of small antelopes in the fauna, 4 percent formal lithic component, and few potsherds. Thus the argument is for quite separate social and economic groups interacting, either amicably (with exchange of pottery), or in enmity (when sheep were stolen).

Once the Dutch colony expanded at the Cape in the eighteenth century, there was pressure for the Khoi to either work for the colonists, or move away. With loss of land and livestock, especially after the smallpox epidemic of 1713, herders were often forced to join foraging bands for survival. The last remaining Khoi lands, which subsequently became common reserves, were focused around mission stations in Namaqualand in the nineteenth century.

[*See also* HUNTER-GATHERERS, AFRICAN; PASTORALISM.]

■ Carmel Schrire, "An Enquiry into the Evolutionary Status and Apparent Identity of San Hunter-Gatherers," *Human Ecology* 8:1 (1980): 9–32. Carmel Schrire and Janette Deacon, "The Indigenous Artifacts from Oudepost 1, a Colonial Outpost of the VOC at Saldanha Bay, Cape," *South African Archaeological Bulletin* 44 (1989): 105–113. Andrew B. Smith, "On Becoming Herders: Khoikhoi and San Ethnicity in Southern Africa," *African Studies* 49:2 (1990): 51–73. John Kinahan, *Pastoral Nomads of the Central Namib Desert* (1991). Alan Barnard, *Hunters and Herders of Southern Africa* (1992). Andrew B. Smith, *Pastoralism in Africa* (1992).

Andrew B. Smith

PENGTOUSHAN. The earliest-dated rice in China, indeed at the moment the earliest anywhere in the world, is contained in pottery from the site of Pengtoushan on the middle reaches of the Yangtze River in Li County, Hunan Province. It is surprising to find the earliest presumably domesticated rice in China up the river rather than nearer the coast where it was expected. The radiocarbon dates, on rice husks and other charcoal within the pottery itself, are too early for the calibration curve, but they probably can be adjusted to about 7000 to 5500 B.C. Carbonized grains were found in lumps of fired clay as well as in the pottery. It is not clear what these lumps are, but they are possibly a part of wattle and daub house construction. The rice grains are large, and are considered to be a form of domesticated rice,

but they have not yet been identified as to subspecies. However, they are said to be the *indica* variety on the basis of their shape. Thus, though there is no question about the association of the rice with the carbon-14 dates, the status of the rice as a domesticate is still in dispute.

The archaeological site is on a low mound rising 10 to 13 feet (3 to 4 m) above the surrounding land, covering about 12,000 square yards (10,000 sq. m). The site lies between a river and a lake, with plenty of water for rice growing. At present the mound is also the location of a modern village. Thus, the site has been only sampled rather than extensively excavated.

The lowest level contained a house floor, ash pits, and graves. The house floor, covering an area of about 44 square yards (37 sq. m), was strewn with yellow sandy soil, and contained postholes. Another house was excavated nearer the surface.

Lithics include large chipped tools, small flaked tools, and small polished tools, a frequent combination in Neolithic China. The large implements include choppers and round, flat stones, while the smaller flint tools, mostly scrapers, points, and gravers, resemble microliths in their production technology but have little edge retouch. Polished tools include small axes, adzes, and chisels. There are also stone ornaments, especially beads.

The red-brown pottery is coarse with thick rounded bases and sides that have been constructed with paddle and anvil. Shapes include bowls, jars, cooking pots, and vessel stands. Only the stands have flat bases. The various containers are for storing, cooking, and serving of foods and beverages. The paste includes other organic matter, such as peat, in addition to rice husks. The exterior is paddled with criss-cross lines of cord marking, and occasionally additional decoration of punctates and incised lines is seen. Some vessels have lug handles.

Sites with similar pottery, including rice husks in the temper, have been located nearby, but have not yet been excavated. These sites are now considered to be related, and collectively represent the Pengtoushan culture.

[*See also* ASIA: PREHISTORY AND EARLY HISTORY OF EAST ASIA; ASIA, ORIGINS OF FOOD PRODUCTION IN: ORIGINS OF FOOD PRODUCTION IN CHINA; CHINA: EARLY CIVILIZATIONS OF CHINA.]

■ Yan Wenming, "China's Earliest Rice Agriculture Remains," *Indo-Pacific Prehistory 1990 1*, Papers from the 14th IPPA Congress, Yokyakarta (1991): 118–126.

Sarah Milledge Nelson

PERSIA, or Iran, a major contributor to the cultural heritage of the ancient Near East, occupies an area of approximately 636,000 square miles (1,648,000 sq. km), bounded to the north by Turkmanistan, the Caspian Sea, and the Republic of Azerbaijan, to the west by Turkey and Iraq, to the south by the Persian Gulf and the Gulf of Oman, and to the east by Pakistan and Afghanistan.

The name Persia was given to the whole country of Iran by the Greeks who were in close contact with the Achaemenid Persians and their homeland Pars. It continued to be known in the West as Persia until 1935, when, at the request of the national government *Iran* became the official name of the country, restoring an ancient geographical terminology.

Iran, or *Eran*, was the land of the Aryans (nobles) or Iranians, a branch of the Indo-European peoples, who, in a number of waves, emigrated from the steppes of Central Asia (see Central Asia, Nomadic Peoples of) to Europe and the Near East during the second and first millennia B.C. The geographical name *Iran* derives from an ancient expression (*Aryana Waejah*, meaning "expanse, territory of the Aryas") found in the *Avesta* (early Iranian religious texts), by which the Iranians designated their own territory. Culturally and linguistically, these Aryans were close relatives of another group of people who also called themselves Aryas, now called Indo-Aryans in contradistinction to the Iranians. The two groups of Aryans were related linguistically and culturally to the extensive family of *Indo-Europeans, whose languages include most of the linguistic groups of Europe as well as those of such ancient Asian groups as the Hittites and Tocharians. The Iranian language, which is very similar to the Vedic of India, is a variety of the same tongue which is inferred to be the parent language of Slavonic, Teutonic, Celtic, Greek, and Latin.

The Paleolithic Periods. The earliest evidence of human occupation in the Iranian Plateau dates to the Lower *Paleolithic Period (ca. 250,000–100 / 80,000 B.P.). Except, however, for a few open sites in the Khurasan region (northeastern Iran), Baluchestan (southeastern Iran), and in the Zagros Mountains, Iran's Lower Paleolithic past is still mainly uncharted. Middle Paleolithic (100 / 80,000–40,000 B.P.) sites are more numerous and evidence about them is much more reliable than of those of the preceding period. Though open sites still existed, many of the sites were now to be found in caves and shelters. Some twenty sites (among them, Ghar-e Khar, at Bisitun; Khunji Cave, Ghamari Cave, and Ghar Arjeneh, near Khurramabad) were found in the Zagros Mountains. Middle Paleolithic (or Mousterian) sites have also been found in Fars (Eshkaft-e Gavi), in Azerbaijan (Tamtama), and Khurasan (Ke-Aram I). The *Levallois* technique of chipping flint blades, common in the Near East, is absent from the Mousterian flint industry found at these sites. The hominid type associated with these sites is identified as *Neanderthal.

The Mousterian flint industry is followed by the Baradostian chipped flint industry of the Upper Paleolithic Period. Remains of the Upper Paleolithic/Epipaleolithic Period (40,000–12,000 B.P.) are primarily found in the Zagros region, at sites such as Yafteh Cave, Ghar Arjeneh, and Pa Sangar, all near Khurramabad. Three sites near Lake Maharlu and Lake Tasht, and one (Eshkaft Gavi) in the Marv Dasht of Fars also date to this period.

The Upper Paleolithic Period must have been a period of experimentation with resource exploitation and accumulation of environmental knowledge for the inhabitants of the Zagros Mountains, for by the end of this period, coinciding with the end of the last ice age, their mastery of the environment enabled these early highland residents to embark on the task of the domestication of native animal (sheep and goats) and plant (wheat and barley) species that ushered in a revolutionary phase in human history. The Neolithic Period (ca. 10,000–4500 B.C.) was a period of the settled life in the lush valleys of the Zagros (the habitat of wild sheep, goats, wheat, and barley) in small villages such as Tappeh Sarab, Tappeh Guran, Tappeh Asiab, and Ganj Dareh.

The Neolithic Period. Archaeological surveys indicate that permanent settlements were rather sparse in the valleys of the Zagros Mountains (Lurestan) from prehistoric times to the Islamic period. Covered by rocky terrain and not suitable for agriculture as primary subsistence economy, these regions provide excellent seasonal pastures and have long been utilized by the pastoral Bakhtyari tribes of the region. A major factor in the symbiotic existence of these communities is the complementary resources to be found in northeastern Khuzestan and in the upper Marv Dasht plain, the site of Persepolis. In these areas, a pastorally based economy could be maintained and developed only through seasonal migration of flocks. Thus, the environmental conditions and geographical features in southwestern Iran necessitated two distinct yet complementary lifestyles and economies based on animal husbandry and on irrigation agriculture.

The earliest evidence for the initial phase of permanent or seasonal settlements is found in the natural habitat of the early domesticates, namely at Ganj Dareh, Tappeh Sarab, Tappeh Asiab, Tappeh Guran, and Tappeh Abdul Hussein, all in the valleys of the Zagros Mountains. This initial sedentization and the ability to control food resources, thanks to the new domesticates, was followed by an increase in the population which resulted in the occupation of lower valleys and the lowland Susiana. Ganj Dareh, near Harsin in Kurdestan, is a good representative of the early highland villages of the eighth millennium B.C. containing early evidence of sophisticated forms of solid architecture with long plano-convex mud bricks and the earliest pottery so far discovered in the Near East. Although Ganj Dareh seems to have been abandoned around 7000 B.C., other Early Neolithic sites such as Zaghe, Sialk, and Sang-e Chakhmaq (central plateau), Haji Firuz (southern Azerbaijan), Tappeh Guran (Lurestan), Ali Kosh (Deh Luran), Chogha Banut (Susiana), Jari and Mushki (in Fars), and Iblis (in Kerman) indicate the development of early settled villages all over Iran.

The central plateau (surrounded by the Zagros and Alburz ranges), Fars, and Susiana are the major cultural provinces in Iran, each with distinct but related cultures. The artistic traditions of these regions are manifest in the art of painted pottery. For instance, excavations at Tappeh Sialk, near Kashan in the central plateau, have revealed an early period (ca. 6000 B.C.) when the inhabitants of the site used stone tools, made use of shell and bone for decoration, and created a pottery with decorative designs that imitated basketry. In a later period (ca. 5000 B.C.) the pottery was more decorative; black paint was used on a dark red surface with rows of animals and plants. Somewhat later (ca. 4000 B.C.) the pottery showed a greater variety of shapes and animal motifs became highly stylized. The potter's wheel was also invented there around this time. Copper smelting and casting were developed as a result of increasing interregional commerce, and an incipient administrative technology manifested itself in the use of button seals.

Fars was also a major cultural province in Iran. The artistic traditions are best represented by the materials from Tall-e Bakun A, near Persepolis, where the painted pottery is arguably the highest manifestation of prehistoric ceramic art. Late prehistoric Fars was also the scene of increasing administrative control, as known from Tall-e Bakun A, where distinctive clay door sealings were used to secure warehouses against unauthorized entry. Only around 3400 B.C., several hundred years after Bakun became deserted, did such practice become common in most major Protoliterate sites in the Near East.

The third major cultural province, Susiana, occupies an important place in the history and archaeology of the Near East. In prehistoric times it was a breeding ground for highly developed cultures and civilizations. In historical periods Susiana retained its importance as both an administrative center and the main grain-producing region for the Achaemenid, Parthian, and Sasanian empires.

Apart from its agricultural importance, lowland Susiana was particularly important for its geographical location. For most of its history, it was a theater of military confrontations not only between rival states based in Mesopotamia and Iran, but also between those states and various highland polities. Occasional hostile contacts notwithstanding, Susiana was especially important as the center of interaction and meeting place of its settled agriculturalist population and the pastoralist tribes who used, and still use, northern Susiana as winter pasture.

Artistic achievements of the prehistoric inhabitants of Susiana are shown by the fine painted pottery of the Susiana sequence. Excavations at the important site of Chogha Mish, the largest prehistoric site in Susiana, documented this sequence from the earliest coarse ware to the highly decorated vessels of fine shapes and elegant designs of the Late Susiana Period (ca. 4000 B.C.).

Urban Development and the Rise of the Elamite State. During the second half of the fourth millennium B.C., Iran and Mesopotamia simultaneously developed essentially distinctive civilizations and written languages. In Susiana a still undeciphered cuneiform writing system, known as Proto-Elamite, was developed. Unlike an earlier period, when the ceramic and glyptic styles of Susiana and lower Mesopotamia shared many features, by 3200 B.C. these styles dramatically diverged from those in Mesopotamia. This period is called Proto-Elamite, a period of colonization of resource-rich regions of the plateau by the inhabitants of Susiana.

During the late fourth and early third millennia B.C. a number of sites on the Iranian Plateau adopted specialized industries presumably to accommodate the needs of the urban centers in lowland Mesopotamia and Susiana, both devoid of many natural resources. Tappeh Qabrestan and Hissar in the central plateau and Tall-e Iblis in Kerman specialized in metallurgy, Tappeh Yahya (in Kerman) in the production of carved steatite vessels, and Shahr-e Sokhteh (in Sistan) in lapis lazuli. Such industrial activities and overland trade coincided with the distribution at a number of sites of Proto-Elamite tablets, indicating, perhaps, that Susiana had an important role in regulating the interregional flow of goods. However, regional diversity persisted even when the Elamite dynasties of Awan and Shimashki (ca. 2600–1900 B.C.) crystallized in the highlands and dominated both Susiana and Fars.

Around 2500 B.C. the Elamite kingdom, the only literate pre-Achaemenid Iranian state, emerged in the highlands of southwestern Iran. The various Elamite dynasties dominated the country well into the first half of the first millennium B.C., when their power was gradually eroded to a great extent by the penetration and establishment of the Medes and Persians in western and south-central Iran, and ancient Anshan in the modern province of Fars, a major Elamite territory. The eclipse of Assyria, Babylonia, and Elam coincides with the arrival and establishment of a number of new peoples in the ancient Near East. The control of most of the highlands by these Iranian tribes must have contributed to the erosion of Elam's influence as a regional power and its political fragmentation.

The Iron Age. Archaeological data are the primary evidence for the early history of the Iranian tribes. These data are complemented by outside (Assyrian and Babylonian) written sources until the advent of Cyrus II, the founder of the Persian Empire. From the mid-sixth century onward, indigenous written sources and the accounts of the Greek historians are the main sources for the history of the Persian Achaemenids. Also important are the traditional Iranian legends and heroic tales (such as *Shahnameh*, the Book of Kings) and the *Avesta*.

The precise routes of penetration and the mechanism and dynamics of the migration of the Iranian tribes into the Iranian Plateau are a matter of scholarly debate. Archaeological data show a clear break in regional traditions during the late second and early first millennia B.C. and indicate that Iran was being penetrated from around 1200–900 B.C. by groups of people from the north. The appearance of a special class of gray-black pottery in the Caspian littoral, the central plateau, and north and central-western Iran has long been seen as the hallmark of the Iron Age culture of Iran and as indicative of the routes of its diffusion into the Iranian Plateau. Most of the archaeological evidence pertaining to this period comes primarily from isolated cemeteries. Since these cemeteries are scattered all over the Iranian Plateau, some scholars have suggested that they mark the migration routes of the Iranian tribes.

From the mid-ninth century B.C. the closely related Medes and the Persians appear prominently in the cuneiform sources from Assyria and Babylonia. These sources leave no doubt about the location of the homeland of the Medes in western Iran, with *Hagmatana* (The Place of Assembly) as its capital. *Hagmatana* is the modern town of Hamadan, known to the Greeks as *Ecbatana*. Since the modern town covers most of the ancient site, it has not yet been possible to excavate this important Median capital systematically. The location of the early territory of the Persians is far less certain. The Persians seem to have settled first in the area around Lake Urmia (in Azerbaijan, northwestern Iran) and gradually moved southeast to Anshan, which later became Persia proper and still retains its name in modern Persian as Fars.

The Medes rose to prominence and established themselves as the ruling tribe in Iran around the middle of the seventh century B.C. In 612 B.C., an alliance of the Medes and Babylonians eliminated the Assyrians and divided the Near East between themselves. In the meantime, the Persians were consolidating their power in the south. In 550 B.C., Cyrus II (Cyrus the Great) defeated the Medes and, in a series of campaigns, forged the largest empire in the region. It was not, however, until the time of Darius I that Persia united all the Near Eastern nations, including Egypt, under its imperial rule.

Cyrus II came from the ruling Persian family of the Achaemenids, which traced its ancestry back to *Hakhamanesh* or Achaemenes, a legendary figure. Traditionally three kings fall between *Hakhamanesh* and Cyrus II: Teispes *(Cheeshpeesh)*, Cyrus I, and Cambyses I *(Kambujieh)*. These early Persian Achaemenid kings were probably the vassals of the Median kings. Whether the marriage of Cambyses I to Astyages' daughter Mandana suggests the need of Media to strengthen its position or vice versa is not known, though the gradual erosion of the Median power and the simultaneous rise of the Persians suggests the former. Whatever the reason, the marriage of his parents gave Cyrus II legitimate rights to claim the Median throne in 550 B.C.

The Achaemenid Empire. Cyrus II first chose as his residence the capital city of the Medes, Hamadan, and then Pasargadae, north of Persepolis. Pasargadae is the site of the first Achaemenid palace built by Cyrus II in Fars. The plan of the palace shows the mature style of the later Achaemenid palaces of Susa and Persepolis. Another main monument at Pasargadae is the tomb of Cyrus II, locally known as "the tomb of the Mother of Solomon." The only free-standing Achaemenid funerary monument, it is placed on a stepped plinth, much like a miniature ziggurat. Although the architecture of the tomb may have been influenced by funerary architecture in Lycia and Phrygia, the general shape and particularly the gabled roof are reminiscent of the early first millennium stone-lined graves at Tappeh Sialk, near Kashan.

With the unification of Media and Persia, as well as other polities of Iranian tribes, Cyrus II embarked on a series of military campaigns to expand his territory, conquering Lydia in 547 B.C., all of Asia Minor by 540 B.C., and Babylon in 539 B.C.

The cosmopolitan and popular measures Cyrus II took in Babylon set the stage for further and future Persian conquests in the Near East. Cyrus's successor, Cambyses II (529–522), set out to conquer Egypt, which was accomplished in 522. After Cambyses's death, Darius, a Persian general of royal blood, ascended to the throne.

Darius relates in detail his early military campaigns in the famous Besitun trilingual (Old Persian, Elamite, Akkadian) inscription, near Kermanshah, in western Iran. The Besitun inscription is one of the most important ancient documents not only because it gives us a detailed account of the early career of Darius, but because it was this trilingual document that provided the key to the decipherment of the cuneiform scripts—in much the same way as the Rosetta Stone did for the decipherment of Egyptian hieroglyphs.

For Darius, Hamadan and Pasargadae must have seemed too remote to serve as administrative centers of his vast empire, and like his Elamite predecessors, he chose Susa as his capital with Hamadan as a provincial capital. Darius also embarked on a large-scale construction of a palace complex at Persepolis in the Marv Dasht area of Fars, the heartland of the Persian Achaemenids. Although the construction of Persepolis was never entirely finished, major ceremonial events took place in this magnificent palace complex.

Despite some painful military setbacks in Greece, when Darius died in 486 B.C. he left a solid empire for his son, Xerxes I (486–465 B.C.). Yet though Cyrus II and Darius had followed a policy of tolerance and evenhandedness with their subject nations, Xerxes abandoned this policy and imposed a heavy-handed rule on the provinces. Although he was successful in capturing and reducing Athens, his military success did not ensure Persian hegemony in mainland Greece and his resources were constantly sapped by the various revolts of the city-states in Asia Minor.

The assassination in 465 B.C. of Xerxes I was a pivotal point in the Persian Achaemenid history. The reigns of his successors were marred by many revolts, harem intrigues, and court corruption. The loss of Egypt to the empire during the reign of Artaxerxes II (404–359 B.C.) and the rise of Macedonia paved the way for the depletion of the empire's resources and eventually led to the downfall of the Achaemenid empire in 330 B.C.

Religion. The structure and characteristics of the religious belief system of the early Iranian tribes and even the Persian Achaemenids are comparatively obscure. The Iranian tribes apparently practiced a polytheistic religion similar to other Indo-European peoples. The gods of their pantheon were hierarchically organized and associated with natural and cultural properties. The basic religious practices included animal sacrifice, worship of fire (probably as the supreme manifestation of truth), and drinking the elixir of the sacred plant *haoma*. Indirect archaeological evidence of cult practices consists primarily of fire altars, rock-cut tombs, and religious implements depicted in the glyptic art and on some stone reliefs. The only religious complex known today of the Persian Achaemenid Period is at Dahaneh Gholaman, north of Zahedan, on the border between Iran and Afghanistan, consisting of a number of large buildings, the most impressive of which is an Achaemenid building with columned porticoes and a central courtyard with three rectangular altars in the middle. The altars were mounted on pedestals and furnished with steps leading to the top.

The extant contemporary cuneiform texts mention principal deities but do not contain any details. Moreover, any speculation on and reconstruction of the religion of the Persian Achaemenids cannot be extended to the popular beliefs beyond the court, for which there is no direct archaeological or written evidence. Nevertheless, sacred texts such as *Avesta, Bundahinsh* (Creation), *Denkard,* and old Iranian legends, augmented by general references in Persian Achaemenid inscriptions to deities and their properties leave some room for discussion.

Social Organization. Little is known about the social structure of the Persian Achaemenid society beyond the royal court. The available evidence, however, suggests a pyramidal structure, the apex of which was occupied by the king of kings (*Shahanshah* in Persian), indicating the degree of regional political autonomy enjoyed by the nobility. Despite the great powers early Achaemenid and other rulers enjoyed throughout the history of Iran, the geography of the country with high rugged mountain ranges and forbidding stretches of desert discouraged a long-lasting powerful central government. The components of the Persian Achaemenid court consisted of powerful landowners (usually of royal blood), military officers, religious officials, harem functionaries, and bureaucrats. Written texts and Persepolis reliefs indicate that both Medes and Persians held important offices. Like many later courts, the Persian Achaemenid court had a seminomadic character, which was to some extent dictated by the country's geography and climate. The court lived in Susa in the winter months, in Hamadan during the summer, and in Persepolis in the spring.

The empire was divided into satrapies (provinces) which were governed by satraps, usually native to the province, chosen by the central court. The power and authority of these satraps depended directly on the strength and weakness of the king. Although the satraps were relatively free in the administration of the internal affairs of the provinces, the king maintained surveillance over them through royal officials (known as the king's eyes and ears) who were attached to the provincial courts. Nevertheless, the Persian Achaemenid rulers, particularly the early ones, were reluctant to practice a heavy-handed policy in the internal affairs of the provinces. The language of the Persian empire was as varied as its subject peoples, but the *lingua franca* was Aramaic, a Semitic language. In Persia proper, Elamite was used as the administrative language, and Old Persian was used primarily in royal and religious inscriptions.

The Seleucid, Parthian, and Sasanian Periods. The overthrow of the Achaemenid empire by the Macedonian Greeks in the fourth century B.C. had profound impact on Near Eastern cultural trends and traditions. Unlike the Persians and their Elamite, Assyrian, and Babylonian predecessors, the Macedonian Greeks were essentially alien to the rich ancient Near Eastern cultural traditions of the region and thus the millennia-old continuity of ancient Near Eastern art, architecture, and cultural traditions took a different course of development after the political hegemony of the Macedonian Greeks in the Near East.

A century of political fragmentation followed the death of Alexander in 312 B.C. The Seleucids preserved the Achaemenid division of the empire into many satrapies, although most of these satrapies became more or less independent kingdoms. Two of these satrapies, Parthia and Fars, were successful in forging large empires (from 210 B.C.–A.D. 225 and A.D. 225–640, respectively) and brought under their control not only the entire Iranian Plateau but large parts of Mesopotamia, Syria, Anatolia, parts of Central Asia, and territories east of the Indus valley.

The Parthians, who spoke Pahlavi, a branch of Old Persian, were an Indo-Iranian tribe who occupied northeastern Iran and parts of the central plateau. They were superb horsemen and archers whose many features of knighthood and chivalry and coats of arms were introduced to the West presumably through their long hostile and non-hostile contacts with Rome. The building form known as *Eivan* (or ivan/iwan), a structure with either a roofed hall open on four sides, or a barrel-vaulted room closed in the back and open in front, was perhaps the most notable architectural contribution of the Parthians.

The rise of the Parthian state coincided with the expansion of Rome. The founder of the dynasty, Arsaces I (Ashk in Persian), was a paramount chief of the Parni, a member tribe of the Dahae confederation. Arsaces crowned himself around 247 B.C. Besides Dara (a strong fortress) Arsaces founded Asaak and Nisa, important cultural and political centers in northeastern Iran. Nisa, the first capital of the Parthians, is located near Ashkabad, in Central Asia. The palace at Nisa consisted of a central court that was surrounded by four eivans, presumably the earliest occurrence of such architectural design which from the Sasanian Period onward became the most dominant architectural plan in western Asia. The monumental palace at Assur is another example of Parthian architecture that undoubtedly influenced the architectural features of the Sasanian palace of Ctesiphon, near Baghdad. At Assur, the facade is made of stucco with rows of engaged colonnettes and framed niches, features that are linked to the *scenae frons* of Roman theaters.

The founder of the Sasanian dynasty, Ardeshir I, who claimed descent from the Achaemenids, was the governor of Fars under the last Parthian king, Ardavan V. Unlike the Parthians, who were still seminomadic when they came to power, the Sasanians had a long history of urban life in Fars. As a result, the Sasanian plans for the development of agriculture, industry, and towns were far larger in scale and more lavish than those of their Parthian predecessors. The Sasanian empire continued the hostilities between Iran and Rome that had begun in the time of the Parthians and their history is marked by many major campaigns against the imperial Rome. When victorious, these campaigns were commemorated in monumental Sasanian reliefs such as those at Naqsh-e Rustam in Fars. Investiture and victory scenes over domestic enemies are also found at Naqsh-e Rajab (near Persepolis), Bishapur and Naqsh-e Bahram (near Kazeroun), Qasr-e Abu Nasr (near Shiraz), Darabgerd (155 miles (250 km) southwest of Shiraz), and at Firuzabad, the ancient Gur, founded by Ardeshir I.

A number of major monumental buildings from the Sasanian Period have survived. Perhaps the most impressive is the palace complex of Ctesiphon (near Baghdad) built by Khosrow II (A.D. 591–628). Still standing is a huge, sweeping barrel vault, made of bricks, known as Taq-e Kasra (Khosrow's vault), a testimony to the great architectural tradition of the Sasanian Period. Among the preserved Sasanian palaces in the Iranian Plateau, the palace of Ardeshir I at Firuzabad is perhaps the most important and best preserved. The circular fortification wall of Firuzabad resembles those of the Parthian towns such as Hatra and Ctesiphon in Mesopotamia. In contrast, the city of Jundi Shapur (in Susiana) with its rectangular grid pattern is traditionally taken as an example of a Sasanian town with a Western (Roman) plan. The city was built by Shapur I, employing Roman prisoners captured in his famous battle with the Roman emperor Valerian. More numerous than palaces, but less monumental, are fire temples, square brick structures that usually consist of a dome supported by four arches.

A number of important and interrelated factors, such as prolonged wars, agricultural overextension, religious schism, exhausted resources, and popular dissatisfaction contributed to the defeat of the Sasanians at the hands of the Arab Muslim invaders. After a token resistance by Yazdgerd III, the last Sasanian king, the empire succumbed to the invading forces in A.D. 637. Despite localized resistance, particularly in the mountainous regions of Iran, after two centuries almost the whole of Iran was converted to Islam. Its cultural development henceforth took a different path, yet characteristic Iranian traditions were incorporated into the new civilization of Islam.

[*See also* ARABIA AND THE PERSIAN / ARABIAN GULF; BABYLON; ISLAMIC CIVILIZATION: INTRODUCTION; NEAR EAST.]

■ A. Alizadeh, "Socio-economic and Political Complexity in Highland Iran During the 5th and 4th Millennia B.C.: The Evidence from Tall-e Bakun A," *Iran* 16 (1988):17–34. E. Carter, and M. W. Stolper, *Elam: Surveys of Political History and Archaeology* (1984). R. Dyson, "Architecture of the Iron I Period at Hasanlu in Western Iran and Its Implications for Theories of Migration on the Iranian Plateau." In J. Deshayes (Organizer) *Le plateau iranien et l'Asie centrale* pp. 155–169. C. Goff, "Luristan in the First Half of the First Millennium B.C.," *Iran* 6:105–134. F. Hole, *The Archaeology of Western Iran: Settlement and Society from Prehistory to the Islamic Conquest* (1987). L. Levine, "Geographical Studies in the Neo-Assyrian Zagros," *Iran* 11 (1973):1–28. K. Schippmann, "The Development of Iranian Fire Temples," *The Memorial Volume of Vth International Congress of Iranian Art and Archaeology, Tehran 1968*, Vol. I (1972), pp. 353–362. Ph.E.L. Smith, 1971. "Iran, 9000–4000 B.C.: The Neolithic," *Expedition* 13 (1971):6–13. Ph.E.L. Smith, *Palaeolithic Archaeology in Iran*, The American Inst. of Iranian Studies Monograph I (1986).

Abbas Alizadeh

PERTHES, Boucher de (1788–1868), was a customs officer with a passion for fossils in the northern French town of Abbeville. During the 1830s, he recovered extinct animal bones, numerous stone axes, and other artifacts from the same layers of the Ice Age gravels of the Somme River. De Perthes declared these were evidence of human existence on earth before the biblical flood, at a time when elephants and hippopotami flourished in Europe. In his rambling *Antiquités Celtiques et Antédiluviennes* (1847), he claimed humanity began much earlier than 6,000 years ago, as in Old Testament genealogies. The scientific establishment ignored his findings, regarding the voluble de Perthes as a nuisance. Eventually, word of his discoveries reached geologist Joseph Prestwich and archaeologist John Evans in

England. They visited de Perthes in 1859. Evans himself removed a stone ax from the same level as the bones of an elephant. De Perthes was vindicated, when the two scientists published accounts of his sites and declared them scientific proof of the antiquity of humankind. De Perthes continued to investigate local gravel pits, but fell into disrepute after some of his workmen found a forged fossil jaw from the Moulin Quignon quarry pit. He declared it a genuine find, but it was soon discredited, much to de Perthes's discomfort. Jacques Boucher de Perthes was too excitable and eccentric to be considered a serious scientist, but his shrewd observations and persistence in the face of scientific skepticism produced the final proof of the antiquity of humankind.

[*See also* ANTIQUITY OF HUMANKIND: ANTIQUITY OF HUMANKIND IN THE OLD WORLD; HISTORY OF ARCHAEOLOGY BEFORE 1900: EUROPEAN ARCHAEOLOGY.]

■ Jacques Boucher de Perthes, *De la Création: Essai sur l'origine et la progression des êtres* (1838–1841). Jacques Boucher de Perthes, *Antiquités Celtiques et Antédiluviennes* (1847). Donald Grayson, *The Establishment of Human Antiquity* (1983).

Brian M. Fagan

PETRIE, Flinders (1853–1942), was educated privately and acquired an interest in archaeology and surveying at an early age. He became obsessed with Egyptian pyramids and carried out the first accurate survey of the *pyramids of Giza in 1880–1882. Between 1883 and 1886, Petrie excavated and surveyed sites in the Nile delta, especially Tanis and Naukratis, for the Egypt Exploration Fund, developing his now-classic excavation methods, which placed great emphasis on pottery and other small finds. In 1887, Petrie worked in the Fayyum Depression, exploring the pyramid of Hawara and excavating a nearby Roman cemetery where the mummies bore portraits of their owners. Thereafter, he excavated in Egypt nearly every winter, investigating el Lahun and the workers' community at el Kahun as well as the town of Ghurab, where he discovered Mycenaean pottery, evidence of contacts between the Nile and Aegean as early as 1700 B.C. One of Petrie's most famous excavations was at el-Amarna, where he unearthed the painted pavements and frescoes of the pharaoh Akhenaton's palace, also the celebrated el-Amarna tablets that described relations between the pharaoh and competing foreign monarchs. In 1892, Petrie became the first Edwards professor of Egyptology at the University of London. Two years later he excavated Pre-Dynastic cemeteries at Naqada and Diospolis Parva. The many grave groups from these cemeteries allowed him to develop his "sequence dating" method for dating prehistoric Egypt, the predecessor of modern seriation techniques. Petrie continued to work along the Nile until 1926, when more stringent antiquities regulations caused him to move his operations to Palestine. There, he excavated three major cities and cross-dated them to Egyptian history. Flinders Petrie was a self-taught archaeologist who brooked no criticism, but his rough-and-ready excavation methods pioneered modern archaeological research in the Near East.

[*See also* HISTORY OF ARCHAEOLOGY BEFORE 1900: NEAR EASTERN ARCHAEOLOGY; HISTORY OF ARCHAEOLOGY FROM 1900 TO 1950: NEAR EASTERN ARCHAEOLOGY.]

■ Flinders Petrie, *Methods and Aims in Archaeology* (1904). Flinders Petrie, *Seventy Years in Archaeology* (1931). W. R. Dawson and E. T. Uphill, *Who Was Who In Egyptology*, 2nd ed. (1972). Margaret S. Drower, *Flinders Petrie: A Life in Archaeology* (1985).

Brian M. Fagan

PITT-RIVERS, A.H.L. Fox, was born in Yorkshire, England, in 1827 and brought up in London. In 1845 he was commissioned into the army and became a specialist in musketry instruction and the history of firearms. He saw active service in the Crimean War, but his postings were mainly of an administrative nature. Inspired by the scientific circles in which he moved after his marriage into the Stanley family, and probably also by the Great Exhibition (1851), he became a collector of ethnographic and antiquarian objects. His reading of Darwin's *On the Origin of Species by Means of Natural Selection* on its publication in 1859 marked a turning point in his career. He developed his parallel theory of the "Evolution of Culture," which was to inform all his later archaeological work. Fascinated by the field monuments that he saw in Ireland and England in the early 1860s, he turned his attention to antiquarian fieldwork, subsequently developing methods of rigorous field investigation and laying foundations for the study of archaeology in Britain. His inheritance of a large estate in 1880 enabled him to increase the scope of his work, and he devoted the last twenty years of his life to large-scale excavation, mainly on his own property, and to his official duties as inspector of ancient monuments under the Ancient Monuments Act (1882). By founding major museum collections and by publishing the results of his researches in unprecedented detail he established standards for the future development of the discipline. After his death in 1900, however, the archaeological community ignored his lead, and it was not until the mid-twentieth century that his contribution began to be appreciated by the new cadre of professional academic archaeologists. He has come to be regarded by many as the "father of British archaeology," by virtue of his pioneering work in excavation, anthropological archaeology, typology, ancient monument protection, and public education; his theoretical stance, that social change is analogous to Darwinian evolution, is recognized but no longer accepted.

[*See also* HISTORY OF ARCHAEOLOGY BEFORE 1900: EUROPEAN ARCHAEOLOGY.]

Mark Bowden

PLANTATION LIFE IN THE SOUTHERN UNITED STATES. The archaeological study of plantations, known simply as plantation archaeology, is broadly defined as the study of material culture found on former sites of plantations that can provide insights into understanding the cultural, economic, and social dimensions of these communities. This research interest was initiated in the southern United States, but is now undertaken on many islands of the Caribbean and work has begun in both Central and South America. Archaeologists have studied many aspects of plantation society, but the primary themes for research on slave-worked plantations include the living conditions of slaves, expressions of African American cultural identity, plantation social structure, and master-slave relationships.

Slavery. Since its inception in the late 1960s, the primary emphasis of plantation archaeology has been the study of slavery. All archaeological studies of slavery contribute information on the living conditions of enslaved people, for example, the characteristics of their housing, diet, household goods, personal possessions, health care, and other aspects of their material world. Some archaeological evidence provides detailed information that supplements contemporary accounts of slave life. Other evidence provides information on undocumented activities of enslaved people such as items they acquired or produced for themselves. Both forms of archaeological data are important to the study of slavery, but the most insightful findings are those that provide an understanding of how enslaved people nurtured and sustained a separate cultural identity or survived the oppressive, dehumanizing conditions of slavery.

Cultural Identity. Archaeologists initially studied plantation slavery to recover artifactual evidence of African American culture in the form of objects suggestive of an African heritage. Few objects of African origin have been recovered, but many archaeological findings suggest ways in which an African heritage was reinterpreted in the Americas. These findings include the recovery of pottery, food remains, African-style housing, and the possible use of homemade, mass-produced, and reworked objects in healing, divination, and other folk practices.

Handcrafted pottery is the most frequently recovered artifact found in association with enslaved African Americans. In the southern United States, this pottery is known as colonoware—a very broad category of open-fired, hand-built earthenwares found primarily on plantations and other sites of the colonial period in South Carolina and Virginia. It is well-documented that Native Americans made some colonowares; however, the evidence from some plantations strongly suggests that African Americans made some colonowares as well, particularly those formed into gobular bowls and pots. Although archaeologists still debate the extent to which African Americans played a role in the production of colonoware, it is clear that enslaved African Americans used this pottery to prepare foods for themselves and for their owners. The foods prepared in colonoware pots blended Native American cultigens such as corn, squash, and beans, African okra and cowpeas, and European turnips and collards.

Recovered food remains further suggest that culinary preferences of enslaved African Americans may have been African in character. Boiling meats possibly in soups or stews was a characteristic way of preparing slave food as indicated from highly fragmented bone, carcasses cut into small portions, or bones from which the meat was apparently sliced. The gobular, colonoware pots and bowls would have been used for preparing and serving such meals.

The presence of African-styled housing was another way in which enslaved people influenced their material world. Excavations at Yaughan and Curriboo, two neighboring, eighteenth-century plantations in South Carolina, uncovered evidence of clay-walled African-styled structures. Although this is the only investigation to date to yield evidence of African-styled housing on a southern plantation, several written descriptions of similar structures suggest that such housing may have been commonplace in colonial South Carolina before planters began to impose their ideals of appropriate slave housing in the nineteenth century.

The most elusive objects to interpret are those suggestive of folk beliefs and practices. Like their African counterparts, many enslaved Africans and their descendants relied upon conjuring or divining to control the world around them. These practices often utilized objects such as crystals, cowrie shells, beads, pierced coins, polished stones and pebbles, reworked glass, and ceramics, which are frequently recovered from sites once occupied by the enslaved. Enslaved people also kept or wore charms to protect them from evil or harm. Archaeologists derive interpretations for the meanings and uses of these objects through ethnographic analogies, oral history, and thoughtful speculation.

Forms of Resistance. In addition to the recovery of material expressions of ethnic identity, the archaeological record also shows how African Americans sought ways to improve their lives under enslavement whenever possible. They supplemented food rations provided to them by planters by gardening and raising livestock, hunting, and fishing. Through these food resources, they not only improved the nutritional content of their diets, but achieved some control over what they ate and how it was prepared. They sold and traded surplus produce and other items to obtain goods for their own use, and recycled discarded materials and made them into tools, gaming pieces, and forms of adornment.

Another approach used for understanding slavery and plantation material culture as a whole lies within the context of plantation social structure. Some archaeologists examine material differences either within the enslaved community or between the major groups of plantation occupants, for example: owners, overseers, artisans, or slaves. By using the cost or the quality of certain recovered materials such as porcelain, cuts of meat, or the size of housing as indicators of social status, these investigators attempt to delineate class distinctions on plantations. This line of investigation has been fruitful in suggesting ways in which plantation resources were utilized, distributed, and recycled by documenting differences in access to resources between specific groups or households. This kind of analysis may be useful in understanding how planter hegemony operated on specific plantations.

Many archaeologists, however, challenge the interpretations derived from the analysis of status differences on plantations. Some archaeologists question whether or not certain status indicators such as cuts of meat or the presence of porcelain are reliable indicators of class differences. Others perceive problems with the use of planter categories of status or planter consumption strategies to understand how enslaved people defined status within their ranks or valued material possessions. For others, the concept status is problematic because it does not adequately explain the master–slave relationship. For these reasons, many archaeologists are increasingly studying the ways in which planters sought to control their charges and how enslaved people responded to their control through acts of resistance.

Through coercion, planters maintained dominance over people they held in bondage, and sought to control both the home and work lives of those enslaved. In the archaeological record, this planter dominance is most evident in the size, location, and arrangement of housing. Slave quarters were often excluded from the formal landscape of the plantation and placed near work areas in order to maximize the cultivation and processing of crops. Most housing was built according to planter specifications and arranged in rows or other patterns that would permit easy access and inspection of premises. These practices served to reinforce planter dominance over the landscape and the subservient position enslaved people held.

Enslaved people resisted planter control of their housing by creating their own sense of space. For example, on many plantations in Virginia, Tennessee, and Kentucky, enslaved people dug storage pits within their dwellings to store food and valuables. Historical accounts indicate that planters knew about these pits and tried to prevent slaves from digging them by raising dwelling quarters above the ground, placing them on building piers and backfilling ones that came to their attention. Enslaved people also created outdoor spaces away from the watchful eye of overseers or masters that gave them some control over their actions.

Planter domination was resisted in other ways as well. Enslaved people's efforts to maintain a separate cultural identity that was expressed archaeologically in foodways, religious beliefs, housing, or the use of space all represent forms of resistance. They also opposed planters by hiding tools and other items they pilfered in storage pits and by actively improving their material lives. Slaveholders responded to acts of resistance by tightening their control, often through cruel forms of punishment. Yet, whenever possible, enslaved people challenged the authority of their white masters choosing forms of resistance that best suited their needs.

Plantation archaeology is one of the most rapidly growing areas of archaeology and continues to provide new and important information. Its greatest contribution is in supplying information on the lives of enslaved people who had few opportunities of documenting their lives through conventional historical sources. This research has been important not only in supplying descriptive details on the material culture of the enslaved, but also in yielding information on the cultural interaction and exchange between planters and slaves.

[See also EUROPEAN COLONIES IN THE NEW WORLD; HISTORICAL ARCHAEOLOGY; NORTH AMERICA: HISTORICAL ARCHAEOLOGY OF NORTH AMERICA.]

■ William Kelso, *Kingsmill Plantations, 1619–1800: Archaeology of Country Life in Colonial Virginia* (1984). John Otto, *Cannon's Point Plantation, 1794–1860: Living Conditions and Status Patterns in the Old South* (1984). Theresa A. Singleton, ed., *The Archaeology of Slavery and Plantation Life* (1985). Douglas Armstrong, *The Old Village and the Great House: An Archaeological and Historical Examination of Drax Hall Plantation, St. Ann's Bay Jamaica* (1990). Charles Orser, "Archaeological Approaches to New World Plantation Slavery," in *Archaeological Method and Theory*, vol. 2, ed. Michael Schiffer (1990), pp. 111–154. Theresa Singleton, "The Archaeology of Slave Life," in *Before Freedom Came: African American Life in the Antebellum South*, ed. Edward D. Campbell III and Kym Rice (1991), pp. 155–175. Leland Ferguson, *Uncommon Ground: Archaeology and Colonial African America, 1650–1800* (1992). Larry McKee, "The Ideals and Realities Behind the Design and Use of 19th Century Virginia Slave Cabins," in *The Art and Mystery of Historical Archaeology: Essays in Honor of Jim Deetz*, ed. Anne Yentsch and Mary Beaudry (1992), pp. 195–213. James Deetz, *Flowerdew Hundred: The Archaeology of a Virginia Plantation, 1619–1864* (1993). Theresa A. Singleton, "The Archaeology of Slavery in North America," *Annual Review of Anthropology* 24 (1995): 119–140.
Theresa A. Singleton

PLANT REMAINS, Analysis of. Despite the view that paleoethnobotany is a new subdiscipline of archaeology, the analysis of plant remains from archaeological sites has its roots in the early part of the nineteenth century. Paleoethnobotany is the study of plants in archaeological contexts, as well as the interaction between humans and these plant resources. These studies have provided insights into the prehistoric utilization of resources, resource procurement, paleoenvironmental conditions, and information on the *domestication of plants.

Not unexpectedly, the earliest archaeological studies of plants occurred in areas with exceptional plant preservation, namely Egypt and Peru, both of which provided the arid environment necessary for the preservation of normally perishable materials. Researchers in Europe in the mid-nineteenth century, however, were quick to explore the potential benefits to be gained from examining both water-logged and carbonized plant materials, and by the middle

part of the twentieth century, analysts in both the Old and New Worlds were actively studying the wealth of plant data coming from excavations throughout the world. The closely related subdiscipline of coprolite analysis, the study of preserved human feces, also begin early in the twentieth century, and by the late 1960s, had demonstrated its scientific validity, becoming routine in nearly all sites where these materials were preserved.

The proper analysis of plant materials is necessarily based on the proper extraction of these materials from the archaeological sites. Historically, three basic techniques have been employed in the collection and extraction of archaeological plant remains: *in situ* collection, flotation extraction of bulk soil sediments, and microscopic analyses.

In the case of *in situ* collection, the archaeologist is responsible for collecting preserved plant remains as they are encountered during excavation. Most radiocarbon samples are collected in this manner. Although this is the most common form of archaeological plant material collection, it is also the least dependable, as many plant remains are quite small and are easily missed during excavation and screening. With this technique, only the largest and most readily recognizable materials might be collected, resulting in an obvious sample bias.

In the late 1960s, archaeologists began experimenting with ways to augment the collection of plant remains from site sediments. Screening of bulk soil sediments for the retrieval of carbonized plant remains had been conducted for years, but an effective technique for the isolation of plant materials from these sediments had not yet been devised. Both chemical and "froth" flotation devices were developed at this time, enabling archaeologists to rapidly and effectively separate lighter organic particles from the heavier inorganic sediments. Chemical flotation devices, now rarely used, made use of a heavy-density medium (for example, zinc chloride) for the differential separation of light organic particles. Frothing devices, currently the mainstay of flotation extraction, employ aerators to separate soils, and are quite effective in liberating the lighter organic particles from their matrices. Modification of flotation machines continues to this day, with the effect being the efficient recovery of plant remains from archaeological sediments. Flotation devices, however, do have their drawbacks. Some of these machines can be quite expensive, and few are very efficient in heavy clay soils. Despite these problems, most professional excavations employ flotation devices for the extraction of carbonized plant remains from their sediments.

With the development of new laboratory techniques comes the development of new analytical applications. The microscopic analysis of pollen from archaeological sites has long been an established practice, and the analysis of biosilicate plant remains, or phytoliths, has recently been exploited by the paleoethnobotanist as well. Modern developments, particularly in the area of genetic and DNA research, have led to the employment of these new techniques in the analysis of archaeological plant remains. For example, for the analysis of residues from ceramic vessels, it is now often possible to identify the original contents through the analyses of plant proteins, isotopes, starches, and lipids. These techniques are relatively expensive, for the most part, ruling out their use by many archaeological projects. Still, future developments will only lead to a refinement of these studies, eventually providing a fuller understanding of how plants were used in the past.

Laboratory analysis is an integral part of the job of the

paleoethnobotanist, and it is here that most significant discoveries are made. Ultimately, all interpretations made by the analyst are based on identification of the archaeological plant remains, thus correct identifications are crucial. The modern paleoethnobotanical laboratory is equipped with both low- and high-powered microscopes, sometimes even scanning electron microscopes, and a modern plant reference collection. This collection is used to confirm plant materials identified from the archaeological sites.

The potential benefits to be gained from the analysis of archaeological plant materials are enormous. The sequence of development of plant domesticates such as maize, wheat, barley, and rice, are known almost entirely from paleoethnobotanical studies. We now know the regions where these plants were first domesticated, as well as the approximate times when these initial domestication processes began. The importance of nondomesticated plants has also been documented through paleoethnobotanical research. Researchers have documented the important role small seed foods (such as *Chenopodium* and *Iva*) played in the subsistence economy of the prehistoric inhabitants of the eastern United States.

Like all aspects of archaeology, the analysis of plant remains does have limitations. Most significant perhaps is the problem of quantification and sample size. How much material should be examined, and when is an archaeobotanical sample adequate? Another problem is that some flotation devices may be more efficient in plant recovery than others. This too may lead to the problem of comparability between studies. These problems must be addressed by the analyst, and considered when making interpretations.

Despite these methodological problems, the potential benefits to be gained from paleoethnobotanical studies are enormous, and future studies will greatly augment our knowledge of the role plants have played in our prehistoric past.

[*See also* DIET, RECONSTRUCTION OF; ENVIRONMENTAL ARCHAEOLOGY; PALEOBOTANY; PALEOENVIRONMENTAL RECONSTRUCTION.]

■ Jane M. Renfrew, *Paleoethnobotany: The Prehistoric Food Plants of the Near East and Europe* (1973). Richard I. Ford, "Paleoethnobotany in American Archaeology" in *Advances in Archaeological Method and Theory* (Volume 2), ed. Michael B. Schiffer (1979), pp. 286–336. W. Van Zeist and W. A. Casparie, eds., *Plants and Ancient Man: Studies in Palaeoethnobotany* (1984). David L. Asch and Nancy B. Asch, "Prehistoric Plant Cultivation in West Central Illinois" in *Prehistoric Food Production in North America*, ed. Richard I. Ford (1985): 149–203. Christine A. Hastorf and Virginia S. Popper, *Current Paleoethnobotany* (1988). Deborah M. Pearsall, *Paleoethnobotany* (1989).

John G. Jones

PLANTS, Domestication of. *See* DOMESTICATION OF PLANTS.

PLEISTOCENE. The Pleistocene epoch spans approximately the last 2.4 million years of geological time. It represents a time interval of great scientific interest owing to the numerous fluctuations in climate that took place and because it represents an important time in hominid evolution. The Pleistocene and Holocene epochs together comprise the Quaternary Period. The Pleistocene is formally regarded as having ended at 10,000 B.P. at the onset of the present Holocene interglacial. The Pleistocene is often subdivided into three sections—Early, Middle, and Late. The boundary between the Early and Middle Pleistocene is usually defined by the prominent Matuyama-Brunhes geomagnetic polarity reversal, considered to have occurred near 790,000 B.P. The boundary between the Middle and Late Pleistocene is generally regarded as equivalent to the beginning of oxygen isotope substage 5e that represents the warmest phase of the last interglacial. The age of this boundary, on the basis of marine oxygen isotope stratigraphy, is considered to be approximately 130,000 B.P.

The beginning of the Pleistocene was marked by the growth of ice sheets in the Northern Hemisphere. The start of glaciation in the Southern Hemisphere took place much earlier, however, perhaps as early as twenty million years ago in the Antarctic. This early phase of cooling was followed by several important geological changes, including, for example, the uplift of the Tibetan plateau and the closure of the Isthmus of Panama, both of which exerted a strong influence on climate and ocean circulation. The progressive cooling of global climate finally gave way at the start of the Pleistocene to remarkable climatic instability. During the ensuing time period, ice sheets waxed and waned, triggering complex changes in sea level. Elsewhere, grassland replaced forest, tree lines were lowered, and arid conditions were widespread. These changes took place at the same time as the development of human culture that began with the use of primitive tools and fire and culminated in the sophisticated human achievements that have taken place during the present interglacial. If the development of human culture is stimulated by the existence of a stable climate, the appearance of people in the Pleistocene landscape could not have taken place at a more inopportune time.

Evidence for Pleistocene Climate Change from Ocean Sediments. The longest and most complete records of Pleistocene climate change are derived from studies of sediments deposited on the floors of the world's oceans. These sediments consist mostly of the skeletal remains of calcareous and siliceous microorganisms that have settled out of the water column. Evidence of the former conditions under which the calcareous microorganisms lived can be determined by the analysis of the stable isotope ratios of the oxygen in the carbonate skeletal remains. The derived oxygen isotope chronology is considered to indicate past fluctuations in global ice volume. Although oxygen isotope studies provide valuable information on the timing of past continental ice sheet growth and decay, however, they cannot provide any information on where the growth and decay of individual ice sheets took place. The most significant limitation of oxygen isotope analysis is caused by the activity of burrowing organisms (bioturbation) on the ocean floor that disturb surface sediments. These limit the accuracy to which sediments in individual cores can be used to define sediment age to $+/-500$ years.

Despite this constraint, Pleistocene oxygen isotope stratigraphy shows that during this period numerous high-magnitude fluctuations in climate took place and were associated with the growth and decay of major ice sheets on at least twenty occasions. Furthermore, many of the periods when global climate switched from glacial to interglacial appear to have been exceptionally rapid indeed, although the rates at which these changes took place cannot be determined owing to the effects of sediment bioturbation. The oxygen isotope curves are also significant in that they demonstrate that most of the Pleistocene has been characterized by glacial age conditions. Only very rarely, for around 5 percent to 10 percent of Pleistocene time, have warm interglacial conditions prevailed. Furthermore, Pleistocene interglacials have rarely been associated with air temperatures significantly higher than present. The most important exception to this pattern was the last interglacial that culminated approximately 130,000–115,000 years ago (oxygen isotope substage 5e).

A popular view is that the Pleistocene glacial and interglacial sequence observed in the oxygen isotope record was caused principally by changes in the nature of the Earth's orbit around the sun. The Milankovitch theory of climate changes is based on the assumption that there has been no absolute annual change in the amount of incoming solar radiation and that Pleistocene climate changes were the result of long-term cyclical changes in the distribution of insolation across both hemispheres. Indeed, many scientists believe that a well-defined 100,000-year glacial/interglacial cycle observed in the oxygen isotope record may be explained by cyclical changes in the eccentricity of the Earth's orbit.

The link between oxygen isotope stratigraphy and ice volume has also permitted estimates to be made of past changes in global sea level, based on the inferred volumes of water stored in the world's oceans. For the Early and Middle Pleistocene, it is not possible to convert ocean water volumes to equivalent sea levels, since plate tectonic processes have caused long-term changes in the shape of ocean basins. Such processes are considered to have been negligible during the Late Pleistocene, however, and attempts have accordingly been made to use oxygen isotope analysis to produce sea-level curves for this time period. These investigations show that during the culmination of the last interglacial, sea level may have been several meters higher than present, and that the end of the interglacial was followed by a number of major climatic oscillations associated with the growth and melting of ice sheets and several major fluctuations in sea level. Sea level fell to its lowest position of −394 feet (−120 m) during the culmination of the last glacial maximum ca. 18,000 B.P.

Evidence for Pleistocene Climate Change from Ice Cores. Detailed information on the nature of Late Pleistocene climate change has also been determined through the study of oxygen isotope ratios in ice cores. The most significant ice cores are those that have been sampled from the Antarctic and Greenland ice sheets. In general, it is possible to calculate the age of ice by counting annual layers of ice; annual layers have now been measured as far back as ca. 14,000 years ago. In "old" ice, where annual layers are indistinct, the age of ice at any given depth is calculated through the use of mathematical models of former ice flow. Until recently, the longest ice core record of climate change was that sampled from Vostok, Antarctica, where a 150,000-year record had been obtained. This record provided, for the first time, a continuous record of past changes in Southern Hemisphere air temperature together with records of past fluctuations in atmospheric CO_2 concentrations, and rates of snow and dust deposition.

More recently, a 9,846-foot (3,000-m) ice core sequence has been drilled and sampled from the central Greenland ice sheet that appears to provide a continuous record of past climate change for the last 250,000 years. In polar glacier ice, the measured oxygen isotope ratios enable detailed estimates to be made of former air temperatures. Remarkably, the results of the Greenland Ice-Core Project (GRIP) show that the last 10,000 years of the Holocene interglacial have

been characterized by sustained climate stability. By contrast, most of Late Pleistocene time as measured in the Greenland ice cores appears to have been characterized by high-magnitude climate oscillations that bear a striking similarity to those evident in the Vostok Antarctic record. The causes of the extreme climate changes that were a feature of the Late Pleistocene are not known.

One of the most extreme and rapid climatic reversals took place during the Younger Dryas, between ca. 11,000 and 10,000 radiocarbon years B.P. The climatic deterioration that accompanied the beginning of this period was associated with large-scale reorganization of Northern Hemisphere atmospheric circulation, dramatic changes in North Atlantic ocean circulation linked to the widespread development of sea ice, extensive ice accumulation in the Northern Hemisphere, and a marked decrease in air temperatures. The warming at the end of this period, at the Pleistocene-Holocene transition, was equally dramatic, with ice core studies indicating that in Greenland there may have been a seven degree (Celsius) warming within about fifty years. The example of the Younger Dryas demonstrates clearly that during numerous critical periods of Pleistocene time, people may have had to adapt to extreme changes in climate within decades, rather than within millennia as has conventionally been believed.

A very important discovery arising from the Greenland ice core research is that very rapid shifts in temperature also occurred during the last interglacial, between ca. 135,000 and 115,000 B.P., most probably reflecting large-scale atmospheric changes over the North Atlantic. The research demonstrates that temperatures may have fluctuated on several occasions from a warm interglacial state with values about two degrees (Celsius) higher than present, to severe cold about ten degrees (Celsius) lower than present within several decades, perhaps even within a single decade—and all of this within a single interglacial! In other words, it is a mistake to use the present interglacial as a climatic analogue for previous Pleistocene interglacials, and it is also fallacious to consider interglacial periods as times of relatively uniform warmth and stable climate. It is a matter of conjecture how *Homo habilis* and *Homo erectus* may have responded to such rapid and high-magnitude climatic fluctuations.

The Greenland and Antarctic ice cores also reveal the presence of volcanic ash at several discrete levels. The influence of large volcanic eruptions on Pleistocene climate has not been studied in any detail, although there is evidence that some of the largest eruptions may have led to global cooling. The most explosive of all Pleistocene eruptions took place in Toba, Sumatra, ca. 75,000 B.P., and it has been suggested that the eruption may have contributed significantly to the onset worldwide of a major period of Late Pleistocene glaciation.

The Last Glacial Maximum: An Analogue for Pleistocene Ice Age Conditions. Numerous reconstructions have been made of the climatic conditions that prevailed during the last glaciation. The most unified attempt has been in the CLIMAP Project, where a detailed reconstruction was made for the Earth's climate around 18,000 B.P. More recently, several numerical models have been developed to simulate the patterns of global atmospheric and oceanic circulation that existed during this period. These general circulation models (GCMs) represent simulations, based on geological evidence, of the response of the atmosphere to inferred distributions of sea surface temperature, the dimensions of former ice sheets, and the former distribution of lakes, sea ice cover, and the like. The models are then tested by the use of other climatic parameters not used in the model (e.g., estimates of former land temperatures). The various models, when considered together with empirical evidence of past changes in climate, demonstrate complex regional responses to the onset of a major ice age. For example, it is now well known that most areas of tropical rain forest disappeared during the last glaciation. In Africa, a significantly weaker monsoonal circulation led to decreased rainfall in many regions, although in certain areas, decreased evaporation rates led to the development of large lakes. A similar situation prevailed in South America, where a northward displacement of the Intertropical Convergence Zone led to the development of a semiarid environment throughout much of Amazonia. In Asia and the Indian subcontinent, glacial age conditions were principally influenced by atmospheric changes resulting from the development of the Eurasian ice sheet. Thus, Ice Age conditions were always associated with permanent high pressure over the continental interior and a weakening of the Indian monsoon. As a result, arid conditions prevailed throughout much of Southeast Asia. Farther east, in China, many areas were affected by increased aridity and by the deposition of large thicknesses of wind-blown loess as a result of the anchoring of a jet stream between the ice sheet to the north and the Tibetan plateau to the south.

In the unglaciated areas south of the large ice sheets in North America, Europe, and Russia, the development of permafrost was very widespread. In the southwestern United States, lower temperatures, decreased evaporation, and the southward displacement of mid-latitude cyclones led to the development of many large lakes. Similar processes affected the Mediterranean region. Here, lowering of sea level led to the virtual separation of the eastern and western Mediterranean basins, while in the eastern Mediterranean, the Nile delta virtually disappeared as a result of diminished rainfall over eastern Africa. Remarkably, the Aegean Sea may have received much of the meltwater from the southern margin of the Eurasian ice sheet owing to the drainage of waters southward through the Caspian Sea, Black Sea, and Sea of Marmara.

Human Evolution and Pleistocene Climate Change. The study of Pleistocene hominid evolution has focused for a long time on whether evolutionary change took place slowly, or in a stepwise manner, with long periods of little change punctuated by short periods of very fast evolutionary development. The recently published ice core record for the last 250,000 years demonstrates very clearly that for this time interval, and probably for the whole of the Pleistocene, climate change was never slow and cyclical but instead was extremely fast and, in many cases, catastrophic. It has always been considered that the development of bipedalism in hominids was related to increased competition between species caused by the replacement during the Miocene and Pliocene of vast forested areas by savanna grasslands. We know also that in low-latitude areas during the last glacial maximum, most tropical rain forest disappeared, leaving only isolated areas of refugia. If it is true that most of the Pleistocene was characterized by cold and cool climate, it may be reasonable to argue that during the Pleistocene most low-latitude environments were only rarely characterized by the expansion of rain forest and for the most part were typified instead by semiarid conditions. The recurrence of such climatic regimes, together with rapid "sawtooth" fluctuations in climate, supports the view that such time intervals may have been associated with considerable stresses and rapid adaptation of species. Thus it is probably not realistic to envisage hominid evolutionary stress and adaptation as having taken place against a background of several slow, cold/warm, interglacial/glacial cycles of climate change but rather against a much harsher climatic background, the hallmark of which were sudden and high-magnitude oscillations.

A recurring feature that also emerges in any consideration of Pleistocene hominid evolution is that the artifact assemblages often exhibit negligible change over long periods of time during which major climate fluctuations have taken place. The hand axes of Acheulian assemblages, for example, appear to have changed little during the last million years. Thus, there is great significance in the observation that whereas at one time the skeletal remains of fossil hominids and their artifacts were used to date Quaternary deposits and events, the reverse is now true.

The study of Paleolithic archaeology has benefited greatly from recent improvements in dating techniques, and the new ice core data now provide a perspective from which to understand the great Late Pleistocene migrations of *Homo sapiens sapiens* and *Homo sapiens neanderthalis*. It is now known, for example, that during the Late Pleistocene in North America and Russia, there may have been at least three major and well-dated periods of ice sheet glaciation separated by lengthy nonglacial intervals. These climatic events must have influenced profoundly the movement of people from eastern Asia into the Americas, although it is not clear what effect such climatic changes may have had on the great *megafaunal extinctions that took place at the close of the Pleistocene. It has been observed that whereas in North America the extinctions coincide with the arrival of human groups, there is no such relationship for Australia, where human colonization at ca. 40,000 B.P. preceded the main extinctions between 26,000 and 15,000 B.P. It may be argued, nonetheless, that even if climatic and natural habitat changes were the predominant factors in the megafaunal extinctions at the end of the last glaciation, hominids may have helped deliver the final coup de grâce to particular species that had already been subject to environmental stresses.

It should not be forgotten that our understanding of Pleistocene archaeology and climate change is ultimately dependent on the application of accurate dating techniques. At present, the accuracy of radiocarbon dating, commonly used in archaeology, is being called into question. Whereas the sidereal and radiocarbon time scales broadly correspond for the majority of the Holocene, the same is not true for the Late Pleistocene. As a result, we should not depend too much upon radiocarbon dating to provide all of the archaeological answers that we require.

[See also AUSTRALOPITHECUS AND HOMO HABILIS; CROMAGNONS; EUROPE, THE FIRST COLONIZATION OF; HOLOCENE *articles on* HOLOCENE ENVIRONMENTS IN EUROPE, HOLOCENE ENVIRONMENTS IN AFRICA, HOLOCENE ENVIRONMENTS IN THE AMERICAS; HOMO ERECTUS; HOMO SAPIENS, ARCHAIC; HUMAN EVOLUTION: INTRODUCTION; HUMANS, MODERN; NEANDERTHALS; PALEOLITHIC.]

■ CLIMAP Project Members, "The Surface of Ice-Age Earth," *Science* 191 (1976): 1131–1137. David Q. Bowen, *Quaternary Geology* (1978). Nicholas J. Shackleton et al., "Oxygen Isotope Calibration of the Onset of Ice-Rafting and History of Glaciation in the North Atlantic Region," *Nature* 307 (1984): 620–623. John E. Kutzbach and H. E. Wright, "Simulation of the Climate of 18,000 years B.P.; Results for the North American / North Atlantic / European Sector and Comparison with the Geological Record of North America," *Quaternary Science Reviews* 4 (1985): 147–187. Nicholas J. Shackleton, "Oxygen Isotopes, Ice Volume and Sea Level," *Quaternary Science Reviews* 6 (1987): 183–190. Wallace S. Broecker and George H. Denton, "What Drives Glacial Cycles?" *Scientific American* January (1990): 43–50. Martin Bell and Michael J. C. Walker, *Late Quaternary Environmental Change: Physical and Human Perspectives* (1992). Alastair G. Dawson, *Ice Age Earth: Late Quaternary Geology and Climate* (1992). Willi Dansgaard et al., "Evidence for General Instability of Past Climate from a 250-kyr Ice-core Record," *Nature* 364 (1993): 218–220. Greenland Ice-Core Project (GRIP) Members, "Climate Instability During the Last Interglacial Period Recorded in the GRIP Ice Core," *Nature* 364 (1993): 203–207.

Alastair G. Dawson

POLITICAL USES OF ARCHAEOLOGY. The political potential of archaeological interpretation stems from its unique relationship with history. Because written history often guides and is reaffirmed by archaeological research, archaeology has been traditionally conceived as a lesser form of historical inquiry. But archaeological evidence is often used to revise history, and it is this capacity that accords it a much less subservient role in the production of historical knowledge. History itself has an intrinsic political value to the state. As a vital component of national and cultural identity, it validates ideology and, consequently, can be used to justify or challenge state policy.

Archaeology can serve a nationalist purpose when it is used to promote patriotic sentiment and a people's pride in their national history. Perhaps the most notorious example of this occurred in Nazi Germany, where the Reich generously funded prehistoric studies that helped create and historically ground the myth of Aryan supremacy. Chronologies were often grossly inflated, and much evidence was selectively presented to demonstrate that civilization was diffused throughout Europe by racially superior Germanic peoples. Nazi leaders justified these histories by arguing that the highest purpose of history was to elevate the morale of the populace.

In modern-day Mexico, archaeology has been used to create a more unified national identity despite a colonial history of divisive ethnic and class tensions. Mexican archaeology has highlighted the glory and achievements of ancient indigenous populations and incorporated these along with Spanish traditions into a unique national heritage. Ancient splendors such as the great city *Teotihuacán, with its awe-inspiring Pyramid of the Sun, now serve as open-air museums that attract a multitude of international tourists. Yet these ruins are equally frequented by Mexican tourists who go there to learn about their history. Thus the legacy of this civilization, which collapsed long before the arrival of the Spanish in Mesoamerica, is appropriated as part of the modern national heritage.

The use of the archaeological record to construct national identity makes its interpretation particularly susceptible to cultural bias. While all archaeological interpretations are a product of their historic contexts, the presentation of historical knowledge can also serve as a method of disseminating the ideology that informs it. Whereas in Mexico, archaeology served to bridge the cultural distance between Europeans and indigenous peoples, in Brazil it has been used to widen it. Traditional studies of Brazilian prehistory have emphasized the primitive nature of native cultures and their reluctance to change. Portuguese colonization, on the other hand, is historically depicted as the civilizing force that forged the modern nation of Brazil. Whereas prehistoric artifacts tend to be displayed in natural history museums, historic artifacts are accorded a more dignified place in fine art museums. National histories and museums have thus fostered a dichotomy of uncivilized natives versus superior and developed Europeans that legitimized exploitation and continues to reflect an ethnic caste system in that country.

In the Soviet Union, marxist social theory guided archaeological interpretation such that all cultural change came to be explained as the resolution of dynamic tensions between the forces and relations of production within societies. Marxist ideology also changed the focus of Soviet archaeology from the lifestyles of historical elites to the conditions of everyday people, peasants, and workers. The attention granted to common dwellings, work spaces, and especially ancient technology in Soviet archaeological investigations reinforced the historic importance of the technoeconomic base of society. In this way theoretical marxist social order was validated and different stages of history were represented as evolutionary steps toward the development of communism.

While archaeological data can be used to substantiate official state history, its openness to interpretation also gives it a latent subversive quality. Challenging dominant ideology is the most basic form of political resistance, and archaeology has contributed to this type of resistance in the Republic of South Africa. The governmental policy of apartheid was in part justified by several widely held historical tenets. Among these, the belief that Boer settlers on the Great Trek reached the Fish River just as Bantu-speaking African populations migrating south reached it had long validated the Dutch claim to most of the land. However, archaeological excavations confirmed Bantu-speaking populations had penetrated as far down as the Cape of Good Hope some 1,500 years before the arrival of the first white settlers. The government's right to confine ethnic groups such as the Venda, Xhosa, and Zulu to tribal homelands, based on the notion that they were being returned to their ancestral territories, was also strongly challenged by archaeological evidence of a complex history of population migration and displacement. As the government of South Africa becomes more democratic, the interpretation of archaeological evidence and the construction of history in this nation is likely to undergo a similar democratization.

Thus, archaeology proves to be a useful tool in the control of history for the state, especially because material evidence is more tangible and compelling than the written word. Material culture invites continual reassessment, yet as the examples above demonstrate, it is no less vulnerable to partisan interpretation.

[*See also* NATIONALISM; NON-WESTERN SOCIETIES, ARCHAEOLOGY AND.]

■ Bruce G. Trigger, "Alternative Archaeologies: Nationalist, Colonialist, Imperialist," *Man* 19 (1984): 355–370. Martin Hall, "Archaeology Under Apartheid," *Archaeology* 41 (1988): 62–64. Neil A. Silberman, "Lure of the Holy Land," *Archaeology* 43 (1990): 28–35.

Julie Ruiz-Sierra

POMPEII. *See* HERCULANEUM AND POMPEII.

POPULAR CULTURE, Portrayal of Archaeology in

Overview
Archaeology in Film and Television
Archaeology in Fiction
Archaeology in Science Fiction

OVERVIEW

Archaeology occupies a central position in popular culture, largely because of Hollywood's preoccupation with adventurous heroes and swashbuckling discoveries. The Indiana Jones movies of recent years have been a powerful focus of popular interest, but are merely the latest manifestation of a long love affair between moviemakers and archaeology, at both the fictional and serious documentary level. Favorite subjects for mass market entertainment movies include mummies and the curse of the pharaohs, the lost continent of Atlantis, and searches for mythic treasures like the Ark of the Covenant and Noah's Ark. In this arena, archaeology and fantasy science sit on either side of a very fine line, which is often blurred in the public arena. Archaeology and archaeologists have long been a favorite topic for fiction writers, especially in the romance, science fiction, and mystery novel genres, although more serious novels like Elizabeth Marshall Thomas's *Reindeer Moon* have attempted reconstructions of the past based on solid scientific data. In recent years, archaeologists have become concerned about the public image of archaeology in popular culture, which often bears little resemblance to reality. They are often portrayed as romantic treasure hunters, preoccupied with pharaohs' gold, when in fact they are highly trained scientists. To counteract these stereotypes, they have embarked on ambitious public education programs, designed to alert the broadest possible audiences to the widespread destruction of the past by looting and industrial activity, and to the importance of archaeology in a world driven in part by the compelling forces of history.

Brian M. Fagan

ARCHAEOLOGY IN FILM AND TELEVISION

Documentaries about archaeological investigations are broadcast to audiences through regular network and cable television programming. The most commercially successful have dealt with human origins and what are popularly perceived to be "mysterious" or "lost" civilizations like the classic Maya. Rarely has an entire series been dedicated to illuminating interdisciplinary approaches to archaeological problem solving. The exceptions include the short-lived American-produced Odyssey series together with a number of outstanding British productions covering subjects as diverse as Troy and the origins of Egyptian civilization.

Despite the wide appeal of documentaries, however, it has been the big screen motion picture that has done the most to shape public perceptions of archaeology. There are two principal ways in which archaeology has been depicted in feature films. The first is by the portrayal of archaeological research in Hollywood-style epics. The second involves the popular fascination with the adventurous lifestyle of archaeologists themselves.

The motion picture industry has been quick to satisfy an innate curiosity about ancient life in science fiction fashion, often substituting the past for some distant universe in order to present Earth's inhabitants with unique technological or social challenges. Although archaeologists have condemned much of Hollywood's vision of the ancient world, motion pictures have been, at times, instrumental in reconstructing lifeways that are simply taken for granted in archaeological reconstructions today.

Although scholars like Robert *Koldewey, Walter Andrae, and Leonard *Woolley succeeded, after years of excavation, in uncovering the ruins of ancient Mesopotamian

ceremonial centers, the ritual life of these civilizations was only dimly perceived until their research inspired D. W. Griffith to experiment with the pageantry of Babylonian religious dramas in *Intolerance* (1916). Later directors even tackled such formidable subject matter as the explanations for Middle Paleolithic cultural variability in *Quest for Fire* (1982) and *Clan of the Cave Bear* (1985), although the resulting reconstructions took simplistic racial or environmentally deterministic points of view. If for no other reason, the field of archaeology owes a debt of gratitude to "epics" for sending people to their libraries by the thousands to research and read about the factual background of the ancient worlds brought to life on the screen.

There have been so many films made about archaeologists themselves that they could qualify as a genre, particularly after the phenomenal success of three features and a television series about a fictional University of Chicago professor named Indiana Jones. It was the discovery of treasure-laden Egyptian tombs during the 1920s and 1930s that inspired innumerable versions of "mummy" pictures, and some featured plausible characterizations of archaeologists, from the ambitious graduate student to the paternalistic professor emeritus. Rather it is the portrayal of archaeologists as treasure hunters that has caused so much consternation among professionals, and films have done little to rectify that stereotype. To date, few words of advice have transcended Sir Joseph Whemple's lecture to his student in *The Mummy* (1932) that "our job is to increase the sum of human knowledge of the past not to satisfy our own curiosity."

Although *Raiders of the Lost Ark* (1981) enlightened audiences on how an archaeologist might integrate ethnohistorical research with a field investigation, the expeditions amounted to little more than thievery, and the paramilitary-style adventures were caused in large part by dismal project planning. Archaeologists may be famous for finding themselves in foreign countries that have erupted in social turmoil, but they are equally reknowned for being able to continue their work unmolested because of their fundamental respect and understanding of the politics and people of the host country. In short, archaeologists have striven to present themselves as the antithesis of their portrayal in most Hollywood-style films.

Part of the problem is that filmmakers are either uninterested or uninformed about the science of archaeology as it has been practiced for the last forty years. Despite the fact that over half of all archaeological fieldwork is now done with large-scale site surveys and not excavation, producers of documentary and feature films alike continue to advise archaeologists that they should contact them only when they "dig something up." This has caused archaeologists who do not excavate to conclude that their work lacks interest for the general public and has driven others to seek public approval by encouraging the media to promote them as the "real" Indiana Joneses.

The solutions to the problem are that, first, archaeologists must take a stronger role in educating film producers about their field by emphasizing the interdisciplinary approach to archaeology, and second, they must take responsibility for educating the general public by learning to communicate through film and television media themselves. The challenge will lie increasingly in affordable visual technology that archaeologists are only now beginning to employ, from the video documentation of their fieldwork to computer modeling of their interpretations of past lifeways.

[*See also* EDUCATION IN ARCHAEOLOGY: POPULAR EDUCATION.]

■ George MacDonald Fraser, *The Hollywood History of the World from One Million Years B.C. to Apocalypse Now* (1988). Baird Searles, *Epic! History on the Big Screen* (1990).

John M. D. Pohl

ARCHAEOLOGY IN FICTION

If the way archaeologists are seen and represented by writers of fiction is any indication, the profession has an identity crisis. Although there have been some notable gains, the problem does not seem to be going away.

Appearances in fiction by archaeologists got off to a shaky start in 1897. *An African Millionaire*, written by Grant Allen, features a rogue of a protagonist named Colonel Clay, who allows intended victims to think he is an archaeologist for the purpose of selling or trading them worthless items.

A sprinkling of romance of adventure novels involving archaeologists appeared in the 1920s to the early 1930s, using themes of mummies, curses (including terrible diseases), tomb robbers, lost worlds, and buried artifacts as enhancements. The archaeologists were one-dimensional, English authority figures, brought on stage to legitimize and authenticate some concocted tomb, site, or valuable cache.

Literary fortunes or archaeologists improved in the mid-1930s when mystery writer Agatha Christie, traveling abroad to overcome the double pain of the death of her mother and the breakup of her marriage, visited *Ur and met a man who would change her life. Max Mallowan, an archaeologist of promise and assistant to the colorful Sir Leonard *Woolley, was as taken by the mystery writer as she was with him. Each subsequently influenced the other. Christie's 1936 novel *Murder in Mesopotamia* featured an archaeologist who struck an agreeable balance between the flamboyant Woolley and the more reserved Mallowan.

Still intrigued by the background potential for archaeology, Christie produced a historical novel, *Death Comes as the End*, set in Thebes at about 2000 B.C. She is clearly using information from Mallowan and her own direct experiences with the current crop of archaeologists being trained in Europe and being sent forth to dig with restraint and consideration. Her characters emerge as role models for her own times and for the waning years of the twentieth century, the notable problem being the fact of their class and gender; women and the middle classes have not been allowed professional momentum. Minorities had to become tomb robbers or opportunistic site guides.

By 1993 an unfortunate paradigm for archaeology had been established. The *New York Times* reported the top money-grossing films of all time for Paramount Pictures: the Indiana Jones films. Based on the Robb MacGregor novels (*Indiana Jones and the Dome of Giants, Indiana Jones and the Pale at Delphi, Indiana Jones and Seven Veils*) the eponymous protagonist, wearing a leather jacket and fedora, became the image of a working archaeologist for millions of readers and viewers. Forget all about his training, his scientific methodology, the reach and brilliance of his conclusions, his approach to the protection of the very sites he dug. Indiana Jones became a comic strip character, bigger than life, democratized and more egalitarian than his predecessors, but considerably more difficult to take with any seriousness.

Such additional fictional portrayals as Virginia Brown's *The Emerald Wizard* and Geoffrey Caine's *The Curse of the Vampire* add to the identity crisis. The profession is made to seem shallow, secretive, hysterical, and worst of all, subject to self-interest.

Unlike their cousins in anthropology, archaeologists have yet to make more than shadowy appearances in the mainstream fiction dealing with serious moral issues of the times. The most popular venue for them is the mystery; adventures and romances are a distant second and third. Although archaeology seems a particularly attractive target for science fiction (and indeed Oliver La Farge published some notable short stories with archaeological themes in the *Magazine of Fantasy and Science Fiction*), only one notable science fiction/fantasy author, Piers Paul Anthony, has produced a large body of work, the *Mercycle*, in which the profession is represented by men and women of varying ethnicity, background, substantial personal dimension, and some kind of scientific and intellectual vector.

This brings us back, nearly full circle, to Tony Hillerman, a mystery/suspense writer of major stature. His readership, if not yet as extensive as Christie's, is still growing and, like Christie's, is apt to endure. Hillerman's protagonists are Native Americans, Joe Leaphorn and Jim Chee, both Navajo tribal policemen. In *Dancehall of the Dead, A Thief of Time*, and others, Hillerman's antagonists are often anthropologists or archaeologists, all of them men so far, who are willing to bend principle for greed.

Subtle in his propaganda, Hillerman readily dramatizes the cost of digs and research, the competition for grants, and the politics of publication primacy. Unlike some of their fictional forebears, Hillerman's archaeologists are convincing, believable individuals. Most readers will believe these individuals are created from some academician, museum curator, or collector the author has observed at close hand.

Help is on the way in the persona of Aaron Elkins's Professor Gideon Oliver, whose text, *A Structuro-Functional Approach to Pleistocene Hominid Phylogeny*, is now in its third edition. Known among the international police community for his expertise in forensic analysis of human skeletal remains, Oliver is described in an ongoing series that puts forth the image of him as a man of wide tastes, culture, and easygoing humor, as well as one who is, as a matter of conscience, available to his students.

Women as protagonists are gaining parity in much genre or category fiction; they have even begun to achieve dominance in the mystery/suspense area, but so far as archaeology goes, Amelia Peabody is the only game in town, with no foreseeable competition through 1994. Appearing in such well-crafted Egyptian outings as *Crocodile on the Sandbank, The Curse of the Pharaohs*, and *The Last Camel Died at Noon*, Peabody combines resourcefulness, wittiness, a concern for establishing a fabric of history, a sense of respect for the dig site, and a determination that artifacts not be removed before their full importance and implications can be assessed. Peabody has short shrift for private collectors and mercenaries who would rob tombs for financial gain or the elitist pleasures of ownership. One major drawback: Peabody is not contemporary, but rather more Victorian, independently wealthy and, thus, above reproach in her motives. She is also free from the politics of the academy.

Some of the negative press given archaeologists may be a throwback to the mad-scientist syndrome, the absent-minded or preoccupied academic stereotype, or the general perception of archaeologists being more interested in artifacts than the people who crafted or caused them to be made.

Democratization of the discipline—moving it from a wealthy man's passionate hobby to a science of commitment—may have opened the literary equivalent of the Mummy's Curse in the form of revealing the bureaucracy, politics, jealousies, and enormous costs of any new undertaking, but archaeologists who turn to morally driven fiction, either in collaboration with novelists or on their own, will be providing the world with quite another kind of artifact from which valid inferences may be made.

■ Allen J. Hubin and Otto Penzler, eds., "The Armchair Detective," various issues (1972–1990). Chris Steinbrunner et al., eds., *Detectionary: A Biographical Dictionary of the Leading Characters in Detective and Mystery Fiction* (1972). Julian Symons, *Mortal Consequences: From the Detective Story to the Crime Novel* (1972). Ian Ousby, *The Bloodhounds of Heaven: The Detective in English Fiction from Godwin to Doyle* (1976). Chris Steinbrunner and Otto Penzler, eds., *Encyclopedia of Mystery and Detection* (1976).

Shelly Lowenkopf

ARCHAEOLOGY IN SCIENCE FICTION

Like archaeology, science fiction, according to Brian Aldiss (1986), is "the search for a definition of man and his status in the universe which will stand in our advanced but confused state of knowledge (science)." Archaeology is now, however, one of the sciences that has greatly exercised writers of science fiction. Two professional anthropologists have written science fiction (Chad Oliver and Leon Stover), but only one archaeologist, and his works are largely unknown in the English-speaking world: the Paleolithic specialist François Bordes, writing such novels as *Ce Monde est Nôtre* (1962) and *La Vermine du Lion* (1967), under the pseudonym Francis Carsac.

A distinction has to be made between those science fiction writers who have used the writings of present-day archaeologists to provide subject matter, and those who have actually written about the discipline of archaeology itself or about archaeologists at work. There are very few of the latter. The profession of archaeology as found practiced in science fiction is usually described by outsiders, with little understanding of its operations or limitations: as such, therefore, it is a useful way of learning about the image of the archaeologist in popular culture. The archaeologist is rarely seen as an excavator (let alone one equipped with all the advanced technology of the future). One of the very few novels to deal with excavation, Robert Silverberg's *Across a Billion Years* (1969), does so in lackluster fashion, despite Silverberg's reputation as an author of a number of well-researched nonfiction books on archaeology. The archaeologist is more often cast as an all-purpose ancient historian or as a Toynbe-esque (or Childeian) cultural analyst. Thus, in the novella *Black Destroyer* by A. E. Van Vogt (1939), the character Korita, although introduced as an archaeologist, is also called a historian. He saves the spaceship by recognizing that the alien civilization they have discovered has died as "a young and vigorous culture, confident, strong with purpose," and thus must have been destroyed, almost overnight, by yet another alien race the explorers have come across.

Frequently, the role model for a science-fictional archaeologist is not Childe or Wheeler but Michael Ventris, a linguist and an amateur. In H. Beam Piper's story *Omnilingual* (1958), an alien language is deciphered by a team of archaeologists and linguists: the "Rosetta Stone," which enables them to succeed, is a periodic table of elements, and the message is that science is a universal language. The best-known amateur archaeologist in science fiction is the captain in the popular TV series *Star Trek: The Next Generation.* Jean-Luc Picard criticizes his lover Vash for selling illegally acquired antiquities on the market (although he himself seems to have a fine antiquities collection), and in the episode "Qpid" he even addresses an international archaeological conference about his investigations of excavations on a planet with a vanished civilization.

In science fiction proper, there are various ways in which writers have introduced archaeology: these have been characterized by Philip Rahtz in *Introduction to Archaeology* (1985). In the first, we have fictional archaeologists investigating past civilizations. Exploring spaceships frequently have archaeologists on their team; numerous far-future stories of Galactic Empire feature archaeologists who are seeking the original home of humanity (as in the later *Foundation* novels of Isaac Asimov), or make much of mysterious ruins and tales of the vanished Old Ones (as in the space adventures of André Norton). In the second, we find archaeologists from other worlds examining the remains of our own extinct civilization. Horace Coon's *43,000 Years Later* (1958) is the most extended treatment; Leo Szilard's "Report on Grand Central Station" and the anonymous *The Motel of the Mysteries* are the funniest. These stories usually act as satire both on the futility of archaeological pretensions to understand past societies, and on the futility of human society itself: the ruined Statue of Liberty stands as a common science fiction version of Ozymandias. Third, there are science fiction interpretations of archaeological evidence: this category can veer toward Von Däniken fringe archaeology, or toward what Michael Moorcock called the Shaggy God story, the likes of which are still written in large numbers by would-be writers, but are seldom published. In its classic adorned form it consists of two survivors from a spaceship wrecked on a virgin planet who turn out in the last line to be called Adam and Eve. In the fourth, a rare category indeed, reconstructions of past history in which the inhabitants of the past have an eye for the future, in which early people talk with a consciousness of future progress: Roy Lewis's extremely witty *The Evolution Man* (1960), a prehistoric romance once published in the Penguin Science Fiction series, is the best example. Finally, there is the large category of time-travel stories, in which archaeologists and historians often figure as competent (or ironically incompetent) participants.

■ Brian W. Aldiss with David Wingrove, *Trillion Year Spree: The History of Science Fiction* (1986). Edward James, *Science Fiction in the Twentieth Century* (1994).

Edward James

POST-PROCESSUAL THEORY.

The term *post-processual* was first used by Ian Hodder in 1985. Since then few writers have adopted it to define their own work. It has become more regularly used in criticism, enabling quite diverse approaches to be caricatured before being dismissed. Such rhetoric avoids detailed engagement with a complex and wide ranging program of ideas and creates a false coherency. Post-processual theory is not a unified body of ideas and it has not given rise to a common methodological program for archaeology. It can be defined only in terms of that divergent body of thinking from whence a critique of processual archaeology has been mounted. This critique found its clearest expression in publications which began to appear in Anglo-American archaeology in the early 1980s.

Post-processual theory has enabled a disenchantment to be voiced with the fundamental positions of the traditional archaeological program. The choice of the term is deliberate; disenchantment does not result in the identification of problems within the traditional program in the hope that their resolution will save that program. Instead it expresses dismay and a loss of faith in the entire enterprise. Post-processual theory finds its common ground in the recognition that all knowledge is strategically employed in social practices; consequently it is suspicious of knowledge claims that are supposedly guaranteed by an unchallengeable external reality or some grand theoretical metanarrative. Post-processual theory expresses instead a disposition toward accepting that an adequate state of knowledge must contain the components of doubt and self-critique.

Post-processual archaeology works against processualism, where the latter has sought to analyze and thus explain social evolution in terms of the adaptation and structural transformation of social systems through time. Such explanations are regarded as having cross-cultural application to the study of human societies which can be ordered into different organizational types. The validity of these explanations is supposedly secured by reference to data of an agreed and objective value. The image is therefore of an archaeology operating scientifically to accrue increasingly sophisticated models of human social evolution which may be tested, via an agreed methodology, against a generally accepted data set.

There are two important points which are challenged by post-processualism: (1) the ontological claim that the real forces of history operate at the level of the social system and its structural transformations (this position has been most simply characterized by Colin Renfrew as "systems thinking"); (2) the epistemological commitment to positivism, in other words, that knowledge claims are substantiated by reference to an external reality, descriptions of which are objectively secure and not contingent upon the position or the status of the observer. We will take these points in turn.

Agency. Post-processual theory seeks to resituate history at the level of human agency. Knowledgeable action, through which agency operates and by which agency is known, controls and directs human life. Resituating history in this way has dramatic implications. The material conditions that archaeologists study can no longer be regarded as having been molded by the operation of some relatively abstract social structure. Instead agency operates within the context of given material conditions, but it does so knowledgeably by drawing both meaning from and imparting meaning to those conditions. Agency thus understands the appropriateness of its actions and is able to communicate its intentions and its authority through its use of material culture. The effectiveness of agency is thus situated in specific readings of material culture. Understanding or interpreting that effectiveness now becomes the central task for archaeology.

A number of theoretical strands are drawn upon to map the post-processual position. From *structuralism has come the recognition that the categories by which the world is known are not inherent within the world (which would make them independent of history) but are the creation of the mind (of "being in the world"). Agency accepts these cultural categories as the real and usable resources necessary to sustain life, but agency can also at times challenge and rethink those categories. Human adaptation to any given set of environmental conditions is therefore mediated through these categorical orders.

Marxism has helped to extend an understanding of the way symbolic orders also sustain and legitimate certain asymmetries of social power by which the life chances of certain groups are enhanced while those of others are diminished. However, in archaeology it has perhaps been feminist writers who have explored most imaginatively the way a dominant symbolic code operates, in this case to sustain gender asymmetries, but may also under certain circumstances be challenged and subverted. Across this wide and at times conflicting political spectrum we find a broad agreement: that dominant codes of meaning are deployed strategically by socially dominant groups. However the point can also be lost when marxist analyses operate at a general and systemic level by equating a particular social structure with a particular set of dominant ideological representations. Feminist studies have been more successful in evoking the local and day-to-day practices by which social authority is negotiated.

By placing history almost literally in the hands of the human agents who created it, post-processual archaeologists would accept that the cultural diversity of human experience, with conflicts over the meaning and value of those experiences, are real historical processes and not the by-products of some deeper structural dynamic. Actions and materials can therefore be conceptualized as texts which were interpreted by the practitioners who made them and who used them. Because the experiences and expectations of those practitioners will have varied, so will their "readings" of these texts. We arrive at the realization that no single meaning can ever be guaranteed for a text that is situated within social practice. To push this point still further, we might accept the strength of Foucault's argument that humans are created out of the positions they occupy in different discourses of power and knowledge.

The primacy given to knowledgeable agency presents archaeology with a serious epistemological challenge. What can we ever know of such foreign and distant pasts, what status do we give our histories of these other periods, and how do we choose between different interpretations of the historical conditions we study?

The Status of Interpretation. For its critics, post-processual theory has mired archaeology in a hopeless relativism. Not only is the meaning of material culture contingent upon past contexts of social discourse, but archaeological interpretations must themselves be similarly situated in contemporary political and social mores. The multiplicity of histories heralded by the post-processual program is intolerable when viewed from a commitment to objectivity. It would appear that any past wished for, perhaps to aid some contemporary political program, need only be accepted as possible or refuted on the basis of political preferences. No independent grounding appears to exist upon which to evaluate conflicting ideas.

Refutation of such criticisms has been slow in coming. The central position of post-processual theory cannot be compromised. There never was a single past, only conflict and diversity in the struggle of other people to interpret their worlds. As we have seen, there need be no single meaning applicable to the materials we study, indeed their historical significance may lie precisely in their ambiguity. It is easier now to think of the archaeological evidence not as a record of a particular process, where the meaning of the record depends upon the archaeologist identifying the processes which created it, but as a *site* or *locale* which was once inhabited by people who sought to interpret it and to act upon those interpretations. The metaphor of the material-as-text helps in our understanding of the implications of this position. The meaning of the text is something recognized by a reader who is guided by his or her own expectations; it is not merely imparted by what the author of the text supposedly "meant." Different readers may differ in their readings of the same text; different historical and cultural conditions may allow for different interpretations of the text.

Post-processual theory thus reroutes the epistemological challenge of archaeology. Historical knowledge cannot be secured by reference to some absolute; the meaning of any assemblage of material culture is always open and cannot be closed by relating it to a single process of production (or, if we stay with our textual analogy, authorship). For us to understand agency as a historical process necessitates understanding something of that agency's ability to interpret its own world. The language of post-processual archaeology thus eschews reference to "explanation" and "testing" in place of a concern with "interpretation."

Interpretation occurs, as Tilley has commented, when we are confronted by things, the significance of which is not obvious, but that puzzle us. Interpretation presents us with a double challenge. First there is the problem of how others may have interpreted their own world. We study the material conditions of those other lives not to discover what they meant but to expose how meanings may have been won from them: who occupied these conditions, what readings may have been possible, what actions arose from those understandings? These questions introduce the second turn in the interpretive strategy: what is the status of our interpretations of those other lives, which we and others have constructed archaeologically and used in our own world? Whose interpretations are before us; which members of our own communities are writing these histories?

The interpretive challenge demands a self-critical control over archaeological analysis, regarding as arrogant claims to have discovered some truth about the lives of other people, even those long dead. An interpretive archaeology should be more restrained, respecting the past and never seeking the final word. It will explore and open up the possibilities of understanding particular material conditions, exposing the richness and diversity of the past. It will also recognize the impositions made upon that past through our own interpretations of it; it will expose the values of our contemporary lives which are drawn into our understandings of the past. The epistemological basis of our historical writings will be explored in terms of their richness and diversity and the strengths of our self-critical awareness (the latter not paraded as a political supremacy but expressed as a humble and ethical awareness of our commitment to other human beings).

These strictures are unlikely to satisfy traditional archaeologists, but the evaluation of historical writing cannot be on an agreed basis given that processual and post-processual archaeologists value the material residues of the human past in quite different ways. Both recognize that these residues are the means by which we practice archaeology; beyond this their paths diverge.

[See also CRITICAL THEORY; CULTURAL ECOLOGY THEORY; CULTURE HISTORICAL THEORY; DARWINIAN THEORY; GENDER, ARCHAEOLOGY OF; GENERAL SYSTEMS THEORY; HISTORY OF ARCHAEOLOGY, INTELLECTUAL; MARXIST THEORY; MIDDLE RANGE THEORY; PROCESSUAL THEORY; SCIENCE IN ARCHAEOLOGY; THEORY IN ARCHAEOLOGY.]

■ Michael Shanks and Christopher Tilley, *Re-constructing Archaeology* (1987). Ian Bapty and Tim Yates, eds., *Archaeology after Structuralism* (1990). Joan M. Gero and Margaret W. Conkey, eds., *Engendering Archaeology* (1991). Ian Hodder, *Theory and Practice in Archaeology* (1992). Christopher Tilley, ed., *Interpretive Archaeology* (1993).

John C. Barrett

POTASSIUM-ARGON DATING. Geologists use the potassium-argon technique to date rocks as much as 2 billion years old and as little as 50,000 years old. The potassium-argon method is one of the few viable ways of dating archaeological sites earlier than 100,000 years old, and has allowed paleoanthropologists to develop an outline chronology for early human evolution and human origins. Potassium (K) is one of the most abundant elements in the earth's crust and is present in nearly every mineral. In its natural form, potassium contains a small proportion of radioactive potassium 40 atoms. For every hundred potassium 40 atoms that decay, eleven become argon 40, an inactive gas that can easily escape from its material by diffusion when lava and other igneous rocks are formed. As volcanic rock forms by crystallization, the concentration of argon 40 drops to almost nothing. But regular and reasonable decay of potassium 40 will continue, with a half-life of 1.3 billion years. It is possible, then, to measure with a spectrometer the concentration of argon 40 that has accumulated since the rock formed. Because many archaeological sites were occupied during a period when extensive volcanic activity occurred, especially in East Africa, it is possible to date them by associations of lava with human settlements.

Potassium-argon dates have been obtained from many igneous minerals, of which the most resistant to later argon diffusion are biotite, muscovite, and sanidine. Microscopic examination of the rock is essential to eliminate the possibility of contamination by recrystallization and other processes. In the standard technique, the samples are processed by crushing the rock, concentrating it, and treating it with hydrofluoric acid to remove any atmospheric argon. The various gases are then removed from the sample and the argon gas is isolated and subjected to mass spectrographic analysis. The age of the sample is then calculated using the argon 40 and potassium 40 content and a standard formula. The resulting date is quoted with a large standard deviation—for Lower Pleistocene sites, on the order of a quarter of a million years. In recent years, computerized argon laser fusion has become the technique of choice. By steering a laser beam over a single irradiated grain of volcanic ash, a potassium-argon specialist can date a lake bed layer, and even a small scatter of tools and animal bones left by an early hominid. The grain glows white hot, gives up a gas, which is purified, and then charged by an electron beam. A powerful magnet accelerates the charged gas and hurls it against a device that counts its argon atoms. By measuring the relative amounts of two isotopes of the element, researchers can calculate the amount of time that has elapsed since the lava cooled and the crystals formed. Potassium-argon dates can be taken only from volcanic rocks, preferably from actual volcanic flows, so the geological associations of fossils and artifacts must be carefully recorded.

Fortunately, many early human settlements in the Old World are found in volcanic areas, where such deposits as lava flows and tuffs are found in profusion. The first archaeological date obtained from this method came from *Olduvai Gorge, Tanzania, where in 1959 Louis and Mary *Leakey found a robust australopithecine skull, *Zinjanthropus boisei*, stone tools, and animal bones in a Lower Pleistocene lake bed of unknown age. Lava samples from the site were dated to about 1.75 million years, doubling the then-assumed date for early humans. Stone flakes and chopping tools of undoubted human manufacture have come from Koobi Fora in northern Kenya, dated to about 2.5 million years, the earliest date for human artifacts. Still earlier *Australopithecus* fossils have been dated at Hadar in Ethiopia to between 3 million and 4 million years ago. Potassium-argon samples have dated the appearance of *Homo erectus* in Africa to about 1.8 million years ago or even earlier. Until recently, paleoanthropologists believed *H. erectus* radiated out of Africa about a million to 700,000 years ago. But a team of Berkeley scientists have used laser fusion to date *H. erectus*-bearing levels at Modjokerto in Southeast Asia to 1.8 million years ago, pushing the radiation date back three quarters of a million years.

[*See also* DATING THE PAST; HUMAN EVOLUTION: FOSSIL EVIDENCE FOR HUMAN EVOLUTION.]

■ G. B. Dalrymple and M. A. Lamphere, *Potassium Argon Dating* (1970). J. W. Michels, *Dating Methods in Archaeology* (1973). S. J. Fleming, *Dating in Archaeology* (1976).

Brian M. Fagan

POVERTY POINT. The Poverty Point site is located just west of the Mississippi River in northeastern Louisiana. The site is significant because its earthworks are the oldest large aboriginal constructions known in mainland North America. They were built between 1730 and 1350 B.C. by Terminal Archaic hunter-gatherers. Today the site is a national historical landmark and a state park.

Poverty Point's earthworks were initially reported in 1873 by Samuel Lockett, of the Louisiana Topographic Survey, but it was not until James Ford of the American Museum of Natural History saw the site on an aerial photograph in 1953 and carried out the first extensive excavations that their large size and geometric layout were recognized.

At the center of the site is a partial elliptical enclosure of six concentric earthen ridges. Five "aisles" radiate through the ridges like spokes of a giant wheel.

Two very large and three smaller mounds occur at various places inside and outside the enclosure. The two largest mounds are thought to be bird figures. Three of the other mounds are platforms, and the remaining one is a conical structure capping an ash bed containing pieces of charred human bone.

The largest mound contains about 98,000 cubic yards (75,000 cu m) of earth, and the total construction amounts to more than 1,960,000 cubic yards (1,500,000 cu m), an unprecedented earth-moving effort, one rarely surpassed during later times.

Artifacts from the site include baked clay objects, which were used in pit baking; untempered and fiber-tempered pottery, representing the earliest kind of ware found in the Lower Mississippi Valley; small solid female figurines of baked clay; tubular clay pipes, and clay plummets, beads, and pendants. Chipped bifacial tools include projectile points, especially types with narrow stem-body junctures; adzes, celts, hoes, drills, and unfinished and broken tools. A core and blade technology produced a variety of microtools, most notably a converging double-backed bladelet called a Jaketown perforator. Ground and polished stone artifacts include: stone vessels, milling stones, whetstones, hammerstones, saws, reamers, polishers, celts, hoes, plummets, gorgets, pipes, bannerstones, narrow-ended tablets, and small geometrical objects—cones, cylinders, spheres, and others. Stone ornaments are common and include tubular and disc beads, owl effigy pendants, bird-head silhouettes, buttons, and Y-shaped, rattle-shaped, claw-shaped geniculate, and geometric pendants.

Poverty Point was a major exchange center. Raw materials, especially rocks from as far away as 990 miles (1,600 km), were imported and traded to contemporary sites within 185 miles (300 km) of the center. The site is thought by some archaeologists to be the largest permanent settlement in mainland North America at its time, the seat of a chiefdom with a population numbering in the thousands. By others, it is seen as a near-vacant ceremonial center or a trade fairgrounds, visited on special occasions by wandering bands.

Poverty Point developed before horticulture. It is a product of Archaic hunter-gatherers, and that makes the degree of cultural complexity evidenced there unique in America north of Mexico.

[*See also* HUNTER-GATHERERS, NORTH AMERICAN ARCHAIC; MOUNDS OF EASTERN NORTH AMERICA, NORTH AMERICA: THE EASTERN WOODLANDS AND THE SOUTH.]

■ James A. Ford and Clarence H. Webb, "Poverty Point: A Late Archaic Site in Louisiana," *American Museum of Natural History, Anthropological Papers* 46 (1956). Jon L. Gibson, "Poverty Point: The First North American Chiefdom," *Archaeology* 27 (1974): 97–105. Clarence H. Webb, "The Poverty Point Culture," *Geoscience and Man* 17 (2nd ed., 1982). Jon L. Gibson, "Poverty Point," *Louisiana Archaeological Survey and Antiquities Commission, Anthropological Study* 7 (1983). H. Edwin Jackson, "The Trade Fair in Hunter-Gatherer Interaction: The Role of Intersocietal Trade in the Evolution of Poverty Point Culture," in *Between Bands and States*, ed. Susan A. Gregg, Southern Illinois University, Center for Archaeological Investigations, *Occasional Paper* 9 (1991), pp. 265–286.

Jon L. Gibson

PREHISTORIC ARCHAEOLOGY is a field of research that encompasses all of the pre-urban societies of the world, which by definition have no written records to provide direct accounts by observers and participants. It therefore has a distinctive set of procedures for analyzing material remains in order to reconstruct their ecological settings, materials procurement and subsistence practices, everyday life, social organization, and the patterning of symbolic codes in such extinct societies. Since this is the "purest" form of archaeology, unaided by other types of evidence, it has been the most lively focus of methodological innovation, in terms both of theory and techniques. Because the interpretation of such indirect traces of complex patterns of activity can only be undertaken in the light of more general notions of how small-scale societies work, it maintains a close relationship with anthropology (and is therefore sometimes termed "anthropological archaeology"). Since it also encompasses the study of premodern human populations, it has close links with biology, biological anthropology, and geology.

This set of disciplines came into existence in the later nineteenth century, and the concept of "prehistory" was a product of evolutionary ideas and the recognition of the long existence of the human species, on a scale not allowed by fundamentalist religious chronologies. It continued a tradition of comparative anthropology with its origins in the Renaissance and the Enlightenment, nourished by the often nationalistic concerns of Romantic historicism in early nineteenth-century Europe. Its fundamental engagement with material remains—and hence the name archaeology—was derived from traditions of classical and oriental scholarship and art history. Because of these many-sided links with other disciplines and areas of discourse, it is still pursued in a variety of different institutional settings and combinations with other subjects. Only in relation to the Paleolithic period can it be considered a truly international community; the prehistory of later periods is usually fragmented by regional and, to some extent, chronological divisions.

The primary centers of prehistoric archaeology in the early stages of its development were museums: either regional and national collections, or international ones that typically existed in the capital cities of the colonial powers. University collections were also important centers of research, as were national archaeological institutes such as the Deutsches Archaeologisches Institut in Germany, operating throughout Europe and the Near East. The scope of such overseas collections varied according to political spheres of influence. In Europe, prehistoric antiquities were often combined with "protohistoric" (early Medieval, i.e., post-Roman) ones, particularly in the countries outside the limits of the former Roman Empire (like Denmark) where their systematic study began. In North America such institutions typically embraced the study of the indigenous peoples of the Americas, often including the urban civilizations of Central America and the Andean region. While these foci continue, they are now complemented by national museums and national antiquities services or monument protection agencies throughout the world.

Of all the branches of archaeology, study of the prehistoric periods most clearly reflects the successive cultural concerns of modern society, showing a tendency to oscillate between comparative and evolutionary interpretations at times of economic growth and political stability, and more introverted issues of cultural interpretation in times of stress and fragmentation. This has most recently been illustrated by the shift from so-called processual to post-processual schools of thought in recent decades. Whereas the former emphasized the kinds of deterministic models current in ecology and geography, the latter has been more sensitive to issues of interpretation arising from humanistic studies. Both aspects are vital to its healthy development as a critical discipline, important both as a scientific study of human origins and a particular account of the development of different cultural traditions and the role of individual men and women within them.

Its future as an international field of research lies in the recognition and pursuit of common themes of the kind at present best exemplified in the Paleolithic. A comparable focus is provided by the patterns of adjustment to ecological change in the early Holocene, and the social factors leading to the emergence of farming and other labor-intensive methods of producing food and organizing social space, and ultimately to the existence of urban civilizations. This also involves the study of colonization of large and important areas such as the Pacific. An important but (since the death of V. Gordon *Childe in 1957) less explicitly considered set of problems concerns the relationship between urban societies and the surrounding communities affected by their growth in Asia, Europe, and the Americas. The incorporation of technologies and ideas originating in urban contexts and their transformation in indigenous cultures is a theme that unites practitioners of archaeology and

other historical disciplines throughout the world, from the fourth millennium B.C. to the second millennium A.D.

[See also ARCHAEOLOGY AS A DISCIPLINE; CLASSICAL ARCHAEOLOGY; HISTORICAL ARCHAEOLOGY; INDUSTRIAL ARCHAEOLOGY.]

■ Glyn Daniel and Colin Renfrew, *The Idea of Prehistory* (1988, rev. ed.). Norman Yoffee and Andrew Sherratt, eds., *Archaeological Theory: Who Sets the Agenda?* (1993).

Andrew Sherratt

PROCESSUAL THEORY, an amalgam of ideas advanced by the "new" or "processual" archaeologists during the 1960s, originated in the United States, mainly at the Universities of Michigan and Chicago. Its major creative force was Lewis R. Binford, an alumnus of Michigan who taught briefly at Chicago and influenced many students who, in turn, became proponents of the program. By the early 1970s processual theory enjoyed a widespread following.

Processual theory includes principles and methods that run the gamut from epistemology, through social theory, to methodology. Its epistemology is uncompromisingly scientific: high on the agenda are the search for laws and theories and the explicit testing of hypotheses.

Certain that the historical processes of *diffusion, independent invention, and migration invoked by culture historians could not rigorously explain cultural variability and change, processualists forged new social theory, drawing inspiration from cultural evolutionists (Leslie White, Elman Service, Morton Fried), cultural ecologists (especially Julian Steward), and systems theorists (such as James Miller). When the uneasy mix of principles obtained from these sources was pitted against the prevailing social theory of culture historians, the latter fell quickly into disfavor.

The processualist views culture in materialist terms as an "extrasomatic adaptation," the linkage between biological organisms (humans) and their environment. At a culture's base, interacting directly with the natural environment, is technology. Resting on the technological foundation is social organization (arrangements of people needed to manage technology), which in turn is capped by ideology (appropriate values and beliefs). The subsystems of a culture, including settlement and subsistence, strive toward mutual integration and stability. Thus, the causes of culture change lie external to the system; most important are environmental stress and population growth. This orientation leads to a series of fundamental research questions, including: (1) how were settlement systems organized in space (and during the annual cycle) to allow a group to exploit critical natural resources? (2) how did groups manage their subsistence and settlement subsystems? and (3) how did changes in the natural environment and in population size affect subsistence, settlement, and social organization?

To facilitate answering their questions, processual archaeologists developed a distinctive methodological theory, consisting of the following postulates: (1) because human behavior (as in subsystems) is highly patterned, artifacts are also highly patterned in their formal (morphological) and spatial properties; (2) given that human behavior and artifacts are markedly patterned, the archaeological record—a product of human behavior—also exhibits strong patterning. Thus, by seeking "patterns" in the formal and spatial properties of artifacts, one can reconstruct the characteristics of subsystems, even social organization. This methodological theory allowed the remains of past cultures to be approached with great optimism. As Lewis Binford put it so memorably, knowledge of the past is limited mainly by our "methodological naïveté."

To accomplish the near-term goal of cultural reconstruction, processualists adopted new methods and techniques, including explicit sampling designs for survey and excavation, a multiplicity of problem-oriented artifact typologies, and quantitative—especially statistical—analyses. Emphasis was also placed on discovering and recovering new kinds of evidence. For example, palynology and flotation analysis became commonplace. Processualists, especially Stuart Struever, insisted that field projects would have to grow in scale, duration, and obviously cost, if the new lines of evidence were to be successfully integrated. His large-scale excavations at the *Koster site in the lower Illinois River Valley (S. Struever and F. A. Holton, *Koster*, 1979) which involved full-time specialists in palynology, geology, malacology, and so on, became a model for the kind of project that processual interests demanded.

In the decade from 1962 to 1972, important case studies in processual archaeology were published. Perhaps the most captivating and controversial were the works of William A. Longacre and James N. Hill, which attempted to reconstruct aspects of social organization—including post-marital residence pattern—at puebloan sites in east-central Arizona. Lewis Binford and Sally Binford also conducted an analysis of variability in Mousterian chipped-stone artifacts; their work touched off heated debates that rage to this day.

Although further research has undermined the findings of some pioneering processual studies, the latter's ingenious arguments and innovative methods opened up new avenues of research, stimulating, for example, the emergence of modern *ethnoarchaeology. Indeed, in the early 1970s Lewis R. Binford and William A. Longacre themselves established ethnoarchaeological projects to better understand artifact patterning in ongoing cultural systems. Their research (Binford among the Nunamiut Eskimo of northern Alaska and Longacre in Kalinga villages in the Philippines) has been productive and influential.

Important principles of processual archaeology were codified in several books in the late 1960s and early 1970s (e.g., P. J. Watson, S. A. LeBlanc, and C. L. Redman, *Explanation in Archaeology*, 1971; M. P. Leone, ed., *Contemporary Archaeology*, 1972; J. N. Woodall, *An Introduction to Modern Archaeology*, 1972) and so became accessible to students. In an archaeology expanding in the 1970s and early 1980s in the United States, under the impacts of cultural resource management studies, many students—most trained in processual theory—became professional archaeologists.

In addition to isolated critiques of processual theory and its early case studies, systematic attacks were launched by distinct schools in opposition to all or part of the processual program. The first was that of "behavioral archaeology," which arose at the University of Arizona under the leadership of J. Jefferson Reid, William L. Rathje, and Michael B. Schiffer. Behavioralists strongly emphasized the need to understand, in all times and all places, the relationships between human behavior and artifacts. They also identified a fatal shortcoming in the processualists' methodological theory: there was no place for explicitly considering how *site formation processes introduce variability into the archaeological record. Patterns attributed to past social organization, for example, may have actually resulted from the patterned action of formation processes, such as reuse, deposition, or disturbance. To assess these possibilities, archaeologists would need new analytic techniques and principles of formation processes, the latter to be obtained through experimentation and from an expanded ethnoarchaeology. The growth of behavioral archaeology along these lines, in the 1970s and 1980s, amended and augmented the processual program, leading to improved theory and method for reconstructing past human behavior.

A second programmatic critique of the processualists arose in England at Cambridge University, where Ian Hodder and his students mounted an aggressive, polemical challenge under the rubric of "post-processual" archaeology. Influenced by post-modernists, neo-Marxists, and mentalist culture theorists in anthropology, post-processualists in the mid-1980s disputed key elements of processualism, including its scientific epistemology, materialist culture theory, ecological-evolutionary models, and emphasis on devising new methods. They called for a shift to questions about the individual in prehistory, internal processes of change, artifacts and the construction of meaning, ideology, power, and class, and the relationships between archaeology and the societies in which it is practiced. In addition to its core at Cambridge, post-processual archaeology has taken limited root in the United States. Although post-processualists remain a tiny minority, the movement has provoked processualists and behavioralists to embrace long-neglected research questions about, for example, ideology, power, and class, and to seek rigorous methods within a scientific epistemology to answer them.

The legacy of processual theory is large and impressive. Most archaeologists in the english-speaking world and, increasingly, in Europe and Latin America, practice what is recognizably a processual program—its rigor improved by the behavioralists and its questioning of the past and present expanded by behavioralists and post-processualists.

[*See also* CRITICAL THEORY; CULTURAL ECOLOGY THEORY; CULTURE HISTORICAL THEORY; GENDER, ARCHAEOLOGY OF; GENERAL SYSTEMS THEORY; HISTORY OF ARCHAEOLOGY, INTELLECTUAL; MARXIST THEORY; METHOD, ARCHAEOLOGICAL; MIDDLE RANGE THEORY; POST-PROCESSUAL THEORY; SCIENCE IN ARCHAEOLOGY; THEORY IN ARCHAEOLOGY.]

■ Lewis R. Binford and Sally R. Binford, "A Preliminary Analysis of Functional Variability in the Mousterian of Levallois Facies," *American Anthropologist* 68:2, Part 2 (1965): 238–295. Sally R. Binford and Lewis R. Binford, eds., *New Perspectives in Archeology* (1968). David L. Clarke, *Analytical Archaeology* (1968). Betty J. Meggers, ed., *Anthropological Archeology in the Americas* (1968). William A. Longacre, "Archaeology as Anthropology," University of Arizona, *Anthropological Papers* 17 (1970). James N. Hill, "Broken K. Pueblo," University of Arizona, *Anthropological Papers* 18 (1970). Lewis R. Binford, *An Archaeological Perspective* (1972). J. Jefferson Reid, Michael B. Schiffer, and William L. Rathje, "Behavioral Archaeology: Four Strategies," *American Anthropologist* 77 (1975): 864–869. Michael B. Schiffer, *Behavioral Archeology* (1976). Ian Hodder, "Postprocessual Archaeology," *Advances in Archaeological Method and Theory* 8 (1985): 1–26.

Michael Brian Schiffer

PSEUDO-ARCHAEOLOGY

INTRODUCTION

The term "pseudo-archaeology" covers a broad spectrum of topics sharing in common a nonscientific misapplication, misinterpretation, and / or misrepresentation of the archaeological record. Subsumed under the pseudo-archaeology rubric are simple, and some not so simple, hoaxes or frauds: the remains of an ostensible, ancient giant man found near Syracuse, New York, in 1869 (the Cardiff Giant); the "discovery" of fragments of a purported fossil human skull with a modern-appearing cranium and an apelike jaw in Sussex, England, beginning in 1911 (Piltdown Man); the discovery in 1898 of a stone covered with Viking runes in Minnesota and dated to the fourteenth century A.D. (the Kensington Stone).

Beyond hoaxes, pseudo-archaeology also includes manufactured mysteries about the human past, as well as their purported solutions. Included in this category of pseudo-archaeology are the myth of an ancient, vanished race responsible for the construction of ancient earthworks in the American Midwest and Southeast; the highly advanced and technologically sophisticated culture of the "Lost Continent of Atlantis" proposed to explain the ostensibly mysterious similarities between the civilizations of the ancient Old and New Worlds; and the allegation that the prehistoric archaeological record bears witness to the visitations of ancient extraterrestrial aliens that, in turn, are used to explain the remarkable achievements of ancient human beings.

Another subset of pseudo-archaeology includes the attempt to force the archaeological record to conform to and provide support for a literal interpretation of the Bible, especially the Old Testament. Here the claim is made that the archaeological record upholds the view that the world was created, more or less as it now appears, sometime within the last 10,000 years. It is also maintained that archaeological evidence supports the view that the world was all but destroyed by a universal flood, that just a handful of people survived that flood, and even that remnants of the boat that served as their refuge—the Ark—still exist on Mount Ararat in Turkey.

These attempts to recast the past in some way often are perpetrated for as simple a reason as money or fame. Some reflect a desire to prove a particular religious perspective. Some are rooted in *nationalism or racism; the Nazis were adept at archaeological frauds in an attempt to provide "scientific" support for their claims of Aryan superiority. Though the specific motives vary, all of these myriad pseudo-archaeologies have in common a lack of objective observation of the archaeological record and an eschewing of the scientific method.

[*See also* POLITICAL USES OF ARCHAEOLOGY.]

■ K. L. Feder, *Frauds, Myths, and Mysteries: Science and Pseudoscience in Archaeology* (1990). S. Williams, *Fantastic Archaeology* (1991).

Kenneth L. Feder

LOST CONTINENTS

Stories of ancient places that were destroyed by catastrophe occur elsewhere, but the tradition of lost continents in Western civilization originates in Plato's two later works *Timaeus* and *Critias*. Critias, descendant of Solon, recounts the lawgiver's report from priests in Egypt telling of a war that took place 9,000 years before between Athens, then ruled by the ideals of Plato's *Republic*, and a great kingdom. Located on a vast island in the Atlantic, divinely constituted Atlantis was ruled by descendants of Poseidon, notably Atlas. On its south coast was built a circular metropolis, a citadel with concentric rings of city and harbor centered on the temple of Poseidon. Growing ambitious, the Atlanteans conquered

Egypt and Tuscany, effectively opposed only by virtuous Athens until both Atlantis and the Athenian army perished in a single night of floods and earthquakes.

A quote of Aristotle said that Atlantis was invented. Most other ancient authors that mentioned Atlantis relied on Plato's word alone. Later, some Neoplatonists accepted it and embellished Plato with tales allegedly from isles in the Atlantic. Disbelief in the ancient gods ended the literal acceptance of Plato's Atlantis. In the Age of Exploration, Atlantis was attached to the Americas, notably by Sir Francis Bacon in his utopian romance *New Atlantis* (1627). A rationalized view maintained considerable respectability into the nineteenth century and was accepted by Alexander von Humboldt. Ignatius Donnelly, the American Populist, vastly elaborated a theory that the civilizations of the Americas (and the rest of the world) derived from Atlantis. Atlantis was adopted by mystics, such as Helena Blavatsky, founder of theosophy, and was exploited by hoaxers, such as Dr. Paul Schliemann, grandson of the archaeologist, but it also excited scholarly interest, for lost continents then played an important role in geological explanation. By 1970, mapping disclosed no scars of lost continents, and the study of plate tectonics made it clear that no large landmasses of the Atlantis type existed in the open ocean. Atlantis was forced to move elsewhere, most often to the Aegean, within reach of the Greek experience. Much reduced in date and size, its city was altered to resemble actual excavated structures. Proposed sites include Troy, but the favorite has been Thera, whose dramatic destruction in the mid-second millennium B.C. has been compared to the sudden end of Atlantis, although the end of Thera was slow enough to permit evacuation. Further, the name Atlantis is firmly connected to the area of the Atlas or the Atlantic, and Aegean places known from both Hittite and Egyptian sources are essentially those of classical times.

Expanding knowledge has progressively driven the Atlantis story away from possible reality. Advocates have had to change its date, location, and description, and would have to alter the name, depriving Atlantis of any existence but that of a composite of experiences and theories. It can be interpreted as Aristotle realized and Plato intended, as a forensic device in a conversation that never took place.

A vast Pacific continent that saw the first human achievements was proposed by James Churchward in *The Lost Continent of Mu* and several other works, based on a hodgepodge of "evidence" made up of incredible personal testimonials, false translations, notably of tablets from Mesoamerica, and spurious reconstructions from archaeological and artistic remains. Although it has attracted some following, it has never received scholarly or scientific support, unlike Atlantis.

■ James Bramwell, *Lost Atlantis* (1937). L. Sprague de Camp, *Lost Continents: The Atlantis Theme in History, Science and Literature* (1970). Warman Welliver, *Character, Plot and Thought in Plato's Timaeus-Critias* (1977). Edwin F. Ramage, ed., *Atlantis, Fact or Fiction?* (1978). Phyllis Young Forsyth, *Atlantis, the Making of a Myth* (1980). Eberhard Zangger, *The Flood from Heaven: Deciphering the Atlantis Legend* (with a foreword by Anthony Snodgrass) (1992).

Bruce B. Williams

ANCIENT ASTRONAUTS

Erich von Daniken is the best-known author to claim a role for space travelers in history. In *Chariots of the Gods* and later works, he asserted that the development of *Homo sapiens* and complex culture were probably due to extraterrestrial intervention. Humankind originated in the selective impregnation of hominids by extraterrestrials. Sometime later, the major ancient civilizations were created or inspired by deliberate interventions that included the use of high technology and mass destruction. He asserted that humanity differs too much from terrestrial forebears to have naturally evolved, that "high civilization" appeared too abruptly to have been achieved without external expertise, that major and many minor artifacts could have been created only with the aid of complex technologies, and that some artifacts were made using knowledge gained by viewing the earth from far above. Ancient literary references to flying, extraterrestrial travel, and extraordinary powers refer to the space travelers, and works of art actually depict them. Von Daniken's books received widespread public attention and inspired some imitators and a film. It became a premise for popular fictional works.

Despite its popularity, the "Chariots" theme never received scholarly support because the conclusions lacked foundation in logic or evidence at the simplest level. Although human development has not followed a smooth or unbroken path, the physical, cultural, and technological developments have not been subject to the abrupt changes von Daniken attributed to outside intervention. Specific arguments misstated or misinterpreted the evidence. For example, maps attributed to the sixteenth-century Turkish admiral Piri Reis are not views from space, but azimuthal projections using data from the voyages of exploration and techniques well known to Arab geographers.

Representations called spacemen from Mesoamerica actually depict well-known ceremonial images. Egypt did not emerge suddenly from a vacuum (ca. 3100 B.C.); its distinctive culture had a long span of prior development. Egypt's pyramids were also developed over a long period, and despite their awe-inspiring scale, the techniques used in their construction are known, at least approximately, today and have been partially used in the recent past to make repairs to temples. Although construction must have been a burden, even the small population (not von Daniken's fifty million) had hundreds of thousands of laborers available for part of the year. The "Chariots" theme fails the most elementary test, for it requires the reader to accept the extraterrestrials as incompetent colonizers who required thousands of years to make less technological change than has occurred globally in the last century without a hint of intervention.

■ Erich von Daniken, *Chariots of the Gods? Unsolved Mysteries of the Past*, trans. Michael Heron (1970). Kenneth Feder, *Frauds, Myths, and Mysteries: Science and Pseudoscience in Archaeology* (1990).
Bruce B. Williams

ANCIENT VOYAGES AND MIGRATIONS

The majority of claims that fall into this category concern the discovery, exploration, and colonization of the New World by ancient peoples of Europe, Asia, and Africa. The consensus of archaeological opinion on this issue is that subsequent to the migration by northeastern Asians across the Bering Land Bridge at the end of the Pleistocene, no further movement of people from the Old to the New World occurred until the Viking exploration of eastern Canada at about A.D. 1000. There, the archaeological site of L'Anse aux Meadows on Newfoundland exhibits indisputable evidence of the presence of the Norse about 500 years before Columbus's voyages to the New World.

Claims of other voyages to the New World usually focus on a number of Old World people: Irish monks led by Saint Brendan of the late fifth and early sixth centuries A.D., Chinese Buddhist monks led by Huishin at around A.D. 500, followers of the Welsh prince Madog in the twelfth century A.D., West African seafarers some 3,000 years ago, and Celts beginning as much as 4,000 years ago.

The evidence provided for these voyages and migrations ordinarily is restricted to myth and legend, linguistic, cultural, and, architectural resemblances, and, especially, the presence of written messages in Old World scripts found in pre-Columbian contexts in the New World.

None of the evidence has been deemed sufficient by most archaeologists to support any of these proposed voyages or migrations. Legends, a handful of similar words in different languages, very generally similar cultural practices, and resemblances in how people pile up stone in construction constitute very weak evidence in support of proposed voyages of exploration and colonization. The epigraphic evidence has largely been dismissed by linguists as based on hoaxes, the misinterpretation of naturally occurring marks on rocks, and the misinterpretation of very recent markings.

Certainly, the evidence most conspicuously missing in support of the claims of these voyages is that which archaeologists would expect to find documenting the presence of an alien people: artifacts, features, and human skeletons clearly of Old World origin in pre-Columbian/pre-Viking archaeological contexts in the New World. In fact, this sort of evidence, when recovered at L'Anse aux Meadows, is precisely what convinced a previously skeptical archaeological community of a pre-Columbian Norse presence in the New World. Unless and until similar evidence is forthcoming, it seems unlikely that many archaeologists will accept the claimed pre-Columbian, pre-Viking voyages and migrations to the New World by people from the Old World.

■ K. L. Feder, *Frauds, Myths, and Mysteries: Science and Pseudoscience in Archaeology* (1990). S. Williams, *Fantastic Archaeology* (1991).
Kenneth L. Feder

PYRAMIDS OF GIZA. Of the Seven Wonders of the World, only the pyramids of Giza remain nearly intact. The awe that they still inspire is perhaps also the source of the fantastic explanations of their construction and function that they have long stimulated among amateur Egyptologists. Yet it is clear to archaeologists after nearly 200 years of scientific study that the pyramids of Giza are part of a continuous ancient building tradition. They were constructed by ingenious but natural methods known to the indigenous people of Egypt. Their symbolism and function were deeply rooted in Egypt's culture and society.

The three pyramid complexes at Giza were built by Kings Khufu (Cheops), Khafre (Chephren), and Menkare (Mykerinos) of the Fourth Dynasty (2613–2494 B.C.) as their tombs and places of eternal worship after their deaths. These complexes are located on the desert plateau, about 2 miles (3 km) west of the modern village of Giza, just west of Cairo. Each complex consists of five major elements, though there are numerous differences in interior detail and plan. In addition to the pyramid itself, each king built a pyramid temple located on the pyramid's eastern side, and a causeway connecting to a valley temple located farther east of the pyramid. The Great Sphinx stands beside the valley temple and causeway of King Khafre. Subsidiary burials are either in the form of a small pyramid probably intended for a queen or in the form of a *mastaba*—a rectangular stone building constructed on top of where a royal official was buried. Khufu had three subsidiary pyramids and three small towns of *mastabas*. There were also villages near the temples that provided housing for the living members of the staff who performed rituals and completed other tasks at the complex.

The three pyramids vary in height: Khufu, 486 feet (148 m); Khafre, 476 feet (145 m); Menkare, 220 feet (67 m). The differing interior plans of pyramids illustrate the evolution of strategies for hiding the grave goods included with the royal mummies. In spite of security measures, however, all the pyramids were plundered in antiquity. Significant finds within the pyramids include Khufu's unfinished granite sarcophagus still *in situ*, Khafre's polished granite sarcophagus and lid still *in situ*, Menkare's wooden coffin constructed for him by priests of the Twenty-sixth Dynasty (664–525 B.C.) now in the British Museum, and Menkare's original basalt sarcophagus, which was lost at sea during shipment to the British Museum in the mid-nineteenth century.

The plans of all three pyramid temples exhibit variations. Though all three include courtyards, colonnades, statue niches, and storage rooms, these elements are disposed in different ways. A foundation course of one wall of Khufu's valley temple has recently been uncovered, but the full plans of Khafre's and Menkare's valley temples are known. Near the entrance of Khafre's temple, the famous statue of him protected by the Horus falcon (now in the Cairo Museum) was found. The numerous statues of Menkare with nome goddesses, presently divided between the Cairo Museum and the Boston Museum of Fine Arts, were also discovered in his valley temple.

Building Methods. The quarries that yielded the majority of the stone to build the pyramids have been located in the vicinity of Giza by Mark Lehner and Zahi Hawass. The Tura limestone used in the pyramid casings was transported both by boat and by sledges and rollers such as those depicted in the Twelfth Dynasty tomb of Djehutihotep at Bersheh (reigns of Sesostris II and III, ca. 1845–1818 B.C.). The stones were lifted by three basic methods: pulling up inclined planes, lifting with ropes and primitive devices, and levering. There is ample archaeological evidence for each of these methods. Chisel marks and illustrations from the Eighteenth Dynasty tomb of Rekhmire (reign of Thutmose III, ca. 1467–1413 B.C.) demonstrate how masons used hammers, chisels, levels, and simple ropes to dress and measure each stone. Many stone, bronze, and wooden tools for measuring, cutting, and moving stone remain from ancient times to show how the Egyptians accomplished these feats of engineering.

Religious Function. Beyond the most basic use of the pyramids as tombs and repositories for the treasures that the Egyptians believed their kings would need in the next world, the pyramid complex as a whole has been interpreted as the official site for royal funerals and for the continuing worship of the deified kings. Though these two uses are sometimes treated as conflicting, they are probably complementary.

The most important sources for determining the original functions of the temples of the Giza funerary complex are the reliefs that once adorned the buildings; the *Pyramid Texts*, which contain details of the royal burial ritual; and the physical layout of each building. However, this evidence is fragmentary and often difficult to interpret. The reliefs were almost entirely destroyed in antiquity and are known only through reused blocks discovered at other sites. They do not provide direct support for the common hypothesis that the valley temple was the embalming site and the pyramid temple was the funeral site. The *Pyramid Texts* are also problematic evidence, since the only preserved copies date to the late Fifth and early Sixth Dynasties (ca. 2345 B.C.), roughly 200 to 300 years after the construction of the pyramids at Giza. In any case, no single spell of the *Pyramid Texts* can unequivocally be associated with a specific room in the pyramid or valley temple. Finally, the plan of each building is distinctive, suggesting that certain rooms cannot be identified with one particular function. Nevertheless, it is clear, as Dieter Arnold has shown, that the complex was used to preserve the king's physical existence in the next world through offerings to statues and memories of the king's triumph over his enemies through sculptured reliefs. The king's continued royal power was guaranteed through rituals such as the coronation and Heb-sed (royal jubilee) cycle. Finally the king's divinity was ensured through depictions of him in the company of the gods.

Role in Society. The rituals required to maintain the king's memory and divinity at the pyramid complexes in Giza required high officials, lower-level bureaucrats, and workers. Houses were provided to these officials in a village attached to the pyramid complex. Since the king distributed these houses and official positions, the pyramids served as a source of political patronage for their builders and for subsequent kings who appointed new high officials. During the Fourth Dynasty, kings insured the future of their younger sons by providing them with positions of importance in the administration of the pyramid complex. By the Fifth Dynasty, however, these men and women and their descendants were overshadowed by the new bureaucracy of commoners. The original administrators who were certainly moved by piety and gratitude toward the king who built the pyramid were now replaced by bureaucrats whose loyalty was to the living king in the palace, the source of the funds and resources available for maintaining the cult. There is evidence for this change in the administrator's titles, which deemphasize the deceased king as time goes on and in the exemption decrees issued by living kings, allowing certain privileges to the workers at the pyramid town.

In addition to being sources of political power, the pyramid complexes were institutions that made a positive contribution to the economy of the Old Kingdom. They were a means for the king to distribute food and clothing to the peasants who were members of the *phyle*—those rotating groups of men who worked for a month each year at the complex. Though the Egyptians did not consciously conceive of the complexes as public works projects, approximately 1,000 workers were employed there throughout the Fifth and Sixth Dynasties.

The performance of rituals at the pyramid complexes seems to have ended with the Old Kingdom. As the pyramids aged, maintenance of their physical structures lapsed. The buildings were not maintained with respect for the architect's original designs or often even for the original purpose of the building. At the pyramid of Menkare the cult was maintained throughout the Old Kingdom, yet the valley temple very quickly became a home for squatters.

Even though the kings of the New Kingdom (ca. 1552–1069 B.C.) demonstrated an interest in restoring the Sphinx, the pyramids and their associated buildings were never again used for the observance of the mortuary cult.

[*See also* EGYPT, *articles on* OLD KINGDOM EGYPT, PREDYNASTIC CULTURES OF EGYPT.]

■ Ahmed Fakhry, *The Pyramids* (1969). I.E.S. Edwards, *The Pyramids of Egypt* (1972). Dieter Arnold, *Building in Egypt: Pharaonic Stone Masonry* (1991).

Edward Bleiberg

R

RADIOCARBON DATING is an isotopic or nuclear decay method of inferring age for organic materials. The radiocarbon (C^{14}) method provides a common chronometric time scale of worldwide applicability for the Late Pleistocene and Holocene. Radiocarbon measurements can be obtained on a wide spectrum of carbon-containing samples including charcoal, wood, marine and freshwater shell, bone and antler, peat and organic-bearing sediments, as well as carbonate deposits such as marl, tufa, and caliche. With a half-life of approximately 5,700 years, the C^{14} method can be routinely employed in the age range of about 300 to between 40,000 to 50,000 years for sample sizes in the range of 1–10 grams of carbon using conventional decay or beta counting. With isotopic enrichment and larger sample sizes, ages up to 75,000 years have been measured. Accelerator mass spectrometry (AMS) for direct or ion counting of C^{14} permits measurements to be obtained routinely on samples of 1–2 milligrams of carbon—and with additional effort on as little as 50–100 micrograms of carbon—with ages up to between 40,000 and 50,000 years. The use of AMS technology may in the future permit a significant extension of the C^{14} time frame to as much as 80,000 to 90,000 years if stringent requirements for the exclusion of microcontamination in samples can be achieved. The C^{14} dating technique was developed at the University of Chicago immediately following World War II by Willard F. Libby (1908–1980) and his collaborators James R. Arnold and Ernest C. Anderson. Libby received the Nobel Prize in chemistry in 1960 for the development of the method.

The natural production of C^{14} is a secondary effect of cosmic-ray bombardment in the upper atmosphere. Following production, C^{14} is oxidized to form $C^{14}O_2$. In this form, C^{14} is distributed throughout the earth's atmosphere. Most of it is absorbed in the oceans, while a small percentage becomes part of the terrestrial biosphere primarily by means of photosynthesis combined with the distribution of carbon compounds through the different pathways of the carbon cycle. In living organisms, metabolic processes maintain the C^{14} content in equilibrium with atmospheric C^{14}. However, once metabolic processes cease—as at the death of an animal or a plant—the amount of C^{14} will begin to decrease by nuclear decay at a rate measured by the C^{14} half-life.

The radiocarbon age of a sample is based on measurement of its residual C^{14} content. For a C^{14} age to be equivalent to its actual or calendar age at a reasonable level of precision, a set of assumptions must hold within relatively narrow limits. These assumptions include (1) the concentration of C^{14} in each carbon reservoir has remained essentially constant over the C^{14} time scale, (2) there has been complete and relatively rapid mixing of C^{14} throughout the various carbon reservoirs on a worldwide basis, (3) carbon isotope ratios in samples have not been altered except by C^{14} decay since these sample materials ceased to be an active part of one of the carbon reservoirs—as at the death of an organism, (4) the half-life of C^{14} is accurately known with a reasonable precision, and (5) natural levels of C^{14} can be measured to appropriate levels of accuracy and precision.

Radiocarbon age estimates are generally expressed in terms of a set of widely accepted parameters that define a conventional radiocarbon age. These parameters include (1) the use of 5,568 (5,570) years as the C^{14} half-life even though the actual value is probably closer to 5,730 years, (2) to define "zero" C^{14} age, the use of specially prepared oxalic acid or sucrose contemporary standards or a modern standard with a known relationship to the primary standards, (3) the use of A.D. 1950 as the zero point from which to count C^{14} time, (4) a normalization of C^{14} in all samples to a common C^{13}/C^{12} value to compensate for fractionation effects, and (5) an assumption that C^{14} in all reservoirs has remained constant over the C^{14} time scale. Radiocarbon ages are typically cited in "radiocarbon years BP" where BP (or sometimes B.P.) indicates "before present" or more specifically "before A.D. 1950." In addition, a conventional understanding is that each C^{14} determination should be accompanied by an expression that provides an estimate of the experimental or analytical uncertainty. Since statistical constraints associated with the measurement of C^{14} is usually the dominant component of the experimental uncertainty, this value is sometimes informally referred to as the "statistical error." This "$\pm$" term is suffixed to all appropriately documented C^{14} age estimates. Typically, a laboratory sample number designation is also included when a C^{14} age is cited.

For most time periods, conventional radiocarbon ages deviate from "real"—that is, calendar, historical, or sidereal—time. A calibrated radiocarbon age takes into consideration the fact that C^{14} activity in living organisms has not remained constant over the C^{14} time scale. Tests of the validity of the assumption of constant C^{14} concentration in living organics over time initially focused on the analyses of the C^{14} activity of a series of historically and dendrochronologically dated samples. Radiocarbon determinations on several species of tree-ring-dated wood from both North America and Europe have documented a long-term trend and shorter, high-frequency variations in the C^{14} activity over time. For the Early and Middle Holocene, the amount of correction required to "calibrate" a C^{14} date, that is, to bring a conventional C^{14} age determination into alignment with calendar time, does not exceed 1,000 years. For the pre-Holocene period, radiocarbon ages compared with uranium-series ages from marine cores suggest deviations in C^{14} ages for the Late Pleistocene of as much as 3,000 years. The C^{14}/tree-ring data also documents shorter-term, higher-frequency variations in C^{14} activity over time superimposed over the long-term trend. These shorter-term variations, which appear as wiggles, kinks, or windings in the calibration curve, add further complexity to the process of calibrating the C^{14} time scale.

For samples from some carbon reservoirs, conventional contemporary standards may not define a zero C^{14} age. A reservoir-corrected radiocarbon age can sometimes be calculated by documenting the apparent age exhibited in known-age control samples and correcting for the observed deviation. Reservoir effects occur when initial C^{14} activities in samples of identical age but from different carbon reservoirs exhibit significantly different C^{14} concentrations. In some cases, living samples from some environments exhibit apparent C^{14} "ages" due to the fact that a significant percentage of the C^{14} in these samples do not draw their carbon directly from the atmosphere. Reservoir effects can occur in mollusk and other shell materials in both fresh water and marine environments. Examples of other samples influenced by reservoir effects include wood and plant materials growing adjacent to active volcanic fumarole vents or where magmatic fossil CO_2 is being injected directly into lake waters and where plants growing in these lake waters derive all or most of their carbon from the lake waters. Reservoir effects can range from a few hundred to a few thousand years depending upon specific circumstances.

In the first decade following its introduction, C^{14} dating documented the geologically late beginning of the postglacial period at about 10,000 C^{14} years B.P. and the antiquity of agriculture and sedentary village societies in southwestern Asia in the eighth–seventh millennium B.C. Applications of AMS C^{14} technology has permitted the dating of human skeletons from various sites in the Western Hemisphere that had previously been assigned ages in the range of 20,000–70,000 years on the basis of previous C^{14} analysis or the application of other dating techniques such as the amino acid racemization method. AMS C^{14} results on well-characterized organic extracts indicate that the age of all of the human skeletons examined to date do not exceed 11,000 C^{14} years. AMS C^{14} measurements have also been crucial in clarifying controversial age assignments of early domesticated or cultivated plants in both the Old and New World as well as documenting that the "Shroud of Turin" was a medieval artifact.

[See also ARCHAEO-PALEOMAGNETIC DATING; DATING THE PAST; DENDROCHRONOLOGY; FISSION-TRACK DATING; LUMINESCENCE DATING; OBSIDIAN HYDRATION DATING; POTASSIUM-ARGON DATING; SERIATION; STRATIGRAPHY.]

■ W. G. Mook and H. T. Waterbolk, eds., C^{14} and Archaeology (1983). R. Gillespie, Radiocarbon User's Handbook (1984). W. G. Mook and H. T. Waterbolk, Radiocarbon Dating, Handbooks for Archaeologists, No. 3 (1985). J.A.J. Gowlett and R.E.M. Hedges, eds., Archaeological Results from Accelerator Dating (1986). R. E. Taylor, Radiocarbon Dating: An Archaeological Perspective (1987). D. Polach, Radiocarbon Dating Literature: The First 21 Years, 1947–1968 (1988). Martin J. Aitken, Science-Based Dating in Archaeology, Chapters 3 and 4 (1990). S. Bowman, Radiocarbon Dating (1990). R. E. Taylor, A. Long, and R. S. Kra, eds., Radiocarbon After Four Decades: An Interdisciplinary Perspective (1992).

R. E. Taylor

RANKING AND SOCIAL INEQUALITY, Theories of.

The study of ranking and social inequality in archaeology, or more specifically, the search for archaeological evidence of prehistoric status differences, is one of the central themes of modern archaeology. Studies of ranking and social inequality in archaeology are founded on Elman Service's *Primitive Social Organization* (1962) and Morton Fried's *The Evolution of Political Society* (1967). These works demonstrated that different kinds of social organizations, population sizes, and economies often could be correlated with distinct types of status differences. It can generally be assumed that there are not, and probably never were, any societies on earth where there was not at least some social inequality based on age and gender, but some societies transcended this type of organization. Most commonly, there are two kinds of status differences that are investigated in the archaeological record: achieved and ascribed status.

Achieved status is founded in the patterns of social inequality generally associated with egalitarian societies. Among groups that can be classified as egalitarian, status is usually based on age, gender, success as a hunter or warrior, artistic abilities, and other characteristics that one can achieve during a single lifetime. The status that is gained is not usually passed on to one's offspring. Social inequalities that are achieved were probably the most common form of status differences in prehistory yet they are the most difficult to identify archaeologically. This is so because there are no obvious differences in material wealth. In fact, archaeologists generally utilize negative data to identify whether or not a prehistoric society was egalitarian or not. If no material indicators of hereditary status inequalities are found, then the prehistoric society in question is considered to be representative of achieved status.

Mortuary remains are perhaps the most useful indicators of achieved social inequalities. If a large number of burials from a single cemetery are analyzed we would expect that the quality and quantity of goods buried with the individuals would be distributed either by age, with some of the elderly having more grave goods than anyone else, or by gender, with some members of one gender having a greater number or quality of items than those of the other gender, or some combination of the two. If egalitarian, then in no case should the burials of children have fancier or more numerous grave goods than adults. This is similar to the conditions identified by Chester King in his study titled the *Evolution of Chumash Society* (1990). He argued that during the Early Phase in the chronology of the Santa Barbara Channel area of California, clear status differences can be identified based on burial goods. Yet, the differences are seen only in adults, not in juveniles, indicating achieved rather than ascribed status.

The second level of social inequality is often referred to as ranking, or a ranked society. In a ranked society one is born with a status greater or lower than other members of the same group or society. So instead of status differences based on achievements, inequalities are ascribed. These hereditary inequalities have been of much interest to archaeologists over the last twenty years and have generated much discussion in the literature. In fact, the transition from achieved to ascribed status, or from egalitarian to ranked societies, forms the foundation of much modern archaeological thought. There are two important issues in the archaeological study of ascribed social inequalities. The most basic and perhaps the simplest is how to identify ranking in the archaeological record. The second is more difficult and consists of investigating the cultural processes by which groups of people make the transition from a society based on achieved status to one based on ascribed status.

There are several methods archaeologists have developed to identify ranking in the archaeological record. The first is the opposite of the pattern described above. In mortuary data archaeologists look for patterns that may be independent of age or gender. For example, in several recent studies of Middle and Late Period cemeteries of the prehistoric Chumash in the Santa Barbara Channel area, clear ranked status differences were seen based on grave goods. Not only did some adults have much greater wealth and prestige, but there were infants and children with greater wealth than most adults.

A second method, and one which has generated more debate, is based on house size. A common tenet of ranked societies is that the highest-ranking individuals tend to be members of the largest kin group, making it the highest-ranked group as well. The largest group, because of its size, tends to have the largest house. Lightfoot and Feinman used this pattern to identify the possibility of hereditary status differences in the Mogollon region of the southwest. Differential house floor areas have also been used to investigate ranking on the Plateau by Ames and on the Northwest Coast by both Coupland and Maschner.

The last method, and the one that has generated the greatest amount of controversy, is based on corporate construction projects. A good example is Sebastian's study of the development of ranking among the Anasazi of the Chaco Canyon area of New Mexico. During the time of the fluorescence of the Chaco culture, large irrigation systems and extensive road networks were constructed. Sebastian argues that it takes a coordinated leadership to generate enough labor to complete these kinds of facilities and thus, combined with data on the trade of exotic items, considers the Chaco phenomenon to be representative of ranked society.

Much more difficult than the identification of hereditary status differences is defining the processes under which they develop. Processual and functional analyses, combined with the notion that the behaviors which cultures manifest must be adaptive, propose that the kinds of changes that led to hereditary status differences were most often population pressure. It was thought that cultures were basically static and it required some kind of external pressure to change their political organization. Binford (*In Pursuit of the Past*, 1982) argues that imbalances between societies and their landscapes induced adaptive change. Thus, a culture would change to ranked system if it were more adaptive. The need for a new adaptation was usually founded in some notion of population pressure. This entire premise was founded in the notion that egalitarian societies were the normal, expected outcome, and ranked societies were somehow special.

More recent archaeological investigations have argued that egalitarian societies are the exception and ranked societies the normal mode of behavior, at least for the last 10,000 years. This change in thought was spurred by the fact that few human–environment imbalances, the conditions predicted by the former models, could be identified archaeologically. Rather, it seems that individuals within societies strive to increase the status and power of themselves and of their kin groups. Our job as archaeologists is to investigate the conditions under which this occurs. A number of variables that influence how quickly societies will become ranked have been identified. The most important are an abundant resource base and a large base population. Another important characteristic is some sort of environmental

or political condition that circumscribes people in a small area, perhaps in large villages. Under these conditions, individuals usually find a means to create hereditary status differences.

[*See also* BURIAL AND BURIAL TOMBS; MORTUARY ANALYSIS; SOCIAL ORGANIZATION, PREHISTORIC.]

■ Elman Service, *Primitive Social Organization* (1962). Morton Fried, *The Evolution of Political Society* (1967). Lewis R. Binford, *In Pursuit of the Past* (1982). Kent Lightfoot and Gary Feinman, "Social Differentiation and Leadership Development in Early Pithouse Villages in the Mogollan Region of the American Southwest," *American Antiquity* 47:1 (1982): 64–86. P. C. Martz, *Social Dimensions of Chumash Mortuary Populations in the Santa Monica Mountains Region* (1984). Gary Coupland, "Household Variability and Status Differentiation at Kitsdas Canyon," *Canadian Journal of Archaeology* 9 (1985): 39–56. T. D. Price and J. A. Brown, eds., *Prehistoric Hunter-Gatherers: The Emergence of Cultural Complexity* (1985). Kenneth Ames, "Storage, Labor, and Sedentism in the Interior Pacific Northwest" (1988). Chester King, *Evolution of Chumash Society* (1990). Lynn Sebastian, "Sociocultural Complexity and the Chaco System," in *Chaco and Hohokam: Prehistoric Regional Systems in the American Southwest*, ed. P. Crown and W. J. Judge (1991), pp. 109–134. Brian Hayden, *A Complex Culture of the British Columbia Plateau* (1992). Herbert D. G. Maschner, *The Origins of Hunter and Gatherer Sedentism and Political Complexity: A Case Study from the Northern Northwest Coast* (1992). P. K. Wason, *The Archaeology of Rank* (1994). T. D. Price and G. M. Feinman, eds., *Foundation of Social Inequality* (1995).

Herbert D. G. Maschner

RAWLINSON, Henry (1810–1895), was born in Oxfordshire, England. He was appointed an officer cadet in the East India Company in 1827, and soon demonstrated a remarkable ability at languages, mastering five Eastern languages in a very short time. In 1833, he was one of a party of British officers sent to reorganize the shah of Persia's army. Posted to Kurdistan, he decided to attempt a decipherment of King Darius's trilingual inscription on the Great Rock of Behistun, commemorating that monarch's victory over five rebel chiefs. Over the next decade, Sir Henry Creswicke Rawlinson copied and deciphered the Old Persian, Elamite, and Babylonian texts, establishing that Babylonian was a Semitic, polyphonic language. Known as the "Father of Cuneiform," Rawlinson shares credit for the decipherment of cuneiform with Irish cleric Edward Hincks and Frenchman Jules Oppert, who worked on vowels, syllables, and word values. He was appointed British consul in Baghdad in 1843. This gave him ample time to work on cuneiform tablets found by Austen Henry *Layard at Nimrud, and *Nineveh, which he identified as Assyrian cities. In 1850–1851, Layard unearthed Assyrian monarch Assurnasirpal's royal archives at Nineveh. It was Rawlinson who realized the crucial importance of this unique library with its grammars and rich archives and arranged for their study in the British Museum. Rawlinson excavated on his own account but once, at Borsippa near Babylon in southern Mesopotamia in 1853, where he unearthed the commemorative cylinders that recorded how Nebuchadnezzar, king of Babylon, had rebuilt and repaired the temple. He resigned from the East India Company in the same year. In later life, he continued to be active in cuneiform research. Rawlinson fostered long-term research on the Assurnasirpal collection, which yielded the celebrated "Deluge Tablets," deciphered by one of his protégés, George Smith, in 1872.

[*See also* HISTORY OF ARCHAEOLOGY BEFORE 1900: NEAR EASTERN ARCHAEOLOGY; WRITING: CUNEIFORM.]

■ Henry Creswicke Rawlinson, *The Persian Cuneiform Inscriptions at Behistun Deciphered and Translated* (1846). Henry Creswicke Rawlinson, *A Commentary on the Cuneiform Inscriptions of Babylonia and Assyria* (1850). George Rawlinson, *Memoir of Major-General Sir Henry Creswicke Rawlinson* (1889). Seton Lloyd, *Foundations in the Dust* (1980).

Brian M. Fagan

REBURIAL AND REPATRIATION. Repatriation refers to the return of human remains, funerary items, sacred objects, or objects of cultural patrimony to a related individual, group, or nation. Reburial can be seen as a subset of repatriation, referring more specifically to remains that had been excavated or collected at an earlier time and then turned over to a related individual, family, or group to be buried (reburial usually includes human remains but can also incorporate associated grave goods).

There are few issues in archaeology that have been as emotional as those of repatriation and reburial, and while media attention has often focused on the United States, the controversy is international in scope. Sir David M. Wilson, director of the British Museum, documents some of this controversy from a museum's perspective in *The British Museum: Purpose and Politics* (1989). Although the controversy has been heated since the mid-1970s, changes in law and practice have accelerated since the mid-1980s (H. Marcus Price III's 1991 book, *Disputing the Dead*, discusses U.S. laws regarding burial). The essential questions of the debate have been summarized as Who owns the past? or Who controls the past? But because these questions often result in dichotomous answers, they can inflame rather than inform the debate. A more useful way to frame the controversy is to acknowledge that there are a number of ways to interpret the past, and that no one group holds exclusive rights to its interpretation or possession.

Although archaeologists have always understood that there was a great public interest in the past, they sometimes ignored the specific interests and concerns of native peoples in the areas in which they conducted work. Reasons for this exclusion include the fact that many early excavators were nothing more than looters whose goal was to acquire more and more items, often for the great museums of the world. Looting and plundering of graves to study craniology was another now-uncomfortable aspect of early anthropological work. These early approaches are frequently used by activists to demonstrate the need for legal protection and bans on archaeological excavations of grave sites, and historical horror stories of relatives being stolen from graves have won widespread public support for restrictions on archaeological research, as well as for the return of archaeological collections to descendants of past groups.

As much as archaeologists may consider themselves and their discipline as apolitical or above politics, archaeology has historically been used for political purposes from building national pride to creating a heritage, and it has been used to denigrate and trivialize groups who are in the way of development and settlement. It is not a coincidence that repatriation issues are most frequently raised by marginalized people who are trying to gain a voice and power over their fate, including Native American groups in the United States, as well as groups in Israel, Australia, and South Africa. A common denominator in these situations is racism and the view that the past is not part of a country's overall heritage, but is instead categorized by association with particular ethnic identities or races.

More recently, archaeology has focused on scientific methods and more systematic approaches to excavation

and research. Unfortunately, these developments were not accompanied by the development of close relationships with native groups. Better archaeology in the present is not sufficient to make up for the perceived sins of the past and ignoring groups in the present. Native groups have increasingly demanded the repatriation of human remains and sacred objects, as well as protection of grave sites. In many parts of the world, it is now illegal for an archaeologist to excavate a grave site without explicit permits and permissions from potentially related native groups. In the United States, federal legislation passed in 1989 and 1990 (the National Museum of the American Indian Act and the Native American Graves Protection and Repatriation Act [NAGPRA]) orders the Smithsonian Institution, federal agencies, and museums that receive federal funds (this includes virtually all American museums, colleges, and universities) to work with Native American tribes to repatriate some of the collections they hold. NAGPRA also places restrictions on the future disturbance of Native American graves and sacred sites on federal and tribal lands. Because the U.S. laws are among the most extensive in any country, they provide a useful example to highlight some of the concerns expressed by archaeologists in this controversy.

The new laws attempt to correct a historical wrong, and few archaeologists would disagree with this goal. Many human remains and other objects were inappropriately or illegally taken from their native tribes. This practice was routine military procedure in the nineteenth century, and the former U.S. Army Medical Museum had the skeletal remains of hundreds of named or tribally identifiable individuals that have been collected off battlefields or from graves. There is no question that the remains of named individuals or someone clearly identified by tribe should be returned to their descendants. Similarly, there is general agreement that remains and objects taken illegally should be returned.

Once clear association of remains with individuals, families, or tribes is lost, repatriating remains and items is difficult. How does one determine cultural affiliation and the appropriate recipient, and if someone makes a claim, how does one determine whether that is the closest and/or most appropriate claimant? Archaeological, biological, ethnographic, geographic, and historical data, as well as information from oral histories, will be used in making these determinations, and native groups act as key players in the decision-making process. Questions of affiliation are being wrestled with now, and in some areas of the United States the answers are easier than in others. The older the remains and objects, the more problematic the assignment. Beyond human remains, there may also be problems in identifying and affiliating funerary objects, objects of cultural patrimony, and sacred objects. Funerary objects are generally identifiable as such, dependent upon the context of collecting and record keeping. Objects of cultural patrimony are clearly defined as objects whose title is held communally such that an individual cannot lawfully transfer this title; examples include Zuñi war gods and Iroquois wampum belts, but there are objects whose identification is less certain. Sacred objects are probably the most problematic category, since they are not clearly defined by law. As of early 1994, the repatriation process was just beginning, and it is still unclear how some of the issues will be resolved.

Another concern is for future study. When something is repatriated, and particularly when it is reburied, it is no longer available for study. One of the ways that science develops is by restudying material. If gone, it cannot be examined or compared with new finds. While data can be recorded, we do not know the questions that may be important in the future. Who would have thought, even ten years ago, that extracting DNA from ancient bone was a realistic possibility? For bones that have been reburied, that possibility is gone.

A final concern is how relationships between archaeologists and native groups can and should develop. Although many on both sides of the issue are skeptical, the repatriation issue has provided a series of opportunities. The protection of graves and sacred sites will allow us to be better stewards of the past, and will save some of that past for future generations. Archaeologists should now focus on sharing their knowledge directly with the people they study, defending their research, and explaining its relevance to native groups. There is much potential for mutual benefit, partnerships, meaningful dialogue, and mutually rewarding interaction. When native groups and archaeologists learn that they have something to teach one another, our understanding of the past is sure to increase.

[See also ARCHAEOLOGY IN THE CONTEMPORARY WORLD; NON-WESTERN SOCIETIES, ARCHAEOLOGY AND, articles on ARCHAEOLOGY AND AFRICAN SOCIETIES, ARCHAEOLOGY AND AUSTRALIAN ABORIGINES, ARCHAEOLOGY AND NATIVE AMERICANS; POLITICAL USES OF ARCHAEOLOGY.]

■ Bruce Trigger, A History of Archaeological Thought (1989). Lynne Goldstein and Keith Kintigh, "Ethics and the Reburial Controversy," American Antiquity 55 (1990): 585–591. Mark P. Leone and Parker B. Potter Jr., "Legitimation and the Classification of Archaeological Sites," American Antiquity 57 (1992): 137–145. Clement W. Meighan, "Some Scholars' Views on Reburial," American Antiquity 57 (1992): 704–710. Anthony Klesert and Shirley Powell, "A Perspective on Ethics and the Reburial Controversy," American Antiquity 58 (1993): 348–354.

Lynne Goldstein

RELIGION is a common if not universal feature of human societies, past and present. Its remains, in the form of icons, shrines, temples, and churches, form a conspicuous part of the archaeological record. It is recognized as one of the most powerful forces operating on individuals and societies, one which can stimulate them to acts of great enterprise or great cruelty. Yet much of what we know of early religions is derived not from archaeology alone, but from the written documents that are associated with it. In a prehistoric context, where textual evidence is unavailable, the archaeologist is faced with the very difficult task of endeavoring to infer religious beliefs from material remains. Thus the archaeological study of religion may properly be divided into two parts: (1) in early historic societies, where archaeology provides valuable information that can be used in association with textual records to provide a richly textured and multidimensional picture of religious beliefs and practices; and (2) in prehistoric contexts, where archaeology may be able to tell us relatively little about specific religious *beliefs*, but can document religious *practices*, insofar as these have left material traces.

Religion may be defined as the belief in, worship of, or obedience to a supernatural power or powers considered to be divine or to have control of human destiny. But while belief lies at the basis of religion, it is the institutionalized expression of that belief which gives religion its form and substance. Most religions involve ceremonies or ritual that take place in specified places, some of which may be specially constructed buildings, although natural features such as rocks and springs are also frequently endowed with religious significance. Wherever regular religious practices are performed, there is the potential for archaeologists to identify and interpret the traces of these activities. This is all the more the case where there are intentional modifications of the landscape such as rock paintings, monuments, or shrines.

Early Evidence for Religious Belief. Despite claims for linguistic competence in chimpanzees, there has been no serious suggestion that these or any other animal species hold beliefs that could be described as religious. The development of religious belief is most likely associated with the cognitive changes involved in the evolution of modern humans. It is difficult to locate the origin of religion in simple chronological terms. We do not know whether it emerged suddenly once a particular cognitive threshold was reached, or whether it formed through a more gradual process as human intellect developed stage by stage. The controversy here parallels the argument over the origin of language, where some argue for a sudden acquisition of language skills within the last 100,000 years, while others prefer to envisage a gradual refinement of modern human language from more primitive forms of communication used by early hominids.

The earliest hard information on the religious dimension to human behavior comes from two categories of archaeological evidence from the Middle and Upper Paleolithic: artistic representations and burial practices. Both are hazardous to interpret.

Paleolithic art includes both portable objects, such as anthropomorphous figurines, and paintings or engravings on the walls of caves or rock shelters. There are claims for early examples of portable Paleolithic art dating back to before 100,000 years ago, but most of the evidence for both portable and mobiliary art comes from within the last 50,000 years. Here are included the so-called *Venus figurines (female figurines) from Europe, painted stone plaques from southern Africa, early engravings at rock shelters in Australia, and the famous Paleolithic decorated caves of western Europe. It is widely accepted that much of this art has religious significance, but the precise nature of that significance is unclear. The Venus figurines have been interpreted as evidence of a cult of human fertility, although they depict the entire spectrum of female anatomical development from young girls through puberty to pregnancy and beyond. Only a few have the distended bellies which might be taken to indicate pregnant individuals.

The cave art of western Europe has most frequently been viewed as a kind of hunting magic, since hunted animals such as bison and horses figure conspicuously among the subjects depicted. A few may even have missiles drawn on them along with marks that may represent wounds. Others, conversely, have interpreted the art in structuralist terms, the different species representing male and female principles, or as a metaphor for human social organization, with particular species serving as the symbols of individual social groups.

Whether the European cave art was the focus for religious ceremonies is uncertain, though there is indeed some evidence which points in that direction. Studies have shown that the places chosen for the most vivid images were often those with particular acoustic properties, suggesting that music or chanting could have played a part in whatever rituals were practiced. On the other hand, it must be recognized that the art is also found in secluded niches and other more private places within the caves which would not have been suitable for group ceremonies.

The second category of Paleolithic evidence relating to religious belief is funerary. The earliest human burials are those from the Qafzeh cave in Israel, where at least three humans of modern type (Homo sapiens sapiens) were laid to rest in shallow pits around 100,000 years ago. Further burials are associated with Neanderthal remains in Europe and the Near East. The act of burial may in itself be considered to have religious significance, although it does not necessarily imply belief in a life after death. These early burials are all inhumations; the first cremation, from the south Australian site of Lake Mungo, dates to around 26,000 B.C. In many cultures, cremation is believed to be necessary in order to free the soul of the deceased from the dead body. Whether the people who cremated their dead at Lake Mungo shared this belief we cannot determine.

Shamanism and Rock Art. Anthropology provides an alternative route for the study of early religious beliefs. The work of Mircea Eliade and others has shown that among hunter-gatherers, the commonest form of religious expression is shamanism. Shamans are ritual specialists who are possessed of special powers and who act as intermediaries between humans and the shadowy world of spirits and the supernatural. In order to communicate with the spirit world the shaman has to enter a trance, sometimes induced by narcotics or hypnotic dance, in order to experience visions or hallucinations.

From ethnographic evidence we know that shamanism may sometimes be directly associated with rock art. The connection has been demonstrated clearly in the case of the rock art of western North America, where the motifs painted on rock faces can be matched specifically with shamanistic beliefs known from the ethnographic literature of the region. In cases such as this, the archaeologist can have reasonable confidence that there has been continuity in belief and religious practice over a period of hundreds, if not thousands, of years. Individual sites and objects can then be interpreted in the light of these ethnographically documented belief systems. A striking example is the appearance in Australian rock art of figures identifiable from current aboriginal beliefs, such as the rainbow serpent Gorrondolmi and his wife depicted at the 6,000-year-old site of Wirlin-Gunyang.

The problem of interpretation becomes much more difficult where there is no directly connected ethnographic information. It has been argued, for instance, that the cave art of the western European Paleolithic also relates to a pattern of shamanistic beliefs concerned with hunting magic. This interpretation has not as yet found general acceptance among cave art specialists.

Shrines and Temples. Among the most obvious material traces of religious activity are the remains of shrines and other specially demarcated areas or buildings intended specifically for religious practice. Here we may distinguish between human-made structures and the concept of the numinous landscape—where natural features such as springs, trees, or rocks are held to have particular religious significance. Australian aborigines, for example, regard particular natural features as some of their most sacred sites. It is only those who have knowledge of these features who can identify them; to those without this knowledge they appear simply as natural features. As an intermediate category between such sites and human-made shrines and temples we may consider natural features that have been intentionally modified as a result of their special significance. Famous examples include the natural cave beneath the Pyramid of the Sun at *Teotihuacán in Mexico, which made the city a center of pilgrimage for the whole region; or the most recent cave-shrine of Lourdes in the French Pyrenees, associated with the Christian cult of the Virgin Mary.

The oldest human-built structures intended for ritual activity date back less than 10,000 years. The recognition of individual ritual sites does however require two major assumptions on the part of the archaeologist: first, that we are correctly recognizing in these sites the traces of ritual behavior; and second, that the nature of these sites was such that they can justifiably be described as largely or exclusively ritual. The whole division of human behavior into a series of subsystems, such as economic, technological, or religious, is a heuristic device made by archaeologists for the sake of convenience. In everyday life, there are no sharp divisions between these different categories of behavior, and many ordinary dwelling houses will contain items or features relating to ritual or religious belief, such as statues or icons. Where we are faced with a major monument such as a Mesopotamian ziggurat or a Mesoamerican temple-pyramid the identification as a shrine may be relatively straightforward. Where a less distinctive structure is concerned, however, it may be difficult to determine with confidence whether it is a shrine.

A good example of this difficulty is provided by the site of *Çatal Hüyük in southern Turkey. Excavations at this large Neolithic tell site occupied around 6000 B.C. exposed a closely packed settlement in which houses were built up against each other, leaving only occasional courtyards open to the sky. Within the complex, almost one third of the rooms had mural decoration or benches suggestive of ritual function. One of the rooms had a wall painting showing a scene of vultures devouring headless corpses; in another was a mural sculpture of a goddess giving birth to a ram. These rooms may have been shrines, implying a very high percentage of ritual space in the settlement as a whole; or they may simply have been richly decorated domestic dwellings in which ritual played a prominent role.

With the emergence of state formations we are on somewhat firmer ground, since most state-level societies devoted considerable effort to the construction of impressive religious monuments. In early Mesopotamia, the city-states were each dedicated to a particular deity or pair of deities, under whose special protection the city was considered to lie. The city of *Ur, for example, was dedicated to the mood god Nanna and his female consort, and it was to Nanna that the famous ziggurat built at Ur around 2100 B.C. was dedicated.

The resources of the state lay behind great building projects such as this, and the temple itself was a wealthy and powerful institution in the early state societies of Mesoamerica, the Near East, and Egypt. The temple was closely associated with the secular power of the ruler, who was also usually high priest, and in some societies was himself regarded as a living god. The division between religious and secular authority was merged in a system where each supported the other. State cults, as well as attracting popular adherents, can also be tools used by secular rulers for propaganda purposes.

Beneath the level of institutionalized state religion, however, lesser cults retained their popularity among the ordinary people, who might leave offerings at small wayside altars or domestic shrines. Excavations at ancient city sites have sometimes enabled archaeologists to document the popularity of these lesser cults in the form of figurines or other tokens. These may be related to beliefs or deities about which the ancient texts are silent. Archaeology is thus able to provide a counterbalance to the emphasis in surviving texts on established state-sponsored cults. The same is true of African religious beliefs, which survived, often in secrecy, alongside official Christianity on North American slave plantations.

Cosmology and Religions. In a world without electric lights, and in regions where cloudless skies are common, the night sky would have made a powerful impression on people's understanding of their place in the cosmos. This is borne out by evidence which shows that astronomical observations played a crucial part in the religious beliefs of many early societies. It has long been established that many important ritual or religious monuments were carefully aligned on solar, lunar, or stellar events, often to an astonishingly high degree of accuracy. The *pyramids of Giza in Egypt, for example, were carefully aligned according to cardinal points, since one version of Egyptian mythology held that the king ascended after death to the circumpolar stars; the shaft from the burial chamber exited in the middle of the pyramid's northern face. Claims for an important astronomical link have also been made with respect to the stone circles of northwestern Europe. According to Alexander Thom and his followers these were carefully constructed so as to include alignments directed toward the rising and setting of the sun, moon, and major stars. Not everybody accepts the postulated lunar and stellar alignments, but the solar alignment is clearly in evidence at some sites. Even today, many people gather at *Stonehenge in southern England at the time of the summer solstice to watch the dawn sun rising above the Heel Stone on the main axis of the stone circle.

Astronomical alignments such as these are probably evidence of a particular set of beliefs concerning human origins and the place of humankind in the whole order of things. This area of belief is closely akin to religion but usually goes under the name of cosmology. In archaeological contexts, cosmology can be inferred—with caution—from the orientation of buildings. This is seen very strikingly in the planning of historical Chinese cities, where rectangular plans were preferred with the principal streets oriented according to the cardinal points. The Chinese view was that, properly organized, earth and heaven formed a geometric and harmonious whole.

Cosmological considerations were also very prominent in urban societies of Central America, and especially in that of the Maya. It has long been known that Maya astronomy was highly sophisticated. Recent work has emphasized how closely this was linked with their mythology. Maya texts tell the mythical story of the creation in terms of stars and constellations visible in the night sky. For example, they believed that the Milky Way as it is visible on August 12 was a vast canoe, paddled by gods who used it to ferry First Father (the maize god) to the place where he would be reborn from the three "hearthstones," which are popularly known today as Orion's belt. Figures from this story from the night sky were regularly depicted in Maya art, but it is only with the aid of the texts and the understanding of Maya cosmology that these can be understood.

Iconography. Religious observances frequently focus on an image or symbol of the supernatural power that is the subject of worship. Furthermore, religious mythology often features prominently in artistic depictions. Together, these tendencies may result in a rich corpus of religious iconography that is open to the archaeologist to study and interpret. Where texts are available, it may be possible to say which being or power is represented; it is most convenient of all where, as in many Egyptian scenes from tombs or temples, the name of the god or goddess is written alongside the depiction. In other cases, detailed studies of the iconography allow a pantheon of deities to be recognized, even though no names can be attached.

The discovery of religious iconography is one of the key categories of evidence that enables archaeologists to identify a room or building as a shrine or temple. In Europe and the Near East, the focus of worship was often a cult image that served as substitute for the deity itself; one of the most splendid examples was the cult statue of Zeus which was made for the temple of the god at Olympia in Greece, home of the original Olympic Games. The seated statue, made of gold and ivory, rose to a height of 43 feet (13 m) in the shadowy rear part of the temple; light from the main door was reflected onto it by a shallow pool of oil at its foot.

In other cases, it may not be so easy to distinguish between divine and human forms. At Tell Asmar in Iraq, a cache of ten alabaster statues was found beneath the floor of a temple. The statues were similar in style and manufacture, and most were interpreted as substitute-figures of worshipers, designed to remind the god of their needs even when they themselves were busy elsewhere. Two of the group were larger, however, and on grounds of their size and of the symbols carved on their bases it was suggested that they might be cult statues of the god and goddess themselves. Others have argued that these too are simply representations of worshipers. This case illustrates once again the difficulty of interpreting religious evidence. Nonetheless, in many religious scenes supernatural figures are carefully distinguished from ordinary mortals by size, by coloring, by the addition of special attributes (such as horns in Mesopotamia, or wings in the Christian tradition), or by their depiction in nonhuman or only partly human guise.

Funerary Beliefs. A final and highly important category of religious evidence is that from burials. One of the major themes of religion is the destiny of humans after death. Most societies possess some belief in a life after death, and this finds reflection in burial rites and cemetery evidence. An extreme case is that of ancient Egypt, where the literal nature of the belief led to extensive efforts to preserve the body of the deceased by mummification. If the body were not preserved, then, according to Egyptian belief, the chances of an afterlife were seriously impaired.

The Egyptian evidence also shows clearly how the form of the burial monument itself can be a powerful religious symbol. The pyramid form beloved of Egyptian rulers during the Old and Middle Kingdoms is thought to have represented the slanting rays of the sun, and indicates the importance of the cult of the sun in the religious beliefs associated with kingship. The Pyramid Texts, magical spells inscribed on the walls of the later Old Kingdom pyramids, suggest that the pyramid was to be seen as a material representation of the sun's rays, on which the dead king would ascend to heaven.

A more contentious subject is the purpose of grave goods

left with the dead. Where these take the form of food remains and feasting equipment, it can be argued that the grave goods were needed for the corpse's sustenance after death. The same applies to burial places that were built to resemble houses, and were presumably regarded as the dwelling place of the dead person's spirit. Many funerary mythologies incorporate the concept of a journey, and here again food or money might be left with the dead people to support them on their journey. A related practice is the placement in the grave of objects signifying the person's rank in society, the intention being to ensure their admission to the correct social rank in the afterlife. At this point, however, interpretation becomes hazardous, since death is an emotive event for those left alive and showing respect to the dead need by no means imply belief in a life after death.

Conclusion. A short account such as this cannot fully do justice to the great diversity of religious belief and the many ways in which it may be manifest in the archaeological record. Where adequate information exists, it is without doubt one of the most fascinating aspects of human behavior. This is particularly the case for more recent, historical periods, where texts and archaeology together form a powerful and mutually reinforcing combination for the study of religious beliefs and practices. It is only archaeology, however, that can document the silent millennia in the early history of religion, stretching back, deep into the prehistoric past.

[*See also* ART; ASTRONOMY; CHRISTIANITY, EARLY; DEAD SEA SCROLLS; IDEOLOGY AND ARCHAEOLOGY; INCA CIVILIZATION: INCA RELIGION; ISLAMIC CIVILIZATION; MAYA CIVILIZATION: MAYA PYRAMIDS AND TEMPLES; ROCK ART: INTRODUCTION; VENUS FIGURINES.]

■ H. Frankfort, H. A. Frankfort, J. A. Wilson, and T. Jacobsen, *Before Philosophy* (1946). I.E.S. Edwards, *The Pyramids of Egypt* (1961). M. Eliade, *Shamanism: Archaic Techniques of Ecstasy* (1964). P. Wheatley, *The Pivot of the Four Quarters* (1971). L. E. Sullivan, *Icanchu's Drum: An Orientation to Meaning in South American Religions* (1988). D. S. Whitley, "Shamanism and Rock Art in Far Western North America," *Cambridge Archaeological Journal* 2 (1992): 89–113. D. Friedel, L. Schele, and J Parker, *Maya Cosmos: Three Thousand Years on the Shaman's Path* (1993). C. E. Orser, "The Archaeology of African American Slave Religion in the Antebellum South," *Cambridge Archaeological Journal* 4 (1994): 33–45.

Chris Scarre

REMOTE SENSING. *See* SITE LOCATION: REMOTE SENSING AND GEOPHYSICAL PROSPECTION.

RESCUE ARCHAEOLOGY. *See* CULTURAL RESOURCE MANAGEMENT.

REPLICATION. *See* EXPERIMENTAL ARCHAEOLOGY.

ROCK ART

INTRODUCTION

Rock art, sensu stricto, denotes any form of artistic activity on rock. Its principal categories are pictographs (applica-

tion of pigment), petroglyphs (motifs carved into rock), and engravings (incisions), but there are also less common types such as petroforms (the laying out of rocks to form patterns) and geoglyphs (the removal of surface material to form patterns on the ground).

Rock art of some kind is known to exist in almost every country, with a few exceptions (such as Holland and Poland). It is found in the open air, in rock shelters, in caves, and inside stone monuments such as the megaliths of western *Europe. The vast majority of surviving rock art is prehistoric, though in many parts of the world it continued to be made into historic times. In a few areas (notably Australia) the tradition still survives, but in most cultures it persists today only in the form of graffiti.

The motifs can generally be divided into four kinds: zoomorphs (animals and birds), anthropomorphs (human or humanlike figures), objects (such as tools or weapons), and nonfigurative or abstract designs. Naturally, all of these may be found on the same panel, though it is not always easy to tell whether they were all produced at the same time and whether they are in association with each other or form meaningful scenes. The figures may be drawn realistically, schematically, or in a highly stylized way. They may be complete, unfinished, or abbreviated; easily accessible or very remote; isolated or grouped together. There is seldom any concern for scale or ground lines, or sometimes even for orientation. In some places, motifs are superimposed on each other, in others they seem to avoid each other.

For most of this century, interpretations of rock art were simplistic, ranging from "art for art's sake" (i.e., meaningless play and doodlings) to sympathetic magic aimed at improving fertility or success in the hunt. A great deal of wishful thinking was involved in such notions; improved ethnographic data together with a more detailed and objective appraisal of the rock art itself have led to the realization that the thought processes behind it were often extraordinarily complex. Scholars around the world are currently pursuing a wide variety of themes, with some focusing on archaeoastronomy or notation and others on evidence for shamanism and trance phenomena, and all relying heavily on extrapolating ethnography through space and time (*see* Astronomy *and* Ethnoarchaeology).

The chronological dimension of rock art was hard to discern until recently. Most rock art could not be dated directly unless a covering archaeological layer provided a minimum age. Stylistic dating was widely used, comparing rock art with dated portable images, and studies of superimposition were the chief means of placing different styles into a temporal sequence. All of this was somewhat subjective and uncertain. Recent advances in science have allowed extremely detailed analyses to be made of tiny amounts of pigment, and the organic materials often revealed by such analyses (in paint, or in the rock varnish covering petroglyphs) can now be placed in time through *radiocarbon dating, thanks to accelerator mass spectrometry, which requires only minute samples. It now seems that the production of rock art (in Australia, at least) stretches back over 40,000 years, and that cave art in western Europe dates back at least 27,000 years. Such analyses and dating will snowball over the next few years, tapping into a huge body of hitherto neglected data. It has already become clear that the accumulation of images on a panel or in a cave is far more complex than had been supposed, often involving multiple artistic episodes and spanning a very long period of time.

Rock art is of enormous importance to archaeology, not

only because of its chronological and geographical spread but also because of its content. It is rock art that provides us with depictions of animal species that are now extinct or no longer inhabit an area, such as elephants in the Sahara, and with depictions and sometimes, as in Australia, even actual-size stencils of tools, weapons, vessels, and vehicles—objects that do not normally survive in the archaeological record. It supplies images of human activities, clothing, and ornamentations as well as stencils of human hands and even human portraits. Rock art provides our most direct insights into the mind and the religion of ancient peoples, into their preoccupations and beliefs.

[*See also* ART; NOTATION, PALEOLITHIC; RELIGION.]

■ Paul G. Bahn, *Rock Art Research* (since 1984). *The International Newsletter of Rock Art* (since 1992). *The Cambridge Illustrated History of Prehistoric Art* (1997).

Paul G. Bahn

ROCK ART OF SOUTHERN AFRICA

Southern Africa has been called the richest storehouse of rock art in the world. Certainly, the number of sites with rock paintings (pictographs) and rock engravings (petroglyphs) run into untold thousands. Rock paintings are found, principally, in the open rock shelters of the mountainous regions skirting the high central plateau. On the plateau, where there are far fewer rock shelters, there are comparatively few rock paintings but large numbers of rock engravings. Rock engravings are hammered, incised, or scraped into rocks and boulders on the tops of low rises or, in some instances, into flat glacial pavements exposed in riverbeds.

Apart from geographical location and technique of manufacture, there are other differences between the two art forms. Generally speaking, among the paintings, depictions of human beings outnumber those of animals; geometric motifs are rare. Human and animal images are often arranged in what appear to be scenes. In contrast, there are very few rock engravings depicting human beings; animal depictions far outnumber them. Moreover, there is a high percentage of geometric motifs among the rock engravings; some sites comprise almost entirely geometrics. Finally, there are very few engraved scenes.

The dating of these rock paintings and engravings has, as in other parts of the world, proved difficult. The oldest date so far obtained for rock paintings comes from southern Namibia, where six portable pieces of stone with paintings were found in an excavated stratum that was dated by radiocarbon to approximately 27,000 B.P. At the other end of the time scale, the most recent art was made at the end of the nineteenth century and perhaps in the first decade of the twentieth century. Various paintings and engravings have been dated to periods between these two extremes. Certainly as far as the rock paintings are concerned, most of those done in the sandstone rock shelters of the southeastern mountains, one of the most densely painted areas, cannot be more than, say, 800 years old. Their deterioration over even a few decades has been noticeable.

The comparatively recent date implied by the deterioration of the paintings suggests that the beliefs and cosmology of the various San (also known as Bushmen) groups will provide a clue to the meaning of the art. By far the majority of the paintings and engravings were made by San hunter-gatherers. Black Bantu-speaking farmers made some clearly different rock art, but some of them probably understood

much about San art. The San who made rock art no longer exist as functioning communities, and the groups that survive in the Kalahari Desert of Namibia and Botswana have no tradition of rock art. However, thanks chiefly to the work of Wilhelm Bleek (1827–1875) and Lucy Lloyd (1834–1914), we know that the southern people who made much of the art had beliefs and rituals very similar to those still surviving among the Kalahari people.

For many decades these records of San beliefs were ignored, and researchers tended to guess what the art meant. Art for art's sake, sympathetic hunting magic, and the chronicling of events were all suggested as possible explanations. Since the late 1970s, when researchers began to study San beliefs, there has been a move away from these explanations and toward acceptance of the religious content and function of both the engravings and the paintings.

San religion is essentially shamanistic. San shamans, who may number as many as half the men and a third of the women in a camp, enter trance at large, communal curing, or "medicine," dances. The shamans of the southern groups were believed to perform various tasks while they were in trance. Some shamans made rain, others cured the sick, while still others guided antelope into the waiting hunters' ambush. A few shamans were believed to shoot "arrows of sickness" into people.

To enter trance, San shamans activated a supernatural potency that was believed to reside in various things, especially in the eland, the largest African antelope and, in many areas, the most frequently painted or engraved animal. The eland was also associated with girls' puberty rituals, boys' first-kill observances, and marriage rites. Depictions of eland thus probably had many associations, though their principal association was shamanistic potency. Other kinds of depictions represent shamanic rituals and hallucinations. Some of the images of visions show shamans partially transformed into animals. The art was thus principally, though not exclusively, associated with the spirit world.

When, toward the end of the nineteenth century, colonial expansion began to destroy the San way of life, traditional beliefs and art helped them to cope with the new threat. Paintings of farmers with horses, rifles, and wagons are sometimes accompanied by shamanic elements. In the face of the rifles, the traditional shaman defenses against evil were impotent and the San communities were destroyed and the art came to an end.

[*See also* ART.]

■ Patricia Vinnicombe, *People of the Eland* (1976). J. David Lewis-Williams, *Believing and Seeing* (1981). J. David Lewis-Williams and Thomas A. Dowson, *Images of Power* (1989). Harald Pager, *Rock Paintings of the Upper Brandberg* (1989). Thomas A. Dowson, *Rock Engravings of Southern Africa* (1992).

J. David Lewis-Williams

ALPINE ROCK ART

Most of the Alpine chain of European mountains is limestone and other calcareous rock, which breaks and cracks under the pressure of ice. In a very few regions, the rock is metamorphic sandstone or schist, the surfaces of which the glaciers have ground smooth, sometimes highly polished and bright red in color. With a warmer climate after the end of the last ice age, the retreat of the glaciers to higher altitudes left these inviting surfaces open to prehistoric people, who carved into them many thousands of little pictures. The figures are usually pecked into the rock by hammering with a stone and the image is built up from a great many tiny pits, and pockmarks. A few are engraved in a thin line, apparently made with a fine metal or flint tool.

The great center of Alpine rock art is Valcamonica, a long and narrow valley of northern Italy that runs south from the high Alps out to the Po plain near Brescia. Along its length are many great panels, a few still exposed, most covered with a natural buildup of earth and mold accumulated since their carving. The Camonica sandstone is dark, nearly black in color; the carvings show up in glancing light, or when specially treated with white pigment for exact recording. Exploration of Valcamonica from the mid-1950s to the 1980s has so far revealed many thousands of figures. There are more figures in the Valtellina, a neighboring valley. A smaller focus is Mont Bégo, on the French–Italian border above Nice, where the carvings are cut into red schist on the high slopes of a 9,520-foot (2,900 m) mountain. One group of figures that were under a sheltered rock on Mont Bégo was painted, suggesting that perhaps all the engravings were colored. Other scattered engravings occur in Switzerland and Austria.

The earliest of the Valcamonica carvings are a few large, elongated animals, characteristic of upper Paleolithic art of the immediate postglacial period. The "Valcamonica cycle" includes artifacts that are characteristic of Neolithic times and the Bronze and Iron Ages that indicate the conquest of the valley and its incorporation into the Roman Empire. With the coming of a literate civilization in Rome, the picture-making tradition died. Among the last scribbled figures are shapes resembling letters, but which are undecipherable.

Outstanding among the Valcamonica figures are pictures of metal objects, especially halberds and daggers of the first metal age in the Alps. In Valcamonica, and also on Mont Bégo, the halberd is the common object—a metal dagger-like blade, but hafted at right angles to the shaft like an axe. Yet the Copper or Bronze Age halberd is rare as a physical artifact unearthed by excavation. Perhaps the pictured halberds were of wood, and have perished. Perhaps the Alpine engravings picture a prehistoric society in images it held important. Both in Valcamonica and on Mont Bégo there are complex geometrical shapes; their lines connect enclosed areas left blank or marked with patterns of dots; suggesting maps of Bronze Age Alpine farmers. Wheeled vehicles are effectively depicted in a kind of broken perspective showing each component from its characteristic direction and representing the earliest evidence for wheeled vehicles in western Europe. Other recurrent images are pairs of feet (a motif shared with the contemporary rock engravings of Scandinavia), but it is hard to know what they stood for in the ancient order of things. The ox team drawing the plow and the ox alone are common motifs in the Bégo figures, showing their power and importance in the peasant life of the valley. Incidentally, the figures give exact pictures of physical structures like the houses, set tall on poles with high ridged roofs, of prehistoric Valcamonica, which closely resemble what we know of *palafitte*, the dwellings built in the shallow waters and swampy edges of the Alpine lakes. The later figures of the Iron Age, commonly only a few centimeters high, are full of conflict and war. Men wearing crested helmets like those known from Etruscan Italy fight in hand-to-hand combat with sword and shield. Other warriors, shown with strong massive bodies, ride horses and brandish long spears.

The imagery of the engravings on these bedrock surfaces is shared by the statue stele, portable stone blocks a meter or two high with engravings carved into them, which concentrate in a little area south of Valcamonica and are found sporadically across the northern Mediterranean region. These, mostly of Copper Age date, help to tide the evidence of the rock engravings into the conventional evidence, the flints, pots, animal bones, and rare metal artifacts, of the region's other archaeological sites. A revival in carving statue stele during the Iron Age, and their occasional association with Christian churches, show that some knowledge of the old ways lingered or was remade.

■ E. Anati, *Camonica Valley* (1961).

Christopher Chippindale

PALEOLITHIC ART

The existence of Paleolithic art was first established and accepted through the discovery of portable decorated objects in a number of caves and rock shelters in southwest France in the early 1860s. There could be no doubt that the objects were ancient, being associated with Paleolithic tools and the bones of Ice Age animals. Some depicted species (e.g., mammoth) that were extinct or others (e.g., reindeer) that had long ago deserted this part of the world.

Distribution. These first discoveries triggered a treasure hunt for ancient art objects in caves and shelters. A small number of people noticed drawings on the cave walls, but thought little of them. The first real claim for the existence of Paleolithic cave art was that made in 1880 for the Spanish cave of *Altamira by a local landowner, de Sautuola. His views were treated with skepticism by the archaeological establishment, because nothing similar had previously been reported, and almost all known portable art had come from France. The rejection of Altamira persisted for twenty years until a breakthrough was made at the cave of La Mouthe (Dordogne) where, in 1895, the removal of some fill had exposed an unknown gallery, the walls of which had engravings including a bison figure. Because of Paleolithic deposits in the blocking fill, it was clear that the pictures must be ancient. Finally, in 1901, engravings were found in the cave of Les Combarelles (Dordogne) and paintings in the nearby cave of Font de Gaume. In 1902 the existence of cave art was officially recognized by the archaeological establishment.

Once again, a kind of "gold rush" ensued, with numerous new sites and galleries being found. Discoveries still continue; in France and Spain, even today, an average of one new site is found every year—most recently the magnificent Grotte Chauvet in the Ardèche, with its unusually numerous and prominent figures of rhinos and big cats. Subsequently, rock art of similar antiquity has been discovered in many other parts of the world as well.

Portable art or *art mobilier* is found from the Iberian Peninsula and North Africa to Siberia, and has notable concentrations in western, central, and eastern Europe. Thousands of specimens are known, and though some sites yield few or none, others contain hundreds or even thousands of items of portable art.

The distribution of cave art (*art pariétal*) is equally patchy, though it is most abundant in areas that are also rich in decorated objects: the Périgord, the French Pyrenees, and Cantabrian Spain. Paleolithic decorated caves are found from Portugal and the very south of Spain to the north of France. Traces have been found in southwest Germany, and there are concentrations in Italy and Sicily. A handful of caves are also known in Yugoslavia, Romania, and Russia.

The current total for Eurasia is about 280 sites. Some contain only one or a few figures on the walls, whereas others like *Lascaux or Les Trois Frères have hundreds. However, in recent years it has become apparent that Paleolithic people also produced rock art in the open air, where it has survived in exceptional circumstances: Six sites have so far been found in Spain, Portugal, and the French Pyrenees with engravings that are Paleolithic in style. So cave art is not typical of the period; caves are merely the places where most art has survived.

Methods of Dating. Dating portable objects is easy, since their position in the stratigraphy of a site, together with the associated tools, gives some idea of the cultural phase involved, and radiocarbon dating of organic material from these levels, or even from the art objects themselves, can give more precise results.

Dating parietal art was, until recently, far more difficult. Where the caves were blocked during or just after the Ice Age, or where parts of the decorated walls themselves are covered by datable Paleolithic deposits, a minimum age can be established. There are also cases where a fragment of decorated wall has fallen and become stratified in the archaeological layers, though this provides an approximate date for the art's fall rather than its execution. Some caves contain occupation deposits that may plausibly be linked with art production (e.g., through the presence of coloring materials). If a site with parietal art has also produced stratified portable art, there are sometimes clear analogies between the two in technique and style, providing a fairly reliable date for the wall decoration.

For the many caves without occupation or portable art, it became necessary to seek stylistic comparison with material from other sites and even other regions, which led inevitably to subjectivity and simplistic schemes of development, since all stylistic arguments are based on an assumption that figures similar in style or technique were roughly contemporaneous in their execution.

The first such scheme was put forward by the abbé Henri *Breuil, who based it primarily on the presence or absence of "twisted perspective," a feature he considered primitive, in which an animal figure in profile still has its horns, antlers, tusks, or hooves facing to the front. Breuil believed this was an archaic feature, associated with early phases of cave art, whereas in the Magdalenian (the last phase of Ice Age culture) everything was drawn in proper perspective. Unfortunately his scheme was inconsistent, since twisted hoofs are known in the Magdalenian (e.g., on the Altamira bison), and true perspective sometimes occurs in early phases.

This scheme was eventually superseded by that of André *Leroi-Gourhan, the French scholar who dominated cave art studies after Breuil's death. Basing himself on securely dated figures, he proposed a series of four styles. Like Breuil, he saw an overall progression from simple, archaic forms to complex, detailed, accurate figures of animals. However, it is now generally recognized that Paleolithic art did not have a single beginning and a single climax; there must have been many of both. Each period probably saw the coexistence of a number of styles and techniques, as well as a wide range of talent and ability.

In recent years it has become possible to analyze minute amounts of pigment from parietal figures and hence learn that many black figures, thought to be manganese, actually contain or consist of charcoal. The development of Accelerator Mass Spectrometry (AMS) has meant that one can now obtain radiocarbon estimates from such tiny samples, and a number of figures in several Paleolithic caves have already been dated in this way (*see* Altamira). In every single case, results suggest that the accumulation of the figures was more episodic and far more complex than envisaged by Leroi-Gourhan's scheme, and sometimes spanned a far longer period than was believed.

Apart from sporadic occurrences of a variety of non-utilitarian objects in earlier periods, the first Eurasian Paleolithic art apparently occurs in the Aurignacian period, around 32,000 years ago; charcoal from two rhinos and a bison in the Chauvet Cave, France, have produced results of approximately this date, making these the earliest dated parietal paintings in the world. For the next ten millennia or so, parietal art seems confined to cave mouths and rock shelters. It was in the Solutrean and, especially, the Magdalenian that deep caves were habitually penetrated and decorated in areas of total darkness, though the Chauvet cave shows that this sometimes happened in much earlier periods as well. Paleolithic art seems to wane with the end of the Ice Age at the close of the Magdalenian, around 11,000˙ years ago.

Techniques and Materials. Portable art comprises a wide variety of materials and forms. The simplest are slightly modified natural objects—fossils, teeth, shells, or bones that were incised, sawn, or perforated to form beads or pendants. Some sites have hundreds of "plaquettes" (slabs of stone with drawings engraved on them), and a few painted specimens are known. Engravings occur on flat bones, and were also done on bone shafts and on batons of antler, not only lengthwise but also around the cylinder, maintaining perfect proportions although the whole figure could not be seen.

In the Magdalenian Period, zoomorphic figures and circular discs were cut out of thin bone. Antler spear-throwers have figures either carved in relief along the shaft, or carved in the round at the hook-end, where the triangular area of antler dictates the posture and size of the carving. Within these constraints, the artists produced a wide variety of images such as fawns, mammoths, or a leaping horse.

A few terra-cotta models have survived in several areas, especially Moravia, but the vast majority of Paleolithic statuettes are made of ivory or soft stone. Ivory was also used to produce beads, bracelets, and armlets.

Cave art itself encompasses an astonishing variety and mastery of techniques. One basic approach was the incorporation of natural rock formations: The shapes of cave walls and stalagmites were employed in countless examples to accentuate or represent parts of figures. The simplest form of marking cave walls was to leave finger traces in the soft clay layer. This technique probably spans the whole period, perhaps inspired by cave-bear claw marks on the walls. In some caves, the finger lines also include some definite animal and humanoid figures. Engraving, as in portable art, is by far the most common technique on cave walls. The tools used for engraving varied from robust picks to sharp flint flakes.

Work in clay was restricted to the Pyrenees; it ranges from finger holes and tracings to engravings in the cave floor, and bas-relief figures in artificial clay banks. The famous clay bison of le d'Audoubert are in haut-relief, and the three-dimensional bear of Montespan comprises about 1,543 pounds (700 kg) of clay.

Parietal sculpture is similarly limited in distribution to the Périgord and Charente regions of France where the limestone could be shaped. But whereas clay figures are known only from the dark depths of caves, sculptures are always in rock shelters or the illuminated front parts of caves. Both bas-relief and haut-relief are found, the figures being created with percussion tools. Almost all parietal sculptures have traces of red pigment and were originally painted, like much portable art.

The red pigment used on cave walls is iron oxide (hematite or ochre); the black is manganese or charcoal. The main coloring materials were usually readily available locally. Recent analyses of pigments, particularly at Niaux, have revealed the use of "recipes" combining paint with extenders like talc or feldspar. Analyses have detected traces of animal and plant oils used as binders.

The simplest way to apply paint to walls was with fingers, but normally some kind of tool was used, though none has survived. Lumps of pigment may have been used as crayons, but since they do not mark the rock well, they were more likely to be sources of powder. Experiments suggest that animal-hair brushes or crushed twigs were the best tools, though occasionally a pad may have been employed on rough surfaces. For hand stencils and some dots and figures, paint was clearly sprayed, either from the mouth or through a tube.

Figures have been found not only on clay floors and on walls, but also on ceilings. Some, like the Altamira ceiling, were within easy reach, but for others a ladder or scaffolding was required. At Lascaux, sockets cut into the wall of one gallery give some idea how the scaffolding was constructed.

Light was sometimes provided by hearths, but portable light was necessary in most cases. Since only a few dozen stone lamps are known from the period, it is likely that burning torches were generally used which left little trace other than a few fragments of charcoal on the walls.

In parietal art, unlike portable, there was no great restriction on size, and figures range from the tiny to the enormous (over 6 feet [2 m]) in some cases, with the great Lascaux bulls exceeding 16 feet (5 m). Small figures are commonly found with large, and there are no groundlines or landscapes.

Types of Images. Paleolithic images are normally grouped into three categories: animals, humans, and non-figurative or abstract (including "signs"). The vast majority of animal figures are adults in profile, most of them recognizable, although many are incomplete or ambiguous, and a few are imaginary, like the Lascaux unicorn.

The animals' age can rarely be estimated, except for the few juveniles known. Their sex is sometimes displayed directly, but almost always discreetly, so that secondary sexual characteristics such as antlers or size and proportions often have to be relied upon. Many figures seem motionless and animated depictions are rare. Scenes as such are very hard to identify in Paleolithic art, since it is often impossible to prove association of figures rather than simple juxtaposition. Only a very few definite scenes are known.

One central fact is the overall dominance of the horse and bison among Paleolithic depictions, although other species (e.g., mammoth or deer) may dominate at particular sites. Carnivores are rare; fish and birds are far more plentiful in portable art than parietal. Insects and recognizable plants are limited to a few examples in portable art. So Paleolithic art is neither a simple bestiary nor a random accumulation of artistic observations of nature. It has meaning and struc-

ture, with different species predominating in different periods and regions.

Apart from hand stencils, definite humans are scarce in parietal art, unlike portable art where the best-known specimens are the poorly named "Venus figurines" depicting females of a wide span of ages and types: they are by no means limited to the handful of obese specimens that are often claimed to be characteristic. Genitalia are rarely depicted, so one usually has to rely on breasts or beards to differentiate the sexes, and most humans have to be left neutral. Clothing is rarely clear, and details such as eyebrows, nostrils, navels, and nipples are extremely uncommon. Few figures have hands or fingers drawn in any detail.

In the past, all composites—figures with elements of both humans and animals—were unjustifiably called sorcerers and assumed to be a shaman or medicine man in a mask or animal costume. But they could simply be people with bestialized faces, or humans with animal heads. In any case, composites (the most famous being the sorcerer of Les Trois Frères) are rare, occurring in only about fifteen sites.

Nonfigurative marks are far more abundant than figurative, and include a tremendously wide range of motifs, from a single dot or line to complex constructions, and to extensive panels of linear marks. Signs can be totally isolated in a cave, clustered on their own panels, or closely associated with the figurative.

The simpler motifs are abundant and widespread. The more complex forms, however, show extraordinary variability and are more restricted in space and time, so they have been seen as ethnic markers, perhaps delineating Paleolithic groups.

Function and Meaning. The first theory attempting to explain this period's art was that it had no meaning; it was simply mindless decoration by hunters with time on their hands. This "art for art's sake" view arose from the first discoveries of portable art, but once parietal art began to be found it became clear that more was involved: The restricted range of species depicted, their frequent inaccessibility and their associations in caves, the palimpsests and undecorated panels, the enigmatic signs, the many purposely incomplete or ambiguous figures, and the caves that were decorated but apparently not inhabited, all combine to suggest that there is complex meaning behind both the subject matter and the location of Paleolithic art.

At the beginning of this century, the functional theory of "Sympathetic Magic" took over: In other words, the depictions of animals were produced in order to control or influence real animals in some way. Ritual and magic were seen in almost every aspect of Paleolithic art—breakage of decorated objects, images "killed" ritually with images of missiles or even physical attack.

Overall, however, there are very few Paleolithic animal figures with missiles on or near them, and many caves have no images of this type at all. Missiles (whatever they are) also occur on some human figures. There are no clear hunting scenes. Moreover, the animal bones found in many decorated caves bear little relation to the species depicted on the walls, and it is clear that the motivations behind the art were different from the environmental factors and economic choices that produced the faunal remains.

Another popular explanation of Ice Age art is that of "fertility magic": The artists depicted animals, hoping they would reproduce and flourish to provide food in the future. Yet few animals have their gender shown, and genitalia are almost always shown discreetly. As for copulation, in the whole of Paleolithic iconography there are only a couple of (very dubious) examples.

It is clear that most Paleolithic art is not about either hunting or sex, at least in an explicit sense. The next major theoretical advance, however, introduced the notion of a symbolic sexual element. In the 1950s two French scholars, Annette Laming-Emperaire and André Leroi-Gourhan concluded that caves had been decorated systematically rather than at random. Parietal art was treated as a carefully laid-out composition within each cave; the animals were not portraits but symbols.

The key advance was the discovery of repeated associations in the art. The numerically dominant horses and bovids, concentrated in the central panels, were thought to represent a basic duality that was assumed to be sexual. Laming-Emperaire believed the horse to be equivalent to the female and the bovids to the male; for Leroi-Gourhan it was vice versa. This idea was then extended to the signs, which were dubbed male (phallic) and female (vulvar).

The most recent work on Paleolithic art is splintering in many directions. One researcher, for example, is seeking detailed and firm criteria by which to recognize the work of individual artists—we do not, of course, know the gender of Paleolithic artists, and there is no justification for assuming that the art was all done by and for men. Others are investigating the acoustics in different parts of the cave, and finding a clear correspondence between the richest panels and the best acoustics, suggesting that sound played an important part in whatever ceremonies accompanied the production of cave art.

No single explanation can suffice for the whole of Paleolithic art: it comprises at least two-thirds of known art history, covering twenty-five millennia and a vast area of the world.

[See also ART; CRO-MAGNONS; EUROPE: THE EUROPEAN PALEOLITHIC PERIOD; NOTATION, PALEOLITHIC; PALEOLITHIC: UPPER PALEOLITHIC; RELIGION; VENUS FIGURINES.]

■ Edouard Lartet and Henry Christy, *Reliquiae Aquitanicae* (1875). Henri Breuil, *Four Hundred Centuries of Cave Art* (1952). Christian Zervos, *L'Art de l'Epoque du Renne en France* (1959). Paolo Graziosi, *Palaeolithic Art* (1960). Annette Laming-Emperaire, *La Signification de l'Art Rupestre Paléolithique* (1962). Peter Ucko and Andrée Rosenfeld, *Palaeolithic Cave Art* (1967). André Leroi-Gourhan, *The Art of Prehistoric Man in Western Europe* (1968). Alexander Marshack, *The Roots of Civilization* (1972). André Leroi-Gourhan, *The Dawn of European Art* (1982). Paul G. Bahn and Jean Vertut, *Images of the Ice Age* (1988).

Paul G. Bahn

SCANDINAVIAN ROCK ART

Scandinavian rock art is found in Denmark, Finland, Norway, and Sweden, and consists mainly of images carved, pecked, polished, or painted onto exposed areas of bedrock. These images are not a homogeneous phenomenon but fall into distinct geographical and formal groups of different ages. Conventionally, rock art is classified as a feature of the Stone and Bronze Ages, and later rock art such as picture stones and runic monuments is, by convention, excluded from the category.

Distribution of Rock Carvings. Scandinavian rock art is found in virtually every region of Norway and Sweden. There are several distinct clusters, however: for example, around the Oslo fjord, in the Trondheim area, and in the Swedish provinces of Östergötland and Uppland. North Scandinavian sites include the enormous concentration at Nämforsen in Sweden and the impressive sites along the Alta fjord in Norway. In Denmark, rock art on bedrock is restricted—for geological reasons—to the island of Bornholm, but it is also found on the widespread megalithic monuments or—as in Sandagergård in North Zealand—on a monument specially built for the purpose.

Rock paintings are known from Finland, Norway, and Sweden, and form a class of their own numbering almost one hundred sites. All paintings are situated on vertical rock faces, often under an overhang or in a cave.

Scandinavian rock art seems to be a discrete phenomenon, though parallels can be identified for rock art of the earlier phases with areas like Karelia, and for the later phases with the rock art of other regions of Bronze Age Europe.

History of Research and Documentation. The oldest pictorial record of Scandinavian rock art is a watercolor, dated 1627, of sites in the district of Brastad in western Sweden. Research proper began at the end of the eighteenth century, on the initiative of private individuals or learned societies, and major contributions were made long before archaeology became an established university discipline. Research efforts have been rather intermittent over the years, but good documentation is now available for Denmark, Sweden, and Norway. There is still no comprehensive scientific record of the rock paintings of Finland, however. New sites or even whole areas of rock art are still being discovered, notably around the Alta fjord in 1973.

Signs, Motifs, Compositions, and Quality. The most frequent and widely distributed sign in Scandinavian rock art is the cupmark, a hemispherical hollow some 2 to 4 inches (5–10 cm) in width. The most common representational motifs are animals such as deer, elk, bear, fish, whales, and birds, human beings, soles of feet, and ships. There are also many signs that are impossible to identify. The scale varies from oversize to natural size to miniature; most of the motifs are rather small (8 to 16 inches [20–40 cm]). The signs may be isolated or in large clusters containing hundreds of motifs. The selection and the principles of combination can vary, as well as style and setting. Clusters of signs can be a result of accumulation, or, alternatively, of conscious scene formation.

Variations in the bedrock material (granite, gneiss, slate, etc.) make the images look different in technical detail. The general impression, however, is a rock art which is clear, well-executed and—up to now—well preserved. To help toward a wider appreciation of the art, conservation and information programs have been established and many of the accessible sites have been painted red.

Chronology. At present, direct dating of Scandinavian rock art has not been attempted, though this could be possible for the paintings if organic binding material can be recovered. Other methods of dating are indirect, and rely on correlations with burial monuments, changes of sea level, stylistic or technical criteria, or comparison with artifacts of known age.

The earliest known sites are in Norway, and have a supposed maximum age of approximately 8000 B.C. These sites are rather few, and the next concentration of rock art comes after a long interval, around 4300 B.C. (e.g., Alta, Nämforsen). The next main body of Scandinavian rock art is the Bronze Age carvings. These are generally dated from 1800 to 500 B.C., though there is a tendency to stretch this period—including the images concerned—back into the later part of the Stone Age and forward into the early part of the Iron Age.

It is evident that total chronological separation of the main bodies of Scandinavian rock art is impossible. On the contrary, there is continuity, especially in the use of individual sites.

Interpretations. Traditionally, Scandinavian rock art was looked upon as historical narrative, giving an account of important past events. Around the turn of the nineteenth century there was strong influence from the history of religion, which saw religious archetypes in the art, transplanted, mainly from the Mediterranean, to a remote northern Europe. Cult and magic as well as ceremonial performances were read into the images.

By creating two opposing image worlds, which were then given contrasting names, such as Southern and Northern, Arctic and South Scandinavian, Farmers' Art and Hunters' Art, a zonal segregation of the landscape was attempted, reflecting different economic systems: mixed farming in southern Scandinavia; hunting and gathering in the north.

In the 1970s, when more quantitative data became available, the settings of the sites came to be viewed within a cultural landscape. Settlements, graves, and traces of production were incorporated into more holistic interpretative hypotheses, and the rock art was seen as a symbolic, ideological reflection of certain social and economic systems. Concentrations of art sites in the wider cultural landscape were interpreted as territories or centers of power. Still more recently, the images have been looked upon as semiotic categories, organized according to belief systems, and gender divisions have entered the analyses.

These more recent interpretations, using hermeneutic theory, have given rock art research within Scandinavia a new direction aimed more at an understanding than an explanation of this world of images.

[See also ART; SCANDINAVIA, articles on EARLY PREHISTORY OF SCANDINAVIA, SCANDINAVIA IN THE BRONZE AGE.]

■ Knut Helskog and Bjørnar Olsen, eds., *Perceiving Rock Art: Social and Political Perspectives* (1966). J-P Taavitsainen, "Recent Rock-Painting Finds in Finland," *Bolletino del Centro di Studi Preistorici* 16 (1977): 148–156. Mats P. Malmer, *A Chronological Study of North European Rock Art* (1981). Gro Steinsland, ed., *Words and Objects: Towards a Dialogue between Archaeology and History of Religion* (1986). Christopher Tilley, *Material Culture and Text: The Art of Ambiguity* (1991). Klavs Randsborg, "Kivik: Archaeology and Iconography," *Acta Archaeologica* 64 (1993): 1–147.

Jarl Nordbladh

NORTH AMERICAN ROCK ART

Graphic imagery on rocks in the natural landscape is found throughout North America. Although to produce a work of art may not have been the original intent, imagery that survives on stone from the prehistoric or recent past is often regarded as *art by the Western world. Painted designs, sometimes called "pictographs," may be simply referred to as rock paintings. Figures cut into the surface of the rock by pecking, incising, scratching, and so forth are known as "petroglyphs." Dating from several thousand years ago into the present century, American Indian rock art comprises a varied body of imagery and styles. The preliterate artist sought to conform to traditional norms as he or she created rock art for religious, social, and political ends. Thus any given style is comprised of a system of selected icons and symbols rendered in a culturally defined manner. Usually any given culture is responsible for one or more discrete styles.

Rock art derives from the ideologies of the authoring cultures, and often contains elements, including supernaturals, from folktales, myths, and cosmologies. Rock art served to identify and maintain significant localities in the landscape, tying people to their mythic beginnings. By its mere presence, rock art functioned to define territoriality. It was also involved with the manipulation of supernatural power and the insurance of general group well-being. In nearly every case it has also to do with the act of communication whether it be with members of the general population, exclusive societies, or with supernatural powers.

Although rock art is more common in the western third of North America, petroglyphs and rock paintings are known from almost every state in the United States and throughout much of Canada. Major regional divisions of rock art based on stylistic and cultural criteria are in turn tied to physiographic regions. The Arctic, the Northwest Coast, the Northern and Eastern Woodlands, the Great Plains, the Columbia Fraser Plateau, California, the Great Basin, and the Southwest are the major geographic provinces into which North American rock art has been divided.

Rock art in deep caves on the North American continent is rare. No rock art has been discovered that is attributable to Paleo-Indians following the end of the Pleistocene. Drawings such as those in Mud Glyph Cave and in other similar true caves in Tennessee, Kentucky, and Virginia, or paintings in limestone caves in New Mexico are later in origin.

The earliest rock art is that of hunter-gatherers or Archaic peoples and is several thousand years old. In the Eastern Woodlands, petroglyphs of atlatls and projectile points at the Jeffers site in Minnesota, the largest rock art site in the Upper Mississippi Valley, have been dated between 3000 B.C. and A.D. 400. Among the oldest pecked rocks in the Great Basin are pit and groove boulders that represent a form of manipulation of rock surfaces but do not involve the creation of graphic images. Other ancient rock art includes the widespread Great Basin Abstract style, found throughout the arid West; this style dates back to at least 1000 B.C. and probably earlier. Ancient representational styles in the Southwest include the Glen Canyon Linear style of the San Juan and Colorado Rivers, with an estimated age of two or three thousand years. There is evidence to suggest that the earliest Barrier Canyon–style paintings of the Green and Colorado River drainages date back to around 3500 or 4000 B.C. The Pecos River style on the Lower Pecos in Texas has been dated by means of radiocarbon to around 1800 B.C. These styles feature large, highly abstracted human forms that may represent shamans or in some cases supernaturals. They are typically represented with elaborate headgear and decorated bodies. In the Barrier Canyon and Pecos River styles, a variety of animals, including small birds, snakes, and plants as well as ritual paraphernalia occur in association. In some of these compositions, ceremonies appear to be in progress.

Rock art made over the last two thousand years of prehistory and into the protohistoric period is more abundant and includes the work of horticulturalists as well as late foraging and hunting groups. Represented in the east is the work of Mississippian prehistoric farmers and ancestors of historic tribes. Petroglyphs in the Upper Ohio Valley are attributed to Algonquian-speaking Eastern Woodland groups between A.D. 1200 and 1750. Likewise, rock art on the Canadian Shield in the Northern Woodlands was made by Algonquian speakers. Rock art on the High Plains includes figures of late prehistoric shield-bearing warriors. Foundations for contemporary Pueblo, Navajo, and Apache ritual art are present among the ceremonial figures, masks, life forms, cloud motifs, and ritual paraphernalia in Southwest rock art where continuities in subject matter and styles indicate a long tradition of continuous ideology and religious beliefs. On the Columbia Plateau a single basic style tradition featuring simple figures of animals, stick men, rayed arcs, and tally marks is dated between 1000 B.C. and A.D. 1800. After A.D. 800 the Yakima Polychrome and Long Narrows styles indicate increasing contact with the Northwest Coast. Many Northwest Coast petroglyphs are related to the ethnographic art of the region and are said to commemorate ongoing myths and legends. Visually outstanding from California is the Santa Barbara Painted style of the southern coastal ranges and the petroglyphs of the desert Coso Range in which bighorn sheep and hunt shamans predominate.

Ethnographic studies along with subject matter and site locations suggest that various rock art styles in western North America, on the High Plains, and in the Northern Woodlands were executed by shamans or by initiates in cult rituals during guardian spirit guests or as part of the ritual acquisition of spirit power. These include, for example, ancestral Chumash and Yokut rock paintings in south-central California, and the Barrier Canyon and Pecos River paintings mentioned above. The Peterborough petroglyph site is a well-known Algonquin shamanistic site in Ontario. Some of the rock art produced in these contexts is thought to represent culturally determined visions acquired during altered states of consciousness aided by hallucinogens. The depiction of mythic beings, spirit helpers, and abstract designs documents these visions. Human and animal elements are sometimes combined, suggesting continuity and transformation between the human and animal world.

Studies of sites where rock art interacts in meaningful ways with sunlight and shadows suggest that this was one means by which various prehistoric people ritually kept track of or formally noted annual rituals or ceremonial occasions. Rock art in locations that interact with shafts of sunlight, such as Anasazi spirals at Chaco Canyon, New Mexico, and Hovenweep in southeastern Utah and elsewhere are thought to have been a means to document or commemorate annual calendric events, important in the ceremonial seasonal round of farming peoples.

Some historic rock art in the Great Plains falls into the category of Biographic Art. Incised and painted pictures of horsemen, tipis, guns, and detailed action scenes were sometimes commemorative records of historic events and personal exploits. These depictions would have served to promote and reinforce individual status. In the majority of cases, however, the rock art of North America is a material legacy of the complex religious systems and ideologies that helped order cosmologies and promoted chances for success and ultimately survival for the diverse peoples and cultures that have made their homes on this continent.

[See also NORTH AMERICA: INTRODUCTION.]

■ Robert Heizer and M. A. Baumhoff, *Prehistoric Rock Art of Nevada and Eastern California* (1962). Selwyn Dewdney and Kenneth E. Kidd, *Indian Rock Paintings of the Great Lakes*, 2d ed. (1967). Campbell Grant, *Rock Art of the American Indian* (1967). Klaus F. Wellman, *A Survey of North American Indian Rock Art* (1979). Polly Schaafsma, *Indian Rock Art of the Southwest* (1980). James Swauger, *Petroglyphs of Ohio* (1984). M. Jane Young, *Signs from the Ancestors: Zuni Cultural Symbolism and Perceptions of Rock Art* (1988). Sally J. Cole, *Legacy on Stone* (1990). James D. Keyser, *Indian Rock Art of the Columbia Plateau* (1992). David S. Whitley, "Shamanism and Rock Art in Far Western North America," *Cambridge Archaeological Journal* 2:1 (1992): 89–113. Solveig A. Turprin, ed., *Shamanism and Rock Art in North America* (1994).

Polly Schaafsma

AUSTRALIAN ROCK ART

Rock art is found in many parts of Australia, but varies in quantity, technique, and style. Where Aboriginal people still paint or engrave on rock, both the images and the activity itself have social and metaphysical meanings. Some signs and symbols may be "owned" or "managed" by members of a particular group but painted by members of another. Different meanings may be ascribed to images, depending on the status of individuals, and full significance may be revealed only to the fully initiated. Such knowledge is extremely important in Aboriginal society, but is inaccessible to archaeological analysis. Earlier research attempted to address questions of specific mythological meaning. Current studies of rock art are concerned with establishing formal patterns in style, motifs, and techniques as indicators of prehistoric developments and relationships or as part of an anthropological assessment of the ways in which art encodes meaning and symbolizes people's relationships to the natural and supernatural world.

There are three main techniques of rock art. Pigments from ochres (yellow, red), pipe clay (white), and charcoal (black) are used both for paintings and for stencil art, in which the pigments are sprayed from the mouth around objects or parts of the body. Pecked or engraved images are chipped into rock surfaces using a hammer stone or a hard, sharp engraving tool. Other techniques, such as modeled beeswax, are occasionally employed. The choice of technique is partially determined by the suitability of appropriate rock surfaces, but there are also significant regional and chronological differences.

There is considerable debate concerning the validity of attempts to date rock engravings either by *radiocarbon dating of minute organic particles trapped below layers of chemical coating (rock varnish) built up on the rock surface or by assays of the chemistry of the varnishes themselves. Claims for ages in excess of 30,000 years up to the present have been made for art in the Olary region of South Australia. These sites have pecked motifs, typically nonfigurative forms (circles, curved lines, sets of dots), and a variety of animal tracks on flat rock exposures. Similar techniques and designs (often referred to as the Panaramitee style) have continued to be employed in many areas of arid Australia to the present. If the early dates are correct, this shows an exceptional degree of continuity in artistic technique and style over extremely long periods of time.

Paintings in the Early Man Shelter in Cape York are securely dated to 13,500 B.P., while there is indirect but generally accepted dating of linear markings deep underground at Koonalda Cave in the Nullarbor of 20,000 B.P. Similar finger fluting and related marks in soft limestone have been identified in other limestone areas in Western Australia, Victoria, and especially southeastern South Australia. Although not directly dated, these have been regarded as part of an early, widespread tradition.

In some areas a local sequence of changes in style and motifs can be shown. In the Kakadu National Park in Northern Australia, changes in the art run parallel to environmental changes, as the sea level rose after about 10,000 B.P., initially forming saline mudflats and later the present freshwater swamps. A series of styles has been suggested for the period before the rise in sea level, with earlier, more naturalistic figures succeeded by smaller, increasingly stylized and schematic forms. Later, Yam figures appear, blending human and animal forms with plants. After about 9,000 years ago, as estuarine conditions developed, fish became the main motif. These are painted in a new, simple X-ray style, where internal anatomical parts are shown. With the development of freshwater swamps, species such as magpie geese become important in the environment, *subsistence, and art. More elaborate forms of X-ray art developed, with a wider array of motifs, including new types of artifacts such as the didjeridoo (drone pipe) and the more recent depictions of Europeans and their introduced animals. This tradition continues to the present.

Elsewhere, sequences are more difficult to establish, and research has concentrated on documenting sites and assessing local and regional stylistic zones. There are broad-scale differences in motif and technique across the continent, with finer-scale variation within each general region. Large outline figures of animals and fish are engraved on sandstone outcrops near Sydney on the southeast coast, while smaller, more complex animal and anthropomorphic figures are pecked on boulders in the northwest region of Western Australia. Paintings vary from very simple linear designs in Victoria to the large-scale, solid-filled naturalistic designs characteristic of Quinkan art in north Queensland. Hand stencils occur in many regions, but stencil art is particularly abundant in the Carnarvon area in southern Queensland, where a wide array of other items, such as wooden dishes, boomerangs, and axes, are also seen stenciled on rock surfaces.

[See also ART; AUSTRALIA AND NEW GUINEA, articles on FIRST SETTLEMENT OF SUNDA AND SAHUL, ABORIGINAL PEOPLES OF AUSTRALIA.]

■ Robert Edwards, Australian Aboriginal Art (1979). Paul Bahn and Andree Rosenfeld, eds., Rock Art and Prehistory (1991). Robert Layton, Australian Rock Art: A New Synthesis (1991). Jo McDonald and Ivan Haskovec, eds., State of the Art: Regional Rock Art: Studies in Australia and Melanesia (1992). Michael J. Morwood, D. R. Hobbs, and Graeme K. Ward, eds., Rock Art and Ethnography (1992).

David Frankel

ROMAN DECORATIVE ARTS

Overview
Roman Sculpture
Roman Glass
Roman Painting
Roman Mosaics
Roman Architecture

OVERVIEW

The archaeological remains of Roman civilization throughout the Mediterranean basin, Western Europe, and the former Near Eastern provinces of the empire are unparalleled in sheer abundance and scale. In striking contrast to the relatively circumscribed regional traditions of arts and craftsmanship of the same regions in the Bronze and Early Iron ages, the artistic and architectural expressions of the Roman imperial age are characterized by their unprecedented geographical *diffusion and, on occasion, by their almost industrial methods of production. Although in the realm of decorative arts—statuary, mosaics, painting, and glassware, for instance—the works of individual artists and

workshops have long been identified by scholars, the economic context of this activity within the developing Roman world system has received increasing archaeological attention in recent years. Likewise, specific production methods and technologies of manufacture are subjects of continuing research. Roman architecture has long been studied as the material conjunction of artistic production, technology, and civic administration; new scholarly perspectives focus on its role as imperial propaganda and, more subtly, on architecture as a means of reshaping the landscape to reflect and reinforce the Roman social order. In the following sections, the various Roman decorative arts are discussed from the standpoint of both decorative and functional characteristics. Special emphasis is placed on their larger significance within Roman society.

Neil Asher Silberman

ROMAN SCULPTURE

The study of Roman sculpture has long been a focus of *Classical archaeology. Roman sculptural monuments can be found throughout the area of the empire, yet many aspects of Roman statuary are poorly understood and continue to be controversial topics despite decades of scholarly debate.

Like Greek sculpture, Roman sculpture is naturalistic in style, encompassing a variety of forms and materials, and was used in several contexts. Commemorative statues included portraits, executed as busts, statues in-the-round, equestrian figures, and historical reliefs. Religious figures included cult statues and temple decoration for pediments and acroteria. Funerary sculpture included carved sarcophagi, sometimes with elaborate relief scenes or reclining figures of the deceased. As an important class of archaeological evidence, Roman sculpture reflects artistic styles, levels of foreign influence, personal taste of patrons, and official policy in art over a period of some twelve centuries. It should be noted that many Roman sculptural remains were not recovered from controlled excavations but are known rather from Renaissance and modern collections and from chance surface finds.

In general, Roman sculpture appears to mirror Greek sculpture in style and composition. The relationship between Greek and Roman art continues to be one of the thorniest problems in classical archaeology. Originally, Roman sculpture and indeed Roman art as a whole was seen as a continuation of the classical tradition. J. J. Winckelmann believed there was no distinction between Greek and Roman art; this view was prevalent until the work of Franz Wickhoff and Alois Riegl, who shifted their focus to identifying the innovations in Roman art.

The origins of Roman sculpture are obscured by Rome's status as an Etruscan city-state. Monumental bronzes such as the Arringatore from Perugia (1st century B.C.), the Mars of Todi (4th to 3rd centuries B.C.), and the Lupa Capitolina (5th century B.C.) are often seen as figures representative of this period of Etruscan political and artistic dominance. The Brutus of the Capitoline (1st century B.C.) is viewed as representative of that most Italian of sculptural genres, the portrait, and although it may in fact represent the influence of Hellenistic portrait herms, this bust and figures like it also reflects the ancient Etruscan and Italic funerary custom of fashioning portrait masks of the deceased from wax. Italic statuary such as the Capestrano Warrior may also testify to the traditional elements of Roman portraiture.

The statuary of the Middle and Late Republican periods is characterized by a surge in Greek influence. The expansion of Rome into Magna Graeca, Illyria, and eventually Greece itself during and after the Punic Wars resulted in the influx of Greek sculptural masterpieces. Greek artists were brought to Rome to execute figures in the Greek style or to produce dutiful reproductions of famous sculptures. Works such as the marble statue of the Roman general from Tivoli (1st century B.C.) show the influence that Greek models had on Roman Republican art: Despite a well-established Roman tradition of togate or armed portrait statues, this figure is heroically draped in the Greek manner, with torso bare, and a slight S-curve to the figure reminiscent of the work of Polykleitos. The careworn face of the general, however, recalls the portraits of Republican Rome.

Imperial sculpture in Rome saw a continuation of Greek influence, and usually reflected Classical models. The Augustus from Prima Porta, for example, resembles the style of Polykleitos in its stance, and it is thought that Greek sculptors worked on the Ara Pacis Augustae, with its famous neo-Attic frieze. Yet both embody uniquely Roman features as well: the Augustus in its breastplate decorated with historical relief, and the altar in its subject matter, a procession of historical figures. This combination of Greek style and Roman subject continued through the Julio-Claudian and Flavian (A.D. 69–98) periods, as typified by the relief sculptures of the Arch of Titus and the Column of Trajan. In the provinces, sculpture was modified through the combination of Roman styles with local materials, artists, and traditions. The period of the Antonines (A.D. 138–192) and Severans (A.D. 193–235) saw a decline in the classical tradition and its replacement by new styles and systems of proportion and composition. This continued through the Tetrarchy, until the time of Constantine, when a more formal, stylized Roman art became the basis for Byzantine and early Christian sculpture, and ultimately, for many of the sculptural traditions of the Middle Ages.

[*See also* BYZANTINE CULTURE: BYZANTINE DECORATIVE ARTS; GREEK ART AND ARCHITECTURE, CLASSICAL: CLASSICAL GREEK SCULPTURE.]

■ E. H. Richardson, "The Etruscan Origins of Early Roman Sculpture," in *Memoirs of the American Academy in Rome, XXI*, (1953). D. E. Strong, *Roman Imperial Sculpture* (1961). C. C. Vermeule, "Greek Sculpture and Roman Taste," in *Bulletin of the Museum of Fine Arts, Boston, LXV*, (1967). H. P. L'Orange, *Likeness and Icon* (1973). M. Bieber, *Ancient Copies* (1977). J.M.C. Toynbee, *Roman Historical Portraits* (1978). J. J. Pollitt, *The Art of Rome, c. 753 BC–AD 377: Sources and Documents* (1983). Brunhilde Sismondo Ridgway, Roman Copies of Greek Sculpture: The Problem of the Originals (1984). D.E.E. Kleiner, *Roman Sculpture* (1992).

Joseph John Basile

ROMAN GLASS

The Romans made a greater variety of glass than any other ancient civilization. Glassblowing was discovered in the Roman Empire, and this led to the production of inexpensive objects for daily use. The Romans manufactured the world's first window panes and they decorated buildings with glass mosaics. They also made dazzling luxury objects such as cameo glasses and cage cups. Roman glass was valued outside the imperial frontier and examples have been found in the Baltic region, the Middle East, India, and eastern Asia.

Roman glassmakers inherited and adapted the techniques of Hellenistic craftsmen in the eastern Mediterranean who produced luxury tableware by casting, grinding, and polishing. Hellenistic products included mosaic glass made from slices of brightly colored canes, and gold-sandwich glass with gold foil laminated between layers of fused colorless glass.

In the late first century B.C. and the first century A.D., the Romans made large numbers of cast, "naturally colored" brown or bluish bowls; bowls with vertical ribs; a wide range of colorless or monochrome tableware; and polychrome vessels consisting of cane slices or strips of different colors. The city of Rome was the largest consumer of fine glassware, but early Roman cast glasses are found (in varying quantities) all over the empire. The taste for colored glass declined between A.D. 50 and 75, after which the finest objects were colorless.

Glassblowing was discovered in the Syro-Palestinian region in the first century B.C. In principle, the technique is simple: The worker gathers molten glass on the end of a blowpipe, then inflates the gather and shapes it by swinging, rolling on a flat surface, and manipulation with tools. By A.D. 50, the technique was used throughout the Mediterranean and in Gaul and Germany. Fifty years later, it was the standard method of glassforming throughout the Roman world.

Blown glass was decorated while hot in three ways: by inflation in molds, application of additional glass, and manipulation with tools. The use of molds enabled glassblowers to produce decorated vessels almost as quickly as plain ones. The technique was pioneered in the eastern Mediterranean, possibly at Sidon. The use of molds spread rapidly to Italy and the outer provinces. Early imperial mold-blown glasses include elegant vessels signed by Ennion and cups that depict gladiators or chariot-racers. Among the later objects are vessels with Christian or Jewish symbols, some of which may have been intended for pilgrimages to Jerusalem and other holy places.

Glass was applied to objects while they were hot by picking up cold fragments or by attaching blobs or trails of molten glass. In the former case, the partly formed object was rolled in chips, which adhered to the surface. Further heating and inflation sometimes produced a mottled effect that may have imitated mosaic glass. In the latter case, molten glass was gathered on the end of a metal rod and applied to the surface as blobs, which could be smoothed by reheating, or as continuous trails, which could be manipulated into patterns. One well-known type has "snakethread" trails embellished by crimping or stamping. Most mottled glass dates from the first century A.D., but objects with trailed decoration were made throughout the Roan imperial period.

The most common method of decorating glass after it had been annealed was to cut and engrave it with wheels fed with an abrasive such as emery. The ornament varies in complexity from simple horizontal grooves, through faceting, to pictorial scenes from Graeco-Roman mythology or the Old and New Testaments. The most meticulous faceted objects were made in the late first century A.D., using colorless glass that imitated rock crystal. Between the late second and the fifth centuries, workshops in several parts of the empire (notably Egypt, Italy, and Germany) produced distinctive varieties of pictorial decoration.

The rarest Roman cut glass consists of cameo glasses and cage cups. Cameos are objects with two or more layers of different colors. The upper layer(s) is carved and cut, leaving relief decoration in one or more colors on a background of contrasting color. The Romans made cameo glasses in two periods: between about 30 B.C., and A.D. 70, and in and around the fourth century. Most early Roman cameo glasses have white decoration on a blue background. They include gems and plaques formed by casting, and vessels generally formed by blowing. In the latter case, a gather of blue glass was dipped into molten white glass to create the overlay. The most famous early Roman cameo glass is the Portland Vase. Later Roman cameo glasses consist almost exclusively of gems and vessels with colorless base glass and colored ornament.

Cage cups were made by taking thick-walled blanks and removing glass mechanically until all that remained was a vessel inside an almost free-standing "cage" of meshes, sometimes accompanied by inscriptions or figures, that is attached to the wall by posts. Most cage cups date from the mid-third to late fourth century A.D. The majority are colorless; but some have colored overlays and at least one, the "Lycurgus Cup," is dichroic.

The Romans made three types of glass with painted ornament. The most common type is painted with enamels designed to melt at low temperatures, so that they can be heated and fused to the surface without the risk of melting the object. The second type is painted with pigments that were not intended to be fired. This "cold painting" has the disadvantage of being more vulnerable to damage. Nevertheless, some objects have a combination of enamels and cold paint applied in several stages. The third, most difficult type of painted ornament is "reverse painting." Designed to be viewed *through* the glass, the decoration is applied in reverse order: highlights first and backgrounds last.

Roman craftsmen decorated glass with gold in two ways: by applying gold to the surface and by laminating it between two fused layers of glass. In both processes, gold foil was attached to the surface with an adhesive, after which the unwanted areas were removed, leaving the decoration as a silhouette. Details were added by scratching the gold with a stylus and sometimes by adding paint or enamel. In the first process, the decoration usually was fixed by firing it at a low temperature. In the second, "gold sandwich" process, a protective layer of glass was affixed either by fusing a preformed cover glass to the decorated surface or by inflating a bubble of hot glass against it, after which the unwanted glass was removed.

The disintegration of the Western Roman Empire was accompanied by reductions in the volume of long-distance trade and the manufacture of luxury articles. Although glass continued to be made, the quantity and quality declined. The most elaborate products of earlier centuries—cameo glass vessels, cage cups, and gold sandwich glass—ceased to be made. Indeed, after the fifth century, the great majority of objects were simple drinking vessels made of "naturally colored" green or brownish glass. In the Eastern Empire, glassmaking continued on a large scale. Indeed, the degree of continuity was such that much early Islamic glass is difficult to distinguish from the latest Roman (Byzantine) glass made in the same regions.

■ Donald B. Harden, Hansgerd Hellenkemper, Kenneth Painter, and David Whitehouse, *Glass of the Caesars* (1987). David Whitehouse, *Glass of the Roman Empire* (1988). Martine Newby and Kenneth Painter, eds., *Roman Glass: Two Centuries of Art and Invention* (1991).

David Whitehouse

ROMAN PAINTING

Two modes of painting were practiced in Greco-Roman antiquity: painting on movable tablets and painting directly on stuccoed walls. Examples of wall painting, found both in tombs and in domestic interiors throughout the Roman world, are all that now survive of a highly prolific art; however, this material comprises a substantial repertoire. In all instances where wall painting is employed, the compositions obey a perceptible decorum of context related to their function as visual signs of status.

The corpus of known painting has expanded steadily with the progress of archaeological exploration. The first discoveries came about in late-fifteenth-century Rome when Raphael and other Florentine painters visited underground chambers of Nero's Golden House (then confused with the Baths of Titus) on the Esquiline Hill and copied figural motifs to be integrated into the ceilings and walls of palaces they decorated "in the antique manner." Having found these images in "grottoes," as tradition goes, they called them "grotesques." Two centuries later, in 1732, excavations began in the Campanian territories buried by the eruption of Mt. Vesuvius in A.D. 79. Paintings preserved in the cities of *Herculaneum and Pompeii as well as in villas in the surrounding territory—Stabiae, Oplontis, and the modern towns Boscotrecase and Boscoreale—comprise the largest and best-known repertoire of painting *in situ*. The oldest paintings at these sites are as early as the late second and early first centuries B.C., while the most recent were executed after the damaging earthquake of A.D. 62, which necessitated extensive reconstruction work on houses and property in Pompeii. Several examples of painting contemporary with those in Campania have been discovered in *Rome, especially in buildings buried within the foundations of later constructions.

Owing to the optimum conditions of preservation in the Vesuvian cities, as well as the imaginative appeal of this arrested culture, Pompeian decoration has enjoyed so large a share of the attention given to Roman painting that the art itself would seem to have died with the city in A.D. 79. This is a highly misleading terminus for the consideration of painting, which, in fact, flourished throughout the rest of the Roman Empire as long as Roman architecture continued to be built. Large multiresidential buildings in the Roman port city of Ostia preserve decoration from the Hadrianic and Early Severan periods. Recent work has been done in reconstructing decorated houses of the same periods in Ephesus. At most ancient sites, painted plaster is recovered only in fragments that require extensive restoration. Such reassembling has, in recent years, been carried out both in northern Europe (especially France, Germany, and England) and throughout the Mediterranean basin in Spain, Israel, Romania, and former Yugoslavia, to mention only a few.

Anonymity of patrons and painters imposes its own conditions of study on Roman painting. Although a few properties have been ascribed to known personages, specifically the emperors Augustus and Nero, most owners are unknown. Likewise, with the exception of one or two persons mentioned in literary sources, the names, social derivation, and training of the painters are unknown. For this reason categorical interpretation with reference to contextual circumstances is the most viable approach to the social relevance of painting. It is appropriately understood as a code of communication serving its patrons' desire for the visual enhancement of prestige. In writing about the necessities of domestic architecture, the Vitruvius, the Augustan author of the *Ten Books on Architecture*, observes that persons of political consequence must provide spaces appropriate for receiving visitors at their houses, while persons of lesser rank go around to pay calls. Conventions of status display can explain not only the practice of painting but also the specific development of patterns and motifs.

Two principles govern the selection of compositions. One is hierarchy by which rooms are decorated with respect to their importance in a program of activities; the other is function, which calls for a practical coordination between activity and appearance. Spaces apt to be crowded, such as reception areas, are painted as backdrops without specific subject interest at eye level. Spaces that facilitate transitional movement—corridors, antechambers, etc.—are given paratactic designs, while those intended for stationary activity— for reading, for sleeping, for the important ritual of social dining—are decorated with symmetrical schemes and subject patterns that invite prolonged inspection.

Two major background sources help to explain the significance of designs. One is the architecture and decoration of public spaces. Paintings that recall the appearance of monumental buildings such as temples and basilicas emphasize the link between public and private spheres of activity for the urban or municipal elite. These designs are particularly prevalent in the Republican period. Also during this period designs based upon the architecture and decoration of theatrical stages are popular, perhaps because the sponsorship of theatrical spectacles as a form of evergetism (civic benefaction) was a prerogative of the upper class.

A second source of patterns is the world of private luxury, including colonnaded porticoes, gardens, and rooms furnished for the display of art objects. This last type makes its appearance during the late Republic, being doubtlessly modeled upon the private galleries of plutocratic collectors, but perhaps also influenced by a newly inaugurated practice of displaying art objects for public view. Simulated picture gallery rooms gain currency during the Augustan period until they become the dominant format for decoration. Their organization centers about subject paintings, either mythological or landscapes, framed within richly decorated columniated housings called *aediculae*. Some paintings may reproduce famous originals, but others are clearly the invention of the painters themselves. Many scholars have written about thematic links and compositional similarities as principles governing the selection and arrangement of pictures within a given room. The components of picture galleries are not limited to framed paintings, but include also a variety of subordinate images imitating statues, gilded ornaments, engraved vessels, candelabra, curtains, or draperies. Small pictures of food items may be taken as allusions to hospitality. Picture gallery schemes persist after the destruction of the Campanian cities and can be seen in both Ostia and Rome. In the northern provinces paratactic arrangements of candelabra and tapestries are especially favored, but columns and *tabellae* are infrequent. Although a predilection for naturalistic representation characterizes Roman wall painting throughout its history, it is clear that each area had its preferred motifs reflecting local valuations of luxury objects. Paintings representing events, especially arena contests, were probably commissioned as commemorations by sponsors. These were employed as megalographic decorations in Campanian gardens, but were also used in tombs.

Formal scholarship on painting has always owed much to the historical and descriptive information offered by ancient literary sources, the most influential authors being C. Plinius Secundus (A.D. 23–79), a scholar and government official of the Flavian Period, and Vitruvius, the architec-tural writer of the Augustan Age. Because natural raw materials furnish the pigments used in painting, Pliny devotes Book 35 of his compendiary *Historia naturalis* to the origins and evolution of the art. Correspondingly, the books dealing with stone and metal incorporate histories of sculpture. Pliny's accounts are historically organized, emphasizing human mastery of nature and highlighting progress in the arts. Most of our information about Greek painters, their patrons, and their subjects derives from Pliny. His information about Roman painting is more sporadic, although he claims an early beginning for indigenous traditions, and talks of paintings that antedate the founding of Rome. The most reliable of his claims on behalf of Roman innovations concern villa landscape paintings, the popularity of which peaked in his own time. Sections of a chapter in Vitruvius's architectural handbook provide an encapsulated history of specifically Roman wall decoration along with technical information on preparing walls for fresco painting and on pigments. Both Pliny and Vitruvius offer some evidence concerning the history of pictorial subjects along with insights into contemporary Roman aesthetics, but a fuller account of figured paintings appears in the ancient rhetorical teacher Philostratus's description of pictures displayed in a gallery near Naples (*Imagines*).

While this primary source material has strongly influenced scholarly perceptions and interpretations of painting, political and practical circumstances surrounding the conduct of excavation campaigns have affected the availability of material for study. The Campanian excavations of the eighteenth century sponsored by the Bourbon kings of Naples and the Two Sicilies had as their purpose the acquisition of antique treasures for the Royal Museum. Figured panels cut from the walls during this period form the basis of the collection now housed in the National Museum in Naples. Because this happened in an era of high reverence for Greek antiquity, it was assumed with reference to ancient sources that mythological subject paintings were copies of Greek masterpieces.

Scholarly attention to painting as a feature of Roman domestic architecture began with the inauguration of the Italian nation in 1862 when Campania assumed the status of an Italian heritage and excavations were reorganized under the state. Paintings were now left in situ with efforts made to preserve them. August Mau, the first to systematize art historical discussion, developed the chronological classification known as the Four Pompeian Styles, based upon the illusionistic treatment of the wall surface as spatially closed or open (*Pompeii: Its Life and Art*, F. Kelsey, trans., 1904). Although Mau attributed the genesis of styles to foreign sources, in the absence of demonstrable proof of such derivations, recent scholars have treated the paintings as products of local tradition. Although much that has been written positing a step-by-step evolution of pictorial motifs is excessively precise, still chronology remains essential to the social historian who wants to link painting with its context. In Pompeii, where many houses retain full decorative programs, some status value seems attached to the retention of old paintings. That redecoration most frequently followed upon structural renovation appears from the fact that the most prevalent compositional style dates from the city's final period when buildings damaged by the earthquake of A.D. 62 underwent repair.

Listed chronologically, the best-preserved examples include: First style—House of Sallust, Pompeii; Second style—Villa Oplontis (at Torre Annunziata), paintings from the Villa Boscoreale in the Metropolitan Museum of Art in New York and the National Museum in Naples, and Houses of Livia and Augustus, Rome; Third style—panels from the Villa Boscotrecase in Naples and New York, walls from the Villa della Farnesina in the National Museum, Rome, and Casa del Fruttetto and House of M. Lucretius Fronto, Pompeii; Fourth style—House of the Vettii and House of Loreius Tiburtinus, Pompeii. The Roman-German Museum of Cologne houses an extensive provincial collection.

■ Nicole Dacos, *La découverte de la Domus Aurea et la Formation des Grotesques à la Renaissance* (1969). Alix Barbet, *La peinture Romaine: Les styles décoratifs Pompéiens* (1985). Laura Anne Laidlaw, *The First Style in Pompeii: Architecture and Painting* (1985). Lawrence Richardson Jr., *Pompeii: An Architectural History* (1988). Andrew Wallace-Hadrill, "The Social Structure of the Roman House," *Publications of the British School in Rome* 56 (1988): 43–97. Peter H. von Blanckenhagen and Christine Alexander, *The Augustan Villa at Boscotrecase*, 2nd ed., with contributions by Joan R. Mertens and C. Faltermeier (1990). Roger Ling, *Roman Painting* (1991). John R. Clark, *The Houses of Roman Italy 100 B.C.–A.D. 200; Ritual, Space and Decoration* (1992). Jacob Isager, *Pliny on Art and Society: The Elder Pliny's Chapters on the History of Art* (1992).

Eleanor Winsor Leach

ROMAN MOSAICS

As a natural development of Hellenistic mosaic tradition, Roman mosaics became a common means of decorating the floors and walls of important or elaborate buildings throughout the Roman Empire. Since they were made of *tesserae* or *tessellae* (small cubes, in Latin), the technical term used for floor mosaics was *opus tessellatum*. The tesserae were usually of stone or marble, but in the finest wall mosaics they were sometimes formed from glass, mother of pearl, or gold. The term for a wall mosaic is *opus musivum*, from the Greek word for Muse, and it is believed that the idea of treating walls in this way was inspired by the decoration of grottos dedicated to the Muses, which incorporated seashells, pieces of pumice stone, and other materials.

Techniques and Treatments. The method of laying mosaic floors is described by two Roman writers, Vitruvius (*De Arch.* 7.1) and Pliny (*Nat. Hist.* 16.186f.); modern archaeological work has shown that mosaicists throughout the empire followed methods roughly similar to those described. Many specialists believe that mosaicists made use of standardized pattern "sketchbooks," from which they or the person commissioning a mosaic could choose the scenes to be represented. This would explain why there are close similarities between mosaics of different periods found in different parts of the empire as well as between mosaics and works of art in other media. Some scholars refute the existence of such sketchbooks, however, mainly because these are neither mentioned in the sources nor otherwise documented. Moreover, two mosaics, however similar, are never identical.

The main development from the mosaics of the Hellenistic Period was a general enrichment of the figured and decorative repertory, and, above all, the acceptance of the fact that mosaic was a medium in its own right and not a means of imitating painting in more durable materials. Regional styles aside, Roman mosaics followed two main trends and were either polychrome or monochrome (black and white). The first was a continuation of Hellenistic tradition and is found throughout the Roman world. In these floors, the background was usually white, and the now enriched pictorial and geometric decoration was polychrome, the variety of colors used depending on the materials available in a given area. Black-and-white mosaics had already made their first, occasional appearances in the Hellenistic Period, but they became a characteristically Roman phenomenon of the first to the third centuries A.D.; they are found mainly in Italy (especially at Ostia), southern France, and Spain. In these, the decoration (figured or geometric) was black, against a white background. Because of this bichrome scheme, and despite the addition of details in white, the black figures of these mosaics remained flat, and little further effort was made to depict the third dimension.

There were also new, fundamental changes in the way the floor space was treated. The Hellenistic tradition in which the mosaic looked more like a carpet in the center of the room, with a central focal point, usually a figured panel framed by a number of bands, continued, especially in the Greek world, where traditions held fast. Yet the decoration of the frames now tended to be more complex, and the proliferation of figured panels within the same floor led to the disappearance of the emphasis on a single focal point in the center. Such floors could be viewed from several different angles, in contrast to those of earlier times, which had a single orientation. Also, the multiple-figured panels, although often occupied by stereotypical scenes and decorative motifs, could be used to represent the symbolic personifications of natural forces, for instance, four compartments for the seasons or the winds, seven for the days of the week or the planets, nine for the muses, or twelve for the months of the year or the signs of the zodiac.

Another important innovation of Roman mosaicists was the occasional treatment of the floor as a single, unified surface. In such cases, a single, figured scene or a repeating geometric pattern, uninterrupted by secondary compartments, and frames, was used to cover an entire floor. Since there was now no primary focal point or any clearly defined center to the composition, these mosaics could be used to decorate rooms of any shape and size, and could be viewed from several different angles.

Motifs and Themes. These new types of composition of mosaic floors brought with them a great enrichment of the decorative repertory. The geometric motifs of the Hellenistic Period were still prevalent, but a vast variety of new motifs was introduced, some of which (like the *pelta* and the Solomon knot) became extremely popular and typical of Roman mosaic decoration.

The variety of figured subjects multiplied in equal measure. Mythological figures still reigned supreme, especially in the Greek East. Some myths were extremely popular throughout the empire, in all types of buildings and locations. In other cases, it is easy to see that themes were linked to room functions. For example, because of their association with water, the Rape of Hylas or Leda and the Swan were popular for the decoration of baths, and the Rape of Ganymede and several Dionysiac themes, due to their association with wine drinking, were ideal subjects for the decoration of dining rooms. The popularity of Orpheus charming the beasts can be attributed to the Romans' love for the exotic. For the same reason, there developed, mainly in the West, another type of mythological scene in which, instead of representing a specific myth, a god or goddess was depicted surrounded by his or her entourage. Thus there is an abundance of Dionysiac Processions, of Triumphs of Aphrodite, and of the *Cortège* of Neptune, all of which offered an opportunity for depicting a rich assortment of strange and exotic creatures and animals.

Although not always associated with mythology, personifications (usually in the shape of a woman) form part of this same group. The city or a geographical location where a myth took place was represented in human form. Much more common were the personifications of the seasons, but other similar themes, like the year or the months, are also found. There are even, especially during Late Antiquity, personifications of abstract ideas, mainly illustrating conceptions associated with life, like Tryphe (luxury) in the House of Menander at Antioch, and Apolausis (enjoyment) in the baths of the same name near Antioch. There are even more difficult concepts like the Theogonia (the birth of a god) present in a scene of the Birth of Dionysus in the House of Aion at Paphos in *Cyprus. In most cases, it would have been impossible to know what these figures personified were it not for the inscriptions that accompany them. Inscriptions became fairly common in Roman mosaics, especially from the third century A.D. onward. Most commonly they give the names of the characters in the scene depicted or address the viewer directly, as in the case of the well-wishing inscriptions sometimes found in the entrance halls of buildings.

Historical subjects were rarely depicted, while portraits, usually of philosophers, poets, and playwrights, were slightly more common. These were often accompanied by depictions of scenes from their works bearing explanatory inscriptions, as seen, for example, in the House of Menander at Mytilene in *Greece.

More characteristic of the Roman West is the depiction of scenes from everyday life, such as hunting scenes or agricultural and other rural activities, which were represented either for their own sake or as accompaniments to personifications of the seasons or the months. Most common among the mosaics of the West, however, are depictions of gladiatorial combats, *Venationes* (staged hunts), and circus scenes, of which there are a great number, especially in North Africa, and which often include the names of the combatants and the animals. It is in these images of human activities, often rendered in minute detail, that Roman mosaics, more perhaps than any other art forms, give us precious information on the daily life, habits, and amusements of the ancients.

Mosaicists and Their Legacy. Only a very small number of Roman mosaics bear the signature of their creator. This is apparently because mosaicists were craftsmen rather than artists who, in the case of sculptors and painters, gave authenticity and value to their work by signing it. In fact, it is generally accepted that the vast majority of mosaics are not original creations but derive from other works of art. The assumption that mosaics were not considered of particularly high artistic value is reflected in the fact that the ancient writers dealing with art hardly speak of either mosaics or mosaicists. Further proof is afforded by the Price Edict of A.D. 301 (through which the emperor Diocletian tried to fix the maximum prices for commodities and salaries throughout the empire), where the standard salary listed for mosaicists was relatively low. The edict defines two types of mosaicist: one is a *tessellarius,* the other, with a slightly higher salary, a *musivarius.* It is a matter of dispute whether the latter is the person who executed the demanding parts of a mosaic panel and the former the one who executed the geometric designs and filled in the background, or whether the *tessellarius* was the mosaicist who decorated floors and the *musivarius* was one who decorated the more demanding walls and vaults.

It appears that wall mosaics made their first appearance toward the end of the Hellenistic or the beginning of the Roman period. Written sources and surviving examples indicate that this development must have taken place in Italy, where, at *Herculaneum and Pompeii, there are some of the earliest and best-preserved examples of the genre, although this may be due to the unusual circumstances that have preserved the Campanian buildings. Few examples survive elsewhere because the walls that these mosaics decorated have long since collapsed, but it appears that wall mosaics were made throughout the empire. These mosaics were generally of finer quality and, as mentioned, formed from *tesserae* of more costly and beautiful materials. Glass in particular was frequently used, for it had the added advantage of being lighter than stone. Wall mosaics were particularly well suited for the decoration of bath buildings, since they were much more resistant to water and humidity than wall paintings.

Mosaics have been found throughout the Roman world, and impressive archaeological publications and reports have provided scholars with important new source material in recent years. Among the sites with important mosaics that have been extensively excavated and studied are Antioch in Turkey, Apamea in Syria, and Ostia in Italy, as well as Pompeii and Herculaneum. The mosaics of the latter two sites, because of their excellent state of preservation and their fixed *terminus ante quem* (the eruption of Vesuvius in A.D. 79), have become points of reference for all subsequent studies. There are also several national mosaic corpora in progress, including those of Italy, France, Spain, and Tunisia.

■ Doro Levi, *Antioch Mosaic Pavements* (1947). Frank Sear, *Roman Wall and Vault Mosaics (Römische Mitteilungen 23)* (1977). Katherine M. D. Dunbabin, *The Mosaics of Roman North Africa* (1978). John R. Clarke, *Roman Black-and-White Figural Mosaics* (1979). Janine Balty, "La mosaique antique au Proche-Orient I," *Aufstieg und Niedergang der römischen Welt II. Principat 12/2 -Künste* (1981): 347–429. Philippe Bruneau, "Tendances de la mosaique en Grèce à l'époque imperiale," *Aufstieg und Niedergang der römischen Welt II. Principat 12/2-Künste* (1981): 320–346. Jean-Pierre Darmon, "Les mosaiques en Occident I," *Aufstieg und Niedergang der römischen Welt II. Principat 12/2 -Künste* (1981): 267–319. Philippe Bruneau, *La Mosaique Antique (Lectures en Sorbonne,* 1) (1987). Michael Donderer, *Die Mozaisten der Antike und ihre wirtschaftliche und soziale Stellung. Eine Quellenstudie (Erlangen Forschungen,* 48) (1989).

Demetrios Michaelides

ROMAN ARCHITECTURE

Roman architecture is the product of a society whose early development was shaped through close contacts with cultures significantly more advanced and sophisticated than its own. It was born into a world of almost perfected forms from which it was free to choose.

Already by the end of the sixth century B.C. monumental temple architecture in *Rome, such as the temple of Jupiter on the Capitoline, was planned and executed under Etruscan guidance. When Pericles was adorning the Athenian Acropolis with monuments that set the standards of classical architecture for centuries to come, Rome was a humble market town. Although a broad view of history compels us to see the fledgling city on the Tiber as a participant in the cultural koiné of the Mediterranean, Rome's position during the first few centuries of its political life was primarily that of a borrower rather than a creator of new forms.

Greece, which became the model par excellence for

Rome, was a self-contained unity of independent city-states. Its artistic horizons could be pure and idealistic as the needs of its institutions were limited, simple, and homogeneous. The unique character of Roman architecture is to be sought in the context of the world empire it represented and in its self-imposed mandate to respond to the complex needs of the pluralistic societies inhabiting its vast dominion.

A few interrelated themes can be isolated in order to review distinguishing characteristics of Roman architecture. Roman architecture was cosmopolitan and ecumenical. Within a highly urban context, it was framed around personal and institutional ritual. It aimed to create cities and bring a broadly based standard of civilization to its citizens. It was practical, utilitarian, and technologically advanced. While it upheld and propagated the norms of classicism, its true contribution to ancient architecture was its ability to transform and transcend these very norms to suit its changing practical and ideological needs.

The Romans created urban systems from Scotland to Syria. At Conimbriga, a small city in central/northern Portugal, the early Augustan restructuring of the pre-Roman town center resulted in a rectangular forum following the 3:2 Vitruvian proportions. It was defined by a colonnade on two sides, a basilica, a curia, shops, and a temple. A more monumental expression of the civic, religious, and commercial bases of Roman life can be seen in the early imperial colony Augusta Raurica (Basel) in Gaul: a forum complex dominated by the official temple framed on three sides by porticoes and shops; a large basilica-curia closed the opposite side and shops. A separate market building, public baths, and a theater slightly askew to the street grid completed the city center. In form and content, such schemes were modeled after experiments already in place by the end of the Republic in Rome or in central and northern Italian colonies such as Cosa, Velleia, and Brescia. Timgad, a military veterans' colony on the highlands of Algeria founded by Trajan in A.D. 100, began as a perfect example of orthogonal planning where no previous settlement pattern existed. However, by the beginning of the third century A.D. the city had outgrown its strictly square plan of 1,200 Roman feet enclosing barely 25 acres (10 ha). Besides the usual civic and religious buildings, the town boasted a very fine library and nearly a dozen large and small public baths. In Asia Minor, with its long history of urban life nurturing Greek and pre-Greek Anatolian civilizations, the Roman contribution was nonetheless significant in imposing an orderly pattern over the irregular growth of old cities. *Ephesus and Sardis with their well-planned civic centers and colonnaded streets replacing earlier thoroughfares are just two of many examples. Equally significant in the eastern provinces was Rome's ability to confront and eventually reconcile with the Greek heritage of the land and its institutions by creating new and hybrid architectural forms, such as the immensely successful bath-gymnasium complex.

Early development of Roman architecture emphasized practical and useful projects: water supply and drainage systems, roads, bridges, harbor structures, circuses, warehouses. There is no doubt that this engineering know-how was primarily inherited from Rome's Etruscan neighbors. The Great Sewer (Cloaca Maxima) of Rome, an immense underground vaulted system, completed under the last Etruscan king in 509 B.C., was just one of these projects. Starting with Aqua Appia built in 312 B.C., Rome had by the second century A.D. nine major aqueducts supplying a total of 35,315,000 cubic feet (1,000,000 cu m) of water daily. The

spectacular remains of this network serving the capital as well as other networks carrying water to the remotest cities of the empire is still visible stretching across the landscape on majestic arches (*Carthage, Segovia, Aspendos). The famous Pont du Gard near Nimes (19 B.C.) crosses the valley of river Gardon on three tiers of arches reaching a height of 162 feet (49 m). The bridge over river Neva at Narni, central Italy, carried the Via Flaminia over a series of arches at a height of 100 feet (30 m).

Much of the success of this bold and functional architecture, which made little or no use of the classical orders, depended on the skillful exploitation of concrete as a building material. Composed of sand and irregular stones mixed in a mortar of lime and a volcanic dust called *pozzolona* (in central Italy and Campania), Roman concrete *(opus caementicium)* took the shape of the form it was poured into and was immensely strong. It required little skilled labor, and it was fast and cheap compared to traditional cut-stone masonry.

The extensive warehouse by the Tiber in Rome known as Porticus Aemilia (ca. 193 B.C.) and the market hall at Ferentinum (early 1st century B.C.) utilize the concrete barrel vault singly or in series. More complex are the multiple vaulted terraces of a number of late Republican sanctuaries such as that of Jupiter Anxur in Terracina, Hercules Victor in Tivoli, and the grandest of them all, the Sanctuary of Fortuna Virilis at Praeneste (ca. 120 B.C.) molding an entire hillside into an architectonic whole. Brick-faced concrete was found to be the ideal material for multistory tenement housing, Rome's solution to the problem of mass housing for large urban populations. Strong and fire resistant, concrete was the preferred mode of building after the Great Fire of Rome in A.D. 64. Some of the most impressive and best-preserved examples of four- to five-story tenements occupying entire city blocks (hence known as *insulae*) come from Ostia, Rome's crowded harbor city.

The mastery of concrete technology enabled the creation of a vaulted-style architecture and produced structures that could cover daring spans and spaces through the imaginative use of arches (round, segmental, flat), barrel and cross-vaults, and endless variations of domes, semidomes, and domical vaults. For many scholars and archaeologists, this represents nothing less than a revolution in ancient architecture over the trabeated systems of the Egyptians and Greeks. The Golden House of Nero with its famous Octagon Suite, the Flavian Palace on the Palatine, and the Markets of Trajan, all in Rome, were moments in the development of this remarkable new vision of space. One might see its culmination in the Pantheon of Hadrian in Rome (ca. A.D. 118–128), an all-concrete circular structure with a dome of 142 feet (43 m) in diameter and equal height.

By the end of the first century A.D. Romans had achieved a dynamic architecture of novel forms through the integration of Greek orders with the new vaulted style. The extensive remains of Hadrian's Villa at Tivoli (A.D. 125–138) provide a textbook example for this exciting and creative synthesis in classicism. The architecture of the great baths and some of the centralized buildings of the late empire, such as the so-called Temple of Minerva Medica or the Mausoleum of Constantine's daughter (Santa Costanza), both in Rome, offer the evidence for the continuation of an architecture of masterful structural and spatial articulations into the late antique and medieval eras. The small, third-century-A.D. Temple of Venus in faraway Baalbek, Syria, with its circular, domed cella and ornate, scalloped podium and entablature, is a highly innovative local exercise in baroque fancy.

Another important manifestation of this tendency to reinvent classicism can be seen in Rome's interest in developing a decorative architecture through novel and unusual combinations of the traditional orders. A practical and resourceful facade motif, the utilization of rows of arches alternating with half-columns is a Roman invention. It can be seen on the Tabularium (Records Building, 78 B.C.) providing a scenic backdrop to the Forum Romanum, the Theater of Marcellus (13 B.C.), and the Colosseum (the Flavian amphitheater, A.D. 80) in Rome. More unorthodox in conception is the fantasy world created in the painted architecture of the Second and Third Pompeian styles during the late Republic. To a conservative critic like Vitruvius, the new creations were an anathema to good taste. Real life examples of this growing trend toward a baroque conception of form appear in the multistory columnar facades—skene frons of theaters, gate structures, nymphaea, tomb facades, honorific halls, and exedrae. Some of the most flamboyant of these all-marble aedicular schemes, such as the facade of the Library of Celsus in Ephesus (ca. A.D. 150), the North Market Gate in Miletus, and the Severan Marble Court of the bath-gymnasium complex in Sardis come from Asia Minor and represent a major change of outlook toward the meaning of classicism and its elements. Although eastern, possibly Ptolemaic Alexandrian, sources for this bold and re-creative approach to classicism have been suggested, existing examples are almost exclusively imperial in date. Many follow an international style (the "Marble Style") made possible by the widespread importation of marble across the Mediterranean.

The uncanonical interpretation of spatial and decorative modes of classical architecture reflect the empire's willingness to embrace the multitude of aesthetic traditions of its widely spread provinces. The degree to which Rome could offer a benign and protective stewardship toward these societies to develop and freely express their artistic will ultimately determined the extent and nature of its architectural contribution on the world stage.

[See also GREEK ART AND ARCHITECTURE, CLASSICAL: CLASSICAL GREEK ARCHITECTURE; ROMAN EMPIRE, articles on ROMAN ROADS, ROMAN AQUEDUCTS.]

■ Axel Boethius, The Golden House of Nero: Some Aspects of Roman Architecture (1960). Frank E. Brown, Roman Architecture (1961). George M. A. Hanfmann, From Croesus to Constantine (1975). George M. A. Hanfmann, Roman Art (1975). Axel Boethius, Etruscan and Early Roman Architecture (1978). John B. Ward-Perkins, Roman Imperial Architecture (1981). William L. MacDonald, The Architecture of the Roman Empire I (revised, 1982). William L. MacDonald, The Architecture of the Roman Empire: An Urban Appraisal II (1986). Jean-Pierre Adam, La Construction Romaine (1989).

Fikret K. Yegül

ROMAN EMPIRE

INTRODUCTION

The Roman Empire in the middle of the second century A.D. extended from Scotland to Arabia and from Morocco to the highlands of Armenia. Its northernmost frontier, the Antonine Wall, ran between the estuaries of the Forth and the Clyde. It embraced western and southern Europe up to the Rhine and Danube, with an ill-defined zone of influence beyond, while the provinces of Upper Germany and Dacia extended beyond those rivers into the Main-Taunus Black Forest region and into Romania respectively. Western Asia belonged to the empire up to the Euphrates and the Syrian or Arabian Desert. Egypt was Roman, as were the North African coast and its hinterland to the edge of the desert zone, and Egypt and North Africa between them supplied Rome with most of its grain. Only in the East, on the frontier with Parthia, was Rome neighbor to an organized power of comparable strength. With the Parthian kings and their successors, the Sassanid Persians, *Rome for centuries contested control of the Armenian highlands and the territory between the upper reaches of the Euphrates and Tigris.

Chronology. Literary sources date Rome's foundation to the middle of the eighth century B.C. (traditionally 753), and archaeological evidence shows this to have been a period of growth when perhaps Iron Age settlements on the Palatine and other hills beside the lowest crossing of the Tiber coalesced to form a single urban community. Rome's geographical position and the aggressive ethos of its republican nobility facilitated its expansion. By the end of the fourth century B.C., Rome dominated Etruria and central Italy, and had sealed its hegemony over the Greek cities to the south by the capture of Tarentum (272 B.C.). Thereafter, involvement in *Sicily brought conflict with *Carthage. During the First Punic War (264–241 B.C.), Rome gained its first overseas provinces, Sicily and Sardinia, and a foothold in Spain. Over the next two centuries, the Second and Third Punic Wars (218–201, 149–146) and successive wars with the Hellenistic powers brought great accretions of territory, culminating in the 60s B.C., when Pompey ended the Seleucid Empire and made Syria a Roman province, and the 50s, with Julius Caesar's conquest of Gaul.

Three major civil wars in less than twenty years thereafter marked the end of republican government, but the Battle of Actium (31 B.C.) left Caesar's adopted son in supreme power. He incorporated *Egypt into the empire the following year, and as the first emperor, Augustus (27 B.C.–A.D. 14) completed the conquest of Spain and extended Rome's direct control in Europe to the Rhine and the Danube. Germany between the Rhine and the Elbe was temporarily conquered, but abandoned after A.D. 9, when the Roman governor Quinctilius Varus fell into an ambush, the site of which has only recently been identified, and lost three legions, nearly a tenth of the army. Augustus could, however, boast on his tomb that he had "extended the territory of all those provinces of the Roman people on whose borders lay peoples not subject to our government" (Res Gestae 26.1). His death marked the end of expansion for a time, until the invasion of Britain in 43. Forty years later, the army was campaigning in northern Scotland, though no permanent occupation resulted. The Romans also advanced into the reentrant angle between the Rhine and the Danube, which was gradually secured with forts and roads and added to the province of Upper Germany. The emperor Trajan subdued Dacia (101–106) and attacked Parthia, but when he died in 117 his acquisitions beyond the Euphrates were promptly abandoned by his successor, Hadrian.

It was Hadrian (117–138) who built the famous wall across northern England, and although Antonius Pius (138–161) sanctioned a new advance into Scotland, the Antonine Wall was abandoned around 164. In the West, the tide of the empire had turned, and the reign of Marcus Aurelius (161–

180) brought trouble on both the eastern and the Rhine-Danube frontiers, revealing the potential weakness of the empire when forced to operate on two fronts. Septimius Severus (193–211) invaded Scotland once more, reaching as far north as the Moray Firth, and is credited with the desire to reconquer the country, but made no lasting gains. His dynasty ended with the murder of Severus Alexander in 235, which ushered in half a century of anarchy. The European frontiers failed, the Goths and other German tribes made vast inroads, even Italy was invaded, and in 271 the emperor Aurelian began to fortify Rome itself. Stretches of the Aurelian walls still stand, most notably behind the Termini railway station, where they can be seen to incorporate the walls of preexisting apartment buildings.

In the East, Septimius Severus actually extended Rome's rule across the Euphrates to the upper Tigris, incorporating two new provinces, Osrhoene, based on Edessa (Urfa), and so-called *Mesopotamia, based on Amida (Diyarbekir). In 224, however, Parthia came under the new Sassanid dynasty, which took the offensive against Rome, destabilizing the frontier, capturing the emperor Valerian (260), and taking the capital of the Syrian province, Antioch. Although Diocletian (284–305) restored order to the empire at large, there remained incessant frontier warfare throughout the next century against the Sassanids, and the Romans' humiliating surrender in 363 of the outlying city of Nisibis, southeast of Mardin, was long remembered. Throughout the fourth and fifth centuries the fates of the eastern and western empires increasingly diverged. The West fell apart as different German tribes carved out portions for themselves. Rome itself was sacked by the Goths in 410. Even North Africa, though protected by the Mediterranean, succumbed to the Vandals, who took Carthage in 439. The deposition of the last western emperor in 476 was more of symbolic than of real political importance, but the eastern empire of Byzantium still had a thousand years to run.

From mud huts to marble, Rome's expansion is reflected in the archaeological record. Its conquests in the third century B.C. brought Rome into close contact with Greek art. The fall of the Greek colonies of Tarentum (272 B.C.), Syracuse (211 B.C.), and Tarentum again (209 B.C.) and the booty acquired in the campaigns against Philip V of Macedon (198–197 B.C.), Antiochus III of Syria (189 B.C.), and Perseus of Macedon (168 B.C.) flooded Rome with Greek art, though this was nothing compared to the sack of Corinth, the richest city in *Greece (146 B.C.). Greek artists settled in Rome, and Roman patrons commissioned public and private works of art. Patronage in the late republic was already considerable, but the scale of it was totally eclipsed by Augustus and some of his successors, who could command both the artists and the resources of the whole empire. Rome, artistically once a remote and barbarous outlier, became the center of artistic activity, but all the provinces of the empire shared in the emperor's patronage, and Roman *art and architecture can be found from Scotland to the Negev. The art historian has the task of elucidating the extent to which local traditions in the different provinces, Celtic in the northwest, Punic and Egyptian in Africa, and a host of traditions in the Near East impinge upon the ubiquitous Roman official art, and upon private art inspired by Roman values.

Contributions of Archaeology. The literary sources for the Roman world are mostly by men of the senatorial class or its dependents, and their interests are those of that class. Lower classes, slaves, and women are better represented in the epigraphic record. Archaeology as a whole casts light on aspects that the writers deal with only tangentially or not at all, or on aspects so familiar to them that they do not bother to describe them. Without archaeology, for instance, we would scarcely know what the cities and countryside of the Roman world looked like. In Italy itself, archaeology has revealed the small towns of *Herculaneum and Pompeii, destroyed by the eruption of Vesuvius in A.D. 79 and under excavation since the eighteenth century. These cities preserve houses and public buildings as in a time capsule, while Ostia, the port of Rome, silted up, gradually abandoned and covered with sand, tells us what a larger commercial center was like. The small towns of North Africa excavated by the French in the late nineteenth and twentieth centuries, like Sabratha and Lepcis Magna (Libya), are a treasury of Roman architecture and everyday life. In Europe, the Romans picked their sites so well that many Roman towns lie beneath modern cities, and it took Second World War bombing to expose the Roman heart of Cologne (Colonia Claudia Ara Agrippinensium) or *London (Londinium). There are, however, sites with no successor, like Wroxeter (Viroconium) in Britain or Glanum (Saint-Rémy-de Provence) in Gaul, where extensive excavation has been possible. Elsewhere, Roman monuments still stand surrounded by contemporary urban life, like the Roman baths in *Paris, the amphitheaters at Nîmes and Arles, or the great monuments of Rome itself. The cities of the eastern half of the empire are less well known. There are some spectacular sites, such as *Ephesus, Palmyra, and Jerash, and individual monuments, like the temples at Baalbek, but in much of the Near East, as in Greece and Egypt, the Roman period has not been the archaeologists' prime concern.

The Roman countryside had until recently attracted less attention than the towns, and over much of the empire this is still the case. It is, for instance, a truism of both ancient and modern writers that Africa was the chief granary of Rome and also a massive producer of olive oil, but no important agricultural site has even been thoroughly excavated in that province, and until recently there had been very little rural survey. In Italy and northwest Europe the countryside has had more attention, and in areas like Britain and northern France, air photography has revealed the hidden landscape. There have been notable villa excavations, as at San Rocco and Settefinestre, and considerable attention has been paid to Roman centuriation, often preserved in the modern field and road system, as in the Carthage area. Archaeology has cast new light on rural aspects of Roman technology, and there has been a recent spate of much-needed research on aqueducts, dams, watermills, water-lifting devices, and the like. Although a certain number of technical manuals survive, most Roman writers took the technological background of their lives for granted.

We are even more indebted to archaeology for our knowledge of the Roman frontiers and the Roman army. What we know about the equipment and uniforms of the army, about the layout of its legionary fortresses, forts, and temporary camps, and about the frontier works and installations comes primarily from excavation, survey and air photography, or sculptural representations on monuments like Trajan's Column or on military gravestones. This knowledge is heavily biased toward northwest Europe, where intensive work continues from the last century. *Hadrian's Wall and the German limes are unarguably the two most intensively researched and best-understood frontiers of the empire, where survey and excavation concern themselves with every signal station. In marked contrast, of the four well-attested legionary fortresses on the upper Euphrates frontier, not one has even been excavated. Much of the early work in northwest Europe on prehistoric and provincial Roman sites was done by local landowners, clergymen, and soldiers, with some academics, and they were all forced to develop relatively sophisticated techniques of excavation and recording, since the structures they were seeking were often built of timber represented only by fugitive postholes. The excavators could not enjoy the Mediterranean technique of gangs of workmen under minimal supervision simply digging until they hit the paved Roman street and the stone walls of solid buildings.

Trade is another area where we owe a debt to archaeology. With some exceptions, ancient writers felt trade to be beneath them, and what literary evidence we have is largely imprecise and anecdotal. Archaeological finds, however, especially of pottery, enable us to reconstruct trade patterns. Studies of the distribution of amphorae have taught us much about trade in wine, oil, and the fish sauce (garum) beloved of the Romans, and surveys in Libya and Tunisia have revealed the extent of olive cultivation in those regions. Meticulous excavation at Pompeii reveals vineyards within the city walls. Studies of the marble trade show how it was organized, with stones cut to predetermined modules and shipped throughout the empire to be stored until needed for some great project. Roman goods spread beyond the imperial boundaries, north into Scandinavia, whether by trade or as booty, and east into India, where the Roman trading station excavated at Arikamedu on the Coromandel coast must be one of many. In the great debate raging since the 1970s on the scope of the ancient economy, the weight of archaeological evidence suggests a more sophisticated and far-flung trade network than the economic minimalists argue for. Indeed, archaeological evidence in general supports a more impressive picture of Roman achievement in many fields than literary evidence suggests, revealing what Sir Mortimer *Wheeler called "the grandest facet of the Roman achievement as a whole: the overall magnitude of its field of thought."

Finally, we must consider Rome's relationship with other societies. Roman literature is somewhat self-centered and complacent, giving the impression that all other peoples existed only to be conquered or to minister to Roman needs. We thus see other cultures only through Roman eyes, and need archaeology to redress the balance. Only now is scholarship coming to appreciate the extent to which other languages and cultural traditions persisted in the East throughout the Roman period, and how much the Romans borrowed from them.

The literary tradition enshrines Punic Carthage as Rome's archetypal enemy, and the Carthaginians are almost unanimously condemned by Greek and Roman authors as perfidious, gloomy, cruel, devoted to money, and devoid of the arts. Recent excavation, however, along with reappraisal of the archaeological evidence, suggests that Carthage participated fully, though with its own traditions, in the Mediterranean culture of the Hellenistic age, and its artistic achievements should be judged on their own terms, not condemned as if trying to be purely Graeco-Roman and not succeeding. The *Celts, too, appear in Greek and Latin literature as archetypal barbarians. Their own voice is lost, and what they thought of the conquering Romans we do not know, except perhaps through the words put into the mouth of a doomed Celtic chieftain by a Roman writer: "Where they

[the Romans] make a desert, they call it peace" (Tacitus, Agricola 30.6). It is archaeology that reveals the artistic wealth and technical skills of the Celtic world at the time the Romans impinged upon the Celts and destroyed their culture. Perhaps the greatest service that archaeology renders is to set the Romans in this wider context and to remind us of the relationships they had with the peoples around them, relationships so often distorted by the Romanocentric tradition.

[See also BRITISH ISLES: ROMAN BRITAIN; EUROPE: ROMAN AND POST-ROMAN EUROPE; GERMANS AND GERMANIC INVASIONS; MEDITERRANEAN WORLD: THE DOMINANCE OF GREECE AND ROME; ROMAN DECORATIVE ARTS: OVERVIEW]

■ Cornelius C. Vermeule III, Roman Imperial Art in Greece and Asia Minor (1968). M. Cary and H. H. Scullard, A History of Rome Down to the Reign of Constantine (3rd ed., 1976). Fergus Millar et al., The Roman Empire and Its Neighbours (2nd ed., 1981). John B. Ward-Perkins, Roman Imperial Architecture (2nd ed., 1981). Peter Garnsey, Keith Hopkins, and C. R. Whittaker, eds., Trade in the Ancient Economy (1983). John Wacher, ed., The Roman World, 2 vols. (1987). Paul Zanker, The Power of Images in the Age of Augustus (1988). Amphores Romaines et Histoire Économique, Dix Ans de Recherches: Actes du Colloque de Sienne (22–24 mai 1986)/Organisé par l'Università degli Studi di Siena (1989). Thomas Blagg and Martin Millet, eds., The Early Roman Empire in the West (1990). Graeme Barker and John Lloyd, eds., Roman Landscapes: Archaeological Survey in the Mediterranean Region (1991). Colin M. Wells, The Roman Empire (2nd ed., 1992). C. R. Whittaker, Frontiers of the Roman Empire: A Social and Economic Study (1994).

Colin M. Wells

THE ROMAN FRONTIER

The Roman word for frontier (limes, plural limites) originally meant "path"; later it referred to the military road, often with signal towers along it, which was built at or near the edge of a zone under Roman military control; and so ultimately it came to mean "frontier" (cf. English "limit," from the same word). Unlike most modern frontiers it was usually a somewhat amorphous geographical zone in which it was difficult to determine exactly where the territory of the Roman Empire began and ended; but occasionally the limes was marked by a continuous single line, as most conspicuously in the example of *Hadrian's Wall in the north of England (and even here the distinction between "Roman" and "barbarian" territory was blurred by the presence of permanently manned outpost forts up to 15.5 miles [25 km] north of the barrier itself). Nor were the frontiers of the Roman Empire static for very long: evolving military strategy, the whims of individual emperors, and threats of attack from beyond the limites, all led to constant troop movements and the shifting of defensive positions. These factors, along with huge variations in the physical geography of the empire's borders, meant that rarely was there at any one time a coherent overall grand strategy blueprint for frontier policy; on the contrary, changes often came about as the result of ad hoc decisions to deal with each frontier problem as it arose. In the late empire, as pressure increased, greater flexibility in defensive capability was provided by the creation of mobile field armies (comitatenses) as a backup to frontier garrisons (limitanei), but simultaneous assault on several frontiers led to total breakdown, and in turn to the gradual dissolution of the western empire.

Augustus's reorganization of provincial administration divided the empire into provinces with troops, where the governor was appointed by himself, and provinces "of the Roman people" without troops, whose governor was appointed by the senate. The principal exception to this rule was Africa, included in the latter category despite being provided with a legion (*Legio III Augusta*) and auxiliaries. In Mauretania to the west of the Roman province of Africa, a client kingdom was established, a means of providing a pro-Roman buffer zone between a Roman province and more hostile territory beyond. Client kingdoms were much used elsewhere in the first century A.D., especially on the eastern frontier. In Gaul and Spain the sea provided natural boundaries, and in Germany and central Europe the Rhine and the Danube were formidable obstacles. A clear intention of Augustus, however, to expand the empire eastward to the river Elbe, marked by forts along the river Lippe at Oberaden, Haltern, and elsewhere, and by other forts along and to the north of the Main, was reversed by withdrawal to the Rhine after the crushing loss of three legions under Varus in a forest ambush in A.D. 9, probably near Osnabrück. Claudius (A.D. 41–54) created new provinces in Raetia (in what is now Bavaria) and Noricum (mostly in Austria), and also started the conquest of Britain, where the initial line of advance was marked approximately by the Roman road from Lincoln to Exeter known as the Fosse Way. Garrison was by means of a network of strategically placed forts linked by roads, with larger bases for legions or mixed legionary and auxiliary garrisons at Colchester, Gloucester, Exeter, and elsewhere. Further advances were made under Nero (A.D. 54–68) and Vespasian (69–79), by which time Wales and northern England were held by a network of forts, and permanent legionary bases were founded at places some way back from the front line, at York, Chester, and Caerleon. Expansion into Scotland as far north of the mouth of the Spey, without entering the highland mass, was achieved under Domitian (A.D. 81–96), with a system of forts and roads based on a legionary fortress at Inchtuthil on the Tay. These impressive advances were, however, soon given up and withdrawal ordered to southern Scotland, when troops were withdrawn to Germany and the Danube, especially to fight the Chattan war (A.D. 85–86).

Furthering plans drawn up by Vespasian, Domitian was also responsible for extending the frontier in Germany east of the Rhine once more, in order to incorporate the reentrant of land defined by the Rhine and the Danube in their upper reaches. About A.D. 90 a line of forts and fortlets was built through the Taunus hills north of Frankfurt, and then southward to the Main and the Neckar, and in advance of the forts a road policed by timber watchtowers every 1640 feet (500 m) or so marked the limes proper. The legionary bases were on the Rhine, at Nijmegen in Holland, Vetera (near Xanten), Neuss, and Mainz, although Vetera was given up before the end of the first century, and Nijmegen a little later.

Germany was by now relatively peaceful, and attention switched to the Danube, where the Dacian chieftain Decebalus's power was increasing in the Carpathian mountains in what is now Romania. The Roman frontier in central Europe was marked by the river Danube, with legionary fortresses at Oescus, Novae, and Durosturum in Lower Moesia and at unknown locations in Upper Moesia. Trajan's Dacian Wars in A.D. 99 to 100 and 104 to 105, commemorated schematically on Trajan's Column in Rome, extended the frontier north of the Danube and brought Rome the new province of Dacia. This was controlled by a legion at Apulum and probably by two other legions, as well as a network of auxiliary forts, watchtowers, and apparently

some short stretches of earth barrier (of uncertain date). With Dacia pacified, Trajan turned his attention to the eastern frontier, controlled by the usual series of key legionary fortresses (Samosata in Commagene, Melitene in Cappadocia, Satala in Pontus [south of the Black Sea], and Jerusalem, for example). Trajan annexed the former Nabataean kingdom (largely in what is now Jordan) as the new province of Arabia, and built a legionary fortress at its capital, Bostra; a road lined with forts ran south to Aqaba on the Red Sea. Trajan planned expansion further east and was campaigning against the Parthians (he took the title Parthicus in 116) when he died in 117.

After Trajan's expansionist policies came the consolidation of Hadrian (117–138). In Germany he ordered the building of a timber palisade, perhaps 10 feet (3 m) high, along the entire frontier from the point where it left the Rhine south of Remagen to its junction with the Danube in Raetia, an astonishing length of some 340 miles (548 km). New forts and fortlets were built to plug gaps, and a program of gradual replacement in stone of the watchtowers behind this palisade, was begun either during or immediately after his reign. In Britain an even more substantial barrier was constructed between Newcastle-upon-Tyne and Bowness-on-Salway, later extended eastward to Wallsend: the whole was 80 Roman miles (79 miles [122 km]) long. It was built of stone in its eastern two-thirds, while the rest was of turf with a timber breastwork. At mile intervals were fortlets ("milecastles") of stone (on the stone wall) or timber, and between each were two turrets of stone throughout. Forts were to the rear of this line, between 2 and 5 miles (3.2 to 8 km) away.

About 124, some two years after building work had started, major changes occurred: forts, at first twelve but later to be sixteen, were brought up to the line of the wall, in some cases replacing turrets or milecastles, and a continuous double earthwork and flat-bottomed ditch (known today as "The Vallum") ran a short distance behind the wall. The Vallum was designed as a clear demarcation of the military zone and reduced the authorized crossing points of the wall from some eighty to a more controllable sixteen; while the placing of garrisons on the wall line presumably indicates the hostility with which the wall was received by local peoples. Never designed to be used as a fighting platform, or even as a totally impregnable barrier (it was no Roman "Maginot line"), Hadrian's Wall served above all as a screen for troop movements if attack was needed, as a means of control of the movement of potentially troublesome peoples, and as an elaborate propaganda exercise. Whether the short stretches of linear barrier in Dacia, or the earliest of the *clausurae*, stretches of walling on the African frontier designed to control the movement of local nomads through mountain passes and valleys, are also of Hadrianic date, is uncertain; but the idea, novel to the Romans, of providing a continuous linear barrier to mark the limites of the empire may well bear the personal imprint of the idiosyncratic emperor himself.

Hadrian's successor, Antoninus Pius (A.D. 138–161), ordered an advance into southern Scotland in 139, barely ten years after the completion of the Hadrianic frontier: the motive was probably military glory rather than any serious threat from the British tribes. The Antonine Wall, which ran for 37 miles (59 km) from Old Kilpatrick on the Clyde to Carriden on the Firth of Forth west of Edinburgh, was of turf on a stone base, with eventually eighteen or nineteen forts and some fortlets (nine are known) in between: no other Roman frontier had such close-spaced garrisons. Six "beacon stances" believed to have been used in signaling are known but no regular system of turrets. Temporarily abandoned less than fifteen years after completion (ca. 155) because of a military crisis (a revolt of the Brigantes tribe) in northern England, it was reoccupied three or four years later, then abandoned definitively by the mid-160s, when permanent withdrawal to Hadrian's Wall took place and the turf section of the latter was rebuilt in stone. Antoninus Pius also ordered in the 150s an advance of the limes eastward in Germany, but only by some 19 miles (30 km), and a new series of forts and watchtowers, and a new palisade, were built. There are no obvious strategic or topographical reasons for the choice of this fresh frontier line, and the advance remains unexplained.

Under Marcus Aurelius, who spent much of his time on the northern frontier in his wars against the Quadi and Marcomanni, significant strengthening of the German and Danube frontiers took place, with new legionary fortresses in Dacia (at Potaissa), Noricum (Lorica), and Raetia (Regensburg). It was probably also now (or at the latest under Caracalla ca. 213) that the German limes was strengthened by the erection of an earth rampart and ditch, running immediately behind the Hadrianic timber palisade—another massive undertaking in view of its sheer length (237 miles [382 km]). In Raetia the palisade was replaced by a stone wall running between the existing stone watchtowers; much narrower than Hadrian's Wall (3.2 to 3.9 feet [1.00–1.20 m] as opposed to 8 to 10 feet [2.50–3.10 m] on Hadrian's Wall), it is unlikely to have had space for the patrol walk usually assumed to have existed on the latter barrier.

Septimius Severus (A.D. 193–211) contemplated the reoccupation of Scotland in his campaigns against the Maeatae—South Shields fort was converted to be his stores base (with twenty-two granaries) and a new fort was built at Carpow in Perthshire—but there were more problems elsewhere and the plans came to nought. The eastern frontier was reorganized following his campaigns in Mesopotamia and a strengthening of the African frontier, with new forts deep in Tripolitania (Bu Ngem is the best known), Numidia (Castellum Dimmidi is one), Mauretania Caesariensis (where a new line of forts pushed the frontier southward nearer to the edge of the Sahara), and Mauretania Tingitana (where a fresh network of forts attempted to guard the province from nomad attacks). But pressures on the frontiers were mounting everywhere in the third century. By 259 to 260, after constant attacks by the Alamanni and others, the entire length of the artificial barriers in Upper Germany and Raetia was abandoned, and the Rhine and the Danube became once more the frontiers. Much of Mauretania Tingitana was given up around A.D. 275 and Dacia was abandoned at the same time, the frontier there becoming once again the Danube.

New forts tended more often than not to follow a different pattern from their predecessors, with loftier, sturdier walls (often without a backing rampart), projecting towers at intervals to give greater control over an attacker, narrower gateways often set back from the line of the defenses, and multiple ditch systems to keep artillery at a safe range. Good examples of the new thinking are the forts built during the third century against Saxon and other pirates round the coast of southeast England, and their counterparts on the other side of the Channel (the "Forts of the Saxon Shore"). The distinction between legions and auxiliaries became more and more blurred, and the size of units

and their internal organization changed: the new legionary fortress built for *Legio I Martia* by Diocletian (A.D. 284–305), for example, at Kaiseraugst near Basle in Switzerland, covered only 11 acres (4.5 ha), rather than the 50 or so acres (21 ha) normal in the early empire, and similar in size is the contemporary legionary fortress at El-Lejjun in Jordan (11.6 acres [4.6 ha]); both were furnished with numerous close-spaced projecting towers. The latter fortress formed part of Diocletian's strengthening of the eastern frontier, which included other fortresses at Trapezus on the Black Sea and Aqaba on the Red Sea.

The history of Roman frontiers in the fourth century is one of a desperate attempt to strengthen existing frontiers with powerful forts in the hope of stemming the barbarian advance. In Britain Hadrian's Wall was maintained until late in the century, while some extra defenses were added elsewhere, such as the signal stations on the Yorkshire coast, and forts at Holyhead and Cardiff. On the Rhine there were new strongholds such as Cologne-Deutz (a fortified bridgehead on the far bank of the river), built by Constantine (A.D. 312–337) and Boppard, built by Valentinian I (364–375). The Danube remained the northern boundary in central Europe. Both here and on the Rhine the garrisons were a mixture of defensive troops and the higher-status strike forces, the *ripenses*: the military frontier mentality was not only one of grim defense behind impregnable walls, but of mobile offensive operations against the enemy as well. In the East the frontier was constantly under threat from the Persians. Only under Julian, who in 363 won a victory at Ctesiphon in Babylonia, did the initiative pass to Rome, and then only briefly, for soon afterward Armenia and part of Mesopotamia were given up.

[*See also* BRITISH ISLES: ROMAN BRITAIN; CELTS; EUROPE: ROMAN AND POST-ROMAN EUROPE; GERMANS AND GERMANIC INVASIONS.]

■ C. M. Wells, *The German Policy of Augustus* (1972). E. N. Luttwak, *The Grand Strategy of the Roman Empire* (1976). I. B. Catanicu, *The Evolution of the System of Defensive Works in Roman Dacia* (1981). D. Breeze, *Northern Frontiers of Roman Britain* (1982). D. L. Kennedy, *Archaeological Explorations on the Roman Frontier in North-east Jordan* (1982). W. S. Hanson and G. S. Maxwell, *Rome's North-west Frontier* (1983). A. Johnson, *Roman Forts* (1983). J. Wacher, ed., *The Roman World* (1987). D. H. French and C. S. Lightfoot, eds., *The Eastern Frontier of the Roman Empire* (1989). B. H. Isaac, *The Limits of Empire: The Roman Army in the East* (1990). C. R. Whittaker, *Frontiers of the Roman Empire* (1994).

Roger Wilson

ROMAN ROADS

One of the most famous road systems known to archaeology is that built by the Romans. The first of their stone-paved all-weather roads, the Via Appia, was built in 312 B.C. to give speedy access from Roman to southern Italy. In the centuries that followed the road system steadily expanded as the Roman Empire grew, until by the first century A.D. it stretched from the Atlantic in the west to the Euphrates in the east. The road system was a vital instrument of the Empire, allowing swift passage of troops and securing the communications on which its survival depended. Several of these roads survive today in their original form as paved highways, but many others have been used and reused over the centuries so that although the road line has been preserved the Roman road itself lies buried beneath more recent surfaces.

After the establishment of a new province, the Romans

built paved roads, probably on the line of older unpaved roads, and created a network of land communications, no doubt for both military and administrative reasons. The provinces of Macedonia and Asia provide illustrations of this policy.

The first Roman roads in Asia Minor were built in 129 B.C., immediately after Rome had inherited the kingdom of Pergamum from Attalus III in 133 B.C. In some new provinces, however, roads were made only after an interval. In Cilicia and Syria (both founded in 63 B.C.) and in Galatia (founded in 25 B.C.) a road network was not constructed until a hundred years later. In Asia Minor the road systems survived, more or less intact, until the Turkish invasions (A.D. 1071). In the provinces of Cilicia, Syria (and its neighbors), Arabia, and Aegyptus, where the Byzantines lost all control after the battle of Yarmuk (A.D. 636), the system disintegrated.

The evidence for this historical summary is based largely on the texts inscribed on milestones. Milestones were erected at an interval of one Roman mile (*milia passuum* = 1,000 Roman paces = 4,872 feet [1,485 m]) along all the roads of the Empire. The basic purpose was to indicate distance. Secondarily they recorded the date of road construction or repair work.

The size of the milestones was never standard or uniform. Only the earliest, Republican milestones had a characteristic shape: a thick, usually tapering shaft and a square plinth, the two cut as a single whole. Some milestones were set on a prepared plinth. The height of the column was usually not more than 4.9 feet (1.5 m). Later milestones varied in dimension; some stood as high as 6 feet (2 m). The inscription was cut on the upper half of the shaft. Recently, evidence for painted inscriptions has come to light in Palaestina.

In form the Republican milestones were massive and imposing, in language, stark and severe. They recorded the road construction of the Roman proconsuls in Asia (in 129 B.C.) and in Macedonia (ca. 125 B.C.). During Imperial times, however, both the form and the language underwent changes. From Augustus onward the texts gave not only the date of construction or repair but also, in elaborate detail, the full or near-full titulature (sometimes including genealogy) of the emperor. The latest milestones naming an emperor are dated to the reign of Anastasius I (A.D. 491–518) and Justin I (A.D. 518–527). Thereafter, although the road system was maintained, the practice of erecting milestones was not.

No Roman road map has been preserved although maps are known to have existed. On the other hand, a medieval copy of an extremely curious depiction of the Roman Empire has survived. Known as the *Tabula Peutingeriana* (the "Map of Peutinger") the map is curious on account of its shape. The Roman world was compressed into a long, narrow strip 22.3 x 1.1 feet (6.82 x 0.34 m). This method of projection, therefore, has distorted the relationships between lands, seas, and islands. Furthermore, there are numerous errors in spelling and location. Nevertheless the *Tabula Peutingeriana* presents valuable information on the cities, towns, and roads of the Roman Empire.

Unlike the *Tabula Peutingeriana*, which illustrates the whole Roman world, the itineraries or road guides treat individual roads, usually by province. The names of Roman roads and cities are listed and then the towns and places on the roads between cities. Distances are indicated in Roman miles.

The most important itinerary, the *Itinerarium Atnonini* (the "Itinerary of Antoninus"), is thought to date from the time of the Emperor Caracalla (A.D. 211–217). The *Itinerarium Hierosolymitanum* (the "Jerusalem Itinerary") refers only to the route from ancient Burdigala (Bordeaux in France) through the Balkans and Asia Minor to Jerusalem in Palestine. It dates from the year A.D. 333 and lists place names, including the small villages and large towns through which the Roman road passed.

Both the *Tabula Peutingeriana* and the *Itinerarium Antonini* indicate some but not all the roads together with the cities, towns, and villages along these roads. The *Itinerarium Hierosolymitanum*, however, categorizes the stopping places: *mansio* (an inn for an overnight stay) or *mutatio* (a posting station where horses could be changed). These stopping places were established at convenient intervals between cities and towns. On average the interval was 6 Roman miles (3.7 miles [9 km]). The remains of inns and posting stations still survive intact in Macedonia, Asia Minor, and Syria.

The roads were organized for military and official personnel and for the imperial post service but they were also used for the transporting of goods and supplies, both governmental and private. Civilian traffic is well documented in ancient sources. In the Byzantine period a new traveler emerged: the Christian pilgrim. In all periods considerable attention was paid by the authorities, both civic and imperial, to law and order on the roads.

No Roman road east of the Adriatic resembles the beautifully constructed roads of Italy, such as the *Via Appia* south of Rome. The much-photographed road west of Aleppo in Syria, generally regarded as Roman and compared with the fine basalt surfaces found in Italy, is demonstrably Byzantine in construction and date (fifth to sixth century A.D.).

The construction of Roman roads from Thrace to the eastern borders of (ancient) Syria was remarkably uniform. There were three elements: large, sometimes huge, edge stones, laid flat, one row on either side of the road; a spine of smaller stones, set vertically on edge, dividing the road into two lanes; and an in-fill of small stones, roughly 3 to 9 inches (0.10–0.30 m) large, between the edge stones and the spine.

There was only one layer of road surface. No bedding or foundations were employed. There is no evidence for digging or excavating a trench for the road surface. The surface stones were laid directly on the ground or topsoil. It is probable that the road was periodically strewn with gravel or sand in order to provide a smooth surface, especially for vehicles.

This type of construction was normal where the terrain was flat and free of rocks. Where the angle of the terrain was laterally steep or where the ground was rocky, different techniques were employed. When the forward (i.e., longitudinal) line of the road was steep, a series of steps was constructed or cut in the rock.

For the crossing of a small stream or shallow marsh, a stone-paved ford was constructed. The typical plan was in the shape of a double "dog-leg," that is with two bends or angles. Major streams and rivers were crossed by bridges built of stone or wood (or both in combination), or by pontoons.

It is important to distinguish between wide and narrow roads, between those roads usable both by foot travelers and by vehicular traffic (highways), and those usable only by foot travelers (roadways). The criterion defining a non-vehicular road is the presence of steps, which, of course, cannot be negotiated by wheeled vehicles. The presence of wheel ruts is an indication that a road was used by carts or wagons.

In the Late Roman/Early Byzantine Period (fourth to sixth centuries A.D.) a fundamental change took place, whereby vehicles were largely displaced in favor of pack animals, principally the camel. As a consequence, when reconstructed some highways became roadways. Thereafter the road systems of the eastern Mediterranean remained virtually intact until the nineteenth century.

[*See also* LAND TRANSPORTATION, *articles on* ROADS AND TRACKS, VEHICLES.]

■ L. Casson, *Travel in the Ancient World* (1974). R. Chevalier, *Roman Roads* (1976). D. Kennedy and D. Riley, *Rome's Desert Frontier from the Air* (1990).

David H. French

ROMAN AQUEDUCTS

Aqueducts were employed by pre-Roman civilizations (such as the Jerwan aqueduct serving Nineveh [built 703–690 B.C.], and *qanats,* the Iranian underground aqueducts), but Roman aqueducts must stand quite apart, from the sheer scale, scope, and magnitude of the achievement. The water supplied to Imperial Rome came to somewhere between 650,000 and 1,300,000 cubic yards (.5 million cu. m and 1 million cu. m) every twenty-four hours, more per capita than modern New York, largely because taps were rare, though known, and with all outlets left permanently running, most of the water, unused, went straight into the drains, helping to keep them scoured clean.

Despite our familiarity with the great arcades and bridges, 90 percent of all aqueducts were underground, some (e.g., the Aqua Appia at *Rome) entirely so. In its usual form, the conduit had concrete walls and a vaulted roof, and was perhaps a meter underground, running at a gradient of 0.15 percent to 0.3 percent with inspection manholes about 246 feet (75 m) apart. It would be around 3 feet (1 m) wide and 5 feet (1.5 m) high, irrespective of the volume of water carried, for the governing factor was human access for maintenance. This usually meant constant chipping away of the calcium carbonate deposit left by the water; accumulating at .04 inches (1 mm) per year, this incrustation could eventually choke the channel, and in the Middle Ages it often did. Interestingly, great plaques of it were then often removed and used in architectural embellishment, especially in Rhineland churches.

In hill country, extensive engineering works were often required to maintain the level of the conduit. Ridges had to be pierced by tunnels, valleys spanned by imposing bridges. The largest of these surviving is the Pont du Gard, carrying the River Gardon the aqueduct serving Nîmes, in southern France. This aqueduct, 161 feet (49 m) high and 903 feet (275 m) long, with a maximum clear span of 80.5 feet (24.52 m), was built ca. 19 B.C. in three superimposed tiers of arches. The bottom and middle tiers are the same size, with a very small one added on top. Its elegant proportions are much admired, despite a suggestion that the top tier is a last-minute addition to correct an error in surveying. Other large bridges are at Tarragona, Segovia, Metz, and Oued Ilelouine (Cherchel, Algeria). Valleys too large to be bridged were spanned by siphons (more properly, "inverted siphons," but "siphon" is the term conventionally used), which conveyed the water through one or more lead pipes—in some cases as many as nine, side by side. The depth of the valley, and hence the static pressure

inside the pipes, was often reduced by spanning its bottom by a low bridge *(venter),* before the pipes rose again and delivered the water into an open tank, whence it continued in the conventional aqueduct. The Romans well understood the problems of pressure and were capable of dealing with them. The common modern belief that they could not make pipes strong enough (based on a misunderstanding of Vitruvius) is sufficiently disproved by the fact that they regularly did, and the main drawback of siphons was their cost, for bridges were cheaper. Lyon in particular had nine siphons on the four aqueducts serving it (at Rome there were few or none), which needed a total of 10,000 to 15,000 tons of lead; the largest siphon is the Beaunant one, about 2 miles (2.6 km) long and 404 feet (123 m) deep, on the Gier (Lyon) aqueduct, being thus two to three times as big as the Pont du Gard bridge. Aspendos (Turkey), which has three consecutive siphons entirely on top of a bridge that zigzags, presents a puzzle not yet convincingly solved.

As the aqueducts approached a lowland city such as Rome or Carthage, they sometimes crossed the plain on long continuous arcades (at Rome up to approx. 7 miles (11 km) long). Being over level ground, these were quite different from the mountain bridges, their purpose being to deliver the water at a high enough level to serve by gravity flow as much as possible of the city. At Rome the opening of new aqueducts to supply increased demand often resulted in a second channel being added on top of the first, and riding it piggyback to the city.

On arrival the water passed through a distribution tank *(castellum divisorium),* of which the two best-preserved examples, at Pompeii and Nîmes, continue to defy scholarly attempts to reconcile their design with the confused description in Vitruvius. Thence most of the water went to feed the great city baths. These voracious consumers were the real *raison d'être* of the aqueduct network, though once it was built the water was naturally also used for drinking and domestic purposes, hitherto supplied, and apparently quite efficiently, by wells and rainwater cisterns. Some cities, such as Ampurias (Spain) and London never had an aqueduct at all. It can thus be argued that the Roman aqueducts were a luxury, not a necessity, and in arid regions, where the scant rainfall was desperately needed for agriculture, were positively wasteful. However, we may at least absolve them from the charge that they encouraged lead poisoning by their extensive use of lead service pipes: The calcium carbonate incrustations formed a lining inside them, insulating the water from the lead, and in any case, without taps, the water was never in the pipe long enough to become contaminated.

A number of Roman-style aqueducts, mostly modeled on that of Segovia, were successfully built in Mexico by the *conquistadores,* but frequent efforts by the colonial French to restore to service Roman aqueducts in North Africa all failed. The authentic Roman evaluation is best left to Nerva's water commissioner, Sextus Julius Frontinus: "I ask you! Just compare with the vast monuments of this vital aqueduct network those useless Pyramids, or the good-for-nothing tourist attractions of the Greeks!"

■ Frontinus, *Stratagems and Aqueducts,* tr. and ed. C. E. Bennett (1925). Thomas Ashby, *The Aqueducts of Ancient of Rome* (1935). Gunther Garbrecht et al., eds., *Die Wasserversorgung Antiker Städte,* vols. 1–3 (1986–1988). A. Trevor Hodge, *Future Currents in Aqueduct Studies* (1990). A. Trevor Hodge, *Roman Aqueducts and Water Supply* (1992).

A. Trevor Hodge

THE COUNTRYSIDE OF THE ROMAN EMPIRE

The Roman landscape was shaped by two fundamental factors. The first was that Rome was an agrarian society with a high percentage of the population dependent on the land. The second was that the relative security of the Pax Romana allowed for dispersed farmsteads established in relation to economic and social rather than defensive needs.

Two characteristic early Roman rural institutions were the colony and the villa. Beginning in the fourth century B.C. colonies of soldier-farmers were established in key defensive locations in Italy. Each had a fortified urban center and tracts of surrounding farmland, which were divided into regular plots by the process known as centuriation and assigned to the colonists. This practice of founding colonies with centuriated land was extended into the provinces as well. Air photographs of field patterns provide evidence of Roman centuriation in Italy, France, Spain, and North Africa.

The villa was the most common form of Roman rural residence. Each villa was a freestanding complex combining residential and agricultural units. Originally, most were simple working farms. From the second century B.C. onward, however, the Roman elite used their villas not only for income production but also as centers of leisure and entertainment. The living quarters were expanded and decorated with statuary, mosaics, and wall painting. This luxury was especially characteristic of the *villae maritimae* located along the Italian coast and the *villae suburbanae* built on the outskirts of major cities and towns.

This growth of luxury villas has been associated with the growth of the great estates known as latifundia. These were slave-based estates that resembled the plantations of the pre–Civil War American South. Their growth was the result of the great wealth and massive influx of slaves that resulted from Rome's wars of conquest of the second and first centuries B.C. Scholars have long argued that the development of the latifundia destroyed the small Roman farmer and heightened tension in the countryside. Many claim now that the role of the latifundia has been exaggerated and that the Roman landscape continued to be inhabited by peasants living on farmsteads of different sizes. The vitality and diversity of Roman rural life was maintained well into the imperial period.

Roman rural archaeologists long concentrated on the mapping, excavation, and dating of larger villa sites and the recovery of art objects such as mosaics and sculpture. Yet the recent debates on the character of Roman rural life have stimulated new types of archaeological research. More emphasis is now placed on the reconstruction of the environment from the evidence of seed and animal bones, the reconstruction of *field systems and land use patterns through aerial photography and geological studies, and the placement of individual sites in the larger landscape through regional surveys. In this research, farmsteads are related to each other, to other types of rural sites such as market centers and shrines, and to the land and its resources. Aerial photography and systematic regional surface surveys, for example, have revealed an unsuspected density of farmsteads in areas of Italy, France, and Britain.

The emphasis on the total landscape has forced a rethinking of the extent of Romanization, especially in northwestern Europe, where the Roman conquest came relatively late. Until recently it was thought that the Romans largely destroyed the former native societies. Now archaeologists are collecting considerable evidence that demonstrates the survival of native shrines and villages and pre-Roman modes of landscape and household organization. Certain aspects of rural activity still remain underrepresented in the archaeological record. We know from written sources that sheep and cattle herding was a major factor in the Roman rural economy. Bone analysis has provided much more evidence for animal breeds and the use of animal products. However, the migratory nature of early *pastoralism means that many archaeological sites connected with this way of life are hard to recover.

Major uncertainties still surround the end of the Roman rural world. Exposed farmsteads did not survive in the growing insecurity of the early medieval period. However, the processes of rural decline were complex and showed considerable regional variation. Farmsteads in some areas of Italy were abandoned by the second century A.D., while others continued to be occupied into the sixth century. The villas in the western provinces, exposed to earlier and more frequent Germanic invasions, show an even more complex pattern of abandonment. Some were deserted by the third century. Others survived into the fourth and fifth centuries and were converted into monasteries and rural churches. The discovery of cemeteries at many villa sites suggests that tenant farmers continued to remain on the land long after the proprietors had left. By the sixth century A.D., however, the characteristic landscape had disappeared, even in Italy.

[*See also* EUROPE: ROMAN AND POST-ROMAN EUROPE.]

■ J. D'Arms, *The Romans on the Bay of Naples* (1970). K. D. White, *Roman Farming* (1970). J. Percival, *The Roman Villa* (1976). T. Pottery, *The Changing Landscape of South Etruria* (1979). E. T. Salmon, *The Making of Roman Italy* (1982). K. Greene, *The Archaeology of the Roman Empire* (1986). T. Pottery, *Roman Italy* (1987). S. L. Dyson, *Community and Society in Roman Italy* (1992).

Stephen L. Dyson

THE EASTERN PROVINCES OF THE ROMAN EMPIRE

The Roman eastern provinces represent the territories of the eastern Mediterranean stretching from mainland Greece to the Euphrates, including Turkey, Syria, Palestine, northern Arabia (Transjordan and the Sinai), and Egypt. In essence, these lands are those conquered by Alexander the Great and consequently where Greek institutions and culture were predominant. In these "Greek-speaking" provinces, the cities were the primary centers for administration, connected by roads that were maintained and protected by military garrisons. Latin was the official language for civil officials and military personnel during the early empire, but it was eventually eclipsed throughout the east by the native Greek language. In contrast, the rural landscape essentially retained its native and indigenous qualities prior to the Christianization of the region. The Aramaic language was widely used throughout the Levant and other native languages were still preserved in the hinterland throughout Roman rule. The revival of the native languages occurred especially in Christian communities, symbolized by the use of Coptic in Egypt and Syriac in the Levant during the late empire. For a limited time, Mesopotamia was embraced as a province after Emperor Trajan's campaign against Parthia (A.D. 114 to 117), but was soon abandoned by his successor Hadrian. The area of Upper Mesopotamia was again occupied by Rome during the campaigns of Lucius Verus (A.D. 162 to 165) and Septimius Severus (A.D. 197 to 199), but its existence as a separate province was again fleeting. In the other regions, the lasting impact of Roman rule is still visible in the remains of civic architecture, numerous inscriptions, well-preserved forts, and occasional stretches of paved roads. Until recently, the archaeology of the region mainly focused on the urban centers and major sites of occupation, but increasing interest in the rural landscape is reflected in the numerous recent surveys and excavations in the hinterland.

Roman occupation of these regions was a slow and complex development over centuries. It began with the Roman conquest of the Greek colonies in southern Italy and *Sicily, often called *Magna Graecia*. One of these colonies, Tarentum, appealed to Pyrrhus, king of Epirus (modern Croatia and Albania), to assist in halting Roman aggression, but in spite of Pyrrhus's victories the Greek cities eventually capitulated to the Romans and became allies (282 to 270 B.C.). At stake in this conflict was commerce between the Adriatic and the eastern Mediterranean. Subsequent piracy in the Adriatic provided Rome with the opportunity to conquer the region and make it a Roman protectorate (228 B.C.). By the late third century B.C., the Greek world was fully aware of the formidable threat posed by Rome. To counter it, Philip V, king of Macedon, entered an alliance with the Gauls north of Italy and Hannibal in Italy, precipitating a conflict with Rome that ended in a military stalemate and a temporary peace treaty in 205 B.C. However, Philip soon entered an alliance with the Seleucid king, Antiochus III, in Syria to protect the Aegean from Roman expansion. When the small mainland kingdom of Pergamum in Asia Minor and the island of Rhodes petitioned Rome in 201 B.C. for assistance against this allied threat, the Romans embarked on the Second Macedonian War (200 through 197), which ended with Rome effectively in control of Greek affairs. This war was the major turning point in the political life of the eastern Mediterranean. After Antiochus III was defeated at Thermopylae in Greece (191 B.C.) and Magnesia in Asia (190 B.C.), a Roman protectorate was eventually established over all of the Greek cities on both sides of the Aegean and the Peace of Apamea levied a war indemnity over the Seleucid kingdom that restrained any further aggression. In 168 B.C., Macedonia was divided into four independent republics and Illyrica into three. By 146 B.C., however, all of Greece was subjected to direct Roman rule. The Hellenistic kingdoms of the east were soon reduced to squabbling principalities that Rome effectively controlled by military intimidation or diplomacy. With the expedition of the military commander Pompey to the east (67 to 63 B.C.) and Augustus's defeat of Antony and Cleopatra at Actium in 31 B.C., the heritage of Alexander the Great came to an end. Archaeological surveys and excavations throughout the Near East and the eastern Mediterranean have uncovered evidence of the far-reaching changes occasioned by the institution of Roman rule in each of the provinces of the region.

Asia. In 133 B.C., the kingdom of Attalus III of Pergamum was bequeathed to Rome and reorganized as the province of Asia. This territorial addition provided Rome with most of the western coastal land of Asia Minor (Anatolia or modern Turkey), extending from the Troad in the north to Caria in the south, including inland Phrygia as well. The fertile agricultural lands and thriving industrial centers of this region were now under Roman control. After Pompey's campaigns against the pirates of Cilicia in 67 B.C. and against Mithridates VI of Pontus in 66 B.C., the territory of Asia was enlarged to include Bithynia on the Black Sea in the north, Galatia to the east, and Lycia and Cilicia on the

southern Anatolian coast. From 49 B.C. to the end of the third century A.D., the Roman province of Asia extending from the Aegean to the Euphrates remained a single territorial unit, divided into twelve or thirteen subdistricts (each called a *conventus*, or *dioikêseis*) named after their chief cities, where provincial courts and assemblies were regularly held. The largely urbanized landscape of the western part of the province was a conglomeration of city territories, ruled by the provincial governor whose seat was at *Ephesus and Pergamum. During the first two centuries of imperial rule, the local temple shrines of Didyma and Aphrodisias were lavishly embellished and the Greek cities in western Asia flourished, as indicated by their impressive architectural remains. The rural interior, in contrast, retained its local character and culture, with the exception of scattered administrative centers. The discovery of the text of the famous *Res Gestae* at the temple of Augustus in Ancyra (modern Ankara) is one of the spectacular Roman finds from the heartland of the province. Throughout most of Roman rule, the eastern frontier was the Euphrates, where legions were stationed at Satala *(XV Apollinaris)*, Melitene *(XII Fulminata)*, and Zeugma *(IV Scythica)*. A far-reaching administrative change came in A.D. 297, when Emperor Diocletian divided Asia into seven autonomous provinces, thereby marking an official end to the economic and political unity of Roman Asia.

Syria. After Pompey's annexation of the region in 64 B.C., the old Seleucid capital of Antioch was transformed into the seat of Roman governors. Their administrative responsibilities included oversight of the affairs of the client kingdoms of Commagene in the north and Arabia in the south. For this reason, internal communications were vital. A road to the east through Aleppo connected Antioch with the Euphrates; another road to the southwest through the Antiochean suburb of Daphne led to the seaport of Laodicea. Another road more than three hundred miles long linked Antioch with Ptolemais (modern Akko) on the seacoast, via the prosperous Phoenician seacoast towns of Byblos, Berytus (modern Beirut), Sidon, and Tyre. Antioch was the province's most important political, economic, and cultural center throughout the imperial period; its population reached almost half a million by the fourth century A.D. Though little of its former grandeur remains, the abundant mosaics from Antioch itself and nearby Daphne now preserved in the Antakya Museum reveal the prosperity and wealth enjoyed by its wealthiest inhabitants. The other Greek cities in northern Syria (Hierapolis, Beroea, Cyrrhus, Chalcis, and Apamea) were also prominent centers of population and wealth, their status and importance attested by their coins. Apamea also has one of the largest theaters known from the Roman world.

The military importance of the province of Syria was dictated by the confrontational policies of the Parthian and later Sassanid dynasties of Iran, who made the frontier region of the Euphrates and Mesopotamia a focal point for diplomacy and conflict between themselves and Rome. As a result, three or four Roman legions were always stationed in Syria, with numerous auxiliary units supplementing their military force. The region from Damascus to Philadelphia (modern Amman) was known as the Decapolis, a league of ten autonomous cities, which was administered as an annex of Syria from the time of Augustus until A.D. 106, when the city territories were divided between the provinces of Syria, Arabia, and perhaps Judaea as well.

During the second and third centuries, the oasis city of

Palmyra rose to prominence as a commercial entrepôt, providing an overlay trading link between the Roman Empire and India and Parthia. Septimius Severus made it a Roman colony, but after the revolt led by the native queen Zenobia (A.D. 268 to 270), and its conquest by Aurelian in 273, its importance gradually declined to that of a desert military outpost. Palmyra's impressive ruins include several temples, a theater, colonnaded streets, and a spectacular necropolis of tower tombs, all of which attest to its ancient wealth and prominence. Another important archaeological site on the imperial frontier is Dura-Europus, located on the Euphrates. It was conquered in A.D. 165 and remained an important Roman military outpost on the eastern border of the empire until its capture by the Sassanians in A.D. 257. Excavations there have provided insight into the local syncretism of Roman and Persian traditions, symbolized by the worship of the deities and cults of Mithras, Bel, Atargatis, and Hadad. The excavated buildings include one of the most important ancient synagogues known from the ancient world, now preserved in the National Museum at Damascus, and the earliest known Christian church building. Parchment documents and papyruses from the site are of importance for our understanding of the administration of the military outpost and represent the fullest documentation we have of any military unit (the *cohortes XX Palmyrenorum*).

Palestine. After the Maccabean revolt against the Seleucid king Antiochus IV in 167 to 164 B.C., Judaea became an independent kingdom under the Hasmonean dynasts. Under these Jewish high priests and monarchs, the territory was enlarged to include the Greek coastal cities, the regions of Samaria, Galilee, Peraea, and Ituraea to the north, and many of the Greek cities in Transjordan. Political rivalry between Hasmonean heirs Aristobulus II and Hyrcanus II brought the intervention of Pompey in 63 B.C., who left Hyrcanus as priestly ruler and ethnarch. The Roman governor of Syria, Gabinius, severely undercut the political autonomy of the Hasmonean monarchy by creating five autonomous districts, leaving Hyrcanus as only spiritual leader. Political power was to some extent regained by Hyrcanus when his minister Antipater assisted Caesar at Alexandria in 48 B.C. After the Parthian invasion of 40 B.C., Antipater's son Herod managed to gain appointment as client king of the region, and under his rule, urbanism in the Hellenistic and Roman model flourished, as attested by excavations at Caesarea Maritima, Samaria-Sebaste, and *Jerusalem. The *Dead Sea Scrolls, discovered near Qumran in 1947 to 1956, provide evidence for Jewish sectarian beliefs and practices in this period. Herod's elaborate rebuilding of the Jerusalem Temple and his construction of magnificent palaces at Masada and Jericho testify to his concentration of wealth. After Herod's death and the deposition of his son and heir Archelaus, however, Judaea, Samaria, and Idumaea became the Roman province of Judaea, administered by Roman governors at Caesarea Maritima. After a brief period of quasi-independence under Herod's grandson Agrippa I (40 to 44 A.D.), Judaea was again placed under direct Roman rule. A national uprising against Roman rule (known as the First Revolt, A.D. 66 to 74) resulted in widespread destruction. After the First Revolt (A.D. 66 to 70), Jerusalem became the headquarter's for the *legio X Fretensis* and, with the destruction of the Temple, the national religious center was shifted to Jamnia and eventually Galilee. After a second revolt against Roman rule led by Bar-Kokhba (A.D. 132 to 135), the emperor Hadrian refounded Jerusalem

as *Colonia Aelia Capitolina,* a pagan city in which Jews were prohibited to enter. The *legio VI Ferrata* was transferred from Syria to Galilee, the province made consular, and its name changed to Syria-Palaestina. Extensive excavations at sites such as Caesarea, Scythopolis (modern Beth Shean), and Cerasa in Jordan testify to the extensive urbanization that occurred over the following century. A major change came to Palestine with the conversion of Constantine to Christianity in the fourth century. Afterward, Christian pilgrimage to Jerusalem and other biblical sites brought a renewed economic vitality to the region.

Arabia. In A.D. 106, the Nabataean Arab kingdom centered at Petra became the last of the Near Eastern client kingdoms to be annexed by Rome. A provincial capital was established at Bostra as the seat of a praetorian legate and garrison of one legion, the *III Cyrenaica.* One of the first administrative acts in this province was the construction of a central highway from Bostra to Aela (modern Aqaba) on the Red Sea, some 267 miles (430 km) of paved road known from its milestones as the *Via Nova* and completed between A.D. 111 to 114. The formal recruitment of six units of the former Nabataean royal army, the *cohortes Ulpiae Petraeorum,* took place at the same time as the construction of the highway and may have been part of the preparations for Emperor Trajan's Parthian War in A.D. 114 to 116. Prior to the Roman annexation, the Nabataean royal capital of Petra had functioned as the emporium for shipping aromatic goods throughout the Levant and Mediterranean world. Its magnificent rock-cut tombs are among the most spectacular archaeological monuments in the world. Even after the annexation, Petra remained the administrative capital of the southern sector of the province and suggestions that Petra declined under Roman rule are belied by its being granted the titles of *metropolis* under Trajan and *colonia* early in the third century, even before similar titles were bestowed on the provincial capital city of Bostra. Moreover, the village settlements increased and flourished in the environs of Petra during the second century.

Farther south, however, the status of the Nabataean port of Leuke Kome in Midian and Hegra (Meda'in Salih) in the Hijaz remain unclear. The latter has magnificent rock-carved tomb facades that rival Petra and are dated from A.D. 1 to 74, but none thereafter. Some evidence exists for Roman military presence in the region into the third century, yet by the Byzantine era it is clear that the Hijaz had come under the control of Arab tribes, some of which were affiliated with the Romans as *foederati.* By this time, the province of Arabia had been reduced in size, with the central region (below the Wadi Mujib) and southern regions (including the Negev and Sinai) becoming a separate province known as Palaestina Tertia. The III Cyrenaica legion remained at Bostra, with the IV Martia now stationed at Lejjun in central Transjordan, and the X Fretensis transferred from Jerusalem to Aela (Aqaba). This string of legionary camps with numerous small forts along the desert periphery has been called the *limes Arabicus,* but the precise meaning of the term *limes* refers simply to the frontier zone, not a clearly defined border, and the function of the troops stationed there seems to be monitoring the internal population of the province, not guarding against an external threat from desert nomads.

Egypt. After Octavian's defeat of Antony and Cleopatra at Actium in 31 B.C., the Hellenistic kingdom of the Ptolemies in Egypt became the private possession of the emperor. Unlike other provinces that were administered by members of the Senate, Egypt was governed by a vice-regal official representing the interests of the emperor, who had the title of prefect and was of non-senatorial status. Senators were allowed to enter the province only with the consent of the emperor. *Alexandria retained its status as the first city; the three regions of the Nile (Delta, Middle Egypt, and the Thebaid) were administered by officials called *epistrategoi*. As in the Hellenistic period, Egyptian society was split between the foreign ruling authorities, merchants, entrepreneurs, and military personnel at the top and the native Egyptian peasantry at the bottom. This division was sharply along racial, social, and economic lines. Roman commercial policies not only exploited the native population, but drained the natural resources of the Nile region even more efficiently and effectively than the Ptolemies had previously. Important information on social life in Roman Egypt has been derived from the Oxyrynchus papyruses.

Egypt was the chief supplier of grain for the gigantic population of Rome, but also supplied masonry from quarries in the eastern desert at Mons Claudianus and Mons Porphyrites. Though few monuments from the Roman period have survived in Alexandria, it is clear that the city flourished and exported goods of local and foreign manufacture all over the Mediterranean. The development of Red Sea trade with Arabia, India, and the Far East expanded during the early Roman imperial era (30 B.C. to A.D. 217). Roads and forts were established between the Nile and the Red Sea ports to facilitate and protect this commerce. A number of these commercial harbors have been the focus of recent archaeological investigation, including Abu Sha'ar (formerly thought to be Myos Hormos), Leukos Limen (Quseir al-Qadim), and Berenice.

Roads and Imperial Patronage. All the eastern provinces of the Roman Empire were linked by a sophisticated road system that is known in some detail from such documents as the Peutinger Table (an elongated road map), the Antonine Itinerary (a road-book without maps), and the *Onomastican* of Eusebius (a gazeteer of sites in Palestine). These sources provide the names and distances of some of the most important roads. These official arteries were utilized for administration and the movement of troops. Travelers along them were offered protection by garrisoned road stations and hospitality by caravanserai and *mansiones* (hostels). Additional archaeological information has come from the discovery of numerous milestones throughout the Near East that provide the dates of construction and sometimes identify the termini of the roads.

Visits by emperors to the east were an additional stimulus to the growth of towns and villages along the main routes. During Emperor Hadrian's tour of the east in A.D. 129 to 130, cities like Antioch, Palmyra, and Bostra gained imperial honors. The visit also kindled great excitement among other Greek cities, provoking numerous construction projects in his honor. City arches and temples dedicated to the emperor dot the eastern landscape from Athens to the Levant; the eastern cities began to revive and create Greek foundation legends to win honors from this Philhellenic ruler; later, Septimius Severus's stay in the east had a similar impact on the region, which was reorganized and revitalized during his reign. In fact, his wife, Julia Domna, was a native Syrian, and mother of the emperors Caracalla and Geta (A.D. 211 to 217), her sister Julia Maesa, the mother of Elagabalus (A.D. 218 to 222), and her niece Julia Mamaea, the mother of the emperor Severus Alexander (A.D. 222 to 235). Under the emperor Philip the Arab (A.D. 244 to 249),

another native of Syria, Rome celebrated its foundation millennium in A.D. 248. After the conversion of Constantine, *Constantinople (formerly the Greek city of Byzantium and modern Istanbul) was founded in A.D. 324 as a "second Rome" and imperial residence for the east. Its importance continued long after the collapse of Rome in A.D. 476, surviving as the capital of the Byzantine Empire until its conquest by the Ottoman Turks in 1453.

[*See also* MEDITERRANEAN TRADE.]

■ A.H.M. Jones, *Cities of the Eastern Roman Provinces*, 2nd ed. (1971). A. N. Sherwin-White, *Roman Foreign Policy in the East, 168 B.C. to A.D. 1* (1983). E. S. Gruen, *The Hellenistic World and the Coming of Rome*, 2 vols. (1984). G. W. Bowersock, *Roman Arabia* (1983). M. Sartre, *L'Orient Romain* (1991). B. Isaac, *The Limits of Empire: The Roman Army in the East*, 2nd ed. (1992). S. Mitchell, *Anatolia: Land, Men, and Gods in Asia Minor* (1993). F. Millar, *The Roman Near East, 31 B.C.–A.D. 337* (1993).

David F. Graf

ROME. The city of Rome, capital of modern Italy, stands above one of the greatest centers of the ancient world. It is perhaps the world's richest and most complex archaeological site, with a continuous occupation spanning almost 3,000 years. Initially a group of farmsteads or small villages, the settlement grew to be the capital of the Roman Empire, and when that declined took on new importance as the residence of the popes. The heart of the modern city is rich in monuments that have been the subject of considerable archaeological and art-historical research over the centuries. Less is known of the residential districts of ancient Rome, but much can be deduced from the available remains and from surviving records and other writings, which refer to many-storied tenement blocks in which most of the population lived.

In archaeological terms, the development of Rome can be divided into five separate stages: the early settlement, the Etruscan city, Rome in the republican period, the imperial centuries, and early Christian Rome.

Tradition held that Rome was founded in 754 B.C. by twin boys, Romulus and Remus, who were abandoned by their parents but suckled by a she-wolf. Archaeology has revealed that it actually began life in the tenth or ninth century B.C. as a series of farmsteads or small villages on the famous Seven Hills (Capitoline, Palatine, Aventine, Caelian, Esquiline, Viminal, and Quirinal) overlooking the River Tiber. Between the hills were marshy valleys where the local people buried their dead in cremation or inhumation cemeteries. They lived in houses of wattle and daub with thatched roofs, like the so-called hut of Romulus preserved as a pattern of postholes on the Palatine. The original appearance of the houses can be judged still better from the pottery hut urns used to contain the ashes of the dead in the cemetery located on the site later occupied by the Forum.

Toward the end of the seventh century, this group of rustic settlements was transformed into a city by Etruscan rulers from the north. In archaeological terms the change takes the form of tiled roofs and stone foundations—more substantial buildings than the earlier huts. The new rulers drained the marshy Forum valley and laid it out as a public square with a gravel-paved surface: a formal city center. The stream that bisected the Forum was canalized as the Cloaca Maxima, and the first bridge, the Pons Sublicius, was built across the River Tiber. It was only of wood, and only wide enough for foot passengers, but it provided the first all-weather link between the Tiber banks.

Rome became an important center under Etruscan rule. Inscriptions in the Etruscan language have been found in the city, and a temple in the Etruscan style—dedicated to Jupiter Capitolinus—was built. There may also have been an agger, or city wall, with a defensive ditch beyond it.

Toward the end of the sixth century B.C., the Romans rose in revolt against their Etruscan rulers and expelled them from the city. In place of the monarchy they set up a new republican constitution, wherein power rested with the senate (the assembly of leading citizens) and two annually elected consuls. The most visible remains of early republican Rome are those of the Servian wall, built in 378 B.C. after the city was attacked by the Gauls. By the end of the fourth century, Rome had grown to such a size that an artificial water supply, the Aqua Appia, had to be built, the first of many aqueducts.

Most of the early buildings of Rome lie buried under later structures. Exceptions are the republican temples in the Largo di Torre Argentina. But the sequence of visible monuments begins really in the second century B.C., when the wealth of empire coupled with new constructional techniques (notably use of brick and concrete) allowed the Romans to embark on a grandiose building program. In the late second century B.C., the temple of Hercules Victor became the first building in Rome to be faced in expensive marble. In the middle of the following century, ambitious generals such as Pompey and Caesar expressed their power through new public buildings, including the city's first stone theater (built by Pompey) and the entirely new forum begun by Julius Caesar.

Caesar's assassination in 44 B.C. was followed by the accession of his adoptive son Augustus as the first Roman emperor in 31 B.C. By this time Rome had grown to be the largest city in the western world, with a population of around a million people, from wealthy senators to shopkeepers, craftsmen, and slaves. Augustus was determined to make Rome a capital worthy of a great empire, and he and his family adorned it with many new and restored monuments. These included structures of an essentially propagandist or dynastic nature, such as the Ara Pacis Augustae (Altar of the Augustan Peace) or the huge circular mausoleum where he and his close relatives were eventually buried, but Augustus also built new aqueducts and took particular pains to reorganize the regular shipment of grain from Egypt, which was distributed free of charge to the urban poor.

The pattern of imperial building set by Augustus was followed by his successors. The policy was a mixture of public service and state propaganda. Thus the Colosseum built by Vespasian (A.D. 69–79) was both a massive auditorium for popular entertainment and a stage set in which the emperor could appear in his proper public setting, surrounded by senators, knights, and common people each in their allotted tiers of seating. The later emperors did depart from Augustus's precedent in one important respect, however, building themselves an imperial residence on Palatine Hill, which has given us the modern word "palace." The greater part of the surviving structure dates to the reigns of Domitian (A.D. 81–96) and Septimius Severus (A.D. 193–211).

Two other categories of imperial buildings at Rome demand special mention: the imperial fora and the huge bath complexes. The original Forum Romanum had been both market and meeting place, but by the first century B.C. was too cramped for the needs of the growing metropolis. The early emperors responded by building a series of adjoining imperial fora, which were both dynastic showpieces and public utilities, providing law courts, offices and libraries. Largest and most splendid was Trajan's Forum, built by the emperor Trajan (A.D. 98–117) from the proceeds of his Dacian conquests. The conquests themselves were celebrated in the spiralling friezes of Trajan's Column, which formed part of the complex. Trajan also built an elaborate baths complex near the Colosseum, and later emperors (notably Caracalla, Diocletian, and Constantine) followed suit. These complexes included not only swimming pools and hot saunalike baths, but libraries, lecture halls, and dining rooms.

While the Roman empire was at the peak of its power, the imperial capital needed no defenses, but by the later third century A.D. the situation had changed, and in A.D. 271 the emperor Aurelian began the construction of the massive walls that are still one of the most conspicuous features of the city's topography. Rome declined in importance during the fourth century, when a new imperial capital was founded at Constantinople (modern Istanbul). Sacked by the Goths in 410, Rome nonetheless retained its preeminence as a religious center (under the papacy) into the Middle Ages, and Roman architectural traditions were preserved in the many early Christian churches, such as Santa Maria Maggiore and Santa Sabina on the Aventine.

No account of ancient Rome would be complete without mention of the cemeteries that lie along the major roads leading out of the city. The most famous, the Via Appia, is still lined by the ruins of elaborate burial monuments. Here too lie some of the major catacombs associated with the early Christian community. Further afield, Rome was linked by road and river with the city of Ostia at the Tiber mouth, and with the artificial harbors built by Claudius (A.D. 41–54) and Trajan a short distance to the north. Here, goods brought from overseas (notably the all-important Egyptian grain) were transferred to smaller vessels for transport up the Tiber to the quaysides of Rome itself.

[See also EUROPE: ROMAN AND POST-ROMAN EUROPE; MEDITERRANEAN WORLD: THE DOMINANCE OF GREECE AND ROME; ROMAN EMPIRE.]

■ J. B. Ward-Perkins, *Roman Imperial Architecture* (1981) T. Cornell and J. Matthews, *Atlas of the Roman World* (1982). L. Richardson, *A New Topographical Dictionary of Ancient Rome* (1992).

Chris Scarre

ROSETTA STONE. Named after the village in the western Egyptian delta where it was found, the trilingual inscription found on the Rosetta Stone provided the key for the decipherment of other Egyptian hieroglyphic discoveries. It was found in mid-July 1799 by a French officer of engineers called Bouchard, one of Napoleon's expedition to Egypt, and was reportedly built into an old wall that was demolished to extend Fort Julien. Accompanying French scholars quickly realized the importance of the inscribed slab of granite but were compelled to cede it to the victorious British army under Article XVI of the Capitulation of Alexandria. In 1802, the stone was installed in the British Museum in London, where it has been on display ever since.

The importance of the Rosetta Stone lies in its being inscribed in three scripts (demotic, Greek, and hieroglyphs) but only two languages (ancient Egyptian and Greek). At the time of the discovery of the Rosetta Stone, the language of ancient Egypt had been extinct for fourteen centuries, although charlatans like the Jesuit Athanasius Kircher in the seventeenth century had erroneously claimed to have deciphered hieroglyphic inscriptions. Yet the Rosetta Stone provided scholars, for the first time, with a Greek translation of an Egyptian language, and the Greek section was found to contain a decree passed on 27 March 196 B.C. by Egyptian priests gathered at Memphis to celebrate the first anniversary of the coronation of Ptolemy V.

Because Greeks formed the upper levels of the Ptolemaic bureaucracy and Egyptian speakers formed the vast majority of the population throughout the Ptolemaic period (305–30 B.C.), royal decrees were routinely issued in both Greek and Egyptian. Thus the text of the Greek section of the Rosetta Stone was repeated in both Egyptian hieroglyphic script, used primarily for monumental inscriptions, and demotic, a script derived from hieroglyphs via cursive hieratic. Demotic was the contemporary documentary script embodying the current form of the language in the Ptolemaic period and was quite different from the hieroglyphs in grammar and vocabulary.

The elongated ovals called *cartouches*, which contained the royal names in hieroglyphs, provided the key to the decipherment of the Rosetta Stone inscription, when compared to the corresponding royal names in the Greek text.

A comparison of the royal names on the Rosetta Stone—in conjunction with the *cartouche* of Cleopatra inscribed on the Bankes' obelisk at Kingston Lacey, Dorset, England—enabled English physician Thomas Young to demonstrate in 1819 in an article in the *Encyclopedia Britannica* that hieroglyphs were basically phonetic, not symbolic, as had previously been thought. This insight offered the French scholar Jean François Champollian the basis for further discoveries. His *Lettre a M. Dacier* in 1822 marked the beginning of the scientific reading of hieroglyphs and the first step toward formulation of a system of ancient Egyptian grammar, the basis of modern Egyptology.

[*See also* WRITING: EGYPTIAN HIEROGLYPHIC.]

■ Carol Andrews, *The Rosetta Stone* (1981). Stephen Quirke and Carol Andrews, *The Rosetta Stone: Facsimile Drawing* (1988).

Carol A. R. Andrews

S

SALVAGE ARCHAEOLOGY. *See* CULTURAL RESOURCE MANAGEMENT.

SAMPLING. Often in archaeological research statistical sampling must be used due to time and funding constraints. For instance, if all sites in a region or an individual site cannot be excavated entirely and complete information is not obtained, archaeologists instead select representative samples from which they make generalizations about the characteristics of a population. In some cases, straightforward methods maximize the potential of acquiring representative samples. At other times, peculiarities of the archaeological work makes it difficult to evaluate the accuracy of the sample.

In formal terms, a "population" is set of things (e.g., the ceramics at a site) about which information (e.g., what percentage is decorated) is sought; an "element" is an individual member of the population (e.g., a potsherd); and a "sample" is a subset of elements drawn from the population.

A sample must be obtained carefully so that it typifies the population without bias, the bane of sampling. Prejudice in the selection process leads to unrepresentative samples and inaccurate population estimates. For example, a researcher could pick up the first one hundred potsherds seen on the surface of a site and, with the information derived from them, generalize about all of the pottery deposited there. Decorated ceramics are more visible than plainware pieces, so the haphazard selection of one hundred potsherds is likely to comprise a sample that includes a disproportionate number of decorated specimens.

To avoid sampling bias, every element in the population must be given an equal and independent chance of being selected. This procedure, called random sampling, maximizes the likelihood of selecting a representative sample. Moreover, it allows the application of statistical models that specify the degree to which an estimate derived from the sample is likely to deviate from the actual value of the population characteristic in question. Random sampling works in situations where every element of the population is known beforehand, such as when the population is the assemblage of all potsherds recovered during an excavation. In this case, a random selection of potsherds could provide estimates about the assemblage as a whole with a known degree of precision, and at a fraction of the cost it would take to analyze the entire assemblage.

Unfortunately, random sampling and its attendant statistical models break down in situations where the complete list of population elements is not available. Frequently in archaeology, the population of interest extends beyond the cultural materials that can be readily enumerated. For example, some potsherds may have been recovered from some sites, but the researcher really desires information about all ceramics in a region (i.e., from all sites). Excavations cannot assure every potsherd an equal and independent chance of being recovered because the locations of artifacts are not known until they are unearthed, and groups of clustered items, not independently selected individuals, are discovered in excavation units.

An idiosyncrasy of archaeological excavations is that the units of investigation (excavation units) do not correspond to the units of measurement (e.g., potsherds). Under this constraint, archaeologists have devised methods to deal effectively with their unorthodox databases, while recognizing that their samples are not ideal. For instance, a random selection of excavation units yields sets of artifact clusters, not independently selected individuals, but at least the sets are randomly chosen. Some statistical techniques can handle random cluster samples, although the estimates derived from them are not as precise as those from unclustered samples. Also, a random selection of excavation units will reveal a sample of buried features, such as subsurface house floors and inhumations. However, the shapes, sizes, and orientations of the excavation units make it likely that features with particular shapes, sizes, and orientations will be found more readily than others. Sophisticated computer simulations that account for these complications have been developed to estimate the population size of buried features at partially excavated sites.

In other situations, random sampling schemes are not appropriate. An example can be taken from regional surveys where field crews walk the landscape to discover prehistoric sites. Sampling a fraction of the regional space in a random way can lead to a sample of sites from which the number of villages in the region can be estimated. However, the scatter of sites found at random locations on a map are not particularly useful for determining the spatial relationships between the villages in the region, or between them and other sites, such as farmsteads and hunting camps. Spatial relationships are best observed when entire tracts of the region are surveyed and all of the sites within them are located.

In practice, archaeologists confront populations of interest from which they may select and study only a portion of the constituent elements. Consequently, sampling strategies are formulated on the basis of research interests, but they are always tempered with a strong dose of pragmatism, as dictated by the practicality of doing archaeological research. Limited resources, other constraining factors, and the unique qualities of archaeological data recovery demand for each project a clear outline of goals, careful decisions about what data must be collected to satisfy these goals, and a thorough assessment of the proposed procedures for collecting the necessary data. As such, a thoughtfully formulated sampling scheme can be a productive design for mediating between research ambitions and limited realities.

[*See also* ANALYSIS, METHODS OF; STATISTICAL ANALYSIS.]

■ Lewis R. Binford, "A Consideration of Archaeological Research Design," *American Antiquity* 29 (1964): 425–441. James W. Mueller, ed., *Sampling in Archaeology* (1975). Bonnie Laird Hole, "Sampling in Archaeology: A Critique," *Annual Review of Anthropology* 9 (1980): 217–234. Jack D. Nance, "Regional Sampling in Archaeological Survey: The Statistical Perspective," in ed. Michael B. Schiffer, *Advances in Archaeological Method and Theory*, Vol. 6 (1983), pp. 289–356. H. Martin Wobst, "We Can't See the Forest for the Trees: Sampling and the Shapes of Archaeological Distributions," in eds. James A. Moore and Arthur S. Keene, *Archaeological Hammers and Theories* (1983), pp. 37–85. David R. Abbott, "Unbiased Estimates of Feature Frequencies with Computer Simulation," *American Archaeology* 5 (1985): 4–11.

David R. Abbott

SAN LORENZO, a large Mesoamerican Formative Period Olmec center, occupies a plateau overlooking the Coatzacoalcos River in southern Veracruz, Mexico. It was initially settled early in the second millennium B.C. and reached its zenith during the San Lorenzo A and B phases (1200–900 B.C.), after which it was abandoned. Palangana phase inhabitants reoccupied the ridge during the period 800–600 B.C. after which it remained uninhabited until the Villa Alta phase (A.D. 900–1100).

The San Lorenzo phase community covered about .4 square miles (1 sq. km) and contained perhaps 1,000 people. Earth mounds supported temples and houses constructed of poles and thatch that faced open plazas, and the pits that provided the mound fill were turned into water reservoirs by lining them with bentonite. Elaborate drain systems constructed of U-shaped stone troughs and stone covers carried excess water from the reservoirs to the plateau edge. Several sculptures displaying water symbols were found associated with one drain line, suggesting that the drains and reservoirs served ritual functions. The Olmecs altered the plateau's natural shape with several large man-made appendages or ridges; one, the Group D ridge, extended 1,640 feet (500 m) and contained artificial fill to a depth of 23 feet (7 m). It has been suggested that the appendages served to reshape the entire settlement into a gigantic bird effigy (Coe and Diehl 1980).

San Lorenzo's glory lies in its seventy Olmec-style stone monuments. These include colossal heads, "altars" (flat-topped thrones), and life-sized seated humans, jaguars, and many other creatures. Most depict motifs and concepts related to rulership and dynastic affairs. Basalt for monuments and drains was quarried in the Tuxtla Mountains more than seventy kilometers away, but apparently the actual sculpting was done at San Lorenzo.

Matthew W. Stirling of the Smithsonian Institution conducted the first excavations at San Lorenzo in 1946 with sponsorship by the National Geographic Society. Michael D. Coe of Yale University directed an extensive research project at the site in 1966–1968, and Mexico's Instituto Nacional de Antropologia e Historia and Universidad Veracruzana also carried out field investigations in 1969. Ann Cyphers G. (Universidad Nacional Autonoma de Mexico) initiated the latest long-term project at the site in 1989.

[*See also* MESOAMERICA; FORMATIVE PERIOD IN MESOAMERICA; MESOAMERICA: INTRODUCTION; OLMEC CIVILIZATION.]

■ Michael D. Coe and Richard A. Diehl, *In the Land of the Olmec*, 2 vols. (1980).

Richard A. Diehl

SARZEC, Ernest de (1832–1901), was a French consular official with considerable experience in Ethiopia and Egypt. While he had visited many archaeological sites along the Nile, he had no experience of excavation, but a profound interest in Oriental art. He was transferred to Basra on the Persian Gulf in 1877, at that time an outpost of the Ottoman Empire. Basra was a sleepy town, so Sarzec passed the time exploring the ancient mounds of southern Mesopotamia and buying clay tablets through local antiquities dealers. Only two months after arriving in Basra, Sarzec dug into the one and a half miles (2.5 km) of mounds at Telloh (ancient Lagash). The excavations soon uncovered the foundations of temples and other mud brick structures, large numbers of clay tablets, terra-cotta cylinders, and terra-cotta statues of a ruler named Gudea. Sarzec realized he had discovered a hitherto unknown Mesopotamian civilization far earlier than that of the Babylonians and Assyrians to the north. He took a leave of absence from his consular post, sailed to Paris, and sold his unique collections to the Louvre. The French government subsidized further excavations at Telloh in 1880–1881, which continued almost every year until 1900. Sarzec was hardly a scientific excavator, but he realized the importance of long-term excavations, of deciphering complex temple foundations, and of recovering as many small objects as possible. In this respect, he was ahead of his time, when most excavators sought clay tablets and little else. Unfortunately, rapacious looters descended on Telloh every time he departed. They found the priceless royal archives of Lagash and dispersed them all over the world. Ernest de Sarzec proved the existence of the Sumerian civilization, the oldest state-organized society in the world, hitherto known only from Babylonian tablets, and identified originally by French cuneiform expert Jules Oppert in 1869.

[*See also* HISTORY OF ARCHAEOLOGY BEFORE 1900: NEAR EASTERN ARCHAEOLOGY; MESOPOTAMIA: SUMER AND AKKAD.]

■ Ernest de Sarzec and Léon Heuzey, *Découvertes en Chaldée* (1884–1912). Brian Fagan, *Return to Babylon* (1979).

Brian M. Fagan

SCANDINAVIA

Early Prehistory of Scandinavia
Scandinavia in the Bronze Age
Scandinavia in the Iron Age
Scandinavia in the Viking Age

EARLY PREHISTORY OF SCANDINAVIA

Most of Scandinavia was covered by ice during the last glaciation. Immediately south of the ice shield reindeer hunters lived throughout the glacial period. As the ice retreated people moved north with the reindeer. During the Allerød, a warmer climatic period (ca. 10,800–ca. 10,000 B.C.), the forest temporarily invaded the area and elk became the dominant game animal.

For the period of the late glacial tundra (ca. 12,500–ca. 9000 B.C.), a sequence of cultures have been identified: Hamburg, Federmesser, Bromme, and Ahrensburg. The material remains consist mainly of a plain lithic inventory based on a good blade technology. Bone and antler tools, however, are also known. Settlements were small and of short duration. There is evidence to suggest a tent-based habitation, as well as a mobile exploitation pattern of the natural resources.

Mesolithic Hunters of the Inland Boreal Forests (ca. 9000–6800 B.C.). After the retreat of the ice, the sea level was 295 feet (90 m) lower than today. It rose gradually until ca. 7000 B.C. when it was 98 feet (30 m) below the present level. In this continental period the southern part of the North Sea across to Great Britain was dry land. Along the rivers and lake shores of this forested flatland, hunters settled in small groups. We have named their culture the Maglemosian. Bogs spreading across the former occupation areas have allowed exceptional preservation of the remains of this culture. The flint technology was "microlithic" with many delicately formed points used as arrowheads. The bone inventory was dominated by barbed bone points for leisters. The habitation consisted of small rectangular huts built of light materials. Summer settlements clustered along the river- and lakebanks, while during the winter the settlements moved to drier ground.

The economy had a broad-spectrum base, with hunting in the forests, extensive fishing in the lakes and rivers, and gathering of fruits, nuts, and plants.

Mesolithic Coastal Fishers and Hunters of the Atlantic Period (6800–3900 B.C.). Around 7000 B.C. the sea began to rise at an astounding pace, some 98.5 feet (30 m) in just 600 years, flooding great tracts of land. The present area of Denmark was changed into a maze of fjords, bays, and islands. Along the protected coastlines a rich hunter-fisher culture evolved. This culture is known in its early stage of development as Kongemose, and subsequently as Ertebølle.

The material remains comprise a many-sided inventory of flint tools, antler and bone implements, and during Ertebølle, for the first time in the Danish cultural sequence, pottery. A rich inventory of wooden artifacts is also known: dugout boats, paddles, bows, arrows, axe handles, leisters, rouses, and complete fish weirs.

Settlements were concentrated in the most favorable fishing positions along the coast. They seem to have been permanent, with individual groups staying within restricted territories. Close to the settlements we find formal burial areas.

Fishing, gathering of mollusks, and hunting were the dominant elements of the economy in coastal regions. Gathering and hunting in the forest is also attested, but C-13 investigations of skeletal material show that the terrestrial component in overall diet was negligible. The many mollusks gathered led to the accumulation of large heaps of debris known as køkkenmøddinger ("kitchen middens").

Neolithic Forest Farmers (3900–2800 B.C.). Farming was first introduced to Denmark with the Funnel-necked Beaker culture. The material culture is very rich, dominated by an abundant and excellent pottery production. The decoration of the pottery is artistically among the best ever produced in northern Europe. Among the flint tools, the huge grounded thin- and thick-butted axes call for particular attention.

Settlements were initially small, dispersed, and temporary. During the Neolithic Period the size and permanency of the settlements grew, and toward the end we find very large permanent settlement sites, tending to concentrate on the coasts.

Farming was based on a combination of cereal growing and livestock husbandry. A swidden agricultural system based on artificially created secondary forests of mainly birch and coppiced hazel is attested. The livestock seem to have been supported by a combination of permanent pastures and forest feeding.

Burials took place in monumental tombs. Initially, timber-built chambers in long barrows were used. Subsequently, *megalithic tombs took over, first dolmens and then passage graves. Huge ritual centers known as causewayed enclosures were constructed and used in a short period around the middle of the Neolithic Period. Extensive offerings, including human beings, were deposited in the bogs.

In central Sweden and south Norway the Pitted Ware culture formed, later spreading into South Sweden and parts of Denmark. It was basically a hunter-gatherer culture, but also incorporated agricultural elements. Settlements had a long duration and were frequently placed in a coastal position.

Late Neolithic Farmers and Stock Herders (2800–1700 B.C.). With the appearance of the Corded Ware tradition in Europe, profound changes occurred in the cultural patterning of the agricultural societies in Scandinavia.

The most prominent elements of the material culture now were tokens of manhood, initially stone battle axes, and later on flint daggers, both manufactured to a very high standard.

Settlements became small and dispersed all across the landscape. The pollen diagrams show an opening of the landscape for agricultural purposes. The agricultural economy was based on cereal growing (mostly barley) and cattle herding.

Burials were individual inhumations with a marked differentiation between men and women. In the western parts of Denmark the graves were placed in small barrows, in the eastern parts mostly in reused megalithic tombs and newly built stone cists, while in Sweden they were flat cemeteries of graves. These changes in Late Neolithic Denmark prefigure many of the features present in the following Bronze Age.

[See also EUROPE, articles on THE EUROPEAN MESOLITHIC PERIOD, THE EUROPEAN NEOLITHIC PERIOD.]

■ Steen Hvass and Birger Storgaard, eds., *Digging into the Past. 25 Years of Archaeology in Denmark* (1993).

Torsten Madsen

SCANDINAVIA IN THE BRONZE AGE

The Bronze Age of Scandinavia, also known as the Nordic Bronze Age, lasted from 1800 to 500 B.C. The period was first defined by C. J. *Thomsen as part of his *Three-Age System, and was later subdivided by the Swedish archaeologist Oscar *Montelius. Based on typology of bronze objects, it is divided into Montelius Periods I–VI, where Periods I–III constitute the Early Bronze Age and Periods IV–VI, the Late Bronze Age. The Scandinavian Bronze Age, as a distinct cultural complex characterized by common features in material culture, ritual activities, and subsistence modes, extended over southern Scandinavia, middle Sweden, and along most of the coastal stretches of Sweden and southern Norway. North of this area, in northern Sweden and Norway, contemporary groups show influences from the southern Bronze Age societies and from Russia, but were hunting communities with a substantially different lifestyle and little use of bronze.

Development of Bronze Use. There are neither copper nor tin sources in Scandinavia, and the area depended on trade and exchange for the metal used so extensively and strikingly in its material culture. Despite this dependency, the Scandinavian Bronze Age developed its own repertoire of bronze objects, whose importance was enhanced by their deposition in hoards and inclusion in graves. The bronze objects range from locally distinct types, such as the elaborate neck collars of the Early Bronze Age, to local copies of central European objects, like swords. They also include imports, such as cauldrons and horse harnesses, in the Late Bronze Age. Bronze objects were imported from all corners of Europe, including Russia, although central and eastern Europe were the main areas of influence. The recent discovery at Fröslunda in western Sweden of a hoard containing at least fourteen Late Bronze Age shields of central European type deserves special mention. The shields were manufactured from thin, hammered bronze sheets and could not have had a defensive purpose. Their nondefensive character is also suggested by the fact that they were manufactured as pairs and deposited together in a lake. Ritual activities often involved such paired items, as is clearly illustrated by the pairs of horned bronze helmets and lures (musical instruments). The latter were even made so that each element of a pair was musically tuned to the other.

The objects from the earliest Bronze Age were pan-European types, but local design and production soon dominated. A rich vocabulary of ornaments, dress fittings, toilet equipment, tools, and weapons developed, and many of these were beautifully ornamented. Bronze, in addition, was used to produce special objects of apparent ritual significance. These were often unique both in their conception and design, and of remarkable technical quality. Examples are the *Trundholm chariot with its horse and sun as well as small acrobatic figurines. But even mundane objects were often of high quality and richly decorated, and the cultural significance of bronze compared to other materials is obvious. Its importance lasted throughout the Bronze Age, and iron, which appeared in the Early Bronze Age, did not replace bronze until several centuries after its introduction, when it was already common in central Europe.

The range of types broadened during the Late Bronze Age, when influences from the central European Urnfield culture intensified the decorative role of bronze (see Urnfields). This period saw, for example, frequent use of bronze rattle attachments on objects and horses. Both size and variability of ornaments and dress fittings increased, and at the end of the Bronze Age the "baroque style" dominated. Metal was also used in new ways for defensive armour and vessels, and objects made from sheet bronze became common. The social importance, as opposed to functional significance, of these objects is attested by the extensive emphasis on display. This is seen in the attachment of bronze to the human body, sometimes permanently, as in the case of certain neck rings. It is also strongly suggested by the emphasis on decoration on many weapons. At times practical use was impossible, and the objects were merely for display like the symbolic battle-axes made of clay covered by bronze sheet.

The striking wealth of bronze in an area without natural access to the raw material, along with the development of a highly visual local bronze industry, has in recent decades caused the Scandinavian Bronze Age to be interpreted as a prestige goods system. Although variation in local surplus production was the basis for fluctuations in wealth, it is suggested that local chiefs came into existence and maintained their position by their access to long-distance ex-

change networks through which the flow of prestigious bronzes was managed. New analyses have investigated the objects in terms of their production and the cultural factors that influenced and were influenced by their use. An understanding of Scandinavian Bronze Age gender distinctions has also begun to emerge, since bronze objects were not merely differently used by men and women but were also involved in distinct distribution systems depending on their gender association. The wealth of objects in graves has furthermore been employed in the analysis of social differences within society, and modest but nonetheless clear ranking seems to be characteristic.

Changes in Material Culture. The changes over time in material culture were due both to internal developments and inventions and to external influences. The earliest Bronze Age, replacing the Late Neolithic or Dagger Period, was largely initiated by external influences that brought new impulses to material culture in the form of ornaments and weapons, while settlements and burial practices show no distinct developments at this time. This changed, however, at the beginning of Period II, when the Scandinavian Bronze Age began to develop its own unique and separate identity. Long-distance influences and imports became restricted to certain types, such as the swords, and the bulk of the material culture developed in close contact with near neighbors such as the Early Bronze Age Sögel-Wohlde culture of northern Germany and later the Lusatian culture of Poland. In the Late Bronze Age, the impact of external influences changed, and a separation between local products and imports was often applied to their use.

After Period I, burial practices also became more distinct. Large burial mounds were erected over stone or oak coffins and the deceased were dressed and accompanied by personal items marking status and identity. The construction of such graves was a considerable undertaking, and their turf mounds show that large areas would have needed to be stripped of surface soil, a practice that had severe agricultural implications. The turf lining of these barrows has in some cases caused superb preservation, and a number of remarkable graves, such as *Egtved, are known. They provide unique insights into details of the burial practice, such as the different stages involved in the wrapping of male and female corpses in the coffin. The former had swords placed on top of the cowhide wrapping, while for the latter all personal objects were deposited under the hide. The unusual preservation also means that organic materials were found, such as woven pieces of clothing, bark containers, and the hair of the deceased. This has made it possible to reconstruct Bronze Age garments that, together with dress fittings and textile fragments from less well preserved graves, show that at least three different costumes were in use. The remains also show that the head and the hair were the focal points for decoration, with elaborate hats and hairnets widely used and hair braided, cut, and styled. The attention to appearance and the suggestion of vanity is also indicated by the common use of razors, tweezers, and combs from the middle of the Early Bronze Age.

At the end of the Early Bronze Age, cremation was introduced through the influence of the central European Urnfield culture, and during the Late Bronze Age this became the dominant burial ritual. At the beginning, cremations might still contain elements of the inhumation rites, such as stone coffins or grave goods, but the new rite gradually affected all elements of the burial process, and by the end of the Bronze Age, the cremated body was buried in an urn under level ground or as secondary grooves in a barrow. At times, the urns were clustered in small cemeteries, apparently unmarked on the surface but clearly recognized by the contemporary community as a special area for the dead. Although cremation became the dominant practice, a few outstandingly rich inhumation graves, such as Voldtofte on Funen, are known; these may have been burials of particular important individuals.

Settlement Evidence. Bronze Age settlements and details of their domestic architecture were barely understood prior to the 1960s, when several large settlement projects were initiated. As a result, hundreds of houses are now known, and their relationship both to their immediate settlement space and the wider cultural landscape have been studied. Only modest changes can be detected during the Bronze Age, but it is nonetheless during this period that the change from the two-aisled longhouse of the Neolithic to the Iron Age villages of three-aisled longhouses took place. The Bronze Age house was a substantial wattle-and-daub, three-aisled longhouse without internal structural divisions. Artifact analysis suggest that there may have been different activity areas both within and around the house, but there are no other traces of these, and the organization of the settlements is still somewhat of an enigma. They have no marked boundaries nor structures such as wells, paths, or fences, although pits and midden deposits may be found. Some settlements in the uplands of Sweden appear to have been more substantial and longer lasting than their southern counterparts, such as the site of Hallunda, where large amounts of debris including molds for bronze casting were found. In these regions settlements often include several so-called burnt mounds composed of fire-cracked stones and settlement debris. These constructions are found by the hundreds, usually in connection with settlements but at times on their own or associated with burial mounds. Their function is not entirely understood, and much research is currently directed toward recording and investigating evidence of the structures, as they may hold important clues to the activities that took place in settlements.

It has been demonstrated that the Bronze Age settlement units together with graves formed territories that sometimes had hoards or rock carving sites along their boundaries. The location of barrows on abandoned fields and the evidence of plowing over former settlements show that occupations were part of a cyclical movement probably caused by exhaustion of the fertility of the fields.

The Scandinavian Bronze Age provides a rewarding subject for archaeological investigation, as its material culture is well recorded and extremely rich. It is ideally suited to the application and development of archaeological theory, and as a result has provided many important case studies for the discipline.

■ Jørgen Jensen, *The Prehistory of Denmark* (1982). Thomas B. Larsson, *The Bronze Age Metalwork of Southern Sweden: Aspects of Social and Spatial Organization 1800–500 B.C.* (1986). Christopher Prescott, "Late Neolithic and Bronze Age Developments on the Periphery of Southern Scandinavia," *Norwegian Archaeological Review* 24 (1991): 36–48. Marie Louise Stig Sørensen, "European Metal Age Culture," in *Encyclopaedia Britannica, Macropaedia*, vol. 18 (1992), pp. 592–604. Marie Louise Stig Sørensen, "Gender Archaeology and Danish Bronze Age Studies," *Norwegian Archaeological Review* 25 (1992): 31–50. Steen Hvass and Birger Storgaard, eds., *Digging into the Past: Twenty-five Years of Archaeology in Denmark* (1993).

Marie Louise Stig Sørensen

SCANDINAVIA IN THE IRON AGE

The Iron Age in Scandinavia is the period between 500 B.C. and A.D. 700, the time span between the Bronze Age and the Viking Age in Northern Europe. The period is divided into three main chronological phases: the Pre-Roman Iron Age (500 B.C.–A.D. 1), the Roman Iron Age (A.D. 1–400), and the Germanic Iron Age (A.D. 400–700), which are respectively contemporary with the Celts, the Romans, and the European mass migrations—including the establishment of the Frankish (Merovingian) kingdom—in central and southwestern Europe.

During this long period of time Scandinavian societies were gradually transformed from their traditional tribal structure based on ties of kinship and alliance into permanently class-divided early states. During the Pre-Roman Iron Age, village organization developed, based on family farms with stalled cattle. A system of "celtic fields" emerged at the same time, reflecting the complete restructuring of society after the decline of the Bronze Age. Social conflict during this period is reflected in *bog bodies such as *Tollund Man. By 150 B.C., with the emergence of Celtic *oppida ("proto-towns") in lands to the south, international trade accelerated and a new warrior elite appeared in Nordic burials. The emergence of large chiefly farms in some of the villages (for example at Hodde) are part of the process. This social structure continued until A.D. 200, by which time Roman imports had replaced Celtic.

At around A.D. 200 village society was reorganized and the enclosed village of the Pre-Roman Iron Age disappeared. The movement toward division into individual farmsteads was completed. The same holds for the smaller farmsteads and buildings without cattle stalls, which were subsumed by the new farmsteads. The system of production was reorganized too: the field systems ("celtic fields") were abandoned and replaced by an infield/outfield system, leading to an intensification of production. The reorganization of the village and of the system of production were concomitant with a redistribution of land, and now at least these were unified. The farmsteads became a productive and legal unity.

In the course of the Germanic Iron Age, royal power was consolidated as a social institution. The consolidation is manifest in the increased specialization and growth in craftsmanship, trade, and agricultural production. Proper trading sites emerged, as can be seen at Gudme/Lundeborg on Funen, at Ribe and Lindholm Høje in Jutland, and at Helgö in Sweden, no doubt under the full control and protection of the king. Craftsmanship blossomed and magnificent jewelry and weaponry (as found in the Vendel and Valsgärde cemeteries in Sweden) are evidence of the importance of gift-giving among the warrior elite.

The consolidation of the new social order also found expression in the redirection of ritual investment, from graves to sacrifices. The elite did not need to demonstrate the legitimacy of their special position through reference to their ancestors; there was however a continued need for the gods' favor. The personal accumulation and burial of valuables is another new feature that demonstrates well the individualized property and legal rights which undoubtedly also permeated the social economy.

Trading and raiding expeditions that brought wealth to the king and the warrior elite escalated, to be followed in the Viking Age by colonization. The Viking Age thus is to be understood against the background of the development that took place in the Germanic Iron Age. But in long-term historical perspective it represents the culmination of a social structure that was founded around A.D. 200–300.

[*See also* EUROPE: THE EUROPEAN IRON AGE.]

■ L. Hedeager, *Iron-Age Societies. From Tribe to State in Northern Europe, 500 BC to AD 700* (1992).

Lotte Hedeager

SCANDINAVIA IN THE VIKING AGE

The "Viking Age" is traditionally defined as the period when Scandinavian raiders terrorized Europe. Historically the era begins with their first recorded attack, in England, in A.D. 793. Defining an end point is less easy, for there is no single momentous event to signal it, although in almost the last, disastrous overseas raid in 1066, the Norwegian king Harald Hadraada was defeated and killed in England. Christianity had already made an impact in Denmark and in Norway by then, though it was to take a little longer before the Swedes also accepted it. The new religion cemented links between Scandinavia and north-west Europe, and encouraged the adoption in Scandinavia of new ideas, artistic impulses, and cultural forms. The eleventh century saw both the definition of nation states in Scandinavia and the end of the Viking Age.

This documentary-inspired view has persistently influenced the interpretation of archaeological discoveries. When fragments of Insular (British and Irish) decorated metalwork were first recognized in Scandinavian graves they were interpreted as Viking booty brought back to Scandinavia after 793. Other items buried in the same graves, particularly weapons (notably swords) and jewelry (notably brooches), were therefore also dated on the basis of this connection to the ninth century or later. But excavations in the 1980s at Ribe (Denmark) and Birka (Sweden), where there are independent chronological frameworks, show that characteristic "Viking Age" brooches were being made from the mid-eighth century onward. Other archaeological discoveries also indicate continuity and evolution from this and earlier centuries. Paradoxically, then, the term "Viking Age" is more usefully applied to the foreign forays of the Scandinavians rather than to their internal development; but since customary usage will probably retain it, its nuances should be kept firmly in mind.

Politics and Culture. Scandinavia's wide variety of terrain, climate, and natural resources ensured that in the eighth century there were considerable differences of emphasis in its economy and society. Political power was wielded on a local or regional, rather than a national or supranational, level. The need for identity generated by these domestic rivalries and foreign pressures may have encouraged raiding, trading, and settlement—the overseas manifestations of the age. Sometimes, as power ebbed and flowed, parts of what today are different countries were linked into a single political unit. Some boundaries were fluid, although others were physically well defined. For example, political power in Jutland extended south into what is now Schleswig-Holstein, as far as an earthwork territorial boundary, the Danevirke, which was constructed before 737.

Beyond the political diversity, there were shared cultural factors throughout the Scandinavian lands. These included communication through the Old Norse language, and the widely available iron-using technology. The technology also embraced a growing mastery of shipbuilding, which probably by the eighth century included sailing boats as well as relatively large oared vessels. These made not only the Baltic Sea but also the eastern Atlantic coastal fringes and the North Sea open to Scandinavian seafarers. This allowed an intensification of long-standing contacts that made prestigious foreign goods available to the Scandinavians.

Viking Ships. The remains of several hundred Viking Age boats have been found in Scandinavia, mostly used as burial chambers. The great majority are small rowing boats, represented only by rusting rivets. Some larger vessels were used for more prestigious burials, and they demonstrate a range of ship types. These include a classic, early tenth-century shallow draft longship, well suited to raiding far up river systems, found at Ladby on Fünen, Denmark, and coastal cruising vessels recovered in a good state of preservation at Gokstad and *Oseberg on Oslo fjord. More recently wrecks have revealed an ever-increasing variety of ferries and cargo ships. They are often recovered partly preserved in harbor silts, as at Hedeby (Schleswig-Holstein), or even where they were deliberately sunk to form blockages in vulnerable water routes as at Skuldelev in Roskilde Fjord, Zealand, Denmark. They show that bigger ships were being built at the end of the Viking Age, although the clinker type of construction remained constant throughout the era. The Skuldelev ships include a vessel built in Viking-controlled Dublin in ca. 1060, offering striking testimony to the vital links the sea provided.

Runic Writing. One form of evidence for Scandinavian Viking Age society, which has been recorded and studied for several hundred years, comprises inscriptions in the runic alphabet. They are reasonably numerous—over thirty-five hundred are known from Sweden alone, although most are from the eleventh century, at the end of the Viking Age. They are usually found on monoliths or rock faces, although even this durable medium is now threatened by atmospheric pollution. Most are memorials to the prosperous dead and to their deeds. They mention expeditions southeastward to Byzantine and Arab lands, and westward to England. They tell of locally famous sailors, warriors, and benefactors, as well as of the women who, when their husbands were abroad, managed the family's estates. Sometimes the rune stones link their memory with public-spirited works undertaken in their home districts, including bridge building, clearing roads, and laying out thing-sites (assembly places).

Art. The rune stones also introduce us to the artistic prowess of the age, for they are often decorated with interlaced designs incorporating stylized animal motifs. Such forms, which had already been the basis for much art in Scandinavia for several centuries, remained typical of Viking Age art. They were common to woodcarvers and textile weavers, whose output has only rarely survived (as at Oseberg), as well as to metalsmiths, whose work provides most of the extant artistic repertoire. A succession of Viking Age styles, evolving one from another, and recognized throughout Scandinavia, has been defined by art historians. The art that survives is elaborate, convoluted, and often applied to small-scale items such as brooches, although at the site of Urnes, Sogn og Fjordane, Norway, which has given its name to the last of these Viking Age styles, an elaborately carved door frame and other wooden panels demonstrate that larger-scale compositions were undertaken.

Religious Practices. Although Christian missionaries

visited Scandinavia in the early ninth century, and despite whatever Christian influences may have been introduced by travelers returning from Christian Europe, Viking Age Scandinavia retained its religious beliefs, cults, and mythology into the eleventh century (*see* Uppsala). Slightly later written sources provide the most specifically detailed insights into a pantheon that was essentially Germanic, but there are important surviving mythological representations, notably on pictorial rune stones such as at Ramsund, in Södermanland, Sweden.

Burials and settlement sites, with their associated objects, are the main sources of archaeological data for the Scandinavian Viking Age. Burials frequently contained everyday items appropriate to the deceased, and this convention suggests a belief in an afterlife. Both inhumation and cremation were practiced, and the details of the grave form and the burial site could greatly vary, reflecting both local custom, influences over time, and the status of the deceased. Some graves were marked, although again there was considerable variation. The use of ship-shaped stone settings, as at Lindholm Høje, Jutland, Denmark, and burial in boats or ships perhaps implies the concept of a voyage to the other world.

Burials that are either monumentally or artifactually impressive can be interpreted as an assertion of royal power. Gravefields such as that at Borre (Vestfold, Norway), with its large burial mounds and richly furnished graves dated ca. 600–900, attest to an important dynasty ostentatiously displaying its authority; so do related ship burials around Oslo Fjord at Tune, Gokstad, and Oseberg.

Occupation Sites. Settlement sites, particularly those in areas where timber rather than stone was the main building resource, have only recently been recognized, thanks to improved archaeological techniques. The discovery and large-scale excavation of villages in Jutland, Denmark, is exemplified at Vorbasse, where the investigation has shown a community periodically moving about within a .4 square mile (1 sq. km) area throughout the first millennium A.D. Such continuity into the Viking Age is not uniform, however; in contrast, the settlement at Forsandmoen, near Stavanger, Norway, disappeared ca. A.D. 800 after an existence of almost two thousand years.

Farming settlements, whatever their form, are the norm, but an increasing variety of other settlement sites are now becoming archaeologically visible. Borg, in the Lofoten Islands of arctic Norway, and Lejre, on Zealand, Denmark, indicate by the impressive scale of their timber buildings and the rich character of associated objects that they were royal or aristocratic manors. These sites both suggest increased specialization and the focusing of resources and assets and they indicate the exercise of regionally centralized authority from the beginning of the Viking Age.

Markets, Manufacture, Towns, and Trade. Marketplaces, established under royal control and often exhibiting evidence for a well-defined and carefully regulated plan, are another important class of site. Ribe, founded ca. 710 on the west coast of Jutland, developed from a seasonal focus for manufacture and exchange into a permanently occupied town. Åhus, in northeast Skåne (southwest Sweden), is another broadly similar early site that flourished in the eighth century. Hedeby, near Schleswig, on the east coast of Jutland, reportedly had merchants settled in it by royal decree in 808, and may have adversely affected Ribe's development. Within the Mälar valley region of Uppland, Sweden, the manufacturing and exchange aspects of the fifth–eighth

century occupation site of Helgö were transferred ca. 800 to Birka, on the nearby island of Bjorkö. On the adjacent mainland, at Adelsö, are traces of a medieval royal manor that had its origins in the seventh century if not before.

To these places came craftsmen who made goods in many of the era's standard forms and materials. Similar archaeological assemblages have been found on different sites, including debris from the working of iron, copper, lead, silver, and gold; bone and antler; wood; amber; glass; and leather. In quantity and quality these remains indicate technically competent mass production. They represent a new departure in the supply of goods to what may have been increasingly wealthy home markets. Overseas contacts also brought wealth to Scandinavia, through both trading and raiding. Enormous quantities of foreign silver coins have been found in Scandinavian hoards. Initially they came predominantly from Arab countries, but in the later tenth century and early eleventh century it was mainly English and German coins that swelled Scandinavian coffers.

The Late Viking Age. Renewed, centralized royal authority in tenth-century Denmark is also shown in rich graves. A princely grave at Mammen, in the Middelsom District of Jutland, which is precisely dated 970–971 by dendrochronology, is one famous example. Most informative of all is the monumental complex at Jelling (Jutland). The north mound, built over an earlier, Bronze Age mound, contained an empty timber burial chamber, dated 958–959; the south mound was not completed until the 970s. An elaborately decorated stone, equidistant between the two great mounds, records in a runic inscription how King Harald made all Denmark Christian. A large timber church, also between the mounds, had within it a grave containing remains, perhaps those of Harald's father, which may initially have been interred within the north mound's chamber.

Harald was probably also responsible for a remarkable series of circular earthworks of geometric precision that functioned as royal regional depots, controlling their vicinity. One at Trelleborg (Zealand) was erected in 980–981, and others are known at Fyrkat (Jutland), Aggersborg (Jutland), Nonnebakken (Fünen), and Trelleborg (Skåne).

Harald's tightening political grip was continued by his descendants and by their contemporary rivals in Norway and Sweden. Kings in all three countries first minted their own silver coins, incorporating their names and titles in the inscription, around the year 1000. They thereby recognized the propaganda value of the medium of exchange. Commerce was fostered with a series of newly founded towns, also dated to around the year 1000, which included Viborg, Odense, and Roskilde (Denmark), Trondheim (Norway), and Lund, Visby, and Sigtuna (Sweden). Several functioned also as the seats of bishops—another indication of the changes signalling an end to the Viking Age.

[See also BRITISH ISLES: VIKING RAIDS AND SETTLEMENT IN BRITAIN AND IRELAND; NORSE IN NORTH AMERICA.]

■ D. M. Wilson and O. Klindt Jensen, *Viking Art* (1966). J. Graham-Campbell, *Viking Artefacts* (1980). K. Randsborg, *The Viking Age in Denmark* (1980). E. Roesdahl, *Viking Age Denmark* (1982). E. Moltke, *Runes and Their Origin: Denmark and Elsewhere* (1987). J. Graham-Campbell, *The Viking World*, rev. ed. (1989). H. Clarke and B. Ambrosiani, *Towns in the Viking Age* (1991). E. Roesdahl, *The Vikings* (1991). E. Roesdahl and D. M. Wilson, eds., *From Viking to Crusader. Scandinavia & Europe 800–1200* (1992). J. Graham-Campbell et al., *Cultural Atlas of the Viking World* (1994). R. I. Page, *Chronicles of the Vikings* (1995).

Richard A. Hall

SCHLIEMANN, Heinrich (1822–1890), the excavator of *Troy, Mycenae, Tiryns, and Orchomenos. Raised in Ankershagen, Mecklenburg, Schliemann attended the *Realschule* in Neustrelitz. After five years as apprentice grocer in Fürstenburg (1836–1841), he set sail for Colombia in November 1841 but was shipwrecked off the coast of Holland. He worked as a clerk in Amsterdam and studied foreign languages to improve his prospects, achieving fluency in about fifteen. In 1846 he was sent to St. Petersburg, where he became a remarkably successful dealer in commodities. After a year in California (1851–1852), he returned to St. Petersburg, married, and raised a family. In 1868 a trip to Italy, Greece, and Troas changed his life. His published account earned him a doctorate in 1869.

Persuaded by Frank Calvert that Hissarlik was the site of Troy, Schliemann excavated there briefly in 1870 and more thoroughly in 1871–1873. His discovery of "Priam's Treasure" in May 1873 caused a sensation. The excavation of the shaft graves at Mycenae in 1876 revealed the wealth and sophistication of Mycenaean civilization, whose existence had previously been completely unknown. This remains his most striking achievement. Excavation at Orchomenos (1880–1881 and 1886) yielded little, but at Tiryns (1884–1885) he found a Mycenaean palace with frescoes. Continued excavation at Troy was the primary focus of the last twelve years of his life, with the campaigns of 1878–1879, 1882, and 1890. He died in Naples in December 1890.

Schliemann's achievements remain controversial. His books are contaminated with untruths. It is now clear, for instance, that his second wife, Sophia, did not witness the discovery of "Priam's Treasure." The whole treasure appears to be a composite. It seems equally clear, however, that his archaeological reporting is usually reliable. Many attribute his misstatements to mistakes or puffery. Schliemann's significance lies in his priority in the field, the importance of the sites he excavated, and his skill in dramatizing his finds to attract media attention, thereby making archaeology a subject of general interest.

[See also HISTORY OF ARCHAEOLOGY BEFORE 1900, *articles on* NEAR EASTERN ARCHAEOLOGY, CLASSICAL ARCHAEOLOGY.]

■ Heinrich Schliemann, Personal Papers, Gennadius Library, American School of Classical Studies, Athens. Heinrich Schliemann, *Ithaque, le Peloponnese et Troie* (1869). Heinrich Schliemann, *Troy and Its Remains* (1875). Heinrich Schliemann, *Mycenae* (1878). Heinrich Schliemann, *Ilios* (1881). Heinrich Schliemann, *Troja* (1884). Heinrich Schliemann, *Tiryns* (1885). George S. Korres, *Bibliographia Herrikou Sleman* (1974). Leo Deuel, *Memoirs of Heinrich Schliemann* (1977). David A. Traill, *Schliemann of Troy: Treasure and Deceit* (1995).

David A. Traill

SCIENCE IN ARCHAEOLOGY. In part as a result of continuing dialogues within archaeology concerning the precise nature of its disciplinary status, terms such as "science in archaeology" and "archaeological science" have come to be used in archaeological literature in at least two senses: (1) when considering the formal use of scientific method and logic in the analysis of the archaeological record and (2) when discussing the use of natural science data in the evaluation and interpretation of archaeological materials and contexts. Due to this dual usage, the role of science in archaeology is considered both in terms of how archaeological data is conceptualized and analyzed and how interdisciplinary interaction with the natural science disciplines including both the physical (e.g., physics, chemistry, geol-

ogy) and biological sciences (e.g., zoology, botany) affects the pursuit of archaeological studies.

Use of Scientific Method and Logic. To some archaeologists, the use of scientific methodologies in archaeology are understood and defined primarily in operational terms (e.g., the adoption of a method of presenting data in a standardized or structured format such as the use of the same terms to define the same artifact or artifact type). To others, a scientific stance may indicate a commitment to a particular approach or conception of the nature of scientific inquiry that concerns formal methodology. For these investigators, the role of a scientific methodology is seen as helpful because it raises to consciousness the need to be explicit about why certain data-collecting or data-analysis strategies are employed.

In some cases, assumptions of a scientific methodology as applied in archaeological studies, including concerns about epistemology (how we know and justify assertions that we know), may need to be considered. For some, such conceptualizations may start with the observation that a scientific world view assumes that a human past and its physical record exists apart from and independently of any socially or culturally conditioned perceptions or conceptions of it. This is the archaeological version of the more general scientific postulate that there is a "real" universe "out there"—a natural reality that exists in spite of the admitted difficulty of a human observer to compensate for perceptual or cultural bias. Other widely accepted characteristics of a scientific approach include an assumption that the human past is knowable and that appropriate techniques can be devised to judge which inferences about the past have higher probabilities of being correct.

Beginning in the 1970s, several leading theoreticians, including Lewis R. Binford, advanced the view that progress within archaeology depended on adopting an explicitly scientific approach. In part, the "New Archaeology" asserted that a scientific framework involved the formulation and empirical testing of hypotheses leading to the development of different types of universal or statistical lawlike generalizations. These generalizations would be designed to describe the interactions of various cultural elements or components and how these interactive patterns changed over time to produce similarities and differences in the archaeological record. Some advocated the formal use of some type of systems theory to structure these studies. Others focused attention on the interaction between cultural and ecological and environmental factors.

Several commentaries concerned with critically examining the nature of a scientific pursuit of archaeological studies have noted analogues between archaeology and other disciplines or academic traditions that are widely considered to be scientific disciplines. For example, it was noted that archaeology shares with other "historical" sciences, such as geology, the problem that no past events, as such, are directly observable. As Binford has noted (*Man* 22 [1987]: 392), an investigator can only observe a set of present "facts" assumed to be relevant to the process of making inferences about past events.

At another level, Joan Schneider has called attention to the comments of Marsden S. Blois (*New England Journal of Medicine* 318 [1988]: 847–851) with regard to the similarity in the processes by which data is evaluated and judgments rendered in archaeology and other human sciences and in the practice of clinical medicine. Both may be considered as scientific undertakings, but they are said to lack "unifying theories" that are unique to or directly emergent from the conduct of their investigations. It is suggested that both undertake a scientific examination using a highly diverse body of observations by means of what Blois called "vertical reasoning." This approach characterizes scientific investigations where a relevant database ranges throughout the whole hierarchical schema of the sciences—from the molecular and atomic levels, up through and including a whole organism possessing the interesting epiphenomenon of "mind."

Use of Natural Science Data. From a historical perspective, archaeological investigations of prehistoric contexts have been closely associated with natural science–based applications and perspectives from essentially the beginning of concern with and knowledge of human prehistory. The demonstration that archaeological materials existed in "deep time" followed from middle and late nineteenth-century geological and paleontological deductions and the expanding discovery of a vastly extended geological and evolutionary time scale that documented the association of human skeletal materials and artifacts with extinct (Pleistocene) fauna.

Although the use of natural science data in archaeological inquiries can be traced as far back as the middle of the eighteenth century, these early studies generally involved incidental, personal interests of physical scientists rather than reflecting a program of formalized investigations. The beginnings of the institutionalization of natural science applications in archaeology dates to the decade following World War II. In the early and middle 1950s, there was a rapid expansion in the development of university- and museum-affiliated basic and applied scientific research laboratories and centers devoted to physical science applications in the pursuit of archaeological and art historic studies. In English-speaking countries, it was suggested that aspects of such research be distinguished as a separate subdiscipline, *archaeometry, a word originally coined by Professor Christopher Hawkes in 1958 as the title of the bulletin of the research laboratory for archaeology and the history of art at Oxford University.

In the early 1960s, other physical science based aspects were organized around the term *"environmental archaeology" and emphasized both geoarchaeological and bioarchaeological reconstruction of environmental contexts for archaeological data. Some investigators suggested the term "archaeological science" as the broadest term to apply to all natural science–based studies in archaeology. In the mid-1970s, the establishment of university chairs in both archaeometry and archaeological science reflect the maturation of the field, as did the appearance in the mid-1970s of specialty publications such as the *Journal of Archaeological Science* and a professional society, the Society for Archaeological Sciences.

Subdivisions of the areas generally subsumed under the rubric of interdisciplinary archaeological science have been variously conceptualized. A compendium assembled by Don Brothwell and Eric Higgs in 1961 under the title *Science in Archaeology: A Survey of Progress and Research* (2nd edition, 1969) considered the subject under seven major topics: dating methods, paleoenvironmental studies (including paleoclimatic, geomorphological, and floral and faunal analyses), osteology, microscopic and radiographic studies, petrographic and spectrographic analyses of artifacts, statistical concepts, and remote sensing techniques. Others have subsumed these seven categories under four more broadly

conceived areas of focus and orientation: archaeological materials analysis, archaeological chronometrics, *paleoenvironmental reconstruction, and remote sensing. Topics associated with data manipulation and processing involving, for example, mathematical modeling, statistical analyses, and data retrieval techniques are generally not subsumed under archaeometry or archaeological science, since these topics are viewed typically as reflecting an overall increase in the quantification of archaeological data in general rather than any specific scientific application in archaeology.

Archaeological dating studies represent the area of natural science applications that has enjoyed the broadest success and well illustrates the role of such applications in archaeological research. There are currently more than twenty physical methods of inferring time relationships—either chronometrically ("real-time") or relative placement—that are used in assigning temporal frameworks for archaeological and hominid paleontological materials spanning a period of as much as five million years. The major physical chronometric techniques currently used in archaeology were developed by physical scientists pursuing physical science agendas. However, several important chronometric dating methods were developed closely within the context of archaeological concerns.

For example, *radiocarbon (carbon-14) dating, which provides, directly or indirectly, the primary temporal controls for much of the prehistoric archaeological record on a worldwide basis for the last 40,000 to 50,000 years, was conceptualized by a physical and nuclear chemist, Willard F. Libby, who was a self-described amateur archaeologist. Radiocarbon dating, like a number of other analytical and technically based methods applied to archaeological materials, provided the basis of making inferences about archaeological phenomena totally independent of assumptions about cultural processes and unrelated to any type of manipulation of strictly archaeological materials. A direct connection between the development and widespread utilization of radiocarbon dating in the 1950s and 1960s and the rise of the "New Archaeology" of the 1970s has been suggested by several commentators.

[*See also* ANALYSIS, METHODS OF; DATING THE PAST; EXPERIMENTAL ARCHAEOLOGY; GENERAL SYSTEMS THEORY; MATERIALS, ANALYSIS OF; METHOD, ARCHAEOLOGICAL; MIDDLE RANGE THEORY; PROCESSUAL THEORY; SCIENTIFIC METHOD; THEORY IN ARCHAEOLOGY.]

■ Patty Jo Watson, Steven A. LeBlanc, and Charles L. Redman, *Archaeological Explanation: The Scientific Method in Archaeology* (1984). P. A. Parkes, *Current Scientific Techniques in Archaeology* (1986). Ulrich Leute, *Archaeometry: An Introduction to Physical Methods in Archaeology and the History of Art* (1987). Ralph O. Allen, ed., *Archaeological Chemistry IV* (1989). G. Gibbon, *Explanation in Archaeology* (1989). Julian Henderson, ed. *Scientific Analysis in Archaeology and Its Interpretation* (1989). Martin J. Aitken, *Science-based Dating in Archaeology* (1990).

R. Ervin Taylor

SCIENTIFIC METHOD. Science is a process of learning and discovery through the systematic study of principles that govern observable phenomena. The basic assumption of all sciences is that there is a real and knowable world and that regularities in it can be reconstructed through the development and testing of hypotheses. Hypotheses are stated relationships between two or more variables in the empirical world that anticipate and explain the interaction between them. Stated relationships are confirmed or rejected by observing the empirical world. Confirmed hypotheses are incorporated into larger theories useful for explaining natural and behavioral phenomena. Scientists are required to be explicit about their assumptions when formulating hypotheses. This allows other scientists to evaluate the foundations of the hypothesis and the validity of the test. Because scientific hypotheses are often dependent upon the accuracy of other confirmed hypotheses and assumptions, they are always open to further evaluation and testing. This is the self-correcting nature of a productive science.

In archaeology, the scientific method has provided a philosophical framework to develop and evaluate ideas that increase our knowledge about prehistoric human behavior. The scientific method was adopted in the 1960s by archaeologists wanting to assign more accurate meaning to archaeological data. Until this time archaeology in the United States was largely descriptive and focused on reconstructing particular cultural chronologies. Unlike scientific archaeology, traditional archaeologists interpreted patterns in the archaeological record largely from personal experience. Interpretations were evaluated on the basis of professional competence rather than testing with empirical data. During the postwar era, change was proposed by a small minority of archaeologists concerned with the way archaeological problems were formulated and analyzed. Walter Taylor (1948) and others (G. R. Willey and P. Phillips 1958) advocated the development and testing of general laws to explain cross-cultural regularities in human behavior, rather than simply describing them. Taylor also proposed using a more scientific approach for reconstructing the prehistoric past involving the formulation of hypotheses and rigorous testing against archaeological data.

The use of scientific method in archaeology was at the core of the "New Archaeology" championed by Lewis Binford and his followers beginning in the 1960s. Binford became dissatisfied with the types of questions being addressed in archaeology as well as the way conclusions were being drawn. He proposed that the process of inquiry into the prehistoric past be modeled after the physical sciences. Initially, proponents of the New Archaeology were interested in testing theories developed by traditional archaeologists. For this reason, Binford turned to the hypothetico-deductive school of scientific explanation that dominated philosophy of science in the United States at that time. This school of thought promoted the deductive testing of hypotheses and the confirmation of general laws. The principal tenets of this approach were adopted quickly by much of the archaeological community and were viewed by some as the only valid framework to describe, explain, and predict human behavior.

Over the past three decades archaeologists have debated which scientific methods are most appropriate for describing and explaining the prehistoric past. Much of this debate has focused on the most legitimate way of developing and testing hypotheses. Hypotheses are usually generated inductively through the observation of patterns and common features in the archaeological record. Ethnographic analogy is also used to inductively establish testable hypotheses about human behavior. In some cases, hypotheses are augmented, or formulated in more creative ways, using personal insight and imagination. Regardless of how hypotheses about past cultural events are developed, they must also be tested. The hypothetico-deductive method of testing hypotheses requires an observational prediction to

be deduced from the hypothesis. If observation of the empirical phenomenon under investigation conforms to the prediction, the hypothesis is said to be confirmed. A hypothesis is strongly supported when several confirming instances are observed.

Many archaeologists have recognized the limitations of the hypothetico-deductive model for explaining prehistoric human behavior. In its purist sense, explanation using this model is attainable only if a particular phenomenon can ultimately be predicted or, in the case of prehistory, postdicted, given a certain set of circumstances. Unfortunately, the complexity of human behavior does not meet the explanatory requirements of prediction. Ethnoarchaeological research clearly indicates that similar archaeological patterns can be produced by different types of human behavior. Therefore, many alternative hypotheses can account for the same pattern in the archaeological record.

Alternative models of scientific confirmation and explanation are generally more inductive. However, the proponents of these models still stress the importance of developing and testing hypotheses. Salmon (1982) argues that the plausibility of all hypothetical accounts of a particular archaeological pattern must be considered. Prior to testing a hypothesis the alternative hypotheses should be evaluated and those with a low probability (prior probability) rejected prior to the test. Statistical rather than universal laws of human behavior can thus be established. This philosophical model is more compatible with the systems approach, which is a more inductive method of scientific inquiry.

The foundations of the scientific method for reconstructing the prehistoric past have recently been questioned. Critiques have been put forward by archaeologists who emphasize the explanatory significance of historical factors for understanding prehistoric culture change. They argue that the complexities of historical trajectories are impossible to predict using scientific reasoning. For this reason, I. Hodder (1984) argues that the scientific method cannot be used to reconstruct prehistoric human behavior and that scientific objectivity is "a false and misleading goal of archaeology." This view is also based on the notion that archaeological theory is influenced by the historical, intellectual, and sociopolitical climate in which it is developed. Therefore, scientific verification of hypotheses is impossible because theory and data cannot be separated. These are valid criticisms of scientific archaeology; however, proponents of this radical school of thought have largely failed to propose a sound alternative approach.

With the exception of the post-processual group, scientific methods continue to be favored in contemporary archaeology. In general, archaeologists agree that the primary goal of archaeological research is to describe and explain behavioral changes in the prehistoric past. Description and explanation are scientific activities. It is also recognized that the scientific method provides a useful guide to archaeological research in that it helps determine what types of data to collect and analyze. However, archaeologists do not yet agree on the best philosophical model for scientific inquiry. Whether verification of hypotheses should be an inductive or a deductive process will undoubtedly be an issue in the field of archaeology for years to come. Regardless, scientific activities should not be undertaken at the expense of ignoring historically unique phenomena. Archaeology is both a scientific and humanistic discipline. The scientific method is only one aspect of exploring the complexity of human behavior. Particular historical events must be considered in all explanations of past events. Historical and scientific approaches should be treated as complementary rather than antithetical and used in parallel to further elucidate the prehistoric past.

[See also METHOD, ARCHAEOLOGICAL; POST-PROCESSUAL THEORY; PROCESSUAL THEORY; SCIENCE IN ARCHAEOLOGY; THEORY IN ARCHAEOLOGY.]

■ G. R. Willey and P. Phillips, *Method and Theory in American Archaeology* (1958). C. G. Hempel and P. Oppenheim, "Studies in the Logic of Explanation," *Philosophy of Science* 15 (1965): 135–175. M. H. Salmon, *Philosophy of Archaeology* (1982). I. Hodder, "Archaeology in 1984," *Antiquity* 58 (1984): 25–32. P. J. Watson, S. A. LeBlanc, and C. L. Redman, *Archaeological Explanation: The Scientific Method in Archaeology* (1984). M. Shanks and C. Tilley, *Re-constructing Archaeology* (1987). J. H. Kelly and M. P. Hanen, *Archaeology and the Methodology of Science* (1988). L. R. Binford, "The 'New Archaeology,' Then and Now," in ed. C. C. Lamberg-Karlovsky, *Archaeological Thought in America* (1989). B. G. Trigger, "History and Contemporary American Archaeology: A Critical Analysis," in C. C. Lamberg-Karlovsky, *Archaeological Thought in America* (1989).

Douglas J. Kennett

SEASONALITY STUDIES. Prehistoric hunter-gatherers and farmers, like their modern counterparts, lived their social, economic, and ritual lives in regular cycles that fluctuated throughout the year. These changes often involved the movement or reorganization of settlements within a large territorial range. Archaeologists are faced with the difficult but fundamental task of reconstructing these dynamic patterns of settlement from the static and incomplete remnants left by prehistoric peoples. Seasonality studies are used to reconstruct the seasonal use of particular locations within larger settlement systems. Studies of seasonality range from the simple presence or absence of seasonally available plants and animals to more complex analytical techniques borrowed from biology and chemistry.

Ethnographers studying indigenous people around the world in the nineteenth and twentieth centuries noted variations in settlement and subsistence through the year as well as cyclical changes in social and religious activities. In many cases these fluctuations occurred in accordance with seasonal changes in the natural environment. For instance, the aboriginal people inhabiting the Pacific Northwest coast of North America aggregated together in large settlements near streams during summer salmon runs. For these people this was a time of collaboration, heightened ritual activity, and socioeconomic interaction (Barnett, 1975).

Archaeological investigations into seasonal variations in prehistoric settlement, *subsistence, and *social organization burgeoned in the 1960s and 1970s as one component of the New Archaeology. Unlike the archaeological investigations of the early twentieth century, which concentrated on the development of culture histories, the New Archaeology focused on reconstructing prehistoric subsistence and settlement patterns. Willey's (1953) seminal work on prehistoric settlement patterns in the Virú Valley of Peru provided the impetus for such investigations. Willey described settlement patterns as "the way people deploy themselves across a landscape." Winters (1969) elaborated upon this idea by making the distinction between *settlement patterns,* the geographic distribution of sites dating to a particular time interval, and *settlement systems,* the functional relationships between sites when the system was extant. Determining the season people lived at particular locations during the year became an integral part of reconstructing functional relationships between sites within prehistoric settlement systems (see Settlement Pattern Analysis).

A number of techniques have been devised to extract seasonal information from the archaeological record. Initially the season of site occupation was determined by the simple presence or absence of seasonally available plants and animals. This is the oldest and most frequently used method for estimating the season of site occupation. Winters (1969) was the first to effectively use seasonally available plants and animals to infer season of site occupation. His study demonstrated that people living in eastern North America during the Archaic Period visited riverine locations during fall and winter months. This estimation was based on the presence of white tail deer, elk, and migratory birds in archaeological deposits dating to this time period. Clearly, this method requires a thorough understanding of the distribution and biology of the plants and animals used by prehistoric people. A strong argument based on *paleoenvironmental reconstruction must also be made for patterns existing in the past. In addition, problems of differential preservation must be accounted for. Difficulties resolving these issues have made such seasonality estimates unreliable. Pike-Tay (1991) suggests that the presence or absence of seasonally available resources should be used as a preliminary measure of seasonality that can be used to develop testable hypotheses.

Beyond the presence or absence of animal remains in archaeological deposits, certain skeletal elements may contain seasonal information. Particular physiological events during the life cycles of animals create visible changes in their skeletons and teeth. These events are often season or age related. Seasonality estimates can be inferred from analogous events in modern populations of animals. Epiphyseal fusion, the joining of cartilage to the articular surface of bone, occurs in different skeletal elements at various times in an animal's life. Estimates of age can then be converted into the season that the animal was killed. Like epiphyseal fusion, the eruption and wear of teeth, the shedding of antler, and the presence of osteoporosis in the bones of birds and mammals are seasonally sensitive. The drawbacks of these techniques is that the diet and health of animals can alter the timing and nature of these physiological events.

A variety of more complex approaches for estimating the season of resource use and site occupation have developed over the last twenty years. Of these, the microscopic analyses of growth increments in teeth, bone, fish otoliths, mollusk shells, and antler pedicles have been the most widely used techniques (Monks 1981). An organism's growth rate is influenced by seasonal changes in the environment. Growth increments in an organism's skeleton (or exoskeleton) record these cyclical changes. Based on studies of modern animals, the season of death can be estimated and inferences about seasonal resource and site use can be made.

Finally, oxygen isotopic analysis of marine mollusk shells is potentially the most accurate, but underutilized, method for making seasonality estimates. The technique was initially recognized as a powerful tool for paleoenvironmental reconstruction because O^{18}/O^{16} ratios in shell contain information about the physical and chemical environment of their growth. Shackleton (1973) showed that the oxygen isotopic ratios in marine shells were temperature dependent and that the O^{18}/O^{16} ratio in the final growth increment of mollusk shells represents the water temperature at the time it was collected by prehistoric people. Kennett and Voorhies (1995) extended the application of this technique to estuarine mollusks, determining that the oxygen isotopic composition of marsh clam shells reflected large-scale salinity fluctuations created by seasonal changes in rainfall.

A great deal of progress has been made in the area of seasonality studies over the last twenty years. It must be remembered, however, that regardless of the method employed to estimate the season of site occupation, a sound interpretive framework is necessary in order to make meaningful statements about the prehistoric past. Successful reconstructions of site seasonality and overall settlement patterns combine ethnographic and ecological analogies to develop multiple working hypotheses. These hypotheses are then augmented with indirect measures of seasonality, such as the location of sites on the landscape or the orientation of dwellings at a particular site. The presence or absence of seasonally available resources can then be used to narrow down the season of site occupation. Finally, more accurate techniques must be employed to test each hypothesis. Multiple lines of evidence will ensure the most accurate seasonality estimates and the best reconstructions of prehistoric subsistence, settlement, and social dynamics.

[See also MIDDLE RANGE THEORY; PALEOBOTANY; ZOO-ARCHAEOLOGY.]

■ G. Willey, *Prehistoric Settlement Patterns in the Virú Valley, Peru* (1953). H. Winters, *The Riverton Culture* (1969). N. J. Shackleton, "Oxygen Isotope Analysis as a Means of Determining Season of Occupation of Prehistoric Midden Sites," *Archaeometry* 15 (1973): 133–141. H. A. Barnett, *The Coast Salish of Canada* (1975). G. G. Monks, "Seasonality Studies," in *Advances in Archaeological Method and Theory*, vol. 4, ed. M. B. Schiffer (1981), pp. 117–240. A. Pike-Tay, *Red Deer Hunting in the Upper Paleolithic of South-West France: A Study of Seasonality* (1991). G. Wefer and W. H. Berger, "Isotope Paleontology: Growth and Composition of Extant Calcereous Species," *Marine Geology* 100 (1991): 207–248. D. J. Kennett and B. Voorhies, "Middle Holocene Periodicities in Rainfall Inferred from Oxygen and Carbon Isotopic Fluctuations in Prehistoric Tropical Estuarine Mollusc Shells," *Archaeometry* 37 (1995).

Douglas J. Kennett

SECHIN ALTO is located in the northern branch of the Casma Valley on the north-central coast of Peru. Its principal feature is a huge rectangular stone platform mound measuring 990 by 825 by 145 feet (300 by 250 by 44 m), making it the largest mound for its time in the Western Hemisphere. Associated with the main mound are four rectangular plazas, which contain three circular courts, stretching 4,600 feet (1,400 m) to the northeast. Sechin Alto is believed to be part of the larger Sechin Alto Complex that covers some 4 square miles (10.5 sq km) and includes three other sites—Sechin Bajo, Taukachi-Konkan, and Cerro Sechin. These sites all share a coincident architectural orientation up the valley and have architectural traits in common, such as rounded corners, circular courts, and the use of cone-shaped adobes.

Sechin Alto was first surveyed by Julio Tello in 1937. In 1956, brief testing by Donald Collier and Donald Thompson yielded two radiocarbon dates of ca. 690 B.C. and ca. 1450 B.C. that were in reverse order compared to the excavation stratigraphy. Nevertheless, architectural and ceramic data from later surveys in 1968 by Rosa Fung and Carlos Williams and in 1980 by Shelia Pozorski and Thomas Pozorski indicate that Sechin Alto and the larger Sechin Alto Complex date to the Initial Period (1800–900 B.C.).

The Sechin Alto Complex was most likely the important center of a larger polity. The coastal site of Las Haldas, 12 miles (20 km) south of the Casma Valley, probably served as a satellite community of the much larger Sechin Alto Complex, likely providing marine resources in return for agricultural products from the inland center. Other early sites in the Casma Valley area, such as Pampa de las Llamas-Moxeke, are more or less contemporary with the Sechin Alto Complex; however, the relationship between Sechin Alto and these other nearby early sites is still unclear.

[See also ANDEAN PRE-INCA CIVILIZATIONS, THE RISE OF: MARITIME FOUNDATIONS OF PRE-INCA CIVILIZATION; SOUTH AMERICA: THE RISE OF COMPLEX SOCIETIES IN SOUTH AMERICA.]

■ Shelia Pozorski and Thomas Pozorski, *Early Settlement and Subsistence in the Casma Valley, Peru* (1987). Shelia Pozorski and Thomas Pozorski, "Early Civilization in the Casma Valley, Peru," *Antiquity* 66 (1992): 845–870.

Shelia Pozorski and Thomas Pozorski

SECONDARY PRODUCTS REVOLUTION. In describing prehistoric ways of life it is necessary to use terms derived from the present, for instance, from recent ethnography. Without some qualification, however, these labels may not be appropriate for earlier times. Although it is possible to describe some Early Holocene populations as "farmers" or "pastoralists," it must be recognized that many of the features now characteristic of these ways of life (either in the ethnographic record or in modern practice) may not have existed at earlier periods (see Pastoralism). When archaeologists and paleozoologists began to reconstruct the character of early farming economies from the intensive study of bone and seed remains in the 1960s, it became clear (for instance, from livestock mortality statistics) that domestic animals had initially been used in a way that was very different from more recent patterns of exploitation. In particular, the early ages at which animals like cattle and sheep were typically killed implied a use for meat rather than any of the other uses to which these species can be put: providers of traction power or transport, or suppliers of material products such as milk or wool. Such usages only appeared some millennia after the initial domestication of the staple food animals—either through changes in the way these species were used, or through the domestication of new ones with specialized roles (like horses and camels)—and these new uses were an important element in economic and cultural change. Many of these innovations were mutually reinforcing, and collectively they greatly enhanced the role of domestic livestock.

This contrast, between an initial "primary" pattern of exploitation for meat and a subsequent "secondary" pattern of more diversified exploitation for secondary applications and products, marked a major biotechnological shift that was in many ways as important as the beginning of farming itself. It was the first employment of sources of energy beyond the human body for cultivation and for overland transport, thereby increasing both productivity and mobility. It was also the source of products which enlarged the scope of material culture (e.g., through the manufacture of woollen textiles) and thus facilitated industrial production. In addition, it made possible the occupation of a range of harsh environments, especially steppes, deserts and mountains, otherwise exploitable only seasonally and at low density by hunters. Finally, it led to new forms of vehicle technology employing the *wheel that were ancestral to many later forms of machinery and provided powerful new media of ostentation and display. To recognize the importance of this transition, the rather cumbersome term Secondary Products Revolution (SPR) was coined by Andrew Sherratt in 1981.

The SPR was primarily a phenomenon of the Old World. Because of the impoverishment of the New World ungulate fauna in the megafaunal extinctions of the Lake Glacial Period, there were far fewer candidates for such forms of exploitation in the Americas. Only in montane South America, where a greater diversity of ungulates survived, did a pattern of animal husbandry based on camelids allow a degree of secondary product use—principally for wool (hair) and pack transport. These were locally important for the development of civilizations culminating in that of the Inca, but the animals and their uses did not spread beyond the Andes. The urban civilizations of Mexico and other parts of Mesoamerica had few domestic animals and no secondary exploitation—demonstrating that the SPR was not a necessary precondition for urban life. In North America, too, animal husbandry played a largely insignificant role in subsistence. In the other half of the globe, however, in the Old World, it is now hard to find groups that keep livestock but do not exploit them in secondary ways, so that the meat-based livestock-rearing systems of early Old World farming groups form an "extinct" way of life that is nowhere represented in the ethnographic record. Moreover, the innovations of secondary animal use, like riding and traction, spread and transformed the lives of certain hunting groups in dry or arctic environments in both hemispheres (though relatively recently in the New World—for example, the use of the ridden horse by Plains Indians, or the dog sledge by the Inuit).

The date at which secondary uses and products appeared among Old World farmers can be inferred from a variety of forms of archaeological evidence. Besides the reconstruction of animal exploitation patterns from mortality statistics derived from bone assemblages, direct evidence exists, such as remains of woollen textiles, or traces of traction activities in the form of plowmarks or wheel ruts. Through all these possess a certain ambiguity, the coincidence of several lines of evidence serves to define a transition. The introduction of wool can illustrate this. Kill-off patterns with large proportions of adult sheep can reflect the use of either wool or milk: a predominance of females suggests milk, and of males, wool. Animal and plant fibers can be distinguished by their micromorphology and by appropriate chemical tests, but wool and hair survive only in acid environments, while plant fibers are better preserved in alkaline ones, so that a broad range of sites must be studied. It is the coincidence between the disappearance of linen cloth fragments in the calcareous sediments of Alpine lakeside villages and the first appearance of wool in the acid bogs of northern Europe that suggests the replacement of linen by wool for most types of clothing in third-millennium Europe. Since spindle whorls can be used for flax as well as for wool, their occurrence is not diagnostic of either fiber, though the appearance of clothespins, suitable for the open weaves of early woollen garments (rather than the dense weave of linen and continuous surface of leather, usually fastened by buttons), is another indication of the change. The proliferation of safety-pin clothing fasteners (fibulae) in the late second millennium may reflect a further expansion in the use of woollen clothing. Although experts are agreed that wool was not used in Europe before the third millennium, the writers of archaeological textbooks (and particularly works on prehistoric farming) have been slow to appreciate this fact.

Another important source of evidence is pictorial or three-dimensional representation. Although formal scenes (with sufficient detail to show milking practices or traction methods) are more characteristic of complex, urban societies, the occurrence of schematic clay figurines affords valuable evidence of earlier practices in less-sophisticated communities. This is the first form of evidence for pack animals—loaded donkeys are seen in east Mediterranean contexts from the fourth millennium—which suggests that they were domesticated at this time specifically for this role. Representations on seals may be a valuable indicator of types of wheeled traction, or of milking—though the biochemical analysis of organic residues in pots will be an even more valuable indicator of the use of milk products when sufficient analyses have been done. The introduction of animal traction to Europe is marked by a coincidence between the occurrence of plowmarks (preserved under earthworks, principally burial mounds) and terra-cotta models of yoked oxen or wheeled wagons. The particular interest generated by these traction animals is itself suggestive of the special character of their new role.

The importance of these innovations has been perceived by archaeologists in different ways. While the primitive character of Early Neolithic exploitation patterns has been generally recognized, some writers on the subject, regarding the appearance of different innovations as responses to specific needs in a particular area, have emphasized the continuous and long drawn-out nature of the introduction of secondary uses. Inherent in the original formulation of the concept, however, was the idea of centricity and punctuation: the emergence of these features in a limited area and their spread to other parts of the Old World as part of a wave of innovations. In this conception, the structure of the SPR would resemble that of the earlier Neolithic (farming) Revolution in the same area of origin—a long period in which individual innovations emerged in different parts of the Near East, and a relatively explosive phase in which they came together, interacted, and spread. The context of this fusion and expansion was the crystallization of urban life in the mid-fourth millennium and the long-distance activity associated with trade networks and *Uruk or Proto-Elamite colonies. The emergence of new forms of animal exploitation coincided with other innovations—in cultivation and diet (tree crops), in manufacturing technology (wheelmade pottery, sheet metal), and in means of transport (boats with sails)—that formed the prelude to what V. Gordon *Childe called the Urban Revolution. This historical, rather than quasi-evolutionary, conception of the nature of the SPR seems to be the most appropriate way of conceptualizing it, and perhaps calls into question whether a separate label is desirable. This point must be evaluated in the context of its immediate intellectual history.

Many of the elements of the secondary exploitation of animals had been included by Childe in *Man Makes Himself* (1936): the plow, cart, donkey, horse, and camel. What was chiefly missing from Childe's account was the European picture (the plow, for instance, was then thought to be an innovation of the Late Bronze Age rather than the fourth millennium) and the broader ecological dimension. As information accumulated concerning the form of agricultural intensification which appeared in Europe after the Neolithic, it seemed desirable to have a common label for these features, and the term SPR has now gained widespread acceptance—even if often interpreted as a purely local development in each of the areas concerned. Yet having achieved recognition for the phenomenon and having emphasized the very different nature of early farming, it may now be more appropriate to stress the cultural and historical significance of secondary animal uses and products. Even using a term such as "the plow" repeats the mistake of "farming" and "pastoralism" in reifying its object and suggesting a false homogeneity, as if pastoralism or plowing were everywhere the same—products of the same calculation of economic or ergonomic rationality. It may in fact be that the economic advantages were not the primary reason why the plow was initially adopted in areas like northern Europe, and that these only became evident in subsequent centuries: certainly it is the case that wool must initially have been a rare and expensive "prestige good" rather than a universal commodity long after the first introduction of woolly sheep. Both innovations thus take their place alongside, for example, alcohol production as elements of more complex culture generated (and spreading) within a particular social as much as an ecological environment and specifically conforming to a pattern of "world-system" phenomena with a strong central focus.

The logic of this model is to see the SPR as a series of "knock-on effects" spreading outward from the initial centers of domestication, transferring known forms of exploitation to new species, and producing further novelty through sharing and interaction between these innovations—together greatly enhancing the role of domestic animals in a whole variety of contexts: in farming, in pastoralism, and ultimately in hunting, too. The whole process was driven as much by an increasing complexity of cultural behavior at the center as by ecological adaptation at the margin. The "revolution" was thus none other than Childe's Urban Revolution—of which the "secondary products complex" was an important but not in itself decisive element—although one which helped to transform not just the Near East but also much of Eurasia. If this is so, then the appearance of the plow and wheel, like the alloy metallurgy which often accompanied them in Europe and the steppes, was ultimately due to events many thousands of miles away.

[See also ANIMAL REMAINS, ANALYSIS OF; CAMEL, DOMESTICATION OF THE; DOMESTICATION OF ANIMALS; HORSE, DOMESTICATION OF THE; LAND TRANSPORTATION: USE OF ANIMALS FOR TRANSPORTATION; TEXTILES.]

■ Sebastian Payne, "Kill-off Patterns of Sheep and Goat at Ashvan Kale," *Anatolian Studies* 23 (1973): 281–303. G. Dahl and A. Hjort, *Having Herds: Pastoral Herd Growth and Household Economy* (1976). Andrew Sherratt, "Plough and Pastoralism: Aspects of the Secondary Products Revolution," in *Pattern of the Past: Studies in Honor of David Clarke*, eds., Ian Hodder, Glyn Isaac, and Norman Hammond (1981), pp. 261–305. J. Chapman, "The 'Secondary Products Revolution' and the Limitations of the Neolithic, *Bulletin of the Institute of Archaeology* (1982): 107–122. Andrew Sherratt, "The Secondary Exploitation of Animals in the Old World," *World Archaeology* 15:1 (1983): 90–104. Andrew Sherratt, "Wool, Wheels and Ploughmarks: Local Developments or Outside Introductions in Neolithic Europe," *Institute of Archaeology Bulletin* 23 (1986): 1–15. Juris Zarins, "Pastoralism in Southwest Asia: The Second Millennium B.C. in *The Walking Larder*, ed. Juliet Clutton-Brock (1989), pp. 127–155. Elizabeth J. W. Barber, *Prehistoric Textiles: The Development of Cloth in the Neolithic and Bronze Ages* (1991). Stuart Piggott, *Wagon, Chariot and Carriage: Symbol and Status in the History of Transport* (1992). Andrew Sherratt, "What Would a Bronze Age World System Look Like? Relations Between Temperate Europe and the Mediterranean in Prehistory," *Journal of European Archaeology* 2:2 (1993): 1–57.

Andrew Sherratt

SEDENTISM. *See* AGRICULTURE.

SERIATION includes a number of relative dating techniques, the first of which was developed in the early 1900s, before the advent of chronometric dating. These techniques are based on a reconstruction of typological or stylistic changes in material culture through time. Ceramics will be used to illustrate the techniques discussed here, but other classes of material can be used as well.

To construct the seriation for an area, stratified sites usually are examined. By examining typological or stylistic shifts from the different strata, these changes can be placed in a relative chronological order. Once the seriation of an area is unraveled at a single or several stratified sites, it can be used to place other sites into a regional temporal ordering through ceramic cross-dating. The following hypothetical example uses three sites, the Deep site, the Shallow site, and the New site, to illustrate. The first site investigated in the region is the Deep site, which contains five strata, the lowest containing ceramic type A, the next type B, and so on to the highest level with type E. Next, the Shallow site is excavated. It has one strata containing ceramic type A. Based on our previous research we can say that the Shallow site is contemporaneous with the earliest occupation at the Deep site. Excavations at the New site reveal two strata with ceramic type E in the lower level and F in the higher level. Because type E is found only at the highest levels of the Deep site we can say that the New site was founded while the Deep site was still being occupied and continued to be occupied after the Deep site was abandoned. Additionally, the New site was occupied after the Shallow site. If chronometric dates can be obtained from the deposits containing ceramics at the Deep site, a date can be assigned to the Shallow and New sites. For example, if the A strata at the Deep site dates to A.D. 900, the Shallow site also dates to A.D. 900.

Seriation can also be undertaken using excavated or surface collections from single component sites. This process assumes that the production of artifact types follows a battleship curve distribution through time. That is, the percentage of the assemblage a type represents is small at the beginning of its production span, widens in the middle as it becomes popular, and is small again at the end as it loses popularity and is eclipsed by another type. The seriation can be determined using a graphical display. In the graph, each site is represented by a line, and the percentage of each ceramic type found at that site is represented by a scaled bar. The lines are rearranged until the bars form battleship curves for each type in the overall display.

In addition to the graphical method, a number of quantitative methods are used to seriate sites. One of the earliest used was the Brainerd-Robinson method, which computes indexes for each unit (either sites or features within a site) and then orders the units based on these indexes. The index is a measure of similarity between two units, computed as the sum of the absolute value of the differences in percentages of each type between units. This figure is then subtracted from 200. The more similar the units, the smaller the differences in percentage of each type and the closer to 200 the index is; the greater the difference between the units, the farther from 200 the index is. A similarity matrix of the indexes is then constructed. The sites are reordered until the highest indexes are on the diagonal and the values decrease consistently with distance from the diagonal. The resulting ordering of the units reflects their chronological ordering.

Today, statistical techniques, such as multidimensional scaling, factor analysis, and cluster analysis, are used in conjunction with computers to determine the correct ordering of the units. Additionally, finer time-scale resolution has been achieved by examining shifts in stylistic elements and motifs in ceramic assemblages rather than types, resulting in a microseriation. The finer resolution of the microseriation is due to the fact that stylistic elements shift through time within a type, and are, therefore, more sensitive to short-term seriations.

Both factor analysis and multidimensional scaling rely on similarity matrices related to the correlation of the ceramic type or stylistic element in the assemblage as a whole. These correlations are used to create new variables representing ceramic or stylistic complexes. Each unit is then scored for these new variables and ordered, with units having similar scores on the new variables being close to each other in the seriation. What these techniques allow the archaeologist to do is look at a large group of variables, which are temporally sensitive, and reduce them to a small set of new variables (the typological or stylistic complexes) that represent the interaction of a number of the original variables. This reduction procedure simplifies the data into a few dimensions on which the units can be sorted.

Cluster analysis uses the similarities and differences between artifact assemblages to group units into chronological periods. Cluster analysis techniques treat each ceramic type or stylistic element as a dimension and the number of sherds of that type, or possessing that element, present in the unit is a measurement on that dimension. This is similar to the way distance is used as a measurement on the dimension of length. If ten types are present, the assemblage can be seen in ten-dimensional space, just as length, width, and height represent three-dimensional space. The closer in space two units are, the more similar their artifact assemblages. Cluster analysis then groups the units that are closest together into temporal periods.

A number of factors can greatly hinder the seriation process, due to their impact on the material culture on which the seriations are based. Aside from obvious problems presented by disturbance, deposit mixing, and inaccurate contextual information, aspects of prehistoric behavior can have an impact. One of the most devastating is the presence of a production curve that does not correspond to a battleship curve. If the production span of a ceramic type or style has more than one period of popularity, or mode on the curve, relative temporal ordering will be confused because it will be unclear as to which mode the unit belongs. The more types or styles this multimodality is present in, the greater the chance of error.

Three additional factors also can affect the seriation. First, if the units of time that correspond to shifts in ceramic production are of very different lengths, the seriation will suffer. Second, if the units are functionally different, the types of artifacts present may vary considerably. If this is the case the ordering or grouping of sites may represent functional similarity rather than temporal relationships. Finally, if the practice of heirlooming objects over long periods of time occurred, the time periods in which the objects were produced and disposed of may not be correlated. If this is true, the similarity matrices and distances used to order or group the units may be inaccurate.

[See also ARCHAEO-PALEOMAGNETIC DATING; ARTIFACT DISTRIBUTION ANALYSIS; DATING THE PAST; DENDROCHRONOLOGY; FISSION-TRACK DATING; LUMINESCENCE DATING; OBSI-

DIAN HYDRATION DATING; RADIOCARBON DATING; STATISTICAL ANALYSIS; STRATIGRAPHY; TYPOLOGICAL ANALYSIS.]

■ Robert Dunnell, "Seriation Method and Its Evaluation," *American Antiquity* 35 (1970): 305–319. Anna O. Shepard, *Ceramics for the Archaeologist* (1976). William Marquardt, "Advances in Archaeological Seriation," in *Advances in Archaeological Method and Theory*, vol. 1, ed. Michael B. Schiffer (1978), pp. 257–314. Prudence Rice, *Pottery Analysis, a Sourcebook* (1987).

Tammy Stone

SERPENT MOUND refers to an earthen ridge that snakes along the crest of a narrow finger ridge on the edge of a cliff overlooking Brush Creek in southern Ohio. In prehistory and today it is remote from population centers. The most famous map of the site is in Squier and Davis's *Ancient Monuments of the Mississippi Valley* published in 1848. Unfortunately, however, it is inaccurate. The most accurate map, which the modern remnant matches closely, was drafted in 1886 by W. H. Holmes. His map shows a spiral on the southern end of the 1,418-foot (432-meter)-long, 4 to 5-foot (1.2 to 1.5-m)-high earthwork, like Squier and Davis. Above the spiral, where Squier and Davis show a weak, undulating line, Holmes has a series of U-shaped curves that give the whole figure a taut effect. At the opposite end, where Squier and Davis show an oval enclosure separate from the sinuous earthwork, Holmes extends the earthwork around the central feature to form a double enclosure.

Viewing the entire figure as a serpent, the enclosure is often said to symbolize an egg, or small animal, which is the target of the serpent's imminent strike. It has also been interpreted as the serpent's eye. This configuration can be seen only from the air, and on the ground trees block the view of the entire figure. It follows the only access route to the enclosure and may have served to mark the location of the ritual place and memorialize the trail to it.

Serpent Mound was excavated between 1888 and 1890 by Frederick W. Putnam, often considered a founder of American anthropology; the property was then deeded to the Ohio Archaeological and Historical Society. The excavation produced few artifacts and no burials. Lacking diagnostic artifacts and datable samples, the site's age is unknown, although the Middle Woodland Period (ca. 200 B.C.–A.D. 400) is favored.

[See also HOPEWELL CULTURE; MOUNDS OF EASTERN NORTH AMERICA; NORTH AMERICA: THE EASTERN WOODLANDS AND THE SOUTH.]

■ F. W. Putnam, "The Serpent Mound of Ohio," *Century Magazine* 39 (1890): 871–888.

William S. Dancey

SETTLEMENT ARCHAEOLOGY refers to that subset of archaeological research that is aimed at entire regions rather than at single sites. While *settlement patterns* is a term sometimes used to refer to intrasite spatial patterning, as used here the term refers to regional approaches. Settlement data are typically collected in the context of regional surveys, and the problems addressed are likewise broadly regional in scope.

Settlement archaeology traces its theoretical underpinnings to the nineteenth-century work of Lewis Henry *Morgan, who was one of the first researchers to discuss the relationship between settlement types and social evolution. The ecological approaches of Julian Steward also form an important component of the theoretical basis for settlement archaeology, specifically as it deals with the relationship between human subsistence settlement systems and the natural landscape.

Archaeological settlement surveys, as they were often done in the past, and are still done in many parts of the world, were typically designed to locate sites for excavation. Other forms of survey were designed to locate particular site types pertaining to a particular time period, for example, Iron Age *hill forts in England. Modern surveys, however, address entire regions and focus on problems of long-term cultural change.

The first truly modern survey is generally considered to be that of the Virúu Valley of Peru, organized by Gordon Willey in the 1940s. There followed a decade in which settlement survey came to play a broader role in archaeological fieldwork, but it was not until the 1960s and 1970s that settlement archaeology came into its own. This was probably the result of two factors. First, with the emergence of the so-called New Archaeology there came an increased emphasis on testing models of cultural change, models that required data from entire regions through long spans of time. The work of Robert Adams and his students in Mesopotamia demonstrated the benefits of taking a broad regional view of the emergence of early states, as well as shifting the research emphasis from studies of urbanism to an examination of the processes involved in the emergence of states. Likewise, William Sanders and Jeffrey Parsons's work in the Valley of Mexico produced data bearing on the emergence of complexity there. And second, the dramatic emergence of *cultural resource management in North America as well as Europe resulted in many limited but intensive surveys of the landscape in order to identify the existence of cultural resources. Rather than being directed at the testing of any particular model, these surveys are conducted with the goal of protecting the cultural resources and mitigating the effects of modern development on those resources.

The major advantage of problem-oriented settlement archaeology is its ability to provide the "big picture," that is, to reveal evidence of broad changes over a wide area through a long span of time. Single-site archaeology cannot provide such data. Settlement archaeology tends to address issues of a regional nature, including such problems as hunter-gatherer subsistence and the emergence of political complexity.

The disadvantages of settlement archaeology are due primarily to the limitations of data collection, which in turn are limited by the visibility and state of preservation of archaeological remains. In the first place, sites with no visible surface traces, because they are either buried or not preserved, remain absent from the regional picture. This results in the underrepresentation of certain site types and sites of certain periods. In the second place, surface data may not be representative of subsurface remains, and in the case of multicomponent sites, earlier phases of occupation may not be visible at all. Thus data tend to be relatively more complete for more recent periods, while earlier periods are underrepresented. Further, survey data tend to be more complete for ceramic periods than for earlier preceramic periods. Ceramic artifacts are relatively indestructible, and they are more visible in surface survey than nonceramic artifacts. Ceramic period settlements tend to be more permanent and substantial than preceramic ones, and therefore more visible on the surface. Finally, the modern environment of the survey region may also contribute substantially to the visibility of the surface remains. It is no

accident that most large regional surveys have been conducted in regions that are arid to semiarid, regions in which visibility of remains is not obscured by vegetation, and those where soil formation is slow. All told, these various factors combine to produce data that can be very incomplete in some cases.

While many sites or periods may go underrepresented, it is also the case that maps of settlement distributions are inclined to be overestimated. Regional chronologies tend not to be very fine grained, being based on artifact style changes, and regional chronologies are usually divided into rather long periods. The sites occupied during those periods may or may not have been occupied for the entire period. It is likewise very difficult to distinguish, on the basis of surface remains, a single long, continuous occupation as opposed to a series of short, separate occupations.

Most settlement research is accomplished by pedestrian survey over all or part of a region. *Sampling plays a key role; some research problems demand 100 percent coverage of a well-defined region, while other problems can be addressed through sample surveys. Increasingly, remote sensing has come to play a role where it is appropriate, especially where visibility is poor or where buried sites are expected. Most recently, archaeological settlement data have been applied to *Geographical Information Systems (GIS), which provide new technology for displaying regional data and producing more elaborate maps of archaeological remains.

[See also ARTIFACT DISTRIBUTION ANALYSIS; CULTURAL RESOURCE MANAGEMENT: SITE MANAGEMENT; SETTLEMENT PATTERN ANALYSIS; SITE LOCATION.]

■ Jeffrey R. Parsons, "Archaeological Settlement Patterns," *Annual Review of Anthropology* 1 (1972): 127–150. William T. Sanders, Jeffrey R. Parsons, and Robert S. Santley, *The Basin of Mexico: Ecological Processes in the Evolution of a Civilization* (1979). Robert McC. Adams, *Heartland of Cities: Surveys of Ancient Settlement and Land Use in the Central Floodplain of the Euphrates* (1981). Albert J. Ammerman, "Surveys and Archaeological Research," *Annual Review of Anthropology* 10 (1981): 63–88. David J. Wilson, *Prehispanic Settlement Patterns in the Lower Santa Valley, Peru: A Regional Perspective on the Origins and Development of Complex North Coast Society* (1988). Suzanne K. Fish and Stephen A. Kowalewski, eds., *The Archaeology of Regions: A Case for Full-Coverage Survey* (1990).

Katharina J. Schreiber

SETTLEMENT PATTERN ANALYSIS. A settlement pattern is the distribution of human activities across the landscape and the spatial relationship between these activities and features of the natural and social environment. By assuming that these relationships are patterned in a predictable manner, the analysis of settlement patterns can be used to reconstruct and explain the organization of human societies and their interactions with the surrounding environment. This analysis can be performed at several levels, from the spatial analysis of small activity sites to the large-scale investigation of human settlement across an entire region. Historically, settlement pattern analysis has centered on the distribution of communities across the landscape, and the following discussion will focus on this scale of analysis. However, many of the methods discussed here are applicable at any level of settlement pattern analysis.

History of Settlement Pattern Analysis. Julian Steward's research in the 1930s on the relationship between regional settlement patterns, population size, and the environment represents one of the first explicit applications of settlement pattern analysis. His work inspired others such as G. R. Willey, whose famous Viru Valley study in the 1940s combined aerial photography, architectural observations, and regional maps of site distributions to reconstruct sociopolitical organization (*Prehistoric Settlement Patterns in the Viru Valley, Peru*, 1953). Although his analyses consisted of simple inferences derived from observations of the settlement data, his work had an important influence on the future of settlement pattern studies. During the 1950s, the analytical techniques employed by settlement archaeologists became increasingly sophisticated. For example, formal sampling methods and different scales of analysis integrating intrasite and intercommunity perspectives were increasingly employed, and ethnographic material began to be used to correlate specific settlement configurations with different types of social organization.

The beginning of the New Archaeology in the mid-1960s profoundly influenced the direction of settlement pattern analysis through its concern with scientific methods and new analytical tools. Quantitative statistics were increasingly used for investigating spatial data, beginning with Lewis and Sally Binford's reconstruction of Paleolithic settlement systems through the application of multivariate statistics (*American Anthropologist*, 68, 1966). Statistical techniques were commonly employed for identifying spatial patterns in the distribution of artifacts and their stylistic attributes, which could then be associated with particular social units. The New Archaeology also encouraged the development of new techniques for producing detailed environmental reconstructions. Through the 1970s and 1980s, archaeologists continued to borrow quantitative models and statistical methods from other disciplines while developing their own tools for analyzing settlement patterns.

The late 1980s and early 1990s have seen the further refinement of the analytical techniques used in settlement patterns. The accessibility of powerful computers has stimulated the use of increasingly sophisticated tools for the analysis of larger regional data sets, which can be managed and manipulated using spatial databases known as *Geographic Information Systems. At the same time, archaeologists rely less on environmental and economic models, diverging into the spatial analysis of other sociocultural domains such as political networking, factionalism, and ethnic behavior. A greater understanding of settlement patterns is being facilitated by ethnoarchaeologists investigating the spatial dimensions of human behavior in living societies and by archaeologists examining the formation processes that have modified the landscape.

Common Analytical Techniques. Before the appropriate techniques for settlement pattern analysis can be selected, the researcher must know how the data were collected. Data may be generated in comprehensive survey programs that record all sites in a region or they may be collected using formal sampling methods. Accurate dates from excavations may be available for the archaeological remains, dates may be derived from disturbed surface assemblages, or the data may have no temporal dimension, instead representing the accumulation of hundreds of years of human behavior. The scale of the data is also important. Most researchers focus on the site as the basic analytical unit. However, recent investigations have noted that the concept of the site is ill-defined and often inherently biased. Some archaeologists therefore advocate the "distributional" approach, which focuses on the distribution of artifacts across the landscape. In any case, archaeologists should be aware of how their data were collected and organized, for many of the tools used in settlement pattern analysis are sensitive to data quality. Settlement pattern analyses are only as accurate and comprehensive as the data used.

The analytical techniques available to the settlement archaeologist can be grouped into four general categories according to their most common application. The first group consists of locational models, which predict where in the landscape a particular activity should be located. These models often assume a least-cost perspective in which humans are seen as situating their activities in such a way as to conserve the amount of energy needed to access or distribute resources. For example, ecotone models predict that humans will locate themselves on the borders between ecological zones, thereby minimizing the effort needed to collect the diverse resources found in each zone. When specific behavioral objectives and constraints can be quantified, location-allocation analyses are useful for determining the optimal locations for human activities. Predictions from these locational models can be compared with actual settlement data to evaluate the influences of economizing behavior and environmental factors on settlement patterns. Because these models focus on environmental characteristics, the researcher should know how modern conditions differ from those encountered in the past.

Other analytical techniques focus on past economic organization. One of the most common methods is catchment analysis, in which estimates of a site's resource base and overall productivity are calculated based on a hypothesized economic range. This technique is especially effective when the results are compared with the actual plant and animal remains recovered from the site. Other analytical techniques are useful for reconstructing regional economic interaction. For example, falloff models and trend surface analyses use regional artifact or resource distributions to identify their sources, delineate economic boundaries, and reconstruct mechanisms of exchange. For societies exhibiting greater sociopolitical complexity, transportation systems can be examined using network analysis. This technique quantifies the linkages between settlements within a defined region and produces indices evaluating the centrality, importance, and accessibility of any given site as well as the general compactness and connectivity of the settlement system. Most of these indices are descriptive and are used only on a comparative basis.

The political organization of past societies can also be derived from settlement data. Central-place models examine the spatial organization of a group of related sites to identify hierarchical networks. The basic expectation is that major centers will be equally spaced from one another and surrounded by a nested hierarchy of increasingly smaller sites. Rank-size analysis, which is derived from central-place theory, evaluates the intensity of centralization in a settlement system by assuming that the degree to which a site is dominant is reflected in its size relative to associated sites. Another analytical tool is the Thiessen polygon, which is used to identify potential territorial boundaries for a group of politically autonomous settlements. Polygons are created by dividing the landscape such that each boundary is equidistant from each pair of adjacent centers. Like many analytical techniques, Thiessen polygons provide a tool for describing settlement data. The resulting descriptions are not always accurate reconstructions of the past, nor do they necessarily explain the human behavior that created the settlement patterns. However, these methods do provide starting points for further investigation.

Ethnographic analogy is also used to develop models for describing and interpreting settlement data. The investigation of how living societies are distributed across the landscape can be especially useful for reconstructing human behaviors that are not the direct result of economizing behavior or for relationships that are not easily quantifiable. For example, the spatial organization of religious activity or ethnic organization can be investigated by deriving archaeological models from ethnographic cases that describe how cosmological symbols or ethnic markers are distributed across the landscape. Although ethnographic analogy possesses its own set of problems and assumptions, it can enhance the archaeologist's understanding of the range of possible settlement behavior.

Conclusions. This discussion has focused on only a few of the important analytical tools available to the settlement archaeologist. Many of the statistical and qualitative approaches used in other archaeological subdisciplines are also applicable to settlement data, and many settlement archaeologists develop their own tools specific to the problems they face. For example, for his study in the basin of Mexico, Vincas Steponaitis (*American Anthropologist*, 83, 1981) created formulas for identifying tribute flow using catchment and settlement data. In another study, Olivier deMontmollin (*The Archaeology of Political Structure*, 1989) developed several simple indices for evaluating Mayan economic and political relationships using regional data. Whatever its origin, every analytical method is based on important assumptions that should be recognized and evaluated. Most quantitative techniques are also sensitive to the accuracy and completeness of the settlement data. As with any archaeological approach, settlement pattern analysis is most effective when combined with explicit theory-driven and goal-oriented research. When it is appropriately used, the analysis of settlement data is a powerful approach for reconstructing and explaining past human behavior.

[*See also* ARTIFACT DISTRIBUTION ANALYSIS; SAMPLING; SETTLEMENT ARCHAEOLOGY; SITE LOCATION: SITE ASSESSMENT; STATISTICAL ANALYSIS.]

▪ Jeffrey R. Parsons, "Archaeological Settlement Patterns," *Annual Review of Anthropology* 1 (1972): 127–150. Kent V. Flannery, ed., *The Early Mesoamerican Village* (1976). Ian Hodder and Clive Orton, *Spatial Analysis in Archaeology* (1976). Gregory A. Johnson, "Aspects of Regional Analysis in Archaeology," *Annual Review of Anthropology* 6 (1977): 479–508. Donna C. Roper, "The Method and Theory of Site Catchment Analysis: A Review," *Advances in Archaeological Method and Theory* 2 (1979): 119–140. J. M. Wagstaff, *Landscape and Culture: Geographical and Archaeological Perspectives* (1987). Charles D. Trombold, ed., *Ancient Road Networks and Settlement Hierarchies in the New World* (1991). Jacqueline Rossignol and LuAnn Wandsnider, eds., *Space, Time, and Archaeological Landscapes* (1992). Edward M. Schortman and Patricia A. Urban, eds., *Resources, Power, and Interregional Interaction* (1992).

John Kantner

SHELL MIDDENS are archaeological middens containing shell. The word *midden* has its roots in the Scandinavian languages, meaning material that accumulates about a dwelling place. Most shell found in archaeological shell middens, however, did not accumulate about a dwelling per se, and therefore the term is inaccurate. People more frequently throw shells aside after extracting, for a variety of purposes, the organic shellfish once inhabiting the shell. The term *shell-bearing site* has been suggested as a more accurate description of sites with remains of shellfish, but because of tradition, the term *shell midden* remains the most frequently used term to describe such sites.

All shell middens have in common their location near water, low densities of artifacts, and large volumes of shell. Shell middens have high probabilities of being saturated by the adjacent body of water. Most oceans or rivers from which shellfish are acquired have fluctuating levels (e.g., tides, storms, floods, or larger-scale changes in worldwide sea level). Shell middens are therefore often found below tide or groundwater level. The shell and the adjacent water bestow on shell middens common characteristics. Sites that contain shell are very porous; the large number of shells creates air spaces throughout the deposits, allowing water (and sometimes small objects) to move rapidly into the lowest portion of the sites. Also, the presence of the shell creates a chemical environment different from that of the surrounding sediment.

The high density of shell in shell middens creates low densities of historically diagnostic artifacts per unit volume of site. The presence of the shell increases the volumes of shell middens by at least a factor of ten, so large volumes of the site must be excavated to obtain even small numbers of artifacts. Shell middens are also places where special food gathering activities took place. People were usually there to collect and to process shellfish. This collecting activity requires few tools, so few artifacts are found in places where the shells are discarded.

Shell middens were first observed by naturalists in the eighteenth century and were examined to determine if their accumulation was cultural or natural. The earliest investigations of shell middens, therefore, concentrated on establishing the human origins of such sites. The discovery of artifacts and hearths with shell led to the eventual determination that the origin of shell middens was cultural; archaeologists then shifted from studying the origins of shell middens to studying their content. For the last century, most research on shell middens focused on the kinds of shell in the sites as indicators of *subsistence and the artifactual remains as indicators of culture history. Although subsistence and culture history are important, the origins of shell middens are equally important. Archaeologists in the last decade have returned to the questions posed first in the eighteenth century: how did shell middens form, and by what means were they altered after prehistoric peoples created them?

The kinds of research done on shell middens is best summarized using a list presented by Ambrose (1967), dividing research into four categories: (1) looking at faunal remains in terms of available food supply, (2) plotting variations in shellfish species acquired from column samples to infer changing ecological conditions in nearby aqueous habitats, (3) delineating ancient shoreline locations by plotting geomorphic positions of shell middens, and (4) ignoring shellfish remains and constructing cultural historical sequences by analyzing the artifacts only. Not considered in his list is the more recent research interest in how shell middens formed, added as a fifth category: examining shell middens in terms of their depositional and postdepositional processes.

Most of the earliest investigations of shell middens fall into the first and fourth categories: analyzing faunal remains in terms of available food supply, and constructing cultural histories. Some of the earliest shell midden analyses in the western United States were conducted in California, where shell midden size became an estimate of site age, prehistoric diet, and population. These studies became the models for research conducted in the following decades, especially on the west coast of North America. In the eastern United States, shell middens were excavated by the Tennessee Valley Authority (TVA) and the Works Progress Administration (WPA) to conserve archaeological material being inundated by flooding and arrange them in a chronological framework. Unlike the California archaeologists, the WPA and TVA researchers never analyzed the shell as dietary evidence, but instead treated it as sediment encasing the objects of historical significance. During this same time period, shell middens were also examined in other parts of the world (Australia, South Africa, Denmark, Britain, Peru, Mexico, and Canada), primarily for purposes of creating culture histories and conducting dietary studies.

Many archaeologists have now begun to examine the appropriateness of using shellfish remains as indicators of diet and seasonality (Claassen, "Gender, Shellfishing, and the Shell Mound Archaic," 1991; Claassen, "Normative Thinking and Shell-Bearing Sites," 1991; Waselkov 1987). They question the reliability of the assumption behind the dietary and seasonality interpretations. Shellfish found in sites may have been used for more than just protein and dietary considerations; they could have been used as bait, construction material, or raw material for tool manufacture. Ethnographic observations concerning the methods of collecting, cooking, and storing shellfish suggest considerable variability in cultural choices and practices. The seasonality assignments are problematic due to local variations in climatic conditions and lack of adequate *sampling. Finally, sampling biases of the archaeological record and of archaeologists themselves influence the results of faunal analyses. All of these considerations have led to skepticism concerning the assumption that the presence of shellfish remains in sites means that the shellfish were exclusively eaten.

Ambrose's second and third categories (inferring changes in ecological conditions within nearby aqueous habitats and delineating ancient shoreline locations by plotting geomorphic positions of shell middens) have been a major focus of research only in the last two decades. The new emphasis reflects an increased interest in environmental reconstruction and geoarchaeology. Archaeologists use shells discovered in shell middens to reconstruct changes in the habitats and the location of ancient shorelines. To infer that shells, which are extracted from shell middens, are indicators of shifts in nearby aquatic habitats or shifts in shoreline locations requires accepting the assumption that the shellfish species found in shell middens are adequate reflections of environmental conditions in adjacent habitats. This assumes that people were selecting shellfish randomly, depositing a random sample of the species inhabiting the body of water.

The assumption that shellfish in middens are indicators of aquatic habitat rather than indicators of shifts in cultural preferences is problematic (Meehan 1982). One of the most serious concerns is the biases that cultural choices could have on the sample; another is that a host of factors unrelated to people could affect the habitat of shellfish, for example, water temperature, salinity, and coastal ecology. The assumption is further complicated by the fact that in most modern coastal environments changes such as sealevel rise, coastal subsidence, urban development, and erosion are all common.

To address these habitat questions adequately, shell middens must be analyzed with other environmental data. For example, Sanger (1981, 1988) has not reconstructed the coastal environments of Maine from the shells found in shell middens alone. His interdisciplinary research at Passamaquoddy Bay, Damariscotta River, and Penobscot Bay used offshore cores, marine geology, and shells from shell middens to reconstruct the complex interplay between environment and cultural preferences. Such independent tests allow archaeologists to evaluate separately the environmental reconstructions and the cultural preferences.

The fifth category, examining shell middens in terms of their depositional and postdepositional processes, has been an important focus of research in the last decade (Stein 1992). This research considers how shell middens are created, including the processes acting to transport and deposit the shell, artifacts, and sediments to the location and the alterations by decomposition, compaction, weathering, and leaching. Stein notes that a small-scale rise in sea level has increased leaching of shell from the lower portions of a shell midden in Washington State. If this process continues, all shell will eventually disappear from the lower half of the site. Many other sites around the world are experiencing this same phenomenon.

Shell middens are found along most coasts and many rivers of the world (Bailey and Parkington 1988). They represent the exploitation of marine and aquatic resources by prehistoric peoples. The discovery of very old shell middens indicates that this exploitation began as early as 25,000 years ago on opposite sides of the world, in Papua New Guinea (Allen, Gosden, and White 1989) and South Africa (Singer and Wymer 1982). By 5,000 years ago, shell middens existed all over the world, indicating a worldwide dependence on such resources. Examining shell middens and unraveling their complex formation is the only way to understand this coastal adaptation.

[See also DIET, RECONSTRUCTION OF; ENVIRONMENTAL ARCHAEOLOGY; PALEOENVIRONMENTAL RECONSTRUCTION; SEASONALITY STUDIES; SITE FORMATION PROCESSES.]

■ Wal R. Ambrose, "Archaeology and Shell Middens," *Archaeology and Physical Anthropology in Oceania* 2 (1967): 169–187. David Sanger, "Unscrambling Messages in the Midden," *Archaeology of Eastern North America* 9 (1981): 37–42. Betty Meehan, *Shell Bed to Shell Midden* (1982). Ronald Singer and John Wymer, eds., *The Middle Stone Age at Klasies River Mouth in South Africa* (1982). Gregory A. Waselkov, "Shellfish Gathering and Shell Midden Archaeology," in *Advances in Archaeological Method and Theory, Vol. 10*, ed. Michael B. Schiffer (1987), pp. 93–210. Geoff Bailey and John Parkington, *The Archaeology of Prehistoric Coastlines* (1988). David Sanger, "Maritime Adaptations in the Gulf of Maine," *Archaeology of Eastern North America* 16 (1988): 81–99. Jim Allen, Chris Gosden, and J. Peter White, "Human Pleistocene Adaptations in the Tropical Island Pacific: Recent Evidence from New Ireland, a Greater Australian Outlier," *Antiquity* 63 (1989): 548–561. Cheryl Claassen, "Gender, Shellfishing, and the Shell Mound Archaic," in *Engendering Archaeology: Women and Prehistory*, ed. Margaret W. Conkey and Joan M. Gero (1991), pp. 276–300. Cheryl Claassen, "Normative Thinking and Shell-Bearing Sites," in *Archaeological Method and Theory, Vol. 3*, ed. Michael B. Schiffer (1991), pp. 249–298. Julie K. Stein, ed., *Deciphering a Shell Midden* (1992).

Julie K. Stein

SHIHUANGDI, Tomb of. King Zheng, "the Tiger of Qin," was the First Sovereign Emperor (Shihuangdi) of China. He became ruler of Qin at the age of thirteen in 246 B.C., unifying China after a series of ruthless military campaigns in 221 B.C. Work may have begun on the emperor's tomb as early as 246 B.C., but intensified with unification. The emperor considered himself unique, so his sepulchre was to be the largest ever built. Later court histories write of more than 700,000 conscripts, many of them convicts, who worked on the tomb, the royal capital, and the royal palace.

The great burial mound measures more than 1,100 feet (335 m) on each side and rises 140 feet (43 m) above the surrounding countryside 25 miles (40 km) east of Xianyang on the banks of the Wei River. Inside is said to lie a replica of the royal domains, with China's great rivers re-created in mercury flowing by some mechanical device into the ocean. The constellations of the heavens appear on the ceiling of the burial chamber, the earth's geography beneath. Scale models of palaces and pavilions contain the emperor's personal possessions, while models of courtiers attend him in death. Many concubines, also laborers who worked on the tomb, were sacrificed and buried inside the tumulus. While Han dynasty historians state that the mound was looted after the fall of the Qin line, Chinese archaeologists have detected unusually high concentrations of mercury in the soil chemistry of the mound and suspect that Shihuangdi's grave goods may be intact. No one has yet excavated the mound, which once lay in the middle of a large funerary park surrounded by a 4-mile (6.5 km) outer wall. In the 1970s, Chinese archaeologists excavated a regiment of terracotta soldiers, armed cavalrymen, kneeling archers, and their officers, perhaps a ceremonial guard assigned to protect the eastern side of the tomb. The molded figures were finished with individual hairstyles, mustaches, and other features and were fully armed. Other finds near the tumulus include two half-scale bronze chariots and their horses as well as underground stables, some with mangers containing horses buried alive.

[*See also* ASIA: PREHISTORY AND EARLY HISTORY OF EAST ASIA; CHINA: EARLY CIVILIZATIONS OF CHINA.]

■ Arthur Cottrell, *The First Emperor of China* (1981). Xueqin Li, *Eastern Zhou and Qin Civilization* (1985). Gina Barnes, *China, Korea, and Japan* (1993).

Brian M. Fagan

SHIPS AND SEAFARING. In the study of water transport, archaeologists investigate the methods used to travel across lakes, down rivers, and over seas, and examine the different vehicles of transport, their construction, and their cultural significance.

Seafaring and the Use of Rivers and Lakes. To a boatman, the rivers and seas of the world are as one: there are no barriers, for example, between Lake Geneva in Switzerland and the Yellow River in China. Seafaring is a natural extension of voyages on inland waters, for before overseas exploration and settlement there was exploration and exploitation of the land by river and by lake.

The evidence. In the absence of excavated water transport early voyages may be recognized in the distribution patterns of artifacts and of those ideas which are archaeologically visible as monuments, rituals or technological innovations, and by the study of past environments, especially former sea levels, coastlines, and river courses. Voyages along or across rivers and lakes can be difficult to prove as overland routes may be a theoretical alternative. Overseas voyages may be similarly difficult to confirm archaeologically, but in certain cases there is supporting evidence. For example, in the third millennium B.C. trade and exchange between the Indus civilization and Mesopotamia could have been by overland route which would not have been more difficult than the medieval Silk Road between China and the Mediterranean. Inscriptions excavated in Mesopotamia and attributed to Sargon of Agade, however, proclaim that overseas ships came to his capital, thereby supporting the overseas route theory. There is a comparable situation in the Red Sea region where inscriptions and paintings from the early third millennium B.C. onward demonstrate that trade and exchange between Egypt and "Punt" which could, in theory, have been by land, was in fact by sea.

With islands, the evidence is clearer and one can be certain, for example, that in approximately 8000 B.C. obsidian was brought by sea from Melos to mainland Greece. The first overseas voyage recognized in this way is remarkably early: the settlement of Greater Australia from Southeast Asia in 50,000 B.C. or earlier. Whether an overseas voyage was also necessary during the first settlement of the Americas is uncertain as there is no universally agreed-upon date for this migration, at an early date this journey could have been overland, whereas after roughly 10,000 B.C., when the Bering Sea had been formed by rising sea levels, water transport would have been needed. Whatever the date, there is no doubt that water transport would have facilitated the subsequent progress southward of these first Americans.

Routes. A river can be an obstacle—hence ferries—or a route. The "natural" use might seem to be to drift downstream, but if this is to be a purposeful voyage some means of steering has to be devised, for example, by the use of a paddle to propel and to steer. An alternative method has been described by Herodotus (2.137): boats on the Nile towed a large weight along the river bed which slowed down the boat relative to the current, thereby making steering possible. There is also the problem of returning upstream against the current. On the Tigris and Euphrates this problem was solved by oarpower, or by towing, either from an oared boat or by men where there was a suitable river bank. Similar methods were used in contemporary Egypt above Aswan, but on the rest of the Nile where the predominant wind was northerly, sail was used: the fact that the predominant wind blew against the Nile current may have been a major stimulus in the introduction of the sail there before 3000 B.C.

Currents, tidal flows, and winds also influence the routes taken on sea voyages: a direct route is not necessarily practicable, especially when under sail. It has been argued that, in the eastern Mediterranean during the second millennium B.C., counterclockwise voyages were undertaken from the Levant to the southern Aegean, to Egypt, and back to the Levant. Such a route had the advantage of fair winds and currents on the Aegean to Egypt leg. There were generally foul winds on the northbound Levant and the westbound Turkish coastal legs, however, which would have made these sections of the voyage lengthy, waiting for the occasional fair wind or using short periods of land and sea breezes to make some progress. Such a route may have suited the "tramp" nature of the mid-second-millennium-B.C. ship wrecked at Ulu Bunin (Kas), off the south coast of Turkey, but if this vessel could have been tacked against the wind, other routes and tactics could have been possible for it and its contemporaries.

It is difficult to determine when sailing vessels could make significant progress against the wind, as mast, sail, and rigging seldom, if ever, survive to be excavated, and iconographic evidence and other enigmatic sources have to be used. Such evidence suggests that Egyptian ships may have been able to sail with the wind forward of the beam, from the mid-second millennium B.C.

Seasonal use. Weather also influences the timing of overseas voyages. The period of stormy seas, strong winds, and obscured skies from mid-October to mid-March was generally avoided in European waters. In other regions different periods were avoided; for example, the coasts of Western India and Sri Lanka from mid-June to mid-September when, as a first- or second-century-A.D. *periplus* (sailing manual) describes, there were particularly stormy seas. Season winds also influenced the timing of voyages. For example, in the Roman period, India-bound ships left their Red Sea ports in July so that they could use the southwest monsoon to cross the Arabian Sea in August and September, and on return they left India in late November with the northeast monsoon.

Pilotage and navigation. Another important determinant in the choice of overseas routes was the ship's master's knowledge in coastal waters and his navigating ability when out of sight of land. The earliest mariners would have remained in sight of land. By the early first millennium B.C., however (and probably much earlier), voyages were intentionally made across open seas in the South Pacific, in the eastern Mediterranean, and possibly in the Indian Ocean.

Early descriptions of coastal landmarks and seamarks, which were probably learned by rote and passed on orally, have survived encapsulated in *periploi* (sailing manuals) of Classical times. Aspects of deep-sea navigation (which is more difficult) are also mentioned in Greek and Latin literature from Homer's time onward and in Chinese, Indian, and Arab accounts of the early medieval period. In many early civilizations there was a sound knowledge of basic astronomy, for example in Egypt and Mesopotamia where there was a vital requirement to forecast the times of annual river floods: such a knowledge of the heavens would have been useful in the open sea. Furthermore, recent studies of the methods used by indigenous twentieth-century navigators of southern India and of the South Pacific have thrown new light on these ancient sources.

The sum of this evidence points toward the use of a form of dead-reckoning navigation, based on environmental observations and without instruments except for the sounding lead. Directions were known relative to the wind, the swell, the sun and moon, constellations, and individual stars; time was measured by the sun and by circumpolar constellations; inherited wisdom and long experience were used to estimate a ship's speed; signs indicating a change in the weather were noted in the sea and the sky; and evidence for land over the horizon was seen in the outflow of great rivers, the flight line of migrating birds, rising crographic clouds and the like.

A crucial and difficult question concerns the date when navigators could measure the altitude (vertical angle) of selected stars as, with this ability, estimates of latitude can be made. On land and aboard a boat in harbor, this can be done using the equinoctial sun's noon shadow cast by a gnomon, a method used in ancient Egypt. This method is, however, impracticable at sea. In the first century A.D., Lucan recorded that Phoenician navigators estimated stars' altitudes against the mast, but this cannot have been with precision. In the Indian Ocean during the eighth century A.D., star altitudes were measured by an outstretched arm, in hand-spans or palms: such a simple, empirical method may have been widely used at a much earlier date, but has gone unrecorded.

The first seagoing, altitude-measuring instrument seems to have been a staff used by ninth-century-A.D. Arabs. This led to the development of the *kamal* (wooden tablets on a knotted string), which was used by Arab seamen from the tenth century. No early examples of this simple but effective instrument are known: they may await excavation. The mariner's compass was first used in the late eleventh century in the seas between India and China. Charts and the sandglass were used in the Mediterranean from the thirteenth century and the mariner's astrolabe and quadrant from the fourteenth century. Columbus had these two instruments on his transatlantic voyage in 1492 yet his log reveals that, apart from the compass and the sandglass, he placed most reliance on noninstrumental methods that had been in use for three thousand years and more.

Landing places. Informal landing places are used today the world over and similar ones must have been used in antiquity. In the mid-second millennium B.C. the soft, muddy foreshore at Ferriby on the river Humber was made suitable for boats by laying a mat of light timbers, while in the first century B.C. at Hengistbury Head in Christchurch Harbour gravel was used for the same purpose. Such informal landing places prevailed worldwide until the ninth to eight century B.C. when, on the Levantine coast, the natural protection that reefs and islands gave to certain havens was reinforced by human-made structures. At around the same time, a breakwater of dressed stone on rubble was built at Delos in the Aegean. These first steps led in due course to the complex harbors of the Roman world with their quays and jetties, warehouses and cargo-handling facilities, shipbuilding and repair sites, fresh water and victuals, lighthouses and so on. Elsewhere, informal landing places persisted until the mid-first millennium A.D., when formal harbors began to be built, for example, in northern Europe.

Water Transport. The evidence for early water transport is sparse, episodic, frequently ambiguous, and biased toward Europe. No rafts or boats earlier than the ninth millennium B.C. have been excavated anywhere in the world, and it is not until the second millennium B.C. that there is direct evidence for seagoing ships. In Europe, logboats have been excavated dating from approximately 8500 B.C. to post-medieval times. The earliest European plank boats are of the mid-second millennium B.C. and from that time onward there are groups of finds with common characteristics that allow certain regional boat building traditions to be identified. It is likely, however, that their origins lie well before the dates usually given to them.

In both northern and southern Europe there are representations and descriptions of boats that can sometimes be used to supplement the excavated evidence, and for barbarian Europe there are the accounts of Classical authors. Within the European traditions, some developments over time can be recognized, as can some regional variants, but other subgroups, and possibly main groups, undoubtedly remain unidentified.

The oldest plank boat known to date was recovered from a pit alongside the pyramid of Cheops (Khufu) at Giza, Egypt: this enormous vessel, 142 feet (43.4 m) in length, 19 feet (5.9 m) maximum beam, and 19.5 to 24.5 feet (6 to 7.5 m) high at the ends, has been dated to roughly 2600 B.C. The remains of another boat have been recognized in a second pit nearby. From the nineteenth-century-B.C. pyramid enclosure of Sesostris III at Dahshur come four small boats, while twelve others, possibly from around 3000 B.C., are presently being excavated at Abydos. There are also models and many early illustrations of bundle rafts and plank boats, including the depiction of sail from around 3200 B.C.

This early use of the sail in Egypt seems to have led to the use of the sail in the eastern Mediterranean from roughly 2000 B.C.; the earliest evidence for the sail in northwest Europe is from the sixth century B.C.

In China, many logboats have been excavated, ranging in date from the fifth millennium B.C. to the present day. Pictograms suggest that sail was used from the second millennium B.C. From the Han period (second century B.C. to third century A.D.) three small plank boats are known but there is no further excavated evidence until the eleventh to fourteenth century A.D., when there are four medieval ships. To supplement this meager record there is illustrative, but enigmatic, evidence from the late-second millennium B.C. onward, descriptions from the first millennium B.C. and a few tomb models from the fourth century B.C.

In the vast area of undoubted early maritime activity which stretches from Arabia and the east coast of Africa to the South Pacific there are just a handful of logboat and plank boat remains, mainly in Southeast Asia. In the later periods some illustrative and written evidence can be added to this sparse excavated material.

Some of the logboats excavated in the Americas have been dated to pre-Columbian times, while fragmentary evidence for hide boats has been excavated in the Arctic region. It seems likely that sails were in use there by the early centuries A.D. "First contact" accounts written, and sometimes illustrated, by fifteenth- to eighteenth-century Europeans can be used to supplement this American evidence and also to amplify the meager evidence from other regions outside Europe. For the Indian Ocean there are similar reports from the Roman period.

Types of water transport. There are four main groups of water transport: floats, rafts, boats, and ships. Floats are personal aids to flotation with the user partly in the water. No remains have been recognized archaeologically, but inflated hide floats are depicted on seventh-century-B.C. reliefs from Assyria and similar ones are in use today in, for example, China and Afghanistan. Blocks of wood and even petrol cans are also used. Rafts are not watertight-like boats, but "flow through" and derive their buoyancy from their individual elements. Boats, on the other hand, derive their buoyancy from the displacement of water by their watertight hull. The distinction between boats and ships may not be clear at the margin but it is generally considered that a vessel over 65.5 feet (20 m) overall in length is a ship, providing that it has a deck under which the crew can rest and feed, and is capable of sustained operations at sea.

Rafts. Two second-century-A.D. log rafts from Strasbourg, France, and three from Viking Age Baltic countries are the only excavated evidence for rafts. Sixteenth-century Europeans found them in use widely in India, Southeast Asia, China, Oceania, and South America, including complex seagoing "freighters" with sails. Bamboo log rafts may have been used by the first migrants to Australia in roughly 50,000 B.C. Two other types of raft are known: bundle rafts and float rafts. Coiled basketry techniques are used to build bundle rafts by binding together bundles of reeds and related species (known worldwide); bark (Tasmania), or poles (central Africa). Depictions of papyrus or reed bundle rafts come from third-millennium-B.C. Egypt and Mesopotamia, and seagoing ones are known to have been used off the east coast of India in the first century A.D. It is likely that, from very early times, bundle rafts were used wherever there were suitable raw materials. Float rafts consisting of a light timber framework supported by inflated hide floats or sealed pots have a limited distribution, mainly on inland waters, although a seagoing hide-float raft of specialized construction is known from post-Columbian Chile. Etruscan engravings depict pot-float rafts with a sail and it is known that hide-float rafts were used in first century A.D. Arabia. The regular and effective use of any type of raft at sea is unlikely outside the zone of warmer seas between approximately 40° N and 40° S because of the risks of hypothermia, whereas use on inland waters is widespread.

Boats. Corresponding to rafts of logs, bundles, and hide floats there are log boats (dugout canoes), bundle boats (known only in the Mesopotamia/Iraq region in recent centuries, where there is a ready supply of tar to waterproof the bundles), and hide or skin boats. There are also bark boats, pottery boats (ancient Egypt and twentieth-century India), basket boats (Southeast Asia in recent centuries), and plank boats. Bundle boats, pottery boats, and basket boats are very restricted in distribution and there are no excavated remains. The evidence for boats of bark, hide, and logs is more substantial. It is plank boats and ships, however, which have left the most impressive remains.

Plank boats and ships. The boat built of wooden planks has become the most widespread type. With the exception of Australia, it appeared in all continents at an early date, although in America it seems to have become established in only two small and widely separated regions: around the Chonos archipelago in Chile, and with the Chumash Indians in the vicinity of the Santa Barbara Channel, north of Los Angeles. The plank boat has proven to be buildable in the greatest range of shapes, to match different functions and operating environments. It has also developed the widest selection of fastenings, including lashing and sewing in a variety of patterns, several types of wooden fastenings, and an even greater range of metal fastenings. Some of these fastening types appear to have cultural significance and to be diagnostic of particular boatbuilding traditions. The plank boat is also the only type of vessel capable of being increased in size to become a ship.

Scholars have sometimes suggested that, at some time in the past, the plank boat was developed from the log raft, the logboat, the hide boat, or the bark boat. Until further evidence is excavated, it seems best to consider the plank boat as a distinct type which may have originated in different ways at various times and places. The plank boats of the Americas, which are generally similar to the other stitched boats of the world but different in detail, appear to have come into being without external stimulus: surely a clear case of indigenous inventiveness.

Specialist techniques. Boatbuilders everywhere face similar problems, such as how to propel a boat or how to finish its ends so that it is watertight and structurally sound. Such problems have been solved by different means, in different cultures, and therein lies the possibility of the identification of different traditions of boatbuilding. Fundamental differences are seen in the way a builder thinks of his or her boat: as a watertight shell or as a waterproof framework, a conceptual difference which is expressed in the sequence of building. In the first case, the shell or "skin" of planks is shaped and fastened together in a watertight manner to produce the hull; then the supporting framework is inserted. In the skeleton sequence of building, the framework is first erected to give the shape, then it is "clothed" with planks and the hull made watertight with caulking. The oldest plank vessel in the world, the royal funeral boat of Cheops of approximately 2650 B.C., was built in the shell sequence, and it seems likely that the earliest boats (hide and bark, as well as plank) were so built, worldwide.

Plank boats built in the skeleton sequence first appear in northwest Europe in a region stretching from Switzerland, the Rhine mouth, Belgium, and northern France and Guernsey, to the river Thames and river Severn in Britain. These sixteen or so Romano-Celtic boats are dated to the first to third century A.D. The skeleton sequence next appears in the eastern Mediterranean region in the period seventh to eleventh century A.D. and, as far as is known, continued in use there to spread to Atlantic Europe sometime in the fourteenth century, around the time that skeleton building is first known in China. Much of the structural strength of the skeleton-built ship lies in the framework. For this reason, the long-term future of ocean-going wooden ships, where size and strength matter, lay with the skeleton-built vessel.

Regional traditions of plank boat building. If we generalize from the known plank boats of Egypt and Europe, we can see a general progression from rope to wooden to metal fastenings. Within those three categories it is the precise stitching pattern or the precise form and usage of the wooden or metal fastening that identifies particular traditions. Using these criteria, eight traditions, described in the following paragraphs, may be identified in this region.

Egyptian stitched boats third millennium B.C.: The planks of the Cheops boat of approximately 2600 B.C. are positioned edge to edge by tenons in mortices within the plank thickness, and are fastened together transversely (and not along the plank edges as seen elsewhere) by ropes of *halfa* grass.

Egyptian / East Mediterranean boats with wooden fastenings (ca. 2000 B.C. to A.D. 1000): Four small boats from the pyramid enclosure of Sesostris III at Dahshur of roughly 1800 B.C. have two types of wooden plank fastenings. tenons in mortices, similar to those in the Cheops boat, and double-dovetail clamps set into the plank faces across the seams. The Egyptian unlocked tenon appears to be a forerunner of the characteristic plank fastenings used in the East Mediterranean tradition in which the tenons are locked within their mortices by treenails, as found in the Kaş wreck of the mid-second millennium B.C., the fourth-century-B.C. Kyrenia wreck, and others up to the seventh century A.D.

Mediterranean boats and ships without plank fastenings from around A.D. 1000: In wrecks from the seventh century A.D., planks above the water line were not fastened together but to the framing (i.e., skeleton-built). Below the waterline, planking was still edge-fastened but the mortices were more widely spaced and were not always locked. An eleventh-century wreck from Serçe Liman off the southern Turkish coast had no plank fastenings and was entirely skeleton-built on a simple framework.

Central Mediterranean stitched boats from around 600 B.C. to A.D. 1100: A number of wrecks from the central Mediterranean, especially in the Adriatic, have stitched-plank fastenings. The earliest known is from the sixth century B.C. and the technique remained in use until at least the eleventh century A.D.

Northwest European stitched boats (ca. 1500 B.C.–300 B.C.): There was a stitched boat tradition from the mid-second millennium B.C. to roughly 300 B.C. in northwest Europe, and later in peripheral regions such as Finland. The earlier ones, such as the three boats from North Ferriby in the Humber estuary, have individual lashings between the planks; the later ones, from around 800 B.C. onward, have continuous sewing.

Romano-Celtic boats without plank fastenings: From the first to third century A.D., in a region stretching from the Swiss lakes to the river Severn in Britain, seagoing and river boats were built in the skeleton sequence with the planking fastened to the framework by large iron nails characteristically clenched by turning the point 180° back into the inboard face of the framing.

Nordic boats and ships with iron fastenings (ca. A.D. 400–1400): From around A.D. 400 to 1400 the Nordic tradition of boatbuilding dominated northern Europe from Scandinavia and the southern Baltic to the Atlantic islands and coasts as far south as northern Spain. The characteristic fastening was an iron nail driven through overlapped (clinker) planking and clenched inboard by deforming the point over a rove, as may be seen in the Viking Age burial ships from *Oseberg and Gokstad in Norway and the wreck of Henry V's *Grace Dieu* of 1418 in the river Hamble, England. In the southern Baltic there was a regional variant in which wooden pegs (treenails) were used instead of iron nails.

Cog tradition boats and ships with iron fastenings (9th to 14th century A.D.): The cog tradition of cargo carriers grew in importance from the twelfth to the fourteenth century, especially in the Rhine / Baltic region. The cog's overlapping planking was fastened together by iron nails similar to those that had been used in the Romano-Celtic tradition to fasten planking to framework.

Plank boat traditions outside Europe. In Southeast Asia there are a number of excavated boats dated to the first millennium A.D. which have stitched planking supplemented by dowels within the seams. Stitched planking also seems to have been the norm in Arabia, India, the South Pacific and the Americas until the advent of Europeans in the sixteenth century, although there is some iconographic evidence for wooden double-dovetail clamps in first-century-B.C. India (as in early Egypt).

In China there is evidence for nail-fastened plank boats from the Han period (second century B.C. to third century A.D.) but an eleventh-century wreck from Wando Island, Korea, which has several Chinese features, has the planking fastened by transverse timbers through the thickness of the planking, and locked tenons inside mortices. Three Song dynasty wrecks of the thirteenth and fourteenth centuries built in the shell sequence with keel, stems, and bulkheads, have obliquely driven metal nails as plank fastenings. The Penglai wreck of around 1376 seems to have been built in the skeleton sequence, yet the planks are still fastened together by angled nails. It seems likely that, from this time, skeleton-built ships became the norm in China, as they are today.

Atlantic Europe—fourteenth to sixteenth centuries A.D. During the fourteenth century, ships began to be built in the skeleton sequence in Atlantic Europe with features from both northern and southern European traditions. With this change from shell to skeleton, shipbuilding may be said to have become more of a science than an art.

In the fifteenth and sixteenth centuries, the traditional single mast with a square sail was replaced by two and then three masts with a combination of lateen and square sails. By this time, too, Atlantic seamen were well accustomed to the use of the mariner's compass and other aids to navigation; navigation had also become more scientific.

From the sixteenth century onward, manuals of navigation and of shipbuilding were compiled in Europe and Arabia and measured drawings and scale models were used in European shipyards. Artists began to portray vessels in greater detail. Thus from this time in Europe, historical sources begin to outweigh archaeological evidence. Furthermore, as Europeans, in their three-masted, multisail, skeleton-built ships, sailed the oceans of the world and encountered other boatbuilding traditions, documentary sources became important worldwide.

[See also LAPITA COMPLEX; MEDITERRANEAN TRADE; NORSE IN NORTH AMERICA; PACIFIC ISLANDS: OVERVIEW; SETTLEMENT OF MELANESIA AND MICRONESIA; SETTLEMENT OF POLYNESIA; PACIFIC ISLANDS NAVIGATION AND WATERCRAFT.]

■ E.G:R. Taylor, *Haven-finding Art* (1971, 2nd ed.). Søren Thirslund, *Navigationens Historie*, vol. 1 (1987). Seán McGrail, *Ancient Boats in N.W. Europe* (1987). Geoffrey Irwin, *Prehistoric Exploration and Colonisation of the Pacific* (1992).

Seán McGrail

SIBERIA, Prehistoric. Pebble tool complexes discovered in the Amur Basin (Filimoshki, Kumara I and Ust'-Tu), the Altai (Ulalinka), and the Lena Basin (Diring Yuriakh) have been attributed to the Lower Paleolithic (Middle or Lower Pleistocene). There is no consensus as to the age of these assemblages, and in the case of Diring Yuriakh, estimates in excess of a million years have been proposed. Nothing is known about which humans were responsible for these sites or how they subsisted.

Mousterian (Middle Paleolithic) sites are confined to the Altai Mountains (e.g., Ust'-Kanskaia cave, Denisova cave, and Kara Bom) and the Minusinsk Depression (Dvuglazka) and contain rich remains of Pleistocene large and small mammals. These sites date to the Kargin Interstadial.

In the Early Upper Paleolithic (34,000–28,000 B.P.) tools were made on large prismatic blades. Animal art and stone dwelling foundations are present at Tolbaga. The Middle Upper Paleolithic (28,000–22,000 B.P.) technology was based on retouched irregular blades, occasional bifacial knives, and bone tools. Large animal bone dwellings and a bone mobilary art similar to the Russian Plain are best exemplified by the remarkable Mal'ta-Buret' culture. The Late Upper Paleolithic technology was based on wedge-shaped microblade cores, microblades, and the composite inset technique. Large side scrapers and pebble tools were also common. Large blade tools (Kokorevo culture), numerous flake tools (Afontova culture), and bifacial knives and points (Diuktai culture) illustrate regional variability. Bone and antler were important, as was decorative art. People lived in light, surface structures and subsisted largely on big game, as in other stages of the Upper and Middle Paleolithic. A fired clay human figurine from Mainskaia (Afontova culture) is a unique art piece. The Final Upper Paleolithic (14,000–10,000 B.P.) is represented by numerous sites in western Siberia, the Bedarevskiia culture of the Tom River, the upper levels of numerous Yenisei sites, Verkholenskaia Gora in the Angara Valley, numerous Trans-Baikal sites, Ustinovka in the Far East, and Berelekh in the Arctic (Indigirka River). The technology had some Mesolithic traits, and the bone-antler component became more elaborate and included different forms of harpoons. The wedge-shaped core and microblade technique remained in force. While good examples of the Late and Final Paleolithic technology are known from Alaska (Denali and Akmak complexes), no good analog exists in Siberia for the older Paleo-Indian complexes of the New World.

The early postglacial Mesolithic cultures of Siberia subsisted on taiga and tundra mammals and fishing. Across Siberia there is strong continuity from the Final Paleolithic. Macrolithic and microblade techniques are found together throughout, and geometric microliths are absent. The wedge-shaped core and microblade technique continues in southern and easternmost reaches of Siberia. Bifacial-point technologies become important in the Far East, particularly in the Amur region and Kamchatka. The microcore technology in the Lena Basin shifts from the wedge-shaped system to small cylindrical and pencil-shaped cores in the distinctive Sumnagin culture.

The Early Neolithic Period in western Siberia began about 7000–6000 B.P. and is marked by the appearance of Neolithic techniques in local Mesolithic contexts. The older hunting and gathering economy continued, with an adjustment to the warmer, milder conditions of the Middle Holocene climatic optimum. The main object of the hunt was elk (*Alces*), which also figures importantly in the art. Fishing was an important economic activity and was executed with nets, stone and bone hooks, and harpoons.

The Early Neolithic culture of western Siberia has pointed-base pottery with straight-line decorations, a trait that links this area to similar cultures west of the Urals. In the middle Irtysh region, comb-stamped pottery occurred with a blade technology. In Middle and Late Neolithic times, the straight-line pottery of the Upper Ob' culture changed from a pointed to a flat base. Polished stone axes and adzes appeared.

In eastern Siberia, the Early Neolithic (ca. 6500–5200 B.P.) is marked by the appearance of pointed-base, net-impressed pottery in the Isakovo culture of the Baikal region and the Syalakh culture of Yakutia. The Syalakh culture spread north to the Taimyr Peninsula and eastward to Chukotka. Both cultures show strong continuity from the preceding Mesolithic background. Based on new carbon-14 data, the Kitoi culture of the Baikal area is also of Early Neolithic age, but appears to be intrusive. Kitoi pottery is spherical or wide bottomed, with stamp and/or stab-and-drag decorations. The Middle Neolithic cultures of these regions show divergence. In the Baikal area, the Serovo culture (5200–4200 B.P.) continued Kitoi pottery traditions with comb stamping, while the northern Bel'kachi culture (5000–3900 B.P.) is characterized by cord-marked pottery added to a lithic tool kit, showing continuity from the Early Neolithic. The Bel'kachi culture spread over a wider territory than the Syalakh and influenced the Gromatukha culture of the Amur Basin. About 4500 B.P., an Aceramic tundra variant of Bel'kachi spread to North America as the Arctic small-tool tradition. The Late Neolithic Glazkovo culture (4200–3200 B.P.) of the Baikal area contains the first copper artifacts in the region. In the north, the Ymyiakhtakh culture (3900–3100 B.P.) continued the Bel'kachi lithic traditions and added a new, "waffle-impressed" (check-stamped) pottery, which became widespread in eastern Siberia. A fully developed Neolithic culture with pottery and polished adzes appeared between 2000 and 1000 B.P. in Chukotka as the North Chukotkan culture and in Kamchatka as the Tar'ya culture.

The Eneolithic lasted for only 500 years (4500–4000 B.P.) and was directly linked to the natural occurrences of copper in the mountains of southern Siberia (Urals, Altai, Sayan, and Trans-Baikal). Elsewhere, Neolithic technology prevailed. While there was a dichotomy between steppe cattle breeding and taiga hunting, the same copper tools were used in both zones.

The Afanasievo culture (4500–4000 B.P.) was intrusive from the west and introduced copper tools. The economy was based on stock breeding (cattle, horse, and sheep), agriculture, and hunting. The pottery had a pointed base and was decorated with a distinctive fir ornamentation and comb stamping. Otherwise, the technology was Neolithic.

About 4000 B.P., a fully developed bronze metallurgy appeared in southern Siberia and was used by both steppe stock breeders and taiga hunters and fishers. In eastern Siberia, copper first appears in the Glazkovo Period in the Bailkal region (3800–3300 B.P.) as copies of stone and bone tools. About 3500 B.P., the powerful stock-breeding and bronze-producing Andronovo culture appeared on the steppe from the Urals to the Yenisei. They penetrated the southern edge of the taiga in search of pastures and were the first horsemen of the Asiatic steppe.

In the Late Bronze Age, about 3000 B.P., the short-horned cattle–breeding Karasuk people replaced the Andronovo culture and exerted tremendous influence across Siberia, from the Ob' to Yakutia. Their switch from pasturing to seasonal transhumance set the stage for nomadic stock breeding. Karasuk culture influenced the Bronze Age Ust'-Mil' culture in Yakutia, although elsewhere in the north, technologies remained essentially Neolithic.

Iron first appeared in the steppe about 3000 B.P. The cattle breeders of the Siberian steppe shifted from pasturing to full-scale nomadic pastoralism, and iron strongly affected warfare. The Early Iron Age (700 B.C. to A.D. 400) is generally subdivided into two historic periods: Scythian and Hun. However, we are now firmly on the doorstep of history.

[See also AMERICAS, FIRST SETTLEMENT OF THE; HUMANS, MODERN: PEOPLING OF THE GLOBE.]

■ Henry N. Michael, *The Neolithic Age in Eastern Siberia* (1958). Mikhail P. Griaznov, *The Ancient Civilization of Southern Siberia* (1969). Aleksei P. Okladnikov, *Yakutia*, ed. Henry N. Michael (1970). Valery N. Chernetsov and Wanda Moszynska, *Prehistory of Western Siberia*, ed. Henry N. Michael (1974). Vitaliy Larichev, Uriy Khol'ushkin, and Inna Laricheva, "The Upper Paleolithic of Northern Asia," *Journal of World Prehistory* 4 (1990): 347–385. Henry N. Michael, "The Neolithic Cultures of Siberia and the Soviet Far East," in *Chronologies in Old World Archaeology*, 2 vols., ed. Robert W. Ehrich (1992). Yuri A. Mochanov, "The Most Ancient Paleolithic of the Diring and the Problem of a Nontropical Origin for Humanity," *Arctic Anthropology* 30 (1993): 22–53.

Wm. Roger Powers

SICILY. From prehistory to the present, the continuous interaction of cultures and peoples on the island of Sicily has formed an extensive and complex record. The Greek Period (eighth to third century B.C.) has left perhaps the most impressive remains, but the earliest archaeological evidence in Sicily is Lower Paleolithic stone tools. Abundant evidence from the Upper Paleolithic includes flint tools and several rockshelter and cave sites, especially in western Sicily. Animals and humans are represented in small stone carvings, and are also incised into the rock at Monte Pellegrino above Palermo (and elsewhere). Hunting and gathering of marine resources sustained the population into the Mesolithic. Cultivation and animal domestication supported the settled villages of the ensuing Neolithic (ca. 6000 B.C.), and handmade pottery was used. Some of the proliferating ceramic styles were influenced or accompanied by mainland Italian types. These signal long-distance contacts, as does the obsidian imported, especially from Lipari; obsidian was by then the dominant material for stone tools.

Bronze Age. The Early Bronze Age Castelluccio culture (named after the type-site near Noto) features complex linear patterns in black on red pottery; among the shapes, very large standed bowls probably had ritual use. The beginning of the Bronze Age may be as early as 2500 B.C. (La Muculufa near Licata). Some Castelluccio villages of circular huts were fortified; cemeteries of rock-cut chamber tombs contain multiple burials. During the Middle Bronze Age (ca. 1400 B.C.), imports and imitations of Mycenaean ceramics and weapons demonstrate wide overseas contacts. At Thapsos near Syracuse, a hut settlement and vast cemetery of rock-cut tombs have been investigated. Thapsos pottery is decorated with incised designs and flanged handles; cups and pedestaled bowls may reach very large size. Pantalica (also near Syracuse), an extensive Late Bronze Age rock-cut chamber tomb cemetery (ca. 1250 B.C.), has no surviving settlement, but a large stone foundation is identified as the dwelling (*anaktoron*) of the local ruler.

In the Late Bronze Age (ca. 1250–650 B.C.), Thapsos ceramic shapes such as the pedestaled forms continue, and influence from southern Italy and the Lipari Islands is seen (as at Morgantina near Enna). Weapons and fibulae from the graves show Mycenaean traits. During the Iron Age (ca. 850–650 B.C.), the greatest resemblances are with the Italian and Iberian peninsulae. Some ceramic forms follow Greek Iron Age pottery, and the final Finocchito period witnesses colonization. In western Sicily, the contemporary Sant'-Angelo Muxaro culture also uses pottery with incised or impressed geometric motifs, and painted wares imitate Greek ceramics. Some of the rock-cut tombs resemble Mycenaean tholos (beehive) tombs.

Greek Period. From the later eighth century B.C., Greeks from Chalkis, Corinth, Megara, Rhodes, and Crete colonized the coasts of Sicily. The fifth-century Athenian historian Thucydides recounts the foundations in relative order and in relation to later datable events. Naxos (modern Taormina) was first, followed by Syracuse, Leontini, Catane, Megara Hyblaia, Zankle (Messina), and Gela. Secondary foundations by the colonies themselves included Leontinoi by Naxos, Selinus (Selinunte) by Megara Hyblaia, Akragas (Agrigento) by Gela, and Himera by Zankle. Historical sources also mention indigenous ethnic groups in the island: eastern Sikels, western Sikans, and Elymians in the northwest. Classical myths of their origins are difficult to integrate with the archaeological evidence for prehistory, but fragmentary inscriptions record their languages. Sikel is related to the Italic languages, but Sikan and Elymian are little understood. From at least the eighth century, Phoenicians settled in the islands as well, first on Motya off western Sicily, and also on Panormus (Palermo) and Soloeis or Solus (Solunto).

Colonization was accompanied by violence, but also by complex processes of acculturation between Greeks and natives. Greek drinking vessels and customs were adopted by indigenous inland communities, and masses of Greek pottery were imported to Sicily for use far beyond the colonies themselves. Local imitations were also produced, while a *ceramics tradition rooted in the Iron Age persisted as well. Burial practices in many communities incorporated Greek customs while retaining the use of chamber tombs.

Unlike their mother cities, many colonies were planned communities with a regular street grid, blocks of houses built around a central courtyard, and clearly defined civic and religious space. Greek cults often assimilated local ones; Demeter and Persephone, concerned with agriculture, were especially important. A pre-Greek cult at Enna was hellenized in this way, while a Sikel sanctuary at Palike (modern Mineo) retained its character and importance into the first century A.D., as did a Punico-Elymian cult of Aphrodite / Astarte at Eryx (Erice near Trapani). Early Greek temples featured roofs decorated with painted terracotta moldings and tiles. Some were simple buildings of mud brick without colonnades (*naiskoi*). The first colonnaded Doric temples of local limestone still have terracotta roofs (e.g., Temple E at Selinus). These stone temples may differ significantly in their plans, proportions, and size from mainland Greek examples. The Temple of Apollo at Syracuse, for example (ca. 600 B.C.), has a double colonnade at the east end. By the mid-sixth century B.C., architectural sculpture had replaced terracotta decoration; Selinus provides some of the best examples (Temples C and E, Palermo Museum). In the late sixth century, the colossal unfinished Temple of Zeus (Olympieion) at Akragas featured an outer wall instead of a colonnade, with applied Doric columns alternating with male statues. These unusual attached columns and screen walls are also used at Selinus (Temples D and F). Aside from the architectural sculpture, Archaic Greek male figures *(kouroi)* come from sites like Megara Hyblaia, Grammichele, and Syracuse; they were grave markers and dedications to divinities. Female figures (e.g., the seated mother suckling twins from Megara) had similar uses. Greek cities produced their own coinage, and later, theaters (such as the famous example of the third century B.C. at Segesta) witness another aspect of Greek culture in Sicily.

Ruled by powerful dynasties, Sicilian cities warred with each other and with the Carthaginians, and were drawn into the Peloponnesian War between *Athens and Sparta. A Doric temple at Himera commemorates the victory of Syracuse and Akragas over *Carthage at Himera in 480 B.C., as does a new Temple of Athena at Syracuse (now incorporated into the Baroque cathedral). They follow mainland architectural norms in plan and detail. At Selinus, however, a contemporary renovation of Temple E was similar to the Athenian Parthenon in scale but used very different proportions. The well-preserved stone and mud-brick walls of Gela, originally from the sixth century, provide an excellent example of defensive measures. Other Archaic fortifications can be seen at Megara Hyblaia, Naxos, and Leontinoi, and Late Classical at Syracuse.

The end of the fifth century B.C. brought violent change in Sicily. In 409, Selinus was taken by the Carthaginians; its massive Temple G remained unfinished. The city was occupied by Punic settlers: the symbol of their goddess Tanit can be found in houses and sanctuaries. Akragas, Himera, Gela, and Camarina fell next. Dionysius I of Syracuse retaliated in 397–396, taking Motya and Solunto. Excavations at these Punic sites have revealed burials, houses, a dye works, and sanctuaries. Motya also yielded a mid-fifth century sculpture of a charioteer, probably taken from a sacked Greek city. Under the hegemony of Syracuse in the Hellenistic Period (fourth to third centuries B.C.), Greek Sicily enjoyed a final period of prosperity. Several devastated cities were rebuilt, and Tindari on the north coast was newly founded.

Roman and Post-Roman Periods. Sicily except for the kingdom of Syracuse became Rome's first province in 241 (First Punic War); Syracuse remained independent and prospered until 211 (Second Punic War). Many cities never recovered from sacking and the enslavement of their populations at this time. The Romans instituted a system of taxation in the form of agricultural tithes. Small- and medium-sized farms continued to exist, especially in the less fertile interior, but large estates run by slaves from the eastern Mediterranean arose, resulting in two revolts during the second century B.C.

The first century brought the famous depradations of the Roman governor Verres, recounted by the orator Cicero, and the civil wars between Octavian (Augustus) and his rivals. Many cities continued to decline, but not all: Solus, Akragas, and Iaitai (Monte Iato) built major new areas of housing and renovated public buildings in the second and first centuries. Roman atrium houses were few, though, and concrete was not widely used until the imperial period. Few Roman temples were built, though the Romans restored many existing shrines. Only when Roman colonists came to cities on the northern and eastern coasts in the first century B.C. did Latin become widespread, but Greek remained in use to the end of antiquity.

With the end of the Republic, the population shifted away from the old towns into the countryside, especially in the interior. In the first two centuries A.D., several Roman building types appeared in Sicily: amphitheaters (e.g., at Syracuse), aqueducts, and baths. Burial practices and domestic architecture, however, remained Hellenistic, except for a few mausolea (Centuripe, Agrigento) and columbaria (Catania) and some Roman wall painting in Solunto. In the countryside, which produced *wine and grain for the empire, a few farms and rural villas have been investigated. The best-known Roman site in Sicily is a late one: the fourth century A.D. villa at Casale (Piazza Armerina). This luxury residence, organized around a peristyle garden with an apsed dining room, living quarters, and bath, has sometimes been thought to have belonged to the emperor Maximian (286–303 A.D.). Though no longer unique in Sicily, it is still notable for the elaborate mosaic floors that decorate all but a few of the four dozen rooms. These show scenes from myth and sport, especially hunting. From the third century, catacombs at Syracuse reflect the spread of Christianity, but it is not until the fourth and fifth centuries that these are found elsewhere. The earliest churches lie beneath later buildings; San Pietro in Syracuse is a known early basilica. In the countryside, most seem to be fifth century, as are telltale lamps with Christian symbols.

Increasing insecurity affected Sicily, especially in the mid-fifth century, when it suffered Vandal and Gothic raids. In 535 Sicily became a Byzantine province, and it remained so until the ninth century, when it was conquered by the Arabs.

[See also MEDITERRANEAN TRADE; MEDITERRANEAN WORLD, *articles on* THE RISE OF AEGEAN AND MEDITERRANEAN STATES, THE DOMINANCE OF GREECE AND ROME.]

■ Luigi Bernabo-Brea, *Sicily before the Greeks* (1957). Margaret Guido, *Sicily: An Archaeological Guide* (1967). Erik Sjöqvist, *Sicily and the Greeks* (1973). Moses Finley, *Ancient Sicily* (2nd ed., 1979). Filippo Coarelli and Mario Torelli, *Sicilia* (Guide archeologiche Laterza) (1984). Jean-Paul Descœudres, ed., *Greek Colonists and Native Populations* (1990). Roger Wilson, *Sicily under the Roman Empire* (1990). Ross Holloway, *The Archaeology of Ancient Sicily* (1991). Maria Aubet, *The Phoenicians and the West* (1993).

Carla M. Antonaccio

SILK ROUTE. The Silk Road, a term that first appeared at the end of the nineteenth century, refers to that network of caravan tracks traversing Central and West Asia, used to carry trade goods between the East and West from approximately the second century B.C. to the fifteenth century A.D.

These tracks were neither a single road nor was silk the only commodity that was carried across them. The termini of the "Road" were said to be Rome in the West and Chang'an in the East. The economic importance of silk for Rome, where it often amounted to as much as 90 percent of their imports from the East, is no doubt responsible for its prominent association by Western scholars with these caravan routes. The technology of silk production had existed in China from as early as 1500 B.C. Silk became one of China's most lucrative exports from at least the second century on, leading the state to institute laws making the technology of silk production a strictly guarded secret. Persons caught attempting to carry out of China this secret or the material for its cultivation (caterpillar eggs of the silk moth, genus *Bombyx,* or mulberry leaves) were subject to execution. This policy was an apparent success, since the Romans were kept unaware even of its material source. Ptolomy wrote that it was made from the hairs on certain tree leaves. Even the Sasanian Persians, who were the primary middlemen in the silk trade for hundreds of years, were unable to produce their own silk until the sixth century A.D. It was then, according to traditional accounts, that a Nestorian Christian monk managed to smuggle caterpillar eggs out of China hidden in his staff, one of the earliest, perhaps legendary, accounts of industrial espionage.

As important as silk was to both Rome and China, it was by no means the only commodity of value passing over the Silk Road. Precious gems and metals, such as jade and gold, were also basic commodities. In addition, horses from Ferghana, foodstuffs and cultigens—such as apricots, melons, and raisins—and manufactured goods such as lacquer from China were in great demand at various points along the Road. Moreover, it is a matter of dispute whether silk was even the most significant or important item of all that changed hands and cultures along the Road, since along with silk and the other commodities, flowed peoples, technologies, and religions. Most significant of the latter were Indian medical technologies, as well as the religions of Buddhism and Islam. Amidst the culturally diverse Buddhist communities across Central Asia, Greek, Indian, and Chinese artistic techniques and sensibilities blended, producing a rich and varied iconography that has come to be associated not just with Central Asia but with China, Korea and Japan as well.

The Routes. Setting out west from Chang'an, Silk Road caravans crossed the Yellow River at Lanzhou, and then passed up the Gansu Corridor to Jiayu Guan Pass, where the Road departed China proper. Due west lay 1,200 miles (1,931 km) of trackless desert, the Gobi and the Takalamakan, bounded much of the way on the north and the south by two parallel mountain ranges, the Tian Shan and the Kun Lun. The width of the desert between these mountain ranges averages 250 miles (402 km). With an average annual rainfall of less than an inch, traversing this barren waste would have been all but impossible except for the existence of a chain of oasis communities, some constituting autonomous states, ringing the deserts on both sides. These oases obtained their water from melting Ice Age glaciers in the surrounding mountain ranges.

At Jiayu Guan the Silk Road split into northern and southern routes, moving between oases. The southern route passed first through Dunhuang, the site of the Maogao Buddhist cave complex, and thence, through Miran, Khotan, and Yarkand before rejoining the northern route in Kashgar at the western edge of the Tarim Basin. The north-

ern route passed through Hami, Turfan, and Kuqa, rejoining the southern route in Kashgar some 1,200 miles (1,931 km) later. From Turfan on the northern route, caravans had the further option of turning northwest and proceeding up through Urumqi, and into the steppe region of Kazakstan, and thence east toward Samarkand. From Yarkand on the southern route or from Kashgar, a primary caravan route turned south across the Karakhoram into the Upper Indus region and on into the Gangetic plain of India.

Caravans continuing west from Kashgar again had the option of taking a northerly or southerly course across the Pamirs, "the Roof of the World." The southern route passed through the Wakan Corridor to Balkh in modern Afghanistan and on to Merv at the eastern edge of the old Persian Empire. The northern route crossed the Pamirs near the Ferghana Valley, and from there continued through Samarkand to Merv. In Persia the Silk Road joined other well-established trade routes, most passing through Ctesiphon (later Baghdad) in the Tigris-Euphrates valley. From there cargoes and travelers continued either to one of several seaports on the eastern Mediterranean, and then by ship to Rome, or overland through modern Turkey to Constantinople and across eastern Europe.

Because of the extreme dryness throughout most of Central Asia, many fabrics, dyes, woods, texts, and even human bodies underwent little deterioration. Consequently, the sites listed above generally all have been extremely rich in artifacts and architectural remains of ancient and medieval Central Asian cultures. Worthy of note are the city remains of Kuqa and Khotan, and those surrounding Turfan: Jiaohe and Gaochang. At the beginning of the twentieth century these sites all yielded rich troves of artifacts to the numerous European and Japanese expeditions that competed with each other in the race to lay claim to the Central Asian heritage. The great preponderance of artifacts were Buddhist paintings, scriptures, and sculpture uncovered in sand-buried caves and ruined monasteries. Also found, though in lesser quantity, were religious artifacts produced for Nestorian Christian, Manichaean, and Zoroastrian communities along the routes.

History. It has traditionally been assumed that trade began in the second century B.C., as the result of a daring journey by a Chinese military commander, Zhang Qien, who was commissioned by the Han Emperor, Wudi, to explore the possibility of an alliance with the Persian Empire against their common nomadic enemy, the Xiongnu. Though captured several times, Zhang was able in each case to escape, eventually establishing contact with the Persians before returning to China. He had traveled over 3,000 miles (4,800 km), and in addition to negotiating a trade agreement with the Persians, he arranged for the import of a powerful new breed of war horse from Ferghana, contributing greatly to China's military strength. He also brought back reports of a country he rendered in Chinese as Li-jian, assumed by most scholars to be Rome. Silk trade was officially sanctioned in the second century B.C. by Wudi, and continued with only minor interruptions until the breakup of the Mongol Empire and the collapse of the Mongol Yuan dynasty in the fifteenth century. Trade was conducted in numerous stages, few if any traders traveling the entire route. The Mongol Empire had extended almost the entire length of the Silk Road, and under its protection, from the thirteenth to the fifteenth centuries, travelers and goods moved across the length of Asia in relative security. It was during this period that Marco Polo traveled the entire route from Italy to Khanbalik (modern Beijing). Also in the thirteenth century Rabban Sauma, a Chinese Nestorian Christian, made the same journey in the opposite direction, from Khanbalik to Rome, and then on into western Europe. The journey accounts of these two figures are rich in data on medieval Asia. With the collapse of the Mongol Empire and the opening of the East-West sea routes, which afforded merchants greater control and far less risk, the Silk Road was almost totally abandoned, and faded almost completely from European consciousness.

Archaeological Discoveries. Whereas this history has generally been borne out by texts and archaeological discoveries, recent findings have greatly extended the time frame during which the Silk Road functioned as a conduit of major importance between East and West. Analysis of strands of silk found in the hair of an Egyptian mummy dating from about 1000 B.C. reveal technologies of weaving and production almost certainly specific to China. This predates earlier assumptions on the beginning of silk trade by at least eight hundred years. Such silk would almost certainly have come by the land route across Central Asia. Similar samples of Chinese silk found in seventh-century B.C. German graves and fifth-century B.C. Greek tombs have provided additional evidence for an earlier commencement of the silk trade than previously assumed. If these current studies are borne out, then all that can be said of the second-century B.C. date is that it marks the beginning of trade officially sanctioned by the Chinese Emperor.

This discovery of silk outside of the immediate Roman world of antiquity extends not only the time frame, it extends the length of the Silk Route, as well. In some respects Nara, Japan, might be regarded as an Eastern terminus. In the twelve-hundred-year-old Shosoin located in Nara there exists a large imperial collection of eastern European, Persian, and Central Asian goods. Unique examples of glass, both silk and non-silk textiles, Buddhist images, and musical instruments are to be found in the collection. These goods, which all arrived in Japan before 752 when they were gathered in the Shosoin, could have come only by the Silk Route. Due to the highly sophisticated preservation technology incorporated in the structure built to house them, they in many cases constitute the sole remaining examples of such goods, and have been the basis for many modern identifications of lost technologies.

Extending the frame even further are contemporary speculations on migrations from Africa into Central Asia and China one million years ago via the routes followed later by the silk trade. Eighty-thousand-year-old artifacts have recently been found in the Pamirs, and others, 20,000 years old, have been found in the deserts of Central Asia. Recent discoveries of twelve-thousand-year-old Caucasian mummies at "Red Hill" near Urumchi on the northern Silk Route suggest a greater ethnic diversity in Central Asian communities than previously suspected.

■ Sir Aurel Stein, *Ruins of Desert Cathay* 2 vols. (1912). Marco Polo, *The Travels* (1958). Edward Schafer, *The Golden Peaches of Samarkand* (1963). Sir Aurel Stein, *On Central Asian Tracks* (1964). Albert von Le Coq, *Buried Treasures of Chinese Turkestan* (1985). David Morgan, *The Mongols* (1986). Morris Rossabi, *Voyager from Xanadu* (1992).

William F. Powell

SIMILAUN MAN. One of the most remarkable archaeological discoveries this century, that of Similaun Man (the "Iceman") was made in September 1991, on the Hauslabjoch in the Tyrolean Alps, close to the Austrian–Italian border. At a height of 10,500 feet (3,200 m), it is one of the highest prehistoric finds in Europe. It takes its name from the associated Similaun glacier, and in conjunction with clothing and a variety of artifacts, provides for the first time frozen evidence not only of a well-preserved Neolithic individual but also a range of organic materials which would have perished under normal conditions.

The discovery of an exposed human head in the ice, as a result of unusual weather conditions, led to an initial forensic inquiry followed later by detailed anatomical and archaeological investigations. The research on the body and the associated finds by an international group still continues. The body, of a man, is remarkably well preserved and even the eyes are intact, although the hair has been separated by the ice. While the exact developmental age of the individual has not been finally agreed, he seems likely to have been in the thirty- to forty-year range (on the evidence of tooth wear and other factors). He appears to have been of slender build and, surprisingly, devoid of obvious deposits of adipocere—derived from body fat, and often seen in recently frozen bodies. There is evidence of ribs broken and healed in life, as well as others which are not healed and may have been fractured some weeks before death. A series of tattoos were found on the trunk and legs and it has been suggested that these may have medical relevance (a Neolithic equivalent of acupuncture!). DNA studies on tissue from the body confirm that he had central or northern European genetic affinities.

Radiocarbon dates strongly suggest that Similaun Man lived within the time range 3350 to 3300 B.C. This makes the clothing and equipment (taken to Mainz for careful conservation) the earliest of its kind in Europe. Reconstruction suggests that seven or eight separate items of clothing, including a cap, were worn on this occasion. As many as eight species of animal had been used in one or another item of clothing. On top of the skin clothing, which included a "bum-bag," loincloth, leggings, deerskin coat, and grass-filled shoes of calfskin, there was probably a thick outer cape of woven grasses or reeds. This latter had historical parallels in the Alps even into the last century. Even though it is the unique dress of a unique individual, the clothing was probably that of a person of no great social standing, but someone who was a farmer and, seasonally, a shepherd.

Some twenty different items were scattered about the body, including a relatively small flanged copper axe about 3.7 inches (9.5 cm) long, hafted in yew wood with leather binding. There was also a damaged yew longbow, and a quiver with fourteen arrows, although only two were ready for use, with flint tips and feather fletching. A flint knife, mounted in a fairly crude bound wooden handle, had an associated string sheath. There was the frame of what appears to have been a rucksack (hazel with larch boards). A lime-wood handle, into which an antler tip was inserted, has been interpreted as a retouching tool for flint shaping. Two fragile birch-bark containers are the kind of finds that survive only in special environmental conditions such as these. Less easy to interpret is a small marble disc hanging on a leather thong, and similarly a piece of net that could have been used in a number of ways.

Two types of fungus were found and were probably used for very different purposes. One is the tinder fungus (*Fomes fomentarius*), but the other, a particular birch bracket fungus, threaded on a leather thong, may have been used as a medicine (on folk medical parallels). Besides the flint tool mentioned, other flints were probably used as a scraper and awl, and small quantities of antler and bone were kept for shaping into points. In all, seventeen different kinds of plant material were utilized, but there was little evidence of food except for a sloe berry, fragments of meat bone (ibex neck vertebrae) and a few cereal grains.

In terms of cultural associations, the copper axe suggests links with the early Remedello culture of northern Italy. Why did Similaun Man die alone in the mountains? Was he in hasty flight from conflict to the south? Broken ribs, and thus the possibility of a fall in the mountains, provides just as likely an explanation. Further research may provide more definitive answers.

[*See also* EUROPE: THE EUROPEAN BRONZE AGE.]

■ Konrad Spindler, *The Man in the Ice* (1994). F. Höpfel, W. Platzer, and K. Spindler, eds. *Der Mann im Eis.* Vol 1. (1992).

Don Brothwell

SIPÁN. The Sipán site is in the lower Lambayeque Valley on the north coast of Peru. It was discovered in 1987 through the monitoring of looting activities and has since been excavated under the direction of Walter Alva of the Bruning Museum. The site consists of the eroded remains of three adobe pyramids with associated ramps, platforms, and other features. Commanding a view of the river and irrigated fields, Sipán likely was the principal administrative, religious, and ceremonial center for elite residents who occupied it when the culture known to archaeologists as Moche was present in the valley.

Three tombs in the smallest pyramid have been excavated, with additional information on two other tombs available from the leavings of looters. The excavated burials come from different phases of construction. Two tombs (Nos. 1 and 2) date to about A.D. 250, while the third (No. 3) was probably built two centuries earlier. The principal interments in the later tombs were clothed in garments that indicate they were priests in a sacrifice ceremony as depicted on Moche pottery and murals, and the earlier burial, less certainly, also was possibly such a priest.

Of the two later burials, Tomb 1 was the most elaborate. An adult male, who was in his late thirties or early forties when he died of natural causes, was found in a plank coffin, accompanied by a wealth of clothing, paraphernalia, and offerings. These included headdresses, bead pectorals, fans, and ornaments, many in gold, silver, and copper alloys. Several other individuals were also in the tomb and likely represent family members, concubines, and sacrificed guards. Tomb 2 also had a principal burial, probably male, in a plank coffin with other burials around it and a sacrificed llama. Tomb 3 contained another male adult, wrapped in a sedge mat and textile shrouds. A single young woman and a sacrificed llama accompanied this burial. Of the three burials, Tomb 3 contained the greatest amount of metal: numerous necklaces, banners, collars, and other items placed in layers under and over the principal burial.

Ceramics were found in all three tombs. In Tomb 3 a few pottery vessels were placed directly next to the burial, but in Tomb 2 many more pots were placed on the floor in a corner of the tomb and in niches in a bench. Tomb 1 had hundreds of vessels placed in surrounding niches. Why pottery was placed in these locales is not known, and it is curious that the general quality of ceramics is not what might be expected in the burials of personages of such apparent high rank. As analysis is still in its early stages, the answer to this question as well as the development of many more await further study.

Research at the Sipán site will add significantly to our understanding of *Moche culture, especially topics related to the social roles of the elite. Insights into iconography and ritual also are plentiful, such as the confirmation that scenes formerly known only through art work were actually staged as rituals. How the individuals buried in these tombs relate to other people and events at the site and in the Moche world remain to be fully investigated. The three burials appear to be the remains of a royal theocracy. Were they the highest echelon, or were there higher-ranking, perhaps secular, rulers above them? Was Sipán an independent polity, or under the rule of a larger political entity? The excavations at Sipán will address such questions as research on some of the most remarkable prehistoric remains found in the Americas continues.

[*See also* ANDEAN PRE-INCA CIVILIZATIONS, RISE OF: INTRODUCTION; SOUTH AMERICA: RISE OF COMPLEX SOCIETIES IN SOUTH AMERICA.]

■ Walter Alva and Christopher B. Donnan, *Royal Tombs of Sipán* (1993). Walter Alva, *Sipán* (1994).

Jeffrey Quilter

SITE FORMATION PROCESSES. How do you know that an object was made by humans? Why did ancient people leave all those things behind? Where did the dirt come from? These are questions that lay visitors to archaeological sites commonly ask the excavators. Until recent decades, archaeologists could not always answer these questions convincingly. Today, however, such questions are of great concern to archaeologists because they focus attention on the processes of people and nature that create—in the landscape—evidence of the cultural past. This evidence, consisting of isolated artifacts, artifact scatters, monuments, sites, and other vestiges of human behavior, is called the archaeological record, and the processes responsible for it are known as formation processes. Variability introduced into the archaeological record by formation processes is now routinely assessed and taken into account as investigators strive to establish well-founded inferences about past human behavior.

Two principal kinds of formation processes are recognized: cultural, where the agency is culturally based activities, and noncultural or environmental, where the agency is a process of the natural environment. The concept of artifact life history helps one to define both kinds of formation processes in relation to the cultural behaviors of most interest. The sequence of specific activities in which artifacts participate during their existence is called a behavioral chain. For analytic purposes, specific activities are often aggregated into stages, such as procurement, manufacture, use, reuse, discard, disturbance, and archaeological recovery. Cultural formation processes are, simply, any and all activities that follow use. Noncultural formation processes designate the environmental agents that impinge upon cultural materials at any stage of their existence.

There are four major types of cultural formation processes, each consisting of myriad distinct activities. (1) *Reuse* processes can take place after an artifact, facility, or structure has served in one set of use activities. Common instances of reuse are recycling (which involves some remanufacture), secondary use (no remanufacture), and lateral cycling (a change in user only). (2) *Cultural deposition,* the transformation of cultural materials from a systemic (behavioral) context to an archaeological (environmental) context, includes discard of broken, worn-out, and obsolete items; accidental loss; ritual deposition, such as disposal of the dead and their accompaniments, caching of artifacts when a structure is dedicated, and placing offerings at a shrine; and leaving behind still-usable artifacts, facilities, and structures upon the abandonment of activity areas and settlements. (3) *Reclamation* processes are the reverse of cultural deposition, transforming cultural materials from an archaeological to a systemic context. Examples of reclamation include scavenging, collecting, gleaning, and looting of previously deposited artifacts; reincorporation of temporarily abandoned artifacts, facilities, and structures; reoccupation of sites; and archaeological recovery. (4) *Disturbance* processes alter the earth's surface and so modify archaeological materials, deposits, and sites. Common examples are trampling, plowing, digging pits and foundations, and land leveling.

Noncultural formation processes are the chemical, physical, and biological processes of the natural environment that impinge upon and modify cultural materials, in systemic and archaeological contexts. The effects of noncultural formation processes are seen at three major scales, which serve as a basis for classification. (1) *Artifact-scale* processes include bacterial or fungal rot of wood, corrosion of metals, and sandblasting of stone and brick, and cause weathering, deterioration, and decay of particular materials. These processes determine what survives, what disappears, and what is modified in the archaeological record. (2) *Site-scale* environmental formation processes are responsible for the disturbance of deposits, as by burrowing animals and tree roots, and for the deterioration of facilities and structures. (3) *Regional-scale* processes affect the regional archaeological record by burial or erosion of sites. By obscuring the ground, wind- and water-lain sediments as well as vegetation hamper site discovery.

In order to make rigorous inferences about past human behavior, archaeologists assess and factor out the influence of formation processes on the observed characteristics of the archaeological record. Distinguishing traces of formation processes from traces of the behaviors of interest can be illustrated by a chipped-stone tool, such as a hand axe. An archaeologist interested in how that tool had been used (mode of action, material worked, etc.) would examine the tool's edges microscopically, taking care to record microflakes, striations, polish, edge rounding, and other alterations that can result from use. In interpreting these traces, however, the archaeologist is mindful that a variety of formation processes—cultural and noncultural—can create similar alterations. For example, trampling produces microflakes as well as striations; sandblasting can lead to polish; and stream transport causes microflaking and edge rounding. What is more, microflaking can also be produced by archaeological recovery and careless handling in the laboratory or museum. With an awareness of such formation processes, the archaeologist turns to other lines of evidence, such as types of microflakes and the distribution of polish and striations on the tool's surface, in order to detect the influence of formation processes. A polish that occurs on a tool's entire surface, for example, was caused by sandblasting and not use. By seeking the traces of formation processes in these additional lines of evidence, investigators identify the causes of the archaeological observations and thereby lay a foundation for behavioral inference.

A second example concerns the role of hominids versus other animals in the creation of faunal accumulations in South African cave deposits. Early sites, like Swartkrans,

that yielded australopithecine remains have also served up controversies galore. During the 1950s, Raymond Dart argued that the australopithecines were hunters, bringing back their prey to the caves. He also claimed that the australopithecines were tool users, exploiting the bones, horns, and teeth of prey to make clubs, awls, scrapers, and so forth. That Dart had not considered the array of natural processes that could modify and deposit these very same bones was demonstrated, beginning in the 1970s, by C. K. Brain. On the basis of ethological studies and experiments, Brain documented the roles of leopards, hyenas, porcupines, and other animals as bone modifiers and accumulators. By seeking the traces of such animals' behaviors in the Swartkrans bone assemblage, Brain showed that the majority of bones were accumulated and modified by nonhominid species. Indeed, telltale traces indicate that some australopithecines, as victims of carnivores, were the hunted, not the hunters. Thus, on the basis of a detailed consideration of formation processes, Brain overturned an inference that for decades had set the agenda for discussions of human origins.

Since the early 1970s, when the systematic study of formation processes intensified, archaeologists—drawing upon the findings of *ethnoarchaeology, geoarchaeology, *experimental archaeology, vertebrate taphonomy, and so on—have been building a firm foundation for inference. It is the rare (and suspect) inference today that has not been established after a thorough analysis of how diverse processes of people and nature created the observed characteristics of the archaeological record.

[*See also* MIDDLE RANGE THEORY.]

■ William L. Rathje and Michael B. Schiffer, *Archaeology* (1982). Lewis R. Binford, *Working at Archaeology* (1983). Kristian Kristiansen, ed., *Archaeological Formation Processes* (1985). Arlene Miller Rosen, *Cities of Clay* (1986). D. T. Nash and M. D. Petraglia, eds., *Natural Formation Processes and the Archaeological Record* British Archaeological Reports, International Series, No. 352 (1987). Michael B. Schiffer, *Formation Processes of the Archaeological Record* (1987). Edward Staski and Livingston D. Sutro, eds., *The Ethnoarchaeology of Refuse Disposal* Anthropological Research Papers, No. 42 (1991). Julie K. Stein, ed., *Deciphering a Shell Midden* (1992). Michael Waters, *Principles of Geoarchaeology* (1992). Catherine Cameron and Steven Tomka, eds., *Abandonment of Settlements and Regions* (1993).

Michael Brian Schiffer

SITE LOCATION

Finding Archaeological Sites
Remote Sensing and Geophysical Prospection
Aerial Photography
Ground Survey
Site Assessment
Surface Collection

FINDING ARCHAEOLOGICAL SITES

After more than 100 years, archaeologists are still vexed by a single important problem. Namely, "How does one efficiently find the full range of archaeological sites present in an area?" With sites such as *Stonehenge, *Tikal, *Cahokia, *Great Zimbabwe, *Mohenjodaro, or *Angkor in mind, one could easily wonder why this should pose a problem.

The record of the human past is not only recorded in these large, quite prominent sites, but also in hundreds of thousands of much smaller, ephemeral sites with every conceivable form, function, and location. These more typical sites document the vast majority of human occupation of the earth, not the larger, more obvious, urban and monumental sites. Even for the relatively brief periods that these larger sites were occupied, any meaningful understanding of the role of those larger sites within regional economic, environmental, and ideological spheres can be attained only through the location and analysis of the myriad smaller habitation and work sites occupying surrounding areas. For earlier periods, the discovery of single-season campsites, quarries, hunting blinds, kill sites, fisheries, and the like is of even more critical importance, for they form the only record of human habitation in most parts of the world for most of human history. Many of these sites consist of thin scatters of stone tools or bones on eroded surfaces, or may be deeply buried under later human or natural deposits. Often, even locating documented historic sites such as farmsteads, mills, and slave quarters can be extremely difficult depending on local conditions of preservation and postdepositional processes such as erosion or alluviation.

To solve the dual problem of representative sampling of sites within a region and the efficient discovery of small sites, archaeologists have focused a substantial amount of attention on several techniques. Ground survey has been a staple of archaeological site discovery since the discipline's beginnings. Enhancements to traditional techniques developed over the past forty years are discussed in the sections on *sampling, ground survey, surface collection, and site assessment in this volume. As an important supplement to ground survey as a primary technique for locating sites, recent years have witnessed several applications of remote sensing applied on a variety of scales. The major remote-sensing techniques used by archaeologists are discussed under that heading and include aerial photography, satellite imagery, side-scanning radar, ground penetrating radar, soil resistivity surveys, and magnetometer surveys.

Other tools and techniques do little good if the locations and characteristics of sites elude archaeologists. Furthermore, simply studying the obvious sites results only in biased and incomplete reconstructions of past human lifeways. Thus, solving the problem of locating the full range of sites present in an area in a thorough but time- and energy-efficient manner is, and will continue to be, a central concern of archaeologists.

[See also SUBSURFACE TESTING, articles on INTRODUCTION, SOIL RESISTIVITY SURVEY, MAGNETOMETER SURVEY, GROUND PENETRATING RADAR.]

George Michaels

REMOTE SENSING AND GEOPHYSICAL PROSPECTION

Archaeological sites may survive the erosion of time and remain recognizable in some form above the ground, even if just as a scatter of masonry, or as a low mound where a village of mud-brick houses once stood. Immeasurably more sites seem to have disappeared literally from the face of the earth. There are reasons, however, for believing that this may not be entirely so. Using remote-sensing techniques, archaeologists can not only rediscover a site but also re-create its plan and provide evidence for some of the ancient activities that took place within it. From the way human action has altered the land in the past, either in the area around a site or especially in the site itself, physical traces are likely to persist. In a small hunter-gatherer settlement of temporary huts, some alteration of the ground will have taken place, even though it may only have been the concentration of refuse in a pit or the setting of a fire in a

hearth. The robbing of stone from the foundations of a Roman villa can leave behind trenches that still preserve the original plan of the building. These features, although altered by weathering, are often buried by a subsequent buildup of soil and survive as hidden evidence. If they are neither buried too deeply nor subsequently destroyed by natural erosion, deep plowing, or a construction project, they await rediscovery by the archaeological geophysicist.

A wide range of geophysical and geochemical techniques have been developed for monitoring the environment and exploring for minerals and oil. Many of these have been adapted to detect and map archaeological sites and features. Instruments also have been designed especially for archaeological prospection. The first geophysical surveys of archaeological sites were undertaken in the 1940s and 1950s, inspired by the need to know more about the sites being discovered by aerial photography. Richard Atkinson first measured the changing electrical resistance of the soil across an archaeological site in England near Oxford in 1947, and the first archaeological use of magnetic measurements was a study in 1957 of the remains of an experimental pottery kiln by a Cambridge group lead by John Belsh.

Every technique depends on distinguishing local differences in the physical or chemical properties of the soil or differences in the growing vegetation that reflect the presence of buried archaeological features. Some devices observe the ground from afar in an aircraft or an orbiting satellite—truly remote sensing. Other instruments are operated close to or in direct contact with the ground and measure such properties as electrical resistance of the soil or the local variation in the earth's magnetic field. The ground-based methods not only define the location of the sites but also can give a precise picture of features within them.

Early satellite instruments were limited in the resolution of their images, with each point (pixel) in the digital image representing tens of meters on the ground. These devices were of limited use in archaeology except for the recognition of very large sites and mapping of the landscape in which they are located, being particularly useful where aerial photography has not been possible. Satellite detectors mainly monitor the ground and vegetation passively, measuring the reflected solar radiation across the wide electromagnetic spectrum from thermal infrared wavelengths to ultraviolet light. By measuring the characteristics of the reflected light at different wavelengths it is possible to identify differences in the soil or vegetation, and at higher resolutions archaeological features may be defined. Active radar from satellites, especially the L-band frequency of 1.225 GHz of the synthetic aperture radar systems, has been used by Richard Adams and colleagues to penetrate the canopy of the Yucatan jungle and discover the pattern of drainage canals associated with Mayan agriculture. Imaging radar has also dramatically probed at least one to two meters deep into the thinner sands of the Saharan and Arabian deserts to reveal relict streams and river courses and associated archaeological sites that were active before the encroachment of the drifting sand.

Archaeological features are increasingly being discovered by airborne thermal imagery, where effectively the temperature of the ground is measured by recording the emitted thermal infrared radiation from the soil and the covering vegetation in the eight- to fourteen-micrometer wavelength range. Temperature differences of less than 33 degrees Fahrenheit (0.25°C) can be detected and archaeological features reveal themselves largely by their thermal capacity differing from that of the surrounding soil. In temperate climates, sediments with a higher water content have a greater thermal capacity and tend to remain cooler in the heat of the day, and plants growing in the more moist soil show less thermal stress in the sun by being able to control their temperature more effectively by transpiration. At night the thermal images are reversed with the moister ground remaining warmer as the heat of the day is radiated away. Sites can be discovered under grassland, which are rarely visible as crop marks. Solid rock has a higher thermal capacity than loose sand, and the ground plans of stone buildings in ancient Egyptian villages under a thin cover of sand thermally "glow" in the dark of the night. In optimal conditions, features less than 1.7 feet (0.5 m) across can be defined.

While airborne and satellite devices efficiently investigate large areas of the landscape, most archaeological geophysical prospection remains firmly on the ground, where a wide range of devices are deployed. These commonly measure either the local change in the electrical resistance of the ground or the local effect of the varying magnetic properties of the archaeological sediments on the earth's magnetic field. The electrical resistance of the soil depends mainly on its ability to retain water and the concentration of dissolved salts in this water. Solid impermeable granitic rocks have a higher resistance than porous limestones, but either as part of a buried wall of an ancient temple are likely to have a higher electrical resistance than the surrounding soil. Waterlogged gravel has a higher resistance than waterlogged peat, and a gravel neolithic burial mound hidden under a waterlogged landscape can be detected by the local increase in electrical resistance, with the organic sediment-filled ditches showing a lower than average resistance. Typical techniques measure the resistance by placing probes a set distance apart into the surface of the ground and comparing the measurement with reference probes at a nearby fixed location. The spacing of the probes determines the depth to which measurements are made. Common features such as buried walls and sediment-filled ditches give different signals depending on the physical arrangement of the probes and require appropriate interpretation, which can be assisted by theoretical modeling. However, archaeological features in general are not simple, uniform structures; they may intersect in a complex way, and so are often not amenable to simple modeling. The best differentiation of features tends to occur when there is differential dying of the ground.

The magnetic characteristics of the soil are largely determined by the concentration and nature of the iron compounds present. The earth's magnetic field may be locally altered by either the soil's magnetic susceptibility being enhanced through past human activity or if there is remanent magnetization of the ground by burning under a hearth, or the survival of a fired structure such as pottery kiln or a metal smelting furnace. These will have taken on a permanent remanent magnetization during their last cooling, which represents the direction and intensity of the earth's magnetic field at that time. The antiquity of an anciently fired structure can often be revealed by difference in orientation of its remanent magnetization from that of the present-day earth's field. The more humic soils associated with human occupation can have a higher iron content, and the rotting vegetation may involve the specific precipitation of microscopic grains of the highly ferrimagnetic mineral magnetite by bacteria such as *Aquaspirillum magnetotacticum*. Nevertheless, the archaeologically related changes in the local magnetic field strength may only be of the order of a ten thousandth of the earth's field, and the measurement is further complicated by the daily variation in the earth's field caused by changes in the strength and direction of electrical currents in the ionosphere. Magnetic surveying therefore either involves the continuous measurement of the earth's field at a fixed reference point during the survey, or the use of a gradiometer where the difference in the field strength is measured simultaneously between a detector close to the ground and one above it monitoring more generally the field strength in the area.

Electromagnetic devices carried over the ground may also measure the soil's electrical conductivity (the inverse of its resistivity) by inducing an electrical current in the ground through a magnetic field generated by the instrument. It then measures the out-of-phase signal associated with the induced current when operating at a high (40 kHz) frequency. At a low frequency (4Hz) the in-phase component of the signal relates to the magnetic susceptibility of the soil. In this way a single electromagnetic instrument can measure both the electrical and magnetic characteristics of the ground. Magnetic susceptibility can also be measured in the laboratory with soil samples that may also be used for defining the presence of sites by geochemical analysis for phosphates and heavy minerals that are known to be associated with human occupation.

In some circumstances, seismic-surveying techniques can detect archaeological sites, but sonic techniques have been principally used archaeologically underwater, where side-scan sonar and sub-bottom profiling have detected not only ancient wrecks but also land-based sites that have been inundated by rising water levels.

A significant advance in recent years has been the automatic recording of geophysical data, measured systematically in a survey on a regular grid in order to create a two-dimensional geophysical digital picture of the site. From this the data can be analyzed and enhanced by computer so that the interrelationship of the archaeological features can be studied and surveys by different techniques compared to give fuller insight into the nature of the site.

The next stage of development in geophysical surveying is the use of either ground-sounding radar or resistivity profiling to obtain vertical geophysical sections across sites which, when placed alongside each other, build a three-dimensional geophysical image of the buried features. Resistivity profiling involves analysis of the resistance measured successively at different separations along an array of probes, where the separation between the probes determines at a first approximation the depth to which the measurement is made. Ground-sounding radar employs antennae operating between 50 and 1,000 MHz, where the penetration achieved by the lower frequencies is offset by a lower resolution. There is a very rapid loss of signal with depth, especially in moist ground, and the detection of a feature or archaeological horizon depends on a strong contrast between the structures and the soil in which they are buried. In optimal conditions a 300 MHz antenna may penetrate to 7 or 10 feet (2 or 3 m) in depth and resolve features larger than 1 foot (0.3 m) in size. The radar record is similar in its formation to a seismic survey, needing expert interpretation, and does not provide an instant picture the archaeologist would prefer.

[See also GEOGRAPHICAL INFORMATION SYSTEMS; SETTLEMENT ANALYSIS.]

■ Anthony J. Clark, *Seeing Beneath the Soil: Prospecting Methods in Archaeology* (1990). I. Scollar, A. Tabbagh, E. Hesse, and I. Herzog, *Archaeological Prospecting and Remote Sensing* (1990). Thomas W. Lillesand and Ralph W. Kiefer, *Remote Sensing and Image Interpretation*, 3rd ed. (1994).

C. A. Shell

AERIAL PHOTOGRAPHY

From the very first photographs taken from balloons in the second half of the nineteenth century, aerial photography's value for recording archaeological sites can be recognized, and with early photography on the ground, form an important historical record. Photographs of the center of Paris taken in 1858 are among the earliest known. Archaeological aerial photography began in the cradle of early military flying. In the summer of 1906 Lt. Sharpe photographed *Stonehenge from a war balloon, recording the monument before the later restoration and straightening of several stones. The need for military survey and reconnaissance in the First World War provided the opportunity to overfly large tracts of terrain previously poorly explored, giving for the first time a coherent overview of the land and leading to the discovery of many new archaeological sites. In southern Palestine the importance of this was recognized to the extent that a Turkish military flying unit was formed under the command of Dr. Theodor Wiegand to photograph archaeological sites for their protection. At the same time Lt. Col. Beazeley recorded not only the city of Samarra by the Tigris in Iraq but also for the first time the extensive network of early irrigation canals, ancient water courses, and associated settlements.

In the 1920s Crawford in England and Poidebard in Syria independently recognized that not only were the slight features of archaeological sites enhanced by low oblique sunlight, but that at certain times of the year vegetation, especially planted crops, would reveal the outline sites for which no evidence survived aboveground. These early crop marks heralded the beginning of the transformation of archaeology from being purely site and artifact-based toward the understanding also of the relationship of sites in a landscape context, with their associated field systems, communication routes, and relationships to the topography and natural resources. From this time the discovery of sites in a number of countries also began to change from the serendipitous to the systematic.

The principles of formation of crop marks are well understood. Indeed, the presence of a parch mark of yellowed grass in the pastures of the *Somerset Levels of England was reported long ago in the seventeenth century, at a meeting of the Royal Society of London, as being due to the trunk of a bog oak lying just below the surface. In temperate climates, where certain crops are growing over archaeological features such as a buried ditch or a stone wall, these buried remains may provide more or less moisture and nutrition for growth than the surrounding soil, and the crop may consequently grow more strongly or weakly in the spring with a resulting difference in its color over the feature, and may ripen more slowly or quickly later in the summer. The heights of the crop may also differ so that in low lighting the site may be visible as if it were still present as earthworks. These crop marks may appear only with certain crops at brief times in the year when the climatic conditions are favorable. The effect of the weather will differ depending on the nature of the soil and the underlying geology. In some circumstances, conditions may very rarely, if ever, suit the formation of these vegetation marks. In warmer climates, extremes of aridity of rainfall may never provide the conditions for the marks to appear.

Sites may also be revealed in their plan by the difference in color of the soil in a plowed field where the top of the underlying masonry of a building has been brought to the surface, or where the soil of the site more effectively retains moisture, making it visible in the differential drying of the topsoil. Slight differences in moisture, and hence the thermal capacity of the soil, may also preferentially melt snow or frost, providing the most ephemeral of marks. The drifting of light snow into hollows and against low walls can dramatically outline field systems and enclosures.

Crop marks and earthworks are often photographed by oblique photography from a light aircraft, with the sites of an area recorded when the weather and crop conditions allow crop marks to form. Digital techniques are routinely used to rectify tracings of sites from oblique photographs so that they can be brought together in a composite plan representing the archaeology of an area. The photographs themselves can also be ortho-rectified and combined in a digital mosaic. If map data are not available, vertical photography has the additional value of being able to provide a digital topographic model of the terrain from photogrammetric analysis of stereopairs, but the verticals often do not record features as clearly as selective use of oblique photography. In areas where ground-based mapping remains difficult, even small-scale vertical photographs may be useful in searching for large sites in remote terrain or tropical forest.

Often monochrome panchromatic film is sufficient to record archaeological features, while color gives a better impression of the landscape relationships. Occasionally false color near infrared film may be used to study differences in the state of the vegetation. Digital image-processing techniques can enhance the appearance of sites, but rarely are able to reveal features not already visible in the original image. The periodicity in the size and shape of modern fields in the Mediterranean region has been investigated, however, by Fourier analysis of vertical photographs to extract the underlying regular structure which survives from the Roman centuration of the landscape two thousand years ago. Photography from space usually has only sufficient resolution to define large sites but occasionally shows interesting large area patterning. The territories of Central Asian pastoralists are clearly visible as differences in the steppe vegetation reveal the differing intensity of grazing.

[See also SCIENCE IN ARCHAEOLOGY.]

■ Raymond V. Schoder, *Ancient Greece from the Air* (1974). D. R. Wilson, *Air Photo Interpretation for Archaeologists* (1982). D. N. Riley, *Air Photography and Archaeology* (1987).

C. A. Shell

GROUND SURVEY

Most regional settlement surveys employ the techniques of ground survey, otherwise known as pedestrian survey, to locate surface remains of archaeological sites. This method is particularly appropriate in regions where there is good surface visibility and sites are well preserved. A regional survey is typically designed around a problem or series of related problems that can be addressed by the collection and interpretation of regional settlement data. The boundaries of the survey region depend primarily on the problem, as the area surveyed must include all relevant aspects of the subsistence-settlement system in question. (In the case of *cultural resource management, however, survey boundaries are defined on the basis of areas to be impacted by modern development.)

Once the research problem and regional boundaries are established, the actual sample of the region to be surveyed and the sample units to be used are defined. While a statistically representative sample of a region might be surveyed, in many cases only full-coverage, 100 percent surveys are adequate. The sample units are typically quadrats or transects; the latter are the most common units used in regional surveys. The spacing of survey transects depends on a variety of factors, including the nature of the remains expected and the visibility of the remains. In cases where sites are small and ephemeral, a relatively narrow spacing of transects is required; where sites are larger, wider spacing of transects will still allow the identification of remains. The wider the spacing of transects, the more ground can be covered with the same investment of labor.

Ground survey requires no specialized equipment, just the feet and eyes of the archaeologist and some familiarity with the sorts of remains expected. Surface remains of sites can range from substantial architectural remains to small scatterings of ceramic and/or lithic artifacts. The definition of exactly what a site is and where its boundaries lie is an issue that is more complicated than it might seem on the face of it. Some researchers prefer a "nonsite" approach; that is, they approach the region as a whole and record significant clusters or concentrations of cultural remains. Other researchers prefer to call such concentrations "sites" and record the surface remains as a single unit. Site boundaries are typically defined as some arbitrary point at which artifact densities decrease in density or simply stop. Recording of a site involves noting the visible cultural features and artifacts on the site, taking measurements of the site, drawing maps or sketch plans of the site, and sometimes making small collections of artifacts. In the case of larger sites or sites with complex internal organization, the site may be divided into segments, or loci, with each locus recorded separately and separate artifact collections made. Some researchers prefer to designate each locus of a site as a separate site, thereby inflating the numbers of sites located, although most prefer to identify the maximum size of a site and subdivide it.

Critical to the interpretation of settlement data and the formulation of maps of settlement patterns for various prehistoric periods is the chronological placement of the site. Artifact collections serve to provide the data on the basis of which such assessments are made. Samples of artifacts from the surface of a site are chosen in two general ways. First, a simple grab sample of diagnostic artifacts might be made from the site or locus within a site. Second, an area of known size might be laid out on the site and every artifact in that area collected. This has the advantage of producing a sample in which one can calculate the relative proportions of different artifact classes or types. In most surveys both types of collections are made.

The accuracy of the ground survey depends on both the visibility and the preservation of prehistoric remains. Visibility can be constrained, in the first place, by the contemporary climate of the region and the resulting vegetation cover on the ground. Not surprisingly, the most successful large-scale surveys have been undertaken in regions such as Mesopotamia, highland Mesoamerica, and the coastal Andean region, where conditions are relatively arid. Few surveys are undertaken in densely forested areas, simply because the ground surface is not visible. In addition, soil formation occurs much more rapidly in wetter, vegetated regions, thus causing sites to be buried, leaving few surface traces. A wet climate and steep terrain can combine to produce areas especially prone to erosion, which in turn buries archaeological remains or causes them to be washed away from their primary context. Climate also determines the degree of preservation of remains that might be expected. Except in completely wet contexts, such as bogs, or very dry contexts, such as the Atacama Desert, organic material does not preserve indefinitely, and this may contribute to the lack of visibility, or existence, of some sites.

Terrain also affects the logistics of ground survey in that sample units and transect layout may be constrained by terrain. For example, while it might be desirable to survey perfectly straight transect lines aligned with some compass bearing, in practice this is rarely possible. In the case of especially steep terrain it is more reasonable to lay out transect lines along elevational contours than according to compass bearings.

The accuracy of ground survey is also constrained by subsequent occupation of sites as well as modern alterations. Multicomponent sites are those sites that were occupied in more than a single defined time period. Evidence of earlier occupation is often obscured by later occupation, so surface remains are more likely to reflect the latest occupations, and earlier remains may not be visible. For example, in surveys of Mesopotamia, where sites form large multilayered tells, later occupations completely cover earlier ones. Artifacts from Sumerian or Uruk periods might occur in the thousands or tens of thousands, but archaeologists seeking evidence of early periods, such as the Úbaid, might be lucky to find a half-dozen Úbaid potsherds, even if the site was large and complex at the time of its earlier occupation. Further, multiple repeated, short occupations of a site are difficult or impossible to distinguish from a single long, continuous occupation based solely on surface remains.

Modern construction has served to wipe away surface evidence of many archaeological sites, and it is not uncommon to find modern settlements located over prehistoric site locations. This also affects the logistics of ground survey, and archaeologists are occasionally faced with an uncooperative, and sometimes armed, property owner. A number of researchers have also had unfortunate encounters with dogs defending their territory.

Ground survey techniques were first developed during the River Basin surveys of the 1930s and 1940s, and were refined during such surveys as the Virú Valley survey in Peru in the 1940s and the Basin of Mexico survey in the 1960s and 1970s. Although settlement surveys have become more sophisticated over the years in terms of problem definition, sampling designs, and interpretive models, and remote sensing increases the ability to find less visible sites, the basic techniques of ground survey continue to employ the feet and eyes of the archaeologist.

[See also SETTLEMENT ARCHAEOLOGY; SETTLEMENT PATTERN ANALYSIS.]

■ Charles L. Redman, "Archaeological Sampling Strategies," in *Addision Modules in Anthropology* (1974). William T. Sanders, Jeffrey R. Parsons, and Robert S. Santley, *The Basin of Mexico: Ecological Processes in the Evolution of a Civilization* (1979). Robert McC. Adams, *Heartland of Cities: Surveys of Ancient Settlement and Land Use in the Central Floodplain of the Euphrates* (1981). David J. Wilson, *Prehispanic Settlement Patterns in the Lower Santa Valley, Peru: A Regional Perspec-

tive on the Origins and Development of Complex North Coast Society (1988).

Katharina J. Schreiber

SITE ASSESSMENT

Once a site has been located, various techniques can be used to learn more about the site and its characteristics which involve less than full-scale excavation. These techniques are directed toward obtaining four kinds of information. First, basic information about the site such as its size, depth, and stratigraphic setting must be obtained. Site size and depth are needed to identify the site boundaries as accurately as possible. Stratigraphic data provide information on the degree of preservation of the site and its contents. Secondly, evidence of the age or ages of site occupation are obtained through site assessment. The archaeologist must know if the site represents a relatively discrete occupation, or a series of overlapping occupations which must be separated during the excavation. Third, the kinds of artifacts and features preserved in the site provide information on the length of the occupation(s), the range of activities performed at the site, and the site plan or layout. Finally, the kinds of environmental data and ecofacts preserved in the site provide information on past environments and the foods used by the site's inhabitants. Once this information has been obtained it is possible to determine whether or not the site can provide data pertaining to questions proposed in the project research design. The techniques for site assessment can be divided into those which disturb the site and those which do not.

Techniques which disturb the site include surface collection, posthole and shovel testing, test pits, and mechanical trenching. Surface collections range from recovering only a few kinds of artifacts to recovering all observed artifacts and from total surface collections to partial surface collections (samples). Randomly generated samples can provide probability estimates (with confidence intervals) of the number of artifacts on the site surface. Systematically generated samples are somewhat easier to use for plotting variations in the density of artifacts across the surface, but they do not provide probability estimates.

Posthole and shovel testing are used to provide information about the artifacts just below the surface of the site. This is particularly important in areas where vegetation completely obscures the ground. Posthole tests involve the use of a posthole digger or a power auger (ca. 8–12 inches [20–30 cm] in diameter) to investigate the site to a depth of 3 to 6 feet (1–2 m). Shovel tests are about 12 to 20 inches (30–50 cm) on a side and are generally excavated to depths of 1.6 to 3 feet (0.5–1 m). The fill from these tests may be screened or simply examined with a trowel. Posthole and shovel tests provide information on site *stratigraphy as well as information about artifacts and ecofacts. They can be used to trace the boundaries of shallowly buried sites and they may provide evidence of buried features or structures. Posthole and shovel testing can use probability or systematic sampling, but the latter is more common.

Coring techniques are useful on sites with deeply buried strata. Hand auger and mechanical cores vary from 1 to 4 inches (3–10 cm) in diameter. They provide very small samples of the sediments 16.4 feet (5 m) or more beneath the surface. The sediment samples can be analyzed for color, organic content, phosphorous, pH, and other characteristics that may indicate a buried soil horizon or a buried midden deposit.

Test pits are larger excavations into a site (usually 3 by 3 feet [1×1 m] or 3 by 6 feet [1×2 m] by 3 to 6 feet [1–2 m] deep) which are used to learn more about the site depth, complexity, degree of preservation, and evidence of subsurface features or structures. They provide better profiles for interpreting the site stratigraphy. Test pits may be excavated in natural or arbitrary levels. Arbitrary levels are somewhat more common since the stratigraphy of the site is unknown. Test pits can be located using probability or systematic sampling.

Mechanical trenching involves the use of a backhoe or other machine to excavate trenches of various lengths and expose profiles (up to about 10 feet [3 m] deep) which provide the best evidence of the site stratigraphy and the presence of buried occupations. Backdirt from the trenches can be screened and artifacts also may be found while scraping the walls of the trench to observe the stratigraphy. Because mechanical trenching can be very disruptive to the site, it is usually employed where structures and features are not present or are very difficult to find by any other means and where the geological setting of the site suggests the potential for buried occupations. In some cases, this kind of trenching may be the only way to determine whether the archaeological deposits are in situ or redeposited and how much erosion has occurred.

Nondestructive site assessment techniques include mapping and various remote-sensing techniques. Site mapping ranges from simple sketch maps of the site boundaries to detailed recording of topography and vegetation, as well as the location of artifacts, features, and structures. Equipment used varies from a Brunton compass and a surveyor's chain to electronic distance measurement systems. Site mapping can help to identify concentrations of artifacts on the site that may indicate activity areas or features. Maps can also help to identify spatially distinct occupations within a site. Contour maps allow superimposition of artifact distributions on topography to study post-depositional disturbances or to locate the strata from which artifacts eroded. For sites with visible structural remains, maps provide evidence of the site layout and orientation which can be used to plan the excavations.

Remote-sensing techniques include aerial photography, soil resistivity, magnetometer, ground-penetrating radar, electromagnetic conductivity, and metal detectors. While aerial photography is usually used to locate sites, it can also provide valuable information during site assessment. Low elevation aerial photographs, including infrared and other special techniques, may reveal crop marks, soil patterns, and structures on a site which can be correlated with the site map. On large urban sites, aerial photographs provide a quick way to develop a site plan to locate surface collections and test units.

Soil resistivity survey involves establishing a grid over the site and inserting electrodes to measure electrical resistance. The technique can locate subsurface features, including walls, pits, and fired areas that increase or decrease electrical resistance in the soil.

Magnetometer survey involves establishing a grid over the site and measuring the strength of the earth's magnetic field at each grid intersection. Small variations in the magnetic field strength can indicate buried features such as fired areas, areas containing ferrous metal objects, or structures (if they are composed of materials which vary in magnetic strength from the surrounding sediments). Better resolution of subsurface features can sometimes be obtained by using two magnetic sensors in a vertical mode called gradiometer survey.

Ground-penetrating radar survey involves establishing a series of transects across the site and dragging a sensor along the ground to generate a subsurface profile. Ideally this profile will help to identify buried walls, pits, or other features which vary in density from the surrounding sediments.

Electromagnetic conductivity survey involves establishing a series of transects across the site and then using a device which induces an electromagnetic field into the earth without requiring the insertion of the electrodes required in resistivity survey. Variation in conductivity can help to locate buried pits, structures, or conductive metals (whereas magnetometers are limited to ferrous metals). Conductivity is also affected by moisture content so that some of the variability in conductivity is related to topography and variation in soils that is unrelated to cultural activity.

Metal detector survey involves establishing a series of transects or a grid across the site and then recording the response of a metal detector along the transect or at each location. Metal detectors are relatively inexpensive and most provide only an auditory signal. They can yield important information about the distribution of metal artifacts buried within about 20 inches (50 cm) of the surface. Metal detectors also afford a relatively economical way of plotting the distribution of metallic objects on a historic site prior to excavation. By knowing the distribution of near-surface metal artifacts, one can better anticipate problems with magnetometer, resistivity, or conductivity surveys.

[See also SUBSURFACE TESTING, articles on SOIL RESISTIVITY SURVEY, MAGNETOMETER SURVEY, GROUND PENETRATING RADAR.]

■ Thomas R. Lyons and Thomas E. Avery, Remote Sensing: A Handbook for Archaeologists and Cultural Resource Managers (1977). Martha Joukowsky, A Complete Manual of Field Archaeology: Tools and Techniques of Fieldwork for Archaeologists (1980). Christopher Carr, Handbook on Soil Resistivity Surveying: Interpretation of Data from Earthen Archaeological Sites (1982). Philip Barker, Techniques of Archaeological Excavation, 2nd ed. (1983). James I. Ebert, "Remote Sensing Applications in Archaeology," Advances in Archaeological Method and Theory 7 (1984): 293–362. Michael B. Schiffer, Formation Processes of the Archaeological Record (1987). E. C. Harris, Principles of Archaeological Stratification, 2nd ed. (1989). I. Scollar, ed., Archaeological Prospecting and Remote Sensing (1990). A. Clark, Seeing Beneath the Soil: Prospecting Methods in Archaeology (1991). Michael R. Waters, Principles of Geoarchaeology (1992).

David L. Carlson

SURFACE COLLECTION

The collection of surface artifacts is one technique used by archaeologists to gather data on past human activities on a particular landscape. However, before deciding what surface artifacts to obtain and how they should be collected, a fundamental decision an archaeologist must make is how a site should be defined. The decision is affected as much by research need as by management concerns. Archaeologists continue to debate the merits of the site as a unit of study. Most argue that human use of the earth has left behind myriad material remains of past human activity across the surface. The number and density of these remains varies greatly from the isolated artifact of the deserts of the American West to the tens of millions of artifacts deposited in large cities of the ancient world, such as Angkor Wat in Cambodia. Opinions differ when higher densities of artifacts are present. For our purposes, sites are real; the people who used the landscape would have recognized certain locations as being bounded in some way.

The surface collection of archaeological materials varies from the illegal and haphazard to the publicly endorsed and controlled. Those illegally collecting artifacts range from persons intent on vandalizing archaeological sites in pursuit of profit to visitors collecting vacation souvenirs. Although archaeologists are bound by the same laws and regulations that all individuals are, the context within which the archaeologist works is guided by a written research design. The research design specifies the reason for the research being conducted; thus what should be collected is clearly defined. The integration of artifact collecting into an explicit research design is the most significant innovation in the surface collection of artifacts over the last thirty years in professional archaeology.

For a long period in archaeology's history, sites with visible architecture or large burial mounds captured the attention and efforts of many early innovators. Consideration of what the distribution of surface artifacts might mean with respect to the excavated deposits was given little attention. However, in many parts of the world, the surface archaeological record is all that exists. Even in these areas, archaeologists collected artifacts haphazardly, often grabbing only time-sensitive artifacts that could date the occupation of the site. Overlooking or underplaying the importance of surface materials led archaeologists to the erroneous interpretations of the past.

Concern for the spatial relationships between artifacts and features, such as hearths, rooms, or entire buildings, that might be present on a site and the significance of these relationships for understanding human behavior reached a critical mass by the late 1960s and early 1970s. A combination of *experimental archaeology and *ethnoarchaeology led to the introduction of more sophisticated field and statistical methods to capture and interpret information that previously was ignored.

The field methods used by archaeologists to record sites are dependent on the research questions contained in the research design. Deciding whether or not artifacts collected from the surface are representative of all the artifacts present directly affects what we can say about the past. Controlling statistical variability is possible through the use of rigorous recording techniques. This might include laying out a square grid over a site, mapping in the artifacts within each square, and then collecting artifacts from certain squares. However, regardless of how precise the spatial information recovered for each artifact may be and the possible association of these artifacts with each other or with features, we cannot ignore how these sites came to be before the archaeologist recorded them.

Archaeologists must understand the dynamic processes that affect sites or risk creating just-so stories or misleading prehistoric narratives. These *site formation processes range from trampling artifacts into the ground or sweeping discarded materials to the side by the site occupants to natural processes such as water and wind transport and soil deposition. Interpreting the surface distribution of artifacts requires an understanding of both human behavior and natural processes that affect the remains of this behavior.

Increasing our understanding of cultural and natural formation processes is possible through the use of *geographical information systems (GIS) and the global positioning system (GPS). Geographical information systems are able to manipulate large quantities of spatial information concerning both natural and cultural variables such as slope and aspect and distance between sites. Correlating site locations with worldwide coordinate systems is possible through the satellite-based global positioning system (GPS). Combining GIS with GPS offers archaeologists new graphical ways of analyzing sites and artifacts. Exploring local, regional, and global spatial relationships in ways not previously possible is on the archaeologist's doorstep.

[See also SETTLEMENT PATTERN ANALYSIS.]

■ Lewis R. Binford, "A Consideration of Archaeological Research Design," *American Antiquity* 29 (1964): 425–441. Daniel Ingersoll, John E. Yellen, and William Macdonald, eds., *Experimental Archeology* (1977). Lewis R. Binford, *Working at Archaeology* (1983). Kathleen M. S. Allen, Stanton Green, and Ezra B. W. Zubrow, eds., *Interpreting Space: GIS and Archaeology* (1990). Michael B. Schiffer, *Formation Processes of the Archaeological Record* (1987).

Marc Kodack

SLAVS. Slavic archaeology covers the period from the point when Slavic peoples first became recognizable to when medieval states formed, roughly the sixth to the eleventh centuries A.D. Fueled by nineteenth and twentieth century instability of national borders in central and eastern Europe, questions of Slavic origins have figured prominently in archaeology. The tradition was undiminished during the half-century of Marxist orthodoxy, when a term was even coined for the study of Slavic ethnic origins—*ethnogenesology*. Much of the literature on Slavic archaeology accepts the equation of ethnic affiliation with archaeological cultures as unproblematic.

Origins. The favored archaeological candidates for Slavic origins are the Przeworsk, Zarubintsy, and Chernyakhov cultures, dating from the second century B.C. to the fourth century A.D., covering much of Poland, the Ukraine, Moldavia, and south of the Carpathians along the Tisza. Excluding the Hungarian area and the eastern Chernyakhov culture extending to the Volga and beyond, the geographical area covered fits not only the best hypothetical linguistic area of early Slavonic speakers, it also coincides with an ecological niche suited to agriculture, avoiding the steppes, which were populated variously by nomads speaking Iranian, Turkic, Magyar, or Asiatic languages, and the heavy forests of the north, to which Baltic and Ugro-Finnish speakers are generally assigned.

The Chernyakhov culture ended around A.D. 400 and the Przeworsk culture shortly thereafter, leaving most of the fifth century curiously devoid of archaeological evidence. The fifth century is also dark through most of western Europe. When archaeological evidence becomes more plentiful in the sixth century, the new Korchak and Pen'kovka cultures in the "homeland" (roughly Poland and Ukraine) are unhesitatingly assumed to be Slavic. Beyond the Przeworsk-Chernyakhov cultural areas, the Kolochin-Tushemlya culture, despite marked similarities, is thought perhaps to be Balto-Slavic, partially because of its geographic position in Byelorussia and further north. In eastern Germany, the Czech Republic and Slovakia, the Sukow-Dziedzice, Feldberg, Tornow, and Prague "cultures" (or pottery styles) of the sixth and seventh centuries are taken to be Slavic, and the result of migration.

Migration into the former Roman Empire certainly occurred. The Slavs mingled along the Danube with the Romanized population of Dacia and lower Moesia, where the Romance language (Romanian) survived, although influenced by the incomers (Romanian contains Slavonic words and syntax). Earlier populations survived in the Carpathians north of the Danube. Incoming Magyars swamped the Slavic peoples settled with Avars in the great basin of the Danube and Tisza at the end of the ninth century. In contrast, further south in the Balkans, Slavonic languages completely replaced the Roman, Greek, and older Thracian languages of the Roman Empire. Unlike the Magyars, the incoming Bulgars dominated politically but ultimately had little effect on the Slavs settled in the former province of Thracia. Although Byzantine texts document repeated Slavic incursions and settlement within regions of the former Roman Empire throughout the fifth century and after, they are little reflected in archaeology, even from the sixth and seventh centuries.

North and east of the Carpathians, the archaeological cultures of the sixth and seventh centuries generally deemed to be "Slavic" are remarkably consistent. Pottery is simple; handmade, biconical shapes predominate, and decoration often takes the form of wavy lines on or above the shoulder. The dead were almost exclusively cremated. Settlements were small, comprising small timber dwellings and outbuildings. The houses were characteristically square and wooden, built of planks or even rough logs. On wetter soils these were built on the ground or on wooden rafts, but elsewhere they were regularly sunken into the ground. Groups of these *Grubenhäuser*, often about 5 by 5 yards square (4 by 4 m sq), make up most of the sixth- and seventh-century settlements known, as at a dozen sites along the Teterev River just east of Kiev, or the seven to ten houses at Dessau-Mosigkau, Saxony, or the near identical hamlet at Březno just north of Prague. Not only were Grubenhäuser much more common than in western, Germanic regions, they persisted well beyond the migration periods. They constituted the eighth-century settlement within the ramparts at Izborsk near Pskov, by the Estonian border. Perhaps 1,000 people dwelled in 13 by 13 feet (4 by 4 m) wooden houses in the annex of the princely fort at Mikulčice in ninth-century Moravia. In the tenth and eleventh centuries, small square log cabins formed the basis of most dwellings at the Polish fortified trading center at Opole on the river Oder. Unlike Germanic Grubenhäuser, Slavic houses often had a clay or stone oven in one corner. This characterized dwellings of the Prague and Korchak cultures. The ninth-century clay ovens of the dozens of Grubenhäuser at the unfortified "hill fort" of Novotroitskoye on the river Psyol, northeast of Kiev, are perfectly preserved.

Society. Archaeology suggests that early Slavic society was fairly egalitarian. Thus the eighth-century hill fort at Klučov in Bohemia contains no extraordinary houses within the timber-and-earth ramparts, nor can they be distinguished from those outside the fortifications. From the seventh to the eleventh century, fortifications were built around all manner of northern Slavic settlements. Among the Wilzi, Obodrites, Sorbs, and smaller tribes that lived in the area of eastern Germany, many hundreds of *hill forts date to this early period. This is exceptional, but a developed social hierarchy (feudalization) and state organization came late to these Slavic peoples. Orthodox Marxist dogma held that in prefeudal society, (so-called gentile society) the elite did not truly exploit fellow peasants, leadership was elective, and many activities were communal. Many Slavic fortifications are interpreted in the literature as built by the people and for the people. At Tornow (Niederlausitz), the early settlement is interpreted as eight independent peasant households of varying sizes, all of whom used the massive circular timber-and-earth fort, 165 feet (50 m) in outer diameter, as a communal "refuge."

When the Tornow fort burned down in the eighth century, it was replaced by a bigger one. Against the interior wall were continuous lean-to buildings, in the center one large house. There was otherwise almost no free room in the fort. The dwellings outside the fort were now more uniform and smaller. One interpretation is that a "village lord" now lived within the fort with storage buildings holding the tribute of the peasants outside. Their servile dependency resulted in a standardization of their homes and presumably plots of land and livestock.

A more conventional and less claustrophobic lordly dwelling is the ninth-century Pohansko by Břeclav (near Brno). In its last phase, a simple palisade enclosed an area roughly 265 by 300 feet (80 by 90 m) within which were a dozen small timber houses or storage buildings, a slightly larger timber building, and a church. It is the "private" church (Eigenkirche), the enclosure, and the scale of the settlement that leads archaeologists to denote it a lord's manor, comparable to Carolingian and Ottonian manors in western Europe.

Although Slavic fortifications are known from the sixth to eighth centuries A.D., they flourished most during the ninth to eleventh centuries. Large ninth-century hill forts are associated with the first Slavic Empire, of Great Moravia (including Staré Město and Mikulčice), and the subsequent tenth-century Bohemian state of the Přemyslid dynasty (including Libušín, Budeč, Levý Hradec, and Kouřim).

In Poland, multiple-enclosure fortifications with great ramparts defending areas even greater than ten hectares appeared in the ninth century (including Gniezno, Ostrów and Poznan). In the middle of the tenth century the Polish state appeared under Miesko I and the Piast dynasty. Most of the great fortified centers throughout the kingdom had become towns by the start of the eleventh century (bishoprics: Poznań, Gniezno, Trzemeszno, Płock, Cracow, Wrocław, Kołobrzeg; towns: Gdańsk, Wolin, Lebus, Iława, Głogów, Giecz, Kalisz, Legnica, Niemcza, Opole, Sieradz, Łęczyca, Kruszwica, Stradów, Wiślica, Sansomierz, Lublin). Kievan Russia followed an almost identical pattern: major fortifications appearing archaeologically, territorial princes appearing textually in the ninth century. Kiev was the largest center; its prince ruled the new state, which by the eleventh century was one of Europe's largest states with some one hundred urban centers. Novgorod is one of the best excavated; its numerous surviving eleventh and twelfth-century letters and documents written on birch bark are among the most important medieval archaeological finds in Europe.

In areas of the former Roman Empire settled by Slavs there were many similar developments. Evidence of sixth- to eighth-century settlement south of the Danube is scarce. In Macedonia, for instance, there is little beyond two excavated villages just northwest of Prilep. Whereas typical handmade seventh-century urns containing cremations occur, as at Kašić near Sadar, traditions of the local populations and Byzantine fashions (especially jewelry, such as earrings) were soon adopted. Slavic settlement within old Roman towns is attested. Two dozen houses have been uncovered at Krivina, Bulgaria (the former Castrum Iatrus). When the Byzantine emperor Constantine Porphyrogenitus wrote in the tenth century of Croatian towns, Nin, Bribir, Knin, Karin, Sidraga, and Skradin, all could trace their origins to antiquity.

Slavic states began forming by the start of the ninth century in the Balkans, earlier than they did north of the Danube. Serbian, Croatian, and Bulgarian dynasties were led by župans (officers), dukes, or tsars. At Rižinice near Solin there is an inscription of prince Trpimir (845–864), at Muć, Nin, Šopot, and Ždrapanj inscriptions of prince Branimir (879–892), calling him Dux Croatorum. A few kilometers east of Šumen there is a 75.5 foot (23 m) high relief sculpture of a mounted warrior, perhaps of an eighth-century Bulgar khan. Despite the early development of a Bulgarian empire (the khan Asparuch ruled 681–701), it was only in the ninth century that Bulgar rulership took on aspects of state organization. Under Krum and Omurtag, Pliska palace and town grew enormously. The town walls enclosed 275 square yards (23 sq km), within which thirty churches have been discovered, mostly dating from the eleventh to fourteenth century. Unlike Byzantine towns, buildings were not built close to one another. A massive church, the largest building in the Balkans, was built in the northern part of the town in the late ninth century. It was connected to the inner citadel, which was defended by a stone wall provided with towers, by a straight paved processional way of almost a mile (1.5 km). The citadel contained the houses of the greater nobles and the royal palace. Its mid-ninth-century hall was immense, 171 by 87 feet (52 by 26.5 m) larger than Charlemagne's at Aachen, built of massive limestone blocks (some of them reused Roman tombstones) in basilican form. The audience room contained inlaid marble. It replaced an earlier, even larger building. A smaller palace complex served as the royal residence. It was provided with heated baths. Rich finds include glazed pottery, weapons, jewelry, iron tools, statuary, and dozens of Greek inscriptions. In the late ninth century, Preslav became the new capital. Comparably impressive, the tsar Symeon built his "golden church" there, a rotunda with twelve semicircular apses.

The economy was overwhelmingly agrarian. Concentrated, specialized iron working is early attested; for example, twenty-four smelting ovens of the early ninth century were found at Želechovice in Moravia. In Cracow a ninth-century wooden chest was discovered containing 4,000 axe-shaped iron bars. These functioned as primitive currency. West European and Arabic silver coins (dirhams) were also used in the ninth and tenth centuries. Some 11,000 dirhams have been found around Kiev alone. Minting began late among the Slavs. The first coins were those of Boleslav (929–967) in Bohemia; Mieszko I (960–992) in Poland; and Vladimir the Great (980–1015) in Russia. Staraya Ladoga, north of Novgorod, is the best excavated emporium of the periods associated with long-distance trade and "proto"-coinage, and comparable to the emporia of the North Sea and Baltic coasts.

Religion. Slavic religious worship of pagan gods (including Svantovit, Triglav, Perun, Svarog, Veles, Stribog, Mokosh, Chors, and Semarg with variant spellings) is attested by about two dozen idols. For obvious reasons the wooden phallus with a carved face found at łęczya has been interpreted as pertaining to fertility cults. But many idols have multiple heads, including a three meter "totem pole" from the river Zbrucz near Husyatin in southern Poland, two similar stone idols found in the Ukraine at Ivankovtsy on the Dniester, and the two-headed idol with drooping mustaches from Lake Tollense, Neubrandenburg, Germany. Multiple-headedness is not only a characteristic shared by many Slavic gods known from texts, but a contemporary,

Saxo Grammaticus, so described the great idol at Arkona on the island of Rügen in the Baltic. It was meant to have held a horn, and two churches on the island have stones with relief carvings of figures with horns who probably represented the god Svantovit. The sites where idols stood have even been excavated. In Russia at Peryn' monastery (named after the god Perun), there was a deep posthole that probably held an idol standing within a circular ditched enclosure. Smaller circular enclosures with postholes were found nearby. Postholes by a village excavated at Tušemlja in the Smolensk region are similarly interpreted as having held idols, as is the great posthole tightly surrounded by eight further postholes, around which was a slight palisade fence, at the lordly manor at Pohansko. This cult site was replaced by a church.

The Christianization of the Moravian lord of Pohansko occurred in the ninth century, a century that saw much of the Slavic territories Christianized. The Balkans were by then largely Christian. The Byzantine city Lychnidos housed a bishop from the fourth to the sixth century. After two hundred dark years an archbishop from the city, now named Ohrid (Macedonia), attended a council at Constantinople. By the tenth century the Balkans had great centers of church learning. John the Exarch worked at Preslav, and the earliest Cyrillic inscriptions appear, for example, the tombstone of tsar Samuel's parents at the village of German, (Macedonia). Poland was primarily Christianized during the tenth century. In the Ukraine, although a bishopric was first founded in Kiev in 864, Christianity suffered several reversals until the end of the tenth century. Exceptionally, the area between the Elbe and Oder in eastern Germany saw extreme resistance to Christian missions. It was only in the twelfth century that Christianity triumphed, but bloodily. A crusade was even launched against the Wends in 1147. Not surprisingly, this area has yielded the most abundant archaeological evidence for pagan practices, including the well-preserved (waterlogged) wooden 23 by 36 foot (7 by 11 m) temple at Groß Raden, Westmecklenberg, Germany. This lay at the edge of a village on a promontory, which was connected by a bridge to a fort on an island in the lake. It has been beautifully reconstructed in an outdoor museum.

Christianization of burial practices can be seen in the abandonment of cremation, which the Church explicitly condemned as pagan. The disappearance of "grave goods"— simply the less perishable appurtenances of the dress and adornment worn by the corpse—is often wrongly interpreted as direct Christian influence. Perhaps indirectly the church had an impact; at death conspicuous wealth was donated to the church rather than buried with the body.

Although the archaeology of the church belongs primarily to medieval archaeology rather than "Slavic archaeology," there are some noteworthy characteristics of Christian archaeology of the early Slavic Period. From the outset, churches were almost exclusively built in stone, rather than the ubiquitous wood. Circular churches were much more common than in western Europe. In Moravia and Bohemia inspiration is often said to have come from the church of St. Donatus at Zadar, following the mission of Methodius and Constantine, but the close relationship of princely palace and round church (e.g., in Poland: Płock, Giecz, Przemyśl, Ostrów Lednicki) is something found in late Carolingian and Ottonian Germany. Despite the Roman orthodoxy of the Polish and Bohemian Church, Byzantine influence is revealed by the early use of cupolas. Indeed, at the Czech

monastery at Sázava, Latin rites had still not been adopted in the eleventh century and archaeology has uncovered there a Byzantine-style tetrafoil-plan church. Thus the Slavic regions of central Europe continued to be pulled between western and eastern cultural and religious allegiance until well into the Middle Ages.

[See also EUROPE: ROMAN AND POST-ROMAN EUROPE.]

Ross Samson

SOCIAL INEQUALITY, Theories of. See RANKING AND SOCIAL INEQUALITY, THEORIES OF.

SOCIAL ORGANIZATION, Prehistoric. In the study of ancient societies, some of the most broadly relevant and stimulating questions that archaeologists examine are social. These queries concern people and their relationships with others, different access patterns to goods and information, the implementation of power, and the composition, size, and boundedness of human groups. The rich intellectual traditions of the social and historical sciences serve as theoretical underpinnings for this examination of similarities, differences, and long-term change in human social organization. Yet, the suite of systematic archaeological methods, procedures, and interpretive frameworks to examine prehistoric social relations is more recent, stemming largely from the latter half of the twentieth century.

As recently as 1954, Christopher Hawkes (in *American Anthropologist* 56: 155–168) outlined a rather narrow vision for archaeology that scripted little potential for the study of prehistoric social organization. Hawkes and others envisioned a hierarchy of inference in which ancient technology and subsistence were viewed as relatively accessible to archaeological discovery, while the sociopolitical and, to an even greater degree, the religious realms were seen as nearly impossible to investigate. In part, Hawkes's problem was a typical one in archaeology: the data do not speak for themselves. To study ancient social organization, archaeologists had to frame the right questions, and devise the means to address them.

A key distinction is notable with the way in which social organization is studied in cultural anthropology, where the investigator can more easily observe living peoples and directly form conclusions about the allocation of power and how a society is organized. For the cultural anthropologist, specific details about kinship, co-residence, and ritual also are generally accessible. In contrast, systematic fieldwork and analysis is essential for the archaeologist to gain even a basic perspective on prehistoric social organization. But, whereas the goal for cultural anthropologists is to understand present societies (and those in the recent past), the archaeological endeavor is broader, aimed at societies over a far longer time span, with all the potential that affords to examine key societal transitions and explain regional processes of long-term change.

Societal Classification. In the late 1950s and 1960s, the study of prehistoric social organization received greater emphasis as social evolutionary frameworks assumed increased prominence in cultural anthropology and archaeology. Stimulated by the evolutionary perspectives of that period, archaeological analyses of social behavior have subsequently focused on key societal transitions, such as the advent of sedentary village life, the institutionalization of inequality, the emergence of formal leadership positions, and the rise of cities and states. In line with these aims, many archaeologists have found utility in the fourfold classification of societies (bands, tribes, chiefdoms, states) developed in *Primitive Social Organization* (1971) by the American anthropologist Elman R. Service.

In this scheme, bands are conceptualized as small-scale societies of mobile hunters and gatherers that generally include no more than a few hundred people. Group boundaries are difficult to define, and specific bands are frequently articulated with neighboring groups into widespread open networks composed of numerous local groups. In bands, leadership positions are individualized and changeable, often depending on personal skills and charisma. Thus, there is no institutionalized government, and the division of labor is based largely on age and gender. Prior to 12,000 years ago, most, if not all, of the world's population lived in bands.

Service defined tribes as larger than bands (rarely more than 2,000 to 3,000 people), having economies dependent on agricultural plants and domesticated animals. Tribes were generally thought to be sedentary, with group boundaries encompassing multiple communities. Tribes, like bands, were considered egalitarian, meaning that age, gender, experience, and personal skills were the principal axes of inequality. In tribes, individuals and households were linked horizontally through kinship, clans, and other sodalities.

In contrast to these egalitarian social forms, chiefdoms are hierarchically structured with inherited differences in access to goods, information, status, and rank. Leadership is ascribed or inherited rather than achieved, as in bands and tribes. Positions of power and rule therefore are institutionalized. Chiefdoms tend to be more internally differentiated than egalitarian societies. Economic specialization typically exists, so that certain households consistently produce more craft and agricultural goods than they require for their own sustenance. Because chiefs often have a nodal role in ritual, military, and economic transactions, chiefly centers (where chiefs reside) tend to be larger and more functionally diverse than other settlements. Chiefdoms are recognized to vary in size, frequently including roughly 10,000 or more inhabitants.

States are more internally differentiated than chiefdoms. Their populations are stratified into distinct socioeconomic classes, while the structure of governmental decision making is hierarchically more complex and less based on kinship ties. Typically, kings, queens, or other state rulers rely on bureaucracies and military power to implement and enforce their legal authority. States also are conceived as demographically and territorially larger than chiefdoms, with many early states associated with central urban settlements that contained thousands of inhabitants. Most archaeologists agree that the world's first states arose in Mesopotamia during the latter half of the fourth millennium B.C.

Service's rather simple typology has provided a basic language and set of concepts for archaeologists to discuss societal variation. Yet its analytical utility is beset with potential pitfalls and problems that belie its often uncritical application. Clearly, to overemphasize or reify the four societal modes outlined by Service would be foolish. Likewise, one should not agonize endlessly over the classification of a specific society in one mode or another. There is much more cross-cultural variation in social organization than can be accommodated by Service's or any similar scheme, in part because societal change does not necessarily occur in the steplike, tightly covarying ways stressed by these frameworks.

More significantly, it is historically inaccurate to presume that all societies inevitably evolve from bands to tribes, or from chiefdoms to states. Rigid adherence to societal taxonomies can blind researchers to the highly variable and sometimes counterintuitive pathways of social change. A key challenge of modern archaeology is to attempt to explain why some societies became larger, more differentiated, and governmentally complex while others did not.

Key Organizational Dimensions. Despite the aforementioned limitations, the works of Service and the other evolutionists serve to highlight several key dimensions for the comparison of social organizational variability and change. The first dimension is scale or size. How many people compose an ancient social system, and how were they distributed over space? Is there evidence of year-round sedentary habitations or only seasonal campsites reflective of more mobile lifeways? Are there centers as might be expected in nonegalitarian societies, and if so, how large, how many, and how differentiated in size and function are they? To examine these issues, archaeological research must be extended beyond the familiar excavation of single sites. Questions of scale have been investigated through systematic settlement pattern surveys, which collectively have concentrated on mapping both regions and specific sites.

By implication, the issue of societal size raises questions about the definition of social system boundaries. For example, to evaluate social organization, archaeologists must consider whether specific communities were autonomous or part of larger polities. Research cannot stop at estimations of the size and number of sites in a given region, but must examine the more difficult issue of how the occupants of those ancient settlements were articulated with each other. To do so requires studying the spatial distributions of specific classes of artifacts and architectural features across archaeological landscapes. For the examination of ancient social organization, it is generally this type of relational data (the spatial distribution of particular classes of artifacts, features, and settlements) that is as or more informative than the specific characteristics of those artifacts and features themselves.

In addition to the parameters of scale and boundedness, comparative analyses of ancient societies also must consider various dimensions of internal organization, including complexity, integration, and differentiation. As noted by Service, chiefdoms and states have more complex, hierarchical forms of decision making or governance than egalitarian societies. Human populations also differ markedly in the ways that their component societal segments are interconnected. Kinship serves a key integratory mode in some populations, while political dominance, territorial proximity, or ethnic identity are more significant in others. The nature and degree of economic articulations between households and communities has been illustrated to vary along a continuum from near self-sufficiency to marked interdependence. Generally, large and hierarchical societies also are socially and economically differentiated, with greater degrees of stratification as well as more numerous specialists. Each of these comparative dimensions of internal organization is accessible to long-term, systematic investigations by social archaeologists.

Analytical Procedures. The significance of settlement patterns for the study of ancient social organization includes estimations of the nature, size, and number of ancient settlements. Yet it also incorporates the distribution of specific economic and ritual activities across the landscape. An illustrative aspect of the latter is the spatial arrangement of monumental features, such as open plazas, earthen platform mounds, stone pyramids, giant storage facilities, and the like. If most contemporaneous communities in a region were associated with comparable ritual features, the implications are decidedly different than if such monuments or storage facilities are limited to the central precincts of the region's largest communities. Archaeologists who examine prehistoric monuments also consider the time and energy costs needed to build these constructions. How much labor was required, and could it have been supplied by the consensual work of the local population alone or were labor drafts necessary?

The specific characteristics of such monumental features and their placement also can inform the archaeologist about the relative openness of access to the activities that were associated with these features. For example, the pyramids of ancient Egypt, which were built and used as richly adorned burial monuments to deceased rulers or pharaohs, provide different clues about the nature of ancient organization than the megalithic henges of middle and late first millennium B.C. western Europe. The latter served as burial crypts (generally with relatively few accompanying goods) for sizable segments of local populations. No serious scholars would deny that Egypt at the time of the pharaohs was a more hierarchical and stratified society than the populations of Late Mesolithic and Early Neolithic Europe.

At prehistoric sites on the plateau of the American Southwest, the most common ritual feature is the kiva. These circular ceremonial features were generally placed within or adjacent to the pueblos to which they were associated. While most kivas were not large enough to service the entire local population, large segments of the community could participate in kiva rituals. In contrast, the accessibility of most ancient Maya temples is strikingly different. Raised off the landscape atop rubble platform mounds in the central precincts of major centers, accessibility to these buildings was generally limited by narrow accessways, closed plazas, and steep stone staircases. The usable ritual or temple space atop these platforms was actually quite small, especially in relation to the total population of the surrounding settlement. Access to these sacred structures was restricted to a relative few. Of course, for each society, understanding ancient social relations requires examination of as complete a corpus of monumental structures as possible.

The study of domestic and community contexts, particularly the comparative analysis of houses, also can provide key insights into wealth and status differences. For a given society, it is revealing whether all houses were basically similar in size and constructed of like materials or not. In many cases, higher-status individuals, such as chiefs, reside in bigger, more elaborate domiciles or elite residences. Some archaeologists view large, grandiose residential structures or palaces as an indicator of status.

Archaeological analyses at the community scale also depend on relational data, the distribution of different artifacts and features across a sample of excavated houses. In egalitarian societies, one might expect each household to have relatively equal access to diverse classes of goods. Prestige-related items and exotics should be evenly dispersed. Alternatively, when such precious and highly crafted artifacts are clustered in the largest or most elaborate residences, the existence of access differentials cannot be ruled out.

Degrees of household self-sufficiency can be investigated through the analysis of storage and economic specialization. In some societies, such as the Inca of late pre-Hispanic

Andes, large food storage facilities were controlled by the state. In other regions, such as ancient Mesoamerica, most food storage apparently was managed by households. Such differences provide important clues regarding the mechanisms of socioeconomic integration. Over the last decades, archaeologists have become adept at identifying the craft manufacture of a wide range of products, such as pottery, stone tools, metals, shell ornaments, and lapidary arts. A degree of economic specialization has been found in many regions of the world following the advent of sedentary life; however, marked global and temporal variation in the scale and intensity of economic specialization also is evident.

Another important archaeological indicator for degrees of social differentiation comes form burials and the accompanying grave goods. The specific context of interment is informative, as is the labor invested in particular tomb settings. For example, marked social disparities are indicated in Egypt, where the highest-ranked segment of society was conspicuously placed in the massive pyramids, while the majority of the population was interred directly in the earth with few associated goods.

Archaeologists generally assume that the treatment of a body at death is at least partially indicative of how an individual was viewed during their lifetime. In less hierarchical societies, the study of ancient cemetery populations has effectively identified status differences based on the quantities and kinds of specific grave goods that were placed with each grave. When properly analyzed, the skeletal remains themselves also can generate information about dietary and health distinctions between different societal segments. In many cases, higher-status individuals have been found to have greater access to protein and have fewer dietary deficiencies than do the rest of the population.

No single analytical procedure provides a foolproof or complete picture of ancient social formations. Solid archaeological interpretations of prehistoric organizational change and diversity must rely on the suite of aforementioned analytical perspectives (settlement patterns, monumental architecture, household archaeology, and burials) often in conjunction with other sources, such as artistic depictions when available. Only when archaeologists can use multiple evidential vantages and look at ancient societies from several analytical scales can they begin to understand the richness of past social systems and describe how these societies changed over time. Although many questions remain, major descriptive and empirical advances in our understanding of past areal and temporal differences in social relations have clearly been made since the 1950s. Nevertheless more work still needs to be done concerning the causality and explanation of these long-term organizational transitions, which archaeologists can now more effectively study and characterize.

[See also IDEOLOGY AND ARCHAEOLOGY; MORTUARY ANALYSIS; RANKING AND SOCIAL INEQUALITY, THEORIES OF; SETTLEMENT PATTERN ANALYSIS.]

■ Morton H. Fried, *The Evolution of Political Society* (1967). Kent V. Flannery, "The Cultural Evolution of Civilizations," *Annual Review of Ecology and Systematics* 3 (1972): 399–426. Marshall Sahlins, *Stone Age Economics* (1972). Elman R. Service, *Origins of the State and Civilization* (1975). Kent V. Flannery, ed., *The Early Mesoamerican Village* (1976). Charles L. Redman et al., eds., *Social Archaeology* (1978). Lewis R. Binford, *In Pursuit of the Past* (1983). Colin Renfrew, *Approaches to Social Archaeology* (1984). Richard E. Blanton et al., *Ancient Mesoamerica*, 2nd ed. (1993). Bruce G. Trigger, *Early Civilizations* (1993).

Gary M. Feinman

SOCIETY ISLANDS. The Society Islands (Tahiti) are located in the southeastern Pacific. Their position is central in relation to other major archipelagos of the region: the southern Cook Islands and Samoa are to the west; the Tuamotus and Marquesas are neighbors to the northeast. The islands are tropical, enjoy abundant rainfall, and once supported an elaborate ancient culture with a highly stratified sociopolitical system. The islands of Tahiti appear to have played a central role in the settlement and continuing interactions of Polynesian populations. Tahiti has also been the subject of detailed anthropological study by Douglas Oliver (reported in the three-volume *Ancient Tahitian Society*, 1974).

Research Background. Despite the significance of Tahiti in Polynesian prehistory, a comparatively small amount of archaeological work has been done in the archipelago. In 1923, Kenneth Emory, from Bishop Museum in Honolulu, began work in Tahiti surveying stone surface structures, particularly religious architecture *(marae)*. In the 1950s and 1960s Emory and his colleagues excavated sites in *Hawaii, the Marquesas, and Tahiti in an effort to build a culture historical sequence for East Polynesia. Emory and Yoshihiko Sinoto's work at the Maupiti burial site in 1962–1963 yielded artifacts important in Polynesian comparisons. Using artifact styles and linguistic data, Emory and Sinoto proposed an East Polynesian settlement sequence in which the Societies played a major part.

Research on Tahitian settlement patterns, initiated by Roger Green in the Opunohu Valley on Mo'orea, began in 1960. Green's approach, departing from the search for culture historical sequences, focused on the archaeology of social organization, demography, land use, and economic adaptations.

Recent work in archaeology has incorporated paleoenvironmental analyses to resolve questions of ecological and landscape change in the islands.

Chronology and Origins. Dating initial colonization of the islands east of Samoa in Polynesia has generated a lively debate among archaeologists. Polynesian traditions have long considered Tahiti a homeland in the settlement of the eastern Pacific from the Samoa-Tonga region. Archaeological research in the Marquesas by Robert Suggs in the 1950s established its apparent primary position in the region's settlement, and additional work in neighboring archipelagos failed to yield dates earlier than those established for the Marquesas. An early, direct colonization of the Marquesas from Samoa or Tonga was considered suspect. Rather, voyagers were likely to have discovered and settled the closer Cook Islands and Tahiti, not the more remote Marquesas.

Recent research in Tahiti and the Cook Islands may now reveal the evidence for postulated early Polynesian settlement. Patrick Kirch and his colleagues have argued, on the basis of pollen and charcoal sequences from lake cores on Mangaia, that the southern Cook Islands were settled as early as 500 B.C., with the implication that colonization included the islands of Tahiti around this time. Some scholars, such as Atholl Anderson, dispute this paleoenvironmental evidence and argue for human colonization much later, around A.D. 800. On Mo'orea Island in Tahiti, Dana Lepofsky and her colleagues have recently recovered coconut remains from a deeply stratified sequence in the interior of Opunohu Valley. The coconuts were identified as domestic, and thus associated with human presence, and dated to about A.D. 650. This is currently the earliest evidence for human colonization of Tahiti. More fieldwork, based on

geologic and geomorphic considerations, may uncover early, perhaps deeply buried deposits in the islands.

Early archaeological assemblages have been excavated from the Maupiti burial ground, the waterlogged village of Vaito'otia-Fa'ahia on Huahine, and the Vaihi site on Ra'iatea. As Sinoto has shown, these sites share several classes of artifacts, which he has designated "Archaic East Polynesian culture." *Radiocarbon dating places these assemblages between about A.D. 800 and 1000. The similarities Sinoto identified in artifacts probably resulted from extensive interaction over the central East Polynesian region (including at least the Cook Islands, Tahiti, and the Marquesas), and not from a colonizing migration. Hawaii and *Easter Island do not appear to share the artifact classes Sinoto saw as diagnostic of Archaic East Polynesian culture. The earliest assemblages in *New Zealand, however, share many of the diagnostic forms, suggesting that central East Polynesia (Cooks-Tahiti-Marquesas) was a source for its colonization, perhaps around A.D. 800 to 1000.

In sum, the paleoenvironmental clues from the region suggest that the earliest sites in Tahiti have yet to be discovered. If found, the earliest materials in Tahiti might date to approximately 500 B.C. The Archaic East Polynesian assemblages seem to provide evidence for interisland contacts centuries after the region had been colonized.

Settlement Patterns and Religious Architecture. Roger Green pioneered *settlement pattern analysis in the Opunohu Valley on Mo'orea. Through field research, he and his colleagues documented a dispersed pattern of domestic complexes, with concentrations in ecologically focal coastal and inland zones. Radiocarbon dates suggest that much of the structural evidence is late in prehistory, dating from the twelfth or thirteenth century to historic times. Green links the Opunohu field evidence with ethnohistorical documentation and reconstructs aspects of social and political organization for the valley.

Emory's early survey recorded a variety of architectural forms in religious structures *(marae)*. These sites are numerous, and some have been the focus of recent restoration work. The *marae* are rectangular courts formed by paving and a low enclosing wall. At one end of the court is a stone platform with upright slabs associated with deities. Emory showed stylistic variability in the *marae* forms between the Windward (Tahiti and Mo'orea) and Leeward Islands, as well as between coastal and inland sites. He saw similarities between Tahitian *marae* and religious sites in Hawaii and the Tuamotu Islands. In addition, Emory recorded other specialized structural forms identified with ethnohistorical sources, including council platforms (for chiefly meetings) and archery platforms.

Future Research. Recent and continuing archaeological research in the Society Islands has placed new emphasis on paleoenvironmental study. This focus will prove important in understanding environmental change in the recent past as well as in reconstructing landscape changes that may conceal the earliest periods of Tahiti's prehistory (see Paleoenvironmental Reconstruction).

[See also PACIFIC ISLANDS: SETTLEMENT OF POLYNESIA; PACIFIC ISLANDS CHIEFDOMS.]

■ Kenneth P. Emory, *Stone Remains in the Society Islands* (1933). Kenneth P. Emory and Yoshihiko H. Sinoto, "Eastern Polynesian Burials at Maupiti," *Journal of the Polynesian Society* 73 (1964): 143–160. Roger C. Green, K. Green, R. Rappaport, A. Rappaport, and J. Davidson, *Archaeology on the Island of Mo'orea, French Polynesia* (1967). Yoshihiko H. Sinoto and Patrick C. McCoy, "Report on the

Preliminary Excavation of an Early Habitation Site on Huahine, Society Islands," *Journal de la Societe des Oceanistes* 31 (1975): 143–186. Kenneth P. Emory, "The Societies," in *The Prehistory of Polynesia*, ed. J. D. Jennings (1979), pp. 200–201. Patrick V. Kirch, "Rethinking East Polynesian Prehistory," *Journal of the Polynesian Society* 95 (1986): 9–40. Dana Lepofsky, Hugh Harries, and Marimari Kellum, "Early Coconuts on Mo'orea Island, French Polynesia," *Journal of the Polynesian Society* 101 (1992): 299–308.

Terry L. Hunt

SOMERSET LEVELS. The Somerset Levels, low-lying wetlands in the southwest of Britain, have been recognized as archaeologically rich since the discovery of the Iron Age Glastonbury Village a century ago. Today, their significance is seen to lie in the combination of archaeological and paleoenvironmental evidence and the presence of organic materials, especially wood, dating from about 4000 B.C. to 1000 A.D., and preserved due to the waterlogged peats that surround them.

Analysis of stratified pollen, beetles, macroscopic plant remains, and structural wood indicates that when the Sweet Track, the earliest known trackway, was built across the Somerset Levels, the surrounding dryland carried thick deciduous forest and the wetland was a dense reed swamp with occasional birch and willow. People felled dryland trees such as oak, elm, ash, lime, and hazel, then split and trimmed the timber to build a raised walkway from the dryland shore to an island in the marsh, a distance of about 1 to 2 miles (2 km). Only stone and wooden tools were available for this task, and the preservation of the Sweet Track enables us to appreciate the woodworking and engineering skills of the builders. Dendrochronology has dated the structure to 3806 B.C., early in the British Neolithic. Associated artifacts such as a jadeite axe brought from overseas and finely made round-based pottery belong within ten years of this date.

From about one thousand years later, hurdles (wattlework) are found. Panels were woven from long, thin, straight stems of hazelwood and laid flat over soft, wet ground to provide safe passage. Occasional long hurdle-built trackways, using many thousands of rods to weave the panels, are indicative of managed coppiced woodland on the dry ground. The hurdles provide direct evidence for a method of construction that was often used but rarely survives on dry ground.

By the later first millennium B.C. much of the wetland swamp had evolved into acid raised bog, with a northeastern zone of richer vegetation and open water. Here two villages developed, that of Glastonbury built on an artificial island out in the water and that of Meare just off the edge of a large natural island.

These Iron Age villages have an exceptionally rich material culture, preserved in the wetland context. There is evidence for manufacture in wood, metal, bone, and antler, for spinning and weaving, and for the production of colorful, intricate glass beads. Remains of food abound, ranging from the common cereals, legumes, and domestic animals of the period to fish, wildfowl, and mammals from the wetlands. Species such as beaver and white-tailed sea eagle were caught as much for fur and feather as for meat.

Glastonbury and Meare provide a counterbalance to dryland evidence, enhancing our understanding of the Iron Age just as the Sweet Track broadens the Neolithic picture.

[*See also* BRITISH ISLES: PREHISTORY OF THE BRITISH ISLES; EUROPE, *articles on* THE EUROPEAN NEOLITHIC PERIOD, THE EUROPEAN IRON AGE.]

■ Bryony Coles and John Coles, *Sweet Track to Glastonbury* (1986). John Coles and Bryony Coles, *Prehistory of the Somerset Levels* (1990). John Coles and Stephen Minnitt, *Industrious and Fairly Civilized: The Glastonbury Lake Village* (1995).

Bryony Coles

SOURCING ARCHAEOLOGICAL MATERIALS. Archaeologists have long been intrigued by artifacts of unusual or exotic material that have clearly originated in regions outside the sites and areas that they are studying. John Evans, in his classic volume, *The Ancient Stone Implements, Weapons, and Ornaments of Great Britain* (New York, 1872) remarked that some chipped stone tools at "manufactories of flint implements . . . were produced, not for immediate use by those who made them, but to be bartered away for some other commodities" (71). In recent decades, a variety of archaeometric techniques have been used to study the procurement and trade of artifacts made of distinctive raw materials. This research has led to a vast literature on the sourcing of artifacts and on the use of these data in examining long-distance exchange and cultural interaction.

In some cases, the sourcing of a material can be done visually. In England and western Europe, distribution maps have been developed for stone axes, the sources of which can be visually distinguished based on the geological characteristics or color of chert or other raw material. Some raw materials, such as the pink and white-striped Alibates chert of the Texas Panhandle, are so distinctive that they can be identified with accuracy, solely by visual identification, over broad areas.

However, in most instances, artifacts of chert, obsidian, jade, copper, steatite, pottery, marble, amber, and other materials have been more precisely sourced using scientific techniques. Petrographic thin-section studies are sometimes sufficient, and have been used for over one hundred years to identify minerals in pottery or stone that might be linked to specific sources. Such studies can often confirm (or invalidate) visual identifications, as has been done successfully in studies of the British Neolithic stone axe trade. In many cases, physico-chemical trace-element analyses are required when petrographic characterization is inconclusive. For example, the sourcing of the quartzite used in the 720-ton Colossi of Memnon of eighteenth-dynasty Egypt was first attempted using petrography. Sources could not be adequately distinguished, and so neutron activation analysis was used (NAA: a technique in which the sample is powdered, irradiated, and trace elements measured via the decay of radioactive isotopes). This linked the Colossi quartzites, and those of other monuments, to their ancient quarry sources along the Nile.

NAA was among the earliest techniques from nuclear chemistry used to do source analysis of ceramics, notably in the research of E. V. Sayre beginning in the late 1950s. I. Perlman and F. Asaro began to apply improved neutron activation techniques to studies of ceramic provenience in the Mediterranean and Egypt in the late 1960s.

Undoubtedly the greatest emphasis on sourcing has involved obsidian. Obsidian is a volcanic glass that was widely used by prehistoric peoples, and was part of long-distance trade as early as the Upper Paleolithic. It was also widely distributed among Mediterranean and Mesoamerican cultures. J. R. Cann and Colin Renfrew published a seminal paper on obsidian sourcing in 1964. They used optical spectrography to identify the ratios of rare trace minerals, in this case barium and zirconium, in parts-per-million. These led to the recognition of discrete obsidian clusters that could be linked to geologic sources. This technique in its updated form is known as optical emission spectrometry (OES); electrons are electrically excited and the different wavelengths of emitted light can be analyzed for trace elements.

In Mesoamerica, the first efforts at sourcing obsidian were made by J. R. Weaver and Fred H. Stross in 1965. They used the x-ray fluorescence technique (XRF) to "fingerprint" obsidian artifacts and noted the striking trace-element differences among them (XRF irradiates a sample with x-ray beams; once the beam is off, the electrons on the sample surface emit wavelengths of fluorescent light that can be identified as to specific trace elements). Many subsequent scholars have been able to trace the distribution of several different types of obsidian across Mesoamerica, linking artifacts to their geologic sources, and shedding much light on long-distance trade among the ancient cultures of that region. The main techniques currently being used, in the western United States as well as Mesoamerica, include NAA and XRF. In the early 1990s, a "Precise XRF" was introduced through the Lawrence Berkeley Laboratory; it yields precision trace-element data averaging 2.3 percent. It has been applied to archaeological obsidian occurring in Texas (where there are no outcrops of artifact-quality obsidian), and has identified artifacts from sources as distant as Malad, Idaho, and central Mexico. It has also allowed more precision in recognizing closely spaced New Mexico outcrops. Another technique, called PIXE (proton-induced x-ray emission), is being used by other obsidian analysts; while it uses a proton beam from a Van de Graaff accelerator to excite a sample, in other ways it is similar to NAA and XRF.

Of concern in carrying out trace-element research has been both the cost of analysis and whether or not it is destructive (i.e., the artifact has to be destroyed, whole or in part, for analysis). NAA is a destructive technique and is generally much more expensive than XRF, which is usually non-destructive.

These, and other trace-element techniques, provide detailed chemical profiles of artifacts, often allowing archaeologists to identify the specific source from which the artifacts are derived. In most cases, successful sourcing projects are long-term, as it is critical that raw material sources are carefully identified, and any trace-element variability within sources be recognized. For example, obsidian sources are generally rather homogenous and discrete from one another in their trace-element patterns; however, several studies have identified intrasource trace-element variability at some source locations. However, most of this research suggests that trace-element sourcing is still accurate in distinguishing specific obsidian outcrops.

Trace element analysis of chert is another matter. While chert clusters of distinctive chemical character might be identified through NAA, chert sources, which are sedimentary in origin, are generally much more broadly distributed and links to specific outcrops are extremely difficult.

[See also ARCHAEOMETRY; MATERIALS, ANALYSIS OF; TRADE, PREHISTORIC, articles on PREHISTORIC AXE TRADE, PREHISTORIC OBSIDIAN TRADE, PREHISTORIC AMBER TRADE.]

■ R. F. Heizer, F. Stross, T. R. Hester, A. Albee, I. Perlman, F. Asaro, and H. Bowman, "The Colossi of Memnon Revisited," Science 182 (1973): 1219–1225. Timothy K. Earle and Jonathan E. Ericson, Exchange Systems in Prehistory (1977). Zui Goffer, Archaeological Chemistry: A Sourcebook on the Applications of Chemistry to Archaeology (1980). Richard E. Hughes, ed., Obsidian Studies in the Great Basin 34 (1984): 14–21. Colin Renfrew and Paul Bahn, Archaeology: Theories, Methods and Practices (1991). Robert D. Giauque, Frank Asaro, Fred H. Stross, and Thomas R. Hester, "High Precision Non-Destructive X-Ray Fluorescence Method Applicable to Establishing the Provenance of Obsidian Artifacts," X-Ray Spectrometry 22 (1993): 44–53.

Thomas R. Hester

SOUTH AMERICA

OVERVIEW

When Pizarro encountered the Inca in 1532, he confronted one of the great civilizations of the New World. The Inca civilization was the culmination of at least 12,000 years of human occupation in South America. The articles in this section describe many aspects of cultural development on this continent, beginning with the earliest sites of Monte Verde in Chile and Pedra Furada in Brazil, which may represent the earliest evidence of human occupation anywhere in the Americas.

The earliest cultural period in South America is known as the Lithic Stage, during which human populations were highly mobile and lived by hunting, fishing, and gathering. By 5000 B.C. there was some use of domesticated plants and animals, marking the beginning of the Archaic way of life. During the Archaic one sees not only the use of domesticated plants but also the introduction of pottery, possibly the earliest in the Amazon, and the beginning of semipermanent villages. By the end of the Archaic, agriculture was a way of life in some areas, such as the Andean highlands, where people lived in permanent villages with ceremonial architecture.

Over the next 3,000 years South American society became increasingly complex while population grew considerably. On the Peruvian coast huge ceremonial centers appeared. In the interior and on the coast powerful chiefdoms and early states, such as Chavín, *Nasca, and *Moche, developed. By the middle of the first millennium the states of *Wari and *Tiwanaku controlled the central Andes and beyond. There is ample evidence of warfare in many parts of South America, and by A.D. 1000 the central Andes was dominated by a number of small regional states. In A.D. 1400 the *Inca civilization rose to power and eventually controlled territory from Ecuador to central Chile. Pizarro and his army fought the Inca for a generation until the Inca fell, weakened by disease.

Charlotte Beck

INTRODUCTION

The European expansion into the Americas that began in the late fifteenth century A.D. represents one of the most dramatic biological and cultural dramas of human history. The European settlers did not comprehend the historical depth or contemporary diversity of the cultures in the areas that they conquered. The vast South American continent, characterized by desert coasts, upland savannas, high mountain chains, and a massive tropical forest, contained thousands of peoples and cultures at the time of European contact. Most of these cultures have since vanished, and the vast majority of surviving cultures have been enculturated. The science of archaeology remains our only means to understand the indigenous cultures of prehistoric South America.

The Earliest Inhabitants. There is little dispute among archaeologists that the first migrants in North America, known as Paleo-Indians, arrived from northeastern Asia by at least 10,000 B.C., and there is consensus that humans rapidly reached the southernmost tip of South America by at least 9000 B.C. While the geographical origin of the first Americans is not disputed, the age of the first migrations is highly controversial. There are two opposing theories among serious scholars. On one side, some Paleo-Indian specialists maintain that the earliest documented human occupation in the Americas is the Clovis culture. Clovis dates to no earlier than 10,000 B.C. or so, a time after the last glaciation. Other specialists, in contrast, argue that glacial-age humans have been in the Americas from as early as 40,000 B.C., or even earlier.

The possible evidence for a glacial-age occupation in the New World includes several sites in South America. The site of *Monte Verde in Chile has yielded C14 dates as early as 31,000 B.C. At Pedra Furada in Brazil, excavators report dates as early as 40,000 B.C. Although compelling, these early dates remain hypothetical and unproven. At present, the evidence suggests that a pre-Clovis occupation no earlier than 13,000 B.C. remains the best candidate for the original migrants to the Americas.

The Lithic Stage. The term "Lithic Stage" is used to refer to the cultures of the first post-glacial hunters and collectors in South America. This lifeway continued until around 5000 B.C. when people adopted the intensive use of domesticated plants and animals. During the Lithic Stage, people lived in relatively small, mobile groups and subsisted on hunting, fishing, and plant collecting. Over millennia, the intensive and continual use of wild plants and animals eventually led to genetic changes in some of these species and ultimately to their domestication by human groups. Throughout South America, there are distinct stone tool traditions of the Lithic Stage, such as the Paijan, the "Fluted Fishtail" and the like, that reflect localized adaptations to the diverse habitats of the continent.

The Archaic Stage (ca. 5000 to 2000 B.C.) Around the sixth millennium B.C., the Lithic Stage lifeways were gradually replaced with those of the Archaic, characterized by the appearance of semipermanent houses, domestication of plants and animals, development of pottery technology, and the beginnings of village life. Hunting and collecting of wild plants were still the dominant economic activities, but population increases combined with the availability of domesticated plants and animals promoted the contraction of the nomadic seasonal rounds and favored more sedentary lifeways. The sites of Paloma and Chilca I, dated to ca. 4500 to 2500 B.C., on the Peruvian coast typify the changes underway in the Archaic. At Paloma, the original Late Lithic/Early Archaic temporary camps gradually grew into a permanent village. People lived in circular, cane-roofed houses. They intensively exploited the sea: mollusks, fish, sea birds, and mammals were complemented with smaller quantities of domesticated plants such as beans and squash.

During the Late Archaic, cultivated plants and marine resources provided the bulk of the diet on the Pacific coast.

Analysis of kitchen refuse from the Late Archaic site of El Paraiso (1800–1500 B.C.) in central Peru has identified squashes, beans, peppers, and fruits, as the major cultigens. People built impressive ceremonial centers at sites such as El Paraiso and Aspero on the Peruvian coast, whereas in the Andean highlands, settlements in the Kotosh tradition had multiroomed ceremonial centers. By the end of the Archaic stage, a stable agricultural system utilized by people living in permanent villages with ceremonial architecture has become the dominant lifeway of Andean South America.

The Rise of Complex Society (2000–600 B.C.). The origins of civilization were found in the profound changes that occurred in several areas of human life in South America. Political and economic organization became much more complex and hierarchical with an ever-increasing distinction between social groups. Economies became increasingly dependent upon stable, intensive agricultural systems and human-altered environments. Population sizes dramatically increased.

On the Peruvian coast, people built huge ceremonial centers such as *Sechin Alto, Huaca de los Reyes, and La Florida. Sechin Alto in the Casma Valley was perhaps the largest architectural monument in the Americas at this time. The site had an enormous "U"-shaped building that enclosed plazas, sunken courts, and other stone structures. Macabre stone stelae or carvings along the walls of Cerro Sechin, a slightly younger site in the region, depict decapitated humans, apparent war captives, and human trophy heads. It appears that another concomitant of the rise of civilization in South America included aggression between communities.

In the Andean highlands, the earlier Kotosh tradition became much more elaborate in some areas and apparently disappeared in others where it was replaced by new architectural styles. In the Lake Titicaca Basin in the south-central Andes, the cultures of Chiripa and Qaluyu developed on the south and north sites of the lake respectively. From ca. 1300 to 500 B.C., Chiripa grew from a small village into a regionally important political and economic center. The people at Chiripa constructed a stone-faced platform mound with an interior sunken court surrounded by masonry structures. By 500 B.C., the Qaluyu peoples had likewise built an elaborate civic and ceremonial center. Qaluyu and Chiripa artisans also produced beautiful ceramic objects and stone stelae.

Early Andean States and Empires (400 B.C. to A.D. 1000) The first millennium B.C. witnessed the general development of powerful chiefdoms and states in western South America. The *Chavín culture, located over 1.9 miles (3 km) above sea level in the eastern flanks of the Cordillera, represents the first art style to expand beyond a single region. For years, Chavín was considered to be the origin of Andean civilization. We now know that Chavín was first occupied around 800 B.C., a date later than cultures such as Sechín on the coast. The site of Chavín itself reached an architectural peak around 300 B.C. with the construction of U-shaped temple buildings, sunken ceremonial courts, and subterranean galleries. The pan-Andean Chavín art style is striking with motifs such as raptorial birds, felines, front-faced staff gods, and serpents. Chavín art, and of more importance the social and political ideas that lay behind it, was a catalyst for the development of the early states throughout western South America.

Farther to the south, the Valley of Nazca is famous for its large ground drawings in the coastal desert plain. The *Nasca lines were made by removing the darker surface layers to expose the lighter subsoils. Built around A.D. 1 to 700 coincident with the development of the *Nazca state, they depict animal and geometric motifs and can reach lengths of 12.4 miles (20 km) or more. The nature and purpose of the lines remain controversial. Some scholars have proposed that the lines correspond to astronomical alignments. Others see the lines as ceremonial roads leading to pilgrimage and political centers in the valley or as part of a pan-Andean set of religious beliefs designed to insure agricultural success.

Around A.D. 300 to 700 in the Moche Valley in northern Peru, two huge pyramid structures were built at the site of Cerro Blanco, the capital of the multivalley Moche state. Moche ceramic art is famous, depicting animals, humans, and fantastic beings. Recent interpretations suggest that this art revolved around a limited number of themes that were used to illustrate epic tales of Moche history. Moche rulers were buried in elaborate tombs, the most famous one being that of *Sipan located north of the Moche Valley (see Moche Culture).

The period from approximately A.D. 400 to 600 marked a dramatic turning point for human civilization in western South America. Two states, known as Wari and Tiwanaku, developed political and economic organizations of such magnitude that they dominated the entire central Andes and beyond. The influence of these two states was so profound that they can justifiably be called empires in the classic sense of the term.

The capital of Tiwanaku is located in the southern Lake Titicaca Basin. At over 12,450 feet (3800 m) above sea level, Tiwanaku ranks as one of the highest ancient imperial capitals in the world. The site was founded around 400 B.C. as a modest village. By A.D. 500, Tiwanaku influence and control extended over 135,150 square miles (350,000 sq km), an area larger than modern Great Britain. During its peak, the capital of Tiwanaku boasted a huge, multiplatformed, stone-faced pyramid, cut stone enclosures, elite residences, exquisitely decorated buildings, a system of subterranean canals, and at least 1.5 square miles (4 sq km) of commoner residential housing. The Tiwanaku imperial economy was based upon the intensive utilization of an agricultural technique known as raised fields, camelid pastoralism, terrace agriculture, an extensive exchange and colonial system, and the organization of large numbers of laborers for state projects. There was a rigid social and political hierarchy expressed in elaborate art and architectural styles.

Sometime around A.D. 1100, Tiwanaku collapsed as an imperial state. The cause or causes of Tiwanaku collapse remain unknown, but climatic changes, provincial revolts, internal political dissension, and invasion by foreigners have all been suggested.

The northern counterpart of Tiwanaku is the *Wari state, located in the central Andean highlands near the town of Ayacucho. Following a modest period of growth as a small settlement, Wari emerged as an expansive state around A.D. 600 spreading its control and influence over a huge area. The Wari capital covers several square kilometers graced by multistoried gallery structures and patio complexes. Beautifully cut stone monuments and finely decorated buildings were built throughout the city.

The Wari imperial economy was structurally similar to Tiwanaku, relying on intensive agriculture, pastoralism, an extensive exchange and colonial system, and the organization of large numbers of laborers for state projects. Unlike Tiwanaku, the Wari peoples relied upon maize agriculture

and did not utilize raised fields. The Wari state also acquired raw materials, such as obsidian and copper, and worked these into valued commodities. They established a number of planned, colonial settlements throughout the central Andes, such as the site of Pikillaqta near modern Cuzco. The establishment of Wari centers in a region was often paralleled by substantial changes in the local culture. In the Carhuarazo Valley near Ayacucho, for instance, recent research has demonstrated that Wari control coincided with the abandonment of local settlements, the construction of roads and bridges, the building of new agricultural terraces, and a new focus on intensive, irrigated maize agriculture.

By A.D. 900, the Wari empire collapsed, curiously paralleling the growth and decline of Tiwanaku. As with its southern counterpart, the cause of Wari decline is not fully known.

The Fluorescence of Amazonian Culture. The traditional view of indigenous Amazonian culture and prehistory was developed by scholars a generation ago. This view assumed a relatively homogeneous biotic community that could not support complex societies. Furthermore, scholars argued that the indigenous peoples of the Amazon had developed an ecological balance with the environment as a result of millennia of natural selection. Finally, they argued that the cultures encountered by the Europeans were typical of the earlier prehistoric cultures.

Recent research in the Amazon has challenged this traditional view. Crude pottery, perhaps the earliest on the continent, has been discovered in the Brazilian Amazon. Millennia later, the elaborate Marajoara culture, located at the mouth of the Amazon, flourished between A.D. 400 and 1300. Marajoara peoples built a society with internal social rankings, intensive agriculture, sophisticated artistic traditions, and mounded settlements. Similar cultures are found throughout the Amazon suggesting a prehistoric cultural complexity far greater than previously imagined. By the time of European contact, the complex Amazonian cultures had collapsed and developed into the shifting agricultural communities typical of the recent past.

Late Andean Regional States and Empire. The collapse of Tiwanaku and Wari at the end of the first millennium A.D. ushered in a new cultural landscape characterized by a variety of smaller state societies. According to the Inca historians, this time period was called the auca runa, or "time of the warriors." Although evidence of warfare is found in much earlier periods, the first centuries of the second millennium A.D. was a time of generalized conflict for most of the Central Andean highlands. Many sites are built on hilltops surrounded by defensive walls, such as the mountainous regions in the north and south-central highlands. In other areas such as the Titicaca Basin, people lived in the lower valleys and constructed massive hilltop refuges for use in times of danger.

The central Andes was home to a number of regional states. The capital of the largest was located near the town of Trujillo in the northern coast of Peru. Known as the Kingdom of Chimor with its capital at *Chan Chan, this state controlled a territory stretching over 620 miles (1,000 km) up the Pacific watershed. The city of Chan Chan was huge, covering 3.7 square miles (6 sq km), and its adobe construction has survived remarkably well in the dry desert climate. About ten monumental compounds were built in this desert city to serve the nobility. These walled ciudadelas or "little cities" are several hundred meters on a side and contained burial platforms, storerooms, elite residences, large wells for water, and administrative buildings. Surrounding the enclosures are vast areas of commoner housing and craft workshops.

The Inca Empire. The empire of Tawantinsuyu or "The Land of the Four Quarters," also known as the Inca Empire, represents one of the great civilizations of the ancient world. At the time of the arrival of the Spaniards in 1532, Tawantinsuyu covered the territories of both the earlier Tiwanaku and Wari Empires and beyond, up and down the Andean spine.

The Inca expanded out of their home in *Cuzco during the Auca Runa, most likely taking advantage of internecine conflict of the time. With difficulty, they conquered the great Kingdom of Chimor and the rich Titicaca Basin, incorporating tens of thousands of new subjects. Over time, the Inca controlled territories in modern Ecuador to the north, and south to central Chile. The famous settlement of *Machu Picchu, for instance, represents an ambitious expansion into the rich forests to the east.

The basis of the Inca imperial economy was a labor tax known as the mit'a. The mit'a was the legal obligation of all households to provide labor to the imperial authorities for the military, agricultural projects, road and bridge building, weaving, and brewing chica or maize beer. Order was maintained by an efficient military organization. At the time of Pizarro's landing in northern Peru, several large armies were in the field composed of thousands of troops. These armies were able to move about the empire on the famous Inca road and bridge system that spanned the entire Andes. In the 1530s, the Inca state was reeling from European diseases and civil war when Pizarro and his native allies launched their attack against Cuzco. After a generation of resistance by the remaining Inca subjects, the Spanish empire firmly established itself as the predominant power in South America.

[*See also* ANDEAN PRE-INCA CIVILIZATIONS, RISE OF; CHIMU STATE; INCA CIVILIZATION; MOUNDS OF THE AMAZON; SOUTH AMERICA, ORIGINS OF FOOD PRODUCTION IN; VALDIVIA CULTURE.]

■ Luis G. Lumbreras, *The Peoples and Cultures of Ancient Peru* (1974). John Hyslop, *Inka Settlement Planning* (1990). Thomas F. Lynch, "Glacial-Age Man in South America? A Critical Review," *American Antiquity*, 55:(1) (1990). Ann Curtenius Roosevelt, *Moundbuilders of the Amazon* (1991). Richard Burger, *Chavín and the Origins of Andean Civilization* (1992). Michael Moseley, *The Incas and Their Ancestors* (1992). Richard F. Townsend, *The Ancient Americas: Art from Sacred Landscapes* (1992).

Charles Stanish

EARLY PREHISTORY OF SOUTH AMERICA

The early prehistory of South America spans from 15,000 to 4,000 B.P. and can be divided into two major periods: Paleo-Indian (15,000–10,000 B.P.) and the Preceramic (or Archaic, 10,000–4,000 B.P.). While these dates are generally valid for most of the continent, in some areas, such as northwestern South America, the Preceramic ends as early as 5,000 B.P., whereas in southern Patagonia, a Preceramic way of life persisted among the ethnographically known foragers such as the Ona and Selk'nam until the end of the nineteenth century. Therefore, it is useful to remember that these terms imply both chronology and lifestyle.

The early prehistory of South America can be organized around three major themes: the entry of humans into the continent; the process of adaptive radiation by hunter-gatherers into different ecological zones; and the emergence of early forms of social complexity within the context of sedentarization and the domestication of indigenous plants and animals.

Human Entry into the Continent. It is generally accepted that the South American continent was occupied by humans no earlier than 15,000 B.P., and possibly no earlier than 13,000–12,000 B.P., but this is a continuing controversy. While a number of sites dating to before 15,000 B.P. have been reported, none has gained widespread acceptance as a valid indicator of early human presence on the continent. The most famous of these sites is Pedra Furada, a rock shelter in northeastern Brazil, with reported dates ranging from 17,000 to 40,000 B.P. The controversy surrounding this site stems from problems similar to those said to exist at other candidates for pre-15,000 B.P. occupations, such as *Monte Verde in southern Chile, Pikimachay in the central Peruvian Andes, and other sites in eastern Brazil such as Esperança Cave and Toca do Sitio do Meio. These include questions about the integrity of site stratigraphy, the origin of the carbonized wood or other materials used to date the reputed human occupation, and finally, skepticism as to whether the artifacts and features at the site are of indisputable human origin.

Sites said to date between 13,000 and 11,000 B.P. are not numerous but are widespread across the continent, and include Taima-Taima in northern Venezuela (11,800 B.P.), Tibitó in Colombia (11,700 B.P.), Los Toldos (12,600 B.P.) in southern Argentina, and Quereo (11,100 B.P.), Cueva del Medio (10,900 B.P.), Tres Arroyos (11,800 B.P.), and Cueva Lago Sophia (11,509 B.P.) in southern Chile. These sites contain a mixture of unifacial and bifacial tools, features such as hearths and other structures, and a wide range of faunal species, including extinct (horse, mastodon, armadillo, and sloth) as well as extant (guanaco, deer, and small mammals) species. One of the most important of these sites is Monte Verde, which is said to contain evidence of wooden log structures, hearths, bifacial and unifacial tools, and the remains of mastodon.

Although much remains to be learned, three observations are clear: (1) there are two distinct routes of entry, one moving down the Pacific coast and the other moving along the Atlantic coast, and humans probably reached the tip of the continent no later than 10,000 B.P.; (2) subsistence adaptations were generalized and local in character, and this appears to be the major cause of observed diversity in stone tool technology in early South America; and (3) early population sizes were very small and the groups were highly mobile; consequently, population growth through the Paleo-Indian period was slow.

Adaptive Radiation and Dispersal. Around 10,000 B.P., human populations began to move into new ecological zones. The causes of this movement are still unclear, but they appear to be related to increasing population growth and new access to significant plant and animal species following the end of the glacial epoch. Ecological zones colonized at this time include the higher elevations of western flanks of the Andes; the major river drainages leading into the interior of the continent, such as the Orinoco, Amazon, and the Parana; and finally, the high altiplano that lies between the two cordillera of the Andes and which runs from northwestern Argentina to southern Colombia. Subsistence and settlement in the early Preceramic (10,000–7,000 B.P.) was generally characterized by broad-spectrum hunting and foraging and decreasing residential mobility through time. Examples of this trend include the Las Vegas Complex of the Ecuadorian littoral, which was based upon the exploitation of fish, shellfish, deer, and small mammals; the Itaparica tradition of the tropical forests of central Brazil, which focused upon deer, tapir, anteater, lizard, fish, fruits, and especially palm; a central Andean highland tradition characterized by a mixed hunting strategy focused upon deer, vicuña, guanaco, as well as some plant use; the Chinchorro Complex of far southern Peru and northern Chile, which was based upon a complex mix of marine resources and numerous others.

Yet another major trend observed during this period was the increasing experimentation with plants and animals destined to be major subsistence domesticates, such as the gourd, squash, potato and the other tubers, palm, avocado, peanut, chili pepper, beans, maize, and the Andean camelids. Some of these species were probably cultivated as early as 8,000 B.P., like gourd and squash. However, none of these species became of critical economic importance until after 7,000 years ago, and in some instances, much later.

Sedentarization, Domestication, and Early Complexity. The late Preceramic (7,000–4,000 B.P.) throughout much of South America witnessed a number of significant changes in adaptive strategy and cultural complexity. As people became more sedentary, human populations grew at both the local and the regional levels, and in some areas, this led to significant resource shortfalls. One response was to intensify the use of particular resources in combination with changes in technology that facilitated this intensification. An area in which this happened was the central coast of Peru during the Cotton Preceramic (4,500–4,000 B.P.). Peoples of this period used domesticated cotton to produce fine nets, which were used to catch prodigious quantities of anchovy well beyond subsistence requirements. Much of this surplus was used to support the construction of monumental architecture at sites such as El Paraíso and Aspero. Because of the scale of architecture, their probable public use, and method of construction, these sites, some archaeologist have concluded, reflect early forms of social hierarchy. If true, these are the earliest true complex societies in South America. Elsewhere, such as on the south-central Andean littoral, Patagonia, and Tierra del Fuego, this form of resource intensification did not lead to the development of social complexity.

Another response to resource shortfalls was to turn to domestication. This was successful in the Andean highlands, for example, and it now seems likely that the Andean camelids were domesticated independently in four places: the Junín puna (6,000 B.P.), the highlands of the Osmore basin (4,400 B.P.), the high deserts of northern Chile (4,000 B.P.), and the northwestern Argentine puna (4,500 B.P.). Reliance upon other domesticates was important in Ecuador (maize) by 5,000 B.P. and in Amazonian and central Brazil (manioc, palm) after 4,000 B.P.

By 4,000 B.P., emergent forms of social complexity appeared in a number of regions of South America, including the central Peruvian littoral and highlands, the Lake Titicaca basin, the Amazon basin, and the riverine lowlands and littoral of western Ecuador.

[See also SOUTH AMERICA, ORIGINS OF FOOD PRODUCTION IN.]

■ Michael J. Moseley, *The Maritime Foundations of Andean Civilization* (1975). John W. Rick, *Prehistoric Hunters of the High Andes* (1980). Pedro I. Schmitz, "Prehistoric Hunters and Gatherers of Brazil," *Journal of World Prehistory* 1 (1987): 53–126. Mark Aldenderfer, "The Archaic Period in the South-Central Andes," *Journal of World Prehistory* 3 (1989): 117–158. Thomas F. Lynch, "Glacial-Age Man in South America? A Critical Review," *American Antiquity* 55 (1990): 12–36. Jeffrey Quilter, "Late Preceramic Peru," *Journal of World Prehistory* 5 (1991): 387–438. T. Dillehay, G. Calderon, G. Politis, and M. Beltrao, "Earliest Hunter-Gatherers of South America," *Journal of World Prehistory* 6 (1992): 145–204. Mark Aldenderfer, *Montane Foragers: Asana and the South-Central Andean Archaic* (1995).

Mark Aldenderfer

THE RISE OF COMPLEX SOCIETIES IN SOUTH AMERICA

Archaeologically, South America can be divided into four principle areas: the central Andes (coastal and highland Peru); the northern Andes (western portion of Ecuador and Colombia); the southern Andes (western Bolivia, northern Chile and northern Argentina); and lowland South America (remainder of the continent). Although some chiefdoms appeared in lowland South America, the most complex prehistoric societies, including state-level organizations, arose in the central, northern, and southern Andes.

Humans have been present in South America for at least 13,000 years. For the first several thousand years, they followed an egalitarian foraging way of life, hunting large and small terrestrial animals, gathering terrestrial plants, and harvesting shellfish, fish, and aquatic mammals from marine and freshwater sources.

Central Andes. By about 3000 B.C. in the central Andes, small, sedentary preceramic villages were established along the coast of Peru. The main subsistence base for these sites was marine fish and shellfish supplemented by crops such as beans, squash, peppers, and avocados—presumably grown using floodplain farming techniques within nearby coastal rivers. A few of these sites exhibit signs of early social complexity, reflected in the construction of moderate-sized stone mounds. The best known is the central-coast site of Aspero which contains seven mounds, twined textiles, and numerous unfired clay figurines, often found in burial contexts.

Between 2500 and 2000 B.C., substantial preceramic sites such as Kotosh and La Galgada also appeared in the Peruvian north-central highlands. These sites are characterized by numerous small ceremonial chambers that contain central hearths vented by horizontal subfloor flues. These ceremonial chambers formed the core element of a widespread religious belief system, known as the Kotosh Religious Tradition, that persisted for the next 1,500 years.

From 2200 to 1100 B.C., the north and central Peruvian coast witnessed a dramatic change in settlement pattern accompanied by significant population growth. With the introduction of irrigation agriculture, major human settlement shifted from the coastline to strategic points 6 to 12 miles (10–20 km) inland where canal intakes were located. Along with irrigation agriculture came true woven textiles that gradually replaced the twined textiles of preceramic times. Pottery making was also introduced, an idea possibly derived from earlier pottery centers in the northern Andes. Most characteristic, however, is the large monumental architecture of the period, consisting of stone-faced platform mounds, which are often U-shaped, accompanied by rectangular and circular plazas. It is the scale and carefully planned nature of these constructions, such as those at *Sechin Alto and Pampa de las Llamas-Moxeke, that lead some scholars to conclude that stratified societies existed by this time.

During the first millennium B.C. the *Chavin culture appeared in the north-central highlands of Peru. The Chavin culture seems to be an amalgamation of ideas derived from earlier coastal, highland, and tropical forest cultures. Centered around the type site of *Chavin de Huantar, this culture reached its maximum extent between 400 and 200 B.C. Most notable is the art style of the culture depicted on stone sculpture, ceramics, gold artifacts, and textiles. The existence of stratified societies is inferred from the discovery of special tombs containing rare and exotic goods. The Chavin culture was perhaps the first widespread horizon style in Peru, but recent fieldwork points to a more restricted areal extent for this culture than previously postulated. The contemporaneous Paracas culture of the Peruvian south coast was partially influenced by the Chavin culture. However, the Paracas culture is most noted for its own accomplishments—fine embroidered textiles that accompanied hundreds of large mummy bundles recovered on the Paracas Peninsula.

Between A.D. 1 and 600, the *Moche culture flourished along the Peruvian north coast. The Moche culture, which possessed a state organization is most noted for its superb modeled and bichromed painted pottery, decorated with scenes from aspects of Moche ritual life. The Moche people were also excellent metallurgists, working with copper, gold, and silver to craft hundreds of delicate pieces of jewelry and body ornaments that were used during ceremonies and were subsequently buried with elite rulers when they died. The Moche people also constructed large adobe platform mounds decorated with painted murals and friezes, most notably at the Moche pyramids and El Brujo.

Contemporary with the Moche culture was the *Nasca (Nazca) state of the south coast of Peru. This culture is particularly noted for its fine polychromed pottery depicting mythical scenes and personages. Unlike Moche settlements, Nasca sites did not house dense populations. The largest Nasca site, Cahuachi, was a relatively empty ceremonial center containing numerous adobe shrines periodically constructed over many decades by visiting pilgrims. The Nasca people also constructed thousands of markings on rocky desert pampas located adjacent to small river drainages. Most are either straight lines or geometric shapes, but a few form large animal figures that are dozens of meters long. The *Nasca lines, shapes, and figures were probably laid down for ritual purposes linked to the worship of supernatural beings controlling water sources in the Nasca drainage.

Between A.D. 600 and 1000, the *Wari state influenced much of central and southern Peru. This culture had a state organization administered from its capital, Wari, in the southern highlands through a series of provincial centers. Most evidence of Wari culture is based on the presence of distinctive polychrome painted pottery, and in northern Peru, Wari presence is only weakly demonstrated at a handful of sites. The Wari probably borrowed iconographic elements and stoneworking techniques from the *Tiwanaku empire centered to the south of Lake Titicaca.

The *Chimu state dominated the entire Peruvian north coast from A.D. 1000 to 1470. The Chimu capital, *Chan Chan, covered over 12.4 square miles (20 sq km) and was one of the largest Precolumbian cities in the New World. Dozens of other centers located in several coastal valleys, along with distinctive blackware pottery, mark the Chimu presence. Extensive expanses of canals and fields along the

desert margins of the coastal valleys testify to Chimu efforts to increase agricultural production to support their capital and administrative centers. Their efforts in this endeavor were not entirely successful. Nevertheless, the Chimu were the most formidable foe of the *Inca civilization, and, according to early Spanish ethnohistoric sources, when the Incas conquered the Chimu in A.D. 1470, they borrowed many Chimu governing principles to help administer their vast empire.

The Inca civilization comprised the largest state organization in all of pre-Columbian America. At its maximum extent, the Inca empire stretched along the Andean mountains and coastal plain from the southern border of Colombia to northern Chile and Argentina. Much of the knowledge about the Incas actually derives from early Spanish ethnohistoric sources such as reports from soldiers and priests, official government censuses, notorial inventories, and land-dispute documents. Nevertheless, archaeological investigations have helped clarify the nature of Inca civilization. The Incas are famous for their superb close-fitting polygonal-stone architecture that is most prevalent within and near the Inca capital of *Cuzco. Also noteworthy is their 24,800-mile-(40,000 km) long road system that facilitated communication throughout their domain. A good portion of this road system was built by earlier peoples, but the Incas successfully connected most disjointed segments into an integrated system. Provincial centers such as Huanuco Pampa were established to administer the empire. Older pre-Inca settlements were sometimes used by the Inca as provincial centers with little or no modification. In these cases, Inca presence is manifested mainly by distinctive Inca pottery painted with geometric patterns and stylized animal and plant designs.

Northern Andes. In the northern Andes, archaeological dating and cultural definition are somewhat problematic due to a relative lack of scientific investigation. Nevertheless, notable archaeological remains exist. The earliest pottery in South America (and the New World as a whole) was produced in northern Colombia (3500–3000 B.C.) at sites like Puerto Hormiga and along the southern Ecuadorian coast by the *Valdivia culture (3000 B.C.). Because the ceramics are quite distinct in the two areas, it seems possible that pottery making was independently invented a number of times. However, exchange of ideas seems reflected in two later coastal Ecuadorian ceramic cultures, Machalilla (2000–1000 B.C.) and Chorrera (1000–500 B.C.), that contain vessel forms like the stirrup spout along with decorative elements which closely resemble contemporary ceramics in northern Peru.

In southern Colombia, the San Agustin culture (A.D. 100–1200) produced distinctive stone sculpture depicting humans, animals, and supernatural beings. This sculpture is usually associated with barrow tombs and stone cists. Central and northern Colombia is noted for the goldwork of its later prehistoric cultures—Sinu and Quimbaya (A.D. 300–1550) and Tairona and Muisca (A.D. 1000–1550). Most of the gold objects, produced by the lost wax method, were small figures of animals, humans, and human/animal combinations used as personal ornaments or religious offerings. The most widespread style was that of the Sinu, pieces of which have been found in tombs as far north as Belize.

The northern Andes also contain abundant remains of raised fields—long ridges and mounds of earth constructed to drain areas for agricultural production. Extensive remnants of raised fields still exist in southern Ecuador near Guayaquil and in northern Colombia along the San Jorge

River drainage. Dating is estimated between A.D. 500 and 1500.

Southern Andes. The southern Andes witnessed the rise and fall of several distinctive cultures. In northern Chile between 4000 and 2000 B.C., the preceramic *Chinchorro culture, with a subsistence base of marine resources, developed elaborate artificial mummification practices to preserve their deceased. The bodies were eviscerated and filled with plant fibers, limbs were supported by inserted reeds and sticks, and the skin was covered with clay and painted.

Much later on the southern shores of Lake Titicaca, the Chiripa culture (1300–100 B.C.) built the first monumental stone architecture in the area—a sunken court surrounded by sixteen precisely laid-out buildings at the type site of Chiripa. The subsequent Pucara culture (100 B.C.–A.D. 100) also had fine stone architecture as well as stone sculpture depicting blocky standing anthropomorphic figures. The Pucara culture is also noted for its distinctive polychromed and incised pottery that features modeled faces of humans and felines.

Southern Andean prehistory is dominated by the Tiwanaku culture, a long-lived culture (400 B.C.–A.D. 1000) that reached its cultural apogee between A.D. 400 and 700. The culture had a state organization centered around its capital of Tiwanaku located just south of Lake Titicaca. The capital city contains several large stone-and-earth constructions and once housed a population of at least 20,000 people. Carved stone statues, gateways, and tenon heads present in the city are rendered in a style possibly inspired by the Pucara culture. Much of the subsistence base for the capital city came from crops produced on the raised fields of Pampa Koani along the shores of Lake Titicaca. The Tiwanaku culture also maintained a series of economic colonies in Bolivia, northern Chile, and the extreme south coast of Peru. Communication and exchange with these colonies was greatly facilitated by the use of llama caravans.

Lowland South America. Judging by early European explorers' reports, lowland South America contained a number of late prehistoric chiefdoms. However, prehistoric use of perishable materials for construction and artifacts, coupled with poor preservation and lack of investigation, hampers current knowledge of the area. Notable exceptions include extensive raised-field systems in northeastern Bolivia and eastern Venezuela, and the late prehistoric mound-building Marajoara culture (400 B.C.–A.D. 1300) near the mouth of the Amazon River.

[*See also* ANDEAN PRE-INCA CIVILIZATIONS, THE RISE OF; INCA CIVILIZATION: INTRODUCTION.]

■ Gordon R. Willey, *An Introduction to American Archaeology,* vol. 2 of *South America* (1971). Luis G. Lumbreras, *The Peoples and Cultures of Ancient Peru* (1974). Jesse D. Jennings, ed., *Ancient South Americans* (1983). Christopher B. Donnan, ed., *Early Ceremonial Architecture in the Andes* (1985). Jonathan Haas, Shelia Pozorski, and Thomas Pozorski, eds., *The Origins and Development of the Andean State* (1987). Richard W. Keatinge, ed., *Peruvian Prehistory* (1988). Michael E. Moseley, *The Incas and their Ancestors* (1992). Craig Morris and Adriana Von Hagen, *The Inka Empire and Its Andean Origins* (1993). Karen Olsen Bruhns, *Ancient South America* (1994).

Thomas Pozorski and Shelia Pozorski

THE AMAZON

Amazonia as a culture area includes almost all of the basin of the Amazon River, as well as the Upper Orinoco and the Guyanas, one-third of South America. It consists of low-lying plains covered by rain forests. The contrast between the poor soils of the huge area of old alluvium (*terra firme*) and the circumscribed rich soils of the new alluvium (*várzea,* less than 3 percent) constitutes an important feature of Amazonia from the point of view of human settlement.

The floodplains constitute a desirable ecological niche both for preagricultural and agricultural peoples. Because of the uniformity of this niche, any innovation in economic strategy, achieved in one part, is bound to spread throughout the niche. Since this represents an immense net of waterways, these innovations could spread far and wide, and populations spawned in Amazonia could penetrate the Central Andes, the Antilles, and ultimately settle coastal Brazil. It is the cultural similarities among the relatively dense populations of the *várzea* that allow us to define Amazonia as a culture area. The complexity of linguistic distribution and the time depth estimated for differentiation of the stocks and linguistic families involved indicate vast human movements, extending over many millennia.

The existence of a notable degree of prehistoric cultural uniformity is indicated by the wide distribution of many ceramic traits. In several instances, particular ceramic styles can be related to the areas represented by the Arawakan (Tutishcaynio / Barrancoid), Tupían (Polychrome), and Karíb (Arauquinoid) linguistic stocks. Only a high degree of human mobility in prehistory could explain the ethnographic and archaeological array. Cultural evolution within Amazonia has involved a continuous buildup of populations of the *várzea,* associated with progressively more effective economic and social structures. Around 600 sites have been reported, of which some 400 have been tested, but none thoroughly excavated. Almost all of them are in the floodplains and constitute *terras pretas* (anthropogenic accumulations of black earth). Some 130 radiocarbon dates are known, but many others have never been published.

B. J. Meggers's model of cultural development postulates that the human occupation of Amazonia was very late and its cultural development very slow and limited by ambiental constraints, most innovations coming from the outside. D. W. Lathrap's model argues for a very early occupation of Central and Lower Amazonia that would develop as a center from which most innovation diffused to the rest of South America. So far, the data strongly supports this model, as has been demonstrated by recent research by A. C. Roosevelt. Both models rest heavily on the displacement or replacement of ceramic styles, explained by human migrations or diffusion. Neither has yet been proven because very little research has been carried out.

The first evidences of human occupation are fine percussion-made stone points and rock paintings in a rock shelter near Santarém (11,000 B.P.) and a chopper industry in another rock shelter on the Guaporé River (12,000 B.P.). The earliest ceramics of the New World (8,000 B.P.), in a shell midden near Santarém, are very simple in form, but complex incised patterns sometimes occur near the rim. Similar ceramics, shell-tempered, red-slipped, and incised, occur in the shell middens at Maranhão (Maiobinha), the mouth of the Amazon (Mina, Areão, Uruá, Tucumã), the lower Trombetas (Castália), Xingu, and even on the Ucayali (5,700–4,000 B.P.), indicating that they were widespread and appeared very early.

From that time on, in Central Amazonia we see a continual merging and branching of styles and the establishment of long-lasting traditions, supporting the model of indigenous development and diffusion proposed by Lathrap rather than the model of successive waves of emigration proposed by Meggers. In contrast, along the Upper Amazon as well as along the upper reaches of its major tributaries, Meggers's model is supported by the superposition of very different ceramic traditions, suggesting successive episodes of colonization from Central Amazonia.

By 4,000 B.P. more developed ceramics, characterized by sharply carinated flanged forms and hachured-zoned incised decoration were present in the Tapajós and Trombetas (Jauari), as well as on the Ucayali; the spread of these forms is attributed to the expansion of the proto-Arawakans. These Tutishcaynio-like wares are widespread from 3,600 B.P. along the tributaries of the Upper Amazon, straddling the boundary with the Andean area. They were also present on the adjacent Pacific coast (Kotosh-Wairajirca, Kotosh-Kotosh, Mácas, Upano, Machalilla), suggesting that they were part of a widespread network of interaction that encompassed not only the eastern slopes of the Andes but also the Pacific coast.

Because of the similarity between a number of traits characteristic of the central Amazonian wares and the later Barrancoide and Saladoide ceramic series on the Orinoco, Lathrap suggests these wares spread up the Rio Negro and down the Orinoco by 2,000 B.P., where they eventually developed into separate entities. These ceramic series became independent about 3,000 B.P. (Ronquín Sombra) and spread successively to the coast, eventually reaching the Antilles.

In Central Amazonia there were apparently three divergent ceramic developments partially paralleling each other in time: Amazonian Barrancoid ceramics, the Amazonian Polychrome Tradition, and Arauquinoid or Itacoatiara Barrancoid ceramics all were characterized by wide flat rims emphasizing modeling and incising, and were found, beginning 2,700 B.P., throughout Central and Upper Amazonia, from Pocó, Itacoatiara, and the Negro to the Ucayali (Hupa-iya), the Napo, Marañón (Upano), Japurá (Mangueiras) Orinoco (Cotua), and Upper Xingu (Diauarum). They were probably carried by waves of Proto-Maipuran Arawakans.

The unfolding of the Amazonian Polychrome tradition is the best understood, and to account for the date distribution we have to model an enormous five-branched and multi-pronged succession of movements embracing not only most of Amazonia but almost all of eastern South America as well. These wares have a complex set of vessel shapes, where red and black or white painting is combined with slipping, incising, excising, and modeling, forming a very sophisticated art style. From 2,000 B.P. (Marajoara) they spread upriver (Guarita, Apuan, Pirapitinga, Tefé, São Joaquim, Miracangüera, Japuré) reaching the upper tributaries (Napo, Maromé, Beni, Caimito, and Caquetá) by 1,000 B.P. (Zebu, Yanayacu). Another late spread was to the Atlantic coast (Maracá, Mazagã, Aristé, Cunani, Koriabo). In Marajó these ceramics are found in large village and burial mounds that represent complex societies.

The Amazonia Polychrome tradition probably marks the upstream and downstream spread of the Tupians. Simplified versions of these wares spread separately southward, out of Amazonia, along the Atlantic coast (Tupinambá) and into Paraguay-Paraná-Uruguay basin (Guaraní). At about the same time, the Itacoatiara ceramics emphasizing incised decoration and sometimes complex forms and modeling spread all the way from the Lower Tapajós and Trombetas, where they represent early historic chiefdoms (Santarém,

Konduri) to the Madeira (Galera), Mamoré (Masicito), Orinoco (Nericagua, Corobal), the Upper Xingu (Ipavu), and the Maranhão coast (Pindaré). Beginning 1,700 B.P. the Pacacocha and Cumancaya ceramic traditions spread along the foot of the Andes, carried by waves of Panoans, from the Ucayali to the Napo (Tivacundo) and Beni (Buturo). Their shape and corrugated finish relate them to the Guaraní ceramics to the south.

According to historic sources (missionaries, conquistadors), much more advanced cultures existed in sixteenth- and seventeenth-century Amazonia than at later times. The entire distance between the Naipo River and Marajó was covered by highly populated villages that dominated each province. The political and social systems of these peoples can be defined as chiefdoms. At the boundaries of the provinces were buffer zones that were sometimes inhabited by other groups.

The political structure of the chiefdoms was characterized by centralized power, hierarchical and differential social status, and elaborate arts (ceramic and lapidary) and rituals. Resource management was intensive and large scale; root and seed crops and fish and turtle corralling supported populations denser and more stable than those living in the area today. Rather sophisticated solutions to the problems of food preservation were invented, such as the grater board, tipiti, casava beiju, alcoholic and non-alcoholic fermented drinks, silos, and agroforestry. These strategies required considerable labor investment; therefore, some chiefdoms maintained alliances or waged wars vying for the dominance of territories, the management of resources, and the maintenance of trade routes. Trade items such as decorated ceramics, textiles, raw materials, food stuffs, utensils, and slaves were produced on a large scale.

[See also MOUNDS OF THE AMAZON.]

■ B. J. Meggers, Archaeological Investigations of the Mouth of Amazon (1957). D. W. Lathrap, The Upper Amazon (1970). G. Willey, An Introduction to American Archaeology, vol. 2 (1971). J. Hemming, Red Gold (1978). J. Brochado and D. W. Lathrap, Amazonia (1980). A. C. Roosevelt, Parmana (1980). A. C. Roosevelt, Moundbuilders of the Amazon (1991). A. C. Roosevelt, et al., "The Earliest Pottery in the Americas from a Shellmound in the Brazilian Amazon," Science (1992).

José Brochado and Francisco S. Noelli

LOWLANDS CULTURES OF SOUTH AMERICA

The prehistoric cultures of lowland South America, as defined in this essay, occupy the northwestern part of the continent, comprised of the coastal lowland regions of western Ecuador, western and northern Colombia, and northwestern Venezuela, as well as the interior llanos of eastern Colombia and western Venezuela. In general terms, the lowlands of northwestern South America share a humid tropical forest or tropical savanna environment characterized by a single season of heavy rains. Exceptions can be found at the geographical extremes in the Santa Elena Peninsula area of western Ecuador and in the Guajira Peninsula area of northwest Venezuela, where arid conditions, ranging from xerophytic scrubland to dry tropical forest, prevail.

The principal physiographic features that unite these diverse culture areas are the littoral zones along the Pacific and Carribean seaboards and the alluvial floodplains of the large river valleys that drain the interior lowlands and adjacent Andean highlands. The rich floral and faunal resources of these littoral and riparian ecosystems made them favorable areas for human settlement throughout the prehistoric era.

While the coastal lowlands of northwestern South America must have played a pivotal role in the initial peopling of the continent between about 14,000 and 8,000 B.P., well-dated archaeological evidence of Paleo-Indian occupations is generally sparse to nonexistent. The best archaeologically documented evidence comes from the Taima-Taima site near the city of Coro in northwestern Venezuela, a water hole kill site where an El Jobo lanceolate point fragment was found in direct association with bones of extinct megafauna (a juvenile mastodon). These remains, along with a diverse assemblage of other faunal material, were dated between 12,600 and 13,400 B.P. Surface finds of Paleo-Indian projectile points have been found on the Paraguana Peninsula to the north as well as on the Caribbean coast of Colombia. Little data exists regarding Paleo-Indian lifeways, but the Venezuelan evidence suggests mobile hunting populations ranging over the humid coastal lowlands in pursuit of large herbivores as well as smaller terrestrial mammals.

The period from 8,000 to 5,500 B.P. in northwestern South America has been characterized as a preceramic littoral tradition extending from Cerro Mangote in Panama and the Atlantic coast of Colombia southward to coastal Ecuador and the Talara region of northern coastal Peru. The Las Vegas site in coastal Ecuador is the earliest and best known of these, although aceramic sites on the Caribbean coast of Colombia are also thought to fall in this time period. Sites of this tradition are characterized by their proximity to the seashore and abundant remains of marine and mangrove estuarine fish and shellfish. Stone tool assemblages are typically simple unifacial industries likely used for woodworking; projectile points are absent. At the Vegas site, ground stone metates and mortars indicate the processing of vegetal foods, and during late Vegas times (8,000–6,600 B.P.), clear botanical evidence exists for incipient horticulture, including maize, squash, and gourds. Ground stone axes suggest forest clearance perhaps for horticultural production. A semisedentary lifeway is indicated by repeated occupation of the site both for habitation and human interment. A notable exception to the settlement-subsistence regime of the preceramic littoral tradition has been documented at the San Jacinto 1 site in the Lower Magdalena Valley about 93 miles (150 km) upriver from the Atlantic coast. Now deeply buried under sterile floodplain alluvium, the site contains a series of occupation floors, hearths, and refuse dating to ca. 6,000–5,700 B.P. Unlike the Vegas site, San Jacinto appears to represent a small sedentary community with an economic orientation based on riverine fishing. The site is also unique for having the earliest well-dated pottery for the lowlands of northwestern South America. The early dating and experimental nature of this pottery suggests an ancestral relationship with the later Formative Period pottery on the Caribbean coast of Colombia.

Between 5,500 and 2,500 B.P. (the Formative Period), settled village life, pottery production, and full reliance on agricultural subsistence became more commonplace in the lowlands of northwestern South America. Agricultural production was based on a diverse array of cultigens that included maize, beans, squash, root crops such as achira, and cotton. In Ecuador, this period begins with the *Valdivia culture, which was centered in coastal Guayas Province but later extended from northern Manabí to El Oro

Province near the Peruvian border. Valdivia culture exhibits considerable cultural change over an eight-phase ceramic sequence lasting approximately 2,000 years. Small villages of flimsy nucleated family dwellings documented for Phase 1 give way to large plaza-type villages of up to 1,500 people by Phase 3, along with evidence for economic specialization, ceremonial architecture, elaborate mortuary practices, and possible hereditary social ranking. By Phase 8 certain sites exhibit large-scale mound building, complex settlement hierarchies, and the production and long-distance exchange of sumptuary items such as worked *spondylus* shell. The Valdivians were succeeded on the coast by the short-lived Machalilla culture and the late Formative Chorrera culture, which represents the first ceramic "horizon style" for the coastal Ecuadorian lowlands. Several regional variants of this style have been identified, but all of them share a diverse range of finely crafted vessel forms, including zoomorphic and phytomorphic effigy vessels, a series of decorative techniques including iridescent painting, and large hollow human-effigy figurines.

In Colombia, the Formative Period has been documented primarily on the Caribbean coast at sites that are characterized by the presence of incised and modeled pottery having both fiber and sand tempering and simple vessel shapes such as the *tecomate*. Unlike the contemporaneous Valdivia culture, however, these groups occupied small ring-shaped mound sites, practiced rudimentary horticulture, and had a generally stable lifeway over a 2,000-year time span. The Late Formative Period of Caribbean Colombia and northwestern Venezuela represents a complete break from the earlier fiber-tempered Tecomate tradition and marks the introduction of the first painted horizon.

Subsequent to the Formative Period, prehistoric occupation of the coastal lowlands of northwestern South America can be conveniently subdivided into two successive periods ending with the Spanish Conquest. The first, spanning from about 2,500 to 1,000 B.P. can be characterized by regional diversification, social ranking, economic specialization, and the emergence of chiefdom societies. In many areas, these developments were associated with the construction of large civic-ceremonial mounds in large plaza-type communities, multitiered site hierarchies, complex mortuary ritual, and specialization in craft production, especially ceramic vessels and figurines.

The second period, spanning from about 1,000 B.P. to the Spanish Conquest, can be characterized by the rise of large complex chiefdoms, massive public works for both ceremonial and agricultural purposes, and extensive territorial control. While some earlier chiefdoms were replaced or displaced by these larger chiefdom polities, in other areas the earlier traditions survived until the Spanish Conquest. In Ecuador, for example, the Manteño culture came to dominate the entire coastal area of Guayas and southern Manabí, establishing large quadripartite regional centers with stone architecture (such as Salangome and Jocay) at various points along the coast.

In Colombia, this period is represented by the emergence of complex chiefdoms in three areas of the Caribbean coast. Sites are associated with extensive raised field agricultural complexes, burial tumuli, and extensive trade.

With the arrival of the Spaniards to the coastal lowlands of northwestern South America in the early part of the sixteenth century, the demise of these complex chiefdom societies was already in progress, perhaps due to rapid depopulation brought on by the early arrival of European diseases such as smallpox. Most of the remnant populations were eventually acculturated into a new mestizo society, some faster than others depending on whether the Spaniards established permanent settlements or religious missions in the immediate vicinity. The late period chiefdoms of northern coastal Ecuador provide a good case of very gradual acculturation to mestizo society, for example. Other groups, such as the Tairona, were able to maintain their ethnic and cultural identity well into the twentieth century (as the modern-day Kogi), in large part due to their isolation in the Sierra Nevada Mountains.

[See also MOUNDS OF THE AMAZON.]

■ Robert A. Feldman and Michael E. Moseley, "The Northern Andes" in ed. J. Jennings, *Ancient South Americans* (1983), pp. 139–177. Warwick Bray, "Across the Darien Gap: A Colombian View of Isthmian Archaeology," ed. F. W. Lange and D. Z. Stone, in *The Archaeology of Lower Central America* (1984), pp. 305–338. Karen E. Stothert, "The Preceramic Las Vegas Culture of Coastal Ecuador," *American Antiquity* 50 (1985): 613–638. Gerardo I. Ardila, "The Peopling of Northern South America" in ed. R. Bonnichsen and K. Turnmire, *Clovis: Origins and Adaptations* (1991), pp. 261–282. Deborah M. Pearsall, "The Origins of Plant Cultivation in South America" in ed. C. W. Cowan and P. J. Watson, *The Origins of Agriculture: An International Perspective* (1992), pp. 173–205. Charles S. Spencer and Elsa M. Redmond, "Prehispanic Chiefdoms of the Western Venezuelan Llanos," *World Archaeology* 24 (1992): 134–157. Jorge G. Marcos, *Ancient Ecuador: Coastal Societies of the Northern Andean Region, 300 B.C.–1500 A.D.* (1993). Karen Olsen Bruhns, *Ancient South America* (1994).

James A. Zeidler

HIGHLANDS CULTURES OF SOUTH AMERICA

The Andes Mountains of South America stretch along the western margin of the continent from the Caribbean coast south to Tierra del Fuego. The Andean landscape with its peaks, steep slopes and infrequent valleys is a challenging one, but the many groups of prehistoric and early historic peoples resident here achieved political and technological complexity and developed rich artistic and ideological traditions. The Inca Empire was the latest and most famous of indigenous highland groups, but many other cultures are known to archaeologists.

Mountain peoples of the northern Andes (Ecuador and Colombia), central Andes (Peru and northern Bolivia) and southern Andes (southern Bolivia, northern Chile, and northwestern Argentina) shared many similarities. Habitation throughout the zone tended to occur in discontinuous pockets. Prehistoric people preferred to build permanent settlements at elevations between 8,000 and 12,000 feet (2,400 and 3,600 m) above sea level (depending on latitude), high enough to benefit from rain-bearing clouds from the east, but low enough to avoid frosts. Highland basins with permanent rivers and relatively gentle slopes were preferred locales, and these valleys became heavily populated.

The earliest settlers of the Andean highlands were hunters and gatherers, but by 8000 B.C. the occupants of *Guitarrero Cave in the central Peruvian highlands were tending beans and oca tubers. Over the next few millennia they and neighboring groups increased their reliance on a variety of crops suited to high altitudes. Plants such as potato, oca, olluco, tarwi, and quinoa served as staples. Of these altitude-adapted plants, only the potato has become popular outside its zone of indigenous use. In later prehistory, maize was everywhere a preferred plant, valued especially for making *chicha*, a fermented beverage that played an important role in ritual and ceremony throughout the Andes. Maize was

difficult to grow at altitudes above 9,900 feet (3,000 m), however.

Andean peoples hunted in the brushy ravines and high-altitude plains away from their settlements. Deer was valued, but the llama and its relatives, high-altitude tolerant members of the camelid family, were critically important. These animals were domesticated as early as 3000 B.C. in the highlands of Junín in central Peru, and gradually were adopted by groups as far north as Ecuador and south far into Chile and Argentina. Llamas were used for meat and for transporting burdens. Alpacas, a closely related species, provided fine wool, which was everywhere spun and woven into textiles. Less spectacular but equally important for subsistence was the guinea pig; this small animal, hardy and prolific, continues to be raised in the kitchens of many Andean houses.

Andean households were extended and multigenerational. Land was owned by the community, and individual households normally held use rights to several plots of land in different locations and altitudes, for the production of different crops. Many households, especially in Peru and Bolivia, also had herds pastured at higher elevations. Complex bonds of kinship and reciprocity bound community members together.

Andean peoples were part of a cosmos in which no boundaries were drawn between natural and supernatural, sacred and profane. Mountain peaks were sacred personalities, and offerings were made to them. Water was sacred, nourishing the earth, which provided for humans. Rain, irrigation water, and rivers descending to the oceans were all part of an unbroken cosmic round in which humans maintained their place through ritual and sacrifice. From Colombia south into Chile and Argentina, recurring similarities in art, myth, ritual, and monument construction underscore important similarities in the ideologies of Andean peoples; Andean ideology was shaped by the mountain environment but flavored by Amazonian influences from the east.

Prehistoric Cultures of the Central and South Andes. The prehistoric cultures of highland South America have drawn considerable attention from archaeologists interested in the evolution of complex societies. The urban sites, monumental architecture, and massive land reclamation projects at which the Spanish marveled in the early 1500s have their antecedents deep in Andean prehistory.

In late preceramic times, 2800 to 1800 B.C., highland peoples of central Peru built ritual structures of modest size that reflect their participation in the Kotosh Religious Tradition. Walled rooms with central fire pits have been found at Kotosh, La Galgada, Huaricoto, and other sites. Carbon from fire pits suggests they were used to burn chili peppers (probably to create an acrid tear-producing smoke) and other offerings. The structures were frequently modified, with replastering and rebuilding marking each new cycle of use. In the Initial Period (1800–1200 B.C.), ritual sites of monumental scale first appear in the sierra. At Pacopampa, Huacaloma, and Kuntur Huasi in northern Peru features such as terraces, stairways, platforms, and sunken plazas define and bound ritual space. Images portrayed on metal, ceramic, and stone link highland religious practices and beliefs to the Peruvian coast as well as to the Amazonia rain forest to the east. Complex beings with feline, serpent, and bird attributes symbolize the cosmological powers attributed to the earth, water, and sky.

The *Chavín culture (1000–500 B.C.) of the central highlands of Peru synthesized many architectural and ideological features already prominent in the sierra. *Chavín de Huantar is an elaborate ritual complex whose mounds and plazas delimit a space ideal for procession and viewing. Low-relief carvings on stone slabs and columns depict Chavín supernaturals, complex beings combining human and animal attributes. The Staff God was a prominent deity; this figure faces forward in a stance of power and authority, clasping a staff in each hand. Chavín images spread widely through the Peruvian sierra and down to the coast, painted on textiles, engraved in stone and shell, modeled on ceramics, and worked in gold. The stylistic uniformity implies widespread adherence to a single ideological system.

The waning of Chavín ideological influence was followed by an era of regional development. The ceramics of Recuay and Cajamarca, the monumental architecture of Huamachuco, and the ceremonial structures at Pucará are highlights of the centuries from 500 B.C. to A.D. 500 in Peru and northern Bolivia. By A.D. 100 *Tiahuanaco (Tiwanaku) was assuming prominence on the southern shore of Lake Titicaca on the Peru-Bolivia border, and by A.D. 500 had grown to be the capital of an empire that controlled surrounding highland and coastal peoples. The economic basis of the Tiahuanaco Empire was intensive cultivation on ridged fields reclaimed from the marshy margins of Lake Titicaca, augmented by fishing in the lake, herding, agricultural production in colonies at lower elevations, and trade with more distant neighbors. Tiwanaku megalithic stonework stirs the imagination of viewers. The dominant image at the site is the Staff God from the so-called Gateway of the Sun, a front-facing anthropomorphic figure holding a staff in each hand.

A few hundred kilometers to the north, the urban site of Wari competed for political, ideological, and economic preeminence. This city spread its influence over much of the central Andes, constructing regional administrative centers to rule subject territory and to channel goods back to the center. Like Tiwanaku, Wari builders worked with stone to create impressive ritual and public spaces. Both cultures produced distinctive polychrome ceramics on which feline and bird imagery recalls the earlier Chavín cult, as does the Staff God, which is painted on oversized urns that have been ritually "killed."

By A.D. 800 the power of the two highland centers had waned, and a new era of regional development followed, marked throughout the central and southern Andes by the emergence of competing chiefdoms, concentration of population in fortified regional centers, and continued reliance on trade networks to provide highland peoples with goods from the Pacific coast to the west and the tropical forest to the east.

Prehistoric Cultures of Ecuador and Colombia. The archaeology of the northern Andes, and the reports of early Spanish chroniclers, suggest that the area was divided into many competing chiefdoms. Chiefs were powerful individuals from high-ranked lineages who were political and military leaders. North Andean cultures boasted artisans, professional merchants, and priests.

The highland cultures of Colombia drew the attention of the Spanish at an early date because of the beauty and abundance of the gold work produced there. Skilled metalworkers from the Tairona, Quimbaya, and Chibcha cultures produced necklaces, nose ornaments, crowns, and other ornaments by a variety of sophisticated techniques, especially lost wax casting and depletion gilding. The San

Agustín culture during the first few centuries of the Christian era produced some sculptures of humans and shamans that celebrate the role of the ritual specialist.

Ecuadorean highland peoples may have defined their ethnicity differently than did their Peruvian neighbors, tolerating less fixed boundaries than those favored by groups to the south. Certainly the many and varied ceramic styles of highland Ecuador attest to much sharing and borrowing of techniques and motifs. The highland topography of Ecuador tended to create pockets of population, but trade relationships and political alliances seem to have worked against isolation.

The Inca Empire. The Inca Empire, the best known of all Andean highland cultures, was a short-lived phenomenon. Around A.D. 1460 the Quechua-speaking group began to expand out of its home territory in the Cuzco Valley of southern Peru. When Francisco Pizarro and his followers arrived in 1532, the empire was the largest ever seen in the New World. Some eight million subjects in a territory extending from the Ecuador-Colombia border south to central Chile answered to the authority of the Inca king. By military power, by alliance, and by negotiation the Inca built their empire. Their astute statecraft allowed them to rule and oversee the activities of a remarkable array of peoples speaking many languages, inhabiting many environments, each group with its own distinctive ethnic tradition and identity.

Much of the Inca infrastructure survives to the present day; megalithic stone construction, extensive agricultural terracing projects, and the road system have withstood natural and human pressures for nearly five centuries. Most of the material wealth of the empire has vanished; fine textiles have rotted, and finely crafted metal has been melted down. The accomplishments of the Inca in the many areas in which they excelled were firmly rooted in millennia of previous Andean highland experience.

[See also ANDEAN PRE-INCA CIVILIZATIONS, THE RISE OF: INTRODUCTION; INCA CIVILIZATION: INTRODUCTION; WARI EMPIRE.]

■ John H. Rowe, "Inca Culture at the Time of the Spanish Conquest," *Handbook of South American Indians*, Vol. 2 (1946). John V. Murra, *The Economic Organization of the Inca State* (1980). Frank Salomon, *Ethnic Lords of Quito in the Age of the Incas: The Political Economy of North Andean Chiefdoms* (1986). William H. Isbell and Gordon F. McEwan, ed., *Huari Administrative Structure: Prehistoric Monumental Architecture and State Government* (1991). Richard L. Burger, *Chavín and the Origins of Andean Civilization* (1992). Michael E. Moseley, *The Inca and Their Ancestors: The Archaeology of Peru* (1992). Alan L. Kolata, *The Tiwanaku: Portrait of an Andean Civilization* (1993). Karen O. Bruhns, *Ancient South America* (1994).

Theresa Lange Topic

HISTORICAL ARCHAEOLOGY OF SOUTH AMERICA

*Historical archaeology is a very recent field of study in South America, and in most South American countries does not yet constitute a distinct subdiscipline within archaeology. The majority of scholars engaged in this field are local, rather than foreign, investigators, and many are specialists in architecture, urban studies, and art history, rather than archaeology. This situation is due largely to two factors. First, historical archaeology tends to emphasize the particular peoples and events that make a nation's history unique, and is less attractive to foreign scholars than prehistoric research, which is often viewed as more "scientific" and generalizing in nature. Second, most South American coun-

tries have limited resources for archaeological research and cannot support a large number of specialized scholars. Historical archaeology is thus best developed in relatively wealthy countries such as Argentina and Brazil where a small number of investigators devote themselves to such research. This is reflected in the publication of an overview of historical archaeology in Argentina, *La arqueología urbana in La Argentina* by Daniel Schávelzon (1992), and the translation of Charles Orser's (1992) introductory volume on historical archaeology into Portuguese for a Brazilian audience. In contract, scholars in the poorest countries, such as Bolivia, have conducted little historical archaeology, and have published almost nothing on the topic.

The Development of Historical Archaeology in South America. The earliest research on historical sites in South America was conducted in the late nineteenth and early twentieth centuries, primarily in Argentina. Two themes run through these early Argentinean studies. A small number of influential publications attempted to distinguish prehistoric from early historic sites, or assessed Spanish influence on indigenous communities in the western provinces of Mendoza and Catamarca. A second group of scholars produced a much larger corpus that was directly tied to the identification, excavation, and restoration of historic places. Most of these were inhabited during the colonial period and were associated primarily with populations of European descent. Examples include the first settlement of Buenos Aires, as well as a series of missions and the Spanish town of Concepción de Bermejo, located to the north of the capital in the Chaco. In neighboring Uruguay similar interests were pursued on a much smaller scale by the Society of Friends of Archaeology, an organization based in Montevideo.

This initial spate of studies was followed by three decades of relative inactivity in Argentina and much of the rest of South America, due, in part, to the repression of scholarly research by military governments. Work resumed in the late 1970s and early 1980s, and while it has been accelerating over the last decade, the absolute number of such investigations is still quite small. With few exceptions, this trend has not resulted in a coherent body of research that is tightly focused on specific issues or is the product of sustained debate among investigators. Most studies are done as a result of salvage projects or in conjunction with research on prehistoric materials. In all South American countries, historical archaeology is closely linked to historic preservation. A variety of properties fall within this category, but most are associated with governments or the Catholic church and include cathedrals, missions, and municipal buildings. While historic preservation projects provide the impetus and much of the funding for excavations, the relationship can also inhibit problem-oriented research that focuses on issues of anthropological interest.

Current Themes in South American Historical Archaeology. Contrary to what Schaedel (1992) claims, however, historical archaeology in South America is not limited to historic preservation. Important exceptions to these general trends do exist and represent the avant-garde of historical archaeology in the region. The publication of a number of articles and books on a related topic is usually linked to the presence of a particular program, or, more rarely, a long-term research project within a country. Examples include the Center for Urban Archaeology in Buenos Aires, which has sponsored a wide range of excavations in that city, and the study of colonial ceramics by scholars associated with the Paul Rivet Foundation in Ecuador. Arno Alvarez Kern's

long-term investigation of Jesuit missions in southern Brazil, and studies of traditional potters in Peru by individuals affiliated with the Center for Rural Andean History in Lima should also be included in this category. A number of different themes have begun to emerge from these investigations as well as those of independent scholars.

Material Culture Studies. Material culture studies are among the most common types of research being done in the region and currently take two forms: art-historical studies of objects that are in museums or private collections, and archaeological analyses of particular artifact classes recovered during excavations. Art-historical studies tend to emphasize complete objects, such as paintings or textiles, that are considered to have artistic merit. The most useful, from an anthropological perspective, provide chronological information or analyze objects in terms of their cultural context.

Archaeological research on particular artifact classes usually focuses on ceramics, although a few analyses of other items, such as bottles and pipes, as well as Fairbanks's important study of glass beads from Nueva Cadiz, Venezuela, have also been conducted. Scholars in Ecuador and Peru have made a notable contribution through their ethnographic studies of traditional potters. One of the primary goals of this research is to document manufacturing techniques, but the initial choice of study sites is related to their potential for yielding archaeological data on ceramic production. For instance, Jaime Miasta excavated deposits near manufacturing locales in Huarochirí, Peru that yielded materials dating from colonial to contemporary times. This research, like most other archaeological studies of material culture, provides data that are essential to the construction of chronologies, a task that has only just begun in most South American countries.

Industrial Archaeology. A recent trend in South American historical archaeology is the examination of manufacturing processes. A number of industrial sites have been excavated, ranging from the first steam engine in Argentina to a colonial silver mill in Potosí, Bolivia. Most of these are isolated studies, but two notable exceptions are the examination of tar-producing locales on Santa Elena Peninsula, Ecuador, by Karen Stothert and the investigation of colonial wineries in Moquegua, Peru. The latter project has generated a wealth of information on the development of viticulture in the valley, as well as data on associated industries such as pottery and lime production.

Contact Period Studies. A more developed field of inquiry is the examination of the contact period and the process of acculturation. The initial establishment of European settlements and the effects of colonization on both indigenous and European populations have been subjects of interest since the inception of historical archaeology in the region. Earlier studies emphasized the impact of European culture on native peoples, but more recent work focuses on interaction among the different groups comprising early colonial society. Excavations have been conducted in many different countries at indigenous settlements and cemeteries, European towns, forts, and missions, and communities inhabited by runaway slaves.

Two general findings have emerged from this work. First, the impact of indigenous cultures on the colonizing population is discernible in a wide variety of contexts. Such influence has been demonstrated at sites ranging from the Governor's Palace in the Colonia del Sacramento, Uruguay, to the frontier garrison Fortín Miñana, Argentina, and the wineries of Moguegua, Peru. Second, the nature of the interaction and its influence on the material record is determined by both the historical and contemporary context of the populations under study. For instance, Myriam Tarragó's analysis of grave goods from two closely related native societies in Argentina revealed very different quantities of European items, probably because of their differing relations with the Inca state prior to the Spanish Conquest.

The relatively large number of such studies is reflected in the publication entitled *Presencia hispánica en la arqueología Argentina*, two volumes that include articles on many aspects of the European presence in Argentina and its effects on native societies. The relatively large amount of research on these issues allows comparison among different cases, but also highlights the importance of understanding the historical conditions affecting specific groups. This concern could provide a means for the creative integration of historical and archaeological data, but most archaeologists are still just mining the historical record for information on the location and dates of sites, rather than using it in a truly interdisciplinary manner.

The most active arena for interdisciplinary research is currently in *urban archaeology, a subfield that is developing under the auspices of the Center for Urban Archaeology in Buenos Aires, directed by architect Daniel Schávelzon. Schávelzon and his colleagues have generated an impressive body of research based on excavations conducted in that city. The range of sites is quite broad, and includes nineteenth-century structures which are seriously underrepresented in the historical archaeology of the region. Most importantly, the close links between archaeology, urban development, and historic preservation are perceived not as a burden, but as an opportunity to make archaeology an integral part of contemporary urban life.

As published studies of historical sites increase, research will undoubtedly crystallize around new themes, and disciplinary boundaries will harden. Discussions of the role of method and theory in historical archaeology and the self-conscious delineation of specialized subfields have already begun in Argentina and Brazil. However, historical archaeology in South America is not simply recapitulating the development of the discipline in industrialized countries. Basic descriptive research is still most common, but processual studies of social change, and innovative approaches to material culture are proceeding at the same time and without apparent conflict. Furthermore, while the field is becoming increasingly professionalized, the involvement of scholars from disciplines outside archaeology is still viewed as an asset, particularly when the research is interdisciplinary in nature. Finally, there is no reason to expect that the discipline will develop in the same way in every country. Intellectual traditions, national histories, and contemporary politics will all influence the outcome, as will interaction with foreign archaeologists.

During the last decade, archaeologists in South America, like their colleagues elsewhere in the world, have been examining the relationship between archaeology and national identity. As the field of historical archaeology develops, archaeologists will have the opportunity to play a role in the development of a more inclusive form of nation building that recognizes the experiences of diverse segments of the population. It is in this arena that some of the more interesting intellectual and political developments will probably emerge.

[See also EUROPEAN COLONIES IN THE NEW WORLD; INDUS-TRIAL ARCHAEOLOGY; MISSION ARCHAEOLOGY; NATIONALISM.]

■ Harry Tschopik, "An Andean Ceramic Tradition in Historial Perspective," *American Antiquity* 15(3) (1950): 196–218. Richard Schaedel, "The Archaeology of the Spanish Colonial Experience in South America," *Antiquity* 66 (1992): 217–242. Pedro A. Funari, "South American Historical Archaeology," *Historical Archaeology in Latin America* 2 (1994): 1–14. Charles Orser, "Toward a Global Historical Archaeology: An Example from Brazil," *Historical Archaeology* 28(1) (1994): 5–22. Prudence Rice, "The Kilns of Moquegua, Peru: Technology, Excavations, and Functions," *Journal of Field Archaeology* 21(3) (1994):325–344.

Mary Van Buren

SOUTH AMERICA, Origins of Food Production in. Within the diverse South American continent, three well-developed agricultural systems existed by the time of European contact: low-altitude systems in the eastern lowlands and western coast, based on cultivation of root crops, such as manioc and maize; mid-elevation Andean systems dominated by maize, beans, and tubers; and high-altitude systems based on the potato and other root crops, quinoa, and herding of llamas and alpacas. When food production began and how these agricultural systems evolved are questions of current debate in South American archaeology.

Antiquity of Domestication. Evidence suggests that by 5000 B.C. a number of plants were being cultivated in South America: maize (*Zea mays*), introduced from Mesoamerica, gourd (*Lagenaria siceraria*), a plant transported by sea from Africa, and native beans (*Phaseolus vulgaris, P. lunatus*), squashes (*Cucurbita*), aji or chili (*Capsicum chinense, Capsicum* sp.), quinoa (*Chenopodium quinoa*), potato (*Solanum tuberosum*), the tree fruit guava (*Psidium guajava*), and, perhaps, the root crops oca (*Oxalis tuberosa*), and *Begonia geraniifolia*. It is important to emphasize, however, that many early finds of cultivated plants are not without interpretive problems. Plant remains from dry caves such as Guitarrero, Ayacucho, Tres Ventanas (Peru), and Huachichocana (Chile) are very difficult to interpret, since strata can be mixed by burrowing animals and later use of caves as burial areas.

Evidence for use of cultivated plants becomes increasingly abundant from 4000 to 1200 B.C. Beans, gourd, squashes, chili peppers, and guava become common on the Peruvian coast. Maize remains, although not widespread, occur at sites in both the Andean mountains and the western coast. A variety of new crops appear: cotton (*Gossypium barbadense*); the tree fruits avocado (*Persea americana*), pacae (*Inga Feuillei*), ciruela (*Bunchosia armeniaca*), cherimoya (*Annona cherimolia*), and lucuma (*Lucuma bifera*); the root crops manioc (*Manihot esculenta*), archira (*Canna edulis*), sweet potato (*Ipomoea batatas*), and jicama (*Pachyrrhizus* sp.); the legumes jackbean (*Canavalia plagiosperma*) and peanut (*Arachis hypogoea*); and the stimulant coca (*Erythroxylon* sp.). It is also during this period that hunting of deer and wild camelids in the Andes is being replaced by herding of domesticated llamas (*Lama glama*) and alpacas (*Lama pacos*). Remains of guinea pigs (*Cavia* spp.) are also present at sites in central Peru.

Evolution of Food Production: Coastal Peru Case. There have been many advances in our understanding of the antiquity of food production in South America since Margaret Towle's seminal work *The Ethnobotany of Pre-Columbian Peru* (Aldine 1961), drew together the plant data from early excavations on the desert coast of Peru. Today the Peruvian coast remains a primary source of data on the origins and evolution of agriculture in South America. Though few South American crops are native to the coast, many were eventually introduced and grown there under irrigation, and their remains were preserved in dried form. With advances in plant recovery techniques, such as fine sieving to recover small seeds, study of dried human feces (coprolites), and analysis of pollen and phytoliths (plant opal silica bodies), recent coastal data spanning the period from 5700 to 400 B.C. provide an informative window into the evolution of food production in the continent.

If the number of cultivated plants present at a site is used to estimate the importance of food production, a pattern of increasing use of cultivated plants over time is exhibited by the coastal Peruvian data. This is not a gradual increase, but a doubling from the earliest sites, La Paloma (5700–3000 B.C.) and Chilca I (3700–2400 B.C.) to the sites of the Cotton Preceramic (2600/2200 B.C.)–1800/1500 B.C. depending on the region), followed by a smaller rise during the Initial period (2000/1500 B.C.–1100/800 B.C. and a leveling off during the Early Horizon (1000–400 B.C. or later).

The earliest cultivated plants to appear in coastal Peru, at the Paloma site, are gourd, squash, bean, and guava. None of these are dietary staples, and all but gourd could have occurred wild in the *lomas* (fog oases) or river valleys of the coast. These plants undergo morphological change or occur in abundance later in time, suggesting they are incidental domesticates at this early date. The next cultivated taxa to appear, at the Chilca I site, are *achira*, jicama (both tubers), and jackbean. The two tubers are not native to the coast and must have been maintained under cultivation. They also represent potential staples. Wild plant and animal resources, especially marine resources, are still the mainstay of diet during this early period, however.

It is during the Cotton Preceramic that cultivated plants become more common at sites and assume a more important role in diet. No one plant dominates archaeological plant assemblages, however; seed crops (beans, chili peppers), root crops (potato, sweet potato, *achira*, jicama), and tree fruits (*lucuma*, avocado, *pacae*, *ciruela*) all occur. Cotton is especially abundant at sites. The dramatic increase in the number of cultivated plants used in the Cotton Preceramic (from seven species to sixteen) suggests that this period marks an important transition in the evolution of food production.

Only three new crops appear on the coast during the Initial Period, the horizon marked by the appearance of pottery: manioc and maize, which are uncommon, and peanut, which is widespread. Overall the pattern is very similar to that of the Cotton Preceramic, that of a broad-based food production system in which no one crop dominates. This pattern occurs in the context of the first evidence for irrigation on the Peruvian coast; for the first time field areas are expanded beyond naturally flooded areas.

During the Early Horizon, the period marked by the artistic style known as Chavín, only one new cultivated plant, the tree fruit *cherimoya*, appears on the coast. Fewer kinds of crops appear at any given site; tree fruits are rarer than at earlier sites. Maize has now become widespread, but is not grown to the exclusion of other dietary staples. This pattern marks the beginning of a narrowing of the food production base: use of some crops declines, others become more widespread. This occurs in the context of increased building of irrigation systems and opening of new agricultural lands.

Evolution of Food Production: Ecuadorian Case. In the Andean mountains and the moist lowlands of eastern and northern South America, preservation of ancient plant remains is limited to those accidentally burned, the inorganic residues of plants (phytoliths), and in certain circumstances, pollen (in bogs, lakes), and dried plant remains (in dry caves). Many fewer data are available than for the arid Peruvian coast. This information is important, however, since the wild ancestors of many South American cultivated plants occur in these regions. An example drawn from recent research in Ecuador will illustrate our understanding of the evolution of food production in the moist lowlands.

Extensive archaeological research has been carried out in southwest Guayas province, Ecuador, where sites dating to the Preceramic Vegas (8000–4600 B.C.) and Formative (pottery-producing) Valdivia periods (3500–1500 B.C.) have been investigated. Vegas culture is known from thirty-one sites that occur in the coastal zone or along intermittent streams. Charred plant remains were not well preserved at the Vegas type site, but phytoliths were recovered. Squash or gourd was identified in early Vegas strata (8000–6000 B.C.,) with maize appearing in late Vegas (6000–4600 B.C.) in association with squash.

Valdivia settlement is riverine and exhibits site hierarchy. A few nucleated village settlements occur   Real Alto is an example—with other smaller settlements appearing late in the Valdivia sequence and in the subsequent Machalilla period (1200–800 B.C.). Real Alto grew from a small village (2.5 acres, ca. 1 ha) to a ceremonial center with two mounds (31 acres, 12.4 ha) by Valdivia III (ca. 2300 B.C.). From the beginning of the Valdivia sequence, cotton, maize, and jackbean occur, along with sedge, cactus, and a variety of wild annuals. *Achira* tubers are added to the assemblage in Valdivia III times. Late Valdivia strata at the San Isidro site in the moister Jama River valley yielded evidence for maize, jackbean, squash or gourd, *achira*, arrowroot (*Maranta*), palm, sedge, and wild annuals.

There is evidence for increasing numbers of cultivated plants used from Early Preceramic through Late Valdivia times in coastal Ecuador (8000–1500 B.C.). This is partially an artifact of preservation or recovery, since no charred plant remains were identified from Vegas. Looking at the Valdivia sequence, however, *achira* is added in Valdivia III times, and arrowroot at the end of Valdivia, suggesting increasing richness of cultivated plants. Maize becomes more common (present in more loci at the Real Alto site) at the time *achira* appears. Subsequent to Valdivia, the same plant assemblage continues in use until European contact in the Jama region. The relative contribution of the various wild and cultivated plants to diet is still unknown, however.

Maize is present in Late Preceramic and Early Formative sites in coastal Ecuador before 4600 B.C. Maize phytoliths and pollen also occur at this time depth in a lake core at Hacienda El Dorado, Colombia. The number of cultivated plants present by middle Valdivia, and the common occurrence of maize at the Real Alto village at that time, suggests food production, including use of maize, was important by 2300 B.C. but was not the mainstay of the diet. This interpretation is based in part on the lack of evidence for extensive environmental manipulation in the Real Alto region. Similarly, the first occurrence of maize in the Colombian sierra is associated with only very slight landscape modification. The appearance of extensive swidden (slash and burn) agriculture occurs there by 3000 B.C. A pollen and phytolith core from Lake Ayauchi in the Ecuadorian Amazon adds information from the eastern lowlands to this picture. From 5100 to 3300 B.C. mature forest indicators dominate, with slight occurrence of disturbance taxa. Maize occurs at 3300 B.C. with increased disturbance indicators and abundant carbon particles, interpreted as the beginning of swiddening. By 500 B.C. maize is increasingly abundant, and vegetation indicators suggest agriculture has intensified.

Status of Research. Many questions remain unanswered concerning the origin and evolution of food production in South America. It is difficult to document early occurrences of domesticated plants since dry cave sites are subject to mixing and early open-air sites are difficult to locate, especially in the forests of the moist lowlands. Rising Holocene sea levels may have covered ancient coastal sites. Archaeological plant remains are usually fragmentary and often lack features necessary to establish whether a plant is domesticated or wild. These problems will continue to limit our understanding of the earliest stages of plant cultivation in South America.

[*See also* DOMESTICATION OF ANIMALS; DOMESTICATION OF PLANTS; MESOAMERICA, ORIGINS OF FOOD PRODUCTION IN; SOUTH AMERICA: EARLY PREHISTORY OF SOUTH AMERICA.]

■ Michael E. Moseley, *The Maritime Foundations of Andean Civilization* (1975). Charles A. Reed, ed., *The Origins of Agriculture* (1977). Jesse Jennings, ed., *Ancient South Americans* (1983). Karen Stothert, "The Preceramic Las Vegas Culture of Coastal Ecuador," *American Antiquity* 50 (1985): 613–637. Deborah M. Pearsall, *Paleoethnobotany* (1989). Robert A. Benfer, "The Preceramic Period Site of Paloma, Peru: Bioindications of Improving Adaptation to Sedentism," *Latin American Antiquity* 1 (1990): 284–318. Dolores R. Piperno, "The Status of Phytolith Analysis in the American Tropics," *Journal of World Prehistory*, 5 (1991): 155–191. Jack R. Harlan, *Crops and Man* 2d ed. (1992). Deborah M. Pearsall, "The Origins of Plant Cultivation in South America," in *The Origins of Agriculture*, ed. C. Wesley Cowan and Patty Jo Watson (1992), pp. 173–205. Jonathan D. Sauer, *Historical Geography of Crop Plants* (1993). James A. Zeidler and Deborah M. Pearsall, eds., *Regional Archaeology in Northern Manabi, Ecuador, vol. 1, Environment, Cultural Chronology, and Prehistoric Subsistence in the Jama River Valley* (1993).

Deborah M. Pearsall

SOUTHEAST ASIA, Kingdoms and Empires of. Before the definition of the degree of cultural complexity attained in the late prehistoric period in Southeast Asia, civilizations there seemed to appear in a vacuum. However, we now know that the last few centuries B.C. saw the development of a number of regional cultures that fall easily within the general definition of chiefdoms. Some specialists dislike using such terms as chiefdom or state in Southeast Asia arguing that they are imported from other regions and do not reflect local cultural characteristics. Bayard, for example, has proposed the use of General Period C and the Thai term *muang* to describe the late prehistoric groups in question, whereas Wolters advocates the Sanskrit word *maṇḍala* for state-like polities.

The Late Prehistoric Period. Between 1500 and about 500 B.C., there were numerous relatively small (less than 12 acres [5 ha]) settlements that included cemeteries. These reveal the use of locally made and exotic artifacts, including bronze and tin jewelry, to denote individual status and achievement. From 500 B.C., the use of forged iron artifacts including spearheads, knives, and billhooks became widespread. Some settlements grew considerably in size, intensive salt extraction commenced, and a wide variety of sumptuary goods in bronze were cast using a variety of

specialized techniques. Some of the larger settlements were ringed by moats, the construction of which may well go back to this period.

It was in the context of such societies that greater social complexity, including many traits associated elsewhere with states, developed. These are almost entirely to be found in lowland, riverine, or coastal areas, and fall naturally into two major groups: those within the Chinese Empire, and those that adopted many features of Indian civilization brought by mercantile contact and the movement of Indian brahmans to Southeast Asia.

The Expansion of the Han Empire. The Chinese imperial ambitions to the south originated with the Chin and reached their fulfillment under the Han dynasty. The objectives were both political and economic, and were achieved by force of arms. After a period of increasing pressure from the north, the Dong Son chiefdom(s) were overcome by a Chinese army under the general Ma Yuan in A.D. 42 and the areas of the lower Red and Ma Rivers were converted into provinces, or commanderies, of the Han Empire. Archaeologically, this period witnessed the end of the *Dong Son culture, which is best known from its rich aristocratic graves such as those from Chau Can and Viet Khe. At Dong Son, the late prehistoric necropolis was succeeded by burials within brick tombs of Han style, and the burial grounds at Lach Truong and Ke Noi represent, archaeologically, an abrupt break. The dead were placed in substantial subterranean brick chambers associated with Chinese items, including typical Han house models. The three commanderies, named Jiaozhi, Jiuzhen, and Rinan, saw the imposition of an extractive imperial economy and alien form of administration quite distinct from the Indianized polities to the south.

These lay along the coast of central and southern Vietnam and east of the Truong Son cordillera, known to the Chinese as the fortress of the sky. Although they never colonized further to the south, they were interested in maritime exchange routes linking their south coast cities with India and the Roman Empire. Indeed, the first historic accounts of Southeast Asia during the period when early kingdoms were forming are found in Chinese archives. These include a description of walled cities, a writing system, taxation, and the presence of Indian visitors in the lands beyond their imperial frontier, and although the location of this particular place cannot be defined, it was probably in the flat lands bordering the lower Mekong River.

Early Civilization in the Mekong Valley. Virtually nothing is known of the prehistoric occupation of this flood-prone region. But it is strategically well placed; it forms a natural landfall for sea-borne traffic from east and west, and sits athwart the lower Mekong, an artery for communication then and for the preceding millennia. Archaeological research there has confirmed Chinese accounts. Canals crisscross the landscape, coming together at nodal centers such as Oc Eo and Angkor Borei. Excavations at Oc Eo have revealed substantial brick structures and many exotic artifacts that evidence participation in an exchange network embracing Rome, India, and China. Some rings and seals were engraved in the *brāhmī* script, stylistically dated between the second and fifth centuries A.D. Glass jewelry was manufactured, a technique with Indian origins, but local methods with a long ancestry were used to cast tin ornaments.

Oc Eo was one of many centers linked by the canal system, and we can learn something of the society represented from a few surviving inscriptions. This tradition of raising stone stelae originated in India, and an example dating to the early sixth century A.D. from Prasat Pram Loven describes the consecration of a footprint of Viṣṇu by a certain Guṇavarman. This prince was involved in the drainage of the local marshes, and his inscription ends with a warning that "whoever subverts these gifts to their own use will suffer with those guilty of the five great crimes." The inscription tells us much about the state of affairs in the lower Mekong: It is written in Sanskrit, the sacerdotal language of Hinduism. The prince bore a Sanskrit name ending in -varman, meaning "the protégé of," and the five great crimes refer to the Indian legal system. The prince was directly involved in marsh drainage, probably by organizing canal construction.

The adoption of the Hindu religion by local leaders is also seen in the construction of temples, some of which have survived from this early period of Funan. Again, a second inscription refers to Rudravarman, a son of Jayavarman who appointed a Brāhman as inspector of royal property. It is apparent that the local overlords adopted Indian political, legal, and religious ideas to further their aims, and employed Sanskrit to describe their achievements. The means and extent to which this trend helped sustain them in power becomes increasingly apparent when we turn to the Zhenla polities.

From the mid-sixth century A.D., the political center of gravity moved north to the middle Mekong and the flat plains surrounding the Great Lake. The polities that rose and fell in this region between 550 and 802 A.D. were named Zhenla by the Chinese, with the implication that it was a state modeled along the Chinese ideal, with a permanent center and ruling dynasty. It is now widely agreed that the reality was more likely to have been a series of competing centers, whose success turned very much on the qualities of the leader and the support he could muster. Vickery has turned from Chinese accounts to the inscriptions raised by the people themselves, and has found that the titles taken by local leaders illustrate a progressive increase in the various levels of rank. The highest title taken by certain overlords was raja and there was clearly a strong element of competitive emulation between them.

The inscriptions also refer to the majority of the population, who worked in the rice fields, as animal herders, weavers, and cooks. Some of the surpluses of food, as well as corvée labor, were taken by the ruling elite, and this energy was converted into palaces, reservoirs, defensive moats, and temples. Siva was the favored deity in the Hindu pantheon, and it is important to appreciate that devotion to him by the ruler permitted him to acquire the god's spiritual and physical power. This route to semidivine status involved the construction of large stone temples surrounded by sacred walled precincts all decorated with reliefs rooted in the religious iconography of India.

The best-known such center is located at Sambor Prei Kuk, the capital of the overlord Īśānavarman and known in antiquity as Īśānapura. The site was enclosed by double walls 1.2 miles (2 km) long, enclosing 988 acres (400 ha), while a substantial reservoir lay outside. Three walled precincts dominate the core, each of which has a central stone temple and satellite temples within the enceinte. The temples have one chamber that contained a liṅga, or stone phallus, which represented the power of the overlord. Religious observance contrasted the darkness and privacy of the inner sanctum with the open space within the surrounding walls.

This period may be characterized as one in which regional overlords competed with each other in the field, in feasting, and for favor with the gods for supremacy. This is characteristically exemplified by inscriptions at Īśānapura that refer to the overlord's military prowess in expanding the territory of his parents. It was critically necessary to attract and maintain followers, and this was assisted by projecting an image of magnificence through impressive buildings and construction of large reservoirs to supply water throughout the dry season for the central populace. This competitive milieu was structurally modified in the early ninth century with the establishment of a great center at Angkor, but before turning to this development, we must first consider the first millennium A.D. in central Thailand, the coastal tract of Vietnam, and the Khorat Plateau.

Central Thailand. The inhabitants of central Thailand were exposed to Indian contact as early as the fourth century B.C., for objects of clear Indian origin, such as a lion carved from carnelian, have been found at the cemetery of Ban Don Ta Phet. Many other sites have revealed artifacts similar to those recovered from Oc Eo, the best-known settlement being Chansen. Here, the second phase yielded an ivory comb decorated with Buddhist symbols dated to the first or second centuries A.D., and tin amulets and pottery stamps from ensuing centuries match those from Oc Eo.

By the seventh century, we encounter persuasive evidence that a polity or polities similar to those of Zhenla were present in this area of rich agricultural potential. Two silver medallions from Nakhon Pathom, for example, proclaim that the sanctuary under which they lay was the "meritorious work of the King of Śrī Dvāravatī." The south Indian script is of seventh-century style. A second Sanskrit inscription from U Thong records that a certain Harṣavarman obtained the lion throne through regular succession. Structurally, these sites of the Dvāravatī polity offer similarities and differences to those of Zhenla. They are moated, but have an irregular plan. They contain large religious edifices, but stress Buddhism rather than Hinduism. The local language contained on some inscriptions was Mon rather than Khmer. The presence of a ruling elite is undoubted. Two toilet trays from Nakhon Pathom bear many symbols of royalty that persist in Thailand to this day. Stucco models from Ku Bua portray a seated royal leader, slaves, soldiers, and Semitic merchants. The Indian legal system is represented by a stone wheel of the law from Lopburi, inscribed in Pāli, the liturgical language of Theravāda Buddhism. This wheel represents that set in motion by the Buddha in Benares.

The religious and ceremonial centers of Dvāravatī ring the Gulf of Siam. Their respective hinterlands include village communities whose rice surpluses sustained the central elite. This pattern is also evident in the valleys of the Mun and Chi rivers on the Khorat Plateau to the northeast. Inscriptions in this region are few, but moated settlements are legion. The larger settlements, such as Muang Sima and Muang Fa Daet contain substantial architectural remains. A seventh-century inscription from the former records in Sanskrit and Khmer the gift of buffalo, cattle, and slaves to a Buddhist community by the lord of Śrī Canāsa. One of the many sacred standing stones from the latter show the walls, and their guards, alongside a fortified gateway. The analysis of landsat images of such sites reveals a sophisticated system of water control, whereby water was diverted into the moats and reservoirs, and then fed by canals into the surrounding rice fields.

Champa. The Cham polities of the coastal plains of central and southern Vietnam have received insufficient attention and are little known. During the late first millennium B.C., this area was home to the Sa Huynh culture. This is documented largely on the basis of extensive urnfield cemeteries in which the cremated dead, along with impressive assemblages of iron and bronze artifacts and exotic items of jewelry, were placed in large mortuary jars. This practice is quite distinct from inhumation, which predominated elsewhere in Southeast Asia, and when we encounter their successors in this area, we find them speaking a distinct language, Cham, which belongs to the Austronesian language family.

The coast, which these people controlled, was an important trade route, and through it, they received a strong exposure to Indians and their ideas. So again we find local leaders adopting the Sanskrit names, Indian architectural principles, and the Hindu religion. According to their own records, the Chams were divided into at least four regional groupings, Amarāvati, Vijaya, Kauthāra, and Paṇḍuraṅga. Each contains a number of major ceremonial centers of which Mi Son in Amarāvati is the best known. Building there began under Bhadravarman, who dedicated a temple there to Śiva which housed the liṅga Bhadreśvara. Construction received further impetus in the seventh century under Vikrāntavarman I and continued at least into the eleventh century. The complex had, as at Isanapura, single-chambered central temples surrounded by sacred walled enclosures.

The Empire of Angkor. The period of competition involving regional overlords in central Cambodia ended with the military success of Jayavarman II toward the end of the eighth century, and his establishment of the cult of the *kamraten jagat ta rāja*, or the god who is king, in 802 A.D. He chose a succession of cult centers in the lands bordering the northern shore of the Great Lake, finally settling upon the site of Hariharāliya. His probable nephew, Indravarman I (877–889) established there a complex of buildings that set a trend that lasted for the next four centuries at least: the construction of a reservoir, a raised temple pyramid to house images of the deified royal ancestors, and a temple mausoleum to take the ashes of the sovereign. The mausoleum represented Mount Meru, the home of the gods, and the reservoir the lakes that surrounded the holy mountain. There was also a leap in scale. Indravarman's reservoir, the *Indratātaka*, was 150 times the area of any earlier example.

It was Indravarman's son, Yasovarman, who moved the cult center to the hill of Bakheng and founded there the complex of Yasodharapura, now known as Angkor. His reservoir, the *Yaśodharatataka* or eastern Baray, has a maximum capacity of 78 million cubic yards (60 million cu m) of water. For the next five centuries, Angkor was to be the focus of a polity that extended its influence over much of the Mekong valley and into central Thailand. Successive overlords added their own monuments and expanded the reservoirs until it became one of the largest cult centers known. Of these overlords, two in particular stand out. Sūryavarman II (1113–1150) ordered the construction of Angkor Wat as his temple mausoleum. It is not only colossal, but imbued with religious symbolism and beauty. His death was followed by a low point in Angkorean history when, in 1177, the Chams brought their navy up the Mekong and sacked the holy center, but the present plan owes its inspiration to Jayavarman VII (1181–1219) who, in a veritable building frenzy, ordered the construction of his own temple mausoleum, the Bayon, that of his son at distant Banteay Chmar, as well as numerous other temples, roads, bridges, way stations, and hospitals. To each major temple he enfeoffed villages to supply the functionaries with food and other consumables, one temple alone being supported by 79,365 people occupying 3,140 villages.

This political system relied to a considerable extent on the readiness of this rural population to provide and deliver the necessary surpluses. In the absence of currency, goods themselves were centralized, and redistributed. While the overlord might control through his army the means of destruction, it was faith in his divine status that bonded the center to the periphery. It may be that the excesses of Jayavarman VII undermined this critical element, for building activity certainly declined after his death and two centuries of relative stagnation ended when the Thais finally destroyed Angkor in the mid-fifteenth century.

In a real sense, the tradition set at Angkor lives on, for many of its ritual procedures, symbols, and the mystical status of royalty are to be found in the Kingdom of Thailand and, until very recently, that of Cambodia itself.

[*See also* ASIA: PREHISTORY AND EARLY HISTORY OF SOUTHEAST ASIA; FUNAN CULTURE; KHMER CIVILIZATION AND THE EMPIRE OF ANGKOR.]

■ B. P. Grosher, *Indochina* (1966). G. Coedes, *The Indianized States of Southeast Asia* (1968). O. W. Wolters, *History, Culture and Region in Southeast Asian Perspectives* (1982). P. Wheatley, *Nagaza and Commandery* (1983). M. Vickery, "Some Remarks on Early State Formation in Cambodia," in *Southeast Asia in the 9th to 14th Centuries*, eds. D. G. Marr and A. P. Milner (1986), pp. 95–115. O.F.W. Higham, *The Archaeology of Mainland Southeast Asia* (1989). N. Zarling, ed., *The Cambridge History of Southeast Asia*, vol. 1 (1992).

Charles Higham

SOUTHERN AFRICA, Later Iron Age Societies of.

Farming societies in southern Africa—communities with mixed economies incorporating plant cultivation and animal husbandry—are grouped together as the "Iron Age." In turn, the Iron Age has been subdivided into an early Iron Age and a later Iron Age. These are more terms of convenience than precise divisions. "Ages" came into use here (as in many parts of the world) before radiometric techniques of dating revolutionized archaeology by replacing such speculative systems of chronology.

Southern Africa's first archaeologists imported the time-honored northern European "age system," dropping the Bronze Age and Neolithic because there was a direct transition from the use of chipped stone tools to forged hoes, axes, and other iron implements. But, as in other parts of the world, radiocarbon chronologies have made unilinear sequences of ages seem a cumbersome way of describing the past. The change from the use of stone technology to ironworking is by no means coterminous in all parts of the subcontinent; in some regions hunter-gatherers carried on using stone tools for many centuries while iron implements were made by neighboring farmers. Furthermore, in some regions there is considerable continuity through the full range of the Iron Age, making divisions such as "early" and "later" difficult to define. Additionally, most farming sites are known for their scatters of broken ceramics, often with distinctive forms and decorative motifs, rather than for the remains of iron technology.

The beginning of the later Iron Age is usually taken to be the marked change in ceramic form and decoration that took place in many areas south of the Zambezi River around

A.D. 1000. For example, in the southeast of the subcontinent (Natal, Zululand, and Transkei) the distinctively incised geometric designs that had characterized pots and bowls made from about A.D. 200 were replaced, apparently abruptly, by differently shaped vessels, usually dark burnished and often undecorated. But in other areas, changes are less clear cut. In eastern Botswana, for instance, there is continuity from initial farming settlement in about A.D. 700 through to about A.D. 1300, while in southern Zimbabwe some archaeologists have argued for continuity, while others have seen in the ceramic assemblages evidence of interrupted sequences.

The end of the later Iron Age is also difficult to define. Many would take it to be the initiation of a "historic" period, when written ethnographic accounts began to become available. However, such descriptions, albeit often vague, start with Arabic writers' references to Azania and the lands of the Waqwaq, and gain momentum from the first Portuguese circumnavigations of the late fifteenth century; most of the later Iron Age is thus part of the historic period. All in all then, archaeological ages should be taken as rough working concepts—loose groupings of information that drag around a fairly heavy burden of past assumptions, but which still seem to have some residual use.

Earlier interpretations of the changes that mark the beginning of the later Iron Age in some areas saw the new ceramics as evidence for a migration southward of cattle keeping warriors, bringing with them the Bantu languages spoken today over most of southern Africa. All later writers, while differing among themselves in detail, now reject the idea of an invasion from the north, and stress instead that developments within the Iron Age were local to the southern African region. The most comprehensive synthesis sees a buildup of population in the well-watered, fertile lands of the southeast and a concomitant increase in cattle herds. Farmers in search of new grazing then spread outward, farther to the south (absorbing the last of the early Iron Age communities), westward onto the high grasslands of the interior plateau (until this time, still the domain of hunter-gatherer bands), and northward across the Limpopo River into modern-day Zimbabwe. The various ceramic assemblages that have been taken as evidence for these movements have been collectively described as the Kutama and Moloko traditions. The Kutama/Moloko model focuses attention on the Mozambican lowlands, which must have been a nucleus for the proposed boom in cattle-keeping, and where comparatively little archaeological fieldwork has yet been completed.

One of the main difficulties with interpretations that rely heavily on the differences and similarities of ceramic assemblages is that we have little idea what such variations mean in terms of real human behavior. For example, it has usually been assumed in southern African archaeology that different pottery styles indicate different "people." But ethnoarchaeological studies have also shown that groups within the same community may use variations in material culture style in complex ways, suggesting that the relationship between ceramic traditions and society may be far more complex than is allowed by many archaeological interpretations. It is thus fortunate that there is evidence other than ceramics for the nature of life in the later Iron Age.

One such source of evidence is settlement pattern. The early Iron Age had been characterized by dispersed villages. These were often small, and there is little evidence that there were hierarchical arrangements. Although some

people were undoubtedly more wealthy and important than others, it seems likely that such differentiation was internal to each village—there is no evidence that any particular sites were structurally more important than others. The later Iron Age is characterized by a marked departure from this pattern. By the twelfth century large towns had been established in eastern Botswana as well as farther down the Limpopo River. Toutswemogala, Bosutswe, Shoshong, Mapungubwe, Mmamgwa, and Mapela were all many times larger than the contemporary sites that have been plotted in the hinterlands of some of these towns. In several cases there is evidence for elite groups: accumulations of wealth in the form of cattle, ornate grave goods, or larger, more widely spaced houses than those allowed the majority of the population. These developments have been seen as evidence for a new, hierarchical form of social and political organization, with the centralization of power and wealth.

These developments along the Limpopo were precursors for early Zimbabwe, for which the southern African later Iron Age is best known. *Great Zimbabwe rose in the thirteenth century, following the decline of the earlier towns to the south, and had itself declined by the time the first Portuguese adventurers arrived off the southeast African coast at the very beginning of the sixteenth century. Many smaller, regional centers, following the same architectural tradition, were built during this period, bringing the eastern Kalahari margins, the Zimbabwe plateau, and much of northern Mozambique directly into the same social and economic frame. After Great Zimbabwe's decline, successor states rose in the south of its former territory, with a capital at the smaller but equally elaborate site of Khami, and also in the north.

Later Iron Age settlement patterns are particularly evident on the high southern grasslands (parts of the Transvaal and the Orange Free State). Here, in the absence of extensive reserves of timber, farmers built enclosures for their livestock from stone—sites that are clearly visible on aerial photographs, allowing their distributions to be accurately plotted. Roughly circular kraals were linked by secondary walling to form complex designs, and the various types of plan have been used by archaeologists in a similar way to pottery decoration, in order to plot the distribution of different "cultures." In some cases, house foundations were also of stone, but in other cases domestic areas were built in mud and thatch, making them less easy to find. Favored areas for occupation were close to rock outcrops (sources of building material) and not too far from the meandering river systems; in this sharply seasonal climate, with little rainfall in the winter months, water supply must have been a major concern. In some areas, settlement units were fairly widely scattered, but in other areas there were dense concentrations of building that comprised loose towns that housed substantial populations. But, in comparison with the Limpopo Valley and Zimbabwe plateau, there is little evidence for the centralization of power and wealth. Although some of the highveld sites are a little larger than others, the air photographs show no evidence of the hierarchies that are a marked feature of early state systems in most parts of the world.

The later Iron Age to the southeast and east of the shield-like plateau that forms the geographical core of South Africa has been less systematically studied. Farmers continued to live in the low-lying areas—long established as the domain of the early Iron Age—and moved to the higher areas, probably to take advantage of the possibilities offered by these uplands for grazing larger herds of livestock. Many stone-built settlements are known, in a wide variety of architectural styles, but only a few have been excavated, and there have been only local studies of distribution patterns. However, the general consequence of the expansion of the farming way of life in the later Iron Age is clear. By A.D. 1500 farmers, depending on various mixes of grain crops and domestic stock, had taken into use almost all the southern African summer rainfall region. The exceptions were the high Drakensburg (where Bushman hunter-gatherers continued to hunt and raid until the end of the nineteenth century) and the western edge of the highveld, where rainfall was too unreliable for crop cultivation, and stone-tool-using pastoralists—the Khoikhoi—continued with a nomadic way of life.

One of the consequences of both more complex political and economic systems and of taking into use the high grasslands with their more limited range of resources was the sacrifice of local self-sufficiency. The complex societies that grew up in, and north of, the Limpopo depended on trade networks, both with the East African coast, where commodities such as gold and ivory were bartered for rarities such as glass beads and cloth, and with other southern African communities. In addition, although the high grasslands provided good grazing, their lack of timber resources made ironworking (which requires large quantities of charcoal) impractical. As a result of factors such as these, a number of craft specializations developed in the later Iron Age. Ironworking is particularly well known because it leaves durable evidence in the archaeological record; it is probable that there were other specializations that have not left such clear evidence for their practice.

One area where there is particularly rich evidence for ironworking is in the vicinity of the eastern Transvaal mining town of Phalaborwa. Here there is evidence for a metal-working industry stretching back to the eighth century A.D. Several hundred smelting sites mark the places where copper and iron were extracted before being forged into wire, beads, bracelets, arrow and spear points, woodworking adzes, and agricultural hoes. A similar center, although not on such a substantial scale, has been studied at Mabhija, in the upper valley of Natal's Thukela River. Iron ore was quarried on an extensive scale, and smelting furnaces were worked in pairs. Products were probably traded up over the escarpment to farmers on the highveld grasslands.

Settlement patterns, domestic economies, crafts, and trade leave material traces in the archaeological record, allowing a reconstruction of some aspects of past ways of life. Belief systems, such as religion and ritual or perceptions of social organization, are more difficult to unravel. Archaeologists working in these areas have taken advantage of the fact that there is demonstrable continuity between the "prehistoric" Iron Age (when verbal information about the past is at best indirect) and the "historic" Iron Age, when the vanguard of European colonization recorded accounts of variable thoroughness and reliability. There are dangers in reading these ethnographies back into the past, since many of their writers carried with them immense prejudices against Africa's indigenous communities, and since to clothe the rather bare bones of archaeological evidence with rich but intangible cultural trappings may be to smother the past with the present, denying the possibilities for change.

The major attempt to integrate the ethnographic and archaeological evidence as a way of reconstructing the "cognitive system" of the later Iron Age has been the case that has been made for a "Bantu Cattle Pattern"—a way of organizing settlement space and house layout that writes structural oppositions such as male/female and headman/commoner into the layout of the village, using oppositions such as left/right and high/low. It has been argued that this way of seeing the world is as much part of the southern African Iron Age as the Bantu languages, and that the emergence of twelfth-century Mapungubwe (followed by Great Zimbabwe, *Khami, and other major centers) was also the emergence of a second, parallel cognitive system that signaled high authority through the positioning of those of importance on the summits of hills. This interpretation shares the strengths and weaknesses of structuralist archaeology in general; cognitive systems are a persuasive marshaling of ethnographic and archaeological evidence as a coherent interpretation, but at the same time such syntheses can become frozen images, unchanging and apparently incapable of explaining change.

The most difficult aspect of southern African Iron Age studies to summarize is that of race. Earlier workers made the simple assumption that biological variation could be represented by simple types—collections of physical attributes—and that Iron Age archaeological sites were part of the debris of a "Negro" invasion southward. Subsequently, biological anthropology has shown that the transmission of physical variability is far more complex, and must be seen in terms of genetic pools, often with complicated patterns of overlap. Such genetic variation can be studied only through statistically viable samples, rendering individual burials and their racial typification of little use. Complicating the matter further is the legacy of the sustained abuse of racial classification in South Africa—the inheritance of apartheid that will affect southern African archaeological research for many years to come.

[See also AFRICA: THE RISE OF KINGDOMS AND STATES IN AFRICA; MAPUNGUBWE AND TOUTSWEMOGALA.]

■ N. J. van der Merwe and R. Scully, "The Phalaborwa Story: Archaeological and Ethnographic Investigation of a South African Iron Age Group," World Archaeology 3 (1971): 178–196. Peter Garlake, Great Zimbabwe (1973). P. V. Tobias, "The Biology of the Southern African Negro," in W. D. Hammond-Tooke, ed., The Bantu-Speaking Peoples of Southern Africa (1974). Tim Maggs, Iron Age Communities of the Southern Highveld (1976). John Parkington and Michael Cronin, "The Size and Layout of Mgungundlovu, 1829–1838," South African Archaeological Society Goodwin Series 3 (1979): 133–148. T. N. Huffman, "Snakes and Birds: Expressive Space at Great Zimbabwe," African Studies 40 (1981): 131–150. T. N. Huffman, "Archaeology and Ethnohistory of the African Iron Age," Annual Review of Anthropology 11 (1982): 133–150. Martin Hall, "Pots and Politics: Ceramic Interpretations in Southern Africa," World Archaeology 15 (1984): 262–273. Tim Maggs, "The Iron Age South of the Zambezi," in Richard Klein, ed., Southern African Prehistory and Palaeoenvironments (1984). Martin Hall, Farmers, Kings and Traders. The People of Southern Africa 200–1860 (1990).

Martin Hall

SOUTHERN CULT. The Southern Cult refers to certain elite art and costumery of *Mississippian culture in the eastern United States, about A.D. 1000–1600. The art occurs in a variety of styles and media, most commonly as embossed sheets of native copper, engraved marine shell, stone statuary and pendants, engraved stone palettes, and painted or engraved pottery. Much of it is portable art meant to be worn or carried as elements of dress indicating special status. Sheet copper artifacts, for instance, often formed elements of elaborate headdresses. Among the most prominent facts concerning these elite artifacts is that they are very often found at Mississippian ceremonial centers hundreds of kilometers distant from the raw materials used in their manufacture, and they are made in distinctive styles that can be traced to various particular Mississippian societies located throughout the culture area. The leaders of these far-flung societies seem to have been linked together in tenuous exchange relationships, in which the acquisition of exotic prestige goods was important to the preservation of hereditary political offices. This limited exchange is believed to have promoted the diffusion of standard religious symbols among societies that otherwise were virtually unconnected and that developed along independent lines.

Although these art styles differ substantially through space and time, and although the pictorial art ranges from realistic to abstract, certain common themes recur. Most of the content centers upon warfare, supernatural beings, or some combination of these two, which suggests that perceived supernatural control over the outcome of actual military conflict among adjacent societies may have been an important message to be conveyed. The military content is exemplified by realistic depictions of maces, flint swords, and bows and arrows, either brandished by human warrior figures or depicted in conjunction with scalps, severed heads, and skeletalized body parts. Supernaturals shown in the art take the form of composite monsters, of which some are vaguely recognizable in the folklore of the historic Native Americans of the Southeast, Caddo, and Central Plains regions of North America. Figuring most prominently are, first, a horned serpent, bearing wings or a feather plume; second, a bird of prey, sometimes transformed into the common theme of the birdman; and third, a panther with reptilian, avian, and sometimes human characteristics. All of these may appear with a distinctive forked motif surrounding the eye, probably derived from the natural eye markings of the peregrine falcon and suggestive of the lightning that was said to flash from the eyes of similar supernaturals in the historic era. Other conventional motifs, for example, those commonly referred to as the ogee, the hand-and-eye, and the bilobed arrow, are difficult to interpret by means of ethnographic analogy and may have an obscure cosmological significance. Given the broad and uneven geographical distribution of this iconography, it seems likely that its meanings varied from place to place, and may have been differently understood by nobles, religious specialists, and commoners.

The concept of the Southern Cult has changed substantially in a half-century of use. A popular thesis in the early twentieth century that the art was directly inspired by Mesoamerican images is, today, discounted by most Southeast specialists, who instead point to developmental antecedents within the region. As developed by Antonio Waring and Preston Holder in the 1940s, the Southern Cult was formalized as a specific trait list consisting of motifs, motif complexes, god-animal representations, and ceremonial objects, with specific reference to materials from the ceremonial centers of Etowah, Georgia, *Moundville, Alabama, and *Spiro Mounds, Oklahoma. They believed it to be a unitary, short-lived cult phenomenon that spread from a Mississippi Valley hearth on the eve of European contact. As the advent of radiocarbon dating discredited this view, more attention has gradually been paid to regional differences in time depth, style zones, and thematic emphases. Modern scholarship acknowledges that the materials in

question do not constitute a unitary phenomenon as was once believed. Rather, the artifacts are interpreted as deriving from several different social institutions within Mississippian societies. The ones most often suggested include hereditary elites, military ranks, and priesthoods concerned with the propitiation of ancestors. As the original concept has yielded to more detailed analyses, the term "Southern Cult" still appears in the literature from time to time, either as a shorthand for the whole corpus of Mississippian ceremonial art and architecture or even more broadly as a label for a postulated common world view attributed to Mississippian religion.

[See also MOUNDS OF EASTERN NORTH AMERICA; NORTH AMERICA: THE EASTERN WOODLANDS AND THE SOUTH.]

■ S. Williams, ed., *The Waring Papers: The Collected Works of Antonio J. Waring, Jr.* (1968). J. A. Brown, "The Southern Cult Reconsidered," *Mid-Continental Journal of Archaeology* 1 (1976): 115–135. P. Phillips and J. A. Brown, *Pre-Columbian Shell Engravings from the Craig Mound at Spiro, Oklahoma*, parts 1 and 2 (1978–1984). J. A. Brown, "The Mississippian Period," *Ancient Art of the American Woodland Indians*, ed. D. S. Brose, J. A. Brown, and D. W. Penney (1985), pp. 92–145. V. J. Knight Jr., "The Institutional Organization of Mississippian Religion," *American Antiquity* 51 (1986): 675–687. P. Galloway, ed., *The Southeastern Ceremonial Complex: Artifacts and Analysis* (1989).

Vernon James Knight

SPEECH AND LANGUAGE. Archaeology and linguistics have two points of contact. The first is the study of the origin of language, in terms of a biologically endowed capacity to acquire a specific language. As our closest relatives, the apes, have such rudimentary linguistic abilities, the evolution of our language capacity must have occurred after the hominid-ape divergence about six million years ago, much of which is within the time frame of the archaeological record. Consequently, we have the task of identifying when the capacity for language arose from the evidence of the archaeological record. A second point of contact between archaeology and linguistics is the study of the origin and spread of languages. The archaeological role in this endeavor is to provide the chronological framework, and the social and economic processes, which have resulted in the modern distribution of languages as understood by historical linguists.

Archaeology and the Origin of Language. Language is widely acknowledged as a uniquely human capacity. The extent to which we attribute linguistic abilities to apes and other nonhuman species depends, of course, on how we define language. Yet in spite of several decades of language experiments, no ape has acquired the two essential features of human language: a vast lexicon of many thousands of words and a series of complex grammatical rules. Language is also widely acknowledged as having a genetic basis and is most appropriately characterized as an instinct, an ability that develops and matures rather than is learned. Noam Chomsky recognized that all languages share the same structure, which he termed the "universal grammar." As a uniquely human capacity, but one that is part of our biological constitution, the capacity for language must have arisen after the phylogenetic divergence of hominids from the apes.

The challenge facing archaeologists is to develop criteria by which a linguistic capacity can be recognized in a Paleolithic archaeological record dominated by stone tools and the waste from their manufacture. The feasibility of this is likely to depend upon the relationship of language to other cognitive processes. If the same cognitive processes are used in "generating" utterances as in "generating" stone tools, then as technology reaches a complexity equivalent to that of modern humans, we can safely assume that language does likewise. On this basis, language would be implied by the appearance of later Acheulian technology about 500,000 years ago, which involved long and complex knapping sequences.

If, on the other hand, language and technology rely on independent cognitive processes, any direct inference about the linguistic capacity from the character of prehistoric technology will be impossible. In light of the recent arguments in psycholinguistics, such as by Noam Chomsky and Jerry Fodor, this appears to be the case: language derives from highly modularized cognitive processes, which are specific to language alone. This is supported by studies of people who have lost their capacity for language due to cognitive pathologies but who retain the capacity for fine motor control.

In light of this, archaeologists require indirect evidence for the appearance of language. This should be forthcoming, since our modern behavior is so structured by language that its appearance in the course of human evolution would have resulted in a restructuring of social and economic relationships. Consequently, when language evolves—and it is often thought to be a rather sudden event—we ought to see a major transformation in the character of the archaeological record, even if there are no direct implications for the form and complexity of stone tools.

This has led several archaeologists to argue that the appearance of fully modern language is a very late evolutionary event, appearing at ca. 50,000 B.P. and fundamentally related to the transition from the Middle to the Upper Paleolithic. Iain Davidson and William Noble, stressing the symbolic aspect of language, have argued that its origin lies in depiction, for this allowed people to recognize that an arbitrary symbol can be used to refer to a distant event. They suggest that the colonization of Australia, requiring the manufacture of boats and crossing of extensive waters, is the earliest indirect evidence for a linguistic capacity. In a similar vein, Robert Whallon has suggested that fully modern language was critical for the Upper Paleolithic colonization of arid environments, such as Siberia, for it was only with language that the extensive social alliance networks essential for survival in such marginal environments could have been maintained. The appearance of representational art, and complex symbolic codes manifest in abstract imagery, by 35,000 B.P. certainly implies that fully modern language had evolved by that date.

If these arguments for a late evolution of language are correct, they raise the issue of the nature of language prior to 50,000 B.P.—the protolanguage capacity possessed by archaic humans, and indeed early *Homo sapiens sapiens*. We must expect this to have been substantially more developed than that of modern apes, partly in light of the behavioral achievements of these hominids, such as colonization of northern latitudes, and partly because, as a biological capacity, language must have an evolutionary history. Moreover, when we examine the endocasts of hominids as early as *Homo habilis* (ca. two million years ago), we find an enlargement of Broca's area, which is known to contain the neuronal structures related to language. More generally, by 1.7 million years ago, *Homo erectus* had a brain capacity of 80 percent that of modern humans, and it is most likely that this had been selected to enable complex social interaction

involving the use of protolanguage. Moreover, fossil evidence suggests that by the time of *H. erectus*, prolonged childhoods emerged that may have facilitated or been essential for the acquisition of protolanguage.

One possibility for the nature of protolanguage, suggested by Michael Corballis, is that it was principally gestural in nature. Indeed, it has long been argued that the origin of language lies in gesture and it is clear from modern sign languages that speech is merely one particular manifestation of the language capacity. As such, protolanguage may have involved all the elements of spoken language, but was simply gestural rather than spoken. Michael Corballis argues that at ca. 50,000–40,000 B.P. there is a change in mode of language from gesture to speech, thus freeing the hands for the technical and artistic developments that occur with the Upper *Paleolithic. While this appears unfairly dismissive of the technological achievements of Archaic humans, Philip Lieberman has indeed argued that *Neanderthals were restricted to a very narrow range of vocal sounds due to the relative positions of the larynx descended into the neck, which appears to be unique to *Homo sapiens sapiens*. Such anatomical change may well have substantially reduced the role of gesture in communication.

Even if Philip Lieberman is correct, it is unlikely that extensive vocalization did not play a substantial role in the protolanguage of Archaic humans. It is clear that the vocalizations of monkeys and apes are intentional and essential to their social interactions with con-specifics. Indeed, if we are to look for the behavioral domain that provided the selective pressures for the elaboration of this incipient capacity for language, this is most likely to be found in social interaction and, more particularly, in the problems resulting from living within large groups.

The biological anthropologist Robin Dunbar has noted that much of our modern communication is "gossip"—talk about the social relations of others—and suggests that this gives us a clue to the evolutionary roots of language. He argues that language evolved to facilitate living in large groups in which it becomes essential to make firm alliances and to keep track of the behaviors, thoughts, and feelings of other individuals. This is an ingenious and convincing argument. The enlargement of the hominid brain during the Pleistocene does indeed suggest that hominids were living in increasingly larger groups, there being a correlation among primates between brain size (as measured by the relative size of the neocortex) and group size. As such, it firmly places the onus on archaeologists to develop means to infer hominid group size from the archaeological record and to explain the social and economic pressures for the increase in hominid group size during the Pleistocene.

Whatever the origin of human language and the archaeological record of its evolution, we can be confident that by 35,000 years ago a fully human linguistic capacity had emerged, and that language had become the structuring force of human social interaction. After this date the relationship between archaeology and language shifts to exploring how the archaeological record can help describe and explain the proliferation and distribution of human languages.

Archaeology and the Origin and Spread of Languages. Today there are perhaps as many as 10,000 languages in the world. Historical linguists have the task of classifying these into families and macro-families, and suggesting the character of early languages that no longer survive. Techniques such as glottochronology focus on identifying the similarities and differences between existing languages and suggesting the date at which they diverged from a common ancestor.

During the 1920s and 1930s it was common for archaeologists to contribute to this field by using the distribution of archaeological cultures to propose patterns of migrations and invasions by ethnic groups, who were assumed to have their own language. Hitler and National Socialists exploited work of this kind, such as that of Gustav *Kossinna, to legitimize their own political agenda. Not surprisingly, in the postwar years, archaeologists shied away from the study of language dispersal. This neglect was exacerbated by the decreased concern with migration and invasion as explanations in archaeology that occurred during the 1960s and 1970s. But the contribution of archaeology to historical linguistics was transformed in 1987 when Colin Renfrew published his seminal book *Archaeology and Language: The Puzzle of Indo-European Origins*. This reintroduced the study of language evolution and dispersal into the mainstream of archaeological thought. Its significance lay as much in the methodological arguments bearing on how language change can be recognized archaeologically as for the specific hypothesis it proposed for the origin of the *Indo-Europeans.

The challenge that archaeologists face when concerned with tracing the spread of languages is to identify correctly the relationship, if any, between the language and the material culture of a group of people. As the equation between an "archaeological culture" and an "ethnic group" has been questioned, if not dismissed, the means by which archaeologists can recognize ethnic, and therefore linguistic, groups become contentious. In some situations there may be a direct relationship between the spread of certain types of material culture and language. For instance, Christopher Ehert has conducted ethnoarchaeological studies among small-scale African groups whose social organization is less complex than a "chiefdom," and recognized that there is a correlation between pottery decoration and ethnicity, which is principally defined by language. Yet in different socioeconomic contexts such a relationship is unlikely, for pottery decoration may spread through trade and imitation.

Colin Renfrew proposed alternative criteria for monitoring the spread of languages in the archaeological record by focusing on demographic and technological variables. The most indicative archaeological pattern, he argued, is when there is the rapid introduction of a new technology and economic basis into an area that leads to substantial increases in population densities, exemplified by agricultural dispersals. Another process of language dispersal with archaeological consequences is "elite dominance"—the intrusion of a relatively small but well-organized group that displaces an existing elite by coercion. In certain cases, this may lead to the language of the new elite becoming dominant. Archaeologically this process can be recognized by the introduction of what Christopher Ehret calls a "status kit"—a coherently maintained prestige suite of cultural traits. When a "status kit" spreads by diffusion to peoples of other languages, it becomes truncated, and only certain elements are adopted. Consequently, to infer the process of elite dominance, with its implications for language change, archaeologists need to recognize the spread of a coherent and discrete package of prestige items.

These approaches to recognizing the movements of people and spread of languages are more processual in character, without a reliance on the contentious notion of archaeological "cultures." Colin Renfrew used them to readdress the origin of the Indo-European languages. The conventional idea had been that these had originated in a "homeland" in the south Russian steppes in the third millennium. Renfrew rejected this on the grounds that there was no sufficiently profound and widespread shift in the archaeological record at that time to indicate large movements of peoples. He substituted for it the claim that the origin of Indo-European languages relates to the dispersal of farming across Europe and Anatolia, some 8,000 years ago.

This was a provocative hypothesis, but one that fitted with the dispersal of Bantu and Polynesian languages, which also appear to have derived from the movement of agriculturalists. Of the various challenges to Renfrew's model the most important was by Marek Zvelebil, who argued that the "wave of advance" model that Renfrew used for the spread of agriculture in Europe is not tenable with the archaeological evidence. In many areas of Europe acculturation and the spread of ideas, rather than the spread of people, played the dominant role in the change from a hunter-gatherer to an agricultural lifestyle. On this basis Marek Zvelebil proposed a revised model for the spread of Indo-European languages, maintaining an initial, but spatially restricted, spread of agriculturalists but adding secondary dispersals and occurrences of elite dominance. The specific explanation about the origin of the Indo-European languages remains to be resolved, but Colin Renfrew's work has demonstrated that archaeology can—indeed it must—play a central role in explaining the modern distribution of languages and language families.

Archaeologists can also turn to historical linguistics to develop their models for the colonization processes of new lands, or to support specific hypotheses. For instance, there is a heated debate concerning the time of entry of humans into the New World from Asia via the Beringia land bridge. Dates as early as 50,000 B.P. have been proposed, while others suggest that New World colonization did not occur until 12,000 B.P. at the earliest. In the context of such controversy evidence from other sources, such as linguistics, may be extremely important. Joseph Greenberg has proposed that Native American languages can be classified into three macro-families. Aleut-Eskimo, Na-Dene, and Amerind, and that these relate to three separate migrations into North America. This threefold division appears to be supported by dental and genetic data. Using glottochronology, Greenberg dates the origin of the diversification of the languages within these groups to ca. 4000 B.P. for Aleut-Eskimo, ca. 4700 B.P. for Na-Dene, and ca. 11,000 B.P. for Amerind. As such this supports those archaeologists who dismiss the evidence for a pre-12,000 B.P. colonization. Greenberg's classification is considered controversial by other linguists of Native American languages.

This last example illustrates how linguistic, genetic, and archaeological data need to be synthesized to understand the movements of past peoples. Colin Renfrew has argued that the recent developments in these three disciplines—in terms of the identification of about twenty macro language families in the world, the developments in microbiology and ancient DNA studies, and a processual approach to prehistoric social and economic change—contain the germs of just such a synthesis. Together with the developments in our understanding of the origin of language, there is likely to be very considerable increase in the interaction between archaeologists and linguists in the next decade.

[See also HUMAN EVOLUTION: THE ORIGINS OF HUMAN BEHAVIOR.]

■ I. Davison, "The Archaeology of Language Origins: A Review," *Antiquity* 65 (1991): 39–48. T. W. Deacon, "The Neural Circuitry Underlying Primate Calls and Human Language," in *Language Origin: A Multidisciplinary Approach*, eds. J. Wind, B. Chiarelli, B. Bichakhian and A. Nocentini (1992), pp. 121–162. R.I.M. Dunbar, "Coevolution of Neocortical Size, Group Size and Language in Humans," *Behavioural and Brain Sciences* 16 (1993): 681–735. L. A. Schepartz, "Language and Modern Human Origins," *Yearbook of Physical Anthropology* 36 (1993): 91–126.

Steven Mithen

SPIRIT CAVE is the name given to a complex of caverns located in karst terrain overlooking the Khong Stream in northern Thailand. The area is under a canopied rain forest, and the site occupies a steep slope above the stream bed. It was discovered by Chester Gorman, who began excavations in 1965. The stratigraphic sequence was divided into four layers, and was less than 3 feet (1 m) in depth. It incorporates a series of ash lenses and hearths which, in conjunction with the shallow cultural deposits, indicate transient occupation episodes. The radiocarbon chronology suggests that this took place over several millennia between 11,000 and 5,500 B.C.

The material culture is dominated by flaked stone implements, including unifacial discoids, which belong to a widespread Southeast Asian tradition usually called *Hoabinhian, after the Vietnamese province where such tools were first encountered and described. A feature of Gorman's excavations was the screening of all deposits, and the dry conditions favored the preservation of animal bone and plant remains. The former includes a few large mammals, such as bovids and deer, but the majority of the species identified represent the canopied forest habitat and include squirrels, small carnivores, and monkeys. No remains of the dog were encountered, an important point since there was no native wolf in Southeast Asia available for domestication. Plants represented include the remains of stimulants, various nuts and plants used today as toxins and adhesives. Some possible food plants were also found, though it is not possible to distinguish between palm and pea remains on the basis of the surviving material. Two possible bean seeds were also recovered. All these plants are compatible with foraging in the forested habitat in the site's vicinity. Fish and shellfish also reflect exploitation of the stream.

The surface of layer two contained a number of potsherds, polished stone adzes of quadrangular shape, and small bifacial slate knives. These have been seen to represent some form of agricultural activity, and since the radiocarbon date from the same surface dates to about 6,000 B.C., such an innovation would appear to be very early in the context of East and Southeast Asian prehistory. Several facts, however, require extreme caution. The surface of layer two is covered only by the very thin layer one, which rarely exceeds 2 inches (5 cm) in depth. The radiocarbon date is extremely questionable according to Spriggs and Anderson's (1993) principles for chronometric hygiene. Finally, excavations of the nearby *Banyan Cave have uncovered a lower layer dated far later than 6000 B.C., which included a Hoabinhian stone industry with no pottery or ground-edge implements. The cultural and chronological contexts for the ceramic assemblage must, therefore, be seriously questioned.

The site represents one of many such rock shelters in tropical Southeast Asia which offered temporary shelter to groups of mobile foragers adapted for millennia to the forested upland habitat.

[See also ASIA: PREHISTORY AND EARLY HISTORY OF SOUTHEAST ASIA; ASIA, ORIGINS OF FOOD PRODUCTION IN: ORIGINS OF FOOD PRODUCTION IN SOUTHEAST ASIA.]

■ C. F. Gorman, "The Hoabinhian and After: Subsistence Patterns in Southeast Asia during the Late Pleistocene and Early Recent Periods," *World Archaeology* 2:3 (1971): 300–20. C. F. Gorman, "Excavations at Spirit Cave, North Thailand: Some Interim Impressions," *Asian Perspectives* 13 (1972): 79–107.

Charles Higham

SPIRO MOUNDS. The Spiro site is the premier ceremonial center of the Arkansas River Valley Caddoan Tradition in eastern Oklahoma, and one of the more impressive late prehistoric religious and political centers in the southeastern United States. Of special import are the massive quantities of exotic prestige goods from Spiro, such as several thousand Gulf coast conch shell cups, beads, and pendants, embossed copper plates, and other ritual paraphernalia representing the Southeastern Ceremonial Complex. These signify the wealth of the Spiroan peoples as well as the status and power of its leaders.

Spiro lies along the Arkansas River near the Ozark highlands and the Ouachita Mountains. The 89-acre (36 ha) site was discovered in 1934 by relic hunters of the Pocola Mining Company, who tunneled into the Craig Mound and uncovered many burials with elaborate grave goods. When the relic hunting was stopped in 1936, Works Progress Administration archaeological crews excavated there until 1941. Their excavations, and subsequent investigations in the 1960s–1980s by the University of Oklahoma and the Oklahoma Archeological Survey, have documented fifteen earthen mounds (used as burial places, for building platforms, and to cover former building locations), a small settlement with a number of rectangular houses, and more than 750 burials, dating to A.D. 850–1450. The corpus of goods found with the burials, particularly from the thirteen cedar litter burials in Craig Mound's Great Mortuary, is unprecedented in the southeastern United States. The Spiroans accumulated these prestige goods through long-distance trade with Mississippi Valley and Southern Plains groups, perhaps through the enterprising exchange of bison hides.

From A.D. 850 to 1250, Spiro was one of at least twelve ceremonial centers in the region, it and the Harlan site preeminent among independent Arkansas River communities. The communities were composed of small hamlets of horticultural folk. By A.D. 1250, Spiro dominated the region, with its leaders wielding considerable political, economic, and social power. After A.D. 1450, the Arkansas River Valley Caddoan peoples had little interaction with other southeastern chiefdoms, and the site was abandoned.

Recent research at Spiro focuses on reevaluating the social and adaptive context of these Caddoan groups. Of particular concern are its biological and cultural affinities with other Caddoan and Mississippian peoples, household integration, and the timing and character of economic, social, and ritual interaction.

The Spiro site now is the Spiro Mounds State Archeological Park, administered by the Oklahoma Department of Tourism and Recreation.

[See also MISSISSIPPIAN CULTURE; MOUNDS OF EASTERN

NORTH AMERICA; NORTH AMERICA: THE EASTERN WOOD-LANDS AND THE SOUTH.]

■ Philip Phillips and James A. Brown, *Pre-Columbian Shell Engravings from the Craig Mound at Spiro, Oklahoma,* Parts 1 and 2, (1978–1984). J. Daniel Rogers, Don G. Wyckoff, and Dennis A. Peterson, eds., *Contributions to Spiro Archeology: Mound Excavations and Regional Perspectives* (1989). Frank F. Schambach, "Some New Interpretations of Spiroan Culture History," in *Archaeology of Eastern North America: Papers in Honor of Stephen Williams,* ed. James B. Stoltman (1993), pp. 187–230.

Timothy K. Perttula

STAR CARR is an early Mesolithic lakeside settlement located on the northern shore of the now-extinct Lake Pickering, near the town of Scarborough in northeast Yorkshire (England). It is dated in conventional radiocarbon terms to around 9,500 B.P., implying an actual age in terms of calibrated radiocarbon dates of around 10,700 B.P.—only a few hundred years after the end of the last Ice Age. Pollen analyses indicate that at the time of occupation the site was surrounded by open birch and pine woodland, enjoying temperatures not very different from those in the same area at the present day. Excavations carried out by Professor Grahame Clark from 1949 to 1952 revealed a dense spread of flint, bone, and antler finds extending over an area of 66 by 82 feet (20 × 25 m) on the immediate shore of the lake, and extending into the adjacent lake-edge deposits. The finds consist of simple forms of *microliths (probably representing tips and barbs of arrows), flint scrapers, burins used for working antler, awls, and transversely sharpened flint axes characteristic of the early Mesolithic Proto-Maglemosian culture of northern Europe. These were associated with over two hundred barbed spearheads manufactured by the so-called groove and splinter technique from red deer antler. There were also elk-antler mattocks (possibly used for digging up roots), scraping tools made of wild oxen bones, and a number of what appear to be masks or headdresses manufactured from pairs of red deer antlers, and possibly used either as hunting disguises or in some ceremonial activities. In addition to these a number of simple perforated beads manufactured from local shale were found and one fragment of what appears to be a wooden paddle.

The associated animal remains indicate the large-scale hunting of red deer, roe deer, wild oxen, elk, and wild pig in the areas around the lake, together with a few remains of waterfowl. Curiously, there are no remains of fish from the site, possibly indicating that the lake had not yet been colonized by fish at this early stage in the Postglacial period. Remains of two domestic dogs represent some of the earliest finds of this animal so far identified in Europe. The season of occupation of the site has been disputed; while the red deer antlers point to hunting mainly during the autumn, winter, and early spring months, the remains of roe deer and pig seem to indicate hunting more during the summer months. It has been suggested that the site would have been occupied by a band of at most twenty-five people, and that the food remains represented by the animal bones alone could have supported a group of this size over a total period of six years—or over a much longer period if (as seems likely) the occupation of the site was more intermittent and seasonal. It has recently been argued that the site is more likely to represent a specialized hunting and butchery site than an occupation location. It is possible that at other seasons of the year the group (or groups) occupying the site

moved either to the adjacent coast, or possibly onto the North York moors immediately to the north.

More recent excavations carried out in 1985 and 1989 have revealed that the site covers a much larger area than previously suspected, probably extending as a series of intermittent, overlapping occupations for at least 328 feet (100 m) along the shore of the lake. Excavations immediately to the east of the original excavations have revealed remnants of a substantial wooden platform, consisting of split and worked planks of poplar or willow, laid down in the waterlogged zone at the edge of the lake. Detailed pollen and sedimentary analyses through the lake edge deposits have revealed concentrations of charcoal particles extending over a total depth of around 12 inches (30 cm), and probably indicating intermittent use of the site over a period of at least 250 to 300 years. Identification of the charcoal particles suggests that these derive from the repeated burning of the reed-swamp vegetation immediately in front of the site, either to improve access to the lake, or conceivably to improve forage supplies for the local animal populations. Concurrent survey work has revealed that Star Carr represents only one of a number of sites of similar age distributed around the shores of the ancient lake Pickering, although as yet no other site has yielded such abundant finds of bone and antler artifacts. Star Carr stands at present as perhaps the riches, best-documented, and most informative early Mesolithic site so far investigated in Europe.

[*See also* BRITISH ISLES: PREHISTORY OF THE BRITISH ISLES; EUROPE: THE EUROPEAN MESOLITHIC PERIOD.]

Paul Mellars

STATES

Theories of the Origins of States
Theories of the Collapse of States

THEORIES OF THE ORIGINS OF STATES

The origin of the state is basically a question of how and why formalized institutions of government first arose in the long trajectory of the evolution of culture in human societies. Theories of the origins of the state can generally be divided into two different schools of thought. One school, often referred to as the "integrative" (or the managerial, benefit, or consensus) school, sees the institutions of state government as evolving in response to societal needs for more effective organization in the face of growing population, economic pressures, and social complexity. The other school, often referred to as the "conflict" (or the coercive, class, or marxist) school, sees the state arising as a means to stabilize a system of social and economic stratification and to resolve social conflicts stemming from the inequalities of stratified societies. Although the "currency" of these two schools of thought has fluctuated over time, they both have deep roots back to the first philosophical writings of Western Civilization, the Middle East, China, and elsewhere.

Today, manifestations of both schools are to be found in the wide range of specific theories that have been offered to explain the origins of the state in the archaeological and ethnohistoric records. These can be grouped into three broad categories depending on the processes that are seen as central agents in the formation of the institutions of government characteristic of state-level society. Generally there are theories based on warfare, production of basic resources, and trade or exchange of resources.

In the warfare models, states emerge in the context of

large-scale and protracted warfare between groups of communities at the tribal or chiefdom level of organization. In this situation warfare may result in the conquest and subordination of one group by another, in which case the institutions of state-level government are the means by which the conquering group rules the vanquished. Warfare may not always result in conquest however, since some kinds of war are aimed at capturing resources or at driving the enemy from a particular area. Under this scenario, the institutions of state-level government arise as means both to organize the society to more competitively engage in combat and also to allocate and administer the captured land or resources.

The production models of state formation see the intensification of agriculture as the primary vehicle for the emergence of the institutions of state government. In these models, population growth and environmental conditions put pressure on a society to produce more agricultural resources through more intensive techniques of production such as irrigation or raised fields. Under these circumstances, the intensification itself requires greater organization and centralized decision making within the social system. With irrigation, for example, there has to be a centralized and coordinated effort to construct and clean canals, assign lands along the canals, and allocate water to fields. There also have to be administrative means to insure that the nonproducing parts of this system, the managers and their bureaucracy, are supported through the centralized collection and reallocation of resources from the producers. In these models, the institutions of government arise to manage agricultural production, make decisions for the system as a whole, and collect and reallocate resources (i.e., taxes) to maintain the system as an effective whole.

In the trade models, the institutions of government develop as a means of organizing either the internal exchange of different kinds of resources within a social system or large-scale trade in basic resources with outside areas. The basic premise in these models is that institutions of state government arise as a more efficient means to both procure and distribute a wide range of resources in a large and complex society. This model works under two somewhat different kinds of circumstances. In the first a large and growing population may obtain significant increases in efficiency through specialization in the production of specific resources. In the second, certain kinds of resources may only be obtained or obtained more efficiently through trade from areas or cultures outside the immediate area. In both of these cases, the institutions of state government are seen to arise as a means to manage the acquisition and distribution of resources within the social system. Decisions about levels of production of various kinds of resources in different parts of the system are made by the apparatus of the state as are decisions about the allocation within the system of resources acquired through trade or exchange. State government also assumes responsibility for physically implementing and supporting the trade or exchange networks including such things as centralized storage facilities, markets, specialized traders, and military protection of caravans.

All of the diverse theories of state formation share certain similar characteristics; namely, growing populations, the need for additional resources to sustain the population, and increasing social, technological, and economic complexity. In all of them there are certain adaptive advantages to be gained for the society as a whole to having a centralized decision-making apparatus in order to more efficiently coordinate the production, procurement, and distribution of resources. In this sense, with the exception of the conquest scenario, all of the models have elements that correspond to the integrative school of thought on state origins.

At the same time, however, elements of the conflict model can be found in each as well. This can be seen directly in the conquest model where a victorious polity uses the institutions of state government to impose rule on vanquished societies. But the seeds of conflict are found in the other models as well. In all of them the individuals in command of the institutions of state government gain greatly increased economic power through control over the production or acquisition of basic resources that are vital to the survival of the society as a whole. With this control over basic resources, the leaders in state-level societies gain a new level of power qualitatively greater than anything seen in preceding simpler forms of sociopolitical organization.

Around the world, the greatly increased power of emergent leaders in the first state societies was directly manifested in a dramatic florescence of monumental communal architecture, state-supported art, specialization in the production of luxury goods, and the appearance of elite palatial architecture. The elaborate art, crafts, and architecture characteristic of all the earliest states was supported or financed through the extraction of taxes in the form of labor or resources. Although there were undoubtedly broad ideological and economic values to the monumental art and architecture of early states, there is ample evidence that the economic power in these societies was being used to support a stratified elite in a lifestyle significantly more luxurious than the rest of the population.

The first states to have arisen in Mesopotamia, China, Egypt, India, Mesoamerica, and the Andes were all quite unique and developed along historically distinct trajectories. None of the various theories that have been offered to explain the "origins of the state" can effectively encompass the individual characteristics of each of these early polities. At the same time, however, the first states to appear around the world also shared basic characteristics of institutional bureaucracies, ruling elites, state religions, standing armies, and centralized economies. These common characteristics, standing at the heart of the state form of organization, represented a cross-cultural response to similar forces of population pressure, resource shortages, and increasing social complexity.

[See also RANKING AND SOCIAL INEQUALITY, THEORIES OF; SOCIAL ORGANIZATION, PREHISTORIC.]

■ Robert Carneiro, "A Theory of the Origin of the State," *Science* 169 (1970): 733–738. Jonathan Haas, *The Evolution of the Prehistoric State* (1982). Elizabeth M. Brumfiel and Timothy Earle, eds., *Specialization, Exchange, and Complex Societies* (1987). Arthur Demarest and Geoffrey W. Conrad, eds., *Ideology and Precolumbian Civilizations* (1992). Steven E. Falconer and Stephen H. Savage, "Heartlands and Hinterlands: Alternative Trajectories of Early Urbanization in Mesopotamia and the Southern Levant," *American Antiquity* 60:1 (1995): 37–58.

Jonathan Haas

THEORIES OF THE COLLAPSE OF STATES

Collapse is a rapid transformation to lower social, political, and economic complexity. Collapse is recurrent: States have been collapsing almost since they began. As costly political organizations requiring high levels of resources, state-organized societies are historically rare and recent, and perhaps none is immune to collapse. Some scholars conclude that collapse is a normal process, but some states do persist for a long time.

Explanations of collapse have a venerable history: Mesopotamian and Chinese writers tried to account for the fall of famous dynasties and many explanations have Greek and Roman antecedents, yet, after 3,000 years, there is no consensus on what causes collapse.

Collapse theories are grouped into seven categories, omitting minor variations. Some theories apply both to states and to simpler political systems. These are preferable, for they incorporate states into the broader phenomenon of political collapse.

Resource Depletion. Two major themes are rapid resource loss from environmental change and resource depletion through mismanagement. Such theories are old: The Western Chou dynasty (ca. 1122–771 B.C.) and Roman writers linked political weakness to environmental deterioration. American geographer Ellsworth Huntington explained the fall of Rome by adverse climate; other writers argue that irrigation intensification weakened Mesopotamian states, as saline groundwater diminished agricultural yields. Some scholars suggest that insufficient Nile floods exacerbated Egyptian political upheavals, including the Old Kingdom collapse (ca. 3100–2181 B.C.); that drought weakened Mycenaean civilization (ca. 1650–1050 B.C.); and that volcanism and climate played a part in Near Eastern collapses. Still others attribute the Classic Maya collapse (ca. A.D. 250–900) to environmental factors, including soil erosion, while some archaeologists implicate soil depletion and savanna formation, consequences of tropical agriculture. Another writer has blamed tectonic uplift in the collapse of the *Chimu state, after A.D. 1000.

Clearly there is logic here: No state can exist without resources. Yet governments always allocate labor and resources, and gather information to do so. These capabilities allow states to ameliorate production shortages. Failure to ease resource deficiencies must therefore be attributed partly to political and economic factors, which the best theories incorporate and which shifts the explanation from resources to the society. Resource depletion alone thus cannot explain collapse.

Catastrophes. Hurricanes, volcanoes, earthquakes, and epidemics are favorite causal candidates. The biblical flood and Plato's Atlantis conveyed early moral lessons. Hurricanes, earthquakes, and epidemics have been implicated in the Maya collapse, and Thera's eruption is said to have doomed Minoan civilization (ca. 2000–1380 B.C.). Though popular, catastrophe explanations are weak. Societies routinely withstand catastrophes, few having succumbed to cataclysms.

Inappropriate Response. Various explanations assume that cultural limitations prevent adaptation, causing collapse. One writer has suggested that environmental productivity limits cultural complexity, so that *Maya civilization, for example, introduced from elsewhere, could not survive in the rain forest and collapsed.

According to some researchers, linkages among parts of complex societies render them unstable, causing disruptions to spread everywhere. Others think that states use resources unwisely, engendering weakness, and that success breeds specialization and inability to change. Some argue that Maya civilization collapsed because its leaders could not respond to stress, and others ascribe similar problems to the Romans: Unable to simplify under duress, administrators increased complexity and costs.

Such theories are superior in that they explain collapse with an understanding of a society's character, yet they fail on a serious count. States are not inherently unstable, or static, or unable to change. In collapsing societies, such as the Roman Empire, people made logical adjustments. Postulating that states are intractable fossils, their leaders incapable of rational action, does not explain collapse.

Intruders. Collapse is commonly explained by invasions of simpler peoples, typically labeled "barbarians." The invasions of the Roman Empire are the classic example. Northern China's vulnerability to nomads is another. Dorian Greeks are thought to have destroyed Mycenaean civilization, and the Mycenaeans to have toppled the Minoans. Some argue that the Harappans, the Hittites, and several Mesopotamian states fell to such invaders. Intruders are frequently implicated in the collapses of the Maya, *Teotihuacán (ca. 150 B.C.–A.D. 700), and *Tula (ca. A.D. 950–1200).

Barbarian invasions offer simple solutions to complex problems, and are therefore popular. Their role in *Rome, *Mesopotamia, and *China is clear. Yet the overthrow of a state by a tribally organized people is an extraordinary event, which itself needs to be explained. Moreover, the intruder theory poses a dilemma: If states are worth invading, why destroy those things that repay conquest?

Conflict. Antagonism between classes is a principal element of conflict theories. Antipathy or revolt of peasants, or elite mismanagement, causes collapse. Marxists are strong proponents.

Conflict theories came naturally to the Greek writers Plato, Aristotle, and Polybius (who, in the second century B.C., foretold the Roman collapse) and to the fourteenth-century Arab historian Ibn Khaldun. Eighteenth-century writers like Giambattista Vico and Comte de Volney indicted social conflict in political disintegration. More recent writers have suggested that irrigation civilizations are weakened when elites seize an excessive share of produce, and that elite self-aggrandizement in imperial systems such as Rome is a major factor in collapse.

Conflict models have been applied to ancient Mexico, Peru, China, Mesopotamia, and the Harappans. One theory suggests that a peasant revolt overthrew Maya civilization, and another postulates that conflict between peasant soldiers and privileged urbanites contributed to the Roman collapse.

Such ideas imply that societies are inherently dysfunctional: States collapse from intrinsic, necessary factors. Yet every government allocates labor and resources; it is a basic capability. Sensible elites should sustain peasant populations as a vital resource. Where this has not happened (the later Roman Empire, or late in Chinese dynasties), it needs to be explained. Otherwise we have only a simplistic dichotomy: Some elites behave rationally and some do not. Thus while conflict is a factor in some collapses, it does not explain them.

Mystical Factors. Mystical explanations are abundant and typically entail unverifiable processes and value judgments. Some are bizarre theories involving numerology and reproductive behavior.

One persistent theme is a biological analogy: Societies progress through a cycle of birth, growth, senescence, and death. Collapse is natural, not needing explanation. The biological analogy is found in Plato, Polybius, and Ammianus Marcellinus (late fourth century A.D.). It was clearly expressed in the nineteenth and early twentieth centuries by Georg Hegel, Nikolay Danilevsky, and Oswald Spengler. American anthropologist Alfred Kroeber wrote of growth and senescence in cultural patterns.

Morality is a second theme: Decadence causes collapse. To Hegel, Sir Flinders Petrie, and English historian Arnold Toynbee, a society is successful while people address adversity. Decline comes when they prefer self-interest. Toynbee's "challenge and response" is the clearest statement, but is only part of his framework. Unmet challenges, in his view, bring discord.

Mystical theories are part of popular discourse, but are clearly valueless. They are vitalistic, asserting that internal forces cause societies to sprout, flower, wither, and die. Their common failing is to rely on intangibles, explaining a mystery with another mystery.

Economics. Economic explanations suggest that states collapse from increasing costliness and declining advantages to complexity. Several authors include economic factors in their explanations of collapse. One characterized the Chinese dynastic cycle as one of rising and falling returns. Another explains the Ottoman Empire's decline as a process of economic weakness, rising military expenditures, and a declining tax base.

Recent research indicates that cultural evolution often leads to increasing then diminishing returns. Complexity is a problem-solving strategy; as easy solutions are exhausted, the cost of solving problems grows, often merely to maintain the status quo. As a society reaches the point of diminishing returns to complexity it becomes vulnerable to collapse from economic weakness, disaffection, or external threat. Ultimately it is disadvantageous to be a complex society, as in the later Roman Empire and Classic Maya.

Economic explanations are rare in the historical sciences, and in collapse studies. Yet they specify mechanisms controlling change, and causal processes. They can incorporate internal weaknesses and external stresses, and are potentially more comprehensive than other approaches. They are quantifiable and refutable. Economic explanations also avoid the following final problem.

Collapse studies exhibit a dilemma: Every writer about states is a member of one. Most value state organization and its traditions of art, architecture, and literature. When these disappear it is natural to consider it a catastrophe, and ask: What went wrong? From this it is logical to search for such things as resource deficits, disasters, inappropriate responses, or class conflict. Such queries arise from a biased perspective, which induces many scholars to ask misguided questions. Hence most explanations of collapse are found wanting. A value-neutral approach asks merely: What causes societies rapidly to decrease in complexity? This question allows very different answers to emerge. Further progress in explaining collapse requires developing an approach as unbiased as possible.

■ T. Patrick Culbert, ed., *The Classic Maya Collapse,* (1973). Robert McC. Adams, *Heartland of Cities* (1981). Joseph A. Tainter, *The Collapse of Complex Societies* (1988). Norman Yoffee and George Cowgill, eds., *The Collapse of Ancient States and Civilizations* (1988).

Joseph A. Tainter

STATISTICAL ANALYSIS. Descriptive and inferential statistics often assist archaeologists in interpreting artifacts and patterns discovered during survey and excavation. The conclusions reached from these methods come from models and theories employed by the archaeologist. The methods are a valuable tool for identifying meaningful patterns in archaeological remains, but they can be misused just as any other technique if they are used uncritically. Descriptive statistics summarize archaeological data in a convenient format, which may be graphical or numeric or a combination of both. In any case, the goal is to summarize a large amount of information in a compact way.

Inferential statistics are based on probability theory and include a number of techniques to allow the archaeologist to make an inference about the whole (the population) by examining only a part of it (the sample). This may involve a conclusion about the site based on excavations of only a part of it or a conclusion about a region based on excavations at only a few sites. Alternatively, it could involve a conclusion about an artifact type (such as its age) based on the examination of a limited number of specimens. Reliable conclusions can be obtained only if the sample observed is chosen randomly. For this reason archaeologists since the mid-1970s have been particularly interested in the development of sampling methods.

Descriptive statistics can be presented as graphs, as in the case of histograms showing the percentage of various types of pottery at a site. Alternatively they may consist of a numeric value, such as the number of sites per square kilometer, the number of lithic flakes per cubic meter, the average length of a projectile point type, or the average age of the artifacts found in a site. Each of these values provides an average or central tendency. Descriptive statistics can also provide information about variability and diversity. For example, the standard error of a radiocarbon age estimate provides evidence on how variable the age of the material might be. The standard deviation of projectile point widths provides evidence on how variable widths might be. Diversity measures include simple counts of the number of kinds of things such as the number of types of pottery or the number of different faunal taxa identified, but they can involve more complex aspects of diversity, such as summary values that compare two regions or time periods in terms of some criterion. The meaning derived from the comparison comes from models or theories that the archaeologist is exploring, not from the numbers or artifacts themselves. Simple summary values have always been used by archaeologists. When they were calculated by hand, before the widespread availability of computers, they tended to be fairly simple. With the expansion of computer use in archaeology, the number and complexity of descriptive statistics has greatly increased.

These more complex descriptive statistics are often referred to as data-reduction or pattern-recognition techniques. They summarize many different variables in numeric or graphical form to help the archaeologist find significant patterns in the data. One of the first techniques to be used in this way was the trait-element method of classifying archaeological sites in the United States in the 1940s and 1950s. The presence or absence of many different traits was determined and then compared to other sites. Sites with many traits in common were considered to belong to the same culture. By the 1960s, although doubts had been raised about the validity of identifying cultures on the basis of trait lists, the basic approach had been modified and applied to other kinds of archaeological questions. These new applications often used a statistical technique called cluster analysis in which artifacts or sites were compared to one another and then grouped on the basis of their similarity. Other techniques were used to produce graphical representations of the similarities and differences between sites or artifacts. For example, multidimensional scaling produces a map in which similar objects are close to one another and different objects are far apart. A third technique tries to identify the unobservable factors (presumably related to past human activities) that produced a particular assemblage of artifacts. Factor analysis uses the correlations between artifact types to identify activity sets or tool kits. The goal is to understand the relative abundance of many different artifacts in terms of a few factors. For example, hunting and butchering activities might lead to the use and disposal of projectile points and knives in greater numbers at a site. A final technique helps the archaeologist to identify differences between artifacts and sites. Discriminant function analysis attempts to locate the variables that help to distinguish the artifacts from different sites, or sites from different time periods. The assumption is that real differences exist, but that they are too subtle to identify without looking at many different variables simultaneously.

Any of the descriptive techniques described above can be the basis for statistical inference. The average length of a collection of projectile points is a descriptive statistic. If the collection is assumed to be a random sample of all of the projectile points of that type (or from a site), the average can be used in statistical inference. Two kinds of inferences are possible, point and interval. A point estimate simply identifies a particular value as the most likely one for the population. An interval estimate provides a range and a confidence level associated with it. A radiocarbon age estimate is a point estimate of the age of a material. An interval estimate can be obtained by adding and subtracting the standard error from the age estimate. For example, if the age estimate is 2,550 ± 50 B.P., the confidence interval is 2,500 B.P. (2,550 − 50) to 2,600 B.P. (2,550 + 50). For this interval, statistical inference allows the conclusion that 68 percent of the time the true age of the material lies within the range (and 32 percent of the time it lies outside this range). Multiplying the standard error by 1.96 before adding and subtracting increases the probability to 95 percent that the true age lies within the range.

Other inferential statistics involve hypothesis testing. A statistical hypothesis is a conclusion that will be evaluated on the basis of one or more samples. In evaluating this hypothesis (referred to as the null hypothesis) the archaeologist balances the chances of rejecting the hypothesis when it is really true (the type I error rate or significance level) against the chances of accepting the hypothesis when it is really false (the type II error rate). Traditionally within the social sciences, a significance level of 0.05 is considered acceptable. This means that 5 percent of the time the archaeologist will mistakenly reject the null hypothesis. Examples of null hypotheses include comparisons of simple descriptive statistics ("The average thickness of pottery vessels at site A is the same as at site B") and measure of association ("Sand-tempered pottery and shell-tempered pottery are equally likely to have incised decorations"). Statistical inference allows archaeologists to test very specific propositions about the archaeological record. As with descriptive statistics, the meaning that they attach to those propositions comes from models and theories, not from the statistical techniques themselves.

[See also ANALYSIS, METHODS OF; SAMPLING; SCIENTIFIC METHOD.]

■ F. R. Hodson, D. G. Kendall, and P. Tâutu, eds., *Mathematics in the Archaeological and Historical Sciences* (1971). J. E. Doran and F. R. Hodson, *Mathematics and Computers in Archaeology* (1975). Clive Orton, *Mathematics in Archaeology* (1980). Robert Whallon and James Brown, eds., *Essays on Archaeological Typology* (1982). Christopher Carr, ed., *For Concordance in Archaeological Analysis: Bridging Data Structure, Quantitative Technique, and Theory* (1985). David Hurst Thomas, *Refiguring Anthropology: First Principles of Probability and Statistics* (1986). Mark S. Aldenderfer, *Quantitative Research in Archaeology: Progress and Prospects* (1987). Torsten Madsen, ed., *Multivariate Archaeology: Numerical Approaches in Scandinavian Archaeology* (1988). Stephen Shennan, *Quantifying Archaeology* (1988). Dwight W. Read, "Statistical Methods and Reasoning in Archaeological Research: A Review of Praxis and Promise," *Journal of Quantitative Anthropology* 1 (1989): 5–78. M. J. Baxter, *Exploratory Multivariate Analysis in Archaeology* (1994).

David L. Carlson

STATUE-MENHIRS are a particular category of standing stone found in parts of southern France, the western Alps, and the islands of Corsica and Sardinia. They consist of a rectangular block of stone, which in most cases has flattened front and back and a roughly rounded top. On this crudely shaped monolith are carved the features of a human or humanlike personage.

Statue-menhir carving may be in relief, leaving features standing in rounded profile, or in sunken relief, or may consist simply of incised lines. The features depicted usually follow a standardized pattern. Lower limbs are rarely shown, but are generally naked when they are shown. Upper limbs, by contrast, are commonly depicted, as is the face, with prominently rounded chin, and the hair, which often continues onto the edges and back of the stone. Occasional elements of clothing or equipment are also shown. The most common is a belt or girdle, sometimes attached to a shoulder strap. Some of the figures grasp in their hands a curved-ended stick resembling a shepherd's crook; others hold axes or bows; but the most famous piece of equipment represented on these stones is the copper dagger, frequently shown hanging from a cord around the neck.

The identity of these mysterious personages is unclear. Of the three regional groups on the French mainland, only one, the Languedoc group, shows any association with settlement site or burial monuments. The others, especially the Rouergue group, are located far from contemporary settlement sites in relatively remote areas of upland. This has led to the suggestion that they represent deities. Breasts on a few examples indicate that some of the statue-menhirs are female; others are considered male from the presence of weapons, though it is quite possible that these were also used by women at this time. The universal absence of a mouth is a feature that may indicate the ritual or belief associated with the monuments.

The south French and Alpine statue-menhirs are dated to the late Neolithic and Chalcolithic Periods (ca. 3500–2500 B.C.). This is shown both by the objects depicted on the stones and by the occasional discovery of a statue-menhir in a sealed archaeological context. At Euzet, Gravas and Montferrand statue-menhirs have been found among the remains of prehistoric farming villages dated to this period. At Sion in western Switzerland, one was found reused in a grave containing Beaker pottery (see Beakers), which probably dates to around 2500 B.C. The majority of the statue-menhirs from southern France have, however, been discovered in isolated upland or forested regions.

In sharp contrast to the statue-menhirs of southern France and the Alpine region are those of Corsica and Sardinia. These date to the second and first millennia B.C. The Sardinian examples generally have little carving, and are merely roughly shaped standing pillars. The earliest of the Corsican statue-menhirs, on the other hand, resemble those of the mainland; they are flat slabs of stone carved with schematic triangular faces and occasional weapons. In date, however, they are probably later than the mainland examples, since the weapons depicted include daggers with T-shaped hilts and cruciform handled swords of Middle or Late Bronze Age type. One theory made these Corsican statue-menhirs the work of Corsican warriors fighting against an invasion of Sardinian "Shardana" during the late second millennium B.C. The "Shardana" are mentioned in Egyptian accounts of the reign of Rameses III as one of the Sea Peoples who invaded Egypt in the twelfth century B.C. There is, however, no firm connection, despite the similarity of name, between the Shardana of Egyptian records and the island of Sardinia.

The later groups of Corsican statue-menhir are carved more completely in the round. One northern series takes the form of a human head carved fully in the round on top of a tapering rectangular pillar. These are dated to the ninth or eighth century B.C. and although they are not grave markers they may be representations of powerful Corsican chieftains.

[See also EUROPE: THE EUROPEAN NEOLITHIC PERIOD.]

■ A. D'Anna, *Les Statues-Menhirs et Stèles Anthropomorphes du Midi Méditerranéen* (1977). N. K. Sandars, *The Sea Peoples* (1978).

Chris Scarre

STEPHENS, John Lloyd. The son of Benjamin and Clemence (Lloyd) Stephens, John Lloyd Stephens was born in Shrewsbury, New Jersey, on 28 November 1805. His life was spent as a traveler, an author, and a steamship and railroad executive. Stephens studied the classics in preparatory school and took his degree at Columbia College in 1822. Later, he attended law school at Litchfield, Connecticut. He returned to New York to practice but found the law unappealing. In 1834 his health slightly deteriorated, and his doctor suggested a sea voyage as a cure. More than glad to get away from the practice of law, Stephens traveled to Egypt, Greece, Turkey, Russia, and Poland. His travels were published in book form as *Incidents of Travel in Egypt, Arabia Petraea, and the Holy Land* (1837) and *Incidents of Travel in Greece, Turkey, Russia, and Poland* (1838).

President Martin Van Buren sent Stephens on a diplomatic mission in 1839 to Central America, where he became acquainted with some of the ancient monuments of Central America. His main archaeological interests were in the ruins of Honduras, Guatemala, and Yucatán. He visited *Copán, Uxmal, *Palenque, and other sites, while his companion Frederick Catherwood, an artist, made pencil drawings of the sites they visited. Although not a scholar, Stephens brought the ancient ruins of Central America to the attention of the public. His trip to sites in Yucatán resulted in his book *Incidents of Travel in Yucatán* (1843).

Stephens was later involved with the Ocean Steam Navigation Company as a company director.

[See also HISTORY OF ARCHAEOLOGY BEFORE 1900: ARCHAEOLOGY OF THE AMERICAS.]

■ John L. Stephens, *Incidents of Travel in Central America, Chiapas, and Yucatán*, 2 vols. (1841). John L. Stephens obituaries: *New York Herald*, October 14 (1852); *New York Tribune*, October 15 (1852). F. L. Hawkes, *Putnam's Monthly Magazine*, January (1853). H. Otis, *Illustrated History of the Panama Railroad* (1861). W. R. Scott, *The Americanist in Panama* (1912). *Dictionary of American Bibliography*, ed. Dumas

Moore, vol. IX (1964). Gordon R. Willey and Jeremy A. Sabloff, *A History of American Archaeology*, 3rd ed. (1975).

Douglas R. Givens

STONE AGE. *See* THREE-AGE SYSTEM.

STONE AGE, Late. *See* AFRICA: PREHISTORY OF AFRICA.

STONE CIRCLES AND ALIGNMENTS. *Stonehenge is not unique. It is just one of more than a thousand stone circles and henges in Britain, Ireland, and Brittany built between 3500 and 1200 B.C. Nor was it one of the first. Its heavy ring of sarsen pillars was erected around 2000 B.C., a thousand years after the ditch and bank of the chalk henge that surrounded it. Lost forever is the timber structure that once stood at its heart.

Stone, earth, and wood were the local materials used by people when they constructed the earliest ritual enclosures in the centuries before 3000 B.C. In the soft soils of the lowlands, they dug the ditches and raised the banks of henges. On the rock-covered hillsides of the west they dragged unshaped boulders to create the circles of stone that are still the wonders of the prehistoric world. Round circuits of postholes, discovered by chance, are the only survivals of tall carved and painted rings of poles put up in forested countryside.

Sometimes such impermanent settings were replaced by durable stone. Excavations at Machrie Moor on the Scottish island of Arran revealed that an irregular circle of sandstones had replaced a larger ring of posts. Similar transformations from wood into stone occurred at the Sanctuary near *Avebury, and maybe from wood to chalk at Woodhenge near Stonehenge.

For more than 2,000 years, communities of the Neolithic and Bronze Age met in such circles on seasonal occasions, and performed rituals of fertility, until a persisting deterioration in the climate weakened the faith that imbued these open-air meeting places. By 1000 B.C. Stonehenge and all the others were deserted.

They ended in one crisis. They had begun in another. Around the middle of the fourth millennium B.C. the egalitarian, stone-using farming families of the Neolithic suffered a disruption to their lives. It may have been caused by worsening weather, or famine, or plague, or overpopulation and soil starvation, but the cult of forebears whose *manes*, or deified souls, sustained people's lives lost its strength. The claustrophobic *megalithic tombs that had been ancestral shrines were abandoned. When, centuries later, societies recovered, they did not return to the tombs but created novel spacious, open-air places of assembly, maneuvering heavy stones upright or trenching the ground to make embanked sacred areas where hundreds could gather.

In *Man Makes Himself* the archaeologist V. Gordon *Childe argued that such new ideas emanated from the civilizations of the East, *ex oriente lux,* but, to the contrary, the circles and henges were indigenous innovations, native monuments whose architecture was unique to western Europe.

These early rings, whether of stone or earth, were huge. Allowing each participant a comfortable body space of outstretched arms around him, a stone circle like Long Meg and Her Daughters in the English Lake District could have held more than 3,000 men and women. Across the Irish Sea, the henge of the Giant's Ring near Belfast had a central area so vast that it could have accommodated a congregation of 10,000.

Such tribal enormities were very different from the tiny ritual centers of the Middle Bronze Age 2,000 years later. Wormy Hillock in northern Scotland had a deep, wide ditch and a high, broad bank, but the space inside this misshapen henge was no more than 19.5 feet (6 m) across. Ten worshipers would have filled it. Cousana, a miniature ring of five stones in southwestern Ireland, could never have accepted more than one. These were family sanctuaries.

Size was not the only difference. There is a basic distinction between henges and stone circles. Henges are plain enclosures surrounded by an earthen bank and ditch. Stone circles are simply rings of standing stones. Where a henge has a stone circle inside it, as at Arbor Low in the Peak District, it is known as a circle-henge. Whether henge or stone circle, every region had its own distinctive architectural style. Henges in the south of England usually had one deep ditch inside the bank, whereas those of the northeast had two shallow ditches, one on either side of the central bank, probably to save the workers from having to dig deeply into resistant gravel. It was a problem avoided by the henge builders of the west, particularly in Ireland, whose ditchless enclosures had awesome banks made up of soil and rubble not dug but scraped up around the rims of the enclosed space, leaving the interior domed like an upturned saucer.

At Mayburgh in northwestern England, workers gathered hundreds of thousands of heavy pebbles and stones to pile up a bank 13 feet (4 m) high and 122 feet (37 m) wide, over 70,000 tons of fist- to pumpkin-sized stones carried, dragged, and sledged from the River Eamont nearly 1,315 feet (400 m) away. Inside the ring, showing how henge and stone circle could combine, there was a rectangle of four stones like others known as Four-Posters in central Scotland. Elsewhere, hybrid monuments known as circle-henges also contained circular or horseshoe-shaped settings.

Similar variety occurred in stone circles. Some in southwestern Scotland and Cornwall had thick and heavy central stones like anthropomorphic versions of the carved megalithic guardians of the dead at the entrances and inside the chambers of massive tombs in Brittany. Along the west coasts of Scotland and southern England there were rings within rings, concentric circles that seem to be stone imitations of the timber framework of the houses of the living. Some circles in areas long hallowed by tradition were built alongside a standing stone that may have preceded them by many centuries. And among the circles there were ovals, "eggs," even rectangles such as King Arthur's Hall on Bodmin Moor, a site that has been compared to much larger oblongs in Brittany.

In that province of France the stone circles, or cromlechs, are gigantic ovals or open-mouthed horseshoes, many with ranks of long lines of stones leading uphill to them (e.g., Carnac, q.v.). Similar double-lined avenues or single rows provided dignified ways for processions to rings, many with internal burials, in southwestern England and northern Ireland. Rows of stones or banks of earth led to a variety of sites, fanlike settings climbing up slopes to cairns in northern Scotland, wandering stretches leading to encircled cairns on Dartmoor, multiple columns of hundreds of stones extending across the landscape toward colossal cromlechs at Carnac in Brittany.

What all these sites—henge, stone circle, cromlech; large or small; circular or oval; early or late—have in common are associations with death, fire, and the sky. Modern archaeo-astronomers such as Alexander Thom and Clive Ruggles have demonstrated the existence of celestial alignments to the sun and, even more, to the moon. At Stonehenge the famous Heel Stone was set up midway between the moon's minor and major risings on the northern skyline. In northeastern Scotland recumbent stone circles had a ponderous prostrate block neatly placed in the arc between the southern moon's rising and setting. Most surprisingly, at a time when there was no Pole Star to assist them, planners of stone circles frequently placed the tallest stone or the entrance at the north or south, less commonly to east or west.

At Woodhenge, the long axis of the six ovals of posts inside the earthwork pointed to the midsummer sunrise. Buried inside the henge were deposits of chalk balls and "cups" and axes nicely aligned on the midsummer and midwinter sunrises and on north and south. Woodhenge also contained a feature common to many stone circles and henges whose solar or lunar sightlines were associated with death. At its heart was the grave of a young child who had been executed and buried exactly on the solstitial axis.

Sacrifices were not unusual. There is a grim side to such enclosures often linked with their entrances. Huge stones in the circles, heightened banks in the henges dominated these entrances, and alongside them the bones of women and children have been found. They may have been killed to give potency to the ring.

The corpse of a female dwarf was laid in the ditch end of Avebury's southern causeway. The burnt bones of women and children were interred in deep pits by both entrances at Stonehenge. Two cremations were put in a central pit at the timber circle of Sarn-y-Bryn-Caled in central Wales. Pathologists deduced that the contorted skeleton in a hollow at the middle of a henge on the Curragh near Dublin was that of a young woman who had volunteered to be buried alive. A female skull was concealed at the entrance of Gorsey Bigbury henge in western England. At the exact east of the inner ring of the sanctuary near Avebury the body of a teenaged girl was buried under one of the circle-stones.

To the modern visitor, stone circles and henges are mysteriously romantic places. To their builders, striving to keep their world stable and secure, the purpose of the rings was harsher. To prehistoric communities their circle may have been a *mandala*, a symbol representing the compass of the human world, a microcosm of physical existence in which the dead could be used to succor and protect the living.

[*See also* ASTRONOMY: ASTRONOMY IN THE OLD WORLD; BRITISH ISLES: PREHISTORY OF THE BRITISH ISLES; EUROPE: THE EUROPEAN NEOLITHIC PERIOD.]

■ Aubrey Burl, *The Stone Circles of the British Isles* (1976). Alexander and Archibald Thom and Aubrey Burl, *Megalithic Rings: Plans and Data for 229 Monuments in Britain* (1980). Douglas Heggie, *Megalithic Science* (1981). Sean O'Nuallain, "A Survey of Stone Circles in Cork and Kerry," *Proceedings of the Royal Irish Academy* 84C (1984): 1–77. Aubrey Burl, *The Stonehenge People* (1987). Anthony Harding with G. E. Lee, *Henge Monuments and Related Sites of Great Britain* (1987). John Barnatt, *Stone Circles of Britain*, 2 vols. (1989). Aubrey Burl, *Prehistoric Henges* (1991). Aubrey Burl, *From Carnac to Callanish. The Prehistoric Stone Avenues and Rows of Britain, Ireland and Brittany* (1993).

Aubrey Burl

STONEHENGE. The most celebrated prehistoric antiquity of Europe, Stonehenge is an upright setting of shaped stones on the open grassland of central Salisbury Plain, southern England.

Seventeen (of a supposed original thirty) immense stone uprights stand close together to make a good circle, about 98.5 feet (30 m) in diameter. They are trimmed into neat rectangular shapes from blocks of sarsen stone, an immensely hard sandstone that occurs naturally near *Avebury about 18.5 miles (30 km) to the north. The uprights support stone lintels, bridging across neighboring stones, that (if complete) once made a complete ring, some 16 feet (5 m) above the ground. It is within a few centimeters of being exactly horizontal, although the ground surface slopes gently—one of many precisions and subtleties in the design of the place. Each lintel is shaped on the curve of the circle, rather than straight-edged, so there is no abrupt angle where it touches its neighbor.

Inside the sarsen circle are five "trilithons," again of sarsen, each of two uprights supporting a single lintel. These blocks weigh up to fifty or sixty tons, and the tallest stands 23 feet (7 m) above ground. Also within the circle are smaller "bluestones," volcanic blocks a few feet long and weighing a few tons, whose origin is the Preseli Mountains of western Wales, nearly 124 miles (200 km) away. About half the stones implied in the design are missing, but enough remains to show the overall layout.

Altogether, Stonehenge has five stone settings, nested one within the other: the outer sarsen circle with its continuous ring of supported lintels (30 uprights plus 30 lintels); then a circle of bluestones without lintels (perhaps 60 originally); then the 5 trilithons with their separate lintels, arranged in a horseshoe and rising taller toward the southwest (10 uprights plus 5 lintels); then a matching horseshoe setting of bluestones without lintels (19 stones); and, at the heart, a single great block of yet another kind of rock, a Welsh sandstone from formations near the origin of the bluestones. This central block is fallen and lies flat in the ground, hidden by the fallen lintel and upright of the tallest trilithon. Stonehenge, then, is a quite small monument in its area, and is composed of less than 150 blocks; yet so grand are the stones, and so powerful in their standing, that it impresses as the most noble of antiquities, even in ruin.

So striking is the appearance of Stonehenge, and so clearly a thing of human creation, that it was recognized as a great curiosity as early as the eleventh century A.D.—long before other ancient monuments had come to scholarly notice. Ever since, it has been the subject of theory, speculation, and mystery, whether caught up into the Arthurian romances of late medieval times or connected in our own time with the habits of extraterrestrial visitors. Great artists like John Constable and J. M. W. Turner painted the spectacle (and in our own century Henry Moore, whose great massive sculptures also evoke the rude power of Stonehenge). Thomas Hardy set the theatrical climax of his most compelling novel, Tess of the d'Urbervilles, in the gray light of dawn at Stonehenge. The twentieth century has seen Stonehenge replicas and pastiches built of concrete, of stone, and (two) of old motorcars(!)—including a full-size and complete replica standing high above the Columbia River, in the wild open landscape of the Pacific Northwest.

The appreciation of Stonehenge is spoiled by two main highways that run close by; the number of visitors is so great that it can be viewed only from a distance, which makes it hard to recognize which stone belongs in which setting, or to see the prehistoric carvings of axes that decorate some of the sarsens. Threatened by its proprietor with export to America at the turn of the century, Stonehenge was sold at auction for £6,600 and given to the British

people in 1918. Its surroundings were saved from development when a public appeal bought them and vested them in the National Trust for safekeeping. As the frontispiece to British prehistory, it has been used as the emblem of archaeology and of Englishness—although the ethnic descendants of its builders, if they are to be identified at all, would be found among the Welsh, Scots, and other Celts of the western British Isles.

Modern archaeological scholarship, and radiocarbon dating, now places the building of the main part of Stonehenge at about 2000 B.C. It is classed among a group of enigmatic ritual monuments, called "henges" after the example of Stonehenge, yet has many special features to itself; in the engineering elegance of its design, it remains unique among the structures of its region and period. The method of building, which uses woodworker's techniques to link the blocks, suggests it belongs with a class of timber structures, now lost or known only from post settings of similar plan. Genuinely unique in several aspects, it has been—and remains—exceptionally difficult to make sense of. The evident unity of the design is as much a wonder as the scale of human labor required to drag the many great blocks so far overland, and then to pound the sarsen, hardest of building stones, into exact shape.

Three centuries of active field research have seen many excavations at Stonehenge, producing not much in the way of finds or evidence for its exact purpose. Pioneering research by John Aubrey, William *Stukeley, and other antiquaries noticed features of the monument less visually compelling—an enclosing ditch and double bank, a great circle of pits containing human cremations, and a long "avenue" across the landscape that makes a fine approach to the site. These features, grand in their own time, are built of soft chalk, so they have decayed into bumps in the fields, whereas the monoliths of Stonehenge stand, many of them, as if untouched by forty centuries of time.

In the archaeological sequence, as we understand it, this famous Stonehenge is comparatively late in a series of earthen and stone works on the site that span perhaps 1,500 years. Long before it, there had been built the enclosing ditch and bank with some settings of unshaped sarsen stones; then there followed a period of abandonment and, in all likelihood, the making of a structure of bluestones before the present design was set upon.

The landscape around Stonehenge—the "Stonehenge environs"—contains several hundred prehistoric sites, older, of much the same age, and younger. Prominent among these are the round barrows, circular burial mounds of broadly the same period. Many of these were explored early in the nineteenth century, and were found to contain burials richly furnished with objects of bronze and gold. These are the graves of the chiefs (or other leaders) who commanded Stonehenge to be built.

Influential in recent public knowledge of Stonehenge are the ideas of Gerald Hawkins, Fred Hoyle, and other astronomers, who think Stonehenge was some kind of prehistoric observatory-cum-computer, intended to celebrate and plot the movement of the sun, the moon, and their eclipses. Archaeologists, reluctant to pretend that Stonehenge was built in the spirit of twentieth-century scientific research, recognize an alignment to the direction of midsummer sunrise in the axis of symmetry that controls the design of Stonehenge. They prefer to think by analogy with the common alignment of Christian churches toward the eastern horizon, where the sun rises; yet Christian churches are neither scientific instruments nor the temples of sun worshipers.

The central stone at Stonehenge is called the "Altar Stone," from an old fancy that it was an ancient altar of sacrifice. A stone outside the main setting is called the "Slaughter Stone," from the idea that the sacrificial victim was butchered there. Another was named the "Heel Stone," from a tale that it was thrown by the devil at a passing friar and caught him on the heel of his foot; because "heel" chances to echo the Greek word for sun, this name was transferred to the pointer stone that stands between the main setting and the direction of midsummer sunrise. In these names, and in the many stories and associations of Stonehenge, one sees how much our contemporary understanding of the place—and of all prehistoric time—is shaped and directed by the ideas of our own age, and of our forebearers' ages. In very recent times, Stonehenge has been the focus of "New Age" beliefs about the ancient powers of earth mysteries. Each summer has seen confrontations between the authorities and the bands of travelers who wish to gather at Stonehenge and celebrate the place in their own manner. Historically erroneous though their woolly ideas about Stonehenge seem to be, one may nonetheless appreciate a profound authenticity in their attitude to the place. This ancient sacred site was not constructed as a tourist attraction nor by people whose understanding of the world was arrived at by the cold logic of analytical science; it was a place of strange power and compelling magic, as it oddly contrives still to be, some 4,000 years and more than 200 human generations after its building.

There are remarkably few ancient finds from Stonehenge, although there is tourist rubbish from every modern age. Among the ancient finds is a complete skeleton, from about the time of its building, of a man who had been shot through the chest with flint arrows, a reminder that this was an ancient place of contest and of conflict, as well as a sacred place.

[See also ASTRONOMY: ASTRONOMY IN THE OLD WORLD; BRITISH ISLES: PREHISTORY OF THE BRITISH ISLES; STONE CIRCLES AND ALIGNMENTS.]

■ R. J. C. Atkinson, *Stonehenge*, rev. ed. (1960). Christopher Chippindale, *Stonehenge Complete* (1983). Julian Richards, *English Heritage Book of Stonehenge* (1991).

Christopher Chippindale

STONE TECHNOLOGY. The human lineage has employed stone technology as a vital part of its adaptive strategy throughout most of the past 2 to 3 million years. The manufacture and use of stone tools appears to have begun in Africa at least 2.5 million years ago, and evidence of this tool tradition remains prominent in the archaeological record throughout the ensuing stages of human evolution until relatively recent times. With the spread of hominids throughout the world, stone tools appear over time in a widening array of archaeological sites, first throughout Africa, then in Europe and Asia, then in Australia, and finally throughout the Americas.

Chronological changes can be seen in stone toolmaking traditions, slowly at first but with a quickening pace over time. Geographic variation in stone tools and toolmaking techniques also becomes more pronounced over time, with distinct tool traditions appearing in many regions of the world and sometimes lasting for relatively long periods of time. Only within the past 50,000 years do tools made in other materials, such as bone or antler, also commonly appear along with stone tools at many archaeological sites. Stone technologies were ultimately replaced by the gradual spread of the use of metals, a process starting several thousand years ago in some parts of the world but not affecting some areas until the past few hundred years. Only a handful of societies, such as some horticulturalists living in remote mountainous regions of New Guinea and Irian Jaya, still maintain indigenous stone tool technologies today.

Origins of Stone Technology. While some tools constitute the first definite, lasting evidence of toolmaking, it is quite possible that other, more perishable materials such as wood or bone were employed as tools by our protohuman ancestors. This seems particularly likely in view of tool use seen in the wild among our closest living relatives, the chimpanzees, for example, their use of twigs or grasses to "fish" for termites or the use of stones and wooden branches as hammers and anvils to crack open hard-shelled nuts. There is no evidence, however, that any species other than our ancestors developed a tradition of making stone implements, modifying naturally occurring rocks in order to use them as tools. This is a novel approach to toolmaking, as it produces tools with sharp edges, properties that are not merely extensions of the stone's natural form.

It is not known how this innovation was discovered, although it is very possible that the earliest stone toolmaking developed as a by-product of some other activity, such as hammering nuts or either offensively or defensively throwing stones that cracked against a hard surface, and then investigating the new properties of the resultant sharp edges. The earliest stone tools were usually made of relatively coarse-grained volcanic and metamorphic rocks common in much of Africa, such as lavas, quartzite, or quartz, although some were made of finer-grained siliceous rocks such as chert. Over time, more selection is seen in the choice of stone materials for many tools, with greater use of obsidian, or volcanic glass, and fine-grained cherts in some regions, as well as transport of materials over greater distances. While the very earliest phases of stone technology may be lost to prehistory, starting about 2.5 million years ago, hominid ancestors in eastern Africa appear to have been sufficiently involved in stone toolmaking to have left distinct concentrations of stone tools in numerous localities, which we now call archaeological sites.

Investigating Prehistoric Stone Technologies. Only relatively recently in human history did people come to realize the great time depth of what is often referred to as the Stone Age—a period in the human past when tools were commonly or even predominantly made in stone. While centuries ago some wondered about strange stones that appeared to be implements of some sort, such as points or axes, it was in nineteenth-century Europe that a long period of human prehistory in which metals were absent and tools were made of stone came to be generally recognized and became the subject of concerted investigations.

Excavations over the past 150 years have produced large quantities of stone artifacts at archaeological sites over much of the world. In some instances, long sequences of deposits in a region or at a single site have revealed a great time depth to local occupation, often with dramatic changes over time in stone technologies. Throughout the first century of archaeological research, a traditional approach to these stone technologies involved assigning the excavated stone tools to particular "types" and then comparing types observed in one site or time period with those observed elsewhere or at other times (see Typological Analysis). Thus, general technological sequences were sometimes established in a particular region, first in western Europe and gradually in other areas (although such sequences are still poorly established in some parts of the world). Such a typological approach was a necessary first step for archaeologists to take, but unfortunately it was not of great use in demonstrating changes in human adaptation over time and space in prehistory. As traditions of stone toolmaking and tool using had largely died out by the time the Stone Age was recognized in historic times, it has often been difficult to understand the full role stone tools played in our ancestors' lives and adaptations, particularly how these tools were made and used. In order to explore such questions, many researchers in the past few decades have turned increasingly to *experimental archaeology, in which investigators attempt to replicate and understand aspects of the technologies, activities, and lifeways of prehistoric peoples.

Experimental investigations of stone technology involve replicating stone tools found at prehistoric sites, especially investigating the techniques and procedures evident, and also exploring the possible uses of stone tools for different activities. Ultimately, archaeologists wish to know not only information about prehistoric stone technologies, but also how tools in stone and other materials fit into the lives and adaptations of prehistoric peoples. Questions of interest to many experimental archaeologists today embrace the entire stone technology system of prehistoric societies, including their acquisition of stone raw materials, initial working of the core, shaping of finished tools, discard of manufacturing by-products or debris, curation and transport of raw materials and tools, reshaping and resharpening of tools, and their ultimate discard or abandonment. Through experiments and studies investigating such problems, archaeologists have gained a great deal of insight into prehistoric stone technologies, particularly how stone tools were made and how they would have been used by prehistoric ancestors, and have thus become better able to interpret the evidence found at archaeological sites.

Modes of Stone Technology. Some differences in stone technologies have been observed throughout the major stages or phases that have been identified within the Stone Age. Not every part of the world has gone through a uniform or synchronous progression of such stages, although there are some common trends observed in many parts of the world over time in the course of the Stone Age. These different recognized stages generally denote not only differences in stone technologies but also important aspects of change in economic or subsistence practices. In Europe and western Asia, for instance, a threefold division of the Stone Age was traditionally made. This paradigm starts with a period called the Paleolithic (Old Stone Age), with hunter-gatherers using flaked-stone tools, followed by a period called the Mesolithic or Epipaleolithic, with even more efficient hunter-gatherers and an improved flaked-stone technology. These were then followed by a period often referred to as the Neolithic (New Stone Age), in which early food producers continued to make flaked-stone tools along with other innovations, for instance, pottery and ground-stone tools such as axes and adzes. There is some difficulty, however, in extending this classification far beyond western Eurasia, although somewhat similar trends in stone technology and economic patterns can be seen elsewhere.

A framework of basic modes of stone technology applied by Grahame Clark to prehistoric Europe can be modified to provide a useful classification system for stone technologies throughout the world. In this system, a general time progression of stone technologies combines aspects of tool form along with some consideration of how they were manufactured. Although all phases or modes are not evident in each geographic area and do not they appear at exactly the same time in one area as in another, this classification helps provide some general sense of overall changes observed in stone technologies through much of the world. Six major modes can be discriminated:

Mode 1: Characterized by simple core forms that have been flaked by percussion, either through direct percussion with a hammer, through anvil technique, or through bipolar technique. Direct percussion flaking is generally done by hard hammer technique or with a hard hammer stone (in contrast to soft hammer percussion, as discussed later). Along with typically simple or casual core forms, sites with Mode 1 technologies usually have a variety of flakes and flake fragments that were produced in flaking these cores. Experimental archaeology has demonstrated that these flakes may in fact constitute a primary tool of many Mode 1 tool kits, as they provide an extremely sharp and efficient cutting edge that could have been used for a variety of purposes, particularly for butchery operations. Many Mode 1 cores may represent the technological by-products of producing such flakes for use as cutting tools.

Mode 2: Characterized by large, bifacially flaked tools such as hand axes or cleavers. In contrast to the simple Mode 1 cores, Mode 2 tools have definitely been deliberately shaped into a predetermined form, often with a great deal of finesse and planning evident in the flaking procedure, and sometimes with very systematic finishing and fine flaking to sharpen the edge. In addition, obtaining the initial stone from which the tool was made often entailed careful selection of a cobble or the skillful manufacture of a large flake from a stone boulder. Later Mode 2 technologies often show the use of soft hammer percussion, in which flaking is carried out with a hammer of bone, wood, or some other material softer than the stone being worked, allowing more refined shaping of the tool. Large Mode 2 tools such as hand axes, cleavers, and picks are believed to have been handheld during use.

Mode 3: Characterized by a variety of shaped tools made from flakes. Mode 3 flake tools are often very well made and have been fashioned into a number of standardized shapes or tool types such as scrapers or points. Many Mode 3 technologies show extensive use of special methods of preparing cores, for instance, the Levallois technique, in which the core is shaped so as to produce a flake of predetermined (usually maximized) size and shape. Mode 3 flake tools are made with hard hammer or, less often, soft hammer technique. It is thought that at least some of the flake tools in Mode 3 industries, particularly those with a base that has either been thinned or shaped into a projecting tang, may have been mounted on a haft (such as a wooden shaft) so as to provide a handle for a scraper or a shaft for a spear. This would constitute the first evidence of composite tools made up of multiple and replaceable parts.

Mode 4: Characterized by relatively long, narrow, parallel-sided flakes called blades, which are usually struck from one of a number of types of specially prepared blade cores. Common tools in Mode 4 or blade industries include end scrapers (with the scraping edge on the end of the blade), chisel-edged burins, awls, and knives. Mode 4 blade technologies are sometimes made with hard hammer percussion, but often involve soft hammer technique or even indirect percussion, in which the flaking blow is directed through an intermediate punch. Another technique of working stone, pressure flaking, working stone by exerting controlled pressure on the edge of a flake, sometimes appears along with Mode 4 blade technologies.

Mode 5: Characterized by a variety of tools made with small blades or bladelets struck from tiny bladelet cores, or alternatively with segments broken from larger blades. Often called microlithic tools, these have commonly been shaped into a variety of standardized and even geometric forms such as crescents or triangles.

Mode 6: Characterized by ground-stone tools such as axes or adzes that have been shaped, or sometimes finished after initially having been flaked, by grinding against an abrasive stone. This toolmaking technique represents a significant investment of time and energy in toolmaking, but produced tough, stable-edged, long-lasting tools. As already noted, ground-stone tools are commonly found among many early food-producing societies, but they are sometimes also found among hunter-gatherers, for instance, some early inhabitants of Australia.

World Patterns in Stone Technology. During the Paleolithic, the earliest and longest phase of the Stone Age in the Old World (Africa, Europe, and Asia), starting with the earliest stone tools and lasting until about 10,000 years ago or later, stone was worked primarily by chipping or "flaking" through percussive blows or by pressure, and subsistence was gained primarily through hunting and gathering activities. The Paleolithic is often further divided in various regions into a sequence of stages. In much of Eurasia and northern Africa, the sequence begins with the Early Paleolithic, which is roughly equivalent to the Early Stone Age in sub-Saharan Africa.

The first Early Stone Age tools appear in Africa, where Mode 1 industries are generally referred to as Oldowan technology, named after the famous site of *Olduvai Gorge in Tanzania, where simple tools nearly two million years old were first discovered several decades ago by Mary and Louis *Leakey. Such sites are commonly associated with early forms of *Homo,* such as *Homo habilis.* Typical core or tool types identified are often called choppers, discoids, or scrapers. More recent site discoveries at Gona in the Hadar region of Ethiopia and in West Turkana in Kenya reveal Mode 1 technologies approximately 2.5 million years old. Somewhat later in the Early Stone Age, Mode 2 technology emerges with the appearance of bifacial hand axes, cleavers, and picks about 1.6 million years ago in eastern Africa, at more or less the time of the emergence of a larger-brained, larger-bodied hominid, *Homo erectus.* This tool tradition, called the *Acheulean tradition after the site of St. Acheul in France, lasts for nearly 1.5 million years, until a couple of hundred thousand years ago. With the spread of hominids out of sub-Saharan Africa starting more than 1 million years ago, Early Paleolithic sites appear in northern Africa, Europe, and western Asia, some characterized by Mode 1 industries and others by Mode 2 biface industries. Interestingly, the Early Paleolithic industries of eastern Asia, such as at *Zhoukoudian Cave and in the Nihewan Basin in China, show only Mode 1 industries composed of simple cores and flakes.

Mode 3 industries begin to appear between 100,000 and 200,000 years ago in the next stone tool phase, called the Middle Paleolithic in Eurasia and northern Africa and the Middle Stone Age in sub-Saharan Africa. Many regional variants appear in the methods used to produce flakes and in the particular standardized, recurring flake-tool types found. Use of the Levallois prepared core technique, which first appeared in late Acheulean times, becomes particularly prominent in many regions of the Old World (except in Southeast Asia) during this phase, which lasts until 30,000 to 40,000 years ago in much of Eurasia and somewhat later in parts of Africa. There are sporadic occurrences in Africa of early blade technologies interbedded within sequences of Mode 3 industries, such as at Haua Fteah in North Africa or in the Howieson's Poort industry at sites such as *Klasies River Cave in South Africa, but these do not appear to be maintained over time. Flakes shaped into points, such as the Aterian points found in much of northern Africa, are often found during this technological phase; some of the points were presumably used as spear points. Mode 3 technologies are found associated with Archaic forms of *Homo sapiens,* such as the *Neanderthals and their contemporaries.

Starting 30,000 to 40,000 years ago in Europe, western Asia, and North Africa, Mode 4 blade technology predominates during the period known as the Upper Paleolithic, a period in which many other tools made in bone, antler, and ivory also become common, as do items of artwork and personal decoration. In the Later Stone Age of sub-Saharan Africa, which begins variably between 40,000 and 20,000 years ago, many sites show well-developed microlithic Mode 5 technologies in addition to other artifacts and tools, such as bone harpoons and shell beads. In eastern Asia as well, microlithic blade technologies begin to appear by about 30,000 years ago in Late Paleolithic times in China, Korea, and Japan. It was apparently during Late Paleolithic times that human populations expanded or migrated to Australia, and apparently somewhat later, probably between 20,000 and 10,000 years ago, that they migrated across the frozen ice bridge of Beringia into the Americas. These late Ice Age inhabitants of America (the Paleo-Indians) hunted mammoth and now extinct forms of bison with a tool kit that included finely made bifacial stone projectile points (such as Clovis and Folsom points).

Mode 5 microlithic technologies also became common in much of western Eurasia during the early Holocene (after the end of the Ice Age or Pleistocene), as in what are often called the Mesolithic and Epipaleolithic cultures of Europe and northern Africa. The bow and arrow, which first appeared during Late Paleolithic times, appears to have become common during the European Mesolithic and in the later Stone Age of sub-Saharan Africa.

In the Americas, the emphasis on bifacial, often pressure-flaked projectile points that was first seen in the Paleo-Indian period continued through most of the Holocene in many stone tool traditions. After the disappearance of the big game animals of the Ice Age, the Paleo-Indian points were replaced by a series of stone industries that generally emphasized new forms of bifacial points, often with distinctive point types specific to a particular region. For a long period of time, most of these were relatively large and were probably mounted on spear shafts and projected with a spear-thrower or atlatl. In the Holocene, microlithic stone tools became characteristic of some peoples in the Arctic region of North America, such as those known as the Paleo-Eskimos. In some parts of the Americas, such as pre-Columbian Mexico, Mode 4 blade technology and fine pressure flaking of obsidian points and other artifacts developed to a high level of proficiency and even artistry. It appears that bow-and-arrow technology became widespread in North America about 1,000 years ago, when small projectile points become common in many tool kits.

New types of stone artifacts were often added to these post–Ice Age tool industries. Chipped-stone axes are found at some Mesolithic European sites, perhaps indicating clearance of forests, and became common during the Neolithic in some areas, such as in northern Europe. Ground-stone bowls and grinding stones (such as mortars and pestles), sometimes found in Middle and Late Stone Age times in Africa, became much more common during the early Holocene in Africa, Eurasia, and the Americas, suggesting intensive use, processing, and even storing of foods as well as greater sedentism among some hunter-gatherer populations (also suggested by early pottery at some sites). Among some of the post–Ice Age societies of western Asia, northeastern Africa, eastern Asia, Mesoamerica and South America, we see early centers of the transition from a hunting-gathering way of life to food production. For a long period following the transition to food production, however, chipped-stone tools continued to be made in many parts of the world, along with ground-stone tools, pottery, and tools in other materials.

Stone tools were gradually replaced among the world's cultures with the introduction of metal tools, at widely different times in different parts of the world. During the Holocene many societies show the development of art forms in various stone materials—figurines, statues, and friezes in materials such as jade, marble, or basalt—and the use of stones such as turquoise or lapis lazuli in artwork and ornaments. An interesting late development in skilled stone technology occurred in many parts of the world with the manufacture of gunflints after flintlock firearms came into use in the seventeenth century. Even long after the initial introduction of metal technology in a number of societies, stone continued to be an important material for making some tools, attesting to the enormous utility of stone technology, the most ancient human tradition.

[See also LITHICS.]

Nicholas Toth and Kathy Schick

STRATIGRAPHY. Archaeological stratigraphy is the study of stratification, which is the physical deposits and other stratigraphic events, such as a pits or post holes, by which a site is composed through time. Stratification is an unintentional result of human behavior and thus an unbiased record of past activities. For societies without written records, the study of archaeological stratification, by the excavation, recording, and analysis of strata, features, and portable artifacts, is the only method by which their history can be recovered. Even for peoples with written records, the study of archaeological stratification provides a unique four-dimensional history of a site that cannot be obtained from documentary sources. Archaeologists have a great responsibility to decipher and record for posterity the latent history of each site as encapsulated in its stratification. As the philosopher Voltaire once stated: "We owe the dead nothing but the truth." In archaeological excavation, the truth about the past can only be obtained by adherence to stratigraphic principles and methods.

Archaeological stratigraphy evolved from geological practices in the last century, but was little refined for some time. The publication of archaeological textbooks by Dame Kathleen Kenyon and Sir Mortimer *Wheeler in the early 1950s underlined the importance of stratigraphy in archaeology. The 1970s saw the establishment of the separate discipline of archaeological stratigraphy, since stratification made by people is different from that formed by natural forces. The first textbook on archaeological stratigraphy appeared in 1979.

Constructing the Stratigraphic Sequence. While several laws of archaeological stratigraphy were then proposed, the Law of Superposition is paramount. It states that "in a series of layers and interfacial features, as originally created, the upper units of stratification are younger and the lower are older, for each must have been deposited on, or created by the removal of, a pre-existing mass of archaeological stratification." This law gives a chronological direction to a body of stratification (generally, early at the bottom and late at the top), and it is the reason for the question always asked about any two contiguous stratigraphic units: Which came first? By attention to the Law of Superposition during an excavation, the units of stratification can be placed in sequential order in relative time, one after the other.

Using the stratigraphic method, a site is excavated by the removal of its deposits according to their unique shapes, and in the reverse order to that in which they were made. Each deposit is given a unique number, which is also assigned to all portable objects taken from it, be they coins, sherds of pottery, animal bones, or samples of soil for pollen analysis. It is axiomatic that each deposit, with its artifacts, is a unique capsule of chronological, cultural, and environmental data, and occupies a unique position in the stratigraphic sequence of a site.

The archaeologist must consider both stratigraphic, or relative, time, by which one event gives way to another, and absolute time, or calendar time, which gives a date in years to stratigraphic data. Stratigraphic time can be ascertained by stratigraphic excavation and recording without any reference to artifacts: a site may contain no artifacts at all, but its stratigraphic sequence can be obtained nonetheless. The basic principles of archaeological stratigraphy are of universal application because they relate to the uniform characteristics of stratification and not to the cultural artifacts found within the deposits. The study of artifacts may assign a calendar date to stratification and thus fix its relative stratigraphic sequence in absolute time. Many artifact specialists will be needed to arrive at such conclusions, but it is the excavating archaeologist who bears the responsibility for the construction of the stratigraphic sequence of the site.

Stratification is a three-dimensional body of archaeological deposits and features, from which a fourth dimension of relative time may be inferred. A stratigraphic sequence is the order, in relative time, of the deposition of layers and the creation of interfacial features, such as pits, through the life of a site. To illustrate such a calendar of relative time, the stratigraphic data is translated into abstract diagrams, with each unit shown in a standardized format. Each unit is placed in its stratigraphic position relative to deposits above and below it, and the box for each unit is connected with lines indicating the order of superposition or correlation. This is the essence of the Harris Matrix system, introduced in 1973, by which the stratigraphic sequence of any site can be illustrated completely in a single diagram. Using this very simple method, which is of universal application, the stratigraphic sequence of any archaeological site can be developed during the course of excavation.

The stratigraphic sequence, not the stratification, is the independent testing pattern against which other analyses of the site, from a reconstruction of its landscape to the study of pottery or pollen, must be proven. Any site that can be excavated is stratified, and its stratigraphic sequence must be demonstrated by such a diagram, as it is not the same as the three-dimensional aspects of stratification shown in profile and plan drawings. The profile drawing is a plane view of the vertical dimensions of stratification, while the plan or map drawing records its surfaces. Such sections illustrate the superimposed pattern of the stratification along the line at which the profile was cut. Plan drawings are records of the surfaces of the stratification and show the horizontal extent of each unit. Modern practice requires single-layer planning, by which each unit is drawn on a separate sheet of tracing paper. Used in conjunction with the stratigraphic sequence of the site, such single-layer plans can be laid down in their order of superimposition, and form one of the most powerful analytical tools in archaeological stratigraphy.

The site notes are another way in which the stratigraphic record of a site can be preserved in a documentary form. Such entries will record the stratigraphic relationships of each unit, the composition of its soil, and related data. Section drawings, plans, and the site notes are all complementary parts of the stratigraphic archive. Used with the stratigraphic sequence, the archaeologist is able to carry out the postexcavation analyses of the portable materials taken from the site.

Dating the Deposits. Stratification is made up partly of deposits with objects that can be taken away for study and preservation. These objects help the archaeologist to fix the stratigraphic sequence in terms of years and centuries. Using the stratigraphic sequence as the testing framework, the objects found within each deposit are analyzed and a determination is made about the date at which the deposit was made. Based upon the date of latest object in the deposit, it is assumed that the stratum could not have been formed any earlier than that date. A date before which the deposit was made may be found by comparing the unit with others in stratigraphic order. Only when a consistent chronological order can be seen throughout the length of the stratigraphic sequence can a final determination of the date of each deposit be made.

The analyses of the artifacts is of paramount importance in obtaining a date in years for units of stratification that are not in superposition, for they cannot be chronologically associated by any other means. This is true not only within a site but applies to comparisons between stratigraphic events of disparate sites, due to the very limited area of most units of stratification.

Having carried out successful analyses of the artifacts, the archaeologist takes up the last stratigraphic task of any archaeological project. This is the reconstruction of the development of the landscape of the site through the course of absolute, or calendar, time (*see* Landscape Archaeology). Having determined the stratigraphic sequence of the site and knowing through artifact data which disparate units or groups of units may be associated, the site can be rebuilt, layer by layer, using the single-layer plans.

The Dual Nature of Stratigraphy. This final process demonstrates the duality of archaeological stratification. Materials are made into deposits, which account for the physical accumulation of stratification on the site, an accretion best viewed in a section drawing. The deposits make surfaces on which people lived, while other surfaces, such as a ditch, were formed by destroying preexisting stratification, thereby significantly changing the stratigraphic sequence. Each deposit has a surface, but some surfaces are without deposits; thus the interfacial, or immaterial, aspects of stratification usually comprise more than half the stratigraphic record. Without the deposits, the surfaces could not be dated in absolute time. Without the surfaces, or breaks in the stratigraphic record, there would be no stratigraphic sequences of relative time on any archaeological site. By applying stratigraphic methods, the archaeologist recovers both aspects of the stratigraphic history of the site, from which the truth about some of its past may be ascertained.

[*See also* ARCHAEO-PALEOMAGNETIC DATING; DATING THE PAST; DENDROCHRONOLOGY; EXCAVATION: INTRODUCTION; FISSION-TRACK DATING; LUMINESCENCE DATING; OBSIDIAN HYDRATION DATING; POTASSIUM-ARGON DATING; RADIOCARBON DATING; SERIATION.]

■ Kathleen M. Kenyon, *Beginning in Archaeology* (1952). Mortimer Wheeler, *Archaeology from the Earth* (1954). Philip Barker, *Techniques of Archaeological Excavation* (1977). Edward C. Harris, *Principles of Archaeological Stratigraphy* (1979; 2nd ed., 1989). Michael B. Schiffer, *Formation Processes of the Archaeological Record* (1987). Edward C. Harris, Marley R. Brown III, and Gregory J. Brown, *Practices of Archaeological Stratigraphy* (1993).

Edward Cecil Harris

STRUCTURALISM. Few theoretical frameworks have had a more profound impact on thinking in the social and historical sciences in the second half of the twentieth century than structuralism. Structuralist approaches and influences have been dominant in many disciplines since the 1960s and 1970s. They have also directly led to the development of entirely new areas of academic study such as media and cultural studies. They have been used in archaeology since the mid-1960s but only really became prominent from the early 1980s onward, forming part of what has become known as "post-processual" archaeology.

Structuralism is a theory of language that has been successfully applied to the study of nonlinguistic cultural forms. This approach has its origins in the work of the Swiss linguist Ferdinand de Saussure (1857–1913) whose theories revolutionized the understanding of language. Before his work, linguists had approached the problem of how languages, as communication systems, worked, by tracing historically changing ways in which people use words. Saussure argued that languages could never be adequately understood by tracing their histories, nor by analyzing individual speech acts. He introduced a crucial distinction between language and speech. The basic characteristic of language is that it is a structure consisting of rules of grammar, syntax, and meaning on which persons draw when they speak. This linguistic structure is socially held in the unconscious minds of a community of speakers. Every individual act of speech is generated by the rules of language, which allow people to communicate with each other, but speakers do not consciously think about these rules when they speak. Language is like a game with rules. To play the game (speak) we have to play by the rules. But these rules cannot be heard ("seen") in speech acts. We can all speak while knowing nothing about language. The task of linguistics is to uncover the rules which we implicitly know in our unconscious mind, but never formalize, in the act of speaking.

The essence of language is that it is a system of difference. It is a sign (word) system. Each sign, or component, of the system has two sides or faces which cannot be separated from each other. These are the signifier and the signified. The signifier is the sound (e.g., "d-o-g"), the signified the four-legged creature, dog, or abstract concept (e.g., time) to which the signifier refers. It is the relationship between signs that matters, not the signs themselves. Meaning is created and maintained by these relationships. In English we use the word dog to refer to a certain class of animal. We use the word cat to refer to another, and so on. In French the words used are different. The choice of which words to use is arbitrary—a matter of tradition and historical convention. In English, we could use the word cat to refer to a dog and vice versa. What is important is that the words used are not the same within any linguistic system. We only know what dogs *are* because they are *not* pigs, cats, rats, and so on.

Saussure's work was exclusively concerned with language but he made the prediction that one day linguistics would form part of a much more general study of sign systems: semiotics. This is precisely what has happened in the latter half of the twentieth century. Two of the most important innovators have been the anthropologist Claude Lévi-Strauss (1908–) and the literary theorist and semiotician Roland Barthes (1915–1980). Lévi-Strauss emphasized universal structuring principles of the human mind, characteristically realizing themselves in the world in a series of binary oppositions (e.g., left/right; back/front; night/day; etc.) by means of which culture is created and can be understood by the analyst. A careful structural analysis of material culture will reveal what these oppositions are and how they may be related to each other. There is enormous practical potential here for using a conceptual framework, based on a principle of binary opposition, for the analysis of archaeological remains. We might find ox bones deposited on the left-hand side of houses with axes, and pig bones on the right-hand side with pots, axes in male graves and pots in female graves. The principles (grammar) structuring the archaeological remains can be understood, in this case, as: ox is to pig as male is to female as left is to right as axe is to pot. Virtually all structural analyses end up listing related series of binary oppositions in this way.

Barthes was concerned with the specific operation of sign systems in everyday Western culture (e.g., clothing and fashion, food, furniture, and cars). For Barthes all human culture constituted an enormous symbolic code and the methods of semiotics provided a tool to crack that code. For example food could be understood in terms of Saussure's distinction between systemness and structure (language) and individual utilization of that system (speech). The speech of food consists of all the events and variations of cooking and eating, the language the underlying system of rules, for example, exclusion or inclusion (edible/inedible), association (what kinds of food can be served together), succession (the sequential ordering of dishes in a meal). A restaurant menu can easily be seen to be a food "grammar" ordering associational relations of difference sequentially: soups before main courses before sweet courses, red wine with dark meats, white wine with fish, and so forth.

Some post-processual archaeologists were attracted to structuralism because it provided a new ontology (theory of existence) and epistemology (theory of knowledge) for the study of material culture running counter to empiricist and functionalist theories that had hitherto dominated the discipline. In order to understand material culture it was necessary to probe beneath the observable surface manifestations of artifacts in the archaeological record to recover an underlying series of principles (rules or "grammars") which themselves could not be seen, but nevertheless could be shown to generate observed contextual associations between things, and therefore, explain them. Structuralism aims, then, at depth analyses.

From a structuralist perspective artifacts are regarded as constituting parts of sign systems that communicate nonverbal meanings in an analogous way to language. An artifact such as a particular type of basket may have, of course, a functional utilitarian use for holding things. On a plane of denotative meaning a basket simply means a basket and is defined in its difference from other types of containers, but on a plane of connotative meaning it can also simultaneously communicate symbolically as part of a sign system (e.g., it can signify femaleness because all women use baskets of this sort as opposed to men who use another type of basket).

Structuralist analyses have been used to study and interpret a wide variety of archaeological evidence, from a study of designs on pots to rock carvings, to the analysis of architecture and house interiors, to the study of entire regions. Such analyses may either identify particular structural grammars (e.g., rules for decorating Greek Neolithic pots), or attempt to link up a whole variety of different types of evidence in order to show that similar principles structure burial practices, settlement space, rubbish disposal, food consumption and so on. The end point of the analysis may be simply to specify the operation of a number of abstract rules structuring the artifacts (e.g., triangular and circular designs never occur together on the rim areas of pots but are regularly associated around the belly) or archaeological deposits (e.g., when axes and pots are left as votive deposits in bogs they are always separated, when they occur in burials they are always together). Further attempts may be made to interpret the meanings of these rules themselves: why associate axes and pots in some contexts and not others? How might this relate to sociopolitical relations? Structuralist analyses in contemporary archaeology are usually linked to such wider considerations.

[See also COGNITIVE ARCHAEOLOGY; CRITICAL THEORY; CULTURE HISTORICAL THEORY; MARXIST THEORY; POST-PROCESSUAL THEORY; PROCESSUAL THEORY; THEORY IN ARCHAEOLOGY.]

■ Ferdinand de Saussure, *Course in General Linguistics* (1974). Dorothy Washburn, ed., *Structure and Cognition in Art* (1983). Ian Hodder, *The Domestication of Europe* (1990). Bjørnar Olsen, "Roland Barthes: From Sign to Text" in *Reading Material Culture*, ed. Christopher Tilley (1990), pp. 163–205. Christopher Tilley, "Claude Lévi-Strauss: Structuralism and Beyond" in *Reading Material Culture*, ed. Christopher Tilley (1990), pp. 3–84. Christopher Tilley, *Material Culture and Text* (1991).

Christopher Tilley

STUKELEY, William (1687–1765), physician and clergyman, was the major eighteenth-century fieldworker in Britain, at a time when unstructured antiquarian collecting began to crystallize into that systematic study which later became the discipline of archaeology.

Stukeley grew up in the low-lying fen country of Lincolnshire, in eastern England; he learned medicine at Cambridge University and in London, and established a practice in Lincolnshire. Beginning in 1710, he took an annual tour on horseback across England, exploring gardens, architectural curiosities, and ancient sites. He moved to London in 1717 and became the first secretary of the Society of Antiquaries of London.

In 1722–1724, his tour took him especially to *Avebury

and *Stonehenge, the great prehistoric monuments of Wilt-shire, where he made detailed field records and sketches. Around Stonehenge, he observed ancient earthworks not before noticed. Around Avebury, he recorded stone settings that were being broken and demolished, so his account has enduring worth. These researches were published in 1740 (*Stonehenge*) and 1743 (*Avebury*), in handsome, well-illustrated volumes that combined fine field observation with ideas about the religion of the ancient Britons that today seem fantastical (in 1730 he had become a clergyman). Other scholars of the age, such as Sir Isaac Newton (who Stukeley knew), show the same combination of convictions, so there is more to this than a sound mind turning inexplicably weak.

Stukeley deserves memory also for the vigor of his writing; as in his account of the approach to Stonehenge:

Stonehenge stands not upon the very summit of a hill, but pretty near it, and for more than three quarters of the circuit you ascend to it very gently from lower ground. At half a mile distance, the appearance of it is stately and awful, really august. As you advance nearer, especially up the avenue, which is to the northeast of it (which side is now most perfect) the greatness of its contour fills the eye in an astonishing manner.

Stukeley is remembered and respected as a pioneer of that intense curiosity and acute observation, which is essential to good archaeological fieldwork.

[*See also* HISTORY OF ARCHAEOLOGY BEFORE 1900: EURO-PEAN ARCHAEOLOGY.]

■ Stuart Piggott, *William Stukeley: An Eighteenth-Century Antiquary,* 2nd ed. (1985).

Christopher Chippindale

SUBSISTENCE. The reconstruction of ancient subsistence systems and the analysis of subsistence change have been the focus of a great deal of primary archaeological research worldwide. The materialist underpinnings of much archaeological theory has emphasized the importance of subsistence studies, and subsistence change has often been invoked as a prime mover in the explanation of general culture change. Furthermore, the relatively good preservation of animal bones and some types of implements used for food acquisition and preparation (e.g., arrowheads, sickle blades, grinding stones) have rendered subsistence systems more accessible to standard methods of archaeological reconstruction than other cultural components, such as social or religious systems.

Subsistence systems can be divided into two general types, not necessarily mutually exclusive: hunting-gathering and food production. These can be further divided according to levels of intensity and organization of exploitation, technologies of exploitation, and actual foodstuffs. Although there is an apparent progression from organizationally and technologically simple to more complex systems on the world scale in the archaeological record, the factors causing subsistence change are, in fact, varied and not self-evident. More complex or intensive modes of production are not necessarily more efficient nor more culturally advanced. Assumptions of progressive linear development of subsistence systems are questionable.

Paleolithic. Reconstruction of the earliest hominid subsistence systems derives from a combination of relatively scant archaeological evidence and analogies with modern hunter-gatherers as well as modern primate groups. The association of stone artifacts and animal bones at early Paleolithic sites such as *Olduvai Gorge, in Kenya, demon-strates that meat acquisition was a significant component of australopithecine and early *Homo* subsistence. Initial appraisals of early hominid subsistence, as conducted, for example by Raymond *Dart, emphasized the importance of hunting both for subsistence and for its effects on the general social order. Studies of modern hunter-gatherers and higher primates in the tropical and subtropical zones have demonstrated that the gathering of vegetal foods is a more important activity than hunting calorically. Reevaluations of early hominid capabilities have cast doubt on systematic hunting as a viable subsistence option and have stressed gathering, scavenging, and small-scale opportunistic hunting. Unfortunately, direct archaeological evidence for gathering in these early periods is virtually absent, due to problems in preservation of organic materials.

Evidence for later Acheulean subsistence seems to reflect a preference for large game, as demonstrated, for example, by the elephant kill sites of *Torralba / Ambrona in Spain and by the association of large fauna with artifactual remains at numerous cave occupation sites throughout the world. As in the earlier period, there is some question as to the effectiveness of Acheulean hunting, and some of the associations between animal bones and human occupations have been attributed to carnivore and scavenger accumulations, especially in cave sites.

Control of fire is first well documented toward the end of the Lower Paleolithic and the beginning of the Middle Paleolithic (ca. 150,000–250,000 B.P.). The effects of this technological development on subsistence must have been considerable. The cooking of both plant and animal foods allows a wider range of foods to be exploited in that it softens previously inedible foods, kills bacteria and increases preservability, and neutralizes some poisons. Direct evidence for these changes is lacking, however.

By the Middle Paleolithic (150,000–40,000 B.P.), the use of Mousterian and Levallois points in Europe and Africa constitutes the earliest evidence for stone projectile points, probably spearheads or lanceheads. Faunal remains reflect a focus on large game, but hunting strategies seem to be more effective than in earlier periods. For example, the open chimney at Tabun Cave in Israel may have been utilized as a game trap in the late Mousterian, as evidenced by the high density and articulation of deer bones in Layer B of the site. Analyses of site location, size, and function seem to reflect seasonal patterns of exploitation. Evidence for gathering is minimal, again due primarily to the vagaries of organic preservation.

Late Paleolithic hunting systems show increasing technological and social sophistication. Evidence for hunting or trapping of small game increases, probably reflecting the development of snares and traps. Specialized hunting systems exploiting specific species, such as reindeer in western Europe, gazelle in the Near Eastern Levant, and perhaps mammoth in North America, reflect close human-animal relationships that may in some cases have resembled ranching. Evidence for vegetal food gathering increases toward the end of the *Pleistocene, in the form of both botanical remains and the implements for processing them (e.g., mortars, pestles, grinders, and sickle blades). Fishing and shellfish collection are reflected in the presence of *shell middens (especially in coastal areas of Africa and Europe), fishbones, and harpoon points. Food storage facilities and preservation techniques are also present among some ancient and recent hunter-gatherer groups, such as Native Americans of the northwest coast and the Natufians of the Mediterranean Levant.

The increased range of late Upper Paleolithic exploitation in the Near East and Mexico has been defined by K. V. Flannery as a "broad spectrum economy." It is this economy, combined with increased specialization focused on specific elements within this spectrum, that provides the background for the emergence of food production.

Neolithic Adaptations. The earliest Neolithic or Archaic subsistence systems were based on the farming of domesticated grains complemented by hunting and the gathering of wild plants. Domestication of these grains seems to have occurred independently in the *Near East (wheat and barley), Southeast Asia (rice), and Central America (maize), according to both the availability of wild progenitors (or assumed progenitors) and earliest archaeological evidence. Secondary crops such as legumes and gourds seem to have been domesticated either concurrently with the grains, as in the Tehuacan Valley in Mexico, or shortly thereafter, as in the Near East. Regardless, these secondary crops seem to have provided vital complementary nutrients, especially in the form of proteins (legumes), to the Neolithic/Archaic diet. Legumes also fix nitrogen in the soil, so crop rotation between grains and legumes can considerably enhance soil productivity.

The *diffusion of these earliest complexes to areas outside the primary ranges of the domesticates is accompanied by an expansion in the number of genera and species domesticated. Thus it is possible to trace the origins and development of various crop complexes in the later stages of the spread of *agriculture, as for example in the Upper and Lower Sonoran Agricultural Complexes adopted in the American Southwest. A key issue concerns the actual mechanisms involved in the adoption of agriculture. It is clear that the process was uneven, and adoption of agricultural systems follows a mosaic of cultural and ecological adaptations. The diffusion of crop complexes is not necessarily associated with the movement of peoples.

The *domestication of animals is tied closely to the development of farming systems. Whereas nineteenth-century evolutionary frameworks predicted a hunting-herding-farming procession, the actual archaeological evidence has demonstrated unequivocally that *pastoralism developed later, as a complement to agricultural societies. The earliest animal domesticates in the Near East (goat, sheep) seem to have been exploited primarily for their meat, but later Neolithic societies in both the Near East and adjacent regions exploited a range of secondary products, including milk, hair, wool, traction, and transport (*see* Secondary Products Revolution).

Like plant domestication, animal domestication was constrained by the need for appropriate progenitors. Thus the only large domesticates in the New World were the Andean camelids, the llama, and the alpaca, more or less the only animals behaviorally appropriate for domestication. In contrast, in the Old World a great range of animal genera and species were domesticated. The types of behavior associated with these domesticates is varied as well, spanning the hunting-ranching of reindeer among modern Laplanders, through ranching of cattle and herding of cattle, sheep, goats, and camels, to the penning of these same species and others (e.g., pigs, fowl).

Pastoralism should not be viewed as a subsistence system per se, but rather as a mode of production within a larger system. Pastoral groups, even when they appear autonomous, are invariably dependent on the products and markets of their agricultural complements. Furthermore, most pastoral economies are based on multiresource exploitation, as opposed to pure pastoralism.

Post-Neolithic Subsistence Systems. With increasing social complexity, subsistence systems also show increased sophistication, in terms of both technology and management. Market systems encouraged agricultural investment in cash crops (e.g., fruit trees) and specialization (e.g., pastoralism). Centralization of authority allowed the construction of large-scale agricultural systems for intensified exploitation, as especially notable in irrigation systems such as those of Mesopotamia, Mesoamerica, and the American Southwest.

The large scale of these systems and the apparent cultural continuity with modern industrial agriculture has tended to obscure the continued existence of numerous less intensive systems, especially on the peripheries of technologically advanced societies. These systems demonstrate that subsistence systems are adaptations to specific social, cultural, and ecological circumstances, and they should not be misconstrued as backward or primitive.

[*See also* AFRICA, ORIGINS OF FOOD PRODUCTION IN; ASIA, ORIGINS OF FOOD PRODUCTION IN: OVERVIEW; DIET, RECONSTRUCTION OF; DOMESTICATION OF PLANTS; FIELD SYSTEMS; MESOAMERICA, ORIGINS OF FOOD PRODUCTION IN; NEW GUINEA, ORIGINS OF FOOD PRODUCTION IN; NORTH AMERICA, ORIGINS OF FOOD PRODUCTION IN; PACIFIC ISLANDS, ORIGINS OF FOOD PRODUCTION IN THE; PALEOBOTANY; PLANT REMAINS, ANALYSIS OF; SEASONALITY STUDIES; SOUTH AMERICA, ORIGINS OF FOOD PRODUCTION IN; ZOOARCHAEOLOGY.]

■ Richard B. Lee and Irven Devors, eds., *Man the Hunter* (1968). Peter J. Ucko and George W. Dimbleby, eds., *The Domestication and Exploitation of Plants and Animals* (1969). Timothy K. Earle and Andrew L. Christenson, eds., *Modeling Change in Prehistoric Subsistence Systems* (1980). Lewis R. Binford, *Bones: Ancient Men and Modern Myths* (1981). Ester Boserup, *Population and Technological Change* (1981). Bruce Winterhalder and Eric A. Smith, eds., *Hunter-Gatherer Foraging Strategies* (1981). Roy Ellen, *Environment, Subsistence and System* (1982). Anatoly M. Khazanov, *Nomads and the Outside World* (1984). David R. Harris and Gordon C. Hillman, eds., *Foraging and Farming* (1989).

Steven Rosen

SUBSURFACE TESTING

Introduction
Soil Resistivity Survey
Magnetometer Survey
Ground Penetrating Radar

INTRODUCTION

The archaeological record is buried beneath the modern surface, and therein lies a dilemma. On the one hand the record is preserved, in a sense, from the ravages of destruction. On the other hand, it is accessible only with great effort. In the ideal world where time and money were of no account, archaeologists would excavate as much as they pleased. But this world is not ideal, and excavation is time-consuming and expensive. As an alternative to full-scale excavation, we often sample the subsurface for the remains that it possesses, either to determine where to dig or to eliminate the need for digging at all.

Archaeologists always use subsurface sampling methods where the surface is vegetated and hence artifacts are not visible, or where the record is buried more than about 1 foot below the surface. We often sample where thorough survey of large areas is impractical. Because these conditions are common, we commonly use subsurface methods. Invasive methods, from coring with small augers to shovel-testing to trenching with heavy equipment, simply are special kinds of excavation that determine what may lie beneath the surface. Noninvasive methods detect elements of the buried record without excavation.

Invasive methods are digging writ small or large, but lacking the fine control ordinarily exercised in excavation. These methods seek artifacts or anthrosols, and are used widely in North America and perhaps elsewhere, often to discover all sites that exist in a region. Some require only simple hand tools, others rather expensive heavy machinery. The simplest versions have been used since the advent of systematic archaeology, but heavy machinery has found wide use only in recent decades. Soil conditions have little effect on invasive methods, which can detect virtually all kinds of sites. But they are very labor-intensive and therefore can sample practically only a microscopic fraction of the subsurface; moreover, those involving hand tools are useful only within several meters of the surface. These qualities do not invalidate invasive methods. They are quite useful in sampling the record at various spatial scales, but not for discovering all sites in a region. Current invasive methods must continue in use until better ones are developed, but only with recognition of their inherent limitations. This means, in practical terms, that we should not expect such methods to discover all or even most sites that exist in a given region.

Noninvasive methods exploit the unusual physical properties of anthrosols. The most common involve the measurement of electrical resistivity (or its complement, conductivity). In addition, magnetic and chemical properties of altered sediments are detectable with appropriate devices, acoustical properties are detectable using ground-penetrating radar, and simple visual ones are detectable using aerial survey. Aerial survey has been used for a century or more, but resistivity and most other methods largely postdate 1950.

Noninvasive methods identify comparatively massive features like ditches and structures. Their chief virtue is that they do not transform the record in the process of investigating it. For simple discovery, they involve much less time and effort than do conventional excavation methods. But they also require special and often costly equipment and the expertise to operate it and to interpret results, and their coverage rate is very low. Consequently, most are practical only at small scales. Aerial survey is the chief exception, but it can detect only the largest-scale features. Natural variation in sediment texture, moisture, and inclusions affects noninvasive methods. The archaeological features they detect are anomalies only in comparison to local sediments, so they require calibration for each set of local conditions. Also, depth sensitivity and horizontal resolution—equally desirable properties—vary inversely such that increasing one reduces the other. Thus results can be difficult to interpret, and sometimes subsequent excavation is required to confirm findings. Because they can detect only large targets, not individual artifacts, non-invasive methods have little value in Paleolithic research, although they can detect buried surfaces on which older sites may lie.

*Sampling never will replace well-controlled excavation, but it has undeniable value for many purposes. No doubt further technical improvements will occur, especially in noninvasive techniques, but our greatest challenge will continue to be appreciating for what purposes various methods are best suited. This requires not technical virtuosity so much as sound archaeological judgment informed by knowledge of how the record formed in geological context and of the sampling theory appropriate to its measurement. Like all tools, subsurface methods are as good as the archaeologists who use them.

[See also EXCAVATION: EXCAVATION STRATEGIES; SITE LOCATION, articles on FINDING ARCHAEOLOGICAL SITES, REMOTE SENSING AND GEOPHYSICAL PROSPECTION, SITE ASSESSMENT.]

■ Christopher Carr, Handbook on Soil Resistivity Surveying: Interpretation of Data from Earthen Archaeological Sites (1982). James J. Krakker, Michael J. Shott, and Paul D. Welch, "Design and Evaluation of Shovel-Test Sampling in Regional Archaeological Survey," Journal of Field Archaeology 10 (1983): 469–480. H. Martin Wobst, "We Can't See the Forest for the Trees: Sampling and the Shapes of Archaeological Distributions," in Archaeological Hammers and Theories, ed. James Moore and Arthur Keene (1983), pp. 32–80. Julie K. Stein, "Coring Archaeological Sites," American Antiquity 51 (1986): 505–527. Anthony Clark, Seeing Beneath the Soil: Prospecting Methods in Archaeology (1990). Don H. Heimmer, Near-Surface, High Resolution Geophysical Methods for Cultural Resource Management and Archaeological Investigations (1992).

Michael J. Shott

SOIL RESISTIVITY SURVEY

Soil resistivity measurements were first collected for archaeological purposes by Richard Atkinson in 1946 at Dorchester on Thames, England. Atkinson used the Wenner array to identify the position of prehistoric features cut into the subsoil. However, the technique has become more commonly used to map the extent of structural features such as walls. Resistivity survey also has been used to infer areas of activity as well as estimating depths to strata or features. Depth work, although traditionally achieved using electrical sounding, is commonly assessed by pseudo or tomographic section.

The technique requires an electric current to be injected into the ground and the soil resistance to be measured at specific points, usually on a regular grid. All systems use four probes, two to apply the AC electric current and two to measure the voltage. The value of the resistance, measured in ohms, is dependent upon the array or configuration of the probes. To compare the results between different arrays, the resistivity of the soil is calculated using a general formula. The resistivity is measured in ohm meters.

Early experimentation revolved around arrays derived from geological geophysics. During the 1960s methodological advances, often charted within the pages of the Italian journal Prospezioni Archeologiche, provided archaeologists with a rapid and efficient technique for area investigation. In Europe, and Britain in particular, the Twin-Probe array has become the most favored arrangement of probes for archaeological prospection. The early equipment was heavy and temperamental, requiring manual recording. Since the early 1980s specialized modern equipment has revolutionized the use of resistivity survey within archaeology. The equipment is now light and robust with automatic logging facilities as standard. A French system allows the equipment to be towed behind a motor vehicle, thus relieving the tedious and fatiguing manual insertion of probes and speeding data collection. The results can be downloaded to a computer in the field and viewed in graphical form. The gridded data can be manipulated with commercially available software to remove erroneous data points or to reduce background trends due to topographical or other factors. The data is commonly presented as XY profiles, dot density, grey-scale, contour, and perspective plots.

Resistivity survey is usually used to prospect for individual features within known sites, or to define a site rather than locate new sites. Once an area has been chosen for survey, perhaps as the result of the analysis of aerial photographs or field-walking data, it is subdivided into convenient collection blocks, usually 60 or 98 square feet (20 or 30 sq m). Within these blocks, the data are systematically collected, usually at one-meter intervals. The sample interval varies depending upon the expected features.

Although the field procedure is very easy to master, the interpretation of the results requires some experience. The resistivity value at a particular point is a bulk measurement and may be related to complex archaeological strata. Features may be masked by later activity at the site and some agricultural regimes, such as plowing, may increase soil noise to the extent that anomalies produced by buried features may not be recognized. The recognition of anomalies depends on a measurable electrical contrast between the archaeological features and the surrounding soil. Thus, some features will be invisible depending on the water content of the soil. Simplistically, negative features are often difficult to locate during wet seasons, and the location of stone walls is often difficult during dry periods. Despite these problems, resistivity survey can aid the understanding of a site prior to, or even without, excavation, particularly when used in conjunction with other complementary geophysical techniques.

[*See also* SITE LOCATION: SITE ASSESSMENT.]

■ A. J. Clark, *Seeing Beneath the Soil* (1990). I. Scollar et al., *Archaeological Geophysics and Remote Sensing* (1990).

C. F. Gaffney

MAGNETOMETER SURVEY

Magnetic surveying (also magnetometry or magnetic prospection) is one of the most popular methods of the several geophysical techniques developed for or adapted to the need for a rapid nondestructive evaluation of archaeological sites. The method was first applied to archaeology in the mid-1950s, when the Oxford Laboratory for Archaeology and the History of Art under Martin Aitken exploited the introduction of a portable magnetometer in 1954 (for historical background, see A. Clark, *Seeing Beneath the Soil*, London, 1990).

In magnetometry the strength of the earth's magnetic field is measured a few centimeters above the surface of a site using very sensitive magnetometers. The magnetic field in mid-northern latitudes is roughly 50,000 nanotesla (nT), while the sensitivity of modern instruments can be 0.01 nT. The most widely used instrument is the proton precession magnetometer, although the fluxgate gradiometer, which measures the vertical magnetic gradient, is gaining acceptance.

The usual procedure is to measure the field on a grid of points spaced a meter or less apart over the site. Since the earth's field changes slightly but significantly throughout the day, it is necessary to correct for this by operating a second, base-station magnetometer. This is particularly necessary during magnetic storms, when the field can change unpredictably and abruptly by several nT. A gradiometer automatically makes this correction. In subsequent analysis, the corrected data are plotted as maps and examined for anomalies or anomalous patterns that can be associated with archaeological sources. It may be necessary to filter the data to remove trends or emphasize short-range features.

Magnetometry provides archaeological information because various human activities can slightly alter the local magnetic content of soils. Examples are pits dug into subsoil and filled in with topsoil, fired hearths, walls or ditches, brick walks, and filled-in privies or cellars. Unfortunately, natural features such as differential soil lenses, varying bedrock depth, or filled-in drainage ditches can also produce magnetic anomalies and must be distinguished from those of archaeological importance by the nature of the anomaly and by utilizing accumulated experience. Modern iron objects on a prehistoric site can produce interfering anomalies and are best removed prior to a survey by visual examination or by using a metal detector. Failing this, it is possible to recognize and discount such intrusive anomalies. On historical sites, modern iron is a greater problem because some of the iron may be of archaeological significance. In this case, the positions and patterns of the objects can give clues as to their relevance.

Magnetometry is unaffected by soil moisture or temperature. The only climatic interference is the decreased performance of batteries in very cold weather. Sloping or undulating terrain can produce trends in the results, but these can usually be removed with mathematical filtering.

Usually magnetometry cannot give a clear picture of the subsurface content of a site but can suggest positions and patterns that may be important. The best utilization of magnetic data occurs when the geophysicist works closely with the archaeologist and both study the data in the light of the archaeological problems and expectations.

[*See also* SITE LOCATION: SITE ASSESSMENT.]

■ Martin J. Aitken, *Physics and Archaeology* (2nd ed., 1974). John W. Weymouth, "Geophysical Methods of Archaeological Site Surveying," Chapter 6 in *Advances in Archaeological Method and Theory*, 9, ed. Michael B. Schiffer (1986), pp. 311–395. Irwin Scollar, ed., *Archaeological Prospecting and Remote Sensing* (1990).

John W. Weymouth

GROUND PENETRATING RADAR

The electronic ground penetrating radar instrument generates images that approximate the cross-sectional appearance of underground features. It is one of the instruments of geophysical exploration that can help archaeologists decide locations for their excavations.

A ground penetrating radar can detect a wider variety of buried materials than probably any other geophysical instrument. It can detect metal, wood, stone, brick, and even air-filled voids. It can also map the undulating interfaces between soil strata and sometimes the depth to bedrock and the water table. The instrument is particularly suitable for locating lenses of debris and also refilled pits and ditches.

The Instrument. The central part of a ground penetrating radar is the antenna, which is probably within a small box, sled, or wheeled cart. This antenna is connected to a low power transmitter and a sensitive receiver. Short pulses of very high frequency radio waves are transmitted from the antenna into the earth. Wherever there is a sharp change in the type of earth, such as that between strata of sand and silt, part of the radio wave is reflected back to the radar's antenna.

The antenna is moved slowly along a line at the earth's surface and the radar echoes are displayed as a two-dimensional image. The length axis of this image indicates the distance along the line of the profile. The vertical axis shows the time delay of the echo; this scale can be converted to show the depth of the objects that cause the echoes.

The images that are created by a ground penetrating radar are very similar to those created by a sonar, which profiles the depth of water and locates fish; the images are also similar to those that are generated during seismic exploration for oil. However, the radar uses a radio pulse rather than a pulse of sound. A radar for locating aircraft is similar to a ground penetrating radar, except that one radar is optimized for detecting distant objects in the air and the other is best for locating nearby objects that are underground.

Radar surveys were first applied to archaeology by Stanford Research Institute in 1974. Ground penetrating radars were first developed for commercial applications by Geophysical Survey Systems, Inc.; their radars were widely available in 1975.

Modern refinements of these instruments have made them more portable and have allowed them to detect smaller features. Most radars now have a computer for the display and recording of the images.

Radar Surveys. A ground penetrating radar can explore for features within soil, rock, shell mounds, walls, peat, fresh water, and ice or snow. It is most suitable where the soil is sandy and is weakly stratified or has horizontal strata. In average soil, a radar can profile to a depth of about 3 meters. If the soil is clay or is saline, the profiling depth of the radar is so shallow as to make it useless. Because the radar antenna operates best when it is very close to the surface of the earth, radar surveys are difficult where there is brush or where there are boulders on the ground.

During a day's survey, a length of about one kilometer can be profiled. This survey is usually done with many parallel lines of profile, perhaps spaced by one meter, so that the three-dimensional shape of underground features can be estimated. While the radar can be excellent for defining features within a known archaeological site, it is not very practical for locating unknown sites, since the area of search can be so large.

A radar is very good for estimating the depth of underground features. However, it is not very good for identifying the materials that are detected: A stone can cause an echo similar to that of a void, and the bedrock interface can look like the water table.

Unlike many other geophysical instruments, the radar has little difficulty with metal objects near the area of survey. A scatter of metallic debris in the soil also causes few problems. However, a layer of rubble at the surface of the ground can hide important archaeological features below it. An intact foundation wall may be hidden by the rubble that surrounds it. Ground penetrating radar is usually not suitable for locating small or thin features, such as postholes or pavements. The features that are detected by a radar survey are generally similar to those found by a resistivity survey, but different from those detected by a magnetic survey.

[See also SITE LOCATION, articles on FINDING ARCHAEOLOGICAL SITES, SITE ASSESSMENT.]

■ Tsuneo Imai, Toshihiko Sakayama, and Takashi Kanemori, "Use of Ground-Probing Radar and Resistivity Surveys for Archaeological Investigations," Geophysics 52 (1987): 137–150. Irwin Scollar et al., Archaeological Prospecting and Remote Sensing (1990). D. Goodman et al., "A Ground Radar Survey of Medieval Kiln Sites in Suzu City, Western Japan," Archaeometry 36 (1994): 317–326.

Bruce W. Bevan

SUNGIR. An Upper *Paleolithic site, Sungir is located at the outskirts of the city of Vladimir, Russia, and has achieved worldwide fame because it contains the most elaborate burials of this period found to date. The cultural remains were discovered on a promontory formed by the Klyazma and Sungir Rivers. Radiocarbon dates indicate occupation between some 26,000 and 22,000 B.P., with the older age being preferred. Deteriorating climatic conditions, which set in after Sungir was abandoned, led to periglacial processes that have greatly disturbed the cultural layer.

About one-half of the site (approximately 5,380 square yards [4,500 sq m]) has been excavated to date. This has revealed five concentrations with surface dwellings, hearths and pits, tool production areas, as well as six burials, only three of which were undisturbed. The nature and structure of the remains suggest that Sungir was occupied over a number of years during the warmer months of the year.

Three undisturbed extended burials were found in a dwelling in the southwestern part of the site. They included a grave of a 45–60-year-old male buried with 2,936 ivory beads, perforated Arctic fox teeth, a stone pendant, and 25 ivory bracelets and rings. Ten feet (3 m) away lay a double grave of a 13-year-old boy and a 9–10-year-old girl interred head-to-head in a single long rectangular grave. The boy's grave contained 4,903 ivory beads, a belt of some 250 drilled Arctic fox teeth, a pin, ivory bracelets and pendants, discs, ivory sculptures of a mammoth and a horse, as well as assorted ivory lances and spears, one of which measured 8 feet (2.4 m) in length. The girl's burial contained 5,274 beads, a pin, many ivory lances, antler shaft straighteners and carved ivory discs. The beads in the three burials were sewn onto clothing, which consisted of shirts, long pants with attached footwear, over-the-knee boots, short outer cloaks, and hats for the males and a hood for the girl. Stratigraphic observations indicate that the adult male was buried a few seasons after the children.

While the burials were not simultaneous, the similarity between the three suggests that all the deceased belonged to the same social group. The wealth of the burial inventory, conservatively estimated as representing some 9,000 hours of work in manufacture of the ivory beads alone, suggests that these individuals held high status in their society, and that the children, because of their age, must have inherited this status. The resulting picture of complex social organization during the Upper Paleolithic must, however, be tempered by the realization that funerary wealth can reflect either high status held in life or one achieved only in death.

Sungir's rich lithic inventory, made on locally available cobbles, features bifacially retouched triangular points, Aurignacian pieces, as well as some archaic Mousterian forms. While this suggests an Early Upper Paleolithic age for the site, scholars are divided on its cultural affiliation, with some classifying it as Aurignacian with leaf points and others as a younger stage in the development of the local Kostenki-Streletskaia archaeological culture.

[See also EUROPE: THE EUROPEAN PALEOLITHIC PERIOD.]

■ Otto N. Bader, Sungir (1978) (in Russian). Otto N. Bader, "Paleoliticheskiie pogrepeniia i paleoantropologicheskii nakhodki na Sungire," in Sungir Antropologicheskoe Issledovanie, ed. Aleksandr A. Zubov (1984).

Olga Soffer

SUTTON HOO is the site of a group of burial mounds (fourteen are currently visible) situated in sandy agricultural land beside the River Deben in southeastern England. One of these mounds was opened in 1939 by Basil Brown and Charles Phillips at the instigation of the landowner. It proved to contain the outline of a clinker-built timber ship 89 feet (27 m) long, in the center of which lay the richest assemblage of grave goods yet discovered in Britain. The deposit included a helmet, sword, and shield; a solid gold buckle; shoulder clasps inset with garnets; a purse decorated with birds of prey rendered in gold and garnet and containing 37 Frankish gold coins, 3 blank flans, and 2 unstruck ingots; silver bowls and a great silver dish from Byzantium, bronze hanging bowls with enameled escutcheons from the Celtic west, a large bronze cauldron with a 11.5-foot (3.5-m)-long suspension chain, and a pile of clothing (much decayed) including a yellow cloak originating from the Near East. The animal ornament on the metal objects features a late "style II" looking forward to the animal patterns found on early Anglo-Celtic gospel books; this and the coins serve to date the obsequies to the early seventh century A.D. The range of objects found in the ship show the burial to be an orthodox if greatly inflated example of the Anglo-Saxon weapon burial rite. The wealth of the assemblage and its location in East Anglia led H. M. Chadwick to propose the ship burial as the grave of Raedwald, a documented king of the East Angles who died ca. A.D. 625.

The ship burial (designated Mound 1), together with the disturbed remains of two earlier mounds (Mounds 2 and 3), excavated by Basil Brown in 1938, were researched and published by R.L.S. Bruce-Mitford and a team at the British Museum between 1945 and 1983. At the instigation of the Society of Antiquaries of London and the British Museum, a new research campaign began in 1983, designed to discover a context for the ship burial and its role in the creation of an early English kingdom. The new campaign, led by M.O.H. Carver, began with a three-year evaluation and continued with a six-year program of excavation and survey. The investigations were divided into four parts: comparative studies of contemporary emergent kingdoms in lands bordering the North Sea; a survey of the putative East Anglian kingdom, using surface collection in sample areas; remote sensing to map the zone containing the barrow cemetery; and excavation at the site itself, 2.5 acres (1 ha) in extent and designed to reveal the sequence of burial rite from the beginning to the end of the cemetery's use.

The fieldwork of this campaign was completed in 1992. Sutton Hoo proved to be the site of an extensive settlement and field system belonging to the Late Neolithic–Early Bronze Age (the Beaker Period). After fitful agricultural exploitation in the Iron Age and the Roman and early Anglo-Saxon periods, it was chosen as the site of a prestigious cemetery reserved for the elite and lasting less than a hundred years, from the late sixth to the late seventh centuries A.D. In the earliest burials, the bodies were cremated and placed in bronze bowls (Mounds 3–7 and 18). Mound 5 was distinguished by being surrounded by satellite burials—bodies (some identified as young men) whose curious position in the grave suggested ritual killing. A series of inhumations followed under other mounds: Mound 14 was the chamber-grave of a woman; beneath Mound 17 lay a young man in a weapon grave, while his horse was placed in a separate but adjacent and parallel grave. Mound 2 contained a weapon burial in a wooden chamber with a clinker-built ship placed on top of the chamber at ground level, both being covered by the mound; in Mound 1 (one of the latest and probably the last), the ship had been placed in a trench and the wooden chamber was inside it. Every burial, except those beneath Mounds 1 and 17, had been disturbed by unrecorded excavations, mainly attributable to the nineteenth century.

Current interpretation of the sequence proposes that the Sutton Hoo cemetery, together with other evidence from East Anglia, reflects the aspiration of the local aristocracy to regional control, culminating in the adoption of kingship and taxation in the late sixth century. The kingship signaled at Sutton Hoo is pagan in its ideology and Scandinavian in its allegiance, as demonstrated by the rites of human sacrifice (Mound 5), late cremation (Mounds 3–7), and ship burial (Mounds 1 and 2). The formation of the kingdom (and its defiant pagan culture) were probably provoked by the proximity of the Christian Merovingian Empire, which had already subjugated Kent. Within fifty years, East Anglia in turn submitted to the new politics and the Sutton Hoo cemetery was abandoned. This episode is seen as the first round in an ideological argument between the benefits of independent enterprise and those of a European union, which has exercised the British ever since.

Following a precedent set by the landowner, all finds from the Sutton Hoo site have been donated to the British Museum. The site has been reconstituted and is open to the public on weekends in summer.

[See also BRITISH ISLES: THE ANGLO-SAXONS.]

■ R.L.S. Bruce-Mitford, The Sutton Hoo Ship Burial, 3 vols. (1975, 1979, 1983). Bulletin of the Sutton Hoo Research Committee 1–9 (1983–1993). M.O.H. Carver, "Kingship and Material Culture in Early Anglo-Saxon East Anglia," in ed. S. Bassett, The Origins of Anglo-Saxon Kingdoms (1989), pp. 141–158. M.O.H. Carver, "Ideology and Allegiance in Early East Anglia," in eds. R. Farrell and C. Neuman de Vegvar, Sutton Hoo: Fifty Years After (1992), pp. 173–182. M.O.H. Carver, "The Anglo-Saxon Cemetery at Sutton Hoo: An Interim Report," in ed. M.O.H. Carver, The Age of Sutton Hoo (1992), pp. 343–371. M.O.H. Carver, ed., The Age of Sutton Hoo (1992). I. Wood, "Frankish Hegemony in England," The Age of Sutton Hoo (1992), pp. 235–242.

Martin Carver

SYSTEMS THEORY. *See* GENERAL SYSTEMS THEORY.

T

TAUTAVEL Also known as the Caune de l'Arago, the cave of Tautavel is located in the foothills of the Pyrénées Orientales, southern France, 265 feet (80 m) above the plain of Roussillon. The site, 115 feet (35 m) long and 35 feet (10 m) wide, was first noted in 1838 for its faunal remains. Prehistoric tools were found there in 1948, and the French prehistorian Henry de Lumley has been excavating the cave since 1964.

The deposits are over 35 feet (10 m) thick, comprising an alternation of sands and sandy clays, with a thick layer of stalagmite at the top. Over twenty ancient living floors have been uncovered, separated from each other by 2 to 8 inches (5–20 cm) of sterile sand, and filled with stone and bone debris, but with no trace of fire. The fauna consists primarily of horse, but also includes bison, aurochs, musk ox, mouflon, chamois, deer, carnivores, rhinoceros, elephant, rabbit, and birds. This faunal assemblage points to the Middle *Pleistocene, while absolute dating techniques (such as amino acid racemization and uranium methods) have produced dates around 450,000, 320,000, and 220,000 B.P., with 95,000 B.P. at the top of the fill.

Over 100,000 stone tools have been recovered. They are archaic, and made mostly of quartz (though some are of flint), and they include numerous side scrapers. There is a great abundance of choppers and chopping tools made from pebbles, but also some microchoppers.

Paleoenvironmental evidence suggests that the contemporary landscape was not too different from the Mediterranean one of today. The cave is considered an ideal site for hunting, with its tremendous view over the plain and its easy access to the plateau above. The occupations appear to have been a mixture of temporary encampments and longer stays.

Tautavel owes its importance primarily to the presence of many fragments of fossil humans, especially "Arago XXI," the incomplete skull of a young (probably male) adult, which is robust and archaic, with a cranial capacity of about 70 cubic inches (1,150 cu cm). Two jawbones have also been found, which are equally archaic. Some researchers assign these finds to *Homo erectus*, while others have pointed to resemblances with *Neanderthals and called them early Neanderthaloids.

[*See also* EUROPE: THE EUROPEAN PALEOLITHIC PERIOD; EUROPE, THE FIRST COLONIZATION OF; HOMO SAPIENS, ARCHAIC.]

■ L'Homme de Tautavel. *Dossiers de l'Archéologie* 36 (1979). *Les Premiers Habitants de l'Europe 1,500,000–100,000 ans.* (1981), pp. 67–82.
Paul G. Bahn

TELL MARDIKH. *See* EBLA.

TEMPLO MAYOR, the Great Temple of the Aztecs, stood inside the sacred precinct in the middle of Tenochtitlán, the Aztec capital city, which was founded in A.D. 1325. Archaeologists excavated this structure between 1978 and 1982, discovering more than one hundred offering caches containing thousands of artifacts such as stone masks, ceramic vessels, knives, and animal remains belonging to jaguars, pumas, eagles, and quails, among others. Aquatic remains were abundant, including those of fish, crocodiles, and turtles. Generally speaking, all of these artifacts reflect the role of the two gods that were worshiped on the two shrines at the top of the Great Temple: Tlaloc, the rain god, and Huitzilopochtli, the Aztec god of war and the sun.

The Great Temple symbolizes two sacred mountains. The Hill of Coatepec was where Huitzilopochtli defeated sister Coyolxauhqui, the moon goddess, in a legendary battle. Tlaloc's side of the temple represents the Hill of Sustenance, where the corn was kept. For this reason, the Great Temple had two flights of stairs leading to the two shrines on top, dedicated to Tlaloc and Huitzilopochtli.

The building's main facade is oriented to the west, where the sun sets. The excavations have revealed that the Great Temple was constructed in seven stages; at the end of the last stage, the temple measured 131 feet (40 m) high and approximately 263 feet (80 m) on each side.

The building was destroyed by the Spaniards after the conquest in 1521. According to sixteenth-century chronicles, the Great Temple was located inside the walled central plaza of the city and was one of seventy-eight buildings that stood in the same location. This main plaza was considered the center of the universe, and the Great Temple symbolized the fundamental center of the Aztec worldview.

Through this structure, one could reach the sky or descend to the underworld. The temple contained in itself the principal Aztec myths and was the expression of their basic needs: agricultural production, represented by the cult of the rain god, and the wealth of conquest provided by Huitzilopochtli, their god of war and the sun.

[*See also* AZTEC CIVILIZATION.]

Eduardo Matos Moctezuma

TENOCHTITLAN (or Tenochtitlán), an island city in Lake Texcoco, Mexico, was the home of the Mexica people and capital of the Aztec Empire. According to Aztec history, the immigrant Mexica founded Tenochtitlan on a swampy island in A.D. 1325 following an omen from their god Huitzilopochtli, an eagle, seated on a cactus, eating a snake (this image is now the national symbol of Mexico). Tenochtitlan's island location in the densely settled basin of Mexico provided excellent opportunities for commerce, and the city prospered and expanded rapidly. It became the imperial capital upon formation of the Aztec Empire in 1428. The Mexica conquered much of Mesoamerica, and the tribute paid by their millions of subjects greatly enriched Tenochtitlan. By the time of the Spanish conquest of 1519, the city covered 5 square miles (13 sq m) with a population of around 200,000. Much of Tenochtitlan was destroyed in the conquest, and Mexico City was built over the ruins.

Tenochtitlan was crossed by numerous canals, which were filled with canoe traffic. Dams and dikes kept the salty waters of Lake Texcoco separate from the fresh water surrounding the city, and the edges of the island were covered with *chinampas,* or raised fields, a highly productive farming system. Urban residents included nobles and commoners engaged in a wide variety of occupations including merchants, craftspersons, farmers, bureaucrats, and priests. The great marketplace at Tlatelolco, Tenochtitlan's smaller twin city, was attended by over 60,000 persons daily. Political and religious activity was concentrated in the Sacred Precinct, a large walled compound filled with temples, palaces, and other civic buildings, including the *Templo Mayor, an impressive temple pyramid that was the symbolic center of the Aztec Empire.

Today Tenochtitlan is buried under Mexico City, making archaeological fieldwork difficult. Prior to 1970, the most important archaeological find from Tenochtitlan was the so-called Aztec calendar stone, a large carved stone disc that symbolized the city's political hegemony. In the past few decades, Mexican archaeologists have made numerous important finds in connection with the expansion of the Mexico City underground subway system. By far the most spectacular results have come from excavations of the Templo Mayor between 1978 and 1988. The Templo Mayor and its museum are open to the public, and other finds from Tenochtitlan can be seen at the National Museum of Anthropology in Mexico City.

[*See also* AZTEC CIVILIZATION.]

■ Edward E. Calnek, "The Internal Structure of Tenochtitlan," in ed. Eric R. Wolf, *The Valley of Mexico* (1976). Jose Luis de Rojas, *Mexico-Tenochtitlan: Economia y Sociedad en el Siglo XVI* (1986).

Michael E. Smith

TEOTIHUACÁN. A visit to the pyramids in the northeastern part of the Valley of Mexico near Mexico City is how most people experience and learn of the site of Teotihuacán. One of the most impressive archaeological sites in the world, it is a place the existence of which has never been forgotten.

The name *Teotihuacán* means "Place of the Gods" and was given by the later Aztecs, as it was believed to be where the current cycle of time began. It was commented on by the Spanish conquistadores of Mexico during the sixteenth century. Today, Teotihuacán is recognized not only as the remains of an impressive pre-Columbian civilization, but also as the earliest city in the New World.

Archaeological work started over a century ago and has continued up to the present. Many large constructions of the central ceremonial / administrative core of the site have been restored, but in the last thirty years, archaeological research has also learned more about the residential and urban nature of Teotihuacán. In 1973, the publication of a map of the city during its florescence from about 100 B.C. to A.D. 750 by the Teotihuacán Mapping Project was able to document its size, density, and complexity. The city covered about 8 square miles (20 sq. km) and had a population of 125,000 to 200,000, making it among the largest cities in the world. The site is dominated by a grid along which all major public buildings and residential compounds are aligned. The city has a major north–south axis, the "Street of the

Dead," with the large Pyramid of the Moon at its northern extension and lined with a series of platform temples and large palaces. Just to the south, facing east, is the monumental Pyramid of the Sun, one of the largest pyramids in the world. At the center of the city, where the major east–west axis crosses, is the Ciudadela, a large, square sunken plaza with large platforms and the Feathered Serpent Pyramid.

The city's population was housed in around 2,000 large rectangular structures called apartment compounds that make up the bulk of the urban grid. Several of these have been reconstructed for visitors. These compounds are a distinctive and practical form of urban housing for Teotihuacán, built to contain an average of sixty to a hundred people organized in lineages, with individual interior plans and privacy from city streets. The compound was apparently the basic administrative and economic unit for the Teotihuacán state. Like other preindustrial cities, Teotihuacán had a variety of occupational specialists, social classes, and ethnic enclaves, which have been discovered by excavations in various compounds. Like other preindustrial cities, it probably was plagued by poor health from poor sanitation and was dependent on emigration to maintain its population numbers.

Teotihuacán had a distinctive art style visible in architecture, murals, ceramic artifacts, figurines, and stone masks. This style is found in many parts of Mesoamerica during the city's florescence and indicates the prestige and preeminence of the city during the Classic Period (ca. A.D. 200–700). While there is really no evidence that Teotihuacán controlled directly a large territory or empire, it wielded immense ideological influence and is invoked in imagery as far away as Guatemala. The power of the city apparently ended about A.D. 750, when the central part of the city was destroyed by fire. The site was never completely abandoned but never again had the same population, prestige, or economic vitality. The significance of Teotihuacán endures as a pre-Columbian preindustrial city, the earliest to appear in the New World.

[*See also* MESOAMERICA, *articles on* INTRODUCTION; FORMATIVE PERIOD IN MESOAMERICA, CLASSIC PERIOD IN MESOAMERICA; OAXACA, VALLEY OF.]

■ René Millon, *Urbanization at Teotihuacan, Mexico,* vol. 1, *The Teotihuacan Map* (1973). William T. Sanders, Jeffrey Parsons, and Robert Santley, *The Basin of Mexico* (1979). Eduardo Matos Moctezuma, *Teotihuacan, City of the Gods* (1990). Janet Berlo, ed., *Art, Ideology, and the City of Teotihuacan* (1992). Rebecca Storey, *Life and Death in the Ancient City of Teotihuacan* (1992). Kathleen Berrin and Esther Pastorzy, eds., *Teotihuacan: Art from the City of the Gods* (1993).

Rebecca Storey

TERRA AMATA. The open-air Paleolithic site of Terra Amata, in southern France, is one of the earliest to have yielded evidence of artificial shelters. The site is located on the Mediterranean coast near Nice, and was excavated in 1966 by Henry de Lumley. He uncovered a lower Paleolithic occupation, dated by the thermoluminescence method to ca. 380,000 B.P., the early part of the Middle Pleistocene Period. The site now has a museum built around it.

Several superimposed occupation floors were discovered on these fossil beaches, containing the very fragmented bones of a variety of animals—wolf, boar, ibex, auroch, red deer, rhinoceros, young elephants, as well as many rabbits, rodents, and birds. About 10,000 stone artifacts were found, mostly choppers and unifacial picks made from pebbles, as well as some flake tools.

The imprints of small wooden posts suggest that temporary huts had been erected, with stones pinning the base of the walls to the ground. Such stones made visible the outline of the dwellings, as did the distribution of tools and food refuse within. The huts were always oval, between 23 feet (7 m) and 49 feet (15 m) in length and four to 20 feet (6 m) wide. One of the oldest was surrounded by a line of large blocks, 12 inches (30 cm) in diameter, sometimes piled on each other, and enclosing a thick layer of organic material and ash. Some of the hut floors appeared to bear the imprint of skin coverings.

Traces of small hearths were found at the center of each hut: Some were dug 6 inches (15 cm) into the sand dune and were 12 to 20 inches (30 to 50 cm) across. Others were paved with pebbles. The fact that many hearths had a small wall of stones at the northwest side indicates not only that the huts were drafty (probably having simple walls of branches) but also that the prevailing wind came from that direction. Together with those of Menez-Dregan, Brittany, and Vertesszöllös, Hungary, these are reckoned to be the oldest constructed hearths known in the world.

In some huts, a blank area indicates where the occupant sat, while all around are the waste products of stoneworking (it was possible to fit many of the pebble flakes back together). Other traces in the site include the imprint in sand of a human right foot, about 9.5 inches (24 cm) in length, and a series of coprolites (fossil feces), some of which may be human, and which contained not only parasites but also pollen grains, which indicated an occupation in the spring and summer.

Terra Amata is also noteworthy for the presence of seventy-five pieces of pigment ranging in color from yellow to brown, red, and purple. Most of them have traces of artificial abrasion and were clearly introduced to the site by the occupants, since they do not occur naturally in the vicinity.

The excavator concluded that the site was used for a series of brief, repeated seasonal stays—perhaps for fifteen successive years—by Acheulean hunter-gatherers, who built fires and erected tent-like structures during the late spring or early summer.

[See also ACHEULEAN TRADITION; EUROPE: THE EUROPEAN PALEOLITHIC PERIOD; PALEOLITHIC: LOWER AND MIDDLE PALEOLITHIC.]

Paul G. Bahn

TEXTILES. In the present context, the term *textiles* is used in the broadest sense and includes not only flexible cloth with continuous-plane surfaces produced on frames or heddle looms (i.e., textiles proper), but also products as diverse as basketry, matting, bags, netting, cordage, sandals, and related so-called perishable fiber artifacts. All of these items can be treated as a unit because they are manually assembled (i.e., woven) from plant or animal components with or without the aid of some sort of auxiliary apparatus or loom.

The production of textiles as defined extends back to nearly 30,000 B.P. and probably beyond, but their exact appearance in the archaeological record may never be known with certainty because of factors of preservation.

As noted in Adovasio (1977: 2), prehistoric textiles, in contrast to lithic or ceramic artifacts, are recovered intact only under special conditions. Environments that are more or less stable (i.e., extremely dry, extremely cold, or extremely wet) retard the decay and disintegration of textiles and other perishables by the exclusion of intermittent moisture, oxygen, bacteria, or a combination of these agents of destruction. Textiles may also be preserved if they are in direct contact with the corrosion by-products of certain metals, notably copper, which act as bactericides. Thoroughly charred or incinerated specimens are insulated from further decay and may also be preserved for long periods if undisturbed.

Textile remains from North America (and from most other parts of the world) have been found almost exclusively in dry caves and rock shelters. Occasionally, however, extensive assemblages of carbonized remains have been recovered from exposed sites in the Americas, Europe, Africa, and Asia. Alaska, parts of Canada, and Eurasia have yielded basketry in permafrost contexts. Waterlogged specimens have been encountered in North America and Mesoamerica, as well as Europe, but this form of preservation is relatively rare. Interestingly, because of this rarity, some of the most spectacular textile remains have come from waterlogged sites like the Windover Bog in Florida, which has yielded the oldest woven cloth in the Americas (Andrews, Adovasio, and Harding 1988).

However, the vast majority of prehistoric textiles have come from sites in the arid and semiarid portions of western North America, including Mexico. Rock shelters and caves in those areas have yielded tens of thousands of specimens, including many complete textiles, baskets, bags, mats, sandals, nets, cords and rope, and other kinds of woven objects. By comparison, the inventory from the remainder of the world is relatively meager. Collections from scattered locations in arid stretches of South America, the Nile Valley, the Near East, and the Indian subcontinent rarely, if ever, approach the staggering mass obtained from the most productive North American sites. Similarly, waterlogged, incinerated, metal-preserved, or permafrozen assemblages from a thousand-odd localities across the planet do not equal in sheer numbers the assemblages from sites in the North American West.

The differential distribution of prehistoric textile remains directly reflects not only conditions of preservation but also the intensity of archaeological research and the methods of excavation and recovery. In many parts of North America (notably, most of the Southeast, Midwest, and Northeast of the United States, as well as Canada), South America, Eurasia, Africa, Australia, and Oceania, the only evidence for textiles of any kind survives in the form of impressions on pottery or living floors, or from the collapsed walls of clay-lined structures or buildings. Where even these clues are lacking, the student of prehistoric textiles must either focus on indirect evidence, such as the presence of awls, loom weights, heddle fragments, frame sections, or other specialized tools that may have been used in the production of textiles, or they must draw inferences from ethnographic or ethnohistoric information.

In short, the extant inventory of prehistoric textiles from all parts of the world is but a dim reflection of the original incidence of manufacture. Furthermore, only in very limited and geographically circumscribed areas can the recovered textile sample be considered representative.

The intimacy of the maker's relationship with any type of basket or textile is predicated on and conditioned by the fact that all of the weaver's "manufacturing choices" are physically represented in the finished specimen. Significantly, this fortuitous condition does not apply to lithics and ceramics, the most durable—and hence most commonly recovered—prehistoric artifact types. The final forms of artifacts from these two classes often embody little or no evidence of their maker's manufacturing options prior to final finishing. Elaborating on this distinction in his preface to the English translation of Balfét's (1952) essay on basketry systematics, Baumhoff (1957) writes:

One of the properties of basketry which makes its analysis attractive lies in the fact that its types may be regarded as discrete elements rather than as arbitrary points on a continuum. The basket weaver may twine with a right hand twist or a left hand twist but he cannot be halfway in between. Furthermore, his method of work is perfectly apparent in the finished product so the craftsman himself need not be observed. Thus for most situations in basket making there is only a finite number of logical alternatives. (2)

Of the greatest importance in the present context, and indeed in any other study of archaeological or ethnographic textiles, is the fact that both the "finite number of logical alternatives" and the "possible combinations" referred to by Baumhoff (1957) are culturally determined to a very high degree. In point of fact, no class of artifacts normally available to the archaeologist for analysis possesses a greater number of culturally bound yet still visible attributes than do the various forms of textiles. By "culturally bound" or "culturally determined" attributes, it is meant simply and explicitly that the range of techno-manipulative alternatives witnessed in the extant attributes of a finished textile or related product is to a very great degree fixed or delimited by the customs or standards of the immediate social entity to which the maker belongs or within which the maker functions. While these standards are subject to idiosyncratic modification and even occasional borrowing of designs or construction attributes, their collective existence is eminently verifiable. Again, this is scarcely a novel observation, nor is its corollary—that no two individuals, bands, tribes, societies, or other social groups ever produced textiles of any kind in exactly the same fashion. Not only has this fact been demonstrated ethnographically for nearly a century, but it is also archaeologically valid as well.

Because of the unique qualities of textiles as artifacts as well as their importance and multifaceted uses in the societies that produced them, the systematic analysis of their nominal and ordinal attributes, method of manufacture, raw material sources, form, decorative motifs, and functions can serve both culture-historical and processual goals (Barber 1991). Textiles can be very sensitive indicators of cultural chronology as they are in the American Great Basin (Adovasio 1974) and Southwest (Morris and Burgh 1941), Peru (Adovasio and Maslowski 1980), and elsewhere. Moreover, they can provide novel and informative insights not only into the general technological milieu of late Paleolithic societies as at Pavlov I (Adovasio, Soffer, and Klima 1994) in central Europe and Monte Verde in Chile but also in countless later populations as well. The analysis of textiles can also provide high-resolution information on such specific topics as prehistoric subsistence practices including food procurement, transport, processing and storage, trade and exchange, social status differentiation, regional, cultural, ethnic, and even family or individual "boundaries" and perforce population movements both in time and through time.

Though among the most fragile products produced by prehistoric and historic societies, textiles are clearly one of the best media for studying their vanished makers. Indeed, no objects show the signature of humanity or better reflect the social and technological matrix of the "hand" that wrote it than do textiles.

■ Earl H. Morris and Robert F. Burgh, *Anasazi Basketry: Basket Maker II Through Pueblo II, A Study Based on Specimens from the San Juan River Country* (1941). Hèléne Balfét, "La Vannerie: Essai de Classification," *L'Anthropologie* 56 (1952): 259–280. Martin A. Baumhoff, "Introduction," in Hèléne Balfét, *Basketry: A Proposed Classification* (1957), pp. 1–21. J. M. Adovasio, "Prehistoric North American Basketry," *The Nevada State Museum Anthropological Papers* 16 (1974): 98–148. J. M. Adovasio, *Basketry Technology: A Guide to Identification and Analysis* (1977). J. M. Adovasio and R. F. Maslowski, "Textiles and Cordage," in T. F. Lunch, *Guitarrero Cave* (1980), pp. 253–290. R. L. Andrews, J. M. Adovasio, and D. G. Harding, "Textile and Related Perishable Remains from the Windover Site (8BR246)," Paper presented at the 53rd Annual Meeting of the Society for American Archaeology, Phoenix, Arizona (1988). E.J.W. Barber, *Prehistoric Textiles: The Development of Cloth in the Neolithic and Bronze Ages, with Special Reference to the Agean* (1991). J. M. Adovasio, Olga Soffer, and I. Klima, "Textile and/or Basketry Impressions from Pavlov I," Ms. on file, Mercyhurst Archaeological Institute, Mercyhurst College, Erie, Pennsylvania (1994).

J. M. Adovasio

THEBES. *See* KARNAK AND LUXOR.

THEORY IN ARCHAEOLOGY. In archaeology and the social sciences more generally, the term "theory" has a greater diversity of meanings than is usual in the natural sciences and the philosophy of science. Usually it means any kind of discourse that is abstract. More narrowly and less frequently it refers, as in the natural sciences and the philosophy of science, to structures of concepts, statements, or models that are intended to make understandable in some way a specified set of phenomena. This brief overview examines both of these meanings of theory in archaeology and the implications for archaeology of the postmodern rejection of theory.

Theory as Abstract Discourse. Common examples of theory as abstract discourse are discussions of foundational issues, methodology, and the proper study of the archaeological record. Foundational issues debated by all disciplines concern fundamental ontological and epistemological questions alike. What exists and can be studied? How can or should it be studied? Familiar and contradictory answers in archaeology are: "only individuals and things exist and can be scientifically studied" / "real but imperceptible structures exist"; "there are universals"; "sensory experience is the only legitimate basis for truth and rationality" / "we cannot rely on our senses alone, for objects have hidden properties." Other foundational issues concern the nature of society or culture and the reasons for change through time. Examples of proposed answers include: "a society is a group of people who regularly interact"; "society is constituted through and made meaningful by symbol systems"; "culture is a real system of action formed by symbol systems"; "the locomotive of history is class struggle."

Still other foundational issues are specific to archaeology and involve questions like, What should archaeology be about? What are the appropriate methods for achieving this goal? Why should the archaeological record be studied? Among answers to the first question are artifacts and archaeological cultures, peoples' past behavior or thought structures, "cultural schemata," and the history of social or cultural structures. A few additional statements illustrate still further the flavor of these kinds of "theoretical" assumptions: "past cultures should be studied in and for themselves"; "the study of the past should serve a social function in the present"; "the past should be investigated in a historical (rather than comparative) manner"; "the primary aim of archaeology should be the discovery of scientific laws"; "since all human behavior is social behavior, the primary task of archaeology must be the interpretive understanding of past understandings." Assumptions like these are considered abstract or theoretical because, being "above experience" or metaphysical, they cannot be demonstrated to be true or false and they are not intended to explain specific instances in the same manner that a theory in the narrow sense is.

Theoretical assumptions or presuppositions like these are important, for they form the conceptual component, the theoretical orientation, of schools of archaeology and they have implications for the activities of archaeologists. Theoretical orientations, or research programs, consist of a usually tacit and fuzzy set of assumptions concerning the nature of the archaeological record and human societies, the proper tasks and procedures of archaeology, and the structure of scholarly inquiry, among other assumptions. Examples include the culture-historical approach, processual archaeology, cultural ecology, interpretative archaeology, and marxist archaeology. Explicit works of "theory" in archaeology are generally of this nature, that is, they are primarily concerned with explicating, defending, or attacking a way of doing archaeology. While the history of archaeology is generally perceived to be about famous archaeologists and their deeds, it is on another level about the development of research programs and their fundamental assumptions, the varying stances that have been taken within a program, and the switch from one to another.

Research programs play a normative role in archaeology, for their assumptions prescribe some activities and goals and not others. For instance, in processual archaeology, where the primary goal of the social sciences is assumed to be the discovery of laws that govern people in groups, the charge is to discover social laws or to show that known laws apply as well to past groups. In addition, since it is assumed that laws are about the constant conjunction of material objects (rather than, for example, about imperceptible social structures), it is human behavior and its material products that are the proper focus of this search. Likewise, if culture is assumed to be a real system of action formed by symbol systems, then archaeologists should study symbol systems, and if social structures are assumed to be real macrocultural arrangements independent of the action of individuals, then they should study social structures.

Theory as Explanatory Structure. An archaeological theory in the narrower, stricter sense is meant to explain archaeological facts. The theory of evolution by natural selection is a well-known example of a theory of this kind in another discipline. It is an explicit attempt to account for fossils, differences among life-forms, and other biological phenomena. Calls for building theories of this kind became part of the rhetoric of processual archaeologists in the 1960s and 1970s, when they decided that the proper approach to the archaeological record was an "explicitly scientific" one. Their attempts to achieve this goal were stymied, however, by their adoption of a syntactic conception of scientific theory that has its roots in logical positivism. According to this conception, a scientific theory is an axiomatic deductive structure that is partially interpreted in terms of definitions called correspondence rules. Correspondence rules define the theoretical terms of the theory by reference to observation terms. For example, a theoretical term like "population pressure" is partially defined by references to certain mea-

sures on the content of the archaeological record and to how those measures are made. Since the meaning of any one term is seldom independent of the meaning of many if not all of the other terms in the theory, changes in the meaning of one term will usually have consequences for the meaning of all other terms. In addition, the basic axioms of the theory are considered laws of the highest generality from which all other laws can be derived. Usually such deductions require numerous subsidiary assumptions. The explanation and prediction of archaeological phenomena and past ways of life consist in demonstrating that they follow logically from the laws of the theory. Since laws, strict axiomatic structures, subsidiary assumptions, correspondence rules, and many other aspects of the syntactic conception of scientific theories have proven difficult, if not impossible, to formulate in a satisfactory manner, explicit theory building in archaeology has been largely avoided. Still, when pressed to give a definition of a scientific theory, most archaeologists refer to some version of this conception.

An alternative conception of theories, called the semantic conception, emerged in physics in the 1970s through detailed examination of the actual practice of science. In this generalized model-based understanding of scientific theories, there is no commitment to particular formal languages, such as mathematics or logic, or even to the widely held view that science is about the discovery of laws of nature and society. The views that theories are well-defined entities, that laws are true statements of universal form, and that science yields knowledge of claims that are universal are all rejected. Instead, the concern is with the construction in more or less everyday language of idealized, abstract systems, called models. The behavior of models is "modeled" according to assumptions about the behavior of real world systems. As an abstract object, a model cannot literally be true or false. Rather the question for a theoretical model is how well it fits the real world system (e.g., geological, cultural, floral, faunal) that are being represented. Models need be similar only to particular real world systems in specified respects and to a limited degree of accuracy—and some models clearly fit better than others. For example, projectile points and sediments may be identified as empirical things that correspond to abstract notions or processes in the model.

It should be clear why in this view theories are illusive in the practice of science and why their testing is an approximation process. In addition, although the focus of a model may be changing ways of life in a particular setting, the model itself is actually composed of a family of models distributed among many scientists operating in diverse specialties, such as geology, archaeology, zoology, and psychology. Here the primary representational relationship is between models and particular real systems, between what ways of life might have been like in a particular setting at a particular time and what they were actually like. In this view of theories, there are principles and generalizations, but no laws; the model applies to this setting and not to all similar settings that have existed and will exist in the future.

A "family of models" conception of theory fits the interdisciplinary nature of archaeological practice and its products much more snugly than does the syntactic conception. Many recent "interpretations" of the past by interpretative archaeologists are theories of this kind. Increased familiarity with the semantic conception of theories should increase the rate and sophistication of theory construction in archaeology.

The Postmodern Challenge. Skeptical postmodernists have challenged modern theory and nearly all of the key foundational assumptions that underlie research programs in archaeology. This critique follows from their rejection of modern views of truth, objectivity, a materialist reality, reason, history, and science, among many other concepts that are integral components of modern inquiry. By modern inquiry is usually meant a set of pervasive Western values, including the methodological suppositions of modern science and philosophical foundationalism that are part of our Enlightenment heritage. Among the reasons postmodernists give for eliminating theory are (1) the idea of a theory implies an absolute truth that does not exist, (2) they assume an epistemological reality that does not exist, (3) no grounds exist for their defensible validation or substantiation, (4) the data and truthful propositions on which they depend are at best contextually relative, (5) they emphasize the unity of wholes over the uniqueness of parts, (6) they deny paradoxical situations where it is never possible to choose one model or interpretation over the other, and (7) they are rarely the basis for action, because they are ad hoc justifications.

Postmodernists deny the possibility of truth, for instance, because truth claims can never be independent of language, that is, of artificial sign systems and socially defined meanings. If language produces and reproduces its own world without reference to reality, then it is impossible to say what is actually present and truth becomes an "effect of discourse." By implication, if no readily accessible external reality exists, then there is no ultimate "arbitrator" that can decide between contending theories. And, because there is no ultimate arbitrator, modern science can have no special or unique logic, for while individuals can employ reasoned arguments, the result can only be preference rather than privileged insight. Although these claims may seem extreme, their rationale and implications cannot be ignored by theory-builders in archaeology. Where David Clarke (1973) once announced a "loss of innocence" in archaeology, postmodernists now point to an "innocence of theory."

Of course, most archaeologists would find archaeology without theory incomprehensible, for it would mean an end to foundational claims and to procedures for adjudicating between truth claims. Fantasy archaeology would reign and the only shared methodological claim would be "anything goes." While acknowledging the indeterminacy of social action and that knowledge is an ongoing social and historical accomplishment, the task for archaeology, then, is to demonstrate how theory in archaeology can still be normative. Among other tasks, this means developing critical standards with which to judge how well theories, explanatory strategies, and research programs fulfill their goals and purposes.

[See also ARCHAEOLOGY AS A DISCIPLINE; CRITICAL THEORY; CULTURAL ECOLOGY THEORY; CULTURE HISTORICAL THEORY; DARWINIAN THEORY; GENDER, ARCHAEOLOGY OF; GENERAL SYSTEMS THEORY; HISTORY OF ARCHAEOLOGY, INTELLECTUAL; MARXIST THEORY; METHOD, ARCHAEOLOGICAL; MIDDLE RANGE THEORY; POST-PROCESSUAL THEORY; PROCESSUAL THEORY; SCIENCE IN ARCHAEOLOGY; SCIENTIFIC METHOD; STRUCTURALISM.]

■ Jane H. Kelley and Marsha P. Hanen, *Archaeology and the Methodology of Science* (1988). Lewis R. Binford, *Debating Archaeology* (1989). Guy E. Gibbon, *Explanation in Archaeology* (1989). Valerie Pinsky and Alison Wylie, eds., *Critical Traditions in Contemporary Archaeology* (1989). Bruce G. Trigger, *A History of Archaeological Thought* (1990).

James Bohman, *New Philosophy of social Science: Problems of Indeterminacy* (1991). Ian Hodder, *Reading the Past: Current Approaches to Interpretation in Archaeology* (2nd ed., 1991). Ian Hodder, ed., *Archaeological Theory in Europe: The Last Three Decades* (1991). Pauline Marie Rosenau, *Post-Modernism and the Social Sciences: Insights, Inroads, and Intrusions* (1992). Michael Shanks, *Experiencing the Past: The Character of Archaeology* (1992). Michael Shanks and Christopher Tilley, *Re-Constructing Archaeology: Theory and Practice* (2nd ed., 1992). Ian Hodder, ed., *Interpreting Archaeology: Finding Meaning in the Past* (1995).

Guy Gibbon

THOMSEN, C. J., (1788–1865), the son of a Copenhagen merchant, followed his father into the family firm, while pursuing a passion for antiquities. In 1816, he became secretary of the Danish Royal Committee for the Preservation and Collection of National Antiquities, succeeding Professor Rasmus Nyerup, librarian of the University of Copenhagen. Nyerup had supervised the fledgling National Museum of Denmark, struggling to classify its growing collections in a meaningful way. "Everything which has come down to us from heathendom is wrapped in a thick fog," he complained. Thomsen brought a businessman's orderly mind to the collections, arranging them into three groups according to the material used to make them. These, he claimed, were three successive prehistoric ages of Stone, Bronze, and Iron. The museum opened to the public in 1819, and expanded into the Palace of Christiansborg a few years later. Here Thomsen was able to expand his displays into separate rooms for the Stone Age, the Age of "Brass," or Bronze, and the Iron Age. Christian Jürgensen Thomsen was a museum man with a passion for classification, for what he called *Museum-ordning*, or museum arrangement. He published a guidebook to the National Museum, *Ledetraad til Nordisk Oldkyndighed*, in 1836, which was translated into English as *A Guide to Northern Antiquities* by Lord Ellesmere in 1848. Thomsen regarded his *Three-Age System as basically conjectural until confirmed by excavation, a task carried out by his successor J. J. A. *Worsaae. It remains a cornerstone of Old World archaeology today.

[See also ANTIQUITY OF HUMANKIND: ANTIQUITY OF HUMANKIND IN THE OLD WORLD; HISTORY OF ARCHAEOLOGY BEFORE 1900: EUROPEAN ARCHAEOLOGY.]

■ Ole Klindt-Jensen, *A History of Scandinavian Archaeology* (1975). Donald K. Grayson, *The Establishment of Human Antiquity* (1983).

Brian M. Fagan

THREE-AGE SYSTEM. The Three-Age System was developed by Christian Jürgensen *Thomsen (1788–1865), curator of the National Museum of Denmark. He classified the museum's collections into three broad groups, creating a separate room each for the Stone Age, Bronze Age, and Iron Age. Thomsen's new system was the first to subdivide the prehistoric past on the basis of archaeological finds. Subsequently, its general stratigraphic validity was established by Jens Jacob Asmussen *Worsaae (1821–1885) by excavations in Danish burial mounds and peat bogs. The Three-Age System was adopted throughout Europe by the 1860s as a technological subdivision of prehistory, giving archaeologists a broad context within which to place their finds. Thomsen's Three Ages were a first attempt at a chronology of relationship for the prehistoric past. By the 1920s, they were widely used as a basis for classifying prehistoric sites not only in Europe, but in Africa and throughout the Old World. The Three-Age System was never used in the

Americas, where archaeology developed close links to anthropology and to Native American studies.

The Stone, Bronze, and Iron Ages are the broadest of technological stages. They are purely arbitrary technological labels, which do not coincide with any levels of social evolution. Victorian archaeologists conceived of prehistory in terms of universal stages of human development, as a form of evolutionary ladder up which all humanity climbed. As more sophisticated theoretical formulations came into being, chronologies became more refined, and archaeologists uncovered evidence of great biological and cultural diversity in the past, the Three Ages assumed lesser importance. Today, they are used as the broadest of technological categories, more labels of convenience than precision. As such, they will always have a place in Old World archaeology, especially in European and Mediterranean archaeology, where bronze and iron technology developed relatively early.

[*See also* ANTIQUITY OF HUMANKIND: ANTIQUITY OF HUMANKIND IN THE OLD WORLD.]

■ Glyn Daniel, *The Idea of Prehistory* (1962). Glyn Daniel, "Stone, Bronze, and Iron," in *To Illustrate the Monuments*, ed. J.V.S. Megaw (1976), pp. 35–42. Donald K. Grayson, *The Establishment of Human Antiquity* (1983).

Brian M. Fagan

TIAHUANACO EMPIRE. The extensive ruins of the capital city of the Tiahuanaco (Tiwanaku) Empire lie high in the Andes, at an elevation of 2.4 miles (3,850 m), making it one of the highest imperial cities in the world, equaled only by centers in the Himalayas. Tiwanaku (the spelling preferred by the Aymara Indians, descendants of its founders) sits near the southern shores of Lake Titicaca, on the altiplano, an extensive tableland with mean elevations between 2.2 and 2.4 miles (3,600 and 3,900 m), and extending 217 miles (350 km) east to west and 497 miles (800 km) north to south at its maximum points.

The high elevation, along with associated environmental conditions, limit the resources for subsistence in the immediate area. While there were some limited groves of small highland tress, the bulk of the Titicaca basin altiplano area was grasslands, ranging from fairly dense growths in the moister northern areas, to dispersed clumps of grass among salt scrub bush in the drier southern areas.

At the time of the Tiwanaku Empire, as well as during the later Inca Empire, and the subsequent Hispanic periods, large herds of domestic llamas and alpacas grazed in the area, with wild guanaco, vicuña, and deer also found in significant numbers. *Textiles were one of the most important luxury goods for several of the pre-Hispanic Andean civilizations; the huge herds of alpaca gave the Tiwanaku folk control of the single most important textile fiber in the Andes. Logistical support of the state functions of Tiwanaku required access to major transportation facilities; the extensive llama herds provided the labor power for the caravans that traveled the Tiwanaku road system. Thus the alpaca and llama herds were a major source of the wealth in Tiwanaku.

The high elevation, with its concomitant low temperatures, frost risk, and the dearth of rainfall in the southern portions of the basin, limited plant agriculture. Agriculture was principally based on frost-resistant tubers (such as certain varieties of potatoes) and grains (mainly quinoa). While maize was a much appreciated foodstuff, only a few sheltered locales near the lake had mild enough conditions to grow this crop, with the result that the major portion of

maize that is recovered archaeobotanically in Tiwanaku sites was imported from lower elevations via the llama caravans, along with other goods.

Tiwanaku began to emerge as paramount among several regional polities about A.D. 350. Its impact as a ruling center extends for several hundreds of years, until A.D. 1050, although the period of its political dominance and most extensive influence on surrounding regions is limited to roughly A.D. 550 to 950.

Tiwanaku had a significant impact on cultures in northwestern Argentina, Bolivia, northern Chile, and Peru during the last half of the first millennium A.D. In Peru, the *Wari (Huari) Empire held sway from A.D. 550 to 850. It is everywhere defined by the presence of a new set of iconography on textiles and ceramics, an iconography that was indisputedly borrowed from Tiwanaku. Thus while Tiwanaku did not rule or control central Peru, the prestige and persuasiveness of its religious manifestation was such that the Wari borrowed and integrated it as the principal vehicle of expression of their political control.

In the areas closer to the Tiwanaku center, economic and political control was manifested in a variety of patterns, suggesting that the very pragmatic flexibility of the Tiwanaku concepts of interactions with their neighbors contributed to the great longevity of the state. Tiwanaku exercised both direct and indirect political control. Direct control methods included physical incorporation into the state by political and military means; enlargement of the state through massive migrations, resettlement, and annexation; and direct economic control of areas through establishment of *mitimae* or *mitmaq*, the local terms for small bands of colonists sent into important resource zones, where they lived in multiethnic communities, in order to directly control access to essential economic resources in the zone, and thus eliminate the need for the home center to acquire such resources via trade. Indirect control was manifested through formation of loosely organized political federations, wherein members might have mutual obligations to provide essential resources, or through the establishment of ports of trade in distant lands. Current evidence suggests that the immediate contiguous Sillumocco polity to the north, and Jachakala polity to the south, were physically annexed and incorporated into the Tiwanaku state, and the various polities in the rich Cochabamba agricultural lands to the east participated differentially in a sort of federation plan.

Tiwanaku presence in neighboring regions is identified principally through items of material culture. Nearly all classes of recovered goods indicate a fascination with or a reverence for the Tiwanaku religious complexes. These artifacts include not just the specific items needed in worship of the gods, such as the stone stela or idols, the hallucinogenic snuff complex, and the libation cup complex, but also depiction of important religious themes on secular clothing and food services. The snuff complex consists of a variety of implements to use hallucinogenic snuffs in religious ceremonies, such as bone tube inhalers, flat snuff trays, and decorated mortars and pestles for processing the snuff. As reflective of the disparate nature of economic and political control, in some areas, such as Azapa and San Pedro de Atacama in Chile, the snuff complex is an important diagnostic of Tiwanaku presence, whereas in other areas, the trait is minor to nonexistent. In Tiwanaku center, the snuff complex is depicted on the major stela in conjunction with libation vessels. These libation vessels, initially in the form of a tall ceramic drinking cup (*kero*), although replaced by a bowl form (tazon) later, are ubiquitous in areas of Tiwanaku influence and contact. In sites where preservation is adequate, Tiwanaku wool textiles, dense with religious motifs, also are a standard artifact. Reconstruction work has begun to identify a colorful pantheon of Tiwanaku gods, with some evidence that differing ceremonies and thus artifacts are associated with individual cults.

The generic south-central Andean resident of A.D. 550 to 950, if not a taxpayer of the Tiwanaku state, probably spoke a bit of Aymara in order to converse with the Tiwanaku traders (much as English is an economic lingua franca today), participated in rituals whose major celebrants at least occasionally wore Tiwanaku wool ceremonial garments and made offerings using local or important copies of Tiwanaku libation vessels, and although perhaps politically independent, was inexorably linked to the Tiwanaku trade networks for access for some subsistence as well as most wealth or sumptuary goods.

[See also ANDEAN PRE-INCA CIVILIZATIONS, THE RISE OF: INTRODUCTION; SOUTH AMERICA, articles on THE RISE OF COMPLEX SOCIETIES IN SOUTH AMERICA, HIGHLANDS CULTURES OF SOUTH AMERICA.]

■ Arthur Posnansky, Tihuanacu: The Cradle of American Man, Vols. 1, 2 (1945), Vols. 3, 4 (1957). Carlos Ponce-Sangines, Tiwanaku: Espacio, Tiempo y Cultura (1972). David L. Browman, "New Light on Andean Tiwanaku," American Scientist 69 (1981): 408–419. Paul S. Goldstein, "Tiwanaku Temples and State Expansion," Latin American Antiquity 4 (1993): 22–47. Alan L. Kolata, The Tiwanaku (1993). Marc Bermann, Lukurmata, Household Archaeology in Prehispanic Bolivia (1994).

David L. Browman

TIKAL. Located in a nature preserve in the lowland region of Guatemala, the ruins of Tikal are covered with tropical rain forest species. This high canopy forest, while testament to the beauty and diversity of the neotropics, nevertheless masks the enormity of Tikal and the extent to which the ancient Maya constructed a built environment from the rolling limestone hills of the central Petén. Obscured are the five towering temple pyramids located at the southern end of an elaborate triangular causeway system, the deep quarries that were converted to reservoirs to supply Tikal with water through the dry season, and the sustaining settlement of Tikal that covers over 23 square miles (60 sq. km).

Possibly the largest of the southern Maya cities, Tikal grew from an initial small settlement of the Middle Formative Period (400–100 B.C.). During the Late Formative (400 B.C.–A.D. 250) and Early Classic (A.D. 250–600) Periods, a burgeoning Tikal supported an elite ruling class many members of which were buried in richly furnished tomb chambers in what has come to be called the North Acropolis. Long-count dates and accompanying hieroglyphic texts on limestone monoliths (stelae), "altars," and wooden lintels that commemorate the rule of these Early and Late Classic kings have allowed the reconstruction of a nearly continuous dynastic history at Tikal from A.D. 376 to 768.

Enduring a hiatus of monumental construction and perhaps of political subjugation by another capital, Tikal reemerged as a formidable political entity in the seventh and eighth centuries (Late Classic). Temples I and II, which frame the east and west sides of the Great Plaza immediately south of the North Acropolis, were built at this time, with Temple I (154 feet [47 m] tall) housing the richly furnished royal burial of a Late Classic ruler of Tikal. The Central Acropolis, thought to have been the royal residence

of Tikal, borders the southern side of the Great Plaza. A possible market area was located to the east of Temple I.

In Classic Maya society, Tikal played a central role. Ancient and venerable, it represented all that was orthodox in the world of Classic Maya elites. The delineation of social classes may have been more institutionalized at Tikal than at many other Maya cities. It was most certainly a political capital, and judging from the distribution of its emblem glyph, Tikal enjoyed hegemony over a large area.

[See also MAYA CIVILIZATION, articles on INTRODUCTION, THE MAYA CALENDAR, MAYA RULERS AND WARFARE, MAYA PYRAMIDS AND TEMPLES, MAYA BALL COURTS, CLASSIC MAYA COLLAPSE; MESOAMERICA: CLASSIC PERIOD IN MESOAMERICA.]

■ Robert J. Sharer, The Ancient Maya, 5th ed. (1983).

Patricia A. McAnany

TIMBER. See WOOD.

TOLLUND MAN. The Iron Age bog body from Tollund Fen in Denmark is one of several well-preserved bodies from that country. The radiocarbon date of ca. 210 B.C. is more recent than some of the other Danish bog finds, and the body is one of the most complete. When found, the Tollund Man was naked except for a well-made leather cap and a belt around the waist. A rope was around his neck, a single length hanging down his back and toward his right hip. The head was in an especially fine state of preservation, and the condition of the trunk was good; the arms and legs displayed varying degrees of decomposition, although both feet had been better preserved.

Since their recovery, Danish *bog bodies have received varying degrees of conservation treatment, but nevertheless some drying and shrinkage have occurred. In the case of Tollund Man, reports indicate that shrinkage has caused a 12 percent reduction in size. Nevertheless, the head is completely lifelike and is probably the most-photographed and -studied part of any bog body. Some slight lateral compression and distortion can be seen in the face, and the nose displays slight deflection to the right. Of note is the fact that the man had shaved two or three days before death, as indicated by the growth of stubble.

The presence of a cap, held in place by a chin strap, is puzzling, as is the belt at the waist. If the man was stripped before or after hanging or strangulation, then why leave the cap in place? And what kind of clothing could be removed that left the belt in position (for surely it was not replaced after death)? The noose—if such it was around his neck— was made of plaited skin rope, and would not have been ideal for hanging. In fact, the bones of the neck were found in normal positions, although rope impressions were visible to the sides of the neck and under the chin.

The intestinal tract of Tollund Man was in a particularly good state of preservation, although it held far less food residue (17 cubic centimeters [275 cu cm]) than in the Grauballe individual (37 cubic centimeters [610 cu cm]). It included seeds of a number of plants, some of which are today regarded as weeds.

Don Brothwell

TOLTEC EMPIRE. The Toltec Empire was the second of three successive pre-Columbian empires in highland central Mexico (*Teotihuacán, the Toltecs, and the Aztecs). *Tula, the Toltec capital, was first settled during the Epiclassic Period (A.D. 750–950), after Teotihuacán's collapse, and reached its apogee during the early Postclassic (950–1275). Xochicalco, Teotenango, and perhaps Cholula all rose to brief prominence during the Epiclassic in central Mexico simultaneously with the climax of Maya culture in southern Mesoamerica. The decline of these central Mexican city-states by the end of the Epiclassic created a political vacuum, which the Toltecs quickly filled.

Tula covered a steep ridge overlooking the juncture of the Tula and Rosas Rivers 43.5 miles (70 km) north of modern Mexico City. The city covered 5.5 square miles (14 sq. km) and contained at least 35,000 inhabitants by the middle of the thirteenth century. The temples, palaces, and ball courts in the center of the city were lavishly decorated with sculptures and facades laden with militaristic symbolism. Stone sculptures depicting warriors outfitted with feathered helmets, shields, protective garments, spear throwers, darts, and stone daggers are especially common. Carved facing tablets on the exterior of Tula's best-preserved temple (Pyramid B) depict jaguars, coyotes, and eagles probably symbolic of elite Toltec military orders analogous to the Aztec Eagle and Jaguar Knights.

Native histories recorded by Spanish chroniclers early in the colonial period contain accounts of a Toltec Empire that collapsed in the thirteenth century. While clearly legendary in nature, they seem to contain a core of authentic history. Archaeological investigations at Tula, *Chichén Itzá in distant Yucatán, and elsewhere provide tantalizing support for these accounts but fail to shed much additional light.

The very limited information on the Toltec Empire has created markedly different interpretations of its nature, geographical extent, and duration. This debate is in turn part of a larger one about the reality of pre-Columbian empires in Mesoamerica. Most scholars believe that large empires existed in the three cases mentioned above and perhaps others as well, but a few maintain that small homogeneous city-states were the most elaborate form of sociopolitical organization in ancient Mesoamerica. The well-documented history of the Aztecs suggests that empires pursued a strategy that involved both economic domination and military conquest and that conquered populations paid tribute to their overlords in foodstuffs, craft products, exotic raw materials, and services.

Mesoamerican empires differed greatly in size, complexity, and degree of internal integration. The Toltec Empire was considerably smaller than those of Teotihuacán and the Aztecs but still incorporated a substantial territory and a population of perhaps 200,000–300,000 people. Since our sources do not reveal how this empire was formed and maintained, we must once again look to the Aztec Empire for possible models. Aztec imperial strategies included both actual territorial control and hegemony, and the Toltecs may have followed similar practices. Territorial empires result from military conquest culminating in the imposition of direct control by the conqueror, while hegemony uses threats and coercion to force voluntary compliance with imperial demands. Although Mesoamerican empires employed both techniques, the problems involved in marshaling large armies and maintaining permanent garrisons in distant lands for long periods of time dictated a preference for the hegemonic approach. It appears that the Toltecs employed both, but direct evidence is lacking.

Mesoamerican city-states frequently established military alliances with friendly powers in order to muster the force needed to overwhelm smaller neighbors. The Aztec Triple Alliance, which united *Tenochtitlán, Texcoco, and Tlaco-pan, is an excellent example of such a strategy. It created a loose federation of autonomous city-states that functioned as a highly effective predatory imperial force. Two Spanish chronicles allude to the existence of an earlier alliance uniting Tula with Culhuacan and Otompan, two smaller communities in the basin of Mexico. If the accounts have any historical validity, this Toltec alliance probably arose in the thirteenth century near the end of the Toltec reign, and Tula would have been the dominant partner.

The Toltec Empire apparently included large sections of central and north-central Mexico in addition to Tula's immediate hinterland. The actual territory under Toltec control is unclear, but the colonial accounts suggest that it included much of Hidalgo and the state of Mexico, plus adjacent portions of Veracruz, Puebla, Queretaro, San Luis Potosí, Guanajuato, Morelos, and Michoacan. In all likelihood the limits were never precise, and they must have varied considerably through time.

The relationship between Chichén Itzá in Yucatán and Tula is one of the most vexing questions about the Toltec Empire. Chichén Itzá flowered during the Epiclassic and early Postclassic Periods (A.D. 800 1200), although it may have been occupied for only a relatively short span during those centuries. Despite the fact that Yucatec Maya clearly comprised the bulk of Chichén Itzá's resident population, many buildings, sculptures, and artifacts show striking similarities to Toltec examples at Tula. Furthermore, numerous sculptures, architectural decorations, and mural paintings depict warriors wearing Toltec costumes and carrying spear throwers and other weapons common at Tula but quite out of place in Yucatán. These depictions suggest that Toltecs from Tula conquered Chichén Itzá and incorporated it into a commercial entrepôt or a tribute state. Colonial documents in Yucatán contain allusions to foreign conquerors at Chichén Itzá, including a man or deity identified as Kukulkan (Feathered Serpent). Toltec history and mythology contain many references to a man and/or god named Quetzalcoatl, the term for Feathered Serpent in the Nahuatl language; unfortunately these references are so vague and contradictory that they add to the confusion rather than help clarify the histories of Tula and Chichén Itzá.

The decline and fall of the Toltec Empire is shrouded in mystery. Documentary sources discuss Tula's abandonment but say nothing about the empire. Climatic changes, population displacements, ethnic conflict, and religious strife have all been put forth as factors in Tula's demise, but the degree to which they affected the larger empire is unknown. In any case, the decline seems to have been rapid and complete, and the former Toltec Empire quickly reverted to a mosaic of abandoned lands and hundreds of tiny independent city-states.

[See also AZTEC CIVILIZATION: THE RISE OF AZTEC CIVILIZATION; MESOAMERICA: POST-CLASSIC PERIOD IN MESOAMERICA.]

■ Nigel Davies, *The Toltecs until the Fall of Tula* (1977). Richard A. Diehl, *Tula: The Toltec Capital of Ancient Mexico* (1983). Ross Hassig, *War and Society in Ancient Mesoamerica* (1992).

Richard A. Diehl

TOMBS. *See* BURIAL AND TOMBS.

TORRALBA/AMBRONA. The Spanish open-air sites of Torralba and Ambrona, in the region of Soria, 93 miles (150 km) northeast of Madrid, are among the most important of lower Paleolithic Europe. Located 1.2 miles (2 km) apart, they were originally lakeshore sites at the time of occupation, which, according to sedimentary evidence, was in the Middle Pleistocene, somewhere between 330,000 and 270,000 years ago. The valley of the River Ambrona is a natural line of communication between the Central Meseta and the Ebro basin.

The first finds were made at Torralba in 1888 during railway construction, and both sites were excavated between 1909 and 1911 by the Marqués de Cerralbo, who demonstrated the stratigraphic association of animal bones with hand axes and other Acheulean artifacts. The American archaeologist F. Clark Howell, working with Aguirre, Freeman, and Butzer, exhausted the 5,900 square yards (5,000 sq. m) of Torralba in 1961–1963 and in 1980–1981—they completed work on the 7,100 square yards (6,000 sq. m) of Ambrona.

The finds at these very complex sites comprise abundant faunal remains together with relatively few tools. The partially dismembered animals include straight-tusked elephant and horse, as well as rhinoceros, deer, aurochs, fallow deer, reindeer, wolf, lion, and much microfauna. The pollen and fragments of wood indicate a relatively open parkland or woodland dominated by pine. The sites are best known for their elephant remains: at least seventy-five individual animals at Torralba, while Ambrona has an almost complete elephant skull.

The tools of flint and quartzite include bifaces and choppers, as well as cores and flakes, and many manuports. The industry is attributed to the middle *Acheulean Tradition. Some of the excavators also claim that large numbers of bone tools and regularly modified tusk-tips are present, whereas other researchers believe that most if not all of these are quite natural, caused by nonhuman bone breakage.

The problem encapsulates the enigma of Torralba and Ambrona as a whole: The sites have traditionally been regarded as accumulations of bones from mass hunts by early Europeans during the animals' spring and autumn migrations, and feature in most popular books on prehistory with vivid depictions of organized hunters driving elephant herds toward marshes with fire. The simple presence of artifacts was enough to convince most researchers that the occupants were very successful big-game hunters who had killed and butchered all these animals.

More recent assessments, however, focusing on the taphonomy of the finds, have produced a much more cautious interpretation, which casts severe doubt on the assumed functional link between the tools and bones. There are no structures or fireplaces in the sites, and the widely scattered charcoal is most likely the product of brush fires. The bones and tools are also very dispersed, and artifacts are extremely rare in some parts of Ambrona.

Many researchers now believe that most if not all the animal remains are present through natural deaths, and that many bones were transported here by water (the frequent rounding and polishing certainly point to this explanation). The tools and the faunal remains may all be associated by chance near old water sources that repeatedly attracted both people and animals. From this viewpoint, the Torralba / Ambrona area probably resembled the margins of a modern-day African stream or waterhole, where the events that produce and disarticulate carcasses can be highly complex, and may span a long time and many different episodes that need not involve people at all.

In other words, the degree of association between the artifacts and the bones remains highly uncertain. Nevertheless, it remains possible that some of the tools were used to kill, or at least to butcher, some of the animals present.

[See also EUROPE: THE EUROPEAN PALEOLITHIC PERIOD.]
Paul G. Bahn

TOURISM. Human curiosity about ancient monuments and artifacts probably dates back beyond the keeping of written records. Early written accounts of mummies and pyramids can be found in the epistles of Greek and Arab travelers to Egypt. Later, beginning in the sixteenth century, wealthy Europeans began to make their way to Italy and Greece, Egypt and Mesopotamia. Tourists of a sort, these early adventurers and antiquaries were among the first foreigners to set eyes on the Great Pyramid at Giza, the lost city of Pompeii, and other spectacular monuments of ancient Western civilizations. Some came merely to view, others to collect. Their writings and collections intrigued a distant public, and their abiding curiosity ultimately gave rise to the discipline of archaeology.

Only recently has the larger public had the leisure, the education, and the means to explore the ancient wonders of the world. Tourism as we now know it probably has its roots in the twentieth century with the development of inexpensive systems of mass transportation and a burgeoning middle class. However, there are intriguing glimpses of a budding tourist industry that predate this period. Over 1,900 people attended the opening day of Giovanni *Belzoni's 1821 Egyptian display in Piccadilly, England. And records of attendance at Stonehenge indicate that this famous English monument has been a tourist destination for over 400 years.

The modern tourist industry is both the boon and the bane of archaeology. On the positive side, tourism is singularly responsible for the salvation of many temple complexes, cave sites, mounds, and other archaeological monuments and landscapes. Urban development is accelerating at an unprecedented rate, and the preservation of the archaeological record is seldom the first concern of a government agency, particularly in developing countries. The monetary value of ancient sites as tourist commodities is often all that protects them from ultimate demise. The money generated by the tourist trade provides for the protection and maintenance of archaeological sites, and often funds new archaeological research. The Jorvik Viking site in York, England, an underground display of tenth-century Viking life that generates over a million dollars for archaeology annually, is a classic example of how successful this exchange can be. Equally important, however, is the opportunity that tourism provides to educate the public about the value of archaeological resources.

Unfortunately, an enthusiastic tourist industry is a double-edged sword. Most archaeological sites were not designed to host thousands of visitors on a daily basis. Most are very fragile, being ancient by definition. The thousands of hands that run moist fingers along crumbling walls, the thousands of feet that crush and shuffle archaeological soils, the thousands of mouths that breath out carbon dioxide and other pollutants into unventilated spaces are destroying many archaeological attractions. The famous cave of *Lascaux in southern France is a case in point. In 1958, ten years after the site was open to the public, colonies of green algae began to appear on walls, blighting the beautiful 17,000 year old paintings that had survived so well in obscurity. So bad was the human-induced air pollution that the cave was forever closed to the general public in 1963. And this is not a unique case. This type of pollution has caused panels and masonry inside poorly ventilated tombs in the *Valley of Kings, Egypt, to deteriorate as well. Outdoor monuments fare no better. The inner circle at *Stonehenge had to be closed off to the public in 1978 when the sheer number of daily visitors so far exceeded the capacity of the stone monument that its safety (not to mention its sanctity) was seriously threatened. Even isolated Chumash Indian rock art sites in the Los Padres National Forest of southern California have had to be fenced off from the public to protect them from would-be artists, collectors, and target shooters.

A new and innovative approach to archaeology-oriented tourism that balances these concerns is the "archaeology vacation." A number of organizations now bring tourists and avocational archaeologists together with professional archaeologists in a highly productive way. The paying participants are provided with the opportunity to take part in an archaeological excavation, often in an exotic setting such as highland Ecuador or East Africa's Rift Valley. The archaeologist is provided with additional labor and funding that might not otherwise be available. More importantly, the lay person learns about the value of proper archaeological excavation, and the archaeologist learns how to communicate the value of archaeology to members of the general public.

At a time when archaeological sites are being decimated at an alarming rate, public support is essential if the few surviving remnants of our cumulative human heritage are to be preserved. The tourist is the developer, pothunter, or politician who will ultimately decide if there is a future for the past.

[See also CULTURAL RESOURCE MANAGEMENT: GLOBAL IS-SUES; DESTRUCTION OF THE PAST; EDUCATION IN ARCHAEOL-OGY: POPULAR EDUCATION; FUTURE OF THE PAST; TRAFFICK-ING IN ANTIQUITIES.]

■ G. Daniel, A Short History of Archaeology (1981). C. Chippindale, "What Future for Stonehenge?," Antiquity 57 (1983): 172–180. B. Del-luc and G. Delluc, "Lascaux II: A Faithful Copy," Antiquity 58 (1984): 194–196. P. Fowler, "What Price the Man-Made Heritage?," Antiq-uity 61 (1987): 409–423. C. Chippindale, "The Heritage Industry," Archaeology 42 (1989): 61–63. E. Herscher, "A Future in Ruins: North America's Threatened Heritage," Archaeology 42 (1989): 67–70.

Patricia M. Lambert

TRADE, African. A major focus of the later archaeology of Africa has been on trade. The huge size of the continent and the scarcity of particular resources led to the development of well-defined routes, trading institutions and systems. European and Asiatic contact along the coasts provided a framework for exploitation of particular commodities, which at different times, supplied and supported the economies of both the Old and New Worlds. The impact of these exchange systems on indigenous African societies has been significant and enduring with the arrival of prestige goods, imported firearms, and technology, while archaeologists have been keen to cite trade and the control of resources as models for indigenous state formation. African trade has also been the subject of classic anthropological studies, such as K. Polyani, et al., Trade, Markets and Early Empires (1957) and Bohannan and Dalton, Markets in Africa (1962). Scientific analysis of trade items and attempts to source raw materials has been confined largely to the study of copper-based metallurgy in West Africa.

African trade can be understood within localized, re-gional, and international perspectives. Localized trade be-came widespread through the development of specialized economic groups, often also defined ethnically. While ex-change took place in commodities, it was normally ex-plained to outsiders as dependency or patron-client rela-tions. Hunter-gatherers (such as in the Kalahari and Namib Deserts, or the rain forest of central Africa) developed com-plex exchange systems with their pastoralist or agricul-turalist neighbors, exchanging forest products, skins, and ivory for grain or manufactured goods. Similar systems operated between pastoralists and agriculturalists in East Africa, mainly in food-based commodities. Specialist groups, with particular skills such as pottery making or ironwork-ing, operated on the margins of larger social units, and were able to survive through their trade relations. In the archae-ological record, such trade is often difficult to identify, as ethnic or economic groups remain largely invisible and our knowledge is often based upon ethnohistorical reconstruc-tions.

Regional trade developed through the activities of spe-cialized traders and the establishment of central places or markets. It relied upon the unequal distribution of particu-lar commodities which were in particular demand. Net-works established for the trade in one essential commodity, such as salt or agricultural products, were often developed for the exchange of other items, in particular prestige goods such as stone axes, beads, and metals.

In East Africa, regional trade can be identified from the second millennium B.C., with the distribution of obsidian from the Rift Valley, and stone bowls, made of gray lava, and probably used for grinding plant remains. Stone beads have been found at burial sites, such as the Njoro River cave; the main materials used were carnelian, jasper, and rock crystal, which have a widespread distribution and thus are difficult to source. Coastal imports (such as cowries and marine gastropods) also occur in graves for a considerable distance inland. Polished stone axes are largely confined to West Africa, and axe factories are known at Buroburo and Rim (Ghana) and on the island of Fernando Po, and are also found throughout the forest zone. Stone rasps made of dolomitic marl are also best explained as exchange goods. Quern stones are also known to have been made at factory sites in West Africa, such as the one excavated at Kintampo (Ghana).

One of the main commodities exchanged throughout the continent was salt, which was essential for agricultural societies with a high carbohydrate diet in a tropical environ-ments with high body perspiration rates. Excavations of several salt-producing sites in the Rift Valley of East Africa have taken place, including Kibero (Uganda) and Uvinza and Ivuna (Tanzania), where salt was obtained from brine springs. At Basanga (Zambia) and Eiland and Harmony (South Africa), salt came from dried-up lake beds. In West Africa, salt came largely from the Sahara, either as mineral resources as at Taghaza and Bilma, or from lake beds. Its trade was in the hands of specialist traders such as the Hausa and Tuareg.

Copper and its alloys were important trade items be-cause of their strong ritual and ceremonial associations throughout the continent, but sources were limited. The earliest record of use comes from Agadez, in Niger, where native copper was exploited by the early second millen-nium B.C., and copper mining and smelting by the early first millennium B.C. In eastern and southern Africa, copper was exploited from around A.D. 500, and in the later Iron Age traded in cross ingots, which have been found as grave goods at *Ingombe Ilede and Sanga. In West Africa, evidence for the use of copper and bronze in ritual contexts comes from graves in the Niger Valley, such as the Tumulus of El Ouladji, which dates to around A.D. 1000, and at Igbo Ukwu, of similar date.

Sources of iron ore—mainly haematite, laterite, and bog iron—are more widespread than copper. Smelting methods are very regional, and it seems probable that the technology was invented at several centers independently during the late first millennium B.C. Phalaborwa (South Africa) has produced the most extensive evidence for iron production, and it is probable that smelted iron was produced almost at an industrial rate, and traded for local reworking. The form of traded iron was normally a roughout hoe; several examples have been found in graves at Sanga.

Gold production seems to have been developed in three main areas, in the upper Niger and Senegal Rivers, in southern Ethiopia, and in northeast Zimbabwe. West African gold was probably exploited largely by alluvial panning; in southern Africa both panning and adit mining was used. Although gold is found only on rare occasions in modern excavations, early finds, including material from the *Mapungubwe burials and the looting of the stone enclosures by the Rhodesia Ancient Ruins Company, suggests that it was important during the later Iron Age in southern Africa.

International trade developed these regional networks, although it also ultimately distorted them, as flow of commodities and cheap manufactured imports increased. This phenomenon can be seen in several areas. In Ethiopia, the rise of the kingdom of *Aksum in the first century A.D. was in part linked to the establishment of trade down the Red Sea. On the East African coast, archaeological evidence for trade dates from around A.D. 500, although the *Periplus of the Erythrean Sea* and the *Geography of Ptolemy* suggest contact with southern Arabia and the Red Sea by A.D. 40 (*see* East Africa: Coastal Towns of East Africa). It is probable that the existing salt trade network between the coast and the interior, extending up to 124 miles (200 km) inland, was developed for other commodities such as ivory, iron, crystal, and gum copal in exchange for copper, cloth, and beads. Coastal communities as far south as Chibuene (Mozambique) seem to have traded inland to the Limpopo; coastal imports such as glass beads are known in quantity from Mapungubwe, Shroda, and the Trowtse sites in the Transvaal and southern Zimbabwe from around A.D. 900. Ivory and gold were the most important export commodities, while Arab sources suggest that considerable numbers of slaves were also obtained. The role of *Great Zimbabwe and other stone enclosures from the thirteenth century remains controversial, with no real evidence that the import of prestige items was of a sufficient scale to develop anything more than regional chieftainships.

In West Africa, trade in the Saharan resources of salt and copper was boosted by Mediterranean input. Attempts have been made to define early routes across the Sahara, on the basis of rock art showing chariots drawn by horses, probably dating from the early part of the first millennium B.C. Actual archaeological evidence for trade during the classical period across the Sahara is very scarce; metalwork from graves in the Fezzan, probably linked to the Garamantes, dating to A.D. 100 to 400 is the most important. The introduction of the camel was clearly a significant factor in the development of the Saharan trade, but when this oc-

curred remains controversial, although domestic camels have been found at Qasr Ibrim in Egyptian Nubia, and dated by radiocarbon to ca. 900 B.C.

Artifactual evidence for the trans-Saharan trade reaching West Africa comes from the medieval period. From Igbo Ukwu, probably dating to the tenth century, large numbers of glass beads (some of which are identifiable as of Egyptian origin) have been found, while some of the copper used in the bronze castings may be of Mediterranean origin. Copper rods from an abandoned caravan have actually been found at Macden Ijafen (western Sahara), dating to the eleventh and twelfth centuries. Excavations at Gao have discovered a hoard of rhinoceros horn, dating to the fourteenth century. It is clear from both numismatic studies and geographical accounts that West Africa became a major supplier of gold to the European and Islamic economies from around A.D. 1000.

With European contact along the African coasts from the late fifteenth century, the patterns of international trade with Africa were modified. On the East African coast, the effects of Portuguese settlement were fairly limited, although attempts were made to intercept traditional trade routes into the interior of southern Africa. In West Africa, the new sea route to the Atlantic coast offered the possibility of closer access to the gold fields and the avoidance of the difficult trans-Saharan route. While the Portuguese were pioneers, other European powers soon established trade castles on the West African coast. Slaves replaced gold as the main export in the seventeenth century, while cheap European copper and brass (often in the form of manillas) were augmented by a package of imported goods, including firearms, wrought iron, pots and pans, tobacco, and cowrie shells. The impact of this trade upon the emerging forest kingdoms of West Africa, such as Ashante, Akan, Benin must have been substantial. This Atlantic trade had a major impact on the developing economies of the New World—with the provision of slave labor for the sugar and tobacco plantations—and as well on the industrialization in Europe.

[*See also* AFRICA, *articles on* INTRODUCTION, THE RISE OF KINGDOMS AND STATES IN AFRICA, HISTORICAL ARCHAEOLOGY OF AFRICA; CAMEL, DOMESTICATION OF THE.]

■ A. W. Lawrence, *Trade Castles and Forts of West Africa* (1963). L. Sundström, *The Exchange Economy of Pre-Colonial Tropical Africa* (1974). E. Herbert, *Red Gold of Africa* (1984). G. Connah, *African Civilisations* (1987). T. Shaw, P. Sinclair, A. Bassey, and A. Okpoko, eds., *The Archaeology of Africa: Food, Metals and Towns* (1993).

Mark Horton

TRADE, Prehistoric

Introduction
Prehistoric Axe Trade
Prehistoric Obsidian Trade
Prehistoric Amber Trade

INTRODUCTION

Prehistoric trade is usually understood in its broadest sense to mean the transfer of goods. Social processes play a major role and in many cases are more important than economic transactions. Although most research has been directed to highly distinctive material objects, such as stone axes, obsidian tools, pots, or metal items, a large number of perishable objects as well as raw materials and food probably circulated within and between prehistoric communities.

The study of prehistoric trade requires two very different kinds of analysis. First, items that have been moved from their points of origin are identified. Second, the mechanism responsible for the distribution of these objects is reconstructed. The former method requires a wide range of techniques grounded in physics and chemistry, and the latter has been heavily influenced by anthropological theory.

Archaeologists use many methods to find out the place of origin for materials found on sites. Transport of animal and plant products is assumed if the species do not occur naturally in the region where they have been found. Artifact form, style of decoration, or methods of manufacture may be distinctive of a source, but local copies of foreign objects can cause confusion. For this reason, a wide range of techniques have been developed to determine the properties of the raw material used to make an object and to match these with the source from which it was obtained. These characterization studies range in sophistication from observations of gross physical properties (e.g., color, size, type of inclusions) to analyses of chemical composition. Identification of sources is most successful when the raw material occurs in a limited number of locations that are spatially restricted. For example, tracing the sources of rocks from volcanic flows is easier than for flint or sandstone that outcrop over a large area. Identifying the raw material source of manufactured items such as pottery and metal can be difficult because raw materials from several sources were sometimes mixed together or artifacts were ground up or melted down and reused.

A fundamental assumption guiding the reconstruction of trade mechanisms is that prehistoric economies operated in a very different way from the commercial markets of the modern world. To emphasize this point, a distinction is made between commercial "trade" and a broader class of behavior called "exchange." Exchange is defined as the transfer of people, food, raw materials, objects, rights and privileges, or ideas between two nodes, which may be individuals, social groups, or, in its loosest sense, places. The goals of the participants are varied and do not necessarily involve economic necessity. In contrast, trade is conceived of as a purely commercial activity in which participants try to maximize profits through the transfer of material goods. One of the important goals for archaeology is to compare and contrast commercial trade with other forms of exchange that are intimately bound to social relationships.

Anthropological definitions of *reciprocity* and *redistribution* have played an influential role in archaeology because these types of exchange take place in different kinds of society. Reciprocity is exchange between two nodes (usually individuals), whereas redistribution is when goods derived from many nodes flow into a central point and are passed back to different persons or places by some form of centralized authority (e.g., a chief). Archaeologists have used redistribution, which has been inferred from the presence of communal storage (e.g., storerooms, large vessels, stone basins), as evidence of the existence of social hierarchy. Redistributive economies have been identified as a phase in the development of civilizations in southwestern Asia, Greece, and Middle and South America.

When looking at reciprocal exchange, archaeologists often make a distinction between commodities, which are utilitarian goods, and primitive valuables (also known as gifts), which have a specific meaning within a social group, circulate in very specific ceremonial contexts, and may also be symbols of social status (sometimes referred to as prestige goods). Whereas commodities are exchanged in all types of society, primitive valuables are commonest where there is competition for status. Polished stone axes, ornaments of amber, jade, and shell, and copper or bronze implements, for example, have been assumed to be primitive valuables and have been used to infer incipient social ranking in Neolithic and Bronze Age Europe, *Hopewell and *Mississippian cultures in North America, and among the *Olmec in Middle America.

The value of an item indicates how it was exchanged. Utilitarian goods are thought to have been commodities, whereas high-value objects are inferred to be valuables or prestige goods. One problem that must be overcome is that value is not intrinsic to an object but is determined by each social context. It has been shown, for example, that the same stone axes that were commodities within communities living near the quarries in northern England functioned as valuables when imported to and reinterpreted by other groups in Yorkshire or East Anglia.

By inference, archaeologists reconstruct value and the kind of reciprocity by analyzing (1) the spatial distribution, (2) the production, and (3) the consumption of items. The distance material travels is often used as a measure of its value. The quantity of items moved is plotted on a graph in relation to the distance from its source for a number of sites. The shape of the fall-off curve has been correlated with the kind of trade, although there are difficulties because different types of trade produce similar curves.

Studies of production are based on the assumption that differing amounts of time, energy, and raw materials invested in acquiring materials and manufacturing items reflect their value, at least for the makers. Studies using this approach have been carried out at such raw material sources as stone quarries and at places of manufacture, such as kilns or craft workshops. Archaeologists in Europe have suggested that the change from labor-intensive methods of ceramic manufacture to the adoption of the potter's wheel or from burnishing to painted decoration indicate that the function of pottery shifted from being a valuable to a mass-produced commodity.

The third method for establishing exchange value is to examine how materials were consumed. Because it is assumed that people conserve valuable goods, frequency of occurrence is used to measure value. The context in which objects are found, however, is the most important method for reconstructing value. Anthropologists have observed that the value of goods is maintained or increased by removing them from circulation. Consequently, grave goods or caches of material are often considered to have been valuables. In contrast, utilitarian commodities are expected to have been discarded in rubbish dumps.

Nonlocal objects were not necessarily exchanged. Some may have been obtained at the source by their users and later discarded at another location. Distribution without exchange is particularly likely for groups that did not reside in permanent settlements or where transport was easy. Raw materials could also have been obtained incidentally while other activities were conducted near a source, a practice called embedded procurement. During the *Pleistocene, in many parts of the world, small amounts of stone were moved over relatively large distances, but this is more likely to represent the movements of people than the result of exchange.

Systematic exchange appears to be primarily associated

with the higher population densities of the *Holocene epoch. In Europe, for example, there is a marked increase in the quantity and variety of imported goods on sites with the onset of the Neolithic Period. Here, as in other areas, the precedent for long-distance exchange of commodities seems to have been the existence of distinct, self-defined social groups. Exchange was an important medium for interaction between these inclusive communities. In contrast, valuables are most common in societies that had some form of social ranking.

Trade is considered an important factor in causing culture change, especially for early states. The exchange of ideas, although invisible to archaeology, may have played as important a role as the transfer of goods. The need for an authority to organize the exchange of necessary commodities has been proposed as a critical factor in the development of *Maya civilization. Competition for valuables is often suggested as causing change from an egalitarian to a hierarchical society. Control over prestige goods obtained through external exchange has been proposed as a key variable in the development of hierarchical societies in the European Iron Age.

Currently, scholars are debating the relevance of the world system model for the noncapitalistic settings witnessed during prehistory. In this view, economic expansion from a more advanced and therefore dominant core area (e.g., southwestern Asia) creates a condition of dependency among the groups in the periphery (e.g., Europe). Although there is great interest among archaeologists in the role of interregional trade and center–periphery relationships, most argue that prehistoric interactions were not limited to relationships based on dependency. In contrast, archaeologists argue that our understanding of prehistoric trade depends on an analysis of the social context in which the exchange of goods took place.

[See also ARTIFACT DISTRIBUTION ANALYSIS; ECONOMIC ARCHAEOLOGY; STATES: THEORIES OF THE ORIGINS OF STATES; TRADE, PREHISTORIC.]

■ Timothy K. Earle and Jonathan E. Ericson, eds., Exchange Systems in Prehistory (1976). Hilary Howard and Elaine L. Morris, eds., Production and Distribution: A Ceramic Viewpoint (1982). Robin Torrence, Production and Exchange of Stone Tools (1986). Jonathan E. Ericson and Timothy K. Earle, eds., Contexts for Prehistoric Exchange (1982). Colin Renfew and Paul Bahn, Archaeology: Theories, Methods and Practice (1991). Catherine Perles, "Systems of Exchange and Organization of Production in Neolithic Greece," Journal of Mediterranean Archaeology 5 (1992): 115–164. Jonathan E. Ericson and Timothy G. Barugh, eds., The American Southwest and Mesoamerica: Systems of Prehistoric Exchange (1993). Andrew Sherratt, "What Would a Bronze-Age World System Look Like? Relations between Temperate Europe and the Mediterranean in Later Prehistory," Journal of European Archaeology 1 (1993): 1–58.

Robin Torrence

PREHISTORIC AXE TRADE

From the earliest days of the discipline, archaeologists have noted a close relationship between the onset of the European Neolithic period and the first appearance of ground and polished axes of flint and stone. Although axes that were flaked into shape had long been a feature of the tool kits of earlier communities, it is only with the Neolithic that we begin to see the consistent use of grinding and polishing in the finishing of flaked or roughed-out axes. Recognized for an equally long period of time is the fact that many stone and flint axes are found at considerable distance from their geological points of origin. This is particularly clear where

examples were made from raw materials that are highly distinctive, such as Alpine jadeite, the orange-colored flint of Grande Pressigny in France, or the "chocolate" flint from deposits in central Europe. Axes made of these materials have been recovered from graves and settlement contexts several hundred kilometers from their respective sources.

Over the past sixty years, the petrological analysis of thin sections cut from many stone axes has confirmed the impression given by tools made from these more visually striking materials. Petrological "fingerprinting" has made it possible to identify groups of stone axes, and to link those groups to their geological sources. Perhaps the best-known example of this work is the research undertaken in Britain. Here the analysis of thin sections from some 10,000 specimens has made it possible to identify the national distribution of stone axes from over twenty-five sources located in western and northern parts of the country.

Traditionally, the production and distribution of axes has been explained as the simple product of an increase in the importance of farming and woodland clearance. That picture is not altogether wrong. But it is now generally acknowledged that the social dimensions of these artifacts may have helped to shape the patterns of dispersal that we see today. Alongside the overall scale of distribution patterns, details of the character and context of many axes suggest that while the vast majority were practical tools, they were also accorded some importance as tokens of identity and value. Many have been found as stray finds, but others occur in hoards, in burials, in ceremonial monuments, and even as deliberate deposits in rivers. Examples include the deposition of axes in graves at Linearbandkeramik sites such as Elsloo, jadeite axe deposits and even carvings of axes at megalithic sites in Brittany, and spectacular axe hoards in bogs in southern Scandinavia. Associated with a variety of tasks, axes may have also embodied concepts of age, gender, and even kinship, and it may have been these symbolic and biographical associations that prompted their use in a variety of forms of exchange. In many societies, exchange was so embedded in social relationships that it often operated as a form of diplomacy. Even in the West today, transactions may serve social as well as purely economic purposes, and this tendency is often more marked in noncapitalist contexts. The giving of the gifts can create long-lasting ties of indebtedness and obligation between giver and receiver, and transactions may play an important role in marriage rites, in cementing alliances and ties of affiliation, and in the creation and maintenance of political authority.

During the 1970s archaeologists attempted to find consistent relationships between different forms of exchange and patterns in the archaeological record. Drawing on mathematical models that charted the relative frequency of artifacts at different distances from their respective sources, various studies attempted to identify the characteristic signatures of different forms of exchange process. More recently, the strength of these mathematical models has been called into question, and it is now accepted that the axe distributions that we see in many parts of Europe reflect the operation of a complex web of local, regional, and even interregional exchange networks. The spatial patterns we see may have taken as much as a millennium to develop, and the significance or value ascribed to axes probably changed during the course of their life histories. As they moved from hand to hand, and from one social context to another, the meanings and biographies of these tools would have been reworked and their passage may have played a part in shaping ties between people at a variety of local and regional levels.

Stone and flint axes remained important as practical tools throughout the Neolithic and for some time during the Chalcolithic and Early Bronze Age. In some parts of Europe, broad continuities in the treatment and context of the earliest copper and bronze axes suggest that these new items came to supplant their stone and flint counterparts. This pattern is not repeated everywhere, but it reminds us that what we often regard as a technical revolution was stimulated as much by the negotiation of social relationships as it was by practical demand.

[See also EUROPE, articles on THE EUROPEAN NEOLITHIC PERIOD, THE EUROPEAN BRONZE AGE.]

■ T. Clough and W. Cummins, eds., Stone Axe Studies. *Council for British Archaeology Research Report* 23 (1979). J. Ericson and T. Earle, *Contexts for Prehistoric Exchange* (1982). A. W. Whittle, *Problems in Neolithic Archaeology* (1988). N. Thomas, *Entangled Objects* (1991). R. Bradley and M. Edmonds, *Interpreting the Axe Trade: Production and Exchange in Neolithic Britain* (1993).

Mark Edmonds

PREHISTORIC OBSIDIAN TRADE

Obsidian is a natural glass found in many parts of the world in areas of recent volcanism that have rhyolitic lavas. Because of its special properties, it has become the focus of numerous studies of prehistoric trade. First, since obsidian flows have a restricted occurrence and their chemical composition is relatively homogeneous, the matching of artifacts found on archaeological sites with their geological source is a relatively straightforward procedure. A large battery of techniques has been used to characterize individual obsidian outcrops. The most common include inductively coupled plasma emission spectrometry (which has replaced optical emission spectroscopy), atomic absorption spectrometry, X-ray fluorescence, proton-induced X-ray emission combined with proton-induced gamma ray emission, and fission track analysis.

Second, the bright, shiny appearance of obsidian means it is easily recognized by excavators and is usually collected and recorded systematically. Third, obsidian was widely used in the past. Due to its isotropic nature, the product of rapid cooling of the lava, obsidian fractures in a predictable manner with little force, making it an ideal raw material for chipping stone tools. Furthermore, a freshly flaked obsidian edge is extremely thin and, although quite brittle, is sharper than a metal blade.

Obsidian was mainly used as cutting tools. Parallel-sided blades dominate assemblages in the Mediterranean, Western Asia, and in Mesoamerica, although other forms were also manufactured, especially in the earlier periods. In contrast, bifacial tools of obsidian were common in prehistoric North America, where these objects circulated because of their ceremonial or symbolic value. Outside North America, obsidian is generally considered to have been primarily a utilitarian commodity, although at certain times and places in Mesoamerica the supply of raw material and/or tools may have been controlled, thereby giving it luxury status.

The earliest evidence for the movement of obsidian a significant distance away from its source area comes from Japan and Papua New Guinea. In both areas, around 20,000 years ago, small quantities of obsidian were transported by sea over considerable distances. The material from Maten-

bec cave in New Ireland has been interpreted as the result of repeated trips between the site and the source areas on the adjacent island of New Britain. Important evidence for early marine voyaging in the Mediterranean also comes from the presence of obsidian, sourced to the Cycladic island of Melos, within archaeological deposits dated to around 12,000 years ago at Franchthi cave on mainland Greece.

These early cases of obsidian transport raise a major question still not completely resolved in analyses of prehistoric trade: How can archaeology differentiate between systematic trade and the distribution of obsidian as part of the normal activities of a mobile population? The issue has generally been ignored in the case of obsidian because by far the largest quantities of material were distributed during times when people practiced some form of horticulture and resided in relatively permanent settlements, or, as in the case of hunter-gatherers in California, maintained territorial boundaries between groups. The widely accepted assumption has therefore been that, whereas people living relatively close to the sources may have obtained their own supplies, others resident more than a day's travel from the outcrops must have acquired their obsidian through some kind of trade. One notable exception may be the Pacific islands, where frequent marine voyaging between settled villages, especially during times of colonization, has been predicted. Consequently, not all archaeologists have accepted unequivocally that trade best explains the distribution of obsidian in the Pacific area, particularly for the Lapita Period (roughly 3500–2000 B.C.), when population appears to have spread into new environments.

Once trade is accepted as the most likely explanation for the distribution of obsidian from its geological origin, the next task is to determine the nature of the economy in which it circulated. Archaeologists have used a wide range of approaches to reconstruct systems of prehistoric obsidian trade. The methods can be roughly divided into those that examine the region over which obsidian was distributed versus those that concentrate on data from single sites. Archaeologists also try to infer how important or valuable obsidian was in each case by studying how obsidian tools were made and used and whether they were discarded as normal household rubbish or only in special contexts, such as in graves during burial ceremonies.

The most basic regional technique is to map the spatial distribution of obsidian from known sources. Some interesting surprises can occur at this stage. For instance, obsidian sourced to outcrops in Idaho and Wyoming has been found in sites belonging to the *Hopewell culture found in the midwestern states but does not occur in archaeological contexts in the intermediate region. Since it seems likely that a special system was used to procure the obsidian and transport it to the area in which it was used, obsidian was probably quite valuable and might have had a ceremonial function at this time.

The distribution of obsidian from a specific source, termed an *interaction zone*, has been interpreted as the area in which people participated in a trading system. When applied in western Asia, Mesoamerica, and the Pacific, the reconstruction of interaction zones has revealed important chronological changes in the nature and scale of trading patterns.

A second type of regional analysis uses graphs that depict the relationship between the quantity of obsidian from a single source at particular sites on the x-axis and distance of these sites from the source on the y-axis. The shape of the resulting fall-off curve is assigned to a particular economic system. This technique has been used in the American Southwest and in the Aegean to distinguish systems where consumers procured their own supplies from those where trade took place. Probably the most common form of prehistoric obsidian trade was based on reciprocal relationships between trading partners or kinsmen. For example, noting that in Europe and Western Asia the curve is exponential, Colin Renfrew proposed that obsidian in these regions had been passed down the line through reciprocal relationships of people residing in adjacent villages. The study of fall-off curves in Mesoamerica has revealed a different type of system called redistribution, in which obsidian moved first into a regional center and was then passed on to smaller villages.

Analyses based on studies of single sites, such as quarries or settlements, are also used to study obsidian trade. By studying how carefully people selected obsidian from among the outcrops; the methods used to extract raw material, produce tools, or prepare partially worked tools for trade; and the quantities of waste generated over time, archaeologists can reconstruct the history of the trading systems in which the obsidian circulated. The most detailed analysis of obsidian quarries was carried out on the island of Melos in the Aegean. Studies of quarries in California, Mexico, and the Pacific have also generated important information about prehistoric trade.

By looking at how obsidian tools from different sources were distributed among households within a site, archaeologists have differentiated between trading systems in which each household obtained its own supplies and those in which obsidian was redistributed by a central agency. In addition, localized concentrations of waste products from making tools have been identified at a number of sites in Mesoamerica and Greece as the products of craft specialist workshops. Their presence in major centers such as *Teotihuacán and Kaminaljuyu has led scholars to propose that the production and trade of obsidian was regulated by a central authority. The recognition and interpretation of workshops has generated much controversy.

Recent analyses of craft specialization combine both regional and single-site approaches. The occurrence of prismatic blades produced by pressure flaking has suggested to some scholars that ordinary householders were not making their own tools, since this specialized technique requires considerable skill and training. Itinerant specialists have been proposed to explain the distribution of obsidian tools in the Greek Neolithic. In Mesoamerica, the existence of specialist obsidian-workers has been used as evidence for the presence of early nonegalitarian societies. For later periods, some archaeologists think that specialists may have operated more freely within a commercialized economy, although the role of the obsidian trade in these times is still a matter of debate.

[See also ARTIFACT DISTRIBUTION ANALYSIS; OBSIDIAN HYDRATION DATING; SOURCING ARCHAEOLOGICAL MATERIALS.]

■ Colin Renfrew, "Trade and Culture Process in European Prehistory," Current Anthropology 10 (1969): 151–169. Timothy K. Earle and Jonathan E. Ericson, eds., Exchange Systems in Prehistory (1976). Jane W. Pires-Ferreira, "Obsidian Exchange in Formative Mesoamerica," in The Early Mesoamerican Village, ed. Kent V. Flannery (1976), pp. 292–305. Jonathan E. Ericson and Timothy K. Earle, eds., Contexts for Prehistoric Exchange (1982). Kenneth G. Hirth, ed., Trade and Exchange in Early Mesoamerica (1984). Robin Torrence, Production and Exchange of Stone Tools (1986). John E. Clark, "Politics, Prismatic Blades, and Mesoamerican Civilization," in The Organization of Core Technology, ed. Jay K. Johnson and Carol A. Morrow (1987), pp. 259–284. J. W. Hatch et al., "Hopewell Obsidian Studies: Behavioral Implications of Recent Sourcing and Dating Research," American Antiquity 55 (1990): 461–479. Colin Renfrew and Paul Bahn, Archaeology: Theories, Methods and Practice (1991). Jean-Christophe Galipaud, ed., Poterie Lapita et Peuplement (1992). Geoffrey Irwin, The Prehistoric Exploration and Colonisation of the Pacific (1992). Catherine Perlès, "Systems of Exchange and Organization of Production in Neolithic Greece," Journal of Mediterranean Archaeology 5 (1992): 115–164.

Robin Torrence

PREHISTORIC AMBER TRADE

The Tertiary fossil resin amber (succinite) was widely prized in prehistoric Europe and the ancient Mediterranean world for ornaments, especially beads, and later—among groups in contact with Greco-Roman civilization—as settings on small bronze items such as brooches. It was valued both for its appearance and for its property of generating static electricity when rubbed, being known to the Greeks as *elektron*. Although occurring in small quantities in association with lignite deposits in several parts of Europe (e.g., Romania, Sicily), its principal source was the Baltic area, where it occurs in abundance as beach pebbles eroded from Oligocene deposits containing remains of the pine tree *Pinus succinifera*. The chief concentrations are in western Jutland (Denmark) and around the mouth of the Vistula (Poland) and along the eastern Baltic coasts, although it can be carried by wave action as far as the coasts of eastern England. The role of other sources may become clearer with the application of more sophisticated methods of characterization (hitherto principally infrared spectroscopy and gas chromatography) and a better understanding of weathering processes; it is generally agreed, however, that the preponderance of European finds are of material from Baltic sources.

While small quantities are known from Upper Paleolithic sites in several parts of Europe, amber came into more frequent use during the Mesolithic Period in the area of its immediate occurrence, where larger pieces (as individual pendants) were sometimes shaped or engraved. During the earlier part of the Neolithic (before 3500 B.C.) it was used locally for beads, which in the later fourth millennium included distinctive forms such as double-axe beads in Middle Neolithic Denmark or flat discs with radial lines of dots in Poland where they are associated with the Globular Amphora culture. In this latter case, they were perhaps obtained in exchange for salt. The first extensive occurrence of finds outside the source areas, however, belongs to the Bronze Age, when Scandinavia and the Baltic coastlands imported finished items of metalwork from the south in exchange for amber, principally in the form of simple biconical beads. These are found in early-second-millennium graves and hoards in central Germany (Únětice culture) and in destruction deposits on fortified settlement sites in the Carpathian Basin (Otomani culture).

Larger quantities of amber, perhaps accompanying northern products such as furs (in exchange for bronze), reached central and western Europe through the intermediacy of the Tumulus cultures (1600–1300 B.C.), where they were used (as in the *Wessex culture in Britain) as beads with complex perforations for collars or pendant groups. Some of these traveled the whole breadth of Europe (probably via Italy) to the Mediterranean, where examples occur, reused, in the shaft graves at Mycenae in Greece.

While not put into graves in Scandinavia, hoards of raw amber (up to 6.5 pounds [3 kg]) have been recovered there. Scandinavian amber continued to be supplied to Italy and the Aegean via the Urnfield cultures in the period from 1300–750 B.C., following a route marked by rich burials in northern Germany and fortifications in the south. In the *Hallstatt period (750–500 B.C.) the supply route shifted eastward, bringing eastern Baltic amber through central Poland (*Biskupin) and around the eastern side of the Alps to Italy, where it was widely used by the *Etruscans and Picenes as an ornamental material. The route was interrupted in the *La Tène period, but resumed in Roman times, when Pliny recorded that the substance was imported "every day of our lives . . . and floods the market."

[See also EUROPE, articles on THE EUROPEAN PALEOLITHIC PERIOD, THE EUROPEAN MESOLITHIC PERIOD, THE EUROPEAN NEOLITHIC PERIOD, THE EUROPEAN BRONZE AGE; HOARDS AND HOARDING.]

■ J. M. De Navarro, "Prehistoric Routes between Northern Europe and Italy Defined by the Amber Trade," *Geographical Journal* 66 (1925): 481–507. Stephen J. Shennan, "Exchange and Ranking: The Role of Amber in Earlier Bronze Age Europe," in *Ranking, Resource and Exchange: Aspects of the Archaeology of Early European Society,* C. Renfrew and S. Shennam, eds. (1982). Andrew Sherratt, "What Would a Bronze Age World System Look Like? Relations between Temperate Europe and the Mediterranean in Prehistory," *Journal of European Archaeology* 1 (1993): 1–57.

Andrew Sherratt

TRAFFICKING IN ANTIQUITIES. A multibillion-dollar business, the trade in antiquities ranks third in monetary terms behind drug smuggling and weapons sales. As the demand for antiquities increases, so do the illicit means to acquire them, either by the plundering of archaeological sites or by the looting of museums. New material continues to enter the market despite the fact that most antiquities-rich countries have strict laws prohibiting the clandestine excavation and export of archaeological material.

International measures to control the illicit trade in antiquities were first taken with the ratification by seventy countries of the UNESCO Convention on the Means of Prohibiting and Preventing the Illicit Import, Export, and Transfer of Ownership of Cultural Property. The Convention, which was adopted by the United Nations Educational, Scientific, and Cultural Organization at its sixteenth session on November 14, 1970, encourages each country to protect its own cultural patrimony as well as to join in an international effort to assist other nations in stopping the illicit traffic. Of the seventy countries that are party to the Convention, the United States is the only one considered to be a major art importer.

Although it is believed that the UNESCO Convention has curbed much of the looting of large-scale antiquities such as temples, pediments, and stelae, the most effective controls have come as a result of import bans effected under the Convention on specific artifacts from specific areas. These bans include pre-Hispanic ceramics and stone artifacts from the Cara Sucia region (occupied 1500 B.C.–A.D. 1500) of El Salvador (ban effective September 11, 1987); antique ceremonial textiles from Coroma, Bolivia (ban effective March 14, 1989); 1,500-year-old gold, silver, copper, and ceramic artifacts of the Moche culture (A.D. 100–800) from the Sipán archaeological region of northern Peru (ban effective May 7, 1990); and Maya (600 B.C.–A.D. 600) ceramic, jade, shell, and bone artifacts from the Petén region of Guatemala (ban effective April 15, 1991). More recently, requests for import bans have been submitted by Canada and Mali. Unfortunately, such import bans are put in place only following the appearance of looted material on the international art market and massive site destruction rather than sufficiently early to prevent such incidents in the first place. However late in coming, the bans do require the importer to prove that antiquities were legally acquired, whereas the Convention relies on a country's ability to report a theft and describe stolen objects—an impossible task when a site has been plundered.

Because of the perceived inadequacy of the UNESCO Convention, new legislation to protect and recover cultural property has been proposed. Known as the Unidroit Convention on the International Protection of Cultural Property (drafted by the International Institute for the Unification of Private Law at Rome), this body of law differs from the UNESCO Convention in providing for the ability to recover stolen property through private law rather than through international treaties and conventions. Although most of the proposed legislation already exists under current United States law, the Unidroit Convention has the added feature of providing the United States and other countries with access to foreign courts. Although few people think of the United States as an art exporter, much Native American material has been lost to countries such as Japan and Germany.

For any international legislation to succeed, it is mandatory that all nations participate in its enforcement. Otherwise, the illicit trade will shift to nonsignatory nations. In addition, it is equally important that collecting institutions, both public and private, as well as individuals reevaluate their collecting policies. Significant measures to amend museum acquisitions policies have already been taken with the adoption of the *Code of Professional Ethics* by the International Council of Museums (ICOM) in 1986. Within the *Code* are guidelines that specifically address the acquisition of illicit material. These guidelines state in part that museums must recognize the connection between the acquisition of illicit material and the often destructive means to obtain it. The guidelines stipulate that for a museum to acquire any object, whether by purchase, gift, bequest, or exchange, the institution's governing body must be able to obtain valid title to the object. The title must ensure that the object was not acquired in or exported from any country in violation of that country's cultural property laws, that recently excavated material is not the product of unscientific investigation or destruction of an ancient monument or site, and that finds were not removed from a site without the knowledge of the landowner or governing authority. The ICOM *Code of Professional Ethics* was adopted by the American Association of Museums in 1991; however, the date by which affiliated museums must comply with the *Code* has not yet been established.

The acquisition of antiquities by illicit means invariably results in the irretrievable loss of information critical to the understanding of both the artifacts in question and the culture that produced them. Accordingly, scholars must not only condemn the illicit commerce in antiquities but refrain from assisting those acquiring antiquities without proper provenance or export permit in order to enhance either the market value or the perceived importance of the objects in question by publishing them for the first time.

[See also CULTURAL RESOURCE MANAGEMENT: GLOBAL ISSUES; DESTRUCTION OF THE PAST; EDUCATION IN ARCHAEOL-

OGY: POPULAR EDUCATION; ETHICS OF ARCHAEOLOGY AND COLLECTING; MUSEUMS AND COLLECTING.]

■ Karl E. Meyer, *The Plundered Past* (1973). Paul M. Bator, *The International Trade in Art* (1983). Jeanette Greenfield, *The Return of Cultural Treasures* (1989). Phyllis Mauch Messenger, ed., *The Ethics of Collecting Cultural Property: Whose Culture? Whose Property?* (1989). United States Information Agency, *Preserving Mankind's Heritage: U.S. Efforts to Prevent the Illicit Trade in Cultural Property* (1991).

Angela M. H. Schuster

TRANSPORTATION. See LAND AND TRANSPORTATION *AND* SHIPS AND SEAFARING.

TREE-RING DATING. See DENDROCHRONOLOGY.

TROY, the Bronze Age and classical site on the mound of Hissarlik, is on the Turkish Aegean coast three miles (4.8 m) south of the Dardanelles. Identification of the site as Homeric Troy cannot be proved, but it was assumed by the Greeks and Romans. Troy was probably a major trading center from the third millennium B.C. It commanded the sea route between the Aegean and the Black Sea and the land route between Asia and Europe. Ships might have brought goods to Troy from the north and east: horses from the Caucasus, gold and grain from Georgia, and tin. Excavations at Besik Bay, 3 miles (5 km) southwest of Troy, suggest that merchant vessels could have beached on the sandy shore of what was in the late Bronze Age a much deeper bay.

When Heinrich *Schliemann first came to northwestern Anatolia in 1868, he became convinced that Hissarlik was Homeric Troy, and in 1870 he began excavations there. In all, Schliemann conducted seven major campaigns at Troy, uncovering remains of nine cities that his assistant, Wilhelm Dörpfeld, designated Troy I–IX (I–VII Bronze Age, VIII Greek, IX Roman). A magnificent treasure discovered by Schliemann in a Troy II level in 1873 consisted of nearly 9,000 objects, including three gold and nine silver vessels and three gold headdresses. Schliemann believed that it was the treasure of the Trojan king Priam, and that Troy II was the Homeric city. (The treasure is in fact from the Early Bronze Age and dates to ca. 2500 B.C.) In 1890, however, Dörpfeld, formerly an architect with the Olympia excavations, recognized Mycenaean pottery in Troy VI levels. Schliemann agreed that Troy VI, not Troy II, was of the proper age to be the Homeric city, but died later that year.

In 1893 and 1894 Dörpfeld confirmed the Late Bronze Age date of Troy VI. Excavations in 1932–1938 under the direction of Carl Blegen of the University of Cincinnati clarified the stratigraphy. Blegen subdivided the nine cities into forty-six strata. Accepting the Trojan War as a historical event, Blegen proposed that Troy VIIA was the city sacked by the Greeks rather than Troy VIh, as Dörpfeld had suggested. There is, however, no unequivocal evidence to support this identification. In 1988 a long-term international expedition, directed by Manfred Korfmann of the University of Tubingen, began a reexamination of the Bronze Age strata, while a team from the University of Cincinnati under C. Brian Rose continued the exploration of the classical remains.

Early Bronze Age Troy (levels 0–V) is characterized by slow and constant cultural development. The earliest signs of Bronze Age settlement have been found directly above bedrock. This level has been designated Troy 0 by the recent German expedition and is comparable to initial Early Bronze Age deposits at nearby Kum Tepe. The initial citadel

wall of Troy I (3000–2500 B.C.), 328 feet (100 m) in diameter, was expanded twice, attaining a diameter of about 369 feet (110 m). In Troy II (2500–2300 B.C.), the wall had a clay superstructure and small projecting towers; its gates were approached by long ramps. Rectangular, freestanding houses are typical of Troy I. Single-room structures, some had porticoes and may be precursors of the Troy II megaron house form. The upper citadel in Troy II was occupied by the great megaron (IIA), flanked by two smaller ones. Elsewhere houses were small, one- or two-room rectangular structures with party walls. In the final phases of the Early Bronze Age (2300–2000 B.C.), there is gradual regularization of the city plan. Closely packed houses with party walls are characteristic of Troy III and IV, but in Troy V the houses are better built and laid out more regularly.

Around 2000 B.C., between Troy V and VI, Troy experienced a dramatic cultural change. Settlement layout, architectural styles, and many artifact types that are characteristic of the Middle Bronze Age begin to appear. The Troy VI citadel wall was thirteen feet (4 m) thick and thirteen feet (4 m) high, excluding a brick superstructure, with three main gates and a postern at the northeastern tower or bastion. From the start of Troy VIA, the characteristic pottery is a gray ware similar to Minyan pottery in Greece. Scattered Mycenaean imports were also found in Troy VI (2000–1350 B.C.). Stone house foundations discovered immediately outside the Troy VI wall suggest that an extramural settlement was an integral part of Late Bronze Age Troy. Recent excavations south of the citadel have revealed a ditch, more than ten feet (3 m) in width, that was cut directly into the bedrock. The ditch is believed to have been a defensive work along the southern edge of the Troy VI lower city. If Troy occupied the entire plateau, it was one of the larger settlements in the Aegean area, and would be five times larger than previously thought.

Troy VI ended catastrophically, with portions of the circuit wall and houses collapsing, but not by fire. Blegen suggested that the destruction was caused by an earthquake (ca. 1350 B.C.). The wall was repaired, and there is no evidence of discontinuity between Troy VI and VIIA. Houses inside the citadel were built in contiguous blocks, and some had many storage pithoi. Troy VIIA ended in a widespread fire (ca. 1250 B.C.), which, together with the numerous storage pithoi and the discovery of miscellaneous human bones, led Blegen to identify it with the Homeric city, destroyed in war. In the succeeding level, Troy VIIB1, houses were rebuilt on old foundations. Troy VIIB2, the final Bronze Age level ending ca. 1000 B.C., saw the addition of rooms to VIIB1 houses.

The principal goals of the excavations of classical Troy include a full study of the city's public monuments and the reconstruction of its political and religious life. The history of Ilion (Roman Ilium Novum) reflects its geographical position and status as Homeric Troy. The site was reoccupied ca. 700 B.C. by Greeks from Lemnos, and as the capital of a league of cities in the Troad formed in 306 B.C., Ilion took on greater importance. Construction of a theater, new Athena temple, and city walls date to this period. A unique feature of Troy's bouleterion (in which representatives of the Troadic League would have met) is the raised platform at the back of the orchestra, which had reserved seating for council leaders.

In 188 B.C., Ilion was recognized as the mother city of Rome and granted a tax exemption. During the Mithridatic Wars, the Roman legate Fimbria sacked the city in 85 B.C.

Perhaps impelled by a visit of Augustus in 20 B.C., the city was rebuilt; The new excavations have clarified the scale of the Julio-Claudian rebuilding, which included restoration of the temple of Athena, theater, and bouleterion. Later imperial visits include Caracalla's in A.D. 214, Constantine's in the early fourth century, and Julian's in 351. The Panathenaia of the Troadic League took place as late as the third century, despite the sack of the city by the Heruli in 267. Notable among the Roman-period structures of Troy is the Odeion, whose original wooden stage, probably built in the first century A.D., was replaced early in the second century with an elaborate two-story building with Corinthian and Ionic orders and walls decorated with multicolored marble. It is blanketed by a thick destruction level, the first solid evidence for the Herulian sack of the city. In the fourth century, the city was an episcopal see. Considerable evidence for Ilium Novum's prosperity in the fourth century is coming to light in the lower city. A large multistory structure proved to be a fourth-century glass factory. A sizable fourth-century house had well-preserved geometric mosaics and wall paintings with floral motifs.

Devastated by a severe earthquake early in the sixth century, the city was abandoned through the ninth century. Little is known of the later Byzantine settlement of the site; it was again abandoned in Ottoman times.

[See also AEGEAN CULTURES: HELLADIC (MYCENAEAN) CULTURE; MYCENAE; HISTORY OF ARCHAEOLOGY BEFORE 1900: NEAR EASTERN ARCHAEOLOGY.]

■ Carl Blegen, et al., Troy I (1950), Troy II (1951), Troy III (1963), Troy IV (1958). Carl Blegen, Troy and the Trojans (1963). George Rapp and John Gifford, eds., Troy: The Archaeological Geology (1982). Lin Foxhall and Jack Davies, eds., The Trojan War, Its Historicity and Context (1984). Michael Wood, In Search of the Trojan War (1985). Machteld Mellink, ed., Troy and the Trojan War (1986). James Ottaway, "New Assault on Troy," Archaeology 44 (1991): 54–59. Time-Life Books, The Wondrous Realms of the Aegean (1993). Studia Troica (annuals).

Mark J. Rose

TRUNDHOLM. The Trundholm sun chariot is a statue of a bronze horse pulling the sun in the shape of a large decorated disk. It dates to the Early Bronze Age in Denmark and with its length of approximately 23 inches (60 cm) it is the longest statue from the Nordic Bronze Age. It is a remarkable and unique object. The splendid craftsmanship has delighted generations, and the intriguing symbol, which seems so obvious, yet beguiling, gives a unique glimpse of Bronze Age beliefs.

The horse and the sun disk are mounted on a six-wheeled base and are attached to each other through a central axis. The wheels are four-spoked, representing one of the earliest examples of this type in Denmark. Remains of loops on the horse's neck and on the side of the disk show that they were originally connected by some kind of chain or string.

The horse is hollow-cast. It is a seminaturalistic plastic representation with incised decoration marking the eyes, the mane, and presumably various pieces of harness. This is one of the oldest figurative horse depictions in Denmark.

The sun, made of two slightly concave bronze disks with a diameter of 10 inches (26 cm), is ornamented with a dense and beautiful pattern of concentric circles similar to those covering contemporary ornaments and weapons. The circles are organized in three bands separated by closely adjoined ribbons with crosshatching. One side is partly covered with a thin gold sheet that was attached by being folded into a groove along the periphery and covered by a

bronze band. This gold was pressed so hard onto the surface that the underlying decoration comes through; a thin pin was used to redraw the decoration on the gold. It is not known whether originally both sides were thus decorated although technical details, such as the presence of a groove for attachment on both sides, have been seen as proof for two-sided decoration. Other interpretations prefer to see the two sides as symbolizing the rising and setting sun respectively, or they describe the chariot as having a day and a night side.

The Trundholm chariot was found in 1902 in a small bog on Zealand, Denmark. It had been deliberately broken apart and placed on a dry bog surface rather than thrown into open water as was the tradition with ritual deposition in Denmark during the Bronze Age.

It is commonly accepted that the statue is composed of two separate parts: one being the horse pulling the sun-disk and the other the chariot upon which the group is placed. This point has been much emphasized since it suggests that the chariot may be a miniature model of real ones used in cultic events. The passive nature of the sun as an object being pulled has also been used to argue that this is not a religious system that involves a personified sun deity, and that the statue refers instead to the celebration of a sun that is part of nature and may represent fertility.

The sun and horse are important motifs in Early Bronze Age society in Scandinavia. They are found in rock carvings, in incised decoration on various objects, and as the horsehead-handles of razors. The association between sun and horse might, furthermore, have been a long-term phenomenon in Northern Europe. The "Trundholm" image, for instance, recurs some two thousand years later in the Viking mythology of Skinfakse, the horse that every morning pulls the daylight up over the world of the humans. The outstanding contribution of the Trundholm chariot is that it provides insights into aspects of Bronze Age belief systems that would otherwise be beyond our reach.

[See also SCANDINAVIA: EARLY PREHISTORY OF SCANDINAVIA.]

■ Peter Gelling and Hilda Ellis Davidson, The Chariot of the Sun and Other Rites and Symbols of the Northern Bronze Age (1969). Peter V. Glob, The Mound People (1974). John M. Coles and Anthony F. Harding, The Bronze Age in Europe (1979).

Marie Louise Stig Sørensen

TULA. Tula, the capital of Mesoamerica's Early Post-Classic Period *Toltec empire, occupied a limestone ridge overlooking the Tula River in Hidalgo State approximately 43 miles (70 km) north of Mexico City. Although farmers occupied the region as early as the first century A.D., Tula was founded in the wake of Teotihuacán's disintegration after A.D. 750. The initial settlers included migrants from nearby communities, groups moving south from the Mesoamerican frontier zone in north-central Mexico, and perhaps refugees from *Teotihuacán. This multiethnic population, believed to include speakers of Nahuatl, Otomi, and perhaps other languages, formed the demographic base for Tula's growth in the Corral, Terminal Corral and Tollan phases (A.D. 800–1200).

In ca. 1100 Tula covered 5.4 square miles (14 sq km) and was home to at least 35,000 souls. Public life focused upon Tula Grande, a large open plaza surrounded by temples, ball courts, palaces and elite residences. Many of these structures were embellished with sculptures, carved friezes, stuccoed and painted walls, and other types of Toltec art.

Excavations in the city's residential zone have uncovered house groups composed of three or more rectangular single-story masonry houses placed around interior courtyards. Although some city dwellers cultivated nearby agricultural fields, many pursued specialized occupations, especially the manufacture of obsidian tools and other craft products.

Tula has never been a "lost city." Fray Bernardino de Sahagun described its ruins in his sixteenth-century treatise on pre-Columbian life and culture, identifying it as the capital of the Toltecs, who preceded the Aztecs in central Mexico. The French explorer Desire Charnay excavated at Tula in the 1880s in an attempt to verify Sahagun's assertion, but many scholars remained skeptical until 1940, when the combined research of ethnohistorian Wigberto Jimenez Moreno and archaeologist Jorge R. Acosta confirmed the identification. Acosta continued to excavate at Tula until 1962 under the auspices of Mexico's Instituto Nacional de Antropologia e Historia (INAH). INAH renewed investigations at the site in 1969 and has continued them sporadically ever since. From 1970 to 1972 the University of Missouri—Columbia conducted excavations and surveys in the urban residential zone, and Tulane University undertook investigation of an obsidian workshop in the 1980s.

[See also CHICHÉN ITZÁ; MESOAMERICA: POST-CLASSIC PERIOD IN MESOAMERICA.]

■ Richard A. Diehl, *Tula: The Toltec Capital of Ancient Mexico* (1983). Dan M. Healan, *Tula of the Toltecs: Excavations and Surveys* (1989).
Richard A. Diehl

TUTANKHAMUN'S TOMB lies in the central area of the *Valley of the Kings at Thebes, where it now bears the number KV 62. It was originally made for a private individual, but pressed into service as a royal tomb when Tutankhamun died with his own intended tomb incomplete. It comprises a passageway leading to an antechamber, off which opens a storeroom. To the right is a large room, running at a right angle to the first chamber, its floor lying around a meter lower. This difference in levels was intended to provide sufficient clearance for the items placed in it, surrounding the king's quartzite sarcophagus.

The sarcophagus itself was closed by a granite lid, apparently broken while being lowered into place. The cause of this accident was probably the discovery that the toes of the outermost gilded wooden anthropoid coffin of the king were higher than the rim of the sarcophagus coffer, and needed adzing down. The middle coffin was also of wood, but elaborately inlaid as well as gilded; it had been made for the burial of Tutankhamun's elder brother, Smenkhkare / Neferneferuaten, in traditional style. It had not apparently been to the revolutionary taste of the latter's co-regent, the sun-worshipping Akhenaten, who was responsible for Smenkhkare / Neferneferuaten's burial, following his premature death. Smenkhkare/Neferneferuaten had thus been interred in an adapted Atenist coffin, leaving his original one in store, along with other pieces, to be employed for his brother a decade later.

Tutankhamun's innermost coffin was made of solid gold. Like the outer coffins it was adorned with a feathered, *rishi*, pattern that represented the king as a kind of human-headed bird. The mummy within was equipped with a gold portrait mask, gold hands, and inlaid bands containing religious formulae. The mummy wrappings contained huge quantities of jewelry, but the cloth was in a very poor state at the time of its discovery, having carbonized through the chemical reaction of the unguents with which the royal body had been drenched at the funeral. These had badly damaged the flesh of the mummy itself, which had also been stuck to the floor of the gold coffin by then.

The sarcophagus was surrounded by four gilded wooden shrines, each covered with visual representations from the various Egyptian funerary texts and a linen pall. The walls of the burial chamber were the only ones of the tomb to be decorated, being adorned with scenes painted on a yellow background. One wall shows the king's mummy receiving the last rites from Tutankhamun's successor, King Ay. Other elements of the decoration include depictions of the king standing before various deities, vignettes from the *Book of Imyduat,* and a depiction of the king's catafalque, drawn by his officials. Like the scene with Ay, this latter depiction seems to be unique for a royal sepulcher, although it is a type common to private tomb chapels.

A doorway opposite the foot of Tutankhamun's sarcophagus led into a small room, dubbed the "Treasury" by the tomb's excavator. A large shrine-shaped chest, upon which rested a canine image of the god Anubis, lay at the threshold of the chamber. The most important item within the room was Tutankhamun's square canopic shrine, which contained the calcite canopic chest, a goddess carved at each corner, and inscribed with formulae associated with the protection of the embalmed internal organs. Inside were four miniature coffinettes of inlaid solid gold. Each of these was of identical design to the full-sized middle coffin, and they too had all been made for Smenkhkare / Neferneferuaten. These coffinettes each held a linen-wrapped bundle of embalmed viscera, heavily anointed with unguents.

The Treasury also held a large number of resin-varnished shrines, containing wooden figures of the king and various deities, overlaid with gold leaf; some of these were also leftovers from earlier reigns, including possibly the early years of Amunhotpe IV. Similar figures have been recovered from other royal tombs, but they were less ornate, being merely covered with black varnish. Other containers in the room held a large number of *shabti* figures. Also present were a model granary, two chariots, model boats, and three miniature nests of coffins, the largest set containing a gold figure of a king and a lock of the hair of Queen Tiy, grandmother of Tutankhamun. The other two nests, with designs appropriate to private persons of the later Eighteenth Dynasty, contained the mummies of two premature infants; both were female, and one had suffered from spina bifida. They almost certainly represent the offspring of Tutankhamun and his sister and wife, Queen Ankhesenamun.

The burial chamber was separated from the antechamber by a false wall and sealed doorway, the latter guarded by a pair of gilded and varnished wooden statues. These are of a type familiar from royal tombs of the Ramesside period. Against one wall of the antechamber three gilded wooden couches were stacked, each with a different pair of animal heads, under and on top of which were piled all kinds of food containers and furniture, including a richly gilded and inlaid throne. Half of the other side of the room was taken up by four dismantled chariots.

A door under one of the stacked couches gave access to the so-called Annex, a storeroom crowded with all kinds of funerary equipment, badly disturbed by tomb robbers and those who had cleared up after them. The tomb had apparently been entered by robbers on two occasions, not long after the funeral, perhaps in the reign of Horemheb, when the tomb of Thutmose IV was certainly plundered. Considerable damage had been done, but the innermost shrines and sarcophagus remained intact, the thieves perhaps being caught in the act.

After the last robbery, and the resealing of the sepulcher, the tomb, which lay in the very bottom of the valley, was progressively covered by debris, in part from the construction of neighboring tombs, until the huts of the artisans working on the tomb of Rameses VI (KV 9) were erected directly above its entrance. Accordingly, the tomb remained undetected during the period of intensive tomb robbing that occurred during the social disorders of the late Twentieth Dynasty. Because of the depth of its burial and its position near the entrance to the much-visited tomb of Rameses VI, Tutankhamun's tomb escaped discovery by the nineteenth-century excavators in the Valley of the Kings, although a number came fairly close. Its entrance was revealed only during the systematic clearance of hitherto-uninvestigated parts of the valley by Howard Carter and Lord Carnarvon after World War I. The first step of the access stairway was uncovered on 4 November 1922, and work on the tomb and its contents continued until the spring of 1932, when the last objects were removed to the Egyptian Museum in Cairo. The royal mummy, the outer coffin, and the sarcophagus remain in the tomb.

The importance of the discovery of the tomb of Tutankhamun lies in the fact that, alone of all New Kingdom royal tombs, it was essentially intact, thus providing detailed evidence on the kind of equipment that accompanied a king of that era to the grave. It also allowed the reconstruction of some of the fragmentary items that had been recovered from the badly robbed tombs of the period, and provided useful comparison with the burial outfits found in the intact Twenty-first Dynasty tomb of King Psusennes I at Tanis, and the partly robbed tomb of Thirteenth Dynasty King Hor, at Dahshûr.

[See also EGYPT: NEW KINGDOM EGYPT; VALLEY OF THE KINGS.]

■ H. Carter and A. C. Mace, *The Tomb of Tut.ankh.Amen*, 3 vols. (1923–1933). C. Desroches-Noblecourt, *Tutankhamen* (1962). H. Beinlich and M. Saleh, *Corpus der Hieroglyphiscen Inschriften aus dem Grab des Tutanchamun* (1989). C. N. Reeves, *The Complete Tutankhamun* (1990). C. N. Reeves, *Valley of the Kings: The Decline of a Royal Necropolis* (1990). A. M. Dodson, *The Coffins and Canopic Equipment from the Tomb of Tutankhamun* (1993). J. Baines, ed., *Stone Vessels, Pottery and Sealings from the Tomb of Tut'ankhamun* (1994).

Aidan Dodson

TYLOR, Sir Edward (1832–1917), was a leading figure in nineteenth-century cultural evolutionism. His father was a successful brass founder in London, but circumstances led the son into the world of scholarship instead of business. Supported by family income, he already had an international reputation for his work on cultural evolution by the time of his first academic position, as keeper of the University Museum at Oxford, in 1883. In 1896 he was appointed the first professor of anthropology at Oxford, a position he held until he retired in 1909.

Initially Tylor was interested in historical as much as evolutionary questions, as illustrated by his *Researches into the Early History of Mankind* (1865). But in his next major work, *Primitive Culture* (1871), his goal was to arrive at scientific laws: he now saw anthropology as a generalizing science that was to seek the causal laws underlying the growth of culture or civilization. His final major book, *Anthropology* (1881), continued his scientific interests. Tylor's evolutionism developed in the context of a vigorous public debate over the relationship between science and religion. He was strongly on the side of science in this debate, and his *Primitive Culture* was widely viewed as an empirical demonstration that religion developed according to naturalistic processes; this work, his most influential, was a keystone in the argument that human affairs reflect the laws of nature, not the will of God.

Tylor's work preceded the modern relativistic, anthropological concept of *culture. In Tylor's view, different peoples had different degrees of culture, and societies could be described as more or less cultured; to be more cultured was both to exhibit greater intelligence and to possess truer and more useful institutions. Tylor did not doubt that Western values were a valid standard by which to judge other peoples or that Western society stood above the rest when this standard was used.

[See also HISTORY OF ARCHAEOLOGY BEFORE 1900: EUROPEAN ARCHAEOLOGY.]

■ George W. Stocking, Jr., *Race, Culture and Evolution: Essays in the History of Anthropology* (1968). George W. Stocking, Jr., *Victorian Anthropology* (1987).

Elvin Hatch

TYPOLOGICAL ANALYSIS is a fundamental process in archaeological research, and is defined as the systematic arrangement of material culture into types based on similarities of form, construction, decoration or style, content, use, or some combination of these. Before the advent of absolute dating techniques, typological analysis, in conjunction with stratigraphic excavation, was the only means by which archaeologists could develop cultural-historical sequences or otherwise measure the passage of time. The assumptions of this approach are that within a region, artifacts of similar form or style are near to one another in time, and that stylistic change is likely to be gradual or evolutionary. Early pioneers of typological analysis include the Swedish scholar Oscar *Montelius, who in the late nineteenth century refined the chronological sequence of the Bronze Age throughout much of Europe with his so-called typological method, the English archaeologist Sir Flinders *Petrie, who in the late nineteenth century developed seriation, and the American archaeologists Nels Nelson and A. V. *Kidder, who in the early twentieth century developed a series of regional chronologies in the American Southwest based on stratigraphic excavation combined with careful description of the stylistic variation of ceramics and their arrangement into types.

Although typological analysis is historically associated with chronology building and the concept of style, it is not limited to these notions. Typologies are arbitrary constructs created by archaeologists to address specific problems encountered in the archaeological record. No single classification of an artifact is its "correct" or "best" type. Typological analysis is based on the recognition that specific *attributes* of the objects under study are important for sorting these materials into types. An attribute is a characteristic of an artifact that cannot be divided into smaller constituent units. Examples include raw material, color, size, and so forth. Attribute states are mutually exclusive instances of attributes. Pottery vessels, for example, can be sorted into use categories such as bowls, jars, plates, and other forms, each of which is an attribute state. Types based on attributes related to use are known as functional types. Stone tools, for instance, can be placed into functional categories using attributes such as the angle of the working edge and patterns of damage found along it. Another common approach to typology is to create descriptive, or morphological types, wherein the goal of classification is to create an exhaustive description of artifacts so that they may be better compared with materials from other sites.

As traditionally practiced, typological analysis is often viewed more as an art than a science. Long familiarity with the materials under study and an intuitive "knack" for distinguishing between relatively small differences in attribute states are often seen as prerequisites for a successful outcome. To some, however, this intuitive approach to typology lacked scientific rigor and worse, was seen as highly arbitrary in the choice of attributes. In response, a number of mathematical, statistical, and formal techniques have been applied to typological analysis. Albert Spaulding in 1953 published an influential paper that introduced archaeology to the chi-square statistic. Since then, other techniques have been used, including cluster analysis, ordination methods, factor analysis, and contingency table analysis. Although in many instances these methods have proved to be of value, there nevertheless continues to be significant debate over the degree to which they are truly useful to or even necessary for typological analysis.

This debate, however, is much deeper than simply an argument about the relative merits of different techniques. It is also an appraisal of the meaning and goals of typological analysis in archaeological research. In his 1953 paper, Spaulding made a strong claim that artifact types were inherent in material culture and could thus be discovered through a statistical analysis of their mutual association. Further, he argued that nominal scale attributes (color, shape, etc.) were more appropriate for analysis than quantitative attributes (size, weight, etc.) since they were likely to be a direct reflection of the ideals and values of those who made the artifacts. The goal of typological analysis, then,

was to discover these ancient folk classifications (labeled by other archaeologists as "mental templates"). Types discovered using this approach to classification are seen as fundamental and immutable.

Reaction to these assertions has centered upon the validity of two assumptions: the logical priority of nominal scale attributes and the reality of types generated by their use. Many have argued that although nominal attributes are often useful, they are not necessarily fundamental to typological analysis, and further, their use does not permit the archaeologist to explore effectively the variability in a collection of artifacts. Vessel size might be of significance to a typology, but the use of nominal attributes does not provide a useful means through which variation in size can be easily defined or observed. As to the reality of types, though it is possible that nominal-scale attributes may well capture aspects of the way ancient peoples perceived some artifact, it is not necessarily the case that this is so, and from a scientific perspective, there is no way in which such an assertion could ever be verified.

No matter how types are constructed, what is of greatest importance to the archaeologist is how they are interpreted and used. Therefore, in typological analysis, it remains the case that the archaeologist must think carefully about the questions being asked and on that basis select the attributes and attribute states most likely to further that end.

[*See also* SERIATION; STATISTICAL ANALYSIS.]

■ Albert C. Spaulding, "Statistical Techniques for the Discovery of Artifact Types," *American Antiquity* 18 (1953): 305–314. Robert C. Dunnell, *Systematics in Prehistory* (1971). Robert Whallon and James A. Brown, eds., *Essays on Archaeological Typology* (1982). Robert C. Dunnell, "Methodological Issues in Americanist Artifact Classification," in *Advances in Archaeological Method and Theory*, ed. Michael B. Schiffer (1986), pp. 149–207. George L. Cowgill, "Artifact Classification and Archaeological Purposes," in *Mathematics and Information Science in Archaeology: A Flexible Framework*, ed. Albertus Voorips (1990), pp. 61–98. William. Y. Adams and Ernest. W. Adams, *Archaeological Typology and Practical Reality* (1991).

Mark Aldenderfer

U

UHLE, Max (b. 1856), linguist and Andean archaeologist. After military service Max Uhle entered the University of Göttingen. In the fall of 1877 he went to Leipzig and took his Ph.D. degree in linguistics in 1880. His dissertation was on Chinese grammar and was Uhle's only work on Chinese philology. After receiving his degree, Uhle became assistant to the director of the Königliches Zoologisches und Anthropologisch-Ethnographisches Museum in Dresden (1881–1888). While at Dresden Uhle read Reiss and Stübel's *Totenfeld von Ancón in Peru*, thus beginning his lifelong interest in Andean archaeology. In 1888 Uhle left the Dresden Museum to become assistant at the Königliches Museum für Völkerkunde in Berlin, which was under the direction of Adolf Bastian, who shared Uhle's interest in Peru.

Uhle's most important work was done in Peru and Boliva in the 1890s and the first part of the twentieth century. Later, he worked in Chile and Ecuador, laying the foundations of Andean archaeology between 1892 and 1905. It was Uhle who applied the principles of *stratigraphy and *seriation to Andean archaeology, in work that was both archaeological and linguistic. Few, if any, have conducted more fieldwork in South America than Uhle.

Most of Uhle's work remains unpublished, as he was never able to get out of the field long enough write up his work. His most extensive Andean collections are found in Philadelphia, Berkeley, Berlin, Quito, Lima, Santiago, Göteborg, and São Paulo.

[See also HISTORY OF ARCHAEOLOGY BEFORE 1900. ARCHAEOLOGY OF THE AMERICAS; HISTORY OF ARCHAEOLOGY FROM 1900 TO 1950: ARCHAEOLOGY OF THE AMERICAS.]

■ Alfred L. Kroeber, "Dr. Max Uhle," *American Anthropologist*, 8(1):202, (1906); John Howland Rowe, "Max Uhle, 1856–1944 (A Memoir of the Father of Peruvian Archaeology)," *University of California Publications in American Archaeology and Ethnology*, 46(1):10–134, (1954); Max Uhle, *Pachacamac* (1903); *The Emeryville Shellmound* (1907); "Über doe Frühkulturen in der Umgebung von Lima," *Sixteenth International Congress of Americanists*, Vienna, pp. 347–370 (1910).

Douglas R. Givens

UNDERWATER ARCHAEOLOGY.

Archaeology is defined as being a subdiscipline of anthropology that studies the human past through its material remains. Underwater archaeology is merely any archaeology that is performed underwater. Some have objected to this definition because it fails to give any coherence to the field of study. Still, the excavation of diverse underwater sites such as Warm Mineral Springs, Florida, the town of Port Royal, Jamaica, and the shipwreck sites of Ulu Burun and Serce Limani in Turkey are archaeological components of Paleo-Indian, Historic, Late Bronze Age, and Byzantine archaeology that make no sense except as related to other comparable sites, on land or underwater, of the same time period and culture. As such they cannot stand alone as an archaeological unit of study, but sites such as these often contribute data obtainable from no other source. The fact that they are underwater is immaterial.

The only differences between sites of any cultural period underwater and those on land are the methods and techniques of excavation. The research questions, analyses, and basic theories are shared with any site of the same cultural manifestation. As such, underwater archaeology has no basic theory unique to itself, except for the specialized studies that surround the evolution and technology of ship construction. The terms "nautical archaeology," "maritime archaeology," and "shipwreck archaeology" are used to describe this latter area of specialization. All involve the scientific study of the material remains of humans and their activities on the sea.

A unique characteristic of many underwater sites is that they happen to be catastrophic sites—sites created within minutes by some disaster that preserves the cultural features and materials and the all-important cultural context. These sites are important because they are valuable time capsules that cover a tightly dated time period and in many instances, preserve a wide array of organic material that is missing from other sites. For this reason underwater excavations are important for the intact assemblages, the controls that they provide to artifact chronologies, and for the organic material, both artifactual and faunal, that is available for study.

Unfortunately, underwater archaeology in both the Old World and the New World is often associated with treasure hunting, for the earliest excavations were performed to recover specimens by trained divers such as at Antikythera, Greece, in 1900, or by individuals excavating Spanish shipwrecks in Bermuda and Florida during the 1950s and 1960s. The title "Father of Underwater Archaeology" is bestowed upon Professor George Bass, not because he was the first person to do underwater excavations, but because as a graduate student in 1960 he directed the underwater excavations of a Late Bronze Age wreck at Cape Gelidonya, Turkey, and because of his continuing nautical archaeology excavations, and his establishment of the Institute of Nautical Archaeology.

The introduction of true underwater archaeology in different parts of the world can be correlated to the time when trained archaeologists actually dive and direct the excavations for scientific reasons. In the New World, underwater archaeology has its tentative beginnings with the excavation of the two shipwreck sites in Canada, the frigate *Machault* and the Browns Bay Vessel from 1966 to 1969, and the excavation at the seventeenth-century sunken town of Port Royal, Jamaica, 1966 to 1968. With the establishment of the

Nautical Archaeology Program at Texas A&M University in 1976 followed by the Program in Maritime History and Nautical Archaeology at East Carolina University in 1981, the first university academic programs were established to train professional archaeologist in nautical or maritime archaeology. It is with the establishment and recognition of formal academic programs at universities that the field of underwater archaeology as an adjunct to archaeological investigations in general becomes an accepted field of specialization.

[See also SHIPS AND SEAFARING.]

■ George F. Bass, ed., A History of Seafaring Based on Underwater Archaeology (1972). Keith Muckelroy, Maritime Archaeology (1978). Keith Muckelroy, ed., Archaeology Under Water (1980). D. L. Hamilton and Robyn Woodward, "A Sunken 17th-Century City: Port Royal, Jamaica," Archaeology 37(1984): 38–45. Peter Throckmorton, ed., The Sea Remembers (1987). George F. Bass, ed., Shipwrecks of the Americas: A History Based on Underwater Archaeology (1988).

Donny L. Hamilton

UPPSALA. In ca. 1076 Adam of Bremen, in his *History of the Archbishops of Hamburg*, described a heathen temple at Uppsala, with a sacred grove, evergreen tree, sacred well, and human sacrifices. This is one of the most explicit near-contemporary references to Viking Age pagan worship. In the seventeenth century it was realized that Adam was not referring to the medieval and modern town of Uppsala, but to the nearby Gamla ("Old") Uppsala, which lies in the county of Uppland, heartland of the Swedish kingdom, 44 miles (70 km) northwest of Stockholm.

Gamla Uppsala is dominated by a row of three large earthen mounds, the "Kings' Mounds," with a slightly smaller "Thing Mound" immediately to the east. Westward, along the Högåsen ("High Ridge"), is a cemetery of several hundred smaller burial mounds. Northeast of the Kings' Mounds are the foreshortened remains of an eleventh-century church, which was once a cathedral housing the relics of King Erik, Sweden's patron saint. It was damaged by a fire in the mid-thirteenth century and was only partially rebuilt; the cathedral was resited in Uppsala in 1273. At the plateau's northern limit lies the Kungsgården terrace. Its name, "Royal demesne," is just one of several medieval indications of regal interests in the site which may have originated much earlier.

The Kings' Mounds were investigated in 1846–1847, 1874, and 1925. Each revealed a stone cairn built over remains from a cremation pyre, and capped by a mound of soil, gravel, and clay. Fragments of high status metalwork, including gold and garnet jewelry and pseudocameos, indicate dates in the sixth century for all three mounds; a wide variety of animal remains also suggests elaborate funeral rites appropriate for aristocratic or royal burials. Only a few of the smaller burial mounds have been excavated; they too are cremation graves, spanning the Iron Age to Viking Age epochs.

In 1926, excavations in and around the church revealed burials thought to relate to an earlier but unrecognized timber church. Earlier still were postholes from a large timber building, initially identified as Adam of Bremen's heathen temple, but really of unknown attribution.

There have been several small-scale excavations, observations, and discoveries among the complex of monuments. Four Viking Age rune stones are recorded. In 1891 a twelfth-century hoard of silver, including bowls, neckchains, and a crucifix, was found immediately north of the plateau. In 1972, four Viking Age boat graves were excavated. Excavation during the late 1980s and into the early 1990s at the south of Kungsgårdsplatån and off its north edge revealed both artifacts and structures that span the first millennium A.D.

In combination, the documentary, place name, and archaeological data demonstrate that Gamla Uppsala was a focus for ritual/religious practices from the Iron Age, and that by the sixth century A.D., if not before, these were clearly linked to the exercise and display of power and prestige, presumably by the Svear kings. This continued into the thirteen century, diminishing but not wholly disappearing thereafter.

[See also SCANDINAVIA: SCANDINAVIA AND THE VIKING AGE.]

■ S. Lindqvist, Uppsala Högar och Ottarshögen (1936). W. Duczko ed., Arkeologi och Miljögeologi i Gamla Uppsala (1993).

Richard A. Hall

UR (Tell al-Muqayyar) lies near the modern city of An Nasiriya in southern Iraq, several kilometers west of the present bed of the Euphrates. In 1854 its ziggurat, or temple tower, was examined by J. E. Taylor on behalf of the British Museum. Beneath the structure's corners he found cuneiform-scribed cylinders that enabled pioneer Assyriologist Henry C. *Rawlinson to identify the site as Ur.

At the end of World War I, the British returned to Ur, mounting expeditions under R. Campbell Thompson in 1918 and H. R. Hall in 1919. These brief forays were followed in 1922 by an expedition jointly conducted by the British Museum and the University of Pennsylvania. Director C. Leonard *Woolley worked at the site until 1934, employing at times as many as 400 workers in what became one of the largest excavations ever carried out in Iraq.

From the presence of sherds in later contexts it can be assumed that Ur was settled during an early phase of the Úbaid Period (late sixth millennium B.C.). The earliest excavated levels are from somewhat later in the Úbaid Period, when Ur appears to have been little more than a marsh village. These remains were covered by a deposit of about 10 feet (3 m) of clean, water-laid silt, in which Woolley saw the universal flood of Noah. This interpretation has been rejected because flood deposits at other Mesopotamian sites do not occur at the same place in the archaeological sequence, which would have to be the case if the Ur flood were of more than local significance.

By about 3000 B.C. (Jamdat Nasr period), Ur occupied about 37 acres (15 ha), and at its center were cone-decorated buildings, apparently temples.

During the following Early Dynastic Period Ur became one of the wealthiest cities of Sumer, approaching its maximum extent of 124 acres (50 ha) in the mid-third millennium. Ur's wealth was largely due to its role as a harbor town at the head of the Persian Gulf. Extensive trade contacts are suggested by burial goods from its Early Dynastic cemetery that were made of raw materials from the Arabian Peninsula, Iran, India, and Afghanistan.

Among 2,000 more modest burials in this mid-third-millennium cemetery, Woolley found sixteen larger interments, each consisting of a built tomb at the bottom of a deep pit. The elite of the city—apparently its rulers—were buried in these graves with their attendants, between six and eighty willing victims, in a ritual that is attested only here in Mesopotamia. These graves yielded some of the most remarkable treasures from Ur: a golden dagger with a gold-studded hilt of lapis luzuli, the sounding box of a musical instrument decorated with inlaid scenes of war and peace, and two gold and lapis statues depicting a male goat with his forelegs resting on the limbs of a tree.

Most of the sixteen tombs were found looted, but that of Puabi, called "queen" on the seal buried with her, was untouched. A woman in her forties, she was interred with twenty-three retainers, surrounded by the finery that had been a part of her privileged life, including a lyre adorned with a golden bull's head, gold and silver vessels, jewelry of precious metals and semiprecious stones, and a spectacular diadem of golden leaves and rosettes.

One of the simpler burials, a wooden coffin in a large hole, turned out to contain numerous vessels and weapons of copper, gold, and electrum, along with hundreds of gold and lapis beads. Most remarkable was a golden helmet in the form of a wig, representing the finest workmanship in the cemetery. The name Meskalamdug was engraved on three vessels from the burial, a name that appears with the title "king" on a seal from a female burial elsewhere in the cemetery. Whether this rich interment was the king's burial remains one of the numerous unanswered questions about the cemetery and the unique practices attested there.

The cult of the moon god Nanna at Ur was one of the most venerable and prestigious in Sumer. Therefore, Sargon of Agade (2334–2279 B.C.) installed his daughter Enheduanna as high priestess of Nanna as part of his program for the unification of southern Mesopotamia. For centuries thereafter, this office was filled by the daughter or sister of the king.

After the fall of Agade, the rulers of Ur reunited southern Mesopotamia into a tightly organized kingdom for about a century (2112–2004 B.C.) and extended Sumerian rule to the plains of Assyria and the mountains of Iran. The founder of this dynasty, Ur-Nammu, and his successors completely rebuilt the center of their capital. Their most impressive architectural legacy is the ziggurat of Nanna, a massive three-stage tower, 205 by 142 feet (63 by 43 m) at its base.

Woolley excavated extensively in the residential districts of Ur dating to the first quarter of the second millennium. The houses that lined the winding, irregular streets typically had a central courtyard off which the other rooms opened. Many of the houses seem to have had a second story; some had private shrines and family burial vaults as well.

Ur became a minor city politically after 2000 B.C., although later kings continued to renovate its temples. The sixth-century B.C. king Nabonidus rebuilt the ziggurat for the last time and installed his daughter as high priestess. In the fourth century B.C., Ur ceased to exist, probably because the Euphrates changed course.

[*See also* MESOPOTAMIA, *articles on* THE RISE OF URBAN CULTURE, SUMER AND AKKAD; NEAR EAST: THE NEOLITHIC AND CHALCOLITHIC (PRE-BRONZE-AGE) PERIODS IN THE NEAR EAST; URUK.]

■ Henry T. Wright, "The Southern Margins of Sumer," in *Heartland of Cities*, by Robert McC. Adams (1981). C. Leonard Woolley and P.R.S. Moorey, "Ur of the Chaldees," rev. ed. (1982).

James A. Armstrong

URARTU, ancient Ararat, was a land of craggy fortresses and rugged terrain, hot in summer, bitterly cold in winter. Within its frontiers stood two great lakes—the salt lake Urmia in modern Iran, and in eastern Turkey the beautiful Lake Van, its translucent turquoise waters surrounded by tall mountains on which small patches of snow remain even at the height of summer. It was on the shores of Lake Van that the Urartian King Sarduri I founded his new capital city of Tushpa around 830 B.C., and in so doing inaugurated the great age of this mountain kingdom, two hundred years during which Urartu was destined to play a leading role in the power politics of the Near East.

The original Urartian capital had been burned by the Assyrians some thirty years before, and Sarduri was anxious to ensure that no such fate befell his new fortress. For this reason he chose for its location a narrow but massive spine of rock rising up out of the marshy land on the very edge of Lake Van. Only 200 yards (183 m) wide, the rock of Van was crowned with a line of mighty fortifications and cut through by a huge rock-cut ditch dividing the core of the citadel from the rest. Later peoples—Seljuks and Ottomans—built on top of the earlier structures, remodeling and restoring the great fortress, but the large stone blocks so typical of Urartian architecture can still be seen at the base of many of the walls. History was to demonstrate that Sarduri's precautions were not in vain; for when the Assyrian armies reached Van a second time, in 735 B.C., the powerful fortifications so deterred them that they made no attempt to storm the citadel.

Van citadel was indeed only one—though probably the greatest—in a whole chain of fortresses on which the Urartians relied for protection from their enemies. These included not only the Assyrians to the south but also fierce bands of horsemen—Scythians and Cimmerians—on the Central Asian steppes to the north. When the Urartian army suffered defeat and failed to hold the frontier, the people would retreat into their strongholds and simply wait for the enemy to depart. The mountainous nature of Urartian territory made it ideal for this strategy, with many a craggy rock easily turned into a near-impregnable fortress.

But the Urartians did not expend all their energies on defence. They were also skilled hydraulic engineers and road builders. The land around Tushpa, the capital, was irrigated by a great canal, known today as the Canal of Semiramis, which brought water 26 miles (42 km) from the Hoşap Valley to the southeast. Dams and canals transformed many of the low-lying basins between the mountains into fertile fields, orchards, and vineyards, a remarkable achievement recorded with pride by Urartian kings in inscriptions on stone monuments and rock faces. Many of the original dams may still be seen, and the Canal of Semiramis has remained in use, with relatively minor repairs, up to the present day. At 2,800 years this must make it one of the oldest operational canals in the world.

Fortresses stood sentinel over these flourishing farmlands and over all the roads leading to the capital. One of the best is Cavustepe, 20 miles (32 km) southeast of Van, where, in contrast to Van citadel, the Urartian remains have not been obscured by later works. Walls, towers, and other buildings are clearly in evidence, strung out along the long thin ridge. Most striking of all is the principal temple, its smooth basalt facade in sharp blue-black contrast with the yellow limestone of the surrounding remains, its freshness belying the centuries which have elapsed. An inscription by the entrance records that it was King Sarduri II who built the temple around the middle of the eighth century B.C. when Urartian power was at its height. Behind stretch rock-cut cisterns and storerooms with rows of huge pottery jars over 5 feet (1 km) in diameter, designed to hold the annual dues of corn and wine from the surrounding countryside.

Other great fortresses stand to the north of Van: at Anzaf, where a pair of mounds, one on either side of the modern road, hold the remains of citadels built by successive Urartian kings, father and son, toward the end of the ninth century, and at Korzut kale near Muradiye at the northeastern extremity of Lake Van, where a massive rocky outcrop stands sentinel over the road as it quits the lakeshore and heads for the mountain pass toward Iran.

The troubled history of Urartu ensured that the kingdom's defenses were several times put to the test. One of the darkest hours came in 714 B.C., when King Rusa I had to face attack on two fronts and mutiny at home. The trouble began when a mighty force of Cimmerian horsemen swept over the Caucasus to devastate the northern provinces of the kingdom. Rusa assembled his army and marched bravely against them, but lost three commanders and their divisions in the ensuing battle, and was forced to retreat back to Van. Spies soon brought news of this reverse to Urartu's southern enemies, the Assyrians, and their Warrior-King Sargon II quickly marched north to take advantage of Rusa's misfortune.

Passing east of Lake Urmia they won a decisive victory over the demoralized Urartian army. Rusa fled homeward on a mare, and, either injured in the battle or simply overcome by adversity, died shortly afterward. The Urartians retreated into the shelter of their fortresses and looked on impotently as the victorious Assyrians burnt and despoiled their houses and lands, destroying crops and felling forests and vineyards in a wanton orgy of vandalism. But the Urartian fortresses held firm, and the Assyrians were unable to conquer or destroy the kingdom. Indeed, what could even the mighty Assyrian army hope to achieve against walls such as Sargon describes, up to 60 feet (18 m) high, standing on the peaks of mountains?

Urartu soon recovered from Sargon's savage raid and regained its former level of power and prosperity. But storm clouds were gathering, and Urartu's days were numbered. The final blow, however, came not from the traditional enemy Assyria but from the rising powers of the Medes on the Iranian plateau to the east. In 612 B.C. they destroyed the great cities of Assyria and soon afterward turned their attention to Urartu. In 585 B.C. the great citadel of Van fell, and the kingdom passed into history. The prophet Jeremiah's appeal to the king of Ararat, or Urartu, for help against a new Iraqi despot, Nebuchadnezzar, came too late to a people already under a foreign yoke.

The following centuries saw a whole succession of foreign powers—Medes, Persians, Greeks, and Romans—in control of Armenia, until at length the very existence of Urartu, high up in its remote mountain fastness, was forgotten. It was only in 1827 that the western scholar Schulz arrived in a van and discovered inscriptions in a hitherto unknown language. But further progress was slow, and fifty years elapsed before the British Museum excavations at Toprakkale near Van first brought the kingdom of Urartu to popular notice. Indeed, it is really only since the Second World War that work by British, Turkish, and Russian archaeologists has begun to reveal once again something of the splendor of the ancient kingdom of Urartu.

[See also ANATOLIA; NEAR EAST: IRON AGE CIVILIZATIONS OF THE NEAR EAST; PERSIA.]

■ C. Burney and D. M. Lang, *The Peoples of the Hills* (1971). P. E. Zimansky, *Ecology and Empire: The Structure of the Urartian State* (1985).

Chris Scarre

URBAN ARCHAEOLOGY. Urban archaeology involves the application of archaeological methods to the study of cities and the process of urbanization. Archaeologists are interested in urban sites in part because of the close link between cities and civilization. Since they first emerged in Mesopotamia about 5,000 years ago, cities share the characteristics of relatively high populations (above 5,000), centralized political and administrative institutions, complex economies with specialization of labor, and social stratification. Archaeologists can recover information about these and other aspects of urbanization using specialized fieldwork methods developed for today's urban environment. Urban archaeology attracts widespread public interest, but sites are still being lost at a rapid rate.

History. Urban archaeology shares the roots of archaeology as a discipline. During the Renaissance, interest in human antiquity motivated early excavations in Rome and other Italian cities. Portions of *Herculaneum and Pompeii were explored more systematically during the eighteenth century. In 1870, Heinrich *Schliemann pioneered basic archaeological methods at Hissarlik, the site of Homeric *Troy in western Turkey. The existence of the Harrappan civilization was revealed through excavations at *Mohenjo-daro and *Harappa by Sir John Marshall in the 1920s. V. Gordon *Childe developed his concept of the Urban Revolution as the second greatest human development after agriculture as based on information from excavations at town sites throughout the Middle East. Excavations at *Anyang in the 1920s revealed the Bronze Age Shange Dynasty Culture of China. *Teotihuacán, the Valley of Mexico site of the largest prehistoric city in the New World (studied by Rene Millon and other archaeologists), represents both a city and a civilization.

Since World War II, the redevelopment of European and American cities has provided a new impetus for urban archaeology. Britain's war-damaged cities provided opportunities for archaeological study of sites dating back to Roman times that otherwise would be inaccessible. In redeveloped districts of *London, Winchester, *York, and Exeter, among many British cities, archaeologists have studied the evolution of urban settlement patterns, architecture, manufacturing, trade, and consumer behavior. The construction of urban transit corridors and underground parking facilities provides opportunities to study deeply buried sites. In Paris, construction of subterranean parking on the Isle de la Cite during the 1970s and 1980s revealed Gallo-Roman, medieval, and post-medieval sites. When the foundations of the castle of Charles V were discovered during construction at the Louvre Museum, planners successfully incorporated them into the design for the new subterranean museum galleries. Museum involvement in urban archaeology in London has facilitated public dissemination of results through exhibits, site tours, and publications.

American urban archaeology is a more recent development. The National Historic Preservation Act of 1966 provides for the protection and study of significant archaeological sites threatened by federal undertakings. Many states and some cities have enacted their own legislation protecting significant archaeological sites. Consequently, archaeologists have had opportunities and resources to investigate urban sites ignored until recently. Construction of transportation corridors through historic sections of Philadelphia, Boston, Atlanta, Knoxville, and Seattle helped to pioneer the archaeological study of those cities. Several American cities, including Alexandria, Virginia, and St.

Augustine, Florida, have active municipal urban archaeology programs.

Methods. Archaeologists have had to develop special methods to work in the urban environment. Sampling strategies, fieldwork, expenses, and public outreach are noticeably different than for rural sites.

Urban archaeologists must be opportunistic in their approach to sampling modern cities. Sites usually become available for excavation due to the exigencies of urban planning, not because of archaeological significance. For this reason, it is especially important that urban archaeologists establish research priorities for sites to be excavated. For example, there has been an ongoing debate about the continuity of the commercial function of towns in post-Roman Britain. The Pirenne thesis, named after historian Henri Pirenne (1862–1935), postulates that urban life in northern Europe all but ended with the expansion of Islam in the eighth century A.D. Redevelopment within the city of London during the 1970s and 1980s enabled archaeologists from the Museum of London to examine the physical evidence for waterfront development and trade for this time period in order to address this thesis. City archaeologists usually identify key research questions and the sites where they can best be addressed, negotiate with project sponsors and research teams, and ensure that the research design is adequately addressed.

Sampling individual urban sites can be problematic from research and curatorial perspectives. These sites often contain large amounts of landfill imported from other areas. During the nineteenth century, the city of Boston, Massachusetts doubled its area in this fashion. What constitutes an adequate sample of this type of fill for archaeological purposes? How can tens or hundreds of thousands of artifacts from these types of sites be processed and curated indefinitely, often at public expense? These are not traditional archaeological problems, and the answers must be decided on a case-by-case basis.

Historical documentation is essential for the sampling and interpretation of urban sites. Most, if not all, modern cities contain public records such as land deeds, probates, tax records, and maps. Private and commercial records may include account books and diaries, as well as drawings, paintings, and photographs of townscapes. This documentation must be carefully evaluated in formulating archaeological research designs. It is usually possible to identify the past owners and users of urban land parcels. This information may be helpful in targeting specific types of historic sites for archaeological investigation. In Alexandria, Virginia, tax and census records were used by urban archaeologist Pamela Cressey to develop an archaeological sampling strategy. In Charlestown, Massachusetts, archaeologists used insurance atlas maps to predict the locations of well-preserved sites in urban renewal areas. Archaeologist William Rathje examines demographic and income data about households whose contemporary garbage he samples. This has led to discoveries about consumer behavior that differ from those based on interviews and questionaires.

The methods of excavating urban sites are varied and often quite costly. Heavy equipment including backhoes and front-end loaders are routinely used for removing deposits lacking archaeological significance. Backdirt usually must be trucked away due to a lack of space on the site. Security measures require fencing and covering urban sites. Pumps are often required to evacuate ground- and rainwater from excavation units. However, equally rigorous recording methods are employed on urban as on rural sites. The Harris Matrix, developed by archaeologist Edward Harris for recording and analyzing complex stratigraphy, is often employed at urban archaeological sites.

Urban sites also provide good opportunities to educate and to involve the public in archaeology because of their proximity to large populations. Urban excavations typically receive considerable media coverage. Often, city dwellers may directly observe or participate in excavation and laboratory analysis. The Toronto Board of Education in Canada has incorporated archaeology into the public school curriculum and conducts excavations for this purpose. Excavated sites that are stabilized and displayed to the public can have didactic value.

Current Status. Urbanization is increasing worldwide and one consequence is the rapid loss of archaeological data. The enactment of legislation protecting urban archaeological resources has proven to be an effective way to slow this attrition of information. Still, there is no consensus among archaeologists about the theoretical orientation and priorities of urban archaeology. Urban archaeology is usually undertaken from a reactive rather than proactive posture. Public dissemination of information from urban excavations is far from adequate.

In both archaeology and anthropology the urban environment represents a relatively new frontier. Despite the difficulties they face, urban archaeologists have contributed to our understanding of the origins of urbanization and of modern urban problems in the areas of sanitation, transportation, housing, and social and material inequality. Urban archaeology has also captured the imagination of the public. As its methods become standardized and a broader comparative perspective is adopted, urban archaeology should make greater contributions to archaeological theory.

[*See also* BRITISH ISLES: THE INDUSTRIAL REVOLUTION; HISTORICAL ARCHAEOLOGY; INDUSTRIAL ARCHAEOLOGY; LANDSCAPE ARCHAEOLOGY; NORTH AMERICA: HISTORICAL ARCHAEOLOGY OF NORTH AMERICA; WASTE MANAGEMENT.]

■ Bert Salwen, "Archeology in Megalopolis," in *Research and Theory in Current Archaeology*, ed. Charles L. Redman (1973), pp. 151–163. Richard P. Schaedel, Jorge Hardoy, and Nora Scott Kinzer, eds., *Urbanization in the Americas from its Beginnings to the Present* (1978). Roy S. Dickens, Jr., ed., *Archaeology of Urban America* (1982). A. R. Hall and H. K. Kenward, eds., *Environmental Archaeology in the Urban Context*, CBA Research Report 43 (1982). Edward Staski, ed., *Living in Cities: Current Research in Urban Archaeology*, Historical Archaeology Special Publication Series 5 (1987).

Steven R. Pendery

URNFIELDS. The name "Urnfield" is applied to the category of site that characterizes the burial aspect of the Late Bronze Age of Europe. As it implies, burial urns, which were used to contain the cremated ashes of the deceased, were placed in pits which were themselves located in a defined cemetery area or "field." Along with the urn would usually be placed a number of other pots and nonceramic objects, typically cups and bowls, bronze ornaments (pins, rings), and personal objects (knives, razors), and beads of glass, bone, or clay. The number of graves in an urnfield also varies, from a few dozen to many hundreds. It is not possible to speak with any confidence of an average number because there are relatively few cases where one can be sure that all graves have been found.

Urnfields mark a major transition in the Bronze Age, from a burial rite that was predominantly by inhumation to one that was predominantly cremation. This change is thought to represent a fundamental change of belief systems from those prevailing in the Early and Middle Bronze Age. In fact, the change was not total, and some cemeteries contained inhumations as well as cremations.

It is usual to talk of an Urnfield Period and Urnfield cultures. The start of the period can be placed at around 1300 B.C., but the end is hard to pin down since the rite continues virtually unchanged into the Early Iron Age. In terms of conventional chronology, the Urnfield Period spans the divisions of the Bronze Age that were made by the German scholar Paul Reinecke, named Bronze D and Hallstatt A and B; the end of Hallstatt B lies around 800 B.C. A number of culture names are in use in central Europe. By far the most widespread group is that named after the Lausitz area of eastern Germany; this group extends from Germany into much of Poland and south to Bohemia and Moravia. Many other more local groups can be distinguished, for instance, the Knovíz group of northern Bohemia, or the Gava group of the Carpathian Basin. The cremation rite also extends far beyond central Europe, to France, Italy, Spain, Yugoslavia, and the Ukraine, even though the name "Urnfields" is not used in all these areas. Divisions between the different cultural groups are as much a matter of archaeological convenience as of prehistoric reality.

The very large numbers of burials known must represent an equally large living population. Statistics for this aspect are only available in crude form: from the area of modern Poland, for instance, there are thousands of known cemeteries and hundreds of graves in each. Allowing for survival factors, it is possible to arrive at a figure of more than one million for the buried population of Poland alone in this period; other areas were hardly less prolific, and strongly suggest a considerable increase in population over the preceding Early and Middle Bronze Age.

Cemetery Evidence. The cemetery at Przeczyce near Bytom in Silesia has been extensively analyzed. On this site there are 874 graves, 727 of which were inhumations and 132 cremations (the proportion of inhumations is unusually high). Analysis of the grave goods shows that though most graves contain at least one pot, there was a marked tendency for adult males to have more pots than other individuals, and for children to have few or no pots. Similarly with ornaments, tools, and weapons: whereas 269 graves contained ornaments of some form (usually simple pendants or rings), diadems (multiple bronze buttons to adorn the temples) occurred in only 15 graves, and tools and weapons in 37, of which 28 were equipped only with arrowheads. These figures suggest that material wealth was unequally distributed through society in the Urnfield world, but the range of goods represented is so much at variance with what is known to have been present from other types of finds that little confidence can be placed in them as true indicators of Urnfield social structure. On the other hand, finds of children's rattles and a set of bone pan-pipes indicate that concerns of sentimentality and artistic production had their place in Urnfield life.

At Sobiejuchy in west-central Poland, 518 cremation graves of a total of around 700 in an area of 1.2 acres (0.5 ha) have been analyzed. Pottery is again the commonest find; 346 graves have a single urn, 62 have two urns, and only a few have more. The entire cemetery produced only 109 bronze and 56 iron objects; there was also stone, glass, clay, and amber. The cemetery appears to have been utilized over time, with distinct chronological zones that are differ-

entially provided for in grave wealth and elaboration; it has been suggested by the excavators that this zonation correlates with phases of occupation and abandonment in the nearby fortified settlement site.

Not all burials in the Urnfield Period were made in cremation cemeteries. The "King's Grave" at Seddin in Brandenburg in northeastern Germany, for instance, was that of a wealthy individual buried with a set of fine metalwork and other objects in a slab-lined chamber sealed by a stone cairn under an enormous mound 262 feet (80 m) in diameter and 36 feet (11 m) high. This grave is one of a small group in the region that contains weapons and other prestige objects. A second group contains knives and a few other ornaments or toilet articles, while a third—the largest—contains only a single object. In this area urnfields as such do not appear; instead the tradition was much more akin to that of the Early Bronze Age, with individuals being buried in marked graves that were scattered thinly across the landscape. This pattern is rather unusual; in most Urnfield cemeteries there are no clear indications of strong social ranking.

Settlement. Large cemetery sites imply large and numerous settlement sites to accompany them. In general, these are much less well known than cemeteries, and have usually been recovered only by chance. They normally consist of numbers of pits and postholes from post-framed houses, as at Lovcicky in Moravia. Here there was a series of forty-eight post-built houses of varying forms; most were rectangular hall-like buildings, whereas one or two that were exceptionally long have been interpreted as belonging to the elite. At Zedau in eastern Germany the houses were smaller but similarly scattered, typical of agricultural villages based on mixed farming. At the same time, fortified settlements came into existence. Hilltop settlement began in a number of areas of Europe, though occupation was rather short-lived, perhaps extending over a few decades. Few such sites have been excavated on any scale. At the Wittnauer Horn in northern Switzerland, the narrow promontory was occupied by two rows of buildings separated by an open area or street. These *hill forts are complemented in certain lowland regions by wooden stockades, usually in wet areas or even on islands. Good examples are the Wasserburg at Bad Buchau, and *Biskupin, but dry-land versions of these are also known, for instance, at Sobiejuchy near Biskupin. Here, an area of 15 acres (6 ha) (four times the size of Biskupin) was surrounded by a rampart which was reinforced by wooden breakwaters. The interior was at one time or another densely populated with domestic occupation; individual houses have not been isolated, but hearths, ovens, and loom emplacements were present. This site, though occupied for only a few generations, served as a major center during its lifetime, with a population running into the thousands.

Economic indicators on this and other similar sites show that a mixed farming economy was being practiced, with the standard range of domesticated plants and animals; cattle and wheat were the favored food sources. An increased range of utilized food plants suggests that risks were being spread, either to counteract the vagaries of the climate or to increase overall food availability, or both: for instance, millet, a species that is drought-resistant and fast-growing, began to be cultivated in significant quantities. Celtic beans and a range of oil-bearing plants were also important.

Symbolism and Religion. Since the Urnfield Period was

prehistoric, we know nothing certain about religion and symbolism, but a large range of objects that have no apparent connection with utilitarian pursuits are known from the Urnfield world. Chief among these are the representations, usually in miniature form, of birds and animals, both as freestanding clay objects, and as appendages to and depictions on pottery and metalwork. Birds, especially water birds, were particularly favored. There are also large cauldrons, sometimes on wheels, believed to be cultic in purpose, and perhaps connected with rites involving water collection and utilization. On the other hand, fixed installations for cult purposes are few and controversial in interpretation.

The urnfields represent the material expression of a widely held set of views both in the field of belief systems and in social and political terms. Although we have no definite information on ethnic make-up, the likelihood is that Urnfield Europe was Celtic, and thus represents the immediate ancestor to the world of the Celtic Iron Age.

[See also BURIAL AND TOMBS; CELTS; EUROPE: THE EUROPEAN BRONZE AGE.]

■ J. M. Coles and A. F. Harding, The Bronze Age in Europe (1979). Archaeological Institute of the Czechoslovak Academy of Sciences, Die Urnenfelderkulturen Mitteleuropas (1987).

Anthony F. Harding

URUK lies in the desert about 9 miles (15 km) east of the present course of the Euphrates, 155 miles (250 km) south of Baghdad. Its mounds, encircled by a 5,000-year-old rampart 6.2 miles (10 km) in circumference, comprise the largest archaeological site in southern Iraq. Although the Sumerians named the city Unu, Akkadian speakers called it Uruk, the name by which it is known today. The Akkadian name appears in the Bible as Erech and is preserved in the Arabic name for its ruins, Warka.

William Kennet Loftus first explored Uruk in the mid-nineteenth century, but systematic excavations were not undertaken until the Deutsche Orient-Gesellschaft began work in 1912. Except during periods of enforced absence the Germans have continued at the site ever since, painstakingly bringing to light evidence of some of the most momentous firsts in human history.

Established during the Úbaid Period (fifth millennium B.C.), Uruk grew to urban proportions during the Early and Middle Uruk Periods (early fourth millennium B.C.). By the Late Uruk period (late fourth millennium B.C.) the city was, at 247 acres (100 ha), the largest settlement in Sumer, the premier city in the world's first urban society.

In Late Uruk times the city encompassed two distinct centers, Eanna, dedicated to the city goddess Inanna, and Kullaba, which, on the basis of much later evidence, was perhaps devoted to the sky god An. The temple platform in Kullaba, first constructed in the Úbaid Period, grew taller with every renovation so that by 3000 B.C. it had become a 43-foot (13-m)-high tower. The temple on top of this proto-ziggurat had a typical tripartite plan, consisting of a long central room, with altar and offering table, flanked on either of its long sides by a row of smaller rooms. This was the White Temple, so named because of its gypsum plaster coating.

At Eanna .3 miles (.5 km) east of Kullaba, repeated demolition and rebuilding during Late Uruk times left only fragmentary walls to represent a stratified series of major buildings (Archaic Levels V–IV). Although nothing was found to indicate their functions, many had features usually associated with early Sumerian temples: tripartite layouts and niche-and-buttress facades. Their walls were frequently decorated with stone or terra-cotta cones arranged so that their flat ends formed a mosaic of multicolored geometric patterns. Although little specific information is known about these buildings, their large size (one measured 263 by 164 feet [80 by 50 m]), their elaborate decoration, and the frequency with which they were demolished and replaced are all indicative of the power and resources available to the city's rulers.

Around 3000 B.C. the White Temple and its high platform were completely buried under a gigantic terrace. At the same time the buildings of Eanna were torn down, filled in, and leveled off, and a new temple platform was erected (Archaic Level III). For nearly 3,000 years thereafter, the precinct of Eanna remained the focus of Uruk's civic existence.

In excavating the debris used to level up Eanna in 3000 B.C., the Germans made one of their most important discoveries, thousands of fragmentary clay tablets bearing pictographs, the earliest written language in the world and the immediate ancestor of cuneiform *writing. Although the tablets were found out of context, it is virtually certain that they originally belonged to the latest phase of Archaic Level IV. Because these earliest signs, about 1,200 in all, were pictographic, they could in theory represent any language. It is most probable, however, that their language was Sumerian, as was demonstrably the case in Archaic Level III. These documents demonstrate that writing was invented to meet the needs of a burgeoning bureaucracy, to keep track of crops, livestock, and other goods. Among the texts are lexical lists, apparently used in the training of scribes. One of these, a list of titles and professions, provides a glimpse into the complexity of Uruk's evolving social hierarchy.

Also attributed to Archaic Level IV, but found in later contexts, are several pieces of sculpture that demonstrate the extraordinary accomplishment of Uruk's early artists: an inlaid limestone mask, perhaps representing the face of Inanna; the statuette of a ruler in an attitude of devotion; and a carved vase showing offerings being brought before Inanna.

Cylinder seals, first appearing in Archaic Level IV, show an equally high level of craftsmanship, depicting scenes of religious processions, the ruler's activities, and animals—domesticated, wild, and mythological. Seals were important new tools for early bureaucrats. When impressed on clay sealings, bullae, or tablets, their complex, individuated scenes could be used to identify those in whose presence or on whose authority a variety of transactions took place.

Uruk expanded in size to 988 acres (400 ha) around 2900 B.C. Regional surveys have shown that dwellers in the immediate vicinity abandoned their villages and moved behind the enormous new rampart that protected what was almost certainly the largest city in the world. In the early third millennium Uruk was at the apex of its trajectory; its rulers, men like Gilgamesh, would appear in later epics as superhuman figures.

At the end of the third millennium Ur-Nammu of *Ur built the ziggurat complex in Eanna that today dominates the ruins of the site, but by this time Uruk's heyday was past. Although later Babylonian and Assyrian rulers continued to maintain the Eanna complex until the sixth century B.C., the city was no longer a major player in Mesopotamian affairs.

Toward the end of its long history, Uruk experienced a brief renaissance under the Seleucids (third–second centuries B.C.). Eanna was renovated, but the Ishtar (Inanna) cult moved to one of two new monumental temples constructed in traditional Babylonian style: the Eshgal, Ishtar's new home, and the Bit Resh, which included the Anu / Antum temple and the Anu ziggurat.

Uruk's final masters, the Parthians, built the small temple to Gareus around A.D. 100. Gareus was a new god at Uruk and his temple was a pastiche of Babylonian and Greco-Roman elements. Thus Uruk, present at the creation of Mesopotamian civilization, likewise witnessed its demise.

[*See also* MESOPOTAMIA, *articles on* THE RISE OF URBAN CULTURE, SUMER AND AKKAD; NEAR EAST: THE NEOLITHIC AND CHALCOLITHIC (PRE-BRONZE-AGE) PERIODS IN THE NEAR EAST; UR.]

■ Robert McC. Adams and Hans J. Nissen, *The Uruk Countryside* (1972). Susan B. Downey, *Mesopotamian Religious Architecture, Alexander Through the Parthians* (1988). Hans J. Nissen, *The Early History of the Ancient Near East, 9000–2000* B.C. (1988). Hans J. Nissen, Peter Damerow, and Robert K. Englund, *Archaic Bookkeeping* (1993).

James A. Armstrong

V

VALDIVIA CULTURE. The Valdivia Culture occupied the western lowlands and coastal region of Ecuador during the Early Formative Period (3500–1500 B.C.) and represents the beginnings of settled village life in that area. Originally identified at the type-site of Valdivia in coastal Guayas Province by Ecuadorian Emilio Estrada, it was subsequently investigated by Smithsonian archaeologists Betty Meggers and Clifford Evans in the early 1960s. The type-site is situated at the mouth of the Valdivia River valley, immediately adjacent to seashore and estuary habitats. Cultural refuse pertaining to the Valdivia occupation covers some 4.2 acres (1.7 ha) on the slope and base of a low spur. Deep excavations were conducted here in 1961 by thick arbitrary levels and yielded abundant remains of Valdivia pottery, "Venus" figurines, chipped stone artifacts, fire-modified rock, and faunal material of terrestrial, fish, and shellfish species. No visible stratigraphy was recognized during excavation, however, and no archaeological features were identified. On the basis of the unique ceramic artifacts and associated radiocarbon dates recovered here, the investigators established a four-phase ceramic sequence (Phases A through D) that was thought to represent slight developmental change through time. Since the Phase A ceramic assemblage was considered at the time to represent the earliest pottery in the New World, its relative sophistication raised the question of origins. This led the investigators to hypothesize a trans-Pacific diffusion of this pottery style from the Neolithic *Jomon tradition of Japan in the latter half of the third millennium B.C. Their argument was subsequently challenged by a number of scholars and was eventually refuted in the early 1970s by the discovery of Valdivia ceramics that predated Phase A both at the Valdivia type-site itself and at Loma Alta, a village site located 5.6 miles (9 km) up the Valdivia Valley. Both the littoral location of the type-site and its obvious reliance on marine and estuarine subsistence resources prompted the investigators to prematurely characterize the entire Valdivia culture as a semisedentary maritime adaptation of egalitarian fishermen and shellfish gatherers having only a marginal reliance on horticulture.

Subsequent research at other important coastal sites, such as San Pablo, Real Alto, and Salango, as well as inland sites, such as Loma Alta, Colimes, and San Lorenzo del Mate, has promoted considerable rethinking on the nature of Valdivia Culture, including its origins, settlement-subsistence system, social organization, and cosmological beliefs. Archaeologist Donald Lathrap has persuasively argued that Valdivia represents a "tropical forest culture" pattern with an essentially inland riverine settlement focus whose ultimate origins are linked to early population dispersals from the Amazon Basin. Newer subsistence data indicate a mixed economy of floodplain horticultural production (based on maize, beans, root crops, cotton, and gourds), hunting, fishing, and the gathering of wild plants and shellfish. Certain shoreline settlements, such as the type-site, are viewed as sites specialized in the exploitation and exchange of maritime and estuarine resources. Perhaps more important, these studies have shed new light on Valdivia chronology and the pace of social change during its 2,000-year time span. An eight-phase ceramic sequence established by Betsy Hill has permitted a more precise delineation of temporal trends in regional settlement patterns and intra-site spatial organization.

Excavations at Real Alto, in particular, have helped transform our understanding of Valdivia society in terms of chronology and social change, community plan and settlement pattern evolution, household organization, and the nature of Valdivia agricultural production. Progressive shifts toward greater population density, increased reliance on cultivated plants, and greater sociopolitical complexity have been identified. The Early Valdivia village was laid out in a horseshoe shape with small flimsy bent-pole dwellings forming a ring around a small open plaza. Each dwelling probably housed a nuclear family. At the opening of the U-shaped plan is evidence of ritual activity, presumably of a communal nature. By Phase 3, the Real Alto village grew to a maximum size of 31 acres (12.4 ha). Dwellings again form a dense ring around a long plaza, but the house structures become much larger and more permanent in their construction, indicating extended family dwellings having considerable longevity. At the center of the new configuration are two small opposing mounds each supporting a ceremonial structure. To the west is a specialized funerary facility or "charnel house," whereas the eastern mound supported a communal structure having ritual functions, judging from its internal midden refuse. By Late Valdivia times (Phases 6–7), the habitation area becomes reduced within the village, as small daughter settlements appear adjacent to floodplain agricultural plots and the ceremonial precinct begins to serve a wider local area.

It is now clear that Valdivia represents a dynamic, fully sedentary society of village horticulturalists characterized by progressive demographic growth and an increasing degree of social ranking and status inequality through time. Beginning as early as Middle Valdivia times, long-distance maritime trade with the complex societies of coastal Peru may have provided an impetus for social change leading to greater complexity in the later Valdivia phases. There is also evidence of a progressive geographic expansion of Valdivia peoples to the north and to the south out of the Guayas Province heartland. Beginning in Middle Valdivia times (Phase 3), when settlements appear on the off-shore islands of La Plata and Puná, this outward colonization culminated in Terminal Valdivia times (Phase 8), when large inland ceremonial centers with satellite communities appear in the wetter environments to the north and to the south. Both the San Isidro site in northern Manabi and the La Emergenciana site in El Oro represent large Phase 8 civic-ceremonial centers with monumental public architecture of a magnitude not seen in earlier Valdivia phases.

[*See also* SOUTH AMERICA: LOWLANDS CULTURES OF SOUTH AMERICA.]

■ Betty J. Meggers, Clifford Evans, and Emilio Estrada, *Early Formative Period of Coastal Ecuador: The Valdivia and Machalilla Phases* (1965). Betsy D. Hill, "A New Chronology of the Valdivia Ceramic Complex from the Coastal Zone of Guayas Province, Ecuador," *Ñawpa Pacha* 10–12 (1972–1974): 1–32. Donald W. Lathrap, *Ancient Ecuador: Culture, Clay, and Creativity, 3000–300 BC* (1975). Donald W. Lathrap, Jorge G. Marcos, and James A. Zeidler, "Real Alto: An Ancient Ceremonial Center," *Archaeology* 30 (1977): 2–13. Jonathan E. Damp, "Architecture of the Early Valdivia Village," *American Antiquity* 49 (1984): 573–585. Deborah M. Pearsall, "An Overview of Formative Period Subsistence in Ecuador: Paleoethnobotanical Data and Perspectives," in *Diet and Subsistence: Current Archaeological Perspectives*, ed. Brenda V. Kennedy and Genevieve M. LeMoine (1988), pp. 149–164. James A. Zeidler, "Maritime Exchange in the Early Formative Period of Ecuador: Geo-political Origins of Uneven Development," *Research in Economic Anthropology* 13 (1991): 247–268.

James A. Zeidler

VALLEY OF THE KINGS, or Wadi el-Biban el-Moluk, lies on the west bank of the Nile, opposite the city of Luxor, behind the curtain of cliffs that rise behind the sites of the royal mortuary temples and private tomb chapels of the Egyptian New Kingdom. Containing the tombs of the kings of that period, it comprises two distinct branches, approached via a long road from the north (the Wadyein) and a pathway over the cliffs from the south. The latter begins at the village of Deir el-Medina, where the state-supported work force responsible for building the royal tombs resided.

Sixty-two tombs have received official numbers, of which the following have been identified with historical figures (listed in chronological order):

Eighteenth Dynasty
20 Thutmose I, usurped by Hatshepsut
42 Thutmose II
34 Thutmose III
38 Thutmose I (reburial)
35 Amunhotpe II
48 Amenemopet (Vizier)
45 Userhat (Overseer of the Fields of Amun)
43 Thutmose IV
36 Maihirpri (Fanbearer)
22 Amunhotpe III
46 Yuya and Tjuiu (parents-in-laws of Amunhotpe III)
55 Smenkhkare / Neferneferuaten (reburial)
62 Tutankhamun
23 Ay
57 Horemheb

Nineteenth Dynasty
16 Rameses I
17 Sethy I
7 Rameses II
5 Amenhirkopshef, Ramesse, Meryatum, and others (sons of Rameses II)
8 Merenptah
15 Sethy II
10 Amenmesse

47 Siptah
14 Tawosret, usurped by Sethnakhte
13 Bay (Chancellor)

Twentieth Dynasty
11 Rameses III
3 Son of Rameses III
2 Rameses IV
9 Rameses V, finished for Rameses VI
1 Rameses VII
6 Rameses IX
19 Montjuhirkopshef (son of Rameses IX)
18 Rameses X
4 Rameses XI

The first tomb certainly known to have been cut in the valley was for Thutmose I of the Eighteenth Dynasty. Like all the royal sepulchers of that dynasty, it was cut in an inconspicuous location, and was covered after the burial. The tomb is uneven in form, later tombs becoming increasingly regular in their design; stone sarcophagi were introduced in the reign of Thutmose II. Tombs down to the reign of Amunhotpe III feature a sharp bend to the left at their midpoints, and a curious decorative scheme in the burial chamber. This included the painting of the walls the color of old papyrus and the inscription of texts from the *Book of Imyduat* with a pen, giving the impression of a gigantic ancient manuscript. Oval burial chambers are a feature of the reigns of Thutmose II and III, but six-pillared rectangular halls, with a sunken crypt at the far end, for the sarcophagus, are then usual until the early Nineteenth Dynasty.

Although the valley was primarily intended for kings, a number of highly placed private individuals had small tombs in the valley, normally consisting of only one or two small rooms, approached by a shaft or passage. Some royal tombs also contained the bodies of family members who had died during the king's reign, but without any particular architectural provision being made for these additional interments.

Amunhotpe III moved the site of his tomb from the previously utilized Eastern branch to the Western. After the hiatus caused by the interment of Akhenaten at Tell el-Amarna, royal burials were moved back to the valley: Tutankhamun was laid to rest in an adapted private tomb in the Eastern branch, but his successor, Ay, was placed in a previously begun sepulcher in the Western arm of the valley, the last king to be buried there.

Eighteenth Dynasty tombs after the early years of Hatshepsut had cartouche-form sarcophagi; however, the last kings of the dynasty possessed rectangular ones, with female divine figures at the corners. Their tombs also differed from earlier ones in having straight axes, a feature that continued to be used for the rest of the valley's history. The last Eighteenth Dynasty tomb, that of Horemheb, replaced painted decoration with decoration in carved relief, a style that continued into later dynasties.

While the tombs of most Eighteenth Dynasty kings were robbed in antiquity, the tomb of Tutankhamun was found largely intact and therefore provides an indication of the characteristic arrangement of funerary goods. A typical royal tomb of the period had its contents centered on the burial chamber, with a number of side rooms opening off it. The sarcophagus was surrounded by several portable shrines, with the canopic chest for the internal organs placed at the foot end. The pillared part of the chamber contained the largest items of funerary equipment, including beds, chairs, and other furniture. Grain and water were housed in a storeroom opposite the foot of the sarcophagus, with offerings of meat placed opposite the head. It seems that figures of the gods, housed in shrines, and items such as chariots were ideally placed in the large columned chamber that usually lay near the midpoint of the tomb's central axis.

A number of major alterations in the overall design of the royal tomb may be seen to have occurred under Rameses II. First, the orientation of the burial chamber changed so that the columns, now numbering eight, ran in two rows across the chamber, rather than in two rows along the axis of the room. The sunken crypt was now placed in the middle of the inner chamber, in contrast to its former position at the far end. Elsewhere, decoration can be seen on the exterior lintel and jambs of the entrance to the tomb: It was only in the previous reign, of Sethy I, that reliefs had been extended out from the innermost chambers to the approach corridors.

Stone sarcophagi were temporarily abandoned by Sethy I and Rameses II in favor of wooden cases, enclosing newly introduced alabaster anthropoid coffins. Stone sarcophagi were, however, reintroduced by Merenptah, whose mummy was encased in a pair of wood and/or gold coffins, an alabaster coffin, and three granite sarcophagi. Later kings, down to the middle of the Twentieth Dynasty, were laid to rest in one stone sarcophagus, one stone coffin, and a pair of gilded wood or cartonnage (linen and plaster composition) inner cases.

As the Ramesside Period progressed, the prominence of the tomb entrance steadily increased, and it is impossible that any sepulchers after the very first part of the Twentieth Dynasty could ever have been concealed. The entrances were protected solely by sealed wooden doors, framed by large rock cuttings that stood a number of meters above the ancient valley floor. Security depended on the vigilance of the necropolis police.

The last tomb begun in the valley was that of Rameses XI, a huge excavation whose decoration was barely begun before being abandoned. The king lived, died, and was probably buried in the north of Egypt. The tomb may have been considered briefly for usurpation by the Twenty-first Dynasty king of Thebes, Pinudjem I, but was never used for royal interment. Later burials in the valley were restricted to intrusive interments in existing tombs.

Robbery of tombs in the valley began fairly early in its history. The first recorded intrusion involved the tomb of Thutmose IV in the reign of Horemheb, but large-scale plundering really got under way in the time of the later Ramesside kings. During the Twenty-first Dynasty, there began a policy of dismantling those burials that had been penetrated, recycling such funerary equipment as survived, and transferring the royal mummies to new communal locations. A considerable number of such transferrals are known to have occurred, until all bodies, except for those whose tomb locations were by now wholly lost, came to rest in two spots. Ten were concealed in the tomb of Amunhotpe II, while some forty corpses were placed in the tomb of the High Priest of Amun, Pinudjem II, near Deir el-Bahari; the latter cache was largely assembled in the second half of the reign of Shoshenq I of the Twenty-second Dynasty.

In addition to its tombs, the valley has also revealed the remains of a number of workmen's huts. Although the village in which tomb workers lived on a permanent basis lay on the opposite side of the cliffs, at Deir el-Medina, the working week was spent in a settlement on the ridge overlooking the valley, with a number of huts for daytime use dotted around the valley floor. It was a group of these, erected in the Twentieth Dynasty, that concealed the entrance of the earlier tomb of Tutankhamun.

The tombs of the Valley of the Kings are all decorated with scenes relating to the various *Books* describing the sun god's nocturnal voyage through the underworld, and are thus key documents for understanding such aspects of the ancient Egyptian religion. The sepulcher contents also provide us with a knowledge of the key items of funerary equipment, likewise of importance from the point of view of understanding mortuary practices. In addition, the superlative artistic quality of many of the paintings, reliefs, and objects in the tombs sheds light on society under the New Kingdom.

A number of tombs in the Valley of the Kings have lain open since ancient times, in particular those of the Nineteenth and Twentieth Dynasties. The remainder have been opened since the early years of the nineteenth century, key names in their exploration being Giovanni *Belzoni, Victor Loret, Theodore Davis, and Howard Carter. After a long hiatus, work has resumed in recent years on reclearing a number of previously partly-known tombs. This work has led to renewed concern about the conservation of the tombs, which is presently being reassessed by the Supreme Council for Antiquities of the Egyptian government.

[*See also* EGYPT: NEW KINGDOM EGYPT; TUTANKHAMUN'S TOMB.]

■ B. Porter and R. B. Moss, *Topographical Bibliography of Ancient Egyptian Hieroglyphic Texts, Reliefs, and Paintings*, 2nd ed., I:2 (1964). E. Thomas, *Royal Necropolis of Thebes* (1966). J. Cerny, *The Valley of the Kings* (1973). J. Romer, *Valley of the Kings* (1981). E. Hornung, *The Valley of the Kings: Horizon of Eternity* (1990). C. N. Reeves, *Valley of the Kings: The Decline of a Royal Necropolis* (1990). C. N. Reeves, ed., *After Tutankhamūn* (1992). A. M. Dodson, *Canopic Equipment of the Kings of Egypt* (1994).

Aidan Dodson

VARNA. The Varna cemetery is located on the outskirts of the Black Sea resort of Varna, Bulgaria. In 1972, drainage operations cut through a grave in the richest area of the cemetery. Since then, excavations by Dr. Ivan Ivanov have uncovered 281 graves. The significance of Varna is that it constitutes the earliest floruit of gold metallurgy in the world, dating to the middle phase of the Balkan Copper Age (early fourth millennium B.C.).

The cemetery comprises flat graves with individuals buried in shallow pits. There are two classes of burial rite: graves with and without skeletons. The former are the commonest, mostly extended inhumations on the back, with goldwork rare: included here are ten poorly furnished contracted inhumations. The second category, graves without skeletons, are of two types: cenotaph graves, where grave goods are laid out as if the body were present, and mask graves, where a life-size clay mask represents the body. Most cenotaph graves are poor, though some have gold- and copper-work, whereas three cenotaphs and three mask graves are extremely rich. Adult females and males are buried with rich or poor artifacts, while children younger than twelve years are not represented.

The grave goods represent the accumulation of more prestige goods than on any other coeval site in eastern Europe. Tombs 4 and 43 each contained over 3.3 pounds (1.5 kg) of gold, Tomb 1 had over 2.2 pounds (1 kg), and Tomb 36 almost 1.7 pounds (0.8 kg) and 853 objects. These sumptuous artifacts indicate a mastery of the techniques of beaten sheet-metal-working, wire production, and gold vessel painting. The majority of gold finds has no parallels anywhere else in Eurasia: the diadem from Tomb 3, appliqués often in the form of a bull, gold-plated axe-shafts, the solid gold astragalus, and the penis sheath from Tomb 43. The copper finds include shaft-hole axes, awls, chisels, and beads. Beads are also made of *Spondylus* and *Dentalium* shells, as well as bone, marble, carnelian, and limestone. Marble rhyta, dishes, axes, and stylized figurines are found, the latter with metal earrings. Obsidian and flint blades up to 16 inches (40 cm) in length were made using pressure-flaking techniques. The ceramics are typically decorated with geometric designs outlined in graphite.

Whereas part of the high status of these grave goods derives from their workmanship and aesthetic qualities, the distance over which they were exchanged provided additional value. Much of the gold derived from southeastern Bulgaria, like the marble and carnelian. Some gold came from Transylvania. The obsidian was from northeastern Hungary. Most of the copper and graphite came from central Bulgarian mines. *Spondylus* and *Dentalium* were from the Aegean, the honey-colored flint from northeastern Bulgaria. The richest graves contained symbols characteristic of different regional communities: the gold astragalus characteristic of northwestern Bulgaria, the gold-painted vase of central Bulgaria and a marble figurine of southern Bulgaria. Products and symbols came from up to 1,543 miles (700 km) away, underlining Varna's integration into wide-ranging exchange and ritual networks covering much of eastern Europe.

The central question raised by Varna is why such an accumulation of finery was concentrated in one cemetery. When Varna was first discovered, there was an overwhelming contrast between the wealth of its finds and the apparently egalitarian nature of contemporary tell settlements. More recently, the excavation of Bulgarian sites such as Ovvcarovo and Poljanica indicates architectural and social differentiation on tells, with the accumulation of household or lineage wealth. Varna takes this process one stage further, for it symbolizes burial not only of local elites but of the leaders of an interregional alliance. The deposition of such wealth in relatively few graves at Varna indicates competitive grave-good deposition by regional lineages to secure the role of alliance leader—a sign of widespread and successful social integration at a time when accumulation of wealth first became possible.

[*See also* EUROPE: THE EUROPEAN COPPER AGE; METALLURGY: METALLURGY IN THE OLD WORLD.]

■ *Studia Praehistorica* (Sofia) vols. 1–2 (collection of articles about Varna) (1975). Ivan Ivanov, *Treasures of the Varna Chalcolithic Necropolis* (1977). Alexander Fol & Jan Lichardus, eds., *Power, Society and Gold: The Varna Cemetery (Bulgaria) and the Start of a New European Civilisation* (1988). National Museums Group Paris, *The First Gold in the World in Bulgaria, 5th Millennium BC* (1989). John Chapman, "The Creation of Social Arenas in the Neolithic and Copper Age of S.E. Europe: The Case of Varna," in *Sacred and Profane*, eds. Paul Garwood, David Jennings, Robin Skeates, and Judith Toms (1991), pp. 152–170.

John Chapman

VENUS FIGURINES. The class of artifacts known as Venus figurines comprises an extremely heterogeneous body of artifactual material from Eurasia, dating to the Upper Paleolithic Period. Venus figurines include, on the one hand, small and easily transportable three-dimensional artifacts or images incised on portable supports, and on the other hand, two-dimensional images deeply carved, light incised, and/or painted onto fixed surfaces such as cave or rock-shelter walls. They range in height from 3 cm to 40 cm or more. While some researchers include in this class abstract images (so-called "vulvae" and forms resembling an elongated "S" or upside-down "P"), these are not discussed here.

The best-studied and most oft-pictured specimens in the "Venus figurine" category are the realistically rendered and almost voluptuous images of the female body, but these are not representative of the class as a whole. There are also clear portrayals of the male body (e.g., from Brassempouy, Laussel, and Dolní Věstonice) as well as numerous generalized anthropomorphs (e.g., examples from Sireuil, Tursac, Grimaldi, Dolní Věstonice, and Malt'a). Many specimens appear to be purposefully androgynous, and those with only faces cannot be sexed at all (e.g., specimens from Brassempouy, Mas d'Azil, Bédeilhac, and Dolní Věstonice). Some may be no more than incomplete rough-outs (or *ébauches*), and a rare few appear to be composite images of anthropomorphs and animals (i.e., Grimaldi, Laussel, Hohlenstein-Städel). There are examples with detailed facial features (e.g., from Malt'a, Buret, and Dolní Věstonice), pronounced coiffures but no facial details (e.g., Brassempouy and Willendorf), and many more with neither face, hair, hands, nor feet rendered in any detail. Some specimens, mostly from the Ukraine and Siberia, have body elaboration interpreted as clothing, belts, and/or tattoos (e.g., especially from the Kostenki group and Buret).

Beyond superficial morphology these artifacts have been worked from many different raw materials, each possessing unique physical qualities that were likely selected for their different attributes of workability, availability, and/or overall surface appearance. Venus figurines were made from ivory, serpentine, schist, limestone, hematite, lignite, calcite, fired clay, steatite, and a few of bone or antler. While they have been the subject of scholarly attention for more than a century, a detailed understanding of the sequence of techniques employed to fabricate them (in all their diversity) has been sorely lacking. Work has only recently been started to study the relationship between raw materials, techniques of fabrication, morphological appearance, and prehistoric significance.

Most coffee-table art books and many well-known studies highlight only what are considered to be the most visually striking specimens. Yet Venus figurines include flat and apparently pre-pubescent female subjects, images interpreted to be in various stages of pregnancy or of the general female life cycle, as well as several obviously male specimens. The preference in allowing such a heterogeneous class of artifacts to be represented by the most voluptuous examples perhaps says more about the analysts than it does about the artifacts. It betrays their extraordinary diversity in morphology, raw materials, technologies of production, and archaeological contexts through time and space. Some theories to explain their prehistoric significance are now questioned because they have overemphasized specimens representing only one side of the morphological system.

Temporal and Spatial Distribution. Venus figurines date to three periods of the Upper Paleolithic. They appear in the archaeological record between approximately 31,000 and 9000 B.P., but chronometric dating is problematic on several counts. Their distribution through both time and space is episodic. *Western Europe:* the earliest examples here date to the Gravettian (ca. 26,000 to 21,000 B.P.) and the Magdalenian (ca. 12,300 to 9000 B.P.), with most specimens associated with cave and rock shelter sites. (The earliest renderings from the French Aurignacian, ca. 31,000 to 28,000 B.P., are the problematic so-called "vulvae" forms not discussed here.) *Central Europe:* specimens are primarily associated with the Pavlovian (ca. 31,000 to 24,000 B.P.); *Ukraine:* anthropomorphic imagery is found throughout the Kostenki-Avdeevo culture period (ca. 26,000 to 12,500 B.P.), and comes almost exclusively from open-air occupation sites; *Siberian* images date to the so-called Eastern Gravettian (primarily ca. 21,000 to 19,000 B.P.). Significantly, some regions with well-established records of Upper Paleolithic human occupation have no evidence of anthropomorphic imagery, including the Cantabrian region of northern Spain and the Mediterranean region of southwestern Europe (with the sole exception of Italy).

Explanatory Theories. Most explanatory theories treat Venus figurines as a homogeneous class of data and collapse together more than 20,000 years of varied production. Portable and immobile specimens are lumped together, and what may be significant regional and temporal differences in technologies, raw materials, and styles are often ignored. Contextual differences between those specimens found at open-air sites, in cave and / or rock shelters, and other geographic locales are typically underestimated.

Functionalist Accounts. Today it is generally thought that Upper Paleolithic visual imagery, including Venus figurines, transmitted through stylistic means ecological and / or social information necessary to group survival. One of the primary explanatory accounts for the appearance and geographic distribution of Venus figurines focuses on ecological stress associated with the ice sheets advancing well into northern Europe 20,000 to 16,000 years ago. According to this account, as resources became more difficult to obtain, areas remaining occupied would have been able to sustain only low population densities. Alliance networks forged by the exchange of marriage partners could have counterbalanced these problems, and some researchers believe that Venus figurines played an important role in symbolizing and communicating information related to mating alliances. The geographically widespread production of Venus figurines as part of a system of information exchange could have permitted small groups of prehistoric hunter-gatherers to remain in areas that, without alliance connections, they might otherwise have had to abandon.

A second and far more questionable set of functionalist interpretations derives from sociobiology. According to several authors, these are representations of female biology that were fabricated and used for erotic and sexual reasons by males and for male gratification and / or education. While some of these explanations highlight the sensuality of the voluptuous three-dimensional images and argue that they were used as prehistoric sex toys or educational aids, others suggest that they served as trophies to mark "brave" acts of rape, kidnapping, and possibly murder. A genetic (and thus evolutionary) advantage was supposedly conferred upon the makers / users, either by teaching and practicing lovemaking skills or by publicizing physical prowess and thereby gaining social advantage among one's peers. The inherently androcentric and heterosexist bias in assumptions underpinning these accounts has now come under close scrutiny and they are today considered far less plausible than when originally proposed.

Gynecological Accounts. According to some, different Venus figurines literally depict physiological processes associated with pregnancy and / or childbirth or else signify the entire female life cycle. Some researchers note that aspects of parturition are well represented, while still others stress that the subject matter is womanhood and not just motherhood. In some ways these (and other related) contemporary theories build on, but also challenge the simplicity of, turn-of-the-century notions that they were symbols of female fertility and magic (hence in part explaining their original appellation—Venus).

Future Directions for Research. The use of multiple lines of evidence is a time-honored way to understand the significance of prehistoric material culture. Attention to different kinds of site context, detailed understanding of various techniques of fabrication, recognition of their diverse morphologies and raw material, site-specific spatial information, and consideration of other classes of artifacts with which Venus figurines were discovered may all help turn attention away from what is compelling today and toward whatever might have made them compelling in prehistory.

[*See also* EUROPE: THE EUROPEAN PALEOLITHIC PERIOD; PALEOLITHIC: UPPER PALEOLITHIC; ROCK ART: PALEOLITHIC ART.]

■ Z. A. Abramova, "Palaeolithic Art in the USSR," *Arctic Anthropology* 4 (1967): 1–179. Desmond Collins and John Onians, "The Origins of Art," *Art History* 1 (1978): 1–25. Randall Eaton, "The Evolution of Trophy Hunting," *Carnivore* 1 (1978): 110–121. Randall Eaton, "Mediations on the Origin of Art as Trophyism," *Carnivore* 2 (1979): 6–8. Patricia Rice, "Prehistoric Venuses: Symbols of Motherhood or Womanhood?" *Journal of Anthropological Archaeology* 37 (1981): 402–414. Marija Gimbutas, *The Goddesses and Gods of Old Europe* (1982). R. Dale Guthrie, "Ethological Observations From Palaeolithic Art," in *La Contribution de la Zoologie et de l'Ethologie à l'Interprétation de l'Art des Peuples Chasseurs Préhistoriques*, eds. Hans-Georg Bandi, et al. (1984), pp. 35–74. Mariana Gvozdover, "Female Imagery in the Palaeolithic," *Soviet Anthropology and Archaeology* 27 (1989): 8–94. Sarah Nelson, "Diversity of the Upper Palaeolithic 'Venus' Figurines and Archaeological Mythology," in *Powers of Observation: Alternative Views in Archaeology*, eds. Sarah Nelson and Alice Kehoe (1990), pp. 11–22. Clive Gamble, "The Social Context for European Palaeolithic Art," *Proceedings of the Prehistoric Society* 57 (1991): 3–15. Marcia-Anne Dobres, "Re-Presentations of Palaeolithic Visual Imagery: Simulacra and Their Alternatives," *Kroeber Anthropological Society Papers* 73–74 (1992): 1–25. Marcia-Anne Dobres, "Reconsidering Venus Figurines: A Feminist Inspired Reanalysis," in *Ancient Images, Ancient Thought: The Archaeology of Ideology*, eds. A. Sean Goldsmith, et al. (1992), pp. 245–262. Henri Delporte, *L'Image de la Femme dans l'Art Préhistorique* (2nd Edition, 1993). Henri Delporte, "Gravettian Female Figurines: A Regional Survey," in *Before Lascaux: The Complex Record of the Early Upper Palaeolithic*, eds. Heidi Knecht, et al. (1993), pp. 243–257. Jean-Pierre Duhard, *Réalisme de l'Image Féminine Paléolithique* (1993).

Marcia-Anne Dobres

VIJAYANAGARA. Located on the southern bank of the Tungabhadra River in the semiarid Deccan Plateau of Southern India, Vijayanagara was the capital of a vast empire that dominated south India from the fourteenth through sixteenth centuries A.D. The city was founded at the site of a small temple center, dated to the eleventh century A.D. From the founding of the empire around 1350, Vijayanagara rapidly grew to a population of some quarter- to a half-million inhabitants. The core of the capital extended over 7.7 square miles (20 sq km) and the fortified suburban zone, containing dispersed settlements, craft production locales, and a diverse range of agricultural fields and irrigation works, was more than 116 square miles (300 sq km) in area. The city was abandoned in A.D. 1565 and has not been extensively reoccupied, resulting in extraordinary archaeological preservation. More than 200 standing-stone buildings are extant, as are monumental fortification walls constructed of locally abundant granite. Documentation began in 1800 with the preparation of the earliest-known site plan and an extraordinary set of seventy photographs was taken by British surveyor Alexander Greenlaw in 1856. Formal work at the site was initiated by the Archaeological Survey of India in the late nineteenth century, though large-scale surface documentation and excavations did not begin until 1980. Research has focused on the study of urban plan, architecture, sculpture and iconography, and domestic material remains including earthenware ceramics and imported East Asian porcelains. Archaeologists have divided the city core into three main spatial zones. These are: a northern sacred zone, containing four large Hindu temple centers and numerous smaller shrines and temples; a central irrigated valley with agricultural fields watered by river-fed canals; and a southern walled urban zone of densely occupied residential areas and a fortified "royal center" with elaborate elite residences, as well as columned halls, platforms, watch towers, water pavilions, and tanks. Other remains include several hundred inscriptions, carved in Sanskrit and Dravidian languages (Kannada and Telugu) on outcropping boulders and temple walls. Additional written resources include contemporary poetry and sacred literature and the accounts of Portuguese, Italian, Russian, and Persian visitors to the city in the fifteenth and sixteenth centuries. Both archaeological and textual evidence attest to the scale and grandeur of the city, which, along with its significance as a major political and military center, was also a center of national and international commerce and the arts.

[See also ASIA: PREHISTORY AND EARLY HISTORY OF SOUTH-EAST ASIA.]

■ A. L. Dallapiccolla, ed., Vijayanagara—City and Empire, 2 vols. (1985). J. M. Fritz, G. A. Michell, and M. S. Nagaraja Rao, Where Kings and Gods Meet: The Royal Centre at Vijayanagara (1985).

Carla M. Sinopoli

VINDOLANDA. After the conquest of northern Britain by the governor Agricola, ca. A.D. 79, a fort was constructed at Vindolanda, on the lateral east-to-west road, the Stanegate, a little over half a mile south of the line of the later *Hadrian's Wall midway between modern Carlisle and Newcastle. Seven successive forts were to be built on the same site, and a substantial civilian settlement grew up nearby.

The first five forts were of timber, designed to hold one or more auxiliary regiments. The use of unseasoned timber in the construction restricted the life of the buildings to a maximum of twelve years, and the process of demolition of old buildings and construction of new ones resulted in layers of turf or clay being laid down over the debris of old sites, to create clean and level conditions for new buildings. The subsoil conditions of acid-free boulder clay, reinforced by the successive layers of turf and clay, created anaerobic conditions among the buried remains, thus preserving all traces of human activity in an almost perfect state. Subsequent construction of successive stone-built forts above the timber remains further protected them.

During the major excavation program of 1970–1973, concerned with the stone-built civilian settlement outside the walls of the stone fort, the early timber remains were revealed 6.5 feet (2 m) below the floors of later civilian buildings. Between 1973 and 1994 excavation of some 21,530 square feet (2,000 sq m) of the early remains was completed, to reveal well-preserved timber structures of five successive forts dating to the period A.D. 85–ca. 130. The anerobic conditions allowed the recovery of very large quantities of artifacts, including leather goods, textiles, wooden objects, metal tools and utensils, a wide range of flora and fauna, and some 2,000 Roman ink documents.

The documents were written in the cursive script, with a carbon-based ink, on specially prepared wafer-thin sheets of wood, no larger than modern postcard size. All the texts found prior to 1990 have been published by Alan K. Bowman and J. David Thomas, and work is progressing on the substantial number of texts found since that date.

The documents can be broadly divided into correspondence (including draft letters), accounts, stores lists, duty rosters, a strength report, duty officers' reports, and miscellaneous military memorabilia. They form an especially valuable archive because they date to a period in Romano-British history that is otherwise devoid of surviving historical sources, and they are also important for information about the spoken Latin of the late first century A.D.

Slightly more than half of the texts are associated with the residence of the prefect of the Ninth Cohort of Batavians, Flavius Cerialis. They include dated material that proves his presence at the site between A.D. 101 and 104. Much of the correspondence relates to commanding officers of the cohorts in garrison, but there are also letters between commanding officers' wives, between slaves, and between ordinary soldiers.

Excavations will continue for many years, with the prospect of more documents being revealed.

[See also BRITISH ISLES: ROMAN BRITAIN; ROMAN EMPIRE: THE ROMAN FRONTIER.]

■ Robin Birley et al., The Vindolanda Research Reports, New Series, vols. I–III (1993, 1994). Alan K. Bowman and J. David Thomas, The Vindolanda Writing Tablets, Tabulae Vindolandenses II (1994). Alan K. Bowman, Life and Letters on the Roman Frontier (1994).

Robin Birley

WARI EMPIRE. The Wari Empire was centered at the site of Wari in the Ayacucho Valley of the central Andean highlands of Peru. During the Middle Horizon Period its political and economic control expanded over most of what is today highland Peru, and perhaps portions of the coast, roughly between A.D. 750 and 1000. For many years Wari culture was thought to be directly derived from Tiwanaku, another important and influential Middle Horizon site, located in Bolivia; it was first called Coast Tiahuanaco or Tiahuanacoid. It was not until the 1930s that the Peruvian archaeologist Julio C. Tello investigated the site of Wari and determined that it was the center of dispersal of the so-called Tiahuanacoid styles.

Prior to the emergence of Wari, during the Early Intermediate Period the Huarpa ceramic tradition characterized the Ayacucho Valley. Toward the end of the Early Intermediate there is stylistic evidence of interaction with the coast, especially with the Nasca culture of the south coast. The latter part of the Early Intermediate seems to have been a time of cultural disruption and increased interregional interaction, perhaps due to climatic deterioration and its negative effects on subsistence pursuits.

Early in the Middle Horizon, Wari emerged as an urban center, the capital of a local state, and it began to expand its political control to the north and south. Wari is characterized by a distinctive style of architecture; this architecture along with the wide dispersal of Wari-style artifacts allows the definition of the limits of Wari control. The typical Wari architectural form was orthogonal in plan: great rectangular enclosures, laid out according to a rigid grid plan and subdivided into square or rectangular units called patio groups. Each patio group comprised a central open patio, surrounded on its perimeter by long, narrow rooms called galleries. Sometimes the galleries were two or three deep, and they were usually two, or even three, stories tall. An interesting characteristic of the architecture is the fact that although doorways allow access between each patio and its associated galleries, there are few doorways allowing access from one patio group to the next. It is clear the Wari architecture was designed to severely restrict movement within each enclosure.

While Wari covers several square kilometers, and the architecture is aligned to conform to the local topography, its provincial centers were much smaller, and each comprised a single rectangular unit. Provincial centers probably served as local political capitals, regional administrative centers within the imperial bureaucracy. The largest provincial center known is Pikillaqta, located just southeast of the city of Cuzco. The great rectangular enclosure there measures some 2,600 feet (800 m) on a side, and is subdivided into many patio groups. While the central portion of the site was occupied for a century or more, other portions of the site were still under construction when the empire collapsed and the site was abandoned.

Another provincial center was Jincamocco, located in southern Ayacucho. This enclosure originally measured about 427 feet (130 m) by 853 feet (260 m), but was expanded during the latter part of the Wari occupation. Archaeological investigations in and around this site indicate that the valley in which it was located was reorganized by Wari to increase maize production. The valley was extensively terraced at the time, probably under Wari direction.

North of Wari, provincial centers were located along the spine of the Andes to as far north as Cajamarca. A very large center was begun at Viracochapampa, but never finished. It is thought that either the local polity capitulated and agreed to cooperate with Wari, making an imposed capital unnecessary, or the Wari never succeeded in conquering the region. There is evidence that all the centers were linked together, and with Wari, by a system of roads. Many of these roads were later incorporated into the well-known royal highways of the Incas.

The case for Wari conquest of the coast is much less clear than in the highlands. On the north coast of Peru, the Moche state fragmented at about the time that Wari influence was first felt. The collapse of Moche might have been due to conquest by Wari, or it may have been entirely independent of Wari expansion. Limited data from several valleys indicate that in the Early Middle Horizon Period old settlements were abandoned, new ones established, and new political organizations formed. The presence of Wari artifacts on the north coast might be explained as the result of trade, rather than conquest.

On the central coast of Peru a major religious center was established at the site of Pachacamac, located just south of the modern city of Lima. Artifacts of Pachacamac style are clearly related to Wari styles, and probably represent a regional variant of Wari-related styles. It is unclear whether Pachacamac was an independent polity, with wide-ranging influence on the coast, or a province within the Wari Empire.

On the south coast several major Wari offerings, but few actual Wari centers, are found. Associated with the Wari expansion was the diffusion of a religious practice that involved the sacrifice and offering of large quantities of high-quality and exquisitely decorated ceramics. Typically, a large pit was dug into the ground, and fancy polychrome pots were smashed and thrown into it. Large vessels depicting supernatural creatures or humans were ritually "killed" with blows aimed first at the head or chest of the being depicted on the pot. Such offering deposits are known in several locations in the highlands, especially in the vicinity of Wari, and at two locations on the south coast: Maymi in the Pisco Valley and Pacheco in the Nasca Valley.

Apparently the site of Pacheco also included a large area of rectilinear architecture, but archaeological investigations in the 1920s were focused on the offering deposit. Since then the site was destroyed to make way for agriculture. Nasca settlement patterns were completely disrupted at the time Pacheco was established, and it is not unlikely that there was some sort of administrative center there.

[See also ANDEAN PRE-INCA CIVILIZATIONS, RISE OF: INTRODUCTION; MOCHE CULTURE; NASCA CIVILIZATION; SOUTH AMERICA, articles on HIGHLANDS CULTURES OF SOUTH AMERICA, THE RISE OF COMPLEX SOCIETIES IN SOUTH AMERICA; TIAHUANACO EMPIRE.]

■ Wendell C. Bennett, Excavations at Wari, Ayachucho, Peru (1953). Gordon F. McEwan, The Middle Horizon in the Valley of Cuzco, Peru: The Impact of the Wari Occupation of the Lucre Basin (1987). William H. Isbell and Gordon F. McEwan, eds., Huari Administrative Structure: Prehistoric Monumental Architecture and State Government (1991). Katharina J. Schreiber, Wari Imperialism in Middle Horizon Peru (1992).

Katharina Schreiber

WASSERBURG. The Wasserburg is the name given to a remarkable fortified site of the Late Bronze Age or Urnfield Period, preserved in the wetlands of the Federseemoor in Baden-Württemberg, southwestern Germany. Discovered in 1920, and excavated between 1921 and 1937, the site is known to be one of the best-preserved Urnfield settlements in Europe. An unfortunate excavation history, however, coupled with the lack of any systematic publication by the excavator, have led to many years of uncertainty about the detail of the site's nature and history. Following the death of the excavator, Hans Reinerth, in 1990, work began on a full examination of the finds and the surviving records, though it will be many years before a full picture is available.

The site is a roughly oval area 495 by 385 feet (151 by 118 m) across, defined by two palisades and enclosing a series of wooden houses. It is known from tree-ring analysis that the palisades were built some 100 to 150 years apart, probably as part of a major remodeling of the site. The outer palisade is a major construction of around 15,000 pine posts, varying in width from 10 to 2 feet (3 m to 60 cm). The excavator believed that bridges connected this palisade (which was supposed to have supported a raised walkway for defenders to stand on) to the dry land some meters behind, but it is just as likely that the posts inside the palisade represent the remains of further houses. The higher ground inside was further ringed by post constructions forming breakwaters. Here the houses were built, mostly in the technique of "Blockbau," that is, of posts lying side by side corduroy-style; there is also some evidence of wattle-and-daub construction, but it is not known whether this is restricted to buildings of particular function.

Reinerth was able to show a major phase of rebuilding in the village plan. In the early phase, the thirty-eight recovered buildings were all simple rectangular one-room affairs containing a hearth; one building was supposed to have a porch and thus be a chieftain's house, but examination of the photographic record suggests instead that two periods of construction were involved. In the site's later phase, there are only nine houses, in the form of large three-winged houses set around a yard. In both phases there was a central area that was not built up. Finds from the site include pottery but also many bronze objects (including some evidence of on-site working), clay fire-dogs, net-sinkers, spindle-whorls, querns, stone axes, clay figurines repre-

senting birds, and a variety of wooden objects, notably canoes and a wagon wheel.

Chronologically, the pottery belongs to three main phases of the Urnfield Period, known as *Hallstatt A2, B1, and B3 (earlier first millennium B.C.). The bronzes mostly belong to the later period, perhaps because earlier ones were effectively gathered up and reused.

Nothing is known about the circumstances of the creation and desertion of the Wasserburg, which shows certain similarities both to Biskupin (which is rather later in date) and to some of the Bronze Age settlements on the Alpine lakes. The remarkable change of house and village plan perhaps reflects a change in social relations and family group affinities, though a more mundane explanation might be the desire to bring under one roof all the various activities that a single habitation unit required, rather than leaving them scattered about within or without the fortified area. In any event, the site represents clear evidence of a move into fortified settlements in what were most likely troubled times in the first millennium B.C.

[See also EUROPE: THE EUROPEAN BRONZE AGE; LAKE DWELLINGS, EUROPEAN; URNFIELDS.]

■ H. Reinerth, Die Wasserburg Buchau: Eine befestigte Inselsiedlung aus der Zeit 1100–800 v. Chr. (1928). W. Kimmig, Die "Wasserburg Buchau"—eine spätbronzezeitliche Siedlung: Forschungsgeschichte—Kleinfunde (1992).

Anthony F. Harding

WASTE MANAGEMENT. Archaeologists have always joked about what they would find if they dug into their own society's refuse, but their rationale was serious: If archaeologists can learn important information about extinct societies from ancient garbage, then archaeologists can learn important information about our own society from fresh garbage.

The first long-term archaeology based on this reasoning was the Garbage Project, initiated at the University of Arizona in 1973. Two decades of analyzing contemporary MSW (municipal solid wastes) have identified some of the advantages and types of such studies.

To collect data on contemporary behaviors, researchers often rely on interview surveys, which may have informant bias. For example, respondents may not be able to accurately recall specific behaviors, such as how many grams of green beans they ate yesterday, and even if they can accurately recall behaviors, such as beer drinking, they may be reluctant to provide specifics. Studies of fresh garbage avoid these biases. Even when people know their refuse is being studied they quickly tire of trying to "sanitize" it. Above all, refuse data are quantitative; packaging and commodity wastes can be weighed, measured for volume, chemically analyzed, and even read for information.

Refuse analysis is, of course, susceptible to its own biases. One is garbage disposals; another is the taking of recyclables to drop-off buy-back centers. The Garbage Project has developed correction factors for both problems.

Fresh Sorts. The first garbage-archaeology format is sampling fresh refuse placed out for collection. The anonymity of sample households is rigorously protected.

Solid waste managers have long characterized waste by material composition. The Garbage Project has added records from package labels (brand, cost, weight or volume, and type of contents, packaging material) and more detailed breakdowns of refuse categories, such as "food waste" ("once-edible food" separated from "food preparation debris" and both identified by specific food type).

Refuse has been collected in this format in short-term studies in five U.S. cities and Mexico City, and in a long-term study in Tucson, Arizona (1973 to present). Analyses have focused on a number of issues, including:

Food Waste. The average U.S. household discards 10 to 15 percent of its edible solid food. One trend: the more pre-prepared foods purchased (e.g., frozen pizzas and micro-wave dinners), the higher the percentage of edible fresh food (e.g., lettuce and grapefruit) wasted.

Diet and Nutrition. Direct interview/refuse compari-sons (with households' permission) have determined that respondents systematically over-report what they believe is good for them and under-report what they believe is not.

Recycling. One Garbage Project discovery is the "surro-gate syndrome": to know whether people will sort their recyclables for curbside collection, don't ask them what they will do; instead, ask them what they believe their neighbors will do.

Household Hazardous Wastes. Respondents have a diffi-cult time reporting on such household hazardous discards as batteries, used motor oil, and unused paints. Such poten-tial toxics are being analyzed to construct algorithms to predict concentrations of each type in refuse from different neighborhoods.

Garbage Census. At the neighborhood level, both the total weight of household solid wastes and the total weight of plastics generated per day are directly related to the size of the population generating the refuse.

Landfill Digs. The second methodological format is ex-cavating refuse from landfills. Refuse is sampled from a series of 3-feet-diameter (1 m) cores drilled by bucket au-gers (well depth up to 105 feet [32 m]) and trenches cut by backhoes. Materials are screened and sorted into forty cate-gories based on material composition and function. Each category is measured for weight and volume. Additional studies record the moisture content of artifacts and the concentrations of hazards such as heavy metals and com-plex organic compounds.

Garbage Project digs at fifteen landfills throughout North America have made an impact on how policy plan-ners and the public perceive what is filling landfills and what happens to buried discards over time.

What Is in Landfills. Before landfill digs, interview sur-veys indicated that many people thought that styrofoam, fast-food packaging, and disposable diapers filled up the most landfill space. In contrast, archaeological data demon-strated that all three of these items *together* account for less than 3 percent of landfill volume. The largest occupant of landfill space turned out to be paper, which fills 40 to 50 percent of landfill space.

One of the future directions of landfill archaeology will be to quantify the impact of public policy. For example, a 1991 Garbage Project study of Metro Toronto landfills esti-mated that the Blue Box curbside recycling program has conserved some 20 percent of landfill space since it began in 1982.

What Happens to Discards over Time. Sanitary landfills are 10 to 100 feet (3–30 m) deep. Below 10 feet, fluids and other environmental factors are often relatively stable and microorganisms are anaerobic. Under these conditions, about 50 percent of food and yard wastes biodegrade in the first 15 years; further biodegradation is slow—the Garbage Project has excavated hot dogs and clumps of grass still recognizable after 30 or 40 years of burial. The biodegrada-tion of paper is generally even slower.

One significant topic for future landfill archaeology will be attempting to trace the sources of hazardous pollutants in escaping fluids (called "leachate") back to specific arti-facts within landfills and finally back to points of discard.

The archaeology of contemporary urban garbage has the unique synergistic potential to record data on a contempo-rary society heretofore undocumented by archaeological techniques, validate traditional method and theory using discards of known origin, and provide hard, quantitative data on current societal problems to policy planners and the public. These uses may be enough reason for even Indiana Jones, now and then, to turn his trowel on his own discards—and then recycle them.

[*See also* ARCHAEOLOGY IN THE CONTEMPORARY WORLD; URBAN ARCHAEOLOGY.]

■ David Macauley, *Motel of the Mysteries* (1979). W. L. Rathje and C. K. Ritenbaugh, eds., "Household Refuse Analysis," *American Behavioral Scientist* 28:1 (1984). D. C. Wilson and W. L. Rathje, "Struc-ture and Dynamics of Household Hazardous Wastes," *Journal of Resource Management and Technology* 17:4 (1989): 200–206. W. L. Rathje, "Once and Future Landfills," *National Geographic* 179:5 (1991): 116–134. W. L. Rathje, W. W. Hughes, D. C. Wilson, M. K. Tani, G. H. Archer, R. G. Hunt, and T. Jones, "The Archaeology of Contemporary Landfills," *American Antiquity* 57:3 (1992): 437–447. W. L. Rathje and C. Murphy, *Rubbish! The Archaeology of Garbage* (1992).

William Rathje

WESSEX takes its name from the kingdom of the West Saxons, but its modern connotations owe more to the writ-ings of Thomas Hardy, who revived the term to provide a setting for his novels. In this sense Wessex can be said to cover the four English counties of Wiltshire, Dorset, Hamp-shire, and Berkshire.

This is a region of central southern England that is domi-nated by chalk downland, and it is because the uplands were used as sheep pasture for many years that such a wide range of prehistoric monuments has survived. On the other hand, it is also true that these include a series of earthworks that were built on a larger scale than their counterparts in other parts of Britain, as well as a few monuments, among them *Stonehenge, that in their developed form are entirely unique. So too is the wealth and variety of the grave goods associated with the Early Bronze Age burial mounds in this region, and for the last fifty years these have been taken to define a "Wessex Culture."

The distinctiveness of Wessex archaeology really extends from the Neolithic Period to the middle years of the Bronze Age, after which it seems to have lost much of its individu-ality. We know very little about hunger-gatherer archaeol-ogy in Wessex, perhaps because the contemporary shore-line has been lost to the sea, and for that reason we can say virtually nothing about the Mesolithic-Neolithic transition in this area. That is particularly unfortunate since the first earthwork monuments conventionally associated with farming groups seem to appear quite suddenly about 4000 B.C. Recent work suggests that initially they were located in seasonal pasture around the upper limits of the settled area.

These monuments had very little to do with the prac-ticalities of agricultural production, and it is not even known whether they were built by a sedentary population. What is quite obvious is that the construction of the first of these monuments established the importance of certain places on the chalk which were to retain their significance as ceremonial centers for almost two thousand years, from the beginning of the Neolithic Period to the end of the Early

Bronze Age. There were at least four of these focal areas in Wessex, each of them associated with a major river that provided access to the more fertile lowland soils.

Types of Monuments. The monuments themselves fall into three main classes—enclosures, alignments, and burial mounds —although each ceremonial complex included one or more examples of each kind of site. The enclosures took two successive forms. The earlier variety, the causewayed enclosure, is characterized by the excavated site at Hambledon Hill. These sites were defined by discontinuous ditches and contained a variety of formal deposits of human and animal remains, together with large quantities of artifacts, some of them obtained from distant parts of the country. With a few exceptions, these enclosures do not seem to have been inhabited, and they are best interpreted as ritual centers serving a wider population. They were located on the edges of the settled landscape, often in areas of woodland. Although these enclosures went out of use by 3300 B.C., similar constructions, known as henge monuments, were adopted in Wessex five hundred years later, although they seem to have originated in northern Britain. Henges may have played a similar role to the causewayed enclosures, but they took a much more complex form. Some of them were such enormous constructions that it may have taken at least half a million worker-hours to build them. Unlike their predecessors, they were defined by continuous earthworks, and inside some of them we find massive post settings, perhaps the remains of circular public buildings. A few of the post settings were later replaced by stone circles. Again, these sites are associated with a range of elaborate and exotic artifacts. They also provide evidence for large-scale feasting. Formal deposits of cultural material are not confined to the interior, and pits containing a range of unusual artifacts are sometimes found in the surrounding area. The best-known of these henge monuments are Stonehenge and *Avebury.

The alignments are less well known. The earliest are the earthwork monuments described as cursuses, which belong to the same period as the causewayed enclosures. They sometimes incorporated burial monuments in their path, and may have been associated with the dead. The largest of these earthworks, the Dorset Cursus, is nearly 6 miles (10 km) long and 109 yards (100 m) wide and seems to have been orientated on the midwinter sunset. Such earthworks retained their significance for a long time, and their last phase of use might even have overlapped with the construction of the stone and earthwork "avenues" leading to the henge monuments at Avebury and Stonehenge. At Avebury two stone circles are connected by an alignment of paired uprights, whereas the Stonehenge avenue is defined by two parallel banks and ditches. As it approaches the site, it swings around to follow the axis of the midsummer sunrise.

Perhaps more revealing are the burial monuments, which show a continuous sequence of development from the Neolithic to the Early Bronze Age. Many of these sites cluster in the vicinity of the causewayed enclosures, cursuses, and henge monuments found in the Wessex landscape. The first funerary monuments to be built were elongated mounds associated with the disarticulated remains of several individuals (long barrows). The bones might be housed in wooden ossuaries, but in the northern part of Wessex there were also sites with stone-built "megalithic" chambers. Very few of these deposits were associated with any grave goods, and it seems as if relics of the dead may

have circulated between these sites and other kinds of monuments, in particular cursuses and causewayed enclosures. Only the latest long barrows contain any individual burials. These are represented by articulated corpses, mostly male, some of them associated with grave goods.

A new tradition of circular mounds (round barrows) were adopted in Wessex from about 3000 B.C. These are associated with individual burials containing grave goods, and are a type of monument more characteristic of other parts of Britain; in Wessex they are rare. On the other hand, they represent the first appearance of a type of funerary monument that became very widespread from the time of the first introduction of metal.

The Early Bronze Age round barrows of Wessex are justly famous. They are found very widely on the chalk uplands, although some of the main groups are located close to major ceremonial monuments such as Stonehenge. It is in the vicinity of the major ceremonial monuments that we find the widest variety of mounds. Sometimes these are arranged in elaborate formal patterns and really constitute a series of elaborate cemeteries, in which other burials were located in between the mounds themselves. Most, but not all, of the richest grave goods of this phase are found in these distinctive cemeteries.

Types of Burials. There were two series of Early Bronze Age burials in Wessex, overlapping in time. The first were inhumations associated with a variety of decorated pottery, personal ornaments of nonlocal raw materials, and finds of metalwork, normally copper and bronze but occasionally gold. These were used to make a series of weapons and personal ornaments, which have close counterparts in Brittany and also in central Europe, and more distant parallels as far afield as Mycenae. These objects were normally associated with individual burials, but well-excavated sites show that any one mound can contain a whole sequence of deposits, some of them successive interments in the same grave. Less elaborately furnished graves may contain cremation burials, but it is not clear whether an equivalent range of grave goods had originally been present on the pyre. The cremation burials are thought to belong to the later years of the "Wessex Culture" when more emphasis may have been placed on creating a monumental mound.

Although so many of these burials were located close to older ceremonial centers, few of those sites had been maintained. Only Stonehenge was rebuilt. The enormous structure that we see today was created during the Early Bronze Age, at the same time as some of the richest burials in its vicinity. Its characteristic architecture owes something to the timber circles associated with large henge monuments, but there is also a direct link with the burials found in the surrounding area, for a metal dagger like those associated with these graves is also depicted in a rock carving at Stonehenge.

Throughout this complex Wessex sequence there is little evidence of contemporary occupation sites. More energy was directed into monuments to the dead than into the settlements of the living. There is little indication of sedentary agriculture. It is only as the distinctive monuments went out of use that we encounter the first signs of intensified food production. Some of the areas around these sites were incorporated into field systems, and in time the remains of older monuments were ploughed out. These changes are all associated with the growth of fixed settlements (some of them enclosed by earthworks) together with the first archaeologically detectable houses and a new range of agricultural facilities. For reasons that still remain obscure it seems as if human effort was gradually directed away from monument building. After the Early Bronze Age the dead occupied insubstantial cremation cemeteries located alongside the settlements and were no longer provided with distinctive grave goods. That transformation not only brings the "Wessex Culture" to an end; it marks a much broader transition that extends throughout the BritishIsles. After that time central southern England was to play a less prominent part in prehistoric archaeology.

[*See also* BRITISH ISLES: PREHISTORY OF THE BRITISH ISLES; CAMPS AND ENCLOSURES, CAUSEWAYED; MEGALITHIC TOMBS; STONE CIRCLES AND ALIGNMENTS.]

■ Roger Mercer, *Hambledon Hill—A Neolithic Landscape* (1979). Colin Burgess, *The Age of Stonehenge* (1980). Julian Richards, *The Stonehenge Environs Project* (1990). John Barrett, Richard Bradley, and Martin Green, *Landscape, Monuments and Society* (1991). John Barrett, *Fragments from Antiquity* (1993). Barry Cunliffe, *Wessex to AD 1000* (1993).

Richard Bradley

WEST AFRICAN FOREST KINGDOMS. Many chiefdom and state-level societies flourished in the tropical rain forest of West Africa during the first and second millennia A.D. Unfortunately, very limited archaeological research has been undertaken and the details of their origins and development remain poorly known. Few sites have been excavated, and neither comprehensive regional surveys nor chronological syntheses have been attempted. Available archaeological evidence indicates that the origins of political complexity in the forest are slightly later than in the northern savanna, but this conclusion can be evaluated in light of future work.

The West African rain forest lies in a narrow swath along the coast between Sierra Leone in the west and Cameroon in the east. In the north it is bordered by transitional forest and the grasslands of the savanna. This open terrain extends southward all the way to the coast between Ghana and Nigeria, dividing the forest into eastern and western segments. The limited information available on the forest kingdoms is, at least in part, a result of the thick vegetation that makes the logistics of archaeological fieldwork challenging. The forest possesses many resources, including iron ore, gold, ivory, and agricultural products. Historically, trade in these materials and other commodities linked societies of the forest with peoples of the drier northern regions.

The earliest archaeological evidence for the rise of forest kingdoms dates to late in the first millennium A.D. While the available information is incomplete, tantalizing clues have been discovered, as illustrated by the site of Igbo Ukwu in southern Nigeria, an area that is today inhabited by the Igbo people. This site, accidentally discovered in 1939, actually incorporates three discrete features interpreted as a shrine, a ritual disposal pit, and a royal burial chamber. Finds include elaborately cast copper alloy objects, elephant tusks, ornate pottery, and over 150,000 imported glass beads. Calibrated radiocarbon dates for the site cluster in the ninth and tenth centuries A.D. The presence of high-status items and exotic trade goods would seem to provide indisputable evidence of the growth of political complexity, but interpretation of these finds is hindered by the fact that the associated settlement remains unstudied.

Other discoveries relevant to the origins of early forest kingdoms have been found in southwestern Nigeria in the portion of the country currently occupied by the Yoruba.

Modern Yoruba settlements include some of the largest urban concentrations in Nigeria, and it is notable that archaeological evidence from this area also presents some of the earliest evidence for urbanization in the West African forest. The southern savanna and the forest margin are dotted with archaeological sites, many characterized by complex networks of walls or earthen banks. Understanding of these sites has been facilitated by oral traditions that recount the origins of many settlements and their continuing ritual importance.

Ile-Ife, the best known early urban center in the Nigerian forest, is described in Yoruba traditions as the place where the world was created. Today it remains central in Yoruba religious life as the location of many ancient shrines that are maintained by the Oni, the ruler of Ife. The modern settlement of Ife is located on top of the ancient site, making archaeological assessment challenging. Excavations suggest that the origins of the settlement may date back to late in the first millennium A.D., the political influence of the polity reaching a peak several centuries later. Archaeological findings include distinctive potsherd pavements constructed from broken ceramic shards placed on edge. Other finds demonstrate the effervescence of metal and terra-cotta art at Ife in the late fourteenth and early fifteenth centuries A.D. Stylistically, some of these figures are reminiscent of the Nok terracottas, found in earlier Iron Age sites in the transitional forest savanna areas of northern Nigeria.

Beginning with the arrival of the Portuguese in coastal Nigeria in the late fifteenth century, oral traditions and archaeological information on the forest kingdoms can be complemented by written accounts. Among the most spectacular are descriptions of Benin City, one of the Yoruba settlements that traces its origins to Ife. Archaeological work at Benin places the initial occupation in the thirteenth century. During the following centuries, Benin became one of the most important kingdoms in the region. European visitors described Benin City as a massive settlement that was the center of a divine kingship ruled by the *oba*, the principal political and religious leader. Archaeological research has revealed a vast complex of walls spanning some 9,900 miles (16,000 km) and covering some 2,500 square miles (6,500 sq km).

Some of the most striking Nigerian discoveries are copper alloy objects produced by a method called cire perdue, or lost-wax casting. Using this technique, craftsmen molded human and animal figures, bracelets, pots, bowls, and ornaments in wax. These forms were then carefully covered with clay and fired, the cavity left by the melted wax forming a mold. The cast objects recovered at sites like Igbo Ukwu, Ife, and Benin provide insights into the wealth and power of the rulers as well as the technological skill of the craftsmen. The bronze and brass used in the casting are not available locally, and so represent substantial accumulations of luxury material. Many of the artistic representations are reminiscent of practices still observable today, including depictions of rulers in ritual regalia.

Evidence for the emergence of kingdoms has also been recovered in the western forest. Excavations around sites such as Adansemanso and Begho in the Akan region of modern-day Ghana demonstrate the presence of settled communities of Iron Age agriculturists during the first millennium A.D. Occupied by the eleventh century A.D., Begho emerged as a trading center near the forest margin, a position that may have allowed the town's inhabitants to capitalize on the exchange of foodstuffs, natural resources, and trade goods from the distinct environmental zones to the north and south. Excavations at the site defined several loci, which oral histories identify as different quarters, including a special section for Muslim merchants.

Trade is a recurrent theme in West African archaeology. Imported metals, glass beads, and occasional other objects underscore the trade linkages that must have brought goods to West Africa from northern and eastern Africa in substantial quantities centuries before the beginning of European coastal trade late in the fifteenth century. The importance of the trans-Saharan trade is noted in Arabic accounts, but this information is limited, providing only tangential references to the societies of the forest. Unfortunately, agricultural produce, wooden objects, gold, ivory, salt, and a host of other forest products are poorly represented in the archaeological record, so the full extent of the trade network remains unknown.

The focus of trade changed with the advent of the Europeans on the West African coast in the late fifteenth century. While the Europeans exploited existing exchange networks, their presence on the coast gave new economic importance to the coastal African traders, who served as middlemen with the peoples of the interior. European documentary accounts and African oral traditions provide vivid, though incomplete, descriptions of states such as Asante in modern Ghana, Dahomey in the Republic of Benin, and Old Oyo in Nigeria. The roots of many of these states may be traced to before the arrival of the Europeans. Yet the arrival of European trade afforded new opportunities and modified political relations.

New states, often focused on European trading enclaves, also emerged, and names like Elmina, in coastal Ghana, and Ouidah, in the Republic of Benin, became increasingly prominent in European descriptions of the region. Although Elmina was described as a "large settlement" by the first Portuguese visitors, it likely numbered only a few hundred people who were subservient to the ruler of one of the neighboring Akan states. Elmina's position became increasingly autonomous with Portuguese and, later, Dutch support, and territory was steadily incorporated into the Elmina state. While tied to the onset of European trade, the Elmina maintain many distinctive Akan rituals and traditions.

In the far western forest, including the countries of Liberia, Sierra Leone, and Guinea, evidence for the rise of political complexity is limited. Iron smelting was introduced into the region by A.D. 700, but there are no indications of large urban concentrations or political stratification. European accounts, beginning in the fifteenth century, record many settlements in the region, and numerous fortified towns and hilltop sites have been identified archaeologically. Oral histories and document records indicate that these settlements often remained autonomous or loosely united under a charismatic or prominent war chief.

[See also AFRICA, articles on PREHISTORY OF AFRICA, THE RISE OF KINGDOMS AND STATES IN AFRICA; TRADE, AFRICAN.]

■ J. F. Ade Ajayi and Michael Crowder, eds., *History of West Africa, Volume 1* (2nd ed., 1976). Graham Connah, *African Civilization* (1987). Christopher R. DeCorse, "Culture Contact, Continuity, and Change on the Gold Coast, A.D. 1400–1900," *African Archaeological Review* 10 (1992): 163–196. Thurstan Shaw, Paul Sinclair, Bassey Andah, and Alex Okpoko, eds., *The Archaeology of Africa* (1993). Ivor Wilks, *Forests of Gold: Essays on the Akan and the Kingdom of Asante* (1993).

Christopher R. DeCorse

WEST AFRICAN SAVANNA KINGDOMS

Introduction
The Sahara, Caravan Trade, and Islam
Benin

INTRODUCTION

From A.D. 800 to 1500, a series of major kingdoms flourished in the Sudanic zone of West Africa between the Niger River and the Atlantic. Archaeology at present informs one only slightly about the origins and development of these kingdoms because research has been spotty at best, often lacking the necessary regional perspective or rigor in excavation.

Ghana, "land of gold," was mentioned in the late eighth century A.D. by an Arab geographer living in Baghdad. A century later, in 872, al-Ya'qubi reckoned Ghana and Gao among the greatest of the black kingdoms. Both arose on the southern margin of the Sahara during the second half of the first millennium A.D. when climate was significantly wetter than at present.

The capital of the Ghana empire (or Wagadu, as the Soninke remember their ancient state) was described by al-Bakri in A.D. 1076, just a few years before it suffered a devastating attack by Berber Almoravids. The capital consisted of two towns, one inhabited by Muslim merchants and one housing the pagan king and local inhabitants. The southwestern Mauritanian site of Kumbi Saleh, where stone-built ruins of houses and mosques extend almost half a square mile, is possibly the Muslim town. Excavations produced glass weights, Mediterranean pottery, and stones with Arabic inscriptions, in addition to local domestic items. The royal town has not yet been definitively located, but there are extensive, still unexplored sites without stone ruins in the area. In al-Bakri's description of the pagan cults of Ghana, one readily recognizes the forest shrines, fetishes, and sorcery that are widespread in Mande religion and elsewhere in West Africa. The royal tumuli of al-Bakri's account have not been located around Kumbi Saleh, but burial mounds with multiple interments and rich furnishings such as al-Bakri described are present in the Lakes region of the Middle Niger, radiocarbon dated to the tenth to twelfth century A.D. The highly stratified nature of society is further detailed by al-Bakri: only the king and crown prince could wear sewn clothes; commoners prostrated themselves and placed dust on their heads in the presence of the king; the king's retinue, his horses, and his pedigreed dogs wore golden ornaments; and a slave class existed, continually augmented by Ghana's slave raiding activities among peoples farther south. The king's power came from his control and taxation of the gold trade, which enabled him to finance a huge standing army estimated by al-Bakri to number 200,000, of which 40,000 were archers.

Many questions remain about Ghana, not the least of which is the nature and chronology of its origins. Paradoxically, excavations in neighboring regions of the Soninké heartland provide a better view of the development of Soninké society and economy in the first millennium than excavations to date in the lowest, pre-ninth-century levels at Kumbi Saleh. To the southeast, research has demonstrated that settlements in favorable areas grew rapidly in the mid-first millennium, with occupation mounds such as Akumbu in the Mema and Jenne-jeno in the Inland Delta reaching 81.5 acres (33 ha). Jenne-jeno's expansion was linked to the development throughout the first millennium of trade networks in iron, stone, and staple commodities along the Niger River and adjacent regions. The extent to which these developments were related to the rise of Ghana remains to be investigated. It has been suggested that the massive slag heaps near ore sources in the Mema resulted from an intensive but short-lived iron industry producing blooms for export to Ghana. Associated charcoal produced later first millennium A.D. dates.

A potentially vital element for understanding the emergence of Sudanic polities such as Ghana is the horse. A pre-Islamic tradition of horsemanship based on a breed of small pony likely existed in the Western Sudan centuries before the introduction of equipment that made cavalry warfare important. The use of mounted horses expanded potential exploitation territories, increasing competition for resources, and offered a new, easily raided source of wealth. The domestic horse is present at Akumbu by the seventh century. A horse figurine was found at Jenné-jeno in a context dated to ca. A.D. 800.

The faunal assemblage at Akumbu from the seventh to thirteenth century documents the disappearance of permanent water in the Mema between 1000 and 1200 as conditions became increasingly dry. After reaching its apogee of power and, apparently, territorial extent ca. A.D. 1000, Ghana began to succumb to the pressure of camel-herding desert nomads, almost certainly related to increasing instabilities in agricultural production and pasturage. A major trading link to the north, Awdaghost, was lost to the Almoravids in 1054. The site of Tegdaoust in south-central Mauritania is identifiable as medieval Awdaghost and has produced rich testimony of its taste for and commerce in North African goods. In 1076, the Almoravids sacked the Ghana capital itself. A century later, according to al-Idrisi, the capital was still occupied, with a Muslim king. But Ghana's power was dissipated among petty former vassal kingdoms to the south, who struggled to consolidate power throughout the twelfth and thirteenth centuries.

Knowledge of the two other early kingdoms of the Western Sudan, Takrur and Gao (known to Arab authors as Kawkaw), is much more limited. From early in the eighth century, Gao had commercial and political relations with the Ibadite state of Tahert in North Africa. As in the case of Ghana, the king of Kawkaw apparently built an empire (dimensions and extent unknown) through control of trade, especially in Saharan salt, and the ability to extract tribute from vassal kings. Some of this early trade may have been oriented east-west, toward Egypt. At Kawkaw, too, twin towns of considerable size, one inhabited by Muslim merchants and one by local Muslim kings, straddled the Niger River, according to Arab chroniclers. The two archaeological sites known at Gao—the old town ("Gao ancien") north of the existing town, and Gao Sané, several miles to the east on the opposite side of a channel (which likely flowed perennially in the late first millennium) leading north to the Tilemsi Valley—correspond to this description. Numerous brick structures are visible on the surface of both sites, some of which have been professionally excavated, revealing a confusing sequence of building and razing episodes. No chronological sequence has been developed for the sites, but research began anew at Gao in 1994. The most notable finds from Gao Sané thus far have been almost three dozen funerary stele with Arabic inscriptions dating to the twelfth century. The fact that some of the earliest stele are of Spanish marble and carved in an Andalusian style underscores Gao's connections with the Almoravid dynasty that ruled throughout the western Sahara and southern Spain at that

time. In the thirteenth and fourteenth centuries, Gao came under the domination of Mali, from which it learned many lessons in hegemonic statecraft. These were implemented in the fifteenth century by Sonni Ali Ber (1464–1492), who founded the great Songhai Empire with its capital at Gao.

Takrur, like early Gao, was involved in salt trade from coastal salt sources, according to al-Bakri, who provides the earliest mention of the town and its first Muslim king, War-jabi. He describes Takrur and Sila as each comprising two towns on either bank of the (Senegal) river. Sila is furthermore described as a vast kingdom where cloth, salt, copper, and sorghum are traded. One hundred years later, al-Idrisi reckons Sila among the domains of the powerful Takrur king, who now traded gold and slaves northward. Presumably the dispersal of Soninké trading clans into the Upper Senegal Valley near gold sources and the disruption of supply routes to Ghana by the Almoravids account for Takrur's improved fortunes. Recent archaeological research in the Middle Senegal Valley indicates that, unlike the Inland Niger Delta, interregional trade along the river was nearly nonexistent prior to the tenth century, when North African imports first appear. The early imports at the sites of Cubalel, Ogo, and Sincu Bara are associated with pottery imitating decorative motifs at Tegdaoust. Sites within the fertile alluvial valley of the Senegal remain small and undifferentiated throughout much of the first millennium. Society on the Middle Senegal seems to have undergone a major and extremely rapid transformation in scale and complexity between A.D. 900 and the period of the Takrur and Sila kingdoms attested to by al-Bakri. It is likely that the tens of thousands of smelting furnaces documented at sites on both sides of the Middle Senegal date largely to the early second millennium. By the thirteenth century, the current division of pastoral peoples (Fulani) and sedentary agriculturalists (Tukolor) along the Middle Senegal is documented historically.

In the thirteenth century, all the regions discussed above became consolidated within the hegemony of the empire of Mali. Of all the early kingdoms, Mali is the best known due to the lasting impression its pilgrim king Mansa Musa made in 1324 while passing through Cairo, where he spent gold so lavishly the price was depressed for years afterward; because of Ibn Battuta's eyewitness account in 1352; and due to a popular translation of the riveting Epic of Sunjata, relating the heroic founding of the empire. Unfortunately, almost no information on Mali comes from archaeology. Claims that the site of Niani in Guinea was the Mali capital visited by Ibn Battuta are problematic due to the lack of any compelling excavated evidence for occupation deposits dating to the thirteenth and fourteenth centuries. The structures interpreted as Mansa Musa's palace and audience room were associated with smoking pipes (a late sixteenth-century introduction) and radiocarbon dates of the fifteenth to seventeenth century A.D. Excavations in the "Arab Quarter" produced mostly material dated to the seventh to eleventh centuries A.D. and a notable lack of imported goods. However, here one can get a glimpse of Malinke society during the period of small villages and petty chiefdoms described by eleventh- and twelfth-century Arab authors in the area called Malal. The presence of small stone tumuli with rock-cut shaft-and-chamber collective graves similar to graves in the southwest of modern Mali indicates strong first millennium cultural connections within this whole area that became the political heartland of the empire of Mali in the thirteenth century.

[See also AFRICA: THE RISE OF KINGDOMS AND STATES IN AFRICA; TRADE, AFRICAN; WEST AFRICAN FOREST KINGDOMS.]

■ Nehemia Levtzion, *Ancient Ghana and Mali* (1973). Nehemia Levtzion, "The Early States of the Western Sudan to 1500," in *History of West Africa,* ed. J. F. Ade Ajayi and Michael Crowder (1974). Roland Oliver and Brian Fagan, *Africa in the Iron Age* (1975). Susan Keech McIntosh and Roderick J. McIntosh, "The Early City in West Africa: Towards an Understanding," *The African Archaeological Review* 2 (1984): 73–98. Graham Connah, *African Civilizations* (1987). Susan Keech McIntosh and Roderick J. McIntosh, "From Stone to Metal: New Perspectives on the Later Prehistory of West Africa," *Journal of World Prehistory* 2 (1988): 89–133. Mohammed el-Fasi, ed., *UNESCO General History of Africa III: VII–XI Century* (1990). Susan Keech McIntosh, "Recent Developments in West African Archaeology," *Journal of Archaeological Research* (forthcoming).

Susan Keech McIntosh and Roderick J. McIntosh

THE SAHARA, CARAVAN TRADE, AND ISLAM

The Origins of the Saharan Trade. With the great trading states of the Phoenicians, Greeks, Egyptians, and, ultimately, Romans arrayed across North Africa in the first millennium B.C., historians and archaeologists have speculated for decades about their role in the development of trading systems in the Sahara and beyond. The linear distribution across the central and western Sahara of rock paintings and engravings depicting horse-drawn chariots led some scholars to propose "chariot routes" linking North and West Africa perhaps as early as the second millennium B.C. More recent work indicates that the rock art reflects the spread, initially among cattle herders of Mediterrannean physical type (paleoberbers) in the Fezzan, of a new fashion of chariot racing made popular by the Greeks in the city of Cyrene (founded 630 B.C.). The chariots thus had nothing to do with long-distance transport or trade. However, the depiction of the chariots in rock art demonstrates contacts with the Mediterrannean world for the first time.

One by-product of that contact, the use of the horse, likely affected Berber societies considerably, increasing their mobility, range, and raiding capacities. Trade between Saharan Berbers and North Africa seems largely limited to precious stones ("carbuncles"), according to classical writers. Copper mines and smelting furnaces dating to the mid-first millennium B.C. have been documented in Mauritania (Akjoujt) and the Air, both in the context of a simple local copper industry that developed very little and disappeared by the first century A.D. Bronze jewelry of Punic style was recovered from Akjoujt, indicating definite contact with North Africa. The small-scale and localized distribution of the copper argues against an organized long-distance commerce. Yet, it is more evidence that the Berber tribes of the Sahara were increasingly operating within a Mediterrannean sphere of influence. Also indicative of this is the spread throughout the Sahara, from the very end of the first millennium B.C., of the alphabetic Berber script called *tifinagh,* developed by North African Berbers.

The Camel and the Intensification of Inter-regional Trade: A.D. 1 to 700. The continuing drying trend restricted the Saharan zones suitable for horses but extended the horse zone southward as the tsetse fly retreated. The introduction of the camel from Egypt in the later centuries B.C. soon had a significant impact. Berber groups emerged who specialized in breeding camels and living on their milk. The prodigious capacity of the camel as a desert pack animal made long-distance trade in heavy commodities such as salt and metals feasible on a significant scale for the first time.

On the southern coast of Mauritania, for example, a concentration of settlements around the salt sources known to later Arab authors as Awlil has been dated to A.D. 400 to 900. Just to the south, camel bones are present on sites in the Middle Senegal Valley by A.D. 400. In Niger, the site of Marandet has produced some mid-first millennium A.D. dates on charcoal associated with crucibles, numbering in the tens of thousands, used for melting and alloying copper. The source and destination of these metals is not currently known.

Much more study of first millennium A.D. Saharan sites is needed to reconstruct the orientation and extent of trade networks. Still, there are a handful of clues indicating that some goods were moving over long distances. The recovery of Gaulish, Italian, and Egyptian pottery in first- and second-century tombs near Garama, capital of the Garamantes (435 miles [700 km] south of Tripoli) is not surprising. But more significant is the presence of Roman oil lamps, glass, coins of Constantine's reign, and over a dozen gold and silver bracelets in the fourth-century tomb of a Berber princess named Ti-n Hinan, located in the Hoggar, 870 miles (1,400 km) from Tripoli. It is unknown whether the gold was West African (indicating the existence of Berber networks extending to both sides of the Sahara) or Spanish or Egyptian. On the southern side of the desert, Saharan copper was reaching Jenné-jeno on the Middle Niger by A.D. 500. Yet there is little else in the way of imported goods to suggest that gold was moving along this route. Still, some argue that the dramatically increased availability of gold for coinage and taxes in North Africa in the fourth and fifth centuries indicates a regular trade in West African gold. At the very least, it is safe to say that the period from A.D. 1 to 700 saw the emergence of long-distance trade in salt, metals, and perhaps slaves in many parts of the Sahara, linking the desert with regions both south and north. These developments were precursors to the integration of these different routes into a single network running from the North African coast to the interior in the ninth and tenth centuries.

Arab Conquest and Islamization. In the wake of Muhammed's death in A.D. 638, Arab groups with conflicting claims to rule as heirs of the prophet spread into North Africa. For several centuries, dynasties (Umayyad, Ibadi, Abbasid, Aghlabid, Fatimid, and Zirid, to name but a few) associated with different schools of Islam (Sunni, Shi'ite and Kharijite) in different regions vied for power. They all needed armies to consolidate power and coinage to legitimate and finance their rule. The establishment of traffic in slaves and gold was a major concern of these early dynasties. Berbers were drawn into the Arab sphere as clients (upon conversion to Islam) and slaves (if nonbelievers).

Beginning in the eighth century, a series of Arab trading towns, including Kairouan ("caravan"), Tahert, and Sijilmassa, were established in the Maghrib. Converted Saharan Berbers procured slaves in exchange for horses from infidel populations to the south, especially in the region of Kanem and Lake Chad. Farther west, the main commodity was gold from sources in the Upper Senegal and Niger Rivers. Trade towns arose on the southern shore ("sahel") of the Sahara, initially controlled by black or Berber populations. For example, the site of Tegdaoust (almost certainly the entrepot of Awdaghost mentioned by Arab authors) appears to have had a predominantly black population in the ninth century, dominated by Sanhaja Berbers who controlled the salt trade from Awlil. Farther east, the polity of Ghana was ruled by a black Soninké dynasty. Excavations at Tegdaoust have revealed that imports of gold, copper, North African glass, and pottery peaked in the tenth century, associated with an influx of North African colonists and merchants. This appears to mark the emergence of a mature trade system capable of transporting prodigious quantities of goods across the Sahara. It is precisely at this time that North African trade goods such as glass beads and brass suddenly appeared throughout the West African savanna, including the Middle Senegal Valley, where stylistic influences from Tegdaoust are apparent. The rapid dispersal of these goods suggests they moved along earlier regional and interregional trade networks that became integrated with the Mediterranean trade. Indispensable to this process was the diaspora of Soninké trading clans throughout the northern savanna beginning in the late first and early second millennia. This diaspora was, in turn, facilitated by the spread of Islam among the merchant and ruling classes, which provided a common language and legal system. Takrur and Gao converted in the eleventh century; the ruler of Ghana held out several decades longer.

A climactic downturn beginning in the late eleventh century coincided with the rise of the powerful Almoravid dynasty from the Sanhaja Berber confederation in the Sahara. Trade continued, but sedentary black populations retreated farther south, where new polities based on the trade arose from the ashes of Ghana. In the fourteenth century, the trade routes reached their maximum extent as the Akan gold fields were opened on the forest margin. While much of the gold trade was redirected to the coast with the arrival of the Europeans in the fifteenth century, the salt and slave trade remained active in the western Sahara until the nineteenth century.

[See also AFRICA: THE RISE OF KINGDOMS AND STATES IN AFRICA; TRADE, AFRICAN; WEST AFRICAN FOREST KINGDOMS.]

■ E. W. Bovill, *The Golden Trade of the Moors*, 2nd ed. (1970). Nehemia Levtzion, *Ancient Ghana and Mali* (1973). Raymond Mauny, "Trans-Saharan Contacts and the Iron Age in West Africa," in *The Cambridge History of Africa*, Vol. 2: *c. 500 B.C.–A.D. 1050*, ed. J. D. Fage (1978), pp. 272–341. Nehemia Levtzion, "The Sahara and the Sudan from the Arab Conquest of the Maghrib to the Rise of the Almoravids," in *The Cambridge History of Africa*, Vol. 2: *c. 500 B.C.–A.D. 1050*, ed. J. D. Fage (1978), pp. 637–684. Jean Devisse, "L'apport de l'archéologie à l'histoire de l'Afrique Occidentale entre le Ve et le XIIe siècle," in *Académie des Inscriptions & Belles-Lettres, Comptes Rendus* (1982), pp. 156–177. Timothy Garrard, "Myth and Metrology: The Early Trans-Saharan Gold Trade," *Journal of African History* 23 (1982): 443–461. Alfred Muzzolini, "The 'Chariot Period' of the Rock Art Chronology in the Sahara and the Maghreb: A Critical Re-appraisal of the Traditional Views," in *Rock Art in the Old World*, ed. Michel Lorblanchet (1988). James Webb, Jr., *Desert Frontier: Ecological and Economic Change along the Western Sahel 1600–1850* (1995).

Susan Keech McIntosh

BENIN

The kingdom of Benin was situated in the rain forest of what is now southern Nigeria, and should not be confused with the modern Republic of Benin, also in West Africa and formerly known as Dahomey. The kingdom developed early in the second millennium A.D., centered on Benin City and ruled by the Oba of Benin, who controlled a powerful army and an extensive network of government officials. It probably reached its greatest extent in the fifteenth century A.D., at the end of which European seafarers first reached Benin City itself. From the sixteenth to the nineteenth century the kingdom profited from trade in slaves, ivory, and other commodities with a succession of European nations,

until in 1897 the British added its territories to their rapidly expanding West African possessions.

Based on the exploitation of the productive rain forest environment, particularly for agriculture, Benin expanded by the conquest of its neighbors, who then became subject populations. Society was organized on a hierarchical basis, consisting of a stratified system of chiefs, officials, priests, and members of the army, all controlled by the Oba. Within Benin City, the population was grouped according to craft specialization, each controlled by a craft guild headed by a chief.

Benin technology was sophisticated: based on the production and use of iron, it included the working of wood, ivory, various alloys of copper, and other materials. There was a distinctive architecture in coursed mud, characterized by horizontally grooved, polished red walls and steepled roofs. Benin is best remembered, however, for its remarkable art, particularly in cast bronze and brass produced by the lost wax technique. This has often been compared to the art of Ife, farther to the west in the Nigerian rain forest, and may have developed from it.

Spiritual and temporal authority were closely combined in Benin, with the Oba the principal officiant in the most important religious ceremonies. Religion played a central part in life, with a pantheon of deities as well as ancestor worship. Each household had its own altars on which stood many of the works of art, particularly heads of copper alloy or wood, that have since become famous. Religious ceremonies included the sacrifice of animals and sometimes humans, in the latter case the victims were asked to carry messages to the gods or ancestors.

This overview of Benin has been mainly constructed from historical and oral traditional sources, but archaeology has also contributed substantially to our understanding of Benin's past. Study of Benin art has provided much information on Benin life and customs. Excavations by Graham Connah in the 1960s established a chronological sequence for Benin pottery and demonstrated occupation of the city by about the thirteenth century A.D. The main site investigated was the site of the Oba's palace, formerly more extensive than now, but a complex system of earthworks around the city was also mapped and partly excavated. Since then Patrick Darling has investigated these earthworks further, demonstrating that half-hidden by the dense vegetation of the surrounding rain forest are some 10,000 miles of ditches and banks. They apparently delimited agricultural land belonging to different lineage groups that were gradually absorbed by the expanding Benin state.

[See also AFRICA: THE RISE OF KINGDOMS AND STATES IN AFRICA; WEST AFRICAN FOREST KINGDOMS.]

■ J. Egharevba, *A Short History of Benin*, 4th ed. (1968). A.F.C. Ryder, *Benin and the Europeans, 1485–1897* (1969). P.J.C. Dark, *An Introduction to Benin Art and Technology* (1973). Graham Connah, *The Archaeology of Benin* (1975). P. J. Darling, *Archaeology and History in Southern Nigeria*, 2 vols. (1984). Graham Connah, *African Civilizations: Precolonial Cities and States in Tropical Africa: An Archaeological Perspective* (1987).

Graham Connah

WEST AFRICAN SCULPTURE. Much of Africa's finest art comes from archaeological excavations. In addition to professionally controlled digs, however, a disturbing amount of illegal digging, with manifold ethical and political problems, has occurred, especially in Mali, in the past twenty years, due primarily to the high prices being paid on the international art market. While recognizing that these activities adulterate the archaeological record, this article will reference some illicit material in the interest of surveying the best-known sculpture.

The earliest corpus of confidently sculptured ceramic art, called Nok, comes from sites distributed unevenly over a roughly 80- by 300-mile (129- by 483-km) area of northern Nigeria. Dated 500 B.C. to A.D. 200, and exhibiting considerable stylistic diversity, this sculpture includes over a hundred ceramic heads, life-size and smaller, one miniature full figure, body fragments, and several animals. Whether or not these finds represent a common culture is still an open question, although temporal, spatial, and style distributions tend to argue for the negative. Many Nok pieces have been stray finds among the alluvial deposits mined for tin, but excavations have also been conducted. The one excavated occupation site, Taruga, indicates that makers of most sculptures were agriculturists; they also smelted iron, as evidenced by furnace slag and tuyeres. Almost nothing is known of the original contexts and meanings, although janus figures and other evidently nonnaturalistic attributes, such as proportions giving exaggerated emphasis to heads, suggest ideological content and ritual contexts.

Ceramics from Yelwa, 200 miles (322 km) northwest of Nok areas and dating from the same era, may be distantly related. Excavations at Daima in northeastern Nigeria yielded human figures and many animals, especially cows. While these too are contemporary with Nok finds, they are distinct in style, simpler, with far less detail.

The meticulous excavations of three adjacent sites in southeastern Nigeria, labeled Igbo Ukwu by Thurstan Shaw, who directed the digs, contrast markedly with the northern Nigerian situation. A stylistically unified, if diverse, corpus of cast and ceramic artifacts number in the hundreds. These have been extensively studied, with chemical and spectrographic analyses of materials. Art works include small human and animal head pendants; a very small equestrian, 2.5 inches (6.4 cm) high; numerous bowls and staff ornaments, some decorated with snakes and insects; two skeuomorphic shells, one featuring a schematic leopard; an elaborate pendant consisting of two eggs with flies in relief and a bird between, plus eleven beaded chains ending in bells. All are lost wax (some possibly euphorbia) castings in leaded bronze.

By analogy to documented Igbo title rituals and regalia and because the sites were once occupied by Nri Igbo peoples, Igbo Ukwu finds are associated by scholars to Nri kingship and ritual practices, which survive in modified form today. One site revealed an elaborate burial of an Nri official or a wealthy titled man wearing copper alloy regalia and thousands of beads. Another was a storehouse or shrine containing dozens of richly ornamented objects in the intricate Igbo Ukwu style, which bears little relationship to other styles from the lower Niger region. Radiocarbon dates cluster in the tenth century A.D., with one in the fifteenth. This is the earliest large corpus of metal arts from West Africa.

Ile Ife, the cradle of Yoruba civilization in southwestern Nigeria, has been excavated in several places, while other ancient objects have been identified in secondary, contemporary ritual sites. The most important excavations have been in sacred groves, at Ita Yemoo, Igbo Obameri, Odo Ogbe Street, and Lafogido. Centering on divine kingship, Ife art includes scores of ceramic heads, animals, and other ritual forms plus about thirty copper alloy pieces, mostly

hollow cast heads with or without fine parallel scarification patterns. Although idealized, many Ife heads are exceptionally naturalistic; some may be imitative portraits. A copper mask, ceremonial vessels and staffs, and a few half and full figures are among the castings, all showing sensitive modeling and superb technical mastery. The hundreds of ceramic finds, made over an extended period, are more varied in style and type. While Ife sites were occupied at least by A.D. 800, the finest sculptures date from the eleventh to fourteenth centuries. Figures depict the Oni, divine king of the city state of Ile Ife, while most other finds are also related to religious organizations and rituals attending kingship.

Owo, another Yoruba city state 60 miles (96 km) from Ile Ife, has yielded heads stylistically close to those of Ife, plus varied other ceramic sculptures, used ritually, excavated by Ekpo Eyo. Dated to around the fifteenth century, Owo art includes pieces related to the art of Benin, capitol of the Edo kingdom south of Owo.

While most Benin art has been found in surface contexts, Graham Connah has conducted excavations that contribute to extensive knowledge about the Benin kingdom and its court art. Much has been passed down in oral traditions and written records beginning in 1485, when the Portuguese first made contact. Copper alloy castings and carved ivories are the primary art forms, dating from around the fourteenth century until the sack of Benin in 1897.

While sculptures recovered by archaeologists in Nigeria are famous and numerous, other important traditions are also known, from Mali, Niger, Ghana, and Cote d'Ivoire. The most extensive of these is ceramic and copper alloy sculpture from the Inland Delta of the Niger river in Mali. Based on excavations by Roderick and Susan McIntosh near the city of Jenne, we know that people occupied this region for about a thousand years, five hundred on either side of A.D. 1000; most fine sculpture dates from the latter half of that period. Much sculpture—several hundred pieces—has been excavated illegally and thus lacks known context. Sculptures include humans and animals in several styles. Human figures predominate, several showing signs of disease, others covered with snakes, the majority depicting persons in iconic, rigid postures or in various lifelike positions. Original contexts and meanings are uncertain, although the McIntosh digs indicate diverse ritual uses. Certain motifs support symbolic interpretations. Overall, the sculpture is accomplished, suggesting a professional class of artists of yet undetermined gender.

Women were ceramic artists in several sculptural traditions in southern Ghana, as well as potters almost universally in Africa, so many sculptures cited here may be women's work, including those excavated in Ghana. A dozen or more stylistically distinct but related ceramic sites are known, both archaeological (seventeenth century and later) and historical. The rather naturalistic figures, some with typical flattened Akan heads, are mostly from royal funerary contexts. A different, unrelated style of ceramic sculpture was recently excavated by James Anquandah in northwestern Ghana. Called Koma, these finds apparently date to between the fifteenth and eighteenth centuries.

[See also AFRICA: THE RISE OF KINGDOMS AND STATES IN AFRICA; WEST AFRICAN FOREST KINGDOMS; WEST AFRICAN SAVANNA KINGDOMS, articles on INTRODUCTION, BENIN.]

■ Frank Willett, Ife in the History of West African Sculpture (1967). Thurstan Shaw, Igbo-Ukwu: An Account of Archaeological Discoveries in Eastern Nigeria, 2 vols., (1970). Graham Connah, The Archaeology of

Benin (1975). Ekpo Eyo, "Igbo 'Laja, Owo," *West African Journal of Archaeology* 6 (1976): 37–58. Oliver Davies, *Excavations at Ahinsan, Ashanti, Ghana: A Seventeenth-Century Site with Ritual Pottery and Terracottas* (1977). Susan K. McIntosh and Roderick J. McIntosh, *Prehistoric Investigations in the Region of Jenne, Mali* (1980).

Herbert M. Cole

WHARRAM PERCY is a deserted medieval village (DMV) on the chalk Yorkshire wolds 18 miles (29 km) east-northeast of York, England. The village was deserted ca. 1500. Its church, now in ruins, was the center for a large parish of five villages, four of them now deserted. Like so many of its neighbors it survived the *Black Death, but the late-medieval reduction in population saw its arable open fields converted to sheep pasture at a time when demand for wool was increasing. Thereafter agricultural operations were managed from a single site next to the vicarage, where, by the late eighteenth century, there was a large courtyard farm, now excavated. The village remains comprise sixteen hectares of grass-covered earthworks, which include roads, a fishpond, the foundation of a manor house, and thirty peasant houses with their backyards (tofts) laid out in regular rows.

The research excavations at Wharram Percy, between 1950 and 1990, made a most important contribution to DMV studies in Britain, and were the inspiration for other medieval village excavations during these years. The open-area method of excavation was introduced to England from continental Europe in 1953 for one of the peasant houses, and the exploration of all aspects of the village helped to change the emphasis of village excavation elsewhere from a study of house types to that of a constantly changing village morphology.

Recent historical research on DMVs was started by William Hoskins and Maurice Beresford in the 1940s. In 1954 Beresford had listed 1,353 sites (*The Lost Villages of England*); by 1968, 2,263 DMVs were recorded (M. W. Beresford and J. G. Hurst, *Deserted Medieval Villages*, 1971); now more than 3,000 have been identified. Beresford first visited Wharram Percy in 1948, and his trial excavations of 1950–1952 led to its being chosen as the major research project of the Deserted Medieval Villages Research Group, which was founded in 1952. Thereafter, excavations took place for three weeks each year under the direction of John Hurst and Maurice Beresford. At first the work was voluntary, but between 1970 and 1990 the Department of the Environment (now English Heritage) provided financial support.

Saxon remains included buildings, fragments from two decorated Anglian stone crosses, smithing slag, molds for interlace-decorated copper-alloy objects, Tating-type ware pottery imported from northern France, and a series of coins, of the eighth and ninth centuries. Two medieval peasant house tofts were excavated, with the aim of discovering how the villagers lived; traditional medieval archaeology had been concerned with the upper classes. A sequence of longhouses, in which villagers lived under the same roof as their animals, was found. The houses were substantially built with curved timbers (crucks) supporting the roof. The walls were flimsy non-load-bearing structures. Houses were rebuilt on different alignments, later buildings thus coming to overlie the earlier ones. In Area 10, peasant houses were built over the site of a late twelfth-century manor house, the fine stone cellar of which, set 10 feet (3 m) deep into the chalk plateau, had been filled with rubble. The peasant houses were kept clean, with the rubbish put on the fields as manure.

From the pottery, bones, wood, leather, and metal objects found, the economy of the medieval peasant could be studied. Medieval external contacts were demonstrated by the pottery, which was made in the Vale of Pickering 14 miles (23 km) away, and fish, which were brought 20 miles (32 km) from the coast. Continental imports included Mayen lave querns from the Rhineland and some fine-quality pottery from southwestern France.

Other aspects of the project included the complete excavation of the parish church of St. Martin with a sample of its churchyard, the medieval water mill and fishpond, and the medieval and postmedieval vicarages. A parish survey has researched the medieval landscape beyond the village boundaries. The arable open fields comprised exceptionally long strips of ridge and furrow of up to 3,280 feet (1,000 m). The main surprise was the discovery that the planned medieval village was laid out (whether in the tenth or the twelfth century is still unresolved) within the framework of a series of Iron Age and Romano-British fields. These farms, about 0.6 miles (1 km) apart, formed a pattern of scattered settlement that continued into the Anglo-Saxon period.

This development, from dispersed prehistoric, Romano British, and Anglo-Saxon settlement to medieval nucleated village, has been demonstrated elsewhere in the Midland belt of England, and has completely overturned the supposition that nucleated villages were introduced by the Anglo-Saxon settlers in the fifth century.

Wharram Percy is now in the care of English Heritage, which has displayed the site to illustrate the complex development of the landscape. The full results are being published in a series of monographs.

[*See also* BRITISH ISLES: MEDIEVAL BRITAIN; MEDIEVAL EUROPE: DESERTED VILLAGES OF MEDIEVAL EUROPE.]

■ David Andrews and Gustav Milne, eds., *Domestic Settlement 1: Areas 10 and 6*, Society Medieval Archaeology, British Archaeological Reports (1979). Robert Bell and Maurice Beresford, *Wharram Percy: The Church of St. Martin*, Society Medieval Archaeology, British Archaeological Reports (1987). Colin Hayfield, *An Archaeological Survey of the Parish of Wharram Percy, 1. The Evolution of the Roman Landscape*, Society Medieval Archaeology, British Archaeological Reports (1987). Stuart Wrathmell, *Domestic Settlement 2: Medieval Peasant Farmsteads*, Society Medieval Archaeology, British Archaeological Reports (1989). Maurice Beresford and John Hurst, *Wharram Percy Deserted Medieval Village* (1990). Gustav Milne and Julian Richards, *Two Anglo-Saxon Buildings and Associated Finds*, Society Medieval Archaeology, British Archaeological Reports (1992).

John G. Hurst

WHEEL, The. Although the principle of rotary motion has been employed almost universally in the material culture of anatomically modern *Homo sapiens* (for instance, in drilling), its application to transport in pre-industrial times was effectively restricted to a group of historically related farming and pastoral cultures in the central belt of the Old World. Wheeled vehicles were not used indigenously in the Americas (though wheels were used on toy animals in Mesoamerica), nor in Africa south of the Sahara; although they were used continuously in Mesopotamia from at least the fourth millennium B.C., they were relatively late introductions even to the civilizations of Egypt (ca. 1700 B.C.) and China (ca. 1400 B.C.). The reason for this is that wheeled vehicles were practical only when used with draught animals and in appropriate terrain; their complex carpentry was developed only in areas where domestic cattle (and, later, horses) were available for traction, and their introduction was often resisted where alternative modes of transport (pack animals, boats) prevailed. Indeed, their persistent popularity in Old World cultures probably owes as much to the use of wheeled vehicles for ostentatious display and warfare as to any practical advantage over other forms of transport such as sledges or animals for riding. The absence of an indigenous form of the wheel among East African pastoralists (who kept domesticated cattle potentially usable for traction in terrain where wheeled vehicles could have been used) supports the view that wheeled vehicles did not appear in parallel in different areas as the result of a common need; the wheel had a single area of origin and spread as part of a traction complex, a classic example of the diffusion of technology.

The first application of animal draught power was to the plow (see Secondary Products Revolution), which probably appeared in northern Mesopotamia by the sixth millennium B.C., and oxen were soon used to pull sledges, for both transport and threshing. For heavy loads, the use of rollers to reduce friction would have been an advantage, perhaps kept in place by pairs of vertical pegs. That sledges were still used in royal ceremonies (ca. 2500 B.C., when wheeled vehicles were already known) is shown by the example recovered by Sir Leonard *Woolley from the Royal Cemetery at Ur. The transition from sledge to wheeled vehicle, however, is indicated a millennium earlier by the addition of two circular marks below the sign for "sledge" in the pictographic script of the late Uruk period in that area. The earliest forms of the wheel were perhaps developed from the captive roller, with a revolving axle to which two separate, solid wheels were permanently attached. This is the simplest and most robust design, requiring less elaborate carpentry than other forms of the wheel. Such a form has the advantage that the body of the vehicle can be lifted clear if the wheels become bogged down or the axle damaged, and this design of cart survives ethnographically in remote (especially mountainous) areas today. The oldest known surviving wheel fragment, from an early Horgen culture (ca. 3400 B.C.) context in Zürich, Switzerland, is of this kind, and may have been characteristic of fourth millennium B.C. vehicles in general. The distribution of wheeled vehicles at this time can be reconstructed from pottery models.

From the third millennium B.C., many more examples of wheels survive through the deposition of vehicles in graves both in Mesopotamia and on the Pontic steppes in the Pit-Grave culture. These show that the more common arrangement had now developed, whereby the axle itself was fixed below the vehicle, and the wheels rotated around it, held in position by a linchpin passing through the axle. This allowed the wheels both to rotate and to be removed individually, which was a particular advantage with four-wheeled vehicles; and this became the dominant design of axle-wheel arrangement thereafter. These early solid-disc wheels typically had a prominent nave (through which the axle fitted), and were usually made from segments of three thick planks, doweled together. Sometimes the nave was made as a separate piece and inserted, and weight could be reduced by cutting lunate perforations in the disc. Leather or rawhide tires, held in position with metal nails around the perimeter of the wheel, were the prerogative of the Mesopotamian elite. As well as the four-wheeled wagons there emerged a range of two-wheeled vehicles specifically adapted for warfare in Mesopotamia.

By the beginning of the second millennium B.C. several attempts had been made to produce a lighter structure of wheel and vehicle suitable for equid traction, especially for use in war. One such was the crossbar wheel, in which the lunate openings were enlarged to occupy most of the disc apart from the rim and a central nave-bearing stem, which was braced with inset crosspieces. Although this survived for millennia as a wheel for country carts, it was superseded by another design based on an entirely different principle: the spoked wheel with a bentwood rim (felloe), as the essential element of a light chariot. In such a wheel, the bentwood felloe was held in tension by a scarf joint, and connected to a nave by a number of spokes. The origins of the new, lighter design of wheel and vehicle must be sought in the interaction between the advanced states of northern Mesopotamia and Syria and the horse-rearing tribes on the other side of the Black Sea through the Assyrian trade-colonies in Anatolia. Four-spoked wheels predominated in Europe and Anatolia, but an early example with ten spokes is known from a grave at Sintashta near Chelyabinsk in the Urals, and later second millennium B.C. examples from the Caucasus and China have up to thirty spokes. A perfectly preserved four-wheeled carriage from the frozen tumulus of Pazyryk (Altai Mountains, mid-first millennium B.C.) has bentwood and multispoked wheels of this type. The most elegant variant of the spoked chariot wheel was perhaps the one developed by Levantine carpenters and used by the Egyptians in the mid-second millennium B.C., using six V-shaped elements back to back in a circle to produce an integrated six-spoke form (famous from chariots on Egyptian reliefs).

During the later second and first millennium B.C. the spoked wheel became more robust, as larger breeds of horses were developed, which allowed the parallel development of cavalry. Their deeper, composite felloes were often shod with iron nails holding rawhide tires, as depicted on Assyrian reliefs. These more substantial wheels were the prototypes from which later wheels for civilian carts and wagons and for military vehicles were to develop. An important contribution to this design was the iron tire—shrunk on while hot, in a skilled operation—that seems to have been developed in temperate Europe in the later first millennium B.C. Together, these provided the essential elements of the wheel as it developed in preindustrial times. During the first millennium A.D., however, use of wheeled vehicles declined, as horses or camels were used for personal transport and as pack animals for carrying goods. This happened in Europe with the decay of the Roman road system, and more markedly in the Near East with the growing predominance of the Arabian *camel (dromedary) on the longer transdesert routes. The greater prestige of riding, with more elaborate saddles and the use of stirrups for horses after the seventh century A.D., reduced the importance of the wheel to such an extent that it was hardly used over large areas of the Near East, allowing the characteristically twisting lanes of the typical Islamic city. Its use revived in temperate Europe during medieval times, with the growth of coaches and carriages that were the ancestors of today's automobile wheeled vehicles. It was the use of steam engines, and more particularly, the invention of the internal combustion engine, that gave the wheel its present absolute predominance as a means of transport.

[See also HORSE, DOMESTICATION OF THE; LAND TRANSPORTATION.]

■ Richard W. Bulliet, The Camel and the Wheel (1975). Mary A. Littauer and Joost Crouwel, Wheeled Vehicles and Ridden Animals in the Ancient Near East (1979). Stuart Piggott, The Earliest Wheeled Transport (1983). P. Roger S. M. Moorey, "The Emergence of the Light, Horse-drawn Chariot in the Near East, c. 2000–1500 B.C.," World

Archaeology 18 (1986): 196–215. Stuart Piggott, *Wagon, Chariot and Carriage: Symbol and Status in the History of Transport* (1992).
Andrew Sherratt

WHEELER, Mortimer (1890–1976), learned archaeology at the University of London. He became director of the National Museum of Wales after distinguished service in World War I. Wheeler adopted General Lane Fox *Pitt-Rivers's scientific digging methods for his excavations at Roman Segontium. He further refined his approach after becoming director of the London Museum in 1926. Wheeler and his first wife, Tessa, revived the fortunes of the museum and were leaders in the founding of the London Institute of Archaeology in 1937. They also excavated Lydney Park, then the Roman town of Verulamium near St. Albans, training a generation of excavators in scientific excavation methods. Wheeler's finest British excavation was the campaign at *Maiden Castle, Dorset, which unraveled the complicated history of one of Britain's finest hill forts.

Wheeler served in the artillery in World War II, attaining the rank of brigadier. In 1944, he was detached from military service to become director general of archaeology for India. During the next four years, he completely overhauled a moribund archaeological organization, trained dozens of Indian archaeologists, and carried out now-classic excavations at the cities of *Harappa and *Mohenjo-daro in the Indus Valley. In his later years, Wheeler became secretary of the British Academy in London, a post he used to support young scholars excavating in many parts of the world. He also became a well-known television personality, and wrote for the general public. His *Archaeology from the Earth* (1954) remains a classic statement on excavation.

[*See also* HISTORY OF ARCHAEOLOGY FROM 1900 TO 1950: EUROPEAN ARCHAEOLOGY.]

■ Jacquetta Hawkes, *Mortimer Wheeler: Adventurer in Archaeology* (1982). R.E.M. Wheeler, *Archaeology from the Earth* (1954). R.E.M. Wheeler, *Still Digging* (1955).

Brian M. Fagan

WINE

Introduction
Wine in the Classical World
Medieval Wine Trade

INTRODUCTION

Archaeological excavations sometimes uncover remains of grapes—berries, seeds, fruit skins, leaves, stems, and fruit stalks (pedicals)—that have been preserved from prehistoric times in a number of different ways. They may have been burned and reduced to charcoal, or waterlogged, or have become mineralized into semifossils, or exist as impressions in clay. They are usually revealed as a minor component in the plant remains recovered from archaeological sites by paleoethnobotanists (the bulk of botanical remains often being composed of the grains of the annual cereal and pulse crops). Careful study of their morphology can reveal whether they represent wild or cultivated wines.

Wines need not be made from cultivated grapes. It is quite possible to use wild grapes, and all that is necessary is to have a suitable container in which to store the wine during and after fermentation. It is possible that the late Paleolithic and Mesolithic finds of grape pips both in the Near East and in the Mediterranean region indicate that wine making may have begun using leather bags well before the beginnings of agriculture. To make wine, all that is needed is for the juice of the ripe grape to come into contact with wild yeast, which is present in the air and in the "bloom" on the grape skins. Grape juice ferments quickly, and wine may be made from ripe wild grapes in a day or so.

Early Finds of Grapes and Wine Residues. Probably the earliest Old World finds of grape seeds are from the site at Terra Amata (modern-day Nice) in southern France, which date to approximately 350,000 B.P. There are other, later Paleolithic finds from the Mediterranean area—for example, from the Franchthi Cave, Greece (ca. 12,000 B.P.), Grotta del'Uzzo, northwestern Sicily (mid-eighth millennium B.C.), and Balma Abeurador, Massif, south-central France (ca, 10,000 B.P.). In the eastern Mediterranean and Near East there are also a number of finds of wild grape pips dating from the eleventh to the seventh millennia B.C. from Abu Hureyra, Jericho, Aswad, Cayonii, and Ras Shamra. It is difficult to know exactly what these finds signify apart from the fact that they were found in remains of human settlements and were presumably used for food if not for wine.

The earliest certain remains of wine so far detected are those of sediment in an amphora dated to 3500 B.C. from Godin Tepe, Iran. The reddish deposit turned out to be formed from tannin and tartrate crystals, similar to those that form on the bottom of red wine bottle corks today.

The remains of grape stalks, seeds, and skins are seldom found in circumstances that suggest wine production, but in prehistoric Greece they do occur associated with spouted vessels on Early Bronze Age sites such as Aghios Kosmas, Attica, and Myrtos on Crete. A number of specialized vessels were developed for the storage and transport of wine in the Bronze Age Aegean, as well as elaborate vessels made of exotic materials that suggest the mixing and drinking of wine was an activity of significance. Other physical residues of wine are known from much later periods: from seventh-century B.C. Cyprus and from Roman finds in amphorae in a shipwreck off Marseilles, and in a Roman glass bottle now in the museum in Speyer, Germany.

Domestication of the Grapevine. It was with the development of economic interest in wine making that the vine itself became domesticated. Collecting berries from the wild and making wine was a more casual activity, and could produce only small quantities. Viticulture, on the other hand, could develop only once a fully sedentary way of life had been established, and in the Old World this occurred as agriculture became the main basis of the economy. The domestication of annual crops came first, ca. 7000 B.C. in the Near East, and this was followed by orchard husbandry with the first fruit trees to be domesticated—fig, date, olive, and the vine. Domestication of these crops is different from that of the annual crops that are propagated from specially selected seeds. The orchard crops are reproduced vegetatively from cuttings, and a later development was by grafting. It seems likely that the domestication of the vine may have taken place by the fourth millennium B.C.

The wild vine *Vitis vinifera sylvestris* was formerly widely distributed throughout the Mediterranean area and in the region between the Black Sea and the Caspian Sea. It differs from the domesticated form in that many of its varieties are dioecious (there are both male and female plants), although there are a few hermaphrodite forms. The cultivated/domesticated vines *Vitus vinifera sativa* are, however, all hermaphrodite. It is not clear how this transition from dioecious to hermaphrodite plants was achieved, or whether the domesticated forms originated from wild hermaphrodite vines. From an archaeological viewpoint it is convenient that the wild and domesticated grapes can usually be distinguished on the basis of the form of their seeds (pips), the wild ones being more or less spherical in shape with a short stalk or beak and a round chalazal scar on the dorsal face, and divergent grooves on either side of the ventral "bridge." In the domesticated grape the pip is larger and pear-shaped, with a longer beak and a large oval chalazal scar and grooves running parallel to the ventral "bridge." It is also the case that the fruit stalks, or pedicels, of bunches of domesticated grapes tend to break off individually and so sometimes survive in archaeological contexts, whereas the stems of wild grape bunches are very robust and do not break up easily in this way.

The domestication of the vine was clearly first undertaken to provide a good, regular supply of large, juicy fruits for wine making. It should also be remembered that fresh and dried fruits would also have an important part to play in the everyday diet, as would grape juice, vinegar, and the light oil obtained by crushing the pips. The planting of a vineyard is a long-term operation: The vines come to fruit in three to five years from planting but then will continue to benefit several generations of farmers living on the same farm. Should a farmer neglect his vineyard and cease to practice the reproduction of his vines by cuttings or grafting, they will quickly revert to the truly wild state, with fruits and pips closely resembling the truly wild grapes.

It seems likely that the domestication of the grapevine first took place in the region between the Caucasus and Armenia, where today the greatest diversity of wild vines are to be found. A unique find from Soviet Georgia, from a burial at Trialeti dated to 3000 B.C., is a number of vine cuttings enveloped in close-fitting silver sleeves reflecting in detail the buds on the enclosed twigs. There are only a few archaeological sites that document the domestication of the vine through time; the sites of Korucutepe and Tepecik excavated as part of the Keban project on the Euphrates span the Chalcolithic to Middle Bronze Age and have a range of grape pips showing a decrease in the breadth/length ratio through time, suggesting that there is a transition from wild to cultivated forms. A similar phenomenon has been observed at a number of sites in East Macedonia (northern Greece), for example, Sitagroi, Dikili Tash, and Dimitra, where the domesticated grape had become established by at least 2500 B.C.

Early Wine Trade. In other areas of the eastern Mediterranean viticulture was established by around 3000 B.C. The ancient Egyptians may have imported cuttings of vines, as well as amphorae full of wine, from Canaan, since the grapevine is not part of the natural flora of Egypt. At any rate remains of grapes have been found on First Dynasty (3100–2890 B.C.) sites in Egypt. It is clear that wine was valued for its keeping qualities, and its alcoholic virtues, and was a valuable trade commodity. In Egypt, Fifth Dynasty lists distinguish six types of wine according to their places of origin and include wine from Asia and from Canaan. The tombs of the nobles on the western side of the Nile Valley opposite Thebes depict in graphic form the processes of wine making from grape picking to pressing and fermenting wine (e.g., the paintings on the walls of the tombs of Rekhmire, Nakht, and Kha'emwese). In Tutankhamun's tomb (1352 B.C.) thirty-six wine amphorae were found, twenty-six of them with labels attached giving the vineyard, the year of production, and the name of the chief vintner. A few were labeled "very good quality" or "sweet,"

many had come from the western Nile Delta, considered the best vine growing area in Egypt even today.

In the Aegean, the Minoans (second millennium B.C.) were producing wine, and oil, in quantity as is shown by the huge pithoi in the storerooms of the Minoan palaces on Crete, and the occasional finds of presses on villa sites such as Vathypetro. The close links between the Minoans and the Egyptians may well indicate that wine was traded between these areas and possibly other parts of the Near East: The wealth of Minoan civilization may well be partly due to trade in wine.

The Mycenaeans on the mainland of Greece (ca. 1600–1150 B.C.) also grew grapes and traded widely in wine—to Syria, Palestine, Egypt, Cyprus, Sicily, and southern Italy—as well as enjoying the fruits of the vintage themselves. It seems from the finds of small Canaanite jars at Mycenae that they may also have imported wine from the Near East.

■ H. F. Lutz, *Viticulture and Brewing in the Ancient Orient* (1922). E. Hyams, *Dionysus: A Social History of the Wine Vine* (1965). J. M. Renfrew, *Palaeoethnobotany: The Prehistoric Foodplants of the Near East and Europe* (1973). W. J. Darby et al., *Food: The Gift of Osiris* (1977). H. Johnson, *The Story of Wine* (1989). W. van Zeist et al., *Progress in Old World Palaeoethnobotony* (1991). J. Robinson, *The Oxford Companion to Wine* (1994). O. Murray and M. Tecusan, *In Vino Veritas* (1995).

Jane M. Renfrew

WINE IN THE CLASSICAL WORLD

Ancient Greece. By the Classical Period, viticulture was well established throughout Greece. Most of the vineyards were small but there are records of larger ones—up to 74 acres (30 ha) on the island of Thasos, north Aegean in the fifth century B.C. and about 30 acres (12 ha) in Attica in fourth century B.C. The Greeks introduced viticulture to Sicily and South Italy (which they called "Oenotria"—the land of trained vines) and to Southern France, and to their colonies on the shores of the Black Sea reaching as far as the Crimea.

The Aegean islands produced most of the wine for the export trade. Most famous, perhaps, was the island of Chios whose characteristic wine amphorae stamped with the emblems of a sphinx, an amphora, and a bunch of grapes are found in eastern Russia, in Scythian tombs on the Dniepr, at Naucratis on the Nile Delta in Egypt, in Cyrenaica, Massilia (Marseille) in southern France and Spain, in Tuscany, and in Bulgaria—in fact in almost all places where the Greeks had trade links from the seventh century B.C. onward.

Another famous, widely traded, wine was produced on the island of Lemnos and this island may also have been the source of the legendary Pramnian wine. The wines of Thasos were lighter in quality with the flavor of apples.

Various "flavorings" were added to the wines of Classical Greece. Brine or sea water was added to the wine from Kos in the fourth century B.C. Besides adding flavor, this may have had preservative qualities. Wines for special occasions on Thasos were improved by the addition of dough and honey. In other places aromatic herbs were added either during the manufacture or by the consumer. Some blending of the wines was also done: Theophrastus describes the blending of the aromatic wine of Heraclea with the soft, salted Erythrean wine which had no bouquet. Wine was almost always drunk diluted with water.

Wines were usually transported and stored in amphorae, of characteristic shapes, that were lined with resin or pitch (which gave an additional flavor to their contents). They held up to 75 liters each and were used commercially for trading. Smaller painted amphorae were used for serving wine. For transport of small amounts over shorter distances, and probably for rapid consumption, wine was put into wineskins made from the skins of sheep or goats.

Wine was drunk after dinner at a symposium with men reclining on couches, propped up on their elbows, sipping wine from a shallow two-handled wine cup. Women, if present, sat on the edge of a couch or on a chair. A light-hearted drinking game known as Kottabos was developed about 600 B.C. when drinkers at a symposium competed with each other to extinguish a lamp on the top of a stand by throwing the dregs of their wine cups at it. Eventually a special disk called a plastinax replaced the lamp, and the aim was to dislodge it and cause it to fall with a clatter onto a lower one called the manes. This game was extremely popular for at least three hundred years.

Wine was associated with the god Dionysus who came to be the symbol of wine. Festivals in Athens in the fifth century B.C. were often concerned with wine. The most important was Anthesteria, held in early spring to mark the opening of the first wine jars of the new vintage in honor of Dionysus. The vintage celebration in early autumn, Oschophoria, was marked by a procession led by young men carrying the vine branches bearing bunches of grapes in honor of Dionysus.

Socrates summed up the role of wine in a civilized society thus: "Wine moistens and tempers the spirits, and lulls the cares of the mind to rest . . . it revives our joys, and is oil to the dying flame of life. If we drink temperately, and small draughts at a time, the wine distills into our lungs like a sweet morning dew . . . it is then the wine commits no rape upon our reason, but pleasantly invites us to agreeable mirth."

Ancient Rome. Viticulture was introduced to southern Italy by the Greeks, possibly already in Mycenaean times but certainly by the establishment of the Greek colonies in Sicily and southern Italy from 800 B.C. onward. Further north, in Tuscany, the Etruscans from the eighth century B.C. cultivated vines and made their own wines which they traded up into Gaul, beyond the Alps, possibly reaching Burgundy even before the Greeks. It is not clear where the Etruscans first obtained their cultivated vines. They imported fine Greek drinking cups and amphorae for use in their symposia and made their own copies of them.

By the time that Hannibal invaded Italy in the late third century B.C., vines were being cultivated throughout the peninsula. We know little about special vintages, however, until 121 B.C. when Opimius was consul and Opimian wine was accepted by Pliny as belonging to one of the greatest vintages: It was so prized that some of it was kept and drunk when it was 125 years old.

The most famous Roman wines were made in the first centuries B.C. and A.D. to serve the huge market of the city of Rome. They were produced in Latium and Campania. Among the most famous were Caecuban (produced in the marshes around Lago di Fondi), Falernian (from the slopes of Monte Massico), and Gauranum (from Monte Barbaro overlooking the northern shores of the Bay of Naples). There were also notable vineyards at Pompeii and on the Sorrento peninsula that produced the light, white surrentium wine. The wines of Alba, just south of Rome, were also highly rated. The streets of towns like Pompeii were well provided with bars and "thermopolia" where snacks and wine could be purchased. The wine was usually served mixed with water and in cold weather the mixture would be served hot. Their marble counters have huge bowls set into them for serving wine, and behind the counters are racks full of amphorae to replenish the supply. One particularly successful Pompeiian wine merchant was Marcus Porcius. Amphorae bearing his trademark seals have been found widely in the western Roman world but are most numerous in southern Gaul from Narbonne, Toulouse, and Bordeaux.

After the destruction of Pompeii and its surrounding vineyards by the eruption of Vesuvius in A.D. 79 there was an unseemly scramble to plant new vineyards on any piece of cultivable land within reach of Rome. Cornfields became vineyards overnight. It was this threat to the production of everyday agricultural produce to feed the capital that probably prompted the emperor Domitian's edict in A.D. 92 whereby he banned the planting of any new vineyards in Italy and ordered the destruction of half the vines in the overseas provinces of the Roman Empire. In another edict he banned the planting of small vineyards within towns in Italy. Though these edicts were never fully enforced they did have the effect of raising the price of wine. They were eventually repealed in A.D. 280 by Probus and this was followed by a burst of vineyard planting throughout the empire, including Britain. The Roman wine trade was well organized by associations of merchants who had their own headquarters on the Tiber with offices and warehouses, and their own ships and lighters specially designed to carry three thousand amphorae, which were replaced in the second and third centuries A.D. by the use of wooden barrels and casks.

The Spread of Wine-Making to the Celtic World. The first signs that wine was being imported to southeast France, southern Germany, and Switzerland occur in the sixth century B.C. when amphorae, drinking vessels made from exotic materials, jugs, strainers, cauldrons, and gigantic craters for mixing wine occur in the archaeological record. They were imported at Massilia (modern Marseilles) and were then shipped upriver into the hinterland probably as part of a gift-exchange system whereby the Greeks and Etruscans established friendly relations with the barbarian elites to the north. Notable finds documenting this relationship are known from Mont Lassois and Vix, on the trade route from Burgundy to Paris, and at the Heuneberg in south Germany around 530 to 520 B.C. This link was interrupted for about a century but from the end of the third century B.C. onward the wine trade with the Celtic world was reestablished. It was a useful way of disposing of the overproduction of wine in Italy, and for the Celtic aristocrats it was a useful way of impressing their followers. The Celts usually drank the wine undiluted. Many of them ensured that amphorae and drinking vessels were buried with them in their graves.

The wine was imported in pottery amphorae. It appears that at several places in the Rhône Valley some sort of transshipment took place and the wine was transferred from amphorae to barrels or wine skins. Huge quantities of discarded amphorae have been found at Toulouse and Châlons-sur-Saône. By the end of the second century B.C., Italian wine was reaching most of France and some amphorae were even trading as far as southern Britain.

The first production of wine in Gaul must have taken place in the coastal regions around Massilia and Narbonne in Provence certainly by the first century A.D. if not before. Resinated wines, which Pliny says were a source of pride and commanded high prices, were being produced in the region of Vienne in the Rhône Valley at that time.

Amphorae were also being made in southwest France at Gaillac in Languedoc for local wine production in the period 27 B.C. to A.D. 14.

By the third century A.D., wine making had become established in both Bordeaux and Burgundy, by A.D. 250 it had reached the Loire Valley, and by 300 had reached the Rhineland and Mosel; within half a century it was established in the Ile de France and Champagne. It seems that Alsace was the only region of France not to have Roman origins for its wine industry.

■ Theophrastus, *Enquiry into Plants* (esp. 3.11–16). Pliny, *Natural History* (Book 14). J. M. Renfrew, *Palaeoethnobotany: The Prehistoric Food Plants of the Near East and Europe* (1973). E. Hyams, *A Social History of Wine* (1987). B. Cunliffe, *Greeks, Romans and Barbarians, Spheres of Interaction* (1988). D. Zohany and M. Hoff *Domestication of Plants in the Old World* (1988). H. Johnson, *The Story of Wine* (1989). W. van Zeist, K. Wasylikowa, and K.-E. Behre, *Progress in Old World Palaeoethnobotany* (1991). J. Robinson, *The Oxford Companion to Wine* (1994).

Jane M. Renfrew

MEDIEVAL WINE TRADE

Wine was an important item in medieval society and was consumed in two main contexts. First, it was a vital part of the Christian ritual and as such was in constant and regular demand within each and every community. Second, it was associated with feasting, and as such its consumption, especially on a large scale, was a symbol of wealth and status. It is reasonable to assume, in addition, that where wine could be obtained at an affordable price it would also have been consumed socially alongside locally produced alcoholic drinks, such as mead and ale, in taverns and alehouses.

Archaeological evidence for the wine trade consists of the pottery amphorae and wooden wine barrels used to transport wine in bulk. Amphorae were used within the Roman Empire to transport many different goods. In Britain and Ireland, sherds of amphorae have been found on what are interpreted as religious or high-status secular settlements from the southwest peninsula through Wales and Ireland to Scotland. These range in date from the fifth to the seventh centuries. Opinion as to the relative importance of religion and status in this trade varies considerably but is perhaps at present favoring the secular interpretation.

No similar finds occur within the area of pagan, Anglo-Saxon settlement, and the first evidence for the wine trade in this area, and in the North Sea littoral, consists of wooden wine barrels from sites such as Dorestad, Hedeby, and London. These sites range in date from the seventh to the eleventh centuries but were at their height in the eighth and ninth centuries. It is to this period that pottery amphorae from the Rhineland can be dated. These Badorf ware amphorae had a wide distribution on both coastal trading settlements and rich secular or religious settlements further inland. Evidence for a slightly later (late tenth to twelfth century) wine trade between the Black Sea and the Baltic consists of finds of ribbed amphorae from the towns of Sigtuna, Lund, and Schleswig.

Other archaeological evidence for the wine trade is much more suspect. The connection between the wine trade specifically and the pottery carried with it is probably not as strong as is often proposed. For example, London-type ware was produced in the London area in the twelfth and thirteenth centuries and has a similar extensive coastal distribution pattern to northwestern French wares (including Rouen ware). In the latter case it has been suggested that the pottery trade was closely linked with that of wine, but there is no indication that London was the center of an export trade in wine at that time, although grapes were grown locally into the fourteenth century.

To summarize, therefore, there was undoubtedly an extensive trade in wine, often over considerable distances, from the fifth century onward. The concentration of evidence in the Christian west suggests that the ritual use of wine was an important consideration in its trade. Later on there is evidence for the trade in wine to southern and eastern England, the Low Countries, and Scandinavia. In the twelfth century, however, this direct archaeological evidence for the wine trade ceases, but in its place we find the development of large-scale trades in both luxury and low-status goods in which areas famed for their wine—Gascony, northern France, and the Rhine Valley—played an important but not overwhelming part.

Alan G. Vince

WOLSTENHOLME TOWNE. *See* MARTIN'S HUNDRED.

WOOD

Introduction
Analysis of Wood
Conservation of Wood

INTRODUCTION

The importance of wood (and woodworkers) in the development of human society cannot be underestimated. Wood is one of the most complex of raw materials, but it can be worked with minimal tools or equipment and is the starting point for so many other crafts and trades. Fuel, usually wood or charcoal, is required by those working in pottery, glass, and metal, for salt production, and for food and heat. Almost all craft tools require wooden hafts and handles; wood is required for spinning equipment and looms and for containers and buildings. Wooden boats need tar distilled from wood to make them watertight, and tree bark produces powerful chemicals for tanning and dying, as well as fibers for ropes and waterproof material for roofing and canoes. The range of qualities possessed by the different species means that wood can be found on an archaeological site not only as part of a mighty building but also as the raw material for the most delicate of fine baskets.

Unfortunately, artifacts made of organic material, such as wood, which play such an important part in the everyday life of any society, need special conditions to survive burial. Therefore, the preservation of archaeological wood is rare, but when it is found in good condition, it is important to get the maximum amount of information out of it. The only way that this can be done is by rapid response to new discoveries by well-trained specialists. Wood is usually preserved only in conditions which are so extreme that the organisms that damage wood—insects, beetles, and fungi, to name just a few—cannot survive. Direct evidence for wood is usually, therefore, found only in conditions of extreme dryness, cold, or wetness. These extremes have to be continuous, or the process of decay may be triggered. The most famous examples of this kind of preservation must be those from Egypt, where a wide range of objects has survived in tombs and pyramids. The natural dryness of the atmosphere in the area, combined with the qualities of the sand, has led to very spectacular preservation of furniture, baskets, musical instruments, and so on. Although the Egyptian example is probably the best known, there are other parts of the world that have produced well-preserved wood. The caves and pueblos of the American Southwest, for example, which were occupied from 9000 B.C. onward, have produced wooden tools, baskets, and handles.

Extreme cold can produce equally spectacular preservation. In the Altai Mountains of southern Siberia at around 400 B.C., people were buried in deep pits lined with logs and covered with stones. The combination of the burial practice and cold climate meant that wooden objects were preserved along with the bodies, clothing, and so on. Similar fine preservation has been found in Alaska and Greenland. The recent find of a prehistoric man, with his wooden arrows and other equipment, frozen in the ice of the Alps, is a rare example from western Europe (*see* Similaun Man).

Preservation of wood through waterlogging may occur on some sites in the limited context of a well or pond. This kind of discovery may mean that some wooden objects are preserved on sites where organic material would not otherwise survive. Extensively preserved sites can occur in lakes, swamps, fens, marshes, and bogs, with clay, mud, and peat helping to seal deposits from the air. Once wood and other organic material has become waterlogged, burial conditions must remain completely, and continuously, wet and airless (anaerobic) or deterioration will be rapid.

Wetlands vary ecologically, which may lead to subtle variations in the quality of preservation and the type of material that is preserved. Peat bogs are very acid, for example, which means that metal and bone may not be preserved, but wood as well as some other plant material may be exceptionally well preserved. The *bog bodies found in countries such as Denmark and Scotland are preserved in these highly acid conditions. In the *Somerset Levels of western England, as well as in Ireland, Holland, and Germany, wooden trackways have been found, constructed to help prehistoric people move about in the treacherous terrain. Acid burial conditions have led to remarkable preservation in parts of northwestern Europe 3,000 years ago. Bodies were buried in oak tree-trunk coffins with grave goods such as birch-bark buckets and were then preserved because of the high level of tannic and other acids produced by the groundwater moving through the wood of the coffin. This kind of discovery generally produces a limited selection of objects, whereas a more extensively waterlogged site, such as a lakeside settlement, may produce a variety of material, covering many aspects of everyday life in the past.

The first, and probably most famous, of all the *lake dwellings were discovered in Switzerland in the nineteenth century. The wooden remains of submerged structures could be seen when the water levels of the lakes dropped to an unusually low level one cold winter. Attempts to examine the wood led to early experiments in underwater archaeology. Since world War II there have been great advances in *underwater archaeology with the development of lightweight and efficient diving equipment. This had led, in particular, to a better understanding of early boats.

The discovery of sequences of wooden waterfronts preserved in *London, New York, and Dublin has led to a greater understanding of the growth of these cities. The London waterfronts, for example, have helped to establish sequences of tree rings going back to the Roman period, which has helped refine and extend tree-ring dating techniques in recent years (*see* Dendrochronology).

Burnt wood, or charcoal, is commonly found on all kinds of archaeological sites, largely because carbon is very resistant to decay. Often it is possible to identify the species of wood in very small pieces of charcoal, when examined under a microscope. Sometimes the examination of charcoal from archaeological deposits can contribute to an understanding of the ancient environment. Wood may be preserved through being in close contact with a toxic substance, such as salt, and is occasionally preserved by mineralization. The most common example of this is where iron or bronze fittings are used on a wooden box. The structure of the wood may be preserved in the corrosion product of the metal where they have been in direct contact, sometimes indicating details of carpentry and joinery in objects, such as coffins, which rarely survive. Examination of mineralized wood with an electron scanning microscope may enable the wood species to be identified.

Wood on archaeological sites does not survive long after excavation without special treatment. Unfortunately, subtle changes in the burial conditions of archaeological wood (by the drainage of a natural wetland, for example) may lead to its destruction while still underground, undetected and unrecorded. The large-scale drainage of the world's wetlands is an archaeological as well as a conservation issue.

■ Bryony and John Coles, *People of the Wetlands: Bogs, Bodies and Lake-dwellers* (1989). Colin Renfrew and Paul Bahn, *Archaeology* (1991).

Maisie Taylor

ANALYSIS OF WOOD

Archaeological wood, once exposed or removed from the burial environment, will immediately begin to deteriorate, and a number of analytical techniques can be destructive. It is important, therefore, that photographs, drawings, and the recording of technological data be completed as soon as possible after excavation and before the wood is transported or stored or any invasive processes are employed. The techniques used in the analysis of archaeological wood will be described, starting with the least invasive, to give some indication of the order in which they should be applied.

Ideally the first examination of ancient wood should be made by a specialist while it is still in the ground. Some cleaning may be done in the field to aid excavation and transportation, but wood may arrive on the specialist's bench in almost any condition from clean to embedded in matrix. Very degraded wood may be difficult to clean simply because of its fragility. The matrix in which it was embedded may be more abrasive or resistant than the surface of the wood. Consequently, even quite well preserved wood may be difficult to clean without damaging the surface; unfortunately it is the wood's surface that carries important clues on woodworking, such as delicate tool marks. The conditions that cause the preservation of wood will also favor the survival of other organic material. It is important, therefore, when cleaning archaeological wood, to be aware that leather or fabric might be preserved with it.

A wooden object should be measured, drawn, and photographed as a first record and to monitor distortion in storage or conservation. Details of woodworking technology, such as how the piece was formed from the original tree or log and whether the artifact was fabricated from sawn, split, or carved wood, must be recorded and described. The grain of the wood should be recorded (this varies depending on the object's original function) and careful notes should be made of surface details that might point to the use of specific tools (e.g., chisel, axe, or gouge marks). Special attention should be paid to the fabrication of joints, sockets, and holes. When the wood is part of a structure or was designed to fit together with another piece, the possible relationship(s) of the various timbers to the rest of the structure must always be borne in mind.

Although the wood of some tree species can be identified with the naked eye, or under low magnification, identifications are best performed with a microscope (magnifications of 100–200 times are usually sufficient). Species identifications can generally be made from a very small sample, but in a small or delicately made artifact, it may be difficult to take an identification sample without damaging the appearance of the object. Care should be taken to avoid areas with evidence of woodworking. It is often possible to take a sample from a broken surface that will be hidden when the piece is conserved or assembled for display. Species identification can be undertaken on wood after conservation, but it is usually much more difficult. If the sample is taken shortly before conservation, it may be possible to replace most of what was removed and to unite the various pieces during conservation for display or storage. Identification of species is done by cutting three very thin (translucent) sections, in three different planes. Identification is performed by examining the cell structure, which differs according to species. The three sections must be cut relative to the grain of the wood: one transversely, across the grain; one radially to the diameter of the original trunk or log; and one tangentially to that diameter. Charcoal has to be identified using reflected light, so thicker sections are required. The recognition of fine detail can be much more difficult, however.

*Dendrochronology is a technique for dating a piece of wood by comparing its growth-ring pattern with that of other pieces and with reference chronologies. The technique is based upon the fact that in favorable seasons trees produce thick annual growth rings, and in poor seasons, growth can be very slight. Reference chronologies (based upon growth-ring widths) have been built up in various parts of the world, and where these data are available, wood from archaeological contexts can be dated to within six months. Tree-ring analysis can also produce useful data on woodland management and similar topics; it does not necessarily always provide absolute dates.

It can be difficult to sample for tree-ring dating without damaging timber or artifacts. The practical details of measuring samples are all very similar whether wet or dry samples are being examined and whether the samples are in the form of cores or slices of wood. Modern microprocessors have made it relatively simple to engineer a piece of mechanical measuring equipment into an electronic recording and analysis system.

Some of the earliest work on tree-ring dating was carried out in the American Southwest on *Pinus ponderosa* (yellow pine) and *Sequoia gigantea* (giant redwood). Early work in Europe was mostly on pines, but the discovery, in Germany, that oak was a suitable wood for tree-ring measurement was important because its timber had been widely used since earliest times for building in northwestern Europe. It is now one of the most widely used species for dendrochronology. Subfossil trees from peat bogs in northern Europe, known as bog oaks, may date back as far as 6000 B.C. In Ireland and Germany there has been much research into

subfossil wood, and this has provided important chronological data.

[*See also* DENDROCHRONOLOGY.]

■ Mike Baillie, *Tree-Ring Dating and Archaeology* (1982). Karl Wilson and Donald White, *The Anatomy of Wood* (1986).

Maisie Taylor

CONSERVATION OF WOOD

The cell walls of plant material are basically made of cellulose, but in wood a secondary layer (lignin) is laid down as the tree grows and matures. Lignin makes the wood stronger, with a greater resistance to decay than most other plant material. Insects, bacteria, and fungi are among the most common organisms that cause deterioration of archaeological wood. The activity of these organisms may be slowed or halted by imbalances in the environment. Preservation of organic material occurs in extreme climatic or environmental conditions: in deserts, under water, or in bogs; under permanent ice or snow; or at high altitude. Wood may also be preserved through contact with toxins. A common example of this preservation is wood within the corrosion products of metal fittings on a box; in these cases the wood has often been replaced by mineral salts. Toxicity may also lead to preservation of wood in copper, lead, or salt mines. Archaeological charcoal survives because burning changes organic material into carbon, which is unaffected by the organisms that destroy wood.

The species of tree, burial conditions, and the quality of the wood when buried all need to be taken into account when selecting the most appropriate conservation procedure. Wood that has been treated with oil in antiquity, or parts of artifacts such as handles that have been polished and greased with use, may behave differently under conservation. Excavated wood can generally be stored only for a very short time without conservation, but storage conditions must be created that lessen the shock of excavation: cool, dark, and wet for waterlogged wood, for example.

The selection of the best conservation technique for an individual piece is possibly the most important stage in the process. The general tendency in recent years has been toward a policy of minimum intervention, but no conservation technique will restore the wood to the full qualities that it possessed when new. The aim of most conservation procedures is to maintain the stability of shape, size, and surface detail while the wood is stored or displayed under normal museum conditions.

There are four general methods that may be applied to accomplish this goal. If the wood is not seriously deteriorated, it may be possible to bring it slowly to a state of equilibrium, without damage. Subsequent storage of this kind of material must be in a carefully controlled environment. Most archaeological wood that is excavated has been affected by burial and may be soft, weak, and brittle. In these cases it will be necessary to impregnate the wood with a consolidant. A reliable and popular technique for waterlogged wood, used over many years, is to replace the water with a water-soluble wax, polyethylene glycol (PEG). The process is long and slow but relatively easy to monitor. Equipment is inexpensive, but the wax may be very expensive. Wood conserved by this method looks very dark and is heavy, and as certain grades of PEG are slightly hygroscopic, subsequent storage must be carefully monitored. Rosin, with alcohol and acetone, has been used as a consolidant but generally has been superseded. Wood can be dehydrated with alcohol and then, using solvents at high temperatures, impregnated with resin. This is potentially dangerous, and laboratories using this technique are very specialized. The impregnation of wood with alum was used in early conservation of boats in Scandinavia. The wood was held, virtually at boiling point, in molten alum. After treatment it was white, hygroscopic, and needed careful finishing and storage. Recent work has tested the possibility of impregnating archaeological wood with various sugars as an inexpensive and simple way of consolidating it. This may well be the most promising of the new methods of conserving archaeological wood.

When waterlogged wood is freeze-dried the water is converted into a vapor in a vacuum at low temperatures and then extracted. Wood is usually pretreated for this method by soaking in PEG. Without pretreatment, freeze-dried wood may be light, brittle, and vulnerable to physical damage. The color of freeze-dried objects is often very good. The freeze-drying equipment is expensive and complex, but the running costs are not high, and the process need take only weeks or months. The size of the vacuum chamber dictates the size of object that can be treated.

Although not a conservation technique, casting of archaeological wood has been done where local conditions or finance have prevented conventional approaches. Carefully made casts may preserve surface detail, and therefore archaeological data, even if the actual piece is lost.

Conservation of wood is expensive and time-consuming, and conserved material must be stored in environmentally controlled conditions. Many techniques cause difficulties in subsequent sampling for *dendrochronology, species identification, and *radiocarbon dating. Some treatments may cause distortion of surface detail. In all cases it is better to complete all recording, drawing, photography, and sampling before the wood goes into conservation.

Maisie Taylor

WOOLLEY, Leonard (1880–1960) was educated at New College, Oxford. He became assistant director of Oxford's Ashmolean Museum in 1905, learning field archaeology at Roman Corbridge and under the American archaeologist Randall MacIver, working on Meroitic cemeteries in the Sudan. Woolley directed excavations on the Hittite city at Carchemish, Syria, from 1911 to 1914, engaging in some intelligence work on the side. He served as an intelligence officer in World War I, was captured by the Turks, and spent two years as a prisoner of war. In 1922, Woolley was appointed director of the joint British Museum and University of Pennsylvania excavations at *Ur, among the largest and most spectacular excavations of the twentieth century. He was the ideal man for the job, having a flair for scientific excavation, a gift for working with Arab laborers, and a genius for publicity. Between 1924 and 1934, he cleared much of the Sumerian city, excavated the lavishly furnished predynastic Ur royal cemetery, and the Third Dynasty royal ziggurat, also probing the base of the great city mound and revealing a small Ubaid village settlement resting on sterile soil. He also claimed, somewhat extravagantly, to have unearthed evidence for the biblical flood, but his claim has subsequently been refuted. Although overshadowed by the discovery of the tomb of Tutankhamun, Leonard Woolley's Ur excavations provided a wealth of information about Sumerian civilization, even if his methods, while scientific, were somewhat rough and ready by today's standards. (*See* Mesopotamia: Sumer and Akkad.)

After Ur, Woolley excavated at Atchana in Syria, immediately before and after World War II, where he recovered evidence of a Bronze Age trading city and later occupation. A small, commanding man, Leonard Woolley ranks among the greatest archaeologists of the twentieth century. As a popularizer of archaeology, he has had few rivals.

[*See also* HISTORY OF ARCHAEOLOGY FROM 1900 TO 1950: NEAR EASTERN ARCHAEOLOGY; MESOPOTAMIA: SUMER AND AKKAD; UR.]

■ C. L. Woolley, *Excavations at Ur*, 10 vols. (1927–1951). C. L. Woolley, *Digging Up the Past*, (1930). C. L. Woolley, *Excavations at Ur*, (1953). C. L. Woolley, *Dead Towns and Living Men* (1954). H.V.F. Winstone, *Woolley of Ur* (1990).

Brian M. Fagan

WORSAAE, Jens Jacob Asmussen (1821–1885) was born in Jutland, Denmark, and from an early age, collected antiquities and excavated burial mounds. While a Copenhagen law student, he assisted Christian Jurgensen *Thomsen with the National Museum collections, succeeding him as director. Later in life, he became inspector general of antiquities in Denmark, king's antiquary, and professor of Archaeology at the University of Copenhagen. Worsaae was the world's first professional archaeologist. At age twenty-two, he published his classic work *Danmarks Oldtid oplyst ved Oldsager og Gravhoje* (1843), in which he took the *Three-Age System out of the National Museum and applied it in the field. Worsaae was an ardent excavator of burial mounds and peat bogs, where artifacts could be recovered in exact stratigraphic contexts. In his excavations, he found Stone Age artifacts underlying Bronze Age sites, which were, in turn, succeeded by Iron Age settlements. Many archaeologists assumed "the bronze objects, which are distinguished by their workmanship, may have been used by the rich; while the iron objects belonged to those less wealthy and those of stone to the poor." Worsaae proved them wrong, by finding associations of architecture, burial customs, and distinctive artifacts associated with Stone Age, Bronze Age, and Iron Age technologies. His excavations proved the stratigraphic validity of the Three-Age System. Worsaae's field research also provided the basis for the spread of the Three-Age System throughout Europe by the 1860s. He was one of the founders of European prehistoric archaeology.

[*See also* HISTORY OF ARCHAEOLOGY BEFORE 1900: EUROPEAN ARCHAEOLOGY; THREE-AGE SYSTEM.]

■ Ole Klint-Jensen, *A History of Scandinavian Archaeology* (1975). Glyn Daniel, *A Short History of Archaeology* (1981).

Brian M. Fagan

WRITING

Introduction
Petroglyphs
Cuneiform
Egyptian Hieroglyphic
Alphabetic Script
Manuscripts and Codices
Writing Materials

INTRODUCTION

Writing is a 5,000-year-old technology for storing, manipulating, and communicating data. Written texts provide a unique source of information for reconstructing the past. They reveal the ancient names of regions, sites, and individuals that have vanished from human memory. Most importantly, they present facts and events in the perspective of extinct cultures. Archaeology considers writing, therefore, as the divide between history and prehistory.

Concerted archaeological and epigraphic research has identified the fountainheads of writing and established the stages of development of various scripts. Accordingly, scholars have determined that writing has been invented independently in three places. The people of Sumer, in the ancient Near East—present-day Iraq—created the first script around 3100 B.C. Chinese script appeared about 1500 B.C. and in Mesoamerica writing existed ca. 300 B.C. In all these instances, writing consisted of a combination of logographs (or pictographs) representing concepts, with phonetic signs standing for the sounds of a language.

The idea of writing as developed in Sumer eventually spread throughout the Near East and surrounding regions. Sumerian cuneiform writing made an increasingly greater use of phonetic syllable signs, evolving into a syllabary in the early third millennium B.C. This system was to be adapted in the following centuries to Akkadian, Eblaite, Elamite, Hittite, Hurrian, and Old Persian. As early as 3100 to 3000 B.C., scribes in Susa in Elam, present-day southwest Iran, used the proto-Elamite script, which later fell into disuse. This was not the case with the Egyptian hieroglyphic script that prevailed with little change from about 3100 to 3000 B.C. until the beginning of the Christian era. The hieratic, and later, the demotic Egyptian script, provided simplified writing forms for everyday business. The peoples of the Indus Valley adopted writing ca. 2500 B.C. Finally, about 2200 B.C., an indigenous hieroglyphic script was initiated in Crete. It was the antecedent of Linear A, used in the Aegean between 1650 and 1450 B.C., before being supplanted by Linear B in the fourteenth century B.C. These earliest writing systems are mostly deciphered except for Elamite, the Indus Valley script, Cretan pictographic, and Linear A.

The earliest known alphabetic inscriptions come from the site of Serabit al-Khadim in Sinai. Dated about 1700 B.C., they encode a western Semitic language, which suggests that the alphabet was invented along the Mediterranean coast of the Levant. The proto-Canaanite, or proto-Sinaitic, alphabet simplified writing by assigning an individual letter to represent each of the consonantal sounds of the language. While other alphabets were invented, such as the Ugaritic, ca. 1500 B.C., the proto-Canaanite script is held to be the direct antecedent of the three main alphabetic families: South Arabian, Phoenician, and Greek. The South Arabian scripts included Sabean and Himyaritic and evolved into Ethiopian. The Phoenician alphabet was the forerunner of the Old Hebrew and the Aramaic alphabets. The latter, in turn, was the progenitor of the modern Jewish, Arabic, and probably the Brahmi and other Indic scripts. The Greek alphabet was first to assign letters for vowels; the Phrygian, Coptic, Etruscan, and Roman, as well as the Cyrilic alphabets were derived from the Greek prototype.

The Chinese writing system is unique in having an uninterrupted literary tradition. The modern script can be tracked backward through the main stages of its 3,500-year evolution: the "clerky script" (li shu) and "lesser seal script" (hsiao chuan) in the Han dynasty after the third century B.C.; the "greater seal script" (ta chuan) during the Western Chou and Shang dynasties, twelfth to eighth centuries B.C.; and finally, in the late Shang dynasty ca. 1500 B.C., pictography (chia-ku wen). The Koreans and Vietnamese adapted Chinese writing to their own languages as did the people of

Japan, where the borrowed Chinese characters (kanji) were supplemented by a syllabary (kana).

The first writing systems of the New World emerged in Mesoamerica during the Late Formative Period, ca. 300 B.C. through A.D. 250. Great strides are now being made in understanding epi-Olmec and Maya. But Oaxacan, a Zapotec script, and Izapan, recovered in present-day Guatemala, remain undeciphered. The four systems began as and remained logosyllabic. They are thought to stem from ancestral Olmec symbols. In turn, the post-Classic, Mixtec, and Aztec scripts, ca. A.D. 900, probably derive from Oaxacan.

Many questions concerning the diffusion of writing remain unanswered. It is not clear why literacy pervaded some societies, whereas others, like the Inca of Peru or the African kingdom of Dahomey, resisted writing, using quipus and pebbles for administrating their states. In fact, at all times, the majority of languages have remained unrecorded.

The preservation and recovery of ancient texts is a function of the medium on which they are recorded. The Near East has produced archives of thousands of cuneiform clay tablets dating from the third to the first millennium B.C. at sites such as Nineveh in Iraq, Ebla and Mari in Syria, Boghazkoy in Turkey, and Persepolis in Iran. Formal funerary or royal hieroglyphic inscriptions of pharaonic Egypt, chiseled on stone monuments such as those of Hierakonpolis, Giza, or Thebes, have survived the millennia. This is not the case for the contemporaneous day-to-day business texts in hieratic or demotic script, traced with ink on ostraca or papyrus scrolls, which, except in special circumstances, have faded or disintegrated. The three Minoan scripts were incised on clay sealings, labels, and tablets. Pictographic linear was identified at *Knossos, Minoan sites such as Aia Triada and Phaistos produced Linear A, and finally, palaces such as that of Knossos, Mycenae, and Pylos on mainland Greece yielded Linear B tablets.

The use of parchment and papyrus is well attested in the ancient Mediterranean world after 300 B.C., but texts in this medium have only rarely been preserved. The extent of our losses is suggested by clay bullae, used to seal tied manuscripts, recovered in layers dating as early as the second millennium B.C. Other difficulties occur in other regions. The decipherment of the Indus Valley script is hindered by the fact that sites such as *Harappa and *Mohenjo-daro have revealed only short inscriptions carved on stone seals. The site of *Anyang, Honan, has produced some 150,000 fragments of turtle shells and bones upon which the earliest Chinese writing was scratched or painted, but little remains from the Chinese tradition of writing on silk and on paper, subsequent to its invention at the Han court in the early second century A.D. Cast bronze vessels, however, have preserved Chia-ku wen inscriptions.

In the New World, the stela of La Mojarra, Veracruz, Mexico, was the key to decoding epi-Olmec, otherwise known from a score of short stone-carved inscriptions. Since only four bark-paper codices have survived their burning by the Spanish conquerers, Maya writing is known principally from approximately one thousand inscriptions carved on stelae and architectural features of religious centers such as Piedras Negras, Guatemala, and *Palenque, Mexico. The Mixtecs first painted pictures of events on large cloth sheets (lienzos) but adopted a leather codex format after A.D. 1400.

Writing and Society. Archaeological enquiry has focused on the functions of writing and its contribution to civilization. It is noteworthy that the three first centers of literacy exploited writing for power, each in a different way. In Sumer, writing was put to work to control the production of goods. The earliest texts recovered in the temples of *Uruk, Mesopotamia, were lists of commodities featuring receipts or disbursements from public storehouses. Epi-Olmec and Maya writing displayed genealogies or royal deeds legitimizing the kings' authority. In China, where writing was deemed a means of communication with the gods, it was the privilege of the ruler to decipher the divine messages.

The storage and the manipulation of economic records remained a main function of writing throughout the millennia. Wherever it was adopted, writing spurred more complex economies, allowing administrations and businesses to perform more elaborate operations. Writing also continued to be used for political ends. It is not by chance that, in most societies, writing coincides with state formation and the levy of taxes. Furthermore, writing fostered the rise of empires by making it possible to maintain contacts with, and domination over, distant groups.

Writing revolutionized communication by making it possible to conduct transactions in the absence of the parties involved. Over the centuries, literacy wove an always tighter network between individuals and nations. Royal edicts were promulgated through the lands, kings wrote to kings, merchants wrote to clients, and fathers wrote to sons. In time, legal documents placed more value on the written word than on face-to-face communication. The connection of writing with magic and the supernatural also persisted. For example, the Egyptians entrusted to texts the incantations regarded as necessary for survival after death.

The capacity of writing to articulate and synthesize information had a profound influence on culture. Collections of proverbs grew into codes of law; lists of kings and their accomplishments expanded into histories; repertories of religious incantations and hymns became canonic scriptures; selections of literary compositions developed into epics. Literacy, therefore, led individuals to conceive of events in a more global and less segmented perspective and allowed nations to realize their past. Moreover, writing paved the way to science. For example, the recording of celestial observations for divination was the first step toward astronomy and mathematics. Finally, a text can be scrutinized and rewritten at will, creating the potential for unprecedented rigor of logic and depth of thought.

Whereas there is a consensus that writing led cultures to higher levels of civilization, there is an enduring debate on the difference of impact the alphabet vs. logographic writing had on society. There are claims and denials that syllabaries, based on about three hundred signs, or alphabets, limited to some thirty letters, make literacy more accessible to the masses while the repertories of thousands of characters of the logographic systems foster a privileged access to knowledge for the benefit of an elite. On the other hand, logography is cited by some as having the advantage of crossing language and cultural boundaries.

Most recently, archaeology has produced the evidence that writing was not a sudden invention, *ex nihilo*, but instead was the outgrowth of many thousands of years' worth of experience in manipulating symbols. The first writing system, Sumerian cuneiform, was linked to a 5,000-year-old system of tokens of multiple shapes used for counting and accounting goods. The Sumerian pictographs inherited from the counters their shapes, meaning, and

method of processing data. In turn, bone tallies and petroglyphs recovered in Paleolithic sites, dating about 15,000 B.C. in the Near East and earlier in Europe, suggest that the token system was preceded by a yet more archaic system of notations.

By identifying the antecedents of the earliest script, archaeology gives an insight into the essence of writing. First, it makes it clear that communication technologies evolved in parallel with economy. Tallies were used by hunters and gatherers, tokens coincided with the beginning of agriculture about 8000 B.C., and writing corresponded to the emergence of city-states about 3100 B.C. Second, each new communication technology denoted an increased mastery of abstraction. Whereas tallies translated quantities of unspecified items, tokens referred to particular sets, and, finally, writing encoded abstract numbers. Third, contradicting the linguistic theory, the background of the cuneiform script elucidates that writing originated as an independent form of communication and developed only to emulate speech. Most importantly, the archaeological data draws attention to the fact that, as in Sumer, societies the world over counted with simple devices, such as pebbles, knotted strings, or cocoa beans, prior to the acquisition of writing. This raises the question whether numeracy is a universal prerequisite for literacy.

[See also MAYA CIVILIZATION: MAYA WRITING; NOTATION, PALEOLITHIC; ROSETTA STONE.]

■ Jack Goody, *The Logic of Writing and the Organization of Society* (1986). Wayne M. Senner, ed., *The Origins of Writing* (1989). John Chadwick, *The Decipherment of Linear B* (1990). J. T. Hooker, ed., *Reading the Past* (1990). Florian Coulmas, *The Writing Systems of the World* (1991). Denise Schmandt-Besserat, *Before Writing* (1992). Joyce Marcus, *Mesoamerican Writing Systems* (1992). William G. Boltz, *The Origin and Early Development of the Chinese Writing System* (1994). Henri-Jean Martin, *The History and Power of Writing* (1994).

Denise Schmandt-Besserat

PETROGLYPHS

People on all the continents and on many major island groups have carved and painted symbols on rock surfaces. The practice boasts an antiquity of at least forty thousand years and is common even today, as attested to by graffiti found decorating the sides of buildings in our current environment.

Those symbols created by carving, incising, rubbing, pitting, pounding, or by other mechanical means, are known as petroglyphs. Those created by painting are known as pictographs. There is no special term for petroglyphs that were painted as well as carved. Any of the three types can be found listed under such terms as "rock art" or "art rupestre."

Many different explanations have been advanced as motives for this worldwide practice. It has been held to be religious in intent, art for art's sake, healing, magic (particularly hunting magic), boundary marking, and the product of idle hands. But except for Native Australians or some western Native Americans, it is impossible for us now to find a reliable informant to give us the meaning or function of a carved or painted design or site—if, indeed, it had a meaning.

It is held that, in Europe, Cro-Magnon people carved and painted designs on walls of caves from as much as forty thousand years ago down until only twelve thousand years ago. On occasion, their sites were further embellished with freestanding sculptures of such animals as bison. In Australia people are said to have been carving and painting symbols on rock surfaces—and presumably other surfaces which perished, whereas the rocks are still with us—at least as long ago as thirty thousand years ago and perhaps even the forty thousand years ago we accept for Cro-Magnon artistry. We are aware that as this is written somewhere people are using spray cans to paint names and designs on walls and sidewalks, while others create similar products by battering with stones or by incising with metal tools.

We can but guess at the motivation of most of those who carved and painted. Modern Native Australians have revealed the meanings of specific designs and groups of designs to researchers. Native Americans in the western United States of America have also imparted such knowledge. Accepting these statements as fact, despite knowing there are those too polite not to give an answer to a query but careful not to give a correct answer, we know that we will never be certain of the meaning of a design or group of designs on the more than 100,000 recorded sites in the worldwide inventory whose total grows even as this is written.

An example of the difficulty of explaining the meaning of a petroglyph/pictograph design was furnished to us by W. J. Hoffman more than a hundred years ago. Cut into a birch-bark scroll used as a pattern for assuring proper performance of an Ojibwa Grand Medicine Society ceremony was a crude but recognizable figure of a bird of prey. Hoffman inquired as to the meaning of the bird. He was informed the design did not represent a bird at all but rather a participant in the ceremony which the scroll recorded who was sitting upright and watching every detail of the ceremony with a concentration equaling that of a hawk watching for its prey. How could the uninitiated reach such a conclusion from what was palpably a crude outline of a hawk?

There are associations of persons interested in recording, studying, and seeking explanations of the meanings of petroglyph and pictograph designs and sites. They range from such an informal group as those who gathered in Natural Bridge State Park in Kentucky in April 1993 to more structured, more formal organizations such as the nationwide American Rock Art Research Association based in California, the Australian Rock Art Research Association, Melbourne, and the International Committee on Rock Art of UNESCO.

There are centers for storing information and learning how to record and study the phenomena. The Centro Camuno di Studi Preistorici in Valcamonica, Italy, offers courses in recording and in seeking explanations for petroglyph and pictograph sites. The University of California at Los Angeles maintains a Rock Art Archive. The Getty Conservation Institute, Marina del Rey, California, trains people to assess needs to assure the preservation of petroglyph and pictograph sites and to form policies for visitor management and site interpretation.

[See also NOTATION, PALEOLITHIC; ROCK ART, *articles on* INTRODUCTION, ROCK ART OF SOUTHERN AFRICA, ALPINE ROCK ART, PALEOLITHIC ART, NORTH AMERICAN ROCK ART, AUSTRALIAN ROCK ART.]

■ William J. Hoffman, *The Midewiwin or "Grand Medicine Society" of the Ojibwa* (1891). Paolo Graziosi, *Palaeolithic Art* (1960). Harald Pager, *Ndedema* (1972). Klaus F. Wellmann, *A Survey of North American Indian Rock Art* (1979).

James L. Swauger

CUNEIFORM

Cuneiform writing, a modern term derived from the Latin words meaning "wedge shaped," denotes a system of writing invented around the end of the fourth millennium B.C., probably in the southern Mesopotamian city of *Uruk. Cuneiform writing continued in use until around A.D. 100 and was the most widely used system of writing prior to the alphabet, which eventually replaced it.

Cuneiform seems to have grown out of an earlier system of recording economic transactions that used tokens or clay counters, which can be traced far back into the Uruk archaeological period, usually dated ca. 3400–3000 B.C. Cuneiform appears toward the end of this period. Cuneiform began as highly stylized pictures of objects drawn on moist clay using a reed stylus, and, though often described as "pictorial," photographs of the earliest tablets datable by archaeological methods clearly reveal the "cuneiform" stylus impressions that characterize the later script, pointing to continuity in the mechanics of writing.

To the eye unaccustomed to reading cuneiform, it looks a bit like mud in which birds have walked about. Ancient Mesopotamian scribes recognized, and probably took pleasure in, the bewildering appearance of cuneiform, because a Sumerian legendary text describes it as looking like pegs or nails. Indeed, the individual strokes of fully developed cuneiform do resemble antique nails, and this resemblance is reflected in the name "nail writing" that occurs in several modern languages (e.g., Dutch and Arabic).

By ca. 2000 B.C., cuneiform seems to have spread from its original home in southern Iraq to most parts of the Mesopotamian basin. Originally created to write the Sumerian language, it was adapted to write Semitic Akkadian (before 2500 B.C.) and the closely related language of *Ebla in northern Syria (variously dated from ca. 2500 to ca. 2250 B.C.). Recent discoveries in Syria and Turkey indicate that its use throughout the third millennium was much more widespread than has generally been thought. It seems safe to assume that by the end of the Third Dynasty of *Ur (ca. 2000 B.C.), cuneiform was known and used from the Zagros Mountains in Iran to the Mediterranean. It achieved its widest distribution in the Middle and Late Bronze Age (ca. 2000–1200 B.C.), being attested in the east from Elam in southwestern Iran to the Mediterranean in the west and in the north from central Turkey to Egypt in the south.

Cuneiform as a writing system was a mixture of word signs (logograms), idea signs (ideograms, used to represent two or more words with more or less similar meanings), and syllabic-phonetic signs. Development of syllable signs was facilitated by the large percentage of monosyllabic words in Sumerian. Sumerian cuneiform relied heavily upon word signs and ideograms, with phonetic signs and rather precise rules for orthography and format being used to make the meaning of these more clear.

Early adaptations (prior to ca. 2200 B.C.) of this system to write Akkadian and the closely related language of Ebla have markedly archaic features in which logograms and ideograms still play a major role. Around 2200 B.C., probably linked with calligraphic and metrological reforms sponsored by one or more of the successors of Sargon of Akkad, syllabograms (phonetic signs) move to the core of the system, and this "Akkad cuneiform" becomes the basis for subsequent adaptations. The tendency toward phonetic writing is perhaps best exemplified in Akkadian letters from the Middle Bronze Age (ca. 2000–1600 B.C.). However, the logographic-ideographic element also continued in certain literary genres.

"Akkad cuneiform" was widely adapted not only to write various dialects of Akkadian but also Elamite, Hittite,

Hurrian, Urartian, and a number of other languages. These adaptations preserve the basic features of the Akkad system, but the specific calligraphic and grammatical rules varied with place, era, and even genre. "Akkad cuneiform" also inspired the invention of two entirely distinct cuneiform scripts: the western Semitic cuneiform alphabet of the Late Bronze Age, known primarily from excavations at Ugarit, and the Old Persian syllabary, used to write monumental inscriptions of the Achaemenid kings in the sixth to fourth centuries B.C.

The modern decipherment of cuneiform writing began in the eighteenth century and was finally achieved in the period 1846–1852. The British army officer Henry *Rawlinson played a major role in this endeavor, copying the almost inaccessible cuneiform inscriptions of Darius I (522–486 B.C.) written in Akkadian, Elamite, and Old Persian high on the cliff face of Behistun on the caravan route leading from Babylonia to the region of Persepolis. Rawlinson also made decisive contributions to the decipherment itself.

Almost simultaneously with decipherment came the explorations at *Nineveh by Austen Henry *Layard and Hormuzd Rassam (1046–1047, 1049–1851), which resulted in discovery of the library of Ashurbanipal (last powerful king of Assyria, 668–ca. 628 B.C.). This cuneiform library, eventually deposited in the British Museum, contained a wide variety of texts, including many Sumerian-Akkadian bilinguals, and has played a major role in subsequent study of these and other languages written in cuneiform.

These discoveries set off a whole series of explorations of tells in Mesopotamia. In the decades that followed, thousands of tablets and other clay or stone artifacts bearing cuneiform writing were dug up by authorized excavations at sites such as Sippar, Girsu, Nippur, *Babylon, and Assur, and made their way into museums in Europe, America, and the Ottoman Empire. These discoveries also had the effect of stimulating the profit-oriented trade in these antiquities to Western collectors, and countless cuneiform economic and administrative tablets were dug up, mostly in Babylonia (for instance, at Girsu, Umma, Larsa, and Puzrish-Dagan) but also in Turkey and Egypt and made their way via the antiquities market into both public and private collections in the late nineteenth and early twentieth centuries.

After the First World War, however, large-scale illicit excavation was gradually stopped, and with the improvement of archaeological methods at authorized excavations the stratigraphic context of newly discovered cuneiform inscriptions began to be reconstructed in a more or less precise way.

[See also ASSYRIAN EMPIRE; MESOPOTAMIA, articles on THE RISE OF URBAN CULTURE, BABYLONIA; NEAR EAST, articles on THE BRONZE AGE IN THE NEAR EAST, IRON AGE CIVILIZATIONS IN THE NEAR EAST.]

■ Marvin A. Powell, ed., "Aspects of Cuneiform Writing," *Visible Language* 15, (1981). Ilya Gershevitch, "Diakonoff on Writing, with an Appendix by Darius," in ed. J. N. Postgate, *Societies and Languages of the Ancient Near East, Studies in Honour of I. M. Diakonoff*, pp. 99–109 (1982). Jerrold S. Cooper, "Cuneiform," in ed. David Noel Freedman et al., *Anchor Bible Dictionary*, Vol. 1 (1992), pp. 1212–1218. Hans J. Nissen, Peter Damerow, Robert K. Englund, *Archaic Bookkeeping, Early Writing and Techniques of Economic Administration in the Ancient Near East* (1993). Denise Schmandt-Besserat, *Before Writing*, 2 vols. (1992). Marvin A. Powell, "Review," *Journal of the American Oriental Society* 114 (1994): 96–97.

Marvin A. Powell

EGYPTIAN HIEROGLYPHIC

Hieroglyphic ("sacred carving") is the term used by Greek authors to describe the pictographic writing of ancient Egypt, probably inspired by the Egyptians' own name for the script, "god's words." Hieroglyphic first appeared toward the end of the fourth millennium B.C. and remained in use until the fourth century A.D. The script was primarily intended for monumental inscriptions; its individual signs, called *hieroglyphs*, were usually carved or painted on stone, wood, or plaster. Handwritten texts employed a cursive form of hieroglyphic, which the Greeks called *hieratic* ("sacerdotal"), and, beginning in the sixth century B.C., a second cursive script, known as *demotic* ("popular"). Both were written with a reed brush and ink on papyrus, leather, or pottery or limestone ostraca.

The last known documents in the ancient script are a hieroglyphic text dated to A.D. 394 and a demotic inscription of A.D. 452. The Egyptian language itself survived until sometime after the twelfth century A.D., written in an alphabet derived from the Greek. This final script, known as *Coptic*, was adopted by early Egyptian Christians to avoid the "pagan" associations of the older writing systems, and is preserved today in the scripture and liturgy of the Coptic church.

Egyptian hieroglyphic was at base a pictographic system. All of its signs represented some object in the ancient Egyptian world, whether natural, man-made, or conceptual. As such, they occasionally reflected historical changes in the objects they depicted: for example, in the form of weapons such as daggers and axes. As elements of the writing system, however, hieroglyphs incorporated several degrees of abstraction from this underlying reality.

Each sign could be used as a logogram or ideogram for individual words or concepts: for instance, the picture of a dagger, for "dagger," or that of a man falling, for the notion "to fall." Many hieroglyphs could also be employed as phonograms to represent sounds of the language rather than (or in addition to) words or concepts. This latter function made it possible to write words or concepts that would otherwise be difficult to depict ideographically. As phonograms, hieroglyphs represented one to three consonants; in common with later Semitic scripts such as Arabic and Hebrew, Egyptian writing reflected the consonantal skeleton of a word, ignoring the vowels. Triconsonantal phonograms were largely associated with single lexical items and their derivations, and as such were essentially logographic. Those representing one or two consonants, however, were used to write not only words associated with the hieroglyphic object but also unrelated words containing the same one or two consonants. Thus, the picture of a tree branch was used not only as the ideogram for *ht* "wood" but also in writing words such as *nht* "successful" and *htht* "throughout."

The uniliteral signs were the most frequent of all hieroglyphs, amounting to an "alphabet" of Egyptian's twenty-four consonants. Nonetheless, Egyptian hieroglyphic never made the transition to a single alphabetic system. In the standard orthography of the Middle Kingdom (early second millennium B.C.), most words were written with one to six signs, biliteral or triliteral phonograms usually being "complemented" by uniliteral signs, and were often marked at the end by an ideogram serving as "determinative" to specify the conceptual class of the word: for example, the sequence *n* + BRANCH + *h* + *t* + MAN BRANDISHING A STICK for *nht* "successful, victorious."

The elements of the hieroglyphic system were analogous to those present in Sumerian cuneiform, although the Egyptians developed consonantal phonograms in place of Sumerian's syllabic signs (representing consonant + vowel combinations). Since cuneiform appeared somewhat earlier than hieroglyphic, it is conceivable that Egypt borrowed at least the idea of writing, if not its details, from ancient Sumer. Opinion is still divided on this question. Those who favor a Sumerian impetus point to the archaeological evidence of Mesopotamian influence in early Egyptian art and architecture. Since the earliest inscriptions already show all the elements of the full system, it has even been suggested that hieroglyphic was the invention of a single individual rather than the product of decades or centuries of development like that traceable for cuneiform.

The origin of Sumerian writing, from clay tokens to cuneiform tablets, is preserved in relatively imperishable materials. Those who argue for a parallel independent development in Egypt note that comparable precursors of hieroglyphic could have been inscribed on less permanent media. This argument is bolstered by later scenes of the gods inscribing the pharaoh's name on tree leaves, and by the Egyptian term for "annals," literally, "collection of branches" (a notched palm rib is the ancestor of the hieroglyph for "year"). Papyrus scrolls occurred almost as early as hieroglyphs themselves.

Historically, the emergence of hieroglyphic was coincident with the formation of the Egyptian state, and the earliest documents were almost exclusively royal. For this reason, it has been suggested that writing developed in Egypt out of the need for administrative record keeping, unlike Sumer, where it had a clear economic origin. The first texts are associated with kings of "Dynasty 0," the period shortly before the beginning of Dynasty 1, and come mostly from two sites: Hierakonpolis, probably the first administrative center to control the entire country; and Abydos, burial place of Dynasties 0–1 kings. The objects on which they are inscribed are of two kinds: (1) grave goods—mostly stelae, jars, jar sealings, and wood or ivory tags attached to other funerary gifts; and (2) royal offerings—primarily decorated maceheads and cosmetic palettes. The inscriptions are short, often no more than proper names and titles. Those on jars identify the contents, place of origin, and donor. Tags and royal offerings are generally more elaborate, with scenes and captions that designate a specific signal year by means of its major events, such as "Smiting Nubia" and "Fashioning (a Statue of) Anubis." Some also contain evidence for a census of livestock and people.

Such year designations form the earliest royal annals, including a biennial census that gave its name to the later term for "regnal year" (ḥsbt, literally, "counting"). In the Fifth Dynasty (ca. 2400 B.C.), these ancient records were compiled into a consecutive history of the kings of Dynasties 0–5, arranged chronologically and carved onto both sides of a stone stela. This monument, now known as the Palermo Stone, has survived in only a few fragments, but these are enough to demonstrate the continuity of hieroglyphic archives: as in the early labels, the stone records the major events of each regnal year, along with the height of the Nile's annual Inundation.

Although the earliest inscriptions contained all the elements of the hieroglyphic system, the script itself was not standardized until Dynasty 3 (ca. 2600 B.C.), both in the form of individual hieroglyphs and in orthography. The first

known consecutive texts date from the reign of Djoser (ca. 2630 to 2611 B.C.) and consist of short statements made by the gods to the king on one of his monuments. Beginning in the New Kingdom (ca. 1500 B.C.), there was an increasing emphasis on the "secret" nature of hieroglyphic writing. This culminated, in the Ptolemaic Period (after 304 B.C.), in the "reinvention" of the script, using older signs with new values based on religious symbolism or acrophony (sound value derived from the first consonant of an associated word). As a result, hieroglyphic texts became increasingly difficult for all but the initiated to read, a factor that no doubt contributed to their eventual illegibility.

The modern recovery of hieroglyphic began in the eighteenth century, but full decipherment became possible only with the discovery of the *Rosetta Stone in 1799. By comparing the stone's hieroglyphic text with both the Greek translation and Coptic equivalents, Jean François Champollion was able to demonstrate that hieroglyphic writing was not only symbolic (ideographic) but also phonographic, representing sounds. The announcement of his discovery in 1822 marks the beginning of the modern science of Egyptology.

[*See also* EGYPT, *articles on* OLD KINGDOM EGYPT, MIDDLE KINGDOM EGYPT, NEW KINGDOM EGYPT.]

■ Hilda Petrie, *Egyptian Hieroglyphs of the First and Second Dynasties* (1927). Alexander Scharff, *Archäologische Beiträge zur Frage der Entstehung der Hieroglyphenschrift* (1942). Siegfried Schott, *Hieroglyphen, Untersuchungen zum Ursprung der Schrift* (1950). Henry George Fischer, "Hieroglyphen" (in English), in *Lexikon der Ägyptologie*, vol. 2, eds. Wolfgang Helck and Wolfhart Westendorf, (1977), pp. 1189–1199. Béatrice André-Leicknam and Christiane Zeigler, eds., *Naissance de l'écriture: cunéiformes et hiéroglyphes* (1982). Wolfgang Schenkel, "Schrift," in *Lexikon der Ägyptologie*, vol. 5, eds. Wolfgang Helck and Wolfhart Westendorf, (1984), pp. 713–735. John D. Ray, "The Emergence of Writing in Egypt," *World Archaeology* 17 (1986): 307–316. Henry George Fischer, "The Origin of Egyptian Hieroglyphs," in *The Origins of Writing* Wayne M. Senner, ed. (1989), pp. 59–76.
James P. Allen

ALPHABETIC SCRIPT

An alphabet is a writing system in which each unit corresponds in principle to a single segment of speech—in which each letter basically corresponds to a sound. It may be more accurate to speak of the alphabet as a family of writing systems, since there are a number of different types of alphabets. All alphabets can be traced to a single original script, invented in the Near East, probably in Syria-Palestine, early in the second millennium B.C. to notate the West Semitic languages. The most important modern members of this original alphabetic group are Hebrew and Arabic; in ancient times Aramaic, Phoenician, and Ugaritic were also important.

The term "alphabet" is used to describe several distinct scripts. The Semitic alphabet is almost purely consonantal at base and did not fully notate vowels prior to the development of a system of diacritical marks that are more or less independent. Other alphabets have full and integrated vowel notation. The earliest of these was the Greek alphabet, which developed from the Semitic alphabet early in the first millennium B.C.; all European scripts are descended from Greek, either directly (e.g., modern Greek) or through the Roman adaptation (in western Europe) or the Cyrillic adaptation (in most of eastern Europe).

The alphabet arose during the Middle Bronze Age (2000–1525 B.C.) and came into increasingly broad use during the succeeding Late Bronze Age (1525–1200 B.C.). The process by which the alphabet came into being is obscure. On the one hand, there can be no doubt that speakers of West Semitic languages were exposed to a variety of writing systems and were influenced in particular by the model of Egyptian hieroglyphics. On the other hand, there is a long-standing tradition of regarding writing as an invention, the work of one person at a particular time.

In Late Bronze Age alphabetic texts two types of signs are used: the linear alphabet, the ancestor of all later forms, and the wedge (or cuneiform) form, used for Ugaritic, the West Semitic language of Ugarit. The wedge form of the alphabet developed under the influence of Mesopotamian cuneiform writing and was adapted for writing on clay. The scribes of Ugarit also adapted it to record vowels in a limited way. Wedge-alphabet writing, unlike most other Semitic forms of the alphabet, was oriented from left to right. Late Bronze Age excavations in the Levant (modern Syria, Lebanon, Israel, and Jordan) have also yielded a small group of linear alphabet texts, the "Proto-Canaanite" texts (also called Canaanite). The Proto-Sinaitic inscriptions, another small body of texts, date from the end of the Middle Bronze Period. They seem to be relevant to the prehistory of the alphabet, but despite various attempts, these rock-cut graffiti from Serābit al-Khadim, a turquoise-mining area in the Sinai peninsula, cannot be said to have been fully deciphered.

During the Iron Age (1200–600 B.C.) the linear alphabet flourished and spread. There are two principal forms, the northern (called in its earliest stages Phoenician) and the southern (best known from South Arabian texts). The southern form of the linear alphabet retained throughout its history the original, purely consonantal orthography, while the northern form over the ninth to fifth centuries B.C. developed various ways of using consonantal signs to indicate the presence of vowels. This development is antecedent to the regular use of vowels in Greek and later alphabets. It was during this period that the Greeks borrowed the Semitic alphabet and adapted it to their language; this new script quickly spread, via Greek colonies in Italy, to the Etruscans and then to the Romans.

As the northern linear alphabet spread through the Levant and neighboring regions and was used to write the various Northwest Semitic languages, it took on different shapes. These new scripts include linear Hebrew (also used for Moabite), and the scripts of Phoenician colonies in the Mediterranean, Punic, and Neo-Punic. A distinctive Aramaic script developed by the mid-eighth century B.C. By 700 Aramaic was the preeminent language of the region; the Persian Empire, established in the mid-sixth century, adopted it as its official language. The Aramaic alphabet replaced the linear Hebrew alphabet among the Jews in the sixth century B.C. The older Hebrew alphabet remained in intermittent use until A.D. 135; during this later phase it is called Paleo-Hebrew script. Post-biblical Hebrew scripts, the Jewish (also called square or Assyrian) scripts, developed from the exilic, Aramaic script.

Aramaic script continued its dominance over a wide area long after the collapse of the Persian Empire. The post-imperial history of script includes, in addition to the Jewish scripts, the Nabatean script (from which Classical Arabic script developed), the Syriac script (still used among eastern Christians), as well as scripts used in Iran and later diffused to South and Central Asia. The many modern South and Southeast Asian alphabets are descended from Aramaic.

The "southern" linear alphabet was the source for the scripts used for the pre-Classical Arabic (e.g., Thamudic), for Old South Arabian languages (e.g., Sabean, Qatabanian), and for inscriptional Ethiopic script. From the last of these developed the syllabary still in use in Ethiopia.

■ I. J. Gelb, *A Study of Writing: The Foundations of Grammatology* (1963). Joseph Naveh, *Early History of the Alphabet* (1982). Peter T. Daniels and William Bright, eds., *The World's Writing Systems* (1994).
M. O'Connor

MANUSCRIPTS AND CODICES

In archaeology, the word "manuscript" commonly refers to a text written in ink or in paint on a thin, pliant and portable object (such as paper, papyrus, or leather). Archaeologists make a clear distinction between a manuscript and an inscription; an inscription generally refers to any text written on a hard surface, whether a plaster wall, a rock-face, or a piece of jewelry.

Manuscripts were made from a surprising variety of materials and were an appropriate writing medium for most contexts (display inscriptions being an obvious exception). The materials from which manuscripts were made varied mainly according to local economic and environmental conditions. Papyrus was overwhelmingly preferred in Egypt because it grew so abundantly there. Papyrus was used alongside animal skins elsewhere in the ancient eastern Mediterranean and the Near East, although papyrus was usually preferred because its sheets were easily trimmed or pasted together, making it easily adaptable to the length of the text being recorded. Parchment—made from animal skins, but far thinner and more highly processed than leather—first became popular in the second century B.C. at Pergamon in Asia Minor, apparently because of an interruption in the supplies of papyrus caused by the wars between the Ptolemies and Seleucids. Over the next several centuries it gradually replaced papyrus in the Mediterranean world as the main manuscript material, owing to a number of advantages: it was more durable than papyrus, it provided a smoother and more even writing surface, and, because it was an animal product, it could be manufactured practically anywhere.

In ancient South and Central Asia, the usual materials for manuscripts were palm leaves or sheets made from the inner bark of birch and aloe trees. In ancient China, manuscripts were most commonly written on silk or bamboo tablets (bamboo tablets are classified as "manuscripts" even though they do not fit the definition given above). True paper, said in early texts to be made of tree bark, old rags, and fishing nets, was invented around A.D. 100, according to traditional accounts. Over the next three centuries, it gradually replaced bamboo tablets and silk as the preferred writing material. The use of paper then spread slowly eastward to Korea and Japan, and westward to India and the Islamic world, eventually reaching Egypt in the tenth century and Europe in the twelfth.

All of the manuscript materials described above are known from archaeological contexts. The greatest proportion of our manuscript material comes from Egypt, which has yielded thousands of papyrus manuscripts in the Egyptian, Greek, and Coptic languages. A vast amount of evidence comes from China as well. In the first half of the twentieth century, archaeologists discovered more than twelve thousand bamboo tablets or fragments of tablets and tens of thousands of paper documents. The paper finds are concentrated in northwestern China, which, like Egypt, is extremely arid; the largest find of paper consists of more than twenty thousand rolls found in the caves at Tun-Huang, ranging in date from A.D. 400 to 1000. The most famous finds of manuscripts written on parchment are undoubtedly the *Dead Sea Scrolls, consisting mainly of copies of the Hebrew Bible and sectarian Jewish religious texts, found in a group of caves near Khirbet Qumran on the shores of the Dead Sea.

The codex is the precursor of the modern book; in antiquity, the word "codex" refers to a document that is written, not on a single sheet or roll, but in leaves that are bound together. In its original use in Latin, the term referred to a multileaved writing tablet or to two or more writing tablets that were bound together. By the second century A.D., however, the term was usually used to designate a book made of parchment leaves sewn together. The leaves of a codex could be of parchment or papyrus, and there are even examples of codices which contain both parchment and papyrus leaves. The codex first came into widespread use among Christians, and it gradually gained in popularity from the second century onward as Christianity spread. By the fifth century, the codex had almost completely replaced the scroll for recording literary and religious texts.

The overwhelming majority of codex manuscripts that have been found in archaeological contexts come from Egypt, though it is very rare that more than a few leaves of a codex are found in an excavation. Although not from a controlled excavation, the most significant find is the twelve nearly complete papyrus codices of gnostic Christian texts found at Nag Hammadi in 1945 and dated to the fourth century. Each of these codices is bound in leather, consists of a single quire (a stack of sheets—usually from twenty to forty in number—folded down the middle and bound together), and is closed by a leather thong wrapped around the covers.

Bamboo and wood writing tablets strung together to form a single document have been found in excavations in China, but there is nothing that could be called a codex in its usual sense. In Mesoamerica, however, codices were commonly used by Maya priests to record religious and ritual texts. These codices were actually long strips of paper that had been folded in the manner of a fan. The manufacture of the paper involved pounding the inner bark of the fig tree into long sheets and then covering them with lime paint to make the surface smooth. Artistic representations show that they were bound in jaguar skin. Only four Maya codices survive, and none are from an archaeological context. However, excavations have uncovered the remains of several completely decayed codices.

[*See also* MAYA CIVILIZATION: MAYA WRITING; NEAR EAST: LATE ANTIQUITY IN THE NEAR EAST.]

■ Jaroslav Černý, *Paper and Books in Ancient Egypt* (1952). Tsuenhsuin Tsien, *Written on Bamboo and Silk: The Beginnings of Chinese Books and Inscriptions* (1962). R. Reed, *Ancient Skins, Parchments, and Leathers* (1972). Michael D. Coe, *The Maya Scribe and His World* (1973). Naphtali Lewis, *Papyrus in Classical Antiquity* (1974; supplement 1989). C. H. Roberts and T. C. Skeat, *The Birth of the Codex* (1983).

William D. Whitt

WRITING MATERIALS

For the archaeologist, writing materials are best studied in relation to the technology of writing. Like any other technology, the many materials and processes involved in

writing—from manufacturing writing implements to producing actual inscriptions—leave distinctive traces in the archaeological record. The tasks of the archaeologist are to connect these distinctive traces to the technology of writing, and to ask questions about the role writing played within the particular society or culture being studied. Archaeologists must also bear in mind that much evidence has been lost through physical decomposition, for in all societies, the vast majority of writing was done with nondurable tools on nondurable objects.

All writing materials can potentially provide information about one or more of the three stages in the technology of writing: preparing inks and paints, manufacturing writing implements (styli and brushes) and inkpots, and producing and preparing writing surfaces. The kinds of inks and paints, the types of writing implements, and the variety of writing surfaces used varied from society to society, owing mainly to environmental, economic, and cultural factors. Tools of wood, metal, or stone could be used to scratch, impress, etch, engrave, or paint inscriptions onto any imaginable surface (stone or rock, wood, metal, clay, textiles, bone, shell, animal skin, plaster, wax- or mud-coatings, and paper made from vegetable fibers) and any imaginable object (jewelry, masonry, pottery, statuary, utensils, etc.).

How a society uses writing is in large part culturally determined, yet the wider contexts in which writing is used are the same in all literate societies: politics, law, religion, economics, literature, and private life. These wider contexts are important when studying writing materials, for they are the major factors in the choice of materials and in the amount of care taken in composition. Because economic documents were by far the most common type of document in all societies, scribes tended to write these on materials that were inexpensive and plentiful, and composition was often careless. In contrast, the main purpose of monumental royal inscriptions was as a display of the king's power and authority. The value and durability of the materials chosen for such documents and the extreme care taken in composition were therefore far greater than those of everyday economic documents.

Whether or not a document leaves any trace in the archaeological record is determined by the durability of the writing material under the environmental conditions in which it was deposited and preserved. Monumental inscriptions, because they are often written on stone or metal, have a much higher probability of surviving in the archaeological record than do economic documents written on animal skins or papyrus.

Most of the inscribed material in the archaeological record comes from excavations in Egypt, Mesopotamia, and northwestern China, not because societies in these regions made greater use of writing than societies in India, Europe, or Mesoamerica, but because the materials most commonly used for writing held up extremely well in their respective climates. Sun-dried clay tablets are quite durable in themselves, but a large percentage of the clay tablets from Mesopotamia were made even more durable by being baked in the conflagrations that destroyed the archives in which they were held. As is well known, the extreme aridity of Egypt is the principal reason why so many papyrus documents and wall-paintings (mainly from tombs) have been preserved there. Likewise in northwestern China, the unusual dryness of the climate is the reason that archaeologists have found huge numbers of paper and wood documents. Yet, almost all of the inscriptions from archaeological contexts in India, Europe, and Mesoamerica were found on pottery, stone, bone, or metal—materials that are durable in most environmental conditions.

Dozens of sites throughout Mesopotamia, Syria, and Asia Minor have yielded clay tablets. *Nineveh, with its thousands of literary tablets from the library of Assurbanipal, is perhaps the single most important site in this respect. There are numerous Egyptian sites noted for finds of papyruses and stone inscriptions (most of them in the south, where it is drier). The most important of these is perhaps ancient Thebes and its vicinity; from this area come the inscriptions of the great temple of *Carnac and large numbers of ostraca and papyruses relating to workmen employed on the royal necropolis on the West Bank of the Nile. Two important sites in China are *Anyang (Honan Province), where a large number of oracle bone inscriptions were found, and Tun-Huang, the site of a huge trove of paper scrolls. Among the other significant sites of the discovery of writing materials are Pompeii and *Athens in the Mediterranean region; *Mohenjo-daro and *Harappa in South Asia; and Copán (Honduras), *Palenque (Mexico), and *Tikal (Guatemala) in Mesoamerica.

Investigation into writing materials and the technology of writing has long tended to be a low priority for archaeologists. Although the situation is now improving, archaeologists in the past were all too quick to hand any inscribed artifact over to the epigraphers, with unfortunately little communication between their two disciplines. As a result, a great deal of information that could have contributed to a deeper understanding of the place of writing in ancient societies remains unpublished or has been lost. A good example is the clay tablets from Mesopotamia; only through the recent analysis of the clays of these tablets has it been possible to determine the area where unprovenanced tablets were manufactured and written. This, in turn, has provided scholars with a clearer picture of patterns of trade and communication within ancient Mesopotamian society.

[See also NEAR EAST: LATE ANTIQUITY IN THE NEAR EAST.]

■ Alfred Lucas, *Ancient Egyptian Materials and Industries* (1926; 4th ed. revised by J. R. Harris, 1962). Tsuen-hsuin Tsien, *Written on Bamboo and Silk: The Beginnings of Chinese Books and Inscriptions* (1962). Stephen D. Houston, *Maya Glyphs* (1989). A. Ghosh, ed., *An Encyclopedia of Indian Archaeology*, 2 vols. (1989). J. T. Hooker, et al., *Reading the Past: Ancient Writing from Cuneiform to the Alphabet* (1990).

William D. Whitt

Y

YANGSHAO CULTURE. The Yangshao culture is represented by a group of sites with painted pottery in the Yellow River basin, in the provinces of Shaanxi, Shanxi, Hebei, Henan, Gansu, and Qinghai, dating from about 5000 to 3000 B.C. The type site, at a village in northwestern Henan, was first excavated by J. G. Andersson in 1921, but it is now known not to be representative of the group as a whole. The sites clearly were dependent on agriculture, with millets, both foxtail and broomcorn, as staples, complemented by domesticated pigs and dogs. Wild plant and animal remains were also found in the sites. Cattle, sheep, and goat remains have been reported from a few sites. Projectile points and bola stones indicate that hunting was common. Stone tools were both chipped and polished, and the pottery included both utilitarian undecorated jars and finer painted vessels in a variety of shapes. Spindle whorls and eyed needles demonstrate that thread was spun and woven and clothing sewn. Silk was already produced at this time, although the everyday clothing was probably made of hempen cloth. While the sites are often characterized as belonging to slash-and-burn cultivators, many of the sites have deep deposits and an investment in facilities, which makes it unlikely that the sites were moved very often or abandoned with regularity. Villages were divided into activity areas: houses were clustered around a central plaza inside a ditch or fence, while cemeteries and pottery-firing locations were placed outside. Groups of houses and burial groups within cemeteries have led to interpretations of social groups such as lineages or clans within each village. Pottery kilns were dug into the ground and exhibit sophisticated heat control. Burials include both primary and secondary burial, often in multiple graves. Infants were buried in urns under house floors.

The considerable archaeological work on Yangshao sites, and the many C[14] dates collected, allow the culture to be divided into regions and phases. Near the Wei and Fen rivers, the sites are divided into an early Banpo phase, a middle Miaodigou phase, and a late Xiwangcun phase. During the Banpo phase the climate was at its warmest and wettest. In central Henan, a site that corresponds in time to Banpo is Shuangmiaogou. A group of sites from this area having rectangular, surface-level, multi-room houses, dating from 4000 to 2500 B.C. are named for the site of Dahecun. Pottery includes both tripod and pedestal vessels, some with geometric cutouts. Sites in northern Henan and southern Hebei, known as the Hougang phase, fall mostly in the 4500 to 3500 B.C. range. In the far west, in Gansu and Qinghai, the phases are called Majiayao, Banshan, and Majang from early to late. Early copper and bronze objects have been found associated with Yangshao pottery in this region, including a bronze knife with about 10 percent tin alloy and the slag of several metals, suggesting that the knife was locally made. No profound changes in the economy or subsistence base is evident in the area. A bronze mirror at Qijia is geometric, related stylistically to the northern bronzes. Some Yangshao sites are found in the upper reaches of tributaries to the Yangtzi River, and a finger stretches to the north to meet the distribution of Hongshan sites, which also have painted pottery.

[*See also* ASIA, *articles on* INTRODUCTION, PREHISTORY AND EARLY HISTORY OF EAST ASIA; CHINA: INTRODUCTION.]

Sarah Milledge Nelson

YORK is a thriving cathedral city and university town on the rivers Ouse and Foss in northeast England. It was the site of a Roman legionary fortress and *Colonia* (Eboracum), an ecclesiastical and trading center of Anglian Northumbria (Eoforwic), a Viking town (Jorvik), headquarters of one faction of the Wars of the Roses, and a prominent player in English medieval politics. Monuments of the city's remarkable history remain above ground: the "Multangular Tower" in Museum Gardens is a Roman construction refurbished in the Middle Ages; St Mary Bishophill Junior is an Anglo-Saxon parish church of the tenth century; York Minster is one of England's finest Gothic cathedrals; medieval secular buildings include the Hall of the Merchant Adventurers and King's Manor, venue for the Council of the North. The city walls, largely resuscitated in Victorian times, preserve the line, appearance, and occasionally the fabric of the medieval defenses, and they also echo parts of the Roman circuit.

The archaeological deposits which lie beneath the pavements are as famous as the buildings which rise above them. Unusually deep and anaerobic, particularly beside the rivers, they preserve extensive stratified sequences of the early city in stone, timber, and other organic materials. The investigations of these deposits by early antiquaries and archaeologists were collected and extended by the Royal Commission on Historical Monuments which established the basic layout of the Roman town. Between 1967 and 1973, the Commission, in collaboration with the Dean and Chapter, undertook a major campaign of excavation at the site of York Minster, when the building was suffering major subsidence. Some 260 separate interventions, directed by A. D. Phillips, revealed a complete sequence at the center of the ancient city, beginning with the construction of the headquarters building (Principia) and three barrack blocks of the Legionary Fortress (A.D. 71), their refurbishment in the Christian era (fourth century), their modification at the end of imperial administration (late fourth to early fifth centuries) and their collapse shortly afterward. Unstratified carved headstones of the seventh to eighth centuries indicated an ecclesiastical center of some status. During the Middle Saxon period, in the ninth to eleventh centuries, a cemetery containing carved Anglo-Scandinavian grave covers in situ and charcoal burials developed within the stub walls of the former principia, while the ruins of the adjacent barrack blocks were modified to host an urban manufacturing center. The site of the Anglo-Saxon minster has not been discovered, but it probably lies immediately to the south off Petergate. The sequence was concluded by vestiges of the Norman cathedral constructed by Thomas of Bayeux in 1070, which lie directly below the present church. Examples of the Roman and Anglo-Saxon buildings and finds are preserved in an undercroft beneath the York Minster where they can be seen by visitors.

From 1972, urban renewal elsewhere in the city prompted a new campaign of archaeological intervention by the York Archaeological Trust, formed and led by P. V. Addyman and chaired by M. W. Barley, which has now excavated and researched the city for more than twenty years. Among their many discoveries may be mentioned second- through fourth-century townhouses and institutional buildings in the Roman Colonia off Mickelgate, Skeldergate, Tanner Row, and Bishophill; an eighth-century helmet with a Christian inscription found at Coppergate; an eighth- to ninth-century trading settlement at Fishergate, probably to be equated with *Eoforwic*; a tenth-century parish church and its graveyard at St. Helen on the Walls; a ninth- through twelfth-century Anglo-Scandinavian residential and manufacturing center in deep anaerobic deposits at Coppergate—associated with the Viking town of *Jorvik*; houses of the late-medieval Vicars Choral at the Bedern and the medieval Jewish cemetery at Jewbury. The Trust has established typologies for the ceramics, building materials, metalwork, leather, cloth, woodwork, and coinage used in the city during the first millennium and later; moreover, it has also pioneered the study of biological remains in urban contexts, applying the new methodology developed by an Environmental Archaeology Unit (now in the University of York) to a rich harvest of bones, seeds, plants, and insects gathered from the anaerobic deposits. Prompt publication of its findings in a fascicule series has helped put the York discoveries at the service of other scholars. Among its other achievements, the Trust has also been responsible for innovative ventures in the presentation of the results of urban archaeology to the public, most famously in the creation of the Jorvik Viking Centre, a reconstruction in situ of the timber buildings found at Coppergate, together with their furnishings and inhabitants.

During the 1980s, in recognition of York's exceptional deposits, and in the face of ever-increasing demands from urban renewal, a new approach to the curation of archaeological strata buried underneath towns was promoted at York. The deposits were mapped and their quality matched to a research agenda to provide a definition of their current value. This in turn is being used to guide town planners to an appropriate mitigation strategy, in which benign engineering solutions are preferred to rescue excavation. The evaluation document included a research program, intended to advance the understanding of York's remarkable history as opportunity and funding allow.

[*See also* BRITISH ISLES, *articles on* ROMAN BRITAIN, THE ANGLO-SAXONS, VIKING RAIDS AND SETTLEMENT IN BRITAIN AND IRELAND.]

■ Royal Commission on Historical Monuments, *An Inventory of the Historical Monuments in the City of York*, vol. I: *Eburacum* (1962). P. V. Addyman, *The Archaeology of York* (1976). P. V. Addyman and V. E. Black, eds., *Archaeological Papers from York presented to M. W. Barley* (1984). G. Andrews, "Archaeology in York: An Assessment Prepared for the Ancient Monuments Inspectorate of the Department of the Environment," in *Archaeological Papers from York presented to M. W. Barley*, ed. P. V. Addyman and V. E. Black (1984): pp. 173–208. R. A. Hall, *The Excavations at York: The Viking Dig* (1984). A. D. Phillips, *Excavations at York Minster*, vol. II: *The Cathedral of Archbishop Thomas of Bayeux* (1985). Ove Arup and Partners and the Department of Archaeology, University of York, *York Development and Archaeology Study* (1991). A. D. Phillips and B. Heywood, *Excavations at York Minster*, vol. I: *Roman to Norman, The Headquarters of the Roman Legionary Fortress at York and Its Exploitation in the Early Middle Ages (71–1070 A.D.)*, ed. M.O.H. Carver (1992).

Martin Carver

Z

ZAPOTEC CIVILIZATION refers to the social and cultural system developed in pre-Hispanic times by the Native American speakers of the Zapotec and related languages. Zapotec civilization evolved in the Southern Highlands region of Mexico, within the modern Mexican state of Oaxaca. Our knowledge of this civilization comes from the work of researchers whose efforts span more than a century. Major contemporary projects, including Kent Flannery's Oaxaca Human Ecology Project, Joyce Marcus's epigraphic studies, John Paddock's research on the later periods of the Valley of Oaxaca and elsewhere, and the settlement pattern research Richard Blanton conducted with several colleagues, all build on a firm intellectual foundation laid down by the great Mexican archaeologists Alfonso Caso (1896–1971) and Ignacio Bernal (1910–1992), among others.

Characterizing Zapotec civilization, its geographical setting, and its historical development is a conceptually problematic task. It is difficult to relate, with clarity, the sociocultural content of this civilization, or even to specify its precise geographical boundaries. Like all social systems we designate as civilizations, Zapotec civilization was large in scale, multiregional, complex, and constantly changing. It was not entirely the product of a particular language group, but instead grew out of interactions among populations carrying diverse cultural traditions, dialects, and even languages.

In tracing the rise of Zapotec civilization, the focal point is the importance of its "core" zone, in the Valley of *Oaxaca, situated roughly in the center of the surrounding more mountainous zones of the Southern Highlands region. A description of the core alone, however, would not stand for the total social system. Other groups speaking Zapotec, and other languages, such as Mixtec, Mixe, and Chinantec, are found in the more peripheral mountainous regions surrounding the central valleys. These groups and were participants, in varying ways, at different times, in the larger civilizational system. An additional complexity derives from the fact that this civilization was embedded within a larger Mesoamerican civilization, with which Zapotecs interacted in varying ways, and from which they derived important components of their suite of sociocultural institutions.

Another problem inherent in any account of Zapotec civilization is the fact that many of its features can be traced to a period prior to the evolution of the Zapotec language as we know it today. Zapotec is one of the recently formed languages of the Otomangean language family that diverged only from Mixtec, the other main language of the Southern Highlands region, after about 4000 B.C., during a period of transition from a foraging to a farming economy. Subsequently, speakers of the Mixtec and Zapotec languages, although sharing a common linguistic and socio-cultural background, and continuing to interact with one another, developed divergent civilizational traditions.

Several important conceptual building blocks of Zapotec civilization antedate the divergence of the Zapotec language. Among them is a cosmology featuring a directionally oriented rectilinear universe divided into four named quarters, with the important east-west axis incised by the daily path of the sun. Each quarter, and the center, were and still are among some contemporary Zapotecs, associated with color symbolism and a manifestation of the Zapotec vital force, *pè*. Similar to Mixtec cosmology, clouds, rain, and especially, lightning *(Cocijo)*, were among the most potent expressions of *pè*. This ancient conceptualization of a four-quartered universe served as a background to many aspects of Zapotec ritual, calendrics, ancestor worship, and architecture. A later addition to Zapotec culture, the 260-day ritual calendar, shared among all the Mesoamerican peoples, was similarly divided into four parts, reflecting this ancient quadrilateral view of the cosmos.

Sometime between about 1900 B.C. and 1400 B.C., populations in the Valley of Oaxaca increased their involvement in agricultural production and began to reside in permanent settlements. These early farmers also produced the first pottery and, shortly after that, fired clay figurines. The earliest well-documented ceramic period (Tierras Largas) dates from 1400 B.C. to 1150 B.C. It is at this time that three institutions basic to later Zapotec civilization are first well documented in the archaeological record: nucleated villages, household units consisting of a dwelling plus associated features such as burial pits, and an early form of public building (although public space may date to the pre-village period). The nucleated village is still present among the Zapotecs, and, although some specific aspects of the domestic-built environment varied over the subsequent pre-Hispanic centuries, a nuclear-family, domestic social structure tended to predominate, with families residing in architecturally free household units (in later urban situations, houses were densely packed but still freestanding).

At the site of San José Mogote, in the northern arm of the Valley of Oaxaca, the Tierras Largas public building consisted of a rectangular plastered room, possibly containing an altar. By the San José phase (1150 B.C. to 855 B.C.), public buildings were erected on stone and earth platforms, fronted by staircases. This basic architectural format was greatly elaborated upon in the subsequent history of Zapotec public construction. The same phase also saw the beginnings of the Zapotec tradition of carved stone monuments, although the first recognizable hieroglyphic writing on a carved stone dates the later Rosario phase (700 B.C. to 500 B.C.).

During the San José phase, 1150 B.C. through 850 B.C., the processes bringing about the evolution of a ruling elite were set in motion, again primarily at the important site of San José Mogote. During this time, elite households participated in long-distance interregional exchange spheres, involving the exchange of exotic goods and ritual items invested with symbols pertaining to the Western Mesoamerican Olmec iconographic system. The control of important ritual, political, and economic activities by an emergent elite during the Early and Middle Formative Periods is later elaborated upon in the evolution of a Zapotec ruling nobility. This process of political centralization is illustrated archaeologically by the establishment of the palace institution by the Terminal Formative Monte Albán II Period (200 B.C. to A.D. 250), at the latest.

Political centralization is related to the development of another important feature of Zapotec civilization, the evolution of a regional hierarchy of centers. Initially, this was seen primarily in the comparatively rapid population growth and architectural elaboration of San José Mogote during the Early and Middle Formative Periods (1400 B.C. to 500 B.C.), but the regional hierarchy of centers was considerably elaborated upon beginning with the subsequent Early Monte Albán I Period (500 B.C. through 350 B.C.), with the foundation of a new regional political capital at *Monte Albán, located near the center of the three arms of the Valley of Oaxaca. The construction of this new capital manifested the origin of the Zapotec state, one of this civilization's most important institutions.

The founding of a regional capital at Monte Albán at about 500 B.C. represented the beginning of a long tradition of city development and city life that were important ingredients of Zapotec civilization in later periods. The beginnings of other important elements of Zapotec civilization can be traced to the periods immediately following Monte Albán's founding, including a characteristic two-chambered temple architecture, a market system, a rubber-ball game, and the anthropomorphic funerary vessels called Zapotec urns. Lastly, imperial expansion outside the Valley of Oaxaca is a characteristic feature of this civilization, and can trace its beginnings to Period I (350 B.C. through 200 B.C.) in the Mixtec region northwest of the Valley at Monte Negro. Notable later episodes occurred in the Cuicatlan Cañada, at the northeast edge of the Southern Highlands region during Period II (200 B.C. to A.D. 250), and in the Isthmus of Tehuantepec in Period V (A.D. 950 to A.D. 1530).

[See also MESOAMERICA, articles on INTRODUCTION, ARCHAIC PERIOD IN MESOAMERICA, FORMATIVE PERIOD IN MESOAMERICA.]

■ Alfonso Caso and Ignacio Bernal, Urnas de Oaxaca (1952). Ignacio Bernal, "Archaeological Synthesis of Oaxaca," in Handbook of Middle American Indians, Volume Three, Part Two: Archaeology of Southern Mesoamerica, Gordon R. Willey, ed. (1965): 788–813. Kent V. Flannery, ed., The Early Mesoamerican Village (1976). Richard E. Blanton, Monte Albán: Settlement Patterns at the Ancient Zapotec Capital (1978). Joyce Marcus, "Archaeology and Religion: A Comparison of the Zapotec and Maya," World Archaeology 10 (1978): 172–189. Joyce Marcus, "Zapotec Writing," Scientific American 242 (1980): 50–64. Richard E. Blanton, Stephen A. Kowalewski, Gary M. Feinman, and Jill Appel, Monte Albán's Hinterland, Part I: The Prehispanic Settlement Patterns of the Central and Southern Parts of the Valley of Oaxaca, Mexico (1982). Kent V. Flannery and Joyce Marcus, eds., The Cloud People: Divergent Evolution of the Zapotec and Mixtec Civilizations (1983). Stephen A. Kowalewski, Gary M. Feinman, Laura M. Finsten, Richard E. Blanton, and Linda M. Nicholas, Monte Albán's Hinterland, Part II: Prehispanic Settlement Patterns in Tlacolula, Etla, and Ocotlan, the Valley of Oaxaca, Mexico, Two Volumes (1989).

Richard E. Blanton

ZHENGZHOU. The Zhengzhou site, also known as Erligang for the region of the city where the first excavations took place, is important in Chinese archaeology as an early site of the Shang dynasty, and the type site for the Zhengzhou Phase or the Erligang Period. First excavated in the 1950s, it is located in the modern city of Zhengzhou, near the Yellow River in Henan Province. The Erligang Phase follows that of Erlitou, a site of the early second millennium B.C. approximately 62 miles (100 km) to the west, assigned to the Xia dynasty. Some artifacts at Zhengzhou are stylistically assignable to the Erlitou and earlier, but the date of the major occupation is the middle second millennium B.C.

The site consists of a massive city wall, palace foundations in the northeast corner of the city, and workshops, ordinary houses, and burials outside the walls. The city was roughly rectangular with one corner cut off. The wall is approximately 4.5 miles (7 km) in circumference, surrounding a 1 square mile (3 sq km) area. The walls, made of stamped earth, persist in a few places to the height of approximately 30 feet (9 m), with 3,118 foot (36 m) bases at the widest. The large buildings—984 feet (300 m) by 492 feet (150 m)—have stamped-earth foundations and large posts, up to 14 inches (35 cm) in diameter, to support the roof. Jade and copper ornaments were found in the foundations, along with sacrificial human skeletons—thus these buildings' designation as royal palaces. In the northwest region of the city another large building with a plastered floor was found, as well as a stamped-earth platform interpreted as an altar. The elite lived within the wall, but the commoners' houses were outside it.

Semisubterranean dwellings and small houses with stamped-earth foundations were found. Of particular interest are two bronze foundries with clay molds for casting both vessels and weapons. Other workshops included bone and pottery areas. Waste from making bone artifacts was determined to be about fifty percent human bone, with the rest coming from cattle, deer, and pigs. The pottery-producing area had fourteen kilns, discarded vessels, paddles, and anvils for shaping the vessels. A possible wine-making district had large coarse jars with a whitish interior residue. Another amenity of the city was its water ditches, about 6.5 feet (2 m) wide and 5 feet (1.5 m) deep. More than two hundred pits contained skeletons of pigs and people as well as trash. Some of these pits may have served for storage, while others may have been disposal pits. Burials differed considerably in size and in both the quantity and the quality of grave goods. Some of the larger ones included subsidiary human burials, presumably sacrificed. One notable discovery was two very large bronze vessels of the type called fang ding, a rectangular open food vessel on four legs. The larger weighs approximately 190 pounds (86 kg).

The site may represent either the Shang city of Ao or the earlier city of Bo, both mentioned in orace bone inscriptions. Scholarly consensus seems to be leaning toward accepting it as Bo, or Early Shang.

[See also ASIA: PREHISTORY AND EARLY HISTORY OF EAST ASIA; CHINA, articles on EARLY CIVILIZATIONS OF CHINA, SHANG CIVILIZATION.]

■ Robert W. Bagley, "The Zhengzhou Phase (The Erligang Period)," in The Great Bronze Age of China, Wen Fong, ed. (1980). An Chin-huai, "The Shang City at Cheng-chou and Related Problems," in Studies of Shang Archaeology, K. C. Chang, ed. (1986).

Sarah Milledge Nelson

ZHOUKOUDIAN. The stratified cave and fissure deposits at Zhoukoudian, 29 miles (47 km) southwest of Beijing, China, were first investigated scientifically in 1927. Years of excavations by both Chinese and Western researchers have yielded numerous human fossils, especially of *Homo erectus*. Locality I at Zhoukoudian is a karst cave site, filled with at least seventeen layers of stratified infilling. The uppermost thirteen contain the remains of at least forty *Homo erectus* individuals and more than 100,000 artifacts, as well as traces of large hearths, animal bones, and some plant remains. Uranium-series, fission-track, and thermoluminescence dates from these horizons assign the Locality I occupations to between 460,000 and 230,000 years ago. The periodic human occupations all occurred during relatively moist and warm periods of the Middle Pleistocene.

The Zhoukoudian fossils provide a clear portrait of *Homo erectus*. The human skulls from Locality I have low profiles and thick walls, and also prominent brow ridges. The occipital bone is sharply curved, with a transverse shelf above the neck-muscle attachment area. Their brain size appears to have increased from about 1100 cc through time, while the post-cranial skeleton was more robust than that of modern humans. Unfortunately, the original fossils were lost during World War II. Scientists have had to rely on anatomist Franz Weidenreich's accurate casts and completed detailed studies of them, to which a growing corpus of more recently excavated fossil material from the site can be added.

A few archaeologists have argued that the stone artifacts and food remains were introduced into the Locality I infilling by natural agencies, including carnivore activity. They also claim that the ash layers which have been interpreted as hearths are the result of natural fires. Chinese archaeologists and other Asian specialists regard such theories as entirely speculative, especially since climatic evidence consistently places *Homo erectus* at the site when climatic conditions were relatively warm and wet.

The stone artifacts from Locality I consist of simple flakes and crude stone choppers, suggesting that the main technology was in wood. Burnt hackberry seeds and large deer bones may give clues to *Homo erectus*'s diet; however, many such finds may result from nonhuman activity. Zhoukoudian's Upper Cave has yielded three *Homo sapiens sapiens* fossils, which display considerable anatomical variation. The Upper Cave deposits have been radiocarbon dated to between 11,000 and 18,000 years ago, to the closing millennia of the last glaciation.

Zhoukoudian provides one of the largest samples of *Homo erectus* fossils from anywhere in the world. While the Zhoukoudian fossils show signs of increasing brain size and a general evolutionary trend toward modern humans, they do not provide unequivocal evidence for the evolution of modern humans in Asia, as has sometimes been claimed, notably by Chinese paleoanthropologists.

[See also ASIA: PREHISTORY AND EARLY HISTORY OF EAST ASIA; CHINA: STONE AGE CULTURES OF CHINA.]

■ R. Wu and S. Lin, "Peking Man," *Scientific American* 243:3 (1983): 86–94. L. Binford and C. K. Ho, "Taphonomy at a Distance: Zhoukoudian the Cave Home of Beijing Man?" *Current Anthropology* 26 (1985): 413–443. R. W. and X. R. Dong, "*Homo erectus* in China," in *Paleoanthropology and Paleolithic Archaeology in the People's Republic of China*, ed. R. W. and J. W. Olsen (1985), pp. 79–88.
Brian M. Fagan

ZHUKAIGOU. Between 1977 and 1984, the remains of a settlement at Zhukaigou, in southwestern Inner Mongolia, yielded cultural remains in five stages, dating from the late third to the mid-second millennium B.C. The excavators, Tian Guangjin and Guo Suxin (Institute of Archaeology, Hohhot), suggested that materials found in the fifth phase at Zhukaigou signal the origins of the Ordos style and that its culture radiated out to other regions with profound effect on the development of steppe culture. Recently other regional groups were identified in the northern corridor, and the role of Zhukaigou in culture formation of the region has been debated.

In Phase I at Zhukaigou, round and square dwellings covered with white ash; vertical, rectangular, or square burial pits and urn burials of children; gray, brown, and polished black pottery; *li-*, *guan-*, *dou-*, and *he*-shaped pots; stone axes, knives, and *chi* as well as bone tools bespeak of already mixed cultural inheritance from the Chinese Longshan, western and northern Asian Neolithic. Burials include articles of everyday use and do not indicate specialization in craft production for the purposes of ritual. These were sedentary people who cultivated grains, kept oxen and sheep, and supplemented their diet through hunting.

During Phases II and III, several new features were added that are identifiable with the Qijia culture known in the upper Wei River Valley, the Yellow River region of Qinghai, in Ningxia and westernmost Inner Mongolia. Added to the Phase I inventory were a large number of flat-bottomed jars with constricted mouths and double handles; cord-marked pottery; remains of fabric (mat) impressions on pots; polished oracle bones; burials with jawbones of sacrificed sheep, pigs, and other animals (also found in Phase I, but now in greatly increased numbers); bronze implements (awls and needles); and personal ornaments. Increased agricultural production is suggested by the introduction of digging tools and sickles.

Taken together, these features show that Levels II and III are the remains of advanced farmers, among whom domesticated animals were of great importance. The numbers of animals offered up in burial and the introduction of human sacrifice marks an intensification of ritual behavior that may indicate differentiation by merit, ethnic background, or honor, as well as efforts to ritualize social control. The snake pattern and the flower-shaped edge that adorn pottery *li*, identified by Tian and Guo as local features in Phase III, are considered hallmarks of the later, nomadic peoples of the area.

The custom of dog sacrifice was added to Phase IV burials following Shang custom, while other forms of sacrifice decreased. A side chamber for burial goods was introduced, while the number of items decreased. This restriction and variation in tomb size suggest the beginnings of interest in customized sets of burial goods based on social differentiation. Oracle bones in Phase IV were polished, burned, and drilled, a treatment known at Middle Shang sites (c. 1300 B.C.), which this level at Zhukaigou predates. Increased care taken with dwellings, including earthen foundations and prepared floors in Phases IV and V, suggests perceived stability.

In Phase V, distinctive burial objects, such as Erligang-style bronze vessels and weapons, imply a different type of arrangement with adjacent cultures. Bronze *ge* halberds, *ding* and *jue* decorated with the *taotie*, and the squared spiral design are comparable to Middle Shang materials; curved bronze and microlithic knives recall Andronovo models from southern Siberia. The edges of the weapons and tools, however, were either annealed after casting or finished by hot hammering. Use of this technique, not preferred by Chinese metalsmiths, and the discovery of an axe mold at the site, infer that these items were manufactured locally.

The political alliances and exchange of items in Phases I to IV were apparently intraregional; acquisition of prestige objects in Phase V, however, were both intraregional and interregional (between Zhukaigou, the steppe, and the central plain). Zhukaigou developed along the lines of other agricultural communities in the northern corridor, except in Phase V. The intensification of burial practices from simple to more elaborate and contact with other bronze-producing societies suggest that Zhukaigou was strategic to metal resources or exotic products. The collapse of such a network may explain the demise of Zhukaigou in the mid-second millennium B.C.

■ Institute of Archaeology, Inner Mongolia, "Zhukaigou Site in Inner Mongolia," *Kaogu xuebao* 3 (1986): 301–331. Tiam Guangjin and Suxin Guo, "The Origins of the Ordos Style," *Kaogu xuebao* 3 (1988): 257–274. Evgenii Chernykh, *Ancient Metallurgy in the USSR* (1992). Katheryn M. Linduff, "Zhukaigou, Steppe Culture and the Rise of Chinese Civilization," *Antiquity* 69 (1995): 133–145.

Katheryn M. Linduff

ZIMBABWE. *See* GREAT ZIMBABWE.

ZOOARCHAEOLOGY is a broad area of study including the analysis of animal remains recovered from prehistoric soil deposits, the analysis of modern hunting and butchering activities, and taphonomy (the study of after-death disposition of animal carcasses). Although prehistoric animal remains are most often recovered from archaeological sites, they need not be. Useful samples have been collected from ancient wood rat and pack rat nests, nonarchaeological dry caves, and exposed river and lake bed deposits—any place where animal remains may have accumulated and been preserved.

Although a relatively recent subfield of archaeology, having its roots in the *middle range theory movement promoted by Lewis Binford, zooarchaeology has proven to be a valuable tool in understanding past human lifeways from earliest through historic times. More detailed explanations of the specific methods employed in zooarchaeology are provided in the section in this volume entitled *Animal Remains, Analysis of. Usually, a statistical or graphical analysis of faunal data can suggest the species of animals present, the parts that were most often collected, the season of collection, hunting and butchering methods, and genetic information on changes in animal species over time.

The results of zooarchaeological analysis have provided archaeologists with valuable reconstructions of prehistoric climate, animal resource exploitation patterns, seasonal occupation of sites, the animal component of prehistoric diet, and the transition from hunting wild animals to raising domesticated animals. For more detailed discussions of the important contributions of zooarchaeology to general archaeology refer to the regional summaries of the history of animal domestication elsewhere in this volume.

George Michaels

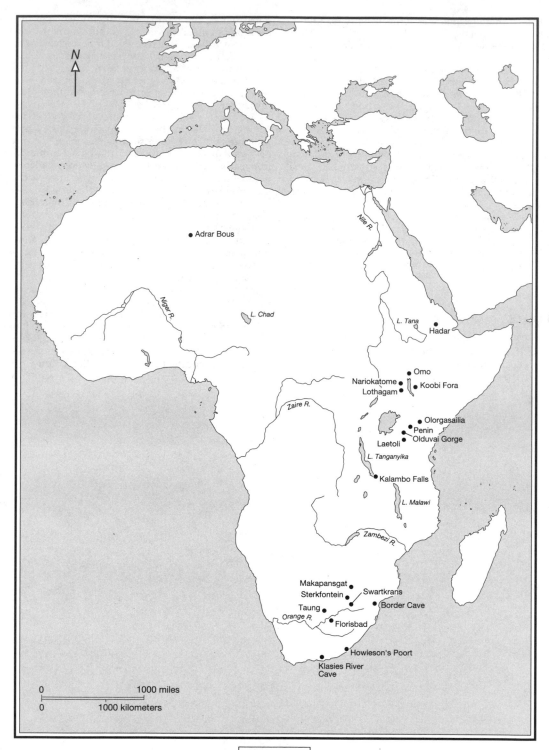

Africa

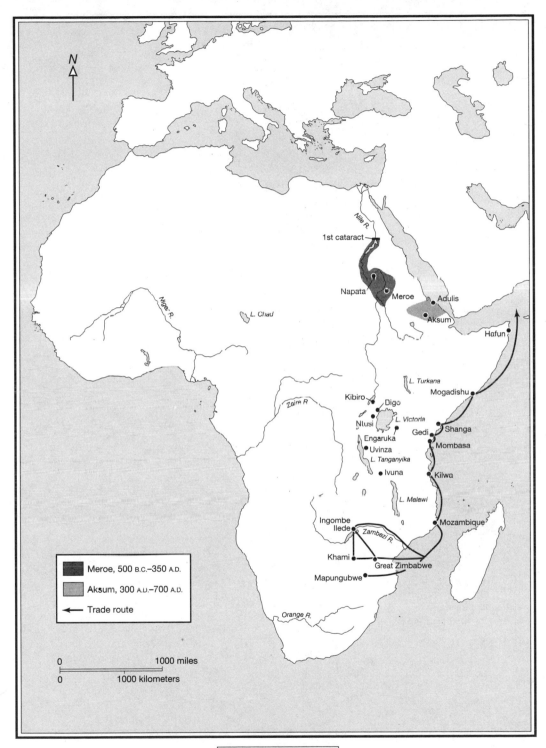

N

1st cataract

Nile R.

Napata
Meroe
Adulis
Aksum
Hafun

Niger R.
L. Chad

Zaire R.
L. Turkana

Kibiro
Digo
Mogadishu

Nlusi
L. Victoria
Gedi
Shanga

Engaruka
Mombasa

Uvinza

Ivuna
L. Tanganyika
Kilwa

L. Malawi

Ingombe
Ilede
Mozambique

Zambezi R.

Khami
Great Zimbabwe

Mapungubwe

Orange R.

Meroe, 500 B.C.–350 A.D.

Aksum, 300 A.D.–700 A.D.

Trade route

0   1000 miles

0   1000 kilometers

East Africa

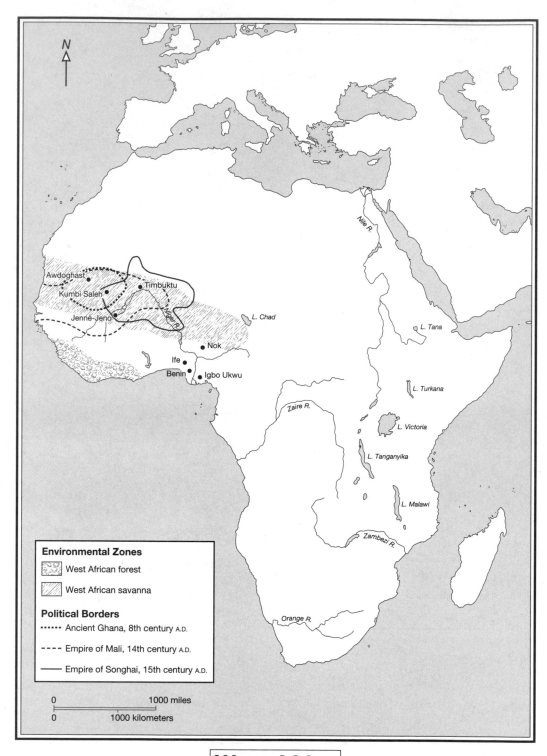

Environmental Zones

West African forest

West African savanna

Political Borders

.... Ancient Ghana, 8th century A.D.

- - - - Empire of Mali, 14th century A.D.

—— Empire of Songhai, 15th century A.D.

| 0 | 1000 miles |
| 0 | 1000 kilometers |

West Africa

Awdoghast

Kumbi Saleh

Timbuktu

Jenné-Jeno

Niger R.

L. Chad

Nok

Ife

Benin • Igbo Ukwu

Nile R.

L. Tana

L. Turkana

L. Victoria

Zaire R.

L. Tanganyika

L. Malawi

Zambezi R.

Orange R.

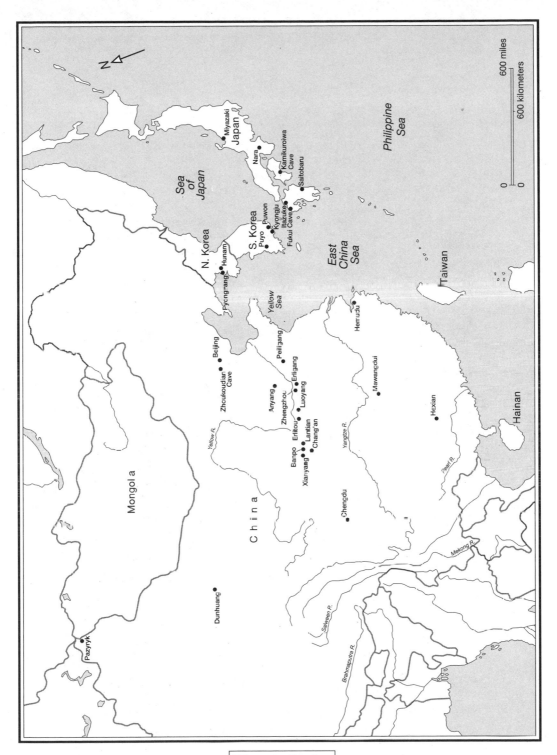

East Asia

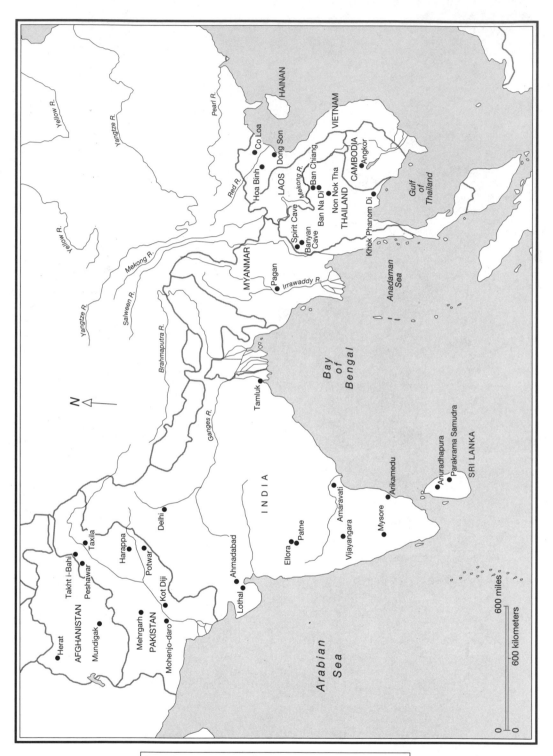

India and Southeast Asia

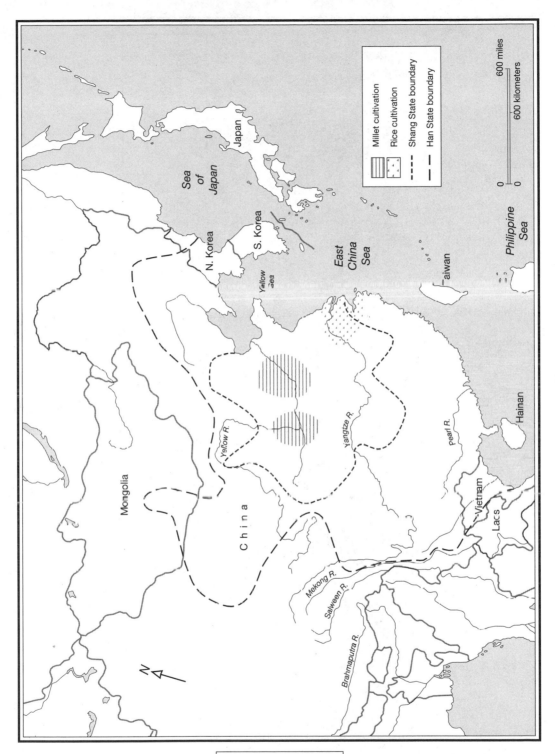

Early China

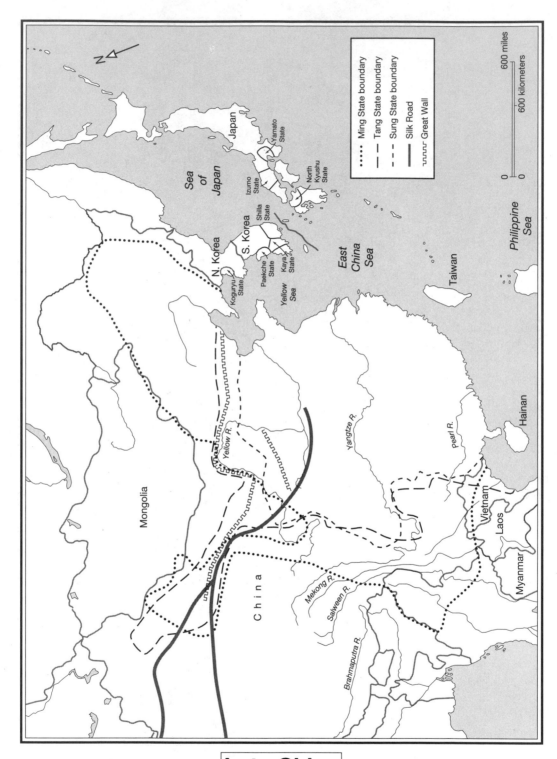

Legend:
- Ming State boundary
- Tang State boundary
- Sung State boundary
- Silk Road
- Great Wall

600 miles
600 kilometers

Japan
Sea of Japan
Yamato State
Izumo State
North Kyushu State
Shilla State
N. Korea
S. Korea
Koguryu State
Paekche State
Kaya State
Yellow Sea
East China Sea
Taiwan
Philippine Sea
Hainan
Mongolia
China
Yellow R.
Yangtze R.
pearl R.
Vietnam
Laos
Myanmar
Mekong R.
Salween R.
Brahmaputra R.

Late China

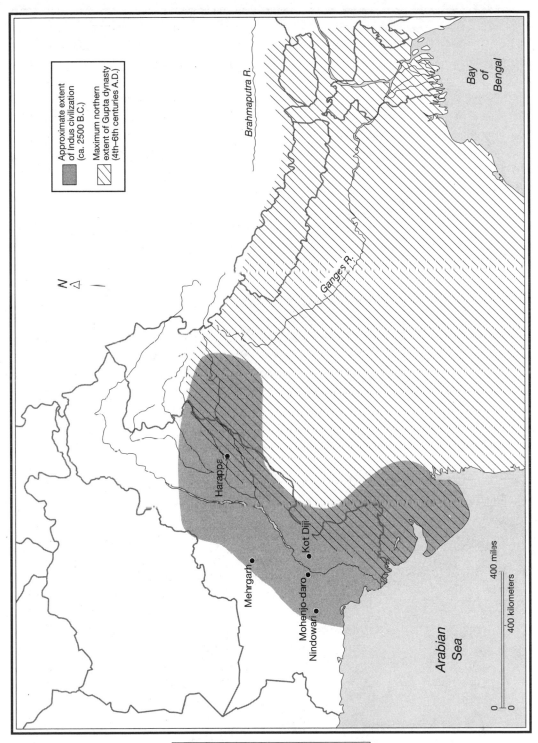

Legend:

Approximate extent
of Indus civilization
(ca. 2500 B.C.)

Maximum northern
extent of Gupta dynasty
(4th–6th centuries A.D.)

Brahmaputra R.

Bay
of
Bengal

Ganges R.

N

Harappa

Mehrgarh

Mohenjo-daro

Kot Diji

Nindowari

Arabian
Sea

400 miles

400 kilometers

0

0

Indus Civilizations

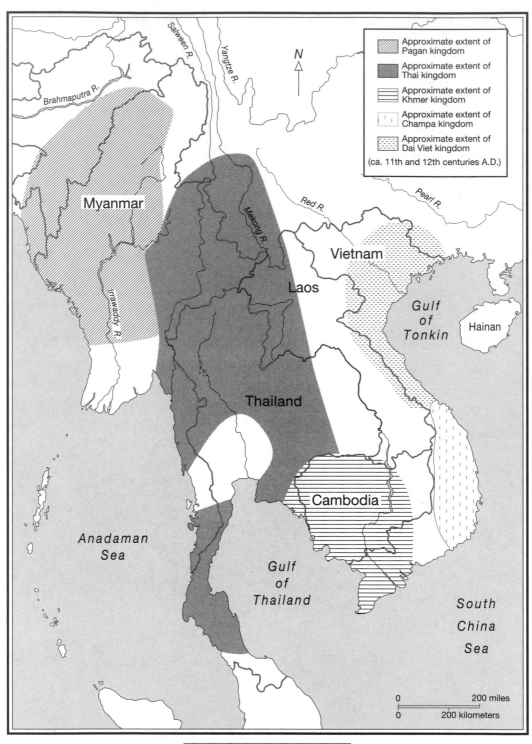

Southeast Asia

N

Skara Brae • • Maes Howe

North Sea

Ertebølle •
Gundestrup •
Grauballe •
Tollund
Egtved •   • Trundholm
             Vedbæk Bøgebakken
Hjortspring •

Mount Sandel •

Great Langdale •

Knowth,
Newgrange •   Star Carr •

Lindow •
Danebury •
Crickley Hill •   Snettisham •
Avebury, West Kennet,   Flag   Grimes Graves •
Windmill Hill •   Fen •   Sutton Hoo •
Glastonbury,   Clacton •
Sweet Track •   Swanscombe •

Maiden Castle •   Boxgrove •
Stonehenge,
Bush Barrow

ATLANTIC
OCEAN

Barnenez •

Téviec •   Mont Lassois, • Pincevent
Carnac • Gavrinis •   Vix   La
Grand Pressigny • Bibracte •   Tène •
                   Châtelperron •
Bougon •

Basse
Yutz •

Hohlenstein-
Stadel •

EUROPE

Lascaux,
Cro-Magnon,   Charavines •   Val
La Chapelle-aux-Saints •   Camonica •   Similaun •

Altamira •   Pech Merle •

Drassempouy •
Le Mas d'Azil • • Tautavel   Terra
                                   Amata •

Torralba,   Tarquinia •
Ambrona •

Muge •

Los Millares •
El Argar •

Mediterranean Sea

AFRICA

Hal Saflieni •
Tarxien •

0 _____ 300 miles
0 _____ 300 kilometers

Western Europe

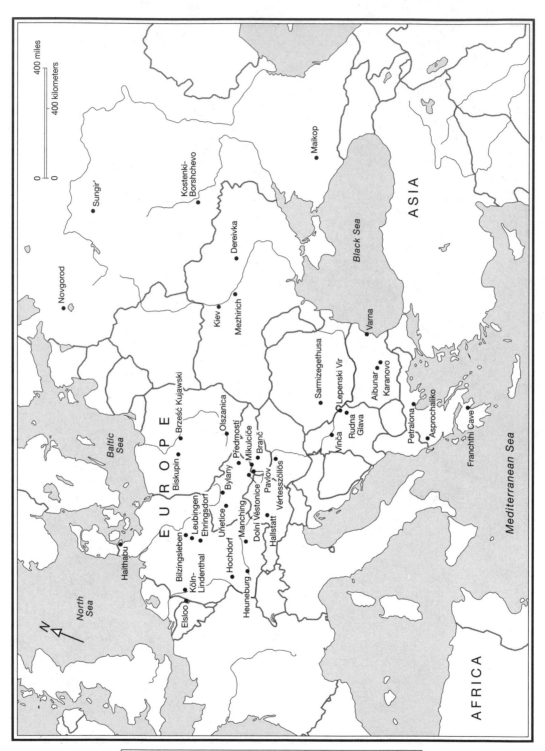

400 miles
400 kilometers
0
0

ASIA

Black Sea

• Maikop

• Sungir'

Kostenki-
Borshchevo •

• Dereivka

• Novgorod

Kiev • • Mezhirich

Baltic Sea

E U R O P E

Brześć Kujawski
•

Olszanica
•

Sarmizegethusa •

Varna •

Lepenski Vir
•

Aibunar •
Karanovo •

Biskupin •

Předmostí •
Bylany • Mikulčice •
• Branč

Vinča •
Rudna
Glava •

Petralona •
Asprochaliko •

Leubingen •
Ehringsdorf •

Unětice •

Pavlov •
Manching • Dolní Věstonice
Vértesszöllős

Franchthi Cave •

Mediterranean Sea

Blizingsleben •

Hochdorf •

Hallstatt

Haithabu •

Köln-
Lindenthal •

Heuneburg •

North
Sea

N

Elsloo •

AFRICA

Central and Eastern Europe

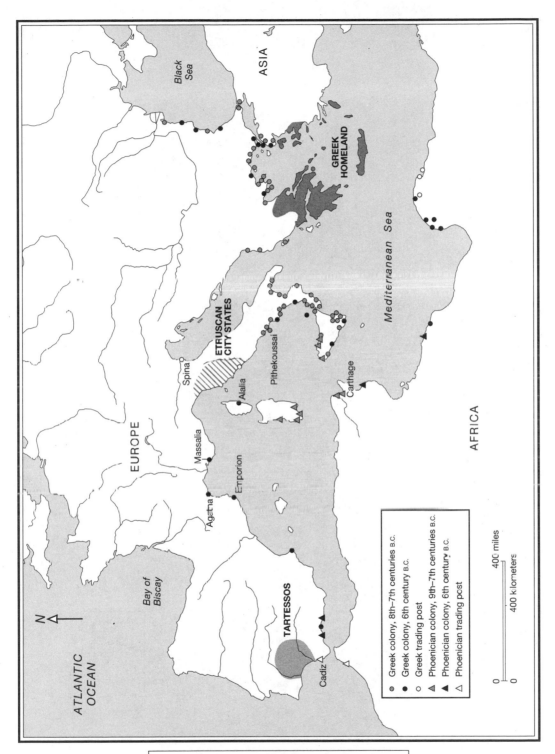

Mediterranean Colonies

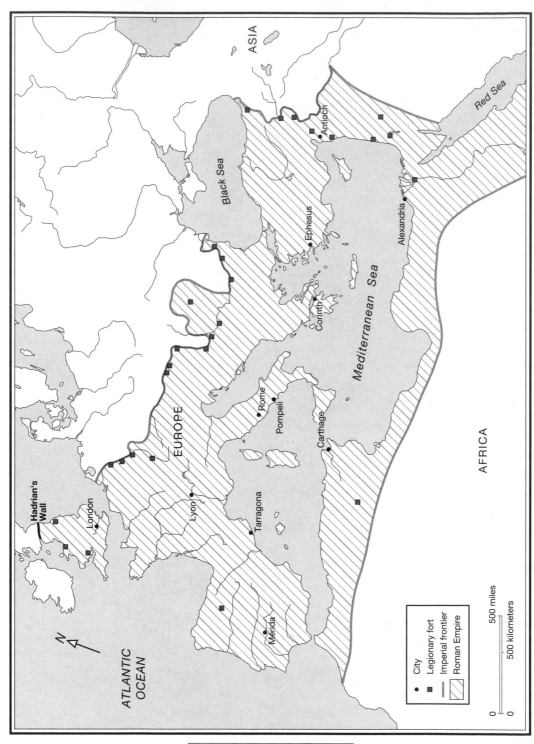

Roman Empire

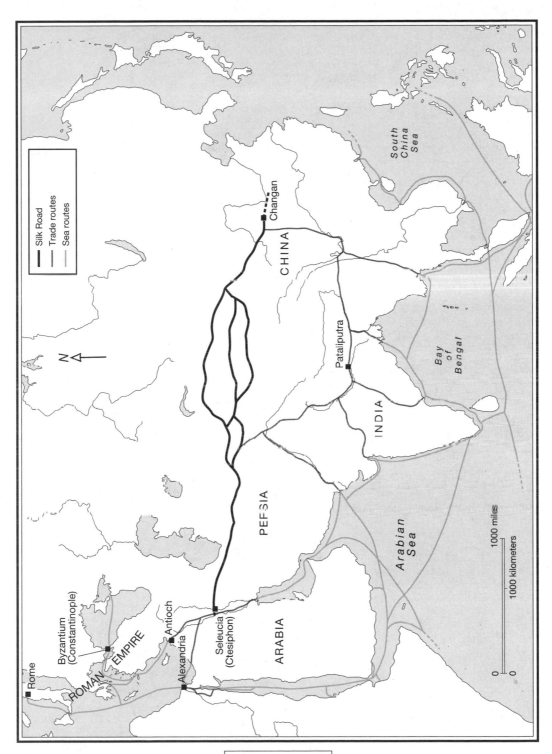

Silk Road

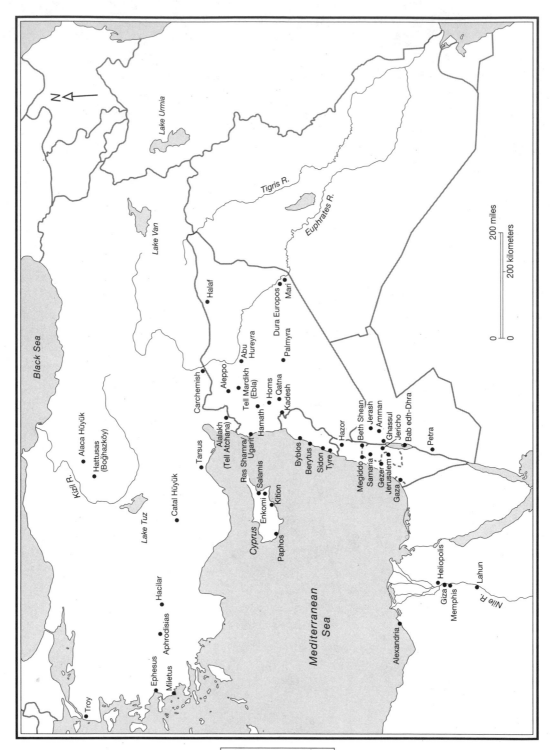

Near East

Classical Greece

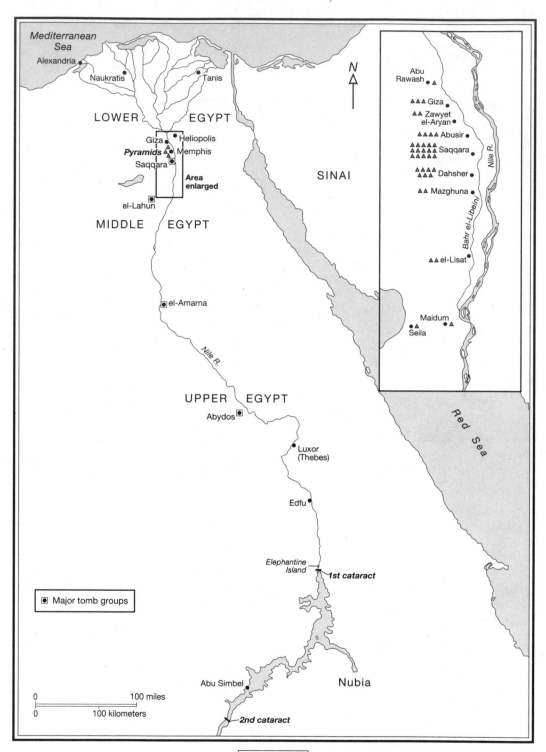

Egypt

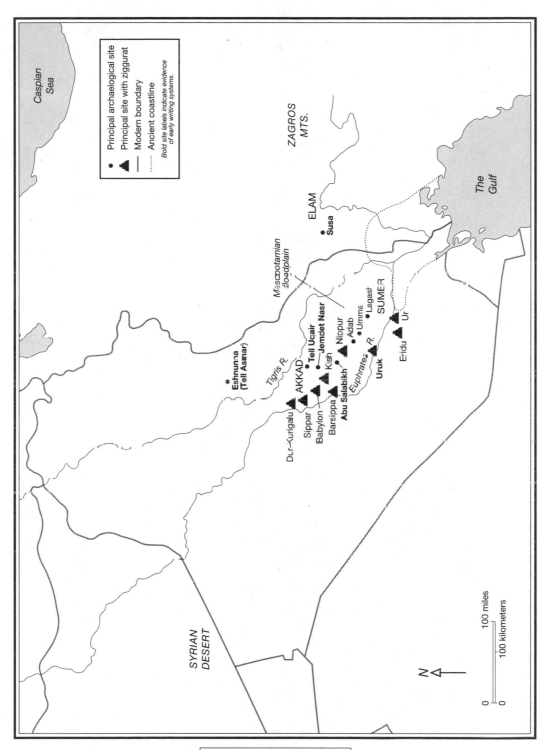

Caspian
Sea

Principal archaelogical site
Principal site with ziggurat
Modern boundary
Ancient coastline
*Bold site labels indicate evidence
of early writing systems.*

ZAGROS
MTS.

ELAM

• Susa

*Mesopotamian
floodplain*

The
Gulf

SUMER

Eshnunna
(Tell Asmar) •

Tell Ucair
Jemdet Nasr

AKKAD
• Nippur
• Adab
Kish •
• Umma
• Lagast

Dur-Kurigalu
Sippar
Babylon
Barsippa
Abu Salabikh

Euphrates R.
Tigris R.

Uruk

Eridu •

Ur

SYRIAN
DESERT

N

100 miles
100 kilometers
0
0

Mesopotamia

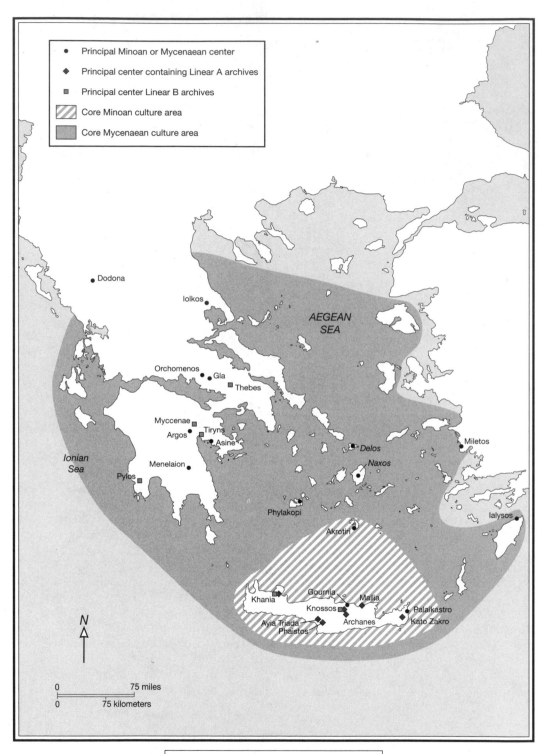

Legend:
- Principal Minoan or Mycenaean center
- Principal center containing Linear A archives
- Principal center Linear B archives
- Core Minoan culture area
- Core Mycenaean culture area

Dodona

Iolkos

AEGEAN SEA

Orchomenos
Gla
Thebes

Myccenae
Argos
Tiryns
Asine

Menelaion

Pylos

Ionian Sea

Delos

Naxos

Miletos

Phylakopi

Ialysos

Akrotiri

Khania
Gournia
Mallia
Knossos
Ayia Triada
Phaistos
Archanes
Palaikastro
Kato Zakro

N

0   75 miles
0   75 kilometers

Aegean Bronze Age

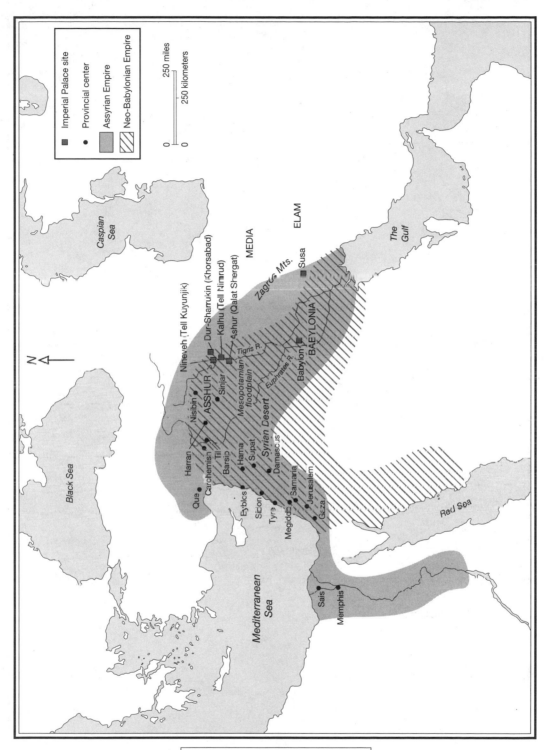

Iron Age Empires

Legend:
- Imperial Palace site ■
- Provincial center ●
- Assyrian Empire (shaded)
- Neo-Babylonian Empire (hatched)

250 miles
250 kilometers

Caspian Sea

MEDIA

ELAM

The Gulf

Zagros Mts.

Nineveh (Tell Kuyunjik)
Dur-Sharrukin (Khorsabad)
Kalhu (Tell Nimrud)
Ashur (Qalat Shergat)

Susa

ASSHUR

Nisibin

Sinjar

Tigris R.

BABYLONIA

Babylon

Euphrates R.

Mesopotamian floodplain

Harran

Til

Barsip

Carchemish

Hama

Supat

Syrian Desert

Damascus

Black Sea

Que

Byblos

Sidon

Tyre

Megiddo

Samaria

Jerusalem

Gaza

Red Sea

Mediterranean Sea

Sais

Memphis

N

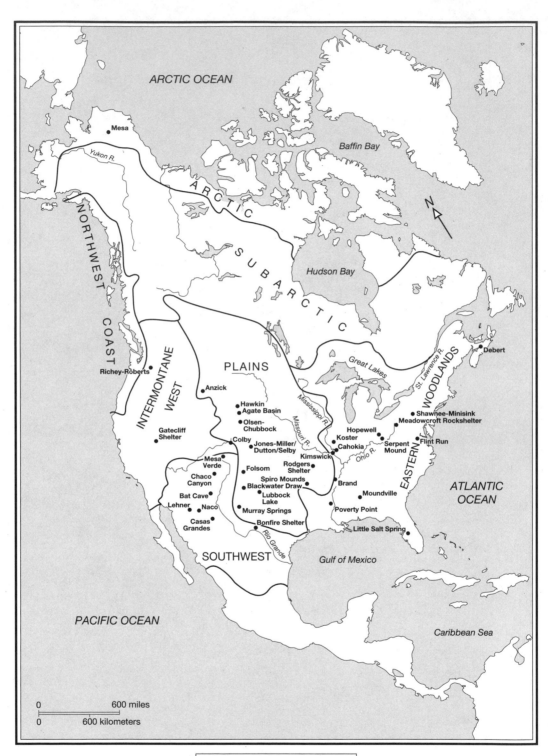

North America

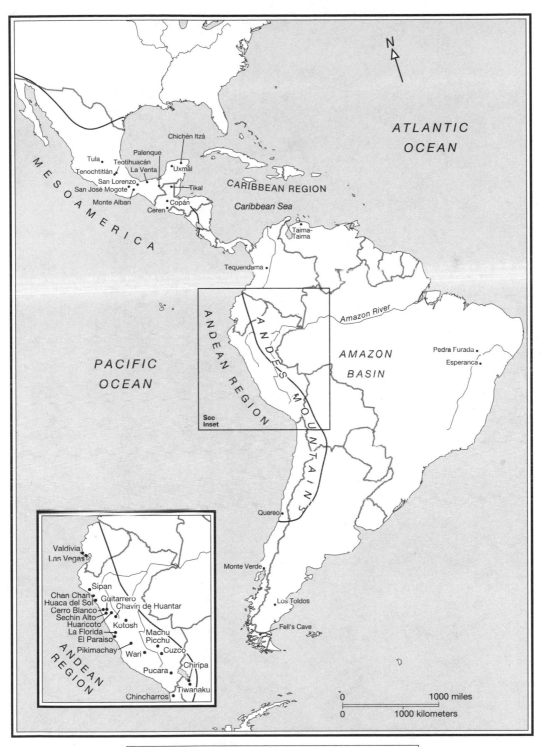

ATLANTIC
OCEAN

Chichén Itzá

Tula
Palenque
Teotihuacán
Tenochtitlán
La Venta
Uxmal
MESOAMERICA
San Lorenzo
San José Mogote
Tikal
Monte Alban
Copán
Ceren

CARIBBEAN REGION

Caribbean Sea

Taima-
Taima

Tequendama

Amazon River

ANDEAN REGION

AMAZON
BASIN

Pedra Furada
Esperanca

PACIFIC
OCEAN

ANDES MOUNTAINS

See
Inset

Quereo

Monte Verde

Valdivia
Las Vegas

Los Toldos

Sipan

Fell's Cave

Chan Chan
Huaca del Sol
Cerro Blanco
Sechin Alto
Huaricoto
La Florida
El Paraiso
Pikimachay
Guitarrero
Chavín de Huantar
Kotosh
Machu
Picchu
Wari
Cuzco
Pucara
Chiripa
ANDEAN
REGION
Chincharros
Tiwanaku

0   1000 miles
0   1000 kilometers

Central and South America

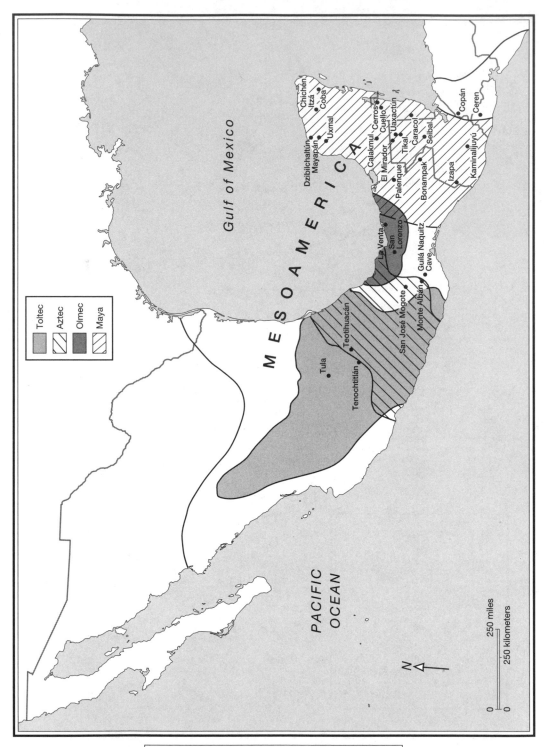

Mesoamerican Empires

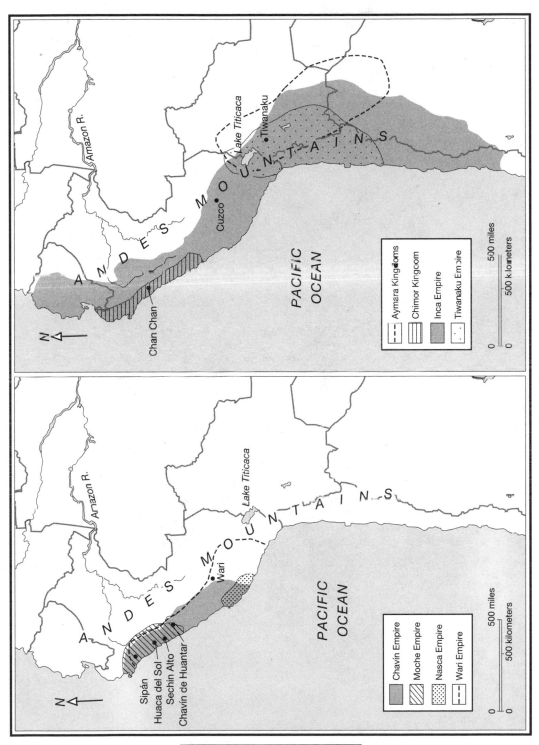

Lake Titicaca
Tiwanaku
Amazon R.
A N D E S   M O U N T A I N S
Cuzco
PACIFIC OCEAN
Chan Chan
N

Aymara Kingdoms
Chimor Kingdom
Inca Empire
Tiwanaku Empire

500 miles
500 kilometers
0
0

Amazon R.
Lake Titicaca
A N D E S   M O U N T A I N S
Wari
PACIFIC OCEAN
Sipán
Huaca del Sol
Sechin Alto
Chavín de Huantar
N

Chavin Empire
Moche Empire
Nasca Empire
Wari Empire

500 miles
500 kilometers
0
0

Andean Empires

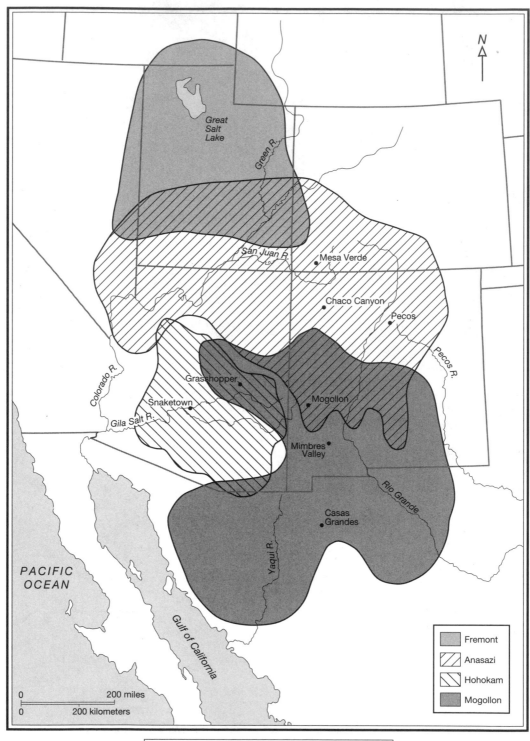

Southwestern America

Fremont

Anasazi

Hohokam

Mogollon

Great Salt Lake

Green R.

San Juan R.

Mesa Verde

Chaco Canyon

Pecos

Pecos R.

Grasshopper

Snaketown

Gila Salt R.

Colorado R.

Mogollon

Mimbres Valley

Casas Grandes

Rio Grande

Yaqui R.

PACIFIC OCEAN

Gulf of California

200 miles

200 kilometers

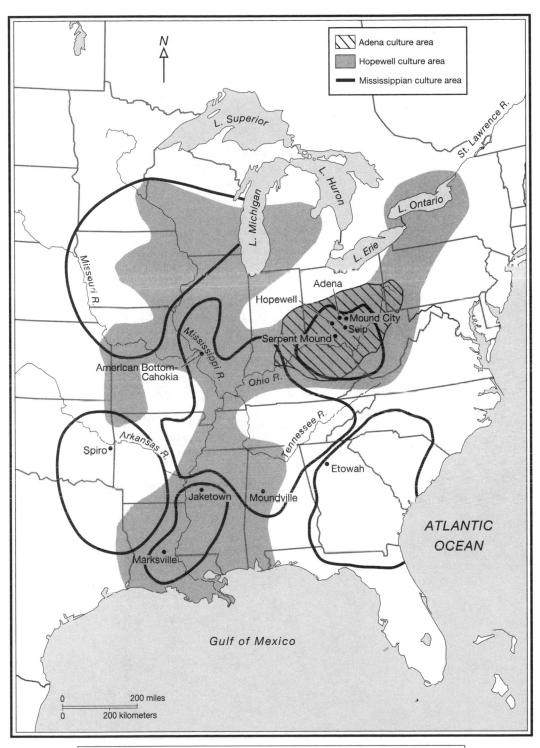

Adena, Hopewell, and Mississippian

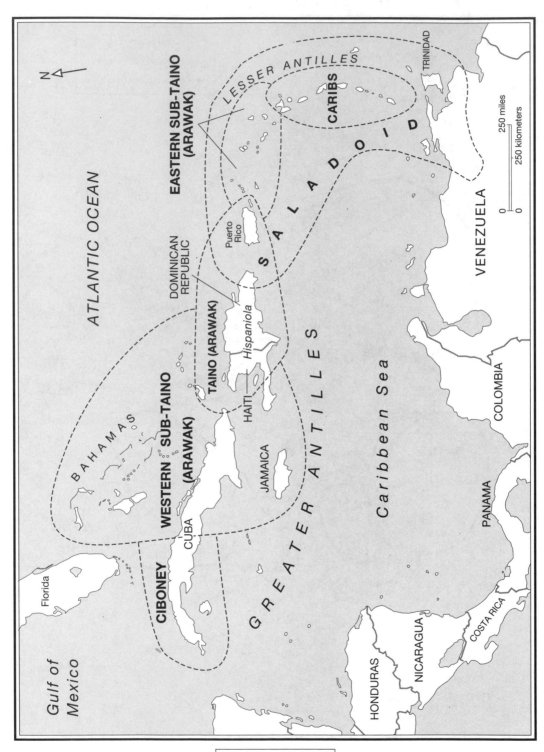

Caribbean

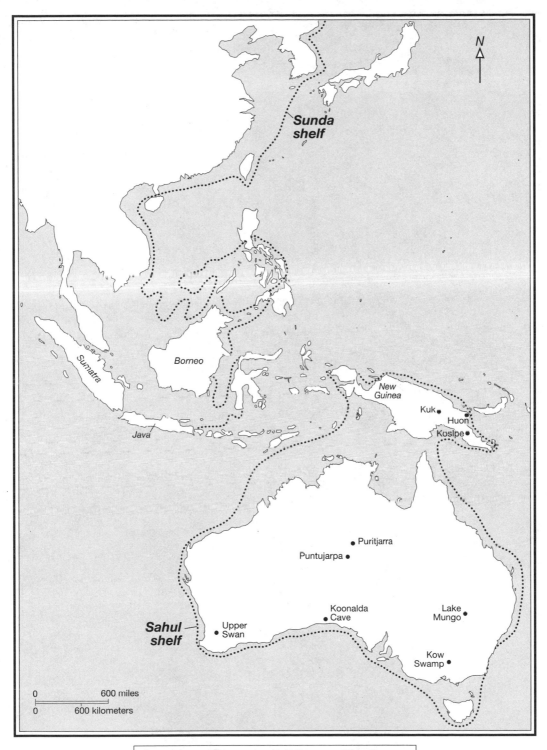

Australia and New Guinea

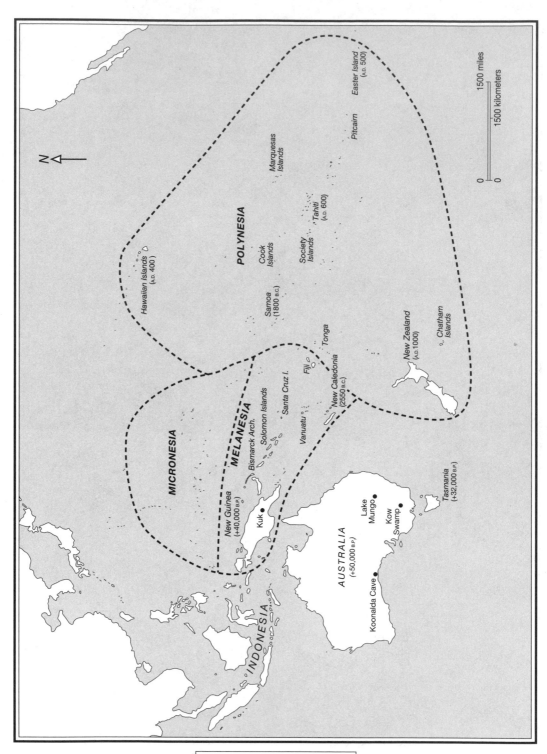

N

POLYNESIA

Easter Island
(A.D. 500)

Pitcairn

Marquesas
Islands

Tahiti
(A.D. 600)

Society
Islands

Cook
Islands

Hawaiian Islands
(A.D. 400)

Samoa
(1800 B.C.)

New Zealand
(A.D. 1000)

Chatham
Islands

Tonga

Fiji

New Caledonia
(2550 B.C.)

Santa Cruz I.

Vanuatu

Solomon Islands

Bismarck Arch.

MELANESIA

MICRONESIA

New Guinea
(+40,000 B.P.)

Kuk

Tasmania
(+32,000 B.P.)

Lake
Mungo

Kow
Swamp

AUSTRALIA
(+50,000 B.P.)

Koonalda Cave

INDONESIA

1500 miles

1500 kilometers

0

0

Pacific Islands

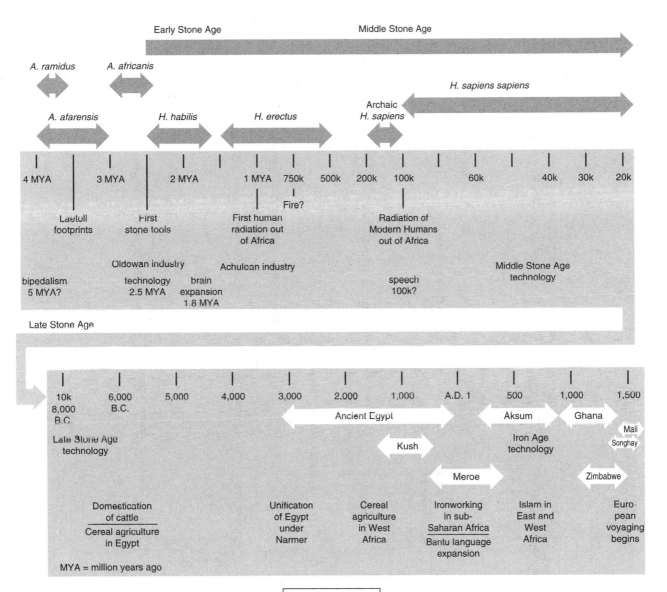

Early Stone Age   Middle Stone Age

A. ramidus   A. africanis

H. sapiens sapiens

A. afarensis   H. habilis   H. erectus   Archaic H. sapiens

| 4 MYA | 3 MYA | 2 MYA | 1 MYA | 750k | 500k | 200k | 100k | 60k | 40k | 30k | 20k |

Fire?

Laetoli footprints   First stone tools   First human radiation out of Africa   Radiation of Modern Humans out of Africa

Oldowan industry   Achulean industry

Middle Stone Age technology

bipedalism 5 MYA?   technology 2.5 MYA   brain expansion 1.8 MYA   speech 100k?

Late Stone Age

| 10k 8,000 B.C. | 6,000 B.C. | 5,000 | 4,000 | 3,000 | 2,000 | 1,000 | A.D. 1 | 500 | 1,000 | 1,500 |

Ancient Egypt   Aksum   Ghana

Mali
Songhay

Late Stone Age technology

Kush   Iron Age technology

Meroe   Zimbabwe

Domestication of cattle   Unification of Egypt under Narmer   Cereal agriculture in West Africa   Ironworking in sub-Saharan Africa   Islam in East and West Africa   Euro-pean voyaging begins

Cereal agriculture in Egypt

Bantu language expansion

MYA = million years ago

Africa

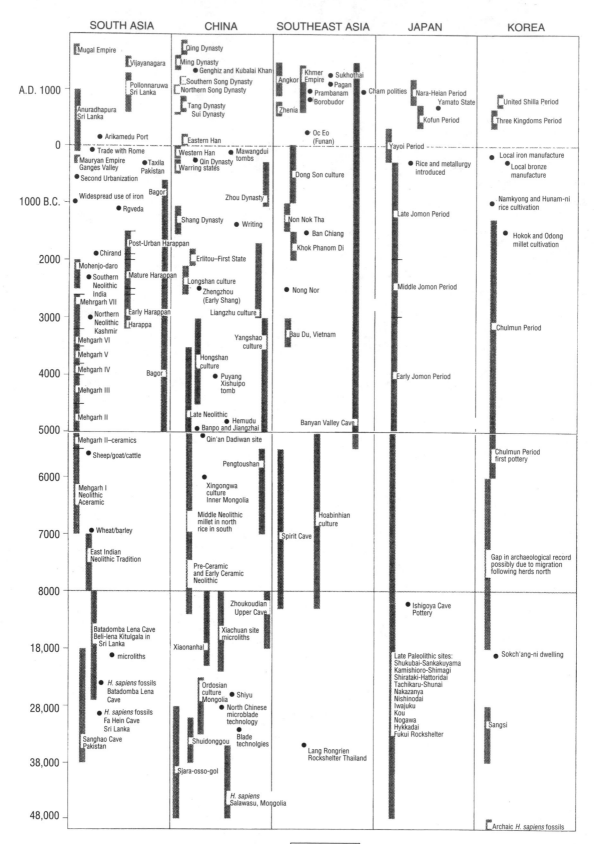

Asia

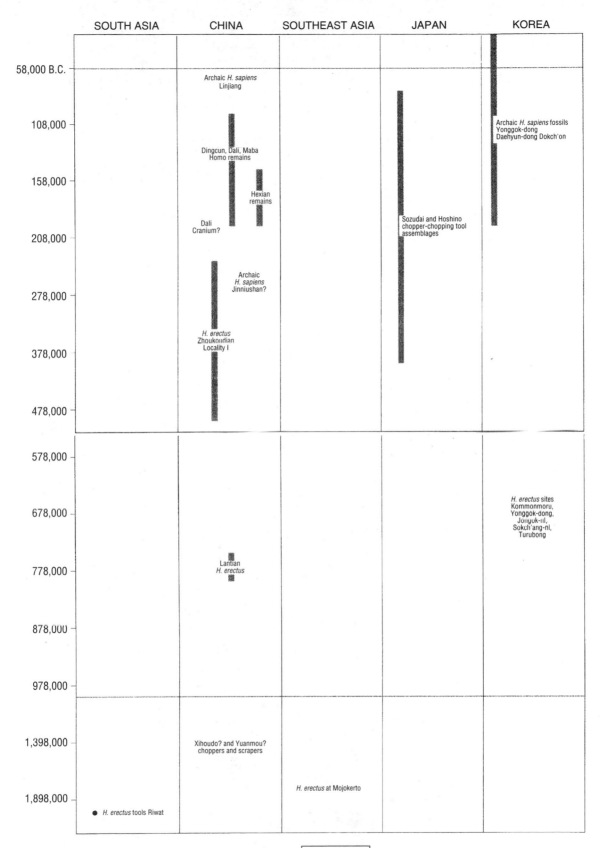

SOUTH ASIA	CHINA	SOUTHEAST ASIA	JAPAN	KOREA

58,000 B.C.

Archaic *H. sapiens*
Linjiang

108,000

Archaic *H. sapiens* fossils
Yonggok-dong
Daehyun-dong Dokch'on

Dingcun, Dali, Maba
Homo remains

158,000

Hexian
remains

Dali
Cranium?

Sozudai and Hoshino
chopper-chopping tool
assemblages

208,000

Archaic
H. sapiens
Jinniushan?

278,000

H. erectus
Zhoukoudian
Locality I

378,000

478,000

578,000

678,000

H. erectus sites
Kommonmoru,
Yonggok-dong,
Jongok-ni,
Sokch'ang-ni,
Turubong

Lantian
H. erectus

778,000

878,000

978,000

1,398,000

Xihoudo? and Yuanmou?
choppers and scrapers

1,898,000

H. erectus at Mojokerto

● *H. erectus* tools Riwat

Asia

	AEGEAN			Neolithic
6500	Early Farmers			
	Crete	Greece	Aegean Turkey	
3000				
2900	Early Minoan (Prepalatial)	Early Helladic	Troy I	Early Bronze Age
2800				
2700				
2600			Troy II	
2500				
2400				
2300				
2200				
2100				
2000				
1900	Middle Minoan (old Palace or First Palace Period)	Middle Helladic		Middle Bronze Age
1800				
1700				
1600				
1500	Late Minoan (old Palace or First Palace period)	Late Helladic (Mycenaean civilization)		Late Bronze Age
1400			Troy VI	
1300	Third Palace Period			
1200	Postpalatial			
1100		Postpalatial		
1000	Protogeometric	First use of iron in Greece		Iron Age
900				
800	Geometric	First Greek colonies overseas / First Olympic Games (776 B.C.)		
700		Greek colonization of Black Sea		
600	Archaic			
500		Persian Wars, 490–479 B.C.		
400	Classical	Parthenon begun, 447 B.C. / Peloponnesian War, 431–404 B.C.		
300		Campaigns of Alexander the Great 335–323 B.C.		
200	Hellenistic			
100		Romans annex Greece, 146 B.C. / Romans annex Aegean Turkey, 133 B.C.		
0	Roman Empire			

Aegean

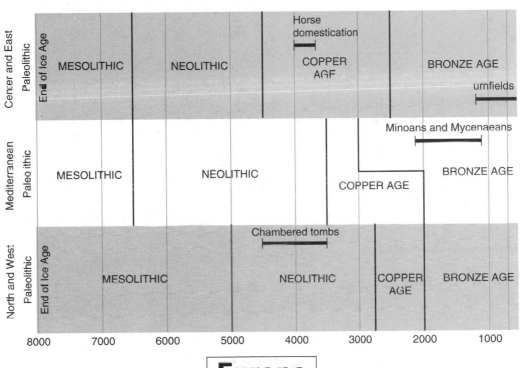

Europe

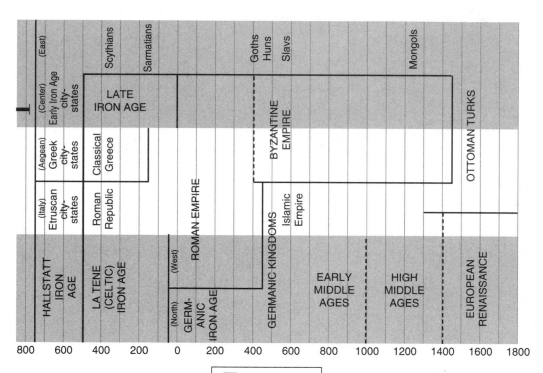

Europe

c. 1,500,000 B.C. LOWER PALEOLITHIC PERIOD

c. 250,000 B.C. MIDDLE PALEOLITHIC PERIOD

c. 45,000 B.C. UPPER PALEOLITHIC PERIOD

c. 18,000 B.C. EPI-PALEOLITHIC PERIOD

c. 8300 B.C. PRE-POTTERY NEOLITHIC

c. 5500 B.C. NEOLOTHIC

c. 4500 B.C. CHALCOLITHIC

c. 3500 B.C. EARLY BRONZE AGE

c. 2200 B.C. MIDDLE BRONZE AGE

c. 1550 B.C. LATE BRONZE AGE

c. 1200 –332 B.C. IRON AGE

Early Iron Age	c.1200 – c. 800 B.C.
Assyrian Period	c. 800 – c. 650 B.C.
Neo-Babylonian Period	c. 650 –539 B.C.
Persian Period	539 –332 B.C.

60 B.C.–c. 640 A.D. ROMAN PERIOD

Early Roman Period	60 B.C.–70 A.D.
Roman Imperial Period	70 –324 A.D.
Byzantine Period	324– c. 640 A.D.

623 –c. 900 A.D. EARLY ISLAMIC PERIOD

Conquest Period	623 –661 A.D.
Umayyad Period	661 –750 A.D.
Early Abbasid Period	749 – c. 900 A.D.

c. 900 –1517 A.D. MIDDLE AGES

Fatimid Period (Egypt, Palestine)	909 –1100 A.D.
Seljuk Period (Iraq, Syria, Turkey)	1000 –1200 A.D.
Crusader Period (Palestine)	1099 –1291 A.D.
Ayyubid Period (Egypt, Syria)	1169 –1260 A.D.
Late Abbasid Period (Iraq)	c. 900 –1258 A.D.
Ikhanid Period (Iran, Iraq)	1256 –1336 A.D.
Mamluk Period (Egypt, Syria)	1250 –1517 A.D.

c. 1517 A.D. OTTOMAN EMPIRE

c. 1917 A.D. MODERN PERIOD

Near East

DATES (B.C.)	DYNASTIES	SELECTED RULERS	CULTURAL/POLITICAL
4000	Predynastic Period		Nagada culture
3500	Protodynastic Period		Stratified society— Political unification of Nile Valley— Foreign military expeditions
3000	Early Dynastic Period		
2900	Dynasties 1–2	Narmer	
2800	*Old Kingdom*		
2700	Dynasty 3	Djoser	Step pyramids
2600	Dynasty 4	Khufu	Giza pyramids
2500	Dynasty 5	Khafre	Pyramid texts
2400	Dynasty 6	Unas	Provincial bureacracy
2300	Dynasties 7–8		Breakdown of central government
2200	*First Intermediate Period (Dynasties 9–10)*		
2100			
2000	*Middle Kingdom (Dynasties 11–12)*	Amenemhet I	Centralization/conquest of Nubia
1900		Senwosret I	Commercial ties to Levant
1800	*Second Intermediate Period (Dynasties 13–17)*		
1700		Salitis	"Hykos" rule
1600	*New Kingdom*	Khian	Close ties to Canaan, trade with Aegean
1500	Dynasty 18	Ahmose I Hatshepsut Thutmosis III	Rise of Theban Dynasty/Valley of Kings
1400		Amenhotep III Akhenaten	tombs—Imperial expansion— Amarna Era
1300		Tutankhamun	
1200	Dynasty 19 Dynasty 20	Ramesses II Ramesses III	War with Hittites— Fea People's attacks
1100			
1000	*Third Intermediate Period (Dynasties 21–23)*	Horemhab Pinudjem I	Rule by local leaders—reunification
900	*Late Dynasties*	Psuennes I Siamun Sheshonk	
800	Dynasty 23	Orsorkon	
700	Dynasties 24–25	Piankhy	
600	*Saite Period (Dynasty 26)*	Psammethicus Necho II	
500	*Persian Period*		Conquest by Persian Empire
400		Achoris	Conquest by Alexander
300	*Ptolemaic Period*	Ptolemy I	
200		Ptolemy II	
100			Hellenistic syncretism
31	*Roman Period*	Cleopatra VII	Conquest by Rome

Egypt

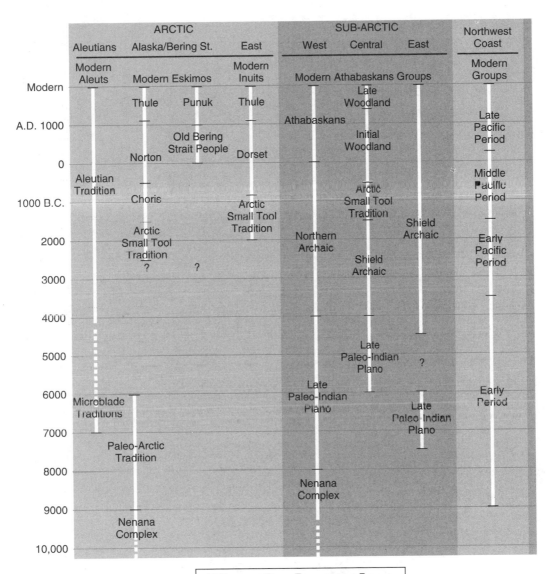

North America

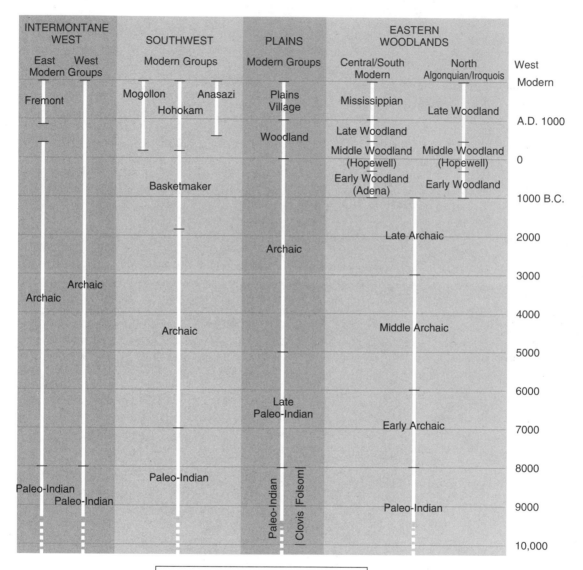

North America

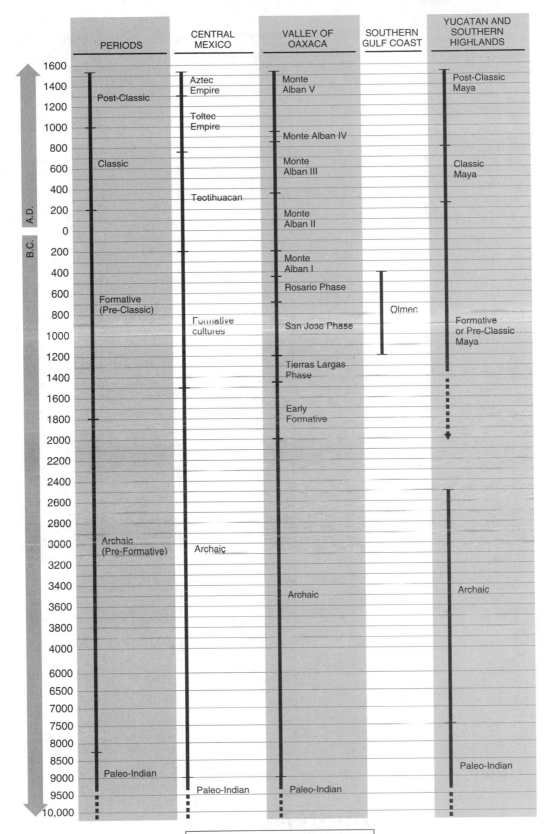

Mesoamerica

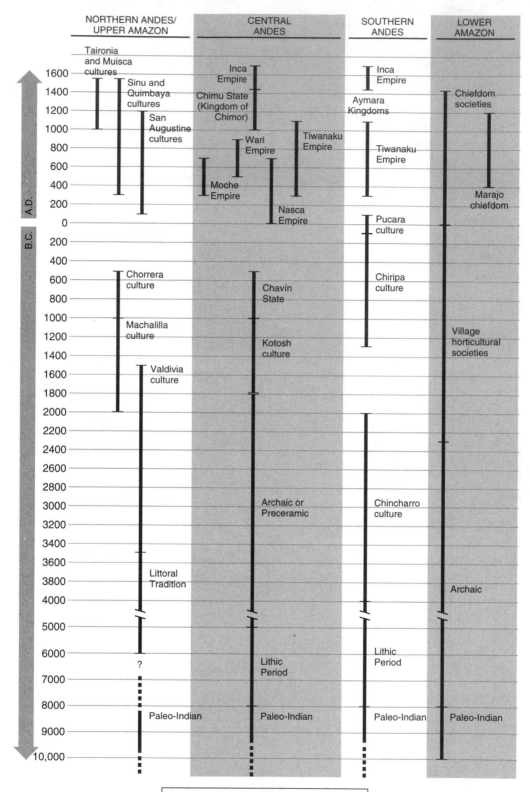

South America

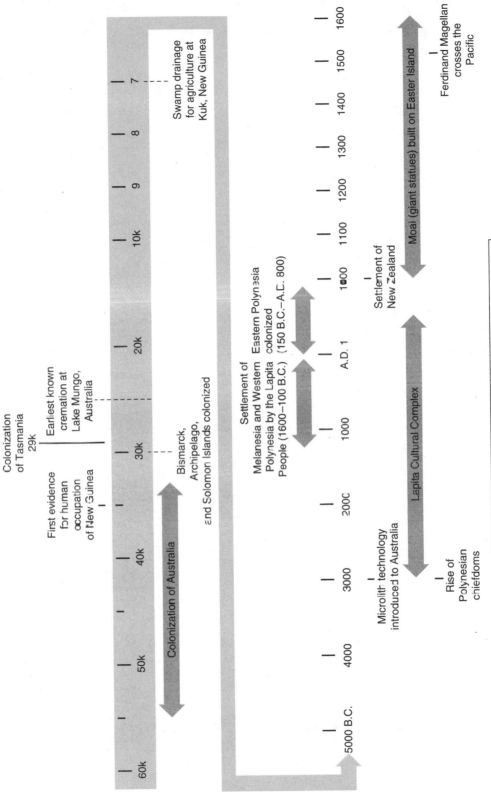

Timeline of the Pacific

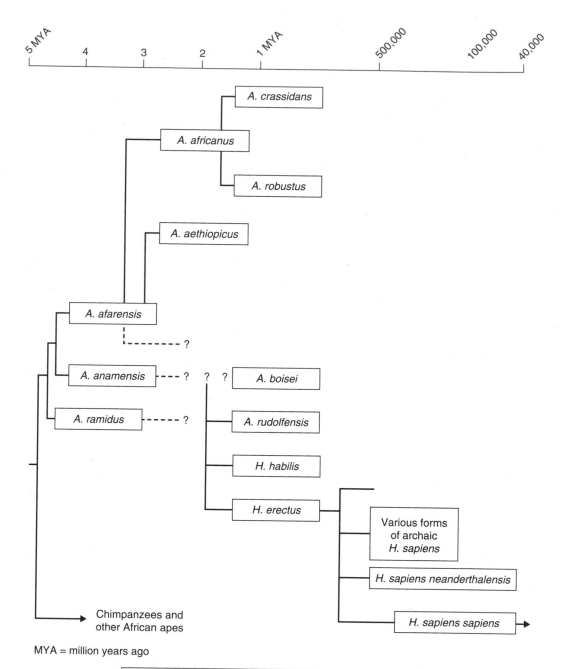

Early Human Evolution

EDITORS

Editor in Chief **BRIAN M. FAGAN** studied archaeology and anthropology at Pembroke College, Cambridge, and spent his early career working in eastern and southern Africa, where he was a pioneer of multidisciplinary African history and archaeology. Since 1967 he has been Professor of Anthropology at the University of California, Santa Barbara, and has specialized in communicating archaeology to general audiences. He is the author of six widely used college textbooks on archaeology, including *In the Beginning* and *People of the Earth*. His general books include *Time Detectives* (1995), *The Adventure of Archaeology* (1985), and *The Rape of the Nile* (1975). Fagan was awarded the Distinguished Service Award of the Society for Professional Archaeologists in 1995 for his efforts to bring archaeology to a wider audience.

CHARLOTTE BECK received her Ph.D. in anthropology from the University of Washington. Since 1986 she has taught in the Department of Anthropology at Hamilton College, where she is now an associate professor. Her area of interest is the Great Basin, where she investigates the earliest human occupations in North America. She works closely with her husband, George T. Jones, with whom she has coauthored numerous articles in journals such as *American Antiquity, Journal of Field Archaeology,* and *Journal of California and Great Basin Anthropology*. Other research interests include surface archaeology and archaeological dating, the subjects of her edited book, *Dating in Exposed and Surface Contexts* (1994).

GEORGE H. MICHAELS is on the staff of the Office of Instructional Consultation at the University of California, Santa Barbara. His research interests include lithic technology and the reconstruction of prehistoric economic systems. He has published several papers and a dissertation on lithic craft specialization as practiced by the prehistoric Lowland Maya of Belize. His most recent work has focused on the uses of cutting-edge multimedia and World Wide Web technologies as teaching and research tools in archaeology.

CHRIS SCARRE studied archaeology at Cambridge University and is Deputy Director of the McDonald Institute for Archaeological Research at the University of Cambridge. A specialist in European archaeology and ancient history, he has edited the widely acclaimed reference books *Timelines of the Ancient World* (1993) and *Past Worlds: The Times Atlas of Archaeology* (1988). His other books include *The Penguin Historical Atlas of Ancient Rome* (1995) and the best-selling *Chronicle of the Roman Emperors* (1995). He is also the editor of the *Cambridge Archaeological Journal*.

NEIL ASHER SILBERMAN is an author and historian with a special interest in the history and politics of modern archaeology. A former Guggenheim Fellow, he is a graduate of Wesleyan University and was trained in Near Eastern archaeology at the Hebrew University of Jerusalem. He is a contributing editor for *Archaeology* magazine and frequent contributor to other archaeological and general-interest periodicals. His books include *Inheriting the Kingdom* (with Richard A. Horsley, 1997), *Invisible America* (with Mark P. Leone, 1995), *The Hidden Scrolls* (1994), *A Prophet from Amongst You: The Life of Yigael Yadin* (1993), *Between Past and Present* (1989), and *Digging for God and Country* (1982).

Index

NOTE: Bold page numbers refer to major discussions of topic.

cover the continent from the Arctic to the Eastern Woodlands to the Northwest Coast; that discuss the Iroquois and Algonquian cultures, the hunters of the North American Plains, and the Norse in North America; and that describe sites such as Mesa Verde, Meadowcroft Rockshelter, Serpent Mound, and Poverty Point. Likewise, the coverage of Europe runs from the Paleolithic period, to the Bronze and Iron Ages, to the Post-Roman era; looks at peoples such as the Celts, the Germans, the Vikings, and the Slavs; and describes sites at Altamira, Pompeii, Stonehenge, Terra Amata, and dozens of other locales. The *Companion* offers equally thorough coverage of Africa, Europe, North America, Mesoamerica, South America, Asia, the Mediterranean, the Near East, Australia, and the Pacific. And finally, the editors have included extensive cross-referencing and thorough indexing, enabling the reader to pursue topics of interest with ease; charts and maps providing additional information; and bibliographies after most entries directing readers to the best sources for further study.

Every Oxford Companion aspires to be the definitive overview of a field of study at a particular moment of time. This superb volume is no exception. Featuring 700 articles written by hundreds of respected scholars from all over the world, *The Oxford Companion to Archaeology* provides authoritative, stimulating entries on everything from bog bodies, to underwater archaeology, to the Pyramids of Giza and the Valley of the Kings.

About the Editor in Chief

Brian M. Fagan is Professor of Anthropology at the University of California, Santa Barbara. He is internationally known for his books and articles on archaeology for general readers, among them *The Rape of the Nile*, *The Adventure of Archaeology*, and *Time Detectives*.

About the Editors

Charlotte Beck is Assistant Professor of Anthropology at Hamilton College. **George Michaels** is a Mayan archaeologist and an Instructional Consultant at the University of California, Santa Barbara. **Chris Scarre** is Deputy Director of the McDonald Institute for Archaeological Research at the University of Cambridge. **Neil Asher Silberman** is an independent scholar and author.